DO NOT CIRCULATE

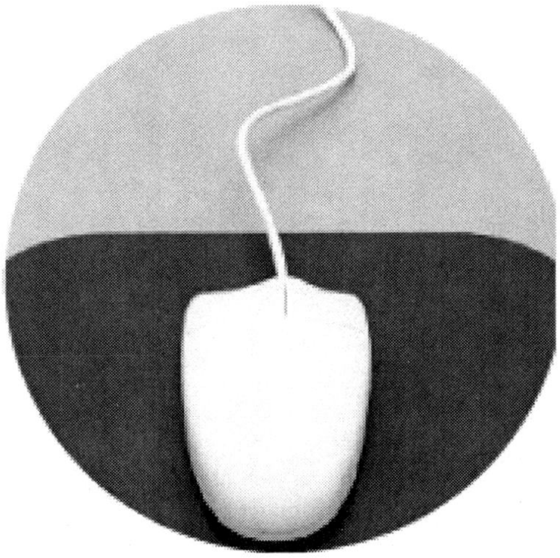

Customer Suppo

AF682848

The Almanac of Ame... Employers 2012

Please register your book immediately...

if you did not purchase it directly from Plunkett Research, Ltd. This will enable us to fulfill your requests for assistance. Also, it will enable us to notify you of future editions.

Your purchase includes access to Book Data and Exports online

As a book purchaser, you can register for free, 1-year, 1-seat online access to the latest data for your book's industry trends, statistics and company profiles. This includes tools to export company data. Simply send us this registration form, and we will send you a user name and password. In this manner, you will have access to our continual updates during the year. Certain restrictions apply.

____ YES, please register me as a purchaser of the book.
I did not buy it directly from Plunkett Research, Ltd.

____ YES, please register me for free online access. I am the actual, original purchaser. (Proof of purchase may be required.)

Customer Name ______________________________

Title ______________________________

Organization ______________________________

Address ______________________________

City ______________ State ________ Zip ____________

Country (if other than USA) ______________________________

Phone ______________ Fax ______________

E-mail ______________________________

Return to: Plunkett Research®, Ltd.
Attn: Registration
P.O. Drawer 541737, Houston, TX 77254-1737 USA
713.932.0000 · Fax 713.932.7080 · www.plunkettresearch.com
customersupport@plunkettresearch.com

* Purchasers of used books are not eligible to register. Use of online access is subject to the terms of the end user license agreement.

33163015872655 C 20111206
R Location: R
331.20973 PLU 2012
The Almanac of American employers.

CENTRAL LIBRARY
IRVING PUBLIC LIBRARY SYSTEM
IRVING, TEXAS 75060

THE ALMANAC OF AMERICAN EMPLOYERS 2012

The Only Guide to America's Hottest, Fastest-Growing Major Corporations

Jack W. Plunkett

Published by:
Plunkett Research®, Ltd., Houston, Texas
www.plunkettresearch.com

3 3163 01587 2655

THE ALMANAC OF AMERICAN EMPLOYERS 2012

Editor and Publisher:
Jack W. Plunkett

Executive Editor and Database Manager:
Martha Burgher Plunkett

Senior Editor and Researcher:
Jill Steinberg

Editors, Researchers and Assistants:
Keith Beeman, III
Kalonji Bobb
Elizabeth Braddock
Xiaowen Chen
Jeremy Faulk
Suzanne Zarosky

Enterprise Accounts Managers:
Emily Hurley
Kelly Burke

Information Technology Manager:
Wenping Guo

Information Technology Intern:
Danil K. Safin

Video & Graphics Manager:
Geoffrey Trudeau

Special Thanks to:
U.S. Department of Labor
Bureau of Labor Statistics
U.S. Department of Commerce
Bureau of Economic Analysis, National Technical Information Service

Plunkett Research®, Ltd.
P. O. Drawer 541737, Houston, Texas 77254 USA
Phone: 713.932.0000 Fax: 713.932.7080
www.plunkettresearch.com

Copyright © 2011, Plunkett Research®, Ltd.
All rights reserved. No part of this book may be reproduced or transmitted in any form by any means, electronic or mechanical, including by photocopying or by any information storage or retrieval system, without the written permission of the publisher.

Published by:
Plunkett Research®, Ltd.
P. O. Drawer 541737
Houston, Texas 77254-1737

Phone: 713.932.0000
Fax: 713.932.7080
Internet: www.plunkettresearch.com

ISBN13 # 978-1-60879-652-6
(eBook Edition # 978-1-60879-914-5)

LIMITED WARRANTY; DISCLAIMER OF LIABILITY:

While Plunkett Research, Ltd. ("PRL") has made an effort to obtain the information presented in this book (the "Data") from sources deemed reliable, PRL makes no warranties, expressed or implied, regarding the Data contained herein. The Data is provided to the End-User "AS IS" without warranty of any kind. No oral or written information or advice given by PRL, its employees, distributors or representatives will create a warranty or in any way increase the scope of this Limited Warranty, and the Customer or End-User may not rely on any such information or advice.

Customer Remedies: PRL's entire liability and your exclusive remedy shall be, at PRL's sole discretion, either (a) return of the price paid, if any, or (b) repair or replacement of the product that does not meet PRL's Limited Warranty and that is returned to PRL with sufficient evidence of or receipt for your original purchase.

NO OTHER WARRANTIES: TO THE MAXIMUM EXTENT PERMITTED BY APPLICABLE LAW, PRL AND ITS DISTRIBUTORS DISCLAIM ALL OTHER WARRANTIES AND CONDITIONS, EITHER EXPRESSED OR IMPLIED, INCLUDING, BUT NOT LIMITED TO, IMPLIED WARRANTIES OR CONDITIONS OF MERCHANTABILITY, FITNESS FOR A PARTICULAR PURPOSE, TITLE AND NON-INFRINGEMENT WITH REGARD TO THE PRODUCT, AND THE PROVISION OF OR FAILURE TO PROVIDE SUPPORT SERVICES.

LIMITATION OF LIABILITY: TO THE MAXIMUM EXTENT PERMITTED BY APPLICABLE LAW, IN NO EVENT SHALL PRL BE LIABLE FOR ANY SPECIAL, INCIDENTAL OR CONSEQUENTIAL DAMAGES WHATSOEVER (INCLUDING, WITHOUT LIMITATION, DAMAGES FOR LOSS OF BUSINESS PROFITS, BUSINESS INTERRUPTION, ABILITY TO OBTAIN OR RETAIN EMPLOYMENT OR REMUNERATION, ABILITY TO PROFITABLY MAKE AN INVESTMENT, OR ANY OTHER PECUNIARY LOSS) ARISING OUT OF THE USE OF, OR RELIANCE UPON, THE DATA, OR THE INABILITY TO USE THIS DATA OR THE FAILURE OF PRL TO PROVIDE SUPPORT SERVICES, EVEN IF PRL HAS BEEN ADVISED OF THE POSSIBILITY OF SUCH DAMAGES. IN ANY CASE, PRL'S ENTIRE LIABILITY UNDER ANY PROVISION OF THIS END-USER LICENSE AGREEMENT SHALL BE LIMITED TO THE AMOUNT ACTUALLY PAID BY YOU FOR THE PRODUCT.

THE ALMANAC OF AMERICAN EMPLOYERS 2012

CONTENTS

Continued on the next page

Continued from the previous page

INTRODUCTION

THE ALMANAC OF AMERICAN EMPLOYERS is an easy-to-use solution to what would otherwise be a complicated problem: How can you tell, among America's giant companies, which firms are most likely to be hiring? Among those firms, which are the best to work for? No other source provides this book's easy-to-understand comparisons of growth, treatment of employees, salaries, benefits, pension plans, profit sharing and many other items of great importance to job seekers.

Especially helpful is the way in which THE ALMANAC OF AMERICAN EMPLOYERS enables readers with no business background to readily compare the growth potential and benefit plans of large employers. You'll see the mid-term financial record of each firm, along with the impact of earnings, sales and growth plans on each company's potential to provide employment opportunities.

Information is presented in a way that addresses the differing interests of individual employees. You'll find separate listings for dozens of categories of data that you may want to consider. While this book is aimed primarily at job seekers, it will also be of tremendous value to researchers, marketing executives and personnel professionals. THE ALMANAC OF AMERICAN EMPLOYERS is the premier guide to the most successful employers in the nation, their policies and their performance.

THE ALMANAC OF AMERICAN EMPLOYERS is your opportunity to gain valuable knowledge in a matter of minutes. Five hundred of the biggest, most successful corporate employers in America are analyzed in this book. Tens of thousands of pieces of information, gathered from a wide variety of sources, have been researched for these corporations and are presented here in a form that can be easily understood by job seekers of all types.

Thanks to THE ALMANAC OF AMERICAN EMPLOYERS' exclusive data system, potentially confusing considerations have been reduced to simple groups of focused data. By scanning the data groups and the long list of unique indexes, you can find the right employers to fit your personal needs.

The AMERICAN EMPLOYERS 500 are among the best major growth companies to work for in America. Which companies offer the best benefits, are the biggest employers or earn the most profits? Where are these companies operating? All of these things and more are made easy for the reader to determine.

Thousands of observations are made that will be of great interest to prospective employees. For many of the firms, you'll find comments about such items as plans for growth, increases or decreases in the number of employees and charitable programs. You'll also find notes about corporate culture and special programs for the convenience of employees, such as health and recreation facilities, on-site child care, job training or career paths. Finally, you'll find basic information on each company, including the home office address and telephone number; regional, national and international locations; a description of the business; and a list of selected subsidiaries and trade names. In addition, you will find fax numbers and Internet addresses.

Whether you are currently employed by one of these corporate giants or are considering applying for a job with one, you will be able to see how each company compares with the others, even if you don't have the slightest understanding of accounting, finance or employee benefits.

Whatever your purpose for researching corporate employers, you'll find this book to be an indispensable guide. Nonetheless, as is true with all resources, this volume has limitations that the reader should be aware of:

- Financial data and other corporate information can change quickly. A book of this type can be no more current than the data that was available as of the time of editing. Consequently, the financial picture, management and ownership of the firm(s) you are studying may have changed since the date of this book. For example, this almanac includes the most up-to-date sales figures and profits available to the editors as of mid-2011. This means that we have typically used corporate financial data as of the end of 2010

- Corporate mergers, changes in corporate financial ratings or stability, acquisitions and downsizing are occurring at a very rapid rate. Such events may have created significant change, subsequent to the publishing of this book, within a company you are studying.

- Some of the companies in THE AMERICAN EMPLOYERS 500 are so large in scope and in variety of business endeavors conducted within a parent organization that we have been unable to completely list all subsidiaries, affiliations, divisions and activities within a firm's corporate structure.

- This volume is intended to be a general guide to major employers in numerous industries. That means that researchers should look to this book for an overview and, when conducting in-depth research, should contact the specific corporations and related industry associations in question for the very latest changes and data. Where possible, we have listed contact information, telephone numbers and Internet addresses for pertinent companies, government agencies and industry associations so that the reader may get further details without unnecessary delay.

- We have used exhaustive efforts to locate and fairly present accurate and complete data. However, when using this book or any other source for business and industry information, the reader should use caution and due diligence by conducting further research where it seems appropriate. We wish you success in your endeavors, and we trust that your experience with this book will be both satisfactory and productive.

- To obtain the best results and to best understand the fields in the company profiles, you should first read the chapter titled "How to Use This Book."

Good luck in your job search. Be patient, do your research and use this book as an important start in the right direction.

Jack W. Plunkett
Houston, Texas
September 2011

HOW TO USE THIS BOOK

Dozens of excellent books already exist to help you choose a career, write a resume, apply for a job and so on. That is not the purpose of THE ALMANAC OF AMERICAN EMPLOYERS. Instead, this book's job is to help you sort through America's giant corporate employers to determine which may be the best for you, or to see how your current employer compares to others. Whether you are entering the job market and looking for your first position, or you are thinking about switching companies in mid-career to find more promising vistas, this book will be a valuable guide.

The two primary sections of the book are devoted first to general information for job seekers (trends analysis and advice on conducting employer research, along with resources, statistics and contacts), followed by the "Individual Data Listings" for THE AMERICAN EMPLOYERS 500. If time permits, you should begin your research in the front chapters of this book. Also, you will find lengthy indexes in Chapter 5 and in the back of the book.

GENERAL INFORMATION FOR JOB SEEKERS

Chapter 1: Major Trends Affecting Job Seekers. This chapter presents an encapsulated view of the major trends in business and the economy that are creating rapid changes in the employment picture at large corporations.

Chapter 2: Statistics. This chapter presents in-depth statistics on employment by education level, sex and race, along with unemployment rates, the fastest-growing occupations and more.

Chapter 3: Research–7 Keys for Job Seekers. This chapter provides a definitive list of items that job seekers should look for when conducting research into major corporate employers.

Chapter 4: Important Contacts for Job Seekers. This chapter covers contacts for important government agencies, professional societies, industry associations, job banks, reference sources and more. Included are Internet sites and contact addresses for a wide variety of job search uses.

THE AMERICAN EMPLOYERS 500

Chapter 5: THE AMERICAN EMPLOYERS 500: Who They Are and How They Were Chosen.

The companies compared in this book were chosen from nearly all industries, on a nationwide basis. They were individually chosen from the largest U.S. employers, based on selected types of business and industry sectors. For a complete description, see Chapter 5.

Individual Data Listings:

Look at one of the companies in THE AMERICAN EMPLOYERS 500's Individual Data Listings. You'll find the following information fields:

Company Name:

The company profiles are in alphabetical order by company name. If you don't find the company you are seeking, it may be a subsidiary or division of one of the firms covered in this book. Try looking it up in the Index by Subsidiaries, Brand Names and Selected Affiliations in the back of the book.

Industry Code:

Industry Group Code: An NAIC code used to group companies within like segments. (See Chapter 4 for a list of codes.)

Suggested Career Paths:

A grid arranged into six major career categories and several sub-categories. A "Y" indicates that the firm is suggested for certain types of employees, by job discipline.

Types of Business:

A listing of the primary types of business specialties conducted by the firm.

Brands/Divisions/Affiliations:

Brand names, operating divisions or subsidiaries of the firm, as well as major corporate affiliations—such as another firm that owns a significant portion of the company's stock. A complete Index by Subsidiaries, Brand Names and Selected Affiliations is in the back of the book.

Contacts:

The names and titles up to 27 top officers of the company are listed, including human resources contacts.

Address:

The firm's full headquarters address, the headquarters telephone, plus toll-free and fax numbers where available. Also provided is the Internet site address.

Financials:

Annual Sales (2010, the latest fiscal year available to the editors, plus up to four previous years): These are stated in thousands of dollars (add three zeros if you want the full number). This figure represents consolidated worldwide sales from all operations. These numbers may be estimates.

Annual Profits (2010, the latest fiscal year available to the editors, plus up to four previous years): These are stated in thousands of dollars (add three zeros if you want the full number). This figure represents consolidated, after-tax net profit from all operations. These numbers may be estimates.

Stock Ticker/Parent Company: When available, the unique stock market symbol used to identify this firm's common stock for trading and tracking purposes is indicated. Where appropriate, this field may contain "private" or "subsidiary" rather than a ticker symbol. If the firm is a subsidiary, its parent company is listed.

Total Number of Employees: The approximate total number of employees, worldwide, as of the end of 2010, or the latest data available to the editors).

Apparent Salaries/Benefits:

(The following descriptions generally apply to U.S. employers only.)

A "Y" in appropriate fields indicates "Yes."

Due to wide variations in the manner in which corporations report benefits to the U.S. Government's regulatory bodies, not all plans will have been uncovered or correctly evaluated during our effort to research this data. Also, the availability to employees of such plans will vary according to the qualifications that employees must meet to become eligible. For example, some benefit plans may be available only to salaried workers—others only to employees who work more than 1,000 hours yearly. Benefits that are available to employees of the main or parent company may not be available to employees of the subsidiaries. In addition, employers frequently alter the nature and terms of plans offered.

NOTE: Generally, employees covered by wealth-building benefit plans do not *fully* own ("vest in") funds contributed on their behalf by the employer until as many as five years of service with that employer have passed. All pension plans are voluntary—that is, employers are not obligated to offer pensions.

Pension Plan: The firm offers a pension plan to qualified employees. In this case, in order for a "Y" to appear, the editors believe that the employer offers a defined benefit or cash balance pension plan (see discussions below). The type and generosity of these plans vary widely from firm to firm. Caution: Some employers refer to plans as "pension" or "retirement" plans when they are actually 401(k) savings plans that require a contribution by the employee.

- Defined Benefit Pension Plans: Pension plans that do not require a contribution from the employee are infrequently offered. However, a few companies, particularly larger employers in high-profit-margin industries, offer defined benefit pension plans where the employee is guaranteed to receive a set pension benefit upon retirement. The amount of the benefit is determined by the years of service with the company and the employee's salary during the later years of employment. The longer a person works for the employer, the higher the retirement benefit. These defined benefit plans are funded entirely by the employer. The benefits, up to a reasonable limit, are guaranteed by the Federal Government's Pension Benefit Guaranty Corporation. These plans are not portable—if you leave the company, you cannot transfer your benefits into a different plan. Instead, upon retirement you will receive the benefits that vested during your service with the company. If your employer offers a pension plan, it must give you a summary plan description within 90 days of the date you join the plan. You can also request a summary annual report of the plan, and once every 12 months you may request an individual benefit statement accounting of your interest in the plan.

- Defined Contribution Plans: These are quite different. They do not guarantee a certain amount of pension benefit. Instead, they set out circumstances under which the employer will make a contribution to a plan on your behalf. The most common example is the 401(k) savings plan. Pension benefits are not guaranteed under these plans.
- Cash Balance Pension Plans: These plans were recently invented. These are hybrid plans—part defined benefit and part defined contribution. Many employers have converted their older defined benefit plans into cash balance plans. The employer makes deposits (or credits a given amount of money) on the employee's behalf, usually based on a percentage of pay. Employee accounts grow based on a predetermined interest benchmark, such as the interest rate on Treasury Bonds. There are some advantages to these plans, particularly for younger workers: a) The benefits, up to a reasonable limit, are guaranteed by the Pension Benefit Guaranty Corporation. b) Benefits are portable—they can be moved to another plan when the employee changes companies. c) Younger workers and those who spend a shorter number of years with an employer may receive higher benefits than they would under a traditional defined benefit plan.

ESOP Stock Plan (Employees' Stock Ownership Plan): This type of plan is in wide use. Typically, the plan borrows money from a bank and uses those funds to purchase a large block of the corporation's stock. The corporation makes contributions to the plan over a period of time, and the stock purchase loan is eventually paid off. The value of the plan grows significantly as long as the market price of the stock holds up. Qualified employees are allocated a share of the plan based on their length of service and their level of salary. Under federal regulations, participants in ESOPs are allowed to diversify their account holdings in set percentages that rise as the employee ages and gains years of service with the company. In this manner, not all of the employee's assets are tied up in the employer's stock.

Savings Plan, 401(k): Under this type of plan, employees make a tax-deferred deposit into an account. In the best plans, the company makes annual matching donations to the employees' accounts, typically in some proportion to deposits made by the employees themselves. A good plan will match one-half of employee deposits of up to 6% of wages. For example, an employee earning $30,000 yearly might deposit $1,800 (6%) into the plan. The company will match one-half of the employee's deposit, or $900. The plan grows on a tax-deferred basis, similar to an IRA. A very generous plan will match 100% of employee deposits. However, some plans do not call for the employer to make a matching deposit at all. Other plans call for a matching contribution to be made at the discretion of the firm's board of directors. Actual terms of these plans vary widely from firm to firm. Generally, these savings plans allow employees to deposit as much as 15% of salary into the plan on a tax-deferred basis. However, the portion that the company uses to calculate its matching deposit is generally limited to a maximum of 6%. Employees should take care to diversify the holdings in their 401(k) accounts, and most people should seek professional guidance or investment management for their accounts.

Stock Purchase Plan: Qualified employees may purchase the company's common stock at a price below its market value under a specific plan. Typically, the employee is limited to investing a small percentage of wages in this plan. The discount may range from 5 to 15%. Some of these plans allow for deposits to be made through regular monthly payroll deductions. However, new accounting rules for corporations, along with other factors, are leading many companies to curtail these plans—dropping the discount allowed, cutting the maximum yearly stock purchase or otherwise making the plans less generous or appealing.

Profit Sharing: Qualified employees are awarded an annual amount equal to some portion of a company's profits. In a very generous plan, the pool of money awarded to employees would be 15% of profits. Typically, this money is deposited into a long-term retirement account. Caution: Some employers refer to plans as "profit sharing" when they are actually 401(k) savings plans. True profit sharing plans are rarely offered.

Highest Executive Salary: The highest executive salary paid, typically a 2010 amount (or the latest year available to the editors) and typically paid to the Chief Executive Officer.

Highest Executive Bonus: The apparent bonus, if any, paid to the above person.

Second Highest Executive Salary: The next-highest executive salary paid, typically a 2010 amount (or the latest year available to the editors) and typically paid to the President or Chief Operating Officer.

Second Highest Executive Bonus: The apparent bonus, if any, paid to the above person.

Other Thoughts:

Apparent Women Officers or Directors: It is difficult to obtain this information on an exact basis, and employers generally do not disclose the data in a public way. However, we have indicated what our best efforts reveal to be the apparent number of women who either are in the posts of corporate officers or sit on the board of directors. There is a wide variance from company to company.

Hot Spot for Advancement for Women/Minorities: A "Y" in appropriate fields indicates "Yes." These are firms that appear either to have posted a substantial number of women and/or minorities to high posts or that appear to have a good record of going out of their way to recruit, train, promote and retain women or minorities. (See the Index of Hot Spots For Women and Minorities in the back of the book.) This information may change frequently and can be difficult to obtain and verify. Consequently, the reader should use caution and conduct further investigation where appropriate.

Growth Plans/ Special Features:

Listed here are observations regarding the firm's strategy, hiring plans, plans for growth and product development, along with general information regarding a company's business and prospects.

Locations:

A "Y" in the appropriate field indicates "Yes."

Primary locations outside of the headquarters, categorized by regions of the United States and by international locations. A complete index by locations is also in the front of this chapter.

Chapter 1

MAJOR TRENDS AFFECTING JOB SEEKERS

Major trends sweeping through business and the economy that affect job seekers of all types:

1) U.S. Job Market Overview
2) Cost Control is a Major Concern at Employers/ Downsizing and Consolidation Through Mergers Continue
3) Unemployment Will Remain High, But Opportunities are Available to Diligent Job Seekers
4) Consumers Spend Less, Save More, Affecting a Wide Variety of Companies
5) Technology Continues to Create Sweeping Changes in the Workplace
6) Continued Growth in Outsourcing, Including Supply Chain and Logistics Services
7) Millions Working as Temps
8) Offshoring and the Globalization of Business
9) Older Americans Will Delay Retirement and Work Longer/Many Employers Find Older Employees Desirable
10) Employment Sectors that Will Offer an Above-Average Number of Job Opportunities in 2012:

- Biotechnology
- Consulting
- Consumer Products
- Cosmetics
- Cruise Lines
- Data Processing Services
- Elder Care, Home Health Care, Nursing Homes and Assisted Living Communities
- Electronic Games, Games for Cell Phones
- Energy Conservation Products and Services
- Food Processing
- Health Care Services
- Health Care Products
- Health Care Technology, Including Computerized Patient Records
- Health Foods, Organic Foods, Enhanced Foods
- Hotels
- Insurance
- Internet Services, Server Hosting, Cloud Computing
- Nanotechnology and MEMS Technologies
- Oil & Gas Exploration and Production
- Oil & Gas Field Services and Technologies
- Online Search Services with Advertising Revenues
- Online-based Business and Consumer Services including Social Media and Software-as-a-Service
- Outsourcing, Including Outsourced Business and Computer Services
- Pharmaceuticals—Generics
- Radio Frequency ID Tags (RFID)
- Restaurants
- Retailing—Basic, Including Drugstores and Supermarkets
- Retailing—Discount and Warehouse Clubs
- Software—Corporate
- Software—Predictive Analytics
- Supply Chain Services That Create Cost-Savings
- Water Filtration and Conservation Equipment
- Wireless and Cellular Communications
- Wireless—Remote Wireless Sensors and Networks

1) U.S. Job Market Overview

Job seekers in 2012 will continue to face a difficult job market, although a higher level of hiring may begin if the economy is stable. Many types of employers restructured and downsized thanks to the deep financial crisis of 2007-09. By 2011, most employers had pushed productivity about as far as they can, and future growth in business will require more employees. That brings up a big question: when, how and where will businesses begin to grow again? Meanwhile, job seekers who want good positions will be forced to be better prepared and to do better research than in the boom years that ended in 2007. They will also have to work harder to find good jobs. The fact remains that there are millions of Americans either out of work or underemployed. Competition for job openings will remain fierce. For example, Southwest Airlines reported that it received 143,143 resumes during 2010 while hiring only 2,188 new employees.

Job seekers in 2012 should be prepared for the fact that nearly all industry sectors suffered ill effects from economic and financial market problems that originated when the housing bubble finally popped in mid-2007 and the financial meltdown accelerated in 2008 and early 2009. America's unemployment level will remain disturbingly high for some time to come.

The good news is that a select set of employers and growth companies will offer good job opportunities. In this period of challenges, a few companies will enjoy booming business. Sectors such as cloud computing and health care will continue to grow and hire. A few companies with exciting new technologies or cost-saving services will see terrific growth. Salesforce.com, a highly innovative provider of online business services, is a good example.

Solid companies that do a terrific job of providing the day-to-day needs of consumers and business will continue to hire—Costco, Amazon.com and Southwest Airlines are good examples. Other industry sectors that fall into this category include insurance firms such as USAA and GEICO along with electric and gas utilities.

Oil and gas exploration and production will continue to be a bright spot for hiring, even if oil prices decline somewhat. Oil field services firm Halliburton recently announced plans to hire 11,000 people, largely to work in America's rapidly expanding shale oil and gas fields. The development of vast new shale oil and shale gas areas in dozens of states is opening up excellent job opportunities, fueling growth at providers of related services and supplies, and encouraging business investment of many kinds. At the same time, this new supply of oil and gas is holding down market prices, providing relief to consumers' budgets.

Other firms will hire only limited numbers of employees, while some will downsize. Many companies that specialize in the manufacture or sale of luxury items have learned to adapt to two big changes. First, many companies have changed their strategies in order to offer a range of products with luxury features that include items with lower price points. Next, companies like Tiffany and Coach have successfully increased their sales of luxury items in emerging markets such as China.

Growing numbers of consumers will prefer to buy from firms that sell goods and services online, offering savings of time, money and car travel. This boosts companies like Amazon.com that offer low prices combined with deep selections and great customer service. Virtually all major retailers, including giants like Wal-Mart and Home Depot, are working hard to provide better online services and choices to their customers.

The travel industry has stabilized to a large degree. Airlines are in better financial shape than they were two and three years ago. Hotels are enjoying higher occupancy rates. Travel firms that do best will be those that have everyday low prices, like JetBlue, along with those that offer all-inclusive prices that seem like bargains, such as popular cruise lines such as Carnival. In fact, the cruise industry did quite well through the recession, and it is likely to create many jobs over the near future as a large number of new ships continue to enter the fleet. Meanwhile, travel has become the single most successful sector at selling products and services via the Internet.

The automobile sector has stabilized, but it now operates at much lower volume than it enjoyed during the boom. New cars have been selling relatively well in recent months, and hiring may be strong at car dealers and car manufacturers alike.

Residential real estate remains very depressed. Homeowners may make repairs or do light remodeling rather than move up to larger homes. The massive number of unsold homes on the market will continue to put a serious damper on the real estate and construction sectors in 2012.

Banking companies will continue to be challenged, and some, like Bank of America, will have lay offs.

Americans who find themselves in the market for a job will need to understand the changes surging through the economy in order to determine which companies to pursue and which to avoid. The U.S. employment market has evolved dramatically, and job seekers must be both knowledgeable and nimble in order to position themselves to find promising careers.

In order to create a robust job market, corporate investment, profits, productivity and revenues must align themselves correctly. These economic indicators were positive during the 2003 to mid-2007 period, and millions of new American jobs were created. As 2007 was winding down, the residential real estate crash, high levels of consumer debt and difficult credit markets were combining to restrain the economy. Millions of workers were laid off, and hiring slowed to a trickle. Unfortunately, 2008-2009 saw these problems spread throughout most U.S. business sectors. The banking, investment, retailing and automobile sectors were under extreme stress, and many major bankruptcies ensued.

One of the results of this tough recession was a new emphasis on increased productivity and cost-effectiveness at employers of most types. Direct results included reduced spending, investment and hiring, and in many cases layoffs.

In 2012, executives will be under the usual pressure to maintain profitability. If the economy begins to improve, they may also start to see some signs of potential growth in selected business sectors, which would encourage hiring. However, better economic conditions may not appear any time soon. Meanwhile, many major corporations are sitting on huge piles of cash. When CEOs become more confident about the future, that cash could fuel job-creating investments. The bottom line: new grads will find it difficult to land their dream jobs, and job seekers of many types will continue to be challenged to find appropriate positions. Nonetheless, there will still be job opportunities for those who are diligent in seeking good employers in stronger business sectors.

Economic Factors Affecting the Job Market

Business Productivity: Productivity has been rising in recent years. That is, business can be produced—whether it is goods or services—by utilizing fewer workers than before. This will be extremely beneficial to the U.S. economy in the long run, but it can hurt the job market over the short term. Productivity is boosted by new technologies, improved management methods and other factors, sometimes as simple as reorganizing the staff and redesigning the workflow to increase output. It can also receive a quick boost from restrained corporate hiring. If rising productivity occurs along with rapidly rising sales and profits, then the job market will improve.

Corporate Sales: A trend of rising sales encourages hiring. The rapid drop in sales at businesses of nearly all types in 2008-2009 caused employers to slash head count. During 2010-2011, the trend was toward somewhat higher sales in most sectors. Reasonable sales growth in 2012 could lead to slightly increased hiring. It remains to be seen whether this will occur.

Corporate Profits: When profits increase sharply, companies are inclined to increase both business investment and hiring. Profitability took a deep downturn in 2008. Many employers were able to post reasonable profits during 2009, but this was generally the result of deep cuts in spending and hiring. The job market suffered as a result. Growth in profits was exceptionally high during 2010 and much of 2011. However, this profitability was often the result of improved business overseas, restrained spending, or both. Hiring will rebound when corporate sales, and accompanying profits, show significant growth, encouraging executives to forecast an extended period of increased demand for their products and services.

In order to compete effectively in today's job market, one of the most important things you can do is arm yourself with knowledge. It is vital for the job seeker to use the best reference tools possible in order to seek out employers that offer a reasonable balance of financial stability, opportunities for advancement and good pay. Excellent job opportunities always exist if you know where to look. Many of America's most successful firms currently need large numbers of new employees.

Thousands of companies, in technical and non-technical sectors, will need large numbers of new hires. In particular, companies that offer products or services that save time and/or money will prosper—for example, many types of companies that offer services that help businesses operate more efficiently, will be hiring. Meanwhile, large companies that are not increasing their overall numbers of employees will be hiring on a regular basis due to normal attrition—that is, the loss of employees due to retirement, relocation or other personal circumstances. For example, massive companies like Walgreen's or Kroger typically need to hire tens of thousands of workers yearly due to normal attrition.

2) Cost Control is a Major Concern at Employers/Downsizing and Consolidation Through Mergers Continue

For most firms during the current, difficult economic environment, executives have been focusing on cost control as a means to maintain profits and financial stability. Throughout the world of business and industry, expenses of virtually all types have been the focus of cuts or better management, from travel budgets to advertising to investments in equipment. Employee costs have been targeted as well. This means that hiring has been restrained at best, since the economic crisis began in late 2007, while many companies have announced big layoffs. Others have cut work hours or even cut pay rates.

Often, companies have merged with others in order to seek operating efficiencies or gain access to needed capital. By 2010, financing was once again available for large corporate mergers and acquisitions, and the number of mergers announced during 2011 was high. This may continue into 2012. A consolidation of companies via a merger may enable the firms to combine customer bases, administrative staff, sales offices and production facilities, while cutting employees who hold duplicated jobs, in hopes of thereby creating more efficient, more profitable firms. These employee reductions often number in the thousands. Mergers may be spurred by economic difficulties and falling profits, or they may involve large firms seeking to acquire companies that have the potential to boost growth and accelerate profits. For example, extreme duress in the home construction market in 2007-2009 instigated the merger of two massive construction firms, Centex and Pulte. On the other hand, prosperous software giant Oracle has been on a buying spree, acquiring companies that it feels will boost Oracle's own growth.

Because they face tough, global competition, manufacturing firms are frequently involved in such mergers. Good jobs in the U.S. manufacturing sector can still be found, despite intense competition from manufacturers in China and other offshore markets. Factories are running with fewer people thanks to immense investments in technology. Output per employee is up spectacularly over the past few decades—to the extent that millions of manufacturing jobs were lost due to a in productivity. In addition, fewer employees are needed to manage non-production functions, such as logistics, administration and marketing. Of course, some American manufacturing industries have been in deep, long term decline, particularly the automobile and textile industries.

Meanwhile, some of the loss in manufacturing employment has been exaggerated by the fact that firms now outsource a good deal of their non-manufacturing operations to services companies. For example, many computer departments, company cafeterias, distribution centers and engineering needs are now outsourced to outside companies that specialize in such work, thus dramatically reducing the number of in-house jobs at manufacturing firms. This is the long term trend of outsourcing in action.

Another extremely important factor in the loss of U.S. manufacturing jobs is the movement of production to foreign nations where costs are often much lower.

Also, companies in both manufacturing and service sectors have caught on to management by teams, vastly enhanced supply chain technology (such as the use of the Internet for ordering and tracking components), along with networked management, distribution and manufacturing systems, which all add up to the fact that fewer mid-management, white-collar types are needed to communicate with the people doing the day-to-day work. Production workers have been encouraged to communicate among themselves. In many cases, workers are taking on unprecedented responsibilities, setting their own goals and schedules, tracking costs and output, thereby boosting profits. Historically, these were the tasks of middle managers. Today, vast numbers of those management jobs have been eliminated.

Businesses without factories are also undergoing re-engineering and leaps in productivity. For example, by upgrading software and linking desktop computers to central databases, a major U.S. insurance firm was able to go from 3,000 employees issuing new policies to only 700. At the same time, it was able to reduce the time necessary to write a new policy from 15 days to only five. Customers applying for insurance policies today are likely to do so online, thus automating the process and reducing the need for employees. Today's corporations are searching hard for innovative ways to get more work done with fewer people. Using online methods is a foundation of this trend.

3) Unemployment Will Remain High, But Opportunities Are Available to Diligent Job Seekers

If you are looking for a job, you might as well face the fact that 2012's employment market will be challenging. Employers will be cautious about hiring new people or investing in new facilities until a reasonable level of confidence in the future emerges.

The U.S. unemployment rate in August 2007 was down to 4.6%. By August 2008, the unemployment rate shot up to 6.1%, and it reached 7.6% in early 2009. By the end of 2009, unemployment had soared to 10%, and 8 million jobs were eliminated during the Great Recession. The job market will take years to recover fully. Nonetheless, many job seekers will be able to find satisfying jobs if they apply themselves to the job hunt, make sure their resumes and self-marketing skills are in superb shape, network effectively and do thorough research. The number of people applying for each job opening is very high. Consequently, it is vital for a job seeker to understand how to best apply for a job online, how to conduct research that will help him or her to shine during an interview and how to create an effective list of prospective employers.

It is also important for job seekers to face the fact that locale has a lot to do with the unemployment rate. Today's dim real estate market exaggerates that factor. That is, one of the reasons that unemployment is so high is that the currently dismal market for homes makes it much more difficult for a job seeker to sell a house in one city in order to relocate to another city for a new job. Meanwhile, there is wide variance in the unemployment rate from state to state and city to city. For example, in August 2011, America's national average unemployment rate was 9.1%. However, it was dramatically higher in many states, including two that were among the hardest hit by the real estate collapse: Florida at 10.7% unemployment and California at 12.1%. Meanwhile, some states have vastly lower unemployment rates, including Nebraska at 4.2%, South Dakota at 4.7% and Louisiana at 7.2%. Job seekers living in states with the lowest unemployment rates are going to face much less competition when applying for job openings.

Internet Research Tip:
The latest rankings of states by unemployment rate can be found at the Bureau of Labor Statistics, www.bls.gov.

4) Consumers Spend Less, Save More, Affecting a Wide Variety of Companies

After piling on debt, running up their credit cards, signing mountains of mortgages and buying new cars at a soaring rate from 2002 through 2007, consumers have completely reversed course. Personal savings rates are much higher. Consumer debt has declined. House sales are dismal, and millions of people continue to face foreclosure on home mortgages. Saving money is in; spending money is out. Welcome to a new era of reduced personal circumstances, increased frugality and worried consumers. Even people with high, steady incomes are spending less. The financial crisis, high levels of consumer debt, high unemployment rates and uncertainty have put the brakes on conspicuous consumption.

While increased personal savings and lower debt levels will be very good for America over the long run, it is a difficult adjustment for the nation to make, and, for the near term at least, it puts a damper on the job market.

These changes have been tough on manufacturers, distributors, personal services providers, transportation companies and retailers alike. In sum, this means that many employers have not only been unable to hire new people, they have cut both work hours and total staff counts.

Smart job seekers will be aware that today's frugal consumer is not a short-term change. It is going to take years for consumers to pay down debts and rebuild personal savings. Hopefully, the housing market will be stabilizing during this period. The end result should be a new era of economic growth, but it will be a lengthy recovery in the meantime. The most successful employers will be those that provide lasting value, low prices, good service, cost-saving strategies and innovative technologies. Excellent examples are Wal-Mart (low prices), Costco (good service and low prices), Amazon (innovative use of technology to provide convenience and cost-savings), travel firms like JetBlue and Carnival Cruise Lines (good service, low prices, high value) and car makers like Honda, Kia and Hundai (lasting value, low prices).

5) Technology Continues to Create Sweeping Changes in the Workplace

Technology has introduced vast changes throughout industries of all types, greatly boosting productivity and reallocating (or eliminating) workers. A major cause of change for employees, and therefore job seekers, is the tidal wave of new technologies that continues to revolutionize the workplace at all levels. Prospering companies are using new technologies to communicate with customers, automate back-office tasks and industrial operations, and push ahead with research and development. There is a never-ending stream of technological innovation. For example, employers have already harnessed the power of networked desktop computers. Today, they are rapidly adopting the use of mobile computing devices such as tablets, Internet-based telephone systems (VOIP and unified communication systems), cloud computing and video conferencing technologies.

The trend of using new practices and technologies while cutting layers of management is largely about communication. This is true whether it is communication between the top offices and the factory floor, communication with customers, communication between the computers in one corporate office with those in another, or communication from desk-to-desk and office-to-office in massive service businesses.

These new technologies mean continuous retraining for much of the workforce. Job seekers who want the best posts must have the training and skills that will let them utilize new technologies effectively. Even in today's era of high unemployment, hundreds of thousands of jobs are remaining unfilled at many companies because of a shortage of technically qualified people. Workforce development is a critical need nationwide.

Jobs in America are shifting to new categories of work based on technologies that didn't exist 20 and 30 years ago. For example, the job title "webmaster" was coined in the 1990s to describe the employee in charge of a firm's Internet sites and intranet operations. Services firms, as well as manufacturers, are placing more and more employees in recently created technical and service positions, while many of the tasks once performed in-house are now provided by outsourced services providers. In the telecommunications industry, digital technology has completely changed the list of job titles while enabling phone service providers to reduce the ratio of employees to customers. In the meantime, hundreds of thousands of jobs have been created at cellular telephone companies. Now, Internet-based telephony, competition from cable providers, fiber to the premises and wireless networks such as Wi-Fi and LTE continue to force telecommunications firms to evolve.

Another excellent example: Retailing, shipping and warehousing are about to see a technology revolution due to the introduction of Radio Frequency Identification Tags (RFID). This breakthrough in inventory management is based on the placement of microchips in product packaging, combined with the use of special sensors in stores and warehouses that alert a central inventory management system of product purchases and the need to restock inventory. From loading docks to shelves to cash registers to parking lots, radio frequency readers will eventually track the movement of each pallet or individual item. Many bar codes will eventually be replaced by RFIDs, with electronic product codes stored on these microchips. The chips can even eliminate the need to scan each item at checkout. Checkout stations will be equipped with readers that automatically calculate purchases. Benefits can include less shoplifting and few inventory errors. Another benefit is that firms will be able to reduce overall inventory thanks to better tracking.

As online ordering, tracking and inventory management continue to become more sophisticated and cost-effective, purchasing executives at firms of all types and sizes will accelerate the use of Internet-based systems for management of their supply chains. There are significant opportunities here for e-commerce services and software companies. Likewise, there is great promise for third-party logistics (3PL) companies that combine the power of Internet-based information with strategically located warehouses to fulfill the inventory needs of manufacturers.

6) Continued Growth in Outsourcing, Including Supply Chain and Logistics Services

Part of the re-engineering process at employers has been a boom in "outsourcing," or the use of outside specialty firms to do chores that firms formerly performed through in-house departments. For example, Pitney Bowes takes over the mailrooms, desktop printers and copiers at major corporations. As part of this turnkey service, Pitney

Bowes supplies its own copiers and desktop printers, and then buys toner and paper by the truckload at the best possible price. It trains its employees to keep track of every single copy so its clients can control costs. Copy department employees are transferred from the client firm to Pitney Bowes, the outsourcing firm. There, these employees learn that the head of a Pitney Bowes' copy department can rise to be a regional manager, a vice president or an even higher position within the company. The client firm's costs are lowered and its profits increase. The outsourcing provider makes a tidy profit through its focused expertise. Xerox offers similar services, to the extent that providing services, instead of selling copiers, is now the major part of this firm's business.

One of the largest fields of outsourcing growth has long been in computer departments. IBM, Accenture and Hewlett-Packard (HP) are among the global leaders in this area. However, many other business functions are commonly outsourced. ServiceMaster takes over janitorial tasks, building management and maintenance functions for giant corporate office campuses and industrial facilities. Another company outsources all of the food warehousing and distribution for nationwide restaurant chains. Why? Because it can run trucks and warehouses more efficiently while its clients concentrate on running restaurants.

While the 1960s, '70s and '80s saw many firms frantically trying to do all tasks in-house, recent trends are quite different. As a period noted for rising productivity and efficiency, the 1990s and 2000s combined were an era of specialization and focus. Companies may do a better job by focusing on their core tasks, while allowing outside firms to provide support and maintenance needs. That trend will continue to be powerful over the long term. Outsourcing, which rapidly gained popularity, will persist in leading the way to higher efficiency and profits. Many outsourced services companies continue to grow, and they will create (and displace) large numbers of jobs.

Some companies combine outsourcing services with temporary workers. Spherion, a major temporary help firm and one of America's largest employers, is also a leading outsourcing company. Spherion's outsourcing division takes over all human resources administration functions for large clients. This means that Spherion's employees do all of the recruiting, employee records management, benefits management and so on for its client companies. This is a logical extension of Spherion's human resources expertise and good cross-marketing to its roster of corporate clients.

One of the fastest-growing fields in outsourcing has been supply chain and logistics management. Companies offering services in this field include giant transportation companies like UPS. "Supply chain" refers to the entire set of providers of supplies and services that are involved in creating and delivering a component or end product. For example, for an automobile manufacturer like Ford, the supply chain includes companies that make tires, batteries, interior components and engine parts, as well as the trucks and trains that ship these parts and the warehouses that hold them. This supply chain supports Ford's own manufacturing and assembly plants. At the end of Ford's business chain lie the automobile dealers that receive completed cars and deliver them to the end customers. Another example: For a clothing store chain like The Gap, the supply chain includes clothing designers, clothing manufacturers and the warehouses and transportation systems that deliver completed clothes to the stores. The Gap's supply chain is located across dozens of nations.

Logistics is the art of moving goods through the supply chain. Supply chains are so complex and so critical to a company's operations that there are countless ways to automate, improve efficiencies and cut costs. Many manufacturers and retailers are outsourcing all or part of their logistics needs to firms that specialize in creating efficiencies and saving costs. Logistics and supply chain companies have been growing rapidly over the past several years, and creating large numbers of jobs. A concept you should be familiar with is Third Party Logistics ("3PL"), a system whereby a specialist firm in logistics provides a variety of transportation, warehousing and logistics-related services to its clients. These tasks were previously performed in-house by the client. When 3PL services are provided within the client's own facilities, it can also be referred to as "Insourcing." In other words, you might find yourself working for UPS at a site within a distribution company that has no other ties to UPS.

7) Millions Working as Temps

More and more, major firms are using temporary workers to fill short-term needs, thereby cutting overall employment costs, since temps usually do not receive extensive benefits, bonuses or training. In addition to employees who are placed in temporary jobs by agencies, there are millions of people employed as "independent contractors" and "contract workers." Temporary staffing companies operate offices throughout the U.S., in cities small and large. To a growing extent, they hire and place workers via their sophisticated Internet sites.

The largest temporary help agencies tend to have vast global operations. Adecco is a Swiss staffing firm with extensive operations in the U.S., Europe and elsewhere, employing hundreds of thousands of people. Manpower, based in the U.S., does a major part of its business in dozens of nations worldwide.

Demand for temporary workers slows dramatically during economic downturns. The use of temps enables employers to increase the workforce quickly when orders from customers increase, and reduce the workforce rapidly when sales decrease. Temporary workers are also an extremely efficient way to meet needs for one-time projects, fill the slots of permanent employees who are on leave and screen potential candidates for full-time positions by first hiring them on a temporary basis.

In addition, some Americans prefer to work as temporary employees, feeling that this gives them more flexibility in their working lives. Unfortunately, many other people who end up working in temporary positions would greatly prefer to be employed full-time. Many of these workers have significant experience as well as college degrees. A large percentage of temps work in professional specialties, such as law, finance, engineering or accounting. Also, the number of information technology temps has increased dramatically in the past several years.

> ***Internet Research Tip:***
> For data on the temporary staffing industry and the temporary workforce in the U.S., see the American Staffing Association (www.americanstaffing.net).

8) Offshoring and the Globalization of Business

Competition from workers in such nations as Mexico, Indonesia, Thailand, and, in particular, China, means that fewer pure manufacturing jobs will be available in the U.S., where pay is high and employee benefit costs are immense compared to those of competing nations. In fact, the costs of Social Security taxes, Medicare taxes, employer-sponsored health care, vacations, holidays, retirement plans and other benefits have risen so high (an amount typically equal to 38% to 45% of wages) that they provide considerable incentive for firms to hold down the number of employees working in U.S. locations. Instead, companies are utilizing workers in other nations. Depending on their experience and job title, a typical factory worker in China may earn only $300 monthly for long hours of hard work. These employees often receive dormitory-style housing and cafeteria meals as well. Otherwise, employee benefit costs are nominal.

While lower employee pay is a factor in some offshoring, proximity to growing foreign markets is another. Giant multinational companies ranging from IBM to Kraft to General Motors find that a vast portion of their business now lies overseas, often in the rapidly-growing, emerging nations that offer lower operating costs. Many of the world's largest companies find that they need to have local operations throughout much of the world.

"Offshoring" is the word used to describe the movement of jobs of all types away from industrialized nations, like America, to less developed countries, like India, the Philippines, Indonesia and China. For example, U.S. financial services companies are sending hundreds of thousands of jobs overseas to India and the Philippines, in such areas as call centers and financial analysis. Moving jobs to other nations poses serious job displacement problems in the U.S. (At the same time, there is a positive factor to the growth of these emerging economies: Increased exports of U.S. goods and services of all types are creating jobs and profits in America.)

Globalization has a profound effect on Americans—consumer prices become lower, while the U.S. job market changes considerably. Consumer goods are quite inexpensive due to the vast variety of items the U.S. imports from other nations, and prices for many categories of these goods have declined dramatically. Americans can purchase consumer electronics like DVD players and color televisions at extremely low prices, and the price of many types of apparel is much lower thanks to globalization. For example, over 90% of the shoes sold in America are manufactured in low cost nations, especially China.

More than ever before, the world is one vast marketplace. Globalization of business supply chains is a strong trend today and will grow even stronger in the future. Consider the rapid globalization of the automobile industry. The entire global automobile sector is dominated by only a handful of companies, including Toyota, GM, Ford, Daimler, Honda, Volkswagen and Nissan, as well as the increasingly successful Korean automakers Kia and Hyundai. Car manufacturers in China are growing more dominant as well. Car manufacturers commonly have engineering teams collaborating from offices in multiple nations, while parts and components may be imported from a wide variety of suppliers in various countries to undergo final assembly at home.

American companies in many industry sectors have been merging and consolidating on a global basis at a rapid clip. That consolidation will continue. One benefit is that U.S. firms can enter into foreign markets through international acquisitions.

Trade is not necessarily always stable. While global economies are undeniably linked, they do not march hand-in-hand. The nose-dive taken by many Asian economies in the late 1990s occurred during one of the biggest economic booms in U.S. history. The strength of America as a consumer market was a platform that helped to stabilize and regenerate Asian businesses that were having difficulties. Likewise, China's economic stimulus during the economic crisis of 2007-2009 helped to boost business in many nations that were undergoing difficult national recessions.

U.S. firms hold leadership positions in several key product and service sectors vital to the rest of the world, including health technology, computers, e-commerce, software and entertainment of all types. The message is clear: global trade and export markets are extremely vital to the health of American business and industry. A study of 2006 results showed that U.S. corporations listed in the Standard & Poor's 500 created, on average, 49% of their revenues from foreign nations, up from 30% in 2001.

A growing middle class in India, China and other emerging nations has been creating demand for goods exported from the U.S., including consumer products bearing desirable brands, as well as luxury automobiles. Also, U.S.-based firms have been enjoying great success in franchising and licensing their methods to startup businesses in China, India and elsewhere, in everything from hotels to fast food to services. American brands such as Nike and Buick are big sellers in China.

Meanwhile, the U.S. is also exporting its newfound expertise in the booming superstore and discount retailing sectors. For instance, hundreds of Wal-Mart's stores are in foreign locations such as Argentina, Brazil, Canada, China,

Korea, Mexico, and the U.K., and Wal-Mart is entering India in a big way through a joint venture. Eventually, Wal-Mart may bring its brand of retailing to virtually all of the world's major markets.

9) Older Americans Will Delay Retirement and Work Longer/Many Employers Find Older Employees Desirable

Certain large employers, particularly national retail chains, have discovered that older workers provide a terrific pool of potential employees. This may be positive for older workers, but to younger job seekers it means more competition for work.

While 2006 marked the year that the first Baby Boomers turned 60, many members of this immense generation are not planning to retire any time soon. The job market has been made more difficult by the fact that many of America's workers who want to retire will be reluctant (or unable) to do so, because the value of their investments in real estate, stocks, bonds or pension plans is down considerably from the levels they saw during the last boom, and these older workers lost confidence in financial markets at the same time that they lost retirement dollars. Some would-be retirees will be working much later in life than they had planned. This trend is also accelerated by the fact that today's senior citizens will enjoy much longer life spans than earlier generations. Many will continue to work simply because they want to remain active, contributing members of society.

The phrase "Baby Boomer" generally refers to the 78 million Americans born from 1946 to 1964. The term evolved to describe the children of soldiers and war industry workers who were involved in World War II. When those veterans and workers returned to civilian life, they started or added to families in large numbers. As a result, this generation is one of the largest demographic segments in the U.S. Baby Boomers make up about 24% of the U.S. population.

Most recently, 2011 marked the year when millions began turning traditional retirement age (65). As Baby Boomers continue to age, America will be experiencing extremely rapid growth in the senior portion of the population. Many Baby Boomers will leave their traditional, long-term jobs and turn to part-time work. Others will continue in their full-time jobs as long as possible.

A survey released in June 2009 by the AARP (a non profit group that represents Americans who are 50 and older) found that 20% of the group's members said they were likely to work until they were in their 70s. 40% of couples surveyed said that one or both spouses will work part-time in retirement. In the first part of 2008, a Bureau of Labor Statistics survey found that 30% of people between the ages of 65 and 69 were either employed or seeking work. This trend is powerful enough that AARP publishes an annual list of "Best Employers for Workers over 50." The 2011 list included several health care firms, including Scripps Health, Kaiser Permanente and West Virginia University Hospitals.

By the early 2000s, many employers were already developing human resources strategies aimed at hiring or retaining older workers. On the lower end of the pay scale, retailers like Home Depot, a firm that has been known to need tens of thousands of new hires in one year, have found older people to be ideal employees. They have knowledge that is extremely useful for providing advice and service to shoppers. They are experienced workers who understand the need to show up on time. Wal-Mart has hundreds of thousands of employees age 55 or older.

On the higher end of the employment scale, older workers with long-term experience in scientific and engineering tasks will be vital in keeping the gears of business and industry turning. During the 2000s boom, when the airline industry saw good growth, rules were altered in the U.S. to enable commercial airline pilots to keep flying until age 65, instead of facing forced retirement at age 60 as they had in the past. A serious shortage of experienced pilots was averted. (Granted, airlines soon went into a tailspin during the Great Recession, along with the rest of the travel industry, and they mothballed a lot of airplanes while cutting the number of routes and flights. Nonetheless, older, experienced pilots will eventually be in high demand.) Heavy industry is an even better example. The National Science Foundation estimated that 38% of America's scientists and engineers were 50+ years old as of 2006. These older workers may not be good at creating the latest electronic games, but they are undeniably the people who have the experience and the knowledge necessary to successfully operate the laboratories, factories, refineries and legacy systems that keep industry humming. They are going to be extremely difficult to replace in America, because younger generations have been shunning degrees in science and engineering for softer disciplines. Energy industry firms like ExxonMobil, Halliburton and Schlumberger, and chemicals firms like global giant BASF, are dealing with this challenge along two lines: First, how to document and pass along the immense treasure of work-related knowledge that these employees have, and second, how to keep these employees interested in working later into their lives. BASF, a firm with about $90 billion in annual revenues and an employee base of 90,000 scattered around the world, estimates that by 2020, 50% or more of its employees will be 50 to 65 years old. It has implemented measures ranging from making the workplace more comfortable and safe for older workers, to an intense knowledge transfer program where older workers mentor younger staff members.

10) Employment Sectors that Will Offer an Above-Average Number of Job Opportunities in 2012

Job seekers should remain aware of the fact that certain industries will have above-average likelihood to offer job openings. This is due to a number of circumstances, including shifts in consumer tastes and requirements, normal employee turnover and attrition, structural changes within industries, global economic conditions and national policies and priorities.

Below is a list of industries particularly recommended to job seekers.

Employment Sectors that Will Offer an Above-Average Number of Job Opportunities in 2012:

- Biotechnology
- Consulting
- Consumer Products
- Cosmetics
- Cruise Lines
- Data Processing Services
- Elder Care, Home Health Care, Nursing Homes and Assisted Living Communities
- Electronic Games, Games for Cell Phones
- Energy Conservation Products and Services
- Food Processing
- Health Care Services
- Health Care Products
- Health Care Technology, Including Computerized Patient Records
- Health Foods, Organic Foods, Enhanced Foods
- Hotels
- Insurance
- Internet Services, Server Hosting, Cloud Computing
- Nanotechnology and MEMS Technologies
- Oil & Gas Exploration and Production
- Oil & Gas Field Services and Technologies
- Online Search Services with Advertising Revenues
- Online-based Business and Consumer Services including Social Media and Software-as-a-Service
- Outsourcing, Including Outsourced Business and Computer Services
- Pharmaceuticals—Generics
- Radio Frequency ID Tags (RFID)
- Restaurants
- Retailing—Basic, Including Drugstores and Supermarkets
- Retailing—Discount and Warehouse Clubs
- Software—Corporate
- Software—Predictive Analytics
- Supply Chain Services That Create Cost-Savings
- Water Filtration and Conservation Equipment
- Wireless and Cellular Communications
- Wireless—Remote Wireless Sensors and Networks

Chapter 2

STATISTICS

Contents:

U.S. Employment Overview: 2010-2011

(Labor Counts In Thousands; Seasonally Adjusted)

	Aug-10	Jan-11	Aug-11
Civilian Labor Force, Total	154,117	153,246	153,594
Employed	139,267	139,323	139,627
Unemployed	14,849	13,863	13,967
Persons 16 Years of Age and Over, Not in Labor Force	83,983	85,518	86,278
Unemployment Rate, All Workers	9.6%	9.0%	9.1%
Adult Men (20 years and over)	9.8%	8.8%	8.9%
Adult Women (20 years and over)	8.0%	7.9%	8.0%
Teenagers (16 to 19 years)	26.2%	25.7%	25.4%
White	8.7%	8.0%	8.0%
Black or African American	16.2%	15.7%	16.7%
Asian (not seasonally adjusted)	7.2%	6.9%	7.1%
Hispanic or Latino	12.1%	11.9%	11.3%
Average Hourly Earnings, Private Industry[P]	$22.67	$22.86	$23.09
Weekly Earnings, Private Industry[P]	$775.31	$781.81	$789.68
Average Work Week, Private Industry (Hours)[P]	34.2	34.2	34.2
Nonfarm Employment[P]	129,873	130,328	131,132
Goods-Producing	17,790	17,835	18,084
Construction	5,520	5,478	5,524
Manufacturing	11,551	11,618	11,757
Private Service-Providing	89,671	90,267	91,086
Retail Trade	14,413	14,478	14,569
Professional & Business Services	16,711	16,953	17,211
Education & Health Services	19,612	19,789	20,024
Leisure & Hospitality	13,051	13,071	13,216
Government	22,412	22,226	21,962

P = Preliminary figures (for August 2011).

Source: U.S. Bureau of Labor Statistics
Plunkett Research, Ltd.
www.plunkettresearch.com

U.S. Civilian Labor Force: 1997-August 2011

(Persons 16 & Older; In Thousands)

Year	Civilian Workforce Level
1997	136,297
1998	137,673
1999	139,368
2000	142,583
2001	143,734
2002	144,863
2003	146,510
2004	147,401
2005	149,320
2006	151,428
2007	153,124
2008	154,287
2009	154,142
2010	153,889
2011	153,594

* As of July; seasonally adjusted.

Source: U.S. Bureau of Labor Statistics
Plunkett Research, Ltd.
www.plunkettresearch.com

Number of People Employed and Unemployed, U.S.: August 2010 vs. August 2011

(Persons 16 & Older; In Thousands; Not Seasonally Adjusted)

Occupation	Employed		Unemployed		Unemp. Rates	
	Aug-10	Aug-11	Aug-10	Aug-11	Aug-10	Aug-11
Total*	**139,919**	**140,335**	**14,759**	**14,008**	**9.5**	**9.1**
Management, professional and related	50,879	51,997	2,762	2,671	5.1	4.9
Management, business and financial	20,741	21,632	1,067	1,037	4.9	4.6
Professional and related	30,138	30,365	1,695	1,634	5.3	5.1
Service	25,228	25,396	2,998	2,924	10.6	10.3
Sales and office	33,429	33,023	3,345	3,182	9.1	8.8
Sales and related	15,367	15,193	1,519	1,424	9	8.6
Office and administrative support	18,062	17,831	1,826	1,757	9.2	9
Natural resources, construction and maintenance	13,743	13,454	2,136	1,718	13.5	11.3
Farming, fishing and forestry	1,092	1,190	117	145	9.6	10.9
Construction and extraction	7,665	7,420	1,498	1,126	16.3	13.2
Installation, maintenance and repair	4,985	4,844	522	447	9.5	8.4
Production, transportation and material moving	16,640	16,464	2,046	2,077	10.9	11.2
Production	8,243	8,130	1,078	984	11.6	10.8
Transportation and material moving	8,397	8,334	968	1,093	10.3	11.6

* Persons with no previous work experience and persons whose last job was in the Armed Forces are included in the unemployed total. Updated population controls are introduced annually with the release of January data.

Note: The labor force includes all persons classified as employed or unemployed. Employed persons include persons 16 years and older in the civilian noninstitutional population who, during a reference week, (a) did any work at all (at least 1 hour) as paid employees, worked in their own business, profession, or on their own farm, or worked 15 hours or more as unpaid workers in an enterprise operated by a member of the family, and (b) all those who were not working but who had jobs or businesses from which they were temporarily absent because of vacation, illness, bad weather, childcare problems, maternity or paternity leave, labor-management dispute, job training, or other family or personal reasons, whether or not they were paid for the time off or were seeking other jobs. Each employed person is counted only once, even if he or she holds more than one job. Excluded are persons whose only activity consisted of work around their own house (painting, repairing, or own home housework) or volunteer work for religious, charitable, and other organizations.

Unemployed persons include persons 16 years and older who had no employment during the reference week, were available for work, except for temporary illness, and had made specific efforts to find employment sometime during the 4-week period ending with the reference week. Persons who were waiting to be recalled to a job from which they had been laid off need not have been looking for work to be classified as unemployed.

Source: U.S. Bureau of Labor Statistics

Plunkett Research, Ltd.

www.plunkettresearch.com

Unemployed Jobseekers by Sex, Reason for Unemployment & Active Job Search Methods Used: 2010 Average

Sex and reason	(Thousands of persons)		Methods used as a percent of total jobseekers							Average number of methods used
	Total unemployed	Total jobseekers	Employer directly	Sent out resumes or filled out applications	Placed or answered ads	Friends or relatives	Public employment agency	Private employment agency	Other	
Total, 16 years and over	**14,825**	**13,394**	**53.6**	**55.2**	**18.4**	**28.8**	**22.2**	**8.9**	**15.4**	**2.03**
Job losers and persons who completed temporary jobs*	9,250	7,819	55.6	54.1	20.5	32.5	26.3	10.7	16.4	2.17
Job leavers	889	889	53.1	58.0	18.6	25.1	20.7	8.3	14.9	2.00
Reentrants	3,466	3,466	50.0	55.9	15.6	23.5	17.0	6.4	14.9	1.84
New entrants	1,220	1,220	51.5	58.4	12.9	22.9	12.3	5.1	11.3	1.75
Men, 16 years and over	**8,626**	**7,638**	**54.9**	**52.7**	**18.1**	**30.4**	**23.0**	**9.0**	**15.7**	**2.04**
Job losers and persons who completed temporary jobs*	5,919	4,932	56.4	51.8	19.7	33.2	26.5	10.5	16.6	2.15
Job leavers	457	457	54.2	56.0	17.9	27.9	19.5	7.9	14.3	1.98
Reentrants	1,608	1,608	51.1	52.6	15.2	25.0	17.2	6.6	15.1	1.84
New entrants	641	641	52.7	57.9	13.4	23.9	12.3	4.7	11.0	1.76
Women, 16 years and over	**6,199**	**5,756**	**52.0**	**58.5**	**18.8**	**26.7**	**21.2**	**8.8**	**15.1**	**2.02**
Job losers and persons who completed temporary jobs*	3,331	2,888	54.3	57.9	21.9	31.2	25.8	11.0	16.1	2.19
Job leavers	432	432	52.0	60.2	19.3	22.2	21.9	8.7	15.7	2.01
Reentrants	1,858	1,858	49.1	58.7	15.8	22.1	16.8	6.2	14.6	1.84
New entrants	579	579	50.1	58.9	12.3	21.7	12.3	5.6	11.5	1.73

Note: Figures are 2010 annual averages, calculated using month-by-month survey data from January through December. The jobseekers total is less than the total unemployed because it does not include persons on temporary layoff. The percent using each met

* Data on the number of jobseekers and the jobsearch methods used exclude persons on temporary layoff.

Source: U.S. Bureau of Labor Statistics
Plunkett Research, Ltd.
www.plunkettresearch.com

U.S. Labor Force Ages 16 to 24 Years Old by School Enrollment, Educational Attainment, Sex, Race & Ethnicity: October 2010

(Numbers in Thousands, Latest Year Available)	Civilian non-institutional population	Total in Labor Force	Percent of Populace	Employed		Unemployed		Not in Labor Force
				Total	Percent of Populace	Number	Rate (%)	
Total, 16 to 24 years	37,616	20,764	55.2	16,945	45.0	3,820	18.4	16,851
Educational Attainment								
Enrolled in school	21,854	8,411	38.5	7,098	32.5	1,314	15.6	13,443
Enrolled in high school[1]	9,612	2,125	22.1	1,576	16.4	548	25.8	7,488
Men	4,965	1,055	21.3	760	15.3	295	28.0	3,910
Women	4,647	1,069	23.0	817	17.6	253	23.6	3,578
White	7,225	1,757	24.3	1,359	18.8	398	22.6	5,468
Black or African American	1,608	266	16.5	141	8.8	125	46.9	1,342
Asian	335	30	8.9	21	6.3	9	(2)	305
Hispanic or Latino ethnicity	1,805	314	17.4	187	10.4	127	40.4	1,491
Enrolled in college	12,242	6,287	51.4	5,521	45.1	766	12.2	5,955
Enrolled in 2-year college	3,512	2,129	60.6	1,772	50.4	358	16.8	1,383
Enrolled in 4-year college	8,729	4,158	47.6	3,750	43.0	408	9.8	4,571
Full-time students	10,680	4,967	46.5	4,331	40.6	635	12.8	5,713
Part-time students	1,562	1,320	84.5	1,190	76.2	130	9.9	242
Men	5,710	2,707	47.4	2,286	40.0	421	15.5	3,003
Women	6,531	3,579	54.8	3,235	49.5	345	9.6	2,952
White	9,461	5,145	54.4	4,569	48.3	576	11.2	4,316
Black or African American	1,630	680	41.7	562	34.5	119	17.4	949
Asian	777	254	32.8	229	29.5	25	9.9	522
Hispanic or Latino ethnicity	1,501	792	52.8	690	46.0	102	12.9	709
Not enrolled in school	15,762	12,353	78.4	9,847	62.5	2,506	20.3	3,409
16 to 19 years	3,134	2,067	65.9	1,357	43.3	710	34.4	1,068
20 to 24 years	12,627	10,286	81.5	8,491	67.2	1,796	17.5	2,341
Sex								
Men	8,274	6,937	83.8	5,341	64.6	1,596	23.0	1,337
Less than a high school diploma	1,731	1,267	73.2	864	49.9	403	31.8	464
High school graduates, no college[3]	3,870	3,193	82.5	2,400	62.0	793	24.8	677
Some college or associate degree	1,784	1,610	90.3	1,328	74.5	282	17.5	174
Bachelor's degree and higher[4]	890	867	97.4	749	84.1	118	13.6	23
Women	7,488	5,416	72.3	4,506	60.2	910	16.8	2,072
Less than a high school diploma	1,299	644	49.6	444	34.2	200	31.0	655
High school graduates, no college[3]	3,125	2,147	68.7	1,671	53.5	476	22.2	978
Some college or associate degree	1,894	1,539	81.2	1,374	72.6	164	10.7	356
Bachelor's degree and higher[4]	1,170	1,087	92.9	1,017	86.9	70	6.5	83
Race								
White	12,330	9,913	80.4	8,140	66.0	1,773	17.9	2,417
Black or African American	2,438	1,679	68.9	1,126	46.2	553	33.0	759
Asian	348	280	80.5	224	64.4	56	20.0	68
Hispanic or Latino ethnicity	3,503	2,631	75.1	2,023	57.7	608	23.1	872

Note: Detail for the above race groups do not sum to totals because data are not presented for all races. Persons whose ethnicity is identified as Hispanic or Latino may be of any race. Because of rounding, sums of individual items may not equal totals.

[1] Includes a small number of persons who are in grades below high school. [2] Data not shown where base is less than 75,000. [3] Includes persons with a high school diploma or equivalent. [4] Includes persons with bachelor's, master's, professional, and doctoral degrees.

Source: U.S. Bureau of Labor Statistics

Plunkett Research, Ltd.

www.plunkettresearch.com

Mean Hourly Earnings & Weekly Hours, Private Industry & State & Local Government: 2010

(By Worker & Establishment Characteristics, Latest Year Available)	Civilian		Private Industry		State & Local Gov't	
	Hourly Earnings[1]	Weekly Hours[2]	Hourly Earnings[1]	Weekly Hours[2]	Hourly Earnings[1]	Weekly Hours[2]
Total	**$21.29**	**35.1**	**$20.47**	**34.9**	**$26.08**	**36.2**
Worker Characteristics[3,4]						
Management, professional & related	34.49	36.7	34.99	37.0	33.02	35.9
Management, business & financial	38.81	39.3	39.42	39.7	35.32	37.4
Professional & related	32.55	35.6	32.57	35.7	32.50	35.6
Service	12.14	30.7	10.62	29.7	19.32	36.4
Sales & office	16.44	34.7	16.35	34.5	17.39	36.4
Sales & related	17.11	32.3	17.11	32.3	16.65	33.9
Office & administrative support	16.09	36.1	15.90	36.0	17.42	36.5
Natural resources, construction & maintenance	21.21	39.0	21.24	39.0	20.97	38.8
Construction & extraction	21.18	39.0	21.31	39.0	20.13	38.7
Installation, maintenance & repair	21.40	39.2	21.34	39.2	21.98	39.2
Production, transportation & material moving	16.00	37.1	15.88	37.2	19.52	34.4
Production	16.26	38.9	16.18	38.8	21.69	39.5
Transportation & material moving	15.73	35.4	15.55	35.6	18.86	33.1
Full time	22.77	39.5	22.01	39.6	26.75	38.9
Part time	12.10	20.7	11.78	21.0	16.39	18.3
Union	26.04	36.6	23.13	36.3	29.72	37.0
Nonunion	20.46	34.8	20.19	34.8	23.12	35.6
Time	21.06	34.9	20.16	34.7	26.07	36.2
Incentive	26.04	38.4	26.03	38.4	--	--
Establishment Characteristics						
Goods producing	--	*(6)*	22.04	39.4	--	*(6)*
Service Producing	--	*(6)*	20.09	34.0	--	*(6)*
1 to 49 workers	17.86	33.5	17.80	33.6	19.61	33.0
50 to 99 workers	19.24	34.3	19.10	34.2	21.40	35.8
100 to 499 workers	20.88	35.9	20.42	35.8	24.31	36.0
500 workers or more	27.02	36.9	26.65	37.0	27.68	36.7

Note: The survey covers all 50 states and the District of Columbia. Data were collected between December 2009 and January 2011. The average month of reference was July 2010. Dashes indicate that data did not meet publication criteria.

[1] Earnings are the straight-time hourly wages or salaries paid to employees. They include incentive pay, cost-of-living adjustments and hazard pay. Excluded are premium pay for overtime, vacations, holidays, nonproduction bonuses and tips. The mean is computed by totaling the pay of all workers and dividing by the number of workers, weighted by hours.

[2] Mean weekly hours are the hours an employee is scheduled to work in a week, exclusive of overtime.

[3] Employees are classified as working either a full-time or a part-time schedule based on the definition used by each establishment. Union workers are those whose wages are determined through collective bargaining. Wages of time workers are based solely on hourly rate or salary; incentive workers are those whose wages are at least partially based on productivity payments such as piece rates, commissions, and production bonuses.

[4] A classification system including about 800 individual occupations is used to cover all workers in the civilian economy.

[5] Estimates for goods-producing and service-providing industries are published for private industry only. Industries are determined by the 2007 North American Industry Classification System (NAICS).

[6] Estimates for goods-producing and service-providing industries are published for private industry only. The NCS uses the 2007 North American Industry Classification System (NAICS) to determine the industry of each sampled establishment.

Source: U.S. Bureau of Labor Statistics

Plunkett Research, Ltd. www.plunkettresearch.com

Medical Care Benefits in the U.S.: Access, Participation and Take-Up Rates, March 2011

(All workers = 100 percent)

Characteristics	Private Industry			State/Local Government		
	Access	Particip-ation	Take-up Rate[1]	Access	Particip-ation	Take-up Rate[1]
All workers	72%	54%	75%	87%	72%	83%
Worker Characteristics						
Management, professional and related	88%	68%	78%	89%	73%	82%
Service	48%	33%	70%	81%	68%	84%
Sales and office	72%	50%	70%	88%	75%	84%
Natural resources, construction and maintenance	77%	57%	80%	95%	82%	86%
Production, transportation and material moving	76%	59%	78%	82%	69%	84%
Full time	88%	67%	77%	99%	82%	83%
Part time	24%	14%	58%	26%	18%	69%
Union	93%	77%	82%	95%	78%	82%
Nonunion	69%	50%	73%	81%	67%	83%
Wage percentiles[2]						
Lowest 10 percent	22%	12%	56%	54%	43%	81%
Lowest 25 percent	39%	24%	62%	69%	57%	82%
Second 25 percent	77%	56%	73%	91%	77%	84%
Third 25 percent	87%	69%	79%	94%	79%	84%
Highest 25 percent	93%	74%	80%	97%	79%	81%
Highest 10 percent	94%	75%	79%	97%	79%	82%
Establishment Characteristics						
1 to 99 workers	57%	42%	73%	74%	63%	85%
1 to 49 workers	53%	38%	72%	67%	57%	85%
50 to 99 workers	69%	51%	74%	84%	72%	86%
100 workers or more	86%	66%	77%	89%	74%	82%
100 to 499 workers	82%	60%	74%	85%	71%	84%
500 workers or more	90%	71%	79%	91%	74%	82%

Note: For this table, a worker with access to medical care benefits is defined as having an employer-provided medical plan available for use, regardless of the worker's decision to enroll or participate in the plan. Farm and private household workers, the self-employed and Federal government workers are excluded from the survey.

[1] The take-up rate is a rounded estimate of the percentage of workers with access to a plan who participate in the plan.

[2] The percentile groupings are based on the average wage for each occupation surveyed, which may include workers both above and below the threshold. The percentile values are based on the estimates published in the "National Compensation Survey: Occupational Earnings in the United States, 2010."

Source: U.S. Bureau of Labor Statistics
Plunkett Research, Ltd.
www.plunkettresearch.com

Retirement Benefits in the U.S.: Access, Participation and Take-Up Rates, March 2011

(All workers = 100 percent)

Characteristics	Private Industry			State/Local Government		
	Access	Particip-ation	Take-up Rate[1]	Access	Particip-ation	Take-up Rate[1]
All workers	64	49	76	90	85	95
Worker Characteristics						
Management, professional and related	80	68	85	92	87	95
Service	40	22	56	84	79	95
Sales and office	69	52	76	90	86	95
Natural resources, construction and maintenance	62	49	79	94	90	96
Production, transportation and material moving	66	51	77	87	84	96
Full time	73	59	80	99	94	95
Part time	37	20	54	41	37	91
Union	90	83	93	97	92	95
Nonunion	61	45	74	84	79	95
Wage percentiles[2]						
Lowest 10 percent	28	10	35	60	56	94
Lowest 25 percent	39	19	50	74	70	94
Second 25 percent	66	48	73	94	89	95
Third 25 percent	74	61	83	95	91	96
Highest 25 percent	84	75	89	98	93	95
Highest 10 percent	87	79	90	97	92	94
Establishment Characteristics						
1 to 99 workers	49	34	69	78	75	96
1 to 49 workers	45	32	70	73	70	95
50 to 99 workers	62	41	66	87	84	97
100 workers or more	81	66	82	91	87	95
100 to 499 workers	77	59	76	87	84	96
500 workers or more	86	76	88	93	88	95

Note: Benefits may include defined benefit pension plans as well as defined contribution retirement plans. Workers are considered as having access or as participating if they have access to or participate in at least one of these plan types. Farm and private household workers, the self-employed and Federal government workers are excluded from the survey.

[1] The take-up rate is a rounded estimate of the percentage of workers with access to a plan who participate in the plan.

[2] The percentile groupings are based on the average wage for each occupation surveyed, which may include workers both above and below the threshold. The percentile values are based on the estimates published in the "National Compensation Survey: Occupational Earnings in the United States, 2010."

Source: U.S. Bureau of Labor Statistics

Plunkett Research, Ltd.

www.plunkettresearch.com

Top 30 U.S. Occupations by Numerical Change in Job Growth: 2008-2018

(By Thousands of Employees)

Occupation	Employment		Change		Training*
	2008	2018	Number	Percent	
Registered nurses	2,619	3,200	**581**	22.2	Associate degree
Home health aides	922	1,383	**461**	50.0	Short-term on-the-job training
Customer service representatives	2,252	2,652	**400**	17.7	Moderate-term on-the-job training
Combined food preparation & serving workers, including fast food	2,702	3,096	**394**	14.6	Short-term on-the-job training
Personal & home care aides	817	1,193	**376**	46.0	Short-term on-the-job training
Retail salespersons	4,489	4,864	**375**	8.4	Short-term on-the-job training
Office clerks, general	3,024	3,383	**359**	11.9	Short-term on-the-job training
Accountants & auditors	1,291	1,570	**279**	21.7	Bachelor's degree
Nursing aides, orderlies & attendants	1,470	1,746	**276**	276.0	Postsecondary vocational award
Postsecondary teachers	1,699	1,956	**257**	15.1	Doctoral degree
Construction laborers	1,249	1,505	**256**	20.5	Moderate-term on-the-job training
Elementary school teachers, except special education	1,550	1,794	**244**	15.8	Bachelor's degree
Truck drivers, heavy & tractor-trailer	1,798	2,031	**233**	13.0	Short-term on-the-job training
Landscaping & groundskeeping workers	1,206	1,423	**217**	18.0	Short-term on-the-job training
Bookkeeping, accounting & auditing clerks	2,064	2,276	**212**	10.3	Moderate-term on-the-job training
Executive secretaries & administrative assistants	1,594	1,799	**205**	12.8	Work experience in a related occupation
Management analysts	747	925	**178**	23.9	Bachelor's or higher degree, plus work experience
Computer software engineers, applications	515	690	**175**	34.0	Bachelor's degree
Receptionists & information clerks	1,139	1,312	**173**	15.2	Short-term on-the-job training
Carpenters	1,285	1,450	**165**	12.9	Long-term on-the-job training
Medical assistants	484	648	**164**	33.9	Moderate-term on-the-job training
Supervisors/managers of office & administrative support workers	1,457	1,618	**161**	11.0	Work experience in a related occupation
Network systems & data communications analysts	292	448	**156**	53.4	Bachelor's degree
Licensed practical/vocational nurses	754	909	**155**	20.7	Postsecondary vocational award
Security guards	1,077	1,229	**152**	14.2	Short-term on-the-job training
Waiters & waitresses	2,382	2,533	**151**	6.4	Short-term on-the-job training
Maintenance & repair workers	1,361	1,509	**148**	10.9	Moderate-term on-the-job training
Physicians & surgeons	661	806	**145**	21.8	First professional degree
Child care workers	1,302	1,444	**142**	10.9	Short-term on-the-job training
Teacher assistants	1,313	1,448	**135**	10.3	Short-term on-the-job training

* An occupation is placed into 1 of 11 categories that best describes the postsecondary education or training needed by most workers to become fully qualified in that occupation. For more information about the categories, see Measures of Education and Training, on the Internet at www.bls.gov/emp/ep_projections_methods.htm.

Source: U.S. Bureau of Labor Statistics
Plunkett Research, Ltd.
www.plunkettresearch.com

Top 30 U.S. Occupations by Percent Change in Job Growth: 2008-2018

(Employment in Thousands)

Occupation	Employment		Change		Training*
	2008	2018	Number	Percent	
Biomedical engineers	16	28	12	**72.0**	Bachelor's degree
Network systems & data communications analysts	292	448	156	**53.4**	Bachelor's degree
Home health aids	922	1,383	461	**50.0**	Short-term on-the-job training
Personal & home care aides	817	1,193	376	**46.0**	Short-term on-the-job training
Financial examiners	27	38	11	**41.2**	Bachelor's degree
Medical scientists, except epidemiologists	109	154	45	**40.4**	Doctoral degree
Physician assistants	75	104	29	**39.0**	Master's degree
Skin care specialists	39	54	15	**37.9**	Postsecondary vocational award
Biochemists & biophysicists	23	32	9	**37.4**	Doctoral degree
Athletic trainers	16	22	6	**37.0**	Bachelor's degree
Physical therapist aides	46	63	17	**36.3**	Short-term on-the-job training
Dental hygienists	174	237	63	**36.1**	Associate degree
Veterinary technologists & technicians	80	108	28	**35.8**	Associate degree
Dental assistants	295	401	106	**35.8**	Moderate-term on-the-job training
Computer software engineers, applications	515	690	175	**34.0**	Bachelor's degree
Medical assistants	484	648	164	**33.9**	Moderate-term on-the-job training
Physical therapist assistants	64	85	21	**33.3**	Associate degree
Veterinarians	60	79	19	**33.0**	First professional degree
Self-enrichment education teachers	254	335	81	**32.1**	Experience in a related occupation
Compliance officers, except agriculture, construction, health and safety, and transportation	260	341	81	**31.1**	Long-term on-the-job training
Occupational therapist aides	8	10	2	**30.7**	Short-term on-the-job training
Environmental engineers	54	71	17	**30.6**	Bachelor's degree
Pharmacy technicians	326	426	100	**30.6**	Moderate-term on-the-job training
Computer software engineers, systems software	395	515	120	**30.4**	Bachelor's degree
Survey researchers	23	31	8	**30.4**	Bachelor's degree
Physical therapists	186	242	56	**30.3**	Master's degree
Personal financial advisors	208	271	63	**30.1**	Bachelor's degree
Environmental engineering technicians	21	28	7	**30.1**	Associate degree
Occupational therapist assistants	27	35	8	**29.8**	Associate degree
Fitness trainers and aerobics instructors	261	338	77	**29.4**	Postsecondary vocational award

* An occupation is placed into 1 of 11 categories that best describes the postsecondary education or training needed by most workers to become fully qualified in that occupation. For more information, see Measures of Education and Training, on the Internet at www.bls.gov/emp/ep_projections_methods.htm.

Source: U.S. Bureau of Labor Statistics
Plunkett Research, Ltd.
www.plunkettresearch.com

Occupations with the Largest Expected Employment Increases, U.S.: 2008-2018

(By Increase in Number Employed, in Thousands)

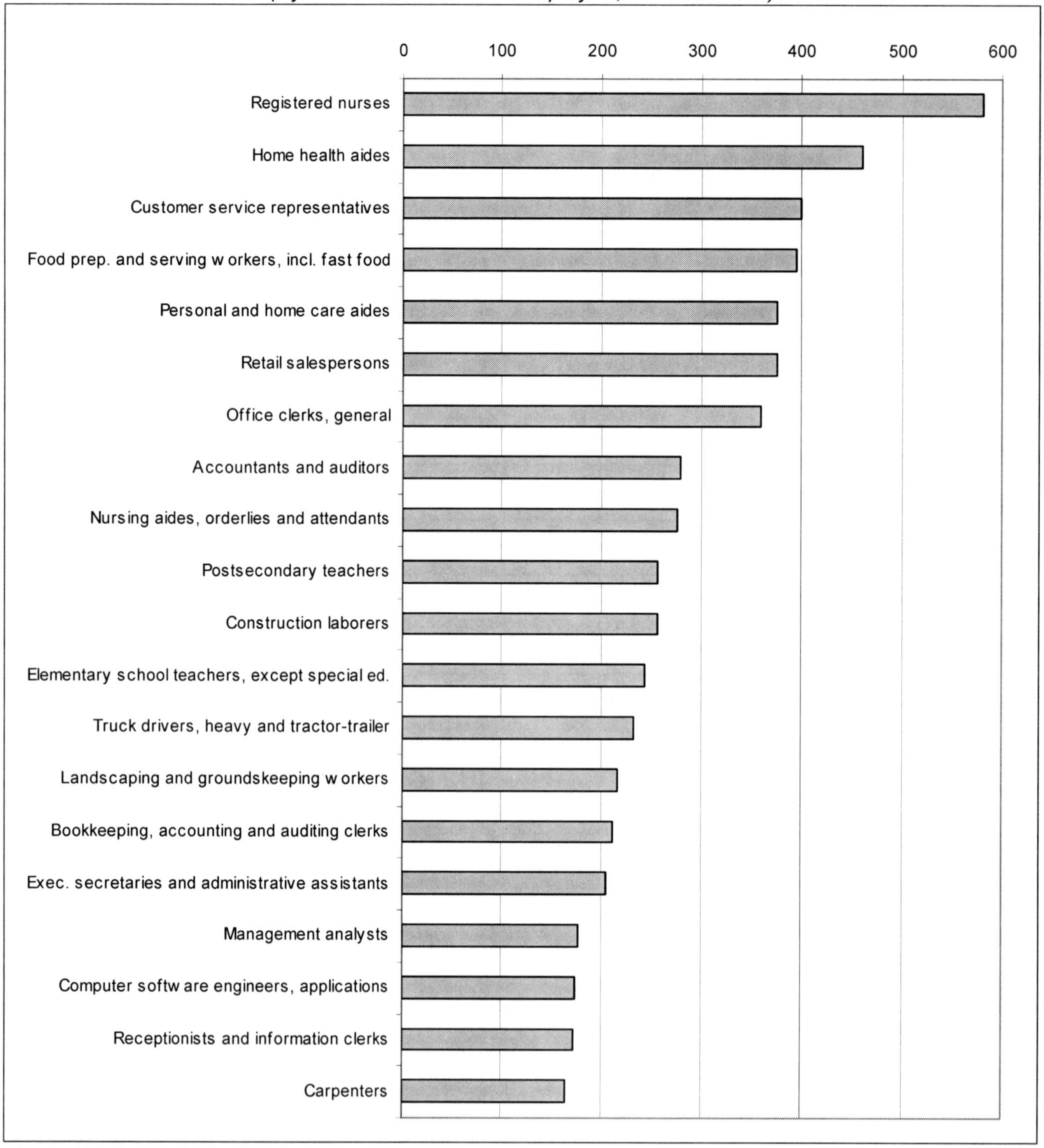

Source: U.S. Bureau of Labor Statistics
Plunkett Research, Ltd.
www.plunkettresearch.com

Occupations with the Fastest Expected Decline, U.S.: 2008-2018

(By Percent Change and Number of Jobs Lost, in Thousands)

Occupation	Change		Wages (May 2008 Median)	Training*
	Percent	Number		
Textile bleaching and dyeing machine operators and tenders	-45%	-7.2	$23,680	Moderate-term on-the-job training
Textile winding, twisting, and drawing out machine setters, operators, and tenders	-41%	-14.2	$23,970	Moderate-term on-the-job training
Textile knitting and weaving machine setters, operators, and tenders	-39%	-11.5	$25,400	Long-term on-the-job training
Shoe machine operators and tenders	-35%	-1.7	$25,090	Moderate-term on-the-job training
Extruding and forming machine setters, operators, and tenders, synthetic and glass fibers	-34%	-4.8	$31,160	Moderate-term on-the-job training
Sewing machine operators	-34%	-4.8	$19,870	Moderate-term on-the-job training
Semiconductor processors	-32%	-10.0	$32,230	Postsecondary vocational award
Textile cutting machine setters, operators, and tenders	-31%	-6.0	$22,620	Moderate-term on-the-job training
Postal Service mail sorters, processors, and processing machine operators	-30%	-54.5	$50,020	Short-term on-the-job training
Fabric menders, except garment	-30%	-0.3	$28,470	Moderate-term on-the-job training
Wellhead pumpers	-28%	-5.3	$37,860	Moderate-term on-the-job training
Fabric and apparel patternmakers	-27%	-2.2	$37,760	Long-term on-the-job training
Drilling & boring machine tool setters, operators, & tenders, metal & plastic	-27%	-8.9	$30,850	Moderate-term on-the-job training
Lathe & turning machine tool setters, operators, & tenders, metal & plastic	-27%	-14.9	$32,940	Moderate-term on-the-job training
Order clerks	-26%	-64.2	$27,990	Short-term on-the-job training
Coil winders, tapers, and finishers	-25%	-5.6	$27,730	Short-term on-the-job training
Photographic processing machine operators	-24%	-12.5	$20,360	Short-term on-the-job training
File clerks	-23%	-49.6	$23,800	Short-term on-the-job training
Derrick operators, oil and gas	-23%	-5.8	$41,920	Moderate-term on-the-job training
Desktop publishers	-23%	-5.9	$36,600	Postsecondary vocational award

* An occupation is placed into 1 of 11 categories that best describes the postsecondary education or training needed by most workers to become fully qualified in that occupation. For more information about the categories, see Measures of Education and Training, on the Internet at www.bls.gov/emp/ep_projections_methods.htm.

Source: U.S. Bureau of Labor Statistics
Plunkett Research, Ltd.
www.plunkettresearch.com

Chapter 3

RESEARCH: 7 KEYS FOR JOB SEEKERS

How to use your library, college placement office, the Internet and other resources to become well-informed about a company and its industry before you ask for an interview

Research is the key to finding appropriate job openings, targeting the best possible employers and performing well when you go to job interviews. Learn what's unique about a company compared to other firms in its industry. Learn why it's prospering–or why it isn't. Where is this company going? Is it favored by stock investors? Is it privately-owned by a family, or has it been acquired by private equity investors who plan to resell it over the mid-term? What are its hottest-selling products and services? Is it investing in research and new facilities so that it may prosper in the future? Also, as many people who have been laid off from failing startup firms have learned the hard way, determining a company's level of financial stability can be one of the most important factors in making a career decision.

The more you're willing to dig deep at the library or your college's career planning office, and the more adept you are at using the Internet for research, the better your chances of success in a job search. If you are willing to ask questions of businesspeople and of employees who currently work for your target employers, you will enhance your job search even further. The two secrets to successful job research are tenacity and focus. Know what to look for and where to find it.

Once you've landed an interview, you should research both the prospective employer and its industry even further. In this manner, you'll know what questions to ask before you agree to take the job, and you'll present yourself as a knowledgeable potential hire who is truly interested in the company and its business.

Here are the seven keys for research that can lead you to a great employer:

1) Financial Stability

Check bond ratings, credit ratings, debt level, growth in sales and growth in profits, along with the views of stock analysts and business journalists.

2) Growth Plans

Look for new plants, stores or offices to be opened; new technologies, products or divisions to be launched; or plans for strategic acquisitions. (See 3, 4 and 5 below.) Is the employer's growth strategy focused primarily on offshoring work to overseas locations or outsourcing work to outside services providers? Or, does it have a balanced growth strategy that will create good opportunities in its American operations?

3) Research and Development Programs

How much does the firm invest in R&D? Is this research and development budget growing? For many types of companies, research is a vital investment in the future.

4) Product Launch and Production

Does the company have the ability to successfully launch new products and services (see 5 below) or to invest in and utilize cutting-edge technologies needed to maintain a competitive edge?

5) Marketing and Distribution Methods

Does the firm utilize an in-house sales force? Does it work through outside dealers and distribution partners? What are its advertising methods? Is it increasing its market share, or are competitors taking customers away? Is the company growing its international sales? Is it adept at using the Internet as a powerful sales tool? Is it successful at selling into growing international markets, such as Brazil, China and India?

6) Employee Benefits

Are wealth-building benefit plans offered? Will the company match all or part of your deposits to a 401(k) savings plan? Check for tuition reimbursement, pension plans, profit sharing, ESOP stock ownership plans, discount stock purchase plans, stock options or performance-based bonuses.

7) Quality-of-Work Factors

Does the company offer continual training, wellness programs, child care, elder care support, promote-from-within policies, flexible work schedules, performance reviews, product discounts or on-site health clubs? Is it a corporate culture that fits your lifestyle?

As a serious job seeker, you should conduct in-depth research and make detailed notes about these key factors for each firm you are considering. Then compare each company's finances, plans and programs to others in the same industry. You'll begin to see what makes some firms outstanding and why those outstanding companies are the best places to make a career investment. For example, if you compare two discount store giants, Wal-Mart and Costco, you will find that Wal-Mart is by far the larger firm, but Costco has an outstanding record of providing superior employee pay and benefits.

Your research goal should be twofold: First, determine whether this is a firm you want to work for. Are the salaries and benefits appealing? Are layoffs likely? Is it planning to expand its workforce in lower-cost nations like India and then lay off U.S. employees? A growing company will offer opportunities for you to advance when it launches new locations, services, technologies or product lines. Second, develop a personal understanding of the company and its industry so you can better sell yourself as a potential employee.

Other Considerations:

Women and Minorities:

Certain industries have a greater tendency to offer advancement opportunities for women or minorities. Historically, the banking and insurance segments have tended to promote both women and minorities, as have retailing, electric utilities, apparel, consumer goods, packaged food and beverages, education, publishing and telephone companies.

Major employers in many other industries are making serious efforts to hire, develop and promote women and minorities for top officers' positions. A study published in September 2011 by Catalyst, a New York-based research group that focuses on women's issues in the workplace, found that 2.8% (14 companies) of the *Fortune 500* firms had female CEOs, up from about 1% in 2001. Some technology companies have been terrific places for women who want to advance, and many tech companies, such as Hewlett-Packard, Xerox and eBay, have been known to post women to CEO spots.

Catalyst reported in another study published in 2011 that 15.7% of members of boards of directors in the Fortune *500* firms were women, up from 9.6% in 1995. (You can access the results of Catalyst studies at www.catalyst.org.) Obviously, women are making slow progress in gaining representation in the highest ranks of corporate America, and they fall far short of parity with men in that regard.

Black Enterprise magazine publishes an annual list of the "Most Powerful African Americans in Corporate America," (see www.blackenterprise.com). Meanwhile, the Executive Leadership Council, www.elcinfo.com, a Washington, D.C.-based nonprofit group that conducts programs aimed at filling more executive posts with African Americans, has a unique statistic to report. Its membership is composed of senior-level black executives who have jobs that are no more than three levels below the CEO spot at Fortune 500 companies. When the group was founded in 1986, it had only a handful of members. Today, its membership is about 380 people employed in high-level executive jobs at major corporations.

The Hispanic Association on Corporate Responsibility (www.hacr.org) promotes Hispanic advancement in the areas of employment, procurement, philanthropy and governance. Another nonprofit agency, National Hispanic Corporate Achievers (hispanicachievers.org), provides an educational forum for Hispanics working for *Fortune 1000* companies.

Tips on Using Business Magazines, Newspapers and Trade Journals to Find Job Leads and Do Employer Research

Many job seekers overlook the tremendous advantages offered by industry magazines (called "trade journals") and other publications when conducting research.

Industry-specific trade journals frequently have classified ads in the back that list job openings. An example of a great magazine to study is *American Banker,* which can be found at major libraries. Additional information is available at www.americanbanker.com.

Journalists at trade journals and business newspapers continuously interview industry-leading executives regarding their companies' growth plans. New projects and company expansion plans described in these articles provide terrific job leads.

You can also get great contact information from these publications. Read the latest business stories about companies and industries that interest you and you will learn vital information. Best of all, you can glean from stories and interviews the names and titles of executives who lead projects, divisions and subsidiaries.

There are literally hundreds of these trade journals—at least one for each industry sector and sometimes dozens covering the largest industries.

Other great resources include business newspapers such as the *Dallas/Ft. Worth Business Journal*, *The Wall Street Journal*, the business pages of major newspapers like *The New York Times* and publications written for major investors like *Investor's Business Daily*. At www.bizjournals.com, you can gain access to news stories from business journals from all over the U.S.

Quality-of-Life Benefits:

Many companies offer benefits that help employees balance their personal and professional lives. The concept is that employees who are healthy and comfortable with their personal and family lives make better, more productive employees. To that end, many companies include fitness programs and family services such as extended maternity leaves and child care or elder care, whether on-site or off-site in the form of referral services. Other popular family-friendly benefits include flextime, flexible benefits spending accounts, adoption assistance and telecommuting. In many cases, benefits are listed on employers' web sites.

Work-Life has become a popular phrase for family-friendly benefits and programs among major employers such as Intel, Abbott Laboratories, Baxter International and Aramark. For additional information, you can study such organizations at the Alliance for Work-Life Progress site at www.awlp.org.

Growth Potential and Job Stability:

A firm's growth potential should be among your top priorities. Companies are always trying to maintain or increase productivity, or the ratio of revenues per employee. If a company's sales are sliding, or if it is running out of cash, the job picture starts to collapse. A little extra research into a company's finances and true potential for growth might save you from a future layoff.

Of course, employers sometimes have to resort to layoffs due to conditions outside of their control. For example, travel industry companies worldwide cut hundreds of thousands of jobs in the revenue slump following the September 11, 2001 attacks on New York City and Washington, D.C.

As a job seeker, you're forced to look out for your own best interests while you sort through thousands of potential employers in dozens of industries. This means that good research is vital. For example, if you put salary at the top of your list, you may have the wrong priorities. From time to time, some of the highest-paying firms have been among those cutting the largest numbers of employees. If you are looking for job stability, your biggest challenge is to pick companies that are more likely to hire now and less likely to have layoffs in the future. That's why a firm's growth outlook should be one of your guiding lights.

However, the goal is *internal* growth caused by expanding sales. Generally less appealing are firms that post a quick spike in growth through big mergers. (In many cases, merged companies lay off people who suddenly find themselves filling jobs duplicated in newly consolidated offices. Also, companies that grow excessively through acquisitions may be taking on loads of debt that can become hard to handle later. However, there are occasional exceptions to this rule, where firms are enjoying soaring demand for products or services and find it difficult to hire quickly enough to keep up.) Companies that are growing rapidly through internal expansion include those opening new stores, distribution centers or offices, developing exciting new products, moving into new markets (including international markets) and creating hot new technologies, retail formats or services. Those types of expansion frequently mean great career opportunities, including the chance for rapid job promotion.

Where can you look for growth companies? If you're tenacious, you can find opportunities where others will find only rejection. Identifying real prospects for growth takes more than a quick glance.

Here's an extremely important point for you to remember: You should look for opportunities in growing divisions that serve special niches, even when the company as a whole is cutting jobs. For example, a firm's online division may be growing, even while its traditional units are shrinking.

Additional key factors for strong corporate growth, and thereby the best job prospects, include:

1) Companies or divisions with a growing share of a promising market.

Management's ability to anticipate or create change in the marketplace makes for a growing company with great prospects. For example, Sam Walton revolutionized the department store business by realizing that consumers want everyday low prices on name-brand merchandise. He created Wal-Mart, while competitor Sears suffered by maintaining an old-fashioned policy of special sales events on private-label goods. Wal-Mart rapidly became one of the largest creators of new jobs in the private sector. Sears was forced to slash its ranks.

Microsoft made its way to the top with unique products serving a soaring market when it developed highly functional software for personal computers. The software giant created thousands of millionaire employees through the immense increase in the value of its stock plans. HEB, an innovative grocer in Texas, has evolved continually over the decades, constantly introducing improvements to store layouts, and even creating an exciting new HEB Marketplace concept that is a retail industry leader. HEB has large numbers of job openings of many types on a continuous basis.

The point to these stories is that you shouldn't invest your career in a company with mediocre prospects. With perseverance, you can target your own list of employers that are posting growth due to competitive advantages or growing market demand. Your best bets are companies taking reasonable risks in order to move ahead. Those risks may include investments in advertising, research and development, new technology, improved techniques on the manufacturing floor, testing of new products and the opening of new retail store formats. For example, Chico's FAS stores scored a hit by filling a niche in the women's apparel market, and Genentech became a leader in the biotechnology field by risking vast amounts on research. Also, don't overlook the potential of the export market—many American firms find much of their growth by creating products and services that enjoy demand overseas as well as in the U.S.

2) Sales and profits: past and present.

The companies most likely to move along at a good clip are those with an exciting mid-term history. Firms with an average annual growth in sales of 10% to 15% or more over the past several years are generally very promising. Companies that managed to get through the recent recession with only minor drops in revenues may be remarkably stable. Many small and mid-size firms grow at much faster rates and find themselves hiring continuously.

3) Beware of fads.

Unfortunately, a few companies post meteoric growth in businesses that turn out to be mere fads. The restaurant industry suffers from this problem on a regular basis. In recent years, companies selling bagels, frozen yogurt, rotisserie chicken and the like enjoyed impressive, nationwide growth only to collapse like a house of cards a couple of years later.

How to Find and Use Expert Opinions:

Superior sources used by sophisticated job researchers include reports written by: 1) stock analysts; 2) professional market research firms; and 3) journalists at business magazines and industry "trade magazines." Many major libraries have large collections of industry-specific trade magazines that can give you clues that competing job seekers will overlook. For example, *Retail Traffic Magazine*, www.retailtrafficmag.com, publishes lists of the fastest-growing retail chains. Virtually every other industry is covered by one or two trade magazines that will give you leads to growing companies. Many articles in these magazines contain the names of executives you may want to contact. Also, most industry trade magazines publish help-wanted ads in the back. The *Gale Directory of Publications and Broadcast Media* is a good index to magazines, organized by industry. You can find this directory in major libraries. Also, it's easy to do an online search for trade magazines, and most of them have terrific web sites that are filled with extremely useful information. For example, a recent search on Google for "pet industry trade magazine" quickly turned up leads to the top magazines for that sector.

Next, move on to reports from experts. Marketing and investment professionals are looking for some of the same clues you should use as a job seeker, and reports written by full-time analysts who cover specific companies or industries can help you find firms that are growing and hiring. You can purchase reports for publicly-traded firms at Yahoo! Finance, http://finance.yahoo.com. First, look up a company by name or ticker symbol. Once you are on the page for that company, look down the left hand column for the link to "Research Reports."

Professionally written market research can be found at Marketresearch.com, www.marketresearch.com. This market research broker charges varying fees for access to the reports. However, many of the reports are reasonably priced, and the insight you gain into industries, markets and leading companies can be extremely helpful. Web sites such as this offer the ability to search for reports by a wide variety of criteria, including company name and industry.

Internet Research Tip:

Be sure to create Google "Alerts" to follow your targeted employers and profession. Google will email results to you daily.

By going to the "more" link at the top of the Google home page, and then selecting "even more" from the drop down list, you can access Google's "Alerts" tool. Here you can arrange to receive email updates on topics of your choice. For example, you can set a general alert about an industry or locale: sales jobs in California, for example. Or something like: opportunities in the American wireless industry. Or even: sales jobs at automobile dealers.

You can use alerts to track specific jobs or employers. For example: openings at Intel. Or: regional sales manager opening Los Angeles. Finally, don't forget that you may want to put a search phrase within quotes to get an exact match to part of your phrase. For example: "loan officer" wanted.

Other Basic Resources:

Annual Reports/10-Ks/S-1s: Companies that sell their stocks to the public, including most of the firms covered in this book, publish annual reports that contain a wealth of information. Annual reports and 10-Ks cover yearly results, financial statements, management practices and other vital information for publicly held firms. S-1s provide the same type of information on companies that are selling stock to the public for the first time. You can find copies of these reports at large libraries. Online, the best place to acquire this information is at the site of the U.S. Securities and Exchange Commission. They have a user-friendly service that enables you to search for companies and access their financial reports at www.sec.gov. (Look for the "Filings & Forms" section, and then see "Search for Company Filings.") Look especially at the five-year "summary financial statement" in the back of these reports. Also, look for growth in sales and earnings. If these are falling, dig deeper to find out why. Faltering sales or profits can lead to layoffs or to a merger with another firm (which could result in deep job cuts).

Also, you can find a wealth of financial information on publicly-traded firms at Yahoo! Finance, http://finance.yahoo.com.

See Chapter 4, "Important Contacts for Job Seekers," for additional places to get basic corporate data.

Tips on Utilizing Financial Documents Filed by Publicly Held Firms

(Access these documents at the Securities Exchange Commission, www.sec.gov.)

10-K (also called Annual Report on Form 10-K): This is an annual filing required by federal law. It follows a standard format. Information includes a complete description of the business, risk factors, historical financial data and much more. It is vital reading for job seekers. You will find that these documents are written in dry, legal language, but they contain a wealth of information.

DEF 14A Proxy Statement: This is an annual document that gives shareholders certain options to consider at their annual meeting. It names the firm's board of directors and top management. It also gives the dollar value and description of salaries, bonuses, pension plans, stock options and other benefits enjoyed by the company's five highest-paid officers. Job seekers can learn a great deal about a firm's management, pay and benefits from this document. Included is a list of the people or organizations that own more than 5% of the company's stock.

S-1: This is a new registration document for companies that are going public for the first time. In other words, they are creating an IPO (initial public offering). The information includes all of the data found in the 10-K and proxy statement filed annually by companies that have been public for more than one year.

10-Q: This is a quarterly report detailing a company's latest sales, profits and balance sheet.

More Ways to Research an Employer's Financial Stability and Growth Plans:

1) Check out its bond rating.

There's no sense in trying to become a financial analyst on your own. Instead, go to your library and turn to the *Bond Guide* published by Standard & Poor's (New York, NY). This monthly booklet rates thousands of corporate bonds, based on a company's ability to pay principal and interest when due. If you're considering a major corporation with a bond rating of less than BB (an indicator that a company's debt is riskier than "investment grade"), you should do a lot more investigating before you continue chasing a job at that company.

2) Talk to vendors and current employees.

Talk to employees who work for the employer, or talk to people who do business with it. No one knows what's really going on better than people who are on the scene. If there are problems that are not yet known by the media, or if there are exciting new developments that have not yet been announced, you may find out a lot just by asking around. While you're at it, ask about corporate culture—how well are employees treated?

Popular Job-Search Internet Sites

CareerBuilder	www.careerbuilder.com
Monster	www.monster.com

Tips on Finding Information on Privately Held Employers

Our subscription service, Plunkett Research Online, and our printed Plunkett's industry almanacs, are among the world's most highly regarded sources of profiles of privately-held companies. Check with your library to see if you have access to these tools.

Study back-issue indexes and archives to major newspapers to see what journalists are reporting about a prospective private employer. Many libraries have recent issues of *The Wall Street Journal, The New York Times* and other important business newspapers. At major public and university libraries, you may be able to access online databases like ProQuest. These databases have excellent search engines that lead you into online archives of the best publications, including *The Wall Street Journal*, as well as many trade magazines and local business journals.

For smaller firms, go online and try American Journalism Review at www.newslink.org, where you'll be able to search news sites including hometown newspapers across the nation. Likewise, search local business newspapers at www.bizjournals.com, where you'll find links to dozens of major business weeklies like the *Houston Business Journal.*

Finally, invest in a credit report. If you really want reassurance, go to Experian SmartBusinessReports, www.smartbusinessreports.com. You can use its links to order a credit report on the employer. These reports are reasonably priced from about $20 to $45, and they can help you determine whether the company is paying its bills on time or has other problems. This could be vital in helping you determine whether to accept a job at a privately-held firm.

3) Use Internet search engines.

Look up your firm and industry in an Internet search engine such as Google. There, you may find unusual articles that were recently written about a company's product breakthroughs, treatment of women or minorities, human interest stories, training programs or stories written from other unique slants.

4) Study other business books and guides.

Search at a library or at an online bookseller like Amazon.com for recent books regarding major companies. For example, if you want to apply to biotech leader Genentech for a job, don't fail to read *The Billion Dollar Molecule: One Company's Quest for the Perfect Drug.* With a little research, you can turn up many other excellent books about specific companies, from banks like Bank of America to publishers like Gannett.

Great Places for Industry Research

Plunkett Research, www.plunkettresearch.com. Go to the specific industry of your choice to see an overview of trends and statistics. At our subscription service, www.plunkettresearchonline.com, subscribers have access to thousands of pages of industry analysis, statistics, contacts and company profiles, along with multiple search and export tools.

Quintessentialcareers.com, www.quintessentialcareers.com. Offers a "Career Resources Toolkit."

Wetfeet.com, www.wetfeet.com. Publishes snapshots of hundreds of employers.

Vault.com, www.vault.com. This site publishes insights about careers with hundreds of leading firms.

5) Explore industry-specific web sites.

See Chapter 4 in this book, "Important Contacts for Job Seekers," for hundreds of sites from dozens of different industry sectors. In particular, study the industry associations for the sector you want to work in.

6) Research benefits and pension plans.

For additional information about corporate pension plans, start with the government agency charged with protecting and regulating pensions: the Pension Benefit Guaranty Corporation, 1200 K St. NW, Washington, D.C. 20005-4026, 202-326-4000, www.pbgc.gov. They can answer certain questions over the telephone.

The U.S. Department of Labor publishes a useful book titled "Protect your Pension." They can be contacted at: U.S. Department of Labor, Employee Benefits Security Administration, 200 Constitution Ave. NW, Room N5635, Washington, D.C. 20210, 866-444-3272 or 202-219-8776, www.dol.gov/ebsa/publications/main.html.

The Social Security Administration, 800-772-1213, www.ssa.gov, can provide you with information regarding your potential Social Security benefits.

NOTE: Generally, employees covered by wealth-building benefit plans do not fully own ("vest in") funds contributed on their behalf by the employer until as many as five years of service with that employer have passed. All pension plans are voluntary—that is, employers are not obligated to offer pensions.

Pension Plans: The type and generosity of these plans vary widely from firm to firm. Caution: Some employers refer to plans as "pension" or "retirement" plans when they are actually 401(k) savings plans that require a contribution by the employee.

Defined Benefit Pension Plans: Pension plans that do not require a contribution from the employee are infrequently offered. However, a few companies, particularly larger employers in high-profit-margin industries, offer defined benefit pension plans where the employee is guaranteed to receive a set pension benefit upon retirement. The amount of the benefit is determined by the years of service with the company and the employee's salary during the later years of employment. The longer a person works for the employer, the higher the retirement benefit. These defined benefit plans are funded entirely by the employer. The benefits, up to a reasonable limit, are guaranteed by the Federal Government's Pension Benefit Guaranty Corporation. These plans are not portable—if you leave the company, you cannot transfer your benefits into a different plan. Instead, upon retirement you will receive the benefits that vested during your service with the company. If your employer offers a pension plan, it must give you a "summary plan description" within 90 days of the date you join the plan. You can also request a "summary annual report" of the plan, and once every 12 months you may request an "individual benefit statement" accounting of your interest in the plan.

Defined Contribution Plans: These are quite different. They do not guarantee a certain amount of pension benefit. Instead, they set out circumstances under which the employer will make a contribution to a plan on your behalf. The most common example is the 401(k) savings plan. Pension benefits are not guaranteed under these plans.

Cash Balance Pension Plans: These plans were recently invented. They are hybrid plans—part defined benefit and part defined contribution. Many employers have converted their older defined benefit plans into cash balance plans. The employer makes deposits (or credits a given amount of money) on the employee's behalf, usually based on a percentage of pay. Employee accounts grow based on a predetermined interest benchmark, such as the interest rate on Treasury Bonds. There are some advantages to these plans, particularly for younger workers: a) The benefits, up to a reasonable limit, are guaranteed by the Pension Benefit Guaranty Corporation. b) Benefits are portable—they can be moved to another plan when the employee changes companies. c) Younger workers and those who spend a shorter number of years with an employer may receive higher benefits than they would under a traditional defined benefit plan.

ESOP Stock Plan (Employees' Stock Ownership Plan): This type of plan is in wide use. Typically, the plan borrows money from a bank and uses those funds to purchase a large block of the corporation's stock. The corporation makes contributions to the plan over a period of time, and the stock purchase loan is eventually paid off. The value of the plan grows significantly as long as the market price of the stock holds up. Qualified employees are allocated a share of the plan based on their length of service and their level of salary. Under federal regulations, participants in ESOPs are allowed to diversify their account holdings in set percentages that rise as the employee ages and gains years of service with the company. In this manner, not all of the employee's assets are tied up in the employer's stock.

Savings Plan, 401(k): Under this type of plan, employees make a tax-deferred deposit into an account. In the best plans, the company makes annual matching donations to the employees' accounts, typically in some proportion to deposits made by the employees themselves. A good plan will match one-half of employee deposits of up to 6% of wages. For example, an employee earning $30,000 yearly might deposit $1,800 (6%) into the plan. The company will match one-half of the employee's deposit, or $900. The plan grows on a tax-deferred basis, similar to an IRA. A very generous plan will match 100% of employee deposits. However, some plans do not call for the employer to make a matching deposit at all. Other plans call for a matching contribution to be made at the discretion of the firm's board of directors. Actual terms of these plans vary widely from firm to firm. Generally, these savings plans allow employees to deposit as much as 15% of salary into the plan on a tax-deferred basis. However, the portion that the company uses to calculate its matching deposit is generally limited to a maximum of 6%. Employees should take care to diversify the holdings in their 401(k) accounts, and most people should seek professional guidance or investment management for their accounts. (Note: when profits are down, many employers exercise their right to suspend their contributions to 401(k)s. Employees may continue to make contributions, but they will not be matched by the employer in these cases.)

Stock Purchase Plan: Qualified employees may purchase the company's common stock at a price below its market value under a specific plan. Typically, the employee is limited to investing a small percentage of wages in this plan. The discount may range from 5% to 15%. Some of these plans allow for deposits to be made through regular monthly payroll deductions. However, new accounting rules for corporations, along with other factors, are leading many companies to curtail these plans—dropping the discount allowed, cutting the maximum yearly stock purchase or otherwise making the plans less generous or appealing.

Profit Sharing: Qualified employees are awarded an annual amount equal to some portion of a company's profits. In a very generous plan, the pool of money awarded to employees would be 15% of profits. Typically, this money is deposited into a long-term retirement account. Caution: Some employers refer to plans as "profit sharing" when they are actually 401(k) savings plans. True profit sharing plans are rarely offered.

Plunkett Research Online and Plunkett's Industry Reference Books:

1) Internet-Based Services: Plunkett Research Online is a reference service that is subscribed to by the nation's leading university placement offices, libraries and information offices. You can use it to filter prospective employers by location, industry, size and more. You can then export contact information for those companies into spreadsheets or text files. In addition, you can use the site to research the latest editions of our industry analysis. Many additional tools for job seekers are included. For an extensive online tour, see www.plunkettresearch.com.

2) Printed Almanacs: Plunkett Research also publishes industry-specific almanacs for the most important industries. These are top-notch resources for job seekers.

Industry-Specific Books from Plunkett Research:

- Plunkett's Advertising & Branding Industry Almanac
- Plunkett's Airline, Hotel & Travel Industry Almanac
- Plunkett's Almanac of Middle Market Companies
- Plunkett's Apparel & Textiles Industry Almanac
- Plunkett's Automobile Industry Almanac
- Plunkett's Banking, Mortgages & Credit Industry Almanac
- Plunkett's Biotech & Genetics Industry Almanac
- Plunkett's Chemicals, Coatings & Plastics Industry Almanac
- Plunkett's Consulting Industry Almanac
- Plunkett's E-Commerce & Internet Business Almanac
- Plunkett's Energy Industry Almanac

- Plunkett's Engineering & Research Industry Almanac
- Plunkett's Entertainment & Media Industry Almanac
- Plunkett's Food Industry Almanac
- Plunkett's Games, Apps & Social Media Industry Almanac
- Plunkett's Green Technology Industry Almanac
- Plunkett's Health Care Industry Almanac
- Plunkett's Insurance Industry Almanac
- Plunkett's InfoTech Industry Almanac
- Plunkett's Investment & Securities Industry Almanac
- Plunkett's Nanotechnology & MEMS Industry Almanac
- Plunkett's Outsourcing & Offshoring Industry Almanac
- Plunkett's Real Estate & Construction Industry Almanac
- Plunkett's Renewable, Alternative & Hydrogen Energy Industry Almanac
- Plunkett's Retail Industry Almanac
- Plunkett's Sports Industry Almanac
- Plunkett's Telecommunications Industry Almanac
- Plunkett's Transportation, Supply Chain & Logistics Industry Almanac
- Plunkett's Wireless & Cellular Telephone Industry Almanac

Publications from Plunkett Research Written Especially for Job Seekers:

- The Almanac of American Employers
- Plunkett's Companion to the Almanac of American Employers

Our books will give you in-depth coverage of specific industries and the leading firms in those industries, along with trends and developments in technology and services. You will find these books in public and academic libraries, college placement offices, human resources offices, corporate libraries and government agency libraries. For sample chapters and additional details, you can preview as well as purchase these books at www.plunkettresearch.com.

The Almanac of American Employers provides profiles and detailed listings of 500 hand-picked, U.S. employers of 2,500 employees or more in size

Plunkett's Companion to The Almanac of American Employers is our book that provides profiles on 500 additional, rapidly growing corporate employers. This companion book covers smaller firms than those in the main volume of *The Almanac of American Employers*.

Chapter 4

IMPORTANT CONTACTS FOR JOB SEEKERS

Contents:

I. Accountants & CPA Associations

American Institute of CPAs (AICPA)
1211 Ave. of the Americas
New York, NY 10036-8775 US
Phone: 212-596-6200
Fax: 1-800-362-5066
Toll Free: 888-777-7077
E-mail Address: *service@aicpa.org*
Web Address: www.aicpa.org
American Institute of CPAs (AICPA) provides information and news for CPAs, news from the organization and a search for accounting firms on its web site.

Council of Petroleum Accountants Societies, Inc. (COPAS)
3900 E. Mexico Ave., Ste. 602
Denver, CO 80210 US
Phone: 303-300-1131
Fax: 303-300-3733
Toll Free: 877-992-6727
E-mail Address: *Execdir@copas.org*
Web Address: www.copas.org
The Council of Petroleum Accountants Societies, Inc. (COPAS) provides a forum for discussing and solving the variety of problems related to accounting for oil and gas. COPAS also provides valuable educational materials related to oil and gas accounting.

International Accounting Standards Board (IASB)
30 Cannon St.
London, EC4M 6XH UK
Phone: 44-20-7246-6410
Fax: 44-20-7246-6411
E-mail Address: *iasb@iasb.org.uk*
Web Address: www.iasb.org
The International Accounting Standards Board (IASB) website hosts an electronic subscription service to the International Financial Reporting (IFRS) Standards as well access to IFRS summaries.

II. Advertising/Marketing Associations

4A's (American Association of Advertising Agencies)
405 Lexington Ave., Fl. 18
New York, NY 10174-1801 US
Phone: 212-682-2500
E-mail Address: *nhill@aaaa.org*
Web Address: www.aaaa.org
The 4A's is the national trade association representing the advertising agency industry in the U.S.

Advertising Women of New York (AWNY)
25 W. 45th St., Ste. 403
New York, NY 10036 US
Phone: 212-221-7969
Fax: 212-221-8296
E-mail Address: *awny@awny.org*
Web Address: www.awny.org
Advertising Women of New York (AWNY) provides a forum for personal and professional growth, serves as a catalyst for the advancement of women in the communications field and promotes and supports philanthropic endeavors through the AWNY Foundation. The web site also provides content from Women Executives in Public Relations (WERP), such as its a dynamic job board.

American Institute of Graphic Arts (AIGA)
164 5th Ave.
New York, NY 10010 US
Phone: 212-807-1990
Fax: 212-807-1799
E-mail Address:
steve_rogenstein@aiga.org
Web Address: www.aiga.org
The American Institute of Graphic Arts (AIGA) strives to further excellence in

communication design, both as a strategic tool for business and as a cultural force.

American Marketing Association (AMA)
311 S. Wacker Dr., Ste. 5800
Chicago, IL 60606 US
Phone: 312-542-9000
Fax: 312-542-9001
Toll Free: 800-262-1150
E-mail Address: *info@ama.org*
Web Address: www.marketingpower.com
The American Marketing Association (AMA) serves marketing professionals in both business and education and serves all levels of marketing practitioners, educators and students.

Cable & Telecommunications Association for Marketing (CTAM)
201 N. Union St., Ste. 440
Alexandria, VA 22314 US
Phone: 703-549-4200
E-mail Address: *info@ctam.com*
Web Address: www.ctam.com
The Cable & Telecommunications Association for Marketing (CTAM) is dedicated to the discipline and development of consumer marketing excellence in cable television, new media and telecommunications services.

Direct Marketing Association (DMA)
1120 Ave. of the Americas
New York, NY 10036-6700 US
Phone: 212-768-7277
Fax: 212-302-6714
E-mail Address: *customerservice@the-dma.org*
Web Address: www.the-dma.org
The Direct Marketing Association (DMA) is the oldest and largest trade association for users and suppliers in the direct, database and interactive marketing fields.

III. Aerospace & Defense Industry Associations

American Institute of Aeronautics and Astronautics (AIAA)
1801 Alexander Bell Dr., Ste. 500
Reston, VA 20191-4344 US
Phone: 703-264-7500
Fax: 703-264-7551
Toll Free: 800-639-2422
E-mail Address: *chrish@aiaa.org*
Web Address: www.aiaa.org
The American Institute of Aeronautics and Astronautics (AIAA) is a nonprofit society aimed at advancing the arts, sciences and technology of aeronautics and astronautics. The institute represents the U.S. in the International Astronautical Federation and the International Council on the Aeronautical Sciences.

IV. Airline & Air Cargo Industry Associations

International Air Transport Association (IATA)
800 Place Victoria
P.O. Box 113
Montreal, QC H4Z 1M1 Canada
Phone: 514-874-0202
Fax: 514-874-9632
E-mail Address: *corpcomms@iata.org*
Web Address: www.iata.org
The International Air Transport Association (IATA) represents about 230 airlines in order to offer the highest standards of passenger and cargo service.

V. Alternative Energy-Ethanol

Renewable Fuels Association (RFA)
425 3rd St. SW, Ste. 1150
Washington, DC 20024 US
Phone: 202-289-3835
Fax: 202-289-7519
Web Address: www.ethanolrfa.org
The Renewable Fuels Association (RFA) is a trade organization representing the ethanol industry. It publishes a wealth of useful information, including a listing of biorefineries and monthly U.S. fuel ethanol production and demand.

VI. Alternative Energy-Solar

Solar Energy Industries Association (SEIA)
575 7th St. NW, Ste. 400
Washington, DC 20004 US
Phone: 202-682-0556
Fax: 202-682-7779
E-mail Address: *info@seia.org*
Web Address: www.seia.org
Established in 1974, the Solar Energy Industries Association is the American trade association of the solar energy industry. Among its operations is a web site that provides news for the solar energy industry, links to related products and companies and solar energy statistics.

VII. Alternative Energy-Wind

American Wind Energy Association (AWEA)
1501 M St. NW, Ste. 1000
Washington, DC 20005 US
Phone: 202-383-2500
Fax: 202-383-2505
E-mail Address: *windmail@awea.org*
Web Address: www.awea.org
The American Wind Energy Association (AWEA) promotes wind energy as a clean source of electricity worldwide. Its website provides excellent resources for research, including an online library, discussions of legislation, and descriptions of wind technologies.

VIII. Banking Industry Associations

American Bankers Association (ABA)
1120 Connecticut Ave. NW
Washington, DC 20036 US
Fax: 202-663-7578
Toll Free: 800-226-5377
E-mail Address: *smarshall@aba.com*
Web Address: www.aba.com
The American Bankers Association (ABA) represents banks of all sizes on issues of national importance for financial institutions and their customers. The site offers financial information and solutions, financial news and member access to further advice and content.

IX. Biotechnology & Biological Industry Associations

Biotechnology Industry Organization (BIO)
1201 Maryland Ave. SW, Ste. 900
Washington, DC 20024 US
Phone: 202-962-9200
Fax: 202-488-6301
E-mail Address: *info@bio.org*
Web Address: www.bio.org
The Biotechnology Industry Organization (BIO) represents members involved in the research and development of health care, agricultural, industrial and environmental biotechnology products. BIO has both small and large member organizations.

X. Booksellers Associations

American Booksellers Association, Inc.
200 White Plains Rd., Ste. 600
Tarrytown, NY 10591 US
Fax: 914-591-2720
Toll Free: 800-637-0037
E-mail Address: *info@bookweb.org*
Web Address: www.bookweb.org
The American Booksellers Association is a nonprofit association representing independent bookstores in the United States.

XI. Broadcasting, Cable, Radio & TV Associations

Academy of Television Arts and Sciences
5220 Lankershim Blvd.
North Hollywood, CA 91601-3109 US
Phone: 818-754-2800
Fax: 818-761-2827
E-mail Address: *support@emmys.org*
Web Address: www.emmys.tv
The Academy of Television Arts and Sciences is a nonprofit corporation devoted to the advancement of telecommunications arts and sciences and to fostering creative leadership in the telecommunications industry. It is one of three organizations that administer the Emmy Awards. It is responsible for prime time Emmys.

American Federation of Television and Radio Artists (AFTRA)
260 Madison Ave., Fl. 7
New York, NY 10016-2401 US
Phone: 212-532-0800
Fax: 212-532-2242
E-mail Address: *info@aftra.org*
Web Address: www.aftra.org
The American Federation of Television and Radio Artists (AFTRA) represents actors and other professional performers and broadcasters in television, radio, sound recordings, non-broadcast/industrial programming and new technologies such as interactive programming and CD-ROMs.

American Women in Radio and Television, Inc. (AWRT)
1760 Old Meadow Rd., Ste. 500
McLean, VA 22102 US
Phone: 703-506-3290
Fax: 703-506-3266
E-mail Address: *info@awrt.org*
Web Address: www.awrt.org
American Women in Radio and Television (AWRT), founded in 1951, is a national nonprofit organization dedicated to advancing the role of women in electronic media and related fields.

Association of America's Public Television Stations (APTS)
2100 Crystal Dr., Ste. 700
Arlington, VA 22202 US
Phone: 202-654-4200
Fax: 202-654-4236
E-mail Address: *jeffrey@apts.org*
Web Address: www.apts.org
The Association of America's Public Television Stations (APTS) is a nonprofit membership organization formed to support the continued growth and development of strong and financially sound noncommercial television service for the American public.

Broadcast Education Association (BEA)
1771 N St. NW
Washington, DC 20036-2891 US
Phone: 202-429-3935
E-mail Address: *tbailey@nab.org*
Web Address: www.beaweb.org
The Broadcast Education Association (BEA) is the professional association for professors, industry professionals and graduate students interested in teaching and research related to electronic media and multimedia enterprises.

National Academy of Television Arts and Sciences
111 W. 57th St., Ste. 600
New York, NY 10019 US
Phone: 212-586-8424
Fax: 212-246-8129
E-mail Address: *info@emmyonline.tv*
Web Address: www.emmyonline.org
The National Academy of Television Arts and Sciences is dedicated to the advancement of the arts and sciences of television and the promotion of creative leadership for artistic, educational and technical achievements within the television industry. It is responsible for awarding the Emmy Awards.

National Association of Broadcasters (NAB)
1771 N St. NW
Washington, DC 20036 US
Phone: 202-429-5300
Fax: 202-429-4199
E-mail Address: *nab@nab.org*
Web Address: www.nab.org
The National Association of Broadcasters (NAB) represents broadcasters for radio and television. The organization also provides benefits to employees of member companies and to individuals and companies that provide products and services to the electronic media industries.

National Association of Television Program Executives (NATPE)
5757 Wilshire Blvd., Penthouse 10
Los Angeles, CA 90036-3681 US
Phone: 310-453-4440
Fax: 310-453-5258
E-mail Address: *info@natpe.org*
Web Address: www.natpe.org
The National Association of Television Program Executives (NATPE) is the leading association for content professionals in the global television industry.

National Cable and Telecommunications Association (NCTA)
25 Massachusetts Ave. NW, Ste. 100
Washington, DC 20001-1413 US
Phone: 202-222-2300
E-mail Address: *rstoddard@ncta.com*
Web Address: www.ncta.com
The National Cable and Telecommunications Association (NCTA) is the principal trade association of the cable television industry in the United States.

Radio Television News Directors Association (RTNDA)
1025 F St. NW, Fl. 7
Washington, DC 20004 US
Phone: 202-659-6510
Fax: 202-223-4007
Toll Free: 800-807-8632
E-mail Address: *stefanib@rtnda.org*
Web Address: www.rtnda.org
The Radio Television News Directors Association (RTNDA) is the world's largest professional organization exclusively committed to professionals in electronic journalism.

Syndication Network Television Association (SNTA)
1 Penn Plz., Ste. 5310
New York, NY 10119 US
Phone: 212-259-3740
Fax: 212-259-3770
E-mail Address: *mburg@snta.com*
Web Address: www.snta.com
The Syndication Network Television Association (SNTA) is an organization of national and independent television stations that syndicate television shows.

Women in Cable & Telecommunications (WICT)
14555 Avion Pkwy., Ste. 250
Chantilly, VA 20151 US
Phone: 703-234-9810
Fax: 703-817-1595
E-mail Address: *lvega@wict.org*
Web Address: www.wict.org
Women in Cable & Telecommunications (WICT) exists to advance the position and influence of women in media through leadership programs and services at both the national and local level.

XII. Careers-Airlines/Flying

Aviation/Aerospace Jobs Page
601 SW 9th St., Stes. J & K
c/o NationJob, Inc.
Des Moines, IA 50309 US
Fax: 515-283-1223
Toll Free: 888-526-5967

E-mail Address: *customerservice@nationjob.com*
Web Address: www.nationjob.com/aviation
The Aviation/Aerospace Jobs Page, a division of NationJob, Inc., features detailed aviation and aerospace job listings and company profiles.

AviationJobSearch.com
London Rd. Sayers Common
West Sussex, BN6 9HS UK
Phone: 01273-837538
Web Address: www.aviationjobsearch.com
AviationJobSearch.com lists jobs related to the airline industry.

Avjobs, Inc.
P.O. Box 630830
Littleton, CO 80163 US
Phone: 303-683-2322
Fax: 888-624-8691
E-mail Address: *info@avjobs.com*
Web Address: www.avjobs.com
Avjobs, Inc. is a group of employers dedicated to helping individuals obtain aviation, airline, aerospace and airport careers.

Flightdeck Recruitment Ltd.
82c E. Hill
Colchester, Essex CO1 2QW UK
Phone: 44-1206-383730
Web Address: www.flightdeckrecruitment.com
Flightdeck Recruitment Ltd. provides a link between aviation recruiters who are looking for flight deck crew and pilots or flight engineers who are seeking employment.

XIII. Careers-Apparel

24 Seven Fashion Recruitment
120 Wooster St., Fl. 4
New York, NY 10012 US
Phone: 212-966-4426
Fax: 212-966-2313
Web Address: www.24seveninc.com
24 Seven Fashion Recruitment is an employment agency serving the fashion, beauty, entertainment, advertising, marketing and retail industries.

Fashion Career Center
E-mail Address: *fashioncc@fashioncareercenter.com*
Web Address: www.fashioncareercenter.com
The Fashion Career Center site provides employees and employers with a place to meet and access information about employment in the fashion industry. The FashionCareerCenter.com web site offers links to fashion jobs and fashion schools, as well as offering fashion career advice.

XIV. Careers-Banking

National Banking & Financial Service Network (NBFSN)
3075 Brickhouse Ct.
Virginia Beach, VA 23452-6860 US
Phone: 757-463-5766
Fax: 757-340-0826
E-mail Address: *susan@nbn-jobs.com*
Web Address: www.banking-financejobs.com
The National Banking & Financial Service Network (NBFSN) is made up of recruiting firms in the banking and financial services marketplace. The web site provides job listings.

XV. Careers-Biotech

BiotechEmployment.com
Phone: 561-630-5201
E-mail Address: *jobs@Biotechemployment.com*
Web Address: www.biotechemployment.com
BiotechEmployment.com is an online resource for job seekers in biotechnology. The site's features includes resume posting, job search agents and employer profiles. It is part of the eJobstores.com, Inc., which includes the Health Care Job Store sites.

Chase Group (The)
Phone: 913-663-3100
Fax: 913-663-3131
E-mail Address: *chase@chasegroup.com*
Web Address: www.chasegroup.com
The Chase Group is an executive search firm specializing in biomedical and pharmaceutical placement.

XVI. Careers-Coatings

CoatingsJobs.com
Web Address: www.coatingsjobs.com
CoatingsJobs.com connects coatings industry job seekers and employers. The web site offers job postings, resume postings, information for job seekers and an employment newsletter.

XVII. Careers-Computers/Technology

ComputerJobs.com, Inc.
1995 N. Park Pl., Ste. 425
Atlanta, GA 30339 US
Toll Free: 800-850-0045
Web Address: www.computerjobs.com
ComputerJobs.com is an employment web site that offers users a links to computer-related job opportunities organized by skill and market.

Dice
4101 NW Urbandale Dr.
Urbandale, IA 50322 US
Phone: 515-280-1144
Fax: 515-280-1452
Toll Free: 877-386-3323
E-mail Address: *dicemedia@dice.com*
Web Address: www.dice.com
Dice.com provides free employment services for IT jobs. The site includes advanced job searches by geographic location and category, availability announcements and resume postings, as well as employer profiles, a recruiter's page and career links. It is maintained by Dice Holdings, Inc., a publicly traded company.

Institute for Electrical and Electronics Engineers (IEEE) Job Site
445 Hoes Ln.
Piscataway, NJ 08855-1331 US
Phone: 732-981-0060
Toll Free: 800-678-4333
E-mail Address: *candidatejobsite@ieee.org*
Web Address: careers.ieee.org
The Institute for Electrical and Electronics Engineers (IEEE) Job Site provides a host of employment services for technical professionals, employers and recruiters. The site offers job listings by geographic area, a resume bank and links to employment services.

Pencom Systems, Inc.
152 Remsen St.
Brooklyn, NY 11201 US
Phone: 718-923-1111
Fax: 718-923-6066
Toll Free: 800-736-2664
E-mail Address: *tom@pencom.com*
Web Address: www.pencom.com
Pencom Systems, Inc., an open systems recruiting company, hosts a career web site geared toward high-technology and scientific professionals, featuring an interactive salary survey, career advisor, job listings and technology resources. Its focus is the financial services industry within the New York City area.

XVIII. Careers-Contract and Freelance

Guru.com
5001 Baum Blvd., Ste. 760
Pittsburgh, PA 15213 US

Phone: 412-687-2228
Fax: 412-687-4466
Toll Free: 888-678-0136
E-mail Address: *pr@guru.com*
Web Address: www.guru.com
Guru.com provides contract job access for freelancers and contract workers, in fields ranging from interior design to architecture, marketing and web design, among others. Employers can post projects, and freelancers can offers bids on prospective jobs. Many tools are provided to enable freelancers to be completely informed about the scope of the work needed.

XIX. Careers-First Time Jobs/New Grads

Alumni-Network Recruitment Corporation
Phone: 905-465-2547
E-mail Address: *karen@alumni-network.com*
Web Address: www.alumni-network.com
Alumni-Network Recruitment Corporation is a professional search and recruiting firm, specializing in ERP, E-Commerce and Engineering.

Black Collegian Online (The)
140 Carondelet St.
New Orleans, LA 70130 US
Phone: 504-523-0154
Web Address: www.blackcollegian.com
The Black Collegian Online features listings for job and internship opportunities, as well as other tools for students of color; it is the web site of The Black Collegian Magazine, published by IMDiversity, Inc. The site includes a list of the top 100 minority corporate employers and an assessment of job opportunities.

CollegeGrad.com, Inc.
234 E. College Ave., Ste. 200
State College, PA 16801 US
Phone: 262-375-6700
Toll Free: 1-800-991-4642
Web Address: www.collegegrad.com
CollegeGrad.com, Inc. offers in-depth resources for college students and recent grads seeking entry-level jobs.

Job Web
62 Highland Ave.
Bethlehem, PA 18017-9085 US
Phone: 610-868-1421
Fax: 610-868-0208
Toll Free: 800-544-5272
E-mail Address: *callen@naceweb.org*
Web Address: www.jobweb.com
Job Web, owned and sponsored by National Association of Colleges and Employers (NACE), displays job openings and employer descriptions for college students and recent graduates. The site also offers a database of career fairs, searchable by state or keyword; sample resumes; and other career related information.

MBAjobs.net
Web Address: www.mbajobs.net
MBAjobs.net is an international service for MBA students and graduates, employers, recruiters and business schools. It aims to match MBA graduates with employers and provides links to online MBA programs.

MonsterCollege
799 Market St., Ste. 500
San Francisco, CA 94103 US
Toll Free: 800-999-8725
E-mail Address: *info@college.monster.com*
Web Address: www.college.monster.com
MonsterCollege provides information about internships and entry-level jobs, as well as career advice and resume tips, to recent college graduates.

National Association of Colleges and Employers (NACE)
62 Highland Ave.
Bethlehem, PA 18017-9085 US
Phone: 610-868-1421
Fax: 610-868-0208
Toll Free: 800-544-5272
E-mail Address: *mcollins@naceweb.org*
Web Address: www.naceweb.org
The National Association of Colleges and Employers (NACE) is a premier U.S. organization representing college placement offices and corporate recruiters who focus on hiring new grads.

XX. Careers-General Job Listings

6FigureJobs
25 3rd St., Ste. 230
Stamford, CT 06905 US
Toll Free: 800-605-5154
Web Address: www.6figurejobs.com
6FigureJobs offers executives a database of high-level positions. Membership is free for qualified individuals.

Career Exposure, Inc.
3934 SW Corbett Ave.
Portland, OR 97239 US
Phone: 503-221-7779
Fax: 503-221-7780
E-mail Address: *pr@careerexposure.com*
Web Address: www.careerexposure.com
Career Exposure, Inc. is an online career center and job placement service, with resources for employers, recruiters and job seekers.

CareerBuilder, Inc.
200 N. LaSalle St., Ste. 1100
Chicago, IL 60601 US
Phone: 773-527-3600
Toll Free: 800-638-4212
Web Address: www.careerbuilder.com
CareerBuilder, Inc. focuses on the needs of companies and also provides a database of job openings. The site has over 1 million jobs posted by 300,000 employers, and receives an average 23 million unique visitors monthly. The company also operates online career centers for 140 newspapers and 9,000 online partners. Resumes are sent directly to the company, and applicants can set up a special e-mail account for job-seeking purposes. CareerBuilder is primarily a joint venture between three newspaper giants: The McClatchy Company, Gannett Co., Inc. and Tribune Company.

CareerOneStop
Toll Free: 877-348-0502
E-mail Address: *info@careeronestop.org*
Web Address: www.careeronestop.org
CareerOneStop is operated by the employment commissions of various state agencies. It contains job listings in both the private and government sectors, as well as a wide variety of useful career resources and workforce information. CareerOneStop is sponsored by the U.S. Department of Labor.

Careers Organization (The)
155 108th Ave. NE, Ste. 810
Bellevue, WA 98004 US
Phone: 510-663-7000
Fax: 510-663-7001
E-mail Address: *support@careers.org*
Web Address: www.careers.org
The Career Organization is an online career resource center with links to jobs and other career-related web sites, as well as information regarding colleges and online degree programs.

CollegeRecruiter.com
3109 W. 50 St., Ste. 121
Minneapolis, MN 55410-2102 US
Phone: 952-848-2211
Fax: 702-537-2227
E-mail Address: *Steven@CollegeRecruiter.com*
Web Address: www.collegerecruiter.com
CollegeRecruiter.com provides college students with internship, part-time and summer job listings. Recent graduates

can search for career opportunities by category and location.

ContractJobHunter
C. E. Publications, Inc.
P.O. Box 3006
Bothell, WA 98041-3006 US
Phone: 425-806-5200
Fax: 425-806-5585
E-mail Address: *staff@cjhunter.com*
Web Address: www.ceweekly.wa.com
ContractJobHunter is a web-based version of the magazine Contract Employment Weekly Online. It posts job listings and links to contract firms in the engineering, IT and technical fields. Libraries for reference materials and resume writing guidelines are also offered. The site is a service of C. E. Publications, Inc.

EmploymentGuide
150 Granby St.
Norfolk, VA 23510 US
Toll Free: 877-876-4039
Web Address:
www.employmentguide.com
EmploymentGuide offers general career resources along with lists of position openings, company profiles and a resume database. It also circulates a free print publication.

EscapeArtist.com Inc.
832-1245 World Trade Ctr.
Panama, WTC-0832 Republic of Panama
Phone: 507-317-6937
Fax: 507-317-6938
Web Address: www.escapeartist.com
EscapeArtist.com provides job searches for overseas positions, as well as international working condition resources and immigration information.

ExecuNet, Inc.
295 Westport Ave.
Norwalk, CT 06851 US
Toll Free: 800-637-3126
E-mail Address:
member.services@execunet.com
Web Address: www.execunet.com
ExecuNet, Inc. is an executive career management information and contact service.

HigherEdJobs.com
328 Innovation Blvd., Ste. 300
State College, PA 16803 US
Phone: 814-861-3080
Fax: 814-861-3082
E-mail Address:
sales@HigherEdJobs.com
Web Address: www.higheredjobs.com
HigherEdJobs.com lists job vacancies in colleges and universities.

IMDiversity, Inc.
140 Carondelet St.
New Orleans, LA 70130 US
Phone: 504-598-3357
Fax: 504-523-0271
E-mail Address:
support@imdiversity.com
Web Address: www.imdiversity.com
IMDiversity, Inc. provides job listings and career development information for minorities in the U.S., with a particular focus on African Americans, Asian Americans and Pacific Islanders, Latino/Hispanic Americans, Native Americans and women.

Indeed.com
177 Broad St., Fl. 6
Stamford, CT 06901 US
Web Address: www.indeed.com
Indeed.com provides extensive lists of jobs of all types, with links directly to the employers. It covers over 50 countries, including the U.S., Canada, India, Mexico.

Job Search USA
E-mail Address:
contactjsu@jobsearchusa.org
Web Address: www.jobsearchusa.org
Job Search USA is a major job posting site that contains job opportunities classified by a variety of keywords.

JobCentral
9002 N. Purdue Rd., Ste. 100
Indianapolis, IN 46268 US
Phone: 317-874-9000
Fax: 317-874-9100
Toll Free: 866-268-6206
Web Address: www.jobcentral.com
JobCentral, operated by the nonprofit DirectEmployers Association, Inc., links users directly to job opportunities posted on the sites of participating employers, thus bypassing the usual job search sites. This saves employers money and allows job seekers to access many more job opportunities.

Jobs in Logistics
Toll Free: 877-562-7678
Web Address: www.jobsinlogistics.com
Jobs in Logistics provides contacts for job seekers in the transportation and logistics fields.

JobsInTheMoney.com
1040 Avenue of the Americas, Ste. 16B
New York, NY 10018 US
Phone: 212-448-8287
Fax: 212-725-9127
Toll Free: 800-380-9040
E-mail Address: *help-usa@efinancialcareers.com*
Web Address:
www.efinancialcareers.com
efinancialcareers.com provides employment listings in the finance industry, as well as job tools such as salary surveys, resume writing assistance and industry news. It is owned by Dice, a part of Dice Holdings, Inc.

LaborMarketInfo (LMI)
P.O. Box 826880, MIC 57
c/o Employment Dev. Dept., Labor Market Info. Div.
Sacramento, CA 94280-0001 US
Phone: 916-262-2162
Fax: 916-262-2352
Toll Free: 800-480-3287
Web Address:
www.labormarketinfo.edd.ca.gov
LaborMarketInfo (LMI) provides job seekers and employers a wide range of resources, namely the ability to find, access and use labor market information and services. It provides statistics for employment demographics on both a local and regional level, as well as career searching tools for California residents. The web site is sponsored by California's Employment Development Office.

MediaBistro.com
475 Park Ave. S., Fl. 4
New York, NY 10016 US
Phone: 212-389-2000
Fax: 866-880-1429
E-mail Address:
laurelT@mediabistro.com
Web Address: www.mediabistro.com
MediaBistro.com provides news and information on current events relating to the media industry. It also offers an array of employment resources, including job listings within the industry.

Monster Worldwide, Inc.
622 Third Ave., Fl. 39
New York, NY 10017 US
Phone: 212-351-7000
Fax: 646-658-0540
E-mail Address:
matthew.henson@monster.com
Web Address: www.monster.com
Monster Worldwide, Inc., parent company of Monster.com, provides online career and personnel services. The firm operates in 50 countries.

MyResumeAgent.com
1 Phoenix Mill Ln., Fl. 3
Kennedy Information, Inc.
Peterborough, NH 03458 US
Phone: 603-924-0900
Toll Free: 800-531-0007
E-mail Address:
feedback@myresumeagent.com

Web Address: www.myresumeagent.com
MyResumeAgent.com allows senior-level professionals to have their resumes sent to executive placement firms for a fee. The site is owned by Kennedy Information, Inc.

NationJob, Inc.
920 Morgan St., Ste. T
Des Moines, IA 50309 US
Fax: 515-243-5384
Toll Free: 888-292-7731
E-mail Address:
customerservice@nationjob.com
Web Address: www.nationjob.com
NationJob.com is an online job search portal. The web site allows users to search through listings or develop a profile of the ideal job based on the criterion of location, industry, salary; and, if they provide an e-mail address, wait for appropriate listings to be sent to them through the firm's PJScout feature.

NETSHARE, Inc.
83 Hamilton Dr., Ste. 202
Novato, CA 94949 US
Toll Free: 800-241-5642
E-mail Address: *netshare@netshare.com*
Web Address: www.netshare.com
Netshare provides access to exclusive listings of executive jobs that pay $100,000 and up.

Net-Temps, Inc.
55 Middlesex St., Ste. 220
North Chelmsford, MA 01863 US
Fax: 978-251-7250
Toll Free: 800-307-0062
E-mail Address: *service@net-temps.com*
Web Address: www.net-temps.com
Net-Temps, Inc. offers a web site, operated by professional career consultants, that features job listings and job seeking tips.

Recruiters Online Network
3599 E. Normandy Park Dr.
Medina, OH 44256 US
E-mail Address:
recruitersonline@earthlink.net
Web Address: www.recruitersonline.com
The Recruiters Online Network provides job postings from thousands of recruiters, Careers Online Magazine, a resume database, as well as other career resources.

True Careers, Inc.
Web Address: www.truecareers.com
True Careers, Inc. offers job listings and provides an array of career resources. It is partnered with CareerBuilder.com, which powers its career information and resume posting functions.

USAJOBS
1900 E St. NW
Washington, DC 20415 US
Phone: 202-606-1800
Web Address: usajobs.opm.gov
USAJOBS, a program of the U.S. Office of Personnel Management, is the official job site for the U.S. Federal Government. It provides a comprehensive list of U.S. government jobs, allowing users to search for employment by location; agency; type of work; or by senior executive positions. It also has special employment sections for individuals with disabilities, veterans and recent college graduates; an information center, offering resume and interview tips and other information; and allows users to create a profile and post a resume.

XXI. Careers-Health Care

Health Care Source
400 TradeCenter, Ste. 3900
Woburn, MA 01801 US
Phone: 781-368-1033
Fax: 800-829-6600
Toll Free: 800-869-5200
E-mail Address:
info@healthcaresource.com
Web Address: www.healthcaresource.com
Health Care Source is a leading provider of talent management, recruitment and employment services for healthcare providers.

MedicalWorkers.com
191 University Blvd., Ste. 252
Denver, CO 80206 US
Phone: 720-227-9364
E-mail Address: *cs@medicalworkers.com*
Web Address: www.medicalworkers.com
MedicalWorkers.com is an employment site for medical and health care professionals.

MedJump.com
7119 E. Shea Blvd., Stes. 109-535
Scottsdale, AZ 85254 US
E-mail Address: *info@medjump.net*
Web Address: www.medjump.com
MedJump.com is dedicated to empowering health care and medical-related professionals with the necessary tools to market their abilities and skills.

Medzilla, Inc.
P.O. Box 1710
Marysville, WA 98270 US
Phone: 360-657-5681
Fax: 775-514-9440
E-mail Address: *info@medzilla.com*
Web Address: www.medzilla.com
Medzilla, Inc.'s web site offers job searches, salary surveys, a search agent and information on employment in the biotech, pharmaceuticals, healthcare and science sectors.

Monster Career Advice-Healthcare
622 3rd Ave., Fl. 39
New York, NY 10017 US
Phone: 212-351-7000
Fax: 646-658-0540
Toll Free: 800-666-7837
Web Address: career-advice.monster.com/Healthcare/job-category-3975.aspx
Monster Career Advice-Healthcare, a service of Monster Worldwide, Inc., provides industry-related articles, job listings, job searches and search agents for the medical field.

NationJob Network-Medical and Health Care Jobs Page
601 SW 9th St., Stes. H&J
Des Moines, IA 50309 US
Fax: 515-243-5384
Toll Free: 800-292-7731
E-mail Address:
customerservice@nationjob.com
Web Address:
www.nationjob.com/medical
The NationJob Network-Medical and Health Care Jobs Page offers information and listings for health care employment.

Nurse-Recruiter.com
36 Washington St., Ste. 170
Wellesley, MA 02481 US
Toll Free: 877-562-7966
E-mail Address:
support@nurserecruiter.com
Web Address: www.nurse-recruiter.com
Nurse-Recruiter.com is a nurse-owned, web-centric company devoted to bringing health care employers and the nursing community together.

PracticeLink
Fax: 877-847-0120
Toll Free: 800-776-8383
E-mail Address:
physicianhelpdesk@practicelink.com
Web Address: www.practicelink.com
PracticeLink, one of the largest physician employment web sites, is a free service used by more than 18,000 practice-seeking physicians annually to quickly search and locate potential career opportunities. PracticeLink is financially supported by more than 700 hospitals, medical groups, private practices and health care systems that advertise more than 5,000 opportunities.

RPh on the Go USA, Inc.
5510 Howard St.
Skokie, IL 60077-2620 US
Phone: 847-588-7170
Fax: 847-588-7060
Toll Free: 800-553-7359
E-mail Address:
lbalaguer@rphonthego.com
Web Address: www.rphonthego.com
RPh on the Go USA, Inc. places temporary and permanent qualified professionals in the pharmacy community.

XXII. Careers-Interview Tips for Consulting Jobs

McKinsey & Company Interviewing Tips
55 E. 52nd St
New York, NY 10022 US
Phone: 212-446-7000
Fax: 212-446-8575
Web Address:
www.mckinsey.com/careers/how_do_i_apply/how_to_do_well_in_the_interview.aspx
The McKinsey & Company Interviewing Tips site is an excellent resource for preparing for a consulting interview.

XXIII. Careers-Job Listings for Seniors

Dinosaur Exchange
Dino-X Ltd., P.O. Box 100
Sydney Vane House Admiral Park
St. Peter Port, Guernsey GY1 3EL
Channel Islands
E-mail Address:
CustomerSupport@dinosaur-exchange.com
Web Address: www.dinosaur-exchange.com
Dinosaur Exchange, opened in 2003, is a job forum for the elderly, which allows seniors to post resumes and be contacted by employers. Dino-X Ltd. owns and operates the web site.

Employment Network for Retired Government Experts (ENRGE)
Zavala, Inc.
P.O. Box 1532
N. Falmouth, MA 02556 US
Phone: 508-564-4140
Web Address: www.enrge.us
The Employment Network for Retired Government Experts (ENRGE) helps government employees to remain active in their professions after retirement. ENERGE is the business name of Zavala, Inc.

Senior Job Bank
NHC Group, Inc.
P.O. Box 508
Marlborough, MA 01752 US
Toll Free: 888-501-0804
Web Address: www.seniorjobbank.org
The Senior Job Bank web site offers an easy, effective and free method for senior citizens to find occasional, part-time, flexible, temporary or full-time jobs. The site is owned and managed by NHC Group, Inc.

Seniors4Hire.org
7071 Warner Ave. F466
Huntington Beach, CA 92647 US
Phone: 714-848-0996
Fax: 714-848-5445
E-mail Address: *info@seniors4hire.org*
Web Address: www.seniors4hire.org
Seniors4Hire.org is an online career center with job postings, employment resources and information on community service employment programs for older workers, retirees and senior citizens. The site is owned and operated by The Forward Group.

YourEncore
20 N. Meridian St., Ste. 800
Indianapolis, IN 46204 US
Phone: 317-226-9301
Fax: 317-226-9312
E-mail Address:
General.Information@yourencore.com
Web Address: www.yourencore.com
YourEncore is a program that seeks to employ retirees by matching them with member companies. The web site utilizes retirees mainly in the areas of engineering, science and product development.

XXIV. Careers-Job Reference Tools

CareerXroads (CXR)
Mark Mehler
P.O. Box 253
Kendall Park, NJ 08824 US
Phone: 732-821-6652
E-mail Address: *mmc@careerxroads.com*
Web Address: www.careerxroads.com
CareerXroads (CXR) publishes an annual guide on job and resume web sites. It was cofounded by Gerry Crispin and Mark Mehler.

Job-Hunt.org
186 Main St.
NETability, Inc.
Marlborough, MA 01752 US
Phone: 508-624-6261
E-mail Address: *info@job-hunt.org*
Web Address: www.job-hunt.org
Job-Hunt.org, rather than collecting resumes or posting job vacancies, offers a vast list of job listing web sites and links to helpful job search tools. It is owned by NETability, Inc.

JobStar
E-mail Address:
electrajobstar@earthlink.net
Web Address: jobstar.org
JobStar has a salary info link to over 300 different salary information and salary survey sites. It also contains job listings focused on the California market.

MBA Career Services Council (CSC)
E-mail Address:
kip.harrell@thunderbird.edu.
Web Address: www.mbacsc.org
The MBA Career Services Council (CSC) is a global professional association for individuals in the field of MBA career services and those that recruit directly from graduate management programs.

NewsVoyager
Web Address: www.newsvoyager.com
NewsVoyager, a service of the Newspaper Association of America (NAA), links individuals to local, national and international newspapers, allowing job seekers to search through thousands of classified sections.

Quintessential Careers (QC)
EmpoweringSites.com
DeLand, Fl 32720 US
Phone: 386-740-8872
Fax: 386-740-9764
E-mail Address:
randall@quintcareers.com
Web Address: www.quintcareers.com
Quintessential Careers (QC) provides a large collection of data and links for job seekers, including advice, tools and job postings; it also offers a guide to researching companies. QC is a subsidiary of EmpoweringSites.com.

Vault.com, Inc.
75 Varick St., Fl. 8
New York, NY 10013 US
Phone: 212-366-4212
Fax: 212-366-6117
Web Address: www.vault.com
Vault.com, Inc. is a comprehensive career web site for employers and employees, with job postings and valuable information on a wide variety of industries. Its features and content are largely geared toward MBA degree holders.

WetFeet.com
Web Address: www.wetfeet.com
WetFeet.com provides an excellent combination of links and resources for job seekers. The site is owned by Universum.

What Color is Your Parachute?
E-mail Address: *rnbolles@jobhuntersbible.com*
Web Address: www.jobhuntersbible.com
The What Color is Your Parachute? official web site, JobHuntersBible.com, is based on the "Job-Hunting on the Internet" chapter of Richard (Dick) Bolle's best-selling book. Designed to aid job hunters and career changers who want to use the Internet as part of their job search, the site provides links to job listing, resume, career counseling, contacts and research sites.

XXV. Careers-Restaurants

FoodService.com
Phone: 678-256-8014
Toll Free: 800-896-4442
E-mail Address: *customercare@Foodservice.com*
Web Address: www.foodservice.com
FoodService.com, managed and run by Food Service Interactive, LLC, offers web site design and job search services for the food service industry.

Resources in Food, Inc. (RIF)
1007 N. Main St.
Columbia, IL 62236 US
Phone: 618-281-3100
Fax: 866-281-7374
Toll Free: 877-743-1100
E-mail Address: *rifchicago@rifood.com*
Web Address: www.rifood.com
Resources in Food (RIF) provides professional management placement for the hospitality industry.

XXVI. Careers-Science

Chem Jobs
730 E. Cypress Ave.
Monrovia, CA 91016 US
Phone: 626-930-0808
Fax: 626-930-0102
E-mail Address: *info@chemindustry.com*
Web Address: www.chemjobs.net
Chem Jobs is a leading Internet site for job seekers in chemistry and related fields, with a particular focus on chemists, biochemists, pharmaceutical scientists and chemical engineers. The web site is powered by Chemindustry.com.

New Scientist Jobs
Quadrant House
84 Theobald's Rd.
Sutton, SM2 5AS UK
E-mail Address: *nssales@elsevier.com.*
Web Address: www.newscientistjobs.com
New Scientist Jobs is a web site produced by the publishers of New Scientist Magazine that connects jobseekers and employers in the bioscience fields. The site includes a job search engine and a free-of-charge e-mail job alert service.

Science Jobs
E-mail Address: *webmaster@science-jobs.org*
Web Address: www.science-jobs.org
Science Jobs is a web site that contains many useful categories of links, including employment newsgroups, scientific journals and placement agencies. It also links to sites containing information regarding internship and fellowship opportunities for high school students and undergrads.

XXVII. Careers-Sports

Jobs in Sports
2506 N. Clark St., Ste. 225
Chicago, IL 60614 US
E-mail Address: *comments@jobsinsports.com*
Web Address: www.jobsinsports.com
Jobs in Sports is an employment web site that provides job listings in areas including sports marketing, sports media, sales, health and fitness, computers and administration, as well as other job resources.

Sports Careers
7010 E. Chauncey Ln., Ste. 115
Phoenix, AZ 85054 US
E-mail Address: *support@sportscareers.com*
Web Address: www.sportscareers.com
Sports Careers offers a range of services to help individuals and employers in the sports industry, including job listings, a resume bank, industry contacts and salary information.

Sports Job Board
Web Address: www.sportsjobboard.com
The Sports Job Board is an employment web site for the sports industry.

WomenSportsJobs.com
Women's Sport Services, LLC
P.O. Box 11
Huntington Beach, CA 92648 US
Phone: 714-848-1201
Fax: 714-848-5111
E-mail Address: *Feedback@WSServices.com*
Web Address: www.womensportsjobs.com
WomenSportsJobs.com is an employment web site specializing in jobs for women in the sports industry. The site is managed by Women's Sport Services, LLC.

Work in Sports LLC
7335 E. Chauncey Ln., Ste. 115
Phoenix, AZ 85054 US
Phone: 480-905-7221
Fax: 480-905-7231
Web Address: www.workinsports.com
Work in Sports LLC is an online employment resource for the sports industry that posts hundreds of jobs on its web site.

XXVIII. Careers-Telecommunications

Call Center Careers
6525 Gunpark Dr.
Ste. 570, PMB 127
Boulder, CO 80301 US
Phone: 303-527-1440
Fax: 303-530-0154
Toll Free: 877-562-8588
E-mail Address: *sales@callcentercareers.com*
Web Address: www.callcentercareers.com
Call Center Careers provides recruiting and staffing services to the call center industry.

XXIX. Careers-Video Games Industry

GameJobs
Web Address: www.gamejobs.com
GameJobs.com is independently owned and operated by the Crest Group, LLC., the managers of the Interactive Entertainment Merchants Association (IEMA), a non-profit retail trade association

Video Game Jobs-About.com Career Planning
Web Address: http://careerplanning.about.com/od/occupations/a/videogamecareer.htm
A useful page on About.com that contains advice and links for people interested in working in the video games industry.

XXX. Chemicals Industry Associations

American Chemical Society (ACS)
1155 16th St. NW
Washington, DC 20036 US
Phone: 202-872-4600

Toll Free: 800-227-5558
E-mail Address: *executivedirector@acs.org*
Web Address: www.acs.org
The American Chemical Society (ACS) is a nonprofit organization aimed at promoting the understanding of chemistry and chemical sciences. It represents a wide range of disciplines including chemistry, chemical engineering and other technical fields.

XXXI. Communications Professional Associations

Association for Women In Communications (AWC)
3337 Duke St.
Alexandria, VA 22314 US
Phone: 703-370-7436
Fax: 703-370-7437
E-mail Address: *info@womcom.org*
Web Address: www.womcom.org
The Association for Women In Communications (AWC) is a professional organization that works for the advancement of women across all communications disciplines by recognizing excellence, promoting leadership and positioning its members at the forefront of the communications industry.

Health and Science Communications Association (HeSCA)
39 Wedgewood Dr., Ste. A
Jewett City, CT 06351 US
Phone: 860-376-5915
Fax: 860-376-6621
E-mail Address: *hesca@hesca.org*
Web Address: www.hesca.org
The Health and Science Communications Association (HeSCA) is an organization of communications professionals committed to sharing knowledge and resources in the health sciences arena.

Health Industry Business Communications Council (HIBCC)
2525 E. Arizona Biltmore Cir., Ste. 127
Phoenix, AZ 85016 US
Phone: 602-381-1091
Fax: 602-381-1093
E-mail Address: *info@hibcc.org*
Web Address: www.hibcc.org
The Health Industry Business Communications Council (HIBCC) seeks to facilitate electronic communications by developing appropriate standards for information exchange among all health care trading partners.

International Association of Business Communicators (IABC)
1 Hallidie Plz., Ste. 600
San Francisco, CA 94102 US
Phone: 415-544-4700
Fax: 415-544-4747
Toll Free: 800-776-4222
E-mail Address: *jugalde@iabc.com*
Web Address: www.iabc.com
The International Association of Business Communicators (IABC) is the leading resource for effective business communication practices.

XXXII. Computer & Electronics Industry Associations

Electronics Technicians Association (ETA)
5 Depot St.
Greencastle, IN 46135 US
Phone: 765-653-8262
Fax: 765-653-4287
Toll Free: 800-288-3824
E-mail Address: *eta@eta-i.org*
Web Address: www.eta-i.org
The Electronics Technicians Association (ETA) is a nonprofit professional association for electronics technicians worldwide. The organization provides recognized professional credentials for electronics technicians.

Semiconductor Industry Association (SIA)
1101 K St. NW, Ste. 450
Washington, DC 20005 US
Phone: 202-446-1700
Fax: 202-216-9745
Toll Free: 866-756-0715
E-mail Address: *mailbox@sia-online.org*
Web Address: www.sia-online.org
The Semiconductor Industry Association (SIA) is a trade association representing the semiconductor industry in the U.S. Through its coalition of more than 60 companies, SIA members represent roughly 80% of semiconductor production in the U.S. The coalition aims to advance the competitiveness of the chip industry and shape public policy on issues particular to the industry.

TechAmerica
601 Pennsylvania Ave. NW
North Bldg., Ste. 600
Washington, DC 20004 US
Phone: 202-682-9110
Fax: 202-682-9111
E-mail Address: *csc@techamerica.org*
Web Address: www.techamerica.org
TechAmerica was formed from the combination of former technology and electronics industry associations AeA and Information Technology Association of America (ITAA). The combined organization represents nearly 1,200 member companies of all sizes from the public and commercial sectors of the industry.

XXXIII. Consulting Industry Associations

American Association of Healthcare Consultants (AAHC)
5938 N. Drake Ave.
Chicago, IL 60659 US
Fax: 773-463-3552
Toll Free: 888-350-2242
E-mail Address: *info@aahcmail.org*
Web Address: www.aahc.net
The American Association of Healthcare Consultants (AAHC) is a professional society for credentialed consultants practicing in health care organization and delivery.

Association of Internal Management Consultants (AIMC)
824 Caribbean Ct.
Marco Island, FL 34145 US
Phone: 239-642-0580
Fax: 239-642-1119
E-mail Address: *info@aimc.org*
Web Address: www.aimc.org
The Association of Internal Management Consultants (AIMC) is a professional association representing in-house management consultants. Members work in for-profit corporations, government agencies, educational institutions and nonprofit organizations.

Institute of Management Consultants USA (IMC)
2025 M St. NW, Ste. 800
Washington, DC 20036-3309 US
Phone: 202-367-1134
Fax: 202-367-2134
E-mail Address: *gail@imcusa.org*
Web Address: www.imcusa.org
The Institute of Management Consultants USA (IMC) certifies management consultants in accordance with the strict international standards of the International Council of Management Consulting Institutes.

Investment Management Consultant Association (IMCA)
5619 DTC Pkwy., Ste. 500
Greenwood Village, CO 80111 US
Phone: 303-770-3377
Fax: 303-770-1812
E-mail Address: *imca@imca.org*
Web Address: www.imca.org

The Investment Management Consultant Association (IMCA) provides information and communication for investment management consultants.

XXXIV. Consulting Industry Resources

Consulting Magazine
1 Washington Park, Ste. 1300
100 Enterprise Dr., Ste. 600
Newark, NJ 07102 US
Phone: 212-563-6054
Fax: 212-564-0465
E-mail Address:
consultingmag@kennedyinfo.com
Web Address: www.consultingmag.com
Consulting Magazine is a leading publication for the consulting industry, and features information on consulting careers, thought leadership and corporate strategies. The magazine is published by Kennedy Information, Inc., a BNA Company.

XXXV. Corporate Information Resources

bizjournals.com
120 W. Morehead St., Ste. 400
Charlotte, NC 28202 US
Web Address: www.bizjournals.com
Bizjournals.com is the online media division of American City Business Journals, the publisher of dozens of leading city business journals nationwide. It provides access to research into the latest news regarding companies both small and large. The organization maintains 42 websites and 64 print publications and sponsors over 700 annual industry events.

Business Wire
44 Montgomery St., Fl. 39
San Francisco, CA 94104 US
Phone: 415-986-4422
Fax: 415-788-5335
Toll Free: 800-227-0845
Web Address: www.businesswire.com
Business Wire offers news releases, industry- and company-specific news, top headlines, conference calls, IPOs on the Internet, media services and access to tradeshownews.com and BW Connect On-line through its informative and continuously updated web site.

Edgar Online, Inc.
11200 Rockville Pike, Ste. 310
Rockville, MD 20852 US
Phone: 301-287-0300
Fax: 301-287-0390
Toll Free: 888-870-2316
Web Address: www.edgar-online.com
Edgar Online, Inc. is a gateway and search tool for viewing corporate documents, such as annual reports on Form 10-K, filed with the U.S. Securities and Exchange Commission.

PR Newswire Association LLC
350 Hudson St., Ste. 300
New York, NY 10014 US
Fax: 800-793-9313
Toll Free: 800-776-8090
E-mail Address:
information@prnewswire.com
Web Address: www.prnewswire.com
PR Newswire Association LLC provides comprehensive communications services for public relations and investor relations professionals, ranging from information distribution and market intelligence to the creation of online multimedia content and investor relations web sites. Users can also view recent corporate press releases from companies across the globe. The Association is owned by United Business Media plc.

Silicon Investor
100 W. Main
P.O. Box 29
Freeman, MO 64746 US
E-mail Address: *bobz@talkzilla.com*
Web Address: siliconinvestor.advfn.com
Silicon Investor is focused on providing information about technology companies. Its web site serves as a financial discussion forum and offers quotes, profiles and charts.

XXXVI. Disabling Conditions

Job Accommodation Network (JAN)
P.O. Box 6080
Morgantown, WV 26506-6080 US
Phone: 304-293-7186
Fax: 304-293-5407
Toll Free: 800-526-7234
E-mail Address: *jan@jan.wvu.edu*
Web Address: janweb.icdi.wvu.edu
The Job Accommodation Network (JAN) is a free consulting service that provides information about job accommodations, the Americans with Disabilities Act and the employability of people with disabilities.

XXXVII. Electronic Health Records/Continuity of Care Records

American Health Information Management Association (AHIMA)
233 N. Michigan Ave., Fl. 21
Chicago, IL 60601-5800 US
Phone: 312-233-1100
Fax: 312-233-1090
E-mail Address:
alan.dowling@ahima.org
Web Address: www.ahima.org
The American Health Information Management Association (AHIMA) is a professional association that consists health information management professionals who work throughout the health care industry.

American Medical Informatics Association (AMIA)
4915 St. Elmo Ave., Ste. 401
Bethesda, MD 20814 US
Phone: 301-657-1291
Fax: 301-657-1296
E-mail Address: *mail@amia.org*
Web Address: www.amia.org
The American Medical Informatics Association (AMIA) is a membership organization of individuals, institutions and corporations dedicated to developing and using information technologies to improve health care.

College of Healthcare Information Management Executives (CHIME)
3300 Washtenaw Ave., Ste. 225
Ann Arbor, MI 48104 US
Phone: 734-665-0000
Fax: 734-665-4922
E-mail Address: *staff@cio-chime.org*
Web Address: www.cio-chime.org
College of Healthcare Information Management Executives (CHIME) was formed with the dual objective of serving the professional development needs of health care CIOs and advocating the more effective use of information management within health care.

Healthcare Information and Management Systems Society (HIMSS)
230 E. Ohio St., Ste. 500
Chicago, IL 60611-3270 US
Phone: 312-664-4467
Fax: 312-664-6143
E-mail Address: *himss@himss.org*
Web Address: www.himss.org
The Healthcare Information and Management Systems Society (HIMSS) provides leadership in the optimal use of technology, information and management systems for the betterment of health care.

XXXVIII. Energy Associations-Electric Power

American Public Power Association (APPA)
1875 Connecticut Ave. NW, Ste. 1200
Washington, DC 20009-5715 US
Phone: 202-467-2900
Fax: 202-467-2910
E-mail Address: *mrufe@appanet.org*
Web Address: www.appanet.org
The American Public Power Association (APPA) is a nonprofit service organization for the country's community-owned electric utilities, dedicated to advancing the public policy interests of its members and their consumers.

Edison Electric Institute (EEI)
701 Pennsylvania Ave. NW
Washington, DC 20004-2696 US
Phone: 202-508-5000
E-mail Address: *feedback@eei.org*
Web Address: www.eei.org
The Edison Electric Institute (EEI) is an association of U.S. shareholder-owned electric companies as well as worldwide affiliates and industry associates. Its web site provides energy news and a link to Electric Perspectives magazine.

Women's International Network of Utility Professionals (WINUP)
P.O. Box 817
Fergus Falls, MN 56538-0817 US
Phone: 218-731-1659
E-mail Address: *tdrexler@otpco.com*
Web Address: www.winup.org
The Women's International Network of Utility Professionals (WINUP) provides networking and support for women in the utility industry.

XXXIX. Energy Associations-Natural Gas

American Gas Association (AGA)
400 N. Capitol St. NW, Ste. 450
Washington, DC 20001 US
Phone: 202-824-7000
E-mail Address: *rshelby@aga.org*
Web Address: www.aga.org
The American Gas Association (AGA) represents a large number of natural gas providers, advocating for these companies and providing a broad range of programs and services for members.

XL. Energy Associations-Other

American Association of Blacks in Energy
1625 K St. NW, Ste. 450
Washington, DC 20006 US
Phone: 202-371-9530
Fax: 202-371-9218
E-mail Address: *info@aabe.org*
Web Address: www.aabe.org
The American Association of Blacks in Energy is dedicated to ensuring the input of African Americans and other minorities in discussions and developments of energy policies, regulations, research and development technologies and environmental issues.

XLI. Energy Associations-Petroleum, Exploration, Production, etc.

American Association of Professional Landmen (AAPL)
4100 Fossil Creek Blvd.
Fort Worth, TX 76137 US
Phone: 817-847-7700
Fax: 817-847-7704
E-mail Address: *aapl@landman.org*
Web Address: www.landman.org
The American Association of Professional Landmen (AAPL) promotes the highest standards of performance for all land professionals and seeks to advance their stature and to encourage sound stewardship of energy and mineral resources.

American Petroleum Institute (API)
1220 L St. NW
Washington, DC 20005-4070 US
Phone: 202-682-8000
Web Address: www.api.org
American Petroleum Institute (API) represents U.S. oil and gas industries and its web site includes in-depth sections for energy consumers and energy professionals.

Independent Petroleum Association of America (IPAA)
1201 15th St. NW, Ste. 300
Washington, DC 20005 US
Phone: 202-857-4722
Fax: 202-857-4799
E-mail Address: *rcarter@ipaa.org*
Web Address: www.ipaa.org
The Independent Petroleum Association of America (IPAA) provides a forum for the exploration and production segment of the independent oil and natural gas business. It also provides information on the domestic exploration and production industry.

International Association of Drilling Contractors (IADC)
10370 Richmond Ave., Ste. 760
Houston, TX 77042 US
Phone: 713-292-1945
Fax: 713-292-1946
E-mail Address: *info@iadc.org*
Web Address: www.iadc.org
The International Association of Drilling Contractors (IADC) represents the worldwide oil and gas drilling industry and promotes commitment to safety, preservation of the environment and advances in drilling technology.

XLII. Engineering, Research & Scientific Associations

American Association of Petroleum Geologists (AAPG)
1444 S. Boulder Ave.
Tulsa, OK 74119 US
Phone: 918-584-2555
Fax: 918-560-2665
Toll Free: 800-364-2274
E-mail Address: *lnation@aapg.org*
Web Address: www.aapg.org
The American Association of Petroleum Geologists (AAPG) is an international geological organization that supports educational and scientific programs and projects related to geosciences.

American Institute of Chemical Engineers (AIChE)
3 Park Ave.
New York, NY 10016-5991 US
Phone: 203-702-7660
Fax: 203-775-5177
Toll Free: 800-242-4363
E-mail Address: *steps@aiche.org*
Web Address: www.aiche.org
The American Institute of Chemical Engineers (AIChE) provides leadership in advancing the chemical engineering profession. The organization, which is comprised of more than 40,000 members from over 90 countries, provides informational resources to chemical engineers.

American Society for Healthcare Engineering (ASHE)
155 N. Wacker Dr., Ste. 400
Chicago, IL 60606 US
Phone: 312-422-3800
Fax: 312-422-4571
E-mail Address: *ashe@aha.org*
Web Address: www.ashe.org

The American Society for Healthcare Engineering (ASHE) is the advocate and resource for continuous improvement in the health care engineering and facilities management professions.

American Society of Agricultural and Biological Engineers (ASABE)
2950 Niles Rd.
St. Joseph, MI 49085 US
Phone: 269-429-0300
Fax: 269-429-3852
E-mail Address: *hq@asabe.org*
Web Address: www.asabe.org
The American Society of Agricultural and Biological Engineers (ASABE) is a nonprofit professional and technical organization interested in engineering knowledge and technology for food and agriculture and associated industries.

American Society of Civil Engineers (ASCE)
1801 Alexander Bell Dr.
Reston, VA 20191-4400 US
Phone: 703-295-6300
Fax: 703-295-6222
Toll Free: 800-548-2723
E-mail Address: *member@asce.org*
Web Address: www.asce.org
The American Society of Civil Engineers (ASCE) is a leading professional organization serving civil engineers. It ensures safer buildings, water systems and other civil engineering works by developing technical codes and standards.

American Society of Safety Engineers (ASSE)
1800 E. Oakton St.
Des Plaines, IL 60018 US
Phone: 847-699-2929
Fax: 847-768-3434
E-mail Address:
customerservice@asse.org
Web Address: www.asse.org
The American Society of Safety Engineers (ASSE) is the world's oldest and largest professional safety organization. It manages, supervises and consults on safety, health and environmental issues in industry, insurance, government and education.

Association of Federal Communications Consulting Engineers (AFCCE)
P.O. Box 19333
Washington, DC 20036 US
E-mail Address: *secretary@afcce.org*
Web Address: www.afcce.org
The Association of Federal Communications Consulting Engineers (AFCCE) is a professional organization of individuals who regularly assist clients on technical issues before the Federal Communications Commission (FCC).

Institute of Industrial Engineers (IIE)
3577 Parkway Ln., Ste. 200
Norcross, GA 30092 US
Phone: 770-449-0460
Fax: 770-441-3295
Toll Free: 800-494-0460
E-mail Address:
executiveoffices@iienet.org
Web Address: www.iienet2.org
The Institute of Industrial Engineers (IIE) is dedicated to the professional needs of industrial engineers.

National Society of Professional Engineers (NSPE)
1420 King St.
Alexandria, VA 22314-2794 US
Phone: 703-684-2800
Fax: 703-836-4875
Toll Free: 888-285-6773
E-mail Address: *memserv@nspe.org*
Web Address: www.nspe.org
The National Society of Professional Engineers (NSPE) represents individual engineering professionals and licensed engineers across all disciplines. NSPE serves approximately 45,000 members and has more than 500 chapters.

Society of Automotive Engineers (SAE)
755 W. Big Beaver, Ste. 1600
Troy, MA 48084 US
Phone: 248-273-2455
Fax: 248-273-2494
Toll Free: 877-606-7323
E-mail Address: *automotive_hq@sae.org*
Web Address: www.sae.org
The Society of Automotive Engineers (SAE) is a resource for technical information and expertise used in designing, building, maintaining and operating self-propelled vehicles for use on land, sea, air or space.

Society of Broadcast Engineers, Inc. (SBE)
9102 N. Meridian St., Ste. 150
Indianapolis, IN 46260 US
Phone: 317-846-9000
Fax: 317-846-9120
E-mail Address: *mclappe@sbe.org*
Web Address: www.sbe.org
The Society of Broadcast Engineers (SBE) exists to increase knowledge of broadcast engineering and promote its interests, as well as to continue the education of professionals in the industry.

Society of Cable Telecommunications Engineers (SCTE)
140 Philips Rd.
Exton, PA 19341-1318 US
Phone: 610-363-6888
Fax: 610-363-5898
Toll Free: 800-542-5040
E-mail Address: *scte@scte.org*
Web Address: www.scte.org
The Society of Cable Telecommunications Engineers (SCTE) is a nonprofit professional association dedicated to advancing the careers and serving the industry of telecommunications professionals by providing technical training, certification and standards.

Society of Hispanic Professional Engineers (SHPE)
5400 E. Olympic Blvd., Ste. 210
Los Angeles, CA 90022 US
Phone: 323-725-3970
Fax: 323-725-0316
E-mail Address: *shpenational@shpe.org*
Web Address: oneshpe.shpe.org
The Society of Hispanic Professional Engineers (SHPE) is a national nonprofit organization that promotes Hispanics in science, engineering and math.

Society of Manufacturing Engineers (SME)
1 SME Dr.
Dearborn, MI 48121 US
Phone: 313-425-3000
Fax: 313-425-3400
Toll Free: 800-733-4763
E-mail Address:
communications@sme.org
Web Address: www.sme.org
The Society of Manufacturing Engineers (SME) is a leading professional organization serving engineers in the manufacturing industries.

Society of Motion Picture and Television Engineers (SMPTE)
3 Barker Ave., Fl. 5
White Plains, NY 10601 US
Phone: 914-761-1100
Fax: 914-761-3115
Web Address: www.smpte.org
The Society of Motion Picture and Television Engineers (SMPTE) is the leading technical society for the motion imaging industry. The firm publishes recommended practice and engineering guidelines, as well the SMPTE Journal.

Society of Women Engineers (SWE)
230 E. Ohio St., Ste. 400
Chicago, IL 60611 US
Phone: 312-596-5223
Toll Free: 877-793-4636
E-mail Address: *hq@swe.org*
Web Address:
societyofwomenengineers.swe.org

The Society of Women Engineers (SWE) is a nonprofit educational and service organization of female engineers.

SPIE
1000 20th St.
Bellingham, WA 98225-6705 US
Phone: 360-676-3290
Fax: 360-647-1445
Toll Free: 888-504-8171
E-mail Address: *CustomerService@spie.org*
Web Address: www.spie.org
SPIE is a nonprofit technical society aimed at the advancement and dissemination of knowledge in optics, photonics and imaging.

XLIII. Entertainment & Amusement Associations-General

International Association of Amusement Parks and Attractions (IAAPA)
1448 Duke St.
Alexandria, VA 22314 US
Phone: 703-836-4800
Fax: 703-836-6742
E-mail Address: *dmandt@iaapa.org*
Web Address: www.iaapa.org
The International Association of Amusement Parks and Attractions (IAAPA) is dedicated to the preservation and prosperity of the amusement industry.

International Special Events Society (ISES)
401 N. Michigan Ave.
Chicago, IL 60611-4267 US
Phone: 312-321-6853
Fax: 312-673-6953
Toll Free: 800-688-4737
E-mail Address: *info@ises.com*
Web Address: www.ises.com
The International Special Events Society (ISES) is comprised of over 7,200 professionals in over 38 countries representing special event planners and producers (from festivals to trade shows), caterers, decorators, florists, destination management companies, rental companies, special effects experts, tent suppliers, audio-visual technicians, event and convention coordinators, balloon artists, educators, journalists, hotel sales managers, specialty entertainers, convention center managers, and many more professional disciplines.

XLIV. Film & Theater Associations

Academy of Motion Picture Arts and Sciences (AMPAS)
8949 Wilshire Blvd.
Beverly Hills, CA 90211-1972 US
Phone: 310-247-3000
Fax: 310-859-9619
Web Address: www.oscars.org
The Academy of Motion Picture Arts and Sciences (AMPAS) is a professional honorary organization, founded to advance the arts and sciences of motion pictures. Besides hosting the Academy Awards and selecting the winners of the Oscars, AMPAS organizes smaller events highlighting the art of filmmaking, including lectures and seminars, and is currently building the Academy Museum of Motion Pictures.

Alliance of Motion Picture and Television Producers (AMPTP)
15301 Ventura Blvd.
Encino, CA 91403 US
Toll Free: 818-995-3600
Web Address: www.amptp.org
The Alliance of Motion Picture and Television Producers (AMPTP) is the primary trade association with respect to labor issues in the motion picture and television industry.

American Cinema Editors, Inc. (ACE)
100 Universal City Plz.
Verna Fields Bldg. 2282, Rm. 190
Universal City, CA 91608 US
Phone: 818-777-2900
Fax: 818-733-5023
E-mail Address: *amercinema@earthlink.net*
Web Address: www.ace-filmeditors.org
American Cinema Editors (ACE) is an honorary society of motion picture editors that seeks to advance the art and science of the editing profession.

American Society of Cinematographers (ASC)
1782 N. Orange Dr.
Hollywood, CA 90028 US
Phone: 323-969-4333
Fax: 323-882-6391
Toll Free: 800-448-0145
E-mail Address: *office@theasc.com*
Web Address: www.theasc.com
The American Society of Cinematographers (ASC) is a trade association for cinematographers in the motion picture industry.

Art Directors Guild (ADG)
11969 Ventura Blvd., Fl. 2
Studio City, CA 91604 US
Phone: 818-762-9995
Fax: 818-762-9997
E-mail Address: *nick@artdirectors.org*
Web Address: www.artdirectors.org
The Art Directors Guild (ADG) represents the creative talents that conceive and manage the background and settings for most films and television projects.

Association of Cinema and Video Laboratories (ACVL)
630 9th Ave.
Chip Wilkinson, Pres., ACVL
New York, NY 10036 US
Phone: 212-586-4822
Fax: 212-582-3744
E-mail Address: *cfw2447@rcn.com*
Web Address: www.acvl.org
The Association of Cinema and Video Laboratories (ACVL) is an international organization whose members are pledged to the highest possible standards of service to the film and video industries.

Independent Film & Television Alliance (IFTA)
10850 Wilshire Blvd., Fl. 9
Los Angeles, CA 90024-4321 US
Phone: 310-446-1000
Fax: 310-446-1600
E-mail Address: *info@ifta-online.org*
Web Address: www.ifta-online.org
The Independent Film & Television Alliance (IFTA), formerly the American Film Marketing Association (AFMA), is a trade association whose mission is to provide the independent film and television industry with high-quality, market-oriented services and worldwide representation.

International Alliance of Theatrical Stage Employees (IATSE)
1430 Broadway, Fl. 20
New York, NY 10018 US
Phone: 212-730-1770
Fax: 212-921-7699
E-mail Address: *webmaster@iatse-intl.org*
Web Address: www.iatse-intl.org
The International Alliance of Theatrical Stage Employees (IATSE) is the labor union representing technicians, artisans and crafts workers in the entertainment industry, including live theater, film and television production and trade shows.

International Animated Film Society (ASIFA-Hollywood)
2114 W. Burbank Blvd.
Burbank, CA 91506 US
Phone: 818-842-4691
E-mail Address: *info@asifa-hollywood.org*

Web Address: www.asifa-hollywood.org
International Animated Film Society (ASIFA-Hollywood) is a nonprofit organization dedicated to the advancement of the art of animation.

International Documentary Association (IDA)
1201 W. 5th St., Ste. M270
Los Angeles, CA 90017 US
Phone: 213-534-3600
Fax: 213-534-3610
E-mail Address: *amina@documentary.org*
Web Address: www.documentary.org
The International Documentary Association (IDA) is a nonprofit member service organization, providing publications, benefits and a public forum to its members for issues regarding nonfiction film, video and multimedia.

Motion Picture Association of America (MPAA)
15301 Ventura Blvd., Bldg. E
Sherman Oaks, CA 91403 US
Phone: 818-995-6600
Fax: 818-285-4403
Web Address: www.mpaa.org
The Motion Picture Association of America (MPAA) serves as the voice and advocate of the U.S. motion picture, home video and television industries.

Motion Picture Editors Guild (MPEG)
7715 Sunset Blvd., Ste. 200
Hollywood, CA 90046 US
Phone: 323-876-4770
Fax: 323-876-0861
Toll Free: 800-705-8700
E-mail Address: *mail@editorsguild.com*
Web Address: www.editorsguild.com
The Motion Picture Editors Guild's (MPEG) web site provides an online directory of editors, a discussion forum and links to related magazines and other organizations that serve the motion picture industry.

Producers Guild of America, Inc. (PGA)
8530 Wilshire Blvd., Ste. 450
Beverly Hills, CA 90211 US
Phone: 310-358-9020
Fax: 310-358-9520
E-mail Address: *info@producersguild.org*
Web Address: www.producersguild.org
The Producers Guild of America, Inc. (PGA) is a nonprofit organization for career professionals who initiate, create, coordinate, supervise and control all aspects of the motion picture and television production processes.

Screen Actors Guild (SAG)
5757 Wilshire Blvd., Fl. 7
Los Angeles, CA 90036-3600 US
Phone: 323-954-1600
Fax: 323-549-6603
Toll Free: 800-724-0767
E-mail Address: *saginfo@sag.org*
Web Address: www.sag.org
The Screen Actors Guild (SAG) represents its members through negotiation and enforcement of collective bargaining agreements that establish equitable levels of compensation, benefits and working conditions for performers. Established in 1933, the guild has 23 branches that represent 120,000 actors worldwide.

Women In Film (WIF)
8857 W. Olympic Blvd.
Ste. 201
Beverly Hills, CA 90211-3605 US
Phone: 310-657-5144
Fax: 310-657-5154
E-mail Address: *info@wif.org*
Web Address: www.wif.org
Women In Film (WIF) strives to empower, promote and mentor women in the entertainment, communication and media industries through a network of contacts, educational programs and events.

XLV. Fitness Industry Associations

American Fitness Professionals and Associates (AFPA)
1601 Long Beach Blvd.
P.O. Box 214
Ship Bottom, NJ 08008 US
Phone: 609-978-7583
Fax: 609-978-7582
Toll Free: 800-494-7782
E-mail Address: *afpa@afpafitness.com*
Web Address: www.afpafitness.com
American Fitness Professionals and Associates (AFPA) offers health and fitness professionals certification programs, continuing education courses, home correspondence courses and regional conventions.

XLVI. Food Industry Associations, General

Institute of Food Technologies (IFT)
525 W. Van Buren, Ste. 1000
Chicago, IL 60607 US
Phone: 312-782-8424
Fax: 312-782-8348
Toll Free: 800-438-3663
E-mail Address: *info@ift.org*
Web Address: www.ift.org
The Institute of Food Technologies (IFT) is devoted to the advancement of the science and technology of food through the exchange of knowledge. The site also provides information and resources for job seekers in the food industry. Members work in food science, food technology and related professions in industry, academia and government.

XLVII. Food Industry Resources, General

Food Manufacturing
1 University, Ste. B6000
Advantage Business Media
Rockaway, NJ 07886-0912 US
Phone: 973-920-7000
Fax: 973-920-7531
E-mail Address: *mbotta@reedbusiness.com*
Web Address: www.foodmanufacturing.com
Food Manufacturing is a trade magazine for companies and employees in the food manufacturing industry. It is published by Advantage Business Media.

XLVIII. Food Processor Industry Associations

Grocery Manufacturers Association (GMA)
1350 I St. NW, Ste. 300
Washington, DC 20005 US
Phone: 202-639-5900
Fax: 202-639-5932
E-mail Address: *info@gmaonline.org*
Web Address: www.gmaonline.org
The Grocery Manufacturers Association (GMA), formerly the National Food Products Association (NFPA), is the voice of the food, beverage and consumer products industry on scientific and public policy issues involving food safety, food security, nutrition, technical and regulatory matters and consumer affairs.

National Frozen and Refrigerated Foods Association (NFRA)
4755 Linglestown Rd., Ste. 300
Harrisburg, PA 17112 US
Phone: 717-657-8601
Fax: 717-657-9862
E-mail Address: *info@nfraweb.org*
Web Address: www.nfraweb.org
The National Frozen and Refrigerated Foods Association (NFRA) promotes the sales and consumption of refrigerated and frozen foods through education, research, training, sales planning and menu

development, providing a forum for industry dialogue.

XLIX. Food Service Industry Associations

International Flight Services Association (IFSA)
1100 Johnson Ferry Rd., Ste. 300
Atlanta, GA 30342 US
Phone: 404-252-3663
Fax: 404-252-0774
E-mail Address: *ifsa@kellencompany.com*
Web Address: www.ifsanet.com
The International Flight Services Association (IFSA), formerly the International Inflight Food Service Association, informs the public with respect to educational and career opportunities within the multi-billion-dollar inflight and railway food service industry.

L. Games Industry Associations

Entertainment Software Association (ESA)
575 7th St. NW, Ste. 300
Washington, DC 20004 US
Phone: 202-223-2400
E-mail Address: *esa@theesa.com*
Web Address: www.theesa.com
The Entertainment Software Association (ESA) is a U.S. trade association for companies that publish video and computer games for consoles, personal computers and the Internet. The ESA owns the E3 Media & Business Summit, a major invitation-only annual trade show for the video game industry.

Fantasy Sports Trade Association (FSTA)
Phone: 312-771-7019
E-mail Address: *megan@fsta.org*
Web Address: www.fsta.org
The Fantasy Sports Trade Association (FSTA) was founded in 1997 to provide a forum for interaction between companies in a unique and growing fantasy sports industry. FSTA represents more than 100 member companies.

Game Manufacturers Association (GAMA)
280 N. High St.
Columbus, OH 43215 US
Phone: 614-255-4500
Fax: 614-255-4499
E-mail Address: *ed@gama.org*
Web Address: www.gama.org
The Game Manufacturers Association (GAMA) is an international nonprofit trade association serving the hobby games industry. It hosts two annual events, the GAMA Trade Show and Origins Game Fair, and publishes a quarterly information newsletter, GAMATimes.

International Game Developers Association (IGDA)
19 Mantua Rd.
Mt. Royal, NJ 08061 US
Phone: 856-423-2990
Fax: 856-423-3420
E-mail Address: *Gordon@igda.org*
Web Address: www.igda.org
The International Game Developers Association (IGDA) represents members involved in the video game production industry. The firm aims to promote professional development within the gaming industry and advocates for issues that affect the game developer community, including anti-censorship issues.

LI. Grocery Industry Associations

Food Marketing Institute (FMI)
2345 Crystal Dr., Ste. 800
Arlington, VA 22202 US
Phone: 202-452-8444
Fax: 202-429-4519
E-mail Address: *fmi@fmi.org*
Web Address: www.fmi.org
The Food Marketing Institute (FMI) is a nonprofit association conducting programs in research, education, industry relations and public affairs on behalf of its 1,500 members.

LII. Health & Nutrition Associations

American Dietetic Association (ADA)
120 S. Riverside Plz., Ste. 2000
Chicago, IL 60606-6995 US
Fax: 312-899-4899
Toll Free: 800-877-1600
E-mail Address: *foundation@eatright.org*
Web Address: www.eatright.org
The American Dietetic Association (ADA) is the world's largest organization of food and nutrition professionals, with nearly 65,000 members. In addition to services for its professional members, this organization's web site offers consumers a respected source for food and nutrition information.

LIII. Health Care Business & Professional Associations

Advanced Medical Technology Association (AdvaMed)
701 Pennsylvania Ave. NW, Ste. 800
Washington, DC 20004-2654 US
Phone: 202-783-8700
Fax: 202-783-8750
E-mail Address: *info@advamed.org*
Web Address: www.advamed.org
The Advanced Medical Technology Association (AdvaMed) strives to be the advocate for a legal, regulatory and economic climate that advances global health care by assuring worldwide access to the benefits of medical technology.

American Academy of Medical Administrators (AAMA)
701 Lee St., Ste. 600
Des Plaines, IL 60016-4516 US
Phone: 847-759-8601
Fax: 847-759-8602
E-mail Address: *info@aameda.org*
Web Address: www.aameda.org
The American Academy of Medical Administrators (AAMA) is an association for health care leaders to enhance their profession and community health.

American Academy of Nursing (AAN)
888 17th St. NW, Ste. 800
Washington, DC 20006 US
Phone: 202-777-1170
Fax: 202-777-0107
E-mail Address: *info@aannet.org*
Web Address: www.aannet.org
The American Academy of Nursing (AAN) works to help nursing leaders transform the health care system in order to optimize public well-being.

American Association of Medical Assistants (AAMA)
20 N. Wacker Dr., Ste. 1575
Chicago, IL 60606 US
Phone: 312-899-1500
Fax: 312-899-1259
Web Address: www.aama-ntl.org
The American Association of Medical Assistants (AAMA) seeks to promote the professional identity and stature of its members and the medical assisting profession through education and credentialing.

American College of Health Care Administrators (ACHCA)
1321 Duke St., Ste. 400
Alexandria, VA 22314 US
Phone: 202-536-5120
Fax: 866-874-1585

E-mail Address: *elollis@achca.org*
Web Address: www.achca.org
The American College of Health Care Administrators (ACHCA) offers educational programming and career development for health care administrators.

American College of Healthcare Executives (ACHE)
1 N. Franklin, Ste. 1700
Chicago, IL 60606-3529 US
Phone: 312-424-2800
Fax: 312-424-0023
E-mail Address: *ache@ache.org*
Web Address: www.ache.org
The American College of Healthcare Executives (ACHE) is an international professional society of health care executives that offers certification and educational programs.

American Dental Association (ADA)
211 E. Chicago Ave.
Chicago, IL 60611-2678 US
Phone: 312-440-2500
E-mail Address: *online@ada.org*
Web Address: www.ada.org
The American Dental Association (ADA) is a professional association of dentists committed to the public's oral health, ethics, science and professional advancement.

American Medical Technologists (AMT)
10700 W. Higgins Rd., Ste. 150
Rosemont, IL 60018 US
Phone: 847-823-5169
Fax: 847-823-0458
Toll Free: 800-275-1268
E-mail Address: *membership@amt1.com*
Web Address: www.amt1.com
American Medical Technologists (AMT) is a nonprofit certification agency and professional membership association representing individuals in health care.

American Medical Women's Association (AMWA)
100 N. 200th St., Fl. 4
Philadelphia, PA 19103 US
Phone: 215-320-3716
Fax: 215-564-2175
Toll Free: 866-564-2483
E-mail Address: *info@amwa-doc.org*
Web Address: www.amwa-doc.org
The American Medical Women's Association (AMWA) is an organization of women physicians and medical students dedicated to serving as the unique voice for women's health and the advancement of women in medicine.

American Occupational Therapy Association, Inc. (AOTA)
4720 Montgomery Ln.
P.O. Box 31220
Bethesda, MD 20824-1220 US
Phone: 301-652-2682
Fax: 301-652-7711
Web Address: www.aota.org
The American Occupational Therapy Association, Inc. (AOTA) advances the quality, availability, use and support of occupational therapy through standard-setting, advocacy, education and research on behalf of its members and the public.

American Organization of Nurse Executives (AONE)
325 7th St. NW
Liberty Pl.
Washington, DC 20004 US
Phone: 202-626-2240
Fax: 202-638-5499
E-mail Address: *aone@aha.org*
Web Address: www.aone.org
The American Organization of Nurse Executives (AONE) is a national organization of nurses who design, facilitate and manage health care.

American Public Health Association (APHA)
800 I St. NW
Washington, DC 20001-3710 US
Phone: 202-777-2742
Fax: 202-777-2534
E-mail Address: *comments@apha.org*
Web Address: www.apha.org
The American Public Health Association (APHA) is an association of individuals and organizations working to improve the public's health and to achieve equity in health status for all.

American School Health Association (ASHA)
7263 State Rte. 43
P.O. Box 708
Kent, OH 44240 US
Phone: 330-678-1601
Fax: 330-678-4526
E-mail Address: *asha@ashaweb.org*
Web Address: www.ashaweb.org
The American School Health Association (ASHA) advocates high-quality school health instruction, health services and a healthy school environment.

Dental Trade Alliance (DTA)
2300 Clarendon Blvd., Ste. 1003
Arlington, VA 22201 US
Phone: 703-379-7755
Fax: 703-931-9429
E-mail Address: *info@dentaltradealliance.org*
Web Address: www.dentaltradealliance.org
The Dental Trade Alliance (DTA) represents dental manufacturers, dental dealers and dental laboratories.

Health Industry Distributors Association (HIDA)
310 Montgomery St.
Alexandria, VA 22314-1516 US
Phone: 703-549-4432
Fax: 703-549-6495
E-mail Address: *rowan@hida.org*
Web Address: www.hida.org
The Health Industry Distributors Association (HIDA) is the international trade association representing medical products distributors.

Healthcare Financial Management Association (HFMA)
2 Westbrook Corporate Ctr., Ste. 700
Westchester, IL 60154 US
Phone: 708-531-9600
Fax: 708-531-0032
Toll Free: 800-252-4362
Web Address: www.hfma.org
The Healthcare Financial Management Association (HFMA) is one of the nation's leading personal membership organizations for health care financial management executives and leaders.

Medical Device Manufacturers Association (MDMA)
1350 I St. NW, Ste. 540
Washington, DC 20005 US
Phone: 202-354-7171
Web Address: www.medicaldevices.org
The Medical Device Manufacturers Association (MDMA) is a national trade association that represents independent manufacturers of medical devices, diagnostic products and health care information systems.

Medical Group Management Association (MGMA)
104 Inverness Ter. E.
Englewood, CO 80112-5306 US
Phone: 303-799-1111
Fax: 303-643-4439
Toll Free: 877-275-6462
E-mail Address: *service@mgma.com*
Web Address: www.mgma.com
Medical Group Management Association (MGMA) is one of the nation's principal voices for medical group practice.

National Association of Health Services Executives (NAHSE)
1140 Connecticut Ave. NW, Ste. 505
Washington, DC 20036 US
Phone: 202-429-6060
Fax: 301-429-6767

E-mail Address: *nahsehq@nahse.org*
Web Address:
www.netforumondemand.com
The National Association of Health Services Executives (NAHSE) is a nonprofit association of black health care executives who promote the advancement and development of black health care leaders and elevate the quality of health care services rendered to minority and underserved communities.

Regulatory Affairs Professionals Society (RAPS)
5635 Fishers Ln., Ste. 550
Rockville, MD 20852 US
Phone: 301-770-2920
Fax: 301-770-2924
E-mail Address: *raps@raps.org*
Web Address: www.raps.org
The Regulatory Affairs Professionals Society (RAPS) is an international professional society representing the health care regulatory affairs profession and individual professionals worldwide.

LIV. Health Insurance Industry Associations

America's Health Insurance Plans (AHIP)
601 Pennsylvania Ave. NW, Ste. 500
Washington, DC 20004 US
Phone: 202-778-3200
Fax: 202-331-7487
E-mail Address: *ahip@ahip.org*
Web Address: www.ahip.org
America's Health Insurance Plans (AHIP) is a prominent trade association representing the private health care insurance system.

LV. Hearing & Speech

Hearing Industries Association (HIA)
1444 I St. NW, Ste. 700
Washington, DC 20005 US
Phone: 202-449-1090
Fax: 202-216-9646
E-mail Address:
mspangler@bostrom.com
Web Address: www.hearing.org
The Hearing Industries Association (HIA) represents and unifies the many aspects of the hearing industry.

LVI. Hotel/Lodging Associations

American Hotel and Lodging Association
1201 New York Ave. NW, Ste. 600
Washington, DC 20005-3931 US
Phone: 202-289-3100
Fax: 202-289-3199
E-mail Address:
informationcenter@ahla.com
Web Address: www.ahla.com
The American Hotel and Lodging Association is a federation of state lodging associations throughout the U.S.

LVII. Human Resources Industry Associations

Society for Human Resource Management (SHRM)
1800 Duke St.
Alexandria, VA 22314 US
Phone: 703-548-3440
Fax: 703-535-6490
Toll Free: 800-283-7476
E-mail Address: *shrm@shrm.org*
Web Address: www.shrm.org
The Society for Human Resource Management (SHRM) addresses the interests and needs of HR professionals through advocacy, publications, research and other resource materials.

LVIII. Industry Research/Market Research

Forrester Research
400 Technology Sq.
Cambridge, MA 02139 US
Phone: 617-497-7090
Toll Free: 866-367-7378
Web Address: www.forrester.com
Forrester Research is a publicly traded company that identifies and analyzes emerging trends in technology and their impact on business. Among the firm's specialties are the financial services, retail, health care, entertainment, automotive and information technology industries.

MarketResearch.com
11200 Rockville Pike, Ste. 504
Rockville, MD 20852 US
Phone: 240-747-3000
Fax: 240-747-3004
Toll Free: 800-298-5699
E-mail Address:
customerservice@marketresearch.com
Web Address: www.marketresearch.com
MarketResearch.com is a leading broker for professional market research and industry analysis. Users are able to search the company's database of research publications including data on global industries, companies, products and trends.

Plunkett Research, Ltd.
P.O. Drawer 541737
Houston, TX 77254-1737 US
Phone: 713-932-0000
Fax: 713-932-7080
E-mail Address:
customersupport@plunkettresearch.com
Web Address: www.plunkettresearch.com
Plunkett Research, Ltd. is a leading provider of market research, industry trends analysis and business statistics. Since 1985, it has served clients worldwide, including corporations, universities, libraries, consultants and government agencies. At the firm's web site, visitors can view product information and pricing and access a large amount of basic market information on industries such as financial services, infotech, e-commerce, health care and biotech.

LIX. Insurance Industry Associations

American Insurance Association (AIA)
1130 Connecticut Ave. NW
Ste. 1000
Washington, DC 20036 US
Phone: 202-828-7100
Fax: 202-293-1219
E-mail Address: *info@aiadc.org*
Web Address: www.aiadc.org
The American Insurance Association (AIA) is a leading property and casualty insurance trade organization, representing companies that offer all types of property and casualty insurance.

LX. Insurance Industry Associations-Agents & Brokers

Council of Insurance Agents & Brokers (CIAB)
701 Pennsylvania Ave. NW, Ste. 750
Washington, DC 20004 US
Phone: 202-783-4400
Fax: 202-783-4410
E-mail Address: *ciab@ciab.com*
Web Address: www.ciab.com
The Council of Insurance Agents & Brokers (CIAB) is an association for commercial insurance and employee benefits intermediaries in the U.S. and abroad.

Independent Insurance Agents & Brokers of America, Inc. (IIABA)
127 S. Peyton St.
Alexandria, VA 22314 US
Fax: 703-683-7556
Toll Free: 800-221-7917
E-mail Address: *info@iiaba.org*

Web Address: www.independentagent.com
Independent Insurance Agents & Brokers of America (IIABA) represents its over 300,000 members who are independent insurance agents and brokers.

Professional Insurance Agents (PIA)
25 Chamberlain St.
P.O. Box 997
Glenmont, NY 12077-0997 US
Fax: 888-225-6935
Toll Free: 800-424-4244
E-mail Address: *pia@pia.org*
Web Address: www.piaonline.org
Professional Insurance Agents (PIA) is a group of voluntary, membership-based trade associations representing professional, independent property and casualty insurance agents.

LXI. Magazines, Business & Financial

Blooomberg Businessweek Online
P.O. Box 8418
Red Oak, IA 51591-1418 US
Fax: 712-623-5229
Toll Free: 800-635-1200
E-mail Address: *bwzcustserv@cdsfulfillment.com*
Web Address: www.businessweek.com
Business Week Online offers an investor service, global business advice, technology news, small business guides, career information, business school advice, daily news briefs and more.

Forbes Online
90 5th Ave.
New York, NY 10011 US
Phone: 212-366-8900
E-mail Address: *dweathers@forbes.net*
Web Address: www.forbes.com
Forbes Online offers varied stock information, news and commentary on business, technology and personal finance, as well as financial calculators and advice.

Fortune
Time & Life Bldg.
Rockefeller Ctr.
New York, NY 10020-1393 US
Phone: 212-522-6724
Fax: 212-522-6412
Toll Free: 800-777-1444
E-mail Address: *Katy_Reitz@timeinc.com*
Web Address: money.cnn.com/magazines/fortune
Fortune, one of the world's premiere business magazines, contains news, business profiles and information on investing, careers, small business, technology and other details of U.S. and international business. Fortune is a publication of Cable News Network (CNN), a Time Warner company.

Investor's Business Daily (IBD)
12655 Beatrice St.
Los Angeles, CA 90066 US
Phone: 310-448-6600
Toll Free: 800-831-2525
E-mail Address: *ibdnews@investors.com*
Web Address: www.investors.com
Investor's Business Daily (IBD) offers subscribers information and articles on the stock market, educational resources, advice from analyst William O'Neil, personal portfolios and updates on events and workshops.

Wall Street Journal Online (The)
200 Liberty St.
New York, NY 10281 US
Phone: 212-416-2000
Toll Free: 800-568-7625
E-mail Address: *onlinejournal@wsj.com*
Web Address: www.wsj.com
The outstanding resources of The Wall Street Journal are available online for a nominal fee.

LXII. MBA Resources

MBA Depot
Web Address: www.mbadepot.com
MBA Depot is an online community and information portal for MBAs, potential MBA program applicants and business professionals.

LXIII. Online Recruiting & Employment ASPs & Solutions

Insala
1331 Airport Fwy., Ste. 313
Euless, TX 76040 US
Phone: 817-355-0939
Fax: 817-355-0746
E-mail Address: *info@insala.com*
Web Address: www.insala.com
Insala provides job search software solutions for the outplacement industry.

Kenexa
650 E. Swedesford Rd., Fl. 2
Wayne, PA 19087 US
Phone: 877-971-9171
Fax: 610-971-9181
Toll Free: 800-391-9557
E-mail Address: *contactus@kenexa.com*
Web Address: www.kenexa.com
Kenexa is a back-end recruiting and job-posting service that is used by many companies in building a workforce. Products and services include recruitment software solutions, talent consulting and recruitment process management.

Workstream, Inc.
2600 Lake Lucien Dr., Ste. 410
Maitland, FL 32751 US
Phone: 407-475-5500
Fax: 407-475-5502
Toll Free: 866-953-8800
E-mail Address: *info@workstreaminc.com*
Web Address: www.workstreaminc.com
Workstream, Inc. creates workforce management solutions through a combination of technology and services designed to integrate an organization.

LXIV. Outsourcing Industry Associations

International Association of Outsourcing Professionals (IAOP)
2600 South Rd., Ste. 44-240
Poughkeepsie, NY 12601 US
Phone: 845-452-0600
Fax: 845-452-6988
E-mail Address: *kim.maneeley@iaop.org*
Web Address: www.outsourcingprofessional.org
The International Association of Outsourcing Professionals (IAOP) represents outsourcing leaders and experts from companies of all sizes and industries around the world.

LXV. Pensions, Benefits & 401(k)s Associations

Profit Sharing/401(k) Council of America (PSCA)
20 N. Wacker Dr., Ste. 3700
Chicago, IL 60606 US
Phone: 312-419-1863
Fax: 312-419-1864
E-mail Address: *psca@psca.org*
Web Address: www.psca.org
The Profit Sharing/401(k) Council of America (PSCA) is a national nonprofit association of 1,200 companies and their 6 million employees. The group expresses its members' interests to federal policymakers and offers practical, cost-effective assistance with profit sharing and 401(k) plan design, administration, investment, compliance and communication. Its web site offers a thorough glossary, statistics and educational material.

LXVI. Pensions, Benefits & 401(k)s Resources

Employee Benefits Security Administration (EBSA)
200 Constitution Ave. NW
Washington, DC 20210 US
Phone: 202-693-8700
Fax: 202-693-8736
Toll Free: 866-444-3272
Web Address: www.dol.gov/ebsa
The Employee Benefits Security Administration (EBSA) is a division of the U.S. Department of Labor, whose web site features a wealth of benefits information for both employers and employees. Included are the answers to such questions as to how a company's bankruptcy will affect its employees and what one should know about pension rights.

Pension Benefit Guarantee Corporation (PBGC)
1200 K St. NW
Washington, DC 20005-4026 US
Phone: 202-326-4000
Fax: 202-326-4344
Toll Free: 800-400-7242
E-mail Address:
participant.pro@pbgc.gov
Web Address: www.pbgc.gov
The Pension Benefit Guarantee Corporation (PBGC) is a U.S. Government agency that guarantees a portion of the retirement incomes of about 44 million American workers in about 30,000 private defined benefit pension plans. Its web site contains information regarding this guarantee, along with information on retirement planning and links to several related organizations.

LXVII. Pharmaceutical Industry Associations (Drug Industry)

American Pharmaceutical Association (APhA)
2215 Constitution Ave. NW
Washington, DC 20037 US
Phone: 202-628-4410
Fax: 202-783-2351
Toll Free: 800-237-2742
E-mail Address: *infocenter@aphanet.org*
Web Address: www.pharmacist.com
American Pharmaceutical Association (APhA) is a national professional society that provides news and information to pharmacists.

Pharmaceutical Research and Manufacturers of America (PhRMA)
950 F St. NW, Ste. 300
Washington, DC 20004 US
Phone: 202-835-3400
Fax: 202-835-3414
Web Address: www.phrma.org
Pharmaceutical Research and Manufacturers of America (PhRMA) represents the nation's leading research-based pharmaceutical and biotechnology companies.

LXVIII. Pilots Associations

Airline Pilots Association (ALPA)
1625 Massachusetts Ave NW
Washington, DC 20036 US
Phone: 703-689-2270
Web Address: www.alpa.org
ALPA is an association for professional airline pilots in the United States, in Canada and internationally.

LXIX. Printers & Publishers Associations

International Publishing Management Association (IPMA)
710 Regency Dr., Ste. 6
Kearney, MO 64060 US
Phone: 816-902-4762
Fax: 816-902-4766
E-mail Address: *ipmainfo@ipma.org*
Web Address: www.ipma.org
The International Publishing Management Association (IPMA) is an exclusive not-for-profit organization dedicated to assisting in-house corporate publishing and distribution professionals.

MPA-The Association of Magazine Media
810 7th Ave., Fl. 24
New York, NY 10019 US
Phone: 212-872-3700
E-mail Address: *mpa@magazine.org*
Web Address: www.magazine.org
MPA-The Association of Magazine Media (formerly the Magazine Publishers of America, Inc.) is the industry association for consumer magazines in all formats, including printed, mobile and online.

National Association of Printers & Lithographers (NAPL)
75 W. Century Rd., Ste. 100
Paramus, NJ 07652 US
Phone: 201-634-9600
Fax: 201-634-0234
Toll Free: 800-642-6275
E-mail Address: *dlospaluto@napl.org*
Web Address: www.napl.org
The National Association of Printers & Lithographers (NAPL) focuses on helping graphic arts professionals increase their expertise.

Newspaper Association of America (NAA)
4401 Wilson Blvd., Ste. 900
Arlington, VA 22203-1867 US
Phone: 571-366-1000
Fax: 571-366-1195
E-mail Address: *Jeff.Sigmund@naa.org*
Web Address: www.naa.org
The Newspaper Association of America (NAA) is a nonprofit organization representing the newspaper industry.

LXX. Real Estate Industry Associations

Institute of Real Estate Management (IREM)
430 N. Michigan Ave.
Chicago, IL 60611 US
Fax: 800-338-4736
Toll Free: 800-837-0706
E-mail Address: *custserv@irem.org*
Web Address: www.irem.org
The Institute of Real Estate Management (IREM) seeks to educate real estate managers, certify their competence and professionalism, serve as an advocate on issues affecting the real estate management industry and enhance its members' professional competence so they can better identify and meet the needs of those who use their services.

National Association of Real Estate Brokers (NAREB)
9831 Greenbelt Rd., Ste. 309
Lanham, MD 20706 US
Phone: 301-552-9340
Fax: 301-552-9216
E-mail Address: *NAREB3@comcast.net*
Web Address: www.nareb.com
The National Association of Real Estate Brokers (NAREB) is a national trade organization dedicated to bringing together the nation's minority professionals in the real estate industry.

National Association of Real Estate Companies (NAREC)
216 W. Jackson Blvd., Ste. 625
Chicago, IL 60606 US
Phone: 312-263-1755
Fax: 312-750-1203
E-mail Address: *info@narec.org*
Web Address: www.narec.org
The National Association of Real Estate Companies (NAREC) is composed of representatives of publicly and privately owned real estate companies, significant

subsidiaries of publicly owned companies and public accounting firms.

National Association of Realtors (NAR)
430 N. Michigan Ave.
Chicago, IL 60611-4087 US
Phone: 202-383-1176
Toll Free: 800-874-6500
E-mail Address: *lsalvant@realtors.org*
Web Address: www.realtor.org
The National Association of Realtors (NAR) is composed of realtors involved in residential and commercial real estate as brokers, salespeople, property managers, appraisers and counselors and in other areas of the industry. NAR also sponsors Realtor.com, operated by Move, Inc.

Women's Council of Realtors (WCR)
430 N. Michigan Ave.
Chicago, IL 60611 US
Toll Free: 800-245-8512
E-mail Address: *wcr@wcr.org*
Web Address: www.wcr.org
The Women's Council of Realtors (WCR) is a community of female real estate professionals.

LXXI. Recording & Music Associations

American Federation of Musicians (AFM)
1501 Broadway, Ste. 600
New York, NY 10036 US
Phone: 212-869-1330
Fax: 212-764-6134
E-mail Address: *presoffice@afm.org*
Web Address: www.afm.org
The American Federation of Musicians (AFM) is the largest union in the world for music professionals, serving musicians throughout the U.S. and Canada.

American Society of Composers, Authors & Publishers (ASCAP)
1 Lincoln Plz.
New York, NY 10023 US
Phone: 212-621-6000
Fax: 212-621-8453
Web Address: www.ascap.com
American Society of Composers, Authors & Publishers (ASCAP) is a membership association of U.S. composers, songwriters and publishers of every kind of music, with hundreds of thousands of members worldwide.

Content Delivery & Storage Association (CDSA)
39 N. Bayles Ave.
Port Washington, NY 11050 US
Phone: 516-767-6720
Fax: 516-883-5793
E-mail Address:
mporter@CDSAonline.org
Web Address: www.cdsaonline.org
The Content Delivery & Storage Association (CDSA), formerly the International Recording Media Association, is a worldwide trade association encompassing organizations involved in every facet of recording media, including entertainment, information and software content storage. CDSA is under the management of the Media & Entertainment Services Alliance (MESA).

International Association of Audio Information Services (IAAIS)
3920 Willshire Dr.
Lawrence, KS 66049 US
Toll Free: 800-280-5325
E-mail Address:
Stuart.Holland@state.mn.us
Web Address: www.iaais.org
International Association of Audio Information Services (IAAIS) is an organization that provides audio access to information for people who are print-disabled.

Music Publisher's Association of the United States (MPA)
243 5th Ave., Ste. 236
New York, NY 10016 US
Phone: 212-327-4044
E-mail Address: *admin@mpa.org*
Web Address: mpa.org
The Music Publisher's Association of the United States (MPA) serves as a forum for publishers to deal with the music industry's vital issues and is actively involved in supporting and advancing compliance with copyright law, combating copyright infringement and exploring the need for further reform.

Recording Industry Association of America (RIAA)
1025 F St. NW, Fl. 10
Washington, DC 20004 US
Phone: 202-775-0101
Web Address: www.riaa.com
The Recording Industry Association of America (RIAA) is the trade group that represents the U.S. recording industry.

Society of Professional Audio Recording Services (SPARS)
9 Music Sq. S., Ste. 222
Nashville, TN 37203 US
Fax: 214-722-1442
Toll Free: 800-771-7727
E-mail Address: *info@spars.com*
Web Address: www.spars.com
The Society of Professional Audio Recording Services (SPARS) is an organization for members of the recording industry to share practical business information about audio and multimedia facility ownership, management and operations.

Songwriters Guild of America
5120 Virginia Way, Ste. C22
Brentwood, TN 37027 US
Phone: 615-742-9945
Fax: 615-630-7501
Toll Free: 800-524-6742
E-mail Address:
corporate@songwritersguild.com
Web Address: www.songwritersguild.com
The Songwriters Guild of America is the nation's largest and oldest songwriters' organization, providing its members with information and programs to further their careers and understanding of the music industry.

LXXII. Satellite-Related Professional Organizations

Satellite Broadcasting & Communications Association (SBCA)
1100 17th St. NW, Ste. 1150
Washington, DC 20036 US
Phone: 202-349-3620
Fax: 202-349-3621
Toll Free: 800-541-5981
E-mail Address: *info@sbca.org*
Web Address: www.sbca.com
The Satellite Broadcasting & Communications Association (SBCA) is the national trade organization representing all segments of the satellite consumer services industry in America.

Society of Satellite Professionals International (SSPI)
55 Broad St., 14th Fl.
The New York Information Technology Ctr.
New York, NY 10004 US
Phone: 212-809-5199
Fax: 212-825-0075
E-mail Address: *rbell@sspi.org*
Web Address: www.sspi.org
The Society of Satellite Professionals International (SSPI) is a nonprofit member-benefit society that serves satellite professionals worldwide.

LXXIII. Securities Industry Associations

North American Securities Administrators Association, Inc. (NASAA)
750 1st St. NE, Ste. 1140
Washington, DC 20002 US
Phone: 202-737-0900
Fax: 202-783-3571
E-mail Address: *bw@nasaa.org*
Web Address: www.nasaa.org
The North American Securities Administrators Association (NASAA) is the oldest international organization committed to investor protection. Its web site provides information on franchising and raising capital, as well as state blue sky securities laws and resources for small investment advisors.

Securities Industry and Financial Markets Association (SIFMA)
120 Broadway, Fl. 35
New York, NY 10271-0080 US
Phone: 212-313-1200
Fax: 212-313-1301
E-mail Address: *inquiry@sifma.org*
Web Address: www.sifma.org
The Securities Industry and Financial Markets Association (SIFMA), formed by the merger of the Securities Industry Association (SIA) and the Bond Market Association, brings together the shared interests of more than 650 securities and bond industry firms to accomplish common goals.

LXXIV. Software Industry Associations

Software & Information Industry Association (SIIA)
1090 Vermont Ave. NW, Fl. 6
Washington, DC 20005-4095 US
Phone: 202-289-7442
Fax: 202-289-7097
E-mail Address: *lgreenback@siia.net*
Web Address: www.siia.net
The Software & Information Industry Association (SIIA) is a principal trade association for the software and digital content industry.

LXXV. Stocks & Financial Markets Data

Reuters.com
3 Times Sq.
New York, NY 10036 US
Phone: 646-223-4000
E-mail Address:
general.info@thomsonreuters.com
Web Address: www.reuters.com
Reuters.com, a service of Thomson Reuters, offers information on business and world markets, political and international news and company-specific stock information.

Yahoo! Finance
701 1st Ave.
Yahoo! Inc.
Sunnyvale, CA 94089 US
Phone: 408-349-5080
Web Address: finance.yahoo.com
Yahoo! Finance provides a wealth of links and a supreme search guide. Users can find just about any financial information concerning both U.S. and world markets. Tax, insurance information, financial news and community research can be conducted through this site, as can searches for other aspects of the financial world.

LXXVI. Telecommunications Industry Associations

CompTel
900 17th St. NW, Ste. 400
Washington, DC 20006 US
Phone: 202-296-6650
Fax: 202-296-7585
E-mail Address: *gnorris@comptel.org*
Web Address: www.comptel.org
CompTel is a trade organization representing voice, data and video communications service providers and their supplier partners. Members are supported through education, networking, policy advocacy and trade shows.

National Association of Telecommunications Officers and Advisors (NATOA)
2121 Eisenhower Ave., Ste. 401
Alexandria, VA 22314 US
Phone: 703-519-8035
Fax: 703-997-7080
E-mail Address: *jharman@natoa.org*
Web Address: www.natoa.org
The National Association of Telecommunications Officers and Advisors (NATOA) works to support and serve the telecommunications industry's interests and the needs of local governments.

Telecommunications Industry Association (TIA)
2500 Wilson Blvd., Ste. 300
Arlington, VA 22201 US
Phone: 703-907-7700
Fax: 703-907-7727
E-mail Address: *gseiffert@tiaonline.org*
Web Address: www.tiaonline.org
The Telecommunications Industry Association (TIA) is a leading trade association in the information, communications and entertainment technology industry. TIA focuses on market development, trade promotion, trade shows, domestic and international advocacy, standards development and enabling e-business.

United States Telecom Association (USTelecom)
607 14th St. NW, Ste. 400
Washington, DC 20005 US
Phone: 202-326-7300
Fax: 202-315-3603
E-mail Address: *osc@ustelecom.org*
Web Address: www.ustelecom.org
The United States Telecom Association (USTelecom) is a trade association representing service providers and suppliers for the telecom industry.

LXXVII. Temporary Staffing Firms

Adecco
Saegereistrasse 10
Glattbrugg, CH-8152 Switzerland
Phone: 41-44-878-88-88
Fax: 41-44-829-89-24
E-mail Address:
investor.relations@adecco.com
Web Address: www.adecco.com
Adecco maintains human resources and staffing services offices in 70 countries. It provides temporary and permanent personnel.

Advantage Resourcing, Inc.
6-10-1 Roppongi, Minato-ku
Roppongi Hills Mori Twr. 35F
Tokyo, 106-6135 Japan
Phone: 81-03-3405-9229
E-mail Address:
info@advantageresourcing.com
Web Address: www.hirethinking.com
Advantage Resourcing, Inc., formerly Radia Holdings, Inc., provides integrated human resources services throughout Asia, North America, Europe and Australia. It is one of the largest staffing providers in Japan, with over 80 branches and satellite offices. In the U.S., the firm maintains over 230 locations in 34 states.

Allegis Group
7301 Parkway Dr.
Hanover, MD 21076 US
Phone: 410-579-4800
Fax: 410-540-7556
Toll Free: 877-388-3823
Web Address: www.allegisgroup.com

The Allegis Group provides technical, professional and industrial recruiting and staffing services. Allegis specializes in information technology staffing services. The firm operates in the United Kingdom, Germany and The Netherlands as Aerotek and TEKsystems, and in India as Allegis Group India. Aerotek provides staffing solutions for aviation, engineering, automotive and scientific personnel markets.

CDI Corporation
1717 Arch St., Fl. 35
Philadelphia, PA 19103-2768 US
Phone: 215-282-8050
Toll Free: 800-996-7566
E-mail Address:
Vince.Webb@cdicorp.com
Web Address: www.cdicorp.com
CDI Corporation specializes in engineering and information technology staffing services. Company segments include CDI IT Solutions, specializing in information technology; CDI Engineering Solutions, specializing in engineering outsourcing services; AndersElite Limited, operating in the United Kingdom and Australia; and MRINetwork, specializing in executive recruitment.

Express Employment Professionals
8516 NW Expressway
Oklahoma, OK 73162 US
Phone: 405-840-5000
Toll Free: 800-222-4057
E-mail Address:
jennifer.anderson@expresspros.com
Web Address: www.expresspros.com
Express Employment Professionals operates through a network of over 550 locations in the United States, Canada, South Africa and Australia. Services include temporary and flexible staffing, evaluation and direct hire, professional and contract staffing, human resource services and online payroll processing (U.S. only).

Glotel Inc.
8700 W. Bryn Mawr Ave., Ste. 400N
Chicago, IL 60631 US
Phone: 312-612-7480
Fax: 312-715-0756
E-mail Address: *info@glotelinc.com*
Web Address: www.glotel.com
Glotel is a global technology staffing and managed projects solutions company specializing in the placement of contract and permanent personnel within all areas of technology. Glotel has a network of offices throughout Europe, the U.S. and Asia-Pacific.

Harvey Nash
1680 Rte. 23 N, Ste. 300
Wayne, NJ 07470 US
Phone: 973-646-2100
Fax: 973-696-3985
E-mail Address: *info@harveynash.com*
Web Address: www.harveynash.com
Harvey Nash provides professional recruitment, interim executive leadership services and outsourcing services. The firm specializes in information technology staffing on a permanent and contract basis in US, UK and Europe. It also offers outsourcing services including offshore software development services, information technology systems management, workforce risk management and managed services for network administration.

Hays plc
250 Euston Rd.
London, NW1 2AF UK
Phone: 44-20-7383-2266
Fax: 44-20-7388-4367
E-mail Address: *feedback@hays.com*
Web Address: www.hays.com
Hays plc is a global leader in specialist recruitment. It places professional candidates in permanent, temporary and interim positions across numerous fields, including accountancy and finance; education; health care; IT and telecom; manufacturing and engineering; pharmaceuticals; professional services; retail, sales and marketing; and support services.

Hudson Highland Group, Inc.
560 Lexington Ave., Floors 4 & 5
New York, NY 10022 US
Phone: 212-351-7400
Fax: 917-256-8592
E-mail Address:
media.relations@hudson.com
Web Address: www.hudson.com
Hudson Highland Group, Inc. provides permanent recruitment, contract and human resources consulting and inclusion solutions. Services range from single placements to total outsourced solutions. The company employs more than 2,000 professionals serving clients and candidates in 20 countries.

Kelly Services, Inc.
999 W. Big Beaver Rd.
Troy, MI 48084-4782 US
Phone: 248-362-4444
E-mail Address: *kfirst@kellyservices.com*
Web Address: www.kellyservices.com
Kelly Services is a staffing solutions company providing approximately 530,000 employees to client companies in more than 25 countries worldwide.

Kforce, Inc.
1001 E. Palm Ave.
Tampa, FL 33605 US
Phone: 813-552-5000
Toll Free: 877-453-6723
Web Address: www.kforce.com
Kforce, Inc. is one of America's largest temporary placement firms, with more than 70 offices in 44 cities across the U.S. It specializes in employees for the following types of jobs: finance and accounting, scientific, technology, health care, clinical research, mortgages, title insurance and real estate.

Labor Ready, Inc.
P.O. Box 2910
Tacoma, WA 98401-2910 US
Phone: 253-383-9101
Fax: 877-733-0399
Toll Free: 877-733-0430
Web Address: www.laborready.com
Labor Ready, Inc. specializes in temporary staffing in construction, manufacturing, hospitality services, transportation, landscaping, warehousing, retail and more with almost 700 branches throughout the U.S., Canada and Puerto Rico.

Manpower, Inc.
100 Manpower Pl.
Milwaukee, WI 53212 US
Phone: 414-961-1000
Web Address: www.manpower.com
One of the largest temporary staffing providers in the world, Manpower places approximately 2 million workers annually in a variety of positions around the world.

Michael Page International plc
Page House, 1 Dashwood Lang Rd.
Addlestone, Weybridge
Surrey, KT15 2QW UK
Phone: 44-1932-264-144
Fax: 44-1932-264-297
E-mail Address: *ukpr@michaelpage.co.uk*
Web Address: www.michaelpage.co.uk
Michael Page International is one of the world's leading professional recruitment consultancies specializing in the placement of candidates in permanent, contract, temporary and interim positions. The Group has operations in the US, UK, Continental Europe, Asia-Pacific and a regional presence in France and Australia. In the US, the firm's focus is on the areas of financial services, supply chain, executive searches, marketing, legal and administrative support.

MPS Group, Inc.
1 Independent Dr.
Jacksonville, FL 32202 US
Phone: 904-360-2000

Fax: 904-360-2972
Web Address: www.mpsgroup.com
MPS Group is a leading provider of staffing, consulting, and human resource solutions with offices throughout the United States, Canada, the United Kingdom and continental Europe. Primary brands include Accounting Principals, Badenoch, Entegee Engineering Technical Group, Soliant Health and Modis International IT solutions.

Pasona Group Inc. (Japan)
Otemachi 2-6-4 Chiyoda-ku
Tokyo, 100-8228 Japan
Web Address: www.pasonagroup.co.jp
Pasona, Inc. provides personnel services, ranging from temporary staffing/contracting, placement/recruiting and outplacement to outsourcing and training.

Randstad USA
2015 S. Park Pl. SE
Atlanta, GA 30339 US
Phone: 770-937-7000
Fax: 770-937-7001
Toll Free: 877-922-2468
Web Address: www.us.randstad.com
Randstad provides staffing services in the office, industrial, technical, creative and professional markets. It specializes in temporary and permanent staffing; recruitment and consultant services; and human resource services. It operates in 83 countries, primarily in Europe, Asia and the U.S. Brands include Capac, Yacht, and Tempo-Team.

Robert Half International Inc. (RHI)
2884 Sand Hill Rd.
Menlo Park, CA 94025 US
Phone: 650-234-6000
E-mail Address: *webmaster@rhi.com*
Web Address: www.rhi.com
Robert Half International Inc. (RHI) specializes in accounting and finance positions. It also places workers in administrative, information technology, legal, advertising and marketing positions on temporary or permanent bases.

Robert Walters plc
55 Strand
London, WC2N 5WR UK
Phone: 44-20-7379-3333
Fax: 44-20-7509-8714
E-mail Address:
contact@robertwalters.com
Web Address: www.robertwalters.com
Robert Walters PLC is a professional recruitment specialist, outsourcing and human resource consultant. The firm provides services for the temporary, contract and permanent placement of individuals in the sectors of finance, operations, legal, information technology, marketing and administration support. It has 43 offices in 20 countries including the US.

Spherion Corporation
2050 Spectrum Blvd.
Fort Lauderdale, FL 33309 US
Phone: 954-308-7600
Toll Free: 800-774-3746
E-mail Address: *help@spherion.com*
Web Address: www.spherion.com
Spherion Corp., a subsidiary of SFN Group, provides temporary staffing, recruitment and employee consulting.

Synergie SA (France)
112 Rue de Chemin Vert
Paris, 75011 France
Phone: 33-1-43-57-22-97
Fax: 33-1-40-21-35-75
Web Address: www.synergie.fr
Synergie provides human resource management services that include temporary placement, consulting and training. The firm is most active in France, but also operates through a network of 550 agencies in throughout Europe and Canada.

Tempstaff Co., Ltd. (Japan)
Shinjuku Maynds Twr. 2-1-1
Yoyogi, Shibuya-ku
Tokyo, 151-0053 Japan
Phone: 81-3-5350-1212
Web Address: www.tempstaff.co.jp
Tempstaff Co., Ltd. provides temporary and permanent placement and recruiting and outsourcing services. It has 263 offices in Japan and 12 overseas offices located in Los Angeles, Seattle, Shanghai, Suzhou, Guangzhou, Hong Kong, Taiwan, Korea, Singapore and Indonesia.

Volt Information Sciences, Inc.
1065 Ave. of the Americas, Fl. 20
New York, NY 10018 US
Phone: 212-704-2400
Fax: 212-704-2413
E-mail Address:
mediarelations@volt.com
Web Address: www.volt.com
Volt Information Sciences, Inc. provides temporary staffing services, professional search, managed services programs, vendor management systems and recruitment process outsourcing, as well as a wealth of additional support services, in North and South America, Europe and Asia through approximately 400 locations.

LXXVIII. Testing Resources

CPP, Inc.
1055 Joaquin Rd., Fl. 2
Mountain View, CA 94043 US
Phone: 650-969-8901
Fax: 650-969-8608
Toll Free: 800-624-1765
E-mail Address: *custserv@cpp.com*
Web Address: www.cpp.com
CPP, Inc. (formerly known as Consulting Psychologists Press) publishes the Meyers-Briggs Type Indicator, Strong Inventory Test and other psychological assessment-related products. CPP also provides information about the tests and, through division Davies-Black Publishing, offers business-related books and services, including those covering career management and leadership development.

LXXIX. Textile & Fabric Associations

International Textile and Apparel Association (ITAA)
6060 Sunrise Vista Dr., Ste. 1300
Citrus Heights, CA 95610 US
Phone: 916-723-1628
Fax: 719-722-8149
E-mail Address: *info@itaaonline.org*
Web Address: www.itaaonline.org
The International Textile and Apparel Association (ITAA) is a nonprofit educational and scientific corporation dedicated to providing opportunities to scholars in the retail, textile and apparel industries.

LXXX. Travel Business & Professional Associations

American Society of Travel Agents (ASTA)
1101 King St., Ste. 200
Alexandria, VA 22314 US
Fax: 703-739-3268
Toll Free: 800-275-2782
E-mail Address: *askasta@astahq.com*
Web Address: www.asta.org
The American Society of Travel Agents (ASTA) is one of the world's largest associations of travel professionals.

Association of Corporate Travel Executives (ACTE)
515 King St., Ste. 440
Alexandria, VA 22314 US
Phone: 703-683-5322
Fax: 703-683-2720
E-mail Address: *info@acte.org*
Web Address: www.acte.org

The Association of Corporate Travel Executives (ACTE) serves the specialized travel interests of corporate purchasers and travel service suppliers from nearly 50 countries.

Association of Retail Travel Agents (ARTA)
4320 North Miller Rd.
c/o Travel Destinations, Inc.
Scottsdale, AZ 85251 US
Fax: 615-985-0600
Toll Free: 800-969-6069
E-mail Address: *info@artaonline.com*
Web Address: www.artaonline.com
The Association of Retail Travel Agents (ARTA) is one of the largest nonprofit associations in North America to exclusively represent travel agents.

Association of Travel Marketing Executives (ATME)
P.O. Box 3176
West Tisbury, MA 02575 US
Phone: 508-693-0550
Fax: 508-693-0115
E-mail Address: *admin@atme.org*
Web Address: www.atme.org
The Association of Travel Marketing Executives (ATME) is a global professional association of senior-level travel marketing executives dedicated to providing cutting-edge information, education and opportunities for meaningful networking with peers.

National Society of Minorities in Hospitality
107 S. West St.
PMB 119
Alexandria, VA 22314 US
Phone: 703-549-9899
Fax: 703-997-7795
E-mail Address: *hq@nsmh.org*
Web Address: www.nsmh.org
The National Society of Minorities in Hospitality strives to establish a working relationship between the hospitality industry and minority students.

Network of Executive Women in Hospitality, Inc. (NEWH)
P.O. Box 322
Shawano, WI 54166 US
Fax: 800-693-6394
Toll Free: 800-593-6394
Web Address: www.newh.org
The Network of Executive Women in Hospitality, Inc. (NEWH) brings together professionals from all facets of the hospitality industry by providing opportunities for education, professional development and networking. Although primarily a U.S.-based organization, NEWH does have international chapters in Toronto and London.

Society of Incentive and Travel Executives
401 N. Michigan Ave.
Chicago, IL 60611 US
Phone: 312-321-5148
Fax: 312-527-6783
E-mail Address: *Marcie_Valerio@site-intl.org*
Web Address: www.site-intl.org
The Society of Incentive and Travel Executives is a worldwide organization of business professionals dedicated to the recognition and development of motivational and performance improvement strategies in the travel industry.

LXXXI. Travel Industry Associations

Destination Marketing Association International
2025 M St. NW, Ste. 500
Washington, DC 20036 US
Phone: 202-296-7888
Fax: 202-296-7889
Toll Free: 888-275-3140
E-mail Address: *info@destinationmarketing.org*
Web Address: www.destinationmarketing.org
The Destination Marketing Association International, formerly the International Association of Convention & Visitor Bureaus, strives to enhance the professionalism, effectiveness and image of destination management organizations worldwide.

International Association of Conference Centers (IACC)
243 N. Lindbergh Blvd.
St. Louis, MO 63141 US
Phone: 314-993-8575
Fax: 314-993-8919
E-mail Address: *info@iacconline.org*
Web Address: www.iacconline.com
The International Association of Conference Centers (IACC) is a nonprofit, facilities-based organization founded to promote a greater awareness and understanding of the unique features of conference centers around the world.

National Tour Association (NTA)
546 E. Main St.
Lexington, KY 40508 US
Phone: 859-226-4444
Fax: 859-226-4414
Toll Free: 800-682-8886
E-mail Address: *questions@ntastaff.com*
Web Address: www.ntaonline.com
The National Tour Association (NTA) is an association for travel professionals who have an interest in the packaged travel sector of the industry.

U.S. Travel Association
1100 New York Ave. NW, Ste. 450
Washington, DC 20005-3934 US
Phone: 202-408-8422
Fax: 202-408-1255
E-mail Address: *feedback@tia.org*
Web Address: www.tia.org
The U.S. Travel Association is the result of a merger between the Travel Industry Association (TIA) and the Travel Business Roundtable. It is a nonprofit association that represents and speaks for the common interests and concerns of all components of the U.S. travel industry.

LXXXII. U.S. Government Agencies

Bureau of Economic Analysis (BEA)
1441 L St. NW
Washington, DC 20230 US
Phone: 202-606-9900
E-mail Address: *customerservice@bea.gov*
Web Address: www.bea.gov
The Bureau of Economic Analysis (BEA), an agency of the U.S. Department of Commerce, is the nation's economic accountant, preparing estimates that illuminate key national, international and regional aspects of the U.S. economy.

Bureau of Labor Statistics (BLS)
2 Massachusetts Ave. NE
Washington, DC 20212-0001 US
Phone: 202-691-5200
Toll Free: 800-877-8339
Web Address: stats.bls.gov
The Bureau of Labor Statistics (BLS) is the principal fact-finding agency for the Federal Government in the field of labor economics and statistics. It is an independent national statistical agency that collects, processes, analyzes and disseminates statistical data to the American public, U.S. Congress, other federal agencies, state and local governments, business and labor. The BLS also serves as a statistical resource to the Department of Labor.

Equal Employment Opportunity Commission (EEOC)
1801 L St. NW
Washington, DC 20507 US
Phone: 202-663-4900
Toll Free: 800-669-4000
E-mail Address: *info@eeoc.gov*

Web Address: www.eeoc.gov
The Equal Employment Opportunity Commission (EEOC) is a Federal Government agency focused on practices and programs that foster equal opportunity at work and elsewhere. Its web site features details about various protective laws regarding employment. It also provides information on how to file a discrimination claim.

FedStats
Web Address: www.fedstats.gov
FedStats compiles information for statistics from over 100 U.S. federal agencies. Visitors can sort the information by agency, geography and topic, as well as perform searches.

National Labor Relations Board (NLRB)
1099 14th St. NW
Washington, DC 20570-0001 US
Phone: 202-208-3000
Fax: 202-208-3013
Toll Free: 866-667-6572
Web Address: www.nlrb.gov
The National Labor Relations Board (NLRB) provides case reports on labor disputes, searchable by company or union.

U.S. Census Bureau
4600 Silver Hill Rd.
Washington, DC 20233-8800 US
Phone: 301-763-4636
Toll Free: 800-923-8282
E-mail Address: *pio@census.gov*
Web Address: www.census.gov
The U.S. Census Bureau is the official collector of data about the people and economy of the U.S. Founded in 1790, it provides official social, demographic and economic information. In addition to the Population & Housing Census, which it conducts every 10 years, the U.S. Census Bureau numerous other surveys annually.

U.S. Department of Commerce (DOC)
1401 Constitution Ave. NW
Washington, DC 20230 US
Phone: 202-482-2000
Fax: 202-482-5168
E-mail Address: *kgriffis@doc.gov*
Web Address: www.commerce.gov
The U.S. Department of Commerce (DOC) regulates trade and provides valuable economic analysis of the economy.

U.S. Department of Labor (DOL)
200 Constitution Ave. NW
Frances Perkins Bldg.
Washington, DC 20210 US
Phone: 202-693-4676
Toll Free: 866-487-2365
Web Address: www.dol.gov
The U.S. Department of Labor (DOL) is the government agency responsible for labor regulations.

U.S. Securities and Exchange Commission (SEC)
100 F St. NE
Washington, DC 20549 US
Phone: 202-942-8088
Toll Free: 888-732-6585
E-mail Address: *publicinfo@sec.gov*
Web Address: www.sec.gov
The U.S. Securities and Exchange Commission (SEC) is a nonpartisan, quasi-judicial regulatory agency responsible for administering federal securities laws. These laws are designed to protect investors in securities markets and ensure that they have access to disclosure of all material information concerning publicly traded securities. Visitors to the web site can access the EDGAR database of corporate financial and business information.

LXXXIII. Waste Industry Associations

Air & Waste Management Association
420 Fort Duquesne Blvd.
1 Gateway Ctr., 3rd Fl.
Pittsburgh, PA 15222-1435 US
Phone: 412-232-3444
Fax: 412-232-3450
Toll Free: 800-270-3444
E-mail Address: *info@awma.org*
Web Address: www.awma.org
The Air & Waste Management Association provides training, information and networking opportunities to environmental professionals worldwide.

LXXXIV. Water Resources Associations

American Water Resources Association (AWRA)
P.O. Box 1626
Middleburg, VA 20118 US
Phone: 540-687-8390
Fax: 540-687-8395
E-mail Address: *info@awra.org*
Web Address: www.awra.org
The American Water Resources Association (AWRA) represents the interests of professionals involved in water resources.

LXXXV. Wireless & Cellular Industry Associations

Cellular Telecommunications & Internet Association (CTIA)
1400 16th St. NW, Ste. 600
Washington, DC 20036 US
Phone: 202-736-3200
Fax: 202-785-0721
E-mail Address: *PChandler@ctia.org*
Web Address: www.ctia.org
The Cellular Telecommunications & Internet Association (CTIA) is an international nonprofit membership organization that represents a variety of wireless communications sectors including cellular service providers, manufacturers, wireless data and Internet companies. CTIA's industry committees study spectrum allocation, homeland security, taxation, safety and emerging technology.

Wireless Communications Association International (WCAI)
1333 H St. NW, Ste. 700 W
Washington, DC 20005-4754 US
Phone: 202-452-7823
E-mail Address: *susan@wcai.com*
Web Address: www.wcai.com
The Wireless Communications Association International (WCAI) is the principal nonprofit trade association representing the wireless broadband industry.

LXXXVI. Writers, Photographers & Editors Associations

American Society of Journalists and Authors, Inc. (ASJA)
1501 Broadway, Ste. 302
New York, NY 10036 US
Phone: 212-997-0947
Fax: 212-937-2315
E-mail Address: *director@asja.org*
Web Address: www.asja.org
The American Society of Journalists and Authors (ASJA) is of the nation's leading organizations of independent nonfiction writers.

American Society of Magazine Editors (ASME)
810 7th Ave., 24th Fl.
c/o Magazine Publishers of America (MPA)
New York, NY 10019 US
Phone: 212-872-3736
E-mail Address: *asme@magazine.org*

Web Address: www.magazine.org/asme
The American Society of Magazine Editors (ASME) is a professional organization for editors of print and online magazines. ASME is part of the Magazine Publishers of America (MPA).

American Society of Newspaper Editors (ASNE)
11690B Sunrise Valley Dr.
Reston, VA 20191-1409 US
Phone: 703-453-1122
Fax: 703-453-1133
E-mail Address: *asne@asne.org*
Web Address: www.asne.org
The American Society of Newspaper Editors (ASNE) is an association that brings together editors of daily newspapers and people directly involved with developing content for daily newspapers.

International Women's Writing Guild (IWWG)
P.O. Box 810
Gracie Sta.
New York, NY 10028-0082 US
Phone: 212-737-7536
Fax: 212-737-9469
E-mail Address: *dirhahn@iwwg.org*
Web Address: www.iwwg.com
The International Women's Writing Guild (IWWG) is a network for the personal and professional empowerment of women through writing.

Media Communications Association International (MCAI)
2810 Crossroads Dr., Ste. 3800
Madison, WI 53718 US
Phone: 608-443-2464
Fax: 608-443-2474
E-mail Address: *execdirect@mca-i.org*
Web Address: www.mca-i.org
The Media Communications Association International (MCAI) is the leading global community for media communications professionals seeking to drive the convergence of communications and technology for the growth of the profession.

National Association of Hispanic Journalists (NAHJ)
529 14th St. NW
1000 National Press Bldg.
Washington, DC 20045-2001 US
Phone: 202-662-7145
Fax: 202-662-7144
Toll Free: 888-346-6245
E-mail Address: *nahj@nahj.org*
Web Address: www.nahj.org
The National Association of Hispanic Journalists (NAHJ) is dedicated to the recognition and professional advancement of Hispanics in the news industry.

National Association of Science Writers, Inc. (NASW)
P.O. Box 890
Hedgesville, WV 25427 US
Phone: 304-754-5077
Fax: 304-754-5076
E-mail Address: *director@nasw.org*
Web Address: www.nasw.org
The National Association of Science Writers (NASW) exists to foster the dissemination of accurate information regarding science through all media devoted to informing the public.

National Conference of Editorial Writers (NCEW)
3899 N. Front St.
Harrisburg, PA 17110 US
Phone: 717-703-3015
Fax: 717-703-3014
E-mail Address: *ncew@pa-news.org*
Web Address: www.ncew.org
The National Conference of Editorial Writers (NCEW) strives to stimulate the conscience and quality of editorial writing.

National Federation of Press Women (NFPW)
P.O. Box 5556
Arlington, VA 22205 US
Fax: 703-812-4555
Toll Free: 800-780-2715
E-mail Address: *presswomen@aol.com*
Web Address: www.nfpw.org
The National Federation of Press Women (NFPW) is an organization of professional journalists and communicators.

National Writers Union (NWU)
113 University Pl., Fl. 6
New York, NY 10003 US
Phone: 212-254-0279
Fax: 212-254-0673
E-mail Address: *nwu@nwu.org*
Web Address: www.nwu.org
The National Writers Union (NWU) is a labor union that represents freelance writers in all genres, formats and media. It is committed to improving the economic and working conditions of freelance writers.

Society of Children's Book Writers and Illustrators (SCBWI)
8271 Beverly Blvd.
Los Angeles, CA 90048 US
Phone: 323-782-1010
Fax: 323-782-1892
E-mail Address: *scbwi@scbwi.org*
Web Address: www.scbwi.org
The Society of Children's Book Writers and Illustrators (SCBWI) serves people who write, illustrate or share a vital interest in children's literature, including publishers, librarians, booksellers and agents.

Chapter 5

THE AMERICAN EMPLOYERS 500: WHO THEY ARE AND HOW THEY WERE CHOSEN

Note: financial data given for each of the AMERICAN EMPLOYERS 500 firms is for the year ended December 31, 2010, a fiscal year ended in 2010 or the latest figures available to the editors. Telephone numbers, addresses, contact names, Internet addresses and other vital facts were collected in the summer of 2011.

The companies chosen to be listed in THE ALMANAC OF AMERICAN EMPLOYERS are not the same as the "Fortune 500" or any other list of corporations. The AMERICAN EMPLOYERS 500 (the actual number is 511) were chosen specifically for their likelihood to provide new job openings to the greatest number of employees. Complete information about each firm can be found in the "Individual Data Listings," beginning about the middle of this book. They are in alphabetical order.

THE AMERICAN EMPLOYERS 500 includes companies from all parts of the United States and from nearly all industry segments: selected financial services firms, retailers, service companies, wholesalers and distributors, and others, as well as industrial companies, technology firms and manufacturers.

Simply stated, the list contains 500 of the largest, most successful employers in the United States today. In particular, the list contains companies that we have hand-selected to have qualities that we feel will be of greatest interest to job seekers of today who are looking for opportunities to obtain employment with major corporations.

Job seekers in America will face a tough market in 2012. Unemployment will remain high, although it may begin to show improvement before 2012 is over.

For the past several years, in order to make this reference guide as useful as possible, we have altered the company selection criteria that were used in early editions. Rather than focusing largely on mid-term growth histories, we are instead focusing more on the type of business, industry sector served and competitive advantage. This is because some sectors may not offer good career prospects today. Consequently, we have deleted some well known companies due to the state of their particular markets.

To be included in our list, the firms were selected based on the following criteria:

1) U.S.-based companies. (However, a small number of companies may be subsidiaries of foreign-based firms. Also, a small number firms are major U.S. employers that utilize headquarters addresses in other nations.)

2) 2,500 employees or more.

3) These are almost exclusively for-profit companies. However, a small number are major, non-profit health care companies.

4) Selected Type of Business and/or Industry Sector. Companies were chosen based on our analysis of the business potential of their products, services and industrial sectors in light of today's economy.

The companies were chosen in this manner for the following reasons:

500 COMPANIES so there is a broad base among which to make comparisons and from which you can study potential employers.

LARGER EMPLOYERS (2,500 or more employees) so the information can pertain to as many employees as reasonably possible, and so the companies ranked will tend to create large numbers of job openings. Also, large companies historically have offered significantly higher wages, better benefits and better training than small employers.

FOR-PROFIT so that job seekers using THE ALMANAC OF AMERICAN EMPLOYERS can choose positions in the profit-seeking, private sector, where incentive plans may be available to motivate and reward them, such as profit sharing, stock ownership, bonuses, stock options and the high pay and prestige of top executive posts.

COMPANIES THAT OPERATE IN PROMISING BUSINESS SECTORS because:

1) Companies that are stable or enjoying growing business are much more likely to have job openings. Corporate stability is more important to job seekers today than ever before due to the wave of layoffs and downsizing that continues to sweep through the U.S. (See Chapter 1, "Major Trends Affecting Job Seekers.")

2) These companies are much more likely to offer advancement opportunities. Current employees will benefit from promote-from-within policies when new plants, new stores, new product lines or new offices are opened.

Obviously, some companies are better to work for than others, depending on what you value. Creating this annual list is an arduous task. Generally, our results are very good, but we do occasionally select a company that soon develops problems or announces a layoff. The world of business constantly goes through major changes, and unforeseen events often occur. Nonetheless, it is not easy for a firm to be selected for the AMERICAN EMPLOYERS 500, and the mere presence of a company on the list can be taken as evidence that it has excelled in many ways. To start with, it has to have generated enough business to employ thousands of people–never a simple task. Also, many of these firms are among the dominant companies in their industries.

20 Largest Employers of the American Employers 500, By Number of Employees

Company	City	State	No. of Employees	Primary Line of Business
WAL-MART STORES INC	Bentonville	AR	2,100,000	Discount Department Stores
KELLY SERVICES INC	Troy	MI	538,000	Staffing & Temporary Help
INTERNATIONAL BUSINESS MACHINES CORP (IBM)	Armonk	NY	436,085	Computer Hardware
UNITED PARCEL SERVICE INC (UPS)	Atlanta	GA	408,600	Express Delivery Service
MCDONALD'S CORP	Oak Brook	IL	400,000	Fast Food Restaurants
YUM! BRANDS INC	Louisville	KY	378,000	Fast Food Restaurants
TARGET CORPORATION	Minneapolis	MN	351,000	Discount Department Stores
KROGER CO (THE)	Cincinnati	OH	334,000	Grocery Stores
PEPSICO INC	Purchase	NY	294,000	Soft Drink Manufacturing
GENERAL ELECTRIC CO (GE)	Fairfield	CT	287,000	Business Leasing & Finance
AT&T INC	Dallas	TX	266,590	Local Telephone Service
BERKSHIRE HATHAWAY INC	Omaha	NE	260,000	Direct Property & Casualty Insurance & Reinsurance
ARAMARK CORPORATION	Philadelphia	PA	254,000	Food Service Contractor
WALGREEN CO	Deerfield	IL	244,000	Drug Stores
SAM'S CLUB	Bentonville	AR	208,800	Warehouse Clubs, Retail
UNITED TECHNOLOGIES CORPORATION	Hartford	CT	208,200	Aerospace Technology
ACCENTURE PLC	Dublin	Ireland	204,000	Technology Consulting Services
GENERAL MOTORS COMPANY (GM)	Detroit	MI	202,000	Automobile, Truck & Engine Manufacturing
CVS CAREMARK CORPORATION	Woonsocket	RI	201,000	Drug Stores
VERIZON COMMUNICATIONS INC	New York	NY	194,400	Local Telephone Service

20 Largest Employers of the American Employers 500, By Revenues

Company	City	State	2010 Sales (in U.S. $ thousands)	Primary Line of Business
WAL-MART STORES INC	Bentonville	AR	405,046,000	Discount Department Stores
EXXON MOBIL CORPORATION (EXXONMOBIL)	Irving	TX	370,125,000	Oil & Gas Exploration & Production
CHEVRON CORPORATION	San Ramon	CA	204,928,000	Oil & Gas Exploration & Production
CONOCOPHILLIPS COMPANY	Houston	TX	189,441,000	Oil & Gas Exploration & Production
GENERAL ELECTRIC CO (GE)	Fairfield	CT	150,211,000	Business Leasing & Finance
BERKSHIRE HATHAWAY INC	Omaha	NE	136,185,000	Direct Property & Casualty Insurance & Reinsurance
GENERAL MOTORS COMPANY (GM)	Detroit	MI	135,592,000	Automobile, Truck & Engine Manufacturing
FORD MOTOR CO	Dearborn	MI	128,954,000	Automobile Manufacturer
AXA FINANCIAL INC	New York	NY	124,819,588	Investment Management
AT&T INC	Dallas	TX	124,280,000	Local Telephone Service
SHELL OIL CO	Houston	TX	120,000,000	Oil & Gas Exploration & Production
MCKESSON CORPORATION	San Francisco	CA	108,702,000	Pharmaceutical Distribution
VERIZON COMMUNICATIONS INC	New York	NY	106,565,000	Local Telephone Service
KOCH INDUSTRIES INC	Wichita	KS	105,000,000	Petroleum Refining
INTERNATIONAL BUSINESS MACHINES CORP (IBM)	Armonk	NY	99,870,000	Computer Hardware
CVS CAREMARK CORPORATION	Woonsocket	RI	96,413,000	Drug Stores
UNITEDHEALTH GROUP INC	Minnetonka	MN	94,155,000	Medical Insurance
PROCTER & GAMBLE CO	Cincinnati	OH	78,938,000	Household Products Manufacturing
AMERISOURCEBERGEN CORP	Chesterbrook	PA	77,953,979	Drug Distribution
KROGER CO (THE)	Cincinnati	OH	76,733,000	Grocery Stores

20 Largest Employers of the American Employers 500, By Profits

Company	City	State	2010 Profits (in U.S. $ thousands)	Primary Line of Business
EXXON MOBIL CORPORATION (EXXONMOBIL)	Irving	TX	30,460,000	Oil & Gas Exploration & Production
MICROSOFT CORP	Redmond	WA	24,098,000	Computer Software
AT&T INC	Dallas	TX	19,864,000	Local Telephone Service
CHEVRON CORPORATION	San Ramon	CA	19,136,000	Oil & Gas Exploration & Production
CELLCO PARTNERSHIP (VERIZON WIRELESS)	Basking Ridge	NJ	18,724,000	Cell Phone Service
INTERNATIONAL BUSINESS MACHINES CORP (IBM)	Armonk	NY	14,833,000	Computer Hardware
WAL-MART STORES INC	Bentonville	AR	14,414,000	Discount Department Stores
APPLE INC	Cupertino	CA	14,013,000	Computer Hardware-PCs
JOHNSON & JOHNSON	New Brunswick	NJ	13,334,000	Personal Health Care & Hygiene Products
BERKSHIRE HATHAWAY INC	Omaha	NE	12,967,000	Direct Property & Casualty Insurance & Reinsurance
PROCTER & GAMBLE CO	Cincinnati	OH	12,736,000	Household Products Manufacturing
COCA-COLA COMPANY (THE)	Atlanta	GA	11,809,000	Soft Drink Manufacturing
GENERAL ELECTRIC CO (GE)	Fairfield	CT	11,644,000	Business Leasing & Finance
INTEL CORP	Santa Clara	CA	11,464,000	Microprocessors
CONOCOPHILLIPS COMPANY	Houston	TX	11,417,000	Oil & Gas Exploration & Production
VERIZON COMMUNICATIONS INC	New York	NY	10,217,000	Local Telephone Service
GOOGLE INC	Mountain View	CA	8,505,000	Search Engine-Internet
CISCO SYSTEMS INC	San Jose	CA	7,767,000	Computer Networking Equipment
GE ENERGY INFRASTRUCTURE	Atlanta	GA	7,271,000	Generation Equipment-Turbines & Generators
PHILIP MORRIS INTERNATIONAL INC	New York	NY	7,259,000	Tobacco Products

INDUSTRY LIST, WITH CODES

This book refers to the following list of unique industry codes, based on the 2007 NAIC code system (NAIC is used by many analysts as a replacement for older SIC codes because NAIC is more specific to today's industry sectors, see www.census.gov/NAICS). Companies profiled in this book are given a primary NAIC code, reflecting the main line of business of each firm.

Agriculture

	Agriculture
11511	Agricultural Crop Production Support, Seeds, Fertilizers

Apparel

	Apparel & Shoe Manufacturing
315	Apparel Manufacturing-General
315211	Apparel Manufacturing-Athletic
315231	Apparel Manufacturing-Women's Lingerie & Underwear
315292	Apparel Manufacturing-Leather & Fur
316213	Shoe Manufacturing-Men's
316219	Shoe Manufacturing-Athletic Shoes & Misc. Shoes, Incl. Children's

Automotive

	Automotive Manufacturing
33611	Automobiles, Manufacturing
336120	Trucks, RVs & Misc. Automotive, Manufacturing
3363	Automobile Parts Manufacturing
	Automotive Services
5321	Automobile, Rental/Leasing
8111	Automotive Repair & Maintenance

Energy

	Fuel Mining & Extraction
211111	Oil & Natural Gas Exploration & Production
21211	Coal Mining
213111	Drilling Services--Oil & Gas Wells
213112	Oil Field Services
	Utilities
221	Utilities-Electric & Gas
2211	Utilities-Electric
221113	Utilities-Nuclear Generation
	Petroleum-Refining & Manufacturing
324110	Petroleum Refineries
325110	Petrochemicals Manufacturing
325120	Industrial Gas Manufacturing
	Manufacturing, Electrical
33591	Battery Manufacturing

Entertainment

	Toys, Sporting Goods & Miscellaneous Manufacturing
339932	Toys, Manufacturing
	Film, Video & Music Recording
512110	TV/Video/Theatrical, Production
	Broadcasting
515120	Television Broadcasting
515210	Cable TV Networks
517110	Cable & Satellite TV & Data Service
	Gambling & Recreation
713940	Fitness Centers/Health Clubs
	Hotels & Accommodations
721110	Hotels/Resorts/Motels
721120	Casino Resorts

Financial Services

	Banking, Credit & Finance
522210	Banking, Credit Cards
522220	Financing--Business
522298	Pawn Shops
522320	Payment & Transaction Processing Services
522320A	Payment & Transaction Processing--Benefits Management
	Stocks & Investments
523110	Investment Banking
523920	Investment Management/Mutual Funds/Pension Funds
	Insurance
524113	Insurance-Life
524114	Insurance-Health, HMO's & PPO's
524126	Insurance--Property & Casualty, Specialty, Surety
524210	Insurance Brokerage, Agencies & Exchanges
	Professional Services, Financial
5412	Accounting Services
	Credit Bureaus
561450	Credit Bureaus

Food & Restaurants

	Food Service
722110	Restaurants
722310	Food Service Contractors

Health Care

	Health Products, Manufacturing
325412	Drugs (Pharmaceuticals), Discovery & Manufacturing
325412A	Drug Delivery Systems
325413	Diagnostic Substances Manufacturing
33911	Medical/Dental/Surgical Equipment & Supplies, Manufacturing
334510	Diagnostic and Other Electromedical Equpment Manufacturing
423450	Medical/Dental/Surgical Equipment & Supplies, Distribution
424210	Drugs (Pharmaceuticals), Distribution
	Health Care-Clinics, Labs and Organizations
6211	Physician Practice Management
621340	Clinics--Physical Rehab Ctr.

6214	Clinics--Outpatient Clinics & Surgery
621511	Laboratories & Diagnostic Services--Medical
6216	Home Health & Hospice Care
	Hospitals
622110	Hospitals/Clinics--General & Specialty Hospitals
622210	Hospitals/Clinics--Psychiatric Clinics
	Nursing
623110	Long-Term Health Care & Assisted Living
	Veterinary Care
541940	Veterinary Clinics

InfoTech

	Computers & Electronics Manufacturing
33411	Computer Networking & Related Equipment, Manufacturing
334111	Computer Hardware, Manufacturing
334112	Computer Storage Equipment & Misc Parts, Manufacturing
334119	Computer Accessories, Monitors, Printers Manufacturing
33441	Semiconductors (Microchips)/Integrated Circuits/Components, Manufacturing
334419	Contract Electronics Manufacturing
3345	Instrument Manufacturing, including Measurement, Control, Test & Navigational
	Electrical Equipment & Wire, Manufacturing
335921	Fiber Optic Cable & Electrical Wire
	Software
511201	Computer Software, Accounting, Banking & Financial
511210B	Computer Software, Network Management, System Testing, & Storage
511210D	Computer Software, Healthcare & Biotechnology
511210E	Computer Software, Security & Anti-Virus
511210F	Computer Software, Multimedia, Graphics & Publishing
511210G	Computer Software, Games & Entertainment
511210H	Computer Software, Business Management & ERP
511210I	Computer Software, Operating Systems, Languages & Development Tools
511210K	Computer Software, Sales & Customer Relationship Management
511210M	Computer Software, E-Commerce & Web Analytics
511210N	Computer Software, Product Lifecycle, Engineering, Design & CAD
	Information & Data Processing Services
518210	Data Processing Services
	Information Services-Professional
541512	Consulting--Computer, Telecommunications & Internet
541513	Computer Programming & Software Design

Internet

519130	Internet Publishing & Web Search Portals

Manufacturing

	Food Products Manufacturing
311	Food Products, Manufacturing
3112	Grain Distribution, Milling & Oilseed Processing
311230	Breakfast Cereal Manufacturing
3113	Sugar & Confectionery Product Manufacturing
311320	Chocolate & Confectionery Manufacturing
3115	Dairy Products, Manufacturing
3118	Bakeries & Tortilla Manufacturing
31191	Snack Products, Manufacturing
	Beverage & Tobacco Manufacturing
3121	Beverages--Soft Drinks & Juices Manufacturing
312140	Beverages--Distilleries
3122	Tobacco Products, Manufacturing
	Paper Products/Forest Products
322	Forest Products/Paper, Manufacturing
3222	Packaging, Manufacturing
	Chemicals
325	Chemicals, Manufacturing
325510	Paints & Coatings, Manufacturing
3256	Soaps, Cleaners, Cosmetics & Toiletries, Manufacturing
325611	Soap & Cleaning Compound Manufacturing
325620	Cosmetics & Toiletries, Manufacturing
	Plastics & Rubber
3262	Rubber Products & Tires Manufacturing
	Machinery & Manufacturing Equipment
333	Machinery, Manufacturing
33313	Machinery-Mining & Oil & Gas Field, Manufacturing
33351	Machine Tools, Manufacturing
333295	Semiconductor Manufacturing Equipment
333313	Business Machines, Manufacturing
	Jewelry, Watch & Other Manufacturing
334518	Watch & Clock Manufacturing
	Electrical Equipment, Appliances, Tools
335	Electrical Equipment, Manufacturing

Real Estate

	Real Estate
531110	Real Estate Investment Trusts - Residential
531120	Real Estate Investment Trusts - Nonresidential

Retailing

	Automobiles & Parts Stores
441110	Auto Dealers, Retail
441310	Auto Parts Stores
	Furniture & Home Furnishings Stores
442299	Linens/Housewares/Art/Framing Stores
	Computers & Electronics Stores
44311	Electronics, Audio & Appliance Stores
	Building Materials & Garden Supplies Stores
444120	Paint & Wallpaper Stores
	Food & Beverage Stores
445110	Grocery Stores/Supermarkets
445120	Convenience Stores
	Drug Stores, Beauty Supply & Health Items Stores
446110	Pharmacies & Drug Stores
	Apparel & Accessories Stores
448	Apparel Stores, General
448120	Apparel Stores, Women's
448310	Jewelry Stores
	Sporting Goods, Hobbies, Books & Music Stores
451110	Sporting Goods Stores

451120	Toys/Hobbies/Games/Crafts Stores
451211E	Book Stores-Online
	Department & Discount Stores
452111	Department Stores
452112	Discount Stores
	Miscellaneous Retailers
453910	Pets/Pet Supplies Stores
454112	Auctions, Retail-Online
	Nonstore Retailers
454113	Mail Order and Non-Store Selling, Incl. TV Shopping
	Personal Services & Salons
446199	Other Health & Personal Care Stores/Weight Management
81211	Hair, Nail & Skin Care Salons

Services

	Construction
237	Construction, Heavy & Civil Engineering
237130	Construction, Power & Communication Lines and Structures
2389	Construction--Other Special Trade Contractors
	Real Estate
5311	Real Estate Operations & Development--General
531210	Real Estate Brokerage
	Consulting & Professional Services
541330	Engineering Services
541360	Surveying & Mapping--Geophysical
54161	Consulting--Management & Business
541612	Consulting-Human Resources
541613	Consulting--Marketing
541614	Logistics Outsourcing
541690	Consulting--Scientific & Technical
541712	Research & Development-Physical, Engineering & Life Sciences
5418	Marketing Agencies & Related Services
541810	Advertising Services/Agencies
541810E	Advertising/Marketing--Online
541910	Market Research
	Management
55111	Management of Companies & Enterprises
	Personnel, Administrative & Support Services
561	Staffing or Outsourcing
561320	Temporary Help/Staffing
812331	Linen/Uniform Supply
	Call Centers
56142	Call Centers and Support Services Outsourcing
	Travel Agencies
5615E	Travel Services-Online
	Waste Management
562	Waste Disposal, Waste Management
	Educational
611410	Business Training, Distance Learning
	Security Services
5616	Security, Protection, Armored Car & Investigation Services

Telecommunications

	Telecommunications Equipment
3342	Communications Equipment, Manufacturing
334210	Telecommunications Equipment Manufacturing
334220	Radio & Wireless Communication, Manufacturing
	Telecommunications
517110	Telecommunications Service Wired, Satellite or Cable
5172	Telecommunications Service Cellular, U.S. & Non-U.S.

Transportation

	Transportation-Manufacturing of Equipment
336214	Travel Trailer & Camper Manufacturing
	Aerospace
33641	Aerospace & Aircraft Related Manufacturing
	Air
481111	Air Transportation
	Rail
48211	Railroad Transportation
	Ships
483111	Shipping-Deep Sea
483112	Cruise Lines
	Truck
484	Truck Transportation
4885	Freight Forwarding & Support Services
4921	Courier/Express Delivery Service
532120	Trucks, Rental/Leasing

Wholesale Distribution-Other

	Distribution-Durable Goods
4238	Machinery, Equipment & Supplies, Distribution

INDEX OF COMPANIES WITHIN INDUSTRY GROUPS

Company	Industry Code	2010 Sales (U.S. $ thousands)	2010 Profits (U.S. $ thousands)
Accounting Services			
DELOITTE & TOUCHE USA LLP	5412	10,938,000	
ERNST & YOUNG LLP	5412	8,373,000	
GRANT THORNTON LLP	5412	1,700,000	
KPMG LLP	5412	6,370,000	
PRICEWATERHOUSECOOPERS	5412	26,600,000	
Advertising Services/Agencies			
INTERPUBLIC GROUP OF COMPANIES INC	541810	6,531,900	281,200
OMNICOM GROUP INC	541810	12,542,500	827,700
Advertising/Marketing--Online			
GROUPON INC	541810E	500,000	
Aerospace & Aircraft Related Manufacturing			
BOEING COMPANY (THE)	33641	64,306,000	3,307,000
SPIRIT AEROSYSTEMS HOLDINGS INC	33641	4,172,000	219,000
TELEDYNE TECHNOLOGIES INC	33641	1,644,200	120,500
UNITED TECHNOLOGIES CORPORATION	33641	54,326,000	4,711,000
Agricultural Crop Production Support, Seeds, Fertilizers			
DUPONT AGRICULTURE & NUTRITION	11511	32,733,000	3,052,000
SCOTTS MIRACLE GROW CO	11511	3,139,900	204,100
Air Transportation			
ALASKA AIR GROUP INC	481111	3,823,300	251,100
AMR CORP (AMERICAN AIRLINES)	481111	22,170,000	-471,000
JETBLUE AIRWAYS CORPORATION	481111	3,779,000	97,000
REPUBLIC AIRWAYS HOLDINGS INC	481111	2,653,651	-13,846
SOUTHWEST AIRLINES CO	481111	12,104,000	459,000
Apparel Manufacturing-Athletic			
DELTA APPAREL INC	315211	424,411	12,187
UNDER ARMOUR INC	315211	1,063,927	68,477
Apparel Manufacturing-General			
HANESBRANDS INC	315	4,326,713	211,293
JARDEN CORP	315	6,022,700	106,700
POLO RALPH LAUREN CORP	315	4,978,900	479,500
Apparel Manufacturing-Leather & Fur			
COACH INC	315292	3,607,636	734,940
Apparel Manufacturing-Women's Lingerie & Underwear			
WARNACO GROUP INC (THE)	315231	2,295,751	138,581
Apparel Stores, General			
BUCKLE INC (THE)	448	898,287	127,303
GUESS? INC	448	2,128,466	242,761
ROSS STORES INC	448	7,184,213	442,757
TJX COMPANIES INC (THE)	448	20,288,444	1,213,572
Apparel Stores, Women's			
ASCENA RETAIL GROUP INC	448120	2,374,571	133,378
CHICO'S FAS INC	448120	1,713,150	69,646
LIMITED BRANDS INC	448120	8,632,000	448,000

Company	Industry Code	2010 Sales (U.S. $ thousands)	2010 Profits (U.S. $ thousands)
VICTORIAS SECRET	448120	5,520,000	
Auctions, Retail-Online			
EBAY INC	454112	9,156,000	1,801,000
Auto Dealers, Retail			
AUTONATION INC	441110	12,461,000	226,600
CARMAX GROUP	441110	7,470,193	281,668
GROUP 1 AUTOMOTIVE INC	441110	5,509,169	50,304
PENSKE AUTOMOTIVE GROUP INC	441110	10,713,585	108,281
Auto Parts Stores			
ADVANCE AUTO PARTS INC	441310	5,925,203	346,053
AUTOZONE INC	441310	7,362,618	738,311
O'REILLY AUTOMOTIVE INC	441310	5,397,525	419,373
Automobile Parts Manufacturing			
CUMMINS INC	3363	13,226,000	1,040,000
EATON CORP	3363	13,715,000	937,000
FEDERAL MOGUL CORP	3363	6,219,000	161,000
GENTEX CORPORATION	3363	816,263	137,734
JOHNSON CONTROLS INC	3363	34,305,000	1,491,000
LEAR CORP	3363	11,954,600	438,300
LKQ CORP	3363	2,469,881	167,118
STONERIDGE INC	3363	635,226	10,809
Automobile, Rental/Leasing			
ENTERPRISE HOLDINGS INC	5321	12,600,000	1,880,000
HERTZ GLOBAL HOLDINGS INC	5321	7,562,500	-30,600
Automobiles, Manufacturing			
FORD MOTOR CO	33611	128,954,000	6,561,000
GENERAL MOTORS COMPANY (GM)	33611	135,592,000	6,503,000
HONDA OF AMERICA MANUFACTURING INC	33611	27,000,000	
PACCAR INC	33611	10,292,900	457,600
Automotive Repair & Maintenance			
MONRO MUFFLER BRAKE INC	8111	564,639	33,191
Bakeries & Tortilla Manufacturing			
SARA LEE CORP	3118	10,793,000	527,000
Banking, Credit Cards			
AMERICAN EXPRESS CO	522210	30,242,000	4,057,000
VISA INC	522210	8,065,000	2,966,000
Battery Manufacturing			
AMERICAN POWER CONVERSION (APC)	33591		
Beverages--Distilleries			
FORTUNE BRANDS INC	312140	7,141,500	496,000
Beverages--Soft Drinks & Juices Manufacturing			
COCA-COLA BOTTLING CO CONSOLIDATED	3121	1,514,599	39,542
COCA-COLA COMPANY (THE)	3121	35,119,000	11,809,000
PEPSICO INC	3121	57,838,000	6,338,000
Book Stores-Online			
AMAZON.COM INC	451211E	34,204,000	1,152,000

Company	Industry Code	2010 Sales (U.S. $ thousands)	2010 Profits (U.S. $ thousands)
Breakfast Cereal Manufacturing			
GENERAL MILLS INC	311230	14,796,500	1,530,500
KELLOGG COMPANY	311230	12,397,000	1,247,000
Burial Caskets and Cases Manufacturing			
HILLENBRAND INC	33911	749,200	92,300
Business Machines, Manufacturing			
XEROX CORP	333313	21,633,000	606,000
Business Training, Distance Learning			
DEVRY INC	611410	1,915,181	279,909
Cable & Satellite TV & Data Service			
AT&T INC	517110	124,280,000	19,864,000
CABLEVISION SYSTEMS CORP	517110	7,231,249	360,948
COMCAST CORP	517110	37,937,000	3,635,000
COX COMMUNICATIONS INC	517110	9,000,000	
DIRECTV	517110	24,102,000	2,198,000
FRONTIER COMMUNICATIONS CORPORATION	517110	3,797,675	152,673
LIBERTY GLOBAL INC	517110	9,016,900	388,200
MEDIACOM COMMUNICATIONS CORP	517110	1,499,000	289,400
TELEPHONE AND DATA SYSTEMS INC (TDS)	517110	4,986,829	188,982
TIME WARNER INC	517110	26,888,000	2,578,000
TW TELECOM INC	517110	1,273,171	271,434
VERIZON COMMUNICATIONS INC	517110	106,565,000	10,217,000
WINDSTREAM CORPORATION	517110	3,712,000	310,700
Cable TV Networks			
WALT DISNEY COMPANY (THE)	515210	38,063,000	4,313,000
Casino Resorts			
BOYD GAMING CORP	721120	2,494,724	183,938
CAESARS ENTERTAINMENT CORPORATION	721120	8,818,600	-823,300
LAS VEGAS SANDS CORP (THE VENETIAN)	721120	6,853,182	781,603
WYNN RESORTS LIMITED	721120	4,184,698	160,127
Chemicals, Manufacturing			
DUPONT (E I DU PONT DE NEMOURS & CO)	325	31,505,000	3,031,000
NALCO HOLDING COMPANY	325	4,250,500	196,200
SENSIENT TECHNOLOGIES CORPORATION	325	1,328,180	107,144
SIGMA-ALDRICH CORP	325	2,271,000	384,000
Chocolate & Confectionery Manufacturing			
HERSHEY CO	311320	5,671,000	509,800
MARS INC	311320	30,000,000	
Clinics--Outpatient Clinics & Surgery			
AMSURG CORP	6214	710,409	49,825
CONCENTRA INC	6214		
DAVITA INC	6214	6,447,391	484,219
HEALTHSOUTH CORP	6214	1,999,300	939,800
UNIVERSAL HEALTH SERVICES INC	6214	5,568,185	230,183
Clinics--Physical Rehab Ctr.			
HANGER ORTHOPEDIC GROUP INC	621340	817,379	21,435
Coal Mining			
CONSOL ENERGY INC	21211	5,236,021	346,781

Company	Industry Code	2010 Sales (U.S. $ thousands)	2010 Profits (U.S. $ thousands)
PEABODY ENERGY CORP	21211	6,860,000	774,000
Communications Equipment, Manufacturing			
HARRIS CORPORATION	3342	5,206,100	561,600
Computer Accessories, Monitors, Printers Manufacturing			
LEXMARK INTERNATIONAL INC	334119	4,199,700	340,000
MOLEX INC	334119	3,007,207	131,489
POLYCOM INC	334119	1,218,489	68,409
Computer Hardware, Manufacturing			
APPLE INC	334111	65,225,000	14,013,000
NCR CORPORATION	334111	4,819,000	137,000
Computer Networking & Related Equipment, Manufacturing			
CISCO SYSTEMS INC	33411	40,040,000	7,767,000
FINISAR CORPORATION	33411	629,880	14,131
JUNIPER NETWORKS INC	33411	4,093,266	619,373
Computer Programming & Software Design			
ACCENTURE PLC	541513	23,094,078	2,060,459
AFFILIATED COMPUTER SERVICES INC	541513		
COGNIZANT TECHNOLOGY SOLUTIONS CORP	541513	4,592,389	733,540
COMPUTER SCIENCES CORPORATION (CSC)	541513	16,128,000	834,000
IGATE CORPORATION	541513	280,597	51,755
INTERNATIONAL BUSINESS MACHINES CORP (IBM)	541513	99,870,000	14,833,000
KEANE INC	541513	1,200,000	
SAIC INC	541513	10,846,000	497,000
SAPIENT CORPORATION	541513	863,519	43,805
SRA INTERNATIONAL INC	541513	1,666,629	18,415
STREAM GLOBAL SERVICES INC	541513	800,173	-53,475
SYNTEL INC	541513	532,133	113,593
Computer Software, Accounting, Banking & Financial			
INTUIT INC	511201	3,455,000	574,000
JACK HENRY & ASSOCIATES INC	511201	836,586	117,870
Computer Software, Business Management & ERP			
BMC SOFTWARE INC	511210H	1,911,200	406,100
CITRIX SYSTEMS INC	511210H	1,874,662	277,065
ORACLE CORP	511210H	26,820,000	6,135,000
SAS INSTITUTE INC	511210H	2,430,000	
TIBCO SOFTWARE INC	511210H	754,007	78,088
Computer Software, E-Commerce & Web Analytics			
GSI COMMERCE INC	511210M	1,357,994	-36,502
Computer Software, Games & Entertainment			
ACTIVISION BLIZZARD INC	511210G	4,447,000	418,000
Computer Software, Healthcare & Biotechnology			
CERNER CORP	511210D	1,850,222	237,272
Computer Software, Multimedia, Graphics & Publishing			
ADOBE SYSTEMS INC	511210F	3,800,000	774,680
Computer Software, Network Management, System Testing, & Storage			
BROCADE COMMUNICATIONS SYSTEMS INC	511210B	2,094,363	118,852

Company	Industry Code	2010 Sales (U.S. $ thousands)	2010 Profits (U.S. $ thousands)
Computer Software, Operating Systems, Languages & Development Tools			
MICROSOFT CORP	511210I	62,484,000	24,098,000
RED HAT INC	511210I	748,236	87,253
Computer Software, Product Lifecycle, Engineering, Design & CAD			
CADENCE DESIGN SYSTEMS INC	511210N	935,954	126,538
NATIONAL INSTRUMENTS CORP	511210N	873,220	109,116
PARAMETRIC TECHNOLOGY CORP	511210N	1,010,049	24,368
Computer Software, Sales & Customer Relationship Management			
SALESFORCE.COM INC	511210K	1,305,583	80,719
Computer Software, Security & Anti-Virus			
SYMANTEC CORP	511210E	5,985,000	714,000
Computer Storage Equipment & Misc Parts, Manufacturing			
EMC CORP	334112	17,015,126	1,969,686
NETAPP INC	334112	3,931,400	400,400
WESTERN DIGITAL CORP	334112	9,850,000	1,382,000
Construction, Heavy & Civil Engineering			
AECOM TECHNOLOGY CORPORATION	237	6,545,791	249,344
BECHTEL GROUP INC	237	32,500,000	
FLUOR CORP	237	20,849,300	441,100
PARSONS BRINCKERHOFF INC	237		
SHAW GROUP INC (THE)	237	7,000,800	92,700
TEAM INC	237	453,869	12,275
Construction, Power & Communication Lines and Structures			
QUANTA SERVICES INC	237130	3,391,218	153,176
Construction--Other Special Trade Contractors			
INSITUFORM TECHNOLOGIES	2389	914,975	60,462
Consulting--Computer, Telecommunications & Internet			
CACI INTERNATIONAL INC	541512	3,149,131	106,515
MANTECH INTERNATIONAL CORP	541512	2,604,038	125,096
MAXIMUS INC	541512	831,749	70,409
Consulting-Human Resources			
MERCER INC	541612	3,478,000	
TOWERS WATSON & CO	541612	2,387,829	120,597
Consulting--Management & Business			
BAIN & COMPANY INC	54161	2,500,000	
BOOZ ALLEN HAMILTON INC	54161	5,122,633	25,419
BOSTON CONSULTING GROUP INC (THE, BCG)	54161	3,050,000	
DELOITTE CONSULTING LLP	54161	7,500,000	
FTI CONSULTING INC	54161	1,401,461	71,890
ICF INTERNATIONAL INC	54161	764,734	27,171
MCKINSEY & COMPANY INC	54161	7,200,000	
NORTH HIGHLAND	54161		
Consulting--Marketing			
INVENTIV HEALTH INC	541613	4,359,700	56,150
Consulting--Scientific & Technical			
TETRA TECH INC	541690	2,201,232	76,819
Contract Electronics Manufacturing			
PLEXUS CORP	334419	2,013,393	89,533

Company	Industry Code	2010 Sales (U.S. $ thousands)	2010 Profits (U.S. $ thousands)
SANMINA-SCI CORPORATION	334419	6,318,691	122,435
TTM TECHNOLOGIES INC	334419	1,179,671	79,899
Convenience Stores			
7-ELEVEN INC	445120	17,000,000	
Cosmetics & Toiletries, Manufacturing			
AVON PRODUCTS INC	325620	10,862,800	606,300
ESTEE LAUDER COMPANIES INC (THE)	325620	7,795,800	478,300
MARY KAY INC	325620	3,000,000	
Courier/Express Delivery Service			
FEDEX CORPORATION	4921	34,734,000	1,184,000
UNITED PARCEL SERVICE INC (UPS)	4921	49,545,000	3,488,000
Credit Bureaus			
EXPERIAN AMERICAS	561450	2,254,000	
FIRST ADVANTAGE CORPORATION	561450	740,000	64,700
Cruise Lines			
CARNIVAL CORPORATION	483112	14,469,000	1,978,000
ROYAL CARIBBEAN CRUISES LTD	483112	6,752,504	547,467
Dairy Products, Manufacturing			
DEAN FOODS CO	3115	12,122,887	146,501
Data Processing Services			
AUTOMATIC DATA PROCESSING INC	518210	8,927,700	1,207,300
RACKSPACE HOSTING INC	518210	780,555	46,358
Department Stores			
MACY'S INC	452111	23,489,000	350,000
Diagnostic and Other Electromedical Equipment Manufacturing			
IDEXX LABORATORIES INC	334510	1,103,392	141,284
Diagnostic Substances Manufacturing			
LIFE TECHNOLOGIES CORP	325413	3,588,094	377,858
Discount Stores			
COSTCO WHOLESALE CORP	452112	76,255,000	1,303,000
DOLLAR GENERAL CORPORATION	452112	11,796,380	339,442
FAMILY DOLLAR STORES INC	452112	7,866,971	358,135
KOHL'S CORP	452112	17,178,000	991,000
PRICESMART INC	452112	1,395,891	49,315
SAM'S CLUB	452112	46,710,000	1,512,000
TARGET CORPORATION	452112	65,357,000	2,488,000
WAL-MART STORES INC	452112	405,046,000	14,414,000
Drilling Services--Oil & Gas Wells			
BAKER HUGHES INC	213111	14,414,000	819,000
DIAMOND OFFSHORE DRILLING INC	213111	3,322,974	955,457
NABORS INDUSTRIES LTD	213111	4,215,540	94,695
PATTERSON-UTI ENERGY INC	213111	1,462,931	116,942
ROWAN COMPANIES INC	213111	1,819,207	279,995
Drug Delivery Systems			
HOSPIRA INC	325412A	3,917,200	357,200
Drugs (Pharmaceuticals), Discovery & Manufacturing			
ALLERGAN INC	325412	4,819,600	600

Company	Industry Code	2010 Sales (U.S. $ thousands)	2010 Profits (U.S. $ thousands)
AMGEN INC	325412	15,053,000	4,627,000
BIOGEN IDEC INC	325412	4,716,400	1,005,300
CELGENE CORP	325412	3,625,745	880,512
CEPHALON INC	325412	2,811,057	417,683
ENDO PHARMACEUTICALS HOLDINGS INC	325412	1,716,229	259,006
FOREST LABORATORIES INC	325412	3,903,524	682,383
GENENTECH INC	325412		
GILEAD SCIENCES INC	325412	7,949,420	2,901,257
JOHNSON & JOHNSON	325412	61,587,000	13,334,000
MYLAN INC	325412	5,450,522	345,542
PERRIGO CO	325412	2,268,870	222,546
WATSON PHARMACEUTICALS INC	325412	3,566,900	184,400
Drugs (Pharmaceuticals), Distribution			
AMERISOURCEBERGEN CORP	424210	77,953,979	636,748
MCKESSON CORPORATION	424210	108,702,000	1,263,000
Electrical Equipment, Manufacturing			
DANAHER CORP	335	13,202,602	1,793,000
DIODES INC	335	612,886	80,264
GE ENERGY INFRASTRUCTURE	335	37,514,000	7,271,000
STANLEY BLACK & DECKER INC	335	8,410,000	198,000
Electronics, Audio & Appliance Stores			
BEST BUY CO INC	44311	49,694,000	1,317,000
Engineering Services			
URS CORPORATION	541330	9,177,051	287,889
Fiber Optic Cable & Electrical Wire			
AMPHENOL CORPORATION	335921	3,554,101	502,413
Financing--Business			
GENERAL ELECTRIC CO (GE)	522220	150,211,000	11,644,000
Fitness Centers/Health Clubs			
HEALTH FITNESS CORP	713940	169,400	
Food Products, Manufacturing			
CAMPBELL SOUP CO	311	7,676,000	844,000
CONAGRA FOODS INC	311	12,079,400	725,800
JM SMUCKER CO	311	4,605,289	494,138
KRAFT FOODS INC	311	49,207,000	4,114,000
RALCORP HOLDINGS INC	311	4,048,500	208,800
SENECA FOODS CORPORATION	311	1,280,110	48,411
TREEHOUSE FOODS INC	311	1,817,024	90,919
Food Service Contractors			
ARAMARK CORPORATION	722310	12,571,676	30,688
SODEXO INC	722310	8,000,000	
Forest Products/Paper, Manufacturing			
KIMBERLY-CLARK CORP	322	19,746,000	1,943,000
Freight Forwarding & Support Services			
CH ROBINSON WORLDWIDE INC	4885	9,274,305	387,026
Grain Distribution, Milling & Oilseed Processing			
ARCHER DANIELS MIDLAND CO	3112	61,682,000	1,930,000
BUNGE LTD	3112	45,707,000	2,354,000

Company	Industry Code	2010 Sales (U.S. $ thousands)	2010 Profits (U.S. $ thousands)
Grocery Stores/Supermarkets			
HE BUTT GROCERY COMPANY (HEB)	445110	16,100,000	
KROGER CO (THE)	445110	76,733,000	70,000
MEIJER INC	445110	14,200,000	
PUBLIX SUPER MARKETS INC	445110	25,100,000	342,100
SAFEWAY INC	445110	41,050,000	589,800
WHOLE FOODS MARKET INC	445110	9,005,794	245,833
Hair, Nail & Skin Care Salons			
REGIS CORPORATION	81211	2,358,434	42,740
Home Health & Hospice Care			
AMEDISYS INC	6216	1,634,319	193,510
CHEMED CORPORATION	6216	1,280,545	81,831
GENTIVA HEALTH SERVICES INC	6216	1,447,029	52,155
LINCARE HOLDINGS INC	6216	1,669,205	181,574
ODYSSEY HEALTHCARE INC	6216	748,093	52,155
Hospitals/Clinics--General & Specialty Hospitals			
ADVENTIST HEALTH SYSTEM	622110		
ASCENSION HEALTH	622110	14,773,000	569,000
CATHOLIC HEALTH INITIATIVES	622110	9,090,555	681,982
COMMUNITY HEALTH SYSTEMS INC	622110	12,986,500	348,441
FAIRVIEW HEALTH SERVICES	622110	2,826,996	101,852
HCA HOLDINGS INC	622110	30,683,000	1,573,000
HEALTH MANAGEMENT ASSOCIATES INC	622110	5,114,997	150,069
KAISER PERMANENTE	622110	44,200,000	2,000,000
MAYO FOUNDATION FOR MEDICAL EDUCATION AND RESEARCH	622110	7,942,000	515,300
METHODIST HEALTH CARE SYSTEM	622110	366,691	9,494
PROVIDENCE HEALTH & SERVICES	622110	8,081,955	330,215
SELECT MEDICAL HOLDINGS CORPORATION	622110	2,390,290	77,644
SPECTRUM HEALTH	622110	3,161,106	121,294
SUTTER HEALTH INC	622110	9,116,000	878,000
TENET HEALTHCARE CORPORATION	622110	9,205,000	1,119,000
Hotels/Resorts/Motels			
CARLSON COMPANIES INC	721110		
HILTON HOTELS CORP	721110	9,000,000	
HYATT HOTELS CORPORATION	721110	3,527,000	66,000
MARRIOTT INTERNATIONAL INC	721110	11,691,000	458,000
STARWOOD HOTELS & RESORTS WORLDWIDE INC	721110	5,071,000	477,000
WYNDHAM WORLDWIDE	721110	3,851,000	379,000
Industrial Gas Manufacturing			
AIR PRODUCTS & CHEMICALS INC	325120	9,026,000	1,029,000
PRAXAIR INC	325120	10,116,000	1,195,000
Instrument Manufacturing, including Measurement, Control, Test & Navigational			
AGILENT TECHNOLOGIES INC	3345	5,444,000	684,000
BECKMAN COULTER INC	3345	3,633,400	230,700
BRUKER CORP	3345	1,304,900	95,400
EMERSON ELECTRIC CO	3345	21,039,000	2,164,000

Company	Industry Code	2010 Sales (U.S. $ thousands)	2010 Profits (U.S. $ thousands)
MILLIPORE CORP	3345	2,352,865	
TEKTRONIX INC	3345		
Insurance Brokerage, Agencies & Exchanges			
ARTHUR J GALLAGHER & CO	524210	1,864,200	174,100
BROWN & BROWN INC	524210	973,492	161,752
MARSH & MCLENNAN COMPANIES INC	524210	10,550,000	855,000
Insurance-Health, HMO's & PPO's			
AFLAC INC	524114	20,732,000	2,344,000
AMERIGROUP CORPORATION	524114	5,806,301	273,371
CIGNA CORP	524114	21,253,000	1,345,000
HEALTH CARE SERVICE CORPORATION (HCSC)	524114	21,784,870	700,000
HUMANA INC	524114	33,868,208	1,099,390
UNITEDHEALTH GROUP INC	524114	94,155,000	4,634,000
Insurance-Life			
AXA FINANCIAL INC	524113	124,819,588	4,243,156
GENWORTH FINANCIAL INC	524113	10,089,000	285,000
JACKSON NATIONAL LIFE INSURANCE COMPANY	524113	18,000,000	509,000
LINCOLN NATIONAL CORPORATION	524113	10,407,000	980,000
MASSACHUSETTS MUTUAL LIFE INSURANCE CO	524113	25,647,100	258,200
METLIFE INC	524113	52,717,000	2,786,000
MUTUAL OF OMAHA COMPANIES (THE)	524113	5,310,958	247,663
NEW YORK LIFE INSURANCE CO	524113	30,168,000	1,436,000
NORTHWESTERN MUTUAL LIFE INSURANCE CO	524113	22,762,608	805,801
PRINCIPAL FINANCIAL GROUP (THE)	524113	9,158,600	666,300
PRUDENTIAL FINANCIAL INC	524113	38,414,000	3,195,000
Insurance--Property & Casualty, Specialty, Surety			
CHUBB CORPORATION (THE)	524126	13,319,000	2,174,000
CNA FINANCIAL CORP	524126	9,209,000	690,000
FM GLOBAL	524126	4,686,800	686,000
LIBERTY MUTUAL GROUP INC	524126	33,200,000	1,678,000
LOEWS CORPORATION	524126	14,615,000	1,288,000
PROGRESSIVE CORPORATION (THE)	524126	14,963,300	1,068,300
SAFECO INSURANCE COMPANY OF AMERICA	524126	1,567,755	93,296
TRAVELERS COMPANIES INC (THE)	524126	25,112,000	3,216,000
USAA	524126	17,946,000	2,637,000
Internet Publishing & Web Search Portals			
BLOOMBERG LP	519130	7,000,000	
FACTSET RESEARCH SYSTEMS INC	519130	641,059	150,211
GOOGLE INC	519130	29,321,000	8,505,000
IAC/INTERACTIVECORP	519130	1,636,815	99,359
THOMSON REUTERS	519130	13,070,000	933,000
Investment Banking			
STIFEL FINANCIAL CORP	523110	1,382,026	1,907
Investment Management/Mutual Funds/Pension Funds			
BLACKROCK INC	523920	8,612,000	2,063,000
FMR CORP (FIDELITY INVESTMENTS)	523920		
Jewelry Stores			
TIFFANY & CO	448310	2,709,704	264,823

Company	Industry Code	2010 Sales (U.S. $ thousands)	2010 Profits (U.S. $ thousands)
Laboratories & Diagnostic Services--Medical			
LABORATORY CORP OF AMERICA HOLDINGS	621511	5,003,900	558,200
Linen/Uniform Supply			
CINTAS CORP	812331	3,547,339	215,620
Linens/Housewares/Art/Framing Stores			
BED BATH & BEYOND INC	442299	7,828,793	600,033
CONTAINER STORE (THE)	442299		
Logistics Outsourcing			
PARK-OHIO HOLDINGS CORP	541614	813,522	15,187
Long-Term Health Care & Assisted Living			
BROOKDALE SENIOR LIVING INC	623110	2,213,264	-48,901
CAPITAL SENIOR LIVING CORP	623110	211,929	4,254
EMERITUS CORP	623110	1,007,065	-57,842
KINDRED HEALTHCARE INC	623110	4,359,697	56,146
SKILLED HEALTHCARE GROUP INC	623110	820,238	-1,041
SUN HEALTHCARE GROUP INC	623110	1,906,861	-4,650
Machine Tools, Manufacturing			
FASTENAL	33351	2,269,471	265,356
Machinery, Equipment & Supplies, Distribution			
WW GRAINGER INC	4238	7,182,158	510,865
Machinery, Manufacturing			
CATERPILLAR INC	333	42,588,000	2,700,000
DEERE & CO	333	26,004,600	1,865,000
ILLINOIS TOOL WORKS INC	333	15,870,376	1,527,193
NACCO INDUSTRIES INC	333	2,687,500	79,500
TEREX CORPORATION	333	4,418,200	362,500
Machinery-Mining & Oil & Gas Field, Manufacturing			
CAMERON INTERNATIONAL CORPORATION	33313	6,134,800	562,900
LUFKIN INDUSTRIES INC	33313	645,643	43,823
Mail Order and Non-Store Selling, Incl. TV Shopping			
COLDWATER CREEK INC	454113	1,038,581	-56,132
Management of Companies & Enterprises			
BERKSHIRE HATHAWAY INC	55111	136,185,000	12,967,000
Market Research			
IMS HEALTH INC	541910	2,321,129	302,392
Marketing Agencies & Related Services			
ACOSTA SALES & MARKETING	5418	1,000,000	
ALLIANCE DATA SYSTEMS CORPORATION	5418	2,791,000	194,000
VALASSIS COMMUNICATIONS INC	5418	2,333,512	385,405
Medical/Dental/Surgical Equipment & Supplies, Distribution			
HENRY SCHEIN INC	423450	7,526,790	325,789
OWENS & MINOR INC	423450	8,123,608	110,579
PATTERSON COMPANIES INC	423450	3,237,376	212,254
THERMO FISHER SCIENTIFIC INC	423450	10,788,700	1,035,600
Medical/Dental/Surgical Equipment & Supplies, Manufacturing			
3M COMPANY	33911	26,662,000	4,085,000
BAUSCH & LOMB INC	33911	2,510,000	

Company	Industry Code	2010 Sales (U.S. $ thousands)	2010 Profits (U.S. $ thousands)
BECTON DICKINSON & CO	33911	7,372,333	1,317,610
BIO RAD LABORATORIES INC	33911	1,927,118	185,490
COOPER COMPANIES INC	33911	1,158,517	112,803
CR BARD INC	33911	2,720,200	509,200
DENTSPLY INTERNATIONAL INC	33911	2,221,014	265,708
EDWARDS LIFESCIENCES CORP	33911	1,447,000	218,000
GENZYME BIOSURGERY	33911	4,050,000	422,100
INTEGRA LIFESCIENCES HOLDINGS CORP	33911	732,068	65,669
KINETIC CONCEPTS INC	33911	2,017,752	256,084
MEDTRONIC INC	33911	15,817,000	3,099,000
RESMED INC	33911	1,092,357	190,085
ST JUDE MEDICAL INC	33911	5,164,771	907,436
STRYKER CORP	33911	7,320,000	1,273,400
VARIAN MEDICAL SYSTEMS INC	33911	2,356,600	360,400
WATERS CORP	33911	1,643,371	381,763
ZIMMER HOLDINGS INC	33911	4,220,200	596,900
Oil & Natural Gas Exploration & Production			
APACHE CORP	211111	12,092,000	3,032,000
CHEVRON CORPORATION	211111	204,928,000	19,136,000
CONOCOPHILLIPS COMPANY	211111	189,441,000	11,417,000
EXXON MOBIL CORPORATION (EXXONMOBIL)	211111	370,125,000	30,460,000
MARATHON OIL CORP	211111	72,321,000	2,568,000
SHELL OIL CO	211111	120,000,000	
WILLIAMS COMPANIES INC (THE)	211111	9,616,000	-1,097,000
Oil Field Services			
BASIC ENERGY SERVICES INC	213112	728,239	-43,563
EXTERRAN HOLDINGS INC	213112	2,461,533	-101,825
FMC TECHNOLOGIES INC	213112	4,125,600	377,900
HALLIBURTON COMPANY	213112	17,973,000	1,842,000
KEY ENERGY SERVICES INC	213112	1,153,684	73,495
NATIONAL OILWELL VARCO INC	213112	12,156,000	1,667,000
OCEANEERING INTERNATIONAL INC	213112	1,917,045	200,531
OIL STATES INTERNATIONAL INC	213112	2,411,984	168,018
SCHLUMBERGER LIMITED	213112	27,447,000	4,267,000
SMITH INTERNATIONAL INC	213112		
TIDEWATER INC	213112	1,168,634	259,476
Other Health & Personal Care Stores/Weight Management			
WEIGHT WATCHERS INTERNATIONAL INC	446199	1,452,037	194,235
Packaging, Manufacturing			
BALL CORP	3222	7,630,000	468,000
BEMIS COMPANY INC	3222	4,835,000	211,500
WEST PHARMACEUTICAL SERVICES INC	3222	1,104,700	65,300
Paint & Wallpaper Stores			
SHERWIN WILLIAMS COMPANY (THE)	444120	7,776,000	462,000
Paints & Coatings, Manufacturing			
VALSPAR CORPORATION (THE)	325510	3,226,687	222,056
Pawn Shops			
CASH AMERICA INTERNATIONAL INC	522298	1,293,339	115,538

Company	Industry Code	2010 Sales (U.S. $ thousands)	2010 Profits (U.S. $ thousands)
Payment & Transaction Processing Services			
FIDELITY NATIONAL INFORMATION SERVICES INC	522320	5,269,500	404,500
HEARTLAND PAYMENT SYSTEMS INC	522320	1,864,337	34,660
TOTAL SYSTEM SERVICES INC (TSYS)	522320	1,717,577	193,947
Payment & Transaction Processing--Benefits Management			
EXPRESS SCRIPTS INC	522320A	44,973,200	1,204,600
MEDCO HEALTH SOLUTIONS INC	522320A	65,968,300	1,427,300
TRUSTMARK COMPANIES	522320A	898,500	44,000
Petrochemicals Manufacturing			
CHEVRON PHILLIPS CHEMICAL COMPANY LLC	325110	11,204,000	1,388,000
EXXONMOBIL CHEMICAL	325110	25,891,000	4,913,000
Petroleum Refineries			
KOCH INDUSTRIES INC	324110	105,000,000	
Pets/Pet Supplies Stores			
PETCO ANIMAL SUPPLIES INC	453910		
PETSMART INC	453910	5,336,392	198,325
Pharmacies & Drug Stores			
CVS CAREMARK CORPORATION	446110	96,413,000	3,424,000
WALGREEN CO	446110	67,420,000	2,091,000
Physician Practice Management			
MEDNAX INC	6211	1,401,559	202,691
TEAM HEALTH HOLDINGS INC	6211	1,519,264	13,337
Radio & Wireless Communication, Manufacturing			
LORAL SPACE & COMMUNICATIONS LTD	334220	1,158,985	487,341
Railroad Transportation			
BURLINGTON NORTHERN SANTA FE LLC	48211	16,850,000	2,459,000
CSX CORP	48211	10,636,000	1,563,000
NORFOLK SOUTHERN CORP	48211	9,516,000	1,496,000
UNION PACIFIC CORP	48211	16,965,000	2,780,000
Real Estate Brokerage			
CB RICHARD ELLIS GROUP INC (CBRE)	531210	5,115,316	156,009
Real Estate Investment Trusts - Nonresidential			
VORNADO REALTY TRUST	531120	2,779,727	647,883
Real Estate Investment Trusts - Residential			
EQUITY LIFESTYLE PROPERTIES INC	531110	511,361	38,354
Real Estate Operations & Development--General			
ABM INDUSTRIES INC	5311	3,495,747	64,121
JONES LANG LASALLE INC	5311	2,925,613	154,439
Research & Development-Physical, Engineering & Life Sciences			
COVANCE INC	541712	2,038,473	68,254
PAREXEL INTERNATIONAL CORP	541712	1,131,039	41,542
PHARMACEUTICAL PRODUCT DEVELOPMENT INC	541712	1,470,570	124,041
Restaurants			
BUFFALO WILD WINGS INC	722110	613,256	38,400
CHIPOTLE MEXICAN GRILL INC	722110	1,835,922	178,981
CRACKER BARREL OLD COUNTRY STORE INC	722110	2,404,515	85,258
DARDEN RESTAURANTS INC	722110	7,113,100	404,500

Company	Industry Code	2010 Sales (U.S. $ thousands)	2010 Profits (U.S. $ thousands)
MCDONALD'S CORP	722110	24,074,600	4,946,300
PANERA BREAD CO	722110	1,542,489	111,866
YUM! BRANDS INC	722110	11,343,000	1,178,000
Rubber Products & Tires Manufacturing			
GOODYEAR TIRE & RUBBER COMPANY (THE)	3262	18,832,000	-216,000
Security, Protection, Armored Car & Investigation Services			
BRINKS COMPANY (THE)	5616	3,121,500	72,800
Semiconductor Manufacturing Equipment			
AMKOR TECHNOLOGY INC	333295	2,939,483	232,147
APPLIED MATERIALS INC	333295	9,548,667	937,866
KLA TENCOR CORP	333295	1,820,760	212,300
LAM RESEARCH CORP	333295	2,133,776	346,669
Semiconductors (Microchips)/Integrated Circuits/Components, Manufacturing			
ADVANCED MICRO DEVICES INC (AMD)	33441	6,494,000	471,000
ANALOG DEVICES INC	33441	2,761,503	712,084
BROADCOM CORP	33441	6,818,319	1,081,800
INTEL CORP	33441	43,623,000	11,464,000
MICROCHIP TECHNOLOGY INC	33441	947,729	217,005
MICRON TECHNOLOGY INC	33441	8,482,000	1,850,000
MULTI-FINELINE ELECTRONIX INC	33441	791,339	29,775
QUALCOMM INC	33441	10,991,000	3,247,000
SANDISK CORP	33441	4,826,807	1,461,574
Shipping-Deep Sea			
SEACOR HOLDINGS INC	483111	2,649,368	244,724
Shoe Manufacturing-Athletic Shoes & Misc. Shoes, Incl. Children's			
CROCS INC	316219	789,695	67,726
NIKE INC	316219	19,014,000	1,906,700
Shoe Manufacturing-Men's			
GENESCO INC	316213	1,574,352	28,813
Snack Products, Manufacturing			
SNYDERS-LANCE INC	31191	979,835	2,512
Soap & Cleaning Compound Manufacturing			
CLOROX CO (THE)	325611	5,534,000	603,000
COLGATE PALMOLIVE CO	325611	15,564,000	2,203,000
Soaps, Cleaners, Cosmetics & Toiletries, Manufacturing			
PROCTER & GAMBLE CO	3256	78,938,000	12,736,000
Sporting Goods Stores			
ACADEMY SPORTS & OUTDOORS LTD	451110	2,400,000	
BASS PRO SHOPS INC	451110		
BIG 5 SPORTING GOODS CORPORATION	451110	896,813	20,562
DICK'S SPORTING GOODS INC	451110	4,412,835	135,359
HIBBETT SPORTS INC	451110	593,492	32,549
RECREATIONAL EQUIPMENT INC (REI)	451110	1,658,751	30,230
Staffing or Outsourcing			
BARRETT BUSINESS SERVICES	561	273,123	7,353
COMPUTER TASK GROUP INC	561	331,400	8,400
Sugar & Confectionery Product Manufacturing			
WM WRIGLEY JR COMPANY	3113		

Company	Industry Code	2010 Sales (U.S. $ thousands)	2010 Profits (U.S. $ thousands)
Surveying & Mapping--Geophysical			
GEOKINETICS INC	541360	558,134	-138,684
Telecommunications Equipment Manufacturing			
CIENA CORP	334210	1,236,636	-331,514
Telecommunications Service Cellular, U.S. & Non-U.S.			
CELLCO PARTNERSHIP (VERIZON WIRELESS)	5172	63,407,000	18,724,000
CLEARWIRE CORP	5172	556,826	-2,303,250
LEAP WIRELESS INTERNATIONAL INC	5172	2,697,203	-785,055
METROPCS COMMUNICATIONS INC	5172	4,069,353	193,415
NII HOLDINGS INC	5172	5,601,316	341,052
UNITED STATES CELLULAR CORP	5172	4,177,681	132,324
Telecommunications Service Wired, Satellite or Cable			
AT&T INC	517110	124,280,000	19,864,000
CABLEVISION SYSTEMS CORP	517110	7,231,249	360,948
COMCAST CORP	517110	37,937,000	3,635,000
COX COMMUNICATIONS INC	517110	9,000,000	
DIRECTV	517110	24,102,000	2,198,000
FRONTIER COMMUNICATIONS CORPORATION	517110	3,797,675	152,673
LIBERTY GLOBAL INC	517110	9,016,900	388,200
MEDIACOM COMMUNICATIONS CORP	517110	1,499,000	289,400
TELEPHONE AND DATA SYSTEMS INC (TDS)	517110	4,986,829	188,982
TIME WARNER INC	517110	26,888,000	2,578,000
TW TELECOM INC	517110	1,273,171	271,434
VERIZON COMMUNICATIONS INC	517110	106,565,000	10,217,000
WINDSTREAM CORPORATION	517110	3,712,000	310,700
Television Broadcasting			
FOX ENTERTAINMENT GROUP INC	515120		
NEWS CORP	515120	32,778,000	2,644,000
UNIVISION COMMUNICATIONS INC	515120	2,245,200	-555,900
Temporary Help/Staffing			
KELLY SERVICES INC	561320	4,950,300	26,100
MANPOWER INC	561320	18,866,500	-263,600
ROBERT HALF INTERNATIONAL INC	561320	3,175,093	66,069
Tobacco Products, Manufacturing			
ALTRIA GROUP INC	3122	24,363,000	3,907,000
PHILIP MORRIS INTERNATIONAL INC	3122	67,713,000	7,259,000
Toys, Manufacturing			
MATTEL INC	339932	5,856,195	684,863
Toys/Hobbies/Games/Crafts Stores			
GAMESTOP CORP	451120	9,077,997	377,265
Travel Services-Online			
EXPEDIA INC	5615E	3,348,109	425,560
SABRE HOLDINGS CORP	5615E	3,400,000	
Travel Trailer & Camper Manufacturing			
THOR INDUSTRIES INC	336214	2,276,557	110,064
Truck Transportation			
CON-WAY INC	484	4,952,000	3,985

Company	Industry Code	2010 Sales (U.S. $ thousands)	2010 Profits (U.S. $ thousands)
JB HUNT TRANSPORT SERVICES INC	484	3,793,000	200,000
Trucks, Rental/Leasing			
AMERCO	532120	2,002,005	65,623
RYDER SYSTEM INC	532120	5,136,400	118,200
Trucks, RVs & Misc. Automotive, Manufacturing			
OSHKOSH CORPORATION	336120	9,842,400	790,000
TV/Video/Theatrical, Production			
LIBERTY MEDIA CORP	512110	8,932,000	1,303,000
Utilities-Electric			
EDISON INTERNATIONAL	2211	12,409,000	1,256,000
FIRSTENERGY CORP	2211	13,339,000	784,000
HAWAIIAN ELECTRIC INDUSTRIES INC	2211	2,664,982	113,535
NEXTERA ENERGY INC	2211	15,317,000	1,957,000
SOUTHERN COMPANY (THE)	2211	17,456,000	1,975,000
Utilities-Electric & Gas			
AES CORPORATION (THE)	221	16,647,000	9,000
DTE ENERGY COMPANY	221	8,557,000	630,000
DUKE ENERGY CORP	221	14,272,000	1,323,000
EXELON CORPORATION	221	18,644,000	2,563,000
MIDAMERICAN ENERGY HOLDINGS CO	221	11,100,000	
PG&E CORPORATION	221	13,841,000	1,099,000
SCANA CORPORATION	221	4,601,000	376,000
SEMPRA ENERGY	221	9,003,000	739,000
Utilities-Nuclear Generation			
ENTERGY CORP	221113	11,487,577	1,270,305
Veterinary Clinics			
VCA ANTECH INC	541940	1,381,468	110,243
Waste Disposal, Waste Management			
STERICYCLE INC	562	1,439,388	207,879
WASTE MANAGEMENT INC	562	12,515,000	953,000
Watch & Clock Manufacturing			
FOSSIL INC	334518	2,030,690	255,205

ALPHABETICAL INDEX

EMERSON ELECTRIC CO
ENDO PHARMACEUTICALS HOLDINGS INC
ENTERGY CORP
ENTERPRISE HOLDINGS INC
EQUITY LIFESTYLE PROPERTIES INC
ERNST & YOUNG LLP
ESTEE LAUDER COMPANIES INC (THE)
EXELON CORPORATION
EXPEDIA INC
EXPERIAN AMERICAS
EXPRESS SCRIPTS INC
EXTERRAN HOLDINGS INC
EXXON MOBIL CORPORATION (EXXONMOBIL)
EXXONMOBIL CHEMICAL
FACTSET RESEARCH SYSTEMS INC
FAIRVIEW HEALTH SERVICES
FAMILY DOLLAR STORES INC
FASTENAL
FEDERAL MOGUL CORP
FEDEX CORPORATION
FIDELITY NATIONAL INFORMATION SERVICES INC
FINISAR CORPORATION
FIRST ADVANTAGE CORPORATION
FIRSTENERGY CORP
FLUOR CORP
FM GLOBAL
FMC TECHNOLOGIES INC
FMR CORP (FIDELITY INVESTMENTS)
FORD MOTOR CO
FOREST LABORATORIES INC
FORTUNE BRANDS INC
FOSSIL INC
FOX ENTERTAINMENT GROUP INC
FRONTIER COMMUNICATIONS CORPORATION
FTI CONSULTING INC
GAMESTOP CORP
GE ENERGY INFRASTRUCTURE
GENENTECH INC
GENERAL ELECTRIC CO (GE)
GENERAL MILLS INC
GENERAL MOTORS COMPANY (GM)
GENESCO INC
GENTEX CORPORATION
GENTIVA HEALTH SERVICES INC
GENWORTH FINANCIAL INC
GENZYME BIOSURGERY
GEOKINETICS INC
GILEAD SCIENCES INC
GOODYEAR TIRE & RUBBER COMPANY (THE)
GOOGLE INC
GRANT THORNTON LLP
GROUP 1 AUTOMOTIVE INC
GROUPON INC
GSI COMMERCE INC
GUESS? INC
HALLIBURTON COMPANY
HANESBRANDS INC
HANGER ORTHOPEDIC GROUP INC
HARRIS CORPORATION
HAWAIIAN ELECTRIC INDUSTRIES INC
HCA HOLDINGS INC
HE BUTT GROCERY COMPANY (HEB)
HEALTH CARE SERVICE CORPORATION (HCSC)
HEALTH FITNESS CORP
HEALTH MANAGEMENT ASSOCIATES INC
HEALTHSOUTH CORP
HEARTLAND PAYMENT SYSTEMS INC
HENRY SCHEIN INC
HERSHEY CO
HERTZ GLOBAL HOLDINGS INC
HIBBETT SPORTS INC
HILLENBRAND INC
HILTON HOTELS CORP
HONDA OF AMERICA MANUFACTURING INC
HOSPIRA INC
HUMANA INC
HYATT HOTELS CORPORATION
IAC/INTERACTIVECORP
ICF INTERNATIONAL INC
IDEXX LABORATORIES INC
IGATE CORPORATION
ILLINOIS TOOL WORKS INC
IMS HEALTH INC
INGRAM MICRO INC
INSITUFORM TECHNOLOGIES
INTEGRA LIFESCIENCES HOLDINGS CORP
INTEL CORP
INTERNATIONAL BUSINESS MACHINES CORP (IBM)
INTERPUBLIC GROUP OF COMPANIES INC
INTUIT INC
INVENTIV HEALTH INC
JACK HENRY & ASSOCIATES INC
JACKSON NATIONAL LIFE INSURANCE COMPANY
JARDEN CORP
JB HUNT TRANSPORT SERVICES INC
JETBLUE AIRWAYS CORPORATION
JM SMUCKER CO
JOHNSON & JOHNSON
JOHNSON CONTROLS INC
JONES LANG LASALLE INC
JUNIPER NETWORKS INC
KAISER PERMANENTE
KEANE INC
KELLOGG COMPANY
KELLY SERVICES INC
KEY ENERGY SERVICES INC
KIMBERLY-CLARK CORP
KINDRED HEALTHCARE INC
KINETIC CONCEPTS INC
KLA TENCOR CORP
KOCH INDUSTRIES INC
KOHL'S CORP
KPMG LLP
KRAFT FOODS INC
KROGER CO (THE)
LABORATORY CORP OF AMERICA HOLDINGS
LAM RESEARCH CORP
LAS VEGAS SANDS CORP (THE VENETIAN)
LEAP WIRELESS INTERNATIONAL INC
LEAR CORP
LEXMARK INTERNATIONAL INC
LIBERTY GLOBAL INC
LIBERTY MEDIA CORP
LIBERTY MUTUAL GROUP INC
LIFE TECHNOLOGIES CORP
LIMITED BRANDS INC
LINCARE HOLDINGS INC
LINCOLN NATIONAL CORPORATION
LKQ CORP
LOEWS CORPORATION
LORAL SPACE & COMMUNICATIONS LTD
LUFKIN INDUSTRIES INC
MACY'S INC
MANPOWER INC
MANTECH INTERNATIONAL CORP
MARATHON OIL CORP
MARRIOTT INTERNATIONAL INC
MARS INC
MARSH & MCLENNAN COMPANIES INC
MARY KAY INC
MASSACHUSETTS MUTUAL LIFE INSURANCE CO
MATTEL INC
MAXIMUS INC
MAYO FOUNDATION FOR MEDICAL EDUCATION AND RESEARCH
MCDONALD'S CORP
MCKESSON CORPORATION
MCKINSEY & COMPANY INC
MEDCO HEALTH SOLUTIONS INC
MEDIACOM COMMUNICATIONS CORP
MEDNAX INC
MEDTRONIC INC
MEIJER INC
MERCER INC
METHODIST HEALTH CARE SYSTEM
METLIFE INC
METROPCS COMMUNICATIONS INC
MICROCHIP TECHNOLOGY INC
MICRON TECHNOLOGY INC
MICROSOFT CORP
MIDAMERICAN ENERGY HOLDINGS CO
MILLIPORE CORP
MOLEX INC
MONRO MUFFLER BRAKE INC
MULTI-FINELINE ELECTRONIX INC
MUTUAL OF OMAHA COMPANIES (THE)
MYLAN INC
NABORS INDUSTRIES LTD
NACCO INDUSTRIES INC
NALCO HOLDING COMPANY
NATIONAL INSTRUMENTS CORP

NATIONAL OILWELL VARCO INC
NCR CORPORATION
NETAPP INC
NEW YORK LIFE INSURANCE CO
NEWS CORP
NEXTERA ENERGY INC
NII HOLDINGS INC
NIKE INC
NORFOLK SOUTHERN CORP
NORTH HIGHLAND
NORTHWESTERN MUTUAL LIFE INSURANCE CO
OCEANEERING INTERNATIONAL INC
ODYSSEY HEALTHCARE INC
OIL STATES INTERNATIONAL INC
OMNICOM GROUP INC
ORACLE CORP
O'REILLY AUTOMOTIVE INC
OSHKOSH CORPORATION
OWENS & MINOR INC
PACCAR INC
PANERA BREAD CO
PARAMETRIC TECHNOLOGY CORP
PAREXEL INTERNATIONAL CORP
PARK-OHIO HOLDINGS CORP
PARSONS BRINCKERHOFF INC
PATTERSON COMPANIES INC
PATTERSON-UTI ENERGY INC
PEABODY ENERGY CORP
PENSKE AUTOMOTIVE GROUP INC
PEPSICO INC
PERRIGO CO
PETCO ANIMAL SUPPLIES INC
PETSMART INC
PG&E CORPORATION
PHARMACEUTICAL PRODUCT DEVELOPMENT INC
PHILIP MORRIS INTERNATIONAL INC
PLEXUS CORP
POLO RALPH LAUREN CORP
POLYCOM INC
PRAXAIR INC
PRICESMART INC
PRICEWATERHOUSECOOPERS
PRINCIPAL FINANCIAL GROUP (THE)
PROCTER & GAMBLE CO
PROGRESSIVE CORPORATION (THE)
PROVIDENCE HEALTH & SERVICES
PRUDENTIAL FINANCIAL INC
PUBLIX SUPER MARKETS INC
QUALCOMM INC
QUANTA SERVICES INC
RACKSPACE HOSTING INC
RALCORP HOLDINGS INC
RECREATIONAL EQUIPMENT INC (REI)
RED HAT INC
REGIS CORPORATION
REPUBLIC AIRWAYS HOLDINGS INC
RESMED INC
ROBERT HALF INTERNATIONAL INC
ROSS STORES INC
ROWAN COMPANIES INC
ROYAL CARIBBEAN CRUISES LTD
RYDER SYSTEM INC
SABRE HOLDINGS CORP
SAFECO INSURANCE COMPANY OF AMERICA
SAFEWAY INC
SAIC INC
SALESFORCE.COM INC
SAM'S CLUB
SANDISK CORP
SANMINA-SCI CORPORATION
SAPIENT CORPORATION
SARA LEE CORP
SAS INSTITUTE INC
SCANA CORPORATION
SCHLUMBERGER LIMITED
SCOTTS MIRACLE GROW CO
SEACOR HOLDINGS INC
SELECT MEDICAL HOLDINGS CORPORATION
SEMPRA ENERGY
SENECA FOODS CORPORATION
SENSIENT TECHNOLOGIES CORPORATION
SHAW GROUP INC (THE)
SHELL OIL CO
SHERWIN WILLIAMS COMPANY (THE)
SIGMA-ALDRICH CORP
SKILLED HEALTHCARE GROUP INC
SNYDERS-LANCE INC
SODEXO INC
SOUTHERN COMPANY (THE)
SOUTHWEST AIRLINES CO
SPECTRUM HEALTH
SPIRIT AEROSYSTEMS HOLDINGS INC
SRA INTERNATIONAL INC
ST JUDE MEDICAL INC
STANLEY BLACK & DECKER INC
STARWOOD HOTELS & RESORTS WORLDWIDE INC
STERICYCLE INC
STIFEL FINANCIAL CORP
STONERIDGE INC
STREAM GLOBAL SERVICES INC
STRYKER CORP
SUN HEALTHCARE GROUP INC
SUTTER HEALTH INC
SYMANTEC CORP
SYNTEL INC
SYSCO CORP
TARGET CORPORATION
TEAM HEALTH HOLDINGS INC
TEAM INC
TECH DATA CORP
TEKTRONIX INC
TELEDYNE TECHNOLOGIES INC
TELEPHONE AND DATA SYSTEMS INC (TDS)
TENET HEALTHCARE CORPORATION
TEREX CORPORATION
TETRA TECH INC
THERMO FISHER SCIENTIFIC INC
THOMSON REUTERS
THOR INDUSTRIES INC
TIBCO SOFTWARE INC
TIDEWATER INC
TIFFANY & CO
TIME WARNER INC
TJX COMPANIES INC (THE)
TOTAL SYSTEM SERVICES INC (TSYS)
TOWERS WATSON & CO
TRAVELERS COMPANIES INC (THE)
TREEHOUSE FOODS INC
TRUSTMARK COMPANIES
TTM TECHNOLOGIES INC
TW TELECOM INC
UNDER ARMOUR INC
UNION PACIFIC CORP
UNITED NATURAL FOODS INC
UNITED PARCEL SERVICE INC (UPS)
UNITED STATES CELLULAR CORP
UNITED TECHNOLOGIES CORPORATION
UNITEDHEALTH GROUP INC
UNIVERSAL HEALTH SERVICES INC
UNIVISION COMMUNICATIONS INC
URS CORPORATION
USAA
VALASSIS COMMUNICATIONS INC
VALSPAR CORPORATION (THE)
VARIAN MEDICAL SYSTEMS INC
VCA ANTECH INC
VERIZON COMMUNICATIONS INC
VICTORIAS SECRET
VISA INC
VORNADO REALTY TRUST
WABTEC CORP
WALGREEN CO
WAL-MART STORES INC
WALT DISNEY COMPANY (THE)
WARNACO GROUP INC (THE)
WASTE MANAGEMENT INC
WATERS CORP
WATSON PHARMACEUTICALS INC
WEIGHT WATCHERS INTERNATIONAL INC
WEST PHARMACEUTICAL SERVICES INC
WESTERN DIGITAL CORP
WHOLE FOODS MARKET INC
WILLIAMS COMPANIES INC (THE)
WINDSTREAM CORPORATION
WM WRIGLEY JR COMPANY
WW GRAINGER INC
WYNDHAM WORLDWIDE
WYNN RESORTS LIMITED
XEROX CORP
YUM! BRANDS INC
ZIMMER HOLDINGS INC

INDEX OF U.S. HEADQUARTERS LOCATION BY STATE

To help you locate members of THE AMERICAN EMPLOYERS 500 geographically, the city and state of the headquarters of each company are in the following index.

ROYAL CARIBBEAN CRUISES LTD; Miami
RYDER SYSTEM INC; Miami
SEACOR HOLDINGS INC; Ft. Lauderdale
TECH DATA CORP; Clearwater

GEORGIA
AFLAC INC; Columbus
COCA-COLA COMPANY (THE); Atlanta
COX COMMUNICATIONS INC; Atlanta
GE ENERGY INFRASTRUCTURE; Atlanta
GENTIVA HEALTH SERVICES INC; Atlanta
NCR CORPORATION; Duluth
NORTH HIGHLAND; Atlanta
SOUTHERN COMPANY (THE); Atlanta
TOTAL SYSTEM SERVICES INC (TSYS); Columbus
UNITED PARCEL SERVICE INC (UPS); Atlanta

HAWAII
HAWAIIAN ELECTRIC INDUSTRIES INC; Honolulu

IDAHO
COLDWATER CREEK INC; Sandpoint
MICRON TECHNOLOGY INC; Boise

ILLINOIS
ARCHER DANIELS MIDLAND CO; Decatur
ARTHUR J GALLAGHER & CO; Itasca
BOEING COMPANY (THE); Chicago
CATERPILLAR INC; Peoria
CDW CORPORATION; Vernon Hills
CNA FINANCIAL CORP; Chicago
DEERE & CO; Moline
DEVRY INC; Downers Grove
EQUITY LIFESTYLE PROPERTIES INC; Chicago
EXELON CORPORATION; Chicago
FORTUNE BRANDS INC; Deerfield
GRANT THORNTON LLP; Chicago
GROUPON INC; Chicago
HEALTH CARE SERVICE CORPORATION (HCSC); Chicago
HOSPIRA INC; Lake Forest
HYATT HOTELS CORPORATION; Chicago
ILLINOIS TOOL WORKS INC; Glenview
JONES LANG LASALLE INC; Chicago
KRAFT FOODS INC; Northfield
LKQ CORP; Chicago
MCDONALD'S CORP; Oak Brook
MOLEX INC; Lisle
NALCO HOLDING COMPANY; Naperville
SARA LEE CORP; Downers Grove
STERICYCLE INC; Lake Forest
TELEPHONE AND DATA SYSTEMS INC (TDS); Chicago
TREEHOUSE FOODS INC; Westchester
TRUSTMARK COMPANIES; Lake Forest
UNITED STATES CELLULAR CORP; Chicago
WALGREEN CO; Deerfield
WM WRIGLEY JR COMPANY; Chicago
WW GRAINGER INC; Lake Forest

INDIANA
CUMMINS INC; Columbus
HILLENBRAND INC; Batesville
REPUBLIC AIRWAYS HOLDINGS INC; Indianapolis
ZIMMER HOLDINGS INC; Warsaw

IOWA
MIDAMERICAN ENERGY HOLDINGS CO; Des Moines
PRINCIPAL FINANCIAL GROUP (THE); Des Moines

KANSAS
KOCH INDUSTRIES INC; Wichita
SPIRIT AEROSYSTEMS HOLDINGS INC; Wichita

KENTUCKY
HUMANA INC; Louisville
KINDRED HEALTHCARE INC; Louisville
LEXMARK INTERNATIONAL INC; Lexington
YUM! BRANDS INC; Louisville

LOUISIANA
AMEDISYS INC; Baton Rouge
ENTERGY CORP; New Orleans
SHAW GROUP INC (THE); Baton Rouge
TIDEWATER INC; New Orleans

MAINE
IDEXX LABORATORIES INC; Westbrook

MARYLAND
CIENA CORP; Linthicum
MARRIOTT INTERNATIONAL INC; Bethesda
SODEXO INC; Gaithersburg
UNDER ARMOUR INC; Baltimore

MASSACHUSETTS
ANALOG DEVICES INC; Norwood
BAIN & COMPANY INC; Boston
BIOGEN IDEC INC; Weston
BOSTON CONSULTING GROUP INC (THE, BCG); Boston
BRUKER CORP; Billerica
EMC CORP; Hopkinton
FMR CORP (FIDELITY INVESTMENTS); Boston
GENZYME BIOSURGERY; Cambridge
KEANE INC; Boston
LIBERTY MUTUAL GROUP INC; Boston
MASSACHUSETTS MUTUAL LIFE INSURANCE CO; Springfield
MILLIPORE CORP; Billerica
PARAMETRIC TECHNOLOGY CORP; Needham
PAREXEL INTERNATIONAL CORP; Waltham
SAPIENT CORPORATION; Boston
STREAM GLOBAL SERVICES INC; Wellesley
THERMO FISHER SCIENTIFIC INC; Waltham
TJX COMPANIES INC (THE); Framingham
WATERS CORP; Milford

MICHIGAN
DTE ENERGY COMPANY; Detroit
FEDERAL MOGUL CORP; Southfield
FORD MOTOR CO; Dearborn
GENERAL MOTORS COMPANY (GM); Detroit
GENTEX CORPORATION; Zeeland
JACKSON NATIONAL LIFE INSURANCE COMPANY; Lansing
KELLOGG COMPANY; Battle Creek
KELLY SERVICES INC; Troy
LEAR CORP; Southfield
MEIJER INC; Grand Rapids
PENSKE AUTOMOTIVE GROUP INC; Bloomfield Hills
PERRIGO CO; Allegan
SPECTRUM HEALTH; Grand Rapids
STRYKER CORP; Kalamazoo
SYNTEL INC; Troy
VALASSIS COMMUNICATIONS INC; Livonia

MINNESOTA
3M COMPANY; St. Paul
BEST BUY CO INC; Richfield
BUFFALO WILD WINGS INC; Minneapolis
CARLSON COMPANIES INC; Minnetonka
CH ROBINSON WORLDWIDE INC; Eden Prairie
CHS INC; Inver Grove Heights
FAIRVIEW HEALTH SERVICES; Minneapolis
FASTENAL; Winona
GENERAL MILLS INC; Minneapolis
HEALTH FITNESS CORP; Minneapolis
MAYO FOUNDATION FOR MEDICAL EDUCATION AND RESEARCH; Rochester
MEDTRONIC INC; Minneapolis
PATTERSON COMPANIES INC; St. Paul
REGIS CORPORATION; Edina
ST JUDE MEDICAL INC; St. Paul
TARGET CORPORATION; Minneapolis

UNITEDHEALTH GROUP INC; Minnetonka
VALSPAR CORPORATION (THE); Minneapolis

MISSOURI
ASCENSION HEALTH; St. Louis
BASS PRO SHOPS INC; Springfield
CERNER CORP; Kansas City
EMERSON ELECTRIC CO; St. Louis
ENTERPRISE HOLDINGS INC; St. Louis
EXPRESS SCRIPTS INC; St. Louis
INSITUFORM TECHNOLOGIES; Chesterfield
JACK HENRY & ASSOCIATES INC; Monett
O'REILLY AUTOMOTIVE INC; Springfield
PANERA BREAD CO; St. Louis
PEABODY ENERGY CORP; St. Louis
RALCORP HOLDINGS INC; St. Louis
SIGMA-ALDRICH CORP; St. Louis
STIFEL FINANCIAL CORP; St. Louis

NEBRASKA
BERKSHIRE HATHAWAY INC; Omaha
BUCKLE INC (THE); Kearney
CONAGRA FOODS INC; Omaha
MUTUAL OF OMAHA COMPANIES (THE); Omaha
UNION PACIFIC CORP; Omaha

NEVADA
AMERCO; Reno
BOYD GAMING CORP; Las Vegas
CAESARS ENTERTAINMENT CORPORATION; Las Vegas
LAS VEGAS SANDS CORP (THE VENETIAN); Las Vegas
WYNN RESORTS LIMITED; Las Vegas

NEW JERSEY
AUTOMATIC DATA PROCESSING INC; Roseland
BECTON DICKINSON & CO; Franklin Lakes
BED BATH & BEYOND INC; Union
CAMPBELL SOUP CO; Camden
CELGENE CORP; Summit
CELLCO PARTNERSHIP (VERIZON WIRELESS); Basking Ridge
CHUBB CORPORATION (THE); Warren
COGNIZANT TECHNOLOGY SOLUTIONS CORP; Teaneck
COVANCE INC; Princeton
CR BARD INC; Murray Hill
HEARTLAND PAYMENT SYSTEMS INC; Princeton
HERTZ GLOBAL HOLDINGS INC; Park Ridge
INTEGRA LIFESCIENCES HOLDINGS CORP; Plainsboro
INVENTIV HEALTH INC; Somerset
JOHNSON & JOHNSON; New Brunswick
MEDCO HEALTH SOLUTIONS INC; Franklin Lakes
PRUDENTIAL FINANCIAL INC; Newark
WYNDHAM WORLDWIDE; Parsippany

NEW YORK
ABM INDUSTRIES INC; New York
AMERICAN EXPRESS CO; New York
ARROW ELECTRONICS INC; Melville
ASCENA RETAIL GROUP INC; Suffern
AVON PRODUCTS INC; New York
AXA FINANCIAL INC; New York
BAUSCH & LOMB INC; Rochester
BLACKROCK INC; New York
BLOOMBERG LP; New York
BUNGE LTD; White Plains
CABLEVISION SYSTEMS CORP; Bethpage
COACH INC; New York
COLGATE PALMOLIVE CO; New York
COMPUTER TASK GROUP INC; Buffalo
DELOITTE & TOUCHE USA LLP; New York
DELOITTE CONSULTING LLP; New York
ERNST & YOUNG LLP; New York
ESTEE LAUDER COMPANIES INC (THE); New York
FOREST LABORATORIES INC; New York
HENRY SCHEIN INC; Melville
IAC/INTERACTIVECORP; New York
INTERNATIONAL BUSINESS MACHINES CORP (IBM); Armonk
INTERPUBLIC GROUP OF COMPANIES INC; New York
JARDEN CORP; Rye
JETBLUE AIRWAYS CORPORATION; Forest Hills
KPMG LLP; New York
LOEWS CORPORATION; New York
LORAL SPACE & COMMUNICATIONS LTD; New York
MARSH & MCLENNAN COMPANIES INC; New York
MCKINSEY & COMPANY INC; New York
MEDIACOM COMMUNICATIONS CORP; Middletown
MERCER INC; New York
METLIFE INC; New York
MONRO MUFFLER BRAKE INC; Rochester
NEW YORK LIFE INSURANCE CO; New York
NEWS CORP; New York
OMNICOM GROUP INC; New York
PARSONS BRINCKERHOFF INC; New York
PEPSICO INC; Purchase
PHILIP MORRIS INTERNATIONAL INC; New York
POLO RALPH LAUREN CORP; New York
PRICEWATERHOUSECOOPERS; New York
SENECA FOODS CORPORATION; Marion
STARWOOD HOTELS & RESORTS WORLDWIDE INC; White Plains
THOMSON REUTERS; New York
TIFFANY & CO; New York
TIME WARNER INC; New York
TOWERS WATSON & CO; New York
TRAVELERS COMPANIES INC (THE); New York
UNIVISION COMMUNICATIONS INC; New York
VERIZON COMMUNICATIONS INC; New York
VORNADO REALTY TRUST; New York
WARNACO GROUP INC (THE); New York
WEIGHT WATCHERS INTERNATIONAL INC; New York

NORTH CAROLINA
COCA-COLA BOTTLING CO CONSOLIDATED; Charlotte
DUKE ENERGY CORP; Charlotte
FAMILY DOLLAR STORES INC; Charlotte
HANESBRANDS INC; Winston-Salem
LABORATORY CORP OF AMERICA HOLDINGS; Burlington
PHARMACEUTICAL PRODUCT DEVELOPMENT INC; Wilmington
RED HAT INC; Raleigh
SAS INSTITUTE INC; Cary
SNYDERS-LANCE INC; Charlotte

OHIO
CHEMED CORPORATION; Cincinnati
CINTAS CORP; Cincinnati
EATON CORP; Cleveland
FIRSTENERGY CORP; Akron
GOODYEAR TIRE & RUBBER COMPANY (THE); Akron
HONDA OF AMERICA MANUFACTURING INC; Marysville
JM SMUCKER CO; Orrville
KROGER CO (THE); Cincinnati
LIMITED BRANDS INC; Columbus
MACY'S INC; Cincinnati
NACCO INDUSTRIES INC; Cleveland
PARK-OHIO HOLDINGS CORP; Cleveland
PROCTER & GAMBLE CO; Cincinnati
PROGRESSIVE CORPORATION (THE); Mayfield Village
SCOTTS MIRACLE GROW CO; Marysville
SHERWIN WILLIAMS COMPANY (THE); Cleveland
STONERIDGE INC; Warren
THOR INDUSTRIES INC; Jackson Center
VICTORIAS SECRET; Reynoldsburg

OKLAHOMA
WILLIAMS COMPANIES INC (THE); Tulsa

OREGON
NIKE INC; Beaverton
TEKTRONIX INC; Beaverton

PENNSYLVANIA
AIR PRODUCTS & CHEMICALS INC; Allentown
AMERISOURCEBERGEN CORP; Chesterbrook
ARAMARK CORPORATION; Philadelphia
CEPHALON INC; Frazer
CIGNA CORP; Philadelphia
COMCAST CORP; Philadelphia
CONSOL ENERGY INC; Canonsburg
DENTSPLY INTERNATIONAL INC; York
DICK'S SPORTING GOODS INC; Coraopolis
ENDO PHARMACEUTICALS HOLDINGS INC; Chadds Ford
GSI COMMERCE INC; King of Prussia
HERSHEY CO; Hershey
LINCOLN NATIONAL CORPORATION; Radnor
MYLAN INC; Canonsburg
SELECT MEDICAL HOLDINGS CORPORATION; Mechanicsburg
UNIVERSAL HEALTH SERVICES INC; King of Prussia
WABTEC CORP; Wilmerding
WEST PHARMACEUTICAL SERVICES INC; Lionville

RHODE ISLAND
AMERICAN POWER CONVERSION (APC); West Kingston
CVS CAREMARK CORPORATION; Woonsocket
FM GLOBAL; Johnston
UNITED NATURAL FOODS INC; Providence

SOUTH CAROLINA
DELTA APPAREL INC; Greenville
SCANA CORPORATION; Columbia

SOUTH DAKOTA
DAKTRONICS INC; Brookings

TENNESSEE
AMSURG CORP; Nashville
AUTOZONE INC; Memphis
BROOKDALE SENIOR LIVING INC; Brentwood
COMMUNITY HEALTH SYSTEMS INC; Franklin
CRACKER BARREL OLD COUNTRY STORE INC; Lebanon
DOLLAR GENERAL CORPORATION; Goodlettsville
FEDEX CORPORATION; Memphis
GENESCO INC; Nashville
HCA HOLDINGS INC; Nashville
TEAM HEALTH HOLDINGS INC; Knoxville

TEXAS
7-ELEVEN INC; Dallas
ACADEMY SPORTS & OUTDOORS LTD; Katy
AFFILIATED COMPUTER SERVICES INC; Dallas
ALLIANCE DATA SYSTEMS CORPORATION; Plano
AMR CORP (AMERICAN AIRLINES); Fort Worth
APACHE CORP; Houston
AT&T INC; Dallas
BAKER HUGHES INC; Houston
BASIC ENERGY SERVICES INC; Midland
BMC SOFTWARE INC; Houston
BURLINGTON NORTHERN SANTA FE LLC; Fort Worth
CAMERON INTERNATIONAL CORPORATION; Houston
CAPITAL SENIOR LIVING CORP; Dallas
CASH AMERICA INTERNATIONAL INC; Fort Worth
CHEVRON PHILLIPS CHEMICAL COMPANY LLC; The Woodlands
CONCENTRA INC; Addison
CONOCOPHILLIPS COMPANY; Houston
CONTAINER STORE (THE); Coppell
DEAN FOODS CO; Dallas
DIAMOND OFFSHORE DRILLING INC; Houston
DIODES INC; Dallas
EXTERRAN HOLDINGS INC; Houston
EXXON MOBIL CORPORATION (EXXONMOBIL); Irving
EXXONMOBIL CHEMICAL; Houston
FLUOR CORP; Irving
FMC TECHNOLOGIES INC; Houston
FOSSIL INC; Richardson
GAMESTOP CORP; Grapevine
GEOKINETICS INC; Houston
GROUP 1 AUTOMOTIVE INC; Houston
HALLIBURTON COMPANY; Houston
HANGER ORTHOPEDIC GROUP INC; Austin
HE BUTT GROCERY COMPANY (HEB); San Antonio
KEY ENERGY SERVICES INC; Houston
KIMBERLY-CLARK CORP; Dallas
KINETIC CONCEPTS INC; San Antonio
LUFKIN INDUSTRIES INC; Lufkin
MARATHON OIL CORP; Houston
MARY KAY INC; Dallas
METHODIST HEALTH CARE SYSTEM; Houston
METROPCS COMMUNICATIONS INC; Richardson
NATIONAL INSTRUMENTS CORP; Austin
NATIONAL OILWELL VARCO INC; Houston
OCEANEERING INTERNATIONAL INC; Houston
ODYSSEY HEALTHCARE INC; Dallas
OIL STATES INTERNATIONAL INC; Houston
PATTERSON-UTI ENERGY INC; Houston
QUANTA SERVICES INC; Houston
RACKSPACE HOSTING INC; San Antonio
ROWAN COMPANIES INC; Houston
SABRE HOLDINGS CORP; Southlake
SCHLUMBERGER LIMITED; Houston
SHELL OIL CO; Houston
SOUTHWEST AIRLINES CO; Dallas
SYSCO CORP; Houston
TEAM INC; Alvin
TENET HEALTHCARE CORPORATION; Dallas
USAA; San Antonio
WASTE MANAGEMENT INC; Houston
WHOLE FOODS MARKET INC; Austin

VIRGINIA
ADVANCE AUTO PARTS INC; Roanoke
AES CORPORATION (THE); Arlington
ALTRIA GROUP INC; Richmond
AMERIGROUP CORPORATION; Virginia Beach
BOOZ ALLEN HAMILTON INC; McLean
BRINKS COMPANY (THE); Richmond
CACI INTERNATIONAL INC; Arlington
CARMAX GROUP; Richmond
COMPUTER SCIENCES CORPORATION (CSC); Falls Church
GENWORTH FINANCIAL INC; Richmond
HILTON HOTELS CORP; McLean
ICF INTERNATIONAL INC; Fairfax
MANTECH INTERNATIONAL CORP; Fairfax
MARS INC; McLean
MAXIMUS INC; Reston
NII HOLDINGS INC; Reston
NORFOLK SOUTHERN CORP; Norfolk
OWENS & MINOR INC; Mechanicsville
SAIC INC; McLean
SRA INTERNATIONAL INC; Fairfax

WASHINGTON
ALASKA AIR GROUP INC; Seattle
AMAZON.COM INC; Seattle
BARRETT BUSINESS SERVICES; Vancouver
CLEARWIRE CORP; Kirkland
COSTCO WHOLESALE CORP; Issaquah
EMERITUS CORP; Seattle

WISCONSIN

OTHER

INDEX BY REGIONS OF THE U.S. WHERE THE FIRMS HAVE LOCATIONS

WEST

CINTAS CORP
CISCO SYSTEMS INC
CITRIX SYSTEMS INC
CLEARWIRE CORP
CLOROX CO (THE)
CNA FINANCIAL CORP
COACH INC
COCA-COLA BOTTLING CO CONSOLIDATED
COCA-COLA COMPANY (THE)
COGNIZANT TECHNOLOGY SOLUTIONS CORP
COLDWATER CREEK INC
COLGATE PALMOLIVE CO
COMCAST CORP
COMMUNITY HEALTH SYSTEMS INC
COMPUTER SCIENCES CORPORATION (CSC)
COMPUTER TASK GROUP INC
CONAGRA FOODS INC
CONCENTRA INC
CONOCOPHILLIPS COMPANY
CONSOL ENERGY INC
CONTAINER STORE (THE)
CON-WAY INC
COOPER COMPANIES INC
COSTCO WHOLESALE CORP
COVANCE INC
COX COMMUNICATIONS INC
CR BARD INC
CRACKER BARREL OLD COUNTRY STORE INC
CROCS INC
CSX CORP
CUMMINS INC
CVS CAREMARK CORPORATION
DANAHER CORP
DARDEN RESTAURANTS INC
DAVITA INC
DEAN FOODS CO
DEERE & CO
DELOITTE & TOUCHE USA LLP
DELOITTE CONSULTING LLP
DELTA APPAREL INC
DENTSPLY INTERNATIONAL INC
DEVRY INC
DICK'S SPORTING GOODS INC
DIODES INC
DIRECTV
DOLLAR GENERAL CORPORATION
DTE ENERGY COMPANY
DUKE ENERGY CORP
DUPONT (E I DU PONT DE NEMOURS & CO)
DUPONT AGRICULTURE & NUTRITION
EATON CORP
EBAY INC
EDISON INTERNATIONAL
EDWARDS LIFESCIENCES CORP
EMC CORP
EMERITUS CORP
EMERSON ELECTRIC CO
ENDO PHARMACEUTICALS HOLDINGS INC
ENTERGY CORP
ENTERPRISE HOLDINGS INC
EQUITY LIFESTYLE PROPERTIES INC
ERNST & YOUNG LLP
ESTEE LAUDER COMPANIES INC (THE)
EXELON CORPORATION
EXPEDIA INC
EXPERIAN AMERICAS
EXPRESS SCRIPTS INC
EXTERRAN HOLDINGS INC
EXXON MOBIL CORPORATION (EXXONMOBIL)
FACTSET RESEARCH SYSTEMS INC
FAIRVIEW HEALTH SERVICES
FAMILY DOLLAR STORES INC
FASTENAL
FEDERAL MOGUL CORP
FEDEX CORPORATION
FIDELITY NATIONAL INFORMATION SERVICES INC
FINISAR CORPORATION
FIRST ADVANTAGE CORPORATION
FIRSTENERGY CORP
FLUOR CORP
FM GLOBAL
FMC TECHNOLOGIES INC
FMR CORP (FIDELITY INVESTMENTS)
FORD MOTOR CO
FOREST LABORATORIES INC
FORTUNE BRANDS INC
FOSSIL INC
FOX ENTERTAINMENT GROUP INC
FRONTIER COMMUNICATIONS CORPORATION
FTI CONSULTING INC
GAMESTOP CORP
GE ENERGY INFRASTRUCTURE
GENENTECH INC
GENERAL ELECTRIC CO (GE)
GENERAL MILLS INC
GENERAL MOTORS COMPANY (GM)
GENESCO INC
GENTIVA HEALTH SERVICES INC
GENWORTH FINANCIAL INC
GILEAD SCIENCES INC
GOODYEAR TIRE & RUBBER COMPANY (THE)
GOOGLE INC
GRANT THORNTON LLP
GROUP 1 AUTOMOTIVE INC
GROUPON INC
GSI COMMERCE INC
GUESS? INC
HALLIBURTON COMPANY
HANESBRANDS INC
HANGER ORTHOPEDIC GROUP INC
HARRIS CORPORATION
HAWAIIAN ELECTRIC INDUSTRIES INC
HCA HOLDINGS INC
HEALTH CARE SERVICE CORPORATION (HCSC)
HEALTH FITNESS CORP
HEALTH MANAGEMENT ASSOCIATES INC
HEALTHSOUTH CORP
HENRY SCHEIN INC
HERSHEY CO
HERTZ GLOBAL HOLDINGS INC
HIBBETT SPORTS INC
HILTON HOTELS CORP
HOSPIRA INC
HUMANA INC
HYATT HOTELS CORPORATION
IAC/INTERACTIVECORP
ICF INTERNATIONAL INC
IDEXX LABORATORIES INC
IGATE CORPORATION
ILLINOIS TOOL WORKS INC
IMS HEALTH INC
INGRAM MICRO INC
INSITUFORM TECHNOLOGIES
INTEGRA LIFESCIENCES HOLDINGS CORP
INTEL CORP
INTERNATIONAL BUSINESS MACHINES CORP (IBM)
INTERPUBLIC GROUP OF COMPANIES INC
INTUIT INC
INVENTIV HEALTH INC
JACK HENRY & ASSOCIATES INC
JACKSON NATIONAL LIFE INSURANCE COMPANY
JARDEN CORP
JB HUNT TRANSPORT SERVICES INC
JETBLUE AIRWAYS CORPORATION
JM SMUCKER CO
JOHNSON & JOHNSON
JOHNSON CONTROLS INC
JONES LANG LASALLE INC
JUNIPER NETWORKS INC
KAISER PERMANENTE
KEANE INC
KELLOGG COMPANY
KELLY SERVICES INC
KEY ENERGY SERVICES INC
KIMBERLY-CLARK CORP
KINDRED HEALTHCARE INC
KLA TENCOR CORP
KOCH INDUSTRIES INC
KOHL'S CORP
KPMG LLP
KRAFT FOODS INC
KROGER CO (THE)
LABORATORY CORP OF AMERICA HOLDINGS
LAM RESEARCH CORP
LAS VEGAS SANDS CORP (THE VENETIAN)
LEAP WIRELESS INTERNATIONAL INC
LEAR CORP
LEXMARK INTERNATIONAL INC
LIBERTY GLOBAL INC
LIBERTY MEDIA CORP
LIBERTY MUTUAL GROUP INC
LIFE TECHNOLOGIES CORP

LIMITED BRANDS INC
LINCARE HOLDINGS INC
LINCOLN NATIONAL CORPORATION
LKQ CORP
LOEWS CORPORATION
LORAL SPACE & COMMUNICATIONS LTD
MACY'S INC
MANPOWER INC
MANTECH INTERNATIONAL CORP
MARATHON OIL CORP
MARRIOTT INTERNATIONAL INC
MARS INC
MARSH & MCLENNAN COMPANIES INC
MARY KAY INC
MASSACHUSETTS MUTUAL LIFE INSURANCE CO
MATTEL INC
MAXIMUS INC
MAYO FOUNDATION FOR MEDICAL EDUCATION AND RESEARCH
MCDONALD'S CORP
MCKESSON CORPORATION
MCKINSEY & COMPANY INC
MEDCO HEALTH SOLUTIONS INC
MEDIACOM COMMUNICATIONS CORP
MEDNAX INC
MEDTRONIC INC
MERCER INC
METHODIST HEALTH CARE SYSTEM
METLIFE INC
METROPCS COMMUNICATIONS INC
MICROCHIP TECHNOLOGY INC
MICRON TECHNOLOGY INC
MICROSOFT CORP
MIDAMERICAN ENERGY HOLDINGS CO
MILLIPORE CORP
MOLEX INC
MULTI-FINELINE ELECTRONIX INC
MUTUAL OF OMAHA COMPANIES (THE)
NABORS INDUSTRIES LTD
NACCO INDUSTRIES INC
NALCO HOLDING COMPANY
NATIONAL INSTRUMENTS CORP
NATIONAL OILWELL VARCO INC
NCR CORPORATION
NETAPP INC
NEW YORK LIFE INSURANCE CO
NEWS CORP
NEXTERA ENERGY INC
NIKE INC
NORTH HIGHLAND
NORTHWESTERN MUTUAL LIFE INSURANCE CO
OCEANEERING INTERNATIONAL INC
ODYSSEY HEALTHCARE INC
OIL STATES INTERNATIONAL INC
OMNICOM GROUP INC
ORACLE CORP
O'REILLY AUTOMOTIVE INC
OSHKOSH CORPORATION
OWENS & MINOR INC
PACCAR INC
PANERA BREAD CO
PARAMETRIC TECHNOLOGY CORP
PAREXEL INTERNATIONAL CORP
PARSONS BRINCKERHOFF INC
PATTERSON COMPANIES INC
PATTERSON-UTI ENERGY INC
PEABODY ENERGY CORP
PENSKE AUTOMOTIVE GROUP INC
PEPSICO INC
PERRIGO CO
PETCO ANIMAL SUPPLIES INC
PETSMART INC
PG&E CORPORATION
PHARMACEUTICAL PRODUCT DEVELOPMENT INC
PLEXUS CORP
POLO RALPH LAUREN CORP
POLYCOM INC
PRAXAIR INC
PRICESMART INC
PRICEWATERHOUSECOOPERS
PRINCIPAL FINANCIAL GROUP (THE)
PROCTER & GAMBLE CO
PROGRESSIVE CORPORATION (THE)
PROVIDENCE HEALTH & SERVICES
PRUDENTIAL FINANCIAL INC
QUALCOMM INC
QUANTA SERVICES INC
RALCORP HOLDINGS INC
RECREATIONAL EQUIPMENT INC (REI)
RED HAT INC
REGIS CORPORATION
REPUBLIC AIRWAYS HOLDINGS INC
RESMED INC
ROBERT HALF INTERNATIONAL INC
ROSS STORES INC
ROWAN COMPANIES INC
ROYAL CARIBBEAN CRUISES LTD
RYDER SYSTEM INC
SAFECO INSURANCE COMPANY OF AMERICA
SAFEWAY INC
SAIC INC
SALESFORCE.COM INC
SAM'S CLUB
SANDISK CORP
SANMINA-SCI CORPORATION
SAPIENT CORPORATION
SARA LEE CORP
SAS INSTITUTE INC
SCANA CORPORATION
SCHLUMBERGER LIMITED
SCOTTS MIRACLE GROW CO
SEACOR HOLDINGS INC
SELECT MEDICAL HOLDINGS CORPORATION
SEMPRA ENERGY
SENECA FOODS CORPORATION
SENSIENT TECHNOLOGIES CORPORATION
SHAW GROUP INC (THE)
SHELL OIL CO
SHERWIN WILLIAMS COMPANY (THE)
SIGMA-ALDRICH CORP
SKILLED HEALTHCARE GROUP INC
SODEXO INC
SOUTHERN COMPANY (THE)
SOUTHWEST AIRLINES CO
SPIRIT AEROSYSTEMS HOLDINGS INC
SRA INTERNATIONAL INC
ST JUDE MEDICAL INC
STANLEY BLACK & DECKER INC
STARWOOD HOTELS & RESORTS WORLDWIDE INC
STERICYCLE INC
STIFEL FINANCIAL CORP
STONERIDGE INC
STREAM GLOBAL SERVICES INC
STRYKER CORP
SUN HEALTHCARE GROUP INC
SUTTER HEALTH INC
SYMANTEC CORP
SYNTEL INC
SYSCO CORP
TARGET CORPORATION
TEAM HEALTH HOLDINGS INC
TEAM INC
TECH DATA CORP
TEKTRONIX INC
TELEDYNE TECHNOLOGIES INC
TELEPHONE AND DATA SYSTEMS INC (TDS)
TENET HEALTHCARE CORPORATION
TEREX CORPORATION
TETRA TECH INC
THERMO FISHER SCIENTIFIC INC
THOMSON REUTERS
THOR INDUSTRIES INC
TIBCO SOFTWARE INC
TIDEWATER INC
TIFFANY & CO
TIME WARNER INC
TJX COMPANIES INC (THE)
TOTAL SYSTEM SERVICES INC (TSYS)
TOWERS WATSON & CO
TRAVELERS COMPANIES INC (THE)
TRUSTMARK COMPANIES
TTM TECHNOLOGIES INC
TW TELECOM INC
UNDER ARMOUR INC
UNION PACIFIC CORP
UNITED NATURAL FOODS INC
UNITED PARCEL SERVICE INC (UPS)
UNITED STATES CELLULAR CORP
UNITED TECHNOLOGIES CORPORATION
UNITEDHEALTH GROUP INC
UNIVERSAL HEALTH SERVICES INC
UNIVISION COMMUNICATIONS INC
URS CORPORATION
USAA
VALASSIS COMMUNICATIONS INC
VALSPAR CORPORATION (THE)
VARIAN MEDICAL SYSTEMS INC

VCA ANTECH INC
VERIZON COMMUNICATIONS INC
VICTORIAS SECRET
VISA INC
VORNADO REALTY TRUST
WABTEC CORP
WALGREEN CO
WAL-MART STORES INC
WALT DISNEY COMPANY (THE)
WARNACO GROUP INC (THE)
WASTE MANAGEMENT INC
WATERS CORP
WATSON PHARMACEUTICALS INC
WEIGHT WATCHERS INTERNATIONAL INC
WESTERN DIGITAL CORP
WHOLE FOODS MARKET INC
WILLIAMS COMPANIES INC (THE)
WW GRAINGER INC
WYNDHAM WORLDWIDE
WYNN RESORTS LIMITED
XEROX CORP
YUM! BRANDS INC
ZIMMER HOLDINGS INC

SOUTHWEST

3M COMPANY
7-ELEVEN INC
ABM INDUSTRIES INC
ACADEMY SPORTS & OUTDOORS LTD
ACCENTURE PLC
ACTIVISION BLIZZARD INC
ADOBE SYSTEMS INC
ADVANCED MICRO DEVICES INC (AMD)
ADVENTIST HEALTH SYSTEM
AECOM TECHNOLOGY CORPORATION
AES CORPORATION (THE)
AFFILIATED COMPUTER SERVICES INC
AFLAC INC
AGILENT TECHNOLOGIES INC
AIR PRODUCTS & CHEMICALS INC
ALASKA AIR GROUP INC
ALLERGAN INC
ALLIANCE DATA SYSTEMS CORPORATION
ALTRIA GROUP INC
AMAZON.COM INC
AMEDISYS INC
AMERCO
AMERICAN EXPRESS CO
AMERICAN POWER CONVERSION (APC)
AMERIGROUP CORPORATION
AMERISOURCEBERGEN CORP
AMKOR TECHNOLOGY INC
AMPHENOL CORPORATION
AMR CORP (AMERICAN AIRLINES)
AMSURG CORP
ANALOG DEVICES INC
APACHE CORP
APPLE INC
APPLIED MATERIALS INC
ARAMARK CORPORATION
ARCHER DANIELS MIDLAND CO
ARROW ELECTRONICS INC
ARTHUR J GALLAGHER & CO
ASCENA RETAIL GROUP INC
ASCENSION HEALTH
AT&T INC
AUTOMATIC DATA PROCESSING INC
AUTONATION INC
AUTOZONE INC
AVNET INC
AXA FINANCIAL INC
BAIN & COMPANY INC
BAKER HUGHES INC
BALL CORP
BARRETT BUSINESS SERVICES
BASIC ENERGY SERVICES INC
BASS PRO SHOPS INC
BECHTEL GROUP INC
BECTON DICKINSON & CO
BED BATH & BEYOND INC
BEMIS COMPANY INC
BERKSHIRE HATHAWAY INC
BEST BUY CO INC
BIG 5 SPORTING GOODS CORPORATION
BIO RAD LABORATORIES INC
BLOOMBERG LP
BMC SOFTWARE INC
BOEING COMPANY (THE)
BOOZ ALLEN HAMILTON INC
BOSTON CONSULTING GROUP INC (THE, BCG)
BRINKS COMPANY (THE)
BROADCOM CORP
BROCADE COMMUNICATIONS SYSTEMS INC
BROOKDALE SENIOR LIVING INC
BROWN & BROWN INC
BUCKLE INC (THE)
BUFFALO WILD WINGS INC
BURLINGTON NORTHERN SANTA FE LLC
CACI INTERNATIONAL INC
CADENCE DESIGN SYSTEMS INC
CAESARS ENTERTAINMENT CORPORATION
CAMERON INTERNATIONAL CORPORATION
CAMPBELL SOUP CO
CAPITAL SENIOR LIVING CORP
CARLSON COMPANIES INC
CARMAX GROUP
CASH AMERICA INTERNATIONAL INC
CATERPILLAR INC
CATHOLIC HEALTH INITIATIVES
CB RICHARD ELLIS GROUP INC (CBRE)
CDW CORPORATION
CELLCO PARTNERSHIP (VERIZON WIRELESS)
CERNER CORP
CH ROBINSON WORLDWIDE INC
CHEMED CORPORATION
CHEVRON CORPORATION
CHEVRON PHILLIPS CHEMICAL COMPANY LLC
CHICO'S FAS INC
CHIPOTLE MEXICAN GRILL INC
CHS INC
CHUBB CORPORATION (THE)
CIENA CORP
CIGNA CORP
CINTAS CORP
CISCO SYSTEMS INC
CITRIX SYSTEMS INC
CLEARWIRE CORP
CLOROX CO (THE)
CNA FINANCIAL CORP
COACH INC
COCA-COLA COMPANY (THE)
COGNIZANT TECHNOLOGY SOLUTIONS CORP
COLDWATER CREEK INC
COLGATE PALMOLIVE CO
COMCAST CORP
COMMUNITY HEALTH SYSTEMS INC
COMPUTER SCIENCES CORPORATION (CSC)
COMPUTER TASK GROUP INC
CONAGRA FOODS INC
CONCENTRA INC
CONOCOPHILLIPS COMPANY
CONTAINER STORE (THE)
CON-WAY INC
COOPER COMPANIES INC
COSTCO WHOLESALE CORP
COVANCE INC
COX COMMUNICATIONS INC
CR BARD INC
CRACKER BARREL OLD COUNTRY STORE INC
CROCS INC
CSX CORP
CUMMINS INC
CVS CAREMARK CORPORATION
DANAHER CORP
DARDEN RESTAURANTS INC
DAVITA INC
DEAN FOODS CO
DEERE & CO
DELOITTE & TOUCHE USA LLP
DELOITTE CONSULTING LLP
DEVRY INC
DIAMOND OFFSHORE DRILLING INC
DICK'S SPORTING GOODS INC
DIODES INC
DIRECTV
DOLLAR GENERAL CORPORATION
DUPONT (E I DU PONT DE NEMOURS & CO)
DUPONT AGRICULTURE & NUTRITION
EATON CORP
EBAY INC
EDISON INTERNATIONAL
EMERITUS CORP

EMERSON ELECTRIC CO
ENTERGY CORP
ENTERPRISE HOLDINGS INC
EQUITY LIFESTYLE PROPERTIES INC
ERNST & YOUNG LLP
EXELON CORPORATION
EXPEDIA INC
EXPERIAN AMERICAS
EXPRESS SCRIPTS INC
EXTERRAN HOLDINGS INC
EXXON MOBIL CORPORATION (EXXONMOBIL)
EXXONMOBIL CHEMICAL
FACTSET RESEARCH SYSTEMS INC
FAMILY DOLLAR STORES INC
FASTENAL
FEDERAL MOGUL CORP
FEDEX CORPORATION
FIDELITY NATIONAL INFORMATION SERVICES INC
FINISAR CORPORATION
FIRST ADVANTAGE CORPORATION
FLUOR CORP
FM GLOBAL
FMC TECHNOLOGIES INC
FMR CORP (FIDELITY INVESTMENTS)
FORD MOTOR CO
FOSSIL INC
FRONTIER COMMUNICATIONS CORPORATION
FTI CONSULTING INC
GAMESTOP CORP
GE ENERGY INFRASTRUCTURE
GENERAL ELECTRIC CO (GE)
GENERAL MILLS INC
GENERAL MOTORS COMPANY (GM)
GENESCO INC
GENTIVA HEALTH SERVICES INC
GENWORTH FINANCIAL INC
GEOKINETICS INC
GOODYEAR TIRE & RUBBER COMPANY (THE)
GOOGLE INC
GRANT THORNTON LLP
GROUP 1 AUTOMOTIVE INC
GUESS? INC
HALLIBURTON COMPANY
HANESBRANDS INC
HANGER ORTHOPEDIC GROUP INC
HARRIS CORPORATION
HCA HOLDINGS INC
HE BUTT GROCERY COMPANY (HEB)
HEALTH CARE SERVICE CORPORATION (HCSC)
HEALTH FITNESS CORP
HEALTH MANAGEMENT ASSOCIATES INC
HEALTHSOUTH CORP
HEARTLAND PAYMENT SYSTEMS INC
HENRY SCHEIN INC
HERSHEY CO
HERTZ GLOBAL HOLDINGS INC
HIBBETT SPORTS INC
HILTON HOTELS CORP
HOSPIRA INC
HUMANA INC
HYATT HOTELS CORPORATION
IAC/INTERACTIVECORP
ICF INTERNATIONAL INC
IDEXX LABORATORIES INC
IGATE CORPORATION
ILLINOIS TOOL WORKS INC
IMS HEALTH INC
INGRAM MICRO INC
INSITUFORM TECHNOLOGIES
INTEL CORP
INTERNATIONAL BUSINESS MACHINES CORP (IBM)
INTERPUBLIC GROUP OF COMPANIES INC
INTUIT INC
INVENTIV HEALTH INC
JACK HENRY & ASSOCIATES INC
JACKSON NATIONAL LIFE INSURANCE COMPANY
JARDEN CORP
JB HUNT TRANSPORT SERVICES INC
JETBLUE AIRWAYS CORPORATION
JM SMUCKER CO
JOHNSON & JOHNSON
JOHNSON CONTROLS INC
JONES LANG LASALLE INC
JUNIPER NETWORKS INC
KEANE INC
KELLOGG COMPANY
KELLY SERVICES INC
KEY ENERGY SERVICES INC
KIMBERLY-CLARK CORP
KINDRED HEALTHCARE INC
KINETIC CONCEPTS INC
KLA TENCOR CORP
KOCH INDUSTRIES INC
KOHL'S CORP
KPMG LLP
KRAFT FOODS INC
KROGER CO (THE)
LABORATORY CORP OF AMERICA HOLDINGS
LAM RESEARCH CORP
LEAP WIRELESS INTERNATIONAL INC
LEAR CORP
LIBERTY MEDIA CORP
LIBERTY MUTUAL GROUP INC
LIFE TECHNOLOGIES CORP
LIMITED BRANDS INC
LINCARE HOLDINGS INC
LINCOLN NATIONAL CORPORATION
LKQ CORP
LOEWS CORPORATION
LUFKIN INDUSTRIES INC
MACY'S INC
MANPOWER INC
MANTECH INTERNATIONAL CORP
MARATHON OIL CORP
MARRIOTT INTERNATIONAL INC
MARS INC
MARSH & MCLENNAN COMPANIES INC
MARY KAY INC
MASSACHUSETTS MUTUAL LIFE INSURANCE CO
MATTEL INC
MAXIMUS INC
MAYO FOUNDATION FOR MEDICAL EDUCATION AND RESEARCH
MCDONALD'S CORP
MCKESSON CORPORATION
MCKINSEY & COMPANY INC
MEDCO HEALTH SOLUTIONS INC
MEDIACOM COMMUNICATIONS CORP
MEDNAX INC
MEDTRONIC INC
MERCER INC
METHODIST HEALTH CARE SYSTEM
METLIFE INC
METROPCS COMMUNICATIONS INC
MICROCHIP TECHNOLOGY INC
MICROSOFT CORP
MIDAMERICAN ENERGY HOLDINGS CO
MILLIPORE CORP
MULTI-FINELINE ELECTRONIX INC
MUTUAL OF OMAHA COMPANIES (THE)
MYLAN INC
NABORS INDUSTRIES LTD
NACCO INDUSTRIES INC
NALCO HOLDING COMPANY
NATIONAL INSTRUMENTS CORP
NATIONAL OILWELL VARCO INC
NEW YORK LIFE INSURANCE CO
NEXTERA ENERGY INC
NIKE INC
NORFOLK SOUTHERN CORP
NORTH HIGHLAND
NORTHWESTERN MUTUAL LIFE INSURANCE CO
OCEANEERING INTERNATIONAL INC
ODYSSEY HEALTHCARE INC
OIL STATES INTERNATIONAL INC
OMNICOM GROUP INC
ORACLE CORP
O'REILLY AUTOMOTIVE INC
OSHKOSH CORPORATION
OWENS & MINOR INC
PACCAR INC
PANERA BREAD CO
PARAMETRIC TECHNOLOGY CORP
PARK-OHIO HOLDINGS CORP
PARSONS BRINCKERHOFF INC
PATTERSON COMPANIES INC
PATTERSON-UTI ENERGY INC
PENSKE AUTOMOTIVE GROUP INC
PEPSICO INC
PETCO ANIMAL SUPPLIES INC
PETSMART INC
PHARMACEUTICAL PRODUCT DEVELOPMENT INC
POLO RALPH LAUREN CORP
POLYCOM INC
PRICEWATERHOUSECOOPERS
PRINCIPAL FINANCIAL GROUP (THE)

PROCTER & GAMBLE CO
PROGRESSIVE CORPORATION (THE)
PRUDENTIAL FINANCIAL INC
QUALCOMM INC
QUANTA SERVICES INC
RACKSPACE HOSTING INC
RALCORP HOLDINGS INC
RECREATIONAL EQUIPMENT INC (REI)
RED HAT INC
REGIS CORPORATION
ROBERT HALF INTERNATIONAL INC
ROSS STORES INC
ROWAN COMPANIES INC
ROYAL CARIBBEAN CRUISES LTD
RYDER SYSTEM INC
SABRE HOLDINGS CORP
SAFECO INSURANCE COMPANY OF AMERICA
SAFEWAY INC
SAIC INC
SAM'S CLUB
SANMINA-SCI CORPORATION
SARA LEE CORP
SAS INSTITUTE INC
SCHLUMBERGER LIMITED
SCOTTS MIRACLE GROW CO
SEACOR HOLDINGS INC
SELECT MEDICAL HOLDINGS CORPORATION
SEMPRA ENERGY
SHAW GROUP INC (THE)
SHELL OIL CO
SHERWIN WILLIAMS COMPANY (THE)
SIGMA-ALDRICH CORP
SKILLED HEALTHCARE GROUP INC
SNYDERS-LANCE INC
SODEXO INC
SOUTHWEST AIRLINES CO
SPIRIT AEROSYSTEMS HOLDINGS INC
SRA INTERNATIONAL INC
ST JUDE MEDICAL INC
STANLEY BLACK & DECKER INC
STARWOOD HOTELS & RESORTS WORLDWIDE INC
STERICYCLE INC
STIFEL FINANCIAL CORP
STONERIDGE INC
STREAM GLOBAL SERVICES INC
STRYKER CORP
SUN HEALTHCARE GROUP INC
SYNTEL INC
SYSCO CORP
TARGET CORPORATION
TEAM HEALTH HOLDINGS INC
TEAM INC
TECH DATA CORP
TEKTRONIX INC
TELEDYNE TECHNOLOGIES INC
TELEPHONE AND DATA SYSTEMS INC (TDS)
TENET HEALTHCARE CORPORATION
TEREX CORPORATION
TETRA TECH INC
THERMO FISHER SCIENTIFIC INC
THOMSON REUTERS
TIDEWATER INC
TIME WARNER INC
TJX COMPANIES INC (THE)
TOTAL SYSTEM SERVICES INC (TSYS)
TOWERS WATSON & CO
TRAVELERS COMPANIES INC (THE)
TRUSTMARK COMPANIES
TW TELECOM INC
UNDER ARMOUR INC
UNION PACIFIC CORP
UNITED PARCEL SERVICE INC (UPS)
UNITED STATES CELLULAR CORP
UNITED TECHNOLOGIES CORPORATION
UNITEDHEALTH GROUP INC
UNIVERSAL HEALTH SERVICES INC
UNIVISION COMMUNICATIONS INC
URS CORPORATION
USAA
VALSPAR CORPORATION (THE)
VCA ANTECH INC
VERIZON COMMUNICATIONS INC
VICTORIAS SECRET
VISA INC
VORNADO REALTY TRUST
WABTEC CORP
WALGREEN CO
WAL-MART STORES INC
WALT DISNEY COMPANY (THE)
WASTE MANAGEMENT INC
WATERS CORP
WEIGHT WATCHERS INTERNATIONAL INC
WEST PHARMACEUTICAL SERVICES INC
WHOLE FOODS MARKET INC
WILLIAMS COMPANIES INC (THE)
WINDSTREAM CORPORATION
WW GRAINGER INC
WYNDHAM WORLDWIDE
XEROX CORP
YUM! BRANDS INC
ZIMMER HOLDINGS INC

MIDWEST

3M COMPANY
7-ELEVEN INC
ABM INDUSTRIES INC
ACADEMY SPORTS & OUTDOORS LTD
ACCENTURE PLC
ACTIVISION BLIZZARD INC
ADVANCE AUTO PARTS INC
ADVANCED MICRO DEVICES INC (AMD)
ADVENTIST HEALTH SYSTEM
AECOM TECHNOLOGY CORPORATION
AES CORPORATION (THE)
AFFILIATED COMPUTER SERVICES INC
AFLAC INC
AGILENT TECHNOLOGIES INC
AIR PRODUCTS & CHEMICALS INC
ALLIANCE DATA SYSTEMS CORPORATION
ALTRIA GROUP INC
AMAZON.COM INC
AMEDISYS INC
AMERCO
AMERICAN EXPRESS CO
AMERICAN POWER CONVERSION (APC)
AMERIGROUP CORPORATION
AMERISOURCEBERGEN CORP
AMPHENOL CORPORATION
AMR CORP (AMERICAN AIRLINES)
AMSURG CORP
ANALOG DEVICES INC
APPLE INC
ARAMARK CORPORATION
ARCHER DANIELS MIDLAND CO
ARROW ELECTRONICS INC
ARTHUR J GALLAGHER & CO
ASCENA RETAIL GROUP INC
ASCENSION HEALTH
AT&T INC
AUTOMATIC DATA PROCESSING INC
AUTONATION INC
AUTOZONE INC
AVON PRODUCTS INC
AXA FINANCIAL INC
BAIN & COMPANY INC
BAKER HUGHES INC
BALL CORP
BASIC ENERGY SERVICES INC
BASS PRO SHOPS INC
BECHTEL GROUP INC
BECTON DICKINSON & CO
BED BATH & BEYOND INC
BEMIS COMPANY INC
BERKSHIRE HATHAWAY INC
BEST BUY CO INC
BLACKROCK INC
BLOOMBERG LP
BMC SOFTWARE INC
BOEING COMPANY (THE)
BOOZ ALLEN HAMILTON INC
BOSTON CONSULTING GROUP INC (THE, BCG)
BOYD GAMING CORP
BRINKS COMPANY (THE)
BROADCOM CORP
BROCADE COMMUNICATIONS SYSTEMS INC
BROOKDALE SENIOR LIVING INC
BROWN & BROWN INC
BRUKER CORP
BUCKLE INC (THE)
BUFFALO WILD WINGS INC
BUNGE LTD
BURLINGTON NORTHERN SANTA FE LLC
CACI INTERNATIONAL INC

CADENCE DESIGN SYSTEMS INC
CAESARS ENTERTAINMENT CORPORATION
CAMERON INTERNATIONAL CORPORATION
CAMPBELL SOUP CO
CAPITAL SENIOR LIVING CORP
CARLSON COMPANIES INC
CARMAX GROUP
CASH AMERICA INTERNATIONAL INC
CATERPILLAR INC
CATHOLIC HEALTH INITIATIVES
CB RICHARD ELLIS GROUP INC (CBRE)
CDW CORPORATION
CELLCO PARTNERSHIP (VERIZON WIRELESS)
CEPHALON INC
CERNER CORP
CH ROBINSON WORLDWIDE INC
CHEMED CORPORATION
CHEVRON CORPORATION
CHEVRON PHILLIPS CHEMICAL COMPANY LLC
CHICO'S FAS INC
CHIPOTLE MEXICAN GRILL INC
CHS INC
CHUBB CORPORATION (THE)
CIENA CORP
CIGNA CORP
CINTAS CORP
CISCO SYSTEMS INC
CITRIX SYSTEMS INC
CLEARWIRE CORP
CLOROX CO (THE)
CNA FINANCIAL CORP
COACH INC
COCA-COLA COMPANY (THE)
COGNIZANT TECHNOLOGY SOLUTIONS CORP
COLDWATER CREEK INC
COLGATE PALMOLIVE CO
COMCAST CORP
COMMUNITY HEALTH SYSTEMS INC
COMPUTER SCIENCES CORPORATION (CSC)
COMPUTER TASK GROUP INC
CONAGRA FOODS INC
CONCENTRA INC
CONOCOPHILLIPS COMPANY
CONTAINER STORE (THE)
CON-WAY INC
COSTCO WHOLESALE CORP
COVANCE INC
COX COMMUNICATIONS INC
CR BARD INC
CRACKER BARREL OLD COUNTRY STORE INC
CROCS INC
CSX CORP
CUMMINS INC
CVS CAREMARK CORPORATION
DANAHER CORP
DARDEN RESTAURANTS INC
DAVITA INC
DEAN FOODS CO
DEERE & CO
DELOITTE & TOUCHE USA LLP
DELOITTE CONSULTING LLP
DELTA APPAREL INC
DENTSPLY INTERNATIONAL INC
DEVRY INC
DICK'S SPORTING GOODS INC
DIODES INC
DIRECTV
DOLLAR GENERAL CORPORATION
DTE ENERGY COMPANY
DUKE ENERGY CORP
DUPONT (E I DU PONT DE NEMOURS & CO)
DUPONT AGRICULTURE & NUTRITION
EATON CORP
EBAY INC
EDISON INTERNATIONAL
EMERITUS CORP
EMERSON ELECTRIC CO
ENTERPRISE HOLDINGS INC
EQUITY LIFESTYLE PROPERTIES INC
ERNST & YOUNG LLP
EXELON CORPORATION
EXPEDIA INC
EXPERIAN AMERICAS
EXPRESS SCRIPTS INC
EXTERRAN HOLDINGS INC
EXXON MOBIL CORPORATION (EXXONMOBIL)
FACTSET RESEARCH SYSTEMS INC
FAIRVIEW HEALTH SERVICES
FAMILY DOLLAR STORES INC
FASTENAL
FEDERAL MOGUL CORP
FEDEX CORPORATION
FIDELITY NATIONAL INFORMATION SERVICES INC
FIRSTENERGY CORP
FLUOR CORP
FM GLOBAL
FMC TECHNOLOGIES INC
FMR CORP (FIDELITY INVESTMENTS)
FORD MOTOR CO
FOREST LABORATORIES INC
FORTUNE BRANDS INC
FOSSIL INC
FRONTIER COMMUNICATIONS CORPORATION
FTI CONSULTING INC
GAMESTOP CORP
GE ENERGY INFRASTRUCTURE
GENERAL ELECTRIC CO (GE)
GENERAL MILLS INC
GENERAL MOTORS COMPANY (GM)
GENESCO INC
GENTEX CORPORATION
GENTIVA HEALTH SERVICES INC
GENWORTH FINANCIAL INC
GOODYEAR TIRE & RUBBER COMPANY (THE)
GOOGLE INC
GRANT THORNTON LLP
GROUP 1 AUTOMOTIVE INC
GROUPON INC
GSI COMMERCE INC
GUESS? INC
HANESBRANDS INC
HANGER ORTHOPEDIC GROUP INC
HARRIS CORPORATION
HCA HOLDINGS INC
HEALTH CARE SERVICE CORPORATION (HCSC)
HEALTH FITNESS CORP
HEALTH MANAGEMENT ASSOCIATES INC
HEALTHSOUTH CORP
HEARTLAND PAYMENT SYSTEMS INC
HENRY SCHEIN INC
HERSHEY CO
HERTZ GLOBAL HOLDINGS INC
HIBBETT SPORTS INC
HILLENBRAND INC
HILTON HOTELS CORP
HONDA OF AMERICA MANUFACTURING INC
HOSPIRA INC
HUMANA INC
HYATT HOTELS CORPORATION
IAC/INTERACTIVECORP
ICF INTERNATIONAL INC
IDEXX LABORATORIES INC
IGATE CORPORATION
ILLINOIS TOOL WORKS INC
INGRAM MICRO INC
INSITUFORM TECHNOLOGIES
INTEGRA LIFESCIENCES HOLDINGS CORP
INTEL CORP
INTERNATIONAL BUSINESS MACHINES CORP (IBM)
INTERPUBLIC GROUP OF COMPANIES INC
INTUIT INC
INVENTIV HEALTH INC
JACK HENRY & ASSOCIATES INC
JACKSON NATIONAL LIFE INSURANCE COMPANY
JARDEN CORP
JB HUNT TRANSPORT SERVICES INC
JETBLUE AIRWAYS CORPORATION
JM SMUCKER CO
JOHNSON & JOHNSON
JOHNSON CONTROLS INC
JONES LANG LASALLE INC
JUNIPER NETWORKS INC
KAISER PERMANENTE
KEANE INC
KELLOGG COMPANY
KELLY SERVICES INC
KEY ENERGY SERVICES INC
KIMBERLY-CLARK CORP
KINDRED HEALTHCARE INC
KLA TENCOR CORP
KOCH INDUSTRIES INC
KOHL'S CORP

KPMG LLP
KRAFT FOODS INC
KROGER CO (THE)
LABORATORY CORP OF AMERICA HOLDINGS
LAM RESEARCH CORP
LEAP WIRELESS INTERNATIONAL INC
LEAR CORP
LEXMARK INTERNATIONAL INC
LIBERTY MEDIA CORP
LIBERTY MUTUAL GROUP INC
LIFE TECHNOLOGIES CORP
LIMITED BRANDS INC
LINCARE HOLDINGS INC
LINCOLN NATIONAL CORPORATION
LKQ CORP
LOEWS CORPORATION
MACY'S INC
MANPOWER INC
MARATHON OIL CORP
MARRIOTT INTERNATIONAL INC
MARS INC
MARSH & MCLENNAN COMPANIES INC
MARY KAY INC
MASSACHUSETTS MUTUAL LIFE INSURANCE CO
MATTEL INC
MAXIMUS INC
MAYO FOUNDATION FOR MEDICAL EDUCATION AND RESEARCH
MCDONALD'S CORP
MCKESSON CORPORATION
MCKINSEY & COMPANY INC
MEDCO HEALTH SOLUTIONS INC
MEDIACOM COMMUNICATIONS CORP
MEDNAX INC
MEDTRONIC INC
MEIJER INC
MERCER INC
METLIFE INC
METROPCS COMMUNICATIONS INC
MICROCHIP TECHNOLOGY INC
MICROSOFT CORP
MIDAMERICAN ENERGY HOLDINGS CO
MILLIPORE CORP
MOLEX INC
MONRO MUFFLER BRAKE INC
MUTUAL OF OMAHA COMPANIES (THE)
MYLAN INC
NABORS INDUSTRIES LTD
NACCO INDUSTRIES INC
NALCO HOLDING COMPANY
NATIONAL INSTRUMENTS CORP
NATIONAL OILWELL VARCO INC
NCR CORPORATION
NEW YORK LIFE INSURANCE CO
NEXTERA ENERGY INC
NIKE INC
NORFOLK SOUTHERN CORP
NORTH HIGHLAND
NORTHWESTERN MUTUAL LIFE INSURANCE CO
ODYSSEY HEALTHCARE INC
OIL STATES INTERNATIONAL INC
OMNICOM GROUP INC
ORACLE CORP
O'REILLY AUTOMOTIVE INC
OSHKOSH CORPORATION
OWENS & MINOR INC
PACCAR INC
PANERA BREAD CO
PARAMETRIC TECHNOLOGY CORP
PARK-OHIO HOLDINGS CORP
PARSONS BRINCKERHOFF INC
PATTERSON COMPANIES INC
PATTERSON-UTI ENERGY INC
PEABODY ENERGY CORP
PENSKE AUTOMOTIVE GROUP INC
PEPSICO INC
PETCO ANIMAL SUPPLIES INC
PETSMART INC
PHARMACEUTICAL PRODUCT DEVELOPMENT INC
PLEXUS CORP
POLO RALPH LAUREN CORP
POLYCOM INC
PRICEWATERHOUSECOOPERS
PRINCIPAL FINANCIAL GROUP (THE)
PROCTER & GAMBLE CO
PROGRESSIVE CORPORATION (THE)
PRUDENTIAL FINANCIAL INC
QUALCOMM INC
QUANTA SERVICES INC
RACKSPACE HOSTING INC
RALCORP HOLDINGS INC
RECREATIONAL EQUIPMENT INC (REI)
RED HAT INC
REGIS CORPORATION
REPUBLIC AIRWAYS HOLDINGS INC
ROBERT HALF INTERNATIONAL INC
ROYAL CARIBBEAN CRUISES LTD
RYDER SYSTEM INC
SAFECO INSURANCE COMPANY OF AMERICA
SAFEWAY INC
SAIC INC
SAM'S CLUB
SANMINA-SCI CORPORATION
SAPIENT CORPORATION
SARA LEE CORP
SAS INSTITUTE INC
SCHLUMBERGER LIMITED
SCOTTS MIRACLE GROW CO
SEACOR HOLDINGS INC
SELECT MEDICAL HOLDINGS CORPORATION
SENECA FOODS CORPORATION
SENSIENT TECHNOLOGIES CORPORATION
SHAW GROUP INC (THE)
SHELL OIL CO
SHERWIN WILLIAMS COMPANY (THE)
SIGMA-ALDRICH CORP
SKILLED HEALTHCARE GROUP INC
SNYDERS-LANCE INC
SODEXO INC
SOUTHWEST AIRLINES CO
SPECTRUM HEALTH
SPIRIT AEROSYSTEMS HOLDINGS INC
SRA INTERNATIONAL INC
ST JUDE MEDICAL INC
STANLEY BLACK & DECKER INC
STARWOOD HOTELS & RESORTS WORLDWIDE INC
STERICYCLE INC
STIFEL FINANCIAL CORP
STONERIDGE INC
STREAM GLOBAL SERVICES INC
STRYKER CORP
SUN HEALTHCARE GROUP INC
SYNTEL INC
SYSCO CORP
TARGET CORPORATION
TEAM HEALTH HOLDINGS INC
TEAM INC
TECH DATA CORP
TELEDYNE TECHNOLOGIES INC
TELEPHONE AND DATA SYSTEMS INC (TDS)
TENET HEALTHCARE CORPORATION
TEREX CORPORATION
TETRA TECH INC
THERMO FISHER SCIENTIFIC INC
THOMSON REUTERS
THOR INDUSTRIES INC
TIME WARNER INC
TJX COMPANIES INC (THE)
TOTAL SYSTEM SERVICES INC (TSYS)
TOWERS WATSON & CO
TRAVELERS COMPANIES INC (THE)
TREEHOUSE FOODS INC
TRUSTMARK COMPANIES
TTM TECHNOLOGIES INC
TW TELECOM INC
UNDER ARMOUR INC
UNION PACIFIC CORP
UNITED NATURAL FOODS INC
UNITED PARCEL SERVICE INC (UPS)
UNITED STATES CELLULAR CORP
UNITED TECHNOLOGIES CORPORATION
UNITEDHEALTH GROUP INC
UNIVERSAL HEALTH SERVICES INC
UNIVISION COMMUNICATIONS INC
URS CORPORATION
VALASSIS COMMUNICATIONS INC
VALSPAR CORPORATION (THE)
VARIAN MEDICAL SYSTEMS INC
VCA ANTECH INC
VERIZON COMMUNICATIONS INC
VICTORIAS SECRET
VISA INC
VORNADO REALTY TRUST
WABTEC CORP
WALGREEN CO
WAL-MART STORES INC

WALT DISNEY COMPANY (THE)
WASTE MANAGEMENT INC
WATERS CORP
WATSON PHARMACEUTICALS INC
WEIGHT WATCHERS INTERNATIONAL INC
WEST PHARMACEUTICAL SERVICES INC
WHOLE FOODS MARKET INC
WILLIAMS COMPANIES INC (THE)
WINDSTREAM CORPORATION
WM WRIGLEY JR COMPANY
WW GRAINGER INC
WYNDHAM WORLDWIDE
XEROX CORP
YUM! BRANDS INC
ZIMMER HOLDINGS INC

SOUTHEAST

3M COMPANY
7-ELEVEN INC
ABM INDUSTRIES INC
ACADEMY SPORTS & OUTDOORS LTD
ACCENTURE PLC
ACTIVISION BLIZZARD INC
ADVANCE AUTO PARTS INC
ADVANCED MICRO DEVICES INC (AMD)
ADVENTIST HEALTH SYSTEM
AECOM TECHNOLOGY CORPORATION
AES CORPORATION (THE)
AFFILIATED COMPUTER SERVICES INC
AFLAC INC
AIR PRODUCTS & CHEMICALS INC
ALTRIA GROUP INC
AMEDISYS INC
AMERCO
AMERICAN EXPRESS CO
AMERICAN POWER CONVERSION (APC)
AMERIGROUP CORPORATION
AMERISOURCEBERGEN CORP
AMGEN INC
AMPHENOL CORPORATION
AMR CORP (AMERICAN AIRLINES)
AMSURG CORP
ANALOG DEVICES INC
APACHE CORP
APPLE INC
ARAMARK CORPORATION
ARCHER DANIELS MIDLAND CO
ARROW ELECTRONICS INC
ARTHUR J GALLAGHER & CO
ASCENA RETAIL GROUP INC
ASCENSION HEALTH
AT&T INC
AUTOMATIC DATA PROCESSING INC
AUTONATION INC
AUTOZONE INC
AVON PRODUCTS INC
AXA FINANCIAL INC
BAIN & COMPANY INC
BAKER HUGHES INC
BALL CORP
BASIC ENERGY SERVICES INC
BASS PRO SHOPS INC
BAUSCH & LOMB INC
BECHTEL GROUP INC
BECKMAN COULTER INC
BECTON DICKINSON & CO
BED BATH & BEYOND INC
BEMIS COMPANY INC
BERKSHIRE HATHAWAY INC
BEST BUY CO INC
BLOOMBERG LP
BMC SOFTWARE INC
BOEING COMPANY (THE)
BOOZ ALLEN HAMILTON INC
BOSTON CONSULTING GROUP INC (THE, BCG)
BOYD GAMING CORP
BRINKS COMPANY (THE)
BROADCOM CORP
BROCADE COMMUNICATIONS SYSTEMS INC
BROOKDALE SENIOR LIVING INC
BROWN & BROWN INC
BUCKLE INC (THE)
BUFFALO WILD WINGS INC
BURLINGTON NORTHERN SANTA FE LLC
CACI INTERNATIONAL INC
CADENCE DESIGN SYSTEMS INC
CAESARS ENTERTAINMENT CORPORATION
CAMERON INTERNATIONAL CORPORATION
CAMPBELL SOUP CO
CAPITAL SENIOR LIVING CORP
CARLSON COMPANIES INC
CARMAX GROUP
CARNIVAL CORPORATION
CASH AMERICA INTERNATIONAL INC
CATERPILLAR INC
CATHOLIC HEALTH INITIATIVES
CB RICHARD ELLIS GROUP INC (CBRE)
CELLCO PARTNERSHIP (VERIZON WIRELESS)
CERNER CORP
CH ROBINSON WORLDWIDE INC
CHEMED CORPORATION
CHEVRON CORPORATION
CHEVRON PHILLIPS CHEMICAL COMPANY LLC
CHICO'S FAS INC
CHIPOTLE MEXICAN GRILL INC
CHS INC
CHUBB CORPORATION (THE)
CIENA CORP
CIGNA CORP
CINTAS CORP
CISCO SYSTEMS INC
CITRIX SYSTEMS INC
CLEARWIRE CORP
CLOROX CO (THE)
CNA FINANCIAL CORP
COACH INC
COCA-COLA BOTTLING CO CONSOLIDATED
COCA-COLA COMPANY (THE)
COLDWATER CREEK INC
COLGATE PALMOLIVE CO
COMCAST CORP
COMMUNITY HEALTH SYSTEMS INC
COMPUTER SCIENCES CORPORATION (CSC)
COMPUTER TASK GROUP INC
CONAGRA FOODS INC
CONCENTRA INC
CONOCOPHILLIPS COMPANY
CONTAINER STORE (THE)
CON-WAY INC
COSTCO WHOLESALE CORP
COVANCE INC
COX COMMUNICATIONS INC
CR BARD INC
CRACKER BARREL OLD COUNTRY STORE INC
CROCS INC
CSX CORP
CUMMINS INC
CVS CAREMARK CORPORATION
DANAHER CORP
DARDEN RESTAURANTS INC
DAVITA INC
DEAN FOODS CO
DEERE & CO
DELOITTE & TOUCHE USA LLP
DELOITTE CONSULTING LLP
DELTA APPAREL INC
DENTSPLY INTERNATIONAL INC
DEVRY INC
DIAMOND OFFSHORE DRILLING INC
DICK'S SPORTING GOODS INC
DIRECTV
DOLLAR GENERAL CORPORATION
DUKE ENERGY CORP
DUPONT (E I DU PONT DE NEMOURS & CO)
DUPONT AGRICULTURE & NUTRITION
EATON CORP
EDISON INTERNATIONAL
EMERITUS CORP
EMERSON ELECTRIC CO
ENTERGY CORP
ENTERPRISE HOLDINGS INC
EQUITY LIFESTYLE PROPERTIES INC
ERNST & YOUNG LLP
EXPEDIA INC
EXPERIAN AMERICAS
EXPRESS SCRIPTS INC
EXTERRAN HOLDINGS INC
EXXON MOBIL CORPORATION (EXXONMOBIL)
FACTSET RESEARCH SYSTEMS INC
FAMILY DOLLAR STORES INC
FASTENAL
FEDERAL MOGUL CORP

FEDEX CORPORATION
FIDELITY NATIONAL INFORMATION SERVICES INC
FIRST ADVANTAGE CORPORATION
FLUOR CORP
FM GLOBAL
FMC TECHNOLOGIES INC
FMR CORP (FIDELITY INVESTMENTS)
FORD MOTOR CO
FOSSIL INC
FRONTIER COMMUNICATIONS CORPORATION
FTI CONSULTING INC
GAMESTOP CORP
GE ENERGY INFRASTRUCTURE
GENERAL ELECTRIC CO (GE)
GENERAL MILLS INC
GENERAL MOTORS COMPANY (GM)
GENESCO INC
GENTIVA HEALTH SERVICES INC
GENWORTH FINANCIAL INC
GOODYEAR TIRE & RUBBER COMPANY (THE)
GOOGLE INC
GRANT THORNTON LLP
GROUP 1 AUTOMOTIVE INC
GSI COMMERCE INC
GUESS? INC
HALLIBURTON COMPANY
HANESBRANDS INC
HANGER ORTHOPEDIC GROUP INC
HARRIS CORPORATION
HCA HOLDINGS INC
HEALTH CARE SERVICE CORPORATION (HCSC)
HEALTH FITNESS CORP
HEALTH MANAGEMENT ASSOCIATES INC
HEALTHSOUTH CORP
HENRY SCHEIN INC
HERSHEY CO
HERTZ GLOBAL HOLDINGS INC
HIBBETT SPORTS INC
HILLENBRAND INC
HILTON HOTELS CORP
HONDA OF AMERICA MANUFACTURING INC
HUMANA INC
HYATT HOTELS CORPORATION
ICF INTERNATIONAL INC
IDEXX LABORATORIES INC
IGATE CORPORATION
ILLINOIS TOOL WORKS INC
INGRAM MICRO INC
INSITUFORM TECHNOLOGIES
INTEL CORP
INTERNATIONAL BUSINESS MACHINES CORP (IBM)
INTERPUBLIC GROUP OF COMPANIES INC
INTUIT INC
INVENTIV HEALTH INC
JACK HENRY & ASSOCIATES INC
JACKSON NATIONAL LIFE INSURANCE COMPANY
JARDEN CORP
JB HUNT TRANSPORT SERVICES INC
JETBLUE AIRWAYS CORPORATION
JM SMUCKER CO
JOHNSON & JOHNSON
JOHNSON CONTROLS INC
JONES LANG LASALLE INC
JUNIPER NETWORKS INC
KAISER PERMANENTE
KEANE INC
KELLOGG COMPANY
KELLY SERVICES INC
KEY ENERGY SERVICES INC
KIMBERLY-CLARK CORP
KINDRED HEALTHCARE INC
KOCH INDUSTRIES INC
KOHL'S CORP
KPMG LLP
KRAFT FOODS INC
KROGER CO (THE)
LABORATORY CORP OF AMERICA HOLDINGS
LEAP WIRELESS INTERNATIONAL INC
LEAR CORP
LIBERTY MEDIA CORP
LIBERTY MUTUAL GROUP INC
LIMITED BRANDS INC
LINCARE HOLDINGS INC
LINCOLN NATIONAL CORPORATION
LKQ CORP
LOEWS CORPORATION
MACY'S INC
MANPOWER INC
MANTECH INTERNATIONAL CORP
MARATHON OIL CORP
MARRIOTT INTERNATIONAL INC
MARS INC
MARY KAY INC
MASSACHUSETTS MUTUAL LIFE INSURANCE CO
MATTEL INC
MAXIMUS INC
MAYO FOUNDATION FOR MEDICAL EDUCATION AND RESEARCH
MCDONALD'S CORP
MCKESSON CORPORATION
MCKINSEY & COMPANY INC
MEDCO HEALTH SOLUTIONS INC
MEDIACOM COMMUNICATIONS CORP
MEDNAX INC
MEDTRONIC INC
MERCER INC
METLIFE INC
METROPCS COMMUNICATIONS INC
MICROCHIP TECHNOLOGY INC
MICROSOFT CORP
MIDAMERICAN ENERGY HOLDINGS CO
MILLIPORE CORP
MOLEX INC
MUTUAL OF OMAHA COMPANIES (THE)
MYLAN INC
NABORS INDUSTRIES LTD
NACCO INDUSTRIES INC
NALCO HOLDING COMPANY
NATIONAL INSTRUMENTS CORP
NATIONAL OILWELL VARCO INC
NCR CORPORATION
NEW YORK LIFE INSURANCE CO
NEXTERA ENERGY INC
NIKE INC
NORFOLK SOUTHERN CORP
NORTH HIGHLAND
NORTHWESTERN MUTUAL LIFE INSURANCE CO
OCEANEERING INTERNATIONAL INC
ODYSSEY HEALTHCARE INC
OIL STATES INTERNATIONAL INC
OMNICOM GROUP INC
ORACLE CORP
O'REILLY AUTOMOTIVE INC
OSHKOSH CORPORATION
OWENS & MINOR INC
PACCAR INC
PANERA BREAD CO
PARAMETRIC TECHNOLOGY CORP
PARK-OHIO HOLDINGS CORP
PARSONS BRINCKERHOFF INC
PATTERSON COMPANIES INC
PATTERSON-UTI ENERGY INC
PENSKE AUTOMOTIVE GROUP INC
PEPSICO INC
PETCO ANIMAL SUPPLIES INC
PETSMART INC
POLO RALPH LAUREN CORP
POLYCOM INC
PRICEWATERHOUSECOOPERS
PRINCIPAL FINANCIAL GROUP (THE)
PROCTER & GAMBLE CO
PROGRESSIVE CORPORATION (THE)
PRUDENTIAL FINANCIAL INC
PUBLIX SUPER MARKETS INC
QUALCOMM INC
QUANTA SERVICES INC
RALCORP HOLDINGS INC
RECREATIONAL EQUIPMENT INC (REI)
RED HAT INC
REGIS CORPORATION
ROBERT HALF INTERNATIONAL INC
ROSS STORES INC
ROWAN COMPANIES INC
ROYAL CARIBBEAN CRUISES LTD
RYDER SYSTEM INC
SAFECO INSURANCE COMPANY OF AMERICA
SAIC INC
SAM'S CLUB
SANMINA-SCI CORPORATION
SAPIENT CORPORATION
SARA LEE CORP
SAS INSTITUTE INC
SCOTTS MIRACLE GROW CO
SEACOR HOLDINGS INC
SELECT MEDICAL HOLDINGS CORPORATION
SEMPRA ENERGY

SHAW GROUP INC (THE)
SHELL OIL CO
SHERWIN WILLIAMS COMPANY (THE)
SIGMA-ALDRICH CORP
SNYDERS-LANCE INC
SODEXO INC
SOUTHERN COMPANY (THE)
SOUTHWEST AIRLINES CO
SRA INTERNATIONAL INC
ST JUDE MEDICAL INC
STANLEY BLACK & DECKER INC
STARWOOD HOTELS & RESORTS WORLDWIDE INC
STERICYCLE INC
STIFEL FINANCIAL CORP
STONERIDGE INC
STREAM GLOBAL SERVICES INC
STRYKER CORP
SUN HEALTHCARE GROUP INC
SYNTEL INC
SYSCO CORP
TARGET CORPORATION
TEAM HEALTH HOLDINGS INC
TEAM INC
TECH DATA CORP
TELEDYNE TECHNOLOGIES INC
TELEPHONE AND DATA SYSTEMS INC (TDS)
TENET HEALTHCARE CORPORATION
TEREX CORPORATION
TETRA TECH INC
THERMO FISHER SCIENTIFIC INC
THOMSON REUTERS
TIDEWATER INC
TIME WARNER INC
TJX COMPANIES INC (THE)
TOTAL SYSTEM SERVICES INC (TSYS)
TOWERS WATSON & CO
TRAVELERS COMPANIES INC (THE)
TRUSTMARK COMPANIES
TW TELECOM INC
UNDER ARMOUR INC
UNION PACIFIC CORP
UNITED NATURAL FOODS INC
UNITED PARCEL SERVICE INC (UPS)
UNITED STATES CELLULAR CORP
UNITED TECHNOLOGIES CORPORATION
UNITEDHEALTH GROUP INC
UNIVERSAL HEALTH SERVICES INC
UNIVISION COMMUNICATIONS INC
URS CORPORATION
USAA
VALSPAR CORPORATION (THE)
VARIAN MEDICAL SYSTEMS INC
VCA ANTECH INC
VERIZON COMMUNICATIONS INC
VICTORIAS SECRET
VISA INC
VORNADO REALTY TRUST
WABTEC CORP
WALGREEN CO
WAL-MART STORES INC
WALT DISNEY COMPANY (THE)
WASTE MANAGEMENT INC
WATERS CORP
WATSON PHARMACEUTICALS INC
WEIGHT WATCHERS INTERNATIONAL INC
WEST PHARMACEUTICAL SERVICES INC
WHOLE FOODS MARKET INC
WILLIAMS COMPANIES INC (THE)
WINDSTREAM CORPORATION
WM WRIGLEY JR COMPANY
WW GRAINGER INC
WYNDHAM WORLDWIDE
XEROX CORP
YUM! BRANDS INC
ZIMMER HOLDINGS INC

NORTHEAST

3M COMPANY
7-ELEVEN INC
ABM INDUSTRIES INC
ACCENTURE PLC
ACTIVISION BLIZZARD INC
ADOBE SYSTEMS INC
ADVANCE AUTO PARTS INC
ADVANCED MICRO DEVICES INC (AMD)
ADVENTIST HEALTH SYSTEM
AECOM TECHNOLOGY CORPORATION
AES CORPORATION (THE)
AFFILIATED COMPUTER SERVICES INC
AFLAC INC
AGILENT TECHNOLOGIES INC
AIR PRODUCTS & CHEMICALS INC
ALLERGAN INC
ALLIANCE DATA SYSTEMS CORPORATION
ALTRIA GROUP INC
AMAZON.COM INC
AMEDISYS INC
AMERCO
AMERICAN EXPRESS CO
AMERICAN POWER CONVERSION (APC)
AMERIGROUP CORPORATION
AMERISOURCEBERGEN CORP
AMGEN INC
AMKOR TECHNOLOGY INC
AMPHENOL CORPORATION
AMR CORP (AMERICAN AIRLINES)
AMSURG CORP
ANALOG DEVICES INC
APPLE INC
ARAMARK CORPORATION
ARCHER DANIELS MIDLAND CO
ARROW ELECTRONICS INC
ARTHUR J GALLAGHER & CO
ASCENA RETAIL GROUP INC
ASCENSION HEALTH
AT&T INC
AUTOMATIC DATA PROCESSING INC
AUTONATION INC
AUTOZONE INC
AVON PRODUCTS INC
AXA FINANCIAL INC
BAIN & COMPANY INC
BAKER HUGHES INC
BALL CORP
BARRETT BUSINESS SERVICES
BASS PRO SHOPS INC
BAUSCH & LOMB INC
BECHTEL GROUP INC
BECTON DICKINSON & CO
BED BATH & BEYOND INC
BEMIS COMPANY INC
BERKSHIRE HATHAWAY INC
BEST BUY CO INC
BIO RAD LABORATORIES INC
BIOGEN IDEC INC
BLACKROCK INC
BLOOMBERG LP
BMC SOFTWARE INC
BOEING COMPANY (THE)
BOOZ ALLEN HAMILTON INC
BOSTON CONSULTING GROUP INC (THE, BCG)
BOYD GAMING CORP
BRINKS COMPANY (THE)
BROADCOM CORP
BROCADE COMMUNICATIONS SYSTEMS INC
BROOKDALE SENIOR LIVING INC
BROWN & BROWN INC
BRUKER CORP
BUCKLE INC (THE)
BUFFALO WILD WINGS INC
BUNGE LTD
CABLEVISION SYSTEMS CORP
CACI INTERNATIONAL INC
CADENCE DESIGN SYSTEMS INC
CAESARS ENTERTAINMENT CORPORATION
CAMERON INTERNATIONAL CORPORATION
CAMPBELL SOUP CO
CAPITAL SENIOR LIVING CORP
CARLSON COMPANIES INC
CARMAX GROUP
CASH AMERICA INTERNATIONAL INC
CATERPILLAR INC
CATHOLIC HEALTH INITIATIVES
CB RICHARD ELLIS GROUP INC (CBRE)
CDW CORPORATION
CELGENE CORP
CELLCO PARTNERSHIP (VERIZON WIRELESS)
CEPHALON INC
CERNER CORP
CH ROBINSON WORLDWIDE INC
CHEMED CORPORATION
CHEVRON CORPORATION
CHEVRON PHILLIPS CHEMICAL COMPANY LLC
CHICO'S FAS INC

CHIPOTLE MEXICAN GRILL INC
CHS INC
CHUBB CORPORATION (THE)
CIENA CORP
CIGNA CORP
CINTAS CORP
CISCO SYSTEMS INC
CITRIX SYSTEMS INC
CLEARWIRE CORP
CLOROX CO (THE)
CNA FINANCIAL CORP
COACH INC
COCA-COLA BOTTLING CO CONSOLIDATED
COCA-COLA COMPANY (THE)
COGNIZANT TECHNOLOGY SOLUTIONS CORP
COLDWATER CREEK INC
COLGATE PALMOLIVE CO
COMCAST CORP
COMMUNITY HEALTH SYSTEMS INC
COMPUTER SCIENCES CORPORATION (CSC)
COMPUTER TASK GROUP INC
CONAGRA FOODS INC
CONCENTRA INC
CONOCOPHILLIPS COMPANY
CONSOL ENERGY INC
CONTAINER STORE (THE)
CON-WAY INC
COOPER COMPANIES INC
COSTCO WHOLESALE CORP
COVANCE INC
COX COMMUNICATIONS INC
CR BARD INC
CRACKER BARREL OLD COUNTRY STORE INC
CROCS INC
CSX CORP
CUMMINS INC
CVS CAREMARK CORPORATION
DANAHER CORP
DARDEN RESTAURANTS INC
DAVITA INC
DEAN FOODS CO
DEERE & CO
DELOITTE & TOUCHE USA LLP
DELOITTE CONSULTING LLP
DELTA APPAREL INC
DENTSPLY INTERNATIONAL INC
DEVRY INC
DICK'S SPORTING GOODS INC
DIODES INC
DIRECTV
DOLLAR GENERAL CORPORATION
DUPONT (E I DU PONT DE NEMOURS & CO)
DUPONT AGRICULTURE & NUTRITION
EATON CORP
EBAY INC
EDISON INTERNATIONAL
EMC CORP
EMERITUS CORP
EMERSON ELECTRIC CO
ENDO PHARMACEUTICALS HOLDINGS INC
ENTERPRISE HOLDINGS INC
EQUITY LIFESTYLE PROPERTIES INC
ERNST & YOUNG LLP
ESTEE LAUDER COMPANIES INC (THE)
EXELON CORPORATION
EXPEDIA INC
EXPERIAN AMERICAS
EXPRESS SCRIPTS INC
EXTERRAN HOLDINGS INC
EXXON MOBIL CORPORATION (EXXONMOBIL)
FACTSET RESEARCH SYSTEMS INC
FAMILY DOLLAR STORES INC
FASTENAL
FEDERAL MOGUL CORP
FEDEX CORPORATION
FIDELITY NATIONAL INFORMATION SERVICES INC
FIRST ADVANTAGE CORPORATION
FIRSTENERGY CORP
FLUOR CORP
FM GLOBAL
FMC TECHNOLOGIES INC
FMR CORP (FIDELITY INVESTMENTS)
FORD MOTOR CO
FOREST LABORATORIES INC
FOSSIL INC
FRONTIER COMMUNICATIONS CORPORATION
FTI CONSULTING INC
GAMESTOP CORP
GE ENERGY INFRASTRUCTURE
GENERAL ELECTRIC CO (GE)
GENERAL MILLS INC
GENERAL MOTORS COMPANY (GM)
GENESCO INC
GENTIVA HEALTH SERVICES INC
GENWORTH FINANCIAL INC
GENZYME BIOSURGERY
GILEAD SCIENCES INC
GOODYEAR TIRE & RUBBER COMPANY (THE)
GOOGLE INC
GRANT THORNTON LLP
GROUP 1 AUTOMOTIVE INC
GSI COMMERCE INC
GUESS? INC
HANESBRANDS INC
HANGER ORTHOPEDIC GROUP INC
HARRIS CORPORATION
HCA HOLDINGS INC
HEALTH CARE SERVICE CORPORATION (HCSC)
HEALTH FITNESS CORP
HEALTH MANAGEMENT ASSOCIATES INC
HEALTHSOUTH CORP
HEARTLAND PAYMENT SYSTEMS INC
HENRY SCHEIN INC
HERSHEY CO
HERTZ GLOBAL HOLDINGS INC
HIBBETT SPORTS INC
HILTON HOTELS CORP
HONDA OF AMERICA MANUFACTURING INC
HOSPIRA INC
HUMANA INC
HYATT HOTELS CORPORATION
IAC/INTERACTIVECORP
ICF INTERNATIONAL INC
IDEXX LABORATORIES INC
IGATE CORPORATION
ILLINOIS TOOL WORKS INC
IMS HEALTH INC
INGRAM MICRO INC
INSITUFORM TECHNOLOGIES
INTEGRA LIFESCIENCES HOLDINGS CORP
INTEL CORP
INTERNATIONAL BUSINESS MACHINES CORP (IBM)
INTERPUBLIC GROUP OF COMPANIES INC
INTUIT INC
INVENTIV HEALTH INC
JACK HENRY & ASSOCIATES INC
JACKSON NATIONAL LIFE INSURANCE COMPANY
JARDEN CORP
JB HUNT TRANSPORT SERVICES INC
JETBLUE AIRWAYS CORPORATION
JM SMUCKER CO
JOHNSON & JOHNSON
JOHNSON CONTROLS INC
JONES LANG LASALLE INC
JUNIPER NETWORKS INC
KAISER PERMANENTE
KEANE INC
KELLOGG COMPANY
KELLY SERVICES INC
KEY ENERGY SERVICES INC
KIMBERLY-CLARK CORP
KINDRED HEALTHCARE INC
KINETIC CONCEPTS INC
KLA TENCOR CORP
KOCH INDUSTRIES INC
KOHL'S CORP
KPMG LLP
KRAFT FOODS INC
KROGER CO (THE)
LABORATORY CORP OF AMERICA HOLDINGS
LAM RESEARCH CORP
LAS VEGAS SANDS CORP (THE VENETIAN)
LEAP WIRELESS INTERNATIONAL INC
LEAR CORP
LIBERTY MEDIA CORP
LIBERTY MUTUAL GROUP INC
LIFE TECHNOLOGIES CORP
LIMITED BRANDS INC
LINCARE HOLDINGS INC
LINCOLN NATIONAL CORPORATION
LKQ CORP
LOEWS CORPORATION

LORAL SPACE & COMMUNICATIONS LTD
LUFKIN INDUSTRIES INC
MACY'S INC
MANPOWER INC
MANTECH INTERNATIONAL CORP
MARATHON OIL CORP
MARRIOTT INTERNATIONAL INC
MARS INC
MARSH & MCLENNAN COMPANIES INC
MARY KAY INC
MASSACHUSETTS MUTUAL LIFE INSURANCE CO
MATTEL INC
MAXIMUS INC
MCDONALD'S CORP
MCKESSON CORPORATION
MCKINSEY & COMPANY INC
MEDCO HEALTH SOLUTIONS INC
MEDIACOM COMMUNICATIONS CORP
MEDNAX INC
MEDTRONIC INC
MERCER INC
METLIFE INC
METROPCS COMMUNICATIONS INC
MICROCHIP TECHNOLOGY INC
MICRON TECHNOLOGY INC
MICROSOFT CORP
MIDAMERICAN ENERGY HOLDINGS CO
MILLIPORE CORP
MOLEX INC
MONRO MUFFLER BRAKE INC
MUTUAL OF OMAHA COMPANIES (THE)
MYLAN INC
NACCO INDUSTRIES INC
NALCO HOLDING COMPANY
NATIONAL INSTRUMENTS CORP
NATIONAL OILWELL VARCO INC
NCR CORPORATION
NETAPP INC
NEW YORK LIFE INSURANCE CO
NEWS CORP
NEXTERA ENERGY INC
NII HOLDINGS INC
NIKE INC
NORFOLK SOUTHERN CORP
NORTH HIGHLAND
NORTHWESTERN MUTUAL LIFE INSURANCE CO
OCEANEERING INTERNATIONAL INC
ODYSSEY HEALTHCARE INC
OMNICOM GROUP INC
ORACLE CORP
O'REILLY AUTOMOTIVE INC
OSHKOSH CORPORATION
OWENS & MINOR INC
PACCAR INC
PANERA BREAD CO
PARAMETRIC TECHNOLOGY CORP
PAREXEL INTERNATIONAL CORP
PARK-OHIO HOLDINGS CORP
PARSONS BRINCKERHOFF INC
PATTERSON COMPANIES INC
PATTERSON-UTI ENERGY INC
PENSKE AUTOMOTIVE GROUP INC
PEPSICO INC
PERRIGO CO
PETCO ANIMAL SUPPLIES INC
PETSMART INC
PG&E CORPORATION
PHARMACEUTICAL PRODUCT DEVELOPMENT INC
PHILIP MORRIS INTERNATIONAL INC
PLEXUS CORP
POLO RALPH LAUREN CORP
POLYCOM INC
PRAXAIR INC
PRICEWATERHOUSECOOPERS
PRINCIPAL FINANCIAL GROUP (THE)
PROCTER & GAMBLE CO
PROGRESSIVE CORPORATION (THE)
PRUDENTIAL FINANCIAL INC
QUALCOMM INC
QUANTA SERVICES INC
RACKSPACE HOSTING INC
RALCORP HOLDINGS INC
RECREATIONAL EQUIPMENT INC (REI)
RED HAT INC
REGIS CORPORATION
REPUBLIC AIRWAYS HOLDINGS INC
RESMED INC
ROBERT HALF INTERNATIONAL INC
ROSS STORES INC
ROYAL CARIBBEAN CRUISES LTD
RYDER SYSTEM INC
SAFECO INSURANCE COMPANY OF AMERICA
SAFEWAY INC
SAIC INC
SAM'S CLUB
SANMINA-SCI CORPORATION
SAPIENT CORPORATION
SARA LEE CORP
SAS INSTITUTE INC
SCANA CORPORATION
SCHLUMBERGER LIMITED
SCOTTS MIRACLE GROW CO
SEACOR HOLDINGS INC
SELECT MEDICAL HOLDINGS CORPORATION
SENECA FOODS CORPORATION
SENSIENT TECHNOLOGIES CORPORATION
SHAW GROUP INC (THE)
SHELL OIL CO
SHERWIN WILLIAMS COMPANY (THE)
SIGMA-ALDRICH CORP
SNYDERS-LANCE INC
SODEXO INC
SOUTHWEST AIRLINES CO
SRA INTERNATIONAL INC
ST JUDE MEDICAL INC
STANLEY BLACK & DECKER INC
STARWOOD HOTELS & RESORTS WORLDWIDE INC
STERICYCLE INC
STIFEL FINANCIAL CORP
STONERIDGE INC
STREAM GLOBAL SERVICES INC
STRYKER CORP
SUN HEALTHCARE GROUP INC
SYNTEL INC
SYSCO CORP
TARGET CORPORATION
TEAM HEALTH HOLDINGS INC
TEAM INC
TECH DATA CORP
TEKTRONIX INC
TELEDYNE TECHNOLOGIES INC
TELEPHONE AND DATA SYSTEMS INC (TDS)
TENET HEALTHCARE CORPORATION
TEREX CORPORATION
TETRA TECH INC
THERMO FISHER SCIENTIFIC INC
THOMSON REUTERS
TIFFANY & CO
TIME WARNER INC
TJX COMPANIES INC (THE)
TOTAL SYSTEM SERVICES INC (TSYS)
TOWERS WATSON & CO
TRAVELERS COMPANIES INC (THE)
TRUSTMARK COMPANIES
TTM TECHNOLOGIES INC
TW TELECOM INC
UNDER ARMOUR INC
UNITED NATURAL FOODS INC
UNITED PARCEL SERVICE INC (UPS)
UNITED STATES CELLULAR CORP
UNITED TECHNOLOGIES CORPORATION
UNITEDHEALTH GROUP INC
UNIVERSAL HEALTH SERVICES INC
UNIVISION COMMUNICATIONS INC
URS CORPORATION
USAA
VALASSIS COMMUNICATIONS INC
VALSPAR CORPORATION (THE)
VARIAN MEDICAL SYSTEMS INC
VCA ANTECH INC
VERIZON COMMUNICATIONS INC
VICTORIAS SECRET
VISA INC
VORNADO REALTY TRUST
WABTEC CORP
WALGREEN CO
WAL-MART STORES INC
WALT DISNEY COMPANY (THE)
WARNACO GROUP INC (THE)
WASTE MANAGEMENT INC
WATERS CORP
WATSON PHARMACEUTICALS INC
WEIGHT WATCHERS INTERNATIONAL INC
WEST PHARMACEUTICAL SERVICES INC
WHOLE FOODS MARKET INC

INDEX OF FIRMS WITH INTERNATIONAL OPERATIONS

COVANCE INC
CR BARD INC
CROCS INC
CSX CORP
CUMMINS INC
CVS CAREMARK CORPORATION
DANAHER CORP
DARDEN RESTAURANTS INC
DEAN FOODS CO
DEERE & CO
DELOITTE & TOUCHE USA LLP
DELOITTE CONSULTING LLP
DELTA APPAREL INC
DENTSPLY INTERNATIONAL INC
DEVRY INC
DIAMOND OFFSHORE DRILLING INC
DIODES INC
DIRECTV
DUKE ENERGY CORP
DUPONT (E I DU PONT DE NEMOURS & CO)
DUPONT AGRICULTURE & NUTRITION
EATON CORP
EBAY INC
EDISON INTERNATIONAL
EDWARDS LIFESCIENCES CORP
EMC CORP
EMERSON ELECTRIC CO
ENTERPRISE HOLDINGS INC
EQUITY LIFESTYLE PROPERTIES INC
ERNST & YOUNG LLP
EXPEDIA INC
EXPRESS SCRIPTS INC
EXTERRAN HOLDINGS INC
EXXON MOBIL CORPORATION (EXXONMOBIL)
EXXONMOBIL CHEMICAL
FACTSET RESEARCH SYSTEMS INC
FASTENAL
FEDERAL MOGUL CORP
FEDEX CORPORATION
FIDELITY NATIONAL INFORMATION SERVICES INC
FINISAR CORPORATION
FIRST ADVANTAGE CORPORATION
FLUOR CORP
FM GLOBAL
FMC TECHNOLOGIES INC
FMR CORP (FIDELITY INVESTMENTS)
FORD MOTOR CO
FOREST LABORATORIES INC
FORTUNE BRANDS INC
FOSSIL INC
FTI CONSULTING INC
GAMESTOP CORP
GE ENERGY INFRASTRUCTURE
GENENTECH INC
GENERAL ELECTRIC CO (GE)
GENERAL MILLS INC
GENERAL MOTORS COMPANY (GM)
GENESCO INC
GENTEX CORPORATION
GENWORTH FINANCIAL INC
GEOKINETICS INC
GILEAD SCIENCES INC
GOODYEAR TIRE & RUBBER COMPANY (THE)
GOOGLE INC
GROUP 1 AUTOMOTIVE INC
GROUPON INC
GSI COMMERCE INC
GUESS? INC
HALLIBURTON COMPANY
HANESBRANDS INC
HANGER ORTHOPEDIC GROUP INC
HARRIS CORPORATION
HCA HOLDINGS INC
HE BUTT GROCERY COMPANY (HEB)
HEALTH FITNESS CORP
HEALTHSOUTH CORP
HENRY SCHEIN INC
HERSHEY CO
HERTZ GLOBAL HOLDINGS INC
HILLENBRAND INC
HILTON HOTELS CORP
HOSPIRA INC
HUMANA INC
HYATT HOTELS CORPORATION
IAC/INTERACTIVECORP
ICF INTERNATIONAL INC
IDEXX LABORATORIES INC
IGATE CORPORATION
ILLINOIS TOOL WORKS INC
IMS HEALTH INC
INGRAM MICRO INC
INSITUFORM TECHNOLOGIES
INTEGRA LIFESCIENCES HOLDINGS CORP
INTEL CORP
INTERNATIONAL BUSINESS MACHINES CORP (IBM)
INTERPUBLIC GROUP OF COMPANIES INC
INTUIT INC
INVENTIV HEALTH INC
JETBLUE AIRWAYS CORPORATION
JM SMUCKER CO
JOHNSON & JOHNSON
JOHNSON CONTROLS INC
JONES LANG LASALLE INC
JUNIPER NETWORKS INC
KEANE INC
KELLOGG COMPANY
KELLY SERVICES INC
KIMBERLY-CLARK CORP
KINETIC CONCEPTS INC
KLA TENCOR CORP
KOCH INDUSTRIES INC
KPMG LLP
KRAFT FOODS INC
LABORATORY CORP OF AMERICA HOLDINGS
LAM RESEARCH CORP
LAS VEGAS SANDS CORP (THE VENETIAN)
LEAR CORP
LEXMARK INTERNATIONAL INC
LIBERTY GLOBAL INC
LIBERTY MEDIA CORP
LIBERTY MUTUAL GROUP INC
LIFE TECHNOLOGIES CORP
LIMITED BRANDS INC
LINCOLN NATIONAL CORPORATION
LOEWS CORPORATION
LORAL SPACE & COMMUNICATIONS LTD
LUFKIN INDUSTRIES INC
MACY'S INC
MANPOWER INC
MANTECH INTERNATIONAL CORP
MARATHON OIL CORP
MARRIOTT INTERNATIONAL INC
MARS INC
MARSH & MCLENNAN COMPANIES INC
MARY KAY INC
MASSACHUSETTS MUTUAL LIFE INSURANCE CO
MATTEL INC
MAXIMUS INC
MAYO FOUNDATION FOR MEDICAL EDUCATION AND RESEARCH
MCDONALD'S CORP
MCKESSON CORPORATION
MCKINSEY & COMPANY INC
MEDCO HEALTH SOLUTIONS INC
MEDNAX INC
MEDTRONIC INC
MERCER INC
METLIFE INC
MICROCHIP TECHNOLOGY INC
MICRON TECHNOLOGY INC
MICROSOFT CORP
MIDAMERICAN ENERGY HOLDINGS CO
MILLIPORE CORP
MOLEX INC
MULTI-FINELINE ELECTRONIX INC
MYLAN INC
NABORS INDUSTRIES LTD
NACCO INDUSTRIES INC
NALCO HOLDING COMPANY
NATIONAL INSTRUMENTS CORP
NATIONAL OILWELL VARCO INC
NCR CORPORATION
NETAPP INC
NEW YORK LIFE INSURANCE CO
NEWS CORP
NEXTERA ENERGY INC
NII HOLDINGS INC
NIKE INC
NORFOLK SOUTHERN CORP
NORTH HIGHLAND
OCEANEERING INTERNATIONAL INC
OIL STATES INTERNATIONAL INC
OMNICOM GROUP INC
ORACLE CORP
OSHKOSH CORPORATION
PACCAR INC
PANERA BREAD CO
PARAMETRIC TECHNOLOGY CORP
PAREXEL INTERNATIONAL CORP
PARK-OHIO HOLDINGS CORP
PARSONS BRINCKERHOFF INC

PATTERSON COMPANIES INC
PATTERSON-UTI ENERGY INC
PEABODY ENERGY CORP
PENSKE AUTOMOTIVE GROUP INC
PEPSICO INC
PERRIGO CO
PETSMART INC
PHARMACEUTICAL PRODUCT DEVELOPMENT INC
PHILIP MORRIS INTERNATIONAL INC
PLEXUS CORP
POLO RALPH LAUREN CORP
POLYCOM INC
PRAXAIR INC
PRICESMART INC
PRICEWATERHOUSECOOPERS
PRINCIPAL FINANCIAL GROUP (THE)
PROCTER & GAMBLE CO
PROGRESSIVE CORPORATION (THE)
PRUDENTIAL FINANCIAL INC
QUALCOMM INC
QUANTA SERVICES INC
RACKSPACE HOSTING INC
RALCORP HOLDINGS INC
RED HAT INC
REGIS CORPORATION
RESMED INC
ROBERT HALF INTERNATIONAL INC
ROSS STORES INC
ROWAN COMPANIES INC
ROYAL CARIBBEAN CRUISES LTD
RYDER SYSTEM INC
SABRE HOLDINGS CORP
SAFECO INSURANCE COMPANY OF AMERICA
SAFEWAY INC
SAIC INC
SALESFORCE.COM INC
SAM'S CLUB
SANDISK CORP
SANMINA-SCI CORPORATION
SAPIENT CORPORATION
SARA LEE CORP
SAS INSTITUTE INC
SCHLUMBERGER LIMITED
SCOTTS MIRACLE GROW CO
SEACOR HOLDINGS INC
SEMPRA ENERGY
SENSIENT TECHNOLOGIES CORPORATION
SHAW GROUP INC (THE)
SHELL OIL CO
SHERWIN WILLIAMS COMPANY (THE)
SIGMA-ALDRICH CORP
SNYDERS-LANCE INC
SODEXO INC
SOUTHWEST AIRLINES CO
SPIRIT AEROSYSTEMS HOLDINGS INC
SRA INTERNATIONAL INC
ST JUDE MEDICAL INC
STANLEY BLACK & DECKER INC
STARWOOD HOTELS & RESORTS WORLDWIDE INC
STERICYCLE INC
STIFEL FINANCIAL CORP
STONERIDGE INC
STREAM GLOBAL SERVICES INC
STRYKER CORP
SYMANTEC CORP
SYNTEL INC
SYSCO CORP
TARGET CORPORATION
TEAM INC
TECH DATA CORP
TEKTRONIX INC
TELEDYNE TECHNOLOGIES INC
TEREX CORPORATION
TETRA TECH INC
THERMO FISHER SCIENTIFIC INC
THOMSON REUTERS
THOR INDUSTRIES INC
TIBCO SOFTWARE INC
TIDEWATER INC
TIME WARNER INC
TJX COMPANIES INC (THE)
TOTAL SYSTEM SERVICES INC (TSYS)
TOWERS WATSON & CO
TRAVELERS COMPANIES INC (THE)
TTM TECHNOLOGIES INC
UNDER ARMOUR INC
UNITED PARCEL SERVICE INC (UPS)
UNITED TECHNOLOGIES CORPORATION
UNITEDHEALTH GROUP INC
UNIVISION COMMUNICATIONS INC
URS CORPORATION
USAA
VALASSIS COMMUNICATIONS INC
VALSPAR CORPORATION (THE)
VARIAN MEDICAL SYSTEMS INC
VERIZON COMMUNICATIONS INC
VICTORIAS SECRET
VISA INC
VORNADO REALTY TRUST
WABTEC CORP
WALGREEN CO
WAL-MART STORES INC
WALT DISNEY COMPANY (THE)
WARNACO GROUP INC (THE)
WASTE MANAGEMENT INC
WATERS CORP
WEIGHT WATCHERS INTERNATIONAL INC
WEST PHARMACEUTICAL SERVICES INC
WESTERN DIGITAL CORP
WHOLE FOODS MARKET INC
WILLIAMS COMPANIES INC (THE)
WM WRIGLEY JR COMPANY
WW GRAINGER INC
WYNDHAM WORLDWIDE
WYNN RESORTS LIMITED
XEROX CORP
YUM! BRANDS INC
ZIMMER HOLDINGS INC

Individual Data Profiles On Each Of The AMERICAN EMPLOYERS 500

3M COMPANY

www.3m.com

Industry Group Code: 33911

Management:		Sales/Marketing:		Liberal Arts:		Information Sys.:		Professionals:		Tech./Scientific:	
Mgmt. Trainees:	Y	Marketing Pros.:	Y	Gen. Writing/Editing:	Y	Info. Mgmt.:	Y	Finance/Acct.:	Y	Engineers, Elec.:	Y
Experienced Mgmt.:	Y	Retail Sales:		Tech. Writing:	Y	Software Dev.:	Y	Law:	Y	Engineers, Other:	Y
Int'l Business:	Y	Comm./Industrial:	Y	Graphic Arts/Photog.:	Y	Hardware Dev.:		HR/Other:	Y	Health/Lab:	Y
MBA Grads:	Y	Sales Trainees:	Y	Music:		Consulting/Other:		Training:	Y	Science/Research:	Y
		Advertising Pros.:	Y	Broadcasting:				Health Care:	Y	Petroleum/Chem.:	
				Other:	Y			Consulting:		Math/Other:	Y

TYPES OF BUSINESS:

Health Care Products
Specialty Materials & Textiles
Industrial Products
Safety, Security & Protection Products
Display & Graphics Products
Consumer & Office Products
Electronics & Communications Products
Fuel Cell Technology

BRANDS/DIVISIONS/AFFILIATES:

Nida-Core Corp.
3M Cogent, Inc.
Hybrivet Systems, Inc.
Cogent, Inc.
Attenti Holdings S.A.
Arizant, Inc.

CONTACTS: *Note: Officers with more than one job title may be intentionally listed here more than once.*

George W. Buckley, CEO
Inge G. Thulin, COO
George W. Buckley, Pres.
Patrick D. Campbell, CFO/Sr. VP
Robert D. MacDonald, Sr. VP-Mktg. & Sales
Angela S. Lalor, Sr. VP-Human Resources
Frederick J. Palensky, Exec. VP-R&D
Frederick J. Palensky, CTO
Marschall I. Smith, General Counsel/Sr. VP-Legal Affairs
Roger H.D. Lacey, Sr. VP-Strategy & Corp. Dev.
David W. Meline, Chief Acct. Officer
Brad T. Sauer, Exec. VP-Health Care Bus.
H.C. Shin, Exec. VP-Industrial & Transportation Bus.
Joaquin Delgado, Exec. VP-Electro & Comm. Bus.
Joe E. Harlan, Exec. VP-Consumer & Office Bus.
George W. Buckley, Chmn.
John K. Woodworth, Sr. VP-Corp. Supply Chain Oper.

Phone: 651-733-1110 **Fax:** 651-733-9973
Toll-Free: 800-364-3577
Address: 3M Center, St. Paul, MN 55144 US

GROWTH PLANS/SPECIAL FEATURES:

3M Company is involved in the research, manufacturing and marketing of a variety of products. The firm is organized into six segments: Health Care; Consumer and Office; Display and Graphics; Electro and Communications; Industrial and Transportation; and Safety, Security and Protection. The Health Care segment's products include medical and surgical supplies, skin infection prevention products, drug delivery systems, orthodontic products, health information systems and veterinary products. The Consumer and Office segment includes office supply, stationery, construction, home improvement, protective material and visual systems products. The Display and Graphics segment's products include optical film and lenses for electronic displays; touch screens and monitors; screen filters; reflective sheeting; and commercial graphics systems. The Electro and Communications segment's products include packaging and interconnection devices (used in circuits); fluids used in computer chips; high-temperature and display tapes; pressure-sensitive tapes and resins; and products for telecommunications systems. The Industrial and Transportation segment's products include vinyl, polyester, tapes, a variety of non-woven abrasives, adhesives, specialty materials, supply chain execution software, filtration systems, paint finishing products, engineering fluids and components for catalytic converters. The Safety, Security and Protection services segment provides products for personal protection, safety and security, energy control, commercial cleaning and protection, passports and secure cards. In October 2010, the firm acquired remote people monitor supplier, Attenti Holdings S.A., and developer of patient warming products for the prevention of hypothermia in surgery settings, Arizant, Inc. In December 2010, the company acquired biometric security systems provider, Cogent, Inc., with the latter subsequently becoming a subsidiary of 3M called 3M Cogent, Inc. In January 2011, the firm opened an innovation center in Dubai and acquired fiber-reinforced foam materials manufacturer, Nida-Core Corp. In February 2011, the company acquired Hybrivet Systems, Inc., provider of toxin detection products.

The company offers employees medical and dental insurance; domestic partner benefits; tuition reimbursement; and adoption assistance.

FINANCIALS: **Sales and profits are in thousands of dollars—add 000 to get the full amount. 2010 Note: Financial information for 2010 was not available for all companies at press time.**

2010 Sales: $26,662,000 — 2010 Profits: $4,085,000
2009 Sales: $23,123,000 — 2009 Profits: $3,193,000
2008 Sales: $25,269,000 — 2008 Profits: $3,460,000
2007 Sales: $24,462,000 — 2007 Profits: $4,096,000
2006 Sales: $22,923,000 — 2006 Profits: $3,851,000

U.S. Stock Ticker: MMM
Int'l Ticker:
Int'l Exchange:
Employees: 80,057 Fiscal Year Ends: 12/31
Parent Company:

SALARIES/BENEFITS:

Pension Plan: | ESOP Stock Plan: | Profit Sharing: | Top Exec. Salary: $5,901,401 | Bonus: $
Savings Plan: Y | Stock Purch. Plan: Y | | Second Exec. Salary: $1,553,068 | Bonus: $

OTHER THOUGHTS:

Apparent Women Officers or Directors: 4
Hot Spot for Advancement for Women/Minorities: Y

LOCATIONS: ("Y" = Yes)

West:	Southwest:	Midwest:	Southeast:	Northeast:	International:
Y	Y	Y	Y	Y	Y

7-ELEVEN INC

www.7-eleven.com

Industry Group Code: 445120

Management:		Sales/Marketing:		Liberal Arts:		Information Sys.:		Professionals:		Tech./Scientific:	
Mgmt. Trainees:	Y	Marketing Pros.:	Y	Gen. Writing/Editing:	Y	Info. Mgmt.:	Y	Finance/Acct.:	Y	Engineers, Elec.:	
Experienced Mgmt.:	Y	Retail Sales:	Y	Tech. Writing:		Software Dev.:	Y	Law:	Y	Engineers, Other:	
Int'l Business:	Y	Comm./Industrial:		Graphic Arts/Photog.:	Y	Hardware Dev.:		HR/Other:	Y	Health/Lab:	
MBA Grads:	Y	Sales Trainees:	Y	Music:		Consulting/Other:		Training:	Y	Science/Research:	
		Advertising Pros.:	Y	Broadcasting:				Health Care:		Petroleum/Chem.:	
				Other:	Y			Consulting:		Math/Other:	

TYPES OF BUSINESS:

Convenience Stores
Gas Stations
Wine

BRANDS/DIVISIONS/AFFILIATES:

Seven & I Holdings Co Ltd
Yosemite Road
Garb-Ko Inc
Handee Marts Inc
Resort Retailers
Prima Marketing
Seven-Eleven Japan Co Ltd
Vcom

CONTACTS: *Note: Officers with more than one job title may be intentionally listed here more than once.*

Joseph DePinto, CEO
Darren Rebelez, COO/Exec. VP
Joseph DePinto, Pres.
Stanley Reynolds, CFO/Exec. VP
Jesus Delgado-Jenkins, Sr. VP-Mktg.
Krystin Mitchell, Sr. VP-Human Resources
Jesus Delgado-Jenkins, Sr. VP-Merch.
Dave Fenton, General Counsel/Sr. VP/Corp. Sec.
Chris Tanaco, Sr. VP-Int'l
Jesus Delgado-Jenkins, Sr. VP-Logistics

Phone: 214-828-7011 | **Fax:** 214-828-7848
Toll-Free:
Address: 1722 Routh St., 1 Arts Plz., Ste. 1000, Dallas, TX 75201 US

GROWTH PLANS/SPECIAL FEATURES:

7-Eleven, Inc. is a wholly-owned subsidiary of Seven-Eleven Japan Co. Ltd., which in turn is a subsidiary of Seven & I Holdings Co. Ltd. The firm franchises and licenses over 8,800 7-Eleven convenience stores throughout the U.S. and Canada and over 42,400 stores in 16 countries including Thailand, Taiwan, Japan, Malaysia, Sweden and Norway. Stores have extended hours and offer products such as beverages, candy, fresh take-out foods, groceries, tobacco items, beer, wine, self-serve gasoline, magazines, specialty items, lottery tickets and certain financial services. 7-Eleven operates a number of additional store chains, including Garb-Ko, Inc. in Michigan, Indiana and Ohio; Handee Marts, Inc. in Pennsylvania and Ohio; Resort Retailers in Utah; and Prima Marketing in West Virginia. The company continues to focus on its point-of-sale automated retail information system, the first of its kind in use in a major convenience store chain. Many 7-Eleven stores offer Vcom kiosks, which offer self service financial transactions including wire transfers, money orders and check cashing, in addition to standard ATM services. The company also offers free ATM access to Citibank customers in most of its stores. In 2011, the firm introduced its first proprietary wine, VitAlma Pinot Grigio, in its Oregon, Washington, Florida and California locations; and agreed to acquire 51 stores in Texas from Exxon Mobile.

7-Eleven offers employees medical, dental, life and AD&D insurance; a 401(k) plan; paid time off; an assistance program; and adoption assistance.

FINANCIALS: **Sales and profits are in thousands of dollars—add 000 to get the full amount. 2010 Note: Financial information for 2010 was not available for all companies at press time.**

2010 Sales: $17,000,000	2010 Profits: $	**U.S. Stock Ticker: Subsidiary**
2009 Sales: $16,681,000	2009 Profits: $	**Int'l Ticker:**
2008 Sales: $15,471,100	2008 Profits: $	Int'l Exchange:
2007 Sales: $15,797,590	2007 Profits: $133,694	Employees: 45,000 Fiscal Year Ends: 2/28
2006 Sales: $15,373,770	2006 Profits: $130,200	Parent Company: SEVEN & I HOLDINGS CO LTD

SALARIES/BENEFITS:

Pension Plan:	ESOP Stock Plan:	Profit Sharing:	Top Exec. Salary: $	Bonus: $870,422
Savings Plan: Y	Stock Purch. Plan:		Second Exec. Salary: $	Bonus: $

OTHER THOUGHTS:

Apparent Women Officers or Directors: 1
Hot Spot for Advancement for Women/Minorities: Y

LOCATIONS: ("Y" = Yes)

West:	Southwest:	Midwest:	Southeast:	Northeast:	International:
Y	Y	Y	Y	Y	Y

ABM INDUSTRIES INC

www.abm.com

Industry Group Code: 5311

Management:		Sales/Marketing:		Liberal Arts:		Information Sys.:		Professionals:		Tech./Scientific:	
Mgmt. Trainees:	Y	Marketing Pros.:	Y	Gen. Writing/Editing:	Y	Info. Mgmt.:	Y	Finance/Acct.:	Y	Engineers, Elec.:	
Experienced Mgmt.:	Y	Retail Sales:		Tech. Writing:		Software Dev.:		Law:	Y	Engineers, Other:	
Int'l Business:	Y	Comm./Industrial:	Y	Graphic Arts/Photog.:		Hardware Dev.:		HR/Other:	Y	Health/Lab:	
MBA Grads:	Y	Sales Trainees:	Y	Music:		Consulting/Other:		Training:	Y	Science/Research:	
		Advertising Pros.:	Y	Broadcasting:				Health Care:		Petroleum/Chem.:	
				Other:				Consulting:		Math/Other:	

TYPES OF BUSINESS:

Janitorial Services
Parking Facilities
Maintenance Personnel
Security Services
Lighting Services
Billing & Accounting Services
Supplier Management
Call Center Services

BRANDS/DIVISIONS/AFFILIATES:

ABM Janitorial Services
ABM Security Services
Security Services of America
Silverhawk Security Specialists
Elite Protection Services
ABM Engineering Services
DHI HOLDINGS, Inc.
Linc Group, LLC (The)

CONTACTS: *Note: Officers with more than one job title may be intentionally listed here more than once.*

Henrik C. Slipsager, CEO
Henrik C. Slipsager, Pres.
James Lusk, CFO/Exec. VP
Erin M. Andre, Sr. VP-Human Resources
Tracy K. Price, Exec. VP/Pres., Eng.
Sarah Hlavinka McConnell, General Counsel/Sr. VP/Corp. Sec.
Tony Mitchell, VP-Corp. Comm.
David L. Farwell, Sr. VP-Investor Rel.
Dean Chin, Chief Acct. Officer/Controller/Sr. VP
James P. McClure, Exec. VP/Pres., ABM Janitorial Svcs.
Steven M. Zaccagnini, Exec. VP/Pres., ABM Facility Svcs.
Maryellen C. Herringer, Chmn.

Phone: 212-297-0200	**Fax:** 415-733-7333
Toll-Free:	
Address: 551 5th Ave., Ste. 300, New York, NY 10176 US	

GROWTH PLANS/SPECIAL FEATURES:

ABM Industries, Inc. is one of the country's largest facility services providers. Founded in California in 1909 as a one-man window cleaning business, today the firm provides janitorial, parking, engineering, security, and mechanical services to commercial, industrial, institutional and retail facilities throughout the U.S., Puerto Rico and Canada. ABM operates through a number of subsidiaries, which are grouped into four segments: janitorial, parking, security and engineering. The company's janitorial services, operated through ABM Janitorial Services, include floor cleaning and finishing; window washing; furniture polishing; and carpet cleaning and dusting. Through Ampco System Parking, the company provides parking and shuttle transportation services in 38 states and Washington D.C. It currently manages more than 1,800 parking operations and offers parking management services to facilities such as airports, universities, office buildings, hotels, retail centers, hospitals and shopping malls. ABM's security services subsidiaries include ABM Security Services, Security Services of America, Silverhawk Security Specialists and Elite Protection Services. Security services offered by these subsidiaries include security officers; investigative services; electronic monitoring of fire, life safety systems and access control devices; and security consulting. ABM Engineering Services is the company's primary engineering subsidiary, offering on-site engineers to operate and maintain mechanical, electrical and plumbing systems at such facilities as high-rise office buildings, schools, computer centers, shopping malls, manufacturing facilities, museums and universities. The engineering segment also provides facility services through ABM Facility Services, which provides streamlined, centralized control and coordination of multiple facility service needs. In addition, this segment also provides an energy management service, which helps clients identify and amend drains on energy efficiency. The company also provides landscaping and golf services through its subsidiary OneSource. In June 2010, ABM Janitorial Services acquired janitorial services firm Diversco, Inc. from DHI HOLDINGS, Inc. In December 2010, the firm acquired The Linc Group, LLC for $300 million.

FINANCIALS: **Sales and profits are in thousands of dollars—add 000 to get the full amount. 2010 Note: Financial information for 2010 was not available for all companies at press time.**

2010 Sales: $3,495,747 — 2010 Profits: $64,121
2009 Sales: $3,481,823 — 2009 Profits: $54,293
2008 Sales: $3,623,590 — 2008 Profits: $45,434
2007 Sales: $2,706,105 — 2007 Profits: $52,440
2006 Sales: $2,579,351 — 2006 Profits: $93,205

U.S. Stock Ticker: ABM
Int'l Ticker:
Int'l Exchange:
Employees: 96,000 Fiscal Year Ends: 10/31
Parent Company:

SALARIES/BENEFITS:

Pension Plan:	ESOP Stock Plan:	Profit Sharing:	Top Exec. Salary: $805,000	Bonus: $1,008,000
Savings Plan: Y	Stock Purch. Plan: Y		Second Exec. Salary: $576,250	Bonus: $270,833

OTHER THOUGHTS:

Apparent Women Officers or Directors: 4
Hot Spot for Advancement for Women/Minorities: Y

LOCATIONS: ("Y" = Yes)

West:	Southwest:	Midwest:	Southeast:	Northeast:	International:
Y	Y	Y	Y	Y	Y

ACADEMY SPORTS & OUTDOORS LTD

www.academy.com

Industry Group Code: 451110

Management:		**Sales/Marketing:**		**Liberal Arts:**		**Information Sys.:**		**Professionals:**		**Tech./Scientific:**	
Mgmt. Trainees:	Y	Marketing Pros.:	Y	Gen. Writing/Editing:	Y	Info. Mgmt.:	Y	Finance/Acct.:	Y	Engineers, Elec.:	
Experienced Mgmt.:	Y	Retail Sales:	Y	Tech. Writing:		Software Dev.:	Y	Law:	Y	Engineers, Other:	
Int'l Business:		Comm./Industrial:		Graphic Arts/Photog.:	Y	Hardware Dev.:		HR/Other:	Y	Health/Lab:	
MBA Grads:	Y	Sales Trainees:	Y	Music:		Consulting/Other:		Training:	Y	Science/Research:	
		Advertising Pros.:	Y	Broadcasting:				Health Care:		Petroleum/Chem.:	
				Other:	Y			Consulting:		Math/Other:	

TYPES OF BUSINESS:

Sporting Goods Stores
Apparel
Footwear
Outdoor Sports Gear
Hunting Licenses

BRANDS/DIVISIONS/AFFILIATES:

CONTACTS: *Note: Officers with more than one job title may be intentionally listed here more than once.*

David Gochman, CEO
Rodney Faldyn, Pres.
Kevin Chapman, VP-Store Oper.
David Gochman, Chmn.

Phone: 281-646-5200	**Fax:** 281-646-5000
Toll-Free: 888-922-2336	
Address: 1800 N. Mason Rd., Katy, TX 77449 US	

GROWTH PLANS/SPECIAL FEATURES:

Academy Sports & Outdoors, Ltd. is one of the largest sporting goods retailers in the U.S. The company operates over 120 stores throughout 11 states including Alabama, Arkansas, Florida, Georgia, Louisiana, Mississippi, Missouri, Oklahoma, South Carolina; Tennessee and Texas. Additionally, the firm plans to further expand its business by opening stores in the southern and southeastern U.S. in the near future. Academy Sports offers a broad selection of sporting equipment, apparel and footwear. The stores, which range in size from 50,000 to 80,000 square feet, are laid out in a racetrack format with soft goods on the inside, including branded and private label athletic and casual apparel, and hard goods, such as camping, hunting, fishing, marine, footwear and fitness and sporting goods, on the outside. The company distributes merchandise to its stores from a 1 million square foot distribution center located in Katy, Texas. The center utilizes radio frequency devices (RFD), automated inventory and replenishment systems and a state-of-the-art warehouse management system to smoothly operate its large processing and inventory space.

The company offers its employees a 401(k) plan; medical, dental and vision insurance; life insurance; short- and long-term disability benefits; tuition reimbursement; merchandise discounts; bereavement leave; continuing education benefits; and business travel accident insurance.

FINANCIALS: **Sales and profits are in thousands of dollars—add 000 to get the full amount. 2010 Note: Financial information for 2010 was not available for all companies at press time.**

2010 Sales: $2,400,000 | 2010 Profits: $
2009 Sales: $2,000,000 | 2009 Profits: $
2008 Sales: $2,000,000 | 2008 Profits: $
2007 Sales: $2,060,000 | 2007 Profits: $
2006 Sales: $1,840,000 | 2006 Profits: $

U.S. Stock Ticker: Private
Int'l Ticker:
Int'l Exchange:
Employees: 15,000 Fiscal Year Ends: 1/31
Parent Company:

SALARIES/BENEFITS:

Pension Plan: | ESOP Stock Plan: | Profit Sharing: | Top Exec. Salary: $ | Bonus: $
Savings Plan: Y | Stock Purch. Plan: | | Second Exec. Salary: $ | Bonus: $

OTHER THOUGHTS:

Apparent Women Officers or Directors:
Hot Spot for Advancement for Women/Minorities:

LOCATIONS: ("Y" = Yes)

West:	Southwest:	Midwest:	Southeast:	Northeast:	International:
	Y	Y	Y		

ACCENTURE PLC

www.accenture.com

Industry Group Code: 541513

Management:		**Sales/Marketing:**		**Liberal Arts:**		**Information Sys.:**		**Professionals:**		**Tech./Scientific:**	
Mgmt. Trainees:	Y	Marketing Pros.:	Y	Gen. Writing/Editing:	Y	Info. Mgmt.:	Y	Finance/Acct.:	Y	Engineers, Elec.:	Y
Experienced Mgmt.:	Y	Retail Sales:		Tech. Writing:	Y	Software Dev.:	Y	Law:	Y	Engineers, Other:	Y
Int'l Business:	Y	Comm./Industrial:	Y	Graphic Arts/Photog.:	Y	Hardware Dev.:	Y	HR/Other:	Y	Health/Lab:	
MBA Grads:	Y	Sales Trainees:		Music:		Consulting/Other:	Y	Training:	Y	Science/Research:	
		Advertising Pros.:	Y	Broadcasting:				Health Care:		Petroleum/Chem.:	
				Other:	Y			Consulting:	Y	Math/Other:	

TYPES OF BUSINESS:

Technology Consulting Services
Computer Operations Outsourcing
Supply Chain Management
Technology Research
Software Development
Human Resources Consulting
Management Consulting
Research & Development

BRANDS/DIVISIONS/AFFILIATES:

Accenture Mobility Operated Services
CadenceQuest Inc
Acceria

CONTACTS:

Note: Officers with more than one job title may be intentionally listed here more than once.

Peter Nanterme, CEO
Johan Deblaere, COO
Pamela J. Craig, CFO
Roxanne Taylor, Chief Mktg. Officer
Jill B. Smart, Chief Human Resources Officer
Kevin M. Campbell, CTO
Gianfranco Casati, Group CEO-Prod.
Julie Spellman Sweet, General Counsel/Corp. Sec./Compliance Officer
Karl-Heinz Floether, Chief Strategy & Corp. Dev. Officer
Roxanne Taylor, Chief Comm. Officer
David P. Rowland, Sr. VP-Finance
Karl-Heinz Floether, Group CEO-Systems Integration, Tech. & Delivery
Martin I. Cole, Group CEO-Comm. & High Tech.
Adrian Lajtha, Chief Leadership Officer
Sander van 't Noordende, Group CEO-Resources
William D. Green, Chmn.
Diego Visconti, Chmn.-Int'l, Strategic Countries

Phone: 353-1-646-2000 **Fax:**
Toll-Free:
Address: 1 Grand Canal Square, Grand Canal Harbor, Dublin, Ireland 2 UK

GROWTH PLANS/SPECIAL FEATURES:

Accenture plc is a leading provider of management consulting, technology and outsourcing services, with operations in over 200 cities in 53 countries. The firm delivers services through five operating groups, which together comprise 20 industry groups. The operating groups are communications and high-tech; financial services; health and public service; products; and resources. Accenture's communications and high-tech group offers technology, consulting and systems integration to the electronics, communications and media industries. Its financial services group provides consulting and outsourcing strategies to the insurance, capital markets and banking industries. Finally, its health and public service group works with local, state, provincial and national governments in the areas of defense; revenue; human services; health; justice; and postal and education authorities. Accenture's products group serves the automotive; life sciences; consumer goods; industrial equipment; retail; and transportation and travel services industries. The company's resources group works with the chemicals; energy; natural resources; and utilities industries. Accenture also offers management consulting services including customer relationship management; supply chain management; human performance; finance and performance management; and strategy. The firm's systems integration and technology services include systems integration consulting, such as information management services and cloud computing; technology consulting, such as enterprise architecture and infrastructure consulting; and IT outsourcing. Accenture offers outsourcing for business processes, applications and infrastructure needs. The company also offers global mobility services through its Accenture Mobility Operated Services. Clients include AT&T; Microsoft; Sony; Bank of America; and the U.S. Department of Commerce. In June 2010, the company acquired CadenceQuest, Inc., which specializes in retail consumer data. In July 2010, the firm purchased Acceria, a French business process firm.

Accenture offers its employees flexible work arrangements and ongoing training and development resources.

FINANCIALS:

Sales and profits are in thousands of dollars—add 000 to get the full amount. 2010 Note: Financial information for 2010 was not available for all companies at press time.

2010 Sales: $23,094,078 — 2010 Profits: $2,060,459
2009 Sales: $23,170,968 — 2009 Profits: $1,589,963
2008 Sales: $25,313,826 — 2008 Profits: $1,691,751
2007 Sales: $21,452,747 — 2007 Profits: $1,243,148
2006 Sales: $18,228,366 — 2006 Profits: $973,329

U.S. Stock Ticker: ACN
Int'l Ticker:
Int'l Exchange:
Employees: 204,000 Fiscal Year Ends: 8/31
Parent Company:

SALARIES/BENEFITS:

Pension Plan: ESOP Stock Plan: Profit Sharing: Top Exec. Salary: $1,250,000 Bonus: $3,040,000
Savings Plan: Stock Purch. Plan: Y Second Exec. Salary: $1,189,500 Bonus: $1,986,465

OTHER THOUGHTS:

Apparent Women Officers or Directors: 6
Hot Spot for Advancement for Women/Minorities: Y

LOCATIONS: ("Y" = Yes)

West:	Southwest:	Midwest:	Southeast:	Northeast:	International:
Y	Y	Y	Y	Y	Y

Sales, profits and employees may be estimates. Financial information, benefits and other data can change quickly and may vary from those stated here.

ACOSTA SALES & MARKETING

www.acosta.com

Industry Group Code: 5418

Management:		Sales/Marketing:		Liberal Arts:		Information Sys.:		Professionals:		Tech./Scientific:	
Mgmt. Trainees:	Y	Marketing Pros.:	Y	Gen. Writing/Editing:	Y	Info. Mgmt.:	Y	Finance/Acct.:	Y	Engineers, Elec.:	
Experienced Mgmt.:	Y	Retail Sales:	Y	Tech. Writing:	Y	Software Dev.:	Y	Law:		Engineers, Other:	
Int'l Business:	Y	Comm./Industrial:		Graphic Arts/Photog.:		Hardware Dev.:		HR/Other:	Y	Health/Lab:	
MBA Grads:	Y	Sales Trainees:		Music:		Consulting/Other:		Training:		Science/Research:	
		Advertising Pros.:	Y	Broadcasting:				Health Care:		Petroleum/Chem.:	
				Other:				Consulting:		Math/Other:	

TYPES OF BUSINESS:

Marketing Services
Consumer Packaged Goods Sales Research
Retail Sales Support
Integrated Marketing Solutions
Outsourcing
Retail Services

BRANDS/DIVISIONS/AFFILIATES:

Acosta Inc
Thomas H Lee Partners LP
L.T. Acosta Company, Inc.

GROWTH PLANS/SPECIAL FEATURES:

Acosta, Inc., which does business as Acosta Sales & Marketing, is an outsourced sales and marketing agency. Founded in 1927 as single-location food broker L.T. Acosta Company, Inc., the firm now serves more than 1,000 consumer packaged goods companies and retail groups through roughly 65 offices across the U.S. and Canada. The company's client roster includes two-thirds of the No. 1 and No. 2 grocery store brands. On behalf of its consumer packaged goods clients, Acosta offers direct sales of new and existing items to retailers such as Safeway and Kroger. As part of this process, the firm provides services such as the negotiation of volume and price levels. For retail clients, the company provides in-store stocking services. It seeks to ensure optimal shelf space location and exposure of its customer's brands in order to maximize the sale of their products. Acosta Sales & Marketing is majority-owned by private equity firm Thomas H. Lee Partners LP.

CONTACTS: *Note: Officers with more than one job title may be intentionally listed here more than once.*

Robert E. Hill, Jr., CEO
Robert E. Hill, Jr., Pres.
Greg Delaney, CFO
Ramin Eivaz, Chief Mktg. Officer
Rebecca Steele, Chief Human Resources Officer
Mark Chaffin, CIO
Drew Prusiecki, General Counsel/Corp. Sec.
Jamie Gronowski, Pres., Oper.
Brian King, Chief Strategy Officer
Woody Norris, Exec. VP-Strategic Initiatives
Jack Parker, Exec. VP-Strategic Initiatives & Bus. Dev.
Gary R. Chartrand, Exec. Chmn.

Phone: 904-281-9800 **Fax:** 904-281-9966
Toll-Free:
Address: 6600 Corp. Ctr. Pkwy., Jacksonville, FL 32216 US

FINANCIALS: **Sales and profits are in thousands of dollars—add 000 to get the full amount. 2010 Note: Financial information for 2010 was not available for all companies at press time.**

2010 Sales: $1,000,000 2010 Profits: $
2009 Sales: $ 2009 Profits: $
2008 Sales: $ 2008 Profits: $
2007 Sales: $ 2007 Profits: $
2006 Sales: $ 2006 Profits: $

U.S. Stock Ticker: Private
Int'l Ticker:
Int'l Exchange:
Employees: 18,000 Fiscal Year Ends:
Parent Company: THOMAS H LEE PARTNERS LP

SALARIES/BENEFITS:

Pension Plan: ESOP Stock Plan: Profit Sharing: Top Exec. Salary: $ Bonus: $
Savings Plan: Stock Purch. Plan: Second Exec. Salary: $ Bonus: $

OTHER THOUGHTS:

Apparent Women Officers or Directors: 1
Hot Spot for Advancement for Women/Minorities:

LOCATIONS: ("Y" = Yes)

West:	Southwest:	Midwest:	Southeast:	Northeast:	International:
Y	Y	Y	Y	Y	Y

ACTIVISION BLIZZARD INC

www.activisionblizzard.com

Industry Group Code: 511210G

Management:		Sales/Marketing:		Liberal Arts:		Information Sys.:		Professionals:		Tech./Scientific:	
Mgmt. Trainees:	Y	Marketing Pros.:	Y	Gen. Writing/Editing:	Y	Info. Mgmt.:	Y	Finance/Acct.:	Y	Engineers, Elec.:	Y
Experienced Mgmt.:	Y	Retail Sales:		Tech. Writing:	Y	Software Dev.:	Y	Law:	Y	Engineers, Other:	
Int'l Business:	Y	Comm./Industrial:		Graphic Arts/Photog.:	Y	Hardware Dev.:		HR/Other:	Y	Health/Lab:	
MBA Grads:	Y	Sales Trainees:		Music:	Y	Consulting/Other:		Training:	Y	Science/Research:	
		Advertising Pros.:	Y	Broadcasting:				Health Care:		Petroleum/Chem.:	
				Other:	Y			Consulting:		Math/Other:	

TYPES OF BUSINESS:

Video Games
Logistics Services

BRANDS/DIVISIONS/AFFILIATES:

Activision Publishing, Inc.
Blizzard Entertainment, Inc.
Vivendi SA
World of Warcraft (WoW)
Guitar Hero
Call of Duty
StarCraft
Diablo

CONTACTS: *Note: Officers with more than one job title may be intentionally listed here more than once.*

Robert A. Kotick, CEO
Thomas Tippl, COO
Robert A. Kotick, Pres.
Thomas Tippl, CFO
Brian Hodous, Chief Customer Officer
Ann Weiser, Chief Human Resources Officer
Chris Walther, Chief Legal Officer
George Rose, Chief Public Policy Officer
Michael Griffith, CEO/Pres., Activision Publishing, Inc.
Michael Morhaime, CEO/Pres., Blizzard Entertainment
Jean-Bernard Levy, Chmn.

Phone: 310-255-2000	**Fax:**
Toll-Free:	
Address: 3100 Ocean Park Blvd., Santa Monica, CA 90405 US	

GROWTH PLANS/SPECIAL FEATURES:

Activision Blizzard, Inc. is a leading international publisher and developer of subscription-based massively multiplayer online role-playing games (MMORPGs) and other PC-based computer games; interactive entertainment software; and peripherals for a variety of game genres. The company was formed with the merger of Vivendi Games, owner of Blizzard Entertainment and its popular game World of Warcraft, and Activision, a leading publisher of interactive entertainment. World of Warcraft has over 12 million subscribers worldwide. Activision and Blizzard persist as separate brands within the company, which organizes its business into the following segments: Activision Publishing; Blizzard Entertainment, Inc. and its subsidiaries; Activision Blizzard Distribution. Activision Publishing publishes interactive entertainment software and peripherals, including certain studios, assets and titles previously included in Vivendi Games' Sierra Entertainment operating segment. Blizzard Entertainment, Inc. and its subsidiaries publish traditional games and MMORPGs. Activision Blizzard Distribution handles the distribution of interactive entertainment software and hardware products. Some of the company's most popular products include Guitar Hero, Call of Duty and Tony Hawk, as well as Spider-Man, James Bond, TRANSFORMERS, StarCraft, Diablo and Warcraft franchise games, including World of Warcraft. Activision Blizzard maintains operations throughout North America, Europe and Asia.

The firm offers its employees medical, dental, vision, life and AD&D insurance; a 401(k) plan; a college savings plan for family members; an employee assistance program; tuition reimbursement; group legal insurance; discounts at the company store; and gym membership discounts.

FINANCIALS: **Sales and profits are in thousands of dollars—add 000 to get the full amount. 2010 Note: Financial information for 2010 was not available for all companies at press time.**

2010 Sales: $4,447,000	2010 Profits: $418,000	**U.S. Stock Ticker: ATVI**
2009 Sales: $4,279,000	2009 Profits: $113,000	**Int'l Ticker:**
2008 Sales: $3,026,000	2008 Profits: $-107,000	Int'l Exchange:
2007 Sales: $1,349,000	2007 Profits: $179,000	Employees: 7,600 Fiscal Year Ends: 12/31
2006 Sales: $1,018,000	2006 Profits: $121,000	Parent Company:

SALARIES/BENEFITS:

Pension Plan:	ESOP Stock Plan:	Profit Sharing:	Top Exec. Salary: $953,654	Bonus: $2,167,250
Savings Plan: Y	Stock Purch. Plan:		Second Exec. Salary: $726,423	Bonus: $664,417

OTHER THOUGHTS:

Apparent Women Officers or Directors: 1
Hot Spot for Advancement for Women/Minorities:

LOCATIONS: ("Y" = Yes)

West:	Southwest:	Midwest:	Southeast:	Northeast:	International:
Y	Y	Y	Y	Y	Y

ADOBE SYSTEMS INC

www.adobe.com

Industry Group Code: 511210F

Management:		Sales/Marketing:		Liberal Arts:		Information Sys.:		Professionals:		Tech./Scientific:	
Mgmt. Trainees:	Y	Marketing Pros.:	Y	Gen. Writing/Editing:	Y	Info. Mgmt.:	Y	Finance/Acct.:	Y	Engineers, Elec.:	Y
Experienced Mgmt.:	Y	Retail Sales:		Tech. Writing:	Y	Software Dev.:	Y	Law:	Y	Engineers, Other:	
Int'l Business:	Y	Comm./Industrial:	Y	Graphic Arts/Photog.:	Y	Hardware Dev.:		HR/Other:	Y	Health/Lab:	
MBA Grads:	Y	Sales Trainees:	Y	Music:		Consulting/Other:	Y	Training:	Y	Science/Research:	
		Advertising Pros.:	Y	Broadcasting:				Health Care:		Petroleum/Chem.:	
				Other:	Y			Consulting:		Math/Other:	

TYPES OF BUSINESS:

Computer Software-Desktop & Publishing
Document Management Software
Photo Editing & Management Software
Graphic Design Software

BRANDS/DIVISIONS/AFFILIATES:

Adobe Acrobat
Adobe Flash Player
Adobe Photoshop
Adobe Creative Suite
Adobe Air
Day Software Holding AG
Omniture Inc
Adobe LiveCycle

CONTACTS: *Note: Officers with more than one job title may be intentionally listed here more than once.*

Shantanu Narayen, CEO
Shantanu Narayen, Pres.
Mark Garrett, CFO/Exec. VP
Ann Lewnes, Sr. VP-Global Mktg.
Donna Morris, Sr. VP-Human Resources
Gerri Martin-Flickinger, CIO/Sr. VP
Kevin Lynch, CTO
Karen Cottle, General Counsel/Sr. VP/Corp. Sec.
Matthew Thompson, Sr. VP-Worldwide Field Oper.
Paul Weiskopf, Sr. VP-Corp. Dev.
David Wadhwani, Sr. VP/Gen. Mgr.-Creative & Interactive Solutions
Christine Castro, VP-Corp. Comm.
Mike Saviage, VP-Investor Rel.
John E. Warnock, Co-Chmn.
Naresh Gupta, Sr. VP-Print & Classic Publishing Solutions Unit
John Loiacono, Sr. VP/Gen. Mgr.-Digital Media Solutions Bus. Unit
Charles M. Geschke, Co-Chmn.
Naresh Gupta, Managing Dir.-R&D, India

Phone: 408-536-6000 | **Fax:** 408-537-6000
Toll-Free: 800-833-6687
Address: 345 Park Ave., San Jose, CA 95110-2704 US

GROWTH PLANS/SPECIAL FEATURES:

Adobe Systems, Inc. is one of the largest software companies in the world. It offers a line of creative, business, web and mobile software and services used by creative professionals, knowledge workers, consumers, original equipment manufacturers, developers and enterprises for creating, managing, delivering, optimizing and engaging with content across multiple operating systems, devices and media. The company operates in six segments: creative solutions; knowledge worker; enterprise; Omniture; platform; and print and publishing. The creative solutions segment focuses primarily on professional creative clients such as graphic designers, production artists, web designers, photographers and prepress professionals. Products include Adobe After Effects Professional, Adobe Creative Suite, Adobe Photoshop and Adobe Dreamweaver. The knowledge worker segment focuses on knowledge clients such as accountants, attorneys, architects, educators, engineers and stock analysts. This segment includes the Adobe Acrobat family of products. The enterprise segment provides server-based Customer Experience Management Solutions, including collaboration, data capture, information assurance, document output, process management and content services, to corporate and government customers. Products include Adobe LiveCycle and Adobe Connect. The Omniture segment, created when Adobe acquired web analytics company Omniture, Inc., provides online business optimization products and services. The platform segment includes client and developer technologies, such as Adobe Flash Player, Adobe AIR and Adobe ColdFusion. Finally, the print and publishing segment addresses market opportunities ranging from technical and business publishing to legacy type printing. In 2010, the firm opened three new data centers in North America, Asia and Europe. In October 2010, Adobe acquired Day Software Holding AG, an Enterprise Content Management (ECM) company. In December 2010, the company announced a strategic alliance with Deloitte Consulting related to enterprise systems.

The firm offers its employees life, disability, medical, dental, vision and prescription drug insurance; health care and dependent care reimbursement accounts; adoption assistance; an assistance program; product discounts; and a 401(k).

FINANCIALS: **Sales and profits are in thousands of dollars—add 000 to get the full amount. 2010 Note: Financial information for 2010 was not available for all companies at press time.**

2010 Sales: $3,800,000	2010 Profits: $774,680	**U.S. Stock Ticker: ADBE**
2009 Sales: $2,945,853	2009 Profits: $386,508	**Int'l Ticker:**
2008 Sales: $3,579,889	2008 Profits: $871,814	Int'l Exchange:
2007 Sales: $3,157,881	2007 Profits: $723,807	Employees: 9,117 Fiscal Year Ends: 11/30
2006 Sales: $2,575,300	2006 Profits: $505,809	Parent Company:

SALARIES/BENEFITS:

Pension Plan:	ESOP Stock Plan:	Profit Sharing:	Top Exec. Salary: $875,000	Bonus: $
Savings Plan: Y	Stock Purch. Plan:		Second Exec. Salary: $510,000	Bonus: $

OTHER THOUGHTS:

Apparent Women Officers or Directors: 5
Hot Spot for Advancement for Women/Minorities: Y

LOCATIONS: ("Y" = Yes)

West:	Southwest:	Midwest:	Southeast:	Northeast:	International:
Y	Y			Y	Y

ADVANCE AUTO PARTS INC

www.advanceautoparts.com

Industry Group Code: 441310

Management:		Sales/Marketing:		Liberal Arts:		Information Sys.:		Professionals:		Tech./Scientific:	
Mgmt. Trainees:	Y	Marketing Pros.:	Y	Gen. Writing/Editing:	Y	Info. Mgmt.:	Y	Finance/Acct.:	Y	Engineers, Elec.:	
Experienced Mgmt.:	Y	Retail Sales:	Y	Tech. Writing:		Software Dev.:	Y	Law:	Y	Engineers, Other:	
Int'l Business:	Y	Comm./Industrial:	Y	Graphic Arts/Photog.:	Y	Hardware Dev.:		HR/Other:	Y	Health/Lab:	
MBA Grads:	Y	Sales Trainees:	Y	Music:		Consulting/Other:		Training:	Y	Science/Research:	
		Advertising Pros.:	Y	Broadcasting:				Health Care:		Petroleum/Chem.:	
				Other:				Consulting:		Math/Other:	

TYPES OF BUSINESS:

Auto Parts & Accessories Stores
Online Sales

BRANDS/DIVISIONS/AFFILIATES:

Autopart International (AI)
Advance Discount Auto Parts
Western Auto

CONTACTS: *Note: Officers with more than one job title may be intentionally listed here more than once.*

Darren R. Jackson, CEO
Kevin Freeland, COO
Jim Wade, Pres.
Mike Norona, CFO/Exec. VP
Greg Johnson, Chief Mktg. Officer
Rick Coro, CIO/Sr. VP-IT
Charles Tyson, Sr. VP-Merch.
Sarah Powell, General Counsel/Sr. VP/Corp. Sec.
Mike Pack, Sr. VP-Oper.
Tami Kozikowski, Chief Dev. Officer
Scott Bauhofer, Sr. VP-eCommerce
Judd Nystrom, Sr. VP-Finance
Mike Marolt, Sr. VP-Store Support
Carl Hauch, Sr. VP-National Oper. & Customer Experience
Randy Young, Sr. VP-Real Estate
Bill Carter, Sr. VP-DIY & Commercial Oper. Support
Jack Brouillard, Chmn.
Jim Durkin, Pres., Autopart Int'l
Chas Scheiderer, Sr. VP-Supply Chain

Phone: 540-362-4911	**Fax:** 540-561-1448
Toll-Free: 877-238-2623	
Address: 5008 Airport Rd., Roanoke, VA 24012 US	

GROWTH PLANS/SPECIAL FEATURES:

Advance Auto Parts, Inc. is a leading specialty retailer of automotive aftermarket parts, accessories, batteries and maintenance items. The firm primarily operates in the U.S. and serves both do-it-yourself (DIY) and do-it-for-me (commercial) customers. It operates in two segments: Advance Auto Parts (AAP) and Autopart International (AI). The AAP segment operates roughly 3,397 stores within the U.S., Puerto Rico and the Virgin Islands. It operates 3,371 stores throughout 39 states in the Northeastern, Southeastern and Midwestern regions of the U.S. The stores operate under the Advance Auto Parts brand, while certain stores in Florida operate under the Advance Discount Auto Parts brand. The company also operates 26 stores under the Western Auto and Advance Auto Parts brands in Puerto Rico and the Virgin Islands. The stores' product categories consist of parts, which include alternators, batteries, clutches, engines and engine parts; accessories, including floor mats, mirrors, vent shades and seat and steering wheel covers; chemicals, including antifreeze, freon, fuel additives and car washes and waxes; and oil and other petroleum products. Its stores also provide a variety of services, including battery charging; oil and battery recycling; battery and wiper installation; and electrical system testing. The AI segment operates approximately 203 stores located primarily throughout the Northeast and Mid-Atlantic regions. Its stores serve the commercial market, with an emphasis on parts for imported cars. In 2010, Advance Auto Parts opened 110 AAP and 38 AI locations; it also closed 5 AAP division stores. In the first half of 2011, the firm opened 28 new AAP and nine new AI locations.

The company offers its employees medical, dental and vision benefits; company-paid life insurance; life and AD&D insurance; short- and long-term disability insurance; store discounts; an employee assistance program; business travel accident insurance; a legal benefits plan; dependent scholarships; and bereavement leave.

FINANCIALS: **Sales and profits are in thousands of dollars—add 000 to get the full amount. 2010 Note: Financial information for 2010 was not available for all companies at press time.**

2010 Sales: $5,925,203	2010 Profits: $346,053
2009 Sales: $5,412,623	2009 Profits: $270,373
2008 Sales: $5,142,255	2008 Profits: $238,038
2007 Sales: $4,844,404	2007 Profits: $238,317
2006 Sales: $4,616,503	2006 Profits: $231,318

U.S. Stock Ticker: AAP
Int'l Ticker:
Int'l Exchange:
Employees: 52,141 Fiscal Year Ends: 12/31
Parent Company:

SALARIES/BENEFITS:

Pension Plan:	ESOP Stock Plan:	Profit Sharing:	Top Exec. Salary: $700,000	Bonus: $2,310,000
Savings Plan: Y	Stock Purch. Plan: Y		Second Exec. Salary: $450,008	Bonus: $816,750

OTHER THOUGHTS:

Apparent Women Officers or Directors: 6
Hot Spot for Advancement for Women/Minorities: Y

LOCATIONS: ("Y" = Yes)

West:	Southwest:	Midwest:	Southeast:	Northeast:	International:
Y		Y	Y	Y	

ADVANCED MICRO DEVICES INC (AMD)

www.amd.com

Industry Group Code: 33441

Management:		Sales/Marketing:		Liberal Arts:		Information Sys.:		Professionals:		Tech./Scientific:	
Mgmt. Trainees:	Y	Marketing Pros.:	Y	Gen. Writing/Editing:		Info. Mgmt.:	Y	Finance/Acct.:	Y	Engineers, Elec.:	Y
Experienced Mgmt.:	Y	Retail Sales:		Tech. Writing:	Y	Software Dev.:	Y	Law:	Y	Engineers, Other:	
Int'l Business:	Y	Comm./Industrial:	Y	Graphic Arts/Photog.:	Y	Hardware Dev.:	Y	HR/Other:	Y	Health/Lab:	
MBA Grads:	Y	Sales Trainees:		Music:		Consulting/Other:		Training:	Y	Science/Research:	Y
		Advertising Pros.:	Y	Broadcasting:				Health Care:		Petroleum/Chem.:	
				Other:				Consulting:		Math/Other:	Y

TYPES OF BUSINESS:

Microprocessors
Semiconductors
Chipsets
Wafer Manufacturing
Multimedia Graphics

BRANDS/DIVISIONS/AFFILIATES:

GLOBALFOUNDRIES, Inc.
Advanced Technology Investment Company LLC
West Coast Hitech L.P.
Broadcom Corp.
Qualcomm, Inc.
ATI Technologies, Inc.
Opteron
Athelon

CONTACTS: *Note: Officers with more than one job title may be intentionally listed here more than once.*

Rory Read, CEO
Thomas Seifert, CFO/Sr. VP
Nigel Dessau, Chief Mktg. Officer/Sr. VP
Allen Sockwell, Sr. VP-Human Resources/Chief Talent Officer
Chekib Akrout, Sr. VP-Tech. Group
Rick Bergman, Sr. VP/Gen. Mgr.-Prod. Div.
Harry A. Wolin, General Counsel/Sr. VP/Sec.
Emilio Ghilardi, Chief Sales Officer/Sr. VP
Donald Newell, VP/CTO-Server
Bruce L. Claflin, Chmn.
David Tang, Sr. VP/Pres., AMD Greater China

Phone: 408-749-4000 **Fax:**
Toll-Free:
Address: 1 AMD Pl., Sunnyvale, CA 94088 US

GROWTH PLANS/SPECIAL FEATURES:

Advanced Micro Devices, Inc. (AMD) is a global semiconductor company that provides processing products for the computing, graphics and consumer electronics markets. The company operates through three segments: Computing Solutions; Graphics; and Foundry. AMD's Computing Solutions segment encompasses microprocessors, chipsets and embedded processors. It supplies microprocessors for the commercial and consumer markets based on the industry standard x86 architecture and its Direct Connect Architecture; chipsets for desktop and notebook PCs, professional workstations and servers; and embedded microprocessors for use in applications that require high to moderate levels of performance. The Graphics segment consists of graphics, video and multimedia products for desktop and notebook computers, home media PCs and professional workstations, as well as royalties from the sale of game consoles that incorporate the firm's graphics technology. It provides customized graphics processing units (GPUs) for graphics in videogame consoles such as the Microsoft Xbox 360 and Nintendo Wii. The Foundry segment consists of the operations of GLOBALFOUNDRIES, Inc., a manufacturing joint venture with Advanced Technology Investment Company LLC and West Coast Hitech L.P. that conducts front end wafer manufacturing and related activities. The firm's products include the Phenom line of processors for desktop PCs; Radeon graphic products for Desktop PCs; Crossfire chipsets; FirePro professional graphics products; Opteron, Athlon and Turion embedded processors; and the Fusion line of accelerated processing units (APUs). AMD has operations across the U.S., Canada, South and Central America, Europe, Africa, the Middle East and the Asia Pacific region.

FINANCIALS: **Sales and profits are in thousands of dollars—add 000 to get the full amount. 2010 Note: Financial information for 2010 was not available for all companies at press time.**

2010 Sales: $6,494,000 — 2010 Profits: $471,000
2009 Sales: $5,403,000 — 2009 Profits: $304,000
2008 Sales: $5,808,000 — 2008 Profits: $-3,129,000
2007 Sales: $5,858,000 — 2007 Profits: $-3,379,000
2006 Sales: $5,627,000 — 2006 Profits: $-166,000

U.S. Stock Ticker: AMD
Int'l Ticker:
Int'l Exchange:
Employees: 11,100 Fiscal Year Ends: 12/31
Parent Company:

SALARIES/BENEFITS:

Pension Plan: ESOP Stock Plan: Profit Sharing: Top Exec. Salary: $925,381 Bonus: $
Savings Plan: Y Stock Purch. Plan: Second Exec. Salary: $625,604 Bonus: $4,000,000

OTHER THOUGHTS:

Apparent Women Officers or Directors: 1
Hot Spot for Advancement for Women/Minorities:

LOCATIONS: ("Y" = Yes)

West:	Southwest:	Midwest:	Southeast:	Northeast:	International:
Y	Y	Y	Y	Y	Y

ADVENTIST HEALTH SYSTEM

www.adventisthealthsystem.com

Industry Group Code: 622110

Management:		Sales/Marketing:		Liberal Arts:		Information Sys.:		Professionals:		Tech./Scientific:	
Mgmt. Trainees:	Y	Marketing Pros.:	Y	Gen. Writing/Editing:	Y	Info. Mgmt.:	Y	Finance/Acct.:	Y	Engineers, Elec.:	
Experienced Mgmt.:	Y	Retail Sales:		Tech. Writing:	Y	Software Dev.:		Law:	Y	Engineers, Other:	
Int'l Business:		Comm./Industrial:	Y	Graphic Arts/Photog.:		Hardware Dev.:		HR/Other:	Y	Health/Lab:	Y
MBA Grads:	Y	Sales Trainees:		Music:		Consulting/Other:		Training:	Y	Science/Research:	
		Advertising Pros.:	Y	Broadcasting:				Health Care:	Y	Petroleum/Chem.:	
				Other:	Y			Consulting:		Math/Other:	

TYPES OF BUSINESS:

Hospitals
Nursing Homes
Home Health Care Services

BRANDS/DIVISIONS/AFFILIATES:

Florida Hospital
Adventist GlenOaks Hospital
Bert Fish Medical Center
University Community Health
Helen Ellis Memorial Hospital

CONTACTS: *Note: Officers with more than one job title may be intentionally listed here more than once.*

Donald L. Jernigan, CEO
Terry D. Shaw, COO
Donald L. Jernigan, Pres.
Terry D. Shaw, CFO
Donald G. Jones, VP-Human Resources
Brent G. Snyder, CIO
Robert R. Henderschedt, Sr. VP-Admin.
Jeffrey S. Bromme, Chief Legal Officer
Gary Skilton, Sr. VP-Treas. Oper.
Sandra K. Johnson, VP-Bus. Dev., Risk Mgmt. & Compliance
Womack H. Rucker, Jr., VP-Corp. Rel.
Amy L. Zbaraschuk, VP-Finance/Controller
Richard K. Reiner, Pres./CEO-Multi-State Div.
John R. Brownlow, Sr. VP-Managed Care
Ted Hamilton, VP-Medical Mission
Carlene Jamerson, Sr. VP/Chief Clinical Officer
Celeste M. West, VP-Supply Chain Mgmt.

Phone: 407-647-4400 **Fax:** 407-975-1469
Toll-Free:
Address: 111 N. Orlando Ave., Winter Park, FL 32789 US

GROWTH PLANS/SPECIAL FEATURES:

Adventist Health System, sponsored by the Seventh-day Adventist Church, is one of the largest not-for-profit Protestant health care organizations in the U.S. The firm operates 43 hospitals in several states, totaling over 7,700 beds; 17 affiliated extended care centers within the long-term care division with over 2,200 beds; and over 26 home health care agencies in 12 states. The company serves about 4 million patients annually. Adventist Health's flagship organization, Florida Hospital, is one of the largest health care providers in central Florida and a national leader in cardiac care. The hospital offers 2,200 beds on seven campuses and provides care in the areas of cancer, neurosciences, orthopedics, kidney disease, limb replantation, sports medicine, rehabilitation and women's medicine programs. Adventist Health is a world leader in the use of tissue-sparing radiation based on proton beams, rather than traditional photon-based radiation. The firm is guided by its Christian mission, combining disease treatment, preventative medicine, education and advocacy of a wholesome lifestyle. The hospitals in the Adventist Health group provide a wide range of free or reduced-price services in their communities, including free medical vans and community clinics, free screening and education programs, debt forgiveness, abuse shelters and programs for the homeless and jobless. In early 2010, the firm began construction on its new eco-friendly, five-story, 150,000-square-foot headquarters in Altamonte Springs, Florida.

FINANCIALS: **Sales and profits are in thousands of dollars—add 000 to get the full amount. 2010 Note: Financial information for 2010 was not available for all companies at press time.**

2010 Sales: $ — 2010 Profits: $
2009 Sales: $6,132,200 — 2009 Profits: $363,600
2008 Sales: $5,496,100 — 2008 Profits: $233,500
2007 Sales: $5,194,800 — 2007 Profits: $360,200
2006 Sales: $4,968,700 — 2006 Profits: $325,400

U.S. Stock Ticker: Nonprofit
Int'l Ticker:
Int'l Exchange:
Employees: 55,000 Fiscal Year Ends: 12/31
Parent Company:

SALARIES/BENEFITS:

Pension Plan: ESOP Stock Plan: Profit Sharing: Top Exec. Salary: $ Bonus: $
Savings Plan: Stock Purch. Plan: Y Second Exec. Salary: $ Bonus: $

OTHER THOUGHTS:

Apparent Women Officers or Directors: 5
Hot Spot for Advancement for Women/Minorities: Y

LOCATIONS: ("Y" = Yes)

West:	Southwest:	Midwest:	Southeast:	Northeast:	International:
Y	Y	Y	Y	Y	

AECOM TECHNOLOGY CORPORATION

www.aecom.com

Industry Group Code: 237

Management:		**Sales/Marketing:**		**Liberal Arts:**		**Information Sys.:**		**Professionals:**		**Tech./Scientific:**	
Mgmt. Trainees:	Y	Marketing Pros.:	Y	Gen. Writing/Editing:		Info. Mgmt.:	Y	Finance/Acct.:	Y	Engineers, Elec.:	Y
Experienced Mgmt.:	Y	Retail Sales:		Tech. Writing:	Y	Software Dev.:	Y	Law:	Y	Engineers, Other:	Y
Int'l Business:	Y	Comm./Industrial:	Y	Graphic Arts/Photog.:	Y	Hardware Dev.:		HR/Other:	Y	Health/Lab:	
MBA Grads:	Y	Sales Trainees:		Music:		Consulting/Other:	Y	Training:	Y	Science/Research:	
		Advertising Pros.:		Broadcasting:				Health Care:		Petroleum/Chem.:	
				Other:				Consulting:	Y	Math/Other:	

TYPES OF BUSINESS:

Engineering & Design Services
Transportation Projects
Environmental Projects
Power & Mining Support
Consulting
Economic Development Consulting

BRANDS/DIVISIONS/AFFILIATES:

AGS
CTE
DMJM Aviation
Faber Maunsell
Tishman Construction Corp.
McNeil Technologies, Inc.
Davis Langdon
RSW Inc

CONTACTS: *Note: Officers with more than one job title may be intentionally listed here more than once.*

John M. Dionisio, CEO
John M. Dionisio, Pres.
Michael S. Burke, CFO/Sr. VP
Ian R. MacLeod, Sr. VP-Human Resources
Raul Cruz, CIO/Sr. VP
James T. Walsh, CTO/Sr. VP
Nancy Laben, General Counsel/Sr. VP-Legal
Bob Pell, Sr. VP-Oper./Chief Integration Officer
Alan P. Krusi, Exec. VP-Corp. Dev.
Paul J. Gennaro, Jr., Chief Comm. Officer
Eric Chen, Sr. VP-Finance
Glenn R. Robson, Chief Strategy Officer/Sr. VP-Finance
Gary Lawrence, Chief Sustainability Officer/VP
Robert Andrews, Global Managing Dir.-Water
Luc Benoit, Global Managing Dir.-Energy
Richard G. Newman, Chmn.
Dickson Lo, CEO-Asia

Phone: 213-593-8000 | **Fax:** 213-593-8730
Toll-Free:
Address: 555 S. Flower St., Ste. 3700, Los Angeles, CA 90071-2300 US

GROWTH PLANS/SPECIAL FEATURES:

AECOM Technology Corporation is a global engineering and design company engaged in facility, transportation, environment and specialty engineering projects for corporate, institutional and government clients. Its operations are divided into two segments: Professional Technical Services (PTS) and Management Support Services (MSS). The PTS segment provides planning; consulting; architectural and engineering design; and program and construction management services to clients in the transportation, facilities, energy, water and government markets. Transportation services include feasibility studies, planning, design, engineering, construction management and asset management for transit and rail, highway, bridge, port, harbor and airport projects. The firm's facility design and construction projects encompass land development assignments and a wide variety of building projects. For the energy sector, it offers design, construction management and commissioning services. AECOM offers water resource, wastewater, wet weather, hazardous waste management and other environmental engineering services. The MSS segment provides program and facilities management and maintenance, training, logistics, consulting, technical assistance and systems integration services, primarily for agencies of the U.S. government. The company operates largely through a network of subsidiaries, including AGS, AECOM's government services arm; CTE, an infrastructure engineering firm; DMJM Aviation, the firm's flagship aviation design and construction management company; Faber Maunsell, a European engineering consultancy firm; Metcalf & Eddy, an environmental engineering group; Hayes, Seay, Mattern & Mattern, Inc., an architectural and engineering firm; and PADCO, a firm that promotes sustainable economic development in more than 100 countries. In July 2010, the firm acquired Tishman Construction Corp. In August 2010, it acquired McNeil Technologies, Inc. In November 2010, AECOM acquired Davis Langdon and RSW Inc.

The company offers its employees medical, dental and life insurance; a stock purchase program with company match; a 401(k) and Roth IRA; and a merit based scholarship program for the children of employees.

FINANCIALS: **Sales and profits are in thousands of dollars—add 000 to get the full amount. 2010 Note: Financial information for 2010 was not available for all companies at press time.**

2010 Sales: $6,545,791 | 2010 Profits: $249,344
2009 Sales: $6,119,465 | 2009 Profits: $189,696
2008 Sales: $5,194,482 | 2008 Profits: $147,226
2007 Sales: $4,237,270 | 2007 Profits: $100,297
2006 Sales: $3,421,492 | 2006 Profits: $53,686

U.S. Stock Ticker: ACM
Int'l Ticker:
Int'l Exchange:
Employees: 48,100 Fiscal Year Ends: 9/30
Parent Company:

SALARIES/BENEFITS:

Pension Plan: Y | ESOP Stock Plan: | Profit Sharing: | Top Exec. Salary: $997,506 | Bonus: $3,000,000
Savings Plan: Y | Stock Purch. Plan: Y | | Second Exec. Salary: $650,021 | Bonus: $1,000,000

OTHER THOUGHTS:

Apparent Women Officers or Directors: 4
Hot Spot for Advancement for Women/Minorities: Y

LOCATIONS: ("Y" = Yes)

West:	Southwest:	Midwest:	Southeast:	Northeast:	International:
Y	Y	Y	Y	Y	Y

AES CORPORATION (THE)

www.aes.com

Industry Group Code: 221

Management:		Sales/Marketing:		Liberal Arts:		Information Sys.:		Professionals:		Tech./Scientific:	
Mgmt. Trainees:	Y	Marketing Pros.:	Y	Gen. Writing/Editing:	Y	Info. Mgmt.:	Y	Finance/Acct.:	Y	Engineers, Elec.:	Y
Experienced Mgmt.:	Y	Retail Sales:		Tech. Writing:	Y	Software Dev.:	Y	Law:	Y	Engineers, Other:	Y
Int'l Business:	Y	Comm./Industrial:	Y	Graphic Arts/Photog.:	Y	Hardware Dev.:		HR/Other:	Y	Health/Lab:	
MBA Grads:	Y	Sales Trainees:		Music:		Consulting/Other:		Training:	Y	Science/Research:	
		Advertising Pros.:	Y	Broadcasting:				Health Care:		Petroleum/Chem.:	
				Other:				Consulting:		Math/Other:	

TYPES OF BUSINESS:

Utilities-Electricity
Wind Generation
Contract Power Generation

BRANDS/DIVISIONS/AFFILIATES:

Indianapolis Power & Light
AES Wind Generation
AES Solar Energy LLC
AES Ballylumford Holdings Limited
China Investment Corporation
AES Eletropaulo
AES Kievoblenergo
DPL, Inc.

CONTACTS: *Note: Officers with more than one job title may be intentionally listed here more than once.*

Paul T. Hanrahan, CEO
Andres Gluski, COO/Exec. VP
Paul T. Hanrahan, Pres.
Victoria Harker, CFO/Exec. VP
Rita Trehan, VP-Human Resources & Internal Comm.
Elizabeth Hackenson, CIO/Sr. VP
Brian Miller, General Counsel/Exec. VP/Corp. Sec.
Gardner W. Walkup, VP-Strategy
Meghan Dotter, Dir.-External Comm.
Joel Abramson, VP-Investor Rel.
Andrew M. Vesey, Exec. VP/Pres., Latin America & Africa
Ned Hall, Exec. VP/Pres., North America
Richard Santoroski, Exec. VP/Chief Risk Officer
Philip Odeen, Chmn.
Andres Gluski, Interim Pres., Asia, Europe & Middle East

Phone: 703-522-1315	**Fax:** 703-528-4510
Toll-Free:	
Address: 4300 Wilson Blvd., Arlington, VA 22203 US	

GROWTH PLANS/SPECIAL FEATURES:

The AES Corporation, through its subsidiaries, operates in the global power industry in 28 countries on five continents. It has a total capacity of roughly 40,500 Megawatts (MW) and over 2,000 MW under construction in six countries. AES operates two primary business lines: power generation and utilities. Utilities operations (55% of the firm's revenues) consist of 14 distribution companies in seven countries that serve over 12 million customers. The segment has integrated utilities in the U.S. through Indianapolis Power & Light and in Cameroon through Sonel; additionally, it has distribution companies in Brazil through AES Eletropaulo and AES Sul; in Chile through AES Gener; and in the Ukraine through AES Kievoblenergo and AES Rivneenergo. AES's generation business (45% of revenues) generates approximately 34,100 MW and sells electricity to wholesale customers through 100 power generation plants in 25 countries. It also has roughly 1,700 MW of capacity under construction in four countries. AES is expanding its wind, solar and other alternative energy operations. The firm's wind power business, AES Wind Generation, has 20 facilities in five countries with a total capacity of roughly 1,800 MW. Joint venture AES Solar Energy LLC (with Riverstone Holdings, LLC) has nine plants in Greece, Spain and France with an output capacity of 37 MW of solar power. In August 2010, subsidiary AES Ballylumford Holdings Limited acquired North Ireland-based Premier Power Limited. In October 2010, AES sold its 55% interest in Ras Laffan to partner Qatar Electricity and Water Company. In April 2011, the firm agreed to acquire DPL, Inc., the parent company of Dayton Power & Light Company, in a transaction worth roughly $4.7 billion.

FINANCIALS: **Sales and profits are in thousands of dollars—add 000 to get the full amount. 2010 Note: Financial information for 2010 was not available for all companies at press time.**

2010 Sales: $16,647,000	2010 Profits: $9,000	**U.S. Stock Ticker: AES**
2009 Sales: $13,954,000	2009 Profits: $658,000	**Int'l Ticker:**
2008 Sales: $15,197,000	2008 Profits: $1,234,000	Int'l Exchange:
2007 Sales: $13,014,000	2007 Profits: $-95,000	Employees: 29,000 Fiscal Year Ends: 12/31
2006 Sales: $11,509,000	2006 Profits: $247,000	Parent Company:

SALARIES/BENEFITS:

Pension Plan: Y	ESOP Stock Plan:	Profit Sharing: Y	Top Exec. Salary: $1,115,400	Bonus: $3,950,000
Savings Plan: Y	Stock Purch. Plan:		Second Exec. Salary: $720,000	Bonus: $1,689,160

OTHER THOUGHTS:

Apparent Women Officers or Directors: 5
Hot Spot for Advancement for Women/Minorities: Y

LOCATIONS: ("Y" = Yes)

West:	Southwest:	Midwest:	Southeast:	Northeast:	International:
Y	Y	Y	Y	Y	Y

AFFILIATED COMPUTER SERVICES INC

www.acs-inc.com

Industry Group Code: 541513

Management:		Sales/Marketing:		Liberal Arts:		Information Sys.:		Professionals:		Tech./Scientific:	
Mgmt. Trainees:	Y	Marketing Pros.:	Y	Gen. Writing/Editing:	Y	Info. Mgmt.:	Y	Finance/Acct.:	Y	Engineers, Elec.:	Y
Experienced Mgmt.:	Y	Retail Sales:		Tech. Writing:	Y	Software Dev.:	Y	Law:	Y	Engineers, Other:	
Int'l Business:	Y	Comm./Industrial:	Y	Graphic Arts/Photog.:	Y	Hardware Dev.:	Y	HR/Other:	Y	Health/Lab:	
MBA Grads:	Y	Sales Trainees:		Music:		Consulting/Other:	Y	Training:	Y	Science/Research:	
		Advertising Pros.:		Broadcasting:				Health Care:		Petroleum/Chem.:	
				Other:	Y			Consulting:	Y	Math/Other:	

TYPES OF BUSINESS:

IT Consulting
Loan Processing Services
Systems Integration
Human Resources Services
IT Outsourcing
Business Process Outsourcing

BRANDS/DIVISIONS/AFFILIATES:

Xerox Corp
Buck Consultants
e-Services Group International
Anix
Pharm/DUR Inc.
ExcellerateHRO, LLP
TMS Health
Spur Information Solutions

CONTACTS: *Note: Officers with more than one job title may be intentionally listed here more than once.*

Lynn Blodgett, CEO
Tom Blodgett, COO
Lynn Blodgett, Pres.
Kevin Kyser, CFO/Exec. VP
Tracy Tolbert, Exec. VP-Sales
Lora Villarreal, Chief People Officer/Exec. VP
Chris Leach, Chief Info. Security Officer
Tom Blodgett, Exec. VP-Commercial Oper.
John Rexford, Exec. VP-Corp. Dev.
Rebecca Scholl, Sr. VP-Corp. Mktg. & Comm.
Ann Vezina, Exec. VP/Pres., Enterprise Solutions & Svcs.
Connie Harvey, Exec. VP/Pres., Healthcare Payer & Insurance
Derrell James, Exec. VP/Pres., IT Outsourcing Solutions
David Amoriell, Exec. VP/Pres., Transportation Solutions

Phone: 214-841-6111 **Fax:** 214-823-9369
Toll-Free:
Address: 2828 N. Haskell Ave., Dallas, TX 75204 US

GROWTH PLANS/SPECIAL FEATURES:

Affiliated Computer Services, Inc. (ACS), a subsidiary of Xerox Corp., provides business process outsourcing and IT services to commercial and government clients. The company operates in two segments: commercial and government. Through the commercial segment, ACS provides business process outsourcing, systems integration services and consulting services to a variety of commercial clients. The commercial segment is focused on markets including communications and consumer goods; healthcare; higher education; transportation; consumer goods and services; and financial services. Its solutions for the commercial segment include IT services; human capital management; finance and accounting; customer care; transaction processing; payment services; and commercial education. Services in the government market include technology and business process based services with a focus on transaction processing, child support payment processing, electronic toll collection, traffic violations processing, program management services (such as Medicaid fiscal agent services) and student loan processing and servicing. ACS serves customers in over 100 countries from more than 425 offices worldwide. Through subsidiary Buck Consultants the firm provides human resources consulting services to corporations. In 2010, it acquired several other IT and consulting services companies, including ExcellerateHRO, LLP in August; TMS Health in October; and Spur Information Solutions in November. In February 2010, Xerox Corporation completed its acquisition of ACS for $6.4 billion.

FINANCIALS: **Sales and profits are in thousands of dollars—add 000 to get the full amount. 2010 Note: Financial information for 2010 was not available for all companies at press time.**

2010 Sales: $	2010 Profits: $	**U.S. Stock Ticker: Subsidiary**
2009 Sales: $6,523,164	2009 Profits: $349,943	**Int'l Ticker:**
2008 Sales: $6,160,550	2008 Profits: $329,010	Int'l Exchange:
2007 Sales: $5,772,479	2007 Profits: $253,090	Employees: 78,000 Fiscal Year Ends: 6/30
2006 Sales: $5,353,661	2006 Profits: $358,806	Parent Company: XEROX CORP

SALARIES/BENEFITS:

Pension Plan:	ESOP Stock Plan:	Profit Sharing:	Top Exec. Salary: $1,013,491	Bonus: $1,228,555
Savings Plan: Y	Stock Purch. Plan:		Second Exec. Salary: $845,769	Bonus: $821,100

OTHER THOUGHTS:

Apparent Women Officers or Directors: 4
Hot Spot for Advancement for Women/Minorities: Y

LOCATIONS: ("Y" = Yes)

West:	Southwest:	Midwest:	Southeast:	Northeast:	International:
Y	Y	Y	Y	Y	Y

AFLAC INC

www.aflac.com

Industry Group Code: 524114

Management:		Sales/Marketing:		Liberal Arts:		Information Sys.:		Professionals:		Tech./Scientific:	
Mgmt. Trainees:	Y	Marketing Pros.:	Y	Gen. Writing/Editing:	Y	Info. Mgmt.:	Y	Finance/Acct.:	Y	Engineers, Elec.:	
Experienced Mgmt.:	Y	Retail Sales:		Tech. Writing:	Y	Software Dev.:	Y	Law:	Y	Engineers, Other:	
Int'l Business:	Y	Comm./Industrial:	Y	Graphic Arts/Photog.:	Y	Hardware Dev.:		HR/Other:	Y	Health/Lab:	
MBA Grads:	Y	Sales Trainees:	Y	Music:		Consulting/Other:		Training:	Y	Science/Research:	
		Advertising Pros.:	Y	Broadcasting:				Health Care:	Y	Petroleum/Chem.:	
				Other:	Y			Consulting:		Math/Other:	

TYPES OF BUSINESS:

Insurance-Supplemental & Specialty Health
Life Insurance
Cancer Insurance
Long-Term Care Insurance
Accident & Disability Insurance
Vision Plans
Dental Plans

BRANDS/DIVISIONS/AFFILIATES:

AFLAC Japan
AFLAC U.S.
American Family Life Assurance Company of Columbus
EVER
Continental American Insurance Company (CAIC)

CONTACTS: *Note: Officers with more than one job title may be intentionally listed here more than once.*

Daniel P. Amos, CEO
Kriss Cloninger III, Pres.
Kriss Cloninger III, CFO
Thomas R. Giddens, Sr. VP/Dir.-Sales
Joseph E. Bohling, Chief Human Resources Officer/Sr. VP
Teresa L. White, Chief Admin. Officer/Exec. VP
Joey M. Loudermilk, General Counsel/Exec. VP/Corp. Sec.
Bob M. Ottman, Sr. VP-Strategic Transformation
Robin Y. Wilkey, Sr. VP-Investor Rel.
Ralph A. Rogers Jr., Sr. VP-Financial Svcs./Chief Acct. Officer
Ron Agypt, Sr. VP-Broker Sales
Paul S. Amos II, Pres./COO-Aflac U.S.
Audrey Boone Tillman, Exec. VP-Corp. Svcs.
Phillip J. Friou, Dir.-Gov't Rel./Sr. VP
Daniel P. Amos, Chmn.
Charles D. Lake II, Chmn.-Aflac Japan

Phone: 706-323-3431 **Fax:** 706-324-6330
Toll-Free: 800-235-2667
Address: 1932 Wynnton Rd., Columbus, GA 31999 US

GROWTH PLANS/SPECIAL FEATURES:

AFLAC, Inc. is a holding company whose principle subsidiary, AFLAC (American Family Life Assurance Company of Columbus), insures more than 50 million people worldwide. The subsidiary is a leading writer of supplemental insurance marketed to employers in the U.S., offering policies for payroll accounts through more than 70,000 licensed agents. AFLAC U.S. sells supplemental insurance products, including accident/disability plans, cancer plans, short-term disability plans, sickness and hospital indemnity plans, hospital intensive care plans, fixed-benefit dental plans, vision care plans, long-term care plans and life insurance products. In addition, AFLAC U.S. offers specified health event coverage for major medical crises such as heart attack and stroke. U.S. insurance products are designed to provide supplemental coverage to individuals who already have major medical or primary insurance coverage. Through Continental American Insurance Company (CAIC), AFLAC U.S. also markets and administers group projects. Another subsidiary, AFLAC Japan, is one of the largest foreign-based insurers in that country. AFLAC Japan's insurance products are designed to help consumers pay for medical and non-medical costs that are not reimbursed under Japan's national health insurance system. EVER, AFLAC Japan's stand-alone medical product, offers a basic level of hospitalization coverage with an affordable premium. AFLAC Japan also sells cancer plans, general medical indemnity plans, medical/sickness riders to its cancer plan, care plans, living benefit life plans, ordinary life insurance plans and annuities. AFLAC Japan accounts for about 75% of AFLAC's insurance earnings.

Employees are offered medical and dental insurance; disability coverage; life insurance; flexible spending accounts; an employee assistance program; a 401(k) plan; a stock purchase program; profit sharing; onsite childcare facilities; a health clinic; onsite fitness centers; health screenings; employee discount programs; and educational scholarships.

FINANCIALS: **Sales and profits are in thousands of dollars—add 000 to get the full amount. 2010 Note: Financial information for 2010 was not available for all companies at press time.**

2010 Sales: $20,732,000	2010 Profits: $2,344,000
2009 Sales: $18,254,000	2009 Profits: $1,497,000
2008 Sales: $16,554,000	2008 Profits: $1,254,000
2007 Sales: $15,393,000	2007 Profits: $1,634,000
2006 Sales: $14,616,000	2006 Profits: $1,483,000

U.S. Stock Ticker: AFL
Int'l Ticker:
Int'l Exchange:
Employees: 7,919 Fiscal Year Ends: 12/31
Parent Company:

SALARIES/BENEFITS:

Pension Plan:	ESOP Stock Plan:	Profit Sharing: Y	Top Exec. Salary: $4,048,361	Bonus: $4,048,361
Savings Plan: Y	Stock Purch. Plan: Y		Second Exec. Salary: $883,500	Bonus: $1,912,601

OTHER THOUGHTS:

Apparent Women Officers or Directors: 8
Hot Spot for Advancement for Women/Minorities: Y

LOCATIONS: ("Y" = Yes)

West:	Southwest:	Midwest:	Southeast:	Northeast:	International:
Y	Y	Y	Y	Y	Y

AGILENT TECHNOLOGIES INC

www.home.agilent.com

Industry Group Code: 3345

Management:		**Sales/Marketing:**		**Liberal Arts:**		**Information Sys.:**		**Professionals:**		**Tech./Scientific:**	
Mgmt. Trainees:	Y	Marketing Pros.:	Y	Gen. Writing/Editing:	Y	Info. Mgmt.:	Y	Finance/Acct.:	Y	Engineers, Elec.:	Y
Experienced Mgmt.:	Y	Retail Sales:		Tech. Writing:	Y	Software Dev.:	Y	Law:	Y	Engineers, Other:	
Int'l Business:	Y	Comm./Industrial:	Y	Graphic Arts/Photog.:	Y	Hardware Dev.:	Y	HR/Other:	Y	Health/Lab:	
MBA Grads:	Y	Sales Trainees:		Music:		Consulting/Other:	Y	Training:	Y	Science/Research:	Y
		Advertising Pros.:	Y	Broadcasting:				Health Care:		Petroleum/Chem.:	
				Other:				Consulting:		Math/Other:	Y

TYPES OF BUSINESS:

Test Equipment
Communications Test Equipment
Integrated Circuits Test Equipment
Bioanalysis Equipment
Image Sensors
Bioinstrumentation
Software Products
Informatics Products

BRANDS/DIVISIONS/AFFILIATES:

Agilent Research Laboratories
Varian, Inc.
A2 Technologies
Lab901
BIOCIUS Life Sciences, Inc.

CONTACTS:

Note: Officers with more than one job title may be intentionally listed here more than once.

William P. Sullivan, CEO
William P. Sullivan, Pres.
Didier Hirsch, CFO/Sr. VP
Jean M. Halloran, Sr. VP-Human Resources
Darlene J.S. Solomon, CTO
Marie Oh Huber, General Counsel/Sec./Sr. VP
Sheila Barr Robertson, VP-Corp. Dev. & Strategy
Amy Flores, Mgr.-Public Rel.
Alicia Rodriguez, VP-Investor Rel.
Hillard C. Terry III, Treas./VP
Ron Nersesian, Sr. VP/Pres., Electronic Measurement Group
Mike McMullen, Sr. VP/Pres., Chemical Analysis Group
Nick Roelofs, Sr. VP/Pres., Life Sciences Solutions
Rick Burdsall, Chief Infrastructure Officer
James G. Cullen, Chmn.

Phone: 408-345-8886 **Fax:** 408-345-8474
Toll-Free: 877-424-4536
Address: 5301 Stevens Creek Blvd., Santa Clara, CA 95051 US

GROWTH PLANS/SPECIAL FEATURES:

Agilent Technologies, Inc. is a measurement technology company with three business segments: electronic measurement, chemical analysis and life sciences. The electronic measurement business provides electronic measurement instruments and systems, software design tools and related services for the design, development, manufacture, installation, deployment and operation of electronics equipment and microscopy products. This business primarily serves customers in the communications and electronics industries. The chemical analysis segment provides instruments, software, consumables and services for substance identification, quantification and analysis to customers in the petrochemical, environmental, forensics and food safety industries. Its main product categories include gas chromatography, mass spectrometry, spectroscopy, vacuum technology, consumables and services. The life sciences business, which serves the pharmaceutical, biotech, academic and government, bio-agriculture and food safety industries, provides liquid chromatography; mass spectrometry; microarrays; Polymerase Chain Reaction (PCR) instrumentation; bioreagents; electrophoresis; laboratory automation and robotics; software and informatics; Nuclear Magnetic Resonance (NMR) and Magnetic Resonance Imaging (MRI) systems; and related services. Subsidiary Agilent Research Laboratories is the firm's central research arm, with offices in California, China, Belgium and the U.K. In February 2010, Agilent agreed to sell its network solutions business to JDSU; and sold Hycor Biomedical, Inc. to Linden LLC. In May 2010, the company acquired Varian, Inc., a scientific equipment manufacturer. In October 2010, the firm opened a life science instruments plant in Singapore. In November 2010, Agilent acquired certain assets from Signametrics related to PXI, VXI, PCI and USB digital multimeters. In February 2011, the firm acquired A2 Technologies, a Fourier transform infrared technology company; and Lab901, a U.K.-based electrophoresis equipment firm. In March 2011, the company acquired BIOCIUS Life Sciences, Inc., a mass spectrometry platform firm.

Agilent offers its employees medical, dental, vision, life and disability plans; an employee assistance plan; onsite fitness centers and vaccinations; and recreational sports leagues.

FINANCIALS:

Sales and profits are in thousands of dollars—add 000 to get the full amount. 2010 Note: Financial information for 2010 was not available for all companies at press time.

2010 Sales: $5,444,000 — 2010 Profits: $684,000
2009 Sales: $4,481,000 — 2009 Profits: $-31,000
2008 Sales: $5,774,000 — 2008 Profits: $693,000
2007 Sales: $5,420,000 — 2007 Profits: $638,000
2006 Sales: $4,973,000 — 2006 Profits: $3,307,000

U.S. Stock Ticker: A
Int'l Ticker:
Int'l Exchange:
Employees: 18,500 Fiscal Year Ends: 10/31
Parent Company:

SALARIES/BENEFITS:

Pension Plan: Y | ESOP Stock Plan: | Profit Sharing: | Top Exec. Salary: $990,000 | Bonus: $2,535,586
Savings Plan: Y | Stock Purch. Plan: Y | Second Exec. Salary: $497,087 | Bonus: $712,505

OTHER THOUGHTS:

Apparent Women Officers or Directors: 5
Hot Spot for Advancement for Women/Minorities: Y

LOCATIONS: ("Y" = Yes)

West:	Southwest:	Midwest:	Southeast:	Northeast:	International:
Y	Y	Y		Y	Y

AIR PRODUCTS & CHEMICALS INC

www.airproducts.com

Industry Group Code: 325120

Management:		Sales/Marketing:		Liberal Arts:		Information Sys.:		Professionals:		Tech./Scientific:	
Mgmt. Trainees:	Y	Marketing Pros.:	Y	Gen. Writing/Editing:	Y	Info. Mgmt.:	Y	Finance/Acct.:	Y	Engineers, Elec.:	Y
Experienced Mgmt.:	Y	Retail Sales:		Tech. Writing:	Y	Software Dev.:	Y	Law:	Y	Engineers, Other:	Y
Int'l Business:	Y	Comm./Industrial:	Y	Graphic Arts/Photog.:		Hardware Dev.:		HR/Other:	Y	Health/Lab:	
MBA Grads:	Y	Sales Trainees:		Music:		Consulting/Other:		Training:	Y	Science/Research:	Y
		Advertising Pros.:		Broadcasting:				Health Care:		Petroleum/Chem.:	Y
				Other:				Consulting:		Math/Other:	

TYPES OF BUSINESS:

Industrial Gases & Chemicals
Respiratory Therapy & Home Medical Equipment
Specialty Resins
Hydrogen Refinery
Natural Gas Liquefaction
Semiconductor Materials

BRANDS/DIVISIONS/AFFILIATES:

Air Products Asia
Air Products Europe
Air Products Japan
Hydrochlor

CONTACTS:

Note: Officers with more than one job title may be intentionally listed here more than once.

John McGlade, CEO
John McGlade, Pres.
Paul Huck, CFO/Sr. VP
Lynn Minella, Sr. VP-Human Resources
Richard Boocock, CIO/VP-Info. Systems
Montgomery Alger, CTO/VP
Deborah A. McCullough, VP-Global Eng.
John D. Stanley, General Counsel/Sr. VP
Joseph M. Pietrantonio, VP-Global Oper.
Lynn Minella, Sr. VP-Corp. Comm.
Simon Moore, Dir.-Investor Rel.
George G. Bitto, Treas./VP/Chief Risk Officer
M. Scott Crocco, Corp. Controller/VP
Robert D. Dixon, Sr. VP/Gen. Mgr.-Merchant Gases
Jeffry L. Byrne, VP/Gen. Mgr-Tonnage Gases
Mary T. Afflerbach, Chief Governance Officer/Corp. Sec.
John McGlade, Chmn.
Ivo Bols, VP/Gen. Mgr.-Merchant Gases Asia
John W. Marsland, Sr. VP-Supply Chain

Phone: 610-481-4911 | **Fax:** 610-481-5900
Toll-Free:
Address: 7201 Hamilton Blvd., Allentown, PA 18195-1501 US

GROWTH PLANS/SPECIAL FEATURES:

Air Products & Chemicals, Inc. serves global technology, energy, industrial and healthcare customers. Products and services include atmospheric gases; process and specialty gases; performance materials; and equipment and services. The company is one of the world's largest suppliers of hydrogen and helium and has built leading positions in growth markets such as semiconductor materials, refinery hydrogen, natural gas liquefaction and advanced coatings and adhesives. It operates in four divisions: merchant gases; tonnage gases; electronics and performance materials; and equipment and energy. The merchant gases segment sells industrial gases such as oxygen, nitrogen, argon, hydrogen and helium, as well as certain medical and specialty gases. It also includes healthcare products such as respiratory therapies, home medical equipment and infusion services, which are provided to patients in their homes, primarily in Europe. The tonnage gases segment provides hydrogen, carbon monoxide, nitrogen, oxygen and syngas, primarily to the petroleum refining, chemical and metallurgical industries worldwide. The electronics and performance materials division provides solutions to a broad range of global industries through chemical synthesis, analytical technology, process engineering and surface science. The equipment and energy segment designs and manufactures cryogenic and gas processing equipment for air separation; hydrocarbon recovery; and purification, natural gas liquefaction and helium distribution. The company has majority or wholly-owned foreign subsidiaries that operate in Canada, 17 European countries, 10 Asian countries and four Latin American countries. International subsidiaries include Air Products Asia; Air Products Europe and Air Products Japan. In January 2011, it established Hydrochlor, a joint venture with Linde Gas North America, to supply high-purity anhydrous hydrochloric acid.

The company offers its employees medical, dental and vision; a 401(k) plan; a profit sharing plan; an employee discount program; and fitness membership reimbursements.

FINANCIALS:

Sales and profits are in thousands of dollars—add 000 to get the full amount. 2010 Note: Financial information for 2010 was not available for all companies at press time.

2010 Sales: $9,026,000	2010 Profits: $1,029,000
2009 Sales: $8,256,000	2009 Profits: $631,000
2008 Sales: $10,415,000	2008 Profits: $910,000
2007 Sales: $9,148,000	2007 Profits: $1,036,000
2006 Sales: $7,885,000	2006 Profits: $723,400

U.S. Stock Ticker: APD
Int'l Ticker:
Int'l Exchange:
Employees: 18,300 Fiscal Year Ends: 9/30
Parent Company:

SALARIES/BENEFITS:

Pension Plan:	ESOP Stock Plan:	Profit Sharing: Y	Top Exec. Salary: $1,200,000	Bonus: $2,746,000
Savings Plan: Y	Stock Purch. Plan:		Second Exec. Salary: $650,000	Bonus: $946,000

OTHER THOUGHTS:

Apparent Women Officers or Directors: 10
Hot Spot for Advancement for Women/Minorities: Y

LOCATIONS: ("Y" = Yes)

West:	Southwest:	Midwest:	Southeast:	Northeast:	International:
Y	Y	Y	Y	Y	Y

ALASKA AIR GROUP INC

www.alaskaair.com

Industry Group Code: 481111

Management:		Sales/Marketing:		Liberal Arts:		Information Sys.:		Professionals:		Tech./Scientific:	
Mgmt. Trainees:		Marketing Pros.:	Y	Gen. Writing/Editing:	Y	Info. Mgmt.:	Y	Finance/Acct.:	Y	Engineers, Elec.:	
Experienced Mgmt.:	Y	Retail Sales:		Tech. Writing:	Y	Software Dev.:	Y	Law:	Y	Engineers, Other:	Y
Int'l Business:	Y	Comm./Industrial:	Y	Graphic Arts/Photog.:	Y	Hardware Dev.:		HR/Other:	Y	Health/Lab:	
MBA Grads:	Y	Sales Trainees:		Music:		Consulting/Other:		Training:	Y	Science/Research:	
		Advertising Pros.:	Y	Broadcasting:				Health Care:	Y	Petroleum/Chem.:	
				Other:	Y			Consulting:		Math/Other:	Y

TYPES OF BUSINESS:

Airlines
Air Cargo

BRANDS/DIVISIONS/AFFILIATES:

Horizon Air Industries Inc
Alaska Airlines, Inc.

CONTACTS: *Note: Officers with more than one job title may be intentionally listed here more than once.*

William S. Ayer, CEO
William S. Ayer, Pres.
Brandon S. Pedersen, CFO/ VP-Finance
Kelley J. Dobbs, VP-Human Resources & Labor Rel.
Keith Loveless, General Counsel/Corp. Sec./VP-Legal Affairs
Benito Minicucci, Exec. VP-Oper./COO-Alaska Airlines, Inc.
Keith Loveless, VP-Corp. Affairs
Shannon K. Alberts, Managing Dir.-Investor Rel.
John F. Schaefer, Jr., VP-Finance/Treas.
Thomas W. Nunn, VP-Safety
Wendy F. Jones, Chief Risk, Compliance & Ethics Officer
Bradley D. Tilden, Pres., Alaska Airlines, Inc.
Glenn S. Johnson, Pres., Horizon Air Industries, Inc.
William S. Ayer, Chmn.

Phone: 206-392-5040	**Fax:**
Toll-Free: 800-252-7522	
Address: 19300 International Blvd., Seattle, WA 98188 US	

GROWTH PLANS/SPECIAL FEATURES:

Alaska Air Group, Inc., through its operating subsidiaries Alaska Airlines, Inc. (Alaska) and Horizon Air Industries, Inc. (Horizon), provides passenger air service to more than 23 million passengers per year to over 90 destinations. The firm also provides freight and mail services, primarily to and within Alaska and on the West Coast. Alaska, founded in 1932, operates an all-jet fleet with an average passenger trip length of 1,232 miles. The subsidiary offers north/south service within the western U.S., Canada and Mexico, as well as passenger and dedicated cargo services to and within Alaska. It also provides long-haul east/west service to Hawaii and twelve cities in the mid-continental and eastern U.S., primarily from Seattle, where it has its largest concentration of departures. Alaska's leading airports are Seattle, Los Angeles, Anchorage and Portland. Its operating fleet consists of 114 jet aircraft. Horizon is a regional airline, operating turboprop and jet aircraft with an average passenger trip length of 359 miles. The subsidiary is one of the largest regional airlines in the Pacific Northwest and serves a number of cities in seven states, five cities in Canada and two cities in Mexico. Approximately 91% of Horizon's revenue passenger miles were flown domestically, primarily in Washington, Oregon, Idaho and California. The Canada market generates 8% of its revenue passenger miles, with Mexico generating the remaining 1%. Horizon's leading airports are Seattle, Portland, Boise and Spokane. Its operating fleet consists of 13 jets and 41 turboprop aircraft.

Both Alaska and Horizon airlines offer employee benefits such as flight privileges; personal time off; health coverage; a 401(k) plan; a profit sharing plan; and performance rewards.

FINANCIALS: **Sales and profits are in thousands of dollars—add 000 to get the full amount. 2010 Note: Financial information for 2010 was not available for all companies at press time.**

2010 Sales: $3,823,300	2010 Profits: $251,100	**U.S. Stock Ticker: ALK**
2009 Sales: $3,399,800	2009 Profits: $121,600	**Int'l Ticker:**
2008 Sales: $3,662,600	2008 Profits: $-135,900	Int'l Exchange:
2007 Sales: $3,506,000	2007 Profits: $125,000	Employees: 12,440 Fiscal Year Ends: 12/31
2006 Sales: $3,334,400	2006 Profits: $-52,600	Parent Company:

SALARIES/BENEFITS:

Pension Plan:	ESOP Stock Plan:	Profit Sharing: Y	Top Exec. Salary: $395,385	Bonus: $745,314
Savings Plan: Y	Stock Purch. Plan:		Second Exec. Salary: $370,961	Bonus: $594,627

OTHER THOUGHTS:

Apparent Women Officers or Directors: 6
Hot Spot for Advancement for Women/Minorities: Y

LOCATIONS: ("Y" = Yes)

West:	Southwest:	Midwest:	Southeast:	Northeast:	International:
Y	Y				Y

ALLERGAN INC

www.allergan.com

Industry Group Code: 325412

Management:		Sales/Marketing:		Liberal Arts:		Information Sys.:		Professionals:		Tech./Scientific:	
Mgmt. Trainees:	Y	Marketing Pros.:	Y	Gen. Writing/Editing:	Y	Info. Mgmt.:	Y	Finance/Acct.:	Y	Engineers, Elec.:	Y
Experienced Mgmt.:	Y	Retail Sales:		Tech. Writing:	Y	Software Dev.:	Y	Law:	Y	Engineers, Other:	Y
Int'l Business:	Y	Comm./Industrial:	Y	Graphic Arts/Photog.:	Y	Hardware Dev.:		HR/Other:	Y	Health/Lab:	Y
MBA Grads:	Y	Sales Trainees:		Music:		Consulting/Other:		Training:	Y	Science/Research:	Y
		Advertising Pros.:	Y	Broadcasting:				Health Care:	Y	Petroleum/Chem.:	Y
				Other:				Consulting:		Math/Other:	Y

TYPES OF BUSINESS:

Pharmaceutical Development
Eye Care Supplies
Dermatological Products
Neuromodulator Products
Obesity Intervention Products
Urologic Products
Medical Aesthetics

BRANDS/DIVISIONS/AFFILIATES:

Restasis
Lumigan
Optive
Latisse
Botox
Juvederm
Ozurdex
Serica Technologies, Inc.

CONTACTS:

Note: Officers with more than one job title may be intentionally listed here more than once.

David E.I. Pyott, CEO
David E.I. Pyott, Pres.
Jeffrey L. Edwards, CFO/Exec. VP-Finance
Scott D. Sherman, Exec. VP-Human Resources
Scott M. Whitcup, Chief Scientific Officer/Exec. VP-R&D
Raymond H. Diradoorian, Exec. VP-Global Tech. Oper.
Samuel J. Gesten, General Counsel/Exec. VP
Jeffrey L. Edwards, Exec. VP-Bus. Dev.
James F. Barlow, Corp. Controller/Sr. VP
David E.I. Pyott, Chmn.
Douglas S. Ingram, Exec. VP/Pres., EMEA

Phone: 714-246-4500	**Fax:** 714-246-6987
Toll-Free: 800-347-4500	
Address: 2525 DuPont Dr., Irvine, CA 92612 US	

GROWTH PLANS/SPECIAL FEATURES:

Allergan, Inc. is a technology-driven global health care company that develops and commercializes specialty pharmaceutical products, biologics and medical devices for the ophthalmic, neurological, medical aesthetics, medical dermatology, breast aesthetics, obesity intervention, urological and other specialty markets in more than 100 countries. The company focuses on treatments for chronic dry eye, glaucoma, retinal disease, psoriasis, acne, movement disorders, neuropathic pain and genitourinary diseases. The company operates in two segments: specialty pharmaceuticals and medical devices. The specialty pharmaceuticals segment includes eye care products, such as Restasis ophthalmic emulsion; Lumigan ophthalmic solution; Optive lubricant eye drops and the Refresh line of artificial tears; Botox, used in the treatment of neuromuscular disorders, pain management, the temporary improvement of wrinkles and for certain other therapeutic and aesthetic indications; skin care products, principally tazarotene products in cream and gel formulations for the treatment of acne, facial wrinkles and psoriasis, marketed under the name Tazorac; eyelash growth solution sold under the name Latisse; and urologics products, including Sanctura XR, a medication for overactive bladder. The medical devices segment includes breast implants for augmentation, revision and reconstructive surgery; obesity intervention products, including the Lap-Band, an adjustable gastric banding system, and the Orbera intragastric balloon system; and facial aesthetics products, including the Juvederm line of dermal filler products. In 2010, the company acquired Serica Technologies, Inc., a medical device company focused on the development of biodegradable silk-based scaffolds for use in tissue regeneration procedures. In October 2010, the FDA approved the use of Botox to treat adult patients that suffer from chronic migraines.

Employees are offered medical, vision and dental insurance; flexible spending accounts; life insurance; disability coverage; adoption assistance; education assistance; an employee assistance program; scholarship awards for employees' children; and group auto and home insurance.

FINANCIALS:

Sales and profits are in thousands of dollars—add 000 to get the full amount. 2010 Note: Financial information for 2010 was not available for all companies at press time.

2010 Sales: $4,819,600	2010 Profits: $ 600	**U.S. Stock Ticker: AGN**
2009 Sales: $4,447,600	2009 Profits: $621,300	**Int'l Ticker:**
2008 Sales: $4,339,700	2008 Profits: $578,600	Int'l Exchange:
2007 Sales: $3,879,000	2007 Profits: $499,300	Employees: 9,200 Fiscal Year Ends: 12/31
2006 Sales: $3,010,100	2006 Profits: $-127,400	Parent Company:

SALARIES/BENEFITS:

Pension Plan: Y	ESOP Stock Plan:	Profit Sharing:	Top Exec. Salary: $1,300,000	Bonus: $1,690,000
Savings Plan: Y	Stock Purch. Plan:		Second Exec. Salary: $673,176	Bonus: $519,500

OTHER THOUGHTS:

Apparent Women Officers or Directors: 2
Hot Spot for Advancement for Women/Minorities: Y

LOCATIONS: ("Y" = Yes)

West:	Southwest:	Midwest:	Southeast:	Northeast:	International:
Y	Y			Y	Y

ALLIANCE DATA SYSTEMS CORPORATION www.alliancedata.com

Industry Group Code: 5418

Management:		Sales/Marketing:		Liberal Arts:		Information Sys.:		Professionals:		Tech./Scientific:	
Mgmt. Trainees:	Y	Marketing Pros.:	Y	Gen. Writing/Editing:	Y	Info. Mgmt.:	Y	Finance/Acct.:	Y	Engineers, Elec.:	
Experienced Mgmt.:	Y	Retail Sales:		Tech. Writing:		Software Dev.:	Y	Law:	Y	Engineers, Other:	
Int'l Business:	Y	Comm./Industrial:	Y	Graphic Arts/Photog.:	Y	Hardware Dev.:		HR/Other:	Y	Health/Lab:	
MBA Grads:	Y	Sales Trainees:		Music:		Consulting/Other:		Training:	Y	Science/Research:	
		Advertising Pros.:	Y	Broadcasting:				Health Care:		Petroleum/Chem.:	
				Other:				Consulting:		Math/Other:	

TYPES OF BUSINESS:

Marketing Services
Credit Services
Transaction Services

BRANDS/DIVISIONS/AFFILIATES:

LoyaltyOne
AIR MILES
LoyaltyOne Consulting
Precima
COLLOQUY
Epsilon
World Financial Network National Bank
Direct Marketing Services

CONTACTS: *Note: Officers with more than one job title may be intentionally listed here more than once.*

Ed Heffernan, CEO
Ed Heffernan, Pres.
Charles Horn, CFO/Exec. VP
Michael D. Kubic, Chief Acct. Officer/Sr. VP/Corp. Controller
Bryan Pearson, Exec. VP/Pres., LoyaltyOne
Ivan Szeftel, Exec. VP/Pres., Retail Credit Svcs.
Bryan Kennedy, Exec. VP/Pres., Epsilon
Robert Minicucci, Chmn.

Phone: 214-494-3000	**Fax:**
Toll-Free:	
Address: 7500 Dallas Pkwy., Ste. 700, Plano, TX 75024 US	

GROWTH PLANS/SPECIAL FEATURES:

Alliance Data Systems Corporation (ADS) is a provider of data-driven and transaction-based marketing and customer loyalty services. It partners with clients to develop unique insight into consumer behavior, and then uses that insight to create and manage customized services that help its clients strengthen their relationship with their customers. The company operates in four segments: loyalty services, operating as LoyaltyOne; Epsilon marketing services; private label services; and private label credit. The loyalty services segment, which includes the Canadian AIR MILES Reward Program, provides loyalty marketing services, including consumer data, customer-centric retail strategies, direct-to-consumer marketing and loyalty consulting services. Other aspects of this segment include LoyaltyOne Consulting; Precima, a strategic analytics firm; Direct Antidote, a loyalty marketing agency; and COLLOQUY, a collection of resources pertaining to the global loyalty-marketing industry. The Epsilon marketing services provides integrated direct marketing solutions that combine database marketing technology and analytics with a broad range of direct marketing services through subsidiary Epsilon. The operations of the private label services segment include transaction processing, customer care and collections services for the company's private label and other retail credit card programs; the private label credit segment provides risk management solutions, account origination and funding services for the same programs. Its primary subsidiaries in this segment are World Financial Network National Bank and World Financial Capital Bank. ADS' client base includes companies in the retail, financial services, hospitality, telecommunications and healthcare markets. In July 2010, the firm acquired the Direct Marketing Services (DMS) division of Equifax, Inc. for $117 million.

The firm offers its employees medical, dental and vision insurance; a 401(k) plan; life insurance; disability coverage; auto and home insurance; backup dependent care; flexible spending accounts; an employee stock purchase program; tuition reimbursement; an employee assistance program; prepaid legal services; and adoption assistance.

FINANCIALS: **Sales and profits are in thousands of dollars—add 000 to get the full amount. 2010 Note: Financial information for 2010 was not available for all companies at press time.**

2010 Sales: $2,791,000	2010 Profits: $194,000	**U.S. Stock Ticker: ADS**
2009 Sales: $1,964,341	2009 Profits: $143,734	**Int'l Ticker:**
2008 Sales: $2,025,300	2008 Profits: $217,400	Int'l Exchange:
2007 Sales: $1,962,200	2007 Profits: $164,061	Employees: 7,600 Fiscal Year Ends: 12/31
2006 Sales: $1,998,742	2006 Profits: $189,605	Parent Company:

SALARIES/BENEFITS:

Pension Plan:	ESOP Stock Plan:	Profit Sharing:	Top Exec. Salary: $889,200	Bonus: $1,001,462
Savings Plan: Y	Stock Purch. Plan: Y		Second Exec. Salary: $719,615	Bonus: $850,000

OTHER THOUGHTS:

Apparent Women Officers or Directors:
Hot Spot for Advancement for Women/Minorities:

LOCATIONS: ("Y" = Yes)

West:	Southwest:	Midwest:	Southeast:	Northeast:	International:
Y	Y	Y		Y	Y

Sales, profits and employees may be estimates. Financial information, benefits and other data can change quickly and may vary from those stated here.

ALTRIA GROUP INC

www.altria.com

Industry Group Code: 3122

Management:		**Sales/Marketing:**		**Liberal Arts:**		**Information Sys.:**		**Professionals:**		**Tech./Scientific:**	
Mgmt. Trainees:	Y	Marketing Pros.:	Y	Gen. Writing/Editing:	Y	Info. Mgmt.:	Y	Finance/Acct.:	Y	Engineers, Elec.:	
Experienced Mgmt.:	Y	Retail Sales:		Tech. Writing:		Software Dev.:	Y	Law:	Y	Engineers, Other:	
Int'l Business:	Y	Comm./Industrial:	Y	Graphic Arts/Photog.:	Y	Hardware Dev.:		HR/Other:	Y	Health/Lab:	
MBA Grads:	Y	Sales Trainees:	Y	Music:		Consulting/Other:		Training:	Y	Science/Research:	
		Advertising Pros.:	Y	Broadcasting:				Health Care:		Petroleum/Chem.:	
				Other:				Consulting:		Math/Other:	

TYPES OF BUSINESS:

Tobacco Products
Wine
Financial Services

BRANDS/DIVISIONS/AFFILIATES:

Phillip Morris USA, Inc.
US Smokeless Tobacco Company
John Middleton Co
Ste. Michelle Wine Estates Ltd
Marlboro
Parliament
Copenhagen
Skoal

CONTACTS: *Note: Officers with more than one job title may be intentionally listed here more than once.*

Michael E. Szymanczyk, CEO
Howard A. Willard, III, CFO/Exec. VP
Craig A. Johnson, Exec. VP-Sales
Charles N. Whitaker, Sr. VP-Human Resources & Compliance
Jane Y. Lewis, Sr. VP-Tobacco Regulatory & Health Sciences
Joseph S. Amado, CIO/Sr. VP
John R. Nelson, Jr., CTO/Exec. VP
Denise F. Keane, General Counsel/Exec. VP
David R. Beran, Vice Chmn./Head-Bus. Oper.
Bruce A. Gates, Sr. VP-External Affairs
Clifford B. Fleet, VP-Investor Rel.
Theodor P. Baseler, Pres./CEO-St. Michelle Wine Estates Ltd.
Peter P. Paoli, Pres.,/CEO-U.S. Smokeless Tobacco Company
Craig G. Schwartz, Pres./CEO-John Middleton Co.
William F. Gifford, Pres./CEO-Philip Morris USA, Inc.
Michael E. Szymanczyk, Chmn.
Craig A. Johnson, Exec. VP-Dist.

Phone: 804-274-2200 **Fax:**

Toll-Free:

Address: 6601 West Broad St., Richmond, VA 23230 US

GROWTH PLANS/SPECIAL FEATURES:

Altria Group, Inc. is the parent company for several consumer goods firms, whose products include cigarettes, cigars, smokeless tobacco, wine and other beverages. The company operates in five segments: cigarettes, smokeless tobacco, cigars, wine and financial services. The cigarettes segment consists of Phillip Morris USA, Inc., one of the largest cigarette manufactures in the U.S. In addition to its market leading brand, Marlboro, it produces the Basic, L&M, Parliament and Virginia Slim brands. The smokeless tobacco segment, through U.S. Smokeless Tobacco Company LLC, markets moist smokeless tobacco products, including the brands Copenhagen, Skoal, Red Seal and Husky, as well as Marlboro snus, a spit-less smokeless product. Cigars are produced by John Middleton Company, which produces machine made cigars such as Prince Albert, Carter Hall, Middleton's and Kentucky Hall. Altria Group's wine unit consists of Ste. Michelle Wine Estates Ltd., one of the top wine producers in the U.S. It operates 11 wineries along the West coast: seven in Washington, three in California and one in Oregon. Its wines are marketed under the brands Chateau Ste. Michelle, Columbia Crest, Snoqualmie and Red Diamond, among others. The financial services unit consists of Phillip Morris Capital Corp., which manages a portfolio consisting primarily of leveraged and direct finance leases. Additionally, Altria Group holds a 27.3% interest in SABMiller plc, owner of the Miller Brewing Company and one of the largest brewers in the world.

The company offers its employees medical, dental, vision and life insurance; flexible spending accounts; cost-free generic prescriptions; orthodontic coverage; short- and long-term disability; a personal health care advocate; and employee assistant plan; a 401(k); a profit sharing plan; tuition assistance; adoption assistance; day care reimbursements; an employee discount program; and an employee stock purchase program.

FINANCIALS: **Sales and profits are in thousands of dollars—add 000 to get the full amount. 2010 Note: Financial information for 2010 was not available for all companies at press time.**

2010 Sales: $24,363,000	2010 Profits: $3,907,000	**U.S. Stock Ticker: MO**
2009 Sales: $23,556,000	2009 Profits: $3,208,000	**Int'l Ticker:**
2008 Sales: $19,356,000	2008 Profits: $4,930,000	Int'l Exchange:
2007 Sales: $73,801,000	2007 Profits: $9,786,000	Employees: 10,000 Fiscal Year Ends: 12/31
2006 Sales: $67,051,000	2006 Profits: $12,022,000	Parent Company:

SALARIES/BENEFITS:

Pension Plan:	ESOP Stock Plan: Y	Profit Sharing: Y	Top Exec. Salary: $1,283,333	Bonus: $3,000,000
Savings Plan: Y	Stock Purch. Plan:		Second Exec. Salary: $759,500	Bonus: $1,200,000

OTHER THOUGHTS:

Apparent Women Officers or Directors: 4
Hot Spot for Advancement for Women/Minorities: Y

LOCATIONS: ("Y" = Yes)

West:	Southwest:	Midwest:	Southeast:	Northeast:	International:
Y	Y	Y	Y	Y	Y

AMAZON.COM INC

www.amazon.com

Industry Group Code: 451211E

Management:		**Sales/Marketing:**		**Liberal Arts:**		**Information Sys.:**		**Professionals:**		**Tech./Scientific:**	
Mgmt. Trainees:	Y	Marketing Pros.:	Y	Gen. Writing/Editing:	Y	Info. Mgmt.:	Y	Finance/Acct.:	Y	Engineers, Elec.:	
Experienced Mgmt.:	Y	Retail Sales:	Y	Tech. Writing:	Y	Software Dev.:	Y	Law:	Y	Engineers, Other:	
Int'l Business:	Y	Comm./Industrial:		Graphic Arts/Photog.:	Y	Hardware Dev.:		HR/Other:	Y	Health/Lab:	
MBA Grads:	Y	Sales Trainees:	Y	Music:		Consulting/Other:		Training:	Y	Science/Research:	
		Advertising Pros.:	Y	Broadcasting:				Health Care:		Petroleum/Chem.:	
				Other:	Y			Consulting:		Math/Other:	

TYPES OF BUSINESS:

Online Retail
Online Books & Music Retail
Online Videos/DVDs Retail
Online Electronics Retail
Online Auctions
Online Household Goods Retail
Online Auto & Industrial Retail
E-Commerce Support & Hosting

BRANDS/DIVISIONS/AFFILIATES:

Amazon Marketplace
Merchants
IMDB.com
Amazon ElastiCache
Amazon Web Services LLC
Woot.com
MyHabit.com

CONTACTS: *Note: Officers with more than one job title may be intentionally listed here more than once.*

Jeffrey P. Bezos, CEO
Jeffrey P. Bezos, Pres.
Thomas J. Szkutak, CFO/Sr. VP
L. Michelle Wilson, General Counsel/Sr. VP/Sec.
Marc A. Onetto, Sr. VP-Worldwide Oper.
Jeffrey Blackburn, Sr. VP-Bus. Dev.
H. Brian Valentine, Sr. VP-eCommerce
Shelley L. Reynolds, Worldwide Controller/Principal Acct. Officer/VP
Sebastian J. Gunningham, Sr. VP-Seller Svcs.
Andrew Jassy, Sr. VP-Amazon Web Svcs.
Steven Kessel, Sr. VP-Worldwide Digital Media
Jeffrey A. Wilke, Sr. VP-North American Retail
Jeffrey P. Bezos, Chmn.
Diego Piacentini, Sr. VP-Int'l Retail

Phone: 206-266-1000 **Fax:** 206-622-2405
Toll-Free:
Address: 410 Terry Ave. N., Seattle, WA 98109-5210 US

GROWTH PLANS/SPECIAL FEATURES:

Amazon.com, Inc. is an Internet consumer-shopping site which offers millions of new, used, refurbished and collectible items in categories such as books, movies, music and games, electronics and computers, home and garden, toys, children's goods, grocery, apparel and jewelry, health and beauty, sports, outdoors, digital downloads, tools and auto and industrial. The company operates in two primary segments: North America and International. In line with this division, the firm operates several international web sites serving the U.K., Germany, Canada, Italy, Japan, China and France. Amazon also maintains fulfillment centers worldwide, which are operated through co-sourced and outsourced arrangements in certain countries. The Amazon Marketplace and Merchants programs allow third parties to integrate their products on Amazon web sites, as well as provide related fulfillment and advertising services to third-party merchants; allow customers to shop for products owned by third parties using Amazon's features and technologies; and allow customers to complete transactions that include multiple sellers in a single checkout process. The firm also offers services such as Amazon Web Services, co-branded credit cards and miscellaneous marketing and promotional offers, such as online advertising. The firm operates IMDB.com, an international movie database offering film reviews and other information; MyHabit.com, a fashion-centered, membership web site featuring various short-term sales; and Woot.com, which features discounted items that are each only available for one sales day. In 2011, Amazon.com agreed to open several new fulfillment facilities in Indiana and Tennessee. In August 2011, the firm acquired the publishing rights to the 4 Hour book series by Timothy Ferris; and Amazon Web Services LLC established new web service Amazon ElastiCache, which allows users to deploy, operate, and scale an in-memory cache for web applications that are running in the Amazon Web Services cloud.

Employee benefits include life, disability, medical, dental and vision insurance; flexible spending accounts; and several discount programs.

FINANCIALS: **Sales and profits are in thousands of dollars—add 000 to get the full amount. 2010 Note: Financial information for 2010 was not available for all companies at press time.**

2010 Sales: $34,204,000	2010 Profits: $1,152,000
2009 Sales: $24,509,000	2009 Profits: $902,000
2008 Sales: $19,166,000	2008 Profits: $645,000
2007 Sales: $14,835,000	2007 Profits: $476,000
2006 Sales: $10,711,000	2006 Profits: $190,000

U.S. Stock Ticker: AMZN
Int'l Ticker:
Int'l Exchange:
Employees: 33,700 Fiscal Year Ends: 12/31
Parent Company:

SALARIES/BENEFITS:

Pension Plan:	ESOP Stock Plan:	Profit Sharing:	Top Exec. Salary: $175,000	Bonus: $
Savings Plan: Y	Stock Purch. Plan: Y		Second Exec. Salary: $160,000	Bonus: $

OTHER THOUGHTS:

Apparent Women Officers or Directors: 4
Hot Spot for Advancement for Women/Minorities: Y

LOCATIONS: ("Y" = Yes)

West:	Southwest:	Midwest:	Southeast:	Northeast:	International:
Y	Y	Y		Y	Y

AMEDISYS INC

www.amedisys.com

Industry Group Code: 6216

Management:		Sales/Marketing:		Liberal Arts:		Information Sys.:		Professionals:		Tech./Scientific:	
Mgmt. Trainees:	Y	Marketing Pros.:	Y	Gen. Writing/Editing:	Y	Info. Mgmt.:	Y	Finance/Acct.:	Y	Engineers, Elec.:	
Experienced Mgmt.:	Y	Retail Sales:		Tech. Writing:	Y	Software Dev.:		Law:	Y	Engineers, Other:	
Int'l Business:		Comm./Industrial:	Y	Graphic Arts/Photog.:	Y	Hardware Dev.:		HR/Other:	Y	Health/Lab:	Y
MBA Grads:	Y	Sales Trainees:		Music:		Consulting/Other:		Training:	Y	Science/Research:	
		Advertising Pros.:		Broadcasting:				Health Care:	Y	Petroleum/Chem.:	
				Other:				Consulting:		Math/Other:	

TYPES OF BUSINESS:

Home Health Care
Home Health Care
Hospice Care

BRANDS/DIVISIONS/AFFILIATES:

Surgery Recovery @ Home
Heart @ Home
Diabetes @ Home
Rehab @ Home
Dysphagia @ Home
Chronic Kidney Disease @ Home
Balanced for Life
Beacon Hospice, Inc.

CONTACTS: *Note: Officers with more than one job title may be intentionally listed here more than once.*

William F. Borne, CEO
Michael D. Snow, COO
Dale E. Redman, CFO
Michael O. Fleming, Chief Medical Officer
G. Patrick Thompson, Jr., CIO
G. Patrick Thompson, Jr., Exec. VP-Admin.
David Bucey, General Counsel/Sr. VP/Corp. Sec.
T.A. Barfield, Chief Dev. Officer
Julie L. Lewis, VP-Gov't Rel. & Health Policy
Robert Yungk, Chief Strategy Officer
Patti Waller, Exec. VP-Clinical Quality
Jim Robinson, Exec. VP-Hospice Div.
Jeffrey Jeter, Chief Compliance Officer
William F. Borne, Chmn.

Phone: 225-292-2031 **Fax:** 225-295-9624
Toll-Free: 800-467-2662
Address: 5959 S. Sherwood Forest Blvd., Baton Rouge, LA 70816 US

GROWTH PLANS/SPECIAL FEATURES:

Amedisys, Inc. provides home health and hospice services in 45 U.S. states, Washington D.C. and Puerto Rico. The firm owns and operates approximately 486 Medicare-certified home health agencies and 67 Medicare-certified hospice agencies. The company also manages the operations of four Medicare-certified home health and two Medicare-certified hospice agencies. In total, Amedisys serves roughly 10 million patients per year. Approximately 86% of the firm's revenue is derived from Medicare payments. Amedisys' services include skilled nursing; home health aides; physical, occupational and speech therapy; medical social workers; oncology; and psychiatric services. In addition, the firm offers several at-home recovery and rehabilitation programs created to meet specific patient needs; these include the Heart @ Home cardiac program; Partners in Wound Care; COPD @ Home; Diabetes @ Home; Behavioral Health @ Home; Stroke Recovery @ Home; Wound Care-a Therapeutic Approach; Pain Management @ Home; Surgery Recovery @ Home; Rehab @ Home; Chronic Kidney Disease @ Home; Balanced for Life; and Dysphagia @ Home. In May 2011, Amedisys agreed to acquire Hackensack University Medical Center's hospice business. In June 2011, the firm acquired Beacon Hospice, Inc., a hospice firm with 23 locations in the northeastern U.S.

Amedisys offers employees benefits including a 401(k) plan; supplemental life, supplemental cancer, disability, medical, dental and vision insurance; eight paid holidays and other paid time off; flexible spending accounts; a stock purchase plan; tuition reimbursement; and an assistance program.

FINANCIALS: **Sales and profits are in thousands of dollars—add 000 to get the full amount. 2010 Note: Financial information for 2010 was not available for all companies at press time.**

2010 Sales: $1,634,319	2010 Profits: $193,510
2009 Sales: $1,513,459	2009 Profits: $230,748
2008 Sales: $1,187,415	2008 Profits: $86,682
2007 Sales: $697,934	2007 Profits: $65,113
2006 Sales: $541,148	2006 Profits: $38,255

U.S. Stock Ticker: AMED
Int'l Ticker:
Int'l Exchange:
Employees: 16,300 Fiscal Year Ends: 12/31
Parent Company:

SALARIES/BENEFITS:

Pension Plan:	ESOP Stock Plan:	Profit Sharing:	Top Exec. Salary: $750,000	Bonus: $
Savings Plan: Y	Stock Purch. Plan: Y		Second Exec. Salary: $461,154	Bonus: $

OTHER THOUGHTS:

Apparent Women Officers or Directors: 1
Hot Spot for Advancement for Women/Minorities: Y

LOCATIONS: ("Y" = Yes)

West:	Southwest:	Midwest:	Southeast:	Northeast:	International:
Y	Y	Y	Y	Y	

AMERCO

Industry Group Code: 532120

www.amerco.com

Management:		Sales/Marketing:		Liberal Arts:		Information Sys.:		Professionals:		Tech./Scientific:	
Mgmt. Trainees:	Y	Marketing Pros.:	Y	Gen. Writing/Editing:		Info. Mgmt.:	Y	Finance/Acct.:	Y	Engineers, Elec.:	
Experienced Mgmt.:	Y	Retail Sales:		Tech. Writing:		Software Dev.:		Law:	Y	Engineers, Other:	
Int'l Business:	Y	Comm./Industrial:	Y	Graphic Arts/Photog.:		Hardware Dev.:		HR/Other:	Y	Health/Lab:	
MBA Grads:	Y	Sales Trainees:	Y	Music:		Consulting/Other:		Training:		Science/Research:	
		Advertising Pros.:		Broadcasting:				Health Care:		Petroleum/Chem.:	
				Other:				Consulting:		Math/Other:	

TYPES OF BUSINESS:

Truck Rental & Leasing Services
Moving & Storage Services & Supplies
Property & Casualty Insurance
Life Insurance
Annuities
Self-Storage Properties

BRANDS/DIVISIONS/AFFILIATES:

U-Haul International, Inc.
Republic Western Insurance Company
Oxford Life Insurance Company
Amerco Real Estate Company
Safemove
Safetow
Safestor

CONTACTS: *Note: Officers with more than one job title may be intentionally listed here more than once.*

Edward J. Shoen, Pres.
Laurence J. De Respino, General Counsel
Jennifer Flachman, Dir.-Investor Rel.
Jason A. Berg, Principal Acct. Officer
Gary B. Horton, Treas.
Edward J. Shoen, CEO/Chmn.-U-Haul
Carlos Vizcarra, Pres., Amerco Real Estate Co.
John C. Taylor, Pres., U-Haul
Edward J. Shoen, Chmn.

Phone: 775-688-6300	**Fax:** 775-688-6338
Toll-Free:	
Address: 1325 Airmotive Way, Ste. 100, Reno, NV 89502 US	

GROWTH PLANS/SPECIAL FEATURES:

AMERCO is a holding company. The firm operates through subsidiaries U-Haul International, Inc.; Amerco Real Estate Company; Republic Western Insurance Company; and Oxford Life Insurance Company. Accordingly, the firm has three reportable business segments: moving and storage; property and casualty insurance; and life insurance. The moving and storage segment consists of U-Haul, with its rental equipment fleet of trucks, trailers and tow dollies being offered by approximately 14,900 independent dealers. It also provides furniture pads, utility dollies and hand trucks; sells a wide selection of other moving supplies; and offers protection packages for moving and storage. U-Haul owns more than 98,000 trucks, 77,000 trailers and 34,000 towing devices. The firm's Emove.com and Uhaul.com online reservation portals are significant drivers of U-Haul's rental transaction volume. The company also offers moving and storage protection packages such as Safemove and Safetow, providing moving and towing customers a damage waiver; cargo protection; and medical and life coverage. Additionally, Safestor protects storage customers from loss on their goods in storage. Amerco Real Estate Company markets commercial properties available for sale or lease. The property and casualty insurance business consists of Republic Western Insurance Company's business activities, which includes coverage for U-Haul customers, independent dealers, fleet owners and employees of AMERCO. The life insurance operating segment consists of Oxford Life Insurance Company, which offers annuities, credit life and disability, critical illness insurance, single premium whole life, group life and disability coverage as well as Medicare supplement insurance. Oxford also administers self-insured group health and dental plans for AMERCO.

Employees are offered medical, dental and vision insurance; life and AD&D insurance; disability coverage; a 401(k) plan; and an employee stock ownership plan.

FINANCIALS: **Sales and profits are in thousands of dollars—add 000 to get the full amount. 2010 Note: Financial information for 2010 was not available for all companies at press time.**

2010 Sales: $2,002,005	2010 Profits: $65,623	**U.S. Stock Ticker: UHAL**
2009 Sales: $1,992,266	2009 Profits: $13,410	**Int'l Ticker:**
2008 Sales: $2,049,174	2008 Profits: $67,784	Int'l Exchange:
2007 Sales: $2,069,298	2007 Profits: $90,553	Employees: 17,600 Fiscal Year Ends: 3/31
2006 Sales: $2,087,525	2006 Profits: $121,154	Parent Company:

SALARIES/BENEFITS:

Pension Plan:	ESOP Stock Plan: Y	Profit Sharing:	Top Exec. Salary: $675,004	Bonus: $
Savings Plan: Y	Stock Purch. Plan:		Second Exec. Salary: $623,077	Bonus: $

OTHER THOUGHTS:

Apparent Women Officers or Directors: 2
Hot Spot for Advancement for Women/Minorities:

LOCATIONS: ("Y" = Yes)

West:	Southwest:	Midwest:	Southeast:	Northeast:	International:
Y	Y	Y	Y	Y	Y

Sales, profits and employees may be estimates. Financial information, benefits and other data can change quickly and may vary from those stated here.

AMERICAN EXPRESS CO

www.americanexpress.com

Industry Group Code: 522210

Management:		**Sales/Marketing:**		**Liberal Arts:**		**Information Sys.:**		**Professionals:**		**Tech./Scientific:**	
Mgmt. Trainees:	Y	Marketing Pros.:	Y	Gen. Writing/Editing:	Y	Info. Mgmt.:	Y	Finance/Acct.:	Y	Engineers, Elec.:	
Experienced Mgmt.:	Y	Retail Sales:		Tech. Writing:		Software Dev.:	Y	Law:	Y	Engineers, Other:	
Int'l Business:	Y	Comm./Industrial:	Y	Graphic Arts/Photog.:	Y	Hardware Dev.:	Y	HR/Other:	Y	Health/Lab:	
MBA Grads:	Y	Sales Trainees:		Music:		Consulting/Other:		Training:	Y	Science/Research:	
		Advertising Pros.:	Y	Broadcasting:				Health Care:		Petroleum/Chem.:	
				Other:	Y			Consulting:		Math/Other:	

TYPES OF BUSINESS:

Credit Card Issuing
Travel-Related Services
Lending & Financing
Transaction Services
Bank Holding Company
International Banking Services
Expense Management
Magazine Publishing

BRANDS/DIVISIONS/AFFILIATES:

Accertify, Inc.
SafeKey
Food & Wine
Travel+Leisure
Departures
Travel Impressions
SkyGuide
American Express Travel Related Services Co

CONTACTS:

Note: Officers with more than one job title may be intentionally listed here more than once.

Kenneth I. Chenault, CEO
Daniel T. Henry, CFO/Exec. VP
John D. Hayes, Chief Mktg. Officer/Head-Global Advertising
L. Kevin Cox, Exec. VP-Human Resources
Stephen Squeri, CIO/Pres., Global Svcs.
Louise M. Parent, General Counsel/Exec. VP
Thomas Schick, Exec. VP-Corp. & External Affairs
Edward P. Gilligan, Vice Chmn.
Ahswini Gupta, Pres., Risk, Info. Mgmt. & Banking Group
Daniel H. Schulman, Pres., Enterprise Growth
William H. Glenn, Pres., Global Merchant Svcs.
Kenneth I. Chenault, Chmn.
Douglas E. Buckminster, Pres., Int'l Consumer & Small Bus. Svcs.

Phone: 212-640-2000 **Fax:** 212-640-0404
Toll-Free: 800-844-4450
Address: 200 Vesey St., World Financial Ctr., New York, NY 10285 US

GROWTH PLANS/SPECIAL FEATURES:

American Express Co. (AmEx), a bank holding company, is a leading global payments and travel firm. Its principal products are charge and credit payment card products and travel-related services. The firm primarily operates through subsidiary American Express Travel Related Services Company, Inc. AmEx's business is organized into four main segments: U.S. Card Services, International Card Services, Global Commercial Services and Global Network & Merchant Services. The U.S. Card Services segment operates through AmEx's U.S. banking subsidiaries, Centurion Bank and American Express Bank, FSB. The division provides a wide array of card products and services to consumers and small businesses in the U.S. The firm's International Card Services division offers these services in countries worldwide. The Global Commercial Services segment offers expense management services to firms and organizations worldwide. Its products and services include corporate purchasing cards, corporate cards, corporate meeting cards, buyer initiated payment programs and business travel accounts. The Global Network & Merchant Services division operates a global general-purpose charge and credit card network for both proprietary and issued cards; manages merchant services internationally, which includes signing merchants to accept cards and processing and settling card transactions for those merchants; and offers merchants point-of-sale, servicing/settlement and marketing/information products and services. The company has a wholesale travel business in the U.S. through subsidiary Travel Impressions. Another division, American Express Publishing, operates several magazines, including Food & Wine, SkyGuide, Black Ink, Departures and Travel+Leisure. In November 2010, AmEx acquired fraud prevention solution provider Accertify, Inc.; and introduced online fraud prevention solution SafeKey. In March 2011, the firm acquired marketing services group Loyalty Partner.

FINANCIALS:

Sales and profits are in thousands of dollars—add 000 to get the full amount. 2010 Note: Financial information for 2010 was not available for all companies at press time.

2010 Sales: $30,242,000 — 2010 Profits: $4,057,000
2009 Sales: $26,730,000 — 2009 Profits: $2,130,000
2008 Sales: $31,920,000 — 2008 Profits: $2,699,000
2007 Sales: $27,559,000 — 2007 Profits: $4,012,000
2006 Sales: $24,826,000 — 2006 Profits: $3,707,000

U.S. Stock Ticker: AXP
Int'l Ticker:
Int'l Exchange:
Employees: 61,000 Fiscal Year Ends: 12/31
Parent Company:

SALARIES/BENEFITS:

Pension Plan: | ESOP Stock Plan: | Profit Sharing: Y | Top Exec. Salary: $1,201,923 | Bonus: $10,450,000
Savings Plan: Y | Stock Purch. Plan: | Second Exec. Salary: $862,019 | Bonus: $5,612,500

OTHER THOUGHTS:

Apparent Women Officers or Directors: 4
Hot Spot for Advancement for Women/Minorities: Y

LOCATIONS: ("Y" = Yes)

West:	Southwest:	Midwest:	Southeast:	Northeast:	International:
Y	Y	Y	Y	Y	Y

AMERICAN POWER CONVERSION (APC)

www.apcc.com

Industry Group Code: 33591

Management:		Sales/Marketing:		Liberal Arts:		Information Sys.:		Professionals:		Tech./Scientific:	
Mgmt. Trainees:	Y	Marketing Pros.:	Y	Gen. Writing/Editing:	Y	Info. Mgmt.:	Y	Finance/Acct.:	Y	Engineers, Elec.:	Y
Experienced Mgmt.:	Y	Retail Sales:		Tech. Writing:	Y	Software Dev.:	Y	Law:	Y	Engineers, Other:	Y
Int'l Business:	Y	Comm./Industrial:	Y	Graphic Arts/Photog.:	Y	Hardware Dev.:	Y	HR/Other:	Y	Health/Lab:	
MBA Grads:	Y	Sales Trainees:	Y	Music:		Consulting/Other:		Training:	Y	Science/Research:	
		Advertising Pros.:	Y	Broadcasting:				Health Care:		Petroleum/Chem.:	
				Other:				Consulting:		Math/Other:	

TYPES OF BUSINESS:

Back-Up Power Supplies
Power Protection & Management Products
Consulting Services
PC Accessories
Power Management Software
Fuel Cell-Based Power Backup

BRANDS/DIVISIONS/AFFILIATES:

Schneider Electric SA
InfraStruXure
Fuel Cell Extended Run (FCXR)

CONTACTS: *Note: Officers with more than one job title may be intentionally listed here more than once.*

Jean-Pascal Tricoire, CEO
Emmanuel Babeau, Exec. VP-Finance

Phone:	**Fax:**
Toll-Free: 800-788-2208	
Address: 132 Fairgrounds Rd., West Kingston, RI 02892 US	

GROWTH PLANS/SPECIAL FEATURES:

American Power Conversion (APC), a subsidiary of Schneider Electric SA, designs, develops, manufactures and markets power protection and management solutions for computer, communications and electronic applications worldwide. The company's products include uninterruptible power supply products, commonly known as UPS; electrical surge protection devices; power distribution products; precision cooling equipment; power management software and accessories; racks and enclosures; and various desktop and notebook personal computer accessories. These products are primarily used with sensitive electronic devices which rely on electric utility power, such as home electronics, PCs, high-performance computer workstations, servers, networking equipment, communications equipment, Internet equipment, data centers, mainframe computers and facilities. APC's UPS products regulate the flow of utility power to the protected equipment and provide seamless back-up power during power interruptions. Back-up power lasts for enough time to continue computer operations, conduct an orderly shutdown, preserve data, work through short power outages or, in some cases, continue operating for several hours or longer. In addition, the firm's Fuel Cell Extended Run (FCXR) product provides hydrogen-based power backup for the firm's InfraStruXure power, cooling, environmental monitoring and management data center for modular and mobile configurations. The company's security and environmental appliances and accessories protect against environmental or human threats and monitor valuable systems with sensors, cameras and accessories. APC's precision cooling equipment regulates temperature and humidity. Lastly, the company provides power management software, consulting services and notebook and PC accessories. In mid 2010, the company formed a new data center software business. The data center software business team will be responsible for software creation and development; sales; service; and marketing programs.

Employees are offered comprehensive health and dental coverage; short- and long-term disability; flexible spending accounts; life insurance; tuition assistance; a relocation program; leaves of absence; holidays; an employee share plan; and a 401(k) plan.

FINANCIALS: **Sales and profits are in thousands of dollars—add 000 to get the full amount. 2010 Note: Financial information for 2010 was not available for all companies at press time.**

2010 Sales: $	2010 Profits: $	**U.S. Stock Ticker: Subsidiary**
2009 Sales: $	2009 Profits: $	**Int'l Ticker:**
2008 Sales: $	2008 Profits: $	Int'l Exchange:
2007 Sales: $	2007 Profits: $	Employees: 11,390 Fiscal Year Ends: 12/31
2006 Sales: $	2006 Profits: $	Parent Company: SCHNEIDER ELECTRIC SA

SALARIES/BENEFITS:

Pension Plan:	ESOP Stock Plan:	Profit Sharing:	Top Exec. Salary: $	Bonus: $230,019
Savings Plan: Y	Stock Purch. Plan: Y		Second Exec. Salary: $	Bonus: $

OTHER THOUGHTS:

Apparent Women Officers or Directors: 1
Hot Spot for Advancement for Women/Minorities:

LOCATIONS: ("Y" = Yes)

West:	Southwest:	Midwest:	Southeast:	Northeast:	International:
	Y	Y	Y	Y	Y

Sales, profits and employees may be estimates. Financial information, benefits and other data can change quickly and may vary from those stated here.

AMERIGROUP CORPORATION

www.amerigroupcorp.com

Industry Group Code: 524114

Management:		Sales/Marketing:		Liberal Arts:		Information Sys.:		Professionals:		Tech./Scientific:	
Mgmt. Trainees:	Y	Marketing Pros.:	Y	Gen. Writing/Editing:	Y	Info. Mgmt.:	Y	Finance/Acct.:	Y	Engineers, Elec.:	
Experienced Mgmt.:	Y	Retail Sales:		Tech. Writing:	Y	Software Dev.:	Y	Law:	Y	Engineers, Other:	
Int'l Business:		Comm./Industrial:		Graphic Arts/Photog.:		Hardware Dev.:	Y	HR/Other:	Y	Health/Lab:	Y
MBA Grads:	Y	Sales Trainees:		Music:		Consulting/Other:		Training:	Y	Science/Research:	
		Advertising Pros.:		Broadcasting:				Health Care:	Y	Petroleum/Chem.:	
				Other:	Y			Consulting:		Math/Other:	

TYPES OF BUSINESS:

Managed Health Care

BRANDS/DIVISIONS/AFFILIATES:

West Regional Service Center

CONTACTS:

Note: Officers with more than one job title may be intentionally listed here more than once.

James G. Carlson, CEO
Richard C. Zoretic, COO/Exec. VP
James G. Carlson, Pres.
James W. Truess, CFO/Exec. VP
Linda Whitley-Taylor, Exec. VP-Human Resources
Mary McCluskey, Chief Medical Officer/Exec. VP
Leon A. Root, Jr., CIO/Exec. VP
Nicholas J. Pace, General Counsel/Exec. VP/Sec.
Tara Wall, Sr. VP-Comm.
Julie Loftus Trudell, Sr. VP-Investor Rel.
Margaret M. Roomsburg, Chief Acct. Officer/Sr. VP
John E. Little, Exec. VP-External Rel.
James G. Carlson, Chmn.

Phone: 757-490-6900	**Fax:** 757-222-2330
Toll-Free: 800-600-4441	
Address: 4425 Corporation Ln., Virginia Beach, VA 23462 US	

GROWTH PLANS/SPECIAL FEATURES:

AMERIGROUP Corporation is a managed health care company focused on serving people who receive health care benefits through publicly sponsored programs, including Medicaid, Medicare Advantage, Family Care and the Children's Health Insurance Program (CHIP). Since the company does not offer Medicare or commercial products, people served by AMERIGROUP are generally younger, tend to access health care in an inefficient manner and have a greater percentage of medical expenses related to obstetrics, diabetes and circulatory and respiratory conditions. The firm reduces costs for families and state governments by combining social and behavioral health services to help members obtain health care. AMERIGROUP's provider networks include approximately 110,000 physicians, including primary care physicians, specialists and ancillary providers, and approximately 700 hospitals across all of its markets. The company currently enrolls 1.93 million members in Texas, Florida, Georgia, Ohio, New Jersey, New York, Maryland, Nevada, New Mexico, Tennessee and Virginia. In April 2011, AMERIGROUP agreed to open the West Regional Service Center in Houston, Texas.

Employees are offered medical, dental and vision insurance; life insurance; disability coverage; a 401(k) plan; an employee stock purchase program; flexible spending accounts; a health savings account; adoption assistance; educational reimbursement; and employee discounts.

FINANCIALS:

Sales and profits are in thousands of dollars—add 000 to get the full amount. 2010 Note: Financial information for 2010 was not available for all companies at press time.

2010 Sales: $5,806,301	2010 Profits: $273,371	**U.S. Stock Ticker: AGP**
2009 Sales: $5,188,070	2009 Profits: $149,279	**Int'l Ticker:**
2008 Sales: $4,437,742	2008 Profits: $-56,606	Int'l Exchange:
2007 Sales: $3,908,774	2007 Profits: $112,227	Employees: 4,500 Fiscal Year Ends: 12/31
2006 Sales: $2,835,089	2006 Profits: $107,106	Parent Company:

SALARIES/BENEFITS:

Pension Plan:	ESOP Stock Plan:	Profit Sharing:	Top Exec. Salary: $789,615	Bonus: $3,809,584
Savings Plan: Y	Stock Purch. Plan: Y		Second Exec. Salary: $535,962	Bonus: $1,505,000

OTHER THOUGHTS:

Apparent Women Officers or Directors: 7
Hot Spot for Advancement for Women/Minorities: Y

LOCATIONS: ("Y" = Yes)

West:	Southwest:	Midwest:	Southeast:	Northeast:	International:
Y	Y	Y	Y	Y	

AMERISOURCEBERGEN CORP

www.amerisourcebergen.com

Industry Group Code: 424210

Management:		Sales/Marketing:		Liberal Arts:		Information Sys.:		Professionals:		Tech./Scientific:	
Mgmt. Trainees:	Y	Marketing Pros.:	Y	Gen. Writing/Editing:	Y	Info. Mgmt.:	Y	Finance/Acct.:	Y	Engineers, Elec.:	
Experienced Mgmt.:	Y	Retail Sales:		Tech. Writing:	Y	Software Dev.:	Y	Law:	Y	Engineers, Other:	
Int'l Business:	Y	Comm./Industrial:	Y	Graphic Arts/Photog.:	Y	Hardware Dev.:		HR/Other:	Y	Health/Lab:	
MBA Grads:	Y	Sales Trainees:	Y	Music:		Consulting/Other:		Training:	Y	Science/Research:	
		Advertising Pros.:	Y	Broadcasting:				Health Care:		Petroleum/Chem.:	
				Other:				Consulting:		Math/Other:	

TYPES OF BUSINESS:

Drug Distribution
Pharmacy Management & Consulting Services
Packaging Solutions
Information Technology
Healthcare Equipment

BRANDS/DIVISIONS/AFFILIATES:

AmerisourceBergen Drug Corporation
AmerisourceBergen Specialty Group
AmerisourceBergen Packaging Group
American Health Packaging
Anderson Packaging
Brecon Pharmaceutical Ltd.
IntrinsiQ, LLC.

CONTACTS: *Note: Officers with more than one job title may be intentionally listed here more than once.*

Steven H. Collis, CEO
R. David Yost, Pres.
Michael D. DiCandilo, CFO/Exec. VP
Jerry Cline, Sr. VP-Mktg. & Retail Sales
June Barry, Sr. VP-Human Resources
Thomas H. Murphy, CIO/Sr. VP
John G. Chou, General Counsel/Sr. VP/Sec.
David M. Senior, Sr. VP-Strategy & Corp. Dev.
Vicki L. Bausinger, Dir.-Shareholder Rel.
Tim G. Guttman, Corp. Controller/VP
David W. Neu, Pres., AmerisourceBergen Drug Corp./Sr. VP
J.F. Quinn, VP/Treas.
James Frary, Pres., AmerisourceBergen Specialty Group/Sr. VP
Richard C. Gozon, Chmn.
Antonio Pera, Sr. VP-Supply Chain Mgmt.

Phone: 610-727-7000 **Fax:** 610-727-3600
Toll-Free: 800-829-3132
Address: 1300 Morris Dr., Chesterbrook, PA 19087 US

GROWTH PLANS/SPECIAL FEATURES:

AmerisourceBergen Corp. is one of the largest wholesale distributors of pharmaceutical products and services to a wide variety of healthcare providers and pharmacies. The firm offers brand name and generic pharmaceuticals, supplies and equipment and serves the U.S., Canada and selected global markets. The company's operations have been consolidated into one reportable segment: Pharmaceutical Distribution. This segment comprises three operating segments, which includes the operations of the AmerisourceBergen Drug Corporation (ABDC), the AmerisourceBergen Specialty Group (ABSG) and the AmerisourceBergen Packaging Group (ABPG). Servicing both healthcare providers and pharmaceutical manufacturers in the pharmaceutical supply channel, the Pharmaceutical Distribution segment's operations provide drug distribution and related services designed to reduce healthcare costs and improve patient outcomes. ABDC provides pharmacy management, staffing and other consulting services, scalable automated pharmacy dispensing equipment, medication and supply dispensing cabinets, and supply management software to a variety of retail and institutional healthcare providers. ABSG provides drug commercialization services, group purchasing, reimbursement consulting, data analytics and physician education. ABPG consists of American Health Packaging, a deliverer of unit dose, punch card and other packaging solutions to institutional and retail health providers; Anderson Packaging, a provider of contract packaging services for pharmaceutical manufacturers; and Brecon Pharmaceuticals Ltd., a U.K.-based provider of contract packaging and clinical trials materials services for pharmaceutical manufacturers. In September 2011, AmerisourceBergen Corp. acquired informatics solutions developer IntrinsiQ, LLC.

Employees are offered medical and dental coverage; disability insurance; life insurance and a 401(k) plan.

FINANCIALS: **Sales and profits are in thousands of dollars—add 000 to get the full amount. 2010 Note: Financial information for 2010 was not available for all companies at press time.**

2010 Sales: $77,953,979 2010 Profits: $636,748
2009 Sales: $71,759,990 2009 Profits: $503,397
2008 Sales: $70,189,733 2008 Profits: $250,559
2007 Sales: $65,672,072 2007 Profits: $469,167
2006 Sales: $56,282,216 2006 Profits: $467,714

U.S. Stock Ticker: ABC
Int'l Ticker:
Int'l Exchange:
Employees: 10,000 Fiscal Year Ends: 9/30
Parent Company:

SALARIES/BENEFITS:

Pension Plan: ESOP Stock Plan: Profit Sharing: Top Exec. Salary: $1,255,514 Bonus: $3,518,510
Savings Plan: Y Stock Purch. Plan: Y Second Exec. Salary: $673,077 Bonus: $1,039,290

OTHER THOUGHTS:

Apparent Women Officers or Directors: 4
Hot Spot for Advancement for Women/Minorities: Y

LOCATIONS: ("Y" = Yes)

West:	Southwest:	Midwest:	Southeast:	Northeast:	International:
Y	Y	Y	Y	Y	

AMGEN INC

www.amgen.com

Industry Group Code: 325412

Management:		Sales/Marketing:		Liberal Arts:		Information Sys.:		Professionals:		Tech./Scientific:	
Mgmt. Trainees:	Y	Marketing Pros.:	Y	Gen. Writing/Editing:	Y	Info. Mgmt.:	Y	Finance/Acct.:	Y	Engineers, Elec.:	Y
Experienced Mgmt.:	Y	Retail Sales:		Tech. Writing:	Y	Software Dev.:	Y	Law:	Y	Engineers, Other:	Y
Int'l Business:	Y	Comm./Industrial:	Y	Graphic Arts/Photog.:	Y	Hardware Dev.:		HR/Other:	Y	Health/Lab:	Y
MBA Grads:	Y	Sales Trainees:	Y	Music:		Consulting/Other:		Training:	Y	Science/Research:	Y
		Advertising Pros.:		Broadcasting:				Health Care:	Y	Petroleum/Chem.:	Y
				Other:				Consulting:		Math/Other:	Y

TYPES OF BUSINESS:

Drugs-Diversified
Oncology Drugs
Nephrology Drugs
Inflammation Drugs
Neurology Drugs

BRANDS/DIVISIONS/AFFILIATES:

Aranesp
EPOGEN
Neulasta
NEUPOGEN
Enbrel
Sensipar
Vectibix
Nplate

CONTACTS: *Note: Officers with more than one job title may be intentionally listed here more than once.*

Kevin W. Sharer, CEO
Kevin W. Sharer, Pres.
Johnathan M. Peacock, CFO/Exec. VP
Brian McNamee, Sr. VP-Human Resources
Roger M. Perlmutter, Exec. VP-R&D
Diana McKenzia, CIO/Sr. VP
David J. Scott, General Counsel/Sr. VP/Corp. Sec.
Fabrizio Bonanni, Exec. VP-Oper.
David Beier, Sr. VP-Corp. Affairs & Global Gov't
Anna Richo, Sr. VP/Chief Compliance Officer
Sean Harper, Sr. VP-Global Dev./Corp. Chief Medical Officer
Kevin W. Sharer, Chmn.
Rolf Hoffmann, Sr. VP-Int'l Commercial Oper.

Phone: 805-447-1000 | **Fax:** 805-447-1010
Toll-Free: 800-772-6436
Address: 1 Amgen Center Dr., Thousand Oaks, CA 91320-1799 US

GROWTH PLANS/SPECIAL FEATURES:

Amgen, Inc. is a global biotechnology medicines company that discovers, develops, manufactures and markets human therapeutics based on cellular and molecular biology. Its products are used for treatment in the fields of supportive cancer care, nephrology and inflammation. Amgen's primary products include Aranesp, EPOGEN, Neulasta, NEUPOGEN and ENBREL, which together represent 91% of the company's sales. Aranesp and EPOGEN stimulate the production of red blood cells to treat anemia and belong to a class of drugs referred to as erythropoiesis-stimulating agents. Aranesp is used for the treatment of anemia both in chronic kidney failure and in concomitant chemotherapy. EPOGEN is used to treat anemia associated with end-stage renal disease. Neulasta and NEUPOGEN selectively stimulate the production of neutrophils, one type of white blood cell that helps the body fight infections. ENBREL inhibits tumor necrosis factor (TNF), a substance induced in response to inflammatory and immunological responses, such as rheumatoid arthritis and psoriasis. Other marketed products include Sensipar/Mimpara, which lowers serum calcium levels; Vectibix, used to treat specific progressions of metastatic colorectal cancer; Prolia, a treatment of steoporosis for postmenopausal women; and Nplate, used to treat low platelet count. Amgen maintains sales and marketing forces primarily in the U.S., Europe and Canada, and markets its products to healthcare providers including physicians or their clinics, dialysis centers, hospitals and pharmacies. Amgen focuses its research and development efforts in the core areas of oncology, hematology, inflammation, bone, nephrology, cardiology and neurology. In March 2011, the firm acquired BioVex Group, Inc., creator of novel investigational oncolytic vaccine OncoVEX(GM-CSF).

Amgen offers its employees health, disability and life insurance; paid time off; a 401(k) plan and a stock purchase plan; voluntary group home and auto insurance; tuition reimbursement; dependent care spending accounts; childcare services; telecommuting and remote work options; and recreation and fitness classes.

FINANCIALS: **Sales and profits are in thousands of dollars—add 000 to get the full amount. 2010 Note: Financial information for 2010 was not available for all companies at press time.**

2010 Sales: $15,053,000 — 2010 Profits: $4,627,000
2009 Sales: $14,642,000 — 2009 Profits: $4,605,000
2008 Sales: $15,003,000 — 2008 Profits: $4,052,000
2007 Sales: $14,771,000 — 2007 Profits: $3,166,000
2006 Sales: $14,268,000 — 2006 Profits: $2,950,000

U.S. Stock Ticker: AMGN
Int'l Ticker:
Int'l Exchange:
Employees: 17,100 Fiscal Year Ends: 12/31
Parent Company:

SALARIES/BENEFITS:

Pension Plan: | ESOP Stock Plan: | Profit Sharing: | Top Exec. Salary: $1,682,308 | Bonus: $3,790,000
Savings Plan: Y | Stock Purch. Plan: Y | | Second Exec. Salary: $991,131 | Bonus: $1,195,000

OTHER THOUGHTS:

Apparent Women Officers or Directors: 4
Hot Spot for Advancement for Women/Minorities: Y

LOCATIONS: ("Y" = Yes)

West:	Southwest:	Midwest:	Southeast:	Northeast:	International:
Y			Y	Y	Y

AMKOR TECHNOLOGY INC

www.amkor.com

Industry Group Code: 333295

Management:		**Sales/Marketing:**		**Liberal Arts:**		**Information Sys.:**		**Professionals:**		**Tech./Scientific:**	
Mgmt. Trainees:		Marketing Pros.:	Y	Gen. Writing/Editing:		Info. Mgmt.:	Y	Finance/Acct.:	Y	Engineers, Elec.:	Y
Experienced Mgmt.:		Retail Sales:		Tech. Writing:	Y	Software Dev.:	Y	Law:	Y	Engineers, Other:	
Int'l Business:	Y	Comm./Industrial:	Y	Graphic Arts/Photog.:		Hardware Dev.:	Y	HR/Other:	Y	Health/Lab:	
MBA Grads:	Y	Sales Trainees:		Music:		Consulting/Other:		Training:		Science/Research:	
		Advertising Pros.:	Y	Broadcasting:				Health Care:		Petroleum/Chem.:	
				Other:				Consulting:		Math/Other:	

TYPES OF BUSINESS:

Semiconductors-Packaging & Testing
Semiconductor Design
Turnkey Solutions

BRANDS/DIVISIONS/AFFILIATES:

Nakaya Microdevices Corporation
Toshiba Corporation

CONTACTS: *Note: Officers with more than one job title may be intentionally listed here more than once.*

Kenneth T. Joyce, CEO
Kenneth T. Joyce, Pres.
Joanne Solomon, CFO/Exec. VP
Mike Lamble, VP-Worldwide Sales
Jooho Kim, Head-Worldwide Mfg.
Gil C. Tily, Chief Admin. Officer/Exec. VP
Gil C. Tily, General Counsel/Corp. Sec./Exec. VP
Jim Fusaro, Exec. VP-Assembly & Test Bus. Unit
James J. Kim, Chmn.
Jooho Kim, Pres., Amkor Technology Korea

Phone: 480-821-5000 **Fax:** 480-821-8276
Toll-Free:
Address: 1900 South Price Rd., Chandler, AZ 85286 US

GROWTH PLANS/SPECIAL FEATURES:

Amkor Technology, Inc. is one of the world's largest subcontractors of semiconductor packaging and test services. The firm offers a range of integrated services, including the final procedures necessary to prepare semiconductor devices for further use. Headquartered in the U.S., the company also has production capabilities in China, Japan, Korea, the Philippines, France, Singapore and Taiwan. The company operates in two segments: packaging and testing. Packaging includes dicing of a semiconductor wafer into separate chips, die bonding, wire bonding and encapsulation of the chip in protective plastic. The testing segment offers turnkey packaging and test solutions including semiconductor wafer bump, wafer probe, wafer backgrind, package design, final test, strip test, system level test, assembly, test and drop shipment and other test-related services. The semiconductors packaged and tested by the firm become components in electrical systems used in computing, wireless, communications, storage, consumer, commercial, industrial, medical, defense and automotive applications. Amkor offers over 1,000 different package types and sizes, and packages are increasingly custom designed for specific chips and specific end-market applications. The company provides customers with leading-edge packaging technologies, including dual and quad leadframe, 2D and 3D thin substrate, flip chip, ball grid array, system-in-package and wafer level solutions. Amkor also offers an extensive range of test engineering services for radio frequency (RF) applications, as well as RF/wireless semiconductor device test development services. The company's customer base consists of more than 200 companies, including many of the world's largest semiconductor companies. The firm maintains a joint venture with Nakaya Microdevices Corporation and Toshiba Corporation that provides semiconductor assembly and final testing services in Japan.

The company offers its employees benefits including an employee assistance program, flexible spending accounts, tuition reimbursement, profit sharing, medical and dental insurance, direct deposit and travel insurance.

FINANCIALS: **Sales and profits are in thousands of dollars—add 000 to get the full amount. 2010 Note: Financial information for 2010 was not available for all companies at press time.**

2010 Sales: $2,939,483 | 2010 Profits: $232,147
2009 Sales: $2,179,109 | 2009 Profits: $156,283
2008 Sales: $2,658,602 | 2008 Profits: $-456,695
2007 Sales: $2,739,445 | 2007 Profits: $219,864
2006 Sales: $2,728,560 | 2006 Profits: $170,084

U.S. Stock Ticker: AMKR
Int'l Ticker:
Int'l Exchange:
Employees: 19,900 Fiscal Year Ends: 12/31
Parent Company:

SALARIES/BENEFITS:

Pension Plan: | ESOP Stock Plan: | Profit Sharing: Y | Top Exec. Salary: $581,539 | Bonus: $
Savings Plan: Y | Stock Purch. Plan: | | Second Exec. Salary: $526,346 | Bonus: $

OTHER THOUGHTS:

Apparent Women Officers or Directors: 1
Hot Spot for Advancement for Women/Minorities:

LOCATIONS: ("Y" = Yes)

West:	Southwest:	Midwest:	Southeast:	Northeast:	International:
Y	Y			Y	Y

AMPHENOL CORPORATION

www.amphenol.com

Industry Group Code: 335921

Management:		**Sales/Marketing:**		**Liberal Arts:**		**Information Sys.:**		**Professionals:**		**Tech./Scientific:**	
Mgmt. Trainees:		Marketing Pros.:	Y	Gen. Writing/Editing:		Info. Mgmt.:	Y	Finance/Acct.:	Y	Engineers, Elec.:	Y
Experienced Mgmt.:		Retail Sales:		Tech. Writing:	Y	Software Dev.:		Law:	Y	Engineers, Other:	Y
Int'l Business:	Y	Comm./Industrial:	Y	Graphic Arts/Photog.:		Hardware Dev.:		HR/Other:	Y	Health/Lab:	
MBA Grads:	Y	Sales Trainees:		Music:		Consulting/Other:		Training:		Science/Research:	
		Advertising Pros.:	Y	Broadcasting:				Health Care:		Petroleum/Chem.:	
				Other:				Consulting:		Math/Other:	

TYPES OF BUSINESS:

Cables & Connectors

BRANDS/DIVISIONS/AFFILIATES:

Times Fiber Communications
Tuchel
Socapex
Sine
Spectra-Strip
Pyle-National
Matrix
Kai-Jack

CONTACTS: *Note: Officers with more than one job title may be intentionally listed here more than once.*

Richard A. Norwitt, CEO
Richard A. Norwitt, Pres.
Diana G. Reardon, CFO/Sr. VP
Jerome F. Monteith, VP-Human Resources
Richard E. Schneider, Sr. VP/Gen. Mgr.-IT & Comm. Prod.
Edward C. Wetmore, General Counsel/Corp. Sec./VP
Gary A. Anderson, Sr. VP/Gen. Mgr.-Aerospace & Industrial Oper.
Craig A. Lampo, Controller/VP
Zachary W. Raley, Sr. VP-Worldwide RF, Microwave & Cable Prod.
David J. Jositas, Treas.
Martin H. Loeffler, Chmn.
Luc Walter, Sr. VP/Group Gen. Mgr.-Int'l Military & Aerospace

Phone: 203-265-8900 **Fax:** 203-265-8516
Toll-Free: 877-267-4366
Address: 358 Hall Ave., Wallingford, CT 06492 US

GROWTH PLANS/SPECIAL FEATURES:

Amphenol Corporation is a leading global designer, manufacturer and marketer of electrical, electronic and fiber optic connectors, interconnect systems and coaxial and flat-ribbon cable. Its operations are divided into three divisions: IT & Communications, which accounted for 60% of its 2010 sales; Industrial & Automotive, 18%; and Commercial Aerospace & Military, 22%. Primary applications of the company's IT and communications products include wireless communication systems, broadband networks, servers, computers, data networking equipment and routers. Amphenol's industrial and automotive products include such applications as factory automation, automobile safety systems, mass transportation, off-road construction, medical equipment and satellite radio systems. Primary applications of Amphenol's commercial aerospace and military products include avionics, engine controls, flight controls, passenger related systems, missile systems, battlefield communications, satellite programs, radar systems and military vehicles. The company is one of the largest producers of military-specification circular environmental connectors. Subsidiary Times Fiber Communications, Inc. is one of the world's largest producers of coaxial cable for the cable TV industry and flat-ribbon cable for computer and telecommunications products. The firm produces two primary varieties of coaxial cable products: semi-flexible, which has an aluminum tubular shield and is used in the trunk and feeder distribution portion of cable television systems; and flexible, which has one or more braided metallic shields and is used in other communications applications. The firm's brands include Amphenol, Times Fiber, Tuchel, Socapex, Sine, Spectra-Strip, Pyle-National, Matrix and Kai-Jack.

FINANCIALS: **Sales and profits are in thousands of dollars—add 000 to get the full amount. 2010 Note: Financial information for 2010 was not available for all companies at press time.**

2010 Sales: $3,554,101 — 2010 Profits: $502,413
2009 Sales: $2,820,065 — 2009 Profits: $317,834
2008 Sales: $3,236,471 — 2008 Profits: $419,151
2007 Sales: $2,851,041 — 2007 Profits: $353,194
2006 Sales: $2,471,430 — 2006 Profits: $255,691

U.S. Stock Ticker: APH
Int'l Ticker:
Int'l Exchange:
Employees: 39,100 Fiscal Year Ends: 12/31
Parent Company:

SALARIES/BENEFITS:

Pension Plan: ESOP Stock Plan: Profit Sharing: Top Exec. Salary: $880,000 Bonus: $1,425,600
Savings Plan: Y Stock Purch. Plan: Second Exec. Salary: $600,000 Bonus: $

OTHER THOUGHTS:

Apparent Women Officers or Directors: 1
Hot Spot for Advancement for Women/Minorities:

LOCATIONS: ("Y" = Yes)

West:	Southwest:	Midwest:	Southeast:	Northeast:	International:
Y	Y	Y	Y	Y	Y

AMR CORP (AMERICAN AIRLINES)

www.aa.com

Industry Group Code: 481111

Management:		Sales/Marketing:		Liberal Arts:		Information Sys.:		Professionals:		Tech./Scientific:	
Mgmt. Trainees:		Marketing Pros.:	Y	Gen. Writing/Editing:	Y	Info. Mgmt.:	Y	Finance/Acct.:	Y	Engineers, Elec.:	
Experienced Mgmt.:	Y	Retail Sales:		Tech. Writing:	Y	Software Dev.:	Y	Law:	Y	Engineers, Other:	Y
Int'l Business:	Y	Comm./Industrial:	Y	Graphic Arts/Photog.:	Y	Hardware Dev.:		HR/Other:	Y	Health/Lab:	
MBA Grads:	Y	Sales Trainees:		Music:		Consulting/Other:		Training:	Y	Science/Research:	
		Advertising Pros.:	Y	Broadcasting:				Health Care:	Y	Petroleum/Chem.:	
				Other:	Y			Consulting:		Math/Other:	Y

TYPES OF BUSINESS:

Airlines
Air Freight
Regional Airline

BRANDS/DIVISIONS/AFFILIATES:

American Airlines Inc
American Eagle Airlines, Inc.
Executive Airlines, Inc.
AMR Eagle Holding Corporation
oneworld Alliance

CONTACTS: *Note: Officers with more than one job title may be intentionally listed here more than once.*

Gerard J. Arpey, CEO
Thomas W. Horton, Pres.
Isabella D. Goren, CFO/Sr. VP
Gary F. Kennedy, General Counsel/Sr. VP/Chief Compliance Officer
Robert W. Reding, Exec. VP-Oper.
Kenneth W. Wimberly, Corp. Sec.
Daniel P. Garton, CEO/Pres., American Eagle Airlines
Gerard J. Arpey, Chmn.

Phone: 817-963-1234	**Fax:** 817-967-9641
Toll-Free:	
Address: 4333 Amon Carter Blvd., Fort Worth, TX 76155 US	

GROWTH PLANS/SPECIAL FEATURES:

AMR Corp. (American Airlines) is an airline holding company. Its principal subsidiary is American Airlines, Inc. (American). American provides scheduled jet service to approximately 160 destinations throughout North America, the Caribbean, Latin America, Europe and Asia. American is also a scheduled air freight carrier, providing a wide range of freight and mail services to shippers through its system. American contracts with an independently-owned regional airline, which does business as AmericanConnection. AMR Eagle Holding Corporation, a wholly-owned subsidiary of AMR, owns two regional airlines that do business under the American Eagle brand: American Eagle Airlines, Inc. and Executive Airlines, Inc. (collectively, the American Eagle carriers). The American Eagle carriers and the AmericanConnection carriers provide connecting service throughout the U.S., Canada, Mexico and the Caribbean. Together, American, AMR Eagle Holding Corporation and the AmericanConnection airline serve approximately 250 cities in roughly 50 countries with an average of 3,400 daily flights. The combined network fleet numbers roughly 900 aircraft. American Airlines is also a founding member of oneworld Alliance, which enables member airlines to offer their customers more services and benefits than any member airline can provide individually. These services include a broader route network, opportunities to earn and redeem frequent flyer miles across the combined oneworld network and more airport lounges. In mid 2010, American announced updates to 76 737-800s, including new cabin interiors, additional storage and improved in-flight entertainment. In August 2011, the company announced plans to spin off AMR Eagle Holding Corporation.

The company offers its employees medical, dental, vision, life and disability plans; long-term care; legal aid; reimbursement accounts; an employee credit union; a 401(k) plan; a profit sharing plan; job-based and personal enrichment training; and travel benefits.

FINANCIALS: **Sales and profits are in thousands of dollars—add 000 to get the full amount. 2010 Note: Financial information for 2010 was not available for all companies at press time.**

2010 Sales: $22,170,000
2009 Sales: $19,917,000
2008 Sales: $23,766,000
2007 Sales: $22,935,000
2006 Sales: $22,563,000

2010 Profits: $-471,000
2009 Profits: $-1,468,000
2008 Profits: $-2,118,000
2007 Profits: $456,000
2006 Profits: $231,000

U.S. Stock Ticker: AMR
Int'l Ticker:
Int'l Exchange:
Employees: 78,250 Fiscal Year Ends: 12/31
Parent Company:

SALARIES/BENEFITS:

Pension Plan:
Savings Plan: Y
ESOP Stock Plan:
Stock Purch. Plan:
Profit Sharing: Y
Top Exec. Salary: $669,646 Bonus: $ 467
Second Exec. Salary: $618,135 Bonus: $ 467

OTHER THOUGHTS:

Apparent Women Officers or Directors: 3
Hot Spot for Advancement for Women/Minorities: Y

LOCATIONS: ("Y" = Yes)

West:	Southwest:	Midwest:	Southeast:	Northeast:	International:
Y	Y	Y	Y	Y	Y

Sales, profits and employees may be estimates. Financial information, benefits and other data can change quickly and may vary from those stated here.

AMSURG CORP

www.amsurg.com

Industry Group Code: 6214

Management:		**Sales/Marketing:**		**Liberal Arts:**		**Information Sys.:**		**Professionals:**		**Tech./Scientific:**	
Mgmt. Trainees:		Marketing Pros.:	Y	Gen. Writing/Editing:		Info. Mgmt.:	Y	Finance/Acct.:	Y	Engineers, Elec.:	
Experienced Mgmt.:		Retail Sales:		Tech. Writing:	Y	Software Dev.:		Law:	Y	Engineers, Other:	
Int'l Business:		Comm./Industrial:	Y	Graphic Arts/Photog.:		Hardware Dev.:		HR/Other:	Y	Health/Lab:	Y
MBA Grads:	Y	Sales Trainees:		Music:		Consulting/Other:		Training:	Y	Science/Research:	
		Advertising Pros.:	Y	Broadcasting:				Health Care:		Petroleum/Chem.:	
				Other:				Consulting:		Math/Other:	

TYPES OF BUSINESS:

Practice-Based Ambulatory Surgery Centers

BRANDS/DIVISIONS/AFFILIATES:

National Surgical Care

CONTACTS: *Note: Officers with more than one job title may be intentionally listed here more than once.*

Christopher A. Holden, CEO
Christopher A. Holden, Pres.
Claire M. Gulmi, CFO/Exec. VP
Claire M. Gulmi, Sec.
Billie A. Payne, Sr. VP-Oper.
David L. Manning, Chief Dev. Officer/Exec. VP
Kevin D. Eastridge, Chief Acct. Officer/Sr. VP-Finance
Phillip A. Clendenin, Chief Compliance Officer/Sr. VP-Corp. Svcs.
Steven I. Geringer, Chmn.

Phone: 615-665-1283 **Fax:** 615-665-0755
Toll-Free: 800-945-2301
Address: 20 Burton Hills Blvd., Ste. 500, Nashville, TN 37215 US

GROWTH PLANS/SPECIAL FEATURES:

AmSurg Corp. develops, acquires and operates ambulatory surgery centers (ASCs) in partnership with physicians throughout the U.S. The company owns a majority interest in 204 ASCs, with more than 580 operating rooms, in 33 states and Washington, D.C. These ASCs are licensed outpatient facilities usually located in or near a partner physician's office. Although the types of procedures performed at each center depend on the specialty of the resident physicians, AmSurg has targeted ownership in centers specializing in gastroenterology, ophthalmology and orthopedic procedures. The most common procedures include colonoscopies, laser eye surgery and carpal tunnel repair. Approximately 90% of the company's centers are equipped and staffed for a single medical specialty (usually gastroenterology or ophthalmology), with the remaining 10% offering more than one of the above specialty areas as well as performing general surgical procedures. Regardless of whether they offer single- or multi-specialty services, all of the centers perform a narrow range of high volume, lower-risk surgical procedures designed with a lower margin cost structure than hospitals. The firm's single-specialty ASCs average 3,000 to 6,000 square feet, while its multi-specialty centers average 5,000 to 10,000 square feet; all feature 2-3 operating rooms that average 6,300 procedures annually. In general, the firm manages the business office, marketing, financial reporting, accreditation and administrative operations of the surgery centers, while physician partners provide the center with a medical director and performance improvement chairman, and may provide certain other services such as billing, collections, transcription and accounts payable processing. In April 2011, the firm agreed to acquire National Surgical Care, a Texas-based operator of 18 ASCs.

Employees of AmSurg receive benefits including medical, prescription, vision and dental insurance; flexible spending accounts; health savings accounts; life and AD&D insurance; short- and long-term disability; a 401(k); fitness reimbursement; discounts at AAA, Dell, AT&T and Verizon; and concierge services.

FINANCIALS: **Sales and profits are in thousands of dollars—add 000 to get the full amount. 2010 Note: Financial information for 2010 was not available for all companies at press time.**

2010 Sales: $710,409 2010 Profits: $49,825
2009 Sales: $658,223 2009 Profits: $52,148
2008 Sales: $588,658 2008 Profits: $47,046
2007 Sales: $518,311 2007 Profits: $44,175
2006 Sales: $441,438 2006 Profits: $37,739

U.S. Stock Ticker: AMSG
Int'l Ticker:
Int'l Exchange:
Employees: 3,100 Fiscal Year Ends: 12/31
Parent Company:

SALARIES/BENEFITS:

Pension Plan: ESOP Stock Plan: Profit Sharing: Top Exec. Salary: $559,000 Bonus: $139,750
Savings Plan: Y Stock Purch. Plan: Second Exec. Salary: $399,400 Bonus: $79,880

OTHER THOUGHTS:

Apparent Women Officers or Directors: 3
Hot Spot for Advancement for Women/Minorities: Y

LOCATIONS: ("Y" = Yes)

West:	Southwest:	Midwest:	Southeast:	Northeast:	International:
Y	Y	Y	Y	Y	

ANALOG DEVICES INC

www.analog.com

Industry Group Code: 33441

Management:		Sales/Marketing:		Liberal Arts:		Information Sys.:		Professionals:		Tech./Scientific:	
Mgmt. Trainees:	Y	Marketing Pros.:	Y	Gen. Writing/Editing:		Info. Mgmt.:	Y	Finance/Acct.:	Y	Engineers, Elec.:	Y
Experienced Mgmt.:	Y	Retail Sales:		Tech. Writing:	Y	Software Dev.:	Y	Law:	Y	Engineers, Other:	
Int'l Business:	Y	Comm./Industrial:	Y	Graphic Arts/Photog.:	Y	Hardware Dev.:	Y	HR/Other:	Y	Health/Lab:	
MBA Grads:	Y	Sales Trainees:		Music:		Consulting/Other:		Training:	Y	Science/Research:	Y
		Advertising Pros.:	Y	Broadcasting:				Health Care:		Petroleum/Chem.:	
				Other:				Consulting:		Math/Other:	Y

TYPES OF BUSINESS:

Integrated Circuits-Analog & Digital
MEMS Products
DSP Products
Accelerometers & Gyroscopes

BRANDS/DIVISIONS/AFFILIATES:

CONTACTS:

Note: Officers with more than one job title may be intentionally listed here more than once.

Jerald G. Fishman, CEO
Jerald G. Fishman, Pres.
David Zinsner, CFO/VP-Finance
Emre Onder, VP-Mktg.
William Matson, VP-Human Resources
Samuel H. Fuller, VP-R&D
Peter Forte, CIO
Samuel H. Fuller, CTO
John Hassett, VP-Worldwide Mfg.
Margaret K. Seif, General Counsel/VP/Sec.
Mark Smrtic, VP-Foundry Oper.
Keith Rutherford, VP-Comm. Bus. Dev.
John Hussey, VP-Corp. Comm.
Seamus Brennan, Chief Acct. Officer/Corp. Controller
Thomas Wessel, VP-European Sales & Mktg.
Pat O'Doherty, VP-Healthcare
David Robertson, VP-Analog Tech.
Ray Stata, Chmn.
Howard Cheng, VP-Asia
Gerry Dundon, VP-Planning & Supply Chain Logistics

Phone: 781-329-4700 **Fax:** 781-326-8703
Toll-Free: 800-262-5643
Address: 3 Technology Way, Norwood, MA 02062 US

GROWTH PLANS/SPECIAL FEATURES:

Analog Devices, Inc. (ADI) designs, manufactures and markets a broad line of high-performance analog, mixed-signal and digital signal processing (DSP) integrated circuits (ICs). The company's products are divided into analog and digital products. Its analog products are then divided into converters; amplifiers and radio frequency (RF); power management and reference; and other analog. Converters translate real-world analog signals into digital data, and vice-versa. Amplifiers are used to condition analog signals and minimize noise, while RF products are designed to operate as wireless devices. Power management products include any device that can be plugged into a wall outlet or run on battery, such as converters, battery chargers, charge pumps and regulators. Other analog products include microelectromechanical devices (MEMS), such as accelerometers, as well as anything else that uses analog technology. ADI's digital signal processor (DSP) products are typically preprogrammed to execute software for applications such as wireless telecommunications or image processing. Its principal products are used in a wide variety of electronic equipment, including industrial process control, factory automation systems, smart munitions, base stations, central office equipment, wireless telephones, computers, cars, CAT scanners, digital cameras and DVD players. The company's product portfolio includes several thousand analog ICs, with as many as several hundred customers per design. ADI's analog technology base also includes an advanced IC technology known in the industry as surface micromachining, which is used to produce micro-electromechanical systems (MEMS) semiconductor products. ADI's customers include Dell, Alcatel, Lucent, Ericsson, Siemens, Sony, Philips, Ford and Volkswagen. The firm has manufacturing facilities in the U.S., Ireland and the Philippines.

The company offers its employees medical, dental and vision coverage; life insurance; dependant and health care spending accounts; a retirement plan; and an education assistance plan.

FINANCIALS:

Sales and profits are in thousands of dollars—add 000 to get the full amount. 2010 Note: Financial information for 2010 was not available for all companies at press time.

2010 Sales: $2,761,503 — 2010 Profits: $712,084
2009 Sales: $2,014,908 — 2009 Profits: $247,772
2008 Sales: $2,582,931 — 2008 Profits: $786,284
2007 Sales: $2,464,721 — 2007 Profits: $496,907
2006 Sales: $2,250,100 — 2006 Profits: $549,482

U.S. Stock Ticker: ADI
Int'l Ticker:
Int'l Exchange:
Employees: 8,500 Fiscal Year Ends: 10/31
Parent Company:

SALARIES/BENEFITS:

Pension Plan: Y | ESOP Stock Plan: | Profit Sharing: | Top Exec. Salary: $930,935 | Bonus: $635,900
Savings Plan: | Stock Purch. Plan: | | Second Exec. Salary: $398,580 | Bonus: $570,498

OTHER THOUGHTS:

Apparent Women Officers or Directors: 1
Hot Spot for Advancement for Women/Minorities:

LOCATIONS: ("Y" = Yes)

West:	Southwest:	Midwest:	Southeast:	Northeast:	International:
Y	Y	Y	Y	Y	Y

APACHE CORP

www.apachecorp.com

Industry Group Code: 211111

Management:		Sales/Marketing:		Liberal Arts:		Information Sys.:		Professionals:		Tech./Scientific:	
Mgmt. Trainees:	Y	Marketing Pros.:	Y	Gen. Writing/Editing:	Y	Info. Mgmt.:	Y	Finance/Acct.:	Y	Engineers, Elec.:	Y
Experienced Mgmt.:	Y	Retail Sales:		Tech. Writing:	Y	Software Dev.:	Y	Law:	Y	Engineers, Other:	Y
Int'l Business:	Y	Comm./Industrial:		Graphic Arts/Photog.:		Hardware Dev.:		HR/Other:	Y	Health/Lab:	
MBA Grads:	Y	Sales Trainees:		Music:		Consulting/Other:		Training:	Y	Science/Research:	
		Advertising Pros.:		Broadcasting:				Health Care:		Petroleum/Chem.:	Y
				Other:				Consulting:		Math/Other:	

TYPES OF BUSINESS:

Oil & Gas Exploration & Production

BRANDS/DIVISIONS/AFFILIATES:

Apache Canada Ltd.
DEK Energy Company
Apache Energy Ltd.
Apache North America, Inc.
Apache Overseas, Inc.
Mariner Energy, Inc.

CONTACTS: *Note: Officers with more than one job title may be intentionally listed here more than once.*

G. Steven Farris, CEO
Rodney J. Eichler, COO/Co-Pres.
Roger B. Plank, Co-Pres./Chief Corp. Officer
Thomas P. Chambers, CFO/Exec. VP
Mark J. Bright, VP-North America Oil & Gas Mktg.
Margery M. Harris, Sr. VP-Human Resources
Michael S. Bahorich, CTO/Exec. VP
W. Kregg Olson, Exec. VP-Corp. Reservoir Eng.
Matthew W. Dundrea, Sr. VP-Admin. & Treasury
P. Anthony Lannie, General Counsel/Exec. VP
Jon A. Jeppesen, Sr. VP-Gulf of Mexico Oper.
David L. French, VP-Bus. Dev.
Robert J. Dye, Sr. VP-Global Comm. & Corp Affairs
Alfonso Leon, VP-Investor Rel., Strategy & Planning
Rebecca A. Hoyt, Controller/Chief Acct. Officer/VP
Dave R. Gilbronson, VP-Int'l Oil & Gas Mktg.
Rodney A. Gryder, VP-Audit
Sarah B. Teslik, Sr. VP-Policy & Governance
G. Steven Farris, Chmn.
Timothy O. Wall, VP-Canada/Pres., Apache Canada

Phone: 713-296-6000	**Fax:** 713-296-6496
Toll-Free: 800-272-2434	
Address: 2000 Post Oak Blvd., Ste. 100, Houston, TX 77056-4400 US	

GROWTH PLANS/SPECIAL FEATURES:

Apache Corp. is an independent energy company that explores, develops and produces natural gas, crude oil and natural gas liquids. The firm currently operates in the U.S., Canada, Egypt, Australia, offshore the United Kingdom in the North Sea, Argentina, and Chile. In North America, Apache's exploration and production interests are focused on the Gulf of Mexico; the Anadarko Basin of western Oklahoma; the Permian Basin of western Texas and New Mexico; the Texas-Louisiana Gulf Coast; East Texas; and the Western Sedimentary basin of Canada. Internationally, Apache has exploration and production interests in Egypt, Australia, Argentina, Chile and the U.K. sector of the North Sea. Crude oil and liquids provide roughly 52% of the firm's production and 77% of its revenue. Natural gas accounts for the remaining 48% of production and 23% of revenues. Apache's estimated proved reserves are balanced at 56% natural gas and 44% crude oil and liquids. Although the company treats all operations as one line of business, interests in many of its properties are through subsidiaries, such as Apache Canada Ltd.; DEK Energy Company; Apache Energy Ltd.; Apache North America, Inc.; and Apache Overseas, Inc. Apache's Canadian natural gas operations have been growing significantly in recent years due to several acquisitions and discoveries. Growth strategies in the U.S. focus on exploiting and expanding established areas, while growth abroad is a mix of exploration and exploitation. In late 2010, Apache Corp. acquired BP plc's (BP) oil and gas operations, acreage and infrastructure in the Permian Basin for $2.5 billion; BP's upstream natural gas business in western Alberta and British Columbia for $3.25 billion; and Mariner Energy, Inc. for roughly $2.7 billion.

Employees of Apache receive health and medical benefits; life insurance; disability coverage; education assistance; alternative work schedules; and flexible spending accounts.

FINANCIALS: **Sales and profits are in thousands of dollars—add 000 to get the full amount. 2010 Note: Financial information for 2010 was not available for all companies at press time.**

2010 Sales: $12,092,000	2010 Profits: $3,032,000	**U.S. Stock Ticker: APA**
2009 Sales: $8,614,826	2009 Profits: $-284,398	**Int'l Ticker:**
2008 Sales: $12,389,750	2008 Profits: $711,954	Int'l Exchange:
2007 Sales: $9,999,752	2007 Profits: $2,806,678	Employees: 4,449 Fiscal Year Ends: 12/31
2006 Sales: $8,309,131	2006 Profits: $2,546,771	Parent Company:

SALARIES/BENEFITS:

Pension Plan: Y	ESOP Stock Plan:	Profit Sharing:	Top Exec. Salary: $1,750,000	Bonus: $3,250,000
Savings Plan: Y	Stock Purch. Plan:		Second Exec. Salary: $634,375	Bonus: $750,000

OTHER THOUGHTS:

Apparent Women Officers or Directors: 5
Hot Spot for Advancement for Women/Minorities: Y

LOCATIONS: ("Y" = Yes)

West:	Southwest:	Midwest:	Southeast:	Northeast:	International:
Y	Y		Y		Y

Sales, profits and employees may be estimates. Financial information, benefits and other data can change quickly and may vary from those stated here.

APPLE INC

www.apple.com

Industry Group Code: 334111

Management:		Sales/Marketing:		Liberal Arts:		Information Sys.:		Professionals:		Tech./Scientific:	
Mgmt. Trainees:	Y	Marketing Pros.:	Y	Gen. Writing/Editing:	Y	Info. Mgmt.:	Y	Finance/Acct.:	Y	Engineers, Elec.:	Y
Experienced Mgmt.:	Y	Retail Sales:	Y	Tech. Writing:	Y	Software Dev.:	Y	Law:	Y	Engineers, Other:	
Int'l Business:	Y	Comm./Industrial:	Y	Graphic Arts/Photog.:	Y	Hardware Dev.:	Y	HR/Other:	Y	Health/Lab:	
MBA Grads:	Y	Sales Trainees:	Y	Music:	Y	Consulting/Other:	Y	Training:	Y	Science/Research:	Y
		Advertising Pros.:	Y	Broadcasting:				Health Care:		Petroleum/Chem.:	
				Other:	Y			Consulting:		Math/Other:	Y

TYPES OF BUSINESS:

Computer Hardware-PCs
Software
Computer Accessories
Retail Stores
Portable Music Players
Online Music Sales and Video Rentals
Cellular Phones
Home Entertainment Software & Systems

BRANDS/DIVISIONS/AFFILIATES:

iLife
iPad
iTunes
Mac OS X
MacBook Air
iPod
iPhone
Safari

CONTACTS: *Note: Officers with more than one job title may be intentionally listed here more than once.*

Timothy D. Cook, CEO
Peter Oppenheimer, CFO/Sr. VP
Philip W. Schiller, Sr. VP-Worldwide Prod. Mktg.
Robert Mansfield, Sr. VP-Mac Hardware Eng.
D. Bruce Sewell, General Counsel/Sr. VP/Sec.
Jeffrey E. Williams, Sr. VP-Oper.
Scott Forstall, Sr. VP-iPhone Software Eng. & Platform Experience
Jonathan Ive, Sr. VP-Industrial Design
Ronald B. Johnson, Sr. VP-Retail
Timothy D. Cook, Chmn.

Phone: 408-996-1010 **Fax:** 408-996-0275
Toll-Free: 800-692-7753
Address: 1 Infinite Loop, Cupertino, CA 95014 US

GROWTH PLANS/SPECIAL FEATURES:

Apple, Inc. designs, manufactures and markets personal computers, portable digital music players and mobile communication devices; and sells a variety of related software, services, peripherals and networking applications. The company's hardware products include the MacBook, MacBook Air and MacBook Pro notebook computers; Mac Pro and iMac desktop computers; Mac minis; and Xserve servers and Xserve RAID Storage Systems. The firm's Mac products feature Intel microprocessors, Mac OS X Leopard operating systems and iLife software. Software products include Mac OS X; iLife '11; iWork '09; Logic Studio; and FileMaker Pro. Additional products include iSight digital video cameras; the iPod line of portable digital music players and accessories; the iPhone, with phone, iPod and Internet services; the iPad notebook; the iPod nano, a flash-memory-based iPod which includes a video camera, microphone, speaker, an FM radio with live pause functionality and a pedometer; Final Cut Studio, a high-definition video production suite of applications; and the iTunes digital entertainment management software for MP3 music files, television shows and movies. The iPhone is available in over 89 countries through 166 individual carrier distribution deals. Peripheral products are sold directly to end-users through its retail and online stores and include printers, storage devices, computer memory, digital video and still camera and other computing products and supplies. Apple's roughly 317 retail stores have been a tremendous success. The firm opened 44 new stores in 2010, and expects to open 40 to 50 in 2011. Apple's average sales per square foot of store space per year were an estimated $4,600 in 2011. In mid 2010, Apple launched the iPhone 4, which features FaceTime, a Retina display and a five-megapixel camera. In January 2011, the company opened Mac App Store, which offers 1,000 paid and free apps. In March 2011, the firm released the iPad 2.

FINANCIALS: **Sales and profits are in thousands of dollars—add 000 to get the full amount. 2010 Note: Financial information for 2010 was not available for all companies at press time.**

2010 Sales: $65,225,000 — 2010 Profits: $14,013,000
2009 Sales: $42,905,000 — 2009 Profits: $8,235,000
2008 Sales: $37,491,000 — 2008 Profits: $6,119,000
2007 Sales: $24,006,000 — 2007 Profits: $3,496,000
2006 Sales: $19,315,000 — 2006 Profits: $1,989,000

U.S. Stock Ticker: AAPL
Int'l Ticker:
Int'l Exchange:
Employees: 49,400 Fiscal Year Ends: 9/30
Parent Company:

SALARIES/BENEFITS:

Pension Plan: ESOP Stock Plan: Profit Sharing: Top Exec. Salary: $800,016 Bonus: $5,900,000
Savings Plan: Y Stock Purch. Plan: Y Second Exec. Salary: $700,014 Bonus: $700,000

OTHER THOUGHTS:

Apparent Women Officers or Directors: 1
Hot Spot for Advancement for Women/Minorities:

LOCATIONS: ("Y" = Yes)

West:	Southwest:	Midwest:	Southeast:	Northeast:	International:
Y	Y	Y	Y	Y	Y

APPLIED MATERIALS INC

www.appliedmaterials.com

Industry Group Code: 333295

Management:		**Sales/Marketing:**		**Liberal Arts:**		**Information Sys.:**		**Professionals:**		**Tech./Scientific:**	
Mgmt. Trainees:		Marketing Pros.:	Y	Gen. Writing/Editing:		Info. Mgmt.:	Y	Finance/Acct.:	Y	Engineers, Elec.:	Y
Experienced Mgmt.:		Retail Sales:		Tech. Writing:	Y	Software Dev.:	Y	Law:	Y	Engineers, Other:	
Int'l Business:	Y	Comm./Industrial:	Y	Graphic Arts/Photog.:		Hardware Dev.:	Y	HR/Other:	Y	Health/Lab:	
MBA Grads:	Y	Sales Trainees:		Music:		Consulting/Other:		Training:		Science/Research:	
		Advertising Pros.:	Y	Broadcasting:				Health Care:		Petroleum/Chem.:	
				Other:				Consulting:		Math/Other:	

TYPES OF BUSINESS:

Semiconductor Manufacturing Equipment
Solar Cells
Photovoltaics (PV)
Global Services
Semiconductor Equipment Manufacturing
Display Technology Equipment
Solar Product Manufacturing
Automation Software

BRANDS/DIVISIONS/AFFILIATES:

Nanomanufacturing Technologies
Silicon Systems Group
Sokudo Company
SunFab
Brooks Software
Semitool, Inc.
Varian Semiconductor Equipment Associates, Inc.

CONTACTS:

Note: Officers with more than one job title may be intentionally listed here more than once.

Michael R. Splinter, CEO
Michael R. Splinter, Pres.
George S. Davis, CFO/Exec. VP
Mary Humiston, VP-Global Human Resources
Ron Kifer, CIO
Mark R. Pinto, CTO
Manfred Kerschbaum, Chief of Staff/Sr. VP
Joseph J. Sweeney, General Counsel/Corp. Sec./Sr. VP
Charlie Pappis, Gen. Mgr.-Applied Global Svcs.
Chris Bowers, VP-Corp. Initiatives
Randhio Thakur, PH.D., Exec. VP/Gen. Mgr.-Silicon Systems
Michael R. Splinter, Chmn.
Joseph Flanagan, VP-Supply Chain

Phone: 408-727-5555 **Fax:** 408-748-9943
Toll-Free:
Address: 3050 Bowers Ave., Santa Clara, CA 95054-3299 US

GROWTH PLANS/SPECIAL FEATURES:

Applied Materials, Inc. (AMI), a global leader in the semiconductor industry, provides solutions for the global semiconductor, flat panel display, solar and related industries, with a portfolio of equipment, service and software products. The firm serves approximately 12,600 people in 11 principle regions including Canada, China, Europe, India, Israel, Japan, Korea, Malaysia, Singapore, Taiwan and the U.S. AMI operates in four reportable segments: Silicon; Applied Global Services; Display; and Energy and Environmental Solutions. The Silicon segment, operated by Silicon Systems Group develops, manufactures and sells a wide range of manufacturing equipment used to fabricate semiconductor chips or integrated circuits. Most chips are built on a silicon wafer base and include a variety of circuit components, such as transistors and other devices, that are connected by multiple layers of wiring (interconnects). The Applied Global Services segment provides products and services designed to improve the performance and productivity and reduce environmental impact of the fab operations of semiconductor, LCD and solar PV manufacturers. The Display segment designs, manufactures, sells and services equipment to fabricate thin film transistor LCDs for televisions, computer displays and other consumer-oriented electronic applications. The Energy and Environmental Solutions segment provides manufacturing solutions for the generation and conservation of energy. AMI's solutions utilize Nanomanufacturing Technology, or the production of ultra-small structures, including the engineering of thin layers of film onto substrates. In April 2010, AMI opened a Singapore Operations Center, its first manufacturing facility in Asia. It is located in Changi North Industrial Park and will manufacture advanced semiconductor equipment as well as support AMI's worldwide supply chain operations and other corporate functions. In May 2011, the firm agreed to acquire Varian Semiconductor Equipment Associates, Inc. for $4.9 billion.

Employees are offered medical insurance; flexible spending accounts; adoption benefits; an employee assistance program; health appraisals; health and fitness education; a 401(k) plan; a stock purchase plan; credit union membership; and tuition reimbursement.

FINANCIALS:

Sales and profits are in thousands of dollars—add 000 to get the full amount. 2010 Note: Financial information for 2010 was not available for all companies at press time.

2010 Sales: $9,548,667	2010 Profits: $937,866
2009 Sales: $5,013,607	2009 Profits: $-305,327
2008 Sales: $8,129,240	2008 Profits: $960,746
2007 Sales: $9,734,856	2007 Profits: $1,710,196
2006 Sales: $9,167,014	2006 Profits: $1,516,663

U.S. Stock Ticker: AMAT
Int'l Ticker:
Int'l Exchange:
Employees: 13,045 Fiscal Year Ends: 10/31
Parent Company:

SALARIES/BENEFITS:

Pension Plan:	ESOP Stock Plan:	Profit Sharing:	Top Exec. Salary: $814,154	Bonus: $
Savings Plan: Y	Stock Purch. Plan: Y		Second Exec. Salary: $493,477	Bonus: $

OTHER THOUGHTS:

Apparent Women Officers or Directors: 2
Hot Spot for Advancement for Women/Minorities: Y

LOCATIONS: ("Y" = Yes)

West:	Southwest:	Midwest:	Southeast:	Northeast:	International:
Y	Y				Y

ARAMARK CORPORATION

www.aramark.com

Industry Group Code: 722310

Management:		Sales/Marketing:		Liberal Arts:		Information Sys.:		Professionals:		Tech./Scientific:	
Mgmt. Trainees:	Y	Marketing Pros.:	Y	Gen. Writing/Editing:	Y	Info. Mgmt.:	Y	Finance/Acct.:	Y	Engineers, Elec.:	
Experienced Mgmt.:	Y	Retail Sales:		Tech. Writing:	Y	Software Dev.:	Y	Law:	Y	Engineers, Other:	
Int'l Business:	Y	Comm./Industrial:	Y	Graphic Arts/Photog.:	Y	Hardware Dev.:		HR/Other:	Y	Health/Lab:	
MBA Grads:	Y	Sales Trainees:	Y	Music:		Consulting/Other:		Training:	Y	Science/Research:	
		Advertising Pros.:	Y	Broadcasting:				Health Care:		Petroleum/Chem.:	
				Other:				Consulting:		Math/Other:	

TYPES OF BUSINESS:

Food Service Contractor
Facilities Management
Uniforms & Career Apparel Rental
Parks & Resorts Concessions & Facilities
Health Care Support Services
Apparel Manufacturing
Clinical Equipment Maintenance

BRANDS/DIVISIONS/AFFILIATES:

Galls
GS Capital Partners
CCMP Capital Advisors
J.P. Morgan Partners
Thomas H. Lee Partners
Warburg Pincus LLC

CONTACTS: *Note: Officers with more than one job title may be intentionally listed here more than once.*

Joseph Neubauer, CEO
L. Frederick Sutherland, CFO/Exec. VP
Lynn B. McKee, Exec. VP-Human Resources
Andrew C. Kerin, Pres., Global Food, Hospitality & Facilities Svcs.
Scott Parrill, Pres., ARAMARK Correctional Svcs.
John Babiarz, Pres., ARAMARK Healthcare
Liza Cartmell, Pres., ARAMARK Sports & Entertainment
Joseph Neubauer, Chmn.

Phone: 215-238-3000 | **Fax:** 215-238-3333
Toll-Free: 800-272-6275
Address: 1101 Market St., ARAMARK Twr., Philadelphia, PA 19107-2988 US

GROWTH PLANS/SPECIAL FEATURES:

ARAMARK Corporation is a leading food, hospitality and facilities management services company. Serving clients in 22 countries, ARAMARK offers services across six broad categories: facilities management; uniforms and work apparel; food service and refreshments; lodging and guest accommodations; clinical technology services; and cleanroom services. ARAMARK's facilities management services include laundry, housekeeping, facilities maintenance, plant operations, landscaping, transportation, clinical equipment maintenance, grounds keeping, custodial services and construction management. Uniform and career apparel services provide both rental and direct marketing services to customers in the manufacturing, transportation, construction, restaurant, hotel, public safety and health care industries, including gear and clothing for emergency response and law enforcement under the Galls brand. The firm operates a fabric cutting plant in Georgia and sewing plants in Puerto Rico and Mexico. Food service and refreshment offerings include dining halls, on-site restaurants, convenience stores, concessions stands, banquet halls, catering and executive dining rooms. Lodging and guest accommodations, including reservations booking and retail services, are provided to parks and resorts, as well as conference and convention centers. Clinical technology services include acquisitions, clinical equipment maintenance services and asset tracking. Cleanroom services are provided to the pharmaceutical, biotechnology and microelectronics manufacturing industries. ARAMARK's clients include numerous domestic and international business and industrial firms; 400 stadiums, arenas, conference and convention centers; 20 state and national parks; over 2,200 healthcare and senior living facilities; 600 correctional facilities; and 2,000 colleges, universities, school districts and private schools. Outside of North America, its largest operations are in the U.K., Germany, Chile, Ireland, Spain and Belgium. ARAMARK is owned by an investor group led by Chairman and CEO Joseph Neubauer and investment funds managed by GS Capital Partners, CCMP Capital Advisors, J.P. Morgan Partners, Thomas H. Lee Partners and Warburg Pincus LLC.

The company offers its employees medical, dental and vision; a 401(k) plan; life and disability insurance; and an employee assistance plan.

FINANCIALS: **Sales and profits are in thousands of dollars—add 000 to get the full amount. 2010 Note: Financial information for 2010 was not available for all companies at press time.**

2010 Sales: $12,571,676	2010 Profits: $30,688	**U.S. Stock Ticker: Private**
2009 Sales: $12,297,869	2009 Profits: $-6,911	**Int'l Ticker:**
2008 Sales: $12,470,200	2008 Profits: $39,500	Int'l Exchange:
2007 Sales: $12,384,300	2007 Profits: $30,900	Employees: 254,000 Fiscal Year Ends: 9/30
2006 Sales: $11,621,173	2006 Profits: $261,098	Parent Company: GS CAPITAL PARTNERS

SALARIES/BENEFITS:

Pension Plan: Y	ESOP Stock Plan:	Profit Sharing:	Top Exec. Salary: $1,250,000	Bonus: $2,100,000
Savings Plan: Y	Stock Purch. Plan:		Second Exec. Salary: $680,577	Bonus: $500,000

OTHER THOUGHTS:

Apparent Women Officers or Directors: 2
Hot Spot for Advancement for Women/Minorities:

LOCATIONS: ("Y" = Yes)

West:	Southwest:	Midwest:	Southeast:	Northeast:	International:
Y	Y	Y	Y	Y	Y

Sales, profits and employees may be estimates. Financial information, benefits and other data can change quickly and may vary from those stated here.

ARCHER DANIELS MIDLAND CO

www.adm.com

Industry Group Code: 3112

Management:		Sales/Marketing:		Liberal Arts:		Information Sys.:		Professionals:		Tech./Scientific:	
Mgmt. Trainees:	Y	Marketing Pros.:	Y	Gen. Writing/Editing:	Y	Info. Mgmt.:	Y	Finance/Acct.:	Y	Engineers, Elec.:	
Experienced Mgmt.:	Y	Retail Sales:		Tech. Writing:	Y	Software Dev.:	Y	Law:	Y	Engineers, Other:	Y
Int'l Business:	Y	Comm./Industrial:	Y	Graphic Arts/Photog.:	Y	Hardware Dev.:		HR/Other:	Y	Health/Lab:	
MBA Grads:	Y	Sales Trainees:		Music:		Consulting/Other:		Training:	Y	Science/Research:	Y
		Advertising Pros.:	Y	Broadcasting:				Health Care:		Petroleum/Chem.:	Y
				Other:				Consulting:		Math/Other:	

TYPES OF BUSINESS:

Food Processing-Oilseeds, Corn & Wheat
Agricultural Services
Nutraceuticals
Transportation Services
Biodiesel
Natural Plastics
Chocolate

BRANDS/DIVISIONS/AFFILIATES:

English River Pellets, Inc.
Alimenta (USA), Inc.
Golden Peanut Company LLC
Elstar Oils S.A.
Eaststarch C.V.
Telles, LLC
Almidones Mexicanos S.A.

CONTACTS: *Note: Officers with more than one job title may be intentionally listed here more than once.*

Patricia A. Woertz, CEO
Juan R. Luciano, COO/Exec. VP
Patricia A. Woertz, Pres.
Steven R. Mills, CFO/Exec. VP
Michael D'Ambrose, Sr. VP-Human Resources
David J. Smith, General Counsel/Exec. VP/Sec.
Kevin L. Hess, VP-Oilseeds Processing Oper.
Ismael Roig, VP-Planning & Bus. Dev.
Victoria A. Podesta, Chief Comm. Officer/VP
Vikram Luthar, VP-Finance/Treas.
Michael R. Baroni, VP-Econmic Policy
Mark A. Bemis, Sr. VP/Pres., Corn Bus. Unit
Craig E. Huss, Chief Risk Officer/Sr. VP
Matthew J. Jansen, Sr. VP/Pres., Oilseeds Bus. Unit
Patricia A. Woertz, Chmn.
Ismael Roig, VP/Pres., APAC

Phone: 217-424-5200 **Fax:** 217-424-6196
Toll-Free: 800-637-5843
Address: 4666 Faries Pkwy., Decatur, IL 62525 US

GROWTH PLANS/SPECIAL FEATURES:

Archer Daniels Midland Co. (ADM) is an agricultural processor that produces and sells oils and corn-based sweeteners. It procures, transports, stores, processes and markets oils and protein meals from soy, canola, sunflower seeds, palm, cotton, peanut and other oilseeds. The company also uses corn to develop sweeteners, such as high fructose corn syrup, citric acid, feed additives and biofuels like ethanol. It produces a variety of other food and feed ingredients, including cocoa, wheat flour, oats, bulgur, starch, soy concentrates, nutraceuticals and industrial flour used to make wallboard. These materials are processed and stored in 265 processing plants and grain elevators in the U.S. and abroad. ADM offers sourcing and distribution services for third parties, making use of the company's network of 24,700 railcars; 700 trucks; 1,600 trailers; and 1,700 barges also used for its own goods. The company has 50% interests in Almidones Mexicanos S.A., which operates a wet corn milling plant in Mexico; Eaststarch C.V., which operates wet corn milling plants in Bulgaria, Hungary, Romania, Slovakia and Turkey; and Telles, LLC, which produces a biodegradable plastic based on corn. In December 2010, ADM opened a new fertilizer blending plant in Paraguay; acquired a soybean storage facility in South Carolina from Carolina Soya; and acquired Alimenta (USA), Inc. from Alimenta S.A. As a result of the transaction, the firm now owns Golden Peanut Company LLC, a major supplier of peanuts and peanut-derived ingredients. In 2011, the firm made several major announcements, including plans to invest in sustainable palm production in Brazil; acquire a soybean crushing and biodiesel facility; acquire a majority share of Elstar Oils S.A.; and acquire four grain storage elevators from Olsen's Mill Acquisition Company/Ag Services of Wisconsin. Also in April 2011, the company opened a bio-based propylene glycol plant in Illinois. In August 2011, ADM acquired English River Pellets, Inc.

FINANCIALS: **Sales and profits are in thousands of dollars—add 000 to get the full amount. 2010 Note: Financial information for 2010 was not available for all companies at press time.**

2010 Sales: $61,682,000 2010 Profits: $1,930,000
2009 Sales: $69,207,000 2009 Profits: $1,684,000
2008 Sales: $69,816,000 2008 Profits: $1,802,000
2007 Sales: $44,018,000 2007 Profits: $2,162,000
2006 Sales: $36,596,111 2006 Profits: $1,312,070

U.S. Stock Ticker: ADM
Int'l Ticker:
Int'l Exchange:
Employees: 30,000 Fiscal Year Ends: 6/30
Parent Company:

SALARIES/BENEFITS:

Pension Plan: Y ESOP Stock Plan: Profit Sharing: Top Exec. Salary: $1,300,000 Bonus: $2,956,454
Savings Plan: Y Stock Purch. Plan: Y Second Exec. Salary: $901,400 Bonus: $803,549

OTHER THOUGHTS:

Apparent Women Officers or Directors: 4
Hot Spot for Advancement for Women/Minorities: Y

LOCATIONS: ("Y" = Yes)

West:	Southwest:	Midwest:	Southeast:	Northeast:	International:
Y	Y	Y	Y	Y	Y

ARROW ELECTRONICS INC

www.arrow.com

Industry Group Code: 423430

Management:		Sales/Marketing:		Liberal Arts:		Information Sys.:		Professionals:		Tech./Scientific:	
Mgmt. Trainees:	Y	Marketing Pros.:	Y	Gen. Writing/Editing:	Y	Info. Mgmt.:	Y	Finance/Acct.:	Y	Engineers, Elec.:	
Experienced Mgmt.:	Y	Retail Sales:		Tech. Writing:	Y	Software Dev.:	Y	Law:	Y	Engineers, Other:	
Int'l Business:	Y	Comm./Industrial:	Y	Graphic Arts/Photog.:	Y	Hardware Dev.:		HR/Other:	Y	Health/Lab:	
MBA Grads:	Y	Sales Trainees:	Y	Music:		Consulting/Other:		Training:	Y	Science/Research:	
		Advertising Pros.:	Y	Broadcasting:				Health Care:		Petroleum/Chem.:	
				Other:				Consulting:		Math/Other:	

TYPES OF BUSINESS:

Electronic Components-Distributor
Computer Products-Distributor
Technical Support Services
Supply Chain Services
Design Services
Materials Planning
Assembly Services
Inventory Management

BRANDS/DIVISIONS/AFFILIATES:

Arrow Enterprise Computing Solutions
Arrow North American Components (NAC)
Converge
Verical, Inc.
Sphinx Group Ltd.
Intechra
Diasa Informatica
Nu Horizons Electronics

CONTACTS: *Note: Officers with more than one job title may be intentionally listed here more than once.*

Michael J. Long, CEO
Michael J. Long, Pres.
Paul J. Reilly, CFO/Exec. VP-Finance
John P. McMahon, Sr. VP-Human Resources
Peter S. Brown, General Counsel/Corp. Sec./Sr. VP
Paul J. Reilly, Exec. VP-Oper.
M. Catherine Morris, Chief Strategy Officer/Sr. VP
John Hourigan, Dir.-Corp. Comm.
Michael Taunton, Treas./VP
Peter T. Kong, Pres., Arrow Global Components
Andrew S. Bryant, Pres., Arrow Enterprise Computing Solutions
Vinnie Vellucci, Pres., Arrow North American Components
Michael J. Long, Chmn.
Simon Yu, Pres., Arrow Asia-Pacific Components

Phone: 631-847-2000	**Fax:** 631-847-2222
Toll-Free: 877-237-8621	
Address: 50 Marcus Dr., Melville, NY 11747-4210 US	

GROWTH PLANS/SPECIAL FEATURES:

Arrow Electronics, Inc. is a global provider of products, services and solutions to industrial and commercial users of electronic components of enterprise computing software. The company offers more than 450,000 products to its clients in the electronic industry products and solutions in materials planning, programming, assembly services and online supply chain tools and design. Arrow serves as a supply channel partner for over 900 suppliers and 125,000 original equipment manufacturers, contract manufacturers and commercial customers through a global network of over 250 locations in 51 countries and territories. Its operations are divided into two segments: enterprise computing solutions and global components. The enterprise computing solutions segment distributes enterprise IT products, such as servers, software and storage devices, to value added retailers (VARs) in North America, Middle East, Africa and Europe. This segment consists primarily of Arrow Enterprise Computing Solutions (ECS), which offers services in North America, Africa and Europe. Additionally, Arrow NAC provides enterprise solutions for contract, aerospace and defense manufacturers. The global components segment, consisting primarily of Arrow North American Components, Arrow EMEA and Arrow Asia/Pacific, distributes electronics components and related products. Its sales are comprised of semiconductors; passive, electro-mechanical and interconnect products such as capacitors, resistors, potentiometers, power supplies, relays, switches, and connectors; and computing, memory and other products. In 2010, Arrow made a number of acquisitions, including Converge and Verical, Inc. in April; Sphinx Group Ltd. in June; and Intechra and Diasa Informatica in December. In March 2010, Arrow ECS established a professional services business unit to offer technical and educational support to clients in North America. In January 2011, it acquired Nu Horizons Electronics.

Employee benefits include a 401(k); an employee stock ownership program; medical, dental and vision coverage; a domestic partner program; an employee assistance program; tuition assistance; volunteer grants; scholarships; and an employee referral program.

FINANCIALS: **Sales and profits are in thousands of dollars—add 000 to get the full amount. 2010 Note: Financial information for 2010 was not available for all companies at press time.**

2010 Sales: $18,744,676	2010 Profits: $479,630	**U.S. Stock Ticker: ARW**
2009 Sales: $14,684,101	2009 Profits: $123,512	**Int'l Ticker:**
2008 Sales: $16,761,009	2008 Profits: $-613,739	Int'l Exchange:
2007 Sales: $15,984,992	2007 Profits: $407,792	Employees: 12,700 Fiscal Year Ends: 12/31
2006 Sales: $13,577,112	2006 Profits: $388,331	Parent Company:

SALARIES/BENEFITS:

Pension Plan:	ESOP Stock Plan: Y	Profit Sharing:	Top Exec. Salary: $1,057,692	Bonus: $1,485,000
Savings Plan: Y	Stock Purch. Plan:		Second Exec. Salary: $666,186	Bonus: $1,198,313

OTHER THOUGHTS:

Apparent Women Officers or Directors: 1
Hot Spot for Advancement for Women/Minorities:

LOCATIONS: ("Y" = Yes)

West:	Southwest:	Midwest:	Southeast:	Northeast:	International:
Y	Y	Y	Y	Y	Y

ARTHUR J GALLAGHER & CO

www.ajg.com

Industry Group Code: 524210

Management:		Sales/Marketing:		Liberal Arts:		Information Sys.:		Professionals:		Tech./Scientific:	
Mgmt. Trainees:	Y	Marketing Pros.:	Y	Gen. Writing/Editing:	Y	Info. Mgmt.:	Y	Finance/Acct.:	Y	Engineers, Elec.:	
Experienced Mgmt.:	Y	Retail Sales:		Tech. Writing:	Y	Software Dev.:	Y	Law:	Y	Engineers, Other:	
Int'l Business:	Y	Comm./Industrial:	Y	Graphic Arts/Photog.:	Y	Hardware Dev.:		HR/Other:	Y	Health/Lab:	
MBA Grads:	Y	Sales Trainees:		Music:		Consulting/Other:		Training:	Y	Science/Research:	
		Advertising Pros.:	Y	Broadcasting:				Health Care:		Petroleum/Chem.:	
				Other:				Consulting:		Math/Other:	

TYPES OF BUSINESS:

Insurance Brokerage & Management
Risk Management Services
Employee Benefit Services
Investment Operations
Claims Management
Information Management
Insurance Software
Reinsurance

BRANDS/DIVISIONS/AFFILIATES:

Old Greenwich Consulting Group
Behnke & Co., Inc.
Premier Risk Services, Inc.
Herbruck, Alder & Company
Continental Excess & Surplus, Inc.
Aviation Insurance Holdings, Inc.
Tribeca Strategic Advisors, LLC
Gleason Agency, Inc. (The)

CONTACTS: *Note: Officers with more than one job title may be intentionally listed here more than once.*

J. Patrick Gallagher, Jr., CEO
J. Patrick Gallagher, Jr., Pres.
Douglas K. Howell, CFO/VP
Susan E. McGrath, Chief Human Resources Officer/VP
Walter D. Bay, General Counsel/VP/Corp. Sec.
James W. Durkin, Jr., VP/Pres., Gallagher Benefit Svcs., Inc.
James S. Gault, VP/Pres./COO-Brokerage Svcs. Div.
Scott R. Hudson, VP/Pres./CEO-Gallagher Basset Svcs., Inc.
David E. McGurn, Jr., VP
J. Patrick Gallagher, Jr., Chmn.

Phone: 630-773-3800	**Fax:** 630-285-4000
Toll-Free:	
Address: 2 Pierce Pl., Itasca, IL 60143-3141 US	

GROWTH PLANS/SPECIAL FEATURES:

Arthur J. Gallagher & Co. and its subsidiaries provide insurance brokerage and third-party claims settlement and administration services to clients in the U.S. and abroad, with Gallagher's brokers, agents and administrators acting as intermediaries between insurers and their customers. The firm operates in three business segments: brokerage, risk management and corporate. The brokerage segment (72% of revenues) is composed of retail and wholesale brokerage operations. Retail operations focus on property/casualty, employer-provided health and welfare insurance and retirement planning on behalf of middle market commercial, industrial, public, religious and not-for-profit clients, while wholesale brokers assist the retail brokers and other non-Gallagher brokers in placing specialized and hard-to-place insurance coverage. The risk management segment (25% of revenues) provides contract claim settlement and administration services for clients that self-insure some or all of their property/casualty coverage and for insurance companies choosing to outsource some or all of their property/casualty claims departments. Gallagher markets its risk management services primarily to Fortune 1000 companies, larger middle market companies, not-for-profit organizations and public entities. The corporate segment (3% of revenues) manages Gallagher's clean energy and tax-advantaged investments and venture capital funds. 87% of the company's revenues are generated in the U.S. In late 2010, Gallagher acquired Old Greenwich Consulting Group; Behnke & Co., Inc.; Premier Risk Services, Inc.; Herbruck, Alder & Company; Continental Excess & Surplus, Inc.; Aviation Insurance Holdings, Inc.; and Tribeca Strategic Advisors, LLC. Some of its 2011 acquisitions include The Gleason Agency, Inc.; James F. Reda & Associates, LLC; Woodbrook Underwriting Agencies, Ltd.; Risk Planners, Inc.; Blue Water Benefits, Inc.; Meyers-Reynolds & Associates, Inc.; HLG Holdings, Ltd.; Fish & Schulkamp, Inc.; Independent Fiduciary Services, Inc.; Bushong Insurance Associates, Inc.; The BeneTex Group, Inc.; and the insurance brokerage business of Robinson-Adams Insurance, Inc.

FINANCIALS: **Sales and profits are in thousands of dollars—add 000 to get the full amount. 2010 Note: Financial information for 2010 was not available for all companies at press time.**

2010 Sales: $1,864,200	2010 Profits: $174,100	**U.S. Stock Ticker: AJG**
2009 Sales: $1,729,300	2009 Profits: $128,600	**Int'l Ticker:**
2008 Sales: $1,645,000	2008 Profits: $77,300	Int'l Exchange:
2007 Sales: $1,623,300	2007 Profits: $138,800	Employees: 10,700 Fiscal Year Ends: 12/31
2006 Sales: $1,470,100	2006 Profits: $128,500	Parent Company:

SALARIES/BENEFITS:

Pension Plan:	ESOP Stock Plan:	Profit Sharing:	Top Exec. Salary: $1,000,000	Bonus: $1,000,000
Savings Plan: Y	Stock Purch. Plan: Y		Second Exec. Salary: $700,000	Bonus: $600,000

OTHER THOUGHTS:

Apparent Women Officers or Directors: 2
Hot Spot for Advancement for Women/Minorities: Y

LOCATIONS: ("Y" = Yes)

West:	Southwest:	Midwest:	Southeast:	Northeast:	International:
Y	Y	Y	Y	Y	Y

Sales, profits and employees may be estimates. Financial information, benefits and other data can change quickly and may vary from those stated here.

ASCENA RETAIL GROUP INC

www.ascenaretail.com

Industry Group Code: 448120

Management:		Sales/Marketing:		Liberal Arts:		Information Sys.:		Professionals:		Tech./Scientific:	
Mgmt. Trainees:	Y	Marketing Pros.:	Y	Gen. Writing/Editing:	Y	Info. Mgmt.:	Y	Finance/Acct.:	Y	Engineers, Elec.:	
Experienced Mgmt.:	Y	Retail Sales:	Y	Tech. Writing:		Software Dev.:	Y	Law:	Y	Engineers, Other:	
Int'l Business:	Y	Comm./Industrial:		Graphic Arts/Photog.:	Y	Hardware Dev.:		HR/Other:	Y	Health/Lab:	
MBA Grads:	Y	Sales Trainees:	Y	Music:		Consulting/Other:		Training:	Y	Science/Research:	
		Advertising Pros.:	Y	Broadcasting:				Health Care:		Petroleum/Chem.:	
				Other:	Y			Consulting:		Math/Other:	

TYPES OF BUSINESS:

Women's Apparel, Retail
Teen Fashion Stores
Fashion Accessories
Private-Label Credit Cards

BRANDS/DIVISIONS/AFFILIATES:

dressbarn
dressbarn woman
Studio Y
Industrial Exchange
Tween Brands Inc
Justice
The Dress Barn, Inc.
maurices

CONTACTS: *Note: Officers with more than one job title may be intentionally listed here more than once.*

David R. Jaffe, CEO
David R. Jaffe, Pres.
Armand Correia, CFO/Sr. VP
Vivian Behrens, Chief Mktg. Officer/Sr. VP
Gene L. Wexler, General Counsel/Sr. VP
Reid Hackney, VP-Finance/Corp. Controller
Michael W. Rayden, CEO-Justice
Elliot S. Jaffe, Chmn.

Phone: 845-369-4500 | **Fax:** 845-369-4829
Toll-Free: 800-373-7722
Address: 30 Dunnigan Dr., Suffern, NY 10901 US

GROWTH PLANS/SPECIAL FEATURES:

Ascena Retail Group, Inc., formerly The Dress Barn, Inc., operates a national chain of value-priced specialty stores offering in-season, moderate- to better-quality career apparel and accessories, primarily to working women in their mid-30's to mid-50's. The majority of Ascena's stores are located in strip malls. The company has three store formats: dressbarn stores, which carry junior and misses sizes; dressbarn woman stores, which feature larger sizes; and combination stores, which carry both. The combination stores are more prevalent, though the company does have some locations that are only either dressbarn or dressbarn women. Ascena's subsidiary, maurices, offers moderately priced, up-to-date fashions designed to appeal to a younger female consumer than the dressbarn and dressbarn woman brands. From its Duluth, Minnesota headquarters, maurices operates primarily within smaller cities of 25,000 to 100,000 in population. maurice's merchandise is sold under three brand names: maurices, Studio Y and Industrial Exchange. Through the company's subsidiary Tween Brands, Inc., the company markets clothing and accessories to tween girls aged 7-14 through its Justice store locations. Ascena operates 833 dressbarn stores in 47 states and Washington, D.C.; 757 maurices stores in 44 states; and 887 Justice stores in 45 states and Puerto Rico. The company offers a dressbarn credit card operated by World Financial Network National Bank, as well as personal and corporate gift cards in a variety of values. Holders of the dressbarn credit card receive targeted promotions including directed mailings and special coupons. In January 2011, The Dress Barn, Inc. completed a reorganization and became Ascena Retail Group, Inc.

The company offers its employees short-term disability; life and accidental death and dismemberment insurance; a 30% merchandise discount; career training; tuition reimbursement; and medical, dental and vision coverage.

FINANCIALS: **Sales and profits are in thousands of dollars—add 000 to get the full amount. 2010 Note: Financial information for 2010 was not available for all companies at press time.**

2010 Sales: $2,374,571 | 2010 Profits: $133,378
2009 Sales: $1,494,236 | 2009 Profits: $69,688
2008 Sales: $1,444,165 | 2008 Profits: $74,088
2007 Sales: $1,426,607 | 2007 Profits: $101,182
2006 Sales: $1,300,277 | 2006 Profits: $78,954

U.S. Stock Ticker: ASNA
Int'l Ticker:
Int'l Exchange:
Employees: 30,000 Fiscal Year Ends: 7/31
Parent Company:

SALARIES/BENEFITS:

Pension Plan: | ESOP Stock Plan: | Profit Sharing: | Top Exec. Salary: $950,000 | Bonus: $153,750
Savings Plan: Y | Stock Purch. Plan: Y | | Second Exec. Salary: $726,923 | Bonus: $2,772,000

OTHER THOUGHTS:

Apparent Women Officers or Directors: 3
Hot Spot for Advancement for Women/Minorities: Y

LOCATIONS: ("Y" = Yes)

West:	Southwest:	Midwest:	Southeast:	Northeast:	International:
Y	Y	Y	Y	Y	Y

ASCENSION HEALTH

www.ascensionhealth.org

Industry Group Code: 622110

Management:		Sales/Marketing:		Liberal Arts:		Information Sys.:		Professionals:		Tech./Scientific:	
Mgmt. Trainees:	Y	Marketing Pros.:		Gen. Writing/Editing:	Y	Info. Mgmt.:	Y	Finance/Acct.:	Y	Engineers, Elec.:	
Experienced Mgmt.:	Y	Retail Sales:		Tech. Writing:	Y	Software Dev.:	Y	Law:	Y	Engineers, Other:	
Int'l Business:		Comm./Industrial:		Graphic Arts/Photog.:	Y	Hardware Dev.:		HR/Other:	Y	Health/Lab:	Y
MBA Grads:	Y	Sales Trainees:		Music:		Consulting/Other:		Training:	Y	Science/Research:	
		Advertising Pros.:	Y	Broadcasting:				Health Care:	Y	Petroleum/Chem.:	
				Other:	Y			Consulting:		Math/Other:	

TYPES OF BUSINESS:

Hospitals
Acute Care Hospitals
Rehabilitation Hospitals
Psychiatric Hospitals
Pharmacy Management

BRANDS/DIVISIONS/AFFILIATES:

Daughters of Charity National Health System
Sisters of St. Joseph Health System
Sisters of St. Joseph of Carondelet
Ascension Health Ventures
Millennium Pharmacy Systems
United Surgical Partners International
Alexian Brothers Health System

CONTACTS:

Note: Officers with more than one job title may be intentionally listed here more than once.

Anthony R. Tersigni, CEO
Robert J. Henkel, COO
Anthony R. Tersigni, Pres.
Anthony J. Speranzo, CFO/Sr. VP
Challis M. Lowe, Sr. VP-Human Resources & Organizational Dev.
David B. Pryor, Chief Medical Officer
Mark D. Barner, CIO/Sr. VP
Joseph R. Impicciche, General Counsel/Sr. VP-Legal Svcs.
John D. Doyle, Chief Strategy Officer
Stephen D. LeResche, VP-Comm.
James K. Beckmann, Jr., Chief Risk Officer/Sr. VP-System Support Svcs.
Laura S. Kaiser, Pres./CEO-Sacred Heart Health System
Charles Barnett, Pres./CEO-Seton Family of Hospitals
Ruth Brinkley, Pres./CEO-Carondelet Health Network
Kathleen Kelly, Chmn.
Scott Caldwell, Chief Supply Chain Officer

Phone: 314-733-8000	**Fax:** 314-733-8013
Toll-Free:	
Address: 4600 Edmundson Rd., St. Louis, MO 63134 US	

GROWTH PLANS/SPECIAL FEATURES:

Ascension Health is a leading not-for-profit health system in the U.S., with more than 500 hospitals and centers in 20 states and the District of Columbia. The Catholic organization was formed in 1999 through the union of the Daughters of Charity National Health System, based in St. Louis, Missouri, and the Sisters of St. Joseph Health System, based in Ann Arbor, Michigan. In 2002, Ascension Health added the hospitals and health facilities of the Sisters of St. Joseph of Carondelet, also based in St. Louis, Missouri. Ascension Health Ventures (AHV), the organization's investment subsidiary, identifies and supports companies that offer potential breakthroughs in healthcare-related products, services and technologies. AHV's investment portfolio includes Impulse Monitoring, which provides intraoperative neurophysiological monitoring; Interventional Spine, which is an early stage developer of a spinal device platform enabling percutaneous approaches for spinal fusion; ISTO Technologies, which is an early stage developer of orthobiologic products for sports medicine and spinal therapy applications; Millennium Pharmacy Systems, which provides pharmaceutical management services to the long-term care industry; and United Surgical Partners International, which operates ambulatory and short-stay surgical facilities in the U.S. and owns private hospitals in Europe. Ascension Health is committed to assisting uninsured and underinsured patients as part of its effort to move the U.S. healthcare toward a more compassionate system. As part of this effort, Ascension Health offers an online resource center that provides information about programs for the uninsured. In April 2011, Ascension Health signed a letter of intent to add Alexian Brothers Health System to its facility network

Ascension Health offers employee benefits such as medical, dental, vision and life insurance; healthcare and dependent care reimbursement accounts; a retirement savings program and a pension plan; tuition reimbursement; and an employee assistance program.

FINANCIALS:

Sales and profits are in thousands of dollars—add 000 to get the full amount. 2010 Note: Financial information for 2010 was not available for all companies at press time.

2010 Sales: $14,773,000	2010 Profits: $569,000	**U.S. Stock Ticker: Nonprofit**
2009 Sales: $14,152,000	2009 Profits: $363,000	**Int'l Ticker:**
2008 Sales: $13,408,273	2008 Profits: $482,592	Int'l Exchange:
2007 Sales: $12,304,000	2007 Profits: $1,223,000	Employees: 113,000 Fiscal Year Ends: 6/30
2006 Sales: $11,405,552	2006 Profits: $802,965	Parent Company:

SALARIES/BENEFITS:

Pension Plan: Y	ESOP Stock Plan:	Profit Sharing:	Top Exec. Salary: $	Bonus: $
Savings Plan: Y	Stock Purch. Plan:		Second Exec. Salary: $	Bonus: $

OTHER THOUGHTS:

Apparent Women Officers or Directors: 10
Hot Spot for Advancement for Women/Minorities: Y

LOCATIONS: ("Y" = Yes)

West:	Southwest:	Midwest:	Southeast:	Northeast:	International:
Y	Y	Y	Y	Y	

Sales, profits and employees may be estimates. Financial information, benefits and other data can change quickly and may vary from those stated here.

AT&T INC

www.att.com

Industry Group Code: 517110

Management:		Sales/Marketing:		Liberal Arts:		Information Sys.:		Professionals:		Tech./Scientific:	
Mgmt. Trainees:	Y	Marketing Pros.:	Y	Gen. Writing/Editing:	Y	Info. Mgmt.:	Y	Finance/Acct.:	Y	Engineers, Elec.:	Y
Experienced Mgmt.:	Y	Retail Sales:	Y	Tech. Writing:	Y	Software Dev.:	Y	Law:	Y	Engineers, Other:	Y
Int'l Business:	Y	Comm./Industrial:	Y	Graphic Arts/Photog.:	Y	Hardware Dev.:		HR/Other:	Y	Health/Lab:	
MBA Grads:	Y	Sales Trainees:	Y	Music:		Consulting/Other:		Training:	Y	Science/Research:	
		Advertising Pros.:	Y	Broadcasting:				Health Care:		Petroleum/Chem.:	
				Other:	Y			Consulting:		Math/Other:	

TYPES OF BUSINESS:

Local Telephone Service
Wireless Telecommunications
Long-Distance Telephone Service
Corporate Telecom, Backbone & Wholesale Services
Directory Publishing
Entertainment & Television via Internet
International Telephone Services
Internet Access via DSL

BRANDS/DIVISIONS/AFFILIATES:

AT&T Mobility LLC
AT&T U-verse
AT&T DIRECT TV
AT&T Wireless Services, Inc.
Yellow Pages
Centennial Communications Corp.
ISIS
AT&T ForHealth

CONTACTS: *Note: Officers with more than one job title may be intentionally listed here more than once.*

Randall L. Stephenson, CEO
Randall L. Stephenson, Pres.
Richard G. Lindner, CFO/Sr. Exec. VP
Catherine M. Coughlin, Global Mktg. Officer/Sr. Exec. VP
William A. Blase Jr., Sr. Exec. VP-Human Resources
Wayne Watts, General Counsel/Sr. Exec. VP
Ronald E. Spears, Sr. Exec. VP-Exec. Oper.
Forest Miller, Group Pres., Corp. Strategy & Dev.
Dru Cessac, Mgr.-Investor Rel.
Rayford Wilkins, Jr., Group Pres., AT&T Diversified Bus.
John T. Stankey, Pres./CEO-AT&T Bus. Solutions
Ralph de la Vega, Pres./CEO-AT&T Mobility & Consumer Markets
James W. Cicconi, Sr. Exec. VP-External & Legislative Affairs
Randall L. Stephenson, Chmn.

Phone: 210-821-4105	**Fax:**
Toll-Free:	
Address: 208 S. Akard St., Dallas, TX 75202 US	

GROWTH PLANS/SPECIAL FEATURES:

AT&T, Inc. is one of the world's largest providers of diversified telecommunications services. The company and its subsidiaries deliver a portfolio of wireless communications; local exchange services; long-distance services; data and broadband and Internet services; video services; telecommunications equipment; managed networking; wholesale services; and directory advertising and publishing services. The company operates through four segments: wireless, wireline, advertising and publishing and other. The wireless segment, operating through AT&T Mobility, provides wireless voice communications services to business and consumer customers. It is one of the nation's largest wireless carriers, serving 85.1 million customers, with service spanning more than 200 countries worldwide. The wireline segment provides retail and wholesale communication services, including voice and data services, domestically and internationally. This segment also includes AT&T's Virtual Private Network (VPN); Voice over IP (VoIP) services; application management; web hosting, security and integration services, outsourcing, government-related services and satellite video services, as well as its AT&T U-Verse high-speed broadband and TV services. The advertising and publishing segment include Yellow and White Pages directories, directory advertising and Internet-based advertising. The other segment primarily includes customer information services and all corporate and other operations. In May 2010, the company sold Sterling Commerce, Inc. to IBM. In June 2010, it agreed to sell AT&T Japan's outsourcing services operations to Internet Initiative Japan, Inc. In August 2010, AT&T sold certain wireless assets of Centennial Communications Corp. to Verizon Wireless. In November of the same year, it established AT&T ForHealth, an initiative to develop innovative technology solutions for the healthcare industry. In March 2011, the firm announced its intent to acquire T-Mobile USA from T-Mobile, in a deal worth $39 billion. If concluded, the acquisition will bring 38,000 employees, 33.7 million wireless subscribers and $21 billion in annual revenues to AT&T.

AT&T offers its employees medical, dental and vision insurance, tuition reimbursement, company discounts, flexible spending accounts and a 401(k) savings and pension plan.

FINANCIALS: **Sales and profits are in thousands of dollars—add 000 to get the full amount. 2010 Note: Financial information for 2010 was not available for all companies at press time.**

2010 Sales: $124,280,000	2010 Profits: $19,864,000	**U.S. Stock Ticker: T**
2009 Sales: $123,018,000	2009 Profits: $12,535,000	**Int'l Ticker:**
2008 Sales: $124,028,000	2008 Profits: $12,867,000	Int'l Exchange:
2007 Sales: $118,928,000	2007 Profits: $11,951,000	Employees: 266,590 Fiscal Year Ends: 12/31
2006 Sales: $63,055,000	2006 Profits: $7,356,000	Parent Company:

SALARIES/BENEFITS:

Pension Plan: Y	ESOP Stock Plan:	Profit Sharing:	Top Exec. Salary: $1,450,000	Bonus: $5,850,000
Savings Plan: Y	Stock Purch. Plan:		Second Exec. Salary: $830,000	Bonus: $1,500,000

OTHER THOUGHTS:

Apparent Women Officers or Directors: 5
Hot Spot for Advancement for Women/Minorities: Y

LOCATIONS: ("Y" = Yes)

West:	Southwest:	Midwest:	Southeast:	Northeast:	International:
Y	Y	Y	Y	Y	Y

AUTOMATIC DATA PROCESSING INC

www.adp.com

Industry Group Code: 518210

Management:		Sales/Marketing:		Liberal Arts:		Information Sys.:		Professionals:		Tech./Scientific:	
Mgmt. Trainees:	Y	Marketing Pros.:	Y	Gen. Writing/Editing:	Y	Info. Mgmt.:	Y	Finance/Acct.:	Y	Engineers, Elec.:	Y
Experienced Mgmt.:	Y	Retail Sales:		Tech. Writing:	Y	Software Dev.:	Y	Law:	Y	Engineers, Other:	
Int'l Business:	Y	Comm./Industrial:	Y	Graphic Arts/Photog.:	Y	Hardware Dev.:		HR/Other:	Y	Health/Lab:	
MBA Grads:	Y	Sales Trainees:	Y	Music:		Consulting/Other:	Y	Training:	Y	Science/Research:	
		Advertising Pros.:	Y	Broadcasting:				Health Care:		Petroleum/Chem.:	
				Other:				Consulting:		Math/Other:	

TYPES OF BUSINESS:

Data Processing Services
Business Outsourcing Solutions
Information Services
Payroll Processing
Automobile Dealer Services

BRANDS/DIVISIONS/AFFILIATES:

ADP TotalSource
MasterTax, LLC
MasterTax Services, LLC
AdvancedMD
Cobalt
Workscape, Inc.
AdvancedMD
Asparity Decision Solutions

CONTACTS: *Note: Officers with more than one job title may be intentionally listed here more than once.*

Gary C. Butler, CEO
Gary C. Butler, Pres.
Christopher R. Reidy, CFO
Michael L. Capone, CIO/VP
Michael A. Bonarti, General Counsel/VP/Sec.
Jan Siegmund, Chief Strategy Officer
Michael C. Eberhard, Treas./VP
Jan Siegmund, Pres., Added Value Svcs.
Edward B. Flynn, III, VP-Employer Svcs., Sales
Regina R. Lee, Pres., Employer Svcs., National Acct. Div.
Carlos Rodriguez, Pres., Employer Svcs., Small Bus. Svcs. Div.

Phone: 973-974-5000	**Fax:** 973-974-5390
Toll-Free: 800-225-5237	
Address: 1 ADP Blvd., Roseland, NJ 07068 US	

GROWTH PLANS/SPECIAL FEATURES:

Automatic Data Processing, Inc. (ADP) is one of the world's largest providers of business outsourcing solutions. The company offers a wide range of human resources, payroll, tax and benefits administration solutions from a single source. The firm also provides integrated computing solutions to automotive, heavy truck, motorcycle, marine and recreational vehicle dealers throughout the world. ADP operates in three segments: employer services; professional employer organization (PEO) services; and dealer services. The employer services segment offers a range of human resources information, payroll processing; and tax and benefits administration products and services, including traditional and web-based outsourcing solutions. The segment assists roughly 537,000 employers in the U.S., Canada, Europe, South America, Australia and Asia to staff, manage, pay and retain their employees. The PEO services segment, which operates as ADP TotalSource, provides small and medium sized businesses with comprehensive employment administration outsourcing solutions (through a co-employment relationship), including payroll, payroll tax filing, human resources guidance, 401(k) plan administration, benefits administration, compliance services, health and workers' compensation coverage and other supplemental benefits for employees. ADP TotalSouce has approximately 54 offices in 23 states; the businesses it serves have a combined total of 241,000 employees. The dealer services division provides integrated dealer management systems and business solutions to 25,000 automotive, heavy truck, motorcycle, marine, RV and heavy machinery retailers in over 90 countries. In August 2010, the company acquired Cobalt and Workscape, Inc. In late 2011, ADP acquired MasterTax, LLC and MasterTax Services, LLC from Consultants in Data Processing , Inc. In March 2011, the firm acquired AdvancedMD. In September 2011, the company acquired Asparity Decision Solutions.

Employees are offered medical, dental and vision insurance; healthcare and dependent care flexible spending accounts; life, AD&D, personal accident and business travel accident insurance; short- and long-term disability; a 529 college bound fund; tuition reimbursement; a scholarship program; a voluntary relocation assistance program; auto and home insurance programs; and on-site child care in some locations.

FINANCIALS: **Sales and profits are in thousands of dollars—add 000 to get the full amount. 2010 Note: Financial information for 2010 was not available for all companies at press time.**

2010 Sales: $8,927,700	2010 Profits: $1,207,300	**U.S. Stock Ticker: ADP**
2009 Sales: $8,838,400	2009 Profits: $1,325,100	**Int'l Ticker:**
2008 Sales: $8,733,700	2008 Profits: $1,155,700	Int'l Exchange:
2007 Sales: $7,800,000	2007 Profits: $1,021,200	Employees: 47,000 Fiscal Year Ends: 6/30
2006 Sales: $6,835,600	2006 Profits: $1,554,000	Parent Company:

SALARIES/BENEFITS:

Pension Plan: Y	ESOP Stock Plan:	Profit Sharing:	Top Exec. Salary: $1,000,000	Bonus: $2,020,000
Savings Plan: Y	Stock Purch. Plan: Y		Second Exec. Salary: $532,400	Bonus: $557,900

OTHER THOUGHTS:

Apparent Women Officers or Directors: 4
Hot Spot for Advancement for Women/Minorities: Y

LOCATIONS: ("Y" = Yes)

West:	Southwest:	Midwest:	Southeast:	Northeast:	International:
Y	Y	Y	Y	Y	Y

Sales, profits and employees may be estimates. Financial information, benefits and other data can change quickly and may vary from those stated here.

AUTONATION INC

www.autonation.com

Industry Group Code: 441110

Management:		**Sales/Marketing:**		**Liberal Arts:**		**Information Sys.:**		**Professionals:**		**Tech./Scientific:**	
Mgmt. Trainees:	Y	Marketing Pros.:	Y	Gen. Writing/Editing:	Y	Info. Mgmt.:	Y	Finance/Acct.:	Y	Engineers, Elec.:	
Experienced Mgmt.:	Y	Retail Sales:	Y	Tech. Writing:		Software Dev.:	Y	Law:	Y	Engineers, Other:	
Int'l Business:		Comm./Industrial:	Y	Graphic Arts/Photog.:	Y	Hardware Dev.:		HR/Other:	Y	Health/Lab:	
MBA Grads:	Y	Sales Trainees:	Y	Music:		Consulting/Other:		Training:	Y	Science/Research:	
		Advertising Pros.:	Y	Broadcasting:				Health Care:		Petroleum/Chem.:	
				Other:				Consulting:		Math/Other:	

TYPES OF BUSINESS:

Auto Dealer
Online Auto Sales
Vehicle Maintenance & Repair Services
Vehicle Parts
Extended Service Contracts
Vehicle Protection Products

BRANDS/DIVISIONS/AFFILIATES:

CONTACTS: *Note: Officers with more than one job title may be intentionally listed here more than once.*

Michael Jackson, CEO
Michael Maroone, COO
Michael Maroone, Pres.
Michael Short, CFO/Exec. VP
Kevin Westfall, Sr. VP-Sales
Jonathan Ferrando, General Counsel/Exec. VP/Corp. Sec.
Donna Parlapiano, Sr. VP-Regional Oper. & Industry Rel.
Marc Cannon, Sr. VP-Corp. Comm. & Public Policy
Michael Jackson, Chmn.

Phone: 954-769-7000 **Fax:** 954-769-6537
Toll-Free:
Address: 200 SW 1st Ave., Ste.1600, Fort Lauderdale, FL 33301 US

GROWTH PLANS/SPECIAL FEATURES:

AutoNation, Inc. is one of the largest automobile retailers in the U.S. It owns and operates 242 new vehicle franchises from 206 stores located in major metropolitan markets, predominantly in the Sunbelt region of the U.S. The company offers a diversified range of automotive products and services, including new vehicles, which generated 54% of the firm's 2010 revenue; used vehicles, 25%; parts and automotive services, 18%; and automotive finance and insurance products, 3%. The firm also arranges financing for vehicle purchases through third-party finance sources. It retailed approximately 370,000 new and used vehicles through its stores in 2010. The company's stores sell 31 different brands of new vehicles. The core brands of vehicles, representing approximately 93% of the new vehicles the firm sold in 2010, are manufactured by Toyota, Ford, Honda, Nissan, General Motors, Mercedes, BMW and Chrysler. AutoNation divides its operations into three segments: Domestic, which is comprised of franchises that sell new General Motors, Ford and Chrysler automobiles; Import, which includes franchises that sell Toyota, Honda and Nissan vehicles; and Premium Luxury, which includes Mercedes, BMW and Lexus franchises. In 2010, The Domestic segment accounted for 31% of the company's total new vehicle unit sales; Import, 52%; and Premium Luxury, 17%. The company's web site allows prospective buyers to evaluate the trade-in value of a current vehicle, explore nearby car lots, read automotive reviews and even arrange for the purchase of an automobile online.

Employees are offered health, dental, life and disability insurance; longevity bonuses; a 401(k) plan; and an employee vehicle purchase program.

FINANCIALS: **Sales and profits are in thousands of dollars—add 000 to get the full amount. 2010 Note: Financial information for 2010 was not available for all companies at press time.**

2010 Sales: $12,461,000 — 2010 Profits: $226,600
2009 Sales: $10,666,000 — 2009 Profits: $198,000
2008 Sales: $13,238,700 — 2008 Profits: $-1,243,100
2007 Sales: $16,385,200 — 2007 Profits: $278,700
2006 Sales: $18,626,500 — 2006 Profits: $316,900

U.S. Stock Ticker: AN
Int'l Ticker:
Int'l Exchange:
Employees: 19,000 Fiscal Year Ends: 12/31
Parent Company:

SALARIES/BENEFITS:

Pension Plan: ESOP Stock Plan: Profit Sharing: Top Exec. Salary: $1,150,000 Bonus: $2,863,039
Savings Plan: Y Stock Purch. Plan: Second Exec. Salary: $1,000,000 Bonus: $1,867,200

OTHER THOUGHTS:

Apparent Women Officers or Directors: 2
Hot Spot for Advancement for Women/Minorities:

LOCATIONS: ("Y" = Yes)

West:	Southwest:	Midwest:	Southeast:	Northeast:	International:
Y	Y	Y	Y	Y	

AUTOZONE INC

www.autozone.com

Industry Group Code: 441310

Management:		**Sales/Marketing:**		**Liberal Arts:**		**Information Sys.:**		**Professionals:**		**Tech./Scientific:**	
Mgmt. Trainees:	Y	Marketing Pros.:	Y	Gen. Writing/Editing:	Y	Info. Mgmt.:	Y	Finance/Acct.:	Y	Engineers, Elec.:	
Experienced Mgmt.:	Y	Retail Sales:	Y	Tech. Writing:		Software Dev.:	Y	Law:	Y	Engineers, Other:	
Int'l Business:	Y	Comm./Industrial:	Y	Graphic Arts/Photog.:	Y	Hardware Dev.:		HR/Other:	Y	Health/Lab:	
MBA Grads:	Y	Sales Trainees:	Y	Music:		Consulting/Other:		Training:	Y	Science/Research:	
		Advertising Pros.:	Y	Broadcasting:				Health Care:		Petroleum/Chem.:	
				Other:				Consulting:		Math/Other:	

TYPES OF BUSINESS:

Auto Parts, Retail
Automotive Software
Online Sales
General Automotive Service

BRANDS/DIVISIONS/AFFILIATES:

Autozone.com
ALLDATA LLC
Loan-a-Tool

CONTACTS:

Note: Officers with more than one job title may be intentionally listed here more than once.

William C. Rhodes, III, CEO
William C. Rhodes, III, Pres.
William T. Giles, CFO/Exec. VP-Finance
Lisa R. Kranc, Sr. VP-Mktg.
Timothy W. Briggs, Sr. VP-Human Resources
Jon A. Bascom, CIO/Sr. VP
Mark A. Finestone, Sr. VP-Merch.
Harry L. Goldsmith, General Counsel/Exec. VP/Corp. Sec.
Thomas B. Newbern, Sr. VP-Store Oper.
Robert D. Olsen, Corp. Dev. Officer/Exec. VP
Charlie Pleas, III, Controller/Sr. VP
William T. Giles, Exec. VP-Store Dev. & IT
Larry Roesel, Sr. VP-Commercial
William C. Rhodes, III, Chmn.
William W. Graves, Sr. VP-Supply Chain

Phone: 901-495-6500	**Fax:** 901-495-8300
Toll-Free: 800-288-6966	
Address: 123 S. Front St., Memphis, TN 38103 US	

GROWTH PLANS/SPECIAL FEATURES:

AutoZone, Inc. is a leading specialty retailer of automotive parts and accessories, targeting do-it-yourself (DIY) customers. With more than 4,425 stores in the U.S. and Puerto Rico and 249 in Mexico, each AutoZone store carries an extensive product line for cars, sport utility vehicles, vans and light trucks, including new and remanufactured automotive parts, maintenance items, accessories and non-automotive products. Many AutoZone stores have a commercial sales program that provides commercial credit and prompt delivery of parts and other products to local, regional and national repair garages, dealers and service stations. Although each of the company's stores carry the same basic product lines, the company does tailor each store's parts inventory to the makes and models of the vehicles in their trade areas. Parts not kept in stock can be ordered and delivered to the store within a few days, or they can be ordered online. AutoZone allows parts ordered online to be returned at any store location. The company also has a Loan-a-Tool program, through which customers can borrow a specialty tool, such as a steering wheel puller, for which they would have little or no use other than for a single job. AutoZone also provides other free services, including check engine light readings; battery charging and installation assistance; and the testing of starters, alternators, batteries, sensors and actuators. In addition, the company offers automotive diagnostic and repair software through its subsidiary ALLDATA LLC.

Employees are offered medical, dental and vision insurance; wellness programs; disability and life insurance; a 401(k) plan; store discounts; tuition reimbursement; ASE certification reimbursement; adoption assistance; and a discount stock purchase plan.

FINANCIALS:

Sales and profits are in thousands of dollars—add 000 to get the full amount. 2010 Note: Financial information for 2010 was not available for all companies at press time.

2010 Sales: $7,362,618	2010 Profits: $738,311
2009 Sales: $6,816,824	2009 Profits: $657,049
2008 Sales: $6,522,706	2008 Profits: $641,606
2007 Sales: $6,169,804	2007 Profits: $595,672
2006 Sales: $5,948,355	2006 Profits: $569,275

U.S. Stock Ticker: AZO
Int'l Ticker:
Int'l Exchange:
Employees: 63,000 Fiscal Year Ends: 8/31
Parent Company:

SALARIES/BENEFITS:

Pension Plan:	ESOP Stock Plan:	Profit Sharing:	Top Exec. Salary: $920,923	Bonus: $1,572,937
Savings Plan: Y	Stock Purch. Plan: Y		Second Exec. Salary: $472,692	Bonus: $605,519

OTHER THOUGHTS:

Apparent Women Officers or Directors: 2
Hot Spot for Advancement for Women/Minorities: Y

LOCATIONS: ("Y" = Yes)

West:	Southwest:	Midwest:	Southeast:	Northeast:	International:
Y	Y	Y	Y	Y	Y

AVNET INC

www.avnet.com

Industry Group Code: 423430

Management:		Sales/Marketing:		Liberal Arts:		Information Sys.:		Professionals:		Tech./Scientific:	
Mgmt. Trainees:	Y	Marketing Pros.:	Y	Gen. Writing/Editing:		Info. Mgmt.:	Y	Finance/Acct.:	Y	Engineers, Elec.:	
Experienced Mgmt.:	Y	Retail Sales:		Tech. Writing:	Y	Software Dev.:		Law:	Y	Engineers, Other:	
Int'l Business:	Y	Comm./Industrial:	Y	Graphic Arts/Photog.:	Y	Hardware Dev.:		HR/Other:	Y	Health/Lab:	
MBA Grads:	Y	Sales Trainees:		Music:		Consulting/Other:		Training:	Y	Science/Research:	
		Advertising Pros.:		Broadcasting:				Health Care:		Petroleum/Chem.:	
				Other:				Consulting:		Math/Other:	

TYPES OF BUSINESS:

Components-Distributor
Marketing Services
Supply Chain Advisory Services

BRANDS/DIVISIONS/AFFILIATES:

Avnet Technology Solutions
Avnet Electronics Marketing
Avnet Logistics
Tallard Technologies SA
Bell Microproducts Inc
Broadband Integrated Resources Ltd
Eurotone Electric Ltd
itX Group Ltd

CONTACTS: *Note: Officers with more than one job title may be intentionally listed here more than once.*

Roy Vallee, CEO
Rick Hamada, COO
Ray Sadowski, CFO/Sr. VP
Harley Feldberg, Pres., Avnet Electronics Mktg. Global
MaryAnn Miller, Chief Human Resources Officer/VP
Steve Phillips, CIO/Sr. VP
David Birk, General Counsel/Sr. VP
Steve Church, Chief Bus. Dev. & Process Officer
Al Maag, Chief Comm. Officer/VP
Vincent Keenan, Investor Rel.
Phil Gallagher, Pres., Avnet Technology Solutions Global
Steve Church, Chief Operational Excellence Officer
Jim Smith, Pres., Avnet Logistics
Patrick Zammit, Pres., Avnet Electronics Mktg., EMEA
Roy Vallee, Chmn.
Graeme Watt, Pres., Avnet Technology Solutions, EMEA

Phone: 480-643-2000	**Fax:** 480-643-7370
Toll-Free: 800-409-1483	
Address: 2211 S. 47th St., Phoenix, AZ 85034 US	

GROWTH PLANS/SPECIAL FEATURES:

Avnet, Inc. is one of the world's largest value-added distributors of electronic components, enterprise computer and storage products, software and embedded subsystems. The company operates through two divisions, Technology Solutions and Electronics Marketing, which operate throughout the Americas, Europe, the Middle East, Africa, Asia and Australia. The firm connects more than 300 suppliers to over 100,000 original equipment manufacturers (OEMs), electronic manufacturing services (EMS) providers, original design manufacturers (ODMs) and value-added resellers (VARs) that design and build the electronic equipment for end-market use, as well as to other industrial customers. Additionally, the firm provides engineering design, materials management and logistics services, system integration and configuration and supply chain services. The Electronics Marketing division markets and sells semiconductors and interconnect, passive and electromechanical devices (IP&E) to a customer base whose end-markets include automotive, communications, computer hardware and peripheral, industrial and manufacturing, medical equipment, military and aerospace. The Technology Solutions division markets and sells servers, data storage, software and related services to resellers and mid to high-end users, as well as focusing on the worldwide OEM market. Avnet generated 44% of its 2010 revenues in the Americas, 25% in the Asia/Pacific region and 31% in the Europe/Middle East/Africa region. In July 2010, the company acquired Tallard Technologies SA, a value-added distributor in Latin America, and Bell Microproducts, Inc., a global distributor. In October 2010, the firm purchased Broadband Integrated Resources, Ltd., which specializes in broadband and cable repair, and Eurotone Electric, Ltd., a Chinese renewable energy company. In January 2011, Avnet acquired itX Group, Ltd., an Australian information technology company.

Employees are offered medical, dental and vision insurance; flexible spending accounts; life and AD&D insurance; travel accident insurance; a pension plan; a 401(k) savings plan; an employee stock purchase plan; short- and long-term disability; and tuition reimbursement, among others.

FINANCIALS: **Sales and profits are in thousands of dollars—add 000 to get the full amount. 2010 Note: Financial information for 2010 was not available for all companies at press time.**

2010 Sales: $19,160,200	2010 Profits: $410,400	**U.S. Stock Ticker: AVT**
2009 Sales: $16,229,900	2009 Profits: $-1,129,700	**Int'l Ticker:**
2008 Sales: $17,952,700	2008 Profits: $499,100	Int'l Exchange:
2007 Sales: $15,681,100	2007 Profits: $393,100	Employees: 14,200 Fiscal Year Ends: 6/30
2006 Sales: $14,253,630	2006 Profits: $204,547	Parent Company:

SALARIES/BENEFITS:

Pension Plan: Y	ESOP Stock Plan: Y	Profit Sharing:	Top Exec. Salary: $1,050,000	Bonus: $2,359,240
Savings Plan: Y	Stock Purch. Plan:		Second Exec. Salary: $610,000	Bonus: $1,235,792

OTHER THOUGHTS:

Apparent Women Officers or Directors: 3
Hot Spot for Advancement for Women/Minorities: Y

LOCATIONS: ("Y" = Yes)

West:	Southwest:	Midwest:	Southeast:	Northeast:	International:
Y	Y				Y

AVON PRODUCTS INC

www.avoncompany.com

Industry Group Code: 325620

Management:		Sales/Marketing:		Liberal Arts:		Information Sys.:		Professionals:		Tech./Scientific:	
Mgmt. Trainees:	Y	Marketing Pros.:	Y	Gen. Writing/Editing:	Y	Info. Mgmt.:	Y	Finance/Acct.:	Y	Engineers, Elec.:	
Experienced Mgmt.:	Y	Retail Sales:	Y	Tech. Writing:		Software Dev.:	Y	Law:	Y	Engineers, Other:	
Int'l Business:	Y	Comm./Industrial:		Graphic Arts/Photog.:	Y	Hardware Dev.:		HR/Other:	Y	Health/Lab:	
MBA Grads:	Y	Sales Trainees:	Y	Music:		Consulting/Other:		Training:	Y	Science/Research:	
		Advertising Pros.:	Y	Broadcasting:				Health Care:		Petroleum/Chem.:	Y
				Other:	Y			Consulting:		Math/Other:	

TYPES OF BUSINESS:

Cosmetics & Beauty Supplies, Direct Selling
Fragrances & Toiletries
Gift & Decorative Items
Apparel & Accessories
Fashion Jewelry
Health & Fitness Products
Online Sales

BRANDS/DIVISIONS/AFFILIATES:

Avon Color
Beyond Color
Anew
Avon Skin-So-Soft
Naturals
Mark
M-The Men's Catalog
Advance Techniques

CONTACTS: *Note: Officers with more than one job title may be intentionally listed here more than once.*

Andrea Jung, CEO
Gina R. Boswell, COO
Elizabeth A. Smith, Pres.
Kimberly A. Ross, CFO/Exec. VP
Lucien Alziari, Sr. VP-Human Resources
Donagh Herlihy, CIO/Sr. VP
Kim Rucker, General Counsel/Sr. VP/Corp. Sec.
John P. Higson, Sr. VP-Global Commercial Oper.
Nancy Glaser, Sr. VP-Global Comm.
Srdjan Mijuskovic, Sr. VP-Central & Eastern Europe
Jorge Martinez Quiroga, Sr. VP/Pres., North America
Geralyn B. Breig, Sr. VP
Jeri B. Finard, Sr. VP/Pres., Global Brand
Andrea Jung, Chmn.
Bob Briddon, Sr. VP/Pres., APAC
John F. Owen, Sr. VP-Global Supply Chain

Phone: 212-282-5000	**Fax:** 212-282-6035
Toll-Free:	
Address: 1345 Ave. of the Americas, New York, NY 10105 US	

GROWTH PLANS/SPECIAL FEATURES:

Avon Products, Inc. is a global manufacturer and marketer of beauty and related products. The firm groups these products into three categories: Beauty, consisting of cosmetics, fragrances, skin care and toiletries, which accounts for roughly 71% of sales; Fashion, which consists of fashion jewelry, watches, apparel, footwear and accessories and accounts for 19% of sales; and Home, which consists of gift and decorative products, housewares, entertainment and leisure products, children's products and nutritional products (10% of sales). The company sells makeup under the Avon Color and Beyond Color brands; skincare products under Anew and Avon Solutions; bath and body products under Avon Skin-So-Soft and Naturals; hair care products under Advance Techniques; health and fitness products under Avon Wellness; skincare products through its Liz Earle brand; Jewelry though its Silpada brand; mom and baby products under the Tiny Tillia brand; and fragrance products under a variety of brands, including Crystal Aura, Derek Jeter Driven, U by Ungaro and Today, Tomorrow, Always. Additionally, Avon has launched a global business targeting teenage girls through the Mark brand name and a portfolio of products for men offered in a publication called M-The Men's Catalog. The company sells products primarily through direct selling and marketing by approximately 6.5 million independent representatives worldwide. The firm's international operations are conducted primarily through subsidiaries in 64 countries and territories outside of the U.S., and its products are distributed in 41 additional countries and territories through distributorships. In December 2010, Avon sold its 74.67% ownership of Avon Japan to TPG Capital for roughly $90 million.

FINANCIALS: **Sales and profits are in thousands of dollars—add 000 to get the full amount. 2010 Note: Financial information for 2010 was not available for all companies at press time.**

2010 Sales: $10,862,800	2010 Profits: $606,300	**U.S. Stock Ticker: AVP**
2009 Sales: $10,205,200	2009 Profits: $625,800	**Int'l Ticker:**
2008 Sales: $10,507,500	2008 Profits: $875,300	Int'l Exchange:
2007 Sales: $9,938,700	2007 Profits: $530,700	Employees: 42,000 Fiscal Year Ends: 12/31
2006 Sales: $8,763,900	2006 Profits: $477,600	Parent Company:

SALARIES/BENEFITS:

Pension Plan:	ESOP Stock Plan:	Profit Sharing:	Top Exec. Salary: $1,375,000	Bonus: $5,362,500
Savings Plan:	Stock Purch. Plan:		Second Exec. Salary: $750,000	Bonus: $1,863,750

OTHER THOUGHTS:

Apparent Women Officers or Directors: 11
Hot Spot for Advancement for Women/Minorities: Y

LOCATIONS: ("Y" = Yes)

West:	Southwest:	Midwest:	Southeast:	Northeast:	International:
Y		Y	Y	Y	Y

AXA FINANCIAL INC

www.axa-equitable.com

Industry Group Code: 524113

Management:		Sales/Marketing:		Liberal Arts:		Information Sys.:		Professionals:		Tech./Scientific:	
Mgmt. Trainees:	Y	Marketing Pros.:	Y	Gen. Writing/Editing:	Y	Info. Mgmt.:	Y	Finance/Acct.:	Y	Engineers, Elec.:	
Experienced Mgmt.:	Y	Retail Sales:		Tech. Writing:		Software Dev.:	Y	Law:	Y	Engineers, Other:	
Int'l Business:	Y	Comm./Industrial:	Y	Graphic Arts/Photog.:	Y	Hardware Dev.:		HR/Other:	Y	Health/Lab:	
MBA Grads:	Y	Sales Trainees:	Y	Music:		Consulting/Other:		Training:	Y	Science/Research:	
		Advertising Pros.:	Y	Broadcasting:				Health Care:		Petroleum/Chem.:	
				Other:	Y			Consulting:		Math/Other:	Y

TYPES OF BUSINESS:

Investment Management
Mutual Funds & Pension Funds
Stock Brokerage
Investment Banking
Securities Underwriting
Annuities
Asset Management
Life Insurance

BRANDS/DIVISIONS/AFFILIATES:

AXA Advisors LLC
AXA Equitable Life Insurance Company
AXA Distributors
AllianceBernstein LP
MONY Group (The)
MONY Life Insurance Company
MONY Life Insurance Company of America
AXA Group

CONTACTS: *Note: Officers with more than one job title may be intentionally listed here more than once.*

Mark Pearson, CEO
Richard S. Dziadzio, CFO/Sr. Exec. VP
Rino Piazzolla, Sr. Exec. VP/Head-Human Resources
Richard V. Silver, Chief Admin. Officer/Sr. Exec. VP
Richard V. Silver, Chief Legal Officer
Mattieu Rouot, Sr. VP/Head-Investor Rel.
Kevin R. Byrne, Chief Investment Officer/Exec. VP
Charles Marino, Chief Actuary/Exec. VP
Nick Lane, Sr. Exec. VP/Pres., Retirement Savings
Andrew McMahon, Pres., AXA Equitable Life insurance
Mark Pearson, Chmn.

Phone: 212-554-1234 | **Fax:** 212-707-1822
Toll-Free: 888-292-4492
Address: 1290 Ave. of the Americas, New York, NY 10104 US

GROWTH PLANS/SPECIAL FEATURES:

AXA Financial, Inc., a wholly-owned subsidiary of AXA Group, is a diversified financial services organization offering a broad spectrum of insurance, investment banking and asset management services. The company's main operating subsidiaries are AXA Advisors LLC, AXA Equitable Life Insurance Company, AXA Distributors, AllianceBernstein LP and The MONY Group. AXA Advisors provides financial, retirement and estate planning; college planning; life insurance; annuities; and mutual funds to individuals and small businesses. AXA Equitable Life Insurance Company offers a variety of traditional variable and interest-sensitive life insurance products, variable and fixed-interest annuity products, mutual funds and other investment products to individuals, small groups, small and medium-size corporations, state and local governments and not-for-profit organizations. AXA Distributors, another of AXA Financial's main operating subsidiaries, distributes managed investment products and services including whole and variable life insurance and fixed and variable annuities, as well as mutual funds to affiliated and independent professional financial intermediaries like brokerages, banks and independent financial planners. AXA Distributors serves over 650 firms and represents over 50,000 individual producers. AllianceBernstein LP provides investment management services and is one of the largest mutual fund sponsors, with approximately $496 billion in assets under management. The MONY Group is a financial services organization that originates and distributes protection, asset accumulation and retail brokerage products and services to individuals, corporations and institutions through advisory and wholesale distribution channels. MONY companies include MONY Life Insurance Company and MONY Life Insurance Company of America. In October 2010, AllianceBernstein acquired the alternative investments group belonging to SunAmerica.

The company offers performance-based compensation including short- and long-term incentive compensation. Employees can build healthcare based on their own specifications, in addition, the company offers dental, vision and retirement plans.

FINANCIALS: **Sales and profits are in thousands of dollars—add 000 to get the full amount. 2010 Note: Financial information for 2010 was not available for all companies at press time.**

2010 Sales: $124,819,588 | 2010 Profits: $4,243,156
2009 Sales: $123,656,076 | 2009 Profits: $5,534,958
2008 Sales: $127,365,758 | 2008 Profits: $1,235,181
2007 Sales: $ | 2007 Profits: $
2006 Sales: $ | 2006 Profits: $

U.S. Stock Ticker: Subsidiary
Int'l Ticker:
Int'l Exchange:
Employees: 10,427 Fiscal Year Ends: 12/31
Parent Company: AXA GROUP

SALARIES/BENEFITS:

Pension Plan: | ESOP Stock Plan: | Profit Sharing: | Top Exec. Salary: $ | Bonus: $
Savings Plan: | Stock Purch. Plan: | | Second Exec. Salary: $ | Bonus: $

OTHER THOUGHTS:

Apparent Women Officers or Directors:
Hot Spot for Advancement for Women/Minorities: Y

LOCATIONS: ("Y" = Yes)

West:	Southwest:	Midwest:	Southeast:	Northeast:	International:
Y	Y	Y	Y	Y	Y

BAIN & COMPANY INC

www.bain.com

Industry Group Code: 54161

Management:		Sales/Marketing:		Liberal Arts:		Information Sys.:		Professionals:		Tech./Scientific:	
Mgmt. Trainees:		Marketing Pros.:	Y	Gen. Writing/Editing:	Y	Info. Mgmt.:	Y	Finance/Acct.:	Y	Engineers, Elec.:	
Experienced Mgmt.:	Y	Retail Sales:		Tech. Writing:	Y	Software Dev.:	Y	Law:	Y	Engineers, Other:	
Int'l Business:	Y	Comm./Industrial:	Y	Graphic Arts/Photog.:	Y	Hardware Dev.:		HR/Other:	Y	Health/Lab:	Y
MBA Grads:	Y	Sales Trainees:		Music:		Consulting/Other:	Y	Training:		Science/Research:	
		Advertising Pros.:		Broadcasting:				Health Care:		Petroleum/Chem.:	
				Other:	Y			Consulting:	Y	Math/Other:	Y

TYPES OF BUSINESS:

Management Consulting
Technology Consulting
Merger & Acquisition Consulting

BRANDS/DIVISIONS/AFFILIATES:

CONTACTS:

Note: Officers with more than one job title may be intentionally listed here more than once.

Steve Ellis, Worldwide Managing Dir.
Leonard Banos, CFO/VP
Vittorio Massone, Head-South Africa Oper.
Cheryl Krauss, Dir.-Public Rel.
Miles Cook, Managing Partner-Global Performance Improvement
Bill Neuenfeldt, Managing Partner-New York Office
Orit Gadiesh, Chmn.
Paolo Bordogna, Head-EMEA Regional Financial Svcs. Practice

Phone: 617-572-2000 **Fax:** 617-572-2427
Toll-Free:
Address: 131 Dartmouth St., Boston, MA 02116 US

GROWTH PLANS/SPECIAL FEATURES:

Bain & Company, Inc. provides business consulting services on a global level. From approximately 42 offices in 27 countries, the firm's consultants work with top management executives from thousands of companies to help them outperform market competitors and create sustained financial growth and stability. Most of the company's offices are located in the heavily industrialized economies of the U.S. and Europe, but offices in locations such as Brazil, Argentina, South Africa, India, China, Japan, Singapore and Australia are also key parts of the firm's business. Consultants typically help executives make important decisions in areas such as corporate strategy, change management, company organization, operations, performance improvement, marketing, revenue sing or sale of a company's unprofitable businesses; the development of strategies to create profitable ones; penetration of new product segments; seizing of new business opportunities; and identification of flawed business strategies. Services are provided to clients in industries such as technology, telecom, financial services, retail, media, consumer products, transportation, nonprofit and public sector, energy and utilities, private equity and health care. In appropriate situations, Bain consultants assist clients in implementing the changes they decide to make to their business structures or processes.

The firm tends to hire college graduates with either liberal arts degrees, MBA degrees or both. Positions often involve extensive travel and sometimes major relocation, the costs of which are reimbursed by Bain.

FINANCIALS:

Sales and profits are in thousands of dollars—add 000 to get the full amount. 2010 Note: Financial information for 2010 was not available for all companies at press time.

2010 Sales: $2,500,000 — 2010 Profits: $
2009 Sales: $2,200,000 — 2009 Profits: $
2008 Sales: $2,400,000 — 2008 Profits: $
2007 Sales: $2,200,000 — 2007 Profits: $
2006 Sales: $1,900,000 — 2006 Profits: $

U.S. Stock Ticker: Private
Int'l Ticker:
Int'l Exchange:
Employees: 5,500 Fiscal Year Ends: 12/31
Parent Company:

SALARIES/BENEFITS:

Pension Plan: ESOP Stock Plan: Profit Sharing: Top Exec. Salary: $ Bonus: $
Savings Plan: Stock Purch. Plan: Second Exec. Salary: $ Bonus: $

OTHER THOUGHTS:

Apparent Women Officers or Directors: 1
Hot Spot for Advancement for Women/Minorities:

LOCATIONS: ("Y" = Yes)

West:	Southwest:	Midwest:	Southeast:	Northeast:	International:
Y	Y	Y	Y	Y	Y

BAKER HUGHES INC

www.bakerhughes.com

Industry Group Code: 213111

Management:		Sales/Marketing:		Liberal Arts:		Information Sys.:		Professionals:		Tech./Scientific:	
Mgmt. Trainees:	Y	Marketing Pros.:	Y	Gen. Writing/Editing:	Y	Info. Mgmt.:	Y	Finance/Acct.:	Y	Engineers, Elec.:	Y
Experienced Mgmt.:	Y	Retail Sales:		Tech. Writing:	Y	Software Dev.:	Y	Law:	Y	Engineers, Other:	Y
Int'l Business:	Y	Comm./Industrial:	Y	Graphic Arts/Photog.:	Y	Hardware Dev.:		HR/Other:	Y	Health/Lab:	
MBA Grads:	Y	Sales Trainees:		Music:		Consulting/Other:		Training:	Y	Science/Research:	
		Advertising Pros.:		Broadcasting:				Health Care:		Petroleum/Chem.:	Y
				Other:				Consulting:		Math/Other:	

TYPES OF BUSINESS:

Oil & Gas Drilling Support Services
Specialty Chemicals
Process Equipment
Geophysical Services
Drilling Fluids
Drill Bits
Data Management

BRANDS/DIVISIONS/AFFILIATES:

Meyer & Associates
JOA Oil & Gas BV
Tanroc

CONTACTS: *Note: Officers with more than one job title may be intentionally listed here more than once.*

Chad C. Deaton, CEO
Martin S. Craighead, COO
Martin S. Craighead, Pres.
Peter A. Ragauss, CFO/Sr. VP
Gary Rich, VP-Global Sales
Didier Charreton, VP-Human Resources
Clifton Triplett, CIO/VP
Derek Mathieson, Pres., Tech.
Derek Mathieson, Pres., Prod.
Alan R. Crain, General Counsel/Sr. VP
Darrell Howard, Pres., Integrated Oper.
David E. Emerson, VP-Corp. Dev.
Adam Anderson, VP-Investor Rel.
Alan J. Keifer, Controller/VP
John A. O'Donnell, Pres., Western Hemisphere Oper.
Sandra E. Alford, Corp. Sec.
Alexander Peng, VP-Tax
Jan Kees Van Gaalen, VP/Treas.
Chad C. Deaton, Chmn.
Belgacem Chariag, VP/Pres., Eastern Hemisphere Oper.
Arthur Soucy, VP-Supply Chain

Phone: 713-439-8600	**Fax:** 713-439-8699
Toll-Free:	
Address: 2929 Allen Pkwy., Ste. 2100, Houston, TX 77019 US	

GROWTH PLANS/SPECIAL FEATURES:

Baker Hughes, Inc. is a major supplier of wellbore-related products and technology services and a provider of drilling, formation evaluation, completion and production products and services to the oil and natural gas industry. The firm operates through two main segments: drilling and evaluation, and completion and production. The drilling and evaluation segment provides products and services used to drill and evaluate oil and natural gas wells, as well as consulting services for the analysis of oil and gas reservoirs. The products and services in this segment include wireline formation evaluation and wireline completion services; data management, processing and analysis services; and real-time drilling, measurement-while-drilling and logging-while-drilling services. Additionally, the firm provides drilling and completion fluids and related services, and is a leading provider of Tricone roller cone drill bits and ream-while-drilling and casing drilling technology. The completion and production segment provides equipment and services used through the productive life of oil and natural gas wells. Baker Hughes' completion and production segment includes equipment for the workover, finishing and completion of wells; oilfield specialty chemicals and chemical technology solutions for petroleum production, transportation and refining; and electric submersible pumps and progressing cavity pumps. Baker Hughes maintains approximately 2,987 on and offshore rigs worldwide and more than 1,000 service locations in 90 countries. In August 2010, the company signed a strategic alliance with the Iraqi South Oil Company to provide technical services for its wireline logging department; and acquired Tanroc, a Canadian oilfield equipment and service supplier. In September 2010, Baker Hughes acquired petroleum industry software developer Meyer & Associates. In October 2010, the firm acquired the remaining 60% interest not already owned in JOA Oil & Gas BV; and opened a new repair and maintenance facility in Pennsylvania. In November 2010, Baker Hughes opened a new facility in Australia.

FINANCIALS: **Sales and profits are in thousands of dollars—add 000 to get the full amount. 2010 Note: Financial information for 2010 was not available for all companies at press time.**

2010 Sales: $14,414,000	2010 Profits: $819,000	**U.S. Stock Ticker: BHI**
2009 Sales: $9,664,000	2009 Profits: $421,000	**Int'l Ticker:**
2008 Sales: $11,864,000	2008 Profits: $1,635,000	Int'l Exchange:
2007 Sales: $10,428,200	2007 Profits: $1,513,900	Employees: 53,100 Fiscal Year Ends: 12/31
2006 Sales: $9,027,400	2006 Profits: $2,419,000	Parent Company:

SALARIES/BENEFITS:

Pension Plan:	ESOP Stock Plan:	Profit Sharing:	Top Exec. Salary: $1,283,461	Bonus: $3,126,755
Savings Plan:	Stock Purch. Plan:		Second Exec. Salary: $711,539	Bonus: $1,254,413

OTHER THOUGHTS:

Apparent Women Officers or Directors: 3
Hot Spot for Advancement for Women/Minorities: Y

LOCATIONS: ("Y" = Yes)

West:	Southwest:	Midwest:	Southeast:	Northeast:	International:
Y	Y	Y	Y	Y	Y

BALL CORP

www.ball.com

Industry Group Code: 3222

Management:		Sales/Marketing:		Liberal Arts:		Information Sys.:		Professionals:		Tech./Scientific:	
Mgmt. Trainees:	Y	Marketing Pros.:	Y	Gen. Writing/Editing:		Info. Mgmt.:	Y	Finance/Acct.:	Y	Engineers, Elec.:	
Experienced Mgmt.:	Y	Retail Sales:		Tech. Writing:		Software Dev.:		Law:	Y	Engineers, Other:	
Int'l Business:	Y	Comm./Industrial:	Y	Graphic Arts/Photog.:		Hardware Dev.:		HR/Other:	Y	Health/Lab:	
MBA Grads:	Y	Sales Trainees:		Music:		Consulting/Other:		Training:	Y	Science/Research:	
		Advertising Pros.:	Y	Broadcasting:				Health Care:		Petroleum/Chem.:	
				Other:				Consulting:		Math/Other:	

TYPES OF BUSINESS:

Packaging Products
Civil Space Systems
Defense Systems
Commercial Space Systems
Metal Food and Household Products Packaging
Radio Frequency and Microwave Technology
Metal Beverage Packaging

BRANDS/DIVISIONS/AFFILIATES:

Ball Aerospace and Technologies Corp.
Ball Europe
Ball Asia Pacific, Ltd.
Rocky Mountain Metal Container LLC
Latapack-Ball Embalagens Ltda.
Neuman Aluminum
Aerocan S.A.S.
Thai Beverage Can Limited

CONTACTS: *Note: Officers with more than one job title may be intentionally listed here more than once.*

John A. Hayes, CEO
John A. Hayes, Pres.
Scott C. Morrison, CFO/Sr. VP
James N. Peterson, VP-Mktg.
Leroy J. Williams, VP-IT & Svcs.
David A. Westerlund, Exec. VP-Admin./Corp. Sec.
Charles E. Baker, General Counsel/VP
James N. Peterson, VP-Corp. Affairs
Ann Scott, Dir.-Investor Rel.
Shawn M. Barker, Controller/VP
Raymond J. Seabrook, Exec. VP/COO-Global Packaging
Michael D. Herdman, Chief Commercial Officer-Global Metal Beverage
David L. Taylor, CEO/Pres., Ball Aerospace & Tech. Corp.
Gerrit Heske, Pres., Ball Europe
R. David Hoover, Chmn.
Gihan Atapattu, Pres., Ball Asia Pacific Ltd.

Phone: 303-469-3131 **Fax:** 303-460-2127
Toll-Free:
Address: 10 Longs Peak Dr., Broomfield, CO 80021 US

GROWTH PLANS/SPECIAL FEATURES:

Ball Corp. is a leading manufacturer of metal packaging for the food and beverage and household products industries. It also supplies aerospace technologies and services to commercial and governmental customers. The company operates in four business segments: metal beverage packaging, Americas and Asia; metal beverage packaging, Europe; metal food and household products packaging, Americas; and aerospace and technologies. The metal beverage packaging segments manufacture and sell aluminum, steel and polyethylene terephthalate (PET) containers. The European packaging division consists of 12 beverage can and can end plants. The metal food and household products packaging unit produces steel food containers, focusing on two-piece and three-piece containers for the packaging of vegetables, fruit, soups, meat, seafood, nutritional products and pet food. This segment also produces aerosol cans and paint cans. The aerospace and technologies business includes defense operations, civil space systems and commercial space operations. Products produced by this segment include spacecraft, sensors, instruments and radio frequency systems. Additional research and development facilities are aimed at producing new sizes and types of containers, as well as finding new uses for current food, beverage and household containers. The company maintains interests in several joint ventures, including Rocky Mountain Metal Container LLC, with MillerCoors; and Latapack-Ball Embalagens Ltda., with Latapack S.A. in Brazil. In 2010, Ball's packaging operations generated 91% of its total revenue, with the aerospace business accounting for the remaining 9%. In July 2010, the company acquired Neuman Aluminum. In August 2010, Ball sold its former plastic packaging operations to Amcor Limited for approximately $280 million. In January 2011, it acquired Aerocan S.A.S., a leading supplier of extruded aluminum aerosol cans and bottles in Europe. In March 2011, it agreed to build a beverage can manufacturing plant in Vietnam in partnership with Thai Beverage Can Limited.

FINANCIALS: **Sales and profits are in thousands of dollars—add 000 to get the full amount. 2010 Note: Financial information for 2010 was not available for all companies at press time.**

2010 Sales: $7,630,000 — 2010 Profits: $468,000
2009 Sales: $6,710,400 — 2009 Profits: $387,900
2008 Sales: $6,826,100 — 2008 Profits: $319,500
2007 Sales: $7,475,300 — 2007 Profits: $281,300
2006 Sales: $6,621,500 — 2006 Profits: $329,600

U.S. Stock Ticker: BLL
Int'l Ticker:
Int'l Exchange:
Employees: 14,000 Fiscal Year Ends: 12/31
Parent Company:

SALARIES/BENEFITS:

Pension Plan: Y ESOP Stock Plan: Profit Sharing: Top Exec. Salary: $1,155,000 Bonus: $4,554,658
Savings Plan: Y Stock Purch. Plan: Y Second Exec. Salary: $725,000 Bonus: $1,885,640

OTHER THOUGHTS:

Apparent Women Officers or Directors: 3
Hot Spot for Advancement for Women/Minorities: Y

LOCATIONS: ("Y" = Yes)

West:	Southwest:	Midwest:	Southeast:	Northeast:	International:
Y	Y	Y	Y	Y	Y

BARRETT BUSINESS SERVICES

www.barrettbusiness.com

Industry Group Code: 561

Management:		Sales/Marketing:		Liberal Arts:		Information Sys.:		Professionals:		Tech./Scientific:	
Mgmt. Trainees:		Marketing Pros.:	Y	Gen. Writing/Editing:	Y	Info. Mgmt.:	Y	Finance/Acct.:	Y	Engineers, Elec.:	
Experienced Mgmt.:		Retail Sales:		Tech. Writing:		Software Dev.:		Law:	Y	Engineers, Other:	
Int'l Business:		Comm./Industrial:	Y	Graphic Arts/Photog.:		Hardware Dev.:		HR/Other:	Y	Health/Lab:	
MBA Grads:	Y	Sales Trainees:		Music:		Consulting/Other:		Training:	Y	Science/Research:	
		Advertising Pros.:	Y	Broadcasting:				Health Care:		Petroleum/Chem.:	
				Other:	Y			Consulting:		Math/Other:	

TYPES OF BUSINESS:

Human Resources Management
Staffing Services
Professional Employer Services (PEO)

BRANDS/DIVISIONS/AFFILIATES:

CONTACTS:

Note: Officers with more than one job title may be intentionally listed here more than once.

Michael L. Elich, Interim CEO
Michael L. Elich, COO/VP
Michael L. Elich, Interim Pres.
James D. Miller, CFO
James D. Miller, Corp. Sec.
James D. Miller, Chief Acct. Officer/VP-Finance/Treas.
Gregory R. Vaughn, VP
Anthony Meeker, Chmn.

Phone: 360-828-0700 **Fax:** 360-828-0701
Toll-Free: 800-494-5669
Address: 8100 NE Parkway Dr., Ste. 200, Vancouver, WA 98662 US

GROWTH PLANS/SPECIAL FEATURES:

Barrett Business Services is a human resources management company that provides staffing services as well as professional employer services (PEO). Originally founded in 1951, Barrett is headquartered in Vancouver, Washington and has 43 offices in California, Oregon, Washington, Idaho, Arizona, Utah, Colorado, Maryland, Delaware and North Carolina. The firm's outsourced services help clients deal with issues concerning employment laws and regulations; payroll processing; employee benefits and administration; worker's compensation coverage; effective risk management; workplace safety programs; and human resource administration. The firm's staffing services include short-term, temporary-to-permanent and permanent placements in areas including clerical/administrative work, light industrial assignments, technical work, on-site management assignments and other specialties. The firm has been offering PEO services since 1990, focusing on human resource management services for small and mid-sized companies. Barrett's PEO services arrangement allows Barrett to enter a contractual agreement with the client's customer(s), thereby becoming a co-employer with the client company. This allows Barrett to assume responsibility for many or all of the human resource management duties such as payroll/taxes, employee benefits, health insurance, worker's compensation, workplace safety, federal/state employment laws, labor regulatory requirements and other administrative tasks. The firm serves customers in a variety of markets, including electronics manufacturers; various light-manufacturing industries; forest products and agriculture-based companies; transportation and shipping enterprises; food processing; telecommunications; public utilities; general contractors in numerous construction-related fields; and various professional services firms.

The company provides its employees medical and dental insurance, as well as a 401(k) plan.

FINANCIALS:

Sales and profits are in thousands of dollars—add 000 to get the full amount. 2010 Note: Financial information for 2010 was not available for all companies at press time.

2010 Sales: $273,123 | 2010 Profits: $7,353
2009 Sales: $236,460 | 2009 Profits: $-4,768
2008 Sales: $280,468 | 2008 Profits: $6,263
2007 Sales: $289,213 | 2007 Profits: $16,806
2006 Sales: $259,184 | 2006 Profits: $16,336

U.S. Stock Ticker: BBSI
Int'l Ticker:
Int'l Exchange:
Employees: 40,935 Fiscal Year Ends: 12/31
Parent Company:

SALARIES/BENEFITS:

Pension Plan: | ESOP Stock Plan: | Profit Sharing: | Top Exec. Salary: $350,000 | Bonus: $
Savings Plan: Y | Stock Purch. Plan: | | Second Exec. Salary: $200,000 | Bonus: $

OTHER THOUGHTS:

Apparent Women Officers or Directors:
Hot Spot for Advancement for Women/Minorities:

LOCATIONS: ("Y" = Yes)

West:	Southwest:	Midwest:	Southeast:	Northeast:	International:
Y	Y			Y	

BASIC ENERGY SERVICES INC

www.basicenergyservices.com

Industry Group Code: 213112

Management:		**Sales/Marketing:**		**Liberal Arts:**		**Information Sys.:**		**Professionals:**		**Tech./Scientific:**	
Mgmt. Trainees:		Marketing Pros.:	Y	Gen. Writing/Editing:		Info. Mgmt.:	Y	Finance/Acct.:	Y	Engineers, Elec.:	Y
Experienced Mgmt.:		Retail Sales:		Tech. Writing:	Y	Software Dev.:		Law:	Y	Engineers, Other:	Y
Int'l Business:		Comm./Industrial:	Y	Graphic Arts/Photog.:		Hardware Dev.:		HR/Other:	Y	Health/Lab:	
MBA Grads:	Y	Sales Trainees:		Music:		Consulting/Other:		Training:	Y	Science/Research:	
		Advertising Pros.:	Y	Broadcasting:				Health Care:		Petroleum/Chem.:	Y
				Other:				Consulting:		Math/Other:	

TYPES OF BUSINESS:

Oil & Gas Well Support Service
Contract Drilling Services

BRANDS/DIVISIONS/AFFILIATES:

Azurite Leasing Company LLC
Azurite Services Company
Freestone Disposal L.P.
Team Snubbing Services, Inc.
Rocky Mountain Cementers, Inc.
New Tech Systems, Inc.
Taylor Rig, LLC

CONTACTS:

Note: Officers with more than one job title may be intentionally listed here more than once.

Ken V. Huseman, CEO
Ken V. Huseman, Pres.
Alen Krenek, CFO/Sr. VP
Doug Rogers, VP-Mktg.
Jim Tyner, VP-Human Resources
Lars Crotwell, VP-IT
Alan Krenek, Sr. VP/Sec.
Alan Krenek, Sr. VP/Treas.
Mark Rankin, VP-Risk Mgmt.
Bobby Adkins, VP-Rental & Fishing Tool Div.
Lynn Wigington, VP-Permian Basin Region
Steve McCoy, VP-Contract Drilling
Steven A. Webster, Chmn.

Phone: 432-620-5500	**Fax:**
Toll-Free:	
Address: 400 W. Illinois, Ste. 800, Midland, TX 79701 US	

GROWTH PLANS/SPECIAL FEATURES:

Basic Energy Services, Inc. (BES) is a well servicing contractor that provides services to oil and gas drilling and production companies. BES provides services during the entire life cycle of a well, from the initial drilling to the final abandonment of the site. The company provides services to over 2,000 oil and gas companies in approximately 100 service points around the country. It is one of the largest well servicing contractors in the U.S., with a service area that focuses primarily on the major oil and gas producing regions, including Texas, Oklahoma, Louisiana, Arkansas, Kansas, New Mexico and the Rocky Mountain states. The company operates in four distinct segments. These segments include well servicing, which operates a fleet of 405 well servicing rigs and related equipment; the fluid service segment operates a fleet of 791 fluid service trucks that aid in transport and disposal of materials to and from well sites; completion and remedial services segment operates the pressure pumping units fleet designed to configure underbalanced drilling operations; and the contract drilling segment operates nine drilling rigs that are contracted out to initiate production of a well. The investment firm DLJ Merchant Banking Partners III, L.P. owns 44.4% of BES. In December 2009, BES acquired Team Snubbing Services, Inc. In March 2010, it acquired Rocky Mountain Cementers, Inc. In April 2010, Basic acquired New Tech Systems, Inc. In May 2010, the firm acquired the assets of Taylor Rig, LLC, adding its operations to the well servicing segment.

FINANCIALS:

Sales and profits are in thousands of dollars—add 000 to get the full amount. 2010 Note: Financial information for 2010 was not available for all companies at press time.

2010 Sales: $728,239	2010 Profits: $-43,563	**U.S. Stock Ticker: BAS**
2009 Sales: $526,627	2009 Profits: $-253,538	**Int'l Ticker:**
2008 Sales: $1,004,942	2008 Profits: $68,238	Int'l Exchange:
2007 Sales: $877,173	2007 Profits: $87,733	Employees: 4,500 Fiscal Year Ends: 12/31
2006 Sales: $	2006 Profits: $	Parent Company:

SALARIES/BENEFITS:

Pension Plan:	ESOP Stock Plan:	Profit Sharing:	Top Exec. Salary: $510,000	Bonus: $
Savings Plan:	Stock Purch. Plan:		Second Exec. Salary: $282,661	Bonus: $

OTHER THOUGHTS:

Apparent Women Officers or Directors:
Hot Spot for Advancement for Women/Minorities:

LOCATIONS: ("Y" = Yes)

West:	Southwest:	Midwest:	Southeast:	Northeast:	International:
Y	Y	Y	Y		

BASS PRO SHOPS INC

www.basspro.com

Industry Group Code: 451110

Management:		Sales/Marketing:		Liberal Arts:		Information Sys.:		Professionals:		Tech./Scientific:	
Mgmt. Trainees:	Y	Marketing Pros.:	Y	Gen. Writing/Editing:	Y	Info. Mgmt.:	Y	Finance/Acct.:	Y	Engineers, Elec.:	
Experienced Mgmt.:	Y	Retail Sales:	Y	Tech. Writing:		Software Dev.:	Y	Law:	Y	Engineers, Other:	
Int'l Business:	Y	Comm./Industrial:		Graphic Arts/Photog.:	Y	Hardware Dev.:		HR/Other:	Y	Health/Lab:	
MBA Grads:	Y	Sales Trainees:	Y	Music:		Consulting/Other:		Training:	Y	Science/Research:	
		Advertising Pros.:	Y	Broadcasting:				Health Care:		Petroleum/Chem.:	
				Other:				Consulting:		Math/Other:	

TYPES OF BUSINESS:

Sporting Goods, Retail
Sport Boats
Hunting & Fishing Equipment
Catalog & Online Sales
Outdoor Apparel
Resort Operations
Television Production

BRANDS/DIVISIONS/AFFILIATES:

Outdoor World
RedHead
Offshore Angler
White River Fly Shops
Tracker Marine
American Rod & Gun
Big Cedar Lodge
Dogwood Canyon

CONTACTS: *Note: Officers with more than one job title may be intentionally listed here more than once.*

James Hagale, COO
James Hagale, Pres.
Stan Lippelman, VP-Mktg.
Leslie Weber, CIO
Larry L. Whiteley, Mgr.-Comm. & Outdoor Education
John L. Morris, Chmn.
Bill Simpson, VP-Supply Chain

Phone: 417-873-5000 | **Fax:** 417-873-5060
Toll-Free: 800-227-7776
Address: 2500 E. Kearney St., Springfield, MO 65898 US

GROWTH PLANS/SPECIAL FEATURES:

Bass Pro Shops, Inc. is a leader in sporting goods retail. The company markets its products through 56 sports superstores in 26 states across the U.S. and Canada, a mail-order catalog and through Internet sites. The firm is dedicated to providing outdoor recreational products, including specialty apparel, and also aims to model and inspire environmental conservation among its customers. The sporting goods superstores operate under the Bass Pro Shop and Outdoor World brand names and range from 100,000 to 600,000 square feet. Products include boats and campers, as well as myriads of fishing, hunting, camping, automobile and marine supplies. Many of these stores have a variety of unique features and attractions to draw more customers, including restaurants, snack bars, archery ranges, indoor fish tanks, waterfalls and video arcades. Aside from its stores, the company sells goods over the Internet and mails more than 125 million catalogs/sales flyers annually under the Bass Pro Shops, RedHead, Offshore Angler and White River Fly Shops brand names. Its wholesale operations consist of Tracker Marine, a leader in sport boat manufacturing; and American Rod & Gun, one of the largest wholesale hunting and fishing distributors in the country. In addition to offering a variety of hunting and fishing trips and contests, Bass Pro runs the Wonders of Wildlife facility, a museum and conservation education center near its corporate headquarters; Big Cedar Lodge, an outdoors-themed vacation spot in Missouri located near the company's own nature park, Dogwood Canyon; and produces a weekly television program on The Outdoor Channel and an international radio show.

FINANCIALS: **Sales and profits are in thousands of dollars—add 000 to get the full amount. 2010 Note: Financial information for 2010 was not available for all companies at press time.**

2010 Sales: $	2010 Profits: $
2009 Sales: $2,800,000	2009 Profits: $
2008 Sales: $2,650,000	2008 Profits: $
2007 Sales: $3,000,000	2007 Profits: $
2006 Sales: $2,660,000	2006 Profits: $

U.S. Stock Ticker: Private
Int'l Ticker:
Int'l Exchange:
Employees: 12,000 Fiscal Year Ends: 12/31
Parent Company:

SALARIES/BENEFITS:

Pension Plan: ESOP Stock Plan: Profit Sharing: Top Exec. Salary: $ Bonus: $
Savings Plan: Stock Purch. Plan: Second Exec. Salary: $ Bonus: $

OTHER THOUGHTS:

Apparent Women Officers or Directors: 1
Hot Spot for Advancement for Women/Minorities:

LOCATIONS: ("Y" = Yes)

West:	Southwest:	Midwest:	Southeast:	Northeast:	International:
Y	Y	Y	Y	Y	Y

BAUSCH & LOMB INC

www.bausch.com

Industry Group Code: 33911

Management:		**Sales/Marketing:**		**Liberal Arts:**		**Information Sys.:**		**Professionals:**		**Tech./Scientific:**	
Mgmt. Trainees:	Y	Marketing Pros.:	Y	Gen. Writing/Editing:	Y	Info. Mgmt.:	Y	Finance/Acct.:	Y	Engineers, Elec.:	Y
Experienced Mgmt.:	Y	Retail Sales:		Tech. Writing:	Y	Software Dev.:	Y	Law:	Y	Engineers, Other:	Y
Int'l Business:	Y	Comm./Industrial:	Y	Graphic Arts/Photog.:	Y	Hardware Dev.:		HR/Other:	Y	Health/Lab:	Y
MBA Grads:	Y	Sales Trainees:	Y	Music:		Consulting/Other:		Training:	Y	Science/Research:	Y
		Advertising Pros.:	Y	Broadcasting:				Health Care:	Y	Petroleum/Chem.:	
				Other:				Consulting:		Math/Other:	Y

TYPES OF BUSINESS:

Supplies-Eye Care
Contact Lens Products
Ophthalmic Pharmaceuticals
Surgical Products

BRANDS/DIVISIONS/AFFILIATES:

Alrex
Warburg Pincus LLC
Zrigan
Ocuvite
Lotemax
Miochol-E
PreserVision
Zyoptic

CONTACTS: *Note: Officers with more than one job title may be intentionally listed here more than once.*

Brent L. Saunders, CEO
Brian J. Harris, CFO/VP
Rick A. Heinick, Corp. VP-Human Resources & Transformation
Alan H. Farnsworth, CIO/Sr. VP-IT & Customer Service/Corp. VP
John W. Sheets, Jr., CTO/Corp. VP
A Robert D. Bailey, General Counsel/Corp. VP
Michael Gowen, Exec. VP-Global Bus. Oper. & Process Excellence
Paul H. Sartori, Corp. VP-Public Affairs
Robert E. Grant, CEO/Pres., Global Surgical Bus.
Rodney W. Unsworth, Pres., APAC
Peter Valenti III, Corp. VP/Global Pres., Vision Care
Flemming Ornskov, Corp. VP/Global Pres., Pharmaceuticals
Fred Hassan, Chmn.
Charl van Zyl, Commercial Leader-EMEA

Phone: 585-338-6000 **Fax:** 585-338-6007
Toll-Free: 800-344-8815
Address: 1 Bausch & Lomb Pl., Rochester, NY 14604-2701 US

GROWTH PLANS/SPECIAL FEATURES:

Bausch & Lomb, Inc. (B&L), owned by private equity firm Warburg Pincus LLC, is a world leader in the development, marketing and manufacturing of eye care products. The firm's products are marketed in more than 100 countries and in five categories: contact lenses; lens care; pharmaceuticals; cataract and vitreoretinal surgery; and refractive surgery. In its contact lens category, B&L's product portfolio includes traditional, planned replacement disposable, daily disposable, continuous wear, toric soft contact lenses and rigid gas-permeable materials. The firm's lens care products include multi-purpose solutions, enzyme cleaners and saline solutions. The firm's pharmaceuticals include generic and branded prescription ophthalmic pharmaceuticals, ocular vitamins, over-the-counter medications and vision accessories. Key pharmaceutical trademarks of the firm are Bausch & Lomb, Alrex, Alaway, Lotemax, Ocuvite, PreserVision and Zylet. B&L's cataract and vitreoretinal division offers a broad line of intraocular lenses and delivery systems, as well as the Millennium and Stellaris lines of phacoemulsification equipment used in the extraction of the patient's natural lens during cataract surgery. The company's refractive surgery products include lasers and diagnostic equipment used in the LASIK surgical procedure under the brand Zyoptic. Eyeonics, Inc., is a subsidiary of the company, specializing in ophthalmic medical devices based in Aliso Viejo, California. Bausch & Lomb Pharmaceuticals specializes in the development and manufacture of products for pharmaceutical companies. B&L's global operations include research and development units on six continents and operating offices in over 43 countries. In June 2010, the company acquired the brand Zrigan, a topical anti-viral for the treatment of corneal ulcers, from Loboratoires Thea. In September 2010, the firm acquired the assets and intellectual property for Miochol-E, an injectable miotic pharmaceutical, from Novartis AG.

Employees are offered medical and dental coverage; various work/life programs; a vacation buy/sell program; domestic partner benefits; flexible spending accounts; and education reimbursement.

FINANCIALS: **Sales and profits are in thousands of dollars—add 000 to get the full amount. 2010 Note: Financial information for 2010 was not available for all companies at press time.**

2010 Sales: $2,510,000 | 2010 Profits: $
2009 Sales: $2,500,000 | 2009 Profits: $
2008 Sales: $2,500,000 | 2008 Profits: $
2007 Sales: $ | 2007 Profits: $
2006 Sales: $2,293,400 | 2006 Profits: $

U.S. Stock Ticker: Private
Int'l Ticker:
Int'l Exchange:
Employees: 13,000 Fiscal Year Ends: 12/31
Parent Company: WARBURG PINCUS LLC

SALARIES/BENEFITS:

Pension Plan: | ESOP Stock Plan: | Profit Sharing: | Top Exec. Salary: $ | Bonus: $
Savings Plan: | Stock Purch. Plan: | | Second Exec. Salary: $ | Bonus: $

OTHER THOUGHTS:

Apparent Women Officers or Directors: 2
Hot Spot for Advancement for Women/Minorities:

LOCATIONS: ("Y" = Yes)

West:	Southwest:	Midwest:	Southeast:	Northeast:	International:
Y			Y	Y	Y

BECHTEL GROUP INC

www.bechtel.com

Industry Group Code: 237

Management:		Sales/Marketing:		Liberal Arts:		Information Sys.:		Professionals:		Tech./Scientific:	
Mgmt. Trainees:	Y	Marketing Pros.:	Y	Gen. Writing/Editing:	Y	Info. Mgmt.:	Y	Finance/Acct.:	Y	Engineers, Elec.:	Y
Experienced Mgmt.:	Y	Retail Sales:		Tech. Writing:	Y	Software Dev.:	Y	Law:	Y	Engineers, Other:	Y
Int'l Business:	Y	Comm./Industrial:	Y	Graphic Arts/Photog.:	Y	Hardware Dev.:		HR/Other:	Y	Health/Lab:	
MBA Grads:	Y	Sales Trainees:	Y	Music:		Consulting/Other:	Y	Training:	Y	Science/Research:	
		Advertising Pros.:		Broadcasting:				Health Care:		Petroleum/Chem.:	Y
				Other:				Consulting:	Y	Math/Other:	Y

TYPES OF BUSINESS:

Engineering, Construction & Project Management Services
Civic Engineering
Outsourcing
Financial Services
Atomic Propulsion Systems Engineering
Airport Construction
Electric Power Plant Construction
Nuclear Power Plant Construction

BRANDS/DIVISIONS/AFFILIATES:

CONTACTS:

Note: Officers with more than one job title may be intentionally listed here more than once.

Riley P. Bechtel, CEO
Bill Dudley, COO
Bill Dudley, Pres.
Peter Dawson, CFO
John MacDonald, Head-Human Resources
Geir Ramleth, Head-Info. Systems
Geir Ramleth, Head-Tech.
Michael Bailey, General Counsel
Anette Sparks, Controller
Steve Katzman, Pres., Asia
Jim Haynes, Pres., Latin America
Susan Kubanis, Head-Sustainability Svcs.
Lorne Parker, Head-Risk Mgmt.
Riley P. Bechtel, Chmn.
David Welch, Pres., EMEA

Phone: 415-768-1234	**Fax:** 415-768-9038
Toll-Free:	
Address: 50 Beale St., San Francisco, CA 94105-1895 US	

GROWTH PLANS/SPECIAL FEATURES:

Bechtel Group, Inc., founded in 1906 by Warren A. Bechtel, is one of the world's largest engineering companies. The privately-owned firm offers engineering, construction and project management services, with a broad project portfolio including road and rail systems, airports and seaports, nuclear power plants, petrochemical facilities, mines, defense and aerospace facilities, environmental cleanup projects, telecommunication networks, pipelines and oil fields development. The firm has participated in such notable endeavors as the construction of the Hoover Dam, the creation of the Bay Area Rapid Transit system in San Francisco, the massive James Bay Hydroelectric Project in Quebec and the quelling of oil field fires in Kuwait following the Persian Gulf War. Bechtel also constructed the Trans-Alaska Oil Pipeline, covering 800 miles between the Prudhoe Bay oil field and Valdez. Bechtel has also been contracted to develop the New Doha International Airport in Qatar, Iraq. An 11-year, multi-billion-dollar project, the new airport will be designed to accommodate six Airbus A380-800's, the largest passenger aircraft in the world.

The firm offers employees benefits including medical, dental and vision coverage; short- and long-term disability; flexible spending accounts; an employee assistance program; life insurance; and a 401(k) plan.

FINANCIALS:

Sales and profits are in thousands of dollars—add 000 to get the full amount. 2010 Note: Financial information for 2010 was not available for all companies at press time.

2010 Sales: $32,500,000	2010 Profits: $
2009 Sales: $30,800,000	2009 Profits: $
2008 Sales: $31,400,000	2008 Profits: $
2007 Sales: $27,000,000	2007 Profits: $
2006 Sales: $20,500,000	2006 Profits: $

U.S. Stock Ticker: Private
Int'l Ticker:
Int'l Exchange:
Employees: 49,000 Fiscal Year Ends: 12/31
Parent Company:

SALARIES/BENEFITS:

Pension Plan: Y	ESOP Stock Plan:	Profit Sharing:	Top Exec. Salary: $	Bonus: $
Savings Plan: Y	Stock Purch. Plan:		Second Exec. Salary: $	Bonus: $

OTHER THOUGHTS:

Apparent Women Officers or Directors: 4
Hot Spot for Advancement for Women/Minorities: Y

LOCATIONS: ("Y" = Yes)

West:	Southwest:	Midwest:	Southeast:	Northeast:	International:
Y	Y	Y	Y	Y	Y

BECKMAN COULTER INC

www.beckmancoulter.com

Industry Group Code: 3345

Management:		Sales/Marketing:		Liberal Arts:		Information Sys.:		Professionals:		Tech./Scientific:	
Mgmt. Trainees:	Y	Marketing Pros.:	Y	Gen. Writing/Editing:	Y	Info. Mgmt.:	Y	Finance/Acct.:	Y	Engineers, Elec.:	Y
Experienced Mgmt.:	Y	Retail Sales:		Tech. Writing:	Y	Software Dev.:	Y	Law:	Y	Engineers, Other:	Y
Int'l Business:	Y	Comm./Industrial:	Y	Graphic Arts/Photog.:	Y	Hardware Dev.:	Y	HR/Other:	Y	Health/Lab:	Y
MBA Grads:	Y	Sales Trainees:		Music:		Consulting/Other:		Training:	Y	Science/Research:	Y
		Advertising Pros.:	Y	Broadcasting:				Health Care:	Y	Petroleum/Chem.:	
				Other:				Consulting:		Math/Other:	Y

TYPES OF BUSINESS:

Equipment-Laboratory Instruments
Chemistry Systems
Genetic Analysis/Nucleic Acid Testing
Biomedical Research Supplies
Immunoassay Systems
Cellular Systems
Discovery & Automation Systems

BRANDS/DIVISIONS/AFFILIATES:

Danaher Corp

CONTACTS:

Note: Officers with more than one job title may be intentionally listed here more than once.

Bob Hurley, Pres.
Chuck McLaughlin, CFO/Sr. VP
Allison Blackwell, Sr. VP-Human resources
Richard Creager, Chief Scientific Officer
Jeff Linton, General Counsel/Sr. VP
JimWildergren, Sr. VP-Global Customer Oper.
Scott Akin, Div. Pres., Life Sciences
Cynthia Collins, Group VP-Cellular Bus. Group
Richard Creager, Sr.VP-Molecular Diagnostics
Clair O'Donovan, Sr.VP-Quality & Regulatory Affairs

Phone: 714-993-5321 **Fax:**

Toll-Free: 877-560-4084

Address: 250 S. Kraemer Blvd., P.O. Box 8000, Brea, CA 92822 US

GROWTH PLANS/SPECIAL FEATURES:

Beckman Coulter, Inc., a wholly-owned subsidiary of Danaher Corp., develops, manufactures and markets biomedical testing instrument systems, tests and supplies that automate complex biomedical tests. The company operates two segmented divisions: Clinical Diagnostics and Life Sciences. The Clinical Diagnostics division focuses on three product categories: chemistry and clinical automation; immunoassay and molecular diagnostics; and cellular analysis. These products span the biomedical testing continuum, from medical research and clinical trials to laboratory diagnostics and point-of-care testing. The company-installed base of over 275,000 systems provides essential biomedical information to enhance health care around the world. The Life Sciences division markets products used in the drug discovery and development process, including centrifuges and the microscale technology capillary electrophoresis, which separates, quantifies and characterizes charged molecules for analysis. The majority of the company's total revenue is generated by the recurring sale of consumable supplies, test kits, services and operating-type lease payments. The firm's revenue is about evenly divided between sales inside and outside the U.S. Its customer base is predominately hospital clinical laboratories, physicians' offices, group practices, commercial reference laboratories, universities, medical research laboratories, pharmaceutical companies and biotechnology firms. Central laboratories of mid- to large-size hospitals represent Beckman Coulter's most significant customer group. Sales to clinical laboratories represent approximately 80% of its total revenue, with the balance coming from the life science research market. In June 2011, the firm was acquired by Danaher Corp.

Beckman Coulter offers its employees health and other insurance benefits, paid vacations and holidays, tuition assistance and retirement savings plans.

FINANCIALS:

Sales and profits are in thousands of dollars—add 000 to get the full amount. 2010 Note: Financial information for 2010 was not available for all companies at press time.

2010 Sales: $3,633,400	2010 Profits: $230,700
2009 Sales: $3,260,600	2009 Profits: $147,100
2008 Sales: $3,098,900	2008 Profits: $186,000
2007 Sales: $2,761,300	2007 Profits: $203,700
2006 Sales: $2,528,500	2006 Profits: $186,900

U.S. Stock Ticker: Subsidiary
Int'l Ticker:
Int'l Exchange:
Employees: 11,900 Fiscal Year Ends: 12/31
Parent Company: DANAHER CORP

SALARIES/BENEFITS:

Pension Plan: Y	ESOP Stock Plan:	Profit Sharing:	Top Exec. Salary: $923,539	Bonus: $794,000
Savings Plan: Y	Stock Purch. Plan: Y		Second Exec. Salary: $500,668	Bonus: $351,700

OTHER THOUGHTS:

Apparent Women Officers or Directors: 2
Hot Spot for Advancement for Women/Minorities: Y

LOCATIONS: ("Y" = Yes)

West:	Southwest:	Midwest:	Southeast:	Northeast:	International:
Y			Y		Y

BECTON DICKINSON & CO

www.bd.com

Industry Group Code: 33911

Management:		**Sales/Marketing:**		**Liberal Arts:**		**Information Sys.:**		**Professionals:**		**Tech./Scientific:**	
Mgmt. Trainees:	Y	Marketing Pros.:	Y	Gen. Writing/Editing:	Y	Info. Mgmt.:	Y	Finance/Acct.:	Y	Engineers, Elec.:	Y
Experienced Mgmt.:	Y	Retail Sales:		Tech. Writing:	Y	Software Dev.:	Y	Law:	Y	Engineers, Other:	Y
Int'l Business:	Y	Comm./Industrial:	Y	Graphic Arts/Photog.:	Y	Hardware Dev.:		HR/Other:	Y	Health/Lab:	Y
MBA Grads:	Y	Sales Trainees:		Music:		Consulting/Other:		Training:	Y	Science/Research:	Y
		Advertising Pros.:	Y	Broadcasting:				Health Care:	Y	Petroleum/Chem.:	
				Other:				Consulting:		Math/Other:	

TYPES OF BUSINESS:

Medical Equipment-Injection/Infusion
Drug Delivery Systems
Infusion Therapy Products
Diabetes Care Products
Surgical Products
Microbiology Products
Diagnostic Products
Consulting Services

BRANDS/DIVISIONS/AFFILIATES:

Becton Dickinson Medical
Becton Dickinson Biosciences
Becton Dickinson Diagnostics
Vacutainer
Hypak
BD Protect
BD Innova
Accuri Cytometers, Inc.

CONTACTS: *Note: Officers with more than one job title may be intentionally listed here more than once.*

Edward J. Ludwig, CEO
Vincent A. Forlenza, COO
Vincent A. Forlenza, Pres.
David V. Elkins, CFO/Exec. VP
Donna M. Boles, Sr. VP-Human Resources
Scott P. Bruder, CTO/Sr. VP
Jeffrey S. Sherman, General Counsel/Sr. VP
Patricia B. Shrader, Sr. VP-Corp., Regulatory & External Affairs
Zachary A. Nagle, VP-Investor Rel.
Richard K. Berman, Treas./VP
Gary M. Cohen, Exec. VP
William A. Kozy, Exec. VP
Patti E. Russell, Chief Ethics & Compliance Officer/VP
David T. Durack, Sr. VP-Corp. Medical Affairs
Edward J. Ludwig, Chmn.

Phone: 201-847-6800 **Fax:** 201-847-6475
Toll-Free: 800-284-6845
Address: 1 Becton Dr., Franklin Lakes, NJ 07417 US

GROWTH PLANS/SPECIAL FEATURES:

Becton, Dickinson & Co. (BD) manufactures and sells a broad line of medical supplies, devices and diagnostic systems used by health care professionals, medical research institutions and the general public. The company operates in three segments: medical, biosciences and diagnostics. The medical segment offers hypodermic products, specially designed devices for diabetes care; prefillable drug delivery systems; and infusion therapy products. It also offers anesthesia and surgical products; ophthalmic surgery devices; critical care systems; elastic support products; and thermometers. The biosciences segment offers industrial microbiology products; cellular analysis systems; research; and clinical reagents for cellular and nucleic acid analysis; cell culture labware and growth media; hematology instruments; and other diagnostic systems, including immunodiagnostic test kits. The diagnostics segment offers specimen collection products and services, consulting services and customized, automated barcode systems for patient identification and point-of-care data capture. Two of BD's most popular products are Hypak prefillable syringes and Vacutainer blood-collection products. Outside of the U.S., BD's products are manufactured and sold in Europe, the Middle East, Africa, Japan, Mexico, Asia Pacific, Canada and Brazil. New products launched in 2010 include the BD Microtainer MAP Microtube for hematology testing, designed for patients with fragile veins that are difficult to access; the BD FACSAria III Cell Sorting System, a flow cytometer that utilizes up to six lasers for the purpose of conducting multicolor experiments; the BD Protect Infection Surveillance and Data Management System, a suite of healthcare management software applications; and the BD Innova Preanalytical Automated Microbiology Specimen Processor. In August 2010, the firm sold its Ophthalmic Systems Unit and Surgical Blades Product Platform to RoundTable Healthcare Partners. In February 2011, it agreed to acquire Accuri Cytometers, Inc.

FINANCIALS: **Sales and profits are in thousands of dollars—add 000 to get the full amount. 2010 Note: Financial information for 2010 was not available for all companies at press time.**

2010 Sales: $7,372,333	2010 Profits: $1,317,610	**U.S. Stock Ticker: BDX**
2009 Sales: $6,986,722	2009 Profits: $1,231,603	**Int'l Ticker:**
2008 Sales: $6,897,619	2008 Profits: $1,126,996	Int'l Exchange:
2007 Sales: $6,282,800	2007 Profits: $890,000	Employees: 28,803 Fiscal Year Ends: 9/30
2006 Sales: $5,738,000	2006 Profits: $752,300	Parent Company:

SALARIES/BENEFITS:

Pension Plan: Y	ESOP Stock Plan:	Profit Sharing:	Top Exec. Salary: $1,070,000	Bonus: $850,000
Savings Plan: Y	Stock Purch. Plan: Y		Second Exec. Salary: $650,000	Bonus: $510,000

OTHER THOUGHTS:

Apparent Women Officers or Directors: 6
Hot Spot for Advancement for Women/Minorities: Y

LOCATIONS: ("Y" = Yes)

West:	Southwest:	Midwest:	Southeast:	Northeast:	International:
Y	Y	Y	Y	Y	Y

BED BATH & BEYOND INC

www.bedbathandbeyond.com

Industry Group Code: 442299

Management:		Sales/Marketing:		Liberal Arts:		Information Sys.:		Professionals:		Tech./Scientific:	
Mgmt. Trainees:	Y	Marketing Pros.:	Y	Gen. Writing/Editing:	Y	Info. Mgmt.:	Y	Finance/Acct.:	Y	Engineers, Elec.:	
Experienced Mgmt.:	Y	Retail Sales:	Y	Tech. Writing:		Software Dev.:	Y	Law:	Y	Engineers, Other:	
Int'l Business:	Y	Comm./Industrial:	Y	Graphic Arts/Photog.:	Y	Hardware Dev.:		HR/Other:	Y	Health/Lab:	
MBA Grads:	Y	Sales Trainees:	Y	Music:		Consulting/Other:		Training:	Y	Science/Research:	
		Advertising Pros.:	Y	Broadcasting:				Health Care:		Petroleum/Chem.:	
				Other:				Consulting:		Math/Other:	

TYPES OF BUSINESS:

Linens & Housewares, Retail
Small Appliances
Home Accessories
Health & Beauty Care
Baby & Toddler Merchandise

BRANDS/DIVISIONS/AFFILIATES:

Bed Bath & Beyond Superstores
Harmon
Christmas Tree Shops
buybuy BABY
Home & More
Harmon Face Values

CONTACTS:

Note: Officers with more than one job title may be intentionally listed here more than once.

Steven H. Temares, CEO
Arthur Stark, Pres.
Eugene A. Castagna, CFO
Scott Hames, VP-Mktg. & Analytics
Arthur Stark, Chief Merch. Officer
Allan N. Rauch, General Counsel/VP-Legal
Richard McMahon, VP-Corp. Oper.
Richard McMahon, Chief Strategy Officer
Eugene A. Castagna, Treas.
Matthew Fiorilli, Sr. VP-Stores
G. William Waltzinger, Jr., VP-Corp. Dev./Pres., Harmon Stores, Inc.
Leonard Feinstein, Co-Chmn.
Warren Eisenberg, Co-Chmn.

Phone: 908-688-0888 **Fax:** 908-688-6483
Toll-Free: 800-462-3966
Address: 650 Liberty Ave., Union, NJ 07083 US

GROWTH PLANS/SPECIAL FEATURES:

Bed Bath & Beyond, Inc. (BBB) is one of the nation's largest operators of domestic superstores, with approximately 1,139 stores in 50 states, as well as Washington D.C., Canada and Puerto Rico. BBB operates four retail entities: Bed Bath & Beyond; Harmon; buybuy BABY; and Christmas Tree Shops. Bed Bath & Beyond stores offer a full line of domestic merchandise and home furnishings. The line includes items such as bed linens, bath accessories and kitchen tiles, while its home furnishings line includes a variety of cookware, dinnerware and glassware. Harmon and Harmon Face Values stores sell beauty care products in 46 stores in four states. Buybuy BABY is a retailer of infant and toddler merchandise, with 45 stores in 20 states including Florida, Georgia, Illinois, Indiana, Maryland, Michigan, New Jersey, New York, Ohio, Texas and Virginia. Christmas Tree Shops offer gifts, household items and furnishings in 66 stores in 18 states. Additionally, the company (through a joint venture) operates two stores in Mexico under the name Home & More. BBB relies on paid advertising and uses circulars and mailing pieces as its primary vehicles. In addition, the company only has three central distribution centers, since the majority of merchandise is shipped to each store from the firm's vendors. BBB is engaged in an ongoing expansion program involving the opening of new stores in both existing and new markets, as well as the expansion or replacement of existing stores with larger ones.

FINANCIALS:

Sales and profits are in thousands of dollars—add 000 to get the full amount. 2010 Note: Financial information for 2010 was not available for all companies at press time.

2010 Sales: $7,828,793 | 2010 Profits: $600,033
2009 Sales: $7,208,340 | 2009 Profits: $425,123
2008 Sales: $7,048,942 | 2008 Profits: $562,808
2007 Sales: $6,617,429 | 2007 Profits: $594,244
2006 Sales: $5,809,562 | 2006 Profits: $572,847

U.S. Stock Ticker: BBBY
Int'l Ticker:
Int'l Exchange:
Employees: 41,000 Fiscal Year Ends: 2/28
Parent Company:

SALARIES/BENEFITS:

Pension Plan: ESOP Stock Plan: Profit Sharing: Top Exec. Salary: $2,288,462 Bonus: $
Savings Plan: Stock Purch. Plan: Second Exec. Salary: $1,212,692 Bonus: $

OTHER THOUGHTS:

Apparent Women Officers or Directors:
Hot Spot for Advancement for Women/Minorities:

LOCATIONS: ("Y" = Yes)

West:	Southwest:	Midwest:	Southeast:	Northeast:	International:
Y	Y	Y	Y	Y	Y

BEMIS COMPANY INC

Industry Group Code: 3222

www.bemis.com

Management:		Sales/Marketing:		Liberal Arts:		Information Sys.:		Professionals:		Tech./Scientific:	
Mgmt. Trainees:		Marketing Pros.:	Y	Gen. Writing/Editing:		Info. Mgmt.:	Y	Finance/Acct.:	Y	Engineers, Elec.:	
Experienced Mgmt.:	Y	Retail Sales:		Tech. Writing:	Y	Software Dev.:		Law:	Y	Engineers, Other:	Y
Int'l Business:	Y	Comm./Industrial:	Y	Graphic Arts/Photog.:		Hardware Dev.:		HR/Other:	Y	Health/Lab:	
MBA Grads:	Y	Sales Trainees:		Music:		Consulting/Other:		Training:		Science/Research:	
		Advertising Pros.:		Broadcasting:				Health Care:		Petroleum/Chem.:	
				Other:				Consulting:		Math/Other:	

TYPES OF BUSINESS:

Flexible Packaging Products
Pressure-Sensitive Materials
Films
Adhesives

BRANDS/DIVISIONS/AFFILIATES:

Curwood, Inc.
Bemis Clysar, Inc.
Milprint, Inc.
Perfecseal, Inc.
MACtac

CONTACTS: *Note: Officers with more than one job title may be intentionally listed here more than once.*

Henry J. Theisen, CEO
Henry J. Theisen, Pres.
Scott B. Ullem, CFO/VP
Timothy S. Fliss, VP-Human Resources
Sheri H. Edison, General Counsel/VP/Sec.
William F. Austen, VP-Oper.
Melanie E. R. Miller, VP-Investor Rel./Treas.
Stanley A. Jaffy, VP-Finance
Gene C. Wulf, Exec. VP
Jerry S. Krempa, Controller/VP
James W. Ransom, VP-Oper.
Robert F. Hawthorne, VP-Oper.
Jeffrey H. Curler, Chmn.

Phone: 920-727-4100 **Fax:**
Toll-Free:
Address: 1 Neenah Ctr., 4th Fl., Neenah, WI 54957 US

GROWTH PLANS/SPECIAL FEATURES:

Bemis Company, Inc. manufactures flexible packaging products and pressure-sensitive materials for customers throughout the U.S., Canada, Europe, Asia, South America and Mexico. Its manufacturing operations are conducted at some 80 facilities in 12 countries. Bemis operates in two business segments: Flexible Packaging, which accounted for 88% of its 2010 revenue; and Pressure Sensitive Materials, 12%. The flexible packaging segment manufactures a range of consumer and industrial packaging, including multilayer flexible polymer film structures, blown and cast stretch film products, carton sealing tapes, thermoformed plastic packaging, paper bags, printed paper roll stock and bag closing materials. These products are used to package products such as meats, liquids, cereals, coffee, cheese, pet food, seed, hygiene products and diapers. Companies operating under this division include Bemis Clysar, Inc., a provider of polyolefin shrink film; Curwood, Inc., a marketer of protective films; Milprint, Inc.; and Perfecseal, Inc., a supplier of medical packaging. The pressure-sensitive materials segment, operating through subsidiaries such as MACtac, manufactures products for the label, graphic and technical markets. Products include pressure-sensitive paper, film and metalized film printing stocks for labeling applications; pressure-sensitive papers and films for decorative signage; tape-based stocks acting as fasteners and mounters; medical grade adhesive tapes; and micro-thin film adhesives used in electronic components. In 2010, roughly 35% of the company's sales were generated outside the U.S. In March 2010, the company acquired the Food Americas flexible packaging facilities of Alcan Packaging Food Americas, which included 23 facilities in the U.S., Canada, Mexico, Brazil, Argentina and New Zealand.

Employees are offered medical and dental insurance; a 401(k); a profit sharing plan; life and travel accident insurance; an employee assistance program; disability coverage; flexible spending accounts; an employee stock purchase plan; employee discounts; and a student scholarship program.

FINANCIALS: **Sales and profits are in thousands of dollars—add 000 to get the full amount. 2010 Note: Financial information for 2010 was not available for all companies at press time.**

2010 Sales: $4,835,000 — 2010 Profits: $211,500
2009 Sales: $3,514,600 — 2009 Profits: $152,500
2008 Sales: $3,779,400 — 2008 Profits: $166,200
2007 Sales: $3,649,300 — 2007 Profits: $181,600
2006 Sales: $3,639,400 — 2006 Profits: $176,300

U.S. Stock Ticker: BMS
Int'l Ticker:
Int'l Exchange:
Employees: 20,000 Fiscal Year Ends: 12/31
Parent Company:

SALARIES/BENEFITS:

Pension Plan: ESOP Stock Plan: Profit Sharing: Y Top Exec. Salary: $900,000 Bonus: $2,106,320
Savings Plan: Y Stock Purch. Plan: Y Second Exec. Salary: $564,000 Bonus: $833,251

OTHER THOUGHTS:

Apparent Women Officers or Directors: 3
Hot Spot for Advancement for Women/Minorities: Y

LOCATIONS: ("Y" = Yes)

West:	Southwest:	Midwest:	Southeast:	Northeast:	International:
Y	Y	Y	Y	Y	Y

BERKSHIRE HATHAWAY INC

www.berkshirehathaway.com

Industry Group Code: 55111

Management:		Sales/Marketing:		Liberal Arts:		Information Sys.:		Professionals:		Tech./Scientific:	
Mgmt. Trainees:	Y	Marketing Pros.:	Y	Gen. Writing/Editing:	Y	Info. Mgmt.:	Y	Finance/Acct.:	Y	Engineers, Elec.:	Y
Experienced Mgmt.:	Y	Retail Sales:	Y	Tech. Writing:	Y	Software Dev.:	Y	Law:	Y	Engineers, Other:	
Int'l Business:	Y	Comm./Industrial:	Y	Graphic Arts/Photog.:	Y	Hardware Dev.:		HR/Other:	Y	Health/Lab:	
MBA Grads:	Y	Sales Trainees:	Y	Music:		Consulting/Other:		Training:	Y	Science/Research:	
		Advertising Pros.:	Y	Broadcasting:				Health Care:		Petroleum/Chem.:	
				Other:	Y			Consulting:		Math/Other:	Y

TYPES OF BUSINESS:

Direct Property & Casualty Insurance & Reinsurance
Retail Operations
Foodservice Operations
Building Products & Services
Apparel & Footwear
Technology Training
Manufactured Housing & RVs
Business Jet Flexible Ownership Services

BRANDS/DIVISIONS/AFFILIATES:

General RE Corporation
GEICO Corporation
Clayton Homes Inc
XTRA Corporation
CORT Business Services Corporation
NetJets Inc
Wesco Financial Corporation
Lubrizol Corporation (The)

CONTACTS: *Note: Officers with more than one job title may be intentionally listed here more than once.*

Warren Buffet, CEO
Marc D. Hamburg, CFO/Sr. VP
Charles Munger, Vice Chmn.
Warren Buffet, Chmn.

Phone: 402-346-1400	**Fax:** 402-346-3375
Toll-Free:	
Address: 3555 Farnam St., Omaha, NE 68131 US	

GROWTH PLANS/SPECIAL FEATURES:

Berkshire Hathaway, Inc. is a holding company that owns subsidiaries engaged in diverse business activities, most importantly insurance and reinsurance. Berkshire provides property and casualty insurance and reinsurance, as well as life accident and health reinsurance, through over 70 U.S. and foreign businesses. General Re Corporation, through its subsidiaries, conducts global reinsurance business in 56 cities and provides reinsurance worldwide. GEICO Corporation mainly provides private passenger auto insurance to individuals in all 50 U.S. states and Washington, D.C. The company's financial subsidiaries include Clayton Homes, Inc., a manufactured housing company; XTRA Corporation, a provider of transportation equipment leases; and furniture rental company CORT Business Services Corporation. Berkshire's apparel and footwear businesses include Fruit of the Loom; Garan; Fechheimer Brothers; H.H. Brown Shoe Group; and Justin Brands. The firm manufactures and distributes building products through Acme Building Brands; Benjamin Moore & Co.; Johns Manville; and MiTek. Subsidiary FlightSafety provides training to aircraft and ship pilots, while NetJets, Inc. offers fractional ownership programs for aircraft. In addition, subsidiary International Dairy Queen services approximately 6,000 Dairy Queen, Orange Julius and Karmelkorn stores. Marmon Holdings, Inc. consists of approximately 250 manufacturing, distribution and service locations. Borsheim Jewelry Company, Inc. is a retailer of fine jewelry, watches, crystal, china, stemware, flatware, gifts and collectibles. Borsheim brands include Helzberg Diamonds and the Ben Bridge Corporation. Other non-insurance operations include grocery and foodservice distribution, furniture retailing, carpet manufacturing, utilities and energy, newspapers, cleaning products, confectioneries, agricultural equipment, kitchen tools and recreational vehicles. In June 2011, Berkshire Hathaway acquired Wesco Financial Corporation. In September 2011, the firm acquired The Lubrizol Corporation.

FINANCIALS: **Sales and profits are in thousands of dollars—add 000 to get the full amount. 2010 Note: Financial information for 2010 was not available for all companies at press time.**

2010 Sales: $136,185,000	2010 Profits: $12,967,000	**U.S. Stock Ticker: BRK.A**
2009 Sales: $112,493,000	2009 Profits: $8,055,000	**Int'l Ticker:**
2008 Sales: $107,786,000	2008 Profits: $4,994,000	Int'l Exchange:
2007 Sales: $118,245,000	2007 Profits: $13,213,000	Employees: 260,000 Fiscal Year Ends: 12/31
2006 Sales: $98,539,000	2006 Profits: $11,015,000	Parent Company:

SALARIES/BENEFITS:

Pension Plan: Y	ESOP Stock Plan:	Profit Sharing:	Top Exec. Salary: $912,500	Bonus: $
Savings Plan: Y	Stock Purch. Plan:		Second Exec. Salary: $100,000	Bonus: $

OTHER THOUGHTS:

Apparent Women Officers or Directors: 2
Hot Spot for Advancement for Women/Minorities: Y

LOCATIONS: ("Y" = Yes)

West:	Southwest:	Midwest:	Southeast:	Northeast:	International:
Y	Y	Y	Y	Y	Y

BEST BUY CO INC

www.bestbuy.com

Industry Group Code: 44311

Management:		Sales/Marketing:		Liberal Arts:		Information Sys.:		Professionals:		Tech./Scientific:	
Mgmt. Trainees:	Y	Marketing Pros.:	Y	Gen. Writing/Editing:	Y	Info. Mgmt.:	Y	Finance/Acct.:	Y	Engineers, Elec.:	
Experienced Mgmt.:	Y	Retail Sales:	Y	Tech. Writing:		Software Dev.:	Y	Law:	Y	Engineers, Other:	
Int'l Business:	Y	Comm./Industrial:	Y	Graphic Arts/Photog.:	Y	Hardware Dev.:		HR/Other:	Y	Health/Lab:	
MBA Grads:	Y	Sales Trainees:	Y	Music:		Consulting/Other:		Training:	Y	Science/Research:	
		Advertising Pros.:	Y	Broadcasting:				Health Care:		Petroleum/Chem.:	
				Other:	Y			Consulting:		Math/Other:	

TYPES OF BUSINESS:

Consumer Electronics Stores
Retail Music & Video Sales
Personal Computers
Office Supplies
Cell Phones and Accessories
Appliances
Cameras
Consumer Electronics Installation & Service

BRANDS/DIVISIONS/AFFILIATES:

Geek Squad
Best Buy Mobile
Napster Inc
Magnolia Audio Video Stores
Pacific Sales
Carphone Warehouse (The)
Phone House (The)
Best Buy Connect

CONTACTS: *Note: Officers with more than one job title may be intentionally listed here more than once.*

Brian J. Dunn, CEO
James L. Muehlbauer, CFO/Exec. VP-Finance
Barry J. Judge, Chief Mktg. Officer/Exec. VP
Carol A. Surface, Exec. VP-Human Capital
Aura Oslapas, Chief Design Officer/Sr. VP
Timothy R. Sheehan, Chief Admin. Officer/Exec. VP
Joseph M. Joyce, General Counsel/Assistant. Sec./Sr. VP
Susan S. Grafton, Chief Acct. Officer/Controller/VP
Shari L. Ballard, Exec. VP/Pres., Americas
Ryan D. Robinson, Sr. VP/CFO-U.S. Strategic Bus. Unit/Treas.
Chris Gould, Treas./VP
Michael A. Vitelli, Exec. VP/Pres., Americas
Richard M. Schulze, Chmn.
Kelandu Patel, Exec. VP/Pres., Asia

Phone: 612-291-1000	**Fax:** 612-292-4001
Toll-Free: 888-237-8289	
Address: 7601 Penn Ave. S., Richfield, MN 55423 US	

GROWTH PLANS/SPECIAL FEATURES:

Best Buy Co., Inc. is one of the leading retailers of name-brand consumer electronics, entertainment software and appliances in the U.S. The company conducts business in both the domestic and international markets. The domestic market includes Best Buy; Best Buy Mobile; Geek Squad, which provides computer repair and installation services; Magnolia Audio Video; Pacific Sales; and Napster, which offers an online music streaming service. The international segment, in Canada, Europe, Mexico and China, includes Best Buy; Geek Squad; Future Shop, an electronics retailer; and Five Star, an appliance retailer. The company's products include home office equipment; cameras; computer and audio/video equipment; computer upgrades; and car audio and security system installation. In Europe, the company focuses primarily on mobile products, operating under the brand names The Carphone Warehouse, The Phone House and Geek Squad. In total, it operates 1,099 Best Buy stores in the U.S., 71 in Canada, eight in China, six in Mexico and two in Turkey (which it plans to close in 2011); as well as 177 U.S. Best Buy mobile stand-alone stores and six Magnolia Audio Video Stores; 35 Pacific Sales stores; 2,440 The Carphone Warehouse and The Phone House stores in Europe; 166 Five Star Stores in China; and 146 Future Shop stores in Canada. Best Buy is rolling out a chain of smaller stores and kiosks that sell cell phones, calling plans and accessories. It hopes to eventually capture a 15% share of the handset market. In June 2010, Best Buy sold its former of broadband, voice and data services provider, Speakeasy, to Covad Communications Group, Inc. In July 2010, it launched Best Buy Connect, a mobile broadband Internet service. Best Buy's average sales per square foot of store space per year were an estimated $900 in 2011.

The firm offers its employees medical, dental, vision and life insurance; disability coverage; 401(k) plans; an employee stock purchase plan; bonus/incentive program; tuition assistance; adoption assistance; and employee discount.

FINANCIALS: **Sales and profits are in thousands of dollars—add 000 to get the full amount. 2010 Note: Financial information for 2010 was not available for all companies at press time.**

2010 Sales: $49,694,000	2010 Profits: $1,317,000
2009 Sales: $45,015,000	2009 Profits: $1,003,000
2008 Sales: $40,023,000	2008 Profits: $1,407,000
2007 Sales: $35,934,000	2007 Profits: $1,377,000
2006 Sales: $30,848,000	2006 Profits: $1,140,000

U.S. Stock Ticker: BBY
Int'l Ticker:
Int'l Exchange:
Employees: 180,000 Fiscal Year Ends: 2/28
Parent Company:

SALARIES/BENEFITS:

Pension Plan:	ESOP Stock Plan:	Profit Sharing:	Top Exec. Salary: $1,247,311	Bonus: $
Savings Plan: Y	Stock Purch. Plan: Y		Second Exec. Salary: $876,926	Bonus: $

OTHER THOUGHTS:

Apparent Women Officers or Directors: 6
Hot Spot for Advancement for Women/Minorities: Y

LOCATIONS: ("Y" = Yes)

West:	Southwest:	Midwest:	Southeast:	Northeast:	International:
Y	Y	Y	Y	Y	Y

BIG 5 SPORTING GOODS CORPORATION

www.big5sportinggoods.com
Industry Group Code: 451110

Management:		Sales/Marketing:		Liberal Arts:		Information Sys.:		Professionals:		Tech./Scientific:	
Mgmt. Trainees:	Y	Marketing Pros.:	Y	Gen. Writing/Editing:	Y	Info. Mgmt.:	Y	Finance/Acct.:	Y	Engineers, Elec.:	
Experienced Mgmt.:	Y	Retail Sales:	Y	Tech. Writing:		Software Dev.:		Law:	Y	Engineers, Other:	
Int'l Business:		Comm./Industrial:		Graphic Arts/Photog.:	Y	Hardware Dev.:		HR/Other:	Y	Health/Lab:	
MBA Grads:	Y	Sales Trainees:	Y	Music:		Consulting/Other:		Training:	Y	Science/Research:	
		Advertising Pros.:	Y	Broadcasting:				Health Care:		Petroleum/Chem.:	
				Other:	Y			Consulting:		Math/Other:	

TYPES OF BUSINESS:
Sporting Goods Stores

BRANDS/DIVISIONS/AFFILIATES:
Court Casuals
Golden Bear
Harsh
Pacifica
Rugged Exposure
Triple Nickel
Big 5 Services Corp.

CONTACTS:
Note: Officers with more than one job title may be intentionally listed here more than once.

Steven G. Miller, CEO
Steven G. Miller, Pres.
Barry Emerson, CFO
Gary Meade, General Counsel/Sr. VP/Corp. Sec.
Shane Starr, Sr. VP-Oper.
Barry Emerson, Sr. VP/Treas.
Richard Johnson, Exec. VP
Steven G. Miller, Chmn.
Thomas Schlauch, Sr. VP-Buying

Phone: 310-536-0611 **Fax:** 310-297-7585
Toll-Free:
Address: 2525 E. El Segundo Blvd., El Segundo, CA 90245 US

GROWTH PLANS/SPECIAL FEATURES:
Big 5 Sporting Goods Corporation is one of the leading sporting goods retailers in the U.S., with 398 locations in 12 states. The company offers more than 25,000 sports products in its stores, including athletic shoes; apparel and accessories for team sports; fitness equipment; camping, hunting and fishing gear; tennis and golf equipment; winter sports gear; and in-line skates. Annually, soft goods, such as apparel and footwear, generate 45% of the firm's total sales, while hard goods, including sporting equipment, generate the remaining 55%. In addition to its private label merchandise, sold under the brands Court Casuals, Golden Bear, Harsh, Pacifica, Rugged Exposure and Triple Nickel, stores offer leading brands such as Adidas, Coleman, Easton, New Balance, Nike, Reebok, Spalding, Under Armour and Wilson. The company practices a systematic method of expansion, opening an average of 16 stores annually, about 66% of which are outside of California. Stores average 11,000 square feet, which is significantly smaller than the average superstore format, allowing stores to cater to smaller markets. Locations, normally freestanding or part of a multi-store shopping center, are chosen in collaboration with local real estate companies, mostly in markets close to those in which the company already has a presence. Big 5 owns a 953,000-square-foot distribution center in Riverside, California from which it operates all of its distribution activities. Through wholly-owned subsidiary Big 5 Services Corp., the firm manages its gift card operations.

Big 5 offers its employees medical and dental insurance; product discounts; and discounts at major theme parks and ski areas.

FINANCIALS:
Sales and profits are in thousands of dollars—add 000 to get the full amount. 2010 Note: Financial information for 2010 was not available for all companies at press time.

2010 Sales: $896,813	2010 Profits: $20,562	**U.S. Stock Ticker: BGFV**
2009 Sales: $895,542	2009 Profits: $21,811	**Int'l Ticker:**
2008 Sales: $864,650	2008 Profits: $13,904	Int'l Exchange:
2007 Sales: $898,292	2007 Profits: $28,091	Employees: 8,900 Fiscal Year Ends: 12/31
2006 Sales: $876,805	2006 Profits: $30,835	Parent Company:

SALARIES/BENEFITS:

Pension Plan:	ESOP Stock Plan:	Profit Sharing:	Top Exec. Salary: $473,000	Bonus: $305,000
Savings Plan: Y	Stock Purch. Plan:		Second Exec. Salary: $325,000	Bonus: $135,000

OTHER THOUGHTS:
Apparent Women Officers or Directors: 2
Hot Spot for Advancement for Women/Minorities:

LOCATIONS: ("Y" = Yes)

West:	Southwest:	Midwest:	Southeast:	Northeast:	International:
Y	Y				

BIO RAD LABORATORIES INC

www.bio-rad.com

Industry Group Code: 33911

Management:		**Sales/Marketing:**		**Liberal Arts:**		**Information Sys.:**		**Professionals:**		**Tech./Scientific:**	
Mgmt. Trainees:	Y	Marketing Pros.:	Y	Gen. Writing/Editing:	Y	Info. Mgmt.:	Y	Finance/Acct.:	Y	Engineers, Elec.:	Y
Experienced Mgmt.:	Y	Retail Sales:		Tech. Writing:	Y	Software Dev.:	Y	Law:	Y	Engineers, Other:	Y
Int'l Business:	Y	Comm./Industrial:	Y	Graphic Arts/Photog.:	Y	Hardware Dev.:		HR/Other:	Y	Health/Lab:	Y
MBA Grads:	Y	Sales Trainees:		Music:		Consulting/Other:		Training:	Y	Science/Research:	Y
		Advertising Pros.:	Y	Broadcasting:				Health Care:	Y	Petroleum/Chem.:	
				Other:				Consulting:		Math/Other:	

TYPES OF BUSINESS:

Equipment-Life Sciences Research
Clinical Diagnostics Products
Analytical Instruments
Laboratory Devices
Biomaterials
Imaging Products
Assays
Software

BRANDS/DIVISIONS/AFFILIATES:

ProteOn
BioPlex 2200
iScript

CONTACTS:

Note: Officers with more than one job title may be intentionally listed here more than once.

Norman Schwartz, CEO
Norman Schwartz, Pres.
Christine Tsingos, CFO/VP
Sanford S. Wadler, General Counsel/VP/Sec.
Tina Cuccia, Mgr.-Corp. Comm.
James R. Stark, Corp. Controller
Ronald W. Hutton, Treas.
Brad Crutchfield, VP/Group Mgr.-Life Science
John Goetz, VP/Group Mgr.-Clinical Diagnostics
David Schwartz, Chmn.
Giovanni Magni, VP/Mgr.-Int'l Sales

Phone: 510-724-7000 **Fax:** 510-741-5815
Toll-Free: 800-424-6723
Address: 1000 Alfred Nobel Dr., Hercules, CA 94547 US

GROWTH PLANS/SPECIAL FEATURES:

Bio-Rad Laboratories, Inc. supplies the life science research, health care and analytical chemistry markets with a broad range of products and systems. These are used to separate complex chemical and biological materials and to identify, analyze and purify components. The company operates in two industry segments: life science and clinical diagnostics. The firm's life science division (34% of revenues) develops products for applications including electrophoresis, image analysis, molecular detection, chromatography, gene transfer, sample preparation and amplification. Products include a range of laboratory instruments, apparatus and consumables used for research in genomics, proteomics and food safety. The Bio-Rad life science division (66% of revenues) provides its services to universities; medical schools; pharmaceutical manufacturers; industrial research organizations; food testing laboratories; government agencies; and biotechnology researchers. The clinical diagnostics division encompasses an array of technologies incorporated into a variety of tests used to detect, identify and quantify substances in blood or other body fluids and tissues. The test results are used as aids for medical diagnosis, detection, evaluation, monitoring and treatment of diseases and other conditions. This division is known for diabetes monitoring products, quality control systems, blood virus testing, blood typing, toxicology, genetic disorders products, molecular pathology and Internet-based software. Bio-Rad is also an international provider of bovine spongiform encephalopathy (mad cow disease) tests. Bio-Rad's brand name systems include the BioPlex 2200 multiplex testing platform; iScript, reverse transcription reagent kits; and ProteOn, a protein interaction analysis system.

FINANCIALS:

Sales and profits are in thousands of dollars—add 000 to get the full amount. 2010 Note: Financial information for 2010 was not available for all companies at press time.

2010 Sales: $1,927,118 — 2010 Profits: $185,490
2009 Sales: $1,784,244 — 2009 Profits: $144,620
2008 Sales: $1,764,365 — 2008 Profits: $89,510
2007 Sales: $1,461,052 — 2007 Profits: $92,994
2006 Sales: $1,273,930 — 2006 Profits: $103,263

U.S. Stock Ticker: BIO
Int'l Ticker:
Int'l Exchange:
Employees: 6,880 Fiscal Year Ends: 12/31
Parent Company:

SALARIES/BENEFITS:

Pension Plan: ESOP Stock Plan: Profit Sharing: Top Exec. Salary: $759,361 Bonus: $620,671
Savings Plan: Y Stock Purch. Plan: Y Second Exec. Salary: $520,130 Bonus: $208,000

OTHER THOUGHTS:

Apparent Women Officers or Directors: 2
Hot Spot for Advancement for Women/Minorities: Y

LOCATIONS: ("Y" = Yes)

West:	Southwest:	Midwest:	Southeast:	Northeast:	International:
Y	Y			Y	Y

BIOGEN IDEC INC

www.biogenidec.com

Industry Group Code: 325412

Management:		Sales/Marketing:		Liberal Arts:		Information Sys.:		Professionals:		Tech./Scientific:	
Mgmt. Trainees:	Y	Marketing Pros.:	Y	Gen. Writing/Editing:		Info. Mgmt.:	Y	Finance/Acct.:	Y	Engineers, Elec.:	Y
Experienced Mgmt.:	Y	Retail Sales:		Tech. Writing:	Y	Software Dev.:	Y	Law:	Y	Engineers, Other:	Y
Int'l Business:	Y	Comm./Industrial:	Y	Graphic Arts/Photog.:		Hardware Dev.:		HR/Other:	Y	Health/Lab:	Y
MBA Grads:	Y	Sales Trainees:		Music:		Consulting/Other:		Training:	Y	Science/Research:	Y
		Advertising Pros.:		Broadcasting:				Health Care:		Petroleum/Chem.:	
				Other:				Consulting:		Math/Other:	

TYPES OF BUSINESS:

Drugs-Immunology, Neurology & Oncology
Autoimmune & Inflammatory Disease Treatments
Drugs-Multiple Sclerosis
Drugs-Cancer

BRANDS/DIVISIONS/AFFILIATES:

AVONEX
TYSABRI
RITUXAN
FUMADERM
Panima Pharmaceuticals AG

CONTACTS: *Note: Officers with more than one job title may be intentionally listed here more than once.*

George A. Scangos, CEO
Paul J. Clancy, CFO/Exec. VP
Craig Eric Schneier, Exec. VP-Human Resources
Douglas E. Williams, Exec. VP-R&D
John G. Cox, Exec. VP-Pharmaceutical Tech.
Susan H. Alexander, General Counsel/Exec. VP/Corp. Sec.
John G. Cox, Exec. VP-Pharmaceutical Oper.
Steven H. Holtzman, Exec. VP-Corp. Dev.
Craig Eric Schneier, Exec. VP-Corp. Comm. & Public Affairs
William D. Young, Chmn.
Francesco Granata, Exec. VP-Global Commercial Oper.

Phone: 781-464-2000	**Fax:** 617-679-2617
Toll-Free:	
Address: 133 Boston Post Rd., Weston, MA 02493 US	

GROWTH PLANS/SPECIAL FEATURES:

Biogen IDEC, Inc. is a biotechnology company that develops, manufactures and markets therapeutic pharmaceuticals in the fields of immunology, neurology and oncology. Biogen currently has four approved products: AVONEX, which is designed to treat relapsing forms of multiple sclerosis (MS) and is used by more than 135,000 patients in 70 countries globally; TYSABRI, which is approved for the treatment of relapsing forms of MS and in the U.S. is approved to treat moderate to severe active Crohn's disease; RITUXAN, which is globally approved for the treatment of relapsed or refractory low-grade or follicular, CD20-positive, B-cell non-Hodgkin's lymphomas (NHLs) and has had over 2.4 million patient exposures worldwide; and FUMADERM, which acts as an immunomodulator and is approved in Germany for the treatment of severe psoriasis. RITUXAN, in combination with methotrexate, is also approved to reduce signs and symptoms in adult patients with moderately-to-severely active rheumatoid arthritis who have had an inadequate response to one or more tumor necrosis factor antagonist therapies. The company is working with Genentech and Roche on the development of RITUXAN in additional oncology and other indications. In addition to its approved drugs, the firm currently has 29 drugs under development, including drugs in the company's core areas of focus as well as in other therapeutic areas such as cardiovascular disease and hemophilia. Biogen also generates revenue by licensing drugs it has developed to other companies, including Schering-Plough, Merck and GlaxoSmithKline. In November 2010, the firm announced plans to reduce its total workforce by 13%. In December 2010, the company acquired Panima Pharmaceuticals AG.

Biogen offers employees medical, dental and vision insurance; tuition reimbursement; commuter benefits; discounts on health clubs and local events; flexible spending accounts; and an employee assistance program.

FINANCIALS: **Sales and profits are in thousands of dollars—add 000 to get the full amount. 2010 Note: Financial information for 2010 was not available for all companies at press time.**

2010 Sales: $4,716,400	2010 Profits: $1,005,300
2009 Sales: $4,377,300	2009 Profits: $977,100
2008 Sales: $4,097,500	2008 Profits: $783,200
2007 Sales: $3,171,600	2007 Profits: $638,172
2006 Sales: $2,683,049	2006 Profits: $217,511

U.S. Stock Ticker: BIIB
Int'l Ticker:
Int'l Exchange:
Employees: 4,850 Fiscal Year Ends: 12/31
Parent Company:

SALARIES/BENEFITS:

Pension Plan:	ESOP Stock Plan:	Profit Sharing:	Top Exec. Salary: $1,204,615	Bonus: $1,440,000
Savings Plan: Y	Stock Purch. Plan: Y		Second Exec. Salary: $657,231	Bonus: $596,160

OTHER THOUGHTS:

Apparent Women Officers or Directors: 3
Hot Spot for Advancement for Women/Minorities: Y

LOCATIONS: ("Y" = Yes)

West:	Southwest:	Midwest:	Southeast:	Northeast:	International:
Y				Y	Y

BLACKROCK INC

Industry Group Code: 523920

www.blackrock.com

Management:		Sales/Marketing:		Liberal Arts:		Information Sys.:		Professionals:		Tech./Scientific:	
Mgmt. Trainees:	Y	Marketing Pros.:	Y	Gen. Writing/Editing:	Y	Info. Mgmt.:	Y	Finance/Acct.:	Y	Engineers, Elec.:	
Experienced Mgmt.:	Y	Retail Sales:		Tech. Writing:		Software Dev.:	Y	Law:	Y	Engineers, Other:	
Int'l Business:	Y	Comm./Industrial:		Graphic Arts/Photog.:		Hardware Dev.:		HR/Other:	Y	Health/Lab:	
MBA Grads:	Y	Sales Trainees:		Music:		Consulting/Other:		Training:	Y	Science/Research:	
		Advertising Pros.:		Broadcasting:				Health Care:		Petroleum/Chem.:	
				Other:				Consulting:		Math/Other:	

TYPES OF BUSINESS:

Investment Management
Risk Management Services
Investment System Services

BRANDS/DIVISIONS/AFFILIATES:

iShares
BlackRock Solutions
Helix Financial Group LLC
Barclays Global Investors

CONTACTS: *Note: Officers with more than one job title may be intentionally listed here more than once.*

Laurence D. Fink, CEO
Charles S. Hallac, COO
Robert S. Kapito, Pres.
Ann Marie Petach, CFO
Jeffrey A. Smith, Head-Human Resources
Robert P. Connolly, General Counsel
Bennett W. Golub, Chief Risk Officer
Robert W. Fairbairn, Head-Global Client Group
J. Richard Kushel, Head-Portfolio Mgmt.
Laurence D. Fink, Chmn.
James J. Charrington, Chmn.-EMEA

Phone: 212-810-5300 | **Fax:** 212-935-1370
Toll-Free:
Address: 40 E. 52nd St., New York, NY 10022 US

GROWTH PLANS/SPECIAL FEATURES:

BlackRock, Inc. and its subsidiaries form one of the largest investment management firms in the U.S., with $3.45 trillion worth of assets under management on behalf of institutional and individual investors worldwide, through a variety of fixed income, cash management, equity and balanced and alternative investment accounts and funds. The company also provides risk management, investment system outsourcing and financial advisory services. Its clients include a diverse group of institutional and retail investors globally. Institutional clients include pension funds, official institutions, foundations, endowments and charities, insurance companies, banks, sub-advisory relationships and private banks. The firm also offers risk management and investment system services through its BlackRock Solutions product line. The firm's exchange traded funds business, iShares, has a 51% market share in the U.S. and a 38% market share in the EMEA. Headquartered in New York, the company maintains offices in 26 countries around the world and a client base in over 100 countries. About 39% of the company's assets are managed on behalf of investors outside the U.S. and Canada, and nearly 40% of its employees live and work outside the U.S. In January 2010, the firm acquired Helix Financial Group LLC.

The company offers employees medical and life insurance; disability coverage; retirement benefits; and tuition assistance.

FINANCIALS: **Sales and profits are in thousands of dollars—add 000 to get the full amount. 2010 Note: Financial information for 2010 was not available for all companies at press time.**

2010 Sales: $8,612,000 | 2010 Profits: $2,063,000
2009 Sales: $4,700,000 | 2009 Profits: $875,000
2008 Sales: $5,064,000 | 2008 Profits: $784,000
2007 Sales: $4,844,655 | 2007 Profits: $995,272
2006 Sales: $2,097,976 | 2006 Profits: $322,602

U.S. Stock Ticker: BLK
Int'l Ticker:
Int'l Exchange:
Employees: 9,127 Fiscal Year Ends: 12/31
Parent Company:

SALARIES/BENEFITS:

Pension Plan: | ESOP Stock Plan: | Profit Sharing: | Top Exec. Salary: $500,000 | Bonus: $9,050,000
Savings Plan: Y | Stock Purch. Plan: | | Second Exec. Salary: $450,000 | Bonus: $1,655,000

OTHER THOUGHTS:

Apparent Women Officers or Directors: 4
Hot Spot for Advancement for Women/Minorities: Y

LOCATIONS: ("Y" = Yes)

West:	Southwest:	Midwest:	Southeast:	Northeast:	International:
Y		Y		Y	Y

BLOOMBERG LP

www.bloomberg.com

Industry Group Code: 519130

Management:		**Sales/Marketing:**		**Liberal Arts:**		**Information Sys.:**		**Professionals:**		**Tech./Scientific:**	
Mgmt. Trainees:	Y	Marketing Pros.:	Y	Gen. Writing/Editing:	Y	Info. Mgmt.:	Y	Finance/Acct.:	Y	Engineers, Elec.:	Y
Experienced Mgmt.:	Y	Retail Sales:		Tech. Writing:	Y	Software Dev.:	Y	Law:	Y	Engineers, Other:	
Int'l Business:	Y	Comm./Industrial:	Y	Graphic Arts/Photog.:	Y	Hardware Dev.:	Y	HR/Other:	Y	Health/Lab:	
MBA Grads:	Y	Sales Trainees:	Y	Music:		Consulting/Other:		Training:	Y	Science/Research:	
		Advertising Pros.:	Y	Broadcasting:				Health Care:		Petroleum/Chem.:	
				Other:	Y			Consulting:		Math/Other:	

TYPES OF BUSINESS:

Financial Data Publishing-Print & Online
Magazine Publishing
Management Software
Multimedia Presentation Services
Broadcast Television
Radio Broadcasting
Electronic Exchange Systems
Software

BRANDS/DIVISIONS/AFFILIATES:

Bloomberg Professional
BusinessWeek
Bloomberg Tradebook
Bloomberg Electronic Trading Systems
Bloomberg New Energy Finance
Bloomberg Television
Bloomberg Magazine
Bureau of National Affairs, Inc. (The)

CONTACTS: *Note: Officers with more than one job title may be intentionally listed here more than once.*

Daniel L. Doctoroff, CEO
Daniel L. Doctoroff, Pres.
Maureen A. McGuire, Chief Mktg. Officer
Richard C. Powell, Jr., Chief Comm. Officer
Matthew Winkler, Editor-in-Chief, Bloomberg News
Thomas Secunda, Vice Chmn./Head-Financial Prod. & Svcs.
Lex Fenwick, CEO-Bloomberg Ventures
Andy Lack, CEO-Bloomberg Media Group
Peter T. Grauer, Chmn.

Phone: 212-318-2000	**Fax:** 917-369-5000
Toll-Free:	
Address: 731 Lexington Ave., New York, NY 10022 US	

GROWTH PLANS/SPECIAL FEATURES:

Bloomberg LP is an information services, news and media company, serving the financial services industry; government offices and agencies; corporations; and news organizations in 160 countries. The company operates in five segments: Bloomberg Professional Service, Bloomberg Tradebook, Bloomberg Enterprise, Bloomberg Business Solutions and Bloomberg News & Media. Bloomberg Professional Service is delivered online to Bloomberg Terminals rented by subscribers. With an average monthly fee around $1,500, these terminals provide traders and asset managers' real-time financial news, market data, analysis, electronic trading and multimedia report capabilities. By the beginning of 2011, the firm had 300,000 terminals in place. Bloomberg Tradebook allows customers to trade on 65 markets in 54 countries. In the Bloomberg Enterprise segment, the company's Electronic Trading Systems allow the firm's professional services to work in conjunction with outside infrastructure and include global risk-management software and a portfolio management system. Additionally, Bloomberg's Data License provides access to the Bloomberg financial database and to more than 4 million financial instruments. Bloomberg Business Solutions include Bloomberg Law, providing legal research tools; Bloomberg Sports, which generates industry-leading analysis; Bloomberg Government; and Bloomberg New Energy Finance, which provides information and analysis on clean energy technologies. Finally, Bloomberg News & Media syndicates information to over 450 newspapers worldwide. This segment also disseminates information across a diverse mix of media outlets, including Bloomberg Television, reaching over 245 million homes worldwide; Bloomberg BusinessWeek, with more than 4.7 million readers in 140 countries; Bloomberg Radio; Bloomberg.com; Bloomberg Mobile; and Bloomberg Markets Magazine. The firm's goal is to grow revenues to $14 billion by 2014. In August 2011, the firm agreed to acquire The Bureau of National Affairs, Inc.

Employees receive tuition reimbursement; adoption assistance; back-up childcare services; short- and long-term disability insurance; medical, dental and vision coverage; onsite medical services; commuter expense saving programs; and flexible spending accounts.

FINANCIALS: **Sales and profits are in thousands of dollars—add 000 to get the full amount. 2010 Note: Financial information for 2010 was not available for all companies at press time.**

2010 Sales: $7,000,000	2010 Profits: $	**U.S. Stock Ticker: Private**
2009 Sales: $6,600,000	2009 Profits: $	**Int'l Ticker:**
2008 Sales: $6,100,000	2008 Profits: $	Int'l Exchange:
2007 Sales: $5,400,000	2007 Profits: $	Employees: 12,500 Fiscal Year Ends: 12/31
2006 Sales: $4,700,000	2006 Profits: $	Parent Company:

SALARIES/BENEFITS:

Pension Plan:	ESOP Stock Plan:	Profit Sharing:	Top Exec. Salary: $	Bonus: $
Savings Plan: Y	Stock Purch. Plan:		Second Exec. Salary: $	Bonus: $

OTHER THOUGHTS:

Apparent Women Officers or Directors: 2
Hot Spot for Advancement for Women/Minorities: Y

LOCATIONS: ("Y" = Yes)

West:	Southwest:	Midwest:	Southeast:	Northeast:	International:
Y	Y	Y	Y	Y	Y

BMC SOFTWARE INC

Industry Group Code: 511210H

www.bmc.com

Management:		Sales/Marketing:		Liberal Arts:		Information Sys.:		Professionals:		Tech./Scientific:	
Mgmt. Trainees:	Y	Marketing Pros.:	Y	Gen. Writing/Editing:	Y	Info. Mgmt.:	Y	Finance/Acct.:	Y	Engineers, Elec.:	Y
Experienced Mgmt.:	Y	Retail Sales:		Tech. Writing:	Y	Software Dev.:	Y	Law:	Y	Engineers, Other:	
Int'l Business:	Y	Comm./Industrial:	Y	Graphic Arts/Photog.:		Hardware Dev.:		HR/Other:	Y	Health/Lab:	
MBA Grads:	Y	Sales Trainees:		Music:		Consulting/Other:		Training:	Y	Science/Research:	
		Advertising Pros.:	Y	Broadcasting:				Health Care:		Petroleum/Chem.:	
				Other:				Consulting:	Y	Math/Other:	

TYPES OF BUSINESS:

Computer Software-Mainframe Related
Systems Management Software
e-Business Software
Consulting & Training Services

BRANDS/DIVISIONS/AFFILIATES:

BMC Atrium
GridApp Systems Inc

CONTACTS: *Note: Officers with more than one job title may be intentionally listed here more than once.*

Robert E. Beauchamp, CEO
Stephen B. Solcher, CFO/Sr. VP
John McMahon, Sr. VP-Worldwide Sales & Svcs.
Hollie Castro, Sr. VP-Admin.
Denise M. Clolery, General Counsel/Sr. VP/Corp. Sec.
Steve Goddard, Sr. VP-Bus. Oper.
Ken Berryman, Sr. VP-Strategy & Corp. Dev.
T. Cory Bleuer, Chief Acct. Officer/Controller/VP
William D. Miller, Pres., Mainframe Service Mgmt.
Robert E. Beauchamp, Chmn.

Phone: 713-918-8800 | **Fax:** 713-918-8000
Toll-Free: 800-841-2031
Address: 2101 Citywest Blvd., Houston, TX 77042 US

GROWTH PLANS/SPECIAL FEATURES:

BMC Software, Inc. is one of the world's largest software vendors. The company provides system management, service management and automation solutions primarily for large companies. Its software products span mainframe and distributed systems, applications, databases and IT process management functions. The company operates in two software business segments: Enterprise Service Management (ESM) and Mainframe Service Management (MSM). The Enterprise Service Management (ESM) segment consists of the company's solutions and related professional services related to a variety of IT management issues, including service support, service assurance and service automation. Also included is the firm's BMC Atrium software package, which helps provide centralized coordination and execution of IT processes. The company's Mainframe Service Management (MSM) segment creates products that address IT challenges for mainframe systems management, data management and enterprise workload automation, with particular focus on streamlining mainframe operations in order to reduce costs and manage large amounts of data without affecting the availability of critical business applications. MSM products are organized into three areas: data and performance management, and enterprise scheduling and output management. The company also operates a professional services segment, consisting of a worldwide team of software consultants who provide implementation, integration, IT process design and re-engineering and education services related to its products. The company's customers include manufacturers, telecommunication companies, financial service providers, educational institutions, retailers, distributors, hospitals, service providers, government agencies and channel partners including resellers, distributors and system integrators. Approximately 16,000 companies worldwide use BMC products, including 90% of the Fortune 100 companies. In December 2010, the company acquired GridApp Systems, Inc., which specializes in cloud-based data applications.

FINANCIALS: **Sales and profits are in thousands of dollars—add 000 to get the full amount. 2010 Note: Financial information for 2010 was not available for all companies at press time.**

2010 Sales: $1,911,200 — 2010 Profits: $406,100
2009 Sales: $1,871,900 — 2009 Profits: $238,100
2008 Sales: $1,731,600 — 2008 Profits: $313,600
2007 Sales: $1,580,400 — 2007 Profits: $215,900
2006 Sales: $1,498,400 — 2006 Profits: $102,000

U.S. Stock Ticker: BMC
Int'l Ticker:
Int'l Exchange:
Employees: 6,100 Fiscal Year Ends: 3/31
Parent Company:

SALARIES/BENEFITS:

Pension Plan: ESOP Stock Plan: Profit Sharing: Top Exec. Salary: $950,000 Bonus: $1,326,675
Savings Plan: Stock Purch. Plan: Second Exec. Salary: $475,000 Bonus: $442,225

OTHER THOUGHTS:

Apparent Women Officers or Directors: 3
Hot Spot for Advancement for Women/Minorities: Y

LOCATIONS: ("Y" = Yes)

West:	Southwest:	Midwest:	Southeast:	Northeast:	International:
Y	Y	Y	Y	Y	Y

Sales, profits and employees may be estimates. Financial information, benefits and other data can change quickly and may vary from those stated here.

BOEING COMPANY (THE)

www.boeing.com

Industry Group Code: 33641

Management:		Sales/Marketing:		Liberal Arts:		Information Sys.:		Professionals:		Tech./Scientific:	
Mgmt. Trainees:	Y	Marketing Pros.:	Y	Gen. Writing/Editing:	Y	Info. Mgmt.:	Y	Finance/Acct.:	Y	Engineers, Elec.:	Y
Experienced Mgmt.:	Y	Retail Sales:		Tech. Writing:	Y	Software Dev.:	Y	Law:	Y	Engineers, Other:	Y
Int'l Business:	Y	Comm./Industrial:	Y	Graphic Arts/Photog.:	Y	Hardware Dev.:	Y	HR/Other:	Y	Health/Lab:	
MBA Grads:	Y	Sales Trainees:		Music:		Consulting/Other:	Y	Training:	Y	Science/Research:	Y
		Advertising Pros.:	Y	Broadcasting:				Health Care:		Petroleum/Chem.:	
				Other:	Y			Consulting:		Math/Other:	Y

TYPES OF BUSINESS:

Commercial Aircraft Manufacturing
Aerospace Technology & Manufacturing
Military Aircraft
Satellite Manufacturing
Communications Products & Services
Air Traffic Management Technology
Financing Services
Research & Development

BRANDS/DIVISIONS/AFFILIATES:

Narus
Argon ST Inc
CDM Technologies
Boeing Capital Corporation
Boeing Military Aircraft
Network & Space Systems
Global Services & Support
787 Dreamliner

CONTACTS: *Note: Officers with more than one job title may be intentionally listed here more than once.*

W. James McNerney, Jr., CEO
W. James McNerney, Jr., Pres.
James A. Bell, CFO/Exec. VP
Richard Stephens, Sr. VP-Human Resources
Kim Hammonds, CIO/VP-IT
John J. Tracy, CTO/Sr. VP-Tech.
John J. Tracy, Sr. VP-Eng.
Richard Stephens, Sr. VP-Admin.
J. Michael Luttig, General Counsel/Exec. VP
John J. Tracy, Sr. VP-Oper.
Shephard W. Hill, Sr. VP-Bus. Dev. & Strategy
Thomas J. Downey, Sr. VP-Comm.
James F. Albaugh, Exec. VP/CEO/Pres., Commercial Airplanes
Wanda K. Denson-Low, Sr. VP-Office of Internal Governance
Timothy Keating, Sr. VP-Gov't Oper.
W. James McNerney, Jr., Chmn.
Shephard W. Hill, Pres., Boeing Int'l

Phone: 312-544-2000 **Fax:** 312-544-2082
Toll-Free:
Address: 100 N. Riverside, Chicago, IL 60606 US

GROWTH PLANS/SPECIAL FEATURES:

The Boeing Company is one of the world's major aerospace firms. The company operates in three segments: commercial airplanes; Boeing Defense, Space & Security; and Boeing Capital Corporation. Commercial airplanes develops, produces and markets commercial jet aircraft and provides related support services. The family of jet aircraft includes the 737 Next-Generation narrow-body model and the 767, 777 and wide-body models. The division also offers aviation support, aircraft modifications, training, maintenance documents and technical advice. Boeing Defense, Space & Security, which comprises Boeing Military Aircraft (BMA), Network & Space Systems (N&SS) and Global Services & Support (GS&S)researches, develops, produces, and supports military aircraft, including fighters, transports, tankers and helicopters; missiles; space systems; missile defense systems; satellites and satellite launch vehicles; and communications, information and battle management systems. The BMA subdivision is focused on the development of military aircraft and precision engagement, as well as mobility products and services. The N&SS subdivision provides products and services to assist customers in transforming operations through network integration, intelligence and surveillance systems, communications and space exploration. The GS&S subdivision is engaged in operations, maintenance, and logistics support functions for military platforms. Boeing Capital Corp. provides financing to commercial airplanes customers. The company's is currently testing its 787 Dreamliner and 747-8 wide-body models. The 787 Dreamliner, manufactured of extremely light components that, combined with advanced technology jet engines, enable the aircraft to enjoy very high fuel efficiency, is expected to enter service in the third quarter of 2011. The company recently acquired Narus, a real-time network traffic intelligence provider for companies and government agencies with large IP networks; Argon ST, Inc.; a C4ISR (Command, Control, Communications, Computers, Intelligence, Surveillance and Reconnaissance) developer; and CDM Technologies, a software engineering company that provides the U.S. military with logistics planning and real-time transportation systems.

FINANCIALS: **Sales and profits are in thousands of dollars—add 000 to get the full amount. 2010 Note: Financial information for 2010 was not available for all companies at press time.**

2010 Sales: $64,306,000 — 2010 Profits: $3,307,000
2009 Sales: $68,281,000 — 2009 Profits: $1,312,000
2008 Sales: $60,909,000 — 2008 Profits: $2,672,000
2007 Sales: $66,387,000 — 2007 Profits: $4,074,000
2006 Sales: $61,530,000 — 2006 Profits: $2,215,000

U.S. Stock Ticker: BA
Int'l Ticker:
Int'l Exchange:
Employees: 160,500 Fiscal Year Ends: 12/31
Parent Company:

SALARIES/BENEFITS:

Pension Plan: Y ESOP Stock Plan: Profit Sharing: Top Exec. Salary: $1,930,000 Bonus: $4,500,300
Savings Plan: Y Stock Purch. Plan: Second Exec. Salary: $952,382 Bonus: $1,314,068

OTHER THOUGHTS:

Apparent Women Officers or Directors: 8
Hot Spot for Advancement for Women/Minorities: Y

LOCATIONS: ("Y" = Yes)

West:	Southwest:	Midwest:	Southeast:	Northeast:	International:
Y	Y	Y	Y	Y	Y

BOOZ ALLEN HAMILTON INC

www.boozallen.com

Industry Group Code: 54161

Management:		Sales/Marketing:		Liberal Arts:		Information Sys.:		Professionals:		Tech./Scientific:	
Mgmt. Trainees:	Y	Marketing Pros.:	Y	Gen. Writing/Editing:	Y	Info. Mgmt.:	Y	Finance/Acct.:	Y	Engineers, Elec.:	
Experienced Mgmt.:	Y	Retail Sales:		Tech. Writing:	Y	Software Dev.:	Y	Law:	Y	Engineers, Other:	
Int'l Business:	Y	Comm./Industrial:	Y	Graphic Arts/Photog.:	Y	Hardware Dev.:		HR/Other:	Y	Health/Lab:	
MBA Grads:	Y	Sales Trainees:		Music:		Consulting/Other:	Y	Training:	Y	Science/Research:	
		Advertising Pros.:	Y	Broadcasting:				Health Care:		Petroleum/Chem.:	
				Other:	Y			Consulting:	Y	Math/Other:	Y

TYPES OF BUSINESS:

Strategy Consulting
Engineering & IT Consulting
Supply Chain Management
Industry Research & Publications
War Gaming & Strategic Simulation

BRANDS/DIVISIONS/AFFILIATES:

Booz Allen Hamiltonn Holding Corp

CONTACTS: *Note: Officers with more than one job title may be intentionally listed here more than once.*

Ralph W. Shrader, CEO
Horacio D. Rozanski, COO/Exec. VP
Ralph W. Shrader, Pres.
Samuel R. Strickland, CFO/Exec. VP
Marie Lerch, VP-Mktg.
Patrick F. Peck, Exec. VP-Tech.
Samuel R. Strickland, Chief Admin. Officer/Exec. VP
Robert S. Osborne, General Counsel/Exec. VP
Marie Lerch, VP-Comm.
Tom Meagher, Dir.-Investor Rel.
C. G. Appleby, Chief Legal Officer/Exec. VP
Joseph Logue, Exec. VP-Defense Bus.
Francis J. Henry, Exec. VP-Civil Bus.
John M. McConnell, Exec. VP-National Security Bus.
Ralph W. Shrader, Chmn.

Phone: 703-902-5000 **Fax:** 703-902-3333
Toll-Free:
Address: 8283 Greensboro Dr., McLean, VA 22102 US

GROWTH PLANS/SPECIAL FEATURES:

Booz Allen Hamilton, Inc. (BAH), founded in 1914, is a strategy and technology consulting firm, providing services to the U.S. government in the defense, intelligence and civil sectors. The company is the primary operating segment of publicly traded Booz Allen Hamilton Holding Corporation (BAHHC). BAH's major areas of expertise include business analytics; information technology; cyber security; operations and logistics; organization and change; service innovation; public sector mission effectiveness; strategy and leadership; and systems engineering and integration. It derives substantially all of its revenue from services provided under contracts and task orders with the U.S. government. The company's work with national governments around the world has included projects to enhance national security, economic well-being and the health and safety of citizens. Some of Booz Allen's largest clients have included the U.S. Department of Defense; the Air Force, Army, Navy and Marine Corps; the U.S. Departments of Energy, Health, Human Services, Homeland Security and several other government agencies. The company's work for other governments includes assignments with the U.K. Department for Work and Pensions as well as government institutions in Abu Dhabi, Australia, Germany, Italy, Jordan and New Zealand. The company also publishes books, reports and studies on industry subjects ranging from information technology to leadership. It maintains offices across the U.S., as well as strategic locations in Russia, Georgia, Kazakhstan and Azerbaijan. BAHHC held an initial public offering (IPO) of stock in November 2010.

FINANCIALS: **Sales and profits are in thousands of dollars—add 000 to get the full amount. 2010 Note: Financial information for 2010 was not available for all companies at press time.**

2010 Sales: $5,122,633 — 2010 Profits: $25,419
2009 Sales: $4,351,218 — 2009 Profits: $-1,284,698
2008 Sales: $4,400,000 — 2008 Profits: $17,900
2007 Sales: $3,147,000 — 2007 Profits: $
2006 Sales: $2,846,000 — 2006 Profits: $

U.S. Stock Ticker: BAH
Int'l Ticker:
Int'l Exchange:
Employees: 25,000 Fiscal Year Ends: 3/31
Parent Company: BOOZ ALLEN HAMILTON HOLDING CORP

SALARIES/BENEFITS:

Pension Plan: ESOP Stock Plan: Profit Sharing: Y Top Exec. Salary: $ Bonus: $
Savings Plan: Y Stock Purch. Plan: Second Exec. Salary: $ Bonus: $

OTHER THOUGHTS:

Apparent Women Officers or Directors: 1
Hot Spot for Advancement for Women/Minorities:

LOCATIONS: ("Y" = Yes)

West:	Southwest:	Midwest:	Southeast:	Northeast:	International:
Y	Y	Y	Y	Y	Y

BOSTON CONSULTING GROUP INC (THE, BCG) www.bcg.com

Industry Group Code: 54161

Management:		**Sales/Marketing:**		**Liberal Arts:**		**Information Sys.:**		**Professionals:**		**Tech./Scientific:**	
Mgmt. Trainees:		Marketing Pros.:	Y	Gen. Writing/Editing:	Y	Info. Mgmt.:	Y	Finance/Acct.:	Y	Engineers, Elec.:	
Experienced Mgmt.:	Y	Retail Sales:		Tech. Writing:	Y	Software Dev.:	Y	Law:	Y	Engineers, Other:	
Int'l Business:	Y	Comm./Industrial:	Y	Graphic Arts/Photog.:	Y	Hardware Dev.:		HR/Other:	Y	Health/Lab:	Y
MBA Grads:	Y	Sales Trainees:		Music:		Consulting/Other:	Y	Training:		Science/Research:	
		Advertising Pros.:		Broadcasting:				Health Care:		Petroleum/Chem.:	
				Other:	Y			Consulting:	Y	Math/Other:	Y

TYPES OF BUSINESS:

Management Consulting
Marketing Consulting
Corporate Strategy Research

BRANDS/DIVISIONS/AFFILIATES:

Strategy Institute (The)

CONTACTS:

Note: Officers with more than one job title may be intentionally listed here more than once.

Hans-Paul Burkner, CEO
Hans-Paul Burkner, Pres.
Debbie Simpson, CFO
Thomas Reichert, Global Leader-IT Practice
Rich Hutchinson, Chief of Staff
Jeremy Barton, General Counsel/Head-Risk Mgmt.
Michel Fredeau, Sr. Partner/Managing Dir.-Paris
Sharon Marcil, Sr. Partner/Managing Dir.-Washington, D.C.
Rich Hutchinson, Partner/Managing Dir.-Atlanta, Georgia
Ivan Marten, Global Leader-Energy Practice
Carl Stern, Chmn.

Phone: 617-973-1200	**Fax:** 617-973-1399
Toll-Free:	
Address: 1 Exchange Pl., 30th & 31st Fl., Boston, MA 02109 US	

GROWTH PLANS/SPECIAL FEATURES:

The Boston Consulting Group, Inc. (BCG) provides international strategy and general management consulting services with the aim of helping businesses create and sustain competitive advantages. With over 65 offices in 40 countries, the firm is one of the world's largest consulting organizations. Most of BCG's offices are located in Europe and Asia, though the firm has a significant North American presence as well. Areas of consulting expertise include automotive, consumer markets, corporate development, the energy industry, e-commerce, financial services, globalization, health care, industrial goods, information technology, operations, organization, pricing, retail, strategy, technology, communications, travel and tourism. BCG also publishes extensive reports on many aspects of multiple industries and is constantly developing new ideas on business structure and efficiency. This written material is stored on the company's web site and can be searched from multiple angles. BCG has established the Strategy Institute, which is a collaboration between certain current BCG consultants and professors and PhDs at higher-education institutions such as Harvard Business School, the National War College, the Said Business School of Oxford University and the University of California, Berkley. The institute is currently doing research on various subjects, such as the relationship between poetry and strategic thinking, as well as projects concerning learning and the relationship between religion and culture in shaping identity. Recently, the Strategy Institute has produced articles on sustainability in business and the importance of public trust in business. In March 2011, the firm opened two offices in Tel Aviv and one in Perth, Israel.

FINANCIALS:

Sales and profits are in thousands of dollars—add 000 to get the full amount. 2010 Note: Financial information for 2010 was not available for all companies at press time.

2010 Sales: $3,050,000	2010 Profits: $	**U.S. Stock Ticker: Private**
2009 Sales: $2,750,000	2009 Profits: $	**Int'l Ticker:**
2008 Sales: $2,670,000	2008 Profits: $	Int'l Exchange:
2007 Sales: $2,400,000	2007 Profits: $	Employees: 6,500 Fiscal Year Ends: 12/31
2006 Sales: $2,000,000	2006 Profits: $	Parent Company:

SALARIES/BENEFITS:

Pension Plan:	ESOP Stock Plan:	Profit Sharing:	Top Exec. Salary: $	Bonus: $
Savings Plan:	Stock Purch. Plan:		Second Exec. Salary: $	Bonus: $

OTHER THOUGHTS:

Apparent Women Officers or Directors: 3
Hot Spot for Advancement for Women/Minorities: Y

LOCATIONS: ("Y" = Yes)

West:	Southwest:	Midwest:	Southeast:	Northeast:	International:
Y	Y	Y	Y	Y	Y

BOYD GAMING CORP

www.boydgaming.com

Industry Group Code: 721120

Management:		**Sales/Marketing:**		**Liberal Arts:**		**Information Sys.:**		**Professionals:**		**Tech./Scientific:**	
Mgmt. Trainees:	Y	Marketing Pros.:	Y	Gen. Writing/Editing:	Y	Info. Mgmt.:	Y	Finance/Acct.:	Y	Engineers, Elec.:	
Experienced Mgmt.:	Y	Retail Sales:		Tech. Writing:		Software Dev.:		Law:	Y	Engineers, Other:	
Int'l Business:		Comm./Industrial:		Graphic Arts/Photog.:	Y	Hardware Dev.:		HR/Other:	Y	Health/Lab:	
MBA Grads:	Y	Sales Trainees:		Music:		Consulting/Other:		Training:	Y	Science/Research:	
		Advertising Pros.:	Y	Broadcasting:				Health Care:		Petroleum/Chem.:	
				Other:				Consulting:		Math/Other:	

TYPES OF BUSINESS:

Casinos & Hotels
Casino Management

BRANDS/DIVISIONS/AFFILIATES:

California Hotel & Casino
Borgata Hotel, Casino, & Spa
Blue Chip Hotel and Casino
Delta Downs Racetrack & Casino
Gold Coast Hotel and Casino
Fremont Hotel & Casino
Club Coast
B Connected

CONTACTS: *Note: Officers with more than one job title may be intentionally listed here more than once.*

Keith E. Smith, CEO
Paul J. Chakmak, COO/Exec. VP
Keith E. Smith, Pres.
John Hirsberg, CFO/Sr. VP/Treas.
Brian A. Larson, General Counsel/Exec. VP/Sec.
Robert L. Boughner, Chief Bus. Dev. Officer/Exec. VP
Rob Meyne, VP-Corp. Comm.
Ellie J. Bowdish, Chief Acct. Officer/VP
Marianne Boyd Johnson, Chief Diversity Officer/Exec. VP
William R. Boyd, VP
William S. Boyd, Exec. Chmn.

Phone: 702-792-7200 **Fax:** 702-792-7313
Toll-Free:
Address: 3883 Howard Hughes Pkwy., 9th Fl., Las Vegas, NV 89169 US

GROWTH PLANS/SPECIAL FEATURES:

Boyd Gaming Corp. is a multi-jurisdictional gaming company and one of the country's leading casino operators. It currently owns and operates 16 casinos totaling 972,787 square feet, and housing 24,536 slot machines, 685 table games and 10,318 hotel rooms. The firm divides its properties into four segments: Las Vegas Locals; Downtown Las Vegas; Midwest and South; and Atlantic City. The Las Vegas Locals properties include The Orleans Hotel and Casino; Sam's Town Hotel & Gambling Hall; Gold Coast Hotel and Casino; Eldorado Casino; Jokers Wild Casino; and Suncoast Hotel and Casino. Downtown Las Vegas facilities consist of the Fremont Hotel & Casino; California Hotel and Casino; and Main Street Casino, Brewery and Hotel. The Midwest and South properties include Sam's Town Hotel and Gambling Hall, in Tunica, Mississippi; the Delta Downs Racetrack and Casino, the Sam's Town Hotel and Casino Shreveport (formerly Shreveport Hotel and Casino) and the Treasure Chest Casino, in Louisiana; the Par-a-Dice Hotel and Casino in East Peoria, Illinois; and the Blue Chip Hotel and Casino in Michigan City, Indiana. The Atlantic City property, Borgata Hotel, Casino and Spa, is jointly owned with Marina District Development Holding Co., LLC. In addition to these properties, the firm owns and operates a jai-alai facility in Dania Beach, Florida; a travel agency; an insurance agency specializing in travel-related insurance; and 85 contiguous acres of land on the Las Vegas Strip. The company maintains a loyalty program which allows customers to use Club Coast or B Connected cards to earn and redeem points at any Boyd gaming property in Nevada, Illinois, Indiana, Louisiana and Mississippi. Boyd has suspended development at its multi-billion dollar Echelon property on the Las Vegas Strip.

Employees are offered medical, dental and vision coverage; a 401(k) plan; short-term disability coverage; and life insurance.

FINANCIALS: **Sales and profits are in thousands of dollars—add 000 to get the full amount. 2010 Note: Financial information for 2010 was not available for all companies at press time.**

2010 Sales: $2,494,724	2010 Profits: $183,938
2009 Sales: $1,824,166	2009 Profits: $156,193
2008 Sales: $1,987,555	2008 Profits: $-153,429
2007 Sales: $1,997,119	2007 Profits: $303,035
2006 Sales: $2,192,634	2006 Profits: $116,778

U.S. Stock Ticker: BYD
Int'l Ticker:
Int'l Exchange:
Employees: 21,300 Fiscal Year Ends: 12/31
Parent Company:

SALARIES/BENEFITS:

Pension Plan:	ESOP Stock Plan:	Profit Sharing:	Top Exec. Salary: $1,100,000	Bonus: $770,000
Savings Plan: Y	Stock Purch. Plan:		Second Exec. Salary: $1,100,000	Bonus: $577,500

OTHER THOUGHTS:

Apparent Women Officers or Directors: 2
Hot Spot for Advancement for Women/Minorities:

LOCATIONS: ("Y" = Yes)

West:	Southwest:	Midwest:	Southeast:	Northeast:	International:
Y		Y	Y	Y	

BRINKS COMPANY (THE)

www.brinkscompany.com

Industry Group Code: 5616

Management:		Sales/Marketing:		Liberal Arts:		Information Sys.:		Professionals:		Tech./Scientific:	
Mgmt. Trainees:	Y	Marketing Pros.:	Y	Gen. Writing/Editing:	Y	Info. Mgmt.:	Y	Finance/Acct.:	Y	Engineers, Elec.:	
Experienced Mgmt.:	Y	Retail Sales:		Tech. Writing:		Software Dev.:	Y	Law:	Y	Engineers, Other:	
Int'l Business:	Y	Comm./Industrial:	Y	Graphic Arts/Photog.:	Y	Hardware Dev.:		HR/Other:	Y	Health/Lab:	
MBA Grads:	Y	Sales Trainees:	Y	Music:		Consulting/Other:		Training:	Y	Science/Research:	
		Advertising Pros.:	Y	Broadcasting:				Health Care:		Petroleum/Chem.:	
				Other:				Consulting:		Math/Other:	

TYPES OF BUSINESS:

Security Services
Armored Car Transport
Document Shredding Services
ATM Servicing
Safe Services
Currency & Deposit Processing

BRANDS/DIVISIONS/AFFILIATES:

Brink's, Inc.
CompuSafe
SCS Technology
Secure Data Solutions
Servicio Pan Americano de Proteccion, S.A. de C.V.
Threshold Financial Technologies, Inc.

CONTACTS: *Note: Officers with more than one job title may be intentionally listed here more than once.*

Michael T. Dan, CEO
Michael T. Dan, Pres.
Joseph W. Dziedzic, CFO/VP
Frank T. Lennon, Chief Admin. Officer/VP
McAlister C. Marshall, General Counsel/VP
Jonathan Leon, Treas.
Arthur E. Wheatley, VP-Risk Mgmt. & Insurance
Matthew A.P. Schumacher, Controller
Lisa M. Landry, VP-Tax
Michael J. McCullough, Sec.
Michael T. Dan, Chmn.
Michael J. Cazer, Pres., Brink's EMEA

Phone: 804-289-9600 **Fax:** 804-289-9770
Toll-Free:
Address: 1801 Bayberry Ct., Richmond, VA 23226 US

GROWTH PLANS/SPECIAL FEATURES:

The Brink's Company, operating through subsidiary Brink's, Inc., provides armored truck and security services. Brink's, Inc. provides armored-car transportation; automated teller machine (ATM) services; currency and deposit processing; coin sorting; check and cash processing services; guarding services, including airport security; and secure air transportation of valuable property, including its patented CompuSafe service. CompuSafe is utilized by a number of the firm's cash-intensive retail customers, including convenience stores, gas stations and restaurants. The service includes installing a specialized safe in the retail establishment that holds safeguarded cassettes. The customer's employees deposit currency into the cassettes, which can only be removed by Brink's Inc.'s armored car personnel. Brinks, Inc. also provides secure document destruction services through its SCS Technology, an advanced size-based shredding system, as well as Secure Data Solutions, which provides customers with domestic and international solutions for transferring, storing and destroying sensitive information. Its North American operations include 181 branches in the U.S. and 52 branches in Canada. The firm's international operations are divided into three regions: Brink's EMEA, with 258 branches in 22 countries; Brink's Latin America, with 217 branches in nine countries; and Brink's Asia-Pacific, with 97 branches in nine countries. In April 2010, the company acquired a majority stake in a Russian cash processing business. In November 2010, it acquired Servicio Pan Americano de Proteccion, S.A. de C.V., a leading secure logistics firm in Mexico. In December of the same year, it acquired Threshold Financial Technologies, Inc., a leading provider of payments solutions, from Versent Corporation.

FINANCIALS: **Sales and profits are in thousands of dollars—add 000 to get the full amount. 2010 Note: Financial information for 2010 was not available for all companies at press time.**

2010 Sales: $3,121,500 | 2010 Profits: $72,800
2009 Sales: $3,135,000 | 2009 Profits: $200,200
2008 Sales: $3,163,500 | 2008 Profits: $183,300
2007 Sales: $2,734,600 | 2007 Profits: $137,300
2006 Sales: $2,354,300 | 2006 Profits: $587,200

U.S. Stock Ticker: BCO
Int'l Ticker:
Int'l Exchange:
Employees: 70,000 Fiscal Year Ends: 12/31
Parent Company:

SALARIES/BENEFITS:

Pension Plan: Y | ESOP Stock Plan: | Profit Sharing: | Top Exec. Salary: $1,107,250 | Bonus: $1,883,400
Savings Plan: Y | Stock Purch. Plan: | | Second Exec. Salary: $450,000 | Bonus: $260,000

OTHER THOUGHTS:

Apparent Women Officers or Directors: 2
Hot Spot for Advancement for Women/Minorities:

LOCATIONS: ("Y" = Yes)

West:	Southwest:	Midwest:	Southeast:	Northeast:	International:
Y	Y	Y	Y	Y	Y

BROADCOM CORP

www.broadcom.com

Industry Group Code: 33441

Management:		**Sales/Marketing:**		**Liberal Arts:**		**Information Sys.:**		**Professionals:**		**Tech./Scientific:**	
Mgmt. Trainees:	Y	Marketing Pros.:	Y	Gen. Writing/Editing:		Info. Mgmt.:	Y	Finance/Acct.:	Y	Engineers, Elec.:	Y
Experienced Mgmt.:	Y	Retail Sales:		Tech. Writing:	Y	Software Dev.:	Y	Law:	Y	Engineers, Other:	
Int'l Business:	Y	Comm./Industrial:	Y	Graphic Arts/Photog.:	Y	Hardware Dev.:	Y	HR/Other:	Y	Health/Lab:	
MBA Grads:	Y	Sales Trainees:		Music:		Consulting/Other:		Training:	Y	Science/Research:	
		Advertising Pros.:	Y	Broadcasting:				Health Care:		Petroleum/Chem.:	
				Other:				Consulting:		Math/Other:	

TYPES OF BUSINESS:

Integrated Circuits-Broadband Transmission
Communications Products
System-on-a-Chip Technology

BRANDS/DIVISIONS/AFFILIATES:

Percello, Ltd.
Teknovus
Beceem Communications, Inc.
Gigle Networks, Inc.

CONTACTS: *Note: Officers with more than one job title may be intentionally listed here more than once.*

Scott A. McGregor, CEO
Scott A. McGregor, Pres.
Eric K. Brandt, CFO/Exec. VP
Thomas F. Lagatta, Exec. VP-Worldwide Sales
Terri Timberman, Exec. VP-Human Resources
Kenneth E. Venner, CIO/Exec. VP-Corp. Svcs.
Henry Samueli, CTO
Neil Y. Kim, Exec. VP-Central Eng.
Arthur Chong, General Counsel/Sec./Sr. VP
Neil Y. Kim, Exec. VP-Oper.
Bob Marsocci, Corp. Comm.
Peter Andrew, Investor Rel.
Robert L. Tirva, Corp. Controller/Principal Acct. Officer/Sr. VP
Ravij Ramaswami, Exec. VP/Gen. Mgr.-Infrastructure & Networking
Daniel A. Marotta, Exec. VP/Gen. Mgr.-Broadband Comm. Group
Robert A. Rango, Exec. VP/Gen. Mgr.-Mobile & Wireless Group
John E. Major, Chmn.

Phone: 949-926-5000 **Fax:** 949-926-5203
Toll-Free:
Address: 5300 California Ave., Irvine, CA 92617-3038 US

GROWTH PLANS/SPECIAL FEATURES:

Broadcom Corp. is a developer of semiconductors for wired and wireless communications. The company's products enable the delivery of voice, video, data and multimedia to mobile devices, consumer electronics devices and business networking products. Broadcom produces system-on-a-chip (SoC) and software solutions for manufacturers of computing and networking equipment, consumer electronics, broadband access products and mobile devices. The firm's products target the broadband communications, enterprise networking and mobile and wireless markets. In the broadband communications market, products incorporating Broadcom's solutions include digital cable, satellite and Internet Protocol (IP) set-top boxes and media servers; cable and digital subscriber line (DSL) modems and residential gateways; high definition televisions (HDTVs); high definition Blu-ray Disc players; and digital video recorders (DVRs). In the enterprise networking markets, products incorporating the firm's solutions include servers; workstations; desktop and notebook computers; wireless infrastructures and wireless access points; switches, hubs and routers; network interface cards; optical networks; and virtual private networks and security appliances. In the mobile and wireless market, products incorporating Broadcom's solutions include wireless-enabled laptop and desktop computers; home broadband gateways; printers; Voice over Internet Protocol (VoIP) phones; handheld media devices; mobile Internet devices; personal navigation devices; TV-enabled mobile devices; and home gaming and entertainment systems. Mobile and wireless products account for approximately 43% of the firm's total revenues; broadband communications products, 31%; enterprise networking products, 23%; and all other, 3%. In March 2010, Broadcom acquired Teknovus, a developer and marketer of Ethernet Passive Optical Network (EPON) solutions. In November 2010, Broadcom Corp. acquired SoC developers Percello, Ltd. and Beceem Communications, Inc. In December 2010, the company acquired SoC developer Gigle Networks, Inc.

Broadcom offers its employees health, dental and vision care; short- and long-term disability coverage; a 401(k) plan; an employee stock purchase plan; credit union membership; and tuition reimbursement.

FINANCIALS: **Sales and profits are in thousands of dollars—add 000 to get the full amount. 2010 Note: Financial information for 2010 was not available for all companies at press time.**

2010 Sales: $6,818,319	2010 Profits: $1,081,800	**U.S. Stock Ticker: BRCM**
2009 Sales: $4,490,323	2009 Profits: $65,261	**Int'l Ticker:**
2008 Sales: $4,658,125	2008 Profits: $214,794	Int'l Exchange:
2007 Sales: $3,776,395	2007 Profits: $213,342	Employees: 8,950 Fiscal Year Ends: 12/31
2006 Sales: $3,667,818	2006 Profits: $379,041	Parent Company:

SALARIES/BENEFITS:

Pension Plan:	ESOP Stock Plan:	Profit Sharing:	Top Exec. Salary: $682,500	Bonus: $1,242,150
Savings Plan: Y	Stock Purch. Plan: Y		Second Exec. Salary: $360,000	Bonus: $500,000

OTHER THOUGHTS:

Apparent Women Officers or Directors:
Hot Spot for Advancement for Women/Minorities:

LOCATIONS: ("Y" = Yes)

West:	Southwest:	Midwest:	Southeast:	Northeast:	International:
Y	Y	Y	Y	Y	Y

BROCADE COMMUNICATIONS SYSTEMS INC www.brocade.com

Industry Group Code: 511210B

Management:		Sales/Marketing:		Liberal Arts:		Information Sys.:		Professionals:		Tech./Scientific:	
Mgmt. Trainees:		Marketing Pros.:	Y	Gen. Writing/Editing:		Info. Mgmt.:	Y	Finance/Acct.:	Y	Engineers, Elec.:	Y
Experienced Mgmt.:	Y	Retail Sales:		Tech. Writing:	Y	Software Dev.:	Y	Law:	Y	Engineers, Other:	Y
Int'l Business:	Y	Comm./Industrial:	Y	Graphic Arts/Photog.:		Hardware Dev.:	Y	HR/Other:	Y	Health/Lab:	
MBA Grads:	Y	Sales Trainees:		Music:		Consulting/Other:	Y	Training:	Y	Science/Research:	
		Advertising Pros.:		Broadcasting:				Health Care:		Petroleum/Chem.:	
				Other:				Consulting:		Math/Other:	

TYPES OF BUSINESS:

Data Storage Equipment
Storage Area Networking (SAN) Equipment
SAN Management Software
IT Infrastructure Management Software

BRANDS/DIVISIONS/AFFILIATES:

Brocade DCX-4S Backbone
Brocade NetIron CER 2000
Brocade One

CONTACTS: *Note: Officers with more than one job title may be intentionally listed here more than once.*

Michael Klayko, CEO
Richard Deranleau, CFO
John McHugh, Chief Mktg. Officer/VP
Lisa McGill, VP-Human Resources
Raymond Lee, VP-IT
Dave Stevens, CTO
Parviz Ghalambor, VP-Eng.
Tyler Wall, General Counsel/Corp. Sec./VP
Raymond Lee, VP-Oper.
T. J. Grewal, VP-Corp. Dev.
Richard Deranleau, VP-Finance
Ian Whiting, Sr. VP-Worldwide Sales
Daniel Fairfax, VP-Global Svcs.
Jason Nolet, VP-Data Center & Enterprise Networking
Barbara Spicek, VP-Worldwide Channels
Dave House, Chmn.
Alberto Soto, Head-Sales, EMEA

Phone: 408-333-8000 **Fax:** 408-333-8101
Toll-Free:
Address: 1745 Technology Dr., San Jose, CA 95110 US

GROWTH PLANS/SPECIAL FEATURES:

Brocade Communication Systems, Inc. is a leading supplier of data center networking hardware and software products and services that help enterprises connect and manage their information. The company is organized into three operating units: Data Center, Global Services and Ethernet Products. The Data Center unit encompasses the Brocade family of Storage Area Network (SAN) infrastructure products and solutions, including directors, switches, routers, fabric-based software applications and distance/extension products. This segment also offers management applications and utilities to centralize data management. The firm's Global Services division offers services related to extended warranty, installation, consulting, break/fix maintenance, network management, telecommunications and related software maintenance and support revenue. The Ethernet Products segment offers Brocade's Open Systems Interconnection Reference Model (OSI) Layer 2-3 switches and routers, which enable efficient use of bandwidth-intensive network business applications and digital entertainment on wide area and local area networks; OSI Layer 4-7 switches, which allow enterprises and service providers to build highly available network infrastructures that efficiently direct the flow of traffic; and file area network products and associated management solutions. Brocade products and services are marketed, sold and supported worldwide through distribution partners, including original equipment manufacturers (OEMs), distributors, systems integrators, value-added resellers (VARs) and by Brocade directly. In February 2010, the company entered a strategic partnership with McAfee, Inc. to offer a broad set of network security products. In June 2010, it unveiled its new Brocade One, a unified network architecture that removes network layers and simplifies network management.

Brocade offers its employees an education reimbursement program, flexible spending accounts, an employee assistance program, a fitness center, paternity leave and medical, dental, vision, life and business travel accident insurance.

FINANCIALS: **Sales and profits are in thousands of dollars—add 000 to get the full amount. 2010 Note: Financial information for 2010 was not available for all companies at press time.**

2010 Sales: $2,094,363 — 2010 Profits: $118,852
2009 Sales: $1,952,926 — 2009 Profits: $-81,384
2008 Sales: $1,466,937 — 2008 Profits: $167,392
2007 Sales: $1,236,863 — 2007 Profits: $76,872
2006 Sales: $750,592 — 2006 Profits: $67,629

U.S. Stock Ticker: BRCD
Int'l Ticker:
Int'l Exchange:
Employees: 4,651 Fiscal Year Ends: 10/31
Parent Company:

SALARIES/BENEFITS:

Pension Plan:	ESOP Stock Plan:	Profit Sharing:	Top Exec. Salary: $726,924	Bonus: $2,421,953
Savings Plan: Y	Stock Purch. Plan:		Second Exec. Salary: $387,693	Bonus: $645,854

OTHER THOUGHTS:

Apparent Women Officers or Directors: 2
Hot Spot for Advancement for Women/Minorities:

LOCATIONS: ("Y" = Yes)

West:	Southwest:	Midwest:	Southeast:	Northeast:	International:
Y	Y	Y	Y	Y	Y

Sales, profits and employees may be estimates. Financial information, benefits and other data can change quickly and may vary from those stated here.

BROOKDALE SENIOR LIVING INC

www.brookdaleliving.com

Industry Group Code: 623110

Management:		Sales/Marketing:		Liberal Arts:		Information Sys.:		Professionals:		Tech./Scientific:	
Mgmt. Trainees:		Marketing Pros.:	Y	Gen. Writing/Editing:	Y	Info. Mgmt.:	Y	Finance/Acct.:	Y	Engineers, Elec.:	
Experienced Mgmt.:	Y	Retail Sales:		Tech. Writing:		Software Dev.:		Law:	Y	Engineers, Other:	
Int'l Business:		Comm./Industrial:		Graphic Arts/Photog.:		Hardware Dev.:		HR/Other:	Y	Health/Lab:	Y
MBA Grads:	Y	Sales Trainees:		Music:		Consulting/Other:		Training:		Science/Research:	
		Advertising Pros.:		Broadcasting:				Health Care:	Y	Petroleum/Chem.:	
				Other:				Consulting:		Math/Other:	

TYPES OF BUSINESS:

Long-Term Health Care & Assisted Living
Retirement Communities
Assisted Living Communities
Continued Care Retirement Communities (CCRCs)
Managed Facilities

BRANDS/DIVISIONS/AFFILIATES:

Innovative Senior Care
Optimum Life
Clare Bridge

CONTACTS:

Note: Officers with more than one job title may be intentionally listed here more than once.

Bill E. Sheriff, CEO
John P. Rijos, COO
John P. Rijos, Co-Pres.
Mark W. Ohlendorf, CFO/Co-Pres.
Bryan D. Richardson, Chief Admin. Officer/Exec. VP
T. Andrew Smith, General Counsel/Sec./Exec. VP
Gregory B. Richard, Exec. VP-Field Oper.
H. Todd Kaestner, Exec. VP-Dev.
Holly Botsford, Mgr.-Public Rel.
George T. Hicks, Exec. VP-Finance
Kristin A. Ferge, Exec. VP/Treas.
Wesley R. Edens, Chmn.

Phone: 615-221-2250 **Fax:** 615-221-2289
Toll-Free: 866-785-9025
Address: 111 Westwood Place, Ste. 200, Brentwood, TN 37027 US

GROWTH PLANS/SPECIAL FEATURES:

Brookdale Senior Living, Inc. (BSL) is one of the largest senior living facility operators in the U.S. It operates 559 owned, leased or managed senior living facilities in 34 states that can serve approximately 51,300 residents. BSL operates four segments, representing different types of facilities. It has 78 retirement centers with 14,620 beds, 427 assisted living communities with 20,988 beds, 35 continuing care retirement communities (CCRCs) with 11,919 beds and it provides management services for 19 third-party facilities with 3,786 beds. At the end of 2010, these facilities were 87.1% occupied. The facilities strive to offer residents a home-like setting and typically feature assistance with daily living, multiple forms of therapy and various home health services. For example, many locations offer the Innovative Senior Care program, which focuses on rehabilitation, fitness and educational offerings in addition to home health services. Additionally, its Optimum Life program is a nationwide wellness initiative that offers a holistic approach to health, life and aging. BSL offers a full spectrum of care options, including independent living, personalized assisted living, rehabilitation and skilled nursing. Additionally, through its Clare Bridge facilities, the firm specializes in the care of Alzheimer's and dementia patients. The company maintains its own culinary arts institute, which offers a training ground for chefs and dining staff. Leased communities generated the largest share (56.1%) of 2010 revenues, followed by owned communities (43.6%) and managed communities (0.3%). BSL generated 81% of its 2010 revenue from private pay customers, with the remainder generated by Medicare, Medicaid and other various third-party payor programs.

Employees are offered medical, dental and vision insurance; flexible spending accounts; disability coverage; an employee assistance plan; a discount stock purchase plan; access to onsite clinics that offer free healthcare services; adoption benefits; legal insurance; and tuition reimbursement.

FINANCIALS:

Sales and profits are in thousands of dollars—add 000 to get the full amount. 2010 Note: Financial information for 2010 was not available for all companies at press time.

2010 Sales: $2,213,264 — 2010 Profits: $-48,901
2009 Sales: $2,023,068 — 2009 Profits: $-66,255
2008 Sales: $1,928,054 — 2008 Profits: $-373,241
2007 Sales: $1,839,296 — 2007 Profits: $-161,979
2006 Sales: $1,309,913 — 2006 Profits: $-108,087

U.S. Stock Ticker: BKD
Int'l Ticker:
Int'l Exchange:
Employees: 38,600 Fiscal Year Ends: 12/31
Parent Company:

SALARIES/BENEFITS:

Pension Plan: ESOP Stock Plan: Profit Sharing: Top Exec. Salary: $587,692 Bonus: $1,012,500
Savings Plan: Y Stock Purch. Plan: Y Second Exec. Salary: $486,962 Bonus: $697,333

OTHER THOUGHTS:

Apparent Women Officers or Directors: 2
Hot Spot for Advancement for Women/Minorities:

LOCATIONS: ("Y" = Yes)

West:	Southwest:	Midwest:	Southeast:	Northeast:	International:
Y	Y	Y	Y	Y	

BROWN & BROWN INC

www.bbinsurance.com

Industry Group Code: 524210

Management:		Sales/Marketing:		Liberal Arts:		Information Sys.:		Professionals:		Tech./Scientific:	
Mgmt. Trainees:	Y	Marketing Pros.:	Y	Gen. Writing/Editing:	Y	Info. Mgmt.:	Y	Finance/Acct.:	Y	Engineers, Elec.:	
Experienced Mgmt.:	Y	Retail Sales:		Tech. Writing:	Y	Software Dev.:	Y	Law:	Y	Engineers, Other:	
Int'l Business:	Y	Comm./Industrial:	Y	Graphic Arts/Photog.:	Y	Hardware Dev.:		HR/Other:	Y	Health/Lab:	
MBA Grads:	Y	Sales Trainees:		Music:		Consulting/Other:		Training:	Y	Science/Research:	
		Advertising Pros.:	Y	Broadcasting:				Health Care:		Petroleum/Chem.:	
				Other:	Y			Consulting:		Math/Other:	

TYPES OF BUSINESS:

Insurance-Property & Casualty
Risk Management Services
Professional Liability Insurance
Third-Party Administration & Consulting
Managed Care & Utilization Management Services
Reinsurance
Life Insurance
Health Insurance

BRANDS/DIVISIONS/AFFILIATES:

Balcos Insurance, Inc.
Comcover Insurance Group, Inc.
Nies Insurance Agency, Inc.
Robert Ellis & Associates, Inc.
Compass Consulting Group, LLC
Fitzharris Agency, Inc.
Global Intermediaries of Eugene, L.L.C.
Thompson, Spears & Associates, Ltd.

CONTACTS: *Note: Officers with more than one job title may be intentionally listed here more than once.*

J. Powell Brown, CEO
J. Powell Brown, Pres.
Cory T. Walker, CFO/Sr. VP
Robert W. Lloyd, General Counsel/VP
Richard Freebourn, Sr., VP-Internal Oper.
Cory T. Walker, Treas.
Kenneth Masters, Regional Exec. VP
J. Scott Penny, Chief Acquisitions Officer/Regional Pres.
Linda S. Downs, Regional Pres.
C. Roy Bridges, Regional Pres.
J. Hyatt Brown, Chmn.

Phone: 386-252-9601 **Fax:** 386-239-5729
Toll-Free:
Address: 220 S. Ridgewood Ave., Daytona Beach, FL 32114 US

GROWTH PLANS/SPECIAL FEATURES:

Brown & Brown, Inc. is a diversified insurance agency and a wholesale brokerage, insurance programs and service organization. The firm markets and sells insurance products and services, primarily in the property, casualty and employee benefit areas. The company is compensated for its services through commissions paid by insurance companies and customer service fess. As an agent and broker, Brown & Brown does not assume underwriting risks. The company operates through 205 locations in 37 states and one location in London. It operates through four segments: retail, wholesale brokerage, national programs and services. The retail segment provides a range of insurance products and services to commercial, public entity, professional and individual customers. The wholesale brokerage division markets and sells excess and surplus commercial and personal insurance and reinsurance, primarily through independent agents and brokers. The national programs division consists of two units: professional programs, which provides professional liability and related package products for certain medical, financial, real estate and law professionals; and special programs, which markets targeted products and services designated for specific industries, trade groups, public entities and market niches. The services division provides clients with third-party claims administration, consulting for the workers' compensation insurance markets, comprehensive medical utilization management services and Medicare Secondary Payer statute compliance-related services. The retail division generates the majority (59.3%) of the company's revenue, followed by the national programs division (19.6%), the wholesale brokerage division (16.2%), the services division (4.8%) and other operations (0.1%). The firm acquired assets from a number of insurance companies in 2011, including Balcos Insurance, Inc.; Comcover Insurance Group, Inc.; Nies Insurance Agency, Inc.; Robert Ellis & Associates, Inc.; Compass Consulting Group, LLC; Fitzharris Agency, Inc.; Fitzharris & Company, Inc.; Fitzharris Administrators, Inc.; Global Intermediaries of Eugene, L.L.C.; Thompson, Spears & Associates, Ltd.; and Public Employee Benefits Solutions, L.L.C.

FINANCIALS: **Sales and profits are in thousands of dollars—add 000 to get the full amount. 2010 Note: Financial information for 2010 was not available for all companies at press time.**

2010 Sales: $973,492 2010 Profits: $161,752
2009 Sales: $967,877 2009 Profits: $153,294
2008 Sales: $977,554 2008 Profits: $166,124
2007 Sales: $959,667 2007 Profits: $190,959
2006 Sales: $878,004 2006 Profits: $172,350

U.S. Stock Ticker: BRO
Int'l Ticker:
Int'l Exchange:
Employees: 5,286 Fiscal Year Ends: 12/31
Parent Company:

SALARIES/BENEFITS:

Pension Plan: ESOP Stock Plan: Profit Sharing: Top Exec. Salary: $565,000 Bonus: $1,179,744
Savings Plan: Y Stock Purch. Plan: Y Second Exec. Salary: $394,215 Bonus: $771,202

OTHER THOUGHTS:

Apparent Women Officers or Directors: 4
Hot Spot for Advancement for Women/Minorities: Y

LOCATIONS: ("Y" = Yes)

West:	Southwest:	Midwest:	Southeast:	Northeast:	International:
Y	Y	Y	Y	Y	Y

BRUKER CORP

www.bruker.com

Industry Group Code: 3345

Management:		**Sales/Marketing:**		**Liberal Arts:**		**Information Sys.:**		**Professionals:**		**Tech./Scientific:**	
Mgmt. Trainees:		Marketing Pros.:	Y	Gen. Writing/Editing:		Info. Mgmt.:	Y	Finance/Acct.:	Y	Engineers, Elec.:	Y
Experienced Mgmt.:		Retail Sales:		Tech. Writing:	Y	Software Dev.:	Y	Law:	Y	Engineers, Other:	
Int'l Business:	Y	Comm./Industrial:	Y	Graphic Arts/Photog.:		Hardware Dev.:	Y	HR/Other:	Y	Health/Lab:	
MBA Grads:	Y	Sales Trainees:		Music:		Consulting/Other:		Training:		Science/Research:	Y
		Advertising Pros.:	Y	Broadcasting:				Health Care:		Petroleum/Chem.:	
				Other:				Consulting:		Math/Other:	Y

TYPES OF BUSINESS:

Scientific Equipment Manufacturing

BRANDS/DIVISIONS/AFFILIATES:

Bruker Energy & Supercon Technologies
Bruker MAT
Bruker BioSpin
Bruker Daltonics
Bruker Optics
Sigma ElectroOptics GmbH
Michrom Bioresources, Inc.
Veeco Metrology, Inc.

CONTACTS: *Note: Officers with more than one job title may be intentionally listed here more than once.*

Frank H. Laukien, CEO
William J. Knight, COO
Frank H. Laukien, Pres.
Brian Monahan, CFO
Richard M. Stein, Corp. Sec.
Collin D'Silva, Pres., Chemical & Applied Markets Div.
Urban Faeh, Pres., Bruker Optics
Frank H. Laukien, Chmn.

Phone: 978-663-3660	**Fax:** 978-667-5993
Toll-Free:	
Address: 40 Manning Rd., Billerica, MA 01821 US	

GROWTH PLANS/SPECIAL FEATURES:

Bruker Corp. is a developer, manufacturer and marketer of proprietary life science and materials research systems/products. The firm serves clients involved in life science, pharmaceutical, biotechnology and molecular diagnostics research. The company also offers materials and chemical analysis for use in various industries and government applications. Bruker's technology platforms include X-ray, magnetic resonance and mass spectrometry technologies; and optical emission, infrared and Raman molecular spectroscopy technologies. In addition, the firm manufactures and distributes superconducting wire products/devices and an array of field analytical systems for chemical, biological, radiological and nuclear detection. The firm has over 70 sales offices on six continents and maintains manufacturing centers in Europe, North America and Japan. The company operates in two divisions: Bruker Scientific Instruments and Bruker Energy & Supercon Technologies (BEST). The Bruker Scientific Instruments division has four subsidiaries: Bruker MAT, which develops and manufactures optical emission spectrometers, atomic force microscopy, analytical X-ray systems and combustion analyzers for elemental analysis; Bruker BioSpin and Bruker Daltronics, both manufacturers of mass spectrometry (MS) instruments and accessories; and Bruker Optics, which offers Fourier transform Infrared/ Near Infrared, terahertz, Raman and time domain low resolution nuclear magnetic resonance spectrometers. The firm's BEST subsidiary develops and manufactures an array of high-performance superconductor wire products and devices for use in rotating machines, transformers, fault current limiters, cables and magnets. In late 2010, the company acquired Veeco Metrology, Inc. and Sigma ElectroOptics GmbH. In April 2011, Bruker acquired Michrom Bioresources, Inc.

FINANCIALS: **Sales and profits are in thousands of dollars—add 000 to get the full amount. 2010 Note: Financial information for 2010 was not available for all companies at press time.**

2010 Sales: $1,304,900	2010 Profits: $95,400	**U.S. Stock Ticker: BRKR**
2009 Sales: $1,114,500	2009 Profits: $81,200	**Int'l Ticker:**
2008 Sales: $1,107,100	2008 Profits: $64,900	Int'l Exchange:
2007 Sales: $1,032,400	2007 Profits: $98,900	Employees: 5,400 Fiscal Year Ends: 12/31
2006 Sales: $	2006 Profits: $	Parent Company:

SALARIES/BENEFITS:

Pension Plan:	ESOP Stock Plan:	Profit Sharing:	Top Exec. Salary: $423,366	Bonus: $752,728
Savings Plan:	Stock Purch. Plan:		Second Exec. Salary: $355,000	Bonus: $215,403

OTHER THOUGHTS:

Apparent Women Officers or Directors: 1
Hot Spot for Advancement for Women/Minorities:

LOCATIONS: ("Y" = Yes)

West:	Southwest:	Midwest:	Southeast:	Northeast:	International:
Y		Y		Y	Y

BUCKLE INC (THE)

www.buckle.com

Industry Group Code: 448

Management:		Sales/Marketing:		Liberal Arts:		Information Sys.:		Professionals:		Tech./Scientific:	
Mgmt. Trainees:	Y	Marketing Pros.:	Y	Gen. Writing/Editing:	Y	Info. Mgmt.:	Y	Finance/Acct.:	Y	Engineers, Elec.:	
Experienced Mgmt.:	Y	Retail Sales:	Y	Tech. Writing:		Software Dev.:	Y	Law:	Y	Engineers, Other:	
Int'l Business:		Comm./Industrial:		Graphic Arts/Photog.:	Y	Hardware Dev.:		HR/Other:	Y	Health/Lab:	
MBA Grads:	Y	Sales Trainees:	Y	Music:		Consulting/Other:		Training:	Y	Science/Research:	
		Advertising Pros.:	Y	Broadcasting:				Health Care:		Petroleum/Chem.:	
				Other:	Y			Consulting:		Math/Other:	

TYPES OF BUSINESS:

Teen Apparel, Retail
Promotional Merchandise
Online Sales

BRANDS/DIVISIONS/AFFILIATES:

Buckle
Buckle [The]
Buckle Screenprinting
Buckle.com
BKE
Lucky Brand Dungarees
Big Star
Silver

CONTACTS: *Note: Officers with more than one job title may be intentionally listed here more than once.*

Dennis Nelson, CEO
Dennis Nelson, Pres.
Karen Rhoads, CFO/VP-Finance
Kari G. Smith, VP-Sales
Patricia K. Whisler, VP-Women's Merch.
Kyle L. Hanson, General Counsel/Corp. Sec.
Thomas B. Heacock, Treas./Controller
Brett P. Milkie, VP-Leasing
Robert M. Carlberg, VP-Men's Merch.
Daniel J. Hirschfeld, Chmn.

Phone: 308-236-8491 **Fax:** 308-236-4493
Toll-Free: 800-626-1255
Address: 2407 W. 24th St., Kearney, NE 68845-4915 US

GROWTH PLANS/SPECIAL FEATURES:

The Buckle, Inc. is a retailer of medium- to high-priced casual apparel, footwear and accessories primarily for young men and women ages 15-30. The company operates roughly 420 stores in 41 states throughout the central, northwest, southwest and southeast U.S. These stores operate under the names Buckle and The Buckle. The majority of the stores are located in regional shopping malls, although some are located in strip centers, downtown areas and lifestyle centers. Buckle markets mostly brand-name casual apparel including denim, tops, sportswear, outerwear, accessories and footwear. Brand names such as Lucky Brand Dungarees, Big Star, Silver, Hurley, Affliction, Fossil, MEK, Billabong, Guess, Quiksilver/Roxy, 7 Diamonds, OBEY and Manchester constitute roughly 67% of total sales. The remaining merchandise consists of items manufactured to the company's specifications by private labels and merchandise marketed under its exclusive BKE label. The firm emphasizes personalized attention to its customers by providing free alterations, free gift-wrapping and a frequent shopper program. Buckle Screenprinting offers promotional merchandising to outside athletic teams, organizations, clubs and individuals. The company tailors individual store inventories to reflect differences in customer buying patterns by shipping new merchandise daily to most stores through its transfer program. This assures that popular merchandise is in stock and reduces the need to lower the price of low-selling merchandise at a particular location.

Employees are offered medical and dental insurance; disability coverage; life insurance; performance bonuses; an employee assistance program; a 40% merchandise discount; a 401(k) plan; and flexible spending accounts.

FINANCIALS: **Sales and profits are in thousands of dollars—add 000 to get the full amount. 2010 Note: Financial information for 2010 was not available for all companies at press time.**

2010 Sales: $898,287 — 2010 Profits: $127,303
2009 Sales: $792,046 — 2009 Profits: $104,409
2008 Sales: $619,888 — 2008 Profits: $75,247
2007 Sales: $530,074 — 2007 Profits: $55,726
2006 Sales: $501,101 — 2006 Profits: $51,906

U.S. Stock Ticker: BKE
Int'l Ticker:
Int'l Exchange:
Employees: 7,000 Fiscal Year Ends: 1/31
Parent Company:

SALARIES/BENEFITS:

Pension Plan: ESOP Stock Plan: Profit Sharing: Top Exec. Salary: $925,000 Bonus: $2,805,377
Savings Plan: Y Stock Purch. Plan: Second Exec. Salary: $335,000 Bonus: $561,075

OTHER THOUGHTS:

Apparent Women Officers or Directors: 3
Hot Spot for Advancement for Women/Minorities: Y

LOCATIONS: ("Y" = Yes)

West:	Southwest:	Midwest:	Southeast:	Northeast:	International:
Y	Y	Y	Y	Y	

BUFFALO WILD WINGS INC

www.buffalowildwings.com

Industry Group Code: 722110

Management:		Sales/Marketing:		Liberal Arts:		Information Sys.:		Professionals:		Tech./Scientific:	
Mgmt. Trainees:	Y	Marketing Pros.:	Y	Gen. Writing/Editing:	Y	Info. Mgmt.:	Y	Finance/Acct.:	Y	Engineers, Elec.:	
Experienced Mgmt.:	Y	Retail Sales:		Tech. Writing:		Software Dev.:	Y	Law:	Y	Engineers, Other:	
Int'l Business:		Comm./Industrial:		Graphic Arts/Photog.:	Y	Hardware Dev.:		HR/Other:	Y	Health/Lab:	
MBA Grads:	Y	Sales Trainees:		Music:		Consulting/Other:		Training:	Y	Science/Research:	
		Advertising Pros.:	Y	Broadcasting:				Health Care:		Petroleum/Chem.:	
				Other:	Y			Consulting:		Math/Other:	

TYPES OF BUSINESS:

Restaurants

BRANDS/DIVISIONS/AFFILIATES:

Buffalo Wild Wings
Wild Flatbreads
Buffalito
Buzztime

CONTACTS: *Note: Officers with more than one job title may be intentionally listed here more than once.*

Sally J. Smith, CEO
James M. Schmidt, COO/Exec. VP
Sally J. Smith, Pres.
Mary J. Twinem, CFO/Exec. VP
Kathleen M. Benning, Exec. VP-Global Mktg. & Brand Dev.
Judith A. Shoulak, Exec. VP-Human Resources
Lee R. Patterson, Sr. VP-IT
Emily C.Decker, General Counsel/Sec./VP
Judith A. Shoulak, Exec. VP-Global Oper.
Mary J. Twinem, Treas.
James M. Damian, Chmn.
Mounir N.Sawda, Managing Dir.-Int'l

Phone: 952-593-9943 | **Fax:** 952-593-9787
Toll-Free: 800-499-9586
Address: 5500 Wayzata Blvd., Ste. 1600, Minneapolis, MN 55416 US

GROWTH PLANS/SPECIAL FEATURES:

Buffalo Wild Wings, Inc., founded in 1982, is the operator of Buffalo Wild Wings restaurants. The company operates over 650 restaurants in 42 states, of which approximately 230 are company-owned and 420 are franchised. The restaurants serve chicken wings in the Buffalo, New York-style spun in 14 signature sauces. The menu also features chicken tenders, salads, Wild Flatbreads, popcorn shrimp, specialty hamburgers and sandwiches, wraps, Buffalito soft tacos and appetizers, which are made to order and are available for dine-in and take-out. The restaurants are geared toward both sports fans and families and feature a full bar, 10 projection screens where sporting events are shown, as well as 50 additional television sets where customers can play Buzztime trivia and video games. Sales at company-owned restaurants represent the majority of the company's total revenue. Food and nonalcoholic beverages account for roughly 77% of restaurant sales, with 23% from alcoholic beverages. The menu item with the highest sales volume is chicken wings, which accounts for 39% of total restaurant sales. In September 2010, the firm opened a new restaurant in Tempe, Arizona.

Employees are offered medical and dental insurance; vision coverage; short- and long-term disability protection; a bonus plan; an employee stock purchase plan; a 401(k) plan; and an employee assistance program.

FINANCIALS: **Sales and profits are in thousands of dollars—add 000 to get the full amount. 2010 Note: Financial information for 2010 was not available for all companies at press time.**

2010 Sales: $613,256 | 2010 Profits: $38,400
2009 Sales: $538,924 | 2009 Profits: $30,671
2008 Sales: $422,417 | 2008 Profits: $24,435
2007 Sales: $329,652 | 2007 Profits: $19,654
2006 Sales: $278,183 | 2006 Profits: $16,273

U.S. Stock Ticker: BWLD
Int'l Ticker:
Int'l Exchange:
Employees: 15,000 Fiscal Year Ends: 12/31
Parent Company:

SALARIES/BENEFITS:

Pension Plan: | ESOP Stock Plan: | Profit Sharing: | Top Exec. Salary: $560,000 | Bonus: $328,104
Savings Plan: Y | Stock Purch. Plan: Y | | Second Exec. Salary: $360,000 | Bonus: $182,404

OTHER THOUGHTS:

Apparent Women Officers or Directors: 5
Hot Spot for Advancement for Women/Minorities: Y

LOCATIONS: ("Y" = Yes)

West:	Southwest:	Midwest:	Southeast:	Northeast:	International:
Y	Y	Y	Y	Y	

Sales, profits and employees may be estimates. Financial information, benefits and other data can change quickly and may vary from those stated here.

BUNGE LTD

www.bunge.com

Industry Group Code: 3112

Management:		Sales/Marketing:		Liberal Arts:		Information Sys.:		Professionals:		Tech./Scientific:	
Mgmt. Trainees:	Y	Marketing Pros.:	Y	Gen. Writing/Editing:		Info. Mgmt.:	Y	Finance/Acct.:	Y	Engineers, Elec.:	
Experienced Mgmt.:	Y	Retail Sales:		Tech. Writing:		Software Dev.:		Law:	Y	Engineers, Other:	Y
Int'l Business:	Y	Comm./Industrial:	Y	Graphic Arts/Photog.:	Y	Hardware Dev.:		HR/Other:	Y	Health/Lab:	
MBA Grads:	Y	Sales Trainees:		Music:		Consulting/Other:		Training:	Y	Science/Research:	Y
		Advertising Pros.:		Broadcasting:				Health Care:		Petroleum/Chem.:	
				Other:				Consulting:		Math/Other:	

TYPES OF BUSINESS:

Crop Production, Soybeans
Oils & Shortening
Oilseed Processing
Ingredients & Prepared Foods
Fertilizer
Milling

BRANDS/DIVISIONS/AFFILIATES:

Serrana
Manah
Ouro Verde
IAP
Vale SA
Morristown Grain Co

CONTACTS:
Note: Officers with more than one job title may be intentionally listed here more than once.

Alberto Weisser, CEO
Drew Burke, Interim CFO
Vicente C. Teixeira, Chief Personnel Officer
Raul Padilla, CEO-Bunge Prod. Lines
Drew Burke, Global Oper. Excellence Officer
Ben Pearcy, Chief Dev. Officer
Jean-Louis Gourbin, CEO-Bunge Europe
Raul Padilla, CEO-Bunge Global Agribusiness
Pedro Parente, CEO/Pres., Bunge Brazil
Soren Schroder, CEO-Bunge North America
Alberto Weisser, Chmn.
Christopher White, CEO-Bunge Asia

Phone: 914-684-2800	**Fax:** 914-684-3499
Toll-Free:	
Address: 50 Main St., White Plains, NY 10606 US	

GROWTH PLANS/SPECIAL FEATURES:

Bunge, Ltd., founded in 1818, is a Bermuda-based agribusiness and food company with operations in oilseed processing; fertilizer production and supply; and edible oil products supply. Through its facilities in North and South America, the company manufactures fertilizer and animal feed for farmers; transporting oilseeds and grains to markets worldwide; processing oilseeds to produce meal for the livestock industry and oil for the food processing, food service and biofuel industries; produces bottled oils, mayonnaise, margarines and other food products for consumers; and mills wheat and corn for food processors, bakeries, brewers and other commercial customers. The company divides its operations into three segments: agribusiness; fertilizer; and food and ingredients. The agribusiness division is involved in the purchase, storage, transport, processing and sale of agricultural commodities and commodity products. This segment also offers financial, risk management and identity preservation services. The company's main focus is soybeans, but it also processes and sells rapeseed, sunseed, corn, wheat and other crops and derivative products. The fertilizer division is engaged in all stages of the fertilizer business, from raw material mining and mixing fertilizer components to product marketing, with activities located primarily in South America. Bunge markets its fertilizers under the Serrana, Manah, Ouro Verde and IAP brand names. The food and ingredients division consists of two divisions: edible oil products and milling products. These divisions include businesses that produce and sell edible oils, shortenings, margarines, mayonnaise and milled products such as wheat flours and corn-based products. The edible oil products division has operations in the U.S., Canada, Brazil, India, China and numerous European countries. In May 2010, the company completed the sale of its fertilizer nutrients business in Brazil to Vale SA for about $3.5 billion. In November 2010, the firm purchased Morristown Grain Co., an owner of grain elevators in Indiana.

FINANCIALS:
Sales and profits are in thousands of dollars—add 000 to get the full amount. 2010 Note: Financial information for 2010 was not available for all companies at press time.

2010 Sales: $45,707,000	2010 Profits: $2,354,000
2009 Sales: $41,926,000	2009 Profits: $361,000
2008 Sales: $52,574,000	2008 Profits: $1,064,000
2007 Sales: $37,842,000	2007 Profits: $778,000
2006 Sales: $26,274,000	2006 Profits: $521,000

U.S. Stock Ticker: BG
Int'l Ticker:
Int'l Exchange:
Employees: 32,000 Fiscal Year Ends: 12/31
Parent Company:

SALARIES/BENEFITS:

Pension Plan:	ESOP Stock Plan:	Profit Sharing:	Top Exec. Salary: $1,200,000	Bonus: $432,000
Savings Plan:	Stock Purch. Plan:		Second Exec. Salary: $700,000	Bonus: $1,250,000

OTHER THOUGHTS:

Apparent Women Officers or Directors: 1
Hot Spot for Advancement for Women/Minorities:

LOCATIONS: ("Y" = Yes)

West:	Southwest:	Midwest:	Southeast:	Northeast:	International:
		Y		Y	Y

BURLINGTON NORTHERN SANTA FE LLC

www.bnsf.com

Industry Group Code: 48211

Management:		Sales/Marketing:		Liberal Arts:		Information Sys.:		Professionals:		Tech./Scientific:	
Mgmt. Trainees:	Y	Marketing Pros.:	Y	Gen. Writing/Editing:		Info. Mgmt.:	Y	Finance/Acct.:	Y	Engineers, Elec.:	Y
Experienced Mgmt.:	Y	Retail Sales:		Tech. Writing:	Y	Software Dev.:	Y	Law:	Y	Engineers, Other:	Y
Int'l Business:	Y	Comm./Industrial:	Y	Graphic Arts/Photog.:		Hardware Dev.:	Y	HR/Other:	Y	Health/Lab:	
MBA Grads:	Y	Sales Trainees:		Music:		Consulting/Other:		Training:	Y	Science/Research:	
		Advertising Pros.:	Y	Broadcasting:				Health Care:		Petroleum/Chem.:	
				Other:				Consulting:		Math/Other:	

TYPES OF BUSINESS:

Rail Transportation
Railroad Infrastructure Management
Locomotive Operation
Intermodal Hubs
Real Estate Development Services

BRANDS/DIVISIONS/AFFILIATES:

Berkshire Hathaway Inc
Burlington Northern Santa Fe Corp
BSNF Railway Company

CONTACTS: *Note: Officers with more than one job title may be intentionally listed here more than once.*

Matthew K. Rose, CEO
Carl R. Ice, COO
Carl R. Ice, Pres.
Thomas N. Hund, CFO/Exec. VP
John P. Lanigan, Jr., Chief Mktg. Officer/Exec. VP
Riz Chand, Chief Human Resources Officer/VP
Jo-ann M. Olsovsky, CIO
Jo-ann M. Olsovsky, VP-Tech. Svcs.
Charles W. Shewmake, General Counsel/VP
Gregory C. Fox, Exec. VP-Oper.
Julie A. Piggott, VP-Planning & Studies
John O. Ambler, VP-Corp. Rel.
Julie A. Piggott, Controller/VP
Roger Norber, Exec. VP-Law/Sec.
Shelley J. Venick, VP/General Tax Counsel
Amy Hawkins, VP-Gov't Affairs
Dean H. Wise, VP-Network Strategy
Matthew K. Rose, Chmn.

Phone: 817-352-1000 **Fax:** 817-352-7171
Toll-Free: 800-795-2673
Address: 2650 Lou Menk Dr., Fort Worth, TX 76131-2830 US

GROWTH PLANS/SPECIAL FEATURES:

Burlington Northern Santa Fe LLC (BNSF), formerly Burlington Northern Santa Fe Corp., is a subsidiary of Berkshire Hathaway, Inc. engaged in the freight rail transportation business. BNSF operates through its primary subsidiary, BNSF Railway Company. BNSF Railway controls one of North America's largest railroad systems, operating approximately 32,000 route miles of track, of which 23,000 are owned route miles, passing through 28 states and two Canadian provinces. BNSF Railway operates various facilities and equipment, including over 6,600 locomotives. It also operates 31 intermodal hubs, as well as 22 automotive distribution facilities and eight port facilities where automobiles are loaded or unloaded from multi-level rail cars. In addition to major cities and ports, the company serves smaller markets through partnerships with numerous shortline partners. The railway transports consumer, industrial and agricultural freight products. Consumer products include truck trailers and containers, canned goods, sugar, automotive goods and low-sulfur coal. Industrial products include construction, building, petroleum, forest products, metals, minerals, chemicals and plastic products, as well as food and beverages. Agricultural products include wheat, corn, bulk foods, soybeans, oil seeds and meals, feeds, barley, oats and rye, flour and mill products, milo, oils, specialty grains, malt, ethanol and fertilizer. As a supplement to railway revenues, the company also offers economic and real estate development services. In February 2010, the firm was acquired by Berkshire Hathaway Corp. Following the acquisition, the company changed its name from Burlington Northern Santa Fe Corporation to Burlington Northern Santa Fe LLC and delisted its stock.

Employees are offered health, dental, vision and life insurance; a prescription drug plan; short- and long-term disability coverage; tuition reimbursement; flexible spending accounts; personal accident insurance; and retiree life insurance.

FINANCIALS: **Sales and profits are in thousands of dollars—add 000 to get the full amount. 2010 Note: Financial information for 2010 was not available for all companies at press time.**

2010 Sales: $16,850,000 — 2010 Profits: $2,459,000
2009 Sales: $14,016,000 — 2009 Profits: $1,721,000
2008 Sales: $18,018,000 — 2008 Profits: $2,115,000
2007 Sales: $15,802,000 — 2007 Profits: $1,829,000
2006 Sales: $14,985,000 — 2006 Profits: $1,887,000

U.S. Stock Ticker: Subsidiary
Int'l Ticker:
Int'l Exchange:
Employees: 38,000 Fiscal Year Ends: 12/31
Parent Company: BERKSHIRE HATHAWAY INC

SALARIES/BENEFITS:

Pension Plan: Y ESOP Stock Plan: Profit Sharing: Top Exec. Salary: $1,183,583 Bonus: $1,679,480
Savings Plan: Y Stock Purch. Plan: Second Exec. Salary: $584,092 Bonus: $546,920

OTHER THOUGHTS:

Apparent Women Officers or Directors: 5
Hot Spot for Advancement for Women/Minorities: Y

LOCATIONS: ("Y" = Yes)

West:	Southwest:	Midwest:	Southeast:	Northeast:	International:
Y	Y	Y	Y		Y

CABLEVISION SYSTEMS CORP

www.cablevision.com

Industry Group Code: 517110

Management:		Sales/Marketing:		Liberal Arts:		Information Sys.:		Professionals:		Tech./Scientific:	
Mgmt. Trainees:	Y	Marketing Pros.:	Y	Gen. Writing/Editing:	Y	Info. Mgmt.:	Y	Finance/Acct.:	Y	Engineers, Elec.:	Y
Experienced Mgmt.:	Y	Retail Sales:		Tech. Writing:	Y	Software Dev.:	Y	Law:	Y	Engineers, Other:	Y
Int'l Business:		Comm./Industrial:	Y	Graphic Arts/Photog.:	Y	Hardware Dev.:		HR/Other:	Y	Health/Lab:	
MBA Grads:	Y	Sales Trainees:	Y	Music:		Consulting/Other:		Training:	Y	Science/Research:	
		Advertising Pros.:	Y	Broadcasting:	Y			Health Care:		Petroleum/Chem.:	
				Other:	Y			Consulting:		Math/Other:	

TYPES OF BUSINESS:

Cable Television Service
Professional Sports Teams
Television Programming
Communications Services
Sports & Music Venues
Voice Over Internet Protocol
High-Speed Internet

BRANDS/DIVISIONS/AFFILIATES:

Rainbow Media Holdings, LLC
Cablevision Lightpath, Inc
Newsday Media Group
Bresnan Communications
Sundance Channel
AMC
We tv
IFC

CONTACTS: *Note: Officers with more than one job title may be intentionally listed here more than once.*

James L. Dolan, CEO
Thomas M. Rutledge, COO
James L. Dolan, Pres.
Michael Huseby, CFO/Exec. VP
Wilt Hildenbrand, Sr. Advisor-Tech.
Wilt Hildenbrand, Sr. Advisor-Eng.
David Ellen, General Counsel/Exec. VP
Charles R. Schueler, Exec. VP-Corp. Comm. & Community Rel.
Patricia Armstrong, Sr. VP-Investor Rel.
Keith Harper, Chief Acct. Officer/Controller/Sr. VP
Joshua Sapan, Pres./CEO-Rainbow Media Holdings LLC
Gregg G. Seibert, Exec. VP
Kevin Watson, Sr. VP/Treas.
Victoria D. Salhus, Sr. VP/Sec.
Charles F. Dolan, Chmn.

Phone: 516-803-2300	**Fax:** 516-803-3134
Toll-Free:	
Address: 1111 Stewart Ave., Bethpage, NY 11714 US	

GROWTH PLANS/SPECIAL FEATURES:

Cablevision Systems Corp. is engaged in cable programming networks, entertainment businesses, a newspaper publishing business and telecommunications companies. It serves about 3.1 million basic video subscribers in and around the New York City metropolitan area, and operates solely through cable operator subsidiary CSC Holdings, LLC. Through wholly-owned subsidiary Rainbow Media Holdings, LLC, the company owns interests in and manages numerous national and regional programming networks, as well as a cable television advertising sales firm. Through another subsidiary, Cablevision Lightpath, Inc., the firm provides telephone services and high-speed Internet access to the business market. CSC also owns approximately 97.2% of newspaper publishing business operator Newsday LLC. The firm operates in three segments: telecommunications services, Rainbow and Newsday. The telecommunications services segment (80% of revenues) oversees the cable television business, including its video, high-speed data and voice over Internet protocol (VoIP) and the operations of the telephone and high-speed data services provided by Lightpath. The Rainbow segment (15% of revenues) consists principally of interests in national programming services (AMC, Sundance Channel, WE tv, IFC and News 12) and regional news programming businesses held by Rainbow Media Holdings. The division also includes a local advertising sales representation business. The Newsday segment (5% of revenues) includes the Newsday daily newspaper, amNew York, Star Community Publishing Group and online web sites such as Newsday.com and ExploreLI.com. In February 2010, the firm spun off its Madison Square Garden operations, including its sports assets, into a separately-traded company. In December 2010, Cablevision Systems acquired Bresnan Communications for approximately $1.365 billion, adding roughly 297,000 basic cable television subscribers to its customer base.

The firm offers employees benefits including medical, dental, vision, life, AD&D and prescription plans; a 401(k); educational assistance; paid time off; and credit union membership.

FINANCIALS: **Sales and profits are in thousands of dollars—add 000 to get the full amount. 2010 Note: Financial information for 2010 was not available for all companies at press time.**

2010 Sales: $7,231,249	2010 Profits: $360,948	**U.S. Stock Ticker: CVC**
2009 Sales: $6,847,301	2009 Profits: $285,572	**Int'l Ticker:**
2008 Sales: $7,230,116	2008 Profits: $-227,576	Int'l Exchange:
2007 Sales: $6,484,481	2007 Profits: $218,456	Employees: 18,138 Fiscal Year Ends: 12/31
2006 Sales: $5,828,493	2006 Profits: $-126,465	Parent Company:

SALARIES/BENEFITS:

Pension Plan: Y	ESOP Stock Plan:	Profit Sharing:	Top Exec. Salary: $1,872,000	Bonus: $9,174,897
Savings Plan: Y	Stock Purch. Plan:		Second Exec. Salary: $1,664,000	Bonus: $8,075,078

OTHER THOUGHTS:

Apparent Women Officers or Directors: 6
Hot Spot for Advancement for Women/Minorities: Y

LOCATIONS: ("Y" = Yes)

West:	Southwest:	Midwest:	Southeast:	Northeast:	International:
Y				Y	

CACI INTERNATIONAL INC

www.caci.com

Industry Group Code: 541512

Management:		Sales/Marketing:		Liberal Arts:		Information Sys.:		Professionals:		Tech./Scientific:	
Mgmt. Trainees:	Y	Marketing Pros.:	Y	Gen. Writing/Editing:	Y	Info. Mgmt.:	Y	Finance/Acct.:	Y	Engineers, Elec.:	Y
Experienced Mgmt.:	Y	Retail Sales:		Tech. Writing:	Y	Software Dev.:	Y	Law:	Y	Engineers, Other:	
Int'l Business:	Y	Comm./Industrial:	Y	Graphic Arts/Photog.:	Y	Hardware Dev.:	Y	HR/Other:	Y	Health/Lab:	
MBA Grads:	Y	Sales Trainees:		Music:		Consulting/Other:	Y	Training:	Y	Science/Research:	
		Advertising Pros.:		Broadcasting:				Health Care:		Petroleum/Chem.:	
				Other:				Consulting:	Y	Math/Other:	

TYPES OF BUSINESS:

Consulting-InfoTech Related
Engineering Simulation Software
Custom Software Engineering
Managed Network Services
Information Management Tools
Knowledge Management
Systems Integration
Radio Frequency Identification (RFID)

BRANDS/DIVISIONS/AFFILIATES:

CACI Ltd.
Wide Area Workflow
Wexford Group International
Athena Innovative Solutions, Inc.
CACI Vision & Solution Center
Applied Systems Research, Inc
TechniGraphics, Inc.

CONTACTS: *Note: Officers with more than one job title may be intentionally listed here more than once.*

Paul M. Cofoni, CEO
Paul M. Cofoni, Pres.
Thomas A. Mutryn, CFO/Exec. VP
H. Robert Boehm, Chief Human Resources Officer/Exec. VP
Deborah B. Dunie, CTO/Exec. VP
Arnold D. Morse, Sec.
Steven H. Weiss, Exec. VP-Gov't Bus. Oper.
Ronald Schneider, Exec. VP-Bus. Dev.
Jody A. Brown, Exec. VP-Public Rel. & Bus. Comm.
David Dragics, Sr. VP-Investor Rel.
Thomas A. Mutryn, Treas.
William M. Fairl, Pres., U.S. Oper.
Daniel D. Allen, COO-U.S. Oper.
Gregory R. Bradford, CEO-CACI Ltd.
Karl Johnson, Exec. VP-Missions Systems Group
J.P. London, Chmn.
Gregory R. Bradford, Pres., U.K. Oper.

Phone: 703-841-7800 | **Fax:** 703-841-7882
Toll-Free:
Address: 1100 N. Glebe Rd., Arlington, VA 22201 US

GROWTH PLANS/SPECIAL FEATURES:

CACI International, Inc. is an information technology (IT) company that provides IT and network services to defense, intelligence and other government departments. Contracts with the U.S. government make up 94.8% of the company's revenue. CACI's domestic operations work through several joint ventures and subsidiaries, including Wexford Group International and Athena Innovative Solutions, Inc. Operations consist of providing data, information and knowledge management programs such as HighView Document Exploitation; business systems like the Wide Area Workflow application; command, control, communications, computers, intelligence, surveillance and reconnaissance (C4ISR) programs such as Rapid Deployment Communications; and information assurance and cyber security; logistics information systems which utilize Radio Frequency Identification (RFID). International operations are conducted through subsidiary CACI Ltd., which is based in the U.K. and accounts for 90% of the company's commercial revenue. The subsidiary focuses on business systems applications; data, information and knowledge management; and enterprise IT and network services. The company also operates the CACI Vision & Solution Center, where customers can test IT solutions before installing them. Another subsidiary, SystemWare, Inc., specializes in cybersecurity and operational security. In November 2010, the company acquired TechniGraphics, Inc. and Applied Systems Research, Inc., two intelligence products companies.

The company offers employees medical, dental and vision insurance; life and AD&D insurance; short- and long-term disability coverage; flexible spending accounts; health club discounts; a 401(k) plan; an employee stock purchase program; a credit union membership; tuition reimbursement; a group legal plan; an employee assistance program; auto and home insurance; a commuter benefit program; pet care discounts; and merchandise discounts.

FINANCIALS: **Sales and profits are in thousands of dollars—add 000 to get the full amount. 2010 Note: Financial information for 2010 was not available for all companies at press time.**

2010 Sales: $3,149,131 | 2010 Profits: $106,515
2009 Sales: $2,730,162 | 2009 Profits: $89,698
2008 Sales: $2,420,537 | 2008 Profits: $77,935
2007 Sales: $1,937,972 | 2007 Profits: $78,532
2006 Sales: $1,755,324 | 2006 Profits: $84,840

U.S. Stock Ticker: CACI
Int'l Ticker:
Int'l Exchange:
Employees: 13,100 Fiscal Year Ends: 6/30
Parent Company:

SALARIES/BENEFITS:

Pension Plan: | ESOP Stock Plan: | Profit Sharing: | Top Exec. Salary: $727,300 | Bonus: $1,756,226
Savings Plan: Y | Stock Purch. Plan: Y | | Second Exec. Salary: $535,085 | Bonus: $660,571

OTHER THOUGHTS:

Apparent Women Officers or Directors: 2
Hot Spot for Advancement for Women/Minorities:

LOCATIONS: ("Y" = Yes)

West:	Southwest:	Midwest:	Southeast:	Northeast:	International:
Y	Y	Y	Y	Y	Y

CADENCE DESIGN SYSTEMS INC

www.cadence.com

Industry Group Code: 511210N

Management:		Sales/Marketing:		Liberal Arts:		Information Sys.:		Professionals:		Tech./Scientific:	
Mgmt. Trainees:		Marketing Pros.:	Y	Gen. Writing/Editing:		Info. Mgmt.:	Y	Finance/Acct.:	Y	Engineers, Elec.:	Y
Experienced Mgmt.:		Retail Sales:		Tech. Writing:	Y	Software Dev.:	Y	Law:	Y	Engineers, Other:	
Int'l Business:	Y	Comm./Industrial:	Y	Graphic Arts/Photog.:		Hardware Dev.:		HR/Other:	Y	Health/Lab:	
MBA Grads:	Y	Sales Trainees:		Music:		Consulting/Other:		Training:		Science/Research:	
		Advertising Pros.:	Y	Broadcasting:				Health Care:		Petroleum/Chem.:	
				Other:				Consulting:		Math/Other:	

TYPES OF BUSINESS:

Software-Electronic Design Automation
Training & Support Services
Design & Methodology Services

BRANDS/DIVISIONS/AFFILIATES:

Incisive Functional Verification Platform
Encounter Digital IC Design Platform
Virtuoso Custom Design Platform
AllegroSystem Interconnect Platform
Denali Software, Inc.

CONTACTS: *Note: Officers with more than one job title may be intentionally listed here more than once.*

Lip-Bu Tan, CEO
Lip-Bu Tan, Pres.
Geoff Ribar, CFO/Sr. VP
John Bruggeman, Chief Mktg. Officer/Sr. VP
Tina Jones, Sr. VP-Global Human Resources
Chi-Ping Hsu, Sr. VP-R&D, Implementation Group
Jim Cowie, General Counsel/Corp. Sec./Sr. VP
Thomas Cooley, Sr. VP-Worldwide Field Oper.
Charlie Huang, Chief Strategy Officer/Sr. VP
Jennifer Jordan, Corp. VP-Investor Rel.
Craig Johnson, Corp. VP-Strategic Planning
Nimish Modi, Sr. VP-R&D, Front End Group
Sanjay Srivastava, Sr. VP-SoC Realization
John B. Shoven, Chmn.

Phone: 408-943-1234	**Fax:** 408-428-5001
Toll-Free: 800-746-6223	
Address: 2655 Seely Ave., San Jose, CA 95134-1931 US	

GROWTH PLANS/SPECIAL FEATURES:

Cadence Design Systems, Inc. (Cadence) is a leading provider of electronic design automation (EDA) software and hardware. Cadence licenses, sells and leases its hardware technology and provides design and methodology services throughout the world to help manage and accelerate electronic product development processes. Cadence combines its design technologies into platforms for four major design activities: functional verification, digital integrated circuit (IC) design, custom IC design and system interconnect. The four Cadence design platforms are Incisive, a program which verifies the function of a logic system; Encounter, a digital IC design program modeled to balance cost and function; Virtuoso, a custom circuit schematic program; and Allegro, a printed circuit board simulation and design system. The company additionally augments its platform product offerings with a set of design for manufacturing (DFM) products that service both the digital and custom IC design flows. Cadence offers a number of fee-based services, including Internet, classroom and custom educational courses; and engineering services and reusable design technologies to aid customers with the design of complex ICs. The company sells software using subscription and term licenses, as well as perpetual licenses for customers who prefer to have the right to use the technology continuously without time restriction. In June 2010, it acquired Denali Software, Inc., a provider of EDA software and intellectual property.

FINANCIALS: **Sales and profits are in thousands of dollars—add 000 to get the full amount. 2010 Note: Financial information for 2010 was not available for all companies at press time.**

2010 Sales: $935,954 | 2010 Profits: $126,538
2009 Sales: $852,632 | 2009 Profits: $-149,871
2008 Sales: $1,038,614 | 2008 Profits: $-1,865,715
2007 Sales: $1,615,013 | 2007 Profits: $286,800
2006 Sales: $1,483,895 | 2006 Profits: $142,592

U.S. Stock Ticker: CDNS
Int'l Ticker:
Int'l Exchange:
Employees: 4,600 Fiscal Year Ends: 12/31
Parent Company:

SALARIES/BENEFITS:

Pension Plan: ESOP Stock Plan: Profit Sharing: Top Exec. Salary: $531,692 Bonus: $11,765
Savings Plan: Y Stock Purch. Plan: Y Second Exec. Salary: $423,135 Bonus: $

OTHER THOUGHTS:

Apparent Women Officers or Directors: 1
Hot Spot for Advancement for Women/Minorities:

LOCATIONS: ("Y" = Yes)

West:	Southwest:	Midwest:	Southeast:	Northeast:	International:
Y	Y	Y	Y	Y	Y

CAESARS ENTERTAINMENT CORPORATION www.caesars.com

Industry Group Code: 721120

Management:		Sales/Marketing:		Liberal Arts:		Information Sys.:		Professionals:		Tech./Scientific:	
Mgmt. Trainees:	Y	Marketing Pros.:	Y	Gen. Writing/Editing:	Y	Info. Mgmt.:	Y	Finance/Acct.:	Y	Engineers, Elec.:	
Experienced Mgmt.:	Y	Retail Sales:		Tech. Writing:		Software Dev.:	Y	Law:	Y	Engineers, Other:	
Int'l Business:	Y	Comm./Industrial:	Y	Graphic Arts/Photog.:	Y	Hardware Dev.:		HR/Other:	Y	Health/Lab:	
MBA Grads:	Y	Sales Trainees:	Y	Music:	Y	Consulting/Other:		Training:	Y	Science/Research:	
		Advertising Pros.:	Y	Broadcasting:				Health Care:		Petroleum/Chem.:	
				Other:	Y			Consulting:		Math/Other:	

TYPES OF BUSINESS:

Casino Hotels
Dockside & Riverboat Casinos
Racing Venues
Casino Management

BRANDS/DIVISIONS/AFFILIATES:

Harrah's Entertainment, Inc.
Caesers
Flamingo
Horseshoe
Total Rewards
World Series of Poker
Rock Ohio Caesars LLC
Hamlet Holdings LLC

CONTACTS: *Note: Officers with more than one job title may be intentionally listed here more than once.*

Gary W. Loveman, CEO
Gary W. Loveman, Pres.
Jonathan S. Halkyard, CFO/Sr. VP/Treas.
David Norton, Chief Mktg. Officer/Sr. VP
Mary Thomas, Sr. VP-Human Resources
Katrina Lane, CTO/Sr. VP
Tim Donovan, General Counsel/Sr. VP
Jan Jones, Sr. VP-Comm. & Gov't Rel.
Tom M. Jenkin, Pres., Western Div.
John Payne, Pres., Central Div.
Don Marrandino, Pres., Eastern Div.
John Baker, Sr. VP-Enterprise Effectiveness
Gary W. Loveman, Chmn.

Phone: 702-407-6000 **Fax:** 702-407-6037
Toll-Free: 800-318-0047
Address: 1 Caesars Palace Dr., Las Vegas, NV 89109 US

GROWTH PLANS/SPECIAL FEATURES:

Caesars Entertainment Corporation, formerly Harrah's Entertainment, Inc., is one of the largest gaming companies in the world. The firm owns or manages approximately 52 casinos throughout the world. It operates casino entertainment facilities primarily under the Harrah's, Caesars and Horseshoe brands in the U.S., including land-based casinos; riverboat or dockside casinos; casino clubs; and three racing venues. Caesars also earns fees from managing three casinos for Indian tribes: Harrah's Phoenix Ak-Chin, located near Phoenix, Arizona; Harrah's Rincon Casino and Resort, near San Diego, California; and Harrah's Cherokee Casino and Hotel, in Cherokee, North Carolina. Its international facilities are located in Canada, Uruguay, England, Scotland, Egypt and South Africa. Additional brands operated and/or owned by Caesars include Bally's; Flamingo; Grand Biloxi; Harveys; Imperial Palace; Paris; Rio; and Showboat. The company also owns and operates the World Series of Poker tournament and brand. Besides casinos, the firm's properties generally include hotel and convention space; restaurants; and non-gaming entertainment facilities. Its facilities contain an aggregate 3 million square feet of gaming space and over 42,000 hotel rooms. For returning customers in the U.S., the firm offers the Total Rewards card plan, allowing holders to earn reward credits for prizes such as vacations, event tickets and cars; Total Rewards currently has over 40 million members. In February 2010, Caesars acquired the Planet Hollywood Resort and Casino in Las Vegas, Nevada. In July 2010, the firm purchased the Thistledown Racetrack, a thoroughbred racing facility located in Cleveland, Ohio. In December 2010, it formed a joint venture with Rock Gaming LLC, Rock Ohio Caesars LLC, in order to develop casinos in Cincinnati and Cleveland.

Employees of Caesars receive medical, dental and vision plans; educational assistance; and health and wellness programs.

FINANCIALS: **Sales and profits are in thousands of dollars—add 000 to get the full amount. 2010 Note: Financial information for 2010 was not available for all companies at press time.**

2010 Sales: $8,818,600 2010 Profits: $-823,300
2009 Sales: $8,907,400 2009 Profits: $846,400
2008 Sales: $9,370,000 2008 Profits: $-5,197,200
2007 Sales: $10,825,200 2007 Profits: $619,400
2006 Sales: $9,673,900 2006 Profits: $535,800

U.S. Stock Ticker: Private
Int'l Ticker:
Int'l Exchange:
Employees: 100,000 Fiscal Year Ends: 12/31
Parent Company: HAMLET HOLDINGS LLC

SALARIES/BENEFITS:

Pension Plan: ESOP Stock Plan: Profit Sharing: Top Exec. Salary: $ Bonus: $
Savings Plan: Y Stock Purch. Plan: Second Exec. Salary: $ Bonus: $

OTHER THOUGHTS:

Apparent Women Officers or Directors: 3
Hot Spot for Advancement for Women/Minorities: Y

LOCATIONS: ("Y" = Yes)

West:	Southwest:	Midwest:	Southeast:	Northeast:	International:
Y	Y	Y	Y	Y	Y

Sales, profits and employees may be estimates. Financial information, benefits and other data can change quickly and may vary from those stated here.

CAMERON INTERNATIONAL CORPORATION

www.c-a-m.com

Industry Group Code: 33313

Management:		Sales/Marketing:		Liberal Arts:		Information Sys.:		Professionals:		Tech./Scientific:	
Mgmt. Trainees:	Y	Marketing Pros.:	Y	Gen. Writing/Editing:		Info. Mgmt.:	Y	Finance/Acct.:	Y	Engineers, Elec.:	Y
Experienced Mgmt.:	Y	Retail Sales:		Tech. Writing:	Y	Software Dev.:	Y	Law:	Y	Engineers, Other:	Y
Int'l Business:	Y	Comm./Industrial:	Y	Graphic Arts/Photog.:	Y	Hardware Dev.:	Y	HR/Other:	Y	Health/Lab:	
MBA Grads:	Y	Sales Trainees:		Music:		Consulting/Other:		Training:	Y	Science/Research:	
		Advertising Pros.:		Broadcasting:				Health Care:		Petroleum/Chem.:	
				Other:				Consulting:		Math/Other:	

TYPES OF BUSINESS:

Oil Field Machinery
Gas Turbines, Compressors & Engines
Oil Field Services
Pressure & Flow Control Equipment

BRANDS/DIVISIONS/AFFILIATES:

Cooper-Bessemer
Cameron
Entech
CSI
Ajax
Vescon Equipamentos Industriais Ltda.
Ring-O
Industrial Machine & Fabrication, LLC

CONTACTS: *Note: Officers with more than one job title may be intentionally listed here more than once.*

Jack B. Moore, CEO
John D. Carne, COO/Exec. VP
Jack B. Moore, Pres.
Charles M. Sledge, CFO/Sr. VP
Ed Will, VP-Mktg. & Strategy
Roslyn Larkey, VP-Human Resources
John Bartos, VP-Tech. & Dev.
William C. Lemmer, General Counsel/Sr. VP
Stephen P. Tomlinson, VP-Oper. Integrity
Hal J. Goldie, VP-Global Bus. Dev.
Jeffrey G. Altamari, VP-Investor Rel.
Christopher A. Krummel, Chief Acct. Officer/Controller/VP
James E. Wright, Sr. VP/Pres., Valves and Measurement
Joseph H. Mongrain, VP/Pres., Process & Compression Systems
Stuart Taylor, VP-Tax
H. Keith Jennings, Treas./VP
Jack B. Moore, Chmn.

Phone: 713-513-3300	**Fax:** 713-513-3456
Toll-Free:	
Address: 1333 West Loop S., Ste. 1700, Houston, TX 77027 US	

GROWTH PLANS/SPECIAL FEATURES:

Cameron International Corporation is an international provider of flow equipment products, systems and services to oil, gas and processing industries. The firm is also a leading manufacturer of centrifugal air compressors, integral and separable gas compressors and turbochargers. The company operates in three segments: drilling and production systems; valves and measurement; and compression systems. The drilling and production systems products include surface and subsea production systems; blowout preventers (BOPs); drilling and production control systems; oil and gas separation equipment; gas conditioning units; membrane separation systems; water processing systems; block valves; gate valves; actuators; chokes; wellheads; drilling riser; and aftermarket parts and services. The division's products are marketed under the brand names Cameron, Entech, Grove, Ring-O, TK and Tom Wheatley. The valves and measurement segment's products include ball valves, butterfly valves, Orbit valves, double block and bleed valves, globe valves and aftermarket parts and services. Measurement products include totalizers, turbine meters, flow computers, chart recorders, sampling systems and ultrasonic flow meters. The segment markets its products under various brand names, including Demco, Navco, Nutron, Techno, Wheatley and WKM. Lastly, the compression systems segment produces reciprocating and integrally geared centrifugal compression equipment and aftermarket parts and services. It markets its products under various brand names, including Ajax, Superior, Cooper-Bessemer, CSI, Texcentric and Enterprise. In 2011, Cameron International acquired aftermarket service provider for reciprocating engines and compressors Industrial Machine & Fabrication, LLC; acquired Brazilian manufacturing firm Vescon Equipamentos Industriais Ltda.; and agreed to acquire Joy Global, Inc.'s LeTourneau Technologies Drillings Systems and Offshore Products segments.

FINANCIALS: **Sales and profits are in thousands of dollars—add 000 to get the full amount. 2010 Note: Financial information for 2010 was not available for all companies at press time.**

2010 Sales: $6,134,800 — 2010 Profits: $562,900
2009 Sales: $5,223,245 — 2009 Profits: $475,519
2008 Sales: $5,848,877 — 2008 Profits: $593,726
2007 Sales: $4,666,368 — 2007 Profits: $500,860
2006 Sales: $3,742,907 — 2006 Profits: $317,816

U.S. Stock Ticker: CAM
Int'l Ticker:
Int'l Exchange:
Employees: 19,500 Fiscal Year Ends: 12/31
Parent Company:

SALARIES/BENEFITS:

Pension Plan: | ESOP Stock Plan: | Profit Sharing: | Top Exec. Salary: $987,654 | Bonus: $1,317,530
Savings Plan: | Stock Purch. Plan: | | Second Exec. Salary: $599,385 | Bonus: $575,533

OTHER THOUGHTS:

Apparent Women Officers or Directors: 2
Hot Spot for Advancement for Women/Minorities:

LOCATIONS: ("Y" = Yes)

West:	Southwest:	Midwest:	Southeast:	Northeast:	International:
Y	Y	Y	Y	Y	Y

Sales, profits and employees may be estimates. Financial information, benefits and other data can change quickly and may vary from those stated here.

CAMPBELL SOUP CO

www.campbellsoup.com

Industry Group Code: 311

Management:		Sales/Marketing:		Liberal Arts:		Information Sys.:		Professionals:		Tech./Scientific:	
Mgmt. Trainees:	Y	Marketing Pros.:	Y	Gen. Writing/Editing:	Y	Info. Mgmt.:	Y	Finance/Acct.:	Y	Engineers, Elec.:	Y
Experienced Mgmt.:	Y	Retail Sales:		Tech. Writing:		Software Dev.:		Law:	Y	Engineers, Other:	Y
Int'l Business:	Y	Comm./Industrial:	Y	Graphic Arts/Photog.:	Y	Hardware Dev.:		HR/Other:	Y	Health/Lab:	Y
MBA Grads:	Y	Sales Trainees:		Music:		Consulting/Other:		Training:	Y	Science/Research:	
		Advertising Pros.:	Y	Broadcasting:				Health Care:		Petroleum/Chem.:	Y
				Other:				Consulting:		Math/Other:	

TYPES OF BUSINESS:

Soup & Sauces-Manufacturing
Pastas
Snack Foods
Packaged Foods
Canned Foods
Cookies
Juice
Frozen Products

BRANDS/DIVISIONS/AFFILIATES:

Pepperidge Farm
V8
Pace Foods
Prego
Swanson
Arnott's
Ecce Panis, Inc.

CONTACTS: *Note: Officers with more than one job title may be intentionally listed here more than once.*

Douglas R. Conant, CEO
Denise Morrison, COO/Exec. VP
Douglas R. Conant, Pres.
B. Craig Owens, CFO/Sr. VP
Nancy A. Reardon, Chief Human Resources & Comm. Officer/Sr. VP
George Dowdie, Sr. VP-Global R&D and Quality
Joseph Spagnoletti, CIO/Sr. VP
B. Craig Owens, Chief Admin. Officer
Ellen Oran Kaden, Sr. VP-Law & Gov't Affairs
Irene Chang Britt, Chief Strategy Officer/Sr. VP
Jerry S. Buckley, Sr. VP-Public Affairs
Jennifer Driscolll, VP-Investor Rel.
Anthony P. DiSilvestro, VP-Finance
Sean Connolly, Pres., Campbell North America
Larry S. Williamsn, Sr. VP-Int'l Bus. Dev.
Patrick J. Callaghan, Pres., Pepperidge Farm
John Sechi, Pres., Greater Europe
Paul R. Charron, Chmn.
Mark Alexander, Pres., Campbell Int'l
David White, Sr. VP-Global Supply Chain

Phone: 856-342-4800 **Fax:** 856-342-3878
Toll-Free: 800-257-8443
Address: 1 Campbell Pl., Camden, NJ 08103 US

GROWTH PLANS/SPECIAL FEATURES:

Campbell Soup Co., with over 20 subsidiaries, is a global manufacturer and marketer of convenience food products. The firm operates in four business segments: U.S. Soup, Sauces and Beverages; Baking and Snacking; International Soup, Sauces and Beverages; and North America Foodservice. The U.S. segment includes Campbell's soups, pasta, gravies, beans and tomato juice; Swanson broth, stocks and canned poultry; Prego pasta sauce; Pace Mexican sauce; and V8 vegetable juices and beverages. The Baking and Snacking segment products include Pepperidge Farm cookies, crackers, bakery and frozen products in the U.S.; and Arnott's biscuits, marketed in Australia and Asia. The International segment includes soup, sauce and beverage businesses in Europe, Latin America, the Asia Pacific region, Russia and China, and a retail business in Canada. Products include Erasco and Heisse Tasse soups in Germany; Devos Lemmens mayonnaise, Campbell's and Royco soups in Belgium; Bla Band soups and sauces in Sweden; Campbell's soup and stock in Asia; and Habitant and Campbell's soups in Canada. The North American Foodservice segment manages the distribution of soup, specialty entrees, beverage products, other prepared foods and Pepperidge Farm products through food service channels in the U.S. and Canada. Recently, the firm acquired artisan bread maker Ecce Panis, Inc. In June 2010, Campbell completed the expansion of its world headquarters; and agreed to sell its German Village Products pasta plant in Ohio. In January 2011, the firm announced plans to launch a line of dry soups and pasta meals in the U.K. in cooperation with Symington's; and formed a joint venture with Swire Pacific, Ltd., to develop its soup business in China.

Employees are offered health, dental and prescription drug coverage; a 401(k) plan; life insurance; disability and business travel accident coverage; tuition reimbursement; adoption assistance; and on-site health clinic, fitness center, cafeteria and dry cleaning facilities.

FINANCIALS: **Sales and profits are in thousands of dollars—add 000 to get the full amount. 2010 Note: Financial information for 2010 was not available for all companies at press time.**

2010 Sales: $7,676,000	2010 Profits: $844,000
2009 Sales: $7,586,000	2009 Profits: $736,000
2008 Sales: $7,998,000	2008 Profits: $1,165,000
2007 Sales: $7,385,000	2007 Profits: $854,000
2006 Sales: $6,894,000	2006 Profits: $766,000

U.S. Stock Ticker: CPB
Int'l Ticker:
Int'l Exchange:
Employees: 18,400 Fiscal Year Ends: 7/31
Parent Company:

SALARIES/BENEFITS:

Pension Plan:	ESOP Stock Plan:	Profit Sharing:	Top Exec. Salary: $1,185,000	Bonus: $1,510,875
Savings Plan: Y	Stock Purch. Plan:		Second Exec. Salary: $780,000	Bonus: $563,550

OTHER THOUGHTS:

Apparent Women Officers or Directors: 7
Hot Spot for Advancement for Women/Minorities: Y

LOCATIONS: ("Y" = Yes)

West:	Southwest:	Midwest:	Southeast:	Northeast:	International:
Y	Y	Y	Y	Y	Y

CAPITAL SENIOR LIVING CORP

www.capitalsenior.com

Industry Group Code: 623110

Management:		Sales/Marketing:		Liberal Arts:		Information Sys.:		Professionals:		Tech./Scientific:	
Mgmt. Trainees:	Y	Marketing Pros.:	Y	Gen. Writing/Editing:	Y	Info. Mgmt.:	Y	Finance/Acct.:	Y	Engineers, Elec.:	
Experienced Mgmt.:	Y	Retail Sales:		Tech. Writing:	Y	Software Dev.:		Law:	Y	Engineers, Other:	
Int'l Business:		Comm./Industrial:		Graphic Arts/Photog.:	Y	Hardware Dev.:		HR/Other:	Y	Health/Lab:	
MBA Grads:	Y	Sales Trainees:		Music:		Consulting/Other:		Training:	Y	Science/Research:	
		Advertising Pros.:	Y	Broadcasting:				Health Care:	Y	Petroleum/Chem.:	
				Other:	Y			Consulting:		Math/Other:	

TYPES OF BUSINESS:

Long-Term Health Care
Nursing Homes
Assisted Living Services
Home Care Services

BRANDS/DIVISIONS/AFFILIATES:

Quality Home Care, Inc.

CONTACTS:

Note: Officers with more than one job title may be intentionally listed here more than once.

Lawrence A. Cohen, CEO
Keith N. Johannessen, COO
Keith N. Johannessen, Pres.
Ralph A. Beattie, CFO/Exec. VP
Rob Goodpaster, VP-Nat'l Mktg.
David R. Brickman, General Counsel/VP/Sec.
David Beathard, Sr., VP-Oper.
Joseph G. Solari, VP-Corp. Dev.
Gloria Holland, VP-Finance
Robert Hollister, Property Controller
Glen H. Campbell, VP-Dev.
James A. Moore, Chmn.

Phone: 972-770-5600	**Fax:** 972-770-5666
Toll-Free:	
Address: 14160 Dallas Pkwy., Ste. 300, Dallas, TX 75254 US	

GROWTH PLANS/SPECIAL FEATURES:

Capital Senior Living Corp. (CSL) is one of the nation's largest operators and developers of residential communities for seniors. The firm operates 77 communities in 23 states, including 32 senior living communities that it either owned or had an ownership interest in and 45 senior living communities that are leased facilities. Its combined facilities can support approximately 11,000 residents. Approximately 95% of the company's annual revenue is generated through private pay parties at these communities. The firm provides senior living services to the elderly in four categories of assistance: independent living, assisted living, continuing care retirement communities and home care services. Its independent living communities provide residents with daily meals, transportation, social and recreational activities, laundry, housekeeping and 24-hour staffing. The firm's assisted living communities, with residents that acquire additional assistance over independent residents, provide personal care services, such as walking, eating, personal hygiene and medication assistance; and special care services for residents with certain forms of dementia. The continuing care retirement communities provide traditional long-term care through 24-hour-per-day skilled nursing care by registered nurses. The company provides home care services to residents at one senior living community through its home care agency, Quality Home Care, Inc., and through third-party providers at a majority of its senior living communities. Many of CSL's communities offer a continuum of care to meet its residents' needs as they change over time. This continuum of care, which integrates independent living, assisted living and home care through independent home care agencies or the company's home care agency, sustains residents' autonomy and independence based on their physical and mental abilities.

Employees are offered medical and dental insurance; life insurance; and a 401(k) plan.

FINANCIALS:

Sales and profits are in thousands of dollars—add 000 to get the full amount. 2010 Note: Financial information for 2010 was not available for all companies at press time.

2010 Sales: $211,929	2010 Profits: $4,254
2009 Sales: $191,991	2009 Profits: $2,759
2008 Sales: $193,274	2008 Profits: $3,724
2007 Sales: $189,052	2007 Profits: $4,360
2006 Sales: $159,070	2006 Profits: $-2,600

U.S. Stock Ticker: CSU
Int'l Ticker:
Int'l Exchange:
Employees: 4,188 Fiscal Year Ends: 12/31
Parent Company:

SALARIES/BENEFITS:

Pension Plan:	ESOP Stock Plan:	Profit Sharing:	Top Exec. Salary: $436,558	Bonus: $406,173
Savings Plan: Y	Stock Purch. Plan:		Second Exec. Salary: $278,538	Bonus: $209,023

OTHER THOUGHTS:

Apparent Women Officers or Directors: 2
Hot Spot for Advancement for Women/Minorities:

LOCATIONS: ("Y" = Yes)

West:	Southwest:	Midwest:	Southeast:	Northeast:	International:
Y	Y	Y	Y	Y	

Sales, profits and employees may be estimates. Financial information, benefits and other data can change quickly and may vary from those stated here.

CARLSON COMPANIES INC

www.carlson.com

Industry Group Code: 721110

Management:		Sales/Marketing:		Liberal Arts:		Information Sys.:		Professionals:		Tech./Scientific:	
Mgmt. Trainees:	Y	Marketing Pros.:	Y	Gen. Writing/Editing:	Y	Info. Mgmt.:	Y	Finance/Acct.:	Y	Engineers, Elec.:	
Experienced Mgmt.:	Y	Retail Sales:		Tech. Writing:		Software Dev.:		Law:	Y	Engineers, Other:	
Int'l Business:	Y	Comm./Industrial:	Y	Graphic Arts/Photog.:		Hardware Dev.:		HR/Other:	Y	Health/Lab:	
MBA Grads:	Y	Sales Trainees:		Music:		Consulting/Other:		Training:	Y	Science/Research:	
		Advertising Pros.:	Y	Broadcasting:				Health Care:		Petroleum/Chem.:	
				Other:	Y			Consulting:		Math/Other:	

TYPES OF BUSINESS:

Hotels & Resorts
Travel Agencies & Services
Marketing Services
Restaurant Chains
Online Travel Services
Business & Government Travel Management

BRANDS/DIVISIONS/AFFILIATES:

Radisson
Park Plaza
Carlson Wagonlit Travel
Park Inn by Radisson
Country Inns and Suites
TGI Friday's
Pick Up Stix
Carlson Hotels Worldwide

CONTACTS: *Note: Officers with more than one job title may be intentionally listed here more than once.*

Hubert Joly, CEO
Hubert Joly, Pres.
Trudy Rautio, CFO
Elizabeth Bastoni, Exec. VP-Human Resources
Trudy Rautio, Chief Admin. Officer/Exec. VP
William A. Van Brunt, General Counsel/Exec. VP
Nick Sheperd, Pres./CEO-Carlson Restaurants Worldwide
Douglas Anderson, Pres./CEO Carlson Wagonlit Travel
Thorsten Kirschke, COO-Carlson Hotels
Gordon McKinnon, Exec. VP/Chief Branding Officer
Marilyn Carlson Nelson, Chmn.
Simon Barlow, Pres., Carlson Hotels APAC

Phone: 763-212-5000	**Fax:** 763-212-2219
Toll-Free:	
Address: 701 Carlson Pkwy., Minnetonka, MN 55305 US	

GROWTH PLANS/SPECIAL FEATURES:

Carlson Companies, Inc. is a firm offering a wide variety of travel, hospitality and marketing services. Carlson Hotels Worldwide operates over 1,080 hotels in more than 77 countries, under brand names such as Radisson; Park Plaza; Park Inn by Radisson; and Country Inns and Suites by CarlsonSM. The firm's restaurant segment, with more than 1,000 locations in more than 60 countries, includes T.G.I. Friday's and Pick Up Stix casual restaurant chains. The company offers franchise opportunities for its various brands of hotels and restaurants. The firm's travel segment, which is comprised of Carlson Wagonlit Travel, offers corporate clients business travel management programs with the objective of maximizing productivity while minimizing cost. In 2010, the company opened several hotels including Radisson Blu Hotel & Conference Centre in Salzburg, Austria; Country Inns & Suites By Carlson in Madison, Alabama; Park Inn Lagos Ikeja in Nigeria; Park Inn Sofia in Bulgaria; Radisson Blu Resort Split in Croatia; and Radisson Hotel Zavidovo in Russia. In mid 2010, the company agreed to develop its first U.S. Radisson Blu hotel which will be located in the Aqua at Lakeshore East Tower in Chicago, Illinois. The new hotel is scheduled to open in the fall of 2011. In December 2010, the firm announced they will open approximately 30 restaurants in the Middle East through a partnership with Americana Group. In 2011, the firm opened several new hotels including Country Inns & Suites By Carlson in San Antonio, Texas; Park Inn by Radisson Sharon, Pennsylvania; a Radisson Hotel in Menomonee Falls, Wisconsin; and Radisson Blu Golden Horn Hotel Istanbul, Turkey.

FINANCIALS: **Sales and profits are in thousands of dollars—add 000 to get the full amount. 2010 Note: Financial information for 2010 was not available for all companies at press time.**

2010 Sales: $	2010 Profits: $	**U.S. Stock Ticker: Private**
2009 Sales: $	2009 Profits: $	**Int'l Ticker:**
2008 Sales: $	2008 Profits: $	Int'l Exchange:
2007 Sales: $	2007 Profits: $	Employees: 50,000 Fiscal Year Ends: 12/31
2006 Sales: $	2006 Profits: $	Parent Company:

SALARIES/BENEFITS:

Pension Plan:	ESOP Stock Plan:	Profit Sharing:	Top Exec. Salary: $	Bonus: $
Savings Plan:	Stock Purch. Plan:		Second Exec. Salary: $	Bonus: $

OTHER THOUGHTS:

Apparent Women Officers or Directors: 4
Hot Spot for Advancement for Women/Minorities: Y

LOCATIONS: ("Y" = Yes)

West:	Southwest:	Midwest:	Southeast:	Northeast:	International:
Y	Y	Y	Y	Y	Y

CARMAX GROUP

www.carmax.com

Industry Group Code: 441110

Management:		Sales/Marketing:		Liberal Arts:		Information Sys.:		Professionals:		Tech./Scientific:	
Mgmt. Trainees:	Y	Marketing Pros.:	Y	Gen. Writing/Editing:	Y	Info. Mgmt.:	Y	Finance/Acct.:	Y	Engineers, Elec.:	
Experienced Mgmt.:	Y	Retail Sales:	Y	Tech. Writing:		Software Dev.:	Y	Law:	Y	Engineers, Other:	
Int'l Business:		Comm./Industrial:	Y	Graphic Arts/Photog.:	Y	Hardware Dev.:		HR/Other:	Y	Health/Lab:	
MBA Grads:	Y	Sales Trainees:	Y	Music:		Consulting/Other:		Training:	Y	Science/Research:	
		Advertising Pros.:	Y	Broadcasting:				Health Care:		Petroleum/Chem.:	
				Other:				Consulting:		Math/Other:	

TYPES OF BUSINESS:

Used Auto Dealers, Retail
New Auto Dealers
Online Sales
Vehicle Repair Services
Financial Services

BRANDS/DIVISIONS/AFFILIATES:

CarMax Foundation (The)
CarMax Auto Finance

CONTACTS:

Note: Officers with more than one job title may be intentionally listed here more than once.

Thomas J. Folliard, CEO
Thomas J. Folliard, Pres.
Thomas W. Reedy, Jr., CFO/Sr. VP
Joseph S. Kunkel, Sr. VP-Mktg. & Strategy
Roberta Douma, VP-Human Resource Dev.
Richard M. Smith, CIO/Sr. VP
Bill Nash, Sr. VP-Merch.
Michael K. Dolan, Chief Admin. Officer/Exec. VP
Eric Margolin, General Counsel/Sr. VP/Corp. Sec.
Lynn Mussatt, VP-Bus. Oper.
Anu Agarwal, VP-Bus. Strategy
Katharine Kenny, VP-Investor Rel.
Keith D. Browning, Exec. VP-Finance
Laura Donahue, VP-Advertising
Angela S. Chattin, Sr. VP-CarMax Auto Finance
Barbara Harvill, VP-IT
Kim Orcutt, VP/Controller
William R. Tiefel, Chmn.
Mark Adams, Asst. VP-Logistics

Phone: 804-747-0422 | **Fax:** 804-967-2918
Toll-Free: 800-519-1511
Address: 12800 Tuckahoe Creek Pkwy., Richmond, VA 23238 US

GROWTH PLANS/SPECIAL FEATURES:

CarMax Group is one of the nation's largest retailers of used cars. The firm purchases, reconditions and sells used vehicles through its 105 used car superstores in 51 metropolitan markets across the U.S. Approximately 85% of the cars in the company's used vehicle inventory are between one and six years old and have less than 60,000 miles. CarMax also sells new vehicles at five of its locations under franchise agreements with three car manufacturers. The company offers a wide selection of makes and models of both domestic and imported vehicles to appeal to diverse consumer preferences and budgets, including popular brands from manufacturers such as Daimler, Chrysler, Ford, General Motors, Honda, Mitsubishi, Subaru, Toyota and Volkswagen. Vehicles purchased through the company's in-store appraisal process that fall short of retail standards are sold at on-site wholesale auctions restricted to licensed automobile dealers. All store locations provide vehicle repair service and used-car warranty service. In addition, through the company's web site, customers can search new and used cars as well as find information on Kelley Blue Book figures, car buying tips, rebates and incentives. CarMax offers financing options through CarMax Auto Finance, including revolving credit and automobile installment loans. The company also works through The CarMax Foundation, which supports community service and philanthropic endeavors. The firm retailed approximately 396,181 used vehicles in 2010, as well as 263,061 wholesale vehicles it sold through on-site auctions.

CarMax offers its employees a benefits package including educational assistance, a daycare savings account, life insurance, adoption assistance, an associate discount program and an employee assistance program. In 2010, CarMax was named by Fortune magazine as one of its 100 Best Companies to Work For, for the seventh consecutive year.

FINANCIALS:

Sales and profits are in thousands of dollars—add 000 to get the full amount. 2010 Note: Financial information for 2010 was not available for all companies at press time.

2010 Sales: $7,470,193	2010 Profits: $281,668
2009 Sales: $6,973,966	2009 Profits: $59,213
2008 Sales: $8,199,571	2008 Profits: $182,025
2007 Sales: $7,465,656	2007 Profits: $198,597
2006 Sales: $6,259,967	2006 Profits: $134,220

U.S. Stock Ticker: KMX
Int'l Ticker:
Int'l Exchange:
Employees: 15,565 Fiscal Year Ends: 2/28
Parent Company:

SALARIES/BENEFITS:

Pension Plan: Y	ESOP Stock Plan:	Profit Sharing:	Top Exec. Salary: $993,077	Bonus: $1,507,500
Savings Plan: Y	Stock Purch. Plan: Y		Second Exec. Salary: $640,347	Bonus: $578,150

OTHER THOUGHTS:

Apparent Women Officers or Directors: 13
Hot Spot for Advancement for Women/Minorities: Y

LOCATIONS: ("Y" = Yes)

West:	Southwest:	Midwest:	Southeast:	Northeast:	International:
Y	Y	Y	Y	Y	

CARNIVAL CORPORATION

www.carnival.com

Industry Group Code: 483112

Management:		Sales/Marketing:		Liberal Arts:		Information Sys.:		Professionals:		Tech./Scientific:	
Mgmt. Trainees:	Y	Marketing Pros.:	Y	Gen. Writing/Editing:	Y	Info. Mgmt.:	Y	Finance/Acct.:	Y	Engineers, Elec.:	
Experienced Mgmt.:	Y	Retail Sales:		Tech. Writing:	Y	Software Dev.:	Y	Law:	Y	Engineers, Other:	Y
Int'l Business:	Y	Comm./Industrial:	Y	Graphic Arts/Photog.:	Y	Hardware Dev.:		HR/Other:	Y	Health/Lab:	
MBA Grads:	Y	Sales Trainees:	Y	Music:	Y	Consulting/Other:		Training:	Y	Science/Research:	
		Advertising Pros.:	Y	Broadcasting:				Health Care:		Petroleum/Chem.:	
				Other:	Y			Consulting:		Math/Other:	

TYPES OF BUSINESS:

Cruise Line
On-Board Casinos
Tours
Resort Hotels

BRANDS/DIVISIONS/AFFILIATES:

Carnival Cruise Lines
Holland America Line
P&O Cruises Australia
Seabourn Cruise Line
Princess Cruises
Costa Cruises
Cunard Line
P&O Cruises

CONTACTS: *Note: Officers with more than one job title may be intentionally listed here more than once.*

Micky Arison, CEO
Howard S. Frank, COO/Vice Chmn.
David Bernstein, CFO/Sr. VP
Arnaldo Perez, General Counsel/Sr. VP/Corp. Sec.
Larry Freedman, Chief Acct. Officer/VP/Controller
David K. Dingle, CEO-Carnival UK
Michael Thamm, Pres., AIDA Cruises
Gerald R. Cahill, CEO/Pres., Carnival Cruise Lines
Ann Sherry, CEO-Carnival Australia
Micky Arison, Chmn.
Pier Luigi Foschi, Chmn./CEO-Costa Crociere SpA

Phone: 305-599-2600	**Fax:** 305-406-4700
Toll-Free:	
Address: 3655 NW 87th Ave., Miami, FL 33178-2428 US	

GROWTH PLANS/SPECIAL FEATURES:

Carnival Corporation is a leading provider of cruises and vacation packages to destinations worldwide. The firm divides its cruise brands into two segments: North America, which includes Carnival Cruise Lines, Princess Cruises, Holland America Line and Seabourn; and Europe, Australia & Asia (EAA), comprised of Costa Crociere, P&O Cruises, Cunard, AIDA and Ibero Cruises. In total, the company operates 100 ships with a capacity for over 191,000 passengers. Carnival Cruise Lines operates 22 ships and is based in North America. Princess is a global cruise and tour company operating 17 ships. Holland America Line serves the industry's premium segment, with 15 ships sailing to all seven continents. Seabourn Cruise Line offers luxury cruises on its six luxury yachts. Costa Crociere is the leading cruise company in Europe and South America, operating a modern fleet of 15 ships. Costa has recently expanded its presence into the Asian market with Costa Asia. P&O Cruises, which operates from the U.K and Australia, sails to destinations in the Caribbean, South America, Scandinavia, the Mediterranean and Atlantic Islands, as well as Round the World cruises. Cunard operates the Queen Mary 2, Queen Elizabeth and Queen Victoria ships. AIDA Cruises operates in the German-speaking cruise market and Ibero Cruises caters to the Spanish-speaking cruise market in Southern Europe. The company also owns Holland America Princess Alaska Tours, a leading tour operator in Alaska and the Canadian Yukon, offering lodging (at 15 owned hotels and lodges), chartered motorcoaches, rail cars, luxury day boats and sightseeing packages. In 2010, the company generated 52% of its revenue in North America, 39% from the European market and the remainder coming mainly from the Australian and Asian market. In January 2011, the firm relocated the port of operations for its Seabourn Cruise Line fleet from Miami to Seattle, Washington.

FINANCIALS: **Sales and profits are in thousands of dollars—add 000 to get the full amount. 2010 Note: Financial information for 2010 was not available for all companies at press time.**

2010 Sales: $14,469,000 — 2010 Profits: $1,978,000
2009 Sales: $13,157,000 — 2009 Profits: $1,790,000
2008 Sales: $14,646,000 — 2008 Profits: $2,330,000
2007 Sales: $13,033,000 — 2007 Profits: $2,408,000
2006 Sales: $11,839,000 — 2006 Profits: $2,279,000

U.S. Stock Ticker: CCL
Int'l Ticker:
Int'l Exchange:
Employees: 85,200 — Fiscal Year Ends: 11/30
Parent Company:

SALARIES/BENEFITS:

Pension Plan: — ESOP Stock Plan: — Profit Sharing: — Top Exec. Salary: $1,296,750 — Bonus: $1,610,464
Savings Plan: Y — Stock Purch. Plan: Y — Second Exec. Salary: $880,000 — Bonus: $2,461,168

OTHER THOUGHTS:

Apparent Women Officers or Directors: 2
Hot Spot for Advancement for Women/Minorities: Y

LOCATIONS: ("Y" = Yes)

West:	Southwest:	Midwest:	Southeast:	Northeast:	International:
Y			Y		Y

CASH AMERICA INTERNATIONAL INC

www.cashamerica.com

Industry Group Code: 522298

Management:		Sales/Marketing:		Liberal Arts:		Information Sys.:		Professionals:		Tech./Scientific:	
Mgmt. Trainees:	Y	Marketing Pros.:	Y	Gen. Writing/Editing:	Y	Info. Mgmt.:	Y	Finance/Acct.:	Y	Engineers, Elec.:	
Experienced Mgmt.:	Y	Retail Sales:	Y	Tech. Writing:		Software Dev.:	Y	Law:	Y	Engineers, Other:	
Int'l Business:	Y	Comm./Industrial:	Y	Graphic Arts/Photog.:	Y	Hardware Dev.:		HR/Other:	Y	Health/Lab:	
MBA Grads:	Y	Sales Trainees:	Y	Music:		Consulting/Other:		Training:	Y	Science/Research:	
		Advertising Pros.:	Y	Broadcasting:				Health Care:		Petroleum/Chem.:	
				Other:				Consulting:		Math/Other:	

TYPES OF BUSINESS:

Pawn Shops
Check Cashing
Payday Loans
Money Orders
Money Transfers
Stored Value Cards

BRANDS/DIVISIONS/AFFILIATES:

Mr. Payroll Corp.
Maxit Financial LLC
Cashland Financial Services, Inc.
Cash America Payday Advance
Prenda Facil
CashNetUSA.com
QuickQuid.co.uk
DollarsDirect.com.au

CONTACTS: *Note: Officers with more than one job title may be intentionally listed here more than once.*

Daniel R. Feehan, CEO
Daniel R. Feehan, Pres.
Thomas A. Bessant, Jr., CFO/Exec. VP
J. Curtis Linscott, General Counsel/Exec. VP/Corp. Sec.
Timothy S. Ho, Pres., e-commerce Div.
Timothy Ho, Pres., Enova Financial
Dennis J. Weese, COO/Pres., Retail Services Div.
Jack R. Daugherty, Chmn.

Phone: 817-335-1100 **Fax:** 817-570-1225
Toll-Free:
Address: 1600 W. 7th St., Fort Worth, TX 76102 US

GROWTH PLANS/SPECIAL FEATURES:

Cash America International, Inc. provides pawn loans, short-term cash advances, check cashing services and other specialty financial services. The company also sells merchandise in its pawnshops, primarily personal property that has been forfeited in connection with its pawn lending operations. The firm provides its specialty financial services via approximately 1,081 locations, including 425 pawnshops in 28 states and 20 jurisdictions in central and southern Mexico (including nine pawnshops that are franchises) under the names Cash America Pawn, SuperPawn and Prenda Facil, as well as via the Internet. The company offers unsecured cash advances to individuals through most of its pawnshops and standalone locations through Cash America Payday Advance and wholly-owned subsidiary Cashland Financial Services, Inc. Cash America also offers short-term loans over the Internet in the U.S. via its CashNetUSA.com web site; in the U.K. via the QuickQuid.co.uk web site; and in Australia with DollarsDirect.com.au. Through Mr. Payroll Corp., the firm offers check cashing services through franchised and company-owned check cashing centers. Many of Cash America's pawn and cash advance locations also offer check cashing services and other retail financial services such as stored value debit cards, money orders and money transfers. In October 2010, the company acquired Maxit Financial, LLC a 39-store chain of pawn lending locations which operate under the names Pawn X-Change and Maxit.

FINANCIALS: **Sales and profits are in thousands of dollars—add 000 to get the full amount. 2010 Note: Financial information for 2010 was not available for all companies at press time.**

2010 Sales: $1,293,339 — 2010 Profits: $115,538
2009 Sales: $1,120,390 — 2009 Profits: $96,678
2008 Sales: $1,030,794 — 2008 Profits: $81,140
2007 Sales: $929,394 — 2007 Profits: $79,346
2006 Sales: $694,514 — 2006 Profits: $60,940

U.S. Stock Ticker: CSH
Int'l Ticker:
Int'l Exchange:
Employees: 6,017 Fiscal Year Ends: 12/31
Parent Company:

SALARIES/BENEFITS:

Pension Plan: ESOP Stock Plan: Profit Sharing: Top Exec. Salary: $792,308 Bonus: $895,771
Savings Plan: Y Stock Purch. Plan: Second Exec. Salary: $420,231 Bonus: $300,181

OTHER THOUGHTS:

Apparent Women Officers or Directors:
Hot Spot for Advancement for Women/Minorities: Y

LOCATIONS: ("Y" = Yes)

West:	Southwest:	Midwest:	Southeast:	Northeast:	International:
Y	Y	Y	Y	Y	Y

CATERPILLAR INC

Industry Group Code: 333

www.cat.com

Management:		Sales/Marketing:		Liberal Arts:		Information Sys.:		Professionals:		Tech./Scientific:	
Mgmt. Trainees:	Y	Marketing Pros.:	Y	Gen. Writing/Editing:	Y	Info. Mgmt.:	Y	Finance/Acct.:	Y	Engineers, Elec.:	Y
Experienced Mgmt.:	Y	Retail Sales:		Tech. Writing:	Y	Software Dev.:	Y	Law:	Y	Engineers, Other:	Y
Int'l Business:	Y	Comm./Industrial:	Y	Graphic Arts/Photog.:	Y	Hardware Dev.:	Y	HR/Other:	Y	Health/Lab:	
MBA Grads:	Y	Sales Trainees:		Music:		Consulting/Other:		Training:	Y	Science/Research:	
		Advertising Pros.:	Y	Broadcasting:				Health Care:		Petroleum/Chem.:	
				Other:				Consulting:		Math/Other:	

TYPES OF BUSINESS:

Machinery-Earth Moving & Agricultural
Diesel and Turbine Engines
Financing
Fuel Cell Manufacturing
Rail Car Maintenance
Engine & Equipment Remanufacturing
Supply Chain Services
Locomotive Manufacturing and Maintenance

BRANDS/DIVISIONS/AFFILIATES:

Progress Rail Services
Solar Turbines
Caterpillar Logistics
Bucyrus International, Inc.
Electro-Motive Diesel

CONTACTS: *Note: Officers with more than one job title may be intentionally listed here more than once.*

Douglas R. Oberhelman, CEO
Ed Rapp, CFO
Greg Folley, Chief Human Resources Officer/VP
John S. Heller, CIO/VP
Tana L. Utley, CTO/VP
James B. Buda, Chief Legal Officer/Sr. VP
Ed Rapp, Pres., Corp. Svcs.
Jananne A. Copeland, Chief Acct. Officer/ Corp. Controller
Rich Lavin, Pres., Construction Industries & Growth Markets
Stu Levenick, Pres., Customer & Dealer Support
Gerard Vittecoq, Pres., Energy & Power Systems
Steve Wunning, Pres., Resource Industries
Douglas R. Oberhelman, Chmn.
Cristiano V. Schena, VP-Europe & South America Oper.
Frank J. Crespo, Chief Procurement Officer/VP

Phone: 309-675-1000 **Fax:** 309-675-4332
Toll-Free:
Address: 100 NE Adams St., Peoria, IL 61629 US

GROWTH PLANS/SPECIAL FEATURES:

Caterpillar, Inc. is a leading manufacturer of construction and mining equipment. The company's three principal lines of business are machinery, engines and financial products. The machinery segment designs, manufactures and markets construction, mining, agricultural and forestry machinery. Its products include pipe layers, motor graders, wheel tractor-scrapers, excavators, backhoe loaders, mining shovels, log skidders and loaders, off-highway trucks, articulated trucks, paving products, telescopic handlers and skid steer loaders, among others. This division, through subsidiary Progress Rail Services, is also responsible for the design, manufacture, remanufacture, maintenance and services of rail-related products. The engines segment designs, manufactures and markets engines for Caterpillar machinery; electric power generation systems; on-highway vehicles and locomotives; marine, petroleum, construction, industrial, agricultural and other applications; and related parts. Caterpillar also manufactures fuel cells, designed to incorporate ethanol, methanol, natural gas, propane, methane, hydrogen and biomass fuels. The firm's Solar Turbines subsidiary is a world leader in industrial gas turbine power system engines. The financial products segment provides financing to customers and dealers for the purchase and lease of Caterpillar and other equipment, financing approximately 60% of equipment sold. Its dealer network consists of nearly 200 dealers worldwide, serving 182 countries. Caterpillar's logistics business provides supply chain services to Caterpillar and 50 other companies worldwide. In August 2010, the company acquired locomotive maker Electro-Motive Diesel. In October 2010, Caterpillar established a joint venture in China with AVIC Liyuan Hydraulics Co. to design and manufacture motors for the construction equipment industry. In November 2010, the firm agreed to acquire mineral equipment producer Bucyrus International, Inc. for $7.6 billion. In January 2011, it announced plans to build a new manufacturing facility in Thailand.

Caterpillar's employees are offered a 401(k) plan; medical insurance; flexible spending accounts; a Healthy Balance program, in which employees receive personalized health information, health club discounts and health improvement programs; and Work.Life.Solutions, a program that offers counseling and legal advice.

FINANCIALS: **Sales and profits are in thousands of dollars—add 000 to get the full amount. 2010 Note: Financial information for 2010 was not available for all companies at press time.**

2010 Sales: $42,588,000
2009 Sales: $32,396,000
2008 Sales: $51,324,000
2007 Sales: $44,958,000
2006 Sales: $41,517,000

2010 Profits: $2,700,000
2009 Profits: $895,000
2008 Profits: $3,557,000
2007 Profits: $3,541,000
2006 Profits: $3,537,000

U.S. Stock Ticker: CAT
Int'l Ticker:
Int'l Exchange:
Employees: 104,490 Fiscal Year Ends: 12/31
Parent Company:

SALARIES/BENEFITS:

Pension Plan: Y
Savings Plan: Y
ESOP Stock Plan:
Stock Purch. Plan:
Profit Sharing:
Top Exec. Salary: $1,550,004 Bonus: $868,001
Second Exec. Salary: $895,957 Bonus: $327,253

OTHER THOUGHTS:

Apparent Women Officers or Directors: 6
Hot Spot for Advancement for Women/Minorities: Y

LOCATIONS: ("Y" = Yes)

West:	Southwest:	Midwest:	Southeast:	Northeast:	International:
Y	Y	Y	Y	Y	Y

Sales, profits and employees may be estimates. Financial information, benefits and other data can change quickly and may vary from those stated here.

CATHOLIC HEALTH INITIATIVES

www.catholichealthinit.org

Industry Group Code: 622110

Management:		Sales/Marketing:		Liberal Arts:		Information Sys.:		Professionals:		Tech./Scientific:	
Mgmt. Trainees:	Y	Marketing Pros.:	Y	Gen. Writing/Editing:	Y	Info. Mgmt.:	Y	Finance/Acct.:	Y	Engineers, Elec.:	
Experienced Mgmt.:	Y	Retail Sales:		Tech. Writing:	Y	Software Dev.:	Y	Law:	Y	Engineers, Other:	
Int'l Business:		Comm./Industrial:		Graphic Arts/Photog.:	Y	Hardware Dev.:		HR/Other:	Y	Health/Lab:	Y
MBA Grads:	Y	Sales Trainees:		Music:		Consulting/Other:		Training:	Y	Science/Research:	
		Advertising Pros.:	Y	Broadcasting:				Health Care:	Y	Petroleum/Chem.:	
				Other:	Y			Consulting:		Math/Other:	

TYPES OF BUSINESS:

Hospitals
Long-Term Care
Assisted & Independent Living Facilities
Community Health Organizations
Home Care Services
Occupational Health Clinic
Cancer Prevention Institute

BRANDS/DIVISIONS/AFFILIATES:

Centura Health
Franciscan Health System
Alegant Health
Good Samaritan Health Systems
Premier Health Partners
PorterCare Adventist Health Care
Consolidated Health Services, Inc.
Immanuel Healthcare System

CONTACTS:

Note: Officers with more than one job title may be intentionally listed here more than once.

Kevin E. Lofton, CEO
Michael T. Rowan, COO/Exec. VP
Kevin E. Lofton, Pres.
Herbert J. Vallier, Chief Human Resource Officer/Sr. VP
Kathleen D. Sanford, Chief Nursing Officer
Michael O'Rourke, CIO/Sr. VP
Mitch H. Melfi, General Counsel/Sr. VP-Legal Affairs
John F. DiCola, Sr. VP-Strategy & Bus. Dev.
Joyce M. Ross, Sr. VP-Comm.
A. Michelle Cooper, Corp. Responsibility Officer/VP
Paul W. Edgett, III, Sr. VP-National Bus. Lines
Susan M. Peach, Sr. VP-Performance Mgmt.
Peter P. Katsampes, VP-CHI Connect Support Centers
Phyllis Hughes, Chmn.
Phillip W. Mears, Sr. VP-Supply Chain

Phone: 303-298-9100 **Fax:** 303-298-9690
Toll-Free:
Address: 198 Inverness Dr. W., Ste. 800, Englewood, CO 80202 US

GROWTH PLANS/SPECIAL FEATURES:

Catholic Health Initiatives (CHI) is a national nonprofit health care organization focused on strengthening and advancing the Catholic health ministry. The organization encompasses over 70 hospitals; more than 40 long-term care, assisted and independent living residential facilities; and two community health organizations, serving approximately 69 urban and rural communities across 20 states. The group's major affiliates include Centura Health, Alegent Health, Good Samaritan Health Systems, Premier Health Partners and Franciscan Health System. Altogether, CHI has over 14,000 beds, and is among the largest Catholic health systems in the U.S. Centura Health, jointly operated by CHI and PorterCare Adventist Health Care, has 12 hospitals and seven senior residences and home care and hospice services. Alegent Health, jointly operated with Immanuel Healthcare System, is made up of nine acute care hospitals with 1,800 beds, two long-term care facilities and a primary care physician network. Good Samaritan Health Systems is a network of hospitals and services serving more than 350,000 customers in the Midwest. Premier Health Partners, jointly operated with MedAmerica Health Systems, includes four hospitals, one assisted living community, a home health care service and a cancer prevention institute. Franciscan Health System includes a number of full-service hospitals, a long-term care facility, a women's health center and midwife service and an occupational health clinic, among other services. In August 2010, CHI agreed to acquire Consolidated Health Services, Inc. from Bethesda, Inc.

FINANCIALS:

Sales and profits are in thousands of dollars—add 000 to get the full amount. 2010 Note: Financial information for 2010 was not available for all companies at press time.

2010 Sales: $9,090,555	2010 Profits: $681,982	**U.S. Stock Ticker: Nonprofit**
2009 Sales: $8,419,601	2009 Profits: $-467,207	**Int'l Ticker:**
2008 Sales: $8,880,989	2008 Profits: $229,696	Int'l Exchange:
2007 Sales: $7,731,500	2007 Profits: $	Employees: 54,000 Fiscal Year Ends: 6/30
2006 Sales: $7,636,233	2006 Profits: $693,701	Parent Company:

SALARIES/BENEFITS:

Pension Plan:	ESOP Stock Plan:	Profit Sharing:	Top Exec. Salary: $	Bonus: $
Savings Plan:	Stock Purch. Plan: Y		Second Exec. Salary: $	Bonus: $

OTHER THOUGHTS:

Apparent Women Officers or Directors: 5
Hot Spot for Advancement for Women/Minorities: Y

LOCATIONS: ("Y" = Yes)

West:	Southwest:	Midwest:	Southeast:	Northeast:	International:
Y	Y	Y	Y	Y	

CB RICHARD ELLIS GROUP INC (CBRE)

www.cbre.com

Industry Group Code: 531210

Management:		Sales/Marketing:		Liberal Arts:		Information Sys.:		Professionals:		Tech./Scientific:	
Mgmt. Trainees:	Y	Marketing Pros.:	Y	Gen. Writing/Editing:		Info. Mgmt.:	Y	Finance/Acct.:	Y	Engineers, Elec.:	
Experienced Mgmt.:	Y	Retail Sales:		Tech. Writing:		Software Dev.:		Law:	Y	Engineers, Other:	
Int'l Business:	Y	Comm./Industrial:	Y	Graphic Arts/Photog.:		Hardware Dev.:		HR/Other:	Y	Health/Lab:	
MBA Grads:	Y	Sales Trainees:		Music:		Consulting/Other:		Training:	Y	Science/Research:	
		Advertising Pros.:		Broadcasting:				Health Care:		Petroleum/Chem.:	
				Other:				Consulting:		Math/Other:	

TYPES OF BUSINESS:

Real Estate Brokerage
Real Estate Management Services
Mortgage Banking
Investment Management
Consulting Services
Real Estate Investment Trust

BRANDS/DIVISIONS/AFFILIATES:

CB Richard Ellis, Inc.
CBRE Capital Markets
CB Richard Ellis Ltd.
CB Richard Ellis Investors, LLC
Trammel Crow Company
CBRE Solar
PropertyOne

CONTACTS:

Note: Officers with more than one job title may be intentionally listed here more than once.

Brett White, CEO
Bob Sulentic, Pres.
Gil Borok, CFO
Chris Kirk, Dir.-Human Resources
Laurence Midler, General Counsel/Exec. VP
Jim Groch, Global Strategy Officer/Chief Investment Officer
Arlin E. Gaffner, Chief Acct. Officer
Ray Torto, Global Chief Economist
Robert Blain, Chmn./Pres./CEO-Asia Pacific
Calvin W. Frese, Jr., Pres., Global Svcs.
Brian F. Stoffers, Pres., Capital Markets
Richard C. Blum, Chmn.
Michael J. Strong, CEO/Pres., EMEA

Phone: 310-405-8900 **Fax:**
Toll-Free:
Address: 11150 Santa Monica Blvd., Ste. 1600, Los Angeles, CA 90025 US

GROWTH PLANS/SPECIAL FEATURES:

CB Richard Ellis Group, Inc. (CBRE) is one of the world's largest commercial real estate services companies, with over 300 offices in more than 50 countries. It offers a full range of services to occupiers, owners, lenders and investors in office, retail, industrial, multi-family and other commercial real estate assets. The firm's core services include commercial property and corporate facilities management; tenant representation; property/agency leasing; property sales; valuation; real estate investment management; commercial mortgage origination and servicing; capital markets (equity and debt); development services; and proprietary research. CBRE operates in five segments: the Americas, which accounted for 62.9% of its 2010 revenue; Europe, Middle East and Africa (EMEA), 18.3%; Asia Pacific, 13.1%; Global Investment Management, 4.2%; and Development Services, 1.5%. The Americas segment operates primarily through CB Richard Ellis, Inc.; CBRE Capital Markets; and CB Richard Ellis Ltd. The EMEA segment has offices in 42 countries, with its largest operations located in the U.K., France, Spain, the Netherlands and Germany. The Asia Pacific segment operates in 12 countries, including China, India, Japan, Korea and Taiwan. In addition, the company has agreements with affiliated offices in the Philippines, Thailand, Indonesia and Vietnam that generate royalty fees and support cross-referral arrangements. Its Global Investment Management business is handled by subsidiary CB Richard Ellis Investors, LLC. Through the Trammel Crow Company, the firm provides development services primarily in the U.S. to users of and investors in commercial real estate. In March 2010, the company launched a solar energy services company, CBRE Solar. In November 2010, it acquired PropertyOne in Hong Kong. In February 2011, the firm agreed to acquire the majority of the real estate investment management business of ING Group NV.

The company offers its employees medical, dental and vision insurance; 401(k); flexible spending accounts; an employee assistance program; and paid vacation and holidays.

FINANCIALS:

Sales and profits are in thousands of dollars—add 000 to get the full amount. 2010 Note: Financial information for 2010 was not available for all companies at press time.

2010 Sales: $5,115,316	2010 Profits: $156,009	**U.S. Stock Ticker: CBG**
2009 Sales: $4,165,820	2009 Profits: $33,341	**Int'l Ticker:**
2008 Sales: $5,128,817	2008 Profits: $-1,012,066	Int'l Exchange:
2007 Sales: $6,034,249	2007 Profits: $390,505	Employees: 31,000 Fiscal Year Ends: 12/31
2006 Sales: $4,032,027	2006 Profits: $318,571	Parent Company:

SALARIES/BENEFITS:

Pension Plan:	ESOP Stock Plan:	Profit Sharing:	Top Exec. Salary: $781,346	Bonus: $843,200
Savings Plan: Y	Stock Purch. Plan:		Second Exec. Salary: $562,038	Bonus: $447,300

OTHER THOUGHTS:

Apparent Women Officers or Directors: 2
Hot Spot for Advancement for Women/Minorities:

LOCATIONS: ("Y" = Yes)

West:	Southwest:	Midwest:	Southeast:	Northeast:	International:
Y	Y	Y	Y	Y	Y

CDW CORPORATION

www.cdw.com

Industry Group Code: 423430

Management:		**Sales/Marketing:**		**Liberal Arts:**		**Information Sys.:**		**Professionals:**		**Tech./Scientific:**	
Mgmt. Trainees:	Y	Marketing Pros.:	Y	Gen. Writing/Editing:	Y	Info. Mgmt.:	Y	Finance/Acct.:	Y	Engineers, Elec.:	
Experienced Mgmt.:	Y	Retail Sales:		Tech. Writing:	Y	Software Dev.:	Y	Law:	Y	Engineers, Other:	
Int'l Business:	Y	Comm./Industrial:	Y	Graphic Arts/Photog.:	Y	Hardware Dev.:		HR/Other:	Y	Health/Lab:	
MBA Grads:	Y	Sales Trainees:	Y	Music:		Consulting/Other:		Training:	Y	Science/Research:	
		Advertising Pros.:	Y	Broadcasting:				Health Care:		Petroleum/Chem.:	
				Other:				Consulting:		Math/Other:	

TYPES OF BUSINESS:

Computer Products, Direct Selling
Online Sales
Custom Installation & Repair-Computers

BRANDS/DIVISIONS/AFFILIATES:

CDW Government Inc
CDW Canada Inc
Providence Equity Partners LLC
Madison Dearborn Partners LLC

CONTACTS: *Note: Officers with more than one job title may be intentionally listed here more than once.*

John A. Edwardson, CEO
Thomas E. Richards, COO
Thomas E. Richards, Pres.
Ann E. Ziegler, CFO/Sr. VP
Neal J. Campbell, Chief Mktg. Officer/Sr. VP
Dennis G. Berger, Chief Coworker Svcs. Officer/Sr. VP
Jonathan J. Stevens, CIO
William T. Weaver, VP-Advanced Tech.
Matthew A. Troka, Sr. VP-Prod. & Partner Mgmt.
Christine A. Leahy, General Counsel/Sr. VP/Corp. Sec.
Jonathan J. Stevens, Sr. VP-Oper.
Douglas E. Eckrote, Sr. VP-Strategic Solutions & Svcs.
Vicky Bunker, Head-Investor Rel.
Virginia L. Seggerman, Controller/VP
Christina V. Rother, Sr. VP-Sales
Anne B. Ireland, VP-Sales Planning & Oper.
Robert J. Welyki, VP/Treas.
Collin B. Kebo, VP-Financial Planning & Analysis
John A. Edwardson, Chmn.

Phone: 847-465-6000 **Fax:** 847-465-6800
Toll-Free: 800-750-4239
Address: 200 N. Milwaukee Ave., Vernon Hills, IL 60061 US

GROWTH PLANS/SPECIAL FEATURES:

CDW Corporation, owned by private equity firms Madison Dearborn Partners LLC and Providence Equity Partners, Inc., is one of the leading providers of multi-branded information technology products and services to business, government and education customers in the U.S. and Canada. The firm offers over 100,000 products from 1,300 leading technology brands, in addition to customized solution design and management, with focus areas including notebooks, desktops, printers, servers and storage, unified communications, security, wireless, power and cooling, networking, software licensing and mobility solutions. The company manages its inventory through a 450,000-square-foot distribution center in Vernon Hills, Illinois, and a 513,000-square-foot distribution center in Las Vegas, Nevada, which ship approximately 2,000 custom-configured systems daily. CDW offers customers free access to certified technicians for telephone support and complete custom installation and repair services via the company's configuration center, in addition to access to a database of frequently asked technical questions and direct links to manufacturers' tech support web sites. Its CDW Government, Inc. subsidiary provides specialized product offerings and services to federal, state and local governments, as well as the educational sector. CDW Canada, Inc. serves commercial and public sector customers in Canada.

The company offers its employees medical, dental and vision insurance; a 401(k) plan; a profit sharing plan; life and AD&D insurance; flexible spending accounts; tuition reimbursement; short- and long-term disability insurance; and an employee assistance program.

FINANCIALS: **Sales and profits are in thousands of dollars—add 000 to get the full amount. 2010 Note: Financial information for 2010 was not available for all companies at press time.**

2010 Sales: $8,801,000 — 2010 Profits: $
2009 Sales: $8,000,000 — 2009 Profits: $
2008 Sales: $8,071,000 — 2008 Profits: $
2007 Sales: $8,145,000 — 2007 Profits: $
2006 Sales: $6,785,473 — 2006 Profits: $266,080

U.S. Stock Ticker: Private
Int'l Ticker:
Int'l Exchange:
Employees: 6,230 Fiscal Year Ends: 12/31
Parent Company: MADISON DEARBORN PARTNERS LLC

SALARIES/BENEFITS:

Pension Plan: ESOP Stock Plan: Profit Sharing: Y Top Exec. Salary: $ Bonus: $1,055,629
Savings Plan: Y Stock Purch. Plan: Second Exec. Salary: $ Bonus: $

OTHER THOUGHTS:

Apparent Women Officers or Directors: 12
Hot Spot for Advancement for Women/Minorities: Y

LOCATIONS: ("Y" = Yes)

West:	Southwest:	Midwest:	Southeast:	Northeast:	International:
Y	Y	Y		Y	Y

Sales, profits and employees may be estimates. Financial information, benefits and other data can change quickly and may vary from those stated here.

CELGENE CORP

Industry Group Code: 325412

www.celgene.com

Management:		Sales/Marketing:		Liberal Arts:		Information Sys.:		Professionals:		Tech./Scientific:	
Mgmt. Trainees:	Y	Marketing Pros.:	Y	Gen. Writing/Editing:		Info. Mgmt.:	Y	Finance/Acct.:	Y	Engineers, Elec.:	Y
Experienced Mgmt.:	Y	Retail Sales:		Tech. Writing:	Y	Software Dev.:	Y	Law:	Y	Engineers, Other:	Y
Int'l Business:	Y	Comm./Industrial:	Y	Graphic Arts/Photog.:	Y	Hardware Dev.:		HR/Other:	Y	Health/Lab:	Y
MBA Grads:	Y	Sales Trainees:		Music:		Consulting/Other:		Training:	Y	Science/Research:	Y
		Advertising Pros.:		Broadcasting:				Health Care:	Y	Petroleum/Chem.:	Y
				Other:				Consulting:		Math/Other:	Y

TYPES OF BUSINESS:

Cancer & Immune-Inflammatory Related Diseases Drugs

BRANDS/DIVISIONS/AFFILIATES:

Revlimid
Thalomid
Vidaza
Focalin
Gloucester Pharmaceuticals
Abraxis Bioscience, Inc.
CC-10004
CC-11050

CONTACTS: *Note: Officers with more than one job title may be intentionally listed here more than once.*

Robert J. Hugin, CEO
Perry Karsen, COO
Robert J. Hugin, Pres.
Jacqualyn A. Fouse, CFO/Sr. VP
Robert J. Hugin, Chmn.

Phone: 908-673-9000 | **Fax:** 732-271-4184
Toll-Free:
Address: 86 Morris Ave., Summit, NJ 07901 US

GROWTH PLANS/SPECIAL FEATURES:

Celgene Corp. is a global integrated biopharmaceutical company primarily engaged in the discovery, development and commercialization of therapies designed to treat cancer and immune-inflammatory related diseases. The company's commercial stage products are Revlimid, Thalomid, Vidaza, Istodax, Abraxane and Focalin. Revlimid has been approved by the U.S. FDA and other regulatory agencies in Europe, Latin America, the Middle East and Asia/Pacific for treatment in combination with dexamethasone for multiple myeloma patients who have received at least one prior therapy. In addition, Revlimid has been approved by the FDA and the Canadian Therapeutics Directorate for treatment of patients with transfusion-dependent anemia due to low- or intermediate-1-risk myelodysplastic syndromes (MDS) associated with a deletion 5q cytogenetic abnormality with or without additional cytogenetic abnormalities. Thalomid has been approved by the FDA for treatment in combination with dexamethasone for patients with newly diagnosed multiple myeloma and is also approved for the treatment and suppression of cutaneous manifestations of erythema nodosum leprosum (ENL), an inflammatory complication of leprosy. Vidaza is approved for treatment in patients with various myelodysplastic syndrome subtypes. Istodax, acquired in early 2010 through the acquisition of Gloucester Pharmaceuticals, is a histone deacetylase (HDAC) inhibitor approved by the FDA for the treatment of CTCL in patients who have received at least one prior systemic therapy. Abraxane is a form of chemotherapy that was acquired through the October 2010 acquisition of Abraxis Bioscience, Inc. Focalin, which is used to treat attention deficit hyperactivity disorder (ADHD), is sold exclusively to Novartis Pharma AG. Its portfolio of drug candidates includes IMiDs compounds, which are proprietary to the firm and have demonstrated certain immunomodulatory and other biologically important properties; CC-10004 and CC-11050, oral anti-inflammatory agents; and kinase inhibitors.

Employees are offered life, business accident, AD&D, medical, dental and vision insurance.

FINANCIALS: **Sales and profits are in thousands of dollars—add 000 to get the full amount. 2010 Note: Financial information for 2010 was not available for all companies at press time.**

2010 Sales: $3,625,745 | 2010 Profits: $880,512
2009 Sales: $2,689,893 | 2009 Profits: $766,747
2008 Sales: $2,254,781 | 2008 Profits: $-1,533,653
2007 Sales: $1,405,820 | 2007 Profits: $226,433
2006 Sales: $898,873 | 2006 Profits: $68,981

U.S. Stock Ticker: CELG
Int'l Ticker:
Int'l Exchange:
Employees: 4,182 Fiscal Year Ends: 12/31
Parent Company:

SALARIES/BENEFITS:

Pension Plan: | ESOP Stock Plan: | Profit Sharing: | Top Exec. Salary: $1,127,000 | Bonus: $3,334,926
Savings Plan: Y | Stock Purch. Plan: | Second Exec. Salary: $889,375 | Bonus: $2,646,999

OTHER THOUGHTS:

Apparent Women Officers or Directors: 3
Hot Spot for Advancement for Women/Minorities: Y

LOCATIONS: ("Y" = Yes)

West:	Southwest:	Midwest:	Southeast:	Northeast:	International:
Y				Y	Y

Sales, profits and employees may be estimates. Financial information, benefits and other data can change quickly and may vary from those stated here.

CELLCO PARTNERSHIP (VERIZON WIRELESS)

www.verizonwireless.com

Industry Group Code: 5172

Management:		Sales/Marketing:		Liberal Arts:		Information Sys.:		Professionals:		Tech./Scientific:	
Mgmt. Trainees:	Y	Marketing Pros.:	Y	Gen. Writing/Editing:	Y	Info. Mgmt.:	Y	Finance/Acct.:	Y	Engineers, Elec.:	Y
Experienced Mgmt.:	Y	Retail Sales:	Y	Tech. Writing:	Y	Software Dev.:	Y	Law:	Y	Engineers, Other:	Y
Int'l Business:		Comm./Industrial:	Y	Graphic Arts/Photog.:	Y	Hardware Dev.:		HR/Other:	Y	Health/Lab:	
MBA Grads:	Y	Sales Trainees:	Y	Music:		Consulting/Other:		Training:	Y	Science/Research:	
		Advertising Pros.:	Y	Broadcasting:				Health Care:		Petroleum/Chem.:	
				Other:	Y			Consulting:		Math/Other:	

TYPES OF BUSINESS:

Cell Phone Service
Retail Sales
Wireless Internet
Media & Ringtones

BRANDS/DIVISIONS/AFFILIATES:

Verizon Wireless
Verizon Communications Inc
Vodafone Group PLC
Alltel Corporation
nPhase
Qualcomm Inc
VCAST
Get It Now

CONTACTS: *Note: Officers with more than one job title may be intentionally listed here more than once.*

Daniel S. Mead, CEO
John Stratton, COO/Exec. VP
Daniel S. Mead, Pres.
Andrew Davies, CFO/VP
Marni Walden, Chief Mktg. Officer/VP
M. Alan Gardner, VP-Human Resources
Ajay Waghray, CIO
David Small, CTO/VP
Steve Zipperstein, General Counsel/VP-Legal & External Affairs
Margaret Feldman, VP-Bus. Dev.
Marquett Smith, VP-Corp. Comm.
Mark Bartolomeo, VP-Global Enterprise Sales
Christopher Felix, VP-Federal Gov't Sales
Mike Lanman, Pres., Enterprise & Govt. Markets
Brian Stacy, VP-Bus. Service Centers & Gov't Support

Phone: 908-559-7000	**Fax:**
Toll-Free: 800-922-0204	
Address: 1 Verizon Way, Basking Ridge, NJ 07920 US	

GROWTH PLANS/SPECIAL FEATURES:

Cellco Partnership, doing business as Verizon Wireless, is a joint venture between Verizon Communications and Vodafone, which own 55% and 45% of Cellco, respectively. Verizon Wireless was formed in 2000 when Vodafone and Bell Atlantic merged their U.S. wireless holdings. The company then acquired the U.S. wireless assets of GTE, when Bell Atlantic bought GTE to create Verizon Communications. The firm has approximately 102.2 million customers and operates over 2,000 company stores and kiosks and 175 switching centers. In addition to wireless voice and messaging services, the company offers mobile broadband plans for laptop, smartphones and other devices; VCAST Music service for downloading music and music videos; VCAST Apps service for downloading smartphone applications; and Get It Now for text and picture messaging, downloading ringtones, ringback tones, games and news alerts. Additionally, the company maintains a joint venture, nPhase, with Qualcomm, Inc. to provide machine-to-machine (M2M) wireless communication solutions. Recently, the firm acquired Alltel Corporation, which significantly expanded its network coverage. As part of the Alltel acquisitions, Verizon divested overlapping properties in 105 operating markets. In March 2010, the company announced an agreement with Skype Mobile to make free Skype international calls available on Verizon smartphones. In August 2010, the firm completed the acquisition of six operating markets in Louisiana and Mississippi, formerly part of Centennial Communications Corp., from AT&T. In December 2010, it launched the initial phase of its 4G LTE network in 38 U.S. markets and 60 airports, with plans to increase its 4G network coverage by 140 markets in 2011.

The company provides its employees with medical, dental, vision and prescription drug coverage; life insurance; adoption assistance; health and dependent care spending accounts; phone discounts; childcare discounts; an employee assistance program; tuition assistance; a 401(k) plan; and a profit sharing plan.

FINANCIALS: **Sales and profits are in thousands of dollars—add 000 to get the full amount. 2010 Note: Financial information for 2010 was not available for all companies at press time.**

2010 Sales: $63,407,000	2010 Profits: $18,724,000
2009 Sales: $62,131,000	2009 Profits: $14,684,000
2008 Sales: $49,332,000	2008 Profits: $13,289,000
2007 Sales: $43,882,000	2007 Profits: $10,860,000
2006 Sales: $38,000,000	2006 Profits: $

U.S. Stock Ticker: Joint Venture
Int'l Ticker:
Int'l Exchange:
Employees: 82,000 Fiscal Year Ends: 12/31
Parent Company:

SALARIES/BENEFITS:

Pension Plan:	ESOP Stock Plan:	Profit Sharing: Y	Top Exec. Salary: $825,000	Bonus: $696,094
Savings Plan: Y	Stock Purch. Plan:		Second Exec. Salary: $526,923	Bonus: $500,084

OTHER THOUGHTS:

Apparent Women Officers or Directors: 6
Hot Spot for Advancement for Women/Minorities: Y

LOCATIONS: ("Y" = Yes)

West:	Southwest:	Midwest:	Southeast:	Northeast:	International:
Y	Y	Y	Y	Y	

CEPHALON INC

www.cephalon.com

Industry Group Code: 325412

Management:		Sales/Marketing:		Liberal Arts:		Information Sys.:		Professionals:		Tech./Scientific:	
Mgmt. Trainees:	Y	Marketing Pros.:	Y	Gen. Writing/Editing:		Info. Mgmt.:	Y	Finance/Acct.:	Y	Engineers, Elec.:	Y
Experienced Mgmt.:	Y	Retail Sales:		Tech. Writing:	Y	Software Dev.:	Y	Law:	Y	Engineers, Other:	Y
Int'l Business:	Y	Comm./Industrial:	Y	Graphic Arts/Photog.:	Y	Hardware Dev.:		HR/Other:	Y	Health/Lab:	Y
MBA Grads:	Y	Sales Trainees:		Music:		Consulting/Other:		Training:	Y	Science/Research:	Y
		Advertising Pros.:		Broadcasting:				Health Care:	Y	Petroleum/Chem.:	Y
				Other:				Consulting:		Math/Other:	Y

TYPES OF BUSINESS:

Pharmaceutical Discovery & Development
Neurological Disorder Treatments
Cancer Treatments
Pain Medications
Addiction Treatment

BRANDS/DIVISIONS/AFFILIATES:

Nuvigil
Provigil
Gabitril
Amrix
Fentora
Actiq
Treanda
Teva Pharmaceutical Industries Ltd

CONTACTS: *Note: Officers with more than one job title may be intentionally listed here more than once.*

J. Kevin Buchi, CEO
Wilco Groenhuysen, CFO/Exec. VP
Jeffry L. Vaught, Chief Scientific Officer/Exec. VP
Peter E. Grebow, Exec. VP-Worldwide Tech. Oper.
Carl A. Savini, Chief Admin. Officer/Exec. VP
Gerald J. Pappert, General Counsel/Exec. VP
Lesley Russell, Chief Medical Officer/Exec. VP
Valli F. Baldassano, Chief Compliance Officer/Exec. VP
William P. Egan, Chmn.
Alain Aragues, Pres., Cephalon Europe/Exec. VP

Phone: 610-344-0200	**Fax:** 610-738-6590
Toll-Free:	
Address: 41 Moores Rd., Frazer, PA 19355 US	

GROWTH PLANS/SPECIAL FEATURES:

Cephalon, Inc. is a biopharmaceutical company. It is focused on the discovery, development and marketing of products in four core areas: central nervous system (CNS) disorders, pain, oncology and inflammatory disease. The company's CNS products include Nuvigil and Provigil for improving wakefulness in patients with excessive sleepiness associated with narcolepsy, obstructive sleep apnea/hypopnea syndrome (OSA/HS) and shift work sleep disorder (SWSD); and Gabitril for use as adjunctive therapy in the treatment of partial seizures in epileptic patients. The firm's pain therapeutics portfolio includes three marketed products in the U.S.: Amrix, a once-a-day, extended release version of cyclobenzaprine hydrochloride for relief of muscle spasms associated with acute, painful musculoskeletal conditions; Fentora for the management of breakthrough pain in patients with cancer; and Actiq and generic OTFC for the management of breakthrough cancer pain in opioid-tolerant patients. Cephalon's oncology products include two marketed products to treat patients with hematologic cancers: Treanda, a bi-functional hybrid cytotoxic; and Trisenox, an intravenous arsenic-based targeted therapy currently marketed in the U.S. and Europe. The firm also has two commercialized oncology products in Europe: Myocet, a cardio-protective chemotherapy agent used to treat metastatic breast cancer; and Targretin, a treatment for cutaneous T-cell lymphoma. Lastly, the firm's inflammatory disease products include Lupuzor, which is currently in a Phase IIb study; CEP-37247, a treatment for patients with sciatica in Phase I and II studies; and Cinquil, an antibody for interleukin-5 (IL-5) in Phase II trials. The firm markets and sells over 150 different branded products in nearly 100 countries. In 2010, the firm acquired Mepha AG, BioAssets Development Corporation and Ception Therapeutics, Inc. In April 2011, Cephalon acquired Gemin X Pharmaceuticals, Inc. In May 2011, the company agreed to be acquired by Israeli firm Teva Pharmaceutical Industries Ltd. for $6.8 billion.

FINANCIALS: **Sales and profits are in thousands of dollars—add 000 to get the full amount. 2010 Note: Financial information for 2010 was not available for all companies at press time.**

2010 Sales: $2,811,057	2010 Profits: $417,683	**U.S. Stock Ticker: CEPH**
2009 Sales: $2,192,308	2009 Profits: $210,727	**Int'l Ticker:**
2008 Sales: $1,974,554	2008 Profits: $171,889	Int'l Exchange:
2007 Sales: $1,772,638	2007 Profits: $-226,429	Employees: 3,726 Fiscal Year Ends: 12/31
2006 Sales: $1,764,069	2006 Profits: $144,816	Parent Company:

SALARIES/BENEFITS:

Pension Plan:	ESOP Stock Plan:	Profit Sharing: Y	Top Exec. Salary: $1,295,093	Bonus: $2,113,200
Savings Plan: Y	Stock Purch. Plan: Y		Second Exec. Salary: $690,800	Bonus: $665,000

OTHER THOUGHTS:

Apparent Women Officers or Directors: 3
Hot Spot for Advancement for Women/Minorities: Y

LOCATIONS: ("Y" = Yes)

West:	Southwest:	Midwest:	Southeast:	Northeast:	International:
Y		Y		Y	Y

CERNER CORP

www.cerner.com

Industry Group Code: 511210D

Management:		Sales/Marketing:		Liberal Arts:		Information Sys.:		Professionals:		Tech./Scientific:	
Mgmt. Trainees:	Y	Marketing Pros.:	Y	Gen. Writing/Editing:	Y	Info. Mgmt.:	Y	Finance/Acct.:	Y	Engineers, Elec.:	Y
Experienced Mgmt.:	Y	Retail Sales:		Tech. Writing:	Y	Software Dev.:	Y	Law:	Y	Engineers, Other:	
Int'l Business:	Y	Comm./Industrial:	Y	Graphic Arts/Photog.:	Y	Hardware Dev.:		HR/Other:	Y	Health/Lab:	
MBA Grads:	Y	Sales Trainees:		Music:		Consulting/Other:	Y	Training:	Y	Science/Research:	Y
		Advertising Pros.:	Y	Broadcasting:				Health Care:	Y	Petroleum/Chem.:	
				Other:				Consulting:	Y	Math/Other:	Y

TYPES OF BUSINESS:

Software-Clinical
Medical Information Systems
Application Hosting
Integrated Delivery Networks
Access Management
Consulting Services
Safety & Risk Management

BRANDS/DIVISIONS/AFFILIATES:

Cerner Millennium
CareAware
CernerWorks
Lights On Network
IMC Health, Inc.

CONTACTS: *Note: Officers with more than one job title may be intentionally listed here more than once.*

Neal Patterson, CEO
Michael Nill, COO/Exec. VP
Neal Patterson, Pres.
Marc G. Naughton, CFO/Exec. VP
Julia M. Wilson, Chief People Officer/Sr. VP
Paul N. Gorup, Chief of Innovation/Sr. VP
Randy Sims, Chief Legal Officer/Sr. VP/Sec.
Kelli Christman, Contact-Media Rel.
Allan Kells, Contact-Investor Rel.
Clifford Illig, Vice Chmn.
Rob Campbell, Chief Learning Officer/VP
Jeffrey A. Townsend, Chief of Staff/Exec. VP
Zane Burke, Exec. VP-Client Organization
Neal Patterson, Chmn.
Bryan Ince, VP-Australia IP Strategy

Phone: 816-221-1024 **Fax:** 816-474-1742
Toll-Free:
Address: 2800 Rockcreek Pkwy., Kansas City, MO 64117 US

GROWTH PLANS/SPECIAL FEATURES:

Cerner Corp. designs, develops, installs and supports information technology and content applications for health care organizations, consumers and physicians. Cerner's applications are designed to help eliminate error, variance and waste in the care process, as well as provide appropriate health information and knowledge to care givers, clinicians and consumers, and appropriate management information to health care administrations. The company's software applications have been designed and developed on the unified Cerner Millennium architecture. The framework combines clinical, financial and management information systems and provides secure access to an individual's electronic medical record at the point of care, and organizes and proactively delivers information to meet the specific needs of the physician, nurse, laboratory technician, pharmacist or other care provider, front- and back-office professionals as well as consumers. Cerner's CareAware device architecture is designed to bridge the gap between medical devices and patient information by connecting information from various devices to the clinician workflow and electronic medical record. Cerner also offers a broad range of services including implementation and training, remote hosting, support and maintenance, healthcare data analysis and clinical process optimization. CernerWorks is the company's remote-hosting business. LightsOn Network, with more than 300 clients, monitors client-hosted and Cerner-hosted systems in near real-time. Roughly 9,000 facilities around the world license the company's products. These facilities include over 2,600 hospitals; 3,500 physician practices covering more than 30,000 physicians; 500 ambulatory facilities such as laboratories, ambulatory centers, cardiac facilities, radiology clinics and surgery centers; 800 home health facilities; and 1,600 retail pharmacies. The firm recently acquired IMC Health, Inc. In May 2011, Cerner Corp. agreed to acquire point-of-care electronic documentation system developer Resource Systems.

The company offers employees life, medical, dental and vision insurance; a 401(k) plan; flexible spending accounts; an employee stock purchase plan; and an employee assistance program.

FINANCIALS: **Sales and profits are in thousands of dollars—add 000 to get the full amount. 2010 Note: Financial information for 2010 was not available for all companies at press time.**

2010 Sales: $1,850,222 | 2010 Profits: $237,272
2009 Sales: $1,671,864 | 2009 Profits: $193,465
2008 Sales: $1,676,028 | 2008 Profits: $188,658
2007 Sales: $1,519,877 | 2007 Profits: $127,125
2006 Sales: $1,378,038 | 2006 Profits: $109,891

U.S. Stock Ticker: CERN
Int'l Ticker:
Int'l Exchange:
Employees: 8,200 Fiscal Year Ends: 12/30
Parent Company:

SALARIES/BENEFITS:

Pension Plan: ESOP Stock Plan: Profit Sharing: Top Exec. Salary: $1,005,385 Bonus: $1,263,450
Savings Plan: Y Stock Purch. Plan: Y Second Exec. Salary: $451,538 Bonus: $494,100

OTHER THOUGHTS:

Apparent Women Officers or Directors: 8
Hot Spot for Advancement for Women/Minorities: Y

LOCATIONS: ("Y" = Yes)

West:	Southwest:	Midwest:	Southeast:	Northeast:	International:
Y	Y	Y	Y	Y	Y

CH ROBINSON WORLDWIDE INC

www.chrobinson.com

Industry Group Code: 4885

Management:		Sales/Marketing:		Liberal Arts:		Information Sys.:		Professionals:		Tech./Scientific:	
Mgmt. Trainees:	Y	Marketing Pros.:	Y	Gen. Writing/Editing:	Y	Info. Mgmt.:	Y	Finance/Acct.:	Y	Engineers, Elec.:	
Experienced Mgmt.:	Y	Retail Sales:		Tech. Writing:	Y	Software Dev.:	Y	Law:	Y	Engineers, Other:	
Int'l Business:	Y	Comm./Industrial:	Y	Graphic Arts/Photog.:		Hardware Dev.:		HR/Other:	Y	Health/Lab:	
MBA Grads:	Y	Sales Trainees:		Music:		Consulting/Other:		Training:	Y	Science/Research:	
		Advertising Pros.:	Y	Broadcasting:				Health Care:		Petroleum/Chem.:	
				Other:				Consulting:		Math/Other:	

TYPES OF BUSINESS:

Freight Logistics
Produce Sourcing
Expedited Services
Fuel Purchasing Management Services
3PL Third Party Logistics

BRANDS/DIVISIONS/AFFILIATES:

T-Chek Systems, Inc.
Fresh 1 (The)
OurWorld
C.H. Robinson Sourcing SAS
Walker Logistics Overseas, Ltd.
Rosemont Farms Corporation, Inc.
Quality Logistics LLC
Transportation Management Center

CONTACTS: *Note: Officers with more than one job title may be intentionally listed here more than once.*

John P. Wiehoff, CEO
Chad M. Lindbloom, CFO/Sr. VP
Laura Gillund, VP-Human Resources
Thomas K. Mahlke, CIO/VP
Ben G. Campbell, General Counsel/VP/Sec.
Angela K. Freeman, VP-Public Rel.
Angela K. Freeman, VP-Investor Rel.
Troy A. Renner, Treas.
James E. Butts, Sr. VP
Bryan D. Foe, Pres., T-Chek
James P. Lemke, Sr. VP-Produce
Timothy P. Manning, VP
John P. Wiehoff, Chmn.

Phone: 952-937-8500 **Fax:** 952-937-6714
Toll-Free:
Address: 14701 Charlson Rd., Eden Prairie, MN 55347 US

GROWTH PLANS/SPECIAL FEATURES:

C.H. Robinson Worldwide, Inc. (CHRW) is one of the largest third-party logistics (3PL) providers and a global provider of multimodal transportation services. It operates through over 230 offices in the U.S., Canada, Mexico, Europe, South America, Australia, the Middle East and Asia. CHRW operates in three sectors: multimodal transportation services; fresh produce sourcing; and information services. In the multimodal transportation services sector, the company (which does not own any of its own equipment) maintains one of the largest global networks of motor carrier capacity through contracts with approximately 47,000 carriers. CHRW serves more than 35,000 customers and handles approximately 9.2 million shipments annually. The group also contracts air carriers, oceans carriers and specialty motor carriers. As part of its transportation solutions, the company also provides value-added logistics services, supply chain analysis, freight consolidation, core carrier program management, and information reporting. The sourcing sector focuses on procuring fresh produce for retailers, wholesalers and foodservice operators nationwide. CHRW has its own brands of produce called The Fresh 1 and OurWorld, which are sourced through various growers and packed through contract agreements with other packaging firms. The information services segment operates primarily through subsidiary T-Chek Systems, Inc., which offers funds transfer, fuel purchasing and online expense management services for motor carriers. Recently, the firm acquired Walker Logistics Overseas, Ltd., a London-based freight forwarder; opened a produce sourcing firm in France, C.H. Robinson Sourcing, SAS; and acquired two jointly-owned produce companies: Rosemont Farms Corporation, Inc., and Quality Logistics LLC. In November 2010, Transportation Management Center (TMC), a division of the company, added a control tower operations center in Mumbai, India.

Employees are offered medical, dental and vision insurance; a 401(k) plan; profit sharing; an employee stock purchase plan; flexible spending accounts; life and disability insurance; an employee assistance plan; and employee discounts.

FINANCIALS: **Sales and profits are in thousands of dollars—add 000 to get the full amount. 2010 Note: Financial information for 2010 was not available for all companies at press time.**

2010 Sales: $9,274,305 — 2010 Profits: $387,026
2009 Sales: $7,577,189 — 2009 Profits: $360,830
2008 Sales: $8,578,614 — 2008 Profits: $359,177
2007 Sales: $7,316,223 — 2007 Profits: $324,261
2006 Sales: $6,556,194 — 2006 Profits: $266,925

U.S. Stock Ticker: CHRW
Int'l Ticker:
Int'l Exchange:
Employees: 7,628 Fiscal Year Ends: 12/31
Parent Company:

SALARIES/BENEFITS:

Pension Plan: — ESOP Stock Plan: — Profit Sharing: Y — Top Exec. Salary: $400,000 — Bonus: $1,322,975
Savings Plan: Y — Stock Purch. Plan: Y — Second Exec. Salary: $260,000 — Bonus: $374,380

OTHER THOUGHTS:

Apparent Women Officers or Directors: 4
Hot Spot for Advancement for Women/Minorities: Y

LOCATIONS: ("Y" = Yes)

West:	Southwest:	Midwest:	Southeast:	Northeast:	International:
Y	Y	Y	Y	Y	Y

CHEMED CORPORATION

www.chemed.com

Industry Group Code: 6216

Management:		Sales/Marketing:		Liberal Arts:		Information Sys.:		Professionals:		Tech./Scientific:	
Mgmt. Trainees:	Y	Marketing Pros.:	Y	Gen. Writing/Editing:	Y	Info. Mgmt.:	Y	Finance/Acct.:	Y	Engineers, Elec.:	
Experienced Mgmt.:	Y	Retail Sales:		Tech. Writing:	Y	Software Dev.:		Law:	Y	Engineers, Other:	
Int'l Business:	Y	Comm./Industrial:	Y	Graphic Arts/Photog.:	Y	Hardware Dev.:		HR/Other:	Y	Health/Lab:	Y
MBA Grads:	Y	Sales Trainees:	Y	Music:		Consulting/Other:		Training:	Y	Science/Research:	
		Advertising Pros.:		Broadcasting:				Health Care:	Y	Petroleum/Chem.:	
				Other:	Y			Consulting:		Math/Other:	

TYPES OF BUSINESS:

Hospice & Home Health Care Services
Plumbing Services

BRANDS/DIVISIONS/AFFILIATES:

Vitas Healthcare Corporation
Roto-Rooter Corporation
Family Comfort Hospice

CONTACTS: *Note: Officers with more than one job title may be intentionally listed here more than once.*

Kevin J. McNamara, CEO
Kevin J. McNamara, Pres.
David P. Williams, CFO/Exec. VP
Lisa A. Reinhard, Chief Admin. Officer/VP
Thomas C. Hutton, VP/Attorney
Arthur V. Tucker, Jr., Controller/VP
Tim S. O'Toole, Exec. VP/CEO-VITAS Healthcare Corp.
Spencer S. Lee, Exec. VP/CEO-Roto-Rooter Mgmt. Company
Naomi C. Dallob, Chief Legal Officer/Sec./VP
Thomas J. Reilly, VP
George J. Walsh, III, Chmn.

Phone: 513-762-6900	**Fax:** 513-762-6919
Toll-Free:	
Address: 255 E. 5th St., 2600 Chemed Ctr., Cincinnati, OH 45202-4726 US	

GROWTH PLANS/SPECIAL FEATURES:

Chemed Corporation, through its wholly-owned subsidiaries VITAS Healthcare Corporation and Roto-Rooter Corporation, offers hospice care and plumbing services, respectively. VITAS, which generates about 72% of Chemed's service revenues, is one of the largest national providers of hospice care and end-of-life services. It cares for approximately 12,000 patients daily either in their own homes or through the subsidiary's 135 leased and 32 inpatient hospice programs at hospitals, nursing homes and assisted-living facilities in 15 states and Washington, D.C. Of this group's revenues, the largest share (72 %) is generated by routine homecare services, followed by continuous care (17%) and general inpatient services (11%). More than 90% of VITAS' service revenues consist of payments from Medicare and Medicaid. Subsidiary Roto-Rooter, 28% of service revenues and sales, supports the maintenance needs of residential and commercial markets by providing services such as plumbing, drain cleaning, high-pressure water jetting, underground leak and line detection, video camera pipe inspections, grease trap and liquid waste pumping, backflow protection, emergency services, automated drain care programs and pipe repair and replacement. One of the largest businesses of its type in North America, Roto-Rooter operates through more than 110 company-owned branch and independent contractors, as well as more than 400 franchisees in 27 U.S. states and Canada, which combined grant it access to almost 90% of the U.S. population and 40% of the Canadian population. Additionally, the subsidiary has licensed master franchisees in Japan, the Philippines, Indonesia and Singapore. Of this group's revenues, the largest share (48%) is generated by plumbing repair and maintenance, followed by sewer and drain cleaning (38%), independent contractors (6%), HVAC (heating, ventilation and air conditioning) repair and maintenance (1%) and other products and services (7%). In April 2011, VITAS acquired Alabama-based hospice provider Family Comfort Hospice.

FINANCIALS: **Sales and profits are in thousands of dollars—add 000 to get the full amount. 2010 Note: Financial information for 2010 was not available for all companies at press time.**

2010 Sales: $1,280,545	2010 Profits: $81,831
2009 Sales: $1,190,236	2009 Profits: $73,784
2008 Sales: $1,148,941	2008 Profits: $71,017
2007 Sales: $1,100,058	2007 Profits: $63,976
2006 Sales: $1,018,587	2006 Profits: $50,651

U.S. Stock Ticker: CHE
Int'l Ticker:
Int'l Exchange:
Employees: 13,058 Fiscal Year Ends: 12/31
Parent Company:

SALARIES/BENEFITS:

Pension Plan: Y	ESOP Stock Plan:	Profit Sharing:	Top Exec. Salary: $783,917	Bonus: $1,400,000
Savings Plan:	Stock Purch. Plan: Y		Second Exec. Salary: $568,833	Bonus: $465,000

OTHER THOUGHTS:

Apparent Women Officers or Directors: 2
Hot Spot for Advancement for Women/Minorities: Y

LOCATIONS: ("Y" = Yes)

West:	Southwest:	Midwest:	Southeast:	Northeast:	International:
Y	Y	Y	Y	Y	

CHEVRON CORPORATION

www.chevron.com

Industry Group Code: 211111

Management:		**Sales/Marketing:**		**Liberal Arts:**		**Information Sys.:**		**Professionals:**		**Tech./Scientific:**	
Mgmt. Trainees:	Y	Marketing Pros.:	Y	Gen. Writing/Editing:	Y	Info. Mgmt.:	Y	Finance/Acct.:	Y	Engineers, Elec.:	Y
Experienced Mgmt.:	Y	Retail Sales:		Tech. Writing:	Y	Software Dev.:	Y	Law:	Y	Engineers, Other:	Y
Int'l Business:	Y	Comm./Industrial:	Y	Graphic Arts/Photog.:	Y	Hardware Dev.:		HR/Other:	Y	Health/Lab:	
MBA Grads:	Y	Sales Trainees:	Y	Music:		Consulting/Other:		Training:	Y	Science/Research:	Y
		Advertising Pros.:	Y	Broadcasting:				Health Care:		Petroleum/Chem.:	Y
				Other:				Consulting:		Math/Other:	Y

TYPES OF BUSINESS:

Oil & Gas Exploration & Production
Power Generation
Petrochemicals
Gasoline Retailing
Coal Mining
Fuel & Oil Additives
Convenience Stores
Pipelines

BRANDS/DIVISIONS/AFFILIATES:

Texaco
Youngs Creek Mining Company LLC
Chevron Phillips Chemical Company
Caltex
Chevron Technology Ventures
Chevron Limited
Atlas Energy, Inc.

CONTACTS: *Note: Officers with more than one job title may be intentionally listed here more than once.*

John S. Watson, CEO
Patricia E. Yarrington, CFO/VP
Joe W. Laymon, VP-Human Resources
John W. McDonald, CTO/VP
R. Hewitt Pate, General Counsel/VP
Jay R. Pryor, VP-Corp. Bus. Dev.
Stephen W. Green, VP-Policy, Gov't & Public Affairs
Pierre R. Breber, Treas./VP
Michael K. Wirth, Exec. VP-Global Downstream & Chemicals
George L. Kirkland, Exec. VP-Global Upstream & Gas/Vice Chmn.
John D. Gass, VP/Pres., Global Gas
Charles A. Taylor, Exec. VP-Strategic Planning
John S. Watson, Chmn.

Phone: 925-842-1000 **Fax:** 925-842-3530
Toll-Free:
Address: 6001 Bollinger Canyon Rd., San Ramon, CA 94583-2324 US

GROWTH PLANS/SPECIAL FEATURES:

Chevron Corporation is an integrated energy company that conducts refining, marketing and transportation operations and, to a lesser degree, chemical operations, mining operations and power generation. Refining operations maintains a refining network capable of processing more than 2 million barrels of crude oil per day. Marketing operations operates primarily under the brands Chevron, Texaco and Caltex. In the U.S., the company markets under the Chevron and Texaco brands. The company supplies directly or through retailers and marketers approximately 8,250 Chevron- and Texaco-branded motor vehicle retail outlets. Outside the U.S., the firm supplies approximately 11,300 branded service stations, including affiliates. Transportation operations maintains the Chevron owned and operated system of crude oil, refined products, chemicals, natural gas liquids and natural gas pipelines in the U.S. The company also has direct or indirect interests in other U.S. and international pipelines. Chemical operations include the manufacturing and marketing of fuel and lubricating oil additives and commodity petrochemicals through Chevron Phillips Chemical Company (CPChem), a joint venture company. CPChem operates manufacturing and research facilities in five countries. Mining operations produces and markets coal and molybdenum. The firm owns three coal mines and controls a 50% interest in Youngs Creek Mining Company LLC. The power generation business develops and operates commercial power projects. The company manages the production of more than 3,100 megawatts (MW) of electricity at 13 facilities it owns through joint ventures. Additionally, Chevron operates gas-fired cogeneration facilities that use waste heat recovery to produce additional electricity or to support industrial thermal hosts. In September 2010, the firm acquired 70% ownership in three deepwater concessions in Liberia; and 50% ownership in a block in the Black Sea. In February 2011, the company acquired Atlas Energy, Inc. for $3.2 billion. In March 2011, Chevron agreed to sell Chevron Limited and the Pembroke Refinery to Valero Energy Corporation.

FINANCIALS: **Sales and profits are in thousands of dollars—add 000 to get the full amount. 2010 Note: Financial information for 2010 was not available for all companies at press time.**

2010 Sales: $204,928,000 — 2010 Profits: $19,136,000
2009 Sales: $171,636,000 — 2009 Profits: $10,483,000
2008 Sales: $273,005,000 — 2008 Profits: $23,931,000
2007 Sales: $220,904,000 — 2007 Profits: $18,688,000
2006 Sales: $210,118,000 — 2006 Profits: $17,138,000

U.S. Stock Ticker: CVX
Int'l Ticker:
Int'l Exchange:
Employees: 62,000 Fiscal Year Ends: 12/31
Parent Company:

SALARIES/BENEFITS:

Pension Plan: Y	ESOP Stock Plan:	Profit Sharing:	Top Exec. Salary: $1,793,750	Bonus: $3,000,000
Savings Plan: Y	Stock Purch. Plan:		Second Exec. Salary: $946,042	Bonus: $1,260,000

OTHER THOUGHTS:

Apparent Women Officers or Directors: 3
Hot Spot for Advancement for Women/Minorities: Y

LOCATIONS: ("Y" = Yes)

West:	Southwest:	Midwest:	Southeast:	Northeast:	International:
Y	Y	Y	Y	Y	Y

Sales, profits and employees may be estimates. Financial information, benefits and other data can change quickly and may vary from those stated here.

CHEVRON PHILLIPS CHEMICAL COMPANY LLC www.cpchem.com

Industry Group Code: 325110

Management:		Sales/Marketing:		Liberal Arts:		Information Sys.:		Professionals:		Tech./Scientific:	
Mgmt. Trainees:	Y	Marketing Pros.:	Y	Gen. Writing/Editing:	Y	Info. Mgmt.:	Y	Finance/Acct.:	Y	Engineers, Elec.:	Y
Experienced Mgmt.:	Y	Retail Sales:		Tech. Writing:	Y	Software Dev.:	Y	Law:	Y	Engineers, Other:	Y
Int'l Business:	Y	Comm./Industrial:	Y	Graphic Arts/Photog.:		Hardware Dev.:		HR/Other:	Y	Health/Lab:	
MBA Grads:	Y	Sales Trainees:		Music:		Consulting/Other:		Training:	Y	Science/Research:	Y
		Advertising Pros.:		Broadcasting:				Health Care:		Petroleum/Chem.:	Y
				Other:				Consulting:		Math/Other:	

TYPES OF BUSINESS:

Petrochemical & Plastics Manufacturing
Olefins & Polyolefins
Aromatics & Styrenics
Specialty Chemicals

BRANDS/DIVISIONS/AFFILIATES:

K-Resin
Aromax
Ryton
TrackTek
Chevron Corporation
ConocoPhillips

CONTACTS: *Note: Officers with more than one job title may be intentionally listed here more than once.*

Peter Cella, CEO
Tim Taylor, COO
Peter Cella, Pres.
Greg Maxwell, CFO/Sr. VP/Controller
Chantal Veevaete, VP-Human Resources
Peggy Colsman, CIO
Mary Jane Hagenson, VP-Tech.
Rick Roberts, Sr. VP-Mfg.
Tim Hill, General Counsel/Sr. VP/Corp. Sec.
Tim Roberts, VP-Corp. Planning & Dev.
Brian Cain, Head-Corp. Comm.
Trevor Roberts, Treas.
Mark Lashier, Sr. VP-Specialties, Aromatics & Styrenics
Mark Haney, Exec. VP-Olefins & Polyolefins
Scott Sharp, VP-Environment, Health, Safety & Security
Dave S. Smith, VP-Polyethylene

Phone: 832-813-4100 **Fax:**
Toll-Free: 800-231-1212
Address: 10001 Six Pines Dr., The Woodlands, TX 77380 US

GROWTH PLANS/SPECIAL FEATURES:

Chevron Phillips Chemical Company LLC (CPChem) is the combined petrochemical businesses of Chevron Corporation and ConocoPhillips, both 50% owners. With 36 production and research centers in nine countries, CPChem is an international producer of olefins and polyolefins. It is also a supplier of aromatics, alpha olefins, styrenics, specialty chemicals, polyethylene pipe and proprietary plastics. The company manufactures chemical products that are vital in the various production processes of over 70,000 consumer and industrial products. Its mix of petrochemical and plastics businesses is segmented into two divisions: olefins and polyolefins; and aromatics, styrenics specialty products. Products in the olefins and polyolefins family consist of ethylene, propylene and their polymer derivatives; olefins and polyalpha olefins; and high-density polyethylene pipe, conduit and pipe fitting. These products are sold as building blocks for other chemicals and as ingredients for use in a variety of end-products including motor oils, lubricants, plastics, coatings, textiles and packaging. CPChem's aromatics and styrenics include cyclohexane, paraxylene, benzene, styrene, polystyrene and K-Resin SBC, a unique type of copolymer. Aromax is the company's proprietary benzene production process. The aromatics and styrenics are used in the manufacturing of insulation products, housewares, food packaging, electronic parts and media enclosures. Its specialty chemicals are used in various applications, including electronics, automobiles, oil and gas well drilling, appliances, agriculture and pharmaceuticals. This division sells TrackTek brand racing fuels and Soltex drill mud additive. Olefins and polyolefins account for roughly 66% of CPChem's sales; specialties, aromatics and styrenics account for 34%.

Employees are offered medical, dental and vision benefits; educational assistance; an employee assistance program; discounts on personal items; and relocation assistance.

FINANCIALS: **Sales and profits are in thousands of dollars—add 000 to get the full amount. 2010 Note: Financial information for 2010 was not available for all companies at press time.**

2010 Sales: $11,204,000 2010 Profits: $1,388,000
2009 Sales: $8,406,000 2009 Profits: $615,000
2008 Sales: $12,646,000 2008 Profits: $276,000
2007 Sales: $12,534,000 2007 Profits: $719,000
2006 Sales: $11,839,000 2006 Profits: $1,349,000

U.S. Stock Ticker: Joint Venture
Int'l Ticker:
Int'l Exchange:
Employees: 4,600 Fiscal Year Ends: 12/31
Parent Company:

SALARIES/BENEFITS:

Pension Plan: ESOP Stock Plan: Profit Sharing: Y Top Exec. Salary: $ Bonus: $
Savings Plan: Y Stock Purch. Plan: Second Exec. Salary: $ Bonus: $

OTHER THOUGHTS:

Apparent Women Officers or Directors: 3
Hot Spot for Advancement for Women/Minorities: Y

LOCATIONS: ("Y" = Yes)

West:	Southwest:	Midwest:	Southeast:	Northeast:	International:
Y	Y	Y	Y	Y	Y

CHICO'S FAS INC

Industry Group Code: 448120

www.chicos.com

Management:		Sales/Marketing:		Liberal Arts:		Information Sys.:		Professionals:		Tech./Scientific:	
Mgmt. Trainees:	Y	Marketing Pros.:	Y	Gen. Writing/Editing:	Y	Info. Mgmt.:	Y	Finance/Acct.:	Y	Engineers, Elec.:	
Experienced Mgmt.:	Y	Retail Sales:	Y	Tech. Writing:		Software Dev.:	Y	Law:	Y	Engineers, Other:	
Int'l Business:	Y	Comm./Industrial:		Graphic Arts/Photog.:	Y	Hardware Dev.:		HR/Other:	Y	Health/Lab:	
MBA Grads:	Y	Sales Trainees:	Y	Music:		Consulting/Other:		Training:	Y	Science/Research:	
		Advertising Pros.:	Y	Broadcasting:				Health Care:		Petroleum/Chem.:	
				Other:	Y			Consulting:		Math/Other:	

TYPES OF BUSINESS:

Women's Apparel, Retail
Online & Catalog Sales
Franchising

BRANDS/DIVISIONS/AFFILIATES:

Chico's
White House/Black Market
Soma by Chico's
Boston Proper, Inc.
Passport Club

CONTACTS:

Note: Officers with more than one job title may be intentionally listed here more than once.

David F. Dyer, CEO
Kent Kleeberger, COO/Exec. VP
David F. Dyer, Pres.
Pamela K. Knous, CFO
Sara K. Stensrud, Chief Human Resources Officer/Exec. VP
Gary A. King, CIO/Exec. VP
Lee Eisenberg, Chief Creative Officer/Exec. VP
A. Alexander (Sandy) Rhodes, General Counsel/Sec./Exec. VP
Robert C. Atkinson, VP-Investor Rel.
Pamela K. Knous, Chief Acct. Officer
Mori MacKenzie, Chief Stores Officer/Exec. VP
Donna M. Colaco, Pres., White House/Black Market Brand
Cynthia S. Murray, Pres., Chico's Brand
Laurie Van Brunt, Pres., Soma Intimates Brand
Ross E. Roeder, Chmn.

Phone: 239-277-6200 **Fax:** 239-277-5237
Toll-Free: 888-550-5559
Address: 11215 Metro Pkwy., Fort Myers, FL 33966 US

GROWTH PLANS/SPECIAL FEATURES:

Chico's FAS, Inc. retails exclusively designed, private label, casual-to-formal clothing, complementary accessories, intimate apparel and gift items for women under the Chico's, White House/Black Market and Soma by Chico's brands. Chico's currently operates 1,151 retail stores in 48 states, Washington, D.C., the U.S. Virgin Islands and Puerto Rico and e-commerce sites for all its brands. Chico's primarily targets women aged 35 and over with moderate and high income levels. There are currently 597 Chico's front-line stores and 63 Chico's outlet stores. The majority of the firm's products are designed and developed by its Product Development Team, headquartered in Fort Myers, Florida. To increase its customer base, the company advertises in national fashion and home and garden magazines such as Martha Stewart Living, Vogue and Vanity Fair, in addition to printing a monthly catalog. The company offers Passport Club membership to women who have spent at least $500 over time, allowing them perks such as a permanent 5% discount on future purchases. Chico's also operates the White House/Black Market chain of 342 women's clothing stores and 21 outlet locations that focuses on women aged 25 and older who lead active work and social lives with moderate to high income levels. White House/Black Market offers clothes predominately in shades of white and black, although the stores do offer a line of denim jeans as well. The White House/Black Market brand contributed 42.3% of the company's total net sales in 2010. The Soma by Chico's intimate wear line currently consists of 120 boutique-style stores and four outlet locations. Soma by Chico's offers foundation products in intimate apparel, sleepwear, bodywear and active wear. The Chico's and Soma brands accounted for 57.7% of 2010 net sales. In August 2011, the firm agreed to acquire Boston Proper, Inc., a women's apparel and accessories retailer.

Chico's employee benefits include merchandise discounts, a retirement savings plan and a stock purchase plan.

FINANCIALS:

Sales and profits are in thousands of dollars—add 000 to get the full amount. 2010 Note: Financial information for 2010 was not available for all companies at press time.

2010 Sales: $1,713,150 | 2010 Profits: $69,646
2009 Sales: $1,582,405 | 2009 Profits: $-19,137
2008 Sales: $1,714,326 | 2008 Profits: $88,875
2007 Sales: $1,640,927 | 2007 Profits: $166,636
2006 Sales: $1,404,575 | 2006 Profits: $193,981

U.S. Stock Ticker: CHS
Int'l Ticker:
Int'l Exchange:
Employees: 16,200 Fiscal Year Ends: 1/31
Parent Company:

SALARIES/BENEFITS:

Pension Plan: | ESOP Stock Plan: | Profit Sharing: | Top Exec. Salary: $950,000 | Bonus: $1,662,500
Savings Plan: Y | Stock Purch. Plan: Y | | Second Exec. Salary: $625,000 | Bonus: $875,000

OTHER THOUGHTS:

Apparent Women Officers or Directors: 6
Hot Spot for Advancement for Women/Minorities: Y

LOCATIONS: ("Y" = Yes)

West:	Southwest:	Midwest:	Southeast:	Northeast:	International:
Y	Y	Y	Y	Y	Y

CHIPOTLE MEXICAN GRILL INC

www.chipotle.com

Industry Group Code: 722110

Management:		Sales/Marketing:		Liberal Arts:		Information Sys.:		Professionals:		Tech./Scientific:	
Mgmt. Trainees:	Y	Marketing Pros.:	Y	Gen. Writing/Editing:	Y	Info. Mgmt.:	Y	Finance/Acct.:	Y	Engineers, Elec.:	
Experienced Mgmt.:	Y	Retail Sales:		Tech. Writing:		Software Dev.:	Y	Law:	Y	Engineers, Other:	
Int'l Business:	Y	Comm./Industrial:		Graphic Arts/Photog.:	Y	Hardware Dev.:		HR/Other:	Y	Health/Lab:	
MBA Grads:	Y	Sales Trainees:		Music:		Consulting/Other:		Training:	Y	Science/Research:	
		Advertising Pros.:	Y	Broadcasting:				Health Care:		Petroleum/Chem.:	
				Other:	Y			Consulting:		Math/Other:	

TYPES OF BUSINESS:

Restaurants

BRANDS/DIVISIONS/AFFILIATES:

CONTACTS:

Note: Officers with more than one job title may be intentionally listed here more than once.

Steve Ells, Co-CEO
John R. Hartung, CFO
Mark Crumpacker, Chief Mktg. Officer
Bob Blessing, Chief Dev. Officer
Robert N. Blessing, Jr., Restaurant Support Officer
Montgomery F. Moran, Co-CEO
Steve Ells, Chmn.

Phone: 303-595-4000 **Fax:**
Toll-Free:
Address: 1543 Wazee St., Ste. 200, Denver, CO 80202 US

GROWTH PLANS/SPECIAL FEATURES:

Chipotle Mexican Grill, Inc. operates Mexican food restaurants serving a relatively focused menu of burritos, tacos, burrito bowls (burrito ingredients without the tortilla) and salads, with an emphasis on fresh and naturally-sourced meats and produce. Chipotle was majority-owned by McDonald's Corporation from 2001 to 2006, when the firm was spun-off and completed its initial public offering. The company operates approximately 1,084 restaurants located across U.S. states, Washington, D.C., Europe and Ontario, Canada. Basic Chipotle ingredients include marinated chicken and steak, carnitas (seasoned and braised pork), barbacoa (spicy shredded beef) and pinto and vegetarian black beans. Customers can customize their food with rice (tossed with lime juice and chopped cilantro), as well as shredded cheese, sour cream, lettuce, peppers and onions. Chipotle also provide a variety of extras such as guacamole, salsas and tortilla chips. In addition to sodas and fruit drinks, most locations also offer a selection of beer and margaritas. Chipotle has used its limited list of ingredients as an opportunity to carefully source the food it serves, part of the company's ongoing Food with Integrity strategy that has helped boost brand image as the chain has grown larger. At its U.S. locations, 86% of its chicken and approximately all of the pork served is naturally raised, from animals on vegetarian diets raised in open pastures or deeply bedded pens without the use of antibiotics and growth hormones. Currently, approximately 80% of the beef served in Chipotle's U.S. restaurants is also naturally raised, while approximately 40% of the beans it buys are organically grown; the company has also committed to purchasing some local produce from small and midsize farms in the regions near its restaurants.

Chipotle offers benefits such as a 401(k) plan and medical insurance.

FINANCIALS:

Sales and profits are in thousands of dollars—add 000 to get the full amount. 2010 Note: Financial information for 2010 was not available for all companies at press time.

2010 Sales: $1,835,922	2010 Profits: $178,981
2009 Sales: $1,518,417	2009 Profits: $126,845
2008 Sales: $1,331,968	2008 Profits: $78,202
2007 Sales: $1,085,782	2007 Profits: $70,563
2006 Sales: $822,930	2006 Profits: $41,423

U.S. Stock Ticker: CMG
Int'l Ticker:
Int'l Exchange:
Employees: 26,500 Fiscal Year Ends: 12/31
Parent Company:

SALARIES/BENEFITS:

Pension Plan:	ESOP Stock Plan:	Profit Sharing:	Top Exec. Salary: $1,180,769	Bonus: $2,448,000
Savings Plan: Y	Stock Purch. Plan:		Second Exec. Salary: $971,154	Bonus: $2,040,000

OTHER THOUGHTS:

Apparent Women Officers or Directors: 1
Hot Spot for Advancement for Women/Minorities:

LOCATIONS: ("Y" = Yes)

West:	Southwest:	Midwest:	Southeast:	Northeast:	International:
Y	Y	Y	Y	Y	Y

CHS INC

www.chsinc.com

Industry Group Code: 4244

Management:		Sales/Marketing:		Liberal Arts:		Information Sys.:		Professionals:		Tech./Scientific:	
Mgmt. Trainees:	Y	Marketing Pros.:	Y	Gen. Writing/Editing:	Y	Info. Mgmt.:	Y	Finance/Acct.:	Y	Engineers, Elec.:	
Experienced Mgmt.:	Y	Retail Sales:		Tech. Writing:		Software Dev.:		Law:	Y	Engineers, Other:	
Int'l Business:	Y	Comm./Industrial:	Y	Graphic Arts/Photog.:	Y	Hardware Dev.:		HR/Other:	Y	Health/Lab:	
MBA Grads:	Y	Sales Trainees:		Music:		Consulting/Other:		Training:	Y	Science/Research:	
		Advertising Pros.:		Broadcasting:				Health Care:		Petroleum/Chem.:	
				Other:				Consulting:		Math/Other:	

TYPES OF BUSINESS:

Food Distribution
Energy Products & Services
Grain Marketing
Convenience Stores

BRANDS/DIVISIONS/AFFILIATES:

Cenex
Country Hedging, Inc.
Ventura Foods, LLC
Horizon Milling, LLC
Agri Point Limited
Central Plains Grain, LLC

CONTACTS: *Note: Officers with more than one job title may be intentionally listed here more than once.*

Carl Casale, CEO
Carl Casale, Pres.
David Kastelic, CFO/Exec. VP
Lisa Zell, General Counsel/Sr. VP
David Christofore, VP/COO-European Grain Oper.
Patrick Kluempke, Exec. VP-Corp. Svcs.
Jay Debertin, Exec. VP/COO-Energy & Foods
Mark Palmquist, Exec. VP/COO-AG Bus.
Lynden Johnson, Sr. VP-Bus. Solutions
Michael Toelle, Chmn.
Claudio Scarrozza, Gen. Mgr./CEO-CHS Europe

Phone: 651-355-6000 **Fax:**
Toll-Free:
Address: 5500 Cenex Dr., Inver Grove Heights, MN 55077 US

GROWTH PLANS/SPECIAL FEATURES:

CHS, Inc. is an agricultural company owned by farmers and ranchers and their member cooperatives across the U.S. The company operates in three segments: energy, Ag business and processing. The energy segment's operations include petroleum refining and pipelines; supply, marketing and distribution of refined fuels (gasoline, diesel fuel and other energy products); blending, sale and distribution of lubricants; and the wholesale supply of propane. Its refined petroleum products are sold under the Cenex brand to member cooperatives and others through a network of roughly 1,450 independent retail sites. The Ag business segment includes agronomy, country operations and grain marketing. The agronomy operations comprise the wholesale crop nutrients business, which sells roughly 5.1 million tons of fertilizer annually. The country operations business, through 386 locations, purchases a variety of grains and provides cooperative members with products and services such as farm supplies and programs for crop and livestock production. The grain marketing operations purchase grain, which is typically contracted for sale for future delivery at a specified location, and arrange for the grain's transportation. It handles nearly 1.9 billion bushels annually. The processing segment converts raw agricultural commodities into ingredients for finished food products or into finished consumer food products. It includes the operations of joint ventures Ventura Foods, LLC, a manufacturer of edible vegetable oil-based products, and Horizon Milling, LLC, a wheat milling joint venture with Cargill, Inc. Through subsidiary Country Hedging, Inc., the company offers brokerage and risk management services. In August 2010, CHS acquired the agronomy and grain operations of Farmers Elevator Co. of Lowder. In November 2010, the firm established Central Plains Grain, LLC, a grain handling joint venture with West Central Ag Services. In January 2011, it acquired the Eastern European grain company Agri Point Limited.

Employees are offered medical, dental and vision coverage; tuition reimbursement; a pension plan; a profit sharing plan; and a 401(k).

FINANCIALS: **Sales and profits are in thousands of dollars—add 000 to get the full amount. 2010 Note: Financial information for 2010 was not available for all companies at press time.**

2010 Sales: $25,267,931 | 2010 Profits: $502,159
2009 Sales: $25,729,916 | 2009 Profits: $381,407
2008 Sales: $32,167,461 | 2008 Profits: $803,045
2007 Sales: $17,215,992 | 2007 Profits: $756,723
2006 Sales: $14,383,835 | 2006 Profits: $505,391

U.S. Stock Ticker: CHSCP
Int'l Ticker:
Int'l Exchange:
Employees: 8,812 Fiscal Year Ends: 8/31
Parent Company:

SALARIES/BENEFITS:

Pension Plan: Y | ESOP Stock Plan: | Profit Sharing: Y | Top Exec. Salary: $900,000 | Bonus: $3,600,000
Savings Plan: Y | Stock Purch. Plan: | Second Exec. Salary: $588,000 | Bonus: $1,637,060

OTHER THOUGHTS:

Apparent Women Officers or Directors: 1
Hot Spot for Advancement for Women/Minorities:

LOCATIONS: ("Y" = Yes)

West:	Southwest:	Midwest:	Southeast:	Northeast:	International:
Y	Y	Y	Y	Y	Y

Sales, profits and employees may be estimates. Financial information, benefits and other data can change quickly and may vary from those stated here.

CHUBB CORPORATION (THE)

www.chubb.com

Industry Group Code: 524126

Management:		**Sales/Marketing:**		**Liberal Arts:**		**Information Sys.:**		**Professionals:**		**Tech./Scientific:**	
Mgmt. Trainees:	Y	Marketing Pros.:	Y	Gen. Writing/Editing:	Y	Info. Mgmt.:	Y	Finance/Acct.:	Y	Engineers, Elec.:	
Experienced Mgmt.:	Y	Retail Sales:		Tech. Writing:	Y	Software Dev.:	Y	Law:	Y	Engineers, Other:	
Int'l Business:	Y	Comm./Industrial:	Y	Graphic Arts/Photog.:	Y	Hardware Dev.:		HR/Other:	Y	Health/Lab:	
MBA Grads:	Y	Sales Trainees:	Y	Music:		Consulting/Other:		Training:	Y	Science/Research:	
		Advertising Pros.:	Y	Broadcasting:				Health Care:		Petroleum/Chem.:	
				Other:	Y			Consulting:		Math/Other:	Y

TYPES OF BUSINESS:

Insurance, Direct Property & Casualty
Reinsurance Services
Consulting Services
Claims Administration Services
Real Estate
Computer Training & Staffing
Luxury Items Insurance

BRANDS/DIVISIONS/AFFILIATES:

Chubb Commercial Insurance
Chubb Specialty Insurance
Chubb Personal Insurance
Federal Insurance Company
Pacific Indemnity Company
Vigilant Insurance Company
Chubb Custom Insurance Company
Chubb Insurance (China) Company Limited

CONTACTS: *Note: Officers with more than one job title may be intentionally listed here more than once.*

John D. Finnegan, CEO
John J. Degnan, COO/Vice Chmn.
John D. Finnegan, Pres.
Richard G. Spiro, CFO/Exec. VP
Dino E. Robusto, Chief Admin. Officer
Maureen Brundage, General Counsel/Exec. VP
Christopher J. Giles, Exec. VP-Int'l Field Oper.
John J. Kennedy, Chief Acct. Officer/Sr. VP
Paul J. Krump, Chief Underwriting Officer/Exec. VP
Kathleen M. Tierney, Exec. VP-Chubb & Son
Dino E. Robusto, Pres., Personal Lines & Claims, Chubb & Son
Mark P. Korsgaard, Exec. VP-Chubb & Son
John D. Finnegan, Chmn.
Harold L. Morrison, Jr., Chief Global Field Officer/Exec. VP

Phone: 908-903-2000 **Fax:** 908-903-2027
Toll-Free:
Address: 15 Mountain View Rd., Warren, NJ 07059 US

GROWTH PLANS/SPECIAL FEATURES:

The Chubb Corporation is a holding company whose subsidiaries provide property and casualty insurance in the U.S., Canada, Europe, Australia and parts of Latin America and Asia. Headquartered in New Jersey, the firm has roughly $50.25 billion in assets and more than 120 offices in 27 countries internationally. The firm's property and casualty group is divided into three units: Chubb Commercial Insurance, which offers a range of insurance solutions for business needs globally; Chubb Specialty Insurance, which offers a variety of specialized professional liability products for privately and publicly owned companies, financial institutions, professional firms and healthcare organizations; and Chubb Personal Insurance, which offers products for individuals who require more coverage choices and higher limits than standard insurance policies. The firm's property and casualty insurance group includes, among others, Federal Insurance Company; Pacific Indemnity Company; Vigilant Insurance Company; Chubb Custom Insurance Company; and Executive Risk Indemnity, Inc. The group underwrites mostly lines of property and casualty insurance and writes non-participating policies. Several members also write participating policies, particularly in the workers' compensation class of business. The firm's other operations include commercial real estate development activities, primarily in New Jersey; residential development activities, primarily in central Florida; consulting and claims administration services; computer training and staffing; and reinsurance services. Chubb offers insurance for primary vacation homes and contents; city homes; valuable possessions including much of the world's individually owned precious jewelry, automobiles and watercraft; and personal liability for some of the wealthiest individuals in the U.S.

Chubb offers its employees flexible spending accounts and medical, dental, vision, life, business travel and disability insurance.

FINANCIALS: **Sales and profits are in thousands of dollars—add 000 to get the full amount. 2010 Note: Financial information for 2010 was not available for all companies at press time.**

2010 Sales: $13,319,000 — 2010 Profits: $2,174,000
2009 Sales: $13,016,000 — 2009 Profits: $2,183,000
2008 Sales: $13,221,000 — 2008 Profits: $1,804,000
2007 Sales: $14,107,000 — 2007 Profits: $2,807,000
2006 Sales: $14,003,000 — 2006 Profits: $2,528,000

U.S. Stock Ticker: CB
Int'l Ticker:
Int'l Exchange:
Employees: 10,100 Fiscal Year Ends: 12/31
Parent Company:

SALARIES/BENEFITS:

Pension Plan: ESOP Stock Plan: Profit Sharing: Top Exec. Salary: $1,312,500 Bonus: $3,600,000
Savings Plan: Stock Purch. Plan: Second Exec. Salary: $874,500 Bonus: $1,789,400

OTHER THOUGHTS:

Apparent Women Officers or Directors: 3
Hot Spot for Advancement for Women/Minorities: Y

LOCATIONS: ("Y" = Yes)

West:	Southwest:	Midwest:	Southeast:	Northeast:	International:
Y	Y	Y	Y	Y	Y

CIENA CORP

www.ciena.com

Industry Group Code: 334210

Management:		Sales/Marketing:		Liberal Arts:		Information Sys.:		Professionals:		Tech./Scientific:	
Mgmt. Trainees:		Marketing Pros.:	Y	Gen. Writing/Editing:		Info. Mgmt.:	Y	Finance/Acct.:	Y	Engineers, Elec.:	Y
Experienced Mgmt.:		Retail Sales:		Tech. Writing:	Y	Software Dev.:	Y	Law:	Y	Engineers, Other:	
Int'l Business:	Y	Comm./Industrial:	Y	Graphic Arts/Photog.:		Hardware Dev.:	Y	HR/Other:	Y	Health/Lab:	
MBA Grads:	Y	Sales Trainees:		Music:		Consulting/Other:		Training:		Science/Research:	
		Advertising Pros.:	Y	Broadcasting:				Health Care:		Petroleum/Chem.:	
				Other:				Consulting:		Math/Other:	Y

TYPES OF BUSINESS:

Communications Networking Equipment
Software & Support Services
Consulting Services
Switching Platforms
Packet Interworking Products
Access Products
Network & Service Management Tools

BRANDS/DIVISIONS/AFFILIATES:

ActivEdge 3000 Series
ActivEdge 5000 Series
ActivFlex 5400 Series
CoreDirector FS
ActivSpan 4200 Series
ActivSpan 5100/5200
ActivFlex 6500
Ciena One Software Suite

CONTACTS: *Note: Officers with more than one job title may be intentionally listed here more than once.*

Gary B. Smith, CEO
Gary B. Smith, Pres.
James E. Moylan, Jr., CFO/Sr. VP-Finance
Thomas Mock, Sr. VP-Corp. Mktg.
Randall Harris, Sr. VP-Global Human Resources
Stephen B. Alexander, CTO/Sr. VP-Tech.
Stephen B. Alexander, Sr. VP-Prod.
David M. Rothenstein, General Counsel/Sr. VP/Corp. Sec.
Michael G. Aquino, Sr. VP-Global Field Oper.
James Frodsham, Chief Strategy Officer/Sr. VP
Andrew Petrik, Controller/VP
Philippe Morin, Sr. VP-Global Prod. Group
Patrick H. Nettles, Chmn.
Rick Dodd, Sr. VP-Global Mktg.

Phone: 410-694-5700	**Fax:** 410-694-5750
Toll-Free: 800-921-1144	
Address: 1201 Winterson Rd., Linthicum, MD 21090 US	

GROWTH PLANS/SPECIAL FEATURES:

Ciena Corp. is a provider of communications networking equipment, software and services that support the transport, switching, aggregation and management of voice, video and data traffic. Its product portfolio includes a range of communications networking equipment and software that is utilized from the core of communications networks, from metropolitan network infrastructures to the network edge, where end users gain access to communications services. Products are offered in four major categories: carrier Ethernet service delivery devices, packet-optical switching devices, packet-optical transport devices and the Ciena One software suite. Carrier Ethernet service delivery devices are designed to provide intelligent access to high-speed Ethernet networks. Products in this category include the ActivEdge 3000 Series, the ActivEdge 5000 Series and the ActivFlex 5400 Series. Packet-optical switching devices are designed to provision and automate bandwidth to prevent slowdowns and overloads. Products in this category include the ActivFlex 5400 Series and the CoreDirector FS multiservice optical switch. Packet-optical transport devices are designed to provide scalable additions to an existing network. These products include the ActivSpan 4200 Series, the ActivSpan 5100/5200 and the ActivFlex 6500. The Ciena One software suite monitors and manages the functions of a network, including switching control and gateway management. Products include the On-Center Network and Services Management Suite and the CatenaView EMS voice, data and video operator. Ciena also offers consulting and technical implementation advice. The firm sells its communications networking equipment, software and services through direct sales efforts and channel relationships. The company services a wide variety of industries, including telecommunications, government, financial services, health care and education.

The company offers its employees medical, dental and vision insurance; short- and long-term disability insurance; flexible spending accounts; business travel accident and life insurance; stock options; a 401(k) plan; an employee stock purchase plan; an employee assistance program; and educational assistance.

FINANCIALS: **Sales and profits are in thousands of dollars—add 000 to get the full amount. 2010 Note: Financial information for 2010 was not available for all companies at press time.**

2010 Sales: $1,236,636	2010 Profits: $-331,514	**U.S. Stock Ticker: CIEN**
2009 Sales: $652,629	2009 Profits: $-581,154	**Int'l Ticker:**
2008 Sales: $902,448	2008 Profits: $38,894	Int'l Exchange:
2007 Sales: $779,769	2007 Profits: $82,788	Employees: 4,201 Fiscal Year Ends: 10/31
2006 Sales: $564,056	2006 Profits: $ 595	Parent Company:

SALARIES/BENEFITS:

Pension Plan:	ESOP Stock Plan:	Profit Sharing:	Top Exec. Salary: $650,000	Bonus: $
Savings Plan: Y	Stock Purch. Plan: Y		Second Exec. Salary: $400,000	Bonus: $

OTHER THOUGHTS:

Apparent Women Officers or Directors: 1
Hot Spot for Advancement for Women/Minorities:

LOCATIONS: ("Y" = Yes)

West:	Southwest:	Midwest:	Southeast:	Northeast:	International:
Y	Y	Y	Y	Y	Y

Sales, profits and employees may be estimates. Financial information, benefits and other data can change quickly and may vary from those stated here.

CIGNA CORP

www.cigna.com

Industry Group Code: 524114

Management:		Sales/Marketing:		Liberal Arts:		Information Sys.:		Professionals:		Tech./Scientific:	
Mgmt. Trainees:	Y	Marketing Pros.:	Y	Gen. Writing/Editing:	Y	Info. Mgmt.:	Y	Finance/Acct.:	Y	Engineers, Elec.:	
Experienced Mgmt.:	Y	Retail Sales:		Tech. Writing:	Y	Software Dev.:	Y	Law:	Y	Engineers, Other:	
Int'l Business:	Y	Comm./Industrial:	Y	Graphic Arts/Photog.:	Y	Hardware Dev.:		HR/Other:	Y	Health/Lab:	
MBA Grads:	Y	Sales Trainees:		Music:		Consulting/Other:		Training:	Y	Science/Research:	
		Advertising Pros.:	Y	Broadcasting:				Health Care:	Y	Petroleum/Chem.:	
				Other:	Y			Consulting:		Math/Other:	

TYPES OF BUSINESS:

Insurance-Medical & Health, HMOs & PPOs
Indemnity Insurance
Investment Management Services
Group Life, Accident & Disability

BRANDS/DIVISIONS/AFFILIATES:

CIGNA HealthCare
Kronos Optimal Health Company
Vanbreda International
International Rehabilitation Associates, Inc.
CIGNA Behavioral Health

CONTACTS: *Note: Officers with more than one job title may be intentionally listed here more than once.*

David M. Cordani, CEO
David M. Cordani, Pres.
Ralph J. Nicoletti, CFO/Exec. VP
John M. Murabito, Exec. VP-Human Resources & Svcs.
Jeffrey Kang, Chief Medical Officer
Mark L. Boxer, CIO
Nicole Jones, General Counsel/Exec. VP
Maggie FitzPatrick, Chief Comm. Officer
Bertram L. Scott, Pres., U.S. Commercial Markets
Matt Manders, Head-U.S. Service, Clinical & Specialty
Isaiah Harris, Jr., Chmn.
William Atwell, Pres., CIGNA Int'l

Phone: 215-761-1000 **Fax:** 215-761-3596
Toll-Free:
Address: 1601 Chestnut St., 2 Liberty Pl., Philadelphia, PA 19192 US

GROWTH PLANS/SPECIAL FEATURES:

CIGNA Corp. and its subsidiaries constitute one of the largest investor-owned employee benefits organizations in the U.S. The group is a major provider of employee benefits, including health care products and services; group life, accident and disability insurance; and workers' compensation case management and related services. CIGNA operates in four segments: health care; disability and life; international; and other operations. The health care segment, which operates as CIGNA HealthCare, offers insured and self-funded medical, dental, behavioral health, vision and prescription drug benefit plans, as well as health advocacy programs and disability and life insurance products. It operates 12 service centers that, together, process approximately119 million medical claims annually. The disability and life segment provides group long-term and short-term disability insurance; group life insurance; worker's compensation and disability case management; and accident and specialty insurance. These products and services are offered in all 50 states and Washington D.C., Puerto Rico, the U.S. Virgin Islands and Canada. The international segment offers life, accident and supplemental health insurance products, as well as international health care products and services in over 27 countries. Lastly, the other operations segment consists of non-leveraged and leveraged corporate-owned life insurance. In 2010, CIGNA Corporation acquired Vanbreda International and Kronos Optimal Health Company. In December 2010, the firm's subsidiary, International Rehabilitation Associates, Inc., sold its workers' compensation and disability case management operations to GENEX Holdings, Inc. In August 2011, CIGNA opened a new office in Turkey.

Employees are offered medical, dental, disability and life insurance; a 401k plan; a discount stock purchase plan; long-term care insurance; flexible work arrangements; elder and childcare assistance; an adoption assistance program; educational reimbursement; wellness and fitness programs; an employee retail discount program; and lactation centers.

FINANCIALS: **Sales and profits are in thousands of dollars—add 000 to get the full amount. 2010 Note: Financial information for 2010 was not available for all companies at press time.**

2010 Sales: $21,253,000	2010 Profits: $1,345,000	**U.S. Stock Ticker: CI**
2009 Sales: $18,414,000	2009 Profits: $1,302,000	**Int'l Ticker:**
2008 Sales: $19,101,000	2008 Profits: $292,000	Int'l Exchange:
2007 Sales: $17,623,000	2007 Profits: $1,115,000	Employees: 30,600 Fiscal Year Ends: 12/31
2006 Sales: $16,547,000	2006 Profits: $1,155,000	Parent Company:

SALARIES/BENEFITS:

Pension Plan:	ESOP Stock Plan:	Profit Sharing:	Top Exec. Salary: $1,000,000	Bonus: $7,356,375
Savings Plan: Y	Stock Purch. Plan: Y		Second Exec. Salary: $592,250	Bonus: $1,740,500

OTHER THOUGHTS:

Apparent Women Officers or Directors: 5
Hot Spot for Advancement for Women/Minorities: Y

LOCATIONS: ("Y" = Yes)

West:	Southwest:	Midwest:	Southeast:	Northeast:	International:
Y	Y	Y	Y	Y	Y

CINTAS CORP

www.cintas.com

Industry Group Code: 812331

Management:		Sales/Marketing:		Liberal Arts:		Information Sys.:		Professionals:		Tech./Scientific:	
Mgmt. Trainees:	Y	Marketing Pros.:	Y	Gen. Writing/Editing:	Y	Info. Mgmt.:	Y	Finance/Acct.:	Y	Engineers, Elec.:	
Experienced Mgmt.:	Y	Retail Sales:		Tech. Writing:		Software Dev.:	Y	Law:	Y	Engineers, Other:	
Int'l Business:	Y	Comm./Industrial:	Y	Graphic Arts/Photog.:	Y	Hardware Dev.:		HR/Other:	Y	Health/Lab:	
MBA Grads:	Y	Sales Trainees:	Y	Music:		Consulting/Other:		Training:	Y	Science/Research:	
		Advertising Pros.:	Y	Broadcasting:				Health Care:		Petroleum/Chem.:	
				Other:				Consulting:		Math/Other:	

TYPES OF BUSINESS:

Linen & Uniform Supply
Uniform Rental, Sales & Cleaning
Uniform Design & Manufacturing
Outsourcing Services
Dust Control Services
Restroom Cleaning Services
Document Shredding & Management
First Aid & Safety Products

BRANDS/DIVISIONS/AFFILIATES:

CONTACTS: *Note: Officers with more than one job title may be intentionally listed here more than once.*

Scott D. Farmer, CEO
J. Phillip Holloman, COO
J. Phillip Holloman, Pres.
William C. Gale, CFO/Sr. VP
Thomas Frooman, General Counsel/VP/Corp. Sec.
J. Michael Hansen, Treas./VP
Robert J. Kohlhepp, Chmn.

Phone: 513-459-1200	**Fax:** 513-573-4130
Toll-Free:	
Address: 6800 Cintas Blvd., Cincinnati, OH 45262-5737 US	

GROWTH PLANS/SPECIAL FEATURES:

Cintas Corp. is a leading uniform supplier in the U.S. that designs, manufactures and implements corporate identity uniform programs. The company's products include entrance mats, restroom supplies, hygiene service supplies, first aid and safety products, fire protection products, document shredding and storage, cleanroom resources and flame resistant clothing. Cintas supplies products and services to more than 900,000 businesses. The firm operates through four segments: Rental Uniforms and Ancillary Products, which accounted for 71% of its fiscal 2011 revenue; Uniform Direct Sales, 11%; First Aid, Safety and Fire Protection Services, 10%; and Document Management Services, 7%. The Rental Uniforms and Ancillary Products segment controls the rental and servicing of uniforms and other garments, as well as supplying mats, mops, shop towels and restroom and hygiene products and services. Rental services include the cleaning of uniforms and providing on-going uniform replacements as required to each customer. The Uniform Direct Sales unit consists of the direct sale of uniforms and related items, as well as branded promotional products. The First Aid, Safety and Fire Protection Services segment consists of on-site defibrillators and accessories, first aid kits and full fire protection systems and maintenance. Lastly, the Document Management Services division offers document destruction, document imaging and document retention services. The company also has specialized services tailored to the requirements of a number of additional industries, including automotive, casino, food processing, healthcare, lawn and garden, lodging, pest control, restaurant, supermarket and veterinary. The firm operates six manufacturing plants and eight distribution centers across North America, as well as more than 400 other facilities in nearly 300 cities nationwide. Cintas supplies its products and services through a national distribution network and approximately 7,700 local delivery routes.

FINANCIALS: **Sales and profits are in thousands of dollars—add 000 to get the full amount. 2010 Note: Financial information for 2010 was not available for all companies at press time.**

2010 Sales: $3,547,339	2010 Profits: $215,620	**U.S. Stock Ticker: CTAS**
2009 Sales: $3,774,685	2009 Profits: $226,357	**Int'l Ticker:**
2008 Sales: $3,937,900	2008 Profits: $335,405	Int'l Exchange:
2007 Sales: $3,706,900	2007 Profits: $334,538	Employees: 30,000 Fiscal Year Ends: 5/31
2006 Sales: $3,403,608	2006 Profits: $323,382	Parent Company:

SALARIES/BENEFITS:

Pension Plan:	ESOP Stock Plan: Y	Profit Sharing: Y	Top Exec. Salary: $725,000	Bonus: $482,000
Savings Plan: Y	Stock Purch. Plan:		Second Exec. Salary: $545,900	Bonus: $357,750

OTHER THOUGHTS:

Apparent Women Officers or Directors:
Hot Spot for Advancement for Women/Minorities:

LOCATIONS: ("Y" = Yes)

West:	Southwest:	Midwest:	Southeast:	Northeast:	International:
Y	Y	Y	Y	Y	Y

CISCO SYSTEMS INC

www.cisco.com

Industry Group Code: 33411

Management:		Sales/Marketing:		Liberal Arts:		Information Sys.:		Professionals:		Tech./Scientific:	
Mgmt. Trainees:	Y	Marketing Pros.:	Y	Gen. Writing/Editing:	Y	Info. Mgmt.:	Y	Finance/Acct.:	Y	Engineers, Elec.:	Y
Experienced Mgmt.:	Y	Retail Sales:		Tech. Writing:	Y	Software Dev.:	Y	Law:	Y	Engineers, Other:	
Int'l Business:	Y	Comm./Industrial:	Y	Graphic Arts/Photog.:	Y	Hardware Dev.:	Y	HR/Other:	Y	Health/Lab:	
MBA Grads:	Y	Sales Trainees:	Y	Music:		Consulting/Other:	Y	Training:	Y	Science/Research:	Y
		Advertising Pros.:	Y	Broadcasting:				Health Care:		Petroleum/Chem.:	
				Other:				Consulting:		Math/Other:	Y

TYPES OF BUSINESS:

Computer Networking Equipment
Routers & Switches
Real-Time Conferencing Technology
Server Virtualization Software
Data Storage Products
Security Products
Teleconference Systems and Technology
Unified Communications Systems

BRANDS/DIVISIONS/AFFILIATES:

Scientific Atlanta Inc
Webex Communications Inc
Tandberg
Cisco United Communications
Flip Video
Unified Computing Systems

CONTACTS: *Note: Officers with more than one job title may be intentionally listed here more than once.*

John T. Chambers, CEO
Gary Moore, COO
Frank A. Calderoni, CFO/Exec. VP
Susan L. Bostrom, Chief Mktg. Officer/Exec. VP
Brian Schipper, Sr. VP-Human Resources
Gregory Akers, Sr. VP-R&D
Rebecca Jacoby, CIO/Sr. VP
Mark Chandler, General Counsel/Sr. VP-Legal Svcs./Sec.
Robert Lloyd, Exec. VP-Worldwide Oper.
Ned Hooper, Chief Strategy Officer/Sr. VP-Consumer Bus.
Blair Christie, Sr. VP-Global Corp. Comm.
Wim Elfrink, Chief Globalization Officer/Exec. VP-Cisco Svcs.
Wendy Bahr, Sr. VP-Global & Transformational Partnerships
Marthin De Beer, Sr. VP-Emerging Tech. Bus. Group
Randy Pond, Exec. VP-Oper., Processes & Systems
John T. Chambers, Chmn.
Edzard Overbeek, Pres., Asia Pacific & Japan

Phone: 408-526-4000 **Fax:** 408-526-4100
Toll-Free: 800-553-6387
Address: 170 W. Tasman Dr., San Jose, CA 95134 US

GROWTH PLANS/SPECIAL FEATURES:

Cisco Systems, Inc. designs, develops, manufactures and markets Internet protocol (IP)-based networking and other products related to the communications and information technology industries, and provides services associated with these products. The firm's products, which include routers, switches and advanced technologies, are installed at large enterprises, public institutions, telecommunications companies, commercial businesses and personal residences. Cisco divides its products into three categories: routing and switching; advanced technologies; and other products. The routing and switching category includes a variety of routers, from core network infrastructure for service providers and enterprises to access routers for branch offices and for telecommuters and consumers at home. The category also includes switching systems, which employ the use of Ethernet, Power over Ethernet, Fibre Channel over Ethernet, Packet over Synchronous Optical Network and Multiprotocol Label Switching. Its Ethernet switching applications include fixed-configuration switches for small and medium-sized businesses to modular switches for enterprises and service providers. The advanced technologies category includes application networking services; video systems; wireless technology products; home networking products, which includes adapters, gateways, modems and home network management software; security products, which include network security, physical and building security, virtual private networks (VPN), firewall and security management solutions; storage area networking products; and Cisco United Communications products, which integrate voice, video, data and mobile applications on fixed and mobile networks. The other products category insists of optical networking products, cable access, the Flip Video family of camcorder lines and service provider voice-over-IP (VoIP) services. Cisco's strategic push is now focused on Unified Computing Systems, which bundle server, storage and networking systems into one new product. Each of Cisco's new servers is capable of running hundreds of virtual servers by utilizing virtualization software. In addition to its product offerings, Cisco provides a range of product support services. The firm's business is divided by region into five segments: the U.S. and Canada, European Markets, Emerging Markets, Asia Pacific and Japan.

FINANCIALS: **Sales and profits are in thousands of dollars—add 000 to get the full amount. 2010 Note: Financial information for 2010 was not available for all companies at press time.**

2010 Sales: $40,040,000	2010 Profits: $7,767,000	**U.S. Stock Ticker: CSCO**
2009 Sales: $36,117,000	2009 Profits: $6,134,000	**Int'l Ticker:**
2008 Sales: $39,540,000	2008 Profits: $8,052,000	Int'l Exchange:
2007 Sales: $34,922,000	2007 Profits: $7,333,000	Employees: 70,700 Fiscal Year Ends: 7/31
2006 Sales: $28,484,000	2006 Profits: $5,580,000	Parent Company:

SALARIES/BENEFITS:

Pension Plan:	ESOP Stock Plan:	Profit Sharing:	Top Exec. Salary: $815,385	Bonus: $1,600,000
Savings Plan:	Stock Purch. Plan:		Second Exec. Salary: $773,762	Bonus: $1,600,000

OTHER THOUGHTS:

Apparent Women Officers or Directors: 13
Hot Spot for Advancement for Women/Minorities: Y

LOCATIONS: ("Y" = Yes)

West:	Southwest:	Midwest:	Southeast:	Northeast:	International:
Y	Y	Y	Y	Y	Y

CITRIX SYSTEMS INC

www.citrix.com

Industry Group Code: 511210H

Management:		Sales/Marketing:		Liberal Arts:		Information Sys.:		Professionals:		Tech./Scientific:	
Mgmt. Trainees:		Marketing Pros.:	Y	Gen. Writing/Editing:		Info. Mgmt.:	Y	Finance/Acct.:	Y	Engineers, Elec.:	Y
Experienced Mgmt.:	Y	Retail Sales:		Tech. Writing:	Y	Software Dev.:	Y	Law:	Y	Engineers, Other:	
Int'l Business:	Y	Comm./Industrial:	Y	Graphic Arts/Photog.:		Hardware Dev.:		HR/Other:	Y	Health/Lab:	
MBA Grads:	Y	Sales Trainees:		Music:		Consulting/Other:	Y	Training:	Y	Science/Research:	
		Advertising Pros.:	Y	Broadcasting:				Health Care:		Petroleum/Chem.:	
				Other:				Consulting:		Math/Other:	

TYPES OF BUSINESS:

Computer Software-Application Server
Consulting Services
Training & Technical Support
Online Services

BRANDS/DIVISIONS/AFFILIATES:

XenApp
XenDesktop
XenServer
NetScaler
GoToMeeting
GoToAssist
GoToMyPC
Netviewer AG

CONTACTS: *Note: Officers with more than one job title may be intentionally listed here more than once.*

Mark B. Templeton, CEO
Mark B. Templeton, Pres.
David J. Henshall, CFO/Sr. VP
Wes R. Wasson, Chief Mktg. Officer/Sr. VP
David R. Friedman, Sr. VP-Human Resources
David R. Friedman, General Counsel
Frank Artale, VP-Bus. Dev.
Brett Caine, Sr. VP/Gen. Mgr.-Online Svcs. Div.
Al J. Monserrat, Sr. VP-Sales & Svcs.
Peter Levine, Sr. VP/Gen. Mgr.-Datacenter & Cloud Div.
Gordon Payne, Sr. VP/Gen. Mgr.-Desktop Div.
Michael Cristinziano, VP-Strategic Dev.
Thomas F. Bogan, Chmn.

Phone: 954-267-3000 **Fax:** 954-267-9319
Toll-Free: 800-424-8749
Address: 851 W. Cypress Creek Rd., Fort Lauderdale, FL 33309 US

GROWTH PLANS/SPECIAL FEATURES:

Citrix Systems, Inc. designs, develops and markets products that allow applications to be delivered, supported and shared on-demand with high performance, enhanced security and improved total cost of ownership. Citrix offers application delivery systems in four product groupings: desktop solutions; online services; datacenter and cloud solutions; and technical services. The firm's desktop solutions, XenApp and XenDesktop, reduce the complexity and cost of administering Windows-based applications and desktops in the enterprise. Citrix XenApp, an application virtualization tool, runs the business logic of applications on a central server, transmitting only screen pixels, keystrokes and mouse movements through an encrypted channel to users' computers. Desktop virtualization is achieved through Citrix XenDesktop, which streams desktop images through multiple virtual machines. The online services division includes products such as GoToMyPC, GoToMeeting, GoToAssist and GoToWebinar which are designed to provide web-based access to office resources for off-site locations. The datacenter and cloud solutions product group includes virtual infrastructure and application networking products. Virtual infrastructure includes the Citrix XenServer, a server virtualization solution that aggregates a pool of computing and storage resources. Citrix Essentials for XenServer adds capabilities such as lab automation, high availability, provisioning, workflow orchestration and seamless integration with storage systems to existing virtualization management systems. Application networking, through products including Citrix NetScalar, Citrix Access Gateway and Citrix Repeater, is designed to improve application performance, access datacenter resources in offsite locations, and deliver local area network-like performance over a wide area network. The technical services division provides consulting services, technical support and product training to support Citrix products. In December 2010, the firm agreed to acquire Netviewer AG.

Citrix offers its employees medical, dental, vision and life insurance; educational assistance; a 401(k) plan; a pension plan; stock options and an employee stock purchase plan; car allowances; an employee assistance plan; and onsite fitness centers.

FINANCIALS: **Sales and profits are in thousands of dollars—add 000 to get the full amount. 2010 Note: Financial information for 2010 was not available for all companies at press time.**

2010 Sales: $1,874,662	2010 Profits: $277,065
2009 Sales: $1,614,088	2009 Profits: $191,017
2008 Sales: $1,583,354	2008 Profits: $178,276
2007 Sales: $1,391,942	2007 Profits: $214,483
2006 Sales: $1,134,319	2006 Profits: $182,997

U.S. Stock Ticker: CTXS
Int'l Ticker:
Int'l Exchange:
Employees: 5,637 Fiscal Year Ends: 12/31
Parent Company:

SALARIES/BENEFITS:

Pension Plan: Y	ESOP Stock Plan:	Profit Sharing:	Top Exec. Salary: $800,000	Bonus: $954,158
Savings Plan: Y	Stock Purch. Plan: Y		Second Exec. Salary: $435,000	Bonus: $325,107

OTHER THOUGHTS:

Apparent Women Officers or Directors:
Hot Spot for Advancement for Women/Minorities:

LOCATIONS: ("Y" = Yes)

West:	Southwest:	Midwest:	Southeast:	Northeast:	International:
Y	Y	Y	Y	Y	Y

CLEARWIRE CORP

www.clearwire.com

Industry Group Code: 5172

Management:		**Sales/Marketing:**		**Liberal Arts:**		**Information Sys.:**		**Professionals:**		**Tech./Scientific:**	
Mgmt. Trainees:	Y	Marketing Pros.:	Y	Gen. Writing/Editing:	Y	Info. Mgmt.:	Y	Finance/Acct.:	Y	Engineers, Elec.:	Y
Experienced Mgmt.:	Y	Retail Sales:		Tech. Writing:	Y	Software Dev.:	Y	Law:	Y	Engineers, Other:	
Int'l Business:	Y	Comm./Industrial:	Y	Graphic Arts/Photog.:	Y	Hardware Dev.:		HR/Other:	Y	Health/Lab:	
MBA Grads:	Y	Sales Trainees:	Y	Music:		Consulting/Other:		Training:	Y	Science/Research:	
		Advertising Pros.:	Y	Broadcasting:				Health Care:		Petroleum/Chem.:	
				Other:	Y			Consulting:		Math/Other:	

TYPES OF BUSINESS:

Wireless Broadband Service
WiMAX Wireless Networks
Voice over Internet Protocol
Wireless Internet Access Service
Mobile Telephone Service

BRANDS/DIVISIONS/AFFILIATES:

CLEAR
Bright House Networks
Time Warner Cable
Intel
Comcast
Google

CONTACTS: *Note: Officers with more than one job title may be intentionally listed here more than once.*

William T. Morrow, CEO
Erik Prusch, CFO
Thomas Enraght-Moony, Sr. VP-Mktg.
Kevin T. Hart, CIO
John Saw, CTO/Sr. VP
Broady R. Hodder, General Counsel/Sr. VP
David Maquera, Chief Strategy Officer/Sr. VP
Hope F. Cochran, Sr. VP-Finance/Treas.
G. Michael Sievert, Chief Commercial Officer
Teresa Elder, Pres., Strategic Partnerships & Wholesale
John W. Stanton, Chmn.
Jim Ryder, Sr. VP-Dist. & Sales

Phone: 425-216-7600	**Fax:** 425-216-7900
Toll-Free: 888-253-2794	
Address: 4400 Carillon Pt., Kirkland, WA 98033 US	

GROWTH PLANS/SPECIAL FEATURES:

Clearwire Corp. builds and operates next-generation wireless broadband networks, including its CLEAR mobile telephone service. The company is one of the largest holders of licensed wireless spectrum in the U.S. Its services consist primarily of wireless broadband connectivity, and Voice over Internet Protocol (VoIP) telephony services. The firm offers its services to in the U.S. and Europe, with network coverage now surpassing 100 million people. These markets range from major metropolitan areas to small, rural communities. Operations in the U.S. are conducted through subsidiary Clearwire U.S., LLC. Internationally, operations are conducted through Clearwire International, LLC, which offers wireless broadband services internationally in Ghent and Brussels, Belgium; Dublin, Ireland; and Malaga and Seville, Spain, with a network covering approximately 3 million people. CLEAR, Clearwire's 4G service, is currently offered by Clearwire in some of its domestic and European pre-WiMAX markets. In recent years, Clearwire and Sprint Nextel Corporation combined their WiMAX businesses into a single company, currently operating as Clearwire. In early 2011, the firm decided to deemphasize its retail operations and focus instead on being a wholesale service company providing 4G network services. For the time being, it will continue operating its 140 retail stores, but probably will not expand them.

The company offers its employees life, AD&D, disability, medical, dental and vision insurance; flexible spending accounts; a 401(k); an assistance program; paid time off; tuition assistance; free CLEAR service for partners; and a 529 college savings plan.

FINANCIALS: Sales and profits are in thousands of dollars—add 000 to get the full amount. 2010 Note: Financial information for 2010 was not available for all companies at press time.

2010 Sales: $556,826	2010 Profits: $-2,303,250
2009 Sales: $274,458	2009 Profits: $-1,253,134
2008 Sales: $20,489	2008 Profits: $-432,626
2007 Sales: $151,440	2007 Profits: $-727,466
2006 Sales: $100,181	2006 Profits: $-284,203

U.S. Stock Ticker: CLWR
Int'l Ticker:
Int'l Exchange:
Employees: 3,500 Fiscal Year Ends: 12/31
Parent Company:

SALARIES/BENEFITS:

Pension Plan:	ESOP Stock Plan:	Profit Sharing:	Top Exec. Salary: $778,846	Bonus: $750,000
Savings Plan: Y	Stock Purch. Plan:		Second Exec. Salary: $726,923	Bonus: $1,154,000

OTHER THOUGHTS:

Apparent Women Officers or Directors: 1
Hot Spot for Advancement for Women/Minorities:

LOCATIONS: ("Y" = Yes)

West:	Southwest:	Midwest:	Southeast:	Northeast:	International:
Y	Y	Y	Y	Y	Y

CLOROX CO (THE)

www.thecloroxcompany.com

Industry Group Code: 325611

Management:		Sales/Marketing:		Liberal Arts:		Information Sys.:		Professionals:		Tech./Scientific:	
Mgmt. Trainees:	Y	Marketing Pros.:	Y	Gen. Writing/Editing:	Y	Info. Mgmt.:	Y	Finance/Acct.:	Y	Engineers, Elec.:	
Experienced Mgmt.:	Y	Retail Sales:		Tech. Writing:		Software Dev.:		Law:	Y	Engineers, Other:	Y
Int'l Business:	Y	Comm./Industrial:	Y	Graphic Arts/Photog.:	Y	Hardware Dev.:		HR/Other:	Y	Health/Lab:	Y
MBA Grads:	Y	Sales Trainees:	Y	Music:		Consulting/Other:		Training:	Y	Science/Research:	
		Advertising Pros.:	Y	Broadcasting:				Health Care:		Petroleum/Chem.:	
				Other:				Consulting:		Math/Other:	

TYPES OF BUSINESS:

Cleaning/Laundry Products-Manufacturing
Automotive Care Products
Pesticides
Cat Litter
Water Filtration Products
Charcoal
Domestic Plastics
Dressings & Sauces

BRANDS/DIVISIONS/AFFILIATES:

Clorox Bleach
Armor All
Kingsford
Glad
Brita
Burt's Bees
Soft Scrub
Pine-Sol

CONTACTS: *Note: Officers with more than one job title may be intentionally listed here more than once.*

Donald R. Knauss, CEO
Lawrence S. Peiros, COO/Exec. VP
Daniel J. Heinrich, CFO/Exec.. VP
Thomas P. Britanik, Chief Mktg. Officer/Sr. VP
Jaqueline P. Kane, Sr. VP-Human Resources & Corp. Affairs
Laura Stein, General Counsel/Sr. VP
Lawrence S. Peiros, COO-Clorox N. America
Frank A. Tataseo, Exec. VP-Strategy & Growth
Aileen Zerudo, Dir.-Corp. Comm.
Steve Austenfeld, VP-Investor Rel.
Tom Johnson, VP-Global Bus. Svcs./Chief Acct. Officer
Benno Dorer, Sr. VP/Gen. Mgr.-Cleaning Div.
Wayne Welker, Chief Innovation Officer/Sr. VP
George C. Roeth, Sr. VP/Gen. Mgr.-Specialty
Grant J. LaMontagne, Sr. VP/Chief Customer Officer
Donald R. Knauss, Chmn.
Michael Costello, Gen. Mgr.-Int'l/VP
James Foster, Sr. VP/Chief Product Supply Officer

Phone: 510-271-7000 **Fax:** 510-832-1463
Toll-Free:
Address: 1221 Broadway, Oakland, CA 94612-1888 US

GROWTH PLANS/SPECIAL FEATURES:

The Clorox Co. produces and markets non-durable consumer products, operating in four business segments: Cleaning, Lifestyle, Household and International. Cleaning consists of laundry, home-care, professional products and auto-care products marketed and sold in the United States. Notable brands in this segment include Clorox Bleach, Formula 409, Pine-Sol, Armor All and Green Works, the company's eco-friendly line of cleaning products. The Lifestyle segment consists of food products, water-filtration systems and filters, as well as all-natural personal care products. Hidden Valley, KC Masterpiece, Brita, and Burt's Bees are some of the important brands in the Lifestyle business. Household consists of charcoal, cat litter, plastic bags, wraps, and container products. Some of the well-known brands in this segment include Glad, Fresh Step, Kingsford and MatchLight. The International segments consists of products sold outside of the U.S., such as home-care, laundry, auto-care, water filtration, charcoal, cat litter products, dressings, plastics bags, container products, and insecticides. International brands include Lemon Tok, Bon Bril, La Negrita, Poett, Mistolin and Sabra. Most of Clorox's consumer products are nationally advertised and sold within the U.S. to grocery stores, mass merchandisers, warehouse clubs, military stores and other retail locations through a direct sales force. Within the U.S., the company also sells institutional, janitorial, healthcare and food-service versions of many of its products through distributors, as well as natural personal care products through the Internet. In early 2010, the company announced a new line of products designed for industrial cleaning known as Green Works Concentrates. In September 2010, the firm introduced Liquid-Plumr Penetrex Gel, a clog remover.

Clorox offers its employees medical, vision and dental insurance; an employee assistance program; dependent care reimbursement; a cash-balance pension plan; and adoption reimbursement.

FINANCIALS: **Sales and profits are in thousands of dollars—add 000 to get the full amount. 2010 Note: Financial information for 2010 was not available for all companies at press time.**

2010 Sales: $5,534,000 — 2010 Profits: $603,000
2009 Sales: $5,450,000 — 2009 Profits: $537,000
2008 Sales: $5,273,000 — 2008 Profits: $461,000
2007 Sales: $4,847,000 — 2007 Profits: $501,000
2006 Sales: $4,644,000 — 2006 Profits: $444,000

U.S. Stock Ticker: CLX
Int'l Ticker:
Int'l Exchange:
Employees: 8,300 Fiscal Year Ends: 6/30
Parent Company:

SALARIES/BENEFITS:

Pension Plan: Y ESOP Stock Plan: Profit Sharing: Y Top Exec. Salary: $1,075,000 Bonus: $1,967,250
Savings Plan: Y Stock Purch. Plan: Second Exec. Salary: $638,750 Bonus: $802,640

OTHER THOUGHTS:

Apparent Women Officers or Directors: 5
Hot Spot for Advancement for Women/Minorities: Y

LOCATIONS: ("Y" = Yes)

West:	Southwest:	Midwest:	Southeast:	Northeast:	International:
Y	Y	Y	Y	Y	Y

CNA FINANCIAL CORP

www.cna.com

Industry Group Code: 524126

Management:		**Sales/Marketing:**		**Liberal Arts:**		**Information Sys.:**		**Professionals:**		**Tech./Scientific:**	
Mgmt. Trainees:	Y	Marketing Pros.:	Y	Gen. Writing/Editing:	Y	Info. Mgmt.:	Y	Finance/Acct.:	Y	Engineers, Elec.:	
Experienced Mgmt.:	Y	Retail Sales:		Tech. Writing:		Software Dev.:	Y	Law:	Y	Engineers, Other:	
Int'l Business:	Y	Comm./Industrial:	Y	Graphic Arts/Photog.:		Hardware Dev.:		HR/Other:	Y	Health/Lab:	
MBA Grads:	Y	Sales Trainees:		Music:		Consulting/Other:		Training:	Y	Science/Research:	Y
		Advertising Pros.:	Y	Broadcasting:				Health Care:	Y	Petroleum/Chem.:	
				Other:				Consulting:		Math/Other:	Y

TYPES OF BUSINESS:

Insurance, Direct Property & Casualty
Life Insurance
Accident & Health Insurance
Claims & Risk Services

BRANDS/DIVISIONS/AFFILIATES:

Continental Casualty Co.
Continental Insurance Co. (The)
Loews Corporation
CNA Specialty
CNA Surety Corporation
CNA Commercial

CONTACTS:

Note: Officers with more than one job title may be intentionally listed here more than once.

Thomas F. Motamed, CEO
D. Craig Mense, CFO/Exec. VP
Thomas Pontarelli, Chief Admin. Officer/Exec. VP
Jonathan D. Kantor, General Counsel/Exec. VP/Sec.
Tim Szerlong, Pres., Worldwide Field Oper.
John Angerami, Sr. VP-CNA Select Risk
Larry A. Haefner, Exec. VP/Chief Actuary
Peter W. Wilson, Pres./COO-CNA Specialty
Bob Lindemann, Pres./COO-CNA Commercial
Thomas F. Motamed, Chmn.
George R. Fay, Exec. VP-Worldwide P&C Claim

Phone: 312-822-5000 **Fax:** 312-822-6419
Toll-Free: 800-262-2000
Address: 333 S. Wabash, Chicago, IL 60604 US

GROWTH PLANS/SPECIAL FEATURES:

CNA Financial Corp. is an insurance holding company. As a U.S. property and casualty insurer, the firm has more than 1 million corporate and professional customers throughout the U.S., Europe and Canada. The core insurance products offered consist of property and casualty coverage, conducted by Continental Casualty Co. and The Continental Insurance Co. These products are reported in two business segments: CNA Commercial and CNA Specialty. Within the CNA Commercial segment, the company offers standard property and casual coverage to small businesses; and commercial insurance and risk management products to large corporations. CNA Specialty provides a range of professional, financial and specialty property and casualty products; surety bonds; and vehicle warranty service contracts. This segment also offers coverage internationally. CNA Financial's non-core operations are managed in two segments: life and group non-core; and corporate and other non-core. The life and group non-core segment includes the life and group lines of business that have been sold or placed in run off. Corporate and other non-core consists of certain corporate expenses and certain property and casualty businesses in run-off. Loews Corporation owns approximately 90% of the company. In 2010, CNA Financial opened new offices in Denver, Chicago, Washington, D.C., New York City, Los Angeles, and Birmingham. In June 2011, the firm acquired CNA Surety Corporation, which now operates as an indirect, wholly-owned subsidiary of the company.

The company offers its employees life, disability, AD&D, medical, dental and vision insurance; flexible spending accounts; a 401(k) savings plan; adoption and tuition reimbursement; domestic partner benefits; university collaboration onsite degree programs; a transit reimbursement incentive program; paid vacation; and an assistance program.

FINANCIALS:

Sales and profits are in thousands of dollars—add 000 to get the full amount. 2010 Note: Financial information for 2010 was not available for all companies at press time.

2010 Sales: $9,209,000	2010 Profits: $690,000	**U.S. Stock Ticker: CNA**
2009 Sales: $8,472,000	2009 Profits: $419,000	**Int'l Ticker:**
2008 Sales: $7,799,000	2008 Profits: $-299,000	Int'l Exchange:
2007 Sales: $10,196,000	2007 Profits: $851,000	Employees: 8,000 Fiscal Year Ends: 12/31
2006 Sales: $10,290,000	2006 Profits: $1,108,000	Parent Company: LOEWS CORPORATION

SALARIES/BENEFITS:

Pension Plan:	ESOP Stock Plan:	Profit Sharing:	Top Exec. Salary: $1,000,000	Bonus: $3,450,000
Savings Plan: Y	Stock Purch. Plan:		Second Exec. Salary: $800,000	Bonus: $2,310,000

OTHER THOUGHTS:

Apparent Women Officers or Directors:
Hot Spot for Advancement for Women/Minorities:

LOCATIONS: ("Y" = Yes)

West:	Southwest:	Midwest:	Southeast:	Northeast:	International:
Y	Y	Y	Y	Y	Y

COACH INC

www.coach.com

Industry Group Code: 315292

Management:		Sales/Marketing:		Liberal Arts:		Information Sys.:		Professionals:		Tech./Scientific:	
Mgmt. Trainees:	Y	Marketing Pros.:	Y	Gen. Writing/Editing:	Y	Info. Mgmt.:	Y	Finance/Acct.:	Y	Engineers, Elec.:	
Experienced Mgmt.:	Y	Retail Sales:	Y	Tech. Writing:		Software Dev.:	Y	Law:	Y	Engineers, Other:	
Int'l Business:	Y	Comm./Industrial:	Y	Graphic Arts/Photog.:	Y	Hardware Dev.:		HR/Other:	Y	Health/Lab:	
MBA Grads:	Y	Sales Trainees:	Y	Music:		Consulting/Other:		Training:	Y	Science/Research:	
		Advertising Pros.:	Y	Broadcasting:				Health Care:		Petroleum/Chem.:	
				Other:	Y			Consulting:		Math/Other:	

TYPES OF BUSINESS:

Leather Accessories
Online & Catalog Sales
Outlet Stores
Purses

BRANDS/DIVISIONS/AFFILIATES:

Coach.com
Coach Japan, Inc.

CONTACTS: *Note: Officers with more than one job title may be intentionally listed here more than once.*

Lew Frankfort, CEO
Jerry Stritzke, COO
Jerry Stritzke, Pres.
Micheal F. Devine, III, CFO/Exec. VP
Sarah Dunn, Sr. VP-Human Resources
Todd Kahn, General Counsel/Sr. VP/Sec.
Michael Tucci, Pres., Retail Div.-North American Retail
Reed Krakoff, Exec. Creative Dir.
Lew Frankfort, Chmn.

Phone: 212-594-1850	**Fax:** 212-594-1682
Toll-Free: 888-262-6224	
Address: 516 W. 34th St., New York, NY 10001 US	

GROWTH PLANS/SPECIAL FEATURES:

Coach, Inc. is a designer, producer and marketer of fine accessories and gifts for men and women, including handbags, women's and men's accessories, footwear, outerwear, business luggage and travel accessories, cases, eyewear, watches, jewelry and fragrance. The firm also licenses its name for watches, shoes and eyewear. The company sells its products through a number of direct channels, accounting for approximately 87% of its sales. The Coach brand is available at over 970 department store locations in the U.S. and 182 international department stores, retail store and duty-free shop locations in over 20 countries. Approximately 63% of the company's sales come from handbags, roughly 27% come from accessories (wristlets, cosmetic cases, money pieces, etc.) and the final 10% of sales derive from all other products (sunglasses, watches, fragrance, etc.). Over the last several years, Coach has successfully transformed itself from a manufacturer of classic leather products to a marketer of more modern, fashionable handbags and accessories, using a broader range of fabrics and materials. Through the firm's web site Coach.com, customers can shop for new products and locate a store nearest to them. In early 2010, the company announced a partnership with BeautyBank and Aramis & Designer Fragrances, to expand Coach Beauty. Coach plans to increase its existing fragrance and beauty line globally, with immediate plans to enter specialty retailers and North American department stores. BeautyBank and Aramis & Designer Fragrances are divisions of The Estee Lauder Companies Inc. At its retail units, Coach's average sales per square foot of store space per year were an estimated $1,800 in 2011. In September 2011, the company opened its first European flagship store in London.

FINANCIALS: **Sales and profits are in thousands of dollars—add 000 to get the full amount. 2010 Note: Financial information for 2010 was not available for all companies at press time.**

2010 Sales: $3,607,636	2010 Profits: $734,940	**U.S. Stock Ticker: COH**
2009 Sales: $3,230,468	2009 Profits: $623,369	**Int'l Ticker:**
2008 Sales: $3,180,757	2008 Profits: $783,055	Int'l Exchange:
2007 Sales: $2,612,456	2007 Profits: $663,665	Employees: 13,000 Fiscal Year Ends: 6/30
2006 Sales: $2,035,085	2006 Profits: $494,277	Parent Company:

SALARIES/BENEFITS:

Pension Plan:	ESOP Stock Plan:	Profit Sharing:	Top Exec. Salary: $2,500,000	Bonus: $4,095,000
Savings Plan:	Stock Purch. Plan:		Second Exec. Salary: $1,214,100	Bonus: $2,428,000

OTHER THOUGHTS:

Apparent Women Officers or Directors: 3
Hot Spot for Advancement for Women/Minorities: Y

LOCATIONS: ("Y" = Yes)

West:	Southwest:	Midwest:	Southeast:	Northeast:	International:
Y	Y	Y	Y	Y	Y

COCA-COLA BOTTLING CO CONSOLIDATED

www.cokeconsolidated.com

Industry Group Code: 3121

Management:		Sales/Marketing:		Liberal Arts:		Information Sys.:		Professionals:		Tech./Scientific:	
Mgmt. Trainees:	Y	Marketing Pros.:	Y	Gen. Writing/Editing:		Info. Mgmt.:	Y	Finance/Acct.:	Y	Engineers, Elec.:	
Experienced Mgmt.:	Y	Retail Sales:		Tech. Writing:		Software Dev.:		Law:	Y	Engineers, Other:	
Int'l Business:		Comm./Industrial:	Y	Graphic Arts/Photog.:		Hardware Dev.:		HR/Other:	Y	Health/Lab:	
MBA Grads:	Y	Sales Trainees:		Music:		Consulting/Other:		Training:	Y	Science/Research:	
		Advertising Pros.:		Broadcasting:				Health Care:		Petroleum/Chem.:	
				Other:				Consulting:		Math/Other:	

TYPES OF BUSINESS:

Beverages-Soft Drink Manufacturing
Bottling Services

BRANDS/DIVISIONS/AFFILIATES:

Coca Cola Company (The)
Dr. Pepper
Country Breeze
Tum-E Yummies
POWERade
Cinnabon Premium Coffee Lattes

CONTACTS: *Note: Officers with more than one job title may be intentionally listed here more than once.*

J. Frank Harrison, III, CEO
William B. Elmore, COO
William B. Elmore, Pres.
James E. Harris, CFO/Sr. VP
Robert G. Chambless, Sr. VP-Mktg. & Sales
Kevin A. Henry, Chief Human Resources Officer/Sr. VP
Umesh M. Kasbekar, Sr. VP-Admin.
Steven D. Westphal, Exec. VP-Oper. & Systems
Umesh M. Kasbekar, Sr. VP-Planning
Lauren C. Steele, VP-Corp. Affairs
William J. Billiard, Chief Acct. Officer/Controller/VP
Henry W. Flint, Vice Chmn.
Robert G. Chambless, Sr. VP-Sales
Clifford M. Deal, III, VP/Treas.
Norman C. George, Pres., ByB Brands, Inc.
J. Frank Harrison, III, Chmn.

Phone: 704-557-4000	**Fax:** 704-551-4646
Toll-Free: 800-777-2653	
Address: 4115 Coca Cola Plz., Charlotte, NC 28211 US	

GROWTH PLANS/SPECIAL FEATURES:

Coca-Cola Bottling Co. Consolidated (CCB), founded in 1902, is a nonalcoholic beverage manufacturer and distributor. The firm primarily produces, markets and distributes products of The Coca-Cola Company, which owns approximately 27.1% of CCB. The company manufactures products in two categories: sparkling beverages, which consist of beverages with carbonation, including energy drinks; and still beverages, including bottled water, tea, ready-to-drink coffee, enhanced water, juices and sports drinks. CCB distributes and markets in certain regions still beverages of The Coca-Cola Company such as POWERade, Minute Maid Adult Refreshments and Minute Maid Juices To Go. It also produces and markets Dr. Pepper, Cinnabon Premium Coffee Lattes and Sundrop in some of its regions. The company's principal soft drink is Coca-Cola classic. The company also markets and distributes certain products which it owns, including Respect, a vitamin and mineral enhanced beverage; Country Breeze tea and diet Country Breeze tea; and Tum-E Yummies, a vitamin C enhanced flavored drink. Products of The Coca-Cola Company generate more than half of CCB's bottle/can volume to retail customers. CCB holds bottling rights from The Coca-Cola Company covering the majority of North Carolina, South Carolina and West Virginia, as well as portions of Alabama, Mississippi, Tennessee, Kentucky, Virginia, Pennsylvania, Georgia and Florida. The main packaging materials for the firm's beverages are plastic bottles and aluminum cans. In addition, the company provides restaurants and other immediate consumption outlets with fountain products. In June 2010, CCB opened a new warehouse in Horry County, South Carolina.

Employees are offered medical, dental and vision insurance, as well as a 401(k) plan.

FINANCIALS: **Sales and profits are in thousands of dollars—add 000 to get the full amount. 2010 Note: Financial information for 2010 was not available for all companies at press time.**

2010 Sales: $1,514,599	2010 Profits: $39,542	**U.S. Stock Ticker: COKE**
2009 Sales: $1,442,986	2009 Profits: $40,543	**Int'l Ticker:**
2008 Sales: $1,463,615	2008 Profits: $9,091	Int'l Exchange:
2007 Sales: $1,435,999	2007 Profits: $19,856	Employees: 5,200 Fiscal Year Ends: 12/31
2006 Sales: $1,431,005	2006 Profits: $23,243	Parent Company:

SALARIES/BENEFITS:

Pension Plan:	ESOP Stock Plan:	Profit Sharing:	Top Exec. Salary: $837,213	Bonus: $1,122,917
Savings Plan: Y	Stock Purch. Plan:		Second Exec. Salary: $680,974	Bonus: $913,360

OTHER THOUGHTS:

Apparent Women Officers or Directors: 3
Hot Spot for Advancement for Women/Minorities: Y

LOCATIONS: ("Y" = Yes)

West:	Southwest:	Midwest:	Southeast:	Northeast:	International:
Y			Y	Y	

COCA-COLA COMPANY (THE)

www.coca-cola.com

Industry Group Code: 3121

Management:		Sales/Marketing:		Liberal Arts:		Information Sys.:		Professionals:		Tech./Scientific:	
Mgmt. Trainees:	Y	Marketing Pros.:	Y	Gen. Writing/Editing:	Y	Info. Mgmt.:	Y	Finance/Acct.:	Y	Engineers, Elec.:	
Experienced Mgmt.:	Y	Retail Sales:		Tech. Writing:	Y	Software Dev.:	Y	Law:	Y	Engineers, Other:	Y
Int'l Business:	Y	Comm./Industrial:	Y	Graphic Arts/Photog.:	Y	Hardware Dev.:		HR/Other:	Y	Health/Lab:	
MBA Grads:	Y	Sales Trainees:	Y	Music:		Consulting/Other:		Training:	Y	Science/Research:	
		Advertising Pros.:	Y	Broadcasting:				Health Care:		Petroleum/Chem.:	
				Other:	Y			Consulting:		Math/Other:	

TYPES OF BUSINESS:

Soft Drink Manufacturing
Concentrates & Syrups
Sports Drinks
Bottled Water
Fruit Juices

BRANDS/DIVISIONS/AFFILIATES:

Dasani
Odwalla
Powerade
Sprite
Evian
Multon
Beverage Partners Worldwide
Ilko Coffee International

CONTACTS:

Note: Officers with more than one job title may be intentionally listed here more than once.

Muhtar Kent, CEO
Gary P. Fayard, CFO/Exec. VP
Joseph V. Tripodi, Chief Mktg. & Commercial Officer/Sr. VP
Ceree Eberly, Chief People Officer/Sr. VP
Eddie R. Hays, VP-Science
Ed Steinikie, CIO/VP
Harry L. Anderson, Sr. VP-Tech. Svcs.
Alexander B. Cummings, Chief Admin. Officer/Exec. VP
Geoffrey J. Kelly, General Counsel/Sr. VP
John M. Farrell, Chief Strategy Officer
Clyde C. Tuggle, Sr. VP-Corp. Affairs & Productivity
Jerry S. Wilson, Chief Customer & Commercial Officer/Sr. VP
Ingrid Saunders Jones, Chmn.-The Coca-Cola Foundation
Bilal Kaafarani, Sr. VP-Global Research & Innovation
Brian P. Kelley, Pres., North America Bus. Integration
Muhtar Kent, Chmn.
Ann T. Taylor, Pres., Global Bus. Svcs.
Rick Frazier, VP-Supply Chain

Phone: 404-676-2121 **Fax:** 404-676-6792
Toll-Free: 800-438-2653
Address: 1 Coca-Cola Plz., Atlanta, GA 30313 US

GROWTH PLANS/SPECIAL FEATURES:

The Coca-Cola Company manufactures, distributes and markets nonalcoholic beverages, beverage concentrates and beverage syrups in over 200 countries. The company sells beverage concentrates and syrups to bottling and canning operations, fountain wholesalers and some fountain retailers. Additionally, it sells finished beverages. Coca-Cola owns or licenses over 500 brands, including diet and light beverages; waters; enhanced waters; juices and juice drinks; teas; coffees; and energy and sports drinks. The firm has ownership interests in numerous joint ventures, bottling operations and canning operations, although most of these operations are independently owned and managed. The company operates through six regional segments in addition to its corporate and bottling segments. Coca-Cola's carbonated products include Coca-Cola Classic, Diet Coke, Coca-Cola Zero, Fanta, Sprite, Diet Sprite, Sprite Zero, Sprite Light, Fresca and Barq's. The firm also produces, distributes and markets juice and juice-drink products including Minute Maid, Simply, Odwalla, Five Alive, Bacardi mixers and Hi-C. Coca-Cola also has a license to manufacture and sell concentrates for Seagram's mixers, a line of sparkling drinks. Multon, a Russian juice business operated as a joint venture with Coca-Cola Hellenic Bottling Company S.A., markets juice products in Russia, Ukraine and Belarus. Beverage Partners Worldwide, a joint venture with Nestle S.A., markets tea products under trademarks including Enviga, Gold Peak, Nestea and Frestea; and coffee products under Nescafé, Taster's Choice and Georgia Club. Other joint ventures include Ilko Coffee International, S.r.l., formed in cooperation with illycafe S.p.A; and Hellenic Partners GmbH, a joint venture between Coca-Cola Hellenic and Ilko Coffee. In February 2010, the firm announced plans to acquire the North American operations of Coca-Cola Enterprises (CCE) and create a new entity named Coca-Cola Refreshments USA, Inc. Concurrently, CCE will acquire bottling operations in Norway and Sweden.

FINANCIALS:

Sales and profits are in thousands of dollars—add 000 to get the full amount. 2010 Note: Financial information for 2010 was not available for all companies at press time.

2010 Sales: $35,119,000	2010 Profits: $11,809,000
2009 Sales: $30,990,000	2009 Profits: $6,824,000
2008 Sales: $31,944,000	2008 Profits: $5,807,000
2007 Sales: $28,857,000	2007 Profits: $5,981,000
2006 Sales: $24,088,000	2006 Profits: $5,080,000

U.S. Stock Ticker: KO
Int'l Ticker:
Int'l Exchange:
Employees: 139,600 Fiscal Year Ends: 12/31
Parent Company:

SALARIES/BENEFITS:

Pension Plan:	ESOP Stock Plan:	Profit Sharing:	Top Exec. Salary: $1,200,000	Bonus: $5,500,000
Savings Plan: Y	Stock Purch. Plan:		Second Exec. Salary: $787,500	Bonus: $1,505,000

OTHER THOUGHTS:

Apparent Women Officers or Directors: 3
Hot Spot for Advancement for Women/Minorities: Y

LOCATIONS: ("Y" = Yes)

West:	Southwest:	Midwest:	Southeast:	Northeast:	International:
Y	Y	Y	Y	Y	Y

COGNIZANT TECHNOLOGY SOLUTIONS CORP www.cognizant.com

Industry Group Code: 541513

Management:		Sales/Marketing:		Liberal Arts:		Information Sys.:		Professionals:		Tech./Scientific:	
Mgmt. Trainees:	Y	Marketing Pros.:	Y	Gen. Writing/Editing:	Y	Info. Mgmt.:	Y	Finance/Acct.:	Y	Engineers, Elec.:	Y
Experienced Mgmt.:	Y	Retail Sales:		Tech. Writing:	Y	Software Dev.:	Y	Law:	Y	Engineers, Other:	
Int'l Business:	Y	Comm./Industrial:	Y	Graphic Arts/Photog.:	Y	Hardware Dev.:	Y	HR/Other:	Y	Health/Lab:	
MBA Grads:	Y	Sales Trainees:		Music:		Consulting/Other:	Y	Training:	Y	Science/Research:	
		Advertising Pros.:		Broadcasting:				Health Care:		Petroleum/Chem.:	
				Other:	Y			Consulting:	Y	Math/Other:	

TYPES OF BUSINESS:

Consulting-IT & Systems
Outsourcing Services
Software Engineering

BRANDS/DIVISIONS/AFFILIATES:

PIPC Group (The)
Process Space
UBS India Service Centre Private Limited
Galileo Performance

CONTACTS: *Note: Officers with more than one job title may be intentionally listed here more than once.*

Fransisco D'Souza, CEO
Gordon J. Coburn, COO
Fransisco D'Souza, Pres.
Gordon J. Coburn, CFO
Gordon J. Coburn, Sec.
Rajeev Mehta, COO-Global Client Svcs.
Gordon J. Coburn, Treas.
John E. Klein, Chmn.
Chandra Sekaran, Pres./Managing Dir.-Global Delivery

Phone: 201-801-0233	**Fax:** 201-801-0243
Toll-Free: 888-937-3277	
Address: 500 Frank W. Burr Blvd., Teaneck, NJ 07666 US	

GROWTH PLANS/SPECIAL FEATURES:

Cognizant Technology Solutions Corp. specializes in custom IT design, development, integration and maintenance services. The firm provides these services primarily to Global 2000 companies located in the U.S., Europe and Asia. The company's core competencies include complex systems development; application maintenance; infrastructure management; enterprise software package implementation and maintenance; technology strategy consulting; data warehousing and business intelligence; application testing; and vertically-oriented business process outsourcing (V-BPO). Cognizant provides its IT services using an integrated on-site/offshore business model. This business model combines technical and account management teams located on-site at the customer location and offshore at dedicated development centers located primarily in India, Argentina, the U.S., the Philippines, China and Hungary. Cognizant operates in four business segments: financial services, which provides services to customers in the banking and insurance industries; healthcare, which provides services to healthcare and life science industries; manufacturing, retail and logistics, which provides services to those industries; and other, which covers communications, information services, media and high technology. The firm has developed proprietary methodologies for integrating on-site and offshore teams, including Cognizant's Process Space software engineering process, which is available to all on-site and offshore programmers. For most projects, Process Space is used as part of an initial assessment that allows the firm to define the scope and risks of the project and subdivide the project into smaller phases with frequent deliverables and feedback from customers. In May 2010, the company acquired U.K.-based program management consulting firm The PIPC Group. In June 2010, the firm acquired French IT testing consulting services provider Galileo Performance.

FINANCIALS: **Sales and profits are in thousands of dollars—add 000 to get the full amount. 2010 Note: Financial information for 2010 was not available for all companies at press time.**

2010 Sales: $4,592,389	2010 Profits: $733,540
2009 Sales: $3,278,663	2009 Profits: $534,963
2008 Sales: $2,816,304	2008 Profits: $430,845
2007 Sales: $2,135,577	2007 Profits: $350,133
2006 Sales: $1,424,267	2006 Profits: $232,795

U.S. Stock Ticker: CTSH
Int'l Ticker:
Int'l Exchange:
Employees: 104,000 Fiscal Year Ends: 12/31
Parent Company:

SALARIES/BENEFITS:

Pension Plan:	ESOP Stock Plan: Y	Profit Sharing:	Top Exec. Salary: $518,400	Bonus: $590,216
Savings Plan: Y	Stock Purch. Plan: Y		Second Exec. Salary: $466,560	Bonus: $531,195

OTHER THOUGHTS:

Apparent Women Officers or Directors: 1
Hot Spot for Advancement for Women/Minorities:

LOCATIONS: ("Y" = Yes)

West:	Southwest:	Midwest:	Southeast:	Northeast:	International:
Y	Y	Y		Y	Y

COLDWATER CREEK INC

www.coldwatercreek.com

Industry Group Code: 454113

Management:		Sales/Marketing:		Liberal Arts:		Information Sys.:		Professionals:		Tech./Scientific:	
Mgmt. Trainees:	Y	Marketing Pros.:	Y	Gen. Writing/Editing:	Y	Info. Mgmt.:	Y	Finance/Acct.:	Y	Engineers, Elec.:	
Experienced Mgmt.:	Y	Retail Sales:	Y	Tech. Writing:		Software Dev.:	Y	Law:	Y	Engineers, Other:	
Int'l Business:		Comm./Industrial:		Graphic Arts/Photog.:	Y	Hardware Dev.:		HR/Other:	Y	Health/Lab:	
MBA Grads:	Y	Sales Trainees:	Y	Music:		Consulting/Other:		Training:	Y	Science/Research:	
		Advertising Pros.:	Y	Broadcasting:				Health Care:		Petroleum/Chem.:	
				Other:	Y			Consulting:		Math/Other:	

TYPES OF BUSINESS:

Upscale Apparel-Women's
Catalog Sales
Gifts, Jewelry & Accessories
Retail & Outlet Stores
Online Sales

BRANDS/DIVISIONS/AFFILIATES:

Coldwatercreek.com
Gifts-To-Go
Northcountry
Spirit
Coldwater Creek, The Spa

CONTACTS: *Note: Officers with more than one job title may be intentionally listed here more than once.*

Dennis C. Pence, CEO
Dennis C. Pence, Pres.
James A. Bell, CFO/Sr. VP
Tim Dilworth, Sr. VP-Mktg.
Kathy McConnell, Sr. VP-Prod. Dev.
John E. Hayes, III, General Counsel/Sr. VP
Gerard El Chaar, Sr. VP-Oper.
Jeffrey Parisian, Chief Strategy Officer/Sr. VP-Real Estate
Georgia Shonk Simmons, Chief Merch.Officer
Jerome Jessup, Chief Creative Officer
Kim Sorenson, Sr. VP-Stores
Waleed Khairzada, Sr. VP-Design & Dev.
Dennis C. Pence, Chmn.

Phone: 208-263-2266 **Fax:** 208-263-1582
Toll-Free: 800-510-2808
Address: 1 Coldwater Creek Dr., Sandpoint, ID 83864 US

GROWTH PLANS/SPECIAL FEATURES:

Coldwater Creek, Inc. retails women's apparel, jewelry, footwear, gift items and home merchandise through three sales channels: a traditional catalog business, an e-commerce web site and retail stores. The company targets professional women who are 35 years of age and older, with household incomes in excess of $75,000. The firm's primary catalog titles and merchandise lines are Northcountry and Spirit. Northcountry is the firm's most established and popular line, offering a broad selection of casual merchandise. Spirit offers a more upscale assortment of apparel, including dresses, jackets and sportswear appropriate for office wear. The Coldwater Creek catalog features merchandise available in the company's stores and is designed to encourage customers to shop in store. Coldwater Creek also sends periodic specialty mailings, such as the Gifts-To-Go holiday catalog. The firm's web site features its entire full-priced, first-line merchandise collection. The company currently has 373 full-line stores and 39 merchandise clearance outlet stores across the U.S. Additionally, the firm operates nine day spas under the name Coldwater Creek The Spa, which offer massages, facials, body treatments, manicures and pedicures and feminine personal care products. Coldwater Creek also maintains a customer contact and technical center in Coeur d'Alene, Idaho, comprising 60,000 square feet, and a 960,000-square-foot customer contact and distribution center in Mineral Wells, West Virginia.

Employees are offered medical, dental and life insurance; a 401(k) plan; an employee stock purchase plan; and discounts on Coldwater Creek products.

FINANCIALS: **Sales and profits are in thousands of dollars—add 000 to get the full amount. 2010 Note: Financial information for 2010 was not available for all companies at press time.**

2010 Sales: $1,038,581 | 2010 Profits: $-56,132
2009 Sales: $1,024,221 | 2009 Profits: $-25,963
2008 Sales: $1,151,472 | 2008 Profits: $-2,488
2007 Sales: $1,054,611 | 2007 Profits: $55,372
2006 Sales: $779,663 | 2006 Profits: $41,570

U.S. Stock Ticker: CWTR
Int'l Ticker:
Int'l Exchange:
Employees: 9,531 Fiscal Year Ends: 1/31
Parent Company:

SALARIES/BENEFITS:

Pension Plan: | ESOP Stock Plan: | Profit Sharing: | Top Exec. Salary: $600,000 | Bonus: $
Savings Plan: Y | Stock Purch. Plan: Y | | Second Exec. Salary: $581,731 | Bonus: $152,100

OTHER THOUGHTS:

Apparent Women Officers or Directors: 5
Hot Spot for Advancement for Women/Minorities: Y

LOCATIONS: ("Y" = Yes)

West:	Southwest:	Midwest:	Southeast:	Northeast:	International:
Y	Y	Y	Y	Y	

COLGATE PALMOLIVE CO

www.colgate.com

Industry Group Code: 325611

Management:		Sales/Marketing:		Liberal Arts:		Information Sys.:		Professionals:		Tech./Scientific:	
Mgmt. Trainees:	Y	Marketing Pros.:	Y	Gen. Writing/Editing:	Y	Info. Mgmt.:	Y	Finance/Acct.:	Y	Engineers, Elec.:	
Experienced Mgmt.:	Y	Retail Sales:		Tech. Writing:	Y	Software Dev.:	Y	Law:	Y	Engineers, Other:	Y
Int'l Business:	Y	Comm./Industrial:	Y	Graphic Arts/Photog.:	Y	Hardware Dev.:		HR/Other:	Y	Health/Lab:	Y
MBA Grads:	Y	Sales Trainees:	Y	Music:		Consulting/Other:		Training:	Y	Science/Research:	Y
		Advertising Pros.:	Y	Broadcasting:				Health Care:		Petroleum/Chem.:	Y
				Other:	Y			Consulting:		Math/Other:	

TYPES OF BUSINESS:

Toothpaste & Oral Care Products Manufacturer
Household Cleaning Products
Soap Products
Baby Care Products
Pet Food
Hair Products
Shaving Products

BRANDS/DIVISIONS/AFFILIATES:

Softsoap
Palmolive
Ajax
Irish Spring
Tom's of Maine
Lady Speed Stick
Hill's Pet Nutrition
Science Diet

CONTACTS: *Note: Officers with more than one job title may be intentionally listed here more than once.*

Ian M. Cook, CEO
Ian M. Cook, Pres.
Dennis Hickey, CFO
Spencer Pingel, VP-Global Mktg.
Daniel B. Marsili, Sr. VP-Global Human Resources
Daniel Bagley, VP-Global R&D
Tom Greene, CIO/VP
Andrew D. Hendry, General Counsel/Sr. VP/Sec.
Jan Guifarro, VP-Corp. Comm.
Bina H. Thompson, VP-Investor Rel.
Joseph M. Bertolini, VP-Global Finance
Nigel B. Burton, Pres., Global Oral Care
Hector I. Erezuma, VP-Taxation
Tom O'Brien, CEO-Tom's of Maine
Neil Thompson, CEO/Pres., Hill's Pet Nutrition
Ian M. Cook, Chmn.
Fabian Garcia, COO-Europe
Manuel Arrese, VP-Global Supply Chain

Phone: 212-310-2000	**Fax:** 212-310-3284
Toll-Free: 800-468-6502	
Address: 300 Park Ave., New York, NY 10022 US	

GROWTH PLANS/SPECIAL FEATURES:

Colgate-Palmolive Co. (Colgate), founded in 1806, is a consumer products company whose products are marketed in over 200 countries and territories throughout the world. The company manages its business in two product segments: oral, personal and home care; and pet nutrition. Colgate oral care products include toothbrushes, toothpaste, tooth whitener, mouth rinses, dental floss and pharmaceutical products for dentists and other oral health professionals. The segment also markets bar and liquid hand soaps; shower gels, shampoos; conditioners; deodorants; antiperspirants; and shave products. The firm's Softsoap and Palmolive brands are two U.S. market leaders in liquid soaps. Other major products include household care products such as Ajax and Palmolive dishwashing liquids and Murphy's Oil Soap. Additional oral, personal and home care brands include Mennen, Irish Spring, Tom's of Maine and Lady Speed Stick. Colgate also supplies specialty pet nutrition products for dogs and cats through subsidiary Hill's Pet Nutrition, with products marketed in over 95 countries. Pet foods are marketed primarily under the Science Diet and Prescription Diet trademarks. Science Diet is sold by authorized pet supply retailers, breeders and veterinarians for everyday nutritional needs, while Prescription Diet includes a range of therapeutic products sold by veterinarians to help nutritionally manage disease conditions in dogs and cats. In March 2011, the company acquired the Sanex Personal Care brand in Europe from Unilever PLC for approximately $940 million. Also in March 2011, the firm divested its laundry detergent business in Colombia.

Colgate offers its employees medical, dental and vision insurance; flexible spending accounts; short- and long-term disability coverage; life, critical illness and pet insurance; a 401(k) and retirement plan; a profit sharing plan; near-site back-up childcare centers; emergency in-home care for dependent children and adults; tuition assistance; academic advisory services; counseling services; and relocation assistance.

FINANCIALS: **Sales and profits are in thousands of dollars—add 000 to get the full amount. 2010 Note: Financial information for 2010 was not available for all companies at press time.**

2010 Sales: $15,564,000	2010 Profits: $2,203,000
2009 Sales: $15,327,000	2009 Profits: $2,291,000
2008 Sales: $15,330,000	2008 Profits: $1,957,200
2007 Sales: $13,789,700	2007 Profits: $1,737,400
2006 Sales: $12,237,700	2006 Profits: $1,353,400

U.S. Stock Ticker: CL
Int'l Ticker:
Int'l Exchange:
Employees: 39,200 Fiscal Year Ends: 12/31
Parent Company:

SALARIES/BENEFITS:

Pension Plan: Y	ESOP Stock Plan:	Profit Sharing: Y	Top Exec. Salary: $1,150,000	Bonus: $3,381,000
Savings Plan: Y	Stock Purch. Plan:		Second Exec. Salary: $838,933	Bonus: $771,076

OTHER THOUGHTS:

Apparent Women Officers or Directors: 36
Hot Spot for Advancement for Women/Minorities: Y

LOCATIONS: ("Y" = Yes)

West:	Southwest:	Midwest:	Southeast:	Northeast:	International:
Y	Y	Y	Y	Y	Y

Sales, profits and employees may be estimates. Financial information, benefits and other data can change quickly and may vary from those stated here.

COMCAST CORP

www.comcast.com

Industry Group Code: 517110

Management:		Sales/Marketing:		Liberal Arts:		Information Sys.:		Professionals:		Tech./Scientific:	
Mgmt. Trainees:	Y	Marketing Pros.:	Y	Gen. Writing/Editing:	Y	Info. Mgmt.:	Y	Finance/Acct.:	Y	Engineers, Elec.:	Y
Experienced Mgmt.:	Y	Retail Sales:		Tech. Writing:	Y	Software Dev.:	Y	Law:	Y	Engineers, Other:	Y
Int'l Business:	Y	Comm./Industrial:	Y	Graphic Arts/Photog.:	Y	Hardware Dev.:		HR/Other:	Y	Health/Lab:	
MBA Grads:	Y	Sales Trainees:	Y	Music:		Consulting/Other:		Training:	Y	Science/Research:	
		Advertising Pros.:	Y	Broadcasting:	Y			Health Care:		Petroleum/Chem.:	
				Other:	Y			Consulting:		Math/Other:	

TYPES OF BUSINESS:

Cable Television
VoIP Service
Cable Network Programming
High-Speed Internet Service
Video-on-Demand
Advertising Services
Interactive Program Schedules
Wireless Services

BRANDS/DIVISIONS/AFFILIATES:

NBC Universal LLC
Philadelphia Flyers
Philadelphia 76ers
Fandango Inc
Global Spectrum LP
Golf Channel (The)
Comcast Interactive Media
Xfinity TV

CONTACTS: *Note: Officers with more than one job title may be intentionally listed here more than once.*

Brian L. Roberts, CEO
Stephen B. Burke, COO
Michael J. Angelakis, CFO
Ken Carrig, Exec. VP-Human Resources, Comcast Cable
Karen D. Buchholz, VP-Admin.
Arthur R. Block, General Counsel/Sr. VP/Corp. Sec.
Robert S. Pick, Sr. VP-Corp. Dev.
Amy L. Banse, Sr. VP/Pres., Comcast Interactive Media
D'Arcy F. Rudnay, Sr. VP-Corp. Comm.
Marlene S. Dooner, Sr. VP-Investor Rel.
Lawrence J. Salva, Chief Acct. Officer/Controller/Sr. VP
Stephen B. Burke, Pres., Comcast Cable
Jeffrey Shell, Sr. VP/Pres., Comcast Programming
Robert S. Victor, Sr. VP-Strategic & Financial Planning
James J. Finnegan, VP-Strategic Intellectual Property
Brian L. Roberts, Chmn.

Phone: 215-286-1700 **Fax:**
Toll-Free: 800-266-2278
Address: 1 Comcast Ctr., Philadelphia, PA 19103-2838 US

GROWTH PLANS/SPECIAL FEATURES:

Comcast Corp. is one of the largest cable operators in the U.S. The company offers a variety of entertainment, information and communications services to residential and commercial customers. The firm's cable systems serve roughly 22.9 million video subscribers, 16.7 million high-speed Internet subscribers and 8.4 million telephone subscribers; it also passes over 51.2 million homes in 39 states and Washington, D.C. Comcast operates in two segments: cable and programming. The cable segment, which generates approximately 95% of revenue, manages and operates the firm's cable systems, including video, high-speed Internet and phone services, as well as the regional sports networks. The programming segment consists primarily of consolidated national programming networks, including E!, The Golf Channel, VERSUS, G4 and Style. Comcast's other business interests include Comcast Spectacor and Comcast Interactive Media. Comcast Spectacor owns the Philadelphia Flyers, the Philadelphia 76ers and the Wachovia Center. It also manages additional facilities for sporting events, concerts and other events. Comcast Interactive Media develops and operates the company's Internet businesses focused on entertainment, information and communication, including Comcast.net, Fandango, Plaxo, Fancast, thePlatform and DailyCandy. In March 2010, the firm partnered with Internet Systems Consortium to launch The Address Family Transition Router, an open source software developed to aid in the transition to and from an IPv4 to an IPv6 global numbering network. In October 2010, Comcast launched Xfinity TV, an online portal for digital subscribers that offers access to some 150,000 video choices including TV shows, full-length movies and other content. In January 2011, Comcast completed its acquisition of 51% of NBC Universal LLC from GE, making Comcast the first U.S. cable company to own a major broadcast network. Though GE will retain a 49% stake in NBC, Comcast will be responsible for its management.

FINANCIALS: **Sales and profits are in thousands of dollars—add 000 to get the full amount. 2010 Note: Financial information for 2010 was not available for all companies at press time.**

2010 Sales: $37,937,000 — 2010 Profits: $3,635,000
2009 Sales: $35,756,000 — 2009 Profits: $3,638,000
2008 Sales: $34,256,000 — 2008 Profits: $2,547,000
2007 Sales: $30,895,000 — 2007 Profits: $2,587,000
2006 Sales: $24,966,000 — 2006 Profits: $2,533,000

U.S. Stock Ticker: CMCSA
Int'l Ticker:
Int'l Exchange:
Employees: 102,000 Fiscal Year Ends: 12/31
Parent Company:

SALARIES/BENEFITS:

Pension Plan:	ESOP Stock Plan:	Profit Sharing:	Top Exec. Salary: $2,908,483	Bonus: $8,234,238
Savings Plan: Y	Stock Purch. Plan: Y		Second Exec. Salary: $2,329,543	Bonus: $9,595,196

OTHER THOUGHTS:

Apparent Women Officers or Directors: 10
Hot Spot for Advancement for Women/Minorities: Y

LOCATIONS: ("Y" = Yes)

West:	Southwest:	Midwest:	Southeast:	Northeast:	International:
Y	Y	Y	Y	Y	Y

COMMUNITY HEALTH SYSTEMS INC

www.chs.net

Industry Group Code: 622110

Management:		Sales/Marketing:		Liberal Arts:		Information Sys.:		Professionals:		Tech./Scientific:	
Mgmt. Trainees:	Y	Marketing Pros.:	Y	Gen. Writing/Editing:	Y	Info. Mgmt.:	Y	Finance/Acct.:	Y	Engineers, Elec.:	
Experienced Mgmt.:	Y	Retail Sales:		Tech. Writing:	Y	Software Dev.:	Y	Law:	Y	Engineers, Other:	
Int'l Business:		Comm./Industrial:		Graphic Arts/Photog.:	Y	Hardware Dev.:		HR/Other:	Y	Health/Lab:	Y
MBA Grads:	Y	Sales Trainees:		Music:		Consulting/Other:		Training:	Y	Science/Research:	
		Advertising Pros.:	Y	Broadcasting:				Health Care:	Y	Petroleum/Chem.:	
				Other:	Y			Consulting:		Math/Other:	

TYPES OF BUSINESS:

Hospitals
Surgical & Emergency Services
Acute Care Services
Internal Medicine
Obstetrics
Emergency Room Services
Diagnostic Services
Ambulatory Surgery Centers

BRANDS/DIVISIONS/AFFILIATES:

Quorum Health Resources, LLC
Forum Health
Bluefield Regional Medical Center
Mercy Health Partners
Moses Taylor Health Care System
Tomball Regional Medical Center

CONTACTS: *Note: Officers with more than one job title may be intentionally listed here more than once.*

Wayne T. Smith, CEO
Wayne T. Smith, Pres.
W. Larry Cash, CFO/Exec. VP
Debra S. Landers, Chief Mktg. Officer/VP
Robert A. Horrar, VP-Human Resources
Barbara R. Paul, Chief Medical Officer/Sr. VP
J. Gary Seay, CIO/Sr. VP
Robert A. Horrar, VP-Admin.
Rachel A. Seifert, General Counsel/Exec. VP/Sec.
Martin G. Schweinhart, Sr. VP-Oper.
Kenneth D. Hawkins, Sr. VP-Acquisitions & Dev.
Tomi Galin, VP-Corp. Comm.
Lizbeth R. Schuler, VP-Investor Rel.
T. Mark Buford, Chief Acct. Officer/Sr. VP
Kathie G. Thomas, Pres., Home Care Div.
Larry M. Carlton, Sr. VP-Revenue Mgmt.
James W. Doucette, Treas./VP
Robert O. Horrar, VP-Bus. Dev.
Wayne T. Smith, Chmn.
Tim G. Marlette, Chief Purchasing Officer/Sr. VP

Phone: 615-465-7000 **Fax:**
Toll-Free:
Address: 4000 Meridian Blvd., Franklin, TN 37067 US

GROWTH PLANS/SPECIAL FEATURES:

Community Health Systems, Inc. is one of the largest operators of hospitals in the U.S. The company owns, leases and operates 131 hospitals in 29 states, with an aggregate of around 19,500 licensed beds. The firm generates revenue by providing a broad range of hospital healthcare services including general acute care services, emergency room services, specialty surgery, critical care, internal medicine, obstetrics and diagnostic services. As part of providing these services, the company also owns imaging centers, physician practices and ambulatory surgery centers. Through Community Health Systems' subsidiary, Quorum Health Resources, LLC (QHR), it also provides management and consulting services to non-affiliated general acute care hospitals. The company's strategy for future growth is acquisition. It targets hospitals in growing, non-urban and select urban healthcare markets for acquisition because of their favorable demographic and economic trends and competitive conditions. In October 2010, Community Health Systems acquired Ohio-based healthcare system Forum Health and West Virginia hospital Bluefield Regional Medical Center. In February 2011, the firm agreed to acquire Mercy Health Partners from Cincinnati-based Catholic Health Partners. In June 2011, the company agreed to sell SouthCrest Hospital and Claremore Regional Hospital, both located in Oklahoma, to Hillcrest HealthCare System. In July 2011, Community Health Systems acquired Moses Taylor Health Care System in Pennsylvania and Tomball Regional Medical Center in Texas.

Employees are offered medical, dental and vision insurance; flexible spending accounts; life insurance and disability insurance; and a 401(k) savings plan.

FINANCIALS: **Sales and profits are in thousands of dollars—add 000 to get the full amount. 2010 Note: Financial information for 2010 was not available for all companies at press time.**

2010 Sales: $12,986,500 | 2010 Profits: $348,441
2009 Sales: $12,107,613 | 2009 Profits: $243,150
2008 Sales: $10,919,095 | 2008 Profits: $218,304
2007 Sales: $7,095,861 | 2007 Profits: $30,289
2006 Sales: $4,180,136 | 2006 Profits: $168,263

U.S. Stock Ticker: CYH
Int'l Ticker:
Int'l Exchange:
Employees: 64,000 Fiscal Year Ends: 12/31
Parent Company:

SALARIES/BENEFITS:

Pension Plan: | ESOP Stock Plan: | Profit Sharing: | Top Exec. Salary: $1,365,000 | Bonus: $4,095,000
Savings Plan: Y | Stock Purch. Plan: Y | | Second Exec. Salary: $735,000 | Bonus: $1,470,000

OTHER THOUGHTS:

Apparent Women Officers or Directors: 18
Hot Spot for Advancement for Women/Minorities: Y

LOCATIONS: ("Y" = Yes)

West:	Southwest:	Midwest:	Southeast:	Northeast:	International:
Y	Y	Y	Y	Y	

Sales, profits and employees may be estimates. Financial information, benefits and other data can change quickly and may vary from those stated here.

COMPUTER SCIENCES CORPORATION (CSC)

www.csc.com

Industry Group Code: 541513

Management:		Sales/Marketing:		Liberal Arts:		Information Sys.:		Professionals:		Tech./Scientific:	
Mgmt. Trainees:		Marketing Pros.:	Y	Gen. Writing/Editing:	Y	Info. Mgmt.:	Y	Finance/Acct.:	Y	Engineers, Elec.:	
Experienced Mgmt.:	Y	Retail Sales:		Tech. Writing:	Y	Software Dev.:	Y	Law:	Y	Engineers, Other:	
Int'l Business:	Y	Comm./Industrial:	Y	Graphic Arts/Photog.:		Hardware Dev.:		HR/Other:	Y	Health/Lab:	
MBA Grads:	Y	Sales Trainees:		Music:		Consulting/Other:	Y	Training:	Y	Science/Research:	
		Advertising Pros.:		Broadcasting:				Health Care:		Petroleum/Chem.:	
				Other:				Consulting:	Y	Math/Other:	Y

TYPES OF BUSINESS:

IT Consulting
Credit Services
Customer Relationship Management
Business Process Reengineering
Management Consulting
Outsourcing
Supply Chain Management
Cloud Computing

BRANDS/DIVISIONS/AFFILIATES:

North American Public Sector
Business Solutions and Services
Managed Services Sector
Bass Company
Vulnerability Research Labs
CenTauri Solutions, LLC

CONTACTS: *Note: Officers with more than one job title may be intentionally listed here more than once.*

Michael W. Laphen, CEO
Michael W. Laphen, Pres.
Michael J. Mancuso, CFO/VP
Peter Allen, Pres., Global Mktg. & Sales
Denise Peppard, VP-Human Resources
William L. Deckelman, Jr., General Counsel/VP/Sec.
Randy E. Phillips, VP-Corp. Dev.
Chris Grandis, Dir.-Media Rel.
Bryan Brady, VP-Investor Rel.
Donald G. DeBuck, VP/Controller
Jim Sheaffer, Pres., North American Public Sector
Jim Cook, Pres., Bus. Solutions & Svcs. Sector
Russ Owen, Pres., Managed Svcs. Sector
Thomas R. Irvin, VP/Treas.
Michael W. Laphen, Chmn.
Guy Hains, Pres., Int'l

Phone: 703-876-1000 **Fax:**
Toll-Free:
Address: 3170 Fairview Park Dr., Falls Church, VA 22042 US

GROWTH PLANS/SPECIAL FEATURES:

Computer Sciences Corporation (CSC) is a leading global provider of information technology and business process outsourcing, consulting and systems integration services and other professional services, specializing in the application of complex information technology (IT). The company delivers its services within three broad service lines: North American Public Sector (NPS), Managed Services Sector (MSS) and Business Services and Solutions (BS&S). The NPS line of business provides a broad spectrum of IT services to the U.S. federal government, ranging from traditional systems integration and outsourcing to complex project management and technical services. Key offerings include enterprise modernization; telecommunications and networking; managed services; base and range operations; and training and simulation. The MSS line of business provides information systems outsourcing services to clients in a broad array of industries including aerospace and defense, automotive, chemical and natural resources, consumer goods, financial services, healthcare, manufacturing, retail and telecommunications. The BS&S line of business provides consulting and systems integration services; business process outsourcing and software maintenance services; credit reporting services, as well as professional technology staffing services in Australia and computer equipment repair and maintenance services in Asia. The company has major operations throughout North America, Europe and the Asia-Pacific region, including India. In April 2010, the firm started offering hosted video services as part of its suite of Unified Communications and Collaboration (UCC) services. Between August and December 2010, CSC acquired three companies: Bass Company; Vulnerability Research Labs; and CenTauri Solutions, LLC.

Employees are offered life, disability, AD&D, medical, dental and vision insurance; flexible spending accounts; a 401(k) plan; an employee assistance program; credit union membership; and educational assistance programs.

FINANCIALS: Sales and profits are in thousands of dollars—add 000 to get the full amount. 2010 Note: Financial information for 2010 was not available for all companies at press time.

2010 Sales: $16,128,000 — 2010 Profits: $834,000
2009 Sales: $16,739,900 — 2009 Profits: $1,115,200
2008 Sales: $16,499,500 — 2008 Profits: $544,600
2007 Sales: $14,854,900 — 2007 Profits: $397,300
2006 Sales: $14,644,800 — 2006 Profits: $495,600

U.S. Stock Ticker: CSC
Int'l Ticker:
Int'l Exchange:
Employees: 94,000 Fiscal Year Ends: 3/31
Parent Company:

SALARIES/BENEFITS:

Pension Plan: ESOP Stock Plan: Profit Sharing: Top Exec. Salary: $1,050,000 Bonus: $2,457,000
Savings Plan: Y Stock Purch. Plan: Second Exec. Salary: $585,000 Bonus: $684,100

OTHER THOUGHTS:

Apparent Women Officers or Directors: 1
Hot Spot for Advancement for Women/Minorities:

LOCATIONS: ("Y" = Yes)

West:	Southwest:	Midwest:	Southeast:	Northeast:	International:
Y	Y	Y	Y	Y	Y

COMPUTER TASK GROUP INC

www.ctg.com

Industry Group Code: 561

Management:		**Sales/Marketing:**		**Liberal Arts:**		**Information Sys.:**		**Professionals:**		**Tech./Scientific:**	
Mgmt. Trainees:		Marketing Pros.:	Y	Gen. Writing/Editing:	Y	Info. Mgmt.:	Y	Finance/Acct.:	Y	Engineers, Elec.:	Y
Experienced Mgmt.:	Y	Retail Sales:		Tech. Writing:	Y	Software Dev.:	Y	Law:	Y	Engineers, Other:	
Int'l Business:	Y	Comm./Industrial:	Y	Graphic Arts/Photog.:		Hardware Dev.:	Y	HR/Other:	Y	Health/Lab:	
MBA Grads:	Y	Sales Trainees:		Music:		Consulting/Other:	Y	Training:	Y	Science/Research:	
		Advertising Pros.:		Broadcasting:				Health Care:		Petroleum/Chem.:	
				Other:				Consulting:		Math/Other:	

TYPES OF BUSINESS:

IT Staffing & Outsourcing
Integration Services
Application Management
Information Security
Help Desk Services
Facilities Management

BRANDS/DIVISIONS/AFFILIATES:

Application Management Outsourcing
CTG Deutschland GmbH
Computer Task Group of Canada, Inc.
Computer Task Group Belgium N.V.
Computer Task Group IT Solutions, S.A.
Computer Task Group Luxembourg PSF
Computer Task Group (U.K.), Ltd.

CONTACTS:

Note: Officers with more than one job title may be intentionally listed here more than once.

James R. Boldt, CEO
James R. Boldt, Pres.
Brendan M. Harrington, CFO/Sr. VP
Peter P. Radetich, General Counsel/Sec./Sr. VP
Arthur W. Crumlish, Sr. VP/Gen. Mgr.-Strategic Staffing Svcs.
Thomas J. Niehaus, Sr. VP/Gen. Mgr.-CTG HealthCare Solutions
Michael Colson, Sr. VP-Solutions Dev.
James R. Boldt, Chmn.
Filip J. L. Gyde, Sr. VP/Gen. Mgr.-CTG Europe

Phone: 716-882-8000	**Fax:** 716-887-7464
Toll-Free: 800-992-5350	
Address: 800 Delaware Ave., Buffalo, NY 14209 US	

GROWTH PLANS/SPECIAL FEATURES:

Computer Task Group, Inc. (CTG) provides consulting and staffing services to information technology (IT) companies in North America and Europe. The firm operates in two segments: IT Solutions, which generated 34% of its 2010 revenue; and IT Staffing, 66%. The IT Solutions segment provides assistance to businesses in selecting and implementing packaged software; designing, constructing, testing and integrating new systems; and other consulting services. CTG offers single or multiple applications support; help desk services; and facilities management. Its solutions also include the Application Management Outsourcing (AMO) project, consisting of the selective outsourcing of IT needs to CTG. CTG is involved in the development and start-up of Health Information Exchanges, which are local partnerships between providers, payors and government agencies to implement secure electronic medical records. IT Staffing services involve recruiting, retaining and managing IT talent for organizations with multiple locations and high-volume IT requirements, as well as firms that need to augment their existing IT staff. The firm can accommodate both short- and long-term staffing arrangements. The firm groups its clients into four categories: Technology Service Providers, which generated 36% of 2010 revenue; Healthcare, including health insurers, life sciences companies and healthcare providers, 27%; Energy, 7%; and Financial Services, 6%. The remaining 24% of revenue was generated by customers in miscellaneous general industries. CTG has an international network of offices located in more than a dozen U.S. states as well as in Belgium, Luxembourg, the U.K., Germany and Canada. Its operating subsidiaries include Computer Task Group of Canada, Inc.; Computer Task Group Belgium N.V.; Computer Task Group IT Solutions, S.A.; Computer Task Group Luxembourg PSF; Computer Task Group (U.K.) Ltd.; and CTG Deutschland GmbH.

Employees are offered medical, dental and vision insurance; tuition reimbursement; short- and long-term disability coverage; and flexible spending accounts.

FINANCIALS:

Sales and profits are in thousands of dollars—add 000 to get the full amount. 2010 Note: Financial information for 2010 was not available for all companies at press time.

2010 Sales: $331,400	2010 Profits: $8,400	**U.S. Stock Ticker: CTGX**
2009 Sales: $275,560	2009 Profits: $5,933	**Int'l Ticker:**
2008 Sales: $353,213	2008 Profits: $7,837	Int'l Exchange:
2007 Sales: $325,285	2007 Profits: $4,246	Employees: 3,400 Fiscal Year Ends: 12/31
2006 Sales: $327,253	2006 Profits: $3,495	Parent Company:

SALARIES/BENEFITS:

Pension Plan:	ESOP Stock Plan:	Profit Sharing:	Top Exec. Salary: $456,233	Bonus: $647,219
Savings Plan: Y	Stock Purch. Plan: Y		Second Exec. Salary: $281,854	Bonus: $167,173

OTHER THOUGHTS:

Apparent Women Officers or Directors:
Hot Spot for Advancement for Women/Minorities:

LOCATIONS: ("Y" = Yes)

West:	Southwest:	Midwest:	Southeast:	Northeast:	International:
Y	Y	Y	Y	Y	Y

CONAGRA FOODS INC

www.conagrafoods.com

Industry Group Code: 311

Management:		Sales/Marketing:		Liberal Arts:		Information Sys.:		Professionals:		Tech./Scientific:	
Mgmt. Trainees:	Y	Marketing Pros.:	Y	Gen. Writing/Editing:	Y	Info. Mgmt.:	Y	Finance/Acct.:	Y	Engineers, Elec.:	
Experienced Mgmt.:	Y	Retail Sales:		Tech. Writing:	Y	Software Dev.:	Y	Law:	Y	Engineers, Other:	Y
Int'l Business:	Y	Comm./Industrial:	Y	Graphic Arts/Photog.:	Y	Hardware Dev.:		HR/Other:	Y	Health/Lab:	
MBA Grads:	Y	Sales Trainees:		Music:		Consulting/Other:		Training:	Y	Science/Research:	
		Advertising Pros.:	Y	Broadcasting:				Health Care:		Petroleum/Chem.:	
				Other:				Consulting:		Math/Other:	

TYPES OF BUSINESS:

Food Products Manufacturing
Food Ingredients
Meat Processing
Foodservice Supply

BRANDS/DIVISIONS/AFFILIATES:

Marie Callender's
Healthy Choice
Hunt's
Chef Boyardee
Peter Pan
Slim Jim
Elan Nutrition, Inc.
American Pie, LLC

CONTACTS: *Note: Officers with more than one job title may be intentionally listed here more than once.*

Gary Rodkin, CEO
Gary Rodkin, Pres.
John Gehring, CFO/Exec. VP
Joan Chow, Chief Mktg. Officer/Exec. VP
Al Bolles, Exec. VP-Research, Quality & Innovation
Brian Keck, Chief Admin. Officer/Exec. VP
Colleen Batcheler, General Counsel/Exec. VP/Corp. Sec.
Doug Knudsen, Pres., ConAgra Food Sales
Andre Hawaux, Pres., Consumer Foods
Paul Maass, Pres., Commercial Foods
Steven F. Goldstone, Chmn.
Greg Smith, Exec. VP-Supply Chain

Phone: 402-595-4000 | **Fax:** 402-595-4709
Toll-Free:
Address: 1 ConAgra Dr., Omaha, NE 68102 US

GROWTH PLANS/SPECIAL FEATURES:

ConAgra Foods, Inc. is a packaged food company serving grocery retailers, as well as restaurants and other food service establishments. It operates in two segments: consumer foods and commercial products. The consumer foods segment includes branded, private label and customized food products that are sold in various retail and foodservice channels in the U.S. and internationally. Products include a variety of categories such as meals, entrees, condiments, sides, snacks and desserts. The segment is further divided into five subsegements. The grocery foods North America subsegment includes label refrigerated or self-stable food products that are sold primarily across the U.S. The division also includes the consumer food businesses in Mexico and Canada. Brands include Chef Boyardee, Egg Beaters, Healthy Choice, Hebrew National, Hunt's, Manwich, PAM, Peter Pan, Reddi-wip and Swiss Miss. The frozen foods division includes frozen food products under the Alexia, Banquet, Healthy Choice, Kid Cuisine and Marie Callender's brands. The snack and store brands subsegment consists of popcorn, meats, seeds and specialty snacks sold under the ACT II, DAVID, Orville Redenbacher's and Slim Jim brands. The enabler brands division includes national and regional branded food products across shelf-stable, refrigerated and frozen temperature classes. Major brands include Blue Bonnet, La Choy, Parkay and Wesson. The domestic export division consists of branded shelf-stable food products sold through distributors in various markets throughout the world. The commercial products segment, includes commercially branded foods and ingredients such as Lamb Weston, a provider of frozen potato products, and ConAgra Mills, a producer of multi-use flours. These brands are sold to foodservice, food manufacturing, and industrial customers. In April 2010, ConAgra acquired Elan Nutrition, Inc., a snack bar manufacturer. In June 2010, the company acquired American Pie, LLC, a pie and pie product manufacturer. In July 2010, the firm sold its Gilroy Foods & Flavors dehydrated food business.

FINANCIALS: **Sales and profits are in thousands of dollars—add 000 to get the full amount. 2010 Note: Financial information for 2010 was not available for all companies at press time.**

2010 Sales: $12,079,400 | 2010 Profits: $725,800
2009 Sales: $12,426,100 | 2009 Profits: $978,400
2008 Sales: $11,248,200 | 2008 Profits: $930,600
2007 Sales: $10,489,500 | 2007 Profits: $764,600
2006 Sales: $10,251,400 | 2006 Profits: $533,800

U.S. Stock Ticker: CAG
Int'l Ticker:
Int'l Exchange:
Employees: 24,000 Fiscal Year Ends: 5/31
Parent Company:

SALARIES/BENEFITS:

Pension Plan: Y | ESOP Stock Plan: | Profit Sharing: | Top Exec. Salary: $1,000,000 | Bonus: $3,200,000
Savings Plan: Y | Stock Purch. Plan: Y | | Second Exec. Salary: $675,000 | Bonus: $1,100,000

OTHER THOUGHTS:

Apparent Women Officers or Directors: 4
Hot Spot for Advancement for Women/Minorities: Y

LOCATIONS: ("Y" = Yes)

West:	Southwest:	Midwest:	Southeast:	Northeast:	International:
Y	Y	Y	Y	Y	Y

CONCENTRA INC

www.concentra.com

Industry Group Code: 6214

Management:		Sales/Marketing:		Liberal Arts:		Information Sys.:		Professionals:		Tech./Scientific:	
Mgmt. Trainees:		Marketing Pros.:	Y	Gen. Writing/Editing:	Y	Info. Mgmt.:	Y	Finance/Acct.:	Y	Engineers, Elec.:	
Experienced Mgmt.:	Y	Retail Sales:		Tech. Writing:	Y	Software Dev.:	Y	Law:	Y	Engineers, Other:	
Int'l Business:		Comm./Industrial:	Y	Graphic Arts/Photog.:		Hardware Dev.:	Y	HR/Other:	Y	Health/Lab:	Y
MBA Grads:		Sales Trainees:		Music:		Consulting/Other:		Training:		Science/Research:	Y
		Advertising Pros.:	Y	Broadcasting:				Health Care:	Y	Petroleum/Chem.:	
				Other:				Consulting:		Math/Other:	Y

TYPES OF BUSINESS:

Health Clinics
Workplace Injury Treatment & Management
Group Health & Automobile Claims Management
Claims Cost Control
Case Management
Medical Advisory Services
Workplace-Based Clinics

BRANDS/DIVISIONS/AFFILIATES:

Humana Inc
Concentra TotalCare
Concentra Auto Injury Solutions
StatCare
Urgent Medical Care of Cumberland
Urgent Medical Care of Smithfield

CONTACTS: *Note: Officers with more than one job title may be intentionally listed here more than once.*

James M. Greenwood, CEO
Ted Bucknam, COO/Exec. VP
Thomas E. Kiraly, CFO/Exec. VP
John A. deLorimier, Chief Mktg. & Sales Officer/Exec. VP
Tammy S. Steele, Sr. VP-Human Resources & Compliance
W. Tom Fogarty, Chief Medical Officer/Exec. VP
Suzanne C. Kosub, CIO/Sr. VP
Mark A. Solls, General Counsel/Corp. Sec./Exec. VP
John R. Anderson, Sr. VP-Medical Oper.
Jay B. Blakey, Sr. VP-Strategic Bus. Dev.
Su Zan Nelson, Sr. VP-Acct. & Finance
William R. Lewis, Sr. VP-Medical Oper.
A. Michael McCollum, Pres., Concentra Health Solutions
Gregory M. Gilbert, Sr. VP-Reimbursement & Gov't Affairs.
Matthew K. Elges, Pres., Auto Injury Solutions
Paul Queally, Chmn.

Phone: 972-364-8211 **Fax:**
Toll-Free: 800-232-3550
Address: 5080 Spectrum Dr., Ste. 1200 W., Addison, TX 75001 US

GROWTH PLANS/SPECIAL FEATURES:

Concentra, Inc. is a national health care company that operates over 310 medical clinics in 40 states. The firm also serves patients at over 240 workplace clinics that it establishes at employer sites as well as programs in which it travels to its customers. Concentra's patient services segment provides services such as primary injury care; urgent care; physical therapy; travel health; physical exams; flu shots; drug screenings; and more. The company's employer services segment offers a vast array of services such as mobile medical services; drug testing and screening; physical therapy; specialist care; clinical and forensic services; medical advisory services (including physician review, education and training, medical directorship, on-site consulting, national medical consultants and medical expert panels); health risk assessments; biometric screenings; vaccinations; health coaching; and medical compliance administration; among other services. Comprehensive services are offered through Concentra TotalCare, an employee health care program delivered at the worksite and customized to the employer's specifications. Subsidiary Concentra Auto Injury Solutions provides products for the property and casualty insurance industry. Concentra became a subsidiary of Humana, Inc. in December 2010 when it was acquired for roughly $790 million. Also in December 2010, Concentra acquired three Rhode Island offices: Urgent Medical Care of Cumberland, Urgent Medical Care of Smithfield and StatCare. In 2011, the firm acquired and/or opened new offices in California, New Jersey, Vermont, Illinois, New York, Texas and Georgia.

FINANCIALS: **Sales and profits are in thousands of dollars—add 000 to get the full amount. 2010 Note: Financial information for 2010 was not available for all companies at press time.**

2010 Sales: $ | 2010 Profits: $
2009 Sales: $752,000 | 2009 Profits: $
2008 Sales: $819,680 | 2008 Profits: $
2007 Sales: $ | 2007 Profits: $
2006 Sales: $1,298,829 | 2006 Profits: $32,737

U.S. Stock Ticker: Subsidiary
Int'l Ticker:
Int'l Exchange:
Employees: 7,800 Fiscal Year Ends: 12/31
Parent Company: HUMANA INC

SALARIES/BENEFITS:

Pension Plan: | ESOP Stock Plan: | Profit Sharing: | Top Exec. Salary: $ | Bonus: $
Savings Plan: | Stock Purch. Plan: Y | | Second Exec. Salary: $ | Bonus: $

OTHER THOUGHTS:

Apparent Women Officers or Directors: 3
Hot Spot for Advancement for Women/Minorities: Y

LOCATIONS: ("Y" = Yes)

West:	Southwest:	Midwest:	Southeast:	Northeast:	International:
Y	Y	Y	Y	Y	

Sales, profits and employees may be estimates. Financial information, benefits and other data can change quickly and may vary from those stated here.

CONOCOPHILLIPS COMPANY

www.conocophillips.com

Industry Group Code: 211111

Management:		Sales/Marketing:		Liberal Arts:		Information Sys.:		Professionals:		Tech./Scientific:	
Mgmt. Trainees:	Y	Marketing Pros.:	Y	Gen. Writing/Editing:	Y	Info. Mgmt.:	Y	Finance/Acct.:	Y	Engineers, Elec.:	Y
Experienced Mgmt.:	Y	Retail Sales:		Tech. Writing:	Y	Software Dev.:	Y	Law:	Y	Engineers, Other:	Y
Int'l Business:	Y	Comm./Industrial:	Y	Graphic Arts/Photog.:	Y	Hardware Dev.:		HR/Other:	Y	Health/Lab:	
MBA Grads:	Y	Sales Trainees:	Y	Music:		Consulting/Other:		Training:	Y	Science/Research:	Y
		Advertising Pros.:	Y	Broadcasting:				Health Care:		Petroleum/Chem.:	Y
				Other:				Consulting:		Math/Other:	Y

TYPES OF BUSINESS:

Oil & Gas Exploration & Production
Natural Gas Distribution
Refining
Pipelines
Oil Sands Operations
Chemical Production
Technology Investment
Gasoline Retail

BRANDS/DIVISIONS/AFFILIATES:

Flying J
Conoco
Phillips 66
DCP Midstream LLC
Chevron Phillips Chemical Company LLC
Alaska Gas Pipe
CFJ Properties
Energy Technology Ventures

CONTACTS: *Note: Officers with more than one job title may be intentionally listed here more than once.*

James J. Mulva, CEO
Jeff Sheets, CFO/Sr. VP
W.C.W. Chiang, Sr. VP-Mktg.
Carin S. Knickel, VP-Human Resources
Greg C. Garland, Sr. VP-Exploration & Prod., Americas
Luc J. Messier, Sr. VP-Project Dev.
Gene L. Batchelder, Chief Admin. Officer/Sr. VP
Janet Langford Kelly, General Counsel/Corp. Sec./Sr. VP-Legal
Larry E. Archibald, Sr. VP-Bus. Dev. & Exploration
Red Cavaney, Sr. VP-Gov't Affairs
Jeff Sheets, Sr. VP-Finance
Robert A. Herman, VP-Health, Safety & Environment
Alan J. Hirshberg, Sr. VP-Planning & Strategy
W.C.W Chiang, Sr. VP-Refining & Transportation
Rand Berney, Sr. VP-Corp. Shared Svcs.
James J. Mulva, Chmn.
Ryan M. Lance, Sr. VP-Exploration & Prod., Int'l
Luc J. Messier, Sr. VP-Procurement

Phone: 281-293-1000 **Fax:**
Toll-Free:
Address: 600 N. Dairy Ashford Rd., Houston, TX 77079 US

GROWTH PLANS/SPECIAL FEATURES:

ConocoPhillips Company is an integrated global energy company. Its business segments include exploration and production; midstream; refining and marketing; chemicals; and emerging businesses. The exploration and production segment explores for, produces, transports and markets crude oil, natural gas and natural gas liquids worldwide. It also mines oil sands to extract bitumen, which it upgrades into synthetic crude oil. The midstream division gathers, processes and markets natural gas produced by the company and others, and also fractionates and markets natural gas liquids. This segment includes the firm's 50% equity investment in DCP Midstream, LLC. The refining and marketing segment purchases, refines, markets and transports crude oil and petroleum products, mainly in the U.S., Europe and Asia. The chemicals group, including the company's 50% equity investment in Chevron Phillips Chemical Company LLC, manufactures and markets petrochemicals and plastics worldwide. The emerging businesses segment oversees businesses such as technologies related to hydrocarbon recovery (including heavy oil), refining, alternative energy, biofuels and the environment. In June 2010, the company sold its 9.03% stake in Syncrude to Sinopec International Petroleum Exploration and Production Company; and sold its 50% ownership of CFJ Properties -Flying J truck stops to Pilot Travel Centers for roughly $626 million. Between late 2010 and early 2011, the firm sold its entire 20% stake in Lukoil (OAO). In January 2011, ConocoPhillips, NRG Energy, Inc. and GE formed joint venture Energy Technology Ventures to invest in alternative venture- and growth-stage firms. In July of the same year, the firm announced plans to split into two publicly traded companies by separating its refining business and its production business. The split is expected to happen in early 2012.

ConocoPhillips' employees receive life, disability, medical and dental insurance; a retirement plan; a savings plan; a health savings account; spending accounts; a Healthy Lifestyle Coach; and scholarships and tuition reimbursement.

FINANCIALS: **Sales and profits are in thousands of dollars—add 000 to get the full amount. 2010 Note: Financial information for 2010 was not available for all companies at press time.**

2010 Sales: $189,441,000 — 2010 Profits: $11,417,000
2009 Sales: $149,341,000 — 2009 Profits: $4,858,000
2008 Sales: $240,842,000 — 2008 Profits: $-16,998,000
2007 Sales: $187,437,000 — 2007 Profits: $11,891,000
2006 Sales: $183,650,000 — 2006 Profits: $15,550,000

U.S. Stock Ticker: COP
Int'l Ticker:
Int'l Exchange:
Employees: 29,900 Fiscal Year Ends: 12/31
Parent Company:

SALARIES/BENEFITS:

Pension Plan: Y | ESOP Stock Plan: Y | Profit Sharing: | Top Exec. Salary: $1,500,000 | Bonus: $1,278,788
Savings Plan: Y | Stock Purch. Plan: | Second Exec. Salary: $1,145,000 | Bonus: $1,474,560

OTHER THOUGHTS:

Apparent Women Officers or Directors: 5
Hot Spot for Advancement for Women/Minorities: Y

LOCATIONS: ("Y" = Yes)

West:	Southwest:	Midwest:	Southeast:	Northeast:	International:
Y	Y	Y	Y	Y	Y

CONSOL ENERGY INC

www.consolenergy.com

Industry Group Code: 21211

Management:		Sales/Marketing:		Liberal Arts:		Information Sys.:		Professionals:		Tech./Scientific:	
Mgmt. Trainees:	Y	Marketing Pros.:	Y	Gen. Writing/Editing:		Info. Mgmt.:	Y	Finance/Acct.:	Y	Engineers, Elec.:	
Experienced Mgmt.:	Y	Retail Sales:		Tech. Writing:	Y	Software Dev.:		Law:	Y	Engineers, Other:	Y
Int'l Business:	Y	Comm./Industrial:	Y	Graphic Arts/Photog.:		Hardware Dev.:		HR/Other:	Y	Health/Lab:	
MBA Grads:	Y	Sales Trainees:		Music:		Consulting/Other:		Training:	Y	Science/Research:	
		Advertising Pros.:		Broadcasting:				Health Care:		Petroleum/Chem.:	Y
				Other:				Consulting:		Math/Other:	

TYPES OF BUSINESS:

Coal Mining
Energy Services
Gas Exploration & Production

BRANDS/DIVISIONS/AFFILIATES:

CNX Gas Corporation
CNX Land Resources Inc
Veolia Water Solutions & Tecchnologies

CONTACTS: *Note: Officers with more than one job title may be intentionally listed here more than once.*

J. Brett Harvey, CEO
Nicholas J. Deluliis, COO/Exec. VP
Nicholas J. Deluliis, Pres.
William J. Lyons, CFO/Exec. VP
Robert Pusateri, Exec. VP-Energy Sales
P. Jerome Richey, Chief Legal Officer/Sec./Exec. VP-Corp. Affairs
Robert P. King, Exec. VP-Bus. Advancement & Support Svcs.
Robert Pusateri, Exec. VP-Transportation Svcs.
J. Brett Harvey, Chmn.

Phone: 724-485-4000 **Fax:** 724-485-4833

Toll-Free:

Address: 1000 Consol Energy Dr., CNX Center, Canonsburg, PA 15317-6506 US

GROWTH PLANS/SPECIAL FEATURES:

CONSOL Energy, Inc. is a multi-fuel energy producer and energy services provider, primarily serving the U.S. electric power generation industry. It produces high-BTU bituminous coal from 13 mining complexes in the U.S., as well as pipeline-quality coalbed methane gas from coal properties in Pennsylvania, Virginia and West Virginia, and conventional gas from Tennessee and Virginia. The company's mining complexes contain an approximate reserve base of 4.4 billion tons of coal. CONSOL is one of the largest producers of bituminous coal in the U.S., as well as one of the largest coal producers from underground mines, one of the largest coal producers east of the Mississippi River and one of the largest coal exporters. The company operates 22 towboats and a fleet of more than 620 barges. It employs transportation specialists who negotiate freight and equipment agreements with railroads, barge lines, terminal operators, ocean vessel brokers and trucking companies. CONSOL's gas operations involve producing coalbed methane and natural gas. The company operates over 12,500 wells and has estimated proved reserves of approximately 1.4 trillion cubic feet of oil equivalent. Through its subsidiary, CNX Land Resources, Inc., the firm has timber and farming operations, as well as commercial development ventures. CNX Gas Corporation, an 83.3% owned subsidiary, produces pipeline-quality coalbed methane gas from coal properties in the Northern and Central Appalachian basin. In addition, the firm provides industrial supply services, terminal services, river and dock services and coal waste disposal services. In April 2011, the firm agreed to partner with Veolia Water Solutions & Technologies to design and build a Zero Liquid Waste Discharge system to treat mine water near Mannington, West Virginia.

CONSOL offers its employees medical, dental, vision and prescription drug coverage; life and AD&D insurance; short- and long-term disability; a 401(k) plan; pension plans; an employee assistance program; relocation assistance; and access to a credit union.

FINANCIALS: **Sales and profits are in thousands of dollars—add 000 to get the full amount. 2010 Note: Financial information for 2010 was not available for all companies at press time.**

2010 Sales: $5,236,021 | 2010 Profits: $346,781
2009 Sales: $4,621,875 | 2009 Profits: $539,717
2008 Sales: $4,652,445 | 2008 Profits: $442,470
2007 Sales: $3,762,197 | 2007 Profits: $267,782
2006 Sales: $3,715,171 | 2006 Profits: $408,882

U.S. Stock Ticker: CNX
Int'l Ticker:
Int'l Exchange:
Employees: 8,630 Fiscal Year Ends: 12/31
Parent Company:

SALARIES/BENEFITS:

Pension Plan: Y ESOP Stock Plan: Profit Sharing: Top Exec. Salary: $1,086,154 Bonus: $2,750,000
Savings Plan: Y Stock Purch. Plan: Second Exec. Salary: $634,462 Bonus: $1,200,000

OTHER THOUGHTS:

Apparent Women Officers or Directors: 1
Hot Spot for Advancement for Women/Minorities:

LOCATIONS: ("Y" = Yes)

West:	Southwest:	Midwest:	Southeast:	Northeast:	International:
Y				Y	Y

Sales, profits and employees may be estimates. Financial information, benefits and other data can change quickly and may vary from those stated here.

CONTAINER STORE (THE)

www.containerstore.com

Industry Group Code: 442299

Management:		**Sales/Marketing:**		**Liberal Arts:**		**Information Sys.:**		**Professionals:**		**Tech./Scientific:**	
Mgmt. Trainees:	Y	Marketing Pros.:	Y	Gen. Writing/Editing:	Y	Info. Mgmt.:	Y	Finance/Acct.:	Y	Engineers, Elec.:	
Experienced Mgmt.:	Y	Retail Sales:	Y	Tech. Writing:		Software Dev.:	Y	Law:	Y	Engineers, Other:	
Int'l Business:		Comm./Industrial:	Y	Graphic Arts/Photog.:	Y	Hardware Dev.:		HR/Other:	Y	Health/Lab:	
MBA Grads:	Y	Sales Trainees:	Y	Music:		Consulting/Other:		Training:	Y	Science/Research:	
		Advertising Pros.:	Y	Broadcasting:				Health Care:		Petroleum/Chem.:	
				Other:	Y			Consulting:		Math/Other:	

TYPES OF BUSINESS:

Home Organization Products, Retail
Luggage
Packing Materials
Specialty Boxes
Online Sales

BRANDS/DIVISIONS/AFFILIATES:

Elfa
Leonard Green & Partners

CONTACTS:

Note: Officers with more than one job title may be intentionally listed here more than once.

Kip Tindell, CEO
Melissa Reiff, Pres.
Kip Tindell, Chmn.

Phone: 972-538-6000	**Fax:** 972-538-7623
Toll-Free: 800-733-3532	
Address: 500 Freeport Pkwy., Coppell, TX 75019 US	

GROWTH PLANS/SPECIAL FEATURES:

The Container Store, owned by private equity firm Leonard Green & Partners, is a national retailer selling organizational and storage products. The company sells drawer and cabinet organizers, luggage, tool racks, packing materials, specialty and shipping boxes and locker organizers, among many other household objects designed to manage space efficiently. Store interiors have an open layout, which is divided into sections with brightly colored banners such as Closet, Kitchen and Laundry. The firm's stores average 25,000 square feet and carry more than 10,000 items, with the company's Elfa brand of wire shelving making up nearly one-fifth of sales. The majority of the company's approximately 50 stores are located in large cities, including locations in Atlanta, Chicago, Houston, Miami, New York and San Diego. The Container Store processes and ships its entire product line from its 725,000-square-foot distribution center near Dallas, Texas. The distribution center uses state-of-the-art warehouse and inventory systems to increase profitability and response time. The company's web site allows customers to view and order store products, plan organizational and storage projects and receive free customized assistance from in-store space planning experts.

The company offers its employees a benefits package that includes a 40% discount on merchandise, a 401(k) savings plan and medical, dental and vision insurance.

FINANCIALS:

Sales and profits are in thousands of dollars—add 000 to get the full amount. 2010 Note: Financial information for 2010 was not available for all companies at press time.

2010 Sales: $	2010 Profits: $	**U.S. Stock Ticker: Private**
2009 Sales: $600,000	2009 Profits: $	**Int'l Ticker:**
2008 Sales: $600,000	2008 Profits: $	Int'l Exchange:
2007 Sales: $500,000	2007 Profits: $	Employees: 4,000 Fiscal Year Ends: 3/31
2006 Sales: $491,000	2006 Profits: $	Parent Company: LEONARD GREEN & PARTNERS

SALARIES/BENEFITS:

Pension Plan:	ESOP Stock Plan:	Profit Sharing:	Top Exec. Salary: $	Bonus: $
Savings Plan: Y	Stock Purch. Plan:		Second Exec. Salary: $	Bonus: $

OTHER THOUGHTS:

Apparent Women Officers or Directors: 1
Hot Spot for Advancement for Women/Minorities:

LOCATIONS: ("Y" = Yes)

West:	Southwest:	Midwest:	Southeast:	Northeast:	International:
Y	Y	Y	Y	Y	

CON-WAY INC

www.con-way.com

Industry Group Code: 484

Management:		Sales/Marketing:		Liberal Arts:		Information Sys.:		Professionals:		Tech./Scientific:	
Mgmt. Trainees:	Y	Marketing Pros.:	Y	Gen. Writing/Editing:		Info. Mgmt.:	Y	Finance/Acct.:	Y	Engineers, Elec.:	
Experienced Mgmt.:		Retail Sales:		Tech. Writing:		Software Dev.:		Law:	Y	Engineers, Other:	
Int'l Business:	Y	Comm./Industrial:	Y	Graphic Arts/Photog.:		Hardware Dev.:		HR/Other:	Y	Health/Lab:	
MBA Grads:	Y	Sales Trainees:		Music:		Consulting/Other:		Training:		Science/Research:	
		Advertising Pros.:	Y	Broadcasting:				Health Care:		Petroleum/Chem.:	
				Other:				Consulting:		Math/Other:	

TYPES OF BUSINESS:

General Trucking
Logistics Services
Time-Sensitive Shipments
Express Delivery Services
E-Business Shipping Solutions

BRANDS/DIVISIONS/AFFILIATES:

Menlo Worldwide
Con-Way Freight
Con-way Truckload
Road Systems
Global LTL

CONTACTS: *Note: Officers with more than one job title may be intentionally listed here more than once.*

Douglas W. Stotlar, CEO
Douglas W. Stotlar, Pres.
Stephen L. Bruffett, CFO/Exec. VP
Thomas Nightingale, Chief Mktg. Officer
Leslie P. Lundberg, Sr. VP-Human Resources
Jacquelyn A. Barretta, CIO/Sr. VP
Jennifer W. Pileggi, General Counsel/Exec. VP/Corp. Sec.
Thomas Nightingale, VP-Comm.
Patrick J. Fossenier, VP-Investor Rel.
John G. Labrie, Pres., Con-Way Freight
Robert L. Bianco, Exec. VP/Pres., Menlo Worldwide Logistics
Herb Schmidt, Exec. VP/Pres., Con-Way Truckload
W. Keith Kennedy, Jr., Chmn.

Phone: 650-378-5200 **Fax:** 650-357-9160
Toll-Free: 800-755-2728
Address: 2855 Campus Dr., Ste. 300, San Mateo, CA 94403 US

GROWTH PLANS/SPECIAL FEATURES:

Con-way, Inc. provides transportation, logistics and supply chain management services for a wide range of manufacturing, industrial and retail customers. Its principal component companies operate in regional and transcontinental less-than-truckload (LTL) and full-truckload freight transportation, contract logistics and supply-chain management, freight brokerage and trailer manufacturing. The company primarily operates through three companies: Con-way Freight; Menlo Worldwide; and Con-way Truckload. Con-way's operations are divided into four segments: freight, logistics, truckload and other. The freight segment consists of the Con-way Freight business unit, which provides regional, inter-regional and transcontinental LTL freight services throughout North America, as well as transborder service to and from Canada, Mexico, Europe, Asia and the Caribbean. Con-way Freight has one of the largest direct delivery networks in the U.S., with hundreds of operating locations across North America. The logistics segment consists of the Menlo Worldwide Logistics business unit, which develops contract-logistics solutions, including the management of complex distribution networks and supply-chain engineering and consulting, and also provides freight brokerage services. The truckload segment includes the Con-way Truckload business unit. Con-way Truckload provides asset-based full-truckload freight services throughout North America, including services into and out of Mexico. The other segment includes the operations of Road Systems, a trailer manufacturer. Con-way and its subsidiaries operate from more than 440 locations across North America and in 18 countries across five continents. In August 2010, Con-way Truckload opened a new driver orientation facility in Ohio. In November 2010, Menlo Worldwide Logistics opened a new office in Illinois.

Employees are offered life, disability, business travel, medical, dental and vision insurance; a 401(k) plan; a bonus program; an employee stock purchase plan; tuition assistance; scholarships for employees' children; flexible spending accounts; business travel insurance; an employee assistance program; and disability coverage.

FINANCIALS: **Sales and profits are in thousands of dollars—add 000 to get the full amount. 2010 Note: Financial information for 2010 was not available for all companies at press time.**

2010 Sales: $4,952,000 | 2010 Profits: $3,985
2009 Sales: $4,269,239 | 2009 Profits: $-110,936
2008 Sales: $5,036,817 | 2008 Profits: $66,961
2007 Sales: $4,387,363 | 2007 Profits: $145,952
2006 Sales: $4,221,478 | 2006 Profits: $258,978

U.S. Stock Ticker: CNW
Int'l Ticker:
Int'l Exchange:
Employees: 27,900 Fiscal Year Ends: 12/31
Parent Company:

SALARIES/BENEFITS:

Pension Plan: | ESOP Stock Plan: | Profit Sharing: | Top Exec. Salary: $644,493 | Bonus: $154,293
Savings Plan: Y | Stock Purch. Plan: Y | | Second Exec. Salary: $411,962 | Bonus: $574,538

OTHER THOUGHTS:

Apparent Women Officers or Directors: 3
Hot Spot for Advancement for Women/Minorities: Y

LOCATIONS: ("Y" = Yes)

West:	Southwest:	Midwest:	Southeast:	Northeast:	International:
Y	Y	Y	Y	Y	Y

Sales, profits and employees may be estimates. Financial information, benefits and other data can change quickly and may vary from those stated here.

COOPER COMPANIES INC

www.coopercos.com

Industry Group Code: 33911

Management:		**Sales/Marketing:**		**Liberal Arts:**		**Information Sys.:**		**Professionals:**		**Tech./Scientific:**	
Mgmt. Trainees:	Y	Marketing Pros.:	Y	Gen. Writing/Editing:		Info. Mgmt.:	Y	Finance/Acct.:	Y	Engineers, Elec.:	
Experienced Mgmt.:	Y	Retail Sales:		Tech. Writing:	Y	Software Dev.:	Y	Law:	Y	Engineers, Other:	Y
Int'l Business:	Y	Comm./Industrial:	Y	Graphic Arts/Photog.:	Y	Hardware Dev.:		HR/Other:	Y	Health/Lab:	Y
MBA Grads:	Y	Sales Trainees:		Music:		Consulting/Other:		Training:	Y	Science/Research:	
		Advertising Pros.:	Y	Broadcasting:				Health Care:	Y	Petroleum/Chem.:	
				Other:				Consulting:		Math/Other:	

TYPES OF BUSINESS:

Medical Devices
Contact Lenses
Gynecological Instruments
Diagnostic Products

BRANDS/DIVISIONS/AFFILIATES:

CooperVision, Inc.
CooperSurgical, Inc.
Proclear
Phosphorylcholine (PC) Technology

CONTACTS: *Note: Officers with more than one job title may be intentionally listed here more than once.*

Robert S. Weiss, CEO
Robert S. Weiss, Pres.
Eugene J. Midlock, CFO/Sr. VP
Carol R. Kaufman, Chief Admin. Officer/Exec. VP/Sec.
Daniel G. McBride, General Counsel/VP/Chief Risk Officer
Albert G. White, III, Chief Strategic Officer
Albert G. White, III, VP-Investor Rel./Treas.
Rodney E. Folden, Controller/VP
Nicholas J. Pichotta, CEO-CooperSurgical, Inc.
Paul L. Remmell, COO/Pres., CooperSurgical, Inc.
John A. Weber, Pres., CooperVision, Inc.
Greg W. Matz, VP-Finance/CFO-CooperVision, Inc.
A. Thomas Bender, Chmn.

Phone: 925-460-3600 **Fax:** 925-460-3649
Toll-Free:
Address: 6140 Stoneridge Mall Rd., Ste. 590, Pleasanton, CA 94588 US

GROWTH PLANS/SPECIAL FEATURES:

Cooper Companies, Inc. develops, manufactures and markets healthcare products, primarily medical devices. The company operates through two business units: CooperVision, Inc. and CooperSurgical, Inc. CooperVision develops, manufactures and markets a broad range of contact lenses, including disposable spherical and specialty contact lenses. It is a leading manufacturer of toric lenses, which correct astigmatism; multifocal lenses for presbyopia, the blurring of vision due to advancing age; and spherical lenses, including hydrogel lenses, which correct the most common near- and farsighted visual defects. The subsidiary uses three different manufacturing processes to produce its lenses: lathing, cast molding and FIPS, a combination of lathing and molding. This manufacturing flexibility allows CooperVision to offer single-use, two-week, monthly and quarterly disposable sphere and toric lenses, as well as custom toric lenses to correct a high degree of astigmatism. Cooper Vision's Proclear line of spherical, toric and multifocal lenses are manufactured with omafilcon A, a material that incorporates its proprietary Phosphorylcholine (PC) Technology to enhance tissue-device compatibility. CooperVision's products are primarily manufactured at its facilities in the U.S., the U.K. and Puerto Rico. It distributes its products out of New York; the U.K.; Belgium; and various smaller international distribution facilities. CooperSurgical develops, manufactures and markets medical devices, diagnostic products and surgical instruments and accessories used primarily by gynecologists and obstetricians. The subsidiary primarily manufactures and distributes its products at its facilities in Trumbull, Connecticut; Pasadena, California; and Stafford, Texas. CooperVision and CooperSurgical represent 84.7% and 15.3%, respectively, of the company's total expenditures for research and development.

FINANCIALS: **Sales and profits are in thousands of dollars—add 000 to get the full amount. 2010 Note: Financial information for 2010 was not available for all companies at press time.**

2010 Sales: $1,158,517 — 2010 Profits: $112,803
2009 Sales: $1,080,421 — 2009 Profits: $100,548
2008 Sales: $1,047,375 — 2008 Profits: $65,476
2007 Sales: $945,240 — 2007 Profits: $-11,192
2006 Sales: $858,960 — 2006 Profits: $66,234

U.S. Stock Ticker: COO
Int'l Ticker:
Int'l Exchange:
Employees: 6,800 Fiscal Year Ends: 10/31
Parent Company:

SALARIES/BENEFITS:

Pension Plan: ESOP Stock Plan: Profit Sharing: Top Exec. Salary: $700,000 Bonus: $1,228,500
Savings Plan: Stock Purch. Plan: Second Exec. Salary: $390,000 Bonus: $410,670

OTHER THOUGHTS:

Apparent Women Officers or Directors: 2
Hot Spot for Advancement for Women/Minorities: Y

LOCATIONS: ("Y" = Yes)

West:	Southwest:	Midwest:	Southeast:	Northeast:	International:
Y	Y			Y	Y

COSTCO WHOLESALE CORP

www.costco.com

Industry Group Code: 452112

Management:		**Sales/Marketing:**		**Liberal Arts:**		**Information Sys.:**		**Professionals:**		**Tech./Scientific:**	
Mgmt. Trainees:	Y	Marketing Pros.:	Y	Gen. Writing/Editing:	Y	Info. Mgmt.:	Y	Finance/Acct.:	Y	Engineers, Elec.:	
Experienced Mgmt.:	Y	Retail Sales:	Y	Tech. Writing:		Software Dev.:	Y	Law:	Y	Engineers, Other:	
Int'l Business:	Y	Comm./Industrial:		Graphic Arts/Photog.:	Y	Hardware Dev.:		HR/Other:	Y	Health/Lab:	
MBA Grads:	Y	Sales Trainees:	Y	Music:		Consulting/Other:		Training:	Y	Science/Research:	
		Advertising Pros.:	Y	Broadcasting:				Health Care:		Petroleum/Chem.:	
				Other:	Y			Consulting:		Math/Other:	

TYPES OF BUSINESS:

Warehouse Clubs, Retail
Food
Health & Beauty Products
Electronics
Furniture
Apparel
Automotive Supplies
Gasoline Sales

BRANDS/DIVISIONS/AFFILIATES:

Costco Wholesale Industries
Costco Mexico

CONTACTS: *Note: Officers with more than one job title may be intentionally listed here more than once.*

James D. Sinegal, CEO
W. Craig Jelinek, COO
W. Craig Jelinek, Pres.
Richard A. Galanti, CFO/Exec. VP
John Matthews, Sr. VP-Human Resources
Paul G. Moulton, Exec. VP-Info. Systems
Doug W. Schutt, Exec. VP/COO-Merch.
Joel Benoliel, Sr. VP-Admin.
Joel Benoliel, Chief Legal Officer
John Thelan, Sr. VP-Depot Oper.
Richard C. Chavez, Sr. VP-Bus. Dev.
Ginnie M. Roeglin, Sr. VP-eCommerce & Publishing
Bob Nelson, VP-Investor Rel.
David S. Petterson, Corp. Controller/Sr. VP
Ali Moayeri, Sr. VP-Construction
Charles V. Burnett, Sr. VP-Pharmacy
Dennis Knapp, Sr. VP-Non-Foods
John Matthews, Sr. VP-Risk Mgmt.
Jeffrey H. Brotman, Chmn.
James P. Murphy, Sr. VP-Int'l Oper.

Phone: 425-313-8100	**Fax:** 425-313-8103
Toll-Free: 800-774-2678	
Address: 999 Lake Dr., Issaquah, WA 98027 US	

GROWTH PLANS/SPECIAL FEATURES:

Costco Wholesale Corp. operates membership warehouses based on the concept that offering members very low prices on a limited selection of branded and private-label products will produce high sales volumes and rapid inventory turnover. This rapid turnover, combined with volume purchasing, efficient distribution and reduced handling of merchandise in self-service warehouse facilities, allows the firm to operate at significantly lower margins than traditional discount retailers. Costco buys the majority of its merchandise directly from manufacturers for shipment to warehouses or to consolidation points, minimizing freight and handling costs. Products include health and beauty aids, cleaning supplies, foods, alcohol, appliances, electronics, tools, office supplies, furniture, automotive supplies, apparel, cameras, house wares and books. Stores contain other features, including pharmacies, print shops, photo labs and gas stations. Memberships are designed to build customer loyalty and cost $40-$100 per year. Costco has approximately 5.8 million business members and approximately 22.5 million Gold Star (individual) members. The firm operates 570 membership warehouses in the U.S., U.K., Canada, Korea, Mexico, Taiwan and Japan, including 32 controlled by the company's joint venture, Costco Mexico. The stores average approximately 140,000 square feet and stock around 4,000 distinct products, including upscale items such as jewelry and wines. Costco Wholesale Industries, a division of the company, operates manufacturing businesses, including special food packaging, optical laboratories, meat processing and jewelry distribution. For 2010, Costco stores averaged $990 in revenues per square foot of store space.

Costco offers its employees health care, dental, vision and prescription coverage; a 401(k) plan; employee assistance plans; care networks; short- and long-term disability; life insurance; an employee stock purchase plan; health care reimbursement; and long-term care insurance.

FINANCIALS: **Sales and profits are in thousands of dollars—add 000 to get the full amount. 2010 Note: Financial information for 2010 was not available for all companies at press time.**

2010 Sales: $76,255,000	2010 Profits: $1,303,000	**U.S. Stock Ticker: COST**
2009 Sales: $69,889,000	2009 Profits: $1,086,000	**Int'l Ticker:**
2008 Sales: $70,977,484	2008 Profits: $1,282,725	Int'l Exchange:
2007 Sales: $63,087,601	2007 Profits: $1,082,772	Employees: 147,000 Fiscal Year Ends: 8/31
2006 Sales: $58,963,180	2006 Profits: $1,103,215	Parent Company:

SALARIES/BENEFITS:

Pension Plan:	ESOP Stock Plan:	Profit Sharing:	Top Exec. Salary: $635,000	Bonus: $95,200
Savings Plan: Y	Stock Purch. Plan: Y		Second Exec. Salary: $600,000	Bonus: $76,160

OTHER THOUGHTS:

Apparent Women Officers or Directors: 4
Hot Spot for Advancement for Women/Minorities: Y

LOCATIONS: ("Y" = Yes)

West:	Southwest:	Midwest:	Southeast:	Northeast:	International:
Y	Y	Y	Y	Y	Y

COVANCE INC

Industry Group Code: 541712

www.covance.com

Management:		Sales/Marketing:		Liberal Arts:		Information Sys.:		Professionals:		Tech./Scientific:	
Mgmt. Trainees:	Y	Marketing Pros.:	Y	Gen. Writing/Editing:		Info. Mgmt.:	Y	Finance/Acct.:	Y	Engineers, Elec.:	
Experienced Mgmt.:	Y	Retail Sales:		Tech. Writing:	Y	Software Dev.:	Y	Law:	Y	Engineers, Other:	
Int'l Business:	Y	Comm./Industrial:	Y	Graphic Arts/Photog.:	Y	Hardware Dev.:		HR/Other:	Y	Health/Lab:	Y
MBA Grads:	Y	Sales Trainees:		Music:		Consulting/Other:	Y	Training:	Y	Science/Research:	Y
		Advertising Pros.:	Y	Broadcasting:				Health Care:	Y	Petroleum/Chem.:	
				Other:				Consulting:	Y	Math/Other:	

TYPES OF BUSINESS:

Pharmaceutical Research & Development
Drug Preclinical/Clinical Trials
Laboratory Testing & Analysis
Approval Assistance
Health Economics & Outcomes Services
Online Tools

BRANDS/DIVISIONS/AFFILIATES:

LabLink
Study Tracker
Trial Tracker
Sanofi-Aventis

CONTACTS: *Note: Officers with more than one job title may be intentionally listed here more than once.*

Joseph L. Herring, CEO
Wendel Barr, COO/Exec. VP
William E. Klitgaard, CFO/Corp. Sr. VP
Lisa Uthgenannt, Corp. VP-Human Resources
Deborah L. Tanner, Sr. VP/Pres., R&D Laboratories
John Repko, CIO/Corp. Sr. VP
James W. Lovett, General Counsel/Corp. Sr. VP/Sec.
Nigel Brown, Corp. VP-Bus. Dev. & Strategy
John Watson, Chief Commercial Officer/Corp. Sr. VP
Richard Cimino, Exec. VP/Pres., Clinical Dev. Svcs.
Joseph L. Herring, Chmn.
Honggang Bi, Corp. VP/Gen. Mgr.-China

Phone: 609-452-4440 **Fax:**
Toll-Free: 888-268-2623
Address: 210 Carnegie Ctr., Princeton, NJ 08540 US

GROWTH PLANS/SPECIAL FEATURES:

Covance, Inc. is a drug development services and contract research firm with operations in over 30 countries. It provides a wide range of product development services to pharmaceutical, biotechnology and medical device industries across the globe. The company also provides laboratory testing services for clients in the chemical, agrochemical and food businesses. Covance operates two business segments: early development services and late-stage development services. Covance's early development services include preclinical services (such as toxicology, pharmaceutical development, research products and a bioanalytical testing service) and Phase I clinical services. Its late-stage development services cover clinical development and support; clinical trials; periapproval and market access; and central laboratory operations. Covance has also introduced several Internet-based products: StudyTracker, an Internet-based client access product, which permits customers of toxicology services to review study data and schedules on a near real-time basis; LabLink, a client access program that allows customers of central laboratory services to review and query lab data; and Trial Tracker, a web-enabled clinical trial project management and tracking tool intended to allow both employees and customers of its late-stage clinical business to review and manage all aspects of clinical-trial projects. In recent years, the company agreed to acquire the Gene Expression Laboratory of Merck & Co., Inc. In June 2010, Covance opened a new biorepository facility in Indiana. In October 2010, the firm became a 10-year research and development partner to Sanofi-Aventis, and acquired from Sanofi-Aventis two facilities in the U.K. and France.

Covance offers its employees medical, dental and vision plans; employee assistance; a 401(k); financial planning services; and tuition reimbursement.

FINANCIALS: **Sales and profits are in thousands of dollars—add 000 to get the full amount. 2010 Note: Financial information for 2010 was not available for all companies at press time.**

2010 Sales: $2,038,473 — 2010 Profits: $68,254
2009 Sales: $1,962,626 — 2009 Profits: $175,882
2008 Sales: $1,827,067 — 2008 Profits: $196,760
2007 Sales: $1,631,516 — 2007 Profits: $175,929
2006 Sales: $1,406,058 — 2006 Profits: $144,998

U.S. Stock Ticker: CVD
Int'l Ticker:
Int'l Exchange:
Employees: 10,528 Fiscal Year Ends: 12/31
Parent Company:

SALARIES/BENEFITS:

Pension Plan: ESOP Stock Plan: Profit Sharing: Top Exec. Salary: $811,667 Bonus: $730,600
Savings Plan: Y Stock Purch. Plan: Y Second Exec. Salary: $471,667 Bonus: $141,600

OTHER THOUGHTS:

Apparent Women Officers or Directors: 2
Hot Spot for Advancement for Women/Minorities:

LOCATIONS: ("Y" = Yes)

West:	Southwest:	Midwest:	Southeast:	Northeast:	International:
Y	Y	Y	Y	Y	Y

COX COMMUNICATIONS INC

ww2.cox.com

Industry Group Code: 517110

Management:		Sales/Marketing:		Liberal Arts:		Information Sys.:		Professionals:		Tech./Scientific:	
Mgmt. Trainees:	Y	Marketing Pros.:	Y	Gen. Writing/Editing:	Y	Info. Mgmt.:	Y	Finance/Acct.:	Y	Engineers, Elec.:	Y
Experienced Mgmt.:	Y	Retail Sales:		Tech. Writing:	Y	Software Dev.:	Y	Law:	Y	Engineers, Other:	Y
Int'l Business:	Y	Comm./Industrial:	Y	Graphic Arts/Photog.:	Y	Hardware Dev.:		HR/Other:	Y	Health/Lab:	
MBA Grads:	Y	Sales Trainees:	Y	Music:		Consulting/Other:		Training:	Y	Science/Research:	
		Advertising Pros.:	Y	Broadcasting:	Y			Health Care:		Petroleum/Chem.:	
				Other:	Y			Consulting:		Math/Other:	

TYPES OF BUSINESS:

Cable TV Service
Digital Cable TV Service
Cable-Based Internet Access
Local & Long-Distance Phone Service
Commercial Telecommunications Services
Data & Video Transport Services

BRANDS/DIVISIONS/AFFILIATES:

Cox Enterprises Inc
Cox Media
Cox Rhapsody
Valpak
AutoTrader.com
Cox Business Services
Travel Channel (The)
Cox Digital Solutions

CONTACTS: *Note: Officers with more than one job title may be intentionally listed here more than once.*

Leo W. Brennan, COO/Exec. VP
Patrick J. Esser, Pres.
Mark F. Bowser, CFO/Exec. VP
Mark Greatrex, Chief Mktg. Officer/Sr. VP
Mae A. Douglas, Chief People Officer/Exec. VP
Kevin Hart, CTO/Exec. VP
Len Barlik, Exec. VP-Prod. Mgmt. & Dev.
Robin H. Sangston, VP-Legal Affairs
Jill Campbell, Sr. VP-Oper.
Andrew Goldberg, VP-Strategic Planning & Analysis
Steve M. Gorman, VP-Web Strategy & Interactive Media
Alexandra M. Wilson, Sr. VP-Public Policy & Regulatory Affairs
William J. Fitzsimmons, Chief Acct. Officer/VP-Corp. Finance
F. William Farina, Sr. VP-Cox Media
Bill Mangen, Exe. Dir.-Strategic Sourcing
Philip G. Meeks, Sr. VP-Cox Bus.
Kelly Williams, VP-Wireless Prod. & Oper.
George Richter, VP-Supply Chain Mgmt.

Phone: 404-843-5000 **Fax:**
Toll-Free: 866-272-5777
Address: 1400 Lake Hearn Dr., Atlanta, GA 30319 US

GROWTH PLANS/SPECIAL FEATURES:

Cox Communications, Inc., owned by Cox Enterprises, Inc., is a multi-service broadband communications and entertainment company serving more than 6 million customers throughout the U.S. Cox offers advanced digital video; digital video recording; high-definition television; high-speed Internet; and local and long distance telephone services over its own nationwide IP network. Cox Business Services provides communications solutions for commercial customers, offering high-speed Internet, Ethernet, Virtual Private Network, voice and long distance, converged access, data and video transport services for businesses. Cox Media offers national and local cable advertising in traditional spot and new media formats, along with promotional opportunities and production services, and owns Valpak, a leading direct marketing company in the U.S. The company also maintains Cox Digital Solutions; Cox Rhapsody; Manheim; Kudzu.com; AutoTrader.com; and the Travel Channel, which operates as a joint venture between Cox and Scripps Networks Interactive, Inc. The firm invests in telecommunications companies such as Sprint PCS. In recent years, Cox acquired the outstanding minority interest in Cox Radio, Inc.; and sold a stake in Travel Channel Media, which operates The Travel Channel, to Scripps. In January 2010, the company announced plans to construct a 60,000-square-foot office complex at its headquarters. In June 2010, Cox Business began offering its Cox Business Security Suite product nationwide. In November 2010, Cox expanded its Internet managed services for small businesses with additional backup, security and e-mail solutions.

The firm offers its employees medical and dental coverage; life and business travel insurance; health and dependent care spending accounts; tuition reimbursement; an employee assistance program; a pension plan; a 401(k) plan; adoption assistance; discounted Cox services such as cable, telephone and internet where available; and employee discounts with Dell, Philips, Ford, GM and others. The firm also operates Cox University, which offers over 150 free online courses.

FINANCIALS: **Sales and profits are in thousands of dollars—add 000 to get the full amount. 2010 Note: Financial information for 2010 was not available for all companies at press time.**

2010 Sales: $9,000,000 — 2010 Profits: $
2009 Sales: $8,500,000 — 2009 Profits: $
2008 Sales: $8,500,000 — 2008 Profits: $
2007 Sales: $8,300,000 — 2007 Profits: $
2006 Sales: $7,300,000 — 2006 Profits: $

U.S. Stock Ticker: Subsidiary
Int'l Ticker:
Int'l Exchange:
Employees: 22,000 Fiscal Year Ends: 12/31
Parent Company: COX ENTERPRISES INC

SALARIES/BENEFITS:

Pension Plan: Y | ESOP Stock Plan: | Profit Sharing: | Top Exec. Salary: $ | Bonus: $1,166,798
Savings Plan: Y | Stock Purch. Plan: | Second Exec. Salary: $ | Bonus: $

OTHER THOUGHTS:

Apparent Women Officers or Directors: 14
Hot Spot for Advancement for Women/Minorities: Y

LOCATIONS: ("Y" = Yes)

West:	Southwest:	Midwest:	Southeast:	Northeast:	International:
Y	Y	Y	Y	Y	

CR BARD INC

www.crbard.com

Industry Group Code: 33911

Management:		Sales/Marketing:		Liberal Arts:		Information Sys.:		Professionals:		Tech./Scientific:	
Mgmt. Trainees:	Y	Marketing Pros.:	Y	Gen. Writing/Editing:	Y	Info. Mgmt.:	Y	Finance/Acct.:	Y	Engineers, Elec.:	
Experienced Mgmt.:	Y	Retail Sales:		Tech. Writing:	Y	Software Dev.:	Y	Law:	Y	Engineers, Other:	Y
Int'l Business:	Y	Comm./Industrial:	Y	Graphic Arts/Photog.:	Y	Hardware Dev.:		HR/Other:	Y	Health/Lab:	Y
MBA Grads:	Y	Sales Trainees:		Music:		Consulting/Other:		Training:	Y	Science/Research:	Y
		Advertising Pros.:	Y	Broadcasting:				Health Care:	Y	Petroleum/Chem.:	
				Other:				Consulting:		Math/Other:	

TYPES OF BUSINESS:

Equipment-Urological Catheters
Diagnostic and Interventional Products
Minimally Invasive Vascular Products
Surgical Specialty Products
Supply Chain and Business Services
Oncology Products
Urology Products

BRANDS/DIVISIONS/AFFILIATES:

Foley
PowerPICC
PowerPort
Ventrio
Sepra
Allomax
Permasorb
SenoRx, Inc.

CONTACTS: *Note: Officers with more than one job title may be intentionally listed here more than once.*

Timothy M. Ring, CEO
John H. Weiland, COO
John H. Weiland, Pres.
Todd C. Schermerhorn, CFO/Sr. VP
Bronwen K. Kelly, VP-Human Resources
John A. DeFord, VP-Science, Tech. & Clinical Affairs
Patrick D. Roche, VP-IT Solutions
Stephen J. Long, General Counsel/Sec./VP
Robert L. Mellen, VP-Bus. Dev. & Strategic Planning
Todd W. Garner, VP-Investor Rel.
Scott T. Lowry, Treas./VP
Gary D. Dolch, Sr. VP-Quality & Regulatory Affairs
Patricia Chirstian, VP-Regulatory Affairs
Frank Lupisella, VP/Controller
Andrea J. Casper, VP-Regulatory Affairs
Timothy M. Ring, Chmn.

Phone: 908-277-8000	**Fax:** 908-277-8240
Toll-Free: 800-367-2273	
Address: 730 Central Ave., Murray Hill, NJ 07974 US	

GROWTH PLANS/SPECIAL FEATURES:

C.R. Bard, Inc. designs, manufactures, packages, distributes and sells medical, surgical and diagnostic devices. The company markets its products in four categories: vascular, urology, oncology and surgical specialties. The company's line of minimally invasive vascular products include percutaneous transluminal angioplasty catheters; guidewires; introducers and accessories; peripheral vascular stents and stent grafts; vena cava filters; and biopsy devices. Additional products include cardiac mapping and electrophysiology laboratory systems, as well as diagnostic and temporary pacing electrode catheters; fabrics and meshes; and implantable blood vessel replacements. The urology segment markets products which include the Foley catheter and the Statlock catheter stabilization line. C.R. Bard's oncology products include the PowerPICC and PowerPort devices, which eliminate the need for unnecessary additional catheters. The firm's surgical specialty products include meshes for vessel and hernia repair; irrigation devices for orthopedic, laparoscopic and gynecological procedures; and products for topical hemostasis. These products include the PerFix plug; Ventralex, Collamend, Ventrio, Sepra and Allomax hernia patches; and the Permasorb fixation device, which attaches hernia patches to host tissue. The company's products are distributed in the U.S. directly to hospitals and other health care institutions, as well as through numerous hospital/surgical supply and other medical specialty distributors. Roughly 74% of C.R. Bard's international sales are generated from products manufactured in the U.S., Puerto Rico or Mexico. In mid 2010, the company acquired SenoRx, Inc., a leading developer of products for breast cancer treatment, including the EnCor biopsy system, Gel Mark tissue marker and Contura balloon catheters.

C.R. Bard offers its employees life, AD&D, disability, medical, prescription drug, dental and vision coverage; flexible spending accounts; an employee stock purchase plan; retirement pensions; 11 paid holidays; and a worldwide travel assistance program.

FINANCIALS: **Sales and profits are in thousands of dollars—add 000 to get the full amount. 2010 Note: Financial information for 2010 was not available for all companies at press time.**

2010 Sales: $2,720,200	2010 Profits: $509,200	**U.S. Stock Ticker: BCR**
2009 Sales: $2,534,900	2009 Profits: $460,100	**Int'l Ticker:**
2008 Sales: $2,452,100	2008 Profits: $416,500	Int'l Exchange:
2007 Sales: $2,202,000	2007 Profits: $406,400	Employees: 11,700 Fiscal Year Ends: 12/31
2006 Sales: $1,979,600	2006 Profits: $272,100	Parent Company:

SALARIES/BENEFITS:

Pension Plan: Y	ESOP Stock Plan:	Profit Sharing:	Top Exec. Salary: $1,050,000	Bonus: $1,320,375
Savings Plan: Y	Stock Purch. Plan: Y		Second Exec. Salary: $852,800	Bonus: $857,917

OTHER THOUGHTS:

Apparent Women Officers or Directors: 4
Hot Spot for Advancement for Women/Minorities: Y

LOCATIONS: ("Y" = Yes)

West:	Southwest:	Midwest:	Southeast:	Northeast:	International:
Y	Y	Y	Y	Y	Y

CRACKER BARREL OLD COUNTRY STORE INC

www.crackerbarrel.com

Industry Group Code: 722110

Management:		Sales/Marketing:		Liberal Arts:		Information Sys.:		Professionals:		Tech./Scientific:	
Mgmt. Trainees:	Y	Marketing Pros.:	Y	Gen. Writing/Editing:	Y	Info. Mgmt.:	Y	Finance/Acct.:	Y	Engineers, Elec.:	
Experienced Mgmt.:	Y	Retail Sales:		Tech. Writing:		Software Dev.:	Y	Law:	Y	Engineers, Other:	
Int'l Business:		Comm./Industrial:		Graphic Arts/Photog.:	Y	Hardware Dev.:		HR/Other:	Y	Health/Lab:	
MBA Grads:	Y	Sales Trainees:	Y	Music:		Consulting/Other:		Training:	Y	Science/Research:	
		Advertising Pros.:	Y	Broadcasting:				Health Care:		Petroleum/Chem.:	
				Other:	Y			Consulting:		Math/Other:	

TYPES OF BUSINESS:

Restaurants-Country Cooking, Food Service
Retail Gifts and Food Products

BRANDS/DIVISIONS/AFFILIATES:

Cracker Barrel Old Country Store

CONTACTS: *Note: Officers with more than one job title may be intentionally listed here more than once.*

Michael A. Woodhouse, CEO
Sandra Cochran, COO
Sandra Cochran, Pres.
Lawrence E. Hyatt, CFO/Sr. VP
Christopher A Ciavarra, Sr. VP-Mktg.
Doug Barber, Chief People Officer/Exec. VP
N. B. Forrest Shoaf, Chief Legal Officer/Sec./Sr. VP
Nicholas V. Flanagan, Sr. VP-Restaurant Oper.
Edward A. Greene, Sr. VP-Strategic Initiatives
Terry Maxwell, Sr. VP-Retail
Michael A. Woodhouse, Chmn.

Phone: 615-444-5533	**Fax:** 615-443-9818
Toll-Free:	
Address: 305 Hartmann Dr., Lebanon, TN 37087 US	

GROWTH PLANS/SPECIAL FEATURES:

Cracker Barrel Old Country Store, Inc., formerly CBRL Group, Inc. is primarily a restaurant chain operator, with 595 Cracker Barrel Old Country Store restaurants in 41 states. Cracker Barrel Old Country Store restaurants resemble turn-of-the-century country stores and offer home-style country cooking featuring its self-developed recipes. Restaurants also feature small retail areas where customers can purchase various products reminiscent of turn-of-the century goods typically found at old-fashioned general stores as well as modern items, such as rocking chairs, seasonal gifts, apparel, toys, music CDs, audio books, cookware, ceramics, figurines and various other gift items, as well as various candies, preserves, syrups and other food items. In 2010, the company's restaurants averaged 7,000 customers per week at typical locations and generated 80% of the firm's total revenue. The retail operations generated the remaining 20% of Cracker Barrel's 2010 revenue.

FINANCIALS: **Sales and profits are in thousands of dollars—add 000 to get the full amount. 2010 Note: Financial information for 2010 was not available for all companies at press time.**

2010 Sales: $2,404,515	2010 Profits: $85,258	**U.S. Stock Ticker: CBRL**
2009 Sales: $2,367,285	2009 Profits: $65,926	**Int'l Ticker:**
2008 Sales: $2,384,521	2008 Profits: $65,553	Int'l Exchange:
2007 Sales: $2,351,576	2007 Profits: $162,065	Employees: 67,000 Fiscal Year Ends: 7/31
2006 Sales: $2,219,475	2006 Profits: $116,291	Parent Company:

SALARIES/BENEFITS:

Pension Plan:	ESOP Stock Plan:	Profit Sharing:	Top Exec. Salary: $1,000,000	Bonus: $2,500,000
Savings Plan: Y	Stock Purch. Plan: Y		Second Exec. Salary: $50,000	Bonus: $1,000,000

OTHER THOUGHTS:

Apparent Women Officers or Directors: 3
Hot Spot for Advancement for Women/Minorities: Y

LOCATIONS: ("Y" = Yes)

West:	Southwest:	Midwest:	Southeast:	Northeast:	International:
Y	Y	Y	Y	Y	

CROCS INC

www.crocs.com

Industry Group Code: 316219

Management:		Sales/Marketing:		Liberal Arts:		Information Sys.:		Professionals:		Tech./Scientific:	
Mgmt. Trainees:		Marketing Pros.:	Y	Gen. Writing/Editing:	Y	Info. Mgmt.:	Y	Finance/Acct.:	Y	Engineers, Elec.:	
Experienced Mgmt.:	Y	Retail Sales:		Tech. Writing:		Software Dev.:		Law:	Y	Engineers, Other:	
Int'l Business:	Y	Comm./Industrial:	Y	Graphic Arts/Photog.:		Hardware Dev.:		HR/Other:	Y	Health/Lab:	
MBA Grads:	Y	Sales Trainees:		Music:		Consulting/Other:		Training:		Science/Research:	
		Advertising Pros.:	Y	Broadcasting:				Health Care:		Petroleum/Chem.:	
				Other:				Consulting:		Math/Other:	

TYPES OF BUSINESS:

Footwear
Hockey & Lacrosse Equipment
Accessories
Apparel

BRANDS/DIVISIONS/AFFILIATES:

Croslite
Ocean Minded
YOU by Crocs
CrocsRX
Jibbitz
Crocs Work
Crocband Sneak
Crocs Tone

CONTACTS: *Note: Officers with more than one job title may be intentionally listed here more than once.*

John McCarvel, CEO
John McCarvel, Pres.
Andrew Davison, Chief Mktg. Officer
Dan Hart, Chief Admin. Officer/Exec. VP
Dan Hart, Chief Legal Officer
Chris Ladd, VP-Global e-commerce
Becky Gebhardt, Sr. Creative Dir.
Thomas Smach, Acting Chmn.
Doug Hayes, VP/Gen. Mgr.-Americas

Phone: 303-848-7000 **Fax:** 303-468-4266
Toll-Free: 866-306-3179
Address: 6328 Monarch Park Pl., Niwot, CO 80503 US

GROWTH PLANS/SPECIAL FEATURES:

Crocs, Inc. is a designer, manufacturer and marketer of footwear for men, women and children under the Crocs brand. All of the company's footwear products incorporate its proprietary closed-cell resin material, known as Croslite, which enables the production of soft, lightweight, non-marking and odor-resistant shoes. To provide maximum comfort and functionality, Crocs shoes are designed around several structural features such as Italian-designed orthotic heels, built-in arch supports and tarsal bars. These properties make the footwear appropriate for casual wear, as well as for recreational uses such as boating, hiking, fishing or gardening. Its shoes are available in either general shoe sizing, ranging from XXS through 4XL, or specific shoe sizing, ranging from children's 6 through men's 13. Apart from its Crocs line of footwear, the company produces the Crocs Work line for the hospital, restaurant and hospitality markets; CrocsRX for the general foot care and diabetic-needs markets; Ocean Minded leather and EVA sandals for beachwear; and YOU by Crocs, a fashion line for women. Crocs' more than 250 models are available in thousands of stores nationwide, with retail price points ranging from $20 to $60. The firm operates nearly 700 retail locations and mall kiosks worldwide (378 of which are in the U.S.). Internationally, Crocs are sold in over 125 countries. In addition to footwear, Crocs markets a line of apparel and accessory items, including Jibbitz accessories, which are specifically suited to snap on to Crocs shoes. The firm produces a line of lightweight kneepads made from Croslite, which it markets to gardening retailers and hardware stores. In 2010, the firm expanded its retail operations into Puerto Rico. In July 2010, Crocs launched its first sneaker, the Crocband Sneak, and in November 2010, it introduced a line of toning shoes under the Crocs Tone label.

FINANCIALS: **Sales and profits are in thousands of dollars—add 000 to get the full amount. 2010 Note: Financial information for 2010 was not available for all companies at press time.**

2010 Sales: $789,695 — 2010 Profits: $67,726
2009 Sales: $645,767 — 2009 Profits: $-42,078
2008 Sales: $721,589 — 2008 Profits: $-185,076
2007 Sales: $847,350 — 2007 Profits: $168,228
2006 Sales: $354,728 — 2006 Profits: $64,417

U.S. Stock Ticker: CROX
Int'l Ticker:
Int'l Exchange:
Employees: 4,000 Fiscal Year Ends: 12/31
Parent Company:

SALARIES/BENEFITS:

Pension Plan: ESOP Stock Plan: Profit Sharing: Top Exec. Salary: $670,191 Bonus: $338,836
Savings Plan: Stock Purch. Plan: Second Exec. Salary: $595,833 Bonus: $240,000

OTHER THOUGHTS:

Apparent Women Officers or Directors: 2
Hot Spot for Advancement for Women/Minorities:

LOCATIONS: ("Y" = Yes)

West:	Southwest:	Midwest:	Southeast:	Northeast:	International:
Y	Y	Y	Y	Y	Y

CSX CORP

www.csx.com

Industry Group Code: 48211

Management:		Sales/Marketing:		Liberal Arts:		Information Sys.:		Professionals:		Tech./Scientific:	
Mgmt. Trainees:	Y	Marketing Pros.:	Y	Gen. Writing/Editing:	Y	Info. Mgmt.:	Y	Finance/Acct.:	Y	Engineers, Elec.:	Y
Experienced Mgmt.:	Y	Retail Sales:		Tech. Writing:	Y	Software Dev.:	Y	Law:	Y	Engineers, Other:	Y
Int'l Business:	Y	Comm./Industrial:	Y	Graphic Arts/Photog.:		Hardware Dev.:	Y	HR/Other:	Y	Health/Lab:	
MBA Grads:	Y	Sales Trainees:		Music:		Consulting/Other:		Training:	Y	Science/Research:	
		Advertising Pros.:	Y	Broadcasting:				Health Care:		Petroleum/Chem.:	
				Other:				Consulting:		Math/Other:	

TYPES OF BUSINESS:

Railroad Transportation
Intermodal Services
Logistics Software & Services
Real Estate
Automotive Distribution & Storage

BRANDS/DIVISIONS/AFFILIATES:

CSX Transportation Inc
CSX Intermodal, Inc.
CSX Real Property, Inc.
CSX Technology
Transflo Terminal Services, Inc.
Total Distribution Services, Inc.

CONTACTS: *Note: Officers with more than one job title may be intentionally listed here more than once.*

Michael J. Ward, CEO
David A. Brown, COO/Exec. VP
Michael J. Ward, Pres.
Oscar Munoz, CFO/Exec. VP
Clarence W. Gooden, Exec. VP-Mktg. & Sales/Chief Commercial Officer
Lisa A. Mancini, Sr. VP-Human Resources & Labor Rel.
Ellen M. Fitzsimmons, General Counsel/Corp. Sec./Sr. VP-Law
Lester M. Passa, VP-Strategic Planning
Ellen M. Fitzsimmons, Sr. VP-Public Affairs
David A. Boor, Treas./VP-Tax
Carolyn T. Sizemore, VP/Controller
Frank A. Lonegro, Pres., CSX Technology, Inc.
Stephen A. Crosby, Pres., CSX Real Property, Inc.
Michael J. Ruehling, VP-Federal Legislation
Michael J. Ward, Chmn.

Phone: 904-359-3200 **Fax:**
Toll-Free:
Address: 500 Water St., 15th Fl., Jacksonville, FL 32202 US

GROWTH PLANS/SPECIAL FEATURES:

CSX Corp. is a rail and intermodal transportation company. The company's largest business unit, CSX Transportation, Inc. (CSXT), is a leading railroad company in the U.S. The division covers roughly 21,000 route miles in 23 states in the eastern half of the U.S., Washington, D.C. and the Canadian provinces Ontario and Quebec. CSXT also serves over 70 ocean, river and lake ports, as well as thousands of production and distribution facilities through track connections to more than 240 short-line and regional railroads. CSXT provides transportation for customers in a wide variety of industries, such as coal, chemicals, automobiles, minerals, agricultural products, food and consumer goods, metals, forest and paper products and phosphates and fertilizer. The firm's intermodal segment, operated through subsidiary CSX Intermodal, Inc., combines rail and truck services with a domestic container fleet to provide a network of intermodal facilities across North America. Other major company subsidiaries include Total Distribution Services, Inc., which operates value-added distribution and storage services to the automotive industry; CSX Real Property, Inc., an organization responsible for the company's real estate sales, leasing, acquisition and management and development activities; CSX Technology, a company providing information technology applications and support services for various shipping needs such as scheduling, tracking and monitoring of freight, data resource management, system architecture and resource management; and Transflo Terminal Services, Inc., which handles intermodal bulk transportation and materials services.

Employees are offered auto, home, life, medical, disability, vision, dental, travel accident, personal accident and domestic partner insurance; flexible spending accounts; an employee assistance plan; a 401(k) plan; a pension plan; tuition reimbursement; pre-paid legal coverage; and employee discounts.

FINANCIALS: **Sales and profits are in thousands of dollars—add 000 to get the full amount. 2010 Note: Financial information for 2010 was not available for all companies at press time.**

2010 Sales: $10,636,000 — 2010 Profits: $1,563,000
2009 Sales: $9,041,000 — 2009 Profits: $1,128,000
2008 Sales: $11,255,000 — 2008 Profits: $1,485,000
2007 Sales: $10,030,000 — 2007 Profits: $1,226,000
2006 Sales: $9,566,000 — 2006 Profits: $1,310,000

U.S. Stock Ticker: CSX
Int'l Ticker:
Int'l Exchange:
Employees: 29,916 Fiscal Year Ends: 12/31
Parent Company:

SALARIES/BENEFITS:

Pension Plan: Y | ESOP Stock Plan: | Profit Sharing: | Top Exec. Salary: $1,100,000 | Bonus: $1,200,000
Savings Plan: Y | Stock Purch. Plan: | Second Exec. Salary: $650,000 | Bonus: $535,000

OTHER THOUGHTS:

Apparent Women Officers or Directors: 5
Hot Spot for Advancement for Women/Minorities: Y

LOCATIONS: ("Y" = Yes)

West:	Southwest:	Midwest:	Southeast:	Northeast:	International:
Y	Y	Y	Y	Y	Y

Sales, profits and employees may be estimates. Financial information, benefits and other data can change quickly and may vary from those stated here.

CUMMINS INC

www.cummins.com

Industry Group Code: 3363

Management:		Sales/Marketing:		Liberal Arts:		Information Sys.:		Professionals:		Tech./Scientific:	
Mgmt. Trainees:	Y	Marketing Pros.:	Y	Gen. Writing/Editing:	Y	Info. Mgmt.:	Y	Finance/Acct.:	Y	Engineers, Elec.:	Y
Experienced Mgmt.:	Y	Retail Sales:		Tech. Writing:	Y	Software Dev.:	Y	Law:	Y	Engineers, Other:	Y
Int'l Business:	Y	Comm./Industrial:	Y	Graphic Arts/Photog.:	Y	Hardware Dev.:	Y	HR/Other:	Y	Health/Lab:	
MBA Grads:	Y	Sales Trainees:		Music:		Consulting/Other:		Training:	Y	Science/Research:	
		Advertising Pros.:	Y	Broadcasting:				Health Care:		Petroleum/Chem.:	
				Other:				Consulting:		Math/Other:	

TYPES OF BUSINESS:

Automotive Products, Motors & Parts Manufacturing
Engines
Filtration Systems
Power Generation Systems
Alternators
Air Handling Systems
Filtration & Emissions Solutions
Fuel Systems

BRANDS/DIVISIONS/AFFILIATES:

Cummins Power Generation
Onan

CONTACTS: *Note: Officers with more than one job title may be intentionally listed here more than once.*

Theodore M. Solso, CEO
N. Thomas Linebarger, COO
N. Thomas Linebarger, Pres.
Patrick J. Ward, CFO/VP
John C. Wall, CTO/VP
Mark R. Gerstle, Chief Admin. Officer/VP
Marya Rose, General Counsel/VP/Sec.
Marsha L. Hunt, Controller/VP
Anant Talaulicar, VP/Pres., Components Group
Richard E. Harris, Chief Investment Officer/VP
Richard Freeland, VP/Pres., Engine Bus.
Livingston Satterthwaite, VP/Pres., Power Generation
Theodore M. Solso, Chmn.
Steven Chapman, VP-China & Russia
Lisa Yoder, VP-Global Supply Chain

Phone: 812-377-5000 **Fax:** 812-377-4937
Toll-Free:
Address: 500 Jackson St., Columbus, IN 47202-3005 US

GROWTH PLANS/SPECIAL FEATURES:

Cummins, Inc. designs, manufactures, distributes and services diesel and natural gas engines; electric power generation systems; and engine-related component products, including filtration and emissions solutions, fuel systems, controls and air handling systems. The company's operations are divided into four segments: engine, power generation, components and distribution. The engine segment, which generates 49% of Cummins' sales, manufactures and markets diesel and natural gas-powered engines, parts, and services under the Cummins brand name for the heavy- and medium-duty truck, bus, recreational vehicle, light-duty automotive, agricultural, construction, mining, marine, oil and gas, rail and governmental equipment markets. The power generation segment, accounting for 18% the firm's revenue, designs and manufactures components of power generation systems, including engines, controls, alternators, transfer switches and switchgear. Products are marketed principally under the Cummins Power Generation and Onan brands and include diesel and alternative-fuel electrical generator sets for commercial, institutional and consumer applications, such as office buildings, hospitals, factories, municipalities, utilities, universities, boats and homes. The components segment (19% of net sales) produces filters, silencers and intake and exhaust systems and commercial turbochargers. The distribution segment (14% of revenue) consists of 19 company-owned and 22 joint ventures that distribute the company's products and services in roughly 70 countries and territories. Cummins serves customers through a network of more than 600 company-owned and independent distributor locations and roughly 6,000 dealer locations in more than 190 countries and territories. In May 2011, the firm opened a new facility in the United Arab Emirates (UAE).

Employees are offered medical and dental insurance; life insurance; a 401(k) plan; a profit sharing plan; a pension plan; flexible spending accounts; an employee stock purchase plan; and disability coverage.

FINANCIALS: **Sales and profits are in thousands of dollars—add 000 to get the full amount. 2010 Note: Financial information for 2010 was not available for all companies at press time.**

2010 Sales: $13,226,000 — 2010 Profits: $1,040,000
2009 Sales: $10,800,000 — 2009 Profits: $428,000
2008 Sales: $14,342,000 — 2008 Profits: $755,000
2007 Sales: $13,048,000 — 2007 Profits: $739,000
2006 Sales: $11,362,000 — 2006 Profits: $715,000

U.S. Stock Ticker: CMI
Int'l Ticker:
Int'l Exchange:
Employees: 39,200 Fiscal Year Ends: 12/31
Parent Company:

SALARIES/BENEFITS:

Pension Plan: Y ESOP Stock Plan: Profit Sharing: Y Top Exec. Salary: $1,139,250 Bonus: $4,452,000
Savings Plan: Y Stock Purch. Plan: Y Second Exec. Salary: $678,125 Bonus: $1,236,800

OTHER THOUGHTS:

Apparent Women Officers or Directors: 5
Hot Spot for Advancement for Women/Minorities: Y

LOCATIONS: ("Y" = Yes)

West:	Southwest:	Midwest:	Southeast:	Northeast:	International:
Y	Y	Y	Y	Y	Y

Sales, profits and employees may be estimates. Financial information, benefits and other data can change quickly and may vary from those stated here.

CVS CAREMARK CORPORATION

info.cvscaremark.com

Industry Group Code: 446110

Management:		Sales/Marketing:		Liberal Arts:		Information Sys.:		Professionals:		Tech./Scientific:	
Mgmt. Trainees:	Y	Marketing Pros.:	Y	Gen. Writing/Editing:	Y	Info. Mgmt.:	Y	Finance/Acct.:	Y	Engineers, Elec.:	
Experienced Mgmt.:	Y	Retail Sales:	Y	Tech. Writing:		Software Dev.:	Y	Law:	Y	Engineers, Other:	
Int'l Business:	Y	Comm./Industrial:		Graphic Arts/Photog.:	Y	Hardware Dev.:		HR/Other:	Y	Health/Lab:	
MBA Grads:	Y	Sales Trainees:	Y	Music:		Consulting/Other:		Training:	Y	Science/Research:	
		Advertising Pros.:	Y	Broadcasting:				Health Care:	Y	Petroleum/Chem.:	
				Other:	Y			Consulting:		Math/Other:	

TYPES OF BUSINESS:

Drug Stores
Pharmacy Benefits Management
Online Pharmacy Services

BRANDS/DIVISIONS/AFFILIATES:

MinuteClinic
SilverScript Insurance Company
CVS Corp.
Accendo Insurance Company
PharmaCare Pharmacy
CVS/pharmacy

CONTACTS: *Note: Officers with more than one job title may be intentionally listed here more than once.*

Larry J. Merlo, CEO
Larry J. Merlo, Pres.
David M. Denton, CFO/Exec. VP
Helena B. Foulkes, Chief Mktg. Officer/Exec. VP
Lisa Bisaccia, Chief Human Resources Officer/Sr. VP
Troyen A. Brennan, Chief Medical Officer/Exec. VP
Stuart M. McGuigan, CIO/Sr. VP
Douglas A. Sgarro, Chief Legal Officer/Exec. VP/Pres., CVS Realty Co.
Laird Daniels, Chief Acct. Officer/Controller/Sr. VP
Jonathan C. Roberts, Exec. VP/COO-PBM Div.
Per Lofberg, Exec. VP/Pres., Caremark Pharmacy Svcs.
David Casey, VP/Diversity Officer
Helena Foulkes, Chief Health Care Strategy Officer
Thomas M. Ryan, Chmn.

Phone: 401-765-1500 **Fax:** 401-762-2137
Toll-Free: 888-746-7287
Address: 1 CVS Dr., Woonsocket, RI 02895 US

GROWTH PLANS/SPECIAL FEATURES:

CVS Caremark Corporation is a leading provider of prescription and related healthcare services in the U.S., filling over 1 billion prescriptions annually. It operates in two segments: retail pharmacy and pharmacy services. The retail pharmacy segment includes over 7,182 retail drugstores, with 7,123 operating a pharmacy; an online retail web site; and retail healthcare clinics. The retail drugstores are located in 41 states and Washington, D.C., operating under the CVS/pharmacy and Longs Drugs names. The firm's drugstores sell prescription drugs and a wide assortment of general merchandise, including over-the-counter drugs, beauty products, photo finishing and other items. The division operates over 569 retail healthcare clinics in 25 states under the MinuteClinic name, predominately located within CVS drugstores. The clinics, staffed by certified nurses and physician assistants, diagnose and treat minor health conditions. The pharmacy services segment provides a full range of pharmacy benefit management services, including mail order pharmacy services, plan design and administration, formulary management, claims processing and health management programs. Through subsidiaries SilverScript Insurance Company and Accendo Insurance Company, the division is a national provider of drug benefits. The segment operates a national retail pharmacy network with over 60,000 participating pharmacies; 44 retail specialty pharmacy stores; 18 specialty mail order pharmacies; and six mail services pharmacies located in 25 states, Puerto Rico and Washington, D.C. Specialty pharmacy stores average 2,000 square feet in size. In December 2010, the firm agreed to acquire the Medicare Part D business from Universal American.

Employee benefits include: Medical and dental insurance; flexible spending accounts; prescription drug plans; 401k; adoption assistance; merchandise discounts; and education reimbursement.

FINANCIALS: **Sales and profits are in thousands of dollars—add 000 to get the full amount. 2010 Note: Financial information for 2010 was not available for all companies at press time.**

2010 Sales: $96,413,000	2010 Profits: $3,424,000
2009 Sales: $98,729,000	2009 Profits: $3,696,000
2008 Sales: $87,471,900	2008 Profits: $3,212,100
2007 Sales: $76,329,500	2007 Profits: $2,637,000
2006 Sales: $43,821,400	2006 Profits: $1,368,900

U.S. Stock Ticker: CVS
Int'l Ticker:
Int'l Exchange:
Employees: 201,000 Fiscal Year Ends: 12/31
Parent Company:

SALARIES/BENEFITS:

Pension Plan:	ESOP Stock Plan: Y	Profit Sharing:	Top Exec. Salary: $1,475,000	Bonus: $2,200,000
Savings Plan: Y	Stock Purch. Plan: Y		Second Exec. Salary: $938,889	Bonus: $1,280,000

OTHER THOUGHTS:

Apparent Women Officers or Directors: 2
Hot Spot for Advancement for Women/Minorities: Y

LOCATIONS: ("Y" = Yes)

West:	Southwest:	Midwest:	Southeast:	Northeast:	International:
Y	Y	Y	Y	Y	Y

DANAHER CORP

www.danaher.com

Industry Group Code: 335

Management:		**Sales/Marketing:**		**Liberal Arts:**		**Information Sys.:**		**Professionals:**		**Tech./Scientific:**	
Mgmt. Trainees:	Y	Marketing Pros.:	Y	Gen. Writing/Editing:	Y	Info. Mgmt.:	Y	Finance/Acct.:	Y	Engineers, Elec.:	Y
Experienced Mgmt.:	Y	Retail Sales:		Tech. Writing:	Y	Software Dev.:	Y	Law:	Y	Engineers, Other:	Y
Int'l Business:	Y	Comm./Industrial:	Y	Graphic Arts/Photog.:	Y	Hardware Dev.:	Y	HR/Other:	Y	Health/Lab:	
MBA Grads:	Y	Sales Trainees:	Y	Music:		Consulting/Other:		Training:	Y	Science/Research:	
		Advertising Pros.:	Y	Broadcasting:				Health Care:		Petroleum/Chem.:	
				Other:				Consulting:		Math/Other:	

TYPES OF BUSINESS:

Power Tools Manufacturing
Environmental Management Products
Test & Calibration Equipment
Medical Tools & Equipment
Motors & Drives
Bar Code Equipment
Security & Defense Products
Automotive Components & Repair Equipment

BRANDS/DIVISIONS/AFFILIATES:

EskoArtwork
Pacific Scientific Aerospace
Beckman Coulter, Inc.

CONTACTS:

Note: Officers with more than one job title may be intentionally listed here more than once.

H. Lawrence Culp, Jr., CEO
H. Lawrence Culp, Jr., Pres.
Daniel L. Comas, CFO/Exec. VP
Jonathan P. Graham, General Counsel/Sr. VP
Daniel A. Raskas, Sr. VP-Corp. Dev.
Matt R. McGrew, VP-Investor Rel.
James H. Ditkoff, Sr. VP-Finance & Tax
Mitchell P. Rales, Chmn.-Exec. Committee
Robert S. Lutz, Sr. VP/Chief Acct. Officer
James A. Lico, Exec. VP
William K. Daniel, II, Exec. VP
Steven M. Rales, Chmn.

Phone: 202-828-0850 **Fax:** 202-828-0860
Toll-Free:
Address: 2099 Pennsylvania Ave. NW, Washington, DC 20006-1813 US

GROWTH PLANS/SPECIAL FEATURES:

Danaher Corp. designs, manufactures and markets professional, medical, industrial, commercial and consumer products. It operates in five business segments: industrial technologies (24% of revenues); test and measurement (22%); environmental (21%); life sciences and diagnostics (17%); and dental (14%). The industrial technologies segment manufactures products and sub-systems generally incorporated into other products by systems integrators, original equipment manufacturers and other customers. It encompasses four business lines: motion, marketing motors and mechanical components; product identification, such as bar code print and read devices; aerospace and defense, manufacturing aircraft and defense equipment; and sensors and controls, used to monitor manufacturing variables. The test and measurement segment provides electronic measurement instruments, monitoring, management and optimization tools for communications networks and related services that are used in the design, development, manufacture, installation, deployment and operation of electronics equipment and communications networks and services. Danaher's environmental segment provides products that help protect water supply and air quality, serving two primary markets: water quality and retail/commercial petroleum. The life sciences and diagnostics segment provides research and clinical tools that are used by scientists to study cells, and the components of cells, to gain a better understanding of complex biological matters; and analytical instruments, reagents, consumables, software and services that are used to diagnose disease, make treatment decisions and monitor patients in hospitals and other critical care settings. The firm's dental segment provides equipment and consumables for the worldwide dental market. By geographic area, North America generates the largest share (49%) of the company's sales, followed by Europe, 28%; Asia/Australia, 17%; and finally other regions, 6%. In January 2011, Danaher agreed to acquire EskoArtwork. In April 2011, the company sold its Pacific Scientific Aerospace operations to Meggitt PLC. In June 2011, the firm acquired Beckman Coulter, Inc. for $5.8 billion

FINANCIALS:

Sales and profits are in thousands of dollars—add 000 to get the full amount. 2010 Note: Financial information for 2010 was not available for all companies at press time.

2010 Sales: $13,202,602 | 2010 Profits: $1,793,000
2009 Sales: $11,184,938 | 2009 Profits: $1,151,704
2008 Sales: $12,697,456 | 2008 Profits: $1,317,631
2007 Sales: $11,025,917 | 2007 Profits: $1,369,904
2006 Sales: $9,466,056 | 2006 Profits: $1,122,029

U.S. Stock Ticker: DHR
Int'l Ticker:
Int'l Exchange:
Employees: 48,200 Fiscal Year Ends: 12/31
Parent Company:

SALARIES/BENEFITS:

Pension Plan: ESOP Stock Plan: Profit Sharing: Top Exec. Salary: $1,117,778 Bonus: $4,400,000
Savings Plan: Stock Purch. Plan: Second Exec. Salary: $600,152 Bonus: $1,200,000

OTHER THOUGHTS:

Apparent Women Officers or Directors:
Hot Spot for Advancement for Women/Minorities:

LOCATIONS: ("Y" = Yes)

West:	Southwest:	Midwest:	Southeast:	Northeast:	International:
Y	Y	Y	Y	Y	Y

Sales, profits and employees may be estimates. Financial information, benefits and other data can change quickly and may vary from those stated here.

DARDEN RESTAURANTS INC

www.dardenrestaurants.com

Industry Group Code: 722110

Management:		Sales/Marketing:		Liberal Arts:		Information Sys.:		Professionals:		Tech./Scientific:	
Mgmt. Trainees:	Y	Marketing Pros.:	Y	Gen. Writing/Editing:	Y	Info. Mgmt.:	Y	Finance/Acct.:	Y	Engineers, Elec.:	
Experienced Mgmt.:	Y	Retail Sales:		Tech. Writing:		Software Dev.:	Y	Law:	Y	Engineers, Other:	
Int'l Business:	Y	Comm./Industrial:		Graphic Arts/Photog.:	Y	Hardware Dev.:		HR/Other:	Y	Health/Lab:	
MBA Grads:	Y	Sales Trainees:		Music:		Consulting/Other:		Training:	Y	Science/Research:	
		Advertising Pros.:	Y	Broadcasting:				Health Care:		Petroleum/Chem.:	
				Other:	Y			Consulting:		Math/Other:	

TYPES OF BUSINESS:

Restaurants-Casual Dining

BRANDS/DIVISIONS/AFFILIATES:

Red Lobster
Olive Garden
Capital Grille (The)
Bahama Breeze
LongHorn Steakhouse
Seasons 52

CONTACTS: *Note: Officers with more than one job title may be intentionally listed here more than once.*

Clarence Otis, Jr., CEO
Andrew H. Madsen, COO
Andrew H. Madsen, Pres.
C. Bradford Richmond, CFO/Sr. VP
JJ Buettgen, Chief Mktg. Officer/Sr. VP
Ronald Bojalad, Sr. VP-Group Human Resources
Patti Reilly-White, CIO/Sr. VP
Teresa Sebastian, General Counsel/Sr. VP/Sec.
Kim Lopdrup, Sr. VP-Bus. Dev.
Valerie K. Collins, Corp. Controller/Sr. VP
John Caron, Pres., Olive Garden
Dave George, Pres., LongHorn Steakhouse
David Pickens, Pres., Red Lobster
Suk Singh, Chief Dev. Officer/Sr. VP
Clarence Otis, Jr., Chmn.
Barry B. Moullet, Chief Supply Chain Officer/Sr. VP

Phone: 407-245-4000 **Fax:**
Toll-Free:
Address: 1000 Darden Ctr. Dr., Orlando, FL 32837 US

GROWTH PLANS/SPECIAL FEATURES:

Darden Restaurants, Inc. is a leading publicly held casual dining company in the U.S. It owns and operates roughly 1,860 restaurants throughout the U.S. and Canada. Darden operates six restaurant chains: Red Lobster, Olive Garden, LongHorn Steakhouse, The Capital Grille, Bahama Breeze and Seasons 52. Red Lobster, with 698 restaurants, is a seafood-specialty restaurant in the U.S. and Canada. Its menu features fresh fish, shrimp, crab, lobster, scallops and other seafood, as well as non-seafood entrees, appetizers and desserts. Olive Garden, with 754 restaurants, is a casual dining Italian restaurant in the U.S. and Canada. Its menu includes a variety of Italian foods, including antipasti; soups, salad and garlic breadsticks; baked pastas; sauteed chicken, seafood and vegetables; grilled meats; and a variety of desserts. It also offers an expanded wine list that includes a broad selection of imported Italian wines, as well as coffee imported from Italy for its espresso and cappuccino. LongHorn Steakhouse restaurants, with 354 locations, are full service establishments serving both lunch and dinner with American West themed decor. The Capital Grille chain of upscale full-service restaurants dry-ages its steaks on the premises and flies in fresh seafood daily to its 44 locations, as well as featuring a 350-selection wine list. Bahama Breeze, which has 26 restaurants, is a Caribbean-themed restaurant that offers guests an island dining experience with a menu featuring Caribbean-style beef, chicken and seafood. Seasons 52, with 17 restaurants, is a fresh grill and wine bar with seasonally inspired menus, offering nutritionally balanced meals lower in calories than comparable restaurant meals. Additionally, the firm operates five franchised LongHorn Steakhouse restaurants in Puerto Rico and 22 franchised Red Lobster restaurants in Japan through unaffiliated companies. In May 2011, Darden Restaurants opened three new restaurants, an Olive Garden, a Red Lobster and a LongHorn Steakhouse, in Maryland.

FINANCIALS: **Sales and profits are in thousands of dollars—add 000 to get the full amount. 2010 Note: Financial information for 2010 was not available for all companies at press time.**

2010 Sales: $7,113,100 — 2010 Profits: $404,500
2009 Sales: $7,217,500 — 2009 Profits: $372,200
2008 Sales: $6,626,500 — 2008 Profits: $377,200
2007 Sales: $5,567,100 — 2007 Profits: $201,400
2006 Sales: $5,353,600 — 2006 Profits: $338,194

U.S. Stock Ticker: DRI
Int'l Ticker:
Int'l Exchange:
Employees: 174,079 Fiscal Year Ends: 5/31
Parent Company:

SALARIES/BENEFITS:

Pension Plan: ESOP Stock Plan: Profit Sharing: Top Exec. Salary: $1,022,169 Bonus: $2,121,000
Savings Plan: Stock Purch. Plan: Second Exec. Salary: $791,596 Bonus: $1,231,900

OTHER THOUGHTS:

Apparent Women Officers or Directors: 7
Hot Spot for Advancement for Women/Minorities: Y

LOCATIONS: ("Y" = Yes)

West:	Southwest:	Midwest:	Southeast:	Northeast:	International:
Y	Y	Y	Y	Y	Y

DAVITA INC

www.davita.com

Industry Group Code: 6214

Management:		Sales/Marketing:		Liberal Arts:		Information Sys.:		Professionals:		Tech./Scientific:	
Mgmt. Trainees:	Y	Marketing Pros.:	Y	Gen. Writing/Editing:	Y	Info. Mgmt.:	Y	Finance/Acct.:	Y	Engineers, Elec.:	
Experienced Mgmt.:	Y	Retail Sales:		Tech. Writing:	Y	Software Dev.:	Y	Law:	Y	Engineers, Other:	
Int'l Business:		Comm./Industrial:	Y	Graphic Arts/Photog.:		Hardware Dev.:		HR/Other:	Y	Health/Lab:	Y
MBA Grads:	Y	Sales Trainees:		Music:		Consulting/Other:		Training:	Y	Science/Research:	Y
		Advertising Pros.:		Broadcasting:				Health Care:	Y	Petroleum/Chem.:	
				Other:				Consulting:		Math/Other:	

TYPES OF BUSINESS:

Renal Care Services
Clinical Research

BRANDS/DIVISIONS/AFFILIATES:

DaVita Rx
DaVita Clinical Research
HomeChoice Partners
Lifeline
DaVita Nephrology Partners
DSI Rentals, Inc.

CONTACTS: *Note: Officers with more than one job title may be intentionally listed here more than once.*

Kent J. Thiry, CEO
Dennis Kogod, COO
Luis Borgen, CFO
Laura Mildenberger, Chief People Officer
Kim Rivera, General Counsel/VP/Corp. Sec.
Bill Myers, VP-Comm.
Jim Gustafson, VP-Investor Rel.
Thomas O. Usilton, Sr. VP
Allen R. Nissenson, Chief Medical Officer
Javier Rodriguez, Sr. VP
LeAnne Zumwalt, VP
Kent J. Thiry, Chmn.

Phone: 303-405-2100 **Fax:**
Toll-Free:
Address: 1551 Wewatta St., Denver, CO 80202 US

GROWTH PLANS/SPECIAL FEATURES:

DaVita, Inc. is a provider of dialysis services in the U.S. for patients suffering from chronic kidney failure, also known as end stage renal disease, or ESRD. The company operates or provides administrative services to 1,612 outpatient dialysis centers located in 42 states and Washington, D.C., serving approximately 125,000 patients. The firm also provides acute inpatient dialysis services in approximately 750 hospitals. The firm's dialysis services include hemodialysis, peritoneal dialysis and pre-ESRD education. In addition, the company provides certain patients the option of home-based hemodialysis. The firm owns two licensed clinical laboratories, located in Florida, which specialize in ERSD patient testing. These specialized laboratories provide routine laboratory tests covered by the Medicare composite payment rate for dialysis and other physician-prescribed laboratory tests for ESRD patients. The company's dialysis and related lab services business accounts for approximately 94% of the company's revenue. Ancillary services and strategic initiatives account for the remaining 6% of revenues and include DaVita Rx, a wholly-owned pharmacy that provides oral medications to DaVita's patients with chronic kidney disease and ERSD; DaVita Clinical Research, which conducts research trials with dialysis patients and provides administrative support for research conducted by DaVita-affiliated nephrology practices; HomeChoice Partners, which offers disease management services; Lifeline, which provides vascular access services; and DaVita Nephrology Partners, which offers physician services. In 2010, DaVita acquired 41 dialysis centers; sold six centers; opened 65 new dialysis centers; closed 18 centers; and made minority equity investments in three centers that were previously under management and administrative service agreements. In September 2011, the firm acquired DSI Rentals, Inc.

Employees are offered medical, dental and vision insurance; short- and long-term disability insurance; flexible spending accounts; life insurance; a 401(k) plan; a stock purchase program; an employee assistance program; and tuition reimbursement.

FINANCIALS: **Sales and profits are in thousands of dollars—add 000 to get the full amount. 2010 Note: Financial information for 2010 was not available for all companies at press time.**

2010 Sales: $6,447,391 | 2010 Profits: $484,219
2009 Sales: $6,108,800 | 2009 Profits: $479,759
2008 Sales: $5,660,173 | 2008 Profits: $374,160
2007 Sales: $5,264,151 | 2007 Profits: $381,778
2006 Sales: $4,880,662 | 2006 Profits: $289,691

U.S. Stock Ticker: DVA
Int'l Ticker:
Int'l Exchange:
Employees: 36,500 Fiscal Year Ends: 12/31
Parent Company:

SALARIES/BENEFITS:

Pension Plan: | ESOP Stock Plan: | Profit Sharing: | Top Exec. Salary: $1,020,000 | Bonus: $3,325,000
Savings Plan: Y | Stock Purch. Plan: Y | | Second Exec. Salary: $727,075 | Bonus: $1,618,000

OTHER THOUGHTS:

Apparent Women Officers or Directors: 4
Hot Spot for Advancement for Women/Minorities: Y

LOCATIONS: ("Y" = Yes)

West:	Southwest:	Midwest:	Southeast:	Northeast:	International:
Y	Y	Y	Y	Y	

Sales, profits and employees may be estimates. Financial information, benefits and other data can change quickly and may vary from those stated here.

DEAN FOODS CO

www.deanfoods.com

Industry Group Code: 3115

Management:		Sales/Marketing:		Liberal Arts:		Information Sys.:		Professionals:		Tech./Scientific:	
Mgmt. Trainees:	Y	Marketing Pros.:	Y	Gen. Writing/Editing:	Y	Info. Mgmt.:	Y	Finance/Acct.:	Y	Engineers, Elec.:	
Experienced Mgmt.:	Y	Retail Sales:		Tech. Writing:		Software Dev.:		Law:	Y	Engineers, Other:	Y
Int'l Business:	Y	Comm./Industrial:	Y	Graphic Arts/Photog.:	Y	Hardware Dev.:		HR/Other:	Y	Health/Lab:	
MBA Grads:	Y	Sales Trainees:	Y	Music:		Consulting/Other:		Training:	Y	Science/Research:	
		Advertising Pros.:	Y	Broadcasting:				Health Care:		Petroleum/Chem.:	
				Other:				Consulting:		Math/Other:	

TYPES OF BUSINESS:

Dairy Products, Manufacturing
Milk Processing & Distribution
Organic Dairy Products
Soy-Based Products
Juices
Coffee Creamers
Powdered Ingredients

BRANDS/DIVISIONS/AFFILIATES:

WhiteWave Foods Company
Creamland
Rachel's Organic
Land O'Lakes
Silk
Horizon Organic
International Delight
Alpro

CONTACTS: *Note: Officers with more than one job title may be intentionally listed here more than once.*

Gregg L. Engles, CEO
Joseph E. Scalzo, COO
Shaun Mara, CFO/Exec. VP
Paul T. Moskowitz, Exec. VP-Human Resources
Kelly Duffin-Maxwell, Exec. VP-R&D
Steven J. Kemps, General Counsel/Exec. VP/Corp. Sec
Gregory A. McKelvey, Chief Strategy & Transformation Officer/Exec. VP
Marguerite Copel, Corp. Comm.
Barry Sievert, Investor Rel.
Scott Vopni, Chief Acct. Officer
Deborah B. Carosella, Sr. VP-Innovation
Blaine E. McPeak, Pres., WhiteWave Foods
Christopher Silva, Chief Commercial Officer
Bernard P.J. Deryckere, CEO-Alpro
Gregg L. Engles, Chmn.

Phone: 214-303-3400 **Fax:**

Toll-Free:

Address: 2711 North Haskell Ave., Ste. 3400, Dallas, TX 75204 US

GROWTH PLANS/SPECIAL FEATURES:

Dean Foods Co. is a leading food and beverage company. The firm operates through two business segments, the Fresh Dairy Direct segment and WhiteWave-Morningstar segment. Generating approximately 76% of the company's net sales, Dean's dairy group manufactures, markets and distributes a variety of branded and private-label dairy-case products to retailers, distributors, foodservice outlets, schools and government entities across the U.S, with 82 manufacturing facilities in 33 states. Products sold by the dairy group include fresh milk, ice cream, flavored milks, buttermilk, half-and-half, whipping cream, coffee creamers, yogurt, cottage cheese, sour cream and dairy based dips, under its more than 60 proprietary and licensed brands, including Berkeley Farms, Brown Cow, Chug, Country Charm, Creamland, Dairy Fresh, Dean's, Hershey's, Land O'Lakes, Meadow Brook, Mountain High, Nature's Pride, Oak Farms, Shenandoah's Pride and Swiss Dairy. Dean purchases its raw milk primarily from farmers' cooperatives. Generating approximately 24% of Dean's net sales, subsidiary WhiteWave-Morningstar Company develops, manufactures, markets and sells a variety of nationally branded soy, dairy and dairy-related products, such as Silk soymilk and cultured soy products; Horizon Organic dairy products; International Delight coffee creamers; Rachel's Organic dairy products; The Organic Cow organic dairy products; and White Wave and Tofu Town branded tofu. The segment also offers branded soy-based beverages and food products in Europe under the Alpro and Provamel brands. Whitewave-Morningstar currently operates 19 domestic and 5 international manufacturing facilities. It purchases 85% of its organic raw milk from a network of over 500 dairy farmers across the U.S., as well as two organic farms that it owns and one organic farm that it leases and manages. WhiteWave-Morningstar sells its products to a variety of customers, including grocery stores, club stores, natural foods stores, mass merchandisers, convenience stores and foodservice outlets.

The company offers employees health and dental insurance; disability coverage; life insurance; and a 401(k) plan.

FINANCIALS: **Sales and profits are in thousands of dollars—add 000 to get the full amount. 2010 Note: Financial information for 2010 was not available for all companies at press time.**

2010 Sales: $12,122,887 | 2010 Profits: $146,501
2009 Sales: $11,113,782 | 2009 Profits: $276,576
2008 Sales: $12,454,613 | 2008 Profits: $183,770
2007 Sales: $11,821,903 | 2007 Profits: $131,353
2006 Sales: $10,098,555 | 2006 Profits: $225,414

U.S. Stock Ticker: DF
Int'l Ticker:
Int'l Exchange:
Employees: 25,780 Fiscal Year Ends: 12/31
Parent Company:

SALARIES/BENEFITS:

Pension Plan: ESOP Stock Plan: Profit Sharing: Top Exec. Salary: $1,133,333 Bonus: $3,335,904
Savings Plan: Y Stock Purch. Plan: Second Exec. Salary: $767,282 Bonus: $1,138,133

OTHER THOUGHTS:

Apparent Women Officers or Directors: 5
Hot Spot for Advancement for Women/Minorities: Y

LOCATIONS: ("Y" = Yes)

West:	Southwest:	Midwest:	Southeast:	Northeast:	International:
Y	Y	Y	Y	Y	Y

DEERE & CO

www.deere.com

Industry Group Code: 333

Management:		Sales/Marketing:		Liberal Arts:		Information Sys.:		Professionals:		Tech./Scientific:	
Mgmt. Trainees:	Y	Marketing Pros.:	Y	Gen. Writing/Editing:	Y	Info. Mgmt.:	Y	Finance/Acct.:	Y	Engineers, Elec.:	Y
Experienced Mgmt.:	Y	Retail Sales:		Tech. Writing:	Y	Software Dev.:	Y	Law:	Y	Engineers, Other:	Y
Int'l Business:	Y	Comm./Industrial:	Y	Graphic Arts/Photog.:	Y	Hardware Dev.:	Y	HR/Other:	Y	Health/Lab:	
MBA Grads:	Y	Sales Trainees:		Music:		Consulting/Other:		Training:	Y	Science/Research:	
		Advertising Pros.:	Y	Broadcasting:				Health Care:		Petroleum/Chem.:	
				Other:				Consulting:		Math/Other:	

TYPES OF BUSINESS:

Construction & Agricultural Equipment
Commercial & Consumer Equipment
Forestry Equipment
Financing

BRANDS/DIVISIONS/AFFILIATES:

John Deere
Ashok Leyland John Deere Construction Eqipment Co.

CONTACTS: *Note: Officers with more than one job title may be intentionally listed here more than once.*

Samuel R. Allen, CEO
James M. Field, CFO/Sr. VP
John D. Lagemann, VP-Mktg. & Sales, U.S.
Mary K. W. Jones, VP-Global Human Resources
Barry W. Schaffter, CIO/VP
Klaus G. Hoehn, VP-Advanced Tech. & Eng.
Michael S. Weinert, VP-Eng.
Michael S. Weinert, VP-Mfg.
James R. Jenkins, General Counsel/Sr. VP
James A. Davlin, VP-Bus. Dev. & Corp. Strategy
Frances B. Emerson, VP-Corp. Comm. & Global Brand Mgmt.
Marie Z. Ziegler, VP-Investor Rel.
Marie Z. Ziegler, Treas./VP
Thomas K. Jarrett, VP-Taxes
Charles R. Stamp, Jr., VP-Public Affairs Worldwide
James A. Israel, Pres., Worldwide Financial Svcs.
Linda E. Newborn, Chief Compliance Officer/VP
Samuel R. Allen, Chmn.
John D. Lagemann, VP-Mktg. & Sales, Canada, Australia & New Zealand
Thomas E. Knoll, VP-Worldwide Supply Mgmt. & Logistics

Phone: 309-765-8000	**Fax:** 309-765-5671
Toll-Free:	
Address: 1 John Deere Pl., Moline, IL 61265 US	

GROWTH PLANS/SPECIAL FEATURES:

Deere & Co. is known for its John Deere brand name. The firm conducts business in three divisions: agricultural and turf equipment; construction and forestry; and credit. The agricultural and turf segment manufactures and distributes farm, lawn and garden equipment including tractors; combines; harvesters; tillage, seeding and soil preparation machinery; sprayers; hay and forage equipment; material handling equipment; integrated agricultural management systems technology; mowers; golf course equipment; utility tractors; landscape and irrigation equipment; and other outdoor power products. The construction and forestry division offers equipment and service parts used in construction, earthmoving, material handling and timber harvesting, including backhoe loaders; crawler dozers and loaders; four-wheel-drive loaders; excavators; and more. The credit segment provides financing services for products offered by the agricultural and turf and construction/forestry segments. It also offers wholesale financing to dealers of the foregoing equipment, finances retail revolving charge accounts, provides operating loans, invests in wind energy generation and offers certain crop risk mitigation products. Sales are generally conducted through the largely independently-owned 2,526 dealer locations, 1,551 of which sell agricultural equipment. The firm has 22 factories located in 16 countries throughout the world. Its products are sold in over 100 countries. Deere & Co. also offers the John Deere University, an online training resource that provides lessons and courses on basic and advanced technology. Ashok Leyland John Deere Construction Equipment Company Private Limited, a joint venture with Ashok Leyland Limited, manufactures and markets backhoes and four-wheel-drive loaders in India. In March 2010, the firm acquired certain assets of Israel-based BHC Manufacturing. In December 2010, Deere & Co. sold its wind energy operations to Exelon Generation Company.

FINANCIALS: **Sales and profits are in thousands of dollars—add 000 to get the full amount. 2010 Note: Financial information for 2010 was not available for all companies at press time.**

2010 Sales: $26,004,600	2010 Profits: $1,865,000	**U.S. Stock Ticker: DE**
2009 Sales: $23,112,400	2009 Profits: $873,500	**Int'l Ticker:**
2008 Sales: $28,438,000	2008 Profits: $2,053,000	Int'l Exchange:
2007 Sales: $24,082,200	2007 Profits: $1,821,700	Employees: 55,700 Fiscal Year Ends: 10/31
2006 Sales: $22,147,800	2006 Profits: $1,693,800	Parent Company:

SALARIES/BENEFITS:

Pension Plan: Y	ESOP Stock Plan:	Profit Sharing:	Top Exec. Salary: $1,512,779	Bonus: $4,864,800
Savings Plan: Y	Stock Purch. Plan: Y		Second Exec. Salary: $795,965	Bonus: $1,606,687

OTHER THOUGHTS:

Apparent Women Officers or Directors: 4
Hot Spot for Advancement for Women/Minorities: Y

LOCATIONS: ("Y" = Yes)

West:	Southwest:	Midwest:	Southeast:	Northeast:	International:
Y	Y	Y	Y	Y	Y

DELOITTE & TOUCHE USA LLP

www.deloitte.com

Industry Group Code: 5412

Management:		Sales/Marketing:		Liberal Arts:		Information Sys.:		Professionals:		Tech./Scientific:	
Mgmt. Trainees:	Y	Marketing Pros.:	Y	Gen. Writing/Editing:	Y	Info. Mgmt.:	Y	Finance/Acct.:	Y	Engineers, Elec.:	
Experienced Mgmt.:	Y	Retail Sales:		Tech. Writing:	Y	Software Dev.:	Y	Law:	Y	Engineers, Other:	
Int'l Business:	Y	Comm./Industrial:	Y	Graphic Arts/Photog.:	Y	Hardware Dev.:		HR/Other:	Y	Health/Lab:	
MBA Grads:	Y	Sales Trainees:		Music:		Consulting/Other:	Y	Training:	Y	Science/Research:	
		Advertising Pros.:	Y	Broadcasting:				Health Care:		Petroleum/Chem.:	
				Other:	Y			Consulting:	Y	Math/Other:	

TYPES OF BUSINESS:

Accounting Services
Management Consulting
Risk Management Services
Financial Advisory Services
Outsourcing Services
Legal & Compliance Advisory Services

BRANDS/DIVISIONS/AFFILIATES:

Deloitte Tax LLP
Deloitte & Touche LLP
Deloitte Consulting LLP
Deloitte Financial Advisory Services LLP
Deloitte Foundation
Deloitte Touche Tohmatsu
ClearCarbon Consulting Inc
DOMANI Sustainability Consulting LLC

CONTACTS: *Note: Officers with more than one job title may be intentionally listed here more than once.*

Barry Salzberg, CEO
Jeff Rohr, CFO
Mitchell L. Glassman, Dir.-Deloitte Consulting LLP
Bob Contri, Head-Banking & Securities Practice
Branko Terzic, Exec. Dir.-Deloitte Center for Energy Solutions
Alison Paul, Head-US Retail Practice
Sharon Allen, Chmn.

Phone: 212-489-1600	**Fax:** 212-489-1687
Toll-Free:	
Address: 1633 Broadway, New York, NY 10019-6754 US	

GROWTH PLANS/SPECIAL FEATURES:

Deloitte & Touche USA LLP (D&T), the U.S. division of global accounting firm Deloitte Touche Tohmatsu (DTT), offers a variety of financial and consulting services. The firm operates through several subsidiaries, including Deloitte & Touche LLP; Deloitte Consulting LLP; Deloitte Financial Advisory Services LLP; and Deloitte Tax LLP. The company divides its services into four categories: audit and enterprise risk, which represented 34% of its 2010 revenue; consulting, 41%; tax, 21%; and financial advisory services, 4%. Additionally, the firm has expertise in offering complementary services such as legal and compliance advising involving litigation, ethics, management and disclosure issues. Industries served by D&T include aerospace and defense; automotive; banking and securities; consumer products; healthcare; insurance; life sciences; media and entertainment; oil and gas; power and utilities; private equity; industrial products; real estate; retail; technology; telecom; tourism, hospitality and leisure; and federal, state and local governments. The firm also funds the Deloitte Foundation, created 80 years ago and dedicated to supporting accounting, business and related fields of study in the U.S. The foundation funds the Deloitte Doctoral Fellowship Program and Trueblood Seminars for Professors, among other higher education initiatives. D&T also conducts and publishes research concerning consumer spending patterns and economic growth. The company maintains offices in nearly 90 U.S. cities and employs more than 8,500 CPAs. In December 2010, D&T acquired ClearCarbon Consulting, Inc. and DOMANI Sustainability Consulting, LLC.

Employees of the firm are offered child care and adoption assistance; flexible work arrangements; medical plans; and a tuition assistance program. In 2011, for the 12th consecutive year, D&T was named to Fortune Magazine's list of 100 Best Companies to Work For.

FINANCIALS: **Sales and profits are in thousands of dollars—add 000 to get the full amount. 2010 Note: Financial information for 2010 was not available for all companies at press time.**

2010 Sales: $10,938,000	2010 Profits: $
2009 Sales: $10,722,000	2009 Profits: $
2008 Sales: $11,042,000	2008 Profits: $
2007 Sales: $9,850,000	2007 Profits: $
2006 Sales: $8,769,000	2006 Profits: $

U.S. Stock Ticker: Subsidiary
Int'l Ticker:
Int'l Exchange:
Employees: 45,730 Fiscal Year Ends: 5/31
Parent Company: DELOITTE TOUCHE TOHMATSU

SALARIES/BENEFITS:

Pension Plan: Y	ESOP Stock Plan:	Profit Sharing:	Top Exec. Salary: $	Bonus: $
Savings Plan: Y	Stock Purch. Plan:		Second Exec. Salary: $	Bonus: $

OTHER THOUGHTS:

Apparent Women Officers or Directors: 2
Hot Spot for Advancement for Women/Minorities:

LOCATIONS: ("Y" = Yes)

West:	Southwest:	Midwest:	Southeast:	Northeast:	International:
Y	Y	Y	Y	Y	Y

DELOITTE CONSULTING LLP

www.deloitte.com

Industry Group Code: 54161

Management:		**Sales/Marketing:**		**Liberal Arts:**		**Information Sys.:**		**Professionals:**		**Tech./Scientific:**	
Mgmt. Trainees:	Y	Marketing Pros.:	Y	Gen. Writing/Editing:	Y	Info. Mgmt.:	Y	Finance/Acct.:	Y	Engineers, Elec.:	
Experienced Mgmt.:	Y	Retail Sales:		Tech. Writing:	Y	Software Dev.:	Y	Law:	Y	Engineers, Other:	
Int'l Business:	Y	Comm./Industrial:	Y	Graphic Arts/Photog.:	Y	Hardware Dev.:		HR/Other:	Y	Health/Lab:	
MBA Grads:	Y	Sales Trainees:		Music:		Consulting/Other:	Y	Training:	Y	Science/Research:	
		Advertising Pros.:	Y	Broadcasting:				Health Care:		Petroleum/Chem.:	
				Other:	Y			Consulting:	Y	Math/Other:	Y

TYPES OF BUSINESS:

Management Consulting
Technology Integration Consulting
Human Resources Consulting
Business Strategy Consulting
Outsourcing Services
Strategic Consulting
Software

BRANDS/DIVISIONS/AFFILIATES:

Deloitte Touche Tohmatsu

CONTACTS: *Note: Officers with more than one job title may be intentionally listed here more than once.*

Punit Renjen, CEO
Suzanne Skipper, Sr. Mgr.-Human Capital
Punit Renjen, Chmn.
John Graves, Global Leader

Phone: 212-489-1600	**Fax:** 212-489-1687
Toll-Free:	
Address: 1633 Broadway, New York, NY 10019 US	

GROWTH PLANS/SPECIAL FEATURES:

Deloitte Consulting LLP, the largest subsidiary of Deloitte Touche Tohmatsu, offers a range of expert consulting services from offices in 40 countries worldwide. It operates through four main service categories: enterprise applications; human capital; strategy and operations; and technology integration. Enterprise applications are software tools that help companies coordinate information, communicate with business partners and utilize customer data better. The company maintains partnerships with business software developers (including Oracle and SAP) that give Deloitte Consulting's consultants the information necessary to help customers implement technological and organizational changes. The firm's human capital expertise provides ways to measure and manage employee productivity, change organizational structure, improve human resource functions and manage isolated groups of employees. The company also analyzes and revises its clients' customer strategies, merger and acquisition strategies, supply chain operations, investment priorities and IT strategies. Lastly, Deloitte Consulting provides technology integration. Since businesses are beginning to integrate desktop and laptop PCs, the firm's consultants help its clients to understand how to use their computerized assets. The technology integration category also provides technological strategies, implementation, management and operations services. In addition, Deloitte Consulting provides market offerings, which are services that are tailored to address client needs and sector priorities. Some of the market offerings that Deloitte Consulting provides are cloud computing, which can help increase IT service delivery capabilities; workforce intelligence, which is a combination of technology experience, strategy and data to help control workforce costs and improve management decisions; and package selection and application strategy, which allows companies to generate more value from their technology segments and portfolios.

Deloitte Consulting offers its employees medical, dental and prescription drug coverage; short- and long-term disability; life and travel accident insurance; a group legal plan; tuition assistance; flexible work arrangements; an employee assistance program; adoption assistance and reimbursement; emergency backup daycare; sabbaticals; flexible spending accounts; and a professional development program.

FINANCIALS: **Sales and profits are in thousands of dollars—add 000 to get the full amount. 2010 Note: Financial information for 2010 was not available for all companies at press time.**

2010 Sales: $7,500,000	2010 Profits: $	**U.S. Stock Ticker: Subsidiary**
2009 Sales: $6,500,000	2009 Profits: $	**Int'l Ticker:**
2008 Sales: $6,300,000	2008 Profits: $	Int'l Exchange:
2007 Sales: $5,200,000	2007 Profits: $	Employees: 40,000 Fiscal Year Ends: 5/31
2006 Sales: $4,500,000	2006 Profits: $	Parent Company: DELOITTE TOUCHE TOHMATSU

SALARIES/BENEFITS:

Pension Plan: Y	ESOP Stock Plan:	Profit Sharing:	Top Exec. Salary: $	Bonus: $
Savings Plan: Y	Stock Purch. Plan:		Second Exec. Salary: $	Bonus: $

OTHER THOUGHTS:

Apparent Women Officers or Directors: 1
Hot Spot for Advancement for Women/Minorities:

LOCATIONS: ("Y" = Yes)

West:	Southwest:	Midwest:	Southeast:	Northeast:	International:
Y	Y	Y	Y	Y	Y

Sales, profits and employees may be estimates. Financial information, benefits and other data can change quickly and may vary from those stated here.

DELTA APPAREL INC

www.deltaapparelinc.com

Industry Group Code: 315211

Management:		Sales/Marketing:		Liberal Arts:		Information Sys.:		Professionals:		Tech./Scientific:	
Mgmt. Trainees:		Marketing Pros.:	Y	Gen. Writing/Editing:	Y	Info. Mgmt.:	Y	Finance/Acct.:	Y	Engineers, Elec.:	
Experienced Mgmt.:	Y	Retail Sales:		Tech. Writing:		Software Dev.:		Law:	Y	Engineers, Other:	
Int'l Business:	Y	Comm./Industrial:	Y	Graphic Arts/Photog.:	Y	Hardware Dev.:		HR/Other:	Y	Health/Lab:	
MBA Grads:	Y	Sales Trainees:		Music:		Consulting/Other:		Training:		Science/Research:	
		Advertising Pros.:	Y	Broadcasting:				Health Care:		Petroleum/Chem.:	
				Other:				Consulting:		Math/Other:	

TYPES OF BUSINESS:

T-Shirts & Sports Clothing
Headwear

BRANDS/DIVISIONS/AFFILIATES:

Delta Pro-Weight
Delta Magnum Weight
Quail Hollow
Soffe
To The Game LLC
Art Gun LLC
Realtree Girl
HPM Apparel, Inc.

CONTACTS:

Note: Officers with more than one job title may be intentionally listed here more than once.

Robert W. Humphreys, CEO
Robert W. Humphreys, Pres.
Deborah H. Merrill, CFO
Martha M. Watson, Corp. Sec./VP
Deborah Merrill, Treas./VP
David Palmer, Assistant Treas./VP
Kenneth Spires, Pres., M.J. Soffe LLC
Steven E. Cochran, Pres., Delta Activewear
Robert W. Humphreys, Chmn.

Phone: 864-232-5200 **Fax:** 864-232-5199
Toll-Free:
Address: 322 S. Main St., Greenville, SC 29601 US

GROWTH PLANS/SPECIAL FEATURES:

Delta Apparel, Inc. designs, manufactures, sources and markets high-quality branded and private label apparel, including casual and athletic wear tops and bottoms, t-shirts and headwear. The firm divides its operations into two segments: activewear apparel and retail-ready apparel. The activewear apparel segment consists of the Delta and FunTees business units, primarily focused on garment styles that are characterized by low fashion risk. The division markets, distributes and manufactures unembellished knit apparel under the brand names Delta Pro-Weight, Delta Magnum Weight, Health Knit, Quail Hollow and Fun Tees. These products are primarily sold to screen printing companies or under private labels for retailers, corporate industry programs, sports licensed apparel marketers and major branded sportswear companies. The retail-ready apparel segment consists of the business units primarily focused on more specialized apparel garments and headwear designed to meet consumer preferences and fashion trends. The division sells these embellished and unembellished products through specialty and boutique stores, high-end and mid-tier retail chains, sporting goods stores, college bookstores and to the U.S. military. The products in this segment are marketed under the brands of Soffe, Intensity Athletics, Junk Food, Kudzu and The Game. Additionally, the retail-ready segment markets licensed products from Realtree Outfitters and Realtree Girl apparel brands. Subsidiaries in this division include M.J. Soffe LLC, To The Game LLC and Art Gun LLC, formerly Art Gun Technologies LLC. The company's manufacturing and cut & sew operations are conducted in North Carolina, El Salvador, Honduras and Mexico. In July 2010, Delta Apparel acquired HPM Apparel, Inc., operating as The Cotton Exchange, which designs and markets casual apparel. In January 2011, the firm signed an exclusive license agreement with beach lifestyle apparel producer Salt Life.

FINANCIALS:

Sales and profits are in thousands of dollars—add 000 to get the full amount. 2010 Note: Financial information for 2010 was not available for all companies at press time.

2010 Sales: $424,411 — 2010 Profits: $12,187
2009 Sales: $355,197 — 2009 Profits: $6,456
2008 Sales: $322,034 — 2008 Profits: $- 508
2007 Sales: $312,438 — 2007 Profits: $6,343
2006 Sales: $270,108 — 2006 Profits: $14,844

U.S. Stock Ticker: DLA
Int'l Ticker:
Int'l Exchange:
Employees: 7,000 Fiscal Year Ends: 6/30
Parent Company:

SALARIES/BENEFITS:

Pension Plan: ESOP Stock Plan: Profit Sharing: Top Exec. Salary: $690,000 Bonus: $735,000
Savings Plan: Y Stock Purch. Plan: Second Exec. Salary: $306,154 Bonus: $95,673

OTHER THOUGHTS:

Apparent Women Officers or Directors: 3
Hot Spot for Advancement for Women/Minorities: Y

LOCATIONS: ("Y" = Yes)

West:	Southwest:	Midwest:	Southeast:	Northeast:	International:
Y		Y	Y	Y	Y

DENTSPLY INTERNATIONAL INC

www.dentsply.com

Industry Group Code: 33911

Management:		Sales/Marketing:		Liberal Arts:		Information Sys.:		Professionals:		Tech./Scientific:	
Mgmt. Trainees:	Y	Marketing Pros.:	Y	Gen. Writing/Editing:	Y	Info. Mgmt.:	Y	Finance/Acct.:	Y	Engineers, Elec.:	Y
Experienced Mgmt.:	Y	Retail Sales:		Tech. Writing:	Y	Software Dev.:	Y	Law:	Y	Engineers, Other:	Y
Int'l Business:	Y	Comm./Industrial:	Y	Graphic Arts/Photog.:	Y	Hardware Dev.:		HR/Other:	Y	Health/Lab:	Y
MBA Grads:	Y	Sales Trainees:		Music:		Consulting/Other:		Training:	Y	Science/Research:	
		Advertising Pros.:	Y	Broadcasting:				Health Care:	Y	Petroleum/Chem.:	
				Other:				Consulting:		Math/Other:	

TYPES OF BUSINESS:

Dental Consumable Products
Dental Specialty Products
Dental Laboratory products

BRANDS/DIVISIONS/AFFILIATES:

Rinn
Golden Gate
Xylocaine
Aquasil
Delton
Elephant
Frialit
Astra Tech AB

CONTACTS:

Note: Officers with more than one job title may be intentionally listed here more than once.

Bret W. Wise, CEO
Christopher T. Clark, COO
Christopher T. Clark, Pres.
William R. Jellison, CFO/Sr. VP
Maureen J. MacInnis, VP-Global Human Resources
Linda C. Niessen, Chief Clinical Officer/VP
Deborah M. Rasin, General Counsel/Sec./VP
James G. Mosch, Exec. VP-Bus. Dev.
Timothy S. Warady, Corp. Controller/VP
James G. Mosch, Exec. VP
William E. Reardon, Treas./VP
Robert J. Winters, VP-Tax
Albert J. Sterkenburg, Sr. VP
Bret W. Wise, Chmn.

Phone: 717-845-7511 **Fax:** 717-845-6377
Toll-Free: 800-877-0020
Address: 221 W. Philadelphia St., Susquehanna Commerce Ctr., York, PA 17405-0872 US

GROWTH PLANS/SPECIAL FEATURES:

DENTSPLY International, Inc. is a global designer, manufacturer and marketer of a broad range of products for the dental market. The company engages in the design, manufacture and distribution of dental products in three principal categories: dental consumables (generating about 35% of sales), dental laboratory products (16%) and specialty dental products (45%). The dental consumables category products consist of dental sundries and small equipment used in dental offices. Dental sundries in this category include dental anesthetics, prophylaxis or prophy paste (used during teeth cleaning), tooth sealants, impression materials, restorative materials, bone grafting materials, tooth whiteners and topical fluoride. Small equipment products include dental diagnostic systems, high and low speed handpieces, intraoral curing light systems and ultrasonic scalers and polishers. The dental laboratory category comprises products and equipment used in preparation of dental appliances by dental laboratories. Products in this category include dental prosthetics (including artificial teeth), precious metal dental alloys, dental ceramics and crown and bridge materials. Equipment includes computer aided machining ceramic systems and porcelain furnaces. Lastly, specialty dental category products, used within dental offices and laboratory settings, include endodontic (root canal) instruments and materials; dental implants and related products; and orthodontic appliances and accessories. Some of DENTSPLY's brand names include Ankylos, Aquasil, Caulk, Delton, Elephant, Friadent, Frialit, Genie, Golden Gate, Interactive Mystique, Midwest, Polocaine, Rinn, Sani-Tip, Sultan and Xylocaine. The firm distributes 55% of its dental products through domestic and foreign distributors, dealers and importers, with certain products sold directly to the dental laboratory or to dental professionals. Through its foreign subsidiaries, the company has operations in over 120 countries, with facilities in more than 40 countries spanning over six continents. Revenues outside the U.S. generate roughly 63% of DENTSPLY's net sales. In August 2011, the firm acquired Astra Tech AB from AstraZeneca.

FINANCIALS:

Sales and profits are in thousands of dollars—add 000 to get the full amount. 2010 Note: Financial information for 2010 was not available for all companies at press time.

2010 Sales: $2,221,014	2010 Profits: $265,708
2009 Sales: $2,159,378	2009 Profits: $274,258
2008 Sales: $2,191,465	2008 Profits: $283,869
2007 Sales: $2,009,833	2007 Profits: $259,654
2006 Sales: $1,810,496	2006 Profits: $223,718

U.S. Stock Ticker: XRAY
Int'l Ticker:
Int'l Exchange:
Employees: 9,700 Fiscal Year Ends: 12/31
Parent Company:

SALARIES/BENEFITS:

Pension Plan:	ESOP Stock Plan:	Profit Sharing:	Top Exec. Salary: $830,000	Bonus: $586,500
Savings Plan: Y	Stock Purch. Plan: Y		Second Exec. Salary: $525,000	Bonus: $296,800

OTHER THOUGHTS:

Apparent Women Officers or Directors: 3
Hot Spot for Advancement for Women/Minorities: Y

LOCATIONS: ("Y" = Yes)

West:	Southwest:	Midwest:	Southeast:	Northeast:	International:
Y		Y	Y	Y	Y

Sales, profits and employees may be estimates. Financial information, benefits and other data can change quickly and may vary from those stated here.

DEVRY INC

www.devryinc.com

Industry Group Code: 611410

Management:		Sales/Marketing:		Liberal Arts:		Information Sys.:		Professionals:		Tech./Scientific:	
Mgmt. Trainees:	Y	Marketing Pros.:	Y	Gen. Writing/Editing:	Y	Info. Mgmt.:	Y	Finance/Acct.:	Y	Engineers, Elec.:	
Experienced Mgmt.:	Y	Retail Sales:		Tech. Writing:		Software Dev.:	Y	Law:	Y	Engineers, Other:	
Int'l Business:	Y	Comm./Industrial:		Graphic Arts/Photog.:	Y	Hardware Dev.:		HR/Other:	Y	Health/Lab:	
MBA Grads:	Y	Sales Trainees:		Music:		Consulting/Other:		Training:	Y	Science/Research:	
		Advertising Pros.:	Y	Broadcasting:				Health Care:		Petroleum/Chem.:	
				Other:	Y			Consulting:		Math/Other:	

TYPES OF BUSINESS:

Higher Education
Online Education
Medical School
Nursing School
Veterinary School
Accounting School

BRANDS/DIVISIONS/AFFILIATES:

DeVry University
Becker Professional Education
Advanced Academics
Ross University
American University of the Caribbean
Chamberlain College of Nursing
Carrington College of California
DeVry Brasil

CONTACTS: *Note: Officers with more than one job title may be intentionally listed here more than once.*

Daniel Hamburger, CEO
Daniel Hamburger, Pres.
Richard M. Gunst, CFO/Sr. VP
Donna N. Jennings, Sr. VP-Human Resources
Eric Dirst, CIO/Sr. VP
Gregory S. Davis, General Counsel/Sr. VP/Sec.
Christopher Caywood, Pres., Online Svcs.
Sharon Thomas Parrott, Sr. VP-External Rel./Chief Compliance Officer
Richard M. Gunst, Treas.
David J. Pauldine, Exec. VP/Pres., DeVry University
Robert Paul, Pres., Carrington Colleges Group
John P. Roselli, Pres., Becker Professional Education
Carlos Filgueiras, Pres., DeVry Brasil
Harold T. Shapiro, Chmn.
Thomas C. Shepherd, Pres., DeVry Medical Int'l

Phone: 630-571-7700 **Fax:**
Toll-Free: 800-733-3879
Address: 3005 Highland Pkwy., Downers Grove, IL 60515 US

GROWTH PLANS/SPECIAL FEATURES:

DeVry, Inc. is a publicly held higher-education company in North America. The firm operates DeVry University, Becker Professional Education, Advanced Academics, Ross University, American University of the Caribbean, Chamberlain College of Nursing, Carrington College, Carrington College of California, Becker Professional Education and DeVry Brasil. DeVry University provides career-oriented, business- and technology-based education to students and graduates at locations in the U.S. and Canada, both in traditional classrooms and online. The university offers associate, bachelor's and master's degree programs in technology, healthcare technology, business and management, with the latter offered through the university's Keller Graduate School of Management. Advanced Academics, which provides online secondary education, is part of the DeVry University segment. Ross University operates two schools: the Ross University School of Medicine, which confers a Doctor of Medicine (MD) degree; and the Ross University School of Veterinary Medicine, which confers a Doctor of Veterinary Medicine (DVM) degree. Over 8,700 graduates have received MD degrees and over 2,000 have received DVM degrees since the university's inception. American University of the Caribbean, acquired in August 2011, offers the same services to students in the Caribbean. Chamberlain College of Nursing offers programs in nursing education at its nine campuses in the U.S. and online. Becker Professional Education is a provider of professional education and training, serving the accounting and finance professions. Carrington College and Carrington College of California prepare students for careers in healthcare through certificate, associate and bachelor's degree programs. DeVry Brasil currently operates five campuses in the cities of Fortaleza and Salvador, Brazil; it offers undergraduate and graduate programs focused on business management, law and engineering.

FINANCIALS: **Sales and profits are in thousands of dollars—add 000 to get the full amount. 2010 Note: Financial information for 2010 was not available for all companies at press time.**

2010 Sales: $1,915,181	2010 Profits: $279,909	**U.S. Stock Ticker: DV**
2009 Sales: $1,461,453	2009 Profits: $165,613	**Int'l Ticker:**
2008 Sales: $1,091,833	2008 Profits: $125,532	Int'l Exchange:
2007 Sales: $933,473	2007 Profits: $76,188	Employees: 12,117 Fiscal Year Ends: 6/30
2006 Sales: $839,513	2006 Profits: $43,053	Parent Company:

SALARIES/BENEFITS:

Pension Plan:	ESOP Stock Plan:	Profit Sharing:	Top Exec. Salary: $751,689	Bonus: $1,339,969
Savings Plan:	Stock Purch. Plan:		Second Exec. Salary: $400,983	Bonus: $514,466

OTHER THOUGHTS:

Apparent Women Officers or Directors: 6
Hot Spot for Advancement for Women/Minorities: Y

LOCATIONS: ("Y" = Yes)

West:	Southwest:	Midwest:	Southeast:	Northeast:	International:
Y	Y	Y	Y	Y	Y

DIAMOND OFFSHORE DRILLING INC

www.diamondoffshore.com

Industry Group Code: 213111

Management:		Sales/Marketing:		Liberal Arts:		Information Sys.:		Professionals:		Tech./Scientific:	
Mgmt. Trainees:	Y	Marketing Pros.:	Y	Gen. Writing/Editing:		Info. Mgmt.:	Y	Finance/Acct.:	Y	Engineers, Elec.:	Y
Experienced Mgmt.:	Y	Retail Sales:		Tech. Writing:	Y	Software Dev.:	Y	Law:	Y	Engineers, Other:	Y
Int'l Business:	Y	Comm./Industrial:	Y	Graphic Arts/Photog.:		Hardware Dev.:		HR/Other:	Y	Health/Lab:	
MBA Grads:	Y	Sales Trainees:		Music:		Consulting/Other:		Training:	Y	Science/Research:	
		Advertising Pros.:		Broadcasting:				Health Care:		Petroleum/Chem.:	Y
				Other:				Consulting:		Math/Other:	

TYPES OF BUSINESS:

Oil & Gas Drilling
Contract Drilling

BRANDS/DIVISIONS/AFFILIATES:

CONTACTS:

Note: Officers with more than one job title may be intentionally listed here more than once.

Lawrence Dickerson, CEO
Lawrence Dickerson, Pres.
Gary T. Krenek, CFO/Sr. VP
Michael D. Acuff, VP-Mktg. & Contracts
R. Lynn Charles, VP-Human Resources
Karl S. Sellers, VP-Eng.
William C. Long, General Counsel/Sr. VP/Sec.
Lyndol L. Dew, Sr. VP-Worldwide Oper.
Beth G. Gordon, Controller
John M. Vecchio, Exec. VP
Steven A. Nelson, VP-Domestic Oper.
Stephen G. Elwood, VP-Tax
Scott L. Kornblau, Treas.
James S. Tisch, Chmn.
Mark F. Baudoin, Sr. VP-South America

Phone: 281-492-5300 | **Fax:** 281-492-5316
Toll-Free: 800-848-1980
Address: 15415 Katy Fwy., Houston, TX 77094 US

GROWTH PLANS/SPECIAL FEATURES:

Diamond Offshore Drilling, Inc. is a leading deepwater drilling contractor. Diamond operates one of the world's largest fleets of offshore drilling units, consisting of 32 semi-submersibles, 13 jack-ups and one drill ship. Its semi-submersible rigs float with their lower hulls between 55 and 90 feet below the water line and are held in position partly with anchors and partly through a special hull characteristic known as wave transparency; five of the rigs also have a special computer-controlled thruster system known as dynamic-positioning. 13 of Diamond's 32 semi-submersibles are high-specification, which means that they are capable of drilling in harsh environments and water depths greater than 4,000 feet; while the other 19 rigs may only work in depths up to 4,000 feet. The company operates in many geographic areas, including the Gulf of Mexico, (in both U.S. and Mexican waters); Europe, principally in the U.K. and Norway; the Mediterranean Basin, primarily in Egypt; South America, principally in Brazil; Australia and Asia, including Malaysia, Indonesia and Vietnam; West Africa, including the Republic of Congo and Angola; and the Middle East, including Kuwait, Qatar and Saudi Arabia.

Employees are offered medical, vision, dental and prescription drug coverage; life and AD&D insurance; disability coverage; an employee assistance plan; flexible spending accounts; a 401(k) plan; and profit sharing.

FINANCIALS:

Sales and profits are in thousands of dollars—add 000 to get the full amount. 2010 Note: Financial information for 2010 was not available for all companies at press time.

2010 Sales: $3,322,974	2010 Profits: $955,457	**U.S. Stock Ticker: DO**
2009 Sales: $3,631,284	2009 Profits: $1,376,219	**Int'l Ticker:**
2008 Sales: $3,544,057	2008 Profits: $1,310,547	Int'l Exchange:
2007 Sales: $2,567,723	2007 Profits: $844,464	Employees: 5,300 Fiscal Year Ends: 12/31
2006 Sales: $2,052,572	2006 Profits: $706,847	Parent Company:

SALARIES/BENEFITS:

Pension Plan:	ESOP Stock Plan:	Profit Sharing: Y	Top Exec. Salary: $827,250	Bonus: $525,000
Savings Plan: Y	Stock Purch. Plan:		Second Exec. Salary: $394,793	Bonus: $220,000

OTHER THOUGHTS:

Apparent Women Officers or Directors: 1
Hot Spot for Advancement for Women/Minorities:

LOCATIONS: ("Y" = Yes)

West:	Southwest:	Midwest:	Southeast:	Northeast:	International:
	Y		Y		Y

DICK'S SPORTING GOODS INC

www.dickssportinggoods.com

Industry Group Code: 451110

Management:		Sales/Marketing:		Liberal Arts:		Information Sys.:		Professionals:		Tech./Scientific:	
Mgmt. Trainees:	Y	Marketing Pros.:	Y	Gen. Writing/Editing:	Y	Info. Mgmt.:	Y	Finance/Acct.:	Y	Engineers, Elec.:	
Experienced Mgmt.:	Y	Retail Sales:	Y	Tech. Writing:		Software Dev.:	Y	Law:	Y	Engineers, Other:	
Int'l Business:		Comm./Industrial:		Graphic Arts/Photog.:	Y	Hardware Dev.:		HR/Other:	Y	Health/Lab:	
MBA Grads:	Y	Sales Trainees:	Y	Music:		Consulting/Other:		Training:	Y	Science/Research:	
		Advertising Pros.:	Y	Broadcasting:				Health Care:		Petroleum/Chem.:	
				Other:	Y			Consulting:		Math/Other:	

TYPES OF BUSINESS:

Sporting Goods Stores
Outdoor Apparel
Footwear
Hunting & Fishing Supplies
Golf Supplies
Bicycles
Online Sales

BRANDS/DIVISIONS/AFFILIATES:

Golf Galaxy LLC
Dick's Sporting Goods
Ativa
PowerBolt
Walter Hagen
Fitness Gear
Acuity
Maxfli

CONTACTS: *Note: Officers with more than one job title may be intentionally listed here more than once.*

Edward W. Stack, CEO
Joseph H. Schmidt, COO
Joseph H. Schmidt, Pres.
Timothy E. Kullman, CFO/Exec. VP-Finance
Lauren Hobart, Chief Mktg. Officer/Sr. VP
Kathy Sutter, Sr. VP-Human Resources
Matthew J. Lynch, CIO/Sr. VP
Peter Whitsett, Exec. VP-Global Merch.
Timothy E. Kullman, Exec. VP-Admin.
David I. Mosse, General Counsel/Sr. VP/Sec.
Lee Belitsky, Sr. VP-Planning, Analysis & Treasury Svcs.
Anne-Marie Megela, Dir.-Investor Rel.
Joe Oliver, Chief Acct. Officer/Controller/Sr. VP
David G. Stanchak, Sr. VP-Real Estate
Peter Whitsett, Pres., Golf Galaxy
Edward W. Stack, Chmn.

Phone: 724-273-3400 **Fax:**
Toll-Free:
Address: 345 Court St., Coraopolis, PA 15108 US

GROWTH PLANS/SPECIAL FEATURES:

Dick's Sporting Goods, Inc. is a retail sporting goods chain with 516 stores in 43 states under the Dick's Sporting Goods and Golf Galaxy names. The company offers a broad assortment of sporting goods equipment, footwear and apparel under national and private-brand labels, including its own Ativa, Power Bolt, Walter Hagen, Fitness Gear, Maxfli and Acuity brands. Each of the 437 Dick's Sporting Goods locations typically contains five store-within-a-store specialty units and offers 27,000 different items. The company seeks to create a distinct look and feel for each specialty department to heighten the customer's interest in the products offered. A typical facility has the following in-store specialty shops: the Pro Shop, a golf shop with a putting green and video monitors displaying programming from the Golf Channel; the Footwear Center, featuring hardwood floors and a track for testing athletic shoes; the Cycle Shop, designed to sell and service bikes, complete with a mechanics' work area and equipment on the sales floor; the Sportsman's Lodge for the hunting and fishing customer, designed to have the look of an authentic bait and tackle shop; and Total Sports, a seasonal sports area displaying sports equipment and athletic apparel. Its stores offer a variety of services such as golf club fitting, repair and grip replacement; tennis and lacrosse racket stringing; ice skate sharpening; scope mounting and bore sighting; and CO2 tank filling for paintball. The 79 Golf Galaxy stores located in 29 states are designed for serious golf enthusiasts and include artificial bent grass putting greens and golf simulators. The company also employs several PGA and LPGA golf professionals to staff its golf departments and Golf Galaxy stores as well as teach private lessons. In addition to its retail locations, the firm maintains separate catalog and e-commerce sites for its chains.

FINANCIALS: **Sales and profits are in thousands of dollars—add 000 to get the full amount. 2010 Note: Financial information for 2010 was not available for all companies at press time.**

2010 Sales: $4,412,835 2010 Profits: $135,359
2009 Sales: $4,130,128 2009 Profits: $-35,094
2008 Sales: $3,888,422 2008 Profits: $155,036
2007 Sales: $3,114,162 2007 Profits: $112,611
2006 Sales: $2,624,987 2006 Profits: $72,980

U.S. Stock Ticker: DKS
Int'l Ticker:
Int'l Exchange:
Employees: 25,200 Fiscal Year Ends: 1/31
Parent Company:

SALARIES/BENEFITS:

Pension Plan: ESOP Stock Plan: Profit Sharing: Top Exec. Salary: $700,000 Bonus: $2,800,000
Savings Plan: Stock Purch. Plan: Second Exec. Salary: $675,000 Bonus: $1,012,500

OTHER THOUGHTS:

Apparent Women Officers or Directors: 3
Hot Spot for Advancement for Women/Minorities: Y

LOCATIONS: ("Y" = Yes)

West:	Southwest:	Midwest:	Southeast:	Northeast:	International:
Y	Y	Y	Y	Y	

DIODES INC

www.diodes.com

Industry Group Code: 335

Management:		**Sales/Marketing:**		**Liberal Arts:**		**Information Sys.:**		**Professionals:**		**Tech./Scientific:**	
Mgmt. Trainees:		Marketing Pros.:	Y	Gen. Writing/Editing:		Info. Mgmt.:	Y	Finance/Acct.:	Y	Engineers, Elec.:	Y
Experienced Mgmt.:	Y	Retail Sales:		Tech. Writing:	Y	Software Dev.:	Y	Law:	Y	Engineers, Other:	Y
Int'l Business:	Y	Comm./Industrial:	Y	Graphic Arts/Photog.:		Hardware Dev.:	Y	HR/Other:	Y	Health/Lab:	
MBA Grads:	Y	Sales Trainees:		Music:		Consulting/Other:	Y	Training:		Science/Research:	
		Advertising Pros.:		Broadcasting:				Health Care:		Petroleum/Chem.:	
				Other:				Consulting:		Math/Other:	Y

TYPES OF BUSINESS:

Semiconductor Manufacturing
Semiconductor Design
Semiconductor Marketing

BRANDS/DIVISIONS/AFFILIATES:

FabTech, Inc.
Shanghai Kaihong Electronics Co., Ltd.
Shanghai Kaihong Technology
DII Taiwan Co, Ltd.
Diodes Hong Kong, Ltd.
Diodes Zetex, Ltd.

CONTACTS:

Note: Officers with more than one job title may be intentionally listed here more than once.

Keh-Shew Lu, CEO
Keh-Shew Lu, Pres.
Richard D. White, CFO/Treas.
Mark A. King, Sr. VP-Sales & Mktg.
Ed Tang, VP-Corp. Admin.
Richard D. White, Sec.
Joseph Liu, Sr. VP-Oper.
Hans Rohrer, Sr. VP-Bus. Dev.
Carl C. Wertz, VP-Investor Rel.
Carl C. Wertz, VP-Finance
Julie Holland, VP-Worldwide Analog Prod.
Francis Tang, VP-Worldwide Discrete Prod.
Raymond Soong, Chmn.
Colin Greene, Pres., Europe/VP-Europe Sales & Mktg.

Phone: 972-385-2810 **Fax:**
Toll-Free:
Address: 15660 N. Dallas Parkway, Ste. 850, Dallas, TX 75248 US

GROWTH PLANS/SPECIAL FEATURES:

Diodes, Inc. designs, manufactures and markets discrete and analogue semiconductor products. The semiconductors are found in a variety of end-user products in the consumer electronics, computing, industrial, communications and automotive sectors. These products include diodes; rectifiers; transistors; metal oxide semiconductor field-effect transistors (MOSFETs); protection devices; functional specific arrays; amplifiers and comparators; Hall effect and temperature sensors; power management devices (including light emitting diode drivers); DC-DC switching and linear voltage regulators; voltage references; special function devices (including USB power switch, load switch, voltage supervisor and motor controllers); and silicon wafers used to manufacture these products. Diodes' product line includes over 6,000 offerings. The company is a global supplier of electronic signal amplification and switching functions, which are basic building-block electronic components incorporated into almost every electronic device. The company conducts a number of operations through its subsidiaries, including FabTech, Inc., which is responsible for wafer fabrication, research and development, engineering and sales; Shanghai Kaihong Electronics Co., Ltd., which handles packaging, assembly, testing, research and development and engineering; Shanghai Kaihong Technology Electronics Company, Ltd., which also handles packaging, assembly, testing, research and development and engineering; DII Taiwan Corporation, Ltd., which handles only sales and marketing; Diodes Hong Kong, Ltd, which contains a logistical center and handles sales and marketing; and Diodes Zetex, Ltd., a U.K.-based semiconductor company. The company has over 250 customers worldwide, including original equipment manufacturers (OEMs). The firm also has approximately 90 distributor customers around the world, through which the firm indirectly serves over 10,000 customers.

FINANCIALS:

Sales and profits are in thousands of dollars—add 000 to get the full amount. 2010 Note: Financial information for 2010 was not available for all companies at press time.

2010 Sales: $612,886 | 2010 Profits: $80,264
2009 Sales: $434,357 | 2009 Profits: $9,848
2008 Sales: $432,785 | 2008 Profits: $30,529
2007 Sales: $401,159 | 2007 Profits: $56,130
2006 Sales: $343,308 | 2006 Profits: $48,143

U.S. Stock Ticker: DIOD
Int'l Ticker:
Int'l Exchange:
Employees: 3,986 Fiscal Year Ends: 12/31
Parent Company:

SALARIES/BENEFITS:

Pension Plan: | ESOP Stock Plan: | Profit Sharing: | Top Exec. Salary: $343,000 | Bonus: $780,000
Savings Plan: Y | Stock Purch. Plan: Y | | Second Exec. Salary: $248,000 | Bonus: $286,000

OTHER THOUGHTS:

Apparent Women Officers or Directors: 1
Hot Spot for Advancement for Women/Minorities:

LOCATIONS: ("Y" = Yes)

West:	Southwest:	Midwest:	Southeast:	Northeast:	International:
Y	Y	Y		Y	Y

DIRECTV

www.directv.com

Industry Group Code: 517110

Management:		Sales/Marketing:		Liberal Arts:		Information Sys.:		Professionals:		Tech./Scientific:	
Mgmt. Trainees:	Y	Marketing Pros.:	Y	Gen. Writing/Editing:	Y	Info. Mgmt.:	Y	Finance/Acct.:	Y	Engineers, Elec.:	Y
Experienced Mgmt.:	Y	Retail Sales:		Tech. Writing:	Y	Software Dev.:	Y	Law:	Y	Engineers, Other:	Y
Int'l Business:	Y	Comm./Industrial:		Graphic Arts/Photog.:	Y	Hardware Dev.:	Y	HR/Other:	Y	Health/Lab:	
MBA Grads:	Y	Sales Trainees:	Y	Music:		Consulting/Other:		Training:	Y	Science/Research:	
		Advertising Pros.:	Y	Broadcasting:	Y			Health Care:		Petroleum/Chem.:	
				Other:	Y			Consulting:		Math/Other:	

TYPES OF BUSINESS:

Satellite Broadcasting
Commercial Satellite Fleet
Satellite-Based Internet Services
Digital Television

BRANDS/DIVISIONS/AFFILIATES:

Liberty Entertainment, Inc.
DIRECTV U.S.
DIRECTV Latin America
DIRECTV Sports Networks LLC
PanAmericana
Sky Brasil Servicos Ltda.
Innova, S. de R.L. de C.V.
FSN Northwest

CONTACTS: *Note: Officers with more than one job title may be intentionally listed here more than once.*

Michael White, CEO
Michael White, Pres.
Patrick T. Doyle, CFO/Exec. VP
Jon Gieselman, Sr. VP-Advertising & Comm.
Joseph A. Bosch, Chief Human Resources Officer/Exec. VP
Romulo G. Pontual, CTO/Exec. VP
Larry D. Hunter, General Counsel/Exec. VP
Michael W. Palkovic, Exec. VP-Oper.
Robert Mercer, Contact-Public Rel.
Darris Gringeri, Contact-Investor Rel.
John F. Murphy, Chief Acct. Officer/Controller/Sr. VP
J. William Little, Treas./Sr. VP
Jan Williamson, Sec.
Michael White, Chmn.
Bruce B. Churchill, Exec. VP/Pres., DIRECTV Latin America

Phone: 212-462-5200 **Fax:** 310-535-5225
Toll-Free:
Address: 2230 E. Imperial Hwy., El Segundo, CA 90245-0956 US

GROWTH PLANS/SPECIAL FEATURES:

DIRECTV, formed by the merger of the DIRECTV Group, Inc. and Liberty Entertainment, Inc. (a former subsidiary of Liberty Media Corporation), is one of the world's top providers of digital television entertainment and wireless systems. The company's three business segments (DIRECTV U.S., DIRECTV Latin America (DTVLA) and DIRECTV Sports Networks LLC) and its subsidiaries are engaged in digital entertainment programming via satellite for residential and commercial subscribers. DIRECTV U.S. provides direct-to-home digital television services, with over 19.1 million U.S. subscribers and 160 national high-definition television channels. It has a fleet of 12 owned satellites, including one leased satellite. The company operates 36 customer service centers. DTVLA is comprised of PanAmericana, which provides services in Venezuela, Argentina, Chile, Colombia, Puerto Rico and certain other countries through wholly-owned subsidiary DIRECTV Latin America, LLC. PanAmericana also operates through 93%-owned subsidiary Sky Brasil Servicos Ltda. (Sky Brazil); and 41%-owned subsidiary Innova, S. de R.L. de C.V. (Sky Mexico). PanAmericana has approximately 2.2 million subscribers; Sky Brazil, 1.6 million; and Sky Mexico, 1.8 million. DIRECTV Sports Networks is comprised primarily of three regional sports television networks based in Washington, Colorado and Pennsylvania, known as FSN Northwest, FSN Rocky Mountain and FSN Pittsburgh. The firm is considering the launch of a massive, wireless voice and data network, probably based on WiMAX, which would offer bundled services including TV, phone and Internet access. Liberty Media Corporation owns 55% of DIRECTV. In 2010, DIRECTV Latin America completed a $604.8 million deal with Globo Comunicacao e Participacoes S.A. to increase the firm's ownership of SKY Brazil to approximately 93%. Globo owns the remaining 7%.

FINANCIALS: **Sales and profits are in thousands of dollars—add 000 to get the full amount. 2010 Note: Financial information for 2010 was not available for all companies at press time.**

2010 Sales: $24,102,000 | 2010 Profits: $2,198,000
2009 Sales: $21,565,000 | 2009 Profits: $942,000
2008 Sales: $19,693,000 | 2008 Profits: $1,521,000
2007 Sales: $17,246,000 | 2007 Profits: $1,451,000
2006 Sales: $14,755,500 | 2006 Profits: $1,420,100

U.S. Stock Ticker: DTV
Int'l Ticker:
Int'l Exchange:
Employees: 16,000 Fiscal Year Ends: 12/31
Parent Company:

SALARIES/BENEFITS:

Pension Plan: Y | ESOP Stock Plan: | Profit Sharing: | Top Exec. Salary: $1,254,178 | Bonus: $
Savings Plan: Y | Stock Purch. Plan: | | Second Exec. Salary: $1,227,965 | Bonus: $2,100,000

OTHER THOUGHTS:

Apparent Women Officers or Directors: 1
Hot Spot for Advancement for Women/Minorities:

LOCATIONS: ("Y" = Yes)

West:	Southwest:	Midwest:	Southeast:	Northeast:	International:
Y	Y	Y	Y	Y	Y

Sales, profits and employees may be estimates. Financial information, benefits and other data can change quickly and may vary from those stated here.

DOLLAR GENERAL CORPORATION

www.dollargeneral.com

Industry Group Code: 452112

Management:		Sales/Marketing:		Liberal Arts:		Information Sys.:		Professionals:		Tech./Scientific:	
Mgmt. Trainees:	Y	Marketing Pros.:	Y	Gen. Writing/Editing:	Y	Info. Mgmt.:	Y	Finance/Acct.:	Y	Engineers, Elec.:	
Experienced Mgmt.:	Y	Retail Sales:	Y	Tech. Writing:		Software Dev.:	Y	Law:	Y	Engineers, Other:	
Int'l Business:		Comm./Industrial:		Graphic Arts/Photog.:	Y	Hardware Dev.:		HR/Other:	Y	Health/Lab:	
MBA Grads:	Y	Sales Trainees:	Y	Music:		Consulting/Other:		Training:	Y	Science/Research:	
		Advertising Pros.:	Y	Broadcasting:				Health Care:		Petroleum/Chem.:	
				Other:	Y			Consulting:		Math/Other:	

TYPES OF BUSINESS:

Discount Stores
Dollar Stores

BRANDS/DIVISIONS/AFFILIATES:

DG Baby
Open Trails
Buck Holdings, L.P.
www.DollarGeneral.com

CONTACTS: *Note: Officers with more than one job title may be intentionally listed here more than once.*

Richard W. Dreiling, CEO
David L. Bere, Pres.
David M. Tehle, CFO/Exec. VP
Bob Ravener, Chief People Officer/Exec. VP
Todd Vasos, Chief Merch. Officer/Div. Pres./Exec. VP
Susan S. Lanigan, General Counsel/Exec. VP
Kathleen R. Guion, Pres., Store Oper. & Dev./Exec. VP
Tawn Earnest, Sr. Dir.-Corp. Comm.
Anita Elliott, Controller/Sr. VP
Richard W. Dreiling, Chmn.
John Flanigan, Exec. VP-Global Supply Chain

Phone: 615-855-4000 **Fax:** 615-855-5252
Toll-Free:
Address: 100 Mission Ridge, Goodlettsville, TN 37072 US

GROWTH PLANS/SPECIAL FEATURES:

Dollar General Corporation owns and operates more than 9,414 discount merchandise stores in 35 states, serving primarily low- and fixed-income families. Additionally, the firm operates nine distribution centers located in several states, including Oklahoma, Virginia, Ohio, South Carolina, Mississippi, Kentucky, Missouri, Florida and Indiana. The traditional Dollar General store has, on average, approximately 7,200 square feet of selling space, which is attractive to the company's target customers who live within five miles of the store. Roughly half of the company's stores serve communities with populations of 20,000 or less. Dollar General stores offer such products as paper and cleaning products; packaged and perishable foods; beverages and snacks; health and beauty aids; pet supplies; various seasonal merchandise; home products, including kitchen supplies, storage items, light bulbs and small appliances; and apparel from private brands DG Baby and Open Trails. The majority of Dollar General's products are priced at $10 or less, with nearly a third of the products priced at $1 or less. The most expensive items generally cost $20. Buck Holdings, L.P. owns 85% of the company's outstanding shares. Sales per square foot of store space averaged $201 in 2010. In August 2011, the firm launched e-commerce site www.DollarGeneral.com. In May 2011, the company announced plans to open stores in California in 2012. In June 2011, the firm began construction on its 10th distribution center, which will be located in Bessemer, Alabama.

Employees of the firm are offered a 401(k) plan; a retirement plan; medical, dental, vision and prescription plans; flexible spending accounts; short- and long-term disability; wellness programs; home and education financing assistance; employee, spouse and dependent life insurance; business travel accident insurance; benefits for part-time employees; and rewards programs.

FINANCIALS: **Sales and profits are in thousands of dollars—add 000 to get the full amount. 2010 Note: Financial information for 2010 was not available for all companies at press time.**

2010 Sales: $11,796,380 | 2010 Profits: $339,442
2009 Sales: $10,457,668 | 2009 Profits: $108,182
2008 Sales: $9,495,300 | 2008 Profits: $-12,800
2007 Sales: $9,169,800 | 2007 Profits: $137,900
2006 Sales: $8,582,237 | 2006 Profits: $350,155

U.S. Stock Ticker: DG
Int'l Ticker:
Int'l Exchange:
Employees: 79,800 Fiscal Year Ends: 1/31
Parent Company:

SALARIES/BENEFITS:

Pension Plan: Y | ESOP Stock Plan: | Profit Sharing: | Top Exec. Salary: $1,143,231 | Bonus: $2,186,595
Savings Plan: Y | Stock Purch. Plan: | Second Exec. Salary: $642,299 | Bonus: $219,450

OTHER THOUGHTS:

Apparent Women Officers or Directors: 3
Hot Spot for Advancement for Women/Minorities: Y

LOCATIONS: ("Y" = Yes)

West:	Southwest:	Midwest:	Southeast:	Northeast:	International:
Y	Y	Y	Y	Y	

DTE ENERGY COMPANY

www.dteenergy.com

Industry Group Code: 221

Management:		Sales/Marketing:		Liberal Arts:		Information Sys.:		Professionals:		Tech./Scientific:	
Mgmt. Trainees:	Y	Marketing Pros.:	Y	Gen. Writing/Editing:	Y	Info. Mgmt.:	Y	Finance/Acct.:	Y	Engineers, Elec.:	Y
Experienced Mgmt.:	Y	Retail Sales:		Tech. Writing:	Y	Software Dev.:	Y	Law:	Y	Engineers, Other:	Y
Int'l Business:		Comm./Industrial:	Y	Graphic Arts/Photog.:	Y	Hardware Dev.:		HR/Other:	Y	Health/Lab:	
MBA Grads:	Y	Sales Trainees:		Music:		Consulting/Other:		Training:	Y	Science/Research:	
		Advertising Pros.:	Y	Broadcasting:				Health Care:		Petroleum/Chem.:	Y
				Other:				Consulting:		Math/Other:	

TYPES OF BUSINESS:

Utilities-Electricity & Natural Gas
Energy Management
Wholesale Energy Trading
Fuel Supply Services
Hydroelectric Power
Nuclear Power
Coal Shipping-Rail & Boat
Consulting Services

BRANDS/DIVISIONS/AFFILIATES:

Detroit Edison Company (The)
Michigan Consolidated Gas Company
DTE Energy Services
DTE Energy Trading

CONTACTS: *Note: Officers with more than one job title may be intentionally listed here more than once.*

Gerard M. Anderson, CEO
Gerard M. Anderson, Pres.
David E. Meador, CFO/Exec. VP
Larry Steward, VP-Human Resources
Lynne Ellyn, CIO/Sr. VP
Bruce Peterson, General Counsel/Sr. VP
Paul Hillegonds, Sr. VP-Corp. Affairs
Peter Oleksiak, VP-Investor Rel.
Peter Oleksiak, Controller/VP/Chief Acct. Officer
Steven E. Kurmas, Pres./COO-Detroit Edison
Gerardo Norcia, Pres./COO-MichCon
Paul C. Hillegonds, Sr. VP
Larry E. Steward, VP
Gerard M. Anderson, Chmn.

Phone: 313-235-4000	**Fax:** 313-235-6743
Toll-Free: 866-966-5555	
Address: 1 Energy Plz., Detroit, MI 48226-1279 US	

GROWTH PLANS/SPECIAL FEATURES:

DTE Energy Company is a diversified energy and energy technology company that develops merchant power and industrial energy projects and works in energy trading, selling electricity, natural gas, coal, chilled water, landfill gas and steam. DTE is one of the nation's largest purchasers, transporters and marketers of coal. The company's principal operating segments include its Electric Utility division, which consists of The Detroit Edison Company, an electric utility in southeastern Michigan that has a generating capacity of 11,000 megawatts (MW) and serves 2.1 million customers; and its Gas Utilities division, represented by Michigan Consolidated Gas Company (MichCon), which distributes natural gas to 1.2 million customers. The firm's Non-Utility Operations segments (which operate in 26 states) include Gas Storage and Pipelines, encompassing DTE's two interstate gas transmission pipelines and storage facilities; Power and Industrial Projects, primarily consisting of energy product delivery, coal transportation and marketing and electricity provided by biomass-fueled energy projects; Unconventional Gas Production, primarily consisting of unconventional gas project development and production; and DTE Energy Trading, which buys, sells and trades electricity, coal and natural gas and provides risk management services consisting of energy marketing and trading operations.

DTE offers its employees medical, dental and vision coverage; comprehensive wellness programs; a 401(k) plan; flexible spending accounts; an employee assistance program; long-term care insurance; life, disability and AD&D insurance; and a cash balance pension.

FINANCIALS: **Sales and profits are in thousands of dollars—add 000 to get the full amount. 2010 Note: Financial information for 2010 was not available for all companies at press time.**

2010 Sales: $8,557,000	2010 Profits: $630,000	**U.S. Stock Ticker: DTE**
2009 Sales: $8,014,000	2009 Profits: $532,000	**Int'l Ticker:**
2008 Sales: $9,329,000	2008 Profits: $546,000	Int'l Exchange:
2007 Sales: $8,506,000	2007 Profits: $971,000	Employees: 9,800 Fiscal Year Ends: 12/31
2006 Sales: $8,159,000	2006 Profits: $433,000	Parent Company:

SALARIES/BENEFITS:

Pension Plan: Y	ESOP Stock Plan:	Profit Sharing:	Top Exec. Salary: $1,219,692	Bonus: $1,870,000
Savings Plan: Y	Stock Purch. Plan:		Second Exec. Salary: $901,538	Bonus: $1,282,000

OTHER THOUGHTS:

Apparent Women Officers or Directors: 5
Hot Spot for Advancement for Women/Minorities: Y

LOCATIONS: ("Y" = Yes)

West:	Southwest:	Midwest:	Southeast:	Northeast:	International:
Y		Y			

DUKE ENERGY CORP

www.duke-energy.com

Industry Group Code: 221

Management:		Sales/Marketing:		Liberal Arts:		Information Sys.:		Professionals:		Tech./Scientific:	
Mgmt. Trainees:	Y	Marketing Pros.:	Y	Gen. Writing/Editing:	Y	Info. Mgmt.:	Y	Finance/Acct.:	Y	Engineers, Elec.:	Y
Experienced Mgmt.:	Y	Retail Sales:		Tech. Writing:	Y	Software Dev.:	Y	Law:	Y	Engineers, Other:	Y
Int'l Business:	Y	Comm./Industrial:	Y	Graphic Arts/Photog.:	Y	Hardware Dev.:		HR/Other:	Y	Health/Lab:	
MBA Grads:	Y	Sales Trainees:		Music:		Consulting/Other:		Training:	Y	Science/Research:	
		Advertising Pros.:	Y	Broadcasting:				Health Care:		Petroleum/Chem.:	Y
				Other:				Consulting:		Math/Other:	

TYPES OF BUSINESS:

Utilities-Electricity & Natural Gas
Merchant Power Generation
Natural Gas Transportation & Storage
Electricity Transmission
Energy Marketing
Real Estate
Telecommunications
Facility & Plant Services

BRANDS/DIVISIONS/AFFILIATES:

Franchised Electric & Gas Service
Duke Energy Generation Services Inc
Duke Energy International LLC
DukeNet Communications LLC
Progress Energy

CONTACTS: *Note: Officers with more than one job title may be intentionally listed here more than once.*

James E. Rogers, CEO
James E. Rogers, Pres.
Lynn J. Good, CFO/Group Exec.
Jennifer L. Weber, Chief Human Resources/Sr. VP
David W. Mohler, CTO/Sr. VP
Marc E. Manly, Chief Legal Officer/Corp. Sec./Group Exec.
Virginia S. Mackin, Chief Comm. Officer/Sr. VP
Stephen G. De May, Sr. VP-Investor Rel./Treas.
Steven K. Young, Controller/Sr. VP
Swati V. Daji, Chief Risk Officer/VP-Global Risk Mgmt.
Roberta B. Bowman, Chief Sustainability Officer/Sr. VP
Gianna M. Manes, Chief Customer Officer/Sr. VP
Jeffrey G. Browning, Chief Ethics & Compliance Officer/Sr. VP
James E. Rogers, Chmn.
Ronald R. Reising, Chief Procurement Officer/Sr. VP

Phone: 704-594-6200 **Fax:** 704-382-3814
Toll-Free: 800-873-3853
Address: 526 S. Church St., Charlotte, NC 28202-1803 US

GROWTH PLANS/SPECIAL FEATURES:

Duke Energy Corp. is an integrated energy and energy services provider that offers delivery and management of electricity and natural gas throughout the U.S. The company's operations can be divided into three segments: franchised electric & gas service; commercial power; and international energy. The franchised electric & gas service segment, with 152,200 miles of distribution lines and a 20,900 mile transmission system, has 4 million customers and has locations in Ohio, Indiana, Kentucky and the Carolinas, covering approximately 50,000 square miles. This segment operates three nuclear power plants; 15 coal-fire plants; 31 hydroelectric stations; 15 combustion turbines that burn natural gas, oil or other fuels; and one combined cycle station that burns natural gas. The commercial power segment owns, operates and manages non-regulated power plants and engages in the marketing and procurement of electric power, fuel and emissions allowances related to the plants. Its plants utilize a variety of fuels such as natural gas, waste coal and wood, and can generate approximately 7,550 MW of power primarily in the Midwestern U.S. The international energy segment owns, operates and manages power generation facilities and sells and markets electric power and natural gas outside the U.S. Subsidiary Duke Energy International, LLC operates power generation plants primarily in Latin America. The firm also operates through Duke Energy Generation Services, Inc., which provides electric generation for municipalities, industrial facilities and other large energy consumers. The subsidiary maintains around 4,400 MW of electric generation at 28 locations in the U.S. In December 2010, Duke Energy sold its 50% interest in DukeNet Communications, LLC to Alinda Capital Partners LLC for roughly $137 million. In August 2011, the firm agreed to merge with Progress Energy by the end of 2011.

Employees are offered life, disability, medical, dental and vision insurance; a 401(k) plan; adoption assistance; flexible spending accounts; a pension plan; and employee discounts.

FINANCIALS: **Sales and profits are in thousands of dollars—add 000 to get the full amount. 2010 Note: Financial information for 2010 was not available for all companies at press time.**

2010 Sales: $14,272,000 — 2010 Profits: $1,323,000
2009 Sales: $12,731,000 — 2009 Profits: $1,075,000
2008 Sales: $13,207,000 — 2008 Profits: $1,362,000
2007 Sales: $12,720,000 — 2007 Profits: $1,500,000
2006 Sales: $10,607,000 — 2006 Profits: $1,863,000

U.S. Stock Ticker: DUK
Int'l Ticker:
Int'l Exchange:
Employees: 18,440 Fiscal Year Ends: 12/31
Parent Company:

SALARIES/BENEFITS:

Pension Plan: Y ESOP Stock Plan: Profit Sharing: Top Exec. Salary: $650,004 Bonus: $656,309
Savings Plan: Y Stock Purch. Plan: Second Exec. Salary: $600,000 Bonus: $653,820

OTHER THOUGHTS:

Apparent Women Officers or Directors: 8
Hot Spot for Advancement for Women/Minorities: Y

LOCATIONS: ("Y" = Yes)

West:	Southwest:	Midwest:	Southeast:	Northeast:	International:
Y		Y	Y		Y

DUPONT (E I DU PONT DE NEMOURS & CO) www.dupont.com

Industry Group Code: 325

Management:		Sales/Marketing:		Liberal Arts:		Information Sys.:		Professionals:		Tech./Scientific:	
Mgmt. Trainees:	Y	Marketing Pros.:	Y	Gen. Writing/Editing:	Y	Info. Mgmt.:	Y	Finance/Acct.:	Y	Engineers, Elec.:	Y
Experienced Mgmt.:	Y	Retail Sales:		Tech. Writing:	Y	Software Dev.:	Y	Law:	Y	Engineers, Other:	Y
Int'l Business:	Y	Comm./Industrial:	Y	Graphic Arts/Photog.:		Hardware Dev.:		HR/Other:	Y	Health/Lab:	Y
MBA Grads:	Y	Sales Trainees:		Music:		Consulting/Other:		Training:	Y	Science/Research:	Y
		Advertising Pros.:		Broadcasting:				Health Care:		Petroleum/Chem.:	Y
				Other:				Consulting:		Math/Other:	

TYPES OF BUSINESS:

Chemicals Manufacturing
Polymers
Performance Coatings
Nutrition & Health Products
Electronics Materials
Agricultural Seeds
Fuel-Cell, Biofuels & Solar Panel Technology
Contract Research & Development

BRANDS/DIVISIONS/AFFILIATES:

Seed Consultants, Inc.,
Teflon
Corian
Kevlar
Tyvek
DuPont Agriculture & Nutrition
Terral Seeds
Danisco A/S

CONTACTS:

Note: Officers with more than one job title may be intentionally listed here more than once.

Ellen J. Kullman, CEO
Nicholas C. Farandakis, CFO/Sr. VP
Douglas Muzyka, Chief Science Officer/Sr. VP
Phuong Tram, CIO/VP-IT
Douglas Muzyka, CTO
Thomas M. Connelly, Jr., Chief Innovation Officer/Exec. VP
Jeffrey A. Coe, Sr. VP-Eng.
Thomas L. Sager, General Counsel/Sr. VP-Legal
Jeffrey A. Coe, Sr. VP-Integrated Oper.
David G. Bills, Sr. VP-Corp. Strategy
Karen A. Fletcher, VP-Investor Rel.
Criag F. Binetti, Sr. VP-DuPont Nutrition & Health
Diane H. Gulyas, Pres., DuPont Performance Polymers
Terry Caloghiris, Pres., DuPont Strategic Initiatives
Linda J. Fisher, Chief Sustainability Officer/VP
Ellen J. Kullman, Chmn.
Donald D. Wirth, VP-Global Oper.
Keith J. Smith, Chief Procurement Officer/VP-Sourcing & Logistics

Phone: 302-774-1000	**Fax:** 302-773-2631
Toll-Free: 800-441-7515	
Address: 1007 Market St., Wilmington, DE 19898 US	

GROWTH PLANS/SPECIAL FEATURES:

E. I. du Pont de Nemours & Co. (DuPont), founded in 1802, develops and manufactures products in the biotechnology, electronics, materials science, synthetic fibers and safety and security sectors. DuPont operates in seven segments: Agriculture and Nutrition (A&N); Electronic and Communications (E&C); Performance Coatings; Performance Chemicals; Performance Materials (PM); Safety and Protection (S&P); and Pharmaceuticals. A&N delivers seed products, insecticides, fungicides, herbicides, soy-based food ingredients, food quality diagnostic testing equipment and liquid food packaging systems. Brands include Pioneer seeds and Solae soy proteins. E&C provides a range of advanced materials for the electronics industry, flexographic printing, color communication systems and a range of fluoropolymer and fluorochemical products. The Performance Coatings segment supplies automotive liquid and powder coatings, and general industrial applications such as coatings for heavy equipment, pipes and appliances and electrical insulation. Brands include DuPont, Standox, Spies Hecker and Nason. PM manufactures polymer-based materials, which include engineered polymers, specialized resins and films for use in food packaging, sealants, adhesives, sporting goods and laminated safety glass. The S&P segment provides protective materials and safety consulting services. Significant brands include Teflon fluoropolymers, films, fabric protectors, fibers and dispersions; Corian surfaces; Kevlar high strength material; and Tyvek protective material. The Pharmaceuticals segment involves the worldwide manufacturing and marketing activities of the antihypertensive drugs, Cozaar and Hyzaar. The company has operations in over 90 countries around the world. In February 2010, the company opened the Meyrin Photovoltaic Application Laboratory at its European Technical Center in Geneva. In December 2010, DuPont acquired Seed Consultants, Inc. and Terral Seed. In January 2011, the firm agreed to buy Danisco A/S a specialty food ingredients and enzyme producer, for $5.8 billion; and acquired MECS.

Employees are offered medical, dental and life insurance; disability coverage; dependent care spending accounts; and adoption assistance.

FINANCIALS:

Sales and profits are in thousands of dollars—add 000 to get the full amount. 2010 Note: Financial information for 2010 was not available for all companies at press time.

2010 Sales: $31,505,000	2010 Profits: $3,031,000	**U.S. Stock Ticker: DD**
2009 Sales: $26,109,000	2009 Profits: $1,755,000	**Int'l Ticker:**
2008 Sales: $30,529,000	2008 Profits: $2,007,000	Int'l Exchange:
2007 Sales: $29,378,000	2007 Profits: $2,988,000	Employees: 60,000 Fiscal Year Ends: 12/31
2006 Sales: $27,421,000	2006 Profits: $3,148,000	Parent Company:

SALARIES/BENEFITS:

Pension Plan: Y	ESOP Stock Plan:	Profit Sharing:	Top Exec. Salary: $1,130,768	Bonus: $1,500,000
Savings Plan: Y	Stock Purch. Plan:		Second Exec. Salary: $625,563	Bonus: $603,000

OTHER THOUGHTS:

Apparent Women Officers or Directors: 7
Hot Spot for Advancement for Women/Minorities: Y

LOCATIONS: ("Y" = Yes)

West:	Southwest:	Midwest:	Southeast:	Northeast:	International:
Y	Y	Y	Y	Y	Y

DUPONT AGRICULTURE & NUTRITION

www.dupont.com/Our_Company/en_US/business/nutrition_health.html

Industry Group Code: 11511

Management:		Sales/Marketing:		Liberal Arts:		Information Sys.:		Professionals:		Tech./Scientific:	
Mgmt. Trainees:		Marketing Pros.:	Y	Gen. Writing/Editing:		Info. Mgmt.:	Y	Finance/Acct.:	Y	Engineers, Elec.:	
Experienced Mgmt.:		Retail Sales:		Tech. Writing:	Y	Software Dev.:		Law:	Y	Engineers, Other:	Y
Int'l Business:	Y	Comm./Industrial:	Y	Graphic Arts/Photog.:		Hardware Dev.:		HR/Other:	Y	Health/Lab:	Y
MBA Grads:	Y	Sales Trainees:		Music:		Consulting/Other:		Training:		Science/Research:	Y
		Advertising Pros.:	Y	Broadcasting:				Health Care:		Petroleum/Chem.:	
				Other:				Consulting:		Math/Other:	Y

TYPES OF BUSINESS:

Agricultural Biotechnology Products & Chemicals Manufacturing
Insecticides
Herbicides
Fungicides
Genetically Modified Plants
Soy Products
Forage & Grain Additives

BRANDS/DIVISIONS/AFFILIATES:

Pioneer Hi-Bred International
DuPont Crop Protection
DuPont Nutrition and Health
Solae Company (The)
DuPont Qualicon
Nandi Seeds Private Limited
MapShots, Inc.
Farms Technology LLC

CONTACTS: *Note: Officers with more than one job title may be intentionally listed here more than once.*

Craig F. Binetti, Pres., DuPont Nutrition & Health
James C. Collins, Pres., DuPont Crop Protection
Paul E. Schickler, Pres., Pioneer Hi-Bred International Inc.
Craig F. Binetti, Pres., Applied Biosciences
John W. Mooney, VP-Supply Chain

Phone: 302-774-1000 **Fax:**

Toll-Free:

Address: 1007 Market St., DuPont Bldg., Wilmington, DE 19898 US

GROWTH PLANS/SPECIAL FEATURES:

DuPont Agriculture & Nutrition (DPAN) is a business unit of global chemical giant DuPont. The company oversees a number of business units covering many aspects of crop protection, genetics, biotechnology, crop chemistry, nutrition science, food quality and safety and protein formulation. Pioneer Hi-Bred International develops advanced plant genetics for a variety of seeds, including alfalfa, corn, hybrid rice, mustard and soybean. DuPont Crop Protection provides herbicide, fungicide and insecticide products and services. DuPont Nutrition and Health provides soy protein, soy fiber and other ingredients under brand names including The Solae Company, a joint venture with Bunge; and DuPont Qualicon. DPAN's major product groups include corn seeds, soybean seeds, other seeds, food ingredients, fungicides, herbicides and insecticides. DPAN has joint ventures in the U.S. and around the world, with projects such as Nandi Seeds Private Limited, an India cotton seeds acquisition company; MapShots, Inc., an agricultural data management company; Farms Technology LLC; GreenLeaf Genetics LLC; and Beijing Kaituo DNA Biotech Research Center Co., Ltd. Regionally, North America accounts for about 50% of the group's sales; Europe, the Middle East and Africa, 23%; Latin America, 17%; and Asia, 10%. Recently a number of new products have been approved for registration by the Environmental Protection Agency (EPA), including the cleaning and personal care product Zemea propanediol and the herbicide Herculex.

FINANCIALS: **Sales and profits are in thousands of dollars—add 000 to get the full amount. 2010 Note: Financial information for 2010 was not available for all companies at press time.**

2010 Sales: $32,733,000
2009 Sales: $27,328,000
2008 Sales: $31,836,000
2007 Sales: $6,842,000
2006 Sales: $

2010 Profits: $3,052,000
2009 Profits: $1,769,000
2008 Profits: $2,010,000
2007 Profits: $894,000
2006 Profits: $

U.S. Stock Ticker: Subsidiary
Int'l Ticker:
Int'l Exchange:
Employees: 60,000 Fiscal Year Ends: 12/31
Parent Company: DUPONT (E I DU PONT DE NEMOURS & CO)

SALARIES/BENEFITS:

Pension Plan: ESOP Stock Plan: Profit Sharing: Top Exec. Salary: $ Bonus: $
Savings Plan: Stock Purch. Plan: Second Exec. Salary: $ Bonus: $

OTHER THOUGHTS:

Apparent Women Officers or Directors:
Hot Spot for Advancement for Women/Minorities:

LOCATIONS: ("Y" = Yes)

West:	Southwest:	Midwest:	Southeast:	Northeast:	International:
Y	Y	Y	Y	Y	Y

EATON CORP

www.eaton.com

Industry Group Code: 3363

Management:		Sales/Marketing:		Liberal Arts:		Information Sys.:		Professionals:		Tech./Scientific:	
Mgmt. Trainees:	Y	Marketing Pros.:	Y	Gen. Writing/Editing:		Info. Mgmt.:	Y	Finance/Acct.:	Y	Engineers, Elec.:	Y
Experienced Mgmt.:	Y	Retail Sales:		Tech. Writing:	Y	Software Dev.:	Y	Law:	Y	Engineers, Other:	Y
Int'l Business:	Y	Comm./Industrial:	Y	Graphic Arts/Photog.:	Y	Hardware Dev.:		HR/Other:	Y	Health/Lab:	
MBA Grads:	Y	Sales Trainees:		Music:		Consulting/Other:		Training:	Y	Science/Research:	Y
		Advertising Pros.:	Y	Broadcasting:				Health Care:		Petroleum/Chem.:	
				Other:				Consulting:		Math/Other:	

TYPES OF BUSINESS:

Hydraulic Products
Electrical Power Distribution & Control Equipment
Truck Transmissions & Axles
Engine Components
Aerospace & Military Components

BRANDS/DIVISIONS/AFFILIATES:

EMC Engineers, Inc.
Wright Line Holding, Inc.
CopperLogic, Inc.
Chloride Phoenixtec Electronics
Tuthill Coupling Group
Internormen Technology Group

CONTACTS: *Note: Officers with more than one job title may be intentionally listed here more than once.*

Alexander M. Cutler, CEO
Alexander M. Cutler, Pres.
Richard H. Fearon, CFO/Chief Planning Officer
Steven M. Boccadoro, Sr. VP-Mktg. & Sales
James W. McGill, Chief Human Resources Officer/Exec. VP
William W. Blausey, Jr., CIO/Sr. VP
Lennart Jonsson, CTO/Exec. VP
Mark M. McGuire, General Counsel/Exec. VP
Thomas S. Gross, COO-Electrical Sector
Kurt B. McMaken, Sr. VP-Corp. Dev. & Treasury
Donald J. McGrath, Sr. VP-Comm.
William C. Hartman, Sr. VP-Investor Rel.
Billie K. Rawot, Controller/Sr. VP
Bradley J. Morton, Pres., Aerospace Group
Curtis J. Hutchins, Pres., Asia-Pacific Region
Craig Arnold, COO-Industrial Sector
Alexander M. Cutler, Chmn.
Yannis P. Tsavalas, Pres., EMEA
Craig Reed, Sr. VP-Supply Chain Mgmt.

Phone: 216-523-5000	**Fax:** 216-523-4787
Toll-Free: 800-386-1911	
Address: 1111 Superior Ave., Cleveland, OH 44114-2584 US	

GROWTH PLANS/SPECIAL FEATURES:

Eaton Corp. is a global designer, manufacturer and marketer of electrical systems and components. The firm operates in two business segments: industrial and electrical. The industrial sector is comprised of three divisions: hydraulics, accounting for 16% of 2010 net sales; aerospace, 11%; and vehicle, 26%. The hydraulics segment develops and sells fluid power products to industrial, mobile equipment and aerospace customers worldwide. The aerospace business unit serves commercial/military aviation, space, military weapon, marine and off-road applications. The vehicle unit focuses on the powertrain and specialized sensor and actuator areas of passenger cars and light trucks; and the drivetrain systems and components for medium-duty and heavy-duty commercial vehicles. Its primary products include engine air management systems such as superchargers, cylinder head modules, engine valves and lifters; manual and automatic transmissions; clutches; driveshafts; drive and trailer axles; brakes; chassis control systems; and collision warning systems. The electrical segment operates in two geographic divisions: electrical Americas, 27% of 2010 net sales; and electrical rest of world, 20%. The segment distributes electrical power and control equipment for industrial, commercial and residential markets. The company sells its products to customers in over 150 countries. In 2010, the firm made several acquisitions, including EMC Engineers, Inc.; Wright Line Holding, Inc.; CopperLogic, Inc.; and Chloride Phoenixtec Electronics. In January 2011, it acquired the Tuthill Coupling Group, a division of the Tuthill Corporation. In the same month, it agreed to acquire ACTOM (Pty) Limited's low-voltage electrical business in South Africa. In March 2011, Eaton agreed to acquire Internormen Technology Group.

FINANCIALS: **Sales and profits are in thousands of dollars—add 000 to get the full amount. 2010 Note: Financial information for 2010 was not available for all companies at press time.**

2010 Sales: $13,715,000 | 2010 Profits: $937,000
2009 Sales: $11,873,000 | 2009 Profits: $383,000
2008 Sales: $15,376,000 | 2008 Profits: $1,058,000
2007 Sales: $13,033,000 | 2007 Profits: $994,000
2006 Sales: $12,232,000 | 2006 Profits: $950,000

U.S. Stock Ticker: ETN
Int'l Ticker:
Int'l Exchange:
Employees: 70,000 Fiscal Year Ends: 12/31
Parent Company:

SALARIES/BENEFITS:

Pension Plan: Y | ESOP Stock Plan: | Profit Sharing: | Top Exec. Salary: $973,248 | Bonus: $575,000
Savings Plan: Y | Stock Purch. Plan: | | Second Exec. Salary: $574,890 | Bonus: $168,906

OTHER THOUGHTS:

Apparent Women Officers or Directors: 1
Hot Spot for Advancement for Women/Minorities: Y

LOCATIONS: ("Y" = Yes)

West:	Southwest:	Midwest:	Southeast:	Northeast:	International:
Y	Y	Y	Y	Y	Y

EBAY INC

Industry Group Code: 454112

www.ebay.com

Management:		Sales/Marketing:		Liberal Arts:		Information Sys.:		Professionals:		Tech./Scientific:	
Mgmt. Trainees:	Y	Marketing Pros.:	Y	Gen. Writing/Editing:	Y	Info. Mgmt.:	Y	Finance/Acct.:	Y	Engineers, Elec.:	Y
Experienced Mgmt.:	Y	Retail Sales:		Tech. Writing:	Y	Software Dev.:	Y	Law:	Y	Engineers, Other:	
Int'l Business:	Y	Comm./Industrial:		Graphic Arts/Photog.:	Y	Hardware Dev.:		HR/Other:	Y	Health/Lab:	
MBA Grads:	Y	Sales Trainees:		Music:		Consulting/Other:		Training:	Y	Science/Research:	
		Advertising Pros.:	Y	Broadcasting:				Health Care:		Petroleum/Chem.:	
				Other:	Y			Consulting:		Math/Other:	

TYPES OF BUSINESS:

Online Retail-Auctions
Online Payment Processing
Memorabilia & Collectibles
E-Commerce Services

BRANDS/DIVISIONS/AFFILIATES:

Half.com
Rent.com
Shopping.com
StubHub
PayPal
Bill Me Later
Critical Path Software
GSI Commerce, Inc.

CONTACTS: *Note: Officers with more than one job title may be intentionally listed here more than once.*

John Donahoe, CEO
John Donahoe, Pres.
Bob Swan, CFO
Elizabeth Axelrod, Sr. VP-Human Resources
Mark Carges, CTO
Mark Carges, Sr. VP-Global Prod., Marketplaces
Michael Jacobson, General Counsel/Sr. VP-Legal Affairs/Sec.
Alan Marks, Sr. VP-Corp. Comm.
Bob Swan, Sr. VP-Finance
Scott Thompson, Pres., PayPal
Pierre M. Omidyar, Chmn.

Phone: 408-376-7400	**Fax:** 408-376-7401
Toll-Free:	
Address: 2145 Hamilton Ave., San Jose, CA 95125 US	

GROWTH PLANS/SPECIAL FEATURES:

eBay, Inc. is an online auction venue that brings together millions of buyers and sellers every day locally, nationally and internationally through its array of web sites. eBay provides online marketplaces for the sale of goods and services, online payments services and online communication offerings. It currently has two primary businesses: marketplaces and payments. The marketplaces segment enables online commerce through a variety of platforms, including the traditional eBay.com web site (which is available in 38 countries) and the company's other online platforms, such as its classifieds web sites, as well as Half.com, Rent.com, Shopping.com and StubHub. Through its eBay.com auction and marketplace site, the company offers fixed-price listings and auction-style listing and provides its users with a number of safeguards against fraud. The payments segment consists of PayPal, which enables individuals and businesses to securely, easily and quickly send and receive payments online in approximately 190 markets worldwide; and Bill Me Later, which enables online U.S. merchants to offer customers transactional credit. In late 2010, eBay acquired mobile application developer Critical Path Software and local shopping engine Milo. In 2011, the firm made several acquisitions, including German online shopping group brands4friends and a 93% interest in Turkish online marketplace GittiGidiyor. Other 2011 acquisitions include GSI Commerce, Inc., an e-commerce products and services firm which was acquired for $2.4 billion; mobile payment provider Zong for $240 million; and ecommerce specialist Magento, Inc.

eBay offers its employees adoption assistance; a pet insurance plan; tuition reimbursement; employee training courses; insurance benefits such as medical, dental, vision, life, accidental death and dismemberment coverage; short- and long-term disability; and business travel accident insurance.

FINANCIALS: **Sales and profits are in thousands of dollars—add 000 to get the full amount. 2010 Note: Financial information for 2010 was not available for all companies at press time.**

2010 Sales: $9,156,000	2010 Profits: $1,801,000	**U.S. Stock Ticker: EBAY**
2009 Sales: $8,727,600	2009 Profits: $2,389,097	**Int'l Ticker:**
2008 Sales: $8,541,261	2008 Profits: $1,779,474	Int'l Exchange:
2007 Sales: $7,672,329	2007 Profits: $348,251	Employees: 17,700 Fiscal Year Ends: 12/31
2006 Sales: $5,969,741	2006 Profits: $1,125,639	Parent Company:

SALARIES/BENEFITS:

Pension Plan:	ESOP Stock Plan:	Profit Sharing:	Top Exec. Salary: $920,673	Bonus: $1,895,113
Savings Plan: Y	Stock Purch. Plan: Y		Second Exec. Salary: $768,606	Bonus: $1,188,811

OTHER THOUGHTS:

Apparent Women Officers or Directors: 2
Hot Spot for Advancement for Women/Minorities: Y

LOCATIONS: ("Y" = Yes)

West:	Southwest:	Midwest:	Southeast:	Northeast:	International:
Y	Y	Y		Y	Y

EDISON INTERNATIONAL

www.edison.com

Industry Group Code: 2211

Management:		Sales/Marketing:		Liberal Arts:		Information Sys.:		Professionals:		Tech./Scientific:	
Mgmt. Trainees:	Y	Marketing Pros.:	Y	Gen. Writing/Editing:	Y	Info. Mgmt.:	Y	Finance/Acct.:	Y	Engineers, Elec.:	Y
Experienced Mgmt.:	Y	Retail Sales:		Tech. Writing:	Y	Software Dev.:	Y	Law:	Y	Engineers, Other:	Y
Int'l Business:	Y	Comm./Industrial:	Y	Graphic Arts/Photog.:	Y	Hardware Dev.:		HR/Other:	Y	Health/Lab:	
MBA Grads:	Y	Sales Trainees:		Music:		Consulting/Other:		Training:	Y	Science/Research:	
		Advertising Pros.:	Y	Broadcasting:				Health Care:		Petroleum/Chem.:	Y
				Other:				Consulting:		Math/Other:	

TYPES OF BUSINESS:

Utilities-Electricity & Natural Gas
Financial Services
Operations Services
Energy Trading

BRANDS/DIVISIONS/AFFILIATES:

Southern California Edison Company
Edison Mission Energy
Edison Capital

CONTACTS: *Note: Officers with more than one job title may be intentionally listed here more than once.*

Theodore F. Craver Jr., CEO
Theodore F. Craver Jr., Pres.
Jim Scilacci, CFO/Exec. VP/Treas.
Daryl David, Sr. VP-Human Resources
Robert L. Adler, General Counsel/Exec. VP
Bertrand Valdman, Sr. VP-Strategic Planning
Janet Clayton, Sr. VP-Corp. Comm.
Scott S. Cunningham, VP-Investor Rel.
Mark Clarke, Controller/VP
Polly Gault, Exec. VP-Public Affairs
Jeff Barnett, VP-Tax
Barbara E. Matthews, Chief Governance Officer/VP/Corp. Sec.
David Heller, Chief Ethics & Compliance Officer/VP-Risk Mgmt.
Theodore F. Craver Jr., Chmn.

Phone: 626-302-2222 **Fax:** 626-302-2517
Toll-Free: 800-655-4555
Address: 2244 Walnut Grove Ave., Rosemead, CA 91770 US

GROWTH PLANS/SPECIAL FEATURES:

Edison International is a California-based holding company with subsidiaries operating primarily in the U.S., with some investments abroad. Major subsidiaries include Southern California Edison Company (SCE), a utility corporation; and non-utility companies Edison Mission Energy (EME) and Edison Capital. SCE is one of the nation's largest electric utilities, providing electric service to a 50,000-square-mile area of California, including over 400 cities and communities, serving over 13 million customers. The energy provided is developed from a range of different kinds of power plants including coal-burning, nuclear, hydroelectric and diesel-burning facilities. SCE also owns over 700 distribution substations, more than 60,000 circuit miles of overhead lines and about 43,500 circuit miles of underground lines. SCE also owns and operates a solar photovoltaic installation on a 600,000 square-foot warehouse roof. Composed of 33,700 advanced thin-film solar panels, the installation has the ability to power 1,300 homes. EME is an independent power producer engaged in the business of developing, acquiring, owning or leasing, operating and selling energy and capacity from independent power production facilities. These operations consist in owning or leasing interests in 39 domestic operating power plants with a capacity of 10,979 megawatts. EME also conducts price risk management and energy trading activities in power markets open to competition. Edison Capital invests in energy and infrastructure projects, including power generation; electric transmission and distribution; transportation; affordable housing; and telecommunications.

Employees are offered medical, dental and vision insurance; disability benefits; an employee assistance program; life insurance; educational reimbursement; credit union membership; and business travel accident insurance.

FINANCIALS: **Sales and profits are in thousands of dollars—add 000 to get the full amount. 2010 Note: Financial information for 2010 was not available for all companies at press time.**

2010 Sales: $12,409,000 — 2010 Profits: $1,256,000
2009 Sales: $12,361,000 — 2009 Profits: $945,000
2008 Sales: $14,112,000 — 2008 Profits: $1,348,000
2007 Sales: $12,868,000 — 2007 Profits: $1,307,000
2006 Sales: $12,622,000 — 2006 Profits: $1,181,000

U.S. Stock Ticker: EIX
Int'l Ticker:
Int'l Exchange:
Employees: 20,117 Fiscal Year Ends: 12/31
Parent Company:

SALARIES/BENEFITS:

Pension Plan: Y | ESOP Stock Plan: | Profit Sharing: | Top Exec. Salary: $1,096,346 | Bonus: $1,633,500
Savings Plan: Y | Stock Purch. Plan: | Second Exec. Salary: $719,758 | Bonus: $659,800

OTHER THOUGHTS:

Apparent Women Officers or Directors: 7
Hot Spot for Advancement for Women/Minorities: Y

LOCATIONS: ("Y" = Yes)

West:	Southwest:	Midwest:	Southeast:	Northeast:	International:
Y	Y	Y	Y	Y	Y

EDWARDS LIFESCIENCES CORP

www.edwards.com

Industry Group Code: 33911

Management:		Sales/Marketing:		Liberal Arts:		Information Sys.:		Professionals:		Tech./Scientific:	
Mgmt. Trainees:	Y	Marketing Pros.:	Y	Gen. Writing/Editing:	Y	Info. Mgmt.:	Y	Finance/Acct.:	Y	Engineers, Elec.:	Y
Experienced Mgmt.:	Y	Retail Sales:		Tech. Writing:	Y	Software Dev.:	Y	Law:	Y	Engineers, Other:	Y
Int'l Business:	Y	Comm./Industrial:	Y	Graphic Arts/Photog.:		Hardware Dev.:		HR/Other:	Y	Health/Lab:	Y
MBA Grads:	Y	Sales Trainees:		Music:		Consulting/Other:		Training:	Y	Science/Research:	
		Advertising Pros.:	Y	Broadcasting:				Health Care:		Petroleum/Chem.:	
				Other:				Consulting:		Math/Other:	

TYPES OF BUSINESS:

Supplies-Cardiovascular Disease Related
Cardiac Surgery Products
Critical Care Products
Vascular Products
Heart Valve Implants

BRANDS/DIVISIONS/AFFILIATES:

PERIMOUNT
ThermaFix
XenoLogiX
Swan-Ganz
FloTrac
PreSep
Edwards SAPIEN
Embrella Cardiovascular, Inc.

CONTACTS: *Note: Officers with more than one job title may be intentionally listed here more than once.*

Michael A. Mussallem, CEO
Thomas M. Abate, CFO/Corp. VP
Robert C. Reindl, Corp. VP-Human Resources
Stanton J. Rowe, Chief Scientific Officer
Stanton J. Rowe, Corp. VP-Advanced Tech.
Aimee S. Weisner, General Counsel/Corp. VP
Paul C. Redmond, Corp. VP-Global Oper.
John H. Kehl, Jr., Corp. VP-Strategy & Corp. Dev.
Bruce P. Garren, Corp. VP-Public Affairs
David K. Erikson, VP-Investor Rel.
Thomas M. Abate, Treas.
Patrick B. Verguet, Corp. VP-EMEA
Larry L. Wood, Corp. VP-Transcatheter Valve Replacement
Carlyn D. Solomon, Corp. VP-Critical Care & Vascular
John P. McGrath, Corp. VP-Quality
Michael A. Mussallem, Chmn.
Huimin Wang, Corp. VP-Japan, APAC & Latin America

Phone: 949-250-2500 **Fax:** 949-250-2525
Toll-Free: 800-424-3278
Address: 1 Edwards Way, Irvine, CA 92614 US

GROWTH PLANS/SPECIAL FEATURES:

Edwards Lifesciences Corp. designs products for cardiovascular diseases, such as heart valve disease, coronary artery disease, peripheral vascular disease (PVD) and congestive heart failure. The firm operates in four main areas: heart valve therapy, critical care, cardiac surgery systems and vascular. Heart valve products include the PERIMOUNT line of pericardial heart valves made from biologically inert porcine tissue, often on a wire-form stent; and valve repair therapies, such as the ThermaFix and XenoLogiX tissue treatment processes. Edwards Lifesciences also offers the Edwards SAPIEN transcatheter heart valve for aortic valve replacement. The company's critical care products include the Swan-Ganz brand hemodynamic monitoring devices used during surgery; FloTrac, a minimally invasive continuous cardiac output monitoring system; and PreSep, a venous oximetry catheter that measures central venous oxygen saturation. Cardiac surgery products include disposable products used in heart surgery procedures such as cannulae (small tubes used to extract fluid); products designed to reduce vascular trauma during cannulae placement, usage and removal; and carbon dioxide laser products used in some heart surgeries. Vascular products include the Fogarty line of embolectomy catheters; balloon-tipped, catheter-based products; surgical clips and inserts; angioscopy equipment; and implantable grafts. Approximately 39% of Edwards Lifesciences' sales come from the U.S. and 61% from international sales. The firm sells its products in approximately 100 countries such as France, the Netherlands, Germany, Italy, Japan, Spain, Australia, Belgium, Canada and U.K. In 2010, Edwards Lifesciences discontinued the MONARC transcatheter mitral repair system line. In March 2011, the firm acquired Embrella Cardiovascular, Inc.

The company offers employee benefits including medical, dental, vision, disability and group life insurance; a stock purchase plan; a 401(k) plan; health and dependent care reimbursement plans; and adoption, tuition and assistance programs.

FINANCIALS: **Sales and profits are in thousands of dollars—add 000 to get the full amount. 2010 Note: Financial information for 2010 was not available for all companies at press time.**

2010 Sales: $1,447,000 2010 Profits: $218,000
2009 Sales: $1,321,400 2009 Profits: $229,100
2008 Sales: $1,237,700 2008 Profits: $128,900
2007 Sales: $1,091,100 2007 Profits: $113,000
2006 Sales: $1,037,000 2006 Profits: $130,500

U.S. Stock Ticker: EW
Int'l Ticker:
Int'l Exchange:
Employees: 7,000 Fiscal Year Ends: 12/31
Parent Company:

SALARIES/BENEFITS:

Pension Plan: ESOP Stock Plan: Profit Sharing: Top Exec. Salary: $796,308 Bonus: $1,600,000
Savings Plan: Y Stock Purch. Plan: Y Second Exec. Salary: $444,202 Bonus: $452,738

OTHER THOUGHTS:

Apparent Women Officers or Directors: 2
Hot Spot for Advancement for Women/Minorities: Y

LOCATIONS: ("Y" = Yes)

West:	Southwest:	Midwest:	Southeast:	Northeast:	International:
Y					Y

EMC CORP

www.emc.com

Industry Group Code: 334112

Management:		Sales/Marketing:		Liberal Arts:		Information Sys.:		Professionals:		Tech./Scientific:	
Mgmt. Trainees:	Y	Marketing Pros.:	Y	Gen. Writing/Editing:		Info. Mgmt.:	Y	Finance/Acct.:	Y	Engineers, Elec.:	Y
Experienced Mgmt.:	Y	Retail Sales:		Tech. Writing:	Y	Software Dev.:	Y	Law:	Y	Engineers, Other:	
Int'l Business:	Y	Comm./Industrial:	Y	Graphic Arts/Photog.:	Y	Hardware Dev.:	Y	HR/Other:	Y	Health/Lab:	
MBA Grads:	Y	Sales Trainees:		Music:		Consulting/Other:		Training:	Y	Science/Research:	Y
		Advertising Pros.:	Y	Broadcasting:				Health Care:		Petroleum/Chem.:	
				Other:				Consulting:		Math/Other:	Y

TYPES OF BUSINESS:

Computer Storage Equipment-Mainframe Disk Memory
Network Storage Systems
Management Protection Software
Consulting Services
Storage Management Services

BRANDS/DIVISIONS/AFFILIATES:

VMware Inc
RSA Security Inc
Captiva Software Corp
Greenplum Inc
Decho Corporation
Isilon Systems Inc
Bus-Tech Inc
Connectrix

CONTACTS: *Note: Officers with more than one job title may be intentionally listed here more than once.*

Joseph M. Tucci, CEO
Joseph M. Tucci, Pres.
David Goulden, CFO/Exec. VP
Jeremy Burton, Chief Mktg. Officer/Exec. VP
John T. (Jack) Mollen, Exec. VP-Human Resources
Sanjay Mirchandani, CIO/Sr. VP
Jeffrey M. Nick, CTO/Sr. VP
Paul T. Dacier, General Counsel/Exec. VP
Pat Gelsinger, COO/Pres., EMC Info. Infrastructure Prod.
Irina Simmons, Treas./Sr. VP
William J. Teuber, Jr., Vice Chmn.
Mark S. Lewis, Pres., Content Mgmt. & Archiving Div.
Howard D. Elias, COO/Pres., EMC Info. Infrastructure & Cloud Svcs
Joseph M. Tucci, Chmn.
Rainer Erlat, Pres., EMEA

Phone: 508-435-1000 **Fax:** 508-435-5222
Toll-Free:
Address: 176 South St., Hopkinton, MA 01748-9103 US

GROWTH PLANS/SPECIAL FEATURES:

EMC Corp., along with its subsidiaries, develops, delivers and supports systems, software and services for the storage, management and protection of electronic information. EMC operates in two business divisions: Information Infrastructure and VMware Virtual Infrastructure. The Information Infrastructure business is divided into three segments, Information Storage; Content Management and Archiving; and RSA Information Security. The information store segment provides a range of networked information storage systems, software and services to support customers' information storage and management strategies. Products include Celerra IP storage systems; Centera content addressed storage systems; Connectrix directors and switches; and LifeLine software for consumers and small and home office users. The segment also maintains Decho Corporation, combination of its Mozy, Inc. and Pi Corp. subsidiaries that is focused on personal information management. The content management and archiving segment helps customers optimize business processes and create, manage and archive information such as documents, e-mail, web pages, records and application data. Its products include the Documentum, Captiva and Document Sciences xPression families. The RSA Information Security segment offers products and services focused on information confidentiality. The RSA Data Security System combines product suites and services for comprehensive data protection, including loss prevention, encryption and key management. EMC Global Services offers consulting services, technology deployment managed services, customer support services, training and certification through more than 14,000 support-service professionals, as well as a global network of alliances and partners. The VMware Virtual Infrastructure division, represented by a majority stake in VMware, Inc. provides virtual infrastructure software from the desktop to the data center, supporting a range of operating systems. In June 2010, the company acquired Greenplum, Inc., which specializes in data storage. In November 2010, the firm acquired Bus-Tech, Inc. and Isilon Systems, Inc., which develop data storage and retrieval systems.

FINANCIALS: **Sales and profits are in thousands of dollars—add 000 to get the full amount. 2010 Note: Financial information for 2010 was not available for all companies at press time.**

2010 Sales: $17,015,126 2010 Profits: $1,969,686
2009 Sales: $14,025,910 2009 Profits: $1,123,971
2008 Sales: $14,880,000 2008 Profits: $2,160,000
2007 Sales: $13,230,205 2007 Profits: $1,665,668
2006 Sales: $11,155,090 2006 Profits: $1,227,601

U.S. Stock Ticker: EMC
Int'l Ticker:
Int'l Exchange:
Employees: 48,500 Fiscal Year Ends: 12/31
Parent Company:

SALARIES/BENEFITS:

Pension Plan: ESOP Stock Plan: Profit Sharing: Top Exec. Salary: $872,308 Bonus: $1,068,420
Savings Plan: Y Stock Purch. Plan: Y Second Exec. Salary: $609,673 Bonus: $655,684

OTHER THOUGHTS:

Apparent Women Officers or Directors: 1
Hot Spot for Advancement for Women/Minorities:

LOCATIONS: ("Y" = Yes)

West:	Southwest:	Midwest:	Southeast:	Northeast:	International:
Y				Y	Y

EMERITUS CORP

www.emeritus.com

Industry Group Code: 623110

Management:		Sales/Marketing:		Liberal Arts:		Information Sys.:		Professionals:		Tech./Scientific:	
Mgmt. Trainees:	Y	Marketing Pros.:	Y	Gen. Writing/Editing:	Y	Info. Mgmt.:	Y	Finance/Acct.:	Y	Engineers, Elec.:	
Experienced Mgmt.:	Y	Retail Sales:		Tech. Writing:	Y	Software Dev.:		Law:	Y	Engineers, Other:	
Int'l Business:	Y	Comm./Industrial:		Graphic Arts/Photog.:	Y	Hardware Dev.:		HR/Other:	Y	Health/Lab:	
MBA Grads:	Y	Sales Trainees:		Music:		Consulting/Other:		Training:	Y	Science/Research:	
		Advertising Pros.:	Y	Broadcasting:				Health Care:	Y	Petroleum/Chem.:	
				Other:	Y			Consulting:		Math/Other:	

TYPES OF BUSINESS:

Long-Term Health Care
Assisted Living Communities

BRANDS/DIVISIONS/AFFILIATES:

Weston Group, Inc.

CONTACTS:

Note: Officers with more than one job title may be intentionally listed here more than once.

Granger Cobb, CEO
Chris Hyatt, COO/Exec. VP
Granger Cobb, Pres.
Robert C. Bateman, CFO/Exec. VP-Finance
Jayne Sallerson, Exec. VP-Mktg. & Sales
Melanie Werdel, Exec. VP-Admin.
Raymond R. Brandstrom, Corp. Sec.
Chris Belford, Sr. VP-Oper.
Eric Mendelsohn, Sr. VP-Corp. Dev.
Jayne Sallerson, Exec. VP-Comm.
Jim L. Hanson, Sr. VP-Financial Svcs./Controller
Budgie Amparo, Exec. VP-Quality Svcs. & Risk Management
Martin D. Roffe, Sr. VP-Financial Planning
John Cincotta, Sr. VP-Sales
Leo Watterson, Sr. VP-Corp. Acct.
Daniel R. Baty, Chmn.

Phone: 206-298-2909 **Fax:** 206-301-4500
Toll-Free: 800-429-4828
Address: 3131 Elliott Ave., Ste. 500, Seattle, WA 98121 US

GROWTH PLANS/SPECIAL FEATURES:

Emeritus Corp. operates assisted living residential communities in the U.S. These communities cater to senior citizens who need help with daily living, but do not require the intensive care provided in skilled nursing facilities. It operates or has an interest in 306 communities, consisting of 28,277 residential rooms or suites with a capacity for 33,265 residents. The firm's communities are located in 42 states and include 165 owned communities and 141 leased communities. Additionally, the company manages 10 facilities for third-parties and 163 facilities through joint ventures. In total, its operating portfolio includes 479 communities, with 42,172 units and a capacity of 49,667 residents. Assisted living generally provides housing and 24-hour personal support services. Seniors reside in a private or semi-private residential unit for a monthly fee based on each resident's individual service needs. The company's specialty is Alzheimer's disease and dementia-related care, for which the company has developed a program that links memory training, familiar environments and personalized care services. In its other assisted living programs, Emeritus business strategy calls for customer service that addresses both physical and social health. The firm's target customers are middle to upper-middle income seniors, 75 and older, living in smaller cities (50,000 to 150,000 persons). In August 2010, Emeritus, through a joint venture with Columbia Pacific Advisors and Blackstone Real Estate Advisors, acquired 144 senior living communities from Sunwest Management. In October 2010, it agreed to acquire Weston Group, Inc., a provider of rehabilitation services and medical equipment. In December 2010, the firm acquired eight additional communities. In January 2011, Emeritus entered into a memorandum of understanding with Columbia Pacific Advisors to begin exploring the potential to develop senior housing in China.

Employees are offered health care benefits; a 401(k) plan; a stock purchase plan; tuition assistance; and sick, vacation and holiday pay.

FINANCIALS:

Sales and profits are in thousands of dollars—add 000 to get the full amount. 2010 Note: Financial information for 2010 was not available for all companies at press time.

2010 Sales: $1,007,065	2010 Profits: $-57,842
2009 Sales: $898,732	2009 Profits: $-53,875
2008 Sales: $772,443	2008 Profits: $-104,751
2007 Sales: $538,874	2007 Profits: $-48,741
2006 Sales: $411,375	2006 Profits: $-14,618

U.S. Stock Ticker: ESC
Int'l Ticker:
Int'l Exchange:
Employees: 29,300 Fiscal Year Ends: 12/31
Parent Company:

SALARIES/BENEFITS:

Pension Plan:	ESOP Stock Plan:	Profit Sharing:	Top Exec. Salary: $641,533	Bonus: $242,850
Savings Plan: Y	Stock Purch. Plan: Y		Second Exec. Salary: $636,952	Bonus: $243,500

OTHER THOUGHTS:

Apparent Women Officers or Directors: 3
Hot Spot for Advancement for Women/Minorities: Y

LOCATIONS: ("Y" = Yes)

West:	Southwest:	Midwest:	Southeast:	Northeast:	International:
Y	Y	Y	Y	Y	

EMERSON ELECTRIC CO

www.emerson.com

Industry Group Code: 3345

Management:		**Sales/Marketing:**		**Liberal Arts:**		**Information Sys.:**		**Professionals:**		**Tech./Scientific:**	
Mgmt. Trainees:	Y	Marketing Pros.:	Y	Gen. Writing/Editing:		Info. Mgmt.:	Y	Finance/Acct.:	Y	Engineers, Elec.:	Y
Experienced Mgmt.:	Y	Retail Sales:		Tech. Writing:	Y	Software Dev.:	Y	Law:	Y	Engineers, Other:	Y
Int'l Business:	Y	Comm./Industrial:	Y	Graphic Arts/Photog.:	Y	Hardware Dev.:	Y	HR/Other:	Y	Health/Lab:	
MBA Grads:	Y	Sales Trainees:		Music:		Consulting/Other:		Training:	Y	Science/Research:	Y
		Advertising Pros.:	Y	Broadcasting:				Health Care:		Petroleum/Chem.:	
				Other:				Consulting:		Math/Other:	Y

TYPES OF BUSINESS:

Engineering & Technology Products & Services
Industrial Automation Products
Power Products
Air Conditioning & Refrigeration Products
Appliances & Tools

BRANDS/DIVISIONS/AFFILIATES:

PlantWeb Digital Plant Architecture
Process Management
Industrial Automation
Network Power
Climate Technologies
Tools and Storage
Chloride Group PLC

CONTACTS:

Note: Officers with more than one job title may be intentionally listed here more than once.

David N. Farr, CEO
Edward L. Monser, COO
Edward L. Monser, Pres.
Frank J. Dellaquila, CFO/Sr. VP
Frank L. Steeves, General Counsel/Sr. VP/Corp. Sec.
Craig W. Ashmore, Exec. VP-Dev. & Planning
Richard J. Schlueter, Chief Acct. Officer/VP
Charles A. Peters, Sr. Exec. VP
David N. Farr, Chmn.

Phone: 314-553-2000 **Fax:** 314-553-3527
Toll-Free:
Address: 8000 W. Florissant Ave., P.O. Box 4100, St. Louis, MO 63136 US

GROWTH PLANS/SPECIAL FEATURES:

Emerson Electric Co. designs and supplies technology products and engineering service to a wide range of industrial, commercial and consumer markets worldwide. The company is organized into five business segments. The Process Management segment, accounting for 28% of sales, provides measurement, control and diagnostic capabilities for automated industrial processes producing items such as foods, medicines, power and fuels. As part of this segment, Emerson offers PlantWeb Digital Plant Architecture, a platform designed to open communication between industrial plant devices and, with its accompanying software, collect and analyze information concerning plant assets and processes. These capabilities give customers the ability to predict changes in equipment and process performance and the impact they can have on plant operations. The Industrial Automation segment (20% of sales) assists clients in automating production lines. Products for this group include motors, transmissions, alternators, fluid controls and materials joining equipment. The Network Power segment (27% of sales) provides power and environmental conditioning systems to help ensure telecommunication systems, data networks and critical business applications operate continuously. The Climate Technologies segment (17% of sales) primarily focuses on household and commercial air-conditioning and refrigeration technologies for comfort and food safety. The Tools and Storage segment (8% of sales) provides motors for a broad range of applications, appliances and integrated appliance solutions; tools for homeowners and professionals; and home and commercial storage systems. Emerson operates approximately 240 manufacturing locations, 80 of which are located in the U.S. In August 2010, the firm agreed to sell its Motors and Appliance Controls operations to Nidec Corporation. In September 2010, the company acquired Chloride Group PLC.

FINANCIALS:

Sales and profits are in thousands of dollars—add 000 to get the full amount. 2010 Note: Financial information for 2010 was not available for all companies at press time.

2010 Sales: $21,039,000	2010 Profits: $2,164,000
2009 Sales: $20,102,000	2009 Profits: $1,724,000
2008 Sales: $23,751,000	2008 Profits: $2,412,000
2007 Sales: $22,131,000	2007 Profits: $2,136,000
2006 Sales: $19,734,000	2006 Profits: $1,845,000

U.S. Stock Ticker: EMR
Int'l Ticker:
Int'l Exchange:
Employees: 127,700 Fiscal Year Ends: 9/30
Parent Company:

SALARIES/BENEFITS:

Pension Plan: Y ESOP Stock Plan: Profit Sharing: Y Top Exec. Salary: $1,187,500 Bonus: $4,062,000
Savings Plan: Y Stock Purch. Plan: Second Exec. Salary: $722,500 Bonus: $2,460,000

OTHER THOUGHTS:

Apparent Women Officers or Directors: 2
Hot Spot for Advancement for Women/Minorities: Y

LOCATIONS: ("Y" = Yes)

West:	Southwest:	Midwest:	Southeast:	Northeast:	International:
Y	Y	Y	Y	Y	Y

ENDO PHARMACEUTICALS HOLDINGS INC

www.endo.com

Industry Group Code: 325412

Management:		Sales/Marketing:		Liberal Arts:		Information Sys.:		Professionals:		Tech./Scientific:	
Mgmt. Trainees:		Marketing Pros.:	Y	Gen. Writing/Editing:		Info. Mgmt.:	Y	Finance/Acct.:	Y	Engineers, Elec.:	
Experienced Mgmt.:		Retail Sales:		Tech. Writing:	Y	Software Dev.:		Law:	Y	Engineers, Other:	
Int'l Business:		Comm./Industrial:	Y	Graphic Arts/Photog.:		Hardware Dev.:		HR/Other:	Y	Health/Lab:	Y
MBA Grads:	Y	Sales Trainees:	Y	Music:		Consulting/Other:		Training:		Science/Research:	Y
		Advertising Pros.:	Y	Broadcasting:				Health Care:		Petroleum/Chem.:	
				Other:				Consulting:		Math/Other:	Y

TYPES OF BUSINESS:

Drugs-Pain Management
Pharmaceutical Preparations

BRANDS/DIVISIONS/AFFILIATES:

Endo Pharmaceuticals, Inc.
Lidoderm
Opana
Percocet
American Medical Systems, Inc.
HealthTronics
Penwest
Qualitest Pharmaceuticals

CONTACTS: *Note: Officers with more than one job title may be intentionally listed here more than once.*

David P. Holveck, CEO
Julie H. McHugh, COO
David P. Holveck, Pres.
Alan G. Levin, CFO/Exec. VP
Larry Cunningham, Sr. VP-Human Resources
Ivan Gergel, Exec. VP-R&D
Caroline B. Manogue, Chief Legal Officer/Corp. Sec./Exec. VP
Kevin Wiggins, Sr. Dir.-Corp. Comm.
Roger H. Kimmel, Chmn.
Denise Hudson, Sr. VP-Supply Chain & Enterprise Quality

Phone: 610-558-9800	**Fax:** 610-558-8979
Toll-Free:	
Address: 100 Endo Blvd., Chadds Ford, PA 19317 US	

GROWTH PLANS/SPECIAL FEATURES:

Endo Pharmaceuticals Holdings, Inc., through subsidiary Endo Pharmaceuticals, Inc., is a specialty pharmaceutical company engaged in the research, development, marketing and sale of branded and generic prescription pharmaceuticals used primarily to treat and manage pain, overactive bladder, central precocious puberty and prostate and bladder cancer. The company has a portfolio of branded products that includes such names as Lidoderm, a topical patch containing lidocaine; Opana and Opana ER, indicated for the relief of moderate to severe pain in patients requiring continuous opioid treatment; Percocet, indicated for the treatment of moderate to moderately severe pain; and Frova, a migraine treatment product. Branded products generate approximately 86% of Endo's net sales in 2010, with 46% of its net sales generated from Lidoderm. Its non-branded generic portfolio currently consists of products primarily focused in pain management. The firm focuses selectively on generics that have one or more barriers to market entry, such as complex formulation, regulatory or legal challenges or difficulty in raw material sourcing. Endo's primary development products include Aveed for the treatment of male hypogonadism; Axomadol, which is currently in Phase II development for the treatment of moderate to severe chronic pain and diabetic peripheral neuropathic pain; and octreotide implant, which is currently in Phase III clinical trials for the treatment of acromegaly and carcinoid syndrome. Endo sells its products to a limited number of large pharmacy chains and through wholesale drug distributors, which supply them to pharmacies, hospitals, governmental agencies and physicians. In 2010, the firm acquired HealthTronics, a provider of healthcare services and manufacturer of medical devices for the urology community; Penwest, a drug development company; and generics company, Qualitest Pharmaceuticals. In June 2011, the firm acquired American Medical Systems, Inc., a supplier of pelvic health products, for $2.9 billion.

FINANCIALS: **Sales and profits are in thousands of dollars—add 000 to get the full amount. 2010 Note: Financial information for 2010 was not available for all companies at press time.**

2010 Sales: $1,716,229	2010 Profits: $259,006
2009 Sales: $1,460,841	2009 Profits: $266,336
2008 Sales: $1,260,536	2008 Profits: $255,336
2007 Sales: $1,085,608	2007 Profits: $227,440
2006 Sales: $909,659	2006 Profits: $137,839

U.S. Stock Ticker: ENDP
Int'l Ticker:
Int'l Exchange:
Employees: 2,947 Fiscal Year Ends: 12/31
Parent Company:

SALARIES/BENEFITS:

Pension Plan:	ESOP Stock Plan:	Profit Sharing:	Top Exec. Salary: $875,000	Bonus: $1,984,500
Savings Plan: Y	Stock Purch. Plan: Y		Second Exec. Salary: $615,000	Bonus: $556,756

OTHER THOUGHTS:

Apparent Women Officers or Directors: 4
Hot Spot for Advancement for Women/Minorities: Y

LOCATIONS: ("Y" = Yes)

West:	Southwest:	Midwest:	Southeast:	Northeast:	International:
Y				Y	

ENTERGY CORP

www.entergy.com

Industry Group Code: 221113

Management:		**Sales/Marketing:**		**Liberal Arts:**		**Information Sys.:**		**Professionals:**		**Tech./Scientific:**	
Mgmt. Trainees:	Y	Marketing Pros.:	Y	Gen. Writing/Editing:	Y	Info. Mgmt.:	Y	Finance/Acct.:	Y	Engineers, Elec.:	Y
Experienced Mgmt.:	Y	Retail Sales:		Tech. Writing:	Y	Software Dev.:	Y	Law:	Y	Engineers, Other:	Y
Int'l Business:	Y	Comm./Industrial:	Y	Graphic Arts/Photog.:	Y	Hardware Dev.:		HR/Other:	Y	Health/Lab:	
MBA Grads:	Y	Sales Trainees:		Music:		Consulting/Other:		Training:	Y	Science/Research:	
		Advertising Pros.:	Y	Broadcasting:				Health Care:		Petroleum/Chem.:	
				Other:				Consulting:		Math/Other:	

TYPES OF BUSINESS:

Utilities-Electric
Energy Management
Energy Trading
Nuclear Generation
Hydroelectric Generation
Wind Generation

BRANDS/DIVISIONS/AFFILIATES:

Entergy Arkansas, Inc.
Entergy Louisiana LLC
Entergy Mississippi, Inc.
Entergy Texas, Inc.
Entergy New Orleans, Inc.
Entergy Gulf States Louisiana LLC
Entergy Nuclear, Inc.

CONTACTS: *Note: Officers with more than one job title may be intentionally listed here more than once.*

J. Wayne Leonard, CEO
Mark T. Savoff, COO/Exec. VP
Richard Smith, Pres.
Leo Denault, CFO/Exec. VP
Renae Conley, Exec. VP-Human Resources & Admin.
Rod West, Chief Admin. Officer/Exec. VP
Robert Sloan, General Counsel/Exec. VP
Gary Taylor, Pres., Utility Oper.
Richard Smith, Pres., Entergy Wholesale Commodity Bus.
Joe Domino, Pres./CEO-Entergy Texas, Inc.
John Herron, Pres./Chief Nuclear Officer-Entergy Nuclear
Haley Fisackerly, Pres./CEO-Entergy Mississippi, Inc.
J. Wayne Leonard, Chmn.

Phone: 504-576-4000 **Fax:** 504-576-4428
Toll-Free: 800-368-3749
Address: 639 Loyola Ave., New Orleans, LA 70113 US

GROWTH PLANS/SPECIAL FEATURES:

Entergy Corp. is an integrated energy company engaged primarily in the electric power production and retail electric distribution operations. The company owns and operates power plants with roughly 30,000 megawatts (MW) of electric general capacity, making it one of the largest nuclear power generators in the U.S. The firm operates in two primary segments, utility and non-utility nuclear. The utility segment, which generates 78% of Entergy Corp.'s revenue, generates, transmits, distributes and sells electric power to 2.7 million customers in a four-state service territory that includes portions of Arkansas, Mississippi, Texas and Louisiana, including New Orleans. The division also operates a small natural gas distribution system. The non-utility nuclear segment, responsible for 22% of revenue, owns and operates six nuclear power plants located in the northeastern U.S. and sells the electric power produced by those plants primarily to wholesale customers. The division also provides services to other nuclear power plant owners. Nuclear operations are carried out by subsidiary, Entergy Nuclear, Inc. The division also sells to wholesale customers the electric power produced by power plants that it owns. The firm has six main regional subsidiaries, all falling under the U.S. utility segment: Entergy Arkansas; Entergy Gulf States of Louisiana; Entergy Louisiana; Entergy Mississippi; Entergy New Orleans; and Entergy Texas.

Employees are offered medical, dental and vision insurance; life insurance; flexible spending accounts; disability coverage; a 401(k) plan; a retirement plan; an employee assistance program; a relocation assistance program; and education reimbursement.

FINANCIALS: **Sales and profits are in thousands of dollars—add 000 to get the full amount. 2010 Note: Financial information for 2010 was not available for all companies at press time.**

2010 Sales: $11,487,577 — 2010 Profits: $1,270,305
2009 Sales: $10,745,650 — 2009 Profits: $1,251,050
2008 Sales: $13,093,756 — 2008 Profits: $1,220,566
2007 Sales: $11,484,398 — 2007 Profits: $1,134,849
2006 Sales: $10,932,158 — 2006 Profits: $1,132,602

U.S. Stock Ticker: ETR
Int'l Ticker:
Int'l Exchange:
Employees: 14,958 Fiscal Year Ends: 12/31
Parent Company:

SALARIES/BENEFITS:

Pension Plan: Y ESOP Stock Plan: Profit Sharing: Top Exec. Salary: $1,291,500 Bonus: $2,665,656
Savings Plan: Y Stock Purch. Plan: Second Exec. Salary: $645,000 Bonus: $776,580

OTHER THOUGHTS:

Apparent Women Officers or Directors: 3
Hot Spot for Advancement for Women/Minorities: Y

LOCATIONS: ("Y" = Yes)

West:	Southwest:	Midwest:	Southeast:	Northeast:	International:
Y	Y		Y		

ENTERPRISE HOLDINGS INC

www.enterpriseholdings.com

Industry Group Code: 5321

Management:		Sales/Marketing:		Liberal Arts:		Information Sys.:		Professionals:		Tech./Scientific:	
Mgmt. Trainees:	Y	Marketing Pros.:	Y	Gen. Writing/Editing:	Y	Info. Mgmt.:	Y	Finance/Acct.:	Y	Engineers, Elec.:	
Experienced Mgmt.:	Y	Retail Sales:		Tech. Writing:		Software Dev.:	Y	Law:	Y	Engineers, Other:	
Int'l Business:	Y	Comm./Industrial:	Y	Graphic Arts/Photog.:	Y	Hardware Dev.:		HR/Other:	Y	Health/Lab:	
MBA Grads:	Y	Sales Trainees:	Y	Music:		Consulting/Other:		Training:	Y	Science/Research:	
		Advertising Pros.:	Y	Broadcasting:				Health Care:		Petroleum/Chem.:	
				Other:	Y			Consulting:		Math/Other:	

TYPES OF BUSINESS:

Car & Truck Rental
Vanpool Services

BRANDS/DIVISIONS/AFFILIATES:

Enterprise Rent-a-Car (ERAC)
National Car Rental
Alamo Rent A Car
RideShare
Enterprise Car Sales
WeCar
Enterprise Fleet Management
Enterprise Truck Rental

CONTACTS: *Note: Officers with more than one job title may be intentionally listed here more than once.*

Andrew C. Taylor, CEO
Pamela Nicholson, COO
Pamela Nicholson, Pres.
William W. Snyder, CFO/Exec. VP
Steve Bloom, Sr. VP-Car Sales
Edward Adams, Sr. VP-Human Resources
Craig Kennedy, CIO/Sr. VP
Lee Kaplan, Chief Admin. Officer/Sr. VP
Matthew G. Darrah, Exec. VP-N. American Oper.
Greg Stubblefield, Chief Strategy Officer/Exec. VP
Laura Bryant, Contact-Corp. Comm.
Lisa Martini, Contact-Investor Rel.
Rose Langhorst, Treas./VP
Steve Bloom, Sr. VP-Enterprise Fleet Mgmt.
Jo Ann Taylor Kindle, Pres., Enterprise Holdings Foundation
Andrew C. Taylor, Chmn.

Phone: 314-512-1000	**Fax:** 314-512-4706
Toll-Free:	
Address: 600 Corporate Park Dr., St. Louis, MO 63105 US	

GROWTH PLANS/SPECIAL FEATURES:

Enterprise Holdings, Inc. is the parent company of Alamo Rent A Car, National Car Rental, and Enterprise Rent-A-Car, along with Enterprise Fleet Management, Enterprise Car Sales, Enterprise Commercial Truck Rental, RideShare vanpooling, and WeCar, a car sharing membership program. Enterprise Holdings was formed in recent years as the final step in the integration of the Alamo and National businesses acquired by Enterprise Rent-A-Car. The company's combined rental fleet is the largest in the world at 1.1 million vehicles. It serves roughly 7,600 retail and airport locations in the U.S., Mexico, the Caribbean, Latin America, Canada, Ireland, the U.K., Germany and Asia. The Enterprise Holdings group of businesses generates roughly $12.6 billion in revenue per year. Alamo Rent A Car is a budget rental car company catering to leisure and vacation customers, particularly international travelers visiting North America. Alamo operates 159 self-service kiosks at 65 U.S. locations. National Car Rental is a premium rental brand that serves frequent business travelers and offers the Emerald Club frequent-renter benefits program. Enterprise Rent-A-Car boasts over 5,000 retail and airport offices in the U.S. Enterprise Car Sales is a used-car reseller that provides non-negotiable pricing and after-market warranties on used cars acquired through trade-in or extracted from the rental fleet. WeCar is a car sharing program that allows customers to rent a car for flexible periods of time through an online membership portal. In November 2010, the firm opened a new Alamo Rent A Car location at the Tampa International Airport in Florida.

Enterprise Holdings offers its employees medical, dental, and vision insurance; prescription drug coverage; flexible spending accounts; life insurance; and long-term disability plans.

FINANCIALS: **Sales and profits are in thousands of dollars—add 000 to get the full amount. 2010 Note: Financial information for 2010 was not available for all companies at press time.**

2010 Sales: $12,600,000	2010 Profits: $1,880,000	**U.S. Stock Ticker: Private**
2009 Sales: $12,100,000	2009 Profits: $	**Int'l Ticker:**
2008 Sales: $12,100,000	2008 Profits: $	Int'l Exchange:
2007 Sales: $	2007 Profits: $	Employees: 68,000 Fiscal Year Ends:
2006 Sales: $	2006 Profits: $	Parent Company:

SALARIES/BENEFITS:

Pension Plan:	ESOP Stock Plan:	Profit Sharing:	Top Exec. Salary: $	Bonus: $
Savings Plan: Y	Stock Purch. Plan:		Second Exec. Salary: $	Bonus: $

OTHER THOUGHTS:

Apparent Women Officers or Directors: 2
Hot Spot for Advancement for Women/Minorities:

LOCATIONS: ("Y" = Yes)

West:	Southwest:	Midwest:	Southeast:	Northeast:	International:
Y	Y	Y	Y	Y	Y

EQUITY LIFESTYLE PROPERTIES INC

www.equitylifestyle.com

Industry Group Code: 531110

Management:		Sales/Marketing:		Liberal Arts:		Information Sys.:		Professionals:		Tech./Scientific:	
Mgmt. Trainees:		Marketing Pros.:		Gen. Writing/Editing:		Info. Mgmt.:	Y	Finance/Acct.:	Y	Engineers, Elec.:	
Experienced Mgmt.:	Y	Retail Sales:		Tech. Writing:		Software Dev.:		Law:	Y	Engineers, Other:	
Int'l Business:	Y	Comm./Industrial:		Graphic Arts/Photog.:		Hardware Dev.:		HR/Other:	Y	Health/Lab:	
MBA Grads:	Y	Sales Trainees:		Music:		Consulting/Other:		Training:		Science/Research:	
		Advertising Pros.:		Broadcasting:				Health Care:		Petroleum/Chem.:	
				Other:				Consulting:		Math/Other:	

TYPES OF BUSINESS:

Real Estate Investment Trust
Manufactured Home & RV Communities

BRANDS/DIVISIONS/AFFILIATES:

MHC Operating Limited Partnership

CONTACTS:

Note: Officers with more than one job title may be intentionally listed here more than once.

Thomas P. Heneghan, CEO
Thomas P. Heneghan, Pres.
Michael B. Berman, CFO/Exec. VP
Seth Rosenberg, Sr. VP-Sales & Mktg.
Barb Itter, VP-Human Resources
Ellen Kelleher, Corp. Sec./Exec. VP
Roger A. Maynard, Exec. VP-Asset Management
Ellen Kelleher, Exec. VP-Property Management
Samuel Zell, Chmn.

Phone: 312-279-1400	**Fax:** 312-279-1710
Toll-Free:	
Address: 2 N. Riverside Plz., Ste. 800, Chicago, IL 60606 US	

GROWTH PLANS/SPECIAL FEATURES:

Equity Lifestyle Properties, Inc. (ELS) is an integrated real estate investment trust (REIT) that owns and operates communities of developed residential sites as well as recreational vehicle (RV) resorts. The company primarily operates through MHC Operating Limited Partnership. The firm owns or has an interest in 307 properties in 27 U.S. states and the Canadian province of British Columbia, consisting of about 111,000 residential sites. The heaviest concentrations of these properties are located in Florida, California and Arizona, with 86 properties, 48 properties and 37 properties, respectively. Additional U.S. sites are located in Texas, Pennsylvania, Washington, Colorado, Oregon, North Carolina, Delaware, New York, Nevada, Virginia, Wisconsin, Indiana, Maine, Illinois, Massachusetts, New Jersey, Michigan, South Carolina, New Hampshire, Ohio, Tennessee, Utah, Alabama and Kentucky. These communities are designed and improved for the placement of detached, single-family manufactured homes that are produced off-site, then installed and set on residential sites within the community. The owner of each home leases the site on which it is located, while the firm handles property infrastructure issues, such as water, sewage and power. Sites typically contain centralized entrances, paved streets, curbs, gutters, parkways, clubhouses for social activities and recreation, swimming pools, shuffleboard courts, tennis courts, laundry facilities and cable television service, among other amenities. Each community is designed to attract, and is marketed to, retirees, empty-nesters, families or first-time homeowners. The company focuses on owning properties in or near large metropolitan markets, as well as popular retirement and vacation destinations.

ELS offers its employees medical coverage, life and disability insurance, a 401(k) plan and a bonus program, among other benefits.

FINANCIALS:

Sales and profits are in thousands of dollars—add 000 to get the full amount. 2010 Note: Financial information for 2010 was not available for all companies at press time.

2010 Sales: $511,361	2010 Profits: $38,354	**U.S. Stock Ticker: ELS**
2009 Sales: $503,221	2009 Profits: $34,005	**Int'l Ticker:**
2008 Sales: $463,586	2008 Profits: $18,303	Int'l Exchange:
2007 Sales: $376,154	2007 Profits: $32,102	Employees: 3,600 Fiscal Year Ends: 12/31
2006 Sales: $346,383	2006 Profits: $16,632	Parent Company:

SALARIES/BENEFITS:

Pension Plan:	ESOP Stock Plan:	Profit Sharing:	Top Exec. Salary: $382,454	Bonus: $573,681
Savings Plan: Y	Stock Purch. Plan:		Second Exec. Salary: $311,428	Bonus: $370,210

OTHER THOUGHTS:

Apparent Women Officers or Directors: 3
Hot Spot for Advancement for Women/Minorities: Y

LOCATIONS: ("Y" = Yes)

West:	Southwest:	Midwest:	Southeast:	Northeast:	International:
Y	Y	Y	Y	Y	Y

Sales, profits and employees may be estimates. Financial information, benefits and other data can change quickly and may vary from those stated here.

ERNST & YOUNG LLP

www.ey.com

Industry Group Code: 5412

Management:		**Sales/Marketing:**		**Liberal Arts:**		**Information Sys.:**		**Professionals:**		**Tech./Scientific:**	
Mgmt. Trainees:	Y	Marketing Pros.:	Y	Gen. Writing/Editing:	Y	Info. Mgmt.:	Y	Finance/Acct.:	Y	Engineers, Elec.:	
Experienced Mgmt.:	Y	Retail Sales:		Tech. Writing:	Y	Software Dev.:	Y	Law:	Y	Engineers, Other:	
Int'l Business:	Y	Comm./Industrial:	Y	Graphic Arts/Photog.:	Y	Hardware Dev.:		HR/Other:	Y	Health/Lab:	
MBA Grads:	Y	Sales Trainees:		Music:		Consulting/Other:	Y	Training:	Y	Science/Research:	
		Advertising Pros.:	Y	Broadcasting:				Health Care:		Petroleum/Chem.:	
				Other:	Y			Consulting:	Y	Math/Other:	

TYPES OF BUSINESS:

Accounting
Risk Management
Tax Preparation Services
Human Resources Management
IT Services
Transaction Support Services
Industry Publications

BRANDS/DIVISIONS/AFFILIATES:

Entrepreneur of the Year Award
Ernst & Young Online
Ernst & Young International
ISA Consulting, LLC

CONTACTS: *Note: Officers with more than one job title may be intentionally listed here more than once.*

James S. Turley, CEO
Gary Belske, COO
Nancy Altobello, Vice Chmn.-People
Steve Howe, Area Managing Partner-Americas
Kate Barton, Vice Chmn.-Tax Svcs.
Tom Hough, Vice Chmn.-Assurance Svcs.
Bryan Segedi, Vice Chmn.-Advisory Svcs.
James S. Turley, Chmn.

Phone: 212-773-3000 **Fax:** 212-773-6350
Toll-Free:
Address: 5 Times Sq., New York, NY 10036-6530 US

GROWTH PLANS/SPECIAL FEATURES:

Ernst & Young, LLP, the U.S. branch of the global accounting firm Ernst & Young International, is a provider of audit, tax, transaction and risk-related services. The firm has offices throughout the U.S. and Puerto Rico. In addition to providing accounting advisory and tax preparation services, the firm offers a number of complementary services such as human resource programs and online/IT services. Ernst & Young serves companies in a number of industry sectors, including the financial services, automotive, consumer products, oil and gas, health care, technology, mining and metals, real estate, retail, communications and entertainment industries. In addition, the company publishes a variety of industry-specific publications and studies providing expertise in quickly-changing markets. Ernst & Young Online is a personalized client portal that provides news and information relating to specific customer needs, a reference library and links to other web resources, as well as access to Ernst & Young staff for answers to direct questions. Additionally, the company oversees the Entrepreneur of the Year Award, a prestigious award given each year for exceptional business acumen and ability. Clients of the firm have included Best Buy, British Petroleum, Coca-Cola, FedEx, Google, Lockheed Martin, McDonald's, Target Corporation and Whole Foods Markets, among others. In April 2011, Ernst & Young, LLP acquired Philadelphia-based consultancy firm ISA Consulting, LLC.

Employees are offered a wide of variety of benefits including medical, dental and vision plans; dependent day care and health care reimbursement accounts. Additional benefits include a health savings account; family medical and parental leave; adoption assistance; a lactation program; a 529 college savings plan; personal financial planning; college coaching for both parents and students; back-up child and adult care services; commuter benefits; and employee discounts at various stores. Moreover, a mortgage referral program; bereavement benefits; business travel accident and life insurance; certification reimbursement and bonuses; higher education matching gifts; and membership in business, professional and civic organizations are also offered.

FINANCIALS: **Sales and profits are in thousands of dollars—add 000 to get the full amount. 2010 Note: Financial information for 2010 was not available for all companies at press time.**

2010 Sales: $8,373,000 | 2010 Profits: $
2009 Sales: $8,647,000 | 2009 Profits: $
2008 Sales: $9,152,000 | 2008 Profits: $
2007 Sales: $ | 2007 Profits: $
2006 Sales: $ | 2006 Profits: $

U.S. Stock Ticker: Subsidiary
Int'l Ticker:
Int'l Exchange:
Employees: 40,318 Fiscal Year Ends: 6/30
Parent Company: ERNST & YOUNG INTERNATIONAL

SALARIES/BENEFITS:

Pension Plan: ESOP Stock Plan: Profit Sharing: Top Exec. Salary: $ Bonus: $
Savings Plan: Stock Purch. Plan: Second Exec. Salary: $ Bonus: $

OTHER THOUGHTS:

Apparent Women Officers or Directors: 6
Hot Spot for Advancement for Women/Minorities: Y

LOCATIONS: ("Y" = Yes)

West:	Southwest:	Midwest:	Southeast:	Northeast:	International:
Y	Y	Y	Y	Y	Y

Sales, profits and employees may be estimates. Financial information, benefits and other data can change quickly and may vary from those stated here.

ESTEE LAUDER COMPANIES INC (THE)

www.elcompanies.com

Industry Group Code: 325620

Management:		Sales/Marketing:		Liberal Arts:		Information Sys.:		Professionals:		Tech./Scientific:	
Mgmt. Trainees:	Y	Marketing Pros.:	Y	Gen. Writing/Editing:	Y	Info. Mgmt.:	Y	Finance/Acct.:	Y	Engineers, Elec.:	
Experienced Mgmt.:	Y	Retail Sales:	Y	Tech. Writing:	Y	Software Dev.:	Y	Law:	Y	Engineers, Other:	Y
Int'l Business:	Y	Comm./Industrial:	Y	Graphic Arts/Photog.:	Y	Hardware Dev.:		HR/Other:	Y	Health/Lab:	
MBA Grads:	Y	Sales Trainees:	Y	Music:		Consulting/Other:		Training:	Y	Science/Research:	Y
		Advertising Pros.:	Y	Broadcasting:				Health Care:		Petroleum/Chem.:	Y
				Other:	Y			Consulting:		Math/Other:	

TYPES OF BUSINESS:

Cosmetics & Toiletries Manufacturing
Cosmetic & Fragrance Sales
Retail Cosmetics Stores
Hair Care Products

BRANDS/DIVISIONS/AFFILIATES:

Aveda
La Mer
Clinique
Prescriptives
Bobbie Brown
AERIN
Origins
Smashbox Beauty Cosmetics, Inc.

CONTACTS: *Note: Officers with more than one job title may be intentionally listed here more than once.*

Fabrizio Freda, CEO
Fabrizio Freda, Pres.
Richard W. Kunes, CFO/Exec. VP
Amy DiGeso, Exec. VP-Global Human Resources
Harvey Gedeon, Exec. VP-Global R&D
Harvey Gedeon, Exec. VP-Corp. Prod. Innovation & Package Dev.
Sara E. Moss, General Counsel/Exec. VP
Alexandra C. Trower, Exec. VP-Global Comm.
John Demsey, Group Pres.
Evelyn H. Lauder, Sr. Corp. VP
William P. Lauder, Chmn.
Cedric Prouve, Group Pres., Int'l
Gregory Polcer, Exec. VP-Global Supply Chain

Phone: 212-572-4200	**Fax:** 212-572-3941
Toll-Free:	
Address: 767 5th Ave., New York, NY 10153 US	

GROWTH PLANS/SPECIAL FEATURES:

The Estee Lauder Companies, Inc. is a global manufacturer and marketer of skin care, cosmetics, fragrance and hair care products. The company's products are sold in over 150 countries and territories under brand names such as Estee Lauder, Aramis, Clinique, Lab Series, Origins, M.A.C., Bobbi Brown, La Mer, Aveda, Jo Malone, Bumble and bumble, Darphin, American Beauty, Flirt!, Good Skin and Grassroots. The firm is also the global licensee for fragrances and cosmetics sold under the Tommy Hilfiger, Donna Karan, Michael Kors, Sean John, Missoni, Daisy Fuentes and Tom Ford brand names. Estee Lauder sells its products principally through 30,000 points of sale including upscale department stores, specialty retailers, upscale perfumeries and pharmacies and prestige salons and spas, as well as freestanding company-owned stores and spas, authorized retailer web sites, stores on cruise ships, television direct marketing, in-flight and duty-free shops and self-select outlets. Estee Lauder has 14 manufacturing factories worldwide and six principle research and development facilities. The founding Lauder family still controls 86.8% of the company's voting shares. The firm operates on a global basis, with over half of its sales generated outside the U.S. Skin care products currently account for roughly 42% of the company's sales; makeup products, 38%; fragrance products, 14%; and hair care items, 5%. In mid 2010, the company acquired Smashbox Beauty Cosmetics, Inc. In April 2011, Estee Lauder partnered with new firm AERIN, LLC to market new luxury lifestyle brand AERIN. In June 2011, the firm opened a new innovation center in Shanghai, China.

FINANCIALS: **Sales and profits are in thousands of dollars—add 000 to get the full amount. 2010 Note: Financial information for 2010 was not available for all companies at press time.**

2010 Sales: $7,795,800	2010 Profits: $478,300	**U.S. Stock Ticker: EL**
2009 Sales: $7,323,800	2009 Profits: $218,400	**Int'l Ticker:**
2008 Sales: $7,910,800	2008 Profits: $473,800	Int'l Exchange:
2007 Sales: $7,037,500	2007 Profits: $449,200	Employees: 31,200 Fiscal Year Ends: 6/30
2006 Sales: $6,463,800	2006 Profits: $244,200	Parent Company:

SALARIES/BENEFITS:

Pension Plan:	ESOP Stock Plan:	Profit Sharing:	Top Exec. Salary: $1,500,000	Bonus: $3,648,950
Savings Plan: Y	Stock Purch. Plan:		Second Exec. Salary: $1,500,000	Bonus: $3,648,950

OTHER THOUGHTS:

Apparent Women Officers or Directors: 10
Hot Spot for Advancement for Women/Minorities: Y

LOCATIONS: ("Y" = Yes)

West:	Southwest:	Midwest:	Southeast:	Northeast:	International:
Y				Y	

EXELON CORPORATION

www.exeloncorp.com

Industry Group Code: 221

Management:		Sales/Marketing:		Liberal Arts:		Information Sys.:		Professionals:		Tech./Scientific:	
Mgmt. Trainees:	Y	Marketing Pros.:	Y	Gen. Writing/Editing:	Y	Info. Mgmt.:	Y	Finance/Acct.:	Y	Engineers, Elec.:	Y
Experienced Mgmt.:	Y	Retail Sales:		Tech. Writing:	Y	Software Dev.:	Y	Law:	Y	Engineers, Other:	Y
Int'l Business:		Comm./Industrial:	Y	Graphic Arts/Photog.:	Y	Hardware Dev.:		HR/Other:	Y	Health/Lab:	
MBA Grads:	Y	Sales Trainees:		Music:		Consulting/Other:		Training:	Y	Science/Research:	
		Advertising Pros.:	Y	Broadcasting:				Health Care:		Petroleum/Chem.:	Y
				Other:				Consulting:		Math/Other:	

TYPES OF BUSINESS:

Utilities-Electricity & Natural Gas
Nuclear Generation
Energy Marketing

BRANDS/DIVISIONS/AFFILIATES:

Commonwealth Edison Company
PECO Energy Company
Exelon Generation Company LLC
Exelon Business Services Company
Wolf Hollow
Exelon Transmission Company
Constellation Energy Group
John Deere Renewables

CONTACTS: *Note: Officers with more than one job title may be intentionally listed here more than once.*

John W. Rowe, CEO
Christopher M. Crane, COO
Christopher M. Crane, Pres.
Matthew F. Helzinger, CFO/Sr. VP
Ruth Ann M. Gillis, Chief Diversity Officer
Ruth Ann M. Gillis, Chief Admin. Officer/Exec. VP
Stacy Frank, VP-Investor Rel.
William A. Von Hoene, Jr., Exec. VP-Finance & Legal
Frank Clark, CEO/Chmn.-ComEd
Denis P. O'Brien, Pres./CEO-PECO Energy
Sonny Garg, Pres., Exelon Power
Ruth Ann M. Gillis, Pres., Exelon Bus. Services Co.
John W. Rowe, Chmn.
Steven P. Breeding, Sr., Exec. Dir.-APAC Bus. Dev.

Phone: 312-394-7398 **Fax:**
Toll-Free: 800-483-3220
Address: 10 S. Dearborn St., 48th Fl., Chicago, IL 60680-5398 US

GROWTH PLANS/SPECIAL FEATURES:

Exelon Corporation is a utility services company. The firm operates through subsidiaries Exelon Generation Company LLC; Exelon Transmission Company; Commonwealth Edison Company (ComEd); and PECO Energy Company. Exelon Generation operates in three business units: Exelon Power, Exelon Generation and Power Team. The business consists of its owned and contracted electric generating facilities; its wholesale energy marketing operations; and its competitive retail supply operations. The subsidiary owns generation assets, which include nuclear, fossil, renewable and hydropower, with an aggregate net capacity of nearly 25.6 gigawatts (GW). ComEd's energy delivery business consists of the purchase and regulated retail sale of electricity and the provision of distribution and transmission services to over 3.8 million retail, commercial and industrial customers in northern Illinois. The subsidiary's retail service territory has an area of roughly 11,300 square miles and an estimated population of 9 million. PECO's energy delivery business consists of the purchase and regulated retail sale of electricity; and the provision of distribution and transmission services to retail customers in southeastern Pennsylvania, including Philadelphia, as well as surrounding counties. The subsidiary's retail service territory has an area of about 2,100 square miles. PECO delivers electricity to roughly 1.6 million customers and natural gas to approximately 490,000 customers. In addition to Exelon Corporation's primary segments, subsidiary Exelon Business Services Company provides financial, human resource, legal, IT, supply management and corporate governance services to Exelon Corporation and its subsidiaries. In December 2010, Exelon Corporation acquired wind power firm John Deere Renewables. In April 2011, the firm agreed to buy utility operator and electricity company, Constellation Energy Group. In August 2011, the company acquired combined-cycle natural gas-fired power plant Wolf Hollow.

FINANCIALS: **Sales and profits are in thousands of dollars—add 000 to get the full amount. 2010 Note: Financial information for 2010 was not available for all companies at press time.**

2010 Sales: $18,644,000	2010 Profits: $2,563,000
2009 Sales: $17,318,000	2009 Profits: $2,707,000
2008 Sales: $18,859,000	2008 Profits: $2,737,000
2007 Sales: $18,916,000	2007 Profits: $2,736,000
2006 Sales: $15,655,000	2006 Profits: $1,592,000

U.S. Stock Ticker: EXC
Int'l Ticker:
Int'l Exchange:
Employees: 19,214 Fiscal Year Ends: 12/31
Parent Company:

SALARIES/BENEFITS:

Pension Plan:	ESOP Stock Plan:	Profit Sharing:	Top Exec. Salary: $1,475,000	Bonus: $2,474,313
Savings Plan: Y	Stock Purch. Plan: Y		Second Exec. Salary: $825,000	Bonus: $1,132,313

OTHER THOUGHTS:

Apparent Women Officers or Directors: 5
Hot Spot for Advancement for Women/Minorities: Y

LOCATIONS: ("Y" = Yes)

West:	Southwest:	Midwest:	Southeast:	Northeast:	International:
Y	Y	Y		Y	

EXPEDIA INC

www.expedia.com

Industry Group Code: 5615E

Management:		Sales/Marketing:		Liberal Arts:		Information Sys.:		Professionals:		Tech./Scientific:	
Mgmt. Trainees:	Y	Marketing Pros.:	Y	Gen. Writing/Editing:	Y	Info. Mgmt.:	Y	Finance/Acct.:	Y	Engineers, Elec.:	Y
Experienced Mgmt.:	Y	Retail Sales:		Tech. Writing:	Y	Software Dev.:	Y	Law:	Y	Engineers, Other:	
Int'l Business:	Y	Comm./Industrial:	Y	Graphic Arts/Photog.:	Y	Hardware Dev.:		HR/Other:	Y	Health/Lab:	
MBA Grads:	Y	Sales Trainees:	Y	Music:		Consulting/Other:		Training:	Y	Science/Research:	
		Advertising Pros.:	Y	Broadcasting:				Health Care:		Petroleum/Chem.:	
				Other:	Y			Consulting:		Math/Other:	

TYPES OF BUSINESS:

Online Travel Services
Online Reservations
Corporate Travel Services
Vacation Packages
Retail Travel Services Kiosks
Destination Activities & Tours
Online Travel Information

BRANDS/DIVISIONS/AFFILIATES:

Hotwire Inc
eLong
Venere
Hotels.com LP
Classic Vacations
Expedia Local Expert
TripAdvisor
Egencia

CONTACTS: *Note: Officers with more than one job title may be intentionally listed here more than once.*

Dara Khosrowshahi, CEO
Dara Khosrowshahi, Pres.
Michael Adler, CFO/Exec. VP
Edmond Mesrobian, CTO
Burke Norton, General Counsel/Exec. VP/Corp. Sec.
Mark Okerstrom, Sr. VP-Corp. Dev.
Patricia L. Zuccotti, Chief Acct. Officer/Sr. VP
Dhiren Fonseca, Co-Pres., Partner Services Group
Gary Fritz, Co-Pres., Partner Services Group
Clem Bason, Pres., Hotwire Group
Stephen Kaufer, Pres./CEO-TripAdvisor.com
Barry Diller, Chmn.
Eric Grosse, Pres., Expedia Worldwide

Phone: 425-679-7200 **Fax:** 425-679-7240
Toll-Free: 800-397-3342
Address: 333 108th Ave. NE, Bellevue, WA 98004 US

GROWTH PLANS/SPECIAL FEATURES:

Expedia, Inc. is an online travel service offering travel shopping and reservation services, publishing schedules, pricing and availability information for numerous airlines, lodging properties, car rental companies, cruise lines and multiple-destination service providers, including restaurants, attractions and tours. The Expedia brand web sites, for both U.S. (Expedia.com) and international travelers, offer a large variety of travel products and services available directly to travelers. Its TripAdvisor Media Network (at www.TripAdvisor.com) is a comprehensive online travel search engine and directory that aggregates traveler opinions and articles about cities, hotels, restaurants and other activities at many diverse destinations. The site's search results also provide links to the websites of TripAdvisor's travel partners through which travelers can make related travel arrangements. Within the TripAdvisor Media Network are several travel media content providers including AirfareWatchDog.com, BookingBuddy.com, CruiseCritic.com, Flipkey.com, and VirtualTourist.com. Expedia receives a commission from travel suppliers for its services as an agent. It also operates as a merchant by directly contracting from suppliers and selling discounted products directly to the consumer. The firm owns Hotels.com, which provides a full portfolio of hotel contacts around the world, and Hotwire.com, a web site that offers travelers discount airfare. Other subsidiaries include Venere, a resource for European hotels; Classic Vacations, a premium vacation packaging agency; eLong, an online travel service based in Beijing, China; Egencia, a travel management service for corporate customers; Expedia CruiseShipCeneters, a network of over 130 cruise vacation retail locations; and Expedia Local Expert, which specializes in local tours and attractions. In late 2010, Expedia acquired mobile travel applications seller Mobiata. In March 2011, the company and AirAsia agreed to form a joint venture to operate the two companies' brands in several Asian markets. In April 2011, the firm announced its plans to spin off TripAdvisor into a free-standing company.

FINANCIALS: **Sales and profits are in thousands of dollars—add 000 to get the full amount. 2010 Note: Financial information for 2010 was not available for all companies at press time.**

2010 Sales: $3,348,109	2010 Profits: $425,560	**U.S. Stock Ticker: EXPE**
2009 Sales: $2,955,426	2009 Profits: $303,623	**Int'l Ticker:**
2008 Sales: $2,937,013	2008 Profits: $-2,429,000	Int'l Exchange:
2007 Sales: $2,665,332	2007 Profits: $295,864	Employees: 8,900 Fiscal Year Ends: 12/31
2006 Sales: $2,237,586	2006 Profits: $244,934	Parent Company:

SALARIES/BENEFITS:

Pension Plan:	ESOP Stock Plan:	Profit Sharing:	Top Exec. Salary: $1,000,000	Bonus: $2,250,000
Savings Plan: Y	Stock Purch. Plan:		Second Exec. Salary: $465,000	Bonus: $2,000,000

OTHER THOUGHTS:

Apparent Women Officers or Directors: 1
Hot Spot for Advancement for Women/Minorities:

LOCATIONS: ("Y" = Yes)

West:	Southwest:	Midwest:	Southeast:	Northeast:	International:
Y	Y	Y	Y	Y	Y

EXPERIAN AMERICAS

www.experian.com

Industry Group Code: 561450

Management:		Sales/Marketing:		Liberal Arts:		Information Sys.:		Professionals:		Tech./Scientific:	
Mgmt. Trainees:	Y	Marketing Pros.:	Y	Gen. Writing/Editing:	Y	Info. Mgmt.:	Y	Finance/Acct.:	Y	Engineers, Elec.:	
Experienced Mgmt.:	Y	Retail Sales:		Tech. Writing:	Y	Software Dev.:	Y	Law:	Y	Engineers, Other:	
Int'l Business:		Comm./Industrial:	Y	Graphic Arts/Photog.:	Y	Hardware Dev.:		HR/Other:	Y	Health/Lab:	
MBA Grads:	Y	Sales Trainees:	Y	Music:		Consulting/Other:		Training:	Y	Science/Research:	
		Advertising Pros.:	Y	Broadcasting:				Health Care:		Petroleum/Chem.:	
				Other:	Y			Consulting:		Math/Other:	Y

TYPES OF BUSINESS:

Credit Bureau
Customer Relationship Software & Solutions
Marketing Software & Solutions
Business & Consumer Internet Sites
Online Services
Risk Management Services, Automotive

BRANDS/DIVISIONS/AFFILIATES:

Experian Group Limited
Prospect Navigator
Credit Migration Solutions
Experian PLC
PriceGrabber.com
BankruptcyPredict
FreeCreditReport.com
LowerMyBills.com

CONTACTS: *Note: Officers with more than one job title may be intentionally listed here more than once.*

Victor Nichols, CEO-Experian North America
Don Robert, CEO-Experian plc
Kerry Williams, Pres., Credit Svcs. & Decisions Analytics
Paul Brooks, CFO-Experian plc

Phone: 714-830-7000 | **Fax:** 714-830-2449
Toll-Free: 888-397-3742
Address: 475 Anton Blvd., Costa Mesa, CA 92626 US

GROWTH PLANS/SPECIAL FEATURES:

Experian Americas is a subsidiary of Experian plc, formerly Experian Group Limited. Experian Americas is a leading credit-reporting agency in the U.S. It also helps organizations find, develop and manage customer relationships by providing information, decision-making solutions and processing services. Experian Americas operates through four segments: credit services, decision analytics, marketing services and interactive. The credit services unit provides clients with solutions that optimize processes in acquiring new customers (Prospect Navigator), maximize customer relationships (Credit Migration Solutions), improve collections (Credit Profile Report), prevent fraud losses (Red Flag Rules), analyze critical data (BankruptcyPredict) and improve business-to-business results (business credit reports). The decision analytics unit is closely related to the credit services segment and provides analytical software and services to help clients optimize their lending strategies. The marketing services unit provides customer acquisition, retention and growth and marketing strategy services to the advertising and media, automotive, banking, catalog, retail, financial services, consumer products and travel and hospitality markets. Finally, the interactive segment offers consumers access to their credit histories through various web tools, including CreditExpert, FreeCreditReport.com, FreeCreditScore.com and LowerMyBills.com. Experian Americas also offers risk management, identity theft protection through ProtectMyID, and customer acquisition and market reporting services tailored to the automotive industry. Through PriceGrabber.com, the company allows consumers to compare prices from over 12,000 merchants online.

Parent Experian offers its employees health, dental and vision care plans; flexible spending accounts; education assistance; credit union membership; employee assistance; referral bonuses; employee discounts; adoption assistance; and fitness reimbursement.

FINANCIALS: **Sales and profits are in thousands of dollars—add 000 to get the full amount. 2010 Note: Financial information for 2010 was not available for all companies at press time.**

2010 Sales: $2,254,000 | 2010 Profits: $
2009 Sales: $2,060,000 | 2009 Profits: $
2008 Sales: $2,000,000 | 2008 Profits: $
2007 Sales: $1,994,000 | 2007 Profits: $
2006 Sales: $1,804,000 | 2006 Profits: $

U.S. Stock Ticker: Subsidiary
Int'l Ticker:
Int'l Exchange:
Employees: 5,553 Fiscal Year Ends: 3/31
Parent Company: EXPERIAN PLC

SALARIES/BENEFITS:

Pension Plan: | ESOP Stock Plan: | Profit Sharing: | Top Exec. Salary: $ | Bonus: $
Savings Plan: Y | Stock Purch. Plan: Y | | Second Exec. Salary: $ | Bonus: $

OTHER THOUGHTS:

Apparent Women Officers or Directors:
Hot Spot for Advancement for Women/Minorities:

LOCATIONS: ("Y" = Yes)

West:	Southwest:	Midwest:	Southeast:	Northeast:	International:
Y	Y	Y	Y	Y	

EXPRESS SCRIPTS INC

www.express-scripts.com

Industry Group Code: 522320A

Management:		Sales/Marketing:		Liberal Arts:		Information Sys.:		Professionals:		Tech./Scientific:	
Mgmt. Trainees:	Y	Marketing Pros.:	Y	Gen. Writing/Editing:	Y	Info. Mgmt.:	Y	Finance/Acct.:	Y	Engineers, Elec.:	
Experienced Mgmt.:	Y	Retail Sales:		Tech. Writing:	Y	Software Dev.:	Y	Law:	Y	Engineers, Other:	
Int'l Business:	Y	Comm./Industrial:	Y	Graphic Arts/Photog.:	Y	Hardware Dev.:		HR/Other:	Y	Health/Lab:	
MBA Grads:	Y	Sales Trainees:		Music:		Consulting/Other:		Training:	Y	Science/Research:	
		Advertising Pros.:	Y	Broadcasting:				Health Care:	Y	Petroleum/Chem.:	
				Other:				Consulting:		Math/Other:	

TYPES OF BUSINESS:

Pharmacy Benefits Management
Mail & Internet Pharmacies
Formulary Management
Integrated Drug & Medical Data Analysis
Market Research Programs
Medical Information Management
Workers' Compensation Programs
Informed-Decision Counseling

BRANDS/DIVISIONS/AFFILIATES:

CuraScript Specialty Distribution
FreedomFP
HealthBridge
ConnectYourCare
DrugDigest.org
NextRx
Rx Outreach

CONTACTS: *Note: Officers with more than one job title may be intentionally listed here more than once.*

George Paz, CEO
Patrick McNamee, COO/Exec. VP
George Paz, Pres.
Jeffrey Hall, CFO/Exec. VP
Edward Ignaczak, Exec. VP-Mktg. & Sales
Steve Miller, Chief Medical Officer/Sr. VP
Gary Wimberly, CIO/Sr. VP
Keith Ebling, General Counsel/Exec. VP/Sec.
Larry Zarin, Sr. VP-Mktg. & Corp. Comm.
George Paz, Chmn.
Agnes Rey-Giraud, Pres., Int'l Oper.
Susan Lang, Chief Supply Chain Officer/Sr. VP

Phone: 314-996-0900	**Fax:** 314-770-0303
Toll-Free:	
Address: 1 Express Way, St. Louis, MO 63121 US	

GROWTH PLANS/SPECIAL FEATURES:

Express Scripts, Inc. is one of the largest independent pharmacy benefit managers in the U.S. The firm provides pharmacy service and pharmacy benefit plan design consultation for clients including HMOs, health insurers, third-party administrators, employers, unions and government health care plans. The company operates in two segments: pharmacy benefit management (PBM) and emerging markets. The PBM division offers retail network pharmacy management and retail drug card programs; home delivery and specialty pharmacy services; patient care contact centers; electronic claims processing and drug utilization review; assistance programs for low-income patients; pharmacogenomics medication therapy and safety; and drug formulary management, compliance and therapy management programs. It dispenses drugs to patients from three home delivery fulfillment pharmacies. The company's public website, www.DrugDigest.org, seeks to aid consumers in making informed decisions about using medications. Express Scripts' emerging markets segment includes the following programs: CuraScript Specialty Distribution, which offers specialty medical supplies and pharmaceutical distribution directly to providers and clinics; FreedomFP, which provides fertility services to both providers and patients; HealthBridge, which offers outsourced distribution and verification services to pharmaceutical manufacturers; and ConnectYourCare, which offers consumer-directed healthcare solutions. The segment also verifies practitioner licensure and offers healthcare account administration/ implementation of consumer-directed healthcare solutions. Recent acquisitions include NextRx, the pharmacy benefits management unit of WellPoint, Inc. In October 2010, the company spun-off its Rx Outreach division to create an independent, non-profit organization that offers prescription drug access to low-income, uninsured U.S. families and individuals. In November 2010, it established Express Scripts Specialty Benefit Services, a comprehensive specialty benefits organization. In July 2011, the company agreed to buy pharmacy benefit manager Medco Health Solutions, Inc. for $29.1 billion.

Employees are offered life, disability, health and dental insurance; adoption assistance; employee assistance programs; and paid time off.

FINANCIALS: **Sales and profits are in thousands of dollars—add 000 to get the full amount. 2010 Note: Financial information for 2010 was not available for all companies at press time.**

2010 Sales: $44,973,200	2010 Profits: $1,204,600
2009 Sales: $24,722,300	2009 Profits: $826,600
2008 Sales: $21,941,200	2008 Profits: $775,900
2007 Sales: $21,824,000	2007 Profits: $567,800
2006 Sales: $21,562,600	2006 Profits: $474,400

U.S. Stock Ticker: ESRX
Int'l Ticker:
Int'l Exchange:
Employees: 83,600 Fiscal Year Ends: 12/31
Parent Company:

SALARIES/BENEFITS:

Pension Plan:	ESOP Stock Plan:	Profit Sharing:	Top Exec. Salary: $971,692	Bonus: $2,528,500
Savings Plan: Y	Stock Purch. Plan: Y		Second Exec. Salary: $507,846	Bonus: $714,000

OTHER THOUGHTS:

Apparent Women Officers or Directors: 2
Hot Spot for Advancement for Women/Minorities:

LOCATIONS: ("Y" = Yes)

West:	Southwest:	Midwest:	Southeast:	Northeast:	International:
Y	Y	Y	Y	Y	Y

EXTERRAN HOLDINGS INC

www.exterran.com

Industry Group Code: 213112

Management:		Sales/Marketing:		Liberal Arts:		Information Sys.:		Professionals:		Tech./Scientific:	
Mgmt. Trainees:		Marketing Pros.:	Y	Gen. Writing/Editing:		Info. Mgmt.:	Y	Finance/Acct.:	Y	Engineers, Elec.:	Y
Experienced Mgmt.:		Retail Sales:		Tech. Writing:	Y	Software Dev.:		Law:	Y	Engineers, Other:	Y
Int'l Business:	Y	Comm./Industrial:	Y	Graphic Arts/Photog.:		Hardware Dev.:		HR/Other:	Y	Health/Lab:	
MBA Grads:	Y	Sales Trainees:		Music:		Consulting/Other:		Training:		Science/Research:	
		Advertising Pros.:	Y	Broadcasting:				Health Care:		Petroleum/Chem.:	Y
				Other:				Consulting:		Math/Other:	

TYPES OF BUSINESS:

Manufacturing-Natural Gas Compression Equipment
Oil & Gas Treatment Facilities
Compressed Natural Gas Fueling Stations
Power Generation Facilities

BRANDS/DIVISIONS/AFFILIATES:

Hanover Compressor Company
Exterran Partners LP
Universal Compression Holdings Inc

CONTACTS:

Note: Officers with more than one job title may be intentionally listed here more than once.

Ernie L. Danner, CEO
Ernie L. Danner, Pres.
J. Michael Anderson, CFO/Sr. VP
J. Michael Anderson, Chief of Staff
Donald C. Wayne, General Counsel/Sr. VP/Sec.
Daniel K. Schlanger, VP-Oper. Svcs.
Kenneth R. Bickett, VP-Finance & Acct.
David Miller, VP
D. Bradley Childers, Pres., North America Oper.
Gordon T. Hall, Chmn.
Joe Kishkill, Pres., Eastern Hemisphere Oper.

Phone: 281-836-7000	**Fax:**
Toll-Free:	
Address: 16666 Northchase Dr., Houston, TX 77060 US	

GROWTH PLANS/SPECIAL FEATURES:

Exterran Holdings, Inc. is a provider of full-service natural gas compression. The firm was formed from the merger of Universal Compression Holdings, Inc., and Hanover Compressor Company. The company's products and services consist of natural gas compression equipment and facilities, such as compression stations; oil and gas production facilities; compressed natural gas (CNG) fueling stations; power generation facilities; and gas plants that can perform fractionation, gas liquids recovery, dewpoint control, treating and dehydration. Exterran Holdings operates in three segments: fabrication, contract operations and aftermarket services. The firm's fabrication operations, which account for roughly 43.1% of revenues, include the fabrication and sale of equipment, as well as engineering, procurement and construction services for refinery/petrochemical facilities, tank farms and desalination plants. Exterran Holdings' contract operations unit (44% of revenues) provides services through approximately 10,433 U.S. and 1,164 international natural gas compression units with a combined aggregate capacity of roughly 5.55 million horsepower. The company's aftermarket unit (12.9% of revenues) sells parts and components; and provides operations, maintenance, overhaul and reconfiguration services. Primary aftermarket clients are owners of production, gas treating, compression and oilfield power generation equipment. The firm's 34%-owned indirect subsidiary Exterran Partners, L.P. operates a fleet of approximately 3,574 compressor units comprising approximately 1.366 million horsepower. Exterran Holdings operates in over 30 countries throughout the Americas, the Middle East, Africa, Australia and Europe. In August 2010, the company sold another 580 compressor units and related contracts to Exterran Partners.

Exterran Holdings offer employees benefits such as life, AD&D, medical, dental and vision insurance; education assistance; paid time off; employee assistance plans; a 401(k); and flexible spending accounts.

FINANCIALS:

Sales and profits are in thousands of dollars—add 000 to get the full amount. 2010 Note: Financial information for 2010 was not available for all companies at press time.

2010 Sales: $2,461,533	2010 Profits: $-101,825	**U.S. Stock Ticker: EXH**
2009 Sales: $2,715,601	2009 Profits: $-549,407	**Int'l Ticker:**
2008 Sales: $3,024,119	2008 Profits: $-947,349	Int'l Exchange:
2007 Sales: $2,540,485	2007 Profits: $34,569	Employees: 10,100 Fiscal Year Ends: 12/31
2006 Sales: $1,593,321	2006 Profits: $86,523	Parent Company:

SALARIES/BENEFITS:

Pension Plan:	ESOP Stock Plan:	Profit Sharing:	Top Exec. Salary: $450,000	Bonus: $303,750
Savings Plan: Y	Stock Purch. Plan:		Second Exec. Salary: $355,000	Bonus: $175,000

OTHER THOUGHTS:

Apparent Women Officers or Directors: 1
Hot Spot for Advancement for Women/Minorities:

LOCATIONS: ("Y" = Yes)

West:	Southwest:	Midwest:	Southeast:	Northeast:	International:
Y	Y	Y	Y	Y	Y

EXXON MOBIL CORPORATION (EXXONMOBIL)

www.exxonmobil.com

Industry Group Code: 211111

Management:		Sales/Marketing:		Liberal Arts:		Information Sys.:		Professionals:		Tech./Scientific:	
Mgmt. Trainees:	Y	Marketing Pros.:	Y	Gen. Writing/Editing:	Y	Info. Mgmt.:	Y	Finance/Acct.:	Y	Engineers, Elec.:	Y
Experienced Mgmt.:	Y	Retail Sales:		Tech. Writing:	Y	Software Dev.:	Y	Law:	Y	Engineers, Other:	Y
Int'l Business:	Y	Comm./Industrial:	Y	Graphic Arts/Photog.:	Y	Hardware Dev.:		HR/Other:	Y	Health/Lab:	
MBA Grads:	Y	Sales Trainees:	Y	Music:		Consulting/Other:		Training:	Y	Science/Research:	Y
		Advertising Pros.:	Y	Broadcasting:				Health Care:		Petroleum/Chem.:	Y
				Other:				Consulting:		Math/Other:	Y

TYPES OF BUSINESS:

Oil & Gas Exploration & Production
Gas Refining & Supply
Fuel Marketing
Power Generation
Chemicals
Petroleum Products
Convenience Stores

BRANDS/DIVISIONS/AFFILIATES:

ExxonMobil Chemical
XTO Energy Inc
Qatargas 2 Train 5
TonenGeneral
ExxonMobil
Esso
Exxon
Mobil

CONTACTS: *Note: Officers with more than one job title may be intentionally listed here more than once.*

Rex W. Tillerson, CEO
L.J. Cavanaugh, VP-Human Resources
C. W. Matthews, General Counsel/VP
W.M. Colton, VP-Corp. Strategic Planning
K.P. Cohen, VP-Public & Gov't Affairs
D. S. Rosenthal, VP-Investor Rel./Sec.
Donald D. Humphreys, Treas./Sr. VP
Andrew P. Swiger, Sr. VP
P.T. Mulva, Controller/VP
Mark W. Albers, Sr. VP
Suzanne M/ McCarron, Pres., ExxonMobil Foundation
Rex W. Tillerson, Chmn.

Phone: 972-444-1000 | **Fax:** 972-444-1505
Toll-Free: 800-252-1800
Address: 5959 Las Colinas Blvd., Irving, TX 75039-2298 US

GROWTH PLANS/SPECIAL FEATURES:

Exxon Mobil Corporation (ExxonMobil) is one of the largest international petroleum and natural gas exploration and production companies in the world. Its principal business is energy, involving exploration for and production of crude oil and natural gas; manufacture of petroleum products; and transportation and sale of crude oil, natural gas and petroleum products. Overall, the firm has eight global business units. The exploration unit manages 72 million exploration acres in 33 countries. The development unit includes a portfolio of 130 major projects expected to develop over 24 billion barrels of oil equivalent (BBOE). The production unit focuses on the recovery of hydrocarbons from oil and gas assets. The natural gas and power marketing unit sells approximately 11 billion cubic feet of natural gas daily and controls 16,000 megawatts (MW) of power generation capacity. The refining and supply unit operates refineries, marine vessels, pipelines and distribution centers with a distillation capacity of 6.3 million barrels per day. The lubricants and specialties unit supplies synthetic lubricants, lube basestocks and asphalt and specialty oil products. The fuels marketing unit serves about 1 million commercial customers through 28,000 service stations. Finally, the chemical unit manufactures olefins, aromatics, polyethylene and polypropylene, as well as specialty hydrocarbon fluids. The company has hundreds of affiliates, many with names that include ExxonMobil, Esso, Exxon or Mobil. The firm owns Qatargas 2 Train 5 in Qatar, one of the largest liquefied natural gas (LNG) production facilities worldwide, and has a joint venture with Toray Industries to develop, manufacture and sell lithium ion battery separator film. In June 2010, ExxonMobil acquired XTO Energy, Inc., a U.S.-based oil and gas producer.

FINANCIALS: **Sales and profits are in thousands of dollars—add 000 to get the full amount. 2010 Note: Financial information for 2010 was not available for all companies at press time.**

2010 Sales: $370,125,000 | 2010 Profits: $30,460,000
2009 Sales: $301,500,000 | 2009 Profits: $19,280,000
2008 Sales: $459,579,000 | 2008 Profits: $45,220,000
2007 Sales: $390,328,000 | 2007 Profits: $40,610,000
2006 Sales: $365,467,000 | 2006 Profits: $39,500,000

U.S. Stock Ticker: XOM
Int'l Ticker:
Int'l Exchange:
Employees: 83,600 Fiscal Year Ends: 12/31
Parent Company:

SALARIES/BENEFITS:

Pension Plan: ESOP Stock Plan: Profit Sharing: Top Exec. Salary: $2,057,000 Bonus: $2,400,000
Savings Plan: Stock Purch. Plan: Second Exec. Salary: $1,010,000 Bonus: $1,418,000

OTHER THOUGHTS:

Apparent Women Officers or Directors: 2
Hot Spot for Advancement for Women/Minorities: Y

LOCATIONS: ("Y" = Yes)

West:	Southwest:	Midwest:	Southeast:	Northeast:	International:
Y	Y	Y	Y	Y	Y

EXXONMOBIL CHEMICAL

www.exxonmobilchemical.com

Industry Group Code: 325110

Management:		Sales/Marketing:		Liberal Arts:		Information Sys.:		Professionals:		Tech./Scientific:	
Mgmt. Trainees:	Y	Marketing Pros.:	Y	Gen. Writing/Editing:	Y	Info. Mgmt.:	Y	Finance/Acct.:	Y	Engineers, Elec.:	Y
Experienced Mgmt.:	Y	Retail Sales:		Tech. Writing:	Y	Software Dev.:	Y	Law:	Y	Engineers, Other:	Y
Int'l Business:	Y	Comm./Industrial:	Y	Graphic Arts/Photog.:		Hardware Dev.:		HR/Other:	Y	Health/Lab:	
MBA Grads:	Y	Sales Trainees:		Music:		Consulting/Other:		Training:	Y	Science/Research:	Y
		Advertising Pros.:		Broadcasting:				Health Care:		Petroleum/Chem.:	Y
				Other:				Consulting:		Math/Other:	

TYPES OF BUSINESS:

Plastics & Rubber Manufacturing
Petrochemicals
Catalyst Technology
Polypropylene

BRANDS/DIVISIONS/AFFILIATES:

Univation Technologies, LLC
Shaw Group (The)
XyMax
PxMax
Exxon Mobil Corporation (ExxonMobil)
Dow Chemical Company (The)
SpectraSyn Elite

CONTACTS: *Note: Officers with more than one job title may be intentionally listed here more than once.*

Stephen D. Pryor, Pres.
Robert Davis, VP-Global Tech.
Bruce Macklin, Sr. VP-Global Oper.

Phone: 281-870-6000	**Fax:** 281-870-6661
Toll-Free:	
Address: 13501 Katy Freeway, Houston, TX 77079-1398 US	

GROWTH PLANS/SPECIAL FEATURES:

ExxonMobil Chemical, a division of Exxon Mobil Corporation, is one of the world's largest petrochemical companies, manufacturing and marketing olefins, aromatics, fluids, synthetic rubber, polyethylene, polypropylene, oriented polypropylene packaging films, plasticizers, synthetic lubricant base-stocks, additives for fuels and lubricants, zeolite catalysts and other petrochemical products. The division has manufacturing locations in roughly 18 countries and markets products in more than 150 countries. ExxonMobil Chemical is one of the only major olefins producer with proprietary pyrolysis-reactor technology, which delivers the highest olefin yields in the industry. The unit's XyMax and PxMax aromatics utilize proprietary zeolite shape-selective catalyst technology. This technology increases conversion and reduces losses versus other technologies in the production of higher olefins. Univation Technologies, LLC, a joint venture company owned by ExxonMobil Chemical and Dow Chemical Co., has developed the UNIPOL PE Process for manufacturing linear low density polyethylene and high density polyethelene. The joint venture also furnishes catalysts for metallocene and bimodal resins. Badger Licensing, LLC, a joint venture with The Shaw Group, licenses alkylation technologies. In 2010, the company and Qatar Petroleum announced plans to build a large petrochemical facility in Ras Laffan Industrial City, Qatar, to take advantage of natural gas resources in the area. In May 2010, ExxonMobil Chemical released a new high-performance, high-viscosity metallocene polyalphaolefin under the brand name SpectraSyn Elite.

FINANCIALS: **Sales and profits are in thousands of dollars—add 000 to get the full amount. 2010 Note: Financial information for 2010 was not available for all companies at press time.**

2010 Sales: $25,891,000	2010 Profits: $4,913,000
2009 Sales: $24,825,000	2009 Profits: $2,309,000
2008 Sales: $24,982,000	2008 Profits: $2,957,000
2007 Sales: $27,480,000	2007 Profits: $4,563,000
2006 Sales: $27,350,000	2006 Profits: $4,382,000

U.S. Stock Ticker: Subsidiary
Int'l Ticker:
Int'l Exchange:
Employees: 31,000 Fiscal Year Ends: 12/31
Parent Company: EXXON MOBIL CORPORATION (EXXONMOBIL)

SALARIES/BENEFITS:

Pension Plan:	ESOP Stock Plan:	Profit Sharing:	Top Exec. Salary: $	Bonus: $
Savings Plan:	Stock Purch. Plan:		Second Exec. Salary: $	Bonus: $

OTHER THOUGHTS:

Apparent Women Officers or Directors:
Hot Spot for Advancement for Women/Minorities:

LOCATIONS: ("Y" = Yes)

West:	Southwest:	Midwest:	Southeast:	Northeast:	International:
	Y				Y

FACTSET RESEARCH SYSTEMS INC

www.factset.com

Industry Group Code: 519130

Management:		Sales/Marketing:		Liberal Arts:		Information Sys.:		Professionals:		Tech./Scientific:	
Mgmt. Trainees:		Marketing Pros.:	Y	Gen. Writing/Editing:	Y	Info. Mgmt.:	Y	Finance/Acct.:	Y	Engineers, Elec.:	
Experienced Mgmt.:	Y	Retail Sales:		Tech. Writing:		Software Dev.:	Y	Law:	Y	Engineers, Other:	
Int'l Business:	Y	Comm./Industrial:	Y	Graphic Arts/Photog.:	Y	Hardware Dev.:		HR/Other:	Y	Health/Lab:	
MBA Grads:	Y	Sales Trainees:		Music:		Consulting/Other:		Training:		Science/Research:	
		Advertising Pros.:	Y	Broadcasting:				Health Care:		Petroleum/Chem.:	
				Other:				Consulting:		Math/Other:	

TYPES OF BUSINESS:

Online Financial & Economic Data
Financial Software
Consulting Services

BRANDS/DIVISIONS/AFFILIATES:

FactSet Fundamentals
FactSet Estimates & Research Connect
Portfolio Analytics
FactSet People
FactSet Global Prices
FactSet Market Aggregates
FactSet Connect
Market Metrics

CONTACTS: *Note: Officers with more than one job title may be intentionally listed here more than once.*

Philip A. Hadley, CEO
Peter Walsh, COO/Exec. VP
Maurizio Nicolelli, Principal Financial Officer/Sr. VP
Michael D. Frankenfield, Exec. VP/Dir.-Global Sales
Jeff Young, CTO/Sr. VP
Chris Ellis, Sr. VP/Dir.-Prod. Dev. FactSet Analytics
Gavin Rush, Sr. VP/Dir.-Software Eng.
Rachel R. Stern, General Counsel/Sec./Sr. VP
Townsend Thomas, Chief Content Officer/Sr. VP
Laura C. Ruhe, Sr. VP/Dir.-Leadership Dev.
Scott L. Beyer, Sr. VP/Dir.-Banking & Brokerage Svcs.
Goran Skoko, Sr. VP/Dir.-Prod. Dev. FactSet Platform
Philip A. Hadley, Chmn.

Phone: 203-810-1000	**Fax:** 203-810-1001
Toll-Free:	
Address: 601 Merritt 7, 3rd Fl., Norwalk, CT 06851 US	

GROWTH PLANS/SPECIAL FEATURES:

FactSet Research Systems, Inc. supplies financial intelligence to the global investment community. It combines content about tens of thousands of companies from multiple sources (stock markets, research firms, governments and others) into a single online platform of information and analytics, which can be downloaded into spreadsheets. The firm's Portfolio Analytics suite includes applications for portfolio attribution, risk management and quantitative analysis. It offers three core data sets: FactSet Fundamentals, a global financial database with coverage of over 50,000 companies from over 70 countries and up to 1,600 data elements on each company record; FactSet Estimates and Research Connect, the firm's global broker estimates database which provides its users with consensus-level estimates/statistics and makes hundreds of full text research reports from approximately 600 contributors, including large investment banks and regional/independent research providers; and FactSet Global Prices, which provides the historic and current number of active issues of worldwide equities, short interest, mutual funds, bonds and derivatives. Some of the additional FactSet databases include: FactSet People, a database of over 500,000 people, including worldwide executives; FactSet Market Aggregates, which derives key ratios and per share values for global equity market indexes and commercial benchmark vendors; Global Private Equity & Venture Capital, a complete survey of any substantial private equity and venture capital firm; and Debt Capital Structure, which provides a breakdown of a company's bank loan and/or corporate bond financing activity for a specific financial reporting period. In May 2010, the firm launched FactSet Connect, which grants users customized content access from any computer, along with FactSet Wireless, which enables clients to use handheld wireless devices to access FactSet content. In June 2010, it acquired Market Metrics, a leading U.S. market research company.

FactSet employee benefits include: medical, dental and vision care; short- and long-term disability insurance; flexible appending accounts; a 401(k); and an employee stock purchase program.

FINANCIALS: **Sales and profits are in thousands of dollars—add 000 to get the full amount. 2010 Note: Financial information for 2010 was not available for all companies at press time.**

2010 Sales: $641,059	2010 Profits: $150,211	**U.S. Stock Ticker: FDS**
2009 Sales: $622,023	2009 Profits: $144,950	**Int'l Ticker:**
2008 Sales: $575,519	2008 Profits: $125,017	Int'l Exchange:
2007 Sales: $475,801	2007 Profits: $109,567	Employees: 4,116 Fiscal Year Ends: 8/31
2006 Sales: $387,350	2006 Profits: $82,916	Parent Company:

SALARIES/BENEFITS:

Pension Plan:	ESOP Stock Plan:	Profit Sharing:	Top Exec. Salary: $275,000	Bonus: $800,000
Savings Plan: Y	Stock Purch. Plan: Y		Second Exec. Salary: $265,000	Bonus: $580,000

OTHER THOUGHTS:

Apparent Women Officers or Directors: 2
Hot Spot for Advancement for Women/Minorities:

LOCATIONS: ("Y" = Yes)

West:	Southwest:	Midwest:	Southeast:	Northeast:	International:
Y	Y	Y	Y	Y	Y

FAIRVIEW HEALTH SERVICES

www.fairview.org

Industry Group Code: 622110

Management:		Sales/Marketing:		Liberal Arts:		Information Sys.:		Professionals:		Tech./Scientific:	
Mgmt. Trainees:		Marketing Pros.:	Y	Gen. Writing/Editing:	Y	Info. Mgmt.:	Y	Finance/Acct.:	Y	Engineers, Elec.:	
Experienced Mgmt.:	Y	Retail Sales:		Tech. Writing:	Y	Software Dev.:	Y	Law:	Y	Engineers, Other:	
Int'l Business:		Comm./Industrial:	Y	Graphic Arts/Photog.:		Hardware Dev.:	Y	HR/Other:	Y	Health/Lab:	Y
MBA Grads:		Sales Trainees:		Music:		Consulting/Other:		Training:		Science/Research:	Y
		Advertising Pros.:	Y	Broadcasting:				Health Care:	Y	Petroleum/Chem.:	
				Other:				Consulting:		Math/Other:	

TYPES OF BUSINESS:

Hospitals
Specialty Clinics
Home Care
Hospice Services
Children's Services
Cancer Care
Senior Care
Academic Teaching Hospital

BRANDS/DIVISIONS/AFFILIATES:

Ebenezer
Fairview Northland Medical Center
Fairview Southdale Hospital
University of Minnesota Medical Center
Fairview Lakes Medical Center
Fairview Maple Grove Hospital Center
Fairview University Medical Center-Mesabi
Fairview Red Wing Medical Center

CONTACTS: *Note: Officers with more than one job title may be intentionally listed here more than once.*

Mark A. Eustis, CEO
Mark A. Eustis, Pres.
Daniel Fromm, CFO
Mark Hansberry, VP-Mktg.
Paula H. Phillippe, Chief Human Resources Officer
Terry Carroll, CIO/Sr. VP-Transformation
George Chresand, General Counsel/Sr. VP
Mark Hansberry, VP-Strategic Planning
Mark Hansberry, VP-Corp. Comm.
Mark F. Thomas, Pres., Senior Svcs.
Daniel K. Anderson, Pres., Fairview Community Hospitals
David Moen, Pres., Fairview Physician Associates
Mark Werner, Chief Clinic Integration Officer
Jon R. Campbell, Chmn.

Phone: 612-672-6000 **Fax:** 612-672-7186
Toll-Free: 800-824-1953
Address: 2450 Riverside Ave., Minneapolis, MN 55454 US

GROWTH PLANS/SPECIAL FEATURES:

Fairview Health Services is an integrated health network. It serves the Minneapolis-St. Paul area of Minnesota and suburbs; the Minnesota Valley; Wyoming; and the Red Wing, Northland, Lakes and Range areas of Minnesota. The system contains eight hospitals; six urgent care clinics; over 40 primary care facilities; over 55 specialty clinics; one children's hospital; home care, hospice and rehabilitation services; and over 30 inpatient and retail pharmacies. The company's hospitals include Fairview Southdale Hospital; Fairview Northland Medical Center; Fairview Maple Grove Hospital Center (25%-owned); Fairview Red Wing Medical Center; Fairview University Medical Center-Mesabi; University of Minnesota Medical Center; University of Minnesota Amplatz Children's Hospital, which opened in April 2011; and Fairview Lakes Medical Center. Through its subsidiary Ebenezer, Fairview provides senior housing facilities including apartments; assisted living complexes; cooperatives; condominiums; a memory care facility for patients living with Alzheimer's or other early-stage dementias; and adult and intergenerational daycare programs. The Fairview Foundation is the group's funding entity for operations, special projects, programs, allocations and endowments.

Fairview offers its employees life, disability, health and dental insurance; an assistance program; wellness, health, disease management, spiritual health, smoking cessation and weight management services; health club discounts; a 529 college savings plan; adoption and day care assistance; a 403(b) and 401(k) plan; on-site continuing education programs; tuition reimbursement; educational initiatives; scholarship opportunities; a Sallie Mae partnership; and medical mission grants.

FINANCIALS: **Sales and profits are in thousands of dollars—add 000 to get the full amount. 2010 Note: Financial information for 2010 was not available for all companies at press time.**

2010 Sales: $2,826,996	2010 Profits: $101,852	**U.S. Stock Ticker: Nonprofit**
2009 Sales: $2,744,562	2009 Profits: $110,242	**Int'l Ticker:**
2008 Sales: $2,566,565	2008 Profits: $20,815	Int'l Exchange:
2007 Sales: $2,332,917	2007 Profits: $48,290	Employees: 90,000 Fiscal Year Ends: 12/31
2006 Sales: $2,114,710	2006 Profits: $35,415	Parent Company:

SALARIES/BENEFITS:

Pension Plan: Y	ESOP Stock Plan:	Profit Sharing:	Top Exec. Salary: $	Bonus: $
Savings Plan: Y	Stock Purch. Plan: Y		Second Exec. Salary: $	Bonus: $

OTHER THOUGHTS:

Apparent Women Officers or Directors: 8
Hot Spot for Advancement for Women/Minorities: Y

LOCATIONS: ("Y" = Yes)

West:	Southwest:	Midwest:	Southeast:	Northeast:	International:
Y		Y			

FAMILY DOLLAR STORES INC

www.familydollar.com

Industry Group Code: 452112

Management:		Sales/Marketing:		Liberal Arts:		Information Sys.:		Professionals:		Tech./Scientific:	
Mgmt. Trainees:	Y	Marketing Pros.:	Y	Gen. Writing/Editing:	Y	Info. Mgmt.:	Y	Finance/Acct.:	Y	Engineers, Elec.:	
Experienced Mgmt.:	Y	Retail Sales:	Y	Tech. Writing:		Software Dev.:	Y	Law:	Y	Engineers, Other:	
Int'l Business:		Comm./Industrial:		Graphic Arts/Photog.:	Y	Hardware Dev.:		HR/Other:	Y	Health/Lab:	
MBA Grads:	Y	Sales Trainees:	Y	Music:		Consulting/Other:		Training:	Y	Science/Research:	
		Advertising Pros.:	Y	Broadcasting:				Health Care:		Petroleum/Chem.:	
				Other:	Y			Consulting:		Math/Other:	

TYPES OF BUSINESS:

Discount Stores
Dollar Stores

BRANDS/DIVISIONS/AFFILIATES:

Family Dollar

CONTACTS: *Note: Officers with more than one job title may be intentionally listed here more than once.*

Howard R. Levine, CEO
R. James Kelly, COO
R. James Kelly, Pres.
Kenneth T. Smith, CFO/Sr. VP
Don Hamblen, Sr. VP-Customer Mktg.
Bryan Venberg, Sr. VP-Human Resources
Joshua R. Jewett, CIO/Sr. VP-IT
Dorlisa K. Flur, Chief Merch. Officer/Exec. VP
James C. Snyder, Jr., General Counsel/Corp. Sec./Sr. VP
Barry Sullivan, Exec. VP-Store Oper.
David R. Styka, VP-Finance
Bryan P. Causey, Sr. VP-Space Mgmt. & Inventory Optimization
Keith M. Gehl, Sr. VP-Real Estate & Facilities
John J. Scanlon, Sr. VP-Merch.
Paul G. White, Sr. VP-Merch.
Howard R. Levine, Chmn.
Kevin Boyanowski, Sr. VP-Global Sourcing
Charles S. Gibson, Jr., Exec. VP-Supply Chain

Phone: 704-847-6961	**Fax:** 704-847-5534
Toll-Free:	
Address: 10401 Old Monroe Rd., Charlotte, NC 28201-1017 US	

GROWTH PLANS/SPECIAL FEATURES:

Family Dollar Stores, Inc. operates a chain of roughly 7,000 general merchandise retail discount stores across 44 states, primarily serving low to lower-middle income consumers. These stores range in size from 7,500 to 9,500 square feet. The goods offered by Family Dollar generally have price points that range from under $1 to $10 and include apparel, food, cleaning products, paper products, home decor, beauty products, health aids, toys, pet products, automotive products, domestics, seasonal goods and electronics. Substantially all of the firm's merchandise is purchased directly from the manufacturer. Family Dollar owns and operates nine distribution centers. Nationally advertised brand name merchandise accounts for approximately 51% of Family Dollar's sales, with the company's private label merchandise accounting for 22% and closeout merchandise accounting for approximately 1%. The company supplements its basic assortment of merchandise with the purchase of certain Treasure Hunt items designed to create more excitement in stores and attract customers throughout the year, with particular emphasis on the holiday seasons. Consumables, such as household chemicals, paper products, food, health and beauty items, hardware, automotive supplies and pet supplies account for roughly 65.1% of Family Dollar Stores' sales; home products, 13.2%; apparel and accessories, 10.7%; and seasonal and electronics, 11%. During 2010, the company opened 200 stores, closed 70 locations, relocated 13 stores renovated 89 locations and expanded 15 stores. In August 2011, the firm opened its 7,000 location in Memphis, Tennessee.

Family Dollar Stores offers its employees medical, vision, dental and prescription drug benefits; life insurance; short- and long-term disability; flexible spending accounts; a 401(k) plan; and an employee stock purchase plan.

FINANCIALS: **Sales and profits are in thousands of dollars—add 000 to get the full amount. 2010 Note: Financial information for 2010 was not available for all companies at press time.**

2010 Sales: $7,866,971	2010 Profits: $358,135	**U.S. Stock Ticker: FDO**
2009 Sales: $7,400,606	2009 Profits: $291,266	**Int'l Ticker:**
2008 Sales: $6,983,628	2008 Profits: $233,073	Int'l Exchange:
2007 Sales: $6,834,305	2007 Profits: $242,854	Employees: 50,000 Fiscal Year Ends: 8/31
2006 Sales: $6,394,772	2006 Profits: $195,111	Parent Company:

SALARIES/BENEFITS:

Pension Plan:	ESOP Stock Plan:	Profit Sharing:	Top Exec. Salary: $998,464	Bonus: $1,560,095
Savings Plan: Y	Stock Purch. Plan: Y		Second Exec. Salary: $708,920	Bonus: $830,773

OTHER THOUGHTS:

Apparent Women Officers or Directors: 3
Hot Spot for Advancement for Women/Minorities: Y

LOCATIONS: ("Y" = Yes)

West:	Southwest:	Midwest:	Southeast:	Northeast:	International:
Y	Y	Y	Y	Y	

FASTENAL

www.fastenal.com

Industry Group Code: 33351

Management:		**Sales/Marketing:**		**Liberal Arts:**		**Information Sys.:**		**Professionals:**		**Tech./Scientific:**	
Mgmt. Trainees:		Marketing Pros.:	Y	Gen. Writing/Editing:		Info. Mgmt.:	Y	Finance/Acct.:	Y	Engineers, Elec.:	Y
Experienced Mgmt.:		Retail Sales:		Tech. Writing:	Y	Software Dev.:		Law:	Y	Engineers, Other:	Y
Int'l Business:	Y	Comm./Industrial:	Y	Graphic Arts/Photog.:		Hardware Dev.:		HR/Other:	Y	Health/Lab:	
MBA Grads:	Y	Sales Trainees:		Music:		Consulting/Other:		Training:		Science/Research:	
		Advertising Pros.:	Y	Broadcasting:				Health Care:		Petroleum/Chem.:	
				Other:				Consulting:		Math/Other:	

TYPES OF BUSINESS:

Fasteners, Tools & Equipment Manufacturing & Retail Sales

BRANDS/DIVISIONS/AFFILIATES:

Fastenal
FNL G9
Holo-Krome
Rock River
Blackstone
Tritan
FMT
PowerPhase

CONTACTS: *Note: Officers with more than one job title may be intentionally listed here more than once.*

Willard D. Oberton, CEO
Willard D. Oberton, Pres.
Daniel L. Florness, CFO/Exec. VP
Nicholas J. Lundquist, Exec. VP-Sales, Eastern US
Reyne K. Wisecup, Exec. VP-Human Resources
Ashok Singh, Exec. VP-IT
Michael Camp, Exec. VP-Prod.
James C. Jansen, Exec. VP-Internal Oper.
Leland J. Hein, Exec. VP-Sales, Western US
Robert A. Kierlin, Chmn.
Steven A. Rucinski, Exec. VP-Sales, Europe, Mexico, Canada & Asia
Michael Camp, Exec. VP-Procurement

Phone: 507-454-5374	**Fax:** 507-453-8049
Toll-Free:	
Address: 2001 Theurer Blvd., Winona, MN 55987-1500 US	

GROWTH PLANS/SPECIAL FEATURES:

Fastenal is a retailer and wholesaler of industrial and construction supplies. The firm operates roughly 2,500 store locations, the majority of which are located in all 50 U.S. states. The other stores are located in Canada, Mexico, Puerto Rico, Singapore, China, The Netherlands, Hungary and Malaysia. The company also operates 14 North American distribution centers from which Fastenal distribute products to its store and in-plant locations. The firm sells 10 types of products: fasteners, sold under the Fastenal, FNL G9, Holo-Krome and Rock River brands; tools through the Fastenal, Rock River and Blackstone brands; cutting tools, marketed under the FMT, Blackstone and Tritan labels; welding supplies through its Blackstone brand; hydraulics and pneumatics through brands Fastenal, Profitter and Dynaflo; janitorial supplies under the Clean Choice brand; material handling items, sold under the Caliber and EquipRite labels; electrical supplies through brand PowerPhase; metals under the Fastenal label; and safety supplies through the Bodyguard and Fastenal brands. Threaded fasteners account for approximately 49.6% of Fastenal's total sales. Of the firm's 996,000 standard stock items, roughly 94.5% are manufactured by other companies; Fastenal manufactures the other 5.5% of its products. In recent years, Fastenal acquired certain assets of socket products manufacturer Holo-Krome Company.

FINANCIALS: **Sales and profits are in thousands of dollars—add 000 to get the full amount. 2010 Note: Financial information for 2010 was not available for all companies at press time.**

2010 Sales: $2,269,471	2010 Profits: $265,356	**U.S. Stock Ticker: FAST**
2009 Sales: $1,930,330	2009 Profits: $184,357	**Int'l Ticker:**
2008 Sales: $2,340,425	2008 Profits: $279,705	Int'l Exchange:
2007 Sales: $2,061,819	2007 Profits: $232,622	Employees: 12,136 Fiscal Year Ends: 12/31
2006 Sales: $	2006 Profits: $	Parent Company:

SALARIES/BENEFITS:

Pension Plan:	ESOP Stock Plan:	Profit Sharing:	Top Exec. Salary: $485,000	Bonus: $
Savings Plan:	Stock Purch. Plan:		Second Exec. Salary: $375,000	Bonus: $

OTHER THOUGHTS:

Apparent Women Officers or Directors:
Hot Spot for Advancement for Women/Minorities:

LOCATIONS: ("Y" = Yes)

West:	Southwest:	Midwest:	Southeast:	Northeast:	International:
Y	Y	Y	Y	Y	Y

FEDERAL MOGUL CORP

www.federalmogul.com

Industry Group Code: 3363

Management:		Sales/Marketing:		Liberal Arts:		Information Sys.:		Professionals:		Tech./Scientific:	
Mgmt. Trainees:		Marketing Pros.:	Y	Gen. Writing/Editing:		Info. Mgmt.:	Y	Finance/Acct.:	Y	Engineers, Elec.:	Y
Experienced Mgmt.:		Retail Sales:		Tech. Writing:	Y	Software Dev.:		Law:	Y	Engineers, Other:	Y
Int'l Business:	Y	Comm./Industrial:	Y	Graphic Arts/Photog.:		Hardware Dev.:		HR/Other:	Y	Health/Lab:	
MBA Grads:	Y	Sales Trainees:		Music:		Consulting/Other:		Training:		Science/Research:	
		Advertising Pros.:	Y	Broadcasting:				Health Care:		Petroleum/Chem.:	
				Other:				Consulting:		Math/Other:	

TYPES OF BUSINESS:

Aftermarket Products & Services
Powertrain Products
Sealing Systems
Vehicle Safety & Performance Products

BRANDS/DIVISIONS/AFFILIATES:

AE
Glyco
National
Goetze
Fel-Pro
FP Diesel
MicroTorq
Daros Group

CONTACTS: *Note: Officers with more than one job title may be intentionally listed here more than once.*

Jose Maria Alapont, CEO
Jose Maria Alapont, Pres.
Alan Haughie, CFO/Sr. VP
William Bowers, Sr. VP-Sales & Mktg.
Pascal Goachet, Sr. VP-Global Human Resources & Organization
Alston German, CIO/VP
Rene Dalleur, Sr. VP-Global Eng.
Rene Dalleur, Sr. VP-Global Mfg. & Customer Satisfaction
Robert L. Katz, General Counsel/Sr. VP
Jean Brunol, Sr. VP-Bus. & Oper. Strategy
Steven K. Gaut, VP-Corp. Comm. & Gov't Rel.
David Bozynksi, Treas./VP
James Burkhart, Sr. VP-Global Aftermarket
Ramzi Hermiz, Sr. VP-Vehicle Safety & Protection
Rainer Jueckstock, Sr. VP-Powertrain Energy
Gerard Chochoy, Sr. VP-Powertrain Sealing & Bearings
Carl C. Icahn, Chmn.
Markus Wermers, Sr. VP-Global Purchasing

Phone: 248-354-7700 **Fax:** 248-354-8548
Toll-Free:
Address: 26555 Northwestern Hwy., Southfield, MI 48033 US

GROWTH PLANS/SPECIAL FEATURES:

Federal-Mogul Corp. is a supplier of vehicle and industrial products for fuel economy, alternative energies, environment and safety systems. The firm sells its products to original equipment manufacturers (OEMs) of automotive, light commercial, heavy-duty, industrial, agricultural, aerospace, marine, rail and off-road vehicles and the worldwide aftermarket. The company operates in five business segments: powertrain energy, accounting for 30% of sales; powertrain sealings and bearings, accounting for 18%; vehicle safety and protection, 15%; global aftermarket, 37%; and corporate. The powertrain energy segment, offers products that include pistons, piston rings, piston pins, cylinder liners, valve seats and guides and transmission components. Brand names include Federal-Mogul, AE, Daros, Champion, Goetze and Nural. The powertrain sealings and bearings segment offers bearings, bushings and thrust washers for engine, transmission and driveline systems. Products are sold under Federal-Mogul, Deva, Fel-Pro, FP Diesel, Glyco, Metafram, Metagliss, National, Payen, and Poral brands. The vehicle safety and protection segment offers brake disc pads, brake linings, brake blocks, element resistant systems protection sleeving products and flexible heat shields. Brand names include Abex, Anco, Bentley-Harris, Beral, Champion, Ferodo, Moog, ThermoQuiet and Wagner. The global aftermarket segment sells engine parts, gaskets, seals, chassis, driveline, hub assemblies, disc pads, linings, rotors, spark plugs, wipers, filters and lighting. These products are manufactured within the firm's other segments and are also purchased from outside suppliers. Federal-Mogul has operations in 34 countries and maintains roughly 173 facilities. In March 2010, the company launched MicroTorq, a crankshaft seal design for vehicles with the ability to reduce friction of up to 70%, and IROX, a polymer coated bearing shell designed to decrease fuel consumption and CO2 emissions. In June 2010, Federal-Mogul acquired piston ring supplier Daros Group.

Employees are offered medical, dental, vision and hearing insurance; flexible spending accounts; life and AD&D insurance; disability coverage; a 401(k) plan; and a pension plan.

FINANCIALS: **Sales and profits are in thousands of dollars—add 000 to get the full amount. 2010 Note: Financial information for 2010 was not available for all companies at press time.**

2010 Sales: $6,219,000 | 2010 Profits: $161,000
2009 Sales: $5,330,000 | 2009 Profits: $-45,000
2008 Sales: $6,865,600 | 2008 Profits: $-467,900
2007 Sales: $6,913,900 | 2007 Profits: $1,412,300
2006 Sales: $6,326,400 | 2006 Profits: $-549,600

U.S. Stock Ticker: FDML
Int'l Ticker:
Int'l Exchange:
Employees: 42,700 Fiscal Year Ends: 12/31
Parent Company:

SALARIES/BENEFITS:

Pension Plan: Y | ESOP Stock Plan: | Profit Sharing: | Top Exec. Salary: $1,500,000 | Bonus: $2,334,252
Savings Plan: Y | Stock Purch. Plan: | | Second Exec. Salary: $556,320 | Bonus: $479,213

OTHER THOUGHTS:

Apparent Women Officers or Directors:
Hot Spot for Advancement for Women/Minorities:

LOCATIONS: ("Y" = Yes)

West:	Southwest:	Midwest:	Southeast:	Northeast:	International:
Y	Y	Y	Y	Y	Y

FEDEX CORPORATION

www.fedex.com

Industry Group Code: 4921

Management:		Sales/Marketing:		Liberal Arts:		Information Sys.:		Professionals:		Tech./Scientific:	
Mgmt. Trainees:	Y	Marketing Pros.:	Y	Gen. Writing/Editing:	Y	Info. Mgmt.:	Y	Finance/Acct.:	Y	Engineers, Elec.:	Y
Experienced Mgmt.:	Y	Retail Sales:		Tech. Writing:	Y	Software Dev.:	Y	Law:	Y	Engineers, Other:	
Int'l Business:	Y	Comm./Industrial:	Y	Graphic Arts/Photog.:	Y	Hardware Dev.:		HR/Other:	Y	Health/Lab:	
MBA Grads:	Y	Sales Trainees:	Y	Music:		Consulting/Other:		Training:	Y	Science/Research:	
		Advertising Pros.:	Y	Broadcasting:				Health Care:		Petroleum/Chem.:	
				Other:	Y			Consulting:		Math/Other:	Y

TYPES OF BUSINESS:

Express Delivery Services
Ground Delivery Services
Freight Services
Document Solutions & Business Services
International Trade Services

BRANDS/DIVISIONS/AFFILIATES:

FedEx Ground Package System Inc
FedEx Freight Corp
FedEx Express Corp
FedEx Custom Critical Inc
FedEx Trade Networks Inc
Unifreight India Pvt. Ltd.
AFL Pvt. Ltd.
Fedex Supply Chain Services Inc

CONTACTS: *Note: Officers with more than one job title may be intentionally listed here more than once.*

Frederick W. Smith, CEO
Frederick W. Smith, Pres.
Alan B. Graf, Jr., CFO/Exec. VP
Laurie A. Tucker, Sr. VP-Corp. Mktg., FedEx Svcs.
Robert B. Carter, CIO/Exec. VP-Info. Svcs.
Christine P. Richards, General Counsel/Exec. VP/Corp. Sec.
T. Michael Glenn, Exec. VP-Market Dev.
T. Michael Glenn, Exec. VP-Corp. Comm.
William G. Margaritis, Sr. VP-Investor Rel.
David J. Bronczek, Pres./CEO-FedEx Express
David F. Rebholz, Pres./CEO-FedEx Ground
William J. Logue, Pres./CEO-FedEx Freight
Brian Philips, Pres./CEO-FedEx Office
Frederick W. Smith, Chmn.
Michael L. Ducker, Pres., FedEx Express Int'l
Craig M. Simon, Pres./CEO-FedEx SupplyChain

Phone: 901-818-7500 **Fax:** 901-395-2000
Toll-Free:
Address: 942 S. Shady Grove Rd., Memphis, TN 38120 US

GROWTH PLANS/SPECIAL FEATURES:

FedEx Corporation provides transportation, e-commerce and business services and operates through Federal Express Corp. (FedEx Express); FedEx Ground Package System, Inc. (FedEx Ground); FedEx Freight Corp. (FedEx Freight); and FedEx Corporate Services, Inc. (FedEx Services). FedEx Express is an express transportation company, offering time-certain delivery within one to three business days. The division also includes FedEx SupplyChain Systems and FedEx Trade Networks, Inc., which provides international trade services, specializing in custom brokerage and global cargo distribution. FedEx Ground offers small-package ground delivery service. It provides service to almost every business address in the U.S. and Canada, as well as residential delivery to nearly 100% of U.S. residents through FedEx Home Delivery. The segment also includes FedEx SmartPost, Inc., which specializes in the consolidation and delivery of high volumes of low-weight, less time-sensitive business-to-consumer packages using the U.S. Postal Service or Canada Post for final delivery to residences. FedEx Freight Corporation provides less-than-truckload (LTL) freight services through its FedEx Freight business (fast-transit LTL freight services) and its FedEx National LTL business (long-haul LTL freight services). The division also includes FedEx Custom Critical, Inc., a time-specific, critical shipment carrier. FedEx Services serves other FedEx companies with sales, marketing and IT support, in addition to customer service through FedEx Customer Information Services, Inc. The unit additionally oversees the company's roughly 1,950 FedEx Office locations (including 135 international locations), which offer a range of printing and business services as well as retail access to FedEx Express and FedEx Ground services. In February 2011, the firm's FedEx Express business completed its acquisition of the distribution, logistics and express transport businesses of Mumbai-based AFL Pvt. Ltd. and its affiliate, Unifreight India Pvt. Ltd.

FedEx employees are offered medical, dental and vision insurance; short- and long-term disability coverage; life insurance; tuition assistance; and reduced-rate shipping.

FINANCIALS: **Sales and profits are in thousands of dollars—add 000 to get the full amount. 2010 Note: Financial information for 2010 was not available for all companies at press time.**

2010 Sales: $34,734,000 2010 Profits: $1,184,000
2009 Sales: $35,497,000 2009 Profits: $747,000
2008 Sales: $37,953,000 2008 Profits: $2,075,000
2007 Sales: $35,214,000 2007 Profits: $3,276,000
2006 Sales: $32,294,000 2006 Profits: $3,014,000

U.S. Stock Ticker: FDX
Int'l Ticker:
Int'l Exchange:
Employees: 141,000 Fiscal Year Ends: 5/31
Parent Company:

SALARIES/BENEFITS:

Pension Plan: Y ESOP Stock Plan: Profit Sharing: Top Exec. Salary: $1,190,029 Bonus: $400,000
Savings Plan: Y Stock Purch. Plan: Y Second Exec. Salary: $879,368 Bonus: $315,907

OTHER THOUGHTS:

Apparent Women Officers or Directors: 6
Hot Spot for Advancement for Women/Minorities: Y

LOCATIONS: ("Y" = Yes)

West:	Southwest:	Midwest:	Southeast:	Northeast:	International:
Y	Y	Y	Y	Y	Y

FIDELITY NATIONAL INFORMATION SERVICES INC

www.fisglobal.com

Industry Group Code: 522320

Management:		Sales/Marketing:		Liberal Arts:		Information Sys.:		Professionals:		Tech./Scientific:	
Mgmt. Trainees:		Marketing Pros.:	Y	Gen. Writing/Editing:	Y	Info. Mgmt.:	Y	Finance/Acct.:	Y	Engineers, Elec.:	
Experienced Mgmt.:	Y	Retail Sales:		Tech. Writing:	Y	Software Dev.:	Y	Law:	Y	Engineers, Other:	
Int'l Business:	Y	Comm./Industrial:	Y	Graphic Arts/Photog.:		Hardware Dev.:		HR/Other:	Y	Health/Lab:	
MBA Grads:	Y	Sales Trainees:		Music:		Consulting/Other:		Training:	Y	Science/Research:	
		Advertising Pros.:		Broadcasting:				Health Care:		Petroleum/Chem.:	
				Other:				Consulting:		Math/Other:	

TYPES OF BUSINESS:

Payment & Transaction Processing Services
IT Consulting
Outsourcing Services
Due Diligence Services
Mortgage Loan Processing

BRANDS/DIVISIONS/AFFILIATES:

GIFTS Software, Inc.
Capco
ValueCentric Marketing Group, Inc.

CONTACTS: *Note: Officers with more than one job title may be intentionally listed here more than once.*

Frank R. Martire, CEO
Gary A. Norcross, COO/Exec. VP
Frank R. Martire, Pres.
Michael D. Hayford, CFO/Exec. VP
Marcia Danzeisen, Sr. VP-Global Mktg.
Michael P. Oates, Chief Human Resources Officer/Exec. VP
Brian Hurdis, Exec. VP-Tech. Svcs.
Michael Gravelle, Chief Legal Officer/Exec. VP/Corp. Sec.
James Susoreny, Exec. VP-Bus. Dev.
Marcia Danzeisen, Sr. VP-Global Comm.
Mary K. Waggoner, Sr. VP-Investor Rel.
Brent Bickett, Exec. VP-Corp. Finance
Ram Chary, Exec. VP-Global Commercial Svcs.
Rob Heyvaert, Exec. VP
Frank D'Angelo, Exec. VP-Payment Solutions
Anthony Jabbour, Exec. VP-Financial Solutions
William P. Foley, II, Chmn.
Mark Davey, Exec. VP-Int'l

Phone: 904-854-5000	**Fax:** 904-357-1105
Toll-Free: 888-323-0310	
Address: 601 Riverside Ave., Jacksonville, FL 32204 US	

GROWTH PLANS/SPECIAL FEATURES:

Fidelity National Information Services, Inc. (FIS) offers banking/payments technology solutions, processing services and information-based services. The firm provides core financial institution processing; card issuer and transaction processing services; and outsourcing services to financial institutions and retailers worldwide. The company has processing and technology relationships with 40 of the top 50 global banks, including nine of the top 10. Headquartered in Jacksonville, Florida, FIS maintains a global presence, serving more than 14,000 financial institutions through offices in over 100 countries worldwide. The company operates in four segments: Financial Solutions, Payment Solutions, International Solutions and Corporate/Other. The Financial Solutions Group offers core processing software applications designed to run critical banking processes; channel, decision and risk management solutions; syndicated loan applications; and global commercial services. The Payment Solutions division offers settlement and card management solutions for financial institution card issuers; check and transaction ticket data capture; healthcare payments solutions; and card issuer services, enabling financial institutions and others to issue VISA and MasterCard branded credit and debit cards, private label cards, and other electronic payment cards for use by both consumer and business accounts. FIS' International Solutions segment provides the firm's services in over 100 countries. The Corporate/Other division includes corporate overhead costs that are not allocated to operating segments. In June 2010, FIS agreed to acquire Compliance Coach, Inc. In October 2010, the firm acquired ValueCentric Marketing Group, Inc. In December 2010, the company acquired Capco. In February 2011, FIS acquired GIFTS Software, Inc.

FINANCIALS: **Sales and profits are in thousands of dollars—add 000 to get the full amount. 2010 Note: Financial information for 2010 was not available for all companies at press time.**

2010 Sales: $5,269,500	2010 Profits: $404,500	**U.S. Stock Ticker: FIS**
2009 Sales: $3,711,100	2009 Profits: $105,900	**Int'l Ticker:**
2008 Sales: $3,446,000	2008 Profits: $214,800	Int'l Exchange:
2007 Sales: $2,892,900	2007 Profits: $561,222	Employees: 32,000 Fiscal Year Ends: 12/31
2006 Sales: $2,416,500	2006 Profits: $259,087	Parent Company:

SALARIES/BENEFITS:

Pension Plan:	ESOP Stock Plan:	Profit Sharing:	Top Exec. Salary: $886,250	Bonus: $2,481,500
Savings Plan: Y	Stock Purch. Plan:		Second Exec. Salary: $627,500	Bonus: $3,067,500

OTHER THOUGHTS:

Apparent Women Officers or Directors: 2
Hot Spot for Advancement for Women/Minorities:

LOCATIONS: ("Y" = Yes)

West:	Southwest:	Midwest:	Southeast:	Northeast:	International:
Y	Y	Y	Y	Y	Y

FINISAR CORPORATION

www.finisar.com

Industry Group Code: 33411

Management:		**Sales/Marketing:**		**Liberal Arts:**		**Information Sys.:**		**Professionals:**		**Tech./Scientific:**	
Mgmt. Trainees:	Y	Marketing Pros.:	Y	Gen. Writing/Editing:		Info. Mgmt.:	Y	Finance/Acct.:	Y	Engineers, Elec.:	Y
Experienced Mgmt.:	Y	Retail Sales:		Tech. Writing:		Software Dev.:		Law:	Y	Engineers, Other:	
Int'l Business:	Y	Comm./Industrial:	Y	Graphic Arts/Photog.:		Hardware Dev.:	Y	HR/Other:	Y	Health/Lab:	
MBA Grads:	Y	Sales Trainees:		Music:		Consulting/Other:		Training:	Y	Science/Research:	Y
		Advertising Pros.:		Broadcasting:				Health Care:		Petroleum/Chem.:	
				Other:				Consulting:		Math/Other:	

TYPES OF BUSINESS:

Optical Subsystems & Components
Network Test & Monitoring Systems
CML Transmitters

BRANDS/DIVISIONS/AFFILIATES:

Quadwire
WaveShaper
Laserwire
C.wire
Broadway Networks, Ltd.

CONTACTS: *Note: Officers with more than one job title may be intentionally listed here more than once.*

Eitan Gertel, CEO
Kurt Adzema, CFO/Exec. VP
Todd Swanson, Exec. VP-Global Mktg. & Sales
John H. Clark, Exec. VP-Global R&D
John H. Clark, Exec. VP-Tech.
Chris Brown, General Counsel/VP
Joseph Young, Exec. VP-Global Oper.
Victoria McDonald, Sr. Mgr.-Corp. Comm.
Jerry S. Rawls, Chmn.

Phone: 408-548-1000 **Fax:** 408-541-6138
Toll-Free:
Address: 1389 Moffett Park Dr., Sunnyvale, CA 94089 US

GROWTH PLANS/SPECIAL FEATURES:

Finisar Corporation is a provider of optical subsystems and components that connect local area networks (LANs), storage area networks (SANs), metropolitan area networks (MANs) and wide area networks (WANs). The company operates in two segments: optical subsystems and components; and network test systems. The firm's optical subsystems consist primarily of transceivers that provide the fundamental optical-electrical interface for connecting the equipment used in building the networks. These products rely on the use of digital semiconductor lasers in conjunction with integrated circuit design and novel packaging technology to provide means for transmitting and receiving digital signals over fiber optic cables using a wide range of network protocols, transmission speeds and physical configurations. The firm's line of optical components consists primarily of packaged lasers and photo-detectors used in transceivers, primarily for LAN and SAN applications. The network test systems allow the generation and capture of data at high speeds; the filtration of data; and the identification of various types of intermittent errors and other network problems for SANs, LANs, wireless networks, voice-over-Internet protocol applications. The firm's key product lines include the WaveShaper family of programmable optical processors and the Laserwire, Quadwire and C.wire brands of optical cables. Finisar sells its optical subsystems and component products to manufacturers of storage and networking equipment such as Brocade, Cisco Systems, EMC, Emulex, Hewlett-Packard Company, Huawei, IBM, QLogic and Siemens. In September 2010, the company acquired transceiver product developer, Broadway Networks, Ltd.

FINANCIALS: **Sales and profits are in thousands of dollars—add 000 to get the full amount. 2010 Note: Financial information for 2010 was not available for all companies at press time.**

2010 Sales: $629,880 — 2010 Profits: $14,131
2009 Sales: $497,058 — 2009 Profits: $-260,343
2008 Sales: $401,625 — 2008 Profits: $-79,013
2007 Sales: $418,548 — 2007 Profits: $-45,399
2006 Sales: $364,293 — 2006 Profits: $-33,029

U.S. Stock Ticker: FNSR
Int'l Ticker:
Int'l Exchange:
Employees: 6,893 Fiscal Year Ends: 4/30
Parent Company:

SALARIES/BENEFITS:

Pension Plan: ESOP Stock Plan: Profit Sharing: Top Exec. Salary: $420,092 Bonus: $133,200
Savings Plan: Stock Purch. Plan: Second Exec. Salary: $420,092 Bonus: $133,200

OTHER THOUGHTS:

Apparent Women Officers or Directors: 1
Hot Spot for Advancement for Women/Minorities:

LOCATIONS: ("Y" = Yes)

West:	Southwest:	Midwest:	Southeast:	Northeast:	International:
Y	Y				Y

Sales, profits and employees may be estimates. Financial information, benefits and other data can change quickly and may vary from those stated here.

FIRST ADVANTAGE CORPORATION

www.fadv.com

Industry Group Code: 561450

Management:		Sales/Marketing:		Liberal Arts:		Information Sys.:		Professionals:		Tech./Scientific:	
Mgmt. Trainees:	Y	Marketing Pros.:	Y	Gen. Writing/Editing:	Y	Info. Mgmt.:	Y	Finance/Acct.:	Y	Engineers, Elec.:	
Experienced Mgmt.:	Y	Retail Sales:		Tech. Writing:	Y	Software Dev.:	Y	Law:	Y	Engineers, Other:	
Int'l Business:	Y	Comm./Industrial:	Y	Graphic Arts/Photog.:	Y	Hardware Dev.:		HR/Other:	Y	Health/Lab:	
MBA Grads:	Y	Sales Trainees:	Y	Music:		Consulting/Other:		Training:	Y	Science/Research:	
		Advertising Pros.:		Broadcasting:				Health Care:		Petroleum/Chem.:	
				Other:				Consulting:		Math/Other:	

TYPES OF BUSINESS:

Credit Reports
Employee Screening

BRANDS/DIVISIONS/AFFILIATES:

First American Corporation (The)
Symphony Technology Group

CONTACTS: *Note: Officers with more than one job title may be intentionally listed here more than once.*

Andy Macdonald, CEO
Andy Macdonald, Pres.
Christopher Wolf, CFO
Paige Vesuvio, VP-Mktg.
Valerie Fulbright, VP-Human Resources
Bret Jardine, General Counsel
Valerie Osinski, Sr. VP/Exec. Gen. Mgr.-Screening Solutions
Josephine Kenney,, Sr. VP-Compliance

Phone: 619-938-7500	**Fax:**
Toll-Free: 866-400-3238	
Address: 100 Carillon Pkwy., St. Petersburg, FL 33716 US	

GROWTH PLANS/SPECIAL FEATURES:

First Advantage Corporation, owned by Symphony Technology Group, provides credit reporting and employee screening marketed primarily to global business customers. The company offers a complete range of hiring services and products designed to reduce costs associated with the process of hiring employees including candidate sourcing, applicant tracking, screening and assessment and post-hire assistance. First Advantage assists in candidate sourcing through strategy development, candidate relationship management, distribution technology, recruitment streamlining and social sourcing. Applicant tracking provides automated new hire forms, task management, virtual personnel files and direct connections to its other products. Screening and assessment services allow clients to test job-related skills and behavioral patterns, in addition to providing background screening, fingerprinting services, substance abuse testing and other services. The post-hire offerings include training, employee assistance programs, employment and income verification, continual screening and training grants. The company has developed specific hiring services for the finance, fleet, gaming & hospitality, petrochemical, retail and staffing industries. It serves companies in North America, Europe, the Middle East, Africa and Asia Pacific. In January 2011, First Advantage was acquired by private equity firm Symphony Technology Group.

First Advantage offers its employees tuition reimbursement; e-learning programs; banking discounts; an employee assistance program; flexible spending accounts; and medical, dental, vision, prescription, life and disability insurance, among other benefits.

FINANCIALS: **Sales and profits are in thousands of dollars—add 000 to get the full amount. 2010 Note: Financial information for 2010 was not available for all companies at press time.**

2010 Sales: $740,000	2010 Profits: $64,700	**U.S. Stock Ticker: Subsidiary**
2009 Sales: $700,000	2009 Profits: $	**Int'l Ticker:**
2008 Sales: $727,276	2008 Profits: $34,857	Int'l Exchange:
2007 Sales: $770,165	2007 Profits: $138,107	Employees: 3,700 Fiscal Year Ends: 12/31
2006 Sales: $797,801	2006 Profits: $66,161	Parent Company: SYMPHONY TECHNOLOGY GROUP

SALARIES/BENEFITS:

Pension Plan:	ESOP Stock Plan:	Profit Sharing:	Top Exec. Salary: $700,000	Bonus: $444,500
Savings Plan: Y	Stock Purch. Plan: Y		Second Exec. Salary: $395,533	Bonus: $238,125

OTHER THOUGHTS:

Apparent Women Officers or Directors: 4
Hot Spot for Advancement for Women/Minorities: Y

LOCATIONS: ("Y" = Yes)

West:	Southwest:	Midwest:	Southeast:	Northeast:	International:
Y	Y		Y	Y	Y

FIRSTENERGY CORP

www.firstenergycorp.com

Industry Group Code: 2211

Management:		Sales/Marketing:		Liberal Arts:		Information Sys.:		Professionals:		Tech./Scientific:	
Mgmt. Trainees:	Y	Marketing Pros.:	Y	Gen. Writing/Editing:	Y	Info. Mgmt.:	Y	Finance/Acct.:	Y	Engineers, Elec.:	Y
Experienced Mgmt.:	Y	Retail Sales:		Tech. Writing:	Y	Software Dev.:	Y	Law:	Y	Engineers, Other:	Y
Int'l Business:		Comm./Industrial:	Y	Graphic Arts/Photog.:	Y	Hardware Dev.:		HR/Other:	Y	Health/Lab:	
MBA Grads:	Y	Sales Trainees:		Music:		Consulting/Other:		Training:	Y	Science/Research:	
		Advertising Pros.:	Y	Broadcasting:				Health Care:		Petroleum/Chem.:	Y
				Other:				Consulting:		Math/Other:	

TYPES OF BUSINESS:

Utilities-Electricity & Natural Gas
Power Generation
Energy Management
Telecommunications

BRANDS/DIVISIONS/AFFILIATES:

Ohio Edison Co.
Cleveland Electric Illuminating Co. (The)
Toledo Edison Co. (The)
Pennsylvania Electric Co.
Jersey Central Power & Light Co.
Metropolitan Edison Co.
Pennsylvania Power Co.
FirstEnergy Service Company

CONTACTS: *Note: Officers with more than one job title may be intentionally listed here more than once.*

Anthony J. Alexander, CEO
Anthony J. Alexander, Pres.
Mark T. Clark, CFO/Exec. VP
Lynn M. Cavalier, Sr. VP-Human Resources
Leila L. Vespoli, General Counsel/Exec. VP
Harvey L. Wagner, Chief Acct. Officer/VP/Controller
Donald R. Schneider, Pres., FirstEnergy Solutions
Gary R. Leidich, Exec. VP
Charles E. Jones, Jr., Pres., First Energy Utilities
James H. Lash, Pres., FirstEnergy Generation
George M. Smart, Chmn.

Phone:	**Fax:** 330-384-3545
Toll-Free: 800-736-3402	
Address: 76 S. Main St., Akron, OH 44308 US	

GROWTH PLANS/SPECIAL FEATURES:

FirstEnergy Corp. is a diversified energy services holding company involved in the generation, transmission and distribution of electricity, energy management and other energy-related services. The firm operates eight principal electric utility subsidiaries: Ohio Edison Co.; The Cleveland Electric Illuminating Co.; The Toledo Edison Co.; Pennsylvania Electric Co.; Jersey Central Power & Light Co.; The Potomac Edison Company; West Penn Power Company; Metropolitan Edison Co.; and Pennsylvania Power Co. FirstEnergy is one of the largest investor-owned electric systems, serving 6 million customers in a service area that ranges over 65,000 square miles of Ohio, Pennsylvania, West Virginia, Maryland and New Jersey. It has more than 23,000 megawatts (MW) of generating capacity. Generation is conducted through a variety of methods including coal, nuclear power, gas and oil and hydroelectric generation. Other FirstEnergy subsidiaries including FirstEnergy Ventures Corp.; FirstEnergy Properties, Inc.; GPU Power, Inc.; GPU Nuclear, Inc.; FirstEnergy Solutions Corp., FirstEnergy Service Company, FirstEnergy Generation Corp. and FirstEnergy Utilities. In February 2011, the company acquired Allegheny Energy, Inc., the parent company of The Potomac Edison Company and West Penn Power Company, for roughly $4.7 billion.

The firm offers employees medical, dental and vision benefits; a 401(k) savings plan; a pension plan; life insurance; flexible spending accounts; adoption assistance; and disability coverage.

FINANCIALS: **Sales and profits are in thousands of dollars—add 000 to get the full amount. 2010 Note: Financial information for 2010 was not available for all companies at press time.**

2010 Sales: $13,339,000 — 2010 Profits: $784,000
2009 Sales: $12,967,000 — 2009 Profits: $1,006,000
2008 Sales: $13,627,000 — 2008 Profits: $1,342,000
2007 Sales: $12,802,000 — 2007 Profits: $1,309,000
2006 Sales: $11,501,000 — 2006 Profits: $1,254,000

U.S. Stock Ticker: FE
Int'l Ticker:
Int'l Exchange:
Employees: 13,330 Fiscal Year Ends: 12/31
Parent Company:

SALARIES/BENEFITS:

Pension Plan: Y | ESOP Stock Plan: | Profit Sharing: | Top Exec. Salary: $1,328,404 | Bonus: $2,468,950
Savings Plan: Y | Stock Purch. Plan: | | Second Exec. Salary: $650,000 | Bonus: $747,338

OTHER THOUGHTS:

Apparent Women Officers or Directors: 6
Hot Spot for Advancement for Women/Minorities: Y

LOCATIONS: ("Y" = Yes)

West:	Southwest:	Midwest:	Southeast:	Northeast:	International:
Y		Y		Y	

FLUOR CORP

www.fluor.com

Industry Group Code: 237

Management:		**Sales/Marketing:**		**Liberal Arts:**		**Information Sys.:**		**Professionals:**		**Tech./Scientific:**	
Mgmt. Trainees:	Y	Marketing Pros.:	Y	Gen. Writing/Editing:	Y	Info. Mgmt.:	Y	Finance/Acct.:	Y	Engineers, Elec.:	Y
Experienced Mgmt.:	Y	Retail Sales:		Tech. Writing:	Y	Software Dev.:	Y	Law:	Y	Engineers, Other:	Y
Int'l Business:	Y	Comm./Industrial:	Y	Graphic Arts/Photog.:	Y	Hardware Dev.:		HR/Other:	Y	Health/Lab:	
MBA Grads:	Y	Sales Trainees:	Y	Music:		Consulting/Other:	Y	Training:	Y	Science/Research:	
		Advertising Pros.:	Y	Broadcasting:				Health Care:		Petroleum/Chem.:	Y
				Other:				Consulting:	Y	Math/Other:	Y

TYPES OF BUSINESS:

Construction, Heavy & Civil Engineering
Power Plant Construction and Management
Facilities Management
Procurement Services
Consulting Services
Project Management
Asset Management
Staffing Services

BRANDS/DIVISIONS/AFFILIATES:

Fluor Constructors International, Inc.

CONTACTS:

Note: Officers with more than one job title may be intentionally listed here more than once.

David T. Seaton, CEO
D. Michael Steuert, CFO/Sr. VP
Glenn Gilkey, Sr. VP-Human Resources
Ray F. Barnard, CIO/VP
Glenn Gilkey, Sr. VP-Admin.
Carlos M. Hernandez, Chief Legal Officer/Corp. Sec.
David E. Constable, Group Pres., Oper.
John L. Hopkins, Group Exec.-Bus. Dev.
Lee Tashjian, VP-Corp. Affairs
Kenneth H. Lockwood, VP-Investor Rel.
Kenneth H. Lockwood, VP-Corp. Finance
Wendy Hallgren, VP-Corp. Compliance
David Marventano, Sr. VP-Gov't Rel.
Joanna M. Oliva, Treas./VP
Richard P. Carter, Pres., Fluor Constructors International, Inc.
Alan L. Boeckmann, Chmn.
Kirk D. Grimes, Pres., Global Svcs.

Phone: 469-398-7000 **Fax:** 469-398-7255
Toll-Free:
Address: 6700 Las Colinas Blvd., Irving, TX 75039 US

GROWTH PLANS/SPECIAL FEATURES:

Fluor Corp. is a global provider of engineering, procurement, construction and maintenance services, with offices in over 25 countries spanning across six continents. The corporation provides logistics services in both Afghanistan and Iraq. As well as being a primary service provider to the U.S. federal government, Fluor serves a diverse set of industries including oil and gas; chemical and petrochemicals; transportation; mining and metals; power; life sciences; and manufacturing. Fluor operates in five business segments: oil and gas; industrial and infrastructure; government; global services; and power. The oil and gas segment offers design, engineering, procurement, construction and project management services to energy-related industries. The industrial and infrastructure segment provides design, engineering and construction services to the transportation, mining, life sciences, telecommunications, manufacturing, microelectronics and healthcare sectors. The government segment provides project management services, including environmental restoration, engineering, construction, site operations and maintenance, to the U.S. government, particularly to the Department of Energy, the Department of Homeland Security and the Department of Defense. The global services segment provides operations, maintenance and construction services, as well as industrial fleet outsourcing, plant turnaround services, temporary staffing, procurement services and construction-related support. The power segment provides such services as engineering, procurement, construction, program management, start-up, commissioning and maintenance to the gas fueled, solid fueled, renewable and nuclear marketplaces. Fluor Constructors International, Inc., which operates separately from the rest of the businesses, provides unionized management and construction services in the U.S. and Canada, both independently.

Employees are offered life, disability, medical, dental, vision, auto and home insurance; a retirement plan; a 401(k) savings plan; an employee assistance program; a tax savings account; education assistance; and legal services.

FINANCIALS:

Sales and profits are in thousands of dollars—add 000 to get the full amount. 2010 Note: Financial information for 2010 was not available for all companies at press time.

2010 Sales: $20,849,300	2010 Profits: $441,100
2009 Sales: $21,990,300	2009 Profits: $732,875
2008 Sales: $22,325,900	2008 Profits: $748,903
2007 Sales: $16,691,000	2007 Profits: $527,961
2006 Sales: $14,078,500	2006 Profits: $263,500

U.S. Stock Ticker: FLR
Int'l Ticker:
Int'l Exchange:
Employees: 39,229 Fiscal Year Ends: 12/31
Parent Company:

SALARIES/BENEFITS:

Pension Plan: Y	ESOP Stock Plan:	Profit Sharing:	Top Exec. Salary: $1,248,042	Bonus: $3,663,280
Savings Plan: Y	Stock Purch. Plan:		Second Exec. Salary: $791,835	Bonus: $1,310,540

OTHER THOUGHTS:

Apparent Women Officers or Directors: 6
Hot Spot for Advancement for Women/Minorities: Y

LOCATIONS: ("Y" = Yes)

West:	Southwest:	Midwest:	Southeast:	Northeast:	International:
Y	Y	Y	Y	Y	Y

FM GLOBAL

www.fmglobal.com

Industry Group Code: 524126

Management:		Sales/Marketing:		Liberal Arts:		Information Sys.:		Professionals:		Tech./Scientific:	
Mgmt. Trainees:		Marketing Pros.:	Y	Gen. Writing/Editing:		Info. Mgmt.:	Y	Finance/Acct.:	Y	Engineers, Elec.:	
Experienced Mgmt.:	Y	Retail Sales:		Tech. Writing:		Software Dev.:		Law:		Engineers, Other:	Y
Int'l Business:	Y	Comm./Industrial:		Graphic Arts/Photog.:		Hardware Dev.:		HR/Other:		Health/Lab:	
MBA Grads:	Y	Sales Trainees:		Music:		Consulting/Other:	Y	Training:		Science/Research:	Y
		Advertising Pros.:		Broadcasting:				Health Care:		Petroleum/Chem.:	
				Other:				Consulting:	Y	Math/Other:	

TYPES OF BUSINESS:

Insurance, Specialty Property & Casualty
Risk Management Services
Property Loss Prevention Engineering
Consulting

BRANDS/DIVISIONS/AFFILIATES:

Affiliated FM
FM Approvals
Mutual Boiler RE
TSB Loss Control Consultants
Corporate Insurance Services
FM Global Cargo
FM Global Research Campus

CONTACTS: *Note: Officers with more than one job title may be intentionally listed here more than once.*

Shivan S. Subramaniam, CEO
Jonathan W. Hall, Exec. VP-Mktg.
Jonathan W. Hall, Exec. VP-Research
Jonathan W. Hall, Exec. VP-Eng.
Thomas A. Lawson, Exec. VP-North America Insurance Oper.
Steven Zenofsky, Mgr.-Public Rel.
Ruud H. Bosman, Vice-Chmn.
Jonathan W. Hall, Exec. VP-Training, Underwriting & Reinsurance
Shivan S. Subramaniam, Chmn.
Thomas A. Lawson, Exec. VP-South America Insurance Oper.

Phone: 401-275-3000	**Fax:** 401-275-3029
Toll-Free: 800-320-6808	
Address: 270 Central Ave., Johnston, RI 02919 US	

GROWTH PLANS/SPECIAL FEATURES:

FM Global, founded in 1835, offers insurance products and property loss prevention engineering services to companies in over 130 countries. Specializing in the chemical, forest products, power generation, education, public entities and health care industries, the firm provides risk management services to avoid property loss and insurance services for when property loss occurs. With a policyholder surplus of approximately $7.3 billion, the company is able to handle claims for businesses around the globe. FM Global operates through a number of business units. Affiliated FM provides middle-market businesses and industries with commercial property insurance and property loss control engineering tailored to the specific needs of each client. Affiliated FM operates in the U.S., Canada, the U.K., France, Germany, the Netherlands and Australia. FM Approvals certifies commercial and industrial property loss prevention products for companies across the globe, publishing over 45,000 products and services in its Approval Guide. Mutual Boiler RE serves the commercial property insurance marketplace, specializing in mechanical, electrical and pressure systems breakdown treaty reinsurance and related support services. FM Global Cargo offers customized cargo insurance coverage, risk engineering services and automated certificate management to the international trade industry. TSB Loss Control Consultants is a consultancy firm that provides training for industrial emergency-response personnel. Corporate Insurance Services (CIS) is a brokerage firm that works with U.S. domestic insurers, specialty companies, surplus/excess line insurers and Lloyd's of London. CIS also offers flood, wind, earthquake, all-risk, inland marine, ocean marine and other lines of insurance. FM Global Research Campus is the company's 1,600 acre facility for property loss prevention, scientific research and product testing. FM Global recently became an admitted reinsurer in Brazil and an admitted insurer in Switzerland.

FM Global offers its employees benefits including travel assistance, a retirement program, educational assistance and medical insurance.

FINANCIALS: **Sales and profits are in thousands of dollars—add 000 to get the full amount. 2010 Note: Financial information for 2010 was not available for all companies at press time.**

2010 Sales: $4,686,800	2010 Profits: $686,000	**U.S. Stock Ticker: Mutual Company**
2009 Sales: $4,312,100	2009 Profits: $839,500	**Int'l Ticker:**
2008 Sales: $3,364,800	2008 Profits: $-318,000	Int'l Exchange:
2007 Sales: $3,355,800	2007 Profits: $927,800	Employees: 5,100 Fiscal Year Ends: 12/31
2006 Sales: $3,321,700	2006 Profits: $736,900	Parent Company:

SALARIES/BENEFITS:

Pension Plan: Y	ESOP Stock Plan:	Profit Sharing:	Top Exec. Salary: $	Bonus: $
Savings Plan:	Stock Purch. Plan:		Second Exec. Salary: $	Bonus: $

OTHER THOUGHTS:

Apparent Women Officers or Directors:
Hot Spot for Advancement for Women/Minorities:

LOCATIONS: ("Y" = Yes)

West:	Southwest:	Midwest:	Southeast:	Northeast:	International:
Y	Y	Y	Y	Y	Y

FMC TECHNOLOGIES INC

www.fmctechnologies.com

Industry Group Code: 213112

Management:		**Sales/Marketing:**		**Liberal Arts:**		**Information Sys.:**		**Professionals:**		**Tech./Scientific:**	
Mgmt. Trainees:	Y	Marketing Pros.:	Y	Gen. Writing/Editing:		Info. Mgmt.:	Y	Finance/Acct.:	Y	Engineers, Elec.:	Y
Experienced Mgmt.:	Y	Retail Sales:		Tech. Writing:	Y	Software Dev.:	Y	Law:	Y	Engineers, Other:	Y
Int'l Business:	Y	Comm./Industrial:	Y	Graphic Arts/Photog.:	Y	Hardware Dev.:		HR/Other:	Y	Health/Lab:	
MBA Grads:	Y	Sales Trainees:		Music:		Consulting/Other:		Training:	Y	Science/Research:	Y
		Advertising Pros.:		Broadcasting:				Health Care:		Petroleum/Chem.:	Y
				Other:				Consulting:		Math/Other:	

TYPES OF BUSINESS:

Oil & Gas Production & Processing Equipment
Airport & Airline Equipment
Food Handling & Processing Systems

BRANDS/DIVISIONS/AFFILIATES:

CONTACTS:

Note: Officers with more than one job title may be intentionally listed here more than once.

John T. Gremp, CEO
John T. Gremp, Pres.
William H. Schumann, III, CFO/Exec. VP
Bradley D. Beitler, VP-Tech.
Mark J. Scott, VP-Admin.
Jeffrey W. Carr, General Counsel/Sr. VP/Corp. Sec.
Jay A. Nutt, Controller/VP
Maryann T. Seaman, Treas./VP
Johan Pfeiffer, VP-Global Surface Wellhead
Tore Halvorsen, Sr. VP-Global Subsea Prod. Systems
Robert L. Potter, Exec. VP-Energy Systems
Peter D. Kinnear, Chmn.

Phone: 281-591-4000	**Fax:** 281-591-4102
Toll-Free:	
Address: 1803 Gears Rd., Houston, TX 77067 US	

GROWTH PLANS/SPECIAL FEATURES:

FMC Technologies, Inc. designs, manufactures and services technologically sophisticated systems and products such as subsea production and processing systems, surface wellhead production systems, high pressure fluid control equipment, measurement solutions and marine loading equipment for the oil and gas industry. The company's business segments are Energy Production Systems and Energy Processing Systems. The Energy Production Systems division, which accounts for roughly 81% of the firm's revenues, designs and manufactures systems and provides services used by the oil and gas companies involved in land and offshore, including deepwater, exploration and production of crude oil gas. The Energy Processing Systems division (19% of revenues) designs, manufactures and supplies technologically advanced high pressure valves and fittings for oilfield service customers, as well as manufacturing liquid and gas measurement and transportation equipment and systems to customers involved in the production, transportation and processing of crude oil, natural gas and petroleum-based refined products. The firm maintains 27 manufacturing facilities in 16 countries. FMC Technologies derives roughly 77% of its revenues outside of the U.S.

Employees are offered life, disability, medical, dental and vision insurance; a 401(k) plan; a pension plan; legal services; educational assistance; an employee assistance plan; adoption assistance; and employee discounts.

FINANCIALS:

Sales and profits are in thousands of dollars—add 000 to get the full amount. 2010 Note: Financial information for 2010 was not available for all companies at press time.

2010 Sales: $4,125,600	2010 Profits: $377,900	**U.S. Stock Ticker: FTI**
2009 Sales: $4,405,400	2009 Profits: $363,300	**Int'l Ticker:**
2008 Sales: $4,550,900	2008 Profits: $361,300	Int'l Exchange:
2007 Sales: $3,648,900	2007 Profits: $302,800	Employees: 11,500 Fiscal Year Ends: 12/31
2006 Sales: $2,915,400	2006 Profits: $276,300	Parent Company:

SALARIES/BENEFITS:

Pension Plan: Y	ESOP Stock Plan:	Profit Sharing:	Top Exec. Salary: $900,000	Bonus: $1,332,900
Savings Plan: Y	Stock Purch. Plan:		Second Exec. Salary: $589,384	Bonus: $523,726

OTHER THOUGHTS:

Apparent Women Officers or Directors: 2
Hot Spot for Advancement for Women/Minorities: Y

LOCATIONS: ("Y" = Yes)

West:	Southwest:	Midwest:	Southeast:	Northeast:	International:
Y	Y	Y	Y	Y	Y

FMR CORP (FIDELITY INVESTMENTS)

www.fidelity.com

Industry Group Code: 523920

Management:		Sales/Marketing:		Liberal Arts:		Information Sys.:		Professionals:		Tech./Scientific:	
Mgmt. Trainees:	Y	Marketing Pros.:	Y	Gen. Writing/Editing:	Y	Info. Mgmt.:	Y	Finance/Acct.:	Y	Engineers, Elec.:	
Experienced Mgmt.:	Y	Retail Sales:	Y	Tech. Writing:		Software Dev.:	Y	Law:	Y	Engineers, Other:	
Int'l Business:	Y	Comm./Industrial:	Y	Graphic Arts/Photog.:	Y	Hardware Dev.:		HR/Other:	Y	Health/Lab:	
MBA Grads:	Y	Sales Trainees:	Y	Music:		Consulting/Other:		Training:	Y	Science/Research:	Y
		Advertising Pros.:	Y	Broadcasting:				Health Care:		Petroleum/Chem.:	
				Other:				Consulting:		Math/Other:	

TYPES OF BUSINESS:

Mutual Funds
Human Resources Administration Services
Employee Benefits Services
Online Brokerage
Outsourced Staffing and Recruiting Services
Clearing and Execution Products and Services
Real Estate Investments
Institutional Account Management and Services

BRANDS/DIVISIONS/AFFILIATES:

Fidelity Investments
Fidelity Management & Research Company (FMR Co.)
Pyramis Global Advisors
Fidelity Employer Services Co.
Fidelity Investments Canada, Ltd.
Fidelity Brokerage Services
Fidelity Investments Life Insurance Company
Strategic Advisers, Inc.

CONTACTS: *Note: Officers with more than one job title may be intentionally listed here more than once.*

Edward C. Johnson, III, CEO
Michael E. Wilens, Pres., Tech.
Michael E. Wilens, Pres., Corp. Oper.
Kevin Uebelein, Pres./CEO-Pyramis Global Advisors
Ronald P. O'Hanley, Head-Asset Management
Jacques Perold, Pres., Fidelity Management & Research Co.
Edward C. Johnson, III, Chmn.
Bill Henderson, CEO-Fidelity Clearing Canada ULC
Abigail Johnson, Pres., Dist.

Phone: 617-563-7000	**Fax:**
Toll-Free: 800-343-3548	
Address: 82 Devonshire St., Boston, MA 02109 US	

GROWTH PLANS/SPECIAL FEATURES:

FMR Corp., operating as Fidelity Investments, is one of the nation's largest mutual fund companies and one of the world's largest providers of financial services. With over $3.5 trillion in assets under administration, the company offers more than 500 mutual funds and numerous other investment vehicles for individual, corporate and other institutional investors. FMR is one of the largest providers of 401(k) retirement savings plans in the U.S. and a leading provider of 403(b), 457 and 401(a) retirement plans for non-profits, colleges, universities, healthcare institutions, state agencies and local governments. In addition, some of the firm provides IRAs, CDs, money market accounts, insurance, bill pay services, checking accounts and annuities, as well as market news and analysis. Fidelity Management & Research Company, with more than 500 analysts and traders, is the investment advisor to Fidelity's funds. Through subsidiary Fidelity Employer Services Co., FMR administers benefit plans for over 15,000 employers and offers human resources administration and employee benefits services. The company also provides investment management products and services such as the Fidelity Advisor family of mutual funds. Through Fidelity Brokerage Services, individual investors can buy and sell stocks, bonds, options, and more than 4,000 mutual funds. FMR's Pyramis Global Advisors unit is a spin-off designed to enhance services and investment products for institutional investors such as corporate and public retirement funds, endowments and foundations. The company serves retail customers by phone and through over 150 investor centers located throughout the U.S. The firm has additional operations in South America, Europe, Asia, the Middle East, Africa and Australia. Outside of the U.S., Fidelity's operations are conducted through its subsidiaries, including Fidelity Investments Canada, Ltd.; Fidelity Investments Management (H.K.), Ltd.; Fidelity Investments Japan; Strategic Advisers, Inc.; Fidelity Investments Life Insurance Company; and Fidelity Brokerage Services Japan LLC.

FINANCIALS: **Sales and profits are in thousands of dollars—add 000 to get the full amount. 2010 Note: Financial information for 2010 was not available for all companies at press time.**

2010 Sales: $	2010 Profits: $	**U.S. Stock Ticker: Private**
2009 Sales: $	2009 Profits: $	**Int'l Ticker:**
2008 Sales: $12,900,000	2008 Profits: $	Int'l Exchange:
2007 Sales: $14,900,000	2007 Profits: $	Employees: 42,000 Fiscal Year Ends: 12/31
2006 Sales: $12,870,000	2006 Profits: $	Parent Company:

SALARIES/BENEFITS:

Pension Plan: Y	ESOP Stock Plan:	Profit Sharing:	Top Exec. Salary: $	Bonus: $
Savings Plan: Y	Stock Purch. Plan:		Second Exec. Salary: $	Bonus: $

OTHER THOUGHTS:

Apparent Women Officers or Directors: 1
Hot Spot for Advancement for Women/Minorities:

LOCATIONS: ("Y" = Yes)

West:	Southwest:	Midwest:	Southeast:	Northeast:	International:
Y	Y	Y	Y	Y	Y

FORD MOTOR CO

www.ford.com

Industry Group Code: 33611

Management:		**Sales/Marketing:**		**Liberal Arts:**		**Information Sys.:**		**Professionals:**		**Tech./Scientific:**	
Mgmt. Trainees:	Y	Marketing Pros.:	Y	Gen. Writing/Editing:	Y	Info. Mgmt.:	Y	Finance/Acct.:	Y	Engineers, Elec.:	Y
Experienced Mgmt.:	Y	Retail Sales:		Tech. Writing:	Y	Software Dev.:	Y	Law:	Y	Engineers, Other:	
Int'l Business:	Y	Comm./Industrial:	Y	Graphic Arts/Photog.:		Hardware Dev.:	Y	HR/Other:	Y	Health/Lab:	Y
MBA Grads:	Y	Sales Trainees:		Music:		Consulting/Other:		Training:	Y	Science/Research:	Y
		Advertising Pros.:	Y	Broadcasting:				Health Care:		Petroleum/Chem.:	
				Other:				Consulting:		Math/Other:	Y

TYPES OF BUSINESS:

Automobile Manufacturer
Automobile Financing
Fuel-Cell & Hybrid Research

BRANDS/DIVISIONS/AFFILIATES:

Lincoln
Motorcraft
Zhejiang Geely Holding Group
Ford Sync
Ford Mustang
Mazda Motor Corporation
Ford Motor Credit Company (The)
MY Ford Mondeo

CONTACTS: *Note: Officers with more than one job title may be intentionally listed here more than once.*

Alan Mulally, CEO
Alan Mulally, Pres.
Lewis W. K. Booth, CFO/Exec. VP
James D. Farley, VP-Mktg. Sales & Service
Felicia J. Fields, VP-Human Resources & Corp. Svcs.
Gerhard Schmidt, VP-Research
Nicholas J. Smither, CIO/VP
Gerhard Schmidt, CTO
Derrick M. Kuzak, VP-Global Prod. Dev.
Gerhard Schmidt, VP-Advanced Eng.
John Fleming, Exec. VP-Mfg. & Labor Affairs
David G. Leitch, General Counsel/Sr. VP
Raymond F. Day, VP-Comm.
Neil M. Schloss, Treas./VP
Michael E. Bannister, Exec. VP/CEO/Chmn.-Ford Motor Credit Co.
Mark Fields, Exec. VP/Pres., Americas
Stephen E. Biegun, VP-Int'l Gov't Affairs
Robert L. Shanks, VP/Controller
William C. Ford, Jr., Exec. Chmn.
Joseph R. Hinrichs, Pres., APAC & Africa
Thomas K. Brown, Sr. VP-Global Purchasing

Phone: 313-322-3000	**Fax:** 313-845-7512
Toll-Free: 800-392-3673	
Address: 1 American Rd., Dearborn, MI 48126 US	

GROWTH PLANS/SPECIAL FEATURES:

Ford Motor Co. is a designer and manufacturer of automobiles and automotive systems. The firm operates in two segments: automotive and financial services. The automotive segment designs, manufactures, sells and services cars and trucks under the brands Ford and Lincoln. The company sells its vehicles to the public via independently owned dealerships, including roughly 10,719 Ford, 284 Lincoln and 997 Ford-Lincoln dealerships. In addition to new car sales, these dealerships offer after-sale vehicle services and products such as maintenance and repair; vehicle accessories; and extended-service warranties. Ford markets these products and services under brands including Ford, Ford Extended Service Plan and Motorcraft. Ford also owns a minority interest in Mazda Motor Corporation. The firm's financial services segment, run through the Ford Motor Credit Company LLC, offers vehicle-related financing, leasing and insurance. Some of Ford's most popular vehicles include the Ford Mustang sports car, the Ford F150 truck, the compact Ford Focus, the Lincoln Navigator SUV and the Ford Escape Hybrid SUV. Through a partnership with Microsoft, the firm offers Ford Sync, a voice-activated in-car communications and entertainment system for mobile phones and music players. The company hopes to quickly introduce fully electric vehicles to the U.S. market. In March 2010, Ford launched the Figo compact car, its first vehicle made specifically for the Indian market. In August 2010, the firm sold its Volvo Cars unit to Zhejiang Geely Holding Group for $1.8 billion. In late 2010, Ford closed its Mercury division. In March 2011, the company released eight models of sedan 2011 MY Ford Mondeo.

The company offers its employees medical, dental and prescription insurance; life and disability insurance; a savings plan; relocation packages; gift matching; dependent scholarships; recreation programs; tuition assistance; and group rates on auto, home, and life insurance.

FINANCIALS: **Sales and profits are in thousands of dollars—add 000 to get the full amount. 2010 Note: Financial information for 2010 was not available for all companies at press time.**

2010 Sales: $128,954,000
2009 Sales: $105,893,000
2008 Sales: $129,165,000
2007 Sales: $154,379,000
2006 Sales: $160,065,000

2010 Profits: $6,561,000
2009 Profits: $2,717,000
2008 Profits: $-14,766,000
2007 Profits: $-2,795,000
2006 Profits: $-12,613,000

U.S. Stock Ticker: F
Int'l Ticker:
Int'l Exchange:
Employees: 164,000 Fiscal Year Ends: 12/31
Parent Company:

SALARIES/BENEFITS:

Pension Plan:	ESOP Stock Plan:	Profit Sharing:	Top Exec. Salary: $1,400,003	Bonus: $
Savings Plan: Y	Stock Purch. Plan:		Second Exec. Salary: $1,300,000	Bonus: $

OTHER THOUGHTS:

Apparent Women Officers or Directors: 5
Hot Spot for Advancement for Women/Minorities: Y

LOCATIONS: ("Y" = Yes)

West:	Southwest:	Midwest:	Southeast:	Northeast:	International:
Y	Y	Y	Y	Y	Y

FOREST LABORATORIES INC

www.frx.com

Industry Group Code: 325412

Management:		Sales/Marketing:		Liberal Arts:		Information Sys.:		Professionals:		Tech./Scientific:	
Mgmt. Trainees:	Y	Marketing Pros.:	Y	Gen. Writing/Editing:	Y	Info. Mgmt.:	Y	Finance/Acct.:	Y	Engineers, Elec.:	Y
Experienced Mgmt.:	Y	Retail Sales:		Tech. Writing:	Y	Software Dev.:	Y	Law:	Y	Engineers, Other:	Y
Int'l Business:	Y	Comm./Industrial:	Y	Graphic Arts/Photog.:	Y	Hardware Dev.:		HR/Other:	Y	Health/Lab:	Y
MBA Grads:	Y	Sales Trainees:		Music:		Consulting/Other:		Training:	Y	Science/Research:	Y
		Advertising Pros.:		Broadcasting:				Health Care:	Y	Petroleum/Chem.:	Y
				Other:				Consulting:		Math/Other:	Y

TYPES OF BUSINESS:

Drugs, Manufacturing
Over-the-Counter Pharmaceuticals
Generic Pharmaceuticals
Antidepressants
Asthma Medications
Cardiovascular Products
OB/Gyn Products
Endocrinology Products

BRANDS/DIVISIONS/AFFILIATES:

Lexapro
Namenda
Bystolic
Forest Research Institute
Forest Pharmaceuticals, Inc.
Clinical Data, Inc.
Inwood Laboratories
Cerexa, Inc.

CONTACTS: *Note: Officers with more than one job title may be intentionally listed here more than once.*

Howard Solomon, CEO
Howard Solomon, Pres.
Francis I. Perier, Jr., CFO
Jerome Lynch, Sr. VP-Sales
Marco Taglietti, Sr. VP-R&D/Pres., Forest Research Institute
Francis I. Perier, Jr., Exec. VP-Admin.
Herschel S. Weinstein, General Counsel/VP/Corp. Sec.
Kevin Walsh, Sr. VP-Oper.
David F. Solomon, Sr. VP-Corp. Dev. & Strategic Planning
Frank J. Murdolo, VP-Investor Rel.
Francis I. Perier, Jr., Exec. VP-Finance
Elaine Hochberg, Chief Commercial Officer/Exec. VP
Howard Solomon, Chmn.

Phone: 212-421-7850	**Fax:**
Toll-Free: 800-947-5227	
Address: 909 3rd Ave., New York, NY 10022-4731 US	

GROWTH PLANS/SPECIAL FEATURES:

Forest Laboratories, Inc. develops, manufactures and sells pharmaceutical products. It currently covers six therapeutic areas, developing treatments for respiratory, pain management, obstetrics and gynecology (ob/gyn) and pediatric, endocrinology, central nervous system and cardiovascular conditions. Forest's four principal brands are Lexapro, an antidepressant; Bystolic, a hypertension treatment; Namenda, a therapy for moderate or severe Alzheimer's disease; and Savella, a dual reuptake inhibitor for the treatment of fibromyalgia. Other products include Daxas for the treatment of chronic obstructive pulmonary disease; Celexa, an antidepressant; Campral, used to treat alcohol dependence; Armour Thyroid, Levothroid and Thyrolar, for treating hypothyroidism; Cervidil, used to prepare the cervix before inducing labor; Aerobid, an asthma medication; AeroChamber Plus, an inhalant delivery system for asthma medications; and Combunox, a pain medication. Forest markets directly to physicians, as well as to pharmacies, hospitals, managed care and other healthcare organizations. The firm's principal customers, which account for 89% of its revenues, include McKesson Drug Company; Cardinal Health, Inc.; and AmeriSource Bergen Corporation. Forest Research Institute, Forest's scientific division, maintains labs on Long Island and in New Jersey. Subsidiary Forest Pharmaceuticals, Inc. manufactures and distributes Forest's branded prescription products in the U.S. Subsidiary Forest Laboratories Europe distributes prescription and over-the-counter drugs in Europe, the Middle East, Australia and Asia. Subsidiary Inwood Laboratories manufactures and supplies generic versions of Forest's medications. Cerexa, Inc. develops and commercializes treatments for life-threatening infections. In December 2010, subsidiary Forest Healthcare B.V. acquired the rights to the colistin products of Gruenenthal GmbH, and sold the rights to Colobreathe to Gruenenthal. In March 2011, Forest subsidiary Magnolia Acquisition Corp. agreed to acquire Clinical Data, Inc.

Employees at Forest receive life, disability, medical, dental, vision and prescription coverage; financial assistance for adoption and fertility treatment; flexible spending accounts; a commuter benefit program; a profit sharing plan; and a 401(k).

FINANCIALS: **Sales and profits are in thousands of dollars—add 000 to get the full amount. 2010 Note: Financial information for 2010 was not available for all companies at press time.**

2010 Sales: $3,903,524	2010 Profits: $682,383	**U.S. Stock Ticker: FRX**
2009 Sales: $3,636,055	2009 Profits: $767,743	**Int'l Ticker:**
2008 Sales: $3,501,802	2008 Profits: $967,933	Int'l Exchange:
2007 Sales: $3,183,324	2007 Profits: $454,103	Employees: 5,200 Fiscal Year Ends: 3/31
2006 Sales: $2,793,934	2006 Profits: $708,514	Parent Company:

SALARIES/BENEFITS:

Pension Plan:	ESOP Stock Plan:	Profit Sharing: Y	Top Exec. Salary: $1,277,500	Bonus: $900,000
Savings Plan: Y	Stock Purch. Plan: Y		Second Exec. Salary: $845,000	Bonus: $550,000

OTHER THOUGHTS:

Apparent Women Officers or Directors: 1
Hot Spot for Advancement for Women/Minorities: Y

LOCATIONS: ("Y" = Yes)

West:	Southwest:	Midwest:	Southeast:	Northeast:	International:
Y		Y		Y	Y

Sales, profits and employees may be estimates. Financial information, benefits and other data can change quickly and may vary from those stated here.

FORTUNE BRANDS INC

www.fortunebrands.com

Industry Group Code: 312140

Management:		Sales/Marketing:		Liberal Arts:		Information Sys.:		Professionals:		Tech./Scientific:	
Mgmt. Trainees:	Y	Marketing Pros.:	Y	Gen. Writing/Editing:	Y	Info. Mgmt.:	Y	Finance/Acct.:	Y	Engineers, Elec.:	
Experienced Mgmt.:	Y	Retail Sales:		Tech. Writing:	Y	Software Dev.:	Y	Law:	Y	Engineers, Other:	Y
Int'l Business:	Y	Comm./Industrial:	Y	Graphic Arts/Photog.:	Y	Hardware Dev.:		HR/Other:	Y	Health/Lab:	
MBA Grads:	Y	Sales Trainees:	Y	Music:		Consulting/Other:		Training:	Y	Science/Research:	
		Advertising Pros.:	Y	Broadcasting:				Health Care:		Petroleum/Chem.:	
				Other:				Consulting:		Math/Other:	

TYPES OF BUSINESS:

Sprits and Wine

BRANDS/DIVISIONS/AFFILIATES:

Jim Beam
Maker's Mark
Canadian Club
Beam Global Spirits & Wine, Inc.
Sauza
Courvoisier
Cruzan

CONTACTS: *Note: Officers with more than one job title may be intentionally listed here more than once.*

Bruce A. Carbonari, CEO
Craig P. Omtvedt, CFO/Sr. VP
Elizabeth R. Lane, VP-Human Resources
Mark A. Roche, General Counsel/Sr. VP/Sec.
Patrick J. Koley, Sr. VP-Strategy & Corp. Dev.
C. Clarkson Hine, VP-Corp. Comm. & Public Affairs
Anthony Diaz, VP-Investor Rel.
Mark Hausberg, Sr. VP-Finance/Treas.
Matt Stanton, VP-Public Affairs
John D. Lee, VP-Strategy
Allan J. Snape, VP-Bus. Dev.
Edward Wiertel, Controller/VP
Bruce A. Carbonari, Chmn.

Phone: 847-484-4400	**Fax:** 847-478-0073
Toll-Free:	
Address: 520 Lake Cook Rd., Deerfield, IL 60015 US	

GROWTH PLANS/SPECIAL FEATURES:

Fortune Brands, Inc. is one of the world's largest distillers of alcoholoc beverages. It is the owner of several premium liquor brands. The premium spirits business operates through holding company Beam Global Spirits & Wine, Inc., whose subsidiaries include Jim Beam Brands Co.; Jim Beam Brands Australia Pty. Ltd.; Beam Global Espana S.L.; Beam Global Spirits & Wine (U.K.) Ltd.; Tequila Sauza S.A. de C.V.; Canadian Club Canada, Inc.; Maker's Mark Distillery, Inc.; Courvoisier S.A.S.; and Alberta Distillers Limited. The company has significant positions in categories including tequila, vodka, bourbon, cognac, rum, Scotch whisky and Canadian whisky. Brands include Courvoisier, EFFEN, Maker's Mark, Cruzan, Sauza, Canadian Club and Laphoaig. It also has significant business in regional and national spirits categories such as German liqueurs and Spanish brandies. In 2011, the firm announced the sale of its golf products businesses. Fortune also proceeded with plans to spin off its home products and security business into a free-standing company.

FINANCIALS: **Sales and profits are in thousands of dollars—add 000 to get the full amount. 2010 Note: Financial information for 2010 was not available for all companies at press time.**

2010 Sales: $7,141,500 — 2010 Profits: $496,000
2009 Sales: $6,694,700 — 2009 Profits: $247,100
2008 Sales: $7,608,900 — 2008 Profits: $145,600
2007 Sales: $8,563,100 — 2007 Profits: $762,600
2006 Sales: $8,769,000 — 2006 Profits: $830,100

U.S. Stock Ticker: FO
Int'l Ticker:
Int'l Exchange:
Employees: 24,600 Fiscal Year Ends: 12/31
Parent Company:

SALARIES/BENEFITS:

Pension Plan: ESOP Stock Plan: Profit Sharing: Top Exec. Salary: $1,100,000 Bonus: $1,529,440
Savings Plan: Stock Purch. Plan: Second Exec. Salary: $630,300 Bonus: $597,524

OTHER THOUGHTS:

Apparent Women Officers or Directors: 4
Hot Spot for Advancement for Women/Minorities: Y

LOCATIONS: ("Y" = Yes)

West:	Southwest:	Midwest:	Southeast:	Northeast:	International:
Y		Y			Y

FOSSIL INC

www.fossil.com

Industry Group Code: 334518

Management:		Sales/Marketing:		Liberal Arts:		Information Sys.:		Professionals:		Tech./Scientific:	
Mgmt. Trainees:	Y	Marketing Pros.:	Y	Gen. Writing/Editing:	Y	Info. Mgmt.:	Y	Finance/Acct.:	Y	Engineers, Elec.:	Y
Experienced Mgmt.:	Y	Retail Sales:	Y	Tech. Writing:	Y	Software Dev.:	Y	Law:	Y	Engineers, Other:	
Int'l Business:	Y	Comm./Industrial:	Y	Graphic Arts/Photog.:	Y	Hardware Dev.:		HR/Other:	Y	Health/Lab:	
MBA Grads:	Y	Sales Trainees:	Y	Music:		Consulting/Other:		Training:	Y	Science/Research:	
		Advertising Pros.:	Y	Broadcasting:				Health Care:		Petroleum/Chem.:	
				Other:	Y			Consulting:		Math/Other:	

TYPES OF BUSINESS:

Watch Manufacturing
Accessories
Online Sales
Leather Goods
Belts
Handbags
Jewelry
Retail Stores

BRANDS/DIVISIONS/AFFILIATES:

Fossil
Relic
Zodiac

CONTACTS:

Note: Officers with more than one job title may be intentionally listed here more than once.

Kosta N. Kartsotis, CEO
Michael W. Barnes, COO
Michael W. Barnes, Pres.
Mike L. Kovar, CFO/Exec. VP
Mike L. Kovar, Treas.
Livio Galanti, Exec. VP
Mark D. Quick, Vice Chmn.
Jennifer Pritchard, Pres., Retail Div.
Kosta N. Karsotis, Chmn.

Phone: 972-234-2525 **Fax:** 972-234-4669
Toll-Free:
Address: 2280 N. Greenville Ave., Richardson, TX 75082 US

GROWTH PLANS/SPECIAL FEATURES:

Fossil, Inc. designs, develops, markets and distributes fashion accessories. The company's principal offerings include a line of men's and women's watches and jewelry sold under proprietary and licensed brands, handbags, leather goods, sunglasses and apparel. In the watch and jewelry product category, Fossil has a diverse portfolio of globally recognized brands such as Fossil, Relic and Zodiac. Also, through license agreements, the company utilizes prestigious brand names such as Burberry, DKNY, Michael Kors, Marc Jacobs, Adidas and Emporio Armani. The company distributes products through various channels including wholesale and export as well as directly to the consumer. Domestically, the company sells its products through a distribution network that includes Neiman Marcus, Nordstrom, Macy's, Dillard's, JCPenney, Kohl's, Sears, Wal-Mart and Target. The firm also sells its products through a network of company-owned stores, which includes 121 retail and 93 outlet stores. Additionally, the company offers an extensive collection of Fossil brand products through its catalog and web site as well as proprietary and licensed watch and jewelry brands through other managed and affiliate web sites. Internationally, products are sold to department stores and specialty stores in over 100 countries through 23 company-owned foreign sales subsidiaries and through approximately 60 independent distributors.

FINANCIALS:

Sales and profits are in thousands of dollars—add 000 to get the full amount. 2010 Note: Financial information for 2010 was not available for all companies at press time.

2010 Sales: $2,030,690 | 2010 Profits: $255,205
2009 Sales: $1,548,093 | 2009 Profits: $139,188
2008 Sales: $1,583,242 | 2008 Profits: $138,097
2007 Sales: $1,432,984 | 2007 Profits: $123,261
2006 Sales: $1,213,965 | 2006 Profits: $77,582

U.S. Stock Ticker: FOSL
Int'l Ticker:
Int'l Exchange:
Employees: 10,500 Fiscal Year Ends: 12/31
Parent Company:

SALARIES/BENEFITS:

Pension Plan: ESOP Stock Plan: Profit Sharing: Top Exec. Salary: $655,558 Bonus: $100,000
Savings Plan: Stock Purch. Plan: Second Exec. Salary: $568,161 Bonus: $43,125

OTHER THOUGHTS:

Apparent Women Officers or Directors: 2
Hot Spot for Advancement for Women/Minorities:

LOCATIONS: ("Y" = Yes)

West:	Southwest:	Midwest:	Southeast:	Northeast:	International:
Y	Y	Y	Y	Y	Y

FOX ENTERTAINMENT GROUP INC

www.fox.com

Industry Group Code: 515120

Management:		Sales/Marketing:		Liberal Arts:		Information Sys.:		Professionals:		Tech./Scientific:	
Mgmt. Trainees:	Y	Marketing Pros.:	Y	Gen. Writing/Editing:	Y	Info. Mgmt.:	Y	Finance/Acct.:	Y	Engineers, Elec.:	Y
Experienced Mgmt.:	Y	Retail Sales:		Tech. Writing:		Software Dev.:	Y	Law:	Y	Engineers, Other:	
Int'l Business:	Y	Comm./Industrial:	Y	Graphic Arts/Photog.:	Y	Hardware Dev.:		HR/Other:	Y	Health/Lab:	
MBA Grads:	Y	Sales Trainees:		Music:	Y	Consulting/Other:		Training:	Y	Science/Research:	
		Advertising Pros.:	Y	Broadcasting:	Y			Health Care:		Petroleum/Chem.:	
				Other:	Y			Consulting:		Math/Other:	

TYPES OF BUSINESS:

Broadcast Television
Film Distribution and Production
Television Programming
Online Communities and Game Sites
Professional Sports
Electronic Games
Cable TV Programming
Online Entertainment

BRANDS/DIVISIONS/AFFILIATES:

News Corp
Fox Filmed Entertainment
Twentieth Century Fox Television
Fox Television Studios
Fox Interactive Media
National Geographic Channel
Twentieth Century Fox Home Entertainment, Inc.
Shine Group

CONTACTS: *Note: Officers with more than one job title may be intentionally listed here more than once.*

K. Rupert Murdoch, CEO
Chase Carey, COO
Chase Carey, Pres.
David DeVoe, CFO/Sr. Exec. VP
Mike Hopkins, Pres., Affiliate Sales & Mktg., FOX Networks
David Haslingden, Pres./COO-FOX Networks Group
David Hill, Chmn./CEO-FOX Sports Media Group
Peter Rice, Chmn.-Entertainment, FOX Networks Group
Jon Hookstratten, Exec. VP-Network Dist.
K. Rupert Murdoch, Chmn.
Hernan Lopez, Pres./CEO-FOX Int'l Channels

Phone: 310-369-1000 **Fax:** 310-969-3300

Toll-Free:

Address: 10201 W. Pico Blvd., Bldg. 100, Ste. 3220, Los Angeles, CA 90035 US

GROWTH PLANS/SPECIAL FEATURES:

Fox Entertainment Group, Inc., a wholly-owned subsidiary of News Corp., is an entertainment conglomerate that operates through four business segments: filmed entertainment, television stations, a television broadcast network and cable network programming. The company engages in feature film and television production and distribution principally through the following businesses: Fox Filmed Entertainment, a leading producer and distributor of feature films; Twentieth Century Fox Television, a producer of network television programming; Fox Television Studios, a leading producer of U.S. broadcast, cable and international programming; and Fox Interactive Media, a network of integrated Internet sites. Twentieth Century Fox Home Entertainment, Inc. distributes motion pictures and other programming produced by units of Fox Entertainment and its affiliates in all home media formats, including digital media available for download from Apple's iTunes Music Store. The company's motion picture and television library consists of varying rights to well over 3,000 previously released motion pictures and many television programs. In television, Fox Television Stations owns and operates 27 stations located in major U.S. market areas. Its television broadcast network, controlled through Fox Broadcasting Company, consists of approximately 203 affiliated stations, including the full-power stations that are owned by subsidiaries of Fox. The company produces television programs through Twentieth Century Fox Television, Fox Television Studios, Fox News Channel, Fox Sports Networks, FX Network, SPEED Channel, FUEL TV, Fox College Sports, Fox Movie Channel, Fox Sports International, National Geographic Channel, Fox Movie Channel and several foreign subsidiaries. The company also owns a 14.6% limited partnership interest in the Colorado Rockies, the baseball franchise in Denver, Colorado. In April 2011, News Corp. acquired Shine Group, a U.K.-based media production company founded by Rupert Murdoch's daughter, Elisabeth Murdoch. In June 2011, it sold its social networking site, Myspace.com, to Specific Media for $35 million.

FINANCIALS: **Sales and profits are in thousands of dollars—add 000 to get the full amount. 2010 Note: Financial information for 2010 was not available for all companies at press time.**

2010 Sales: $
2009 Sales: $
2008 Sales: $
2007 Sales: $
2006 Sales: $

2010 Profits: $
2009 Profits: $
2008 Profits: $
2007 Profits: $
2006 Profits: $

U.S. Stock Ticker: Subsidiary
Int'l Ticker:
Int'l Exchange:
Employees: 12,500 Fiscal Year Ends: 6/30
Parent Company: NEWS CORP

SALARIES/BENEFITS:

Pension Plan: ESOP Stock Plan: Profit Sharing: Top Exec. Salary: $ Bonus: $21,175,000
Savings Plan: Stock Purch. Plan: Second Exec. Salary: $ Bonus: $

OTHER THOUGHTS:

Apparent Women Officers or Directors:
Hot Spot for Advancement for Women/Minorities:

LOCATIONS: ("Y" = Yes)

West:	Southwest:	Midwest:	Southeast:	Northeast:	International:
Y	Y	Y	Y	Y	Y

Sales, profits and employees may be estimates. Financial information, benefits and other data can change quickly and may vary from those stated here.

FRONTIER COMMUNICATIONS CORPORATION www.frontier.com

Industry Group Code: 517110

Management:		Sales/Marketing:		Liberal Arts:		Information Sys.:		Professionals:		Tech./Scientific:	
Mgmt. Trainees:	Y	Marketing Pros.:	Y	Gen. Writing/Editing:	Y	Info. Mgmt.:	Y	Finance/Acct.:	Y	Engineers, Elec.:	Y
Experienced Mgmt.:	Y	Retail Sales:		Tech. Writing:	Y	Software Dev.:	Y	Law:	Y	Engineers, Other:	Y
Int'l Business:		Comm./Industrial:	Y	Graphic Arts/Photog.:	Y	Hardware Dev.:		HR/Other:	Y	Health/Lab:	
MBA Grads:	Y	Sales Trainees:		Music:		Consulting/Other:		Training:	Y	Science/Research:	
		Advertising Pros.:	Y	Broadcasting:				Health Care:		Petroleum/Chem.:	
				Other:				Consulting:		Math/Other:	

TYPES OF BUSINESS:

Telecommunications
Internet Services
Long-Distance Phone Services
Directory Service
Access Services
Wireless Internet Services

BRANDS/DIVISIONS/AFFILIATES:

Frontier Pages
IPConnect

CONTACTS:

Note: Officers with more than one job title may be intentionally listed here more than once.

Maggie Wilderotter, CEO
Daniel McCarthy, COO/Exec. VP
Maggie Wilderotter, Pres.
Donald R. Shassian, CFO/Exec. VP
Peter B. Hayes, Exec. VP-Commercial Sales
Cecilia K. McKenney, Exec. VP-Human Resources
Melinda White, Exec. VP-Prod. Mktg.
Joy Eldred, Central Region VP-Eng.
Kathleen Quinn Abernathy, Chief Legal Officer/Exec. VP
Melinda White, Exec. VP-Revenue Dev.
Ann Burr, Pres., Northeast Region
Cecilia K. McKenney, Exec. VP-Call Center Sales & Service
John Lass, Pres., Central Region
Denise Baumbach, Pres., West Region
Maggie Wilderotter, Chmn.

Phone: 203-614-5600 **Fax:** 203-614-4602
Toll-Free:
Address: 3 High Ridge Pk., Stamford, CT 06905 US

GROWTH PLANS/SPECIAL FEATURES:

Frontier Communications Corporation provides communication services to homes and business, primarily in rural areas. The firm operates as an incumbent local exchange carrier in 27 states. The company provides access, local, long distance, data/Internet, directory, television and wireless services. The firm has approximately 7.44 million access lines and 8 million broadband and voice connections. Access services allow other carriers the use of Frontier facilities for long distance voice and data transmissions. Local services include basic telephone wireline services, as well as call forwarding, conference calling, caller identification, voicemail and call waiting. Long distance services use external interexchange carrier facilities. Data and Internet services include Internet access via high-speed or dial up connections, frame relay, Metro Ethernet and asynchronous transfer mode (ATM) switching services, as well as data transmission services to other carriers and commercial customers with dedicated high-capacity circuits. Directory services include white and yellow page directories of residential and business listings; and the Frontier Pages, an online directory service. Television services are offered in partnership with Echostar's DISH Network, including access to local channels, digital television channels and high-definition programming. Wireless services include wireless data WIFI networks in 19 municipalities, five colleges/universities and over 360 businesses. In July 2010, Frontier acquired roughly 4.8 million access lines in 14 states, primarily in rural locations and small towns, from Verizon Communications, in a transaction valued at approximately $8.6 billion. Frontier gained approximately 7 million customers in the transaction.

Frontier employee benefits include medical, dental and vision coverage; flexible spending accounts; life, disability and accident insurance; a legal plan; corporate discounts; and tuition reimbursement.

FINANCIALS:

Sales and profits are in thousands of dollars—add 000 to get the full amount. 2010 Note: Financial information for 2010 was not available for all companies at press time.

2010 Sales: $3,797,675 — 2010 Profits: $152,673
2009 Sales: $2,117,894 — 2009 Profits: $120,783
2008 Sales: $2,237,018 — 2008 Profits: $182,660
2007 Sales: $2,288,015 — 2007 Profits: $214,654
2006 Sales: $2,025,367 — 2006 Profits: $344,555

U.S. Stock Ticker: FTR
Int'l Ticker:
Int'l Exchange:
Employees: 14,900 Fiscal Year Ends: 12/31
Parent Company:

SALARIES/BENEFITS:

Pension Plan: ESOP Stock Plan: Profit Sharing: Y Top Exec. Salary: $974,167 Bonus: $1,922,163
Savings Plan: Y Stock Purch. Plan: Second Exec. Salary: $478,333 Bonus: $979,850

OTHER THOUGHTS:

Apparent Women Officers or Directors: 8
Hot Spot for Advancement for Women/Minorities: Y

LOCATIONS: ("Y" = Yes)

West:	Southwest:	Midwest:	Southeast:	Northeast:	International:
Y	Y	Y	Y	Y	

Sales, profits and employees may be estimates. Financial information, benefits and other data can change quickly and may vary from those stated here.

FTI CONSULTING INC

www.fticonsulting.com

Industry Group Code: 54161

Management:		**Sales/Marketing:**		**Liberal Arts:**		**Information Sys.:**		**Professionals:**		**Tech./Scientific:**	
Mgmt. Trainees:	Y	Marketing Pros.:	Y	Gen. Writing/Editing:	Y	Info. Mgmt.:	Y	Finance/Acct.:	Y	Engineers, Elec.:	
Experienced Mgmt.:	Y	Retail Sales:		Tech. Writing:	Y	Software Dev.:	Y	Law:	Y	Engineers, Other:	
Int'l Business:	Y	Comm./Industrial:	Y	Graphic Arts/Photog.:	Y	Hardware Dev.:		HR/Other:	Y	Health/Lab:	
MBA Grads:	Y	Sales Trainees:		Music:		Consulting/Other:	Y	Training:	Y	Science/Research:	
		Advertising Pros.:		Broadcasting:				Health Care:		Petroleum/Chem.:	
				Other:	Y			Consulting:	Y	Math/Other:	

TYPES OF BUSINESS:

Bankruptcy & Restructuring Consulting
Interim Management Staffing
Corporate Recovery Services
Litigation Assistance
Forensic Accounting
Data Mining
Technology Consulting
Software Development

BRANDS/DIVISIONS/AFFILIATES:

Baker Tilly Hong Kong Business Recovery Ltd.
Compass Lexecon
Network Industries Strategies
FS Asia Advisory Limited

CONTACTS: *Note: Officers with more than one job title may be intentionally listed here more than once.*

Jack B. Dunn, IV, CEO
Dominic DiNapoli, COO/Exec. VP
Jack B. Dunn, IV, Pres.
David G. Bannister, CFO/Exec. VP
Liz Nickles, Chief Mktg. Officer/Sr. VP
Roger Carlile, Chief Admin. Officer/Exec. VP
Eric Miller, General Counsel/Exec. VP
David G. Bannister, Chief Dev. Officer
Catherine Freeman, Chief Acct. Officer/Controller/Sr. VP
John MacColl, Chief Risk Officer/Exec. VP
Eric Miller, Chief Ethics Officer
Joanne Catanese, Sec./Associate General Counsel
Dennis J. Shaugnessy, Chmn.

Phone: 561-515-1900 **Fax:**
Toll-Free: 800-334-5701
Address: 777 Flagler Dr., Ste. 1500, West Palm Beach, FL 33401 US

GROWTH PLANS/SPECIAL FEATURES:

FTI Consulting, Inc. is a global consulting firm that provides turnaround, restructuring, bankruptcy and other related consulting services. The firm works in 12 industries ranging from retail to insurance and from media and entertainment to energy and utilities, operating in 33 U.S. cities and 22 foreign countries, including the U.K., Russia, the France, Japan and China. The firm operates in five segments: Corporate Finance/Restructuring; Forensic and Litigation Consulting; Economic Consulting; Technology; and Strategic Communications. The Corporate Finance/Restructuring segment's services include turnaround and restructuring services, which consists of providing advisory services to debtors, creditors and stakeholders confronted with liquidity problems, underperformance and over-expansion; interim key executive staffing; and mergers and acquisitions services, which includes financial accounting, investment banking and tax advice. Forensic and Litigation Consulting includes forensic accounting and financial investigations; trial services, which includes providing advice and support for clients in complex civil trials; and pre-, in- and post-trial dispute advisory services. Economic Consulting, offered through Compass Lexecon, Network Industries Strategies and Auction Solutions, includes analyses of complex economic issues in legal and regulatory proceedings. The Technology segment includes FTI's proprietary Ringtail software for document review, litigation support and information management; Attenext technology, which is used to collect, search and manage data; and other software products and services. Strategic Communications includes financial and brand communications, media relations, public affairs and business consulting. In April 2010, FTI acquired Hong Kong-based Baker Tilly Hong Kong Business Recovery Ltd. In August 2010, the firm acquired Hong Kong-based firm FS Asia Advisory Limited. In early 2011, the company acquired the International Arbitration and Airline Competition operations and agreed to acquire the majority of the European business of LECG Corporation.

Employees are offered life, disability, AD&D, medical, dental and vision insurance; health and dependent care flexible spending accounts; a 401(k); and an employee assistance program.

FINANCIALS: **Sales and profits are in thousands of dollars—add 000 to get the full amount. 2010 Note: Financial information for 2010 was not available for all companies at press time.**

2010 Sales: $1,401,461 — 2010 Profits: $71,890
2009 Sales: $1,399,946 — 2009 Profits: $143,026
2008 Sales: $1,293,145 — 2008 Profits: $120,906
2007 Sales: $1,001,270 — 2007 Profits: $86,334
2006 Sales: $707,933 — 2006 Profits: $42,024

U.S. Stock Ticker: FCN
Int'l Ticker:
Int'l Exchange:
Employees: 3,527 Fiscal Year Ends: 12/31
Parent Company:

SALARIES/BENEFITS:

Pension Plan: | ESOP Stock Plan: | Profit Sharing: | Top Exec. Salary: $2,000,000 | Bonus: $650,000
Savings Plan: Y | Stock Purch. Plan: | | Second Exec. Salary: $1,500,000 | Bonus: $1,040,000

OTHER THOUGHTS:

Apparent Women Officers or Directors: 4
Hot Spot for Advancement for Women/Minorities: Y

LOCATIONS: ("Y" = Yes)

West:	Southwest:	Midwest:	Southeast:	Northeast:	International:
Y	Y	Y	Y	Y	Y

GAMESTOP CORP

www.gamestop.com

Industry Group Code: 451120

Management:		Sales/Marketing:		Liberal Arts:		Information Sys.:		Professionals:		Tech./Scientific:	
Mgmt. Trainees:	Y	Marketing Pros.:	Y	Gen. Writing/Editing:	Y	Info. Mgmt.:	Y	Finance/Acct.:	Y	Engineers, Elec.:	
Experienced Mgmt.:	Y	Retail Sales:	Y	Tech. Writing:		Software Dev.:	Y	Law:	Y	Engineers, Other:	
Int'l Business:	Y	Comm./Industrial:		Graphic Arts/Photog.:	Y	Hardware Dev.:		HR/Other:	Y	Health/Lab:	
MBA Grads:	Y	Sales Trainees:	Y	Music:		Consulting/Other:		Training:	Y	Science/Research:	
		Advertising Pros.:	Y	Broadcasting:				Health Care:		Petroleum/Chem.:	
				Other:	Y			Consulting:		Math/Other:	

TYPES OF BUSINESS:

Video Games-Retail
PC Software Sales
Game Accessories
Online Sales
Magazine Publication

BRANDS/DIVISIONS/AFFILIATES:

EB Games
GameStop.com
EBGames.com
Game Informer
Micromania
Casual Digital Store
www.GameStop.co.uk
Spawn Labs

CONTACTS: *Note: Officers with more than one job title may be intentionally listed here more than once.*

J. Paul Raines, CEO
Tony Bartel, Pres.
Robert A. Lloyd, CFO
Michael N. Rosen, Sec.
R. Richard Fontaine, Chmn.

Phone: 817-424-2000 | **Fax:** 817-424-2002
Toll-Free: 800-883-8895
Address: 625 Westport Pkwy., Grapevine, TX 76051 US

GROWTH PLANS/SPECIAL FEATURES:

GameStop Corp. is a retailer of video games and PC games. The company operates 6,670 retail stores throughout U.S., Canada, Australia and Europe under the names GameStop, EB Games and Micromania. Approximately 4,536 stores are included in the U.S. segment with 345 stores in Canada, 405 in Australia and 1,384 in the European segment. The firm's retail outlets offer new and used video game products and accessories. New video game software sales represented the largest portion of the firm's 2010 sales, comprising 41.9%. By purchasing used products, the company provides its customers with an opportunity to trade in used video games and peripherals for store credits and apply those credits towards other merchandise, which increases sales. Stores also typically feature several video game sampling areas, which provide customers the opportunity to play games before purchase, as well as equipment to play video game clips. Additionally, GameStop operates multiple e-commerce web sites, including GameStop.com and EBGames.com, as well as publishing Game Informer, one of the largest multi-platform video game magazines in the U.S., based on its 5.7 million subscribers. Paid Game Informer subscribers receive a GameStop loyalty card, which offers discounts on selected merchandise in the company's stores. The firm operates the Casual Digital Store, an online game download service powered by RealNetworks, Inc., that allows users to download PC games directly. In March 2011, the firm acquired Spawn Labs, a streaming technology company. In July 2011, the company launched the web site www.gamestop.co.uk in the U.K.

GameStop offers its employees medical, dental, vision and prescription drug coverage; paid holidays and vacation; flexible spending accounts; short- and long-term disability; a 401(k) plan; tuition reimbursement; and employee discounts of 15%.

FINANCIALS: **Sales and profits are in thousands of dollars—add 000 to get the full amount. 2010 Note: Financial information for 2010 was not available for all companies at press time.**

2010 Sales: $9,077,997 | 2010 Profits: $377,265
2009 Sales: $8,805,897 | 2009 Profits: $398,282
2008 Sales: $7,093,962 | 2008 Profits: $288,291
2007 Sales: $5,318,900 | 2007 Profits: $158,250
2006 Sales: $3,091,783 | 2006 Profits: $100,784

U.S. Stock Ticker: GME
Int'l Ticker:
Int'l Exchange:
Employees: 59,000 Fiscal Year Ends: 1/31
Parent Company:

SALARIES/BENEFITS:

Pension Plan: | ESOP Stock Plan: | Profit Sharing: | Top Exec. Salary: $1,250,000 | Bonus: $1,354,000
Savings Plan: Y | Stock Purch. Plan: | | Second Exec. Salary: $1,200,000 | Bonus: $1,354,000

OTHER THOUGHTS:

Apparent Women Officers or Directors: 1
Hot Spot for Advancement for Women/Minorities:

LOCATIONS: ("Y" = Yes)

West:	Southwest:	Midwest:	Southeast:	Northeast:	International:
Y	Y	Y	Y	Y	Y

Sales, profits and employees may be estimates. Financial information, benefits and other data can change quickly and may vary from those stated here.

GE ENERGY INFRASTRUCTURE

www.gepower.com

Industry Group Code: 335

Management:		Sales/Marketing:		Liberal Arts:		Information Sys.:		Professionals:		Tech./Scientific:	
Mgmt. Trainees:		Marketing Pros.:	Y	Gen. Writing/Editing:		Info. Mgmt.:	Y	Finance/Acct.:	Y	Engineers, Elec.:	Y
Experienced Mgmt.:	Y	Retail Sales:		Tech. Writing:	Y	Software Dev.:		Law:	Y	Engineers, Other:	Y
Int'l Business:	Y	Comm./Industrial:	Y	Graphic Arts/Photog.:		Hardware Dev.:		HR/Other:	Y	Health/Lab:	
MBA Grads:	Y	Sales Trainees:		Music:		Consulting/Other:		Training:		Science/Research:	
		Advertising Pros.:	Y	Broadcasting:				Health Care:		Petroleum/Chem.:	
				Other:				Consulting:		Math/Other:	

TYPES OF BUSINESS:

Generation Equipment-Turbines & Generators
Water Processing Technologies and Products
Generators-Wind, Hydro, Geothermal & Turbo
Nuclear Fuel Systems
Pumps & Pipelines
Metering & Control Systems
Energy Management Systems
Consulting-Energy

BRANDS/DIVISIONS/AFFILIATES:

General Electric Co (GE)
GE Energy Services
GE Power & Water
GE Oil & Gas

CONTACTS:

Note: Officers with more than one job title may be intentionally listed here more than once.

John Krenicki, Jr., CEO
John Krenicki, Jr., Pres.
Daniel Janki, CFO
James Suciu, Pres., Global Sales & Mktg.
Daniel C. Heintzelman, Pres./CEO-Energy Svcs.
Claudi Santiago, Pres./CEO-Oil & Gas
Kishore Hayaraman, Pres./CEO-India

Phone: 678-844-6000 **Fax:** 678-844-6690
Toll-Free:
Address: 4200 Wildwood Pkwy., Atlanta, GA 30339 US

GROWTH PLANS/SPECIAL FEATURES:

GE Energy Infrastructure, a subsidiary of the General Electric Co. (GE), designs and supplies energy technology. The division, which accounts for roughly 25% of GE's total revenues, operates in three segments: Energy Services, Oil & Gas and Power & Water. The Energy Services segment serves power generation, industrial, government and other customers worldwide with products and services related to energy production, distribution and management. The firm is a leading provider of Integrated Gasification Combined Cycle (IGCC) technology design and development. IGCC systems convert coal and other hydrocarbons into synthetic gas that is used as the primary fuel for gas turbines in combined-cycle systems. The segment sells steam turbines and generators to the electric utility industry and to private industrial customers for cogeneration applications. Nuclear reactors, fuel and support services for both new and installed boiling water reactors are offered through joint ventures with Hitachi and Toshiba. The Oil & Gas segment designs and manufactures surface and subsea drilling and production systems; equipment for floating production platforms; compressors; turbines; turboexpanders; high pressure reactors; industrial power generation; and a broad portfolio of ancillary equipment. The segment also provides services relating to installing and maintaining this equipment. The Power & Water division designs and manufactures motors and control systems used in industrial applications primarily for oil and gas extraction and mining. Its renewable energy portfolio offers wind turbines solar technology. In addition, it offers water treatment solutions for industrial and municipal water systems including the supply and related services of specialty chemicals, water purification systems, pumps, valves, filters and fluid handling equipment for improving the performance of water, wastewater and process systems, including mobile treatment systems and desalination processes. The segment also sells aircraft engine derivatives for use as industrial power sources. In March 2011, the firm acquired Lineage Power Holdings, Inc.

FINANCIALS:

Sales and profits are in thousands of dollars—add 000 to get the full amount. 2010 Note: Financial information for 2010 was not available for all companies at press time.

2010 Sales: $37,514,000	2010 Profits: $7,271,000
2009 Sales: $37,134,000	2009 Profits: $6,842,000
2008 Sales: $38,570,000	2008 Profits: $6,080,000
2007 Sales: $30,698,000	2007 Profits: $4,817,000
2006 Sales: $25,221,000	2006 Profits: $3,518,000

U.S. Stock Ticker: Subsidiary
Int'l Ticker:
Int'l Exchange:
Employees: 67,000 Fiscal Year Ends: 12/31
Parent Company: GENERAL ELECTRIC CO (GE)

SALARIES/BENEFITS:

Pension Plan: ESOP Stock Plan: Profit Sharing: Top Exec. Salary: $ Bonus: $
Savings Plan: Y Stock Purch. Plan: Second Exec. Salary: $ Bonus: $

OTHER THOUGHTS:

Apparent Women Officers or Directors:
Hot Spot for Advancement for Women/Minorities:

LOCATIONS: ("Y" = Yes)

West:	Southwest:	Midwest:	Southeast:	Northeast:	International:
Y	Y	Y	Y	Y	Y

GENENTECH INC

www.gene.com

Industry Group Code: 325412

Management:		**Sales/Marketing:**		**Liberal Arts:**		**Information Sys.:**		**Professionals:**		**Tech./Scientific:**	
Mgmt. Trainees:	Y	Marketing Pros.:	Y	Gen. Writing/Editing:	Y	Info. Mgmt.:	Y	Finance/Acct.:	Y	Engineers, Elec.:	Y
Experienced Mgmt.:	Y	Retail Sales:		Tech. Writing:	Y	Software Dev.:	Y	Law:	Y	Engineers, Other:	Y
Int'l Business:	Y	Comm./Industrial:	Y	Graphic Arts/Photog.:	Y	Hardware Dev.:		HR/Other:	Y	Health/Lab:	Y
MBA Grads:	Y	Sales Trainees:	Y	Music:		Consulting/Other:		Training:	Y	Science/Research:	Y
		Advertising Pros.:	Y	Broadcasting:				Health Care:	Y	Petroleum/Chem.:	Y
				Other:				Consulting:		Math/Other:	Y

TYPES OF BUSINESS:

Drug Development & Manufacturing
Genetically Engineered Drugs

BRANDS/DIVISIONS/AFFILIATES:

Avastin
TNKase
Herceptin
Rituxan
Activase
Pulmozyme
Nutropin
Roche Group

CONTACTS: *Note: Officers with more than one job title may be intentionally listed here more than once.*

Ian T. Clark, CEO
Steve Krognes, CFO/Sr. VP
Denise Smith-Hams, Sr. VP-Human Resources
Richard H. Scheller, Exec. VP-Research/Chief Scientific Officer
Frederick C. Kentz, Sec./Sr. VP/Chief Compliance Officer
Hal Barron, Head-Global Dev.
Andrew C. Chan, Sr. VP-Immunology
Hal Barron, Chief Medical Officer
Jennifer E. Cook, Sr. VP-Genetech Immunology & Ophthalmology
Troy Cox, Sr. VP-Metabolism & Primary Care
Arthur D. Levinson, Chmn.

Phone: 650-225-1000	**Fax:** 650-225-6000
Toll-Free:	
Address: 1 DNA Way, South San Francisco, CA 94080-4990 US	

GROWTH PLANS/SPECIAL FEATURES:

Genentech, Inc., a wholly-owned subsidiary of the Roche Group, makes medicines by splicing genes into fast-growing bacteria that then produce therapeutic proteins and combat diseases on a molecular level. Genentech uses cutting-edge technologies such as computer visualization of molecules, micro arrays and sensitive assaying techniques to develop, manufacture and market pharmaceuticals for unmet medical needs. Genentech's research is directed toward the oncology, immunology and vascular biology fields. The company's products consist of a variety of cardio-centric medications, as well as cancer, growth hormone deficiency (GHD) and cystic fibrosis treatments. Biotechnology products offered by Genentech include Herceptin, used to treat metastatic breast cancers; Avastin, used to inhibit angiogenesis of solid-tumor cancers; Nutropin, a growth hormone for the treatment of GHD in children and adults; TNKase, for the treatment of acute myocardial infarction; and Pulmozyme, for the treatment of cystic fibrosis. The company also produces the Rituxan antibody, used for the treatment of patients with non-Hodgkin's lymphoma. Through its long-standing Genentech Access to Care Foundation, Genentech assists those without sufficient health insurance to receive its medicines.

FINANCIALS: Sales and profits are in thousands of dollars—add 000 to get the full amount. 2010 Note: Financial information for 2010 was not available for all companies at press time.

2010 Sales: $	2010 Profits: $	**U.S. Stock Ticker: Subsidiary**
2009 Sales: $	2009 Profits: $	**Int'l Ticker:**
2008 Sales: $13,418,000	2008 Profits: $3,427,000	Int'l Exchange:
2007 Sales: $11,724,000	2007 Profits: $2,769,000	Employees: 11,000 Fiscal Year Ends: 12/31
2006 Sales: $9,284,000	2006 Profits: $2,113,000	Parent Company: ROCHE HOLDING LTD

SALARIES/BENEFITS:

Pension Plan:	ESOP Stock Plan:	Profit Sharing:	Top Exec. Salary: $	Bonus: $
Savings Plan: Y	Stock Purch. Plan: Y		Second Exec. Salary: $	Bonus: $

OTHER THOUGHTS:

Apparent Women Officers or Directors: 18
Hot Spot for Advancement for Women/Minorities: Y

LOCATIONS: ("Y" = Yes)

West:	Southwest:	Midwest:	Southeast:	Northeast:	International:
Y					Y

GENERAL ELECTRIC CO (GE)

www.ge.com

Industry Group Code: 522220

Management:		Sales/Marketing:		Liberal Arts:		Information Sys.:		Professionals:		Tech./Scientific:	
Mgmt. Trainees:	Y	Marketing Pros.:	Y	Gen. Writing/Editing:	Y	Info. Mgmt.:	Y	Finance/Acct.:	Y	Engineers, Elec.:	Y
Experienced Mgmt.:	Y	Retail Sales:		Tech. Writing:	Y	Software Dev.:	Y	Law:	Y	Engineers, Other:	
Int'l Business:	Y	Comm./Industrial:	Y	Graphic Arts/Photog.:	Y	Hardware Dev.:		HR/Other:	Y	Health/Lab:	
MBA Grads:	Y	Sales Trainees:		Music:		Consulting/Other:		Training:	Y	Science/Research:	Y
		Advertising Pros.:	Y	Broadcasting:				Health Care:		Petroleum/Chem.:	
				Other:	Y			Consulting:		Math/Other:	Y

TYPES OF BUSINESS:

Business Leasing & Finance
Energy Systems & Consulting
Financial Services
Industrial & Electrical Equipment & Consumer Products
Television & Film Production & Distribution
Real Estate Investments & Finance
Medical Equipment
Transportation, Aircraft Engines, Rail Systems & Truck Fleet Management

BRANDS/DIVISIONS/AFFILIATES:

GE Energy Infrastructure
GE Technology Infrastructure
GE Capital
NBC Universal LLC
Orbotech Medical Solutions Ltd.
Dresser, Inc.
GE Healthcare
GE Capital Aviation Services

CONTACTS: *Note: Officers with more than one job title may be intentionally listed here more than once.*

Jeffrey R. Immelt, CEO
Keith S. Sherin, CFO
Beth Comstock, Chief Mktg. Officer/Sr. VP
John Lynch, Sr. VP-Corp. Human Resources
Mark M. Little, Sr. VP/Dir.-Global Research
Charlene Begley, CIO/Sr. VP
Brackett B. Denniston, III, General Counsel/Sr. VP
Wayne Hewett, VP-Oper.
Pamela Daley, Sr. VP-Corp. Bus. Dev.
Trevor Schauenberg, VP-Corp. Investor Comm.
Kathryn A. Cassidy, Treas./Sr. VP
John Krenicki, Jr., CEO/Pres., GE Energy Infrastructure
Michael A. Neal, Chmn./CEO-GE Capital
John G. Rice, CEO/Pres., GE Technology Infrastructure
Susan P. Peters, Chief Learning Officer/VP-Exec. Dev.
Jeffrey R. Immelt, Chmn.
Ferdinando Beccalli-Falco, CEO/Pres., GE Europe & North Asia/CEO-GE Germany

Phone: 203-373-2211 **Fax:** 203-373-3131
Toll-Free:
Address: 3135 Easton Turnpike, Fairfield, CT 06828-0001 US

GROWTH PLANS/SPECIAL FEATURES:

General Electric Co. (GE) is one of the largest technology, media, and financial services corporations in the world. The company's products, which range from aircraft engines, power generation, water processing, and security technology to medical imaging, business financing, media content and industrial products, are designed and manufactured by GE's five operating divisions: Energy Infrastructure, Technology Infrastructure, NBC Universal, GE Capital and Home & Business Solutions. The Energy Infrastructure division serves power generation, industrial, government and other customers worldwide with products and services related to energy production, distribution and management. The Technology Infrastructure division comprises the firm's aviation, enterprise solutions, healthcare technology and transportation technology operations. NBC Universal, 49%-owned by GE and 51% owned by Comcast, is engaged in the production and distribution of film and television programming; the operation of cable/satellite television networks around the world; the broadcast of network television; and investment and programming activities in digital media and the Internet. GE Capital manages all of the lending and financial services units of GE, including commercial lending and leasing; consumer lending; real estate activities; energy financial services; and commercial aircraft leasing and finance (through GE Capital Aviation Services). GE's Home & Business division manufactures, sells and services major home appliances, including refrigerators, freezers and residential water systems; and lighting products such as automotive, decorative and specialty bulbs. In March 2010, GE announced plans to expand its wind turbine manufacturing, engineering and service facilities in Norway, Sweden, Germany and the U.K. In January 2011, Comcast completed its acquisition of 51% of NBC Universal from GE. Though GE will retain a 49% stake in NBC, Comcast will be responsible for its operations and management. In February 2011, GE acquired Orbotech Medical Solutions Ltd. and Dresser, Inc., a global energy infrastructure technology firm.

FINANCIALS: **Sales and profits are in thousands of dollars—add 000 to get the full amount. 2010 Note: Financial information for 2010 was not available for all companies at press time.**

2010 Sales: $150,211,000
2009 Sales: $156,783,000
2008 Sales: $182,515,000
2007 Sales: $172,488,000
2006 Sales: $151,568,000

2010 Profits: $11,644,000
2009 Profits: $11,025,000
2008 Profits: $17,410,000
2007 Profits: $22,208,000
2006 Profits: $20,742,000

U.S. Stock Ticker: GE
Int'l Ticker:
Int'l Exchange:
Employees: 287,000 Fiscal Year Ends: 12/31
Parent Company:

SALARIES/BENEFITS:

Pension Plan:	ESOP Stock Plan:	Profit Sharing:	Top Exec. Salary: $3,300,000	Bonus: $
Savings Plan: Y	Stock Purch. Plan:		Second Exec. Salary: $1,750,000	Bonus: $2,900,000

OTHER THOUGHTS:

Apparent Women Officers or Directors: 11
Hot Spot for Advancement for Women/Minorities: Y

LOCATIONS: ("Y" = Yes)

West:	Southwest:	Midwest:	Southeast:	Northeast:	International:
Y	Y	Y	Y	Y	Y

Sales, profits and employees may be estimates. Financial information, benefits and other data can change quickly and may vary from those stated here.

GENERAL MILLS INC

www.generalmills.com

Industry Group Code: 311230

Management:		Sales/Marketing:		Liberal Arts:		Information Sys.:		Professionals:		Tech./Scientific:	
Mgmt. Trainees:	Y	Marketing Pros.:	Y	Gen. Writing/Editing:	Y	Info. Mgmt.:	Y	Finance/Acct.:	Y	Engineers, Elec.:	
Experienced Mgmt.:	Y	Retail Sales:		Tech. Writing:	Y	Software Dev.:	Y	Law:	Y	Engineers, Other:	Y
Int'l Business:	Y	Comm./Industrial:	Y	Graphic Arts/Photog.:	Y	Hardware Dev.:		HR/Other:	Y	Health/Lab:	
MBA Grads:	Y	Sales Trainees:	Y	Music:		Consulting/Other:		Training:	Y	Science/Research:	
		Advertising Pros.:	Y	Broadcasting:				Health Care:		Petroleum/Chem.:	
				Other:				Consulting:		Math/Other:	

TYPES OF BUSINESS:

Cereal Manufacturing
Snack Foods
Frozen Foods
Baking Products
Yogurt
Organic Foods
Convenience Meal Products
Canned and Frozen Vegetables

BRANDS/DIVISIONS/AFFILIATES:

Big G Cereals
Cheerios
Betty Crocker
Progresso
Pillsbury
Yoplait
Bisquick
Cascadian Farm

CONTACTS: *Note: Officers with more than one job title may be intentionally listed here more than once.*

Kendall J. Powell, CEO
Kendall J. Powell, Pres.
Donal L. Mulligan, CFO/Exec. VP
Mark W. Addicks, Chief Mktg. Officer/Sr. VP
Michael L. Davis, Sr. VP-Global Human Resources
Peter C. Erickson, Sr. VP-Tech., Innovation & Quality
Roderick A. Palmore, General Counsel/Chief Corp. & Risk Officer/Sec.
Ian R. Friendly, Exec. VP/COO-U.S. Retail
Y. Marc Belton, Exec. VP-Global Strategy & Growth
Christina L. Shea, Exec. VP-External Rel.
Kristen S. Wenker, VP-Investor Rel.
Richard O. Lund, Controller/VP
Gary Chu, Sr. VP-Greater China
Peter J. Capell, Sr. VP-Wholesome Snacks
Luis Gabriel Merizalde, Pres., EMEA
Samir Behl, VP/Pres., Asia Pacific Region
Kendall J. Powell, Chmn.
Christopher D. O'Leary, Exec. VP/COO-Int'l
John Church, VP-Supply Chain

Phone: 763-764-7600 **Fax:** 763-764-7384
Toll-Free: 800-248-7310
Address: 1 General Mills Blvd., Minneapolis, MN 55426 US

GROWTH PLANS/SPECIAL FEATURES:

General Mills, Inc. is a leading global producer of packaged consumer foods. The company manufactures its products in 15 countries and markets them in more than 100. Its joint ventures manufacture and market products in over 130 countries. The firm operates under three main divisions: U.S. Retail, accounting for 70% of 2010 sales, International, accounting for 18% of sales and Bakeries & Food Service, accounting for 12%. The U.S. retail division consists of seven segments: Big G Cereals, which controls Cheerios, Chex and Lucky Charms; meals, with products such as Betty Crocker, Hamburger Helper and Progresso; Pillsbury, including frozen dough products and frozen breakfast products; Yogurt, including Yoplait, Go-GURT and Yoplait Kids; snacks, which includes Fruit Roll-Ups and Bugles; baking products, including Bisquick baking mix and Warm Delights microwaveable desserts; and small planet foods and other, featuring Cascadian Farm cereal and granola bars and Larabar fruit and nut energy bars. The bakeries and food service segment consists of products marketed to retail and wholesale bakeries; and offered to commercial and noncommercial food service sectors, such as restaurants and school cafeterias, throughout the U.S. and Canada, under the Pillsbury and Gold Medal trademarks. The international segment is made up of retail and food services businesses outside the U.S. and Canada, with major product categories including super-premium ice cream; grain snacks; shelf-stable and frozen vegetables; refrigerated and frozen dough products; and dry dinners. The firm, along with Nestle SA, has a 50% interest in Cereal Partners Worldwide (CPW), which manufactures ready-to-eat cereal products outside the U.S. and Canada. It also has a 50% stake in Haagen-Dazs Japan, Inc. which manufactures and produces Haagen Dazs ice cream products and frozen novelties.

The company offers employees medical and dental insurance; legal, auto and homeowners insurance; disability coverage; educational assistance; and domestic partner benefits.

FINANCIALS: **Sales and profits are in thousands of dollars—add 000 to get the full amount. 2010 Note: Financial information for 2010 was not available for all companies at press time.**

2010 Sales: $14,796,500 — 2010 Profits: $1,530,500
2009 Sales: $14,691,300 — 2009 Profits: $1,304,400
2008 Sales: $13,652,100 — 2008 Profits: $1,294,700
2007 Sales: $12,442,000 — 2007 Profits: $1,143,900
2006 Sales: $11,712,000 — 2006 Profits: $1,090,300

U.S. Stock Ticker: GIS
Int'l Ticker:
Int'l Exchange:
Employees: 33,000 Fiscal Year Ends: 5/31
Parent Company:

SALARIES/BENEFITS:

Pension Plan: | ESOP Stock Plan: Y | Profit Sharing: | Top Exec. Salary: $973,042 | Bonus: $1,926,622
Savings Plan: Y | Stock Purch. Plan: | Second Exec. Salary: $555,832 | Bonus: $733,698

OTHER THOUGHTS:

Apparent Women Officers or Directors: 14
Hot Spot for Advancement for Women/Minorities: Y

LOCATIONS: ("Y" = Yes)

West:	Southwest:	Midwest:	Southeast:	Northeast:	International:
Y	Y	Y	Y	Y	Y

Sales, profits and employees may be estimates. Financial information, benefits and other data can change quickly and may vary from those stated here.

GENERAL MOTORS COMPANY (GM)

www.gm.com

Industry Group Code: 33611

Management:		Sales/Marketing:		Liberal Arts:		Information Sys.:		Professionals:		Tech./Scientific:	
Mgmt. Trainees:	Y	Marketing Pros.:	Y	Gen. Writing/Editing:	Y	Info. Mgmt.:	Y	Finance/Acct.:	Y	Engineers, Elec.:	Y
Experienced Mgmt.:	Y	Retail Sales:		Tech. Writing:	Y	Software Dev.:	Y	Law:	Y	Engineers, Other:	
Int'l Business:	Y	Comm./Industrial:	Y	Graphic Arts/Photog.:	Y	Hardware Dev.:	Y	HR/Other:	Y	Health/Lab:	Y
MBA Grads:	Y	Sales Trainees:		Music:		Consulting/Other:	Y	Training:	Y	Science/Research:	Y
		Advertising Pros.:	Y	Broadcasting:				Health Care:		Petroleum/Chem.:	
				Other:				Consulting:		Math/Other:	Y

TYPES OF BUSINESS:

Automobile, Truck & Engine Manufacturing
Security & Information Services
Automotive Electronics
Financing & Insurance
Parts & Service
Transmissions
Engines
Locomotives

BRANDS/DIVISIONS/AFFILIATES:

Chevrolet
Buick
Cadillac
GMC
Opel
AmeriCredit Corp.
FinanciaLinx Corporation
General Motors Financial Company Inc

CONTACTS: *Note: Officers with more than one job title may be intentionally listed here more than once.*

Daniel F. Akerson, CEO
Daniel Ammann, CFO/Sr. VP
Joel Ewanick, Global Chief Mktg. Officer/VP
Cynthia J. Brinkley, VP-Global Human Resources
Terry Kline, CIO/VP-IT
Thomas G. Stephens, Global CTO/Vice Chmn.
Mary T. Barra, Sr. VP-Global Prod. Dev.
Michael P. Millikin, General Counsel/Sr. VP
Stephen J. Girsky, Vice Chmn.-Bus. Dev. & Corp. Strategy
Selim Bingol, VP-Global Comm.
Nick S. Cyprus, Chief Acct. Officer/Controller/VP
Jaime Ardila, Pres., GM South America
Mark L. Reuss, Pres., North America
David N. Reilly, Pres., GM Europe
Robert E. Ferguson, VP-Global Public Policy
Daniel F. Akerson, Chmn.
Timothy E. Lee, Pres., GM Int'l Oper.
Stephen J. Girsky, Vice Chmn.-Global Purchasing & Supply Chain

Phone: 313- 556-5000	**Fax:**
Toll-Free:	
Address: 300 Renaissance Ctr., Detroit, MI 48265-3000 US	

GROWTH PLANS/SPECIAL FEATURES:

General Motors Company (GM), formerly General Motors Corp., is engaged in the worldwide development, production and marketing of cars, trucks, automotive systems and locomotives. The firm's major North American brands include Chevrolet, Buick, Cadillac and GMC. Besides its North American brands, GM markets vehicles internationally under the following brands: Opel, Vauxhall, Daewoo, Isuzu and Holden. GM is organized into four geographically-based segments: General Motors North America (GMNA), which generated 31% of 2010 vehicle sales; General Motors International Operations (GMIO), 37% (more than two-thirds of which originated in China); General Motors Europe (GME), 20%; and General Motors South America (GMSA), 12%. Recently, the firm emerged from bankruptcy after shedding $79 billion in existing debt, while receiving $30 billion in additional government funding. The U.S. government controls a 26.5% stake in the company. In 2010, GM sold its Saab division to Spyker Cars NV; and completed the wind down of its Pontiac, Saturn and HUMMER brands. In October 2010, in an effort to return to the auto lending business, the firm acquired loan provider AmeriCredit Corp. for $3.5 billion. Following the acquisition, the company was renamed General Motors Financial Company, Inc. (GM Financial). In November 2010, after undergoing an extensive restructuring, the firm completed an IPO. In January 2011, subsidiary GM Daewoo announced it would change its name to GM Korea and begin selling most of its cars under the Chevrolet brand. In April 2011, GM Financial acquired FinanciaLinx Corporation, a leading independent auto leasing company in Canada. In September 2011, GM completed the construction of a new $200 million dollar diesel engine factory in Thailand.

FINANCIALS: **Sales and profits are in thousands of dollars—add 000 to get the full amount. 2010 Note: Financial information for 2010 was not available for all companies at press time.**

2010 Sales: $135,592,000 | 2010 Profits: $6,503,000
2009 Sales: $104,589,000 | 2009 Profits: $104,690,000
2008 Sales: $148,979,000 | 2008 Profits: $-30,860,000
2007 Sales: $179,984,000 | 2007 Profits: $-38,732,000
2006 Sales: $204,467,000 | 2006 Profits: $-1,978,000

U.S. Stock Ticker: GM
Int'l Ticker:
Int'l Exchange:
Employees: 202,000 Fiscal Year Ends: 12/31
Parent Company:

SALARIES/BENEFITS:

Pension Plan: Y | ESOP Stock Plan: | Profit Sharing: | Top Exec. Salary: $1,133,333 | Bonus: $
Savings Plan: Y | Stock Purch. Plan: Y | | Second Exec. Salary: $900,000 | Bonus: $

OTHER THOUGHTS:

Apparent Women Officers or Directors: 8
Hot Spot for Advancement for Women/Minorities: Y

LOCATIONS: ("Y" = Yes)

West:	Southwest:	Midwest:	Southeast:	Northeast:	International:
Y	Y	Y	Y	Y	Y

GENESCO INC

www.genesco.com

Industry Group Code: 316213

Management:		Sales/Marketing:		Liberal Arts:		Information Sys.:		Professionals:		Tech./Scientific:	
Mgmt. Trainees:	Y	Marketing Pros.:	Y	Gen. Writing/Editing:	Y	Info. Mgmt.:	Y	Finance/Acct.:	Y	Engineers, Elec.:	
Experienced Mgmt.:	Y	Retail Sales:	Y	Tech. Writing:		Software Dev.:	Y	Law:	Y	Engineers, Other:	
Int'l Business:	Y	Comm./Industrial:	Y	Graphic Arts/Photog.:	Y	Hardware Dev.:		HR/Other:	Y	Health/Lab:	
MBA Grads:	Y	Sales Trainees:	Y	Music:		Consulting/Other:		Training:	Y	Science/Research:	
		Advertising Pros.:	Y	Broadcasting:				Health Care:		Petroleum/Chem.:	
				Other:	Y			Consulting:		Math/Other:	

TYPES OF BUSINESS:

Shoes, Retail
Retail Stores
Men's Accessories
Wholesale Operations
Hats, Retail
Catalog & Online Operations
Athletic Team Products

BRANDS/DIVISIONS/AFFILIATES:

Johnston & Murphy
Journeys
Underground Station
Journeys Kidz
Schuh Group Ltd.
Dockers
Lids
Schuh Group Ltd

CONTACTS: *Note: Officers with more than one job title may be intentionally listed here more than once.*

Robert J. Dennis, CEO
Robert J. Dennis, Pres.
James S. Gulmi, CFO/Sr. VP-Finance
Roger G. Sisson, General Counsel/Corp. Sec./Sr. VP
Mimi E. Vaughn, Sr. VP-Strategy & Shared Svcs.
Paul D. Williams, Chief Acct. Officer/VP
Kenneth J. Kocher, Sr. VP/Pres., Hat World
James C. Estepa, Sr. VP/CEO/Pres., Genesco Retail
Jonathan D. Caplan, Sr. VP/CEO-Genesco Branded Group
Jonathan D. Caplan, Pres., Johnston & Murphy
Robert J. Dennis, Chmn.

Phone: 615-367-7000	**Fax:** 615-367-8579
Toll-Free:	
Address: 1415 Murfreesboro Rd., Nashville, TN 37217-2895 US	

GROWTH PLANS/SPECIAL FEATURES:

Genesco, Inc. is a leading specialty retailer of footwear, headwear, licensed sportswear and accessories through 2,309 retail stores in the U.S., Canada and Puerto Rico. The company operates five business segments: Journeys Group; Underground Station Group; Lids Sports Group; Johnston & Murphy Group; and Licensed Brands. The Journey's Group segment operates 1,017 stores, including Journeys, Journeys Kidz and Shi by Journeys, and markets products through a catalog and Journeys.com. Journeys stores target customers in the 13-22 year age group. Shi carries shoes targeted at women in their mid 20s to early 30s. The Underground Station Group segment operates 151 stores, including Underground Station and Jarman. The Lids Sports Group segment operates 985 stores, including Hat World, Lids, Hat Shack, Hat Zone, Head Quarters, Cap Connection, Lids Kids and Lids Locker Room, and also markets products online. Through LIDS Team Sports and Impact Sports, the company provides full-service team uniform and apparel production, custom screen printing and sporting goods distribution. The Johnston & Murphy Group segment operates 156 retail and factory stores, as well as JohnstonMurphy.com, and sells footwear, luggage and accessories primarily targeting male business and professional customers. Retail prices for Johnston & Murphy footwear generally range from $110 to $250. The Licensed Brands segment is comprised primarily of Dockers footwear, marketed under a license from Levi Strauss & Company. In June 2011, the firm acquired Schuh Group Ltd., a United Kingdom-based casual and athletic footwear retailer.

Employee benefits include educational assistance, flexible spending accounts, adoption assistance, scholarships, healthcare and dental plans, company discounts, an employee credit association, child care and fitness classes.

FINANCIALS: **Sales and profits are in thousands of dollars—add 000 to get the full amount. 2010 Note: Financial information for 2010 was not available for all companies at press time.**

2010 Sales: $1,574,352	2010 Profits: $28,813
2009 Sales: $1,551,562	2009 Profits: $150,756
2008 Sales: $1,502,119	2008 Profits: $5,171
2007 Sales: $1,460,478	2007 Profits: $67,646
2006 Sales: $1,283,876	2006 Profits: $62,686

U.S. Stock Ticker: GCO
Int'l Ticker:
Int'l Exchange:
Employees: 13,900 Fiscal Year Ends: 1/31
Parent Company:

SALARIES/BENEFITS:

Pension Plan:	ESOP Stock Plan:	Profit Sharing:	Top Exec. Salary: $778,500	Bonus: $149,472
Savings Plan: Y	Stock Purch. Plan: Y		Second Exec. Salary: $408,972	Bonus: $58,892

OTHER THOUGHTS:

Apparent Women Officers or Directors: 2
Hot Spot for Advancement for Women/Minorities:

LOCATIONS: ("Y" = Yes)

West:	Southwest:	Midwest:	Southeast:	Northeast:	International:
Y	Y	Y	Y	Y	Y

GENTEX CORPORATION

www.gentex.com

Industry Group Code: 3363

Management:		**Sales/Marketing:**		**Liberal Arts:**		**Information Sys.:**		**Professionals:**		**Tech./Scientific:**	
Mgmt. Trainees:		Marketing Pros.:	Y	Gen. Writing/Editing:		Info. Mgmt.:	Y	Finance/Acct.:	Y	Engineers, Elec.:	Y
Experienced Mgmt.:		Retail Sales:		Tech. Writing:	Y	Software Dev.:		Law:	Y	Engineers, Other:	Y
Int'l Business:	Y	Comm./Industrial:	Y	Graphic Arts/Photog.:		Hardware Dev.:		HR/Other:	Y	Health/Lab:	
MBA Grads:	Y	Sales Trainees:		Music:		Consulting/Other:		Training:	Y	Science/Research:	
		Advertising Pros.:	Y	Broadcasting:				Health Care:		Petroleum/Chem.:	
				Other:				Consulting:		Math/Other:	

TYPES OF BUSINESS:

Specialty Automobile Parts Manufacturer
Electro-Optic Technology
Rearview Mirrors & Mirror Sub-Assemblies
Headlight Systems
Smoke Alarms & Smoke Detectors

BRANDS/DIVISIONS/AFFILIATES:

SmartBeam

CONTACTS:

Note: Officers with more than one job title may be intentionally listed here more than once.

Fred Bauer, CEO
Steve Dykman, CFO/VP
Bruce Los, VP-Human Resources
Tom Guarr, VP-Chemical Research
Jeremy Fogg, VP-Mechanical Eng. & Program Mgmt.
Connie Hamblin, Corp. Sec.
John Arnold, VP-Oper.
Connie Hamblin, VP-Corp. Comm.
Connie Hamblin, VP-Investor Rel.
Steve Dykman, VP-Finance
Enoch Jen, Sr. VP
Bill Tonar, VP-Advanced Materials & Process Dev.
Scott Edwards, VP-Fire Protection Prod.
Mark Newton, Sr. VP
Fred Bauer, Chmn.

Phone: 616-772-1800 **Fax:** 616-772-7348
Toll-Free:
Address: 600 N. Centennial St., Zeeland, MI 49464 US

GROWTH PLANS/SPECIAL FEATURES:

Gentex Corporation designs, develops, manufactures and markets proprietary products. The firm employs electro-optic technology including automatic-dimming rearview mirrors for the automotive industry and fire protection products primarily for the commercial building industry. Its interior auto-dimming mirror uses electrochromic technology and continually varies and automatically darkens to eliminate rearview headlight glare. The company has also introduced an exterior auto-dimming mirror sub-assembly, which works as a complete glare-control system with the interior mirror. Gentex supplies automatic-dimming rearview mirrors for Cadillac, Buick, Chevrolet, Saturn, Ford, Kia, Hummer, BMW, Fiat and other manufacturers. The mirrors are standard or option equipment in over 150 vehicles, including the Ford Expedition, Ford F150, Lincoln Navigator, Lincoln Mark LT, Mazda CX-9 and Toyota Camry. SmartBeam, the company's headlamp control system, automatically turns vehicle high beams on and off according to surrounding traffic conditions. Customers for this product include Opel/Vauxhall, BMW, Toyota, Rolls Royce, Tata/Land Rover and Audi. Gentex is currently making three exterior mirror sub-assembly products: thin glass flat, convex and aspheric. The company also manufactures LED turn signals for side-view mirrors, as well as roughly 60 different models of smoke alarms and smoke detectors, combined with more than 150 different models of signaling appliances. All of its smoke detectors and alarms rely on a photoelectric principle to detect smoke. Gentex also develops dimmable aircraft windows for the passenger compartment of the new Boeing 787 Dreamliner. In December 2010, Gentex acquired a new manufacturing facility in Holland, Michigan.

Gentex offers its employees health, dental, life and disability insurance; a 401(k) plan; tuition reimbursement; quarterly profit sharing; stock options; access to a wellness center; an employee stock purchase plan; and free coffee, tea and soft drinks.

FINANCIALS:

Sales and profits are in thousands of dollars—add 000 to get the full amount. 2010 Note: Financial information for 2010 was not available for all companies at press time.

2010 Sales: $816,263 2010 Profits: $137,734
2009 Sales: $544,523 2009 Profits: $64,637
2008 Sales: $623,800 2008 Profits: $62,088
2007 Sales: $653,933 2007 Profits: $122,130
2006 Sales: $572,267 2006 Profits: $108,761

U.S. Stock Ticker: GNTX
Int'l Ticker:
Int'l Exchange:
Employees: 2,908 Fiscal Year Ends: 12/31
Parent Company:

SALARIES/BENEFITS:

Pension Plan: ESOP Stock Plan: Profit Sharing: Y Top Exec. Salary: $428,979 Bonus: $39,727
Savings Plan: Y Stock Purch. Plan: Y Second Exec. Salary: $242,896 Bonus: $57,389

OTHER THOUGHTS:

Apparent Women Officers or Directors: 1
Hot Spot for Advancement for Women/Minorities:

LOCATIONS: ("Y" = Yes)

West:	Southwest:	Midwest:	Southeast:	Northeast:	International:
		Y			Y

GENTIVA HEALTH SERVICES INC

www.gentiva.com

Industry Group Code: 6216

Management:		Sales/Marketing:		Liberal Arts:		Information Sys.:		Professionals:		Tech./Scientific:	
Mgmt. Trainees:	Y	Marketing Pros.:	Y	Gen. Writing/Editing:		Info. Mgmt.:	Y	Finance/Acct.:	Y	Engineers, Elec.:	
Experienced Mgmt.:	Y	Retail Sales:		Tech. Writing:		Software Dev.:		Law:	Y	Engineers, Other:	Y
Int'l Business:		Comm./Industrial:	Y	Graphic Arts/Photog.:		Hardware Dev.:		HR/Other:	Y	Health/Lab:	
MBA Grads:	Y	Sales Trainees:		Music:		Consulting/Other:		Training:	Y	Science/Research:	
		Advertising Pros.:		Broadcasting:				Health Care:		Petroleum/Chem.:	
				Other:				Consulting:		Math/Other:	

TYPES OF BUSINESS:

Home Health Care Services
Administrative Services

BRANDS/DIVISIONS/AFFILIATES:

Gentiva Neurorehabilitation
Gentiva Safe Strides
Gentiva Orthopedics
Gentiva Cardiopulmonary
Gentive Rehab Without Walls
Gentiva Senior Health
CareCentrix Holdings, Inc.
Odyssey HealthCare, Inc.

CONTACTS: *Note: Officers with more than one job title may be intentionally listed here more than once.*

Tony Strange, CEO
Tony Strange, Pres.
Eric R. Slusser, CFO/Exec. VP/Treas.
John N. Camperlengo, General Counsel/Sr. VP/Sec.
David Gieringer, Controller/VP
Charlotte Weaver, Chief Clinical Officer/Sr. VP
John N. Camperlengo, Chief Compliance Officer
Jeff Shaner, Sr. VP/Pres., Hospice Div.
David Causby, Sr. VP/Pres., Home Health Div.
Tony Strange, Chmn.

Phone: 770-951-6450 **Fax:**
Toll-Free:
Address: 3350 Riverwood Pkwy., Ste. 1400, Atlanta, GA 30339-3314 US

GROWTH PLANS/SPECIAL FEATURES:

Gentiva Health Services, Inc. is a leading home health care service provider. The company's focus is on providing comprehensive in-home geriatric care services. To this end, the firm operates two divisions, home health and hospice. The home health division, through licensed and Medicare-certified agencies, provides various combinations of nursing and therapy services; paraprofessional nursing services; and homemaker services to adult and elderly patients in over 300 locations in 39 states. The division also operates focused specialty programs, including Gentiva Orthopedics, providing individualized home orthopedic rehabilitation services to patients recovering from joint replacement or other major orthopedic surgery; Gentiva Safe Strides, providing therapies for patients with balance issues; Gentiva Cardiopulmonary, helping patients manage heart and lung health in a home-base environment; Gentiva Neurorehabilitation, which helps patients with neurological injuries and conditions heal in their own home; Gentiva Senior Health, which addresses the needs of patients with age-related diseases and helps them safely stay in their homes; and Gentiva Rehab Without Walls, providing home and community-based neurorehabilitation therapies for patients with traumatic brain injury, cerebrovascular accident injury and acquired brain injury. The home health division offers various consulting services to home health agencies. Additionally, the firm conducts hospice services for terminally ill patients in the southeast U.S. For hospice patients, Gentiva assigns an interdisciplinary team of healthcare professionals, dependent on the individual's needs, at over 150 locations in 30 states. These teams can include physicians, nurses, home health aides, medical social workers, dietary counselors and bereavement specialists. In August 2010, the firm acquired home health company Odyssey HealthCare, Inc. for $1 billion. In August 2011, Gentiva Health agreed to sell its interest in CareCentrix Holdings, Inc.

Employees are offered medical, dental and vision insurance; life and disability insurance; a 401(k) plan; an employee stock purchase plan; and tuition assistance.

FINANCIALS: **Sales and profits are in thousands of dollars—add 000 to get the full amount. 2010 Note: Financial information for 2010 was not available for all companies at press time.**

2010 Sales: $1,447,029	2010 Profits: $52,155	**U.S. Stock Ticker: GTIV**
2009 Sales: $1,152,460	2009 Profits: $59,182	**Int'l Ticker:**
2008 Sales: $1,239,536	2008 Profits: $153,450	Int'l Exchange:
2007 Sales: $1,171,349	2007 Profits: $32,828	Employees: 15,350 Fiscal Year Ends: 12/31
2006 Sales: $1,106,588	2006 Profits: $20,776	Parent Company:

SALARIES/BENEFITS:

Pension Plan:	ESOP Stock Plan:	Profit Sharing:	Top Exec. Salary: $753,753	Bonus: $120,000
Savings Plan: Y	Stock Purch. Plan: Y		Second Exec. Salary: $721,096	Bonus: $1,435,000

OTHER THOUGHTS:

Apparent Women Officers or Directors: 1
Hot Spot for Advancement for Women/Minorities:

LOCATIONS: ("Y" = Yes)

West:	Southwest:	Midwest:	Southeast:	Northeast:	International:
Y	Y	Y	Y	Y	

GENWORTH FINANCIAL INC

www.genworth.com

Industry Group Code: 524113

Management:		**Sales/Marketing:**		**Liberal Arts:**		**Information Sys.:**		**Professionals:**		**Tech./Scientific:**	
Mgmt. Trainees:	Y	Marketing Pros.:	Y	Gen. Writing/Editing:	Y	Info. Mgmt.:	Y	Finance/Acct.:	Y	Engineers, Elec.:	
Experienced Mgmt.:	Y	Retail Sales:		Tech. Writing:	Y	Software Dev.:	Y	Law:	Y	Engineers, Other:	
Int'l Business:	Y	Comm./Industrial:	Y	Graphic Arts/Photog.:	Y	Hardware Dev.:		HR/Other:	Y	Health/Lab:	
MBA Grads:	Y	Sales Trainees:	Y	Music:		Consulting/Other:		Training:	Y	Science/Research:	
		Advertising Pros.:	Y	Broadcasting:				Health Care:	Y	Petroleum/Chem.:	
				Other:	Y			Consulting:		Math/Other:	Y

TYPES OF BUSINESS:

Life Insurance
Annuities
Group Health, Life, Dental & Disability Insurance
Payment Protection Insurance
Mortgage Insurance
Retirement Income & Investment Products & Services
Long-Term Care Insurance

BRANDS/DIVISIONS/AFFILIATES:

CONTACTS:

Note: Officers with more than one job title may be intentionally listed here more than once.

Michael D. Fraizer, CEO
Jerome T. Upton, COO-Int'l
Michael D. Fraizer, Pres.
Martin P. Klein, CFO/Sr. VP
Michael S. Laming, Sr. VP-Human Resources
Scott J. McKay, CIO/Sr. VP
Leon E. Roday, General Counsel/Sr. VP/Sec.
Joseph J. Pehota, Sr. VP-Corp. Dev.
Al Orendorff, VP-Public Rel.
Thomas M. Stinson, Pres., Insurance Prod.
Kevin Schneider, Sr. VP/Pres./CEO-US Mortgage Insurance
Ronald Joelson, Chief Investment Officer/Sr. VP
Patrick B. Kelleher, Exec. VP/Pres./CEO-Retirement & Protection
Michael D. Fraizer, Chmn.
Robert J. Brannock, Pres., Europe

Phone: 804-281-6000 **Fax:** 804-662-2414
Toll-Free: 888-436-9678
Address: 6620 W. Broad St., Richmond, VA 23230 US

GROWTH PLANS/SPECIAL FEATURES:

Genworth Financial, Inc. is a financial security and insurance company focused on developing products that help the investment, protection, homeownership, retirement and independent lifestyle needs of more than 15 million customers. Genworth Financial has with a presence in more than 25 countries. The company, which has roughly $112.4 billion in assets, operates in three segments: retirement and protection; international; and U.S. mortgage insurance. The retirement and protection segment provides protection, wealth accumulation, retirement income and institutional products, such as life insurance; long-term care insurance; a linked-benefits product that combines long-term care insurance with universal life insurance; and Medicare supplement insurance. The segment also offers wellness and care coordination services for its long-term care policyholders; a variety of annuities; managed account programs, financial planning services and mutual funds; funding agreements and funding agreements backing notes; and guaranteed investment contracts. The international division provides structured, or bulk, mortgage insurance products as well as analytical tools and technology in Canada, Australia, New Zealand, Mexico and various European countries. This division also provides payment protection in North America and Europe. The U.S. mortgage insurance segment offers flow, or prime-based, individually underwritten residential mortgage loans. Genworth Financial also has corporate and other activities, which consist primarily of unallocated corporate income and expenses, results of a small, non-core business and most interest and other financing expenses.

Employees are offered medical, dental and vision insurance; life insurance; disability coverage; flexible spending accounts; child care subsidies; pension plans; 401(k) plans; an employee discount program; and tuition reimbursement.

FINANCIALS:

Sales and profits are in thousands of dollars—add 000 to get the full amount. 2010 Note: Financial information for 2010 was not available for all companies at press time.

2010 Sales: $10,089,000 | 2010 Profits: $285,000
2009 Sales: $9,069,000 | 2009 Profits: $-399,000
2008 Sales: $9,948,000 | 2008 Profits: $-572,000
2007 Sales: $11,125,000 | 2007 Profits: $1,154,000
2006 Sales: $10,285,000 | 2006 Profits: $1,283,000

U.S. Stock Ticker: GNW
Int'l Ticker:
Int'l Exchange:
Employees: 6,500 Fiscal Year Ends: 12/31
Parent Company:

SALARIES/BENEFITS:

Pension Plan: Y | ESOP Stock Plan: | Profit Sharing: | Top Exec. Salary: $1,121,403 | Bonus: $1,000,000
Savings Plan: Y | Stock Purch. Plan: | Second Exec. Salary: $647,922 | Bonus: $425,000

OTHER THOUGHTS:

Apparent Women Officers or Directors: 4
Hot Spot for Advancement for Women/Minorities: Y

LOCATIONS: ("Y" = Yes)

West:	Southwest:	Midwest:	Southeast:	Northeast:	International:
Y	Y	Y	Y	Y	Y

GENZYME BIOSURGERY

www.genzyme.com/business/biosurgery/biosurg_home.asp

Industry Group Code: 33911

Management:		Sales/Marketing:		Liberal Arts:		Information Sys.:		Professionals:		Tech./Scientific:	
Mgmt. Trainees:	Y	Marketing Pros.:	Y	Gen. Writing/Editing:	Y	Info. Mgmt.:	Y	Finance/Acct.:	Y	Engineers, Elec.:	Y
Experienced Mgmt.:	Y	Retail Sales:		Tech. Writing:	Y	Software Dev.:	Y	Law:	Y	Engineers, Other:	Y
Int'l Business:		Comm./Industrial:	Y	Graphic Arts/Photog.:		Hardware Dev.:	Y	HR/Other:	Y	Health/Lab:	
MBA Grads:	Y	Sales Trainees:		Music:		Consulting/Other:		Training:	Y	Science/Research:	
		Advertising Pros.:	Y	Broadcasting:				Health Care:		Petroleum/Chem.:	
				Other:				Consulting:		Math/Other:	

TYPES OF BUSINESS:

Equipment-Surgery & Orthopedic Products
Burn Treatment Products
Biomaterials & Biotherapeutics

BRANDS/DIVISIONS/AFFILIATES:

Genzyme Corp
Synvisc
Seprafilm
Seprapack
Sepragel ENT
Carticel
Epicel
Sanofi-Aventis SA

CONTACTS: *Note: Officers with more than one job title may be intentionally listed here more than once.*

Alison Lawton, Gen. Mgr./Sr. VP
Christopher Viehbacher, CEO-Sanofi-Aventis SA

Phone: 617-768-1000	**Fax:** 617-591-5986
Toll-Free:	
Address: 55 Cambridge Pkwy., Cambridge, MA 02142 US	

GROWTH PLANS/SPECIAL FEATURES:

Genzyme Biosurgery (GB), a division of Genzyme Corp., develops and markets a portfolio of devices, biomaterials and biotherapeutics primarily for the general surgery market. GB's products are used for osteoarthritis relief, adhesion prevention, hernia repair, cartilage repair and burn treatment. It derives much of its revenue from Synvisc and Synvisc-One (hylan G-F 20) and Sepra. Synvisc and Synvisc-One are biomaterial-based products derived from hyaluronan that are used to treat the pain associated with osteoarthritis (OA) of the knee. Synvisc-One, a single-injection product, has been approved by the European Union, the U.S. and various Asian and Latin American countries. Synvisc is sold commercially in approximately 40 countries, and Synvisc-One is sold in 20 countries. The Sepra family of products consists of the Sepramesh IP, which is manufactured and marketed by Davol, Inc. under a license agreement; Seprafilm, one of the only FDA-approved products clinically proven to reduce the incidence, extent and severity of postsurgical adhesions following abdominal and pelvic surgery; Seprapack, which is indicated for use in patients undergoing nasal/sinus surgery; and Sepragel ENT. The firm also produces Carticel, which helps repair damaged knee cartilage; Epicel, a permanent skin replacement product for patients with life-threatening burns; and the HyluMed product line, which consists of medical-grade and sterile HA powder. The company markets its products directly to physicians and hospital administrators throughout the U.S. and Europe. It also uses Genzyme Corp.'s network of distributors to sell certain products in the U.S., Europe, Asia and Latin America. In April 2011, Sanofi-Aventis S.A. acquired Genzyme Corp., which is now a wholly-owned subsidiary of Sanofi-Aventis.

FINANCIALS: **Sales and profits are in thousands of dollars—add 000 to get the full amount. 2010 Note: Financial information for 2010 was not available for all companies at press time.**

2010 Sales: $4,050,000	2010 Profits: $422,100	**U.S. Stock Ticker: Subsidiary**
2009 Sales: $4,515,525	2009 Profits: $422,300	**Int'l Ticker:**
2008 Sales: $4,605,039	2008 Profits: $99,553	Int'l Exchange:
2007 Sales: $426,647	2007 Profits: $60,082	Employees: 10,000 Fiscal Year Ends: 12/31
2006 Sales: $	2006 Profits: $	Parent Company: SANOFI-AVENTIS SA

SALARIES/BENEFITS:

Pension Plan:	ESOP Stock Plan:	Profit Sharing:	Top Exec. Salary: $	Bonus: $
Savings Plan: Y	Stock Purch. Plan: Y		Second Exec. Salary: $	Bonus: $

OTHER THOUGHTS:

Apparent Women Officers or Directors: 1
Hot Spot for Advancement for Women/Minorities:

LOCATIONS: ("Y" = Yes)

West:	Southwest:	Midwest:	Southeast:	Northeast:	International:
				Y	

GEOKINETICS INC

www.geokinetics.com

Industry Group Code: 541360

Management:		Sales/Marketing:		Liberal Arts:		Information Sys.:		Professionals:		Tech./Scientific:	
Mgmt. Trainees:		Marketing Pros.:	Y	Gen. Writing/Editing:		Info. Mgmt.:	Y	Finance/Acct.:	Y	Engineers, Elec.:	Y
Experienced Mgmt.:		Retail Sales:		Tech. Writing:	Y	Software Dev.:	Y	Law:	Y	Engineers, Other:	Y
Int'l Business:	Y	Comm./Industrial:	Y	Graphic Arts/Photog.:		Hardware Dev.:		HR/Other:	Y	Health/Lab:	
MBA Grads:	Y	Sales Trainees:		Music:		Consulting/Other:		Training:		Science/Research:	
		Advertising Pros.:	Y	Broadcasting:				Health Care:		Petroleum/Chem.:	
				Other:				Consulting:		Math/Other:	Y

TYPES OF BUSINESS:

Seismic Data Acquisition & Processing
Seismic Data Software

BRANDS/DIVISIONS/AFFILIATES:

Geokinetics USA, Inc.
Geokinetics Exploration, Inc.
Geokinetics International Holdings, Inc.
Geophysical Development Corporation

CONTACTS: *Note: Officers with more than one job title may be intentionally listed here more than once.*

Richard Miles, CEO
Richard Miles, Pres.
Gary L. Pittman, CFO
Jim White, Exec. VP-Tech.
Lee Parker, Exec. VP-Oper.
Jim White, Exec. VP-Bus. Dev.
William R. Ziegler, Chmn.

Phone: 713-850-7600	**Fax:** 713-850-7330
Toll-Free:	
Address: 1500 City West Blvd., Ste. 800, Houston, TX 77042 US	

GROWTH PLANS/SPECIAL FEATURES:

Geokinetics, Inc. is a global provider of seismic acquisition services, which include high-end seismic data processing and interpretation services, to the oil and gas industry worldwide. The company is organized into three segments: North American seismic data acquisition, International seismic data acquisition and data processing and interpretation. The company's seismic data acquisition operations are conducted primarily by three wholly-owned subsidiaries: Geokinetics USA, Inc.; Geokinetics Exploration, Inc.; and Geokinetics International Holdings, Inc. Geokinetics' seismic acquisition service is engaged in land, transition zone and shallow water environments seismic acquisition services on a contract basis for its customers. Geokinetics' equipment is capable of collecting 2D, 3D and multi-component seismic acquisition data with a combined recording capacity of approximately 206,000 channels and capabilities of operating up to 38 crews worldwide. Most of the company's land and transition zone acquisition services involve 3D surveys. Crew count, configuration and location can change depending upon industry demand and requirements. The firm's data processing and interpretation operations are conducted by its subsidiary Geophysical Development Corporation (GDC). GDC provides geophysical processing, interpretation, software and consultation services to the oil and gas industry. The company has domestic offices in Texas and international offices in the U.K., Canada, Central and South America, Europe, the Middle East, Australia and Asia. The firm's customers include national oil companies, major international oil companies and smaller independent E&P companies. In February 2010, the firm acquired PGS Onshore, Petroleum Geo-Services' multi-client data library and seismic data acquisition business, for $210 million.

The company offers employee benefits including medical insurance, dental insurance, life insurance, disability benefits, tuition assistance and a 401(k) plan with company match.

FINANCIALS: **Sales and profits are in thousands of dollars—add 000 to get the full amount. 2010 Note: Financial information for 2010 was not available for all companies at press time.**

2010 Sales: $558,134	2010 Profits: $-138,684	**U.S. Stock Ticker: GOK**
2009 Sales: $510,966	2009 Profits: $-5,011	**Int'l Ticker:**
2008 Sales: $474,598	2008 Profits: $ 986	Int'l Exchange:
2007 Sales: $357,677	2007 Profits: $-15,936	Employees: 5,200 Fiscal Year Ends: 7/31
2006 Sales: $225,183	2006 Profits: $-4,176	Parent Company:

SALARIES/BENEFITS:

Pension Plan: Y	ESOP Stock Plan:	Profit Sharing:	Top Exec. Salary: $375,000	Bonus: $220,000
Savings Plan: Y	Stock Purch. Plan:		Second Exec. Salary: $300,000	Bonus: $102,000

OTHER THOUGHTS:

Apparent Women Officers or Directors:
Hot Spot for Advancement for Women/Minorities:

LOCATIONS: ("Y" = Yes)

West:	Southwest:	Midwest:	Southeast:	Northeast:	International:
	Y				Y

Sales, profits and employees may be estimates. Financial information, benefits and other data can change quickly and may vary from those stated here.

GILEAD SCIENCES INC

www.gilead.com

Industry Group Code: 325412

Management:		Sales/Marketing:		Liberal Arts:		Information Sys.:		Professionals:		Tech./Scientific:	
Mgmt. Trainees:	Y	Marketing Pros.:	Y	Gen. Writing/Editing:		Info. Mgmt.:	Y	Finance/Acct.:	Y	Engineers, Elec.:	Y
Experienced Mgmt.:	Y	Retail Sales:		Tech. Writing:	Y	Software Dev.:	Y	Law:	Y	Engineers, Other:	Y
Int'l Business:	Y	Comm./Industrial:	Y	Graphic Arts/Photog.:	Y	Hardware Dev.:		HR/Other:	Y	Health/Lab:	Y
MBA Grads:	Y	Sales Trainees:		Music:		Consulting/Other:		Training:	Y	Science/Research:	Y
		Advertising Pros.:		Broadcasting:				Health Care:	Y	Petroleum/Chem.:	Y
				Other:				Consulting:		Math/Other:	Y

TYPES OF BUSINESS:

Viral & Bacterial Infections Drugs
Respiratory & Cardiopulmonary Diseases Drugs

BRANDS/DIVISIONS/AFFILIATES:

CGI Pharmaceuticals, Inc.
Arresto Biosciences, Inc.
Calistoga Pharmaceuticals, Inc.
Atripla
Hepsera
Viread
Lexiscan
Ranexa

CONTACTS: *Note: Officers with more than one job title may be intentionally listed here more than once.*

John C. Martin, CEO
John F. Milligan, COO
John F. Milligan, Pres.
Robin L. Washington, CFO/Sr. VP
Kristen M. Metza, Sr. VP-Human Resources
Norbert W. Bischofberger, Exec. VP-R&D/Chief Scientific Officer
Kevin Young, Exec. VP-Commercial Oper.
Gregg H. Alton, Exec. VP-Corp. & Medical Affairs
John C. Martin, Chmn.

Phone: 650-574-3000	**Fax:** 650-578-9264
Toll-Free: 800-445-3235	
Address: 333 Lakeside Dr., Foster City, CA 94404 US	

GROWTH PLANS/SPECIAL FEATURES:

Gilead Sciences, Inc. is a biopharmaceutical company that discovers, develops and commercializes therapeutics for the treatment of life-threatening diseases such as viral and bacterial infections. The company expanded its efforts to include respiratory and cardiopulmonary diseases. The firm maintains research, development, manufacturing, sales and marketing facilities in the U.S., Europe and Australia and operates marketing subsidiaries in another 12 countries. Gilead currently has 10 products on the market: Viread, Truvada and Emtriva, which are oral medicines used as part of a combination therapy to treat HIV; Atripla, an oral formulation for treatment of HIV; Hespera, an oral medication used for treatment of Hepatitis B; AmBisome, an antifungal agent to treat serious invasive fungal infections; Vistide, an antiviral medication for the treatment of cytomegalovirus retinitis in patients with AIDS; Ranexa, a treatment for chronic angina; Letairis, for the treatment of pulmonary arterial hypertension; and Cayston, an inhaled antibiotic as a treatment to improve respiratory systems in cystic fibrosis patients with Pseudomonas aeruginosa. The firm has a number of products in development, including treatments for hypertension, heart failure, hepatitis C, HIV/AIDS, and others. The company also derives revenues from licensing agreements for Macugen, a macular degeneration treatment developed by OSI Pharmaceuticals, Inc.; Lexiscan, an injection used as a pharmacologic stress agent in radionuclide myocardial perfusion imaging; and Tamiflu, an influenza medication sold by F. Hoffman-LaRoche. In July 2010, Gilead acquired CGI Pharmaceuticals, Inc. In January 2011, the firm acquired Arresto Biosciences, Inc. In Febraury 2011, the company agreed to acquire Calistoga Pharmaceuticals, Inc. for roughly $375 million.

The company offers its employees medical, vision, dental, disability, life and AD&D insurance; a 401(k); a stock purchase plan; an entertainment discount program; an employee assistance plan; and tuition reimbursement.

FINANCIALS: **Sales and profits are in thousands of dollars—add 000 to get the full amount. 2010 Note: Financial information for 2010 was not available for all companies at press time.**

2010 Sales: $7,949,420	2010 Profits: $2,901,257
2009 Sales: $7,011,383	2009 Profits: $2,635,755
2008 Sales: $5,335,750	2008 Profits: $1,978,899
2007 Sales: $4,230,045	2007 Profits: $1,584,902
2006 Sales: $3,026,139	2006 Profits: $-1,189,957

U.S. Stock Ticker: GILD
Int'l Ticker:
Int'l Exchange:
Employees: 4,000 Fiscal Year Ends: 12/31
Parent Company:

SALARIES/BENEFITS:

Pension Plan:	ESOP Stock Plan:	Profit Sharing:	Top Exec. Salary: $1,242,095	Bonus: $2,187,500
Savings Plan: Y	Stock Purch. Plan: Y		Second Exec. Salary: $805,008	Bonus: $850,500

OTHER THOUGHTS:

Apparent Women Officers or Directors: 4
Hot Spot for Advancement for Women/Minorities: Y

LOCATIONS: ("Y" = Yes)

West:	Southwest:	Midwest:	Southeast:	Northeast:	International:
Y				Y	Y

GOODYEAR TIRE & RUBBER COMPANY (THE) www.goodyear.com

Industry Group Code: 3262

Management:		Sales/Marketing:		Liberal Arts:		Information Sys.:		Professionals:		Tech./Scientific:	
Mgmt. Trainees:	Y	Marketing Pros.:	Y	Gen. Writing/Editing:		Info. Mgmt.:	Y	Finance/Acct.:	Y	Engineers, Elec.:	
Experienced Mgmt.:	Y	Retail Sales:	Y	Tech. Writing:		Software Dev.:		Law:	Y	Engineers, Other:	
Int'l Business:	Y	Comm./Industrial:		Graphic Arts/Photog.:		Hardware Dev.:		HR/Other:	Y	Health/Lab:	
MBA Grads:	Y	Sales Trainees:	Y	Music:		Consulting/Other:		Training:	Y	Science/Research:	
		Advertising Pros.:	Y	Broadcasting:				Health Care:		Petroleum/Chem.:	
				Other:				Consulting:		Math/Other:	

TYPES OF BUSINESS:

Tire Manufacturing
Automotive Service Shops
Resins & Latex
Synthetic Polymers
Industrial Chemicals
Belts & Hoses
Blimps
Retail Sales

BRANDS/DIVISIONS/AFFILIATES:

Goodyear
Kelly
Lee
Fulda
Sava
Dunlop

CONTACTS: *Note: Officers with more than one job title may be intentionally listed here more than once.*

Richard J. Kramer, CEO
Richard J. Kramer, Pres.
Darren Wells, CFO/Exec. VP
Joseph B. Ruocco, Sr. VP-Human Resources
Jean-Claude Kihn, CTO/Sr. VP
David L. Bialoski, General Counsel/Sr. VP/Sec.
John D. Fish, Sr. VP- Global Oper.
Isabel H. Jasinowsky, VP-Gov't Rel.
Scott Honnold, Treas./VP
Curt Andersson, Pres., North American Tire
Pierre E. Cohade, Pres., Asia Pacific
Jamie C. Szulc, Pres., Latin America
Richard J. Noechel, Controller/VP
Richard J. Kramer, Chmn.
Arthur de Bok, Pres., EMEA
Mark W. Purtilar, Chief Procurement Officer/VP

Phone: 330-796-2121	**Fax:** 330-796-2222
Toll-Free:	
Address: 1144 E. Market St., Akron, OH 44316-0001 US	

GROWTH PLANS/SPECIAL FEATURES:

The Goodyear Tire & Rubber Company is one of the world's leading manufacturers of tires and rubber-related chemicals for various applications. Goodyear is also one of the world's largest operators of commercial truck service and tire retreading centers. It operates approximately 1,500 tire and auto service center outlets, and manufactures products in 55 manufacturing facilities in 22 countries. Goodyear operates through four business segments: North American Tire, EMEA Tire, Latin American Tire and Asia Pacific Tire. Goodyear manufactures rubber tires for automobiles, trucks, buses, aviation, motorcycles, farm implements, earthmoving equipment, industrial equipment and other applications. The company sells tires under brands including Goodyear, Dunlop, Kelly, Fulda, Debica, Sava, various other Goodyear-owned brands and the private-label brands of certain customers. It also retreads truck, aviation and heavy equipment tires, manufactures and sells tread rubber and other tire retreading materials; provides automotive repair services; and manufactures and sells flaps for truck tires and other types of tires. The company also operates three blimps located in Ohio, California and Florida. Approximately 84% of net sales are from the sale of new tires. In April 2011, the company sold its Latin American farm tire operations to Titan International, Inc.'s subsidiary, Titan Tire Corporation, for approximately $99 million.

Employees are offered medical and welfare benefits, as well as a pension plan.

FINANCIALS: **Sales and profits are in thousands of dollars—add 000 to get the full amount. 2010 Note: Financial information for 2010 was not available for all companies at press time.**

2010 Sales: $18,832,000	2010 Profits: $-216,000	**U.S. Stock Ticker: GT**
2009 Sales: $16,301,000	2009 Profits: $-375,000	**Int'l Ticker:**
2008 Sales: $19,488,000	2008 Profits: $-77,000	Int'l Exchange:
2007 Sales: $19,644,000	2007 Profits: $602,000	Employees: 72,000 Fiscal Year Ends: 12/31
2006 Sales: $18,751,000	2006 Profits: $-330,000	Parent Company:

SALARIES/BENEFITS:

Pension Plan: Y	ESOP Stock Plan:	Profit Sharing:	Top Exec. Salary: $929,924	Bonus: $5,653,500
Savings Plan:	Stock Purch. Plan:		Second Exec. Salary: $922,500	Bonus: $8,522,974

OTHER THOUGHTS:

Apparent Women Officers or Directors: 4
Hot Spot for Advancement for Women/Minorities: Y

LOCATIONS: ("Y" = Yes)

West:	Southwest:	Midwest:	Southeast:	Northeast:	International:
Y	Y	Y	Y	Y	Y

GOOGLE INC

www.google.com

Industry Group Code: 519130

Management:		**Sales/Marketing:**		**Liberal Arts:**		**Information Sys.:**		**Professionals:**		**Tech./Scientific:**	
Mgmt. Trainees:	Y	Marketing Pros.:	Y	Gen. Writing/Editing:	Y	Info. Mgmt.:	Y	Finance/Acct.:	Y	Engineers, Elec.:	Y
Experienced Mgmt.:	Y	Retail Sales:		Tech. Writing:	Y	Software Dev.:	Y	Law:	Y	Engineers, Other:	
Int'l Business:	Y	Comm./Industrial:	Y	Graphic Arts/Photog.:	Y	Hardware Dev.:	Y	HR/Other:	Y	Health/Lab:	
MBA Grads:	Y	Sales Trainees:		Music:		Consulting/Other:		Training:	Y	Science/Research:	
		Advertising Pros.:	Y	Broadcasting:				Health Care:		Petroleum/Chem.:	
				Other:	Y			Consulting:		Math/Other:	

TYPES OF BUSINESS:

Search Engine-Internet
Paid Search Listing Advertising Services
Online Software and Productivity Tools
Online Video and Photo Services
E-Book Services
Analytical Tools
Search and Advertising on Cell Phones
Online Maps

BRANDS/DIVISIONS/AFFILIATES:

Admeld, Inc.
Google Maps
Google News
Gmail
YouTube LLC
Picasa
Chrome
Android

CONTACTS: *Note: Officers with more than one job title may be intentionally listed here more than once.*

Larry Page, CEO
Patrick Pichette, CFO/Sr. VP
Alan Eustace, Sr. VP-Research
Sergey Brin, Pres., Tech./Co-Founder
Alan Eustace, Sr. VP-Eng.
David C. Drummond, Chief Legal Officer
Shona Brown, Sr. VP-Bus. Oper.
Nikesh Arora, Chief Bus. Officer
Jonathan Rosenberg, Sr. VP-Prod. Mgmt.
David C. Drummond, Sr. VP-Corp. Dev.
Eric Schmidt, Chmn.

Phone: 650-253-0000 **Fax:** 650-253-0001
Toll-Free:
Address: 1600 Amphitheatre Pkwy., Mountain View, CA 94043 US

GROWTH PLANS/SPECIAL FEATURES:

Google, Inc. operates Google.com, one of the world's largest and most used search engines, which indexes the content of billions of Internet pages. While Google charges nothing for its search engine, it charges fees to other sites that use its search technology, and has a lucrative program that enables business clients to bid for ad space. Businesses use the AdWords program to promote their products and services. In addition, third-party web sites that comprise the Google Network use the AdSense program to deliver ads that generate revenue and are relevant to search results. The company's applications include office productivity and content sharing tools, such as Google Docs, Gmail, Blogger and YouTube. Client products mostly serve desktop needs, such as the Google Toolbar browser add-on, the Google Chrome browser, the Google Chrome OS operating system and the Picasa photo sharing service. Google's GEO services encompass the company's cartographical and other similar tools, including Google Maps, Google Local Search, Google Earth and Google SketchUp, a three dimensional modeling tool. Google Mobile operations include Android, a free and open source smart phone operating system, and related mobile applications. Additional service categories include Google Checkout, an online shopping and payment service, and Google Labs, an experimental testing service. Google provides its services in 112 different languages, with more than 50% of its searches coming from outside the U.S. In June 2011, the company agreed to purchase Admeld, Inc., a firm specializing in online ads. In August 2011, Google announced plans to acquire Android phone manufacturer Motorola Mobility for $12.5 billion as part of its efforts to compete with Apple's iPhone.

Employee benefits include medical, dental and vision insurance; flexible spending accounts; a college savings plan; adoption assistance; tuition reimbursement; free on-site lunches and dinners; recreation facilities; on-site dry cleaning; and oil change and car wash facilities.

FINANCIALS: **Sales and profits are in thousands of dollars—add 000 to get the full amount. 2010 Note: Financial information for 2010 was not available for all companies at press time.**

2010 Sales: $29,321,000	2010 Profits: $8,505,000	**U.S. Stock Ticker: GOOG**
2009 Sales: $23,650,563	2009 Profits: $6,520,448	**Int'l Ticker:**
2008 Sales: $21,795,550	2008 Profits: $4,226,858	Int'l Exchange:
2007 Sales: $16,593,986	2007 Profits: $4,203,720	Employees: 24,400 Fiscal Year Ends: 12/31
2006 Sales: $10,604,917	2006 Profits: $3,077,446	Parent Company:

SALARIES/BENEFITS:

Pension Plan: Y	ESOP Stock Plan:	Profit Sharing:	Top Exec. Salary: $450,000	Bonus: $2,524,038
Savings Plan: Y	Stock Purch. Plan:		Second Exec. Salary: $450,000	Bonus: $3,214,738

OTHER THOUGHTS:

Apparent Women Officers or Directors: 1
Hot Spot for Advancement for Women/Minorities:

LOCATIONS: ("Y" = Yes)

West:	Southwest:	Midwest:	Southeast:	Northeast:	International:
Y	Y	Y	Y	Y	Y

GRANT THORNTON LLP

www.grantthornton.com

Industry Group Code: 5412

Management:		**Sales/Marketing:**		**Liberal Arts:**		**Information Sys.:**		**Professionals:**		**Tech./Scientific:**	
Mgmt. Trainees:	Y	Marketing Pros.:	Y	Gen. Writing/Editing:	Y	Info. Mgmt.:	Y	Finance/Acct.:	Y	Engineers, Elec.:	
Experienced Mgmt.:	Y	Retail Sales:		Tech. Writing:	Y	Software Dev.:	Y	Law:	Y	Engineers, Other:	
Int'l Business:		Comm./Industrial:	Y	Graphic Arts/Photog.:	Y	Hardware Dev.:		HR/Other:	Y	Health/Lab:	
MBA Grads:	Y	Sales Trainees:		Music:		Consulting/Other:	Y	Training:	Y	Science/Research:	
		Advertising Pros.:	Y	Broadcasting:				Health Care:		Petroleum/Chem.:	
				Other:	Y			Consulting:	Y	Math/Other:	

TYPES OF BUSINESS:

Accounting & Auditing Services
Financial Services
Administration Consulting

BRANDS/DIVISIONS/AFFILIATES:

Grant Thornton International
On The Horizon
Getting in the Game
Huron Consulting Group

CONTACTS:

Note: Officers with more than one job title may be intentionally listed here more than once.

Stephen Chipman, CEO
Lou Grabowsky, COO
Russ Wieman, CFO
Ken Cunningham, Chief Legal Officer
Mike McGuire, Managing Partner-Industry & Market Dev.
Trent Gazzaway, Managing Partner-Audit Svcs.
Mark Stutman, Managing Partner-Tax Svcs.
Steve Lukens, Managing Partner-Advisory Svcs.

Phone: 312-856-0200	**Fax:** 312-602-8099
Toll-Free:	
Address: 175 W. Jackson Blvd., Chicago, IL 60604 US	

GROWTH PLANS/SPECIAL FEATURES:

Grant Thornton LLP is the U.S. arm of Grant Thornton International, a global accounting, tax and business advisory organization. The firm has approximately 50 offices across the country, providing specialist financial, tax and advisory services to both public and private corporations. Some of Grant Thornton's key audit and assurance services include integrated auditing, benefits management and public finance. The company's investment banking services involve sell side advisory, buy side advisory, management buyouts, restructurings and capital raising. It also offers more general administrative consulting services, such as Sarbanes-Oxley compliance; services for Chief Information Officers and Chief Financial Officers; project management office strategies; and performance improvement. Grant Thornton serves customers in the construction, real estate, consumer products, food and beverage, health care, energy, technology, manufacturing, retail, transportation, non-profit and financial services industries. Grant Thornton offers audit and assurance services tailored to particular needs, as well as providing the public with a series of publications, including On the Horizon, which publishes weekly news on developments in the accounting world. With support from Grant Thornton International's investment banking teams, the company can assist international clients with cross-border merger and acquisition activities. Grant Thornton's advisory services cover information technology security, strategy and assessment; financial valuation; corporate governance and restructuring; merger integration; and fraudulent activity detection. The company also provides international tax services and transfer pricing. In early 2010, the company and Lewis & Roca jointly released Getting in the Game: A Guide to Successful Gaming Company Compliance, a business guide for gaming firms. In October 2010, Grant Thornton acquired the disputes and investigations business of Huron Consulting Group.

Grant Thornton's employee benefits include medical and dental plans; reimbursement accounts; and a 401(k) plan.

FINANCIALS:

Sales and profits are in thousands of dollars—add 000 to get the full amount. 2010 Note: Financial information for 2010 was not available for all companies at press time.

2010 Sales: $1,700,000	2010 Profits: $	**U.S. Stock Ticker: Private**
2009 Sales: $1,300,000	2009 Profits: $	**Int'l Ticker:**
2008 Sales: $1,220,000	2008 Profits: $	Int'l Exchange:
2007 Sales: $1,075,000	2007 Profits: $	Employees: 6,500 Fiscal Year Ends: 7/31
2006 Sales: $886,000	2006 Profits: $	Parent Company:

SALARIES/BENEFITS:

Pension Plan:	ESOP Stock Plan:	Profit Sharing:	Top Exec. Salary: $	Bonus: $
Savings Plan: Y	Stock Purch. Plan:		Second Exec. Salary: $	Bonus: $

OTHER THOUGHTS:

Apparent Women Officers or Directors:
Hot Spot for Advancement for Women/Minorities:

LOCATIONS: ("Y" = Yes)

West:	Southwest:	Midwest:	Southeast:	Northeast:	International:
Y	Y	Y	Y	Y	

GROUP 1 AUTOMOTIVE INC

www.group1auto.com

Industry Group Code: 441110

Management:		Sales/Marketing:		Liberal Arts:		Information Sys.:		Professionals:		Tech./Scientific:	
Mgmt. Trainees:	Y	Marketing Pros.:	Y	Gen. Writing/Editing:	Y	Info. Mgmt.:	Y	Finance/Acct.:	Y	Engineers, Elec.:	
Experienced Mgmt.:	Y	Retail Sales:	Y	Tech. Writing:		Software Dev.:	Y	Law:	Y	Engineers, Other:	
Int'l Business:	Y	Comm./Industrial:	Y	Graphic Arts/Photog.:	Y	Hardware Dev.:		HR/Other:	Y	Health/Lab:	
MBA Grads:	Y	Sales Trainees:	Y	Music:		Consulting/Other:		Training:	Y	Science/Research:	
		Advertising Pros.:	Y	Broadcasting:				Health Care:		Petroleum/Chem.:	
				Other:				Consulting:		Math/Other:	

TYPES OF BUSINESS:

Auto Dealers
Auto Repair Services
Insurance Services
Automotive Replacement Parts
Financing Services
Collision Service Centers

BRANDS/DIVISIONS/AFFILIATES:

Metro Volkswagen
Sterling McCall Ford
Harrelson Toyota/Scion

CONTACTS: *Note: Officers with more than one job title may be intentionally listed here more than once.*

Earl J. Hesterberg, CEO
Earl J. Hesterberg, Pres.
John C. Rickel, CFO/Sr. VP
David W. Hult, VP-Mktg.
J. Brooks O'Hara, VP-Human Resources
James R. Druzbik, VP-Info. Systems
Darryl M. Burman, General Counsel/VP/Corp. Sec.
Wade D. Hubbard, VP-Fixed Oper.
Mark J. Iuppenlatz, VP-Corp. Dev.
Peter C. DeLongchamps, VP-Public Affairs & Manufacturer Rel.
Kim Paper Canning, Mgr.-Investor Rel.
Lance A. Parker, Corp. Controller/VP
Michael D. Welch, Treas.
Daryl Kenningham, VP-East Region
Frank Grese Jr., VP-West Region
Ronald W. Barnhill, VP-Taxes
John L. Adams, Chmn.
Gigi L. Myung, VP-Purchasing

Phone: 713-647-5700 **Fax:** 713-647-5858
Toll-Free:
Address: 800 Gessner, Ste. 500, Houston, TX 77024 US

GROWTH PLANS/SPECIAL FEATURES:

Group 1 Automotive, Inc. is a leading operator in the U.S. and U.K. automotive retailing industry. The company, through its subsidiaries, sells new and used cars and light trucks; provides maintenance and repair services; sells replacement parts; and arranges vehicle financing and insurance through its 101 dealership locations (totaling 136 franchises). The dealerships offer 32 different brands, including Toyota, Honda, Nissan, Ford, BMW, Chevrolet, Dodge, Jeep and Mercedes-Benz. Import and luxury vehicles account for over 85% of the firm's car sales, while domestic vehicles account for less than15%. Group 1 Automotive dealerships have taken several steps toward building customer confidence in their used vehicle inventory, including participation in manufacturer certification processes. These processes make used vehicles eligible for new vehicle benefits such as new vehicle finance rates and extended manufacturer warranties. In addition to its dealerships, the company owns 25 collision service centers. Group 1 Automotive uses American Auto Exchange's vehicle management software to identify vehicle sales trends, conduct local market analyses and perform current market appraisals. In March 2010, the company acquired two BMW/Mini dealerships located in the U.K. In April 2010, the firm acquired Harrelson Toyota/Scion (now known as Toyota/Scion of Rock Hill) in South Carolina. In June 2010, Group I Automotive acquired a new Mini franchise in Texas and sold its Pines Ford Lincoln Mercury dealership located in Florida.

FINANCIALS: **Sales and profits are in thousands of dollars—add 000 to get the full amount. 2010 Note: Financial information for 2010 was not available for all companies at press time.**

2010 Sales: $5,509,169 — 2010 Profits: $50,304
2009 Sales: $4,525,707 — 2009 Profits: $34,845
2008 Sales: $5,654,087 — 2008 Profits: $-48,013
2007 Sales: $6,392,997 — 2007 Profits: $63,415
2006 Sales: $6,083,484 — 2006 Profits: $88,390

U.S. Stock Ticker: GPI
Int'l Ticker:
Int'l Exchange:
Employees: 7,454 Fiscal Year Ends: 12/31
Parent Company:

SALARIES/BENEFITS:

Pension Plan: ESOP Stock Plan: Profit Sharing: Top Exec. Salary: $950,000 Bonus: $1,000,000
Savings Plan: Stock Purch. Plan: Y Second Exec. Salary: $427,500 Bonus: $485,000

OTHER THOUGHTS:

Apparent Women Officers or Directors: 4
Hot Spot for Advancement for Women/Minorities: Y

LOCATIONS: ("Y" = Yes)

West:	Southwest:	Midwest:	Southeast:	Northeast:	International:
Y	Y	Y	Y	Y	Y

GROUPON INC

www.groupon.com

Industry Group Code: 541810E

Management:		Sales/Marketing:		Liberal Arts:		Information Sys.:		Professionals:		Tech./Scientific:	
Mgmt. Trainees:		Marketing Pros.:	Y	Gen. Writing/Editing:		Info. Mgmt.:	Y	Finance/Acct.:	Y	Engineers, Elec.:	
Experienced Mgmt.:	Y	Retail Sales:		Tech. Writing:		Software Dev.:		Law:	Y	Engineers, Other:	
Int'l Business:	Y	Comm./Industrial:	Y	Graphic Arts/Photog.:		Hardware Dev.:		HR/Other:	Y	Health/Lab:	
MBA Grads:	Y	Sales Trainees:		Music:		Consulting/Other:		Training:		Science/Research:	
		Advertising Pros.:	Y	Broadcasting:				Health Care:		Petroleum/Chem.:	
				Other:				Consulting:		Math/Other:	

TYPES OF BUSINESS:

Online Marketing Services

BRANDS/DIVISIONS/AFFILIATES:

Citydeal
Ludic Labs

CONTACTS:

Note: Officers with more than one job title may be intentionally listed here more than once.

Andrew Mason, CEO
Margo Georgiadis, COO
Margo Georgiadis, Pres.
Jason Child, CFO
Aaron Cooper, Sr. VP-Customer Mktg.
Ken Pelletier, CTO
David Jesse, VP-Prod.
Brian Totty, Sr. VP-Eng.
Sean Smyth, VP-Bus. Dev.
Darren Schwartz, Sr. VP-Sales

Phone:	**Fax:**
Toll-Free: 877-788-7858	
Address: 600 W. Chicago Ave., Ste. 620, Chicago, IL 60654 US	

GROWTH PLANS/SPECIAL FEATURES:

Groupon, Inc., launched in 2008, is an online retailer, offering daily coupons to various local restaurants, activities and attractions in over 500 markets and 44 countries. The firm partners with local companies in cities across the globe to offer discounts on products and services, with the assumption that enough subscribers will be interested in buying their coupons. The site works by selling a coupon that only becomes valid after a certain amount of users purchase it; if an inadequate number of users purchase the coupon, it is canceled and those who bought the coupon are not charged. The average discount on a Groupon deal is around 50-90%. Its daily coupons consist of a diverse range of products and services, including spa treatments; tickets to various sporting and cultural events; discounts at bars and restaurants; teeth cleanings; discounted admissions at museums and other local attractions; and gyms, among others. The firm has over 60 million subscribers worldwide, delivering more than 600 offers daily. It has received approximately $950 million in venture funding. In May 2010, the company acquired Citydeal, a similar company with operations in 16 countries and over 1 million users. In December 2010, it acquired Ludic Labs, a developer of local online marketing and advertising solutions.

FINANCIALS:

Sales and profits are in thousands of dollars—add 000 to get the full amount. 2010 Note: Financial information for 2010 was not available for all companies at press time.

2010 Sales: $312,000	2010 Profits: $	**U.S. Stock Ticker: Private**
2009 Sales: $	2009 Profits: $	**Int'l Ticker:**
2008 Sales: $	2008 Profits: $	Int'l Exchange:
2007 Sales: $	2007 Profits: $	Employees: 6,000 Fiscal Year Ends:
2006 Sales: $	2006 Profits: $	Parent Company:

SALARIES/BENEFITS:

Pension Plan:	ESOP Stock Plan:	Profit Sharing:	Top Exec. Salary: $	Bonus: $
Savings Plan:	Stock Purch. Plan:		Second Exec. Salary: $	Bonus: $

OTHER THOUGHTS:

Apparent Women Officers or Directors:
Hot Spot for Advancement for Women/Minorities:

LOCATIONS: ("Y" = Yes)

West:	Southwest:	Midwest:	Southeast:	Northeast:	International:
Y		Y			Y

GSI COMMERCE INC

www.gsicommerce.com

Industry Group Code: 511210M

Management:		Sales/Marketing:		Liberal Arts:		Information Sys.:		Professionals:		Tech./Scientific:	
Mgmt. Trainees:		Marketing Pros.:	Y	Gen. Writing/Editing:		Info. Mgmt.:	Y	Finance/Acct.:	Y	Engineers, Elec.:	Y
Experienced Mgmt.:		Retail Sales:		Tech. Writing:	Y	Software Dev.:	Y	Law:	Y	Engineers, Other:	
Int'l Business:	Y	Comm./Industrial:	Y	Graphic Arts/Photog.:		Hardware Dev.:		HR/Other:	Y	Health/Lab:	
MBA Grads:	Y	Sales Trainees:		Music:		Consulting/Other:	Y	Training:		Science/Research:	
		Advertising Pros.:	Y	Broadcasting:				Health Care:		Petroleum/Chem.:	
				Other:	Y			Consulting:	Y	Math/Other:	

TYPES OF BUSINESS:

E-Commerce Consulting
Web Site Design Services
Managed Hosting Services
Customer Service Operations
Online Marketing
Merchandising Services
Order Fulfillment

BRANDS/DIVISIONS/AFFILIATES:

gsi interactive
e-Dialog Inc
ShipQuik
Retail Convergence, Inc.
VendorNet
RueLaLa.com
ShopRunner.com
SmartBargains.com

CONTACTS:

Note: Officers with more than one job title may be intentionally listed here more than once.

Michael G. Rubin, CEO
Michael G. Rubin, Pres.
Michael R. Conn, CFO
Fiona Dias, Exec. VP-Mktg.
Jim Flanagan, Exec. VP-Human Resources
Jim Macintyre, Chief-eCommerce Tech.
Bob Liewald, Exec. VP-Merch.
Arthur H. Miller, General Counsel/Exec. VP
Robert Wuesthoff, Exec. VP-Global Oper.
Fiona Disa, Exec. VP-Strategy
Michael R. Conn, Exec. VP-Finance
Scott Hardy, Exec. VP-Bus. Mgmt.
Damon Mintzer, Exec. VP-Sales
Ronald C. Williamsion, Sr. VP-Customer Care
Steven Davis, Exec. VP/Pres., Rue La La
Michael G. Rubin, Chmn.

Phone: 610-491-7000	**Fax:**
Toll-Free:	
Address: 935 First Ave., King of Prussia, PA 19406 US	

GROWTH PLANS/SPECIAL FEATURES:

GSI Commerce, Inc. is a provider of e-commerce products and services that enable retailers, branded manufacturers, entertainment companies and professional sports organizations to operate e-commerce businesses both domestically and internationally. The company operates in three segments: e-commerce services, interactive marketing services and consumer engagement The e-commerce services segment delivers customized products and services to clients through an integrated e-commerce platform, which is made up of three components: technology, fulfillment and call center services. Technology services include an e-Commerce Engine, a software product that provides configurable features that enable the buying and selling of products online, such as product presentation, merchandising, shopping cart and checkout. The fulfillment component offers fulfillment and drop shipping services through sevenfulfillment centers (five in the U.S., one in Canada and one in Europe). Call center services are also provided through three customer care centers in the U.S. and one in the U.K. The interactive marketing services segment provides interactive marketing, online advertising and design services through its in-house digital marketing agency, TrueAction. The segment also offers e-mail marketing services through subsidiary, e-Dialog, Inc. The consumer engagement segment consists of exclusive membership shopping sites such as ShopRunner.com, RueLaLa.com and SmartBargains.com. The company also operates ShipQuik, a package-delivery program in partnership with UPS. In May 2010, GSI acquired Vendornet, a provider of multichannel ecommerce supply chain solutions. In March 2011, the firm agreed to be acquired by Ebay, Inc. for $2.4 billion.

Employees are offered medical, dental and vision insurance; flexible spending accounts; life insurance; disability coverage; an employee assistance program; auto and home insurance; pet insurance; and group legal insurance.

FINANCIALS:

Sales and profits are in thousands of dollars—add 000 to get the full amount. 2010 Note: Financial information for 2010 was not available for all companies at press time.

2010 Sales: $1,357,994	2010 Profits: $-36,502	**U.S. Stock Ticker: GSIC**
2009 Sales: $1,004,215	2009 Profits: $-11,028	**Int'l Ticker:**
2008 Sales: $966,926	2008 Profits: $-16,923	Int'l Exchange:
2007 Sales: $749,957	2007 Profits: $3,039	Employees: 5,304 Fiscal Year Ends: 12/31
2006 Sales: $609,553	2006 Profits: $53,701	Parent Company:

SALARIES/BENEFITS:

Pension Plan:	ESOP Stock Plan:	Profit Sharing:	Top Exec. Salary: $474,000	Bonus: $
Savings Plan: Y	Stock Purch. Plan:		Second Exec. Salary: $444,158	Bonus: $296,474

OTHER THOUGHTS:

Apparent Women Officers or Directors: 2
Hot Spot for Advancement for Women/Minorities: Y

LOCATIONS: ("Y" = Yes)

West:	Southwest:	Midwest:	Southeast:	Northeast:	International:
Y		Y	Y	Y	Y

GUESS? INC

www.guessinc.com

Industry Group Code: 448

Management:		Sales/Marketing:		Liberal Arts:		Information Sys.:		Professionals:		Tech./Scientific:	
Mgmt. Trainees:	Y	Marketing Pros.:	Y	Gen. Writing/Editing:	Y	Info. Mgmt.:	Y	Finance/Acct.:	Y	Engineers, Elec.:	
Experienced Mgmt.:	Y	Retail Sales:	Y	Tech. Writing:		Software Dev.:	Y	Law:	Y	Engineers, Other:	
Int'l Business:	Y	Comm./Industrial:		Graphic Arts/Photog.:	Y	Hardware Dev.:		HR/Other:	Y	Health/Lab:	
MBA Grads:	Y	Sales Trainees:	Y	Music:		Consulting/Other:		Training:	Y	Science/Research:	
		Advertising Pros.:	Y	Broadcasting:				Health Care:		Petroleum/Chem.:	
				Other:	Y			Consulting:		Math/Other:	

TYPES OF BUSINESS:

Casual Clothing Stores
Accessories
Fragrances
Footwear
Online Sales
Jeans

BRANDS/DIVISIONS/AFFILIATES:

Baby GUESS
Guess? Jeans
Triangle Design
Question Mark
GUESS by Marciano
GUESS Kids
GUESS U.S.A.
Yes

CONTACTS: *Note: Officers with more than one job title may be intentionally listed here more than once.*

Paul Marciano, CEO
J. Michael Prince, COO
Dennis Secor, CFO/Sr. VP
Michael Relich, CIO/Sr. VP
Nancy Shachtman, Pres., North America
Maurice Marciano, Chmn.

Phone: 213-765-3100 **Fax:** 213-765-5927
Toll-Free: 800-224-8377
Address: 1444 S. Alameda St., Los Angeles, CA 90021 US

GROWTH PLANS/SPECIAL FEATURES:

Guess?, Inc. designs, markets, distributes and licenses collections of contemporary apparel and accessories for men, women and children that reflect the American lifestyle and European fashion sensibilities. The company's apparel is marketed under trademarks including GUESS, GUESS?, GUESS U.S.A., GUESS Jeans, Triangle Design, Question Mark, a stylized G, GUESS Kids, Baby GUESS, YES and GUESS by Marciano. The lines include full collections of denim and cotton clothing, including jeans, pants, overalls, skirts, dresses, shorts, blouses, shirts, jackets and knitwear. The firm also grants licenses to manufacture and distribute a broad range of products that complement its apparel lines, including eyewear, watches, handbags, footwear, infants' and children's apparel, leather apparel, fragrance, jewelry and other fashion accessories. Guess products are sold through three primary distribution channels: its own stores in the U.S. and Canada; a network of wholesale accounts in the U.S.; and via the Internet. The company operates 481 stores in U.S. and Canada, consisting of 192 full-price retail stores, 118 factory outlet stores, 54 G by GUESS stores, 57 GUESS by MARCIANO stores and 60 Guess Accessories stores. Guess also directly operates 125 stores in Europe and the Middle East, 43 stores in Asia and 10 stores in Central and South America. The firm's European headquarters is located in Lugano, Switzerland.

Guess offers its employees medical, dental and vision insurance; flexible spending accounts; an employee assistance program; life and AD&D insurance; short- and long-term disability; an employee stock purchase plan; a corporate wellness program; access to a credit union; and tuition reimbursement.

FINANCIALS: **Sales and profits are in thousands of dollars—add 000 to get the full amount. 2010 Note: Financial information for 2010 was not available for all companies at press time.**

2010 Sales: $2,128,466 | 2010 Profits: $242,761
2009 Sales: $2,093,390 | 2009 Profits: $213,562
2008 Sales: $1,749,916 | 2008 Profits: $186,472
2007 Sales: $1,252,664 | 2007 Profits: $131,172
2006 Sales: $1,185,184 | 2006 Profits: $123,168

U.S. Stock Ticker: GES
Int'l Ticker:
Int'l Exchange:
Employees: 12,700 Fiscal Year Ends: 12/31
Parent Company:

SALARIES/BENEFITS:

Pension Plan: | ESOP Stock Plan: | Profit Sharing: | Top Exec. Salary: $1,000,000 | Bonus: $4,837,155
Savings Plan: | Stock Purch. Plan: Y | | Second Exec. Salary: $800,000 | Bonus: $900,000

OTHER THOUGHTS:

Apparent Women Officers or Directors:
Hot Spot for Advancement for Women/Minorities: Y

LOCATIONS: ("Y" = Yes)

West:	Southwest:	Midwest:	Southeast:	Northeast:	International:
Y	Y	Y	Y	Y	Y

HALLIBURTON COMPANY

www.halliburton.com

Industry Group Code: 213112

Management:		Sales/Marketing:		Liberal Arts:		Information Sys.:		Professionals:		Tech./Scientific:	
Mgmt. Trainees:	Y	Marketing Pros.:	Y	Gen. Writing/Editing:	Y	Info. Mgmt.:	Y	Finance/Acct.:	Y	Engineers, Elec.:	Y
Experienced Mgmt.:	Y	Retail Sales:		Tech. Writing:	Y	Software Dev.:	Y	Law:	Y	Engineers, Other:	Y
Int'l Business:	Y	Comm./Industrial:	Y	Graphic Arts/Photog.:	Y	Hardware Dev.:		HR/Other:	Y	Health/Lab:	
MBA Grads:	Y	Sales Trainees:		Music:		Consulting/Other:		Training:	Y	Science/Research:	Y
		Advertising Pros.:	Y	Broadcasting:				Health Care:		Petroleum/Chem.:	Y
				Other:				Consulting:		Math/Other:	

TYPES OF BUSINESS:

Oil & Gas Drilling Support Services
Software Information Systems

BRANDS/DIVISIONS/AFFILIATES:

Landmark
Security DBS Drill Bits
Sperry Drilling Services
Baroid Fluid Services
Multi-Chem Group LLC
Boots & Coots Inc

CONTACTS: *Note: Officers with more than one job title may be intentionally listed here more than once.*

David J. Lesar, CEO
David J. Lesar, Pres.
Mark A. McCollum, CFO/Exec. VP
Lawrence Pope, Chief Human Resources Officer
Lawrence Pope, VP-Admin.
Albert Cornelison, General Counsel/Exec. VP
Tim Probert, Exec. VP-Strategy & Corp. Dev.
Christian Garcia, VP-Investor Rel.
Evelyn M Angelle, Chief Acct. Officer/Sr. VP
Sherry D. Williams, Chief Ethics & Compliance Officer/Sr. VP
Robert Moran, VP-Gov't Affairs
Joseph F. Andolino, Sr.VP-Tax
James S. Brown, Pres., Western Hemisphere
David J. Lesar, Chmn.
Joe D. Rainey, Pres., Eastern Hemisphere

Phone: 281-575-3000	**Fax:**
Toll-Free: 888-669-3920	
Address: 3000 N. Sam Houston Pkwy. E., Houston, TX 77032 US	

GROWTH PLANS/SPECIAL FEATURES:

Halliburton Company provides products and services to the upstream oil and gas industry. The firm serves major national and independent oil and gas companies around the world, operating in approximately 70 countries. Halliburton operates through two business segments: Drilling and Evaluation and Completion and Production. The Drilling and Evaluation segment provides field and reservoir modeling, drilling, evaluation and precise well-bore placement systems that enable customers to model, measure, and optimize their well construction activities. This segment consists of Baroid Fluid Services; Sperry Drilling Services; Security DBS Drill Bits; wireline and perforating services; software services subsidiary Landmark; and project management. The Completion and Production segment delivers cementing, stimulation, intervention and completion services. This segment consists of production enhancement services, completion tools and services and cementing services. Completion tools and services include subsurface safety valves and flow control equipment, surface safety systems, packers and specialty completion equipment, intelligent completion systems, expandable liner hanger systems, sand control systems, well servicing tools and reservoir performance services. Production covers stimulation services, pipeline process services, sand control services and well intervention services. Cementing services involve bonding the well and well casing while isolating fluid zones and maximizing wellbore stability. In September 2010, the firm acquired Boots & Coots, Inc., which provides well intervention services and pressure control product service line. In April 2011, the company announced plans to build a 200,000 square foot manufacturing facility in Lafayette, Louisiana. In September 2011, the firm agreed to acquire Multi-Chem Group, LLC, an oilfield production and completion chemicals and services provider.

FINANCIALS: **Sales and profits are in thousands of dollars—add 000 to get the full amount. 2010 Note: Financial information for 2010 was not available for all companies at press time.**

2010 Sales: $17,973,000	2010 Profits: $1,842,000	**U.S. Stock Ticker: HAL**
2009 Sales: $14,675,000	2009 Profits: $1,155,000	**Int'l Ticker:**
2008 Sales: $18,279,000	2008 Profits: $2,215,000	Int'l Exchange:
2007 Sales: $15,264,000	2007 Profits: $3,536,000	Employees: 58,000 Fiscal Year Ends: 12/31
2006 Sales: $12,955,000	2006 Profits: $2,348,000	Parent Company:

SALARIES/BENEFITS:

Pension Plan: Y	ESOP Stock Plan:	Profit Sharing:	Top Exec. Salary: $1,358,500	Bonus: $6,838,800
Savings Plan: Y	Stock Purch. Plan: Y		Second Exec. Salary: $600,000	Bonus: $1,762,500

OTHER THOUGHTS:

Apparent Women Officers or Directors: 5
Hot Spot for Advancement for Women/Minorities: Y

LOCATIONS: ("Y" = Yes)

West:	Southwest:	Midwest:	Southeast:	Northeast:	International:
Y	Y		Y		Y

HANESBRANDS INC

www.hanesbrands.com

Industry Group Code: 315

Management:		Sales/Marketing:		Liberal Arts:		Information Sys.:		Professionals:		Tech./Scientific:	
Mgmt. Trainees:		Marketing Pros.:	Y	Gen. Writing/Editing:	Y	Info. Mgmt.:	Y	Finance/Acct.:	Y	Engineers, Elec.:	
Experienced Mgmt.:	Y	Retail Sales:		Tech. Writing:		Software Dev.:		Law:	Y	Engineers, Other:	
Int'l Business:	Y	Comm./Industrial:	Y	Graphic Arts/Photog.:		Hardware Dev.:		HR/Other:	Y	Health/Lab:	
MBA Grads:	Y	Sales Trainees:		Music:		Consulting/Other:		Training:		Science/Research:	
		Advertising Pros.:	Y	Broadcasting:				Health Care:		Petroleum/Chem.:	
				Other:				Consulting:		Math/Other:	

TYPES OF BUSINESS:

Underwear
Outerwear
Hosiery
Internet Sales
Catalogs

BRANDS/DIVISIONS/AFFILIATES:

Champion
Hanes
Playtex
barely there
Just My Size
Wonderbra
GearCo Inc
Gear For Sports

CONTACTS: *Note: Officers with more than one job title may be intentionally listed here more than once.*

Rich Noll, CEO
E. Lee Wyatt, Jr., CFO/Exec. VP
Kevin W. Oliver, Chief Human Resources Officer
Joia M. Johnson, General Counsel/Exec. VP/Corp. Sec.
Joan McReynolds, Chief Customer Officer/Exec. VP
Kevin D. Hall, Exec. VP-Outerwear Strategic Bus. Unit
W. Howard Upchurch, Jr., Exec. VP/Gen. Mgr.-Domestic Innerwear
William J. Nictakis, Pres., U.S. Bus.
Rich Noll, Chmn.
Gerald Evans, Pres., Int'l Bus.
Gerald Evans, Pres., Global Supply Chain

Phone: 336-519-4400	**Fax:**
Toll-Free:	
Address: 1000 E. Hanes Mill Rd., Winston-Salem, NC 27105 US	

GROWTH PLANS/SPECIAL FEATURES:

Hanesbrands, Inc. designs, manufactures, sources and sells apparel including t-shirts, bras, panties, men's underwear, kids' underwear, socks, hosiery, casualwear and activewear. The company is organized into five operating segments: Innerwear, Outerwear, Hosiery, Direct-to-Consumer and International. Hanesbrands' innerwear segment, which accounted for 46% of its 2010 net sales, produces bras, panties, men's underwear, kids' underwear, socks, marketed under the Hanes, Playtex, Bali, barely there, Just My Size and Wonderbra brands. Hanesbrands also maintains a licensing agreement with Polo Ralph Lauren to produce underwear. The outerwear segment of the firm, representing 29% of its net sales, produces t-shirts, fleece, athletic uniforms, thermals sleepwear and casualwear marketed under the Hanes, Champion and Just My Size brands. Hanesbrands' hosiery segment produces hosiery under the Hanes, L'eggs and Just My Size brands, generating 4% of its net sales. The direct-to-consumer segment, 9% of sales, operates 228 outlet stores as well as having catalogs and Internet sales. The international segment, 12% of net sales, includes sales in Asia, Canada, Europe and Latin America. The design, research and product development activities are primarily located in North Carolina facility, with some activities in New York City and the U.K. The company sells its products through multiple distribution channels, including mass merchants (44% of 2010 sales), national chains and department stores (15%), the company's international segment (12%), direct to consumer (9%) and other retail channels such as specialty retailers and sporting goods stores (20%). Hanesbrands engages in manufacturing through both company-owned and operated facilities and third-party contractors. In November 2010, the company acquired GearCo, Inc., known as Gear For Sports, a leading seller of licensed logo apparel in collegiate bookstores and other channels.

Employees are offered medical, dental and vision insurance; life insurance; disability coverage; a retirement savings plan; adoption assistance; and an employee assistance program.

FINANCIALS: **Sales and profits are in thousands of dollars—add 000 to get the full amount. 2010 Note: Financial information for 2010 was not available for all companies at press time.**

2010 Sales: $4,326,713	2010 Profits: $211,293	**U.S. Stock Ticker: HBI**
2009 Sales: $3,891,275	2009 Profits: $51,283	**Int'l Ticker:**
2008 Sales: $4,248,770	2008 Profits: $127,169	Int'l Exchange:
2007 Sales: $4,474,537	2007 Profits: $126,127	Employees: 55,500 Fiscal Year Ends: 12/31
2006 Sales: $2,250,473	2006 Profits: $74,139	Parent Company:

SALARIES/BENEFITS:

Pension Plan:	ESOP Stock Plan:	Profit Sharing:	Top Exec. Salary: $800,000	Bonus: $280,440
Savings Plan: Y	Stock Purch. Plan:		Second Exec. Salary: $650,000	Bonus: $151,905

OTHER THOUGHTS:

Apparent Women Officers or Directors: 4
Hot Spot for Advancement for Women/Minorities: Y

LOCATIONS: ("Y" = Yes)

West:	Southwest:	Midwest:	Southeast:	Northeast:	International:
Y	Y	Y	Y	Y	Y

HANGER ORTHOPEDIC GROUP INC

www.hanger.com

Industry Group Code: 621340

Management:		**Sales/Marketing:**		**Liberal Arts:**		**Information Sys.:**		**Professionals:**		**Tech./Scientific:**	
Mgmt. Trainees:	Y	Marketing Pros.:	Y	Gen. Writing/Editing:		Info. Mgmt.:	Y	Finance/Acct.:	Y	Engineers, Elec.:	Y
Experienced Mgmt.:	Y	Retail Sales:	Y	Tech. Writing:	Y	Software Dev.:	Y	Law:	Y	Engineers, Other:	Y
Int'l Business:	Y	Comm./Industrial:	Y	Graphic Arts/Photog.:		Hardware Dev.:		HR/Other:	Y	Health/Lab:	
MBA Grads:	Y	Sales Trainees:		Music:		Consulting/Other:		Training:	Y	Science/Research:	
		Advertising Pros.:		Broadcasting:				Health Care:	Y	Petroleum/Chem.:	
				Other:				Consulting:		Math/Other:	

TYPES OF BUSINESS:

Orthotic & Prosthetic Patient Care Centers
Orthotic & Prosthetic Devices & Components Distribution

BRANDS/DIVISIONS/AFFILIATES:

Hanger Prosthetics and Orthotics
Southern Prosthetic Supply, Inc.
Innovative Neurotronics, Inc.
Linkia LLC
Dynamic Orthotics and Prosthetics
Nebraska Orthotic and Prosthetic Services
Spectrum Prosthetics and Orthotics of Iowa
Accelerated Care Plus

CONTACTS: *Note: Officers with more than one job title may be intentionally listed here more than once.*

Thomas F. Kirk, CEO
Vinit K. Asar, COO
Vinit K. Asar, Pres.
George E. McHenry, CFO/Exec. VP/Sec.
Drew Morton, VP-Human Resources
Walt Meffert, CIO/VP
Thomas E. Hartman, General Counsel/VP
Jennifer Bittner, Contact-Press
Thomas C. Hofmeister, VP-FinanceChief Acct. Officer
Richmond L. Taylor, Pres./COO-Hanger Prosthetics & Orthotics, Inc.
Ronald N. May, Pres./COO-Southern Prosthetic Supply, Inc.
Rebecca Hast, Pres., Linkia, LLC
Ivan R. Sabel, Chmn.

Phone: 512-777-3800	**Fax:**
Toll-Free:	
Address: 10910 Domain Dr., Ste. 300, Austin, TX 78758 US	

GROWTH PLANS/SPECIAL FEATURES:

Hanger Orthopedic Group, Inc., through its primary business, Hanger Prosthetics and Orthotics, owns and operates orthotic and prosthetic (O&P) patient care centers. The firm operates over 675 O&P patient care centers in 45 states and Washington, D.C. It offers patient care services to over 650,000 patients annually. Through subsidiary Southern Prosthetic Supply, Inc. (SPS), the company also distributes branded and private label O&P devices and components in the U.S., all of which are manufactured by third parties. The firm also manufactures and distributes therapeutic footwear for diabetic patients in the podiatric market. Approximately 36.1% of SPS' distribution sales are to third-party O&P services providers. Hanger also creates new products through subsidiary Innovative Neurotronics, Inc. (IN) for patients who have had a loss of mobility due to strokes, multiple sclerosis or other similar conditions. IN specializes in product development principally in the field of functional electrical stimulation. Another subsidiary, Linkia LLC, develops programs to manage all aspects of O&P patient care for large private payors. Each of the company's patient care centers are closely managed by one or more practitioners, substantially all of which are certified by the O&P industry certifying boards. Its patient care centers also employ highly trained technical personnel who assist in the provision of services to patients and who fabricate various O&P devices, as well as office administrators who schedule patient visits, obtain approvals from payors and bill and collect for services rendered. Patient care services account for roughly 87.5% of the firm's revenues; distribution, 11.7%; and therapeutic solutions, 0.8%. In 2010, Hanger acquired Dynamic Orthotics and Prosthetics of Texas; Nebraska Orthotic and Prosthetic Services; Spectrum Prosthetics and Orthotics of Iowa; and Accelerated Care Plus, based in Nevada. In August 2011, the company acquired the following four firms: BioConcepts, Inc.; US Orthotics & Prosthetics, Inc.; Team Post-Op, Inc.; and MK Prosthetic & Orthotic Services, Inc.

Employees are offered medical, dental, vision and life insurance; disability coverage; and flexible spending accounts.

FINANCIALS: **Sales and profits are in thousands of dollars—add 000 to get the full amount. 2010 Note: Financial information for 2010 was not available for all companies at press time.**

2010 Sales: $817,379	2010 Profits: $21,435	**U.S. Stock Ticker: HGR**
2009 Sales: $760,070	2009 Profits: $36,093	**Int'l Ticker:**
2008 Sales: $703,129	2008 Profits: $26,746	Int'l Exchange:
2007 Sales: $637,350	2007 Profits: $17,602	Employees: 4,273 Fiscal Year Ends: 12/31
2006 Sales: $598,766	2006 Profits: $3,434	Parent Company:

SALARIES/BENEFITS:

Pension Plan:	ESOP Stock Plan:	Profit Sharing:	Top Exec. Salary: $619,398	Bonus: $559,540
Savings Plan: Y	Stock Purch. Plan: Y		Second Exec. Salary: $399,614	Bonus: $258,865

OTHER THOUGHTS:

Apparent Women Officers or Directors: 3
Hot Spot for Advancement for Women/Minorities: Y

LOCATIONS: ("Y" = Yes)

West:	Southwest:	Midwest:	Southeast:	Northeast:	International:
Y	Y	Y	Y	Y	Y

HARRIS CORPORATION

www.harris.com

Industry Group Code: 3342

Management:		Sales/Marketing:		Liberal Arts:		Information Sys.:		Professionals:		Tech./Scientific:	
Mgmt. Trainees:	Y	Marketing Pros.:	Y	Gen. Writing/Editing:	Y	Info. Mgmt.:	Y	Finance/Acct.:	Y	Engineers, Elec.:	Y
Experienced Mgmt.:	Y	Retail Sales:		Tech. Writing:	Y	Software Dev.:	Y	Law:	Y	Engineers, Other:	
Int'l Business:	Y	Comm./Industrial:	Y	Graphic Arts/Photog.:	Y	Hardware Dev.:	Y	HR/Other:	Y	Health/Lab:	
MBA Grads:	Y	Sales Trainees:		Music:		Consulting/Other:	Y	Training:	Y	Science/Research:	Y
		Advertising Pros.:	Y	Broadcasting:				Health Care:		Petroleum/Chem.:	
				Other:				Consulting:		Math/Other:	Y

TYPES OF BUSINESS:

Communications Equipment Manufacturing
Wireless Communications Equipment
Broadcasting Equipment
Microwave Equipment

BRANDS/DIVISIONS/AFFILIATES:

Falcon III
CapRock Communications
Core180, Inc.

CONTACTS: *Note: Officers with more than one job title may be intentionally listed here more than once.*

Howard L. Lance, CEO
Robert K. Henry, COO/Exec. VP
Howard L. Lance, Pres.
Gary L. McArthur, CFO/Sr. VP
Jeffrey S. Shuman, Chief Human Resources Officer/Sr. VP
R. Kent Buchanan, CTO
R. Kent Buchanan, VP-Eng.
Jeffrey S. Shuman, Chief Admin. Officer
Scott Mikuen, General Counsel/VP/Sec.
Ricardo A. Navarro, VP-Corp. Dev.
Pamela Padgett, VP-Corp. Comm.
Pamela Padgett, VP-Investor Rel.
Charles J. Greene, Treas.
Sheldon J. Fox, Pres., Gov't Comm. Systems Div.
Lewis Schwartz, VP/Chief Acct. Officer
Harris Morris, Jr., Pres., Broadcast Comm.
Peter Challan, VP-Gov't Rel.
Howard L. Lance, Chmn.
Andy Start, Pres., Int'l Tactical Radio Comm.
Leon V. Shivamber, VP-Supply Chain Mgmt.

Phone: 321-727-9100 **Fax:**
Toll-Free: 800-442-7747
Address: 1025 W. NASA Blvd., Melbourne, FL 32919-0001 US

GROWTH PLANS/SPECIAL FEATURES:

Harris Corporation is an international communications and information technology company. The firm, along with its subsidiaries, provides sales and services to government and commercial markets in over 150 countries. Harris operates through three divisions: RF Communications, Government Communications Systems and Integrated Network Solutions. The RF Communications segment is a global supplier of secure radio communications products and systems for defense and government operations; and also performs advanced research, primarily for the U.S. Department of Defense and for international customers in government, defense and peacekeeping organizations. Its products include the Falcon III multiband manpack radio. The firm's Government Communications Systems segment designs, develops and supplies communications and information networks and equipment; develops integrated intelligence, surveillance and reconnaissance solutions; develops, designs and supports information systems for image and other data collection, processing, analysis, interpretation, display, storage and retrieval; offers enterprise IT and communications engineering, operations and support services; and conducts advanced research studies, primarily for various agencies of the U.S. government and other aerospace and defense companies. The Integrated Network Solutions segment serves the global digital and analog media markets, providing infrastructure and networking products and solutions; media and workflow solutions; and television and radio transmission equipment and systems. In February 2010, Harris acquired the land-based, situational awareness technology assets of OSI Geospatial, Inc. In July 2010, the firm acquired CapRock Communications for roughly $525 million. In November 2010, the company agreed to acquire the Global Connectivity Services operations of Schlumberger Information Solutions from Schlumberger Limited. In March 2011, Harris acquired infrastructure assets from Core180, Inc.

The firm offers employees benefits including medical, dental and vision insurance; a 401(k); paid time off; tuition reimbursement; and health and dependent care spending accounts.

FINANCIALS: **Sales and profits are in thousands of dollars—add 000 to get the full amount. 2010 Note: Financial information for 2010 was not available for all companies at press time.**

2010 Sales: $5,206,100 | 2010 Profits: $561,600
2009 Sales: $5,005,000 | 2009 Profits: $37,900
2008 Sales: $4,596,100 | 2008 Profits: $444,200
2007 Sales: $3,737,900 | 2007 Profits: $480,400
2006 Sales: $3,474,800 | 2006 Profits: $237,900

U.S. Stock Ticker: HRS
Int'l Ticker:
Int'l Exchange:
Employees: 15,800 Fiscal Year Ends: 6/30
Parent Company:

SALARIES/BENEFITS:

Pension Plan: | ESOP Stock Plan: | Profit Sharing: | Top Exec. Salary: $1,050,000 | Bonus: $2,004,492
Savings Plan: Y | Stock Purch. Plan: | | Second Exec. Salary: $560,000 | Bonus: $884,895

OTHER THOUGHTS:

Apparent Women Officers or Directors: 3
Hot Spot for Advancement for Women/Minorities: Y

LOCATIONS: ("Y" = Yes)

West:	Southwest:	Midwest:	Southeast:	Northeast:	International:
Y	Y	Y	Y	Y	Y

HAWAIIAN ELECTRIC INDUSTRIES INC

www.hei.com

Industry Group Code: 2211

Management:		Sales/Marketing:		Liberal Arts:		Information Sys.:		Professionals:		Tech./Scientific:	
Mgmt. Trainees:	Y	Marketing Pros.:	Y	Gen. Writing/Editing:	Y	Info. Mgmt.:	Y	Finance/Acct.:	Y	Engineers, Elec.:	Y
Experienced Mgmt.:	Y	Retail Sales:		Tech. Writing:	Y	Software Dev.:	Y	Law:	Y	Engineers, Other:	Y
Int'l Business:		Comm./Industrial:	Y	Graphic Arts/Photog.:	Y	Hardware Dev.:		HR/Other:	Y	Health/Lab:	
MBA Grads:	Y	Sales Trainees:		Music:		Consulting/Other:		Training:	Y	Science/Research:	
		Advertising Pros.:	Y	Broadcasting:				Health Care:		Petroleum/Chem.:	
				Other:				Consulting:		Math/Other:	

TYPES OF BUSINESS:

Utilities-Electricity
Savings Bank
Renewable Energy
Biofuels

BRANDS/DIVISIONS/AFFILIATES:

Hawaiian Electric Company
Hawaiian Electric Light Company
Maui Electric Company, Limited
Renewable Hawaii, Inc.
American Savings Bank, F.S.B.
HEI Diversified
Pacific Energy Conservation Services, Inc.
Uluwehiokama Biofuels Corp.

CONTACTS: *Note: Officers with more than one job title may be intentionally listed here more than once.*

Constance H. Lau, CEO
Constance H. Lau, Pres.
James A. Ajello, CFO/Sr. VP-Financial/Treas.
Chet A. Richardson, Chief Admin. Officer
Chet A. Richardson, General Counsel/Sr. VP/Sec.
Andrew I. T. Chang, VP-External Affairs
Shelee M.T. Kimura, Mgr.-Investor Rel.
David M. Kostecki, VP-Finance/Controller/Chief Acct. Officer
Richard M. Rosenblum, CEO/Pres., Hawaiian Electric Company, Inc.
Jay M. Ignacio, Pres., Hawaii Electric Light Company, Inc.
Richard F. Wacker, Pres., American Savings Bank, F.S.B.
Edward L. Reinhardt, Pres., Maui Electric Company, Ltd.
Jeffrey N. Watanabe, Chmn.

Phone: 808-543-5662	**Fax:** 808-543-7966
Toll-Free:	
Address: 900 Richards St., Honolulu, HI 96813 US	

GROWTH PLANS/SPECIAL FEATURES:

Hawaiian Electric Industries, Inc. (HEI) is a diversified holding company engaged in independent power and utility services and the operation of a savings bank. HEI's Hawaiian Electric Company (HECO) subsidiary, founded in 1891, is a regulated electric public utility company, along with its subsidiaries Hawaiian Electric Light Company (HELCO) and Maui Electric Company, Limited (MECO). HECO's Renewable Hawaii, Inc. subsidiary invests in renewable energy projects, while Uluwehiokama Biofuels Corp. invests in a Maui-based biofuel refining plant. HECO, HELCO and MECO are regulated operating electric public utilities engaged in the production, purchase, transmission, distribution and sale of electricity on the islands of Oahu, Maui, Lanai, Molokai and Hawaii. These islands have a combined population of approximately 1.2 million, or approximately 95% of the Hawaii population, and comprise a service area of 5,766 square miles. The principle communities served include Honolulu on Oahu; Wailuku and Kahului on Maui; and Hilo and Kona on Hawaii. Each island has its own generation and transmission system that is not connected to any other grid, which results in the company maintaining a larger amount of surplus capacity than most utilities. HEI's electric utility operations generate approximately 89% of its revenues. Additional HEI subsidiaries include HEI Diversified (HEIDI), a holding company; Pacific Energy Conservation Services, Inc. (PECS), a contract services company; HEI Properties, Inc. (HEIPI); HEI Investments, Inc.; Hawaiian Electric Industries Capital Trusts II and III; and The Old Oahu Tug Service, Inc. (TOOTS). HEIDI's American Savings Bank, F.S.B. subsidiary is a leading financial institution in Hawaii, with more than 60 branch offices offering investment products, financial planning services, insurance, deposit accounts and consumer loans. It manages assets of $4.8 billion and deposits of $4.0 billion.

FINANCIALS: **Sales and profits are in thousands of dollars—add 000 to get the full amount. 2010 Note: Financial information for 2010 was not available for all companies at press time.**

2010 Sales: $2,664,982 | 2010 Profits: $113,535
2009 Sales: $2,309,590 | 2009 Profits: $83,011
2008 Sales: $3,218,920 | 2008 Profits: $90,278
2007 Sales: $2,090,548 | 2007 Profits: $84,779
2006 Sales: $2,460,904 | 2006 Profits: $108,001

U.S. Stock Ticker: HE
Int'l Ticker:
Int'l Exchange:
Employees: 3,427 Fiscal Year Ends: 12/31
Parent Company:

SALARIES/BENEFITS:

Pension Plan: Y | ESOP Stock Plan: | Profit Sharing: | Top Exec. Salary: $787,267 | Bonus: $2,575,164
Savings Plan: | Stock Purch. Plan: | | Second Exec. Salary: $584,667 | Bonus: $282,037

OTHER THOUGHTS:

Apparent Women Officers or Directors: 7
Hot Spot for Advancement for Women/Minorities: Y

LOCATIONS: ("Y" = Yes)

West:	Southwest:	Midwest:	Southeast:	Northeast:	International:
Y					

HCA HOLDINGS INC

www.hcahealthcare.com

Industry Group Code: 622110

Management:		**Sales/Marketing:**		**Liberal Arts:**		**Information Sys.:**		**Professionals:**		**Tech./Scientific:**	
Mgmt. Trainees:	Y	Marketing Pros.:	Y	Gen. Writing/Editing:	Y	Info. Mgmt.:	Y	Finance/Acct.:	Y	Engineers, Elec.:	
Experienced Mgmt.:	Y	Retail Sales:		Tech. Writing:	Y	Software Dev.:	Y	Law:	Y	Engineers, Other:	
Int'l Business:	Y	Comm./Industrial:		Graphic Arts/Photog.:	Y	Hardware Dev.:		HR/Other:	Y	Health/Lab:	Y
MBA Grads:	Y	Sales Trainees:		Music:		Consulting/Other:		Training:	Y	Science/Research:	
		Advertising Pros.:	Y	Broadcasting:				Health Care:	Y	Petroleum/Chem.:	
				Other:	Y			Consulting:		Math/Other:	

TYPES OF BUSINESS:

Hospitals-General
Outpatient Surgery Centers
Sub-Acute Care
Psychiatric Hospitals
Rehabilitation Services
Hospital Management Services

BRANDS/DIVISIONS/AFFILIATES:

Mercy Hospital
Parallon Business Solutions
HCA-HealthONE LLC

CONTACTS: *Note: Officers with more than one job title may be intentionally listed here more than once.*

Richard M. Bracken, CEO
R. Milton Johnson, CFO/Exec. VP
John M. Steele, Sr. VP-Human Resources
Jonathan B. Perlin, Chief Medical Officer/Pres., Clinical Svcs.
Noel B. Williams, CIO/Sr. VP
Robert A. Waterman, General Counsel/Sr. VP
Samuel N. Hazen, Pres., Oper.
Joe Sowell, Chief Dev. Officer/Sr. VP
Jana J. Davis, Sr. VP-Corp. Comm.
Mark Kimbrough, VP-Investor Rel.
David G. Anderson, Sr. VP-Finance/Treas.
Chuck J. Hall, Pres., National Group
Donald W. Stinnett, Sr. VP/Controller
Victor L. Campbell, Sr. VP
Paul Rutledge, Pres., Central Group
Richard M. Bracken, Chmn.

Phone: 615-344-9551 **Fax:**
Toll-Free:
Address: 1 Park Plz., Nashville, TN 37203 US

GROWTH PLANS/SPECIAL FEATURES:

HCA Holdings, Inc. owns and operates approximately 164 hospitals and 106 outpatient surgery centers in 20 states and the U.K. The company's acute care hospitals provide a full range of services, including internal medicine, general surgery, neurosurgery, orthopedics, obstetrics, cardiac care, diagnostic and emergency services, radiology, respiratory therapy, cardiology and physical therapy. The psychiatric hospitals provide therapeutic programs including child, adolescent and adult psychiatric care and adult and adolescent alcohol and drug abuse treatment and counseling. The outpatient health care facilities operated by HCA Holdings include surgery centers, diagnostic and imaging centers, comprehensive outpatient rehabilitation and physical therapy centers. The company's hospitals do not engage in extensive medical research and education programs; however, some facilities are affiliated with medical schools and may participate in the clinical rotation of medical interns and residents. In addition, HCA Holdings provides a variety of management services to health care facilities such as patient safety programs; ethics and compliance programs; national supply contracts; equipment purchasing and leasing contracts; and accounting, financial and clinical systems. Other services include governmental reimbursement assistance; construction planning and coordination; information technology systems; legal counsel; human resource services; and internal audit. In May 2011, the firm acquired the 473-bed Mercy Hospital, located in Miami, Florida; and established new subsidiary Parallon Business Solutions to offer business services to healthcare providers. In June 2011, HCA Holdings agreed to buy the remaining 40% interest in its joint venture with The Colorado Health Foundation, HCA-HealthONE LLC, for roughly $1.45 billion.

HCA offers its employees a day care flexible spending account; child care center discounts; an adoption assistance program; a ConSern student loan program; laser surgery discounts at LaserVision; a healthcare flexible spending account; and medical, dental and vision coverage.

FINANCIALS: **Sales and profits are in thousands of dollars—add 000 to get the full amount. 2010 Note: Financial information for 2010 was not available for all companies at press time.**

2010 Sales: $30,683,000 | 2010 Profits: $1,573,000
2009 Sales: $30,052,000 | 2009 Profits: $1,375,000
2008 Sales: $28,374,000 | 2008 Profits: $673,000
2007 Sales: $26,900,000 | 2007 Profits: $
2006 Sales: $25,477,000 | 2006 Profits: $1,036,000

U.S. Stock Ticker: HCA
Int'l Ticker:
Int'l Exchange:
Employees: 194,000 Fiscal Year Ends: 12/31
Parent Company:

SALARIES/BENEFITS:

Pension Plan: Y | ESOP Stock Plan: | Profit Sharing: | Top Exec. Salary: $1,324,975 | Bonus: $2,614,824
Savings Plan: Y | Stock Purch. Plan: | Second Exec. Salary: $849,984 | Bonus: $1,032,267

OTHER THOUGHTS:

Apparent Women Officers or Directors: 2
Hot Spot for Advancement for Women/Minorities:

LOCATIONS: ("Y" = Yes)

West:	Southwest:	Midwest:	Southeast:	Northeast:	International:
Y	Y	Y	Y	Y	Y

HE BUTT GROCERY COMPANY (HEB)

www.heb.com

Industry Group Code: 445110

Management:		Sales/Marketing:		Liberal Arts:		Information Sys.:		Professionals:		Tech./Scientific:	
Mgmt. Trainees:	Y	Marketing Pros.:	Y	Gen. Writing/Editing:	Y	Info. Mgmt.:	Y	Finance/Acct.:	Y	Engineers, Elec.:	
Experienced Mgmt.:	Y	Retail Sales:	Y	Tech. Writing:		Software Dev.:	Y	Law:	Y	Engineers, Other:	
Int'l Business:	Y	Comm./Industrial:		Graphic Arts/Photog.:	Y	Hardware Dev.:		HR/Other:	Y	Health/Lab:	
MBA Grads:	Y	Sales Trainees:	Y	Music:		Consulting/Other:		Training:	Y	Science/Research:	
		Advertising Pros.:	Y	Broadcasting:				Health Care:		Petroleum/Chem.:	
				Other:	Y			Consulting:		Math/Other:	

TYPES OF BUSINESS:

Supermarkets
Grocery Stores
Gourmet Food Stores
Dairy Processing
Bakery
Pharmacy Services

BRANDS/DIVISIONS/AFFILIATES:

H-E-B
Central Market
H-E-B plus!
H-E-B Insurance Agency
H-E-B Wireless
Temple Retail Support Center
Joe V's Smart Shop

CONTACTS: *Note: Officers with more than one job title may be intentionally listed here more than once.*

Charles C. Butt, CEO
Craig Boyan, COO
Craig Boyan, Pres.
Tina James, Sr. VP-Human Resources
Winell Herron, VP-Public Affairs & Diversity
Scott McClelland, Pres., Houston Food & Drug Stores Div.
Suzanne Wade, Pres., San Antonio Food & Drug Stores Div.

Phone: 210-938-8000 **Fax:** 210-938-8169
Toll-Free: 800-432-3113
Address: 646 S. Main Ave, San Antonio, TX 78204 US

GROWTH PLANS/SPECIAL FEATURES:

H.E. Butt Grocery Company (HEB) is one of the largest regional food retailers in the southwestern U.S. and Mexico. It operates over 329 grocery stores in 155 communities in Texas and Mexico under H-E-B brand names. The firm owns one of the largest milk plants in Texas, as well as a large bread bakery, a meat plant, a pastry bakery, an ice cream plant, a chip plant and a photo processing lab. The stores carry a wide variety of merchandise, including a line of products under the H-E-B brand name. HEB also operates Central Market stores, with single locations in Houston, Dallas, Fort Worth, Plano, San Antonio and Southlake, as well as two locations in Austin. Central Markets are gourmet specialty stores featuring large prepared foods-to-go areas, eat-in areas, comprehensive wine departments, specialty butcher and fish counters, a European bakery, a deli with meats, a large selection of cheeses from around the globe and a juice and ice cream bar. H-E-B plus! stores offer additional departments including Cook & Grill, Card & Party and a Tortilleria. H-E-B Insurance Agency offers automobile, life, health, travel, homeowners and renters insurance with locations in six Texas cities. H-E-B Wireless offers cell phone plans in partnership with providers such as Sprint and T-Mobile. The company owns and operates a $30-million retail support center in Monterrey, Mexico. In 2010, the firm opened the Temple Retail Support Center, a 450,000 sq. ft. warehouse and transportation facility in central Texas; and opened Joe V's Smart Shop, a new small grocery store concept in Houston, Texas.

Employees of the firm are offered medical, life and disability insurance; a dental and vision plan; disability protection; a leadership development program; dependent day care spending accounts; adoption assistance; paid time off; retirement and saving plans; an employee assistance plan; scholarship programs; flexible spending accounts; credit union membership, discounts on groceries and a prescription plan.

FINANCIALS: **Sales and profits are in thousands of dollars—add 000 to get the full amount. 2010 Note: Financial information for 2010 was not available for all companies at press time.**

2010 Sales: $16,100,000 — 2010 Profits: $
2009 Sales: $16,000,000 — 2009 Profits: $
2008 Sales: $15,100,000 — 2008 Profits: $
2007 Sales: $13,500,000 — 2007 Profits: $
2006 Sales: $13,500,000 — 2006 Profits: $

U.S. Stock Ticker: Private
Int'l Ticker:
Int'l Exchange:
Employees: 76,000 Fiscal Year Ends: 10/31
Parent Company:

SALARIES/BENEFITS:

Pension Plan: Y ESOP Stock Plan: Profit Sharing: Top Exec. Salary: $ Bonus: $
Savings Plan: Y Stock Purch. Plan: Second Exec. Salary: $ Bonus: $

OTHER THOUGHTS:

Apparent Women Officers or Directors: 2
Hot Spot for Advancement for Women/Minorities: Y

LOCATIONS: ("Y" = Yes)

West:	Southwest:	Midwest:	Southeast:	Northeast:	International:
	Y				Y

HEALTH CARE SERVICE CORPORATION (HCSC) www.hcsc.com

Industry Group Code: 524114

Management:		Sales/Marketing:		Liberal Arts:		Information Sys.:		Professionals:		Tech./Scientific:	
Mgmt. Trainees:	Y	Marketing Pros.:	Y	Gen. Writing/Editing:	Y	Info. Mgmt.:	Y	Finance/Acct.:	Y	Engineers, Elec.:	
Experienced Mgmt.:	Y	Retail Sales:		Tech. Writing:	Y	Software Dev.:	Y	Law:	Y	Engineers, Other:	
Int'l Business:		Comm./Industrial:	Y	Graphic Arts/Photog.:	Y	Hardware Dev.:		HR/Other:	Y	Health/Lab:	
MBA Grads:	Y	Sales Trainees:		Music:		Consulting/Other:		Training:	Y	Science/Research:	
		Advertising Pros.:		Broadcasting:				Health Care:	Y	Petroleum/Chem.:	
				Other:	Y			Consulting:		Math/Other:	

TYPES OF BUSINESS:

Insurance-Medical & Health, HMOs & PPOs
Traditional Indemnity Plans
Medicare Supplemental Health
Life Insurance
Dental & Vision Insurance
Electronic Claims & Information Network
Workers' Compensation
Retirement Services

BRANDS/DIVISIONS/AFFILIATES:

Blue Cross and Blue Shield of Illinois
Blue Cross and Blue Shield of Texas
Blue Cross and Blue Shield of New Mexico
Blue Cross and Blue Shield of Oklahoma
Preferred Financial Group
Colorado Bankers Life Insurance Company
Dental Network of America, Inc.
TMG Health

CONTACTS: *Note: Officers with more than one job title may be intentionally listed here more than once.*

Patricia A. Hemingway Hall, CEO
Colleen F. Reitan, COO/Exec. VP
Patricia A. Hemingway Hall, Pres.
Kenneth S. Avner, CFO/Sr. VP
Paul B. Handel, Chief Medical Officer/Sr. VP
Martin G. Foster, Exec. VP/Pres., Plan Oper.
Ross Blackstone, Contact-Media
Anthony F. Trani, Pres., Ancillary Svcs.
Elizabeth A. Watrin, Pres., New Mexico Div.
Karen M. Atwood, Pres., Illinois Div.
Bert E. Marshall, Pres., Oklahoma Div.

Phone: 312-653-6000 | **Fax:** 312-819-1220
Toll-Free:
Address: 300 E. Randolph St., Chicago, IL 60601-5099 US

GROWTH PLANS/SPECIAL FEATURES:

Health Care Service Corporation (HCSC) is a non-investor-owned mutual insurance company that operates through its Blue Cross and Blue Shield divisions in Illinois, Texas, New Mexico and Oklahoma. It also has several subsidiaries that offer a variety of health and life insurance products and related services to employers and individuals. It provides PPOs, HMOs, POS plans, traditional indemnity and Medicare supplemental health plans to over 13 million members through Blue Cross and Blue Shield of Illinois (BCBSI), Blue Cross and Blue Shield of Oklahoma (BCBSO), Blue Cross and Blue Shield of Texas (BCBST) and Blue Cross and Blue Shield of New Mexico (BCBSNM). Through its non-Blue Cross and Blue Shield subsidiaries, the company offers prescription drug plans, Medicare supplemental insurance, dental and vision coverage, life and disability insurance, workers' compensation, retirement services and medical financial services. One such subsidiary, Preferred Financial Group, is made up of HSCS's various life insurance subsidiaries, including Fort Dearborn Life Insurance Company of Illinois (FDL) and Colorado Bankers Life Insurance Company. Another subsidiary, Dental Network of America, Inc., functions as a third-party administrator for all company dental programs and is registered in every state except Florida. It also offers a dental discount card program. MedConnect, LLC is an online resource for medical professionals. Hallmark Services Corporation provides administration and claim adjudication services for individual policies to the direct markets divisions of BCBSI and BCBST. Availity, L.L.C., a partially-owned subsidiary, operates a health care clearinghouse and provides Internet-based health information services. TMG Health offers business process outsourcing (BPO) for Medicare and Medicaid.

Employees of the firm are offered educational assistance, a transportation reimbursement account, an employee assistance program, a wellness program, flextime, credit union membership, a savings bond program, adoption assistance, flexible spending accounts and medical, vision, life and disability insurance.

FINANCIALS: **Sales and profits are in thousands of dollars—add 000 to get the full amount. 2010 Note: Financial information for 2010 was not available for all companies at press time.**

2010 Sales: $21,784,870	2010 Profits: $700,000
2009 Sales: $17,505,700	2009 Profits: $514,500
2008 Sales: $16,269,300	2008 Profits: $742,600
2007 Sales: $14,348,400	2007 Profits: $
2006 Sales: $12,971,600	2006 Profits: $1,115,400

U.S. Stock Ticker: Mutual Company
Int'l Ticker:
Int'l Exchange:
Employees: 16,000 Fiscal Year Ends: 12/31
Parent Company:

SALARIES/BENEFITS:

Pension Plan: Y	ESOP Stock Plan:	Profit Sharing:	Top Exec. Salary: $	Bonus: $
Savings Plan: Y	Stock Purch. Plan: Y		Second Exec. Salary: $	Bonus: $

OTHER THOUGHTS:

Apparent Women Officers or Directors: 4
Hot Spot for Advancement for Women/Minorities: Y

LOCATIONS: ("Y" = Yes)

West:	Southwest:	Midwest:	Southeast:	Northeast:	International:
Y	Y	Y	Y	Y	

HEALTH FITNESS CORP

www.hfit.com

Industry Group Code: 713940

Management:		**Sales/Marketing:**		**Liberal Arts:**		**Information Sys.:**		**Professionals:**		**Tech./Scientific:**	
Mgmt. Trainees:	Y	Marketing Pros.:	Y	Gen. Writing/Editing:	Y	Info. Mgmt.:	Y	Finance/Acct.:	Y	Engineers, Elec.:	
Experienced Mgmt.:	Y	Retail Sales:		Tech. Writing:		Software Dev.:		Law:	Y	Engineers, Other:	
Int'l Business:	Y	Comm./Industrial:	Y	Graphic Arts/Photog.:	Y	Hardware Dev.:		HR/Other:	Y	Health/Lab:	
MBA Grads:	Y	Sales Trainees:	Y	Music:		Consulting/Other:		Training:	Y	Science/Research:	
		Advertising Pros.:	Y	Broadcasting:				Health Care:		Petroleum/Chem.:	
				Other:	Y			Consulting:		Math/Other:	

TYPES OF BUSINESS:

Fitness Center Management
Consulting Services
Corporate & Hospital-Based Fitness Centers
Fitness Center Design
Wellness Programs
Health & Fitness Assessment
On-Site Physical Therapy Services

BRANDS/DIVISIONS/AFFILIATES:

INSIGHT Health Risk Assessment
HFC Wellness Programs
HFC Fitness Programs
JOBFIT
Science Advisory Board
Trustmark Companies

CONTACTS: *Note: Officers with more than one job title may be intentionally listed here more than once.*

Paul Lotharius, CEO
Brian Gagne, COO
Paul Lotharius, Pres.
Wes Winnekins, CFO/Exec. VP
Debra Marshall, VP-Mktg.
Tina Loskota, VP-Human Resources
Sean Katz, CIO
Mark Totts, VP-Prod. Dev.
J.Mark McConnell, Sr. VP-Bus. & Corp. Dev.
Gregory Siedschlag, VP-Finance
David Hurt, VP-Fitness Mgmt. Account Svcs.
Katherine Meacham, VP-Account Svcs.
Brian Gagne, Sr. VP-Account Mgmt. & Program Dev.
Dennis Richling, Chief Medial & Wellness Officer

Phone: 952-831-6830 **Fax:** 952-897-5173
Toll-Free: 800-639-7913
Address: 1650 W. 82nd St., Ste. 1100, Minneapolis, MN 55431 US

GROWTH PLANS/SPECIAL FEATURES:

HealthFitness Corp. (HFC) and its subsidiaries provide fitness and wellness management services and programs to Fortune 500 companies, as well as hospitals, communities and universities in the U.S. and Canada. The firm also provides injury prevention programs and on-site physical therapy services. Currently, HFC serves over 300 corporate clients across 400 locations. It manages approximately 215 corporate, hospital, community and university fitness centers; 170 corporate health management sites; and 100 unstaffed health management locations. Through its two business segments, Fitness Management Services and Health Management Services, the company provides a full range of development, management, marketing and consulting services, including demographic analysis; interior/floor plan and fitness program design; and occupational health consulting services. HFC Wellness Programs feature a menu of lifestyle programs addressing the specific needs of a company's workforce, including weight loss, stress management and HFC Fitness Programs, which offer customized exercise-based programs including personal training and specialty group classes. Specific programs include INSIGHT Health Risk Assessment, a full range of tools to assess the health and well-being of individuals, and JOBFIT, a series of resources for on-the-job injury prevention and treatment. In 2010, the company became a subsidiary of Trustmark Companies.

The firm offers its employees medical, dental and vision coverage; flexible spending accounts; life and AD&D insurance; a 401(k) plan; an employee stock purchase plan; long-term disability insurance; and an employee assistance program.

FINANCIALS: **Sales and profits are in thousands of dollars—add 000 to get the full amount. 2010 Note: Financial information for 2010 was not available for all companies at press time.**

2010 Sales: $169,400 | 2010 Profits: $
2009 Sales: $79,473 | 2009 Profits: $3,279
2008 Sales: $77,676 | 2008 Profits: $2,722
2007 Sales: $69,958 | 2007 Profits: $ 910
2006 Sales: $63,578 | 2006 Profits: $1,352

U.S. Stock Ticker: Subsidiary
Int'l Ticker:
Int'l Exchange:
Employees: 3,472 Fiscal Year Ends: 12/31
Parent Company: TRUSTMARK COMPANIES

SALARIES/BENEFITS:

Pension Plan: | ESOP Stock Plan: | Profit Sharing: | Top Exec. Salary: $319,431 | Bonus: $95,031
Savings Plan: Y | Stock Purch. Plan: Y | | Second Exec. Salary: $217,308 | Bonus: $36,250

OTHER THOUGHTS:

Apparent Women Officers or Directors: 3
Hot Spot for Advancement for Women/Minorities: Y

LOCATIONS: ("Y" = Yes)

West:	Southwest:	Midwest:	Southeast:	Northeast:	International:
Y	Y	Y	Y	Y	Y

HEALTH MANAGEMENT ASSOCIATES INC

www.hma.com

Industry Group Code: 622110

Management:		Sales/Marketing:		Liberal Arts:		Information Sys.:		Professionals:		Tech./Scientific:	
Mgmt. Trainees:	Y	Marketing Pros.:	Y	Gen. Writing/Editing:	Y	Info. Mgmt.:	Y	Finance/Acct.:	Y	Engineers, Elec.:	
Experienced Mgmt.:	Y	Retail Sales:		Tech. Writing:	Y	Software Dev.:	Y	Law:	Y	Engineers, Other:	
Int'l Business:		Comm./Industrial:		Graphic Arts/Photog.:	Y	Hardware Dev.:		HR/Other:	Y	Health/Lab:	Y
MBA Grads:	Y	Sales Trainees:		Music:		Consulting/Other:		Training:	Y	Science/Research:	
		Advertising Pros.:	Y	Broadcasting:				Health Care:	Y	Petroleum/Chem.:	
				Other:	Y			Consulting:		Math/Other:	

TYPES OF BUSINESS:

Acute Care Hospitals

BRANDS/DIVISIONS/AFFILIATES:

Brooksville Regional Hospital
Barrow Regional Medical Center
Natchez Community Hospital
Twin Rivers Regional Medical Center
Heart of Lancaster Regional Medical Center
Williamson Memorial Hospital
Wuesthoff Health System
Tri-Lakes Medical Center

CONTACTS: *Note: Officers with more than one job title may be intentionally listed here more than once.*

Gary D. Newsome, CEO
Gary D. Newsome, Pres.
Kelly E. Curry, CFO/Exec. VP
Eric L. Waller, Chief Mktg. Officer
Patrick E. Lombart, Sr. VP-Human Resources
Ronald N. Riner, Chief Medical Officer
Ken Chatfield, CIO
Timothy R. Parry, General Counsel/Sr. VP/Corp. Sec.
Peter M. Lawson, Exec. VP-Dev.
Alan Levine, Sr. VP-Gov't Rel.
John C. Merriwether, VP-Financial Rel.
Robert E. Farnham, Chief Acct. Officer/Sr. VP-Finance
Joseph C. Meek, VP/Treas.
Britt T. Reynolds, Pres., Div. 1
Ann M. Barnhart, Pres., Div. 2
Alan Levine, Pres., Div. 3
William J. Schoen, Chmn.

Phone: 239-598-3131	**Fax:** 239-598-2705
Toll-Free:	
Address: 5811 Pelican Bay Blvd., Ste. 500, Naples, FL 34108 US	

GROWTH PLANS/SPECIAL FEATURES:

Health Management Associates, Inc. (HMA) owns and operates acute care hospitals in non-urban communities. The company operates approximately 59 hospitals with roughly 8,864 licensed beds. The firm operates facilities in Arkansas, Kentucky, Mississippi, Florida, Alabama, Georgia, Missouri, North Carolina, Oklahoma, Pennsylvania, South Carolina, Tennessee, Texas, Washington and West Virginia. These hospitals offer services such as general surgery; internal medicine; obstetrics; radiology; oncology; and emergency room, diagnostic, coronary and pediatric care. HMA also provides outpatient services which include cardiology, one-day surgery, respiratory therapy, laboratory, X-ray and physical therapy. In addition, certain HMA hospitals provide specialty services in areas like magnetic resonance imaging, radiation therapy, neurosurgery, computer-assisted tomography scanning and lithotripsy. The facilities benefit from centralized corporate resources such as finance and control systems; purchasing; physicians recruitment services; administrative personnel management; information technology; legal services; facilities planning; marketing; and public relations. Some of the company's hospitals provide services to retired and certain other military personnel and their families, pursuant to the Civilian Health and Medical Program of Uniformed Services (CHAMPUS). HMA hospitals include Brooksville Regional Hospital, Barrow Regional Medical Center, Natchez Community Hospital, Twin Rivers Regional Medical Center, Heart of Lancaster Regional Medical Center and Williamson Memorial Hospital. In October 2010, HMA acquired Wuesthoff Health System, a two hospital, 413-bed system in Florida. In December 2010, the firm sold its 140-bed Riley Hospital in Mississippi to Anderson Regional Medical Center. In May 2011, the company acquired 95% ownership and operational control of Tri-Lakes Medical Center, a 112-bed facility in Mississippi.

The company offers its employees life, disability, critical illness, medical, dental and vision coverage; flexible spending accounts; a 401(k) plan; and vacation and holiday plans.

FINANCIALS: **Sales and profits are in thousands of dollars—add 000 to get the full amount. 2010 Note: Financial information for 2010 was not available for all companies at press time.**

2010 Sales: $5,114,997 — 2010 Profits: $150,069
2009 Sales: $4,617,143 — 2009 Profits: $138,182
2008 Sales: $4,360,466 — 2008 Profits: $168,149
2007 Sales: $4,185,819 — 2007 Profits: $117,508
2006 Sales: $4,050,425 — 2006 Profits: $182,749

U.S. Stock Ticker: HMA
Int'l Ticker:
Int'l Exchange:
Employees: 35,800 Fiscal Year Ends: 12/31
Parent Company:

SALARIES/BENEFITS:

Pension Plan: ESOP Stock Plan: Profit Sharing: Top Exec. Salary: $900,000 Bonus: $1,897,500
Savings Plan: Y Stock Purch. Plan: Second Exec. Salary: $675,000 Bonus: $1,075,219

OTHER THOUGHTS:

Apparent Women Officers or Directors: 2
Hot Spot for Advancement for Women/Minorities: Y

LOCATIONS: ("Y" = Yes)

West:	Southwest:	Midwest:	Southeast:	Northeast:	International:
Y	Y	Y	Y	Y	

Sales, profits and employees may be estimates. Financial information, benefits and other data can change quickly and may vary from those stated here.

HEALTHSOUTH CORP

www.healthsouth.com

Industry Group Code: 6214

Management:		**Sales/Marketing:**		**Liberal Arts:**		**Information Sys.:**		**Professionals:**		**Tech./Scientific:**	
Mgmt. Trainees:	Y	Marketing Pros.:	Y	Gen. Writing/Editing:		Info. Mgmt.:	Y	Finance/Acct.:	Y	Engineers, Elec.:	
Experienced Mgmt.:	Y	Retail Sales:		Tech. Writing:		Software Dev.:		Law:	Y	Engineers, Other:	Y
Int'l Business:	Y	Comm./Industrial:	Y	Graphic Arts/Photog.:		Hardware Dev.:		HR/Other:	Y	Health/Lab:	
MBA Grads:	Y	Sales Trainees:		Music:		Consulting/Other:		Training:	Y	Science/Research:	
		Advertising Pros.:	Y	Broadcasting:				Health Care:		Petroleum/Chem.:	
				Other:				Consulting:		Math/Other:	

TYPES OF BUSINESS:

Inpatient Rehabilitation Facilities
Long-term Care Hospitals
Home Health Programs

BRANDS/DIVISIONS/AFFILIATES:

Sugar Land Rehabilitation Hospital

CONTACTS:

Note: Officers with more than one job title may be intentionally listed here more than once.

Jay Grinney, CEO
Mark J. Tarr, COO/Exec. VP
Jay Grinney, Pres.
Cheryl Levy, Chief Human Resources Officer
Dexanne B. Clohan, Chief Medical Officer
Rusty Yeager, CIO/Sr. VP
John P. Whittington, General Counsel/Exec. VP/Corp. Sec.
Stephen L. Royal, Chief Dev. Officer
Mary Ann Arico, Sr. VP-Corp. Comm.
Mary Ann Arico, Chief Investor Rel. Officer
Edmund Fay, Treas./Sr. VP
Terry Maxhimer, Pres., Central Region
Frank Brown, Pres., Southwest Region
Jerry Gray, Pres., West Region
Justin Hunter, Sr. VP-Public Policy, Legislation & Regulations
Jon F. Hanson, Chmn.

Phone: 205-967-7116	**Fax:** 205-969-3543
Toll-Free: 800-765-4772	
Address: 3660 Grandview Pkwy., Ste. 200, Birmingham, AL 35243 US	

GROWTH PLANS/SPECIAL FEATURES:

HealthSouth Corp. operates inpatient rehabilitative health care and long-term acute care hospitals and provides treatment to more than 250,000 people annually on both an inpatient and an outpatient basis. It operates 97 inpatient rehabilitation hospitals, one long-term care facility, 32 outpatient rehabilitation satellites and 25 licensed, hospital-based home health agencies. The facilities are located in 26 states, with a concentration in Texas, Pennsylvania, Florida, Tennessee, Arizona and Alabama. The company also has a facility in Puerto Rico. HealthSouth provides rehabilitation services to patients with physical disabilities due to various conditions such as head injury, spinal cord injury, certain orthopedic problems and neuromuscular disease. In total, the company's facilities operate approximately 6,879 beds. The firm is focused primarily on operating inpatient rehabilitation facilities and growing the inpatient rehabilitation business through bed expansion, consolidation in existing markets (through joint venturing or acquisition), de-novo projects in existing and new markets and acquisitions. Although its focus is the enhancement of its position in the inpatient rehabilitation industry, HealthSouth intends to expand its share in the long-term acute care, home health and hospice markets. In September 2010, the firm acquired Sugar Land Rehabilitation Hospital in Texas. In October 2010, HealthSouth acquired a 30-bed inpatient rehabilitation unit in Arkansas from Health Management Associates. In August 2011, the company sold five long-term care facilities to LifeCare Holdings, Inc. for roughly $117.5 million.

Employees are offered medical, dental and vision insurance; flexible spending accounts; life and disability insurance; a 401(k) plan; a 529 college savings plan; pre-paid legal services; and an employee assistance plan.

FINANCIALS:

Sales and profits are in thousands of dollars—add 000 to get the full amount. 2010 Note: Financial information for 2010 was not available for all companies at press time.

2010 Sales: $1,999,300	2010 Profits: $939,800	**U.S. Stock Ticker: HLS**
2009 Sales: $1,911,100	2009 Profits: $68,800	**Int'l Ticker:**
2008 Sales: $1,829,500	2008 Profits: $226,400	Int'l Exchange:
2007 Sales: $1,723,500	2007 Profits: $627,400	Employees: 23,000 Fiscal Year Ends: 12/31
2006 Sales: $1,711,600	2006 Profits: $-647,200	Parent Company:

SALARIES/BENEFITS:

Pension Plan:	ESOP Stock Plan:	Profit Sharing:	Top Exec. Salary: $1,000,000	Bonus: $1,436,800
Savings Plan: Y	Stock Purch. Plan: Y		Second Exec. Salary: $527,000	Bonus: $455,581

OTHER THOUGHTS:

Apparent Women Officers or Directors: 7
Hot Spot for Advancement for Women/Minorities: Y

LOCATIONS: ("Y" = Yes)

West:	Southwest:	Midwest:	Southeast:	Northeast:	International:
Y	Y	Y	Y	Y	Y

HEARTLAND PAYMENT SYSTEMS INC

www.heartlandpaymentsystems.com

Industry Group Code: 522320

Management:		Sales/Marketing:		Liberal Arts:		Information Sys.:		Professionals:		Tech./Scientific:	
Mgmt. Trainees:		Marketing Pros.:	Y	Gen. Writing/Editing:	Y	Info. Mgmt.:	Y	Finance/Acct.:	Y	Engineers, Elec.:	
Experienced Mgmt.:	Y	Retail Sales:		Tech. Writing:	Y	Software Dev.:	Y	Law:	Y	Engineers, Other:	
Int'l Business:		Comm./Industrial:	Y	Graphic Arts/Photog.:	Y	Hardware Dev.:		HR/Other:	Y	Health/Lab:	
MBA Grads:	Y	Sales Trainees:		Music:		Consulting/Other:		Training:		Science/Research:	
		Advertising Pros.:		Broadcasting:				Health Care:		Petroleum/Chem.:	
				Other:				Consulting:		Math/Other:	

TYPES OF BUSINESS:

Financial Processing Services
Credit/Debit Processing
Payroll Processing Services
Processing Equipment Provider

BRANDS/DIVISIONS/AFFILIATES:

HPS Exchange
Chockstone, Inc.

CONTACTS: *Note: Officers with more than one job title may be intentionally listed here more than once.*

Robert O. Carr, CEO
Conan Lane, COO
Robert H.B. Baldwin Jr., Pres.
Maria Rueda, CFO
Heidi Goff, Chief Mktg. Officer
Steven M. Elefant, CIO
Kristopher T. Herrin, CTO
Charles H.N. Kallenbach, General Counsel/Chief Legal Officer
Joseph E. White, Chief Acct. Officer
Bryan Thompson, Chief Enterprise Officer
Marty A. Moretti, Chief Service Officer
John R. South, Chief Security Officer
Robert O. Carr, Chmn.

Phone: 609-683-3831 **Fax:** 609-683-3815
Toll-Free: 888-798-3131
Address: 90 Nassau St., Princeton, NJ 08542 US

GROWTH PLANS/SPECIAL FEATURES:

Heartland Payment Systems, Inc. (HPS) is a provider of credit/debit card, payroll and other associated processing services to approximately 173,860 U.S. bankcard merchants. Heartland primarily serves restaurant, hospitality, hotel and retail merchants throughout the U.S. Headquartered in Princeton, New Jersey, the firm also maintains offices in Ohio, Indiana, Tennessee, Texas, Oregon, Colorado and Ontario, Canada. The firm's services include credit/debit card processing, payroll services and the HPS Exchange, while products include gift cards (with company logos), terminals, printers and other processing equipment. HPS' credit/debit card processing services allow clients to extend a variety of payment options to customers; the firm processes all major credit cards, including Visa, MasterCard, American Express, Diners Club, JCB and Discover, 24 hours per day, 365 days a year. HPS' payroll services entail calculation of payroll checks (which includes taxes, voluntary reductions, retirement plans and direct deposit), tax returns/filing concerns and additional services, such as reimbursement checks and automated check signing. The HPS Exchange is a company-developed transaction processing platform with added features unique to HPS. The HPS Exchange features fast transaction processing, customized reports/receipts and online merchant management, which allows retailers to immediately view transaction processing details in real time. HPS' products include gift cards tailored to each of its retail clients; cards contain stored value which is read on the card's magnetic strip, as well as company logo information. Processing equipment available for clients include a PIN pad, wireless and hand-held terminals, all of which is installed by HPS' local managers. HPS additionally publishes brochures and articles related to fraud control, interchange rates and other information specific to the industries it serves.

Heartland offers its employees health, dental and life insurance; short- and long-term disability; flexible spending and dependent care accounts; and the option to add additional life insurance for spouses and dependents.

FINANCIALS: **Sales and profits are in thousands of dollars—add 000 to get the full amount. 2010 Note: Financial information for 2010 was not available for all companies at press time.**

2010 Sales: $1,864,337 — 2010 Profits: $34,660
2009 Sales: $1,652,139 — 2009 Profits: $-51,796
2008 Sales: $1,544,902 — 2008 Profits: $41,840
2007 Sales: $1,313,846 — 2007 Profits: $35,870
2006 Sales: $1,097,041 — 2006 Profits: $28,544

U.S. Stock Ticker: HPY
Int'l Ticker:
Int'l Exchange:
Employees: 2,612 Fiscal Year Ends: 12/31
Parent Company:

SALARIES/BENEFITS:

Pension Plan: ESOP Stock Plan: Profit Sharing: Top Exec. Salary: $715,000 Bonus: $143,000
Savings Plan: Y Stock Purch. Plan: Second Exec. Salary: $430,000 Bonus: $43,000

OTHER THOUGHTS:

Apparent Women Officers or Directors: 2
Hot Spot for Advancement for Women/Minorities:

LOCATIONS: ("Y" = Yes)

West:	Southwest:	Midwest:	Southeast:	Northeast:	International:
	Y	Y		Y	

HENRY SCHEIN INC

www.henryschein.com

Industry Group Code: 423450

Management:		Sales/Marketing:		Liberal Arts:		Information Sys.:		Professionals:		Tech./Scientific:	
Mgmt. Trainees:	Y	Marketing Pros.:	Y	Gen. Writing/Editing:	Y	Info. Mgmt.:	Y	Finance/Acct.:	Y	Engineers, Elec.:	
Experienced Mgmt.:	Y	Retail Sales:		Tech. Writing:	Y	Software Dev.:	Y	Law:	Y	Engineers, Other:	
Int'l Business:	Y	Comm./Industrial:	Y	Graphic Arts/Photog.:	Y	Hardware Dev.:		HR/Other:	Y	Health/Lab:	
MBA Grads:	Y	Sales Trainees:	Y	Music:		Consulting/Other:		Training:	Y	Science/Research:	
		Advertising Pros.:	Y	Broadcasting:				Health Care:	Y	Petroleum/Chem.:	
				Other:				Consulting:		Math/Other:	

TYPES OF BUSINESS:

Health Care Products Distribution
Dental Supplies Distribution
Veterinary Products Distribution
Electronic Catalogs

BRANDS/DIVISIONS/AFFILIATES:

AVImark
Dentrix
Easy Dental
MicroMD
Butler Schein Animal Health
Provet Holdings Limited.
Sogim Grimouille
Alpha Scientific, Inc.

CONTACTS: *Note: Officers with more than one job title may be intentionally listed here more than once.*

Stanley M. Bergman, CEO
James P. Breslawski, COO
James P. Breslawski, Pres.
Steven Paladino, CFO/Exec. VP
James A. Harding, CTO/Sr. VP
Michael Racioppi, Chief Merch. Officer/Sr. VP
Gerald A. Benjamin, Chief Admin. Officer/Exec. VP
Mark E. Mlotek, Exec. VP-Corp. Bus. Dev.
Susan Vassallo, VP-Corp. Comm.
Leonard A. David, Chief Compliance Officer/Sr. VP
Stanley Komaroff, Sr. Advisor
Lonnie Shoff, Pres., Henry Schein Global Healthcare Specialties
Stanley M. Bergman, Chmn.
Michael Zack, Pres., Int'l Group

Phone: 631-843-5500 **Fax:** 631-843-5658
Toll-Free:
Address: 135 Duryea Rd., Melville, NY 11747 US

GROWTH PLANS/SPECIAL FEATURES:

Henry Schein, Inc. distributes products and services to office-based healthcare practitioners in North America and Europe. The firm has over 700,000 customers in more than 200 countries, including dental practitioners and laboratories; physician practices; government institutions; and animal health clinics. The company operates in two segments: healthcare distribution and technology. The healthcare distribution segment aggregates the dental, medical and international operating segments. This segment distributes branded and generic pharmaceuticals; small equipment; laboratory products; large dental equipment; consumable products; infection-control products; vaccines; diagnostic tests; surgical products; and vitamins. The technology segment provides software, technology and other value-added services to healthcare practitioners, primarily in the U.S. and Canada. Value-added solutions include practice-management software systems for dental and medical practitioners and animal health clinics. Its practice-management software solutions include Oasis, Dentrix, EXACT and Easy Dental for dental practices; DVM Manager and AVImark for veterinary clinics; and MicroMD for physician usage. The technology group also provides financial services and continuing education for practitioners. Henry Schein offers more than 190,000 branded and Henry Schein private-brand products. The firm distributes approximately 30.8 million pieces of direct marketing material annually through its electronic catalog and ordering system. Butler Schein Animal Health, a joint venture 50.1%-owned by Henry Schein and 49.9%-owned by Butler Animal Health Supply, is a combination of each firm's U.S. animal health operations. In January 2011, Henry Schein acquired Provet Holdings Limited. In February 2011, Butler Schein Animal Health acquired majority ownership of McAllister Software Systems, LLC and ImproMed, Inc. In April 2011, Henry Schein acquired Alpha Scientific, Inc. In May 2011, the firm acquired Sogim Grimouille.

The company offers its employees medical, dental, vision, life, AD&D and disability insurance; flexible spending accounts; a 401(k); a 529 college savings plan; tuition assistance; paid time off; and on-site wellness programs.

FINANCIALS: **Sales and profits are in thousands of dollars—add 000 to get the full amount. 2010 Note: Financial information for 2010 was not available for all companies at press time.**

2010 Sales: $7,526,790	2010 Profits: $325,789	**U.S. Stock Ticker: HSIC**
2009 Sales: $6,538,336	2009 Profits: $333,157	**Int'l Ticker:**
2008 Sales: $6,380,413	2008 Profits: $261,374	Int'l Exchange:
2007 Sales: $5,889,884	2007 Profits: $229,176	Employees: 13,500 Fiscal Year Ends: 12/31
2006 Sales: $5,048,191	2006 Profits: $163,759	Parent Company:

SALARIES/BENEFITS:

Pension Plan:	ESOP Stock Plan:	Profit Sharing:	Top Exec. Salary: $1,150,000	Bonus: $1,791,000
Savings Plan: Y	Stock Purch. Plan: Y		Second Exec. Salary: $600,000	Bonus: $500,750

OTHER THOUGHTS:

Apparent Women Officers or Directors: 3
Hot Spot for Advancement for Women/Minorities: Y

LOCATIONS: ("Y" = Yes)

West:	Southwest:	Midwest:	Southeast:	Northeast:	International:
Y	Y	Y	Y	Y	Y

HERSHEY CO

www.hersheys.com

Industry Group Code: 311320

Management:		Sales/Marketing:		Liberal Arts:		Information Sys.:		Professionals:		Tech./Scientific:	
Mgmt. Trainees:	Y	Marketing Pros.:	Y	Gen. Writing/Editing:	Y	Info. Mgmt.:	Y	Finance/Acct.:	Y	Engineers, Elec.:	Y
Experienced Mgmt.:	Y	Retail Sales:		Tech. Writing:		Software Dev.:		Law:	Y	Engineers, Other:	Y
Int'l Business:	Y	Comm./Industrial:	Y	Graphic Arts/Photog.:	Y	Hardware Dev.:		HR/Other:	Y	Health/Lab:	
MBA Grads:	Y	Sales Trainees:		Music:		Consulting/Other:		Training:	Y	Science/Research:	
		Advertising Pros.:	Y	Broadcasting:				Health Care:		Petroleum/Chem.:	Y
				Other:				Consulting:		Math/Other:	

TYPES OF BUSINESS:

Candy Manufacturing
Baking Supplies
Chocolate Products
Confectionaries & Snacks
Amusement Parks
Resorts/Hotels

BRANDS/DIVISIONS/AFFILIATES:

Hershey North America
Reese's
Hershey International
HERSHEYPARK
Scharffen Berger
Artisan Confections Company
Van Houten
Hershey Entertainment and Resorts Company

CONTACTS: *Note: Officers with more than one job title may be intentionally listed here more than once.*

John P. Bilbrey, CEO
John P. Bilbrey, Pres.
Humberto P. Alfonso, CFO/Sr. VP
Michele G. Buck, Global Chief Mktg. Officer/Sr. VP
C. Daniel Azzara, VP-Global R&D
George F. Davis, CIO/Sr. VP
Burton H. Snyder, General Counsel/Sr. VP/Corp. Sec.
Terence L. O'Day, Sr. VP-Global Oper.
Javier H. Idrovo, Sr. VP-Bus. Dev. & Strategy
James E. Nevels, Chmn.
Thaddeus J. Jastrzebski, Sr. VP/Pres., Hershey Int'l

Phone: 717-534-4200	**Fax:** 717-534-7873
Toll-Free: 800-468-1714	
Address: 100 Crystal A Dr., Hershey, PA 17033-0810 US	

GROWTH PLANS/SPECIAL FEATURES:

Hershey Co. (formerly Hershey Foods Corp.) is one of the largest candy makers in the U.S., manufacturing more than 80 brands. The firm sells and markets through three main divisions: Hershey North America; Global Marketing Group; and Hershey International, which oversees the corporation's international interests and exports to more than 50 countries worldwide. Hershey's principal product groups include chocolate and non-chocolate confectionery products such as Reese's, Kit Kat, Hershey Bars and Hershey Kisses; packaged items; and grocery products such as baking ingredients, chocolate drink mixes, peanut butter, dessert toppings and beverages. Wholly-owned subsidiary Artisan Confections Company produces Scharffen Berger high-cacao dark chocolate products and Dagoba natural and organic chocolate products. Its products are sold primarily to wholesale distributors, chain grocery stores, mass merchandisers, chain drug stores, vending companies, wholesale clubs, convenience stores, dollar stores, concessionaires, department stores and natural food stores. The company maintains manufacturing operations in the U.S., Mexico, Brazil and India. Hershey also produces products in China through Lotte Confectionery Co., Ltd. (with 44% Hershey ownership). In addition, the firm markets its Van Houten brand products in the Middle East and Asia. Most company operations occur in Hershey, Pennsylvania where the company runs HERSHEYPARK, an amusement park operated by subsidiary Hershey Entertainment and Resorts Company.

Employees are offered health, dental and vision insurance; an employee assistance program; life insurance; disability coverage; on-site fitness centers; gym membership reimbursement; a 401(k) plan; retirement contributions; an employee stock purchase plan; health care and dependant care spending accounts; store discounts; adoption assistance; and tuition reimbursement.

FINANCIALS: **Sales and profits are in thousands of dollars—add 000 to get the full amount. 2010 Note: Financial information for 2010 was not available for all companies at press time.**

2010 Sales: $5,671,000	2010 Profits: $509,800	**U.S. Stock Ticker: HSY**
2009 Sales: $5,298,668	2009 Profits: $435,994	**Int'l Ticker:**
2008 Sales: $5,132,768	2008 Profits: $311,405	Int'l Exchange:
2007 Sales: $4,946,716	2007 Profits: $214,154	Employees: 13,500 Fiscal Year Ends: 12/31
2006 Sales: $4,944,230	2006 Profits: $559,061	Parent Company:

SALARIES/BENEFITS:

Pension Plan: Y	ESOP Stock Plan: Y	Profit Sharing:	Top Exec. Salary: $1,000,000	Bonus: $2,267,730
Savings Plan: Y	Stock Purch. Plan:		Second Exec. Salary: $550,000	Bonus: $711,022

OTHER THOUGHTS:

Apparent Women Officers or Directors: 2
Hot Spot for Advancement for Women/Minorities: Y

LOCATIONS: ("Y" = Yes)

West:	Southwest:	Midwest:	Southeast:	Northeast:	International:
Y	Y	Y	Y	Y	Y

HERTZ GLOBAL HOLDINGS INC

www.hertz.com

Industry Group Code: 5321

Management:		Sales/Marketing:		Liberal Arts:		Information Sys.:		Professionals:		Tech./Scientific:	
Mgmt. Trainees:	Y	Marketing Pros.:	Y	Gen. Writing/Editing:	Y	Info. Mgmt.:	Y	Finance/Acct.:	Y	Engineers, Elec.:	
Experienced Mgmt.:	Y	Retail Sales:	Y	Tech. Writing:		Software Dev.:	Y	Law:	Y	Engineers, Other:	
Int'l Business:	Y	Comm./Industrial:	Y	Graphic Arts/Photog.:	Y	Hardware Dev.:		HR/Other:	Y	Health/Lab:	
MBA Grads:	Y	Sales Trainees:	Y	Music:		Consulting/Other:		Training:	Y	Science/Research:	
		Advertising Pros.:	Y	Broadcasting:				Health Care:		Petroleum/Chem.:	
				Other:	Y			Consulting:		Math/Other:	

TYPES OF BUSINESS:

Automobile Rental
Truck Rental
Claims Management
Heavy Equipment Rental
Used Automobile Sales
Leasing
Actuarial Services
Franchising

BRANDS/DIVISIONS/AFFILIATES:

Prestige Collection
Hertz Fun Collection
Green Collection
Hertz Equipment Rental Corporation
1st Call Studio Equipment
Dollar Thrifty Automotive Group, Inc.
Forces, Inc.
24/7 Studio Equipment

CONTACTS: *Note: Officers with more than one job title may be intentionally listed here more than once.*

Mark P. Frissora, CEO
Elyse Douglas, CFO/Exec. VP
Michael P. Senackerib, Chief Mktg. Officer/Sr. VP
LeighAnne Baker, Chief Human Resources Officer/Sr. VP
Joseph F. Eckroth, CIO/Sr. VP-Global Customer Care
Jeffrey Zimmerman, General Counsel/Sr. VP/Sec.
Richard Broome, Sr. VP-Corp. Comm. & Affairs
Jatindar Kapur, Sr. VP-Finance/Controller
Scott Sider, Exec. VP/Pres., Vehicle Renting & Leasing
Scott Massengill, VP/Treas.
Lois Boyd, Sr. VP-Advantage Rent A Car
Robert J. Stuart, Sr. VP-Global Sales
Mark P. Frissora, Chmn.
Michael Taride, Exec. VP/Pres., Hertz Int'l
Todd Poste, VP-Global Procurement

Phone: 201-307-2000 **Fax:** 201-307-2644
Toll-Free: 800-654-3131
Address: 225 Brae Blvd., Park Ridge, NJ 07656-0713 US

GROWTH PLANS/SPECIAL FEATURES:

Hertz Global Holdings, Inc. owns one of the largest worldwide airport general use car rental brands and one of the largest equipment rental businesses in the U.S. and Canada. The company operates in two segments: car rental and equipment rental. In the car rental business segment, Hertz and its independent licensees accept reservations for car rentals at approximately 8,500 locations in approximately 146 countries. The company generally accepts reservations only for a class of vehicles, but it also accepts reservations for specific makes and models of vehicles in its Prestige Collection national-scale luxury rental program; its Hertz Fun Collection rental program; its Green Collection environmentally friendly rental program; and a limited number of models in high-volume, leisure-oriented destinations. The firm has approximately 2,360 staffed rental locations in the U.S., of which approximately 20% are airport locations and 80% are off-airport locations. It also rents cars from 1,340 other locations that are not staffed. Hertz has 1,120 staffed rental locations internationally, of which 20% are airport locations and 80% are off-airport locations, and it rents cars from 120 other locations that are not staffed. The equipment rental business segment, which operates through Hertz Equipment Rental Corporation, rents equipment through 320 branches in the U.S., Canada, France, Spain and China. It offers a broad range of equipment, including earthmoving equipment; material handling equipment; aerial and electrical equipment; air compressors; pumps; generators; small tools; compaction equipment; and construction-related trucks. The car rental segment accounts for roughly 85.8% of the company's revenue, while equipment rental accounts for the remaining 14.2%. In 2010, the firm acquired 1st Call Studio Equipment; Rent One Italy; and 24/7 Studio Equipment. In 2011, Hertz Global acquired Forces, Inc. and WGI Rentals; and opened new offices in Bangladesh and North Carolina.

FINANCIALS: **Sales and profits are in thousands of dollars—add 000 to get the full amount. 2010 Note: Financial information for 2010 was not available for all companies at press time.**

2010 Sales: $7,562,500	2010 Profits: $-30,600
2009 Sales: $7,101,500	2009 Profits: $-111,300
2008 Sales: $8,525,100	2008 Profits: $-1,206,700
2007 Sales: $8,685,600	2007 Profits: $264,500
2006 Sales: $8,058,400	2006 Profits: $115,900

U.S. Stock Ticker: HTZ
Int'l Ticker:
Int'l Exchange:
Employees: 22,900 Fiscal Year Ends: 12/31
Parent Company:

SALARIES/BENEFITS:

Pension Plan: Y	ESOP Stock Plan:	Profit Sharing:	Top Exec. Salary: $1,131,250	Bonus: $2,657,968
Savings Plan:	Stock Purch. Plan:		Second Exec. Salary: $536,250	Bonus: $580,619

OTHER THOUGHTS:

Apparent Women Officers or Directors: 3
Hot Spot for Advancement for Women/Minorities: Y

LOCATIONS: ("Y" = Yes)

West:	Southwest:	Midwest:	Southeast:	Northeast:	International:
Y	Y	Y	Y	Y	Y

HIBBETT SPORTS INC

www.hibbett.com

Industry Group Code: 451110

Management:		**Sales/Marketing:**		**Liberal Arts:**		**Information Sys.:**		**Professionals:**		**Tech./Scientific:**	
Mgmt. Trainees:	Y	Marketing Pros.:	Y	Gen. Writing/Editing:	Y	Info. Mgmt.:	Y	Finance/Acct.:	Y	Engineers, Elec.:	
Experienced Mgmt.:	Y	Retail Sales:	Y	Tech. Writing:		Software Dev.:	Y	Law:	Y	Engineers, Other:	
Int'l Business:		Comm./Industrial:		Graphic Arts/Photog.:	Y	Hardware Dev.:		HR/Other:	Y	Health/Lab:	
MBA Grads:	Y	Sales Trainees:	Y	Music:		Consulting/Other:		Training:	Y	Science/Research:	
		Advertising Pros.:	Y	Broadcasting:				Health Care:		Petroleum/Chem.:	
				Other:				Consulting:		Math/Other:	

TYPES OF BUSINESS:

Sporting Goods Stores
Sports Apparel
Athletic Shoes
Training Equipment

BRANDS/DIVISIONS/AFFILIATES:

Hibbett Sports
Sports & Co.
Sports Additions
Hibbett Team Sales Inc

CONTACTS: *Note: Officers with more than one job title may be intentionally listed here more than once.*

Jeffry O. Rosenthal, CEO
Jeffry O. Rosenthal, Pres.
Gary A. Smith, CFO/Sr. VP
Rebecca Jones, Sr. VP-Merch.
Cathy E. Pryor, Sr. VP-Store Oper.
Gary A. Smith, Chief Acct. Officer
Michael J. Newsome, Chmn.

Phone: 205-942-4292 **Fax:** 205-912-7290
Toll-Free:
Address: 451 Industrial Ln., Birmingham, AL 35211 US

GROWTH PLANS/SPECIAL FEATURES:

Hibbett Sports, Inc. is an operator of sporting goods stores in small to mid-sized markets predominantly in the Sunbelt, Mid-Atlantic and Midwest. Its stores offer a broad assortment of athletic equipment, footwear and apparel. The company's merchandise assortment features a broad selection of brand name merchandise emphasizing team sports complemented by localized apparel and accessories designed to appeal to a wide range of customers. Hibbett operates a total of 789 stores in 24 states, including 770 Hibbett Sports stores, 16 Sports Additions stores and three Sports & Co. superstores. The firm's primary retail format is Hibbett Sports, a 5,000-square-foot store located in enclosed malls or in strip centers that are generally the center of commerce within an area and that are usually anchored by a Wal-Mart store. Hibbett's Sports Additions stores are small, mall-based stores averaging 2,500 square feet with roughly 90% of merchandise consisting of athletic footwear and the remainder consisting of caps and a limited assortment of apparel. Sports Additions stores offer a broader assortment of athletic footwear, with a greater emphasis on fashion than the athletic footwear choices offered by traditional Hibbett Sports stores. The firm's Sports & Co. superstores average 25,000 square feet and offer a broader assortment of athletic footwear, apparel and equipment than the Hibbett Sports stores. Subsidiary Hibbett Team Sales, Inc. supplies customized athletic apparel, equipment and footwear to school, athletic and youth programs in Alabama and northern Georgia. It sells its merchandise directly to educational institutions and youth associations.

Employees are offered life, disability, medical and dental insurance; a vision care plan; a stock purchase plan; a 401(k) plan; employee discounts; and a 529 college savings plan.

FINANCIALS: **Sales and profits are in thousands of dollars—add 000 to get the full amount. 2010 Note: Financial information for 2010 was not available for all companies at press time.**

2010 Sales: $593,492 — 2010 Profits: $32,549
2009 Sales: $564,188 — 2009 Profits: $29,448
2008 Sales: $520,720 — 2008 Profits: $30,329
2007 Sales: $512,094 — 2007 Profits: $38,073
2006 Sales: $440,269 — 2006 Profits: $33,624

U.S. Stock Ticker: HIBB
Int'l Ticker:
Int'l Exchange:
Employees: 5,900 Fiscal Year Ends: 1/31
Parent Company:

SALARIES/BENEFITS:

Pension Plan: ESOP Stock Plan: Profit Sharing: Top Exec. Salary: $541,000 Bonus: $595,100
Savings Plan: Y Stock Purch. Plan: Y Second Exec. Salary: $325,000 Bonus: $321,750

OTHER THOUGHTS:

Apparent Women Officers or Directors: 2
Hot Spot for Advancement for Women/Minorities:

LOCATIONS: ("Y" = Yes)

West:	Southwest:	Midwest:	Southeast:	Northeast:	International:
Y	Y	Y	Y	Y	

HILLENBRAND INC

www.hillenbrandinc.com

Industry Group Code: 339995

Management:		Sales/Marketing:		Liberal Arts:		Information Sys.:		Professionals:		Tech./Scientific:	
Mgmt. Trainees:		Marketing Pros.:	Y	Gen. Writing/Editing:	Y	Info. Mgmt.:	Y	Finance/Acct.:	Y	Engineers, Elec.:	
Experienced Mgmt.:		Retail Sales:		Tech. Writing:		Software Dev.:		Law:	Y	Engineers, Other:	
Int'l Business:	Y	Comm./Industrial:	Y	Graphic Arts/Photog.:		Hardware Dev.:		HR/Other:	Y	Health/Lab:	
MBA Grads:	Y	Sales Trainees:		Music:		Consulting/Other:		Training:		Science/Research:	
		Advertising Pros.:	Y	Broadcasting:				Health Care:		Petroleum/Chem.:	
				Other:				Consulting:		Math/Other:	

TYPES OF BUSINESS:

Burial Caskets and Cases Manufacturing
Conveying Equipment
Size Reduction Equipment

BRANDS/DIVISIONS/AFFILIATES:

Batesville Casket Company
K-Tron International Inc
K-Tron Feeders
K-Tron Premier
K-Tron Colormax
Pennsylvania Crusher
Gundlach
Rotex Global LLC

CONTACTS: *Note: Officers with more than one job title may be intentionally listed here more than once.*

Kenneth A. Camp, CEO
Kenneth A. Camp, Pres.
Cynthia L. Lucchese, CFO/Sr. VP
P. Douglas Wilson, Chief Admin. Officer/Sr. VP
John R. Zerkle, General Counsel/Sec/Sr. VP
Diane R. Bohman, VP-Corp. Strategy
Elizabeth E. Dreyer, Chief Acct. Officer/Controller/VP
Joe A. Raver, Sr. VP/Pres., K-Tron Int'l, Inc.
Kimberly K. Dennis, Sr. VP/Pres., Batesville Svcs., Inc.
Kevin C. Bowen, Pres., K-Tron Process Group
Jan M. Santerre, VP-Lean Bus.
Ray J. Hillenbrand, Chmn.

Phone: 812-934-7000	**Fax:** 812-934-7613
Toll-Free:	
Address: 1 Batesville Blvd., Batesville, IN 47006 US	

GROWTH PLANS/SPECIAL FEATURES:

Hillenbrand, Inc. is a holding company involved in funeral products and bulk solid material handling equipment. The firm operates through two primary subsidiaries: Batesville Casket Company and K-Tron International, Inc. Batesville Casket manufactures and sells non-gasketed steel, hardwood and veneer hardwood caskets, as well as cloth-covered and all-wood caskets. Additional products include urns, containers and other similar products. The company's hardwood caskets are made from mahogany, cherry, walnut, maple, pile, oak, pecan, poplar and sycamore woods, and are manufactured to resist the entrance of outside elements as well as rust and corrosion. Urns and containers are primarily made of hardwoods, fiberboard, bronze, acrylic and marble. This segment maintains 86 customer service centers and six rapid deployment centers throughout North America, along with other facilities in Puerto Rico, Canada, Mexico, the U.K., Australia and South Africa. Hillenbrand's K-Tron segment, which it acquired in 2010, is comprised of two units: the Process Group, which designs, produces, markets, sells and services feeders and pneumatic conveying equipment; and the Size Reduction Group, which designs, manufactures, markets, and sells equipment that is used to reduce materials in size, such as coal-crushing tools. Process Group products can be used across several industries, including plastic; resin production; and food, chemical and pharmaceutical production. Brands in this subdivision include K-Tron Feeders, K-Tron Premier and K-Tron Colormax. Size Reduction Group product brands include Pennsylvania Crusher and Gundlach, which serve mining, quarrying, glass making, salt processing and fertilizer production; while the Jeffrey Rader brand equipment is used in pulp and paper, wood, forest and biomass industries. Much of the revenues generated by this group come from the sale of replacement parts. K-Tron manufactures its products in facilities in the U.S., Switzerland and China. In September 2011, Hillenbrand acquired Rotex Global LLC, a leading manufacturer of dry material separation machines.

FINANCIALS: **Sales and profits are in thousands of dollars—add 000 to get the full amount. 2010 Note: Financial information for 2010 was not available for all companies at press time.**

2010 Sales: $749,200	2010 Profits: $92,300	**U.S. Stock Ticker: HI**
2009 Sales: $649,100	2009 Profits: $102,300	**Int'l Ticker:**
2008 Sales: $678,100	2008 Profits: $93,200	Int'l Exchange:
2007 Sales: $667,200	2007 Profits: $99,500	Employees: 3,200 Fiscal Year Ends: 9/30
2006 Sales: $	2006 Profits: $	Parent Company:

SALARIES/BENEFITS:

Pension Plan: Y	ESOP Stock Plan:	Profit Sharing:	Top Exec. Salary: $690,068	Bonus: $1,000,000
Savings Plan:	Stock Purch. Plan:		Second Exec. Salary: $424,041	Bonus: $450,000

OTHER THOUGHTS:

Apparent Women Officers or Directors: 5
Hot Spot for Advancement for Women/Minorities: Y

LOCATIONS: ("Y" = Yes)

West:	Southwest:	Midwest:	Southeast:	Northeast:	International:
		Y	Y	Y	Y

Sales, profits and employees may be estimates. Financial information, benefits and other data can change quickly and may vary from those stated here.

HILTON HOTELS CORP

www.hiltonworldwide.com

Industry Group Code: 721110

Management:		Sales/Marketing:		Liberal Arts:		Information Sys.:		Professionals:		Tech./Scientific:	
Mgmt. Trainees:	Y	Marketing Pros.:	Y	Gen. Writing/Editing:	Y	Info. Mgmt.:	Y	Finance/Acct.:	Y	Engineers, Elec.:	
Experienced Mgmt.:	Y	Retail Sales:		Tech. Writing:		Software Dev.:	Y	Law:	Y	Engineers, Other:	
Int'l Business:	Y	Comm./Industrial:	Y	Graphic Arts/Photog.:	Y	Hardware Dev.:		HR/Other:	Y	Health/Lab:	
MBA Grads:	Y	Sales Trainees:	Y	Music:		Consulting/Other:		Training:	Y	Science/Research:	
		Advertising Pros.:	Y	Broadcasting:				Health Care:		Petroleum/Chem.:	
				Other:	Y			Consulting:		Math/Other:	

TYPES OF BUSINESS:

Hotels & Resorts
Timeshare Properties
Conference Centers
Franchising
Management Services
Online Reservations

BRANDS/DIVISIONS/AFFILIATES:

Hilton
Hilton Garden Inn
Hampton Inn
Conrad Hotels and Resorts
Waldorf Astoria Collection
Embassy Suites
Hilton Garden Vacations Company LLC
Home2 Suites by Hilton

CONTACTS:

Note: Officers with more than one job title may be intentionally listed here more than once.

Christopher Nassetta, CEO
Christopher J. Nassetta, Pres.
Tom Kennedy, CFO/Exec. VP
Matthew W. Schuyler, Chief Human Resources Officer/Exec. VP
Ian R. Carter, Pres., Global Oper. & Dev.
Kevin Jacobs, Sr. VP-Corp. Strategy
Ellen Gonda, Sr. VP-Global Corp. Comm.
Kevin Jacobs, Treas.
Paul Brown, Pres., Global Brands & Commercial Svcs.
Mark Wang, Pres., Hilton Grand Vacations Co., LLC
Matt Richardson, Head-Architecture/Design/Construction/Real Estate

Phone: 703-883-1000 **Fax:**
Toll-Free: 800-445-8667
Address: 7930 Jones Branch Dr., Ste. 1100, McLean, VA 22102 US

GROWTH PLANS/SPECIAL FEATURES:

Hilton Hotels Corp. (HHC), founded in 1919, owns, manages and develops hotels, resorts and timeshare properties; and franchises lodging properties. HHC consists of 10 hotel brands and more than 3,600 hotels in 81 countries around the world. Its hotel brands include Hilton, Hilton Garden Inn, Doubletree, Embassy Suites, Homewood Suites, Home2 Suites, Hampton Inn, Conrad Hotels and Resorts and The Waldorf Astoria Collection. HHC owns the worldwide rights to develop and market Hilton and Conrad brands. Although the majority of the company's hotels are located within the U.S., the company also operates luxury lodgings in locations such as Thailand, Ireland, Singapore, Uruguay, Indonesia and Egypt. Hilton Worldwide Resorts offers 54 self-contained resorts in the Middle East, Asia Pacific, Europe, the Americas, the Indian Ocean and the Caribbean. Through Hilton Garden Vacations Company, LLC, the firm also owns and manages several vacation timeshare properties with three more under development. HHonors, the firm's loyalty enrollment program for returning customers, has over 25 million members and includes partner benefits with JetBlue Airlines. The firm is investing in technologies such as check-in kiosks to facilitate an easier and faster check-in process for its customers in partnership with IBM. HHC, in separate deals with three real estate groups, is developing over 55 properties in Russia, the U.K. and Central America, all planned to be completed by 2012. In July 2010, AT&T agreed to provide a fully-managed suite of Wi-Fi and Internet services to all Hilton brand hotels. In October 2010, the firm opened to national sales office in Abu Dhabi and Dubai. In February 2011, Home2 Suites by Hilton opened its first property in Fayetteville, North Carolina. In March 2011, Doubletree opened a hotel in Aqaba, Jordan.

FINANCIALS:

Sales and profits are in thousands of dollars—add 000 to get the full amount. 2010 Note: Financial information for 2010 was not available for all companies at press time.

2010 Sales: $9,000,000 | 2010 Profits: $
2009 Sales: $8,000,000 | 2009 Profits: $
2008 Sales: $7,770,000 | 2008 Profits: $
2007 Sales: $8,090,000 | 2007 Profits: $121,000
2006 Sales: $7,438,000 | 2006 Profits: $572,000

U.S. Stock Ticker: Private
Int'l Ticker:
Int'l Exchange:
Employees: 135,000 Fiscal Year Ends: 12/31
Parent Company: BLACKSTONE GROUP LP (THE)

SALARIES/BENEFITS:

Pension Plan:	ESOP Stock Plan:	Profit Sharing:	Top Exec. Salary: $	Bonus: $
Savings Plan: Y	Stock Purch. Plan:		Second Exec. Salary: $	Bonus: $

OTHER THOUGHTS:

Apparent Women Officers or Directors: 1
Hot Spot for Advancement for Women/Minorities:

LOCATIONS: ("Y" = Yes)

West:	Southwest:	Midwest:	Southeast:	Northeast:	International:
Y	Y	Y	Y	Y	Y

Sales, profits and employees may be estimates. Financial information, benefits and other data can change quickly and may vary from those stated here.

HONDA OF AMERICA MANUFACTURING INC www.ohio.honda.com

Industry Group Code: 33611

Management:		Sales/Marketing:		Liberal Arts:		Information Sys.:		Professionals:		Tech./Scientific:	
Mgmt. Trainees:		Marketing Pros.:	Y	Gen. Writing/Editing:	Y	Info. Mgmt.:	Y	Finance/Acct.:	Y	Engineers, Elec.:	Y
Experienced Mgmt.:	Y	Retail Sales:		Tech. Writing:	Y	Software Dev.:	Y	Law:	Y	Engineers, Other:	Y
Int'l Business:		Comm./Industrial:	Y	Graphic Arts/Photog.:		Hardware Dev.:		HR/Other:	Y	Health/Lab:	
MBA Grads:	Y	Sales Trainees:		Music:		Consulting/Other:		Training:	Y	Science/Research:	
		Advertising Pros.:	Y	Broadcasting:				Health Care:		Petroleum/Chem.:	
				Other:				Consulting:		Math/Other:	

TYPES OF BUSINESS:

Automobile Manufacturing
Engine & Parts Manufacturing
Motorcycle Manufacturing

BRANDS/DIVISIONS/AFFILIATES:

Honda Motor Co Ltd
Accord
Acura
Civic
CR-V
Honda of Canada Manufacturing, Inc.
Honda Transmission Manufacturing of America

CONTACTS: *Note: Officers with more than one job title may be intentionally listed here more than once.*

Hidenobu Iwata, CEO
Hidenobu Iwata, Pres.
Tom Shoupe, Pres., Honda Mftg. of Alabama, LLC
Nobuyuki Sanui, Pres., Honda of Canada Mftg.
Mike Wallace, Mgr.-Honda MRO Purchasing

Phone: 937-642-5000	**Fax:** 937-644-6575
Toll-Free:	
Address: 24000 Honda Pkwy., Marysville, OH 43040 US	

GROWTH PLANS/SPECIAL FEATURES:

Honda of America Manufacturing, Inc. (HAM), a subsidiary of Honda Motor Co., Ltd., manufactures engines, transmissions, motorcycles, cars and light trucks for the North American market. The firm's five main plants are in Marysville, Anna and East Liberty, Ohio. The Marysville auto plant builds approximately 440,000 vehicles per year, including more than 90% of Honda Accord Sedans sold in the U.S. The Anna engine plant produces engine blocks and heads, camshafts, crankshafts, driveshafts, cylinder sleeves and brakes, producing more than 1.18 million V-6 and four-cylinder engines annually. This plant also performs engine testing. The East Liberty auto plant produces Accord Crosstour, Honda Element and CR-V vehicles. The 1.9 million square foot plant produces 240,000 cars and light trucks annually, as well as exporting stamped parts to Honda of Canada Manufacturing, Inc. for the production of its Civic models. The Ohio plants produce the Accord Coupe and Sedan; the Acura TL and RDX; and the CR-V. Honda Motor Co. has other subsidiaries and operations based in Ohio, including Honda Transmission Manufacturing of America, Inc., which operates a transmission manufacturing plant that produces 800,000 automatic transmissions per year, and research and development and engineering facilities. The company has additional manufacturing operations in Georgia, North Carolina, Indiana, Alabama and South Carolina. The company's Honda plants in Ohio have produced more than 14 million automobiles, 1 million motorcycles, 2 million all-terrain vehicles (ATVs), 17 million engines and over 13 million automatic transmissions.

Employees are offered medical, dental, vision and prescription drug insurance; a post-retirement medical plan; education reimbursement; relocation assistance; credit union membership; a pension plan; a 401(k) plan; a stock purchase plan; and a college savings program.

FINANCIALS: **Sales and profits are in thousands of dollars—add 000 to get the full amount. 2010 Note: Financial information for 2010 was not available for all companies at press time.**

2010 Sales: $27,000,000	2010 Profits: $	**U.S. Stock Ticker: Subsidiary**
2009 Sales: $	2009 Profits: $	**Int'l Ticker:**
2008 Sales: $	2008 Profits: $	Int'l Exchange:
2007 Sales: $	2007 Profits: $	Employees: 13,500 Fiscal Year Ends: 3/31
2006 Sales: $	2006 Profits: $	Parent Company: HONDA MOTOR CO LTD

SALARIES/BENEFITS:

Pension Plan: Y	ESOP Stock Plan:	Profit Sharing:	Top Exec. Salary: $	Bonus: $
Savings Plan: Y	Stock Purch. Plan: Y		Second Exec. Salary: $	Bonus: $

OTHER THOUGHTS:

Apparent Women Officers or Directors:
Hot Spot for Advancement for Women/Minorities:

LOCATIONS: ("Y" = Yes)

West:	Southwest:	Midwest:	Southeast:	Northeast:	International:
		Y	Y	Y	

HOSPIRA INC

www.hospira.com

Industry Group Code: 325412A

Management:		Sales/Marketing:		Liberal Arts:		Information Sys.:		Professionals:		Tech./Scientific:	
Mgmt. Trainees:		Marketing Pros.:	Y	Gen. Writing/Editing:		Info. Mgmt.:	Y	Finance/Acct.:	Y	Engineers, Elec.:	Y
Experienced Mgmt.:	Y	Retail Sales:		Tech. Writing:	Y	Software Dev.:		Law:	Y	Engineers, Other:	Y
Int'l Business:	Y	Comm./Industrial:	Y	Graphic Arts/Photog.:	Y	Hardware Dev.:		HR/Other:	Y	Health/Lab:	Y
MBA Grads:	Y	Sales Trainees:		Music:		Consulting/Other:		Training:		Science/Research:	
		Advertising Pros.:		Broadcasting:				Health Care:	Y	Petroleum/Chem.:	Y
				Other:	Y			Consulting:		Math/Other:	Y

TYPES OF BUSINESS:

Pharmaceutical Development
Generic Pharmaceuticals
Medication Delivery Systems
Anesthetics
Injectable Medications
Diagnostic Imaging Agents
Contract Manufacturing

BRANDS/DIVISIONS/AFFILIATES:

One2One
TheraDoc
LifeCare PCA
Symbiq
Retacrit
GemStar
LifeShield
CLAVE

CONTACTS: *Note: Officers with more than one job title may be intentionally listed here more than once.*

Christopher B. Begley, CEO
Terrence C. Kearney, COO
Thomas E. Werner, CFO
Anil G. D'Souza, VP-Global Mktg.
Ken Meyers, Sr. VP-Organizational Transformation & People Dev.
Sumant Ramachandra, Chief Science Officer/Sr. VP-R&D & Medical Affairs
Daphne E. Jones, CIO/Sr. VP
Brian J. Smith, General Counsel/Sr. VP/Sec.
James H. Hardy, Sr. VP-Oper.
Anil G. D'Souza, VP-Corp. Dev.
Thomas E. Werner, Sr. VP-Finance
Francois Dubois, Sr. VP-Quality
Ron Squarer, Sr. VP/Chief Commercial Officer
Christopher B. Begley, Chmn.

Phone: 224-212-2000 **Fax:** 224-212-3350
Toll-Free: 877-946-7747
Address: 275 N. Field Dr., Lake Forest, IL 60045 US

GROWTH PLANS/SPECIAL FEATURES:

Hospira, Inc. is a global specialty pharmaceutical and medication delivery company. The company's primary operations involve the research and development of generic pharmaceuticals, pharmaceuticals based on proprietary pharmaceuticals whose patents have expired. The company's activities include the development, manufacture and marketing of generic acute-care and oncology injectables, as well as integrated infusion therapy and medication management systems. Hospira divides its products into three categories: specialty injectable pharmaceuticals, other pharmaceuticals and medication management systems. The specialty injectable pharmaceuticals segment consists of approximately 200 injectable generic drugs; the proprietary sedation drug Precedex; Nivestim, a biosimilar filgrastim used for the treatment of low white blood cells in patients who have received a chemotherapeutic agent; and Retacrit, a biogeneric version of erythropoietin, used primarily in the treatment of anemia in dialysis and in certain oncology applications. The other pharmaceuticals segment consists primarily of large volume I.V. solutions and nutritional products. Through its One2One manufacturing services group, this segment also offers contract manufacturing services to proprietary pharmaceutical and biotechnology companies for formulation development, filling and finishing of injectable and oral drugs worldwide. The medication management systems segment's products include electronic drug delivery pumps under the Symbiq, LifeCare PCA, GemStar and Plum A+ brands; safety software; and administration sets that are used to deliver I.V. fluids and medications. Other devices include gravity administration sets and other device products, which include needlestick safety products. Products in this segment are sold under the LifeShield, CLAVE and MicroClave brands. In March 2010, the company acquired the generic injectable pharmaceuticals business of Indian firm Orchid Chemicals & Pharmaceuticals Ltd. for $400 million. In December 2010, the firm acquired Javelin Pharmaceuticals, Inc. through subsidiary Discus Acquisition Corporation.

Employees are offered life, disability, medical and dental insurance; flexible spending accounts; an employee assistance plan; adoption assistance; and tuition assistance.

FINANCIALS: **Sales and profits are in thousands of dollars—add 000 to get the full amount. 2010 Note: Financial information for 2010 was not available for all companies at press time.**

2010 Sales: $3,917,200	2010 Profits: $357,200
2009 Sales: $3,879,300	2009 Profits: $403,900
2008 Sales: $3,629,500	2008 Profits: $320,900
2007 Sales: $3,436,238	2007 Profits: $136,758
2006 Sales: $2,688,505	2006 Profits: $237,679

U.S. Stock Ticker: HSP
Int'l Ticker:
Int'l Exchange:
Employees: 14,000 Fiscal Year Ends: 12/31
Parent Company:

SALARIES/BENEFITS:

Pension Plan: Y	ESOP Stock Plan:	Profit Sharing:	Top Exec. Salary: $1,050,000	Bonus: $2,100,000
Savings Plan: Y	Stock Purch. Plan:		Second Exec. Salary: $625,000	Bonus: $1,000,000

OTHER THOUGHTS:

Apparent Women Officers or Directors: 3
Hot Spot for Advancement for Women/Minorities: Y

LOCATIONS: ("Y" = Yes)

West:	Southwest:	Midwest:	Southeast:	Northeast:	International:
Y	Y	Y		Y	Y

Sales, profits and employees may be estimates. Financial information, benefits and other data can change quickly and may vary from those stated here.

HUMANA INC

www.humana.com

Industry Group Code: 524114

Management:		Sales/Marketing:		Liberal Arts:		Information Sys.:		Professionals:		Tech./Scientific:	
Mgmt. Trainees:	Y	Marketing Pros.:	Y	Gen. Writing/Editing:	Y	Info. Mgmt.:	Y	Finance/Acct.:	Y	Engineers, Elec.:	
Experienced Mgmt.:	Y	Retail Sales:		Tech. Writing:	Y	Software Dev.:	Y	Law:	Y	Engineers, Other:	
Int'l Business:	Y	Comm./Industrial:	Y	Graphic Arts/Photog.:	Y	Hardware Dev.:		HR/Other:	Y	Health/Lab:	
MBA Grads:	Y	Sales Trainees:		Music:		Consulting/Other:		Training:	Y	Science/Research:	
		Advertising Pros.:	Y	Broadcasting:				Health Care:	Y	Petroleum/Chem.:	
				Other:	Y			Consulting:		Math/Other:	

TYPES OF BUSINESS:

Insurance-Medical & Health, HMOs & PPOs
Insurance-Dental
Employee Benefit Plans
Insurance-Group Life
Wellness Programs

BRANDS/DIVISIONS/AFFILIATES:

HumanaDental
HumanaOne
Humana Ventures
Humana Medicare
Concentra, Inc.
Arcadian Management Services

CONTACTS: *Note: Officers with more than one job title may be intentionally listed here more than once.*

Michael B. McCallister, CEO
James E. Murray, COO/Sr. VP
Michael B. McCallister, Pres.
James H. Bloem, CFO/Sr. VP/Treas.
Raja Rajamannar, Chief Innovation & Mktg. Officer/Sr. VP
Bonita C. Hathcock, Chief Human Resources Officer/Sr. VP
Brian LeClaire, CIO/Sr. VP
Thomas J. Liston, Sr. VP-Senior Prod.
Christopher M. Todoroff, General Counsel/Sr. VP
Paul B. Kusserow, Chief Strategy & Corp. Dev. Officer/Sr. VP
Heidi S. Margulis, Sr. VP-Public Affairs
Steven E. McCulley, Principal Acct. Officer/VP/Controller
Brian LeClaire, Chief Service Officer
Michael B. McCallister, Chmn.

Phone: 502-580-1000	**Fax:** 502-580-3639
Toll-Free:	
Address: 500 W. Main St., Louisville, KY 40202 US	

GROWTH PLANS/SPECIAL FEATURES:

Humana, Inc. is a leading health benefits company in the U.S., serving approximately 10.2 million medical benefit plan members and 7.1 million specialty products members in the U.S. and Puerto Rico. It operates in two segments: government and commercial. The government segment consists of beneficiaries of government benefit programs and includes three lines of business: Medicare, Military and Medicaid. The company offers at least one type of Medicare plan in all 50 states. Approximately 76% of the firm's premiums and administrative services fees are derived from contracts with the federal government, including 17% related to its Medicare Advantage contracts in Florida with the Centers for Medicare and Medicaid Services and 11% related to its military services contracts. Humana's commercial operations, which are offered to both employer groups and individuals, consist of medical and specialty services. HumanaDental covers 3.9 million customers, making it one of the largest dental carriers in the U.S. HumanaOne offers insurance coverage to individuals. Humana Ventures is a capital investing branch of Humana. Finally, Humana Medicare offers plans for Medicare patients to help them with drug and medical coverage. The company also offers a wide variety of services to employers, such as workers' compensation, dental plans, group life plans and an administrative-services-only plan. Humana provides health benefits and related services to companies ranging from fewer than 10 to over 10,000 employees. Many of its products are offered through HMOs (health maintenance organizations), Private Fee-For-Service (PFFS) and preferred provider organizations (PPOs). In December 2010, Human acquired health care company Concentra, Inc. for roughly $790 million. In August 2011, the firm agreed to acquire HMO Arcadian Management Services.

Employees are offered medical, dental and life insurance; long-term care benefits; healthcare spending accounts; a 401(k) and retirement plan; short- and long-term disability coverage; short-term income protection (STIP) for illness; tuition reimbursement; adoption assistance; dependent care flexible spending accounts; and a work-life program.

FINANCIALS: **Sales and profits are in thousands of dollars—add 000 to get the full amount. 2010 Note: Financial information for 2010 was not available for all companies at press time.**

2010 Sales: $33,868,208	2010 Profits: $1,099,390	**U.S. Stock Ticker: HUM**
2009 Sales: $30,960,414	2009 Profits: $1,039,675	**Int'l Ticker:**
2008 Sales: $28,946,372	2008 Profits: $647,154	Int'l Exchange:
2007 Sales: $25,289,989	2007 Profits: $833,684	Employees: 35,200 Fiscal Year Ends: 12/31
2006 Sales: $21,416,537	2006 Profits: $487,423	Parent Company:

SALARIES/BENEFITS:

Pension Plan: Y	ESOP Stock Plan:	Profit Sharing:	Top Exec. Salary: $1,026,182	Bonus: $2,052,364
Savings Plan: Y	Stock Purch. Plan: Y		Second Exec. Salary: $676,087	Bonus: $1,014,131

OTHER THOUGHTS:

Apparent Women Officers or Directors: 3
Hot Spot for Advancement for Women/Minorities: Y

LOCATIONS: ("Y" = Yes)

West:	Southwest:	Midwest:	Southeast:	Northeast:	International:
Y	Y	Y	Y	Y	Y

Sales, profits and employees may be estimates. Financial information, benefits and other data can change quickly and may vary from those stated here.

HYATT HOTELS CORPORATION

www.hyatt.com

Industry Group Code: 721110

Management:		Sales/Marketing:		Liberal Arts:		Information Sys.:		Professionals:		Tech./Scientific:	
Mgmt. Trainees:	Y	Marketing Pros.:	Y	Gen. Writing/Editing:	Y	Info. Mgmt.:	Y	Finance/Acct.:	Y	Engineers, Elec.:	
Experienced Mgmt.:	Y	Retail Sales:		Tech. Writing:		Software Dev.:	Y	Law:	Y	Engineers, Other:	
Int'l Business:	Y	Comm./Industrial:	Y	Graphic Arts/Photog.:	Y	Hardware Dev.:		HR/Other:	Y	Health/Lab:	
MBA Grads:	Y	Sales Trainees:	Y	Music:		Consulting/Other:		Training:	Y	Science/Research:	
		Advertising Pros.:	Y	Broadcasting:				Health Care:		Petroleum/Chem.:	
				Other:	Y			Consulting:		Math/Other:	

TYPES OF BUSINESS:

Hotel Ownership & Management
Timeshares
Golf Courses
Gaming
Retirement Communities
Motels & Inns
Hotel Franchising

BRANDS/DIVISIONS/AFFILIATES:

Hyatt Regency
Grand Hyatt
Hyatt Resorts
Hyatt Summerfield Suites
Andaz
Hyatt Vacation Club
Hyatt Gold Passport
Park Hyatt

CONTACTS: *Note: Officers with more than one job title may be intentionally listed here more than once.*

Mark S. Hoplamazian, CEO
Mark S. Hoplamazian, Pres.
Harmit J. Singh, CFO
John Wallis, Global Head-Mktg. & Brand Strategy
Robert W. K. Webb, Chief Human Resources Officer
Rena Hozore Reiss, General Counsel/Sec.
H. Charles Floyd, COO-North America Oper.
Stephen G. Haggerty, Global Head-Dev. & Real Estate
Katie Meyer, VP-Corp. Comm.
Atish Shah, Sr. VP-Investor Rel.
Steve Sokal, Sr. VP-Global Asset Mgmt.
Sal Mendoza, VP-Diversity & Inclusion
Thomas J. Pritzker, Chmn.
Rakesh Sarna, COO-Int'l Oper.

Phone: 312-750-1234 **Fax:** 312-750-8550
Toll-Free:
Address: 71 S. Wacker Dr., 12th Fl., Chicago, IL 60606 US

GROWTH PLANS/SPECIAL FEATURES:

Hyatt Hotels Corporation (Hyatt) owns, operates, manages and franchises full-service luxury hotels in 45 countries across the globe. Its portfolio of 453 Hyatt-branded properties includes 177 managed hotels for third-party owners; 132 franchised hotels; 90 owned properties; 24 properties managed by Hyatt owned by unconsolidated hospitality ventures; 15 managed vacation ownership properties; and nine residential properties. Hyatt's operations consist of eight brands. Its best known brand, Hyatt Regency, caters mainly to corporate travel clients. Grand Hyatt hotels cater to leisure and business travelers and include accommodations for banquets and conferences. Hyatt Resorts often feature professional, PGA golf courses; adventure travel opportunities, such as scuba diving, biking, hot air balloon trips or horseback riding; Hyatt Pure spas; and activities for kids and families. Hyatt Summerfield Suites, an all-suites hotel concept designed to feel more like home, offers 32-inch HDTVs, a full kitchen and complementary shopping service for its outdoor BBQ-pits. Hyatt Place hotels feature high-tech amenities such as 42-inch HDTVs in every room, free Wi-Fi Internet access and a 24-hour, touch-screen room service ordering system. Park Hyatt hotels are smaller, full-service luxury hotels featuring world class art and restaurants in a few of the world's most visited cities. The Andaz branded hotels are boutique-style hotels that feature restaurants and bars aimed at local clientele as well as single travelers. Hyatt Vacation Club offers vacation ownership and vacation rental opportunities, offering members timeshare or points-based resort vacation opportunities. Hyatt's rewards program, Hyatt Gold Passport, has over 10 million members. In October 2010, Hyatt announced management agreements for 11 new Hyatt-branded hotels in China. In March 2011, it signed management agreements for nine new hotels in India, bringing total development in the country to 38 properties.

Employees of Hyatt receive complementary hotel rooms; medical, dental, vision and prescription drug coverage; tuition assistance; and life insurance.

FINANCIALS: **Sales and profits are in thousands of dollars—add 000 to get the full amount. 2010 Note: Financial information for 2010 was not available for all companies at press time.**

2010 Sales: $3,527,000	2010 Profits: $66,000	**U.S. Stock Ticker: H**
2009 Sales: $3,330,000	2009 Profits: $-43,000	**Int'l Ticker:**
2008 Sales: $3,835,000	2008 Profits: $168,000	Int'l Exchange:
2007 Sales: $3,750,000	2007 Profits: $	Employees: 130,000 Fiscal Year Ends: 12/31
2006 Sales: $3,500,000	2006 Profits: $	Parent Company:

SALARIES/BENEFITS:

Pension Plan:	ESOP Stock Plan:	Profit Sharing:	Top Exec. Salary: $979,167	Bonus: $983,000
Savings Plan: Y	Stock Purch. Plan:		Second Exec. Salary: $581,000	Bonus: $370,000

OTHER THOUGHTS:

Apparent Women Officers or Directors: 2
Hot Spot for Advancement for Women/Minorities:

LOCATIONS: ("Y" = Yes)

West:	Southwest:	Midwest:	Southeast:	Northeast:	International:
Y	Y	Y	Y	Y	Y

IAC/INTERACTIVECORP

www.iac.com

Industry Group Code: 519130

Management:		**Sales/Marketing:**		**Liberal Arts:**		**Information Sys.:**		**Professionals:**		**Tech./Scientific:**	
Mgmt. Trainees:	Y	Marketing Pros.:	Y	Gen. Writing/Editing:	Y	Info. Mgmt.:	Y	Finance/Acct.:	Y	Engineers, Elec.:	Y
Experienced Mgmt.:	Y	Retail Sales:		Tech. Writing:		Software Dev.:	Y	Law:	Y	Engineers, Other:	
Int'l Business:	Y	Comm./Industrial:	Y	Graphic Arts/Photog.:	Y	Hardware Dev.:		HR/Other:	Y	Health/Lab:	
MBA Grads:	Y	Sales Trainees:		Music:		Consulting/Other:		Training:	Y	Science/Research:	
		Advertising Pros.:	Y	Broadcasting:	Y			Health Care:		Petroleum/Chem.:	
				Other:	Y			Consulting:		Math/Other:	

TYPES OF BUSINESS:

E-Commerce, Online Advertising & Search Engines
Online Personals & Dating Services
Online Entertainment & Shopping Directories
Service Provider Listings Online

BRANDS/DIVISIONS/AFFILIATES:

Ask.com
PeopleMedia
Evite
Shoebuy
Pronto
Meetic
Match.com
Excite.com

CONTACTS:

Note: Officers with more than one job title may be intentionally listed here more than once.

Greg Blatt, CEO
Thomas J. McInerney, CFO/Exec. VP
Jason Stewart, Chief Admin. Officer/Sr. VP
Gregg Winiarski, General Counsel/Sr. VP
Mark Stein, Sr. VP-Corp. Dev.
Stacy Simpson, Sr. VP-Global Comm. & Brand Mktg.
Nick Stoumpas, Sr. VP-Investor Rel./Treas.
Michael Schwerdtman, Controller/Sr. VP
Shana Fisher, Sr. VP-Strategy, Mergers & Acquisitions
Joanne Hawkins, Sr. VP/Deputy General Counsel
Mandy Ginsberg, Exec. VP/Gen. Mgr.-Match.com
Greg Morrow, Sr. VP-Tax
Barry Diller, Chmn./Sr. Exec.

Phone: 212-314-7300	**Fax:** 212-314-7309
Toll-Free:	
Address: 555 W. 18th St., New York, NY 10011 US	

GROWTH PLANS/SPECIAL FEATURES:

IAC/InterActiveCorp. operates more than 50 Internet brands serving over 247.3 million unique visitors in over 30 countries. The firm operates through four segments: Search, Media & Other, Match and ServiceMagic. The Search segment consists of the firm's search business, which includes Ask.com and other destination search web sites through which the firm provides search and related advertising services; and Citysearch, a leading online local city guide. The Media & Other segment includes Shoebuy, an Internet retailer of footwear and related apparel and accessories and generally acts as an agent in connection with the purchase of merchandise through its various web sites, passing purchases made by customers through its various web sites on to the relevant vendors for fulfillment and shipping; Pronto, a comparison search engine through which consumers can search and compare prices for a range of merchandise offered by online retailers; and Evite, an online social planning web site. Additional web sites in this segment include Gifts.com, Connected Ventures, InstantAction.com, Electus and The Daily Beast. The Match segment provides subscription-based online personals services in the U.S. and various international countries, primarily through Match.com. The division provides online personals services to approximately 1.3 million subscribers. The Match segment also includes the operations of PeopleMedia, a recently acquired targeted dating site operator; and other dating sites, such as SinglesNet.com, Chemistry.com, BlackPeopleMeet.com and SeniorPeopleMeet.com. ServiceMagic is an online marketplace that connects consumers, by way of various patented and patent-pending proprietary technologies, with 67,000 service professionals covering over 700 specialties. Other IAC portals include MyWay.com, Excite.com, Dictionary.com, GirlSense.com and iWon.com. In March 2010, Match.com and Meetic formed a joint venture to provide personals services in Latin America.

FINANCIALS:

Sales and profits are in thousands of dollars—add 000 to get the full amount. 2010 Note: Financial information for 2010 was not available for all companies at press time.

2010 Sales: $1,636,815	2010 Profits: $99,359	**U.S. Stock Ticker: IACI**
2009 Sales: $1,346,695	2009 Profits: $-978,822	**Int'l Ticker:**
2008 Sales: $1,410,078	2008 Profits: $-156,201	Int'l Exchange:
2007 Sales: $1,332,600	2007 Profits: $-144,069	Employees: 3,200 Fiscal Year Ends: 12/31
2006 Sales: $5,908,902	2006 Profits: $187,065	Parent Company:

SALARIES/BENEFITS:

Pension Plan:	ESOP Stock Plan:	Profit Sharing:	Top Exec. Salary: $650,000	Bonus: $1,200,000
Savings Plan: Y	Stock Purch. Plan:		Second Exec. Salary: $650,000	Bonus: $1,200,000

OTHER THOUGHTS:

Apparent Women Officers or Directors: 4
Hot Spot for Advancement for Women/Minorities: Y

LOCATIONS: ("Y" = Yes)

West:	Southwest:	Midwest:	Southeast:	Northeast:	International:
Y	Y	Y		Y	Y

ICF INTERNATIONAL INC

www.icfi.com

Industry Group Code: 54161

Management:		Sales/Marketing:		Liberal Arts:		Information Sys.:		Professionals:		Tech./Scientific:	
Mgmt. Trainees:		Marketing Pros.:	Y	Gen. Writing/Editing:	Y	Info. Mgmt.:	Y	Finance/Acct.:	Y	Engineers, Elec.:	
Experienced Mgmt.:	Y	Retail Sales:		Tech. Writing:	Y	Software Dev.:	Y	Law:	Y	Engineers, Other:	
Int'l Business:	Y	Comm./Industrial:	Y	Graphic Arts/Photog.:		Hardware Dev.:		HR/Other:	Y	Health/Lab:	
MBA Grads:	Y	Sales Trainees:		Music:		Consulting/Other:	Y	Training:		Science/Research:	
		Advertising Pros.:		Broadcasting:				Health Care:		Petroleum/Chem.:	
				Other:				Consulting:	Y	Math/Other:	

TYPES OF BUSINESS:

Consulting Services
Information Technology Services
Management Services
Government Program Implementation and Management

BRANDS/DIVISIONS/AFFILIATES:

ICF Consulting
Jacob & Sundstrom, Inc.
Marbek Resource Consultants Ltd

CONTACTS: *Note: Officers with more than one job title may be intentionally listed here more than once.*

Sudhakar Kesavan, CEO
John Wasson, COO
John Wasson, Pres.
Sandra Murray, Interim CFO
Isabel Reiff, Exec. VP-Bus. Dev. & Mktg
Candice Mendenhall, Sr. VP-Human Resources
Ellen Glover, Exec. VP-Tech. & Mgmt. Solutions
Sandra Murray, Sr. VP-Admin. & Contracts
Douglas Beck, Sr. VP/Dir.-Corp. Dev.
Gerald Croan, Exec. VP-Corp. Strategy
Frank Abramcheck, Sr. VP-Market Research & Bus. Processing
Jeanne Townend, Sr. VP-Health, Education & Social Programs
Philip Mihlmester, Sr. VP-Energy, Climate & Transportation
Sudhakar Kesavan, Chmn.
Christina Cameron, Sr. VP-Int'l Bus., Europe & Asia

Phone: 703-934-3603	**Fax:** 703-934-3740
Toll-Free: 800-532-4783	
Address: 9300 Lee Highway, Fairfax, VA 22031-1207 US	

GROWTH PLANS/SPECIAL FEATURES:

ICF International, Inc. (ICFI) provides management, consulting, technology and implementation services to the U.S. government and other governmental, commercial and international clients. ICFI organizes its services around three primary markets: energy, environment and infrastructure; health, human services and social programs; and homeland security and defense. Within the energy, environment and infrastructure market, ICFI assists energy firms in the development, analysis and implementation of business operation strategies that take the natural environment and related government legislation into account, as well as providing advisory services related to climate change. The firm advises clients on a range of topics related to electric power, traditional fuels and renewable sources of energy, with special areas of focus including power market analysis and modeling; transmissions analysis; electric system reliability standards; energy asset valuation; regulatory and litigation support; fuels market analysis; air regulatory strategy; and renewable energy and green power. Through its health, human services and social programs segment, ICFI provides research, consulting, development, implementation support and improvement services for a variety of programs at the national, regional and local levels, including programs sponsored by the U.S. Department of Health and Human Services, the National Institutes of Health, the Centers for Disease Control, the Department of Justice and the Department of Housing and Urban Development. Through its homeland security and defense division, the company develops infrastructure protection plans, provides strategic planning and technology solutions and manages programs designed to test the emergency preparedness of local communities, such as those near nuclear power plants. Recent acquisitions include Jacob & Sundstrom, Inc., a technology security firm specializing in cyber-security and identity management; and in January 2011, Marbek Resource Consultants Ltd.

ICFI offers employees flexible spending accounts; tuition reimbursement; medical, dental and vision coverage; life and disability insurance; a 401(k) plan; on-site massage therapy; and commuter benefits for public transportation.

FINANCIALS: **Sales and profits are in thousands of dollars—add 000 to get the full amount. 2010 Note: Financial information for 2010 was not available for all companies at press time.**

2010 Sales: $764,734	2010 Profits: $27,171
2009 Sales: $674,399	2009 Profits: $22,356
2008 Sales: $697,426	2008 Profits: $28,723
2007 Sales: $727,120	2007 Profits: $40,556
2006 Sales: $331,279	2006 Profits: $11,867

U.S. Stock Ticker: ICFI
Int'l Ticker:
Int'l Exchange:
Employees: 3,700 Fiscal Year Ends: 12/31
Parent Company:

SALARIES/BENEFITS:

Pension Plan:	ESOP Stock Plan:	Profit Sharing:	Top Exec. Salary: $480,002	Bonus: $469,440
Savings Plan: Y	Stock Purch. Plan:		Second Exec. Salary: $400,005	Bonus: $312,960

OTHER THOUGHTS:

Apparent Women Officers or Directors: 7
Hot Spot for Advancement for Women/Minorities: Y

LOCATIONS: ("Y" = Yes)

West:	Southwest:	Midwest:	Southeast:	Northeast:	International:
Y	Y	Y	Y	Y	Y

Sales, profits and employees may be estimates. Financial information, benefits and other data can change quickly and may vary from those stated here.

IDEXX LABORATORIES INC

www.idexx.com

Industry Group Code: 334510

Management:		Sales/Marketing:		Liberal Arts:		Information Sys.:		Professionals:		Tech./Scientific:	
Mgmt. Trainees:	Y	Marketing Pros.:	Y	Gen. Writing/Editing:		Info. Mgmt.:	Y	Finance/Acct.:	Y	Engineers, Elec.:	Y
Experienced Mgmt.:	Y	Retail Sales:		Tech. Writing:	Y	Software Dev.:	Y	Law:	Y	Engineers, Other:	Y
Int'l Business:	Y	Comm./Industrial:	Y	Graphic Arts/Photog.:		Hardware Dev.:		HR/Other:	Y	Health/Lab:	Y
MBA Grads:	Y	Sales Trainees:		Music:		Consulting/Other:		Training:	Y	Science/Research:	Y
		Advertising Pros.:		Broadcasting:				Health Care:	Y	Petroleum/Chem.:	
				Other:				Consulting:		Math/Other:	

TYPES OF BUSINESS:

Veterinary Laboratory Testing Products
Point-of-Care Diagnostic Products
Veterinary Pharmaceuticals
Information Management Software
Food & Water Testing Products
Laboratory Testing Services
Consulting

BRANDS/DIVISIONS/AFFILIATES:

VetTest
VetLyte
VetStat
LaserCyte
SNAPshot DX
Coag Dx
Colisure
ProCyte Dx Hematology Analyzer

CONTACTS: *Note: Officers with more than one job title may be intentionally listed here more than once.*

Jonathan W. Ayers, CEO
Jonathan W. Ayers, Pres.
Merilee Raines, CFO/VP
Giovani Twigge, VP-Human Resources
William E. Brown, III, Chief Scientific Officer/VP
Conan R. Deady, General Counsel/Corp. VP/Sec.
Dan Meyaard, VP-Worldwide Oper.
Merilee Raines, Treas.
James Polewaczyck, Corp. VP-Rapid Assay & Digital Radiography
Michael Williams, VP-Instrument Diagnostics
Thomas J. Dupree, VP-Companion Animal Group
Johnny D. Powers, VP-IDEXX Reference Laboratories
Jonathan W. Ayers, Chmn.
Ali Naqui, Corp. VP-Int'l

Phone: 207-556-0300	**Fax:** 207-556-4286
Toll-Free: 800-548-6733	
Address: 1 Idexx Dr., Westbrook, ME 04092 US	

GROWTH PLANS/SPECIAL FEATURES:

IDEXX Laboratories, Inc. develops, manufactures and distributes products and provides services for the veterinary and the food and water testing markets. The company operates in two business segments: The Companion Animal Group, which provides products and services for the veterinary market; Water Quality; and the Production Animal Segment, which provides products for production animal health. The company also operated two smaller segments: Dairy, comprising products for dairy quality, and OPTI Medical, comprising products for the human medical diagnostic market. Its primary business focus is on animal health. IDEXX currently markets an integrated and flexible suite of in-house laboratory analyzers for use in veterinary practices, which is referred to as the VetLab suite of analyzers. The suite includes several instrument systems, as well as associated proprietary consumable products such as VetTest, VetLyte, VetStat and LaserCyte analyzers; the IDEXX SNAPshot Dx; ProCyte Dx Hematology Analyzer; and the Coag Dx Analyzer, among other offerings. In addition, it also provides assay kits, software and instrumentation for accurate assessment of infectious disease in production animals, such as cattle, swine and poultry. The company currently offers commercial veterinary laboratory and consulting services throughout the U.S. The Water Quality segment's products include Colilert-18 and Colisure tests, which simultaneously detect total coliforms and E. coli in water. IDEXX's principal product for use in testing for antibiotic residue in milk is the SNAP Beta-Lactam test.

IDEXX offers its employee health, dental and life insurance; a 401(k) plan; short- and long-term disability programs; flexible spending accounts; sick days; vacation and paid holidays; an employee stock purchase plan; and employee assistance programs.

FINANCIALS: **Sales and profits are in thousands of dollars—add 000 to get the full amount. 2010 Note: Financial information for 2010 was not available for all companies at press time.**

2010 Sales: $1,103,392	2010 Profits: $141,284	**U.S. Stock Ticker: IDXX**
2009 Sales: $1,031,633	2009 Profits: $122,225	**Int'l Ticker:**
2008 Sales: $1,024,030	2008 Profits: $116,169	Int'l Exchange:
2007 Sales: $922,555	2007 Profits: $94,014	Employees: 4,800 Fiscal Year Ends: 12/31
2006 Sales: $739,117	2006 Profits: $93,678	Parent Company:

SALARIES/BENEFITS:

Pension Plan:	ESOP Stock Plan:	Profit Sharing:	Top Exec. Salary: $700,000	Bonus: $900,000
Savings Plan: Y	Stock Purch. Plan: Y		Second Exec. Salary: $316,558	Bonus: $270,000

OTHER THOUGHTS:

Apparent Women Officers or Directors: 3
Hot Spot for Advancement for Women/Minorities: Y

LOCATIONS: ("Y" = Yes)

West:	Southwest:	Midwest:	Southeast:	Northeast:	International:
Y	Y	Y	Y	Y	Y

Sales, profits and employees may be estimates. Financial information, benefits and other data can change quickly and may vary from those stated here.

IGATE CORPORATION

www.igate.com

Industry Group Code: 541513

Management:		**Sales/Marketing:**		**Liberal Arts:**		**Information Sys.:**		**Professionals:**		**Tech./Scientific:**	
Mgmt. Trainees:	Y	Marketing Pros.:	Y	Gen. Writing/Editing:	Y	Info. Mgmt.:	Y	Finance/Acct.:	Y	Engineers, Elec.:	Y
Experienced Mgmt.:	Y	Retail Sales:		Tech. Writing:	Y	Software Dev.:	Y	Law:	Y	Engineers, Other:	
Int'l Business:	Y	Comm./Industrial:	Y	Graphic Arts/Photog.:	Y	Hardware Dev.:	Y	HR/Other:	Y	Health/Lab:	
MBA Grads:	Y	Sales Trainees:		Music:		Consulting/Other:	Y	Training:	Y	Science/Research:	
		Advertising Pros.:		Broadcasting:				Health Care:		Petroleum/Chem.:	
				Other:				Consulting:	Y	Math/Other:	

TYPES OF BUSINESS:

IT Consulting
Data Management & Integration
Business Process Outsourcing
Web Integration Services
Software Design Services
Call Center Consulting
Process Investment Strategies
Call Center Operations

BRANDS/DIVISIONS/AFFILIATES:

iGATE Global Solutions Limited
Patni Computer Systems, Ltd.

CONTACTS: *Note: Officers with more than one job title may be intentionally listed here more than once.*

Phaneesh Murthy, CEO
Phaneesh Murthy, Pres.
Sujit Sircar, CFO
Robert Massie, Chief Sales Officer
Srinivas Kandula, Head-Global Human Resources
Amit Goyal, Head-Info. Systems
Nagasamy Pitchai, Sr. VP-Mfg., Logistics & Retail Svcs. Delivery
Mukund Srinath, VP-Legal/Corp. Sec.
Prabhanjan Deshpande, Head-Corp. Comm. & Media Rel.
Araceli Roiz, Mgr.-Investor Rel.
Prashanth Idgunji, VP-Finance
Sunil Wadhwani, Co-Chmn.
David A. Kruzner, Sr. VP-Consulting Solutions
Arun Varadarajan, Sr. VP-Client Servicing
Murali Raghavan, Sr. VP/Head-Horizontal Svcs.
Ashok Trivedi, Co-Chmn.
Jason Trussell, VP/Regional Mgr.-Canada
Sean Narayanan, Chief Delivery Officer

Phone: 510-896-3000 **Fax:** 510-896-3010
Toll-Free: 877-924-4283
Address: 6528 Kaiser Dr., Fremont, CA 94555 US

GROWTH PLANS/SPECIAL FEATURES:

iGATE Corporation is an outsourcing provider of information technology (IT) and IT-enabled operations and services. The firm focuses on large and mid-sized customers in industries such as financial services, insurance, manufacturing, media and healthcare. Together with its subsidiary, iGATE Global Solutions Limited, the company offers a combination of process investment strategies, technology leverage and business process outsourcing (BPO). iGATE's enterprise offerings include outsourcing of IT and BPO services using an offshore/onsite delivery model, wherein the balance between onsite and offshore presence is calculated on a case-by-case basis. IT services include software application development and maintenance; implementation and support of enterprise applications, as well as data management and systems integration. BPO services include call center services and transaction processing services. Call center services consist of consulting, implementation and operations, including everything from designing call centers to training representatives to developing measurement tools. While iGATE's call center offerings are marketed to clients across a range of industries, its transaction processing services are generally focused on clients in the mortgage banking, financial services, insurance and capital market industries. iGATE is active worldwide, with operations in India, Canada, Europe, Mexico, China, Singapore, Malaysia, Japan, Australia and the U.S. In January 2011, the firm agreed to acquire Indian company Patni Computer Systems, Ltd.

FINANCIALS: **Sales and profits are in thousands of dollars—add 000 to get the full amount. 2010 Note: Financial information for 2010 was not available for all companies at press time.**

2010 Sales: $280,597 2010 Profits: $51,755
2009 Sales: $193,099 2009 Profits: $28,575
2008 Sales: $218,798 2008 Profits: $30,904
2007 Sales: $201,734 2007 Profits: $15,585
2006 Sales: $170,414 2006 Profits: $8,704

U.S. Stock Ticker: IGTE
Int'l Ticker:
Int'l Exchange:
Employees: 15,846 Fiscal Year Ends: 12/31
Parent Company:

SALARIES/BENEFITS:

Pension Plan: ESOP Stock Plan: Profit Sharing: Top Exec. Salary: $500,000 Bonus: $40,385
Savings Plan: Y Stock Purch. Plan: Second Exec. Salary: $300,000 Bonus: $60,750

OTHER THOUGHTS:

Apparent Women Officers or Directors: 1
Hot Spot for Advancement for Women/Minorities:

LOCATIONS: ("Y" = Yes)

West:	Southwest:	Midwest:	Southeast:	Northeast:	International:
Y	Y	Y	Y	Y	Y

ILLINOIS TOOL WORKS INC

www.itw.com

Industry Group Code: 333

Management:		Sales/Marketing:		Liberal Arts:		Information Sys.:		Professionals:		Tech./Scientific:	
Mgmt. Trainees:	Y	Marketing Pros.:	Y	Gen. Writing/Editing:		Info. Mgmt.:	Y	Finance/Acct.:	Y	Engineers, Elec.:	
Experienced Mgmt.:	Y	Retail Sales:		Tech. Writing:	Y	Software Dev.:		Law:	Y	Engineers, Other:	
Int'l Business:	Y	Comm./Industrial:	Y	Graphic Arts/Photog.:	Y	Hardware Dev.:		HR/Other:	Y	Health/Lab:	
MBA Grads:	Y	Sales Trainees:		Music:		Consulting/Other:		Training:	Y	Science/Research:	
		Advertising Pros.:	Y	Broadcasting:				Health Care:		Petroleum/Chem.:	
				Other:				Consulting:		Math/Other:	

TYPES OF BUSINESS:

Industrial Products & Equipment
Steel, Plastic & Paper Products
Power Systems & Electronics
Transportation-Related Components, Fasteners, Fluids & Polymers
Construction-Related Fasteners & Tools
Food Equipment & Adhesives
Decorative Surfacing Materials
Adhesives, Sealants & Lubrication

BRANDS/DIVISIONS/AFFILIATES:

Elro Group
Panreac Group

CONTACTS:

Note: Officers with more than one job title may be intentionally listed here more than once.

David B. Speer, CEO
Ronald D. Kropp, CFO/Sr. VP
Sharon M. Brady, Sr. VP-Human Resources
Lei Z. Schlitz, VP-R&D
Mark W. Croll, VP-Patents & Tech.
James H. Wooten, Jr., General Counsel/Sr. VP/Corp. Sec.
John L. Brooklier, VP-Investor Rel.
Randall J. Scheuneman, Chief Acct. Officer/VP
Craig Hindman, Exec. VP-Decorative Surfaces
Robert E. Brunner, Exec. VP-Construction Prod.
Timothy J. Gardner, Exec. VP-Consumer Packaging Bus.
Steven L. Martindale, Exec. VP-Test & Measurement Bus.
David B. Speer, Chmn.

Phone: 847-724-7500 **Fax:** 847-657-4261
Toll-Free:
Address: 3600 W. Lake Ave., Glenview, IL 60026-1215 US

GROWTH PLANS/SPECIAL FEATURES:

Illinois Tool Works, Inc. (ITW) is a multinational manufacturer of a diversified range of industrial products and equipment with approximately 825 operations in 52 countries. It operates in eight segments: industrial packaging; power systems and electronics; transportation; construction products; food equipment; decorative services; polymers and fluids; and other. The industrial packaging segment produces steel, plastic and paper products used for bundling, shipping and protecting transported goods. Products include steel and plastic strapping and related tools and equipment; plastic stretch film; and metal jacketing and other insulation products. The power systems and electronics segment produces equipment and consumables associated with specialty power conversion, metallurgy and electronics. Products include welding equipment and airport ground support equipment. The transportation division produces components, fasteners, fluids and polymers for transportation-related applications. Products include metal and plastic components for automobiles; fillers and putties for auto body repair; and polyester coatings and repair products for the marine industry. The construction products segment produces tools, fasteners and other products for construction applications. Products include packaged hardware, fasteners, anchors and other products for retail. The food equipment division provides commercial food equipment and related services. Products include warewashing equipment; cooking and refrigeration equipment; food processing equipment; and kitchen exhaust, ventilation and pollution control systems. The decorative services segment produces decorative surfacing laminate for furniture, office and retail space, countertops and flooring applications. The polymer and fluids segment offers adhesives, sealants, lubrication and cutting fluids and hygiene products. Products include hand wipes and cleaners for industrial applications; and adhesives for industrial, construction and consumer purposes. Products offered by the other segment include plastic reclosable bags; metal and plastic fasteners; product coding and marking equipment; and static and contamination control equipment. In September 2010, ITW acquired Elro Group and Panreac Group. In March 2011, the firm acquired the car care business of SOPUS Products.

FINANCIALS:

Sales and profits are in thousands of dollars—add 000 to get the full amount. 2010 Note: Financial information for 2010 was not available for all companies at press time.

2010 Sales: $15,870,376	2010 Profits: $1,527,193	**U.S. Stock Ticker: ITW**
2009 Sales: $13,877,068	2009 Profits: $969,490	**Int'l Ticker:**
2008 Sales: $17,100,341	2008 Profits: $1,691,093	Int'l Exchange:
2007 Sales: $16,110,267	2007 Profits: $1,869,862	Employees: 61,000 Fiscal Year Ends: 12/31
2006 Sales: $12,784,342	2006 Profits: $1,717,746	Parent Company:

SALARIES/BENEFITS:

Pension Plan:	ESOP Stock Plan:	Profit Sharing:	Top Exec. Salary: $1,100,000	Bonus: $1,256,640
Savings Plan:	Stock Purch. Plan:		Second Exec. Salary: $500,000	Bonus: $449,600

OTHER THOUGHTS:

Apparent Women Officers or Directors: 4
Hot Spot for Advancement for Women/Minorities: Y

LOCATIONS: ("Y" = Yes)

West:	Southwest:	Midwest:	Southeast:	Northeast:	International:
Y	Y	Y	Y	Y	Y

IMS HEALTH INC

www.imshealth.com

Industry Group Code: 541910

Management:		Sales/Marketing:		Liberal Arts:		Information Sys.:		Professionals:		Tech./Scientific:	
Mgmt. Trainees:	Y	Marketing Pros.:	Y	Gen. Writing/Editing:	Y	Info. Mgmt.:	Y	Finance/Acct.:	Y	Engineers, Elec.:	Y
Experienced Mgmt.:	Y	Retail Sales:		Tech. Writing:	Y	Software Dev.:	Y	Law:	Y	Engineers, Other:	
Int'l Business:	Y	Comm./Industrial:	Y	Graphic Arts/Photog.:	Y	Hardware Dev.:		HR/Other:	Y	Health/Lab:	Y
MBA Grads:	Y	Sales Trainees:		Music:		Consulting/Other:		Training:	Y	Science/Research:	
		Advertising Pros.:	Y	Broadcasting:				Health Care:	Y	Petroleum/Chem.:	
				Other:	Y			Consulting:	Y	Math/Other:	

TYPES OF BUSINESS:

Market Research - Pharmaceuticals
Pharmaceutical Sales Tracking
Health Care Databases
Software-Sales Management & Market Research
Physician Profiling
Industry Audits
Prescription Tracking Reporting Services

BRANDS/DIVISIONS/AFFILIATES:

TPG Capital
SDI Health LLC
TPG Inc
IMS Institute for Healthcare Informatics

CONTACTS:

Note: Officers with more than one job title may be intentionally listed here more than once.

Ari Bousbib, CEO
Harshan Bhangdia, Acting CFO/VP
Paul Thomson, Sr. VP-Human Resources
Paul Thomson, Sr. VP-Admin.
Harvey A. Ashman, General Counsel/Sr. VP-External Affairs
Kevin McKay, Sr. VP-Global Oper.
Stefan Linn, Sr. VP-Strategy, Innovation & Dev.
Harshan Bhangdia, Controller
Michael Brogan, Pres., IMS Brogan
Deborah Kobewka, Pres., Asia Pacific
Adel Al-Saleh, Sr. VP-Global Pharma Solutions
William Nelligan, Pres., U.S.
Ari Bousbib, Chmn.
Elisabeth Beck, Pres., East Europe
Kevin Knightly, Sr. VP-Supply Mgmt.

Phone: 203-845-5200	**Fax:**
Toll-Free:	
Address: 901 Main Ave., Ste. 612, Norwalk, CT 06851-1187 US	

GROWTH PLANS/SPECIAL FEATURES:

IMS Health, Inc., formerly TPG, Inc., is a business intelligence firm serving the healthcare and pharmaceutical industries. IMS Health serves clients in more than 100 countries from its 75 offices, located on six continents. It offers services in three areas: market measurement; commercial effectiveness; portfolio planning; medicine valuation; and consulting and services. The company's market measurement takes stock of the global health care market, patient-centered treatments, emerging models, disease patterns, product lifecycles, medical device tracking, consumer health investments, managed markets and new market forecasting. Its commercial effectiveness services consist of intelligence designed to support the planning, development and execution of critical business processes such as sales territory reporting; promotion management, brand performance management, strategies for optimal product launches, commercial workshops and end-to-end service models. The firm's portfolio planning services asses market opportunities, conduct market research, analyze portfolios and explore licensing and partnership deals. Medicine valuation services are conducted through cost-of-illness analyses and market access inquiries. Its consulting and services functions conduct market research and analyze the best paths to achieve commercial success. IMS Health offers its services to pharmaceutical and medical device manufacturers; ad agencies; managed care organizations; distributors; chemical suppliers; academic institutions; government agencies; and public policy organizations. In January 2011, the company announced plans to acquire SDI Health LLC, which specializes in health care market analysis. In March 2011, the firm launched the IMS Institute for Healthcare Informatics to research global health trends and health care products.

FINANCIALS:

Sales and profits are in thousands of dollars—add 000 to get the full amount. 2010 Note: Financial information for 2010 was not available for all companies at press time.

2010 Sales: $2,321,129	2010 Profits: $302,392	**U.S. Stock Ticker: Private**
2009 Sales: $2,189,745	2009 Profits: $258,455	**Int'l Ticker:**
2008 Sales: $2,329,528	2008 Profits: $311,250	Int'l Exchange:
2007 Sales: $2,192,571	2007 Profits: $234,040	Employees: 7,250 Fiscal Year Ends: 12/31
2006 Sales: $1,958,588	2006 Profits: $315,511	Parent Company: TPG CAPITAL

SALARIES/BENEFITS:

Pension Plan:	ESOP Stock Plan:	Profit Sharing:	Top Exec. Salary: $850,000	Bonus: $567,500
Savings Plan:	Stock Purch. Plan:		Second Exec. Salary: $725,000	Bonus: $364,400

OTHER THOUGHTS:

Apparent Women Officers or Directors: 2
Hot Spot for Advancement for Women/Minorities: Y

LOCATIONS: ("Y" = Yes)

West:	Southwest:	Midwest:	Southeast:	Northeast:	International:
Y	Y			Y	Y

Sales, profits and employees may be estimates. Financial information, benefits and other data can change quickly and may vary from those stated here.

INGRAM MICRO INC

www.ingrammicro.com

Industry Group Code: 423430

Management:		Sales/Marketing:		Liberal Arts:		Information Sys.:		Professionals:		Tech./Scientific:	
Mgmt. Trainees:	Y	Marketing Pros.:	Y	Gen. Writing/Editing:	Y	Info. Mgmt.:	Y	Finance/Acct.:	Y	Engineers, Elec.:	
Experienced Mgmt.:	Y	Retail Sales:		Tech. Writing:	Y	Software Dev.:	Y	Law:	Y	Engineers, Other:	
Int'l Business:	Y	Comm./Industrial:	Y	Graphic Arts/Photog.:	Y	Hardware Dev.:		HR/Other:	Y	Health/Lab:	
MBA Grads:	Y	Sales Trainees:	Y	Music:		Consulting/Other:		Training:	Y	Science/Research:	
		Advertising Pros.:	Y	Broadcasting:				Health Care:		Petroleum/Chem.:	
				Other:				Consulting:		Math/Other:	

TYPES OF BUSINESS:

Microcomputers, Distribution
Networking Equipment
Software & Accessories Distribution
Supply Chain Management Services
Online Marketing Services

BRANDS/DIVISIONS/AFFILIATES:

Micro Logistics
Arete Sistemas
Arkenova Sistemas

CONTACTS: *Note: Officers with more than one job title may be intentionally listed here more than once.*

Gregory M.E. Spierkel, CEO
William D. Humes, CFO/Exec. VP
Lynn Jolliffe, Exec. VP-Human Resources
Mario Leone, CIO/Exec. VP
Larry C. Boyd, General Counsel/Sr. VP/Sec.
G. Sam Kamel, Sr. VP-Corp. Strategy
Ria M. Carlson, Sr. VP-Comm. & Brand Mgmt.
Shailendra Gupta, Sr. Exec. VP/Pres., Ingram Micro Asia-Pacific
Keith W. F. Bradley, Sr. Exec. VP/Pres., Ingram Micro North America
Eduardo Araujo, Sr. Exev. VP/Pres., Ingram Micro Latin America
Dale R. Laurance, Chmn.
Alain Maquet, Sr. VP/Pres., EMEA
Robert Gifford, Sr. Exec. VP-Global Logistics

Phone: 714-566-1000	**Fax:**
Toll-Free:	
Address: 1600 E. St. Andrew Pl., Santa Ana, CA 92705-4926 US	

GROWTH PLANS/SPECIAL FEATURES:

Ingram Micro, Inc. is a global distributor of technology products and supply chain management services. The company markets microcomputer hardware, networking equipment and software products to nearly 180,000 resellers in approximately 150 countries. Ingram provides a comprehensive inventory of hundreds of thousands of distinct items from nearly 1,300 suppliers. Its products are sold in four primary segments: IT Peripheral, Systems, Software and Networking. Peripherals include printers, scanners, displays, projectors, monitors, mass storage and tape. Systems products include servers, desktops, laptop computers and personal digital assistants. Software products include operating systems, entertainment software, security tools and business applications. Networking products include routers, switches, hubs, wireless networks, networking cards, video conferencing, storage area networks and software products such as business application, operating system, entertainment and security software. In terms of revenue, peripherals account for 40% to 45% of revenue, systems for 25% to 30%, software for 15% to 20% and networking products for 10% to 15%. In addition, the company offers components, such as processors, motherboards, hard drives and memory; supplies and accessories, including ink and toner supplies, paper, carrying cases and anti-glare screens; and consumer electronic products, such as cell phones, digital cameras, DVD players and televisions. Ingram also offers supply chain management services such as sales and marketing, customer care, financial services and logistics to suppliers and resellers. Its Micro Logistics division provides end-to-end order management and fulfillment, retail logistics merchandising, warehousing and storage, contract manufacturing, distribution center services, product procurement, reverse logistics, transportation management, marketing services and other outsourcing services. Through its web site, Ingram also offers online account management, a vast resource library and advanced marketing tools. In December 2010, the company acquired Arete Sistemas and Arkenova Sistemas, two Spanish wholesale providers.

Ingram Micro offers its employees medical, dental and vision coverage; a 401(k) plan; adoption assistance; tuition reimbursement; an employee assistance program; and product discounts.

FINANCIALS: **Sales and profits are in thousands of dollars—add 000 to get the full amount. 2010 Note: Financial information for 2010 was not available for all companies at press time.**

2010 Sales: $34,588,984	2010 Profits: $318,060	**U.S. Stock Ticker: IM**
2009 Sales: $29,515,446	2009 Profits: $202,138	**Int'l Ticker:**
2008 Sales: $34,362,152	2008 Profits: $-394,921	Int'l Exchange:
2007 Sales: $35,047,089	2007 Profits: $275,908	Employees: 15,650 Fiscal Year Ends: 12/31
2006 Sales: $31,357,477	2006 Profits: $265,766	Parent Company:

SALARIES/BENEFITS:

Pension Plan:	ESOP Stock Plan:	Profit Sharing:	Top Exec. Salary: $850,000	Bonus: $1,807,950
Savings Plan: Y	Stock Purch. Plan:		Second Exec. Salary: $650,000	Bonus: $829,530

OTHER THOUGHTS:

Apparent Women Officers or Directors: 5
Hot Spot for Advancement for Women/Minorities: Y

LOCATIONS: ("Y" = Yes)

West:	Southwest:	Midwest:	Southeast:	Northeast:	International:
Y	Y	Y	Y	Y	Y

Sales, profits and employees may be estimates. Financial information, benefits and other data can change quickly and may vary from those stated here.

INSITUFORM TECHNOLOGIES

www.insituform.com

Industry Group Code: 2389

Management:		**Sales/Marketing:**		**Liberal Arts:**		**Information Sys.:**		**Professionals:**		**Tech./Scientific:**	
Mgmt. Trainees:		Marketing Pros.:	Y	Gen. Writing/Editing:		Info. Mgmt.:	Y	Finance/Acct.:	Y	Engineers, Elec.:	Y
Experienced Mgmt.:	Y	Retail Sales:		Tech. Writing:	Y	Software Dev.:		Law:	Y	Engineers, Other:	Y
Int'l Business:	Y	Comm./Industrial:	Y	Graphic Arts/Photog.:		Hardware Dev.:		HR/Other:	Y	Health/Lab:	
MBA Grads:	Y	Sales Trainees:		Music:		Consulting/Other:		Training:		Science/Research:	
		Advertising Pros.:		Broadcasting:				Health Care:		Petroleum/Chem.:	
				Other:				Consulting:		Math/Other:	

TYPES OF BUSINESS:

Construction, Heavy & Civil Engineering
Sewer & Pipe Rehabilitation Services

BRANDS/DIVISIONS/AFFILIATES:

Insituform CIPP Process
Insituform Blue
United Pipeline Systems
Corrpro Companies, Inc.
Bayou Companies (The)
Insitu Envirotech (S.E. Asia) Pte Ltd.

CONTACTS: *Note: Officers with more than one job title may be intentionally listed here more than once.*

J. Joseph Burgess, CEO
J. Joseph Burgess, Pres.
David A. Martin, CFO/VP
Holly Sharp, VP-Human Resources
David F. Morris, Chief Admin. Officer/Sr. VP
David F. Morris, General Counsel/Corp. Sec.
Kenneth Young, Treas./VP
Holly Sharp, VP-Environmental, Health & Safety
Charles Voltz, Sr. VP-North American Rehabilitation
Dorwin Hawn, Sr. VP-Energy & Mining
Daniel Cowan, VP-APAC
Alfred L. Woods, Chmn.
Alex Buehler, VP-Europe

Phone: 636-530-8000 **Fax:** 636-519-8010
Toll-Free: 800-234-2992
Address: 17988 Edison Ave., Chesterfield, MO 63005-3700 US

GROWTH PLANS/SPECIAL FEATURES:

Insituform Technologies is provider of proprietary technologies and pipeline rehabilitation services to the sewer, water, energy and mining infrastructure markets. The firm's products are sold in over 70 countries on six continents. Most of Insituform's installation operations are project-oriented contracts for municipal entities, concerning the maintenance of municipal sewers, commercial pipes and water mains. The company and its subsidiaries operate principally in the U.S., Canada, the Netherlands, the U.K., Portugal France, Switzerland, Chile, Spain, Poland, Mexico, Belgium, Romania and India. The firm's operations comprise the five following operating segments: North American Sewer Rehabilitation; European Sewer Rehabilitation; Asia-Pacific Sewer Rehabilitation; Water Rehabilitation; and Energy and Mining. Sewer rehabilitation services include the firm's proprietary Insituform Cured-In-Place Pipe (CIPP) process, a trenchless technology allowing pipeline to be repaired without digging and major service disruptions. Insituform's CIPP process involves saturating a synthetic fiber tube with a thermosetting resin, installing the tube into a host pipe and then hardening the resin, forming a new rigid pipe-within-a-pipe. Water rehabilitation activities are focused on pipelines carrying drinking water and include the firm's Insituform Blue brand of potable water pipe restoration services. The company's subsidiaries include United Pipeline Systems, a provider of high-density polyethylene (HDPE) lining systems used for the protection of internal pipelines; Corrpro Companies, Inc., a provider of corrosion protection and pipeline maintenance services in North America; and The Bayou Companies, a provider of pipeline services to energy and infrastructure firms, primarily in the Gulf of Mexico and North America. In early 2010, the firm acquired its former Singaporean licensee, Insitu Envirotech (S.E. Asia) Pte Ltd., for $1.3 million.

Employees are offered retirement plans; a 401(k) plan; disability coverage; and life insurance.

FINANCIALS: **Sales and profits are in thousands of dollars—add 000 to get the full amount. 2010 Note: Financial information for 2010 was not available for all companies at press time.**

2010 Sales: $914,975 — 2010 Profits: $60,462
2009 Sales: $726,866 — 2009 Profits: $26,171
2008 Sales: $536,664 — 2008 Profits: $21,640
2007 Sales: $495,570 — 2007 Profits: $2,543
2006 Sales: $527,419 — 2006 Profits: $24,678

U.S. Stock Ticker: INSU
Int'l Ticker:
Int'l Exchange:
Employees: 3,200 Fiscal Year Ends: 12/31
Parent Company:

SALARIES/BENEFITS:

Pension Plan: Y ESOP Stock Plan: Profit Sharing: Top Exec. Salary: $565,000 Bonus: $882,768
Savings Plan: Y Stock Purch. Plan: Second Exec. Salary: $345,000 Bonus: $349,151

OTHER THOUGHTS:

Apparent Women Officers or Directors: 3
Hot Spot for Advancement for Women/Minorities: Y

LOCATIONS: ("Y" = Yes)

West:	Southwest:	Midwest:	Southeast:	Northeast:	International:
Y	Y	Y	Y	Y	Y

INTEGRA LIFESCIENCES HOLDINGS CORP

www.integra-ls.com

Industry Group Code: 33911

Management:		Sales/Marketing:		Liberal Arts:		Information Sys.:		Professionals:		Tech./Scientific:	
Mgmt. Trainees:		Marketing Pros.:	Y	Gen. Writing/Editing:		Info. Mgmt.:	Y	Finance/Acct.:	Y	Engineers, Elec.:	Y
Experienced Mgmt.:	Y	Retail Sales:		Tech. Writing:	Y	Software Dev.:		Law:	Y	Engineers, Other:	Y
Int'l Business:	Y	Comm./Industrial:	Y	Graphic Arts/Photog.:		Hardware Dev.:		HR/Other:	Y	Health/Lab:	
MBA Grads:	Y	Sales Trainees:		Music:		Consulting/Other:		Training:		Science/Research:	
		Advertising Pros.:		Broadcasting:				Health Care:	Y	Petroleum/Chem.:	
				Other:				Consulting:		Math/Other:	

TYPES OF BUSINESS:

Medical Equipment Manufacturing
Implants & Biomaterials
Absorbable Medical Products
Tissue Regeneration Technology
Neurosurgery Products
Skin Replacement Products

BRANDS/DIVISIONS/AFFILIATES:

DuraGen Plus Dural Regeneration Matrix
Suturable DuraGen Dural Regeneration Matrix
DuraGen XS Dural Regeneration Matrix
AccuDrain External Ventricular Drainage Systems
Jarit
Luxtec
Miltex
Total Wrist Fusion System

CONTACTS: *Note: Officers with more than one job title may be intentionally listed here more than once.*

Stuart M. Essig, CEO
Peter J. Arduini, COO
Peter J. Arduini, Pres.
John B. Henneman III, CFO/Exec. VP-Finance
Deborah A. Leonetti, Chief Mktg. Officer
Richard D. Gorelick, Sr. VP-Human Resources
Simon J. Archibald, Chief Scientific Officer
Robert Perrett, CIO/Sr. VP
John B. Henneman, III, Exec. VP-Admin.
Richard D. Gorelick, General Counsel/Sec.
James A. Oti, Sr. VP-Global Oper.
Maria Platsis, Sr. VP-Corp. Dev.
Gianna Sabella, Dir.-Corp. Comm.
Angela Steinway, Mgr.-Investor Rel.
John Bostjancic, Sr. VP-Finance
Nora Brennan, VP/Treas.
Judith E. O'Grady, Sr. VP-Quality, Regulatory & Clinical Affairs
Robert D. Paltridge, Pres., Extremity Reconstruction
Jerry E. Corbin, VP/Controller
Richard E. Caruso, Chmn.
Debbie Leonetti, Pres., Int'l

Phone: 609-275-0500 **Fax:** 609-275-5363
Toll-Free: 800-654-2873
Address: 311 Enterprise Dr., Plainsboro, NJ 08536 US

GROWTH PLANS/SPECIAL FEATURES:

Integra Lifesciences Holdings Corp. develops, manufactures and markets surgical implants and medical instruments primarily for use in neurosurgery, orthopedics and general surgery. The company divides its products into three groups: neurosciences, orthopedics and medical instruments. The neurosciences group's products include duraplasty products such as the DuraGen Plus, Suturable DuraGen and DuraGen XS Dural Regeneration Matrices; tissue ablation equipment, which features the company's CUSA tissue ablation system; cerebral spinal fluid (CSF) management devices; cranial stabilization equipment, which features the MAYFIELD system; and intracranial monitoring equipment including the Camino ICP monitor, the LICOX brain tissue monitoring system and the AccuDrain External Ventricular Drainage Systems. The orthopedics group includes specialty metal implants for surgery of the extremities and spine; orthobiologics products for repair and grafting of bone; dermal regeneration products; tissue engineered wound dressings; and nerve and tendon repair products. The medical instruments group includes operating room instrumentation and surgical lighting. The Jarit instrument line offers reusable surgical instruments for laparoscopic, general, cardiovascular, neuro, gynecological, and orthopedic surgical specialties. Luxtec provides products for the surgical illumination market such as Xenon illumination systems, fiber optic cables and surgical loupes. Miltex provides dental instruments for oral surgery and periodontal and endodontic instrumentation. In August 2010, Integra opened a new facility in Irvine, California. In October 2010, the firm released Integra Endoscopic Gastroc Release System, a disposable that allows for selective cutting of soft tissues. In April 2011, the company opened a new facility in Medina, Ohio. In May 2011, Integra acquired spine fusion specialist SeaSpine, Inc.

Integra offers its employees life, dependent life, disability, AD&D, medical, dental and vision insurance; flexible spending accounts; an employee assistance program; an employee stock purchase plan; a 401(k); and educational assistance.

FINANCIALS: **Sales and profits are in thousands of dollars—add 000 to get the full amount. 2010 Note: Financial information for 2010 was not available for all companies at press time.**

2010 Sales: $732,068	2010 Profits: $65,669	**U.S. Stock Ticker: IART**
2009 Sales: $682,487	2009 Profits: $50,955	**Int'l Ticker:**
2008 Sales: $654,604	2008 Profits: $27,727	Int'l Exchange:
2007 Sales: $550,459	2007 Profits: $25,749	Employees: 3,000 Fiscal Year Ends: 12/31
2006 Sales: $419,297	2006 Profits: $29,407	Parent Company:

SALARIES/BENEFITS:

Pension Plan:	ESOP Stock Plan:	Profit Sharing:	Top Exec. Salary: $614,808	Bonus: $
Savings Plan: Y	Stock Purch. Plan: Y		Second Exec. Salary: $457,404	Bonus: $

OTHER THOUGHTS:

Apparent Women Officers or Directors: 8
Hot Spot for Advancement for Women/Minorities: Y

LOCATIONS: ("Y" = Yes)

West:	Southwest:	Midwest:	Southeast:	Northeast:	International:
Y		Y		Y	Y

Sales, profits and employees may be estimates. Financial information, benefits and other data can change quickly and may vary from those stated here.

INTEL CORP

www.intel.com

Industry Group Code: 33441

Management:		Sales/Marketing:		Liberal Arts:		Information Sys.:		Professionals:		Tech./Scientific:	
Mgmt. Trainees:	Y	Marketing Pros.:	Y	Gen. Writing/Editing:	Y	Info. Mgmt.:	Y	Finance/Acct.:	Y	Engineers, Elec.:	Y
Experienced Mgmt.:	Y	Retail Sales:		Tech. Writing:	Y	Software Dev.:	Y	Law:	Y	Engineers, Other:	
Int'l Business:	Y	Comm./Industrial:	Y	Graphic Arts/Photog.:	Y	Hardware Dev.:	Y	HR/Other:	Y	Health/Lab:	
MBA Grads:	Y	Sales Trainees:		Music:		Consulting/Other:	Y	Training:	Y	Science/Research:	Y
		Advertising Pros.:	Y	Broadcasting:				Health Care:		Petroleum/Chem.:	
				Other:	Y			Consulting:		Math/Other:	Y

TYPES OF BUSINESS:

Microprocessors
Semiconductors
Circuit Boards
Flash Memory Products
Software Development
Home Network Equipment
Digital Imaging Products
Healthcare Products

BRANDS/DIVISIONS/AFFILIATES:

Pentium
Dual Core
Numonyx B.V.
SySDSoft
Intel Mobile Communications
McAfee Inc
Wind River Systems, Inc.
Intel Research Labs

CONTACTS: *Note: Officers with more than one job title may be intentionally listed here more than once.*

Paul S. Otellini, CEO
Paul S. Otellini, Pres.
Stacy J. Smith, CFO/Sr. VP
Thomas M. Kilroy, Sr. VP-Mktg. & Sales
Patricia Murray, Sr. VP/Dir.-Human Resources
Justin R. Rattner, VP/Dir.-Intel Labs
Diane M. Bryant, CIO/VP
Justin R. Rattner, CTO
Robert J. Baker, Sr. VP/Gen. Mgr.-Mfg. & Tech. Group
Andy D. Bryant, Chief Admin. Officer/Exec. VP
A. Douglas Melamed, General Counsel/Sr. VP
Leslie S. Culbertson, VP/Dir.-Finance
Ravi Jacob, VP/Treas.
Arvind Sodhani, Exec. VP/Pres., Intel Capital
William M. Holt, Sr. VP/Gen. Mgr.-Mfg. & Tech. Group
David Perlmutter, Exec. VP/Gen. Mgr.-Intel Architecture Group
Jane E. Shaw, Chmn.
Brain M. Krzanich, VP/Gen. Mgr.-Supply Chain & Mfg.

Phone: 408-765-8080	**Fax:**
Toll-Free:	
Address: 2200 Mission College Blvd., Santa Clara, CA 95054-1549 US	

GROWTH PLANS/SPECIAL FEATURES:

Intel Corp. is a global semiconductor chip maker that develops advanced integrated digital technology platforms for the computing and communications industries. It operates in nine segments: PC Client Group; Data Center Group; Embedded and Communications Group; Digital Home Group; Ultra-Mobility Group; NAND Solutions Group; Wind River Software Group; Software and Services Group; and Digital Health Group. The PC Client Group (72% of revenues) provides Intel architecture-based products and platforms for notebooks, netbooks and desktops. The Data Center Group (20% of revenues) delivers server, storage and workstation platforms. The Embedded Communications Group's products include solutions for applications through long life-cycle support, platform integration and software and architectural scalability. The Digital Home Group provides products for next-generation consumer electronics with interactive Internet content and traditional broadcast programming. The Ultra-Mobility Group offers energy-efficient Intel Atom processors and related chipsets designed for mobile Internet devices (MIDs) within the handheld market segment. The NAND Solutions Group produces flash memory products used in portable memory storage devices, digital camera memory cards and solid-state drives. The Wind River Software Group develops and licenses device software optimization products, including operating systems, for customers in the embedded and handheld market segments. The Software and Services Group promotes Intel architecture as the platform of choice for software applications and operating systems. Lastly, the Digital Health Group offers technology products for healthcare providers and for use in personal healthcare. The Embedded Communications Group, Digital Home Group and Ultra-Mobility Group together account for 4% of revenues; and NAND Solutions Group, Wind River Software Group, Software and Services Group and Digital Health Group, 4%. In February 2011, the company acquired security-software company McAfee, Inc. for $7.68 billion. In March 2011, Intel Mobile Communications acquired Egyptian firm SySDSoft.

The firm offers its employees life, AD&D, disability, medical and dental coverage; an employee assistance program; and flexible spending accounts.

FINANCIALS: **Sales and profits are in thousands of dollars—add 000 to get the full amount. 2010 Note: Financial information for 2010 was not available for all companies at press time.**

2010 Sales: $43,623,000	2010 Profits: $11,464,000	**U.S. Stock Ticker: INTC**
2009 Sales: $35,127,000	2009 Profits: $4,369,000	**Int'l Ticker:**
2008 Sales: $37,586,000	2008 Profits: $5,292,000	Int'l Exchange:
2007 Sales: $38,334,000	2007 Profits: $6,976,000	Employees: 82,500 Fiscal Year Ends: 12/31
2006 Sales: $35,382,000	2006 Profits: $5,044,000	Parent Company:

SALARIES/BENEFITS:

Pension Plan: Y	ESOP Stock Plan:	Profit Sharing: Y	Top Exec. Salary: $1,000,000	Bonus: $5,251,500
Savings Plan: Y	Stock Purch. Plan: Y		Second Exec. Salary: $500,000	Bonus: $1,857,300

OTHER THOUGHTS:

Apparent Women Officers or Directors: 8
Hot Spot for Advancement for Women/Minorities: Y

LOCATIONS: ("Y" = Yes)

West:	Southwest:	Midwest:	Southeast:	Northeast:	International:
Y	Y	Y	Y	Y	Y

INTERNATIONAL BUSINESS MACHINES CORP (IBM)

www.ibm.com

Industry Group Code: 541513

Management:		Sales/Marketing:		Liberal Arts:		Information Sys.:		Professionals:		Tech./Scientific:	
Mgmt. Trainees:	Y	Marketing Pros.:	Y	Gen. Writing/Editing:	Y	Info. Mgmt.:	Y	Finance/Acct.:	Y	Engineers, Elec.:	Y
Experienced Mgmt.:	Y	Retail Sales:		Tech. Writing:	Y	Software Dev.:	Y	Law:	Y	Engineers, Other:	Y
Int'l Business:	Y	Comm./Industrial:	Y	Graphic Arts/Photog.:	Y	Hardware Dev.:	Y	HR/Other:	Y	Health/Lab:	
MBA Grads:	Y	Sales Trainees:	Y	Music:		Consulting/Other:	Y	Training:	Y	Science/Research:	Y
		Advertising Pros.:	Y	Broadcasting:				Health Care:		Petroleum/Chem.:	
				Other:	Y			Consulting:	Y	Math/Other:	Y

TYPES OF BUSINESS:

Computer Hardware
Supercomputers
Microelectronic Technology
Software Development
Networking Systems
IT Consulting & Outsourcing
Financial Services

BRANDS/DIVISIONS/AFFILIATES:

Intelliden, Inc.
Lombardi
Sterling Commerce
BigFix, Inc.
Unica Corporation
Storwize
Netezza Corporation
Datacap

CONTACTS: *Note: Officers with more than one job title may be intentionally listed here more than once.*

Samuel J. Palmisano, CEO
Samuel J. Palmisano, Pres.
Mark Loughridge, CFO/Sr. VP
Virginia M Rometty, Sr. VP-Mktg. & Sales
J. Randall MacDonald, Sr. VP-Human Resources
John E. Kelly, III, Sr. VP/Dir.-IBM Research
Linda S. Sanford, Sr. VP-IT & Enterprise On Demand Transformation
Robert C. Weber, General Counsel/Sr. VP-Legal & Regulatory Affairs
Virginia M Rometty, Sr. VP-Strategy
Jon C. Iwata, Sr. VP-Comm. & Mktg.
Linda S. Sanford, Sr. VP-IT & Enterprise On Demand Transformation
Michael E. Daniels, Sr. VP-Svcs.
Rodney C. Adkins, Sr. VP-IBM Systems and Tech Group.
Samuel J. Palmisano, Chmn.
R. Frankin Kern, Sr. VP-IBM Global Bus. Svcs.

Phone: 914-499-1900	**Fax:** 800-314-1092
Toll-Free: 800-426-4968	
Address: 1 New Orchard Rd., Armonk, NY 10504-1722 US	

GROWTH PLANS/SPECIAL FEATURES:

International Business Machines Corp. (IBM) produces computer hardware and software, and is one of the largest technology consulting businesses in the world. It operates in five primary segments: global technology services; systems and technology; global business services; software; and global financing. The global technology services segment primarily includes IT infrastructure services and business process services. The systems and technology division provides IBM's clients with business solutions built on advanced computing power and storage capabilities. Offerings include servers and infrastructure storage products; microelectronics for IBM systems and for sale to original equipment manufacturers; and retail store solutions, such as network-connected cash registers. The global business services segment primarily reflects professional services and application outsourcing services. Capabilities include consulting, systems integration and application management services. The software segment consists primarily of middleware and operating systems software. Middleware software enables clients to integrate systems, processes and applications across a standard software platform. Offerings include information management software; operating systems; and Tivoli software for infrastructure management, including security and storage management. The global financing division's capabilities include commercial financing, client financing and remarketing. IBM is active in over 170 countries worldwide. In 2010, the firm acquired several companies, including IT solutions provider National Interest Security Company, LLC; data integrity software firm Initiate Systems, Inc.; cloud integration company Cast Iron Systems; IT infrastructure management provider BigFix, Inc.; former AT&T subsidiary Sterling Commerce; marketing firm Unica Corporation; the assets of Wilshire Credit Corporation; data compression technology firm Storwize; business analytics company Netezza Corporation; Canadian firm Clarity Systems; and software developers Lombardi, Intelliden, Inc., Coremetrics; BLADE Network Technologies, OpenPages, PSS Systems and Datacap.

FINANCIALS: **Sales and profits are in thousands of dollars—add 000 to get the full amount. 2010 Note: Financial information for 2010 was not available for all companies at press time.**

2010 Sales: \$99,870,000 — 2010 Profits: \$14,833,000
2009 Sales: \$95,758,000 — 2009 Profits: \$13,425,000
2008 Sales: \$103,600,000 — 2008 Profits: \$12,300,000
2007 Sales: \$98,786,000 — 2007 Profits: \$10,418,000
2006 Sales: \$91,424,000 — 2006 Profits: \$9,492,000

U.S. Stock Ticker: IBM
Int'l Ticker:
Int'l Exchange:
Employees: 436,085 Fiscal Year Ends: 12/31
Parent Company:

SALARIES/BENEFITS:

Pension Plan:	ESOP Stock Plan:	Profit Sharing:	Top Exec. Salary: \$1,800,000	Bonus: \$4,750,000
Savings Plan: Y	Stock Purch. Plan: Y		Second Exec. Salary: \$720,000	Bonus: \$975,000

OTHER THOUGHTS:

Apparent Women Officers or Directors: 4
Hot Spot for Advancement for Women/Minorities: Y

LOCATIONS: ("Y" = Yes)

West:	Southwest:	Midwest:	Southeast:	Northeast:	International:
Y	Y	Y	Y	Y	Y

INTERPUBLIC GROUP OF COMPANIES INC www.interpublic.com

Industry Group Code: 541810

Management:		Sales/Marketing:		Liberal Arts:		Information Sys.:		Professionals:		Tech./Scientific:	
Mgmt. Trainees:	Y	Marketing Pros.:	Y	Gen. Writing/Editing:	Y	Info. Mgmt.:	Y	Finance/Acct.:	Y	Engineers, Elec.:	
Experienced Mgmt.:	Y	Retail Sales:		Tech. Writing:	Y	Software Dev.:	Y	Law:	Y	Engineers, Other:	
Int'l Business:	Y	Comm./Industrial:	Y	Graphic Arts/Photog.:	Y	Hardware Dev.:		HR/Other:	Y	Health/Lab:	
MBA Grads:	Y	Sales Trainees:		Music:	Y	Consulting/Other:		Training:	Y	Science/Research:	
		Advertising Pros.:	Y	Broadcasting:				Health Care:		Petroleum/Chem.:	
				Other:	Y			Consulting:	Y	Math/Other:	

TYPES OF BUSINESS:

Advertising Services
Marketing & Branding
Market Research
Public Relations
Online Marketing
Direct Marketing
Promotions & Events
Sports & Entertainment Marketing

BRANDS/DIVISIONS/AFFILIATES:

Draftfcb
Lowe Worldwide
McCann Erickson Worldwide
Campbell Mithun
Campbell-Ewald
Constituency Management Group
CUBOCC
Delaney Lund Knox Warren

CONTACTS: *Note: Officers with more than one job title may be intentionally listed here more than once.*

Michael I. Roth, CEO
Frank Mergenthaler, CFO/Exec. VP
Timothy A. Sompolski, Chief Human Resources Officer/Exec. VP
Joseph W. Farrelly, CIO/Sr. VP
Nicholas J. Camera, General Counsel/Sr. VP/Sec.
David I. Weiss, Sr. VP-Bus. Dev.
Jerome J. Leshne, Sr. VP-Investor Rel.
Christopher Carroll, Chief Acct. Officer/Controller
Julie M. Connors, Chief Risk Officer/Sr. VP-Audit
Philippe Krakowsky, Chief Strategy & Talent Officer/Exec. VP
Heide Gardner, Chief Diversity Officer/Sr. VP
Anthony G. Alexandrou, Sr. VP-Global Taxation
Michael I. Roth, Chmn.

Phone: 212-704-1200 **Fax:** 212-704-1201
Toll-Free:
Address: 1114 Ave. of the Americas, New York, NY 10036 US

GROWTH PLANS/SPECIAL FEATURES:

Interpublic Group of Companies, Inc. (IPG) is a group comprising hundreds of advertising and specialized marketing and communications services companies that combined represent one of the largest resources of advertising and marketing expertise in the world, with offices and affiliations in over 100 countries. The firm operates in two primary segments: Integrated Agency Network, which consists of its global brands Draftfcb, Lowe Worldwide and McCann Erickson Worldwide, as well as Mediabrands and various domestic integrated agencies; and the Constituency Management Group (CMG), which includes the firm's specialist marketing services agencies. Draftfcb provides consumer advertising and behavioral, data-driven direct marketing. Lowe Worldwide is focused on delivering and sustaining high-value ideas in such markets as the U.K., the U.S., India, Sweden and Latin America. McCann Erickson Worldwide provides best-in-class communications tools and resources in all regions of the world with operations in over 110 countries. Mediabrands oversees its independently operated global media networks, Initiative and Universal McCann. IPG's domestic agency brands include Campbell-Ewald; Campbell Mithun; Deutsch, Inc., a Lowe & Partners Company; Hill Holliday; The Martin Agency; and Mullen. The CMG division includes MRM Worldwide, providing relationship marketing and digital expertise; Momentum Worldwide, providing experiential marketing; and McCann Healthcare Worldwide, providing healthcare communications. Other subsidiaries include FutureBrand; Jack Morton Worldwide; Octagon; Reprise Media, Inc.; Translation, LLC; and WeberShandwick. The company also has a joint venture mobile marketing company, Ansible, formed with Velti, a leading mobile technology provider. IPG's largest clients include General Motors Corporation; Johnson & Johnson; Microsoft; Unilever; and Verizon. In March 2010, the firm acquired CUBOCC, a digital marketing company based in Brazil. In July 2010, it acquired Delaney Lund Knox Warren (DLKW), merging its operations into Lowe & Partners.

The firm offers its employees medical and dental insurance; adoption benefits; life insurance; disability coverage; tuition reimbursement; flexible spending accounts; and transportation accounts.

FINANCIALS: **Sales and profits are in thousands of dollars—add 000 to get the full amount. 2010 Note: Financial information for 2010 was not available for all companies at press time.**

2010 Sales: $6,531,900	2010 Profits: $281,200	**U.S. Stock Ticker: IPG**
2009 Sales: $6,027,600	2009 Profits: $143,400	**Int'l Ticker:**
2008 Sales: $6,962,700	2008 Profits: $265,200	Int'l Exchange:
2007 Sales: $6,554,200	2007 Profits: $167,600	Employees: 41,000 Fiscal Year Ends: 12/31
2006 Sales: $6,190,800	2006 Profits: $-31,700	Parent Company:

SALARIES/BENEFITS:

Pension Plan:	ESOP Stock Plan:	Profit Sharing:	Top Exec. Salary: $1,332,500	Bonus: $2,500,000
Savings Plan: Y	Stock Purch. Plan:		Second Exec. Salary: $1,285,000	Bonus: $1,600,000

OTHER THOUGHTS:

Apparent Women Officers or Directors: 6
Hot Spot for Advancement for Women/Minorities: Y

LOCATIONS: ("Y" = Yes)

West:	Southwest:	Midwest:	Southeast:	Northeast:	International:
Y	Y	Y	Y	Y	Y

Sales, profits and employees may be estimates. Financial information, benefits and other data can change quickly and may vary from those stated here.

INTUIT INC

www.intuit.com

Industry Group Code: 511201

Management:		**Sales/Marketing:**		**Liberal Arts:**		**Information Sys.:**		**Professionals:**		**Tech./Scientific:**	
Mgmt. Trainees:	Y	Marketing Pros.:	Y	Gen. Writing/Editing:	Y	Info. Mgmt.:	Y	Finance/Acct.:	Y	Engineers, Elec.:	Y
Experienced Mgmt.:	Y	Retail Sales:		Tech. Writing:	Y	Software Dev.:	Y	Law:	Y	Engineers, Other:	
Int'l Business:	Y	Comm./Industrial:	Y	Graphic Arts/Photog.:	Y	Hardware Dev.:		HR/Other:	Y	Health/Lab:	
MBA Grads:	Y	Sales Trainees:		Music:		Consulting/Other:		Training:	Y	Science/Research:	
		Advertising Pros.:	Y	Broadcasting:				Health Care:		Petroleum/Chem.:	
				Other:				Consulting:		Math/Other:	

TYPES OF BUSINESS:

Computer Software-Financial Management
Business Accounting Software
Consumer Finance Software
Tax Preparation Software
Online Financial Services

BRANDS/DIVISIONS/AFFILIATES:

QuickBooks
Intuit Health
Medfusion
Quicken
LaCerte
Intuit Real Estate Solutions
TurboTax
Mint.com

CONTACTS: *Note: Officers with more than one job title may be intentionally listed here more than once.*

Brad D. Smith, CEO
Brad D. Smith, Pres.
R. Neil Williams, CFO/Sr. VP
Caroline Donahue, Sr. VP-Sales & Channel Mktg.
Sherry Whiteley, Chief Human Resources Officer/Sr. VP
Ginny T. Lee, CIO/Sr. VP
Tayloe Stansbury, CTO/Sr. VP
Laura A. Fennell, General Counsel/Sr. VP/Corp. Sec.
Kris Halvorsen, Chief Innovation Officer/Sr. VP
Harry Pforzheimer, Chief Comm. Officer
Scott D. Cook, Chmn.-Exec. Committee
Nora Denzel, Sr. VP/Gen. Mgr.-Employee Mgmt. Solutions
Kiran Patel, Exec. VP/Gen. Mgr.-Small Bus. Group
Sasan Goodarzi, Pres., Intuit Financial Services
Bill Campbell, Chmn.
Alexander M. Lintner, Pres., Global Bus. Div.

Phone: 650-944-6000 **Fax:** 650-944-3699
Toll-Free: 800-446-8848
Address: 2632 Marine Way, Mountain View, CA 94043 US

GROWTH PLANS/SPECIAL FEATURES:

Intuit, Inc. is a provider of software and web-based services. The firm specializes in providing financial management and tax solutions to consumers; small and medium-sized businesses; financial institutions; and accounting professionals. The company has four business segments: Small Business Group; Tax; Accounting Professionals; Financial Services; Other Businesses. The Small Business Group includes three smaller divisions: Financial Management Solutions, Employee Management Solutions and Payment Solutions. Financial Management Solutions includes QuickBooks financial and business management software and services, technical support, financial supplies, as well as Intuit Websites, which provides website design and hosting services for small and medium-sized businesses. The Employee Management Solutions division provides payroll products and services for small businesses. Payment Solutions offers merchant services for small businesses, including credit and debit card processing, electronic check conversion and automated clearing house services. The Tax segment operates in two divisions: Consumer Tax, which includes TurboTax income tax preparation products and services for consumers and small businesses; and the Accounting Professionals division, which includes LaCerte and ProSeries professional tax products and services. The Financial Services segment consists of outsourced online services for banks and credit unions provided by Intuit Financial Services Business. Other Businesses includes Quicken personal finance products and services; Mint.com online personal finance services; Intuit Health online patient-to-provider communication solutions; and the company's businesses in Canada and the UK. In January 2010, the company sold Intuit Real Estate Solutions to Vista Equity Partners for approximately $128 million. In May 2010, Intuit acquired Medfusion, a North Carolina based patient-to-provider communications company, for approximately $91 million. In July 2010, the firm combined Medfusion with its Quicken Health Group to form a new business unit called Intuit Health.

FINANCIALS: **Sales and profits are in thousands of dollars—add 000 to get the full amount. 2010 Note: Financial information for 2010 was not available for all companies at press time.**

2010 Sales: $3,455,000 | 2010 Profits: $574,000
2009 Sales: $3,109,000 | 2009 Profits: $447,000
2008 Sales: $2,993,000 | 2008 Profits: $476,762
2007 Sales: $2,672,947 | 2007 Profits: $440,003
2006 Sales: $2,293,010 | 2006 Profits: $416,963

U.S. Stock Ticker: INTU
Int'l Ticker:
Int'l Exchange:
Employees: 7,700 Fiscal Year Ends: 7/31
Parent Company:

SALARIES/BENEFITS:

Pension Plan: ESOP Stock Plan: Profit Sharing: Top Exec. Salary: $800,000 Bonus: $1,428,000
Savings Plan: Y Stock Purch. Plan: Y Second Exec. Salary: $700,000 Bonus: $1,025,000

OTHER THOUGHTS:

Apparent Women Officers or Directors: 5
Hot Spot for Advancement for Women/Minorities: Y

LOCATIONS: ("Y" = Yes)

West:	Southwest:	Midwest:	Southeast:	Northeast:	International:
Y	Y	Y	Y	Y	Y

Sales, profits and employees may be estimates. Financial information, benefits and other data can change quickly and may vary from those stated here.

INVENTIV HEALTH INC

www.ventiv.com

Industry Group Code: 541613

Management:		Sales/Marketing:		Liberal Arts:		Information Sys.:		Professionals:		Tech./Scientific:	
Mgmt. Trainees:	Y	Marketing Pros.:	Y	Gen. Writing/Editing:	Y	Info. Mgmt.:	Y	Finance/Acct.:	Y	Engineers, Elec.:	
Experienced Mgmt.:	Y	Retail Sales:		Tech. Writing:	Y	Software Dev.:	Y	Law:	Y	Engineers, Other:	
Int'l Business:	Y	Comm./Industrial:	Y	Graphic Arts/Photog.:	Y	Hardware Dev.:		HR/Other:	Y	Health/Lab:	
MBA Grads:	Y	Sales Trainees:		Music:		Consulting/Other:	Y	Training:	Y	Science/Research:	
		Advertising Pros.:		Broadcasting:				Health Care:	Y	Petroleum/Chem.:	
				Other:	Y			Consulting:	Y	Math/Other:	

TYPES OF BUSINESS:

Marketing-Life Sciences & Pharmaceuticals
Sales & Marketing Outsourcing
Clinical Staffing
Health Care Communications
Advertising Services
Data Services
Sales Force Deployment
Clinical & Statistical Research

BRANDS/DIVISIONS/AFFILIATES:

inVentiv Commercial Services
inVentiv Communications
inVentiv Clinical Services
inVentiv Patient Outcomes
GSW Worldwide
Stonefly Communications Group LLC
Thomas H Lee Partners LP
Substrat'Homme SA

CONTACTS: *Note: Officers with more than one job title may be intentionally listed here more than once.*

Paul Meister, CEO
Joe Massaro, CFO
Tristen Herrstrom, Chief Resource Officer
Tony Jerig, CIO
Dan Twibell, Chief Client Dev. Officer
Marcia Frederick, Chief Comm. Officer
Paul Mignon, COO-inVentiv Commercial/Pres., Selling Solutions
William O'Donnell, COO/Pres., inVentiv Communications
Dan Rubin, Pres., inVentiv Patient Outcomes
Tricia Glover, Chief Compliance Officer
Paul Meister, Chmn.
Rick Finnegan, Exec. VP-Int'l, inVentiv Commercial

Phone: 732-537-4800	**Fax:** 732-537-4912
Toll-Free: 800-416-0555	
Address: 500 Atrium Dr., Somerset, NJ 08873 US	

GROWTH PLANS/SPECIAL FEATURES:

inVentiv Health, Inc. is a clinical services and marketing services provider for the pharmaceutical and life sciences industry. inVentiv's services include sales and marketing; clinical staffing; planning and analytics; marketing support; professional development and training; and data collection and management. It operates in four business units: inVentiv Commercial, inVentiv Communications, inVentiv Clinical and inVentiv Patient Outcomes. inVentiv Commercial is comprised of inVentiv Selling Solutions, which encompass activities related to sales teams and sales support services; and inVentiv Advance Insights, which focuses on strategic and tactical planning, market research and commercial analytics. inVentiv Communications provides advertising, business communications, branding, medical education and contract marketing services via subsidiaries GSW Worldwide; Palio Communications LLC; Navicor Group LLC; Stonefly Communications Group LLC; Angela Liedler GmbH; Chamberlain Communications LLC; and Jeffrey Simbrow and Associates. inVentiv Clinical consists of subsidiaries Smith Hanley Associates LLC; Smith Hanley Consulting Group LLC; and MedFocus LLC (collectively Smith Hanley), as well as recently acquired ParagonRx. Other subsidiaries include HHI Clinical & Statistical Research Services LLC and Anova Clinical Resources LLC. This segment provides services related to recruitment, clinical staffing and data collection and management. inVentiv Patient Outcomes provides services related to patient adherence, assistance and reimbursement; clinical educator teams; and medical cost containment and disease management. The segment includes Adheris, Inc.; The Franklin Group; The Therapeutics Institute; AWAC LLC; and Patient Marketing Group LLC. In August 2010, the company was acquired by a group of private investors that included Thomas H. Lee Partners, L.P., Liberty Lane Partners, LLP and others. In September 2010, the firm acquired Substrat'Homme SA. In January 2011, it agreed to acquire the i3 clinical development businesses from Ingenix. In February 2011, inVentiv acquired Campbell Alliance.

The firm offers its employees health and life insurance, as well as a 401(k) plan.

FINANCIALS: **Sales and profits are in thousands of dollars—add 000 to get the full amount. 2010 Note: Financial information for 2010 was not available for all companies at press time.**

2010 Sales: $4,359,700	2010 Profits: $56,150	**U.S. Stock Ticker: Private**
2009 Sales: $4,270,010	2009 Profits: $62,610	**Int'l Ticker:**
2008 Sales: $1,119,812	2008 Profits: $-128,021	Int'l Exchange:
2007 Sales: $977,300	2007 Profits: $47,484	Employees: 6,400 Fiscal Year Ends: 12/31
2006 Sales: $766,245	2006 Profits: $51,235	Parent Company: THOMAS H LEE PARTNERS LP

SALARIES/BENEFITS:

Pension Plan:	ESOP Stock Plan:	Profit Sharing:	Top Exec. Salary: $541,874	Bonus: $574,602
Savings Plan: Y	Stock Purch. Plan:		Second Exec. Salary: $505,385	Bonus: $

OTHER THOUGHTS:

Apparent Women Officers or Directors: 3
Hot Spot for Advancement for Women/Minorities: Y

LOCATIONS: ("Y" = Yes)

West:	Southwest:	Midwest:	Southeast:	Northeast:	International:
Y	Y	Y	Y	Y	Y

JACK HENRY & ASSOCIATES INC

www.jackhenry.com

Industry Group Code: 511201

Management:		Sales/Marketing:		Liberal Arts:		Information Sys.:		Professionals:		Tech./Scientific:	
Mgmt. Trainees:		Marketing Pros.:	Y	Gen. Writing/Editing:		Info. Mgmt.:	Y	Finance/Acct.:	Y	Engineers, Elec.:	Y
Experienced Mgmt.:	Y	Retail Sales:		Tech. Writing:	Y	Software Dev.:	Y	Law:	Y	Engineers, Other:	
Int'l Business:		Comm./Industrial:	Y	Graphic Arts/Photog.:		Hardware Dev.:	Y	HR/Other:	Y	Health/Lab:	
MBA Grads:	Y	Sales Trainees:		Music:		Consulting/Other:		Training:	Y	Science/Research:	
		Advertising Pros.:	Y	Broadcasting:				Health Care:		Petroleum/Chem.:	
				Other:				Consulting:		Math/Other:	

TYPES OF BUSINESS:

Software-Data Processing
Financial Services Software
Consulting Services
Hardware Sales

BRANDS/DIVISIONS/AFFILIATES:

Silverlake System
CIF 20/20
Core Director
Episys
Symitar
ProfitStars
iPay Technologies
Cruise

CONTACTS:

Note: Officers with more than one job title may be intentionally listed here more than once.

John F. Prim, CEO
Tony L. Wormington, Pres.
Kevin D. Williams, CFO
Mark Forbis, CTO/VP
Janet E. Gray, Sec.
Kevin D. Williams, Treas.
Jerry D. Hall, Exec. VP/Vice Chmn.
Michael E. Henry, Chmn.

Phone: 417-235-6652 **Fax:** 417-235-4281
Toll-Free: 800-299-4222
Address: 663 W. Hwy. 60, Monett, MO 65708 US

GROWTH PLANS/SPECIAL FEATURES:

Jack Henry & Associates, Inc. (JHA) is a leading provider of integrated computer systems relating to data processing and management information for banks, credit unions and other financial institutions in the U.S. The company serves more than 11,200 financial institutions and corporate entities. It provides its products and services through three marketed brands: Jack Henry Banking, Symitar, Profit Stars and iPay Technologies. Jack Henry Banking currently supports over 1,500 commercial banks with information and transaction processing platforms that provide enterprise-wide automation. Its core banking software platforms include SilverLake, an IBM System i-based product designed for commercial-focused banks with assets ranging from $500 million to $30 million; CIF 20/20, an IBM-System i-based system that supports 780 banks ranging from new institutions to those with assets exceeding $2 billion; and Core Director, a Windows-based client/server system that serves more than 250 banks ranging from new institutions to banks with assets over $1 billion. The Symitar brand supports credit unions through its two core platforms: Episys, an IBM System p-based program designed for credit unions with more than $50 million in assets; and Cruise, a Window-based client/server system designed for credit unions with less than $50 million in assets. ProfitStars provides approximately 65 specialized products and services to over 9,600 financial services organizations. Products include business intelligence and management applications; retail delivery products; business banking systems; electronic funds transfer products; Internet banking products; risk management and protection programs; document imaging products; and professional services and education products. iPay Technologies provides electronic bill pay services. The firm also sells re-marketed hardware products that support its software, such as IBM Power Systems, Lenovo workstations, Dell Servers and Canon check scanners. In June 2010, the company completed its acquisition of iPay Technologies.

The firm offers employees medical, dental and vision insurance; flexible spending accounts; and education assistance.

FINANCIALS:

Sales and profits are in thousands of dollars—add 000 to get the full amount. 2010 Note: Financial information for 2010 was not available for all companies at press time.

2010 Sales: $836,586	2010 Profits: $117,870
2009 Sales: $745,593	2009 Profits: $103,102
2008 Sales: $742,926	2008 Profits: $104,222
2007 Sales: $666,467	2007 Profits: $104,681
2006 Sales: $590,877	2006 Profits: $89,923

U.S. Stock Ticker: JKHY
Int'l Ticker:
Int'l Exchange:
Employees: 4,528 Fiscal Year Ends: 6/30
Parent Company:

SALARIES/BENEFITS:

Pension Plan:	ESOP Stock Plan:	Profit Sharing:	Top Exec. Salary: $495,733	Bonus: $625,430
Savings Plan: Y	Stock Purch. Plan: Y		Second Exec. Salary: $408,484	Bonus: $394,094

OTHER THOUGHTS:

Apparent Women Officers or Directors: 1
Hot Spot for Advancement for Women/Minorities:

LOCATIONS: ("Y" = Yes)

West:	Southwest:	Midwest:	Southeast:	Northeast:	International:
Y	Y	Y	Y	Y	

JACKSON NATIONAL LIFE INSURANCE COMPANY www.jnl.com

Industry Group Code: 524113

Management:		Sales/Marketing:		Liberal Arts:		Information Sys.:		Professionals:		Tech./Scientific:	
Mgmt. Trainees:		Marketing Pros.:	Y	Gen. Writing/Editing:	Y	Info. Mgmt.:	Y	Finance/Acct.:	Y	Engineers, Elec.:	
Experienced Mgmt.:		Retail Sales:		Tech. Writing:		Software Dev.:		Law:	Y	Engineers, Other:	
Int'l Business:		Comm./Industrial:		Graphic Arts/Photog.:		Hardware Dev.:		HR/Other:	Y	Health/Lab:	
MBA Grads:	Y	Sales Trainees:	Y	Music:		Consulting/Other:		Training:	Y	Science/Research:	
		Advertising Pros.:	Y	Broadcasting:				Health Care:	Y	Petroleum/Chem.:	
				Other:	Y			Consulting:		Math/Other:	

TYPES OF BUSINESS:

Life Insurance
Financial Services
Annuities
Asset Management
Retail Brokerage Services

BRANDS/DIVISIONS/AFFILIATES:

Prudential plc
Jackson National Life Distributors LLC
Curian Capital LLC
PPM America, Inc.
JNL Southeast Agency LLC
National Planning Holdings, Inc.
Jackson National Asset Management LLC
PPM Finance, Inc.

CONTACTS: *Note: Officers with more than one job title may be intentionally listed here more than once.*

Michael A. Wells, CEO
James R. Sopha, COO
Michael A. Wells, Pres.
P. Chad Myers, CFO/Exec. VP
J. Mark Clark, CIO/Sr. VP
Laura L. Prieskorn, Chief Admin. Officer/Sr. VP
Thomas Meyer, General Counsel/Sr. VP/Sec.
Kenneth H. Stewart, Sr. VP-Corp. Dev.
Clifford J. Jack, Head-Retail/Exec. VP
Lisa Drake, Chief Actuary/Sr. VP

Phone: 517-381-5500	**Fax:** 517-706-5521
Toll-Free:	
Address: 1 Corporate Way, Lansing, MI 48951 US	

GROWTH PLANS/SPECIAL FEATURES:

Jackson National Life Insurance Company, an indirect wholly-owned subsidiary of U.K. firm Prudential plc, offers life insurance and financial services such as fixed, indexed and variable annuities. In addition, the company offers life insurance and institution products and, through subsidiaries and affiliated firms, asset management and retail brokerage services. The firm has nearly $107 billion in total assets. Jackson National markets its products throughout the U.S. through wholesalers and broker/dealers. Jackson National Life Distributors LLC, a wholesale distributor subsidiary, operates in two groups: registered wholesalers, which target independent broker-dealers whose representatives are registered securities brokers; and guaranteed wholesalers, which market fixed and fixed index annuities and life insurance products. The company's Institutional Products Group markets annuity and life insurance products to financial institutions. The group also offers specialized education programs to financial institutions. Curian Capital LLC is the firm's asset management subsidiary, providing customized investment solutions. National Planning Holdings, Inc. is Jackson's National affiliated network of independent broker-dealers. Subsidiary JNL Southeast Agency LLC, based in Atlanta, Georgia, is a career agency that sells the company's traditional life insurance and fixed annuity products. With more than 100 area sales representatives, JNL provides these products to customers in Arkansas, Florida, Georgia, North Carolina, Mississippi, Virginia, South Carolina and Tennessee. Subsidiary Jackson National Asset Management LLC provides fund account and reporting for Jackson National's variable funds. Subsidiary PPM America, Inc. and affiliate PPM Finance, Inc. manage the company's investment portfolio.

Jackson National offers employees benefits such as health dental and vision plans, flexible spending accounts, short- and long-term disability coverage and product discounts.

FINANCIALS: **Sales and profits are in thousands of dollars—add 000 to get the full amount. 2010 Note: Financial information for 2010 was not available for all companies at press time.**

2010 Sales: $18,000,000	2010 Profits: $509,000
2009 Sales: $14,200,000	2009 Profits: $670,000
2008 Sales: $2,340,061	2008 Profits: $-981,863
2007 Sales: $4,110,144	2007 Profits: $619,279
2006 Sales: $3,712,167	2006 Profits: $541,565

U.S. Stock Ticker: Subsidiary
Int'l Ticker:
Int'l Exchange:
Employees: 3,000 Fiscal Year Ends: 12/31
Parent Company: PRUDENTIAL PLC

SALARIES/BENEFITS:

Pension Plan:	ESOP Stock Plan:	Profit Sharing:	Top Exec. Salary: $	Bonus: $
Savings Plan: Y	Stock Purch. Plan:		Second Exec. Salary: $	Bonus: $

OTHER THOUGHTS:

Apparent Women Officers or Directors: 3
Hot Spot for Advancement for Women/Minorities: Y

LOCATIONS: ("Y" = Yes)

West:	Southwest:	Midwest:	Southeast:	Northeast:	International:
Y	Y	Y	Y	Y	

JARDEN CORP

www.jarden.com

Industry Group Code: 315

Management:		Sales/Marketing:		Liberal Arts:		Information Sys.:		Professionals:		Tech./Scientific:	
Mgmt. Trainees:		Marketing Pros.:	Y	Gen. Writing/Editing:	Y	Info. Mgmt.:	Y	Finance/Acct.:	Y	Engineers, Elec.:	
Experienced Mgmt.:	Y	Retail Sales:		Tech. Writing:		Software Dev.:		Law:	Y	Engineers, Other:	Y
Int'l Business:		Comm./Industrial:	Y	Graphic Arts/Photog.:	Y	Hardware Dev.:		HR/Other:	Y	Health/Lab:	
MBA Grads:	Y	Sales Trainees:	Y	Music:		Consulting/Other:		Training:		Science/Research:	
		Advertising Pros.:	Y	Broadcasting:				Health Care:		Petroleum/Chem.:	
				Other:				Consulting:		Math/Other:	

TYPES OF BUSINESS:

Manufacturing - Consumer Products
Manufacturing - Outdoor Products
Manufacturing - Sports Equipment
Manufacturing - Consumables

BRANDS/DIVISIONS/AFFILIATES:

VillaWare
K2
Coleman
Marmot
Crock-Pot
Bee
FoodSaver
Oster

CONTACTS: *Note: Officers with more than one job title may be intentionally listed here more than once.*

Martin E. Franklin, CEO
James E. Lillie, COO
James E. Lillie, Pres.
Ian G. H. Ashken, CFO/Vice Chmn.
J. David Tolbert, Sr. VP-Human Resources & Corp. Risk
John E. Capps, General Counsel/Corp. Sec./Exec. VP
Patricia J. Gaglione, Sr. VP-Bus. Oper.
Patricia A. Mount, Chief Transition Officer/Sr. VP
Richard T. Sansone, Chief Acct. Officer/Sr. VP
Martin E. Franklin, Chmn.
Patricia J. Gaglione, Sr. VP-Supply Chain

Phone: 914-967-9400	**Fax:** 914-967-9405
Toll-Free:	
Address: 555 Theodore Fremd Ave., Rye, NY 10580 US	

GROWTH PLANS/SPECIAL FEATURES:

Jarden Corp. is a leading global manufacturer, marketer and distributor of niche consumer products. It operates in three segments: outdoor solutions, consumer solutions and branded consumables. In its outdoor solutions segment, Jarden provides camping, backpacking, tailgating and outdoor cooking products under its Campingaz and Coleman brands; water sports equipment and all-terrain vehicle equipment under its Stearns, Sevylor and Mad Dog Gear brands; fishing equipment under brands such as Abu Garcia, All Star, Berkley, Fenwick, Gulp!, JRC, Mitchell, Penn, Stren, Trilene, Pure Fishing and Ugly Stik brands; baseball, softball, football, basketball and lacrosse products under its deBeer, Gait, Miken, Rawlings and Worth brands; skiing, snowboarding, snowshoeing and in-line skating products under its K2, Marker and Volkl brands; and technical outdoor apparel and equipment under its Marmot and Planet Earth brands. In its consumer solutions segment, the company provides coffeemakers, bedding, home vacuum packaging machines, heating pads, slow cookers, air cleaning products, fans, heaters, pet care products and personal grooming products. Its kitchen products are sold under such brands as Crock-Pot, FoodSaver, Mr. Coffee, Oster, Rival, Seal-a-Meal, Sunbeam and VillaWare. Personal care products include such brands as Health o meter, Oster and Sunbeam. Jarden's air conditioning brands include Bionaire, Holmes and Patton. In its branded consumables segment, the company provides such products as arts and crafts items; collectible tins; playing cards; clothespins; toothpicks; plastic cutlery; home canning supplies; rope, cord and twine; firelogs and firestarters; kitchen matches; and home safety equipment. Brand names in this segment include Ball, Bee, Bicycle, Crawford, Diamond, Dicon, First Alert, Forster, Hoyle, Java-Log, Kerr, Lehigh, Leslie-Lock, Loew-Cornell and Pine Mountain. In April 2010, Jarden acquired the Mapa Spontex Home Care and Baby Care businesses of Total S.A. for $500 million.

FINANCIALS: **Sales and profits are in thousands of dollars—add 000 to get the full amount. 2010 Note: Financial information for 2010 was not available for all companies at press time.**

2010 Sales: $6,022,700	2010 Profits: $106,700	**U.S. Stock Ticker: JAH**
2009 Sales: $5,152,600	2009 Profits: $128,700	**Int'l Ticker:**
2008 Sales: $5,383,300	2008 Profits: $-58,900	Int'l Exchange:
2007 Sales: $4,660,100	2007 Profits: $28,100	Employees: 24,000 Fiscal Year Ends: 12/31
2006 Sales: $3,846,300	2006 Profits: $106,000	Parent Company:

SALARIES/BENEFITS:

Pension Plan:	ESOP Stock Plan:	Profit Sharing:	Top Exec. Salary: $2,034,728	Bonus: $4,069,456
Savings Plan:	Stock Purch. Plan:		Second Exec. Salary: $939,105	Bonus: $1,878,210

OTHER THOUGHTS:

Apparent Women Officers or Directors: 2
Hot Spot for Advancement for Women/Minorities:

LOCATIONS: ("Y" = Yes)

West:	Southwest:	Midwest:	Southeast:	Northeast:	International:
Y	Y	Y	Y	Y	

JB HUNT TRANSPORT SERVICES INC

www.jbhunt.com

Industry Group Code: 484

Management:		Sales/Marketing:		Liberal Arts:		Information Sys.:		Professionals:		Tech./Scientific:	
Mgmt. Trainees:	Y	Marketing Pros.:	Y	Gen. Writing/Editing:		Info. Mgmt.:	Y	Finance/Acct.:	Y	Engineers, Elec.:	
Experienced Mgmt.:	Y	Retail Sales:		Tech. Writing:	Y	Software Dev.:	Y	Law:	Y	Engineers, Other:	
Int'l Business:	Y	Comm./Industrial:	Y	Graphic Arts/Photog.:		Hardware Dev.:		HR/Other:	Y	Health/Lab:	
MBA Grads:	Y	Sales Trainees:		Music:		Consulting/Other:		Training:	Y	Science/Research:	
		Advertising Pros.:		Broadcasting:				Health Care:		Petroleum/Chem.:	
				Other:				Consulting:		Math/Other:	

TYPES OF BUSINESS:

General Trucking
Logistics Services
Intermodal Services

BRANDS/DIVISIONS/AFFILIATES:

CONTACTS:

Note: Officers with more than one job title may be intentionally listed here more than once.

John N. Roberts, III, CEO
Craig Harper, COO
John N. Roberts, III, Pres.
David G. Mee, CFO/Exec. VP-Finance
Paul R. Bergant, Chief Mktg. Officer/Exec. VP/Pres., Intermodal
Kay Palmer, CIO/Exec. VP
David G. Mee, Exec. VP-Admin.
David G. Mee, Corp. Sec.
Craig Harper, Exec. VP-Oper.
Donald G. Cope, Chief Acct. Officer/Controller/Sr. VP
Bob D. Ralston, Exec. VP-Equipment & Properties
Nick Hobbs, Exec. VP/Pres., Dedicated Contract Svcs.
Terrence D. Matthews, Exec. VP-Sales & Mktg.
David Chelette, VP/Treas.
Kirk Thompson, Chmn.

Phone: 479-820-0000 **Fax:** 479-659-6297
Toll-Free: 800-643-3622
Address: 615 J.B. Hunt Corporate Dr., Lowell, AR 72745 US

GROWTH PLANS/SPECIAL FEATURES:

J.B. Hunt Transport Services, Inc. is a North American truckload transportation and logistics company servicing the U.S., Canada and Mexico. J.B. Hunt's operations are organized into four business segments: Full truckload dry-van freight, intermodal, dedicated contract services and integrated capacity solutions. The full truckload dry-van freight segment (14% of revenues) consists of conventional truck transport services in which company-controlled tractors pick up, transport and deliver cargo. J.B. Hunt dedicates 1,698 company-controlled tractors to this segment. The segment also has 1,163 independent contractors, some of whom lease company-owned tractors. The intermodal business segment (55% of revenues) utilizes agreements with rail carriers under which those carriers provide for railway movement of goods while J.B. Hunt provides for the drayage (i.e. transport of goods by truck to and from rail terminals). The segment operates 40,170 company-controlled containers system wide. It also manages a fleet of 2,303 company-owned tractors. The dedicated contract services segment (24% of revenues) involves the provision of customized services governed by long-term contracts and currently includes dry-van, flatbed, temperature-controlled, dump trailers and local inner-city operations. This segment essentially specializes in the design, development and execution of customer-specific fleet services, including private fleet conversion, dedicated fleet creation and transportation system augmentation. It operates 3,969 company-controlled trucks, 358 customer-owned trucks and 31 independent contractor trucks. The integrated capacity solutions division (7% of revenues) provides non-asset and asset-light transportation solutions to customers through relationships with third-party carriers and integration with company owned equipment.

Employees are offered life, disability, auto, home, medical, dental and vision insurance; a 401(k) plan; and healthcare and dependent care reimbursement accounts.

FINANCIALS:

Sales and profits are in thousands of dollars—add 000 to get the full amount. 2010 Note: Financial information for 2010 was not available for all companies at press time.

2010 Sales: $3,793,000	2010 Profits: $200,000
2009 Sales: $3,203,321	2009 Profits: $136,435
2008 Sales: $3,731,943	2008 Profits: $200,593
2007 Sales: $3,489,899	2007 Profits: $213,134
2006 Sales: $3,327,987	2006 Profits: $219,952

U.S. Stock Ticker: JBHT
Int'l Ticker:
Int'l Exchange:
Employees: 15,223 Fiscal Year Ends: 12/31
Parent Company:

SALARIES/BENEFITS:

Pension Plan: ESOP Stock Plan: Profit Sharing: Top Exec. Salary: $695,000 Bonus: $
Savings Plan: Y Stock Purch. Plan: Second Exec. Salary: $530,000 Bonus: $

OTHER THOUGHTS:

Apparent Women Officers or Directors: 2
Hot Spot for Advancement for Women/Minorities:

LOCATIONS: ("Y" = Yes)

West:	Southwest:	Midwest:	Southeast:	Northeast:	International:
Y	Y	Y	Y	Y	

JETBLUE AIRWAYS CORPORATION

www.jetblue.com

Industry Group Code: 481111

Management:		Sales/Marketing:		Liberal Arts:		Information Sys.:		Professionals:		Tech./Scientific:	
Mgmt. Trainees:	Y	Marketing Pros.:	Y	Gen. Writing/Editing:	Y	Info. Mgmt.:	Y	Finance/Acct.:	Y	Engineers, Elec.:	Y
Experienced Mgmt.:	Y	Retail Sales:		Tech. Writing:	Y	Software Dev.:	Y	Law:	Y	Engineers, Other:	Y
Int'l Business:	Y	Comm./Industrial:		Graphic Arts/Photog.:	Y	Hardware Dev.:		HR/Other:	Y	Health/Lab:	
MBA Grads:	Y	Sales Trainees:		Music:		Consulting/Other:		Training:	Y	Science/Research:	
		Advertising Pros.:	Y	Broadcasting:				Health Care:	Y	Petroleum/Chem.:	
				Other:	Y			Consulting:		Math/Other:	

TYPES OF BUSINESS:

Airline
In-Flight Entertainment

BRANDS/DIVISIONS/AFFILIATES:

JetBlue Getaways
Jet Blue Features
PlusTV

CONTACTS: *Note: Officers with more than one job title may be intentionally listed here more than once.*

David Barger, CEO
Robert Maruster, COO/Exec. VP
David Barger, Pres.
Ed Barnes, CFO/Exec. VP
Robin Hayes, Chief Commercial Officer/Exec. VP
Joanna Geraghty, Chief People Officer/Exec. VP
Joseph Eng, CIO/Exec. VP
James Hnat, General Counsel/Corp. Sec.
Jenny Dervin, VP-Corp. Comm.
Don Daniels, Chief Acct. Officer/VP
Harry L. Spencer, VP-Compensation & Benefits
James Hnat, Exec. VP-Corp. Affair
Jeffrey Goodell, VP-Gov't Affairs
Warren Christie, VP-JetBlue University
Joel Peterson, Chmn.

Phone: 718-286-7900	**Fax:**
Toll-Free: 800-538-2583	
Address: 118-29 Queens Blvd., Forest Hills, NY 11375 US	

GROWTH PLANS/SPECIAL FEATURES:

JetBlue Airways Corporation is a low-fare, low-cost passenger airline. It primarily operates on point-to-point routes with its fleet of 115 Airbus A320 aircraft and 45 EMBRAER 190 aircraft. It serves 63 destinations in 21 states, Puerto Rico and eleven countries in the Caribbean and Latin America. The majority of its average 650 daily flights have as an origin or destination one of the company's four focus cities: Boston, Ft. Lauderdale, Los Angeles/Long Beach, New York and Orlando. The company's flights are single-class, but feature leather seats and seat-back televisions with 36 channels of live DirecTV programming, 41 channels on its proprietary PlusTV network, 100 stations of free SiriusXM satellite radio and movie channel offerings from Jet Blue Features. In 2010, the firm completed 98.1% of scheduled flights. JetBlue sells vacation packages through JetBlue Getaways, a one-stop website designed to meet customers' demand for packaged travel planning. The firm also participates in four major global distribution systems: Sabre, Galileo, Worldspan and Amadeus; and four major online travel agents (OTAs): Expedia, Travelocity, Orbitz and Priceline. The company consistently receives top marks in consumer surveys conducted by JD Power & Associates.

JetBlue offers employees medical, dental, vision and life insurance; short- and long-term disability insurance; a group legal plan; flexible spending accounts; pilot loss of license; health risk assessments; disease management programs; a 401(k) plan; a Roth 401(k) plan; self-directed accounts; a profit sharing plan; a stock purchase plan; and free and reduced rate standby travel on JetBlue flights.

FINANCIALS: **Sales and profits are in thousands of dollars—add 000 to get the full amount. 2010 Note: Financial information for 2010 was not available for all companies at press time.**

2010 Sales: $3,779,000	2010 Profits: $97,000	**U.S. Stock Ticker: JBLU**
2009 Sales: $3,292,000	2009 Profits: $61,000	**Int'l Ticker:**
2008 Sales: $3,388,000	2008 Profits: $-85,000	Int'l Exchange:
2007 Sales: $2,842,000	2007 Profits: $12,000	Employees: 11,609 Fiscal Year Ends: 12/31
2006 Sales: $2,363,000	2006 Profits: $-1,000	Parent Company:

SALARIES/BENEFITS:

Pension Plan:	ESOP Stock Plan:	Profit Sharing: Y	Top Exec. Salary: $600,000	Bonus: $300,000
Savings Plan: Y	Stock Purch. Plan: Y		Second Exec. Salary: $400,000	Bonus: $200,000

OTHER THOUGHTS:

Apparent Women Officers or Directors: 4
Hot Spot for Advancement for Women/Minorities: Y

LOCATIONS: ("Y" = Yes)

West:	Southwest:	Midwest:	Southeast:	Northeast:	International:
Y	Y	Y	Y	Y	Y

JM SMUCKER CO

www.smucker.com

Industry Group Code: 311

Management:		Sales/Marketing:		Liberal Arts:		Information Sys.:		Professionals:		Tech./Scientific:	
Mgmt. Trainees:	Y	Marketing Pros.:	Y	Gen. Writing/Editing:	Y	Info. Mgmt.:	Y	Finance/Acct.:	Y	Engineers, Elec.:	
Experienced Mgmt.:	Y	Retail Sales:		Tech. Writing:		Software Dev.:		Law:	Y	Engineers, Other:	Y
Int'l Business:	Y	Comm./Industrial:	Y	Graphic Arts/Photog.:	Y	Hardware Dev.:		HR/Other:	Y	Health/Lab:	
MBA Grads:	Y	Sales Trainees:	Y	Music:		Consulting/Other:		Training:	Y	Science/Research:	
		Advertising Pros.:	Y	Broadcasting:				Health Care:		Petroleum/Chem.:	
				Other:				Consulting:		Math/Other:	

TYPES OF BUSINESS:

Food Products, Manufacturing
Fruit Spreads
Dessert Toppings
Peanut Butter
Beverages
Shortening and Oils
Baking Mixes
Condiments

BRANDS/DIVISIONS/AFFILIATES:

Smuckers
Jif
Crisco
Uncrustables
Adams
Pillsbury
Knott's Berry Farm
Folgers

CONTACTS:

Note: Officers with more than one job title may be intentionally listed here more than once.

Timothy P. Smucker, Co-CEO
Mark R. Belgya, CFO/Sr. VP
Christopher P. Resweber, VP-Mktg. Svcs.
Andrew G. Platt, CIO/VP-Info. Svcs.
M. Ann Harlan, General Counsel/VP-Legal
Dennis J. Armstrong, Sr. VP-Oper.
Barry C. Dunaway, Sr. VP-Corp. & Organization Dev.
John W. Denman, Controller/VP
Richard K. Smucker, Co-CEO/Exec. Chmn.
Vincent C. Byrd, Pres., U.S. Retail-Coffee
Paul Smucker Wagstaff, Pres., U.S. Retail-Oils & Baking
Steven Oakland, Pres., U.S. Retail-Smucker's Jif & Hungry Jack
Timothy P. Smucker, Chmn.
Dennis J. Armstrong, Sr. VP-Logistics

Phone: 330-682-3000 **Fax:** 330-684-6410
Toll-Free: 888-550-9555
Address: 1 Strawberry Ln., Orrville, OH 44667-0280 US

GROWTH PLANS/SPECIAL FEATURES:

J.M. Smucker Co. (Smuckers) manufactures and markets branded food products on a worldwide basis, with the majority of its sales in the U.S. and Canada. Products offered by Smuckers include peanut butter; shortening and oils; flour and baking ingredients; fruit spreads; baking mixes and ready-to-spread frostings; fruit and vegetable juices; beverages; coffee; dessert toppings; syrups; frozen sandwiches; pickles and condiments; and canned milk. Products are sold through brokers to food retailers, food wholesalers, club stores, mass merchandisers, discount stores and military commissaries. The company sells to food service distributors and operators including restaurants, schools and universities; health care operators; and health/natural food stores. The raw fruit materials used by Smuckers in the production of its food products are purchased from independent growers and suppliers. The company's major trademarks include Smuckers, Jif, Crisco, Dutch Girl, White Lily, Hungry Jack, Uncrustables, Adams, Laura Scudder's, Goober, Pet, R. W. Knudsen Family, and Magic Shell. Smuckers also uses the Pillsbury trademark under a royalty-free license. The company owns the brands Knott's Berry Farm and Folgers coffee. Knott's Berry Farm sells jellies and preserves and Folgers coffee sells coffee by flavors, decaf and instant coffee. Products are also available to customers through Smucker's web site.

Employees are offered medical, dental, life and disability insurance; a pension plan; a 401(k) plan; and an employee stock ownership plan.

FINANCIALS:

Sales and profits are in thousands of dollars—add 000 to get the full amount. 2010 Note: Financial information for 2010 was not available for all companies at press time.

2010 Sales: $4,605,289	2010 Profits: $494,138
2009 Sales: $3,757,933	2009 Profits: $265,953
2008 Sales: $2,524,774	2008 Profits: $170,379
2007 Sales: $2,148,017	2007 Profits: $157,219
2006 Sales: $2,154,726	2006 Profits: $143,354

U.S. Stock Ticker: SJM
Int'l Ticker:
Int'l Exchange:
Employees: 4,850 Fiscal Year Ends: 4/30
Parent Company:

SALARIES/BENEFITS:

Pension Plan: Y	ESOP Stock Plan: Y	Profit Sharing:	Top Exec. Salary: $820,000	Bonus: $1,574,400
Savings Plan: Y	Stock Purch. Plan:		Second Exec. Salary: $820,000	Bonus: $1,574,400

OTHER THOUGHTS:

Apparent Women Officers or Directors: 6
Hot Spot for Advancement for Women/Minorities: Y

LOCATIONS: ("Y" = Yes)

West:	Southwest:	Midwest:	Southeast:	Northeast:	International:
Y	Y	Y	Y	Y	Y

JOHNSON & JOHNSON

www.jnj.com

Industry Group Code: 325412

Management:		Sales/Marketing:		Liberal Arts:		Information Sys.:		Professionals:		Tech./Scientific:	
Mgmt. Trainees:	Y	Marketing Pros.:	Y	Gen. Writing/Editing:	Y	Info. Mgmt.:	Y	Finance/Acct.:	Y	Engineers, Elec.:	Y
Experienced Mgmt.:	Y	Retail Sales:		Tech. Writing:	Y	Software Dev.:	Y	Law:	Y	Engineers, Other:	Y
Int'l Business:	Y	Comm./Industrial:	Y	Graphic Arts/Photog.:	Y	Hardware Dev.:		HR/Other:	Y	Health/Lab:	Y
MBA Grads:	Y	Sales Trainees:	Y	Music:		Consulting/Other:		Training:	Y	Science/Research:	Y
		Advertising Pros.:	Y	Broadcasting:				Health Care:	Y	Petroleum/Chem.:	Y
				Other:				Consulting:		Math/Other:	Y

TYPES OF BUSINESS:

Personal Health Care & Hygiene Products
Sterilization Products
Surgical Products
Pharmaceuticals
Skin Care Products
Baby Care Products
Contact Lenses
Medical Equipment

BRANDS/DIVISIONS/AFFILIATES:

Alza Corp
Cordis Corp
DePuy Inc
Ethicon Inc
LifeScan Inc
Mentor Corp
Micrus Endovascular
Crucell N.V.

CONTACTS: *Note: Officers with more than one job title may be intentionally listed here more than once.*

William C. Weldon, CEO
Dominic J. Caruso, CFO
Peter M. Fasolo, VP-Human Resources
Russell C. Deyo, General Counsel/VP
Jeffrey Leebaw, VP-Media Rel.
Dominic J. Caruso, VP-Finance
Sheri McCoy, Vice Chmn.
Alex Gorsky, Vice Chmn.
William C. Weldon, Chmn.

Phone: 732-524-0400 **Fax:** 732-214-0332
Toll-Free:
Address: 1 Johnson & Johnson Plz., New Brunswick, NJ 08933 US

GROWTH PLANS/SPECIAL FEATURES:

Johnson & Johnson, founded in 1886, is one of the world's most comprehensive and well-known developers and manufacturers of health care products. The firm owns more than 250 companies in over 60 countries and markets its products in almost every country in the world. Johnson & Johnson's worldwide operations are divided into three segments: consumer; pharmaceuticals; and medical devices and diagnostics. The company's principal consumer goods are personal care and hygiene products, including baby care, skin care, oral care, wound care and women's health care products, as well as nutritional and over-the-counter pharmaceutical products. Major consumer brands include Motrin, Band-Aid, Listerine, Clean & Clear, Tylenol, Listerine, Neosporin, Aveeno and Pepcid AC. The pharmaceutical segment covers a wide spectrum of health fields, including anti-infective, antipsychotic, contraceptive, dermatology, gastrointestinal, hematology, immunology, neurology, oncology, pain management and virology. Among its pharmaceutical products are Risperdal, an antipsychotic used to treat schizophrenia, and Remicade for the treatment of immune mediated inflammatory diseases. In the medical devices and diagnostics segment, Johnson & Johnson makes a number of products including orthopedic joint reconstruction devices, surgical care, advanced sterilization products, blood glucose monitoring devices, diagnostic products and disposable contact lenses. Subsidiaries include Alza Corp.; CentoCor, Inc.; Cordis Corp.; DePuy, Inc.; Ethicon, Inc.; Lifescan, Inc.; Mentor Corp.; and Scios, Inc. Recently, Johnson & Johnson acquired an 18.4% stake in Elan Corporation, an Irish biotechnology firm; and acquired Elan's Alzheimer's drug development program. In January 2010, the firm's subsidiary Ethicon acquired Acclarent, Inc., a California-based medical device company. In September 2010, the company acquired Micrus Endovascular, a developer of minimally invasive medical products. In October 2010, Johnson & Johnson agreed to acquire Crucell N.V., a vaccine production company. In June 2011, the firm announced plans to exit its stents (used to open clogged arteries) business.

Johnson & Johnson offers its employees benefits that include medical coverage; an employee assistance program; and on-site fitness centers.

FINANCIALS: **Sales and profits are in thousands of dollars—add 000 to get the full amount. 2010 Note: Financial information for 2010 was not available for all companies at press time.**

2010 Sales: $61,587,000 — 2010 Profits: $13,334,000
2009 Sales: $61,897,000 — 2009 Profits: $12,266,000
2008 Sales: $63,747,000 — 2008 Profits: $12,949,000
2007 Sales: $61,095,000 — 2007 Profits: $10,576,000
2006 Sales: $53,324,000 — 2006 Profits: $11,053,000

U.S. Stock Ticker: JNJ
Int'l Ticker:
Int'l Exchange:
Employees: 114,000 Fiscal Year Ends: 1/31
Parent Company:

SALARIES/BENEFITS:

Pension Plan: ESOP Stock Plan: Profit Sharing: Top Exec. Salary: $1,802,500 Bonus: $12,831,146
Savings Plan: Y Stock Purch. Plan: Y Second Exec. Salary: $831,838 Bonus: $3,608,760

OTHER THOUGHTS:

Apparent Women Officers or Directors: 4
Hot Spot for Advancement for Women/Minorities: Y

LOCATIONS: ("Y" = Yes)

West:	Southwest:	Midwest:	Southeast:	Northeast:	International:
Y	Y	Y	Y	Y	Y

JOHNSON CONTROLS INC

www.johnsoncontrols.com

Industry Group Code: 3363

Management:		**Sales/Marketing:**		**Liberal Arts:**		**Information Sys.:**		**Professionals:**		**Tech./Scientific:**	
Mgmt. Trainees:	Y	Marketing Pros.:	Y	Gen. Writing/Editing:	Y	Info. Mgmt.:	Y	Finance/Acct.:	Y	Engineers, Elec.:	Y
Experienced Mgmt.:	Y	Retail Sales:		Tech. Writing:	Y	Software Dev.:	Y	Law:	Y	Engineers, Other:	Y
Int'l Business:	Y	Comm./Industrial:	Y	Graphic Arts/Photog.:	Y	Hardware Dev.:	Y	HR/Other:	Y	Health/Lab:	
MBA Grads:	Y	Sales Trainees:		Music:		Consulting/Other:		Training:	Y	Science/Research:	Y
		Advertising Pros.:	Y	Broadcasting:				Health Care:		Petroleum/Chem.:	
				Other:				Consulting:		Math/Other:	Y

TYPES OF BUSINESS:

Automobile Parts & Controls
Automotive Batteries
Facilities Management
Automotive Interior Components
Energy Management Services
Building Security, Lighting & HVAC Systems

BRANDS/DIVISIONS/AFFILIATES:

National Energy Services
Johnson Controls-Saft Advanced Power Solutions
C. Rob. Hammerstein Group
KEIPER
Varta
Metasys Sustainability Manager
Heliar
LTH

CONTACTS: *Note: Officers with more than one job title may be intentionally listed here more than once.*

Stephen A. Roell, CEO
Keith Wandell, COO
Stephen A. Roell, Pres.
R. Bruce McDonald, CFO/Exec. VP
Susan F. Davis, Exec. VP-Human Resources
Colin Boyd, CIO/VP-IT
Jerome D. Okarma, General Counsel/VP/Sec.
Jacqueline F. Strayer, VP-Corp. Comm.
Glen Ponczak, Exec. Dir.-Investor Rel.
Frank A. Voltolina, Corp. Treas./VP
C. David Meyers, VP/Pres., Building Efficiency
Jeffrey G. Augustin, VP-Finance, Building Efficiency
Alex A. Molinaroli, VP/Pres., Power Solutions
Charles A. Harvey, VP-Public Affairs & Diversity
Stephen A. Roell, Chmn.
Jeffrey S. Edwards, VP-Automotive Experience, Japan & APAC

Phone: 414-524-1200 **Fax:** 414-524-2070
Toll-Free: 800-524-6220
Address: 5757 N. Green Bay Ave., Milwaukee, WI 53209 US

GROWTH PLANS/SPECIAL FEATURES:

Johnson Controls, Inc. is a leader in automotive interiors/batteries, building efficiency and facility management. The firm's Automotive Experience segment, which accounts for roughly 49% of the company's sales, designs and manufactures concept cars; complete seat systems; seating components; electronics; instrument panels; overhead, door and cargo management systems; cockpits; and interior trim for manufacturers of cars and light trucks. The division operates approximately 175 wholly- and majority-owned manufacturing/assembly plants in 27 countries. Johnson Control's Power Solutions division (14% of sales) manufactures and replaces automotive batteries, focusing on innovations for hybrid electric vehicles. Its battery brands include Optima, Varta, Heliar (in South America), and LTH (in Mexico). The segment produces roughly 120 million lead-acid batteries annually in approximately 55 wholly- and majority-owned manufacturing/assembly facilities in 18 countries. The Building Efficiency division (37% of sales) operates in 59 countries, supplying systems designed for heating; ventilation; air conditioning; lighting; security; and fire management. The U.S. Department of Defense utilizes Johnson Controls for the Pentagon's energy management and environmental control systems. Global WorkPlace Solutions, part of Building Efficiency, provides companies with a real-estate based approach to shareholder value. The Building Efficiency division also does facility management, using its patented Metasys Building Management System. It handles school districts, hospitals, factories, airports and government facilities. Johnson Controls has a joint venture with Saft SA, a battery company, called Johnson Controls-Saft Advanced Power Solutions. In March 2010, Johnson Controls acquired lighting services firm National Energy Services. In December 2010, the firm agreed to acquire German recliner system technology group KEIPER and the automotive sport and specialty seat operations of Recaro. In February 2011, Johnson Controls acquired metal seat manufacturer C. Rob. Hammerstein Group.

The firm offers employees benefits including health care coverage, tuition reimbursement and a 401(k) plan.

FINANCIALS: **Sales and profits are in thousands of dollars—add 000 to get the full amount. 2010 Note: Financial information for 2010 was not available for all companies at press time.**

2010 Sales: $34,305,000 — 2010 Profits: $1,491,000
2009 Sales: $28,497,000 — 2009 Profits: $-338,000
2008 Sales: $38,062,000 — 2008 Profits: $979,000
2007 Sales: $34,624,000 — 2007 Profits: $1,252,000
2006 Sales: $32,235,000 — 2006 Profits: $1,028,000

U.S. Stock Ticker: JCI
Int'l Ticker:
Int'l Exchange:
Employees: 137,000 Fiscal Year Ends: 9/30
Parent Company:

SALARIES/BENEFITS:

Pension Plan: ESOP Stock Plan: Profit Sharing: Top Exec. Salary: $1,365,000 Bonus: $6,317,000
Savings Plan: Y Stock Purch. Plan: Second Exec. Salary: $835,000 Bonus: $1,826,000

OTHER THOUGHTS:

Apparent Women Officers or Directors: 4
Hot Spot for Advancement for Women/Minorities: Y

LOCATIONS: ("Y" = Yes)

West:	Southwest:	Midwest:	Southeast:	Northeast:	International:
Y	Y	Y	Y	Y	Y

JONES LANG LASALLE INC

www.joneslanglasalle.com

Industry Group Code: 5311

Management:		Sales/Marketing:		Liberal Arts:		Information Sys.:		Professionals:		Tech./Scientific:	
Mgmt. Trainees:	Y	Marketing Pros.:	Y	Gen. Writing/Editing:		Info. Mgmt.:	Y	Finance/Acct.:	Y	Engineers, Elec.:	
Experienced Mgmt.:	Y	Retail Sales:		Tech. Writing:		Software Dev.:		Law:	Y	Engineers, Other:	
Int'l Business:	Y	Comm./Industrial:	Y	Graphic Arts/Photog.:		Hardware Dev.:		HR/Other:	Y	Health/Lab:	
MBA Grads:	Y	Sales Trainees:		Music:		Consulting/Other:		Training:	Y	Science/Research:	
		Advertising Pros.:		Broadcasting:				Health Care:		Petroleum/Chem.:	
				Other:				Consulting:		Math/Other:	

TYPES OF BUSINESS:

Real Estate Rental, Leasing & Management
Investment Management
Project Management
Consulting Services
Real Estate Investment Banking
Properties Brokerage

BRANDS/DIVISIONS/AFFILIATES:

LaSalle Investment Management, Inc.

CONTACTS: *Note: Officers with more than one job title may be intentionally listed here more than once.*

Colin Dyer, CEO
Lauralee E. Martin, COO
Colin Dyer, Pres.
Lauralee E. Martin, CFO
Charles Doyle, Chief Mktg. Officer
Nazneen Razi, Chief Human Resources Officer
David Johnson, CIO
Mark Ohringer, General Counsel/Corp. Sec.
Joe Romenesko, Global Treas.
Jeff Jacobson, CEO-LaSalle Investment Mgmt.
Peter C. Roberts, CEO-Americas
Christian Ulbrich, CEO-EMEA
James Jasionowski, Global Dir.-Tax
Sheila A. Penrose, Chmn.
Alastair Hughes, CEO-APAC

Phone: 312-782-5800 | **Fax:** 312-782-4339
Toll-Free:
Address: 200 E. Randolph Dr., Chicago, IL 60601 US

GROWTH PLANS/SPECIAL FEATURES:

Jones Lang LaSalle, Inc. (JLL) is a real estate money management firm that provides integrated real estate and investment management expertise on a local, regional and global level to owner, occupier and investor clients. The firm is active in the area of property and corporate facility management services, with a portfolio encompassing roughly 1.6 billion square feet worldwide. JLL offers its real estate services across three geographically-aligned business segments: the Americas; Europe, the Middle East and Africa; and Asia Pacific. The company's range of real estate service areas includes agency leasing; property management; project and development management; valuations; brokerage of properties; capital markets; real estate investment banking and merchant banking; corporate finance; hotel advisory; space acquisition and disposition; facilities management; strategic consulting; energy management and sustainability; value recovery and receivership services; and money management. These services are offered to for-profit and not-for-profit firms, as well as to governmental entities and public-private partnerships, across a wide variety of property categories including offices, hotels, industrial, retail, multi-family residential, hospitals, data centers, sporting facilities, cultural institutions and transportation centers. A fourth business segment encompasses the operations of subsidiary LaSalle Investment Management, a leading diversified real estate investment management firm with over $41 billion in assets under management globally. JLL has operations in over 1,000 locations in 60 countries worldwide, including 185 corporate offices.

JLL offers employee benefits including medical, dental and vision coverage; health savings accounts and flexible spending accounts; discounted gym memberships; life and disability insurance; a 401(k) plan; a discount stock purchase plan; an education assistance program; adoption assistance; and an employee assistance program.

FINANCIALS: **Sales and profits are in thousands of dollars—add 000 to get the full amount. 2010 Note: Financial information for 2010 was not available for all companies at press time.**

2010 Sales: $2,925,613	2010 Profits: $154,439
2009 Sales: $2,480,736	2009 Profits: $-3,595
2008 Sales: $2,697,586	2008 Profits: $84,883
2007 Sales: $2,652,075	2007 Profits: $257,832
2006 Sales: $2,013,578	2006 Profits: $176,401

U.S. Stock Ticker: JLL
Int'l Ticker:
Int'l Exchange:
Employees: 40,300 Fiscal Year Ends: 12/31
Parent Company:

SALARIES/BENEFITS:

Pension Plan:	ESOP Stock Plan:	Profit Sharing:	Top Exec. Salary: $750,000	Bonus: $1,162,500
Savings Plan: Y	Stock Purch. Plan: Y		Second Exec. Salary: $425,000	Bonus: $880,000

OTHER THOUGHTS:

Apparent Women Officers or Directors: 5
Hot Spot for Advancement for Women/Minorities: Y

LOCATIONS: ("Y" = Yes)

West:	Southwest:	Midwest:	Southeast:	Northeast:	International:
Y	Y	Y	Y	Y	Y

JUNIPER NETWORKS INC

www.juniper.net

Industry Group Code: 33411

Management:		Sales/Marketing:		Liberal Arts:		Information Sys.:		Professionals:		Tech./Scientific:	
Mgmt. Trainees:	Y	Marketing Pros.:	Y	Gen. Writing/Editing:	Y	Info. Mgmt.:	Y	Finance/Acct.:	Y	Engineers, Elec.:	Y
Experienced Mgmt.:	Y	Retail Sales:		Tech. Writing:	Y	Software Dev.:	Y	Law:	Y	Engineers, Other:	
Int'l Business:	Y	Comm./Industrial:	Y	Graphic Arts/Photog.:	Y	Hardware Dev.:	Y	HR/Other:	Y	Health/Lab:	
MBA Grads:	Y	Sales Trainees:	Y	Music:		Consulting/Other:		Training:	Y	Science/Research:	Y
		Advertising Pros.:	Y	Broadcasting:				Health Care:		Petroleum/Chem.:	
				Other:				Consulting:		Math/Other:	Y

TYPES OF BUSINESS:

Networking Equipment
IP Networking Systems
Internet Routers
Network Security Products
Internet Software
Intrusion Prevention
Application Acceleration

BRANDS/DIVISIONS/AFFILIATES:

Junos Platform
E-Series
J-Series
M-Series
T-Series
MX-Series
Junos Innovation Fund
Junos OS

CONTACTS: *Note: Officers with more than one job title may be intentionally listed here more than once.*

Kevin Johnson, CEO
Robyn Denholm, CFO/Exec. VP
Lauren P. Flaherty, Chief Mktg. Officer/Exec. VP
Steven Rice, Exec. VP-Human Resources
Pradeep Sindhu, CTO
Mitchell Gaynor, General Counsel/Sr. VP/Sec.
Michael Rose, Exec. VP-Oper., Service & Support
Luis Avila-Marco, Sr. VP-Corp. Dev. & Strategy
Cindy Ta, Contact-Media Rel.
Kathleen Bela, Contact-Investor Rel.
Gene Zamiska, VP-Finance/Controller
Stefan Dyckerhoff, Exec. VP/Gen. Mgr.-Infrastructure Prod. Group
David Yen, Exec. VP/Gen. Mgr.-Fabric & Switching Tech. Group
Mark Bauhaus, Exec. VP/Gen. Mgr.-Service Layer Tech. Bus. Group
Gerri Elliott, Exec. VP-Strategic Alliances
Scott Kriens, Chmn.
John Morris, Exec. VP-Worldwide Field Oper.

Phone: 408-745-2000 **Fax:** 408-745-2100
Toll-Free: 888-586-4737
Address: 1194 N. Mathilda Ave., Sunnyvale, CA 94089-1206 US

GROWTH PLANS/SPECIAL FEATURES:

Juniper Networks, Inc. is a provider of custom-designed Internet protocol (IP) networking platforms for Internet service providers, enterprises, governments and educational institutions. Its operations are organized into two segments: infrastructure and service layer technologies (SLT). The infrastructure segment primarily offers scalable router products used to control and direct network traffic. Product families offered by the firm include the M-Series, T-Series, E-Series, EX-Series and MX-Series. The SLT segment offers services that protect networks as well as maximize existing bandwidth and acceleration of applications across a distributed network. The SLT product families include firewall services, virtual private network systems, intrusion detection/prevention and application acceleration platforms. In addition, Junos Platform, the company's extended software portfolio, offers Junos Space, a network application platform; the Junos OS operating system; and Junos Pulse, an integrated, multi-service network client. The firm outsources manufacturing to companies including IBM, Flextronics, Celestica and Plexus. Juniper Networks maintains several strategic alliances with companies including IBM, Avaya, Ericsson, NEC and Motorola. The company's customers include wireline, wireless and cable ISPs; private enterprises; federal, state and local government agencies; and research and education institutions. The firm maintains sales offices in 47 countries worldwide. Juniper Networks owns over 500 issued or pending technology patents. In February 2010, the company launched $50 million corporate venture Junos Innovation Fund. In April 2010, Juniper Networks acquired video delivery specialist Ankeena Networks, Inc. In July 2010, the firm acquired software company SMobile Systems, Inc. In November 2010, the company acquired Internet video storage and delivery infrastructure firm Blackwave's intellectual property. In December 2010, Juniper Networks acquired virtualization security technology provider Altor Networks.

The firm offers its employees benefits including medical, dental and vision insurance; a 401(k); paid time off and holidays; and a stock purchase plan.

FINANCIALS: **Sales and profits are in thousands of dollars—add 000 to get the full amount. 2010 Note: Financial information for 2010 was not available for all companies at press time.**

2010 Sales: $4,093,266	2010 Profits: $619,373
2009 Sales: $3,315,900	2009 Profits: $115,200
2008 Sales: $3,572,376	2008 Profits: $511,749
2007 Sales: $2,836,100	2007 Profits: $360,800
2006 Sales: $2,303,580	2006 Profits: $-1,001,437

U.S. Stock Ticker: JNPR
Int'l Ticker:
Int'l Exchange:
Employees: 8,772 Fiscal Year Ends: 12/31
Parent Company:

SALARIES/BENEFITS:

Pension Plan:	ESOP Stock Plan:	Profit Sharing:	Top Exec. Salary: $740,000	Bonus: $2,074,425
Savings Plan: Y	Stock Purch. Plan: Y		Second Exec. Salary: $481,250	Bonus: $224,984

OTHER THOUGHTS:

Apparent Women Officers or Directors: 7
Hot Spot for Advancement for Women/Minorities: Y

LOCATIONS: ("Y" = Yes)

West:	Southwest:	Midwest:	Southeast:	Northeast:	International:
Y	Y	Y	Y	Y	Y

KAISER PERMANENTE

www.kaiserpermanente.org

Industry Group Code: 622110

Management:		**Sales/Marketing:**		**Liberal Arts:**		**Information Sys.:**		**Professionals:**		**Tech./Scientific:**	
Mgmt. Trainees:	Y	Marketing Pros.:	Y	Gen. Writing/Editing:	Y	Info. Mgmt.:	Y	Finance/Acct.:	Y	Engineers, Elec.:	
Experienced Mgmt.:	Y	Retail Sales:		Tech. Writing:	Y	Software Dev.:	Y	Law:	Y	Engineers, Other:	
Int'l Business:		Comm./Industrial:	Y	Graphic Arts/Photog.:	Y	Hardware Dev.:		HR/Other:	Y	Health/Lab:	Y
MBA Grads:	Y	Sales Trainees:		Music:		Consulting/Other:		Training:	Y	Science/Research:	
		Advertising Pros.:	Y	Broadcasting:				Health Care:	Y	Petroleum/Chem.:	
				Other:	Y			Consulting:		Math/Other:	

TYPES OF BUSINESS:

Hospitals & Clinics
General & Specialty Hospitals
Outpatient Facilities
HMO
Health Insurance
Integrated Health Care System
Physician Networks

BRANDS/DIVISIONS/AFFILIATES:

Kaiser Foundation Health Plan Inc
Kaiser Foundation Hospitals
Permanente Medical Groups
KP HealthConnect
Kaiser Permanente Health Research

CONTACTS: *Note: Officers with more than one job title may be intentionally listed here more than once.*

George C. Halvorson, CEO
Bernard J. Tyson, COO
Bernard J. Tyson, Pres.
Kathy Lancaster, CFO/Exec. VP
Paul B. Records, Chief Human Resources Officer/Sr. VP
Raymond J. Baxter, Sr. VP-Research
Phil Fasano, CIO/Sr. VP
Steven Zatkin, General Counsel/Sr. VP
Arthur M. Southam, Exec. VP-Health Plan Oper.
Diane Gage Lofgren, Sr. VP-Brand Strategy
Diane Gage Lofgren, Sr. VP-Corp. Comm. & Public Rel.
John H. Cochran, Exec. Dir.-Permanente Federation
Raymond J. Baxter, Sr. VP-Community Benefit & Health Policy
Peter Andruszkiewicz, Pres., Georgia
Jed Weissberg, Sr. VP-Quality
George C. Halvorson, Chmn.

Phone: 510-271-5800 **Fax:** 510-267-7524
Toll-Free:
Address: 1 Kaiser Plz., Oakland, CA 94612 US

GROWTH PLANS/SPECIAL FEATURES:

Kaiser Permanente is a nonprofit company dedicated to providing integrated health care coverage. The firm operates in Washington, D.C. and nine states: California, Colorado, Georgia, Hawaii, Maryland, Ohio, Oregon, Virginia and Washington. The company's headquarters are in Oakland, California. It serves over 8.8 million members, of which over 6.5 million are in California. Kaiser has three main operating divisions: Kaiser Foundation Health Plan, Inc., which contracts with individuals and groups to provide medical coverage; Kaiser Foundation Hospitals and their subsidiaries, operating community hospitals and outpatient facilities in several states; and Permanente Medical Groups, the company's network of physicians providing health care to its members. The company's resources include approximately 35 medical centers, including hospitals and outpatient facilities; 454 medical offices; and 15,129 physicians. Kaiser Foundation Hospitals also fund medical and health-related research. In addition, Kaiser Permanente Health Research has eight research centers across the country that conduct clinical trials of new drugs, medical devices and specializes in epidemiological studies. The firm, as a participant in the Medicare program, cares for over 880,000 Medicare members, making it one of the largest health plans serving the Medicare program. The KP HealthConnect program integrates clinical records with appointments, registration and billing, thereby significantly improving care delivery and patient satisfaction. In 2011, Kaiser Permanente opened two new facilities in Washington, D.C.

Employees of the firm are offered medical, vision, dental and life insurance; a prescription plan; paid time off for vacations; designated holidays; sick leave; disability benefits; retirement plans; tuition reimbursement; employee assistance programs; and transit spending account options. Kaiser Permanente's employee health care coverage extends to spouses, domestic partners and unmarried children.

FINANCIALS: **Sales and profits are in thousands of dollars—add 000 to get the full amount. 2010 Note: Financial information for 2010 was not available for all companies at press time.**

2010 Sales: $44,200,000	2010 Profits: $2,000,000	**U.S. Stock Ticker: Nonprofit**
2009 Sales: $42,100,000	2009 Profits: $	**Int'l Ticker:**
2008 Sales: $40,300,000	2008 Profits: $	Int'l Exchange:
2007 Sales: $37,800,000	2007 Profits: $1,700,000	Employees: 167,300 Fiscal Year Ends: 12/31
2006 Sales: $34,600,000	2006 Profits: $	Parent Company:

SALARIES/BENEFITS:

Pension Plan: Y	ESOP Stock Plan:	Profit Sharing:	Top Exec. Salary: $	Bonus: $
Savings Plan: Y	Stock Purch. Plan: Y		Second Exec. Salary: $	Bonus: $

OTHER THOUGHTS:

Apparent Women Officers or Directors: 8
Hot Spot for Advancement for Women/Minorities: Y

LOCATIONS: ("Y" = Yes)

West:	Southwest:	Midwest:	Southeast:	Northeast:	International:
Y		Y	Y	Y	

KEANE INC

www.keane.com

Industry Group Code: 541513

Management:		Sales/Marketing:		Liberal Arts:		Information Sys.:		Professionals:		Tech./Scientific:	
Mgmt. Trainees:	Y	Marketing Pros.:	Y	Gen. Writing/Editing:	Y	Info. Mgmt.:	Y	Finance/Acct.:	Y	Engineers, Elec.:	Y
Experienced Mgmt.:	Y	Retail Sales:		Tech. Writing:	Y	Software Dev.:	Y	Law:	Y	Engineers, Other:	
Int'l Business:	Y	Comm./Industrial:	Y	Graphic Arts/Photog.:	Y	Hardware Dev.:	Y	HR/Other:	Y	Health/Lab:	
MBA Grads:	Y	Sales Trainees:		Music:		Consulting/Other:	Y	Training:	Y	Science/Research:	
		Advertising Pros.:	Y	Broadcasting:				Health Care:		Petroleum/Chem.:	
				Other:	Y			Consulting:	Y	Math/Other:	

TYPES OF BUSINESS:
IT Consulting
Business Management Software
Software Development & Integration
System Design & Implementation
Applications Outsourcing
Health Care Consulting

BRANDS/DIVISIONS/AFFILIATES:
ShoreWise Adaptive Delivery
Keane Optimum
CyberFicient Technologies, Inc.
AMTEC Consulting plc

CONTACTS: *Note: Officers with more than one job title may be intentionally listed here more than once.*
John McCain, CEO
John McCain, Pres.
David Kaminsky, CFO/Exec. VP
David Vice, Chief Sales & Mktg. Officer/Exec. VP
Dean Williams, Sr. VP-Global Human Capital
Thomas S. Gary, CIO
John M. Dick, General Counsel
Leanne Orphanos, Sr. Dir.-Bus. Oper.
John M. Dick, Exec. VP-Corp. Dev.
Tara Jantzen, Sr. Dir.-Corp. Comm. & Public Rel.
Marv Mouchawar, Exec. VP-Global Delivery
James T. Milde, Exec. VP-Financial Svcs. & Insurance
Michael Thomas, Exec. VP-Healthcare & Life Science Svcs.
Robert W. Gray, Exec. VP-Commercial Svcs.
Mani Subramanian, Chmn.
Ian Miller, Exec. VP-EMEA

Phone: 617-241-9200	**Fax:** 617-241-9507
Toll-Free: 877-885-3263	
Address: 100 City Sq., Boston, MA 02129 US	

GROWTH PLANS/SPECIAL FEATURES:
Keane, Inc. is a global services company specializing in enabling the transformation of businesses and IT functions. The firm's global delivery approach, branded ShoreWise Adaptive Delivery, offers onsite, offsite, near shore and offshore options. In addition, the company offers Keane Optimum, a one-source solution intended to aid healthcare organizations improve patient care and financial performance. Keane has partnerships with several firms, including BMC Software; Business Objects; CIDEON; Compuware; Curam Software; Siemens; Ariba; Informatica; HP Software; IBM; Lombardi Software; Microsoft; Oracle; PlanetSoft; PlanView; SAP; and Vertica. The firm provides business services including consulting, process outsourcing, strategy and program and performance management services, and technology services including application, architecture, enterprise application, infrastructure, quality assurance and testing. The company serves the financial services, insurance, healthcare, manufacturing, public sector, telecom, life sciences, energy/utilities, hospitality, transportation and retail industries. Keane has operations in the U.S., Australia, Canada, China, France, India, New Zealand, Switzerland, Singapore, United Arab Emirates and the U.K. In April 2010, the firm acquired CyberFicient Technologies, Inc., a Texas-based provider of staffing services, enterprise Java consulting and human service solutions; and AMTEC Consulting plc, a U.K.-based independent advisory consulting firm.

Keane offers its employees tuition assistance; a 401(k); discounted home and auto insurance; an employee assistance program; adoption assistance; paid time off; a 529 College Savings Plan; mortgage discounts; and a variety of healthcare options.

FINANCIALS: **Sales and profits are in thousands of dollars—add 000 to get the full amount. 2010 Note: Financial information for 2010 was not available for all companies at press time.**

2010 Sales: $1,200,000	2010 Profits: $	**U.S. Stock Ticker: Private**
2009 Sales: $1,200,000	2009 Profits: $	**Int'l Ticker:**
2008 Sales: $1,200,000	2008 Profits: $	Int'l Exchange:
2007 Sales: $1,100,000	2007 Profits: $	Employees: 12,500 Fiscal Year Ends: 12/31
2006 Sales: $948,306	2006 Profits: $34,514	Parent Company:

SALARIES/BENEFITS:

Pension Plan:	ESOP Stock Plan:	Profit Sharing:	Top Exec. Salary: $	Bonus: $309,750
Savings Plan: Y	Stock Purch. Plan:		Second Exec. Salary: $	Bonus: $

OTHER THOUGHTS:
Apparent Women Officers or Directors: 2
Hot Spot for Advancement for Women/Minorities:

LOCATIONS: ("Y" = Yes)

West:	Southwest:	Midwest:	Southeast:	Northeast:	International:
Y	Y	Y	Y	Y	Y

KELLOGG COMPANY

www.kelloggs.com

Industry Group Code: 311230

Management:		Sales/Marketing:		Liberal Arts:		Information Sys.:		Professionals:		Tech./Scientific:	
Mgmt. Trainees:	Y	Marketing Pros.:	Y	Gen. Writing/Editing:	Y	Info. Mgmt.:	Y	Finance/Acct.:	Y	Engineers, Elec.:	
Experienced Mgmt.:	Y	Retail Sales:		Tech. Writing:	Y	Software Dev.:	Y	Law:	Y	Engineers, Other:	Y
Int'l Business:	Y	Comm./Industrial:	Y	Graphic Arts/Photog.:	Y	Hardware Dev.:		HR/Other:	Y	Health/Lab:	
MBA Grads:	Y	Sales Trainees:	Y	Music:		Consulting/Other:		Training:	Y	Science/Research:	
		Advertising Pros.:	Y	Broadcasting:				Health Care:		Petroleum/Chem.:	
				Other:				Consulting:		Math/Other:	

TYPES OF BUSINESS:

Cereal Manufacturing
Frozen Foods
Snack Foods
Convenience Foods
Processed Foods

BRANDS/DIVISIONS/AFFILIATES:

Keebler
Pop-Tarts
Nutri-Grain
Eggo
Rice Krispies
Special K
Corn Pops
Frosted Mini-Wheats

CONTACTS:

Note: Officers with more than one job title may be intentionally listed here more than once.

John A. Bryant, CEO
John A. Bryant, Pres.
Ronald L. Dissinger, CFO
Mark Baynes, Global Chief Mktg. Officer/VP
Margaret Bath, VP-Research & Quality
Brian S. Rice, CIO/Sr. VP
Margaret Bath, VP-Tech.
Gary H. Pilnick, General Counsel/Corp. Sec.
Gary H. Pilnick, Sr. VP-Corp. Dev.
Celeste A. Clark, Sr. VP-Global Public Policy & External Rel.
David Denholm, Pres., Kellogg APAC
Celeste Clark, Chief Sustainability Officer
Brad J. Davidson, Sr. VP/Pres., Kellogg North America
Todd Penegor, VP/Pres., U.S. Snacks
James M. Jenness, Chmn.
Paul Norman, Sr. VP/Pres., Kellogg Int'l

Phone: 269-961-2000 **Fax:** 269-961-2871
Toll-Free: 800-962-1413
Address: 1 Kellogg Sq., Battle Creek, MI 49016-3599 US

GROWTH PLANS/SPECIAL FEATURES:

Kellogg Company is one of the world's largest producers of cereal and through Kellog Snacks Division, a major producer of convenience and snack foods, including cookies, crackers, toaster pastries, fruit snacks, cereal bars, frozen waffles, meat alternatives, pie crusts and ice cream cones. The firm's products are manufactured in 18 countries and marketed in over 180 countries worldwide. Kellogg's two major divisions are U.S. and international, which is further divided into Europe, Latin America and Asia Pacific. Kellogg owns a number of familiar cereal trademarks including Apple Jacks, Corn Pops, Corn Flakes, Crispix, Froot Loops, Frosted Mini-Wheats, Rice Krispies and Special K. Other Kellogg trademarks and products include Eggo frozen waffles, Rice Krispies Treats, Nutri-Grain convenience foods, Pop-Tarts toaster pastries, Kashi nutritional foods and Morningstar Farms meat and dairy alternatives. Cookie and cracker trademarks include Cheez-It, E.L. Fudge, Famous Amos, Chips Deluxe, Murray, Town House, Vienna Fingers, Wheatables and Zesta. The company also owns the Keebler line of snack food products. Kellogg offers a number of products with a focus on health and wellness. These products include: Smart Start, a cold cereal with ingredients that may help lower blood pressure and cholesterol; Special K Protein Meal and Snack Bars; and Special K20 Protein Waters, which contain five grams of protein and come in three flavors. Kellogg's largest customer is Wal-Mart, which accounts for roughly 21% of consolidated net sales.

Employees are offered life, medical, dental and vision insurance; a 401(k) plan; tuition reimbursement; flexible spending accounts; disability coverage; health screenings and flu shots; an employee assistance program; a college savings program; adoption assistance; a discount employee stock purchase plan; and employee discount programs.

FINANCIALS:

Sales and profits are in thousands of dollars—add 000 to get the full amount. 2010 Note: Financial information for 2010 was not available for all companies at press time.

2010 Sales: $12,397,000 | 2010 Profits: $1,247,000
2009 Sales: $12,575,000 | 2009 Profits: $1,212,000
2008 Sales: $12,822,000 | 2008 Profits: $1,148,000
2007 Sales: $11,776,000 | 2007 Profits: $1,103,000
2006 Sales: $10,906,700 | 2006 Profits: $1,004,100

U.S. Stock Ticker: K
Int'l Ticker:
Int'l Exchange:
Employees: 30,645 Fiscal Year Ends: 12/31
Parent Company:

SALARIES/BENEFITS:

Pension Plan: | ESOP Stock Plan: | Profit Sharing: | Top Exec. Salary: $1,194,237 | Bonus: $2,760,000
Savings Plan: Y | Stock Purch. Plan: Y | | Second Exec. Salary: $830,763 | Bonus: $1,508,800

OTHER THOUGHTS:

Apparent Women Officers or Directors: 4
Hot Spot for Advancement for Women/Minorities: Y

LOCATIONS: ("Y" = Yes)

West:	Southwest:	Midwest:	Southeast:	Northeast:	International:
Y	Y	Y	Y	Y	Y

KELLY SERVICES INC

www.kellyservices.com

Industry Group Code: 561320

Management:		Sales/Marketing:		Liberal Arts:		Information Sys.:		Professionals:		Tech./Scientific:	
Mgmt. Trainees:	Y	Marketing Pros.:	Y	Gen. Writing/Editing:	Y	Info. Mgmt.:	Y	Finance/Acct.:	Y	Engineers, Elec.:	
Experienced Mgmt.:	Y	Retail Sales:		Tech. Writing:	Y	Software Dev.:	Y	Law:	Y	Engineers, Other:	
Int'l Business:	Y	Comm./Industrial:	Y	Graphic Arts/Photog.:	Y	Hardware Dev.:		HR/Other:	Y	Health/Lab:	
MBA Grads:	Y	Sales Trainees:	Y	Music:		Consulting/Other:		Training:	Y	Science/Research:	
		Advertising Pros.:	Y	Broadcasting:				Health Care:		Petroleum/Chem.:	
				Other:	Y			Consulting:		Math/Other:	

TYPES OF BUSINESS:

Staffing & Temporary Help
Human Resources Consulting
Outsourcing Solutions
Permanent Hiring Programs
Call Center Services
Benefits & Payroll Outsourcing

BRANDS/DIVISIONS/AFFILIATES:

Kelly Office Services
KellyConnect
KellyDirect
Kelly Catering and Hospitality
Kelly Industrial
Kelly Selection
Kelly Executive

CONTACTS: *Note: Officers with more than one job title may be intentionally listed here more than once.*

Carl T. Camden, CEO
George S. Corona, COO
Carl T. Camden, Pres.
Patricia Little, CFO
Michael S. Morrow, Sr. VP-Global Mktg.
Nina M. Ramsey, Sr. VP-Global Human Resources
Joseph Drouin, CIO
James H. Bradley, Sr. VP- Global Admin.
Daniel T. Lis, General Counsel/Corp. Sec.
Steve S. Armstrong, Sr. VP/Gen. Mgr.-Oper.
Michael E. Debs, Chief Acct. Officer/Controller/Sr. VP
Michael S. Webster, Gen. Mgr.-Americas
Rolf E. Kleiner, Sr. VP-Outsourcing & Consulting Group
Peter W. Quigley, Sr. VP-Global Client Rel.
Pamela M. Berklich, Sr. VP-Global Solutions & Svcs.
Terence E. Adderley, Chmn.
Leif Agneus, Gen. Mgr.-EMEA/Sr. VP

Phone: 248-362-4444 **Fax:** 248-362-2258
Toll-Free:
Address: 999 W. Big Beaver Rd., Troy, MI 48084 US

GROWTH PLANS/SPECIAL FEATURES:

Kelly Services, Inc. is a staffing and services company that offers temporary staffing services, staff leasing, outsourcing and full-time placement. Kelly's workforce solutions are provided to customers through offices in three regions: the Americas; Europe, the Middle East and Africa (EMEA); and Asia Pacific (APAC). It operates in seven segments: Americas Commercial; Americas Professional and Technical (Americas PT); EMEA Commercial; EMEA Professional and Technical (EMEA PT); APAC Commercial; APAC Professional and Technical (APAC PT); and the Outsourcing and Consulting Group (OCG). Some of the services that the Americas Commercial segment include are Kelly Office Services, an administrative support staff; KellyConnect, which offers staff for contact centers, technical support hotlines and telemarketing units; and KellyDirect, a permanent placement service for people of all business areas. The Americas PT segment includes various industry-specific services, some of which include CGR/seven, which places employees in creative services positions; and Kelly Healthcare Resources, which provides all levels of healthcare specialists and professionals for work in hospitals, HMOs and other health companies. The EMEA Commercial segment includes Kelly Catering and Hospitality, which provides chefs, porters and hospitality representatives; and Kelly Industrial, which supplies manual workers to semi-skilled professionals in a variety of trade, non-trade and operational positions. The EMEA PT segment provides many of the same services as the Americas PT segment. The APAC Commercial segment offers services similar to the Americas PT and EMEA Commercial segments through staffing solutions that include permanent placement, temporary staffing and vendor on-site. The APAC PT segment provides Kelly Selection and Kelly Executive (only in Australia and New Zealand), which offer mid- to senior-level search and selection to identify leaders in human resources, sales and marketing, finance and management. The OCG segment delivers integrated talent management solutions, such as recruitment, outsourcing and human resources consulting.

FINANCIALS: **Sales and profits are in thousands of dollars—add 000 to get the full amount. 2010 Note: Financial information for 2010 was not available for all companies at press time.**

2010 Sales: $4,950,300	2010 Profits: $26,100
2009 Sales: $4,314,800	2009 Profits: $-104,500
2008 Sales: $5,517,290	2008 Profits: $-82,239
2007 Sales: $5,667,589	2007 Profits: $61,016
2006 Sales: $5,546,778	2006 Profits: $63,491

U.S. Stock Ticker: KELYA
Int'l Ticker:
Int'l Exchange:
Employees: 538,000 Fiscal Year Ends: 12/31
Parent Company:

SALARIES/BENEFITS:

Pension Plan:	ESOP Stock Plan:	Profit Sharing:	Top Exec. Salary: $934,650	Bonus: $538,200
Savings Plan:	Stock Purch. Plan:		Second Exec. Salary: $552,750	Bonus: $238,800

OTHER THOUGHTS:

Apparent Women Officers or Directors: 7
Hot Spot for Advancement for Women/Minorities: Y

LOCATIONS: ("Y" = Yes)

West:	Southwest:	Midwest:	Southeast:	Northeast:	International:
Y	Y	Y	Y	Y	Y

KEY ENERGY SERVICES INC

www.keyenergy.com

Industry Group Code: 213112

Management:		Sales/Marketing:		Liberal Arts:		Information Sys.:		Professionals:		Tech./Scientific:	
Mgmt. Trainees:		Marketing Pros.:	Y	Gen. Writing/Editing:		Info. Mgmt.:	Y	Finance/Acct.:	Y	Engineers, Elec.:	Y
Experienced Mgmt.:		Retail Sales:		Tech. Writing:	Y	Software Dev.:		Law:	Y	Engineers, Other:	Y
Int'l Business:		Comm./Industrial:	Y	Graphic Arts/Photog.:		Hardware Dev.:		HR/Other:	Y	Health/Lab:	
MBA Grads:	Y	Sales Trainees:		Music:		Consulting/Other:		Training:	Y	Science/Research:	
		Advertising Pros.:	Y	Broadcasting:				Health Care:		Petroleum/Chem.:	Y
				Other:				Consulting:		Math/Other:	

TYPES OF BUSINESS:

Oil & Gas Drilling Support Services
Well Servicing & Workovers
Oilfield Trucking & Fluid Hauling
Drilling Services
Storage & Disposal Services
Equipment Rental

BRANDS/DIVISIONS/AFFILIATES:

GeoStream

CONTACTS:

Note: Officers with more than one job title may be intentionally listed here more than once.

Richard Alario, CEO
Newton W. Wilson III, COO/Exec. VP
Richard Alario, Pres.
T. M. Whichard III, CFO/Sr. VP
Kim B. Clarke, Chief People Officer
Don D. Weinheimer, Sr. VP-Prod. Dev. & Quality
Kim B. Clarke, Sr. VP-Admin.
Kimberly R. Frye, General Counsel/Sr. VP
Don D. Weinheimer, Sr. VP-Strategic Planning
Tommy Pipes, Sr. VP-Industry Rel.
Gary L. Russell, VP-Investor Rel.
Jeff Skelly, Sr. VP-Rig Svcs.
Richard Alario, Chmn.

Phone: 713-651-4300 | **Fax:** 713-652-4005
Toll-Free:
Address: 1301 McKinney St., Ste. 1800, Houston, TX 77010 US

GROWTH PLANS/SPECIAL FEATURES:

Key Energy Services, Inc. is one of the world's leading onshore, rig-based well servicing contractors. Key operations are located throughout the U.S. and in Canada, Argentina, Mexico and Russia. The company operates in two segments: well servicing and production services. The well services segment is comprised of two subdivisions: rig-based services, which include the maintenance and workover of existing oil and gas wells and well plugging and abandonment solutions; and fluid management services, which include oilfield transportation and produced water disposal services for operators of saltwater and other fluid-producing wells. The production services segment is composed of three subdivisions: pressure pumping services, including fracturing, nitrogen, acidizing, cementing and coiled tubing services, used to enhance oil and natural gas well production; wireline services, including well perforating, completion logging, production logging and casing integrity services; and fishing and rental services. Fishing services involve recovering lost or stuck equipment in the wellbore. The division's rental equipment includes drill pipe, tubulars, handling tools, pressure-control equipment, power swivels and foam air units. In March 2010, Key Energy formed a joint venture with AlMansoori Specialized Engineering to provide well intervention services in the Middle East and North Africa. In June 2010, the company acquired five large diameter coiled tubing units from Express Energy Services CT, LP. In October 2010, the firm acquired certain subsidiaries and assets from OFS Energy Services and sold its pressure pumping and wireline businesses to Patterson-UTI Energy.

The company offers its employees medical, vision and dental coverage; a 401(k) plan; a retirement plan; educational assistance; and life and disability insurance.

FINANCIALS:

Sales and profits are in thousands of dollars—add 000 to get the full amount. 2010 Note: Financial information for 2010 was not available for all companies at press time.

2010 Sales: $1,153,684 | 2010 Profits: $73,495
2009 Sales: $955,699 | 2009 Profits: $-156,121
2008 Sales: $1,624,446 | 2008 Profits: $84,058
2007 Sales: $1,662,012 | 2007 Profits: $169,289
2006 Sales: $1,546,177 | 2006 Profits: $171,033

U.S. Stock Ticker: KEG
Int'l Ticker:
Int'l Exchange:
Employees: 7,400 Fiscal Year Ends: 12/31
Parent Company:

SALARIES/BENEFITS:

Pension Plan: Y | ESOP Stock Plan: | Profit Sharing: | Top Exec. Salary: $764,800 | Bonus: $
Savings Plan: Y | Stock Purch. Plan: | | Second Exec. Salary: $422,740 | Bonus: $

OTHER THOUGHTS:

Apparent Women Officers or Directors: 4
Hot Spot for Advancement for Women/Minorities: Y

LOCATIONS: ("Y" = Yes)

West:	Southwest:	Midwest:	Southeast:	Northeast:	International:
Y	Y	Y	Y	Y	

KIMBERLY-CLARK CORP

www.kimberly-clark.com

Industry Group Code: 322

Management:		**Sales/Marketing:**		**Liberal Arts:**		**Information Sys.:**		**Professionals:**		**Tech./Scientific:**	
Mgmt. Trainees:	Y	Marketing Pros.:	Y	Gen. Writing/Editing:	Y	Info. Mgmt.:	Y	Finance/Acct.:	Y	Engineers, Elec.:	
Experienced Mgmt.:	Y	Retail Sales:		Tech. Writing:		Software Dev.:	Y	Law:	Y	Engineers, Other:	
Int'l Business:	Y	Comm./Industrial:	Y	Graphic Arts/Photog.:	Y	Hardware Dev.:		HR/Other:	Y	Health/Lab:	
MBA Grads:	Y	Sales Trainees:	Y	Music:		Consulting/Other:		Training:	Y	Science/Research:	
		Advertising Pros.:	Y	Broadcasting:				Health Care:		Petroleum/Chem.:	
				Other:	Y			Consulting:		Math/Other:	

TYPES OF BUSINESS:

Personal Care Products-Paper
Consumer Tissue Products
Safety Products
Healthcare Products

BRANDS/DIVISIONS/AFFILIATES:

Kleenex
Scott
Huggies
Kotex
Depend
Pull-Ups
Viva
ON-Q

CONTACTS: *Note: Officers with more than one job title may be intentionally listed here more than once.*

Thomas J. Falk, CEO
Thomas J. Falk, Pres.
Mark A. Buthman, CFO/Sr. VP
Anthony J. Palmer, Chief Mktg. Officer/Sr. VP
Lizanne C. Gottung, Chief Human Resources Officer/Sr. VP
Thomas J. Mielke, Chief Compliance Officer/Sr. VP-Law
Elane B. Stock, Chief Strategy Officer/Sr. VP
Thomas J. Mielke, Sr. VP-Gov't Affairs
Paul J. Alexander, VP-Investor Rel.
Christian A. Brickman, Pres., KC Professional
Joanne B. Bauer, Pres., Health Care Bus.
Robert. E. Abernathy, Pres., North Atlantic Consumer Prod.
Jan B. Spencer, Sr. VP-Continuous Improvement & Sustainability
Thomas J. Falk, Chmn.
Robert W. Black, Pres., Int'l
Jan B. Spencer, Sr. VP-Sourcing

Phone: 972-281-1200	**Fax:** 972-281-1490
Toll-Free:	
Address: P.O. Box 619100, Dallas, TX 75261 US	

GROWTH PLANS/SPECIAL FEATURES:

Kimberly-Clark Corp. (KC) is a health and hygiene company that manufactures and markets a wide range of health and hygiene products in 39 countries. KC operates in four segments: KC professional and other; personal care; consumer tissue; and healthcare. The KC professional and other segment manufactures and markets paper towels; napkins; wipers; facial and bathroom tissue; and a range of safety products for the away-from-home marketplace. Brand names in this segment include Kimberly-Clark, Kimtech, Kleenguard, Scott, WypAll, Kleenex and Kimcare. The personal care segment manufactures and markets products such as feminine and incontinence care products; baby wipes; training, youth and swim pants; and disposable diapers. Items in this segment are sold under brand names such as Kotex, Depend, Poise, Little-Swimmers, Pull-Ups, Huggies and GoodNites. The consumer tissue segment manufactures and markets napkins; paper towels; facial and bathroom tissue; and related products for household use. Products in this division are sold under brands such as Scott, Kleenex, Viva, Andrex, Scottex, Cottonelle, Page and Hakle. The healthcare segment manufactures and markets sterilization wrap; drapes; surgical gowns; disposable face masks and exam gloves; respiratory products; infection control products; and other disposable medical items. Products in this division are sold under brand names such as ON-Q, Kimberly-Clark and Ballard. Sales to KC's largest customer, Wal-Mart Stores, Inc., account for approximately 13% of its sales. The firm's products are sold in over 150 countries. In August 2011, KC agreed to open a new global innovation center in Bogota, Colombia.

FINANCIALS: **Sales and profits are in thousands of dollars—add 000 to get the full amount. 2010 Note: Financial information for 2010 was not available for all companies at press time.**

2010 Sales: $19,746,000	2010 Profits: $1,943,000	**U.S. Stock Ticker: KMB**
2009 Sales: $19,115,000	2009 Profits: $1,994,000	**Int'l Ticker:**
2008 Sales: $19,415,000	2008 Profits: $1,690,000	Int'l Exchange:
2007 Sales: $18,266,000	2007 Profits: $1,822,900	Employees: 57,000 Fiscal Year Ends: 12/31
2006 Sales: $16,746,900	2006 Profits: $1,499,500	Parent Company:

SALARIES/BENEFITS:

Pension Plan: Y	ESOP Stock Plan:	Profit Sharing:	Top Exec. Salary: $1,281,249	Bonus: $1,307,280
Savings Plan:	Stock Purch. Plan: Y		Second Exec. Salary: $718,750	Bonus: $537,883

OTHER THOUGHTS:

Apparent Women Officers or Directors: 6
Hot Spot for Advancement for Women/Minorities: Y

LOCATIONS: ("Y" = Yes)

West:	Southwest:	Midwest:	Southeast:	Northeast:	International:
Y	Y	Y	Y	Y	Y

Sales, profits and employees may be estimates. Financial information, benefits and other data can change quickly and may vary from those stated here.

KINDRED HEALTHCARE INC

www.kindredhealthcare.com

Industry Group Code: 623110

Management:		Sales/Marketing:		Liberal Arts:		Information Sys.:		Professionals:		Tech./Scientific:	
Mgmt. Trainees:	Y	Marketing Pros.:	Y	Gen. Writing/Editing:	Y	Info. Mgmt.:	Y	Finance/Acct.:	Y	Engineers, Elec.:	
Experienced Mgmt.:	Y	Retail Sales:		Tech. Writing:	Y	Software Dev.:	Y	Law:	Y	Engineers, Other:	
Int'l Business:		Comm./Industrial:		Graphic Arts/Photog.:	Y	Hardware Dev.:		HR/Other:	Y	Health/Lab:	Y
MBA Grads:	Y	Sales Trainees:		Music:		Consulting/Other:		Training:	Y	Science/Research:	
		Advertising Pros.:	Y	Broadcasting:				Health Care:	Y	Petroleum/Chem.:	
				Other:	Y			Consulting:		Math/Other:	

TYPES OF BUSINESS:

Hospitals
Nursing Centers
Contract Rehabilitation Services

BRANDS/DIVISIONS/AFFILIATES:

RehabCare Group
Professional HealthCare, LLC
RehabCare

CONTACTS: *Note: Officers with more than one job title may be intentionally listed here more than once.*

Paul J. Diaz, CEO
Benjamin A. Breier, COO
Paul J. Diaz, Pres.
Richard A. Lechleiter, CFO/Exec. VP
Richard E. Chapman, CIO/Exec. VP
Richard E. Chapman, Chief Admin. Officer
M. Suzanne Riedman, General Counsel/Chief Diversity Officer
Gregory C. Miller, Chief Dev. Officer
Jeffrey P. Winter, Exec. VP/Pres., Hospital Div.
Lane M. Bowen, Exec. VP/Pres., Nursing Center Div.
William M. Altman, Sr. VP-Strategy & Public Policy
Joseph L. Landenwich, Sr. VP-Corp. Legal Affairs/Corp. Sec.
Edward L. Kuntz, Chmn.

Phone: 502-596-7300	**Fax:**
Toll-Free: 800-545-0749	
Address: 680 S. 4th St., Louisville, KY 40202-2412 US	

GROWTH PLANS/SPECIAL FEATURES:

Kindred Healthcare, Inc. is a healthcare services company that operates hospitals, nursing centers and a contract rehabilitation services business across 46 U.S. states. The company runs three operating divisions. The hospital division operates 120 long-term acute care hospitals (8,609 licensed beds) and five inpatient rehabilitation hospitals (183 beds) in 26 states. The firm treats medically complex patients, including the critically ill, suffering from multiple organ system failures, most commonly the cardiovascular, pulmonary, kidney, gastrointestinal and cutaneous systems. A number of hospitals in this division offer skilled nursing, sub-acute and outpatient services, which may include diagnostic services, rehabilitation therapy, CT scanning, one-day surgery and laboratory. The health service division operates 224 nursing/rehabilitation centers and six assisted living facilities (27,585 licensed beds) in 27 states. Through its nursing centers, Kindred Healthcare provides long-term care services; a full range of pharmacy, medical and clinical services; and routine services, including daily dietary, social and recreational services. A number of nursing centers offer specialized programs for residents suffering from Alzheimer's disease and other types of dementia. The contract rehabilitation services business provides rehabilitative services under the name RehabCare in 1,760 nursing centers, hospitals and other locations. In addition to standard physical, occupational and speech therapies, the company provides specialized care programs for wound care, pain management, cognitive deficit, neurologic, orthopedic and pulmonary rehabilitation therapies. In November 2010, Kindred Healthcare acquired five long-term acute care hospitals (250 total beds) from Vista Healthcare, LLC for roughly $179 million. In April 2011, the firm acquired four California facilities from CareSouth HHA Holdings, LLC. In June 2011, the company acquired RehabCare Group. In September 2011, Kindred Healthcare acquired Professional HealthCare, LLC for $51 million.

Employees are offered medical, dental and vision coverage; flexible spending accounts; and a 401(k) plan.

FINANCIALS: **Sales and profits are in thousands of dollars—add 000 to get the full amount. 2010 Note: Financial information for 2010 was not available for all companies at press time.**

2010 Sales: $4,359,697	2010 Profits: $56,146	**U.S. Stock Ticker: KND**
2009 Sales: $4,270,007	2009 Profits: $40,111	**Int'l Ticker:**
2008 Sales: $4,093,864	2008 Profits: $36,285	Int'l Exchange:
2007 Sales: $4,128,649	2007 Profits: $-46,870	Employees: 56,800 Fiscal Year Ends: 12/31
2006 Sales: $4,266,661	2006 Profits: $78,711	Parent Company:

SALARIES/BENEFITS:

Pension Plan:	ESOP Stock Plan:	Profit Sharing:	Top Exec. Salary: $1,040,839	Bonus: $2,461,940
Savings Plan: Y	Stock Purch. Plan: Y		Second Exec. Salary: $675,000	Bonus: $1,149,038

OTHER THOUGHTS:

Apparent Women Officers or Directors: 3
Hot Spot for Advancement for Women/Minorities: Y

LOCATIONS: ("Y" = Yes)

West:	Southwest:	Midwest:	Southeast:	Northeast:	International:
Y	Y	Y	Y	Y	

KINETIC CONCEPTS INC

www.kci1.com

Industry Group Code: 33911

Management:		Sales/Marketing:		Liberal Arts:		Information Sys.:		Professionals:		Tech./Scientific:	
Mgmt. Trainees:	Y	Marketing Pros.:	Y	Gen. Writing/Editing:	Y	Info. Mgmt.:	Y	Finance/Acct.:	Y	Engineers, Elec.:	Y
Experienced Mgmt.:	Y	Retail Sales:		Tech. Writing:	Y	Software Dev.:	Y	Law:	Y	Engineers, Other:	Y
Int'l Business:	Y	Comm./Industrial:	Y	Graphic Arts/Photog.:	Y	Hardware Dev.:		HR/Other:	Y	Health/Lab:	Y
MBA Grads:	Y	Sales Trainees:	Y	Music:		Consulting/Other:		Training:	Y	Science/Research:	
		Advertising Pros.:	Y	Broadcasting:				Health Care:	Y	Petroleum/Chem.:	
				Other:				Consulting:		Math/Other:	

TYPES OF BUSINESS:

Equipment-Specialized Mattresses & Beds
Kinetic Therapy Products
Therapeutic Support Surfaces
Wound Closure Devices
Circulatory Devices

BRANDS/DIVISIONS/AFFILIATES:

LifeCell Corporation
KinAir
FirstStep
InterCell
AtmosAir
TechniMotion Medical
Negative Pressure Technology Platform

CONTACTS: *Note: Officers with more than one job title may be intentionally listed here more than once.*

Cathy Burzik, CEO
Cathy Burzik, Pres.
Martin J. Landon, CFO/Exec. VP
Stephen D. Seidel, General Counsel/Sec.
Mike Genau, Global Pres., Active Healing Solutions
Lisa Colleran, Pres., LifeCell
Stephen D. Seidel, Pres., Global Therapeutic Support Systems
Ronald W. Dollens, Chmn.

Phone: 210-524-9000 **Fax:** 210-255-6998
Toll-Free: 800-275-4524
Address: 8023 Vantage Dr., San Antonio, TX 78230-4726 US

GROWTH PLANS/SPECIAL FEATURES:

Kinetic Concepts, Inc. (KCI) is a global medical technology company that designs, develops, manufactures and markets high-technology therapies and products for the advanced wound care, regenerative medicine and therapeutic support system markets. The company operates through a network of over 100 U.S. and more than 50 international service centers that are able to rapidly deliver its products to major hospitals in the U.S., Canada, Australia, Singapore, South Africa and most major European countries. KCI's Active Healing Solutions business is involved in the development and commercialization of advanced wound care therapies based on the company's Negative Pressure Technology Platform. Negative pressure therapy is used on serious trauma wounds, failed surgical closures, amputations, burns covering a large portion of the body, serious pressure ulcers and other difficult wounds. The Regenerative Medicine business operates primarily through its wholly-owned subsidiary, LifeCell Corporation, which develops products and techniques to treat tissue in reconstructive, orthopedic and urogynecologic surgical procedures. The Therapeutic Support Systems segment focuses on hospital beds, mattress replacements and overlays for critical care, wound care and bariatric needs. The therapeutic surfaces for wound treatment and prevention treat pressure sores, burns, ulcers, skin grafts and other skin conditions. They also help prevent the formation of pressure sores in certain immobile individuals by reducing friction between skin and bed and by using surfaces supported by air, foam, silicon beads or viscous fluid. These include the KinAir beds, FirstStep and InterCell overlays and AtmosAir seating surfaces. In January 2011, the acquired most of the assets andintellectual property of TechniMotion Medical, a Texas-based that designs and develops patient handling systems for acute and post-acute patient care.

KCI offers its employees health insurance; life and AD&D coverage; short- and long-term disability; flexible reimbursement accounts; a 401(k) plan; an employee stock purchase plan; education assistance; and referral bonuses.

FINANCIALS: **Sales and profits are in thousands of dollars—add 000 to get the full amount. 2010 Note: Financial information for 2010 was not available for all companies at press time.**

2010 Sales: $2,017,752	2010 Profits: $256,084
2009 Sales: $1,992,644	2009 Profits: $228,702
2008 Sales: $1,877,909	2008 Profits: $166,444
2007 Sales: $1,609,944	2007 Profits: $237,144
2006 Sales: $1,371,636	2006 Profits: $195,468

U.S. Stock Ticker: KCI
Int'l Ticker:
Int'l Exchange:
Employees: 6,900 Fiscal Year Ends: 12/31
Parent Company:

SALARIES/BENEFITS:

Pension Plan: ESOP Stock Plan: Profit Sharing: Top Exec. Salary: $882,500 Bonus: $883,097
Savings Plan: Y Stock Purch. Plan: Y Second Exec. Salary: $490,000 Bonus: $30,831

OTHER THOUGHTS:

Apparent Women Officers or Directors: 2
Hot Spot for Advancement for Women/Minorities: Y

LOCATIONS: ("Y" = Yes)

West:	Southwest:	Midwest:	Southeast:	Northeast:	International:
	Y			Y	Y

KLA TENCOR CORP

www.kla-tencor.com

Industry Group Code: 333295

Management:		Sales/Marketing:		Liberal Arts:		Information Sys.:		Professionals:		Tech./Scientific:	
Mgmt. Trainees:		Marketing Pros.:	Y	Gen. Writing/Editing:		Info. Mgmt.:	Y	Finance/Acct.:	Y	Engineers, Elec.:	Y
Experienced Mgmt.:		Retail Sales:		Tech. Writing:	Y	Software Dev.:	Y	Law:	Y	Engineers, Other:	
Int'l Business:	Y	Comm./Industrial:	Y	Graphic Arts/Photog.:		Hardware Dev.:	Y	HR/Other:	Y	Health/Lab:	
MBA Grads:	Y	Sales Trainees:		Music:		Consulting/Other:		Training:		Science/Research:	
		Advertising Pros.:	Y	Broadcasting:				Health Care:		Petroleum/Chem.:	
				Other:				Consulting:		Math/Other:	

TYPES OF BUSINESS:

Semiconductor Test Equipment
Process Control & Yield Management Software & Services
Support Services

BRANDS/DIVISIONS/AFFILIATES:

ICOS Vision Systems Corporation NV

CONTACTS: *Note: Officers with more than one job title may be intentionally listed here more than once.*

Richard P. Wallace, CEO
Richard P. Wallace, Pres.
Mark P. Dentinger, CFO/Exec. VP
Ben Tsai, CTO/Exec. VP
Robert P. Akins, Chmn.

Phone: 408-875-3000	**Fax:** 408-875-4144
Toll-Free:	
Address: 1 Technology Dr., Milpitas, CA 95035 US	

GROWTH PLANS/SPECIAL FEATURES:

KLA Tencor Corp. is one of the world's largest suppliers of process control and yield management products to the semiconductor and related nanoelectronics industries. The firm's portfolio of products, software, services and expertise is designed to help integrated circuit manufacturers manage yield throughout the entire fabrication process, from research and development to final volume production. The company markets and sells products to semiconductor, wafer, disk and reticle manufacturers worldwide. Its products are categorized into the following groups: chip manufacturing, wafer manufacturing, reticle manufacturing, complementary metal-oxide-semiconductor (CMOS) image sensor manufacturing, data storage media/head manufacturing, solar manufacturing, high-brightness LED manufacturing, microelectromechanical (MEMS) manufacturing and general purpose and lab applications. Chip manufacturing products and services encompass defect inspection, review, metrology, in-situ process monitoring and lithography modeling tools designed to help chip manufacturers manage yield. The company's wafer manufacturing tools include inspection, metrology and data-management systems. It offers inspection and metrology systems for reticle manufacturing and data storage media/ head manufacturing. The firm's CMOS sensors convert light to electrical signals and are primarily used in digital cameras. In the solar manufacturing category, the firm offers surface profilers and solar wafer and cell inspection modules, which are integrated in different stages of the solar wafer and cell production lines to increase yield and lower production costs. High Brightness LED manufacturing products include the ICOS wafer inspector for automated inspection of HB-LED wafers. KLA-Tencor's MEMS manufacturing products are tools and techniques for the manufacturing of complete systems-on-a-chip. The firm's general purpose and lab applications tools measure surface topography for a variety of industries. Subsidiaries include ICOS Vision Systems Corporation NV.

KLA-Tencor offers its employees medical, dental and vision coverage; life and disability insurance; flexible spending accounts; profit sharing; an employee stock purchase plan; a 401(k) plan; an employee assistance program; tuition reimbursement; pet insurance; and commuter assistance.

FINANCIALS: **Sales and profits are in thousands of dollars—add 000 to get the full amount. 2010 Note: Financial information for 2010 was not available for all companies at press time.**

2010 Sales: $1,820,760	2010 Profits: $212,300	**U.S. Stock Ticker: KLAC**
2009 Sales: $1,520,216	2009 Profits: $-523,368	**Int'l Ticker:**
2008 Sales: $2,521,716	2008 Profits: $359,083	Int'l Exchange:
2007 Sales: $2,731,229	2007 Profits: $528,098	Employees: 5,000 Fiscal Year Ends: 6/30
2006 Sales: $2,070,627	2006 Profits: $380,452	Parent Company:

SALARIES/BENEFITS:

Pension Plan:	ESOP Stock Plan:	Profit Sharing: Y	Top Exec. Salary: $780,769	Bonus: $3,130,494
Savings Plan: Y	Stock Purch. Plan: Y		Second Exec. Salary: $400,000	Bonus: $891,000

OTHER THOUGHTS:

Apparent Women Officers or Directors: 1
Hot Spot for Advancement for Women/Minorities:

LOCATIONS: ("Y" = Yes)

West:	Southwest:	Midwest:	Southeast:	Northeast:	International:
Y	Y	Y		Y	Y

KOCH INDUSTRIES INC

www.kochind.com

Industry Group Code: 324110

Management:		**Sales/Marketing:**		**Liberal Arts:**		**Information Sys.:**		**Professionals:**		**Tech./Scientific:**	
Mgmt. Trainees:	Y	Marketing Pros.:	Y	Gen. Writing/Editing:	Y	Info. Mgmt.:	Y	Finance/Acct.:	Y	Engineers, Elec.:	Y
Experienced Mgmt.:	Y	Retail Sales:		Tech. Writing:	Y	Software Dev.:	Y	Law:	Y	Engineers, Other:	Y
Int'l Business:	Y	Comm./Industrial:	Y	Graphic Arts/Photog.:	Y	Hardware Dev.:		HR/Other:	Y	Health/Lab:	
MBA Grads:	Y	Sales Trainees:		Music:		Consulting/Other:		Training:	Y	Science/Research:	
		Advertising Pros.:		Broadcasting:				Health Care:		Petroleum/Chem.:	Y
				Other:				Consulting:		Math/Other:	

TYPES OF BUSINESS:

Petroleum Refining
Chemicals
Textiles
Pipelines
Fertilizer Production
Chemical Equipment
Asphalt & Paving Supplies
Beef Production

BRANDS/DIVISIONS/AFFILIATES:

Flint Hills Resources
Koch Mineral Services
Matador Cattle Company
Koch Pipeline Company
Koch Chemical Technologies Group, LLC
Koch Nitrogen Company, LLC
INVISTA
Georgia-Pacific Corp

CONTACTS: *Note: Officers with more than one job title may be intentionally listed here more than once.*

Charles G. Koch, CEO
David L. Robertson, COO
David L. Robertson, Pres.
Steve Feilmeier, CFO
Katie Stavinoha, Dir.-Public Affairs
Charles G. Koch, Chmn.

Phone: 316-828-5500	**Fax:** 316-828-5739
Toll-Free:	
Address: 4111 E. 37th St. N., Wichita, KS 67220 US	

GROWTH PLANS/SPECIAL FEATURES:

Koch Industries, Inc. is a diversified group of companies with operations in markets as diverse as refining and chemicals; process and pollution control equipment and technologies; minerals and fertilizers; polymers and fibers; commodity and financial trading and services; and forest and consumer products. It also conducts operations in venture capital investments, municipal finance, capital market investments and business development. Subsidiary Flint Hills Resources operates petroleum refineries in Alaska, Minnesota and Texas, with a combined crude oil processing capacity of more than 800,000 barrels per day. These plants produce aromatics, olefins, polymers and intermediate chemicals. The subsidiary obtains its supply from purchasing offices in Houston, Denver, and Calgary, Canada. Subsidiary Koch Mineral Services supplies coal and petroleum coke as well as cement, pulp and paper, sulfur and related products internationally. Koch Nitrogen Company and its affiliates own or have interests in nitrogen fertilizer plants capable of manufacturing more than 9 million metric tons of nitrogen products annually. Koch's ranching subsidiary, Matador Cattle Company, operates three ranches in Kansas, Montana, and Texas. Subsidiary Koch Pipeline Company, LP and its affiliates operate a 4,000-mile network of pipelines. Subsidiary Koch Chemical Technology Group and its affiliates design, manufacture, sell, install and service process and pollution control equipment. Subsidiary INVISTA is a global producer and marketer of polymers and fibers, primarily for nylon, spandex and polyester applications. Subsidiary Georgia-Pacific manufactures and markets tissue, packaging, paper, building products, related chemicals and fluff, filter and market pulp under such brand names as Quilted Northern, Angel Soft, Brawny and Dixie.

Employees are offered medical and dental insurance; a 401(k) plan; a pension plan; flexible spending accounts; life insurance; business travel accident insurance; disability coverage; and educational assistance.

FINANCIALS: **Sales and profits are in thousands of dollars—add 000 to get the full amount. 2010 Note: Financial information for 2010 was not available for all companies at press time.**

2010 Sales: $105,000,000	2010 Profits: $	**U.S. Stock Ticker: Private**
2009 Sales: $100,000,000	2009 Profits: $	**Int'l Ticker:**
2008 Sales: $100,000,000	2008 Profits: $	Int'l Exchange:
2007 Sales: $98,000,000	2007 Profits: $	Employees: 80,000 Fiscal Year Ends: 12/31
2006 Sales: $90,000,000	2006 Profits: $	Parent Company:

SALARIES/BENEFITS:

Pension Plan: Y	ESOP Stock Plan:	Profit Sharing:	Top Exec. Salary: $	Bonus: $
Savings Plan: Y	Stock Purch. Plan:		Second Exec. Salary: $	Bonus: $

OTHER THOUGHTS:

Apparent Women Officers or Directors: 1
Hot Spot for Advancement for Women/Minorities:

LOCATIONS: ("Y" = Yes)

West:	Southwest:	Midwest:	Southeast:	Northeast:	International:
Y	Y	Y	Y	Y	Y

KOHL'S CORP

www.kohls.com

Industry Group Code: 452112

Management:		Sales/Marketing:		Liberal Arts:		Information Sys.:		Professionals:		Tech./Scientific:	
Mgmt. Trainees:	Y	Marketing Pros.:	Y	Gen. Writing/Editing:	Y	Info. Mgmt.:	Y	Finance/Acct.:	Y	Engineers, Elec.:	
Experienced Mgmt.:	Y	Retail Sales:	Y	Tech. Writing:		Software Dev.:	Y	Law:	Y	Engineers, Other:	
Int'l Business:		Comm./Industrial:		Graphic Arts/Photog.:	Y	Hardware Dev.:		HR/Other:	Y	Health/Lab:	
MBA Grads:	Y	Sales Trainees:	Y	Music:		Consulting/Other:		Training:	Y	Science/Research:	
		Advertising Pros.:	Y	Broadcasting:				Health Care:		Petroleum/Chem.:	
				Other:	Y			Consulting:		Math/Other:	

TYPES OF BUSINESS:

Discount Department Stores
Online Sales

BRANDS/DIVISIONS/AFFILIATES:

Kohls.com

CONTACTS:

Note: Officers with more than one job title may be intentionally listed here more than once.

Kevin Mansell, CEO
Kevin Mansell, Pres.
Wes McDonald, CFO/Exec. VP
Peggy Eskenasi, Sr. Exec. VP-Prod. Dev.
John Worthington, Sr. Exec. VP-Store Admin.
John Worthington, Sr. Exec. VP-Store Oper.
Donald Brennan, Chief Merch. Officer
Kevin Mansell, Chmn.
John Worthington, Sr. Exec. VP-Purchasing

Phone: 262-703-1440 **Fax:**
Toll-Free:
Address: N56 W17000 Ridgewood Dr., Menomonee Falls, WI 53051 US

GROWTH PLANS/SPECIAL FEATURES:

Kohl's Corp. operates family-oriented specialty department stores. The company currently operates 1,089 stores in 49 states, with three store formats: prototype (approximately 88,000 square feet of retail space), small (approximately 68,000 square feet of retail space) and urban (approximately 125,000 square feet of retail space). Kohl's stores offer apparel, shoes and accessories for women, children and men; soft home products, such as sheets and pillows; and other home products such as small electronics and luggage. The stores' brands include Dockers, Lee, Levi's, Jockey, Candie's, Nike, Dana Buchman, LC Lauren Conrad, Simply Vera Vera Wang, Dana Buchman Food Network and FILA Sport. Approximately 32% of Kohl's' merchandise is marketed towards women; 19% is marketed towards men; 18% is comprised of home furnishing products; 13% is designed for children; 10% is comprised of accessories; and 8% is comprised of footwear. In addition to its physical retail locations, the company also markets its products through its e-commerce site, Kohls.com. The company maintains nine distribution centers located in Ohio, Texas, Virginia, Missouri, New York, California, Georgia and Illinois; and e-commerce fulfillment centers in Monroe, Ohio and San Bernardino, California. In March 2011, the firm opened in nine new stores in seven states: Illinois, New York, South Dakota, Texas, Virginia, Washington and Wisconsin.

The company offers its employees medical, dental and vision insurance; long-term disability and life insurance; a 401(k) plan; tuition reimbursement; and merchandise discounts.

FINANCIALS:

Sales and profits are in thousands of dollars—add 000 to get the full amount. 2010 Note: Financial information for 2010 was not available for all companies at press time.

2010 Sales: $17,178,000 — 2010 Profits: $991,000
2009 Sales: $16,389,000 — 2009 Profits: $885,000
2008 Sales: $16,473,734 — 2008 Profits: $1,083,851
2007 Sales: $15,596,910 — 2007 Profits: $1,108,681
2006 Sales: $13,402,217 — 2006 Profits: $841,960

U.S. Stock Ticker: KSS
Int'l Ticker:
Int'l Exchange:
Employees: 133,000 Fiscal Year Ends: 1/31
Parent Company:

SALARIES/BENEFITS:

Pension Plan: ESOP Stock Plan: Profit Sharing: Top Exec. Salary: $1,300,000 Bonus: $2,600,000
Savings Plan: Y Stock Purch. Plan: Second Exec. Salary: $900,833 Bonus: $1,575,000

OTHER THOUGHTS:

Apparent Women Officers or Directors: 1
Hot Spot for Advancement for Women/Minorities:

LOCATIONS: ("Y" = Yes)

West:	Southwest:	Midwest:	Southeast:	Northeast:	International:
Y	Y	Y	Y	Y	

KPMG LLP

www.us.kpmg.com

Industry Group Code: 5412

Management:		Sales/Marketing:		Liberal Arts:		Information Sys.:		Professionals:		Tech./Scientific:	
Mgmt. Trainees:	Y	Marketing Pros.:	Y	Gen. Writing/Editing:	Y	Info. Mgmt.:	Y	Finance/Acct.:	Y	Engineers, Elec.:	
Experienced Mgmt.:	Y	Retail Sales:		Tech. Writing:	Y	Software Dev.:	Y	Law:	Y	Engineers, Other:	
Int'l Business:	Y	Comm./Industrial:	Y	Graphic Arts/Photog.:	Y	Hardware Dev.:		HR/Other:	Y	Health/Lab:	
MBA Grads:	Y	Sales Trainees:		Music:		Consulting/Other:	Y	Training:	Y	Science/Research:	
		Advertising Pros.:	Y	Broadcasting:				Health Care:		Petroleum/Chem.:	
				Other:	Y			Consulting:	Y	Math/Other:	

TYPES OF BUSINESS:

Accounting Services
Human Resource Advisory Services
Accounting Technology
Publications
Risk Management

BRANDS/DIVISIONS/AFFILIATES:

KPMG International
Audit Committee Institute
KPMG TaxWatch Thought Leadership Series
Japanese Practice
Tax Governance Institute
EquaTerra Inc

CONTACTS:

Note: Officers with more than one job title may be intentionally listed here more than once.

John Veihmeyer, CEO
Henry R. Keizer, COO
George Ledwith, Exec. Dir.-External Comm.
Harley Duncan, Managing Dir.
John Veihmeyer, Chmn.

Phone: 212-758-9700	**Fax:** 212-751-2109
Toll-Free:	
Address: 757 3rd Ave., New York, NY 10017 US	

GROWTH PLANS/SPECIAL FEATURES:

KPMG LLP, the U.S. subsidiary of global accounting cooperative KPMG International, is a leading provider of audit, advisory and tax services across the U.S. The firm's audit operations are based on a multidisciplinary approach focused on compliance tools, technological assistance and cultural values central to clients' companies. KPMG founded and maintains the Audit Committee Institute, designed to educate audit committee members about governance, accounting, financial reporting and other audit issues. KPMG's tax services segment provides tax assistance in the following areas: economic and valuation services; exempt organizations tax; federal tax; inbound tax services; international corporate tax; international executive services; legislative and regulatory services; mergers and acquisitions; state and local tax; and trade and customs. The company also provides tax-related news through its KPMG TaxWatch Thought Leadership Series and tax-related newsletters and publications. The firm's advisory services division assists its clients in achieving strengthened governance, reporting and internal controls; early identification and assessment of risk and control issues that affect performance; improved efficiency and effectiveness of key business processes; and informed responses to existing and proposed regulatory requirements. With approximately 90 offices across the U.S., KPMG serves companies and organizations in such major industry sectors as financial services; industrial markets; consumer markets; information, communications and entertainment; government; and health care. The firm also maintains a special focus group that has industry experience with the issues Japanese companies face in the U.S., as well as both Japanese and American business cultures, practices and standards. In February 2011, the company announced an agreement to acquire EquaTerra, Inc., a business advisory firm.

KPMG offers employees medical, dental and vision coverage; short- and long-term disability; life and long-term care insurance; a 401(k) plan; a pension plan; flexible spending accounts; and discounts on cars, insurance; jewelry, retailers, transit passes and other programs.

FINANCIALS:

Sales and profits are in thousands of dollars—add 000 to get the full amount. 2010 Note: Financial information for 2010 was not available for all companies at press time.

2010 Sales: $6,370,000	2010 Profits: $	**U.S. Stock Ticker: Subsidiary**
2009 Sales: $6,310,000	2009 Profits: $	**Int'l Ticker:**
2008 Sales: $7,000,000	2008 Profits: $	Int'l Exchange:
2007 Sales: $6,000,000	2007 Profits: $	Employees: 25,000 Fiscal Year Ends: 9/30
2006 Sales: $5,000,000	2006 Profits: $	Parent Company: KPMG INTERNATIONAL

SALARIES/BENEFITS:

Pension Plan: Y	ESOP Stock Plan:	Profit Sharing:	Top Exec. Salary: $	Bonus: $
Savings Plan: Y	Stock Purch. Plan:		Second Exec. Salary: $	Bonus: $

OTHER THOUGHTS:

Apparent Women Officers or Directors:
Hot Spot for Advancement for Women/Minorities:

LOCATIONS: ("Y" = Yes)

West:	Southwest:	Midwest:	Southeast:	Northeast:	International:
Y	Y	Y	Y	Y	Y

KRAFT FOODS INC

www.kraftfoodscompany.com

Industry Group Code: 311

Management:		Sales/Marketing:		Liberal Arts:		Information Sys.:		Professionals:		Tech./Scientific:	
Mgmt. Trainees:	Y	Marketing Pros.:	Y	Gen. Writing/Editing:	Y	Info. Mgmt.:	Y	Finance/Acct.:	Y	Engineers, Elec.:	
Experienced Mgmt.:	Y	Retail Sales:		Tech. Writing:	Y	Software Dev.:	Y	Law:	Y	Engineers, Other:	Y
Int'l Business:	Y	Comm./Industrial:	Y	Graphic Arts/Photog.:	Y	Hardware Dev.:		HR/Other:	Y	Health/Lab:	
MBA Grads:	Y	Sales Trainees:	Y	Music:		Consulting/Other:		Training:	Y	Science/Research:	
		Advertising Pros.:	Y	Broadcasting:				Health Care:		Petroleum/Chem.:	
				Other:				Consulting:		Math/Other:	

TYPES OF BUSINESS:

Food Manufacturing
Snack Foods
Beverages
Prepared Foods
Convenience Meals
Cheese Products
Energy & Nutrition Products
Processed Meats

BRANDS/DIVISIONS/AFFILIATES:

Knudsen
Jacobs
Maxwell House
Velveeta
Oscar Mayer
Jell-O
Oreo
Cadbury plc

CONTACTS: *Note: Officers with more than one job title may be intentionally listed here more than once.*

Irene Rosenfeld, CEO
Timothy McLevish, CFO/Exec. VP
Mary Beth West, Chief Mktg. Officer
Karen May, Exec. VP-Global Human Resources
Jean Spence, Exec. VP-R&D and Quality
Marc Firestone, General Counsel/Exec. VP-Legal Affairs
David Brearton, Exec. VP-Oper. & Bus. Svcs.
Sam Rovit, Exec. VP-Strategy
Sanjay Khosla, Exec. VP/Pres., Developing Markets
Mary Beth West, Chief Category Officer
W. Anthony Vernon, Exec. VP/Pres., Kraft Foods North America
Marc Firestone, Exec. VP-Corp. Affairs
Irene Rosenfeld, Chmn.
Michael Clarke, Exec. VP/Pres., Kraft Foods Europe
Franz-Josef H. Vogelsang, Exec. VP-Global Supply Chain

Phone: 847-646-2000 **Fax:** 847-646-6005
Toll-Free:
Address: 3 Lakes Dr., Northfield, IL 60093 US

GROWTH PLANS/SPECIAL FEATURES:

Kraft Foods, Inc., one of the largest food companies in the U.S, manufactures and markets packaged food products and beverages. The company's products consist principally of desserts and confectionary products, generating 29% of revenue; snacks, generating 22%; beverages, 17%; cheese, 14%; convenient meals, 10%; and various packaged grocery products, 8%. Kraft has operations in more than 70 countries and sells its products in approximately 160 countries. The company markets many of the world's leading food brands, more than 50 of which have revenues of at least $100 million and nine of which have revenues exceeding $1 billion. These nine brands include Kraft cheeses, dinners and dressings; Oscar Mayer meats; Philadelphia cream cheese; Maxwell House and Jacobs coffee; Nabisco cookies and crackers, including its Oreo cookie brand; Milka chocolates; and LU biscuits. Other major brands include Gevalia, Kool-Aid, Crystal Light and Country Time beverages; Cracker Barrel, Athenos, Velveeta, Cheez Whiz, Knudsen and Deli Deluxe cheese products; Lunchables, Boca and Deli Creations convenient meal products; Jell-O, Cool Whip, Miracle Whip, A.1., Grey Poupon and Shake N' Bake grocery products; and Newtons, Nutter Butter, Ritz, Wheat Thins, Cheese Nips, Teddy Grahams, Planters and Easy Cheese snacks. These products are generally sold to supermarket chains, wholesalers, club stores, masss merchandisers, distributors, convenience stores, gasoline stations and other retail food outlets. In January 2010, Kraft agreed to sell its pizza business, including the DiGiorno, Tombstone, Jack's, Delisso and California Pizza Kitchen brands, to Nestle. In February 2010, the company acquired British confectionery company Cadbury plc. Following the acquisition, the firm agreed to sell Cadbury's E. Wendel chocolates brand and its Kandia-Excelent chocolate and soft cake business in Romania. In October 2010, Kraft completed construction of a new candy and gum research and development center in Switzerland. In August, 2011, the firm announced plans to split off into two businesses—Global Snacks and North American Grocery.

FINANCIALS: **Sales and profits are in thousands of dollars—add 000 to get the full amount. 2010 Note: Financial information for 2010 was not available for all companies at press time.**

2010 Sales: $49,207,000 2010 Profits: $4,114,000
2009 Sales: $38,754,000 2009 Profits: $3,021,000
2008 Sales: $41,932,000 2008 Profits: $2,884,000
2007 Sales: $35,858,000 2007 Profits: $2,724,000
2006 Sales: $34,356,000 2006 Profits: $3,060,000

U.S. Stock Ticker: KFT
Int'l Ticker:
Int'l Exchange:
Employees: 125,000 Fiscal Year Ends: 12/31
Parent Company:

SALARIES/BENEFITS:

Pension Plan: Y ESOP Stock Plan: Profit Sharing: Top Exec. Salary: $1,470,000 Bonus: $10,584,125
Savings Plan: Y Stock Purch. Plan: Second Exec. Salary: $720,000 Bonus: $1,950,583

OTHER THOUGHTS:

Apparent Women Officers or Directors: 7
Hot Spot for Advancement for Women/Minorities: Y

LOCATIONS: ("Y" = Yes)

West:	Southwest:	Midwest:	Southeast:	Northeast:	International:
Y	Y	Y	Y	Y	Y

KROGER CO (THE)

www.kroger.com

Industry Group Code: 445110

Management:		Sales/Marketing:		Liberal Arts:		Information Sys.:		Professionals:		Tech./Scientific:	
Mgmt. Trainees:	Y	Marketing Pros.:	Y	Gen. Writing/Editing:	Y	Info. Mgmt.:	Y	Finance/Acct.:	Y	Engineers, Elec.:	
Experienced Mgmt.:	Y	Retail Sales:	Y	Tech. Writing:		Software Dev.:	Y	Law:	Y	Engineers, Other:	
Int'l Business:		Comm./Industrial:		Graphic Arts/Photog.:	Y	Hardware Dev.:		HR/Other:	Y	Health/Lab:	
MBA Grads:	Y	Sales Trainees:	Y	Music:		Consulting/Other:		Training:	Y	Science/Research:	
		Advertising Pros.:	Y	Broadcasting:				Health Care:		Petroleum/Chem.:	
				Other:	Y			Consulting:		Math/Other:	

TYPES OF BUSINESS:

Grocery Stores
Convenience Stores
Jewelry Stores
Pharmacies
Food Processing
Gas Stations
Department Stores

BRANDS/DIVISIONS/AFFILIATES:

Smith's Food & Drug Centers Inc
Fry's
Barclay
QFC
Ralph's
Smith's
King Soopers
Quik Stop

CONTACTS:

Note: Officers with more than one job title may be intentionally listed here more than once.

David Dillon, CEO
Rodney W. McMullen, COO
Rodney W. McMullen, Pres.
J. Michael Schlotman, CFO/Sr. VP
Kathleen S. Barclay, Sr. VP-Human Resources
Christopher Hjelm, CIO/Sr. VP
Michael J. Donnelly, Sr. VP-Merch.
Paul W. Heldman, General Counsel/Exec. VP/Sec.
Geoffrey J. Covert, Sr. VP-Retail Oper.
R. Pete Williams, Sr. VP
M. Marnette Perry, Sr. VP
David Dillon, Chmn.

Phone: 513-762-4000 **Fax:** 513-762-1160
Toll-Free: 866-221-4141
Address: 1014 Vine St., Cincinnati, OH 45202-1100 US

GROWTH PLANS/SPECIAL FEATURES:

The Kroger Co. is one of the largest supermarket operators in the U.S. The company operates 2,460 supermarkets in 31 states under a variety of names: Kroger; Kroger Fresh Fare; Kroger Marketplace; Ralphs; Food 4 Less; King Soopers; Smith's; Smith's Marketplace; Fry's; Fry's Marketplace; Dillons; Dillons Marketplace; QFC; Baker's; Owen's; Hilander; Scott's; Gerbe's Jay C; Pay Less; Fred Meyer; Foods Co.; and City Market. Of these stores, 1,014 have fuel centers. Kroger's supermarkets operate under one of four store formats: combination food and drug stores; multi-department stores; marketplace stores; or price-impact warehouse stores. Kroger's stores offer one-stop shopping, including whole health sections, pharmacies, pet centers and world-class perishables, such as fresh seafood and organic produce. Kroger also operates 784 convenience stores under the Quik Stop; Loaf N' Jug; Tom Thumb; Turkey Hill; Kwik Shop and Smith's Express names. In addition, the company operates 361 fine jewelry stores under the banners Fred Meyer Jewelers, Littman Jewelers, Barclay Jewelers and Fox's Jewelers. Moreover, the firm offers financial services such as credit cards loans, and theft protection under Kroger Personal Finance. Kroger manages a number of walk-in medical clinics located in its stores under the name The Little Clinic. The company operates 40 food processing or manufacturing plants, which are primarily bakeries and dairies and supply approximately 39% of the corporate brand units sold in its retail outlets. These plants consisted of 18 dairies, 10 deli or bakery plants, five grocery product plants, three beverage plants, two meat plants and two cheese plants.

Employees are offered medical, dental, vision, life and personal accident insurance; disability coverage; flexible spending accounts; home owners and auto insurance; an employee assistance plan; credit union membership; a continuing education program; and professional liability coverage.

FINANCIALS:

Sales and profits are in thousands of dollars—add 000 to get the full amount. 2010 Note: Financial information for 2010 was not available for all companies at press time.

2010 Sales: $76,733,000 — 2010 Profits: $70,000
2009 Sales: $76,148,000 — 2009 Profits: $1,249,000
2008 Sales: $70,235,000 — 2008 Profits: $1,181,000
2007 Sales: $66,111,000 — 2007 Profits: $1,115,000
2006 Sales: $60,553,000 — 2006 Profits: $958,000

U.S. Stock Ticker: KR
Int'l Ticker:
Int'l Exchange:
Employees: 334,000 Fiscal Year Ends: 1/31
Parent Company:

SALARIES/BENEFITS:

Pension Plan: ESOP Stock Plan: Profit Sharing: Top Exec. Salary: $1,256,548 Bonus: $808,020
Savings Plan: Y Stock Purch. Plan: Y Second Exec. Salary: $887,562 Bonus: $538,680

OTHER THOUGHTS:

Apparent Women Officers or Directors: 6
Hot Spot for Advancement for Women/Minorities: Y

LOCATIONS: ("Y" = Yes)

West:	Southwest:	Midwest:	Southeast:	Northeast:	International:
Y	Y	Y	Y	Y	

LABORATORY CORP OF AMERICA HOLDINGS www.labcorp.com

Industry Group Code: 621511

Management:		Sales/Marketing:		Liberal Arts:		Information Sys.:		Professionals:		Tech./Scientific:	
Mgmt. Trainees:	Y	Marketing Pros.:	Y	Gen. Writing/Editing:	Y	Info. Mgmt.:	Y	Finance/Acct.:	Y	Engineers, Elec.:	
Experienced Mgmt.:	Y	Retail Sales:		Tech. Writing:	Y	Software Dev.:	Y	Law:	Y	Engineers, Other:	
Int'l Business:	Y	Comm./Industrial:	Y	Graphic Arts/Photog.:	Y	Hardware Dev.:		HR/Other:	Y	Health/Lab:	Y
MBA Grads:	Y	Sales Trainees:		Music:		Consulting/Other:		Training:	Y	Science/Research:	Y
		Advertising Pros.:		Broadcasting:				Health Care:	Y	Petroleum/Chem.:	
				Other:				Consulting:		Math/Other:	

TYPES OF BUSINESS:

Clinical Laboratory Testing
Diagnostics
Urinalyses
Blood Cell Counts
Blood Chemistry Analysis
HIV Tests
Genetic Testing
Specialty & Niche Tests

BRANDS/DIVISIONS/AFFILIATES:

Center for Molecular Biology and Pathology (CMBP)
National Genetics Institute, Inc. (NGI)
Viro-Med Laboratories, Inc.
DIANON Systems, Inc.
US LABS
Esoterix
Orchid Cellmark, Inc.
Genzyme Genetics

CONTACTS: *Note: Officers with more than one job title may be intentionally listed here more than once.*

David P. King, CEO
James T. Boyle, COO/Exec. VP
William B. Hayes, CFO/Exec. VP
Lisa Hoffman Starr, Sr. VP-Human Resources
Lidia L. Fonseca, CIO/Sr. VP
F. Samuel Eberts, III, Chief Legal Officer/Sr. VP
Mark E. Brecher, Chief Medical Officer
Andrew S. Walton, Exec. VP-Esoteric Bus.
David P. King, Chmn.

Phone: 336-229-1127 **Fax:** 336-513-4510
Toll-Free:
Address: 358 S. Main St., Burlington, NC 27215 US

GROWTH PLANS/SPECIAL FEATURES:

Laboratory Corp. of America Holdings (LabCorp) is a leading independent clinical laboratory company in the U.S., offering health-related laboratory tests to the medical industry. Its tests are used primarily for routine screening, patient diagnosis and the monitoring and treatment of disease. The company operates a nationwide network of 51 primary testing facilities and over 1,700 service centers, consisting of branches, patient service centers and STAT labs, which can perform routine tests quickly and report results to the physician immediately. LabCorp's testing services include routine testing, specialty testing and new test development. The most frequently requested routine tests offered by the firm include blood chemistry analyses, thyroid tests, urinalyses, blood cell counts, Pap tests, HIV tests, microbiology cultures and substance-abuse tests. Specialty testing businesses in which LabCorp offers testing and related services include infectious diseases, diagnostic genetics, oncology testing, clinical trials testing, identity testing, allergy testing and occupational testing. Its Center for Molecular Biology and Pathology (CMBP) is a leading molecular diagnostics and polymerase chain reaction (PCR) technology firm. The company's National Genetics Institute, Inc. (NGI) subsidiary is a leading developer of PCR assays for Hepatitis C. Subsidiary Viro-Med Laboratories, Inc. provides molecular microbial testing using real time PCR platforms. Additional specialty testing subsidiaries include pathology testing firm DIANON Systems, Inc.; anatomic pathology and oncology testing firm US LABS; specialty reference testing firm Esoterix; and kidney stone analysis laboratory Litholink Corporation. The company processes an average of over 440,000 specimens per day and provides clinical laboratory services in all 50 states, Washington, D.C., Puerto Rico, Belgium and Canada. In December 2010, LabCorp acquired Genzyme Genetics from Genzyme Corporation. In April 2011, the firm acquired Orchid Cellmark, Inc. In June 2011, the company agreed to acquire Clearstone Central Laboratories.

Employees are offered life, disability, medical, dental and vision insurance.

FINANCIALS: **Sales and profits are in thousands of dollars—add 000 to get the full amount. 2010 Note: Financial information for 2010 was not available for all companies at press time.**

2010 Sales: $5,003,900 — 2010 Profits: $558,200
2009 Sales: $4,694,700 — 2009 Profits: $543,300
2008 Sales: $4,505,200 — 2008 Profits: $464,500
2007 Sales: $4,068,200 — 2007 Profits: $476,800
2006 Sales: $3,590,800 — 2006 Profits: $431,600

U.S. Stock Ticker: LH
Int'l Ticker:
Int'l Exchange:
Employees: 31,000 Fiscal Year Ends: 12/31
Parent Company:

SALARIES/BENEFITS:

Pension Plan: | ESOP Stock Plan: Y | Profit Sharing: | Top Exec. Salary: $885,333 | Bonus: $1,902,675
Savings Plan: Y | Stock Purch. Plan: Y | | Second Exec. Salary: $450,000 | Bonus: $702,782

OTHER THOUGHTS:

Apparent Women Officers or Directors: 4
Hot Spot for Advancement for Women/Minorities: Y

LOCATIONS: ("Y" = Yes)

West:	Southwest:	Midwest:	Southeast:	Northeast:	International:
Y	Y	Y	Y	Y	Y

Sales, profits and employees may be estimates. Financial information, benefits and other data can change quickly and may vary from those stated here.

LAM RESEARCH CORP

www.lamrc.com

Industry Group Code: 333295

Management:		Sales/Marketing:		Liberal Arts:		Information Sys.:		Professionals:		Tech./Scientific:	
Mgmt. Trainees:		Marketing Pros.:	Y	Gen. Writing/Editing:		Info. Mgmt.:	Y	Finance/Acct.:	Y	Engineers, Elec.:	Y
Experienced Mgmt.:		Retail Sales:		Tech. Writing:	Y	Software Dev.:	Y	Law:	Y	Engineers, Other:	
Int'l Business:	Y	Comm./Industrial:	Y	Graphic Arts/Photog.:		Hardware Dev.:	Y	HR/Other:	Y	Health/Lab:	
MBA Grads:	Y	Sales Trainees:		Music:		Consulting/Other:		Training:		Science/Research:	
		Advertising Pros.:	Y	Broadcasting:				Health Care:		Petroleum/Chem.:	
				Other:				Consulting:		Math/Other:	

TYPES OF BUSINESS:

Semiconductor Manufacturing Equipment
Etch Processing Systems
Chemical Mechanical Planarization Systems
Wafer Cleaning Equipment & Services
Support Services

BRANDS/DIVISIONS/AFFILIATES:

2300 Exelan Flex
2300 Versys Kiyo
Transformer Coupled Plasma
TCP 9400DSiE Deep Silicon Etch System
2300 Syndion Through-Silicon Via Etch System

CONTACTS: *Note: Officers with more than one job title may be intentionally listed here more than once.*

Stephen G. Newberry, CEO
Martin Anstice, COO
Martin Anstice, Pres.
Ernest E. Maddock, CFO/Sr. VP
Thomas J. Bondur, VP/Gen. Mgr.-Mktg. & Sales
Sarah A. O'Dowd, VP-Human Resources
Sarah A. O'Dowd, Chief Legal Officer
Ernest E. Maddock, Chief Acct. Officer
Richard A. Gottscho, VP/Gen. Mgr.-Etch Bus.
Jeffrey Marks, VP/Gen. Mgr.-Clean Bus.
James W. Bagley, Chmn.

Phone: 510-572-0200 **Fax:** 510-572-2935
Toll-Free: 800-526-7678
Address: 4650 Cushing Pkwy., Fremont, CA 94538 US

GROWTH PLANS/SPECIAL FEATURES:

Lam Research Corp. is a supplier of wafer fabrication equipment and services. The firm designs, manufactures, markets and services semiconductor processing equipment used in semiconductor device fabrication. The company's etch products are used to deposit special films on silicon wafers and to selectively etch away portions of various films, creating an integrated circuit. The firm also offers wafer cleaning services and equipment that employs proprietary technology and can be used throughout the semiconductor manufacturing process. Lam Research Corp.'s etch products selectively remove portions of various films from the wafer in the creation of semiconductor devices by utilizing various plasma-based technologies to create critical device features at current and future technology nodes. The firm's etch products include the 2300 Exelan Flex series for dielectric etch, the 2300 Versys Kiyo series for conductor etch, the Transformer Coupled Plasma (TCP) 9400DSiE Deep Silicon Etch System for micro-electromechanical systems and the 2300 Syndion Through-Silicon Via Etch System for three-dimensional integrated circuits. In addition, Lam provides technical support, training, spares and service. The company maintains more than 20 customer support centers in the U.S., Europe and the Asia-Pacific region. Lam developed several industry firsts including: the patented TCP source technology, the first inductive plasma source technology with a planar coil; introducing the dual frequency confined (DFC) technology for dielectric etch; developing the first 200/300mm capable etch product line with a 200mm comparable footprint; decoupling plasma density and bias power for conductor etch; and providing technologies to control parameters that impact critical dimension uniformity.

Employees are offered life, disability, AD&D, medical, dental and vision insurance; flexible spending accounts; group legal service plans; educational assistance; gym membership reimbursements; an employee assistance program; adoption aid; and a credit union.

FINANCIALS: **Sales and profits are in thousands of dollars—add 000 to get the full amount. 2010 Note: Financial information for 2010 was not available for all companies at press time.**

2010 Sales: $2,133,776 — 2010 Profits: $346,669
2009 Sales: $1,115,946 — 2009 Profits: $-302,148
2008 Sales: $2,474,911 — 2008 Profits: $439,349
2007 Sales: $2,566,576 — 2007 Profits: $685,815
2006 Sales: $1,642,171 — 2006 Profits: $335,755

U.S. Stock Ticker: LRCX
Int'l Ticker:
Int'l Exchange:
Employees: 3,232 Fiscal Year Ends: 6/30
Parent Company:

SALARIES/BENEFITS:

Pension Plan: | ESOP Stock Plan: | Profit Sharing: | Top Exec. Salary: $737,473 | Bonus: $3,211,287
Savings Plan: Y | Stock Purch. Plan: Y | | Second Exec. Salary: $425,141 | Bonus: $1,385,442

OTHER THOUGHTS:

Apparent Women Officers or Directors: 3
Hot Spot for Advancement for Women/Minorities: Y

LOCATIONS: ("Y" = Yes)

West:	Southwest:	Midwest:	Southeast:	Northeast:	International:
Y	Y	Y		Y	Y

LAS VEGAS SANDS CORP (THE VENETIAN) www.lasvegassands.com

Industry Group Code: 721120

Management:		Sales/Marketing:		Liberal Arts:		Information Sys.:		Professionals:		Tech./Scientific:	
Mgmt. Trainees:	Y	Marketing Pros.:	Y	Gen. Writing/Editing:	Y	Info. Mgmt.:	Y	Finance/Acct.:	Y	Engineers, Elec.:	
Experienced Mgmt.:	Y	Retail Sales:		Tech. Writing:		Software Dev.:	Y	Law:	Y	Engineers, Other:	
Int'l Business:	Y	Comm./Industrial:	Y	Graphic Arts/Photog.:	Y	Hardware Dev.:		HR/Other:	Y	Health/Lab:	
MBA Grads:	Y	Sales Trainees:	Y	Music:	Y	Consulting/Other:		Training:	Y	Science/Research:	
		Advertising Pros.:	Y	Broadcasting:				Health Care:		Petroleum/Chem.:	
				Other:	Y			Consulting:		Math/Other:	

TYPES OF BUSINESS:

Hotel Casinos
Convention & Conference Centers
Shopping Center Development
Casino Property Development

BRANDS/DIVISIONS/AFFILIATES:

Venetian Resort Hotel Casino (The)
Sands Expo and Convention Center (The)
Congress Center (The)
Sands Macao Casino (The)
Palazzo Resort Hotel Casino (The)
Venetian Macao Resort Hotel (The)
Marina Bay Sands
Cotai Strip

CONTACTS: *Note: Officers with more than one job title may be intentionally listed here more than once.*

Sheldon G. Adelson, CEO
Michael A. Leven, COO
Michael A. Leven, Pres.
Kenneth J. Kay, CFO/Sr. VP
Gayle M. Hyman, General Counsel/Sr. VP
Robert G. Goldstein, Pres., Gaming Oper.
Leonard DeAngelo, Sr. VP-Asia Oper., Marina Bay Sands
Nigel Roberts, Pres., Marina Bay Sands
Sheldon G. Adelson, Chmn.
Steven C. Jacobs, CEO-Sands China Ltd.

Phone: 702-414-1000 **Fax:** 702-414-4884
Toll-Free:
Address: 3355 Las Vegas Blvd. S., Las Vegas, NV 89109 US

GROWTH PLANS/SPECIAL FEATURES:

Las Vegas Sands Corp. (The Venetian) (LVSC) is an international hotel, resort and casino firm. Its flagship property is The Venetian Resort Hotel Casino, which is connected to the firm's The Palazzo Resort Hotel Casino. Together, The Venetian and The Palazzo offer 225,000 square feet (sq. ft.) of gaming space with 230 table games and 2,640 slot machines; 7,100 hotel suites; and 840,000 sq. ft. of dining, retail and entertainment space, including The Shoppes at The Palazzo. LVSC also runs the 1.2 million sq. ft. convention and trade show facility, The Sands Expo and Convention Center, and a supplemental event and conference center, The Congress Center, that connects to The Venetian. These properties feature 1.2 million sq. ft. of meeting, exhibition and convention space; 1 million sq. ft. of retail and dining space; and the 15,000 seat Venetian Arena. The company's largest development project, the multi-billion dollar Cotai Strip, is a collection of hotel properties, casinos and entertainment venues in Macao, China, the resort and gaming hub for China's population. The firm runs The Sands Macao and The Venetian Macao Resort Hotel, the anchor property on the Cotai Strip. Other properties on the Cotai Strip include the Four Seasons Hotel Macao and the Plaza Casino. One of the company's newest properties is the Sands Casino Resort Bethlehem, Philadelphia, featuring 3,000 slot machines and various entertainment options. Construction on the tower of the Sands Casino Resort Bethlehem is to be completed by mid-2011. The firm's newest international hotel and casino, Marina Bay Sands, opened in April 2010, in Singapore, Malaysia. In October 2010, it signed a ten-year license agreement with InterContinental Hotels Group plc to affiliate The Venetian and The Palazzo with the InterContinental's global portfolio.

FINANCIALS: **Sales and profits are in thousands of dollars—add 000 to get the full amount. 2010 Note: Financial information for 2010 was not available for all companies at press time.**

2010 Sales: $6,853,182 | 2010 Profits: $781,603
2009 Sales: $4,929,444 | 2009 Profits: $-368,743
2008 Sales: $4,735,126 | 2008 Profits: $-168,325
2007 Sales: $3,104,422 | 2007 Profits: $116,688
2006 Sales: $2,340,178 | 2006 Profits: $442,003

U.S. Stock Ticker: LVS
Int'l Ticker:
Int'l Exchange:
Employees: 34,000 Fiscal Year Ends: 12/31
Parent Company:

SALARIES/BENEFITS:

Pension Plan: | ESOP Stock Plan: | Profit Sharing: | Top Exec. Salary: $1,561,539 | Bonus: $
Savings Plan: Y | Stock Purch. Plan: | | Second Exec. Salary: $1,000,000 | Bonus: $

OTHER THOUGHTS:

Apparent Women Officers or Directors: 1
Hot Spot for Advancement for Women/Minorities:

LOCATIONS: ("Y" = Yes)

West:	Southwest:	Midwest:	Southeast:	Northeast:	International:
Y				Y	Y

LEAP WIRELESS INTERNATIONAL INC

www.leapwireless.com

Industry Group Code: 5172

Management:		Sales/Marketing:		Liberal Arts:		Information Sys.:		Professionals:		Tech./Scientific:	
Mgmt. Trainees:	Y	Marketing Pros.:	Y	Gen. Writing/Editing:	Y	Info. Mgmt.:	Y	Finance/Acct.:	Y	Engineers, Elec.:	Y
Experienced Mgmt.:	Y	Retail Sales:		Tech. Writing:		Software Dev.:	Y	Law:	Y	Engineers, Other:	
Int'l Business:		Comm./Industrial:	Y	Graphic Arts/Photog.:	Y	Hardware Dev.:		HR/Other:	Y	Health/Lab:	
MBA Grads:	Y	Sales Trainees:	Y	Music:		Consulting/Other:		Training:	Y	Science/Research:	
		Advertising Pros.:	Y	Broadcasting:				Health Care:		Petroleum/Chem.:	
				Other:	Y			Consulting:		Math/Other:	

TYPES OF BUSINESS:

Cell Phone Service
Retail Sales
Music Downloads

BRANDS/DIVISIONS/AFFILIATES:

Cricket Communications, Inc.
LCW Wireless Operations, LLC
Denali Spectrum Operations, LLC
Cricket Wireless
Cricket Broadband
Cricket PAYGo
STX Wireless Operations, LLC
Muve Music

CONTACTS: *Note: Officers with more than one job title may be intentionally listed here more than once.*

S. Douglas Hutcheson, CEO
Raymond J. Roman, COO/Exec. VP
S. Douglas Hutcheson, Pres.
Walter Z. Berger, CFO/Exec. VP
Leonard C. Stephens, Sr. VP-Human Resources
Dave Truzinski, CIO/Sr. VP
Collin Holland, Sr. VP-Tech. Oper.
Collin Holland, Sr. VP-Eng.
Robert J. Irving, Jr., General Counsel/Sr. VP/Corp. Sec.
Robert A. Young, Exec. VP-Field Oper.
William D. Ingram, Sr. VP-Strategy
Jeffery E. Nachbor, Chief Acct. Officer/Sr. VP-Financial Oper.
David B. Davis, Chief Sales Officer/Sr. VP
Aaron P. Maddox, Sr. VP-Finance, Wireless Oper.
Mark H. Rachesky, Chmn.

Phone: 858-882-6000 **Fax:** 858-882-6010
Toll-Free: 800-274-2538
Address: 5887 Copley Dr., San Diego, CA 92111 US

GROWTH PLANS/SPECIAL FEATURES:

Leap Wireless International, Inc. provides mobile wireless services targeted to meet the needs of younger and lower-income customers under-served by traditional communications companies. Leap operates under the Cricket brand, which is distributed through subsidiary Cricket Communications, Inc. and is also offered in Oregon by LCW Wireless Operations, LLC, and in the upper Midwest by Denali Spectrum Operations, LLC. Cricket, through a variety of flat-rate service plans, offers a choice of unlimited anytime local voice minutes; unlimited anytime domestic long distance voice minutes; unlimited text, instant and picture messaging; and additional related services. In addition to Cricket Wireless voice and data services, the company offers Cricket Broadband, an unlimited mobile broadband service; and the Cricket PAYGo service, which allows customers to pay a flat daily fee only on days they wish to use their phone. Over half of Cricket customers are younger than 35, and roughly half earn less than $35,000 per year. Cricket currently operates in 35 states and Washington D.C. and has approximately 5.5 million customers. Leap sells Cricket products and service through two channels: retail locations and kiosks; and authorized dealers and distributors. Leap, LCW and Denali together have approximately 350 direct retail locations and 3,700 indirect distributors. In August 2010, Cricket Communications acquired all the outstanding shares of LCW Wireless, and in September, it acquired the outstanding interest in Denali. In October 2010, Leap established STX Wireless Operations, LLC, a joint venture with Pocket Communications to provide service in the south Texas region. In January 2011, the company introduced Muve Music, an unlimited music download service designed specifically for mobile handsets.

Leap offers its employees benefits including tuition assistance; an employee assistance program; adoption assistance; fitness reimbursement; a 401(k) plan; and medical, dental and vision insurance with domestic partner coverage.

FINANCIALS: **Sales and profits are in thousands of dollars—add 000 to get the full amount. 2010 Note: Financial information for 2010 was not available for all companies at press time.**

2010 Sales: $2,697,203 2010 Profits: $-785,055
2009 Sales: $2,383,162 2009 Profits: $-237,963
2008 Sales: $1,958,862 2008 Profits: $-147,823
2007 Sales: $1,630,803 2007 Profits: $-75,927
2006 Sales: $1,167,187 2006 Profits: $-24,357

U.S. Stock Ticker: LEAP
Int'l Ticker:
Int'l Exchange:
Employees: 4,262 Fiscal Year Ends: 12/31
Parent Company:

SALARIES/BENEFITS:

Pension Plan: ESOP Stock Plan: Profit Sharing: Top Exec. Salary: $750,000 Bonus: $
Savings Plan: Y Stock Purch. Plan: Second Exec. Salary: $530,000 Bonus: $156,000

OTHER THOUGHTS:

Apparent Women Officers or Directors:
Hot Spot for Advancement for Women/Minorities:

LOCATIONS: ("Y" = Yes)

West:	Southwest:	Midwest:	Southeast:	Northeast:	International:
Y	Y	Y	Y	Y	

LEAR CORP

www.lear.com

Industry Group Code: 3363

Management:		Sales/Marketing:		Liberal Arts:		Information Sys.:		Professionals:		Tech./Scientific:	
Mgmt. Trainees:	Y	Marketing Pros.:	Y	Gen. Writing/Editing:	Y	Info. Mgmt.:	Y	Finance/Acct.:	Y	Engineers, Elec.:	Y
Experienced Mgmt.:	Y	Retail Sales:		Tech. Writing:	Y	Software Dev.:	Y	Law:	Y	Engineers, Other:	
Int'l Business:	Y	Comm./Industrial:	Y	Graphic Arts/Photog.:	Y	Hardware Dev.:	Y	HR/Other:	Y	Health/Lab:	Y
MBA Grads:	Y	Sales Trainees:		Music:		Consulting/Other:	Y	Training:	Y	Science/Research:	
		Advertising Pros.:		Broadcasting:				Health Care:		Petroleum/Chem.:	
				Other:				Consulting:		Math/Other:	

TYPES OF BUSINESS:

Automobile Components
Automotive Interiors
Electrical Systems
Instrument Panels
Seat Systems
Flooring Systems
Entertainment & Wireless Systems
Keyless Entry Systems

BRANDS/DIVISIONS/AFFILIATES:

Dynamic Environmental Comfort System
SoyFoam

CONTACTS: *Note: Officers with more than one job title may be intentionally listed here more than once.*

Robert E. Rossiter, CEO
Robert E. Rossiter, Pres.
Matthew J. Simoncini, CFO/Sr. VP
Melvin Stephens, Sr. VP-Human Resources
Terrence B. Larkin, General Counsel/Sr. VP/Corp. Sec.
Melvin Stephens, Sr. VP-Corp. Rel. & Comm.
Melvin Stephens, Sr. VP-Investor Rel.
Wendy L. Foss, Controller/VP
Shari Burgess, VP/Treas.
Louis R. Salvatore, Sr. VP/Pres., Global Seating Systems
Ray E Scott, Sr. VP/Pres., Global Electrical Power Systems
Henry D. G. Wallace, Chmn.

Phone: 248-447-1500	**Fax:** 248-447-1722
Toll-Free: 800-413-5327	
Address: 21557 Telegraph Rd., Southfield, MI 48033 US	

GROWTH PLANS/SPECIAL FEATURES:

Lear Corp. is one of the world's largest automotive interior systems suppliers. The firm serves every major automotive manufacturer, including General Motors, Ford, Daimler, BMW, Fiat, Volkswagen, Renault-Nissan, Hyundai and PSA Peugeot Citroen. The company currently operates 200 facilities in 34 countries. Its business is conducted through two segments: seating and electrical power management systems. The seating segment, accounting for 80% of the firm's revenues, consists of the manufacture, assembly and supply of vehicle seating requirements. Products include the Dynamic Environmental Comfort System, which is 30-40% lighter than standard seats; and SoyFoam seating made from recyclable materials and designs. The electronic power management segment, accounting for 20% of revenue comprises four categories: electrical distribution systems; smart junction boxes and body control modules; wireless systems; and specialty electronics. New electronic technology allows the integration of wiring and electronic products within the overall electrical architecture of the vehicle. Lear has the ability to integrate engineering, research, design, development and validation testing of all automotive interior systems with its research and development studio, its six advanced technology centers and its product engineering centers worldwide.

Employees are offered medical, dental and vision insurance; flexible spending accounts; an employee assistance program; life insurance; disability coverage; a 401(k) plan; a pension plan; a financial planning program; and tuition reimbursement.

FINANCIALS: **Sales and profits are in thousands of dollars—add 000 to get the full amount. 2010 Note: Financial information for 2010 was not available for all companies at press time.**

2010 Sales: $11,954,600	2010 Profits: $438,300	**U.S. Stock Ticker: LEA**
2009 Sales: $9,739,600	2009 Profits: $826,700	**Int'l Ticker:**
2008 Sales: $13,570,500	2008 Profits: $-689,900	Int'l Exchange:
2007 Sales: $15,995,000	2007 Profits: $241,500	Employees: 86,757 Fiscal Year Ends: 12/31
2006 Sales: $17,838,900	2006 Profits: $-707,500	Parent Company:

SALARIES/BENEFITS:

Pension Plan: Y	ESOP Stock Plan:	Profit Sharing:	Top Exec. Salary: $1,240,530	Bonus: $5,404,375
Savings Plan: Y	Stock Purch. Plan:		Second Exec. Salary: $635,152	Bonus: $1,494,202

OTHER THOUGHTS:

Apparent Women Officers or Directors: 2
Hot Spot for Advancement for Women/Minorities:

LOCATIONS: ("Y" = Yes)

West:	Southwest:	Midwest:	Southeast:	Northeast:	International:
Y	Y	Y	Y	Y	Y

LEXMARK INTERNATIONAL INC

www.lexmark.com

Industry Group Code: 334119

Management:		Sales/Marketing:		Liberal Arts:		Information Sys.:		Professionals:		Tech./Scientific:	
Mgmt. Trainees:	Y	Marketing Pros.:	Y	Gen. Writing/Editing:	Y	Info. Mgmt.:	Y	Finance/Acct.:	Y	Engineers, Elec.:	Y
Experienced Mgmt.:	Y	Retail Sales:		Tech. Writing:	Y	Software Dev.:	Y	Law:	Y	Engineers, Other:	
Int'l Business:	Y	Comm./Industrial:	Y	Graphic Arts/Photog.:	Y	Hardware Dev.:	Y	HR/Other:	Y	Health/Lab:	
MBA Grads:	Y	Sales Trainees:	Y	Music:		Consulting/Other:		Training:	Y	Science/Research:	
		Advertising Pros.:	Y	Broadcasting:				Health Care:		Petroleum/Chem.:	
				Other:				Consulting:		Math/Other:	

TYPES OF BUSINESS:

Computer Accessories-Printers
Laser & Inkjet Printers
Printer Consumables
Typewriters & Supplies
Connectivity Products
Document Software
Managed Print Services Outsourcing

BRANDS/DIVISIONS/AFFILIATES:

Perceptive Software Inc

CONTACTS:

Note: Officers with more than one job title may be intentionally listed here more than once.

Paul Rooke, CEO
Paul Rooke, Pres.
John W. Gamble Jr., CFO/Exec. VP
Jeri Isbell, VP-Human Resources
Robert J. Patton, General Counsel/Sec./VP
Gary Stromquist, Corp. Finance
Paul A. Rooke, Exec. VP/Pres., Imaging Solutions & Svcs.
Scott Coons, VP/CEO/Pres., Perceptive Software
Paul J. Curlander, Chmn.
Ronaldo Foresti, VP-Asia Pacific & Latin America

Phone: 859-232-2000	**Fax:** 859-232-2403
Toll-Free: 800-539-6275	
Address: 740 W. New Circle Rd., Lexington, KY 40550 US	

GROWTH PLANS/SPECIAL FEATURES:

Lexmark International, Inc. is a global developer, manufacturer and supplier of laser and inkjet printers and associated consumable supplies for the office and home markets. Its products are sold in over 150 countries across the Americas, Europe, the Middle East, Africa, Asia, the Pacific Rim and the Caribbean. The firm has four manufacturing sites and approximately 70 sales offices. Lexmark is divided into two segments: the Printing Solutions and Services Division, and the Imaging Solutions Division. The Printing Solutions and Services Division markets the company's lines of workgroup monochrome laser printers, color laser printers and laser multifunction printers to small and medium businesses, large corporations and the general public sector. The Imaging Solutions Division focuses on marketing inkjet and laser printers to the small office and home office (SOHO) markets. Lexmark also offers include outsourced managed print services, a service where Lexmark takes over ownership and/or operation of a client's printers, copiers and fax machines with the goal of savings substantial operating costs for the client. International sales, including exports from the U.S., accounted for approximately 57% of the firm's revenue. In June 2010, the company acquired Perceptive Software, Inc., a developer of enterprise content management software, for $280 million.

Employees are offered a 401(k) plan; flexible spending accounts; a stock purchase plan; and health benefits.

FINANCIALS:

Sales and profits are in thousands of dollars—add 000 to get the full amount. 2010 Note: Financial information for 2010 was not available for all companies at press time.

2010 Sales: $4,199,700	2010 Profits: $340,000
2009 Sales: $3,879,900	2009 Profits: $145,900
2008 Sales: $4,528,400	2008 Profits: $240,200
2007 Sales: $4,973,900	2007 Profits: $300,800
2006 Sales: $5,108,100	2006 Profits: $338,400

U.S. Stock Ticker: LXK
Int'l Ticker:
Int'l Exchange:
Employees: 13,200 Fiscal Year Ends: 12/31
Parent Company:

SALARIES/BENEFITS:

Pension Plan:	ESOP Stock Plan:	Profit Sharing:	Top Exec. Salary: $1,003,846	Bonus: $1,073,200
Savings Plan: Y	Stock Purch. Plan: Y		Second Exec. Salary: $572,192	Bonus: $552,520

OTHER THOUGHTS:

Apparent Women Officers or Directors: 3
Hot Spot for Advancement for Women/Minorities: Y

LOCATIONS: ("Y" = Yes)

West:	Southwest:	Midwest:	Southeast:	Northeast:	International:
Y		Y			Y

LIBERTY GLOBAL INC

www.lgi.com

Industry Group Code: 517110

Management:		**Sales/Marketing:**		**Liberal Arts:**		**Information Sys.:**		**Professionals:**		**Tech./Scientific:**	
Mgmt. Trainees:	Y	Marketing Pros.:	Y	Gen. Writing/Editing:	Y	Info. Mgmt.:	Y	Finance/Acct.:	Y	Engineers, Elec.:	Y
Experienced Mgmt.:	Y	Retail Sales:		Tech. Writing:	Y	Software Dev.:	Y	Law:	Y	Engineers, Other:	Y
Int'l Business:	Y	Comm./Industrial:	Y	Graphic Arts/Photog.:	Y	Hardware Dev.:		HR/Other:	Y	Health/Lab:	
MBA Grads:	Y	Sales Trainees:		Music:		Consulting/Other:		Training:	Y	Science/Research:	
		Advertising Pros.:	Y	Broadcasting:				Health Care:		Petroleum/Chem.:	
				Other:				Consulting:		Math/Other:	

TYPES OF BUSINESS:

Video, Voice & Broadband Internet Access Services
Telephony Services
VoIP Services
Mobile Telephony Services
Video on Demand Services

BRANDS/DIVISIONS/AFFILIATES:

UPC Broadband Holding BV
Unitymedia GmbH
VTR Global Com S.A.
Telenet Group Holding NV
Chellomedia BV
Austar United Communications Limited
Aster Sp. Z.o.o
Kabel BW Erste Beteiligungs GmbH

CONTACTS: *Note: Officers with more than one job title may be intentionally listed here more than once.*

Michael T. Fries, CEO
Michael T. Fries, Pres.
Charles H. R. Bracken, Co-CFO/Principal Financial Officer/Sr. VP
Amy M. Blair, Sr. VP-Global Human Resources
Balan Nair, CTO/Sr. VP
Elizabeth M. Markowski, General Counsel/Sec./Sr. VP
Shane O'Neill, Chief Strategy Officer/Sr. VP
Rick Westerman, Sr. VP-Corp. Comm.
Rick Westerman, Sr. VP-Investor Rel.
Bernard G. Dvorak, Co-CFO/Principle Acct. Officer/Sr. VP
Mauricio Ramos, CEO-VTR GlobalCom SA
Diederik Karsten, Managing Dir.-European Broadband
Shane O'Neill, Pres., Chellomedia
Robert M. Leighton, Sr. VP-Programming
John C. Malone, Chmn.
Mauricio Ramos, Pres., Liberty Global Latin America

Phone: 303-220-6600 **Fax:** 303-220-6601
Toll-Free:
Address: 12300 Liberty Blvd., Englewood, CO 80112 US

GROWTH PLANS/SPECIAL FEATURES:

Liberty Global, Inc. (LGI) is an international provider of video, voice and broadband Internet services, with consolidated broadband communications and/or direct-to-home (DTH) satellite operations in 14 countries around the world, primarily in Europe, Australia and Chile. LGI has roughly 17.6 million customers and 27.1 million video, voice and/or Internet subscribers. Its products include Video on Demand, high definition TV, Digital Video Recorders (DVRs), VoIP telephony services and broadband Internet speeds higher than 100 megabytes per second (Mbps). The firm conducts its business operations through various subsidiaries. Through indirect wholly-owned subsidiary UPC Holding BV, the firm provides video, voice and broadband Internet services in nine European countries and in Chile. The European broadband communications operations and DTH operations of UPC Holding, along with the German broadband communications operations of subsidiary Unitymedia GmbH, are collectively referred to as the UPC Broadband Division. UPC Broadband Holding's broadband communication operations in Chile are provided through VTR Global Com S.A., an 80%-owned subsidiary. Through LGI's 50.2% indirect majority interest in Telenet Group Holding NV, the firm provides broadband communications services in Belgium. Through its 54.2% indirect majority-owned subsidiary Austar United Communications Limited, the firm provides DTH satellite services in Australia. LGI also has consolidated broadband communications operations in Puerto Rico; consolidated programming business interests in Europe and Argentina; and DTH operations in Germany, part of Unitymedia. The firm's consolidated programming interests in Europe are primarily held through Chellomedia BV, which owns or manages investments in various businesses. Certain of Chellomedia's subsidiaries and affiliates provide programming services to LGI's broadband communications operations. In December 2010, the firm agreed to acquire Polish cable operator Aster Sp. Z.o.o. In March 2011, the company agreed to acquire German cable operator Kabel BW Erste Beteiligungs GmbH.

FINANCIALS: **Sales and profits are in thousands of dollars—add 000 to get the full amount. 2010 Note: Financial information for 2010 was not available for all companies at press time.**

2010 Sales: $9,016,900 — 2010 Profits: $388,200
2009 Sales: $7,497,400 — 2009 Profits: $-412,100
2008 Sales: $10,497,700 — 2008 Profits: $-788,900
2007 Sales: $9,003,300 — 2007 Profits: $-422,600
2006 Sales: $6,483,900 — 2006 Profits: $706,200

U.S. Stock Ticker: LBTYA
Int'l Ticker:
Int'l Exchange:
Employees: 20,000 Fiscal Year Ends: 3/31
Parent Company:

SALARIES/BENEFITS:

Pension Plan: | ESOP Stock Plan: | Profit Sharing: | Top Exec. Salary: $985,554 | Bonus: $2,559,000
Savings Plan: Y | Stock Purch. Plan: | | Second Exec. Salary: $663,692 | Bonus: $804,000

OTHER THOUGHTS:

Apparent Women Officers or Directors: 3
Hot Spot for Advancement for Women/Minorities: Y

LOCATIONS: ("Y" = Yes)

West:	Southwest:	Midwest:	Southeast:	Northeast:	International:
Y					Y

LIBERTY MEDIA CORP

www.libertymedia.com

Industry Group Code: 512110

Management:		Sales/Marketing:		Liberal Arts:		Information Sys.:		Professionals:		Tech./Scientific:	
Mgmt. Trainees:	Y	Marketing Pros.:	Y	Gen. Writing/Editing:		Info. Mgmt.:	Y	Finance/Acct.:	Y	Engineers, Elec.:	Y
Experienced Mgmt.:	Y	Retail Sales:		Tech. Writing:		Software Dev.:	Y	Law:	Y	Engineers, Other:	
Int'l Business:	Y	Comm./Industrial:	Y	Graphic Arts/Photog.:	Y	Hardware Dev.:		HR/Other:	Y	Health/Lab:	
MBA Grads:	Y	Sales Trainees:		Music:		Consulting/Other:		Training:	Y	Science/Research:	
		Advertising Pros.:	Y	Broadcasting:	Y			Health Care:		Petroleum/Chem.:	
				Other:	Y			Consulting:		Math/Other:	

TYPES OF BUSINESS:

Television Shopping Network
Television Production
Video Distribution
Online Retail
Satellite Television
Satellite Radio

BRANDS/DIVISIONS/AFFILIATES:

QVC Inc
Starz Entertainment
Provide Commerce Inc.
Atlanta Braves
Sirius XM Radio Inc.
TruePosition, Inc.
WildBlue Communications, Inc.
Leisure Arts Inc.

CONTACTS: *Note: Officers with more than one job title may be intentionally listed here more than once.*

Gregory B. Maffei, CEO
Gregory B. Maffei, Pres.
Charles Y. Tanabe, General Counsel/Exec. VP
David J.A. Flowers, Treas./Sr. VP
Christopher W. Shean, Controller/Sr. VP
John C. Malone, Chmn.

Phone: 720-875-5400 **Fax:** 720-875-7469
Toll-Free:
Address: 12300 Liberty Blvd., Englewood, CO 80112 US

GROWTH PLANS/SPECIAL FEATURES:

Liberty Media Corp. is a holding company that is primarily involved in e-commerce, entertainment, media and communications operations in the U.S., Europe and Asia. The firm divides its operations into three groups: the interactive group, the Starz group and the capital group. The interactive group is mostly engaged in e-commerce, and includes subsidiaries such as QVC, Inc.; Provide Commerce, Inc.; Backcountry.com, Inc.; Bodybuilding.com, LLC; and BuySeasons, Inc. Liberty Media also holds interests in Expedia, Inc.; LOCKERZ; HSN, Inc.; Interval Leisure Group, Inc.; Ticketmaster Entertainment, Inc.; and Tree.com, Inc. The Starz group is involved with U.S. video programming distributed by cable, satellite, Internet and other distributors. Assets within the group include Starz Entertainment, LLC, a collection of premium movie channels and services; Pickspal, Inc., which specializes in online games; and a 37% ownership stake in WildBlue Communications, Inc., which provides satellite Internet access. The capital group represents the company's interests that fall outside of the interactive and entertainment groups, and includes subsidiaries such as Starz Media, LLC; Atlanta National League Baseball Club, Inc.; Leisure Arts, Inc.; TruePosition, Inc; WFRV and WJMN Television Station, Inc.; and interests in Time Warner Inc. and Sprint Nextel Corporation. In June 2010, the company announced plans to split-off Liberty Capital and Liberty Starz.

FINANCIALS: **Sales and profits are in thousands of dollars—add 000 to get the full amount. 2010 Note: Financial information for 2010 was not available for all companies at press time.**

2010 Sales: $8,932,000 — 2010 Profits: $1,303,000
2009 Sales: $8,305,000 — 2009 Profits: $1,050,000
2008 Sales: $8,079,000 — 2008 Profits: $-758,000
2007 Sales: $7,802,000 — 2007 Profits: $758,000
2006 Sales: $8,613,000 — 2006 Profits: $1,021,000

U.S. Stock Ticker: LINTA
Int'l Ticker:
Int'l Exchange:
Employees: 24,073 Fiscal Year Ends: 12/31
Parent Company:

SALARIES/BENEFITS:

Pension Plan: ESOP Stock Plan: Profit Sharing: Top Exec. Salary: $1,000,000 Bonus: $5,062,500
Savings Plan: Y Stock Purch. Plan: Second Exec. Salary: $875,500 Bonus: $1,050,600

OTHER THOUGHTS:

Apparent Women Officers or Directors:
Hot Spot for Advancement for Women/Minorities:

LOCATIONS: ("Y" = Yes)

West:	Southwest:	Midwest:	Southeast:	Northeast:	International:
Y	Y	Y	Y	Y	Y

LIBERTY MUTUAL GROUP INC

www.libertymutualgroup.com

Industry Group Code: 524126

Management:		Sales/Marketing:		Liberal Arts:		Information Sys.:		Professionals:		Tech./Scientific:	
Mgmt. Trainees:	Y	Marketing Pros.:	Y	Gen. Writing/Editing:	Y	Info. Mgmt.:	Y	Finance/Acct.:	Y	Engineers, Elec.:	
Experienced Mgmt.:	Y	Retail Sales:		Tech. Writing:	Y	Software Dev.:	Y	Law:	Y	Engineers, Other:	
Int'l Business:	Y	Comm./Industrial:	Y	Graphic Arts/Photog.:	Y	Hardware Dev.:		HR/Other:	Y	Health/Lab:	
MBA Grads:	Y	Sales Trainees:		Music:		Consulting/Other:		Training:	Y	Science/Research:	
		Advertising Pros.:	Y	Broadcasting:				Health Care:		Petroleum/Chem.:	
				Other:	Y			Consulting:		Math/Other:	

TYPES OF BUSINESS:

Insurance, Direct Property & Casualty
Rehabilitation Services
Disability Care Management
Homeowners' Insurance
Auto Insurance
Group Life Insurance
Asset Management & Investment Products
Workers' Compensation

BRANDS/DIVISIONS/AFFILIATES:

Liberty Life Assurance Company of Boston
Liberty Mutual Property
Liberty Mutual Reinsurance
Liberty International Underwriters
Research Institute for Safety
Liberty Insurance Company Ltd.
Videocon Industries Ltd.

CONTACTS: *Note: Officers with more than one job title may be intentionally listed here more than once.*

David H. Long, CEO
David H. Long, Pres.
Dennis J. Langwell, CFO/Sr. VP
Helen E.R. Sayles, Sr. VP-Human Resources
A. Alexander Fontanes, CIO/Exec. VP
Helen E.R. Sayles, Sr. VP-Admin.
Christopher C. Mansfield, General Counsel/Sr. VP
Paul G. Alexander, Sr. VP/Mgr.-Comm.
Laurance H.S. Yahia, Treas./VP
J. Eric Brosius, Sr. VP/Corp. Actuary
John D. Doyle, VP/Comptroller
Christopher L. Peirce, Exec. VP/Prs., Comm. Markets
Timothy M. Sweeney, Exec. VP-Personal Markets
Edmund F. Kelly, Chmn.
Luis Bonell, Exec. VP-Liberty Int'l

Phone: 617-357-9500	**Fax:** 617-350-7648
Toll-Free: 800-837-5254	
Address: 175 Berkeley St., Boston, MA 02116 US	

GROWTH PLANS/SPECIAL FEATURES:

Liberty Mutual Group, Inc. is a group of insurance companies with over 900 offices worldwide and $109.5 billion in assets. Liberty Mutual has four strategic business units: Personal Markets, Commercial Markets, Agency Markets and Liberty International. The company's Personal Markets business unit provides private passenger automobile, homeowners, valuable possessions, identity theft and personal liability coverage through more than 350 U.S. offices. This unit also offers traditional and variable life insurance and annuity products through subsidiary Liberty Life Assurance Company of Boston. The company's Commercial Markets business unit provides risk and disability management and risk transfer products and services through six smaller units: National Market, Middle Market, Liberty Mutual Property, Specialty Lines, Group Benefits and Liberty Mutual Reinsurance. Liberty Mutual's Agency Markets business unit consists of specialty, property and casualty insurance carriers that sell products primarily through independent agents and brokers. The company's Liberty International business unit provides personal and commercial insurance through operations in Venezuela, Argentina, Colombia, Brazil, Chile, Singapore, Thailand, Vietnam, China, Hong Kong, Spain, Portugal, Turkey and Poland. Subsidiary Liberty International Underwriters provides casualty, specialty casualty, marine, energy, engineering and aviation insurance through 36 offices in Asia, Europe, the Middle East and the Americas. Liberty Mutual also operates the Research Institute for Safety, which conducts original investigations of job-related accidents and publishes its findings in a range of peer-reviewed journals. In November 2010, the firm and Videocon Industries, Ltd. announced plans to establish a non-life insurance joint venture in India which will provide personal and commercial insurance products.

Employees are offered medical, dental and vision insurance; a 401(k) plan; a pension plan; tuition reimbursement; savings on fitness club memberships; flexible spending accounts; disability insurance; life insurance; and disability coverage.

FINANCIALS: **Sales and profits are in thousands of dollars—add 000 to get the full amount. 2010 Note: Financial information for 2010 was not available for all companies at press time.**

2010 Sales: $33,200,000 | 2010 Profits: $1,678,000
2009 Sales: $31,094,000 | 2009 Profits: $1,023,000
2008 Sales: $28,855,000 | 2008 Profits: $1,140,000
2007 Sales: $25,961,000 | 2007 Profits: $1,518,000
2006 Sales: $23,520,000 | 2006 Profits: $1,626,000

U.S. Stock Ticker: Mutual Company
Int'l Ticker:
Int'l Exchange:
Employees: 45,000 Fiscal Year Ends: 12/31
Parent Company:

SALARIES/BENEFITS:

Pension Plan: Y | ESOP Stock Plan: | Profit Sharing: | Top Exec. Salary: $ | Bonus: $
Savings Plan: Y | Stock Purch. Plan: | Second Exec. Salary: $ | Bonus: $

OTHER THOUGHTS:

Apparent Women Officers or Directors: 4
Hot Spot for Advancement for Women/Minorities: Y

LOCATIONS: ("Y" = Yes)

West:	Southwest:	Midwest:	Southeast:	Northeast:	International:
Y	Y	Y	Y	Y	Y

LIFE TECHNOLOGIES CORP

www.lifetechnologies.com

Industry Group Code: 325413

Management:		Sales/Marketing:		Liberal Arts:		Information Sys.:		Professionals:		Tech./Scientific:	
Mgmt. Trainees:	Y	Marketing Pros.:	Y	Gen. Writing/Editing:		Info. Mgmt.:	Y	Finance/Acct.:	Y	Engineers, Elec.:	Y
Experienced Mgmt.:	Y	Retail Sales:		Tech. Writing:	Y	Software Dev.:	Y	Law:	Y	Engineers, Other:	Y
Int'l Business:	Y	Comm./Industrial:	Y	Graphic Arts/Photog.:	Y	Hardware Dev.:	Y	HR/Other:	Y	Health/Lab:	Y
MBA Grads:	Y	Sales Trainees:		Music:		Consulting/Other:		Training:	Y	Science/Research:	Y
		Advertising Pros.:		Broadcasting:				Health Care:	Y	Petroleum/Chem.:	
				Other:				Consulting:		Math/Other:	Y

TYPES OF BUSINESS:

Equipment-Gene Cloning Kits
Microarrays
Reagents
RNA & DNA Libraries

BRANDS/DIVISIONS/AFFILIATES:

AcroMetrix
Invitrogen MAGic Sample Processor
Applied Biosystems ViiA 7 Real-Time PCR System
Synthetic Genomics, Inc.
Invitrogen Corp.
Ion Torrent

CONTACTS: *Note: Officers with more than one job title may be intentionally listed here more than once.*

Gregory T. Lucier, CEO
Mark P. Stevenson, COO
Mark P. Stevenson, Pres.
David F. Hoffmeister, CFO
Amanda Clardy, Chief Mktg. Officer
Peter Leddy, Sr. VP-Global Human Resources
Brian Pollok, Chief Scientific Officer/Head-Global R&D
Joe Beery, CIO
John A. Cottingham, Chief Legal Officer
Mark O'Donnell, Sr. VP-Global Oper. & Svcs.
Paul Grossman, Sr. VP-Strategy & Corp. Dev.
Tim Ingersoll, Contact-Media Rel.
Eileen Pattinson, Sr. Dir.-Investor Rel.
Kelli A. Richard, VP-Finance/Chief Acct. Officer
Nicolas M. Barthelemy, Pres., Comm. Oper.
Paul Billings, Chief Medical Officer
Susan Crawford, VP-Bus. Transformation
Claude D. Benchimol, Sr. VP-Biological Info. Systems
Gregory T. Lucier, Chmn.

Phone: 760-603-7200 **Fax:** 760-603-6500
Toll-Free:
Address: 5791 Van Allen Way, Carlsbad, CA 92008 US

GROWTH PLANS/SPECIAL FEATURES:

Life Technologies Corp., formerly Invitrogen Corporation, is a global biotechnology tools company focused on developing research systems, instruments, reagents, software, and custom services. The company's product portfolio includes technologies for sample preparation, cell culture, RNA interference analysis, functional genomics research, proteomics, cell biology, capillary electrophoresis-based sequencing and next generation sequencing applications, as well as clinical diagnostic applications, forensics, animal, food, pharmaceutical and water testing analysis. The company divides its operations into three segments: molecular biology systems (MBS); cell systems (CS); and genetic systems (GS). The MBS segment includes molecular biology-based technologies, with applications including basic and real-time PCR, RNAi, DNA synthesis, sample preparation, transfection, cloning and protein expression profiling and protein analysis. The CS segment includes product lines used in the study of cell function, including cell culture media and sera; stem cells and related tools; cellular imaging products; antibodies; drug discovery services; and cell therapy related products. The GS division includes next generation sequencing systems and reagents, including capillary electrophoresis, the SOLiD and Ion Torrent systems, as well as reagent kits developed specifically for applied markets. The company has a presence in 160 countries, and its intellectual property portfolio contains over 4,000 patents and exclusive licenses. In January 2010, the fir, agreed to acquire AcroMetrix. In February 2010, Life Technologies sold its mass spectroscopy operations to Danaher Corporation. In April 2010, the company debuted the Invitrogen MAGic Sample Processor, a proteomic and epigenetic sample preparation system; and introduced the Applied Biosystems ViiA 7 Real-Time PCR System, which integrates a variety of genotyping and quantitative PCR applications. In June 2010, the firm announced an investment in Synthetic Genomics, Inc., which aims to commercialize synthetic genomic advances. In October 2010, the company acquired Ion Torrent. In February 2011, Life Technologies launched a distribution hub in Singapore.

FINANCIALS: **Sales and profits are in thousands of dollars—add 000 to get the full amount. 2010 Note: Financial information for 2010 was not available for all companies at press time.**

2010 Sales: $3,588,094 | 2010 Profits: $377,858
2009 Sales: $3,280,344 | 2009 Profits: $144,594
2008 Sales: $1,620,323 | 2008 Profits: $5,714
2007 Sales: $1,281,747 | 2007 Profits: $119,149
2006 Sales: $1,151,175 | 2006 Profits: $-191,049

U.S. Stock Ticker: LIFE
Int'l Ticker:
Int'l Exchange:
Employees: 11,000 Fiscal Year Ends: 12/31
Parent Company:

SALARIES/BENEFITS:

Pension Plan: ESOP Stock Plan: Profit Sharing: Top Exec. Salary: $1,129,808 Bonus: $2,874,813
Savings Plan: Y Stock Purch. Plan: Y Second Exec. Salary: $678,462 Bonus: $1,215,000

OTHER THOUGHTS:

Apparent Women Officers or Directors: 5
Hot Spot for Advancement for Women/Minorities: Y

LOCATIONS: ("Y" = Yes)

West:	Southwest:	Midwest:	Southeast:	Northeast:	International:
Y	Y	Y		Y	Y

Sales, profits and employees may be estimates. Financial information, benefits and other data can change quickly and may vary from those stated here.

LIMITED BRANDS INC

www.limitedbrands.com

Industry Group Code: 448120

Management:		**Sales/Marketing:**		**Liberal Arts:**		**Information Sys.:**		**Professionals:**		**Tech./Scientific:**	
Mgmt. Trainees:	Y	Marketing Pros.:	Y	Gen. Writing/Editing:	Y	Info. Mgmt.:	Y	Finance/Acct.:	Y	Engineers, Elec.:	
Experienced Mgmt.:	Y	Retail Sales:	Y	Tech. Writing:		Software Dev.:	Y	Law:	Y	Engineers, Other:	
Int'l Business:	Y	Comm./Industrial:		Graphic Arts/Photog.:	Y	Hardware Dev.:		HR/Other:	Y	Health/Lab:	
MBA Grads:	Y	Sales Trainees:	Y	Music:		Consulting/Other:		Training:	Y	Science/Research:	
		Advertising Pros.:	Y	Broadcasting:				Health Care:		Petroleum/Chem.:	
				Other:	Y			Consulting:		Math/Other:	

TYPES OF BUSINESS:

Apparel, Retail
Contract Manufacturing
Apparel Importing
Catalog & Online Sales
Lingerie
Cosmetics
Fragrances
Candles

BRANDS/DIVISIONS/AFFILIATES:

Limited, Inc. (The)
Victoria's Secret
Henri Bendel
Bath & Body Works
White Barn Candle Company
C.O. Bigelow
La Senza Corporation
Mast Industries

CONTACTS: *Note: Officers with more than one job title may be intentionally listed here more than once.*

Leslie H. Wexner, CEO
Stuart Burgdoerfer, CFO/Exec. VP
Jane L. Ramsey, Exec. VP-Human Resources
Martyn R. Redgrave, Chief Admin. Officer/Exec. VP
Sharen J. Turney, CEO/Pres., Victoria's Secret Megabrand
Diane Neal, CEO-Bath & Body Works
Leslie H. Wexner, Chmn.

Phone: 614-415-7000	**Fax:** 614-415-7094
Toll-Free:	
Address: 3 Limited Pkwy., Columbus, OH 43230 US	

GROWTH PLANS/SPECIAL FEATURES:

Limited Brands, Inc., formerly The Limited, Inc., is an apparel, lingerie, personal care products, accessories and fragrances retailer under brand names including Victoria's Secret, Bath & Body Works, Express and Limited. The company operates nearly 3,000 retail stores. Victoria's Secret and Victoria's Secret Beauty, with approximately 1,028 stores in the U.S., are specialty retailers of women's intimate apparel, beauty products and related accessories. Victoria's Secret's direct marketing segment is in charge of the catalog, of which 300 million copies are produced annually. Bath & Body Works, with 1,606 stores, features personal care products and also operates White Barn Candle Company to supply its candle needs and C.O. Bigelow for body products. C.O. Bigelow has brand specific stores in Ohio, Massachusetts, Illinois and New Jersey. Limited Brands also retains full ownership of the approximately 11 Henri Bendel women's personal care, apparel and accessory stores. In addition, the firm owns Mast Industries, a contract manufacturer and apparel importer, which supplies merchandise to Victoria's Secret, Express and Limited Stores. Finally, the company operates La Senza, a Canadian lingerie company. La Senza operates approximately 252 stores. Limited Brands runs four e-commerce sites: VictoriasSecret.com, HenriBendel.com, LaSenza.com and bathandbodyworks.com.

Limited Brands offers its employees medical, dental and vision insurance; product discounts; tuition assistance; paid time off; and adoption assistance.

FINANCIALS: **Sales and profits are in thousands of dollars—add 000 to get the full amount. 2010 Note: Financial information for 2010 was not available for all companies at press time.**

2010 Sales: $8,632,000	2010 Profits: $448,000	**U.S. Stock Ticker: LTD**
2009 Sales: $9,043,000	2009 Profits: $220,000	**Int'l Ticker:**
2008 Sales: $10,134,000	2008 Profits: $718,000	Int'l Exchange:
2007 Sales: $10,671,000	2007 Profits: $675,000	Employees: 90,000 Fiscal Year Ends: 1/31
2006 Sales: $9,699,000	2006 Profits: $683,000	Parent Company:

SALARIES/BENEFITS:

Pension Plan:	ESOP Stock Plan:	Profit Sharing:	Top Exec. Salary: $1,924,000	Bonus: $6,302,351
Savings Plan: Y	Stock Purch. Plan: Y		Second Exec. Salary: $1,250,000	Bonus: $3,998,400

OTHER THOUGHTS:

Apparent Women Officers or Directors: 5
Hot Spot for Advancement for Women/Minorities: Y

LOCATIONS: ("Y" = Yes)

West:	Southwest:	Midwest:	Southeast:	Northeast:	International:
Y	Y	Y	Y	Y	Y

LINCARE HOLDINGS INC

www.lincare.com

Industry Group Code: 6216

Management:		Sales/Marketing:		Liberal Arts:		Information Sys.:		Professionals:		Tech./Scientific:	
Mgmt. Trainees:	Y	Marketing Pros.:	Y	Gen. Writing/Editing:	Y	Info. Mgmt.:	Y	Finance/Acct.:	Y	Engineers, Elec.:	
Experienced Mgmt.:	Y	Retail Sales:		Tech. Writing:	Y	Software Dev.:		Law:	Y	Engineers, Other:	
Int'l Business:		Comm./Industrial:	Y	Graphic Arts/Photog.:	Y	Hardware Dev.:		HR/Other:	Y	Health/Lab:	Y
MBA Grads:	Y	Sales Trainees:		Music:		Consulting/Other:		Training:	Y	Science/Research:	
		Advertising Pros.:		Broadcasting:				Health Care:	Y	Petroleum/Chem.:	Y
				Other:				Consulting:		Math/Other:	

TYPES OF BUSINESS:

Home Health Care-Oxygen & Other Respiratory Therapy Services
Durable Medical Equipment
Home Infusion Therapies

BRANDS/DIVISIONS/AFFILIATES:

CONTACTS:

Note: Officers with more than one job title may be intentionally listed here more than once.

John P. Byrnes, CEO
Shawn S. Schabel, COO
Shawn S. Schabel, Pres.
Paul G. Gabos, CFO
Paul G. Gabos, Corp. Sec.
John P. Byrnes, Chmn.

Phone: 727-530-7700	**Fax:** 727-532-9692
Toll-Free:	
Address: 19387 US 19 N., Clearwater, FL 33764 US	

GROWTH PLANS/SPECIAL FEATURES:

Lincare Holdings, Inc. provides oxygen and other respiratory therapy services to in-home patients. The firm serves over 750,000 customers in 48 states through 1,090operating centers. The company also provides durable medical equipment and home infusion therapies in certain geographic markets. The firm's customers typically suffer from chronic obstructive pulmonary diseases (COPD), such as emphysema, chronic bronchitis or asthma, and require supplemental oxygen or other respiratory therapy services in order to alleviate the symptoms and discomfort of respiratory dysfunction. Lincare's home oxygen equipment comes in two variations: oxygen concentrators and liquid oxygen systems. Oxygen concentrators are stationary units that provide a continuous flow of oxygen by filtering ordinary room air and are often supplemented with portable gaseous oxygen cylinders or liquid oxygen systems to meet the ambulatory or emergency needs of the customer. Liquid oxygen systems are thermally insulated containers of liquid oxygen; they generally consist of a stationary unit and a portable unit, and are most commonly used by customers with significant ambulatory requirements. Other respiratory therapy services offered by the company include nebulizers and associated respiratory medications, which provide aerosol therapy for customers suffering from COPD and asthma; non-invasive ventilation, which provides nocturnal ventilatory support for customers with neuromuscular disease and COPD; ventilators, which support respiratory function in severe cases of respiratory failure where the customer can no longer sustain the mechanics of breathing without the assistance of a machine; and continuous positive airway pressure devices, which maintain open airways in customer suffering from obstructive sleep apnea by providing airflow at prescribed pressures during sleep. Lincare's home infusion therapy products and services include chemotherapy; continuous pain management; intravenous antibiotic therapy; parenteral nutrition; dobutamine infusions; enteral nutrition; immunoglobulin therapy; and central catheter management.

FINANCIALS:

Sales and profits are in thousands of dollars—add 000 to get the full amount. 2010 Note: Financial information for 2010 was not available for all companies at press time.

2010 Sales: $1,669,205 | 2010 Profits: $181,574
2009 Sales: $1,550,477 | 2009 Profits: $136,096
2008 Sales: $1,664,580 | 2008 Profits: $227,266
2007 Sales: $1,595,990 | 2007 Profits: $224,489
2006 Sales: $1,409,795 | 2006 Profits: $212,981

U.S. Stock Ticker: LNCR
Int'l Ticker:
Int'l Exchange:
Employees: 10,225 Fiscal Year Ends: 12/31
Parent Company:

SALARIES/BENEFITS:

Pension Plan: | ESOP Stock Plan: | Profit Sharing: | Top Exec. Salary: $921,030 | Bonus: $1,013,134
Savings Plan: Y | Stock Purch. Plan: Y | | Second Exec. Salary: $614,328 | Bonus: $675,759

OTHER THOUGHTS:

Apparent Women Officers or Directors:
Hot Spot for Advancement for Women/Minorities:

LOCATIONS: ("Y" = Yes)

West:	Southwest:	Midwest:	Southeast:	Northeast:	International:
Y	Y	Y	Y	Y	

LINCOLN NATIONAL CORPORATION

www.lfg.com

Industry Group Code: 524113

Management:		Sales/Marketing:		Liberal Arts:		Information Sys.:		Professionals:		Tech./Scientific:	
Mgmt. Trainees:	Y	Marketing Pros.:	Y	Gen. Writing/Editing:	Y	Info. Mgmt.:	Y	Finance/Acct.:	Y	Engineers, Elec.:	
Experienced Mgmt.:	Y	Retail Sales:		Tech. Writing:	Y	Software Dev.:	Y	Law:	Y	Engineers, Other:	
Int'l Business:	Y	Comm./Industrial:	Y	Graphic Arts/Photog.:	Y	Hardware Dev.:		HR/Other:	Y	Health/Lab:	
MBA Grads:	Y	Sales Trainees:	Y	Music:		Consulting/Other:		Training:	Y	Science/Research:	
		Advertising Pros.:	Y	Broadcasting:				Health Care:	Y	Petroleum/Chem.:	
				Other:	Y			Consulting:		Math/Other:	Y

TYPES OF BUSINESS:

Life Insurance
Investment Management
Retirement Plans
Mutual Funds
Financial Planning
Annuities

BRANDS/DIVISIONS/AFFILIATES:

MoneyGuard
Lincoln DentalConnect
Lincoln InStep
MoneyGuard Reserve Plus
Lincoln Financial Group

CONTACTS: *Note: Officers with more than one job title may be intentionally listed here more than once.*

Dennis R. Glass, CEO
Dennis R. Glass, Pres.
Randal J. Freitag, CFO/Exec. VP
Heather Dzielak, Chief Mktg. Officer/Sr. VP
Lisa M. Buckingham, Chief Human Resources Officer/Sr. VP
Nicole S. Jones, General Counsel/Sr. VP
Frederick J. Crawford, Exec. VP/Head-Corp. Dev. & Investments
Laurel O'Brien, Contact-Media
Jim Sjoreen, VP-Investor Rel.
Robert W. Dineen, CEO-Lincoln Financial Advisors/Securities Corp.
Will H. Fuller, Pres./CEO-Lincoln Financial Distributors
Mark E. Konen, Pres., Insurance & Retirement Solutions
Charles C. Cornelio, Pres., Defined Contribution

Phone: 484-583-1400 **Fax:** 484-583-3962
Toll-Free: 877-275-5462
Address: 150 N. Radnor Chester Rd., Ste. A305, Radnor, PA 19087 US

GROWTH PLANS/SPECIAL FEATURES:

Lincoln National Corporation is a holding company operating multiple insurance and investment businesses. The operations of the firm's subsidiaries, collectively known as Lincoln Financial Group, are divided into two operating businesses: Retirement Solutions and Insurance Solutions. The Retirement Solutions business operates in two segments: the annuities segment, which provides tax-deferred growth and lifetime income opportunities for its clients by offering individual fixed annuities; and the defined contribution segment, which provides employer-sponsored fixed/variable annuities and 401(k), 403(b) and 457 mutual fund-based programs. Lincoln Financial's Insurance Solutions division is also divided into two segments: the life insurance segment, which provides wealth protection, transfer opportunities, term insurance and a linked-benefit product called MoneyGuard; and the group protection segment, which offers group term life, disability income and dental insurance primarily to small and mid-sized employers. The company's other operations include financial data for operations that are not directly related to the business segments, investment income and its run-off institutional pension business. New products released in 2011 by Lincoln National include dental health maintenance organization (DHMO) option Lincoln DentalConnect, which is available in Texas, California and Florida; MoneyGuard Reserve Plus; and retirement planning solution Lincoln InStep.

Lincoln National offers employee benefits including disability, life, AD&D, medical, dental and vision insurance; domestic partner benefits; training programs; tuition reimbursement; educational and adoption assistance; and counseling services.

FINANCIALS: **Sales and profits are in thousands of dollars—add 000 to get the full amount. 2010 Note: Financial information for 2010 was not available for all companies at press time.**

2010 Sales: $10,407,000
2009 Sales: $8,499,000
2008 Sales: $9,224,000
2007 Sales: $9,614,000
2006 Sales: $8,962,000

2010 Profits: $980,000
2009 Profits: $-485,000
2008 Profits: $57,000
2007 Profits: $1,215,000
2006 Profits: $1,316,000

U.S. Stock Ticker: LNC
Int'l Ticker:
Int'l Exchange:
Employees: 8,270 Fiscal Year Ends: 12/31
Parent Company:

SALARIES/BENEFITS:

Pension Plan: ESOP Stock Plan: Profit Sharing: Y Top Exec. Salary: $1,995,233 Bonus: $1,253,655
Savings Plan: Y Stock Purch. Plan: Second Exec. Salary: $875,753 Bonus: $324,628

OTHER THOUGHTS:

Apparent Women Officers or Directors: 4
Hot Spot for Advancement for Women/Minorities: Y

LOCATIONS: ("Y" = Yes)

West:	Southwest:	Midwest:	Southeast:	Northeast:	International:
Y	Y	Y	Y	Y	Y

LKQ CORP

www.lkqcorp.com

Industry Group Code: 3363

Management:		Sales/Marketing:		Liberal Arts:		Information Sys.:		Professionals:		Tech./Scientific:	
Mgmt. Trainees:	Y	Marketing Pros.:	Y	Gen. Writing/Editing:		Info. Mgmt.:	Y	Finance/Acct.:	Y	Engineers, Elec.:	
Experienced Mgmt.:	Y	Retail Sales:		Tech. Writing:	Y	Software Dev.:		Law:	Y	Engineers, Other:	Y
Int'l Business:		Comm./Industrial:	Y	Graphic Arts/Photog.:		Hardware Dev.:		HR/Other:	Y	Health/Lab:	
MBA Grads:	Y	Sales Trainees:		Music:		Consulting/Other:		Training:	Y	Science/Research:	
		Advertising Pros.:		Broadcasting:				Health Care:		Petroleum/Chem.:	
				Other:				Consulting:		Math/Other:	

TYPES OF BUSINESS:

Remanufactured OEM Parts
Aftermarket Replacement Parts
Vehicle Salvage
Scrap/Bulk Automotive Parts
Refurbished Aluminum Wheels

BRANDS/DIVISIONS/AFFILIATES:

AkzoNobel Coatings, Inc.

CONTACTS: *Note: Officers with more than one job title may be intentionally listed here more than once.*

Joseph M. Holsten, Co-CEO
Robert L. Wagman, Pres./Co-CEO
John S. Quinn, CFO/Exec. VP
Victor M. Casini, General Counsel/Sr. VP/Corp. Sec.
Walter P. Hanley, Sr. VP-Dev.
Michael Clark, VP-Finance/Controller
Leonard A. Damron, Sr. VP-Southeast Region
H. Bradley Willen, VP-Midwest Region
Steven H. Jones, VP-Central Region & Core Oper.
Donald F. Flynn, Chmn.

Phone: 312-621-1950 **Fax:** 312-621-1969
Toll-Free: 877-557-2677
Address: 500 W. Madison St., Ste. 2800, Chicago, IL 60661 US

GROWTH PLANS/SPECIAL FEATURES:

LKQ Corp. is one of the largest providers of recycled OEM (original equipment manufacturer) automotive parts and related services in the U.S. LKQ operates over 325 facilities around the world. In the U.S. and Canada, the company has 97 locations that supply wholesale recycled OEM parts, 80 of which include a combination of processing, sales and redistribution operations, and 17 of which are primarily redistribution facilities. The firm's aftermarket parts business operates from facilities that serve as sales, warehousing or distribution centers, with a total of 166 facilities in the U.S. and Canada. LKQ also has locations providing self-service retail recycled vehicle products. The company refurbishes bumpers and wheels at 53 locations in the U.S. and Canada and one location in northeast Mexico. It also refurbishes head lamps and tail lamps at a facility in Michigan. The firm procures salvage vehicles, primarily at auctions, using its local professionals and centralized purchasing systems, and directly from insurance companies, automobile manufacturers and other suppliers. Once LKQ has received the proper title, assuring that the vehicles have not been stolen, it dismantles it for recycled parts. The firm's customers include collision and mechanical repair shops and, indirectly, insurance companies, including extended-warranty companies. LKQ's most popular products include engines, vehicle front-end assemblies, doors, transmissions, trunk lids, bumper assemblies, wheels, head and tail lamp assemblies and mirrors. In its 23 year history, the company has acquired over 100 firms. In 2010, LKQ acquired 16 wholesale products businesses, one recycled heavy-duty truck products business, two self service retail operations and one tire recycling business. In early 2011, the firm acquired an engine remanufacturer, an automotive heating and cooling component distributor, a wholesale recycled products business and a recycled heavy-duty truck company. In May 2011, LKQ acquired the paint distribution operations of AkzoNobel Coatings, Inc.

FINANCIALS: **Sales and profits are in thousands of dollars—add 000 to get the full amount. 2010 Note: Financial information for 2010 was not available for all companies at press time.**

2010 Sales: $2,469,881 2010 Profits: $167,118
2009 Sales: $2,047,942 2009 Profits: $127,521
2008 Sales: $1,908,532 2008 Profits: $99,899
2007 Sales: $1,112,351 2007 Profits: $65,901
2006 Sales: $789,381 2006 Profits: $44,395

U.S. Stock Ticker: LKQX
Int'l Ticker:
Int'l Exchange:
Employees: 12,000 Fiscal Year Ends: 12/31
Parent Company:

SALARIES/BENEFITS:

Pension Plan: ESOP Stock Plan: Profit Sharing: Top Exec. Salary: $650,000 Bonus: $1,620,093
Savings Plan: Y Stock Purch. Plan: Second Exec. Salary: $366,575 Bonus: $625,951

OTHER THOUGHTS:

Apparent Women Officers or Directors:
Hot Spot for Advancement for Women/Minorities:

LOCATIONS: ("Y" = Yes)

West:	Southwest:	Midwest:	Southeast:	Northeast:	International:
Y	Y	Y	Y	Y	

LOEWS CORPORATION

www.loews.com

Industry Group Code: 524126

Management:		Sales/Marketing:		Liberal Arts:		Information Sys.:		Professionals:		Tech./Scientific:	
Mgmt. Trainees:	Y	Marketing Pros.:	Y	Gen. Writing/Editing:	Y	Info. Mgmt.:	Y	Finance/Acct.:	Y	Engineers, Elec.:	
Experienced Mgmt.:	Y	Retail Sales:		Tech. Writing:	Y	Software Dev.:	Y	Law:	Y	Engineers, Other:	
Int'l Business:	Y	Comm./Industrial:	Y	Graphic Arts/Photog.:	Y	Hardware Dev.:		HR/Other:	Y	Health/Lab:	
MBA Grads:	Y	Sales Trainees:	Y	Music:		Consulting/Other:		Training:	Y	Science/Research:	
		Advertising Pros.:	Y	Broadcasting:				Health Care:		Petroleum/Chem.:	
				Other:	Y			Consulting:		Math/Other:	Y

TYPES OF BUSINESS:

Direct Property & Casualty Insurance
Natural Gas Exploration & Production
Offshore Oil & Gas Drilling
Hotel Operation
Pipelines

BRANDS/DIVISIONS/AFFILIATES:

CNA Financial Corp
Boardwalk Pipeline Partners LP
Loews Hotels Holding Corp
Diamond Offshore Drilling Inc
HighMount Exploration & Production LLC
CNA Specialty
Continental Casualty Co
CNA Commercial

CONTACTS: *Note: Officers with more than one job title may be intentionally listed here more than once.*

James S. Tisch, CEO
James S. Tisch, Pres.
Peter W. Keegan, CFO/Sr. VP
Alan Momeyer, VP-Human Resources
Robert D. Fields, CIO/VP
Gary W. Garson, General Counsel/Sr. VP/Sec.
Candace Leeds, VP-Public Rel.
Darren Daugherty, Head-Investor Rel.
John J. Kenny, Treas.
Jonathan M. Tisch, Co-Chmn.
Jonathan M. Tisch, CEO/Chmn.-Loews Hotels
Mark S. Schwartz, Controller
Richard W. Scott, Chief Investment Officer/Sr. VP
Andrew H. Tisch, Co-Chmn.

Phone: 212-521-2000	**Fax:** 212-521-2525
Toll-Free:	
Address: 667 Madison Ave., New York, NY 10065-8087 US	

GROWTH PLANS/SPECIAL FEATURES:

Loews Corporation is a holding firm for companies involved in various industries. The company operates primarily through five subsidiaries: CNA Financial Corp., which accounted for 63% of the firm's consolidated revenue; Boardwalk Pipeline Partners, LP, 7.7%; Diamond Offshore Drilling, Inc., 23%; Loews Hotels Holdings Corp., 2.1%; and HighMount Exploration & Production, LLC, 2.9%. CNA Financial, a 90%-owned subsidiary, is an insurance holding company; its property and casualty insurance businesses are conducted by Continental Casualty Co. and The Continental Insurance Co. CAN Financial's core business includes two operating segments: CNA Specialty, which provides domestic and international professional liability coverage for clients including architects, lawyers, accountants, healthcare professionals, financial intermediaries and public and private companies; and CNA Commercial, which markets a broad range of property and casualty insurance products and services to small, middle-market and large businesses and organizations. Boardwalk Pipeline Partners, a 66%-owned subsidiary, specializes in the interstate transportation and storage of natural gas. The subsidiary conducts its operations through three companies: Texas Gas Transmission LLC, Gulf Crossing Pipeline Company LLC and Gulf South Pipeline, LP. Diamond Offshore Drilling, a 50.4%-owned subsidiary, owns and operates offshore oil and gas drilling rigs that are used by companies exploring for and producing hydrocarbons. The subsidiary owns 46 offshore rigs, of which 32 are semi-submersible. Loews Hotels, a wholly-owned subsidiary, operates 18 hotels, including Loews Annapolis; Hard Rock Hotel in Orlando, Florida; The Regency in New York; and Loews Hotel Vogue in Montreal, Canada. HighMount Exploration, another wholly-owned subsidiary, explores, produces and markets natural gas, with total proved reserves of 741 billion cubic feet of natural gas equivalents.

FINANCIALS: **Sales and profits are in thousands of dollars—add 000 to get the full amount. 2010 Note: Financial information for 2010 was not available for all companies at press time.**

2010 Sales: $14,615,000	2010 Profits: $1,288,000
2009 Sales: $14,117,000	2009 Profits: $564,000
2008 Sales: $13,247,000	2008 Profits: $4,530,000
2007 Sales: $14,302,000	2007 Profits: $2,488,000
2006 Sales: $17,702,000	2006 Profits: $2,491,300

U.S. Stock Ticker: L
Int'l Ticker:
Int'l Exchange:
Employees: 18,400 Fiscal Year Ends: 12/31
Parent Company:

SALARIES/BENEFITS:

Pension Plan:	ESOP Stock Plan:	Profit Sharing:	Top Exec. Salary: $990,000	Bonus: $1,710,000
Savings Plan: Y	Stock Purch. Plan:		Second Exec. Salary: $975,000	Bonus: $2,725,000

OTHER THOUGHTS:

Apparent Women Officers or Directors: 5
Hot Spot for Advancement for Women/Minorities: Y

LOCATIONS: ("Y" = Yes)

West:	Southwest:	Midwest:	Southeast:	Northeast:	International:
Y	Y	Y	Y	Y	Y

LORAL SPACE & COMMUNICATIONS LTD

www.loral.com

Industry Group Code: 334220

Management:		Sales/Marketing:		Liberal Arts:		Information Sys.:		Professionals:		Tech./Scientific:	
Mgmt. Trainees:	Y	Marketing Pros.:	Y	Gen. Writing/Editing:		Info. Mgmt.:	Y	Finance/Acct.:	Y	Engineers, Elec.:	Y
Experienced Mgmt.:	Y	Retail Sales:		Tech. Writing:		Software Dev.:	Y	Law:	Y	Engineers, Other:	
Int'l Business:	Y	Comm./Industrial:	Y	Graphic Arts/Photog.:		Hardware Dev.:	Y	HR/Other:	Y	Health/Lab:	
MBA Grads:	Y	Sales Trainees:		Music:		Consulting/Other:		Training:	Y	Science/Research:	
		Advertising Pros.:	Y	Broadcasting:				Health Care:		Petroleum/Chem.:	
				Other:				Consulting:		Math/Other:	

TYPES OF BUSINESS:

Satellite Equipment
Communications & Weather Satellite Systems
Fixed Satellite & Network Services
Information Delivery Systems
Managed Communications Networks
Internet Services

BRANDS/DIVISIONS/AFFILIATES:

Telesat Canada
Space Systems/Loral, Inc.
XTAR, LLC

CONTACTS: *Note: Officers with more than one job title may be intentionally listed here more than once.*

Michael B. Targoff, CEO/Vice Chmn.
Michael B. Targoff, Pres.
Harvey B. Rein, CFO/Sr. VP
Avi Katz, General Counsel/Sec./Sr. VP
Richard P. Mastoloni, Sr. VP-Finance/Treas.
John Capogrossi, VP/Controller
Barry J. Sitler, VP-Tax
Mark H. Rachesky, Chmn.

Phone: 212-697-1105	**Fax:** 212-338-5662
Toll-Free:	
Address: 600 3rd Ave., New York, NY 10016 US	

GROWTH PLANS/SPECIAL FEATURES:

Loral Space & Communications, Ltd. is a leader in satellite communications. The company is divided into two segments: Satellite Manufacturing and Satellite Services. Its subsidiary, Telesat Canada, manages and operates the firm's Satellite Services business. It maintains 12 satellites in geosynchronous orbits, approximately 22,000 miles above the equator, which provide high-bandwidth services and serve as the backbone for many forms of telecommunications. Customers lease transponder capacity for distribution of cable television programming, for direct-to-home (DTH) video transmission, live video feeds from breaking news and sporting events and broadband data distribution. Subsidiary Space Systems/Loral, Inc. designs and manufactures satellites and space system components for commercial and government broadcasting applications including fixed satellite services, direct to home broadcasting, broadband data distribution, wireless telephony, digital radio, military communications, weather monitoring and air traffic management. Loral also owns 56% of XTAR, LLC, a joint venture with Spanish telecommunications company HISDESAT. XTAR provides X-band services to government users in the U.S., Spain and other allied countries, including the U.S. Department of State, the Spanish Ministry of Defense and the Danish armed forces.

FINANCIALS: **Sales and profits are in thousands of dollars—add 000 to get the full amount. 2010 Note: Financial information for 2010 was not available for all companies at press time.**

2010 Sales: $1,158,985
2009 Sales: $993,400
2008 Sales: $869,398
2007 Sales: $882,454
2006 Sales: $797,333

2010 Profits: $487,341
2009 Profits: $231,702
2008 Profits: $-692,916
2007 Profits: $29,659
2006 Profits: $-22,720

U.S. Stock Ticker: LORL
Int'l Ticker:
Int'l Exchange:
Employees: 2,700 Fiscal Year Ends: 12/31
Parent Company:

SALARIES/BENEFITS:

Pension Plan: ESOP Stock Plan: Profit Sharing: Top Exec. Salary: $957,308 Bonus: $1,445,188
Savings Plan: Stock Purch. Plan: Second Exec. Salary: $488,731 Bonus: $256,389

OTHER THOUGHTS:

Apparent Women Officers or Directors:
Hot Spot for Advancement for Women/Minorities:

LOCATIONS: ("Y" = Yes)

West:	Southwest:	Midwest:	Southeast:	Northeast:	International:
Y				Y	Y

LUFKIN INDUSTRIES INC

www.lufkin.com

Industry Group Code: 33313

Management:		Sales/Marketing:		Liberal Arts:		Information Sys.:		Professionals:		Tech./Scientific:	
Mgmt. Trainees:		Marketing Pros.:	Y	Gen. Writing/Editing:		Info. Mgmt.:	Y	Finance/Acct.:	Y	Engineers, Elec.:	Y
Experienced Mgmt.:		Retail Sales:		Tech. Writing:	Y	Software Dev.:		Law:	Y	Engineers, Other:	Y
Int'l Business:	Y	Comm./Industrial:	Y	Graphic Arts/Photog.:		Hardware Dev.:		HR/Other:	Y	Health/Lab:	
MBA Grads:	Y	Sales Trainees:		Music:		Consulting/Other:		Training:		Science/Research:	
		Advertising Pros.:	Y	Broadcasting:				Health Care:		Petroleum/Chem.:	
				Other:				Consulting:		Math/Other:	

TYPES OF BUSINESS:

Oil Pump Manufacturing
Gearbox Manufacturing

BRANDS/DIVISIONS/AFFILIATES:

International Lift Systems LLC.
Rotating Machinery Technology, Inc.

CONTACTS:

Note: Officers with more than one job title may be intentionally listed here more than once.

John F. Glick, CEO
John F. Glick, Pres.
Christopher L. Boone, CFO/VP
Brian Gifford, VP-Human Resources
Scott H. Semlinger, VP-Mfg. Tech.
Paul G. Perez, General Counsel/VP/Sec.
Christopher L. Boone, Treas.
Terry L. Orr, VP-Power Transmission Div.
Mark E. Crews, VP-Oilfield Div.
Douglas V. Smith, Chmn.

Phone: 936-634-2211	**Fax:** 936-637-5272
Toll-Free:	
Address: 601 S. Raguet St., Lufkin, TX 75902-0849 US	

GROWTH PLANS/SPECIAL FEATURES:

Lufkin Industries, Inc. is a leading manufacturer of global supplier of oil field and power transmission products. The firm operates through two business segments: oil field and power transmission. The oil field division manufactures, designs, installs and services artificial lift products, including reciprocating rod lift (also called pumping units), gas lift, plunger lift equipment and related products. Pumping units manufactured include air-balanced units; beam-balanced units; crank-balanced units; and a Mark II Unitorque unit. In addition, the company designs, manufactures, installs and services computer control equipment and analytical services for artificial lift equipment; and operates an iron foundry to produce castings for new pumping units. The power transmission segment designs, manufactures and services speed increasing and reducing gearboxes for industrial applications. Speed increasers are those that convert from low-speed and high torque input to high-speed and lower torque output, while the speed reducing gearboxes do the reverse. This segment also manufactures spare parts and parts for aftermarket service; and operates an industrial gear repair facility devoted to the rebuild, repair and overhaul needs of the aftermarket end-user. The company also produces medium to large, low to mid-volume ductile and gray iron castings. These are used in a wide range of applications, including valves, machine tools, pump and compressors, construction equipment and special machinery. In July 2010, the company announced plans for the construction of an oilfield and power transmission manufacturing facility in Romania.

The company offers employees medical, dental and vision insurance; 401(k); a pension plan; a dependant scholarship program; and tuition reimbursement.

FINANCIALS:

Sales and profits are in thousands of dollars—add 000 to get the full amount. 2010 Note: Financial information for 2010 was not available for all companies at press time.

2010 Sales: $645,643	2010 Profits: $43,823	**U.S. Stock Ticker: LUFK**
2009 Sales: $521,359	2009 Profits: $22,026	**Int'l Ticker:**
2008 Sales: $741,194	2008 Profits: $88,239	Int'l Exchange:
2007 Sales: $555,806	2007 Profits: $74,211	Employees: 3,000 Fiscal Year Ends: 12/31
2006 Sales: $605,492	2006 Profits: $72,994	Parent Company:

SALARIES/BENEFITS:

Pension Plan: Y	ESOP Stock Plan:	Profit Sharing:	Top Exec. Salary: $520,000	Bonus: $
Savings Plan: Y	Stock Purch. Plan:		Second Exec. Salary: $255,000	Bonus: $

OTHER THOUGHTS:

Apparent Women Officers or Directors: 1
Hot Spot for Advancement for Women/Minorities:

LOCATIONS: ("Y" = Yes)

West:	Southwest:	Midwest:	Southeast:	Northeast:	International:
	Y			Y	Y

MACY'S INC

www.macysinc.com

Industry Group Code: 452111

Management:		**Sales/Marketing:**		**Liberal Arts:**		**Information Sys.:**		**Professionals:**		**Tech./Scientific:**	
Mgmt. Trainees:	Y	Marketing Pros.:	Y	Gen. Writing/Editing:	Y	Info. Mgmt.:	Y	Finance/Acct.:	Y	Engineers, Elec.:	
Experienced Mgmt.:	Y	Retail Sales:	Y	Tech. Writing:		Software Dev.:	Y	Law:	Y	Engineers, Other:	
Int'l Business:	Y	Comm./Industrial:		Graphic Arts/Photog.:	Y	Hardware Dev.:		HR/Other:	Y	Health/Lab:	
MBA Grads:	Y	Sales Trainees:	Y	Music:		Consulting/Other:		Training:	Y	Science/Research:	
		Advertising Pros.:	Y	Broadcasting:				Health Care:		Petroleum/Chem.:	
				Other:	Y			Consulting:		Math/Other:	

TYPES OF BUSINESS:

Department Stores
Bridal & Formalwear Stores
Direct Marketing
Online Sales
Catalogs
Wedding Planning & Bridal Registries
Credit Services
Furniture Stores

BRANDS/DIVISIONS/AFFILIATES:

Holiday Lane
Bloomingdale's By Mail
FDS Bank
Macy's Credit & Customer Service Inc
Macy's Systems & Technology Inc
Macy's Merchandising Group Inc
Macy's Logistics & Operations
Alfani

CONTACTS: *Note: Officers with more than one job title may be intentionally listed here more than once.*

Terry J. Lundgren, CEO
Terry J. Lundgren, Pres.
Karen M. Hoguet, CFO
Peter Sachse, Chief Mktg. Officer
Julie Greiner, Chief Merch. Planning Officer
Thomas L. Cole, Chief Admin. Officer
Ronald Klein, Chief Stores Officer
Timothy M. Adams, Chief Private Brand Officer
Jeffrey Gennette, Chief Merch. Officer
Mark S. Cosby, Pres., Stores
Terry J. Lundgren, Chmn.

Phone: 513-579-7000 **Fax:** 513-579-7555
Toll-Free: 800-261-5385
Address: 7 W. 7th St., Cincinnati, OH 45202 US

GROWTH PLANS/SPECIAL FEATURES:

Macy's, Inc. is a U.S. operator of full-line department stores. The firm currently has approximately 850 stores in 45 states, Washington D.C., Guam and Puerto Rico. Macy's department stores, which operate under the brand names Macy's and Bloomingdale's, offer men's, women's and children's apparel and accessories; cosmetics; home furnishings; and other consumer goods. Through its stores, the firm conducts direct-to-customer catalog and e-commerce businesses under the names Bloomingdale's By Mail, Bloomingdales.com and Macys.com. Additionally, the company offers online bridal registry and gift purchase facilities. The firm's owned brands include Charter Club; Alfani; Epic Threads; first impressions; and Holiday Lane. It also licenses brands American Rag and Martha Stewart Collection from third parties. Feminine accessories, intimate apparel, shoes and cosmetics generate approximately 36% of Macy's revenues; feminine apparel account for 26%; 23% is derived from men's and children's apparel; and home and miscellaneous products account for 15%. The company conducts many of its support functions through direct/indirect subsidiary firms and divisions. These include FDS Bank and Macy's Credit and Customer Service, Inc., which both offer credit processing, certain collections, customer service and credit marketing services; Macy's Systems and Technology, Inc., which offers operational electronic data processing and management information services; Macy's Merchandising Group, Inc., which designs, develops and markets the firm's private label brands; and Macy's Logistics and Operations, which operates warehouses and distribution services. In September 2010, the company announced plans to expand its fulfillment center in Robertson County, Tennessee. In May 2011, the company opened stores in Chicago, Illinois and Milwaukee, Wisconsin.

Macy's offers its employees medical and dental coverage; flexible spending accounts; wellness programs, including health screenings and Weight Watchers; disability protection; a 401(k) plan; a cash account pension plan; life, AD&D and travel insurance; and a merchandise discount.

FINANCIALS: **Sales and profits are in thousands of dollars—add 000 to get the full amount. 2010 Note: Financial information for 2010 was not available for all companies at press time.**

2010 Sales: $23,489,000
2009 Sales: $24,892,000
2008 Sales: $26,313,000
2007 Sales: $26,970,000
2006 Sales: $22,390,000

2010 Profits: $350,000
2009 Profits: $-4,803,000
2008 Profits: $893,000
2007 Profits: $995,000
2006 Profits: $1,406,000

U.S. Stock Ticker: M
Int'l Ticker:
Int'l Exchange:
Employees: 161,000 Fiscal Year Ends: 1/31
Parent Company:

SALARIES/BENEFITS:

Pension Plan: Y ESOP Stock Plan: Profit Sharing: Top Exec. Salary: $1,500,000 Bonus: $5,252,400
Savings Plan: Y Stock Purch. Plan: Second Exec. Salary: $1,000,000 Bonus: $1,750,800

OTHER THOUGHTS:

Apparent Women Officers or Directors: 5
Hot Spot for Advancement for Women/Minorities: Y

LOCATIONS: ("Y" = Yes)

West:	Southwest:	Midwest:	Southeast:	Northeast:	International:
Y	Y	Y	Y	Y	Y

Sales, profits and employees may be estimates. Financial information, benefits and other data can change quickly and may vary from those stated here.

MANPOWER INC

www.manpower.com

Industry Group Code: 561320

Management:		**Sales/Marketing:**		**Liberal Arts:**		**Information Sys.:**		**Professionals:**		**Tech./Scientific:**	
Mgmt. Trainees:	Y	Marketing Pros.:	Y	Gen. Writing/Editing:	Y	Info. Mgmt.:	Y	Finance/Acct.:	Y	Engineers, Elec.:	
Experienced Mgmt.:	Y	Retail Sales:		Tech. Writing:	Y	Software Dev.:	Y	Law:	Y	Engineers, Other:	
Int'l Business:	Y	Comm./Industrial:	Y	Graphic Arts/Photog.:	Y	Hardware Dev.:		HR/Other:	Y	Health/Lab:	
MBA Grads:	Y	Sales Trainees:	Y	Music:		Consulting/Other:		Training:	Y	Science/Research:	
		Advertising Pros.:	Y	Broadcasting:				Health Care:		Petroleum/Chem.:	
				Other:	Y			Consulting:		Math/Other:	

TYPES OF BUSINESS:

Staffing & Temporary Help
Employee Testing, Training & Development
Internal Audit, Accounting & Tax Services
Organizational Performance Consulting
IT Recruitment & Managed Services
Business Function Outsourcing
Market Research

BRANDS/DIVISIONS/AFFILIATES:

Manpower Professional
Elan
Right Management
Manpower Business Solutions
World of Work Insight
COMSYS IT Partners, Inc.

CONTACTS: *Note: Officers with more than one job title may be intentionally listed here more than once.*

Jeffrey A. Joerres, CEO
Jeffrey A. Joerres, Pres.
Mike Van Handel, CFO/Exec. VP
Emma van Rooyen, Chief Mktg. Officer/Sr. VP
Mara Swan, Exec. VP-Global Talent
Denis Edwards, Global CIO/Sr. VP
Ken C. Hunt, Chief Legal Officer/Sr. VP
Mara Swan, Exec. VP-Global Strategy
David Arkless, Pres., Corp. & Gov't Affairs
Michael Van Handel, Contact-Investor Rel.
Owen J. Sullivan, Exec. VP/CEO-Right Mgmt. & Jefferson Wells
Francoise Gri, Exec. VP/Pres., Southern Europe
Darryl Green, Exec. VP/Pres., APAC & Middle East
Jonas Prising, Exec. VP/Pres., Americas
Jeffrey A. Joerres, Chmn.
Hans Leentjes, Exec. VP/Pres., Northern Europe

Phone: 414-961-1000 | **Fax:** 414-906-7985
Toll-Free:
Address: 100 Manpower Pl., Milwaukee, WI 53212 US

GROWTH PLANS/SPECIAL FEATURES:

Manpower, Inc. is a world leader in the employment services industry, with a global network of nearly 3,900 offices in 82 countries and territories. Manpower offers permanent, temporary and contract recruitment; employee assessment and selection; training; outplacement; outsourcing; consulting; and professional services. The permanent, temporary and contract recruitment segment finds people for all jobs at both the staff and professional levels under the Manpower, Manpower Professional and Elan brands. The employee assessment and selection segment assesses candidate skills to ensure a good fit between clients and employees. The training segment offers training and development solutions to improve employees' skills and gain qualifications. In the outplacement segment, the company uses its Right Management brand to help provide employees transition to future career paths. Through its Manpower Business Solutions brand, the outsourcing segment provides clients with large-scale recruiting, vendor management and onsite human resources services. The consulting segment helps clients attract and retain employees, while also furthering employees' growth. Through its Jefferson Wells brand, the professional services segment delivers risk advisory, tax, finance and accounting services. During 2010, Manpower found permanent and temporary jobs for 3.5 million people who work to help the company's 400,000 clients. The firm primarily supplies workers to the office (representing 32% of recruitment revenues), industrial (38%) and technical (30%) markets. In April 2010, Manpower entered into a partnership with the Ministry of Youth and Sport, Republic of Serbia, to provide programs to promote social inclusion and economic opportunity for young people. Also in April 2010, the company acquired COMSYS IT Partners, Inc. In January 2011, Manpower launched iPad app World of Work Insight.

Employees are offered medical and dental insurance; life insurance; an employee stock purchase plan; a 401(k) plan; a profit sharing plan; short- and long-term disability coverage; and tuition reimbursement.

FINANCIALS: **Sales and profits are in thousands of dollars—add 000 to get the full amount. 2010 Note: Financial information for 2010 was not available for all companies at press time.**

2010 Sales: $18,866,500	2010 Profits: $-263,600
2009 Sales: $16,038,700	2009 Profits: $-9,200
2008 Sales: $21,537,100	2008 Profits: $205,500
2007 Sales: $20,486,100	2007 Profits: $473,700
2006 Sales: $17,562,500	2006 Profits: $398,000

U.S. Stock Ticker: MAN
Int'l Ticker:
Int'l Exchange:
Employees: 30,000 Fiscal Year Ends: 12/31
Parent Company:

SALARIES/BENEFITS:

Pension Plan:	ESOP Stock Plan:	Profit Sharing: Y	Top Exec. Salary: $1,000,000	Bonus: $2,305,521
Savings Plan: Y	Stock Purch. Plan: Y		Second Exec. Salary: $550,000	Bonus: $845,358

OTHER THOUGHTS:

Apparent Women Officers or Directors: 5
Hot Spot for Advancement for Women/Minorities: Y

LOCATIONS: ("Y" = Yes)

West:	Southwest:	Midwest:	Southeast:	Northeast:	International:
Y	Y	Y	Y	Y	Y

MANTECH INTERNATIONAL CORP

www.mantech.com

Industry Group Code: 541512

Management:		Sales/Marketing:		Liberal Arts:		Information Sys.:		Professionals:		Tech./Scientific:	
Mgmt. Trainees:		Marketing Pros.:	Y	Gen. Writing/Editing:		Info. Mgmt.:	Y	Finance/Acct.:	Y	Engineers, Elec.:	Y
Experienced Mgmt.:		Retail Sales:		Tech. Writing:	Y	Software Dev.:	Y	Law:	Y	Engineers, Other:	
Int'l Business:	Y	Comm./Industrial:	Y	Graphic Arts/Photog.:		Hardware Dev.:		HR/Other:	Y	Health/Lab:	
MBA Grads:	Y	Sales Trainees:		Music:		Consulting/Other:	Y	Training:		Science/Research:	
		Advertising Pros.:	Y	Broadcasting:				Health Care:		Petroleum/Chem.:	
				Other:				Consulting:		Math/Other:	

TYPES OF BUSINESS:

Information Technology Services
Technology and Software Development

BRANDS/DIVISIONS/AFFILIATES:

MTSC, Inc.

CONTACTS:

Note: Officers with more than one job title may be intentionally listed here more than once.

George J. Pedersen, CEO
Kevin M. Phillips, CFO/Exec. VP
Carlos S. Echalar, Exec. VP-Human Resources
Terry M. Ryan, Pres./COO-Eng. & Advanced Tech. Group
Jeffrey S. Brown, General Counsel/Exec./VP/Sec.
Matthew E. Candy, Sr. VP-Corp. Dev.
M. Stuart Davis, Exec. VP-Comm. & Strategy
Sherill I. Daily, Jr., VP-Portfolio Analysis
Sally Sullivan, VP-Bus. Dev.
Judith L. Bjornass, Sr. VP
George J. Pedersen, Chmn.

Phone: 703-218-6000	**Fax:** 703-218-8296
Toll-Free:	
Address: 12015 Lee Jackson Hwy., Fairfax, VA 22033 US	

GROWTH PLANS/SPECIAL FEATURES:

ManTech International Corp. is a provider of technologies and services for mission- critical security programs for the U.S. Intelligence Community, the U.S. Department of Defense, Homeland Security; and other U.S. federal government agencies. Services include engineering, systems integration, software services, cyber security, enterprise architecture, information operations and computer forensics, information technology, communications integration, engineering support and global logistics and supply chain management. The company operates in 40 countries. The company's services fall into three categories: Mission Support, Systems Engineering and Technical Services. The Mission Support category provides cyber warfare and cyber defense applications and services to the U.S. Department of Defense, agencies in the Intelligence Community, the Department of State and the Department of Justice. The firm also designs, develops, implements, tests and maintains security applications for information systems and network infrastructures. In addition, the Mission Support Category also offers enterprise systems engineering; intelligence operations and analysis support; and secrecy management and program security architecture services. The Systems Engineering segment in addition to providing systems engineering and support services, offers system analysis, modeling and testing of technologies and systems, particular those that are being deployed to identify and detect nuclear and radiological sources that are attempting entry into the U.S. The segment also performs certification tests of new and upgraded systems for confirmation of their operation in accordance with design requirements. The Technical Services division provides communication systems and infrastructure support; global and domestic mission-critical logistics support; global property management; and global IT modernization. In December 2010, the firm acquired MTSC, Inc., a provider of systems integration, cyber security and networking engineering services to U.S. government agencies, for $75 million.

The company offers employees medical, dental and vision insurance; flexible spending accounts; tuition assistance; life insurance; disability coverage; an employee assistance program; and a retail discount program.

FINANCIALS:

Sales and profits are in thousands of dollars—add 000 to get the full amount. 2010 Note: Financial information for 2010 was not available for all companies at press time.

2010 Sales: $2,604,038	2010 Profits: $125,096
2009 Sales: $2,020,334	2009 Profits: $111,764
2008 Sales: $1,870,879	2008 Profits: $90,292
2007 Sales: $1,148,098	2007 Profits: $67,207
2006 Sales: $1,137,178	2006 Profits: $50,701

U.S. Stock Ticker: MANT
Int'l Ticker:
Int'l Exchange:
Employees: 10,100 Fiscal Year Ends: 12/31
Parent Company:

SALARIES/BENEFITS:

Pension Plan:	ESOP Stock Plan: Y	Profit Sharing:	Top Exec. Salary: $1,666,394	Bonus: $1,056,250
Savings Plan: Y	Stock Purch. Plan:		Second Exec. Salary: $500,001	Bonus: $1,350,000

OTHER THOUGHTS:

Apparent Women Officers or Directors: 3
Hot Spot for Advancement for Women/Minorities: Y

LOCATIONS: ("Y" = Yes)

West:	Southwest:	Midwest:	Southeast:	Northeast:	International:
Y	Y		Y	Y	Y

MARATHON OIL CORP

www.marathon.com

Industry Group Code: 211111

Management:		Sales/Marketing:		Liberal Arts:		Information Sys.:		Professionals:		Tech./Scientific:	
Mgmt. Trainees:	Y	Marketing Pros.:	Y	Gen. Writing/Editing:		Info. Mgmt.:	Y	Finance/Acct.:	Y	Engineers, Elec.:	Y
Experienced Mgmt.:	Y	Retail Sales:		Tech. Writing:	Y	Software Dev.:	Y	Law:	Y	Engineers, Other:	Y
Int'l Business:	Y	Comm./Industrial:	Y	Graphic Arts/Photog.:		Hardware Dev.:		HR/Other:	Y	Health/Lab:	
MBA Grads:	Y	Sales Trainees:		Music:		Consulting/Other:		Training:	Y	Science/Research:	
		Advertising Pros.:		Broadcasting:				Health Care:		Petroleum/Chem.:	Y
				Other:				Consulting:		Math/Other:	

TYPES OF BUSINESS:

Oil & Gas Exploration & Production
Oil Sands
Integrated Gas Operations

BRANDS/DIVISIONS/AFFILIATES:

CONTACTS:

Note: Officers with more than one job title may be intentionally listed here more than once.

Clarence P. Cazalot, Jr., CEO
Clarence P. Cazalot, Jr., Pres.
Janet F. Clark, CFO/Exec. VP
Thomas M. Kelley, Sr. VP-Mktg.
Robert L. Sovine, VP-Human Resources
Thomas K. Sneed, CIO
Sylvia J. Kerrigan, General Counsel/VP/Sec.
Robert E. Estill, VP-Strategic Planning & Portfolio Mgmt.
Howard J. Thill, VP-Investor Rel. & Public Affairs
Paul C. Reinbolt, VP-Finance/Treas.
Gary R. Heminger, Exec. VP-Downstream
David E. Roberts, Jr., Exec. VP-Upstream
Eileen M. Campbell, VP-Public Policy
Annel R. Bay, Sr. VP-Exploration
Thomas J. Usher, Chmn.
Steve D. L. Reynish, Pres., Marathon Oil Canada Corp.
George P. Shaffner, Sr. VP-Logistics & Transportation

Phone: 713-629-6600 **Fax:**
Toll-Free: 866-462-7284
Address: 5555 San Felipe Rd., Houston, TX 77056-2723 US

GROWTH PLANS/SPECIAL FEATURES:

Marathon Oil Corp. explores for crude oil and natural gas worldwide. It operates in three segments: Exploration and products (E&P); oil sands mining (OSM);; and integrated gas (IG). The E&P segment explores for, produces and markets liquid hydrocarbons and natural gas on a worldwide basis. Principal exploration, development or exploration activities are in the U.S., Angola, Canada, Equatorial Guinea, Indonesia, Libya, Norway, Poland, Iraq and the U.K. In 2010, the company's U.S. operations drilled 77 wells, 73 of which were commercially viable. Internationally, it drilled 10 wells, 7 of which were commercially viable. The division's 2010 net sales averaged about 390,000 barrels of oil equivalent per day. In total, U.S. operations account for 29% of worldwide hydrocarbon sales and 41% of natural gas sales. The OSM segment mines, extracts and transports bitumen from oil sands deposits in Alberta, Canada, and upgrades the bitumen to produce and market synthetic crude oil and by-products. The IG segments markets and transports products manufactured from natural gas, such as liquefied natural gas and methanol, on a worldwide basis. During 2011, the company spun off its downstream business into the independent Marathon Petroleum Corp., headquartered in Findlay, Ohio. The firm will continue its upstream business as Marathon Oil Corp.

FINANCIALS:

Sales and profits are in thousands of dollars—add 000 to get the full amount. 2010 Note: Financial information for 2010 was not available for all companies at press time.

2010 Sales: $72,321,000 | 2010 Profits: $2,568,000
2009 Sales: $53,287,000 | 2009 Profits: $1,463,000
2008 Sales: $76,589,000 | 2008 Profits: $3,528,000
2007 Sales: $64,751,000 | 2007 Profits: $3,956,000
2006 Sales: $64,896,000 | 2006 Profits: $5,234,000

U.S. Stock Ticker: MRO
Int'l Ticker:
Int'l Exchange:
Employees: 29,677 Fiscal Year Ends: 12/31
Parent Company:

SALARIES/BENEFITS:

Pension Plan: Y | ESOP Stock Plan: | Profit Sharing: | Top Exec. Salary: $1,400,000 | Bonus: $2,500,000
Savings Plan: Y | Stock Purch. Plan: | Second Exec. Salary: $918,750 | Bonus: $120,000

OTHER THOUGHTS:

Apparent Women Officers or Directors: 4
Hot Spot for Advancement for Women/Minorities: Y

LOCATIONS: ("Y" = Yes)

West:	Southwest:	Midwest:	Southeast:	Northeast:	International:
Y	Y	Y	Y	Y	Y

MARRIOTT INTERNATIONAL INC

www.marriott.com

Industry Group Code: 721110

Management:		Sales/Marketing:		Liberal Arts:		Information Sys.:		Professionals:		Tech./Scientific:	
Mgmt. Trainees:	Y	Marketing Pros.:	Y	Gen. Writing/Editing:	Y	Info. Mgmt.:	Y	Finance/Acct.:	Y	Engineers, Elec.:	
Experienced Mgmt.:	Y	Retail Sales:		Tech. Writing:		Software Dev.:	Y	Law:	Y	Engineers, Other:	
Int'l Business:	Y	Comm./Industrial:	Y	Graphic Arts/Photog.:	Y	Hardware Dev.:		HR/Other:	Y	Health/Lab:	
MBA Grads:	Y	Sales Trainees:	Y	Music:		Consulting/Other:		Training:	Y	Science/Research:	
		Advertising Pros.:	Y	Broadcasting:				Health Care:		Petroleum/Chem.:	
				Other:	Y			Consulting:		Math/Other:	

TYPES OF BUSINESS:

Hotels & Resorts
Suites Hotels
Corporate Apartments
Extended Stay Lodging
Luxury Hotels
Business Hotels

BRANDS/DIVISIONS/AFFILIATES:

Marriott Hotels and Resorts
Ritz-Carlton (The)
Bulgari Hotel and Resort
Renaissance Hotels, Resorts and ClubSport
Courtyard Residence Inn
Fairfield Inn
ExecuStay
TownePlace Suites

CONTACTS: *Note: Officers with more than one job title may be intentionally listed here more than once.*

J. W. Marriott, Jr., CEO
Arne M. Sorenson, COO
Arne M. Sorenson, Pres.
Carl T. Berquist, CFO/Exec. VP
David A. Rodriguez, Exec. VP-Global Human Resources
Carl Wilson, CIO/Exec. VP
Edward A. Ryan, General Counsel/Exec. VP
Anthony G. Capuano, Exec. VP-Global Dev.
Kathleen Matthews, Exec. VP-Global Comm. & Public Affairs
Laura E. Paugh, Sr. VP-Investor Rel.
David J. Grissen, Pres., Americas
Robert J. McCarthy, Pres., Americas & Global Lodging Svcs.
Simon F. Cooper, Pres., Asia Pacific
Amy C. McPherson, Pres., Europe
J. W. Marriott, Jr., Chmn.
Edwin D. Fuller, Pres./Managing Dir.-Marriott Lodging Int'l

Phone: 301-380-3000 **Fax:** 301-380-3967
Toll-Free: 800-721-7033
Address: 10400 Fernwood Rd., Bethesda, MD 20817 US

GROWTH PLANS/SPECIAL FEATURES:

Marriott International, Inc. operates 3,545 hotels and related lodging facilities in the U.S. and about 70 other countries and territories. Though primarily known for the firm's various hotel brands, Marriot also has operations in time shares. The company operates through five segments: North American Full-Service; North American Limited-Service; International; Luxury; and Timeshare. Marriott develops, operates and franchises hotels under various brand names, including Marriott Hotels and Resorts; JW Marriott Hotels and Resorts; the Ritz-Carlton, featuring luxury hotels and resorts; Bulgari Hotel and Resort; Renaissance Hotels, Resorts and ClubSport; Courtyard; Residence Inn, the firm's extended-stay brand; Fairfield Inn; SpringHill Suites; and TownePlace Suites. The firm also provides furnished corporate housing units in 41 major markets through its ExecuStay brand, as well as operating 20 upscale serviced apartments through Marriott Executive Apartments. The company also develops, markets and operates timeshare, fractional ownership and residential properties under four separate brand names in over 70 locations. The resorts are usually adjacent to the firm's hotels, bearing the brand names Marriott Vacation Club International, Horizons by Marriott Vacation Club International, Ritz-Carlton Club and Grand Residences by Marriott. Additionally, Marriott manages approximately 43 golf resorts worldwide. The company also operates 14 systemwide hotel reservation centers: eight in the U.S. and Canada, and six in other countries and territories. In late 2010, the firm announced a joint venture with AC Hotels of Spain to launch the AC Hotels by Marriott brand in Spain, Italy and Portugal. Marriott plans to spin-off its timeshare business as a free-standing company.

Employees are offered medical, dental and disability insurance; a 401(k) plan; tuition reimbursement; discounts on hotel rooms, food and beverages; and work/family programs and services. Marriot was named one of the 100 Best Companies to Work For and one of the Best Companies for Hourly Workers by Working Mother Magazine.

FINANCIALS: **Sales and profits are in thousands of dollars—add 000 to get the full amount. 2010 Note: Financial information for 2010 was not available for all companies at press time.**

2010 Sales: $11,691,000 | 2010 Profits: $458,000
2009 Sales: $10,908,000 | 2009 Profits: $-346,000
2008 Sales: $12,879,000 | 2008 Profits: $359,000
2007 Sales: $12,990,000 | 2007 Profits: $696,000
2006 Sales: $11,995,000 | 2006 Profits: $608,000

U.S. Stock Ticker: MAR
Int'l Ticker:
Int'l Exchange:
Employees: 129,000 Fiscal Year Ends: 12/31
Parent Company:

SALARIES/BENEFITS:

Pension Plan: | ESOP Stock Plan: | Profit Sharing: | Top Exec. Salary: $1,253,063 | Bonus: $2,268,419
Savings Plan: Y | Stock Purch. Plan: | | Second Exec. Salary: $1,018,750 | Bonus: $1,298,296

OTHER THOUGHTS:

Apparent Women Officers or Directors: 7
Hot Spot for Advancement for Women/Minorities: Y

LOCATIONS: ("Y" = Yes)

West:	Southwest:	Midwest:	Southeast:	Northeast:	International:
Y	Y	Y	Y	Y	Y

Sales, profits and employees may be estimates. Financial information, benefits and other data can change quickly and may vary from those stated here.

MARS INC

www.mars.com

Industry Group Code: 311320

Management:		**Sales/Marketing:**		**Liberal Arts:**		**Information Sys.:**		**Professionals:**		**Tech./Scientific:**	
Mgmt. Trainees:	Y	Marketing Pros.:	Y	Gen. Writing/Editing:	Y	Info. Mgmt.:	Y	Finance/Acct.:	Y	Engineers, Elec.:	
Experienced Mgmt.:	Y	Retail Sales:		Tech. Writing:	Y	Software Dev.:	Y	Law:	Y	Engineers, Other:	Y
Int'l Business:	Y	Comm./Industrial:	Y	Graphic Arts/Photog.:	Y	Hardware Dev.:		HR/Other:	Y	Health/Lab:	
MBA Grads:	Y	Sales Trainees:	Y	Music:		Consulting/Other:		Training:	Y	Science/Research:	
		Advertising Pros.:	Y	Broadcasting:				Health Care:		Petroleum/Chem.:	
				Other:				Consulting:		Math/Other:	

TYPES OF BUSINESS:

Chocolate & Confectionery Manufacturing
Snack Foods & Candy Bars
Pet Nutrition
Drink Vending Systems
Prepared Foods
Information Technology Services

BRANDS/DIVISIONS/AFFILIATES:

M&Ms
M&M'S World
Milky Way
Twix
Sheba
Cesar
Uncle Ben's
Wm Wrigley Jr Company

CONTACTS: *Note: Officers with more than one job title may be intentionally listed here more than once.*

Paul S. Michaels, CEO
Paul S. Michaels, Pres.
Olivier Goudet, CFO/Exec. VP
Aileen Richards, VP-Personnel & Organization
Richard Ware, VP-R&D
Alberto Mora, General Counsel/VP/Sec.
Frank Mars, Pres., Symbioscience
Dushan Petrovich, Pres., Wrigley Gum & Confections
Grant Reid, Pres., Chocolate
Brian Camastral, Pres., Food
John Franklyn Mars, Chmn.
Richard Ware, VP-Supply & Procurement

Phone: 703-821-4900 **Fax:** 703-448-9678
Toll-Free: 800-627-7852
Address: 6885 Elm St., McLean, VA 22101 US

GROWTH PLANS/SPECIAL FEATURES:

Mars, Inc., founded in 1911, is family-owned company that operates through six business divisions: chocolate, pet care, food, drinks, Symbioscience and Wm. Wrigley Jr. Company, which produces Wrigley Gum and Sugar. One of the world's largest family-owned companies, Mars operates approximately 135 manufacturing facilities and distributes products to over 68 countries. The company, has a branded retail store called M&M World, it has three locations in the U.S. The company's chocolate segment makes some of the world's most popular and widely available snacks and confectionery products, including M&Ms, Mars, Snickers, Milky Way, Twix, and Dove, Combos snacks, 3 Musketeers and Kudos bars. The pet care unit offers products for cats and dogs include such brands as Sheba, Cesar, Whiskas, Pedigree, Royal Canin, My Dog, Kitekat, Buckeye, Frolic, Chappi, Winergy, Trill, Waltham, Aquarian, Rena and Nutro. In the food division, Mars produces rice, entrees, sauces and condiments under brand names including Uncle Ben's, Dolmio, Suzi-Wan, Seeds of Change and Ebly. The firm's drink's segment distributes Mars' KLIX and FLAVIA drink vending machine systems, which are industry leading products that provide in-cup drinks such as fresh ground coffee, leaf tea and hot chocolate. The Symbioscience unit offers products such as Mars Botanical Cocoapro; Mars Plantcare - Seramis; Mars Veterinary - Wisdom Panel MX; and Mars Sustainable Solutions. The Wrigley Gum and Sugar division offers snacks such as Starburst, Skittles, Juicy Fruit gum, Life Savers and Altoids. In addition, the company manufactures nutritional foods, snacks and beverages under the Cocoa Via brand. In January 2010, the firm introduced Snickers Peanut Butter Squared, which features peanuts, caramel, nougat, peanut butter and milk chocolate.

The firm offers its employees medical and dental coverage.

FINANCIALS: **Sales and profits are in thousands of dollars—add 000 to get the full amount. 2010 Note: Financial information for 2010 was not available for all companies at press time.**

2010 Sales: $30,000,000 2010 Profits: $
2009 Sales: $28,000,000 2009 Profits: $
2008 Sales: $30,000,000 2008 Profits: $
2007 Sales: $27,000,000 2007 Profits: $
2006 Sales: $21,500,000 2006 Profits: $

U.S. Stock Ticker: Private
Int'l Ticker:
Int'l Exchange:
Employees: 65,000 Fiscal Year Ends: 12/31
Parent Company:

SALARIES/BENEFITS:

Pension Plan: Y ESOP Stock Plan: Profit Sharing: Top Exec. Salary: $ Bonus: $
Savings Plan: Y Stock Purch. Plan: Second Exec. Salary: $ Bonus: $

OTHER THOUGHTS:

Apparent Women Officers or Directors: 1
Hot Spot for Advancement for Women/Minorities:

LOCATIONS: ("Y" = Yes)

West:	Southwest:	Midwest:	Southeast:	Northeast:	International:
Y	Y	Y	Y	Y	Y

MARSH & MCLENNAN COMPANIES INC

www.marshmac.com

Industry Group Code: 524210

Management:		Sales/Marketing:		Liberal Arts:		Information Sys.:		Professionals:		Tech./Scientific:	
Mgmt. Trainees:	Y	Marketing Pros.:	Y	Gen. Writing/Editing:	Y	Info. Mgmt.:	Y	Finance/Acct.:	Y	Engineers, Elec.:	
Experienced Mgmt.:	Y	Retail Sales:		Tech. Writing:	Y	Software Dev.:	Y	Law:	Y	Engineers, Other:	
Int'l Business:	Y	Comm./Industrial:	Y	Graphic Arts/Photog.:	Y	Hardware Dev.:		HR/Other:	Y	Health/Lab:	
MBA Grads:	Y	Sales Trainees:		Music:		Consulting/Other:		Training:	Y	Science/Research:	
		Advertising Pros.:	Y	Broadcasting:				Health Care:		Petroleum/Chem.:	
				Other:	Y			Consulting:	Y	Math/Other:	

TYPES OF BUSINESS:

Insurance Brokerage
Consulting Services
Risk Management
Benefits Administration
Human Resources Services

BRANDS/DIVISIONS/AFFILIATES:

Marsh, Inc.
Guy Carpenter & Company LLC
Marsh & McLennan Risk Capital Holdings
Mercer Inc
Oliver Wyman Group
NERA Economic Consulting
Lippincott

CONTACTS: *Note: Officers with more than one job title may be intentionally listed here more than once.*

Brian Duperreault, CEO
Daniel S. Glaser, COO/Group Pres.
Brian Duperreault, Pres.
Vanessa A. Wittman, CFO/Exec. VP
Orlando D. Ashford, Chief Human Resources Officer/Sr. VP
Ben Allen, CIO/Sr. VP/Chief Innovation Officer
Peter J. Beshar, General Counsel/Exec. VP
Orlando D. Ashford, Chief Comm. Officer
E. Scott Gilbert, Chief Risk & Compliance Officer/Sr. VP
M. Michele Burns, CEO/Chmn.-Mercer, Inc.
John P. Drzik, CEO/Pres., Oliver Wyman Group
Alexander S. Moczarsk, Pres./CEO-Guy Carpenter
Lang of Monkton, Chmn.-Exec. Committee

Phone: 212-345-5000 **Fax:** 212-345-4838
Toll-Free:
Address: 1166 Ave. of the Americas, New York, NY 10036-2774 US

GROWTH PLANS/SPECIAL FEATURES:

Marsh & McLennan Companies, Inc. (MMC) is a global professional services firm. The company provides insurance and management and consulting services in the areas of risk, strategy and human capital to clients in over 100 countries. It is the parent company of a number of leading risk experts and specialty consultants, including: Marsh, Inc., the insurance broker, intermediary and risk advisor; Guy Carpenter & Company LLC, the risk and reinsurance specialist; Mercer, Inc., the provider of HR and related financial advice and services; and Oliver Wyman Group, the management consultancy. MMC operates in two divisions: Risk and Insurance Services and Consulting. The Risk and Insurance Services segment is primarily composed of two companies and their subsidiaries: Marsh, Inc., which operates through hundreds of offices in 100 countries; and Guy Carpenter & Company LLC. This segment also owns investments in private equity funds and other firms through Marsh & McLennan Risk Capital Holdings. The Consulting segment operates through Mercer, Inc. and Oliver Wyman Group. The Mercer division offers investment consulting services, and specialized management and economic consulting services, as well as human resources consulting and related outsourcing. Oliver Wyman Group is a full service management consulting firm. The group includes Lippincott, a consulting firm that helps clients with branding and corporate image; and NERA Economic Consulting, one of the world's largest consulting groups that focuses on economics and deploys professional economists. In August 2010, MMC sold risk consulting subsidiary, Knoll, Inc., to security and international screening firm Altegrity, Inc. for $1.13 billion.

MMC offers employees medical, dental and vision insurance; spending accounts; life insurance; business travel accident insurance; disability coverage; an employee stock purchase plan; a 401(k) plan; a retirement plan; tuition assistance; auto and home insurance; pet insurance; a legal assistance plan; and an employee assistance program.

FINANCIALS: **Sales and profits are in thousands of dollars—add 000 to get the full amount. 2010 Note: Financial information for 2010 was not available for all companies at press time.**

2010 Sales: $10,550,000	2010 Profits: $855,000	**U.S. Stock Ticker: MMC**
2009 Sales: $9,831,000	2009 Profits: $227,000	**Int'l Ticker:**
2008 Sales: $10,730,000	2008 Profits: $-73,000	Int'l Exchange:
2007 Sales: $11,350,000	2007 Profits: $2,475,000	Employees: 51,000 Fiscal Year Ends: 12/31
2006 Sales: $10,547,000	2006 Profits: $990,000	Parent Company:

SALARIES/BENEFITS:

Pension Plan: Y	ESOP Stock Plan:	Profit Sharing:	Top Exec. Salary: $1,000,000	Bonus: $4,650,000
Savings Plan: Y	Stock Purch. Plan: Y		Second Exec. Salary: $1,000,000	Bonus: $3,500,000

OTHER THOUGHTS:

Apparent Women Officers or Directors: 4
Hot Spot for Advancement for Women/Minorities: Y

LOCATIONS: ("Y" = Yes)

West:	Southwest:	Midwest:	Southeast:	Northeast:	International:
Y	Y	Y		Y	Y

MARY KAY INC

www.marykay.com

Industry Group Code: 325620

Management:		Sales/Marketing:		Liberal Arts:		Information Sys.:		Professionals:		Tech./Scientific:	
Mgmt. Trainees:	Y	Marketing Pros.:	Y	Gen. Writing/Editing:	Y	Info. Mgmt.:	Y	Finance/Acct.:	Y	Engineers, Elec.:	
Experienced Mgmt.:	Y	Retail Sales:	Y	Tech. Writing:		Software Dev.:	Y	Law:	Y	Engineers, Other:	
Int'l Business:	Y	Comm./Industrial:		Graphic Arts/Photog.:	Y	Hardware Dev.:		HR/Other:	Y	Health/Lab:	
MBA Grads:	Y	Sales Trainees:	Y	Music:		Consulting/Other:		Training:	Y	Science/Research:	
		Advertising Pros.:	Y	Broadcasting:				Health Care:		Petroleum/Chem.:	Y
				Other:	Y			Consulting:		Math/Other:	

TYPES OF BUSINESS:

Cosmetics & Beauty Supplies, Direct Selling
Online Retail
Fragrances
Over-the-Counter Drugs
Cosmetics & Beauty Supplies, Manufacturing

BRANDS/DIVISIONS/AFFILIATES:

Embrace
TimeWise
Belara
Domain
Velocity
Journey
Angelfire
Elige

CONTACTS:

Note: Officers with more than one job title may be intentionally listed here more than once.

Yvette Franco, VP-Mktg.
Beth Lange, Chief Scientific Officer
Terry Jacks, VP-R&D
Anne Crews, VP-Gov't Rel.

Phone: 972-687-6300	**Fax:** 972-687-1611
Toll-Free: 800-627-9529	
Address: 16251 Dallas Pkwy., Dallas, TX 75001 US	

GROWTH PLANS/SPECIAL FEATURES:

Mary Kay, Inc. is one of the largest direct sellers of skin care products in the U.S. Mary Kay Ash, the company's founder, launched the company in 1963 along with her son. The company's merchandise includes more than 200 products across several categories, including skin care, color cosmetics, spa and body care and fragrances. Skin care includes anti-aging creams, cleansers, moisturizers, basic skin care for different skin types, products for specific needs such as acne treatment and oil control, and lip and eye care. Color cosmetics products include lip, eyes, cheeks, nails, foundations and powder color enhancers, as well as travel sets and applicators. The Mary Kay fragrance line has specialty scents for both men and women, including Journey, Belara and Elige for women and Domain, MK High Intensity and Velocity for men. Mary Kay develops, tests, manufactures and packages the majority of its products at its own plants. Most inventory is manufactured at the Dallas site, where the company headquarters and the Mary Kay Museum are located. An additional manufacturing facility is located in China. With FDA approval, the company also manufactures and distributes certain products classified as over-the-counter drugs, such as sunscreens and acne treatment products. There are over 1.8 million Mary Kay independent beauty consultants serving customers in more than 30 countries worldwide. Independent beauty consultants may eventually become independent sales directors and/or independent national sales directors. Since its inception, the family of Mary Kay Ash has owned the majority of the company.

Mary Kay's independent sales consultants, who serve as the company's front-line sales force, generally work out of their homes and set their own working schedules.

FINANCIALS:

Sales and profits are in thousands of dollars—add 000 to get the full amount. 2010 Note: Financial information for 2010 was not available for all companies at press time.

2010 Sales: $3,000,000	2010 Profits: $	**U.S. Stock Ticker: Private**
2009 Sales: $2,600,000	2009 Profits: $	**Int'l Ticker:**
2008 Sales: $2,600,000	2008 Profits: $	Int'l Exchange:
2007 Sales: $2,400,000	2007 Profits: $	Employees: 3,500 Fiscal Year Ends: 12/31
2006 Sales: $2,250,000	2006 Profits: $	Parent Company:

SALARIES/BENEFITS:

Pension Plan:	ESOP Stock Plan:	Profit Sharing:	Top Exec. Salary: $	Bonus: $
Savings Plan:	Stock Purch. Plan:		Second Exec. Salary: $	Bonus: $

OTHER THOUGHTS:

Apparent Women Officers or Directors: 3
Hot Spot for Advancement for Women/Minorities:

LOCATIONS: ("Y" = Yes)

West:	Southwest:	Midwest:	Southeast:	Northeast:	International:
Y	Y	Y	Y	Y	Y

MASSACHUSETTS MUTUAL LIFE INSURANCE CO

www.massmutual.com

Industry Group Code: 524113

Management:		Sales/Marketing:		Liberal Arts:		Information Sys.:		Professionals:		Tech./Scientific:	
Mgmt. Trainees:	Y	Marketing Pros.:	Y	Gen. Writing/Editing:	Y	Info. Mgmt.:	Y	Finance/Acct.:	Y	Engineers, Elec.:	
Experienced Mgmt.:	Y	Retail Sales:	Y	Tech. Writing:	Y	Software Dev.:	Y	Law:	Y	Engineers, Other:	
Int'l Business:	Y	Comm./Industrial:	Y	Graphic Arts/Photog.:		Hardware Dev.:		HR/Other:	Y	Health/Lab:	
MBA Grads:	Y	Sales Trainees:	Y	Music:		Consulting/Other:		Training:	Y	Science/Research:	Y
		Advertising Pros.:	Y	Broadcasting:				Health Care:	Y	Petroleum/Chem.:	
				Other:				Consulting:		Math/Other:	Y

TYPES OF BUSINESS:

Life Insurance
Pension Products
Real Estate Equity Management
Disability Insurance
Investment Management Products
Mutual Fund Management
Investor Services

BRANDS/DIVISIONS/AFFILIATES:

MassMutual Holding Company, Inc.
First Mercantile Trust Company
Yingda Taihe Life Insurance Company
Cornerstone Real Estate Advisers
Babson Capital Management LLC
MassMutual Global Funding, LLC
Oppenheimer Funds, Inc.
Vantage Term

CONTACTS: *Note: Officers with more than one job title may be intentionally listed here more than once.*

Roger W. Crandall, CEO
Roger W. Crandall, Pres.
Michael T. Rollings, CFO/Exec. VP
Robert J. Casale, CIO/Exec. VP
Mark D. Roellig, General Counsel/Exec. VP/Corp. Sec.
Sharmaine Miller, VP-New Bus. Oper.
Elizabeth A. Ward, Chief Enterprise Risk Officer/Sr. VP
Debra A. Palermino, Exec. VP
M. Timothy Corbett, Chief Investment Officer/Exec. VP
Douglas G. Russell, Sr. VP
Roger W. Crandall, Chmn.

Phone: 413-744-1000 **Fax:** 413-744-6005
Toll-Free: 800-7671000
Address: 1295 State St., Springfield, MA 01111-0001 US

GROWTH PLANS/SPECIAL FEATURES:

Massachusetts Mutual Life Insurance Co. (MassMutual) is a global, growth oriented, diversified financial services organization. With its affiliates, it boasts more than 13 million clients and over $448 billion in managed assets. The mutually owned company offers financial protection, accumulation and income management by providing life insurance, annuities, disability income insurance, long term care insurance, retirement planning products, income management and other products and services for individuals, business owners, corporations and institutions. It operates through several subsidiaries. MassMutual's investment group provides investment management products, such as securities and real estate, as well as mutual fund management and real estate equities management services primarily through subsidiary Oppenheimer Funds, Inc. and Cornerstone Real Estate Advisers. Subsidiary Babson Capital Management LLC offers individual and institutional investor services. MassMutual, with the aim of expanding globally, has established subsidiaries in Argentina, Bermuda, Chile, Hong Kong and Luxembourg to market products that emphasize the company's individual coverage and institutional money management businesses. The firm also maintains a joint venture with State Grid Corporation of China called Yingda Taihe Life Insurance Company with the intention of expanding the life insurance business in the Chinese market. In September 2010, MassMutual introduced a new life insurance product portfolio, dubbed Vantage Term, featuring both a 10-year and 20-year level premium product, as well as an annually renewable term product.

MassMutual offers employee benefits such as health, dental, vision, disability and life coverage; flexible spending accounts; 401(k) and pension plans; educational assistance; flexible scheduling and flextime; child care and adoption assistance; an on-site credit union; a matching gift program; and discounted auto and homeowner's insurance.

FINANCIALS: **Sales and profits are in thousands of dollars—add 000 to get the full amount. 2010 Note: Financial information for 2010 was not available for all companies at press time.**

2010 Sales: $25,647,100 — 2010 Profits: $258,200
2009 Sales: $18,274,000 — 2009 Profits: $-283,000
2008 Sales: $19,301,000 — 2008 Profits: $-1,060,000
2007 Sales: $18,744,000 — 2007 Profits: $201,000
2006 Sales: $18,020,000 — 2006 Profits: $810,000

U.S. Stock Ticker: Mutual Company
Int'l Ticker:
Int'l Exchange:
Employees: 11,000 Fiscal Year Ends: 12/31
Parent Company:

SALARIES/BENEFITS:

Pension Plan: Y ESOP Stock Plan: Profit Sharing: Top Exec. Salary: $ Bonus: $
Savings Plan: Y Stock Purch. Plan: Second Exec. Salary: $ Bonus: $

OTHER THOUGHTS:

Apparent Women Officers or Directors: 6
Hot Spot for Advancement for Women/Minorities: Y

LOCATIONS: ("Y" = Yes)

West:	Southwest:	Midwest:	Southeast:	Northeast:	International:
Y	Y	Y	Y	Y	Y

Sales, profits and employees may be estimates. Financial information, benefits and other data can change quickly and may vary from those stated here.

MATTEL INC

Industry Group Code: 339932

www.mattel.com

Management:		Sales/Marketing:		Liberal Arts:		Information Sys.:		Professionals:		Tech./Scientific:	
Mgmt. Trainees:	Y	Marketing Pros.:	Y	Gen. Writing/Editing:	Y	Info. Mgmt.:	Y	Finance/Acct.:	Y	Engineers, Elec.:	Y
Experienced Mgmt.:	Y	Retail Sales:		Tech. Writing:	Y	Software Dev.:	Y	Law:	Y	Engineers, Other:	
Int'l Business:	Y	Comm./Industrial:	Y	Graphic Arts/Photog.:	Y	Hardware Dev.:		HR/Other:	Y	Health/Lab:	
MBA Grads:	Y	Sales Trainees:		Music:		Consulting/Other:		Training:	Y	Science/Research:	
		Advertising Pros.:	Y	Broadcasting:				Health Care:		Petroleum/Chem.:	
				Other:	Y			Consulting:		Math/Other:	

TYPES OF BUSINESS:

Toy Manufacturing

BRANDS/DIVISIONS/AFFILIATES:

Fisher-Price
American Girl LLC
Barbie
Polly Pocket!
Disney Classics
Hot Wheels
Matchbox
Kung Fu Panda

CONTACTS:

Note: Officers with more than one job title may be intentionally listed here more than once.

Robert A. Eckert, CEO
Bryan G. Stockton, COO
Kevin M. Farr, CFO
Alan Kaye, Chief Human Resources Officer/Exec. VP
Robert Normile, Chief Legal Officer/Exec. VP/Sec.
Thomas A. Debrowski, Exec. VP-Worldwide Oper.
Dianne Douglas, Sr. VP-Investor Rel.
Mandana Sadigh, Treas./Sr. VP
H. Scott Topman, Sr. VP/Corp. Controller
Ellen L. Brothers, Exec. VP/Pres., American Girl Brands
Christopher P. Schaden, Exec. VP-North America
David Allmark, Exec. VP-Fisher-Price Brands
Robert A. Eckert, Chmn.
Geoff Massingberd, Exec. VP-Int'l

Phone: 310-252-2000 **Fax:** 310-252-2179
Toll-Free:
Address: 333 Continental Blvd., El Segundo, CA 90245 US

GROWTH PLANS/SPECIAL FEATURES:

Mattel, Inc. designs, manufactures and markets a variety of toy products worldwide. Mattel's product portfolio of brands and products are grouped into three categories: Mattel Girls & Boys Brands; Fisher-Price Brands; and American Girl Brands. The Mattel Girls & Boys Brands include Barbie fashion dolls and accessories; Polly Pocket; Little Mommy; Disney Classics; High School Musical; Hot Wheels; Matchbox; Battle Force 5; Speed Racer; Tyco R/C vehicles and playsets; CARS; Radica; Toy Story; Max Steel; Batman; Kung Fu Panda; and games and puzzles. Fisher-Price brands include Fisher-Price; LittlePeople; BabyGear; View-Master; Sesame Street; Dora the Explorer; Go Diego Go!; See 'N Say; and Power Wheels. American Girl Brands include Just Like You, the historical collection and Bitty Baby. The firm's sells its products in the domestic segment through various retailers, including chain stores, department stores and free-standing toy stores, in addition to several company-operated small retail outlets. The company's international sales represent approximately 46% of its total sales, of which sales in Europe represent approximately 52%, sales in Latin America represent approximately 30%, sales in Asia Pacific represent approximately 11% and sales in other regions represent approximately 7%. Products marketed internationally are generally the same as those developed and marketed domestically, with the exception of American Girl Brands. However, some American Girl Brand products are developed or adapted for particular markets. Mattel's principal manufacturing facilities are located in China, Indonesia, Thailand, Malaysia and Mexico. Wal-Mart, Toys R Us and Target, Mattel's largest customers, account for approximately 41% of worldwide net sales.

Mattel offers its employees medical, dental and prescription drug coverage; life, accident and business travel insurance; short- and long-term disability; retirement plans; a stock purchase plan; product discounts; adoption assistance; and an employee assistance program.

FINANCIALS:

Sales and profits are in thousands of dollars—add 000 to get the full amount. 2010 Note: Financial information for 2010 was not available for all companies at press time.

2010 Sales: $5,856,195	2010 Profits: $684,863
2009 Sales: $5,430,846	2009 Profits: $528,704
2008 Sales: $5,918,002	2008 Profits: $379,636
2007 Sales: $5,970,090	2007 Profits: $599,993
2006 Sales: $5,650,156	2006 Profits: $592,927

U.S. Stock Ticker: MAT
Int'l Ticker:
Int'l Exchange:
Employees: 31,000 Fiscal Year Ends: 12/31
Parent Company:

SALARIES/BENEFITS:

Pension Plan: Y | ESOP Stock Plan: | Profit Sharing: | Top Exec. Salary: $1,250,000 | Bonus: $3,250,000
Savings Plan: | Stock Purch. Plan: Y | Second Exec. Salary: $1,000,000 | Bonus: $1,700,000

OTHER THOUGHTS:

Apparent Women Officers or Directors: 5
Hot Spot for Advancement for Women/Minorities: Y

LOCATIONS: ("Y" = Yes)

West:	Southwest:	Midwest:	Southeast:	Northeast:	International:
Y	Y	Y	Y	Y	Y

Sales, profits and employees may be estimates. Financial information, benefits and other data can change quickly and may vary from those stated here.

MAXIMUS INC

www.maximus.com

Industry Group Code: 541512

Management:		Sales/Marketing:		Liberal Arts:		Information Sys.:		Professionals:		Tech./Scientific:	
Mgmt. Trainees:		Marketing Pros.:	Y	Gen. Writing/Editing:	Y	Info. Mgmt.:	Y	Finance/Acct.:	Y	Engineers, Elec.:	
Experienced Mgmt.:	Y	Retail Sales:		Tech. Writing:	Y	Software Dev.:	Y	Law:	Y	Engineers, Other:	
Int'l Business:	Y	Comm./Industrial:	Y	Graphic Arts/Photog.:		Hardware Dev.:		HR/Other:	Y	Health/Lab:	
MBA Grads:	Y	Sales Trainees:		Music:		Consulting/Other:	Y	Training:		Science/Research:	
		Advertising Pros.:		Broadcasting:				Health Care:		Petroleum/Chem.:	
				Other:				Consulting:	Y	Math/Other:	

TYPES OF BUSINESS:

Consulting-Government Agencies
Outsourced Program Management
IT Systems Management
Consulting

BRANDS/DIVISIONS/AFFILIATES:

CONTACTS:

Note: Officers with more than one job title may be intentionally listed here more than once.

Richard A. Montoni, CEO
Richard A. Montoni, Co-Pres.
David N. Walker, CFO
David Casey, Chief Mktg. Officer/Co-Pres.
Mark Andrekovich, Chief Human Capital Officer
David R. Francis, General Counsel/Corp. Sec.
David N. Walker, Treas.
Deanne M. Wertin, Pres., Consulting
Bruce L. Caswell, Pres., Health Svcs.
Akbar Piloti, Pres., Human Svcs.
John F. Boyer, Pres., MAXIMUS Federal Svcs., Inc.
Peter B. Pond, Chmn.

Phone: 703-251-8500 **Fax:** 703-251-8240
Toll-Free: 800-629-4687
Address: 11419 Sunset Hills Rd., Reston, VA 20190 US

GROWTH PLANS/SPECIAL FEATURES:

Maximus, Inc. provides consulting, systems solutions and operations management, primarily to federal, state and local government agencies. The firm has held contracts with government agencies in all 50 states and operates in the U.S., Australia, the U.K., Canada and Israel. The company is divided into two segments: health services and human services. The health services segment, which generated 62% of 2010 revenue, provides business process outsourcing; administrative support services; and consulting services for state, provincial and federal government programs, such as Medicaid, CHIP (Children's Health Insurance Programs), SNAP (Supplemental Nutrition Assistance Program), Medicare and Health Insurance BC (British Columbia). The business process outsourcing services include government health insurance program administration, health insurance enrollment services, consumer outreach, payment processing, multilingual customer contact centers, independent medical reviews, health plan oversight and specialized program consulting services. The human services segment, which generated 38% of 2010 revenue, provides a variety of administrative support and case management services for federal, national, state and county human services agencies including welfare-to-work programs, child support enforcement, higher education services and K-12 special education services. Over half of the segment's revenue is generated outside of the U.S, primarily in Australia and the U.K. The division also provides primarily seasonal business and tax credit services for employers. In July 2010, Maximus expanded its health services segment to include a health insurance exchange consulting service in order to help its customers become compliant with new federal regulatory requirements set down by the Affordable Care Act. In September 2010, the company sold its enterprise resource planning division to CherryRoad Technologies, Inc.

The company offers its employees medical, dental, vision, life and AD&D insurance; a flexible spending account; a long-term care policy; legal services; an employee assistance program; a 401(k); paid time off; METLIFE discounts; GlobalFit discounts; Aflac policies; and a Northwest Federal Credit Union account.

FINANCIALS:

Sales and profits are in thousands of dollars—add 000 to get the full amount. 2010 Note: Financial information for 2010 was not available for all companies at press time.

2010 Sales: $831,749	2010 Profits: $70,409
2009 Sales: $720,108	2009 Profits: $46,540
2008 Sales: $699,552	2008 Profits: $6,677
2007 Sales: $583,020	2007 Profits: $-8,255
2006 Sales: $583,571	2006 Profits: $2,460

U.S. Stock Ticker: MMS
Int'l Ticker:
Int'l Exchange:
Employees: 6,834 Fiscal Year Ends: 9/30
Parent Company:

SALARIES/BENEFITS:

Pension Plan:	ESOP Stock Plan:	Profit Sharing:	Top Exec. Salary: $700,000	Bonus: $700,000
Savings Plan: Y	Stock Purch. Plan:		Second Exec. Salary: $431,000	Bonus: $400,000

OTHER THOUGHTS:

Apparent Women Officers or Directors: 2
Hot Spot for Advancement for Women/Minorities:

LOCATIONS: ("Y" = Yes)

West:	Southwest:	Midwest:	Southeast:	Northeast:	International:
Y	Y	Y	Y	Y	Y

Sales, profits and employees may be estimates. Financial information, benefits and other data can change quickly and may vary from those stated here.

MAYO FOUNDATION FOR MEDICAL EDUCATION AND RESEARCH

www.mayo.edu

Industry Group Code: 622110

Management:		Sales/Marketing:		Liberal Arts:		Information Sys.:		Professionals:		Tech./Scientific:	
Mgmt. Trainees:	Y	Marketing Pros.:	Y	Gen. Writing/Editing:	Y	Info. Mgmt.:	Y	Finance/Acct.:	Y	Engineers, Elec.:	
Experienced Mgmt.:	Y	Retail Sales:		Tech. Writing:	Y	Software Dev.:	Y	Law:	Y	Engineers, Other:	
Int'l Business:	Y	Comm./Industrial:		Graphic Arts/Photog.:	Y	Hardware Dev.:		HR/Other:	Y	Health/Lab:	Y
MBA Grads:	Y	Sales Trainees:		Music:		Consulting/Other:		Training:	Y	Science/Research:	
		Advertising Pros.:	Y	Broadcasting:				Health Care:	Y	Petroleum/Chem.:	
				Other:	Y			Consulting:		Math/Other:	

TYPES OF BUSINESS:

Hospitals/Clinics-General & Specialty Hospitals
Physician Practice Management
Medical Research
Health Care Education

BRANDS/DIVISIONS/AFFILIATES:

Mayo Clinic
St. Marys Hospital
Rochester Medical Hospital
Mayo Clinic Hospital
Mayo Health System
Mayo Clinic College of Medicine
Dan Abraham Healthy Living Center
Birdsall Medical Research Building

CONTACTS: *Note: Officers with more than one job title may be intentionally listed here more than once.*

John H. Noseworthy, CEO
John H. Noseworthy, Pres.
Jeffrey W. Bolton, CFO
Shirley A. Weis, Chief Admin. Officer/VP
Jonathan J. Oviatt, Chief Legal Officer/Sec.
Harry N. Hoffman, Treas.
William C. Rupp, VP
Victor Trastek, VP
Marilyn Carlson Nelson, Chmn.

Phone: 507-284-2511	**Fax:** 507-284-0161
Toll-Free:	
Address: 200 First St. S.W., Rochester, MN 55905 US	

GROWTH PLANS/SPECIAL FEATURES:

The Mayo Foundation for Medical Education and Research is a not-for-profit health care organization providing medical treatment, physician management, health care education, research and other specialized medical services through a network of clinics and hospitals in Minnesota, Arizona and Florida. The three primary clinics, which house physician group practices, are located in Rochester, Minnesota; Jacksonville, Florida; and Scottsdale and Phoenix, Arizona. The Rochester, Minnesota campus is comprised of the Mayo, The Hilton and Stabile buildings, as well as St. Mary's Hospital, with 1,265 beds, and the Rochester Methodist Hospital, with 794 beds. This facility is a fully integrated medical research and education center. The Dan Abraham Healthy Living Center, located in the Rochester campus, is a four-story, 127,000 square foot state-of-the-art wellness and fitness facility. The Jacksonville, Florida campus is centered around the Davis and Mayo buildings, in conjunction with the Birdsall Medical Research Building. This facility focuses on neurological diseases. The Mayo Clinic Hospital, located on the Jacksonville campus, offers 214 beds and 22 operating rooms. In addition, it offers care in more than 35 medical and surgical specialties. The Scottsdale, Arizona campus is centered around a five-story outpatient clinic. The Mayo Clinic Hospital, located in Phoenix, Arizona, contains 244 beds, 18 operating rooms, an outpatient surgery center, a patient education library, a pharmacy, a full service laboratory, an endoscopy suite and a 188-seat auditorium for patients, staff and students. The Mayo Clinic Specialty Building is an outpatient clinic building connected to the Mayo Clinic Hospital on the Phoenix campus. In addition, the Mayo Foundation has international locations in Canada, United Arab Emirates–Dubai, Mexico and Guatemala.

Employees of the firm are offered medical, dental, vision and prescription drug plans; flexible spending accounts; tuition assistance; a scholarship plan; relocation reimbursement and a variety of other benefits. Benefits may vary by location.

FINANCIALS: **Sales and profits are in thousands of dollars—add 000 to get the full amount. 2010 Note: Financial information for 2010 was not available for all companies at press time.**

2010 Sales: $7,942,000
2009 Sales: $7,582,100
2008 Sales: $7,221,800
2007 Sales: $6,897,600
2006 Sales: $6,291,600

2010 Profits: $515,300
2009 Profits: $333,200
2008 Profits: $
2007 Profits: $198,000
2006 Profits: $117,500

U.S. Stock Ticker: Nonprofit
Int'l Ticker:
Int'l Exchange:
Employees: 56,100 Fiscal Year Ends: 12/31
Parent Company:

SALARIES/BENEFITS:

Pension Plan: Y ESOP Stock Plan: Profit Sharing: Top Exec. Salary: $ Bonus: $
Savings Plan: Y Stock Purch. Plan: Y Second Exec. Salary: $ Bonus: $

OTHER THOUGHTS:

Apparent Women Officers or Directors: 4
Hot Spot for Advancement for Women/Minorities: Y

LOCATIONS: ("Y" = Yes)

West:	Southwest:	Midwest:	Southeast:	Northeast:	International:
Y	Y	Y	Y		Y

MCDONALD'S CORP

www.mcdonalds.com

Industry Group Code: 722110

Management:		Sales/Marketing:		Liberal Arts:		Information Sys.:		Professionals:		Tech./Scientific:	
Mgmt. Trainees:	Y	Marketing Pros.:	Y	Gen. Writing/Editing:	Y	Info. Mgmt.:	Y	Finance/Acct.:	Y	Engineers, Elec.:	
Experienced Mgmt.:	Y	Retail Sales:		Tech. Writing:		Software Dev.:	Y	Law:	Y	Engineers, Other:	
Int'l Business:	Y	Comm./Industrial:		Graphic Arts/Photog.:	Y	Hardware Dev.:		HR/Other:	Y	Health/Lab:	
MBA Grads:	Y	Sales Trainees:		Music:		Consulting/Other:		Training:	Y	Science/Research:	
		Advertising Pros.:	Y	Broadcasting:				Health Care:		Petroleum/Chem.:	
				Other:	Y			Consulting:		Math/Other:	

TYPES OF BUSINESS:

Fast Food Restaurants
Home-Meal Replacement Restaurants
Franchising

BRANDS/DIVISIONS/AFFILIATES:

Big Mac
Quarter Pounder
Filet O'Fish
Happy Meal
Egg McMuffin

CONTACTS:

Note: Officers with more than one job title may be intentionally listed here more than once.

Jim Skinner, CEO
Don Thompson, COO
Don Thompson, Pres.
Peter J. Bensen, CFO/Exec. VP
Richard Floersch, Chief Human Resources Officer/Exec. VP
Gloria Santona, General Counsel/Exec. VP/Corp. Sec.
Jose Armario, Pres., McDonald's Latin America & Canada
Jan Fields, Pres., McDonald's USA, LLC
Denis Hannequin, Pres., Europe
Jeff Stratton, Worldwide Chief Restaurant Officer/Exec. VP
Andrew J. McKenna, Chmn.
Tim Fenton, Pres., McDonald's Middle East, APAC & Africa

Phone: 630-623-3000 **Fax:** 630-623-5700
Toll-Free: 800-244-6227
Address: 1 McDonald's Plz., Oak Brook, IL 60523 US

GROWTH PLANS/SPECIAL FEATURES:

McDonald's Corp. operates more than 33,000 fast-food restaurants in 118 countries, serving approximately 64 million customers per day. McDonald's has expanded primarily based on its successful franchising model, whereby independent businessmen and women provide capital by initially investing in equipment, signs, seating and decor of restaurants and personally operating them. The company shares the investment by owning or leasing the land and buildings. Approximately 80% of McDonald's worldwide restaurants are franchises, the rest being operated directly by the company or under joint-venture agreements. The McDonald's menu includes items such as hamburgers, cheeseburgers, fish and chicken sandwiches, chicken nuggets, french fries, salads, milkshakes, desserts and soft drinks. McDonald's restaurants are also open during breakfast hours and offer egg sandwiches, hotcakes, biscuit and bagel sandwiches and muffins. Brand names include the Big Mac, Quarter Pounder, Filet O'Fish and Egg McMuffin. As part of a multi-year beverage business strategy designed to take advantage of the significant and growing beverage category, the company is introducing hot specialty coffee offerings on a market-by-market basis, all of which serve as a platform for the recent introduction of smoothies, frappes and other beverage options in a number of markets. McDonalds averaged about $2.5 million in sales per store during 2011. The company is working to provide nutritious additions to its menu, including salads, apple slices, oatmeal and low fat yogurt.

The firm offers qualified employees medical, dental and vision insurance; short- and long-term disability; profit sharing and savings plans; adoption assistance; vacation and holiday pay; and a child care discount. McDonald's U.S. employees at corporate division and regional offices may receive benefits including a bonus program, educational assistance, credit union membership and sabbaticals of eight weeks every 10 years. Hamburger University is McDonald's worldwide management training center located in Illinois.

FINANCIALS:

Sales and profits are in thousands of dollars—add 000 to get the full amount. 2010 Note: Financial information for 2010 was not available for all companies at press time.

Sales	Profits
2010 Sales: $24,074,600	2010 Profits: $4,946,300
2009 Sales: $22,744,700	2009 Profits: $4,551,000
2008 Sales: $23,522,400	2008 Profits: $4,313,200
2007 Sales: $22,786,600	2007 Profits: $2,395,100
2006 Sales: $20,895,200	2006 Profits: $3,544,200

U.S. Stock Ticker: MCD
Int'l Ticker:
Int'l Exchange:
Employees: 400,000 Fiscal Year Ends: 12/31
Parent Company:

SALARIES/BENEFITS:

Pension Plan:	ESOP Stock Plan:	Profit Sharing: Y	Top Exec. Salary: $1,433,333	Bonus: $4,500,000
Savings Plan: Y	Stock Purch. Plan:		Second Exec. Salary: $794,952	Bonus: $1,855,000

OTHER THOUGHTS:

Apparent Women Officers or Directors: 3
Hot Spot for Advancement for Women/Minorities: Y

LOCATIONS: ("Y" = Yes)

West:	Southwest:	Midwest:	Southeast:	Northeast:	International:
Y	Y	Y	Y	Y	Y

MCKESSON CORPORATION

www.mckesson.com

Industry Group Code: 424210

Management:		Sales/Marketing:		Liberal Arts:		Information Sys.:		Professionals:		Tech./Scientific:	
Mgmt. Trainees:	Y	Marketing Pros.:	Y	Gen. Writing/Editing:	Y	Info. Mgmt.:	Y	Finance/Acct.:	Y	Engineers, Elec.:	
Experienced Mgmt.:	Y	Retail Sales:		Tech. Writing:	Y	Software Dev.:	Y	Law:	Y	Engineers, Other:	
Int'l Business:	Y	Comm./Industrial:	Y	Graphic Arts/Photog.:	Y	Hardware Dev.:		HR/Other:	Y	Health/Lab:	
MBA Grads:	Y	Sales Trainees:	Y	Music:		Consulting/Other:	Y	Training:	Y	Science/Research:	
		Advertising Pros.:	Y	Broadcasting:				Health Care:		Petroleum/Chem.:	
				Other:				Consulting:		Math/Other:	

TYPES OF BUSINESS:

Pharmaceutical Distribution
Medical-Surgical Products Distribution
Health Care Management Software
Consulting
Outsourcing

BRANDS/DIVISIONS/AFFILIATES:

Nadro, S.A. de C.V.
Parata Systems LLC
McKesson Health Solutions
McKesson Pharmacy Systems and Automation
InterQual
Portico Systems
Zee Medical
U.S. Oncology

CONTACTS: *Note: Officers with more than one job title may be intentionally listed here more than once.*

John H. Hammergren, CEO
John H. Hammergren, Pres.
Jeffrey C. Campbell, CFO/Exec. VP
Jorge L. Figueredo, Exec. VP-Human Resources
Randall N. Spratt, CIO/Exec. VP
Randall N. Spratt, CTO/Exec. VP
Laureen E. Seeger, General Counsel/Exec. VP/Chief Compliance Officer
Marc E. Owen, Exec. VP-Corp. Strategy & Bus. Dev.
Ana Schrank, VP-Investor Rel.
Paul C. Julian, Exec. VP/Group Pres., McKesson Corporation
Patrick J. Blake, Exec. VP/Pres., McKesson Technology Solutions
John H. Hammergren, Chmn.

Phone: 415-983-8300	**Fax:**
Toll-Free: 800-826-9360	
Address: 1 Post St., San Francisco, CA 94104 US	

GROWTH PLANS/SPECIAL FEATURES:

McKesson Corporation provides medicines, pharmaceutical supplies, information and care management products and services to the healthcare industry. The company operates in two segments: McKesson distribution solutions and McKesson technology solutions. The McKesson distribution solutions segment distributes ethical and proprietary drugs, medical-surgical supplies and equipment and health and beauty care products throughout North America. This segment also provides specialty pharmaceutical solutions to biotech and pharmaceutical manufacturers, sells pharmacy software and provides consulting and outsourcing services. It also maintains a 49% interest in Nadro, S.A. de C.V., a leading pharmaceutical distributor in Mexico, and a 39% interest in Parata Systems LLC, which sells automated pharmacy and supply management systems and services to retail and institutional outpatient pharmacies. The McKesson technology solutions segment delivers clinical, patient care, financial, supply chain and strategic management software solutions, as well as pharmacy automation for hospitals and connectivity and outsourcing services. The firm's payor group of businesses, which includes InterQual, provides clinical auditing and compliance systems, claims payment solutions, medical management software and care management programs. Customers of this segment include hospitals, physicians, homecare providers, retail pharmacies and payors from North America, Europe and the Asia Pacific region. The company's subsidiaries include U.S. Pharmaceutical Distribution; McKesson Canada; Medical-Surgical Distribution; McKesson Pharmacy Systems and Automation; Zee Medical; and RelayHealth. In December 2010, the company acquired U.S. Oncology, an integrated oncology company. In July 2011, the firm acquired Portico Systems, an integrated provider of management solutions.

FINANCIALS: **Sales and profits are in thousands of dollars—add 000 to get the full amount. 2010 Note: Financial information for 2010 was not available for all companies at press time.**

2010 Sales: $108,702,000	2010 Profits: $1,263,000	**U.S. Stock Ticker: MCK**
2009 Sales: $106,632,000	2009 Profits: $823,000	**Int'l Ticker:**
2008 Sales: $101,703,000	2008 Profits: $990,000	Int'l Exchange:
2007 Sales: $92,977,000	2007 Profits: $913,000	Employees: 32,500 Fiscal Year Ends: 3/31
2006 Sales: $86,983,000	2006 Profits: $751,000	Parent Company:

SALARIES/BENEFITS:

Pension Plan:	ESOP Stock Plan: Y	Profit Sharing: Y	Top Exec. Salary: $1,580,000	Bonus: $12,828,150
Savings Plan:	Stock Purch. Plan: Y		Second Exec. Salary: $986,000	Bonus: $6,289,000

OTHER THOUGHTS:

Apparent Women Officers or Directors: 1
Hot Spot for Advancement for Women/Minorities: Y

LOCATIONS: ("Y" = Yes)

West:	Southwest:	Midwest:	Southeast:	Northeast:	International:
Y	Y	Y	Y	Y	Y

MCKINSEY & COMPANY INC

www.mckinsey.com

Industry Group Code: 54161

Management:		**Sales/Marketing:**		**Liberal Arts:**		**Information Sys.:**		**Professionals:**		**Tech./Scientific:**	
Mgmt. Trainees:	Y	Marketing Pros.:	Y	Gen. Writing/Editing:	Y	Info. Mgmt.:	Y	Finance/Acct.:	Y	Engineers, Elec.:	
Experienced Mgmt.:	Y	Retail Sales:		Tech. Writing:	Y	Software Dev.:	Y	Law:	Y	Engineers, Other:	
Int'l Business:	Y	Comm./Industrial:	Y	Graphic Arts/Photog.:	Y	Hardware Dev.:		HR/Other:	Y	Health/Lab:	
MBA Grads:	Y	Sales Trainees:		Music:		Consulting/Other:	Y	Training:	Y	Science/Research:	
		Advertising Pros.:	Y	Broadcasting:				Health Care:		Petroleum/Chem.:	
				Other:	Y			Consulting:	Y	Math/Other:	Y

TYPES OF BUSINESS:

Management Consulting
Strategic & Logistics Consulting
Industry-Specific Consulting
Business Research
Business Publications

BRANDS/DIVISIONS/AFFILIATES:

McKinsey & Co.
McKinsey Global Institute
McKinsey Quarterly (The)

CONTACTS: *Note: Officers with more than one job title may be intentionally listed here more than once.*

Dominic Barton, Managing Dir.
Andrew Whitehouse, External Relations Dir.-EMEA
Ian Gleeson, External Relations Dir.-UK & Ireland
Kai Peter Rather, External Relations Dir.-Germany
Michael Halbye, Chmn.-EMEA

Phone: 212-446-7000 **Fax:** 212-446-8575
Toll-Free:
Address: 55 E. 52nd St., 21st Fl., New York, NY 10022 US

GROWTH PLANS/SPECIAL FEATURES:

McKinsey & Company, Inc. is a privately held international business consulting firm that was established in 1926. Headquartered in New York, the firm maintains more than 90 offices in over 50 countries, as well as a cross-functional global business technology office. The firm provides consulting services for companies seeking functional assistance or market insights. Through a variety of leadership and financial consulting services, McKinsey helps clients sustain growth and maximize revenue. The firm serves companies within a wide range of industries including banking, insurance, telecom, information services, media/entertainment, industrial, health care, public sector and retail/consumer. It helps clients achieve functional efficiency with consulting services such as outsourcing, information technology (IT) services, financial strategy, operations strategy, organization and leadership. McKinsey's consultants publish a variety of books and articles with topics ranging from company productivity and structural engineering to accentuating the positive. The firm also publishes a quarterly magazine called The McKinsey Quarterly, which is regarded as required reading for those who aspire to be at the top of the consulting game. Through the McKinsey Global Institute (MGI), the company conducts business research and develops points of view relating to the economic issues faced by businesses and governments.

FINANCIALS: **Sales and profits are in thousands of dollars—add 000 to get the full amount. 2010 Note: Financial information for 2010 was not available for all companies at press time.**

2010 Sales: $7,200,000 2010 Profits: $
2009 Sales: $6,600,000 2009 Profits: $
2008 Sales: $5,500,000 2008 Profits: $
2007 Sales: $4,500,000 2007 Profits: $
2006 Sales: $4,200,000 2006 Profits: $

U.S. Stock Ticker: Private
Int'l Ticker:
Int'l Exchange:
Employees: 18,000 Fiscal Year Ends: 12/31
Parent Company:

SALARIES/BENEFITS:

Pension Plan: ESOP Stock Plan: Profit Sharing: Top Exec. Salary: $ Bonus: $
Savings Plan: Stock Purch. Plan: Second Exec. Salary: $ Bonus: $

OTHER THOUGHTS:

Apparent Women Officers or Directors:
Hot Spot for Advancement for Women/Minorities:

LOCATIONS: ("Y" = Yes)

West:	Southwest:	Midwest:	Southeast:	Northeast:	International:
Y	Y	Y	Y	Y	Y

MEDCO HEALTH SOLUTIONS INC

www.medco.com

Industry Group Code: 522320A

Management:		Sales/Marketing:		Liberal Arts:		Information Sys.:		Professionals:		Tech./Scientific:	
Mgmt. Trainees:	Y	Marketing Pros.:	Y	Gen. Writing/Editing:	Y	Info. Mgmt.:	Y	Finance/Acct.:	Y	Engineers, Elec.:	
Experienced Mgmt.:	Y	Retail Sales:		Tech. Writing:	Y	Software Dev.:	Y	Law:	Y	Engineers, Other:	
Int'l Business:	Y	Comm./Industrial:	Y	Graphic Arts/Photog.:	Y	Hardware Dev.:		HR/Other:	Y	Health/Lab:	
MBA Grads:	Y	Sales Trainees:		Music:		Consulting/Other:		Training:	Y	Science/Research:	
		Advertising Pros.:	Y	Broadcasting:				Health Care:	Y	Petroleum/Chem.:	
				Other:				Consulting:		Math/Other:	

TYPES OF BUSINESS:

Pharmacy Benefits Management
Payment & Transaction Processing
Online Services

BRANDS/DIVISIONS/AFFILIATES:

Accredo Health Group Inc
Europa Apotheek Venlo
Therapeutic Resource Centers
DNA Direct, Inc.
United BioSource Corporation

CONTACTS:

Note: Officers with more than one job title may be intentionally listed here more than once.

David Snow, CEO
Kenneth O. Klepper, COO
Kenneth O. Klepper, Pres.
Richard J. Rubino, CFO/Sr. VP-Finance
Jack A. Smith, Chief Mktg. Officer/Sr. VP
Karin Princivalle, Sr. VP-Human Resources
Glen Stettin, Chief Medical Officer
Thomas Moriarty, General Counsel/Corp. Sec./Sr. VP
Gabriel Cappucci, Chief Acct. Officer/Sr. VP/Controller
Mary T. Daschner, Group Pres., Gov't PBM Group
Timothy Wentworth, Group Pres., Employer & Key Accounts
Glenn C. Taylor, Group Pres., Health Plans
Laizer D. Kornwasser, Sr. VP-Retail, Mail & Diabetes Markets
David B. Snow, Jr., Chmn.
Brian T. Griffin, Pres., Int'l

Phone: 201-269-3400 **Fax:** 201-269-1109
Toll-Free:
Address: 100 Parsons Pond Dr., Franklin Lakes, NJ 07417-2603 US

GROWTH PLANS/SPECIAL FEATURES:

Medco Health Solutions, Inc. is a national pharmacy benefit manager with over 65 million members. Its prescription drug benefit programs are designed to drive down the cost of pharmacy healthcare for private and public employers, health plans, labor unions, government agencies of all sizes and individuals served by the Medicare Part D Prescription Drug Program. Medco collaborates with retail pharmacies, physicians, pharmaceutical manufacturers, the Centers for Medicare & Medicaid Services for Medicare and state Medicaid agencies. It provides its services through a national network of retail pharmacies, its mail-order pharmacies and its Specialty Pharmacy segment, Accredo Health Group. The firm maintains Medco Therapeutic Resource Centers, staffed with hundreds of pharmacists trained and certified in specific complex and chronic conditions and associated medications. The company's services include mail order services, which provide cost savings through a high degree of automation; systems for identifying generic substitution for brand-name medicines; cooperative services with physicians, clients and members to offer personalized medicine in order to maximize safety and cost reductions; a flexible array of Medicare Part D products; and methods to manage drug utilization in order to minimize waste and fraud. The firm holds a majority interest in Europa Apotheek Venlo, a provider of clinical health care and mail-order pharmacy services in Germany. Medco is a leading purchaser of generic prescription drugs, with a 71% utilization rate among its members. In early 2010, the company acquired DNA Direct, Inc., which specializes in providing personalized care through genomic medicine. In September 2010, Medco acquired United BioSource Corporation for roughly $730 million. In July 2011, Medco agreed to be acquired by Express Scripts, Inc. for $29.1 billion.

FINANCIALS:

Sales and profits are in thousands of dollars—add 000 to get the full amount. 2010 Note: Financial information for 2010 was not available for all companies at press time.

2010 Sales: $65,968,300 — 2010 Profits: $1,427,300
2009 Sales: $59,804,200 — 2009 Profits: $1,280,300
2008 Sales: $51,258,000 — 2008 Profits: $1,102,900
2007 Sales: $44,506,200 — 2007 Profits: $912,000
2006 Sales: $42,543,700 — 2006 Profits: $630,200

U.S. Stock Ticker: MHS
Int'l Ticker:
Int'l Exchange:
Employees: 23,425 Fiscal Year Ends: 12/31
Parent Company:

SALARIES/BENEFITS:

Pension Plan: ESOP Stock Plan: Profit Sharing: Top Exec. Salary: $1,300,000 Bonus: $2,700,000
Savings Plan: Y Stock Purch. Plan: Y Second Exec. Salary: $821,700 Bonus: $1,400,000

OTHER THOUGHTS:

Apparent Women Officers or Directors: 4
Hot Spot for Advancement for Women/Minorities: Y

LOCATIONS: ("Y" = Yes)

West:	Southwest:	Midwest:	Southeast:	Northeast:	International:
Y	Y	Y	Y	Y	Y

Sales, profits and employees may be estimates. Financial information, benefits and other data can change quickly and may vary from those stated here.

MEDIACOM COMMUNICATIONS CORP

www.mediacomcc.com

Industry Group Code: 517110

Management:		**Sales/Marketing:**		**Liberal Arts:**		**Information Sys.:**		**Professionals:**		**Tech./Scientific:**	
Mgmt. Trainees:	Y	Marketing Pros.:	Y	Gen. Writing/Editing:	Y	Info. Mgmt.:	Y	Finance/Acct.:	Y	Engineers, Elec.:	Y
Experienced Mgmt.:	Y	Retail Sales:		Tech. Writing:		Software Dev.:	Y	Law:	Y	Engineers, Other:	
Int'l Business:		Comm./Industrial:		Graphic Arts/Photog.:	Y	Hardware Dev.:		HR/Other:	Y	Health/Lab:	
MBA Grads:	Y	Sales Trainees:		Music:		Consulting/Other:		Training:	Y	Science/Research:	
		Advertising Pros.:	Y	Broadcasting:	Y			Health Care:		Petroleum/Chem.:	
				Other:				Consulting:		Math/Other:	

TYPES OF BUSINESS:

Cable TV Service
Internet Service
Digital Cable
Telephone Service

BRANDS/DIVISIONS/AFFILIATES:

Mediacom Online
Mediacom Online Ultra
Mediacom Phone
Rocco B. Commisso

CONTACTS: *Note: Officers with more than one job title may be intentionally listed here more than once.*

Rocco B. Commisso, CEO
Mark E. Stephan, CFO/Exec. VP
Michael Rahimi, Sr. VP-Mktg. & Consumer Svcs.
Italia Commisso Weinand, Sr. VP-Human Resources & Programming
J.R. Walden, Sr. VP-Tech.
Joseph E. Young, General Counsel/Sr. VP/Sec.
John G. Pascarelli, Exec. VP-Oper.
Calvin G. Craib, Sr. VP-Bus. Dev.
Thomas J. Larsen, VP-Public & Legal Affairs
Calvin G. Craib, Sr. VP-Corp. Finance
Charles J. Bartolotta, Sr. VP-Enterprise Solutions & Field Service Oper.
Brian M. Walsh, Sr. VP/Corp. Controller
Tapan Dandnaik, Sr. VP-Customer Service & Financial Oper.
Steve Litwer, Sr. VP-Advertising Sales, OnMedia Div.
Rocco B. Commisso, Chmn.

Phone: 845-695-2600 **Fax:** 845-695-2699
Toll-Free:
Address: 100 Crystal Run Rd., Middletown, NY 10941 US

GROWTH PLANS/SPECIAL FEATURES:

Mediacom Communications Corp., a leading local cable company, supplies an array of broadband products and services to approximately 1.24 million basic subscribers, 678,000 digital video customers, 778,000 high speed data (HSD) customers and 287,000 telephone customers. The firm offers its customers a full array of traditional video services, which includes basic service, digital video service, pay-per-view service, high definition television, digital video recorders and video-on-demand. In addition, the company offers Mediacom Online, which offers three levels of high-speed Internet access, ranging from 3 Mbps to 20 Mpbs. Mediacom's premium Internet service, Mediacom Online Ultra, allows maximum downstream and upstream speeds of 105 Mbps and 10 Mbps, respectively. Mediacom Online Ultra is available to 25% of the firm's service territory, or 700,000 homes, and the firm plans to expand this to 1.4 million homes. The firm's Mediacom Phone offers customers unlimited local, regional and long-distance calling within the U.S., Puerto Rico, U.S. Virgin Islands and Canada. It is delivered over Voice over Internet Protocol (VoIP) that digitizes voice signals and routes them as data packets through Mediacom's controlled broadband cable systems. It includes features such as Caller ID with name and number, call waiting, three-way calling and enhanced Emergency 911 dialing. Mediacom also offers video, HSD, phone, network and transport services to commercial and large enterprise customers. It also offers large enterprise customers who require high-bandwidth connections solutions such as the point-to-point circuits required by wireless communications providers. The firm generates additional revenues from the sale of advertising time on its satellite-delivered channels. In March 2011, Mediacom was taken private by its founder, CEO and chairman, Rocco B. Commisso.

FINANCIALS: **Sales and profits are in thousands of dollars—add 000 to get the full amount. 2010 Note: Financial information for 2010 was not available for all companies at press time.**

2010 Sales: $1,499,000	2010 Profits: $289,400
2009 Sales: $1,460,359	2009 Profits: $774,067
2008 Sales: $1,401,894	2008 Profits: $-77,494
2007 Sales: $1,293,375	2007 Profits: $-95,129
2006 Sales: $1,210,400	2006 Profits: $-124,922

U.S. Stock Ticker: Private
Int'l Ticker:
Int'l Exchange:
Employees: 4,520 Fiscal Year Ends: 12/31
Parent Company:

SALARIES/BENEFITS:

Pension Plan:	ESOP Stock Plan:	Profit Sharing:	Top Exec. Salary: $850,000	Bonus: $956,000
Savings Plan: Y	Stock Purch. Plan: Y		Second Exec. Salary: $350,000	Bonus: $130,000

OTHER THOUGHTS:

Apparent Women Officers or Directors: 1
Hot Spot for Advancement for Women/Minorities:

LOCATIONS: ("Y" = Yes)

West:	Southwest:	Midwest:	Southeast:	Northeast:	International:
Y	Y	Y	Y	Y	

MEDNAX INC

www.mednax.com

Industry Group Code: 6211

Management:		Sales/Marketing:		Liberal Arts:		Information Sys.:		Professionals:		Tech./Scientific:	
Mgmt. Trainees:		Marketing Pros.:	Y	Gen. Writing/Editing:		Info. Mgmt.:	Y	Finance/Acct.:	Y	Engineers, Elec.:	
Experienced Mgmt.:		Retail Sales:		Tech. Writing:	Y	Software Dev.:		Law:	Y	Engineers, Other:	
Int'l Business:	Y	Comm./Industrial:	Y	Graphic Arts/Photog.:		Hardware Dev.:		HR/Other:	Y	Health/Lab:	
MBA Grads:	Y	Sales Trainees:		Music:		Consulting/Other:		Training:	Y	Science/Research:	
		Advertising Pros.:	Y	Broadcasting:				Health Care:	Y	Petroleum/Chem.:	
				Other:				Consulting:		Math/Other:	

TYPES OF BUSINESS:

Hospital-Based Pediatrician Practice Management
Pediatric Intensive Care Unit Management
Neonatal Intensive Care Unit Management
Perinatal Physician Services
Staffing Services
Laboratory Services

BRANDS/DIVISIONS/AFFILIATES:

Pediatrix Medical Group Inc
Pediatrix University
American Anesthesiology
Pediatrix Screening
Obstetrix Medical Group
UltraHealthCare, P.A.
Neonatal Medical Associates, Inc.
Pinnacle Anesthesia

CONTACTS: *Note: Officers with more than one job title may be intentionally listed here more than once.*

Roger J. Medel, CEO
Joseph M. Calabro, COO
Joseph M. Calabro, Pres.
Vivian Lopez-Blanco, CFO
Alan R. Spitzer, Sr. VP-Center for Research, Education & Quality
Robert C. Bryant, CIO/Sr. VP
Thomas W. Hawkins, General Counsel/Sr. VP/Sec.
Steve C. Collins, Sr. VP-Bus. Dev.
Bob Kneeley, VP-Investor Rel.
Vivian Lopez-Blanco, Treas.
William C. Hawk, Sr. VP-American Anesthesiology
Frederick V. Miller, Pres., Pediatrix Div.
Karl Wagner, Pres., American Anesthesiology
David Clark, COO-Pediatrix Div.
Cesar L. Alvarez, Chmn.
Carlos A. Perez, Regional Pres., Caribbean Region

Phone: 954-384-0175	**Fax:** 954-838-9961
Toll-Free: 800-243-3839	
Address: 1301 Concord Terr., Sunrise, FL 33323 US	

GROWTH PLANS/SPECIAL FEATURES:

MEDNAX, Inc., formerly Pediatrix Medical Group, Inc., is a holding company which operates primarily through two subsidiaries: Pediatrix Medical Group and American Anesthesiology. Pediatrix provides physician services to ensure comprehensive clinical care to babies born prematurely or with medical complications and to expectant mothers experiencing complicated pregnancies. Pediatrix's network is composed of over 1,675 affiliated physicians, including 968 neonatal physician subspecialists who provide clinical care in 33 states and Puerto Rico. The company also works with other pediatric subspecialists, including roughly 172 maternal-fetal physicians, 104 pediatric cardiologists, 84 pediatric intensivists and 39 pediatric hospitalists. Pediatrix operates through three primary divisions: Obstetrix Medical Group specializes in maternal-fetal medicine, providing care for woman and their unborn babies during high risk pregnancies; Pediatrix Screening operates the nation's largest independent laboratory specializing in newborn hearing and metabolic screening; and Pediatrix University focuses on clinical research and on offering neonatal medical education through its virtual classrooms and online journals. American Anesthesiology is a national group practice specializing in anesthesia services. The group comprises over 325 anesthesiologists and more than 400 certified registered nurse anesthetists and anesthesia assistants throughout Georgia, Florida, North Carolina and Virginia. These anesthesia professionals work in both hospitals and offices. In 2010, the firm acquired four neonatal practices in Idaho, Louisiana and Washington; Maryland Perinatal Associates, PC; Roberto Villarreal M.D., P.A. and UltraHealthCare, P.A. in Texas; Neonatology Associates, PC and Southeast Anesthesiology Consultants, P.A. in Florida; and Wilmington Maternal-Fetal Medicine, PLLC, in North Carolina. In 2011, MEDNAX acquired Neonatal Medical Associates, Inc. and Pinnacle Anesthesia through American Anesthesiology in Florida; Center for Maternal Fetal Care, P.A. and Hill Country Maternal Fetal Medicine in Texas; and Northwest Newborn Specialists, P.C. in Oregon.

The firm offers employee benefits including life, AD&D, health and disability insurance.

FINANCIALS: **Sales and profits are in thousands of dollars—add 000 to get the full amount. 2010 Note: Financial information for 2010 was not available for all companies at press time.**

2010 Sales: $1,401,559	2010 Profits: $202,691	**U.S. Stock Ticker: MD**
2009 Sales: $1,288,264	2009 Profits: $175,804	**Int'l Ticker:**
2008 Sales: $1,068,277	2008 Profits: $169,201	Int'l Exchange:
2007 Sales: $917,644	2007 Profits: $142,722	Employees: 6,270 Fiscal Year Ends: 12/31
2006 Sales: $804,696	2006 Profits: $124,465	Parent Company:

SALARIES/BENEFITS:

Pension Plan:	ESOP Stock Plan:	Profit Sharing:	Top Exec. Salary: $950,000	Bonus: $1,140,000
Savings Plan: Y	Stock Purch. Plan: Y		Second Exec. Salary: $600,000	Bonus: $480,000

OTHER THOUGHTS:

Apparent Women Officers or Directors: 2
Hot Spot for Advancement for Women/Minorities:

LOCATIONS: ("Y" = Yes)

West:	Southwest:	Midwest:	Southeast:	Northeast:	International:
Y	Y	Y	Y	Y	Y

MEDTRONIC INC

www.medtronic.com

Industry Group Code: 33911

Management:		Sales/Marketing:		Liberal Arts:		Information Sys.:		Professionals:		Tech./Scientific:	
Mgmt. Trainees:	Y	Marketing Pros.:	Y	Gen. Writing/Editing:	Y	Info. Mgmt.:	Y	Finance/Acct.:	Y	Engineers, Elec.:	Y
Experienced Mgmt.:	Y	Retail Sales:		Tech. Writing:	Y	Software Dev.:	Y	Law:	Y	Engineers, Other:	Y
Int'l Business:	Y	Comm./Industrial:	Y	Graphic Arts/Photog.:	Y	Hardware Dev.:	Y	HR/Other:	Y	Health/Lab:	Y
MBA Grads:	Y	Sales Trainees:	Y	Music:		Consulting/Other:		Training:	Y	Science/Research:	Y
		Advertising Pros.:	Y	Broadcasting:				Health Care:	Y	Petroleum/Chem.:	
				Other:				Consulting:		Math/Other:	Y

TYPES OF BUSINESS:

Equipment-Defibrillators & Pacing Products
Neurological Devices
Diabetes Management Devices
Ear, Nose & Throat Surgical Equipment
Pain Management Devices
Cardiac Surgery Equipment

BRANDS/DIVISIONS/AFFILIATES:

ATS Medical, Inc
Invatec
Osteotech

CONTACTS: *Note: Officers with more than one job title may be intentionally listed here more than once.*

Omar Ishrak, CEO
Gary Ellis, CFO/Sr. VP
Caroline Stockdale, Sr. VP-Human Resources
Richard E. Kuntz, Chief Scientific, Clinical & Regulatory Officer
Stephen N. Oesterle, Sr. VP-Medicine & Tech.
D. Cameron Findlay, General Counsel/Corp. Sec./Sr. VP
H. James Dallas, Sr. VP-Quality & Oper.
Susan Alpert, Chief Regulatory Officer/Sr. VP
Bob Blankenmeyer, Sr. VP/Pres., Surgical Tech.
Scott R. Ward, Sr. VP/Pres., Cardiovascular
Michael J. Coyle, Exec. VP/Pres., Cardiac & Vascular Group.
Omar Ishrak, Chmn.
Jean-Luc Butel, Exec. VP/Pres., Int'l

Phone: 763-514-4000 **Fax:** 763-514-4879
Toll-Free: 800-633-8766
Address: 710 Medtronic Pkwy., Minneapolis, MN 55432 US

GROWTH PLANS/SPECIAL FEATURES:

Medtronic, Inc. is a global leader in medical technology marketing its products in over 120 companies. The firm operates in seven business sectors: cardiac rhythm disease management (CRDM); surgical technologies; neuromodulation; spinal; cardiovascular; physio-control; and diabetes. Products in the CRDM segment manage cardiac rhythm disorders and include pacemakers, implantable defibrillators, ablation products and products for the treatment of atrial fibrillation (AF). The surgical technologies division develops and manufactures minimally invasive products to treat ear, nose and throat (ENT) and neurological diseases. The neuromodulation division develops devices for the treatment of neurological, urological and gastroenterological disorders. The spinal division offers medical devices used to treat spinal and cranial conditions. The cardiovascular segment offers medical devices and technology used to treat chronic diseases affecting the vascular system. The physio-control segment develops, manufactures and maintains monitor and defibrillator products for use in and out of hospitals, as well as for public access use. The diabetes unit integrated diabetes management systems, insulin pump therapy, continuous glucose monitoring systems and therapy management software. In April 2010, Medtronic acquired Invatec, a developer of cardiovascular disease interventional treatment technologies, and two affiliated companies. In August 2010, the firm acquired ATS Medical, Inc. for roughly $370 million; and opened a patient care facility in Beijing, China. In November 2010, Medtronic acquired biotechnology company Osteotech for roughly $123 million. In March 2011, the company opened a new manufacturing facility in Singapore.

Employees are offered healthcare and disability coverage; flexible work hours; adoption and elder care assistance; retirement plans; stock ownership options; and volunteer opportunities through the Medtronic Foundation.

FINANCIALS: **Sales and profits are in thousands of dollars—add 000 to get the full amount. 2010 Note: Financial information for 2010 was not available for all companies at press time.**

Sales	Profits
2010 Sales: $15,817,000	2010 Profits: $3,099,000
2009 Sales: $14,599,000	2009 Profits: $2,169,000
2008 Sales: $13,515,000	2008 Profits: $2,231,000
2007 Sales: $12,299,000	2007 Profits: $2,802,000
2006 Sales: $11,292,000	2006 Profits: $2,546,700

U.S. Stock Ticker: MDT
Int'l Ticker:
Int'l Exchange:
Employees: 43,321 Fiscal Year Ends: 4/30
Parent Company:

SALARIES/BENEFITS:

Pension Plan: Y	ESOP Stock Plan: Y	Profit Sharing:	Top Exec. Salary: $1,118,150	Bonus: $2,334,858
Savings Plan:	Stock Purch. Plan: Y		Second Exec. Salary: $604,200	Bonus: $859,964

OTHER THOUGHTS:

Apparent Women Officers or Directors: 4
Hot Spot for Advancement for Women/Minorities: Y

LOCATIONS: ("Y" = Yes)

West:	Southwest:	Midwest:	Southeast:	Northeast:	International:
Y	Y	Y	Y	Y	Y

MEIJER INC

Industry Group Code: 445110

www.meijer.com

Management:		Sales/Marketing:		Liberal Arts:		Information Sys.:		Professionals:		Tech./Scientific:	
Mgmt. Trainees:	Y	Marketing Pros.:	Y	Gen. Writing/Editing:	Y	Info. Mgmt.:	Y	Finance/Acct.:	Y	Engineers, Elec.:	
Experienced Mgmt.:	Y	Retail Sales:	Y	Tech. Writing:		Software Dev.:	Y	Law:	Y	Engineers, Other:	
Int'l Business:		Comm./Industrial:		Graphic Arts/Photog.:	Y	Hardware Dev.:		HR/Other:	Y	Health/Lab:	
MBA Grads:	Y	Sales Trainees:	Y	Music:		Consulting/Other:		Training:	Y	Science/Research:	
		Advertising Pros.:	Y	Broadcasting:				Health Care:		Petroleum/Chem.:	
				Other:	Y			Consulting:		Math/Other:	

TYPES OF BUSINESS:

Grocery Stores
General Merchandise
Hardware
Photo Services
Pharmacies
In-Store Restaurants
Gasoline, Retail
Home Decor

BRANDS/DIVISIONS/AFFILIATES:

Meijer Naturals
Meijer Organics
Meijer Gold
Meijer Real Estate
Meijer MarketPlace

CONTACTS: *Note: Officers with more than one job title may be intentionally listed here more than once.*

Hendrik G. Meijer, CEO
Mark Murray, Pres.
Stacie Behler, VP-Corp. Comm. & Public Rel.
Doug Meijer, Co-Chmn.
Frank Guglielmi, Contact-Media
Hendrik G. Meijer, Co-Chmn.

Phone: 616-453-6711 | **Fax:** 616-791-2572
Toll-Free: 877-363-4537
Address: 2929 Walker Ave. NW, Grand Rapids, MI 49544-9424 US

GROWTH PLANS/SPECIAL FEATURES:

Meijer, Inc. is a leading grocery retailer in the Midwest, with over 200 superstores throughout Illinois, Indiana, Kentucky, Michigan and Ohio. 177 of these stores offer gas stations, while two have car washes. The firm's combination grocery and general merchandise stores range in size from 200,000 to 250,000 square feet, which is about four times the size of typical grocery stores. Each Meijer store carries about 120,000 brand-name and private-label products, including bulk foods, fresh produce, frozen items, seafood and meat products. Most stores feature nearly 40 departments, such as electronics, hardware, toys, garden, entertainment, jewelry, photo, banking, pharmacy, books, apparel, automotive and furniture. Meijer Real Estate provides leasing and internal licenses on adjacent properties, former Meijer properties and in-store tenant space. In addition, some stores offer a discount gas station, Meijer prepaid Mastercard and business gift cards. Company brands include Meijer Naturals, Meijer Organics and Meijer Gold. The superstores also offer several in-store restaurants, including delis and cafes. Meijer stores are open 24-hours-a-day and close only on Christmas. In addition to its retail stores, the firm operates a web site that features a baby club, wine guides, contests, advertisements, pharmaceutical help and gardening tips. In August 2010, Meijer announced plans to open six new stores. In August 2011, the firm opened Meijer MarketPlace in Chicago. The new store concept is 96,000 square feet in size, about half the size of most Meijer supercenters.

Employees are offered medical, dental, vision and life insurance; flexible spending accounts; disability protection; workers compensation; paid time off; employee discount; adoption assistance; a pension plan; and a 401(k) plan.

FINANCIALS: **Sales and profits are in thousands of dollars—add 000 to get the full amount. 2010 Note: Financial information for 2010 was not available for all companies at press time.**

2010 Sales: $14,200,000 — 2010 Profits: $
2009 Sales: $14,321,000 — 2009 Profits: $
2008 Sales: $13,880,000 — 2008 Profits: $
2007 Sales: $13,900,000 — 2007 Profits: $
2006 Sales: $12,500,000 — 2006 Profits: $

U.S. Stock Ticker: Private
Int'l Ticker:
Int'l Exchange:
Employees: 72,200 Fiscal Year Ends: 1/31
Parent Company:

SALARIES/BENEFITS:

Pension Plan: Y | ESOP Stock Plan: | Profit Sharing: | Top Exec. Salary: $ | Bonus: $
Savings Plan: Y | Stock Purch. Plan: | | Second Exec. Salary: $ | Bonus: $

OTHER THOUGHTS:

Apparent Women Officers or Directors: 1
Hot Spot for Advancement for Women/Minorities:

LOCATIONS: ("Y" = Yes)

West:	Southwest:	Midwest:	Southeast:	Northeast:	International:
		Y			

MERCER INC

www.mercer.com

Industry Group Code: 541612

Management:		Sales/Marketing:		Liberal Arts:		Information Sys.:		Professionals:		Tech./Scientific:	
Mgmt. Trainees:	Y	Marketing Pros.:	Y	Gen. Writing/Editing:	Y	Info. Mgmt.:	Y	Finance/Acct.:	Y	Engineers, Elec.:	
Experienced Mgmt.:	Y	Retail Sales:		Tech. Writing:	Y	Software Dev.:	Y	Law:	Y	Engineers, Other:	
Int'l Business:	Y	Comm./Industrial:	Y	Graphic Arts/Photog.:	Y	Hardware Dev.:		HR/Other:	Y	Health/Lab:	
MBA Grads:	Y	Sales Trainees:		Music:		Consulting/Other:	Y	Training:	Y	Science/Research:	
		Advertising Pros.:	Y	Broadcasting:				Health Care:		Petroleum/Chem.:	
				Other:	Y			Consulting:	Y	Math/Other:	

TYPES OF BUSINESS:

Consulting-Human Resources
Investment/Financial Consulting
Health and Benefits Management
Human Capital Consulting
Outsourced Human Resources Services (BPO)
Investment Management
Retirement Plan Administration
Merger/Acquisition Consulting

BRANDS/DIVISIONS/AFFILIATES:

Mercer Sentinel
Mercer Retirement Solutions
ePRISM
Marsh & McLennan Companies Inc
Global HR Monitor

CONTACTS: *Note: Officers with more than one job title may be intentionally listed here more than once.*

M. Michele Burns, CEO
Terry Thompson, COO
Bob Van Pelt, CFO
Norbert Englert, Chief Human Resources Officer
Caroline Cheng, General Counsel
Tom Elliott, Pres., Health & Benefits
Phil de Cristo, Pres., Investment Mgmt.
Jeff Miller, Pres., Outsourcing
Simon O'Regan, Pres., Retirement, Risk & Finance Consulting
M. Michele Burns, Chmn.
David Anderson, Managing Dir.-Australia & New Zealand

Phone: 212-345-7000 **Fax:** 212-345-7414
Toll-Free:
Address: 1166 Ave. of the Americas, New York, NY 10036 US

GROWTH PLANS/SPECIAL FEATURES:

Mercer, Inc., a subsidiary of Marsh & McLennan Companies, Inc., offers a broad range of human resource advice and solutions in 40 countries. The firm has eight lines of business: Consulting; Health and Benefits; Human Capital; Surveys and Products; Mergers/Acquisitions; Investment Management; Workforce Communication; and Outsourcing. The Consulting segment handles retirement, risk, financial and investment issues; programs include Mercer Retirement Solutions and Mercer Sentinel. The Health and Benefits segment offers advice/solutions for health care strategy and funding; pharmacy; and disease and absentee management. The Human Capital business analyzes clients' compensation and performance management systems, including executive and broad-based employee compensation programs, and offers additional compensation administration services. The Surveys and Products division offers human resources tools like ePRISM and Global HR Monitor. The Mergers/Acquisitions unit helps clients through each step of every type of business reorganization and transformation. Mercer's Investment Management team offers its services in the U.S., Europe, Australia and Canada. The Workforce Communication division helps businesses reorganize at every operating level (e.g. benefit packages, mergers/acquisitions, employee retention, executive responsibility, etc.). The Outsourcing segment provides outsourced human resources administration, technology and business process solutions. The majority of the firm's clients are Fortune 1,000 and FTSE 100 companies.

The company offers benefits including life, disability, medical, dental and vision insurance; paid time off; tuition reimbursement; employee discounts; a stock purchase plan; and retirement savings plans.

FINANCIALS: **Sales and profits are in thousands of dollars—add 000 to get the full amount. 2010 Note: Financial information for 2010 was not available for all companies at press time.**

2010 Sales: $3,478,000 — 2010 Profits: $
2009 Sales: $3,327,000 — 2009 Profits: $
2008 Sales: $3,642,000 — 2008 Profits: $
2007 Sales: $3,368,000 — 2007 Profits: $
2006 Sales: $3,021,000 — 2006 Profits: $

U.S. Stock Ticker: Subsidiary
Int'l Ticker:
Int'l Exchange:
Employees: 20,000 Fiscal Year Ends: 12/31
Parent Company: MARSH & MCLENNAN COMPANIES INC

SALARIES/BENEFITS:

Pension Plan: ESOP Stock Plan: Profit Sharing: Top Exec. Salary: $ Bonus: $
Savings Plan: Y Stock Purch. Plan: Y Second Exec. Salary: $ Bonus: $

OTHER THOUGHTS:

Apparent Women Officers or Directors: 3
Hot Spot for Advancement for Women/Minorities: Y

LOCATIONS: ("Y" = Yes)

West:	Southwest:	Midwest:	Southeast:	Northeast:	International:
Y	Y	Y	Y	Y	Y

METHODIST HEALTH CARE SYSTEM

www.methodisthealth.com

Industry Group Code: 622110

Management:		**Sales/Marketing:**		**Liberal Arts:**		**Information Sys.:**		**Professionals:**		**Tech./Scientific:**	
Mgmt. Trainees:	Y	Marketing Pros.:		Gen. Writing/Editing:	Y	Info. Mgmt.:	Y	Finance/Acct.:	Y	Engineers, Elec.:	
Experienced Mgmt.:	Y	Retail Sales:		Tech. Writing:	Y	Software Dev.:	Y	Law:	Y	Engineers, Other:	
Int'l Business:		Comm./Industrial:		Graphic Arts/Photog.:	Y	Hardware Dev.:		HR/Other:	Y	Health/Lab:	Y
MBA Grads:	Y	Sales Trainees:		Music:		Consulting/Other:		Training:	Y	Science/Research:	
		Advertising Pros.:	Y	Broadcasting:				Health Care:	Y	Petroleum/Chem.:	
				Other:	Y			Consulting:		Math/Other:	

TYPES OF BUSINESS:

Hospitals

BRANDS/DIVISIONS/AFFILIATES:

Methodist Hospital (The)
Methodist Sugar Land Hospital
Methodist Willowbrook Hospital
San Jacinto Methodist Hospital
Weill Medical College of Cornell University
Baylor College of Medicine
Methodist Hospital Physician Organization
Methodist International

CONTACTS: *Note: Officers with more than one job title may be intentionally listed here more than once.*

Ronald G. Girotto, CEO
Ronald G. Girotto, Pres.
Mauro Ferrari, Pres./CEO-Methodist Hospital Research Institute
Richard J. Robbins, Dir.-Medicine Dept.
Miguel Quinones, Dir.-Cardiology Dept.
Alan Lumsden, Dir.-Cardiovascular Surgery Dept.
Ewing Werlein, Jr., Chmn.
Valter Aleixo, Mgr.-Oper., Methodist Int'l

Phone: 713-790-3311	**Fax:**
Toll-Free:	
Address: 6565 Fannin St., Houston, TX 77030 US	

GROWTH PLANS/SPECIAL FEATURES:

Methodist Health Care System, operating as The Methodist Hospital, is a not-for-profit health care organization that owns and operates several hospitals located in Houston, Texas. Its hospitals include The Methodist Hospital, Methodist Sugar Land Hospital, Methodist Willowbrook Hospital and San Jacinto Methodist Hospital. Some of The Methodist Hospital's areas of focus include breast care, heart care, neuroscience, orthopedics and oncology. The Methodist Hospital location is an adult teaching hospital affiliated with Weill Medical College of Cornell University. It also maintains joint programs with Baylor College of Medicine. The Methodist Sugar Land Hospital serves the Fort Bend and surrounding communities, providing such medical services as inpatient and outpatient medical care; inpatient and outpatient surgery; cancer treatment services; emergency care; and diagnostic and therapeutic medical imaging. The Methodist Willowbrook Hospital consists of a 139,000-square-foot professional building and a 173,000-square-foot hospital with inpatient and outpatient treatment areas. Services offered by the hospital include a diagnostic center, surgery center, a birthing center, a pharmacy, a laboratory, a blood bank, wellness services, pastoral services and an education and conference center. Located in Baytown, The San Jacinto Methodist Hospital is one of the only not-for-profit church-affiliated hospitals in the area. Methodist Health Care System conducts translational and clinical research through the Methodist Hospital Research Institute. The organization also manages the Methodist Hospital Physician Organization, which focuses on engaging physicians in an academic environment while maintaining clinical practice autonomy; and Methodist International, which offers international patient services, administrative healthcare consulting and health professional services through international partnerships.

FINANCIALS: **Sales and profits are in thousands of dollars—add 000 to get the full amount. 2010 Note: Financial information for 2010 was not available for all companies at press time.**

2010 Sales: $366,691	2010 Profits: $9,494	**U.S. Stock Ticker: Private**
2009 Sales: $345,767	2009 Profits: $64,133	**Int'l Ticker:**
2008 Sales: $	2008 Profits: $	Int'l Exchange:
2007 Sales: $	2007 Profits: $	Employees: 13,392 Fiscal Year Ends:
2006 Sales: $	2006 Profits: $	Parent Company:

SALARIES/BENEFITS:

Pension Plan:	ESOP Stock Plan:	Profit Sharing:	Top Exec. Salary: $	Bonus: $
Savings Plan:	Stock Purch. Plan: Y		Second Exec. Salary: $	Bonus: $

OTHER THOUGHTS:

Apparent Women Officers or Directors: 5
Hot Spot for Advancement for Women/Minorities: Y

LOCATIONS: ("Y" = Yes)

West:	Southwest:	Midwest:	Southeast:	Northeast:	International:
Y	Y				

METLIFE INC

www.metlife.com

Industry Group Code: 524113

Management:		**Sales/Marketing:**		**Liberal Arts:**		**Information Sys.:**		**Professionals:**		**Tech./Scientific:**	
Mgmt. Trainees:	Y	Marketing Pros.:	Y	Gen. Writing/Editing:	Y	Info. Mgmt.:	Y	Finance/Acct.:	Y	Engineers, Elec.:	
Experienced Mgmt.:	Y	Retail Sales:		Tech. Writing:	Y	Software Dev.:	Y	Law:	Y	Engineers, Other:	
Int'l Business:	Y	Comm./Industrial:	Y	Graphic Arts/Photog.:	Y	Hardware Dev.:		HR/Other:	Y	Health/Lab:	
MBA Grads:	Y	Sales Trainees:	Y	Music:		Consulting/Other:		Training:	Y	Science/Research:	
		Advertising Pros.:	Y	Broadcasting:				Health Care:	Y	Petroleum/Chem.:	
				Other:	Y			Consulting:		Math/Other:	Y

TYPES OF BUSINESS:

Insurance
Banking
Investment Products
Mutual Funds
Life Insurance
Property & Casualty Insurance
Auto Insurance

BRANDS/DIVISIONS/AFFILIATES:

MetLife Bank
Simple Solutions Variable Annuity
Metropolitan Property and Casualty Insurance Co
American Life Insurance Company
Delaware American Life Insurance Company

CONTACTS: *Note: Officers with more than one job title may be intentionally listed here more than once.*

Steven A. Kandarian, CEO
Steven A. Kandarian, Pres.
William J. Wheeler, CFO/Exec. VP
Frans Hijkoop, Exec. VP-Human Resources
Martin Lippert, Exec. VP-Global Tech.
Exec. VP-Tech. & Oper.
Nicholas D. Latrenta, General Counsel
Maria R. Morris, Exec. VP-Global Oper. & Integration
John McCallion, VP/Head-Investor Rel.
Marlene Debel, Treas./Sr. VP
Steven J. Goulart, Chief Investment Officer/Exec. VP
William J. Mullaney, Pres., U.S.
Gwenn L. Carr, Exec. VP
William J. Mullaney, Pres., U.S. Bus.
C. Robert Henrikson, Chmn.
William J. Toppeta, Pres., Int'l

Phone: 212-578-2211 **Fax:** 212-578-3320
Toll-Free: 800-638-5433
Address: 200 Park Ave., New York, NY 10166-0188 US

GROWTH PLANS/SPECIAL FEATURES:

MetLife, Inc. is a provider of insurance and other financial services with operations throughout the U.S. and regions of Latin America, Europe and Asia Pacific. Through its domestic and international subsidiaries and affiliates, the company offers life insurance; annuities; automobile and homeowners insurance; retail banking; and other financial services to individuals, as well as group insurance and retirement and savings products and services to corporations and other institutions. The firm operates in two main segments: U.S. and International. The U.S. segment, which serves over 60,000 group customers, combines the operations of four units: insurance products, which cover group life, individual life and non-medical health insurance products; retirement products, including individual and institutional annuity products; corporate benefit funding, which provides pension closeouts, structured settlements and other benefit funding solutions; and the auto and home group, which operates through the Metropolitan Property and Casualty Insurance Co. subsidiary and offers personal lines property and casualty insurance including renters', homeowners', car and recreational vehicle insurance. The international segment provides accident and health insurance; credit insurance; annuities; and savings and retirement products to customers in 64 countries in Latin America, Europe and Asia Pacific. In addition, the company maintains the banking, corporate and other segment, which consists primarily of excess capital not allocated to the business segments; and various start-up entities, including MetLife Bank, National Association. In November 2010, MetLife acquired American Life Insurance Company from ALICO Holdings LLC, a subsidiary of American International Group, Inc. Also in November 2010, the firm acquired Delaware American Life Insurance Company from AIG. The company paid roughly $16.4 billion combined for these companies.

Employees are offered medical and dental insurance; disability coverage; life insurance; flexible spending accounts; prepaid legal services; wellness and fitness programs; adoption assistance; a pension plan; and a 401(k).

FINANCIALS: **Sales and profits are in thousands of dollars—add 000 to get the full amount. 2010 Note: Financial information for 2010 was not available for all companies at press time.**

2010 Sales: $52,717,000 — 2010 Profits: $2,786,000
2009 Sales: $41,057,000 — 2009 Profits: $-2,278,000
2008 Sales: $50,982,000 — 2008 Profits: $3,278,000
2007 Sales: $47,152,000 — 2007 Profits: $4,465,000
2006 Sales: $48,254,000 — 2006 Profits: $6,293,000

U.S. Stock Ticker: MET
Int'l Ticker:
Int'l Exchange:
Employees: 66,000 Fiscal Year Ends: 12/31
Parent Company:

SALARIES/BENEFITS:

Pension Plan: Y ESOP Stock Plan: Profit Sharing: Top Exec. Salary: $1,000,000 Bonus: $4,500,000
Savings Plan: Y Stock Purch. Plan: Second Exec. Salary: $646,667 Bonus: $1,700,000

OTHER THOUGHTS:

Apparent Women Officers or Directors: 7
Hot Spot for Advancement for Women/Minorities: Y

LOCATIONS: ("Y" = Yes)

West:	Southwest:	Midwest:	Southeast:	Northeast:	International:
Y	Y	Y	Y	Y	Y

METROPCS COMMUNICATIONS INC

www.metropcs.com

Industry Group Code: 5172

Management:		Sales/Marketing:		Liberal Arts:		Information Sys.:		Professionals:		Tech./Scientific:	
Mgmt. Trainees:	Y	Marketing Pros.:	Y	Gen. Writing/Editing:	Y	Info. Mgmt.:	Y	Finance/Acct.:	Y	Engineers, Elec.:	Y
Experienced Mgmt.:	Y	Retail Sales:		Tech. Writing:		Software Dev.:	Y	Law:	Y	Engineers, Other:	
Int'l Business:		Comm./Industrial:	Y	Graphic Arts/Photog.:	Y	Hardware Dev.:		HR/Other:	Y	Health/Lab:	
MBA Grads:	Y	Sales Trainees:	Y	Music:		Consulting/Other:		Training:	Y	Science/Research:	
		Advertising Pros.:	Y	Broadcasting:				Health Care:		Petroleum/Chem.:	
				Other:	Y			Consulting:		Math/Other:	

TYPES OF BUSINESS:

Mobile Phone Service

BRANDS/DIVISIONS/AFFILIATES:

TravelTalk
Binary Runtime Environment for Wireless (BREW)
Samsung Finesse.
GroupLINE
MetroPCS

CONTACTS:

Note: Officers with more than one job title may be intentionally listed here more than once.

Roger D. Linquist, CEO
Thomas C. Keys, COO
Roger D. Linquist, Pres.
J. Braxton Carter, CFO/Exec. VP
Phillip R. Terry, Sr. VP-Corp. Mktg.
Tom Currier, VP-Human Resources
John J. Olsen, CIO/Sr. VP
Malcom M. Lorang, CTO/Sr. VP
Ed Chao, Sr. VP-Eng. & Network Oper.
Mark A. Stachiw, General Counsel/Exec. VP/Corp. Sec.
Greg Pressly, VP-Customer Oper.
Douglas S. Glen, Sr. VP-Corp. Dev.
Jim Mathias, Dir.-Investor Rel.
Keith D. Terreri, VP-Finance/Treas.
Terri Smith, VP-Revenue Assistance & Acct.
Jimmy Sartain, VP-Bus. Analytics
David Walker, VP-Network Oper.
Christine B. Kornegay, Sr. VP/Chief Acct. Officer/Controller
Roger D. Linquist, Chmn.

Phone: 214-570-5800 **Fax:**
Toll-Free: 888-863-8768
Address: 2250 Lakeside Blvd., Richardson, TX 75082-4304 US

GROWTH PLANS/SPECIAL FEATURES:

MetroPCS Communications, Inc. is a wireless broadband personal communication services provider. It offers pre-paid, no long-term contract, flat rate, unlimited usage basis in selected major metropolitan markets in the U.S. These markets include San Francisco; Miami; Los Angeles; Atlanta; New York; Philadelphia; Sacramento; Tampa/Sarasota; Jacksonville/Orlando; Dallas/Ft. Worth; Detroit; Las Vegas; and Boston. The company provides services to more than 8.1 million customers; it has access to wireless coverage for over 11,000 U.S. cities, totaling approximately 142 million people. Through roaming agreements, MetroPCS offers services (through the Metro USA brand) to an area that includes over 280 million people. The firm's service allows its customers to place unlimited local calls from within the service area and to receive unlimited calls from any area while in the local service areas under a flat monthly rate plan. For additional fees, MetroPCS provides unlimited long distance calls from within the service area, unlimited voicemail, caller ID, call waiting, text messaging, mobile Internet browsing, ringtones, ring back tones, downloads, games, content applications and international long distance/text messaging. The firm offers data services, such as ringtones, games and content applications, through its Binary Runtime Environment for Wireless (BREW) platform. The company offers TravelTalk, a service option that allows customers to use their MetroPCS service when traveling to major metropolitan areas within the U.S.; there is no extra charge when traveling to other MetroPCS markets. In April 2010, MetroPCS began offering direct voice mail-to-text service, which converts voice mail content to text form. In September 2010, the firm introduced commercial 4G LTE services, the first company to do so in the U.S.

MetroPCS offers employees life, AD&D, disability, medical, dental and vision insurance; a 401(k); an employee phone plan; and flexible spending accounts.

FINANCIALS:

Sales and profits are in thousands of dollars—add 000 to get the full amount. 2010 Note: Financial information for 2010 was not available for all companies at press time.

Sales	Profits
2010 Sales: $4,069,353	2010 Profits: $193,415
2009 Sales: $3,840,515	2009 Profits: $176,844
2008 Sales: $2,751,516	2008 Profits: $149,438
2007 Sales: $2,235,734	2007 Profits: $100,403
2006 Sales: $1,546,863	2006 Profits: $53,806

U.S. Stock Ticker: PCS
Int'l Ticker:
Int'l Exchange:
Employees: 3,600 Fiscal Year Ends: 12/31
Parent Company:

SALARIES/BENEFITS:

Pension Plan:	ESOP Stock Plan:	Profit Sharing:	Top Exec. Salary: $804,470	Bonus: $2,119,400
Savings Plan: Y	Stock Purch. Plan:		Second Exec. Salary: $513,711	Bonus: $821,700

OTHER THOUGHTS:

Apparent Women Officers or Directors: 1
Hot Spot for Advancement for Women/Minorities:

LOCATIONS: ("Y" = Yes)

West:	Southwest:	Midwest:	Southeast:	Northeast:	International:
Y	Y	Y	Y	Y	

MICROCHIP TECHNOLOGY INC

www.microchip.com

Industry Group Code: 33441

Management:		Sales/Marketing:		Liberal Arts:		Information Sys.:		Professionals:		Tech./Scientific:	
Mgmt. Trainees:	Y	Marketing Pros.:	Y	Gen. Writing/Editing:		Info. Mgmt.:	Y	Finance/Acct.:	Y	Engineers, Elec.:	Y
Experienced Mgmt.:	Y	Retail Sales:		Tech. Writing:	Y	Software Dev.:	Y	Law:	Y	Engineers, Other:	
Int'l Business:	Y	Comm./Industrial:	Y	Graphic Arts/Photog.:	Y	Hardware Dev.:	Y	HR/Other:	Y	Health/Lab:	
MBA Grads:	Y	Sales Trainees:		Music:		Consulting/Other:		Training:	Y	Science/Research:	Y
		Advertising Pros.:	Y	Broadcasting:				Health Care:		Petroleum/Chem.:	
				Other:				Consulting:		Math/Other:	

TYPES OF BUSINESS:

Semiconductors-Specialized
Microcontrollers
Battery Management & Interface Devices
Development Tools
Memory Products

BRANDS/DIVISIONS/AFFILIATES:

PIC
dsPIC
Digital Signal Controllers
EEPROM
EPROM
Silicon Storage Technology Inc

CONTACTS: *Note: Officers with more than one job title may be intentionally listed here more than once.*

Steve Sanghi, CEO
Ganesh Moorthy, COO/Exec. VP
Steve Sanghi, Pres.
J. Eric Bjornholt, CFO/VP
Mitchell R. Little, VP-Worldwide Sales & Applications
Lauren A. Carr, VP-Human Resources
Robert H. Owen, VP-Info. Svcs.
Stephen V. Drehobl, VP-Tech, Security & Microcontroller Div.
Randall L. Drwinga, VP-Memory Prod. Div.
Kenneth N. Pye, VP-Worldwide Applications Eng.
David S. Lambert, VP-Fab Oper.
Kimberly van Herk, Corp. Sec.
Gordon W. Parnell, VP-Bus. Dev.
Gordon W. Parnell, VP-Investor Rel.
William Yang, VP-Pacific Rim Finance
Joseph R. Krawczyk, VP-Asia Sales
Mitchel Obolsky, VP-Advanced Microcontroller Architecture Div.
Dan L. Termer, VP-Vertical Markets Group
Steve Sanghi, Chmn.
Gary P. Marsh, VP-European Sales

Phone: 480-792-7200	**Fax:** 480-899-9210
Toll-Free:	
Address: 2355 W. Chandler Blvd., Chandler, AZ 85224-6199 US	

GROWTH PLANS/SPECIAL FEATURES:

Microchip Technology, Inc. develops and manufactures specialized semiconductor products used for a wide variety of embedded control applications. In addition, the company offers a broad spectrum of high-performance linear, mixed-signal, power management, thermal management, battery management and interface devices. The firm focuses on embedded control functions, including microcontrollers; development tools; analog and interface products; and memory products. Microchip offers a broad family of microcontroller products featuring the proprietary architecture PIC with a variety of memory technology configurations, low voltage and power and small footprint. The company targets the 8-bit , 16-bit and 32-bit microcontroller markets. Additionally, the scalable product architecture allows it to target both the entry-level of the 32-bit microcontroller markets, as well as the 4-bit microcontroller marketplace. The firm is able to incorporate non-volatile memory, such as Flash, EEPROM and EPROM Memory, into the microcontroller and offers reprogrammable microcontroller products. The development tools enable system designers to program a PIC microcontroller and dsPIC Digital Signal Controllers for specific applications. Microchip's family of development tools operate in the standard Windows environment on standard PC hardware. These tools range from entry-level systems, which include an assembler and programmer or in-circuit debugging hardware, to fully configured systems that provide in-circuit emulation hardware. Analog and interface products consist of several families with over 600 power management, linear, mixed-signal, thermal management and interface products. Memory products consists primarily of serial electrically erasable programmable read only memory, referred to as Serial EEPROMs. Serial EEPROM products are used for non-volatile program and data storage systems where such data must be either modified frequently or retained for long periods. In April 2010, the company acquired Silicon Storage Technology, Inc., a developer of memory and other similar products.

FINANCIALS: **Sales and profits are in thousands of dollars—add 000 to get the full amount. 2010 Note: Financial information for 2010 was not available for all companies at press time.**

2010 Sales: $947,729 | 2010 Profits: $217,005
2009 Sales: $903,297 | 2009 Profits: $248,820
2008 Sales: $1,035,737 | 2008 Profits: $297,748
2007 Sales: $1,039,671 | 2007 Profits: $357,029
2006 Sales: $927,893 | 2006 Profits: $242,369

U.S. Stock Ticker: MCHP
Int'l Ticker:
Int'l Exchange:
Employees: 5,418 Fiscal Year Ends: 3/31
Parent Company:

SALARIES/BENEFITS:

Pension Plan: | ESOP Stock Plan: | Profit Sharing: Y | Top Exec. Salary: $505,762 | Bonus: $1,378,720
Savings Plan: Y | Stock Purch. Plan: Y | | Second Exec. Salary: $242,483 | Bonus: $204,922

OTHER THOUGHTS:

Apparent Women Officers or Directors: 3
Hot Spot for Advancement for Women/Minorities: Y

LOCATIONS: ("Y" = Yes)

West:	Southwest:	Midwest:	Southeast:	Northeast:	International:
Y	Y	Y	Y	Y	Y

MICRON TECHNOLOGY INC

www.micron.com

Industry Group Code: 33441

Management:		Sales/Marketing:		Liberal Arts:		Information Sys.:		Professionals:		Tech./Scientific:	
Mgmt. Trainees:	Y	Marketing Pros.:	Y	Gen. Writing/Editing:		Info. Mgmt.:	Y	Finance/Acct.:	Y	Engineers, Elec.:	Y
Experienced Mgmt.:	Y	Retail Sales:		Tech. Writing:	Y	Software Dev.:	Y	Law:	Y	Engineers, Other:	
Int'l Business:	Y	Comm./Industrial:	Y	Graphic Arts/Photog.:	Y	Hardware Dev.:	Y	HR/Other:	Y	Health/Lab:	
MBA Grads:	Y	Sales Trainees:		Music:		Consulting/Other:		Training:	Y	Science/Research:	Y
		Advertising Pros.:	Y	Broadcasting:				Health Care:		Petroleum/Chem.:	
				Other:				Consulting:		Math/Other:	

TYPES OF BUSINESS:

Components-Semiconductor Memory
PCs & Peripherals
Flash Memory Devices
CMOS Image Sensors
FLCOS Displays
Photovoltaic Solar Panels

BRANDS/DIVISIONS/AFFILIATES:

Lexar Media, Inc.
Crucial
Aptina Imaging Corporation
RealSSD
Numonyx BV

CONTACTS: *Note: Officers with more than one job title may be intentionally listed here more than once.*

Steven R. Appleton, CEO
D. Mark Durcan, COO
D. Mark Durcan, Pres.
Ronald C. Foster, CFO/VP-Finance
Mark W. Adams, VP-Worldwide Sales
Patrick T. Otte, VP-Human Resources
Scott J. DeBoer, VP-Process R&D
James E. Mahoney, VP-Info. Systems
Roderic W. Lewis, General Counsel/VP-Legal Affairs/Corp. Sec.
Brian J. Shields, VP-Worldwide Oper.
Michael W. Sadler, VP-Corp. Dev.
Kipp A. Bedard, VP-Investor Rel.
Philippe Morali, Treas.
John F. Schreck, VP-DRAM Dev.
Brian M. Shirley, VP-DRAM Solutions
Mario Licciardello, VP-Wireless Solutions
Frankie F. Roohparvar, VP-NAND Dev.
Steven R. Appleton, Chmn.
Steven L. Thorsen, Jr., Chief Procurement Officer/VP

Phone: 208-368-4000	**Fax:** 208-368-4435
Toll-Free:	
Address: 8000 S. Federal Way, Boise, ID 83707-0006 US	

GROWTH PLANS/SPECIAL FEATURES:

Micron Technology, Inc. designs, develops, manufactures and markets semiconductor memory products and personal computer systems. Its products are used in a range of electronic devices, including personal computers, workstations, servers, cell phones, digital cameras and other consumer and industrial products. Micron has three segments: Memory, producing dynamic random access memory (DRAM) and NAND flash memory, accounting for 89% of 2010 sales; Numonyx, acquired in May 2010 and representing 7% of 2010 sales; and all other, which includes various equity interests and joint developments. Micron offers double data rate (DDR), DDR2 and DDR3 DRAM, primarily used for the main system memory in computers; and synchronous DRAM (SDRAM), used in networking devices, servers, consumer electronics, communications equipment and computer peripherals. NAND products are re-writable, non-volatile semiconductor devices used in mobile devices such as digital cameras, MP3 players, USB Flash Drives and cellular phones. The firm also offers RealSSD solid-state drives for applications that require lower power consumption and higher reliability standards than traditional hard drives. Numonyx's chief products are NOR flash memory and Phase Change Memory (PCM) devices, which offer speed and other enhancements over earlier generations of memory drives. The all other segment includes its interest in Aptina Imaging Corp., which manufactures CMOS image sensors, as well as various development projects for FLCOS microdisplays and solar products. The company's Lexar Media, Inc. subsidiary markets digital media and flash-based products to retail and original equipment manufacturing markets, while the Crucial brand focuses on web-based direct sales. The firm's manufacturing facilities are located in the U.S., Italy, Japan, Puerto Rico, Singapore and China. In January 2010, the company established a joint venture with Origin Energy Ltd. to develop advanced photovoltaic technology. In May 2010, it acquired Numonyx BV for $1.2 billion.

Employees are offered medical, dental, vision and life insurance; short- and long-term disability coverage, business travel accident coverage; and educational assistance.

FINANCIALS: **Sales and profits are in thousands of dollars—add 000 to get the full amount. 2010 Note: Financial information for 2010 was not available for all companies at press time.**

2010 Sales: $8,482,000	2010 Profits: $1,850,000	**U.S. Stock Ticker: MU**
2009 Sales: $4,803,000	2009 Profits: $-1,882,000	**Int'l Ticker:**
2008 Sales: $5,841,000	2008 Profits: $-1,655,000	Int'l Exchange:
2007 Sales: $5,688,000	2007 Profits: $-320,000	Employees: 25,900 Fiscal Year Ends: 8/31
2006 Sales: $5,272,000	2006 Profits: $408,000	Parent Company:

SALARIES/BENEFITS:

Pension Plan:	ESOP Stock Plan:	Profit Sharing:	Top Exec. Salary: $806,405	Bonus: $2,090,000
Savings Plan: Y	Stock Purch. Plan:		Second Exec. Salary: $507,692	Bonus: $1,068,000

OTHER THOUGHTS:

Apparent Women Officers or Directors:
Hot Spot for Advancement for Women/Minorities:

LOCATIONS: ("Y" = Yes)

West:	Southwest:	Midwest:	Southeast:	Northeast:	International:
Y				Y	Y

MICROSOFT CORP

www.microsoft.com

Industry Group Code: 511210I

Management:		Sales/Marketing:		Liberal Arts:		Information Sys.:		Professionals:		Tech./Scientific:	
Mgmt. Trainees:	Y	Marketing Pros.:	Y	Gen. Writing/Editing:	Y	Info. Mgmt.:	Y	Finance/Acct.:	Y	Engineers, Elec.:	Y
Experienced Mgmt.:	Y	Retail Sales:		Tech. Writing:	Y	Software Dev.:	Y	Law:	Y	Engineers, Other:	
Int'l Business:	Y	Comm./Industrial:	Y	Graphic Arts/Photog.:	Y	Hardware Dev.:		HR/Other:	Y	Health/Lab:	
MBA Grads:	Y	Sales Trainees:		Music:	Y	Consulting/Other:	Y	Training:	Y	Science/Research:	Y
		Advertising Pros.:	Y	Broadcasting:				Health Care:		Petroleum/Chem.:	
				Other:	Y			Consulting:		Math/Other:	Y

TYPES OF BUSINESS:

Computer Software
Personal Communications Services
Video Games Systems
Mobile Communications
Voice-Enabled Mobile Search
Internet Search Engine
E-Mail Services
Instant Messaging

BRANDS/DIVISIONS/AFFILIATES:

Xbox 360
Microsoft Windows 7
Microsoft Office
Xbox Kinect
Microsoft Windows Phone 7
MSN
Microsoft Windows XP
Microsoft Dynamics

CONTACTS: *Note: Officers with more than one job title may be intentionally listed here more than once.*

Steve Ballmer, CEO
B. Kevin Turner, COO
Peter Klein, CFO
Mich Mathews, Sr. VP-Central Mktg. Group
Lisa Brummel, Sr. VP-Human Resources
Craig Mundie, Chief Research Officer
Eric Rudder, Sr. VP-Tech. Strategy
Brad Smith, General Counsel/Sr. VP-Legal/Sec.
Craig Mundie, Chief Strategy Officer
Qi Lu, Pres., Online Svcs. Div.
Steven Sinofsky, Pres., Windows & Windows Live Div.
Kurt DelBane, Pres., Microsoft Office Div.
Andrew Lees, Pres., Mobile Comm. Bus.
Don A. Mattrick, Pres., Interactive Entertainment Bus.
Bill Gates, Chmn.
Jean-Philippe Courtois, Pres., Microsoft Int'l

Phone: 425-882-8080 **Fax:**
Toll-Free: 800-642-7676
Address: 1 Microsoft Way, Redmond, WA 98052-7329 US

GROWTH PLANS/SPECIAL FEATURES:

Microsoft Corp. develops, manufactures and supports software for a wide range of computing devices. The company operates in five segments: Windows and Windows Live; Server and Tools; Online Services Business; Microsoft Business Division; and Entertainment and Devices Division. The Windows and Windows Live segment provides the premium and standard-edition Windows operating systems; maintains the Windows Live service; and develops the Internet Explorer browser. The company's latest operating system is Windows 7. Other products in this segment include Windows Vista, Windows XP and Tablet PC Edition. The Server and Tools segment licenses products, applications, tools, content and services related to Windows server products and operating systems. The division offers the Windows Server operating system, Microsoft SQL Server, Visual Studio and System Center products, among others. The Online Services Business segment consists of an online advertising platform and provides personal services including Bing; Microsoft adCenter; MSN; and Atlas online tools for advertisers and publishers. The Microsoft Business Division offers the Microsoft Office and Office Web Apps systems, as well as Microsoft Dynamics business services. The Entertainment and Devices Division is responsible for developing, producing and marketing Xbox 360 video game systems, including consoles and accessories; Xbox LIVE; the Zune digital music and entertainment platform; PC software games; the Mediaroom Internet television software; and Windows Automotive. In October 2010, the company acquired Canesta, Inc., a developer of 3D sensing technologies. In November 2010, the company launched the Xbox Kinect, an advanced camera-based accessory for the Xbox 360; and Windows Phone 7, a new operating system for smartphone devices. In May 2011, the company agreed to acquire Skype for $8.5 billion.

Microsoft offers its employees health, dental and vision coverage; on-site health screenings; health club memberships; cigarette smoking cessation programs; adoption assistance; childcare service discounts; autism behavioral therapy; a 401(k) plan; an employee stock purchase plan; charitable gift matching; tuition assistance; and online training programs.

FINANCIALS: **Sales and profits are in thousands of dollars—add 000 to get the full amount. 2010 Note: Financial information for 2010 was not available for all companies at press time.**

2010 Sales: $62,484,000 | 2010 Profits: $24,098,000
2009 Sales: $58,437,000 | 2009 Profits: $14,569,000
2008 Sales: $60,420,000 | 2008 Profits: $17,681,000
2007 Sales: $51,122,000 | 2007 Profits: $14,065,000
2006 Sales: $44,282,000 | 2006 Profits: $12,599,000

U.S. Stock Ticker: MSFT
Int'l Ticker:
Int'l Exchange:
Employees: 89,000 Fiscal Year Ends: 6/30
Parent Company:

SALARIES/BENEFITS:

Pension Plan: | ESOP Stock Plan: | Profit Sharing: | Top Exec. Salary: $670,000 | Bonus: $670,000
Savings Plan: Y | Stock Purch. Plan: Y | | Second Exec. Salary: $645,000 | Bonus: $1,960,000

OTHER THOUGHTS:

Apparent Women Officers or Directors: 4
Hot Spot for Advancement for Women/Minorities: Y

LOCATIONS: ("Y" = Yes)

West:	Southwest:	Midwest:	Southeast:	Northeast:	International:
Y	Y	Y	Y	Y	Y

Sales, profits and employees may be estimates. Financial information, benefits and other data can change quickly and may vary from those stated here.

MIDAMERICAN ENERGY HOLDINGS CO

www.midamerican.com

Industry Group Code: 221

Management:		Sales/Marketing:		Liberal Arts:		Information Sys.:		Professionals:		Tech./Scientific:	
Mgmt. Trainees:	Y	Marketing Pros.:	Y	Gen. Writing/Editing:	Y	Info. Mgmt.:	Y	Finance/Acct.:	Y	Engineers, Elec.:	Y
Experienced Mgmt.:	Y	Retail Sales:		Tech. Writing:	Y	Software Dev.:	Y	Law:	Y	Engineers, Other:	Y
Int'l Business:	Y	Comm./Industrial:	Y	Graphic Arts/Photog.:	Y	Hardware Dev.:		HR/Other:	Y	Health/Lab:	
MBA Grads:	Y	Sales Trainees:		Music:		Consulting/Other:		Training:	Y	Science/Research:	
		Advertising Pros.:		Broadcasting:				Health Care:		Petroleum/Chem.:	Y
				Other:				Consulting:		Math/Other:	

TYPES OF BUSINESS:

Utilities-Electricity & Natural Gas
Pipelines
Wind Generation
Hydroelectric Generation
Thermal Generation
Real Estate Brokerage

BRANDS/DIVISIONS/AFFILIATES:

PacifiCorp
BYD COMPANY LIMITED
Northern Natural Gas Company
Kern River Gas Transmission Company
CE Electric UK
CalEnergy Generation
HomeServices of America Inc
Berkshire Hathaway Inc

CONTACTS: *Note: Officers with more than one job title may be intentionally listed here more than once.*

Gregory E. Abel, CEO
Gregory E. Abel, Pres.
Patrick J. Goodman, CFO/Sr. VP
Maureen E. Sammon, Chief Admin. Officer/Sr. VP
Douglas L. Anderson, General Counsel/Sr. VP/Sec.
David L. Sokol, Chmn.

Phone: 515-242-4300 **Fax:**
Toll-Free:
Address: 666 Grand Ave., Ste. 500, Des Moines, IA 50309-2580 US

GROWTH PLANS/SPECIAL FEATURES:

MidAmerican Energy Holdings Co. (MEHC), with over $45 billion in assets, generates, transmits, stores, distributes and supplies energy through its subsidiaries to over 6.9 million customers. The company has six primary subsidiaries. PacifiCorp serves more than 1.7 million customers, operating in three business units: Pacific Power, delivering electricity in Oregon, Washington and California; Rocky Mountain Power, delivery electricity in Wyoming, Utah and Idaho; and PacifiCorp Energy, which constitutes the company's electric generation, energy trading and coal mining operations. MidAmerican Energy Company generates, transmits and sells electricity to 725,000 customers and supplies natural gas to an additional 707,000 customers. It operates in Iowa, Illinois, Nebraska and South Dakota. Northern Natural Gas Company owns largest 15,000-mile interstate natural gas pipeline system extending from Texas to the upper Midwest. Kern River Gas Transmission Company owns 1,680 miles of interstate pipeline and delivers more than 1.9 billion cubic feet of natural gas per day to Nevada, Utah and California. CE Electric U.K., a holding company for Northern Electric and Yorkshire Electric, distributes electricity to 3.8 million customers in the U.K. Through another subsidiary, Integrated Utility Services, CE Electric provides strategic and technical engineering design services. CalEnergy Generation is an international leader in energy production and development from diversified fuel sources, including geothermal, natural gas and hydroelectric. MEHC also owns Homeservices of America, Inc., a leading U.S. residential real estate brokerage firm. MEHC is one of America's largest operators of wind energy. It has invested billions of dollars in wind farms, particularly in Iowa. The firm also owns about 9.9% of Chinese battery maker BYD Co. MEHC is owned by Berkshire Hathaway, Inc.

The company offers its employees medical, dental, vision and life insurance; a 401 (k) plan; a profit sharing plan; an employee assistance program; flexible spending accounts; tuition reimbursement; and adoption assistance.

FINANCIALS: **Sales and profits are in thousands of dollars—add 000 to get the full amount. 2010 Note: Financial information for 2010 was not available for all companies at press time.**

2010 Sales: $11,100,000 | 2010 Profits: $
2009 Sales: $11,200,000 | 2009 Profits: $
2008 Sales: $12,700,000 | 2008 Profits: $
2007 Sales: $12,376,000 | 2007 Profits: $
2006 Sales: $10,300,700 | 2006 Profits: $916,100

U.S. Stock Ticker: Subsidiary
Int'l Ticker:
Int'l Exchange:
Employees: 15,800 Fiscal Year Ends: 12/31
Parent Company: BERKSHIRE HATHAWAY INC

SALARIES/BENEFITS:

Pension Plan: | ESOP Stock Plan: | Profit Sharing: Y | Top Exec. Salary: $1,000,000 | Bonus: $13,000,000
Savings Plan: Y | Stock Purch. Plan: | Second Exec. Salary: $822,917 | Bonus: $5,000,000

OTHER THOUGHTS:

Apparent Women Officers or Directors: 1
Hot Spot for Advancement for Women/Minorities:

LOCATIONS: ("Y" = Yes)

West:	Southwest:	Midwest:	Southeast:	Northeast:	International:
Y	Y	Y	Y	Y	Y

MILLIPORE CORP

www.millipore.com

Industry Group Code: 3345

Management:		**Sales/Marketing:**		**Liberal Arts:**		**Information Sys.:**		**Professionals:**		**Tech./Scientific:**	
Mgmt. Trainees:	Y	Marketing Pros.:	Y	Gen. Writing/Editing:		Info. Mgmt.:	Y	Finance/Acct.:	Y	Engineers, Elec.:	Y
Experienced Mgmt.:	Y	Retail Sales:		Tech. Writing:	Y	Software Dev.:	Y	Law:	Y	Engineers, Other:	
Int'l Business:	Y	Comm./Industrial:	Y	Graphic Arts/Photog.:	Y	Hardware Dev.:	Y	HR/Other:	Y	Health/Lab:	Y
MBA Grads:	Y	Sales Trainees:		Music:		Consulting/Other:		Training:	Y	Science/Research:	Y
		Advertising Pros.:	Y	Broadcasting:				Health Care:		Petroleum/Chem.:	
				Other:				Consulting:		Math/Other:	Y

TYPES OF BUSINESS:

Biotechnology Instruments
Fluid Analysis, Identification & Purification Equipment
Chromatography Technologies

BRANDS/DIVISIONS/AFFILIATES:

EMD Millipore
Merck KGaA

CONTACTS: *Note: Officers with more than one job title may be intentionally listed here more than once.*

Toni Spinazzola, Head-Human Resources
David Hutchinson, General Counsel
Peter C. Kershaw, Head-Global Oper.
Amanda Turton, Head-Corp. Comm.
Joerg Hornstein, Controller
Jonathan DiVincenzo, Head-Bioscience Bus. Unit
Bernd Reckmann, Head-Chemicals
Jean-Paul Mangeolle, Head-Process Solutions
Klaus Bischoff, Head-Lab Solutions Bus. Unit

Phone: 978-715-4321 **Fax:** 800-645-5439
Toll-Free: 800-645-5476
Address: 290 Concord Rd., Billerica, MA 01821 US

GROWTH PLANS/SPECIAL FEATURES:

Millipore Corp. (known in the U.S. as EMD Millipore) is a multinational bioscience company that provides technologies, tools and services for research, development and production. The company's products and services are based on technologies such as filtration, chromatography, cell culture supplements, antibodies and cell lines. The firm operates in three divisions: bioscience, lab solutions and process solutions. The bioscience division is organized around four specific market segments: biotools for the separation, isolation and purification of biological samples; research reagents such as antibodies, dyes and biochemical reagents; drug discovery reagent for the analysis of drug candidates; and laboratory water purification systems that remove contaminants for critical laboratory analysis. The lab solutions segment offers lab water equipment, laboratory chemicals and consumables. It offers inorganic chemistry products such as reagents of high purity such as salts, acids and caustics; volumetric solutions; buffers; reference materials for instrumental analysis; and products for inorganic trace analysis. Its organic chemistry products include building blocks, reagents and solvents commonly used in organic synthesis. The company's process solutions division offers products utilized by biotechnology and pharmaceutical firms in order to develop and manufacture biopharmaceutical drugs. Millipore Corp. is a division of German pharmaceutical and chemical firm Merck KGaA. In May 2011, the firm opened a new training facility in Shanghai, China.

Millipore offers employees flexible spending accounts, tuition reimbursement, employee assistance programs and adoption assistance.

FINANCIALS: **Sales and profits are in thousands of dollars—add 000 to get the full amount. 2010 Note: Financial information for 2010 was not available for all companies at press time.**

2010 Sales: $2,352,865 — 2010 Profits: $
2009 Sales: $1,654,410 — 2009 Profits: $179,190
2008 Sales: $1,602,138 — 2008 Profits: $145,801
2007 Sales: $1,531,555 — 2007 Profits: $136,472
2006 Sales: $1,255,371 — 2006 Profits: $96,984

U.S. Stock Ticker: Subsidiary
Int'l Ticker:
Int'l Exchange:
Employees: 6,100 Fiscal Year Ends: 12/31
Parent Company: MERCK KGAA

SALARIES/BENEFITS:

Pension Plan: ESOP Stock Plan: Profit Sharing:
Savings Plan: Y Stock Purch. Plan:
Top Exec. Salary: $850,962 Bonus: $655,666
Second Exec. Salary: $375,587 Bonus: $217,096

OTHER THOUGHTS:

Apparent Women Officers or Directors: 2
Hot Spot for Advancement for Women/Minorities: Y

LOCATIONS: ("Y" = Yes)

West:	Southwest:	Midwest:	Southeast:	Northeast:	International:
Y	Y	Y	Y	Y	Y

MOLEX INC

www.molex.com

Industry Group Code: 334119

Management:		Sales/Marketing:		Liberal Arts:		Information Sys.:		Professionals:		Tech./Scientific:	
Mgmt. Trainees:	Y	Marketing Pros.:	Y	Gen. Writing/Editing:		Info. Mgmt.:	Y	Finance/Acct.:	Y	Engineers, Elec.:	Y
Experienced Mgmt.:	Y	Retail Sales:		Tech. Writing:	Y	Software Dev.:	Y	Law:	Y	Engineers, Other:	
Int'l Business:	Y	Comm./Industrial:	Y	Graphic Arts/Photog.:		Hardware Dev.:	Y	HR/Other:	Y	Health/Lab:	
MBA Grads:	Y	Sales Trainees:		Music:		Consulting/Other:		Training:	Y	Science/Research:	
		Advertising Pros.:	Y	Broadcasting:				Health Care:		Petroleum/Chem.:	
				Other:				Consulting:		Math/Other:	

TYPES OF BUSINESS:

Electronic Components
Transportation Products
Commercial Products
Micro Products
Automation & Electrical Products
Integrated Products
Global Sales & Marketing Organization

BRANDS/DIVISIONS/AFFILIATES:

CONTACTS:

Note: Officers with more than one job title may be intentionally listed here more than once.

Martin P. Slark, CEO
Liam McCarthy, COO
Liam McCarthy, Pres.
David D. Johnson, CFO/Exec. VP
Graham C. Brock, Exec. VP/Pres., Global Sales & Mktg. Div.
Ana G. Rodriguez, Sr. VP-Global Human Resources
Gary J. Matula, CIO/Sr. VP-IS
David D. Johnson, Treas.
James E. Fleischhacker, Exec. VP/Pres., Global Commercial Prod. Div.
John H. Krehbiel, Jr., Co-Chmn.
J. Michael Nauman, Exec. VP/Pres., Global Integrated Prod. Div.
Katsumi Hirokawa, Exec. VP/Pres., Global Micro Prod. Div.
Frederick A. Krehbiel, Co-Chmn.

Phone: 630-969-4550 **Fax:** 630-968-8356
Toll-Free: 800-786-6539
Address: 2222 Wellington Ct., Lisle, IL 60532-1682 US

GROWTH PLANS/SPECIAL FEATURES:

Molex, Inc. is a manufacturer of electronic components. It designs, manufactures and sells more than 100,000 products, including terminals, connectors, planar cables, cable assemblies, interconnection systems, backplanes, integrated products and mechanical and electronic switches. The company also provides manufacturing services to integrate specific components into a customer's product. The firm is organized into four divisions: commercial products; micro products; integrated products; and global sales and marketing organization. The commercial products segment specializes in products that cater to multiple markets, especially to those that require high speed and quality parts, and components for engine and cockpit applications in the transportation industry. The micro products segment focuses on small-size connectors for portable electronics. The integrated products segment creates printed circuit boards and flexible circuits. Businesses that this division caters to include factories and automated facilities, as well as structured cabling for offices, universities and government buildings. The global sales and marketing organization segment comprises regional sales and industry marketing support teams, which provide customers with access to the Molex products. Molex operates 39 manufacturing facilities in 16 countries including Italy, Poland, Japan, South Korea, Vietnam, Thailand, China, the U.S. and Mexico.

FINANCIALS:

Sales and profits are in thousands of dollars—add 000 to get the full amount. 2010 Note: Financial information for 2010 was not available for all companies at press time.

2010 Sales: $3,007,207 — 2010 Profits: $131,489
2009 Sales: $2,581,841 — 2009 Profits: $-321,287
2008 Sales: $3,328,347 — 2008 Profits: $215,437
2007 Sales: $3,265,874 — 2007 Profits: $240,768
2006 Sales: $2,861,289 — 2006 Profits: $236,091

U.S. Stock Ticker: MOLX
Int'l Ticker:
Int'l Exchange:
Employees: 35,519 Fiscal Year Ends: 6/30
Parent Company:

SALARIES/BENEFITS:

Pension Plan: ESOP Stock Plan: Y Profit Sharing: Top Exec. Salary: $873,392 Bonus: $900,000
Savings Plan: Y Stock Purch. Plan: Y Second Exec. Salary: $565,250 Bonus: $500,000

OTHER THOUGHTS:

Apparent Women Officers or Directors: 1
Hot Spot for Advancement for Women/Minorities:

LOCATIONS: ("Y" = Yes)

West:	Southwest:	Midwest:	Southeast:	Northeast:	International:
Y		Y	Y	Y	Y

MONRO MUFFLER BRAKE INC

www.monro.com

Industry Group Code: 8111

Management:		Sales/Marketing:		Liberal Arts:		Information Sys.:		Professionals:		Tech./Scientific:	
Mgmt. Trainees:	Y	Marketing Pros.:	Y	Gen. Writing/Editing:	Y	Info. Mgmt.:	Y	Finance/Acct.:	Y	Engineers, Elec.:	
Experienced Mgmt.:	Y	Retail Sales:		Tech. Writing:	Y	Software Dev.:	Y	Law:	Y	Engineers, Other:	
Int'l Business:		Comm./Industrial:		Graphic Arts/Photog.:	Y	Hardware Dev.:		HR/Other:	Y	Health/Lab:	
MBA Grads:	Y	Sales Trainees:		Music:		Consulting/Other:		Training:	Y	Science/Research:	
		Advertising Pros.:	Y	Broadcasting:				Health Care:		Petroleum/Chem.:	
				Other:				Consulting:		Math/Other:	

TYPES OF BUSINESS:

Automotive Repair & Maintenance
Under-Car Repair Services
Inspection Services
Tires

BRANDS/DIVISIONS/AFFILIATES:

Monro Muffler Brake & Service
Mr. Tire
Tread Quarters Discount Tire
Monro Muffler Brake & Service
Monro Service Corporation

CONTACTS: *Note: Officers with more than one job title may be intentionally listed here more than once.*

Robert G. Gross, CEO
John W. Van Heel, Pres.
Catherine D'Amico, CFO
John W. Van Heel, Sec.
Joseph Tomarchio, Jr., Exec. VP-Store Oper.
Catherine D'Amico, Exec. VP-Finance/Treas.
Craig L. Hoyle, Div. VP-Southern Oper.
Christopher R. Hoornbeck, Div. VP-Western Oper.
Robert G. Gross, Chmn.

Phone: 585-647-6400	**Fax:** 585-647-0945
Toll-Free:	
Address: 200 Holleder Pkwy., Rochester, NY 14615 US	

GROWTH PLANS/SPECIAL FEATURES:

Monro Muffler Brake, Inc., based in Rochester, New York, operates through a chain of 781 company-operated stores and 14 dealer-operated stores providing automotive under-car repair and tire services in the U.S. These stores are typically located in high-visibility locations in suburban and small towns in New York, Pennsylvania, Ohio, Connecticut, Massachusetts, West Virginia, Virginia, Maryland, Vermont, New Hampshire, New Jersey, North Carolina, South Carolina, Indiana, Rhode Island, Delaware and Maine. The stores operate under the names Monro Muffler Brake & Service, Tread Quarters Discount Tire and Mr. Tire. The firm's stores service approximately 3.9 million vehicles annually. Monro provides a range of services on passenger cars, light trucks and vans for brakes; mufflers and exhaust systems; and steering, drive train, suspension and wheel alignment. Other products and services offered by the company include tires and routine maintenance services, such as state inspections. The company specializes in the repair and replacement of parts that must be periodically replaced due to normal wear and tear. Typically, the firm does not perform under-the-hood repair, except for oil change services, heating and cooling system flush and fill services and some minor tune-ups. Monro operates one subsidiary, Monro Service Corporation, which provides purchasing, distribution, merchandising, advertising, accounting and other store support functions.

Monro offers its employees ASE certification reimbursement, recreational discounts, an employee assistance program, tool insurance and medical, dental, life and disability insurance.

FINANCIALS: **Sales and profits are in thousands of dollars—add 000 to get the full amount. 2010 Note: Financial information for 2010 was not available for all companies at press time.**

2010 Sales: $564,639 | 2010 Profits: $33,191
2009 Sales: $476,106 | 2009 Profits: $24,088
2008 Sales: $439,389 | 2008 Profits: $21,921
2007 Sales: $417,226 | 2007 Profits: $22,271
2006 Sales: $368,727 | 2006 Profits: $22,666

U.S. Stock Ticker: MNRO
Int'l Ticker:
Int'l Exchange:
Employees: 4,926 Fiscal Year Ends: 3/31
Parent Company:

SALARIES/BENEFITS:

Pension Plan: | ESOP Stock Plan: Y | Profit Sharing: | Top Exec. Salary: $769,125 | Bonus: $150,000
Savings Plan: Y | Stock Purch. Plan: | | Second Exec. Salary: $360,000 | Bonus: $

OTHER THOUGHTS:

Apparent Women Officers or Directors: 1
Hot Spot for Advancement for Women/Minorities:

LOCATIONS: ("Y" = Yes)

West:	Southwest:	Midwest:	Southeast:	Northeast:	International:
		Y		Y	

MULTI-FINELINE ELECTRONIX INC

www.mflex.com

Industry Group Code: 33441

Management:		Sales/Marketing:		Liberal Arts:		Information Sys.:		Professionals:		Tech./Scientific:	
Mgmt. Trainees:		Marketing Pros.:	Y	Gen. Writing/Editing:		Info. Mgmt.:	Y	Finance/Acct.:	Y	Engineers, Elec.:	Y
Experienced Mgmt.:	Y	Retail Sales:		Tech. Writing:	Y	Software Dev.:	Y	Law:	Y	Engineers, Other:	Y
Int'l Business:	Y	Comm./Industrial:	Y	Graphic Arts/Photog.:		Hardware Dev.:	Y	HR/Other:	Y	Health/Lab:	
MBA Grads:	Y	Sales Trainees:		Music:		Consulting/Other:		Training:		Science/Research:	
		Advertising Pros.:		Broadcasting:				Health Care:		Petroleum/Chem.:	
				Other:				Consulting:		Math/Other:	

TYPES OF BUSINESS:

Flexible Printed Circuit Boards
Flexible Printed Circuit Board Assemblies

BRANDS/DIVISIONS/AFFILIATES:

MFLEX U.K. Limited

CONTACTS:

Note: Officers with more than one job title may be intentionally listed here more than once.

Reza Meshgin, CEO
Reza Meshgin, Pres.
Thomas Liguori, CFO/Exec. VP
Don Pucci, VP-Mktg. & Sales
Hedley Lawson, Jr., VP-Global Human Resources
Bill Beckenbaugh, CTO/VP
Christine Besnard, General Counsel/VP/Sec.
Thomas A. Lee, VP-Oper. & Program Mgmt.
Matthew Wolk, Chief Strategy Officer/VP-Corp. Dev.
Craig Riedel, Corp. Treas./VP
Philip A. Harding, Chmn.
Lance Jin, VP/Managing Dir.-China Oper.

Phone: 714-238-1488 **Fax:** 714-996-3834
Toll-Free:
Address: 3140 E. Coronado St., Anaheim, CA 92806 US

GROWTH PLANS/SPECIAL FEATURES:

Multi-Fineline Electronix, Inc. is one of the world's largest producers of flexible printed circuits and flexible printed circuit assemblies. Flexible printed circuits, which consist of copper conductive patterns that have been etched or printed while affixed to flexible substrate materials such as polyimide or polyester, are used to provide connections between electronic components and as a substrate to support these electronic devices. Flexible printed circuits can be enhanced by attaching electronic components, such as connectors, switches, resistors, capacitors, light emitting devices, integrated circuits, cameras and optical sensors, to the circuit. With operations in the U.S., China, Singapore, the U.K. and Malaysia, the firm offers a global service and support base for the design and manufacture of flexible interconnect products. The company has control over every aspect of its circuit production, from design and application engineering and prototyping through high-volume fabrication, component assembly and testing. The firm targets its efforts within the electronics market and focuses particularly on applications where flexible printed circuits facilitate human interaction with an electronic device and are the enabling technology in achieving a desired size, shape, weight or functionality of the device. Current applications for its products include mobile phones, consumer electronic devices, portable bar code scanners, computer storage devices and medical devices. Multi-Fineline Electronix provides its products to original equipment manufacturers (OEMs) such as Motorola, Inc. and Sony Ericsson; to electronic manufacturing services providers such as Foxconn Electronics, Inc. and Flextronics International, Ltd.; and to display manufacturers. The company also produces printed segmented electroluminescent displays and keyboards through its U.K. subsidiary, MFLEX U.K. Limited.

The firm offers employees in the U.S. medical, dental and vision insurance; life and AD&D insurance; disability coverage; a 401(k) plan; educational reimbursement; and an employee assistance program.

FINANCIALS:

Sales and profits are in thousands of dollars—add 000 to get the full amount. 2010 Note: Financial information for 2010 was not available for all companies at press time.

2010 Sales: $791,339 — 2010 Profits: $29,775
2009 Sales: $764,432 — 2009 Profits: $46,068
2008 Sales: $728,805 — 2008 Profits: $40,479
2007 Sales: $508,147 — 2007 Profits: $3,038
2006 Sales: $504,204 — 2006 Profits: $40,357

U.S. Stock Ticker: MFLX
Int'l Ticker:
Int'l Exchange:
Employees: 17,100 Fiscal Year Ends: 9/30
Parent Company:

SALARIES/BENEFITS:

Pension Plan: | ESOP Stock Plan: | Profit Sharing: | Top Exec. Salary: $570,000 | Bonus: $601,113
Savings Plan: Y | Stock Purch. Plan: | Second Exec. Salary: $340,000 | Bonus: $239,039

OTHER THOUGHTS:

Apparent Women Officers or Directors: 2
Hot Spot for Advancement for Women/Minorities:

LOCATIONS: ("Y" = Yes)

West:	Southwest:	Midwest:	Southeast:	Northeast:	International:
Y	Y				Y

MUTUAL OF OMAHA COMPANIES (THE) www.mutualofomaha.com

Industry Group Code: 524113

Management:		Sales/Marketing:		Liberal Arts:		Information Sys.:		Professionals:		Tech./Scientific:	
Mgmt. Trainees:		Marketing Pros.:	Y	Gen. Writing/Editing:	Y	Info. Mgmt.:	Y	Finance/Acct.:	Y	Engineers, Elec.:	
Experienced Mgmt.:		Retail Sales:		Tech. Writing:		Software Dev.:		Law:	Y	Engineers, Other:	
Int'l Business:		Comm./Industrial:		Graphic Arts/Photog.:		Hardware Dev.:		HR/Other:	Y	Health/Lab:	
MBA Grads:	Y	Sales Trainees:	Y	Music:		Consulting/Other:		Training:	Y	Science/Research:	
		Advertising Pros.:	Y	Broadcasting:				Health Care:	Y	Petroleum/Chem.:	
				Other:	Y			Consulting:		Math/Other:	

TYPES OF BUSINESS:

Life Insurance
Asset Management
Annuities
Medical & Dental Insurance
Supplemental Health Insurance
IT Services & Consulting

BRANDS/DIVISIONS/AFFILIATES:

Companion Life Insurance Company
United of Omaha Life Insurance Company
United World Life Insurance Company
Mutual of Omaha Investors Services, Inc.
Continuum Worldwide Corporation
East Campus Realty, LLC
Retirement Marketing Solutions Inc
Omaha Financial Holdings, Inc.

CONTACTS: *Note: Officers with more than one job title may be intentionally listed here more than once.*

Daniel P. Neary, CEO
David A. Diamond, CFO/Exec. VP
James T. Blackledge, Exec. VP-Info. Svcs.
Richard C. Anderl, General Counsel/Exec. VP
David A. Diamond, Treas.
Daniel P. Martin, Exec. VP-Group Benefit Svcs.
Michael C. Weekly, Exec. VP-Individual Financial Svcs.
Richard A. Witt, Chief Investment Officer/Exec. VP
Stacy A. Scholtz, Exec. VP-Corp. Svcs.
Daniel P. Neary, Chmn.

Phone: 402-342-7600 **Fax:** 402-351-2775
Toll-Free: 800-775-6000
Address: Mutual of Omaha Plz., Omaha, NE 68175 US

GROWTH PLANS/SPECIAL FEATURES:

The Mutual of Omaha Companies provide insurance, annuities and asset management products through several affiliated companies. These firms include Companion Life Insurance Company; Mutual of Omaha Investor Services, Inc.; United of Omaha Life Insurance Company; United World Life Insurance Company; Omaha Financial Holdings, Inc.; Continuum Worldwide Corporation; Retirement Marketing Solutions, Inc.; and East Campus Realty, LLC. Companion Life Insurance Company provides insurance, annuities and investment services to New York residents. Mutual of Omaha Investor Services, Inc. is a registered broker dealer that offers mutual funds and asset management to affiliate companies and directly to consumers. United of Omaha Life Insurance Company provides life insurance, annuities and financial services through the Mutual of Omaha network of sales representatives. United World Life Insurance Company offers specialty life plans, as well as health and accident coverage, through independent agents. Omaha Financial Holdings, Inc. is a holding company that handles Mutual of Omaha's banking operation. Continuum Worldwide Corporation provides operational risk management services. Retirement Marketing Solutions, Inc. is a wholesaler that offers retirement products across the U.S. East Campus Realty, LLC is in the process of developing Midtown Crossing at Turner Park, a mixed-use development offering condominiums, apartments, services, dining and entertainment adjacent to Mutual of Omaha's headquarters.

The firm offers employees benefits including medical, dental, vision, life and disability insurance; flexible spending accounts; and a 401(k).

FINANCIALS: **Sales and profits are in thousands of dollars—add 000 to get the full amount. 2010 Note: Financial information for 2010 was not available for all companies at press time.**

2010 Sales: $5,310,958 2010 Profits: $247,663
2009 Sales: $4,554,266 2009 Profits: $143,793
2008 Sales: $4,072,790 2008 Profits: $47,048
2007 Sales: $4,241,677 2007 Profits: $217,027
2006 Sales: $4,204,837 2006 Profits: $165,710

U.S. Stock Ticker: Mutual Company
Int'l Ticker:
Int'l Exchange:
Employees: 4,200 Fiscal Year Ends: 12/31
Parent Company:

SALARIES/BENEFITS:

Pension Plan: ESOP Stock Plan: Profit Sharing: Top Exec. Salary: $ Bonus: $
Savings Plan: Y Stock Purch. Plan: Second Exec. Salary: $ Bonus: $

OTHER THOUGHTS:

Apparent Women Officers or Directors: 2
Hot Spot for Advancement for Women/Minorities:

LOCATIONS: ("Y" = Yes)

West:	Southwest:	Midwest:	Southeast:	Northeast:	International:
Y	Y	Y	Y	Y	

MYLAN INC

www.mylan.com

Industry Group Code: 325412

Management:		Sales/Marketing:		Liberal Arts:		Information Sys.:		Professionals:		Tech./Scientific:	
Mgmt. Trainees:	Y	Marketing Pros.:	Y	Gen. Writing/Editing:		Info. Mgmt.:	Y	Finance/Acct.:	Y	Engineers, Elec.:	Y
Experienced Mgmt.:	Y	Retail Sales:		Tech. Writing:	Y	Software Dev.:	Y	Law:	Y	Engineers, Other:	Y
Int'l Business:	Y	Comm./Industrial:	Y	Graphic Arts/Photog.:		Hardware Dev.:		HR/Other:	Y	Health/Lab:	Y
MBA Grads:	Y	Sales Trainees:		Music:		Consulting/Other:		Training:	Y	Science/Research:	Y
		Advertising Pros.:		Broadcasting:				Health Care:	Y	Petroleum/Chem.:	Y
				Other:				Consulting:		Math/Other:	Y

TYPES OF BUSINESS:

Drugs-Generic
Generic Pharmaceuticals
Active Pharmaceutical Ingredients

BRANDS/DIVISIONS/AFFILIATES:

UDL Laboratories, Inc.
Mylan Pharmaceuticals, Inc.
Mylan Technologies, Inc.
Matrix Laboratories Limited
Dey
Mylan S.A.S.
Mylan-Nifedipine Extended Release Tablets
Mylan Pharmaceuticals S.L

CONTACTS: *Note: Officers with more than one job title may be intentionally listed here more than once.*

Robert J. Coury, CEO
Rajiv Malik, COO/Exec. VP
Heather Bresch, Pres.
John D. Sheehan, CFO/Exec. VP
Harry A. Korman, Pres., North America
Robert J. Coury, Chmn.
Didier Barret, Pres., EMEA

Phone: 724-514-1800	**Fax:** 724-514-1870
Toll-Free:	
Address: 1500 Corporate Dr., Canonsburg, PA 15317 US	

GROWTH PLANS/SPECIAL FEATURES:

Mylan, Inc. develops, licenses, manufactures, distributes and markets generic/branded generic pharmaceutical products, specialty pharmaceuticals and active pharmaceutical ingredients (APIs). The company has two operating segments: generics and specialty. The generics segment operates in the U.S., Canada, Europe, the Middle East, Africa, Australia, New Zealand, India and Japan. In the U.S., this segment markets roughly 270 products through three subsidiaries: Mylan Pharmaceuticals Inc. (MPI), which sells solid oral dosage products; Mylan Institutional, which re-packages and markets products obtained from MPI and third parties; and Mylan Technologies, Inc., which develops and markets transdermal patches. The firm also manufactures and markets generic pharmaceuticals in Canada through Mylan Pharmaceuticals ULC, which offers 120 products. Sales in EMEA are generated through operations in 21 countries. In France, Mylan markets 200 products through its wholly-owned subsidiaries Mylan S.A.S. and Qualimed S.A.S.; in Italy, 120 products through Mylan S.p.A; in Spain, 85 products through Mylan Pharmaceuticals S.L.; and in Germany, 130 products through Mylan dura. The company also markets 160 products in the U.K. In Asia Pacific, the firm markets products in Australia through Alphapharm; in New Zealand through Mylan New Zealand; in India through Matrix, which additionally has eight API and intermediate manufacturing facilities; and in Japan through Mylan Seiyaku. The firm also has a manufacturing facility located in Japan. The specialty segment is conducted through Dey, which focuses on the respiratory, psychiatry and severe allergy markets. Its principal product is EpiPen, which is used for severe allergic reactions.

FINANCIALS: **Sales and profits are in thousands of dollars—add 000 to get the full amount. 2010 Note: Financial information for 2010 was not available for all companies at press time.**

2010 Sales: $5,450,522	2010 Profits: $345,542	**U.S. Stock Ticker: MYL**
2009 Sales: $5,092,785	2009 Profits: $247,748	**Int'l Ticker:**
2008 Sales: $5,137,585	2008 Profits: $-181,215	Int'l Exchange:
2007 Sales: $1,611,819	2007 Profits: $217,284	Employees: 13,000 Fiscal Year Ends: 12/31
2006 Sales: $1,257,164	2006 Profits: $184,542	Parent Company:

SALARIES/BENEFITS:

Pension Plan: Y	ESOP Stock Plan:	Profit Sharing:	Top Exec. Salary: $1,700,000	Bonus: $3,293,750
Savings Plan: Y	Stock Purch. Plan: Y		Second Exec. Salary: $787,019	Bonus: $1,240,000

OTHER THOUGHTS:

Apparent Women Officers or Directors: 1
Hot Spot for Advancement for Women/Minorities: Y

LOCATIONS: ("Y" = Yes)

West:	Southwest:	Midwest:	Southeast:	Northeast:	International:
	Y	Y	Y	Y	Y

NABORS INDUSTRIES LTD

www.nabors.com

Industry Group Code: 213111

Management:		Sales/Marketing:		Liberal Arts:		Information Sys.:		Professionals:		Tech./Scientific:	
Mgmt. Trainees:	Y	Marketing Pros.:	Y	Gen. Writing/Editing:		Info. Mgmt.:	Y	Finance/Acct.:	Y	Engineers, Elec.:	Y
Experienced Mgmt.:	Y	Retail Sales:		Tech. Writing:		Software Dev.:		Law:	Y	Engineers, Other:	
Int'l Business:	Y	Comm./Industrial:	Y	Graphic Arts/Photog.:		Hardware Dev.:		HR/Other:	Y	Health/Lab:	
MBA Grads:	Y	Sales Trainees:		Music:		Consulting/Other:		Training:		Science/Research:	
		Advertising Pros.:		Broadcasting:				Health Care:		Petroleum/Chem.:	Y
				Other:				Consulting:		Math/Other:	

TYPES OF BUSINESS:

Contract Drilling Services
Oil Field Management
Site Construction
Drilling Instrumentation & Software
Marine & Land Transportation Services
Drilling Systems, Manufacturing

BRANDS/DIVISIONS/AFFILIATES:

Nabors International
Canrig Drilling Technologies
Ryan Energy Technologies
Peak Oilfield Services Company
Superior Well Services Inc

CONTACTS: *Note: Officers with more than one job title may be intentionally listed here more than once.*

Eugene M. Isenberg, CEO
Anthony G. Petrello, COO
Anthony G. Petrello, Pres.
R. Clark Wood, CFO
Mark D. Andrews, Corp. Sec.
Dennis A. Smith, Dir.-Bus. Dev.
R. Clark Wood, Chief Acct. Officer
Eugene M. Isenberg, Chmn.

Phone: 441-292-1510 **Fax:** 441-292-1334
Toll-Free:
Address: 8 Par-La-Ville Rd., Mintflower Pl., Hamilton, HM08 Bermuda

GROWTH PLANS/SPECIAL FEATURES:

Nabors Industries, Ltd. is one of the largest land-drilling contractors in the world. The company's operations include approximately 730 land workover rigs in the U.S. and Canada; 542 actively marketed land-drilling rigs; 40 offshore platform rigs; and three inland barge rigs. The company conducts oil, gas and geothermal land-drilling operations in the continental U.S., Alaska, Canada, South America, Mexico, the Caribbean, Russia, Africa, Asia and the Middle East. In addition, Nabors is one of the largest land-well-servicing and workover contractors in the U.S. and Canada. The company provides a number of services in select domestic and international markets, including oil field management, engineering, transportation, construction, maintenance, well logging, directional drilling, rig instrumentation, data collection and other support services. The firm also operates through several subsidiaries. Canrig Drilling Technology, Ltd., manufacturers, markets and supplies a range of portable and fixed top drive drilling systems for oil and gas exploration. Ryan Energy Technologies, Inc. is a leader in the development and provision of drilling technology and services. Ryan Energy specializes in downhole and surface technologies and equipment. In addition, Nabors Industries owns 50%-interest in Peak Oilfield Services Company, a joint venture with Cook Inlet Region, Inc., which primarily provides rig moving, site construction, custom heavy hauling, crane and rigging services and general freight services. Peak Oilfield Services conducts its business through multiple terminals within Texas. In September 2010, Nabors Industries acquired Superior Well Services, Inc. for roughly $900 million.

FINANCIALS: **Sales and profits are in thousands of dollars—add 000 to get the full amount. 2010 Note: Financial information for 2010 was not available for all companies at press time.**

2010 Sales: $4,215,540 — 2010 Profits: $94,695
2009 Sales: $3,553,585 — 2009 Profits: $-85,546
2008 Sales: $5,336,406 — 2008 Profits: $475,737
2007 Sales: $4,940,681 — 2007 Profits: $930,691
2006 Sales: $4,942,714 — 2006 Profits: $1,020,736

U.S. Stock Ticker: NBR
Int'l Ticker:
Int'l Exchange:
Employees: 23,412 Fiscal Year Ends: 12/31
Parent Company:

SALARIES/BENEFITS:

Pension Plan: ESOP Stock Plan: Profit Sharing: Top Exec. Salary: $1,141,750 Bonus: $19,891,275
Savings Plan: Stock Purch. Plan: Second Exec. Salary: $965,806 Bonus: $7,886,551

OTHER THOUGHTS:

Apparent Women Officers or Directors:
Hot Spot for Advancement for Women/Minorities:

LOCATIONS: ("Y" = Yes)

West:	Southwest:	Midwest:	Southeast:	Northeast:	International:
Y	Y	Y	Y		Y

NACCO INDUSTRIES INC

www.nacco.com

Industry Group Code: 333

Management:		Sales/Marketing:		Liberal Arts:		Information Sys.:		Professionals:		Tech./Scientific:	
Mgmt. Trainees:	Y	Marketing Pros.:	Y	Gen. Writing/Editing:		Info. Mgmt.:	Y	Finance/Acct.:	Y	Engineers, Elec.:	
Experienced Mgmt.:	Y	Retail Sales:	Y	Tech. Writing:		Software Dev.:		Law:	Y	Engineers, Other:	
Int'l Business:	Y	Comm./Industrial:		Graphic Arts/Photog.:		Hardware Dev.:		HR/Other:	Y	Health/Lab:	
MBA Grads:	Y	Sales Trainees:	Y	Music:		Consulting/Other:		Training:	Y	Science/Research:	
		Advertising Pros.:	Y	Broadcasting:				Health Care:		Petroleum/Chem.:	
				Other:				Consulting:		Math/Other:	

TYPES OF BUSINESS:

Forklift Truck Manufacturing, Dealerships & Rental
Electrical Appliance Manufacturing
Kitchen Appliance Stores, Retail
Coal/Lignite Mining
Online Sales

BRANDS/DIVISIONS/AFFILIATES:

North American Coal Corp.
NACCO Materials Handling Group, Inc.
NACCO Housewares Group
North American Coal
Yale
Hyster
Hamilton Beach Brands, Inc.
Kitchen Collection, Inc. (The)

CONTACTS: *Note: Officers with more than one job title may be intentionally listed here more than once.*

Alfred M. Rankin, Jr., CEO
Alfred M. Rankin, Jr., Pres.
Charles A. Bittenbender, General Counsel/Corp. Sec./VP
J. C. Butler, Jr., VP-Corp. Dev.
Kenneth C. Schilling, Controller
Lauren E. Miller, VP-Consulting Services
J. C. Butler, Jr., Treas.
Alfred M. Rankin, Jr., Chmn.

Phone: 440-449-9600 **Fax:**
Toll-Free:
Address: 5875 Landerbrook Dr., Ste. 300, Cleveland, OH 44124 US

GROWTH PLANS/SPECIAL FEATURES:

NACCO Industries, Inc. is a holding company with four principle businesses: housewares distribution, housewares retail, lift trucks and mining. NACCO Materials Handling Group (NMGH), NACCO's lift trucks operations, consists of subsidiary NMHG Holding Co., which is engaged in the design, engineering, manufacturing, selling, servicing and leasing of a line of lift trucks and aftermarket parts marketed globally under the Hyster and Yale brand names. NMHG operates 14 manufacturing and assembly facilities worldwide, with five plants in the Americas, three in Europe and five in Asia-Pacific. The subsidiary also offers retail dealerships. NACCO Housewares Group, the firm's housewares operations, consists of subsidiaries Hamilton Beach Brands, Inc., and The Kitchen Collenction, Inc. Hamilton Beach is a leading designer, marketer and distributor of small electric household appliances, as well as commercial products for restaurants, bars and hotels. The Kitchen Collection (KC) is a national specialty retailer of kitchenware and gourmet foods operating under the Kitchen Collection and Le Gourmet Chef names in outlet and traditional malls nationwide. KC operates approximately 296 retail stores. North American Coal, NACCO's mining operations, mines and markets lignite coal primarily as fuel for power generation and provides selected value-added mining services for other natural resources companies.

The company offers its employees a 401(k) plan, a profit sharing plan and a health benefits.

FINANCIALS: **Sales and profits are in thousands of dollars—add 000 to get the full amount. 2010 Note: Financial information for 2010 was not available for all companies at press time.**

2010 Sales: $2,687,500	2010 Profits: $79,500	**U.S. Stock Ticker: NC**
2009 Sales: $2,310,600	2009 Profits: $31,100	**Int'l Ticker:**
2008 Sales: $3,680,300	2008 Profits: $-437,600	Int'l Exchange:
2007 Sales: $3,602,700	2007 Profits: $89,300	Employees: 8,700 Fiscal Year Ends: 12/31
2006 Sales: $3,349,000	2006 Profits: $106,200	Parent Company:

SALARIES/BENEFITS:

Pension Plan:	ESOP Stock Plan:	Profit Sharing: Y	Top Exec. Salary: $1,138,798	Bonus: $554,168
Savings Plan: Y	Stock Purch. Plan:		Second Exec. Salary: $584,196	Bonus: $

OTHER THOUGHTS:

Apparent Women Officers or Directors: 3
Hot Spot for Advancement for Women/Minorities: Y

LOCATIONS: ("Y" = Yes)

West:	Southwest:	Midwest:	Southeast:	Northeast:	International:
Y	Y	Y	Y	Y	Y

NALCO HOLDING COMPANY

www.nalco.com

Industry Group Code: 325

Management:		Sales/Marketing:		Liberal Arts:		Information Sys.:		Professionals:		Tech./Scientific:	
Mgmt. Trainees:		Marketing Pros.:	Y	Gen. Writing/Editing:		Info. Mgmt.:	Y	Finance/Acct.:	Y	Engineers, Elec.:	Y
Experienced Mgmt.:		Retail Sales:		Tech. Writing:	Y	Software Dev.:		Law:	Y	Engineers, Other:	Y
Int'l Business:	Y	Comm./Industrial:	Y	Graphic Arts/Photog.:		Hardware Dev.:		HR/Other:	Y	Health/Lab:	
MBA Grads:	Y	Sales Trainees:		Music:		Consulting/Other:		Training:		Science/Research:	Y
		Advertising Pros.:	Y	Broadcasting:				Health Care:		Petroleum/Chem.:	Y
				Other:				Consulting:		Math/Other:	

TYPES OF BUSINESS:

Water Treatment Chemicals & Services
Energy Services
Paper Services
Air Pollution Control
Consulting Services

BRANDS/DIVISIONS/AFFILIATES:

Nalco Mobotec, Inc.
TIORCO
OOO Kogalym Chemicals Plant
Nalco Fab-Tech, LLC
Fabrication Technologies, Inc.

CONTACTS: *Note: Officers with more than one job title may be intentionally listed here more than once.*

J. Erik Fyrwald, CEO
J. Erik Fyrwald, Pres.
Kathryn Mikells, CFO/Exec. VP
Mary Kay Kaufmann, Chief Mktg. Officer
Laurie M. Marsh, VP-Human Resources
Stewart H. McCutcheon, CIO
Manian Ramesh, CTO
Stephen N. Landsman, General Counsel/VP/Corp. Sec.
Scott Hinkle, Controller
Rich Bendure, Group VP-Water Mktg. & Dev.
Steve M. Taylor, Exec. VP/Pres., Energy Svcs. Div.
Eric G. Melin, Exec. VP/Pres., APAC
David E. Flitman, Sr. Exec. VP/Pres., Water & Process Svcs.
J. Erik Fyrwald, Chmn.
David Johnson, Exec. VP-EMEA
Mark R. Stoll, VP-Energy Svcs. Supply Chain

Phone: 630-305-1000	**Fax:** 630-305-2900
Toll-Free:	
Address: 1601 W. Diehl Rd., Naperville, IL 60563-1198 US	

GROWTH PLANS/SPECIAL FEATURES:

Nalco Holding Company provides integrated water treatment and process improvement services, chemicals and equipment programs for industrial and institutional applications. The company's products and services are typically used in water treatment applications to prevent corrosion, contamination and the build-up of harmful deposits, or in production processes to enhance process efficiency and improve customers' end products. The firm operates in three primary divisions: Water Services, Energy Services and Paper Services. The Water Services segment, which accounts for roughly 42% of Nalco's sales, provides products and services utilized in water treatment applications such as wastewater treatment, cooling programs, boiler treatment programs and pollutant control systems. The Energy Services division (40% of sales) provides on-site chemicals and systems to the global natural gas, petroleum and petrochemical industries. In addition to recovery, production and process enhancements, energy service products deliver a range of water treatment offerings to refineries and petrochemical plants. The Paper Services division (18% of sales) offers programs that are used in all principal steps of the papermaking process and across all grades of paper, including graphic grades; board and packaging; and tissue and towel. Paper service programs include programs that manage organic and inorganic contaminants, programs that increase pulp cleanliness and programs that deliver brightness and whiteness. Additionally, subsidiary Nalco Mobotec, Inc. is a supplier of emission reduction products and services addressing customers' air pollution challenges. Another subsidiary, TIORCO, internationally markets custom-engineered chemical solutions that increase production of crude oil and gas from existing fields. Nalco serves almost 50,000 customer locations in 150 countries. In August 2011, the firm acquired Fabrication Technologies, Inc. (now known as Nalco Fab-Tech, LLC); and opened a new office in India. In December 2010, the company and Russian oil group OAO LUKOIL formed joint venture OOO Kogalym Chemicals Plant. In January 2011, Nalco sold its performance products division to Lubrizol Corporation.

FINANCIALS: **Sales and profits are in thousands of dollars—add 000 to get the full amount. 2010 Note: Financial information for 2010 was not available for all companies at press time.**

2010 Sales: $4,250,500	2010 Profits: $196,200	**U.S. Stock Ticker: NLC**
2009 Sales: $3,746,800	2009 Profits: $60,500	**Int'l Ticker:**
2008 Sales: $4,212,400	2008 Profits: $-342,600	Int'l Exchange:
2007 Sales: $3,912,500	2007 Profits: $129,000	Employees: 12,400 Fiscal Year Ends: 12/31
2006 Sales: $3,602,600	2006 Profits: $98,900	Parent Company:

SALARIES/BENEFITS:

Pension Plan:	ESOP Stock Plan:	Profit Sharing:	Top Exec. Salary: $875,000	Bonus: $1,105,000
Savings Plan:	Stock Purch. Plan:		Second Exec. Salary: $482,419	Bonus: $234,000

OTHER THOUGHTS:

Apparent Women Officers or Directors: 4
Hot Spot for Advancement for Women/Minorities: Y

LOCATIONS: ("Y" = Yes)

West:	Southwest:	Midwest:	Southeast:	Northeast:	International:
Y	Y	Y	Y	Y	Y

NATIONAL INSTRUMENTS CORP

www.ni.com

Industry Group Code: 511210N

Management:		Sales/Marketing:		Liberal Arts:		Information Sys.:		Professionals:		Tech./Scientific:	
Mgmt. Trainees:		Marketing Pros.:	Y	Gen. Writing/Editing:		Info. Mgmt.:	Y	Finance/Acct.:	Y	Engineers, Elec.:	Y
Experienced Mgmt.:		Retail Sales:		Tech. Writing:	Y	Software Dev.:	Y	Law:	Y	Engineers, Other:	
Int'l Business:	Y	Comm./Industrial:	Y	Graphic Arts/Photog.:		Hardware Dev.:		HR/Other:	Y	Health/Lab:	
MBA Grads:	Y	Sales Trainees:		Music:		Consulting/Other:		Training:		Science/Research:	
		Advertising Pros.:	Y	Broadcasting:				Health Care:		Petroleum/Chem.:	
				Other:				Consulting:		Math/Other:	

TYPES OF BUSINESS:

Software-Instrumentation
Virtual Instrumentation
Signal Conditioning Hardware
Test & Measurement Software
Motion Control Products
Analysis & Visualization Software
Automation Software
Image Acquisition Products

BRANDS/DIVISIONS/AFFILIATES:

LabVIEW
LabWindows
LabVIEW FPGA
TestStand
Measurement Studio
LabVIEW Real-Time
FieldPoint

CONTACTS: *Note: Officers with more than one job title may be intentionally listed here more than once.*

James Truchard, CEO
Alex Davern, COO/Exec. VP
James Truchard, Pres.
Alex Davern, CFO
Pete Zogas, Sr. VP-Sales & Mktg.
Mark Finger, VP-Human Resources
Phil Hester, Sr. VP-R&D
Arleene Porterfield, VP-Global IT
Tony Vento, VP-Systems & Applications Eng.
Rob Porterfield, VP-Mfg.
David Hugley, General Counsel/VP/Sec.
John Pasquarette, VP-eCommerce
John Roiko, VP-Finance
Ray Almgren, VP-Prod. Mktg., Core Platforms
Andrew Krupp, VP-Quality & Continuous Improvement
Ron Wolfe, VP-Semiconductor Test
Kevin Schultz, VP-R&D, Data Acquisition & Distributed I/O
James Truchard, Chmn.
Scott Rust, VP-R&D, NI Penang

Phone: 512-338-9119 **Fax:** 512-683-5759
Toll-Free: 800-433-3488
Address: 11500 N. Mopac Expwy., Austin, TX 78759-3504 US

GROWTH PLANS/SPECIAL FEATURES:

National Instruments Corp. (NI) supplies test, measurement and automation products used by engineers and scientists from numerous industries. Its key markets range from the automotive, aerospace, electronics, semiconductors and defense sectors, to the education, government, medical research and telecommunications industries, among others. The company provides flexible application software and modular, multifunction hardware that users combine with computers, networks and third party devices to create measurement, automation and embedded systems, or virtual instruments. Virtual instrumentation is a shift from traditional hardware-centered systems to software-centered systems that exploit the computational, display, productivity and connectivity capabilities of computers, networks and the Internet. NI's application software products include the LabVIEW, LabVIEW Real-Time, LabWindows and Measurement Studio programs that allow users to develop graphical user interfaces, control instruments and acquire, analyze and present data. Other applications include LabVIEW FPGA, which allows users to configure applications to execute directly in silicon via a field programmable gate array (FPGA); TestStand, targeted for T&M applications; and Multisim, a type of circuit simulation software used for electronic circuit design, board layout and electrical engineering training programs. The firm's hardware and related driver software products include data acquisition (DAQ), which help convert analog data into digital format; PCI hardware extensions for instrumentation chassis and controllers (PXI); and image acquisition and motion control products that integrate vision and motion into measurement applications. Additional products include the Compact FieldPoint distributed I/O application; modular instruments and embedded control hardware/software; industrial communications interfaces for communicating with serial devices; general purpose interface buses (GPIBs); and VXI computer controllers.

The firm offers its employees a 401(k) plan, stock purchase and profit sharing plans; health, dental and vision coverage; life and disability insurance; tuition assistance; and an on-site fitness center.

FINANCIALS: **Sales and profits are in thousands of dollars—add 000 to get the full amount. 2010 Note: Financial information for 2010 was not available for all companies at press time.**

2010 Sales: $873,220 | 2010 Profits: $109,116
2009 Sales: $676,594 | 2009 Profits: $17,085
2008 Sales: $820,537 | 2008 Profits: $84,827
2007 Sales: $740,378 | 2007 Profits: $107,033
2006 Sales: $660,407 | 2006 Profits: $72,708

U.S. Stock Ticker: NATI
Int'l Ticker:
Int'l Exchange:
Employees: 5,280 Fiscal Year Ends: 12/31
Parent Company:

SALARIES/BENEFITS:

Pension Plan: | ESOP Stock Plan: | Profit Sharing: Y | Top Exec. Salary: $296,562 | Bonus: $73,169
Savings Plan: Y | Stock Purch. Plan: Y | | Second Exec. Salary: $237,250 | Bonus: $37,741

OTHER THOUGHTS:

Apparent Women Officers or Directors: 1
Hot Spot for Advancement for Women/Minorities:

LOCATIONS: ("Y" = Yes)

West:	Southwest:	Midwest:	Southeast:	Northeast:	International:
Y	Y	Y	Y	Y	Y

Sales, profits and employees may be estimates. Financial information, benefits and other data can change quickly and may vary from those stated here.

NATIONAL OILWELL VARCO INC

www.nov.com

Industry Group Code: 213112

Management:		Sales/Marketing:		Liberal Arts:		Information Sys.:		Professionals:		Tech./Scientific:	
Mgmt. Trainees:	Y	Marketing Pros.:	Y	Gen. Writing/Editing:		Info. Mgmt.:	Y	Finance/Acct.:	Y	Engineers, Elec.:	Y
Experienced Mgmt.:	Y	Retail Sales:		Tech. Writing:	Y	Software Dev.:	Y	Law:	Y	Engineers, Other:	Y
Int'l Business:	Y	Comm./Industrial:	Y	Graphic Arts/Photog.:		Hardware Dev.:		HR/Other:	Y	Health/Lab:	
MBA Grads:	Y	Sales Trainees:		Music:		Consulting/Other:		Training:	Y	Science/Research:	
		Advertising Pros.:		Broadcasting:				Health Care:		Petroleum/Chem.:	Y
				Other:				Consulting:		Math/Other:	

TYPES OF BUSINESS:

Oil & Gas Drilling Equipment & Systems
Distribution & Logistics Services
IT Services

BRANDS/DIVISIONS/AFFILIATES:

NOV IntelliServ
Voest-Alpine Tubulars
Advanced Production and Loading PLC
STSA
Ameron International Corporation

CONTACTS: *Note: Officers with more than one job title may be intentionally listed here more than once.*

Merrill (Pete) Miller, Jr., CEO
Merrill (Pete) Miller, Jr., Pres.
Clay C. Williams, CFO/Sr. VP
Dwight W. Rettig, General Counsel/VP
Robert Blanchard, Chief Acct. Officer/Corp. Controller/VP
Merrill (Pete) Miller, Jr., Chmn.

Phone: 713-375-3700	**Fax:**
Toll-Free: 888-262-8645	
Address: 7909 Parkwood Circle Dr., Houston, TX 77036 US	

GROWTH PLANS/SPECIAL FEATURES:

National Oilwell Varco, Inc. designs, manufactures and sells equipment and components used in oil and gas drilling and production operations, and provides oilfield services and supply chain integration services to the upstream oil and gas industry. The company has operations in over 800 locations on six continents. National Oilwell Varco operates through three business segments: rig technology, which accounts for 57.3% of revenue; petroleum services and supplies, 34.4%; and distribution services, 12.3%. The firm's rig technology segment designs, manufactures, sells and services offshore and onshore drilling rigs; derricks; rig instrumentation systems; coiled tubing equipment and pressure pumping units; wireline winches; and cranes. Its operations extend to Canada, Norway, the U.K., India, China and Belarus. The petroleum services and supplies segment manufactures, rents and sells drill pipe, wired drill pipe, transfer pumps, solids control systems, drilling motors, drill bits and mud pump consumables. Its operations extend to Canada, the U.K., China, Kazakhstan, Mexico, Russia, Argentina, India, Bolivia, the Netherlands, Singapore, Malaysia, Vietnam and the United Arab Emirates. The distribution services segment provides maintenance, repair and operating supplies and spare parts to drill site and production locations throughout North America, Mexico, the Middle East, Europe, Southeast Asia and South America. Through its information technology platforms and processes, this segment provides complete procurement, inventory management and logistics services. The firm also maintains interests in several joint ventures including NOV IntelliServ, which provides wellbore data transmission services; and Voest-Alpine Tubulars, a manufacturer of green tubing. In December 2010, the company acquired Advanced Production and Loading PLC, which designs and manufactures turret mooring systems and other products for offshore vessels and terminals. In July 2011, the firm acquired STSA, a Singapore-based blowout preventer service and pressure control equipment provider for offshore drilling; and agreed to acquire Ameron International Corporation.

FINANCIALS: **Sales and profits are in thousands of dollars—add 000 to get the full amount. 2010 Note: Financial information for 2010 was not available for all companies at press time.**

2010 Sales: $12,156,000	2010 Profits: $1,667,000	**U.S. Stock Ticker: NOV**
2009 Sales: $12,712,000	2009 Profits: $1,469,000	**Int'l Ticker:**
2008 Sales: $13,431,400	2008 Profits: $1,952,000	Int'l Exchange:
2007 Sales: $9,789,000	2007 Profits: $1,337,100	Employees: 41,027 Fiscal Year Ends: 12/31
2006 Sales: $7,025,800	2006 Profits: $684,000	Parent Company:

SALARIES/BENEFITS:

Pension Plan: Y	ESOP Stock Plan:	Profit Sharing:	Top Exec. Salary: $950,000	Bonus: $2,280,000
Savings Plan: Y	Stock Purch. Plan:		Second Exec. Salary: $600,000	Bonus: $960,000

OTHER THOUGHTS:

Apparent Women Officers or Directors:
Hot Spot for Advancement for Women/Minorities:

LOCATIONS: ("Y" = Yes)

West:	Southwest:	Midwest:	Southeast:	Northeast:	International:
Y	Y	Y	Y	Y	Y

NCR CORPORATION

www.ncr.com

Industry Group Code: 334111

Management:		Sales/Marketing:		Liberal Arts:		Information Sys.:		Professionals:		Tech./Scientific:	
Mgmt. Trainees:	Y	Marketing Pros.:	Y	Gen. Writing/Editing:	Y	Info. Mgmt.:	Y	Finance/Acct.:	Y	Engineers, Elec.:	Y
Experienced Mgmt.:	Y	Retail Sales:		Tech. Writing:	Y	Software Dev.:	Y	Law:	Y	Engineers, Other:	
Int'l Business:	Y	Comm./Industrial:	Y	Graphic Arts/Photog.:	Y	Hardware Dev.:	Y	HR/Other:	Y	Health/Lab:	
MBA Grads:	Y	Sales Trainees:	Y	Music:		Consulting/Other:	Y	Training:	Y	Science/Research:	
		Advertising Pros.:	Y	Broadcasting:				Health Care:		Petroleum/Chem.:	
				Other:				Consulting:		Math/Other:	

TYPES OF BUSINESS:

Point-of-Sale Computer Systems
Barcode Scanning Equipment
Automatic Teller Machines (ATMs)
Transaction Processing Equipment
Point-of-Sale & Store Automation
Data Warehousing
Printer Consumables
Consulting Services

BRANDS/DIVISIONS/AFFILIATES:

NCI Ltd

CONTACTS:

Note: Officers with more than one job title may be intentionally listed here more than once.

Bill Nuti, CEO
Robert Fishman, CFO/Sr. VP
Peter Leav, Sr. VP-Global Sales
Andrea Ledford, Sr. VP-Human Resources
Jennifer Daniels, General Counsel/Corp. Sec.
Peter Dorsman, Sr. VP-Global Oper.
Richard Bravman, VP-Corp. Dev./Chief Mktg. Officer
Dan Bogan, Sr. VP/Gen. Mgr.-NCR Consumables
Bill Nuti, Chmn.

Phone: 937-445-5000	**Fax:** 937-445-1682
Toll-Free: 800-225-5627	
Address: 2651 Satellite Blvd., Duluth, GA 30096 US	

GROWTH PLANS/SPECIAL FEATURES:

NCR Corporation provides information technology and related services to various industries, enabling client companies to interact more efficiently with customers. The company offers financial institutions, retailers and independent deployers financial-oriented self-service technologies, such as ATMs, cash dispensers, software solutions and consulting services relating to ATM security, software and bank branch optimization. Financial self-service solutions are designed to quickly and reliably process consumer transactions and incorporate advanced features such as automated check cashing/deposit, automated cash deposit, web-enablement, bill payment and the dispensing of non-cash items. NCR provides retail store automation solutions for the general merchandise, food, drug, travel, hospitality, health care, entertainment, gaming and public sector segments. The company has focused its investments and resources on self-service technologies with expanded offerings to include self-ticketing and self-check-in/out systems for the travel industry; self-service food ordering; and patient management check-in/out in the health care sector. The firm provides maintenance and support services for its products, including complete systems management and site assessment and site preparation, staging, installation and implementation. NCR is also involved in the resale and service of third-party computer hardware from select manufacturers, such as Cisco Systems. NCR Consumables develops, produces and markets a line of printer consumables for various print technologies, including paper rolls for receipts in ATMs and point of sale (POS) solutions; inkjet and laser printer supplies; thermal transfer and ink ribbons; labels; laser documents; business forms; and specialty media items such as photo and presentation papers and two-sided thermal paper. The firm's business segments are organized into three geographical groups: Americas; Europe, Middle East and Africa (EMEA); and Asia Pacific and Japan (APJ).

FINANCIALS:

Sales and profits are in thousands of dollars—add 000 to get the full amount. 2010 Note: Financial information for 2010 was not available for all companies at press time.

2010 Sales: $4,819,000	2010 Profits: $137,000
2009 Sales: $4,612,000	2009 Profits: $-30,000
2008 Sales: $5,315,000	2008 Profits: $228,000
2007 Sales: $4,970,000	2007 Profits: $274,000
2006 Sales: $4,582,000	2006 Profits: $382,000

U.S. Stock Ticker: NCR
Int'l Ticker:
Int'l Exchange:
Employees: 21,000 Fiscal Year Ends: 12/31
Parent Company:

SALARIES/BENEFITS:

Pension Plan:	ESOP Stock Plan:	Profit Sharing:	Top Exec. Salary: $1,000,000	Bonus: $1,500,000
Savings Plan:	Stock Purch. Plan:		Second Exec. Salary: $471,250	Bonus: $420,560

OTHER THOUGHTS:

Apparent Women Officers or Directors: 3
Hot Spot for Advancement for Women/Minorities: Y

LOCATIONS: ("Y" = Yes)

West:	Southwest:	Midwest:	Southeast:	Northeast:	International:
Y		Y	Y	Y	Y

NETAPP INC

www.netapp.com

Industry Group Code: 334112

Management:		Sales/Marketing:		Liberal Arts:		Information Sys.:		Professionals:		Tech./Scientific:	
Mgmt. Trainees:	Y	Marketing Pros.:	Y	Gen. Writing/Editing:	Y	Info. Mgmt.:	Y	Finance/Acct.:	Y	Engineers, Elec.:	Y
Experienced Mgmt.:	Y	Retail Sales:		Tech. Writing:	Y	Software Dev.:	Y	Law:	Y	Engineers, Other:	
Int'l Business:	Y	Comm./Industrial:	Y	Graphic Arts/Photog.:		Hardware Dev.:	Y	HR/Other:	Y	Health/Lab:	
MBA Grads:	Y	Sales Trainees:		Music:		Consulting/Other:		Training:	Y	Science/Research:	
		Advertising Pros.:	Y	Broadcasting:				Health Care:		Petroleum/Chem.:	
				Other:				Consulting:		Math/Other:	

TYPES OF BUSINESS:

Data Management Solutions
Storage Solutions
Data Protection Software Products
Data Protection Platform Products
Storage Security Products
Data Retention & Archive Software Products
Storage Management & Application Software
Management Tools

BRANDS/DIVISIONS/AFFILIATES:

Data ONTAP
Bycast, Inc.
NetCache
NetStore
NearStore
MetroCluster
FlexVol
DataFort

CONTACTS: *Note: Officers with more than one job title may be intentionally listed here more than once.*

Tom Georgens, CEO
Tom Georgens, Pres.
Steve Gomo, CFO/Exec. VP
Christine Heckart, Chief Mktg. Officer
Gwen McDonald, Exec. VP-Human Resources
Steve Kleiman, Chief Scientist/Sr. VP
Marina Levinson, CIO/Sr. VP
Brian Pawlowsku, CTO/Sr. VP
Manish Goel, Exec. VP-Product Oper.
Matthew Fawcett, General Counsel/Exec. VP/Sec.
Rob Salmon, Exec. VP-Field Oper.
Vic Mahadevan, Chief Strategy Officer
Tara Dhillon, VP-Investor Rel.
Eric Mann, Sr. VP-Americas Sales
Ed Deenihan, Exec. VP-Customer Advocacy
Tom Gerstenberger, Sr. VP-Bus. Oper.
Mark Jon Bluth, Sr. VP-Oper.
Dan Warmenhoven, Chmn.
Andreas Konig, Sr. VP/Gen. Mgr.-EMEA

Phone: 408-822-6000 **Fax:** 408-822-4501
Toll-Free: 877-263-8277
Address: 495 E. Java Dr., Sunnyvale, CA 94089 US

GROWTH PLANS/SPECIAL FEATURES:

NetApp, Inc. is a provider of storage and data management products. Its products include data management software; storage management and integration software; fabric-attached storage (FAS) products; V-Series products; virtual tape library (VTL) Data Protection Systems; data protection software products; data retention and archive products; storage security products; and the NetApp Performance Acceleration Module (PAM). The FAS and V-Series storage product lines are based on Data ONTAP, an optimized, scalable and flexible operating system that supports any mix of storage area network (SAN), network-attached storage (NAS) and Internet protocol SAN (IP SAN) environments concurrently in UNIX, Linux, Windows and Web environments. NetApp data management software includes FlexVol, FlexClone, Deduplication, FlexShare, FlexCache and MultiStore technology designed to enhance the efficiency of storage architecture. The company's storage management and application integration software is divided into four suites of products targeted to different IT administrative roles: Storage Suite, Server Suite, Database Suite and Application Suite. VTL Data Protection Systems is a disk-to-disk backup application that can be used by any heterogeneous primary storage environment. The company's data protection products include business continuance and disk backup solutions for enterprise customers including MetroCluster, SnapMirror, SyncMirror, SnapRestore, and SnapVault brands. Its data retention and archive products are designed to meet regulatory demands faced by enterprises and are marketed under the SnapLock brand name. Storage security products consist of the DataFort security appliance, which combines wire-speed encryption, access controls, authentication and automated key management tools. The PAM is designed to enhance the performance of random read intensive workloads such as file services and messaging. In May 2010, the company acquired Bycast, Inc., which specializes in mass data storage.

The firm offers its employees medical, dental and vision coverage; short- and long-term disability; a 401(k) plan; an employee stock purchase program; flexible spending accounts; an employee assistance program; and tuition reimbursement.

FINANCIALS: **Sales and profits are in thousands of dollars—add 000 to get the full amount. 2010 Note: Financial information for 2010 was not available for all companies at press time.**

2010 Sales: $3,931,400 | 2010 Profits: $400,400
2009 Sales: $3,406,393 | 2009 Profits: $64,600
2008 Sales: $3,303,167 | 2008 Profits: $309,738
2007 Sales: $2,804,282 | 2007 Profits: $297,735
2006 Sales: $2,066,456 | 2006 Profits: $266,452

U.S. Stock Ticker: NTAP
Int'l Ticker:
Int'l Exchange:
Employees: 8,333 Fiscal Year Ends: 4/30
Parent Company:

SALARIES/BENEFITS:

Pension Plan: | ESOP Stock Plan: | Profit Sharing: | Top Exec. Salary: $754,038 | Bonus: $2,001,750
Savings Plan: Y | Stock Purch. Plan: Y | | Second Exec. Salary: $599,999 | Bonus: $1,467,692

OTHER THOUGHTS:

Apparent Women Officers or Directors: 3
Hot Spot for Advancement for Women/Minorities: Y

LOCATIONS: ("Y" = Yes)

West:	Southwest:	Midwest:	Southeast:	Northeast:	International:
Y				Y	Y

NEW YORK LIFE INSURANCE CO

www.newyorklife.com

Industry Group Code: 524113

Management:		Sales/Marketing:		Liberal Arts:		Information Sys.:		Professionals:		Tech./Scientific:	
Mgmt. Trainees:	Y	Marketing Pros.:	Y	Gen. Writing/Editing:	Y	Info. Mgmt.:	Y	Finance/Acct.:	Y	Engineers, Elec.:	
Experienced Mgmt.:	Y	Retail Sales:	Y	Tech. Writing:		Software Dev.:	Y	Law:	Y	Engineers, Other:	
Int'l Business:	Y	Comm./Industrial:	Y	Graphic Arts/Photog.:		Hardware Dev.:		HR/Other:	Y	Health/Lab:	
MBA Grads:	Y	Sales Trainees:	Y	Music:		Consulting/Other:		Training:	Y	Science/Research:	Y
		Advertising Pros.:	Y	Broadcasting:				Health Care:	Y	Petroleum/Chem.:	
				Other:				Consulting:		Math/Other:	Y

TYPES OF BUSINESS:

Life Insurance
Annuities
Mutual Funds
Asset Management
Life Insurance
Real Estate

BRANDS/DIVISIONS/AFFILIATES:

New York Life Investment Management
New York Life International LLC
New York Life Investments Real Estate Group
Madison Capital Funding
MainStay Investments
ACE Group

CONTACTS: *Note: Officers with more than one job title may be intentionally listed here more than once.*

Theodore A. Mathas, CEO
Theodore A. Mathas, Pres.
Michael E. Sproule, CFO/Exec. VP
Barry Schub, Sr. VP-Human Resources
Eileen T. Slevin, CIO/Sr. VP
Sue Ericksen, CTO/Sr. VP-Corp. Info. Dept.
Frank M. Boccio, Chief Admin. Officer/Exec. VP
Sheila K. Davidson, General Counsel/Exec. VP/Chief Legal Officer
Gary Wendlandt, Vice Chmn./Chief Investment Officer
Christopher O. Blunt, Exec. VP-Retirement Income Security
John Y. Kim, Chief Investment Officer/Exec. VP
Susan A. Thrope, Deputy General Counsel/Sec./Sr. VP
Theodore A. Mathas, Chmn.

Phone: 212-576-7000 **Fax:** 212-576-8145
Toll-Free: 800-692-3086
Address: 51 Madison Ave., New York, NY 10010 US

GROWTH PLANS/SPECIAL FEATURES:

New York Life Insurance Co. provides life insurance policies, annuities, mutual funds and third-party asset management services. The company has more than $283 billion assets under management. New York Life operates in all 50 U.S. states; and through New York Life International, LLC, it operates in India, Thailand, Argentina, Bermuda, China, Mexico and Taiwan. New York Life markets fixed and variable life insurance and annuity products that provide protection in the form of death benefits, savings and retirement income. The company offers five- and 20-year term life insurance; family protection insurance; survivorship life insurance and increased premium term life and term life to age 90 insurance. Other lines of business include long-term care insurance and special group policies sold through AARP and other affinity groups or professional associations. The firm maintains a virtual service center on its web site that enables policyholders to obtain information on their policies and premiums. Through its New York Life Investment Management subsidiary, the company provides a broad range of asset management products and services for individuals, corporations, foundations and municipalities. The primary distribution channel for its products is the firm's agency force. In addition, the company provides individual health, group health and impaired risk life and disability income through third party services. Some of the subsidiaries of the firm include New York Life Investments Fixed Income Investors Group (FIIG) which manages investments in the institutional market; New York Life Investments Real Estate Group, which manages a portfolio of real estate debt and equity; Madison Capital Funding, which is a finance company that serves the financing needs of private equity sponsors; and MainStay Investments, which provides investment advisory services to individual investors. In October 2010, the firm agreed to sell its life insurance operation in South Korea and Hong Kong to ACE Group for approximately $425 million in cash.

FINANCIALS: **Sales and profits are in thousands of dollars—add 000 to get the full amount. 2010 Note: Financial information for 2010 was not available for all companies at press time.**

2010 Sales: $30,168,000 | 2010 Profits: $1,436,000
2009 Sales: $22,246,000 | 2009 Profits: $1,327,000
2008 Sales: $16,830,000 | 2008 Profits: $-1,016,000
2007 Sales: $21,123,000 | 2007 Profits: $
2006 Sales: $20,980,000 | 2006 Profits: $2,298,000

U.S. Stock Ticker: Mutual Company
Int'l Ticker:
Int'l Exchange:
Employees: 17,000 Fiscal Year Ends: 12/31
Parent Company:

SALARIES/BENEFITS:

Pension Plan: Y | ESOP Stock Plan: | Profit Sharing: | Top Exec. Salary: $ | Bonus: $
Savings Plan: | Stock Purch. Plan: | | Second Exec. Salary: $ | Bonus: $

OTHER THOUGHTS:

Apparent Women Officers or Directors: 9
Hot Spot for Advancement for Women/Minorities: Y

LOCATIONS: ("Y" = Yes)

West:	Southwest:	Midwest:	Southeast:	Northeast:	International:
Y	Y	Y	Y	Y	Y

NEWS CORP

www.newscorp.com

Industry Group Code: 515120

Management:		Sales/Marketing:		Liberal Arts:		Information Sys.:		Professionals:		Tech./Scientific:	
Mgmt. Trainees:	Y	Marketing Pros.:	Y	Gen. Writing/Editing:	Y	Info. Mgmt.:	Y	Finance/Acct.:	Y	Engineers, Elec.:	Y
Experienced Mgmt.:	Y	Retail Sales:		Tech. Writing:		Software Dev.:	Y	Law:	Y	Engineers, Other:	
Int'l Business:	Y	Comm./Industrial:	Y	Graphic Arts/Photog.:	Y	Hardware Dev.:		HR/Other:	Y	Health/Lab:	
MBA Grads:	Y	Sales Trainees:		Music:	Y	Consulting/Other:		Training:	Y	Science/Research:	
		Advertising Pros.:	Y	Broadcasting:	Y			Health Care:		Petroleum/Chem.:	
				Other:	Y			Consulting:		Math/Other:	

TYPES OF BUSINESS:

Television Broadcasting & Distribution
Film & Television Production
Newspaper Publishing
Online Media
Advertising Services
Magazine & Book Publishing
Satellite Television

BRANDS/DIVISIONS/AFFILIATES:

BRITISH SKY BROADCASTING GROUP PLC (BSKYB)
STAR Group Limited
MyNetworkTV
Fox Broadcasting Company
HarperCollins Publishers Inc
Wall Street Journal (The)
IGN.com
Dow Jones & Co., Inc

CONTACTS:

Note: Officers with more than one job title may be intentionally listed here more than once.

K. Rupert Murdoch, CEO
Chase Carey, COO
Chase Carey, Pres.
David DeVoe, CFO/Sr. Exec. VP
Beryl Cook, Chief Human Resources Officer
Lawrence A. Jacobs, General Counsel/Sr. Exec. VP
Teri Everett, Sr. VP-Corp. Affairs & Comm.
Reed Nolte, Sr. VP-Investor Rel.
Roger Ailes, Chmn./CEO-FOX News Channel & FOX Bus. Network
Tom Mockridge, CEO-European Television
Michael Regan, Exec. VP-Gov't Affairs
James Murdoch, Deputy COO
K. Rupert Murdoch, Chmn.

Phone: 212-852-7000 **Fax:** 212-852-7147
Toll-Free:
Address: 1211 Ave. of the Americas, New York, NY 10036 US

GROWTH PLANS/SPECIAL FEATURES:

News Corp. is a media and entertainment company with roughly $55.9 billion in assets. The firm operates in six segments: filmed entertainment; television; cable network programming; direct broadcast satellite television; publishing; and other. The filmed entertainment segment produces and acquires live-action and animated motion pictures for distribution and licensing in all formats; and produces and licenses television programming worldwide. Subsidiaries include Twentieth Century Fox and Fox Searchlight Pictures. The television segment operates broadcast television stations; broadcasts network programming in the U.S.; and develops, produces and broadcasts television programming in Asia. News Corp. owns 27 Fox and MyNetworkTV television stations. The cable networking programming division produces and licenses news, sports, general entertainment and movie programming for distributors worldwide. News Corp.'s U.S. cable network operations include the Fox News Channel, the FX Network and the National Geographic Channels; its international cable interests consist primarily of STAR Group Limited. The direct broadcast satellite television segment operates through SKY Italia, which currently distributes services via satellite and broadband to subscribers in Italy. The publishing division offers book publishing through HarperCollins Publishers, which primarily publishes fiction and non-fiction for the general consumer; the publication of free standing inserts and the provision of in-store marketing products and services; and newspapers and magazines in the U.K., Ireland, Australia and the U.S., including The Sun, The Wall Street Journal (Dow Jones & Co., Inc) and the New York Post. The other segment includes News' Internet businesses, including IGN.com; News Outdoor; Fox Mobile Entertainment for mobile phones; and others. In 2011, the firm sold its MySpace unit after disappointing results. In mid 2011, News Corp was involved in a deep controversy in the UK when it was alleged that a tabloid owned by the firm, News of the World, had illegally gathered personal details from private voice mail accounts, and private investigators used by the firm were accused of using illicit methods to gather information. News Corp promptly closed the newspaper.

FINANCIALS:

Sales and profits are in thousands of dollars—add 000 to get the full amount. 2010 Note: Financial information for 2010 was not available for all companies at press time.

2010 Sales: $32,778,000	2010 Profits: $2,644,000	**U.S. Stock Ticker: NWS**
2009 Sales: $30,423,000	2009 Profits: $-3,310,000	**Int'l Ticker:**
2008 Sales: $32,996,000	2008 Profits: $5,518,000	Int'l Exchange:
2007 Sales: $28,655,000	2007 Profits: $3,426,000	Employees: 51,000 Fiscal Year Ends: 6/30
2006 Sales: $25,327,000	2006 Profits: $2,314,000	Parent Company:

SALARIES/BENEFITS:

Pension Plan:	ESOP Stock Plan:	Profit Sharing:	Top Exec. Salary: $8,100,000	Bonus: $15,000,000
Savings Plan: Y	Stock Purch. Plan:		Second Exec. Salary: $8,100,000	Bonus: $4,368,800

OTHER THOUGHTS:

Apparent Women Officers or Directors: 3
Hot Spot for Advancement for Women/Minorities: Y

LOCATIONS: ("Y" = Yes)

West:	Southwest:	Midwest:	Southeast:	Northeast:	International:
Y				Y	Y

Sales, profits and employees may be estimates. Financial information, benefits and other data can change quickly and may vary from those stated here.

NEXTERA ENERGY INC

www.nexteraenergy.com

Industry Group Code: 2211

Management:		**Sales/Marketing:**		**Liberal Arts:**		**Information Sys.:**		**Professionals:**		**Tech./Scientific:**	
Mgmt. Trainees:	Y	Marketing Pros.:	Y	Gen. Writing/Editing:	Y	Info. Mgmt.:	Y	Finance/Acct.:	Y	Engineers, Elec.:	Y
Experienced Mgmt.:	Y	Retail Sales:		Tech. Writing:	Y	Software Dev.:	Y	Law:	Y	Engineers, Other:	Y
Int'l Business:	Y	Comm./Industrial:	Y	Graphic Arts/Photog.:	Y	Hardware Dev.:		HR/Other:	Y	Health/Lab:	
MBA Grads:	Y	Sales Trainees:		Music:		Consulting/Other:		Training:	Y	Science/Research:	
		Advertising Pros.:	Y	Broadcasting:				Health Care:		Petroleum/Chem.:	Y
				Other:				Consulting:		Math/Other:	

TYPES OF BUSINESS:

Utilities-Electricity & Natural Gas
Fiber-Optic Services
Financial Services
Nuclear Power
Energy Trading & Marketing
Wind Power
Solar Power

BRANDS/DIVISIONS/AFFILIATES:

Florida Power & Light Company
NextEra Energy Resources LLC
FPL FiberNet, LLC
NextEra Energy Power Marketing LLC
FPL Group, Inc.

CONTACTS: *Note: Officers with more than one job title may be intentionally listed here more than once.*

Lewis Hay, III, CEO
James L. Robo, COO
James L. Robo, Pres.
Armando Pimentel, Jr., CFO/Exec. VP-Finance
Shaun J. Francis, Exec. VP-Human Resources
Robert L. McGrath, Exec. VP-Eng., Construction & Corp. Svcs.
Charles E. Sieving, General Counsel/Exec. VP
Christopher A. Bennett, Chief Strategy, Policy & Bus. Officer/Exec. VP
K. Michael Davis, Chief Acct. Officer/Controller/VP
Carmen Perez, Pres., FPL FiberNet LLC
F. Mitchell Davidson, CEO/Pres., NextEra Energy Resources
Armando J. Olivera, CEO/Pres., Florida Power & Light Company
Alissa E. Ballot, VP/Corp. Sec.
Lewis Hay, III, Chmn.

Phone: 561-694-4000	**Fax:**
Toll-Free:	
Address: 700 Universe Blvd., Juno Beach, FL 33408 US	

GROWTH PLANS/SPECIAL FEATURES:

NextEra Energy, Inc., formerly FPL Group, Inc., is a public utility holding company. Its primary subsidiaries are Florida Power & Light Company (FPL), which generates, transmits, distributes, buys and sells electricity; and NextEra Energy Resources LLC, a leading renewable energy generator. FPL supplies electric service to over 8.7 million people throughout the east and lower west coasts of Florida and has 4.5 million customer accounts. Approximately 58% of the company's power is produced by natural gas fueled plants; 20% by nuclear plants; 4% by oil plants and 5% by coal plants, while 13% is purchased from other companies. In all, FPL operates 79 plants that burn natural gas, oil or a combination of both; and ownership in three coal plants. FPL also has one solar generation facility in operation and two under construction. NextEra Energy Resources has a capacity of roughly 18,866 megawatts (MW), utilizing 44% wind, 35% natural gas, 14% nuclear, 4% oil, 2% hydro and 1% combined solar and coal. The subsidiary's portfolio includes more than 100 operating projects in 26 states and Canada. NextEra Energy Power Marketing LLC, a subsidiary of NextEra Energy Resources, buys and sells wholesale energy commodities, such as natural gas, oil and electricity, and manages the fuel needs of NextEra Energy Resources' power generation fleet. Additionally, NextEra Energy operates FPL FiberNet LLC, which leases wholesale fiber-optic network capacity and dark fiber to various clients.

NextEra Energy offers medical, dental and vision benefits; flexible spending plans; life insurance and dependant life insurance; and education and adoption assistance.

FINANCIALS: **Sales and profits are in thousands of dollars—add 000 to get the full amount. 2010 Note: Financial information for 2010 was not available for all companies at press time.**

2010 Sales: $15,317,000	2010 Profits: $1,957,000	**U.S. Stock Ticker: NEE**
2009 Sales: $15,643,000	2009 Profits: $1,615,000	**Int'l Ticker:**
2008 Sales: $16,410,000	2008 Profits: $1,639,000	Int'l Exchange:
2007 Sales: $15,263,000	2007 Profits: $1,312,000	Employees: 14,690 Fiscal Year Ends: 12/31
2006 Sales: $15,710,000	2006 Profits: $1,281,000	Parent Company:

SALARIES/BENEFITS:

Pension Plan: Y	ESOP Stock Plan: Y	Profit Sharing:	Top Exec. Salary: $1,293,500	Bonus: $2,328,300
Savings Plan: Y	Stock Purch. Plan:		Second Exec. Salary: $831,600	Bonus: $1,144,282

OTHER THOUGHTS:

Apparent Women Officers or Directors: 6
Hot Spot for Advancement for Women/Minorities: Y

LOCATIONS: ("Y" = Yes)

West:	Southwest:	Midwest:	Southeast:	Northeast:	International:
Y	Y	Y	Y	Y	Y

NII HOLDINGS INC

www.nii.com

Industry Group Code: 5172

Management:		Sales/Marketing:		Liberal Arts:		Information Sys.:		Professionals:		Tech./Scientific:	
Mgmt. Trainees:	Y	Marketing Pros.:	Y	Gen. Writing/Editing:	Y	Info. Mgmt.:	Y	Finance/Acct.:	Y	Engineers, Elec.:	Y
Experienced Mgmt.:	Y	Retail Sales:		Tech. Writing:	Y	Software Dev.:	Y	Law:	Y	Engineers, Other:	Y
Int'l Business:	Y	Comm./Industrial:	Y	Graphic Arts/Photog.:	Y	Hardware Dev.:		HR/Other:	Y	Health/Lab:	
MBA Grads:	Y	Sales Trainees:		Music:		Consulting/Other:		Training:	Y	Science/Research:	
		Advertising Pros.:	Y	Broadcasting:				Health Care:		Petroleum/Chem.:	
				Other:				Consulting:		Math/Other:	

TYPES OF BUSINESS:

Cell Phone Service
GPS Technologies
Internet Service

BRANDS/DIVISIONS/AFFILIATES:

CONTACTS:

Note: Officers with more than one job title may be intentionally listed here more than once.

Steven P. Dussek, CEO
Gokul V. Hemmady, CFO/Exec. VP
Gregory J. Santoro, Chief Mktg. Officer/ExecVP
Alfonso Martinez, Exec. VP-Human Resources
Alan Strauss, CTO/Exec. VP
Gary Begeman, General Counsel/Exec. VP
John M. McMahon, Exec. VP-Bus. Oper.
Gregory J. Santoro, Chief Strategy Officer
Daniel E. Freiman, Treas./VP
Miguel E. Rivera, Pres., Nextel Peru
Sergio Borges Chaia, CEO/Pres., Nextel Brazil
Ruben Butvilofsky, Pres., Nextel Argentina
Claudio Hidalgo, Pres., Nextel Chile
Steven M. Shindler, Chmn.
Peter A. Foyo, Pres., Nextel Mexico

Phone: 703-390-5100	**Fax:** 703-547-5269
Toll-Free:	
Address: 1875 Explorer St., Ste. 1000, Reston, VA 20190 US	

GROWTH PLANS/SPECIAL FEATURES:

NII Holdings, Inc., provides digital wireless communication services through operating companies located in selected Latin American markets. Based in Virginia, the firm operates through five major divisions named for their geographic area: Nextel Mexico, Nextel Chile, Nextel Brazil, Nextel Argentina and Nextel Peru. The company uses a transmission technology developed by Motorola, Inc., called integrated digital enhanced network (iDEN), to provide its digital mobile services on 800 MHz spectrum holdings throughout its market area. This technology allows NII to use its spectrum efficiently and to offer multiple wireless services integrated into a variety of handset devices. Services offered by NII include mobile telephone, Nextel Direct Connect, international roaming, International Direct Connect, global positioning system (GPS) technologies, text messaging and e-mail. The company's mobile telephone service includes such features as speakerphone, conference calling, voice mail, call forwarding and additional line service. Nextel Direct Connect is a long-range walkie-talkie service enabling users to set up a conference more quickly than would be possible with a traditional mobile telephone call. International Direct Connect allows subscribers to communicate instantly across national borders with other subscribers in Mexico, Brazil, Argentina, Peru and Chile; any Sprint Nextel Corporation subscriber in the U.S. and TELUS subscriber in Canada using a compatible handset. NII's operating companies have approximately 9.03 million digital handsets in commercial service. In May 2010, the firm, through Nextel Argentina, Nextel Mexico and Nextel Brazil, released the Motorola i1 Android-based smartphone; the product offers a Push-to-Talk feature and several other multimedia capabilities.

FINANCIALS:

Sales and profits are in thousands of dollars—add 000 to get the full amount. 2010 Note: Financial information for 2010 was not available for all companies at press time.

2010 Sales: $5,601,316	2010 Profits: $341,052	**U.S. Stock Ticker: NIHD**
2009 Sales: $4,397,599	2009 Profits: $381,491	**Int'l Ticker:**
2008 Sales: $4,269,380	2008 Profits: $341,955	Int'l Exchange:
2007 Sales: $3,296,295	2007 Profits: $378,418	Employees: 13,500 Fiscal Year Ends: 12/31
2006 Sales: $2,371,340	2006 Profits: $294,490	Parent Company:

SALARIES/BENEFITS:

Pension Plan:	ESOP Stock Plan:	Profit Sharing:	Top Exec. Salary: $771,520	Bonus: $503,525
Savings Plan:	Stock Purch. Plan:		Second Exec. Salary: $750,677	Bonus: $1,059,660

OTHER THOUGHTS:

Apparent Women Officers or Directors: 2
Hot Spot for Advancement for Women/Minorities:

LOCATIONS: ("Y" = Yes)

West:	Southwest:	Midwest:	Southeast:	Northeast:	International:
				Y	Y

NIKE INC

www.nike.com

Industry Group Code: 316219

Management:		Sales/Marketing:		Liberal Arts:		Information Sys.:		Professionals:		Tech./Scientific:	
Mgmt. Trainees:	Y	Marketing Pros.:	Y	Gen. Writing/Editing:	Y	Info. Mgmt.:	Y	Finance/Acct.:	Y	Engineers, Elec.:	
Experienced Mgmt.:	Y	Retail Sales:	Y	Tech. Writing:		Software Dev.:	Y	Law:	Y	Engineers, Other:	
Int'l Business:	Y	Comm./Industrial:	Y	Graphic Arts/Photog.:	Y	Hardware Dev.:		HR/Other:	Y	Health/Lab:	
MBA Grads:	Y	Sales Trainees:	Y	Music:		Consulting/Other:		Training:	Y	Science/Research:	
		Advertising Pros.:	Y	Broadcasting:				Health Care:		Petroleum/Chem.:	
				Other:	Y			Consulting:		Math/Other:	

TYPES OF BUSINESS:

Athletic Shoes/Apparel Manufacturing
Athletic Equipment
Sports Accessories
Retail Stores
Sports Apparel
Plastic Products
Hockey Products
Swimwear

BRANDS/DIVISIONS/AFFILIATES:

Cole Haan Holdings Inc
Star Chevron
Jack Purcell
Converse Inc
Hurley International LLC
Umbro Ltd
Chuck Taylor
All Star

CONTACTS: *Note: Officers with more than one job title may be intentionally listed here more than once.*

Mark Parker, CEO
Mark Parker, Pres.
Donald Blair, CFO/VP
John Slusher, VP-Global Sports Mktg.
David Ayre, VP-Global Human Resources
Hans van Alebeek, VP-Tech.
Eric Sprunk, VP-Merch. & Prod.
Ernie Rose, VP-Mfg. & Sourcing
John F. Colburn III, Corp. Sec.
Gary M. DeStefano, VP/Pres., Global Oper.
Thomas E. Clarke, VP-New Bus. Dev.
Chris Shimojima, VP-eCommerce
Nigel Powell, VP-Global Comm.
Bernard Pliska, VP/Corp. Controller
Maria S. Eitel, Pres., NIKE Foundation
Charlie Denson, Pres., NIKE Brand
Roger Wyett, Pres., NIKE Affiliates
Bob Wood, Pres., SPARQ/SST
Philip H. Knight, Chmn.
Jan Singer, VP-Global Apparel
Nick Athanasakos, VP-Global Supply Chain

Phone: 503-671-6453 **Fax:**
Toll-Free: 800-344-6453
Address: 1 Bowerman Dr., Beaverton, OR 97005 US

GROWTH PLANS/SPECIAL FEATURES:

Nike, Inc. designs, develops and markets footwear, apparel, equipment and accessories. It is one of the largest sellers of athletic footwear and athletic apparel in the world. The company's athletic footwear products are designed primarily for specific athletic use, although a large percentage of the products are worn for casual or leisure purposes. Running, training, basketball, soccer, sport-inspired urban shoes and children's shoes are the firm's top-selling product categories. Nike also markets shoes designed for tennis, golf, baseball, football, lacrosse, walking, outdoor activities, skateboarding, bicycling, volleyball, wrestling, cheerleading, aquatic activities and other athletic and recreational uses. The firm maintains several wholly-owned subsidiaries, including Cole Haan, which designs and distributes a line of casual footwear, apparel and accessories for men and women under the Cole Haan brand name; Converse, Inc., which distributes and licenses footwear, apparel and accessories through brand names Converse, All Star, One Star, Chuck Taylor, Star Chevron and Jack Purcell; Hurley International LLC, which is headquartered in the U.K. and designs/distributes a collection of action sports apparel sold under the Hurley brand; and Umbro Ltd., which markets a line of athletic and casual footwear, apparel and equipment (primarily for soccer) under the trademark name Umbro. Nike sells its products to retail accounts, through Nike-owned retail stores and through a mix of independent distributors and licensees, in more than 150 countries. Within the U.S., the firm operates 346 Nike Brand and subsidiary retail stores: 171 Nike locations, 106 Cole Haan stores, 51 Converse factory stores and 18 Hurley locations. U.S. sales generate approximately 42% of the firm's total revenues. In the international market, which includes several countries within Europe, Asia, South America, and Africa, the firm maintains 343 retail stores (274 Nike, 68 Cole Haan and one Hurley). The international market accounts for 58% of Nike's total revenues.

FINANCIALS: **Sales and profits are in thousands of dollars—add 000 to get the full amount. 2010 Note: Financial information for 2010 was not available for all companies at press time.**

2010 Sales: $19,014,000 | 2010 Profits: $1,906,700
2009 Sales: $19,176,100 | 2009 Profits: $1,486,700
2008 Sales: $18,627,000 | 2008 Profits: $1,883,400
2007 Sales: $16,325,900 | 2007 Profits: $1,491,500
2006 Sales: $14,954,900 | 2006 Profits: $1,392,000

U.S. Stock Ticker: NKE
Int'l Ticker:
Int'l Exchange:
Employees: 34,400 Fiscal Year Ends: 5/31
Parent Company:

SALARIES/BENEFITS:

Pension Plan: | ESOP Stock Plan: | Profit Sharing: Y | Top Exec. Salary: $1,475,000 | Bonus: $4,441,875
Savings Plan: Y | Stock Purch. Plan: Y | Second Exec. Salary: $1,260,000 | Bonus: $3,238,000

OTHER THOUGHTS:

Apparent Women Officers or Directors: 18
Hot Spot for Advancement for Women/Minorities: Y

LOCATIONS: ("Y" = Yes)

West:	Southwest:	Midwest:	Southeast:	Northeast:	International:
Y	Y	Y	Y	Y	Y

Sales, profits and employees may be estimates. Financial information, benefits and other data can change quickly and may vary from those stated here.

NORFOLK SOUTHERN CORP

www.nscorp.com

Industry Group Code: 48211

Management:		Sales/Marketing:		Liberal Arts:		Information Sys.:		Professionals:		Tech./Scientific:	
Mgmt. Trainees:	Y	Marketing Pros.:	Y	Gen. Writing/Editing:	Y	Info. Mgmt.:	Y	Finance/Acct.:	Y	Engineers, Elec.:	Y
Experienced Mgmt.:	Y	Retail Sales:		Tech. Writing:	Y	Software Dev.:	Y	Law:	Y	Engineers, Other:	Y
Int'l Business:	Y	Comm./Industrial:	Y	Graphic Arts/Photog.:		Hardware Dev.:	Y	HR/Other:	Y	Health/Lab:	
MBA Grads:	Y	Sales Trainees:		Music:		Consulting/Other:		Training:	Y	Science/Research:	
		Advertising Pros.:	Y	Broadcasting:				Health Care:		Petroleum/Chem.:	
				Other:				Consulting:		Math/Other:	

TYPES OF BUSINESS:

Railroad Transportation
Cargo Services
Logistics Services
Business Process Automation

BRANDS/DIVISIONS/AFFILIATES:

Norfolk Southern Railway Co.
CSX Corp
Conrail, Inc.
Pocahontas Land Corporation
Triple Crown Services Co.
RoadRailer
Lambert's Point Docks, Inc.
TransWorks

CONTACTS:
Note: Officers with more than one job title may be intentionally listed here more than once.

Charles W. Moorman, CEO
Mark D. Manion, COO
Charles W. Moorman, Pres.
James A. Squires, CFO/Exec. VP
Donald W. Seale, Chief Mktg. Officer/Exec. VP
Deborah H. Butler, CIO
John P. Rathbone, Exec. VP-Admin.
James A. Hixon, Exec. VP-Law
Mark D. Manion, Exec. VP-Oper.
Deborah H. Butler, Exec. VP-Planning
James Hixon, Exec. VP-Corp. Rel.
Leanne Marilley, Dir.-Investor Rel.
James A. Squires, Exec. VP-Finance
Charles W. Moorman, Chmn.

Phone: 757-823-5567	**Fax:** 757-629-2361
Toll-Free: 800-635-5738	
Address: 3 Commercial Pl., Box 227, Norfolk, VA 23510 US	

GROWTH PLANS/SPECIAL FEATURES:

Norfolk Southern Corp., based in Norfolk, Virginia, controls a major freight railroad through Norfolk Southern Railway Co. Norfolk Southern Railway Co. is principally engaged in the rail transportation of raw materials, intermediate products and finished goods in the Southeast, East and Midwest and, via interchange with rail carriers, the rest of the U.S. Norfolk Southern also transports overseas freight through several Atlantic and Gulf Coast ports. The company's general merchandise traffic is composed of five major commodity groupings: automotive; chemicals; metals and construction; agriculture, consumer products and government; and paper, clay and forest products. The firm also provides logistics services and offers an intermodal network in the eastern U.S. Norfolk Southern operates about 21,000 route miles in 22 eastern states and Washington, D.C. The firm owns and leases nearly 4,000 locomotives and 90,000 freight cars. Its lines reach many individual industries, electric generating facilities, mines, warehouses, paper and steel mills, automobile assembly plants, rail auto parts centers, vehicle mixing centers, distribution centers, transload facilities and other businesses located in smaller communities. Through a limited liability company, the firm and CSX Corp. jointly own Conrail, Inc., whose primary subsidiary is Consolidated Rail Corp. Other subsidiaries of Norfolk Southern include the Triple Crown Services Co., which offers door-to-door truckload service using RoadRailer equipment; Lambert's Point Docks, Inc., which provides important export transloading services; Pocahontas Land Corporation, which owns and manages coal-containing land in several Southern and Midwestern states; and TransWorks, which provides modular transportation management systems, business process automation products and financial management solutions. Recently, Norfolk Southern opened a new intermodal terminal in Titusville, Florida.

The company offers its employees medical, dental and vision coverage; a 401(k) plan; railroad retirement, which includes an additional benefit based on railroad earnings; and education assistance.

FINANCIALS:
Sales and profits are in thousands of dollars—add 000 to get the full amount. 2010 Note: Financial information for 2010 was not available for all companies at press time.

2010 Sales: $9,516,000	2010 Profits: $1,496,000	**U.S. Stock Ticker: NSC**
2009 Sales: $7,969,000	2009 Profits: $1,034,000	**Int'l Ticker:**
2008 Sales: $10,661,000	2008 Profits: $1,716,000	Int'l Exchange:
2007 Sales: $9,432,000	2007 Profits: $1,464,000	Employees: 28,559 Fiscal Year Ends: 12/31
2006 Sales: $9,407,000	2006 Profits: $1,481,000	Parent Company:

SALARIES/BENEFITS:

Pension Plan: Y	ESOP Stock Plan:	Profit Sharing:	Top Exec. Salary: $950,000	Bonus: $613,700
Savings Plan: Y	Stock Purch. Plan:		Second Exec. Salary: $500,000	Bonus: $201,900

OTHER THOUGHTS:

Apparent Women Officers or Directors: 2
Hot Spot for Advancement for Women/Minorities: Y

LOCATIONS: ("Y" = Yes)

West:	Southwest:	Midwest:	Southeast:	Northeast:	International:
	Y	Y	Y	Y	Y

NORTH HIGHLAND

Industry Group Code: 54161

www.northhighland.com

Management:		Sales/Marketing:		Liberal Arts:		Information Sys.:		Professionals:		Tech./Scientific:	
Mgmt. Trainees:		Marketing Pros.:	Y	Gen. Writing/Editing:		Info. Mgmt.:	Y	Finance/Acct.:	Y	Engineers, Elec.:	
Experienced Mgmt.:		Retail Sales:		Tech. Writing:	Y	Software Dev.:	Y	Law:	Y	Engineers, Other:	
Int'l Business:	Y	Comm./Industrial:	Y	Graphic Arts/Photog.:		Hardware Dev.:		HR/Other:	Y	Health/Lab:	
MBA Grads:	Y	Sales Trainees:		Music:		Consulting/Other:	Y	Training:		Science/Research:	
		Advertising Pros.:	Y	Broadcasting:				Health Care:		Petroleum/Chem.:	
				Other:	Y			Consulting:	Y	Math/Other:	

TYPES OF BUSINESS:

Management & Technology Consulting Services
Human Resources Consulting Services
Supply Chain Optimization
Marketing Consulting Services
Financial Reporting Consulting Services

BRANDS/DIVISIONS/AFFILIATES:

HBC Consulting
Insight Solutions Group, Inc.

CONTACTS:

Note: Officers with more than one job title may be intentionally listed here more than once.

Dan Reardon, CEO
David Deiters, Pres.
Kirk Hancock, CFO
Michael Lee, Pres.
Jeff Busch, Exec. VP
David Peterson, Chmn.

Phone: 404-233-1015 **Fax:** 404-233-4930
Toll-Free:
Address: 550 Pharr Rd., Ste. 850, Atlanta, GA 30305 US

GROWTH PLANS/SPECIAL FEATURES:

North Highland is a global consulting firm that serves clients locally through 48 offices across the U.S. and worldwide. The firm serves corporate, government and nonprofit clients through eight service categories: operations; strategy and advisory; information technology; customer experience and engagement; human capital; finance and accounting; and execution. Operations services encompass operational strategy, process and performance improvement consulting and supply chain optimization services. Strategy and advisory services include strategic planning and implementation; enterprise performance management; merger planning and integration; and outsourcing and shared services. Information technology solutions include infrastructure, architecture and design for VoIP and workflow platforms; sourcing strategy; solution planning and integration; and business intelligence and information management. Customer experience and engagement services include brand interaction strategy, marketing operations, customer analytics and segmentation, sales and contact center strategy and multichannel brand execution services. Human capital services encompass human resources and workforce strategy consulting, human resource performance improvement, workforce performance advisory and organizational design services. Finance and accounting services include finance function transformation; resource planning; and planning, budgeting and financial reporting solutions. Finally, the firm's execution operations include program and project management and change management services. In addition to the U.S., North Highland's offices are located in Australia, the Netherlands, Portugal, Austria, Belgium, Romania, China, Singapore, France, Spain, Germany, Switzerland, the United Arab Emirates, the U.K., Italy and Hungary. Recently opened offices are located in Jacksonville, Florida, and St. Louis, Missouri. In September 2010, the company acquired a majority interest in HBC Consulting, a China-based consulting firm to expand its services in China. In January 2011, North Highland acquired Insight Solutions Group, Inc., a management consulting firm.

North Highland offers its employees medical, dental, life and disability insurance; health and child care spending accounts; education reimbursement; career coaching; 3 - 4 weeks vacation and an employee assistance program.

FINANCIALS:

Sales and profits are in thousands of dollars—add 000 to get the full amount. 2010 Note: Financial information for 2010 was not available for all companies at press time.

2010 Sales: $ | 2010 Profits: $
2009 Sales: $ | 2009 Profits: $
2008 Sales: $ | 2008 Profits: $
2007 Sales: $ | 2007 Profits: $
2006 Sales: $ | 2006 Profits: $

U.S. Stock Ticker: Private
Int'l Ticker:
Int'l Exchange:
Employees: 3,200 Fiscal Year Ends:
Parent Company:

SALARIES/BENEFITS:

Pension Plan: | ESOP Stock Plan: Y | Profit Sharing: | Top Exec. Salary: $ | Bonus: $
Savings Plan: Y | Stock Purch. Plan: | Second Exec. Salary: $ | Bonus: $

OTHER THOUGHTS:

Apparent Women Officers or Directors: 1
Hot Spot for Advancement for Women/Minorities:

LOCATIONS: ("Y" = Yes)

West:	Southwest:	Midwest:	Southeast:	Northeast:	International:
Y	Y	Y	Y	Y	Y

Sales, profits and employees may be estimates. Financial information, benefits and other data can change quickly and may vary from those stated here.

NORTHWESTERN MUTUAL LIFE INSURANCE CO

www.northwesternmutual.com

Industry Group Code: 524113

Management:		Sales/Marketing:		Liberal Arts:		Information Sys.:		Professionals:		Tech./Scientific:	
Mgmt. Trainees:		Marketing Pros.:	Y	Gen. Writing/Editing:	Y	Info. Mgmt.:	Y	Finance/Acct.:	Y	Engineers, Elec.:	
Experienced Mgmt.:	Y	Retail Sales:		Tech. Writing:	Y	Software Dev.:	Y	Law:		Engineers, Other:	
Int'l Business:		Comm./Industrial:	Y	Graphic Arts/Photog.:		Hardware Dev.:		HR/Other:	Y	Health/Lab:	
MBA Grads:	Y	Sales Trainees:		Music:		Consulting/Other:	Y	Training:		Science/Research:	
		Advertising Pros.:	Y	Broadcasting:				Health Care:		Petroleum/Chem.:	
				Other:				Consulting:	Y	Math/Other:	Y

TYPES OF BUSINESS:

Life Insurance
Disability Insurance
Employee Benefit Plans
Long-Term Care Insurance
Investment Products & Services
Financial Planning Services

BRANDS/DIVISIONS/AFFILIATES:

Northwestern Long Term Care Insurance Company
Northwestern Mutual Investment Services, LLC
Northwestern Mutual Financial Network
Northwestern Mutual Trust Company
Estate Strategies Group
Network Planning Advisors
Strategic Employee Benefit Services

CONTACTS: *Note: Officers with more than one job title may be intentionally listed here more than once.*

John E. Schlifske, CEO
John M. Bremer, COO
Gary A. Poliner, Pres.
Michael G. Carter, CFO/VP
Conrad C. York, VP-Mktg.
Susan A. Lueger, VP-Human Resources
Timothy G. Schaefer, CIO
Jean M. Maier, Exec. VP-Tech.
Gregory C. Oberland, Exec. VP-Insurance & Investment Prod.
Marcia Rimai, Chief Admin. & Compliance Officer/Exec. VP
Raymond J. Manista, General Counsel/Sec.
Jean M. Maier, Exec. VP-Enterprise Oper.
Bethany M. Rodenhuis, VP-Corp. Planning
Kimberley Goode, VP-Comm. & Corp. Affairs
Gary M. Hewitt, Treas./VP
Gary A. Poliner, Chief Risk Officer
Mark G. Doll, Exec. VP/Chief Investment Officer
Eric P. Christophersen, VP-Wealth Mgmt.
John E. Schlifske, Chmn.
Meridee J. Maynar, Sr. VP-Prod. Dist.

Phone: 414-271-1444	**Fax:** 414-299-7022
Toll-Free:	
Address: 720 E. Wisconsin Ave., Milwaukee, WI 53202-4797 US	

GROWTH PLANS/SPECIAL FEATURES:

Northwestern Mutual Life Insurance Co. (NMLIC) is a financial network company. It offers network services, insurance products, investment products and advisory services to 3.3 million policy owners with 5.2 million policies nationwide and a total of roughly $1.24 trillion of life insurance coverage in force. Its network services include asset and income protection, personal needs analysis, investment services, education funding and retirement products. The firm also offers permanent, term and combination life insurance plans; providing individual and group disability plans to approximately 420,000 policy holders. Long-term care insurance is offered to 112,000 policy holders through NMLIC's Northwestern Long Term Care Insurance Company subsidiary, while investment services are provided by subsidiary Northwestern Mutual Investment Services, LLC. Under its marketing name, Northwestern Mutual Financial Network, NMLIC offers a wide range of products and services through 350 offices across the U.S. Network affiliates include Strategic Employee Benefit Services, which provides custom-designed employee benefit programs; Network Planning Advisors, which offers financial planning services; Estate Strategies Group, an investment advising group specializing in estate and business succession planning; and Northwestern Mutual Trust Company, which offers a full range of investment and trust services. NMLIC manages approximately $180 billion in total assets.

NMLIC offers its employees flexible spending accounts, training programs, flexible work schedules, adoption assistance, an on-site fitness center, credit union membership, educational assistance and a business-casual work environment.

FINANCIALS: **Sales and profits are in thousands of dollars—add 000 to get the full amount. 2010 Note: Financial information for 2010 was not available for all companies at press time.**

2010 Sales: $22,762,608	2010 Profits: $805,801
2009 Sales: $21,152,574	2009 Profits: $321,000
2008 Sales: $21,923,000	2008 Profits: $483,200
2007 Sales: $21,355,000	2007 Profits: $1,000,000
2006 Sales: $19,733,000	2006 Profits: $829,000

U.S. Stock Ticker: Mutual Company
Int'l Ticker:
Int'l Exchange:
Employees: 5,000 Fiscal Year Ends: 12/31
Parent Company:

SALARIES/BENEFITS:

Pension Plan: Y	ESOP Stock Plan:	Profit Sharing:	Top Exec. Salary: $	Bonus: $
Savings Plan: Y	Stock Purch. Plan:		Second Exec. Salary: $	Bonus: $

OTHER THOUGHTS:

Apparent Women Officers or Directors: 5
Hot Spot for Advancement for Women/Minorities: Y

LOCATIONS: ("Y" = Yes)

West:	Southwest:	Midwest:	Southeast:	Northeast:	International:
Y	Y	Y	Y	Y	

OCEANEERING INTERNATIONAL INC

www.oceaneering.com

Industry Group Code: 213112

Management:		Sales/Marketing:		Liberal Arts:		Information Sys.:		Professionals:		Tech./Scientific:	
Mgmt. Trainees:	Y	Marketing Pros.:	Y	Gen. Writing/Editing:		Info. Mgmt.:	Y	Finance/Acct.:	Y	Engineers, Elec.:	Y
Experienced Mgmt.:	Y	Retail Sales:		Tech. Writing:	Y	Software Dev.:	Y	Law:	Y	Engineers, Other:	Y
Int'l Business:	Y	Comm./Industrial:	Y	Graphic Arts/Photog.:		Hardware Dev.:		HR/Other:	Y	Health/Lab:	
MBA Grads:	Y	Sales Trainees:		Music:		Consulting/Other:		Training:	Y	Science/Research:	
		Advertising Pros.:		Broadcasting:				Health Care:		Petroleum/Chem.:	Y
				Other:				Consulting:		Math/Other:	

TYPES OF BUSINESS:

Oil & Gas Drilling Support Services
Subsea Construction
Engineered Services & Hardware
Maintenance & Repair Services
Production Systems
Remotely Operated Vehicles
Robotic Systems

BRANDS/DIVISIONS/AFFILIATES:

Oceaneering Intervention Engineering
Grayloc Products
Oceaneering Multiflex
Oceaneering Rotator
Advanced Technologies
Deepwater Technical Solutions
Ocean Legend
SMX International Canada Inc

CONTACTS: *Note: Officers with more than one job title may be intentionally listed here more than once.*

M. Kevin McEvoy, CEO
M. Kevin McEvoy, Pres.
W. Cardon Gerner, CFO/Sr. VP
Janet G. Charles, VP-Human Resources
Gregg K. Farris, CIO/VP
F. Richard Frisbie, Sr. VP-Deepwater Tech.
George R. Haubenreich, Jr., General Counsel/Sr. VP/Sec.
Stephen E. Bradshaw, VP-Bus. Dev.
Jack Jurkoshek, Dir.-Investor Rel.
W. Cardon Gerner, Chief Acct. Officer/VP
Marvin J. Migura, Exec. VP
Kevin Kerins, Sr. VP-Remotely Operated Vehicles
Robert P. Mingoia, Treas./VP
Robert P. Moschetta, VP-Health Safety Environment
John R. Huff, Chmn.
Todd Hoefler, VP-Supply Chain Mgmt.

Phone: 713-329-4500 | **Fax:** 713-329-4951

Toll-Free:

Address: 11911 FM 529, Houston, TX 77041 US

GROWTH PLANS/SPECIAL FEATURES:

Oceaneering International, Inc. primarily provides oilfield products and services worldwide to the oil and gas industry. The oil and gas business of the company has five segments: Remotely Operated Vehicles (ROVs), Subsea Products, Subsea Projects, Inspection and Mobile Offshore Production Systems (MOPS). Oceaneering uses submersible ROVs to support drilling and construction; pipeline inspection; and subsea production facility operation and maintenance. It designs and builds ROVs, owning a total of 260, one of the largest ROV fleets worldwide. The firm is an industry leader in providing ROV services on deepwater wells, a technically demanding operation. Its Subsea Products segment generally manufactures built-to-order items including hydraulic hoses, ROV tooling, control valves, production control equipment and pipeline repair systems. These products are manufactured mainly by the Oceaneering Intervention Engineering; Grayloc Products; Oceaneering Multiflex; and Oceaneering Rotator divisions. The Subsea Projects segment primarily operates in the Gulf of Mexico, offering subsea installation, inspection, maintenance and repair services. The Inspection segment provides nondestructive testing and inspection services to the power generation, engineering and petrochemical industries. The MOPS segment functions through the Ocean Legend unit, which operates offshore of Western Australia. Oceaneering's non-oilfield business is accomplished by its Advanced Technologies unit, which manufactures remotely operated diving vessels used extensively by the U.S. Navy, as well as life-support and robotic systems for use in government space programs. In August 2010, the firm acquired SMX International Canada, Inc., which specializes in manufacturing clamp connectors, check valves and universal ball joints.

Oceaneering offers its employees medical, dental, vision, life and AD&D insurance; flexible spending accounts; an employee assistance program; and a 401(k) program.

FINANCIALS: **Sales and profits are in thousands of dollars—add 000 to get the full amount. 2010 Note: Financial information for 2010 was not available for all companies at press time.**

2010 Sales: $1,917,045	2010 Profits: $200,531
2009 Sales: $1,822,081	2009 Profits: $188,353
2008 Sales: $1,977,421	2008 Profits: $199,386
2007 Sales: $1,743,080	2007 Profits: $180,374
2006 Sales: $1,280,198	2006 Profits: $124,494

U.S. Stock Ticker: OII
Int'l Ticker:
Int'l Exchange:
Employees: 8,200 Fiscal Year Ends: 12/31
Parent Company:

SALARIES/BENEFITS:

Pension Plan: | ESOP Stock Plan: | Profit Sharing: | Top Exec. Salary: $662,500 | Bonus: $3,280,560
Savings Plan: Y | Stock Purch. Plan: | | Second Exec. Salary: $450,000 | Bonus: $1,512,640

OTHER THOUGHTS:

Apparent Women Officers or Directors: 1
Hot Spot for Advancement for Women/Minorities:

LOCATIONS: ("Y" = Yes)

West:	Southwest:	Midwest:	Southeast:	Northeast:	International:
Y	Y		Y	Y	Y

ODYSSEY HEALTHCARE INC

www.odyshealth.com

Industry Group Code: 6216

Management:		**Sales/Marketing:**		**Liberal Arts:**		**Information Sys.:**		**Professionals:**		**Tech./Scientific:**	
Mgmt. Trainees:	Y	Marketing Pros.:	Y	Gen. Writing/Editing:	Y	Info. Mgmt.:	Y	Finance/Acct.:	Y	Engineers, Elec.:	
Experienced Mgmt.:	Y	Retail Sales:		Tech. Writing:	Y	Software Dev.:		Law:	Y	Engineers, Other:	
Int'l Business:		Comm./Industrial:		Graphic Arts/Photog.:	Y	Hardware Dev.:		HR/Other:	Y	Health/Lab:	Y
MBA Grads:	Y	Sales Trainees:		Music:		Consulting/Other:		Training:	Y	Science/Research:	
		Advertising Pros.:		Broadcasting:				Health Care:	Y	Petroleum/Chem.:	
				Other:	Y			Consulting:		Math/Other:	

TYPES OF BUSINESS:

Hospice Care Services
Medical Supplies & Equipment

BRANDS/DIVISIONS/AFFILIATES:

Gentiva Health Services Inc

CONTACTS:

Note: Officers with more than one job title may be intentionally listed here more than once.

Sandra Banfield, Chief Compliance Officer
Tony Strange, Pres./CEO-Gentiva Health Services

Phone: 214-922-9711	**Fax:** 214-922-9752
Toll-Free: 888-922-9711	
Address: 717 N. Harwood St., Ste. 1500, Dallas, TX 75201 US	

GROWTH PLANS/SPECIAL FEATURES:

Odyssey HealthCare, Inc. is a leading provider of hospice care in the U.S. The firm operates approximately 100 Medicare-certified hospice programs in 30 states and caters to roughly 12,456 patients per day. Odyssey assigns each of its hospice patients to an interdisciplinary team, composed of a physician, a patient care manager, one or more registered nurses, one or more certified home health aides, a medical social worker, a chaplain, a homemaker and one or more specially trained volunteers. The team assesses the clinical, psychosocial and spiritual needs of the patient and his or her family; develops a plan of care; and delivers, monitors and coordinates that plan of care with the goal of providing appropriate care for the patient and his or her family. Services provided by the company include nursing care; medical social services, physician services, dietary, spiritual and other patient counseling; general inpatient care; medical supplies and equipment; drugs for pain control and symptom management; home health aide services; homemaker services; physical, occupational and speech therapy; respite inpatient care; and family bereavement counseling. Services provided under the Medicare and Medicaid program represent approximately 97% of Odyssey's net patient service revenues. In August 2010, the firm was acquired by Gentiva Health Services, Inc. for $1 billion.

Employees are offered life, short-term disability, medical, dental and vision insurance; a 401(k); tuition reimbursement; paid time off; and flexible spending accounts.

FINANCIALS:

Sales and profits are in thousands of dollars—add 000 to get the full amount. 2010 Note: Financial information for 2010 was not available for all companies at press time.

2010 Sales: $748,093	2010 Profits: $52,155	**U.S. Stock Ticker: Subsidiary**
2009 Sales: $598,930	2009 Profits: $59,182	**Int'l Ticker:**
2008 Sales: $616,050	2008 Profits: $14,426	Int'l Exchange:
2007 Sales: $398,232	2007 Profits: $12,111	Employees: 6,094 Fiscal Year Ends: 12/31
2006 Sales: $379,218	2006 Profits: $19,729	Parent Company: GENTIVA HEALTH SERVICES INC

SALARIES/BENEFITS:

Pension Plan:	ESOP Stock Plan:	Profit Sharing:	Top Exec. Salary: $671,322	Bonus: $812,500
Savings Plan: Y	Stock Purch. Plan:		Second Exec. Salary: $383,451	Bonus: $370,000

OTHER THOUGHTS:

Apparent Women Officers or Directors: 2
Hot Spot for Advancement for Women/Minorities:

LOCATIONS: ("Y" = Yes)

West:	Southwest:	Midwest:	Southeast:	Northeast:	International:
Y	Y	Y	Y	Y	

OIL STATES INTERNATIONAL INC

www.oilstatesintl.com

Industry Group Code: 213112

Management:		Sales/Marketing:		Liberal Arts:		Information Sys.:		Professionals:		Tech./Scientific:	
Mgmt. Trainees:	Y	Marketing Pros.:	Y	Gen. Writing/Editing:		Info. Mgmt.:	Y	Finance/Acct.:	Y	Engineers, Elec.:	Y
Experienced Mgmt.:	Y	Retail Sales:		Tech. Writing:	Y	Software Dev.:	Y	Law:	Y	Engineers, Other:	Y
Int'l Business:	Y	Comm./Industrial:	Y	Graphic Arts/Photog.:		Hardware Dev.:		HR/Other:	Y	Health/Lab:	
MBA Grads:	Y	Sales Trainees:		Music:		Consulting/Other:		Training:	Y	Science/Research:	
		Advertising Pros.:		Broadcasting:				Health Care:		Petroleum/Chem.:	Y
				Other:				Consulting:		Math/Other:	

TYPES OF BUSINESS:

Oil & Gas Drilling Support Services
Offshore Products
Well Site Services
Tubular Services
Drilling Services
Catering & Logistics Services
Construction Services
Equipment Rental

BRANDS/DIVISIONS/AFFILIATES:

Sooner, Inc.
Oil States Energy Services, Inc.
HWC Energy Services, Inc.
PTI Group, Inc.
Acute Technological Services, Inc.
Mountain West Oilfield Service and Supplies
Ufford Leasing LLC (Mountain West)
MAC Services Group Limited (The)

CONTACTS: *Note: Officers with more than one job title may be intentionally listed here more than once.*

Cindy B. Taylor, CEO
Cindy B. Taylor, Pres.
Bradley J. Dodson, CFO/Treas./Sr. VP
Lias J. Steen, VP-Human Resources
Lias J. Steen, VP-Legal
Christopher E. Cragg, Sr. VP-Oper.
Robert W. Hampton, Sr. VP-Acct.
Ron R. Green, CEO/Pres., PTI Group, Inc.
Charles Moses, Sr. VP-Offshore Products
Robert W. Hampton, Corp. Sec.
Stephen A. Wells, Chmn.

Phone: 713-652-0582 **Fax:** 713-652-0499
Toll-Free:
Address: 333 Clay St., 3 Allen Ctr., Ste. 4620, Houston, TX 77002 US

GROWTH PLANS/SPECIAL FEATURES:

Oil States International, Inc. is a leading provider of specialty products and services to oil and gas drilling/production companies worldwide. Areas of operation include West Africa, the North Sea, South America, Australia, Central Asia, Southeast Asia and onshore/offshore U.S. Oil States operates in four principal business segments: offshore products, tubular services, accommodations and well site services. Its offshore products segment designs and manufactures products for the offshore energy industry, such as flexible bearings and connector products; subsea pipeline products; marine winches, mooring and lifting systems and rig equipment; drilling riser repair; and blowout preventer stack assembly, integration, testing and repair services. Oil States' tubular services segment offers casing, premium tubing and line pipe, which are purchased from manufacturers and sold to oil/gas companies and drilling contractors. It has also developed an e-commerce portal for pricing, ordering and tracking tubular products, operating under Sooner, Inc. Oil States' accommodations segment offers temporary and permanent accommodations services for people working in remote locations in the U.S., Canada and Australia. These services include catering/food services, housekeeping, laundry, facility management, water/wastewater treatment, power generation, communications and redeployment logistics. The firm's well site services segment provides worker services, drilling services, rental equipment, remote site accommodations, catering and logistics services and modular building construction services. Subsidiary Oil States Energy Services, Inc. (formerly HWC Energy Services, Inc.) provides worldwide well control services, drilling services and rental equipment to the oil and gas industry, while subsidiary PTI Group, Inc. is a supplier of integrated housing, food, site management and logistics support services to remote sites. In October 2010, Oil States acquired Acute Technological Services, Inc. In December 2010, the firm acquired Mountain West Oilfield Service and Supplies, Inc., Ufford Leasing LLC (Mountain West) and The MAC Services Group Limited.

Oil States offers its employees benefits including medical, dental and vision coverage.

FINANCIALS: **Sales and profits are in thousands of dollars—add 000 to get the full amount. 2010 Note: Financial information for 2010 was not available for all companies at press time.**

2010 Sales: $2,411,984 — 2010 Profits: $168,018
2009 Sales: $2,108,250 — 2009 Profits: $59,612
2008 Sales: $2,948,457 — 2008 Profits: $222,710
2007 Sales: $2,088,235 — 2007 Profits: $203,372
2006 Sales: $1,923,357 — 2006 Profits: $197,634

U.S. Stock Ticker: OIS
Int'l Ticker:
Int'l Exchange:
Employees: 6,904 Fiscal Year Ends: 12/31
Parent Company:

SALARIES/BENEFITS:

Pension Plan: ESOP Stock Plan: Profit Sharing: Top Exec. Salary: $526,308 Bonus: $842,092
Savings Plan: Y Stock Purch. Plan: Second Exec. Salary: $346,424 Bonus: $282,516

OTHER THOUGHTS:

Apparent Women Officers or Directors: 1
Hot Spot for Advancement for Women/Minorities:

LOCATIONS: ("Y" = Yes)

West:	Southwest:	Midwest:	Southeast:	Northeast:	International:
Y	Y	Y	Y		Y

OMNICOM GROUP INC

www.omnicomgroup.com

Industry Group Code: 541810

Management:		Sales/Marketing:		Liberal Arts:		Information Sys.:		Professionals:		Tech./Scientific:	
Mgmt. Trainees:	Y	Marketing Pros.:	Y	Gen. Writing/Editing:	Y	Info. Mgmt.:	Y	Finance/Acct.:	Y	Engineers, Elec.:	
Experienced Mgmt.:	Y	Retail Sales:		Tech. Writing:		Software Dev.:	Y	Law:	Y	Engineers, Other:	
Int'l Business:	Y	Comm./Industrial:	Y	Graphic Arts/Photog.:	Y	Hardware Dev.:		HR/Other:	Y	Health/Lab:	
MBA Grads:	Y	Sales Trainees:		Music:		Consulting/Other:		Training:	Y	Science/Research:	
		Advertising Pros.:	Y	Broadcasting:				Health Care:		Petroleum/Chem.:	
				Other:				Consulting:	Y	Math/Other:	

TYPES OF BUSINESS:

Advertising Services
Public Relations
Market Research
Marketing & Brand Consulting
Interactive & Search Engine Marketing
Media Planning & Buying
Health Care Communications

BRANDS/DIVISIONS/AFFILIATES:

BBDO Worldwide
DDB Worldwide Communications Group Inc
TBWA Worldwide Inc
Ketchum Inc
Porter Novelli
Goodby Silverstein & Partners
Omnicom Digital
Arnell Group

CONTACTS: *Note: Officers with more than one job title may be intentionally listed here more than once.*

John D. Wren, CEO
John D. Wren, Pres.
Randall J. Weisenburger, CFO/Exec. VP
Michael J. O'Brien, General Counsel/Sr. VP/Corp. Sec.
Philip J. Angelastro, Sr. VP-Finance/Controller
Asit Mehra, Exec. VP
Janet Riccio, Exec. VP
Serge Dumont, Sr. VP/Pres., Omnicom APIMA
Dennis E. Hewitt, Treas.
Bruce Crawford, Chmn.
Tim Love, CEO- Asia-Pacific, India, Middle East & Africa

Phone: 212-415-3600 **Fax:** 212-415-3530
Toll-Free:
Address: 437 Madison Ave., New York, NY 10022 US

GROWTH PLANS/SPECIAL FEATURES:

Omnicom Group, Inc. is a holding company that, through its subsidiaries, is one of the largest advertising, marketing and corporate communications companies in the world. The firm owns subsidiary agencies that operate in over 100 countries worldwide. Its agencies provide an extensive range of services, mainly focusing on four fundamental disciplines, including traditional media advertising, customer relationship management, public relations and specialty communications. The company's holdings are managed by the Diversified Agency Services (DAS) division; this sector includes over 100 public relations, marketing, consulting and special communications firms, such as Ketchum, Inc. and Porter Novelli. Omnicom's traditional media advertising is based in three areas: global advertising brands, national advertising agencies and media services. Global advertising brands include BBDO Worldwide, DDB Worldwide and TBWA Worldwide. National advertising agencies include Arnell Group; Goodby Silverstein & Partners; GSD&M; Martin/Williams; Merkley and Partners; and Zimmerman Advertising. Media services operate as the Omnicom Media Group (OMG), which include two full service media companies, OMD Worldwide and PHD Network, and several media specialist companies. Other group activities of note include experiential marketing, mobile marketing, package design, custom printing, reputation consulting and search engine marketing. Omnicom digital oversees the company's digital operations. Traditional media advertising accounted for about 45.3% if the company's 2010 revenue, while customer relationship management made up 36.3%, public relations contributed 9.1% and specialty communications supplied 9.3%. The U.S. accounted for 53% of revenue, with the rest of the world generating 47%. In July 2010, the company's subsidiary, Agency.com, relaunched as Signal to Noise, and will specialize in digital marketing. In October 2010, Omnicom acquired Sales Power, a China-based promotional company, and its Diversified Agency Services division acquired Excerpta Medica, a medical communications company. Also in October 2010, the firm's Ketchum subsidiary purchased the Russian public relations firm Maslov.

FINANCIALS: **Sales and profits are in thousands of dollars—add 000 to get the full amount. 2010 Note: Financial information for 2010 was not available for all companies at press time.**

2010 Sales: $12,542,500 | 2010 Profits: $827,700
2009 Sales: $11,720,700 | 2009 Profits: $793,000
2008 Sales: $13,359,900 | 2008 Profits: $1,000,300
2007 Sales: $12,694,000 | 2007 Profits: $975,700
2006 Sales: $11,376,900 | 2006 Profits: $864,000

U.S. Stock Ticker: OMC
Int'l Ticker:
Int'l Exchange:
Employees: 65,500 Fiscal Year Ends: 12/31
Parent Company:

SALARIES/BENEFITS:

Pension Plan: ESOP Stock Plan: Profit Sharing: Top Exec. Salary: $1,000,000 Bonus: $5,000,000
Savings Plan: Stock Purch. Plan: Second Exec. Salary: $975,000 Bonus: $3,700,000

OTHER THOUGHTS:

Apparent Women Officers or Directors: 2
Hot Spot for Advancement for Women/Minorities:

LOCATIONS: ("Y" = Yes)

West:	Southwest:	Midwest:	Southeast:	Northeast:	International:
Y	Y	Y	Y	Y	Y

ORACLE CORP

www.oracle.com

Industry Group Code: 511210H

Management:		Sales/Marketing:		Liberal Arts:		Information Sys.:		Professionals:		Tech./Scientific:	
Mgmt. Trainees:	Y	Marketing Pros.:	Y	Gen. Writing/Editing:	Y	Info. Mgmt.:	Y	Finance/Acct.:	Y	Engineers, Elec.:	Y
Experienced Mgmt.:	Y	Retail Sales:		Tech. Writing:	Y	Software Dev.:	Y	Law:	Y	Engineers, Other:	
Int'l Business:	Y	Comm./Industrial:	Y	Graphic Arts/Photog.:	Y	Hardware Dev.:		HR/Other:	Y	Health/Lab:	
MBA Grads:	Y	Sales Trainees:		Music:		Consulting/Other:	Y	Training:	Y	Science/Research:	Y
		Advertising Pros.:	Y	Broadcasting:				Health Care:		Petroleum/Chem.:	
				Other:	Y			Consulting:		Math/Other:	Y

TYPES OF BUSINESS:

Computer Software-Database Management
e-Business Applications Software
Internet-Based Software
Consulting Services
Human Resources Management Software
CRM Software
Middleware

BRANDS/DIVISIONS/AFFILIATES:

Oracle Database
Sun Microsystems
Solaris
Oracle Exadata
Oracle On Demand
Phase Forward, Inc.
Silver Creek Systems, Inc.
Art Technology Group Inc

CONTACTS: *Note: Officers with more than one job title may be intentionally listed here more than once.*

Lawrence J. Ellison, CEO
Safra A. Catz, Co-Pres.
Safra A. Catz, CFO
Judith Sim, Chief Mktg. Officer/Sr. VP
Thomas Kurian, Exec. VP-Prod. Dev.
Dorian Daley, General Counsel/Sr. VP/Sec.
Cindy Reese, Sr. VP-Worldwide Oper.
William C. West, Chief Acct. Officer/Sr. VP/Corp. Controller
Mark V. Hurd, Co-Pres.
Mary Ann Davidson, Chief Security Officer
Luiz Meisler, Exec. VP-Latin America
Edward Screven, Chief Corp. Architect
Jeffrey O. Henley, Chmn.
Takao Endo, Pres./CEO-Oracle Japan

Phone: 650-506-7000 **Fax:** 650-506-7200
Toll-Free: 800-672-2531
Address: 500 Oracle Pkwy., Redwood Shores, CA 94065 US

GROWTH PLANS/SPECIAL FEATURES:

Oracle Corp. is one of the largest enterprise software companies in the world. The firm markets its software directly to corporations rather than dealing in the consumer market. Oracle's products can be categorized into three broad areas: software, which represented 77% of its 2010 revenue; hardware systems (through the acquisition of Sun Microsystems), 9%; and services, 14%. The company's core software business segment is based upon its prepackaged enterprise data management software and Internet applications including Oracle Database, Oracle Fusion Middleware, Oracle Enterprise Manager, Oracle Collaboration Suite, Oracle Developer Suite and Oracle E-Business Suite. The firm's flagship Oracle Database software is used to securely manage the retrieval and manipulation of all forms of data. Oracle Database is available in four different versions: Express Edition, which is the most basic offering; Standard Edition One, which includes Unix and 64-bit support; Standard Edition, which supports four CPU sockets and offers enhanced workload management; and the fully-loaded Enterprise Edition. The hardware systems segment consists of hardware products and systems support. Its offerings include a wide variety of innovative products, such as servers and storage products, networking components, the Solaris operating system and Oracle Exadata, a family of integrated software and hardware products. Oracle's services business is comprised of Oracle Consulting, specializing in the design, deployment and migration of database technology and applications software; and Oracle On Demand, which offers distributed application services including E-Business Suite On Demand, Technology On Demand and other Software-as-a-Service (SaaS) products. The services segment also provides education and training to its customers. Oracle actively acquires complimentary businesses and has made numerous acquisitions in recent years, including Sun Microsystems for $7.3 billion in January 2010. Other firms acquired in 2010 include Silver Creek Systems, Inc.; DataScaler; AmberPoint; Convergin; and Phase Forward, Inc. In January 2011, Oracle acquired Art Technology Group, Inc. for $1.1 billion.

FINANCIALS: **Sales and profits are in thousands of dollars—add 000 to get the full amount. 2010 Note: Financial information for 2010 was not available for all companies at press time.**

2010 Sales: $26,820,000	2010 Profits: $6,135,000	**U.S. Stock Ticker: ORCL**
2009 Sales: $23,252,000	2009 Profits: $5,593,000	**Int'l Ticker:**
2008 Sales: $22,430,000	2008 Profits: $5,521,000	Int'l Exchange:
2007 Sales: $17,996,000	2007 Profits: $4,274,000	Employees: 105,000 Fiscal Year Ends: 5/31
2006 Sales: $14,380,000	2006 Profits: $3,381,000	Parent Company:

SALARIES/BENEFITS:

Pension Plan:	ESOP Stock Plan:	Profit Sharing:	Top Exec. Salary: $800,000	Bonus: $3,871,953
Savings Plan: Y	Stock Purch. Plan: Y		Second Exec. Salary: $800,000	Bonus: $3,871,953

OTHER THOUGHTS:

Apparent Women Officers or Directors: 5
Hot Spot for Advancement for Women/Minorities: Y

LOCATIONS: ("Y" = Yes)

West:	Southwest:	Midwest:	Southeast:	Northeast:	International:
Y	Y	Y	Y	Y	Y

O'REILLY AUTOMOTIVE INC

www.oreillyauto.com

Industry Group Code: 441310

Management:		Sales/Marketing:		Liberal Arts:		Information Sys.:		Professionals:		Tech./Scientific:	
Mgmt. Trainees:	Y	Marketing Pros.:	Y	Gen. Writing/Editing:	Y	Info. Mgmt.:	Y	Finance/Acct.:	Y	Engineers, Elec.:	
Experienced Mgmt.:	Y	Retail Sales:	Y	Tech. Writing:		Software Dev.:	Y	Law:	Y	Engineers, Other:	
Int'l Business:		Comm./Industrial:	Y	Graphic Arts/Photog.:	Y	Hardware Dev.:		HR/Other:	Y	Health/Lab:	
MBA Grads:	Y	Sales Trainees:	Y	Music:		Consulting/Other:		Training:	Y	Science/Research:	
		Advertising Pros.:	Y	Broadcasting:				Health Care:		Petroleum/Chem.:	
				Other:				Consulting:		Math/Other:	

TYPES OF BUSINESS:

Auto Parts, Retail
Tools
Auto Accessories

BRANDS/DIVISIONS/AFFILIATES:

O'Reilly Auto Parts
Power Torque
BrakeBest
Prestone
Master Pro
Omnispark
Super Start
Ultima

CONTACTS: *Note: Officers with more than one job title may be intentionally listed here more than once.*

Greg L. Henslee, CEO/Co-Pres.
Ted F. Wise, COO
Ted F. Wise, Co-Pres.
Tom McFall, CFO/Exec. VP
Tony Bartholomew, VP-Sales
Phillip Thompson, VP-Human Resources
Steve Jasinski, VP-Info. Systems
Mike Swearengin, Sr. VP-Merch.
Phyllis Evans, VP-Store Admin.
Tricia Headley, Corp. Sec./VP
Jeff Shaw, Sr. VP-Oper. & Store Sales
Jeremy Fletcher, VP-Finance/Controller
Doug Ruble, VP-Advertising & Mktg.
Alan Fears, VP-Store Acquisitions & Expansion
Greg Johnson, Sr. VP-Dist. Oper.
Brett Heintz, VP-Retail Systems
David E. O'Reilly, Chmn.
Greg Beck, VP-Purchasing

Phone: 417-829-5727	**Fax:**
Toll-Free: 800-755-6759	
Address: 233 S. Patterson Ave., Springfield, MO 65802 US	

GROWTH PLANS/SPECIAL FEATURES:

O'Reilly Automotive, Inc., founded in 1957, is one of the largest specialty retailers of automotive aftermarket parts, tools, supplies, equipment and accessories in the U.S., selling products to both do-it-yourself (DIY) customers and professional installers. The company operates 3,570 stores in 38 states across the U.S. Stores carry an average of 22,000 Stock-Keeping Units (SKUs) with an extensive product line consisting of new and remanufactured automotive hard parts, such as alternators, starters, brake system components, batteries, chassis parts and engine parts; maintenance items, such as oil, antifreeze, fluids, wiper blades, lighting, engine additives and appearance products; accessories, such as floor mats, truck accessories and seat covers; and a complete line of auto body paint and related materials, automotive tools and professional service equipment. Store merchandise generally consists of nationally recognized, well-advertised, name-brand products such as AC Delco, Moog, Wagner, Gates Rubber, Federal Mogul, Monroe, Prestone, Quaker State, Pennzoil, Castrol, Valvoline, STP, BWD, Cardone, Wix, Armor All and Turtle Wax. In addition to name-brand products, stores carry a wide variety of high-quality private-label products under the BestTest, BrakeBest, Master Pro, MicroGard, Murray, Power Torque, Super Start, Ultima and Omnispark brands. O'Reilly operates 23 distribution centers, each equipped with highly automated material handling equipment that expedites the movement of products to loading areas for shipment to individual stores on a nightly basis.

O'Reilly offers its employees a benefits package that includes medical, dental, vision, pharmacy and life insurance; a credit union membership; a 401(k) plan; a profit sharing plan; a discount stock purchase plan; and an employee assistance program.

FINANCIALS: **Sales and profits are in thousands of dollars—add 000 to get the full amount. 2010 Note: Financial information for 2010 was not available for all companies at press time.**

2010 Sales: $5,397,525	2010 Profits: $419,373	**U.S. Stock Ticker: ORLY**
2009 Sales: $4,847,062	2009 Profits: $307,498	**Int'l Ticker:**
2008 Sales: $3,576,553	2008 Profits: $186,232	Int'l Exchange:
2007 Sales: $2,522,319	2007 Profits: $193,988	Employees: 31,070 Fiscal Year Ends: 12/31
2006 Sales: $2,283,222	2006 Profits: $178,085	Parent Company:

SALARIES/BENEFITS:

Pension Plan:	ESOP Stock Plan:	Profit Sharing: Y	Top Exec. Salary: $842,308	Bonus: $3,429,089
Savings Plan: Y	Stock Purch. Plan: Y		Second Exec. Salary: $605,385	Bonus: $1,968,700

OTHER THOUGHTS:

Apparent Women Officers or Directors: 3
Hot Spot for Advancement for Women/Minorities: Y

LOCATIONS: ("Y" = Yes)

West:	Southwest:	Midwest:	Southeast:	Northeast:	International:
Y	Y	Y	Y	Y	

OSHKOSH CORPORATION

www.oshkoshcorporation.com

Industry Group Code: 336120

Management:		Sales/Marketing:		Liberal Arts:		Information Sys.:		Professionals:		Tech./Scientific:	
Mgmt. Trainees:	Y	Marketing Pros.:	Y	Gen. Writing/Editing:	Y	Info. Mgmt.:	Y	Finance/Acct.:	Y	Engineers, Elec.:	Y
Experienced Mgmt.:	Y	Retail Sales:		Tech. Writing:	Y	Software Dev.:	Y	Law:	Y	Engineers, Other:	Y
Int'l Business:	Y	Comm./Industrial:	Y	Graphic Arts/Photog.:	Y	Hardware Dev.:	Y	HR/Other:	Y	Health/Lab:	
MBA Grads:	Y	Sales Trainees:		Music:		Consulting/Other:		Training:	Y	Science/Research:	
		Advertising Pros.:	Y	Broadcasting:				Health Care:		Petroleum/Chem.:	
				Other:				Consulting:		Math/Other:	

TYPES OF BUSINESS:

Fire & Emergency Vehicles
Military Trucks
Truck Bodies
Specialty Trucks
Cement Mixers
Refuse Trucks

BRANDS/DIVISIONS/AFFILIATES:

Oshkosh
JLG
Pierce
JerrDan

CONTACTS: *Note: Officers with more than one job title may be intentionally listed here more than once.*

Charles L. Szews, CEO
Charles L. Szews, Pres.
David M. Sagehorn, CFO/Exec. VP
Michael K. Rohrkaste, Chief Human Resources Officer
Michael S. Guzowski, VP-IT
Gary W. Schmiedel, Exec. VP-Tech.
Josef Matosevic, Exec. VP-Global Mfg. Oper.
Michael K. Rohrkaste, Chief Admin. Officer/Exec. VP
Bryan J. Blankfield, General Counsel/Exec. VP/Sec.
Mark M. Radue, VP-Bus. Dev.
John Daggett, VP-Corp. Comm.
Patrick N. Davidson, VP-Investor Rel.
Thomas J. Polnaszek, Sr. VP-Finance/Controller
R. Scott Grennier, VP/Treas.
Wilson R. Jones, Exec. VP/Pres., Access Equipment
James W. Johnson, Exec. VP/Pres., Fire & Emergency
Frank R. Nerenhausen, Exec. VP/Pres., Commercial
Richard M. Donnelly, Chmn.
Gregory L. Fredericksen, Chief Procurement Officer/Exec. VP

Phone: 920-235-9150	**Fax:** 920-233-9250
Toll-Free:	
Address: 2307 Oregon St., Oshkosh, WI 54902 US	

GROWTH PLANS/SPECIAL FEATURES:

Oshkosh Corporation is a leading designer, manufacturer and marketer of specialty vehicles and vehicle bodies. The company operates in four segments: defense; access equipment; fire and emergency; and commercial. The defense segment, accounting for roughly 73% of the company's sales, supplies severe-duty, heavy-payload tactical trucks to the U.S. Department of Defense (DoD). The access equipment segment, through subsidiary JLG, manufactures aerial work platforms, telehandlers, scissor lifts and vertical masts used in construction, agricultural, industrial, institutional and general maintenance applications. JLG markets its products in over 3,500 locations worldwide. This segment accounts for approximately 13% of sales. The fire and emergency segment, through subsidiary Pierce, is a leading domestic manufacturer of fire apparatus assembled on custom chassis. It also manufactures fire apparatus assembled on commercially-available chassis, snow removal vehicles and emergency vehicles, including pumpers; aerial and ladder trucks; tankers; light-, medium- and heavy-duty rescue vehicles; rough terrain response vehicles; mobile command and control centers; bomb squad vehicles; and hazardous materials control vehicles. The segment sells aircraft rescue and fire fighting (ARFF) vehicles to domestic and international airports. Through its JerrDan subsidiary, the segment also manufactures towing and recovery equipment in the U.S. The segment accounts for roughly 9% of sales. The commercial segment, representing 5% of sales, manufactures rear- and front-discharge concrete mixers; refuse collection vehicles; mobile and stationary compactors and waste transfer units; portable and stationary concrete batch plants; and vehicle components. In October 2010, Oshkosh opened a new manufacturing facility in Tianjin, China.

Employees are offered medical, dental and life insurance; disability coverage; and a pension plan.

FINANCIALS: **Sales and profits are in thousands of dollars—add 000 to get the full amount. 2010 Note: Financial information for 2010 was not available for all companies at press time.**

2010 Sales: $9,842,400	2010 Profits: $790,000	**U.S. Stock Ticker: OSK**
2009 Sales: $5,295,200	2009 Profits: $-1,098,800	**Int'l Ticker:**
2008 Sales: $6,936,400	2008 Profits: $79,300	Int'l Exchange:
2007 Sales: $6,139,300	2007 Profits: $268,100	Employees: 12,400 Fiscal Year Ends: 9/30
2006 Sales: $3,427,388	2006 Profits: $205,529	Parent Company:

SALARIES/BENEFITS:

Pension Plan: Y	ESOP Stock Plan:	Profit Sharing:	Top Exec. Salary: $1,184,501	Bonus: $2,369,004
Savings Plan:	Stock Purch. Plan: Y		Second Exec. Salary: $684,950	Bonus: $1,095,920

OTHER THOUGHTS:

Apparent Women Officers or Directors: 4
Hot Spot for Advancement for Women/Minorities: Y

LOCATIONS: ("Y" = Yes)

West:	Southwest:	Midwest:	Southeast:	Northeast:	International:
Y	Y	Y	Y	Y	Y

OWENS & MINOR INC

www.owens-minor.com

Industry Group Code: 423450

Management:		Sales/Marketing:		Liberal Arts:		Information Sys.:		Professionals:		Tech./Scientific:	
Mgmt. Trainees:	Y	Marketing Pros.:	Y	Gen. Writing/Editing:	Y	Info. Mgmt.:	Y	Finance/Acct.:	Y	Engineers, Elec.:	
Experienced Mgmt.:	Y	Retail Sales:		Tech. Writing:	Y	Software Dev.:	Y	Law:	Y	Engineers, Other:	
Int'l Business:		Comm./Industrial:	Y	Graphic Arts/Photog.:	Y	Hardware Dev.:		HR/Other:	Y	Health/Lab:	
MBA Grads:	Y	Sales Trainees:	Y	Music:		Consulting/Other:		Training:	Y	Science/Research:	
		Advertising Pros.:	Y	Broadcasting:				Health Care:	Y	Petroleum/Chem.:	
				Other:				Consulting:		Math/Other:	

TYPES OF BUSINESS:

Distribution-Medical & Surgical Equipment
Supply Chain Management

BRANDS/DIVISIONS/AFFILIATES:

OMSolutions
PANDAC
SurgiTrack
WISDOM Gold

CONTACTS:

Note: Officers with more than one job title may be intentionally listed here more than once.

Craig R. Smith, CEO
Charles C. Colpo, COO/Exec. VP
Craig R. Smith, Pres.
James L. Bierman, CFO/Sr. VP
W. Marshall Simpson, Sr. VP-Sales
Erika T. Davis, Sr. VP-Human Resources
Richard W. Mears, CIO/Sr. VP
Grace R. den Hartog, General Counsel/Sr. VP/Corp. Sec.
W. Marshall Simpson, Sr. VP-Oper.
Mark A. Van Sumeren, Sr. VP-Strategic Planning & Bus. Dev.
Hugh F. Gouldthorpe, Jr., VP-Comm. & Quality
Chuck Graves, Dir.-Investor Rel.
D. Andrew Edwards, VP-Finance/Chief Acct. Officer
G. Gilmer Minor, III, Chmn.
E. V. Clarke, Exec. VP-Supply Chain

Phone: 804-723-7000 **Fax:** 804-723-7100
Toll-Free:
Address: 9120 Lockwood Blvd., Mechanicsville, VA 23116 US

GROWTH PLANS/SPECIAL FEATURES:

Owens & Minor, Inc. (OMI), founded in 1882, is a distributor of medical and surgical supplies to the acute-care market and a healthcare supply-chain management company. In its acute-care supply distribution business, the company distributes 200,000 finished medical and surgical products produced by over 1,400 suppliers to roughly 4,100 healthcare provider customers from 52 distribution and service centers nationwide. The firm's primary distribution customers are acute-care hospitals, which account for more than 95% of the company's revenue. Other customers include the U.S. government, for which OMI serves as a vendor for medical and surgical supply distribution services for the U.S. Department of Defense. On a more limited basis, the company serves alternate care providers including clinics, home healthcare organizations, nursing homes, physicians' offices, rehabilitation facilities and surgery centers. The firm typically provides its distribution services under contractual arrangements with terms ranging from 3-5 years. Most of OMI's sales consist of consumable goods such as disposable gloves; dressings; endoscopic products; intravenous products; needles and syringes; sterile procedure trays; surgical products and gowns; urological products; and wound closure products. The company also offers a number of supply chain services, including OMSolutions, comprising OMI's supply chain consulting, customer technology and resource management teams; PANDAC, an operating room-focused inventory management program to help healthcare providers reduce and control suture and endo-mechanical inventory; SurgiTrack, a customizable surgical supply service; and WISDOM Gold, an Internet-based spending management, data normalization and contract management system.

OMI offers its employees educational assistance; incentive pay; flexible benefit plans; and medical, dental, vision, life and disability insurance.

FINANCIALS:

Sales and profits are in thousands of dollars—add 000 to get the full amount. 2010 Note: Financial information for 2010 was not available for all companies at press time.

2010 Sales: $8,123,608	2010 Profits: $110,579
2009 Sales: $8,037,624	2009 Profits: $104,658
2008 Sales: $7,243,237	2008 Profits: $93,327
2007 Sales: $6,800,466	2007 Profits: $72,710
2006 Sales: $5,533,736	2006 Profits: $48,752

U.S. Stock Ticker: OMI
Int'l Ticker:
Int'l Exchange:
Employees: 4,800 Fiscal Year Ends: 12/31
Parent Company:

SALARIES/BENEFITS:

Pension Plan:	ESOP Stock Plan:	Profit Sharing:	Top Exec. Salary: $829,339	Bonus: $269,739
Savings Plan: Y	Stock Purch. Plan: Y		Second Exec. Salary: $518,336	Bonus: $112,391

OTHER THOUGHTS:

Apparent Women Officers or Directors: 3
Hot Spot for Advancement for Women/Minorities: Y

LOCATIONS: ("Y" = Yes)

West:	Southwest:	Midwest:	Southeast:	Northeast:	International:
Y	Y	Y	Y	Y	

PACCAR INC

www.paccar.com

Industry Group Code: 33611

Management:		Sales/Marketing:		Liberal Arts:		Information Sys.:		Professionals:		Tech./Scientific:	
Mgmt. Trainees:	Y	Marketing Pros.:	Y	Gen. Writing/Editing:		Info. Mgmt.:	Y	Finance/Acct.:	Y	Engineers, Elec.:	Y
Experienced Mgmt.:	Y	Retail Sales:		Tech. Writing:	Y	Software Dev.:	Y	Law:	Y	Engineers, Other:	Y
Int'l Business:	Y	Comm./Industrial:	Y	Graphic Arts/Photog.:	Y	Hardware Dev.:		HR/Other:	Y	Health/Lab:	
MBA Grads:	Y	Sales Trainees:		Music:		Consulting/Other:		Training:	Y	Science/Research:	
		Advertising Pros.:	Y	Broadcasting:				Health Care:		Petroleum/Chem.:	
				Other:				Consulting:		Math/Other:	

TYPES OF BUSINESS:

Truck Manufacturer
Premium Truck Manufacturer
Parts Distribution
Finance, Lease and Insurance Services

BRANDS/DIVISIONS/AFFILIATES:

PACCAR International
DAF Trucks
Peterbilt Motors
Kenworth Truck Company
PacLease
PACCAR Financial Services

CONTACTS: *Note: Officers with more than one job title may be intentionally listed here more than once.*

Mark C. Pigott, CEO
Ronald E. Armstrong, Pres.
T. Kyle Quinn, CIO/VP
David C. Anderson, General Counsel/VP
Michael T. Barkley, Controller/VP
Thomas E. Plimpton, Vice Chmn.
Robert J. Christensen, Sr. VP
Daniel D.Sobic, Exec. VP
Mark C. Pigott, Chmn.

Phone: 425-468-7400	**Fax:** 425-468-8216
Toll-Free:	
Address: 777 106th Ave. NE, Bellevue, WA 98004 US	

GROWTH PLANS/SPECIAL FEATURES:

PACCAR, Inc. is a leading manufacturer of premium light-, medium- and heavy-duty trucks. The firm operates in two major divisions: trucks and financing/leasing. The truck subsidiaries include Kenworth Truck Company, Peterbilt Motors and DAF Trucks. The vehicles are used worldwide for over-the-road and off-highway hauling of freight, petroleum, wood products, construction and other materials. The Kenworth and Peterbilt nameplates are manufactured and distributed by separate divisions in the U.S. and foreign plants in Canada, Mexico and Australia. Headquartered in the Netherlands, DAF Trucks comprises the European component of PACCAR, with distribution throughout Europe, Asia and Africa. Another group, PACCAR International, is based in the U.S. and offers the Kenworth, Peterbilt and DAF brands outside of their primary markets. Products and services are available worldwide through a network of approximately 1,800 locations in more than 100 countries, with customer call centers operating continuously. Substantially all trucks and related parts are sold to independent dealers. The company's financing/leasing segment, which operates through wholly-owned subsidiaries PACCAR Financial and PacLease, maintains a presence in over 18 countries and owns a fleet of over 150,000 vehicles. This division provides financing and leasing arrangements, mainly for its manufactured trucks. The company's share of the U.S. and Canadian Class 8 truck market is roughly 25.1%. Commercial trucks and related replacement parts comprise the largest segment of the company's business, accounting for approximately 86.5% of net sales. In January 2010, the firm launched the new PACCAR MX diesel engine for its Kenworth and Peterbilt models in order to meet more stringent emissions requirements.

PACCAR offers its employees medical, dental, vision, life, AD&D and disability insurance; a 401(k) plan; a pension plan; flexible spending accounts; an employee assistance program; tuition reimbursement; charitable gift matching; college scholarship; an employee stock purchase plan; and an employee computer purchase plan.

FINANCIALS: **Sales and profits are in thousands of dollars—add 000 to get the full amount. 2010 Note: Financial information for 2010 was not available for all companies at press time.**

2010 Sales: $10,292,900	2010 Profits: $457,600	**U.S. Stock Ticker: PCAR**
2009 Sales: $8,086,500	2009 Profits: $111,900	**Int'l Ticker:**
2008 Sales: $14,972,500	2008 Profits: $1,017,900	Int'l Exchange:
2007 Sales: $15,221,700	2007 Profits: $1,227,300	Employees: 17,700 Fiscal Year Ends: 12/31
2006 Sales: $16,454,100	2006 Profits: $1,496,000	Parent Company:

SALARIES/BENEFITS:

Pension Plan: Y	ESOP Stock Plan:	Profit Sharing:	Top Exec. Salary: $1,350,000	Bonus: $
Savings Plan: Y	Stock Purch. Plan: Y		Second Exec. Salary: $800,000	Bonus: $

OTHER THOUGHTS:

Apparent Women Officers or Directors: 1
Hot Spot for Advancement for Women/Minorities:

LOCATIONS: ("Y" = Yes)

West:	Southwest:	Midwest:	Southeast:	Northeast:	International:
Y	Y	Y	Y	Y	Y

PANERA BREAD CO

www.panerabread.com

Industry Group Code: 722110

Management:		**Sales/Marketing:**		**Liberal Arts:**		**Information Sys.:**		**Professionals:**		**Tech./Scientific:**	
Mgmt. Trainees:	Y	Marketing Pros.:	Y	Gen. Writing/Editing:	Y	Info. Mgmt.:	Y	Finance/Acct.:	Y	Engineers, Elec.:	
Experienced Mgmt.:	Y	Retail Sales:		Tech. Writing:		Software Dev.:	Y	Law:	Y	Engineers, Other:	
Int'l Business:	Y	Comm./Industrial:		Graphic Arts/Photog.:	Y	Hardware Dev.:		HR/Other:	Y	Health/Lab:	
MBA Grads:	Y	Sales Trainees:		Music:		Consulting/Other:		Training:	Y	Science/Research:	
		Advertising Pros.:	Y	Broadcasting:				Health Care:		Petroleum/Chem.:	
				Other:				Consulting:		Math/Other:	

TYPES OF BUSINESS:

Restaurants
Bakery-cafes

BRANDS/DIVISIONS/AFFILIATES:

Panera Bread
Saint Louis Bread Co.
Paradise Bakery & Cafe
Panera Cares
MyPanera

CONTACTS: *Note: Officers with more than one job title may be intentionally listed here more than once.*

William W. Moreton, CEO
Cedric Vanzura, Co-COO/Exec. VP
William W. Moreton, Pres.
Jeffrey Kip, CFO/Sr. VP
Michael Simon, Chief Mktg. Officer/Sr. VP
Liz Dunlap, Chief People Officer/Sr. VP
Thomas Kish, CIO/Sr. VP
Scott Blair, General Counsel/Chief Legal Officer/Sr. VP
Michael Nolan, Chief Dev. Officer/Sr. VP
Scott Davis, Chief Concept Officer/Exec. VP
John Maguire, Co-COO/Exec. VP
Michael Kupstas, Chief Franchise Officer/Sr. VP
William H. Simpson, Chief Company & Joint Venture Oper. Officer/Sr. VP
Ronald M. Shaich, Chmn.
Mark Borland, Chief Supply Chain Officer/Sr. VP

Phone: 314-984-1000 **Fax:** 314-909-3300
Toll-Free:
Address: 3630 S. Geyer Rd., Ste. 100, St. Louis, MO 63127 US

GROWTH PLANS/SPECIAL FEATURES:

Panera Bread Co., along with its subsidiaries, is a national bakery-cafe concept with approximately 1,453 company-owned and franchise-operated bakery-cafe locations in 40 states and Ontario, Canada. The company serves nearly six million customers weekly and operates under the Panera Bread, Saint Louis Bread Co. and Paradise Bakery & Cafe brands. The firm's menu's key groups are fresh baked goods, including a variety of bagels, breads, muffins, scones, rolls and sweets; made-to-order sandwiches, in addition to soups and salads; and custom roasted coffees and beverages including espresso, cappuccino drinks and smoothies. The company operates in three segments: company bakery-cafe operations, franchise operations and fresh dough operations. The company bakery-cafe operations segment consists of 662 company-owned bakery-cafes, which are located in the U.S. Its bakery-cafes are principally located in suburban, strip mall and regional mall locations. The franchise operations segment consists of 791 franchise-operated bakery-cafes, which are located throughout the U.S. and in Ontario, Canada. Lastly, its fresh dough operations segment, which supplies fresh dough items daily to most company-owned and franchise-operated bakery-cafes, consists of 26 fresh dough facilities, 22 of which are company-owned and four of which are franchise-operated. In November 2010, the firm introduced a new loyalty program, MyPanera, which offers members exclusive experiential opportunities, invitations, preview tastings of new menu items, recipes and more. In late 2010 and early 2011, Panera opened its second and third non-profit cafes, called Panera Cares, in Michigan and Oregon. The first Panera Cares cafe was opened in early 2010 in Missouri.

Employees are offered medical, dental and vision insurance; a flexible spending account; a 401(k) plan; an employee stock purchase plan; incentive programs; life insurance; a disability program; and an employee discount program.

FINANCIALS: **Sales and profits are in thousands of dollars—add 000 to get the full amount. 2010 Note: Financial information for 2010 was not available for all companies at press time.**

2010 Sales: $1,542,489	2010 Profits: $111,866	**U.S. Stock Ticker: PNRA**
2009 Sales: $1,353,494	2009 Profits: $86,050	**Int'l Ticker:**
2008 Sales: $1,298,853	2008 Profits: $67,436	Int'l Exchange:
2007 Sales: $1,066,691	2007 Profits: $57,456	Employees: 15,900 Fiscal Year Ends: 12/31
2006 Sales: $	2006 Profits: $	Parent Company:

SALARIES/BENEFITS:

Pension Plan:	ESOP Stock Plan:	Profit Sharing:	Top Exec. Salary: $618,000	Bonus: $2,333,820
Savings Plan: Y	Stock Purch. Plan: Y		Second Exec. Salary: $574,740	Bonus: $794,334

OTHER THOUGHTS:

Apparent Women Officers or Directors: 1
Hot Spot for Advancement for Women/Minorities:

LOCATIONS: ("Y" = Yes)

West:	Southwest:	Midwest:	Southeast:	Northeast:	International:
Y	Y	Y	Y	Y	Y

PARAMETRIC TECHNOLOGY CORP

www.ptc.com

Industry Group Code: 511210N

Management:		**Sales/Marketing:**		**Liberal Arts:**		**Information Sys.:**		**Professionals:**		**Tech./Scientific:**	
Mgmt. Trainees:	Y	Marketing Pros.:	Y	Gen. Writing/Editing:	Y	Info. Mgmt.:	Y	Finance/Acct.:	Y	Engineers, Elec.:	Y
Experienced Mgmt.:	Y	Retail Sales:		Tech. Writing:	Y	Software Dev.:	Y	Law:	Y	Engineers, Other:	Y
Int'l Business:	Y	Comm./Industrial:	Y	Graphic Arts/Photog.:		Hardware Dev.:		HR/Other:	Y	Health/Lab:	
MBA Grads:	Y	Sales Trainees:		Music:		Consulting/Other:		Training:	Y	Science/Research:	
		Advertising Pros.:	Y	Broadcasting:				Health Care:		Petroleum/Chem.:	
				Other:				Consulting:		Math/Other:	

TYPES OF BUSINESS:

Computer Software-Engineering & Manufacturing
Engineering Consulting Services
Enterprise Publishing Software
Product Data Management

BRANDS/DIVISIONS/AFFILIATES:

Windchill
Arbortext
Creo Elements/View
Relex Reliability
InSight
Creo Elements/Pro
Creo Elements/Direct
Mathcad

CONTACTS: *Note: Officers with more than one job title may be intentionally listed here more than once.*

James E. Heppelmann, CEO
James E. Heppelmann, Pres.
Jeffrey D. Glidden, CFO/Exec. VP
Paul Cunningham, Exec. VP-Worldwide Sales
Tom Kearns, CIO/Sr. VP
Brian Shepherd, Exec. VP-Prod. Dev.
Aaron C. von Staats, General Counsel/Corp. VP
Barry F. Cohen, Exec. VP-Strategy
Rob Gremley, Exec. VP-Mktg.
Mark Hodges, Chief Customer Officer/Div. VP
Marc Diouane, Exec. VP-Global Svcs.
C. Richard (Dick) Harrison, Chmn.
Anthony Paul DiBona, Exec. VP-Global Maintenance Support
Paul Cunningham, Exec. VP-Dist.

Phone: 781-370-5000	**Fax:** 781-370-6000
Toll-Free: 877-275-4782	
Address: 140 Kendrick St., Needham, MA 02494 US	

GROWTH PLANS/SPECIAL FEATURES:

Parametric Technology Corp. (PTC) develops, markets and supports product development software and related services, designed to aid companies in designing products and managing product information. It competes in the product lifecycle management (PLM) market with product lines in product data management, collaboration and related fields. It also offers computer-aided design (CAD), manufacturing (CAM) and engineering (CAE) products that compete in the computer aided technologies (CAx) market. The company divides its product offerings into two categories: PLM and Desktop. PLM product lines include Windchill product content management, product development and project collaboration programs; Arbortext data management and delivery tools; Creo Elements/View visualization, verification, annotation and automated comparison tools for documents as well as MCAD (2D and 3D) and ECAD formats; Relex Reliability planning and safety management software; and InSight product analytics tools. Desktop software includes CAx products as well as document authoring tools, including Creo Elements/Pro, a line of three-dimensional design products; CreoElements/Direct CAD and collaboration software; Arbortext authoring and illustration tools; and Mathcad engineering calculation software. The firm also offers maintenance, consulting and training services. PTC serves customers in the aerospace and defense; airlines; automotive; consumer products; electronics; footwear & apparel; industrial equipment; medical devices; and retail industries.

The firm provides its employees with tuition reimbursement; medical, dental and vision plans; life insurance; a 401(k) plan; and short- and long-term disability coverage.

FINANCIALS: **Sales and profits are in thousands of dollars—add 000 to get the full amount. 2010 Note: Financial information for 2010 was not available for all companies at press time.**

2010 Sales: $1,010,049	2010 Profits: $24,368	**U.S. Stock Ticker: PMTC**
2009 Sales: $938,185	2009 Profits: $31,522	**Int'l Ticker:**
2008 Sales: $1,070,330	2008 Profits: $79,702	Int'l Exchange:
2007 Sales: $941,279	2007 Profits: $143,656	Employees: 5,317 Fiscal Year Ends: 9/30
2006 Sales: $847,983	2006 Profits: $56,804	Parent Company:

SALARIES/BENEFITS:

Pension Plan:	ESOP Stock Plan:	Profit Sharing:	Top Exec. Salary: $600,000	Bonus: $
Savings Plan: Y	Stock Purch. Plan:		Second Exec. Salary: $521,650	Bonus: $

OTHER THOUGHTS:

Apparent Women Officers or Directors:
Hot Spot for Advancement for Women/Minorities:

LOCATIONS: ("Y" = Yes)

West:	Southwest:	Midwest:	Southeast:	Northeast:	International:
Y	Y	Y	Y	Y	Y

PAREXEL INTERNATIONAL CORP

www.parexel.com

Industry Group Code: 541712

Management:		Sales/Marketing:		Liberal Arts:		Information Sys.:		Professionals:		Tech./Scientific:	
Mgmt. Trainees:	Y	Marketing Pros.:	Y	Gen. Writing/Editing:	Y	Info. Mgmt.:	Y	Finance/Acct.:	Y	Engineers, Elec.:	Y
Experienced Mgmt.:	Y	Retail Sales:		Tech. Writing:	Y	Software Dev.:	Y	Law:	Y	Engineers, Other:	
Int'l Business:	Y	Comm./Industrial:	Y	Graphic Arts/Photog.:	Y	Hardware Dev.:		HR/Other:	Y	Health/Lab:	Y
MBA Grads:	Y	Sales Trainees:		Music:		Consulting/Other:	Y	Training:	Y	Science/Research:	Y
		Advertising Pros.:		Broadcasting:				Health Care:	Y	Petroleum/Chem.:	
				Other:				Consulting:	Y	Math/Other:	Y

TYPES OF BUSINESS:

Clinical Trial & Data Management
Biostatistical Analysis & Reporting
Medical Communications Services
Clinical Pharmacology Services
Consulting Services

BRANDS/DIVISIONS/AFFILIATES:

Clinical Research Services
PAREXEL Consulting & Medical Communications Svcs.
Perceptive Informatics Inc

CONTACTS: *Note: Officers with more than one job title may be intentionally listed here more than once.*

Josef H. von Rickenbach, CEO
Mark A. Goldberg, COO
James F. Winschel, Jr., CFO/Sr. VP
Anita Cooper, MA, D.Phil, Corp. Sr. VP/Gen. Mgr.-Clinical Research Svcs.
Ulf Schneider, Chief Admin. Officer/Sr. VP
Douglas A. Batt, General Counsel/Sr. VP/Corp. Sec.
Jennifer Baird, Sr. Dir.-Public Rel.
Jill L. Baker, VP-Investor Rel.
Kurt A. Brykman, Pres., PAREXEL Consulting & Medical Comm. Svcs.
Steve Kent, Pres., Perceptive Informatics
Josef H. von Rickenbach, Chmn.

Phone: 781-487-9900	**Fax:** 781-768-5512
Toll-Free:	
Address: 195 West St., Waltham, MA 02451 US	

GROWTH PLANS/SPECIAL FEATURES:

PAREXEL International Corp. is a biopharmaceutical services company. The firm provides clinical research, medical communications services, consulting and informatics and advanced technology products and services to the international biotechnology, pharmaceutical and medical device industries. Operating in approximately 70 locations throughout 54 countries, PAREXEL has three business segments: Clinical Research Services (CRS); PAREXEL Consulting and Medical Communications Services (PCMS); and Perceptive Informatics, Inc. PAREXEL's core business, CRS, accounts for roughly 77% of its revenues. It provides clinical trials management and biostatistics; data management; clinical pharmacology; and related medical advisory, patient recruitment and investigator site services. PCMS (13.5% of revenues) provides technical expertise and advice for drug development, regulatory affairs and biopharmaceutical process consulting; offers product launch support, including market development, product development and targeted communications services; identifies alternatives and solutions regarding product development, registration and commercialization; and provides health policy consulting and strategic reimbursement services. Lastly, Perceptive Informatics (9.5% of revenues) provides information technology designed to improve clients' product development processes, including medical imaging services, integrated voice response products, CTMS, web-based portals, systems integration, and patient diary applications. In 2010, the firm opened new facilities in South Africa, China, Singapore and Russia; and established new strategic relationships with Bristol-Myers Squibb and Eli Lilly and Company.

FINANCIALS: **Sales and profits are in thousands of dollars—add 000 to get the full amount. 2010 Note: Financial information for 2010 was not available for all companies at press time.**

2010 Sales: $1,131,039 — 2010 Profits: $41,542
2009 Sales: $1,050,755 — 2009 Profits: $39,307
2008 Sales: $964,283 — 2008 Profits: $64,640
2007 Sales: $741,955 — 2007 Profits: $37,289
2006 Sales: $614,947 — 2006 Profits: $23,544

U.S. Stock Ticker: PRXL
Int'l Ticker:
Int'l Exchange:
Employees: 9,720 Fiscal Year Ends: 6/30
Parent Company:

SALARIES/BENEFITS:

Pension Plan: ESOP Stock Plan: Profit Sharing: Top Exec. Salary: $650,000 Bonus: $754,000
Savings Plan: Stock Purch. Plan: Second Exec. Salary: $450,000 Bonus: $409,913

OTHER THOUGHTS:

Apparent Women Officers or Directors: 4
Hot Spot for Advancement for Women/Minorities: Y

LOCATIONS: ("Y" = Yes)

West:	Southwest:	Midwest:	Southeast:	Northeast:	International:
Y				Y	Y

PARK-OHIO HOLDINGS CORP

www.pkoh.com

Industry Group Code: 541614

Management:		Sales/Marketing:		Liberal Arts:		Information Sys.:		Professionals:		Tech./Scientific:	
Mgmt. Trainees:		Marketing Pros.:	Y	Gen. Writing/Editing:		Info. Mgmt.:	Y	Finance/Acct.:	Y	Engineers, Elec.:	
Experienced Mgmt.:		Retail Sales:		Tech. Writing:	Y	Software Dev.:	Y	Law:	Y	Engineers, Other:	
Int'l Business:	Y	Comm./Industrial:	Y	Graphic Arts/Photog.:		Hardware Dev.:		HR/Other:	Y	Health/Lab:	
MBA Grads:	Y	Sales Trainees:		Music:		Consulting/Other:		Training:		Science/Research:	
		Advertising Pros.:	Y	Broadcasting:				Health Care:	Y	Petroleum/Chem.:	
				Other:				Consulting:		Math/Other:	

TYPES OF BUSINESS:

Logistics & Supply Chain Services
Automobile Parts Manufacturing
Aluminum Components
Industrial Equipment Manufacturing

BRANDS/DIVISIONS/AFFILIATES:

Park-Ohio Industries, Inc.
Ajax Tocco Magnethermic
Pillar Induction
Assembly Component Systems

CONTACTS: *Note: Officers with more than one job title may be intentionally listed here more than once.*

Edward F. Crawford, CEO
Matthew V. Crawford, COO
Matthew V. Crawford, Pres.
Jeffrey L. Rutherford, CFO/VP
Robert D. Vilsack, General Counsel/Corp. Sec.
Patrick W. Fogarty, Dir.-Corp. Dev.
Edward F. Crawford, Chmn.

Phone: 440-947-2000	**Fax:** 440-947-2099
Toll-Free:	
Address: 6065 Parkland Blvd., Cleveland, OH 44124 US	

GROWTH PLANS/SPECIAL FEATURES:

Park-Ohio Holdings Corp., through its subsidiary Park-Ohio Industries, Inc., is an industrial supply chain logistics and diversified manufacturing business. The company operates through three segments: the Supply Technologies segment, the Aluminum Products segment and the Manufactured Products segment. The Supply Technologies segment, which accounts for approximately 49% of the firm's sales, provides integrated supply chain and logistics services for a broad range of high-volume, specialty production components. Supply Technologies provides various value-added services, such as engineering and design; part usage; cost analysis; supplier selection; quality assurance; bar coding; product packaging and tracking; just-in-time and point-of-use delivery; electronic billing services; and ongoing technical support. This segment operates 49 logistics service centers in the U.S., Puerto Rico, Scotland, Ireland, Mexico, Canada, Hungary, China, Taiwan, Singapore and India. It also maintains production sourcing and support centers in Asia. The segment's primary customers are in the heavy-duty truck; automotive and vehicle parts; electrical distribution and controls; power sports/fitness equipment; heating, ventilation and air conditioning; aerospace and defense; electrical components; appliance; and semiconductor industries. Park-Ohio's Aluminum Products segment (18% of sales) casts and machines aluminum engine, transmission, brake, suspension and other components for automotive, agricultural equipment, construction equipment, heavy-duty truck and marine equipment used by original equipment manufacturers, primarily on a sole-source basis. The Manufactured Products segment (33% of sales) operates a diverse group of niche manufacturing businesses that design and manufacture a range of highly engineered products, including induction heating and melting systems, pipe threading systems, rubber products and forged and machined products. This segment operates 22 facilities in the U.S., the U.K., Canada, Mexico, Belgium, Germany, China and Japan. In September 2010, the Supply Technologies segment acquired Assembly Component Systems from Lawson Products, Inc. In January 2011, Park-Ohio subsidiary Ajax Tocco Magnethermic acquired Pillar Induction from ABP Induction.

FINANCIALS: **Sales and profits are in thousands of dollars—add 000 to get the full amount. 2010 Note: Financial information for 2010 was not available for all companies at press time.**

2010 Sales: $813,522	2010 Profits: $15,187	**U.S. Stock Ticker: PKOH**
2009 Sales: $701,047	2009 Profits: $-5,209	**Int'l Ticker:**
2008 Sales: $1,068,757	2008 Profits: $-119,803	Int'l Exchange:
2007 Sales: $1,071,441	2007 Profits: $21,197	Employees: 3,200 Fiscal Year Ends: 12/31
2006 Sales: $1,056,246	2006 Profits: $24,179	Parent Company:

SALARIES/BENEFITS:

Pension Plan: Y	ESOP Stock Plan:	Profit Sharing:	Top Exec. Salary: $731,250	Bonus: $742,000
Savings Plan:	Stock Purch. Plan: Y		Second Exec. Salary: $390,000	Bonus: $260,000

OTHER THOUGHTS:

Apparent Women Officers or Directors: 1
Hot Spot for Advancement for Women/Minorities:

LOCATIONS: ("Y" = Yes)

West:	Southwest:	Midwest:	Southeast:	Northeast:	International:
	Y	Y	Y	Y	Y

Sales, profits and employees may be estimates. Financial information, benefits and other data can change quickly and may vary from those stated here.

PARSONS BRINCKERHOFF INC

www.pbworld.com

Industry Group Code: 237

Management:		Sales/Marketing:		Liberal Arts:		Information Sys.:		Professionals:		Tech./Scientific:	
Mgmt. Trainees:	Y	Marketing Pros.:	Y	Gen. Writing/Editing:	Y	Info. Mgmt.:	Y	Finance/Acct.:	Y	Engineers, Elec.:	Y
Experienced Mgmt.:	Y	Retail Sales:		Tech. Writing:	Y	Software Dev.:	Y	Law:	Y	Engineers, Other:	Y
Int'l Business:	Y	Comm./Industrial:	Y	Graphic Arts/Photog.:	Y	Hardware Dev.:		HR/Other:	Y	Health/Lab:	
MBA Grads:	Y	Sales Trainees:	Y	Music:		Consulting/Other:	Y	Training:	Y	Science/Research:	
		Advertising Pros.:		Broadcasting:				Health Care:		Petroleum/Chem.:	Y
				Other:				Consulting:	Y	Math/Other:	Y

TYPES OF BUSINESS:

Engineering Services
Planning, Design & Construction
Civic Construction Projects
Commercial Construction
Transportation Consulting
Program Management Services
Telecommunications & Environmental Projects

BRANDS/DIVISIONS/AFFILIATES:

Balfour Beatty PLC
PB Research Library

CONTACTS: *Note: Officers with more than one job title may be intentionally listed here more than once.*

George J. Pierson, CEO
Lisa M. Palumbo, General Counsel
Judy Cooper, Sr. VP/Dir.-Corp. Comm.
Paul Skoutelas, Market Leader-Transit, PB Americas
Gay Knipper, Dir.-National Program Mgmt., PB Americas
Richard A. Schrader, Chmn.

Phone: 212-465-5000	**Fax:** 212-465-5096
Toll-Free:	
Address: 1 Penn Plz., New York, NY 10119 US	

GROWTH PLANS/SPECIAL FEATURES:

Parsons Brinckerhoff, Inc., a subsidiary of Balfour Beatty PLC, provides engineering, consulting, and management services to local governments and the transportation, energy, and commercial market sectors. The company also offers construction services, program and project management, and facilities management. Parsons Brinckerhoff has taken on projects for clients such as Bangkok Mass Transit System Corporation and the City of Austin, Texas; and its signature works include the design of New York City's first subway and the reconfiguration of the Fort Washington Way interstate connector in Cincinnati. The company also worked with the Delhi Metro Rail Corporation to build a mass transit system designed as an urban transport system to move over 3 million passengers a day. Other relevant projects have included a gas fired power station in Kuwait; a web site and communications plan for lower Manhattan, known as lowermanhatten.info; and designing and engineering the Greater Cairo Metro system. Potential clients can view the company's work through the PB Research Library, a body that showcases and publishes the details of important projects. The firm is organized into three divisions: Americas, International and Facilities. The company is employee-owned with 150 offices worldwide.

FINANCIALS: **Sales and profits are in thousands of dollars—add 000 to get the full amount. 2010 Note: Financial information for 2010 was not available for all companies at press time.**

2010 Sales: $	2010 Profits: $	**U.S. Stock Ticker: Subsidiary**
2009 Sales: $2,300,000	2009 Profits: $	**Int'l Ticker:**
2008 Sales: $2,343,117	2008 Profits: $73,882	Int'l Exchange:
2007 Sales: $1,853,741	2007 Profits: $62,117	Employees: 13,000 Fiscal Year Ends: 10/31
2006 Sales: $1,689,964	2006 Profits: $46,386	Parent Company: BALFOUR BEATTY PLC

SALARIES/BENEFITS:

Pension Plan:	ESOP Stock Plan:	Profit Sharing:	Top Exec. Salary: $	Bonus: $
Savings Plan:	Stock Purch. Plan:		Second Exec. Salary: $	Bonus: $

OTHER THOUGHTS:

Apparent Women Officers or Directors: 3
Hot Spot for Advancement for Women/Minorities: Y

LOCATIONS: ("Y" = Yes)

West:	Southwest:	Midwest:	Southeast:	Northeast:	International:
Y	Y	Y	Y	Y	Y

PATTERSON COMPANIES INC

www.pattersoncompanies.com

Industry Group Code: 423450

Management:		Sales/Marketing:		Liberal Arts:		Information Sys.:		Professionals:		Tech./Scientific:	
Mgmt. Trainees:	Y	Marketing Pros.:	Y	Gen. Writing/Editing:	Y	Info. Mgmt.:	Y	Finance/Acct.:	Y	Engineers, Elec.:	
Experienced Mgmt.:	Y	Retail Sales:		Tech. Writing:	Y	Software Dev.:	Y	Law:	Y	Engineers, Other:	
Int'l Business:	Y	Comm./Industrial:	Y	Graphic Arts/Photog.:	Y	Hardware Dev.:		HR/Other:	Y	Health/Lab:	Y
MBA Grads:	Y	Sales Trainees:	Y	Music:		Consulting/Other:		Training:	Y	Science/Research:	
		Advertising Pros.:	Y	Broadcasting:				Health Care:	Y	Petroleum/Chem.:	
				Other:				Consulting:		Math/Other:	

TYPES OF BUSINESS:

Dental Products & Related Services
Veterinary Products
Non-Wheelchair Assistive Products

BRANDS/DIVISIONS/AFFILIATES:

Patterson Dental Holdings, Inc.
Direct Dental Supply Co.
Webster Management LP
Patterson Medical Holdings, Inc.
Accu-Bite, Inc.
Physio Med Services Limited.
Mobilis Healthcare Group Ltd
American Veterinary Supply Corporation

CONTACTS: *Note: Officers with more than one job title may be intentionally listed here more than once.*

Scott P. Anderson, CEO
Scott P. Anderson, Pres.
R. Stephen Armstrong, CFO/Exec. VP
Jerome E. Thygesen, VP-Human Resources
Ranell Hamm, CIO
Matthew L. Levitt, Sec.
R. Stephen Armstrong, Treas.
George L. Henriques, Pres., Webster Veterinary Supply, Inc.
David P. Sproat, Pres., Patterson Medical
Paul A. Guggenheim, Pres., Patterson Dental
Peter L. Frechette, Chmn.

Phone: 651-686-1600	**Fax:** 651-686-9331
Toll-Free: 800-328-5536	
Address: 1031 Mendota Heights Rd., St. Paul, MN 55120 US	

GROWTH PLANS/SPECIAL FEATURES:

Patterson Companies, Inc. is a firm engaged in the distribution of products to the dental, veterinary and medical industries. The company operates in three segments: dental supply, veterinary supply and rehabilitation supply. The dental supply segment, Patterson Dental, is one of the largest distributors of dental products in North America. The division provides consumable products, including X-ray film, restorative materials, hand instruments and sterilization products; basic and advanced technology dental equipment; practice management and clinical software; patient education systems; and office forms and stationery. Patterson Dental also offers related services including dental equipment installation; maintenance and repair; dental office design; and equipment financing. The veterinary supply segment, Webster Veterinary, provides products for the diagnosis, treatment and/or prevention of diseases in companion pets and equine animals. Webster offers over 11,000 products that are sold by about 235 field sales representatives. The segment also has an agency commission business with several pharmaceutical manufacturers. The rehabilitation supply segment, Patterson Medical, distributes rehabilitation medical supplies and non-wheelchair assistive products. Patterson Medical operates as Medco Sports Medicine and Sammons Preston Rolyan in North America; and as Mobilis, Rolyan, Ausmedic and Homecraft in international markets. Patterson Companies' subsidiaries include Patterson Dental Holdings, Inc.; Dolphin Imaging Systems, LLC; Direct Dental Supply Co.; Webster Management LP; Patterson Medical Holdings, Inc.; Mobilis Healthcare Group Ltd.; Halo Healthcare Ltd.; County Footwear Ltd.; Accu-Bite, Inc.; and Physio Med Services Limited. In August 2011, Webster Veterinary acquired veterinary distribution firm American Veterinary Supply Corporation.

The company offers employee benefits including life, disability, medical, dental and vision insurance; stock purchase/ownership plans; a 401(k); discounts; and assistance programs.

FINANCIALS: **Sales and profits are in thousands of dollars—add 000 to get the full amount. 2010 Note: Financial information for 2010 was not available for all companies at press time.**

2010 Sales: $3,237,376	2010 Profits: $212,254	**U.S. Stock Ticker: PDCO**
2009 Sales: $3,094,227	2009 Profits: $199,635	**Int'l Ticker:**
2008 Sales: $2,998,729	2008 Profits: $224,858	Int'l Exchange:
2007 Sales: $2,798,398	2007 Profits: $208,336	Employees: 6,890 Fiscal Year Ends: 4/30
2006 Sales: $2,615,123	2006 Profits: $198,425	Parent Company:

SALARIES/BENEFITS:

Pension Plan:	ESOP Stock Plan: Y	Profit Sharing:	Top Exec. Salary: $286,491	Bonus: $147,211
Savings Plan: Y	Stock Purch. Plan: Y		Second Exec. Salary: $275,324	Bonus: $165,052

OTHER THOUGHTS:

Apparent Women Officers or Directors: 2
Hot Spot for Advancement for Women/Minorities:

LOCATIONS: ("Y" = Yes)

West:	Southwest:	Midwest:	Southeast:	Northeast:	International:
Y	Y	Y	Y	Y	Y

Sales, profits and employees may be estimates. Financial information, benefits and other data can change quickly and may vary from those stated here.

PATTERSON-UTI ENERGY INC

www.patenergy.com

Industry Group Code: 213111

Management:		Sales/Marketing:		Liberal Arts:		Information Sys.:		Professionals:		Tech./Scientific:	
Mgmt. Trainees:	Y	Marketing Pros.:	Y	Gen. Writing/Editing:		Info. Mgmt.:	Y	Finance/Acct.:	Y	Engineers, Elec.:	Y
Experienced Mgmt.:	Y	Retail Sales:		Tech. Writing:	Y	Software Dev.:	Y	Law:	Y	Engineers, Other:	Y
Int'l Business:	Y	Comm./Industrial:	Y	Graphic Arts/Photog.:		Hardware Dev.:		HR/Other:	Y	Health/Lab:	
MBA Grads:	Y	Sales Trainees:		Music:		Consulting/Other:		Training:	Y	Science/Research:	
		Advertising Pros.:		Broadcasting:				Health Care:		Petroleum/Chem.:	Y
				Other:				Consulting:		Math/Other:	

TYPES OF BUSINESS:

Oil & Gas Services
Onshore Contract Drilling Services
Drilling & Completion Fluid Services
Pressure Pumping Services
Oil & Gas Production

BRANDS/DIVISIONS/AFFILIATES:

Key Energy Services

CONTACTS:

Note: Officers with more than one job title may be intentionally listed here more than once.

Douglas J. Wall, CEO
Douglas J. Wall, Pres.
John E. Vollmer, III, CFO/Treas.
Seth D. Wexler, General Counsel/Sec.
John E. Vollmer, III, Sr. VP-Corp. Dev.
Greg Pipkin, Chief Acct. Officer
Kenneth N. Berns, Sr. VP
Mark S. Siegel, Chmn.

Phone: 281-765-7100 **Fax:** 281-765-7175
Toll-Free:
Address: 450 Gears Rd., Ste. 500, Houston, TX 77067 US

GROWTH PLANS/SPECIAL FEATURES:

Patterson-UTI Energy, Inc. serves land-based oil and natural gas exploration and production companies with drilling and related services. The company operates in 14 U.S. states and western Canada through three business segments: contract drilling; pressure pumping; and oil and natural gas. Patterson-UTI operates approximately 356 currently marketable contract drilling rigs, with a maximum drilling depth capacity ranging from 5,000 to 25,000 feet; of these rigs, 232 are mechanical and 124 are silicon-controlled rectifier (SCR) electric. Under turnkey contracts, the company will drill a well to a certain depths under specified conditions for a fixed fee. Patterson-UTI dug 2,919 wells in 2010, each dug on average in about 21 days. It operates 317 trucks and 402 trailers used to transport and support its rigs. Pressure pumping services include stimulation, which enhances well flow by pumping corrosive acid, nitrogen gas or highly pressurized fracturing fluid into a well; and cementing, which involves inserting a substance between a wellbore and its casing to add support. The oil and gas segment operates in Texas and New Mexico as a working interest owner. Contract drilling provides roughly 74% of the company's revenue; pressure pumping, 23.9%; and oil and natural gas, 2.1%. In October 2010, Patterson-UTI acquired the pressure pumping and wireline business of Key Energy Services for $238 million. In January 2011, the firm sold its electric wireline subsidiary, Universal Wireline, Inc., to Gray Wireline Services, Inc. for roughly $25.5 million.

FINANCIALS:

Sales and profits are in thousands of dollars—add 000 to get the full amount. 2010 Note: Financial information for 2010 was not available for all companies at press time.

2010 Sales: $1,462,931	2010 Profits: $116,942
2009 Sales: $781,946	2009 Profits: $-38,290
2008 Sales: $2,063,880	2008 Profits: $347,069
2007 Sales: $1,986,096	2007 Profits: $438,639
2006 Sales: $2,546,586	2006 Profits: $673,254

U.S. Stock Ticker: PTEN
Int'l Ticker:
Int'l Exchange:
Employees: 7,000 Fiscal Year Ends: 12/31
Parent Company:

SALARIES/BENEFITS:

Pension Plan: ESOP Stock Plan: Profit Sharing: Top Exec. Salary: $600,000 Bonus: $893,611
Savings Plan: Y Stock Purch. Plan: Second Exec. Salary: $350,000 Bonus: $595,741

OTHER THOUGHTS:

Apparent Women Officers or Directors:
Hot Spot for Advancement for Women/Minorities:

LOCATIONS: ("Y" = Yes)

West:	Southwest:	Midwest:	Southeast:	Northeast:	International:
Y	Y	Y	Y	Y	Y

PEABODY ENERGY CORP

www.peabodyenergy.com

Industry Group Code: 21211

Management:		**Sales/Marketing:**		**Liberal Arts:**		**Information Sys.:**		**Professionals:**		**Tech./Scientific:**	
Mgmt. Trainees:	Y	Marketing Pros.:	Y	Gen. Writing/Editing:		Info. Mgmt.:	Y	Finance/Acct.:	Y	Engineers, Elec.:	
Experienced Mgmt.:	Y	Retail Sales:		Tech. Writing:	Y	Software Dev.:		Law:	Y	Engineers, Other:	Y
Int'l Business:	Y	Comm./Industrial:	Y	Graphic Arts/Photog.:		Hardware Dev.:		HR/Other:	Y	Health/Lab:	
MBA Grads:	Y	Sales Trainees:		Music:		Consulting/Other:		Training:	Y	Science/Research:	
		Advertising Pros.:		Broadcasting:				Health Care:		Petroleum/Chem.:	Y
				Other:				Consulting:		Math/Other:	

TYPES OF BUSINESS:

Coal Production
Energy Trading & Marketing
Transportation Services
Carbon Capture
Coal Conversion Technologies

BRANDS/DIVISIONS/AFFILIATES:

Peabody-Winsway Resources

CONTACTS: *Note: Officers with more than one job title may be intentionally listed here more than once.*

Gregory H. Boyce, CEO
Eric Ford, COO/Exec. VP
Richard A. Navarre, Pres.
Michael C. Crews, CFO/Exec. VP
Lina Young, VP-IT
Jeane Hull, Exec. VP-Tech. Svcs.
Scott P. Lawson, Sr. VP-Eng. Svcs.
Sharon D. Fiehler, Chief Admin. Officer/Exec. VP
Alexander C. Scoch, Chief Legal Officer/Exec. VP-Law/Sec.
Vic Svec, Sr. VP-Corp. Comm.
Vic Svec, Sr. VP-Investor Rel.
Richard A. Navarre, Chief Commercial Officer
Fredrick D. Palmer, Sr. VP-Gov't Rel.
Keith Downham, VP-Resource Dev., Indonesia
Randy M. Tucker, VP-IT Svcs.
Gregory H. Boyce, Chmn.
Zhenchun Shi, Pres., Asia

Phone: 314-342-3400	**Fax:** 314-342-7799
Toll-Free:	
Address: 701 Market St., St. Louis, MO 63101 US	

GROWTH PLANS/SPECIAL FEATURES:

Peabody Energy Corp. is a private-sector coal company with operations worldwide. The firm sells approximately 245.9 million tons of coal annually to a clientele of nearly 345 electricity generating and industrial plants in 25 countries. It has 28 coal mining operations in the U.S. and Australia. In 2010, the firm produced 218.4 million tons of coal. The company has approximately 9 billion tons of proven and probable coal reserves. The mining operations consist of three principal operating segments: western U.S. mining, Midwestern U.S. mining and Australian mining. In addition to mining operations, the firm markets, brokers and trades coal through a trading and brokerage operations segment. Peabody Energy has international trading locations in London, U.K.; Newcastle, Australia; Beijing, China; Jakarta, Indonesia; and Singapore. Other energy-related commercial activities include the development of mine-mouth coal-fueled generating plants; the management of vast coal reserve and real estate holdings; the advancement of carbon capture sequestration initiatives; and Btu conversion technologies, which are designed to convert coal to natural gas and transportation fuels. In mid 2010, the company formed a joint venture in Mongolia with Winsway Coking Coal Holdings, Ltd. called Peabody-Winsway Resources. This joint venture maintains uranium and coal licenses in Mongolia and is currently heading an exploration program in the country.

FINANCIALS: **Sales and profits are in thousands of dollars—add 000 to get the full amount. 2010 Note: Financial information for 2010 was not available for all companies at press time.**

2010 Sales: $6,860,000	2010 Profits: $774,000	**U.S. Stock Ticker: BTU**
2009 Sales: $6,012,400	2009 Profits: $463,000	**Int'l Ticker:**
2008 Sales: $6,593,400	2008 Profits: $953,500	Int'l Exchange:
2007 Sales: $4,574,712	2007 Profits: $264,285	Employees: 7,200 Fiscal Year Ends: 12/31
2006 Sales: $4,108,396	2006 Profits: $600,697	Parent Company:

SALARIES/BENEFITS:

Pension Plan:	ESOP Stock Plan:	Profit Sharing:	Top Exec. Salary: $1,110,250	Bonus: $2,359,306
Savings Plan:	Stock Purch. Plan:		Second Exec. Salary: $747,250	Bonus: $1,210,784

OTHER THOUGHTS:

Apparent Women Officers or Directors: 4
Hot Spot for Advancement for Women/Minorities: Y

LOCATIONS: ("Y" = Yes)

West:	Southwest:	Midwest:	Southeast:	Northeast:	International:
Y		Y			Y

PENSKE AUTOMOTIVE GROUP INC www.penskeautomotive.com

Industry Group Code: 441110

Management:		Sales/Marketing:		Liberal Arts:		Information Sys.:		Professionals:		Tech./Scientific:	
Mgmt. Trainees:	Y	Marketing Pros.:	Y	Gen. Writing/Editing:	Y	Info. Mgmt.:	Y	Finance/Acct.:	Y	Engineers, Elec.:	
Experienced Mgmt.:	Y	Retail Sales:	Y	Tech. Writing:		Software Dev.:		Law:	Y	Engineers, Other:	
Int'l Business:	Y	Comm./Industrial:		Graphic Arts/Photog.:		Hardware Dev.:		HR/Other:	Y	Health/Lab:	
MBA Grads:	Y	Sales Trainees:	Y	Music:		Consulting/Other:		Training:	Y	Science/Research:	
		Advertising Pros.:	Y	Broadcasting:				Health Care:		Petroleum/Chem.:	
				Other:				Consulting:		Math/Other:	

TYPES OF BUSINESS:

Auto Dealers, Retail
Automotive Leasing
Online Car Retail

BRANDS/DIVISIONS/AFFILIATES:

Penske Corporation
Penske Truck Leasing Co.
Mercedes-Benz of Greenwich
Crevier BMW
Crevier MINI
Fred Baker Porsche
Fred Baker Audi

CONTACTS: *Note: Officers with more than one job title may be intentionally listed here more than once.*

Roger S. Penske, CEO
Robert H. Kurnick, Jr., Pres.
David K. Jones, CFO
Calvin C. Sharp, Exec. VP-Human Resources
Shane M. Spradlin, General Counsel/Exec. VP/Corp. Sec.
R. Whitfield Ramonat, Exec. VP-Central Oper. & Financial Svcs.
Anthony R. Pordon, Exec. VP-Corp. Dev.
Anthony R. Pordon, Exec. VP-Investor Rel.
David K. Jones, Exec. VP-Finance
Bernie Wolfe, Exec. VP-East Oper.
George Brochick, Exec. VP-West Oper.
J.D. Carlson, Sr. VP/Controller
Gerard Nieuwenhuys, Managing Dir.-Synter Group
Roger S. Penske, Chmn.

Phone: 248-648-2500 **Fax:** 248-648-2525
Toll-Free:
Address: 2555 Telegraph Rd., Bloomfield Hills, MI 48302 US

GROWTH PLANS/SPECIAL FEATURES:

Penske Automotive Group, Inc. (PAG), formerly called United Auto Group, is a leading automotive retailer, owning and operating 172 franchises in the U.S. and 151 franchises outside of the U.S., primarily in the U.K. The firm offers a full range of vehicle brands, with approximately 95% of its total revenue generated from brands of non-U.S. based manufacturers and 66% generated from premium brands, including Audi, BMW, Cadillac and Porsche. Typically, customers can choose from an inventory of over 1,250 new and used vehicles and have access to approximately 253 service bays with the capacity to service approximately 1,000 vehicles per day. Every PAG dealership maintains a web site where customers can review vehicle inventories and obtain photos, prices, promotions, specifications, reviews, financial information and tools to schedule service appointments. PAG has also partnered with CarsDirect.com, a leading online car buying service that provides consumers with a full menu of research features. The firm previously offered distribution services through wholly-owned subsidiary smart USA Distributor, LLC, as the exclusive distributor of the smart fortwo vehicle in the U.S. and Puerto Rico via a network of over 75 smart dealerships. However, PAG exited this business in early 2011. The firm derives 55% of its revenue from the sale of new vehicles; 29% from used vehicles; 13% from parts and services; and 13% from financing and interest. Penske Corporation and its affiliates own approximately 51% of the stock of PAG. PAG owns 9% limited partnership interest in Penske Truck Leasing Co. In December 2010, the firm acquired the Fred Baker Porsche and Audi franchises in Ohio. In July 2011, the company acquired Mercedes-Benz of Greenwich in Connecticut and the Crevier BMW and MINI franchises in California.

FINANCIALS: **Sales and profits are in thousands of dollars—add 000 to get the full amount. 2010 Note: Financial information for 2010 was not available for all companies at press time.**

2010 Sales: $10,713,585 | 2010 Profits: $108,281
2009 Sales: $9,523,105 | 2009 Profits: $76,920
2008 Sales: $11,637,136 | 2008 Profits: $-418,903
2007 Sales: $12,781,717 | 2007 Profits: $122,233
2006 Sales: $11,126,719 | 2006 Profits: $124,701

U.S. Stock Ticker: PAG
Int'l Ticker:
Int'l Exchange:
Employees: 14,800 Fiscal Year Ends: 12/31
Parent Company:

SALARIES/BENEFITS:

Pension Plan: | ESOP Stock Plan: | Profit Sharing: | Top Exec. Salary: $1,000,000 | Bonus: $
Savings Plan: Y | Stock Purch. Plan: | | Second Exec. Salary: $600,000 | Bonus: $

OTHER THOUGHTS:

Apparent Women Officers or Directors: 1
Hot Spot for Advancement for Women/Minorities:

LOCATIONS: ("Y" = Yes)

West:	Southwest:	Midwest:	Southeast:	Northeast:	International:
Y	Y	Y	Y	Y	Y

PEPSICO INC

Industry Group Code: 3121

www.pepsico.com

Management:		**Sales/Marketing:**		**Liberal Arts:**		**Information Sys.:**		**Professionals:**		**Tech./Scientific:**	
Mgmt. Trainees:	Y	Marketing Pros.:	Y	Gen. Writing/Editing:	Y	Info. Mgmt.:	Y	Finance/Acct.:	Y	Engineers, Elec.:	
Experienced Mgmt.:	Y	Retail Sales:		Tech. Writing:	Y	Software Dev.:	Y	Law:	Y	Engineers, Other:	Y
Int'l Business:	Y	Comm./Industrial:	Y	Graphic Arts/Photog.:	Y	Hardware Dev.:		HR/Other:	Y	Health/Lab:	
MBA Grads:	Y	Sales Trainees:	Y	Music:		Consulting/Other:		Training:	Y	Science/Research:	
		Advertising Pros.:	Y	Broadcasting:				Health Care:		Petroleum/Chem.:	
				Other:	Y			Consulting:		Math/Other:	

TYPES OF BUSINESS:

Soft Drink Manufacturing
Snack Food Manufacturing
Juice & Sports Drink Manufacturing
Cereal Manufacturing
Rice & Pasta Product Manufacturing
Oatmeal Product Manufacturing
Bottled Water Production
Cereal Bar Manufacturing

BRANDS/DIVISIONS/AFFILIATES:

Frito-Lay Inc
PepsiCo Beverages North America
PepsiCo International
Quaker Foods North America
Tropicana Products Inc
Pepsi-Cola Metropolitan Bottling Co Inc
Cheetos
Doritos

CONTACTS: *Note: Officers with more than one job title may be intentionally listed here more than once.*

Indra K. Nooyi, CEO
Hugh F. Johnston, CFO
A. Salman Amin, Chief Mktg. Officer/Exec. VP
Cynthia M. Trudell, Chief Personnel Officer/Exec. VP
Mehmood Khan, Chief Scientific Officer
Robert Dixon, CIO/Sr. VP
Larry D. Thompson, General Counsel/Sec.
Richard Goodman, Exec. VP-Global Oper.
Julie Hamp, Chief Communications Officer/Sr. VP
Alfred P. Carey, CEO-PepsiCo Americas Beverages
Saad Abdul-Latif, CEO-PepsiCo Asia, Middle East, Africa
John C. Compton, CEO-PepsiCo Americas Foods
Neil Campbell, Pres., Tropicana Beverages North America
Indra K. Nooyi, Chmn.
Zein Abdalla, CEO-PepsiCo Europe
Rich Beck, Sr. VP-Global Supply Chain Oper.

Phone: 914-253-2000 **Fax:** 914-253-2070
Toll-Free:
Address: 700 Anderson Hill Rd., Purchase, NY 10577 US

GROWTH PLANS/SPECIAL FEATURES:

PepsiCo, Inc. is a leading global food, snack and beverage company. The company operates in four business units: PepsiCo Americas Foods (PAF); PepsiCo Americas Beverages (PAB); PepsiCo Europe; and PepsiCo Asia, Middle East and Africa. PAF includes Frito-Lay North America (FLNA), Quaker Foods North America (QFNA) and all of the firm's Latin American food and snack businesses (LAF). FLNA manufactures or uses contract manufacturers, markets, sells and distributes branded snacks. Brands offered include Lay's potato chips, Doritos, Cheetos, Fritos, Ruffles, Quaker Chewy granola bars and SunChips. Approximately 23% of the firm's 2010 total net revenue was derived from this division. QFNA, which accounted for 3% of 2010 revenue, offers products including Aunt Jemima mixes and syrups; Quaker grits; Life cereal; Rice-a-Roni; and Near East side dishes. LAF offers a number of snack foods including Gamesa, Doritos, Ruffles, Lay's and Sabritas as well as Quaker brand cereals and snacks. Latin American foods made up 11% of 2010 revenue. PAB includes PepsiCo Beverages North America and all of the company's Latin American beverage businesses and offers brands including Pepsi, Gatorade, Tropicana, Mirinda, Mug, Propel, SoBe Lifewater, Dole, Amp Energy, Naked juice and Izze as well as ready-to-drink coffee, water and tea products under the Unilever/Lipton and Starbucks brands. This segment accounted for 35% of 2010 revenue. PepsiCo International, which includes all PepsiCo businesses in Europe, Asia, Middle East and Africa, distributes products including Lay's, Doritos, Cheetos, Ruffles, Quaker, Kurkure, Chipsy, Smith's and Red Rock Deli. International sales contributed 28% of 2010 revenue. In February 2010, the firm completed the merger of The Pepsi Bottling Group, Inc. and PepsiAmericas, Inc. with wholly-owned subsidiary Pepsi-Cola Metropolitan Bottling Company, Inc. (Metro), with Metro as the surviving company. In September 2011, the company completed the acquisition of Wimm-Bill-Dann Dairy and Juice Company for about $3.8 billion.

FINANCIALS: **Sales and profits are in thousands of dollars—add 000 to get the full amount. 2010 Note: Financial information for 2010 was not available for all companies at press time.**

2010 Sales: $57,838,000 | 2010 Profits: $6,338,000
2009 Sales: $43,232,000 | 2009 Profits: $5,979,000
2008 Sales: $43,251,000 | 2008 Profits: $6,935,000
2007 Sales: $39,474,000 | 2007 Profits: $5,658,000
2006 Sales: $35,137,000 | 2006 Profits: $5,642,000

U.S. Stock Ticker: PEP
Int'l Ticker:
Int'l Exchange:
Employees: 294,000 Fiscal Year Ends: 12/31
Parent Company:

SALARIES/BENEFITS:

Pension Plan: Y | ESOP Stock Plan: | Profit Sharing: | Top Exec. Salary: $1,300,000 | Bonus: $3,000,000
Savings Plan: Y | Stock Purch. Plan: | Second Exec. Salary: $846,154 | Bonus: $1,404,000

OTHER THOUGHTS:

Apparent Women Officers or Directors: 5
Hot Spot for Advancement for Women/Minorities: Y

LOCATIONS: ("Y" = Yes)

West:	Southwest:	Midwest:	Southeast:	Northeast:	International:
Y	Y	Y	Y	Y	Y

PERRIGO CO

www.perrigo.com

Industry Group Code: 325412

Management:		Sales/Marketing:		Liberal Arts:		Information Sys.:		Professionals:		Tech./Scientific:	
Mgmt. Trainees:	Y	Marketing Pros.:	Y	Gen. Writing/Editing:		Info. Mgmt.:	Y	Finance/Acct.:	Y	Engineers, Elec.:	Y
Experienced Mgmt.:	Y	Retail Sales:		Tech. Writing:	Y	Software Dev.:	Y	Law:	Y	Engineers, Other:	Y
Int'l Business:	Y	Comm./Industrial:	Y	Graphic Arts/Photog.:		Hardware Dev.:		HR/Other:	Y	Health/Lab:	Y
MBA Grads:	Y	Sales Trainees:		Music:		Consulting/Other:		Training:	Y	Science/Research:	Y
		Advertising Pros.:		Broadcasting:				Health Care:	Y	Petroleum/Chem.:	Y
				Other:				Consulting:		Math/Other:	Y

TYPES OF BUSINESS:

Generic Prescription Drugs
Over-the-Counter Pharmaceuticals
Nutritional Products
Active Pharmaceutical Ingredients
Consumer Products

BRANDS/DIVISIONS/AFFILIATES:

Perrigo U.K.
Wrafton Laboratories, Ltd.
Perrigo Co. of South Carolina
Perrigo New York, Inc.
Perrigo Israel Pharmaceuticals, Ltd.
Orion Laboratories Pty, Ltd.
Quimica Y Farmacia S.A. de C.V.
PBM Holdings, Inc.

CONTACTS: *Note: Officers with more than one job title may be intentionally listed here more than once.*

Joseph C. Papa, CEO
Joseph C. Papa, Pres.
Judy L. Brown, CFO/Exec. VP
James Tomshack, Sr. VP-Consumer Healthcare Sales
Michael Stewart, Sr. VP-Global Human Resources
Jatin Shah, Chief Scientific Officer/Sr. VP
Thomas M. Farrington, CIO/Sr. VP
Todd W. Kingma, General Counsel/Exec. VP/Sec.
John T. Hendrickson, Exec. VP-Global Oper.
Jeffrey R. Needham, Sr. VP-Global Bus. Dev.
Arthur J. Shannon, VP-Corp. Comm.
Arthur J. Shannon, VP-Investor Rel.
Sharon Kochan, Exec. VP-U.S. Generics
Louis Yu, Sr. VP-Global Quality & Compliance
Jeffrey R. Needham, Exec. VP/Gen. Mgr.-Consumer Healthcare
Joseph C. Papa, Chmn.
Refael Lebel, Exec. VP/Pres., Perrigo Israel
John T. Hendrickson, Exec. VP-Supply Chain

Phone: 269-673-8451 **Fax:** 269-673-7534
Toll-Free:
Address: 515 Eastern Ave., Allegan, MI 49010 US

GROWTH PLANS/SPECIAL FEATURES:

Perrigo Co. is a global healthcare supplier and one of the world's largest manufacturers of over-the-counter pharmaceutical and nutritional products for the store brand market. The company also develops and manufactures generic prescription drugs, active pharmaceutical ingredients (API) and consumer products. The firm operates through three segments: consumer healthcare, prescription pharmaceuticals and API. The consumer healthcare segment makes a broad line of products including analgesics, cough/cold/allergy/sinus, gastrointestinal, smoking cessation, first aid, vitamin and nutritional supplements. The pharmaceuticals segment's primary activity is the development, manufacture and sale of generic prescription drug products, generally for the U.S. market. The company currently markets roughly 300 generic prescription products to approximately 120 customers. The API segment, through subsidiary Chemagis, develops, manufactures and markets API for the drug industry and branded pharmaceutical companies. Perrigo's operations also include the Israel pharmaceutical and diagnostic products segment, which includes the marketing and manufacturing of branded prescription drugs under long-term exclusive licenses and the importation of pharmaceutical, diagnostics and other medical products into Israel. Perrigo operates through several wholly-owned subsidiaries. In the U.S., these subsidiaries consist primarily of L. Perrigo Co.; Perrigo Co. of South Carolina; and Perrigo New York, Inc. International subsidiaries include Perrigo Israel Pharmaceuticals, Ltd.; Quimica Y Farmacia S.A. de C.V.; Wrafton Laboratories, Ltd.; and Perrigo U.K., Ltd. In June 2011, the firm agreed to acquire pharmaceutical manufacturer Paddock Laboratories, Inc.

FINANCIALS: **Sales and profits are in thousands of dollars—add 000 to get the full amount. 2010 Note: Financial information for 2010 was not available for all companies at press time.**

2010 Sales: $2,268,870 — 2010 Profits: $222,546
2009 Sales: $2,006,862 — 2009 Profits: $144,049
2008 Sales: $1,729,921 — 2008 Profits: $135,773
2007 Sales: $1,368,351 — 2007 Profits: $73,797
2006 Sales: $1,366,821 — 2006 Profits: $71,400

U.S. Stock Ticker: PRGO
Int'l Ticker:
Int'l Exchange:
Employees: 7,700 Fiscal Year Ends: 6/30
Parent Company:

SALARIES/BENEFITS:

Pension Plan: ESOP Stock Plan: Profit Sharing: Top Exec. Salary: $918,750 Bonus: $1,837,500
Savings Plan: Stock Purch. Plan: Second Exec. Salary: $457,177 Bonus: $548,612

OTHER THOUGHTS:

Apparent Women Officers or Directors: 3
Hot Spot for Advancement for Women/Minorities: Y

LOCATIONS: ("Y" = Yes)

West:	Southwest:	Midwest:	Southeast:	Northeast:	International:
Y				Y	Y

PETCO ANIMAL SUPPLIES INC

www.petco.com

Industry Group Code: 453910

Management:		**Sales/Marketing:**		**Liberal Arts:**		**Information Sys.:**		**Professionals:**		**Tech./Scientific:**	
Mgmt. Trainees:	Y	Marketing Pros.:	Y	Gen. Writing/Editing:	Y	Info. Mgmt.:	Y	Finance/Acct.:	Y	Engineers, Elec.:	
Experienced Mgmt.:	Y	Retail Sales:	Y	Tech. Writing:		Software Dev.:	Y	Law:	Y	Engineers, Other:	
Int'l Business:		Comm./Industrial:		Graphic Arts/Photog.:	Y	Hardware Dev.:		HR/Other:	Y	Health/Lab:	
MBA Grads:	Y	Sales Trainees:	Y	Music:		Consulting/Other:		Training:	Y	Science/Research:	
		Advertising Pros.:	Y	Broadcasting:				Health Care:		Petroleum/Chem.:	
				Other:	Y			Consulting:		Math/Other:	

TYPES OF BUSINESS:

Pets & Pet Supplies, Retail
Online Sales
Pet Grooming
Veterinary Services
Obedience Training
Pet Photography

BRANDS/DIVISIONS/AFFILIATES:

Petco Foundation (The)
P.A.L.S.
Think Adoption First
Leonard Green & Partners LP
TPG Capital
Complete Petmart

CONTACTS: *Note: Officers with more than one job title may be intentionally listed here more than once.*

James M. Myers, CEO
Bruce C. Hall, COO
Bruce C. Hall, Pres.
Michael E. Foss, CFO/Exec. VP
Marc Brown, VP-Human Resources
Herman Nell, CIO
Thomas A. Farello, Sr. VP-Oper.
Lisa Epstein, Dir.-Corp. Comm.
Reginald Holden, VP-Procurement

Phone: 858-453-7845	**Fax:**
Toll-Free:	
Address: 9125 Rehco Rd., San Diego, CA 92121 US	

GROWTH PLANS/SPECIAL FEATURES:

Petco Animal Supplies, Inc. is a leading specialty retailer of premium pet food, supplies and services. The company currently operates over 1,000 stores and 11 distribution centers in 50 states and Washington, D.C. Petco's superstores carry more than 10,000 products, including premium pet food and treats; small animals such as fish, birds, reptiles and related supplies; collars and leashes; grooming products; toys; pet carriers; cat furniture; dog houses and beds; vitamins; and veterinary supplies. Most stores also provide a variety of pet services, including professional grooming, veterinary clinics, vaccinations, obedience training and pet photography. Several services are performed in glass-walled stations in order to increase customer awareness and confidence in the services. In light of overpopulation problems, Petco chooses not to sell dogs and cats, though it does support adoption programs such as Petfinder.com through in-store Think Adoption First kiosks in many stores. The firm also operates the P.A.L.S. (Petco Animal Lovers Save) customer loyalty program. Members receive special benefits and savings through the use of the P.A.L.S. card, which allows Petco to target customers and track shopping habits. In addition to its retail stores, the company operates an e-commerce site, which offers Petco merchandise, pet tips, a community forum, online specials and information about the Petco Foundation, an animal welfare and rights group. The company is owned by Leonard Green & Partners LP and TPG Capital, two private equity investment firms. In June 2011, the firm acquired Ohio-based Complete Petmart, a pet specialty chain.

Petco offers its employees health insurance plans, discounted pet insurance, a 401(k) retirement savings plan and merchandise discounts.

FINANCIALS: **Sales and profits are in thousands of dollars—add 000 to get the full amount. 2010 Note: Financial information for 2010 was not available for all companies at press time.**

2010 Sales: $	2010 Profits: $	**U.S. Stock Ticker: Private**
2009 Sales: $2,600,000	2009 Profits: $	**Int'l Ticker:**
2008 Sales: $2,600,000	2008 Profits: $	Int'l Exchange:
2007 Sales: $2,400,000	2007 Profits: $	Employees: 22,000 Fiscal Year Ends: 1/31
2006 Sales: $1,996,089	2006 Profits: $75,170	Parent Company: TPG CAPITAL

SALARIES/BENEFITS:

Pension Plan:	ESOP Stock Plan:	Profit Sharing:	Top Exec. Salary: $	Bonus: $
Savings Plan: Y	Stock Purch. Plan:		Second Exec. Salary: $	Bonus: $

OTHER THOUGHTS:

Apparent Women Officers or Directors: 1
Hot Spot for Advancement for Women/Minorities:

LOCATIONS: ("Y" = Yes)

West:	Southwest:	Midwest:	Southeast:	Northeast:	International:
Y	Y	Y	Y	Y	

PETSMART INC

www.petsmart.com

Industry Group Code: 453910

Management:		**Sales/Marketing:**		**Liberal Arts:**		**Information Sys.:**		**Professionals:**		**Tech./Scientific:**	
Mgmt. Trainees:	Y	Marketing Pros.:	Y	Gen. Writing/Editing:	Y	Info. Mgmt.:	Y	Finance/Acct.:	Y	Engineers, Elec.:	
Experienced Mgmt.:	Y	Retail Sales:	Y	Tech. Writing:		Software Dev.:	Y	Law:	Y	Engineers, Other:	
Int'l Business:	Y	Comm./Industrial:		Graphic Arts/Photog.:	Y	Hardware Dev.:		HR/Other:	Y	Health/Lab:	
MBA Grads:	Y	Sales Trainees:	Y	Music:		Consulting/Other:		Training:	Y	Science/Research:	
		Advertising Pros.:	Y	Broadcasting:				Health Care:		Petroleum/Chem.:	
				Other:	Y			Consulting:		Math/Other:	

TYPES OF BUSINESS:

Pets & Pet Supplies, Retail
Online & Catalog Sales
Pet Training
In-Store Adoption Centers
Veterinary Services
Pet Boarding
Pet Grooming

BRANDS/DIVISIONS/AFFILIATES:

Medical Management International, Inc.
Banfield, The Pet Hospital
PetsHotels
PetPerks
PetSmart.com
Doggie Day Camp
GNC Pets

CONTACTS: *Note: Officers with more than one job title may be intentionally listed here more than once.*

Robert F. Moran, CEO
Robert F. Moran, Pres.
Lawrence Molloy, CFO/Sr. VP
John Alpaugh, Chief Mktg. Officer/Sr. VP
Neil Stacey, Sr. VP-Human Resources
Donald Beaver, CIO/Sr. VP
Joseph O'Leary, Exec. VP-Merch., Supply Chain & Mktg.
Emily Dickinson, General Counsel/Sr. VP/Sec.
David K. Lenhardt, Sr. VP-Svcs. & Store Oper.
Jaye Perricone, Sr. VP-Real Estate
David K. Lenhardt, Sr. VP-Info. Systems & Human Resources
Philip L. Francis, Chmn.
Bruce Thorn, Sr. VP-Supply Chain

Phone: 623-580-6100 **Fax:** 623-395-6517
Toll-Free: 800-738-1385
Address: 19601 N. 27th Ave., Phoenix, AZ 85027 US

GROWTH PLANS/SPECIAL FEATURES:

PetSmart, Inc. is a leading operator of superstores specializing in pet food, supplies and services. The company operates over 1,192 stores in the U.S. and Canada, which offer an assortment of pet services and products. PetSmart stores also offer value-added pet services, including grooming, training, boarding and day camp, and the firm operates full-service veterinary hospitals in 768 stores. Medical Management International, Inc., an operator of veterinary hospitals, operates 757 of PetSmart's hospitals under the name Banfield, The Pet Hospital. The remaining hospitals are located in Canada and operated by other third parties. PetSmart offers pet boarding in more than 184 stores through its PetSmart PetsHotels. These PetsHotels offer Doggie Day Camp, which offers climate-controlled daycare for dogs and cats. The company opened 46 and closed eight stores during 2010. Its stores range in size from 12,000 to 27,500 square feet and carry roughly 10,000 distinct items, including nationally recognized brand names and a selection of proprietary or private label brands. PetSmart stores sell supplies for dogs, cats, fresh-water tropical fish, birds and other small pets, such as hamsters, gerbils and guinea pigs. The company also actively supports pet adoption through its in-store adoption centers. The firm offers a PetPerks loyalty program and sells its products online through PetSmart.com. In August 2010, the company expanded into New York, opening two stores. In March 2011, PetSmart began offering multi-vitamin line GNC Pets.

PetSmart offers its employees medical, dental and vision insurance; a health reimbursement account; an employee assistance program; flexible spending accounts; life and AD&D insurance; short- and long-term disability; a 401(k) plan; an employee stock purchase plan; adoption assistance; an educational assistance program; an associate discount; and a travel assistance program.

FINANCIALS: **Sales and profits are in thousands of dollars—add 000 to get the full amount. 2010 Note: Financial information for 2010 was not available for all companies at press time.**

2010 Sales: $5,336,392 — 2010 Profits: $198,325
2009 Sales: $5,065,293 — 2009 Profits: $192,670
2008 Sales: $4,672,656 — 2008 Profits: $258,684
2007 Sales: $4,233,857 — 2007 Profits: $185,069
2006 Sales: $3,760,499 — 2006 Profits: $182,490

U.S. Stock Ticker: PETM
Int'l Ticker:
Int'l Exchange:
Employees: 45,000 Fiscal Year Ends: 1/31
Parent Company:

SALARIES/BENEFITS:

Pension Plan: ESOP Stock Plan: Profit Sharing: Top Exec. Salary: $1,038,363 Bonus: $2,363,314
Savings Plan: Y Stock Purch. Plan: Y Second Exec. Salary: $998,942 Bonus: $2,273,592

OTHER THOUGHTS:

Apparent Women Officers or Directors: 3
Hot Spot for Advancement for Women/Minorities: Y

LOCATIONS: ("Y" = Yes)

West:	Southwest:	Midwest:	Southeast:	Northeast:	International:
Y	Y	Y	Y	Y	Y

PG&E CORPORATION

www.pgecorp.com

Industry Group Code: 221

Management:		**Sales/Marketing:**		**Liberal Arts:**		**Information Sys.:**		**Professionals:**		**Tech./Scientific:**	
Mgmt. Trainees:	Y	Marketing Pros.:	Y	Gen. Writing/Editing:	Y	Info. Mgmt.:	Y	Finance/Acct.:	Y	Engineers, Elec.:	Y
Experienced Mgmt.:	Y	Retail Sales:		Tech. Writing:	Y	Software Dev.:	Y	Law:	Y	Engineers, Other:	Y
Int'l Business:	Y	Comm./Industrial:	Y	Graphic Arts/Photog.:	Y	Hardware Dev.:		HR/Other:	Y	Health/Lab:	
MBA Grads:	Y	Sales Trainees:		Music:		Consulting/Other:		Training:	Y	Science/Research:	
		Advertising Pros.:	Y	Broadcasting:				Health Care:		Petroleum/Chem.:	Y
				Other:				Consulting:		Math/Other:	

TYPES OF BUSINESS:

Utilities-Electricity & Natural Gas
Energy Trading
Electricity Generation
Pipelines
Hydroelectric & Nuclear Generation
Natural Gas

BRANDS/DIVISIONS/AFFILIATES:

Pacific Gas and Electric Co

CONTACTS:

Note: Officers with more than one job title may be intentionally listed here more than once.

Anthony F. Earley, Jr., CEO
John S. Keenan, COO/Sr. VP-Pacific Gas & Electric Co.
Anthony F. Earley, Jr., Pres.
Kent M. Harvey, CFO/Sr. VP
Hyun Park, General Counsel/Sr. VP
Rand L. Rosenberg, Sr. VP-Corp. Strategy & Dev.
Greg S. Pruett, Sr. VP-Corp. Affairs
Gabriel B. Togneri, VP-Investor Rel.
Dinyar B. Mistry, Controller/VP
Geisha J. Williams, Exec. VP-Electric Oper., Pacific Gas & Electric Co
John R. Simon, Sr. VP-Human Resources, Pacific Gas & Electric
Linda Y.H. Cheng, VP-Corp. Governance/Corp. Sec.
Edward T. Bedwell, VP-Gov't Oper., Pacific Gas & Electric Co.
Anthony F. Earley, Jr., Interim Chmn.
Desmond A. Bell, Chief Procurement Officer/Sr. VP-Shared Svcs.

Phone: 415-267-7000 **Fax:** 415-267-7268
Toll-Free: 800-719-9056
Address: 1 Market, Spear Twr, Ste. 2400, San Francisco, CA 94105 US

GROWTH PLANS/SPECIAL FEATURES:

PG&E Corporation is a holding company that markets energy services and products in northern and central California through subsidiary Pacific Gas and Electric Co. The subsidiary is one of the largest electric and natural gas utilities in the U.S., serving roughly 5.2 million electric and 4.3 million natural gas customers. With approximately 141,000 circuit miles of distribution lines, the company's electricity distribution network extends through most of northern and central California. Pacific owns and operates power plants producing nearly half of the power it sells, including 110 hydroelectric, two nuclear and 11 fossil fuel facilities. The company's hydroelectric generation system covers 16 counties in northern and central California. It includes 99 reservoirs; 44 miles of flumes; 170 dams; 172 miles of canals; 56 diversions; 54 miles of pipe; 130 miles of tunnels; and five miles of natural waterways. The company's natural gas operations consist of an integrated transportation, storage and distribution system throughout 39 counties, including most of northern and central California. This system consists of approximately 6,000 miles of backbone and local transmission pipelines; 43,000 miles of distribution pipelines; and three storage facilities. Through interconnections with various interstate pipelines, the company receives gas from every major natural gas basin in western North America, including basins in Canada, the southwestern U.S. and the Rocky Mountains.

The company offers employees supplemental life, medical, dental and vision insurance; health care and dependent care reimbursement accounts; paid time off; a retirement savings plan; adoption reimbursement; and tuition refund opportunities.

FINANCIALS:

Sales and profits are in thousands of dollars—add 000 to get the full amount. 2010 Note: Financial information for 2010 was not available for all companies at press time.

2010 Sales: $13,841,000	2010 Profits: $1,099,000	**U.S. Stock Ticker: PCG**
2009 Sales: $13,399,000	2009 Profits: $1,220,000	**Int'l Ticker:**
2008 Sales: $14,628,000	2008 Profits: $1,185,000	Int'l Exchange:
2007 Sales: $13,237,000	2007 Profits: $1,006,000	Employees: 19,424 Fiscal Year Ends: 12/31
2006 Sales: $12,539,000	2006 Profits: $2,108,000	Parent Company:

SALARIES/BENEFITS:

Pension Plan: Y	ESOP Stock Plan:	Profit Sharing:	Top Exec. Salary: $1,182,160	Bonus: $
Savings Plan: Y	Stock Purch. Plan:		Second Exec. Salary: $672,500	Bonus: $

OTHER THOUGHTS:

Apparent Women Officers or Directors: 10
Hot Spot for Advancement for Women/Minorities: Y

LOCATIONS: ("Y" = Yes)

West:	Southwest:	Midwest:	Southeast:	Northeast:	International:
Y				Y	

PHARMACEUTICAL PRODUCT DEVELOPMENT INC www.ppdi.com

Industry Group Code: 541712

Management:		Sales/Marketing:		Liberal Arts:		Information Sys.:		Professionals:		Tech./Scientific:	
Mgmt. Trainees:	Y	Marketing Pros.:	Y	Gen. Writing/Editing:		Info. Mgmt.:	Y	Finance/Acct.:	Y	Engineers, Elec.:	Y
Experienced Mgmt.:	Y	Retail Sales:		Tech. Writing:	Y	Software Dev.:	Y	Law:	Y	Engineers, Other:	
Int'l Business:	Y	Comm./Industrial:	Y	Graphic Arts/Photog.:	Y	Hardware Dev.:		HR/Other:	Y	Health/Lab:	Y
MBA Grads:	Y	Sales Trainees:		Music:		Consulting/Other:	Y	Training:	Y	Science/Research:	Y
		Advertising Pros.:		Broadcasting:				Health Care:	Y	Petroleum/Chem.:	
				Other:				Consulting:	Y	Math/Other:	

TYPES OF BUSINESS:

Contract Research
Drug Discovery & Development Services
Clinical Data Consulting Services
Medical Marketing & Information Support Services
Drug Discovery Services
Medical Device Development

BRANDS/DIVISIONS/AFFILIATES:

Furiex Pharmaceuticals, Inc.
Taijitu Biologics Limited

CONTACTS: *Note: Officers with more than one job title may be intentionally listed here more than once.*

David L. Grange, CEO
William J. Sharbaugh, COO
Daniel G. Darazsdi, CFO
Christine A. Dingivan, Chief Medical Officer/Exec. VP
Michael O. Wilkinson, CIO/Exec. VP
B. Judd Hartman, General Counsel/Corp. Sec.
William W. Richardson, Sr. VP-Global Bus. Dev.
Louise Caudle, Dir.-Corp. Comm.
Luke Heagle, Dir.-Investor Rel.
Daniel G. Darazsdi, Treas./Assistant Sec.
Lee E. Babiss, Exec. VP-Global Laboratory Svcs.
Paul Colvin, Exec. VP-Global Clinical Dev.
Fred N. Eshelman, Chmn.

Phone: 910-251-0081 **Fax:** 910-762-5820
Toll-Free:
Address: 929 N. Front St., Wilmington, NC 28401 US

GROWTH PLANS/SPECIAL FEATURES:

Pharmaceutical Product Development, Inc. (PPD) provides drug discovery and development services to pharmaceutical, biotechnology, medical device, academic and government organizations. PPD's services are divided into two segments: Discovery Sciences and Development. Through the combined services of these segments, PPD helps pharmaceutical companies through all stages of clinical testing. The stages of testing can be specifically divided into discovery and preclinical, phase I, phase II-IIIb and post-approval. In the discovery and preclinical stages of drug testing, PPD helps clients accelerate drug discovery and provides information concerning the pharmaceutical composition of a new drug, its safety, its formulaic design and how it will be administered. During phase I testing, PPD conducts healthy volunteer clinics, provides data and project management services and offers regulatory affairs assistance. In phase II and III tests, PPD oversees the later stages of product development and government approval, providing project management, clinical quality assurance, patient recruitment, medical device development and clinical monitoring. In the post-approval stage, PPD provides technology, approval and marketing services intended to maximize the new drug's lifecycle. PPD has experience conducting research and drug development in the areas of central nervous system diseases, cardiovascular diseases, critical care studies, dermatological disorders, endocrine/metabolic studies, infectious disease treatment, hematology/oncology studies and pulmonary/allergy treatment, among others. The firm conducts its operations through 86 offices in 43 countries, and recently opened labs and offices in China, India and Russia. In June 2010, PPD spun-off subsidiary Furiex Pharmaceuticals, Inc., which is now an independent company. In January 2011, the company and Taijitu Biologics Limited established novel biotherapeutics discovery joint venture Taijitu Biologics Limited.

FINANCIALS: **Sales and profits are in thousands of dollars—add 000 to get the full amount. 2010 Note: Financial information for 2010 was not available for all companies at press time.**

2010 Sales: $1,470,570 | 2010 Profits: $124,041
2009 Sales: $1,416,770 | 2009 Profits: $159,295
2008 Sales: $1,551,384 | 2008 Profits: $187,519
2007 Sales: $1,414,465 | 2007 Profits: $163,401
2006 Sales: $1,247,682 | 2006 Profits: $156,652

U.S. Stock Ticker: PPDI
Int'l Ticker:
Int'l Exchange:
Employees: 11,000 Fiscal Year Ends: 12/31
Parent Company:

SALARIES/BENEFITS:

Pension Plan: | ESOP Stock Plan: | Profit Sharing: | Top Exec. Salary: $740,000 | Bonus: $300,000
Savings Plan: | Stock Purch. Plan: Y | | Second Exec. Salary: $380,519 | Bonus: $150,000

OTHER THOUGHTS:

Apparent Women Officers or Directors: 2
Hot Spot for Advancement for Women/Minorities:

LOCATIONS: ("Y" = Yes)

West:	Southwest:	Midwest:	Southeast:	Northeast:	International:
Y	Y	Y		Y	Y

PHILIP MORRIS INTERNATIONAL INC

www.pmi.com

Industry Group Code: 3122

Management:		**Sales/Marketing:**		**Liberal Arts:**		**Information Sys.:**		**Professionals:**		**Tech./Scientific:**	
Mgmt. Trainees:		Marketing Pros.:	Y	Gen. Writing/Editing:	Y	Info. Mgmt.:	Y	Finance/Acct.:	Y	Engineers, Elec.:	Y
Experienced Mgmt.:	Y	Retail Sales:		Tech. Writing:		Software Dev.:	Y	Law:	Y	Engineers, Other:	Y
Int'l Business:	Y	Comm./Industrial:	Y	Graphic Arts/Photog.:	Y	Hardware Dev.:		HR/Other:	Y	Health/Lab:	
MBA Grads:	Y	Sales Trainees:	Y	Music:		Consulting/Other:		Training:	Y	Science/Research:	Y
		Advertising Pros.:	Y	Broadcasting:				Health Care:		Petroleum/Chem.:	
				Other:				Consulting:		Math/Other:	

TYPES OF BUSINESS:

Tobacco Products

BRANDS/DIVISIONS/AFFILIATES:

Morven Gold
Marlboro
L&M
Chesterfield
Parliament
Virginia Slims
Bond Street
Parliament

CONTACTS:

Note: Officers with more than one job title may be intentionally listed here more than once.

Louis C. Camilleri, CEO
Andre Calantzopoulos, COO
Hermann Waldemer, CFO
Daniele Regorda, Sr. VP-Human Resources
Doug Dean, Sr. VP-R&D
Kevin Click, CIO/Sr. VP
David Bernick, General Counsel/Sr. VP
Martin King, Sr. VP-Oper.
Even Hurwitz, Sr. VP-Corp. Affairs
Joachim Psotta, VP/Controller
Jacek Olczak, Pres., European Union
Miroslaw Zielinski, Pres., PMI Duty Free
Miroslaw Zielinski, Pres., Eastern Europe, Middle East & Africa
Jerry Whitson, Corp. Sec./Deputy General Counsel
Louis C. Camilleri, Chmn.
Matteo Pellegrini, Pres., Asia

Phone: 917-663-2000	**Fax:**
Toll-Free:	
Address: 120 Park Ave., New York, NY 10017 US	

GROWTH PLANS/SPECIAL FEATURES:

Philip Morris International, Inc. (PMI) is a holding company specializing in tobacco. The firm's subsidiaries and affiliates, along with their licensees, are engaged in the manufacture and sale of cigarettes and other tobacco products in roughly 160 countries. Formerly a business unit of Altria Group, Inc., Philip Morris International was fully spun-off in recent years to create a separate, publicly-traded company focused on the international tobacco business. The firm's corporate headquarters is in New York City, while its primary operations center is located in Lausanne, Switzerland. PMI's business is managed in four geographic segments: European Union; Eastern Europe, Middle East and Africa; Asia; and Latin America & Canada. The European Union segment represents approximately 43.9% of the company's revenues; the Eastern Europe, Middle East and Africa segment, 25.9%; the Asia segment, 23.7%; and the Latin America & Canada segment, 6.5%. The company's product portfolio contains approximately 150 distinct brands and over 1,900 variants, led by Marlboro, the world's best selling cigarette brand. Other major brands include L&M, Chesterfield, Philip Morris, Parliament, Virginia Slims and Bond Street. PMI also owns a variety of local brands in various markets, including Dji Sam Soe, in Indonesia; Diana, in Italy; Apollo-Soyuz, in Russia; Morven Gold, in Pakistan; Boston, in Columbia; Classic, in Serbia; f6, in Germany; Delicados, in Mexico; Assos, in Greece; and Petra, in the Czech Republic and Slovakia. The company maintains approximately 58 production factories worldwide. PMI recently acquired Swedish Match South Africa (Proprietary) Limited.

FINANCIALS:

Sales and profits are in thousands of dollars—add 000 to get the full amount. 2010 Note: Financial information for 2010 was not available for all companies at press time.

2010 Sales: $67,713,000 — 2010 Profits: $7,259,000
2009 Sales: $62,080,000 — 2009 Profits: $6,342,000
2008 Sales: $63,640,000 — 2008 Profits: $6,890,000
2007 Sales: $55,243,000 — 2007 Profits: $6,026,000
2006 Sales: $49,260,000 — 2006 Profits: $6,146,000

U.S. Stock Ticker: PM
Int'l Ticker:
Int'l Exchange:
Employees: 78,300 Fiscal Year Ends: 12/31
Parent Company:

SALARIES/BENEFITS:

Pension Plan: ESOP Stock Plan: Profit Sharing: Top Exec. Salary: $1,500,000 Bonus: $7,560,000
Savings Plan: Stock Purch. Plan: Second Exec. Salary: $1,264,582 Bonus: $3,770,130

OTHER THOUGHTS:

Apparent Women Officers or Directors:
Hot Spot for Advancement for Women/Minorities:

LOCATIONS: ("Y" = Yes)

West:	Southwest:	Midwest:	Southeast:	Northeast:	International:
				Y	Y

PLEXUS CORP

www.plexus.com

Industry Group Code: 334419

Management:		**Sales/Marketing:**		**Liberal Arts:**		**Information Sys.:**		**Professionals:**		**Tech./Scientific:**	
Mgmt. Trainees:	Y	Marketing Pros.:	Y	Gen. Writing/Editing:		Info. Mgmt.:	Y	Finance/Acct.:	Y	Engineers, Elec.:	Y
Experienced Mgmt.:	Y	Retail Sales:		Tech. Writing:	Y	Software Dev.:	Y	Law:	Y	Engineers, Other:	
Int'l Business:	Y	Comm./Industrial:	Y	Graphic Arts/Photog.:	Y	Hardware Dev.:	Y	HR/Other:	Y	Health/Lab:	
MBA Grads:	Y	Sales Trainees:		Music:		Consulting/Other:	Y	Training:	Y	Science/Research:	
		Advertising Pros.:	Y	Broadcasting:				Health Care:		Petroleum/Chem.:	
				Other:				Consulting:		Math/Other:	

TYPES OF BUSINESS:

Contract Electronics Manufacturing-Diversified
Hardware & Software Design
Printed Circuit Board Design
Prototyping Services
Material Procurement & Management
Logistics Services

BRANDS/DIVISIONS/AFFILIATES:

CONTACTS:

Note: Officers with more than one job title may be intentionally listed here more than once.

Dean Foate, CEO
Dean Foate, Pres.
Ginger Jones, CFO/VP
Joe Mauthe, VP-Global Human Resources
Steve Frisch, Sr. VP-Global Eng. Svcs.
Mike Buseman, Sr. VP-Global Mfg. Oper.
Angelo Ninivaggi, General Counsel/VP/Sec.
Mike Verstegen, Sr. VP-Global Market Dev.
George Setton, Corp. Treas.
Todd Kelsey, Sr. VP-Global Customer Svcs.
John L. Nussbaum, Chmn.
Yong Jin Lim, Regional Pres., Plexus Asia Pacific

Phone: 920-722-3451 **Fax:** 920-751-5395
Toll-Free:
Address: 1 Plexus Way, Neenah, WI 54957-0156 US

GROWTH PLANS/SPECIAL FEATURES:

Plexus Corp. is a global provider of electronic manufacturing services (EMS). The company also provides global logistics management, aftermarket service and repair. It provides these services to original equipment manufacturers (OEMs) and other technology companies in the wireline and networking, wireless infrastructure, medical, industrial and commercial and defense, security and aerospace market sectors. The company's customers may outsource all stages of the product realization process, including product specifications; development, design and design verification; regulatory compliance support; prototyping and new product introduction; manufacturing test equipment development; materials sourcing, procurement and supply-chain management; product assembly, manufacturing, configuration and test; order fulfillment; logistics; and service and repair. Plexus's services include product development and design services, such as project management, feasibility studies, product conceptualization and product verification testing; prototyping and new product introduction services, including prototype assembly; test equipment development services, including testing for printed circuit assemblies, subassemblies, system assemblies and finished products; material sourcing and procurement services; agile manufacturing services, including printed circuit board assembly, basic assembly, system integration and mechatronic integration; fulfillment and logistic services; and aftermarket support. Plexus has 22 active facilities in 15 locations in the U.S., Europe and Asia. In November 2010, the firm announced plans to expand its engineering capacity in Germany. In December 2010, the company announced plans for the construction of a new manufacturing facility in China.

The company offers employees medical, dental and vision insurance; flexible spending accounts; life and AD&D insurance; travel accident insurance; disability coverage; a 401(k) plan; on-site financial planning free of charge; tuition reimbursement; relocation assistance; an employee assistance program; and employee discounts.

FINANCIALS:

Sales and profits are in thousands of dollars—add 000 to get the full amount. 2010 Note: Financial information for 2010 was not available for all companies at press time.

2010 Sales: $2,013,393	2010 Profits: $89,533
2009 Sales: $1,616,622	2009 Profits: $46,327
2008 Sales: $1,841,622	2008 Profits: $84,144
2007 Sales: $1,546,264	2007 Profits: $65,718
2006 Sales: $1,460,557	2006 Profits: $100,025

U.S. Stock Ticker: PLXS
Int'l Ticker:
Int'l Exchange:
Employees: 8,700 Fiscal Year Ends: 9/30
Parent Company:

SALARIES/BENEFITS:

Pension Plan:	ESOP Stock Plan:	Profit Sharing:	Top Exec. Salary: $766,632	Bonus: $1,527,627
Savings Plan: Y	Stock Purch. Plan:		Second Exec. Salary: $349,537	Bonus: $347,308

OTHER THOUGHTS:

Apparent Women Officers or Directors: 1
Hot Spot for Advancement for Women/Minorities:

LOCATIONS: ("Y" = Yes)

West:	Southwest:	Midwest:	Southeast:	Northeast:	International:
Y		Y		Y	Y

POLO RALPH LAUREN CORP

www.polo.com

Industry Group Code: 315

Management:		**Sales/Marketing:**		**Liberal Arts:**		**Information Sys.:**		**Professionals:**		**Tech./Scientific:**	
Mgmt. Trainees:	Y	Marketing Pros.:	Y	Gen. Writing/Editing:	Y	Info. Mgmt.:	Y	Finance/Acct.:	Y	Engineers, Elec.:	
Experienced Mgmt.:	Y	Retail Sales:	Y	Tech. Writing:		Software Dev.:	Y	Law:	Y	Engineers, Other:	
Int'l Business:	Y	Comm./Industrial:	Y	Graphic Arts/Photog.:	Y	Hardware Dev.:		HR/Other:	Y	Health/Lab:	
MBA Grads:	Y	Sales Trainees:	Y	Music:		Consulting/Other:		Training:	Y	Science/Research:	
		Advertising Pros.:	Y	Broadcasting:				Health Care:		Petroleum/Chem.:	
				Other:	Y			Consulting:		Math/Other:	

TYPES OF BUSINESS:

Men's & Women's Branded Fashions
Apparel Design & Marketing
Accessories
Fragrances
Home Furnishings
Cosmetics
Retail Stores

BRANDS/DIVISIONS/AFFILIATES:

Polo
Ralph by Ralph Lauren
Club Monaco
Black Label
Chaps
Blue Label
Rugby
Polo.com

CONTACTS: *Note: Officers with more than one job title may be intentionally listed here more than once.*

Ralph Lauren, CEO
Roger N. Farah, COO
Roger N. Farah, Pres.
Tracey T. Travis, CFO
Mitchell A. Kosh, Sr. VP-Human Resources
Mitchell A. Kosh, Sr. VP-Legal
Ralph Lauren, Chmn.

Phone: 212-318-7000	**Fax:** 212-318-7690
Toll-Free: 800-377-7656	
Address: 650 Madison Ave., New York, NY 10022 US	

GROWTH PLANS/SPECIAL FEATURES:

Polo Ralph Lauren Corp. (Polo) designs, markets and distributes premium lifestyle products. Polo licenses the manufacturing of its products to companies worldwide. Capitalizing on the creative force of its founder, Ralph Lauren, the firm's various brand names have become recognizable cultural symbols across the globe. The firm offers four categories of lifestyle products: apparel products (including extensive collections of men's, women's and children's clothing); home products (including bedding and bath products, furniture, fabric, wallpaper, paints, tabletop and giftware); accessories (including footwear, eyewear, jewelry, leather goods, handbags and luggage); and fragrance products (consisting of fragrances and skin care products). The company markets its products through department, specialty, golf and Polo Ralph Lauren stores, as well as via the Internet and mail order catalogs. Polo also offers wholesale products to upscale (and certain mid-tier) department stores, specialty stores and golf/pro shops worldwide. Its brands include Ralph by Ralph Lauren, Glamorous, Romance, Polo, Lauren for Men, Purple Label, Blue Label, Black Label, Polo Jeans Co., Pink Pony, Polo Sport and Club Monaco. It currently operates 259 Ralph Lauren, Club Monaco and Rugby stores (as well as 10,000 shops-within-shops) in North America, Japan, Europe and Latin America. Polo also operates Impact 21 stores in Japan. The company formed Ralph Lauren Media in a joint venture with NBC in order to reach consumers through various media outlets, including the Internet, television, cable and print. Its first initiative was the creation of Polo.com, a web site that brings products and information to consumers in an online magazine format.

FINANCIALS: **Sales and profits are in thousands of dollars—add 000 to get the full amount. 2010 Note: Financial information for 2010 was not available for all companies at press time.**

2010 Sales: $4,978,900	2010 Profits: $479,500	**U.S. Stock Ticker: RL**
2009 Sales: $5,018,900	2009 Profits: $406,000	**Int'l Ticker:**
2008 Sales: $4,880,100	2008 Profits: $419,800	Int'l Exchange:
2007 Sales: $4,295,400	2007 Profits: $400,900	Employees: 19,000 Fiscal Year Ends: 3/31
2006 Sales: $3,746,300	2006 Profits: $308,000	Parent Company:

SALARIES/BENEFITS:

Pension Plan: Y	ESOP Stock Plan:	Profit Sharing:	Top Exec. Salary: $1,250,000	Bonus: $19,500,000
Savings Plan: Y	Stock Purch. Plan:		Second Exec. Salary: $900,000	Bonus: $9,900,000

OTHER THOUGHTS:

Apparent Women Officers or Directors:
Hot Spot for Advancement for Women/Minorities:

LOCATIONS: ("Y" = Yes)

West:	Southwest:	Midwest:	Southeast:	Northeast:	International:
Y	Y	Y	Y	Y	Y

POLYCOM INC

www.polycom.com

Industry Group Code: 334119

Management:		**Sales/Marketing:**		**Liberal Arts:**		**Information Sys.:**		**Professionals:**		**Tech./Scientific:**	
Mgmt. Trainees:		Marketing Pros.:	Y	Gen. Writing/Editing:		Info. Mgmt.:	Y	Finance/Acct.:	Y	Engineers, Elec.:	Y
Experienced Mgmt.:		Retail Sales:		Tech. Writing:	Y	Software Dev.:	Y	Law:	Y	Engineers, Other:	
Int'l Business:	Y	Comm./Industrial:	Y	Graphic Arts/Photog.:		Hardware Dev.:	Y	HR/Other:	Y	Health/Lab:	
MBA Grads:	Y	Sales Trainees:		Music:		Consulting/Other:		Training:		Science/Research:	
		Advertising Pros.:	Y	Broadcasting:				Health Care:		Petroleum/Chem.:	
				Other:				Consulting:		Math/Other:	Y

TYPES OF BUSINESS:

Communications Equipment & Software
Network Management Software
Professional Service & Support

BRANDS/DIVISIONS/AFFILIATES:

Polycom Architected Telepresence Experience
Polycom HDX
Polycom VoiceStation
Polycom VVX 1500
Polycom SoundStructure
Polycom Vortex
Polycom SoundPoint
Accordent Technologies, Inc.

CONTACTS: *Note: Officers with more than one job title may be intentionally listed here more than once.*

Andrew M. Miller, CEO
Andrew M. Miler, Pres.
Michael R. Kourey, CFO/Sr. VP-Finance & Admin.
Kate Huchison, Chief Mktg. Officer/Exec. VP
Ashley D. Goldsmith, Exec. VP-Human Resources
Arijit Bose, CIO/Sr. VP-IT
Sayed M. Darwish, Chief Admin. Officer
Sayed M. Darwish, General Counsel/Exec.. VP/Corp. Sec.
Robert B. Steele, Sr. VP-Worldwide Oper.
Laura J. Durr, Principal Acct. Officer/Worldwide Controller/VP
Thomas B. Johnson, Pres., Polycom Americas
Ron Myers, Sr. VP-Global Channels
Donald J. Floyd, VP-Internal Audit
Sudhakar Ramakrishna, Chief Dev. Officer
David G. DeWalt, Chmn.
Gary Rider, Pres., EMEA

Phone: 925-924-6000	**Fax:** 925-924-6100
Toll-Free: 800-765-9266	
Address: 4750 Willow Rd., Pleasanton, CA 94588 US	

GROWTH PLANS/SPECIAL FEATURES:

Polycom, Inc. is a global provider of unified communications (UC) applications that enable users to conduct video, voice, data and web communications. The company's products are organized into three groups: UC Group Systems, which includes immersive telepresence, group video and group voice systems; UC Personal Devices, which include desktop video devices, desktop voice and wireless local area network (LAN) products; and Network Infrastructure, which includes conferencing infrastructure, distributed media applications, management applications, recording and streaming security and remote access. Specific products in the UC Group Systems division include the Polycom RealPresence Experience room environment (RPX), Polycom Open Telepresence Experience suite (OTX), Polycom Architected Telepresence Experience (Polycom ATX) and Polycom HDX personal room based telepresence applications. The division also includes the Polycom CX5000 Unified Conference Station, which adds group collaboration to Microsoft Office Live Meeting 2007 and Microsoft Office Communications Server 2007; Polycom VoiceStation products for smaller rooms; and Polycom Soundstation conference phones for midsize rooms. Products in the UC Personal Devices group include the Polycom VVX 1500 business media phone, which combines advanced telephony, one-touch video and integrated business applications; the Polycom SoundPoint series of standards-based Session Initiation Protocol (SIP) desktop devices; and the Polycom Communicator speakerphone, which uses PC-based Voice and Video over IP (V2oIP) and Voice over instant Messaging (VoIM) technologies. The Network Infrastructure group includes the Polycom RMX 200 platform, which provides a multi-network unified HD conference infrastructure to support real-time voice and video applications; the Polycom Video Border Proxy (VBP) NAT/Firewall traversal application; and the Polycom SoundStructure and Polycom Vortex series of installed voice conferencing products for larger high-end conferences rooms, auditoriums, courtrooms and classrooms. In March 2011, the company acquired video content management services provider, Accordent Technologies, Inc. for $50 million.

FINANCIALS: **Sales and profits are in thousands of dollars—add 000 to get the full amount. 2010 Note: Financial information for 2010 was not available for all companies at press time.**

2010 Sales: $1,218,489	2010 Profits: $68,409	**U.S. Stock Ticker: PLCM**
2009 Sales: $966,984	2009 Profits: $49,879	**Int'l Ticker:**
2008 Sales: $1,069,320	2008 Profits: $75,696	Int'l Exchange:
2007 Sales: $929,908	2007 Profits: $62,881	Employees: 3,230 Fiscal Year Ends: 12/31
2006 Sales: $682,385	2006 Profits: $71,924	Parent Company:

SALARIES/BENEFITS:

Pension Plan:	ESOP Stock Plan:	Profit Sharing:	Top Exec. Salary: $529,167	Bonus: $303,000
Savings Plan: Y	Stock Purch. Plan: Y		Second Exec. Salary: $437,700	Bonus: $180,992

OTHER THOUGHTS:

Apparent Women Officers or Directors: 5
Hot Spot for Advancement for Women/Minorities: Y

LOCATIONS: ("Y" = Yes)

West:	Southwest:	Midwest:	Southeast:	Northeast:	International:
Y	Y	Y	Y	Y	Y

PRAXAIR INC

www.praxair.com

Industry Group Code: 325120

Management:		Sales/Marketing:		Liberal Arts:		Information Sys.:		Professionals:		Tech./Scientific:	
Mgmt. Trainees:	Y	Marketing Pros.:	Y	Gen. Writing/Editing:		Info. Mgmt.:	Y	Finance/Acct.:	Y	Engineers, Elec.:	Y
Experienced Mgmt.:	Y	Retail Sales:		Tech. Writing:	Y	Software Dev.:	Y	Law:	Y	Engineers, Other:	Y
Int'l Business:	Y	Comm./Industrial:	Y	Graphic Arts/Photog.:		Hardware Dev.:		HR/Other:	Y	Health/Lab:	
MBA Grads:	Y	Sales Trainees:		Music:		Consulting/Other:		Training:	Y	Science/Research:	Y
		Advertising Pros.:		Broadcasting:				Health Care:		Petroleum/Chem.:	Y
				Other:				Consulting:		Math/Other:	

TYPES OF BUSINESS:

Industrial Gases
Atmospheric & Process Gases
Coatings & Powders
On-Site Production Plants
Distribution

BRANDS/DIVISIONS/AFFILIATES:

Praxair Surface Technologies, Inc.

CONTACTS: *Note: Officers with more than one job title may be intentionally listed here more than once.*

Stephen F. Angel, CEO
Stephen F. Angel, Pres.
James S. Sawyer, CFO/Exec. VP
Sunil Mattoo, VP-Mktg.
Sally A. Savoia, VP-Human Resources
Marc A. Franciosa, VP-IT Svcs.
Raymond P. Roberge, CTO/Sr. VP
James T. Breedlove, General Counsel/Sr. VP/Corp. Sec.
Eduardo Galvan, VP-Global Oper. Excellence
Sunil Mattoo, VP-Strategic Planning
Susan M. Neumann, VP-Corp. Comm. & Public Rel.
Kelcey E. Hoyt, Dir.-Investor Rel.
Elizabeth T. Hirsch, Controller/VP
Eduardo Menezes, Sr. VP/Pres., North American Industrial Gases
Todd A. Skare, Pres., Praxair Europe
Ricardo S. Malfitano, Exec. VP
Anne K. Roby, Pres., Praxair Asia
Stephen F. Angel, Chmn.
Domingos H. G. Bulus, Pres., Praxair South America
Murray G. Covello, VP-Global Supply Systems

Phone: 203-837-2000 | **Fax:**

Toll-Free: 800-772-9247

Address: 39 Old Ridgebury Rd., Danbury, CT 06810-5113203-8 US

GROWTH PLANS/SPECIAL FEATURES:

Praxair, Inc. is an industrial gas supplier in North America, South America, Asia and Europe. Praxair's primary products are atmospheric gases, which include oxygen, nitrogen, argon and rare gases, and process gases, which include carbon dioxide, helium, hydrogen, electronic gases, specialty gases and acetylene. The company also designs, engineers, and builds equipment that produces industrial gases for internal use and external sale. Praxair serves approximately 25 industries including healthcare, petroleum refining, computer chip manufacturing, beverage carbonation, fiber-optics, steel making, aerospace, chemicals, and water treatment. Approximately 94% of the firm's sales are generated in four regional segments (North America, Europe, South America and Asia) primarily from the sale of industrial gases; the remaining 6% is generated from the surface technologies segment. Atmospheric gases are the highest volume products produced by Praxair. Using air as its raw material, Praxair produces oxygen, nitrogen and argon through several air separation processes of which cryogenic air separation is the most prevalent. Process gases, including carbon dioxide, hydrogen, carbon monoxide, helium and acetylene are produced by methods other than air separation. Praxair uses three distribution methods for industrial gases: on-site or tonnage; merchant liquid; and packaged or cylinder gases. Through its subsidiary Praxair Surface Technologies, the company supplies wear-resistant and high-temperature corrosion-resistant metallic and ceramic coatings and powders to the aircraft, printing, textile, plastics, primary metals and petrochemical industries. It also manufactures a complete line of electric arc, plasma and high-velocity oxygen fuel spray equipment, as well as arc and flame wire equipment used for the application of wear resistant coatings. In February 2011, Praxair agreed to sell its U.S. homecare operations to Apria Healthcare, Inc. In April 2011, the firm agreed to open a new facility in Argentina. In May 2011, Praxair Surface Technologies opened a new manufacturing facility in Singapore.

FINANCIALS: **Sales and profits are in thousands of dollars—add 000 to get the full amount. 2010 Note: Financial information for 2010 was not available for all companies at press time.**

2010 Sales: $10,116,000 | 2010 Profits: $1,195,000
2009 Sales: $8,956,000 | 2009 Profits: $1,254,000
2008 Sales: $10,796,000 | 2008 Profits: $1,211,000
2007 Sales: $9,402,000 | 2007 Profits: $1,177,000
2006 Sales: $8,324,000 | 2006 Profits: $988,000

U.S. Stock Ticker: PX
Int'l Ticker:
Int'l Exchange:
Employees: 26,261 Fiscal Year Ends: 12/31
Parent Company:

SALARIES/BENEFITS:

Pension Plan: ESOP Stock Plan: Profit Sharing: Top Exec. Salary: $1,083,750 Bonus: $3,105,000
Savings Plan: Stock Purch. Plan: Second Exec. Salary: $600,000 Bonus: $1,086,874

OTHER THOUGHTS:

Apparent Women Officers or Directors: 7
Hot Spot for Advancement for Women/Minorities: Y

LOCATIONS: ("Y" = Yes)

West:	Southwest:	Midwest:	Southeast:	Northeast:	International:
Y				Y	Y

Sales, profits and employees may be estimates. Financial information, benefits and other data can change quickly and may vary from those stated here.

PRICESMART INC

www.pricesmart.com

Industry Group Code: 452112

Management:		Sales/Marketing:		Liberal Arts:		Information Sys.:		Professionals:		Tech./Scientific:	
Mgmt. Trainees:	Y	Marketing Pros.:	Y	Gen. Writing/Editing:	Y	Info. Mgmt.:	Y	Finance/Acct.:	Y	Engineers, Elec.:	
Experienced Mgmt.:	Y	Retail Sales:	Y	Tech. Writing:		Software Dev.:	Y	Law:	Y	Engineers, Other:	
Int'l Business:	Y	Comm./Industrial:		Graphic Arts/Photog.:	Y	Hardware Dev.:		HR/Other:	Y	Health/Lab:	
MBA Grads:	Y	Sales Trainees:	Y	Music:		Consulting/Other:		Training:	Y	Science/Research:	
		Advertising Pros.:	Y	Broadcasting:				Health Care:		Petroleum/Chem.:	
				Other:	Y			Consulting:		Math/Other:	

TYPES OF BUSINESS:

Warehouse Clubs, Retail

BRANDS/DIVISIONS/AFFILIATES:

CONTACTS:

Note: Officers with more than one job title may be intentionally listed here more than once.

Jose Luis Laparte, CEO
William J. Naylon, COO/Exec. VP
Jose Luis Laparte, Pres.
John M. Heffner, CFO/Exec. VP
Jose Luis Marin, Sr. VP-Mktg.
Thomas D. Martin, Exec. VP-Merch.
Robert M. Gans, General Counsel/Exec. VP/Corp. Sec.
John D. Hildebrandt, Exec. VP-Oper.
Michael L. McCleary, Corp. Controller/Sr. VP
Brud E. Drachman, Exec. VP-Construction Mgmt.
Rodrigo Calvo, Sr. VP-Real Estate.
Ernesto Grijalva, Sr. VP-Latin America & Caribbean Legal Affairs
Atul Patel, Sr. VP/Treas.
Robert Price, Chmn.
Chris Souhadra, Exec. VP-Central American Oper.

Phone: 858-404-8800 **Fax:** 858-404-8848
Toll-Free:
Address: 9740 Scranton Rd., San Diego, CA 92121-1745 US

GROWTH PLANS/SPECIAL FEATURES:

PriceSmart, Inc. is one of the largest operators of warehouse membership clubs in Central America and the Caribbean. It currently operates 27warehouse clubs in 11 countries and one U.S. territory, including Aruba (one), Barbados (one), the Dominican Republic (two), El Salvador (two), Guatemala (three), Honduras (two), Jamaica (one), Nicaragua (one), Panama (four), Costa Rica (five), Trinidad (four) and the U.S. Virgin Islands (one). In addition, there is one warehouse club in operation in Micronesia licensed to and operated by local business people, from which the company earns a royalty fee. The firm's operations are managed by subsidiary companies in each of the countries in which it has stores. These subsidiaries typically begin as joint ventures with local businesspeople. The company then purchases the portion it doesn't already own if the stores in the area show promise. These stores provide basic consumer goods, with an emphasis on quality, low prices and efficiency. PriceSmart's merchandise, offered under both brand names and private labels, includes various food items, consumer electronics, appliances, home furnishings, office supplies, apparel, automotive supplies and garden and seasonal goods. Sales are typically comprised of approximately 48% U.S. and Asian sourced merchandise, with around 52% locally sourced merchandise. The company's stores feature several in-store member services and conveniences, including auto/tire centers, bakeries, banking services, coffee bars, one-hour photo processing, optical centers, pharmacies and rotisserie chicken. A typical store ranges in size from 48,000 to 78,000 square feet, smaller than U.S. warehouse clubs, and are located in urban areas. The average annual membership fee for business customers is $25, and for individual members (referred to as Diamond members), $20. In May 2010, the company announced the opening of its fourth store in Trinidad. In November 2010, Pricesmart opened its third warehouse in the Dominican Republic.

PriceSmart offers its employees medical, dental and vision insurance; life insurance; and short- and long-term disability.

FINANCIALS:

Sales and profits are in thousands of dollars—add 000 to get the full amount. 2010 Note: Financial information for 2010 was not available for all companies at press time.

2010 Sales: $1,395,891	2010 Profits: $49,315
2009 Sales: $1,251,628	2009 Profits: $42,319
2008 Sales: $1,119,876	2008 Profits: $38,106
2007 Sales: $888,801	2007 Profits: $12,926
2006 Sales: $734,673	2006 Profits: $11,858

U.S. Stock Ticker: PSMT
Int'l Ticker:
Int'l Exchange:
Employees: 4,728 Fiscal Year Ends: 8/31
Parent Company:

SALARIES/BENEFITS:

Pension Plan: ESOP Stock Plan: Profit Sharing: Top Exec. Salary: $405,333 Bonus: $125,000
Savings Plan: Stock Purch. Plan: Second Exec. Salary: $354,667 Bonus: $

OTHER THOUGHTS:

Apparent Women Officers or Directors: 1
Hot Spot for Advancement for Women/Minorities:

LOCATIONS: ("Y" = Yes)

West:	Southwest:	Midwest:	Southeast:	Northeast:	International:
Y					Y

Sales, profits and employees may be estimates. Financial information, benefits and other data can change quickly and may vary from those stated here.

PRICEWATERHOUSECOOPERS

www.pwcglobal.com

Industry Group Code: 5412

Management:		**Sales/Marketing:**		**Liberal Arts:**		**Information Sys.:**		**Professionals:**		**Tech./Scientific:**	
Mgmt. Trainees:	Y	Marketing Pros.:	Y	Gen. Writing/Editing:	Y	Info. Mgmt.:	Y	Finance/Acct.:	Y	Engineers, Elec.:	
Experienced Mgmt.:	Y	Retail Sales:		Tech. Writing:	Y	Software Dev.:	Y	Law:	Y	Engineers, Other:	
Int'l Business:	Y	Comm./Industrial:	Y	Graphic Arts/Photog.:	Y	Hardware Dev.:		HR/Other:	Y	Health/Lab:	
MBA Grads:	Y	Sales Trainees:		Music:		Consulting/Other:	Y	Training:	Y	Science/Research:	
		Advertising Pros.:	Y	Broadcasting:				Health Care:		Petroleum/Chem.:	
				Other:	Y			Consulting:	Y	Math/Other:	

TYPES OF BUSINESS:

Accounting Services
Business Advisory
Corporate Finance Services
Employee Benefits Services
Tax Services
Business Publications

BRANDS/DIVISIONS/AFFILIATES:

BearingPoint

CONTACTS:

Note: Officers with more than one job title may be intentionally listed here more than once.

Dennis J. Finn, Head-U.S. & Global Human Capital
Javier H. Rubinstein, General Counsel
Paul Boorman, Head-Global Oper.
Christopher Kelkar, Head-Global Strategy & Transformation
Moira Elms, Head-Global Comm. & Brand
Robert E. Moritz, Sr. Partner-U.S.
Donald A. McGovern Jr., Head-Global Assurance Svcs.
Pierre Coll, Head-Global Risk & Quality
Ian Powell, Sr. Partner-U.K.
Dennis M. Nally, Chmn.
Silas S. S. Yang, Sr. Partner-China & Hong Kong

Phone: 646-471-4000 **Fax:** 813-286-6000
Toll-Free:
Address: 300 Madison Ave., 24th Fl., New York, NY 10017 US

GROWTH PLANS/SPECIAL FEATURES:

PricewaterhouseCoopers (PwC) is a global accounting firm with offices in 766 cities across 154 countries. Locations of PwC offices include Africa, the Americas, Asia/Asia Pacific, Europe and the Middle East. PwC provides accounting and advisory services to a large number of mid-sized and small companies and caters to 415 of the companies in the FT Global 500 and 415 of Fortune magazine's Global 500 companies in 21 industries that include entertainment and media, aerospace and defense, and chemicals. The firm provides industry-focused services for public and private clients primarily in five areas: audit and assurance; consulting; deals; human resources; and tax. Audit and assurance provides financial statement audits, regulatory and Sarbanes-Oxley compliance and financial accounting, while a crisis management sector offers business recovery services with dispute analysis and investigations. The consulting sector offers services in technology, operations, sustainability, investigations and finance. The deals sector specializes in acquisitions and mergers; strategic and valuation advice; and growth and divestments in addition to developing exit strategies. The human resources services segment has over 6,000 professionals in more than 100 countries and helps clients with international assignments; HR management; and employee growth, benefits and rewards. Lastly, the tax sector helps businesses reduce tax risks; improve operating efficiency; and manage total tax contributions to governments. PwC also produces a number of publications that provide authoritative information on better business practices and emerging issues facing management and breaking trends in the business world. In recent years, the firm acquired several assets from global technology and management consulting company BearingPoint.

FINANCIALS:

Sales and profits are in thousands of dollars—add 000 to get the full amount. 2010 Note: Financial information for 2010 was not available for all companies at press time.

2010 Sales: $26,600,000 2010 Profits: $
2009 Sales: $26,171,000 2009 Profits: $
2008 Sales: $28,185,000 2008 Profits: $
2007 Sales: $24,729,000 2007 Profits: $
2006 Sales: $22,000,000 2006 Profits: $

U.S. Stock Ticker: Private
Int'l Ticker:
Int'l Exchange:
Employees: 162,000 Fiscal Year Ends: 6/30
Parent Company:

SALARIES/BENEFITS:

Pension Plan: Y ESOP Stock Plan: Profit Sharing: Top Exec. Salary: $ Bonus: $
Savings Plan: Y Stock Purch. Plan: Second Exec. Salary: $ Bonus: $

OTHER THOUGHTS:

Apparent Women Officers or Directors: 1
Hot Spot for Advancement for Women/Minorities:

LOCATIONS: ("Y" = Yes)

West:	Southwest:	Midwest:	Southeast:	Northeast:	International:
Y	Y	Y	Y	Y	Y

Sales, profits and employees may be estimates. Financial information, benefits and other data can change quickly and may vary from those stated here.

PRINCIPAL FINANCIAL GROUP (THE)

www.principal.com

Industry Group Code: 524113

Management:		Sales/Marketing:		Liberal Arts:		Information Sys.:		Professionals:		Tech./Scientific:	
Mgmt. Trainees:	Y	Marketing Pros.:	Y	Gen. Writing/Editing:	Y	Info. Mgmt.:	Y	Finance/Acct.:	Y	Engineers, Elec.:	
Experienced Mgmt.:	Y	Retail Sales:		Tech. Writing:	Y	Software Dev.:	Y	Law:	Y	Engineers, Other:	
Int'l Business:	Y	Comm./Industrial:	Y	Graphic Arts/Photog.:	Y	Hardware Dev.:		HR/Other:	Y	Health/Lab:	
MBA Grads:	Y	Sales Trainees:	Y	Music:		Consulting/Other:		Training:	Y	Science/Research:	
		Advertising Pros.:	Y	Broadcasting:				Health Care:	Y	Petroleum/Chem.:	
				Other:	Y			Consulting:		Math/Other:	Y

TYPES OF BUSINESS:

Asset Management
Life Insurance
Health Insurance
Annuities
Disability Insurance
Investment Services
Specialty Benefits Insurance

BRANDS/DIVISIONS/AFFILIATES:

Principal Life Insurance Co.
Principal Financial Services, Inc.
Principal International, Inc.
Finisterre Capital LLP
HSBC AFORE, S.A. de C.V
Finisterre Holdings Limited
Origin Asset Management, LLP

CONTACTS:

Note: Officers with more than one job title may be intentionally listed here more than once.

Larry D. Zimpleman, CEO
Larry D. Zimpleman, Pres.
Terrance Lillis, CFO/Sr. VP
Mary A. O'Keefe, Chief Mktg. Officer/Sr. VP
Ralph C. Eucher, Sr. VP-Human Resources
Gary P. Scholten, CIO/Sr. VP
Karen E. Shaff, General Counsel/Exec. VP
Timothy M. Dunbar, Sr. VP-Strategy
Susan Houser, Contact-Media
John Egan, VP-Investor Rel.
Timothy M. Dunbar, Sr. VP-Finance
James P. McCaughan, Pres., Principal Global Investors
Julia M. Lawler, Chief Investment Officer/Sr. VP
Nora M. Everett, Sr. VP-Retirement & Investor Svcs.
Rex Auyeung, Sr. VP/Pres., Principal Financial Group-Asia
Larry D. Zimpleman, Chmn.
Ned A. Burmeister, Sr. VP/COO-Principal Int'l, Inc.
Timothy J. Minard, Sr. VP-Dist.

Phone: 515-247-5111	**Fax:** 515-246-5475
Toll-Free: 800-986-3343	
Address: 711 High St., Des Moines, IA 50392 US	

GROWTH PLANS/SPECIAL FEATURES:

The Principal Financial Group is a leading provider of retirement savings, investment and insurance products and services. It holds a total of $318.8 billion in assets, which it manages for approximately 19.1 million customers throughout the world. Principal Financial Group focuses primarily on small and medium sized businesses, which it defines as companies with less than 1,000 employees. The company is organized into four primary business segments: retirement and investor services; Principal Global Investors; Principal International; and U.S. Insurance Solutions. The firm's retirement and investor services operations concentrate on asset accumulation and management, additionally offering individual and group life insurance; group health insurance; and individual and group disability insurance. The Principal Global Investors segment focuses on providing a range of asset management services covering a broad range of asset classes, investment styles and portfolio structures to Principle Financial Group's other segments and third-party institutional clients. Principal International has operations in Chile, Mexico, Hong Kong, Brazil, Thailand, India, Indonesia, China, Singapore and Malaysia. The U.S. Insurance Solutions segment offers individual life and disability insurance as well as group health insurance, group dental, group vision, group life and group long-term and short-term disability insurance in the U.S. Principal Financial Group provides full service accumulation products to over 30,000 defined contribution pension plans covering 3.1 million plan participants; and to over 2,500 defined benefit pension plans, covering over 319,000 plan members. In April 2011, the firm agreed to acquire HSBC AFORE, S.A. de C.V. from Grupo Financiero HSBC, S.A. de C.V. for roughly $198 million; and majority interest in Finisterre Capital LLP and Finisterre Holdings Limited. In July 2011, the company agreed to acquire 74% interest in Origin Asset Management, LLP for roughly $66 million.

The firm offers employees medical, dental and vision insurance; adoption reimbursement; and domestic partner benefits.

FINANCIALS:

Sales and profits are in thousands of dollars—add 000 to get the full amount. 2010 Note: Financial information for 2010 was not available for all companies at press time.

2010 Sales: $9,158,600	2010 Profits: $666,300
2009 Sales: $8,849,100	2009 Profits: $589,700
2008 Sales: $9,935,900	2008 Profits: $425,100
2007 Sales: $10,906,500	2007 Profits: $860,300
2006 Sales: $9,873,100	2006 Profits: $1,064,300

U.S. Stock Ticker: PFG
Int'l Ticker:
Int'l Exchange:
Employees: 13,627 Fiscal Year Ends: 12/31
Parent Company:

SALARIES/BENEFITS:

Pension Plan: Y	ESOP Stock Plan:	Profit Sharing:	Top Exec. Salary: $781,538	Bonus: $1,547,446
Savings Plan: Y	Stock Purch. Plan: Y		Second Exec. Salary: $539,269	Bonus: $1,617,807

OTHER THOUGHTS:

Apparent Women Officers or Directors: 11
Hot Spot for Advancement for Women/Minorities: Y

LOCATIONS: ("Y" = Yes)

West:	Southwest:	Midwest:	Southeast:	Northeast:	International:
Y	Y	Y	Y	Y	Y

PROCTER & GAMBLE CO

Industry Group Code: 3256 | **www.pg.com**

Management:		Sales/Marketing:		Liberal Arts:		Information Sys.:		Professionals:		Tech./Scientific:	
Mgmt. Trainees:	Y	Marketing Pros.:	Y	Gen. Writing/Editing:	Y	Info. Mgmt.:	Y	Finance/Acct.:	Y	Engineers, Elec.:	
Experienced Mgmt.:	Y	Retail Sales:		Tech. Writing:	Y	Software Dev.:	Y	Law:	Y	Engineers, Other:	Y
Int'l Business:	Y	Comm./Industrial:	Y	Graphic Arts/Photog.:	Y	Hardware Dev.:		HR/Other:	Y	Health/Lab:	Y
MBA Grads:	Y	Sales Trainees:	Y	Music:		Consulting/Other:		Training:	Y	Science/Research:	Y
		Advertising Pros.:	Y	Broadcasting:				Health Care:		Petroleum/Chem.:	Y
				Other:	Y			Consulting:		Math/Other:	

TYPES OF BUSINESS:

Household Products Manufacturing
Beauty Products
Foods & Beverages
Personal Care Products
Fabric Care Products
Franchising, Dry Cleaners and Car Washes
Pet Products

BRANDS/DIVISIONS/AFFILIATES:

Cover Girl
Crest
Tide
Head & Shoulders
Gillete
Pantene
Charmin
Oral-B

CONTACTS: *Note: Officers with more than one job title may be intentionally listed here more than once.*

Robert A. McDonald, CEO
Robert A. McDonald, Pres.
Jon R. Moeller, CFO
Moheet Nagrath, Global Human Resources Officer
Filippo Passerini, CIO/Pres., Global Bus. Svcs.
Bruce Brown, CTO
Valarie L. Sheppard, Global Acct. Officer
Deborah P. Majoras, Chief Legal Officer/Sec.
Werner Geissler, Vice Chmn.-Global Oper.
Robert L. Fregolle, Jr., Global Customer Bus. Dev. Officer
Christopher D. Hassall, Global External Rel. Officer
Teri L. List, Treas./Sr. VP
Valarie L. Sheppard, Comptroller/VP
Nancy K. Swanson, VP-Corporate
Shannan Stevenson, Pres., Greater China
Marc S. Pritchard, Global Brand Building Officer
Robert A. McDonald, Chmn.
Giovanni Ciserani, Pres., Western Europe
R. Keith Harrison Jr., Global Prod. Supply Officer

Phone: 513-983-1100	**Fax:** 513-983-4381
Toll-Free:	
Address: 1 Procter & Gamble Plz., Cincinnati, OH 45202 US	

GROWTH PLANS/SPECIAL FEATURES:

Procter & Gamble Co. develops and manufactures a wide range of consumer packaged goods, including home care, baby care, beauty care and personal care products, which it markets in over 180 countries. The firm operates in two segments: beauty and grooming, which includes cosmetics, hair care products, razors, deodorants, oral care products and feminine products; and household care, which includes fabric care, home care (dish care and batteries), baby care (baby wipes and diapers) and family care (bath and facial tissue and paper towels), as well as pet care products, snacks and over the counter medications. Its brands include Head & Shoulders, Olay, Pantene, Braun, Gillette, Crest, Oral-B, Iams, Dawn, Downy, Duracell, Tide, Bounty, Charmin and Pampers. The firm's products are primarily distributed through mass merchandisers, grocery stores, membership club stores and drug stores, with Wal-Mart accounting for about 16% of sales. In the U.S., Procter & Gamble operates 36 manufacturing facilities in 22 states, and also owns and operates 102 facilities in 41 other countries. Sales in North America account for about 41% of the company's revenue; Western Europe, 20%; Asia, 16%; Latin America, 9%; and Central and Eastern Europe, the Middle East and Africa, 14%. The company is expanding its franchise division with Mr. Clean car washes and Tide Dry Cleaners. In February 2011, the firm consolidated its three business divisions into two, eliminating its health and well being unit and splitting that unit's portfolio between the beauty and grooming and household care segments. In April 2011, the firm agreed to sell its Pringles brand to Diamond Foods, Inc. for roughly $2.35 billion dollars.

FINANCIALS: **Sales and profits are in thousands of dollars—add 000 to get the full amount. 2010 Note: Financial information for 2010 was not available for all companies at press time.**

2010 Sales: $78,938,000	2010 Profits: $12,736,000	**U.S. Stock Ticker: PG**
2009 Sales: $76,694,000	2009 Profits: $13,436,000	**Int'l Ticker:**
2008 Sales: $79,257,000	2008 Profits: $12,075,000	Int'l Exchange:
2007 Sales: $74,832,000	2007 Profits: $10,340,000	Employees: 127,000 Fiscal Year Ends: 4/30
2006 Sales: $68,222,000	2006 Profits: $8,684,000	Parent Company:

SALARIES/BENEFITS:

Pension Plan:	ESOP Stock Plan:	Profit Sharing:	Top Exec. Salary: $1,600,000	Bonus: $2,632,000
Savings Plan:	Stock Purch. Plan: Y		Second Exec. Salary: $985,000	Bonus: $886,490

OTHER THOUGHTS:

Apparent Women Officers or Directors: 15
Hot Spot for Advancement for Women/Minorities: Y

LOCATIONS: ("Y" = Yes)

West:	Southwest:	Midwest:	Southeast:	Northeast:	International:
Y	Y	Y	Y	Y	Y

Sales, profits and employees may be estimates. Financial information, benefits and other data can change quickly and may vary from those stated here.

PROGRESSIVE CORPORATION (THE)

www.progressive.com

Industry Group Code: 524126

Management:		Sales/Marketing:		Liberal Arts:		Information Sys.:		Professionals:		Tech./Scientific:	
Mgmt. Trainees:	Y	Marketing Pros.:	Y	Gen. Writing/Editing:	Y	Info. Mgmt.:	Y	Finance/Acct.:	Y	Engineers, Elec.:	
Experienced Mgmt.:	Y	Retail Sales:		Tech. Writing:	Y	Software Dev.:	Y	Law:	Y	Engineers, Other:	
Int'l Business:	Y	Comm./Industrial:		Graphic Arts/Photog.:	Y	Hardware Dev.:		HR/Other:	Y	Health/Lab:	
MBA Grads:	Y	Sales Trainees:	Y	Music:		Consulting/Other:		Training:	Y	Science/Research:	
		Advertising Pros.:	Y	Broadcasting:				Health Care:		Petroleum/Chem.:	
				Other:	Y			Consulting:		Math/Other:	Y

TYPES OF BUSINESS:

Insurance, Direct Property & Casualty
Automobile Insurance

BRANDS/DIVISIONS/AFFILIATES:

ProgressiveResponds.com
Progressive Direct

CONTACTS:

Note: Officers with more than one job title may be intentionally listed here more than once.

Glenn M. Renwick, CEO
Glenn M. Renwick, Pres.
Brian C. Domeck, CFO/VP
M. Jeffrey Charney, Chief Mktg. Officer
Valerie Krasowski, Chief Human Resources Officer
Raymond M. Voelker, CIO
Charles E. Jarrett, Chief Legal Officer/Sec./VP
Jeffrey W. Basch, Chief Acct. Officer/VP
Thomas A. King, VP/Treas.
John Barbagallo, Pres., Commercial Lines Group
William M. Cody, Chief Investment Officer
Susan Patricia Griffith, Pres., Claims
Peter B. Lewis, Chmn.

Phone: 440-461-5000	**Fax:** 440-446-7436
Toll-Free: 800-776-4737	
Address: 6300 Wilson Mills Rd., Mayfield Village, OH 44143 US	

GROWTH PLANS/SPECIAL FEATURES:

The Progressive Corporation, together with its 54 subsidiaries and one affiliated mutual insurance company, is one of the largest auto insurers in the U.S., with more than 10 million policies in force. Progressive is divided into three business areas: personal lines, commercial auto and claims. The firm's personal lines segment writes insurance for private passenger automobiles and recreational and other vehicles, motorcycles, ATVs, RVs, mobile homes, watercraft and snowmobiles. The personal lines business accounts for 90% of total net premiums. The commercial auto business writes physical damage insurance for automobiles and trucks owned by small businesses and represents 10% of Progressive's total net premiums. The firm manages its claims business on a companywide basis through approximately 320 claims offices located throughout the U.S. The company has 54 service centers in 41 metropolitan areas across the country; these centers provide end-to-end resolution for auto physical damage losses. Customers can choose to bring their vehicles to one of these sites for evaluation, where they can pick up a rental vehicle. Progressive's representatives will then write the estimate, select a qualified repair shop, arrange the vehicle's repair, pick-up and delivery and inspect the vehicle once the repairs are complete. Progressive maintains a catastrophe web site, ProgressiveResponds.com, to provide consumers with information about how to stay safe and protect their vehicles and boats during a catastrophic event. The company also has provides policy issuance and claims adjusting services for Commercial Auto Insurance Procedures/Plans (CAIP), which are state-supervised plans active in 43 states. In addition, the firm offers car insurance in Australia through Progressive Direct.

Progressive offers its employees health, dental, vision and life insurance; tuition assistance; flexible spending accounts; an employee assistance program; on-site fitness and health centers; adoption assistance; and a 401(k) plan.

FINANCIALS:

Sales and profits are in thousands of dollars—add 000 to get the full amount. 2010 Note: Financial information for 2010 was not available for all companies at press time.

2010 Sales: $14,963,300	2010 Profits: $1,068,300	**U.S. Stock Ticker: PGR**
2009 Sales: $14,563,600	2009 Profits: $1,057,500	**Int'l Ticker:**
2008 Sales: $12,840,100	2008 Profits: $-70,000	Int'l Exchange:
2007 Sales: $14,686,800	2007 Profits: $1,182,500	Employees: 24,638 Fiscal Year Ends: 12/31
2006 Sales: $14,786,400	2006 Profits: $1,647,500	Parent Company:

SALARIES/BENEFITS:

Pension Plan:	ESOP Stock Plan:	Profit Sharing:	Top Exec. Salary: $750,000	Bonus: $1,265,625
Savings Plan: Y	Stock Purch. Plan:		Second Exec. Salary: $421,538	Bonus: $592,788

OTHER THOUGHTS:

Apparent Women Officers or Directors: 6
Hot Spot for Advancement for Women/Minorities: Y

LOCATIONS: ("Y" = Yes)

West:	Southwest:	Midwest:	Southeast:	Northeast:	International:
Y	Y	Y	Y	Y	Y

Sales, profits and employees may be estimates. Financial information, benefits and other data can change quickly and may vary from those stated here.

PROVIDENCE HEALTH & SERVICES

www2.providence.org

Industry Group Code: 622110

Management:		**Sales/Marketing:**		**Liberal Arts:**		**Information Sys.:**		**Professionals:**		**Tech./Scientific:**	
Mgmt. Trainees:	Y	Marketing Pros.:	Y	Gen. Writing/Editing:	Y	Info. Mgmt.:	Y	Finance/Acct.:	Y	Engineers, Elec.:	
Experienced Mgmt.:	Y	Retail Sales:		Tech. Writing:	Y	Software Dev.:	Y	Law:	Y	Engineers, Other:	
Int'l Business:		Comm./Industrial:		Graphic Arts/Photog.:		Hardware Dev.:	Y	HR/Other:	Y	Health/Lab:	Y
MBA Grads:	Y	Sales Trainees:		Music:		Consulting/Other:		Training:	Y	Science/Research:	Y
		Advertising Pros.:		Broadcasting:				Health Care:	Y	Petroleum/Chem.:	
				Other:	Y			Consulting:		Math/Other:	

TYPES OF BUSINESS:

Hospitals-General
Assisted Living Facilities
Low Income Living Facilities
Counseling

BRANDS/DIVISIONS/AFFILIATES:

Providence Services
Providence Health System
Sisters of Providence
Little Company of Mary
Providence Alaska Medical Center
Providence Kodiak Island Medical Center
Providence St. Peter Hospital
Providence Centralia Hospital

CONTACTS: *Note: Officers with more than one job title may be intentionally listed here more than once.*

John Koster, CEO
Mike Butler, COO/Exec. VP
John Koster, Pres.
Jan Jones, Chief Admin. Officer/Sr. VP
Colleen Wadden, Dir.-External Comm.
Greg Van Pelt, Exec. VP
Jack Mudd, Sr. VP-Mission Leadership
Lucille Dean, Chmn.

Phone: 425-525-3355	**Fax:**
Toll-Free:	
Address: 1801 Lind Avenue SW, Renton, WA 98057 US	

GROWTH PLANS/SPECIAL FEATURES:

Providence Health & Services, the result of a recent merger between Providence Services and Providence Health System, is a not-for-profit collection of health facilities in the Pacific Northwest run by two Catholic religious orders: the Sisters of Providence and the Little Company of Mary. Providence has 27 hospitals in the group that offer acute and primary care, home and hospice care, substance abuse programs, mental health treatment and various communities outreach programs. The group also has 35 non-acute care facilities, physician clinics, a health plan, a liberal arts university, a high school and numerous other health, housing and educational services. Providence focuses on providing care for poor and vulnerable patients by providing medical care as well as spiritual support. In addition, the group runs an advocacy program on the federal and state levels focused on creating a more equitable, accessible health care system. Some hospitals under the system include Providence Alaska Medical Center and Providence Kodiak Island Medical Center in Alaska; Providence St. Peter Hospital and Providence Centralia Hospital in Washington; Providence Hood River Memorial Hospital, Providence Seaside Hospital and Providence Newberg Hospital in Oregon; and Providence Little Company of Mary Medical Center Torrance, Providence Tarzana Medical Center and Providence Holy Cross Medical Center in California. Providence also provides its patients with a 24-hour-a-day Nurse Advice line, a physician referral program and online bill pay services. Providence Health International (PHI), formerly called Providence International Missions, provides support for employees and institutions in economically developing countries. The system office is located in Renton, Washington.

Employees of the firm are offered medical, dental and vision insurance; disability and life coverage; tuition reimbursement; an employee assistance program; flexible savings accounts; wellness programs; free parking; fitness center discounts; pharmacy discounts; a credit union; and recognition and service awards.

FINANCIALS: **Sales and profits are in thousands of dollars—add 000 to get the full amount. 2010 Note: Financial information for 2010 was not available for all companies at press time.**

2010 Sales: $8,081,955	2010 Profits: $330,215	**U.S. Stock Ticker: Nonprofit**
2009 Sales: $7,670,182	2009 Profits: $323,381	**Int'l Ticker:**
2008 Sales: $7,026,141	2008 Profits: $	Int'l Exchange:
2007 Sales: $6,348,037	2007 Profits: $	Employees: 45,000 Fiscal Year Ends: 12/31
2006 Sales: $5,821,293	2006 Profits: $	Parent Company:

SALARIES/BENEFITS:

Pension Plan:	ESOP Stock Plan:	Profit Sharing:	Top Exec. Salary: $	Bonus: $
Savings Plan: Y	Stock Purch. Plan: Y		Second Exec. Salary: $	Bonus: $

OTHER THOUGHTS:

Apparent Women Officers or Directors: 5
Hot Spot for Advancement for Women/Minorities: Y

LOCATIONS: ("Y" = Yes)

West:	Southwest:	Midwest:	Southeast:	Northeast:	International:
Y					

PRUDENTIAL FINANCIAL INC

www.prudential.com

Industry Group Code: 524113

Management:		Sales/Marketing:		Liberal Arts:		Information Sys.:		Professionals:		Tech./Scientific:	
Mgmt. Trainees:	Y	Marketing Pros.:	Y	Gen. Writing/Editing:	Y	Info. Mgmt.:	Y	Finance/Acct.:	Y	Engineers, Elec.:	
Experienced Mgmt.:	Y	Retail Sales:		Tech. Writing:	Y	Software Dev.:	Y	Law:	Y	Engineers, Other:	
Int'l Business:	Y	Comm./Industrial:	Y	Graphic Arts/Photog.:	Y	Hardware Dev.:		HR/Other:	Y	Health/Lab:	
MBA Grads:	Y	Sales Trainees:	Y	Music:		Consulting/Other:		Training:	Y	Science/Research:	
		Advertising Pros.:	Y	Broadcasting:				Health Care:	Y	Petroleum/Chem.:	
				Other:	Y			Consulting:		Math/Other:	Y

TYPES OF BUSINESS:

Insurance-Life
Property & Casualty Insurance
Asset Management, Pension & Benefit Plans
Brokerage Services
Relocation Services

BRANDS/DIVISIONS/AFFILIATES:

Prudential Insurance Company of America (The)
Prudential Real Estate and Relocation Services
Prudential Real Estate Affiliates, Inc.
AIG Edison Life Insurance Company
AIG Star Life Insurance Co., Ltd.

CONTACTS: *Note: Officers with more than one job title may be intentionally listed here more than once.*

John Strangfeld, CEO
John Strangfeld, Pres.
Richard J. Carbone, CFO/Exec. VP
Sharon C. Taylor, Sr. VP-Corp. Human Resources
Barbara G. Koster, CIO/Sr. VP
Susan L. Blount, General Counsel/Sr. VP
Bob DeFillippo, Head-Global Comm.
Charles F. Lowrey, Exec. VP/COO-U.S. Bus.
Helen M. Galt, Chief Risk Officer/Sr. VP
John Strangfeld, Chmn.
Edward P. Baird, Exec. VP-Int'l Bus.

Phone: 973-802-6000 | **Fax:** 973-367-6476
Toll-Free: 877-998-7625
Address: 751 Broad St., Newark, NJ 07102 US

GROWTH PLANS/SPECIAL FEATURES:

Prudential Financial, Inc. provides insurance, investment management and other financial products and services to individual and institutional customers worldwide. It operates in three divisions: U.S. Retirement Solutions and Investment Management; U.S. Individual Life and Group Insurance; and International Insurance and Investments. The Retirement Solutions and Investment division is composed of three segments: individual annuities, which manufactures and distributes individual variable and fixed annuity products; retirement, which provides retirement investment and income products; and asset management, which provides investment management and advisory services. The Individual Life and Group Insurance division is composed of two segments: individual life, which manufactures and distributes individual variable life, term life and universal life insurance products; and group insurance, which manufactures and distributes group life, long-term and short-term group disability, long-term care and group corporate- and trust-owned life insurance products. This division operates through The Prudential Insurance Company of America, the firm's major subsidiary. The International division operates through two divisions: international insurance, which distributes individual life insurance products in Japan, Korea and other countries outside the U.S.; and international investments, which offers proprietary and non-proprietary asset management, investment advice and services to international retail and institutional clients. The firm also operates Prudential Real Estate and Relocation Services, a real estate brokerage and relocation services business. All of the company's operations are divided into either Financial Services Businesses, which are publicly traded on the New York Stock Exchange, or Closed Block Businesses, which represent a former operating division. The company has approximately $883 billion in assets under management. In February 2011, the firm acquired Japanese companies AIG Edison Life Insurance Company and AIG Star Life Insurance Co., Ltd. from American International Group, Inc. (AIG). In July 2011, the company sold its global commodities operations to Jefferies Group, Inc. for roughly $419.5 million.

FINANCIALS: **Sales and profits are in thousands of dollars—add 000 to get the full amount. 2010 Note: Financial information for 2010 was not available for all companies at press time.**

2010 Sales: $38,414,000 | 2010 Profits: $3,195,000
2009 Sales: $32,566,000 | 2009 Profits: $3,124,000
2008 Sales: $29,275,000 | 2008 Profits: $-1,073,000
2007 Sales: $34,377,000 | 2007 Profits: $3,729,000
2006 Sales: $32,268,000 | 2006 Profits: $3,428,000

U.S. Stock Ticker: PRU
Int'l Ticker:
Int'l Exchange:
Employees: 41,044 Fiscal Year Ends: 12/31
Parent Company:

SALARIES/BENEFITS:

Pension Plan: Y | ESOP Stock Plan: | Profit Sharing: | Top Exec. Salary: $1,000,000 | Bonus: $6,100,000
Savings Plan: Y | Stock Purch. Plan: | Second Exec. Salary: $850,000 | Bonus: $5,200,000

OTHER THOUGHTS:

Apparent Women Officers or Directors: 6
Hot Spot for Advancement for Women/Minorities: Y

LOCATIONS: ("Y" = Yes)

West:	Southwest:	Midwest:	Southeast:	Northeast:	International:
Y	Y	Y	Y	Y	Y

PUBLIX SUPER MARKETS INC

www.publix.com

Industry Group Code: 445110

Management:		**Sales/Marketing:**		**Liberal Arts:**		**Information Sys.:**		**Professionals:**		**Tech./Scientific:**	
Mgmt. Trainees:	Y	Marketing Pros.:	Y	Gen. Writing/Editing:	Y	Info. Mgmt.:	Y	Finance/Acct.:	Y	Engineers, Elec.:	
Experienced Mgmt.:	Y	Retail Sales:	Y	Tech. Writing:		Software Dev.:	Y	Law:	Y	Engineers, Other:	
Int'l Business:		Comm./Industrial:		Graphic Arts/Photog.:	Y	Hardware Dev.:		HR/Other:	Y	Health/Lab:	
MBA Grads:	Y	Sales Trainees:	Y	Music:		Consulting/Other:		Training:	Y	Science/Research:	
		Advertising Pros.:	Y	Broadcasting:				Health Care:		Petroleum/Chem.:	
				Other:	Y			Consulting:		Math/Other:	

TYPES OF BUSINESS:

Grocery Stores
Dairy, Deli & Bakery Products
Convenience Stores
Liquor Stores
Restaurants

BRANDS/DIVISIONS/AFFILIATES:

Crisper's
Publix GreenWise Market

CONTACTS:

Note: Officers with more than one job title may be intentionally listed here more than once.

William E. Crenshaw, CEO
Randall Jones, Pres.
David P. Phillips, CFO
Laurie Douglas, CIO/Sr. VP
John A. Attaway, Jr., General Counsel/Sec./Sr. VP
David P. Phillips, Treas.
Charles Jenkins, Chmn.

Phone: 863-688-1188 | **Fax:** 863-616-9649
Toll-Free: 800-242-1227
Address: 3300 Publix Corporate Pkwy., Lakeland, FL 33811 US

GROWTH PLANS/SPECIAL FEATURES:

Publix Super Markets, Inc. is a leading operator of supermarkets, with 1,034 locations in Alabama, Florida, Georgia, South Carolina and Tennessee. The company also operates 11 convenience stores, 128 liquor stores and 36 Crisper's restaurants. The firm's supermarkets sell groceries, dairy products, produce, deli foods, bakery items, meat, seafood, housewares and health and beauty care merchandise. Many stores also feature pharmacies, floral departments, photo labs and in-store banking areas. Publix's lines of merchandise include a variety of nationally advertised and private label brands, as well as some unbranded merchandise, such as produce, meat and seafood. In addition to its retail operations, Publix manufactures dairy, bakery and deli products through manufacturing facilities located in Jacksonville, Lakeland and Deerfield Beach, Florida and Lawrenceville and Atlanta, Georgia. The firm is one of the largest employee-owned grocery stores in the U.S. Additionally, the firm operates Publix GreenWise Market in Lakeland, Florida which sells all-natural and organic products, combined with conventional products.

Publix offers its employees health, dental and vision coverage; quarterly retail bonuses; an employee stock ownership plan; holiday bonuses; free hot lunches; prescription discounts; a 401(k) plan; access to a credit union; tuition reimbursement; and an employee assistance plan.

FINANCIALS:

Sales and profits are in thousands of dollars—add 000 to get the full amount. 2010 Note: Financial information for 2010 was not available for all companies at press time.

2010 Sales: $25,100,000 | 2010 Profits: $342,100
2009 Sales: $24,319,716 | 2009 Profits: $284,200
2008 Sales: $23,929,064 | 2008 Profits: $1,089,770
2007 Sales: $23,016,568 | 2007 Profits: $1,183,925
2006 Sales: $21,654,774 | 2006 Profits: $1,097,209

U.S. Stock Ticker: PUSH
Int'l Ticker:
Int'l Exchange:
Employees: 148,000 Fiscal Year Ends: 12/31
Parent Company:

SALARIES/BENEFITS:

Pension Plan: Y | ESOP Stock Plan: Y | Profit Sharing: Y | Top Exec. Salary: $777,400 | Bonus: $195,635
Savings Plan: Y | Stock Purch. Plan: | Second Exec. Salary: $635,099 | Bonus: $156,921

OTHER THOUGHTS:

Apparent Women Officers or Directors: 1
Hot Spot for Advancement for Women/Minorities: Y

LOCATIONS: ("Y" = Yes)

West:	Southwest:	Midwest:	Southeast:	Northeast:	International:
			Y		

QUALCOMM INC

www.qualcomm.com

Industry Group Code: 33441

Management:		Sales/Marketing:		Liberal Arts:		Information Sys.:		Professionals:		Tech./Scientific:	
Mgmt. Trainees:	Y	Marketing Pros.:	Y	Gen. Writing/Editing:	Y	Info. Mgmt.:	Y	Finance/Acct.:	Y	Engineers, Elec.:	Y
Experienced Mgmt.:	Y	Retail Sales:		Tech. Writing:	Y	Software Dev.:	Y	Law:	Y	Engineers, Other:	
Int'l Business:	Y	Comm./Industrial:	Y	Graphic Arts/Photog.:	Y	Hardware Dev.:	Y	HR/Other:	Y	Health/Lab:	
MBA Grads:	Y	Sales Trainees:		Music:		Consulting/Other:		Training:	Y	Science/Research:	Y
		Advertising Pros.:	Y	Broadcasting:				Health Care:		Petroleum/Chem.:	
				Other:				Consulting:		Math/Other:	Y

TYPES OF BUSINESS:

Telecommunications Equipment
Digital Wireless Communications Products
Integrated Circuits
Mobile Communications Systems
Wireless Software & Services
E-Mail Software
Code Division Multiple Access

BRANDS/DIVISIONS/AFFILIATES:

FLO TV Incoroporated
Qualcomm Flarion Technologies Inc
Qualcomm MEMS Technologies Inc
Qualcomm Innovation Center Inc
Qualcomm Austria Research Center GmbH
Atheros Communications Inc
GPSNet Technologies, Inc.
Sylectus

CONTACTS: *Note: Officers with more than one job title may be intentionally listed here more than once.*

Paul E. Jacobs, CEO
Steven R. Altman, Pres.
William E. Keitel, CFO/Exec. VP
William F. Davidson, Jr., Sr. VP-Global Mktg.
Daniel L. Sullivan, Exec. VP-Human Resources
Norm Fjeldheim, CIO/Sr. VP
Roberto Padovani, CTO/Exec. VP
Donald J. Rosenberg, General Counsel/Exec. VP/Corp. Sec.
Jing Wang, Exec. VP/Pres., Global Bus. Oper.
Margaret L. Johnson, Exec. VP/Pres., Global Market Dev.
William Bold, Sr. VP-Gov't Affairs
William F. Davidson, Jr., Sr. VP-Investor Rel.
James Lederer, Exec. VP/Gen. Mgr.-Qualcomm CDMA Tech.
Derek Aberle, Exec. VP/Pres., Qualcomm Tech. Licensing
Steve Mollenkopf, Exec. VP/Pres., Qualcomm CDMA Tech.
Paul E. Jacobs, Chmn.
Andrew Gilbert, Exec. VP-European Innovation Dev.

Phone: 858-587-1121	**Fax:** 858-658-2100
Toll-Free:	
Address: 5775 Morehouse Dr., San Diego, CA 92121-1714 US	

GROWTH PLANS/SPECIAL FEATURES:

Qualcomm, Inc. provides digital wireless communications products, technologies and services. It designs application-specific integrated circuits based on Code Division Multiple Access (CDMA) technology and licenses its technology to domestic and international telecommunications equipment suppliers. CDMA technology is an industry standard for all forms of digital wireless communications networks. The company also sells Binary Runtime Environment for Wireless (BREW) software to network operators, handset manufacturers and application developers. BREW is an open-standard platform that can interface with many different wireless applications. The firm's wireless business services, which consist of satellite and terrestrial-based two-way data messaging and position reporting, serve transportation companies, private and construction equipment fleets and U.S. government agencies through its government technologies division. Subsidiary Qualcomm MEMS Technologies develops improved graphical systems for handheld devices. Subsidiary FLO TV Incorporated offers services over a nationwide multicast network based on the MediaFLO Media Distribution System (MDS) and Forward Link Only (FLO) technology. This network is utilized as a shared resource for wireless operators and partners. Subsidiary Qualcomm Flarion Technologies is a developer and provider of FLASH-OFDM (Orthogonal Frequency Division Multiplexing Access). The firm offers mobile entertainment services via partnerships with a variety of media networks including NBC, CBS, FOX, ESPN and MTV. In March 2010, Qualcomm established the Qualcomm Austria Research Center GmbH to design and develop augmented reality. In May 2011, the firm opened a new research and development facility in China. In January 2011, the firm agreed to acquire technology company Atheros Communications, Inc. for $3.1 billion. In February 2011, the company acquired, through subsidiary Qualcomm Canada, Inc., GPSNet Technologies, Inc., operator of Sylectus fleet management software.

Employees are offered medical, dental and vision insurance; dependent/health care reimbursement accounts; tuition reimbursement; and a 401(k).

FINANCIALS: **Sales and profits are in thousands of dollars—add 000 to get the full amount. 2010 Note: Financial information for 2010 was not available for all companies at press time.**

2010 Sales: $10,991,000	2010 Profits: $3,247,000	**U.S. Stock Ticker: QCOM**
2009 Sales: $10,416,000	2009 Profits: $1,592,000	**Int'l Ticker:**
2008 Sales: $11,142,000	2008 Profits: $3,160,000	Int'l Exchange:
2007 Sales: $8,871,000	2007 Profits: $3,303,000	Employees: 17,500 Fiscal Year Ends: 9/30
2006 Sales: $7,526,000	2006 Profits: $2,470,000	Parent Company:

SALARIES/BENEFITS:

Pension Plan:	ESOP Stock Plan:	Profit Sharing:	Top Exec. Salary: $1,146,644	Bonus: $3,377,500
Savings Plan: Y	Stock Purch. Plan: Y		Second Exec. Salary: $810,014	Bonus: $1,225,000

OTHER THOUGHTS:

Apparent Women Officers or Directors: 4
Hot Spot for Advancement for Women/Minorities: Y

LOCATIONS: ("Y" = Yes)

West:	Southwest:	Midwest:	Southeast:	Northeast:	International:
Y	Y	Y	Y	Y	Y

QUANTA SERVICES INC

www.quantaservices.com

Industry Group Code: 237130

Management:		Sales/Marketing:		Liberal Arts:		Information Sys.:		Professionals:		Tech./Scientific:	
Mgmt. Trainees:	Y	Marketing Pros.:	Y	Gen. Writing/Editing:		Info. Mgmt.:	Y	Finance/Acct.:	Y	Engineers, Elec.:	Y
Experienced Mgmt.:	Y	Retail Sales:		Tech. Writing:	Y	Software Dev.:		Law:	Y	Engineers, Other:	Y
Int'l Business:	Y	Comm./Industrial:	Y	Graphic Arts/Photog.:		Hardware Dev.:		HR/Other:	Y	Health/Lab:	
MBA Grads:	Y	Sales Trainees:		Music:		Consulting/Other:		Training:	Y	Science/Research:	
		Advertising Pros.:		Broadcasting:				Health Care:		Petroleum/Chem.:	
				Other:				Consulting:		Math/Other:	

TYPES OF BUSINESS:

Construction, Power & Communication Lines
Network Installation & Support Services
Network Design Services
Electric Power Transmission Systems
Gas Pipeline Systems

BRANDS/DIVISIONS/AFFILIATES:

Valard Construction, LP

CONTACTS:

Note: Officers with more than one job title may be intentionally listed here more than once.

James F. O'Neil, III, CEO
James H. Haddox, CFO
Darren B. Miller, VP-IT
Darren B. Miller, VP-Admin.
Tana L. Pool, General Counsel/VP
Benadetto G. Bosco, Sr. VP-Bus. Dev. & Outsourcing
Derrick A. Jensen, VP-Finance & Admin./Chief Acct. Officer
Earl C. Austin, Jr., Pres., Natural Gas & Pipeline Div.
Kenneth W. Trawick, Pres., Telecomm. & Renewables Div.
Nicholas M. Grindstaff, VP-Finance/Treas.
Earl C. Austin, Jr., Pres., Electric Power Div.
John R. Colson, Exec. Chmn.

Phone: 713-629-7600 **Fax:** 713-629-7676
Toll-Free:
Address: 1360 Post Oak Blvd., Ste. 2100, Houston, TX 77056 US

GROWTH PLANS/SPECIAL FEATURES:

Quanta Services, Inc. is a specialty contract provider of network services, with operations in all 50 states and parts of Canada. The company designs, installs and maintains networks for the electric power, telecommunications and broadband cable and gas industries. The firm also handles control systems for traffic networks and cable and control systems for light rail lines, airports and highways. Quanta Services operates in four segments: Electric Power Infrastructure Services (EPIS), Natural Gas and Pipeline Infrastructure Services (NGPIS), Telecommunications Infrastructure Services (TIS) and Fiber Optic Licensing (FOL). The EPIS segment, which accounts for roughly 52% of the firm's revenues, provides services such as the design, installation, upgrade, repair and maintenance of electric power transmission and distribution networks; and emergency restoration services. The NGPIS division (36% of revenues) offers services including the design, installation, repair and maintenance of compressor/pump stations, natural gas and oil transmission/distribution systems and gas gathering systems; related trenching, directional boring and automatic welding services; pipeline protection and integrity; emergency restoration services; and rehabilitation and fabrication of pipeline support systems and related facilities. Quanta Services' TIS segment (9% of revenues) designs, installs, repairs and maintenances copper, fiber optic and coaxial cable networks used for data, video and voice transmission; it also designs and installs wireless communications towers and switching systems. The FOL division (3% of revenues) designs, procures, builds and maintains fiber optic telecommunications infrastructure in certain U.S. markets. It also licenses the rights to its point-to-point fiber optic telecommunications facilities. In October 2010, Quanta Services acquired Canadian firm Valard Construction, LP.

FINANCIALS:

Sales and profits are in thousands of dollars—add 000 to get the full amount. 2010 Note: Financial information for 2010 was not available for all companies at press time.

2010 Sales: $3,391,218	2010 Profits: $153,176
2009 Sales: $3,318,126	2009 Profits: $163,535
2008 Sales: $3,780,213	2008 Profits: $157,565
2007 Sales: $2,656,036	2007 Profits: $121,865
2006 Sales: $2,109,632	2006 Profits: $17,483

U.S. Stock Ticker: PWR
Int'l Ticker:
Int'l Exchange:
Employees: 13,751 Fiscal Year Ends: 12/31
Parent Company:

SALARIES/BENEFITS:

Pension Plan: Y ESOP Stock Plan: Profit Sharing: Top Exec. Salary: $844,482 Bonus: $466,752
Savings Plan: Y Stock Purch. Plan: Second Exec. Salary: $506,688 Bonus: $492,796

OTHER THOUGHTS:

Apparent Women Officers or Directors: 1
Hot Spot for Advancement for Women/Minorities:

LOCATIONS: ("Y" = Yes)

West:	Southwest:	Midwest:	Southeast:	Northeast:	International:
Y	Y	Y	Y	Y	Y

RACKSPACE HOSTING INC

www.rackspace.com

Industry Group Code: 518210

Management:		**Sales/Marketing:**		**Liberal Arts:**		**Information Sys.:**		**Professionals:**		**Tech./Scientific:**	
Mgmt. Trainees:		Marketing Pros.:	Y	Gen. Writing/Editing:	Y	Info. Mgmt.:	Y	Finance/Acct.:	Y	Engineers, Elec.:	Y
Experienced Mgmt.:	Y	Retail Sales:		Tech. Writing:		Software Dev.:	Y	Law:	Y	Engineers, Other:	
Int'l Business:	Y	Comm./Industrial:	Y	Graphic Arts/Photog.:		Hardware Dev.:		HR/Other:	Y	Health/Lab:	
MBA Grads:	Y	Sales Trainees:		Music:		Consulting/Other:		Training:		Science/Research:	
		Advertising Pros.:	Y	Broadcasting:				Health Care:		Petroleum/Chem.:	
				Other:				Consulting:		Math/Other:	

TYPES OF BUSINESS:

Web Hosting Services

BRANDS/DIVISIONS/AFFILIATES:

Cloud Servers
Cloud Files
Cloud Sites
Rackspace Cloud Drive
Cloudkick, Inc.

CONTACTS:

Note: Officers with more than one job title may be intentionally listed here more than once.

Lanham Napier, CEO
Mark Roenigk, COO
Lanham Napier, Pres.
Bruce R. Knooihuizen, CFO
Klee Kleber, Sr. VP-Mktg.
Wayne Roberts, VP-Human Resources
John Engates, CTO
Klee Kleber, Sr. VP-Prod.
Alan Schoenbaum, General Counsel/Sr. VP/Sec.
Lew Moorman, Chief Strategy Officer
Bruce R. Knooihuizen, Treas./Sr. VP
Lew Moorman, Pres., The Rackspace Cloud
Jim Lewandowski, Sr. VP-Worldwide Sales
Graham Weston, Chmn.
David Kelly, Sr. VP-Int'l Rackspace Hosting

Phone: 210-312-4000 **Fax:** 210-312-4300
Toll-Free: 800-961-2888
Address: 5000 Walzem Rd., San Antonio, TX 78218 US

GROWTH PLANS/SPECIAL FEATURES:

Rackspace Hosting, Inc. specializes in hosting services for businesses, delivering web sites, web-based information technology (IT) systems and computing-as-a-service. It actively offers four service categories: Dedicated Hosting, Cloud Hosting, Cloud Applications and Hybrid Hosting. Dedicated Hosting delivers a customer-specific server, located in secure, business-class data centers and allows customers to have full administrator privileges. Services within this division include Managed Hosting, the division's core service offering, which manages customers' data centers, network, hardware devices, and operating system software; Private Clouds, which allows virtualized dedicated IT environments; and Managed Colocation, which offers data centers and hardware for customers' applications. Dedicated Hosting also offers platform hosting, which provides customers with ordering and provisioning support and is often combined with traditional managed services. Cloud Hosting services assist businesses in running custom applications using the technologies of cloud computing (where applications and files are stored remotely rather than on a user's computer). This division offers Cloud Servers, which allow customers to purchase pieces of virtual servers, load their applications onto the server and pay only for the capacity they use; Cloud Files, which allows customers to purchase storage services by the gigabyte and Cloud Sites, which allows customers to deploy applications to a cluster of servers that will scale processing on demand and as required by the application. Cloud Applications offer e-mail, collaboration and file back-up cloud applications. It currently hosts over 1.6 million paid mailboxes. Hybrid Hosting consists of a suite of services that combine dedicating hosting and cloud computing features. Rackspace serves 90,000 customers in more than 120 countries. The firm has operations in the U.S., the U.K. and Hong Kong. In December 2010, the company acquired Cloudkick, Inc., a cloud computing software company.

Employees are offered medical, dental and vision insurance; a 401(k) plan; profit sharing; employee training; and an on-site fitness facility.

FINANCIALS:

Sales and profits are in thousands of dollars—add 000 to get the full amount. 2010 Note: Financial information for 2010 was not available for all companies at press time.

2010 Sales: $780,555	2010 Profits: $46,358	**U.S. Stock Ticker: RAX**
2009 Sales: $628,987	2009 Profits: $30,218	**Int'l Ticker:**
2008 Sales: $531,933	2008 Profits: $21,703	Int'l Exchange:
2007 Sales: $362,017	2007 Profits: $17,829	Employees: 3,492 Fiscal Year Ends: 12/31
2006 Sales: $223,966	2006 Profits: $19,820	Parent Company:

SALARIES/BENEFITS:

Pension Plan:	ESOP Stock Plan:	Profit Sharing: Y	Top Exec. Salary: $351,955	Bonus: $224,217
Savings Plan: Y	Stock Purch. Plan:		Second Exec. Salary: $351,955	Bonus: $173,885

OTHER THOUGHTS:

Apparent Women Officers or Directors: 2
Hot Spot for Advancement for Women/Minorities:

LOCATIONS: ("Y" = Yes)

West:	Southwest:	Midwest:	Southeast:	Northeast:	International:
	Y	Y		Y	Y

RALCORP HOLDINGS INC

www.ralcorp.com

Industry Group Code: 311

Management:		Sales/Marketing:		Liberal Arts:		Information Sys.:		Professionals:		Tech./Scientific:	
Mgmt. Trainees:	Y	Marketing Pros.:	Y	Gen. Writing/Editing:	Y	Info. Mgmt.:	Y	Finance/Acct.:	Y	Engineers, Elec.:	
Experienced Mgmt.:	Y	Retail Sales:		Tech. Writing:		Software Dev.:		Law:	Y	Engineers, Other:	Y
Int'l Business:	Y	Comm./Industrial:	Y	Graphic Arts/Photog.:	Y	Hardware Dev.:		HR/Other:	Y	Health/Lab:	
MBA Grads:	Y	Sales Trainees:		Music:		Consulting/Other:		Training:	Y	Science/Research:	
		Advertising Pros.:		Broadcasting:				Health Care:		Petroleum/Chem.:	
				Other:				Consulting:		Math/Other:	

TYPES OF BUSINESS:

Food Processing-Store Brand Products
Crackers & Cookies
Dressings & Sauces
Nuts & Candy
Breakfast Cereal

BRANDS/DIVISIONS/AFFILIATES:

American Italian Pasta Company
North American Baking, Ltd.
J.T. Bakeries, Inc.
Sepp's Gourmet Foods, Ltd.
Krusteaz
Bloomfield Bakers
Post Cereals
Honey Bunches of Oats

CONTACTS: *Note: Officers with more than one job title may be intentionally listed here more than once.*

Kevin J. Hunt, Co-CEO/Co-Pres.
David P. Skarie, Co-Pres./Co-CEO
Gregory Billhartz, General Counsel/VP/Sec.
Scott Monette, Chief Dev. Officer/Treas./VP
Thomas G. Granneman, Chief Acct. Officer/VP
Richard R. Koulouris, VP/Pres., Snacks, Sauces & Spreads
Charles Huber, Pres., Frozen Bakery Prod.
Ronald D. Wilkinson, VP/Pres., Cereal Prod.
Walt George, VP/Pres., American Italian Pasta Co.
William P. Stiritz, Chmn.

Phone: 314-877-7000	**Fax:** 314-877-7900
Toll-Free:	
Address: 800 Market St., St. Louis, MO 63101 US	

GROWTH PLANS/SPECIAL FEATURES:

Ralcorp Holdings, Inc. manufactures, distributes and markets Post brand and private-label food products. The company's products are marketed through the grocery, mass merchandise, drugstore and foodservice channels. The firm's business consists of five operating segments: branded cereal products; other cereal products; snacks, sauces and spreads; frozen bakery products; and pasta. The branded cereal products segment consists of the Post brand of ready-to-eat cereals, including Honey Bunches of Oats, Pebbles, Post Selects, Great Grains, Spoon Size Shredded Wheat, Post Raisin Bran, Grape-Nuts and Honeycomb. The other cereal products segment includes ready-to-eat cereals and hot cereals; and the Bloomfield Bakers line of nutritional bars, natural and organic specialty cookies, crackers and cereals. The snacks, sauces and spreads segment includes the firm's cracker and cookie business; jarred, canned and bagged snack nuts; chocolate candy; chips; and dressings, syrups, peanut butter, jellies, salad dressings, salsas, sauces and non-alcoholic drink mixes. Ralcorp's frozen bakery products segment offers frozen griddle products such as pancakes, waffles and French toast; frozen bread products such as breads, rolls and biscuits; dessert products such as frozen cookies and frozen cookie dough, muffins and Danishes; and dry mixes for bakery foods. These items are sold through brands Krusteaz, Panne Provincio, Lofthouse and Parco. Finally, the pasta segment produces over 300 different shapes and sizes of pasta products, including spaghetti, linguine, fettuccine, angel hair, lasagna, elbow macaroni, rigatoni, rotini and egg noodles. Recently, Ralcorp sold its interest in Vail Resorts, Inc. In June 2010, the company acquired North American Baking, Ltd., and J.T. Bakeries, Inc., two cracker manufacturers; and Sepp's Gourmet Foods, Ltd., a frozen breakfast foods manufacturer. In July 2010, the firm acquired pasta manufacturer American Italian Pasta Company.

The company offers employees benefits including life, personal accident, disability, medical and dental insurance; flexible spending accounts; a 401(k); and educational assistance.

FINANCIALS: **Sales and profits are in thousands of dollars—add 000 to get the full amount. 2010 Note: Financial information for 2010 was not available for all companies at press time.**

2010 Sales: $4,048,500	2010 Profits: $208,800	**U.S. Stock Ticker: RAH**
2009 Sales: $3,891,900	2009 Profits: $290,400	**Int'l Ticker:**
2008 Sales: $2,824,400	2008 Profits: $167,800	Int'l Exchange:
2007 Sales: $2,233,400	2007 Profits: $31,900	Employees: 10,800 Fiscal Year Ends: 9/30
2006 Sales: $1,850,200	2006 Profits: $68,300	Parent Company:

SALARIES/BENEFITS:

Pension Plan:	ESOP Stock Plan:	Profit Sharing:	Top Exec. Salary: $610,000	Bonus: $632,500
Savings Plan: Y	Stock Purch. Plan:		Second Exec. Salary: $610,000	Bonus: $632,500

OTHER THOUGHTS:

Apparent Women Officers or Directors:
Hot Spot for Advancement for Women/Minorities:

LOCATIONS: ("Y" = Yes)

West:	Southwest:	Midwest:	Southeast:	Northeast:	International:
Y	Y	Y	Y	Y	Y

RECREATIONAL EQUIPMENT INC (REI)

www.rei.com

Industry Group Code: 451110

Management:		Sales/Marketing:		Liberal Arts:		Information Sys.:		Professionals:		Tech./Scientific:	
Mgmt. Trainees:	Y	Marketing Pros.:	Y	Gen. Writing/Editing:	Y	Info. Mgmt.:	Y	Finance/Acct.:	Y	Engineers, Elec.:	
Experienced Mgmt.:	Y	Retail Sales:	Y	Tech. Writing:		Software Dev.:		Law:	Y	Engineers, Other:	
Int'l Business:	Y	Comm./Industrial:		Graphic Arts/Photog.:	Y	Hardware Dev.:		HR/Other:	Y	Health/Lab:	
MBA Grads:	Y	Sales Trainees:	Y	Music:		Consulting/Other:		Training:	Y	Science/Research:	
		Advertising Pros.:	Y	Broadcasting:				Health Care:		Petroleum/Chem.:	
				Other:				Consulting:		Math/Other:	

TYPES OF BUSINESS:

Outdoor Gear & Clothing, Retail
Sporting Equipment Retail & Rental
Adventure Travel Services
Catalog & Online Sales

BRANDS/DIVISIONS/AFFILIATES:

REI
REI Adventures
REI-Outlet.com
REI.com

CONTACTS: *Note: Officers with more than one job title may be intentionally listed here more than once.*

Sally Jewell, CEO
Sally Jewel, Pres.
Ivar Chhina, CFO/Exec. VP
Tom Vogl, Sr. VP-Mktg.
Michelle Clements, Sr. VP-Human Resources
Bill Baumann, VP-IT
Angela Owen, Sr. VP-Merch.
Catherine Walker, General Counsel/Corp. Sec./Sr. VP-Legal
Brad Brown, VP-eCommerce & Direct Sales
Michael Collins, VP-Public Affairs
Sue Sallee, VP-Finance & Acct.
Tim Spangler, Sr. VP-Retail
Lee Fromson, VP-REI Gear & Apparel
Janet Hopkins, VP-Customer Experience
Matt Hyde, Exec. VP
Anne Farrell, Chmn.
David Presley, VP-Logistics & Dist.

Phone: 253-891-2500 **Fax:** 253-891-2523
Toll-Free: 800-999-4734
Address: 6750 S. 228th St., Kent, WA 98032 US

GROWTH PLANS/SPECIAL FEATURES:

Recreational Equipment, Inc. (REI) is one of the largest consumer cooperatives in the U.S. The firm offers quality gear, clothing and footwear selected for performance and durability in outdoor recreation, including hiking, climbing, camping, bicycling, paddling and winter sports. Today, REI has more than 3.8 million active members served by approxiamtely 110 retail stores in roughly 30 states. Stores include a variety of facilities for testing equipment, including bike test trails, climbing pinnacles and camp stove demonstration tables. In addition, the company offers Eco Sensitive clothing, which has a high percentage of organic, rapidly renewable and recycled fibers. The firm also operates several Internet sites: REI.com and REI-Outlet.com; it also operates an adventure travel company, REI Adventures. While anyone may shop at the stores, customers who pay a small fee to become members receive special discounts and a share in the company's profits through an annual patronage refund based on their purchases. REI's e-commerce site is one of the biggest outdoor online stores, offering a comprehensive library of product information, expert gear advice and outdoor recreation information. REI-Outlet.com offers brand-name closeouts, overstocks and seconds at discounts of 30% to 60%. REI Adventures has been operating small group tours throughout the world for more than 20 years, avoiding standard tourist routes and emphasizing outdoor activities. Each year, REI Adventures plans more than 90 domestic and international bicycling, trekking, kayaking, hiking, camping and mountaineering adventures. The firm invests millions of dollars on an annual basis to build trails, clean up the environment and teach children outdoor ethics.

Employees are offered health, life and disability plans, tuition reimbursement, adoption and relocation assistance, an employee discount program and a public transit subsidy. REI has been selected as one of the 100 best companies to work for by Fortune Magazine for 13 years in a row.

FINANCIALS: **Sales and profits are in thousands of dollars—add 000 to get the full amount. 2010 Note: Financial information for 2010 was not available for all companies at press time.**

2010 Sales: $1,658,751 — 2010 Profits: $30,230
2009 Sales: $1,455,351 — 2009 Profits: $29,807
2008 Sales: $1,434,569 — 2008 Profits: $14,465
2007 Sales: $1,342,024 — 2007 Profits: $41,427
2006 Sales: $1,181,531 — 2006 Profits: $40,273

U.S. Stock Ticker: Private
Int'l Ticker:
Int'l Exchange:
Employees: 9,137 Fiscal Year Ends: 12/31
Parent Company:

SALARIES/BENEFITS:

Pension Plan: Y ESOP Stock Plan: Profit Sharing: Y Top Exec. Salary: $ Bonus: $
Savings Plan: Stock Purch. Plan: Second Exec. Salary: $ Bonus: $

OTHER THOUGHTS:

Apparent Women Officers or Directors: 9
Hot Spot for Advancement for Women/Minorities: Y

LOCATIONS: ("Y" = Yes)

West:	Southwest:	Midwest:	Southeast:	Northeast:	International:
Y	Y	Y	Y	Y	

RED HAT INC

www.redhat.com

Industry Group Code: 511210I

Management:		Sales/Marketing:		Liberal Arts:		Information Sys.:		Professionals:		Tech./Scientific:	
Mgmt. Trainees:		Marketing Pros.:	Y	Gen. Writing/Editing:		Info. Mgmt.:	Y	Finance/Acct.:	Y	Engineers, Elec.:	Y
Experienced Mgmt.:		Retail Sales:		Tech. Writing:	Y	Software Dev.:	Y	Law:	Y	Engineers, Other:	
Int'l Business:	Y	Comm./Industrial:	Y	Graphic Arts/Photog.:		Hardware Dev.:		HR/Other:	Y	Health/Lab:	
MBA Grads:	Y	Sales Trainees:		Music:		Consulting/Other:		Training:		Science/Research:	
		Advertising Pros.:	Y	Broadcasting:				Health Care:		Petroleum/Chem.:	
				Other:	Y			Consulting:		Math/Other:	

TYPES OF BUSINESS:

Computer Software-Linux Operating Systems
Open-Source Software

BRANDS/DIVISIONS/AFFILIATES:

Red Hat Cloud Foundations
JBoss Enterprise Middleware Suite
Red Hat Network Satellite
JBoss Operations Network
Red Hat Enterprise Virtualization

CONTACTS: *Note: Officers with more than one job title may be intentionally listed here more than once.*

Jim Whitehurst, CEO
Jim Whitehurst, Pres.
Charlie Peters, CFO/Exec. VP
Alex Pinchev, Exec. VP/Pres., Global Sales, Svcs. & Field Mktg.
DeLisa Alexander, Sr. VP-People & Brand
Lee Congdon, CIO
Brian Stevens, CTO
Paul Cormier, Exec. VP/Pres., Prod. & Tech.
Brian Stevens, VP-Worldwide Eng.
Michael Cunningham, General Counsel/Exec. VP/Sec.
Tom Rabon, Exec. VP-Corp. Affairs
Jim Totton, VP-Platform Bus. Unit
Scott Crenshaw, VP-Cloud Bus. Unit
Michael Tiemann, VP-Open Source Affairs
Craig Muzilla, VP-Middleware Bus. Unit
Matthew J. Szulik, Chmn.

Phone: 919-754-3700 **Fax:** 919-754-3701
Toll-Free: 888-733-4281
Address: 1801 Varsity Dr., Raleigh, NC 27606 US

GROWTH PLANS/SPECIAL FEATURES:

Red Hat, Inc. is a provider of open source software solutions. The firm's solutions include its core enterprise operating system platform Red Hat Enterprise Linux, virtual solutions, the enterprise middleware platform JBoss Enterprise Middleware Suite and other Red Hat enterprise technologies. The company offers a choice of operating system platforms for servers, work stations and desktops that support multiple application areas, including the data center, edge-of-the-network applications, IT infrastructure, corporate desktop and technical/developer workstation. Red Hat Enterprise Linux 5 offers additional technology enhancements, including integrated virtualization. The enterprise middleware platform, JBoss Enterprise Middleware, delivers a suite of middleware products for service-oriented architectures, permitting web-enabled applications to run on open source and other platforms. JBoss Enterprise Middleware provides an application infrastructure for building and deploying distributed applications that are accessible via the Internet, corporate intranets, extranets and virtual private networks. Examples of applications deployed on JBoss include online e-business; hotel and airline reservations; online banking; credit card processing; securities trading; healthcare systems; customer and partner portals; retail and point of sale systems; telecommunications network infrastructure; and grid-based systems. The integrated management services, Red Hat Network Satellite and JBoss Operations Network, permit Red Hat enterprise technologies to be updated and configured and the performance of these and other technologies to be monitored and managed in an automated fashion. The firm's suite of training and other professional service offerings enable enterprise customers to adapt Red Hat's technologies to their needs. In June 2010, Red Hat introduced Red Hat Cloud Foundations, a series of comprehensive solutions for the planning, building and managing of and platform-as-a-service and infrastructure-as-a-service public and private clouds. Also in June 2010, the firm integrated its Red Hat Enterprise Virtualization product with Cisco's Virtual Network Link.

FINANCIALS: **Sales and profits are in thousands of dollars—add 000 to get the full amount. 2010 Note: Financial information for 2010 was not available for all companies at press time.**

2010 Sales: $748,236 — 2010 Profits: $87,253
2009 Sales: $652,572 — 2009 Profits: $78,721
2008 Sales: $523,016 — 2008 Profits: $76,667
2007 Sales: $400,624 — 2007 Profits: $59,907
2006 Sales: $278,330 — 2006 Profits: $79,685

U.S. Stock Ticker: RHT
Int'l Ticker:
Int'l Exchange:
Employees: 3,200 Fiscal Year Ends: 2/28
Parent Company:

SALARIES/BENEFITS:

Pension Plan: ESOP Stock Plan: Profit Sharing: Top Exec. Salary: $700,000 Bonus: $595,000
Savings Plan: Y Stock Purch. Plan: Second Exec. Salary: $425,000 Bonus: $270,938

OTHER THOUGHTS:

Apparent Women Officers or Directors: 3
Hot Spot for Advancement for Women/Minorities: Y

LOCATIONS: ("Y" = Yes)

West:	Southwest:	Midwest:	Southeast:	Northeast:	International:
Y	Y	Y	Y	Y	Y

REGIS CORPORATION

www.regiscorp.com

Industry Group Code: 81211

Management:		**Sales/Marketing:**		**Liberal Arts:**		**Information Sys.:**		**Professionals:**		**Tech./Scientific:**	
Mgmt. Trainees:	Y	Marketing Pros.:	Y	Gen. Writing/Editing:	Y	Info. Mgmt.:	Y	Finance/Acct.:	Y	Engineers, Elec.:	
Experienced Mgmt.:	Y	Retail Sales:	Y	Tech. Writing:		Software Dev.:	Y	Law:	Y	Engineers, Other:	
Int'l Business:	Y	Comm./Industrial:		Graphic Arts/Photog.:	Y	Hardware Dev.:		HR/Other:	Y	Health/Lab:	
MBA Grads:	Y	Sales Trainees:		Music:		Consulting/Other:		Training:	Y	Science/Research:	
		Advertising Pros.:	Y	Broadcasting:				Health Care:		Petroleum/Chem.:	
				Other:				Consulting:		Math/Other:	

TYPES OF BUSINESS:

Hair Salons
Hair Care Products
Beauty Schools
Hair Restoration Services

BRANDS/DIVISIONS/AFFILIATES:

Regis Salons
MasterCuts
Sassoon
SmartStyle
SuperCuts
Cost Cutters

CONTACTS: *Note: Officers with more than one job title may be intentionally listed here more than once.*

Paul D. Finkelstein, CEO
David Bortnem, COO/Exec. VP
Randy L. Pearce, Pres.
Brent Moen, CFO/Sr. VP
Norma Knudsen, Exec. VP-Merch.
Eric A. Bakken, General Counsel/Sr. VP/Sec.
Eric A. Bakkan, Exec. VP-Bus. Dev.
Mark Fosland, Sr. VP-Investor Rel.
Mark Fosland, Sr. VP-Finance
Gordon Nelson, Exec. VP-Fashion & Education
Darryll Porter, CEO/Pres., Hair Club-Men & Women
Andy Cohen, Pres., Regis Salon Div.
John Exline, Pres., SmartStyle Family Hair Salons
Paul D. Finkelstein, Chmn.
Jackie Lang, Sr. VP/Int'l Managing Dir.-U.K.

Phone: 952-947-7000	**Fax:** 952-947-7700
Toll-Free:	
Address: 7201 Metro Blvd., Edina, MN 55439 US	

GROWTH PLANS/SPECIAL FEATURES:

Regis Corporation is a global owner, operator, franchiser and consolidator of hair and retail product salons. The company owns, franchises or holds ownership interests in over 12,700 worldwide locations. Regis' locations consist of 9,819 company-owned and franchise salons, 96 hair restoration centers and 2,786 locations in which the company maintains an ownership interest of less than 100%. Salon operations are managed based on two geographic areas, North America and International. The company's North American salon operations comprise 7,483 company-owned salons and 1,936 franchise salons. International operations comprise 400 company-owned salons. The firm's worldwide salon locations operate primarily under the trade names of Regis Salons, MasterCuts, SmartStyle, Supercuts, Cost Cutters and Sassoon.

FINANCIALS: **Sales and profits are in thousands of dollars—add 000 to get the full amount. 2010 Note: Financial information for 2010 was not available for all companies at press time.**

2010 Sales: $2,358,434
2009 Sales: $2,429,787
2008 Sales: $2,481,391
2007 Sales: $2,373,338
2006 Sales: $2,430,864

2010 Profits: $42,740
2009 Profits: $-124,466
2008 Profits: $85,204
2007 Profits: $83,170
2006 Profits: $109,578

U.S. Stock Ticker: RGS
Int'l Ticker:
Int'l Exchange:
Employees: 56,000 Fiscal Year Ends: 6/30
Parent Company:

SALARIES/BENEFITS:

Pension Plan:	ESOP Stock Plan:	Profit Sharing:	Top Exec. Salary: $1,421,461	Bonus: $1,064,278
Savings Plan:	Stock Purch. Plan:		Second Exec. Salary: $717,705	Bonus: $357,500

OTHER THOUGHTS:

Apparent Women Officers or Directors: 5
Hot Spot for Advancement for Women/Minorities: Y

LOCATIONS: ("Y" = Yes)

West:	Southwest:	Midwest:	Southeast:	Northeast:	International:
Y	Y	Y	Y	Y	Y

REPUBLIC AIRWAYS HOLDINGS INC

www.rjet.com

Industry Group Code: 481111

Management:		Sales/Marketing:		Liberal Arts:		Information Sys.:		Professionals:		Tech./Scientific:	
Mgmt. Trainees:	Y	Marketing Pros.:	Y	Gen. Writing/Editing:	Y	Info. Mgmt.:	Y	Finance/Acct.:	Y	Engineers, Elec.:	
Experienced Mgmt.:	Y	Retail Sales:		Tech. Writing:		Software Dev.:		Law:	Y	Engineers, Other:	
Int'l Business:		Comm./Industrial:		Graphic Arts/Photog.:		Hardware Dev.:		HR/Other:	Y	Health/Lab:	
MBA Grads:	Y	Sales Trainees:		Music:		Consulting/Other:		Training:	Y	Science/Research:	
		Advertising Pros.:	Y	Broadcasting:				Health Care:		Petroleum/Chem.:	
				Other:				Consulting:		Math/Other:	

TYPES OF BUSINESS:

Regional Airline

BRANDS/DIVISIONS/AFFILIATES:

Chautauqua Airlines, Inc.
Republic Airline, Inc.
Shuttle America Corporation
Frontier Airlines, Inc.
Lynx Airlines, Inc.
Frontier Airlines Holdings

CONTACTS: *Note: Officers with more than one job title may be intentionally listed here more than once.*

Bryan Bedford, CEO
Wayne C. Heller, COO/Exec. VP
Bryan Bedford, Pres.
Tim Dooley, CFO/Sr. VP
Aaron Workman, VP-IT
Thomas Duffy, VP-Tech. Svcs.
Jeff Domrese, VP-Tech. Oper. & Maintenance
Lars-Eric Arnell, VP-Corp. Dev.
Joe Allman, Controller/VP
Scott Durgin, VP-Strategic Alliances
Jerry Balsano, VP-Customer Service
Brad Elstad, VP-Safety & Regulatory Compliance
Don Osmundson, VP-Flight Oper.
Bryan Bedford, Chmn.
Drew Skaff, VP-Supply Chain

Phone: 317-484-6000	**Fax:**
Toll-Free:	
Address: 8909 Purdue Rd., Ste. 300, Indianapolis, IN 46268 US	

GROWTH PLANS/SPECIAL FEATURES:

Republic Airways Holdings, Inc. is a holding company that offers scheduled passenger services through its wholly-owned subsidiaries. These subsidiaries include Chautauqua Airlines, Inc. (Chautauqua Airlines); Shuttle America Corporation (Shuttle America); Republic Airline, Inc. (Republic Airline); Frontier Airlines, Inc.; and Lynx Airlines, Inc. (Lynx). The firm's hubs and focus cities include Cleveland, Atlanta, Cincinnati, New York, Chicago, Denver, Charlotte, Philadelphia and Washington D. C. Republic's subsidiaries offer scheduled passenger service on approximately 1,540 flights daily to 128 cities in 41 states, Canada, Mexico and Costa Rica under operations as Frontier and Midwest; and through fixed-fee code share agreements with AMR Corp., the parent of American Airlines, Inc.; Continental Airlines, Inc.; Delta Air Lines, Inc.; United Air Lines, Inc.; and US Airways, Inc. The company provides its partners with fixed-fee regional airline services, operating as AmericanConnection, Continental Express, Delta Connection, US Airways Express and United Express. Its fleet currently consists of 275 aircraft: 50 Airbus aircraft ranging from 120-162 seats; 144 EJet aircraft ranging from 70-99 seats; 3 Q400 aircraft with 74 seats; and 78 Embraer aircraft ranging from 37-50 seats.

FINANCIALS: **Sales and profits are in thousands of dollars—add 000 to get the full amount. 2010 Note: Financial information for 2010 was not available for all companies at press time.**

2010 Sales: $2,653,651 | 2010 Profits: $-13,846
2009 Sales: $1,642,218 | 2009 Profits: $36,385
2008 Sales: $1,479,755 | 2008 Profits: $84,580
2007 Sales: $1,292,677 | 2007 Profits: $82,758
2006 Sales: $1,143,078 | 2006 Profits: $79,510

U.S. Stock Ticker: RJET
Int'l Ticker:
Int'l Exchange:
Employees: 10,500 Fiscal Year Ends: 12/31
Parent Company:

SALARIES/BENEFITS:

Pension Plan: | ESOP Stock Plan: | Profit Sharing: | Top Exec. Salary: $450,000 | Bonus: $
Savings Plan: Y | Stock Purch. Plan: | | Second Exec. Salary: $236,540 | Bonus: $250,000

OTHER THOUGHTS:

Apparent Women Officers or Directors: 1
Hot Spot for Advancement for Women/Minorities:

LOCATIONS: ("Y" = Yes)

West:	Southwest:	Midwest:	Southeast:	Northeast:	International:
Y		Y		Y	

RESMED INC

www.resmed.com

Industry Group Code: 33911

Management:		Sales/Marketing:		Liberal Arts:		Information Sys.:		Professionals:		Tech./Scientific:	
Mgmt. Trainees:		Marketing Pros.:	Y	Gen. Writing/Editing:	Y	Info. Mgmt.:	Y	Finance/Acct.:	Y	Engineers, Elec.:	Y
Experienced Mgmt.:		Retail Sales:		Tech. Writing:	Y	Software Dev.:	Y	Law:	Y	Engineers, Other:	
Int'l Business:	Y	Comm./Industrial:	Y	Graphic Arts/Photog.:		Hardware Dev.:	Y	HR/Other:	Y	Health/Lab:	Y
MBA Grads:	Y	Sales Trainees:		Music:		Consulting/Other:		Training:		Science/Research:	
		Advertising Pros.:	Y	Broadcasting:				Health Care:	Y	Petroleum/Chem.:	
				Other:				Consulting:		Math/Other:	

TYPES OF BUSINESS:

Sleep Disordered Breathing Medical Equipment
Diagnosis & Treatment Products

BRANDS/DIVISIONS/AFFILIATES:

BiancaMed Ltd.
MAP Medizin-Technologie GmbH
AutoSet Spirit
AutoSet CS2
ResMed S8 Series I
ResMed S8 Series II
C-Series Tango
S9 Series

CONTACTS: *Note: Officers with more than one job title may be intentionally listed here more than once.*

Peter C. Farrell, CEO
Robert Douglas, COO
Brett Sandercock, CFO
Michael Zill, CIO
David Pendarvis, Chief Admin. Officer
David Pendarvis, Global General Counsel/Corp. Sec.
Jim Hollingshead, Chief Strategy Officer
Constance Bienfait, Dir.-Investor Rel.
Michael Farrell, Pres., Americas
Geoff Neilson, Pres., Respiratory Care Strategic Bus. Unit
Peter C. Farrell, Chmn.
Stein Jacobsen, COO-Europe

Phone: 858-836-5000 **Fax:** 858-836-5501
Toll-Free: 800-424-0737
Address: 9001 Spectrum Ctr. Blvd., San Diego, CA 92123 US

GROWTH PLANS/SPECIAL FEATURES:

ResMed, Inc. develops, manufactures and distributes medical equipment for treating, diagnosing and managing sleep disordered breathing (SDB) and other respiratory disorders. SDB includes obstructive sleep apnea (OSA) and other related respiratory disorders that occur during sleep. The company was originally founded to commercialize a Continuous Positive Airway Pressure (CPAP) treatment for OSA, which delivers pressurized air, typically through a nasal mask, to prevent collapse of the upper airway during sleep. Since the introduction of nasal CPAP, the company has developed a number of innovative products for SDB, including mask systems, headgear, airflow generators, diagnostic products and other accessories. The company's business strategy includes expanding into new clinical applications by seeking to identify new uses for its technologies. It also hopes to increase consumer awareness of the little-known condition, which may afflict up to 20% of Americans. The firm sells products in over 70 countries through both wholly-owned subsidiaries and independent distributors. ResMed's major international locations include Australia, France, Germany, Norway, Sweden, Switzerland and the U.K. Air flow generators, which deliver positive airway pressure to patients through masks, account for roughly 56% of the firm's net revenues. These generators include the AutoSet Respond, AutoSet CS2, ResMed S8 Series I & II, C-Series Tango and AutoSet Spirit. Through subsidiaries ResMed, Ltd., ResMed Motor Technologies Inc., MAP Medizin-Technologie GmbH, and ResMed Paris SAS, the company owns approximately 1,300 patents and another 1,300 pending internationally. In July 2011, ResMed acquired Irish medical technology firm BiancaMed Ltd.

The company offer employees life, AD&D, disability, health, dental, vision and long-term care insurance; flexible spending accounts; retirement savings plans; and domestic partnership benefits.

FINANCIALS: **Sales and profits are in thousands of dollars—add 000 to get the full amount. 2010 Note: Financial information for 2010 was not available for all companies at press time.**

2010 Sales: $1,092,357 | 2010 Profits: $190,085
2009 Sales: $920,735 | 2009 Profits: $146,448
2008 Sales: $835,397 | 2008 Profits: $110,303
2007 Sales: $716,332 | 2007 Profits: $66,302
2006 Sales: $606,996 | 2006 Profits: $88,211

U.S. Stock Ticker: RMD
Int'l Ticker:
Int'l Exchange:
Employees: 3,200 Fiscal Year Ends: 6/30
Parent Company:

SALARIES/BENEFITS:

Pension Plan: | ESOP Stock Plan: | Profit Sharing: | Top Exec. Salary: $736,625 | Bonus: $958,113
Savings Plan: Y | Stock Purch. Plan: | | Second Exec. Salary: $466,875 | Bonus: $607,255

OTHER THOUGHTS:

Apparent Women Officers or Directors: 1
Hot Spot for Advancement for Women/Minorities:

LOCATIONS: ("Y" = Yes)

West:	Southwest:	Midwest:	Southeast:	Northeast:	International:
Y				Y	Y

ROBERT HALF INTERNATIONAL INC

www.rhi.com

Industry Group Code: 561320

Management:		Sales/Marketing:		Liberal Arts:		Information Sys.:		Professionals:		Tech./Scientific:	
Mgmt. Trainees:	Y	Marketing Pros.:	Y	Gen. Writing/Editing:	Y	Info. Mgmt.:	Y	Finance/Acct.:	Y	Engineers, Elec.:	
Experienced Mgmt.:	Y	Retail Sales:		Tech. Writing:	Y	Software Dev.:	Y	Law:	Y	Engineers, Other:	
Int'l Business:	Y	Comm./Industrial:	Y	Graphic Arts/Photog.:	Y	Hardware Dev.:		HR/Other:	Y	Health/Lab:	
MBA Grads:	Y	Sales Trainees:	Y	Music:		Consulting/Other:		Training:	Y	Science/Research:	
		Advertising Pros.:	Y	Broadcasting:				Health Care:		Petroleum/Chem.:	
				Other:	Y			Consulting:		Math/Other:	

TYPES OF BUSINESS:

Staffing
Risk Consulting
Internal Audit Services
Litigation Consulting & Forensic Accounting

BRANDS/DIVISIONS/AFFILIATES:

Accountemps
Robert Half Finance & Accounting
Robert Half Management Resources
Robert Half Technology
OfficeTeam
Robert Half Legal
Creative Group (The)
Protiviti Inc

CONTACTS: *Note: Officers with more than one job title may be intentionally listed here more than once.*

Harold M. Messmer, Jr., CEO
M. Keith Waddell, Pres./Vice Chmn.
M. Keith Waddell, CFO
Michael Buckley, Chief Admin. Officer
Steven Karel, General Counsel/Exec. VP/Corp. Sec.
Robert W. Glass, Exec. VP-Corp. Dev.
Michael Buckley, Treas./Exec. VP
Paul F. Gentzkow, COO/Pres., Staffing Svcs.
Harold M. Messmer, Jr., Chmn.

Phone: 650-234-6000	**Fax:** 650-234-6999
Toll-Free:	
Address: 2884 Sand Hill Rd., Menlo Park, CA 94025 US	

GROWTH PLANS/SPECIAL FEATURES:

Robert Half International, Inc. (RHI) is a global staffing firm that provides professional staffing and risk consulting services. RHI operates through more than 400 company operated or owned locations in 42 states and 18countries around the world. The company provides temporary, project and full-time workers to firms in areas such as accounting, finance, administrative and legal support, information technology, advertising and marketing. RHI consists of eight staffing divisions: Accountemps for the staffing of accounting and finance professionals; Robert Half Finance and Accounting and Robert Half Management Resources for senior-level accounting and financing professionals; OfficeTeam, a division for highly skilled temporary administrative support; Robert Half Technology for information technology professionals; Robert Half Legal, a staffing sector for attorneys, paralegals and legal support personnel; and the Creative Group for advertising, marketing and web design professionals. RHI has increased its focus on providing workers for small to mid-size businesses, and it has a growing number of highly-experienced, older workers on its list. The company's wholly-owned subsidiary, Protiviti, Inc., provides internal audit and risk consulting services by aiding clients in identifying, measuring and managing operational and technology-related risks in areas such as the media, hospitality, communications, energy, financial services, real estate, healthcare, government, education, non-profit, manufacturing, distribution and technology industries. Business risk consultations involve areas such as anti-money laundering, capital projects and construction, energy commodity risks, fraud investigation and forensic accounting. Technology risk consultations provide solutions for security and privacy, continuity, change management, IT assets and application effectiveness. Protiviti's consulting practice includes assistance to firms facing bankruptcy or restructuring.

Employees are offered medical, dental, vision and life insurance; a savings plan; short- and long-term disability coverage; an employee assistance program; and travel accident insurance.

FINANCIALS: **Sales and profits are in thousands of dollars—add 000 to get the full amount. 2010 Note: Financial information for 2010 was not available for all companies at press time.**

2010 Sales: $3,175,093	2010 Profits: $66,069	**U.S. Stock Ticker: RHI**
2009 Sales: $3,036,547	2009 Profits: $37,263	**Int'l Ticker:**
2008 Sales: $4,600,554	2008 Profits: $250,181	Int'l Exchange:
2007 Sales: $4,645,666	2007 Profits: $296,212	Employees: 10,400 Fiscal Year Ends: 12/31
2006 Sales: $4,013,546	2006 Profits: $283,178	Parent Company:

SALARIES/BENEFITS:

Pension Plan:	ESOP Stock Plan:	Profit Sharing:	Top Exec. Salary: $525,000	Bonus: $1,515,762
Savings Plan: Y	Stock Purch. Plan:		Second Exec. Salary: $265,000	Bonus: $758,818

OTHER THOUGHTS:

Apparent Women Officers or Directors: 1
Hot Spot for Advancement for Women/Minorities:

LOCATIONS: ("Y" = Yes)

West:	Southwest:	Midwest:	Southeast:	Northeast:	International:
Y	Y	Y	Y	Y	Y

ROSS STORES INC

www.rossstores.com

Industry Group Code: 448

Management:		**Sales/Marketing:**		**Liberal Arts:**		**Information Sys.:**		**Professionals:**		**Tech./Scientific:**	
Mgmt. Trainees:	Y	Marketing Pros.:	Y	Gen. Writing/Editing:	Y	Info. Mgmt.:	Y	Finance/Acct.:	Y	Engineers, Elec.:	
Experienced Mgmt.:	Y	Retail Sales:	Y	Tech. Writing:		Software Dev.:	Y	Law:	Y	Engineers, Other:	
Int'l Business:	Y	Comm./Industrial:		Graphic Arts/Photog.:	Y	Hardware Dev.:		HR/Other:	Y	Health/Lab:	
MBA Grads:	Y	Sales Trainees:	Y	Music:		Consulting/Other:		Training:	Y	Science/Research:	
		Advertising Pros.:	Y	Broadcasting:				Health Care:		Petroleum/Chem.:	
				Other:	Y			Consulting:		Math/Other:	

TYPES OF BUSINESS:

Discount Apparel Stores
Home Furnishings

BRANDS/DIVISIONS/AFFILIATES:

dd's DISCOUNTS
Ross Dress for Less

CONTACTS:

Note: Officers with more than one job title may be intentionally listed here more than once.

Michael A. Balmuth, CEO
Michael B. O'Sullivan, COO
Michael B. O'Sullivan, Pres.
John G. Call, CFO/Sr. VP
Ken Caruana, Exec. VP-Mktg.
Ken Caruana, Exec. VP-Human Resources
Michael K. Kobayashi, CIO/Exec. VP
Barbara Rentler, Chief Merch. Officer
Mark LeHocky, General Counsel/Corp. Sec./Sr. VP
James S. Fassio, Chief Dev. Officer
Douglas Baker, Gen. Merch.Officer/Sr. VP
Ken Caruana, Exec. VP-Strategy
Gary L. Cribb, Exec. VP-Stores & Loss Prevention
Michael Balmuth, Vice Chmn.
Norman A. Ferber, Chmn.
Michael K. Kobayashi, Sr. VP-Supply Chain

Phone: 925-965-4400 **Fax:**
Toll-Free:
Address: 4440 Rosewood Dr., Pleasanton, CA 94588-3050 US

GROWTH PLANS/SPECIAL FEATURES:

Ross Stores, Inc. operates 1,055 off-price retail apparel and home accessories stores in 27 states and Guam, 953 of which operate under the Ross Dress for Less brand. The company also operates 67 dd's DISCOUNTS locations in California, Florida, Texas and Arizona. Most of the stores are located in predominantly community and neighborhood strip shopping centers in heavily populated urban and suburban areas. The company's chains target value-conscious women and men ages 18-54. Ross offers new, in-season, name-brand and designer apparel, accessories, footwear and home merchandise at savings of 20%-60% off department and specialty store regular prices, while dd's DISCOUNTS, targeting lower-income customers, offers similar merchandise, but at savings of up to 70% off department and specialty store prices. The company's stores are supplied by four distribution processing facilities. Ross has combined a network of approximately 7,700 vendors and manufacturers, purchasing the vast majority of its merchandise directly from the manufacturer. By purchasing later in the merchandise buying cycle than department and specialty stores, Ross takes advantage of imbalances between retailers' demand for products and manufacturers' supply of those products. In addition, the company typically does not require that manufacturers provide promotional and markdown allowances, return privileges, split shipments, drop shipments to stores or delayed deliveries of merchandise, further enabling Ross to provide significant discounts on in-season merchandise. Sales of women's products account for approximately 29% of the firm's revenues; home accents/bed and bath, 25%; men's products, 13%; accessories, lingerie, jewelry and fragrances,12%; shoes, 21%; and children's products, 12%.

Ross offers its employees medical, dental, vision and life insurance; sick pay; health care spending accounts; a commuter reimbursement account; a 401 (k) plan; and an employee stock purchasing plan.

FINANCIALS:

Sales and profits are in thousands of dollars—add 000 to get the full amount. 2010 Note: Financial information for 2010 was not available for all companies at press time.

2010 Sales: $7,184,213	2010 Profits: $442,757
2009 Sales: $6,486,139	2009 Profits: $305,441
2008 Sales: $5,975,212	2008 Profits: $261,051
2007 Sales: $5,570,210	2007 Profits: $241,634
2006 Sales: $4,944,179	2006 Profits: $199,632

U.S. Stock Ticker: ROST
Int'l Ticker:
Int'l Exchange:
Employees: 45,600 Fiscal Year Ends: 1/31
Parent Company:

SALARIES/BENEFITS:

Pension Plan:	ESOP Stock Plan:	Profit Sharing:	Top Exec. Salary: $1,147,427	Bonus: $2,320,478
Savings Plan: Y	Stock Purch. Plan: Y		Second Exec. Salary: $942,133	Bonus: $1,601,626

OTHER THOUGHTS:

Apparent Women Officers or Directors: 3
Hot Spot for Advancement for Women/Minorities: Y

LOCATIONS: ("Y" = Yes)

West:	Southwest:	Midwest:	Southeast:	Northeast:	International:
Y	Y		Y	Y	Y

ROWAN COMPANIES INC

www.rowancompanies.com

Industry Group Code: 213111

Management:		**Sales/Marketing:**		**Liberal Arts:**		**Information Sys.:**		**Professionals:**		**Tech./Scientific:**	
Mgmt. Trainees:		Marketing Pros.:	Y	Gen. Writing/Editing:		Info. Mgmt.:	Y	Finance/Acct.:	Y	Engineers, Elec.:	Y
Experienced Mgmt.:	Y	Retail Sales:		Tech. Writing:		Software Dev.:		Law:	Y	Engineers, Other:	Y
Int'l Business:	Y	Comm./Industrial:	Y	Graphic Arts/Photog.:		Hardware Dev.:		HR/Other:	Y	Health/Lab:	
MBA Grads:	Y	Sales Trainees:		Music:		Consulting/Other:		Training:	Y	Science/Research:	
		Advertising Pros.:		Broadcasting:				Health Care:		Petroleum/Chem.:	Y
				Other:				Consulting:		Math/Other:	

TYPES OF BUSINESS:

Drilling-Offshore & Land
Steel Production
Heavy Equipment Manufacturing

BRANDS/DIVISIONS/AFFILIATES:

LeTourneau Technologies, Inc.

CONTACTS:

Note: Officers with more than one job title may be intentionally listed here more than once.

W. Matt Ralls, CEO
W. Matt Ralls, Pres.
William H. Wells, CFO/Sr. VP-Finance/Treas.
Terry Woodall, VP-Human Resources
Lisa Gauthier, CIO/VP
Mike Dowdy, VP-Eng.
John L. Buvens, Exec. VP-Legal
David P. Russell, Exec. VP-Drilling Oper.
Mark A. Keller, Exec. VP-Bus. Dev.
Suzanne M. McLeod, Dir.-Investor Rel.
Gregory M. Hatfield, Controller/VP
Thomas P. Burke, Pres./CEO-LeTourneau Technologies, Inc.
J. Kevin Bartol, VP-Corp. Dev.
Barbara Carroll, VP-Health, Safety & Environment
Melanie M. Trent, Corp. Sec./VP
H.E. Lentz, Chmn.

Phone: 713-621-7800 | **Fax:** 713-960-7660
Toll-Free:
Address: 2800 Post Oak Blvd., Ste. 5450, Houston, TX 77056 US

GROWTH PLANS/SPECIAL FEATURES:

Rowan Companies, Inc. is a provider of international and domestic contract drilling services. The company also manufactures equipment for the drilling, mining and timber industries. Rowan operates through three segments: Drilling Services, Drilling Products and Systems, and Mining, Forestry and Steel Products. Drilling Services, the firm's largest segment, provides contract drilling services utilizing a fleet of 23 self-elevating mobile offshore drilling platforms (called jack-up rigs) and 29 deep-well land drilling rigs. The offshore drilling fleet includes 20 premium cantilever jack-up rigs, featuring three harsh environment Gorilla class rigs, four enhanced Super Gorilla class rigs, four Tarzan Class rigs, seven 116-C class rigs and two 240C class rigs; and three conventional jack-up rigs, with skid-off capability. Rowan operates larger, deep-water type jack-up rigs capable of drilling to depths of up to 35,000 feet in maximum water depths range from 250-550 feet. Rowan's drilling operations are conducted primarily in the Gulf of Mexico, Texas, Oklahoma, Louisiana and Alaska, as well as internationally primarily in the Middle East, the North Sea, West Africa, Canada, Mexico and Egypt. The Drilling Products and Systems and Mining, Forestry and Steel Products segments operate through subsidiary LeTourneau Technologies, Inc. The Drilling Products segment manufactures jack-up rigs, rig kits and related components, mud pumps, drawworks, top drives, rotary tables, variable-speed motors, drives and other electrical components for the drilling industry. The Mining, Forestry and Steel Products segment manufactures heavy equipment such as large-wheeled front-end loaders, diesel-electric powered log stackers and steel plate products. In July 2010, Rowan announced its intention to acquire Norwegian company Skeie Drilling & Production ASA, an owner and manufacturer of high-spec jack-up rigs.

Employees are offered medical, dental, vision and prescription drug coverage; life and AD&D insurance; disability coverage; an employee assistance program; a 401(k) plan; and a pension plan.

FINANCIALS:

Sales and profits are in thousands of dollars—add 000 to get the full amount. 2010 Note: Financial information for 2010 was not available for all companies at press time.

2010 Sales: $1,819,207	2010 Profits: $279,995	**U.S. Stock Ticker: RDC**
2009 Sales: $1,770,180	2009 Profits: $367,504	**Int'l Ticker:**
2008 Sales: $2,212,736	2008 Profits: $427,628	Int'l Exchange:
2007 Sales: $2,095,021	2007 Profits: $483,800	Employees: 5,217 Fiscal Year Ends: 12/31
2006 Sales: $1,510,734	2006 Profits: $318,246	Parent Company:

SALARIES/BENEFITS:

Pension Plan: Y	ESOP Stock Plan:	Profit Sharing:	Top Exec. Salary: $800,000	Bonus: $1,134,440
Savings Plan: Y	Stock Purch. Plan:		Second Exec. Salary: $400,000	Bonus: $365,000

OTHER THOUGHTS:

Apparent Women Officers or Directors: 3
Hot Spot for Advancement for Women/Minorities: Y

LOCATIONS: ("Y" = Yes)

West:	Southwest:	Midwest:	Southeast:	Northeast:	International:
Y	Y		Y		Y

ROYAL CARIBBEAN CRUISES LTD

www.royalcaribbean.com

Industry Group Code: 483112

Management:		**Sales/Marketing:**		**Liberal Arts:**		**Information Sys.:**		**Professionals:**		**Tech./Scientific:**	
Mgmt. Trainees:	Y	Marketing Pros.:	Y	Gen. Writing/Editing:	Y	Info. Mgmt.:	Y	Finance/Acct.:	Y	Engineers, Elec.:	
Experienced Mgmt.:	Y	Retail Sales:		Tech. Writing:	Y	Software Dev.:	Y	Law:	Y	Engineers, Other:	Y
Int'l Business:	Y	Comm./Industrial:	Y	Graphic Arts/Photog.:	Y	Hardware Dev.:		HR/Other:	Y	Health/Lab:	
MBA Grads:	Y	Sales Trainees:	Y	Music:	Y	Consulting/Other:		Training:	Y	Science/Research:	
		Advertising Pros.:	Y	Broadcasting:				Health Care:		Petroleum/Chem.:	
				Other:	Y			Consulting:		Math/Other:	

TYPES OF BUSINESS:

Cruise Line
Rail Tours
Online Travel Services
Academic Tours

BRANDS/DIVISIONS/AFFILIATES:

Royal Caribbean International
Celebrity Cruises
Pullmantur
Azamara Club Cruises
CDF Croisieres de France
TUI Cruises
Oasis of the Seas
Celebrity Xpedition

CONTACTS: *Note: Officers with more than one job title may be intentionally listed here more than once.*

Richard D. Fain, CEO
Brian J. Rice, CFO/Exec. VP
Harri Kulovaara, Exec. VP-Maritime
Adam M. Goldstein, CEO/Pres., Royal Caribbean Int'l
William Wright, Sr. VP-Marine Oper., Royal Caribbean Int'l
Craig Milan, Pres., Royal Celebrity Tours
Richard D. Fain, Chmn.
Michael Bayley, Exec. VP-Int'l

Phone: 305-539-6000	**Fax:** 305-374-7354
Toll-Free:	
Address: 1050 Caribbean Way, Miami, FL 33132 US	

GROWTH PLANS/SPECIAL FEATURES:

Royal Caribbean Cruises, Ltd. is a global cruise vacation firm serving the contemporary, premium and deluxe cruise markets, including the budget and luxury segments. With 40 ships offering 92,300 berths, the firm operates five brand names: Royal Caribbean International; Celebrity Cruises; Pullmantur; Azamara Club Cruises; and CDF Croisieres de France. It also has a 50% joint venture investment in TUI Cruises with TUI AG. Royal Caribbean's ships have itineraries that call on approximately 420 destinations worldwide. Royal Caribbean International operates 22 ships with 62,000 berths, offering cruise itineraries that range from 2-18 nights. Its destinations include Alaska, Asia, Australia, Bermuda, Canada, Hawaii, Latin America and New Zealand. Its ships offer surf simulators; an interactive water park called the H2O Zone; Royal Promenades, which are boulevards with shopping and dining venues; and ice skating rinks. The Celebrity Cruises brand targets the higher-end segment of the industry. It operates 10 ships with 20,500 berths, and its destinations include Alaska, Bermuda and the Panama Canal. Its ships include spa facilities and a glass-blowing studio. It also operates Celebrity Xpedition, a ship that travels to the Galapagos Islands. Pullmantur serves the Spanish, Portuguese and Latin American cruise markets, and it operates five ships with 7,650 berths. The ships' onboard activities include exercise facilities, swimming pools, beauty salons, gaming facilities and dining venues. Azamara Club Cruises consists of two smaller ships, of about 700 passengers each, that focus on cruises to unique destinations, with an emphasis on on-board lectures and fine dining. Its ships sail in Asia, the Mediterranean and the Panama Canal. CDF Croisieres de France serves the French market and operates one ship, Bleu de France. It offers seasonal itineraries to the Mediterranean and the Caribbean. In September 2010, Royal Caribbean opened a new office in Mexico.

FINANCIALS: **Sales and profits are in thousands of dollars—add 000 to get the full amount. 2010 Note: Financial information for 2010 was not available for all companies at press time.**

2010 Sales: $6,752,504	2010 Profits: $547,467	**U.S. Stock Ticker: RCL**
2009 Sales: $5,889,826	2009 Profits: $162,421	**Int'l Ticker:**
2008 Sales: $6,532,525	2008 Profits: $573,722	Int'l Exchange:
2007 Sales: $6,149,139	2007 Profits: $603,405	Employees: 60,000 Fiscal Year Ends: 12/31
2006 Sales: $5,229,584	2006 Profits: $633,922	Parent Company:

SALARIES/BENEFITS:

Pension Plan: Y	ESOP Stock Plan:	Profit Sharing:	Top Exec. Salary: $1,000,000	Bonus: $4,066,000
Savings Plan:	Stock Purch. Plan: Y		Second Exec. Salary: $700,000	Bonus: $1,797,250

OTHER THOUGHTS:

Apparent Women Officers or Directors: 3
Hot Spot for Advancement for Women/Minorities: Y

LOCATIONS: ("Y" = Yes)

West:	Southwest:	Midwest:	Southeast:	Northeast:	International:
Y	Y	Y	Y	Y	Y

RYDER SYSTEM INC

www.ryder.com

Industry Group Code: 532120

Management:		Sales/Marketing:		Liberal Arts:		Information Sys.:		Professionals:		Tech./Scientific:	
Mgmt. Trainees:	Y	Marketing Pros.:	Y	Gen. Writing/Editing:		Info. Mgmt.:	Y	Finance/Acct.:	Y	Engineers, Elec.:	
Experienced Mgmt.:	Y	Retail Sales:	Y	Tech. Writing:		Software Dev.:	Y	Law:	Y	Engineers, Other:	
Int'l Business:	Y	Comm./Industrial:	Y	Graphic Arts/Photog.:		Hardware Dev.:		HR/Other:	Y	Health/Lab:	
MBA Grads:	Y	Sales Trainees:	Y	Music:		Consulting/Other:		Training:	Y	Science/Research:	
		Advertising Pros.:	Y	Broadcasting:				Health Care:		Petroleum/Chem.:	
				Other:				Consulting:		Math/Other:	

TYPES OF BUSINESS:

Truck Rental & Leasing
Trucking
Logistics & Consulting Services
Supply Chain Management
Dedicated Fleet Services
Fleet Management Services

BRANDS/DIVISIONS/AFFILIATES:

Carmenita Leasing, Inc.
Ryder Supply Chain Solutions Asia
Total Logistic Control
Scully Companies, Inc. (The)

CONTACTS: *Note: Officers with more than one job title may be intentionally listed here more than once.*

Gregory T. Swienton, CEO
Art A. Garcia, CFO/Exec. VP
Gregory F. Greene, Chief Admin. Officer/Exec. VP
Robert D. Fatovic, Chief Legal Officer/Exec. VP/Corp. Sec.
Bob Brunn, VP-Public Affairs
Bob Brunn, VP-Investor Rel.
Robert E. Sanchez, Pres., Global Fleet Mgmt. Solutions
Gregory T. Swienton, Chmn.
David Hunt, Managing Dir.-Fleet Management Solutions Europe/VP
John H. Williford, Pres., Global Supply Chain Solutions

Phone: 305-500-3726 **Fax:** 305-500-3203
Toll-Free:
Address: 11690 NW 105th St., Miami, FL 33178 US

GROWTH PLANS/SPECIAL FEATURES:

Ryder System, Inc. is a global provider of transportation and supply chain management solutions. It operates in three segments: fleet management solutions, supply chain solutions and dedicated contract carriage. The fleet management solutions segment, which accounts for approximately 67% of Ryder's revenues, provides full service leasing, contract maintenance, contract-related maintenance and commercial renal of trucks, tractors and trailers to customers principally in the U.S., Canada and the U.K. The division also offers transaction fleet solutions including commercial truck rental; maintenance services; and value-added fleet support services such as insurance, vehicle administration and fuel services. In addition, it provides customers with access to a large selection of used trucks, tractors and trailers through the used vehicle sales program. The supply chain solutions segment, from which Ryder derives roughly 23% of its revenues, provides supply chain solutions including distribution and transportation services throughout North America and Asia. The division's products are organized into three primary categories: professional services, distribution management and transportation management. Additionally, the firm offers customers a variety of information technology solutions, or e-fulfillment. The dedicated contract carriage segment, which accounts for approximately 10% of Ryder's revenues, combines equipment, maintenance and administrative services with additional services such as driver hiring and training; routing and scheduling; fleet sizing; safety; regulatory compliance; risk management; technology and communication systems support, including on-board computers; and other technical support. In February 2010, Ryder and Asian logistics solutions provider Cargo Services Far East Limited agreed to form joint venture Ryder Supply Chain Solutions Asia to offer services such as inland transport, vendor/purchase order management, export consolidation and order fulfillment from Asia to North America. In January 2011, the firm acquired Total Logistic Control; Carmenita Leasing, Inc.; and The Scully Companies, Inc.

FINANCIALS: **Sales and profits are in thousands of dollars—add 000 to get the full amount. 2010 Note: Financial information for 2010 was not available for all companies at press time.**

2010 Sales: $5,136,400 — 2010 Profits: $118,200
2009 Sales: $4,887,254 — 2009 Profits: $61,945
2008 Sales: $5,999,041 — 2008 Profits: $199,881
2007 Sales: $6,363,130 — 2007 Profits: $253,861
2006 Sales: $6,306,643 — 2006 Profits: $248,959

U.S. Stock Ticker: R
Int'l Ticker:
Int'l Exchange:
Employees: 22,900 Fiscal Year Ends: 12/31
Parent Company:

SALARIES/BENEFITS:

Pension Plan: ESOP Stock Plan: Profit Sharing: Top Exec. Salary: $900,000 Bonus: $639,956
Savings Plan: Y Stock Purch. Plan: Second Exec. Salary: $525,000 Bonus: $159,989

OTHER THOUGHTS:

Apparent Women Officers or Directors: 3
Hot Spot for Advancement for Women/Minorities: Y

LOCATIONS: ("Y" = Yes)

West:	Southwest:	Midwest:	Southeast:	Northeast:	International:
Y	Y	Y	Y	Y	Y

SABRE HOLDINGS CORP

www.sabre-holdings.com

Industry Group Code: 5615E

Management:		Sales/Marketing:		Liberal Arts:		Information Sys.:		Professionals:		Tech./Scientific:	
Mgmt. Trainees:	Y	Marketing Pros.:	Y	Gen. Writing/Editing:	Y	Info. Mgmt.:	Y	Finance/Acct.:	Y	Engineers, Elec.:	Y
Experienced Mgmt.:	Y	Retail Sales:		Tech. Writing:	Y	Software Dev.:	Y	Law:	Y	Engineers, Other:	
Int'l Business:	Y	Comm./Industrial:	Y	Graphic Arts/Photog.:	Y	Hardware Dev.:		HR/Other:	Y	Health/Lab:	
MBA Grads:	Y	Sales Trainees:		Music:		Consulting/Other:		Training:	Y	Science/Research:	
		Advertising Pros.:		Broadcasting:				Health Care:		Petroleum/Chem.:	
				Other:	Y			Consulting:		Math/Other:	

TYPES OF BUSINESS:

Online Travel Reservations
Travel Marketing Solutions
Distribution & Technology Solutions
Consulting Services

BRANDS/DIVISIONS/AFFILIATES:

Silver Lake Partners
TPG Inc
Sabre Travel Network
Travelocity.com LP
LastMinute.com
Moneydirect
GetThere.com
TRAMS

CONTACTS: *Note: Officers with more than one job title may be intentionally listed here more than once.*

Sam Gilliland, CEO
Thomas Klein, Pres.
Mark Miller, CFO/Exec. VP
Paul Rostron, Exec. VP-Human Resources
Barry Vandevier, CIO
Sterling L. Miller, General Counsel/Exec. VP/Corp. Sec.
Jeffery Jackson, Exec. VP-Corp. Bus. Dev.
Hugh Jones, Pres./CEO-Travelocity Global
Greg Webb, Pres., Sabre Travel Network
Sam Gilliland, Chmn.

Phone: 682-605-1000 **Fax:**
Toll-Free:
Address: 3150 Sabre Dr., Southlake, TX 76092 US

GROWTH PLANS/SPECIAL FEATURES:

Sabre Holdings Corp., owned by private equity companies Silver Lake Partners and Texas Pacific Group, is a provider of travel products and services through its four businesses: Travelocity, Sabre Travel Network, Sabre Airline Solutions and Sabre Hospitality Solutions. Travelocity markets and distributes travel-related products and services directly to individuals, including leisure travelers and business travelers, through the Travelocity.com, LastMinute.com, IgoUgo.com, HolidayAutos.com, WorldChoiceTravel.com and Zuji.com web sites and contact centers. Travelers can access offerings, pricing and information about airlines, hotels, car rental companies, cruise lines, vacation and last-minute travel packages and other travel-related services. For business travelers, Travelocity Business provides GetThere products and other travel services. Sabre Travel Network segment markets and distributes travel-related products and services through online and traditional travel agencies and corporate channels. Users of the Sabre system can access information about, book reservations for and purchase a variety of travel offerings, including airline trips, hotel stays, car rentals, cruises and tour packages through its key brands, GetThere, Moneydirect, and TRAMS. Sabre tools allow travel agencies to book travel online, automate certain processes and manage reservations. Additionally, the firm offers distribution and technology services to hotels. The company's online booking portal for agents, MySabre, offers agents and suppliers merchandising opportunities at the point of sale. Buyers and sellers of travel products may also connect through Sabre GDS, an online portal with over 400 airlines, 76,000 hotels, 28 car rental companies, 13 cruise lines, 35 railroads and 220 tour operators. Sabre Travel Network also provides travel services to government agencies. The Sabre Airline Solutions segment provides passenger management services; software products and consulting services to airlines. These products and services target areas such as planning and scheduling; pricing, revenue and crew management; airline reservations; and border security. The Sabre Hospitality Solution segment offers hotel suppliers marketing, distribution and consulting services.

FINANCIALS: **Sales and profits are in thousands of dollars—add 000 to get the full amount. 2010 Note: Financial information for 2010 was not available for all companies at press time.**

2010 Sales: $3,400,000 — 2010 Profits: $
2009 Sales: $3,200,000 — 2009 Profits: $
2008 Sales: $3,000,000 — 2008 Profits: $
2007 Sales: $3,000,000 — 2007 Profits: $
2006 Sales: $2,823,797 — 2006 Profits: $155,638

U.S. Stock Ticker: Private
Int'l Ticker:
Int'l Exchange:
Employees: 9,000 Fiscal Year Ends: 12/31
Parent Company: SILVER LAKE PARTNERS

SALARIES/BENEFITS:

Pension Plan: ESOP Stock Plan: Profit Sharing: Top Exec. Salary: $ Bonus: $
Savings Plan: Stock Purch. Plan: Second Exec. Salary: $ Bonus: $

OTHER THOUGHTS:

Apparent Women Officers or Directors:
Hot Spot for Advancement for Women/Minorities:

LOCATIONS: ("Y" = Yes)

West:	Southwest:	Midwest:	Southeast:	Northeast:	International:
	Y				Y

SAFECO INSURANCE COMPANY OF AMERICA www.safeco.com

Industry Group Code: 524126

Management:		Sales/Marketing:		Liberal Arts:		Information Sys.:		Professionals:		Tech./Scientific:	
Mgmt. Trainees:	Y	Marketing Pros.:	Y	Gen. Writing/Editing:	Y	Info. Mgmt.:	Y	Finance/Acct.:	Y	Engineers, Elec.:	
Experienced Mgmt.:	Y	Retail Sales:		Tech. Writing:	Y	Software Dev.:	Y	Law:	Y	Engineers, Other:	
Int'l Business:	Y	Comm./Industrial:	Y	Graphic Arts/Photog.:	Y	Hardware Dev.:		HR/Other:	Y	Health/Lab:	
MBA Grads:	Y	Sales Trainees:	Y	Music:		Consulting/Other:		Training:	Y	Science/Research:	
		Advertising Pros.:	Y	Broadcasting:				Health Care:		Petroleum/Chem.:	
				Other:	Y			Consulting:		Math/Other:	

TYPES OF BUSINESS:

Direct Property & Casualty Insurance
Personal Insurance

BRANDS/DIVISIONS/AFFILIATES:

Liberty Mutual Insurance Co
Liberty Mutual Group Inc
Safeco Corp
Safeco Package (The)
Liberty Northwest
Colorado Casualty
America First Insurance
Golden Eagle Insurance

CONTACTS:

Note: Officers with more than one job title may be intentionally listed here more than once.

Matthew D. Nickerson, COO/Exec. VP
Michael Hughes, Pres.
Loralie Levenhagen, Mgr.-Human Resources/Assistant VP
James M. MacPhee, Chief Prod. Officer/Sr. VP
Donald J. DeShaw, General Counsel/VP-Corp. Legal
Kris L. Hill, Mgr.-Finance/Sr. VP
Glenn Shapiro, Mgr.-Claims/Sr. VP

Phone: 206-545-5000 **Fax:**
Toll-Free:
Address: 1001 Fourth Ave., Safeco Plz., Seattle, WA 98154 US

GROWTH PLANS/SPECIAL FEATURES:

Safeco Insurance Company of America (Safeco), formerly Safeco Corp., is a property and casualty insurance provider for homeowners and drivers. The company is a subsidiary of life, auto and home insurance provider Liberty Mutual Group. The firm's personal insurance services include auto, homeowners, condo, rental, and specialty insurance products for individuals. Its specialty insurance products include umbrella, classic car, motorcycle, recreational vehicle and boat/watercraft owners' insurance coverage for individuals. The personal insurance division also offers individual surety bonds. The company also offers The Safeco Package, a combined auto and home property insurance product. Safeco maintains regional offices in California, Texas, Indiana, Ohio, Colorado, Washington, New Hampshire and Georgia. It also has service facilities in Missouri Oregon, Illinois and Connecticut; and customer care centers in Indianapolis, Washington and Colorado. The firm's business insurance activities are operated by Safeco's sister companies, such as Liberty Northwest; Colorado Casualty; America First Insurance; Golden Eagle Insurance; Ohio Causality; Indiana Insurance; Montgomery Insurance; and Peerless Insurance. These companies provide business-owner policies, surety bonds, commercial auto, commercial multi-peril, workers' compensation, commercial property and general liability policies for small- and mid-sized businesses.

Through Liberty Mutual Group, Safeco offers its employees benefits including a 401(k) plan; flexible spending accounts; medical, vision, disability, life, AD&D, dependent life and long-term care insurance; and tuition reimbursement.

FINANCIALS:

Sales and profits are in thousands of dollars—add 000 to get the full amount. 2010 Note: Financial information for 2010 was not available for all companies at press time.

2010 Sales: $1,567,755 | 2010 Profits: $93,296
2009 Sales: $1,592,432 | 2009 Profits: $104,390
2008 Sales: $ | 2008 Profits: $
2007 Sales: $6,208,800 | 2007 Profits: $707,800
2006 Sales: $6,289,900 | 2006 Profits: $880,000

U.S. Stock Ticker: Subsidiary
Int'l Ticker:
Int'l Exchange:
Employees: 7,200 Fiscal Year Ends: 12/31
Parent Company: LIBERTY MUTUAL GROUP INC

SALARIES/BENEFITS:

Pension Plan: | ESOP Stock Plan: | Profit Sharing: | Top Exec. Salary: $ | Bonus: $1,250,000
Savings Plan: Y | Stock Purch. Plan: | | Second Exec. Salary: $ | Bonus: $

OTHER THOUGHTS:

Apparent Women Officers or Directors: 2
Hot Spot for Advancement for Women/Minorities: Y

LOCATIONS: ("Y" = Yes)

West:	Southwest:	Midwest:	Southeast:	Northeast:	International:
Y	Y	Y	Y	Y	Y

Sales, profits and employees may be estimates. Financial information, benefits and other data can change quickly and may vary from those stated here.

SAFEWAY INC

www.safeway.com

Industry Group Code: 445110

Management:		Sales/Marketing:		Liberal Arts:		Information Sys.:		Professionals:		Tech./Scientific:	
Mgmt. Trainees:	Y	Marketing Pros.:	Y	Gen. Writing/Editing:	Y	Info. Mgmt.:	Y	Finance/Acct.:	Y	Engineers, Elec.:	
Experienced Mgmt.:	Y	Retail Sales:	Y	Tech. Writing:		Software Dev.:	Y	Law:	Y	Engineers, Other:	
Int'l Business:	Y	Comm./Industrial:		Graphic Arts/Photog.:	Y	Hardware Dev.:		HR/Other:	Y	Health/Lab:	
MBA Grads:	Y	Sales Trainees:	Y	Music:		Consulting/Other:		Training:	Y	Science/Research:	
		Advertising Pros.:	Y	Broadcasting:				Health Care:		Petroleum/Chem.:	
				Other:	Y			Consulting:		Math/Other:	

TYPES OF BUSINESS:

Grocery Stores
Food Processing & Packaging
Online Grocery Sales & Home Delivery
Pharmacies
Gift Cards & Payment Processing Technology

BRANDS/DIVISIONS/AFFILIATES:

Carr-Gottstein Foods Co
Randall's Food Markets Inc.
Vons Companies Inc. (The)
Canada Safeway Limited
GroceryWorks
Safeway SELECT
Casa Ley, S.A. de C.V.
Blackhawk Network

CONTACTS: *Note: Officers with more than one job title may be intentionally listed here more than once.*

Steven A. Burd, CEO
Steven A. Burd, Pres.
Robert L. Edwards, CFO/Exec. VP
Diane M. Deitz, Chief Mktg. Officer/Exec. VP
Russell M. Jackson, Sr. VP-Human Resources
David T. Ching, CIO/Sr. VP
Kelly Griffith, Pres., Merch.
Donald P. Wright, Sr. VP-Eng. & Real Estate
Larree M. Renda, Chief Admin. Officer/Exec. VP
Robert A. Gordon, General Counsel/Sec./Chief Governance Officer
Bruce L. Everette, Exec. VP-Retail Oper.
Larree M. Renda, Chief Strategist Officer
Melissa C. Plaisance, Sr. VP-Investor Rel. & Finance
David F. Bond, Chief Acct. Officer/Sr. VP-Finance & Control
Kenneth M. Shachmut, Sr. VP-Strategic & Health Initiatives
David R. Stern, Sr. VP-Planning & Bus. Dev.
Steven A. Burd, Chmn.
Jerry Tidwell, Sr. VP-Supply Oper.

Phone: 925-467-3000 | **Fax:** 925-467-3323
Toll-Free: 877-723-3929
Address: 5918 Stoneridge Mall Rd., Pleasanton, CA 94588 US

GROWTH PLANS/SPECIAL FEATURES:

Safeway, Inc., originally incorporated as SSI Holdings Corporations and then Safeway Stores, is one of the largest food retailers in North America, operating 1,694 stores located principally in California, Oregon, Washington, Alaska, Colorado, Arizona, Texas, the Chicago metropolitan area and the Mid-Atlantic region. The company's Canadian retail operations are located principally in British Columbia, Alberta, Manitoba and Saskatchewan. These stores operate regionally under the names Safeway, Carrs, Genuardi's, Pavilions, Tom Thumb, Dominick's, Randall's and Vons, each of which offer a wide selection of both food and general merchandise and feature a variety of special departments such as bakery, delicatessen, pharmacy and floral departments. In addition, the company offers online grocery shopping and home delivery through its wholly-owned subsidiary, GroceryWorks. Safeway has developed a line of hundreds of Safeway SELECT brand products, ranging from packaged foods to laundry detergent, and offers corporate-branded products under the Safeway and subsidiary labels. The company recently expanded its O Organics line of certified organic foods and beverages to over 400 exclusive products. Safeway operates 32 processing plants and 17 distribution/warehousing centers in the U.S. and Canada. The firm also owns a 49% interest in Casa Ley, S.A. de C.V., which operates about 168 general merchandise and food stores in Mexico. Beyond these operations, Safeway manages its Blackhawk Network subsidiary, which is one of the largest providers of third-party prepaid gift cards in the country with a gift card offering of more than 100 brands from retailers such as Best Buy, Pizza Hut and Starbucks Coffee.

Safeway offers its employees medical, prescription drug, vision and dental coverage; an employee assistance plan; flexible spending accounts; life insurance; short- and long-term disability; a retirement plan; and a 401(k) plan.

FINANCIALS: **Sales and profits are in thousands of dollars—add 000 to get the full amount. 2010 Note: Financial information for 2010 was not available for all companies at press time.**

2010 Sales: $41,050,000 | 2010 Profits: $589,800
2009 Sales: $40,850,700 | 2009 Profits: $-1,097,500
2008 Sales: $44,104,000 | 2008 Profits: $965,300
2007 Sales: $42,286,000 | 2007 Profits: $888,400
2006 Sales: $40,185,000 | 2006 Profits: $870,600

U.S. Stock Ticker: SWY
Int'l Ticker:
Int'l Exchange:
Employees: 180,000 Fiscal Year Ends: 12/31
Parent Company:

SALARIES/BENEFITS:

Pension Plan: Y | ESOP Stock Plan: | Profit Sharing: | Top Exec. Salary: $1,491,173 | Bonus: $750,000
Savings Plan: Y | Stock Purch. Plan: Y | | Second Exec. Salary: $687,098 | Bonus: $326,371

OTHER THOUGHTS:

Apparent Women Officers or Directors: 3
Hot Spot for Advancement for Women/Minorities: Y

LOCATIONS: ("Y" = Yes)

West:	Southwest:	Midwest:	Southeast:	Northeast:	International:
Y	Y	Y		Y	Y

SAIC INC

Industry Group Code: 541513

www.saic.com

Management:		Sales/Marketing:		Liberal Arts:		Information Sys.:		Professionals:		Tech./Scientific:	
Mgmt. Trainees:	Y	Marketing Pros.:	Y	Gen. Writing/Editing:	Y	Info. Mgmt.:	Y	Finance/Acct.:	Y	Engineers, Elec.:	Y
Experienced Mgmt.:	Y	Retail Sales:		Tech. Writing:	Y	Software Dev.:	Y	Law:	Y	Engineers, Other:	Y
Int'l Business:	Y	Comm./Industrial:	Y	Graphic Arts/Photog.:	Y	Hardware Dev.:	Y	HR/Other:	Y	Health/Lab:	
MBA Grads:	Y	Sales Trainees:		Music:		Consulting/Other:	Y	Training:	Y	Science/Research:	Y
		Advertising Pros.:		Broadcasting:				Health Care:		Petroleum/Chem.:	
				Other:	Y			Consulting:	Y	Math/Other:	

TYPES OF BUSINESS:

Systems Integration Services
Consulting Services
Research & Development
Software Development
Engineering
Cybersecurity
IT Infrastructure Management

BRANDS/DIVISIONS/AFFILIATES:

Atlan, Inc.
R.W. Beck Group, Inc.
Beck Disaster Recovery, Inc.
Spectrum San Diego
CloudShield Technologies, Inc.
Science, Engineering & Technology Associates Corp.
Reveal Imaging Technologies, Inc.
Science Applications International Corporation

CONTACTS: *Note: Officers with more than one job title may be intentionally listed here more than once.*

Walter P. Havenstein, CEO
Mark W. Sopp, CFO/Exec. VP
Brian F. Keenan, Exec. VP-Human Resources
Larry D. Cox, Gen. Mgr.-Info. Sys. & Intelligence Bus. Unit
Amy E. Alving, CTO
Vincent A. Maffio, General Counsel/Exec. VP-Audit
Anthony J. Moraco, Exec. VP-Oper. & Performance Excellence
James E. Cuff, Exec. VP-Bus. Dev. & Strategy
Deborah L. James, Exec. VP-Comm. & Gov't Affairs
Paul Levi, Sr. VP-Investor Rel.
K. Stuart Shea, Pres., Intelligence & Surveillance Group
Deborah H. Alderson, Pres., Defense Solutions Group
James E. Cuff, Exec. VP-Mergers & Acquisitions
Joseph W. Craver, III, Pres., Energy, Heath & Infrastructure Group
A. Thomas Young, Chmn.
Donald H. Foley, Exec. VP-Special Int'l Assignment

Phone: 703-676-4300 | **Fax:** 703-676-2269
Toll-Free: 800-430-7629
Address: 1710 SAIC Dr., McLean, VA 22102 US

GROWTH PLANS/SPECIAL FEATURES:

SAIC, Inc., formerly Science Applications International Corporation, provides scientific, engineering, systems integration and technical services primarily to government customers. The company's clients include all branches of the U.S. military, the U.S. Department of Defense, intelligence agencies, the U.S. Department of Homeland Security, other U.S. government agencies, foreign governments and customers in select commercial markets. SAIC operates in three segments: government, commercial and corporate. The government segment, which generates 96% of the firm's revenues, offers services in the areas of systems integration; software development; IT outsourcing; cyber security; secure information sharing; data processing; communications; logistics; research and development; environmental consulting; energy and utilities; design and construction; homeland security; and geospatial solutions. SAIC's commercial segment, which generates 5% of its revenue, primarily targets commercial customers worldwide in the oil and gas; utilities; and life sciences industries. While the commercial segment provides a number of IT systems integration and advanced technical services, the focused offerings include applications and IT infrastructure management, data lifecycle management and business transformation services. The corporate segment handles issues relating to the company's internal real estate management subsidiary. SAIC's recent acquisitions includes Atlan, Inc., which provides cyber security product testing; R.W. Beck Group, Inc., a consulting firm; Beck Disaster Recovery, Inc., an emergency management consultant company; Spectrum San Diego, a producer of vehicle X-ray security scanners; CloudShield Technologies, Inc., a cyber security solutions company; Science, Engineering and Technology Associates Corporation, a technology company; and Reveal Imaging Technologies, Inc., a developer of threat detection products. In September 2010, the firm opened the Cyber Innovation Center in Maryland; the center is intended to help develop and deliver cyber security solutions.

SAIC offers its employees medical, dental and vision coverage; flexible spending accounts; life and disability insurance; a 401(k) plan; a wellness program; back-up childcare; an employee assistance program; tuition reimbursement; and a long-term care program.

FINANCIALS: **Sales and profits are in thousands of dollars—add 000 to get the full amount. 2010 Note: Financial information for 2010 was not available for all companies at press time.**

2010 Sales: $10,846,000 | 2010 Profits: $497,000
2009 Sales: $10,070,000 | 2009 Profits: $452,000
2008 Sales: $8,926,000 | 2008 Profits: $416,000
2007 Sales: $8,060,000 | 2007 Profits: $390,000
2006 Sales: $7,518,000 | 2006 Profits: $927,000

U.S. Stock Ticker: SAI
Int'l Ticker:
Int'l Exchange:
Employees: 46,200 Fiscal Year Ends: 1/31
Parent Company:

SALARIES/BENEFITS:

Pension Plan: | ESOP Stock Plan: | Profit Sharing: | Top Exec. Salary: $1,000,000 | Bonus: $1,444,500
Savings Plan: Y | Stock Purch. Plan: | Second Exec. Salary: $547,117 | Bonus: $560,000

OTHER THOUGHTS:

Apparent Women Officers or Directors: 6
Hot Spot for Advancement for Women/Minorities: Y

LOCATIONS: ("Y" = Yes)

West:	Southwest:	Midwest:	Southeast:	Northeast:	International:
Y	Y	Y	Y	Y	Y

SALESFORCE.COM INC

www.salesforce.com

Industry Group Code: 511210K

Management:		**Sales/Marketing:**		**Liberal Arts:**		**Information Sys.:**		**Professionals:**		**Tech./Scientific:**	
Mgmt. Trainees:		Marketing Pros.:	Y	Gen. Writing/Editing:		Info. Mgmt.:	Y	Finance/Acct.:	Y	Engineers, Elec.:	Y
Experienced Mgmt.:	Y	Retail Sales:		Tech. Writing:	Y	Software Dev.:	Y	Law:	Y	Engineers, Other:	
Int'l Business:	Y	Comm./Industrial:	Y	Graphic Arts/Photog.:		Hardware Dev.:		HR/Other:	Y	Health/Lab:	
MBA Grads:	Y	Sales Trainees:		Music:		Consulting/Other:	Y	Training:	Y	Science/Research:	
		Advertising Pros.:	Y	Broadcasting:				Health Care:		Petroleum/Chem.:	
				Other:				Consulting:		Math/Other:	

TYPES OF BUSINESS:

Software-Sales & Marketing Automation
Customer Relationship Management Software
Software Subscription Services

BRANDS/DIVISIONS/AFFILIATES:

AppExchange
Force.com
Salesforce Chatter
Service Cloud
Heroku
Jigsaw
Premier Training
Vmforce

CONTACTS: *Note: Officers with more than one job title may be intentionally listed here more than once.*

Marc Benioff, CEO
Steve Cakebread, Pres.
Graham Smith, CFO/Exec. VP
George Hu, Exec. VP-Mktg. & Platform
J.P. Rangaswami, Chief Scientist
Parker Harris, Exec. VP-Tech.
David Schellhase, Exec. VP-Legal
Polly Sumner, Chief Adoption Officer
Jim Steele, Chief Customer Officer
Maria Martinez, Exec. VP-Customers For Life
Hilarie Koplow-McAdams, Exec. VP-Worldwide Sales
Marc Benioff, Chmn.
Frank van Veenendaal, Pres., Worldwide Sales & Svcs.

Phone: 415-901-7000 **Fax:** 415-901-7040
Toll-Free: 800-667-6389
Address: 1 Market St., Ste. 300, The Landmark, San Francisco, CA 94105 US

GROWTH PLANS/SPECIAL FEATURES:

SalesForce.com, Inc. builds and delivers customer relationship management (CRM) applications through an on-demand web services platform. The firm's web-based services enable clients to track sales and marketing by delivering enterprise software as an online service, making software purchases similar to paying for a utility as opposed to a packaged product. Its product suite provides integrated online sales force automation, customer service and support automation, partner relationship management and marketing automation applications. The company's AppExchange program allows businesses to access hundreds of on-demand business software applications developed by third parties. The company's products are scalable and can be mixed and matched with services such as system integration, data management, employee training and customer support. SalesForce.com also sponsors the Force.com online platform, which enables existing customers and third-party developers to develop and deliver software-as-a-service applications which they build within the platform's existing technology environment. Through Force.com, applications can be created, published, and run. In addition, these applications can be listed on the AppExchange marketplace. The firm also offers Premier Training, a subscription-based training model for the use of its platform; Service Cloud and Service Cloud 2, which are customer service solutions that uses cloud computing technology to capture the conversations and expertise of Google, Facebook and Amazon.com; and Contact Manager Edition, a subscription service aimed at individuals and small businesses. In 2010, SalesForce.com released several new products, including Force.com Visual Process Manager, a visual design tool; Salesforce Chatter, a real-time enterprise collaboration solution and platform; Chatter Mobile for mobile applications; Chatter Free, a free version of Salesforce Chatter; enterprise Java cloud VMforce; and crowd-sourced business data solution Jigsaw for Salesforce CRM. In May 2010, the company acquired crowd-sourced data services provider Jigsaw. In December 2010, SalesForce.com agreed to acquire Ruby-based cloud application platform Heroku for roughly $212 million.

FINANCIALS: **Sales and profits are in thousands of dollars—add 000 to get the full amount. 2010 Note: Financial information for 2010 was not available for all companies at press time.**

2010 Sales: $1,305,583 | 2010 Profits: $80,719
2009 Sales: $1,076,769 | 2009 Profits: $43,428
2008 Sales: $748,700 | 2008 Profits: $18,356
2007 Sales: $497,098 | 2007 Profits: $ 481
2006 Sales: $309,857 | 2006 Profits: $28,474

U.S. Stock Ticker: CRM
Int'l Ticker:
Int'l Exchange:
Employees: 3,969 Fiscal Year Ends: 1/31
Parent Company:

SALARIES/BENEFITS:

Pension Plan: ESOP Stock Plan: Profit Sharing: Top Exec. Salary: $750,000 Bonus: $600,000
Savings Plan: Stock Purch. Plan: Second Exec. Salary: $420,000 Bonus: $252,000

OTHER THOUGHTS:

Apparent Women Officers or Directors: 4
Hot Spot for Advancement for Women/Minorities: Y

LOCATIONS: ("Y" = Yes)

West:	Southwest:	Midwest:	Southeast:	Northeast:	International:
Y					Y

SAM'S CLUB

Industry Group Code: 452112

www.samsclub.com

Management:		Sales/Marketing:		Liberal Arts:		Information Sys.:		Professionals:		Tech./Scientific:	
Mgmt. Trainees:	Y	Marketing Pros.:	Y	Gen. Writing/Editing:	Y	Info. Mgmt.:	Y	Finance/Acct.:	Y	Engineers, Elec.:	
Experienced Mgmt.:	Y	Retail Sales:	Y	Tech. Writing:		Software Dev.:	Y	Law:	Y	Engineers, Other:	
Int'l Business:	Y	Comm./Industrial:		Graphic Arts/Photog.:	Y	Hardware Dev.:		HR/Other:	Y	Health/Lab:	
MBA Grads:	Y	Sales Trainees:	Y	Music:		Consulting/Other:		Training:	Y	Science/Research:	
		Advertising Pros.:	Y	Broadcasting:				Health Care:		Petroleum/Chem.:	
				Other:	Y			Consulting:		Math/Other:	

TYPES OF BUSINESS:

Warehouse Clubs, Retail

BRANDS/DIVISIONS/AFFILIATES:

Wal-Mart Stores Inc
Member's Mark
Bakers & Chefs
Business Membership
Advantage Membership
Plus Membership Card
Sam's Cafe
Mas Club

CONTACTS: *Note: Officers with more than one job title may be intentionally listed here more than once.*

Brian C. Cornell, CEO
Brian C. Cornell, Pres.
Ann Bordelon, CFO
John Boswell, Sr. VP-Mktg.
Linda Hefner, Chief Merch. Officer/Exec. VP
Tim Yatsko, Chief Admin. Officer/Sr. VP
P. Todd Harbaugh, Exec. VP-Oper.
John Boswell, Sr. VP-e-Commerce
Susan Koehler, Contact-Media
Michael W. Turner, Sr. VP-Sam's Club Membership
Tom Waaldron, Sr. VP-Sam's Club People

Phone: 479-277-7000	**Fax:**
Toll-Free: 800-331-0085	
Address: 608 SW 8th St., Bentonville, AR 72716-0745 US	

GROWTH PLANS/SPECIAL FEATURES:

Sam's Club, a subsidiary of Wal-Mart Stores, Inc. and one of the nation's largest members-only warehouse clubs, operates over 590 stores in the U.S. with approximately 47 million members. Additionally, Wal-Mart's International division operates over 120 Sam's Clubs in Brazil, Canada, China, Mexico and Puerto Rico. Sam's Club offers discounted prices on over 4,000 items, including appliances and electronics, office supplies, food, clothing, optical and pharmacy services, home furnishings, books and auto supplies. It also sells selected private-label items under the Member's Mark, Bakers & Chefs and Sam's Club brands. Most locations also offer photo processing, pharmaceuticals, optical departments, gasoline stations and fresh departments, including bakery, meat, produce, floral and Sam's Cafe. Sam's Club requires a customer to become a member, providing two options: Business Membership or Advantage Membership. Both member groups pay an annual fee. In addition, Sam's Club offers a PLUS Membership Card, which offers extra benefits on either level, and a Golden Key membership, which allows business members priority shopping hours. In addition to merchandise discounts, Sam's Club offers its members discounted services that include various types of insurance, a travel club, an auto purchase program, discount credit card processing, software training, mail-order pharmacy services, Internet access and long-distance services. Sam's Club stores, averaging 72,000-190,000 square feet, are designed to resemble a warehouse, with merchandise displayed on shipping pallets or in large freezer/cooler units. The company's merchandise consists of five categories: grocery and consumables; fuel and other categories; technology, office and entertainment; home and apparel; and health and wellness. For 2010, Sam's Club revenues averaged $618 per square foot of store space.

Sam's Club offers its employees medical, dental and life insurance; merchandise discounts; education assistance; GED reimbursement; and scholarships.

FINANCIALS: **Sales and profits are in thousands of dollars—add 000 to get the full amount. 2010 Note: Financial information for 2010 was not available for all companies at press time.**

2010 Sales: $46,710,000	2010 Profits: $1,512,000
2009 Sales: $46,854,000	2009 Profits: $1,610,000
2008 Sales: $44,357,000	2008 Profits: $1,618,000
2007 Sales: $41,582,000	2007 Profits: $1,480,000
2006 Sales: $39,798,000	2006 Profits: $

U.S. Stock Ticker: Subsidiary
Int'l Ticker:
Int'l Exchange:
Employees: 208,800 Fiscal Year Ends: 1/31
Parent Company: WAL-MART STORES INC

SALARIES/BENEFITS:

Pension Plan:	ESOP Stock Plan: Y	Profit Sharing:	Top Exec. Salary: $	Bonus: $
Savings Plan: Y	Stock Purch. Plan:		Second Exec. Salary: $	Bonus: $

OTHER THOUGHTS:

Apparent Women Officers or Directors: 3
Hot Spot for Advancement for Women/Minorities: Y

LOCATIONS: ("Y" = Yes)

West:	Southwest:	Midwest:	Southeast:	Northeast:	International:
Y	Y	Y	Y	Y	Y

SANDISK CORP

www.sandisk.com

Industry Group Code: 33441

Management:		Sales/Marketing:		Liberal Arts:		Information Sys.:		Professionals:		Tech./Scientific:	
Mgmt. Trainees:		Marketing Pros.:	Y	Gen. Writing/Editing:		Info. Mgmt.:	Y	Finance/Acct.:	Y	Engineers, Elec.:	Y
Experienced Mgmt.:	Y	Retail Sales:		Tech. Writing:	Y	Software Dev.:	Y	Law:	Y	Engineers, Other:	Y
Int'l Business:	Y	Comm./Industrial:	Y	Graphic Arts/Photog.:		Hardware Dev.:	Y	HR/Other:	Y	Health/Lab:	
MBA Grads:	Y	Sales Trainees:		Music:		Consulting/Other:		Training:		Science/Research:	
		Advertising Pros.:		Broadcasting:				Health Care:		Petroleum/Chem.:	
				Other:				Consulting:		Math/Other:	

TYPES OF BUSINESS:

Flash-Based Data Storage Products
Flash Memory Cards

BRANDS/DIVISIONS/AFFILIATES:

SanDisk Ultra II
SanDisk Extreme
miniSD
microSD
CompactFlash
Flash Partners Ltd.
Flash Alliance Ltd.
Memory Stick PRO

CONTACTS:

Note: Officers with more than one job title may be intentionally listed here more than once.

Eli Harari, CEO
Sanjay Mehrotra, COO
Sanjay Mehrotra, Pres.
Judy Bruner, CFO/Exec. VP
Yoram Cedar, CTO/Exec. VP
Yoram Cedar, Exec. VP-Corp. Eng.
Eli Harari, Chmn.

Phone: 408-801-1000	**Fax:** 408-801-8657
Toll-Free:	
Address: 601 McCarthy Blvd., Milpitas, CA 95035 US	

GROWTH PLANS/SPECIAL FEATURES:

SanDisk Corp. is a supplier of flash-based data storage products for the consumer, mobile communications and industrial markets. It designs, develops, markets and manufactures products in a variety of form factors using flash memory, controller and firmware technologies. The firm's products are used in a wide range of consumer electronics devices such as digital camera, mobile phones, gaming consoles, MP3 players and other digital devices. SanDisk's products are also embedded in a variety of systems for the enterprise, industrial, military and other markets. The company manufactures and sells every major flash card format including CompactFlash; Secure Digital (SD); MultiMediaCard; Reduced Size MultiMediaCard; Secure Digital High Capacity (SDHC); miniSD; microSD; Memory Stick PRO (which it co-owns with Sony Corp.); and other Memory Stick products such as USB flash drives. In addition to its standard grade products, SanDisk offers Ultra II and SanDisk Extreme memory cards, designed for faster write times and improved operation in harsh conditions. The company does not operate fabrication facilities but does control a significant portion of its flash memory wafer manufacturing through its Flash Partners Ltd. and Flash Alliance Ltd. joint ventures with Toshiba, as well as through sourcing agreements. SanDisk's customers include retailers such as Best Buy and original equipment manufacturers (OEMs) such as Canon. SanDisk also licenses its technologies to several companies, including Intel, Sony and Toshiba. The firm currently holds over 1,100 U.S. and 600 foreign patents. In July 2010, the company agreed to enter into a new joint venture with Toshiba Corporation to manufacture NAND flash memory. In August 2010, the firm introduced the SanDisk integrated solid slate drives (iSSD) for use in tablet PCs and ultra-thin notebooks.

SanDisk Corp. offers employees benefits including medical, dental, life, AD&D and vision insurance; an employee assistance program; tuition reimbursement; and a 401(k) savings plan.

FINANCIALS:

Sales and profits are in thousands of dollars—add 000 to get the full amount. 2010 Note: Financial information for 2010 was not available for all companies at press time.

2010 Sales: $4,826,807	2010 Profits: $1,461,574	**U.S. Stock Ticker: SNDK**
2009 Sales: $3,566,806	2009 Profits: $519,390	**Int'l Ticker:**
2008 Sales: $3,351,352	2008 Profits: $-1,973,480	Int'l Exchange:
2007 Sales: $3,896,366	2007 Profits: $276,514	Employees: 3,469 Fiscal Year Ends: 12/31
2006 Sales: $3,257,525	2006 Profits: $198,896	Parent Company:

SALARIES/BENEFITS:

Pension Plan:	ESOP Stock Plan:	Profit Sharing:	Top Exec. Salary: $848,000	Bonus: $1,696,000
Savings Plan: Y	Stock Purch. Plan: Y		Second Exec. Salary: $561,000	Bonus: $1,000,000

OTHER THOUGHTS:

Apparent Women Officers or Directors: 1
Hot Spot for Advancement for Women/Minorities:

LOCATIONS: ("Y" = Yes)

West:	Southwest:	Midwest:	Southeast:	Northeast:	International:
Y					Y

SANMINA-SCI CORPORATION

www.sanmina-sci.com

Industry Group Code: 334419

Management:		Sales/Marketing:		Liberal Arts:		Information Sys.:		Professionals:		Tech./Scientific:	
Mgmt. Trainees:	Y	Marketing Pros.:	Y	Gen. Writing/Editing:		Info. Mgmt.:	Y	Finance/Acct.:	Y	Engineers, Elec.:	Y
Experienced Mgmt.:	Y	Retail Sales:		Tech. Writing:	Y	Software Dev.:	Y	Law:	Y	Engineers, Other:	Y
Int'l Business:	Y	Comm./Industrial:	Y	Graphic Arts/Photog.:	Y	Hardware Dev.:	Y	HR/Other:	Y	Health/Lab:	
MBA Grads:	Y	Sales Trainees:		Music:		Consulting/Other:		Training:	Y	Science/Research:	
		Advertising Pros.:	Y	Broadcasting:				Health Care:		Petroleum/Chem.:	
				Other:				Consulting:		Math/Other:	

TYPES OF BUSINESS:

Contract Electronics Manufacturing
Assembly & Testing
Logistics Services
Support Services
Product Design & Engineering
Repair & Maintenance Services

BRANDS/DIVISIONS/AFFILIATES:

Viking Modular Solutions

CONTACTS:

Note: Officers with more than one job title may be intentionally listed here more than once.

Jure Sola, CEO
Hari Pillai, COO
Hari Pillai, Pres.
Bob Eulau, CFO/Exec. VP
Dennis Young, Exec. VP-Worldwide Sales & Mktg.
David Pulatie, Exec. VP-Human Resources
Michael R. Tyler, General Counsel/Corp. Sec./Exec. VP
Michael Kovacs, Dir.-Public Rel. & Worldwide Mktg.
Paige Bombino, Dir.-Investor Rel.
Hamid Shokrgozar, Pres., Viking Modular Solutions
Dave Dutkowsky, Exec. VP-Comm. Infrastructure
Jure Sola, Chmn.

Phone: 408-964-3500 **Fax:** 408-964-3636
Toll-Free:
Address: 2700 N. First St., San Jose, CA 95134 US

GROWTH PLANS/SPECIAL FEATURES:

Sanmina-SCI Corporation is an independent global provider of customized, integrated electronics manufacturing services (EMS). With production facilities in 18 countries, the firm is one of the largest global EMS providers. Its services include product design and engineering; manufacturing; final assembly and test; direct order fulfillment; and global supply chain management. The product design and engineering segment provides services for initial product development, detailed product design, prototyping, validation and pre-production services. The company designs high speed digital, analog, radio frequency, wired, wireless, optical and electro-mechanical products. Its manufacturing services are vertically integrated, allowing the company to manufacture key system components and subassemblies, such as circuit boards; printed circuit board assemblies; backplanes and backplane assemblies; enclosures; cable assemblies; precision machining; optical components and modules; and memory modules. This segment includes the operations of Viking Modular Solutions, a manufacturer of flash memory and related storage products. The final assembly and test unit combines the company's assemblies and modules to form finished products, and then tests these products for functionality, environmental impact, conformity to applicable industry, product integrity and regulatory standards. The direct order fulfillment segment receives customer orders, configures products to quickly fill the orders and delivers the products either to original equipment manufacturers (OEMs), a distribution channel (such as a retail outlet) or directly to the end customer. The global supply chain management segment plans, purchases and warehouses product components. It provides these services, as well as after-market support, primarily to OEMs in the communications; defense and aerospace; industrial and medical instrumentation; multimedia; computing and storage; and automotive technology sectors. In March 2010, the firm established a manufacturing facility in the Tamil Nadu state of India.

Sanmina-SCI offers its employees a 401(k) plan; tuition reimbursement; credit union membership; an employee assistance program; business travel accident insurance; and medical, dental, vision, life and AD&D insurance.

FINANCIALS:

Sales and profits are in thousands of dollars—add 000 to get the full amount. 2010 Note: Financial information for 2010 was not available for all companies at press time.

2010 Sales: $6,318,691 — 2010 Profits: $122,435
2009 Sales: $5,177,481 — 2009 Profits: $-136,222
2008 Sales: $7,202,403 — 2008 Profits: $-486,349
2007 Sales: $7,137,793 — 2007 Profits: $-1,134,657
2006 Sales: $7,645,118 — 2006 Profits: $-141,557

U.S. Stock Ticker: SANM
Int'l Ticker:
Int'l Exchange:
Employees: 44,199 Fiscal Year Ends: 9/30
Parent Company:

SALARIES/BENEFITS:

Pension Plan: ESOP Stock Plan: Profit Sharing: Top Exec. Salary: $804,385 Bonus: $1,401,918
Savings Plan: Y Stock Purch. Plan: Second Exec. Salary: $510,795 Bonus: $737,000

OTHER THOUGHTS:

Apparent Women Officers or Directors:
Hot Spot for Advancement for Women/Minorities:

LOCATIONS: ("Y" = Yes)

West:	Southwest:	Midwest:	Southeast:	Northeast:	International:
Y	Y	Y	Y	Y	Y

Sales, profits and employees may be estimates. Financial information, benefits and other data can change quickly and may vary from those stated here.

SAPIENT CORPORATION

www.sapient.com

Industry Group Code: 541513

Management:		Sales/Marketing:		Liberal Arts:		Information Sys.:		Professionals:		Tech./Scientific:	
Mgmt. Trainees:	Y	Marketing Pros.:	Y	Gen. Writing/Editing:	Y	Info. Mgmt.:	Y	Finance/Acct.:	Y	Engineers, Elec.:	Y
Experienced Mgmt.:	Y	Retail Sales:		Tech. Writing:	Y	Software Dev.:	Y	Law:	Y	Engineers, Other:	
Int'l Business:	Y	Comm./Industrial:	Y	Graphic Arts/Photog.:	Y	Hardware Dev.:	Y	HR/Other:	Y	Health/Lab:	
MBA Grads:	Y	Sales Trainees:		Music:		Consulting/Other:	Y	Training:	Y	Science/Research:	
		Advertising Pros.:		Broadcasting:				Health Care:		Petroleum/Chem.:	
				Other:	Y			Consulting:	Y	Math/Other:	

TYPES OF BUSINESS:

Information Technology Consulting
Internet Strategy Consulting

BRANDS/DIVISIONS/AFFILIATES:

Sapient Government Services
Sapient Global Markets
SapientNitro

CONTACTS:

Note: Officers with more than one job title may be intentionally listed here more than once.

Alan Herrick, CEO
Preston B. Bradford, COO/Sr. VP
Alan Herrick, Pres.
Joe Tibbetts, CFO/Sr. VP
William Kanarick, Chief Mktg. Officer
Preston B. Bradford, Chief Admin. Officer
Jane Owens, General Counsel/Sr. VP/Sec.
Gaston Legorburu, Worldwide Creative Officer-SapientNitro
Alan Wexler, Sr. VP/Lead-North America
Karandeep Singh, Managing Dir.-India
Chris Clarke, Worldwide Creative Officer-SapientNitro
Darius W. Gaskins, Jr., Chmn.
Christian Oversohl, Sr. VP/Lead-Europe

Phone: 617-621-0200 **Fax:** 617-621-1300
Toll-Free:
Address: 131 Dartmouth St., Boston, MA 02116 US

GROWTH PLANS/SPECIAL FEATURES:

Sapient Corporation is a business consulting and technology services firm that designs and manages information technology to improve business performance for clients in the U.S. and abroad. Sapient has offices in the U.S., Canada, the U.K., Germany, Russia, the Netherlands, Switzerland, Sweden, India, United Arab Emirates, Singapore, Australia and China. The firm operates through three primary divisions: SapientNitro, Sapient Global Markets and Sapient Government Services. SapientNitro, a leading global interactive marketing agency, provides interactive marketing and creative services; web site and interactive development; media planning and buying; strategic planning and market analytics; and marketing technologies. Sapient Global Markets offers financial and commodity market customers advisory services, analytics, technology, and business process solutions. Sapient Government Services provide consulting, technology, and marketing services to several agencies of the U.S. government, including the Library of Congress, Federal Bureau of Investigation, National Institutes of Health and United States Department of Homeland Security. The group also serves provincial and other governmental entities in Canada and Europe. Sapient works on both long and short-term consulting projects. Sapient operates through a proprietary Global Distributed Delivery (GDD) model, which allows associates in widely disparate locations to work together efficiently. The company's clients consist of companies within the following industries: technology, communications, energy and utilities, financial services, media and entertainment, automotive, transportation, health care and life sciences, education, consumer/retail products, travel and hospitality. In April 2010, Sapient Corp. opened its first office in Dubai, United Arab Emirates.

The firm has been listed in Capital Magazine's Best Workplaces in Germany, Financial Times' U.K.'s 50 Best Work Places, Globe 100's Top Places to Work in Boston, Globe & Mail's Top 100 Best Places to Work in Canada and Florida Trend's Top 100 Places to Work in Florida.

FINANCIALS:

Sales and profits are in thousands of dollars—add 000 to get the full amount. 2010 Note: Financial information for 2010 was not available for all companies at press time.

2010 Sales: $863,519 — 2010 Profits: $43,805
2009 Sales: $666,678 — 2009 Profits: $88,126
2008 Sales: $687,488 — 2008 Profits: $62,476
2007 Sales: $565,989 — 2007 Profits: $15,216
2006 Sales: $421,643 — 2006 Profits: $3,136

U.S. Stock Ticker: SAPE
Int'l Ticker:
Int'l Exchange:
Employees: 9,015 Fiscal Year Ends: 12/31
Parent Company:

SALARIES/BENEFITS:

Pension Plan: ESOP Stock Plan: Profit Sharing: Top Exec. Salary: $550,000 Bonus: $310,000
Savings Plan: Stock Purch. Plan: Second Exec. Salary: $350,000 Bonus: $136,400

OTHER THOUGHTS:

Apparent Women Officers or Directors: 2
Hot Spot for Advancement for Women/Minorities:

LOCATIONS: ("Y" = Yes)

West:	Southwest:	Midwest:	Southeast:	Northeast:	International:
Y		Y	Y	Y	Y

SARA LEE CORP

www.saralee.com

Industry Group Code: 3118

Management:		Sales/Marketing:		Liberal Arts:		Information Sys.:		Professionals:		Tech./Scientific:	
Mgmt. Trainees:	Y	Marketing Pros.:	Y	Gen. Writing/Editing:	Y	Info. Mgmt.:	Y	Finance/Acct.:	Y	Engineers, Elec.:	
Experienced Mgmt.:	Y	Retail Sales:		Tech. Writing:	Y	Software Dev.:	Y	Law:	Y	Engineers, Other:	Y
Int'l Business:	Y	Comm./Industrial:	Y	Graphic Arts/Photog.:	Y	Hardware Dev.:		HR/Other:	Y	Health/Lab:	
MBA Grads:	Y	Sales Trainees:	Y	Music:		Consulting/Other:		Training:	Y	Science/Research:	
		Advertising Pros.:	Y	Broadcasting:				Health Care:		Petroleum/Chem.:	
				Other:				Consulting:		Math/Other:	

TYPES OF BUSINESS:

Food & Beverage, Manufacturing
Processed Meats
Bakery Products
Foodservice Distribution
Coffee & Tea

BRANDS/DIVISIONS/AFFILIATES:

JBS SA
Rainbo
Douwe Egberts
Cafe Damasco
Maison du Cafe
Sun-Maid
Senseo
National Textiles LLC

CONTACTS: *Note: Officers with more than one job title may be intentionally listed here more than once.*

Marcel H. M. Smits, Interim CEO/Exec. VP
Mark A. Garvey, Interim CFO/Sr. VP-Finance
Stephen J. Cerrone, Exec. VP-Human Resources
Paulette Dodson, Interim General Counsel/Sec.
B. Thomas Hansson, Sr. VP-Strategic Planning & Corp. Dev.
John Zyck, Interim Controller
Michael A. Feder, Interim CEO-Sara Lee North American Fresh Bakery
Christopher J. Fraleigh, Exec. VP/CEO-North America
James S. Crown,
Frank van Oers, Exec. VP/CEO-Beverage & Bakery, Sara Lee Int'l

Phone: 630-598-8100	**Fax:** 630-598-8482
Toll-Free:	
Address: 3500 Lacey Rd., Downers Grove, IL 60515 US	

GROWTH PLANS/SPECIAL FEATURES:

Sara Lee Corp. manufactures and markets brand-name meat, bakery and beverage products worldwide. The company operates in five segments: North American retail, North American fresh bakery, North American foodservice, international beverage and international bakery. The North American retail segment sells packaged meat and frozen bakery products. Products include hot dogs, sausages, breakfast sandwiches, deli meats, bacon, cooked hams and frozen pies, cakes and cheesecakes. This segment also includes the firm's U.S. retail coffee business. The North American fresh bakery segment sells fresh bakery products and specialty items, such as bread, buns, bagels, rolls, muffins, specialty bread and cakes, under the Sara Lee, Colonial, Rainbo and Sun-Maid brands, among others. Customers include supermarkets, mass merchandisers, warehouse clubs, restaurants and schools. The North American foodservice segment sells meat, bakery and beverage products to foodservice customers; and private label refrigerated dough to retail customers. The international beverage segment sells coffee and tea products primarily in Europe, Australia and Brazil under the Douwe Egberts, Senseo, Maison du Cafe and Cafe do Ponto brands. Finally, the international bakery segment sells bakery and dough products to retail and foodservice customers in Europe (primarily Spain and France) and Australia. Products include bread, buns, rolls, specialty bread, refrigerated dough and frozen desserts, marketed under the Bimbo, CroustiPate and BonGateaux brands. Recently, the firm sold its deodorants and skin-care business to Unilever. During 2010, Sara Lee sold its 51% stake in Godrej Sara Lee, its Indian household insecticides joint venture; sold its air care business to Procter & Gamble; acquired Cafe Damasco, a Brazilian coffee business; launched the Douwe Egberts espresso coffee brand in the Netherlands; and agreed to sell its White King and Janola cleaning brands to Symex Holdings Ltd. In November 2010, the firm agreed to sell its North American fresh bakery operations to Grupo Bimbo. In early 2011, Sara Lee announced plans to split its food and beverage businesses into two separate companies.

FINANCIALS: **Sales and profits are in thousands of dollars—add 000 to get the full amount. 2010 Note: Financial information for 2010 was not available for all companies at press time.**

2010 Sales: $10,793,000	2010 Profits: $527,000	**U.S. Stock Ticker: SLE**
2009 Sales: $10,882,000	2009 Profits: $380,000	**Int'l Ticker:**
2008 Sales: $10,949,000	2008 Profits: $-64,000	Int'l Exchange:
2007 Sales: $11,983,000	2007 Profits: $504,000	Employees: 33,000 Fiscal Year Ends: 6/30
2006 Sales: $11,175,000	2006 Profits: $555,000	Parent Company:

SALARIES/BENEFITS:

Pension Plan:	ESOP Stock Plan:	Profit Sharing:	Top Exec. Salary: $1,150,000	Bonus: $3,105,934
Savings Plan:	Stock Purch. Plan:		Second Exec. Salary: $579,600	Bonus: $1,099,884

OTHER THOUGHTS:

Apparent Women Officers or Directors: 2
Hot Spot for Advancement for Women/Minorities: Y

LOCATIONS: ("Y" = Yes)

West:	Southwest:	Midwest:	Southeast:	Northeast:	International:
Y	Y	Y	Y	Y	Y

SAS INSTITUTE INC

www.sas.com

Industry Group Code: 511210H

Management:		Sales/Marketing:		Liberal Arts:		Information Sys.:		Professionals:		Tech./Scientific:	
Mgmt. Trainees:	Y	Marketing Pros.:	Y	Gen. Writing/Editing:	Y	Info. Mgmt.:	Y	Finance/Acct.:	Y	Engineers, Elec.:	Y
Experienced Mgmt.:	Y	Retail Sales:		Tech. Writing:	Y	Software Dev.:	Y	Law:	Y	Engineers, Other:	
Int'l Business:	Y	Comm./Industrial:	Y	Graphic Arts/Photog.:	Y	Hardware Dev.:		HR/Other:	Y	Health/Lab:	
MBA Grads:	Y	Sales Trainees:		Music:		Consulting/Other:	Y	Training:	Y	Science/Research:	Y
		Advertising Pros.:	Y	Broadcasting:				Health Care:		Petroleum/Chem.:	
				Other:	Y			Consulting:	Y	Math/Other:	Y

TYPES OF BUSINESS:

Software-Statistical Analysis
Business Intelligence Software
Data Warehousing
Online Bookstore

BRANDS/DIVISIONS/AFFILIATES:

SAS 9.2
SAS Enterprise BI Server
DataFlux
IDeaS
JMP Software
Memex
RiskAdvisory
SAS Curriculum Pathways

CONTACTS: *Note: Officers with more than one job title may be intentionally listed here more than once.*

James Goodnight, CEO
James Goodnight, Pres.
Don Parker, CFO/Sr. VP
Jim Davis, Chief Mktg. Officer/Sr. VP
Jennifer Mann, VP-Human Resources
Suzanne Gordon, CIO/VP-IT
Keith Collins, CTO/Sr. VP
Carl Farrell, Exec. VP-SAS Americas
James Goodnight, Chmn.
Mikael Hagstrom, Exec. VP-EMEA & APAC

Phone: 919-677-8000 **Fax:** 919-677-4444
Toll-Free: 800-727-0025
Address: 100 SAS Campus Dr., Cary, NC 27513-2414 US

GROWTH PLANS/SPECIAL FEATURES:

SAS Institute, Inc. provides statistical analysis software. The company's products are designed to extract, manage and analyze large volumes of data, often assisting in financial reporting and credit analysis. Individual contracts can be tailored to specific global and local industries, such as banking, manufacturing and government. SAS's top products are SAS 9.2 and SAS Enterprise BI (Business Intelligence) Server. The SAS 9.2 platform is centered on providing extensive data management and analytics integration. It also features predictive applications, a highly adaptable interface and unique grid computing capabilities. SAS Enterprise BI Server is an enhanced reporting and analysis system for the organization and reporting of business intelligence. SAS also provides data warehousing services for large amounts of data, as well as consulting, training and technical support through its SAS Services unit. The company's DataFlux subsidiary helps it deliver quality capabilities in SAS Data Integration solutions. In addition, the firm operates an online bookstore offering a library of SAS-produced books, documentation and training materials. SAS serves more than 50,000 business, government and university sites in over 100 different countries, including 93 of the top 100 companies on the Fortune Global 500 list. The firm's software is used in a number of industries, including aerospace, defense, banking, government, financial services, insurance, manufacturing and retail. Other subsidiaries and divisions include IDeaS Revenue Optimization; JMP Software; DataFlux; RiskAdvisory; and SAS Curriculum Pathways. In June 2010, SAS Institute acquired intelligence management solutions provider Memex.

SAS offers its employees life, disability, medical, dental, auto, home and vision insurance; flexible spending accounts; on-site health care and fitness centers; an employee assistance program; adoption assistance; scholarship programs; and a casual work environment. The firm has been listed in Fortune's Top 100 Companies to Work For in America for 13 consecutive years, and was ranked number 1 in January 2010.

FINANCIALS: **Sales and profits are in thousands of dollars—add 000 to get the full amount. 2010 Note: Financial information for 2010 was not available for all companies at press time.**

2010 Sales: $2,430,000	2010 Profits: $	**U.S. Stock Ticker: Private**
2009 Sales: $2,200,000	2009 Profits: $	**Int'l Ticker:**
2008 Sales: $2,260,000	2008 Profits: $	Int'l Exchange:
2007 Sales: $2,150,000	2007 Profits: $	Employees: 11,398 Fiscal Year Ends: 12/31
2006 Sales: $1,900,000	2006 Profits: $	Parent Company:

SALARIES/BENEFITS:

Pension Plan:	ESOP Stock Plan:	Profit Sharing: Y	Top Exec. Salary: $	Bonus: $
Savings Plan: Y	Stock Purch. Plan:		Second Exec. Salary: $	Bonus: $

OTHER THOUGHTS:

Apparent Women Officers or Directors: 2
Hot Spot for Advancement for Women/Minorities: Y

LOCATIONS: ("Y" = Yes)

West:	Southwest:	Midwest:	Southeast:	Northeast:	International:
Y	Y	Y	Y	Y	Y

SCANA CORPORATION

www.scana.com

Industry Group Code: 221

Management:		Sales/Marketing:		Liberal Arts:		Information Sys.:		Professionals:		Tech./Scientific:	
Mgmt. Trainees:	Y	Marketing Pros.:	Y	Gen. Writing/Editing:	Y	Info. Mgmt.:	Y	Finance/Acct.:	Y	Engineers, Elec.:	Y
Experienced Mgmt.:	Y	Retail Sales:		Tech. Writing:	Y	Software Dev.:	Y	Law:	Y	Engineers, Other:	Y
Int'l Business:		Comm./Industrial:	Y	Graphic Arts/Photog.:	Y	Hardware Dev.:		HR/Other:	Y	Health/Lab:	
MBA Grads:	Y	Sales Trainees:		Music:		Consulting/Other:		Training:	Y	Science/Research:	
		Advertising Pros.:	Y	Broadcasting:				Health Care:		Petroleum/Chem.:	Y
				Other:				Consulting:		Math/Other:	

TYPES OF BUSINESS:

Electricity & Natural Gas
Telecommunications Services
Ethernet Services & Data Center Facilities
Communications Towers Management
Management & Maintenance Services
Service Contracts
Risk Management Services

BRANDS/DIVISIONS/AFFILIATES:

South Carolina Electric & Gas Co.
South Carolina Generating Co., Inc.
South Carolina Fuel Co., Inc.
Public Service Co. of North Carolina, Inc.
Carolina Gas Transmission Corp.
SCANA Communications, Inc.
SCANA Energy Marketing, Inc.
ServiceCare, Inc.

CONTACTS: *Note: Officers with more than one job title may be intentionally listed here more than once.*

William B. Timmerman, CEO
Kevin B. Marsh, COO
Kevin B. Marsh, Pres.
Jimmy Addison, CFO/Sr. VP
George J. Bullwinkel, Jr., Pres./COO-Scana Energy Mktg.
Ronald Lindsey, General Counsel/Sr. VP
Mark R. Cannon, Treas./Risk Mgmt. Officer
Kevin B. Marsh, Pres./COO-South Carolina Electric & Gas Co.
Charles McFadden, Sr. VP-Gov't Affairs & Economic Dev.
Paul V. Fant, Pres./COO-Carolina Gas Transmission
Gina S. Champion, Corp. Sec./Associate General Counsel
William B. Timmerman, Chmn.
Sarena D. Burch, Sr. VP-Fuel Procurement & Asset Mgmt.

Phone: 803-217-9000 **Fax:** 803-217-8119
Toll-Free: 800-763-5891
Address: 100 SCANA Pkwy., Cayce, SC 29033 US

GROWTH PLANS/SPECIAL FEATURES:

SCANA Corporation is an energy-based holding company that operates through wholly-owned subsidiaries. South Carolina Electric & Gas Company (SCE&G) generates, transmits, distributes and sells electricity to about 660,600 retail and wholesale customers, as well as purchasing, selling and transporting natural gas to about 313,500 customers. South Carolina Generating Company, Inc. owns and operates Williams Station and sells electricity exclusively to SCE&G. South Carolina Fuel Company, Inc. acquires, owns and provides financing for SCE&G's nuclear fuel, fossil fuel and emission allowances. Public Service Company of North Carolina, Inc. purchases, sells and transports natural gas for 482,000 residential, commercial and industrial customers. Carolina Gas Transmission Corp. (CGTC) transports natural gas in southeastern Georgia and South Carolina. SCANA Communications, Inc. (SCI) provides fiber optic communications, Ethernet services and data center facilities through a 500-mile fiber optic and Ethernet telecommunications network. SCI also provides communication tower site construction, management and rental services in South Carolina, North Carolina and Georgia. SCANA Energy Marketing, Inc. (SEMI) markets natural gas, primarily in the Southeast, and provides energy-related risk management services. Through its SCANA Energy division, SEMI markets natural gas in Georgia's retail market. ServiceCare, Inc. provides service contracts on home appliances and heating and air conditioning units. SCANA Services, Inc. provides administrative and management services to SCANA's subsidiaries. The firm also owns three smaller energy-related companies. SCANA's electrical service operations primarily serve the chemicals, educational services, textile manufacturing, paper products, food products, lumber and wood products, health services, food and retail industries; the company markets natural gas to automobile manufacturers and the pharmaceuticals, chemicals, ceramics, food products and steel industries. The firm's natural gas operations include liquefied natural gas liquefaction and storage facilities.

The company offers its employees medical, dental and vision insurance; a retirement plan; and a 401(k) plan.

FINANCIALS: **Sales and profits are in thousands of dollars—add 000 to get the full amount. 2010 Note: Financial information for 2010 was not available for all companies at press time.**

2010 Sales: $4,601,000 | 2010 Profits: $376,000
2009 Sales: $4,237,000 | 2009 Profits: $348,000
2008 Sales: $5,319,000 | 2008 Profits: $346,000
2007 Sales: $4,621,000 | 2007 Profits: $320,000
2006 Sales: $4,563,000 | 2006 Profits: $310,000

U.S. Stock Ticker: SCG
Int'l Ticker:
Int'l Exchange:
Employees: 5,877 Fiscal Year Ends: 12/31
Parent Company:

SALARIES/BENEFITS:

Pension Plan: Y | ESOP Stock Plan: | Profit Sharing: | Top Exec. Salary: $1,099,000 | Bonus: $934,150
Savings Plan: Y | Stock Purch. Plan: | | Second Exec. Salary: $580,000 | Bonus: $377,000

OTHER THOUGHTS:

Apparent Women Officers or Directors: 5
Hot Spot for Advancement for Women/Minorities: Y

LOCATIONS: ("Y" = Yes)

West:	Southwest:	Midwest:	Southeast:	Northeast:	International:
Y				Y	

SCHLUMBERGER LIMITED

www.slb.com

Industry Group Code: 213112

Management:		Sales/Marketing:		Liberal Arts:		Information Sys.:		Professionals:		Tech./Scientific:	
Mgmt. Trainees:	Y	Marketing Pros.:	Y	Gen. Writing/Editing:	Y	Info. Mgmt.:	Y	Finance/Acct.:	Y	Engineers, Elec.:	Y
Experienced Mgmt.:	Y	Retail Sales:		Tech. Writing:	Y	Software Dev.:	Y	Law:	Y	Engineers, Other:	Y
Int'l Business:	Y	Comm./Industrial:	Y	Graphic Arts/Photog.:	Y	Hardware Dev.:		HR/Other:	Y	Health/Lab:	
MBA Grads:	Y	Sales Trainees:		Music:		Consulting/Other:		Training:	Y	Science/Research:	Y
		Advertising Pros.:	Y	Broadcasting:				Health Care:		Petroleum/Chem.:	Y
				Other:				Consulting:		Math/Other:	Y

TYPES OF BUSINESS:

Oil & Gas Drilling Support Services
Seismic Services
Reservoir Imaging
Data & IT Consulting Services
Outsourcing
Stimulation Services

BRANDS/DIVISIONS/AFFILIATES:

Schlumberger Oilfield Services
WesternGeco
Framo Engineering
M-I Drilling Fluids
Wilson International Inc

CONTACTS:

Note: Officers with more than one job title may be intentionally listed here more than once.

Andrew Gould, CEO
Paal Kibsgaard, COO
Simon Ayat, CFO/Exec. VP
Stephanie Cox, VP-Personnel
Ram Shenoy, VP-Research
Alexander Juden, General Counsel/Sec.
Kjell-Erik Oestdahl, VP-Oper.
Rod Nelson, VP-Corp. Comm.
Malcolm Theobald, VP-Investor Rel.
Hatem Soliman, Pres., Latin America
Aaron Gatt Floridia, Pres., Middle East
Robert Drummond, Pres., North America
Maurice Dijols, Pres., Russia
Andrew Gould, Chmn.
Mark Corrigan, Pres., Europe & Africa

Phone: 713-513-2000 **Fax:**

Toll-Free:

Address: 5599 San Felipe St., Fl. 17, Houston, TX 77056 US

GROWTH PLANS/SPECIAL FEATURES:

Schlumberger Limited (SLB) is a leading oil field service company offering technology, project management and information solutions for customers in the international oil and gas industry. SLB operates in 80 countries throughout North America, Latin America, Europe, Africa, the Middle East and Asia. It also maintains 25 research and engineering facilities worldwide. The SLB Oilfield Services segment is divided into eight technology-based service lines, which include wireline; drilling and measurements; well testing; well services; completions; artificial lift; data and consulting services; and SLB information services. The overall purpose of the Oilfield Services sector is to provide proper exploration with production services and technologies throughout the entire life cycle of a reservoir. Another SLB service is its Integrated Project Management (IPM) line, which provides consulting, project management and engineering services for well construction using SLB technology. The company owns 40% of M-I SWACO, which offers drilling and completion fluids to stabilize rock and minimize formation damage. In addition, the firm owns a majority stake in Framo Engineering, a Norwegian-based company that provides multiphase booster pumps, flow metering equipment and swivel stack systems. WesternGeco, another subsidiary, offers worldwide marine and seismic reservoir imaging, data processing centers and a multi-client seismic library for monitoring and development services. Smith Oilfield, which the company merged with in August 2010, supplies advanced engineering and related services to oil and gas sites. The company's wholly-owned subsidiary, Wilson International, Inc., provides substantial distribution operations. In October 2010, the firm entered into an agreement with Eurasia Drilling Company to buy and sell each other's drilling and service assets and form a strategic alliance in Eastern Europe.

FINANCIALS:

Sales and profits are in thousands of dollars—add 000 to get the full amount. 2010 Note: Financial information for 2010 was not available for all companies at press time.

2010 Sales: $27,447,000 | 2010 Profits: $4,267,000
2009 Sales: $22,702,000 | 2009 Profits: $3,134,000
2008 Sales: $27,163,000 | 2008 Profits: $5,435,000
2007 Sales: $23,277,000 | 2007 Profits: $5,177,000
2006 Sales: $19,230,000 | 2006 Profits: $3,710,000

U.S. Stock Ticker: SLB
Int'l Ticker:
Int'l Exchange:
Employees: 108,000 Fiscal Year Ends: 12/31
Parent Company:

SALARIES/BENEFITS:

Pension Plan: Y | ESOP Stock Plan: | Profit Sharing: | Top Exec. Salary: $2,500,000 | Bonus: $2,800,000
Savings Plan: Y | Stock Purch. Plan: Y | | Second Exec. Salary: $1,287,654 | Bonus: $1,088,100

OTHER THOUGHTS:

Apparent Women Officers or Directors: 2
Hot Spot for Advancement for Women/Minorities:

LOCATIONS: ("Y" = Yes)

West:	Southwest:	Midwest:	Southeast:	Northeast:	International:
Y	Y	Y		Y	Y

SCOTTS MIRACLE GROW CO

www.scotts.com

Industry Group Code: 11511

Management:		Sales/Marketing:		Liberal Arts:		Information Sys.:		Professionals:		Tech./Scientific:	
Mgmt. Trainees:	Y	Marketing Pros.:	Y	Gen. Writing/Editing:	Y	Info. Mgmt.:	Y	Finance/Acct.:	Y	Engineers, Elec.:	
Experienced Mgmt.:	Y	Retail Sales:	Y	Tech. Writing:	Y	Software Dev.:		Law:	Y	Engineers, Other:	Y
Int'l Business:	Y	Comm./Industrial:	Y	Graphic Arts/Photog.:	Y	Hardware Dev.:		HR/Other:	Y	Health/Lab:	
MBA Grads:	Y	Sales Trainees:	Y	Music:		Consulting/Other:		Training:	Y	Science/Research:	Y
		Advertising Pros.:	Y	Broadcasting:				Health Care:		Petroleum/Chem.:	Y
				Other:				Consulting:		Math/Other:	

TYPES OF BUSINESS:

Horticulture & Turf Products Manufacturer
Fertilizers
Herbicides
Plant Foods
Lawn Services
Outdoor & Garden Products
Plants & Seeds
Mowers & Tractors

BRANDS/DIVISIONS/AFFILIATES:

Turf Builder
Miracle-Gro
Scotts Professional Seed
Ortho
Weedol
EverGreen
Scotts LawnService
Peters Professional

CONTACTS: *Note: Officers with more than one job title may be intentionally listed here more than once.*

James Hagedorn, CEO
Barry W. Sanders, Pres.
David C. Evans, CFO/Exec. VP
James Lyski, Chief Mktg. Officer/Exec. VP
Denise Stump, Exec. VP-Global Human Resources
Jeff Garascia, Sr. VP-Global R&D
Vince Brockman, General Counsel/Exec. VP/Chief Ethics Officer
Mike Lukemire, Sr. VP-Oper.
Pete Supron, Sr. VP-Bus. Dev.
Jim King, Sr. VP-Corp. Affairs
Jim King, Sr. VP-Investor Rel.
Randy Coleman, Sr. VP-Global Operating Finance
Mike Lukemire, Pres., Southeast Region
Mike Carbonara, Pres., Northeast Region
Phil Jones, Pres., West Region
Andy Coogle, Sr. VP-Legal Compliance
James Hagedorn, Chmn.
Michel Gasnier, Pres., Int'l Region
Dave Swihart, Sr. VP-Global Supply Chain

Phone: 937-644-0011 **Fax:** 937-578-5754
Toll-Free: 888-270-3714
Address: 14111 Scottslawn Rd., Marysville, OH 43041 US

GROWTH PLANS/SPECIAL FEATURES:

Scotts Miracle-Gro Co. (SMG) is a marketer of do-it-yourself lawn, garden and home protection products in North America and Europe. Its products include consumer fertilizers, plant foods, soils and mulches, pest controls, grass seed and bird food. The company's principal brands in North America are Scotts, Miracle-Gro and Ortho. International consumer brands include Miracle-Gro, Evergreen, Fertiligene, Celaflor, KB, Substral, Levington and Weedol. SMG operates through the following business segments: Global Consumer and Scotts LawnService. The Global Consumer segment sells products in the following categories: Lawn Care, including lawn fertilizer, crabgrass control, weed control, pest control; Gardening and Landscape, which offers a line of plant foods marketed under the Miracle-Gro brand name; Outdoor Living, which includes wild bird feed products sold under the Morning Song and Scotts brands; and Home Protection, which includes a broad line of weed control, indoor and outdoor pest control and plant disease control products. The Scotts LawnService segment provides residential lawn care, lawn aeration, tree and shrub care and external pest control services in the U.S. through 78 company-operated locations and 87 independently-franchised locations. In March 2011, SMG sold its Global Professional segment, which included brands such as Agroblen, Scotts Professional Seed, Peters Professional and Scotts Turfseed, to ICL for roughly $270 million.

FINANCIALS: **Sales and profits are in thousands of dollars—add 000 to get the full amount. 2010 Note: Financial information for 2010 was not available for all companies at press time.**

2010 Sales: $3,139,900 | 2010 Profits: $204,100
2009 Sales: $2,980,700 | 2009 Profits: $153,300
2008 Sales: $2,823,200 | 2008 Profits: $-10,900
2007 Sales: $2,871,800 | 2007 Profits: $113,400
2006 Sales: $2,697,100 | 2006 Profits: $132,700

U.S. Stock Ticker: SMG
Int'l Ticker:
Int'l Exchange:
Employees: 6,750 Fiscal Year Ends: 9/30
Parent Company:

SALARIES/BENEFITS:

Pension Plan: ESOP Stock Plan: Profit Sharing: Top Exec. Salary: $1,000,000 Bonus: $1,652,400
Savings Plan: Y Stock Purch. Plan: Y Second Exec. Salary: $900,000 Bonus: $1,013,186

OTHER THOUGHTS:

Apparent Women Officers or Directors: 4
Hot Spot for Advancement for Women/Minorities: Y

LOCATIONS: ("Y" = Yes)

West:	Southwest:	Midwest:	Southeast:	Northeast:	International:
Y	Y	Y	Y	Y	Y

SEACOR HOLDINGS INC

www.seacorholdings.com

Industry Group Code: 483111

Management:		Sales/Marketing:		Liberal Arts:		Information Sys.:		Professionals:		Tech./Scientific:	
Mgmt. Trainees:	Y	Marketing Pros.:	Y	Gen. Writing/Editing:	Y	Info. Mgmt.:	Y	Finance/Acct.:	Y	Engineers, Elec.:	Y
Experienced Mgmt.:	Y	Retail Sales:		Tech. Writing:	Y	Software Dev.:	Y	Law:	Y	Engineers, Other:	Y
Int'l Business:	Y	Comm./Industrial:	Y	Graphic Arts/Photog.:		Hardware Dev.:		HR/Other:	Y	Health/Lab:	
MBA Grads:	Y	Sales Trainees:		Music:		Consulting/Other:		Training:	Y	Science/Research:	
		Advertising Pros.:		Broadcasting:				Health Care:		Petroleum/Chem.:	Y
				Other:				Consulting:		Math/Other:	

TYPES OF BUSINESS:

Offshore Oil Platform Logistics
Inland Shipping
Aviation Services
Environmental Services
Helicopter Services

BRANDS/DIVISIONS/AFFILIATES:

SEACOR Commodity Trading LLC
EraMed LLC
National Response Corporation
SCF Marine, Inc.
SES-Kazakhstan LLP
Era Helicopters LLC

CONTACTS: *Note: Officers with more than one job title may be intentionally listed here more than once.*

Oivind Lorentzen, CEO
Richard Ryan, CFO/Sr. VP
Paul Robinson, General Counsel/Sr. VP/Corp. Sec.
Dick Fagerstal, Sr. VP-Corp. Dev. & Finance
Molly Hottinger, VP-Corp. Comm.
Molly Hottinger, VP-Investor Rel.
Matthew Cenac, Chief Acct. Officer/VP
John Gellert, Sr. VP
Randall Blank, Pres./CEO-Environmental Svcs./Sr. VP
Timothy Power, Pres., SCF Marine, Inc.
Peter Coxon, Pres., SEACOR Smit, Inc.
Charles Fabrikant, Chmn.

Phone: 954-523-2200	**Fax:** 954-524-9185
Toll-Free:	
Address: 2200 Eller Dr., Ft. Lauderdale, FL 33316 US	

GROWTH PLANS/SPECIAL FEATURES:

SEACOR Holdings, Inc. owns, operates, invests in and markets equipment primarily in the offshore oil and gas, industrial aviation and marine transportation industries, as well as providing environmental remediation and crisis response services. The company's operations are divided into six business segments. The firm's offshore marine services segment operates a diversified fleet of support vessels primarily servicing offshore oil and gas exploration, development and production facilities worldwide. This segment accounts for about 19% of the firm's annual revenue. The marine transportation services segment (3% of revenue) operates a fleet of eight U.S.-flag tankers providing marine transportation services for petroleum products and chemicals moving in the U.S. domestic coastwise trade. The inland river services division (6%), operating as SCF Marine, Inc., operates a fleet of 1,527 dry cargo vessels, which transport dry and liquid bulk cargo on U.S. inland waterways, including the Mississippi River, its tributaries and Gulf Intracoastal Waterways. The aviation services segment (9%) operates 176 helicopters providing transportation services to the offshore oil and gas exploration, development and production industry, through Era Helicopters LLC; aircraft leasing; transportation services to hospitals, through EraMED LLC; and flightseeing tours in Alaska. The firm's commodity trading and logistics services (28%) subsidiary, SEACOR Commodity Trading LLC, has operations in the purchase, storage, transportation and sale of agricultural and energy commodities, such as rice, sugar, ethanol and clean blendstocks. Finally, the environmental services group (3%), which comprises various subsidiaries including National Response Corporation, provides emergency preparedness and response services to oil, chemical, industrial and marine transportation customers and government agencies. In August 2010, SEACOR acquired SES Borkit LLP, which is now called SES-Kazakhstan LLP.

SEACOR offers its employees medical, dental, life and AD&D insurance; short- and long-term disability coverage; a 401(k) plan; and a stock purchase plan.

FINANCIALS: **Sales and profits are in thousands of dollars—add 000 to get the full amount. 2010 Note: Financial information for 2010 was not available for all companies at press time.**

2010 Sales: $2,649,368 | 2010 Profits: $244,724
2009 Sales: $1,711,338 | 2009 Profits: $145,103
2008 Sales: $1,655,956 | 2008 Profits: $219,423
2007 Sales: $1,359,230 | 2007 Profits: $236,819
2006 Sales: $1,323,445 | 2006 Profits: $234,394

U.S. Stock Ticker: CKH
Int'l Ticker:
Int'l Exchange:
Employees: 6,045 Fiscal Year Ends: 12/31
Parent Company:

SALARIES/BENEFITS:

Pension Plan: ESOP Stock Plan: Profit Sharing: Top Exec. Salary: $700,000 Bonus: $4,500,000
Savings Plan: Y Stock Purch. Plan: Y Second Exec. Salary: $350,000 Bonus: $500,000

OTHER THOUGHTS:

Apparent Women Officers or Directors: 1
Hot Spot for Advancement for Women/Minorities:

LOCATIONS: ("Y" = Yes)

West:	Southwest:	Midwest:	Southeast:	Northeast:	International:
Y	Y	Y	Y	Y	Y

SELECT MEDICAL HOLDINGS CORPORATION

www.selectmedicalcorp.com

Industry Group Code: 622110

Management:		Sales/Marketing:		Liberal Arts:		Information Sys.:		Professionals:		Tech./Scientific:	
Mgmt. Trainees:	Y	Marketing Pros.:	Y	Gen. Writing/Editing:	Y	Info. Mgmt.:	Y	Finance/Acct.:	Y	Engineers, Elec.:	
Experienced Mgmt.:	Y	Retail Sales:		Tech. Writing:	Y	Software Dev.:	Y	Law:	Y	Engineers, Other:	
Int'l Business:	Y	Comm./Industrial:		Graphic Arts/Photog.:	Y	Hardware Dev.:		HR/Other:	Y	Health/Lab:	Y
MBA Grads:	Y	Sales Trainees:		Music:		Consulting/Other:		Training:	Y	Science/Research:	
		Advertising Pros.:	Y	Broadcasting:				Health Care:	Y	Petroleum/Chem.:	
				Other:	Y			Consulting:		Math/Other:	

TYPES OF BUSINESS:

Specialty Acute Care Hospitals
Long-Term Acute Care
Outpatient Rehabilitation Clinics
Contract Therapy Services
Medical Equipment Distribution
Billing Services
Recruiting

BRANDS/DIVISIONS/AFFILIATES:

Kessler Institute for Rehabilitation
Kentucky Orthopedic Rehab Team
Select Medical Corporation
Select Physical Therapy
Kessler Rehabilitation Centers

CONTACTS:

Note: Officers with more than one job title may be intentionally listed here more than once.

Robert A. Ortenzio, CEO
Patricia A. Rice, COO/Co-Pres.
David S. Chernow, Co-Pres.
Martin F. Jackson, CFO/Exec. VP
John A. Saich, Chief Human Resources Officer/Exec. VP
James J. Talalai, CIO/Exec. VP
Michael E. Tarvin, Chief Legal Officer/Exec. VP/Corp. Sec.
David S. Chernow, Chief Dev. & Statregy Officer
Scott A. Romberger, Chief Acct. Officer/Controller/Sr. VP
Robert G. Breighner, Jr., VP-Compliance & Audit Svcs.
Robert G. Breighner, Jr., Corp. Compliance Officer
Rocco A. Ortenzio, Exec. Chmn.

Phone: 717-972-1100 **Fax:**

Toll-Free: 888-735-6332

Address: 4714 Old Gettysburg Rd., Mechanicsburg, PA 17055 US

GROWTH PLANS/SPECIAL FEATURES:

Select Medical Holdings Corporation, through its subsidiary Select Medical Corporation, operates specialty acute care hospitals for long-term stay patients in the U.S. The firm operates 944 outpatient rehabilitation clinics in 36 states; 111 long-term acute care hospitals in 25 states; and seven medical rehabilitation hospitals in 3 states. The company also provides medical rehabilitation services on a contract basis at assisted living centers, nursing homes, hospitals, schools, senior care centers and worksites. Select Medical's business is divided between specialty hospitals and outpatient rehabilitation. The company's hospitals treat patients with serious, often complex medical conditions, such as respiratory failure; neuromuscular disorders; cardiac disorders; non-healing wounds; renal disorders; and cancer. Kessler Institute for Rehabilitation, one of Select Medical's most well known hospitals, specializes in treating amputation, spinal cord, stroke and traumatic brain injuries. The majority of Select Medical's specialty hospitals are located in leased space within a host general hospital. The firm's outpatient rehabilitation segment is designed to help patients minimize physical and cognitive impairments and maximize functional ability. Services at its clinics include physical, occupational and speech rehabilitation programs; work injury prevention and management; sports performance; women's health; vestibular rehabilitation; and athletic training services. This segment operates through brand names such as Kentucky Orthopedic Rehab Team, Select Physical Therapy and Kessler Rehabilitation Centers. In addition, the company provides clinical program development; billing support; staff retention strategies; recruiting; training; and assistance with equipment. In April 2011, the firm and Baylor Institute for Rehabilitation created a new joint venture regional rehabilitation network to serve the Dallas-Fort Worth metroplex.

Employees of the firm are offered benefits that include life, health, dental, vision and prescription insurance; a 401(k); personal and family medical leave; short- and long-term disability coverage; continuing education; and tuition reimbursement.

FINANCIALS:

Sales and profits are in thousands of dollars—add 000 to get the full amount. 2010 Note: Financial information for 2010 was not available for all companies at press time.

2010 Sales: $2,390,290 | 2010 Profits: $77,644
2009 Sales: $2,239,871 | 2009 Profits: $78,888
2008 Sales: $2,153,362 | 2008 Profits: $25,834
2007 Sales: $1,991,666 | 2007 Profits: $36,957
2006 Sales: $1,851,498 | 2006 Profits: $94,879

U.S. Stock Ticker: SEM
Int'l Ticker:
Int'l Exchange:
Employees: 18,100 Fiscal Year Ends: 12/31
Parent Company:

SALARIES/BENEFITS:

Pension Plan: | ESOP Stock Plan: | Profit Sharing: | Top Exec. Salary: $848,720 | Bonus: $
Savings Plan: Y | Stock Purch. Plan: | | Second Exec. Salary: $848,720 | Bonus: $

OTHER THOUGHTS:

Apparent Women Officers or Directors: 1
Hot Spot for Advancement for Women/Minorities:

LOCATIONS: ("Y" = Yes)

West:	Southwest:	Midwest:	Southeast:	Northeast:	International:
Y	Y	Y	Y	Y	

SEMPRA ENERGY

www.sempra.com

Industry Group Code: 221

Management:		Sales/Marketing:		Liberal Arts:		Information Sys.:		Professionals:		Tech./Scientific:	
Mgmt. Trainees:	Y	Marketing Pros.:	Y	Gen. Writing/Editing:	Y	Info. Mgmt.:	Y	Finance/Acct.:	Y	Engineers, Elec.:	Y
Experienced Mgmt.:	Y	Retail Sales:		Tech. Writing:	Y	Software Dev.:	Y	Law:	Y	Engineers, Other:	Y
Int'l Business:	Y	Comm./Industrial:	Y	Graphic Arts/Photog.:	Y	Hardware Dev.:		HR/Other:	Y	Health/Lab:	
MBA Grads:	Y	Sales Trainees:		Music:		Consulting/Other:		Training:	Y	Science/Research:	
		Advertising Pros.:	Y	Broadcasting:				Health Care:		Petroleum/Chem.:	Y
				Other:				Consulting:		Math/Other:	

TYPES OF BUSINESS:

Utilities-Electricity & Natural Gas
Energy Management
Energy Marketing
Power Generation-Natural Gas Plants
LNG Pipelines, Storage & Terminals
Power Generation-Solar Power Plants
Power Generation-Wind Farms

BRANDS/DIVISIONS/AFFILIATES:

Southern California Gas Company
San Diego Gas & Electric Company
Sempra Generation
Sempra LNG
Sempra Pipeline & Storage
RBS Sempra Commodities
Pacific Enterprises

CONTACTS: *Note: Officers with more than one job title may be intentionally listed here more than once.*

Debra L. Read, CEO
Neal E. Schmale, COO
Neal E. Schmale, Pres.
Mark A. Snell, CFO/Exec. VP
G. Joyce Rowland, Sr. VP-Human Resources
Javade Chaudhri, General Counsel/Exec. VP
Monica Haas, VP-Corp. Planning
Randall L. Clark, VP-Corp. Rel./Corp. Sec.
Steven D. Davis, VP-Investor Rel. & Corp. Comm.
Joseph A. Householder, Chief Acct. Officer/Controller/Sr. VP
Richard A. Vaccari, Treas./VP
Amy Chiu, VP-Risk Analysis & Mgmt.
Paul Young, Chief Tax Counsel/VP-Tax
Lisa Urick, VP-Audit Svcs.
Donald E. Felsinger, Chmn.

Phone: 619-696-2034 **Fax:** 619-696-2374
Toll-Free: 877-866-2066
Address: 101 Ash St., San Diego, CA 92101 US

GROWTH PLANS/SPECIAL FEATURES:

Sempra Energy provides electric, natural gas and other energy products and services primarily in California as well as internationally. The company operates through two main branches: Sempra Utilities and Sempra Global. Sempra Utilities is comprised of two main companies: Southern California Gas Company, which is a natural gas distribution utility that supplies natural gas to a population of over 20 million in a 20,000-square-mile service territory in southern and central California; and San Diego Gas & Electric Company, which provides electricity distribution and transmission and natural gas distribution services to more than 1.4 million customers across 4,100 square miles in southern Orange County and San Diego, California. The division also includes Pacific Enterprises, the holding company for Southern California Gas Company. Sempra Global is primarily composed of subsidiaries not subject to California utility regulations, including Sempra Generation, Sempra Pipeline & Storage and Sempra LNG. Sempra Generation develops, owns and operates electric power plants in the U.S. and Mexico, including one of the largest thin-film solar power facilities in North America. Sempra Pipeline & Storage develops and operates natural gas pipelines and storage facilities in Mexico and the U.S. Sempra LNG develops liquefied natural gas (LNG) receipt terminals in North America. In November 2010, RBS Sempra Commodities, a joint venture between Sempra Energy and The Royal Bank of Scotland, sold its Sempra Energy Solutions division to Noble Group, Ltd. for roughly $318 million.

Sempra offers its employees medical, dental and vision care; life and AD&D insurance; a pension plan; tuition reimbursement; an employee assistance program; a health club membership subsidy; volunteer/giving incentive programs; and a mass-transit/parking subsidy.

FINANCIALS: **Sales and profits are in thousands of dollars—add 000 to get the full amount. 2010 Note: Financial information for 2010 was not available for all companies at press time.**

2010 Sales: $9,003,000 | 2010 Profits: $739,000
2009 Sales: $8,106,000 | 2009 Profits: $1,119,000
2008 Sales: $10,758,000 | 2008 Profits: $1,113,000
2007 Sales: $11,438,000 | 2007 Profits: $1,099,000
2006 Sales: $11,761,000 | 2006 Profits: $1,406,000

U.S. Stock Ticker: SRE
Int'l Ticker:
Int'l Exchange:
Employees: 13,504 Fiscal Year Ends: 12/31
Parent Company:

SALARIES/BENEFITS:

Pension Plan: Y | ESOP Stock Plan: | Profit Sharing: | Top Exec. Salary: $1,184,300 | Bonus: $2,171,300
Savings Plan: Y | Stock Purch. Plan: | Second Exec. Salary: $833,900 | Bonus: $1,111,900

OTHER THOUGHTS:

Apparent Women Officers or Directors: 5
Hot Spot for Advancement for Women/Minorities: Y

LOCATIONS: ("Y" = Yes)

West:	Southwest:	Midwest:	Southeast:	Northeast:	International:
Y	Y		Y		Y

SENECA FOODS CORPORATION

www.senecafoods.com

Industry Group Code: 311

Management:		Sales/Marketing:		Liberal Arts:		Information Sys.:		Professionals:		Tech./Scientific:	
Mgmt. Trainees:		Marketing Pros.:	Y	Gen. Writing/Editing:	Y	Info. Mgmt.:	Y	Finance/Acct.:	Y	Engineers, Elec.:	
Experienced Mgmt.:	Y	Retail Sales:		Tech. Writing:		Software Dev.:		Law:	Y	Engineers, Other:	Y
Int'l Business:		Comm./Industrial:	Y	Graphic Arts/Photog.:	Y	Hardware Dev.:		HR/Other:	Y	Health/Lab:	
MBA Grads:	Y	Sales Trainees:	Y	Music:		Consulting/Other:		Training:		Science/Research:	
		Advertising Pros.:	Y	Broadcasting:				Health Care:		Petroleum/Chem.:	
				Other:				Consulting:		Math/Other:	

TYPES OF BUSINESS:

Food Products-Manufacturing
Canned and Frozen Foods
Food Processing
Food Service Supply

BRANDS/DIVISIONS/AFFILIATES:

Aunt Nellie's
Read
Libby's
Festal
Seneca
Stokely's
Lebanon Valley Cold Storage, LP
Unilink, LLC

CONTACTS: *Note: Officers with more than one job title may be intentionally listed here more than once.*

Kraig Kayser, CEO
Paul Palmby, COO/Exec. VP
Kraig Kayser, Pres.
Roland Breunig, CFO/Sr. VP/Treas.
Dean E. Erstad, Sr. VP-Sales
Carl Cichetti, CIO
Cynthia Fohrd, Chief Admin. Officer
John Exner, General Counsel
Jeffery L. Van Riper, VP/Controller/Sec.
Arthur Wolcott, Chmn.

Phone: 315-926-8100	**Fax:** 315-926-8300
Toll-Free:	
Address: 3736 S. Main St., Marion, NY 14505 US	

GROWTH PLANS/SPECIAL FEATURES:

Seneca Foods Corporation (SFC) is a producer of canned, bottled, frozen, and packaged vegetables and fruit products. The company sells products under its own brands, but the majority of its business derives from the processing and packing of food for institutional food distributors and private label customers. SFC has two principal operations: the food operation and the non-food operation. The food operation constitutes 99% of total sales, of which 82% is vegetable processing, 16% is fruit processing and 2% is fruit chip processing. The non-food operation, accounting for 1% of sales, is primarily related to the sale of cans and ends and outside revenue generated from the firm's trucking and aircraft operations. The company's products include Libby's canned vegetables and canned and bottled fruit; Aunt Nellie's canned vegetables and salads; Read canned bean and German potato salads; Stokely's canned vegetables; Festal canned pumpkin and squash; and Seneca apple and sweet potato chips. SFC's most significant business alliance is a 20-year agreement with General Mills Operations, Inc. (GMOI). Under this agreement, which was signed in 1995, SFC packs and cans vegetables carrying GMOI's Green Giant brand name. The firm utilizes 27 facilities in Minnesota, Washington, Idaho, New York, California, Illinois and Wisconsin. In addition to retail sales, the firm offers its fruit and vegetable products to the food service industry in institutional size cans, in bulk and in frozen packaging. The food service branch serves schools, hospitals, restaurants and other institutional settings. SFC products are available throughout the U.S. as well as internationally. In August 2010, the firm acquired Lebanon Valley Cold Storage, LP and its subsidiary, Lebanon Valley Cold Storage, LLC; and acquired Unilink, LLC.

Employees are offered medical and dental insurance; disability coverage; a 401(k) and pension plan; group auto and home owners insurance; an assistance program; and flexible spending accounts.

FINANCIALS: **Sales and profits are in thousands of dollars—add 000 to get the full amount. 2010 Note: Financial information for 2010 was not available for all companies at press time.**

2010 Sales: $1,280,110	2010 Profits: $48,411	**U.S. Stock Ticker: SENEA**
2009 Sales: $1,280,684	2009 Profits: $18,765	**Int'l Ticker:**
2008 Sales: $1,080,724	2008 Profits: $8,019	Int'l Exchange:
2007 Sales: $1,024,853	2007 Profits: $32,067	Employees: 3,300 Fiscal Year Ends: 3/31
2006 Sales: $883,823	2006 Profits: $21,993	Parent Company:

SALARIES/BENEFITS:

Pension Plan: Y	ESOP Stock Plan:	Profit Sharing:	Top Exec. Salary: $473,982	Bonus: $237,658
Savings Plan: Y	Stock Purch. Plan:		Second Exec. Salary: $473,538	Bonus: $237,658

OTHER THOUGHTS:

Apparent Women Officers or Directors: 3
Hot Spot for Advancement for Women/Minorities: Y

LOCATIONS: ("Y" = Yes)

West:	Southwest:	Midwest:	Southeast:	Northeast:	International:
Y		Y		Y	

SENSIENT TECHNOLOGIES CORPORATION www.sensient-tech.com

Industry Group Code: 325

Management:		**Sales/Marketing:**		**Liberal Arts:**		**Information Sys.:**		**Professionals:**		**Tech./Scientific:**	
Mgmt. Trainees:	Y	Marketing Pros.:	Y	Gen. Writing/Editing:	Y	Info. Mgmt.:	Y	Finance/Acct.:	Y	Engineers, Elec.:	
Experienced Mgmt.:	Y	Retail Sales:		Tech. Writing:	Y	Software Dev.:	Y	Law:	Y	Engineers, Other:	Y
Int'l Business:	Y	Comm./Industrial:	Y	Graphic Arts/Photog.:	Y	Hardware Dev.:		HR/Other:	Y	Health/Lab:	
MBA Grads:	Y	Sales Trainees:		Music:		Consulting/Other:		Training:	Y	Science/Research:	Y
		Advertising Pros.:		Broadcasting:				Health Care:		Petroleum/Chem.:	Y
				Other:				Consulting:		Math/Other:	

TYPES OF BUSINESS:

Flavor, Fragrance & Color Chemicals
Inks & Pigments
Pharmaceutical & Cosmetic Ingredients
Specialty Chemicals
Dehydrated Vegetables

BRANDS/DIVISIONS/AFFILIATES:

Sensient Food Colors
Sensient Pharmaceutical Technologies
Sensient Paper Colors
Sensient Cosmetic Technologies
Sensient Flavors
Sensient Dehydrated Flavors LLC
Sensient Fragrances

CONTACTS: *Note: Officers with more than one job title may be intentionally listed here more than once.*

Kenneth P. Manning, CEO
Douglas S. Pepper, COO
Douglas S. Pepper, Pres.
Richard F. Hobbs, CFO/Sr. VP
Gordon Hering, VP-Mktg.
Gordon Hering, VP-Tech.
Stephen J. Rolfs, VP-Admin.
John L. Hammond, General Counsel/Sec./VP
Jeffrey T. Makal, Chief Acct. Officer/Controller/VP
John F. Collopy, VP/Treas.
Richard J. Malin, Assistant Controller
Paul Manning, Pres., Color Group
James P. McCarthy, Pres., Flavors & Fragrances Group
Kenneth P. Manning, Chmn.
Robert J. Wilkins, Pres., APAC

Phone: 414-271-6755 **Fax:** 414-347-3785
Toll-Free: 800-558-9892
Address: 777 E. Wisconsin Ave., Milwaukee, WI 53202-5304 US

GROWTH PLANS/SPECIAL FEATURES:

Sensient Technologies Corporation, incorporated in 1882, manufactures and markets fragrances, flavors and colors worldwide. Its operations include producing specialty food and beverage systems; cosmetic and pharmaceutical ingredient systems; and inkjet and specialty inks and colors. The company's customers include major international manufacturers representing some of the world's best-known brands. Sensient is composed of three segments: Flavors & Fragrances Group, Color Group, and Asia Pacific Group. The Flavors & Fragrances Group manufactures and markets flavor and fragrance systems for food, beverage, household and personal care products. Dehydrated flavors generate roughly 29% of this segment's revenue; dairy flavors, 20%; savory flavors, 19%; beverage flavors, 9%; confectionary & bakery flavors, 5%; all other flavors, 9%; and all fragrances combined, 10%. This group's subsidiaries include Sensient Dehydrated Flavors, LLC, Sensient Flavors, LLC and Sensient Fragrances. The Color group manufactures and markets natural and synthetic colors, including those for textiles and papers. Food and beverage colors generate approximately 59% of this segment's revenue; cosmetics, 20%; inkjet & specialty inks and colors, 11%; pharmaceuticals, 4%; and other technical colors, 6%. Trade names within the group include Sensient Food Colors, Sensient Pharmaceutical Technologies, Sensient Cosmetic Technologies and Sensient Paper Colors. Headquartered in Australia, the Asia Pacific Group markets the full line of products for Pacific Rim countries, as well as specialty products designed to appeal to local preferences. It maintains manufacturing facilities in Australia, New Zealand and the Philippines. Sensient has roughly 70 offices located across 30 countries, and 59% of its revenue is generated outside the U.S. In October 2010, the firm opened a new facility in Guangzhou, China.

FINANCIALS: **Sales and profits are in thousands of dollars—add 000 to get the full amount. 2010 Note: Financial information for 2010 was not available for all companies at press time.**

2010 Sales: $1,328,180 — 2010 Profits: $107,144
2009 Sales: $1,201,412 — 2009 Profits: $86,561
2008 Sales: $1,252,620 — 2008 Profits: $90,861
2007 Sales: $1,184,778 — 2007 Profits: $77,786
2006 Sales: $1,098,774 — 2006 Profits: $66,425

U.S. Stock Ticker: SXT
Int'l Ticker:
Int'l Exchange:
Employees: 3,618 Fiscal Year Ends: 12/31
Parent Company:

SALARIES/BENEFITS:

Pension Plan: ESOP Stock Plan: Profit Sharing: Top Exec. Salary: $913,500 Bonus: $1,164,713
Savings Plan: Stock Purch. Plan: Second Exec. Salary: $458,000 Bonus: $446,550

OTHER THOUGHTS:

Apparent Women Officers or Directors: 1
Hot Spot for Advancement for Women/Minorities:

LOCATIONS: ("Y" = Yes)

West:	Southwest:	Midwest:	Southeast:	Northeast:	International:
Y		Y		Y	Y

SHAW GROUP INC (THE)

www.shawgrp.com

Industry Group Code: 237

Management:		Sales/Marketing:		Liberal Arts:		Information Sys.:		Professionals:		Tech./Scientific:	
Mgmt. Trainees:	Y	Marketing Pros.:	Y	Gen. Writing/Editing:		Info. Mgmt.:	Y	Finance/Acct.:	Y	Engineers, Elec.:	Y
Experienced Mgmt.:	Y	Retail Sales:		Tech. Writing:	Y	Software Dev.:		Law:	Y	Engineers, Other:	Y
Int'l Business:	Y	Comm./Industrial:	Y	Graphic Arts/Photog.:	Y	Hardware Dev.:		HR/Other:	Y	Health/Lab:	
MBA Grads:	Y	Sales Trainees:		Music:		Consulting/Other:		Training:	Y	Science/Research:	
		Advertising Pros.:		Broadcasting:				Health Care:		Petroleum/Chem.:	
				Other:				Consulting:		Math/Other:	

TYPES OF BUSINESS:

Pipe Manufacturing
Construction & Engineering
Consulting Services
Environmental Services
Facilities Management
Power Plant Construction
Nuclear Power Plant Construction

BRANDS/DIVISIONS/AFFILIATES:

Westinghouse
Shaw Rolta Limited
Coastal Planning & Engineering, Inc.

CONTACTS: *Note: Officers with more than one job title may be intentionally listed here more than once.*

James M. Bernhard, Jr., CEO
Gary P. Graphia, COO/Exec. VP
James M. Bernhard, Jr., Pres.
Brian K. Ferraioli, CFO/Exec. VP
David L. Chapman, Sr., Pres., Fabrication & Mfg. Group
John Donofrio, General Counsel/Exec. VP/Corp. Sec.
Gentry Brann, VP-Corp. Comm.
Gentry Brann, VP-Investor Rel.
Michael J. Kershaw, Chief Acct. Officer/Sr. VP
Clarence L. Ray Jr., CEO-Power Group
Louis J. Pucher, Pres., Energy & Chemicals Group
George P. Bevan, Pres., Environmental & Infrastructure Group
Ron Barnes, Pres., Fossil, Renewables & Nuclear Div.
James M. Bernhard, Jr., Chmn.

Phone: 225-932-2500	**Fax:** 225-987-3328
Toll-Free:	
Address: 4171 Essen Ln., Baton Rouge, LA 70809 US	

GROWTH PLANS/SPECIAL FEATURES:

The Shaw Group, Inc. is a construction and engineering contractor firm. It is involved in engineering; technology; construction; fabrication; and environmental and industrial services. The company operates in seven segments: power; energy & chemicals (E&C); environmental & infrastructure (E&I); plant services; fabrication & manufacturing (F&M); investment in Westinghouse; and corporate. The power segment provides a range of project-related services, primarily to the global fossil and nuclear power generation industries. The E&C division's offerings include design, engineering, construction, procurement, technology and consulting services, primarily to the oil and gas, refinery, petrochemical and chemical industries. The E&I segment designs and executes remediation solutions involving contaminants in soil, air and water. It also provides project/facilities management for non-environmental construction, watershed restoration, emergency response services, program management and solutions to support and enhance domestic and global land, water and air transportation systems. The maintenance segment performs routine and outage/turnaround maintenance, engineering, construction, recovery and specialty services. The plant services sector' services include fossil/nuclear maintenance and turbine generator repair. The F&M segment supplies fabricated piping systems. Shaw's Investment in Westinghouse division includes its 20% equity interest in Westinghouse, which offers advanced licensing, nuclear plant designs, engineering services, equipment, fuel and other products and services to the international nuclear electric power industry. The corporate segment includes the corporate management and expenses associated with managing the firm. The company's customer base includes multinational oil companies and industrial corporations; regulated utilities; independent and merchant power producers; government agencies; and other equipment manufacturers. In January 2011, Shaw agreed to acquire the additional 50% interest in joint venture Shaw Rolta Limited from partner Rolta India Limited for roughly $23 million. In March 2011, the firm acquired coastal engineering and restoration specialist Coastal Planning & Engineering Inc. for roughly $26 million.

FINANCIALS: **Sales and profits are in thousands of dollars—add 000 to get the full amount. 2010 Note: Financial information for 2010 was not available for all companies at press time.**

2010 Sales: $7,000,800	2010 Profits: $92,700	**U.S. Stock Ticker: SHAW**
2009 Sales: $7,279,690	2009 Profits: $14,995	**Int'l Ticker:**
2008 Sales: $6,998,011	2008 Profits: $140,717	Int'l Exchange:
2007 Sales: $5,723,712	2007 Profits: $-19,000	Employees: 27,000 Fiscal Year Ends: 8/31
2006 Sales: $4,775,649	2006 Profits: $50,226	Parent Company:

SALARIES/BENEFITS:

Pension Plan:	ESOP Stock Plan:	Profit Sharing:	Top Exec. Salary: $1,972,768	Bonus: $580,800
Savings Plan: Y	Stock Purch. Plan:		Second Exec. Salary: $853,679	Bonus: $482,933

OTHER THOUGHTS:

Apparent Women Officers or Directors: 1
Hot Spot for Advancement for Women/Minorities:

LOCATIONS: ("Y" = Yes)

West:	Southwest:	Midwest:	Southeast:	Northeast:	International:
Y	Y	Y	Y	Y	Y

SHELL OIL CO

www.shell.us

Industry Group Code: 211111

Management:		Sales/Marketing:		Liberal Arts:		Information Sys.:		Professionals:		Tech./Scientific:	
Mgmt. Trainees:	Y	Marketing Pros.:	Y	Gen. Writing/Editing:	Y	Info. Mgmt.:	Y	Finance/Acct.:	Y	Engineers, Elec.:	Y
Experienced Mgmt.:	Y	Retail Sales:		Tech. Writing:	Y	Software Dev.:	Y	Law:	Y	Engineers, Other:	Y
Int'l Business:	Y	Comm./Industrial:		Graphic Arts/Photog.:	Y	Hardware Dev.:		HR/Other:	Y	Health/Lab:	
MBA Grads:	Y	Sales Trainees:		Music:		Consulting/Other:		Training:	Y	Science/Research:	Y
		Advertising Pros.:	Y	Broadcasting:				Health Care:		Petroleum/Chem.:	Y
				Other:				Consulting:		Math/Other:	Y

TYPES OF BUSINESS:

Oil & Gas Exploration & Production
Chemicals
Power Generation
Nanocomposites
Nanocatalysts
Refineries
Pipelines & Shipping
Hydrogen Storage Technology

BRANDS/DIVISIONS/AFFILIATES:

Shell Oil Products US
Shell Chemicals Limited
Shell Gas and Power
Shell Exploration and Production
Royal Dutch Shell (Shell Group)
Motiva Enterprises LLC
Shell Hydrogen
Shell Wind Energy

CONTACTS: *Note: Officers with more than one job title may be intentionally listed here more than once.*

Marvin E. Odum, Pres.
Bill Lowrey, General Counsel/Sr. VP/Corp. Sec.
Curtis R. Frasier, Exec. VP-Americas Shell Gas & Power
Marvin E. Odum, Dir.-Shell-Upstream Americas
Mark Quartermain, Pres., Shell Energy North America (US) LP

Phone: 713-241-6161	**Fax:** 713-241-4044
Toll-Free:	
Address: 910 Louisiana St., Houston, TX 77002 US	

GROWTH PLANS/SPECIAL FEATURES:

Shell Oil Co., an affiliate of the Shell Group, is a chemical, oil and natural gas producer in the U.S., with operations in all 50 states. Shell Oil has a number of divisions, joint ventures and operations, including Shell Oil Products U.S., Motiva Enterprises, Shell Chemicals, Shell Gas and Power, Shell Exploration and Production (SEPCo) and others. These companies discover, develop, manufacture, transport and market crude oil, natural gas and chemical products. Specifically, Motiva Enterprises has three refineries which produce a total of 740,000 barrels of oil per day, as well as a network of approximately 7,700 Shell-branded stations in the eastern and southern U.S. Shell Chemicals is involved in manufacturing chemicals, including ethylene and propylene, for use in cars, computers, packaging and paints. It manufactures 15 billion pounds of chemicals annually for industrial use through three plants. SEPCo explores and develops natural gas in the U.S, with interests in five states and the Gulf of Mexico. Shell Oil's Gas and Power business is involved in power generation, gas pipeline transmission, receiving terminals, liquefied natural gas (LNG), shipping and coal gasification. Other divisions include Shell Hydrogen, focused on the development of hydrogen and fuel cell technologies from regional bases in Houston and Tokyo; and Shell Wind Energy, with eight wind farms in the U.S. and 11 in total.

Employees are offered medical and vision insurance; flexible spending accounts; disability coverage; group auto and home insurance; a group legal plan; a pension plan; a savings plan; and an employee assistance program.

FINANCIALS: **Sales and profits are in thousands of dollars—add 000 to get the full amount. 2010 Note: Financial information for 2010 was not available for all companies at press time.**

2010 Sales: $120,000,000	2010 Profits: $	**U.S. Stock Ticker: Subsidiary**
2009 Sales: $100,000,000	2009 Profits: $	**Int'l Ticker:**
2008 Sales: $100,818,000	2008 Profits: $	Int'l Exchange:
2007 Sales: $87,548,000	2007 Profits: $	Employees: 22,000 Fiscal Year Ends: 12/31
2006 Sales: $80,974,000	2006 Profits: $	Parent Company: ROYAL DUTCH SHELL PLC

SALARIES/BENEFITS:

Pension Plan: Y	ESOP Stock Plan:	Profit Sharing:	Top Exec. Salary: $	Bonus: $
Savings Plan: Y	Stock Purch. Plan: Y		Second Exec. Salary: $	Bonus: $

OTHER THOUGHTS:

Apparent Women Officers or Directors:
Hot Spot for Advancement for Women/Minorities:

LOCATIONS: ("Y" = Yes)

West:	Southwest:	Midwest:	Southeast:	Northeast:	International:
Y	Y	Y	Y	Y	Y

SHERWIN WILLIAMS COMPANY (THE) www.sherwin-williams.com

Industry Group Code: 444120

Management:		Sales/Marketing:		Liberal Arts:		Information Sys.:		Professionals:		Tech./Scientific:	
Mgmt. Trainees:	Y	Marketing Pros.:	Y	Gen. Writing/Editing:	Y	Info. Mgmt.:	Y	Finance/Acct.:	Y	Engineers, Elec.:	
Experienced Mgmt.:	Y	Retail Sales:	Y	Tech. Writing:	Y	Software Dev.:	Y	Law:	Y	Engineers, Other:	
Int'l Business:	Y	Comm./Industrial:	Y	Graphic Arts/Photog.:	Y	Hardware Dev.:		HR/Other:	Y	Health/Lab:	
MBA Grads:	Y	Sales Trainees:	Y	Music:		Consulting/Other:		Training:	Y	Science/Research:	Y
		Advertising Pros.:	Y	Broadcasting:				Health Care:		Petroleum/Chem.:	Y
				Other:				Consulting:		Math/Other:	

TYPES OF BUSINESS:

Paints & Coatings Manufacturing
Retail Paint Stores
Wall Coverings
Automotive Finishing Products
Design Consulting

BRANDS/DIVISIONS/AFFILIATES:

Duron Inc
Martin-Senour
Dutch Boy
Thompson's
Becker Powder Coatings, Inc
Minwax
Pratt & Lambert
Sayerlack Industrial Wood Coatings

CONTACTS: *Note: Officers with more than one job title may be intentionally listed here more than once.*

Christopher M. Connor, CEO
John G. Morikis, COO
John G. Morikis, Pres.
Sean P. Hennessy, CFO/Sr. VP-Finance
Thomas E. Hopkins, Sr. VP-Human Resources
Richard M. Weaver, VP-Admin.
Louis E. Stellato, General Counsel/Sec./Sr. VP
Steven J. Oberfeld, Sr. VP-Corp. Planning & Dev.
Robert J. Wells, VP-Corp. Comm. & Public Affairs
Cynthia D. Brogan, Treas./VP
Michael T. Cummins, VP-Taxes
Mark J. Dvoroznak, VP-Corp. Audit & Loss Prevention
Allen J. Mistysyn, VP/Controller
Christopher M. Connor, Chmn.

Phone: 216-566-2200 **Fax:** 216-566-2947
Toll-Free: 800-474-3794
Address: 101 Prospect Ave. NW, Cleveland, OH 44115-1075 US

GROWTH PLANS/SPECIAL FEATURES:

The Sherwin-Williams Company is one of the largest international manufacturers, distributors and retailers of paint and related products to professional, industrial, commercial and retail customers. The company operates in three segments: Paint Stores Group, Consumer Group and Global Finishes group. The Paint Stores group consists of 3,390 company-operated stores, which sell Sherwin-Williams brand architectural paint, coating and other associated products and brands. Several subsidiaries operate under this division, including Duron, Inc., a Maryland paint producer. In 2010, this segment opened 36 new stores. It has operations in the U.S., Canada, Puerto Rico, Jamaica, Trinidad and Tobago and the Virgin Islands. This division also sells industrial products, marine products and finishes for original equipment manufacturers (OEM). The Consumer Group produces and distributes paint, coatings and related products to third-party customers and to the Paint Stores Group (which represents 53% of the consumer group's sales). The Global Finishes Group, through 564 branches, manufactures, licenses, distributes and sells paints and coatings; industrial and marine products, automotive finishes; refinish products; and OEM coatings. In all three segments, the company's varnish, applicators, paint, finishes and coatings are marketed under various name brands, including several private labels such as Sherwin-Williams, Sayerlack, Pratt & Lambert, Martin-Senour, Dutch Boy, Thompson's, Minwax and Krylon. In September 2010, Sherwin-Williams acquired Becker Industrial Products, AB.

Sherwin-Williams offers its employees medical, vision and dental insurance; a pension plan; a stock purchase plan; tuition aid; adoption assistance; short- and long-term disability coverage; and life insurance.

FINANCIALS: **Sales and profits are in thousands of dollars—add 000 to get the full amount. 2010 Note: Financial information for 2010 was not available for all companies at press time.**

2010 Sales: $7,776,000 | 2010 Profits: $462,000
2009 Sales: $7,094,000 | 2009 Profits: $436,000
2008 Sales: $7,980,000 | 2008 Profits: $477,000
2007 Sales: $8,005,000 | 2007 Profits: $616,000
2006 Sales: $7,810,000 | 2006 Profits: $576,000

U.S. Stock Ticker: SHW
Int'l Ticker:
Int'l Exchange:
Employees: 32,228 Fiscal Year Ends: 12/31
Parent Company:

SALARIES/BENEFITS:

Pension Plan: Y | ESOP Stock Plan: | Profit Sharing: | Top Exec. Salary: $1,221,987 | Bonus: $2,085,000
Savings Plan: Y | Stock Purch. Plan: Y | | Second Exec. Salary: $748,953 | Bonus: $910,000

OTHER THOUGHTS:

Apparent Women Officers or Directors: 2
Hot Spot for Advancement for Women/Minorities: Y

LOCATIONS: ("Y" = Yes)

West:	Southwest:	Midwest:	Southeast:	Northeast:	International:
Y	Y	Y	Y	Y	Y

SIGMA-ALDRICH CORP

www.sigmaaldrich.com

Industry Group Code: 325

Management:		**Sales/Marketing:**		**Liberal Arts:**		**Information Sys.:**		**Professionals:**		**Tech./Scientific:**	
Mgmt. Trainees:	Y	Marketing Pros.:	Y	Gen. Writing/Editing:		Info. Mgmt.:	Y	Finance/Acct.:	Y	Engineers, Elec.:	Y
Experienced Mgmt.:	Y	Retail Sales:		Tech. Writing:	Y	Software Dev.:	Y	Law:	Y	Engineers, Other:	Y
Int'l Business:	Y	Comm./Industrial:	Y	Graphic Arts/Photog.:		Hardware Dev.:		HR/Other:	Y	Health/Lab:	
MBA Grads:	Y	Sales Trainees:		Music:		Consulting/Other:		Training:	Y	Science/Research:	Y
		Advertising Pros.:		Broadcasting:				Health Care:		Petroleum/Chem.:	Y
				Other:				Consulting:		Math/Other:	

TYPES OF BUSINESS:

Chemicals Manufacturing
Biotechnology Equipment
Pharmaceutical Ingredients
Fine Chemicals
Chromatography Products

BRANDS/DIVISIONS/AFFILIATES:

Research Essentials
Research Specialties
Research Biotech
SAFC
Cerilliant Corp
Resource Technology Corp
Vetec Quimica Fina Ltda

CONTACTS: *Note: Officers with more than one job title may be intentionally listed here more than once.*

Rakesh Sachdev, CEO
Rakesh Sachdev, Pres.
Kirk Richter, Interim CFO/VP
Gerrit van den Dool, VP-Sales
Doug Rau, VP-Human Resources
Magnus Borg, CIO/VP
Rakesh Sachdev, Chief Admin. Officer
George Miller, General Counsel/Sr. VP/Sec.
Karen Miller, VP-Strategy & Corp. Dev.
Kirk Richter, Treas.
Gilles Cottier, Pres., SAFC
Frank Wicks, Pres., Research Specialties & Essentials
David Smoller, Pres., Research Biotech
Steve Walton, VP-Quality & Safety
Barret A. Toan, Chmn.
Joseph Porwoll, Pres., Supply Chain

Phone: 314-771-5765 **Fax:** 314-771-5757
Toll-Free: 800-521-8956
Address: 3050 Spruce St., St. Louis, MO 63103 US

GROWTH PLANS/SPECIAL FEATURES:

Sigma-Aldrich Corp. is a life science and technology company that develops, manufactures, purchases and distributes a broad range of biochemicals and organic chemicals. The company offers roughly 147,000 chemicals (including 48,000 chemicals manufactured in-house) and 40,000 equipment products used for scientific and genomic research; biotechnology; pharmaceutical development; disease diagnosis; and pharmaceutical and high technology manufacturing. Sigma-Aldrich is structured into four units: research essentials, research specialties, research biotech and SAFC. The research essentials unit sells biological buffers; cell culture reagents; biochemicals; chemicals; solvents; and other reagents and kits. The research specialties unit provides organic chemicals, biochemicals, analytical reagents, chromatography consumables, reference materials and high-purity products. The research biotech unit supplies immunochemical, molecular biology, cell signaling and neuroscience biochemicals and kits used in biotechnology, genomic, proteomic and other life science research applications. The SAFC (fine chemicals) unit offers large-scale organic chemicals and biochemicals used in development and production by pharmaceutical, biotechnology, industrial and diagnostic companies. The company operates in 40 countries, sells its products in nearly 160 countries and services over 1 million customers. Customers include commercial laboratories; pharmaceutical and industrial companies; universities; diagnostics, chemical and biotechnology companies and hospitals; non-profit organizations; and governmental institutions. In December 2010, Sigma-Aldrich acquired Cerilliant Corp. in Round Rock, Texas, which added about 2,800 products to the company's portfolio. In January 2011, the firm purchased Resource Technology Corp., which specializes in analytical chemistry products. In May 2011, Sigma-Aldrich obtained the Brazil-based Vetec Quimica Fina Ltda., which produces over 3,000 products. In April 2011, the company unveiled its new European headquarters in St. Gallen, Switzerland.

FINANCIALS: **Sales and profits are in thousands of dollars—add 000 to get the full amount. 2010 Note: Financial information for 2010 was not available for all companies at press time.**

2010 Sales: $2,271,000 | 2010 Profits: $384,000
2009 Sales: $2,147,600 | 2009 Profits: $346,700
2008 Sales: $2,200,700 | 2008 Profits: $341,500
2007 Sales: $2,038,700 | 2007 Profits: $311,100
2006 Sales: $1,797,500 | 2006 Profits: $276,800

U.S. Stock Ticker: SIAL
Int'l Ticker:
Int'l Exchange:
Employees: 7,890 Fiscal Year Ends: 12/31
Parent Company:

SALARIES/BENEFITS:

Pension Plan: Y | ESOP Stock Plan: | Profit Sharing: | Top Exec. Salary: $809,711 | Bonus: $1,052,700
Savings Plan: Y | Stock Purch. Plan: | Second Exec. Salary: $488,846 | Bonus: $443,352

OTHER THOUGHTS:

Apparent Women Officers or Directors: 2
Hot Spot for Advancement for Women/Minorities: Y

LOCATIONS: ("Y" = Yes)

West:	Southwest:	Midwest:	Southeast:	Northeast:	International:
Y	Y	Y	Y	Y	Y

Sales, profits and employees may be estimates. Financial information, benefits and other data can change quickly and may vary from those stated here.

SKILLED HEALTHCARE GROUP INC www.skilledhealthcaregroup.com

Industry Group Code: 623110

Management:		Sales/Marketing:		Liberal Arts:		Information Sys.:		Professionals:		Tech./Scientific:	
Mgmt. Trainees:	Y	Marketing Pros.:	Y	Gen. Writing/Editing:		Info. Mgmt.:	Y	Finance/Acct.:	Y	Engineers, Elec.:	
Experienced Mgmt.:		Retail Sales:		Tech. Writing:	Y	Software Dev.:		Law:	Y	Engineers, Other:	
Int'l Business:		Comm./Industrial:	Y	Graphic Arts/Photog.:		Hardware Dev.:		HR/Other:	Y	Health/Lab:	
MBA Grads:	Y	Sales Trainees:		Music:		Consulting/Other:		Training:	Y	Science/Research:	
		Advertising Pros.:	Y	Broadcasting:				Health Care:		Petroleum/Chem.:	
				Other:				Consulting:		Math/Other:	

TYPES OF BUSINESS:

Operating Skilled Nursing & Assisted Living Facilities
Rehabilitation Therapy
Hospice Care

BRANDS/DIVISIONS/AFFILIATES:

Onex Corporation
Express Recovery
Hallmark Rehabilitation, Inc.
Hospice Care of the West
St. Joseph Transitional Rehabilitation Center
Luke Healthcare and Rehabilitation Center
Woodland Care Center

CONTACTS: *Note: Officers with more than one job title may be intentionally listed here more than once.*

Boyd W. Hendrickson, CEO
Jose C. Lynch, COO
Jose C. Lynch, Pres.
Devasis Ghose, CFO/Exec. VP
Roland Rapp, Chief Admin. Officer/Exec. VP
Roland Rapp, General Counsel/Sec.
Christopher N. Felfe, Chief Acct. Officer/Sr. VP-Finance
Matthew Moore, Exec. VP-Inpatient Svcs.
Susan Thomas Whittle, Chief Compliance Officer/Sr. VP
Boyd W. Hendrickson, Chmn.

Phone: 949-282-5800 **Fax:** 949-282-5889
Toll-Free:
Address: 27442 Portola Pkwy., Ste. 200, Foothill Ranch, CA 92610 US

GROWTH PLANS/SPECIAL FEATURES:

Skilled Healthcare Group, Inc. owns and operates skilled nursing and assisted living facilities. Its 78 skilled nursing facilities are in located suburban and large urban markets in California, Kansas, Iowa, Missouri, Nevada, New Mexico and Texas. These facilities, which in total have approximately 9,566 beds, typically target high-acuity patients, recovering from strokes; cardiovascular ailments; joint replacements; and other neurological, muscular or skeletal conditions. These facilities often include the Express Recovery program for patients recovering form joint replacement surgery as well as cardiac and respiratory ailments. These units feature an extensive rehabilitation therapy regimen, a separate entrance and 12-36 beds. The company's 22 assisted living facilities have approximately 1,264 licensed beds, and provide simple services such as meals, activities and security at a lower level of nursing care than available in the nursing homes. Skilled Healthcare owns roughly 77% of its facilities. The company also operates several independent living units. The firm's subsidiary, Hallmark Rehabilitation, Inc., contracts with nursing homes to provide rehabilitation therapy services typically to high-acuity patients. Skilled Healthcare endeavors to meet the spiritual, physical and mental needs of terminally ill patients and their families through Hospice Care of the West, providing counseling, education, clinical and palliative care (which can offer pain relief but no cure). The firm derives approximately 88.2% of its revenues from long-term care services, with ancillary services accounting for the remaining 11.8%. Onex Corporation owns a majority of the company's stock. In December 2010, the firm sold its Westside Campus of Care skilled nursing facility in Texas; it also acquired three previously leased facilities: St. Joseph Transitional Rehabilitation Center, located in Nevada; and Luke Healthcare and Rehabilitation Center and Woodland Care Center, located in California. In March 2011, Skilled Healthcare agreed to transfer operations of five facilities to Brius Healthcare, LLC.

FINANCIALS: **Sales and profits are in thousands of dollars—add 000 to get the full amount. 2010 Note: Financial information for 2010 was not available for all companies at press time.**

2010 Sales: $820,238 2010 Profits: $-1,041
2009 Sales: $759,751 2009 Profits: $-133,181
2008 Sales: $733,330 2008 Profits: $34,096
2007 Sales: $634,607 2007 Profits: $7,928
2006 Sales: $531,657 2006 Profits: $17,337

U.S. Stock Ticker: SKH
Int'l Ticker:
Int'l Exchange:
Employees: 9,489 Fiscal Year Ends: 12/31
Parent Company: ONEX CORPORATION

SALARIES/BENEFITS:

Pension Plan: ESOP Stock Plan: Profit Sharing: Top Exec. Salary: $650,000 Bonus: $380,000
Savings Plan: Stock Purch. Plan: Second Exec. Salary: $520,000 Bonus: $230,750

OTHER THOUGHTS:

Apparent Women Officers or Directors: 3
Hot Spot for Advancement for Women/Minorities: Y

LOCATIONS: ("Y" = Yes)

West:	Southwest:	Midwest:	Southeast:	Northeast:	International:
Y	Y	Y			

Sales, profits and employees may be estimates. Financial information, benefits and other data can change quickly and may vary from those stated here.

SNYDERS-LANCE INC

www.lance.com

Industry Group Code: 31191

Management:		Sales/Marketing:		Liberal Arts:		Information Sys.:		Professionals:		Tech./Scientific:	
Mgmt. Trainees:	Y	Marketing Pros.:	Y	Gen. Writing/Editing:		Info. Mgmt.:	Y	Finance/Acct.:	Y	Engineers, Elec.:	
Experienced Mgmt.:	Y	Retail Sales:		Tech. Writing:		Software Dev.:		Law:	Y	Engineers, Other:	
Int'l Business:	Y	Comm./Industrial:	Y	Graphic Arts/Photog.:		Hardware Dev.:		HR/Other:	Y	Health/Lab:	
MBA Grads:	Y	Sales Trainees:		Music:		Consulting/Other:		Training:	Y	Science/Research:	
		Advertising Pros.:		Broadcasting:				Health Care:		Petroleum/Chem.:	
				Other:				Consulting:		Math/Other:	

TYPES OF BUSINESS:

Snack Foods, Manufacturing
Distribution Services

BRANDS/DIVISIONS/AFFILIATES:

Lance, Inc.
Snyder's of Hanover, Inc.
Cape Cod Potato Chips
Captain's Wafers
O-Ke-Doke
Tom's
Stella D'oro
Krunchers!

CONTACTS: *Note: Officers with more than one job title may be intentionally listed here more than once.*

David V. Singer, CEO
Carl E. Lee, Jr., COO
Carl E. Lee, Jr., Pres.
Rick D. Puckett, CFO/Exec. VP/Treas.
Kevin A. Henry, Chief Human Resources Officer/Sr. VP
Rick D. Puckett, Corp. Sec.
Margaret E. Wicklund, Controller/Principal Acct. Officer/VP
Michael A. Warehime, Chmn.
Blake W. Thompson, Sr. VP-Supply Chain

Phone: 704-554-1421 **Fax:** 704-554-5562
Toll-Free: 800-438-1880
Address: 14120 Ballantyne Corporate Pl., Ste. 350, Charlotte, NC 28277 US

GROWTH PLANS/SPECIAL FEATURES:

Snyder's-Lance, Inc., formerly Lance, Inc., manufactures, markets and distributes snack food products. The combined company was formed in December 2010 following a merger of equals transaction between Snyder's of Hanover, Inc. and Lance. Snyder's is a leading manufacturer of pretzels and other snack foods available throughout the U.S., Canada, Europe, Asia and the Middle East. The new company now produces numerous varieties of snacks, including sandwich crackers and cookies; restaurant style crackers; potato chips and pretzels; tortilla chips; cookies; sugar wafers; nuts; candy; and other salty snacks. The company sells these products under such brands as Lance, Snyder's of Hanover, Cape Cod, Grande, Tom's, Jays, O-Ke-Doke, Stella D'oro, Krunchers!, Archway and Naturals. Additionally, the firm produces various private label snacks for third-party retailers. It also purchases a small percentage of products for resale, manufacturing roughly 97% of the products it sells. The company's direct-store delivery (DSD) system consists of approximately 1,100 sales routes in 24 states, mostly located within the southeastern and mid-Atlantic states. Each sales route is served by one sales representative, with the company using its own vehicle fleet to make weekly deliveries. Its customers include convenience stores, grocery stores, distributors, mass merchandisers, food service establishments, club stores, discount stores, drug stores, school, recreational facilities, independent retailers and military and government facilities. The combined company has manufacturing facilities in Goodyear, Arizona; Charlotte, North Carolina; Burlington, Iowa; Jeffersonville, Indiana; Columbus, Georgia; Hanover, Pennsylvania; Hyannis, Massachusetts; Corsicana, Texas; Perry, Florida; Cambridge, Ontario; Guelph, Ontario; and Waterloo, Ontario. In December 2010, Lance, Inc. and Snyder's of Hanover, Inc. completed their merger transaction.

FINANCIALS: **Sales and profits are in thousands of dollars—add 000 to get the full amount. 2010 Note: Financial information for 2010 was not available for all companies at press time.**

2010 Sales: $979,835	2010 Profits: $2,512
2009 Sales: $918,163	2009 Profits: $35,794
2008 Sales: $852,468	2008 Profits: $17,706
2007 Sales: $762,736	2007 Profits: $23,838
2006 Sales: $730,116	2006 Profits: $18,478

U.S. Stock Ticker: LNCE
Int'l Ticker:
Int'l Exchange:
Employees: 7,000 Fiscal Year Ends: 12/31
Parent Company:

SALARIES/BENEFITS:

Pension Plan:	ESOP Stock Plan:	Profit Sharing: Y	Top Exec. Salary: $660,000	Bonus: $719,400
Savings Plan: Y	Stock Purch. Plan: Y		Second Exec. Salary: $401,310	Bonus: $218,800

OTHER THOUGHTS:

Apparent Women Officers or Directors: 1
Hot Spot for Advancement for Women/Minorities:

LOCATIONS: ("Y" = Yes)

West:	Southwest:	Midwest:	Southeast:	Northeast:	International:
	Y	Y	Y	Y	Y

SODEXO INC

www.sodexousa.com

Industry Group Code: 722310

Management:		**Sales/Marketing:**		**Liberal Arts:**		**Information Sys.:**		**Professionals:**		**Tech./Scientific:**	
Mgmt. Trainees:	Y	Marketing Pros.:	Y	Gen. Writing/Editing:	Y	Info. Mgmt.:	Y	Finance/Acct.:	Y	Engineers, Elec.:	
Experienced Mgmt.:	Y	Retail Sales:		Tech. Writing:		Software Dev.:		Law:	Y	Engineers, Other:	
Int'l Business:	Y	Comm./Industrial:	Y	Graphic Arts/Photog.:		Hardware Dev.:		HR/Other:	Y	Health/Lab:	
MBA Grads:	Y	Sales Trainees:		Music:		Consulting/Other:		Training:	Y	Science/Research:	
		Advertising Pros.:	Y	Broadcasting:				Health Care:		Petroleum/Chem.:	
				Other:				Consulting:		Math/Other:	

TYPES OF BUSINESS:

Food Service Outsourcing
Facilities Management
Laundry Services
Sports Arena Management
Plant Management
Grounds Keeping
Asset Management
Outsourced Procurement Services

BRANDS/DIVISIONS/AFFILIATES:

Sodexho Group
Sodexho Foundation
Sodexho Alliance
Entegra Procurement Services

CONTACTS: *Note: Officers with more than one job title may be intentionally listed here more than once.*

George Chavel, CEO
Lorna Donatone, COO
George Chavel, Pres.
Debbie White, CFO/Sr. VP
Peri Bridger, Sr. VP-Human Resources
Tony Tocco, CIO/Sr. VP
Michael Montelongo, Chief Admin. Officer/Sr. VP
Jessica P. Montoya, Assistant General Counsel/VP-Gov't Affairs
Stephen J. Brady, Sr. VP-Corp. Comm.
Jaya K. Bohlmann, Sr. VP-Public Rel.
Lorna Donatone, Pres., Education Market
Rohini Anand, Sr. VP/Global Chief Diversity Officer

Phone: 301-987-4500 **Fax:** 301-987-4438
Toll-Free: 800-763-3946
Address: 9801 Washingtonian Blvd., Gaithersburg, MD 20878 US

GROWTH PLANS/SPECIAL FEATURES:

Sodexo, Inc. is the North American subsidiary of French firm the Sodexo Group, a global contract foodservice supplier. The company is one of the largest providers of contract food and facilities management services in the U.S., Mexico and Canada, with more than 6,000 clients and 700 facilities management sites. In total, it serves 9.3 million meals to 10 million consumers each year. Sodexo offers a wide variety of outsourcing solutions in food service, housekeeping, grounds keeping, facilities management, business strategy, laundry services and asset and materials management. The company provides these services to corporations; health care, long term care and retirement centers; conference centers; schools; college campuses; military bases; and government and remote sites. Services to college stadiums and arenas involve concession stands, catering, physical plant management and sports field management. The firm also has a contract to manage the food operations for the U.S. Marine Corps, which includes meal preparation, operation of clean dining facilities and bringing national brands to Navy bases, Army bases and international locations. In addition, the company sponsors the Sodexo Foundation, an independent charitable organization that supports initiatives addressing the problems of hunger in children and families. In February 2010, the firm joined with First Lady Michelle Obama's campaign to eliminate childhood obesity within a generation. The Entegra Procurement Services unit provides food and supplies purchasing management for 10,000 clients in hospitality and other industries.

Employees of the firm are offered a 401(k) savings plan; health and family care spending accounts; employee assistance; tuition reimbursement; medical, dental and vision plans; and an employee stock purchase program (ESPP).

FINANCIALS: **Sales and profits are in thousands of dollars—add 000 to get the full amount. 2010 Note: Financial information for 2010 was not available for all companies at press time.**

2010 Sales: $8,000,000	2010 Profits: $	**U.S. Stock Ticker: Subsidiary**
2009 Sales: $	2009 Profits: $	**Int'l Ticker:**
2008 Sales: $	2008 Profits: $	Int'l Exchange:
2007 Sales: $	2007 Profits: $	Employees: 120,000 Fiscal Year Ends: 8/31
2006 Sales: $	2006 Profits: $	Parent Company: SODEXO GROUP

SALARIES/BENEFITS:

Pension Plan: Y	ESOP Stock Plan:	Profit Sharing:	Top Exec. Salary: $	Bonus: $
Savings Plan: Y	Stock Purch. Plan: Y		Second Exec. Salary: $	Bonus: $

OTHER THOUGHTS:

Apparent Women Officers or Directors: 6
Hot Spot for Advancement for Women/Minorities: Y

LOCATIONS: ("Y" = Yes)

West:	Southwest:	Midwest:	Southeast:	Northeast:	International:
Y	Y	Y	Y	Y	Y

SOUTHERN COMPANY (THE)

www.southerncompany.com

Industry Group Code: 2211

Management:		Sales/Marketing:		Liberal Arts:		Information Sys.:		Professionals:		Tech./Scientific:	
Mgmt. Trainees:	Y	Marketing Pros.:	Y	Gen. Writing/Editing:	Y	Info. Mgmt.:	Y	Finance/Acct.:	Y	Engineers, Elec.:	Y
Experienced Mgmt.:	Y	Retail Sales:		Tech. Writing:	Y	Software Dev.:	Y	Law:	Y	Engineers, Other:	Y
Int'l Business:		Comm./Industrial:	Y	Graphic Arts/Photog.:	Y	Hardware Dev.:		HR/Other:	Y	Health/Lab:	
MBA Grads:	Y	Sales Trainees:		Music:		Consulting/Other:		Training:	Y	Science/Research:	
		Advertising Pros.:	Y	Broadcasting:				Health Care:		Petroleum/Chem.:	Y
				Other:				Consulting:		Math/Other:	

TYPES OF BUSINESS:

Utilities-Electricity & Natural Gas
Wireless Communications Services
Fiber Optic Solutions
Nuclear Power Operating Services
Consulting Services
Power Generation Construction

BRANDS/DIVISIONS/AFFILIATES:

Alabama Power Company
Georgia Power Company
Mississippi Power Company
Gulf Power Company
Southern Power
SEGCO
Southern Nuclear
SouthernLINC Wireless

CONTACTS:

Note: Officers with more than one job title may be intentionally listed here more than once.

Thomas A. Fanning, CEO
Anthony J. Topazi, COO/Exec. VP
Thomas A. Fanning, Pres.
Art P. Beattie, CFO/Exec. VP
G. Edison Holland, Jr., General Counsel/Exec. VP/Sec.
Chris Womack, Pres., External Affairs
Michael D. Garrett, CEO/Pres., Georgia Power
Mark A. Crosswhite, Pres./CEO-Gulf Power Company
Charles D. McCrary, Exec. VP
James H. Miller, III, Chmn./CEO/Pres., Southern Nuclear
Thomas A. Fanning, Chmn.

Phone: 404-506-5000	**Fax:** 404-506-0455
Toll-Free:	
Address: 30 Ivan Allen Jr. Blvd., NW, Atlanta, GA 30308 US	

GROWTH PLANS/SPECIAL FEATURES:

The Southern Company, through its subsidiaries, is a producer and distributor of electricity in the U.S. Its four main subsidiaries (Alabama Power Company, Georgia Power Company, Mississippi Power Company and Gulf Power Company) have a combined service territory of 120,000 square miles. It also owns Southern Power, which constructs, acquires and manages power generation assets and sells electricity. Southern Power owns 7,880 megawatts (MW) of generating capacity through a total of 10 power plants, and serves investor-owned utilities, independent power producers, municipalities and electric cooperatives across five states. Alabama Power and Georgia Power each own 50% of SEGCO, which operates a power generation plant and 230,000 miles of transmission lines in Alabama, supplying electricity to both Alabama and Georgia. Combined, Southern Company's utility subsidiaries have a generating capacity of over 42,000 MW and serve more than 4.4 million residential, commercial and industrial electricity customers in the southeastern U.S. through 80 fossil and hydro generation plants. Its sources of generation consist of 55% coal; 23.7% oil and gas; 14.1% nuclear; 4.7% purchased power; and 2.5% hydro. The firm also owns Southern Nuclear, which operates the company's nuclear power plants; SouthernLINC Wireless, which provides digital wireless communications and wholesale fiber optic solutions; and Southern Renewable Energy, formed in early 2010 to acquire, own and construct renewable generation assets.

The Southern Company offers its employees medical, dental and prescription drug coverage; an employee assistance program; life insurance; flexible spending accounts; tuition reimbursement; adoption assistance; a pension plan; and a savings plan.

FINANCIALS:

Sales and profits are in thousands of dollars—add 000 to get the full amount. 2010 Note: Financial information for 2010 was not available for all companies at press time.

2010 Sales: $17,456,000	2010 Profits: $1,975,000	**U.S. Stock Ticker: SO**
2009 Sales: $15,743,000	2009 Profits: $1,643,000	**Int'l Ticker:**
2008 Sales: $17,127,000	2008 Profits: $1,742,000	Int'l Exchange:
2007 Sales: $15,353,000	2007 Profits: $1,734,000	Employees: 25,940 Fiscal Year Ends: 12/31
2006 Sales: $14,356,000	2006 Profits: $1,573,000	Parent Company:

SALARIES/BENEFITS:

Pension Plan: Y	ESOP Stock Plan:	Profit Sharing:	Top Exec. Salary: $1,077,522	Bonus: $5,147,627
Savings Plan: Y	Stock Purch. Plan:		Second Exec. Salary: $809,892	Bonus: $1,951,986

OTHER THOUGHTS:

Apparent Women Officers or Directors: 3
Hot Spot for Advancement for Women/Minorities: Y

LOCATIONS: ("Y" = Yes)

West:	Southwest:	Midwest:	Southeast:	Northeast:	International:
Y			Y		

SOUTHWEST AIRLINES CO

www.southwest.com

Industry Group Code: 481111

Management:		Sales/Marketing:		Liberal Arts:		Information Sys.:		Professionals:		Tech./Scientific:	
Mgmt. Trainees:	Y	Marketing Pros.:	Y	Gen. Writing/Editing:	Y	Info. Mgmt.:	Y	Finance/Acct.:	Y	Engineers, Elec.:	Y
Experienced Mgmt.:	Y	Retail Sales:		Tech. Writing:	Y	Software Dev.:	Y	Law:	Y	Engineers, Other:	Y
Int'l Business:	Y	Comm./Industrial:		Graphic Arts/Photog.:	Y	Hardware Dev.:		HR/Other:	Y	Health/Lab:	
MBA Grads:	Y	Sales Trainees:	Y	Music:		Consulting/Other:		Training:	Y	Science/Research:	
		Advertising Pros.:	Y	Broadcasting:				Health Care:	Y	Petroleum/Chem.:	
				Other:	Y			Consulting:		Math/Other:	

TYPES OF BUSINESS:

Airline-Domestic
Air Freight

BRANDS/DIVISIONS/AFFILIATES:

EarlyBird Check-in
AirTran

CONTACTS:

Note: Officers with more than one job title may be intentionally listed here more than once.

Gary C. Kelly, CEO
Michael G. Van De Ven, COO/Exec. VP
Gary Kelly, Pres.
Laura H. Wright, CFO/Sr. VP-Finance
Dave Ridley, Sr. VP-Mktg.
Jeff Lamb, Chief People Officer
Jan Marshall, CIO/VP-Tech
Bob Young, CTO/VP-Tech
Jim Sokol, VP-Eng. & Maintenance
Jeff Lamb, Sr. VP-Admin.
Madeleine Johnson, General Counsel/VP
Greg Wells, Sr. VP-Oper.
Robert E. Jordan, Exec. VP-Strategy & Planning
Ginger C. Hardage, Sr. VP-Corp. Comm. & Culture
Scott E. Topping, Treas./VP
Matt Hafner, VP-Ground Oper./VP-In-flight & Provisioning
Ron Ricks, Exec. VP-Corp. Svcs./Sec.
Chuck Magill, VP-Flight Oper.
Kevin M. Krone, VP-Mktg., Sales & Dist.
Gary C. Kelly, Chmn.
Daryl Krause, Sr. VP-Procurement

Phone: 214-792-4000	**Fax:** 214-792-5015
Toll-Free: 800-435-9792	
Address: 2702 Love Field Dr., Dallas, TX 75235 US	

GROWTH PLANS/SPECIAL FEATURES:

Southwest Airlines Co. is a low-fare domestic airline that provides primarily short haul, high-frequency airline services. Southwest is one of the largest carriers in the U.S. based on number of domestic passengers. The firm operates 547 Boeing 737 planes, serving 72 cities in 37 states throughout the U.S. The firm operates over 3,100 flights daily. Its busiest routes include those to Las Vegas, Phoenix, Baltimore, Houston, Los Angeles, Chicago, Denver, Oakland, San Diego and Dallas. Using only one type of airplane simplifies the company's scheduling, maintenance, flight operations and training activities. Southwest primarily flies to many conveniently located secondary or downtown airports such as Houston-Hobby, Dallas-Love Field and Chicago-Midway, which are typically less congested than other airlines' hub airports. Southwest primarily employs a point-to-point route system, which allows for more direct nonstop routing, thereby minimizing connections, delays, and total trip time. It also offers the EarlyBird Check-in service, which allows customers to reserve a boarding position prior to general check-in for a fee. In November 2010, the company began offering service to five Mexican cities: Cancun, Guadalajara, Morelia, Toluca/Mexico City and Zacatecas. In May 2011, the firm acquired AirTran Holdings. and its operating subsidiary, AirTran Airways, Inc. for $1.4 billion, adding significantly to its presence in important markets. In August 2011, the firm announced plans to launch 15 daily flights from Atlanta beginning in early 2012.

Employees of the firm are offered medical, dental, vision and life insurance; health and dependent care spending accounts; adoption assistance; an employee assistance program; a 401(k) plan; a profit sharing plan; an employee stock purchase plan; free flights with Southwest Airlines and discounted flights with other carriers; various travel-related discounts; access to the University for People; the Manager in Training Program (MIT); and personal development and leadership training.

FINANCIALS:

Sales and profits are in thousands of dollars—add 000 to get the full amount. 2010 Note: Financial information for 2010 was not available for all companies at press time.

2010 Sales: $12,104,000	2010 Profits: $459,000	**U.S. Stock Ticker: LUV**
2009 Sales: $10,350,000	2009 Profits: $99,000	**Int'l Ticker:**
2008 Sales: $11,023,000	2008 Profits: $178,000	Int'l Exchange:
2007 Sales: $9,860,000	2007 Profits: $645,000	Employees: 34,901 Fiscal Year Ends: 12/31
2006 Sales: $9,086,000	2006 Profits: $499,000	Parent Company:

SALARIES/BENEFITS:

Pension Plan:	ESOP Stock Plan:	Profit Sharing: Y	Top Exec. Salary: $465,000	Bonus: $930,000
Savings Plan: Y	Stock Purch. Plan: Y		Second Exec. Salary: $370,000	Bonus: $475,000

OTHER THOUGHTS:

Apparent Women Officers or Directors: 13
Hot Spot for Advancement for Women/Minorities: Y

LOCATIONS: ("Y" = Yes)

West:	Southwest:	Midwest:	Southeast:	Northeast:	International:
Y	Y	Y	Y	Y	Y

SPECTRUM HEALTH

www.spectrum-health.org

Industry Group Code: 622110

Management:		Sales/Marketing:		Liberal Arts:		Information Sys.:		Professionals:		Tech./Scientific:	
Mgmt. Trainees:	Y	Marketing Pros.:	Y	Gen. Writing/Editing:	Y	Info. Mgmt.:	Y	Finance/Acct.:	Y	Engineers, Elec.:	
Experienced Mgmt.:	Y	Retail Sales:		Tech. Writing:	Y	Software Dev.:		Law:	Y	Engineers, Other:	
Int'l Business:		Comm./Industrial:	Y	Graphic Arts/Photog.:		Hardware Dev.:		HR/Other:	Y	Health/Lab:	Y
MBA Grads:	Y	Sales Trainees:		Music:		Consulting/Other:		Training:	Y	Science/Research:	
		Advertising Pros.:	Y	Broadcasting:				Health Care:	Y	Petroleum/Chem.:	
				Other:	Y			Consulting:		Math/Other:	

TYPES OF BUSINESS:

Hospitals-General
Trauma Center
Neonatal Center
Burn Center
Poison Center
HMO
Long-Term Care
Children's Hospital

BRANDS/DIVISIONS/AFFILIATES:

Renucci Hospitality House
Helen DeVos Children's Hospital
Kent Community Campus
Priority Health
Spectrum Health Laboratory Outreach Services
Lemmen-Holton Cancer Pavilion
Meijer Heart Center
Butterworth Hospital

CONTACTS: *Note: Officers with more than one job title may be intentionally listed here more than once.*

Richard C. Breon, CEO
Richard C. Breon, Pres.
Michael P. Freed, CFO/Exec. VP
Patrick O'Hare, CIO/Sr. VP
Elias J. Neujahr, VP-Oper.
Tina Freese-Decker, Interim Pres., Spectrum Health United Memorial

Phone: 616-391-1774 | **Fax:** 616-391-2780
Toll-Free: 866-989-7999
Address: 100 Michigan St. N.E., Grand Rapids, MI 49503 US

GROWTH PLANS/SPECIAL FEATURES:

Spectrum Health is one of the largest health systems in western Michigan. The firm serves approximately 580,000 Priority Health Plan members and 11,000 employers in 39 counties. Additionally, Spectrum Health operates more than 140 service areas with a total of 1,983 beds, including a Level 1 trauma center, a neonatal center, a burn center and a poison center. The company is comprised of Helen DeVos Children's Hospital, Butterworth Hospital, Lemmen-Holton Cancer Pavilion, Meijer Heart Center, Kent Community Campus and the Renucci Hospitality House. The Helen DeVos Children's Hospital is the only children's hospital in west Michigan. Kent Community Campus provides long-term care for patients recovering from major illnesses and complex medical conditions. In addition to Spectrum's primary care locations, the firm operates over 80 outpatient sites for diagnostics, treatment, imaging services, surgery, rehabilitation and laboratory services. Spectrum also operates a continuing care division that provides a complete continuum of specialized services for adults and seniors recovering from illness and complex medical conditions, including sub acute care; long-term acute care; rehabilitation; outpatient; and residential and home care; as well as specialized units for patients with brain or spinal cord injuries. Spectrum Health Laboratory Outreach Services, with 21 board-certified pathologists, provides CT Scanning, diagnostic imaging, an endoscopy center, forensic pathology, interventional radiology, mammography, MRI, neurodiagnostics, nuclear medicine, PET imaging, ultrasound, vascular imaging, X-ray and fluoroscopy services. Additional services offered include breastfeeding services; grief and loss support; pastoral care; childcare resources; a poison center; postpartum depression programs; and more. The company's operations also include Priority Health, an HMO which serves more than 500,000 members throughout Michigan. In August 2011, the firm began construction on a new pavilion that will house approximately five Spectrum offices in Grand Rapids, Michigan.

FINANCIALS: **Sales and profits are in thousands of dollars—add 000 to get the full amount. 2010 Note: Financial information for 2010 was not available for all companies at press time.**

2010 Sales: $3,161,106 — 2010 Profits: $121,294
2009 Sales: $2,700,000 — 2009 Profits: $-50,910
2008 Sales: $2,595,495 — 2008 Profits: $
2007 Sales: $2,322,354 — 2007 Profits: $
2006 Sales: $2,102,835 — 2006 Profits: $

U.S. Stock Ticker: Nonprofit
Int'l Ticker:
Int'l Exchange:
Employees: 17,800 Fiscal Year Ends: 6/30
Parent Company:

SALARIES/BENEFITS:

Pension Plan: ESOP Stock Plan: Profit Sharing: Top Exec. Salary: $ Bonus: $
Savings Plan: Stock Purch. Plan: Second Exec. Salary: $ Bonus: $

OTHER THOUGHTS:

Apparent Women Officers or Directors: 1
Hot Spot for Advancement for Women/Minorities:

LOCATIONS: ("Y" = Yes)

West:	Southwest:	Midwest:	Southeast:	Northeast:	International:
		Y			

SPIRIT AEROSYSTEMS HOLDINGS INC

www.spiritaero.com

Industry Group Code: 33641

Management:		Sales/Marketing:		Liberal Arts:		Information Sys.:		Professionals:		Tech./Scientific:	
Mgmt. Trainees:		Marketing Pros.:	Y	Gen. Writing/Editing:		Info. Mgmt.:	Y	Finance/Acct.:	Y	Engineers, Elec.:	Y
Experienced Mgmt.:	Y	Retail Sales:		Tech. Writing:	Y	Software Dev.:	Y	Law:	Y	Engineers, Other:	Y
Int'l Business:	Y	Comm./Industrial:	Y	Graphic Arts/Photog.:		Hardware Dev.:		HR/Other:	Y	Health/Lab:	
MBA Grads:	Y	Sales Trainees:		Music:		Consulting/Other:		Training:		Science/Research:	
		Advertising Pros.:		Broadcasting:				Health Care:		Petroleum/Chem.:	
				Other:				Consulting:		Math/Other:	

TYPES OF BUSINESS:

Aircraft Manufacturing
Aerostructures
Fuselages
Wings & Flight Control Components
Engineering, Design & Materials Testing
Custom Tool Fabrication
Spare Parts & Maintenance Services
Supply Chain Management

BRANDS/DIVISIONS/AFFILIATES:

Taikoo Spirit AeroSystems (Jinjiang) Composite Co.

CONTACTS:

Note: Officers with more than one job title may be intentionally listed here more than once.

Jeff Turner, CEO
Buck Buchanan, COO/Sr. VP
Jeff Turner, Pres.
Philip Anderson, CFO/Sr. VP
Gloria Flentje, Sr. VP-Human Resources
Peter Wu, Chief Scientist/VP
H.D. Walker, CTO
Gloria Flentje, Sr. VP-Corp. Admin.
Michelle Russell, General Counsel/Sr. VP/Sec.
H.D. Walker, Sr. VP-Bus. Dev.
Debbie Gann, Head-Corp. Comm.
Alan Hermanson, Head-Investor Rel.
Steve Sharp, Treas./Controller/VP
Ron Brunton, Sr. VP-Special Assignments
Mike King, Sr. VP/Gen. Mgr.-Fuselage Segment
John Lewelling, Sr. VP/Gen. Mgr.-AeroStructures Segment
John Pilla, Sr. VP/Gen. Mgr.-Propulsion Segment
Robert Johnson, Chmn.

Phone: 316-526-9000 **Fax:**
Toll-Free: 800-501-7597
Address: 3801 S. Oliver St., Wichita, KS 67210 US

GROWTH PLANS/SPECIAL FEATURES:

Spirit Aerosystems Holdings, Inc. is an independent original parts designer and manufacturer of aerostructures. Aerostructures are structural components such as fuselages, propulsion systems and wing systems for commercial and military aircraft. The firm operates through three principal segments: fuselages, propulsion systems and wing systems. The fuselages segment produces forward, mid and rear fuselage sections and offers services that include numerical control programming, materials testing, on-site planning and global supply chain management. The propulsion systems segment primarily produces nacelles (aerodynamic engine enclosures which enhance propulsion installation efficiency, dampen engine noise and provide thrust reversing capabilities), struts/pylons (structures that attach engines to airplane wings) and engine structural components. Propulsion system services include engineering design, numerical control programming, materials testing, on-site planning, process improvement consulting and global supply chain management. The wing systems segment produces wings, wing components and flight control components. Spirit Aerosystems is also engaged in tooling, which is the fabrication of custom tools. The firm's tooling capabilities include tool design, CNC programming, machining, composite, aluminum and invar tooling. The company offers spare parts and components for all items of which it is the original production supplier and provides maintenance, repair and overhaul work for nacelles, fuselage doors, structural components and modification kits. Spirit Aerosystems primarily supplies its products to Boeing and Airbus. Taikoo Spirit AeroSystems (Jinjiang) Composite Co. Ltd., a joint venture between the firm, Hong Kong Aircraft Engineering Company Limited (HAECO) and HAECO's subsidiary Taikoo (Xiamen) Aircraft Engineering Co. Ltd. repair station in China. In July 2010, Spirit Aerosystems opened a new manufacturing plant in Kingston, North Carolina. In September 2010, the company opened a new spare parts sales office in Shannon, Ireland.

FINANCIALS:

Sales and profits are in thousands of dollars—add 000 to get the full amount. 2010 Note: Financial information for 2010 was not available for all companies at press time.

2010 Sales: $4,172,000 — 2010 Profits: $219,000
2009 Sales: $4,078,500 — 2009 Profits: $191,700
2008 Sales: $3,771,800 — 2008 Profits: $265,400
2007 Sales: $3,860,800 — 2007 Profits: $296,900
2006 Sales: $3,207,700 — 2006 Profits: $16,800

U.S. Stock Ticker: SPR
Int'l Ticker:
Int'l Exchange:
Employees: 13,918 Fiscal Year Ends: 12/31
Parent Company:

SALARIES/BENEFITS:

Pension Plan: ESOP Stock Plan: Profit Sharing: Top Exec. Salary: $430,228 Bonus: $
Savings Plan: Y Stock Purch. Plan: Second Exec. Salary: $375,003 Bonus: $

OTHER THOUGHTS:

Apparent Women Officers or Directors: 3
Hot Spot for Advancement for Women/Minorities: Y

LOCATIONS: ("Y" = Yes)

West:	Southwest:	Midwest:	Southeast:	Northeast:	International:
Y	Y	Y			Y

SRA INTERNATIONAL INC

www.sra.com

Industry Group Code: 541513

Management:		Sales/Marketing:		Liberal Arts:		Information Sys.:		Professionals:		Tech./Scientific:	
Mgmt. Trainees:	Y	Marketing Pros.:	Y	Gen. Writing/Editing:	Y	Info. Mgmt.:	Y	Finance/Acct.:	Y	Engineers, Elec.:	Y
Experienced Mgmt.:	Y	Retail Sales:		Tech. Writing:	Y	Software Dev.:	Y	Law:	Y	Engineers, Other:	
Int'l Business:	Y	Comm./Industrial:	Y	Graphic Arts/Photog.:	Y	Hardware Dev.:	Y	HR/Other:	Y	Health/Lab:	
MBA Grads:	Y	Sales Trainees:		Music:		Consulting/Other:	Y	Training:	Y	Science/Research:	
		Advertising Pros.:	Y	Broadcasting:				Health Care:		Petroleum/Chem.:	
				Other:	Y			Consulting:	Y	Math/Other:	Y

TYPES OF BUSINESS:

Technology Consulting
Strategic Consulting
Systems Design
Systems Integration
Managed Services
Outsourcing

BRANDS/DIVISIONS/AFFILIATES:

GangNet
NetOwl
One View Analyst
Sentech
Platinum Solutions, Inc.
Providence Equity Partners

CONTACTS: *Note: Officers with more than one job title may be intentionally listed here more than once.*

Stanton D. Sloane, CEO
Timothy J. Atkin, COO/Exec. VP
Stanton D. Sloane, Pres.
Richard J. Nadeau, CFO/Exec. VP
Patrick Burke, Sr. VP-Mktg. & Sales
Mary E. Good, Sr. VP-Human Resources
Brian Michl, CIO/VP
David L. Matthews, Sr. VP-Tech. Oper. & Quality
Mark D. Schultz, General Counsel
Sheila S. Blackwell, VP-Comm. & Public Affairs
David Keffer, VP-Investor Rel.
Stewart Simonson, VP-Gov't Affairs
Scott F. Large, Sr. VP-Intelligence & Space
Steve Tolbert, Sr. VP-Health & Civil Svcs. Sector
Jeffrey Rydant, Sr. VP-National Security Sector
Ernst Volgenau, Chmn.
Jim McClave, VP-EMEA

Phone: 703-803-1500	**Fax:** 703-803-1509
Toll-Free:	
Address: 4300 Fair Lakes Ct., Fairfax, VA 22033 US	

GROWTH PLANS/SPECIAL FEATURES:

SRA International, Inc. provides technology and strategic consulting services and solutions to a broad range of clients involved in national security, civil government and global health. The firm's business strategy focuses primarily on the U.S. federal government, with a portfolio of clients in national security, including defense, homeland security, intelligence and law enforcement; and civil government, including health, environmental, aviation and other domestic customers. The company's services across all sectors include strategic consulting; systems design, development and integration; cyber security and information assurance; outsourcing and managed services; and business solutions. The strategic consulting service helps clients form and execute business plans. The systems design, development and integration service includes security engineering, software development, and database design. The cyber security and information assurance service offers various cyber security approaches such as security architecture, information operations, and training services. The outsourcing and managed services segment helps clients consolidate infrastructures and reduce operational costs. The business solutions segment includes text and data mining; enterprise resource planning; control systems; disaster planning; and business intelligence. SRA also develops and sells software and hardware products in each market. Some of the firm's software products include One View Analyst, which helps clients sift through gigabytes of information, store the most relevant pieces and search through each piece; NetOwl, which applies advanced natural language understanding technologies to Chinese, English, Arabic, Farsi, French, Korean and Spanish texts to extract content; and GangNet, a database system that helps law enforcement officials record and track gang member information and activities. In July 2010, the firm acquired Sentech. In October 2010, SRA agreed to acquire Platinum Solutions, Inc. In April 2011, the company agreed to be acquired by Providence Equity Partners.

Employees are offered life, disability, medical, vision and dental insurance; health and dependent care flexible spending programs; educational and financial planning assistance; commuter expense reimbursement; and college savings plans.

FINANCIALS: **Sales and profits are in thousands of dollars—add 000 to get the full amount. 2010 Note: Financial information for 2010 was not available for all companies at press time.**

2010 Sales: $1,666,629	2010 Profits: $18,415
2009 Sales: $1,540,556	2009 Profits: $58,000
2008 Sales: $1,506,933	2008 Profits: $73,264
2007 Sales: $1,268,872	2007 Profits: $63,430
2006 Sales: $1,179,267	2006 Profits: $62,520

U.S. Stock Ticker: SRX
Int'l Ticker:
Int'l Exchange:
Employees: 7,100 Fiscal Year Ends: 6/30
Parent Company:

SALARIES/BENEFITS:

Pension Plan:	ESOP Stock Plan:	Profit Sharing:	Top Exec. Salary: $680,000	Bonus: $626,441
Savings Plan: Y	Stock Purch. Plan: Y		Second Exec. Salary: $401,667	Bonus: $334,466

OTHER THOUGHTS:

Apparent Women Officers or Directors: 3
Hot Spot for Advancement for Women/Minorities: Y

LOCATIONS: ("Y" = Yes)

West:	Southwest:	Midwest:	Southeast:	Northeast:	International:
Y	Y	Y	Y	Y	Y

Sales, profits and employees may be estimates. Financial information, benefits and other data can change quickly and may vary from those stated here.

ST JUDE MEDICAL INC

www.sjm.com

Industry Group Code: 33911

Management:		**Sales/Marketing:**		**Liberal Arts:**		**Information Sys.:**		**Professionals:**		**Tech./Scientific:**	
Mgmt. Trainees:	Y	Marketing Pros.:	Y	Gen. Writing/Editing:	Y	Info. Mgmt.:	Y	Finance/Acct.:	Y	Engineers, Elec.:	Y
Experienced Mgmt.:	Y	Retail Sales:		Tech. Writing:	Y	Software Dev.:	Y	Law:	Y	Engineers, Other:	Y
Int'l Business:	Y	Comm./Industrial:	Y	Graphic Arts/Photog.:	Y	Hardware Dev.:		HR/Other:	Y	Health/Lab:	Y
MBA Grads:	Y	Sales Trainees:	Y	Music:		Consulting/Other:		Training:	Y	Science/Research:	Y
		Advertising Pros.:	Y	Broadcasting:				Health Care:	Y	Petroleum/Chem.:	
				Other:				Consulting:		Math/Other:	

TYPES OF BUSINESS:

Cardiovascular Medical Devices
Cardiac Rhythm Management Devices
Cardiac Surgery Devices
Cardiology Devices
Atrial Fibrillation Devices

BRANDS/DIVISIONS/AFFILIATES:

AGA Medical Holdings, Inc.
LightLab Imaging, Inc.
St. Jude Medical Advanced Technology Center
St. Jude Medical Neuromodulation

CONTACTS: *Note: Officers with more than one job title may be intentionally listed here more than once.*

Daniel J. Starks, CEO
Daniel J. Starks, Pres.
John C. Heinmiller, CFO/Exec. VP
Angela D. Craig, VP-Human Resources
Mark D. Carlson, Chief Medical Officer/Sr. VP-Research
Thomas R. Northenscold, CIO/VP-IT
Pamela S. Krop, General Counsel/VP/Sec.
Angela D. Craig, VP-Corp. Rel.
Jane J. Song, Pres., Atrial Fibrillation Div.
Michael T. Rousseau, Group Pres.
Eric S. Fain, Pres., Cardiac Rhythm Mgmt. Div.
Frank J. Callaghan, Pres., Cardiovascular Div.
Daniel J. Starks, Chmn.
Denis M. Gestin, Pres., Int'l Div.

Phone: 651-756-2000 **Fax:** 651-756-3301
Toll-Free: 800-328-9634
Address: 1 St. Jude Medical Dr., St. Paul, MN 55117 US

GROWTH PLANS/SPECIAL FEATURES:

St. Jude Medical, Inc. is a developer, manufacturer and distributor of cardiovascular medical devices and neurostimulation medical devices. The company operates in four segments: cardiac rhythm management, with products including tachycardia implantable cardioverter defibrillator systems (ICDs) and bradycardia pacemaker systems; cardiovascular, with products including vascular closure devices, heart valve replacement and repair products and pressure measurement guidewires; neuromodulation, with products including neurostimulation devices; and atrial fibrillation, with products including electrophysiology (EP) introducers and catheters, advanced cardiac mapping, navigation and recording systems and ablation systems. St. Jude's neuromodulation division focuses its efforts on the related therapy areas. Neuromodulation is the delivery of very small, precise doses of electric current or drugs directly to nerve sites and is aimed at treating patients suffering from chronic pain or other disabling nervous system disorders. The firm markets and sells its products through a direct sales force and independent distributors. Principal geographic markets for its products are the U.S., Europe, Japan and the Asia-Pacific region. St. Jude also sells products in Canada and Latin America. Cardiac rhythm management products generate approximately 58.9% of St. Jude Medical's revenues; cardiovascular, 20.1%; atrial fibrillation, 13.7%; and neuromodulation, 7.3%. In mid 2010, St. Jude Medical acquired LightLab Imaging, Inc., a developer of coronary imaging technology. LightLab has been incorporated into the firm's cardiovascular division. In November 2010, the company acquired AGA Medical Holdings, Inc. In March 2011, St. Jude opened the St. Jude Medical Advanced Technology Center Asia Pacific in Beijing, China.

The company offers its employees benefits including medical, dental and vision coverage; flexible spending accounts; an employee assistance program; access to a credit union; life and disability insurance; a physical fitness program; a matching gift program; a scholarship program; and tuition reimbursement.

FINANCIALS: **Sales and profits are in thousands of dollars—add 000 to get the full amount. 2010 Note: Financial information for 2010 was not available for all companies at press time.**

2010 Sales: $5,164,771	2010 Profits: $907,436	**U.S. Stock Ticker: STJ**
2009 Sales: $4,681,273	2009 Profits: $777,226	**Int'l Ticker:**
2008 Sales: $4,363,251	2008 Profits: $353,018	Int'l Exchange:
2007 Sales: $3,779,277	2007 Profits: $537,756	Employees: 15,000 Fiscal Year Ends: 12/31
2006 Sales: $3,302,447	2006 Profits: $548,251	Parent Company:

SALARIES/BENEFITS:

Pension Plan:	ESOP Stock Plan:	Profit Sharing:	Top Exec. Salary: $995,000	Bonus: $1,408,920
Savings Plan: Y	Stock Purch. Plan: Y		Second Exec. Salary: $678,300	Bonus: $800,394

OTHER THOUGHTS:

Apparent Women Officers or Directors: 5
Hot Spot for Advancement for Women/Minorities: Y

LOCATIONS: ("Y" = Yes)

West:	Southwest:	Midwest:	Southeast:	Northeast:	International:
Y	Y	Y	Y	Y	Y

STANLEY BLACK & DECKER INC

www.stanleyblackanddecker.com

Industry Group Code: 335

Management:		Sales/Marketing:		Liberal Arts:		Information Sys.:		Professionals:		Tech./Scientific:	
Mgmt. Trainees:	Y	Marketing Pros.:	Y	Gen. Writing/Editing:	Y	Info. Mgmt.:	Y	Finance/Acct.:	Y	Engineers, Elec.:	Y
Experienced Mgmt.:	Y	Retail Sales:		Tech. Writing:	Y	Software Dev.:	Y	Law:	Y	Engineers, Other:	Y
Int'l Business:	Y	Comm./Industrial:	Y	Graphic Arts/Photog.:	Y	Hardware Dev.:	Y	HR/Other:	Y	Health/Lab:	
MBA Grads:	Y	Sales Trainees:	Y	Music:		Consulting/Other:		Training:	Y	Science/Research:	
		Advertising Pros.:	Y	Broadcasting:				Health Care:		Petroleum/Chem.:	
				Other:	Y			Consulting:		Math/Other:	

TYPES OF BUSINESS:

Power Tools & Accessories Manufacturer
Security Solutions
Household Appliances
Home Improvement Products
Fastening & Assembly Systems
Plumbing Products
Automotive Machinery

BRANDS/DIVISIONS/AFFILIATES:

Black & Decker Corp. (The)
Stanley Works (The)
Price Pfister
Kwikset
Porter-Cable
DeWALT
CRC Evans Pipeline International
Niscayah Group AB

CONTACTS: *Note: Officers with more than one job title may be intentionally listed here more than once.*

John F. Lundgren, CEO
James M. Loree, COO/Exec. VP
John F. Lundgren, Pres.
Donald Allan, Jr., CFO/Sr. VP
Mark J. Mathieu, Sr. VP-Human Resources
Hubert W. Davis, Jr., CIO/Sr. VP-Bus. Transformation
Bruce H. Beatt, General Counsel/Sr. VP/Sec.
Tim Perra, Dir.-Global Comm.
Kate White, Dir.-Investor Rel.
Craig A. Douglas, Treas./VP
Jeffrey D. Ansell, Sr. VP/Pres., Construction & DIY
Jaime Ramirez, Pres., Latin America
Ben S. Sihota, Pres., Emerging Markets Pacific Group
Massimo Grassi, Pres., Industrial & Auto Repair
Nolan D. Archibald, Exec. Chmn.
Jeff Hung-Tse Chen, VP/Pres., Asia

Phone: 860-225-5111 **Fax:**
Toll-Free:
Address: 1000 Stanley Dr., New Britain, CT 06053 US

GROWTH PLANS/SPECIAL FEATURES:

Stanley Black & Decker, Inc., formerly The Black & Decker Corp., is a global manufacturer and marketer of power tools and accessories; hardware and home improvement products; security solutions; and technology-based fastening systems. The firm is also a global supplier of engineered fastening and assembly systems. Stanley Black & Decker products and services are marketed in over 100 countries in hardware and home improvement stores around the globe. The firm operates in three business segments: construction and do it yourself (CDIY), security and industrial. The CDIY segment includes consumer power tools and accessories; lawn and garden tools; plumbing products; consumer mechanics tools; storage systems; and pneumatic tools and fasteners. The security segment provides both mechanical and electric access and security systems primarily for retailers, educational, financial and healthcare institutions, as well as commercial, government and industrial customers. The industrial segment manufactures and markets professional industrial and automotive mechanics tools and storage systems; metal and plastic fasteners and engineered fastening systems; hydraulic tools and accessories; plumbing, heating and air conditioning tools; assembly tools and systems; and specialty tools. The company sells these products to industrial clients in the automotive, transportation, aerospace, electronics and machine tool industries primarily through third party distributors. Product names include DeWALT, Porter-Cable, Delta Machinery and Black & Decker, as well as Price Pfister plumbing products, Kwikset security hardware, Mac Tools, Stanley and Sargent and Greenleaf. Stanley Black & Decker, Inc. was formed in 2010 when Black & Decker merged with The Stanley Works company. In mid 2010, the firm acquired CRC Evans Pipeline International. In September 2011, the firm acquired Swedish company Niscayah Group AB.

FINANCIALS: **Sales and profits are in thousands of dollars—add 000 to get the full amount. 2010 Note: Financial information for 2010 was not available for all companies at press time.**

2010 Sales: $8,410,000 — 2010 Profits: $198,000
2009 Sales: $3,737,000 — 2009 Profits: $227,000
2008 Sales: $4,426,000 — 2008 Profits: $219,000
2007 Sales: $6,563,200 — 2007 Profits: $518,100
2006 Sales: $6,447,300 — 2006 Profits: $486,100

U.S. Stock Ticker: SWK
Int'l Ticker:
Int'l Exchange:
Employees: 36,700 Fiscal Year Ends: 12/31
Parent Company:

SALARIES/BENEFITS:

Pension Plan: Y ESOP Stock Plan: Y Profit Sharing: Top Exec. Salary: $1,208,433 Bonus: $4,342,800
Savings Plan: Y Stock Purch. Plan: Second Exec. Salary: $1,187,500 Bonus: $1,875,000

OTHER THOUGHTS:

Apparent Women Officers or Directors: 2
Hot Spot for Advancement for Women/Minorities:

LOCATIONS: ("Y" = Yes)

West:	Southwest:	Midwest:	Southeast:	Northeast:	International:
Y	Y	Y	Y	Y	Y

STARWOOD HOTELS & RESORTS WORLDWIDE INC

www.starwoodhotels.com

Industry Group Code: 721110

Management:		Sales/Marketing:		Liberal Arts:		Information Sys.:		Professionals:		Tech./Scientific:	
Mgmt. Trainees:	Y	Marketing Pros.:	Y	Gen. Writing/Editing:	Y	Info. Mgmt.:	Y	Finance/Acct.:	Y	Engineers, Elec.:	
Experienced Mgmt.:	Y	Retail Sales:		Tech. Writing:		Software Dev.:	Y	Law:	Y	Engineers, Other:	
Int'l Business:	Y	Comm./Industrial:	Y	Graphic Arts/Photog.:	Y	Hardware Dev.:		HR/Other:	Y	Health/Lab:	
MBA Grads:	Y	Sales Trainees:	Y	Music:		Consulting/Other:		Training:	Y	Science/Research:	
		Advertising Pros.:	Y	Broadcasting:				Health Care:		Petroleum/Chem.:	
				Other:	Y			Consulting:		Math/Other:	

TYPES OF BUSINESS:

Hotels & Resorts
Financial Services
Hotel Management & Franchising
Spa Services
Online Auction Web Site
Preferred Guest Club

BRANDS/DIVISIONS/AFFILIATES:

Sheraton
W
Four Points
Westin
Le Meridien
St. Regis
Luxury Collection
Aloft

CONTACTS: *Note: Officers with more than one job title may be intentionally listed here more than once.*

Frits van Paasschen, CEO
Frits van Paasschen, Pres.
Vasant M. Prabhu, CFO
Christie Hicks, Sr. VP-Global Sales
Jeffrey M. Cava, Chief Human Resources Officer/Exec. VP
Phil McAveety, Chief Brand Officer/Exec. VP
Kenneth S. Siegel, Chief Admin. Officer
Kenneth S. Siegel, General Counsel
Simon Turner, Pres., Global Dev.
Alan Schnaid, Controller/Sr. VP
Roeland Vos, Pres., EMEA
Denise M. Coll, Pres., North America
Osvaldo V. Librizzi, Pres., Latin America
Matthew E. Avril, Pres., Hotel Group
Bruce W. Duncan, Chmn.
Miguel Ko, Chmn./Pres., APAC

Phone: 914-640-8100 **Fax:** 914-640-8310
Toll-Free:
Address: 1111 Westchester Ave., White Plains, NY 10604 US

GROWTH PLANS/SPECIAL FEATURES:

Starwood Hotels & Resorts Worldwide, Inc. manages the global operation of hotels and resorts, primarily in the luxury and upscale segments of the industry. It owns, leases, manages or franchises approximately 1,041 hotels containing about 308,700 rooms in roughly 100 countries. The company's hotel brand names include St. Regis, The Luxury Collection, W, Westin, Sheraton, Four Points, Le Meridien, Aloft and Element. The firm's earnings are derived mainly from its hotel and leisure operations; the receipt of franchise fees; and the development, ownership and operation of vacation ownership resorts. Additionally, Starwood provides financing to customers who purchase interests in resorts. The firm's frequent guest loyalty program, Starwood Preferred Guest, is unique in the hotel industry for its lack of capacity controls and blackout dates. Starwood's property portfolio includes the St. Regis in New York, New York; The Phoenician in Scottsdale, Arizona; the Hotel Gritti Palace in Venice, Italy; and the St. Regis in Beijing, China. In early 2010, the company sold Bliss, a spa and related product firm, to Steiner Leisure Limited for $100 million. In 2010, Starwood Hotels opened approximately 62 new hotels in locations such as New York, North Carolina, Virginia, Florida, Ohio, Oklahoma, Texas, Arizona, Connecticut, Tennessee, Canada and India. In March 2011, the firm opened a new Westin in Houston, Texas.

The company offers its employees life, disability, medical, dental and vision insurance; a 401(k) plan; an employee stock purchase plan; an employee assistance program; and domestic partner benefits.

FINANCIALS: **Sales and profits are in thousands of dollars—add 000 to get the full amount. 2010 Note: Financial information for 2010 was not available for all companies at press time.**

2010 Sales: $5,071,000 | 2010 Profits: $477,000
2009 Sales: $4,696,000 | 2009 Profits: $73,000
2008 Sales: $5,754,000 | 2008 Profits: $329,000
2007 Sales: $5,999,000 | 2007 Profits: $542,000
2006 Sales: $5,979,000 | 2006 Profits: $1,043,000

U.S. Stock Ticker: HOT
Int'l Ticker:
Int'l Exchange:
Employees: 145,000 Fiscal Year Ends: 12/31
Parent Company:

SALARIES/BENEFITS:

Pension Plan: | ESOP Stock Plan: | Profit Sharing: | Top Exec. Salary: $1,208,333 | Bonus: $3,000,000
Savings Plan: Y | Stock Purch. Plan: Y | | Second Exec. Salary: $747,292 | Bonus: $902,100

OTHER THOUGHTS:

Apparent Women Officers or Directors: 7
Hot Spot for Advancement for Women/Minorities: Y

LOCATIONS: ("Y" = Yes)

West:	Southwest:	Midwest:	Southeast:	Northeast:	International:
Y	Y	Y	Y	Y	Y

Sales, profits and employees may be estimates. Financial information, benefits and other data can change quickly and may vary from those stated here.

STERICYCLE INC

www.stericycle.com

Industry Group Code: 562

Management:		Sales/Marketing:		Liberal Arts:		Information Sys.:		Professionals:		Tech./Scientific:	
Mgmt. Trainees:		Marketing Pros.:	Y	Gen. Writing/Editing:		Info. Mgmt.:	Y	Finance/Acct.:	Y	Engineers, Elec.:	
Experienced Mgmt.:		Retail Sales:		Tech. Writing:	Y	Software Dev.:		Law:	Y	Engineers, Other:	
Int'l Business:	Y	Comm./Industrial:	Y	Graphic Arts/Photog.:		Hardware Dev.:		HR/Other:	Y	Health/Lab:	
MBA Grads:	Y	Sales Trainees:		Music:		Consulting/Other:		Training:		Science/Research:	
		Advertising Pros.:	Y	Broadcasting:				Health Care:		Petroleum/Chem.:	
				Other:				Consulting:		Math/Other:	

TYPES OF BUSINESS:

Medical Waste Treatment

BRANDS/DIVISIONS/AFFILIATES:

Steri-Safe
Steri-Tub
Healthcare Waste Solutions, Inc..

CONTACTS:

Note: Officers with more than one job title may be intentionally listed here more than once.

Mark C. Miller, CEO
Richard T. Kogler, COO/Exec. VP
Frank J.M. ten Brink, CFO/Exec. VP
Frank J.M. ten Brink, Chief Admin. Officer
Michael J. Collins, Pres., Return Mgmt. Svcs.
Charles A. Alutto, Pres., Serticycle USA
Mark C. Miller, Chmn.
Richard L. Foss, Exec. VP-Int'l

Phone: 847-367-5910 **Fax:** 847-367-9493
Toll-Free: 800-643-0240
Address: 28161 N. Keith Dr., Lake Forest, IL 60045 US

GROWTH PLANS/SPECIAL FEATURES:

Stericycle, Inc. is engaged in the business of medical waste disposal. Through its national networks of 136 processing or combined processing and collection sites and 129 additional transfer sites, the firm is able to serve the U.S., Canada, Mexico, Argentina, Brazil, Chile, the U.K., Ireland, Romania, Portugal and Japan. In order to dispose of medical waste, Stericycle utilizes various technologies, including autoclaving, an electro-thermal-deactivation system (ETD), chemical treatment and incineration. While Stericycle's customers are mainly hospitals, clinics, acute care facilities and dental offices, it also handles disposal of expired or surplus products from pharmacies and pharmaceutical manufacturers. The company generally provides its customers with its own waste containers, such as the plastic Steri-Tub and Bio Systems containers, to avoid needle sticks and leakages; it then scans all containers on arrival at treatment facilities to detect radioactive materials. After treatment, the residual ash is passed on to a third-party landfill and the containers are returned to customers. Stericycle utilizes its own branded methodologies, which include Steri-Safe, a compliance program designed to familiarize clients with regulatory policies, mail-back programs, product recalls, returns and on-site waste disposal services. The company serves more than 485,000 customers worldwide, of which over 13,000 are large-quantity generators, such as hospitals, blood banks and pharmaceutical manufacturers; and more than 472,000 small-quantity generators, such as outpatient clinics, medical and dental offices, long-term and sub-acute care facilities and retail pharmacies. In April 2011, Stericycle acquired Healthcare Waste Solutions, Inc.

The company offers its employees medical, dental and vision insurance; flexible spending accounts; an employee assistance program; tuition reimbursement; short- and long-term disability; life, AD&D, long-term care, auto and home insurance; a prepaid legal program; a 401(k) plan; an employee stock purchase plan; and paid vacation, holidays and funeral leave.

FINANCIALS:

Sales and profits are in thousands of dollars—add 000 to get the full amount. 2010 Note: Financial information for 2010 was not available for all companies at press time.

2010 Sales: $1,439,388	2010 Profits: $207,879
2009 Sales: $1,177,736	2009 Profits: $175,691
2008 Sales: $1,083,679	2008 Profits: $148,708
2007 Sales: $932,767	2007 Profits: $118,378
2006 Sales: $789,637	2006 Profits: $105,270

U.S. Stock Ticker: SRCL
Int'l Ticker:
Int'l Exchange:
Employees: 9,078 Fiscal Year Ends: 12/31
Parent Company:

SALARIES/BENEFITS:

Pension Plan: ESOP Stock Plan: Profit Sharing: Top Exec. Salary: $305,964 Bonus: $573,683
Savings Plan: Y Stock Purch. Plan: Y Second Exec. Salary: $259,401 Bonus: $344,250

OTHER THOUGHTS:

Apparent Women Officers or Directors:
Hot Spot for Advancement for Women/Minorities:

LOCATIONS: ("Y" = Yes)

West:	Southwest:	Midwest:	Southeast:	Northeast:	International:
Y	Y	Y	Y	Y	Y

Sales, profits and employees may be estimates. Financial information, benefits and other data can change quickly and may vary from those stated here.

STIFEL FINANCIAL CORP

www.stifel.com

Industry Group Code: 523110

Management:		**Sales/Marketing:**		**Liberal Arts:**		**Information Sys.:**		**Professionals:**		**Tech./Scientific:**	
Mgmt. Trainees:	Y	Marketing Pros.:	Y	Gen. Writing/Editing:	Y	Info. Mgmt.:	Y	Finance/Acct.:	Y	Engineers, Elec.:	
Experienced Mgmt.:	Y	Retail Sales:		Tech. Writing:		Software Dev.:	Y	Law:	Y	Engineers, Other:	
Int'l Business:	Y	Comm./Industrial:		Graphic Arts/Photog.:		Hardware Dev.:		HR/Other:	Y	Health/Lab:	
MBA Grads:	Y	Sales Trainees:		Music:		Consulting/Other:		Training:	Y	Science/Research:	
		Advertising Pros.:		Broadcasting:				Health Care:		Petroleum/Chem.:	
				Other:				Consulting:		Math/Other:	

TYPES OF BUSINESS:

Stock Brokerage/Investment Banking
Underwriting
Broker-Dealer
Investment Advisory Services
Research
Insurance
Annuities

BRANDS/DIVISIONS/AFFILIATES:

Stifel Nicolaus & Company Inc
Century Securities Associates Inc
Stifel Nicolaus Ltd
Stifel Bank & Trust
Thomas Weisel Partners Canada, Inc.
Missouri Valley Partners
Thomas Weisel Partners Group, Inc.
Stifel Nicolaus Weisel

CONTACTS: *Note: Officers with more than one job title may be intentionally listed here more than once.*

Ronald J. Kruszewski, CEO
Ronald J. Kruszewski, Pres.
James M. Zemlyak, CFO/Sr. VP
David D. Sliney, Sr. VP-Tech., Stifel Nicolaus
David M. Minnick, General Counsel/Sr. VP/Corp. Sec.
David D. Sliney, Sr. VP-Oper., Stifel Nicolaus
David D. Sliney, Sr. VP-Strategic Planning, Stifel Nicolaus
James M. Zemlyak, Treas.
Thomas W. Weisel, Co-Chmn.
Victor Nesi, Co-Head-Capital Investments
Thomas P. mulroy, Sr. VP/Co-Head-Capital Markets
Scott B. McCuaig, Sr. VP/Pres./Co-COO-Stifel Nicolaus
Ronald J. Kruszewski, Co-Chmn.

Phone: 314-342-2000	**Fax:** 314-342-2097
Toll-Free: 800-679-5446	
Address: 501 N. Broadway, St. Louis, MO 63102 US	

GROWTH PLANS/SPECIAL FEATURES:

Stifel Financial Corp. is a financial services holding company that provides, through its subsidiaries, retail brokerage, securities trading, investment banking, investment advisory, retail, consumer and commercial banking and related financial services throughout the U.S. Its principal subsidiary is Stifel Nicolaus & Company, Inc., a full service retail/institutional brokerage and investment banking firm. Other subsidiaries include Century Securities Associates, Inc., an independent contractor broker-dealer firm; Stifel Nicolaus Limited and Thomas Weisel Partners Canada, Inc., international subsidiaries; and Stifel Bank & Trust, a retail and commercial bank. The firm operates in three business segments: Global Wealth Management, Institutional Group and Other. The Global Wealth Management segment includes two businesses: the Private Client Group, which provides brokerage services through roughly 310 branch offices and independent contractor offices in 43 states and Washington, D.C.; and Stifel Bank, which provides residential, consumer and commercial lending. The Institutional Group segment offers institutional sales and trading services, as well as corporate and public finance underwriting. The Other segment includes revenues and expenses associated with certain corporate activities. Internationally, Stifel Financial operates in Canada, the U.K. and Europe. In April 2010, Stifel Financial acquired Missouri Valley Partners, an investment advisory company. In July 2010, the company acquired Thomas Weisel Partners Group, Inc., an investment bank. Following the merger, the investment banking platform of Stifel Nicolaus operates under the Stifel Nicolaus Weisel name.

The company offers its employees medical, dental, vision and prescription drug coverage; healthcare, dependent care and commuter flexible spending accounts; life insurance; short- and long-term disability benefits; tuition assistance; business travel accident insurance; an employee assistance program; a 401(k) plan; profit sharing; and a stock ownership plan.

FINANCIALS: **Sales and profits are in thousands of dollars—add 000 to get the full amount. 2010 Note: Financial information for 2010 was not available for all companies at press time.**

2010 Sales: $1,382,026	2010 Profits: $1,907	**U.S. Stock Ticker: SF**
2009 Sales: $1,090,636	2009 Profits: $75,798	**Int'l Ticker:**
2008 Sales: $870,337	2008 Profits: $55,502	Int'l Exchange:
2007 Sales: $763,065	2007 Profits: $32,170	Employees: 4,906 Fiscal Year Ends: 12/31
2006 Sales: $471,388	2006 Profits: $15,431	Parent Company:

SALARIES/BENEFITS:

Pension Plan:	ESOP Stock Plan: Y	Profit Sharing: Y	Top Exec. Salary: $250,000	Bonus: $1,572,500
Savings Plan: Y	Stock Purch. Plan:		Second Exec. Salary: $250,000	Bonus: $1,470,000

OTHER THOUGHTS:

Apparent Women Officers or Directors:
Hot Spot for Advancement for Women/Minorities:

LOCATIONS: ("Y" = Yes)

West:	Southwest:	Midwest:	Southeast:	Northeast:	International:
Y	Y	Y	Y	Y	Y

STONERIDGE INC

www.stoneridge.com

Industry Group Code: 3363

Management:		Sales/Marketing:		Liberal Arts:		Information Sys.:		Professionals:		Tech./Scientific:	
Mgmt. Trainees:		Marketing Pros.:	Y	Gen. Writing/Editing:		Info. Mgmt.:	Y	Finance/Acct.:	Y	Engineers, Elec.:	Y
Experienced Mgmt.:		Retail Sales:		Tech. Writing:	Y	Software Dev.:	Y	Law:	Y	Engineers, Other:	
Int'l Business:	Y	Comm./Industrial:	Y	Graphic Arts/Photog.:		Hardware Dev.:		HR/Other:	Y	Health/Lab:	
MBA Grads:	Y	Sales Trainees:		Music:		Consulting/Other:		Training:		Science/Research:	
		Advertising Pros.:	Y	Broadcasting:				Health Care:		Petroleum/Chem.:	
				Other:				Consulting:		Math/Other:	

TYPES OF BUSINESS:

Automotive Electronic Components
Vehicle Power Distribution Systems
Actuator & Sensor Products
Instrumentation & Display Products
Wiring Systems
Switch Products

BRANDS/DIVISIONS/AFFILIATES:

Stoneridge Hi-Stat Manufacturing
Stoneridge Pollak
Stoneridge Electronics North America
Stoneridge Electronics Europe
PST Eletronica
Minda Stoneridge Instruments Ltd.
Bolton Conductive Systems, LLC
Stoneridge Electronics North America-Wiring

CONTACTS: *Note: Officers with more than one job title may be intentionally listed here more than once.*

John C. Corey, CEO
John C. Corey, Pres.
George E. Strickler, CFO
Thomas A. Beaver, VP-Global Sales
Thomas A. Beaver, VP-Systems Eng.
Richard Adante, VP-Oper.
George E. Strickler, Treas./Exec. VP
Mark J. Tervalon, VP/Pres., Stoneridge Electronics Div.
Steven J. Syzdek, VP/Gen. Mgr.-Stoneridge APAC
Mike Carnahan, VP/Gen. Mgr.-Electronics, North America
Michael D. Sloan, VP/Pres., Control Devices Div.
William M. Lasky, Chmn.
Peter Kruk, Managing Dir.-Stoneridge Electronics, Europe

Phone: 330-856-2443	**Fax:** 330-856-3618
Toll-Free:	
Address: 9400 E. Market St., Warren, OH 44484 US	

GROWTH PLANS/SPECIAL FEATURES:

Stoneridge, Inc. is a leading independent designer and manufacturer of highly engineered electrical and electronic components, modules and systems focused principally on the automotive, medium- and heavy-duty truck, agricultural and off-road vehicle markets. Stoneridge has 18 manufacturing and design centers and several sales and engineering support offices at various locations around the world. The company operates in two segments: electronics and control devices. Core electronics products include vehicle electrical power and distribution systems; electronic instrumentation; and information display products. These products collect, store and display vehicle information such as speed, pressure, maintenance data, operator performance, temperature and distance traveled. The power distribution systems regulate, coordinate and direct the operation of the entire electrical system within a vehicle compartment. The firm's control devices segment manufactures products that monitor, measure or activate a specific function within a vehicle. These products include electronic switches and sensors that control emissions, braking, steering and suspension systems. Stoneridge operates five divisions under its two reportable segments. The electronics division includes Stoneridge Electronics North America-Wiring, Stoneridge Electronics North America-Transportation and Stoneridge Electronics Europe. The control devices division includes Stoneridge Pollak and Stoneridge Hi-Stat Manufacturing. The electronics segment generates approximately 63% of Stoneridge's sales, while control devices account for 37%. The company also operates through joint ventures, including PST Eletronica of Brazil, in which it holds a 50% interest; and Minda Stoneridge Instruments Ltd. of India, in which it holds a 49% stake. The firm also owns a 51% stake in Bolton Conductive Systems, LLC, a military and specialty vehicle wiring and electronics supplier.

Stoneridge offers its employees health and life insurance; a 401(k); savings plans; flexible spending accounts; and long-term disability coverage.

FINANCIALS: **Sales and profits are in thousands of dollars—add 000 to get the full amount. 2010 Note: Financial information for 2010 was not available for all companies at press time.**

2010 Sales: $635,226	2010 Profits: $10,809	**U.S. Stock Ticker: SRI**
2009 Sales: $475,152	2009 Profits: $-32,326	**Int'l Ticker:**
2008 Sales: $752,698	2008 Profits: $-97,527	Int'l Exchange:
2007 Sales: $727,120	2007 Profits: $16,671	Employees: 6,800 Fiscal Year Ends: 12/31
2006 Sales: $708,699	2006 Profits: $14,513	Parent Company:

SALARIES/BENEFITS:

Pension Plan:	ESOP Stock Plan:	Profit Sharing:	Top Exec. Salary: $655,000	Bonus: $1,056,000
Savings Plan: Y	Stock Purch. Plan:		Second Exec. Salary: $340,688	Bonus: $378,400

OTHER THOUGHTS:

Apparent Women Officers or Directors: 1
Hot Spot for Advancement for Women/Minorities:

LOCATIONS: ("Y" = Yes)

West:	Southwest:	Midwest:	Southeast:	Northeast:	International:
Y	Y	Y	Y	Y	Y

STREAM GLOBAL SERVICES INC

www.stream.com

Industry Group Code: 541513

Management:		Sales/Marketing:		Liberal Arts:		Information Sys.:		Professionals:		Tech./Scientific:	
Mgmt. Trainees:		Marketing Pros.:	Y	Gen. Writing/Editing:	Y	Info. Mgmt.:	Y	Finance/Acct.:	Y	Engineers, Elec.:	
Experienced Mgmt.:	Y	Retail Sales:		Tech. Writing:	Y	Software Dev.:	Y	Law:	Y	Engineers, Other:	
Int'l Business:	Y	Comm./Industrial:	Y	Graphic Arts/Photog.:		Hardware Dev.:		HR/Other:	Y	Health/Lab:	
MBA Grads:	Y	Sales Trainees:		Music:		Consulting/Other:		Training:		Science/Research:	
		Advertising Pros.:		Broadcasting:				Health Care:		Petroleum/Chem.:	
				Other:				Consulting:	Y	Math/Other:	

TYPES OF BUSINESS:

Customer Service Outsourcing
Technical Support
Contact Centers

BRANDS/DIVISIONS/AFFILIATES:

CONTACTS:

Note: Officers with more than one job title may be intentionally listed here more than once.

Kathryn Marinello, CEO
Brian J. Delaney, COO/Exec. VP
Dennis J. Lacey, CFO/Exec. VP
Robert Dechant, Exec. VP-Global Mktg. & Sales
Andrew J. Suchoff, Exec. VP-Global Human Resources
Jim Radzicki, CTO/Exec. VP
Sally Comollo, Dir.-Mktg. Comm.
Barbara Weyl, Exec. VP-Global Recruiting & Training
Stephen Loynd, Dir.-Vertical Mktg. Strategies
Kathryn Marinello, Chmn.
Cormac Twomey, Sr. VP-Sales & Client Management, EMEA

Phone: 781-304-1800	**Fax:**
Toll-Free: 888-284-5834	
Address: 20 William St., Ste. 310, Wellesley, MA 02481 US	

GROWTH PLANS/SPECIAL FEATURES:

Stream Global Services, Inc. is a global provider of customer relationship management (CRM) and other business process outsourcing (BPO) services to companies in the technology, software, consumer electronics and communications industries. The firm's systems and processes deliver contact center solutions, including an integrated suite of e-mail, voice and chat solutions. Stream has more than 50 contact centers located in 22 countries around the world and is active in six primary industries: telecommunications; technology; entertainment and media; retail; healthcare; and financial services. Its telecommunications services include technical support, warranty support, surveys, pre- and post-paid activation, upgrades, predictive modeling, direct mailing and data entry. Technology services include inbound and outbound sales; customer service; low-level technical support; product explanation; set-up assistance; and web chat. The company's entertainment and media offerings focus on customer loyalty and retention; customer support functions such as billing duties, service feature inquiries, repairs and installation services; and certain levels of technical support. Its retail offerings focus on customer billing issues, post-sale service and assisting with peak shopping season call volume. For the healthcare industry, Stream offers customer care support, back-office processing, medical billing services and Medicare enrollment services. The firm's financial services are dedicated to account enrollments, back-office duties, consumer loans, credit cards, financial planning, fraud identification and online banking. The company operates across the world, with offices in the U.S., Latin America, Canada, Europe, India, the Philippines, Africa and the Middle East. In 2010, the firm's two largest clients, Dell, Inc. and Hewlett-Packard Company, accounted for 16% and 12% of its annual revenue, respectively.

FINANCIALS:

Sales and profits are in thousands of dollars—add 000 to get the full amount. 2010 Note: Financial information for 2010 was not available for all companies at press time.

2010 Sales: $800,173	2010 Profits: $-53,475
2009 Sales: $584,769	2009 Profits: $-28,573
2008 Sales: $211,373	2008 Profits: $-11,659
2007 Sales: $483,569	2007 Profits: $-14,679
2006 Sales: $405,547	2006 Profits: $-5,349

U.S. Stock Ticker: SGS
Int'l Ticker:
Int'l Exchange:
Employees: 30,000 Fiscal Year Ends: 12/31
Parent Company:

SALARIES/BENEFITS:

Pension Plan:	ESOP Stock Plan:	Profit Sharing:	Top Exec. Salary: $595,000	Bonus: $107,100
Savings Plan:	Stock Purch. Plan:		Second Exec. Salary: $300,000	Bonus: $91,500

OTHER THOUGHTS:

Apparent Women Officers or Directors: 2
Hot Spot for Advancement for Women/Minorities:

LOCATIONS: ("Y" = Yes)

West:	Southwest:	Midwest:	Southeast:	Northeast:	International:
Y	Y	Y	Y	Y	Y

STRYKER CORP

www.stryker.com

Industry Group Code: 33911

Management:		Sales/Marketing:		Liberal Arts:		Information Sys.:		Professionals:		Tech./Scientific:	
Mgmt. Trainees:	Y	Marketing Pros.:	Y	Gen. Writing/Editing:	Y	Info. Mgmt.:	Y	Finance/Acct.:	Y	Engineers, Elec.:	
Experienced Mgmt.:	Y	Retail Sales:		Tech. Writing:	Y	Software Dev.:	Y	Law:	Y	Engineers, Other:	Y
Int'l Business:	Y	Comm./Industrial:	Y	Graphic Arts/Photog.:	Y	Hardware Dev.:		HR/Other:	Y	Health/Lab:	Y
MBA Grads:	Y	Sales Trainees:		Music:		Consulting/Other:		Training:	Y	Science/Research:	Y
		Advertising Pros.:	Y	Broadcasting:				Health Care:	Y	Petroleum/Chem.:	
				Other:				Consulting:		Math/Other:	

TYPES OF BUSINESS:

Equipment-Orthopedic Implants
Powered Surgical Instruments
Endoscopic Systems
Patient Care & Handling Equipment
Imaging Software

BRANDS/DIVISIONS/AFFILIATES:

Stryker Orthopaedics
Stryker Osteosynthesis
OtisMed Corporation
Mutoh Co., Ltd.
Stryker Instruments
Memometal Technologies S.A.
Concentric Medical, Inc.
Orthovita, Inc.

CONTACTS: *Note: Officers with more than one job title may be intentionally listed here more than once.*

Stephen P. MacMillan, CEO
Stephen P. MacMillan, Pres.
Curt R. Hartman, CFO/VP
Michael W. Rude, VP-Human Resources
Curtis E. Hall, General Counsel/Sec./VP
Lonny Carpenter, Group Pres., Oper. & Global Quality
Katherine A. Owen, VP-Strategy
Katherine A. Owen, VP-Investor Rel.
Tony McKinney, Chief Acct. Officer/VP
Michael P. Mogul, Group Pres., Orthopaedics
Eric Lum, VP-Tax
Tim Scannell, Group Pres., MedSurg & Spine
Kevin A. Lobo, Group Pres., Orthopaedics
Stephen P. MacMillan, Chmn.
Ramesh Subrahmanian, Group Pres., Int'l

Phone: 269-385-2600 **Fax:** 269-385-1062
Toll-Free:
Address: 2825 Airview Blvd., Kalamazoo, MI 49002 US

GROWTH PLANS/SPECIAL FEATURES:

Stryker Corp. develops, manufactures and markets specialty surgical and medical products for the global market. These products include orthopedic implants, patient care and handling equipment, powered surgical instruments and endoscopic systems. The firm's products are produced by two segments: Orthopedic Implants (59% of revenues) and MedSurg equipment (41% of revenues). The Orthopedic Implant segment's products include reconstructive implants for knee, hip, elbow, shoulder and other joint surgeries; nailing, plating and external fixation systems to mend trauma injuries; spine implants; micro implants for craniomaxillofacial and hand surgery; and bone cement. Bone implants are typically made from cobalt chromium, titanium alloys, ceramics or ultrahigh molecular weight polyethylene. This segment's products are designed and manufactured by subsidiaries Stryker Orthopaedics, Stryker Osteosynthesis, Stryker Spine and Stryker Biotech. The MedSurg Equipment segment includes powered surgical instruments (including bone saws, drills and rasps), surgical navigation systems (including navigation software), hospital beds and stretchers, endoscopic products, emergency medical equipment and medical video imaging equipment. These devices are produced by Stryker Instruments, Stryker Endoscopy and Stryker Medical. The company maintains administrative, sales, warehousing and distribution sites in 41 countries in Europe, Asia, Africa and the Americas, as well as exporting products to numerous international destinations. In November 2010, Stryker acquired medical instrument developers OtisMed Corporation and Mutoh Co., Ltd. In December 2010, the company purchased Ascent Healthcare Solutions, which reprocesses and remanufactures medical devices. In January 2011, Stryker acquired the neurovascular operations of Boston Scientific. In February 2011, the firm sold its OP-1 product family to Olympus. 2011 acquisitions include Orthovita, Inc., Memometal Technologies S.A. and Concentric Medical, Inc.

Stryker offers its employees healthcare benefits; retirement programs; tuition reimbursement, an onsite cafeteria and fitness center; wellness programs; and discount purchase programs.

FINANCIALS: **Sales and profits are in thousands of dollars—add 000 to get the full amount. 2010 Note: Financial information for 2010 was not available for all companies at press time.**

2010 Sales: $7,320,000	2010 Profits: $1,273,400
2009 Sales: $6,723,100	2009 Profits: $1,107,400
2008 Sales: $6,718,200	2008 Profits: $1,147,800
2007 Sales: $6,000,500	2007 Profits: $1,017,400
2006 Sales: $5,147,200	2006 Profits: $777,700

U.S. Stock Ticker: SYK
Int'l Ticker:
Int'l Exchange:
Employees: 20,036 Fiscal Year Ends: 12/31
Parent Company:

SALARIES/BENEFITS:

Pension Plan:	ESOP Stock Plan:	Profit Sharing:	Top Exec. Salary: $1,200,000	Bonus: $1,375,734
Savings Plan: Y	Stock Purch. Plan: Y		Second Exec. Salary: $490,000	Bonus: $470,064

OTHER THOUGHTS:

Apparent Women Officers or Directors: 6
Hot Spot for Advancement for Women/Minorities: Y

LOCATIONS: ("Y" = Yes)

West:	Southwest:	Midwest:	Southeast:	Northeast:	International:
Y	Y	Y	Y	Y	Y

SUN HEALTHCARE GROUP INC

www.sunh.com

Industry Group Code: 623110

Management:		**Sales/Marketing:**		**Liberal Arts:**		**Information Sys.:**		**Professionals:**		**Tech./Scientific:**	
Mgmt. Trainees:	Y	Marketing Pros.:	Y	Gen. Writing/Editing:	Y	Info. Mgmt.:	Y	Finance/Acct.:	Y	Engineers, Elec.:	
Experienced Mgmt.:	Y	Retail Sales:		Tech. Writing:	Y	Software Dev.:		Law:	Y	Engineers, Other:	
Int'l Business:		Comm./Industrial:		Graphic Arts/Photog.:	Y	Hardware Dev.:		HR/Other:	Y	Health/Lab:	
MBA Grads:	Y	Sales Trainees:		Music:		Consulting/Other:		Training:	Y	Science/Research:	
		Advertising Pros.:	Y	Broadcasting:				Health Care:	Y	Petroleum/Chem.:	
				Other:	Y			Consulting:		Math/Other:	

TYPES OF BUSINESS:

Long-Term Care
Sub-Acute Care
Assisted Living Services
Temporary Medical Staffing
Mobile Radiology
Medical Laboratory Services
Home Health Care Services
Physical Therapy

BRANDS/DIVISIONS/AFFILIATES:

SunDance Rehabilitation Corporation
CareerStaff Unlimited Inc
SunPlus Home Health Services
SunBridge Healthcare Corp
Sabra Health Care REIT Inc
SolAmor Hospice Corporation
Countryside Hospice Care Inc

CONTACTS: *Note: Officers with more than one job title may be intentionally listed here more than once.*

William A. Mathies, CEO
L. Bryan Shaul, CFO/Exec. VP
Cindy Chrispell, Sr. VP-Human Resources
Michael Newman, General Counsel/Exec. VP
Raymond L. Thivierge, Chief Dev. Officer
Jeffrey M. Kreger, Corp. Controller/VP
Brandi Riddle, VP/Treas.
Chauncey J. Hunker, Sr. VP/Chief Compliance Officer/Chief Risk Officer
Sue Gwyn, Pres., SunDance Rehabilitation Corp.
Logan Sexton, Pres., SunBridge Healthcare, LLC
William A. Mathies, Chmn.

Phone: 949-255-7100 **Fax:**
Toll-Free: 800-729-6600
Address: 18831 Von Karman, Ste. 400, Irvine, CA 92612 US

GROWTH PLANS/SPECIAL FEATURES:

Sun Healthcare Group, Inc., through its subsidiaries, is a nationwide provider of long-term, sub-acute and related specialty healthcare services primarily to the senior population in the U.S. The firm operates in three principal business segments: inpatient services (which accounts for 89% of total revenues), rehabilitation therapy services (6.3%) and medical staffing services (4.7%). Its core business is providing inpatient services, primarily through subsidiary SunBridge Healthcare Corp. SunBridge Healthcare has approximately 164 skilled nursing facilities, 16 combined skilled nursing, assisted and independent living centers; 10 assisted living centers; eight mental health centers; and two independent living centers, with a combined 23,053 licensed beds located in 25 states. These facilities provide inpatient skilled nursing and custodial services including therapeutic rehabilitation; housekeeping; daily nursing; social services; and dietary and administrative services for individuals requiring certain assistance for activities in daily living. Specialized care is available for patients with Alzheimer's disease. The firm's rehabilitation services are provided at approximately 508 facilities in 36 states through SunDance Rehabilitation Corporation. These services include physical therapy, speech pathology and occupational therapy. Sun Healthcare's medical staffing services, through CareerStaff Unlimited, Inc., operates in 39 states and provides licensed therapists skilled in physical, occupational and speech therapy; the subsidiary also provides nurses, pharmacists, pharmacist technicians, medical imaging technicians, physicians and related medical personnel. CareerStaff customers include hospitals, skilled nursing facilities, schools and prisons. In November 2010, the firm split into two publicly traded companies: Sun Healthcare Group, which includes all of the group's current subsidiaries; and Sabra Health Care REIT, Inc., which includes the firm's real estate portfolio. In January 2011, Sun Healthcare subsidiary SolAmor Hospice Corporation acquired Countryside Hospice Care, Inc.

FINANCIALS: **Sales and profits are in thousands of dollars—add 000 to get the full amount. 2010 Note: Financial information for 2010 was not available for all companies at press time.**

2010 Sales: $1,906,861 — 2010 Profits: $-4,650
2009 Sales: $1,881,799 — 2009 Profits: $38,671
2008 Sales: $1,823,503 — 2008 Profits: $109,287
2007 Sales: $1,557,756 — 2007 Profits: $57,510
2006 Sales: $1,004,897 — 2006 Profits: $27,118

U.S. Stock Ticker: SUNH
Int'l Ticker:
Int'l Exchange:
Employees: 29,992 Fiscal Year Ends: 12/31
Parent Company:

SALARIES/BENEFITS:

Pension Plan: ESOP Stock Plan: Profit Sharing: Top Exec. Salary: $786,491 Bonus: $735,944
Savings Plan: Y Stock Purch. Plan: Y Second Exec. Salary: $622,960 Bonus: $575,364

OTHER THOUGHTS:

Apparent Women Officers or Directors: 4
Hot Spot for Advancement for Women/Minorities: Y

LOCATIONS: ("Y" = Yes)

West:	Southwest:	Midwest:	Southeast:	Northeast:	International:
Y	Y	Y	Y	Y	

SUTTER HEALTH INC

www.sutterhealth.org

Industry Group Code: 622110

Management:		**Sales/Marketing:**		**Liberal Arts:**		**Information Sys.:**		**Professionals:**		**Tech./Scientific:**	
Mgmt. Trainees:	Y	Marketing Pros.:	Y	Gen. Writing/Editing:	Y	Info. Mgmt.:	Y	Finance/Acct.:	Y	Engineers, Elec.:	
Experienced Mgmt.:	Y	Retail Sales:		Tech. Writing:	Y	Software Dev.:		Law:	Y	Engineers, Other:	
Int'l Business:		Comm./Industrial:	Y	Graphic Arts/Photog.:		Hardware Dev.:		HR/Other:	Y	Health/Lab:	Y
MBA Grads:	Y	Sales Trainees:		Music:		Consulting/Other:		Training:	Y	Science/Research:	
		Advertising Pros.:	Y	Broadcasting:				Health Care:	Y	Petroleum/Chem.:	
				Other:	Y			Consulting:		Math/Other:	

TYPES OF BUSINESS:

Hospitals-General
Neonatal Care
Pregnancy & Birth
Training Programs
Medical Research Facilities
Home Health Services
Hospice Networks
Long-Term Care

BRANDS/DIVISIONS/AFFILIATES:

Samuel Merritt University
Sutter Institute for Medical Research
Sutter Health Institute for Research & Education
Palo Alto Medical Foundation Research Institute
California Pacific Medical Center Research
Jordan Research & Education Institute (The)

CONTACTS: *Note: Officers with more than one job title may be intentionally listed here more than once.*

Patrick Fry, CEO
Patrick Fry, Pres.
Robert D. Reed, CFO/Sr. VP
Jim Gray, Chmn.

Phone: 916-733-8800 **Fax:**
Toll-Free:
Address: 2200 River Plaza Dr., Sacramento, CA 95833 US

GROWTH PLANS/SPECIAL FEATURES:

Sutter Health, Inc. is one of the nation's largest not-for-profit health care systems. Through its affiliates, the firm serves 100 Northern California communities. Sutter Health operates approximately 24 hospitals; four trauma centers; 20 ambulatory surgery Centers; 11 home and hospice centers; nine behavioral health centers; one express care center; four long-term care centers and nine cancer centers. Many of the group's hospitals operate charitable foundations. The company has 4,946 affiliated doctors and approximately 5,000 volunteers. Sutter Health also operates physician and nurse training programs including Samuel Merritt University, formerly Samuel Merritt College for Nursing and Health Professional Training; clinical trial locations; home health companies; hospice and occupational health networks; comprehensive outpatient clinics; and long-term care centers. It is a regional leader in labor and delivery, neonatology, orthopedics, pediatrics and cancer care services. Specialty services include pregnancy information and classes; cancer survival and heart health services; visiting nurse and hospice care; and direct medical billing services. Sutter Health operates five research institutes: Sutter Institute for Medical Research; Sutter Health Institute for Research & Education; Palo Alto Medical Foundation Research Institute; The Jordan Research & Education Institute; and California Pacific Medical Center Research Institute. The company was one of the first health networks in its area to implement two eICU (electronic ICU) centers, which allow more comprehensive and consistent monitoring of ICU patients by feeding monitoring data to a central location.

Employees are offered medical, dental, vision and life insurance and flexible spending accounts.

FINANCIALS: **Sales and profits are in thousands of dollars—add 000 to get the full amount. 2010 Note: Financial information for 2010 was not available for all companies at press time.**

2010 Sales: $9,116,000 — 2010 Profits: $878,000
2009 Sales: $8,772,000 — 2009 Profits: $697,000
2008 Sales: $8,270,000 — 2008 Profits: $187,000
2007 Sales: $7,651,000 — 2007 Profits: $471,000
2006 Sales: $7,123,000 — 2006 Profits: $452,000

U.S. Stock Ticker: Nonprofit
Int'l Ticker:
Int'l Exchange:
Employees: 41,000 Fiscal Year Ends: 12/31
Parent Company:

SALARIES/BENEFITS:

Pension Plan: Y ESOP Stock Plan: Profit Sharing: Top Exec. Salary: $ Bonus: $
Savings Plan: Y Stock Purch. Plan: Y Second Exec. Salary: $ Bonus: $

OTHER THOUGHTS:

Apparent Women Officers or Directors:
Hot Spot for Advancement for Women/Minorities: Y

LOCATIONS: ("Y" = Yes)

West:	Southwest:	Midwest:	Southeast:	Northeast:	International:
Y					

SYMANTEC CORP

www.symantec.com

Industry Group Code: 511210E

Management:		Sales/Marketing:		Liberal Arts:		Information Sys.:		Professionals:		Tech./Scientific:	
Mgmt. Trainees:	Y	Marketing Pros.:	Y	Gen. Writing/Editing:	Y	Info. Mgmt.:	Y	Finance/Acct.:	Y	Engineers, Elec.:	Y
Experienced Mgmt.:	Y	Retail Sales:		Tech. Writing:	Y	Software Dev.:	Y	Law:	Y	Engineers, Other:	
Int'l Business:	Y	Comm./Industrial:	Y	Graphic Arts/Photog.:	Y	Hardware Dev.:		HR/Other:	Y	Health/Lab:	
MBA Grads:	Y	Sales Trainees:		Music:		Consulting/Other:	Y	Training:	Y	Science/Research:	
		Advertising Pros.:	Y	Broadcasting:				Health Care:		Petroleum/Chem.:	
				Other:				Consulting:		Math/Other:	Y

TYPES OF BUSINESS:

Software-Security
Remote Management Products
IT Consulting Services

BRANDS/DIVISIONS/AFFILIATES:

Norton360
Norton Utilities
Norton AntiVirus
Norton Internet Security
GuardianEdge
PGP Corporation
Symantec Data Insight for Storage
Ubiquity

CONTACTS:

Note: Officers with more than one job title may be intentionally listed here more than once.

Enrique T. Salem, CEO
Enrique T. Salem, Pres.
James Beer, CFO/Exec. VP
Carine Clark, Chief Mktg. Officer/Sr. VP
Rebecca Ranninger, Chief Human Resources Officer/Exec. VP
Deepak Mohan, Sr. VP-Info. Mgmt. Group
Mark Bregman, CTO/Exec. VP
Scott Taylor, General Counsel/Exec. VP/Sec.
Ken Berryman, Sr. VP-Strategy
Genevieve Haldeman, VP-Corp. Comm.
Bill Robbins, Exec. VP-Worldwide Sales
Janice Chaffin, Pres., Consumer Bus. Unit
Bernard Kwok, Sr. VP-APAC & Japan
Francis deSouza, Sr. VP-Enterprise Security Group
John W. Thompson, Chmn.
John Brigden, Sr. VP-EMEA

Phone: 650-527-8000 **Fax:**
Toll-Free:
Address: 350 Ellis St., Mountain View, CA 94043 US

GROWTH PLANS/SPECIAL FEATURES:

Symantec Corp. provides a range of software, appliances and services designed to secure and manage information technology (IT) infrastructure. The company provides customers worldwide with software and services that protect, manage and control information risks related to security, data protection, storage, compliance, and systems management. The firm has five operating segments: consumer products; security and compliance; storage and service management; services; and other. The consumer products segment delivers Internet security, PC tuneup and backup products. The company's Norton brand provides protection for Windows and Macintosh platforms. Primary consumer products include Norton Antivirus, Norton360, and Norton Internet Security, which help defend home and home office users by blocking online identity theft, detecting and eliminating spyware and protecting against hackers from entering a user's system. The security and compliance segment provides solutions for compliance and security management, endpoint security, messaging management and data protection management software solutions that allow customers to secure, provision, backup and remotely access laptops, PCs, mobile devices and servers. The storage and service management division provides storage and server management, data protection, and application performance services that manage IT risk on an ongoing basis. Symantec's services division offers technical support, managed services, consulting, support and education. The other segment includes sunset products and products nearing the end of their life cycle. Symantec Corp. operates in over 40 countries and maintains more than 40,000 partnerships worldwide. In January 2010, the firm agreed to acquire information security solutions provider Gideon Technologies, Inc. In June 2010, the company acquired email and data encryption firms GuardianEdge and PGP Corporation. In August 2010, Symantec Corp. acquired the identity and authentication operations of VeriSign. In late 2010, the company released evolving malware fighting product Ubiquity. In December 2010, the firm launched new unstructured data organizing tool Symantec Data Insight for Storage.

FINANCIALS:

Sales and profits are in thousands of dollars—add 000 to get the full amount. 2010 Note: Financial information for 2010 was not available for all companies at press time.

2010 Sales: $5,985,000 | 2010 Profits: $714,000
2009 Sales: $6,149,854 | 2009 Profits: $-6,728,870
2008 Sales: $5,874,419 | 2008 Profits: $463,850
2007 Sales: $5,199,370 | 2007 Profits: $404,380
2006 Sales: $4,143,392 | 2006 Profits: $156,852

U.S. Stock Ticker: SYMC
Int'l Ticker:
Int'l Exchange:
Employees: 17,400 Fiscal Year Ends: 3/31
Parent Company:

SALARIES/BENEFITS:

Pension Plan: | ESOP Stock Plan: | Profit Sharing: | Top Exec. Salary: $660,000 | Bonus: $747,120
Savings Plan: Y | Stock Purch. Plan: Y | | Second Exec. Salary: $625,000 | Bonus: $3,092,969

OTHER THOUGHTS:

Apparent Women Officers or Directors: 4
Hot Spot for Advancement for Women/Minorities: Y

LOCATIONS: ("Y" = Yes)

West:	Southwest:	Midwest:	Southeast:	Northeast:	International:
Y					Y

SYNTEL INC

www.syntelinc.com

Industry Group Code: 541513

Management:		Sales/Marketing:		Liberal Arts:		Information Sys.:		Professionals:		Tech./Scientific:	
Mgmt. Trainees:	Y	Marketing Pros.:	Y	Gen. Writing/Editing:	Y	Info. Mgmt.:	Y	Finance/Acct.:	Y	Engineers, Elec.:	Y
Experienced Mgmt.:	Y	Retail Sales:		Tech. Writing:	Y	Software Dev.:	Y	Law:	Y	Engineers, Other:	
Int'l Business:	Y	Comm./Industrial:	Y	Graphic Arts/Photog.:	Y	Hardware Dev.:	Y	HR/Other:	Y	Health/Lab:	
MBA Grads:	Y	Sales Trainees:		Music:		Consulting/Other:	Y	Training:	Y	Science/Research:	
		Advertising Pros.:		Broadcasting:				Health Care:		Petroleum/Chem.:	
				Other:	Y			Consulting:	Y	Math/Other:	

TYPES OF BUSINESS:

IT Consulting
Outsourcing Services
e-Business Solutions
Application Development & Management

BRANDS/DIVISIONS/AFFILIATES:

TeamSourcing
Identeon

CONTACTS:

Note: Officers with more than one job title may be intentionally listed here more than once.

Prashant Ranade, CEO
Prashant Ranade, Pres.
Arvind Godbole, CFO
Lakshmanan Chidambaram, VP-Sales
Srikanth Karra, Head-Global Human Resources
Arvind Godbole, Chief Info. Security Officer
Daniel Moore, Chief Admin. Officer
Daniel Moore, General Counsel/Sec.
Murlidhar Reddy, VP-Oper., Healthcare & Life Sciences Vertical
Neerja Sethi, VP
V.S. Raj, CEO-State Street Syntel Svcs. Private Ltd.
Anil Jain, Sr. VP-Insurance Bus. Unit
Rakesh Khanna, Pres., Banking & Finance Bus. Unit
Bharat Desai, Chmn.
Amit Chatterjee, Sr. VP/Head-Europe
R.S. Ramdas, Head-Global Procurement/Sr. VP-Corp. Svcs.

Phone: 248-619-2800 **Fax:** 248-619-2888
Toll-Free:
Address: 525 E. Big Beaver Rd., Ste. 300, Troy, MI 48083 US

GROWTH PLANS/SPECIAL FEATURES:

Syntel, Inc. delivers flexible, custom information technology (IT) and business process outsourcing (BPO) services to its Global 2000 companies and government entities. The firm caters to 124 customers in the U.S. and Europe. Services are divided into four segments: Applications Outsourcing, e-Business, Knowledge Process Outsourcing (KPO) and TeamSourcing. The Applications Outsourcing division outsources services for ongoing management, development and maintenance of business applications; this division contributes 76% of consolidated revenues. The e-Business unit provides customized technology services in web solutions (including architecture, web-enablement of legacy applications and portal development), customer relationship management services and maintains alliances with major IT application software infrastructure providers (such as IBM and Oracle); this division accounts for 7% of revenues. The KPO division focuses on transaction processing, loan servicing, retirement processing and collections; operating through the use of proprietary tool Identeon, which assists in strategic assessments of business processes, this business unit accounts for 15% of revenue. TeamSourcing provides professional IT consulting services including systems specification, design, development, implementation and maintenance of applications involving diverse computer hardware, software and networking technologies; it accounts for 2% of total revenues. Syntel holds strategic partnerships with approximately 22 technology companies, including Jaspersoft Corp.; MEGA International; Hewlett-Packard; Microsoft Corp.; and Oracle.

FINANCIALS:

Sales and profits are in thousands of dollars—add 000 to get the full amount. 2010 Note: Financial information for 2010 was not available for all companies at press time.

2010 Sales: $532,133	2010 Profits: $113,593
2009 Sales: $419,006	2009 Profits: $118,495
2008 Sales: $410,426	2008 Profits: $86,681
2007 Sales: $337,673	2007 Profits: $62,860
2006 Sales: $270,229	2006 Profits: $50,916

U.S. Stock Ticker: SYNT
Int'l Ticker:
Int'l Exchange:
Employees: 17,383 Fiscal Year Ends: 12/31
Parent Company:

SALARIES/BENEFITS:

Pension Plan:	ESOP Stock Plan:	Profit Sharing:	Top Exec. Salary: $284,418	Bonus: $
Savings Plan: Y	Stock Purch. Plan: Y		Second Exec. Salary: $256,602	Bonus: $

OTHER THOUGHTS:

Apparent Women Officers or Directors:
Hot Spot for Advancement for Women/Minorities:

LOCATIONS: ("Y" = Yes)

West:	Southwest:	Midwest:	Southeast:	Northeast:	International:
Y	Y	Y	Y	Y	Y

SYSCO CORP

www.sysco.com

Industry Group Code: 4244

Management:		Sales/Marketing:		Liberal Arts:		Information Sys.:		Professionals:		Tech./Scientific:	
Mgmt. Trainees:	Y	Marketing Pros.:	Y	Gen. Writing/Editing:	Y	Info. Mgmt.:	Y	Finance/Acct.:	Y	Engineers, Elec.:	
Experienced Mgmt.:	Y	Retail Sales:		Tech. Writing:		Software Dev.:	Y	Law:	Y	Engineers, Other:	
Int'l Business:	Y	Comm./Industrial:	Y	Graphic Arts/Photog.:	Y	Hardware Dev.:		HR/Other:	Y	Health/Lab:	
MBA Grads:	Y	Sales Trainees:	Y	Music:		Consulting/Other:		Training:	Y	Science/Research:	
		Advertising Pros.:	Y	Broadcasting:				Health Care:		Petroleum/Chem.:	
				Other:				Consulting:		Math/Other:	

TYPES OF BUSINESS:

Food-Wholesale Distribution
Restaurant Supplies Distribution
Medical & Surgical Supplies Distribution
Cleaning Supplies Distribution

BRANDS/DIVISIONS/AFFILIATES:

SYGMA Network
Baugh Supply Chain Cooperative Inc
SYSCO Natural
SYSCO Reliance
SYSCO Imperial
SYSCO Classic
SYSCO Supreme
Goldberg & Solovy Foods Inc

CONTACTS: *Note: Officers with more than one job title may be intentionally listed here more than once.*

William J. DeLaney, III, CEO
William J. DeLaney, III, Pres.
John T. McIntyre, VP-Sales & Brand Dev.
Paul T. Moskowitz, Sr. VP-Human Resources
John D. Holzem, VP-IT
Alan E. Hasty, Sr. VP-Merch.
Michael C. Nichols, Sr. VP-Admin.
Michael C. Nichols, General Counsel
Gregory S. Keller, VP-Corp. Bus. Dev.
Mark A. Palmer, VP-Corp. Comm.
Neil A. Russell, II, VP-Investor Rel.
G. Mitchell Elmer, Chief Acct. Officer/Controller/Sr. VP
Barbara B. Green, VP-Tax
D. Michael Downs, VP-Real Estate & Construction
Albert L. Gaylor, VP-Industry Rel. & Diversity
Kathy O. Gish, Treas./VP
Manuel A. Fernandez, Chmn.
Joel T. Grade, VP-Foodservice Oper., Canada
Robert E. Howell, VP-Supply Chain Svcs. & Sourcing

Phone: 281-584-1390	**Fax:** 281-584-2721
Toll-Free:	
Address: 1390 Enclave Pkwy., Houston, TX 77077-2099 US	

GROWTH PLANS/SPECIAL FEATURES:

SYSCO Corp., through its subsidiaries, is one of the largest distributors of food and food-related products to the foodservice industry in North America. The firm provides products and services to more than 400,000 customers, including restaurants, healthcare companies, educational facilities and lodging establishments. Restaurants account for approximately 62% of the company's sales; hospitals and nursing homes, 11%; schools and colleges, 5%; hotels and motels, 6%; and other sources, 16%. SYSCO distributes a wide variety of frozen and imported foods; fresh meats and seafood; dairy items; fresh produce; and nonfood items, including tableware, restaurant/kitchen equipment, medical/surgical supplies and cleaning supplies. Subsidiary SYGMA Network specializes in serving chain restaurants, especially Wendy's, which accounts for 31% of its sales. Subsidiary Baugh Supply Chain Cooperative, Inc. covers the purchasing and marketing of SYSCO-brand merchandise, as well as private-label and national-brand merchandise. The firm operates 177 distribution facilities throughout the U.S. and Canada, with a fleet of approximately 8,900 delivery vehicles (consisting of tractor and trailer combinations, vans and panel trucks); about 90% of these vehicles are company owned. SYSCO's brands include SYSCO Natural, its produce line; SYSCO Reliance low-cost food items; SYSCO Classic, featuring higher quality foods; and SYSCO Imperial and SYSCO Supreme, both of which offer the company's highest quality and most expensive products. In May 2011, the firm acquired foodservice distributor acquired Goldberg & Solovy Foods, Inc.

Employees of the firm are offered life, disability, medical, dental and vision insurance; annual performance incentives; an assistance program; tuition assistance; a stock purchase plan; matching charity gifts; a 401(k); direct deposit; product discounts; and business casual work attire.

FINANCIALS: **Sales and profits are in thousands of dollars—add 000 to get the full amount. 2010 Note: Financial information for 2010 was not available for all companies at press time.**

2010 Sales: $37,243,495	2010 Profits: $1,179,983	**U.S. Stock Ticker: SYY**
2009 Sales: $36,853,330	2009 Profits: $1,055,948	**Int'l Ticker:**
2008 Sales: $37,522,111	2008 Profits: $1,106,151	Int'l Exchange:
2007 Sales: $35,042,075	2007 Profits: $1,001,076	Employees: 46,000 Fiscal Year Ends: 6/30
2006 Sales: $32,628,438	2006 Profits: $855,325	Parent Company:

SALARIES/BENEFITS:

Pension Plan: Y	ESOP Stock Plan:	Profit Sharing:	Top Exec. Salary: $800,000	Bonus: $1,638,230
Savings Plan: Y	Stock Purch. Plan: Y		Second Exec. Salary: $730,000	Bonus: $1,830,363

OTHER THOUGHTS:

Apparent Women Officers or Directors: 7
Hot Spot for Advancement for Women/Minorities: Y

LOCATIONS: ("Y" = Yes)

West:	Southwest:	Midwest:	Southeast:	Northeast:	International:
Y	Y	Y	Y	Y	Y

TARGET CORPORATION

www.target.com

Industry Group Code: 452112

Management:		Sales/Marketing:		Liberal Arts:		Information Sys.:		Professionals:		Tech./Scientific:	
Mgmt. Trainees:	Y	Marketing Pros.:	Y	Gen. Writing/Editing:	Y	Info. Mgmt.:	Y	Finance/Acct.:	Y	Engineers, Elec.:	
Experienced Mgmt.:	Y	Retail Sales:	Y	Tech. Writing:		Software Dev.:	Y	Law:	Y	Engineers, Other:	
Int'l Business:	Y	Comm./Industrial:		Graphic Arts/Photog.:	Y	Hardware Dev.:		HR/Other:	Y	Health/Lab:	
MBA Grads:	Y	Sales Trainees:	Y	Music:		Consulting/Other:		Training:	Y	Science/Research:	
		Advertising Pros.:	Y	Broadcasting:				Health Care:		Petroleum/Chem.:	
				Other:	Y			Consulting:		Math/Other:	

TYPES OF BUSINESS:

Discount Department Stores
Online Sales
Catalog Sales
Groceries
Credit Cards

BRANDS/DIVISIONS/AFFILIATES:

SuperTarget
Target.com
Market Pantry
Archer Farms
Merona
Xhilaration
Choxie
REDcards

CONTACTS: *Note: Officers with more than one job title may be intentionally listed here more than once.*

Gregg W. Steinhafel, CEO
Gregg W. Steinhafel, Pres.
Douglas A. Scovanner, CFO/Exec. VP
Michael R. Francis, Chief Mktg. Officer/Exec. VP
Jodeen A. Kozlak, Exec. VP-Human Resources
Beth M. Jacob, CIO/Sr. VP-Tech. Svcs.
Jane P. Windmeier, Sr. VP-Tech.
Kathryn A. Tesija, Exec. VP-Merch.
Timothy R. Baer, General Counsel/Exec. VP/Corp. Sec.
Janna Adair-Potts, Sr. VP-Store Oper.
John D. Griffith, Exec. VP-Property Dev.
Stephen Eastman, Pres., Target.com
Susan KahnSusan Kahn, Sr. VP-Corp. Comm.
Jane P. Windmeier, Sr. VP-Global Fianace Systems
Sid Keswani, Sr. VP-Stores
Terrence J. Scully, Pres., Target Financial & Retail Svcs.
Bryan Everett, Sr. VP-Stores
Derek Jenkins, Sr. VP-Stores
Gregg W. Steinhafel, Chmn.
Lalit Ahuja, Chmn./Pres., Target India
Mitchell L. Stover, Sr. VP-Dist.

Phone: 612-304-6073	**Fax:** 612-696-3731
Toll-Free:	
Address: 1000 Nicollet Mall, Minneapolis, MN 55403 US	

GROWTH PLANS/SPECIAL FEATURES:

Target Corporation operates large-format general merchandise and food discount stores in the U.S., which include Target and SuperTarget stores. The firm operates in two segments: retail operations and credit cards. Target operates approximately 1,750 stores in 49 states, as well as 37 distribution centers. Over 240 of these locations are SuperTarget stores, which combine grocery and general merchandise in a single format. SuperTarget stores feature coffee bars, bakeries, banking areas, pharmacies and photo services. The company operates three stores in India as well as those in the U.S. Target carries brands such as Play Wonder; Smith & Hawken; Room Essentials; Durabuilt; Embark; Garden Place; Boots & Barkley; Choxie; Circo; Gilligan & O'Malley; Kaori; and Sutton and Dodge. In addition, Target sells merchandise under its own private-label brands, including Market Pantry, Archer Farms, Merona, Xhilaration, Choxie, Trutech, Target and Target Limited Edition. Target stores derive the largest percentage of sales from household essentials (approximately 24%); while electronics, sporting goods, toys and entertainment accounts for 20%; apparel and accessories for 20%; home furniture and decor for 19%; and food and pet supplies for 17%. The company's proprietary credit card products, called REDcards, provide discounts in an attempt to gain customer loyalty. REDcards are sold under the Target Visa and Target Card names. Target also sells merchandise via its e-commerce site, Target.com. The average Target customer is 40 years old, with an annual household income of roughly $64,000. The firm plans to eventually open 3,000 new stores in the U.S. and will test small urban-store designs, ranging from 60,000 to 100,000 square feet.

Target offers employees life, disability, medical, dental and prescription drug insurance; educational loans; tuition reimbursement; home loans; childcare, tax preparation and adoption assistance; and several discount plans.

FINANCIALS: **Sales and profits are in thousands of dollars—add 000 to get the full amount. 2010 Note: Financial information for 2010 was not available for all companies at press time.**

2010 Sales: $65,357,000	2010 Profits: $2,488,000	**U.S. Stock Ticker: TGT**
2009 Sales: $64,948,000	2009 Profits: $2,214,000	**Int'l Ticker:**
2008 Sales: $63,367,000	2008 Profits: $2,849,000	Int'l Exchange:
2007 Sales: $59,490,000	2007 Profits: $2,787,000	Employees: 351,000 Fiscal Year Ends: 1/31
2006 Sales: $52,620,000	2006 Profits: $2,408,000	Parent Company:

SALARIES/BENEFITS:

Pension Plan:	ESOP Stock Plan:	Profit Sharing:	Top Exec. Salary: $1,500,000	Bonus: $5,301,000
Savings Plan: Y	Stock Purch. Plan: Y		Second Exec. Salary: $995,000	Bonus: $1,469,814

OTHER THOUGHTS:

Apparent Women Officers or Directors: 20
Hot Spot for Advancement for Women/Minorities: Y

LOCATIONS: ("Y" = Yes)

West:	Southwest:	Midwest:	Southeast:	Northeast:	International:
Y	Y	Y	Y	Y	Y

TEAM HEALTH HOLDINGS INC

www.teamhealth.com

Industry Group Code: 6211

Management:		Sales/Marketing:		Liberal Arts:		Information Sys.:		Professionals:		Tech./Scientific:	
Mgmt. Trainees:	Y	Marketing Pros.:	Y	Gen. Writing/Editing:		Info. Mgmt.:	Y	Finance/Acct.:	Y	Engineers, Elec.:	
Experienced Mgmt.:	Y	Retail Sales:		Tech. Writing:		Software Dev.:		Law:	Y	Engineers, Other:	
Int'l Business:		Comm./Industrial:		Graphic Arts/Photog.:		Hardware Dev.:		HR/Other:	Y	Health/Lab:	Y
MBA Grads:		Sales Trainees:		Music:		Consulting/Other:	Y	Training:	Y	Science/Research:	Y
		Advertising Pros.:		Broadcasting:				Health Care:	Y	Petroleum/Chem.:	
				Other:				Consulting:	Y	Math/Other:	

TYPES OF BUSINESS:

Hospital Staffing
Emergency Department Administration
Pediatrics
Radiology & Teleradiology Services
Urgent Care

BRANDS/DIVISIONS/AFFILIATES:

Daniel & Yeager, Inc.
Spectrum Healthcare Resources
After Hours Pediatrics
Morningstar Emergency Physicians
TeamHealth Medical Call Center
Medical Management Resources of TeamHealth
Health Care Financial Services
Healthcare Revenue Recovery Group

CONTACTS: *Note: Officers with more than one job title may be intentionally listed here more than once.*

Gregory Roth, CEO
Gregory Roth, Pres.
David Jones, CFO/Exec. VP
Dan Wilbanks, Sr. VP-Mktg.
Gar LaSalle, Chief Medical Officer
Joe Carman, Chief Admin. Officer
Heidi Allen, General Counsel/Sr. VP
Kent Bristow, Sr. VP-Oper.
Dan Wilbanks, Sr. VP-Bus. Dev.
Paul Gleis, Chief Compliance Officer
Oliver Rogers, Pres., Hospital Based Svcs.
David Grinbergs, Pres., Emergency Medicine Div.
Barbara Blevins, COO-Hospital Based Svcs.
Lynn Massingale, Exec. Chmn.

Phone: 865-693-1000 **Fax:** 865-539-3073
Toll-Free: 800-818-1498
Address: 265 Brookview Ctr. Way, Ste. 400, Knoxville, TN 37919 US

GROWTH PLANS/SPECIAL FEATURES:

Team Health Holdings, Inc. is a provider of clinical outsourcing services such as emergency department administration and staffing. The firm, operating through subsidiaries and affiliates, offers services that include emergency, hospital and intensivist medicine; radiology and teleradiology services; pediatrics; military hospital staffing; medical call center services; occupational medicine; and urgent care. In addition, Team Health also manages recruiting, hiring, payroll, billing, collection and benefits functions. The firm has more than 5,600 health care professionals, including physicians, physician assistants, nurse practitioners and nurses who serve at 530 hospitals and affiliated clinics in 44 states. The company provides both permanent and as temporary assistance to its clients. Health care professionals are trained in a variety of different areas, specializing in anesthesia, emergency medicine, radiology, urgent care and pediatrics. Clients include civilian and military hospitals; surgical centers; imaging centers; and private clinics, which are concentrated mainly in Florida, the Midwest and California, the regions where Team Health is most active. The Team Health network operates through a series of specialty affiliates, organized regionally. For instance, Daniel & Yeager, Inc. provide locum tenens, otherwise known as temporary workers; Spectrum Healthcare Resources offers military medical staffing; After Hours Pediatrics provides urgent care facilities for infants, children and young adults in concert with local pediatricians; and Health Care Financial Services and Healthcare Revenue Recovery Group provide billing and collections services. In August 2010, Team Health acquired Morningstar Emergency Physicians, which operates 15 facilities in Texas and Oklahoma.

Employees are offered health, dental and vision insurance; life insurance; and flexible spending accounts, among other benefits.

FINANCIALS: **Sales and profits are in thousands of dollars—add 000 to get the full amount. 2010 Note: Financial information for 2010 was not available for all companies at press time.**

2010 Sales: $1,519,264 | 2010 Profits: $13,337
2009 Sales: $1,423,441 | 2009 Profits: $40,705
2008 Sales: $2,291,812 | 2008 Profits: $44,666
2007 Sales: $2,106,152 | 2007 Profits: $43,270
2006 Sales: $ | 2006 Profits: $

U.S. Stock Ticker: TMH
Int'l Ticker:
Int'l Exchange:
Employees: 5,700 Fiscal Year Ends: 12/31
Parent Company:

SALARIES/BENEFITS:

Pension Plan: | ESOP Stock Plan: | Profit Sharing: | Top Exec. Salary: $664,615 | Bonus: $647,000
Savings Plan: Y | Stock Purch. Plan: | | Second Exec. Salary: $600,832 | Bonus: $534,222

OTHER THOUGHTS:

Apparent Women Officers or Directors: 2
Hot Spot for Advancement for Women/Minorities:

LOCATIONS: ("Y" = Yes)

West:	Southwest:	Midwest:	Southeast:	Northeast:	International:
Y	Y	Y	Y	Y	

TEAM INC

www.teaminc.com

Industry Group Code: 237

Management:		**Sales/Marketing:**		**Liberal Arts:**		**Information Sys.:**		**Professionals:**		**Tech./Scientific:**	
Mgmt. Trainees:	Y	Marketing Pros.:	Y	Gen. Writing/Editing:		Info. Mgmt.:	Y	Finance/Acct.:	Y	Engineers, Elec.:	
Experienced Mgmt.:	Y	Retail Sales:		Tech. Writing:	Y	Software Dev.:		Law:	Y	Engineers, Other:	Y
Int'l Business:	Y	Comm./Industrial:	Y	Graphic Arts/Photog.:		Hardware Dev.:		HR/Other:	Y	Health/Lab:	
MBA Grads:	Y	Sales Trainees:		Music:		Consulting/Other:		Training:	Y	Science/Research:	
		Advertising Pros.:		Broadcasting:				Health Care:		Petroleum/Chem.:	
				Other:				Consulting:		Math/Other:	

TYPES OF BUSINESS:

Piping System Maintenance & Construction Services

BRANDS/DIVISIONS/AFFILIATES:

Quest Integrity Group, LLC

CONTACTS: *Note: Officers with more than one job title may be intentionally listed here more than once.*

Philip J. Hawk, CEO
Pete W. Wallace, COO/Exec. VP
Ted W. Owen, CFO/Exec. VP
John P. Kearns, Sr. VP-Eng.
John P. Kearns, Sr. VP-Mfg.
Andre C. Bouchard, Sr. VP-Admin.
Andre C. Bouchard, General Counsel/Sec.
David C. Palmore, Sr. VP-TMS Div.
Art Victorson, Sr. VP-TCM Div.
Philip J. Hawk, Chmn.

Phone: 281-331-6154	**Fax:**
Toll-Free: 800-662-8326	
Address: 200 Hermann Dr., Alvin, TX 77511 US	

GROWTH PLANS/SPECIAL FEATURES:

Team, Inc. is a provider of specialty maintenance and construction services related primarily to the maintenance of high temperature and high pressure piping systems utilized in heavy industries. The company's offerings encompass a range of services, including leak repair, hot tapping, fugitive emissions control, field machining, technical bolting, field valve repair, non-destructive testing and field heat treating. Team's services are available 24-hours-a-day, seven-days-a-week, and are marketed to companies in a broad range of industries, including petrochemicals, refining, power, pipeline, pulp and paper, steel, shipbuilding, original equipment manufacturers (OEMs), municipalities and large engineering and construction firms. Team's leak repair services consist of on-stream repairs of leaks in pipes, valves, flanges and other parts of piping systems and related equipment, utilizing both standard and custom-designed clamps and enclosures for piping systems. The company's hot tapping services involve utilizing special equipment to cut holes in pressurized pipelines so that new branch pipes can be connected without interrupting operations. Emissions control services are focused on volatile organic chemical leaks, and include identification, monitoring, data management and reporting services, primarily for the chemical, refining and natural gas processing industries. Field machining services include flange facing, pipe cutting, line boring, journal turning, drilling and milling, while technical bolting services help to maintain leak-free connections. Field valve services encompass on-site repairs for a variety of valves, as well as diagnostics and repair for specialty valve actuators. The company maintains over 100 locations throughout the U.S. and internationally in Canada, Aruba, Belgium, Singapore, the Netherlands, Trinidad and Venezuela. 71.3% of the firm's revenues are generated by business in the U.S., while Canada accounts for approximately 19.7% and Europe 5.5%; the remaining 3.5% coming from other foreign locations. In November 2010, Team acquired a 95% interest in Quest Integrity Group, LLC for roughly $42.6 million.

FINANCIALS: **Sales and profits are in thousands of dollars—add 000 to get the full amount. 2010 Note: Financial information for 2010 was not available for all companies at press time.**

2010 Sales: $453,869	2010 Profits: $12,275	**U.S. Stock Ticker: TISI**
2009 Sales: $497,559	2009 Profits: $22,911	**Int'l Ticker:**
2008 Sales: $478,475	2008 Profits: $23,623	Int'l Exchange:
2007 Sales: $318,348	2007 Profits: $15,515	Employees: 3,100 Fiscal Year Ends: 5/31
2006 Sales: $259,838	2006 Profits: $10,636	Parent Company:

SALARIES/BENEFITS:

Pension Plan:	ESOP Stock Plan:	Profit Sharing:	Top Exec. Salary: $525,000	Bonus: $300,000
Savings Plan: Y	Stock Purch. Plan:		Second Exec. Salary: $300,000	Bonus: $170,000

OTHER THOUGHTS:

Apparent Women Officers or Directors:
Hot Spot for Advancement for Women/Minorities:

LOCATIONS: ("Y" = Yes)

West:	Southwest:	Midwest:	Southeast:	Northeast:	International:
Y	Y	Y	Y	Y	Y

TECH DATA CORP

www.techdata.com

Industry Group Code: 423430

Management:		Sales/Marketing:		Liberal Arts:		Information Sys.:		Professionals:		Tech./Scientific:	
Mgmt. Trainees:	Y	Marketing Pros.:	Y	Gen. Writing/Editing:	Y	Info. Mgmt.:	Y	Finance/Acct.:	Y	Engineers, Elec.:	
Experienced Mgmt.:	Y	Retail Sales:		Tech. Writing:	Y	Software Dev.:	Y	Law:	Y	Engineers, Other:	
Int'l Business:	Y	Comm./Industrial:	Y	Graphic Arts/Photog.:	Y	Hardware Dev.:		HR/Other:	Y	Health/Lab:	
MBA Grads:	Y	Sales Trainees:	Y	Music:		Consulting/Other:		Training:	Y	Science/Research:	
		Advertising Pros.:	Y	Broadcasting:				Health Care:		Petroleum/Chem.:	
				Other:				Consulting:		Math/Other:	

TYPES OF BUSINESS:

Computer & Software Products, Distribution
Training
Assembly Services

BRANDS/DIVISIONS/AFFILIATES:

Cisco Solutions Group
Triade Holding BV

CONTACTS:

Note: Officers with more than one job title may be intentionally listed here more than once.

Robert M. Dutkowsky, CEO
Jeffery P. Howells, CFO/Exec. VP
John O'Shea, VP-Network Prod. Mktg.
John Tonnison, CIO/Exec. VP
David R. Vetter, General Counsel/Sr. VP/Sec.
Jarred LeFebvre, Mgr.-Public Rel.
Charles V. Dannewitz, Treas./Sr. VP
Joseph B. Trepani, Sr. VP/Controller
Murray Wright, Pres., The Americas
Steven A. Raymund, Chmn.
Nestor Cano, Pres., Europe
Darryl Branch, Sr. VP-Logistics & Integration Svcs.

Phone: 727-539-7429 | **Fax:** 727-538-5860
Toll-Free: 800-292-7906
Address: 5350 Tech Data Dr., Clearwater, FL 33760 US

GROWTH PLANS/SPECIAL FEATURES:

Tech Data Corp. is a worldwide distributor of information technology (IT) products, logistics management and other value-added services. The company serves more than 125,000 value-added resellers (VARs), direct marketers, retailers and corporate resellers in over 100 countries throughout Europe, Latin America and North America. It offers a variety of products from manufacturers and publishers including Fujitsu-Siemens, Apple, Autodesk, Symantec, Hewlett-Packard, Canon, Nortel Networks, Cisco Systems, Acer, Adobe, IBM, Intel, Kingston, McAfee, Lexmark, Microsoft, Samsung, Sony, Toshiba, Western Digital and Xerox. Products are typically purchased directly from manufacturers or software publishers on a non-exclusive basis, and then shipped to customers from one of Tech Data's 24 regionally located logistics centers. The company's vendor agreements do not restrict it from selling similar products manufactured by competitors. The firm also provides resellers with extensive pre- and post-sale training, service and support, as well as configuration and assembly services and e-commerce tools. Tech Data provides products and services to the online reseller channel and does business with thousands of resellers through its web site. The firm's entire electronic catalog is available online, and its electronic software distribution initiative allows resellers and vendors to easily access software titles directly from a secure location on the web site. Tech Data's Cisco Solutions Group business unit supports the firm's entire solutions offering from networking firm Cisco Systems. In October 2010, the firm acquired electronics and information technology company Triade Holding B.V.

FINANCIALS:

Sales and profits are in thousands of dollars—add 000 to get the full amount. 2010 Note: Financial information for 2010 was not available for all companies at press time.

2010 Sales: $22,099,876 | 2010 Profits: $180,155
2009 Sales: $24,080,484 | 2009 Profits: $117,278
2008 Sales: $23,423,078 | 2008 Profits: $102,129
2007 Sales: $21,440,445 | 2007 Profits: $-96,981
2006 Sales: $20,482,851 | 2006 Profits: $26,586

U.S. Stock Ticker: TECD
Int'l Ticker:
Int'l Exchange:
Employees: 7,600 Fiscal Year Ends: 1/31
Parent Company:

SALARIES/BENEFITS:

Pension Plan: | ESOP Stock Plan: | Profit Sharing: | Top Exec. Salary: $957,000 | Bonus: $1,914,000
Savings Plan: Y | Stock Purch. Plan: Y | | Second Exec. Salary: $709,500 | Bonus: $993,300

OTHER THOUGHTS:

Apparent Women Officers or Directors: 1
Hot Spot for Advancement for Women/Minorities:

LOCATIONS: ("Y" = Yes)

West:	Southwest:	Midwest:	Southeast:	Northeast:	International:
Y	Y	Y	Y	Y	Y

TEKTRONIX INC

www.tek.com

Industry Group Code: 3345

Management:		Sales/Marketing:		Liberal Arts:		Information Sys.:		Professionals:		Tech./Scientific:	
Mgmt. Trainees:	Y	Marketing Pros.:	Y	Gen. Writing/Editing:		Info. Mgmt.:	Y	Finance/Acct.:	Y	Engineers, Elec.:	Y
Experienced Mgmt.:	Y	Retail Sales:		Tech. Writing:	Y	Software Dev.:	Y	Law:	Y	Engineers, Other:	Y
Int'l Business:	Y	Comm./Industrial:	Y	Graphic Arts/Photog.:	Y	Hardware Dev.:	Y	HR/Other:	Y	Health/Lab:	
MBA Grads:	Y	Sales Trainees:		Music:		Consulting/Other:		Training:	Y	Science/Research:	Y
		Advertising Pros.:	Y	Broadcasting:				Health Care:		Petroleum/Chem.:	
				Other:				Consulting:		Math/Other:	Y

TYPES OF BUSINESS:

Test & Measurement Equipment
Support Services
Oscilloscopes
Logic analyzers
Video test equipment
Communications test equipment

BRANDS/DIVISIONS/AFFILIATES:

MAXTEK
TEKTRONIX
Danaher Corp
Mixed Signals, Inc.

CONTACTS: *Note: Officers with more than one job title may be intentionally listed here more than once.*

Amir Aghdaei, CEO
Amir Aghdaei, Pres.
Chuck McLaughlin, CFO/VP
Robert W. Blaskowsky, CIO/VP
Fuki Yoneyama, Pres., Japan Region/VP-Japan Sales

Phone: 503-627-7111 **Fax:** 503-627-6108
Toll-Free: 800-833-9200
Address: 14200 SW Karl Braun Dr., Beaverton, OR 97077 US

GROWTH PLANS/SPECIAL FEATURES:

Tektronix, Inc. develops, manufactures and markets test, measurement and monitoring products to a wide variety of customers in the computing, communications semiconductors, education, computer, military/aerospace, research and consumer electronics industries. The company provides general purpose testing products and video test, measurement and monitoring products, which includes oscilloscopes, logic analyzers, signal sources and spectrum analyzers. Additional video products include waveform monitors, video signal generators, compressed digital video test products and other test and measurement for video equipment manufacturers, content developers and traditional television broadcasters. The general testing products are designed to capture, display and analyze streams of electrical data, while video products ensure the delivery of the best possible video experience to the viewer. The firm also offers telecommunications network management and network diagnostics products. Network management products consist of network monitoring systems that actively test networks and provide troubleshooting, provisioning and automated service quality monitoring. The firm's products are sold under the TEKTRONIX and MAXTEK brand names. The company is a subsidiary of Danaher Corporation, a designer and manufacturer of a variety of professional, medical, industrial and consumer products. In mid 2010, Tektronix acquired digital content monitoring firm Mixed Signals, Inc.

Employees are offered medical and dental insurance; disability coverage; life insurance; and retirement plans.

FINANCIALS: **Sales and profits are in thousands of dollars—add 000 to get the full amount. 2010 Note: Financial information for 2010 was not available for all companies at press time.**

2010 Sales: $
2009 Sales: $
2008 Sales: $
2007 Sales: $1,105,172
2006 Sales: $1,039,870

2010 Profits: $
2009 Profits: $
2008 Profits: $
2007 Profits: $90,408
2006 Profits: $92,355

U.S. Stock Ticker: Subsidiary
Int'l Ticker:
Int'l Exchange:
Employees: 5,028 Fiscal Year Ends: 12/31
Parent Company: DANAHER CORP

SALARIES/BENEFITS:

Pension Plan: ESOP Stock Plan: Profit Sharing: Top Exec. Salary: $ Bonus: $472,900
Savings Plan: Stock Purch. Plan: Second Exec. Salary: $ Bonus: $

OTHER THOUGHTS:

Apparent Women Officers or Directors:
Hot Spot for Advancement for Women/Minorities:

LOCATIONS: ("Y" = Yes)

West:	Southwest:	Midwest:	Southeast:	Northeast:	International:
Y	Y			Y	Y

TELEDYNE TECHNOLOGIES INC

www.teledyne.com

Industry Group Code: 33641

Management:		Sales/Marketing:		Liberal Arts:		Information Sys.:		Professionals:		Tech./Scientific:	
Mgmt. Trainees:	Y	Marketing Pros.:	Y	Gen. Writing/Editing:		Info. Mgmt.:	Y	Finance/Acct.:	Y	Engineers, Elec.:	Y
Experienced Mgmt.:	Y	Retail Sales:		Tech. Writing:	Y	Software Dev.:	Y	Law:	Y	Engineers, Other:	Y
Int'l Business:	Y	Comm./Industrial:	Y	Graphic Arts/Photog.:	Y	Hardware Dev.:	Y	HR/Other:	Y	Health/Lab:	
MBA Grads:	Y	Sales Trainees:		Music:		Consulting/Other:		Training:	Y	Science/Research:	Y
		Advertising Pros.:	Y	Broadcasting:				Health Care:		Petroleum/Chem.:	
				Other:				Consulting:		Math/Other:	Y

TYPES OF BUSINESS:

Electronics & Communications Products
Systems Engineering Solutions
Aerospace Engines & Components
Energy Systems

BRANDS/DIVISIONS/AFFILIATES:

Teledyne Isco Inc
Teledyne Brown Engineering Inc
Teledyne ODI Inc
Teledyne Tekmar Co
Teledyne Energy Systems Inc
CML Group Ltd
DALSA Corporation
Nova Research Inc

CONTACTS: *Note: Officers with more than one job title may be intentionally listed here more than once.*

Robert Mehrabian, CEO
Robert Mehrabian, Pres.
Dale A. Schnittjer, CFO/Sr. VP
Robyn E. McGowan, VP-Human Resources
Patrick Neville, CIO/VP
Robert W. Steenberge, CTO/VP
Robyn E. McGowan, VP-Admin.
John T. Kuelbs, General Counsel/Exec. VP/Sec.
Jason VanWees, VP-Corp. Dev.
Jason VanWees, VP-Investor Rel.
Susan L. Main, Controller/VP
Ivars R. Blukis, Chief Bus. Risk Assurance Officer
Aldo Pichelli, COO/Pres., Electronics & Comm. Segment
Stephen F. Blackwood, Treas./VP
Rex Geveden, Pres., Teledyne Brown Eng.
Robert Mehrabian, Chmn.

Phone: 805-373-4545 **Fax:** 805-373-4775
Toll-Free:
Address: 1049 Camino Dos Rios, Thousand Oaks, CA 91360 US

GROWTH PLANS/SPECIAL FEATURES:

Teledyne Technologies, Inc., together with its subsidiaries, is a leading manufacturer of electronic components, instruments and communications products. The firm operates in four segments: Instrumentation, which generated 35% of 2010 sales; Digital Imaging, 8%; Aerospace & Defense Electronics, 37%; and Engineered Systems, 20%. Among its many precision instruments are defense electronics, monitoring and control instrumentation for marine, environmental and industrial applications; data acquisition and communications equipment for airlines and business aircraft and components; and subsystems for wireless and satellite communications. The company also provides systems engineering and IT services for defense, space and environmental applications, and manufactures general aviation engines and components, supply energy generation, energy storage and small propulsion products. Subsidiaries include Teledyne Isco, Inc., a producer of water quality monitoring products such as wastewater samplers and open channel flow meters; Teledyne Brown Engineering, Inc. (TBE), a full-service missile defense contractor; Teledyne Solutions, Inc., a missile defense systems engineering contractor for the U.S. Army; Teledyne Energy Systems, Inc., a provider of Teledyne Titan hydrogen gas generators and thermoelectric and fuel cell-based power sources; and Teledyne Tekmar Co., a manufacturer of instruments that automate the preparation and concentrations of drinking water and wastewater. In August 2010, TBE acquired U.K.-based CML Group, Ltd. In February 2011, the firm completed the acquisition of DALSA Corporation, a designer and manufacturer of digital imaging products and semiconductor wafers and components. In March 2011, it acquired a majority stake in Nova Research, Inc. In April 2011, the company divested its former piston engine businesses.

Teledyne Technologies offers its employees medical, dental and vision coverage; life insurance; a 401(k); a discount stock purchase plan; tuition reimbursement; and paid holidays and vacations.

FINANCIALS: **Sales and profits are in thousands of dollars—add 000 to get the full amount. 2010 Note: Financial information for 2010 was not available for all companies at press time.**

2010 Sales: $1,644,200	2010 Profits: $120,500
2009 Sales: $1,652,100	2009 Profits: $113,300
2008 Sales: $1,722,000	2008 Profits: $111,300
2007 Sales: $1,622,300	2007 Profits: $98,500
2006 Sales: $1,433,200	2006 Profits: $80,300

U.S. Stock Ticker: TDY
Int'l Ticker:
Int'l Exchange:
Employees: 9,200 Fiscal Year Ends: 12/31
Parent Company:

SALARIES/BENEFITS:

Pension Plan: Y	ESOP Stock Plan:	Profit Sharing:	Top Exec. Salary: $847,808	Bonus: $1,765,100
Savings Plan: Y	Stock Purch. Plan: Y		Second Exec. Salary: $433,974	Bonus: $507,200

OTHER THOUGHTS:

Apparent Women Officers or Directors: 4
Hot Spot for Advancement for Women/Minorities: Y

LOCATIONS: ("Y" = Yes)

West:	Southwest:	Midwest:	Southeast:	Northeast:	International:
Y	Y	Y	Y	Y	Y

Sales, profits and employees may be estimates. Financial information, benefits and other data can change quickly and may vary from those stated here.

TELEPHONE AND DATA SYSTEMS INC (TDS) www.teldta.com

Industry Group Code: 517110

Management:		Sales/Marketing:		Liberal Arts:		Information Sys.:		Professionals:		Tech./Scientific:	
Mgmt. Trainees:	Y	Marketing Pros.:	Y	Gen. Writing/Editing:	Y	Info. Mgmt.:	Y	Finance/Acct.:	Y	Engineers, Elec.:	Y
Experienced Mgmt.:	Y	Retail Sales:		Tech. Writing:	Y	Software Dev.:	Y	Law:	Y	Engineers, Other:	Y
Int'l Business:		Comm./Industrial:	Y	Graphic Arts/Photog.:	Y	Hardware Dev.:		HR/Other:	Y	Health/Lab:	
MBA Grads:	Y	Sales Trainees:	Y	Music:		Consulting/Other:		Training:	Y	Science/Research:	
		Advertising Pros.:	Y	Broadcasting:				Health Care:		Petroleum/Chem.:	
				Other:				Consulting:		Math/Other:	

TYPES OF BUSINESS:

Local Telephone Service
Cellular Telephone Services
Internet Access
Printing Services
Long-Distance Telephone Service
Data Networks
Broadband Service

BRANDS/DIVISIONS/AFFILIATES:

United States Cellular Corporation
TDS Telecom
TDS Metrocom
Suttle Straus Inc
VISI Inc
United States Cellular Corp
TEAM Technologies, LLC

CONTACTS: *Note: Officers with more than one job title may be intentionally listed here more than once.*

LeRoy T. Carlson, Jr., CEO
LeRoy T. Carlson, Jr., Pres.
Kenneth R. Meyers, CFO/Exec. VP
C. Theodore Herbert, VP-Human Resources
Kurt Thaus, CIO/Sr. VP
Joseph R. Hanley, VP-Tech., Planning & Svcs.
Kevin C. Gallagher, Sr. VP/Corp. Sec.
Scott H. Williamson, Sr. VP-Corp. Dev. & Acquisitions
Jane W. McCahon, VP-Corp. Rel.
James W. Twesme, VP-Finance
Frieda E. Ireland, VP-Internal Audit
Kenneth M. Kotylo, VP-Corp. Dev. & Acquisitions
Peter L. Sereda, VP/Treas.
Douglas D. Shuma, Corp. Controller/Sr. VP
Walter C.D. Carlson, Chmn.

Phone: 312-630-1900 **Fax:** 312-630-1908
Toll-Free:
Address: 30 N. LaSalle St., Ste. 4000, Chicago, IL 60602 US

GROWTH PLANS/SPECIAL FEATURES:

Telephone and Data Systems, Inc. (TDS) is a diversified telecommunications service company with wireless telephone and wireline telephone operations. It has approximately 6.1 million wireless customers and 1.1 million wireline equivalent access lines in 36 states. TDS has three subsidiary companies through which it operates: United States Cellular Corporation (U.S. Cellular), which generates 84% of revenue; TDS Telecommunications Corporation (TDS Telecom), generating 16% of revenue; and Suttle-Strauss, Inc, accounting for less than 1%. The firm owns approximately 82% of U.S. Cellular, which is one of the U.S.'s largest wireless telecommunications providers, with approximately 6.1 million customers in five major regions in 26 states. TDS conducts its wireline telephone operations through wholly-owned subsidiary TDS Telecom. This subsidiary provides voice, Internet and entertainment services, including local exchange service, long-distance telephone service and broadband access, to rural and suburban communities in 28 states through its incumbent local exchange carrier (ILEC) business; and its competitive local exchange carrier (CLEC) business, which operates under the brand TDS Metrocom. Majority-owned subsidiary (80%) Suttle-Straus is a full-service printing and communications company that offers corporate communications, direct mail and advertising materials to customers in the Chicago, Illinois, and Wisconsin markets. In March 2010, TDS acquired VISI, Inc., a provider of colocation, dedicated hosting, Internet and virtual computing services to small and medium-sized companies. VISI is included in the ILEC business division. In December of the same year, the firm acquired TEAM Technologies, LLC, a data center services provider, for $47 million. TDS Telecom gained direct control of the newly purchased company.

The firm offers employees medical, dental and vision insurance; life insurance; a pension plan; a 401(k) savings plan; disability coverage; domestic partner benefits; flexible spending accounts; stock purchase plans; an employee assistance plan; and product and entertainment discounts.

FINANCIALS: **Sales and profits are in thousands of dollars—add 000 to get the full amount. 2010 Note: Financial information for 2010 was not available for all companies at press time.**

2010 Sales: $4,986,829 — 2010 Profits: $188,982
2009 Sales: $5,019,943 — 2009 Profits: $247,109
2008 Sales: $5,091,388 — 2008 Profits: $117,895
2007 Sales: $4,829,000 — 2007 Profits: $386,100
2006 Sales: $4,364,500 — 2006 Profits: $161,800

U.S. Stock Ticker: TDS
Int'l Ticker:
Int'l Exchange:
Employees: 12,400 Fiscal Year Ends: 12/31
Parent Company:

SALARIES/BENEFITS:

Pension Plan: Y ESOP Stock Plan: Profit Sharing: Top Exec. Salary: $1,275,000 Bonus: $1,480,000
Savings Plan: Y Stock Purch. Plan: Y Second Exec. Salary: $882,000 Bonus: $935,000

OTHER THOUGHTS:

Apparent Women Officers or Directors: 4
Hot Spot for Advancement for Women/Minorities: Y

LOCATIONS: ("Y" = Yes)

West:	Southwest:	Midwest:	Southeast:	Northeast:	International:
Y	Y	Y	Y	Y	

TENET HEALTHCARE CORPORATION

www.tenethealth.com

Industry Group Code: 622110

Management:		**Sales/Marketing:**		**Liberal Arts:**		**Information Sys.:**		**Professionals:**		**Tech./Scientific:**	
Mgmt. Trainees:	Y	Marketing Pros.:	Y	Gen. Writing/Editing:		Info. Mgmt.:	Y	Finance/Acct.:	Y	Engineers, Elec.:	
Experienced Mgmt.:	Y	Retail Sales:		Tech. Writing:		Software Dev.:		Law:	Y	Engineers, Other:	Y
Int'l Business:		Comm./Industrial:		Graphic Arts/Photog.:		Hardware Dev.:		HR/Other:	Y	Health/Lab:	
MBA Grads:	Y	Sales Trainees:		Music:		Consulting/Other:		Training:	Y	Science/Research:	
		Advertising Pros.:		Broadcasting:				Health Care:	Y	Petroleum/Chem.:	
				Other:				Consulting:		Math/Other:	

TYPES OF BUSINESS:

Hospitals-General
Specialty Care Facilities
Outpatient Centers
Diagnostic Imaging Centers
Rural Health Care Clinics
HMOs

BRANDS/DIVISIONS/AFFILIATES:

CONTACTS:

Note: Officers with more than one job title may be intentionally listed here more than once.

Trevor Fetter, CEO
Stephen Newman, COO
Trevor Fetter, Pres.
Biggs C. Porter, CFO
Cathy Fraser, Sr. VP-Human Resources
Stephen F. Brown, CIO/Exec. VP
Gary Ruff, General Counsel/Sr. VP
Drew Kahn, VP-Oper.-Southern States Region
Edward Kangas, Chmn.

Phone: 469-893-2200 **Fax:** 469-893-8600
Toll-Free:
Address: 13737 Noel Rd., Dallas, TX 75240 US

GROWTH PLANS/SPECIAL FEATURES:

Tenet Healthcare Corporation specializes in the provision of health care services, primarily through the operation of general hospitals. All of Tenet's operations are conducted through its subsidiaries. The company's 49 general hospitals and a single critical access hospital, located in 11 states, together contain 13,428 licensed beds. Tenet's operations are structured into four regions and one separate market: the California region, which includes the hospitals in California and Nebraska; the Central region, which includes the hospitals in Missouri, Tennessee and Texas; the Southern States region, which includes the hospitals in Alabama, Georgia, North Carolina and South Carolina; the Florida Region, which includes the hospitals in Florida; and the separate market, which includes two hospitals in Philadelphia, Pennsylvania. Each of the company's general hospitals offers acute care services, operating and recovery rooms, radiology services, respiratory therapy services, clinical laboratories and pharmacies. In addition, most offer intensive care, critical care or coronary care units, physical therapy and orthopedic, oncology and outpatient services. Some of the hospitals also offer tertiary care services such as open-heart surgery, neonatal intensive care and neuroscience. Along with hospitals, Tenet's subsidiaries own or lease physician practices, captive insurance companies and other ancillary health care businesses, including outpatient surgery centers, diagnostic imaging centers and occupational and rural health care clinics. Its subsidiaries also own interests in a health maintenance organization (HMO).

The company offers its employees medical, dental and vision insurance; life and AD&D insurance; a 401(k) plan; an employee stock purchase plan; and credit union membership.

FINANCIALS:

Sales and profits are in thousands of dollars—add 000 to get the full amount. 2010 Note: Financial information for 2010 was not available for all companies at press time.

2010 Sales: $9,205,000 | 2010 Profits: $1,119,000
2009 Sales: $9,014,000 | 2009 Profits: $538,000
2008 Sales: $8,585,000 | 2008 Profits: $311,000
2007 Sales: $8,083,000 | 2007 Profits: $276,000
2006 Sales: $8,453,000 | 2006 Profits: $-732,000

U.S. Stock Ticker: THC
Int'l Ticker:
Int'l Exchange:
Employees: 43,020 Fiscal Year Ends: 12/31
Parent Company:

SALARIES/BENEFITS:

Pension Plan: | ESOP Stock Plan: | Profit Sharing: | Top Exec. Salary: $1,081,000 | Bonus: $4,075,825
Savings Plan: Y | Stock Purch. Plan: Y | | Second Exec. Salary: $720,800 | Bonus: $1,644,119

OTHER THOUGHTS:

Apparent Women Officers or Directors: 1
Hot Spot for Advancement for Women/Minorities: Y

LOCATIONS: ("Y" = Yes)

West:	Southwest:	Midwest:	Southeast:	Northeast:	International:
Y	Y	Y	Y	Y	

TEREX CORPORATION

www.terex.com

Industry Group Code: 333

Management:		Sales/Marketing:		Liberal Arts:		Information Sys.:		Professionals:		Tech./Scientific:	
Mgmt. Trainees:		Marketing Pros.:	Y	Gen. Writing/Editing:		Info. Mgmt.:	Y	Finance/Acct.:	Y	Engineers, Elec.:	Y
Experienced Mgmt.:		Retail Sales:		Tech. Writing:	Y	Software Dev.:		Law:	Y	Engineers, Other:	Y
Int'l Business:	Y	Comm./Industrial:	Y	Graphic Arts/Photog.:		Hardware Dev.:		HR/Other:	Y	Health/Lab:	
MBA Grads:	Y	Sales Trainees:		Music:		Consulting/Other:		Training:		Science/Research:	
		Advertising Pros.:	Y	Broadcasting:				Health Care:		Petroleum/Chem.:	
				Other:				Consulting:		Math/Other:	

TYPES OF BUSINESS:

Heavy Equipment
Cranes
Mining Equipment
Aerial Work Platforms
Road Building Equipment
Utility Products
Construction Equipment
Materials Handling Equipment

BRANDS/DIVISIONS/AFFILIATES:

Terex
Terex Cranes
Terex Atlas
Terex Aerial Work Platforms
Terex Construction
Terex Materials Processing

CONTACTS:

Note: Officers with more than one job title may be intentionally listed here more than once.

Ronald M. DeFeo, CEO
Phillip C. Widman, CFO/Sr. VP
Kevin A. Barr, Sr. VP-Human Resources
Eric I. Cohen, General Counsel/Sr. VP/Corp. Sec.
Brian J. Henry, Sr. VP-Bus. Dev.
Tom Gelston, VP-Investor Rel.
Brian J. Henry, Sr. VP-Finance
Tim Ford, Pres., Terex Aerial Work Platforms
Mark Clair, VP/Controller/Chief Acct. Officer
George Ellis, Pres., Terex Construction
Kieran Hegarty, Pres., Terex Materials Processing
Ronald M. DeFeo, Chmn.

Phone: 203-222-7170 **Fax:** 203-222-7976
Toll-Free:
Address: 200 Nyala Farm Rd., Westport, CT 06880 US

GROWTH PLANS/SPECIAL FEATURES:

Terex Corporation is a diversified global manufacturer of capital equipment. The company specializes in providing solutions for the construction, infrastructure, quarrying, shipping, transportation and utility industries. The company operates in four business segments: Terex Aerial Work Platforms; Terex Construction; Terex Cranes; and Terex Materials Processing. The Terex Aerial Work Platforms segment designs, manufactures and markets products such as material lifts, portable aerial work platforms, trailer-mounted articulating booms, self-propelled articulating and telescopic booms, scissor lifts, construction trailers and related components and parts. The Terex Construction segment designs, manufactures and markets roadbuilding, heavy and compact construction equipment. Roadbuilding equipment includes asphalt and concrete pavers, transfer devices, reclaimers/stabilizers, plants, mixers, placers and cold planers; landfill compactors; and bridge inspection equipment. Heavy equipment includes hydraulic excavators, off-highway trucks, large wheel loaders and material handlers. Compact equipment includes excavators, site dumpers, loader backhoes, compaction equipment and skid steer loaders. The Terex Cranes segment produces mobile telescopic cranes, tower cranes, lattice boom crawler cranes and truck-mounted cranes, as well as their related replacement parts and components. It also offers specialized port and rail equipment such as straddle carriers; gantry cranes; mobile harbor cranes; ship-to-shore cranes; telescopic container stackers; lift trucks; and forklifts, as well as related replacement parts and components. The Terex Materials Processing segment produces crushers, apron feeders, washing systems, screens and related components and replacement parts. Terex sells its products worldwide and operates manufacturing facilities in North America, South America, Europe, Australia and Asia. In February 2010, the company sold its mining division to Bucyrus International, Inc. for $1.3 billion. In April 2010, Terex Corporation sold its Germany-based Terex Atlas heavy construction equipment/knuckle-boom crane manufacturing business to Atlas Maschinen GmbH. In August 2010, the firm agreed to acquire 65% ownership of Chinese lattice boom crawler crane manufacturer Shandong Topower Heavy Machinery Company.

FINANCIALS:

Sales and profits are in thousands of dollars—add 000 to get the full amount. 2010 Note: Financial information for 2010 was not available for all companies at press time.

2010 Sales: $4,418,200	2010 Profits: $362,500	**U.S. Stock Ticker: TEX**
2009 Sales: $3,858,400	2009 Profits: $-398,400	**Int'l Ticker:**
2008 Sales: $8,387,000	2008 Profits: $71,900	Int'l Exchange:
2007 Sales: $7,976,100	2007 Profits: $613,900	Employees: 16,300 Fiscal Year Ends: 12/31
2006 Sales: $	2006 Profits: $	Parent Company:

SALARIES/BENEFITS:

Pension Plan:	ESOP Stock Plan:	Profit Sharing:	Top Exec. Salary: $1,058,958	Bonus: $782,000
Savings Plan:	Stock Purch. Plan:		Second Exec. Salary: $727,458	Bonus: $200,000

OTHER THOUGHTS:

Apparent Women Officers or Directors: 1
Hot Spot for Advancement for Women/Minorities:

LOCATIONS: ("Y" = Yes)

West:	Southwest:	Midwest:	Southeast:	Northeast:	International:
Y	Y	Y	Y	Y	Y

TETRA TECH INC

www.tetratech.com

Industry Group Code: 541690

Management:		Sales/Marketing:		Liberal Arts:		Information Sys.:		Professionals:		Tech./Scientific:	
Mgmt. Trainees:		Marketing Pros.:	Y	Gen. Writing/Editing:	Y	Info. Mgmt.:	Y	Finance/Acct.:	Y	Engineers, Elec.:	Y
Experienced Mgmt.:	Y	Retail Sales:		Tech. Writing:	Y	Software Dev.:	Y	Law:	Y	Engineers, Other:	
Int'l Business:	Y	Comm./Industrial:	Y	Graphic Arts/Photog.:	Y	Hardware Dev.:		HR/Other:	Y	Health/Lab:	
MBA Grads:	Y	Sales Trainees:		Music:		Consulting/Other:	Y	Training:		Science/Research:	
		Advertising Pros.:		Broadcasting:				Health Care:		Petroleum/Chem.:	
				Other:				Consulting:	Y	Math/Other:	

TYPES OF BUSINESS:

Consulting-Engineering & Technical
Water Resource Management
Infrastructure Consulting
Communications Infrastructure
Research & Development
Alternative Energy Development

BRANDS/DIVISIONS/AFFILIATES:

EBA Engineering Consultants Ltd
BPR Inc
Fransen Engineering Ltd

CONTACTS: *Note: Officers with more than one job title may be intentionally listed here more than once.*

Dan L. Batrack, CEO
Dan L. Batrack, Pres.
Steven M. Burdick, CFO/Sr. VP-Finance
Craig L. Christensen, CIO/Sr. VP
Ronald J. Chu, Exec. VP-Technical Support Svcs.
James R. Pagenkopf, Exec. VP-Eng. & Consulting Svcs.
Richard A. Lemmon, Sr. VP-Corp. Admin.
Janis B. Salin, General Counsel/Sec./VP
Michael A. Bieber, VP-Corp. Dev.
Sam W. Box, Sr. VP-Project Risk Mgmt.
Donald I. Rogers, Sr. VP-Remediation & Construction Group
Leslie L. Shoemaker, Sr. VP-Corp. Strategy
Wiliam R. Brownlie, Sr. VP-Eng.
Dan L. Batrack, Chmn.

Phone: 626-351-4664 **Fax:** 626-351-5291
Toll-Free:
Address: 3475 E. Foothill Blvd., Pasadena, CA 91107-6024 US

GROWTH PLANS/SPECIAL FEATURES:

Tetra Tech, Inc. provides consulting, engineering, program management, construction management and technical services focused on resource management, infrastructure and environmental impact. It operates four principal segments: Environmental Consulting Services (ECS), which generates about 33% of the firm's revenue; Technical Support Services (TSS), 24%; Engineering and Architecture Services (EAS), 13%; and Remediation and Construction Management (RCM), 35% (with 5% intersegment elimination). The ECS segment is concentrated on water resource management and provides services focused on the following areas: surface water, stormwater management and watershed management projects conducted for federal, state and local agencies, as well as commercial clients; groundwater projects, typically investigating contamination; waste management, including consulting and engineering services for hazardous waste contamination; mining and geotechnical science, for managing mining projects; and information technology and modeling, for data management and communications. The TSS segment provides solutions in the areas of environmental planning, cleanup, and reuse of contaminated sites; disaster management, including emergency response and public health preparedness; carbon footprint management through alternative fuel development and carbon capture; international development, primarily for nongovernmental organizations; and facility planning and operational support for federal government clients. The EAS segment provides design and construction services for water and wastewater treatment plants, combined sewer storage and separation facilities, environmentally sensitive buildings, commuter railway stations, bridges and major highways, and restores parks and river corridors. Finally, the RCM segment provides environmental remediation and reconstruction services, such as the construction of energy efficient facilities; and alternative energy development services, including site evaluation, biological assessment and construction services for wind, geothermal, solar, biogeneration and hydropower energy sites. Tetra has 330 offices across 13 countries. Recent company acquisitions include the international development business of PA Consulting Group; EBA Engineering Consultants, Ltd.; BPR, Inc.; and Fransen Engineering, Ltd.

FINANCIALS: **Sales and profits are in thousands of dollars—add 000 to get the full amount. 2010 Note: Financial information for 2010 was not available for all companies at press time.**

2010 Sales: $2,201,232	2010 Profits: $76,819
2009 Sales: $2,287,484	2009 Profits: $87,028
2008 Sales: $2,145,254	2008 Profits: $60,906
2007 Sales: $1,553,888	2007 Profits: $46,353
2006 Sales: $1,414,704	2006 Profits: $36,604

U.S. Stock Ticker: TTEK
Int'l Ticker:
Int'l Exchange:
Employees: 12,000 Fiscal Year Ends: 9/30
Parent Company:

SALARIES/BENEFITS:

Pension Plan: Y | ESOP Stock Plan: | Profit Sharing: | Top Exec. Salary: $638,846 | Bonus: $960,000
Savings Plan: | Stock Purch. Plan: Y | Second Exec. Salary: $442,153 | Bonus: $320,000

OTHER THOUGHTS:

Apparent Women Officers or Directors: 3
Hot Spot for Advancement for Women/Minorities: Y

LOCATIONS: ("Y" = Yes)

West:	Southwest:	Midwest:	Southeast:	Northeast:	International:
Y	Y	Y	Y	Y	Y

Sales, profits and employees may be estimates. Financial information, benefits and other data can change quickly and may vary from those stated here.

THERMO FISHER SCIENTIFIC INC

www.thermofisher.com

Industry Group Code: 423450

Management:		**Sales/Marketing:**		**Liberal Arts:**		**Information Sys.:**		**Professionals:**		**Tech./Scientific:**	
Mgmt. Trainees:	Y	Marketing Pros.:	Y	Gen. Writing/Editing:		Info. Mgmt.:	Y	Finance/Acct.:	Y	Engineers, Elec.:	
Experienced Mgmt.:	Y	Retail Sales:		Tech. Writing:	Y	Software Dev.:	Y	Law:	Y	Engineers, Other:	
Int'l Business:	Y	Comm./Industrial:	Y	Graphic Arts/Photog.:	Y	Hardware Dev.:		HR/Other:	Y	Health/Lab:	
MBA Grads:	Y	Sales Trainees:		Music:		Consulting/Other:		Training:	Y	Science/Research:	
		Advertising Pros.:		Broadcasting:				Health Care:		Petroleum/Chem.:	
				Other:				Consulting:		Math/Other:	

TYPES OF BUSINESS:

Laboratory Equipment & Supplies Distribution
Contract Manufacturing
Equipment Calibration & Repair
Clinical Trial Services
Laboratory Workstations
Clinical Consumables
Diagnostic Reagents
Custom Chemical Synthesis

BRANDS/DIVISIONS/AFFILIATES:

BRAHMS AG
Ahura Scientific
Finnzymes
Thermo Electron Industries
Fermentas International Inc
Thermo Scientific
Dharmacon
Dionex Corporation

CONTACTS: *Note: Officers with more than one job title may be intentionally listed here more than once.*

Marc N. Casper, CEO
Marc N. Casper, Pres.
Peter M. Wilver, CFO/Sr. VP
Seth H. Hoogasian, General Counsel/Sr. VP/Sec.
Kenneth J. Apicerno, VP-Investor Rel.
Peter E. Hornstra, Chief Acct. Officer/VP
Alan J. Malus, Sr. VP/Pres., Laboratory Prod.
Gregory J. Herrema, Sr. VP/Pres., Analytical Instruments
Edward A. Pesicka, Sr. VP/Pres., Customer Channels
Ken Berger, Sr. VP/Pres., Specialty Diagnostics
Jim Manzi, Chmn.

Phone: 781-622-1000	**Fax:** 781-622-1207
Toll-Free: 800-678-5599	
Address: 81 Wyman St., Waltham, MA 02454 US	

GROWTH PLANS/SPECIAL FEATURES:

Thermo Fisher Scientific, Inc. is a distributor of products and services principally to the scientific-research and clinical laboratory markets. The firm serves over 350,000 customers including biotechnology and pharmaceutical companies; colleges and universities; medical-research institutions; hospitals; reference, quality control, process-control and research and development labs in various industries; and government agencies. It operates in two segments: Analytical Technologies and Laboratory Products and Services. The Analytical Technologies segment has three primary growth platforms: analytical instruments, specialty diagnostics and biosciences; and through them, provides a broad range of instruments, software and services, bioscience reagents, and diagnostic assays. Thermo Fisher's products include analytical instruments; automation and robotics; life science research supplies; chemicals; disposable laboratory supplies; diagnostic supplies; laboratory equipment; furniture; software; and custom products. The company's services include asset management, instrument standards compliance services, education, technical support and professional assistance. The company's brands include ABGene, BioImage, Cellomics, Consolidated Technologies, Fisher Diagnostics, Microgenics, Owl Separation Systems, Inc, and Nalgene Outdoor. The company has over 600 subsidiaries, including Alchematrix, Echochem N.B., Flux Instruments, LambTrack Ltd., Fermentas International, Inc. and Thermo Electron Industries. In May 2011, Thermo Fisher acquired Dionex Corporation.

ThermoFisher offers its employees comprehensive benefits, paid time off, tuition reimbursement, retirement plans and employee recognition awards.

FINANCIALS: **Sales and profits are in thousands of dollars—add 000 to get the full amount. 2010 Note: Financial information for 2010 was not available for all companies at press time.**

2010 Sales: $10,788,700	2010 Profits: $1,035,600	**U.S. Stock Ticker: TMO**
2009 Sales: $10,109,700	2009 Profits: $850,300	**Int'l Ticker:**
2008 Sales: $10,498,000	2008 Profits: $980,900	Int'l Exchange:
2007 Sales: $9,746,400	2007 Profits: $748,400	Employees: 37,000 Fiscal Year Ends: 12/31
2006 Sales: $3,791,617	2006 Profits: $168,935	Parent Company:

SALARIES/BENEFITS:

Pension Plan: Y	ESOP Stock Plan:	Profit Sharing:	Top Exec. Salary: $981,970	Bonus: $1,610,000
Savings Plan: Y	Stock Purch. Plan:		Second Exec. Salary: $611,879	Bonus: $646,800

OTHER THOUGHTS:

Apparent Women Officers or Directors: 1
Hot Spot for Advancement for Women/Minorities: Y

LOCATIONS: ("Y" = Yes)

West:	Southwest:	Midwest:	Southeast:	Northeast:	International:
Y	Y	Y	Y	Y	Y

THOMSON REUTERS

www.thomsonreuters.com

Industry Group Code: 519130

Management:		**Sales/Marketing:**		**Liberal Arts:**		**Information Sys.:**		**Professionals:**		**Tech./Scientific:**	
Mgmt. Trainees:		Marketing Pros.:	Y	Gen. Writing/Editing:	Y	Info. Mgmt.:	Y	Finance/Acct.:	Y	Engineers, Elec.:	
Experienced Mgmt.:	Y	Retail Sales:		Tech. Writing:		Software Dev.:	Y	Law:	Y	Engineers, Other:	
Int'l Business:	Y	Comm./Industrial:	Y	Graphic Arts/Photog.:	Y	Hardware Dev.:		HR/Other:	Y	Health/Lab:	
MBA Grads:	Y	Sales Trainees:		Music:		Consulting/Other:		Training:	Y	Science/Research:	
		Advertising Pros.:	Y	Broadcasting:				Health Care:		Petroleum/Chem.:	
				Other:	Y			Consulting:		Math/Other:	

TYPES OF BUSINESS:

Information Services & Software
Legal & Regulatory Information Services
Financial Information & Technology
Health Care Information Tools
Scientific Data Tools

BRANDS/DIVISIONS/AFFILIATES:

Reuters Group PLC
Thomson Corporation
Reuters
Thomson Elite
Thomson Reuters Healthcare
Physicians' Desk Reference, Inc.
Thomson Reuters Group Limited
Breakingviews Limited

CONTACTS:

Note: Officers with more than one job title may be intentionally listed here more than once.

Thomas H. Glocer, CEO
Robert D. Daleo, CFO/Exec. VP
Gustav Carlson, Chief Mktg. Officer/Exec. VP
Stephen Dando, Chief Human Resources Officer/Exec. VP
Peter Jackson, Chief Scientist/VP-R&D
James Powell, CTO/Exec. VP
Andy Martens, Sr. VP-New Prod. Dev.
Deidre Stanley, General Counsel/Exec. VP
David Craig, Chief Strategy Officer
Frank Golden, Sr. VP-Investor Rel.
James C. Smith, Pres./CEO-Professional Div.
Devin Wenig, Pres./CEO-Markets Div.
Chris Ahearn, Pres., Reuters Media
Mark Redwood, Pres., Sales & Trading, Markets Div.
David Thomson, Chmn.

Phone: 646-223-4000	**Fax:**
Toll-Free:	
Address: 3 Times Square, New York, NY 10036 US	

GROWTH PLANS/SPECIAL FEATURES:

Thomson Reuters, formerly the Thomson Corporation, provides specialized information in digital and print formats, with operations in 100 countries. The company is organized in two divisions: Markets, which consists of the previous Reuters business combined with Thomson Financial; and Professional, which consists of Thomson's previous non-financial business segments. The Markets division includes four units: Sales & Trading, which provides information, trading and post-trade connectivity requirements of buy-side and sell-side customers in the foreign exchange, fixed income, equities and other exchange-traded instruments, and commodities and energy markets; Enterprise, which offers information and software supporting business automation within capital markets; Investment & Advisory, which provides information, decision support tools and integration services to portfolio managers, wealth managers, investment bankers, research analysts and corporate executives; and Media, which offers global information and news to print and digital media outlets, as well as directly to consumers through Reuters-branded digital services online, mobile and IPTV platforms. The Professional division includes three units: Legal, providing information, decision support tools and research services to legal, intellectual property, compliance, business and government professionals worldwide; Tax & Accounting, serving tax and accounting professionals in North America; and Healthcare & Science, serving physicians, scientists, researchers and other professionals in the healthcare, academic, corporate and government marketplaces. Approximately 90% of the company's revenues are derived from electronic products, software and online services. 86% of its revenue is in the form of recurring, subscription based activities. Thomson Reuters was formed in a merger-acquisition transaction between Thomson Corporation and Reuters Group PLC for $17.5 billion. In 2010, Thomson Reuters agreed to acquire a number of companies including ProfSoft, Inc.; Revista dos Tribunais; Point Carbon A/S; Complinet; Mace Advisers Limited; Highline Financial; Pangea3; and GeneGo.

FINANCIALS:

Sales and profits are in thousands of dollars—add 000 to get the full amount. 2010 Note: Financial information for 2010 was not available for all companies at press time.

2010 Sales: $13,070,000	2010 Profits: $933,000
2009 Sales: $12,997,000	2009 Profits: $1,575,000
2008 Sales: $13,441,000	2008 Profits: $1,942,000
2007 Sales: $7,296,000	2007 Profits: $4,062,000
2006 Sales: $6,641,000	2006 Profits: $1,143,000

U.S. Stock Ticker: TRI
Int'l Ticker:
Int'l Exchange:
Employees: 55,000 Fiscal Year Ends: 12/31
Parent Company:

SALARIES/BENEFITS:

Pension Plan:	ESOP Stock Plan:	Profit Sharing:	Top Exec. Salary: $1,550,000	Bonus: $2,976,000
Savings Plan:	Stock Purch. Plan:		Second Exec. Salary: $1,000,000	Bonus: $1,200,000

OTHER THOUGHTS:

Apparent Women Officers or Directors: 2
Hot Spot for Advancement for Women/Minorities: Y

LOCATIONS: ("Y" = Yes)

West:	Southwest:	Midwest:	Southeast:	Northeast:	International:
Y	Y	Y	Y	Y	Y

THOR INDUSTRIES INC

www.thorindustries.com

Industry Group Code: 336214

Management:		Sales/Marketing:		Liberal Arts:		Information Sys.:		Professionals:		Tech./Scientific:	
Mgmt. Trainees:	Y	Marketing Pros.:	Y	Gen. Writing/Editing:	Y	Info. Mgmt.:	Y	Finance/Acct.:	Y	Engineers, Elec.:	Y
Experienced Mgmt.:	Y	Retail Sales:		Tech. Writing:	Y	Software Dev.:		Law:	Y	Engineers, Other:	
Int'l Business:	Y	Comm./Industrial:	Y	Graphic Arts/Photog.:	Y	Hardware Dev.:		HR/Other:	Y	Health/Lab:	
MBA Grads:	Y	Sales Trainees:		Music:		Consulting/Other:		Training:	Y	Science/Research:	
		Advertising Pros.:	Y	Broadcasting:				Health Care:		Petroleum/Chem.:	
				Other:				Consulting:		Math/Other:	

TYPES OF BUSINESS:

Recreational Vehicle Manufacturing
Motor Homes
Automotive Parts & Accessories
Buses

BRANDS/DIVISIONS/AFFILIATES:

Airstream, Inc.
Dutchmen Manufacturing, Inc.
Thor Motor Coach
Keystone RV Company
SJC Industries
Champion Bus, Inc.
Towables Holdings, Inc.
Thor Motor Coach.

CONTACTS:

Note: Officers with more than one job title may be intentionally listed here more than once.

Peter B. Orthwein, CEO
Jeff Kime, Pres.
Christian G. Farman, CFO/Sr. VP
Walter L. Bennett, Chief Admin. Officer
Walter L. Bennett, Corp. Sec./Exec. VP
Richard E. Riegel, III, Sr. Group Pres., Investor Rel.
Christian G. Farman, Treas.
Richard E. Riegel, II, Sr. Group Pres., Bus Group
Ron Fenech, Sr. Group Pres., RV Group
Peter B. Orthwein, Chmn.

Phone: 937-596-6849 **Fax:** 937-596-6539
Toll-Free:
Address: 419 W. Pike St., Jackson Center, OH 45334 US

GROWTH PLANS/SPECIAL FEATURES:

Thor Industries, Inc. is a leading manufacturer of a wide range of recreation vehicles (RVs) and small and midsize commercial buses. In addition, the firm provides related parts, services and accessories for all vehicles they manufacture. The company's primary RV subsidiaries are Airstream, Inc.; Dutchmen Manufacturing, Inc.; Crossroads RV; Keystone RV Company; Komfort Corp; Citair, Inc.; and Thor Motor Coach. Together they produce conventional travel trailers, fifth wheels, park models, which are mobile homes designed for recreational living, and Class A, B and C motor homes. Towable RVs generate approximately 68% of the firm's sales, while motorized RVs account for roughly 13%. The firm markets its recreational vehicles through approximately 1,418 dealers throughout the U.S. and Canada. Thor Industries' small and midsize bus operating subsidiaries are Champion Bus, Inc.; SJC Industries, Corp.; El Dorado National California, Inc.; El Dorado National Kansas, Inc; General Coach, Inc.; and Goshen Coach, Inc. Product applications include transit buses, airport car rental and hotel shuttles, paramedical transit for hospitals and nursing homes and tour and charter buses. Bus sales generate roughly 19% of the firm's sales. Thor also has a joint venture with Cruise America, Inc. called CAT Joint Venture LLC, which makes short-term rentals of motorized recreation vehicles to the public. In September 2010, Thor Industries acquired Towables Holdings, Inc., the parent company of Heartland Recreation Vehicles, LLC. Also in September 2010, the firm combined subsidiaries Four Winds International, Inc. and Damon Corporation, Inc. to form Thor Motor Coach.

FINANCIALS:

Sales and profits are in thousands of dollars—add 000 to get the full amount. 2010 Note: Financial information for 2010 was not available for all companies at press time.

2010 Sales: $2,276,557	2010 Profits: $110,064
2009 Sales: $1,521,896	2009 Profits: $17,143
2008 Sales: $2,640,680	2008 Profits: $92,706
2007 Sales: $2,856,308	2007 Profits: $134,731
2006 Sales: $3,066,276	2006 Profits: $163,405

U.S. Stock Ticker: THO
Int'l Ticker:
Int'l Exchange:
Employees: 6,950 Fiscal Year Ends: 7/31
Parent Company:

SALARIES/BENEFITS:

Pension Plan: ESOP Stock Plan: Profit Sharing: Top Exec. Salary: $600,000 Bonus: $6,719,345
Savings Plan: Y Stock Purch. Plan: Second Exec. Salary: $500,000 Bonus: $726,625

OTHER THOUGHTS:

Apparent Women Officers or Directors:
Hot Spot for Advancement for Women/Minorities:

LOCATIONS: ("Y" = Yes)

West:	Southwest:	Midwest:	Southeast:	Northeast:	International:
Y		Y			Y

TIBCO SOFTWARE INC

www.tibco.com

Industry Group Code: 511210H

Management:		Sales/Marketing:		Liberal Arts:		Information Sys.:		Professionals:		Tech./Scientific:	
Mgmt. Trainees:		Marketing Pros.:	Y	Gen. Writing/Editing:		Info. Mgmt.:	Y	Finance/Acct.:	Y	Engineers, Elec.:	Y
Experienced Mgmt.:		Retail Sales:		Tech. Writing:	Y	Software Dev.:	Y	Law:	Y	Engineers, Other:	
Int'l Business:	Y	Comm./Industrial:	Y	Graphic Arts/Photog.:		Hardware Dev.:		HR/Other:	Y	Health/Lab:	
MBA Grads:	Y	Sales Trainees:		Music:		Consulting/Other:		Training:		Science/Research:	
		Advertising Pros.:	Y	Broadcasting:				Health Care:		Petroleum/Chem.:	
				Other:	Y			Consulting:		Math/Other:	

TYPES OF BUSINESS:

Software-Business Process
Data Management Software
Consulting & Support Services

BRANDS/DIVISIONS/AFFILIATES:

Netrics, Inc.
Proginet Corp.
OpenSpirit Corp.
Loyalty Lab, Inc.

CONTACTS: *Note: Officers with more than one job title may be intentionally listed here more than once.*

Vivek Y. Ranadive, CEO
Murray Rode, COO
Sydney Carey, CFO/Exec. VP
Ram Menon, Exec. VP-Worldwide Mktg.
Tom Laffey, Exec. VP-Tech.
Tom Laffey, Exec. VP-Prod. Dev.
William Hughes, General Counsel/Exec. VP/Corp. Sec.
Murat Sonmez, Exec. VP-Global Field Oper.
Vivek Y. Ranadive, Chmn.

Phone: 650-846-1000 **Fax:** 650-846-1005
Toll-Free: 800-420-8450
Address: 3303 Hillview Ave., Palo Alto, CA 94304 US

GROWTH PLANS/SPECIAL FEATURES:

TIBCO Software, Inc. is a provider of infrastructure software, focused on creating and marketing software for use in the integration of business information, processes and applications. The company offers a range of standards-based infrastructure software products that help customers to streamline business process management by offering real-time access to information. TIBCO's software products are capable of instantly correlating information about an organization's operations and performance with information about expected behavior and business rules, allowing customers to anticipate and respond to business developments. While its products can be sold individually to address specific technical challenges, the overall emphasis of the firm's development and sales efforts is to create products that interoperate and can be sold together as a suite. TIBCO's products are designed to address three primary areas of operational efficiency: Service Oriented Architecture (SOA), Business Process Management (BPM) and Business Optimization. The firm's SOA offerings enable organizations to migrate their IT infrastructure to a common framework by turning information and functions into discrete and reusable components that can be invoked from across the business and aggregated with other such services to create composite applications. BPM products enable the automation and coordination of the assets and tasks that make up business processes. The firm's Business Optimization software automatically converts and analyzes data, and can also initiate appropriate notifications or adaptation of business processes. The company also offers professional services, including consulting, planning, maintenance and support of information systems. In 2010, TIBCO acquired Netrics, Inc., which specializes in data matching algorithms; Proginet Corp., which focuses on file transfer technologies; OpenSpirit Corp., which develops oil and gas software; and Loyalty Lab, Inc., which produces marketing software.

TIBCO offers its employees medical, dental and vision coverage; life and AD&D insurance; a 401(k) program; short- and long-term disability; an employee assistance program; and tuition reimbursement.

FINANCIALS: **Sales and profits are in thousands of dollars—add 000 to get the full amount. 2010 Note: Financial information for 2010 was not available for all companies at press time.**

2010 Sales: $754,007	2010 Profits: $78,088	**U.S. Stock Ticker: TIBX**
2009 Sales: $621,388	2009 Profits: $62,302	**Int'l Ticker:**
2008 Sales: $644,471	2008 Profits: $52,411	Int'l Exchange:
2007 Sales: $577,386	2007 Profits: $51,888	Employees: 2,540 Fiscal Year Ends: 11/30
2006 Sales: $517,279	2006 Profits: $72,864	Parent Company:

SALARIES/BENEFITS:

Pension Plan:	ESOP Stock Plan:	Profit Sharing:	Top Exec. Salary: $488,750	Bonus: $488,750
Savings Plan: Y	Stock Purch. Plan:		Second Exec. Salary: $355,416	Bonus: $277,974

OTHER THOUGHTS:

Apparent Women Officers or Directors:
Hot Spot for Advancement for Women/Minorities:

LOCATIONS: ("Y" = Yes)

West:	Southwest:	Midwest:	Southeast:	Northeast:	International:
Y					Y

TIDEWATER INC

www.tdw.com

Industry Group Code: 213112

Management:		Sales/Marketing:		Liberal Arts:		Information Sys.:		Professionals:		Tech./Scientific:	
Mgmt. Trainees:		Marketing Pros.:	Y	Gen. Writing/Editing:		Info. Mgmt.:	Y	Finance/Acct.:	Y	Engineers, Elec.:	Y
Experienced Mgmt.:		Retail Sales:		Tech. Writing:		Software Dev.:		Law:	Y	Engineers, Other:	Y
Int'l Business:	Y	Comm./Industrial:	Y	Graphic Arts/Photog.:		Hardware Dev.:		HR/Other:	Y	Health/Lab:	
MBA Grads:	Y	Sales Trainees:		Music:		Consulting/Other:		Training:	Y	Science/Research:	
		Advertising Pros.:	Y	Broadcasting:				Health Care:		Petroleum/Chem.:	Y
				Other:				Consulting:		Math/Other:	

TYPES OF BUSINESS:

Offshore Drilling Support Vessels
Supply Vessels
Marine Services
Shipbuilding

BRANDS/DIVISIONS/AFFILIATES:

Quality Shipyards, LLC

CONTACTS: *Note: Officers with more than one job title may be intentionally listed here more than once.*

Dean E. Taylor, CEO
Jeffrey M. Platt, COO
Dean E. Taylor, Pres.
Quinn P. Fanning, CFO/Exec. VP
Chris Orth, VP-Sales, Western Hemisphere
Debbie Willingham, Chief Human Resources Officer/VP
Matthew Mancheski, CIO/VP
William R. Brown, IV, Mgr.-Eng. & Tech. Svcs. Group
Bruce D. Lundstrom, General Counsel/Exec. VP/Sec.
Matthew Mancheski, Chief Strategic Planning Officer
Joseph M. Bennett, Chief Investor Rel. Officer/Exec. VP
Craig J. Demarest, Principal Acct. Officer/Controller/VP
Stephen W. Dick, Exec. VP-Domestic Div.
Kevin Carr, VP-Taxation
William R. Brown, IV, VP/Gen. Mgr.-Quality Shipyards LLC
Monty Orr, VP-Int'l Sales, Eastern Hemisphere
Dean E. Taylor, Chmn.
Gerard P. Kehoe, Sr. VP/Regional Mgr.-Latin America

Phone: 504-568-1010 **Fax:** 504-566-4559
Toll-Free: 800-678-8433
Address: 601 Poydras St., Ste. 1900, New Orleans, LA 70130 US

GROWTH PLANS/SPECIAL FEATURES:

Tidewater, Inc., through its subsidiaries and joint ventures, provides offshore service vessels and marine support services to the international offshore energy industry through the operation of one of the world's largest fleets of offshore marine service vessels. The company operates in two reportable segments: U.S. and International. Principal areas of international operation include the Persian Gulf, the Arabian Gulf, and areas offshore Australia, Brazil, Egypt, India, Indonesia, Malaysia, Mexico, Trinidad and West Africa. Through offices in over 30 countries, Tidewater's international operations provide approximately 89% of the company's revenue. The firm's fleet of 398 vessels includes deepwater vessels; towing supply and supply vessels; crewboats and utility vessels; platform supply vessels; offshore and inshore tugs; and production, line-handling, platform maintenance, diving support and various other special purpose vessels. The vessels provide services supporting all phases of offshore exploration, development and production, including towing and anchor handling for mobile offshore drilling units; transporting supplies and personnel necessary to sustain drilling, workover and production activities; offshore construction and seismic support; and a variety of specialized services, such as pipe and cable laying. Subsidiary Quality Shipyards LLC constructs, modifies and repairs vessels for Tidewater's own operations and third-party operations though two shipyards in Houma, Louisiana. The shipyard operation delivered two 266-foot platform supply vessels to Tidewater in December 2009 and March 2010, and is currently constructing one additional 266-foot platform supply vessel, expected to be delivered in February 2012.

Tidewater offers its employees medical and dental coverage, disability insurance, life insurance, business travel accident coverage, a 401(k) plan and a retirement plan.

FINANCIALS: **Sales and profits are in thousands of dollars—add 000 to get the full amount. 2010 Note: Financial information for 2010 was not available for all companies at press time.**

2010 Sales: $1,168,634 | 2010 Profits: $259,476
2009 Sales: $1,390,835 | 2009 Profits: $406,898
2008 Sales: $1,270,171 | 2008 Profits: $348,763
2007 Sales: $1,125,260 | 2007 Profits: $256,646
2006 Sales: $877,617 | 2006 Profits: $235,756

U.S. Stock Ticker: TDW
Int'l Ticker:
Int'l Exchange:
Employees: 7,900 Fiscal Year Ends: 3/31
Parent Company:

SALARIES/BENEFITS:

Pension Plan: Y | ESOP Stock Plan: | Profit Sharing: | Top Exec. Salary: $615,940 | Bonus: $493,477
Savings Plan: Y | Stock Purch. Plan: | | Second Exec. Salary: $332,072 | Bonus: $189,231

OTHER THOUGHTS:

Apparent Women Officers or Directors: 3
Hot Spot for Advancement for Women/Minorities: Y

LOCATIONS: ("Y" = Yes)

West:	Southwest:	Midwest:	Southeast:	Northeast:	International:
Y	Y		Y		Y

Sales, profits and employees may be estimates. Financial information, benefits and other data can change quickly and may vary from those stated here.

TIFFANY & CO

www.tiffany.com

Industry Group Code: 448310

Management:		**Sales/Marketing:**		**Liberal Arts:**		**Information Sys.:**		**Professionals:**		**Tech./Scientific:**	
Mgmt. Trainees:	Y	Marketing Pros.:	Y	Gen. Writing/Editing:	Y	Info. Mgmt.:	Y	Finance/Acct.:	Y	Engineers, Elec.:	
Experienced Mgmt.:	Y	Retail Sales:	Y	Tech. Writing:		Software Dev.:	Y	Law:	Y	Engineers, Other:	
Int'l Business:	Y	Comm./Industrial:		Graphic Arts/Photog.:	Y	Hardware Dev.:		HR/Other:	Y	Health/Lab:	
MBA Grads:	Y	Sales Trainees:	Y	Music:		Consulting/Other:		Training:	Y	Science/Research:	
		Advertising Pros.:	Y	Broadcasting:				Health Care:		Petroleum/Chem.:	
				Other:	Y			Consulting:		Math/Other:	

TYPES OF BUSINESS:

Jewelry & Other Luxury Items, Retail
Catalog & Online Sales
Jewelry
Fragrance
Timepieces
Stationery
Home Décor

BRANDS/DIVISIONS/AFFILIATES:

Tiffany and Company
Mitsukoshi Ltd.
Tiffany & Co. Japan, Inc.

CONTACTS: *Note: Officers with more than one job title may be intentionally listed here more than once.*

Michael J. Kowalski, CEO
James E. Quinn, Pres.
James N. Fernandez, CFO/Exec. VP
Caroline D. Naggiar, Chief Mktg. Officer
Victoria Berger-Gross, Sr. VP-Global Human Resources
Pamela H. Cloud, Sr. VP-Merch.
Patrick B. Dorsey, General Counsel/Sec./Sr. VP
John S. Petterson, Sr. VP-Oper.
Patrick F. McGuiness, Sr. VP-Finance
Beth O. Canavan, Exec. VP
Jon M. King, Exec. VP
Michael J. Kowalski, Chmn.

Phone: 212-755-8000 **Fax:** 212-605-4465
Toll-Free:
Address: 727 Fifth Ave., New York, NY 10022 US

GROWTH PLANS/SPECIAL FEATURES:

Tiffany & Co. is a holding company that operates through its principle subsidiary, Tiffany and Company, founded in 1837, a retail firm primarily selling jewelry, but also selling timepieces, sterling silver goods, china, crystal, stationery, fragrances and personal accessories. Its products are sold through U.S. and international Tiffany & Co. stores; as well as through direct marketing, including business-to-business, mail-order, Internet and wholesale sales. The firm operates approximately 84 branch stores in the U.S. The company also operates approximately 129 international retail locations: 56 located in Japan; 11 in Korea; 14 in China; nine in the U.K.; eight in Hong Kong; six in Taiwan; five in Germany and Australia; five in Singapore; four in France; two each in Malaysia and Macau; one each in Ireland, Austria and Belgium; two in Spain; and one each in the Netherlands and Switzerland. Operations in the Americas account for roughly 70% of the firm's sales (most of which are derived from the U.S.); Asia-Pacific activities, 18% (the majority of which are derived from Japan); and European operations, 12% (primarily the U.K.). Approximately 91% of net sales are derived from Tiffany & Co. jewelry, while the remaining 9% of sales came from all other brand products. Tiffany & Co. Japan, Inc. has a partnership with Mitsukoshi Ltd., which operates several Mitsukoshi department stores and other retail locations in Japan. While the typical store has traditionally measured approximately 10,000 square feet in size; the company has recently opened several 2,500 to 5,000 square-foot Tiffany & Co. branch stores. Tiffany & Co.'s average sales per square foot of store space per year were an estimated $3,100 in 2011.

Tiffany & Co. offers its employees benefits including flexible spending accounts; medical, dental and vision insurance; and employee assistance programs.

FINANCIALS: **Sales and profits are in thousands of dollars—add 000 to get the full amount. 2010 Note: Financial information for 2010 was not available for all companies at press time.**

2010 Sales: $2,709,704 — 2010 Profits: $264,823
2009 Sales: $2,848,859 — 2009 Profits: $220,022
2008 Sales: $2,927,751 — 2008 Profits: $323,478
2007 Sales: $2,560,734 — 2007 Profits: $272,897
2006 Sales: $2,312,792 — 2006 Profits: $254,655

U.S. Stock Ticker: TIF
Int'l Ticker:
Int'l Exchange:
Employees: 8,400 Fiscal Year Ends: 1/31
Parent Company:

SALARIES/BENEFITS:

Pension Plan: ESOP Stock Plan: Profit Sharing: Top Exec. Salary: $958,957 Bonus: $1,550,000
Savings Plan: Stock Purch. Plan: Second Exec. Salary: $746,452 Bonus: $800,000

OTHER THOUGHTS:

Apparent Women Officers or Directors: 4
Hot Spot for Advancement for Women/Minorities: Y

LOCATIONS: ("Y" = Yes)

West:	Southwest:	Midwest:	Southeast:	Northeast:	International:
Y				Y	

TIME WARNER INC

www.timewarner.com

Industry Group Code: 517110

Management:		**Sales/Marketing:**		**Liberal Arts:**		**Information Sys.:**		**Professionals:**		**Tech./Scientific:**	
Mgmt. Trainees:	Y	Marketing Pros.:	Y	Gen. Writing/Editing:	Y	Info. Mgmt.:	Y	Finance/Acct.:	Y	Engineers, Elec.:	Y
Experienced Mgmt.:	Y	Retail Sales:		Tech. Writing:	Y	Software Dev.:	Y	Law:	Y	Engineers, Other:	Y
Int'l Business:	Y	Comm./Industrial:	Y	Graphic Arts/Photog.:	Y	Hardware Dev.:		HR/Other:	Y	Health/Lab:	
MBA Grads:	Y	Sales Trainees:		Music:	Y	Consulting/Other:		Training:	Y	Science/Research:	
		Advertising Pros.:	Y	Broadcasting:	Y			Health Care:		Petroleum/Chem.:	
				Other:	Y			Consulting:		Math/Other:	

TYPES OF BUSINESS:

Cable TV Networks
Television Production
Cable TV Service
Magazine Publishing
Entertainment Investments
Film Production

BRANDS/DIVISIONS/AFFILIATES:

Home Box Office, Inc.
Central European Media Company
Warner Bros Entertainment Inc
Time Inc
New Line Cinema
Turner Broadcasting System Inc
TNT
Flixster Inc

CONTACTS: *Note: Officers with more than one job title may be intentionally listed here more than once.*

Jeffrey L. Bewkes, CEO
Jeffrey L. Bewkes, Pres.
John K. Martin, CFO/Exec. VP
Gary L. Ginsberg, Exec. VP-Corp. Mktg.
John K. Martin, Chief Admin. Officer/Exec. VP
Paul T. Cappuccio, General Counsel/Exec. VP
Gary L. Ginsberg, Exec. VP-Comm.
Doug Shapiro, Sr. VP-Investor Rel.
Carol Melton, Exec. VP-Global Public Policy
Olaf Olafsson, Exec. VP
Philip I. Kent, Chmn./CEO-Turner Broadcasting System
Bill Nelson, Chmn./CEO-HBO
Jeffrey L. Bewkes, Chmn.

Phone: 212-484-8000	**Fax:**
Toll-Free:	
Address: 1 Time Warner Ctr., New York, NY 10019 US	

GROWTH PLANS/SPECIAL FEATURES:

Time Warner, Inc. is a global media and entertainment conglomerate, with interests across television, cinema and publishing. The firm operates in three primary segments: that include networks, filmed entertainment and publishing. The networks segment consists principally of domestic and international basic cable networks and pay television programming services. This division consists of basic cable networks owned by subsidiary Turner Broadcasting System, Inc. (TBS), including TNT, CNN, Cartoon Network, TruTV and Turner Classic Movies; and pay television programming, such as the HBO and Cinemax channels, operated by Home Box Office, Inc. The segment also produces original programming for its networks, including past hit shows such as Sex and the City and The Sopranos. Additionally, the firm holds a 29.5% interest in Central Media Enterprises Ltd., a broadcasting company that operates networks in six Central and Eastern European countries. The filmed entertainment segment, operated principally through subsidiary Warner Bros. Entertainment Group, produces and distributes theatrical motion pictures, television shows, animation and digital media and videogames; distributes home video products; and licenses rights to the company's feature films, television programming and characters. Time Warner's publishing business consists principally of magazine publishing and related web sites, as well as a number of direct-marketing and direct-selling businesses. Time, Inc. publishes 22 magazines in the U.S., including People, Sports Illustrated, Time, InStyle, Real Simple, Southern Living and Fortune, and over 70 magazines outside the U.S., primarily through IPC Media in the U.K. and Grupo Editorial Expansion in Mexico. Recently, the firm spun off AOL, its former subsidiary, as an independent company.

Time Warner offers its employees healthcare packages for families and domestic partners; disability, life and long-term care benefits; an employee assistance program; reimbursement for wellness activities; onsite fitness center and health services; onsite child care options; and career development programs.

FINANCIALS: **Sales and profits are in thousands of dollars—add 000 to get the full amount. 2010 Note: Financial information for 2010 was not available for all companies at press time.**

2010 Sales: $26,888,000	2010 Profits: $2,578,000	**U.S. Stock Ticker: TWX**
2009 Sales: $25,388,000	2009 Profits: $2,477,000	**Int'l Ticker:**
2008 Sales: $26,434,000	2008 Profits: $-13,398,000	Int'l Exchange:
2007 Sales: $26,211,000	2007 Profits: $4,387,000	Employees: 31,000 Fiscal Year Ends: 12/31
2006 Sales: $43,690,000	2006 Profits: $6,552,000	Parent Company:

SALARIES/BENEFITS:

Pension Plan:	ESOP Stock Plan:	Profit Sharing:	Top Exec. Salary: $2,000,000	Bonus: $14,420,000
Savings Plan:	Stock Purch. Plan:		Second Exec. Salary: $1,500,000	Bonus: $5,450,000

OTHER THOUGHTS:

Apparent Women Officers or Directors: 3
Hot Spot for Advancement for Women/Minorities: Y

LOCATIONS: ("Y" = Yes)

West:	Southwest:	Midwest:	Southeast:	Northeast:	International:
Y	Y	Y	Y	Y	Y

Sales, profits and employees may be estimates. Financial information, benefits and other data can change quickly and may vary from those stated here.

TJX COMPANIES INC (THE)

www.tjx.com

Industry Group Code: 448

Management:		Sales/Marketing:		Liberal Arts:		Information Sys.:		Professionals:		Tech./Scientific:	
Mgmt. Trainees:	Y	Marketing Pros.:	Y	Gen. Writing/Editing:	Y	Info. Mgmt.:	Y	Finance/Acct.:	Y	Engineers, Elec.:	
Experienced Mgmt.:	Y	Retail Sales:	Y	Tech. Writing:		Software Dev.:	Y	Law:	Y	Engineers, Other:	
Int'l Business:	Y	Comm./Industrial:		Graphic Arts/Photog.:	Y	Hardware Dev.:		HR/Other:	Y	Health/Lab:	
MBA Grads:	Y	Sales Trainees:	Y	Music:		Consulting/Other:		Training:	Y	Science/Research:	
		Advertising Pros.:	Y	Broadcasting:				Health Care:		Petroleum/Chem.:	
				Other:	Y			Consulting:		Math/Other:	

TYPES OF BUSINESS:

Discount Apparel Stores
Domestics
Footwear
Jewelry
Home Furnishings
Accessories

BRANDS/DIVISIONS/AFFILIATES:

T.J. Maxx
Marshalls
HomeGoods
A.J. Wright
Winners
T.K. Maxx
HomeSense

CONTACTS: *Note: Officers with more than one job title may be intentionally listed here more than once.*

Carol Meyrowitz, CEO
Ernie Herrman, Pres.
Jeffrey G. Naylor, CFO/Sr. Exec. VP
Jeffrey G. Naylor, Chief Admin. Officer
Michael MacMillan, Sr. Exec. VP/Group Pres.
Jerome R. Rossi, Sr. Exec. VP/Group Pres.
Nan Stutz, Sr. Exec. VP/Group Pres.
Bernard Cammarata, Chmn.
Paul Sweetenham, Sr. Exec. VP/Group Pres., Europe

Phone: 508-390-1000	**Fax:** 508-390-2091
Toll-Free:	
Address: 770 Cochituate Rd., Framingham, MA 01701 US	

GROWTH PLANS/SPECIAL FEATURES:

The TJX Companies, Inc. is a low-price apparel and home fashions retailer, operating over 2,700 stores. The firm operates through eight chains: T.J. Maxx, Marshalls and HomeGoods in the U.S. and Canada; Winners and HomeSense in Canada; and HomeSense and T.K. Maxx in Europe. TJX's 1,753 T.J. Maxx stores and Marshalls stores offer brand-name family apparel, including footwear and accessories, and home fashions, including home basics, accent furniture and giftware, in 48 U.S. states, Washington, D.C. and Puerto Rico. The chains are similar, although Marshalls features a full-line shoe department and larger men's and juniors' departments while T.J. Maxx carries an extended line of jewelry and accessories. TJX's stores offer merchandise sold at 20% to 60% below department and specialty store regular prices. TJX also operates 336 U.S. HomeGoods stores, which sell low-priced home fashions. The chain offers a broad array of home basics, giftware, accent furniture, lamps, rugs, wall decor, decorative accessories, children's furniture and seasonal merchandise. Its 82 international HomeSense stores resemble the HomeGoods chain. In addition, TJX's 150 A.J. Wright stores, catering to moderate-income customers, provide family apparel and home fashions. Moreover, the firm operates the 215-store Winners chain, patterned after T.J. Maxx, in Canada. The company's 307 T.K. Maxx stores in the U.K., Ireland and Germany resemble its domestic stores, although with a slight name change. The company purchases its inventory from over 12,000 vendors worldwide. In March 2011, the firm opened its first Marshalls store in Canada. It plans to open six more Canadian Marshalls locations in 2012. Also in 2011, TJX converted 90 of its A.J. Wright locations to the T.J. Maxx, Marshalls and HomeGoods brands; while it closed the remaining 72 A.J. Wright stores.

TJX offers its employees medical, dental, vision, disability and life insurance; a 401(k) plan; a profit sharing plan; group auto and home insurance; a college savings program; store discounts; a mortgage discount program; a tuition assistance program; and flexible spending accounts. Corporate employees have access to basketball courts, a credit union, fitness classes and indoor golf driving ranges.

FINANCIALS: **Sales and profits are in thousands of dollars—add 000 to get the full amount. 2010 Note: Financial information for 2010 was not available for all companies at press time.**

2010 Sales: $20,288,444	2010 Profits: $1,213,572	**U.S. Stock Ticker: TJX**
2009 Sales: $18,999,505	2009 Profits: $880,617	**Int'l Ticker:**
2008 Sales: $18,336,726	2008 Profits: $771,750	Int'l Exchange:
2007 Sales: $14,104,013	2007 Profits: $738,039	Employees: 154,000 Fiscal Year Ends: 1/31
2006 Sales: $15,955,943	2006 Profits: $689,834	Parent Company:

SALARIES/BENEFITS:

Pension Plan:	ESOP Stock Plan:	Profit Sharing: Y	Top Exec. Salary: $1,575,000	Bonus: $4,127,571
Savings Plan: Y	Stock Purch. Plan:		Second Exec. Salary: $987,021	Bonus: $1,839,085

OTHER THOUGHTS:

Apparent Women Officers or Directors: 3
Hot Spot for Advancement for Women/Minorities: Y

LOCATIONS: ("Y" = Yes)

West:	Southwest:	Midwest:	Southeast:	Northeast:	International:
Y	Y	Y	Y	Y	Y

Sales, profits and employees may be estimates. Financial information, benefits and other data can change quickly and may vary from those stated here.

TOTAL SYSTEM SERVICES INC (TSYS)

www.tsys.com

Industry Group Code: 522320

Management:		Sales/Marketing:		Liberal Arts:		Information Sys.:		Professionals:		Tech./Scientific:	
Mgmt. Trainees:	Y	Marketing Pros.:	Y	Gen. Writing/Editing:	Y	Info. Mgmt.:	Y	Finance/Acct.:	Y	Engineers, Elec.:	
Experienced Mgmt.:	Y	Retail Sales:		Tech. Writing:		Software Dev.:	Y	Law:	Y	Engineers, Other:	
Int'l Business:	Y	Comm./Industrial:	Y	Graphic Arts/Photog.:	Y	Hardware Dev.:		HR/Other:	Y	Health/Lab:	
MBA Grads:	Y	Sales Trainees:	Y	Music:		Consulting/Other:		Training:	Y	Science/Research:	
		Advertising Pros.:	Y	Broadcasting:				Health Care:		Petroleum/Chem.:	
				Other:				Consulting:		Math/Other:	

TYPES OF BUSINESS:

Credit Card Processing
Risk Management Tools
Fraud Detection
Debt Collection Services
Printing Services
Customer Relationship Management
Business Process Management

BRANDS/DIVISIONS/AFFILIATES:

TSYS Canada Inc
Columbus Depot Equipment Company
Total System Services de Mexico
TSYS Acquiring Solutions
UnionPay Data Co Ltd
TSYS Merchant Solutions

CONTACTS: *Note: Officers with more than one job title may be intentionally listed here more than once.*

Philip W. Tomlinson, CEO
M. Troy Woods, COO
M. Troy Woods, Pres.
James B. Lipham, CFO/Sr. Exec. VP
Ryland L. Harrelson, Chief Human Resources Officer/Exec. VP
Kenneth L. Tye, CIO/Sr. Exec. VP
Stephen W. Humber, CTO/Exec. VP
Connie C. Dudley, Exec. VP-Prod. & Client Dev.
G. Sanders Griffith, III, General Counsel/Sr. Exec. VP/Sec.
Paul Todd, Exec. VP-Strategy, Mergers & Acquisitions
Cyle Mims, Contact-Media Rel. & External Comm.
Shawn Roberts, Contact-Investor Rel.
Dorenda K. Weaver, Chief Acct. Officer/Exec. VP
William A. Pruett, Sr. Exec. VP
Colleen W. Kynard, Exec. VP-Customer Care
Mark D. Pyke, Pres., TSYS Acquiring Solutions
Philip W. Tomlinson, Chmn.
Gaylon Jowers, Jr., Pres., Int'l/Exec. VP

Phone: 706-649-2310	**Fax:** 706-649-4266
Toll-Free:	
Address: 1 TSYS Way, Columbus, GA 31901 US	

GROWTH PLANS/SPECIAL FEATURES:

Total System Services, Inc. (TSYS) is one of the world's largest electronic payment processors of consumer credit, retail, debit, stored value, government services and commercial card accounts for financial and non-financial institutions. TSYS serves 400 clients in 85 countries throughout the Americas, Africa, Europe, the Middle East and the Asia Pacific region. The company also offers value-added products and services, including risk management tools and techniques like fraud detection and prevention and behavior analysis tools, as well as revenue enhancement tools, such as customer relationship management and client advising. TSYS's operations are divided into three segments: North America Services, accounting for approximately 60.2% of revenues; International Services, accounting for 19.9%; and Merchant Services, accounting for 19.9%. Merchant services include processing services, acquiring applications, related systems and integrated support services. The company also offers additional services such as business process management, mail and correspondence processing, teleservicing, data documentation, offset printing, collections and account solicitation and client services. The firm's subsidiaries include Columbus Productions, which provides commercial printing and finishing solutions; TSYS Acquiring Solutions, a supplier of transaction processing, related systems and integrated support services; and TSYS Canada, Inc. The company also owns a 49% equity interest in a joint venture company called Total System Services de Mexico, as well as a 44.5% interest in China UnionPay Data Co., Ltd. In January 2011, the firm acquired the remaining 49% of joint venture, National Merchant Solutions, from First National Bank of Omaha, and consequently rebranded it as TSYS Merchant Solutions.

The company offers U.S. employees medical, dental and vision insurance; flexible spending accounts; life and AD&D insurance; disability coverage; discounted banking services; and adoption assistance.

FINANCIALS: **Sales and profits are in thousands of dollars—add 000 to get the full amount. 2010 Note: Financial information for 2010 was not available for all companies at press time.**

2010 Sales: $1,717,577	2010 Profits: $193,947	**U.S. Stock Ticker: TSS**
2009 Sales: $1,677,483	2009 Profits: $215,213	**Int'l Ticker:**
2008 Sales: $1,711,534	2008 Profits: $250,100	Int'l Exchange:
2007 Sales: $1,805,836	2007 Profits: $237,443	Employees: 7,788 Fiscal Year Ends: 12/31
2006 Sales: $1,787,171	2006 Profits: $249,163	Parent Company:

SALARIES/BENEFITS:

Pension Plan:	ESOP Stock Plan:	Profit Sharing:	Top Exec. Salary: $840,000	Bonus: $
Savings Plan:	Stock Purch. Plan:		Second Exec. Salary: $610,000	Bonus: $

OTHER THOUGHTS:

Apparent Women Officers or Directors: 5
Hot Spot for Advancement for Women/Minorities: Y

LOCATIONS: ("Y" = Yes)

West:	Southwest:	Midwest:	Southeast:	Northeast:	International:
Y	Y	Y	Y	Y	Y

TOWERS WATSON & CO

www.towerswatson.com

Industry Group Code: 541612

Management:		Sales/Marketing:		Liberal Arts:		Information Sys.:		Professionals:		Tech./Scientific:	
Mgmt. Trainees:	Y	Marketing Pros.:	Y	Gen. Writing/Editing:	Y	Info. Mgmt.:	Y	Finance/Acct.:	Y	Engineers, Elec.:	
Experienced Mgmt.:	Y	Retail Sales:		Tech. Writing:	Y	Software Dev.:	Y	Law:	Y	Engineers, Other:	
Int'l Business:	Y	Comm./Industrial:	Y	Graphic Arts/Photog.:	Y	Hardware Dev.:		HR/Other:	Y	Health/Lab:	
MBA Grads:	Y	Sales Trainees:		Music:		Consulting/Other:	Y	Training:	Y	Science/Research:	
		Advertising Pros.:	Y	Broadcasting:				Health Care:		Petroleum/Chem.:	
				Other:	Y			Consulting:	Y	Math/Other:	

TYPES OF BUSINESS:

Human Resources Consulting
Benefit Plan & Compensation Consulting
Actuarial & Management Consulting
Reinsurance Consulting
Human Resources Outsourcing
Human Resources Consulting

BRANDS/DIVISIONS/AFFILIATES:

Towers Perrin
Towers Watson Danismanlik Ltd. Sti

CONTACTS: *Note: Officers with more than one job title may be intentionally listed here more than once.*

John Haley, CEO
Mark Mactas, COO
Mark Mactas, Pres.
Roger F. Millay, CFO/VP
Sharon Clark, Head-Mktg.
Gail McKee, Chief Human Resources Officer
Tony Candito, CIO
Anne Bodnar, Chief Admin. Officer
Walter Bardenwerper, General Counsel/VP/Sec.
Gordon L. Gould, Head-Strategy & Corp. Dev.
Michael McNamara, Contact-Media
Roger F. Millay, Head-Finance
Tricia Guinn, Head-Risk & Financial Svcs.
James K. Foreman, Head-North America
Julie Gebauer, Head-Talent & Rewards Bus. Unit
Gene Wickes, Head-Benefits Bus. Unit
John Haley, Chmn.
Bob Charles, VP-Sales, APAC

Phone: 212-725-7550	**Fax:** 212-644-7432
Toll-Free:	
Address: 875 3rd Ave., New York, NY 10022 US	

GROWTH PLANS/SPECIAL FEATURES:

Towers Watson & Co., formerly Towers Perrin, provides human resources, benefit plan and compensation consultation. The firm has worked with 85% of the world's 500 largest companies and 84% of the Fortune 1,000 U.S. companies. Towers Watson's services include third-party administration for retirement, health and welfare plans and compensation administration; human resources consulting, including communication training; employee hiring research; and rewards and performance management. The company is divided into three sections: benefits; risk and financial services; and talent and rewards. The benefits business unit provides international human resources consulting and related services; mergers and acquisitions; retirement; technology and administrative services. The risk and financial business unit, provides finance modeling software; insurance consulting; investments; reinsurance and risk management. The talent and rewards business unit, provides consulting on communication, change of management issues; data services; employee surveys; executive compensation, human resources effectiveness; reward programs; sales effectiveness; talent management and organization alignment. Services include assistance with employee benefits, compensation, and communication and change management. The firm has offices worldwide in 34 countries. In early 2010, Towers Perrin and Wyatt Worldwide merged to form Towers Watson & Co. In March 2011, the firm established new subsidiary Towers Watson Danismanlik Ltd. Sti in Turkey.

FINANCIALS: **Sales and profits are in thousands of dollars—add 000 to get the full amount. 2010 Note: Financial information for 2010 was not available for all companies at press time.**

2010 Sales: $2,387,829	2010 Profits: $120,597	**U.S. Stock Ticker: TW**
2009 Sales: $1,676,029	2009 Profits: $146,458	**Int'l Ticker:**
2008 Sales: $1,760,055	2008 Profits: $155,441	Int'l Exchange:
2007 Sales: $1,486,520	2007 Profits: $116,280	Employees: 12,750 Fiscal Year Ends: 6/30
2006 Sales: $1,271,810	2006 Profits: $86,120	Parent Company:

SALARIES/BENEFITS:

Pension Plan:	ESOP Stock Plan:	Profit Sharing:	Top Exec. Salary: $457,500	Bonus: $571,875
Savings Plan:	Stock Purch. Plan: Y		Second Exec. Salary: $350,000	Bonus: $503,125

OTHER THOUGHTS:

Apparent Women Officers or Directors: 6
Hot Spot for Advancement for Women/Minorities: Y

LOCATIONS: ("Y" = Yes)

West:	Southwest:	Midwest:	Southeast:	Northeast:	International:
Y	Y	Y	Y	Y	Y

TRAVELERS COMPANIES INC (THE)

www.travelers.com

Industry Group Code: 524126

Management:		Sales/Marketing:		Liberal Arts:		Information Sys.:		Professionals:		Tech./Scientific:	
Mgmt. Trainees:	Y	Marketing Pros.:	Y	Gen. Writing/Editing:	Y	Info. Mgmt.:	Y	Finance/Acct.:	Y	Engineers, Elec.:	
Experienced Mgmt.:	Y	Retail Sales:		Tech. Writing:	Y	Software Dev.:	Y	Law:	Y	Engineers, Other:	
Int'l Business:	Y	Comm./Industrial:	Y	Graphic Arts/Photog.:	Y	Hardware Dev.:		HR/Other:	Y	Health/Lab:	
MBA Grads:	Y	Sales Trainees:	Y	Music:		Consulting/Other:		Training:	Y	Science/Research:	
		Advertising Pros.:	Y	Broadcasting:				Health Care:		Petroleum/Chem.:	
				Other:	Y			Consulting:		Math/Other:	Y

TYPES OF BUSINESS:

Direct Property & Casualty Insurance
Reinsurance
Automobile & Homeowners' Insurance
General Liability & Commercial Multi-Peril Insurance
Marine Insurance
Risk Management Services

BRANDS/DIVISIONS/AFFILIATES:

JMalucelli Participaces em Seguros e Resseguros SA
Lloyd's
Specialty Liability Group

CONTACTS: *Note: Officers with more than one job title may be intentionally listed here more than once.*

Jay S. Fishman, CEO
Brian W. MacLean, COO
Brian W. MacLean, Pres.
Jay S. Benet, CFO
Lisa Caputo, Exec. VP-Mktg.
John P. Clifford, Jr., Exec. VP-Human Resources
Madelyn Lankton, CIO/Exec. VP
Andy F. Bessette, Chief Admin. Officer/Exec. VP
Kenneth F. Spence III, General Counsel/Exec. VP
Maria Olivo, Exec. VP-Strategic Dev.
Lisa Caputo, Exec. VP-Corp. Comm.
Gabriella Nawi, Sr. VP-Investor Rel.
Maria Olivo, Treas.
William H. Heyman, Chief Investment Officer
John J. Albano, Exec. VP-Field Mgmt.
Alan D. Schnitzer, Chief Legal Officer
Joan Kois Woodward, Exec. VP-Public Policy
Jay S. Fishman, Chmn.
Kevin C. Smith, Pres., Int'l

Phone: 917-778-6000 **Fax:** 917-778-7007
Toll-Free:
Address: 485 Lexington Ave., New York, NY 10017 US

GROWTH PLANS/SPECIAL FEATURES:

The Travelers Companies, Inc. is a holding company principally engaged in providing commercial and personal property and casualty insurance products and services to businesses, government units, associations and individuals. The company operates in three segments: business insurance; financial, professional and international insurance; and personal insurance. The business insurance segment offers a broad array of property and casualty insurance and insurance-related services primarily in the U.S. The division is organized in six groups: select accounts, commercial accounts, national accounts, industry-focused underwriting, target risk underwriting and specialized distribution. These groups provide a wide array of insurance coverage, including commercial multi-peril, property, general liability, commercial auto, workers' compensation and marine, as well as providing risk management, claims handling, reinsurance, healthcare and other services. The business insurance group also includes the Specialty Liability Group, which manages the company's asbestos and environmental liabilities. The financial, professional and international insurance segment includes surety and financial liability coverage, which require a primarily credit-based underwriting process, as well as property and casualty products marketed on an international basis. This division operates through two groups: bond and financial products, which provides bond and insurance products and risk management services; and International, which offers specialized insurance and risk management services marketed in the U.K., Ireland and Canada and on a wider international basis through Lloyd's. The personal insurance segment writes virtually all types of property and casualty insurance covering personal risks. The primary coverage plans in this segment are automobile and homeowner's insurance. In June 2011, Travelers acquired 43% ownership of Brazilian surety insurance firm JMalucelli Participaces em Seguros e Resseguros S.A. for roughly $410 million.

Employees of the firm are offered medical and dental coverage; an educational assistance plan; up to 20 days of paid time off (PTO); an insurance program; flexible work hours; and a pension plan.

FINANCIALS: **Sales and profits are in thousands of dollars—add 000 to get the full amount. 2010 Note: Financial information for 2010 was not available for all companies at press time.**

2010 Sales: $25,112,000 — 2010 Profits: $3,216,000
2009 Sales: $24,680,000 — 2009 Profits: $3,622,000
2008 Sales: $24,477,000 — 2008 Profits: $2,924,000
2007 Sales: $26,017,000 — 2007 Profits: $4,601,000
2006 Sales: $25,090,000 — 2006 Profits: $4,208,000

U.S. Stock Ticker: TRV
Int'l Ticker:
Int'l Exchange:
Employees: 32,000 Fiscal Year Ends: 12/31
Parent Company:

SALARIES/BENEFITS:

Pension Plan: Y — ESOP Stock Plan: — Profit Sharing: — Top Exec. Salary: $1,000,000 — Bonus: $6,250,000
Savings Plan: Y — Stock Purch. Plan: — Second Exec. Salary: $812,500 — Bonus: $3,350,000

OTHER THOUGHTS:

Apparent Women Officers or Directors: 8
Hot Spot for Advancement for Women/Minorities: Y

LOCATIONS: ("Y" = Yes)

West:	Southwest:	Midwest:	Southeast:	Northeast:	International:
Y	Y	Y	Y	Y	Y

TREEHOUSE FOODS INC

www.treehousefoods.com

Industry Group Code: 311

Management:		Sales/Marketing:		Liberal Arts:		Information Sys.:		Professionals:		Tech./Scientific:	
Mgmt. Trainees:	Y	Marketing Pros.:	Y	Gen. Writing/Editing:		Info. Mgmt.:	Y	Finance/Acct.:	Y	Engineers, Elec.:	
Experienced Mgmt.:	Y	Retail Sales:		Tech. Writing:		Software Dev.:		Law:	Y	Engineers, Other:	Y
Int'l Business:		Comm./Industrial:	Y	Graphic Arts/Photog.:	Y	Hardware Dev.:		HR/Other:	Y	Health/Lab:	
MBA Grads:	Y	Sales Trainees:		Music:		Consulting/Other:		Training:	Y	Science/Research:	
		Advertising Pros.:		Broadcasting:				Health Care:		Petroleum/Chem.:	
				Other:				Consulting:		Math/Other:	

TYPES OF BUSINESS:

Food Manufacturing & Distribution

BRANDS/DIVISIONS/AFFILIATES:

Bay Valley Foods LLC
E. D. Smith Valley Foods LTD
Sturm Foods, Inc.
S.T. Specialty Foods
Hoffman House
Nalley's
Nature's Goodness
Peter Piper

CONTACTS:

Note: Officers with more than one job title may be intentionally listed here more than once.

Sam K. Reed, CEO
David B. Vermylen, COO
Sam K. Reed, Pres.
Dennis F. Riordan, CFO/Sr. VP
Thomas E. O'Neill, Chief Admin. Officer/Sr. VP
Thomas E. O'Neill, General Counsel
Erik T. Kahler, Sr. VP-Corp. Dev.
Sharon M. Flanagan, Sr. VP-Strategy
Harry J. Walsh, Pres., Bay Valley Foods LLC/Exec. VP
Alan T. Gambrel, Chief Admin. Officer-Bay Valley Foods LLC
Sam K. Reed, Chmn.

Phone: 708-483-1300	**Fax:**
Toll-Free:	
Address: 2 Westbrook Corporate Ctr., Ste. 1070, Westchester, IL 60154 US	

GROWTH PLANS/SPECIAL FEATURES:

TreeHouse Foods Inc. is a food manufacturer servicing primarily the retail grocery and foodservice distribution industry. The firm operates in the U.S. through its wholly-owned subsidiary, Bay Valley Foods LLC; and in Canada through Bay Valley Foods' wholly-owned subsidiary, E.D. Smith Valley Foods LTD. The company's products include salad dressings and sauces; non-dairy powdered coffee creamer; Mexican sauces; pickles; private label soup; and jams and pie fillings. The firm manufactures these products under private labels to retailers such as mass merchandisers and supermarkets. Products are resold under either the retailers' own or controlled brand names. TreeHouse Foods also markets its products to the foodservice industry, including foodservice distributors and national restaurant operators, under its own labels and brands; sells to industrial customers who use the firm's products as ingredients in other products or repackage them in portion control packages; and sells items under its own brands, primarily on a regional basis to retail customers. The company operates in three segments: North American Retail Grocery; Food Away From Home; and Industrial and Export. The North American Retail Grocery division sells branded and private label products to customers within the United States and Canada under brand names such as Hoffman House, Nalley's, Nature's Goodness, Peter Piper, Second Nature and Steinfeld. The Food Away From Home segment sells products such as pickles, salsas, non-dairy powdered creamers, aseptic and refrigerated products to the U.S. and Canadian food service industry under the labels Schwartz and Saucemaker. TreeHouse Foods' Industrial and Export group offers co-pack business and non-dairy powdered creamers for use in industrial applications. In October 2010, the firm acquired S.T. Specialty Foods for approximately $180 million. In February 2011, Bay Valley Foods announced plans to close its pickle facility in Springfield, Missouri.

FINANCIALS:

Sales and profits are in thousands of dollars—add 000 to get the full amount. 2010 Note: Financial information for 2010 was not available for all companies at press time.

2010 Sales: $1,817,024	2010 Profits: $90,919
2009 Sales: $1,511,653	2009 Profits: $81,314
2008 Sales: $1,500,650	2008 Profits: $28,224
2007 Sales: $1,157,902	2007 Profits: $41,622
2006 Sales: $939,396	2006 Profits: $44,856

U.S. Stock Ticker: THS
Int'l Ticker:
Int'l Exchange:
Employees: 4,000 Fiscal Year Ends: 12/31
Parent Company:

SALARIES/BENEFITS:

Pension Plan:	ESOP Stock Plan:	Profit Sharing:	Top Exec. Salary: $880,167	Bonus: $2,506,884
Savings Plan:	Stock Purch. Plan:		Second Exec. Salary: $588,333	Bonus: $1,262,107

OTHER THOUGHTS:

Apparent Women Officers or Directors: 1
Hot Spot for Advancement for Women/Minorities:

LOCATIONS: ("Y" = Yes)

West:	Southwest:	Midwest:	Southeast:	Northeast:	International:
		Y			

TRUSTMARK COMPANIES

Industry Group Code: 522320A

www.trustmarkins.com

Management:		Sales/Marketing:		Liberal Arts:		Information Sys.:		Professionals:		Tech./Scientific:	
Mgmt. Trainees:		Marketing Pros.:	Y	Gen. Writing/Editing:	Y	Info. Mgmt.:	Y	Finance/Acct.:	Y	Engineers, Elec.:	
Experienced Mgmt.:		Retail Sales:		Tech. Writing:		Software Dev.:	Y	Law:	Y	Engineers, Other:	
Int'l Business:		Comm./Industrial:	Y	Graphic Arts/Photog.:		Hardware Dev.:		HR/Other:	Y	Health/Lab:	
MBA Grads:	Y	Sales Trainees:		Music:		Consulting/Other:		Training:		Science/Research:	
		Advertising Pros.:	Y	Broadcasting:				Health Care:		Petroleum/Chem.:	
				Other:	Y			Consulting:		Math/Other:	

TYPES OF BUSINESS:

Employee Benefits Management

BRANDS/DIVISIONS/AFFILIATES:

CoreSource
Trustmark Group Benefits
Trustmark Voluntary Benefit Solutions
Starmark
Trustmark Affinity Markets
Health Contact Partners
HealthFitness Corporation
Trustmark Disability Advisors

CONTACTS: *Note: Officers with more than one job title may be intentionally listed here more than once.*

David M. McDonough, CEO
Joseph L. Pray, COO
Joseph L. Pray, Pres.
Phil Goss, CFO/Sr. VP
Kate Martine, Sr. VP-Human Resources
Dennis Richling, Chief Medical and Wellness Officer
Kate Martine, Sr. VP-Admin.
Dennis L. Schoff, General Counsel/Sr. VP/Corp. Sec.
Rich Olejniczak, VP-Trustmark Voluntary Benefit Solutions Oper.
Donna Hirsch, VP-Organizational Dev.
Kate Martine, Sr. VP-Corp. Comm.
Yasmin Thompson, VP-Finance
Warren R. Schreier, Exec. VP-Individual Medical
Warren R. Schreier, Exec. VP-Consumer Health Advice Bus. Integration
Nancy Eckrich, Sr. VP
Paul Lotharius, CEO-Health Fitness
J. Grover Thomas, Jr., Chmn.

Phone: 847-615-1500	**Fax:** 847-615-3910
Toll-Free:	
Address: 400 Field Dr., Lake Forest, IL 60045 US	

GROWTH PLANS/SPECIAL FEATURES:

Trustmark Companies offer health and life insurance and benefits administration services to employer groups through nine major operating divisions. These subsidiaries are CoreSource, Trustmark Group Benefits, Trustmark Affinity Markets, Starmark, HealthFitness Corporation, Health Contact Partners, Trustmark Disability Advisors, Trustmark Individual Medical and Trustmark Voluntary Benefit Solutions. CoreSource is one of the nation's largest employee benefit administrators, managing health care for over 2.5 million people across the U.S. It serves self-insured employers with claims administration, case management, provider network development, information management, fraud detection, COBRA administration and prescription-drug benefit administration. Trustmark Group Benefits, a division of Trustmark Life Insurance Company, serves the health and life insurance needs of employers with between 51 and 500 employees. The company provides standard and custom medical, dental, life and disability plans; administrative services; stop-loss insurance; experience rated refunds; and minimum premium plans. Trustmark Affinity Markets serves insurance policies to associations and other affiliated organizations. Starmark provides substantially the same services as Trustmark Group, for businesses with 2-50 employees. HealthFitness offers on-site and web-based workplace programs that help improve employee health and fitness. HealthFitness programs include medical screenings, risk assessment, fitness management, and coaching. Health Contact Partners provides a telephone line to a nurse, who is on call 24 hours, seven days a week; customer service with inbound and outbound surveys and assessments; and health consulting. Trustmark Disability Advisors specializes in disability claims, providing service in negotiated settlements when and if appropriate; adjudication and appeals; and financial consulting. Trustmark Individual Medical offer pharmacy and drug cards, claim processing, appeals and adjudication. Trustmark Voluntary Benefit Solutions offers voluntary dental, universal life, disability and critical illness plans through businesses and credit unions. In June 2008, the company acquired Health Contact Partners, a company offering contact and call center services to the healthcare industry.

FINANCIALS: **Sales and profits are in thousands of dollars—add 000 to get the full amount. 2010 Note: Financial information for 2010 was not available for all companies at press time.**

2010 Sales: $898,500 | 2010 Profits: $44,000
2009 Sales: $794,400 | 2009 Profits: $51,300
2008 Sales: $830,400 | 2008 Profits: $53,000
2007 Sales: $887,996 | 2007 Profits: $39,013
2006 Sales: $1,008,963 | 2006 Profits: $110,910

U.S. Stock Ticker: Mutual Company
Int'l Ticker:
Int'l Exchange:
Employees: 6,200 Fiscal Year Ends: 12/31
Parent Company:

SALARIES/BENEFITS:

Pension Plan: ESOP Stock Plan: Profit Sharing: Top Exec. Salary: $ Bonus: $
Savings Plan: Stock Purch. Plan: Second Exec. Salary: $ Bonus: $

OTHER THOUGHTS:

Apparent Women Officers or Directors: 5
Hot Spot for Advancement for Women/Minorities: Y

LOCATIONS: ("Y" = Yes)

West:	Southwest:	Midwest:	Southeast:	Northeast:	International:
Y	Y	Y	Y	Y	

Sales, profits and employees may be estimates. Financial information, benefits and other data can change quickly and may vary from those stated here.

TTM TECHNOLOGIES INC

www.ttmtech.com

Industry Group Code: 334419

Management:		Sales/Marketing:		Liberal Arts:		Information Sys.:		Professionals:		Tech./Scientific:	
Mgmt. Trainees:		Marketing Pros.:	Y	Gen. Writing/Editing:		Info. Mgmt.:	Y	Finance/Acct.:	Y	Engineers, Elec.:	Y
Experienced Mgmt.:		Retail Sales:		Tech. Writing:	Y	Software Dev.:		Law:	Y	Engineers, Other:	
Int'l Business:	Y	Comm./Industrial:	Y	Graphic Arts/Photog.:		Hardware Dev.:	Y	HR/Other:	Y	Health/Lab:	
MBA Grads:	Y	Sales Trainees:		Music:		Consulting/Other:		Training:		Science/Research:	
		Advertising Pros.:	Y	Broadcasting:				Health Care:		Petroleum/Chem.:	
				Other:				Consulting:		Math/Other:	

TYPES OF BUSINESS:

Printed Circuit Board Manufacturing
Backplane Assemblies
Quick-Turn Manufacturing Services

BRANDS/DIVISIONS/AFFILIATES:

CONTACTS:

Note: Officers with more than one job title may be intentionally listed here more than once.

Kenton K. Alder, CEO
Shane Whiteside, COO/Exec. VP
Kenton K. Alder, Pres.
Steven W. Richards, CFO/Exec. VP
Grace Lee, Sr. VP-Human Resources
Dale Knecht, VP-IT
Douglas L. Soder, Exec. VP
Robert Klatell, Chmn.
Canice T. K. Chung, CEO-Asia Pacific Region

Phone: 714-241-0300	**Fax:** 714-241-0708
Toll-Free:	
Address: 2630 S. Harbor Blvd., Santa Ana, CA 92704 US	

GROWTH PLANS/SPECIAL FEATURES:

TTM Technologies, Inc. is a provider of complex printed circuit boards (PCBs) used in electronic equipment and provides backplane assembly services for both standard and specialty products in defense and commercial operations. The primary raw materials that the firm uses in PCB manufacturing include copper-clad laminate; chemical solutions such as copper and gold for plating operations; photographic film; carbide drill bits; and plastic for testing fixtures. The firm is capable of manufacturing high-layer count PCBs, stacked microvias (small conducting pathways between layers of a circuit board), copper and epoxy-filled vias, flex and rigid flex circuits, multiple surface finishes, fine line traces, embedded passives and oversize panel formats, among others. TTM also offers thermal management and custom assembly services, as well as design, modeling and simulation services. The company can function as a one-stop manufacturing service because its facilities are specialized and integrated, each focusing on a different stage of an electronic product's life cycle. TTM's specialty is quick-turn services, which enable customers to shorten the time required to develop new products and bring them to market. The company serves high-end commercial markets and aerospace markets, providing PCBs and backplane assemblies for applications including networking/communications infrastructure; high-end computing; defense systems; industrial controls; and medical testing equipment. Customers include both OEMs and electronic manufacturing services (EMS) providers. In March 2010, the firm combined its business with Meadville Holdings Limited's PCB business.

TTM offers its employees medical, dental and vision coverage; life and AD&D insurance; short- and long-term disability; a 401(k) plan; and access to a credit union.

FINANCIALS:

Sales and profits are in thousands of dollars—add 000 to get the full amount. 2010 Note: Financial information for 2010 was not available for all companies at press time.

2010 Sales: $1,179,671	2010 Profits: $79,899	**U.S. Stock Ticker: TTMI**
2009 Sales: $582,476	2009 Profits: $4,857	**Int'l Ticker:**
2008 Sales: $680,981	2008 Profits: $-35,270	Int'l Exchange:
2007 Sales: $669,458	2007 Profits: $34,683	Employees: 17,448 Fiscal Year Ends: 12/31
2006 Sales: $369,316	2006 Profits: $35,039	Parent Company:

SALARIES/BENEFITS:

Pension Plan:	ESOP Stock Plan:	Profit Sharing:	Top Exec. Salary: $586,000	Bonus: $324,058
Savings Plan: Y	Stock Purch. Plan:		Second Exec. Salary: $345,000	Bonus: $149,903

OTHER THOUGHTS:

Apparent Women Officers or Directors: 1
Hot Spot for Advancement for Women/Minorities:

LOCATIONS: ("Y" = Yes)

West:	Southwest:	Midwest:	Southeast:	Northeast:	International:
Y		Y		Y	Y

TW TELECOM INC

www.twtelecom.com

Industry Group Code: 517110

Management:		**Sales/Marketing:**		**Liberal Arts:**		**Information Sys.:**		**Professionals:**		**Tech./Scientific:**	
Mgmt. Trainees:	Y	Marketing Pros.:	Y	Gen. Writing/Editing:	Y	Info. Mgmt.:	Y	Finance/Acct.:	Y	Engineers, Elec.:	Y
Experienced Mgmt.:	Y	Retail Sales:		Tech. Writing:	Y	Software Dev.:	Y	Law:	Y	Engineers, Other:	
Int'l Business:		Comm./Industrial:	Y	Graphic Arts/Photog.:	Y	Hardware Dev.:		HR/Other:	Y	Health/Lab:	
MBA Grads:	Y	Sales Trainees:		Music:		Consulting/Other:		Training:	Y	Science/Research:	
		Advertising Pros.:	Y	Broadcasting:				Health Care:		Petroleum/Chem.:	
				Other:				Consulting:		Math/Other:	

TYPES OF BUSINESS:

Voice & Data Networking Solutions
Ethernet Services
Internet Access

BRANDS/DIVISIONS/AFFILIATES:

Integrated NLAN
Switched NLAN
Elite NLAN
Extended NLAN

CONTACTS:

Note: Officers with more than one job title may be intentionally listed here more than once.

Larissa L. Herda, CEO
John T. Blount, COO
Larissa L. Herda, Pres.
Mark A. Peters, CFO/Exec. VP
Graham Taylor, Sr. VP-Mktg.
Steve Hardardt, Sr. VP-Human Resources
Harold W. Teets, Sr. VP-IT & Network Tech.
Steve Hardardt, Sr. VP-Bus. Admin.
Paul B. Jones, General Counsel/Exec. VP-Regulatory Policy
Marc Willency, Sr. VP-Corp. Oper.
Michael A. Rouleau, Sr. VP-Bus. Dev. & Strategy
Bob Meldrum, VP-Corp. Comm.
Carole Curtin, VP-Investor Rel.
Jill R. Stuart, Sr. VP-Finance & Acct./Chief Acct. Officer
Robert W. Gaskins, Sr. VP-Corp. Dev. & Strategy
Larissa L. Herda, Chmn.

Phone: 303-566-1000 **Fax:** 303-566-1010
Toll-Free:
Address: 10475 Park Meadows Dr., Littleton, CO 80124 US

GROWTH PLANS/SPECIAL FEATURES:

TW Telecom, Inc. provides managed network services, including Ethernet and data networking, Internet access, local and long distance voice, virtual private network (VPN), voice over Internet protocol (VoIP) and network security services, to enterprise organizations and communications services throughout the U.S, as well as to global locations for the company's IP VPN services. Through its subsidiaries the company operates in 75 metropolitan areas in 30 states and D.C. over its 28,000 route-mile network of fiber-optic cable, directly connecting roughly 11,876 buildings served directly by its metropolitan fiber facilities. The firm's customers are principally long-distance carriers, Internet service providers, incumbent & competitive local exchange carriers, wireless communications companies, telecommunications-intensive enterprise organizations in the distribution, health care, finance, service and manufacturing industries, as well as state, local and federal government entities. The company's data services allow customers to connect their own internal computer networks and access external computer networks at very high speeds using the Ethernet protocol. Those data solutions include the Switched NLAN service, Elite NLAN, Extended NLAN, Integrated NLAN, IP VPN Services, and Regional Ethernet. TW's Internet Services include offerings of Ethernet speeds up to 10 gigabytes per second (Gbps). The company provides managed solutions for its IP VPN and Internet access services; as well Distributed Denial of Service Mitigation, which monitors, identifies and mitigates denial of service attacks; and network security services such as firewalls, spam relay, integrated URL filtering, anti-virus and encrypted VPN functionality. In November 2010, TW added roughly 600 buildings in Atlanta to its network.

TW offers its employees medical, vision and dental insurance; life and disability insurance; flexible spending accounts; an employee assistance program; and a stock option plan.

FINANCIALS:

Sales and profits are in thousands of dollars—add 000 to get the full amount. 2010 Note: Financial information for 2010 was not available for all companies at press time.

2010 Sales: $1,273,171	2010 Profits: $271,434	**U.S. Stock Ticker: TWTC**
2009 Sales: $1,211,390	2009 Profits: $27,586	**Int'l Ticker:**
2008 Sales: $1,159,019	2008 Profits: $8,525	Int'l Exchange:
2007 Sales: $1,083,679	2007 Profits: $-40,269	Employees: 2,975 Fiscal Year Ends: 12/31
2006 Sales: $812,375	2006 Profits: $-98,819	Parent Company:

SALARIES/BENEFITS:

Pension Plan:	ESOP Stock Plan:	Profit Sharing:	Top Exec. Salary: $862,750	Bonus: $1,669,000
Savings Plan: Y	Stock Purch. Plan: Y		Second Exec. Salary: $500,500	Bonus: $553,000

OTHER THOUGHTS:

Apparent Women Officers or Directors: 3
Hot Spot for Advancement for Women/Minorities: Y

LOCATIONS: ("Y" = Yes)

West:	Southwest:	Midwest:	Southeast:	Northeast:	International:
Y	Y	Y	Y	Y	

UNDER ARMOUR INC

www.underarmour.com

Industry Group Code: 315211

Management:		**Sales/Marketing:**		**Liberal Arts:**		**Information Sys.:**		**Professionals:**		**Tech./Scientific:**	
Mgmt. Trainees:		Marketing Pros.:	Y	Gen. Writing/Editing:	Y	Info. Mgmt.:	Y	Finance/Acct.:	Y	Engineers, Elec.:	
Experienced Mgmt.:	Y	Retail Sales:		Tech. Writing:		Software Dev.:		Law:	Y	Engineers, Other:	
Int'l Business:	Y	Comm./Industrial:	Y	Graphic Arts/Photog.:	Y	Hardware Dev.:		HR/Other:	Y	Health/Lab:	
MBA Grads:	Y	Sales Trainees:		Music:		Consulting/Other:		Training:		Science/Research:	
		Advertising Pros.:	Y	Broadcasting:				Health Care:		Petroleum/Chem.:	
				Other:				Consulting:		Math/Other:	

TYPES OF BUSINESS:

Compression Performance Apparel
Outdoor and Sports Apparel
Shirts
Footwear
Gloves

BRANDS/DIVISIONS/AFFILIATES:

HEATGEAR
COLDGEAR
ALLSEASONGEAR

CONTACTS: *Note: Officers with more than one job title may be intentionally listed here more than once.*

Kevin A. Plank, CEO
Wayne A. Marino, COO
Kevin A. Plank, Pres.
Brad Dickerson, CFO
J. Scott Plank, Exec. VP-Bus. Dev.
John S. Rogers, VP/Gen. Mgr.-eCommerce
Dan J. Sawall, VP-Retail
Gene McCarthy, Sr. VP-Footwear
Henry B. Stafford, Sr. VP-Apparel
Kip J. Fulks, Exec. VP-Prod.
Kevin Plank, Chmn.
Mark Dowley, Pres., Int'l/Exec. VP-Global Brand

Phone: 410-454-6428 | **Fax:** 410-454-6535
Toll-Free: 888-727-6687
Address: 1020 Hull St., Fl. 3, Baltimore, MD 21230 US

GROWTH PLANS/SPECIAL FEATURES:

Under Armour, Inc. (UA) develops, markets and distributes branded performance apparel, footwear and accessories for men, women and youth. It offers several lines of apparel and accessories that utilize a variety of synthetic microfiber fabrications engineered to replace traditional cotton products in the world of athletics and fitness. UA's active wear and sports apparel accessories are designed to wick perspiration away from the skin; help regulate body temperature; enhance comfort and mobility; and improve performance regardless of weather conditions. Its products are designed and merchandised along three gear lines: HEATGEAR, for hot weather; COLDGEAR, for cold weather; and ALLSEASONGEAR, for weather between the extremes. Within each product line, UA's garments come in three fit types: compression (tight fitting), fitted (athletic cut) and loose (relaxed). Apparel represents about 80% of the firm's net revenues, while footwear and accessories (such as gloves for baseball batting, football, golf and running) account for 12% and 4%, respectively. Licensing arrangements for the sale of UA products represent the remaining 4% of revenue. The firm's products are offered worldwide in over 23,000 retail stores, including Academy Sports and Outdoors, Dick's Sporting Goods, Hibbett Sporting Goods, Modell's Sporting Goods, The Sports Authority and Cabela's. UA products also can be purchased across the U.S., Canada and Western Europe through national, regional, independent and specialty retailers. Additional international revenues are generated through third-party distributors selling UA's products internationally, along with revenues from the firm's licensee in Japan. Unaffiliated manufacturers operating in 22 countries manufacture virtually all of the company's products. International professional football, baseball, basketball, hockey, rugby and soccer players, as well as athletes in major collegiate sports and junior athletes of all levels use UA's products. The company is the official supplier of footwear to the NFL (National Football League).

FINANCIALS: **Sales and profits are in thousands of dollars—add 000 to get the full amount. 2010 Note: Financial information for 2010 was not available for all companies at press time.**

2010 Sales: $1,063,927	2010 Profits: $68,477	**U.S. Stock Ticker: UA**
2009 Sales: $856,411	2009 Profits: $46,785	**Int'l Ticker:**
2008 Sales: $725,244	2008 Profits: $38,229	Int'l Exchange:
2007 Sales: $606,561	2007 Profits: $52,558	Employees: 3,900 Fiscal Year Ends: 12/31
2006 Sales: $430,689	2006 Profits: $38,979	Parent Company:

SALARIES/BENEFITS:

Pension Plan:	ESOP Stock Plan:	Profit Sharing:	Top Exec. Salary: $650,000	Bonus: $316,875
Savings Plan: Y	Stock Purch. Plan:		Second Exec. Salary: $400,000	Bonus: $150,000

OTHER THOUGHTS:

Apparent Women Officers or Directors:
Hot Spot for Advancement for Women/Minorities:

LOCATIONS: ("Y" = Yes)

West:	Southwest:	Midwest:	Southeast:	Northeast:	International:
Y	Y	Y	Y	Y	Y

UNION PACIFIC CORP

www.up.com

Industry Group Code: 48211

Management:		Sales/Marketing:		Liberal Arts:		Information Sys.:		Professionals:		Tech./Scientific:	
Mgmt. Trainees:	Y	Marketing Pros.:	Y	Gen. Writing/Editing:		Info. Mgmt.:	Y	Finance/Acct.:	Y	Engineers, Elec.:	Y
Experienced Mgmt.:	Y	Retail Sales:		Tech. Writing:	Y	Software Dev.:	Y	Law:	Y	Engineers, Other:	Y
Int'l Business:		Comm./Industrial:	Y	Graphic Arts/Photog.:		Hardware Dev.:	Y	HR/Other:	Y	Health/Lab:	
MBA Grads:	Y	Sales Trainees:		Music:		Consulting/Other:		Training:	Y	Science/Research:	
		Advertising Pros.:	Y	Broadcasting:				Health Care:		Petroleum/Chem.:	
				Other:				Consulting:		Math/Other:	

TYPES OF BUSINESS:

Railroad

BRANDS/DIVISIONS/AFFILIATES:

Union Pacific Railroad Company
UMAX

CONTACTS: *Note: Officers with more than one job title may be intentionally listed here more than once.*

James R. Young, CEO
James R. Young, Pres.
Robert M. Knight, Jr., CFO/Exec. VP-Finance
John J. Koraleski, Exec. VP-Mktg. & Sales
Barbara W. Schaefer, Sr. VP-Human Resources/Corp. Sec.
Lynden Tennison, CIO/Sr. VP
Charles R. Eisele, Sr. VP-Admin.
J. Michael Hemmer, General Counsel/Sr. VP-Law
Lance Fritz, Exec. VP-Oper.
Charles R. Eisele, Sr. VP-Strategic Planning
Robert W. Turner, Sr. VP-Corp. Rel.
Mary S. Jones, Treas./VP
Richard R. McClish, VP-Continuous Improvement
William Turner, VP-Labor Rel.
Mike Rock, VP-External Rel.
James R. Young, Chmn.
Joseph E. O'Connor, Jr., VP-Purchasing

Phone: 402-544-5000 **Fax:** 402-501-2133
Toll-Free: 888-870-8777
Address: 1400 Douglas St., Omaha, NE 68179 US

GROWTH PLANS/SPECIAL FEATURES:

Union Pacific Corp. is a provider of rail transportation. The company operates primarily through Union Pacific Railroad Company, which is one of the largest railroads in North America, covering 23 states across the western two-thirds of the U.S. Union Pacific Railroad is a Class I railroad with approximately 31,953 route miles linking Pacific Coast and Gulf Coast ports with the Midwest and Eastern U.S. gateways and providing several north/south corridors to key Mexican gateways. The firm handles freight in six commodity groups: agriculture, including grains, food products, beverages and sweeteners, accounts for approximately 19% of the firm's revenues; automotive, which accounts for roughly 8% of revenues; chemicals, including liquid and dry chemicals, plastics and liquid petroleum products, accounts for roughly 15% of revenues; energy, including coal transportation, accounts for 22% of revenues; industrial products account for 16% of revenues and includes stone, cement, lumber, paper and government and consumer goods; and intermodal products (international and domestic shipments), from which Union Pacific derives roughly 20% of revenues. The firm spent approximately $2.5 billion throughout 2010 to enhance the safety and efficiency of the Union Pacific Railroad network. In February 2010, Union Pacific Railroad Company and CSX Intermodal agreed to jointly launch UMAX, a new domestic interline container program featuring access to over 20,000 containers and over 600 service lanes supported by faster and more frequent train schedules. In December 2010, the firm opened a new office in Des Moines, Iowa.

The firm offers employees benefits including disability, medical, dental, vision and life insurance; wellness and fitness programs; paid vacation; a pension plan; a 401(k) plan; a transportation spending account; tuition reimbursement; and employee discounts on automobiles, computers, mortgage services, home appliances, wireless phone services and personal banking services.

FINANCIALS: **Sales and profits are in thousands of dollars—add 000 to get the full amount. 2010 Note: Financial information for 2010 was not available for all companies at press time.**

2010 Sales: $16,965,000	2010 Profits: $2,780,000	**U.S. Stock Ticker: UNP**
2009 Sales: $14,143,000	2009 Profits: $1,898,000	**Int'l Ticker:**
2008 Sales: $17,970,000	2008 Profits: $2,338,000	Int'l Exchange:
2007 Sales: $16,283,000	2007 Profits: $1,855,000	Employees: 42,884 Fiscal Year Ends: 12/31
2006 Sales: $15,578,000	2006 Profits: $1,606,000	Parent Company:

SALARIES/BENEFITS:

Pension Plan: Y	ESOP Stock Plan:	Profit Sharing:	Top Exec. Salary: $1,150,000	Bonus: $2,500,000
Savings Plan: Y	Stock Purch. Plan:		Second Exec. Salary: $600,000	Bonus: $955,000

OTHER THOUGHTS:

Apparent Women Officers or Directors: 3
Hot Spot for Advancement for Women/Minorities: Y

LOCATIONS: ("Y" = Yes)

West:	Southwest:	Midwest:	Southeast:	Northeast:	International:
Y	Y	Y	Y		

UNITED NATURAL FOODS INC

www.unfi.com

Industry Group Code: 4244

Management:		Sales/Marketing:		Liberal Arts:		Information Sys.:		Professionals:		Tech./Scientific:	
Mgmt. Trainees:	Y	Marketing Pros.:	Y	Gen. Writing/Editing:	Y	Info. Mgmt.:	Y	Finance/Acct.:	Y	Engineers, Elec.:	
Experienced Mgmt.:	Y	Retail Sales:		Tech. Writing:		Software Dev.:	Y	Law:	Y	Engineers, Other:	
Int'l Business:		Comm./Industrial:	Y	Graphic Arts/Photog.:	Y	Hardware Dev.:		HR/Other:	Y	Health/Lab:	
MBA Grads:	Y	Sales Trainees:	Y	Music:		Consulting/Other:		Training:	Y	Science/Research:	
		Advertising Pros.:		Broadcasting:				Health Care:		Petroleum/Chem.:	
				Other:				Consulting:		Math/Other:	

TYPES OF BUSINESS:

Food Distribution
Natural & Organic Foods Distribution
Nutritional Supplements Distribution
Personal Care Products Distribution
Retail Stores

BRANDS/DIVISIONS/AFFILIATES:

Natural Retail Group Inc
Woodstock Farms
Albert's Organics
Blooming Prairie
Select Nutrition
Harvest Bay
Organic Baby
UNFI Specialty

CONTACTS: *Note: Officers with more than one job title may be intentionally listed here more than once.*

Steven L. Spinner, CEO
Steven L. Spinner, Pres.
Mark E. Shamber, CFO/Sr. VP
Thomas A. Dziki, Chief Human Resources Officer/Sr. VP
John Stern, CIO/Sr. VP
Joseph J. Traficanti, General Counsel/Sr. VP/Chief Compliance Officer
Mark E. Shamber, Treas.
Craig H. Smith, Pres., Eastern Region
Thomas A. Dziki, Sr. VP-Sustainable Dev.
Kurt Luttecke, Pres., Western Region
Thomas A. Dziki, Chief Sustainability Officer
Michael S. Funk, Chmn.
David A. Matthews, Pres., UNFI Int'l
Sean Griffin, Sr. VP-National Dist.

Phone: 401-528-8634 **Fax:**
Toll-Free: 800-877-8898
Address: 313 Iron Horse Way, Providence, RI 02908 US

GROWTH PLANS/SPECIAL FEATURES:

United Natural Foods, Inc. (UNFI) is a national distributor of natural and organic foods and related products. The company, which is a Certified Organic Distributor, carries more than 60,000 natural and organic products; these are sold under regional brand, national brand, private and master distribution labels. The firm offers six types of products: grocery and general merchandise; personal care items; produce; nutritional supplements; perishables and frozen foods; and bulk and food service products. UNFI serves over 23,000 customers, including supernatural chains (large chains of natural foods supermarkets), independently owned natural products retailers and conventional supermarkets located across the U.S. The company also distributes through the food service, international and buying club channels. The company has been the primary distributor to one of the largest natural foods chain in the U.S., Whole Foods Market, Inc., for more than 10 years. UNFI is also the primary distributor for another major organic chain, Wild Oats Market, which is owned by Whole Foods. The company's operations comprise three principal divisions: wholesale, which includes the operations of its 28 distribution centers; retail, which consists of UNFI's 13 owned and managed retail stores (through subsidiary Natural Retail Group, Inc.); and manufacturing, which is comprised of its subsidiary, United Natural Trading Co. (which does business as Woodstock Farms), and its branded product lines. Woodstock Farms is an importer, processor, packager, and wholesale distributors of natural and organic products; trail mixes; nuts; seeds; dried fruit; and confections. Distribution members of UNFI include Albert's Organics, UNFI Specialty and Select Nutrition. UNFI's brands include Woodstock Farms, Harvest Bay and Organic Baby. In June 2011, the firm agreed to divest its specialty non-foods and general merchandise business operations.

UNFI offers employees medical, dental, life and disability insurance; an assistance program; a stock ownership plan; and educational assistance.

FINANCIALS: **Sales and profits are in thousands of dollars—add 000 to get the full amount. 2010 Note: Financial information for 2010 was not available for all companies at press time.**

2010 Sales: $3,757,139	2010 Profits: $68,321
2009 Sales: $3,454,900	2009 Profits: $59,184
2008 Sales: $3,365,857	2008 Profits: $48,479
2007 Sales: $2,754,280	2007 Profits: $50,153
2006 Sales: $2,433,594	2006 Profits: $43,277

U.S. Stock Ticker: UNFI
Int'l Ticker:
Int'l Exchange:
Employees: 6,500 Fiscal Year Ends: 7/31
Parent Company:

SALARIES/BENEFITS:

Pension Plan:	ESOP Stock Plan: Y	Profit Sharing:	Top Exec. Salary: $775,000	Bonus: $456,320
Savings Plan: Y	Stock Purch. Plan:		Second Exec. Salary: $343,885	Bonus: $207,305

OTHER THOUGHTS:

Apparent Women Officers or Directors: 1
Hot Spot for Advancement for Women/Minorities:

LOCATIONS: ("Y" = Yes)

West:	Southwest:	Midwest:	Southeast:	Northeast:	International:
Y		Y	Y	Y	

UNITED PARCEL SERVICE INC (UPS)

www.ups.com

Industry Group Code: 4921

Management:		Sales/Marketing:		Liberal Arts:		Information Sys.:		Professionals:		Tech./Scientific:	
Mgmt. Trainees:	Y	Marketing Pros.:	Y	Gen. Writing/Editing:	Y	Info. Mgmt.:	Y	Finance/Acct.:	Y	Engineers, Elec.:	Y
Experienced Mgmt.:	Y	Retail Sales:		Tech. Writing:	Y	Software Dev.:	Y	Law:	Y	Engineers, Other:	
Int'l Business:	Y	Comm./Industrial:	Y	Graphic Arts/Photog.:	Y	Hardware Dev.:		HR/Other:	Y	Health/Lab:	
MBA Grads:	Y	Sales Trainees:		Music:		Consulting/Other:		Training:	Y	Science/Research:	
		Advertising Pros.:	Y	Broadcasting:				Health Care:		Petroleum/Chem.:	
				Other:	Y			Consulting:		Math/Other:	Y

TYPES OF BUSINESS:

Express Delivery Service
Logistics Services
Supply Chain Services
International Products & Services
Ground & Air Delivery Services
Visibility & Technology Services

BRANDS/DIVISIONS/AFFILIATES:

UPS Freight
UPS Supply Chain Solutions
UPS WorldShip
Quantum View
UPS Next Day Air
UPS Hundredweight Services
Flex Global View
UPS Billing Analysis Tool

CONTACTS: *Note: Officers with more than one job title may be intentionally listed here more than once.*

D. Scott Davis, CEO
David Abney, COO
Kurt Kuehn, CFO
Alan Gershenhorn, Chief Mktg. & Sales Officer
Allen E. Hill, Sr. VP-Human Resources
David Barnes, CIO/Sr. VP
Teri Plummer McClure, General Counsel/Sr. VP-Legal/Corp. Sec.
Myron Gray, Pres., US Oper.
Christine M. Owens, Sr. VP-Comm. & Brand Mgmt.
John McDevitt, Sr. VP-Global Transportation Svcs. & Labor Rel.
David Abney, Pres., UPS Airlines
Terri Plummer McClure, Sr. VP-Compliance & Public Affairs
Glenn Rice, Pres., UPS East Region
D. Scott Davis, Chmn.
Daniel J. Brutto, Pres., UPS Int'l

Phone: 404-828-6000 **Fax:** 404-828-6562
Toll-Free: 800-874-5877
Address: 55 Glenlake Pkwy. NE, Atlanta, GA 30328 US

GROWTH PLANS/SPECIAL FEATURES:

United Parcel Service, Inc. (UPS) is one of the world's largest package delivery companies and a global provider of supply chain management. It delivers packages each business day for 1.8 million shipping customers to 6.1 million consignees in over 215 countries. The company delivers an average of 15.6 million pieces per day worldwide. In addition, the supply chain solutions capabilities are available in over 200 countries. The firm is also a major provider of less-than-truckload transportation (LTL) services. Offerings include domestic and international package products and services; and supply chain and freight services. The U.S. domestic package products and services business delivers packages traveling by ground or air transportation. In addition to the standard ground delivery products, UPS Hundredweight Services offers guaranteed, time-definite service to customers sending multiple packages shipments. UPS Next Day Air offers several service options guaranteeing next business day delivery by 8:00AM, 10:30AM, noon, 3-4:30PM or by the end of the day in the 48 contiguous U.S. states and limited areas of Alaska. International services include guaranteed early morning, morning and noon delivery to major cities around the world, as well as scheduled day-definite air and ground services. Supply chain and freight segment consists of its forwarding and logistics operations, UPS Freight and other related businesses. The division provides services in more than 175 countries and territories and includes supply chain design and management; freight distribution; customs brokerage; mail; and consulting services. UPS freight offers a variety of LTL/truckload services to customers in North America. Other business units within this segment include Mail Boxes, Etc.; UPS Supply Chain Solutions; and UPS Capital. In January 2011, UPS opened new healthcare-dedicated facilities in Singapore, the Netherlands, Canada and Kentucky to serve the special needs of the health care industry, including the shipment of drugs and supplies, bringing its health care support locations to a global total of 30.

The company offers its employees life, disability, medical, dental and vision insurance; child and elder care spending accounts; and assistance and discount programs.

FINANCIALS: **Sales and profits are in thousands of dollars—add 000 to get the full amount. 2010 Note: Financial information for 2010 was not available for all companies at press time.**

2010 Sales: $49,545,000 — 2010 Profits: $3,488,000
2009 Sales: $45,297,000 — 2009 Profits: $2,152,000
2008 Sales: $51,486,000 — 2008 Profits: $3,003,000
2007 Sales: $49,700,000 — 2007 Profits: $382,000
2006 Sales: $47,547,000 — 2006 Profits: $4,202,000

U.S. Stock Ticker: UPS
Int'l Ticker:
Int'l Exchange:
Employees: 408,600 Fiscal Year Ends: 12/31
Parent Company:

SALARIES/BENEFITS:

Pension Plan: Y ESOP Stock Plan: Profit Sharing: Top Exec. Salary: $1,000,000 Bonus: $130,523
Savings Plan: Y Stock Purch. Plan: Y Second Exec. Salary: $462,500 Bonus: $62,900

OTHER THOUGHTS:

Apparent Women Officers or Directors: 4
Hot Spot for Advancement for Women/Minorities: Y

LOCATIONS: ("Y" = Yes)

West:	Southwest:	Midwest:	Southeast:	Northeast:	International:
Y	Y	Y	Y	Y	Y

Sales, profits and employees may be estimates. Financial information, benefits and other data can change quickly and may vary from those stated here.

UNITED STATES CELLULAR CORP

www.uscellular.com

Industry Group Code: 5172

Management:		Sales/Marketing:		Liberal Arts:		Information Sys.:		Professionals:		Tech./Scientific:	
Mgmt. Trainees:	Y	Marketing Pros.:	Y	Gen. Writing/Editing:	Y	Info. Mgmt.:	Y	Finance/Acct.:	Y	Engineers, Elec.:	Y
Experienced Mgmt.:	Y	Retail Sales:	Y	Tech. Writing:	Y	Software Dev.:	Y	Law:	Y	Engineers, Other:	Y
Int'l Business:		Comm./Industrial:	Y	Graphic Arts/Photog.:	Y	Hardware Dev.:		HR/Other:	Y	Health/Lab:	
MBA Grads:	Y	Sales Trainees:	Y	Music:		Consulting/Other:		Training:	Y	Science/Research:	
		Advertising Pros.:	Y	Broadcasting:				Health Care:		Petroleum/Chem.:	
				Other:				Consulting:		Math/Other:	

TYPES OF BUSINESS:

Cell Phone Service
PCS Service

BRANDS/DIVISIONS/AFFILIATES:

Telephone and Data Systems Inc (TDS)
easyedge
Qualcomm Inc
Mobile Broadband
TEAM Technologies LLC

CONTACTS:

Note: Officers with more than one job title may be intentionally listed here more than once.

Mary N. Dillon, CEO
Mary N. Dillon, Pres.
Steven T. Campbell, CFO/Exec. VP-Finance/Treas.
Edward Perez, VP-Mktg. & Sales Oper.
Jeffrey J. Childs, Chief Human Resources Officer/Exec. VP
John M. Cregier, VP-IT
Michael S. Irizarry, CTO/Exec. VP
John C. Gockley, VP-Legal & Regulatory Affairs
Alan D. Ferber, Chief Strategy & Brand Officer
Karen C. Ehlers, VP-Public Affairs & Comm.
Thomas S. Weber, VP-Financial Strategy
Rochelle J. Boersma, VP-Agent Effectiveness
Thomas P. Catani, VP-Sales, East
Nick B. Wright, VP-Sales, West
Katherine L. Hust, VP-Sales, Mid-Central
LeRoy T. Carlson, Jr., Chmn.

Phone: 773-399-8900 **Fax:** 773-399-7054
Toll-Free: 888-944-9400
Address: 8410 W. Bryn Mawr Ave., Ste. 700, Chicago, IL 60631 US

GROWTH PLANS/SPECIAL FEATURES:

United States Cellular Corp. (U.S. Cellular), a majority-owned subsidiary of Telephone and Data Systems, Inc., is a leading wireless service provider in the U.S., serving more than 6 million customers in 26 states. The company owns interests in consolidated wireless markets that cover portions of 35 states and a total population of roughly 90.5 million. The company's products are divided into two segments: wireless devices and wireless services. The wireless devices segment offers a range of wireless handset devices, laptop cards and such accessories as carrying cases, hands-free devices, memory cards, batteries and battery chargers. The firm has also installed service repair programs at certain facilities which assist customers with over-the-counter exchanges, smartphone advance exchanges, loaner phones, device recycling and device returns. The firm maintains a repair facility in Tulsa, Oklahoma to handle such issues. U.S. Cellular sells wireless devices to agents and other third-party distributors for resale. The second segment, wireless services, provides a variety of packaged voice and data pricing plans, including both postpay and prepay options. The company's easyedge brand of enhanced data services uses a binary runtime environment for wireless (BREW) technology, licensed from Qualcomm, and adds limited computer-like functionality to handsets, enabling applications to be downloaded over-the-air directly to the customer's wireless device. These enhanced data services include downloading news, weather, sports information, games, ring tones and other services. Telephone and Data Systems owns approximately 83% of the company. In early 2010, the company expanded networks near St. Joseph, Missouri; northwest Omaha; Palmyra, Missouri; and Sapulpa, Oklahoma. In December 2010, U.S. Cellular acquired data center services provider TEAM Technologies, LLC.

The firm offers its employees medical, dental and vision insurance; life and AD&D insurance; short- and long-term disability; flexible spending accounts; a 401(k) plan; a pension plan; an employee stock purchase plan; an associate scholar program; a PC purchase program; and adoption assistance.

FINANCIALS:

Sales and profits are in thousands of dollars—add 000 to get the full amount. 2010 Note: Financial information for 2010 was not available for all companies at press time.

2010 Sales: $4,177,681 — 2010 Profits: $132,324
2009 Sales: $4,213,880 — 2009 Profits: $206,732
2008 Sales: $4,243,185 — 2008 Profits: $32,990
2007 Sales: $3,946,264 — 2007 Profits: $314,734
2006 Sales: $3,473,155 — 2006 Profits: $179,490

U.S. Stock Ticker: USM
Int'l Ticker:
Int'l Exchange:
Employees: 8,993 Fiscal Year Ends: 12/31
Parent Company: TELEPHONE AND DATA SYSTEMS INC (TDS)

SALARIES/BENEFITS:

Pension Plan: Y ESOP Stock Plan: Profit Sharing: Top Exec. Salary: $521,287 Bonus: $189,531
Savings Plan: Y Stock Purch. Plan: Y Second Exec. Salary: $458,583 Bonus: $222,325

OTHER THOUGHTS:

Apparent Women Officers or Directors: 5
Hot Spot for Advancement for Women/Minorities: Y

LOCATIONS: ("Y" = Yes)

West:	Southwest:	Midwest:	Southeast:	Northeast:	International:
Y	Y	Y	Y	Y	

UNITED TECHNOLOGIES CORPORATION

www.utc.com

Industry Group Code: 33641

Management:		Sales/Marketing:		Liberal Arts:		Information Sys.:		Professionals:		Tech./Scientific:	
Mgmt. Trainees:	Y	Marketing Pros.:	Y	Gen. Writing/Editing:	Y	Info. Mgmt.:	Y	Finance/Acct.:	Y	Engineers, Elec.:	Y
Experienced Mgmt.:	Y	Retail Sales:		Tech. Writing:	Y	Software Dev.:	Y	Law:	Y	Engineers, Other:	Y
Int'l Business:	Y	Comm./Industrial:	Y	Graphic Arts/Photog.:	Y	Hardware Dev.:	Y	HR/Other:	Y	Health/Lab:	
MBA Grads:	Y	Sales Trainees:		Music:		Consulting/Other:	Y	Training:	Y	Science/Research:	Y
		Advertising Pros.:	Y	Broadcasting:				Health Care:		Petroleum/Chem.:	
				Other:				Consulting:		Math/Other:	Y

TYPES OF BUSINESS:

Aerospace Technology
Elevator & Escalator Systems
HVAC Systems
Fuel Cells & Power Generation
Industrial Systems
Aircraft Parts & Maintenance
Flight Systems
Security Products & Services

BRANDS/DIVISIONS/AFFILIATES:

Otis Elevator Company
Carrier Corp.
Sikorsky
Pratt & Whitney Canada Corp
Hamilton Sundstrand
UTC Power
United Technologies Research Centre Ireland

CONTACTS: *Note: Officers with more than one job title may be intentionally listed here more than once.*

Louis R. Chenevert, CEO
Gregory J. Hayes, CFO/Sr. VP
J. Thomas Bowler, Jr., Sr. VP-Human Resources & Organization
J. Michael McQuade, Sr. VP-Science & Tech.
Nancy Davis, CIO/VP
Charles D. Gill, General Counsel/Sr. VP
Eileen Drake, VP-Oper.
David P. Hess, Pres., Pratt & Whitney
William M. Brown, Pres., UTC Fire & Security
Geraud Darnis, Pres., Carrier
Didier Michaud-Daniel, Pres., Otis
Louis R. Chenevert, Chmn.
Jothi Purushotaman, Pres., UTC India

Phone: 860-728-7000 **Fax:** 860-728-7028
Toll-Free:
Address: 1 Financial Plz., Hartford, CT 06103 US

GROWTH PLANS/SPECIAL FEATURES:

United Technologies Corporation (UTC) provides high-technology products and services to the building systems and aerospace industries worldwide. The company operates through six principle segments: Carrier Corp.; Hamilton Sundstrand; Otis Elevator Company; Pratt & Whitney; Sikorsky; and UTC Fire & Security. Carrier manufactures commercial and residential heating, ventilation and air conditioning (HVAC) systems and equipment. It also produces, sells, services and provides components for commercial and transport refrigeration equipment. Hamilton Sundstrand serves commercial, military, regional and corporate aviation, as well as space and undersea applications. Its products include power generation management and distribution systems, flight systems, engine control systems, environmental control systems, fire protection and detection systems, auxiliary power units and propeller systems. Otis is one of the world's largest elevator and escalator manufacturing, installation and maintenance companies. Otis designs, manufactures, sells and installs a wide range of passenger and freight elevators for low, medium and high speed applications, as well as a broad line of escalators and moving walkways. Pratt & Whitney produces and services commercial, general aviation and military aircraft engines. It also handles rocket engine production for commercial and government space applications. Sikorsky is a world leader in helicopter manufacture and design, with customers including the U.S. military and 40 other countries. UTC Fire & Security offers fire and special hazard detection and suppression systems; fire fighting equipment; electronic security, monitoring and rapid response systems; and service and security personnel services. In March 2010, the firm acquired the GE security business from General Electric Co. In April 2010, the company opened an R&D hub in Ireland called United Technologies Research Centre Ireland. Also in 2010, UTC acquired a 49.5% stake in Clipper Windpower, a manufacturer of electricity-creating wind turbines, for $271 million.

UTC offers employees medical and dental insurance; health care and dependent care reimbursement accounts; vision care discounts; and a 401(k) plan.

FINANCIALS: **Sales and profits are in thousands of dollars—add 000 to get the full amount. 2010 Note: Financial information for 2010 was not available for all companies at press time.**

2010 Sales: $54,326,000 | 2010 Profits: $4,711,000
2009 Sales: $52,425,000 | 2009 Profits: $4,179,000
2008 Sales: $59,757,000 | 2008 Profits: $5,053,000
2007 Sales: $55,716,000 | 2007 Profits: $4,548,000
2006 Sales: $47,829,000 | 2006 Profits: $3,732,000

U.S. Stock Ticker: UTX
Int'l Ticker:
Int'l Exchange:
Employees: 208,200 Fiscal Year Ends: 12/31
Parent Company:

SALARIES/BENEFITS:

Pension Plan: | ESOP Stock Plan: | Profit Sharing: | Top Exec. Salary: $1,435,000 | Bonus: $2,980,447
Savings Plan: Y | Stock Purch. Plan: | | Second Exec. Salary: $950,000 | Bonus: $1,836,510

OTHER THOUGHTS:

Apparent Women Officers or Directors: 4
Hot Spot for Advancement for Women/Minorities: Y

LOCATIONS: ("Y" = Yes)

West:	Southwest:	Midwest:	Southeast:	Northeast:	International:
Y	Y	Y	Y	Y	Y

UNITEDHEALTH GROUP INC

www.unitedhealthgroup.com

Industry Group Code: 524114

Management:		Sales/Marketing:		Liberal Arts:		Information Sys.:		Professionals:		Tech./Scientific:	
Mgmt. Trainees:	Y	Marketing Pros.:	Y	Gen. Writing/Editing:	Y	Info. Mgmt.:	Y	Finance/Acct.:	Y	Engineers, Elec.:	
Experienced Mgmt.:	Y	Retail Sales:		Tech. Writing:	Y	Software Dev.:	Y	Law:	Y	Engineers, Other:	
Int'l Business:	Y	Comm./Industrial:	Y	Graphic Arts/Photog.:	Y	Hardware Dev.:		HR/Other:	Y	Health/Lab:	
MBA Grads:	Y	Sales Trainees:		Music:		Consulting/Other:		Training:	Y	Science/Research:	
		Advertising Pros.:	Y	Broadcasting:				Health Care:	Y	Petroleum/Chem.:	
				Other:	Y			Consulting:		Math/Other:	

TYPES OF BUSINESS:

Medical Insurance
Wellness Plans
Dental & Vision Insurance
Health Information Technology

BRANDS/DIVISIONS/AFFILIATES:

United Healthcare
Ovations
AmeriChoice
OptumHealth
Ingenix
Ingenix Life Sciences

CONTACTS: *Note: Officers with more than one job title may be intentionally listed here more than once.*

Stephen J. Hemsley, CEO
Stephen J. Hemsley, Pres.
David S. Wichmann, CFO/Exec. VP
Lori Sweere, Exec. VP-Human Capital
Christopher J. Walsh, General Counsel/Exec. VP
Don Nathan, Chief Comm. Officer/Sr. VP
Eric S. Rangen, Chief Acct. Officer/Sr. VP
Gail K. Boudreaux, Exec. VP/CEO-UnitedHealthcare
William A. Munsell, Exec. VP/Pres., Enterprise Services Group
Larry C. Renfro, Exec. VP/CEO-Optum
William A. Munsell, Exec. VP
Richard T. Burke, Chmn.
Simon Stevens, Pres., Global Health/Exec. VP

Phone: 952-936-1300 **Fax:** 952-936-1819
Toll-Free: 800-328-5979
Address: 9900 Bren Rd. E., Minnetonka, MN 55343 US

GROWTH PLANS/SPECIAL FEATURES:

UnitedHealth Group, Inc. is a diversified health and insurance firm that serves over 75 million Americans. The company provides individuals with access to healthcare services and resources through 730,000 physicians and other care providers and 5,300 hospitals across the U.S. The company has four operating segments: Health Benefits; OptumHealth; Ingenix; and Prescription Solutions. The Health Benefits segment, which includes UnitedHealthcare, Ovations and AmeriChoice, provides consumer-oriented health benefit plans and services for large national employers, public sector employers, mid-sized employers, small businesses and individuals nationwide; health and well-being services for individuals age 50 and older; and network-based health services for beneficiaries of government-sponsored health care programs. The OptumHealth segment is engaged in care services, behavioral solutions, specialty benefits and financial services in fields such as dental, vision, disability, therapy and stop-loss coverage. The Ingenix segment offers database and data management services; software products; publications; consulting and actuarial services; business process outsourcing services; pharmaceutical data consulting and research; and pharmaceutical development services in the U.S. and internationally. Ingenix's customers include 6,200 hospitals; 246,000 physicians; 2,000 payers and intermediaries; 205 Fortune 500 companies; 270 government entities; and 2,200 life sciences companies. The Prescription Solutions segment offers a comprehensive suite of integrated pharmacy benefit management (PBM) services to over 12 million people through over 66,000 retail network pharmacies as well as mail order service facilities. In January 2011, Ingenix established new division Ingenix Life Sciences and agreed to sell its i3 clinical development division to inVentiv Health.

The company offers its employees medical, vision and dental insurance; flexible spending accounts; life and AD&D insurance; an employee assistance program; adoption assistance; and tuition reimbursement.

FINANCIALS: **Sales and profits are in thousands of dollars—add 000 to get the full amount. 2010 Note: Financial information for 2010 was not available for all companies at press time.**

2010 Sales: $94,155,000	2010 Profits: $4,634,000
2009 Sales: $87,138,000	2009 Profits: $3,822,000
2008 Sales: $81,186,000	2008 Profits: $2,977,000
2007 Sales: $75,431,000	2007 Profits: $4,654,000
2006 Sales: $71,542,000	2006 Profits: $4,159,000

U.S. Stock Ticker: UNH
Int'l Ticker:
Int'l Exchange:
Employees: 87,000 Fiscal Year Ends: 12/31
Parent Company:

SALARIES/BENEFITS:

Pension Plan: ESOP Stock Plan: Profit Sharing: Top Exec. Salary: $1,300,000 Bonus: $3,400,000
Savings Plan: Y Stock Purch. Plan: Y Second Exec. Salary: $700,000 Bonus: $1,400,000

OTHER THOUGHTS:

Apparent Women Officers or Directors: 3
Hot Spot for Advancement for Women/Minorities: Y

LOCATIONS: ("Y" = Yes)

West:	Southwest:	Midwest:	Southeast:	Northeast:	International:
Y	Y	Y	Y	Y	Y

UNIVERSAL HEALTH SERVICES INC

www.uhsinc.com

Industry Group Code: 6214

Management:		Sales/Marketing:		Liberal Arts:		Information Sys.:		Professionals:		Tech./Scientific:	
Mgmt. Trainees:	Y	Marketing Pros.:	Y	Gen. Writing/Editing:		Info. Mgmt.:	Y	Finance/Acct.:	Y	Engineers, Elec.:	
Experienced Mgmt.:	Y	Retail Sales:		Tech. Writing:	Y	Software Dev.:	Y	Law:	Y	Engineers, Other:	
Int'l Business:	Y	Comm./Industrial:		Graphic Arts/Photog.:		Hardware Dev.:		HR/Other:	Y	Health/Lab:	Y
MBA Grads:	Y	Sales Trainees:		Music:		Consulting/Other:		Training:	Y	Science/Research:	
		Advertising Pros.:		Broadcasting:				Health Care:	Y	Petroleum/Chem.:	
				Other:				Consulting:		Math/Other:	

TYPES OF BUSINESS:

Acute Care Hospitals
Radiation Oncology Centers
Behavioral Health Hospitals
Surgical Hospitals
Administrative Services
Physician Recruitment
Facilities Planning

BRANDS/DIVISIONS/AFFILIATES:

Psychiatric Solutions Inc

CONTACTS: *Note: Officers with more than one job title may be intentionally listed here more than once.*

Alan B. Miller, CEO
Marc D. Miller, Pres.
Steve G. Filton, CFO/Sr. VP/Sec.
Gerry Johnson Geckle, VP-Human Resources
Michael S. Nelson, VP-Info. Svcs.
Matthew D. Klein, General Counsel/VP
Richard C. Wright, VP-Dev.
Cheryl K. Ramagano, Treas./VP
Charles F. Boyle, Controller/VP
Marvin G. Pember, Sr. VP
Debra K. Osteen, Sr. VP
Larry Harrod, VP-Behavioral Finance
Alan B. Miller, Chmn.

Phone: 610-768-3300 **Fax:** 610-992-4545
Toll-Free:
Address: 367 S. Gulph Rd., King of Prussia, PA 19406-0958 US

GROWTH PLANS/SPECIAL FEATURES:

Universal Health Services, Inc. (UHS) owns and operates, through its subsidiaries, acute care hospitals, behavioral health centers, surgical hospitals, ambulatory surgery centers and radiation oncology centers. UHS has 25 acute care hospitals and 206 behavioral health centers located in 37 states, Washington, D.C., the U.S. Virgin Islands and Puerto Rico. As part of its ambulatory treatment centers division, the firm manages or partially/wholly owns seven surgical hospitals and surgery and radiation oncology centers located in five states and Puerto Rico. UHS hospitals provide general surgery, pharmaceutical services, internal medicine, pediatric services, obstetrics, emergency room care, radiology, oncology, diagnostic care, coronary care and behavioral health services. The company also provides non-medical services to its facilities, including a variety of management services such as central purchasing; facilities planning; administrative personnel management; finance and control systems; information services; physician recruitment services; marketing; and public relations. Acute care hospitals, surgery centers, surgical hospitals and radiation oncology centers make up approximately 70% of the firm's revenue, with behavioral health care facilities accounting for roughly 30%. In November 2010, UHS acquired Psychiatric Solutions, Inc., an operator of 105 facilities in 32 states, Puerto Rico and the U.S. Virgin Islands, for roughly $3.04 billion.

The company offers its employees medical, dental, vision, life, AD&D and disability insurance; paid time off; a 401(k) plan; an employee stock purchase plan; and flexible spending accounts.

FINANCIALS: **Sales and profits are in thousands of dollars—add 000 to get the full amount. 2010 Note: Financial information for 2010 was not available for all companies at press time.**

2010 Sales: $5,568,185 — 2010 Profits: $230,183
2009 Sales: $5,202,379 — 2009 Profits: $260,373
2008 Sales: $5,022,417 — 2008 Profits: $199,377
2007 Sales: $4,751,005 — 2007 Profits: $170,387
2006 Sales: $4,191,300 — 2006 Profits: $259,458

U.S. Stock Ticker: UHS
Int'l Ticker:
Int'l Exchange:
Employees: 49,700 Fiscal Year Ends: 12/31
Parent Company:

SALARIES/BENEFITS:

Pension Plan: ESOP Stock Plan: Profit Sharing: Top Exec. Salary: $1,377,053 Bonus: $1,170,495
Savings Plan: Y Stock Purch. Plan: Y Second Exec. Salary: $499,313 Bonus: $

OTHER THOUGHTS:

Apparent Women Officers or Directors: 3
Hot Spot for Advancement for Women/Minorities: Y

LOCATIONS: ("Y" = Yes)

West:	Southwest:	Midwest:	Southeast:	Northeast:	International:
Y	Y	Y	Y	Y	

UNIVISION COMMUNICATIONS INC

www.univision.com

Industry Group Code: 515120

Management:		Sales/Marketing:		Liberal Arts:		Information Sys.:		Professionals:		Tech./Scientific:	
Mgmt. Trainees:	Y	Marketing Pros.:	Y	Gen. Writing/Editing:	Y	Info. Mgmt.:	Y	Finance/Acct.:	Y	Engineers, Elec.:	Y
Experienced Mgmt.:	Y	Retail Sales:		Tech. Writing:		Software Dev.:	Y	Law:	Y	Engineers, Other:	
Int'l Business:	Y	Comm./Industrial:	Y	Graphic Arts/Photog.:	Y	Hardware Dev.:		HR/Other:	Y	Health/Lab:	
MBA Grads:	Y	Sales Trainees:		Music:	Y	Consulting/Other:		Training:	Y	Science/Research:	
		Advertising Pros.:	Y	Broadcasting:	Y			Health Care:		Petroleum/Chem.:	
				Other:	Y			Consulting:		Math/Other:	

TYPES OF BUSINESS:

Spanish Television Broadcasting
Cable Television Programming
Online Portal
Radio Broadcasting

BRANDS/DIVISIONS/AFFILIATES:

Univision Television Group
Galavision
TeleFutura
Univision Interactive Media
Univision Radio Inc
Broadcasting Media Partners, Inc
Univision Movil
Univision Interactive Self-Service

CONTACTS: *Note: Officers with more than one job title may be intentionally listed here more than once.*

Randy Falco, CEO
Randy Falco, Pres.
Andrew W. Hobson, CFO/Sr. Exec. VP
Ruth Gaviria, Sr. VP-Corp. Mktg.
Roberto Llamas, Chief Human Resources Officer/Exec. VP
C. Douglas Kranwinkle, General Counsel/Exec. VP
Charlie Echeverry, Exec. VP-Interactive Media Sales
Monica Talan, VP-Corp. Comm.
Peter H. Lori, Chief Acct. Officer/Controller/Exec. VP
Cesar Conde, Pres., Univision Networks
Jose Valle, Pres., Univision Radio
Kevin Conroy, Pres., Univision Interactive Media, Inc.
Issac Lee, Pres., News
Tonia O'Connor, Pres., Dist. Sales & Mktg.

Phone: 212-455-5200	**Fax:** 212-867-6710
Toll-Free:	
Address: 605 3rd Ave., 12th Fl., New York, NY 10158 US	

GROWTH PLANS/SPECIAL FEATURES:

Univision Communications, Inc. is one of the leading Spanish-language media companies in the U.S. The firm currently operates in three business segments: television, radio and interactive media. The television segment consists of the Univision, TeleFutura and the Galavision cable television networks. Univision's radio segment is operated through Univision Radio, Inc., an owner of 68 radio stations in 16 of the top 25 U.S. Hispanic markets and five stations in Puerto Rico. The Interactive media division, which is operated by Univision Interactive Media, consists of Univision.com, a web portal; and Univision Movil, a Spanish-language suite of mobile offerings. Each of these three segments represents the largest Spanish-language media application in their respective fields within the U.S. The firm is able to reach 97% of all U.S. Hispanic households via its nationwide Univision broadcast and cable channels. TeleFutura is the company's 24-hour Spanish-language broadcast television network, reaching 86% of U.S. Hispanic households. TeleFutura Television Group is the owner and operator of 18 full-power and 14 low-power Spanish-language stations. The company's Galavision network is the leading Spanish-language cable television network, which covers approximately 82% of U.S. Hispanic cable households. Broadcast is supported by the Univision Television Group, which owns and operates 20 full-power and 9 low-power Univision Network stations. The firm is majority-owned by Broadcasting Media Partners, Inc., a consortium of private-equity investors. In December 2010, Grupo Televisa, S.A.B. acquired a minority interest in Univision Communications; and the firm launched financial advice web site UnivisionDinero.com

FINANCIALS: **Sales and profits are in thousands of dollars—add 000 to get the full amount. 2010 Note: Financial information for 2010 was not available for all companies at press time.**

2010 Sales: $2,245,200	2010 Profits: $-555,900
2009 Sales: $1,972,500	2009 Profits: $-252,100
2008 Sales: $2,032,400	2008 Profits: $-5,127,300
2007 Sales: $2,196,000	2007 Profits: $-314,900
2006 Sales: $2,166,652	2006 Profits: $349,174

U.S. Stock Ticker: Subsidiary
Int'l Ticker:
Int'l Exchange:
Employees: 4,233 Fiscal Year Ends: 12/31
Parent Company: BROADCASTING MEDIA PARTNERS INC

SALARIES/BENEFITS:

Pension Plan:	ESOP Stock Plan:	Profit Sharing:	Top Exec. Salary: $	Bonus: $
Savings Plan:	Stock Purch. Plan:		Second Exec. Salary: $	Bonus: $

OTHER THOUGHTS:

Apparent Women Officers or Directors: 5
Hot Spot for Advancement for Women/Minorities: Y

LOCATIONS: ("Y" = Yes)

West:	Southwest:	Midwest:	Southeast:	Northeast:	International:
Y	Y	Y	Y	Y	Y

URS CORPORATION

www.urscorp.com

Industry Group Code: 541330

Management:		Sales/Marketing:		Liberal Arts:		Information Sys.:		Professionals:		Tech./Scientific:	
Mgmt. Trainees:	Y	Marketing Pros.:	Y	Gen. Writing/Editing:	Y	Info. Mgmt.:	Y	Finance/Acct.:	Y	Engineers, Elec.:	Y
Experienced Mgmt.:	Y	Retail Sales:		Tech. Writing:	Y	Software Dev.:	Y	Law:	Y	Engineers, Other:	Y
Int'l Business:	Y	Comm./Industrial:	Y	Graphic Arts/Photog.:	Y	Hardware Dev.:		HR/Other:	Y	Health/Lab:	
MBA Grads:	Y	Sales Trainees:		Music:		Consulting/Other:	Y	Training:	Y	Science/Research:	
		Advertising Pros.:		Broadcasting:				Health Care:		Petroleum/Chem.:	
				Other:				Consulting:	Y	Math/Other:	

TYPES OF BUSINESS:

Engineering Design Services
Systems Engineering & Technical Assistance
Operations & Maintenance Services
Construction

BRANDS/DIVISIONS/AFFILIATES:

Scott Wilson Group plc
BP Barber
Apptis Holdings, Inc.

CONTACTS:

Note: Officers with more than one job title may be intentionally listed here more than once.

Martin M. Koffel, CEO
Martin M. Koffel, Pres.
H. Thomas Hicks, CFO/VP-Finance
Joseph Masters, General Counsel/Sec./VP
Thomas W. Bishop, VP-Strategy/Sr. VP-Construction Svcs.
Susan B. Kilgannon, VP-Comm.
Reed N. Brimhall, Chief Acct. Officer/Controller/VP
Robert Zaist, Pres., Energy & Construction
Gary V. Jandegian, VP/Pres., Infrastructure & Environment
Randall A. Wotring, VP/Pres., Federal
Thomas W. Bishop, Sr. VP-Infrastructure & Environment
Martin M. Koffel, Chmn.
Hugh Blackwood, Sr. VP-Int'l Oper.

Phone: 415-774-2700 **Fax:** 415-398-1905
Toll-Free:
Address: 600 Montgomery St., Fl. 26, San Francisco, CA 94111 US

GROWTH PLANS/SPECIAL FEATURES:

URS Corporation is a worldwide engineering design services firm and a U.S. federal government contractor for systems engineering, technical assistance, operations and maintenance services. The company focuses primarily on providing fee-based professional and technical services in the engineering and construction services and defense markets. The firm operates in three divisions: Infrastructure & Environment, Federal Services and Energy & Construction. The Infrastructure & Environment division provides professional planning and design; program management; construction management; and operations and maintenance services to various government agencies and departments in the U.S. and internationally, as well as to private industry clients. The Federal Services division provides planning; systems engineering and technical assistance; operations and maintenance; and program management services to various U.S. government agencies, including the Departments of Defense and Homeland Security. The Energy & Construction division builds transportation infrastructure, including airports, mass transit systems and tolls roads. The unit also performs complex tasks such as nuclear waste disposal, mining, engineering and facility management. The company has a network of offices and job sites across the U.S. and in more than 30 foreign countries in the Americas, Europe, the Middle East and Asia-Pacific. In 2010, earnings from the firm's two largest customers, the U.S. Army and the Department of Energy (DOE), represented 21% and 13% of consolidated revenues respectively. In September 2010, URS acquired Scott Wilson Group plc, a U.K.-based infrastructure engineering and design firm. In April 2011, the firm acquired BP Barber, a privately held civil engineering firm based in South Carolina. In June 2011, it acquired Apptis Holdings, Inc., a leading provider of IT services to the federal government.

URS offers its employees medical, vision and dental insurance; short- and long-term insurance; life and AD&D insurance; an employee assistance program; flexible spending accounts; and tuition reimbursement.

FINANCIALS:

Sales and profits are in thousands of dollars—add 000 to get the full amount. 2010 Note: Financial information for 2010 was not available for all companies at press time.

2010 Sales: $9,177,051 — 2010 Profits: $287,889
2009 Sales: $9,249,088 — 2009 Profits: $269,120
2008 Sales: $10,086,289 — 2008 Profits: $219,791
2007 Sales: $5,383,007 — 2007 Profits: $132,243
2006 Sales: $4,222,869 — 2006 Profits: $113,012

U.S. Stock Ticker: URS
Int'l Ticker:
Int'l Exchange:
Employees: 47,000 Fiscal Year Ends: 12/31
Parent Company:

SALARIES/BENEFITS:

Pension Plan: Y ESOP Stock Plan: Profit Sharing: Top Exec. Salary: $1,000,002 Bonus: $1,862,503
Savings Plan: Y Stock Purch. Plan: Y Second Exec. Salary: $711,250 Bonus: $542,219

OTHER THOUGHTS:

Apparent Women Officers or Directors: 2
Hot Spot for Advancement for Women/Minorities:

LOCATIONS: ("Y" = Yes)

West:	Southwest:	Midwest:	Southeast:	Northeast:	International:
Y	Y	Y	Y	Y	Y

Sales, profits and employees may be estimates. Financial information, benefits and other data can change quickly and may vary from those stated here.

USAA

Industry Group Code: 524126

www.usaa.com

Management:		Sales/Marketing:		Liberal Arts:		Information Sys.:		Professionals:		Tech./Scientific:	
Mgmt. Trainees:	Y	Marketing Pros.:	Y	Gen. Writing/Editing:	Y	Info. Mgmt.:	Y	Finance/Acct.:	Y	Engineers, Elec.:	
Experienced Mgmt.:	Y	Retail Sales:		Tech. Writing:	Y	Software Dev.:	Y	Law:	Y	Engineers, Other:	
Int'l Business:	Y	Comm./Industrial:		Graphic Arts/Photog.:	Y	Hardware Dev.:		HR/Other:	Y	Health/Lab:	
MBA Grads:	Y	Sales Trainees:	Y	Music:		Consulting/Other:		Training:	Y	Science/Research:	
		Advertising Pros.:	Y	Broadcasting:				Health Care:		Petroleum/Chem.:	
				Other:	Y			Consulting:		Math/Other:	Y

TYPES OF BUSINESS:

Insurance, Direct Property & Casualty
Banking
Life Insurance
Real Estate Development
Discount Brokerage
Investment Management
Mutual Funds

BRANDS/DIVISIONS/AFFILIATES:

USAA Investment Management Company
USAA Alliance Services LLC
USAA Educational Foundation
United Services Automobile Association

CONTACTS: *Note: Officers with more than one job title may be intentionally listed here more than once.*

Josue Robles, Jr., CEO
Josue Robles, Jr., Pres.
Kristi A. Matus, CFO/Exec. VP
Roger V. Chacko, Chief Mktg. Officer/Exec. VP
Shon Manasco, Exec. VP-People Svcs.
Kevin J. Bergner, Chief Admin. Officer/Exec. VP
Steven A. Bennett, General Counsel/Corp. Sec./Exec. VP
Wayne Peacock, Exec. VP-Enterprise Bus. Oper.
Stephen M. Speakes, Exec. VP-Enterprise Strategy & Planning
Wendi E. Strong, Exec. VP-Corp. Comm.
F. David Bohne, Pres., USAA Fed. Savings Bank
Stuart Parker, Pres., USAA Property & Casualty Insurance Group
Christopher W. Claus, Pres., USAA Financial Advice & Solutions Group
Wayne Peacock, Exec. VP-Member Experience
John H. Moellering, Chmn.

Phone: 210-498-2211 **Fax:** 210-498-9940
Toll-Free: 800-531-8722
Address: 9800 Fredericksburg Rd., San Antonio, TX 78288 US

GROWTH PLANS/SPECIAL FEATURES:

USAA (United Services Automobile Association) is a mutual insurance company that serves over 8 million members, comprising exclusively U.S. military personnel and their families. It owns and manages over $147.86 billion in assets from offices in Texas, Colorado, Arizona and Florida; and international offices in London and Frankfurt. USAA offers more than 150 financial services and products, primarily automobile, homeowner's and renter's insurance as well as automobile, mortgage and home equity loans. The company also manages checking accounts, savings accounts, credit cards and personal loans for its military customers. In addition, customers have access to mutual funds and brokerage services through USAA Investment Management Company. Members can access their accounts and conduct investing, banking and insurance business online. Additionally, subsidiary USAA Alliance Services, LLC has formed a series of partnerships to provide members with discounts on home security, travel services and insurance, floral services, car rentals and diamond and fine jewelry. The firm's USAA Educational Foundation division, a nonprofit entity, provides consumer education to the general public on topics including personal finance, safety and quality of life. In August 2010, the company opened another financial center in San Antonio, Texas. In 2011, USAA opened new financial centers in Virginia, Maryland; San Diego, California; and Fayetteville, North Carolina.

USAA employee benefits include educational assistance, flextime, flexible spending accounts, wellness benefits and blood pressure screenings. Company employees called to active military duty receive their accustomed pay for four weeks, and pay differential for up to two years after deployment. USAA employees are eligible to receive benefits, holiday bonuses and corporate performance bonuses during the time they are deployed. Women account for 62% of USAA's employees.

FINANCIALS: **Sales and profits are in thousands of dollars—add 000 to get the full amount. 2010 Note: Financial information for 2010 was not available for all companies at press time.**

2010 Sales: $17,946,000 — 2010 Profits: $2,637,000
2009 Sales: $17,558,000 — 2009 Profits: $3,020,000
2008 Sales: $12,912,000 — 2008 Profits: $423,000
2007 Sales: $14,417,900 — 2007 Profits: $1,855,500
2006 Sales: $13,416,000 — 2006 Profits: $2,330,000

U.S. Stock Ticker: Mutual Company
Int'l Ticker:
Int'l Exchange:
Employees: 22,600 Fiscal Year Ends: 12/31
Parent Company:

SALARIES/BENEFITS:

Pension Plan: Y ESOP Stock Plan: Profit Sharing: Top Exec. Salary: $ Bonus: $
Savings Plan: Y Stock Purch. Plan: Second Exec. Salary: $ Bonus: $

OTHER THOUGHTS:

Apparent Women Officers or Directors: 4
Hot Spot for Advancement for Women/Minorities: Y

LOCATIONS: ("Y" = Yes)

West:	Southwest:	Midwest:	Southeast:	Northeast:	International:
Y	Y		Y	Y	Y

VALASSIS COMMUNICATIONS INC

www.valassis.com

Industry Group Code: 5418

Management:		Sales/Marketing:		Liberal Arts:		Information Sys.:		Professionals:		Tech./Scientific:	
Mgmt. Trainees:		Marketing Pros.:	Y	Gen. Writing/Editing:	Y	Info. Mgmt.:	Y	Finance/Acct.:	Y	Engineers, Elec.:	
Experienced Mgmt.:	Y	Retail Sales:		Tech. Writing:		Software Dev.:	Y	Law:	Y	Engineers, Other:	
Int'l Business:	Y	Comm./Industrial:	Y	Graphic Arts/Photog.:	Y	Hardware Dev.:		HR/Other:	Y	Health/Lab:	
MBA Grads:	Y	Sales Trainees:		Music:		Consulting/Other:		Training:		Science/Research:	
		Advertising Pros.:		Broadcasting:				Health Care:		Petroleum/Chem.:	
				Other:				Consulting:		Math/Other:	

TYPES OF BUSINESS:

Marketing Products & Services
Direct Mail
Newspaper Advertising
Sampling
Software

BRANDS/DIVISIONS/AFFILIATES:

NCH Marketing Services, Inc.
Valassis Canada, Inc.
Promotion Watch, Inc.
Valassis Direct Mail, Inc.
RedPlum

CONTACTS: *Note: Officers with more than one job title may be intentionally listed here more than once.*

Alan F. Schultz, CEO
Alan F. Schultz, Pres.
Robert L. Recchia, CFO/Exec. VP
Rob Mason, Exec. VP-Mktg. & Sales
Ron Goolsby, Exec. VP-Mfg. & Client Svcs.
Richard P. Herpich, Exec. VP-Strategic Initiatives
Mary Broaddus, Dir.-Corp. Comm.
Mary Broaddus, Dir.-Investor Rel.
Brian J. Husselbee, CEO/Pres., NHC Marketing Services, Inc.
Gabrielle Austin, VP-New Account Dev.
Alan F. Schultz, Chmn.

Phone: 734-591-3000	**Fax:** 734-591-4994
Toll-Free: 800-437-0479	
Address: 19975 Victor Pkwy., Livonia, MI 48152 US	

GROWTH PLANS/SPECIAL FEATURES:

Valassis Communications, Inc. provides a wide range of marketing products and services to more than 15,000 premier manufacturers, direct marketers, retailers, telecommunications companies, franchisees and other advertisers. Its offerings are divided into four segments: free-standing inserts (FSI); neighborhood targeted products; international digital media & services; and shared mail (ADVO). FSI consists of four-color promotional booklets containing the coupons of multiple advertisers that are distributed to roughly 59 million households on 42 publishing dates. Neighborhood targeted products, targeted based on geographic and demographic targeting characteristics, include preprinted inserts, which are specialized print promotion programs in a variety of formats for single advertisers; newspaper-delivered product sampling, which are customer product samples inserted into newspapers or placed in a polybag with the newspapers; newspaper polybag advertising, full-color advertising message on a newspaper polybag without a sample; and door hangers, or product samples and advertisements delivered directly to the consumer's door. The international, digital media and services segment, through subsidiary NCH Marketing Services, Inc., provides coupon clearing, promotion information management and marketing services with operations in the U.S., Canada, Mexico, and Poland. Valassis Canada, Inc. provides promotional products to over 5 million Canadian households. Promotion Watch, Inc. offers a variety of promotion security and consulting services, including the execution of sweepstakes and contests. The segment also includes direct mail, analytics, digital and in-store services. Shared Mail (ADVO), through Valassis Direct Mail, Inc. distributes shared mail advertising products to approximately 70 million households on a weekly basis. With a total base of more than 112 million U.S. households, the segment's client base consists primarily of national and local grocers; restaurants; drugstores; discount and department stores; and home furnishing retailers. The segment's core program is published under the consumer brand name RedPlum.

The firm offers its employees an assistance plan and disability, medical, dental, vision and life insurance.

FINANCIALS: **Sales and profits are in thousands of dollars—add 000 to get the full amount. 2010 Note: Financial information for 2010 was not available for all companies at press time.**

2010 Sales: $2,333,512	2010 Profits: $385,405	**U.S. Stock Ticker: VCI**
2009 Sales: $2,244,248	2009 Profits: $66,768	**Int'l Ticker:**
2008 Sales: $2,381,907	2008 Profits: $-207,491	Int'l Exchange:
2007 Sales: $2,242,171	2007 Profits: $58,002	Employees: 6,735 Fiscal Year Ends: 12/31
2006 Sales: $1,043,491	2006 Profits: $51,282	Parent Company:

SALARIES/BENEFITS:

Pension Plan:	ESOP Stock Plan:	Profit Sharing: Y	Top Exec. Salary: $1,000,000	Bonus: $2,000,000
Savings Plan: Y	Stock Purch. Plan:		Second Exec. Salary: $515,000	Bonus: $515,000

OTHER THOUGHTS:

Apparent Women Officers or Directors: 3
Hot Spot for Advancement for Women/Minorities: Y

LOCATIONS: ("Y" = Yes)

West:	Southwest:	Midwest:	Southeast:	Northeast:	International:
Y		Y		Y	Y

VALSPAR CORPORATION (THE)

www.valspar.com

Industry Group Code: 325510

Management:		Sales/Marketing:		Liberal Arts:		Information Sys.:		Professionals:		Tech./Scientific:	
Mgmt. Trainees:	Y	Marketing Pros.:	Y	Gen. Writing/Editing:	Y	Info. Mgmt.:	Y	Finance/Acct.:	Y	Engineers, Elec.:	
Experienced Mgmt.:	Y	Retail Sales:		Tech. Writing:	Y	Software Dev.:	Y	Law:	Y	Engineers, Other:	Y
Int'l Business:	Y	Comm./Industrial:	Y	Graphic Arts/Photog.:	Y	Hardware Dev.:		HR/Other:	Y	Health/Lab:	
MBA Grads:	Y	Sales Trainees:		Music:		Consulting/Other:		Training:	Y	Science/Research:	Y
		Advertising Pros.:	Y	Broadcasting:				Health Care:		Petroleum/Chem.:	Y
				Other:				Consulting:		Math/Other:	

TYPES OF BUSINESS:

Coatings & Paints
Packaging Coating Products
Specialty Polymers
General Industrial, Coil & Wood Products
Colorants & Gelcoats
Furniture Protection Plans

BRANDS/DIVISIONS/AFFILIATES:

Isocoat Tintas e Vernizes Ltda.
De Beer
House of Kolor
Quikrete
Wattyl Limited
Hua Run Paints Holdings Limited

CONTACTS: *Note: Officers with more than one job title may be intentionally listed here more than once.*

Gary E. Hendrickson, CEO
Gary E. Hendrickson, Pres.
Lori A. Walker, CFO/Sr. VP
Anthony L. Blaine, Sr. VP-Human Resources
Cynthia A. Arnold, CTO/Sr. VP
Rolf Engh, General Counsel/Exec. VP/Sec.
Tracy Jokinen, Controller/VP
Steven L. Erdahl, Exec. VP
Howard C. Heckes, Sr. VP-Consumer Div.
William L. Mansfield, Chmn.

Phone: 612-851-7000	**Fax:** 612-851-7408
Toll-Free:	
Address: 901 3rd Ave., S., Minneapolis, MN 55402 US	

GROWTH PLANS/SPECIAL FEATURES:

The Valspar Corporation is a global provider of paints, coatings and related products. The company operates in two segments: coatings and paints. The coatings segment includes a range of decorative and protective coatings for metal, wood, plastic and glass, primarily sold to original equipment manufacturers (OEM). Products within this segment include primers, top coats, varnishes, inks, sprays, stains, fillers and other coatings used in manufacturing industries such as building products, appliances, furniture, transportation, agricultural and construction equipment, metal packaging and metal fabrication. This segment includes the firm's packaging product line and three industrial product lines: general industrial, coil and wood. The packaging product line includes coatings for the interior and exterior of metal packaging containers, principally food containers and beverage cans. The firm also produces coatings for aerosol and paint cans; bottle crowns for glass; plastic packaging; and bottle closures. The wood coatings unit includes an 86% interest in Hua Run Paints Holdings Company Limited. The paints segment offers interior and exterior paints; stains; primers; varnishes; high performance floor paints; and specialty decorative products. This segment also markets automotive refinish paints and aerosol spray paints under brand names Valspar Refinish, De Beer and House of Kolor. Valspar also makes and sells specialty polymers, colorants, gelcoats and furniture protection plans. The company's gelcoats and related products are sold to boat manufacturers, shower and tub manufacturers and others. Valspar's consumer product line is the largest part of its paint segment and is sold primarily to the do-it-yourself and professional construction markets. In September 2010, Valspar acquired Wattyl Limited, an Australian paint manufacturer. In February 2011, the firm acquired Brazilian powder coatings manufacturer Isocoat Tintas e Vernizes Ltda.

Valspar offers employees medical, dental and life insurance; education assistance; and an employee assistance program.

FINANCIALS: **Sales and profits are in thousands of dollars—add 000 to get the full amount. 2010 Note: Financial information for 2010 was not available for all companies at press time.**

2010 Sales: $3,226,687	2010 Profits: $222,056	**U.S. Stock Ticker: VAL**
2009 Sales: $2,879,042	2009 Profits: $160,153	**Int'l Ticker:**
2008 Sales: $3,482,378	2008 Profits: $150,766	Int'l Exchange:
2007 Sales: $3,249,287	2007 Profits: $172,115	Employees: 10,180 Fiscal Year Ends: 10/31
2006 Sales: $2,978,062	2006 Profits: $175,252	Parent Company:

SALARIES/BENEFITS:

Pension Plan: Y	ESOP Stock Plan: Y	Profit Sharing:	Top Exec. Salary: $920,000	Bonus: $1,981,680
Savings Plan: Y	Stock Purch. Plan:		Second Exec. Salary: $541,000	Bonus: $1,057,113

OTHER THOUGHTS:

Apparent Women Officers or Directors: 4
Hot Spot for Advancement for Women/Minorities: Y

LOCATIONS: ("Y" = Yes)

West:	Southwest:	Midwest:	Southeast:	Northeast:	International:
Y	Y	Y	Y	Y	Y

VARIAN MEDICAL SYSTEMS INC

www.varian.com

Industry Group Code: 33911

Management:		Sales/Marketing:		Liberal Arts:		Information Sys.:		Professionals:		Tech./Scientific:	
Mgmt. Trainees:	Y	Marketing Pros.:	Y	Gen. Writing/Editing:	Y	Info. Mgmt.:	Y	Finance/Acct.:	Y	Engineers, Elec.:	Y
Experienced Mgmt.:	Y	Retail Sales:		Tech. Writing:	Y	Software Dev.:	Y	Law:	Y	Engineers, Other:	Y
Int'l Business:	Y	Comm./Industrial:	Y	Graphic Arts/Photog.:	Y	Hardware Dev.:	Y	HR/Other:	Y	Health/Lab:	Y
MBA Grads:	Y	Sales Trainees:		Music:		Consulting/Other:		Training:	Y	Science/Research:	Y
		Advertising Pros.:	Y	Broadcasting:				Health Care:	Y	Petroleum/Chem.:	
				Other:				Consulting:		Math/Other:	Y

TYPES OF BUSINESS:

Radiation Oncology Systems
X-Ray Equipment
Software Systems
Security & Inspection Products

BRANDS/DIVISIONS/AFFILIATES:

RapidArc
Ginzton Technology Center
Varian Particle Therapy
Linatron
TrueBeam
Augmenix, Inc.

CONTACTS: *Note: Officers with more than one job title may be intentionally listed here more than once.*

Timothy E. Guertin, CEO
Timothy E. Guertin, Pres.
Elisha W. Finney, CFO/Sr. VP
Wendy S. Reitherman, VP-Human Resources
Jessica Denecour, CIO/VP
George A. Zdasiuk, CTO/VP
John W. Kuo, General Counsel/VP/Corp. Sec.
Lester Boeh, VP-Emerging Bus.
Spencer R. Sias, VP-Corp. Comm.
Spencer R. Sias, VP-Investor Rel.
Tai-Yun Chen, VP-Finance/Controller
Franco N. Palomba, VP-Finance/Treas.
Robert H. Kluge, VP/Pres., X-Ray Prod.
Dow R. Wilson, Exec. VP/Pres., Oncology Systems
George A. Zdasiuk, Dir.-Ginzton Tech. Center
Richard M. Levy, Chmn.

Phone: 650-493-4000 **Fax:**
Toll-Free: 800-544-4636
Address: 3100 Hansen Way, Palo Alto, CA 94304-1030 US

GROWTH PLANS/SPECIAL FEATURES:

Varian Medical Systems, Inc. designs, manufactures, sells and services equipment and software products for treating cancer with radiotherapy, stereotactic radiosurgery and brachytherapy. The firm operates in three segments: oncology systems; X-ray products; and security and inspection products (SIP). The oncology systems segment provides software and hardware for treating cancer with radiation, including linear accelerators; brachytherapy afterloaders; treatment simulation and verification equipment and accessories; and information management, treatment planning and image processing software. The RapidArc radiotherapy planning and treatment delivery products, which were recently developed, delivers image-guided, intensity-modulated radiation therapy (IMRT) two to eight times faster than conventional IMRT. The X-ray products segment manufactures and sells X-ray imaging components and subsystems, namely X-ray tubes for use in a range of applications including computed tomography (CT) scanning; radioscopic/fluoroscopic imaging; mammography; special procedures. X-ray products also have industrial applications; including flat panel detectors for digital X-ray image capture, which is an alternative to image intensifier tubes for fluoroscopy and X-ray film for radiography. The SIP segment provides Linatron X-ray accelerators to original equipment manufacturers. It also includes the Varian Particle Therapy business, which designs and manufactures products and systems for delivering proton therapy; and technologies developed by the Ginzton Technology Center, including digital X-ray imaging technology, volumetric/functional imaging, improved X-ray sources and technology for security and cargo screening applications. In April 2011, Varian Medical received approval to sell its TrueBeam system for image-guided radiotherapy in China. In May 2011, the firm acquired minority interest in Augmenix, Inc.

Varian offers employees medical, dental and vision plans; educational reimbursement; an employee assistance program; and a stock purchase plan.

FINANCIALS: **Sales and profits are in thousands of dollars—add 000 to get the full amount. 2010 Note: Financial information for 2010 was not available for all companies at press time.**

2010 Sales: $2,356,600
2009 Sales: $2,214,100
2008 Sales: $2,069,700
2007 Sales: $1,776,600
2006 Sales: $1,597,800

2010 Profits: $360,400
2009 Profits: $319,000
2008 Profits: $279,500
2007 Profits: $239,500
2006 Profits: $245,100

U.S. Stock Ticker: VAR
Int'l Ticker:
Int'l Exchange:
Employees: 5,300 Fiscal Year Ends: 8/31
Parent Company:

SALARIES/BENEFITS:

Pension Plan: Y ESOP Stock Plan: Profit Sharing: Top Exec. Salary: $875,005 Bonus: $1,379,077
Savings Plan: Y Stock Purch. Plan: Y Second Exec. Salary: $606,008 Bonus: $802,886

OTHER THOUGHTS:

Apparent Women Officers or Directors: 5
Hot Spot for Advancement for Women/Minorities: Y

LOCATIONS: ("Y" = Yes)

West:	Southwest:	Midwest:	Southeast:	Northeast:	International:
Y		Y	Y	Y	Y

VCA ANTECH INC

www.vcaantech.com

Industry Group Code: 541940

Management:		**Sales/Marketing:**		**Liberal Arts:**		**Information Sys.:**		**Professionals:**		**Tech./Scientific:**	
Mgmt. Trainees:	Y	Marketing Pros.:	Y	Gen. Writing/Editing:	Y	Info. Mgmt.:	Y	Finance/Acct.:	Y	Engineers, Elec.:	
Experienced Mgmt.:	Y	Retail Sales:		Tech. Writing:	Y	Software Dev.:	Y	Law:	Y	Engineers, Other:	
Int'l Business:		Comm./Industrial:		Graphic Arts/Photog.:	Y	Hardware Dev.:		HR/Other:	Y	Health/Lab:	Y
MBA Grads:	Y	Sales Trainees:		Music:		Consulting/Other:		Training:	Y	Science/Research:	
		Advertising Pros.:		Broadcasting:				Health Care:	Y	Petroleum/Chem.:	
				Other:				Consulting:		Math/Other:	

TYPES OF BUSINESS:

Animal Health Care Services
Veterinary Diagnostic Laboratories
Full-Service Animal Hospitals
Veterinary Equipment
Ultrasound Imaging

BRANDS/DIVISIONS/AFFILIATES:

Antech Diagnostics
VCA Animal Hospitals
Pet DRx Corporation
BrightHeart Veterinary Centers
MediMedia Animal Health, LLC
Vetstreet
Sound Technologies, Inc.
Zoasis.com

CONTACTS: *Note: Officers with more than one job title may be intentionally listed here more than once.*

Robert Antin, CEO
Arthur J. Antin, COO/Sr. VP
Robert Antin, Pres.
Tomas W. Fuller, CFO/VP
Neil Tauber, Sr. VP-Dev.
Dawn R. Olsen, Principal Acct. Officer/Controller/VP
Josh Drake, Pres., Antech Diagnostics
Robert Antin, Chmn.

Phone: 310-571-6500 **Fax:** 310-571-6700
Toll-Free: 800-966-1822
Address: 12401 W. Olympic Blvd., Los Angeles, CA 90064-1022 US

GROWTH PLANS/SPECIAL FEATURES:

VCA Antech, Inc. (VCA) provides animal health services and operates one of the largest networks of veterinary diagnostic laboratories and freestanding, full-service animal hospitals in the U.S. The firm's 50 veterinary diagnostic laboratories, operated through Antech Diagnostics, provide numerous testing services, as well as consulting services to veterinarians who use these services in the detection, diagnosis, evaluation, monitoring, treatment and prevention of diseases and other conditions. The laboratories provide testing services daily to over 17,000 animal hospitals and zoos across the U.S., as well as government agencies, and it offers clients access to results online through Zoasis.com. The VCA Animal Hospitals division operates more than 525 animal hospitals in 41 states, offering a full range of general medical and surgical services for animals, as well as specialized treatments including advanced diagnostic services, internal medicine, oncology, ophthalmology, dermatology and cardiology. The division is supported by more than 2,100 veterinarians. VCA animal hospitals typically have three to five full-time veterinarians on staff, and are open 10-15 hours per day, six or seven days a week. The company's medical technology subsidiary, Sound Technologies, Inc., sells medical imaging equipment, primarily ultrasound and digital radiography tools, and related software and services. In July 2010, VCA acquired a 70.4% interest in Pet DRx Corporation, which operates 23 animal hospitals in California. In November 2010, it acquired the remaining 29.6% interest in Pet DRx. In July 2011, the firm agreed to acquire BrightHeart Veterinary Centers. In August 2011, it acquired MediMedia Animal Health, LLC (operating as Vetstreet), a leading provider of online communications and professional education services to the veterinary sector.

VCA offers its employees health, life, dental and vision insurance; tuition reimbursement; disability coverage; and veterinary care discounts.

FINANCIALS: **Sales and profits are in thousands of dollars—add 000 to get the full amount. 2010 Note: Financial information for 2010 was not available for all companies at press time.**

2010 Sales: $1,381,468 — 2010 Profits: $110,243
2009 Sales: $1,314,507 — 2009 Profits: $131,428
2008 Sales: $1,277,470 — 2008 Profits: $132,984
2007 Sales: $1,156,145 — 2007 Profits: $121,012
2006 Sales: $983,313 — 2006 Profits: $105,529

U.S. Stock Ticker: WOOF
Int'l Ticker:
Int'l Exchange:
Employees: 9,400 Fiscal Year Ends: 12/31
Parent Company:

SALARIES/BENEFITS:

Pension Plan: ESOP Stock Plan: Profit Sharing: Top Exec. Salary: $910,167 Bonus: $928,013
Savings Plan: Y Stock Purch. Plan: Second Exec. Salary: $579,197 Bonus: $531,498

OTHER THOUGHTS:

Apparent Women Officers or Directors: 1
Hot Spot for Advancement for Women/Minorities:

LOCATIONS: ("Y" = Yes)

West:	Southwest:	Midwest:	Southeast:	Northeast:	International:
Y	Y	Y	Y	Y	

VERIZON COMMUNICATIONS INC

www22.verizon.com

Industry Group Code: 517110

Management:		**Sales/Marketing:**		**Liberal Arts:**		**Information Sys.:**		**Professionals:**		**Tech./Scientific:**	
Mgmt. Trainees:	Y	Marketing Pros.:	Y	Gen. Writing/Editing:	Y	Info. Mgmt.:	Y	Finance/Acct.:	Y	Engineers, Elec.:	Y
Experienced Mgmt.:	Y	Retail Sales:	Y	Tech. Writing:	Y	Software Dev.:	Y	Law:	Y	Engineers, Other:	Y
Int'l Business:	Y	Comm./Industrial:	Y	Graphic Arts/Photog.:	Y	Hardware Dev.:		HR/Other:	Y	Health/Lab:	
MBA Grads:	Y	Sales Trainees:	Y	Music:		Consulting/Other:		Training:	Y	Science/Research:	
		Advertising Pros.:	Y	Broadcasting:				Health Care:		Petroleum/Chem.:	
				Other:	Y			Consulting:		Math/Other:	

TYPES OF BUSINESS:

Local Telephone Service
Telecommunications Services
Wireless Services
Long-Distance Services
High-Speed Internet Access
Video-on-Demand Services
e-Commerce & Online Services

BRANDS/DIVISIONS/AFFILIATES:

Verizon Wireless
Verizon Business
Verizon Telecom
Alltel Corporation
Terremark Worldwide, Inc.

CONTACTS: *Note: Officers with more than one job title may be intentionally listed here more than once.*

Ivan G. Seidenberg, CEO
Lowell McAdam, COO
Lowell McAdam, Pres.
Francis J. Shammo, CFO/Exec. VP
Marc C. Reed, Exec. VP-Human Resources
Roger Gurnani, CIO/Exec. VP
Anthony J. Melone, CTO/Exec. VP
Randal S. Milch, General Counsel/Exec. VP
Virginia P. Ruesterholz, Pres., Verizon Svcs. Oper.
John W. Diercksen, Exec. VP-Strategy, Dev. & Planning
Peter W. Thonis, Chief Comm. Officer
John N. Doherty, Sr. VP-Investor Rel.
Robert J. Barish, Controller/Sr. VP
Daniel S. Mead, Pres./CEO-Verizon Wireless
William L. Horton, Jr., Sr. VP/Corp. Sec.
Thomas J. Tauke, Exec. VP-Public Affairs, Policy & Comm.
Ivan G. Seidenberg, Chmn.

Phone: 212-395-1000	**Fax:** 212-571-1897
Toll-Free: 800-621-9900	
Address: 140 West St., New York, NY 10007 US	

GROWTH PLANS/SPECIAL FEATURES:

Verizon Communications, Inc. is one of the world's largest providers of communications services. It operates in two segments: wireline and domestic wireless. The wireline segment, operating in over 150 countries, comprises four units: Mass Markets; Global Enterprise; Global Wholesale; and Other. The Mass Markets unit provides local exchange, long distance, broadband services and FiOS TV services to residential and small business subscribers. Global Enterprise offers voice, data and Internet communications services to medium and large business customers, multi-national corporations and state and federal government customers. Global Wholesale provides switched access and special access services to long distance and other carriers. Lastly, the Other segment provides local exchange and long distance services from former MCI mass market customers, operator services, pay phone, card services and supply sales. The domestic wireless segment's products and services include wireless voice, data products and other value added services and equipment sales across the U.S. The division includes Verizon Wireless, in which Verizon holds a 55% controlling interest, with Vodafone holding the rest. The segment's network covers a population of 292 million and provides services to a customer base of nearly 94.1 million. Verizon Wireless'4G LTE network is deployed in 38 major metropolitan areas in the U.S. The primary network technology platform is CDMA, based on spread-spectrum digital radio technology. The wireline segment accounts for roughly 40% of revenues, while the domestic wireless segment accounts for 60%. In November 2010, Verizon Wireless, AT&T Mobility LLC and T-Mobile USA agreed to form a joint venture to build national mobile commerce network ISIS. In April 2011, Verizon Communications acquired Terremark Worldwide, Inc.

Verizon offers its employees life, AD&D, disability, medical, dental and vision insurance; health and dependent care spending accounts; fitness centers at certain locations; commuter spending accounts; employee, adoption and tuition assistance; and discounts on Verizon products.

FINANCIALS: **Sales and profits are in thousands of dollars—add 000 to get the full amount. 2010 Note: Financial information for 2010 was not available for all companies at press time.**

2010 Sales: $106,565,000 — 2010 Profits: $10,217,000
2009 Sales: $107,808,000 — 2009 Profits: $3,651,000
2008 Sales: $97,354,000 — 2008 Profits: $6,428,000
2007 Sales: $93,469,000 — 2007 Profits: $5,521,000
2006 Sales: $88,182,000 — 2006 Profits: $6,197,000

U.S. Stock Ticker: VZ
Int'l Ticker:
Int'l Exchange:
Employees: 194,400 — Fiscal Year Ends: 12/31
Parent Company:

SALARIES/BENEFITS:

Pension Plan: — ESOP Stock Plan: — Profit Sharing: — Top Exec. Salary: $2,100,000 — Bonus: $3,937,500
Savings Plan: Y — Stock Purch. Plan: — Second Exec. Salary: $913,462 — Bonus: $1,736,538

OTHER THOUGHTS:

Apparent Women Officers or Directors: 3
Hot Spot for Advancement for Women/Minorities: Y

LOCATIONS: ("Y" = Yes)

West:	Southwest:	Midwest:	Southeast:	Northeast:	International:
Y	Y	Y	Y	Y	Y

VICTORIAS SECRET

www.victoriassecret.com

Industry Group Code: 448120

Management:		Sales/Marketing:		Liberal Arts:		Information Sys.:		Professionals:		Tech./Scientific:	
Mgmt. Trainees:	Y	Marketing Pros.:	Y	Gen. Writing/Editing:	Y	Info. Mgmt.:	Y	Finance/Acct.:	Y	Engineers, Elec.:	
Experienced Mgmt.:	Y	Retail Sales:	Y	Tech. Writing:		Software Dev.:	Y	Law:	Y	Engineers, Other:	
Int'l Business:	Y	Comm./Industrial:		Graphic Arts/Photog.:	Y	Hardware Dev.:		HR/Other:	Y	Health/Lab:	
MBA Grads:	Y	Sales Trainees:	Y	Music:		Consulting/Other:		Training:	Y	Science/Research:	
		Advertising Pros.:	Y	Broadcasting:				Health Care:		Petroleum/Chem.:	
				Other:	Y			Consulting:		Math/Other:	

TYPES OF BUSINESS:

Intimate Apparel-Women's, Retail
Cosmetics
Fragrances
Personal Care Products
Online Sales
Catalogs
Women's Shoes
General Women's Apparel

BRANDS/DIVISIONS/AFFILIATES:

PINK
Victoria's Secret Direct
Victoria's Secret Beauty
Angels
IPEX
Body by Victoria
La Senza
Limited Brands Inc

CONTACTS:

Note: Officers with more than one job title may be intentionally listed here more than once.

Sharen Jester Turney, CEO
Sharen Jester Turney, Pres.
Jill Beraud, Chief Mktg. Officer/Exec. VP
Larry Fultz, Exec. VP-Human Resources
Shashi Batra, Pres., Victoria's Secret Beauty
Leslie H. Wexner, Chmn./CEO-Limited Brands Inc.

Phone: 614-577-7111 **Fax:**
Toll-Free: 800-411-5116
Address: 4 Limited Pkwy. E, Reynoldsburg, OH 43068 US

GROWTH PLANS/SPECIAL FEATURES:

Victoria's Secret, a wholly-owned subsidiary of Limited Brands, Inc., purchases, distributes and sells lingerie, personal care products and women's apparel through over 1,000 retail stores, the Internet and direct mail channels. The stores offer branded merchandise such as IPEX, PINK, Very Sexy, Body by Victoria, VS Cotton, BioFit, Dream Angels, Beauty Rush and Angels. The firm also owns several standalone PINK stores in the U.S. and Canada, which sell intimate apparel, denim, casual apparel and body products targeted to young women ages 13-25. Victoria's Secret Beauty offers a complete line of fragrance, cosmetics and body products for skin and hair. In addition to its retail stores, the company operates Victoria's Secret Direct, which consists of the famous Victoria's Secret Catalog and an e-commerce site, VictoriasSecret.com. The firm's widely distributed catalog offers women's fashion apparel, lingerie, swimwear and footwear through its over 390 million annually distributed copies. Street apparel such as dresses, pants, skirts, shorts, tops and shoes are available from the catalog and online, but not in stores. Once each year, Victoria's Secret conducts a televised fashion show featuring some of the world's top models and performances by pop stars such as Justin Timberlake and Seal. The Victoria's Secret group also includes the operations of La Senza, a Canadian lingerie store chain owned by Limited Brands.

Employees are offered merchandise discounts, education assistance, school loans, adoption assistance, bonus programs and an annual retirement contribution.

FINANCIALS:

Sales and profits are in thousands of dollars—add 000 to get the full amount. 2010 Note: Financial information for 2010 was not available for all companies at press time.

2010 Sales: $5,520,000 — 2010 Profits: $
2009 Sales: $5,604,000 — 2009 Profits: $
2008 Sales: $5,601,046 — 2008 Profits: $
2007 Sales: $5,606,993 — 2007 Profits: $
2006 Sales: $5,138,741 — 2006 Profits: $

U.S. Stock Ticker: Subsidiary
Int'l Ticker:
Int'l Exchange:
Employees: 45,000 Fiscal Year Ends: 1/31
Parent Company: LIMITED BRANDS INC

SALARIES/BENEFITS:

Pension Plan: ESOP Stock Plan: Profit Sharing: Top Exec. Salary: $1,909,769 Bonus: $1,523,192
Savings Plan: Y Stock Purch. Plan: Second Exec. Salary: $1,240,385 Bonus: $1,090,500

OTHER THOUGHTS:

Apparent Women Officers or Directors: 4
Hot Spot for Advancement for Women/Minorities: Y

LOCATIONS: ("Y" = Yes)

West:	Southwest:	Midwest:	Southeast:	Northeast:	International:
Y	Y	Y	Y	Y	Y

VISA INC

www.visa.com

Industry Group Code: 522210

Management:		Sales/Marketing:		Liberal Arts:		Information Sys.:		Professionals:		Tech./Scientific:	
Mgmt. Trainees:	Y	Marketing Pros.:	Y	Gen. Writing/Editing:	Y	Info. Mgmt.:	Y	Finance/Acct.:	Y	Engineers, Elec.:	
Experienced Mgmt.:	Y	Retail Sales:		Tech. Writing:		Software Dev.:	Y	Law:	Y	Engineers, Other:	
Int'l Business:	Y	Comm./Industrial:	Y	Graphic Arts/Photog.:	Y	Hardware Dev.:		HR/Other:	Y	Health/Lab:	
MBA Grads:	Y	Sales Trainees:		Music:		Consulting/Other:		Training:	Y	Science/Research:	
		Advertising Pros.:	Y	Broadcasting:				Health Care:		Petroleum/Chem.:	
				Other:	Y			Consulting:		Math/Other:	

TYPES OF BUSINESS:

Credit Cards
Debit Cards
Prepaid Cards

BRANDS/DIVISIONS/AFFILIATES:

Fundamo
Visa USA Inc
Visa International Service Association
Visa Canada Association
Visa International
Inovant LLC
CyberSource Corporation
PlaySpan, Inc.

CONTACTS: *Note: Officers with more than one job title may be intentionally listed here more than once.*

Joseph W. Saunders, CEO
John M. Partridge, Pres.
Byron H. Pollitt, CFO
Antonio J. Lucio, Global Chief Mktg. Officer
Scott Sullivan, Global Head-Human Resources
Michael L. Dreyer, Global Head-Tech.
James McCarthy, Global Head-Prod.
Joshua R. Floum, General Counsel
Antonio J. Lucio, Chief Strategy & Corp. Dev. Officer
Doug Michelman, Global Head-Corp. Rel.
Jack Carsky, Global Head-Investor Rel.
Una Somerville, Global Head-Client Support Svcs.
Ellen Richey, Chief Enterprise Risk Officer
William M. Sheedy, Group Pres., The Americas
Darren Parslow, Global Head-Processing
Joseph W. Saunders, Chmn.
Elizabeth Buse, Pres., APAC, Central Europe, Middle East & Africa

Phone: 415-932-2100	**Fax:**
Toll-Free: 800-847-2911	
Address: P.O. Box 8999, San Francisco, CA 94128-8999 US	

GROWTH PLANS/SPECIAL FEATURES:

Visa, Inc. operates one of the largest consumer payment systems in the world, with approximately 1.87 billion Visa cards in use and money transfer operations in over 200 countries. Visa's payment platforms include credit, debit, prepaid and personal consumption expenditure. In 2011, Visa sales volume across these platforms grew to over $5.6 trillion. The company operates through regional organizations covering Central and Eastern Europe, the Middle East and Africa (CEMEA); the U.S.; Latin America and the Caribbean; Canada; and the Asia Pacific region. Through the Visa brand, the firm's products include credit, debit and prepaid cards; Internet payment systems; traveler's checks and fund transfers; and programs and benefits for commercial and governmental enterprises. Visa offers several types of credit card for individuals and for commercial and governmental offices, with various benefits and credit limits. The company has 15,500 financial institution customers and 1.8 million ATMs. It does not issue cards, set fees or determine the interest rates consumers will be charged. The firm earns revenues by charging banks to issue Visa-branded cards and merchants to accept Visa-branded cards. Subsidiaries of the company include Visa Canada Association; Visa U.S.A., Inc.; CyberSource Corporation; Visa International Service Association; and Inovant LLC. Visa Europe, which recently split off into a separate organization, remains a membership association; it is a licensee of (and owns a minority interest in) Visa. In January 2011, Visa International sold its 10% interest in CBSS to Banco do Brasil and Bradesco. In March 2011, Visa acquired digital payment processor PlaySpan, Inc. In June 2011, the firm acquired mobile financial services delivery company Fundamo.

Visa offers its employees health care coverage; life insurance; retirement and savings plans; on-site fitness facilities; employee discounts; commuter benefits; and spot awards.

FINANCIALS: **Sales and profits are in thousands of dollars—add 000 to get the full amount. 2010 Note: Financial information for 2010 was not available for all companies at press time.**

2010 Sales: $8,065,000	2010 Profits: $2,966,000	**U.S. Stock Ticker: V**
2009 Sales: $6,911,000	2009 Profits: $2,353,000	**Int'l Ticker:**
2008 Sales: $6,263,000	2008 Profits: $804,000	Int'l Exchange:
2007 Sales: $3,589,796	2007 Profits: $-1,076,095	Employees: 6,800 Fiscal Year Ends: 9/30
2006 Sales: $2,948,126	2006 Profits: $454,561	Parent Company:

SALARIES/BENEFITS:

Pension Plan: Y	ESOP Stock Plan:	Profit Sharing:	Top Exec. Salary: $950,037	Bonus: $4,203,750
Savings Plan: Y	Stock Purch. Plan:		Second Exec. Salary: $750,029	Bonus: $1,990,000

OTHER THOUGHTS:

Apparent Women Officers or Directors: 6
Hot Spot for Advancement for Women/Minorities: Y

LOCATIONS: ("Y" = Yes)

West:	Southwest:	Midwest:	Southeast:	Northeast:	International:
Y	Y	Y	Y	Y	Y

VORNADO REALTY TRUST

www.vno.com

Industry Group Code: 531120

Management:		Sales/Marketing:		Liberal Arts:		Information Sys.:		Professionals:		Tech./Scientific:	
Mgmt. Trainees:		Marketing Pros.:		Gen. Writing/Editing:		Info. Mgmt.:	Y	Finance/Acct.:	Y	Engineers, Elec.:	
Experienced Mgmt.:	Y	Retail Sales:		Tech. Writing:		Software Dev.:		Law:	Y	Engineers, Other:	
Int'l Business:	Y	Comm./Industrial:		Graphic Arts/Photog.:		Hardware Dev.:		HR/Other:	Y	Health/Lab:	
MBA Grads:	Y	Sales Trainees:		Music:		Consulting/Other:		Training:		Science/Research:	
		Advertising Pros.:		Broadcasting:				Health Care:		Petroleum/Chem.:	
				Other:				Consulting:		Math/Other:	

TYPES OF BUSINESS:

Real Estate Investment Trust
Office Properties
Retail Properties
Toys
Merchandise

BRANDS/DIVISIONS/AFFILIATES:

Merchandise Mart
Toys-R-Us Inc
Alexander's
Hotel Pennsylvania
Vornado Retail Portfolio
LNR Property Corporation
J.C. Penney Company Inc

CONTACTS: *Note: Officers with more than one job title may be intentionally listed here more than once.*

Michael D. Fascitelli, CEO
Michael D. Fascitelli, Pres.
Joseph Macnow, CFO
Joseph Macnow, Exec. VP-Admin.
Joseph Macnow, Exec. VP-Finance
David R. Greenbaum, Pres., New York Office Div.
Christopher Kennedy, Pres., Merch. Mart Div.
Micheal J. Franco, Exec. VP/Co-Head-Acquisitions & Capital Markets
Wendy Silverstein, Exec. VP/Co-Head-Acquisitions & Capital Markets
Steven Roth, Chmn.

Phone: 212-894-7000	**Fax:** 201-587-0600
Toll-Free:	
Address: 888 7th Ave., New York, NY 10019 US	

GROWTH PLANS/SPECIAL FEATURES:

Vornado Realty Trust, which conducts its business through 93.2%-owned Vornado Realty L.P., is a fully integrated real estate investment trust (REIT). It is one of the largest property owners in New York City, primarily in Manhattan. The firm has four different platforms: office, retail, merchandise mart and toys. The office portfolio is made up of 111 wholly- or partially-owned office properties (40.3 million square feet) in the New York City metropolitan area; Washington, D.C.; northern Virginia; and San Francisco. The Vornado Retail Portfolio controls and/or manages 161properties (25.6 million square feet) in 21 states, Puerto Rico and Washington, D.C. The Merchandise Mart division includes six properties in four states and Washington, D.C., with 6.9 million square feet of showroom and office space. The toys division holds a 32.7% interest in Toys-R-Us, Inc., which owns and/or operates approximately 1,589 stores worldwide. Vornado's additional properties include the Hotel Pennsylvania in Manhattan, containing 1 million square feet with 1,700 rooms and 400,000 square feet of retail and office space; a 32.4% interest in Alexander's, which owns seven properties in the greater New York metropolitan area; and 9.9% ownership of J.C. Penney Company, Inc. In July 2010, the firm acquired 26.2% interest in commercial mortgage loan provider LNR Property Corporation. In October 2010, Vornado sold 45% interest in a Washington, D.C., property to The Canada Pension Plan Investment Board (the firm retains the remaining 55% interest). In January 2011, the company agreed to sell two office buildings in Washington, D.C., totaling 319,000 square feet for roughly $107 million.

FINANCIALS: **Sales and profits are in thousands of dollars—add 000 to get the full amount. 2010 Note: Financial information for 2010 was not available for all companies at press time.**

2010 Sales: $2,779,727	2010 Profits: $647,883	**U.S. Stock Ticker: VNO**
2009 Sales: $2,696,692	2009 Profits: $160,169	**Int'l Ticker:**
2008 Sales: $2,697,051	2008 Profits: $395,043	Int'l Exchange:
2007 Sales: $2,405,243	2007 Profits: $607,833	Employees: 4,780 Fiscal Year Ends: 12/31
2006 Sales: $1,909,100	2006 Profits: $560,140	Parent Company:

SALARIES/BENEFITS:

Pension Plan:	ESOP Stock Plan:	Profit Sharing:	Top Exec. Salary: $1,000,000	Bonus: $750,000
Savings Plan:	Stock Purch. Plan:		Second Exec. Salary: $1,000,000	Bonus: $750,000

OTHER THOUGHTS:

Apparent Women Officers or Directors: 2
Hot Spot for Advancement for Women/Minorities:

LOCATIONS: ("Y" = Yes)

West:	Southwest:	Midwest:	Southeast:	Northeast:	International:
Y	Y	Y	Y	Y	Y

WABTEC CORP

www.wabtec.com

Industry Group Code: 336510

Management:		Sales/Marketing:		Liberal Arts:		Information Sys.:		Professionals:		Tech./Scientific:	
Mgmt. Trainees:	Y	Marketing Pros.:	Y	Gen. Writing/Editing:		Info. Mgmt.:	Y	Finance/Acct.:	Y	Engineers, Elec.:	Y
Experienced Mgmt.:	Y	Retail Sales:		Tech. Writing:	Y	Software Dev.:	Y	Law:	Y	Engineers, Other:	Y
Int'l Business:	Y	Comm./Industrial:	Y	Graphic Arts/Photog.:	Y	Hardware Dev.:	Y	HR/Other:	Y	Health/Lab:	
MBA Grads:	Y	Sales Trainees:		Music:		Consulting/Other:		Training:	Y	Science/Research:	
		Advertising Pros.:		Broadcasting:				Health Care:		Petroleum/Chem.:	
				Other:				Consulting:		Math/Other:	

TYPES OF BUSINESS:

Railroad Equipment Manufacturing
Bus and Subway Equipment Manufacturing

BRANDS/DIVISIONS/AFFILIATES:

Swiger Coil Systems
Brush Traction Group
Hunan CSR Wabtec Railway Transportation
Hubei Dengfeng Unifin Electrical Equipment
Westinghouse Air Brake Technologies Corporation

CONTACTS:

Note: Officers with more than one job title may be intentionally listed here more than once.

Albert J. Neupayer, CEO
Raymond T. Betler, COO
Albert J. Neupayer, Pres.
Alvaro Garcia-Tunon, CFO/Sr. VP
Scott E. Wahlstrom, VP-Human Resources
Charles F. Kovac, Sr. VP-Freight Prod.
Alvaro Garcia-Tunon, Corp. Sec.
R. Mark Cox, VP-Corp. Dev.
Timothy R. Wesley, VP-Corp. Comm.
Timothy R. Wesley, VP-Investor Rel.
Patrick D. Dugan, Controller/VP
Richard A. Mathes, VP-Strategic Planning
Robert D. Dimsa, VP/Gen. Mgr.-Locomotive Prod.
Mark S. Warner, VP/Gen. Mgr.-MotivePower
Ekhard Herrmann, Managing Dir.-Wabtec South Africa
William E. Kassling, Chmn.
Danny Dolzadelli, Managing Dir.-Wabtec Australia
John D. Whiteford, VP-Global Sourcing

Phone: 412-825-1000 **Fax:** 412-825-1019
Toll-Free:
Address: 1001 Air Brake Ave., Wilmerding, PA 15148 US

GROWTH PLANS/SPECIAL FEATURES:

Westinghouse Air Brake Technologies Corporation, doing business as Wabtec Corp., is a provider of technology-based equipment and services for the global rail industry. It develops products such as railway braking equipment; freight car truck components; draft gears; air compressors; railway electronics; brake shoes and pads; rail and bus door assemblies; accessibility lifts and ramps; heat exchangers and cooling products; and commuter and switcher locomotives. The company operates in two business segments: the Freight Group and the Transit Group. The Freight Group, accounting for 52% of sales, manufactures and services components for new existing freight cars and locomotives, builds new switcher locomotives and rebuilds freight locomotives. Its customers are traded railroads; leasing companies; and manufacturers of locomotives and freight cars. The Transit Group, accounting for 48% of the company's sales, produces components for new and existing transit vehicles, typically subway cars and buses, builds new commuter locomotives and refurbishes subway cars. Customers include transit authorities, leasing companies and manufacturers of subway cars and buses. The company owns over 1,250 active patents worldwide (500 in the U.S.). Wabtec has around 50 manufacturing plants and operations in the U.S., Canada, Mexico, Europe, Asia, Australia and South America. Customers outside the U.S. account for roughly 46% of sales. In October 2010, Wabtec and Dengfer formed Chinese joint venture Hubei Dengfeng Unifin Electrical Equipment Cooling System Co., Ltd., to manufacture transformer oil coolers and generator coolers. In November 2010, the firm acquired traction motors and electric coil manufacturer Swiger Coil Systems. In February 2011, the company acquired U.K. locomotive overhauls, services and aftermarket components provider Brush Traction Group. In June 2011, Wabtec Corp. and Zhuzhou CSR Times Electric Co., Ltd. formed service brake equipment manufacturing joint venture Hunan CSR Wabtec Railway Transportation Technology Co., Ltd.; and acquired a transit aftermarket parts business from GE Transportation.

FINANCIALS:

Sales and profits are in thousands of dollars—add 000 to get the full amount. 2010 Note: Financial information for 2010 was not available for all companies at press time.

2010 Sales: $1,507,012	2010 Profits: $123,099
2009 Sales: $1,401,616	2009 Profits: $115,055
2008 Sales: $1,574,749	2008 Profits: $130,551
2007 Sales: $1,360,088	2007 Profits: $109,570
2006 Sales: $	2006 Profits: $

U.S. Stock Ticker: WAB
Int'l Ticker:
Int'l Exchange:
Employees: 6,654 Fiscal Year Ends: 12/31
Parent Company:

SALARIES/BENEFITS:

Pension Plan:	ESOP Stock Plan:	Profit Sharing:	Top Exec. Salary: $815,000	Bonus: $1,270,795
Savings Plan:	Stock Purch. Plan:		Second Exec. Salary: $370,000	Bonus: $461,540

OTHER THOUGHTS:

Apparent Women Officers or Directors: 1
Hot Spot for Advancement for Women/Minorities:

LOCATIONS: ("Y" = Yes)

West:	Southwest:	Midwest:	Southeast:	Northeast:	International:
Y	Y	Y	Y	Y	Y

WALGREEN CO

www.walgreens.com

Industry Group Code: 446110

Management:		Sales/Marketing:		Liberal Arts:		Information Sys.:		Professionals:		Tech./Scientific:	
Mgmt. Trainees:	Y	Marketing Pros.:	Y	Gen. Writing/Editing:	Y	Info. Mgmt.:	Y	Finance/Acct.:	Y	Engineers, Elec.:	
Experienced Mgmt.:	Y	Retail Sales:	Y	Tech. Writing:		Software Dev.:	Y	Law:	Y	Engineers, Other:	
Int'l Business:	Y	Comm./Industrial:		Graphic Arts/Photog.:	Y	Hardware Dev.:		HR/Other:	Y	Health/Lab:	
MBA Grads:	Y	Sales Trainees:	Y	Music:		Consulting/Other:		Training:	Y	Science/Research:	
		Advertising Pros.:	Y	Broadcasting:				Health Care:	Y	Petroleum/Chem.:	
				Other:	Y			Consulting:		Math/Other:	

TYPES OF BUSINESS:

Drug Stores
Mail-Order Pharmacy Services
Pharmacy Benefit Management
Health Care Center Management
Online Pharmacy Services
Photo Printing Services
Specialty Pharmacy Services
Home Infusion Services

BRANDS/DIVISIONS/AFFILIATES:

Walgreen's Health Services
Take Care Health Systems Inc
Carle RxExpress
DrugStore.com
Intercom Plus

CONTACTS:

Note: Officers with more than one job title may be intentionally listed here more than once.

Gregory D. Wasson, CEO
Gregory D. Wasson, Pres.
Wade D. Miquelon, CFO/Exec. VP
Kimberly L. Feil, Chief Mktg. Officer/VP
Kathleen Wilson-Thompson, Chief Human Resources Officer/Sr. VP
Cheryl Pegus, Chief Medical Officer
Timothy J. Theriault, CIO/Sr. VP
W. Bryan Pugh, VP-Merch.
Dana I. Green, General Counsel/Exec. VP/Corp. Sec.
Sona Chawla, Sr. VP-eCommerce
Rick J. Hans, VP-Investor Rel.
Rick J. Hans, VP-Finance
Donald C. Huonker, Sr. VP-Healthcare Innovation
Hal F. Rosenbluth, Pres., Walgreens Health & Wellness
Kermit R. Crawford, Pres., Pharmacy Svcs.
Mark A. Wagner, Pres., Community Mgmt.
Alan G. McNally, Chmn.
J. Randolph Lewis, Sr. VP-Supply Chain Mgmt.

Phone: 847-914-2500	**Fax:** 847-914-2804
Toll-Free: 800-925-4733	
Address: 200 Wilmot Rd., Deerfield, IL 60015 US	

GROWTH PLANS/SPECIAL FEATURES:

Walgreen Co. operates one of the largest chains of U.S. drug stores. The company has approximately 8,046 locations in all 50 U.S. states, Washington, D.C., Guam and Puerto Rico; 16 full-service distribution centers; and two prescription mail service facilities. Stores offer prescription and non-prescription drugs, as well as general merchandise. To coordinate its operations, the firm uses Intercom Plus, a proprietary computer system for filling prescriptions, linking all stores into a single network. A large percentage of the company's stores have drive-through pharmacies, and most stores offer one-hour photo processing. The firm also accepts prescription refill orders online through its web site. Prescription sales accounted for approximately 65.2% of total sales; non-prescription drugs, roughly 10%; and general merchandise, nearly 25%. The company also operates Walgreen's Health Services, a benefit management, mail service, home care and specialty pharmacy services business. A new growth strategy is Walgreen's plan to provide health clinics within the premises of major employers. The company also operates 352 care clinics operated by Take Care Health Systems, Inc. within its drugstores. Approximately 5.9 million customers shop at Walgreen's stores each day. In addition, Walgreens.com receives approximately 15 million visits each month. In April 2011, the firm agreed to acquire 10 Carle RxExpress pharmacy locations in Illinois from The Carle Foundation. In June 2011, Walgreen acquired DrugStore.com for roughly $409 million.

Employees are offered medical, prescription and dental coverage; life and accident insurance; a profit sharing plan; an employee purchase program; and on-site childcare at the corporate office.

FINANCIALS:

Sales and profits are in thousands of dollars—add 000 to get the full amount. 2010 Note: Financial information for 2010 was not available for all companies at press time.

2010 Sales: $67,420,000	2010 Profits: $2,091,000
2009 Sales: $63,335,000	2009 Profits: $2,006,000
2008 Sales: $59,034,000	2008 Profits: $2,157,000
2007 Sales: $53,762,000	2007 Profits: $2,041,300
2006 Sales: $47,409,000	2006 Profits: $1,750,600

U.S. Stock Ticker: WAG
Int'l Ticker:
Int'l Exchange:
Employees: 244,000 Fiscal Year Ends: 8/31
Parent Company:

SALARIES/BENEFITS:

Pension Plan:	ESOP Stock Plan:	Profit Sharing: Y	Top Exec. Salary: $1,066,667	Bonus: $1,653,334
Savings Plan: Y	Stock Purch. Plan: Y		Second Exec. Salary: $709,333	Bonus: $659,680

OTHER THOUGHTS:

Apparent Women Officers or Directors: 5
Hot Spot for Advancement for Women/Minorities: Y

LOCATIONS: ("Y" = Yes)

West:	Southwest:	Midwest:	Southeast:	Northeast:	International:
Y	Y	Y	Y	Y	Y

WAL-MART STORES INC

www.walmartstores.com

Industry Group Code: 452112

Management:		Sales/Marketing:		Liberal Arts:		Information Sys.:		Professionals:		Tech./Scientific:	
Mgmt. Trainees:	Y	Marketing Pros.:	Y	Gen. Writing/Editing:	Y	Info. Mgmt.:	Y	Finance/Acct.:	Y	Engineers, Elec.:	
Experienced Mgmt.:	Y	Retail Sales:	Y	Tech. Writing:		Software Dev.:	Y	Law:	Y	Engineers, Other:	
Int'l Business:	Y	Comm./Industrial:		Graphic Arts/Photog.:	Y	Hardware Dev.:		HR/Other:	Y	Health/Lab:	
MBA Grads:	Y	Sales Trainees:	Y	Music:		Consulting/Other:		Training:	Y	Science/Research:	
		Advertising Pros.:	Y	Broadcasting:	Y			Health Care:		Petroleum/Chem.:	
				Other:	Y			Consulting:		Math/Other:	

TYPES OF BUSINESS:

Discount Department Stores
Supermarkets
Warehouse Membership Clubs
Online Sales
Pharmacies
Vision Centers
Auto Repair Centers

BRANDS/DIVISIONS/AFFILIATES:

Sam's Club
Wal-Mart Supercenter
Marketside
Best Price
Massmart Holdings Limited
Yihaodian
Neighborhood Market

CONTACTS: *Note: Officers with more than one job title may be intentionally listed here more than once.*

Michael T. Duke, CEO
Michael T. Duke, Pres.
Charles Holley, Jr., CFO/Exec. VP
Stephen Quinn, Chief Mktg. Officer/Exec. VP-Wal-Mart U.S.
M. Susan Chambers, Exec. VP-People
Rollin L. Ford, CIO/Exec. VP
Jeffrey J. Gearhart, General Counsel/Exec. VP/Sec.
Leslie A. Dach, Exec. VP-Corp. Affairs
Carol Schumacher, VP-Investor Rel.
Steven P. Whaley, Controller/Sr. VP
Ignacio Perez Lizuar, Exec. VP-Oper., Sam's Club
Eduardo Solorzano, Pres./CEO-Wal-Mart Latin America
Brian C. Cornell, CEO/Pres., Sam's Club
William S. Simon, CEO/Pres., Wal-Mart U.S.
S. Robson Walton, Chmn.
C. Douglas McMillon, CEO/Pres., Wal-Mart Int'l
Ed Kolodzieski, Exec. VP-Global Sourcing

Phone: 479-273-4000 **Fax:** 479-277-1830
Toll-Free: 800-925-6278
Address: 702 SW 8th St., Bentonville, AR 72716 US

GROWTH PLANS/SPECIAL FEATURES:

Wal-Mart Stores, Inc., one of the world's largest retailers, operates through a massive base of Wal-Mart stores, Wal-Mart Supercenters, Sam's Clubs, Marketside, Neighborhood Markets and WalMart.com. The company operates in three business segments: Wal-Mart Stores, representing roughly 62.1% of sales; Sam's Club, 11.8%; and International, 26.1%. The company serves over 200 million weekly customers in over 9,600 stores in 28 countries, with 69 different banners. Wal-Mart offers a wide variety of discount merchandise in six merchandise units, including family apparel; grocery, consisting of meat, produce, deli, bakery, dairy, frozen foods, beauty aids, household chemicals, paper goods and pet supplies; entertainment, such as electronics, toys and photo-processing services; hardlines, which consists of fabrics, books, hardware, sporting goods and seasonal merchandise; health and wellness, including pharmacy and optical services; and home, including home furnishings, housewares and small appliances. Wal-Mart Supercenters, located in 48 states, are larger stores that combine a full-line supermarket with a discount department store. Sam's Club is a members-only warehouse club that sells merchandise at warehouse prices to consumers and small businesses. The International segment includes wholly-owned subsidiaries in Argentina, Brazil, Canada, Japan, Puerto Rico and the U.K.; majority-owned subsidiaries in Central America, Chile, South Africa and Mexico; joint ventures in India and China; and minority-owned subsidiaries in China. The company is currently shifting its focus away from its supercenters. New stores will focus more on small formats, including the Marketside concept. Wal-Mart is expanding into India with a joint venture opening several Best Price wholesale distribution centers. In September 2010, the company partnered with T-Mobile to offer the Walmart Family Mobile post-paid cell phone service. In May 2011, Wal-Mart agreed to acquire minority interest in Chinese e-commerce firm Yihaodian. In June 2011, the firm acquired 51% of South African company Massmart Holdings Limited.

FINANCIALS: **Sales and profits are in thousands of dollars—add 000 to get the full amount. 2010 Note: Financial information for 2010 was not available for all companies at press time.**

2010 Sales: $405,046,000 | 2010 Profits: $14,414,000
2009 Sales: $401,087,000 | 2009 Profits: $13,254,000
2008 Sales: $373,821,000 | 2008 Profits: $12,863,000
2007 Sales: $344,992,000 | 2007 Profits: $11,284,000
2006 Sales: $308,945,000 | 2006 Profits: $11,231,000

U.S. Stock Ticker: WMT
Int'l Ticker:
Int'l Exchange:
Employees: 2,100,000 Fiscal Year Ends: 1/31
Parent Company:

SALARIES/BENEFITS:

Pension Plan: ESOP Stock Plan: Profit Sharing: Y Top Exec. Salary: $1,232,670 Bonus: $3,852,059
Savings Plan: Y Stock Purch. Plan: Y Second Exec. Salary: $1,035,385 Bonus: $1,901,977

OTHER THOUGHTS:

Apparent Women Officers or Directors: 7
Hot Spot for Advancement for Women/Minorities: Y

LOCATIONS: ("Y" = Yes)

West:	Southwest:	Midwest:	Southeast:	Northeast:	International:
Y	Y	Y	Y	Y	Y

WALT DISNEY COMPANY (THE)

corporate.disney.go.com

Industry Group Code: 515210

Management:		Sales/Marketing:		Liberal Arts:		Information Sys.:		Professionals:		Tech./Scientific:	
Mgmt. Trainees:	Y	Marketing Pros.:	Y	Gen. Writing/Editing:	Y	Info. Mgmt.:	Y	Finance/Acct.:	Y	Engineers, Elec.:	Y
Experienced Mgmt.:	Y	Retail Sales:		Tech. Writing:		Software Dev.:	Y	Law:	Y	Engineers, Other:	
Int'l Business:	Y	Comm./Industrial:	Y	Graphic Arts/Photog.:	Y	Hardware Dev.:		HR/Other:	Y	Health/Lab:	
MBA Grads:	Y	Sales Trainees:	Y	Music:	Y	Consulting/Other:		Training:	Y	Science/Research:	
		Advertising Pros.:	Y	Broadcasting:	Y			Health Care:		Petroleum/Chem.:	
				Other:	Y			Consulting:		Math/Other:	

TYPES OF BUSINESS:

Cable TV Networks, Broadcasting & Entertainment
Filmed Entertainment
Merchandising
Television Networks
Music & Book Publishing
Online Entertainment Programs
Theme Parks, Resorts & Cruise Lines
Comic Book Publishing

BRANDS/DIVISIONS/AFFILIATES:

Walt Disney Parks & Resorts
ESPN Inc
ABC Inc
Walt Disney Studios (The)
Playdom
ABC Entertainment Group
Walt Disney Pictures
Marvel Entertainment, Inc.

CONTACTS: *Note: Officers with more than one job title may be intentionally listed here more than once.*

Robert A. Iger, CEO
Robert A. Iger, Pres.
Jay Rasulo, CFO/Sr. Exec. VP
Jayne Parker, Chief Human Resources Officer/Exec. VP
Kevin Mayer, Exec. VP-Tech. Group
Alan Braverman, General Counsel/Sr. Exec. VP/Corp. Sec.
Kevin Mayer, Exec. VP-Corp. Strategy & Bus. Dev.
Zenia Mucha, Exec. VP-Corp. Comm.
Christine M. McCarthy, Exec. VP-Corp. Finance & Real Estate/Treas.
Ronald L. Iden, Sr. VP-Global Security
Preston Padden, Exec. VP-Worldwide Gov't Rel.
Rich Ross, Chmn., Walt Disney Studios
Thomas O. Staggs, Chmn., Walt Disney Parks & Resorts
John E. Pepper, Jr., Chmn.
Andy Bird, Chmn., Walt Disney Int'l

Phone: 818-560-1000	**Fax:** 818-560-1930
Toll-Free:	
Address: 500 S. Buena Vista St., Burbank, CA 91521 US	

GROWTH PLANS/SPECIAL FEATURES:

The Walt Disney Company is an international entertainment company operating in five primary business segments: media networks; studio entertainment; consumer products; parks and resorts; and interactive media. The media networks segment, which operates ABC Television Network, is involved in domestic broadcast television networks and stations; cable/satellite networks; international broadcast operations; television production and distribution; domestic broadcast radio networks and stations; and Internet operations. The company also owns interest in and/or operates numerous cable networks, including ESPN, ABC Family, the History Channel and A&E. The studio entertainment segment produces and acquires feature films, direct-to-video programming, musical recordings and live stage plays. Its motion picture subsidiaries include Walt Disney Pictures, Touchstone Pictures, Pixar and Dimension. The consumer products segment designs, promotes and sells merchandise based on the firm's intellectual property. The parks and resorts segment owns and operates Florida's Walt Disney World Resort; Disney Cruise Line; the Disneyland resort in California; Adventures by Disney; and the Disney Vacation Club. It also holds interest in the Disneyland Paris and Hong Kong Disneyland resorts, and licenses the Tokyo Disney Resort in Japan. The Walt Disney World Resort includes Magic Kingdom, Epcot, Disney's Hollywood Studios and Disney's Animal Kingdom. Lastly, the interactive media segment creates and delivers company-branded entertainment and lifestyle content across interactive media platforms. The group's primary operating businesses are Disney Interactive Studios, which produces video games, and Disney Online, which produces web sites and online virtual worlds. Additionally, Disney owns the comic book publisher Marvel Entertainment, Inc. In August 2010, it acquired Playdom, Inc., a developer of online games for social networking sites. In December 2010, Disney sold Mirmax Film Corp. to Filmyard Holdings, LLC for $663 million. The firm plans to open a new theme near Shanghai, China at a cost of about $4.6 billion.

Employees are offered health, dental and life insurance; educational reimbursement; complimentary theme park passports; an employee stock purchase program; a personal assistant network; and childcare centers in certain locations.

FINANCIALS: **Sales and profits are in thousands of dollars—add 000 to get the full amount. 2010 Note: Financial information for 2010 was not available for all companies at press time.**

2010 Sales: $38,063,000 — 2010 Profits: $4,313,000
2009 Sales: $36,149,000 — 2009 Profits: $3,307,000
2008 Sales: $37,843,000 — 2008 Profits: $4,427,000
2007 Sales: $35,510,000 — 2007 Profits: $4,687,000
2006 Sales: $33,747,000 — 2006 Profits: $3,374,000

U.S. Stock Ticker: DIS
Int'l Ticker:
Int'l Exchange:
Employees: 149,000 — Fiscal Year Ends: 9/30
Parent Company:

SALARIES/BENEFITS:

Pension Plan:	ESOP Stock Plan:	Profit Sharing:	Top Exec. Salary: $2,780,063	Bonus: $9,260,000
Savings Plan: Y	Stock Purch. Plan: Y		Second Exec. Salary: $1,317,824	Bonus: $2,450,000

OTHER THOUGHTS:

Apparent Women Officers or Directors: 8
Hot Spot for Advancement for Women/Minorities: Y

LOCATIONS: ("Y" = Yes)

West:	Southwest:	Midwest:	Southeast:	Northeast:	International:
Y	Y	Y	Y	Y	Y

Sales, profits and employees may be estimates. Financial information, benefits and other data can change quickly and may vary from those stated here.

WARNACO GROUP INC (THE)

www.warnaco.com

Industry Group Code: 315231

Management:		**Sales/Marketing:**		**Liberal Arts:**		**Information Sys.:**		**Professionals:**		**Tech./Scientific:**	
Mgmt. Trainees:		Marketing Pros.:	Y	Gen. Writing/Editing:	Y	Info. Mgmt.:	Y	Finance/Acct.:	Y	Engineers, Elec.:	
Experienced Mgmt.:	Y	Retail Sales:		Tech. Writing:		Software Dev.:		Law:	Y	Engineers, Other:	
Int'l Business:	Y	Comm./Industrial:	Y	Graphic Arts/Photog.:	Y	Hardware Dev.:		HR/Other:	Y	Health/Lab:	
MBA Grads:	Y	Sales Trainees:		Music:		Consulting/Other:		Training:	Y	Science/Research:	
		Advertising Pros.:	Y	Broadcasting:				Health Care:		Petroleum/Chem.:	
				Other:	Y			Consulting:		Math/Other:	

TYPES OF BUSINESS:

Lingerie Manufacturing
Swimwear
Sportswear
Retail Stores
Online Sales

BRANDS/DIVISIONS/AFFILIATES:

Warnaco Swimwear Inc
Olga
Calvin Klein
Speedo
Chaps
CalvinKleinJeans.com
CKU.com
SpeedoUSA.com

CONTACTS: *Note: Officers with more than one job title may be intentionally listed here more than once.*

Joseph R. Gromek, CEO
Helen McCluskey, COO
Joseph R. Gromek, Pres.
Lawrence R. Rutkowski, CFO/Exec. VP
Elizabeth Wood, Sr. VP-Human Resources
Jay Dubliner, General Counsel/Sr. VP/Corp. Sec.
Stanley P. Silverstein, Exec. VP-Bus. Dev.
Frank Tworecke, Pres., Sportswear Group
Martha Olson, Pres., Intimate Apparel & Swimwear
Hans Schmitt, Managing Dir.-Europe
Charles R. Perrin, Chmn.
Stanley P. Silverstein, Exec. VP-Int'l Strategy
Dwight Meyer, Pres., Global Sourcing, Dist. & Logistics

Phone: 212-287-8000	**Fax:**
Toll-Free:	
Address: 501 7th Ave., New York, NY 10018 US	

GROWTH PLANS/SPECIAL FEATURES:

The Warnaco Group, Inc. designs, sources, markets, licenses and distributes a broad line of intimate apparel, sportswear and swimwear worldwide. The company sells its products under several highly recognized brand names, including Warner's, Olga, Calvin Klein, Speedo and Chaps. Warnaco operates in three business segments: intimate apparel, sportswear and swimwear. The intimate apparel group accounts for approximately 36% of revenue; the sportswear group, 53%; and the swimwear group, 11%. The firm relies on its highly recognizable brands to sell at a broad range of price points and across consumer age groups. The company's products are distributed domestically and internationally in over 100 countries, with domestic and international sales generating approximately 43.9% and 56.1% of revenue, respectively. Warnaco sells its products through major department stores, independent retailers, chain stores, membership clubs, specialty, off-price and other stores, mass merchandisers and the Internet. Its customers include such leading retailers as Macy's, J.C. Penney, Kohl's, Sears, Target, and Costco. Warnaco operates approximately 1,360 Calvin Klein retail stores worldwide, including 189 free-standing stores; 118 outlet free-standing stores; two online stores, CalvinKleinJeans.com and CKU.com; and 1,050 shop-in-shop/concession stores. Additionally, 619 Calvin Klein retail stores are operated by third parties or distributor agreements. The firm also operates SpeedoUSA.com, an online Speedo store marketing swimwear, accessories and aquatic exercise equipment. The company focuses its advertising on brand and/or product-specific advertising, primarily through point-of-sale displays, visuals and in-store promotions. In October 2010, Warnaco acquired 22 franchised Calvin Klein Jeans retail stores in Italy from L'Innominato S.p.A.

FINANCIALS: **Sales and profits are in thousands of dollars—add 000 to get the full amount. 2010 Note: Financial information for 2010 was not available for all companies at press time.**

2010 Sales: $2,295,751 | 2010 Profits: $138,581
2009 Sales: $2,019,625 | 2009 Profits: $98,998
2008 Sales: $2,065,023 | 2008 Profits: $47,254
2007 Sales: $1,819,579 | 2007 Profits: $79,107
2006 Sales: $1,611,201 | 2006 Profits: $50,750

U.S. Stock Ticker: WRC
Int'l Ticker:
Int'l Exchange:
Employees: 6,400 Fiscal Year Ends: 12/31
Parent Company:

SALARIES/BENEFITS:

Pension Plan: ESOP Stock Plan: Profit Sharing: Top Exec. Salary: $1,100,000 Bonus: $2,062,500
Savings Plan: Stock Purch. Plan: Second Exec. Salary: $800,000 Bonus: $1,020,000

OTHER THOUGHTS:

Apparent Women Officers or Directors: 5
Hot Spot for Advancement for Women/Minorities: Y

LOCATIONS: ("Y" = Yes)

West:	Southwest:	Midwest:	Southeast:	Northeast:	International:
Y				Y	Y

WASTE MANAGEMENT INC

www.wm.com

Industry Group Code: 562

Management:		Sales/Marketing:		Liberal Arts:		Information Sys.:		Professionals:		Tech./Scientific:	
Mgmt. Trainees:	Y	Marketing Pros.:	Y	Gen. Writing/Editing:	Y	Info. Mgmt.:	Y	Finance/Acct.:	Y	Engineers, Elec.:	
Experienced Mgmt.:	Y	Retail Sales:		Tech. Writing:	Y	Software Dev.:	Y	Law:	Y	Engineers, Other:	Y
Int'l Business:	Y	Comm./Industrial:	Y	Graphic Arts/Photog.:	Y	Hardware Dev.:		HR/Other:	Y	Health/Lab:	
MBA Grads:	Y	Sales Trainees:	Y	Music:		Consulting/Other:		Training:	Y	Science/Research:	
		Advertising Pros.:	Y	Broadcasting:				Health Care:		Petroleum/Chem.:	
				Other:				Consulting:		Math/Other:	

TYPES OF BUSINESS:

Waste Disposal
Recycling Services
Landfill Operation
Hazardous Waste Management
Transfer Stations
Recycled Commodity Trading
Waste Methane Generation

BRANDS/DIVISIONS/AFFILIATES:

Think Green
Agnion Energy, Inc.
Peninsula Compost Company, LLC
Wheelbrator Technologies, Inc.
Recycle America Alliance
TOSS
Bio-In-A-Box
BioSite

CONTACTS: *Note: Officers with more than one job title may be intentionally listed here more than once.*

David P. Steiner, CEO
David P. Steiner, Pres.
Robert G. Simpson, CFO/Sr. VP
David A. Aardsma, Sr. VP-Mktg. & Sales
Jay Romans, Sr. VP-People
Puneet Bhasin, CIO/Sr. VP
Rick L. Wittenbraker, General Counsel/Chief Compliance Officer/Sr. VP
William Caesar, Chief Strategy Officer
Barry H. Caldwell, Sr. VP-Gov't Affairs & Corp. Comm.
Cherie C. Rice, VP-Finance/Treas.
Patrick J. DeRueda, Pres., Waste Management Recycle America
Mark A. Weidman, Pres., Wheelabrator Technologies, Inc.
Carl Rush, VP-Organic Growth
Jeff Harris, Sr. VP-Midwestern Group
John Pope, Chmn.

Phone: 713-512-6200	**Fax:** 713-512-6299
Toll-Free:	
Address: 1001 Fannin St., Ste. 4000, Houston, TX 77002 US	

GROWTH PLANS/SPECIAL FEATURES:

Waste Management, Inc. provides comprehensive waste management services to municipal, commercial, industrial and residential customers throughout North America. The company utilizes a number of transfer stations when it is not economical to transport solid waste generated from urban markets directly to landfills. Within these transfer stations, waste is consolidated, compacted and loaded onto long-haul trailers for transport to landfills. Waste Management is the nation's largest collector of recyclables from businesses and households, collecting recyclable materials through subsidiary Recycle America Alliance and depositing them at about a hundred local materials recovery facilities. The firm recycles several different materials, including plastics, rubber, electronics and commodities. The company also has a pulp and paper trading group that reduces paper's overall long-term commodity price exposure. Waste Management operates about 271 solid waste landfills and five secure hazardous waste landfills. Its hazardous waste management services include geosynthetic manufacturing, radioactive waste services and landfill liner installation. The company has developed TOSS, Bio-In-A-Box and BioSite, which are bioremediation systems for materials contaminated with petrochemicals, pesticides, explosives or hazardous organics. Through the subsidiary Wheelbrator Technologies, Inc., the company operates 22 waste-to-energy facilities, which produce electricity through burning solid waste at high temperatures. Additionally, Waste Management promotes environmental initiatives such as Keep America Beautiful, Habitat for Humanity, Red Cross/FEMA and Wildlife Habitat Council, as well as its own Think Green. In March 2011, subsidiary Waste Management Recycle America acquired three recycling facilities in Virginia and Maryland from Canusa Hershman Recycling Company. In 2011, Waste Management opened new facilities in Pennsylvania, Illinois, New Jersey and Texas. It also invested in Agnion Energy, Inc. and Peninsula Compost Company, LLC.

Waste Management offers its employees life, AD&D, medical, dental and vision insurance; prescription drug coverage; family assistance programs; flexible spending accounts; adoption assistance; education savings accounts; an employee stock purchase plan; and tuition reimbursement.

FINANCIALS: **Sales and profits are in thousands of dollars—add 000 to get the full amount. 2010 Note: Financial information for 2010 was not available for all companies at press time.**

2010 Sales: $12,515,000	2010 Profits: $953,000	**U.S. Stock Ticker: WM**
2009 Sales: $11,791,000	2009 Profits: $994,000	**Int'l Ticker:**
2008 Sales: $13,388,000	2008 Profits: $1,087,000	Int'l Exchange:
2007 Sales: $13,310,000	2007 Profits: $1,163,000	Employees: 42,800 Fiscal Year Ends: 12/31
2006 Sales: $13,363,000	2006 Profits: $1,149,000	Parent Company:

SALARIES/BENEFITS:

Pension Plan:	ESOP Stock Plan:	Profit Sharing:	Top Exec. Salary: $1,073,077	Bonus: $1,407,514
Savings Plan: Y	Stock Purch. Plan: Y		Second Exec. Salary: $566,298	Bonus: $487,875

OTHER THOUGHTS:

Apparent Women Officers or Directors: 2
Hot Spot for Advancement for Women/Minorities: Y

LOCATIONS: ("Y" = Yes)

West:	Southwest:	Midwest:	Southeast:	Northeast:	International:
Y	Y	Y	Y	Y	Y

Sales, profits and employees may be estimates. Financial information, benefits and other data can change quickly and may vary from those stated here.

WATERS CORP

www.waters.com

Industry Group Code: 33911

Management:		Sales/Marketing:		Liberal Arts:		Information Sys.:		Professionals:		Tech./Scientific:	
Mgmt. Trainees:	Y	Marketing Pros.:	Y	Gen. Writing/Editing:		Info. Mgmt.:	Y	Finance/Acct.:	Y	Engineers, Elec.:	Y
Experienced Mgmt.:	Y	Retail Sales:		Tech. Writing:	Y	Software Dev.:	Y	Law:	Y	Engineers, Other:	Y
Int'l Business:	Y	Comm./Industrial:	Y	Graphic Arts/Photog.:	Y	Hardware Dev.:		HR/Other:	Y	Health/Lab:	Y
MBA Grads:	Y	Sales Trainees:		Music:		Consulting/Other:		Training:	Y	Science/Research:	Y
		Advertising Pros.:	Y	Broadcasting:				Health Care:		Petroleum/Chem.:	
				Other:				Consulting:		Math/Other:	

TYPES OF BUSINESS:

Equipment-Liquid Chromatography Instruments
Mass Spectrometry Systems
Thermal Analyzers
Rheometry Equipment
Software Development
Food Safety Technology

BRANDS/DIVISIONS/AFFILIATES:

Waters Division
TA Instruments
Waters Xevo TQ MS System
Waters Acquity UPLC H-Class Method Development
Waters Synapt G2 System
Synapt High Definition MS
Waters ACQUITY UPLC I-Class System
Xevo TQD

CONTACTS: *Note: Officers with more than one job title may be intentionally listed here more than once.*

Douglas A. Berthiaume, CEO
Douglas A. Berthiaume, Pres.
John Ornell, CFO
Elizabeth B. Rae, VP-Human Resources
John Ornell, VP-Admin.
Mark T. Beaudouin, General Counsel/VP/Corp. Sec.
Jeff Tarmy, Mgr.-Corp. Comm.
Gene Cassis, VP-Investor Rel.
John Ornell, VP-Finance
Arthur G. Caputo, Exec. VP/Pres., Waters Div.
Terrence P. Kelly, Pres., TA Instruments, Inc.
Douglas A. Berthiaume, Chmn.

Phone: 508-478-2000 **Fax:** 508-872-1990
Toll-Free: 800-252-4752
Address: 34 Maple St., Milford, MA 01757 US

GROWTH PLANS/SPECIAL FEATURES:

Waters Corp. designs, manufactures and markets analytical instruments. The firm operates in two segments: the Waters division and TA Instruments, Inc. The Waters division offers high-performance liquid chromatography (HPLC) and mass spectrometry instrument systems and associated service and support products, including chromatography columns and laboratory informatics software. HPLC equipment detects, identifies, monitors and measures the chemical, physical and biological composition of materials. Waters Corp.'s liquid chromatography instruments allow for different degrees of automation, from component-configured systems to its fully-automated Alliance systems. Mass spectrometry is an analytical technique that identifies unknown compounds and quantifies known materials. These instruments are used primarily in conjunction with the firm's HPLC products by a wide array of industries, particularly the life sciences pharmaceutical, biomedical, clinical and environmental market segments. The firm's mass spectrometer products include the Waters Xevo TQ MS System, Waters Synapt G2-S System; and Synapt High Definition MS. Through its TA Instruments division, the company designs, manufactures, services and sells thermal analysis instruments that measure the physical characteristics of materials as a function of temperature. In addition to thermal analyzers, TA Instruments produces rheometry instruments, which complement thermal analyzers by characterizing materials' viscosities and fluid behavior. TA Instruments is also a developer and supplier of software-based products that interface with the company's instruments. The thermal analytic and rheometry instruments are used by material testing laboratories for the development and production of materials used in plastics, automobiles, electronics and chemicals. In January 2011, Waters Corporation agreed to build its new mass spectrometry headquarters in Manchester, U.K. In June 2011, the firm released mass spectrometer Waters ACQUITY UPLC I-Class System and tandem quadrupole mass detector Xevo TQD.

FINANCIALS: **Sales and profits are in thousands of dollars—add 000 to get the full amount. 2010 Note: Financial information for 2010 was not available for all companies at press time.**

2010 Sales: $1,643,371 — 2010 Profits: $381,763
2009 Sales: $1,051,978 — 2009 Profits: $323,313
2008 Sales: $1,139,886 — 2008 Profits: $322,479
2007 Sales: $1,087,592 — 2007 Profits: $268,072
2006 Sales: $922,532 — 2006 Profits: $222,200

U.S. Stock Ticker: WAT
Int'l Ticker:
Int'l Exchange:
Employees: 5,381 Fiscal Year Ends: 12/31
Parent Company:

SALARIES/BENEFITS:

Pension Plan: Y ESOP Stock Plan: Profit Sharing: Top Exec. Salary: $757,050 Bonus: $1,483,269
Savings Plan: Stock Purch. Plan: Y Second Exec. Salary: $463,500 Bonus: $792,652

OTHER THOUGHTS:

Apparent Women Officers or Directors: 3
Hot Spot for Advancement for Women/Minorities: Y

LOCATIONS: ("Y" = Yes)

West:	Southwest:	Midwest:	Southeast:	Northeast:	International:
Y	Y	Y	Y	Y	Y

WATSON PHARMACEUTICALS INC

www.watson.com

Industry Group Code: 325412

Management:		Sales/Marketing:		Liberal Arts:		Information Sys.:		Professionals:		Tech./Scientific:	
Mgmt. Trainees:	Y	Marketing Pros.:	Y	Gen. Writing/Editing:	Y	Info. Mgmt.:	Y	Finance/Acct.:	Y	Engineers, Elec.:	Y
Experienced Mgmt.:	Y	Retail Sales:		Tech. Writing:	Y	Software Dev.:	Y	Law:	Y	Engineers, Other:	Y
Int'l Business:	Y	Comm./Industrial:	Y	Graphic Arts/Photog.:	Y	Hardware Dev.:		HR/Other:	Y	Health/Lab:	Y
MBA Grads:	Y	Sales Trainees:		Music:		Consulting/Other:		Training:	Y	Science/Research:	Y
		Advertising Pros.:		Broadcasting:				Health Care:	Y	Petroleum/Chem.:	Y
				Other:				Consulting:		Math/Other:	Y

TYPES OF BUSINESS:

Generic Pharmaceuticals
Branded Drugs
Urology Drugs
Anti-Hypertensive Drugs
Nephrology Drugs
Anti-Inflammatory Drugs
Oral Contraceptive Drugs
Pain Management Drugs

BRANDS/DIVISIONS/AFFILIATES:

Watson Laboratories
Watson Pharma
Arrow Group
Anda Pharmaceuticals
Anda
Valmed
Trelstar Depot
Gelnique

CONTACTS: *Note: Officers with more than one job title may be intentionally listed here more than once.*

Paul M. Bisaro, CEO
Paul M. Bisaro, Pres.
R. Todd Joyce, CFO/Exec. VP
David A. Buchen, General Counsel/Exec. VP/Sec.
Robert A. Stewart, Exec. VP-Global Oper.
Charles M. Mayr, Sr. VP-Corp. Affairs
Patricia L. Eisenhauer, VP-Investor Rel.
G. Frederick Wilkinson, Exec. VP-Global Brands
Albert Paonessa III, Exec. VP/COO-Anda, Inc.
Andrew L. Turner, Chmn.
Sigurdur Oli Olafsson, Exec. VP-Global Generics

Phone: 951-493-5300	**Fax:**
Toll-Free:	
Address: 311 Bonnie Cir., Corona, CA 92880-2882 US	

GROWTH PLANS/SPECIAL FEATURES:

Watson Pharmaceuticals, Inc. develops, manufactures, markets, sells and distributes roughly 30 branded and 160 generic pharmaceutical products. The firm operates through three segments: global generics, global brands and distribution. The global generics segment includes pharmaceutical products that are bioequivalent to proprietary products. These generic products address the therapeutic areas of antibiotics, anti-inflammatories, depression, hypertension, oral contraceptives, pain management and smoking cessation. Generic products accounted for roughly 66% of net revenues. The global brands segment develops, manufactures, markets, sells and distributes products primarily through two core areas: specialty products and nephrology. The specialty products include urology and a number of non-promoted products. The nephrology product line concerns products for the treatment of iron deficiency anemia. Brands include Trelstar Depot and Trelstar LA, treatments for advanced prostate cancer; Gelnique, a treatment for overactive bladder symptoms; Rapaflo, a treatment for symptoms of benign prostatic hyperplasia; and Ferrlecit and INFeD, iron replacement therapies for patients with iron deficiency anemia. The company markets its brand products through 350 sales professionals. Brand products accounted for roughly 11% of total revenues. The distribution segment distributes generic products and select brand products to independent pharmacies, pharmacy chains, alternative care facilities and physicians' offices in the U.S. The company's distribution business subsidiaries (23% of revenues) include Anda, Anda Pharmaceuticals and Valmed.

The company offers employees life, AD&D, business travel accident, disability, medical, dental and vision insurance; domestic partner coverage; flexible spending accounts; and tuition reimbursement.

FINANCIALS: **Sales and profits are in thousands of dollars—add 000 to get the full amount. 2010 Note: Financial information for 2010 was not available for all companies at press time.**

2010 Sales: $3,566,900	2010 Profits: $184,400	**U.S. Stock Ticker: WPI**
2009 Sales: $2,793,000	2009 Profits: $222,000	**Int'l Ticker:**
2008 Sales: $2,535,501	2008 Profits: $238,379	Int'l Exchange:
2007 Sales: $2,496,651	2007 Profits: $141,030	Employees: 6,030 Fiscal Year Ends: 12/31
2006 Sales: $1,979,244	2006 Profits: $-445,005	Parent Company:

SALARIES/BENEFITS:

Pension Plan:	ESOP Stock Plan:	Profit Sharing:	Top Exec. Salary: $1,000,000	Bonus: $1,500,000
Savings Plan: Y	Stock Purch. Plan:		Second Exec. Salary: $604,846	Bonus: $398,057

OTHER THOUGHTS:

Apparent Women Officers or Directors: 1
Hot Spot for Advancement for Women/Minorities: Y

LOCATIONS: ("Y" = Yes)

West:	Southwest:	Midwest:	Southeast:	Northeast:	International:
Y		Y	Y	Y	

WEIGHT WATCHERS INTERNATIONAL INC

www.weightwatchers.com
Industry Group Code: 446199

Management:		Sales/Marketing:		Liberal Arts:		Information Sys.:		Professionals:		Tech./Scientific:	
Mgmt. Trainees:	Y	Marketing Pros.:	Y	Gen. Writing/Editing:	Y	Info. Mgmt.:	Y	Finance/Acct.:	Y	Engineers, Elec.:	
Experienced Mgmt.:	Y	Retail Sales:		Tech. Writing:		Software Dev.:	Y	Law:	Y	Engineers, Other:	
Int'l Business:	Y	Comm./Industrial:		Graphic Arts/Photog.:	Y	Hardware Dev.:		HR/Other:	Y	Health/Lab:	
MBA Grads:	Y	Sales Trainees:	Y	Music:		Consulting/Other:		Training:	Y	Science/Research:	
		Advertising Pros.:	Y	Broadcasting:				Health Care:	Y	Petroleum/Chem.:	
				Other:	Y			Consulting:		Math/Other:	

TYPES OF BUSINESS:

Weight Management Programs
Franchising
Branded Diet Products

BRANDS/DIVISIONS/AFFILIATES:

Flex Plan
Core Plan
Weight Watchers Online
Weight Watchers eTools
WeightWatchers.com

CONTACTS: *Note: Officers with more than one job title may be intentionally listed here more than once.*

David P. Kirchhoff, CEO
David P. Kirchhoff, Pres.
Ann M. Sardini, CFO
Michael Basone, CTO
Jeffrey A. Fiarman, General Counsel/Sec./Exec. VP
Michael Basone, Pres., WeightWatchers.com
Donna Fontana, VP-Public Rel.
David Burwick, Co-Pres., North America
Raymond Debbane, Chmn.
Melanie Stack Stubbing, Pres., Int'l

Phone: 212-589-2700	**Fax:** 212-589-2600
Toll-Free:	
Address: 11 Madison Ave., 17th Fl., New York, NY 10010 US	

GROWTH PLANS/SPECIAL FEATURES:

Weight Watchers International, Inc. is a global weight management services provider, operating through a network of company-owned and franchise operations. The firm has two operating segments: Weight Watchers International and the company's web site, WeightWatchers.com. Weight management plans consist of Flex Plans and Core Plans. The Flex Plan offers customers a list of foods graded on a POINTS scale, which takes into consideration calories, fat and dietary fiber. This plan allows the dieter to eat any food from the list up to a weekly POINTS total. The Core Plan offers the dieter a list of low calorie density core foods which they can eat freely, without limit; and allows the dieter to eat certain non-core foods up to a POINTS limit. Weight Watchers' weekly meetings are one hour long and promote weight loss through diet, exercise, behavior modification and group support. Each week, 1.2 million people attend 50,000 meetings worldwide. These are run by 12,000 classroom leaders, all of whom have participated in the company's weight loss program. The firm's franchised operations draw in more than 12 million people a year, representing roughly 17% of the company's total attendance. Besides these services, the firm offers various products primarily sold at Weight Watchers meetings and to franchises. These products include nutrition bars, snacks, cookbooks, POINTS value guides and Weight Watchers magazines. Through WeightWatchers.com, the company offers two subscription weight management products to consumers: Weight Watchers Online and Weight Watchers eTools. Weight Watchers Online provides interactive and personalized resources that allow users to follow the company's weight management plans via the Internet. Weight Watchers eTools is the Internet weight management companion for Weight Watchers meetings members who want to interactively manage the day-to-day aspects of their weight management plans on the Internet.

FINANCIALS: **Sales and profits are in thousands of dollars—add 000 to get the full amount. 2010 Note: Financial information for 2010 was not available for all companies at press time.**

2010 Sales: $1,452,037 — 2010 Profits: $194,235
2009 Sales: $1,398,900 — 2009 Profits: $177,300
2008 Sales: $1,535,812 — 2008 Profits: $204,331
2007 Sales: $1,467,167 — 2007 Profits: $201,180
2006 Sales: $1,233,300 — 2006 Profits: $209,800

U.S. Stock Ticker: WTW
Int'l Ticker:
Int'l Exchange:
Employees: 26,000 Fiscal Year Ends: 12/31
Parent Company:

SALARIES/BENEFITS:

Pension Plan:	ESOP Stock Plan:	Profit Sharing:	Top Exec. Salary: $730,385	Bonus: $471,098
Savings Plan:	Stock Purch. Plan: Y		Second Exec. Salary: $412,496	Bonus: $232,493

OTHER THOUGHTS:

Apparent Women Officers or Directors: 3
Hot Spot for Advancement for Women/Minorities: Y

LOCATIONS: ("Y" = Yes)

West:	Southwest:	Midwest:	Southeast:	Northeast:	International:
Y	Y	Y	Y	Y	Y

WEST PHARMACEUTICAL SERVICES INC

www.westpharma.com

Industry Group Code: 3222

Management:		Sales/Marketing:		Liberal Arts:		Information Sys.:		Professionals:		Tech./Scientific:	
Mgmt. Trainees:	Y	Marketing Pros.:	Y	Gen. Writing/Editing:		Info. Mgmt.:	Y	Finance/Acct.:	Y	Engineers, Elec.:	
Experienced Mgmt.:	Y	Retail Sales:		Tech. Writing:	Y	Software Dev.:	Y	Law:	Y	Engineers, Other:	Y
Int'l Business:	Y	Comm./Industrial:	Y	Graphic Arts/Photog.:	Y	Hardware Dev.:		HR/Other:	Y	Health/Lab:	Y
MBA Grads:	Y	Sales Trainees:		Music:		Consulting/Other:		Training:	Y	Science/Research:	Y
		Advertising Pros.:	Y	Broadcasting:				Health Care:	Y	Petroleum/Chem.:	
				Other:				Consulting:		Math/Other:	

TYPES OF BUSINESS:

Injectable Drug Delivery Systems Components
Plastic Packaging Systems Components
Elastomer & Metal Components

BRANDS/DIVISIONS/AFFILIATES:

Medimop Medical Projects, Ltd.
West Analytical Services
La Model Ltd.

CONTACTS: *Note: Officers with more than one job title may be intentionally listed here more than once.*

Donald E. Morel, Jr., CEO
Donald E. Morel, Jr., Pres.
William J. Federici, CFO/VP
Richard D. Luzzi, VP-Human Resources
John R. Gailey, III, General Counsel/Corp. Sec./VP
Michael A. Anderson, Treas./VP
John Paproski, Pres., Pharmaceutical Delivery Systems
Jeffrey C. Hunt, Pres., Pharmaceutical Packaging Systems
Donald A. McMillan, Pres., Americas Pharmaceutical Packaging Systems
Heino Lennartz, Pres., Europe Pharmaceutical Packaging Systems
Donald E. Morel, Jr., Chmn.
Warwick Bedwell, Pres., APAC Pharmaceutical Packaging Systems

Phone: 610-594-2900	**Fax:** 610-594-3000
Toll-Free:	
Address: 101 Gordon Dr., Lionville, PA 19341-0645 US	

GROWTH PLANS/SPECIAL FEATURES:

West Pharmaceutical Services, Inc. manufactures components and systems for injectable drug delivery and plastic packaging, as well as delivery system components for the healthcare, pharmaceutical and consumer products industries. The firm operates in two segments: pharmaceutical packaging systems and pharmaceutical delivery systems. The pharmaceutical packaging systems segment focuses on primary container solutions, including components for drug packaging and pre-fillable syringe systems. It also includes pharmaceutical packaging products, disposable medical components and laboratory and other services. The pharmaceutical delivery systems segment focuses on safety and administration systems and multi-component systems for drug administration. It consists of injection molding services and advanced injection systems. Medimop Medical Projects, Ltd., the firm's wholly-owned subsidiary, provides transfer, mixing and administration systems for injectable pharmaceuticals. The firm has a long-standing partnership with Japan-based Daikyo Seiko, Ltd. West Pharmaceutical also owns 49% of West Pharmaceutical Services Mexico S.A de C.V. and its manufacturing subsidiaries, PharmaTap and AluPlast. In July 2010, the firm acquired La Model Ltd., a developer of an electronic patch injector system using pre-filled cartridge technology. In December 2010, West Pharmaceutical agreed to shut down its manufacturing facility in Pennsylvania. In March 2011, the company agreed to partner with CareFusion to jointly develop a new needle-free vial access device.

The company offers employees medical, dental, life and disability coverage; a retirement plan; a stock purchase plan; an employee assistance program; education assistance; a scholarship program; and flexible spending accounts.

FINANCIALS: **Sales and profits are in thousands of dollars—add 000 to get the full amount. 2010 Note: Financial information for 2010 was not available for all companies at press time.**

2010 Sales: $1,104,700 | 2010 Profits: $65,300
2009 Sales: $1,055,700 | 2009 Profits: $73,600
2008 Sales: $1,051,100 | 2008 Profits: $86,000
2007 Sales: $1,020,100 | 2007 Profits: $70,700
2006 Sales: $913,300 | 2006 Profits: $67,100

U.S. Stock Ticker: WST
Int'l Ticker:
Int'l Exchange:
Employees: 6,600 Fiscal Year Ends: 12/31
Parent Company:

SALARIES/BENEFITS:

Pension Plan: Y	ESOP Stock Plan:	Profit Sharing:	Top Exec. Salary: $825,028	Bonus: $890,091
Savings Plan: Y	Stock Purch. Plan:		Second Exec. Salary: $512,782	Bonus: $435,132

OTHER THOUGHTS:

Apparent Women Officers or Directors: 1
Hot Spot for Advancement for Women/Minorities:

LOCATIONS: ("Y" = Yes)

West:	Southwest:	Midwest:	Southeast:	Northeast:	International:
	Y	Y	Y	Y	Y

WESTERN DIGITAL CORP

www.westerndigital.com

Industry Group Code: 334112

Management:		Sales/Marketing:		Liberal Arts:		Information Sys.:		Professionals:		Tech./Scientific:	
Mgmt. Trainees:	Y	Marketing Pros.:	Y	Gen. Writing/Editing:		Info. Mgmt.:	Y	Finance/Acct.:	Y	Engineers, Elec.:	Y
Experienced Mgmt.:	Y	Retail Sales:		Tech. Writing:	Y	Software Dev.:	Y	Law:	Y	Engineers, Other:	
Int'l Business:	Y	Comm./Industrial:	Y	Graphic Arts/Photog.:	Y	Hardware Dev.:	Y	HR/Other:	Y	Health/Lab:	
MBA Grads:	Y	Sales Trainees:		Music:		Consulting/Other:		Training:	Y	Science/Research:	Y
		Advertising Pros.:	Y	Broadcasting:				Health Care:		Petroleum/Chem.:	
				Other:				Consulting:		Math/Other:	Y

TYPES OF BUSINESS:

Data Storage Hardware
Hard Drives

BRANDS/DIVISIONS/AFFILIATES:

SiliconEdge
Caviar
S25
SiliconDrive
VelociRaptor
My Passport
My Book
GreenPower

CONTACTS: *Note: Officers with more than one job title may be intentionally listed here more than once.*

John F. Coyne, CEO
Timothy M. Leyden, COO
John F. Coyne, Pres.
Wolfgang U. Nickl, CFO/Sr. VP
James J. Murphy, Exec. VP-Worldwide Sales & Sales Oper.
James D. Morris, Exec. VP/Gen. Mgr.-Storage Prod.
James K. Welsh, Exec. VP/Gen. Mgr.-Branded Prod.
Thomas E. Pardun, Chmn.

Phone: 949-672-7000 **Fax:** 949-672-5490
Toll-Free:
Address: 20511 Lake Forest Dr., Lake Forest, CA 92630-7741 US

GROWTH PLANS/SPECIAL FEATURES:

Western Digital Corp. (WD) designs, develops, manufactures and sells hard drives. Hard drives are storage devices that are key components of computers including desktop and notebook computers; data storage subsystems; and other consumer electronic devices. WD hard drives include 3.5-inch and 2.5-inch form factor drives and have capacities ranging from 80 gigabytes to 3 terabytes with nominal rotation speeds up to 10,000 RPM. The company also sells external hard drives, stand alone storage products, compatible with most new PC systems, which allow users to supplement the storage space of their computers. Hard drive products include desktop hard drives, designed for desktop PCs; mobile hard drives, designed for use with notebook computers; enterprise hard drive products, designed for business use and the high-end PC market; consumer electronics, hard drives that may be used in products such as DVRs and karaoke systems; and other branded products. The company has recently expanded its offerings to include solid state drives and media players. Solid-state drives, constructed with semiconductor material and marketed under the SiliconEdge and SiliconDrive brands, are used in embedded systems markets, which include network-communications; industrial, embedded-computing; medical; military; aerospace; media appliance and data streaming applications. WD media players can be used to play digital movies music and photos from WD storage devices. WD brand names include the WD S25, WD RE, WD Velociraptor, WD Scorpio, My Passport, My Book, My DVR Expander and WD Greenpower Technology, designed to consume substantially less power than standard drives. In June 2010, the company acquired Hoya Corporation's magnetic media business for about $233 million. In October 2010, the firm commenced manufacturing operations in Brazil.

The firm offers its employees a 401(k) plan; health, dental and vision coverage; life and AD&D insurance; educational reimbursements; adoption assistance; and an employee assistance program.

FINANCIALS: **Sales and profits are in thousands of dollars—add 000 to get the full amount. 2010 Note: Financial information for 2010 was not available for all companies at press time.**

2010 Sales: $9,850,000	2010 Profits: $1,382,000	**U.S. Stock Ticker: WDC**
2009 Sales: $7,453,000	2009 Profits: $470,000	**Int'l Ticker:**
2008 Sales: $8,074,000	2008 Profits: $867,000	Int'l Exchange:
2007 Sales: $5,468,000	2007 Profits: $564,000	Employees: 62,500 Fiscal Year Ends: 6/30
2006 Sales: $4,341,300	2006 Profits: $395,900	Parent Company:

SALARIES/BENEFITS:

Pension Plan:	ESOP Stock Plan:	Profit Sharing:	Top Exec. Salary: $807,692	Bonus: $3,645,673
Savings Plan: Y	Stock Purch. Plan:		Second Exec. Salary: $507,692	Bonus: $1,122,275

OTHER THOUGHTS:

Apparent Women Officers or Directors: 1
Hot Spot for Advancement for Women/Minorities:

LOCATIONS: ("Y" = Yes)

West:	Southwest:	Midwest:	Southeast:	Northeast:	International:
Y					Y

WHOLE FOODS MARKET INC

www.wholefoodsmarket.com

Industry Group Code: 445110

Management:		**Sales/Marketing:**		**Liberal Arts:**		**Information Sys.:**		**Professionals:**		**Tech./Scientific:**	
Mgmt. Trainees:	Y	Marketing Pros.:	Y	Gen. Writing/Editing:	Y	Info. Mgmt.:	Y	Finance/Acct.:	Y	Engineers, Elec.:	
Experienced Mgmt.:	Y	Retail Sales:	Y	Tech. Writing:		Software Dev.:	Y	Law:	Y	Engineers, Other:	
Int'l Business:	Y	Comm./Industrial:		Graphic Arts/Photog.:	Y	Hardware Dev.:		HR/Other:	Y	Health/Lab:	
MBA Grads:	Y	Sales Trainees:	Y	Music:		Consulting/Other:		Training:	Y	Science/Research:	
		Advertising Pros.:	Y	Broadcasting:				Health Care:		Petroleum/Chem.:	
				Other:	Y			Consulting:		Math/Other:	

TYPES OF BUSINESS:

Natural Foods Grocery Stores
Nutritional Supplements
Seafood Processing
Coffee Roasting

BRANDS/DIVISIONS/AFFILIATES:

365 Organic Everyday Value
365 Everyday Value
Whole Kitchen
Whole Pantry
Allegro Coffee Company
Pigeon Cove
Select Fish
Produce Field Inspection Office

CONTACTS: *Note: Officers with more than one job title may be intentionally listed here more than once.*

John P. Mackey, Co-CEO
A.C. Gallo, COO
A.C. Gallo, Pres.
Glenda Jane Flanagan, CFO/Exec. VP
Michael Besancon, Sr. Global VP-Mktg.
Mike Clifford, CIO/VP
Roberta Lang, General Counsel/Global VP-Legal Affairs
Brian O'Connell, Global VP-Oper. Finance
Jim Sud, Exec. VP-Growth & Bus. Dev.
Margaret Wittenberg, Global VP-Public Affairs & Quality Standards
Cindy McCann, Global VP-Investor Rel.
Sam Ferguson, Global VP-Acct./Controller
Walter Robb, Co-CEO
Bart Beilman, Global VP-Dist.
Lee Matecko, Global VP-Construction & Store Dev.
Laura Derba, Pres., North America Region
John B. Elstrott, Chmn.
Jeff Turnas, Pres., U.K. Region
Michael Besancon, Sr. Global VP-Purchasing & Dist.

Phone: 512-477-4455	**Fax:** 512-482-7000
Toll-Free:	
Address: 550 Bowie St., Austin, TX 78703-4644 US	

GROWTH PLANS/SPECIAL FEATURES:

Whole Foods Market, Inc. owns and operates a chain of natural organic food supermarkets in the U.S. and internationally. The firm's stores generally feature foods made from natural ingredients and free of chemical additives. Whole Foods' merchandise line of over 20,500 items includes organically grown and high-grade commercial produce; grocery products; environmentally safe household items; hormone- and antibiotic-free meats; bulk foods; fresh bakery goods; soups, salads, entrees and sandwiches; vitamins; cosmetics; and miscellaneous items. Merchandise is sold through four private-label brands: 365 Everyday Value; 365 Organic Everyday Value; and Whole Kitchen and Whole Pantry, which are chef quality, all natural foods. The company owns about 288 store locations in 39 states and Washington, D.C., as well as five stores in the U.K. and six stores in Canada. Its stores, which average 37,600 square feet in size, are supplemented by regional distribution centers, bakeries, commissary kitchens, seafood-processing facilities, produce procurement centers and a coffee roasting operation. The company operates a web site that offers features such as online recipes, health information and environmental issue information. The firm's subsidiaries include Allegro Coffee Company; Pigeon Cove and Select Fish, both seafood processing facilities; and Produce Field Inspection Office. As part of a renewable energy initiative, the company has converted 20 locations to either use or host solar power to supplement traditional power, and plans to convert as many as 70 locations. Whole Foods has 52 new stores in development that will average 39,000 square feet in size. In 2010, the firm opened 16 new store locations.

Whole Foods has been named one of the 100 Best Companies to Work For in America by Fortune Magazine for 13 consecutive years. Employees are offered benefits including life, disability, medical, dental and vision insurance; a 401(k); store discounts; paid time off; a personal wellness account; profit sharing; and stock purchase/option plans.

FINANCIALS: **Sales and profits are in thousands of dollars—add 000 to get the full amount. 2010 Note: Financial information for 2010 was not available for all companies at press time.**

2010 Sales: $9,005,794	2010 Profits: $245,833	**U.S. Stock Ticker: WFMI**
2009 Sales: $8,031,620	2009 Profits: $146,804	**Int'l Ticker:**
2008 Sales: $7,953,912	2008 Profits: $114,524	Int'l Exchange:
2007 Sales: $6,591,773	2007 Profits: $182,740	Employees: 64,100 Fiscal Year Ends: 9/30
2006 Sales: $5,607,376	2006 Profits: $203,828	Parent Company:

SALARIES/BENEFITS:

Pension Plan: Y	ESOP Stock Plan:	Profit Sharing: Y	Top Exec. Salary: $402,620	Bonus: $348,348
Savings Plan: Y	Stock Purch. Plan: Y		Second Exec. Salary: $370,918	Bonus: $380,050

OTHER THOUGHTS:

Apparent Women Officers or Directors: 7
Hot Spot for Advancement for Women/Minorities: Y

LOCATIONS: ("Y" = Yes)

West:	Southwest:	Midwest:	Southeast:	Northeast:	International:
Y	Y	Y	Y	Y	Y

WILLIAMS COMPANIES INC (THE)

www.williams.com

Industry Group Code: 211111

Management:		Sales/Marketing:		Liberal Arts:		Information Sys.:		Professionals:		Tech./Scientific:	
Mgmt. Trainees:	Y	Marketing Pros.:	Y	Gen. Writing/Editing:		Info. Mgmt.:	Y	Finance/Acct.:	Y	Engineers, Elec.:	Y
Experienced Mgmt.:	Y	Retail Sales:		Tech. Writing:	Y	Software Dev.:	Y	Law:	Y	Engineers, Other:	Y
Int'l Business:	Y	Comm./Industrial:	Y	Graphic Arts/Photog.:		Hardware Dev.:		HR/Other:	Y	Health/Lab:	
MBA Grads:	Y	Sales Trainees:		Music:		Consulting/Other:		Training:	Y	Science/Research:	
		Advertising Pros.:		Broadcasting:				Health Care:		Petroleum/Chem.:	Y
				Other:				Consulting:		Math/Other:	

TYPES OF BUSINESS:

Gas Exploration & Production
Natural Gas Transportation
Pipelines
Wholesale Power

BRANDS/DIVISIONS/AFFILIATES:

Williams Production Co LLC
Williams Production RMT Company
Williams Gas Pipeline Co LLC
Williams Field Services Group LLC
Laurel Mountain Midstream LLC
Williams Partners LP
Southern Union Company
Midstream Gas & Liquids

CONTACTS:

Note: Officers with more than one job title may be intentionally listed here more than once.

Alan Armstrong, CEO
Alan Armstrong, Pres.
Don R. Chappel, CFO/Sr. VP
Ralph A. Hill, Pres., Exploration
Ralph A. Hill, Pres., Prod.
Robyn L. Ewing, Chief Admin. Officer/Sr. VP-Admin.
James J. Bender, General Counsel/Sr. VP
Phil Wright, Sr. VP-Corp. Dev.
Chris Stockton, Contact-Media Rel.
Richard George, Contact-Investor Rel.
Rory Miller, Pres., Midstream Gathering & Processing
Robyn L. Ewing, Sr. VP-Strategic Svcs.
Randy Barnard, Pres., Gas Pipeline
Sharna Reingold, Contact-Investor Rel.
Steven J. Malcolm, Chmn.

Phone: 918-573-2000	**Fax:** 918-573-6714
Toll-Free: 800-945-5426	
Address: 1 Williams Ctr., Tulsa, OK 74172 US	

GROWTH PLANS/SPECIAL FEATURES:

The Williams Companies, Inc. finds, produces, gathers, processes and transports natural gas. The firm operates in five segments: exploration and production; gas pipeline; midstream gas and liquids; gas marketing services; and other. The exploration and production segment produces, develops and manages natural gas reserves primarily located in the Rocky Mountain and Mid-Continent regions of the U.S. It is operated through subsidiaries such as Williams Production RMT Company and Williams Production Company LLC. The gas pipeline segment includes natural gas pipelines and pipeline joint venture investments organized under subsidiary Williams Gas Pipeline Co., LLC. The midstream and gas liquids segment includes its natural gas gathering, treating and processing business; it is comprised of several subsidiaries including Williams Natural Gas Liquids, Inc.; Midstream Gas & Liquids; Williams Field Services Group LLC; and Williams Partners L.P. The gas marketing services segment manages the firm's natural gas commodity risk through purchases, sales and other related transactions through subsidiary Williams Gas Marketing, Inc. The other segment primarily consists of corporate operations. The company has holdings in several production basins, including the Piceance Basin in Colorado, the San Juan Basin in New Mexico, Barnett Shale in Texas, the Powder River Basin in Wyoming and the Arkoma Basin in Arkansas and Oklahoma. In November 2010, the firm sold its Piceance Basin to Williams Partners for $782 million. In 2011, the firm agreed to acquire Southern Union Company for $8.7 billion.

FINANCIALS:

Sales and profits are in thousands of dollars—add 000 to get the full amount. 2010 Note: Financial information for 2010 was not available for all companies at press time.

2010 Sales: $9,616,000	2010 Profits: $-1,097,000	**U.S. Stock Ticker: WMB**
2009 Sales: $8,255,000	2009 Profits: $285,000	**Int'l Ticker:**
2008 Sales: $11,890,000	2008 Profits: $1,418,000	Int'l Exchange:
2007 Sales: $10,239,000	2007 Profits: $990,000	Employees: 5,022 Fiscal Year Ends: 12/31
2006 Sales: $9,376,000	2006 Profits: $309,000	Parent Company:

SALARIES/BENEFITS:

Pension Plan: Y	ESOP Stock Plan:	Profit Sharing:	Top Exec. Salary: $1,100,000	Bonus: $1,276,378
Savings Plan: Y	Stock Purch. Plan:		Second Exec. Salary: $610,154	Bonus: $559,052

OTHER THOUGHTS:

Apparent Women Officers or Directors: 2
Hot Spot for Advancement for Women/Minorities: Y

LOCATIONS: ("Y" = Yes)

West:	Southwest:	Midwest:	Southeast:	Northeast:	International:
Y	Y	Y	Y	Y	Y

WINDSTREAM CORPORATION

www.windstream.com

Industry Group Code: 517110

Management:		Sales/Marketing:		Liberal Arts:		Information Sys.:		Professionals:		Tech./Scientific:	
Mgmt. Trainees:		Marketing Pros.:	Y	Gen. Writing/Editing:	Y	Info. Mgmt.:	Y	Finance/Acct.:	Y	Engineers, Elec.:	Y
Experienced Mgmt.:		Retail Sales:		Tech. Writing:	Y	Software Dev.:		Law:	Y	Engineers, Other:	
Int'l Business:		Comm./Industrial:	Y	Graphic Arts/Photog.:		Hardware Dev.:		HR/Other:	Y	Health/Lab:	
MBA Grads:	Y	Sales Trainees:		Music:		Consulting/Other:		Training:		Science/Research:	
		Advertising Pros.:	Y	Broadcasting:				Health Care:		Petroleum/Chem.:	
				Other:	Y			Consulting:		Math/Other:	

TYPES OF BUSINESS:

Telephone Service--Local Exchange Carrier & Diversified
Network Access Services
High-Speed Internet Access

BRANDS/DIVISIONS/AFFILIATES:

Q-Comm Corp.
Kentucky Data Link Inc
Norlight Inc
Hosted Solutions Acquisition LLC
Iowa Telecommunications Services, Inc.

CONTACTS: *Note: Officers with more than one job title may be intentionally listed here more than once.*

Jeffrey R. Gardner, CEO
Brent Whittington, COO
Jeffrey R. Gardner, Pres.
Tony Thomas, CFO
Ric Crane, Chief Mktg. Officer/Exec. VP
Susan Bradley, Sr. VP-Human Resources
Cindy Nash, CIO
John P. Fletcher, General Counsel/Exec. VP
Grant Raney, Exec. VP-Network Oper.
Mary Michaels, Dir.-Investor Rel. & Capital Markets
Robert G. Clancy, Treas./Sr. VP
John Eichler, VP/Controller
Mike Rhoda, Sr. VP-Governmental Affairs
John Leach, Sr. VP-Bus. Sales
Christopher Turco, Data Center Oper.
Dennis E. Foster, Chmn.

Phone: 501-748-7000 **Fax:**
Toll-Free: 866-445-5880
Address: 4001 Rodney Parham Rd., Little Rock, AR 72212 US

GROWTH PLANS/SPECIAL FEATURES:

Windstream Corporation is a provider of telecommunications services in rural communities in the U.S. Windstream is one of the largest local telecommunications carriers in the U.S. as well as one of the largest primarily focused on rural markets. Windstream has approximately 3 million access lines and 1 million Internet customers spanning Alabama, Arkansas, Florida, Georgia, Kentucky, Mississippi, Missouri, Nebraska, New Mexico, New York, North Carolina, Ohio, Oklahoma, Pennsylvania, South Carolina and Texas. The company offers local telephone, high-speed Internet, long distance, network access and video services. Voice services consist of traditional telephone services, as well as enhanced services such as call waiting, call forwarding, caller identification, three-way calling, no-answer transfer and voicemail. Long distance services include switched interstate, intrastate and international long distance as well as operator services. Data and special access services primarily consist of high-speed Internet services and the provision of special access dedicated circuits. The company also offers enhanced Internet services to business customers, which include obtaining Internet protocol addresses, web site design and hosting. Windstream also has a co-branded agreement with DISH networks through which it offers cable television services. In February 2010, the company acquired NuVox, a South Carolina based competitive local exchange carrier, for approximately $647 million. In June 2010, Windstream acquired Iowa Telecommunications Services, Inc. for $1.2 billion.

Windstream offers its employees medical, prescription drug, dental and vision coverage; flexible spending accounts; life and AD&D insurance; a 401(k) program; an employee stock purchase program; a U.S. Bond program; short- and long-term disability; employee discounts; an educational assistance program; an adoption program; and paid time off.

FINANCIALS: **Sales and profits are in thousands of dollars—add 000 to get the full amount. 2010 Note: Financial information for 2010 was not available for all companies at press time.**

2010 Sales: $3,712,000 | 2010 Profits: $310,700
2009 Sales: $2,996,600 | 2009 Profits: $334,500
2008 Sales: $3,171,500 | 2008 Profits: $412,700
2007 Sales: $3,245,900 | 2007 Profits: $917,100
2006 Sales: $3,033,300 | 2006 Profits: $545,300

U.S. Stock Ticker: WIN
Int'l Ticker:
Int'l Exchange:
Employees: 10,086 Fiscal Year Ends: 12/31
Parent Company:

SALARIES/BENEFITS:

Pension Plan: ESOP Stock Plan: Profit Sharing: Top Exec. Salary: $991,000 Bonus: $2,242,347
Savings Plan: Y Stock Purch. Plan: Y Second Exec. Salary: $593,269 Bonus: $868,881

OTHER THOUGHTS:

Apparent Women Officers or Directors: 2
Hot Spot for Advancement for Women/Minorities:

LOCATIONS: ("Y" = Yes)

West:	Southwest:	Midwest:	Southeast:	Northeast:	International:
	Y	Y	Y	Y	

WM WRIGLEY JR COMPANY

www.wrigley.com

Industry Group Code: 3113

Management:		Sales/Marketing:		Liberal Arts:		Information Sys.:		Professionals:		Tech./Scientific:	
Mgmt. Trainees:	Y	Marketing Pros.:	Y	Gen. Writing/Editing:	Y	Info. Mgmt.:	Y	Finance/Acct.:	Y	Engineers, Elec.:	
Experienced Mgmt.:	Y	Retail Sales:		Tech. Writing:		Software Dev.:	Y	Law:	Y	Engineers, Other:	
Int'l Business:	Y	Comm./Industrial:	Y	Graphic Arts/Photog.:	Y	Hardware Dev.:		HR/Other:	Y	Health/Lab:	
MBA Grads:	Y	Sales Trainees:	Y	Music:		Consulting/Other:		Training:	Y	Science/Research:	
		Advertising Pros.:	Y	Broadcasting:				Health Care:		Petroleum/Chem.:	
				Other:				Consulting:		Math/Other:	

TYPES OF BUSINESS:

Chewing Gum Manufacturing
Candy & Confections
Breath Mints
Packaging Materials
Flavorings

BRANDS/DIVISIONS/AFFILIATES:

Wrigley's Spearmint
Doublemint
Juicy Fruit
Life Savers
Big Red
Altoids
Mars Inc
Northwestern Flavors, LLC

CONTACTS: *Note: Officers with more than one job title may be intentionally listed here more than once.*

Dushan Petrovich, Pres.
Reuben Gamoran, CFO/Exec. VP
Martin Schlatter, Chief Mktg. Officer/Sr. VP
Maureen Jones, Mgr.-Corp. Comm.
Paul Chibe, VP/Gen. Mgr.-U.S. Gum & Mints

Phone: 312-644-2121 | **Fax:** 312-644-0097
Toll-Free:
Address: 410 N. Michigan Ave., Chicago, IL 60611 US

GROWTH PLANS/SPECIAL FEATURES:

Wm. Wrigley Jr. Company, founded as a partnership in 1891, is one of the world's largest gum makers and has products distributed in over 180 countries and territories. The firm has manufacturing locations in 14 countries and offices in over 40 countries to market its products globally. Flavors and product benefits are tailored to fit local market needs and desires. In addition to selling gum, the company is also sells non-gum items, including mints, breath strips and candies, both through internal brand development and acquisitions. Its brands include Wrigley's Spearmint, Juicy Fruit, Altoids, Doublemint, Life Savers, Big Red, Boomer, Pim Pom, Winterfresh, Extra, Freedent, 5, Hubba Bubba, Orbit, Excel, Creme Savers, Eclipse, Airwaves, Solano, Sugus, P.K., and Cool Air. The firm also has two associated companies: L. A. Dreyfus Company, which manufactures chewing gum base for Wrigley and associated companies; and Northwestern Flavors, LLC, a manufacturer of flavorings and rectified mint oil for the firm's production facilities. The company markets its products through distributors, wholesalers, corporate chains and cooperative buying groups that distribute the products through retail outlets. Additional direct customers are vending distributors, concessionaires and other established customers purchasing in wholesale quantities. Wm. Wrigley Jr. Company is owned by major candy group Mars, Inc.

FINANCIALS: **Sales and profits are in thousands of dollars—add 000 to get the full amount. 2010 Note: Financial information for 2010 was not available for all companies at press time.**

2010 Sales: $
2009 Sales: $
2008 Sales: $5,500,000
2007 Sales: $5,389,100
2006 Sales: $4,683,437

2010 Profits: $
2009 Profits: $
2008 Profits: $
2007 Profits: $632,005
2006 Profits: $529,377

U.S. Stock Ticker: Subsidiary
Int'l Ticker:
Int'l Exchange:
Employees: 16,000 Fiscal Year Ends: 12/31
Parent Company: MARS INC

SALARIES/BENEFITS:

Pension Plan: ESOP Stock Plan: Profit Sharing: Top Exec. Salary: $ Bonus: $
Savings Plan: Stock Purch. Plan: Second Exec. Salary: $ Bonus: $

OTHER THOUGHTS:

Apparent Women Officers or Directors:
Hot Spot for Advancement for Women/Minorities:

LOCATIONS: ("Y" = Yes)

West:	Southwest:	Midwest:	Southeast:	Northeast:	International:
		Y	Y	Y	Y

WW GRAINGER INC

Industry Group Code: 4238

www.grainger.com

Management:		Sales/Marketing:		Liberal Arts:		Information Sys.:		Professionals:		Tech./Scientific:	
Mgmt. Trainees:	Y	Marketing Pros.:	Y	Gen. Writing/Editing:	Y	Info. Mgmt.:	Y	Finance/Acct.:	Y	Engineers, Elec.:	
Experienced Mgmt.:	Y	Retail Sales:		Tech. Writing:	Y	Software Dev.:	Y	Law:	Y	Engineers, Other:	
Int'l Business:	Y	Comm./Industrial:	Y	Graphic Arts/Photog.:	Y	Hardware Dev.:		HR/Other:	Y	Health/Lab:	
MBA Grads:	Y	Sales Trainees:	Y	Music:		Consulting/Other:		Training:	Y	Science/Research:	
		Advertising Pros.:	Y	Broadcasting:				Health Care:		Petroleum/Chem.:	
				Other:				Consulting:		Math/Other:	

TYPES OF BUSINESS:

Industrial Equipment & Products-Wholesale
Maintenance & Repair Products
Online Sales
Safety Products
Logistics Services

BRANDS/DIVISIONS/AFFILIATES:

Acklands-Grainger
Grainger Industrial Supply India Private Limited
Grainger Caribe, Inc.
SafetyCertified, Inc.
Wolseley Industrial Products Group
Ranson Industrial and Safety Supplies, Inc.
Grainger, S.A. de C.V.
Fabory Group

CONTACTS: *Note: Officers with more than one job title may be intentionally listed here more than once.*

James T. Ryan, CEO
James T. Ryan, Pres.
Ronald L. Jadin, CFO/Sr. VP
Lawrence J. Pilon, Sr. VP-Human Resources
John L. Howard, General Counsel/Sr. VP
Laura D. Brown, Sr. VP-Corp. Comm.
Laura D. Brown, Sr. VP-Investor Rel.
Gregory S. Irving, Controller/VP
Michael A. Pulick, Sr. VP/Pres., Grainger US
Vernon O'Donnell, Mgr.-Strategic Brand Comm.
Sara Granack, Dir.-Int'l Comm.
Erin Ptacek, Dir.-Corp. Brand & Reputation
James T. Ryan, Chmn.
Court Carruthers, Sr. VP/Pres., Grainger Int'l
Donald Macpherson, Sr. VP-Global Supply Chain

Phone: 847-535-1000 **Fax:** 847-535-0878
Toll-Free: 800-323-0620
Address: 100 Grainger Pkwy., Lake Forest, IL 60045-5201 US

GROWTH PLANS/SPECIAL FEATURES:

W. W. Grainger, Inc. (Grainger) offers facilities maintenance products and related services and information solutions to approximately 2 million businesses and institutions. The company is divided into two segments: United States and Canada. The U.S. segment markets over 700,000 products, including material handling equipment, safety and security supplies, lighting and electrical products, power and hand tools, pumps and plumbing supplies, cleaning and maintenance supplies, forestry and agriculture equipment, building and home inspection supplies and vehicle and fleet components. The U.S. business operates through over 400 branches in all 50 states, as well as a network of 14 distribution centers. The Canada segment, operating as Acklands-Grainger, is a leading broad-line distributor of industrial and safety supplies, including tools, fasteners, safety supplies, instruments and welding and shop equipment. This business operates through over 170 branches and six distribution centers across Canada. Grainger maintains additional operations internationally, including Grainger, S.A. de C.V. in Mexico; Grainger Industrial Supply India Private Limited in India; Grainger Caribe, Inc. in Puerto Rico; Grainger Colombia SAS in Columbia; Grainger China LLC in China; Grainger Panama S.A. in Panama; and a 53% interest in MonotaRO Co., Ltd., in Japan. In 2010, Grainger acquired SafetyCertified, Inc.; and Acklands-Grainger acquired Ranson Industrial and Safety Supplies, Inc., Solus Securite, Inc. and Wolseley Industrial Products Group. In December 2010, the firm sold its Highsmith brand to DEMCO, Inc. In August 2011, the company acquired Dutch fastener specialist Fabory Group.

Employee benefits at Grainger include health, dental, vision and prescription drug benefits; life insurance; disability benefits; employee discounts; an employee assistance program; an adoption benefit program; an educational assistance program; auto and homeowners insurance; and tuition reimbursement.

FINANCIALS: **Sales and profits are in thousands of dollars—add 000 to get the full amount. 2010 Note: Financial information for 2010 was not available for all companies at press time.**

2010 Sales: $7,182,158 — 2010 Profits: $510,865
2009 Sales: $6,221,991 — 2009 Profits: $430,466
2008 Sales: $6,850,032 — 2008 Profits: $475,355
2007 Sales: $6,418,014 — 2007 Profits: $420,120
2006 Sales: $5,883,654 — 2006 Profits: $383,399

U.S. Stock Ticker: GWW
Int'l Ticker:
Int'l Exchange:
Employees: 17,000 Fiscal Year Ends: 12/31
Parent Company:

SALARIES/BENEFITS:

Pension Plan: Y ESOP Stock Plan: Profit Sharing: Y Top Exec. Salary: $887,000 Bonus: $1,980,000
Savings Plan: Stock Purch. Plan: Second Exec. Salary: $500,000 Bonus: $700,000

OTHER THOUGHTS:

Apparent Women Officers or Directors: 5
Hot Spot for Advancement for Women/Minorities: Y

LOCATIONS: ("Y" = Yes)

West:	Southwest:	Midwest:	Southeast:	Northeast:	International:
Y	Y	Y	Y	Y	Y

WYNDHAM WORLDWIDE

www.wyndhamworldwide.com

Industry Group Code: 721110

Management:		Sales/Marketing:		Liberal Arts:		Information Sys.:		Professionals:		Tech./Scientific:	
Mgmt. Trainees:	Y	Marketing Pros.:	Y	Gen. Writing/Editing:	Y	Info. Mgmt.:	Y	Finance/Acct.:	Y	Engineers, Elec.:	
Experienced Mgmt.:	Y	Retail Sales:		Tech. Writing:		Software Dev.:	Y	Law:	Y	Engineers, Other:	
Int'l Business:	Y	Comm./Industrial:	Y	Graphic Arts/Photog.:	Y	Hardware Dev.:		HR/Other:	Y	Health/Lab:	
MBA Grads:	Y	Sales Trainees:	Y	Music:		Consulting/Other:		Training:	Y	Science/Research:	
		Advertising Pros.:	Y	Broadcasting:				Health Care:		Petroleum/Chem.:	
				Other:	Y			Consulting:		Math/Other:	

TYPES OF BUSINESS:

Hotels, Motels & Resorts
Property Management
Hotel Development
Vacation Property Exchange and Rental
Timeshare Resorts
Franchising
Vacation Ownership

BRANDS/DIVISIONS/AFFILIATES:

Hoseasons
Wingate Inns
Ramada
Days Inn
Tryp
Howard Johnson
AmeriHost
Trendwest

CONTACTS: *Note: Officers with more than one job title may be intentionally listed here more than once.*

Stephen P. Holmes, CEO
Thomas G. Conforti, CFO/Exec. VP
Betsy O'Rourke, Sr. VP-Mktg.
Mary R. Falvey, Chief Human Resources Officer/Exec. VP
Scott G. McLester, General Counsel/Exec. VP
Betsy O'Rourke, Sr. VP-Comm.
Nicola Rossi, Sr. VP/Chief Acct. Officer
Franz S. Hanning, Pres./CEO-Wyndham Vacation Ownership
Eric A. Danziger, Pres./CEO-Wyndham Hotel Group
Geoff Ballotti, Pres./CEO-Wyndham Exchange & Rentals
Tom Anderson, Exec. VP/Chief Real Estate Dev. Officer
Stephen P. Holmes, Chmn.

Phone: 973-753-6000	**Fax:**
Toll-Free:	
Address: 22 Sylvan Way, Parsippany, NJ 07054 US	

GROWTH PLANS/SPECIAL FEATURES:

Wyndham Worldwide (WW) is a hospitality company offering individual consumers and business customers an array of hospitality products and services, as well as various accommodation alternatives and price ranges through its portfolio of world-renowned brands. The company encompasses over 7,210 hotels representing over 612,700 rooms on six continents and more than 900 hotels representing 102,700 rooms in development. Wyndham Hotel Group offers the TripRewards loyalty program. Group RCI, the firm's vacation exchange business, offers its 3.8 million members access for specified periods to over 4,000 vacation properties in 100 countries around the world. WW also offers Wyndham Vacation Ownership, which includes marketing and sales of vacation ownership interests, consumer financing in conjunction with the purchase of vacation ownership interests, property management services to property owners' associations and development and acquisition of vacation ownership resorts. Wyndham Vacation has over 160 vacation ownership resorts in U.S., Canada, Mexico, the Caribbean and the South Pacific that represent over 814,000 owners of vacation ownership interests. WW's extensive portfolio of brands includes Wyndham Hotels and Resorts; Ramada; Days Inn; Super 8; Wyndham Rewards; Wingate by Wyndham; Microtel; RCI; The Registry Collection; Endless Vacation Rentals; Landal GreenParks; Cottages4You; Novasol; Wyndham Vacation Resorts; and WorldMark by Wyndham. In March 2010, WW announced that its Registry Collection program welcomed 24 new resort destinations, increasing its total number of properties to 175. In 2010, the firm acquired four hotel brands: Tryp, ResortQuest, James Villa Holidays and Hoseasons.

Employees are offered business travel accident, long-term disability, life, personal accident, medical, dental and vision insurance; flexible spending accounts; a 401(k) plan; an educational assistance program; an employee assistance program; adoption reimbursement; flexible work arrangements; and travel discounts.

FINANCIALS: **Sales and profits are in thousands of dollars—add 000 to get the full amount. 2010 Note: Financial information for 2010 was not available for all companies at press time.**

2010 Sales: $3,851,000	2010 Profits: $379,000	**U.S. Stock Ticker: WYN**
2009 Sales: $3,750,000	2009 Profits: $293,000	**Int'l Ticker:**
2008 Sales: $4,281,000	2008 Profits: $-1,074,000	Int'l Exchange:
2007 Sales: $4,360,000	2007 Profits: $403,000	Employees: 26,400 Fiscal Year Ends: 12/31
2006 Sales: $3,842,000	2006 Profits: $287,000	Parent Company:

SALARIES/BENEFITS:

Pension Plan:	ESOP Stock Plan:	Profit Sharing:	Top Exec. Salary: $1,085,011	Bonus: $2,712,528
Savings Plan: Y	Stock Purch. Plan:		Second Exec. Salary: $606,008	Bonus: $825,000

OTHER THOUGHTS:

Apparent Women Officers or Directors: 4
Hot Spot for Advancement for Women/Minorities: Y

LOCATIONS: ("Y" = Yes)

West:	Southwest:	Midwest:	Southeast:	Northeast:	International:
Y	Y	Y	Y	Y	Y

WYNN RESORTS LIMITED

www.wynnresorts.com

Industry Group Code: 721120

Management:		**Sales/Marketing:**		**Liberal Arts:**		**Information Sys.:**		**Professionals:**		**Tech./Scientific:**	
Mgmt. Trainees:	Y	Marketing Pros.:	Y	Gen. Writing/Editing:	Y	Info. Mgmt.:	Y	Finance/Acct.:	Y	Engineers, Elec.:	
Experienced Mgmt.:	Y	Retail Sales:		Tech. Writing:		Software Dev.:	Y	Law:	Y	Engineers, Other:	
Int'l Business:	Y	Comm./Industrial:	Y	Graphic Arts/Photog.:	Y	Hardware Dev.:		HR/Other:	Y	Health/Lab:	
MBA Grads:	Y	Sales Trainees:	Y	Music:	Y	Consulting/Other:		Training:	Y	Science/Research:	
		Advertising Pros.:	Y	Broadcasting:				Health Care:		Petroleum/Chem.:	
				Other:	Y			Consulting:		Math/Other:	

TYPES OF BUSINESS:

Hotel Casinos

BRANDS/DIVISIONS/AFFILIATES:

Wynn Las Vegas, LLC
Wynn Resorts (Macau), S.A.
Encore Suites at Wynn Las Vegas
Encore Suites at Wynn Macau
PokerStarsWynn.com

CONTACTS: *Note: Officers with more than one job title may be intentionally listed here more than once.*

Stephen A. Wynn, CEO
Marc D. Schorr, COO
Matt Maddox, CFO
Linda Chen, Pres., Wynn Int'l Mktg., Ltd.
John Strzemp, Chief Admin. Officer/Exec. VP
Kim Sinatra, General Counsel/Sec./Sr. VP
Matt Maddox, Treas.
Marilyn W. Spiegel, Pres., Wynn Las Vegas, LLC
Maurice Wooden, COO-Wynn Las Vegas, LLC
Scott Peterson, Sr. VP/CFO-Wynn Las Vegas, LLC
Stephen A. Wynn, Chmn.
Ian M. Coughlan, Pres., Wynn Resorts (Macau), S.A.

Phone: 702-770-7555 **Fax:**
Toll-Free:
Address: 3131 Las Vegas Blvd. S., Las Vegas, NV 89109 US

GROWTH PLANS/SPECIAL FEATURES:

Wynn Resorts Limited is a developer, owner and operator of destination casino resorts. It owns and operates two destination casino resorts: The Wynn Las Vegas on the Strip in Las Vegas, Nevada, which includes Encore at Wynn Las Vegas; and the Wynn Macau in the Macau Special Administrative Region of China. Wynn Las Vegas offers 2,716 rooms and suites. The 111,000-square-foot casino features 147 table games, a baccarat salon, private VIP gaming rooms, a poker room, 1,842 slot machines, and a race and sports book. The resort's 22 food and beverage outlets feature five fine dining restaurants. Other amenities include two nightclubs; a spa and salon; a Ferrari and Maserati automobile dealership; wedding chapels; an 18-hole golf course; 223,000 square feet of meeting space; and a 74,000 square foot retail promenade featuring boutiques from Alexander McQueen, Cartier, Chanel, and Louis Vuitton. Wynn Las Vegas also has a showroom which features Le Reve, a water-based theatrical production. The Encore at Wynn Las Vegas features 2,034 suites, a 76,000 square feet casino with 95 table games, a baccarat salon, 778 slot machines and a sports book. It also features 13 food and beverage outlets; two night clubs; a spa and salon; meeting space; and 27,000 square feet of upscale retail outlets. The Wynn Macau features 595 hotel rooms and suites; 410 table games, 935 slot machines; a poker room; six restaurants; a spa and salon; lounges; meeting facilities; and 48,000 square feet of retail space. The company's newest hotel, the Encore at Wynn Macau, features 410 luxury suites; four villas; approximately 34,000 square feet of casino gaming space, including a sky casino, containing 60 table games and 80 slot machines; two restaurants; a luxury spa; and retail brands Chanel, Piaget and Cartier. In March 2011, Wynn Resorts and PokerStars agreed to launch Internet poker site PokerStarsWynn.com.

FINANCIALS: **Sales and profits are in thousands of dollars—add 000 to get the full amount. 2010 Note: Financial information for 2010 was not available for all companies at press time.**

2010 Sales: $4,184,698 | 2010 Profits: $160,127
2009 Sales: $3,045,611 | 2009 Profits: $20,654
2008 Sales: $2,987,324 | 2008 Profits: $210,479
2007 Sales: $2,687,519 | 2007 Profits: $196,336
2006 Sales: $1,432,257 | 2006 Profits: $628,728

U.S. Stock Ticker: WYNN
Int'l Ticker:
Int'l Exchange:
Employees: 16,405 Fiscal Year Ends: 12/31
Parent Company:

SALARIES/BENEFITS:

Pension Plan: | ESOP Stock Plan: | Profit Sharing: | Top Exec. Salary: $2,953,125 | Bonus: $4,062,500
Savings Plan: Y | Stock Purch. Plan: | Second Exec. Salary: $1,817,308 | Bonus: $2,000,000

OTHER THOUGHTS:

Apparent Women Officers or Directors: 5
Hot Spot for Advancement for Women/Minorities: Y

LOCATIONS: ("Y" = Yes)

West:	Southwest:	Midwest:	Southeast:	Northeast:	International:
Y					Y

Sales, profits and employees may be estimates. Financial information, benefits and other data can change quickly and may vary from those stated here.

XEROX CORP

www.xerox.com

Industry Group Code: 333313

Management:		Sales/Marketing:		Liberal Arts:		Information Sys.:		Professionals:		Tech./Scientific:	
Mgmt. Trainees:	Y	Marketing Pros.:	Y	Gen. Writing/Editing:	Y	Info. Mgmt.:	Y	Finance/Acct.:	Y	Engineers, Elec.:	Y
Experienced Mgmt.:	Y	Retail Sales:		Tech. Writing:	Y	Software Dev.:	Y	Law:	Y	Engineers, Other:	Y
Int'l Business:	Y	Comm./Industrial:	Y	Graphic Arts/Photog.:	Y	Hardware Dev.:	Y	HR/Other:	Y	Health/Lab:	
MBA Grads:	Y	Sales Trainees:	Y	Music:		Consulting/Other:		Training:	Y	Science/Research:	Y
		Advertising Pros.:	Y	Broadcasting:				Health Care:		Petroleum/Chem.:	
				Other:				Consulting:		Math/Other:	

TYPES OF BUSINESS:

Business Machines-Copiers, Printers & Scanners
Managed Print Services Outsourcing
Software
Multipurpose Office Machines
Consulting Services
Desktop Printers

BRANDS/DIVISIONS/AFFILIATES:

Fuji Xerox
DocuColor
Global Imaging Systems Inc
ColorQube
WorkCentre
Phaser
iGen
Affiliated Computer Services

CONTACTS: *Note: Officers with more than one job title may be intentionally listed here more than once.*

Ursula M. Burns, CEO
Ursula M. Burns, Pres.
Lawrence A. Zimmerman, CFO/Vice Chmn.
Christa Carone, Chief Mktg. Officer/VP
Tom Maddison, VP-Human Resources
John E. McDermott, CIO/VP
Sophie V. Vandebroek, CTO/VP/Pres., Xerox Innovation Group
Anthony M. Federico, Chief Engineer/VP
Don H. Liu, General Counsel/Sr. VP/Sec.
James A. Firestone, Exec. VP-Corporate Oper.
Uta Werner, Chief Strategy Officer/VP
James H. Lesko, VP-Investor Rel.
Gary R. Kabureck, Chief Acct. Officer/VP
John M. Kelly, Corp. VP-Xerox Global Services North America
Leslie F. Varon, VP-Finance/Controller
Jule Limoli, Pres., North American Agent Oper.
Rhonda L. Seegal, VP/Treas.
Ursula M. Burns, Chmn.
Jacques Guers, VP-Europe

Phone: 203-968-3000	**Fax:** 203-968-3218
Toll-Free:	
Address: 45 Glober Ave., Norwalk, CT 06856 US	

GROWTH PLANS/SPECIAL FEATURES:

Xerox Corp. is a document systems and services company operating in the global document market. It operates in three segments: Production, Office, and Other. The Production segment manufactures high-end digital monochrome and color systems designed for customers in the graphic communications industry and for large enterprises. These products enable digital on-demand printing, digital full-color printing and enterprise printing. The division offers a complete family of monochrome production systems from 65-288 pages per minute (ppm) and color production systems from 40-110 ppm. Additionally, it offers a variety of pre-press and post-press options, as well as workflow software. Key products in this segment include FreeFlow digital workflow software, the iGen family of digital production presses and the DocuColor digital presses. The Office segment develops and manufactures a range of color and black-and-white multifunction, printer, copier and fax products used by global, national, and small to mid-size commercial customers, as well as government, education and other public sectors. Office systems and services, which include monochrome devices at speeds up to 95 ppm and color devices up to 85 ppm, include the family of ColorQube, WorkCentre multifunction printers and Phaser desktop printers and multifunction printers. The Other segment primarily includes revenue from paper sales, value-added services, wide-format systems and Global Imaging Systems (GIS) network integration and electronic presentation systems. The firm receives about 50% of its revenues from services such as managed printing. Fuji Xerox, an unconsolidated entity of which Xerox owns 25%, develops, manufactures and distributes document management system, supplies and services. In February 2010, the company acquired Affiliated Computer Services, a leading provider of business process outsourcing and information technology services.

The company offers employees medical, dental and vision insurance; health care and dependent care accounts; life insurance; disability coverage; a 401(k) plan; an employee assistance program; childcare assistance; mortgage assistance; tuition assistance; and credit union membership.

FINANCIALS: **Sales and profits are in thousands of dollars—add 000 to get the full amount. 2010 Note: Financial information for 2010 was not available for all companies at press time.**

2010 Sales: $21,633,000	2010 Profits: $606,000	**U.S. Stock Ticker: XRX**
2009 Sales: $15,179,000	2009 Profits: $485,000	**Int'l Ticker:**
2008 Sales: $17,608,000	2008 Profits: $230,000	Int'l Exchange:
2007 Sales: $17,228,000	2007 Profits: $1,135,000	Employees: 136,500 Fiscal Year Ends: 12/31
2006 Sales: $15,895,000	2006 Profits: $1,210,000	Parent Company:

SALARIES/BENEFITS:

Pension Plan:	ESOP Stock Plan:	Profit Sharing:	Top Exec. Salary: $1,160,000	Bonus: $2,331,350
Savings Plan: Y	Stock Purch. Plan:		Second Exec. Salary: $900,000	Bonus: $1,884,375

OTHER THOUGHTS:

Apparent Women Officers or Directors: 12
Hot Spot for Advancement for Women/Minorities: Y

LOCATIONS: ("Y" = Yes)

West:	Southwest:	Midwest:	Southeast:	Northeast:	International:
Y	Y	Y	Y	Y	Y

YUM! BRANDS INC

www.yum.com

Industry Group Code: 722110

Management:		**Sales/Marketing:**		**Liberal Arts:**		**Information Sys.:**		**Professionals:**		**Tech./Scientific:**	
Mgmt. Trainees:	Y	Marketing Pros.:	Y	Gen. Writing/Editing:	Y	Info. Mgmt.:	Y	Finance/Acct.:	Y	Engineers, Elec.:	
Experienced Mgmt.:	Y	Retail Sales:		Tech. Writing:		Software Dev.:	Y	Law:	Y	Engineers, Other:	
Int'l Business:	Y	Comm./Industrial:		Graphic Arts/Photog.:	Y	Hardware Dev.:		HR/Other:	Y	Health/Lab:	
MBA Grads:	Y	Sales Trainees:		Music:		Consulting/Other:		Training:	Y	Science/Research:	
		Advertising Pros.:	Y	Broadcasting:				Health Care:		Petroleum/Chem.:	
				Other:	Y			Consulting:		Math/Other:	

TYPES OF BUSINESS:

Fast Food Restaurants

BRANDS/DIVISIONS/AFFILIATES:

Pizza Hut
KFC
Taco Bell
Long John Silver's
A&W All-American Food
Yum! Restaurants International
Yum! China
WingStreet

CONTACTS: *Note: Officers with more than one job title may be intentionally listed here more than once.*

David C. Novak, CEO
Emil J. Brolick, COO
David C. Novak, Pres.
Richard T. Carucci, CFO
Anne P. Byerlein, Chief People Officer
Christian L. Campbell, General Counsel/Corp. Sec./Sr. VP
Jonathan D. Blum, Chief Public Affairs Officer/Sr. VP
Timothy P. Jerzyk, Sr. VP-Investor Rel./Treas.
Larry Gathof, Treas./VP
Scott O. Bergren, Pres./Chief Concept Officer-Pizza Hut
Roger Eaton, Pres./Chief Concept Officer-KFC
Greg Creed, Pres./Chief Concept Officer-Taco Bell
Samuel Su, Chmn./CEO-Yum! China Div.
David C. Novak, Chmn.
Graham D. Allan, Pres., Yum Restaurants Int'l

Phone: 502-874-8300	**Fax:** 502-874-8790
Toll-Free:	
Address: 1441 Gardiner Ln., Louisville, KY 40213 US	

GROWTH PLANS/SPECIAL FEATURES:

Yum! Brands, Inc. is a fast-food restaurant company with over 38,000 restaurants in more than 110 countries and territories. The firm's brands include KFC, Pizza Hut, WingStreet, Taco Bell, A&W and Long John Silver's. KFC, Pizza Hut, Taco Bell and Long John Silver's are global leaders, respectively, in the chicken, pizza, Mexican-style and seafood fast-food segments. The restaurants are operated by the company, independent third-party franchisees, or by affiliates in which it owns a non-controlling equity interest. The firm also utilizes multi-branding, where at least two of its restaurants are operated as a single unit. In all six chains, customers are offered dine in and carry out options; all but Pizza Hut and WingStreet offer drive-through options at certain locations. WingStreet is a delivery-based wing chain and has more than 2,200 locations in the United States, Australia and Canada. The WingStreet brand is within many Pizza Hut restaurants. Yum! Brands has three operating divisions: U.S., International and China. Yum! Brands own approximately 4,958 multi-branded locations worldwide, of which 4,629 are in the U.S. The Yum! Restaurants International division comprises roughly 14,300 restaurants, which are primarily KFCs and Pizza Huts. Yum! China has approximately 3,200 KFC restaurants and 520 Pizza Hut locations, in addition to 120 Pizza Hut Home Service delivery units. In 2010, Yum! Restaurants International opened 884 new restaurants in more than 75 countries, while Yum! China opened more than 500 new restaurants. In January 2011, the company announced plans to sell its Long John Silver's and A&W restaurants in order to focus on global expansion, particularly expansion in mainland China. Taco Bell units averaged about $1.2 million in sales during 2011, KFC about $1.1 million and Pizza Hut about $800,000.

Employees of the firm are offered benefits including life, disability, medical, dental, vision and hearing insurance; flexible spending accounts; an assistance program; discount programs; and tuition reimbursement.

FINANCIALS: **Sales and profits are in thousands of dollars—add 000 to get the full amount. 2010 Note: Financial information for 2010 was not available for all companies at press time.**

2010 Sales: $11,343,000	2010 Profits: $1,178,000	**U.S. Stock Ticker: YUM**
2009 Sales: $10,836,000	2009 Profits: $1,083,000	**Int'l Ticker:**
2008 Sales: $11,304,000	2008 Profits: $964,000	Int'l Exchange:
2007 Sales: $10,435,000	2007 Profits: $909,000	Employees: 378,000 Fiscal Year Ends: 12/31
2006 Sales: $9,561,000	2006 Profits: $824,000	Parent Company:

SALARIES/BENEFITS:

Pension Plan:	ESOP Stock Plan:	Profit Sharing:	Top Exec. Salary: $1,400,000	Bonus: $2,993,760
Savings Plan: Y	Stock Purch. Plan: Y		Second Exec. Salary: $811,923	Bonus: $1,718,917

OTHER THOUGHTS:

Apparent Women Officers or Directors: 3
Hot Spot for Advancement for Women/Minorities: Y

LOCATIONS: ("Y" = Yes)

West:	Southwest:	Midwest:	Southeast:	Northeast:	International:
Y	Y	Y	Y	Y	Y

ZIMMER HOLDINGS INC

www.zimmer.com

Industry Group Code: 33911

Management:		**Sales/Marketing:**		**Liberal Arts:**		**Information Sys.:**		**Professionals:**		**Tech./Scientific:**	
Mgmt. Trainees:	Y	Marketing Pros.:	Y	Gen. Writing/Editing:	Y	Info. Mgmt.:	Y	Finance/Acct.:	Y	Engineers, Elec.:	
Experienced Mgmt.:	Y	Retail Sales:		Tech. Writing:	Y	Software Dev.:	Y	Law:	Y	Engineers, Other:	Y
Int'l Business:	Y	Comm./Industrial:	Y	Graphic Arts/Photog.:	Y	Hardware Dev.:		HR/Other:	Y	Health/Lab:	Y
MBA Grads:	Y	Sales Trainees:	Y	Music:		Consulting/Other:		Training:	Y	Science/Research:	
		Advertising Pros.:	Y	Broadcasting:				Health Care:	Y	Petroleum/Chem.:	
				Other:				Consulting:		Math/Other:	

TYPES OF BUSINESS:

Orthopedic Supplies
Orthopedic Reconstructive Implants
Dental Implants
Spinal Surgery Products
Trauma Management Products
Orthopedic Surgical Products
Orthobiological Products
Healthcare Consulting

BRANDS/DIVISIONS/AFFILIATES:

NexGen
VerSys
Anatomical Shoulder
Tapered Screw-Vent
Puros
CopiOs
Beijing Montagne Medical Device Co., Ltd.
Sodem Diffusion S.A.

CONTACTS: *Note: Officers with more than one job title may be intentionally listed here more than once.*

David C. Dvorak, CEO
David C. Dvorak, Pres.
James T. Crines, CFO/Exec. VP-Finance
William P. Fisher, VP-Global Human Resources
Cheryl R. Blanchard, Sr. VP-R&D/Chief Scientific Officer
Chad F. Phipps, General Counsel/Sec./Sr. VP
Richard C. Stair, Sr. VP-Global Oper.
Paul G. Blair, VP-Investor Rel.
Derek Davis, VP-Finance/Corp. Controller/Chief Acct. Officer
Jeffery A. McCaulley, Pres., Zimmer Reconstructive
Stephen H. L. Ooi, Pres., APAC
Jefferey B. Paulsen, Group Pres., Global Bus.
Norman D. Finch Jr., Chief Compliance Officer/VP
John L. McGoldrick, Chmn.
Bruno A. Melzi, Chmn.-EMEA
Richard C. Stair, Sr. VP-Logistics

Phone: 574-267-6131 **Fax:**
Toll-Free: 800-613-6131
Address: 345 E. Main St., Warsaw, IN 46580 US

GROWTH PLANS/SPECIAL FEATURES:

Zimmer Holdings, Inc., founded in 1927, primarily designs, develops, manufactures and markets implants and related surgical products. Zimmer's main products comprise orthopedic reconstructive implants, spine products, trauma products and orthopedic surgical products. Orthopedic reconstructive implants include: knee replacement products, including NexGen, Innex and Natural-Knee II; hip implants VerSys and Fitmore; extremity implants Anatomical Shoulder, Biglian/Flatow and Coonrad/Morrey Total Elbow; dental reconstructive implants Tapered Screw-Vent teeth; dental restorative products Zimmer Hex-Lock abutments; and dental regenerative products Puros allograft materials. Spine products cover stabilization equipment for spinal surgery, implants for correcting spinal deformations (including scoliosis) and CopiOs bone void filler. Trauma products are used primarily to reattach or stabilize damaged bone or tissue to support the body's natural healing process. Specific products include Zimmer Universal Locking System plates and the Zimmer Intertrochanteric/Subtrochanteric (ITST) Nailing System, a hip fracture treatment. Lastly, orthopedic surgical products include the Pulsavac Plus wound cleaning and debridement (dead tissue removal) system and the Automatic Tourniquet System (ATS). Besides the above-mentioned products, Zimmer also develops orthobiological materials, including tissue regeneration products, and it provides hospital-focused consulting services to help member institutions design, implement and manage orthopedic programs. Its primary customers include orthopedic surgeons, neurosurgeons, oral surgeons, dentists, hospitals, stocking distributors, healthcare dealers and healthcare purchasing organizations or buying groups. Zimmer has operations in over 25 countries and markets its products in over 100 countries. The Americas generate roughly 58% of the firm's net sales, followed by Europe (26%) and Asia-Pacific (16%). In December 2010, Zimmer acquired China-based firm Beijing Montagne Medical Device Co., Ltd. and Swiss company Sodem Diffusion S.A.

Zimmer offers its employees medical, dental and vision care plans; life and AD&D insurance; flexible spending accounts; disability income protection plans; and tuition reimbursement.

FINANCIALS: **Sales and profits are in thousands of dollars—add 000 to get the full amount. 2010 Note: Financial information for 2010 was not available for all companies at press time.**

2010 Sales: $4,220,200 — 2010 Profits: $596,900
2009 Sales: $4,095,400 — 2009 Profits: $717,400
2008 Sales: $4,121,100 — 2008 Profits: $848,600
2007 Sales: $3,897,500 — 2007 Profits: $773,200
2006 Sales: $3,495,400 — 2006 Profits: $834,500

U.S. Stock Ticker: ZMH
Int'l Ticker:
Int'l Exchange:
Employees: 8,000 Fiscal Year Ends: 12/31
Parent Company:

SALARIES/BENEFITS:

Pension Plan: ESOP Stock Plan: Profit Sharing: Top Exec. Salary: $833,654 Bonus: $1,039,475
Savings Plan: Y Stock Purch. Plan: Y Second Exec. Salary: $563,026 Bonus: $426,016

OTHER THOUGHTS:

Apparent Women Officers or Directors: 3
Hot Spot for Advancement for Women/Minorities: Y

LOCATIONS: ("Y" = Yes)

West:	Southwest:	Midwest:	Southeast:	Northeast:	International:
Y	Y	Y	Y	Y	Y

ADDITIONAL INDEXES

CONTENTS:

INDEX OF FIRMS NOTED AS HOT SPOTS FOR ADVANCEMENT FOR WOMEN & MINORITIES

INTEGRA LIFESCIENCES HOLDINGS CORP
INTEL CORP
INTERNATIONAL BUSINESS MACHINES CORP (IBM)
INTERPUBLIC GROUP OF COMPANIES INC
INTUIT INC
INVENTIV HEALTH INC
JACKSON NATIONAL LIFE INSURANCE COMPANY
JETBLUE AIRWAYS CORPORATION
JM SMUCKER CO
JOHNSON & JOHNSON
JOHNSON CONTROLS INC
JONES LANG LASALLE INC
JUNIPER NETWORKS INC
KAISER PERMANENTE
KELLOGG COMPANY
KELLY SERVICES INC
KEY ENERGY SERVICES INC
KIMBERLY-CLARK CORP
KINDRED HEALTHCARE INC
KINETIC CONCEPTS INC
KRAFT FOODS INC
KROGER CO (THE)
LABORATORY CORP OF AMERICA HOLDINGS
LAM RESEARCH CORP
LEXMARK INTERNATIONAL INC
LIBERTY GLOBAL INC
LIBERTY MUTUAL GROUP INC
LIFE TECHNOLOGIES CORP
LIMITED BRANDS INC
LINCOLN NATIONAL CORPORATION
LOEWS CORPORATION
MACY'S INC
MANPOWER INC
MANTECH INTERNATIONAL CORP
MARATHON OIL CORP
MARRIOTT INTERNATIONAL INC
MARSH & MCLENNAN COMPANIES INC
MASSACHUSETTS MUTUAL LIFE INSURANCE CO
MATTEL INC
MAYO FOUNDATION FOR MEDICAL EDUCATION AND RESEARCH
MCDONALD'S CORP
MCKESSON CORPORATION
MEDCO HEALTH SOLUTIONS INC
MEDTRONIC INC
MERCER INC
METHODIST HEALTH CARE SYSTEM
METLIFE INC
MICROCHIP TECHNOLOGY INC
MICROSOFT CORP
MILLIPORE CORP
MYLAN INC
NACCO INDUSTRIES INC
NALCO HOLDING COMPANY
NCR CORPORATION
NETAPP INC
NEW YORK LIFE INSURANCE CO
NEWS CORP
NEXTERA ENERGY INC
NIKE INC
NORFOLK SOUTHERN CORP
NORTHWESTERN MUTUAL LIFE INSURANCE CO
ORACLE CORP
O'REILLY AUTOMOTIVE INC
OSHKOSH CORPORATION
OWENS & MINOR INC
PAREXEL INTERNATIONAL CORP
PARSONS BRINCKERHOFF INC
PEABODY ENERGY CORP
PEPSICO INC
PERRIGO CO
PETSMART INC
PG&E CORPORATION
POLYCOM INC
PRAXAIR INC
PRINCIPAL FINANCIAL GROUP (THE)
PROCTER & GAMBLE CO
PROGRESSIVE CORPORATION (THE)
PROVIDENCE HEALTH & SERVICES
PRUDENTIAL FINANCIAL INC
PUBLIX SUPER MARKETS INC
QUALCOMM INC
RECREATIONAL EQUIPMENT INC (REI)
RED HAT INC
REGIS CORPORATION
ROSS STORES INC
ROWAN COMPANIES INC
ROYAL CARIBBEAN CRUISES LTD
RYDER SYSTEM INC
SAFECO INSURANCE COMPANY OF AMERICA
SAFEWAY INC
SAIC INC
SALESFORCE.COM INC
SAM'S CLUB
SARA LEE CORP
SAS INSTITUTE INC
SCANA CORPORATION
SCOTTS MIRACLE GROW CO
SEMPRA ENERGY
SENECA FOODS CORPORATION
SHERWIN WILLIAMS COMPANY (THE)
SIGMA-ALDRICH CORP
SKILLED HEALTHCARE GROUP INC
SODEXO INC
SOUTHERN COMPANY (THE)
SOUTHWEST AIRLINES CO
SPIRIT AEROSYSTEMS HOLDINGS INC
SRA INTERNATIONAL INC
ST JUDE MEDICAL INC
STARWOOD HOTELS & RESORTS WORLDWIDE INC
STRYKER CORP
SUN HEALTHCARE GROUP INC
SUTTER HEALTH INC
SYMANTEC CORP
SYSCO CORP
TARGET CORPORATION
TELEDYNE TECHNOLOGIES INC
TELEPHONE AND DATA SYSTEMS INC (TDS)
TENET HEALTHCARE CORPORATION
TETRA TECH INC
THERMO FISHER SCIENTIFIC INC
THOMSON REUTERS
TIDEWATER INC
TIFFANY & CO
TIME WARNER INC
TJX COMPANIES INC (THE)
TOTAL SYSTEM SERVICES INC (TSYS)
TOWERS WATSON & CO
TRAVELERS COMPANIES INC (THE)
TRUSTMARK COMPANIES
TW TELECOM INC
UNION PACIFIC CORP
UNITED PARCEL SERVICE INC (UPS)
UNITED STATES CELLULAR CORP
UNITED TECHNOLOGIES CORPORATION
UNITEDHEALTH GROUP INC
UNIVERSAL HEALTH SERVICES INC
UNIVISION COMMUNICATIONS INC
USAA
VALASSIS COMMUNICATIONS INC
VALSPAR CORPORATION (THE)
VARIAN MEDICAL SYSTEMS INC
VERIZON COMMUNICATIONS INC
VICTORIAS SECRET
VISA INC
WALGREEN CO
WAL-MART STORES INC
WALT DISNEY COMPANY (THE)
WARNACO GROUP INC (THE)
WASTE MANAGEMENT INC
WATERS CORP
WATSON PHARMACEUTICALS INC
WEIGHT WATCHERS INTERNATIONAL INC
WHOLE FOODS MARKET INC
WILLIAMS COMPANIES INC (THE)
WW GRAINGER INC
WYNDHAM WORLDWIDE
WYNN RESORTS LIMITED
XEROX CORP
YUM! BRANDS INC
ZIMMER HOLDINGS INC

INDEX OF SUBSIDIARIES, BRAND NAMES AND AFFILIATIONS

INDEX OF SUBSIDIARIES, BRAND NAMES AND AFFILIATIONS, CONT.

INDEX OF SUBSIDIARIES, BRAND NAMES AND AFFILIATIONS, CONT.

INDEX OF SUBSIDIARIES, BRAND NAMES AND AFFILIATIONS, CONT.

INDEX OF SUBSIDIARIES, BRAND NAMES AND AFFILIATIONS, CONT.

INDEX OF SUBSIDIARIES, BRAND NAMES AND AFFILIATIONS, CONT.

INDEX OF SUBSIDIARIES, BRAND NAMES AND AFFILIATIONS, CONT.

INDEX OF SUBSIDIARIES, BRAND NAMES AND AFFILIATIONS, CONT.

INDEX OF SUBSIDIARIES, BRAND NAMES AND AFFILIATIONS, CONT.

INDEX OF SUBSIDIARIES, BRAND NAMES AND AFFILIATIONS, CONT.

INDEX OF SUBSIDIARIES, BRAND NAMES AND AFFILIATIONS, CONT.

INDEX OF SUBSIDIARIES, BRAND NAMES AND AFFILIATIONS, CONT.

INDEX OF SUBSIDIARIES, BRAND NAMES AND AFFILIATIONS, CONT.

INDEX OF SUBSIDIARIES, BRAND NAMES AND AFFILIATIONS, CONT.

INDEX OF SUBSIDIARIES, BRAND NAMES AND AFFILIATIONS, CONT.

INDEX OF SUBSIDIARIES, BRAND NAMES AND AFFILIATIONS, CONT.

INDEX OF SUBSIDIARIES, BRAND NAMES AND AFFILIATIONS, CONT.

INDEX OF SUBSIDIARIES, BRAND NAMES AND AFFILIATIONS, CONT.

INDEX OF SUBSIDIARIES, BRAND NAMES AND AFFILIATIONS, CONT.

INDEX OF SUBSIDIARIES, BRAND NAMES AND AFFILIATIONS, CONT.

INDEX OF SUBSIDIARIES, BRAND NAMES AND AFFILIATIONS, CONT.

INDEX OF SUBSIDIARIES, BRAND NAMES AND AFFILIATIONS, CONT.

INDEX OF SUBSIDIARIES, BRAND NAMES AND AFFILIATIONS, CONT.

INDEX OF SUBSIDIARIES, BRAND NAMES AND AFFILIATIONS, CONT.

INDEX OF SUBSIDIARIES, BRAND NAMES AND AFFILIATIONS, CONT.

INDEX OF SUBSIDIARIES, BRAND NAMES AND AFFILIATIONS, CONT.

INDEX OF SUBSIDIARIES, BRAND NAMES AND AFFILIATIONS, CONT.

INDEX OF SUBSIDIARIES, BRAND NAMES AND AFFILIATIONS, CONT.

INDEX OF SUBSIDIARIES, BRAND NAMES AND AFFILIATIONS, CONT.

INDEX BY COMPANIES FOR SPECIFIC TYPES OF JOB SEEKERS

Indexed by the following categories:

Information Systems

KLA TENCOR CORP
LAM RESEARCH CORP
LEAR CORP
LEXMARK INTERNATIONAL INC
LIFE TECHNOLOGIES CORP
LORAL SPACE & COMMUNICATIONS LTD
MEDTRONIC INC
MICROCHIP TECHNOLOGY INC
MICRON TECHNOLOGY INC
MILLIPORE CORP
MOLEX INC
MULTI-FINELINE ELECTRONIX INC
NCR CORPORATION
NETAPP INC
NORFOLK SOUTHERN CORP
OSHKOSH CORPORATION
PLEXUS CORP
POLYCOM INC
PROVIDENCE HEALTH & SERVICES
QUALCOMM INC
RESMED INC
SAIC INC
SANDISK CORP
SANMINA-SCI CORPORATION
SAPIENT CORPORATION
SRA INTERNATIONAL INC
STANLEY BLACK & DECKER INC
SYNTEL INC
TEKTRONIX INC
TELEDYNE TECHNOLOGIES INC
TTM TECHNOLOGIES INC
UNION PACIFIC CORP
UNITED TECHNOLOGIES CORPORATION
VARIAN MEDICAL SYSTEMS INC
WABTEC CORP
WESTERN DIGITAL CORP
XEROX CORP

Information Management

3M COMPANY
7-ELEVEN INC
ABM INDUSTRIES INC
ACADEMY SPORTS & OUTDOORS LTD
ACCENTURE PLC
ACOSTA SALES & MARKETING
ACTIVISION BLIZZARD INC
ADOBE SYSTEMS INC
ADVANCE AUTO PARTS INC
ADVANCED MICRO DEVICES INC (AMD)
ADVENTIST HEALTH SYSTEM
AECOM TECHNOLOGY CORPORATION
AES CORPORATION (THE)
AFFILIATED COMPUTER SERVICES INC
AFLAC INC
AGILENT TECHNOLOGIES INC
AIR PRODUCTS & CHEMICALS INC
ALASKA AIR GROUP INC
ALLERGAN INC
ALLIANCE DATA SYSTEMS CORPORATION
ALTRIA GROUP INC
AMAZON.COM INC
AMEDISYS INC
AMERCO
AMERICAN EXPRESS CO
AMERICAN POWER CONVERSION (APC)
AMERIGROUP CORPORATION
AMERISOURCEBERGEN CORP
AMGEN INC
AMKOR TECHNOLOGY INC
AMPHENOL CORPORATION
AMR CORP (AMERICAN AIRLINES)
AMSURG CORP
ANALOG DEVICES INC
APACHE CORP
APPLE INC
APPLIED MATERIALS INC
ARAMARK CORPORATION
ARCHER DANIELS MIDLAND CO
ARROW ELECTRONICS INC
ARTHUR J GALLAGHER & CO
ASCENA RETAIL GROUP INC
ASCENSION HEALTH
AT&T INC
AUTOMATIC DATA PROCESSING INC
AUTONATION INC
AUTOZONE INC
AVNET INC
AVON PRODUCTS INC
AXA FINANCIAL INC
BAIN & COMPANY INC
BAKER HUGHES INC
BALL CORP
BARRETT BUSINESS SERVICES
BASIC ENERGY SERVICES INC
BASS PRO SHOPS INC
BAUSCH & LOMB INC
BECHTEL GROUP INC
BECKMAN COULTER INC
BECTON DICKINSON & CO
BED BATH & BEYOND INC
BEMIS COMPANY INC
BERKSHIRE HATHAWAY INC
BEST BUY CO INC
BIG 5 SPORTING GOODS CORPORATION
BIO RAD LABORATORIES INC
BIOGEN IDEC INC
BLACKROCK INC
BLOOMBERG LP
BMC SOFTWARE INC
BOEING COMPANY (THE)
BOOZ ALLEN HAMILTON INC
BOSTON CONSULTING GROUP INC (THE, BCG)
BOYD GAMING CORP
BRINKS COMPANY (THE)
BROADCOM CORP
BROCADE COMMUNICATIONS SYSTEMS INC
BROOKDALE SENIOR LIVING INC
BROWN & BROWN INC
BRUKER CORP
BUCKLE INC (THE)
BUFFALO WILD WINGS INC
BUNGE LTD
BURLINGTON NORTHERN SANTA FE LLC
CABLEVISION SYSTEMS CORP
CACI INTERNATIONAL INC
CADENCE DESIGN SYSTEMS INC
CAESARS ENTERTAINMENT CORPORATION
CAMERON INTERNATIONAL CORPORATION
CAMPBELL SOUP CO
CAPITAL SENIOR LIVING CORP
CARLSON COMPANIES INC
CARMAX GROUP
CARNIVAL CORPORATION
CASH AMERICA INTERNATIONAL INC
CATERPILLAR INC
CATHOLIC HEALTH INITIATIVES
CB RICHARD ELLIS GROUP INC (CBRE)

CDW CORPORATION
CELGENE CORP
CELLCO PARTNERSHIP (VERIZON WIRELESS)
CEPHALON INC
CERNER CORP
CH ROBINSON WORLDWIDE INC
CHEMED CORPORATION
CHEVRON CORPORATION
CHEVRON PHILLIPS CHEMICAL COMPANY LLC
CHICO'S FAS INC
CHIPOTLE MEXICAN GRILL INC
CHS INC
CHUBB CORPORATION (THE)
CIENA CORP
CIGNA CORP
CINTAS CORP
CISCO SYSTEMS INC
CITRIX SYSTEMS INC
CLEARWIRE CORP
CLOROX CO (THE)
CNA FINANCIAL CORP
COACH INC
COCA-COLA BOTTLING CO CONSOLIDATED
COCA-COLA COMPANY (THE)
COGNIZANT TECHNOLOGY SOLUTIONS CORP
COLDWATER CREEK INC
COLGATE PALMOLIVE CO
COMCAST CORP
COMMUNITY HEALTH SYSTEMS INC
COMPUTER SCIENCES CORPORATION (CSC)
COMPUTER TASK GROUP INC
CONAGRA FOODS INC
CONCENTRA INC
CONOCOPHILLIPS COMPANY
CONSOL ENERGY INC
CONTAINER STORE (THE)
CON-WAY INC
COOPER COMPANIES INC
COSTCO WHOLESALE CORP
COVANCE INC
COX COMMUNICATIONS INC
CR BARD INC
CRACKER BARREL OLD COUNTRY STORE INC
CROCS INC
CSX CORP

CUMMINS INC
CVS CAREMARK CORPORATION
DANAHER CORP
DARDEN RESTAURANTS INC
DAVITA INC
DEAN FOODS CO
DEERE & CO
DELOITTE & TOUCHE USA LLP
DELOITTE CONSULTING LLP
DELTA APPAREL INC
DENTSPLY INTERNATIONAL INC
DEVRY INC
DIAMOND OFFSHORE DRILLING INC
DICK'S SPORTING GOODS INC
DIODES INC
DIRECTV
DOLLAR GENERAL CORPORATION
DTE ENERGY COMPANY
DUKE ENERGY CORP
DUPONT (E I DU PONT DE NEMOURS & CO)
DUPONT AGRICULTURE & NUTRITION
EATON CORP
EBAY INC
EDISON INTERNATIONAL
EDWARDS LIFESCIENCES CORP
EMC CORP
EMERITUS CORP
EMERSON ELECTRIC CO
ENDO PHARMACEUTICALS HOLDINGS INC
ENTERGY CORP
ENTERPRISE HOLDINGS INC
EQUITY LIFESTYLE PROPERTIES INC
ERNST & YOUNG LLP
ESTEE LAUDER COMPANIES INC (THE)
EXELON CORPORATION
EXPEDIA INC
EXPERIAN AMERICAS
EXPRESS SCRIPTS INC
EXTERRAN HOLDINGS INC
EXXON MOBIL CORPORATION (EXXONMOBIL)
EXXONMOBIL CHEMICAL
FACTSET RESEARCH SYSTEMS INC
FAIRVIEW HEALTH SERVICES
FAMILY DOLLAR STORES INC
FASTENAL

FEDERAL MOGUL CORP
FEDEX CORPORATION
FIDELITY NATIONAL INFORMATION SERVICES INC
FINISAR CORPORATION
FIRST ADVANTAGE CORPORATION
FIRSTENERGY CORP
FLUOR CORP
FM GLOBAL
FMC TECHNOLOGIES INC
FMR CORP (FIDELITY INVESTMENTS)
FORD MOTOR CO
FOREST LABORATORIES INC
FORTUNE BRANDS INC
FOSSIL INC
FOX ENTERTAINMENT GROUP INC
FRONTIER COMMUNICATIONS CORPORATION
FTI CONSULTING INC
GAMESTOP CORP
GE ENERGY INFRASTRUCTURE
GENENTECH INC
GENERAL ELECTRIC CO (GE)
GENERAL MILLS INC
GENERAL MOTORS COMPANY (GM)
GENESCO INC
GENTEX CORPORATION
GENTIVA HEALTH SERVICES INC
GENWORTH FINANCIAL INC
GENZYME BIOSURGERY
GEOKINETICS INC
GILEAD SCIENCES INC
GOODYEAR TIRE & RUBBER COMPANY (THE)
GOOGLE INC
GRANT THORNTON LLP
GROUP 1 AUTOMOTIVE INC
GROUPON INC
GSI COMMERCE INC
GUESS? INC
HALLIBURTON COMPANY
HANESBRANDS INC
HANGER ORTHOPEDIC GROUP INC
HARRIS CORPORATION
HAWAIIAN ELECTRIC INDUSTRIES INC
HCA HOLDINGS INC
HE BUTT GROCERY COMPANY (HEB)
HEALTH CARE SERVICE CORPORATION (HCSC)

HEALTH FITNESS CORP
HEALTH MANAGEMENT ASSOCIATES INC
HEALTHSOUTH CORP
HEARTLAND PAYMENT SYSTEMS INC
HENRY SCHEIN INC
HERSHEY CO
HERTZ GLOBAL HOLDINGS INC
HIBBETT SPORTS INC
HILLENBRAND INC
HILTON HOTELS CORP
HONDA OF AMERICA MANUFACTURING INC
HOSPIRA INC
HUMANA INC
HYATT HOTELS CORPORATION
IAC/INTERACTIVECORP
ICF INTERNATIONAL INC
IDEXX LABORATORIES INC
IGATE CORPORATION
ILLINOIS TOOL WORKS INC
IMS HEALTH INC
INGRAM MICRO INC
INSITUFORM TECHNOLOGIES
INTEGRA LIFESCIENCES HOLDINGS CORP
INTEL CORP
INTERNATIONAL BUSINESS MACHINES CORP (IBM)
INTERPUBLIC GROUP OF COMPANIES INC
INTUIT INC
INVENTIV HEALTH INC
JACK HENRY & ASSOCIATES INC
JACKSON NATIONAL LIFE INSURANCE COMPANY
JARDEN CORP
JB HUNT TRANSPORT SERVICES INC
JETBLUE AIRWAYS CORPORATION
JM SMUCKER CO
JOHNSON & JOHNSON
JOHNSON CONTROLS INC
JONES LANG LASALLE INC
JUNIPER NETWORKS INC
KAISER PERMANENTE
KEANE INC
KELLOGG COMPANY
KELLY SERVICES INC
KEY ENERGY SERVICES INC
KIMBERLY-CLARK CORP

KINDRED HEALTHCARE INC
KINETIC CONCEPTS INC
KLA TENCOR CORP
KOCH INDUSTRIES INC
KOHL'S CORP
KPMG LLP
KRAFT FOODS INC
KROGER CO (THE)
LABORATORY CORP OF AMERICA HOLDINGS
LAM RESEARCH CORP
LAS VEGAS SANDS CORP (THE VENETIAN)
LEAP WIRELESS INTERNATIONAL INC
LEAR CORP
LEXMARK INTERNATIONAL INC
LIBERTY GLOBAL INC
LIBERTY MEDIA CORP
LIBERTY MUTUAL GROUP INC
LIFE TECHNOLOGIES CORP
LIMITED BRANDS INC
LINCARE HOLDINGS INC
LINCOLN NATIONAL CORPORATION
LKQ CORP
LOEWS CORPORATION
LORAL SPACE & COMMUNICATIONS LTD
LUFKIN INDUSTRIES INC
MACY'S INC
MANPOWER INC
MANTECH INTERNATIONAL CORP
MARATHON OIL CORP
MARRIOTT INTERNATIONAL INC
MARS INC
MARSH & MCLENNAN COMPANIES INC
MARY KAY INC
MASSACHUSETTS MUTUAL LIFE INSURANCE CO
MATTEL INC
MAXIMUS INC
MAYO FOUNDATION FOR MEDICAL EDUCATION AND RESEARCH
MCDONALD'S CORP
MCKESSON CORPORATION
MCKINSEY & COMPANY INC
MEDCO HEALTH SOLUTIONS INC
MEDIACOM COMMUNICATIONS CORP
MEDNAX INC
MEDTRONIC INC

MEIJER INC
MERCER INC
METHODIST HEALTH CARE SYSTEM
METLIFE INC
METROPCS COMMUNICATIONS INC
MICROCHIP TECHNOLOGY INC
MICRON TECHNOLOGY INC
MICROSOFT CORP
MIDAMERICAN ENERGY HOLDINGS CO
MILLIPORE CORP
MOLEX INC
MONRO MUFFLER BRAKE INC
MULTI-FINELINE ELECTRONIX INC
MUTUAL OF OMAHA COMPANIES (THE)
MYLAN INC
NABORS INDUSTRIES LTD
NACCO INDUSTRIES INC
NALCO HOLDING COMPANY
NATIONAL INSTRUMENTS CORP
NATIONAL OILWELL VARCO INC
NCR CORPORATION
NETAPP INC
NEW YORK LIFE INSURANCE CO
NEWS CORP
NEXTERA ENERGY INC
NII HOLDINGS INC
NIKE INC
NORFOLK SOUTHERN CORP
NORTH HIGHLAND
NORTHWESTERN MUTUAL LIFE INSURANCE CO
OCEANEERING INTERNATIONAL INC
ODYSSEY HEALTHCARE INC
OIL STATES INTERNATIONAL INC
OMNICOM GROUP INC
ORACLE CORP
O'REILLY AUTOMOTIVE INC
OSHKOSH CORPORATION
OWENS & MINOR INC
PACCAR INC
PANERA BREAD CO
PARAMETRIC TECHNOLOGY CORP
PAREXEL INTERNATIONAL CORP
PARK-OHIO HOLDINGS CORP
PARSONS BRINCKERHOFF INC
PATTERSON COMPANIES INC
PATTERSON-UTI ENERGY INC

PEABODY ENERGY CORP
PENSKE AUTOMOTIVE GROUP INC
PEPSICO INC
PERRIGO CO
PETCO ANIMAL SUPPLIES INC
PETSMART INC
PG&E CORPORATION
PHARMACEUTICAL PRODUCT DEVELOPMENT INC
PHILIP MORRIS INTERNATIONAL INC
PLEXUS CORP
POLO RALPH LAUREN CORP
POLYCOM INC
PRAXAIR INC
PRICESMART INC
PRICEWATERHOUSECOOPERS
PRINCIPAL FINANCIAL GROUP (THE)
PROCTER & GAMBLE CO
PROGRESSIVE CORPORATION (THE)
PROVIDENCE HEALTH & SERVICES
PRUDENTIAL FINANCIAL INC
PUBLIX SUPER MARKETS INC
QUALCOMM INC
QUANTA SERVICES INC
RACKSPACE HOSTING INC
RALCORP HOLDINGS INC
RECREATIONAL EQUIPMENT INC (REI)
RED HAT INC
REGIS CORPORATION
REPUBLIC AIRWAYS HOLDINGS INC
RESMED INC
ROBERT HALF INTERNATIONAL INC
ROSS STORES INC
ROWAN COMPANIES INC
ROYAL CARIBBEAN CRUISES LTD
RYDER SYSTEM INC
SABRE HOLDINGS CORP
SAFECO INSURANCE COMPANY OF AMERICA
SAFEWAY INC
SAIC INC
SALESFORCE.COM INC
SAM'S CLUB
SANDISK CORP
SANMINA-SCI CORPORATION
SAPIENT CORPORATION
SARA LEE CORP

SAS INSTITUTE INC
SCANA CORPORATION
SCHLUMBERGER LIMITED
SCOTTS MIRACLE GROW CO
SEACOR HOLDINGS INC
SELECT MEDICAL HOLDINGS CORPORATION
SEMPRA ENERGY
SENECA FOODS CORPORATION
SENSIENT TECHNOLOGIES CORPORATION
SHAW GROUP INC (THE)
SHELL OIL CO
SHERWIN WILLIAMS COMPANY (THE)
SIGMA-ALDRICH CORP
SKILLED HEALTHCARE GROUP INC
SNYDERS-LANCE INC
SODEXO INC
SOUTHERN COMPANY (THE)
SOUTHWEST AIRLINES CO
SPECTRUM HEALTH
SPIRIT AEROSYSTEMS HOLDINGS INC
SRA INTERNATIONAL INC
ST JUDE MEDICAL INC
STANLEY BLACK & DECKER INC
STARWOOD HOTELS & RESORTS WORLDWIDE INC
STERICYCLE INC
STIFEL FINANCIAL CORP
STONERIDGE INC
STREAM GLOBAL SERVICES INC
STRYKER CORP
SUN HEALTHCARE GROUP INC
SUTTER HEALTH INC
SYMANTEC CORP
SYNTEL INC
SYSCO CORP
TARGET CORPORATION
TEAM HEALTH HOLDINGS INC
TEAM INC
TECH DATA CORP
TEKTRONIX INC
TELEDYNE TECHNOLOGIES INC
TELEPHONE AND DATA SYSTEMS INC (TDS)
TENET HEALTHCARE CORPORATION
TEREX CORPORATION
TETRA TECH INC
THERMO FISHER SCIENTIFIC INC

THOMSON REUTERS
THOR INDUSTRIES INC
TIBCO SOFTWARE INC
TIDEWATER INC
TIFFANY & CO
TIME WARNER INC
TJX COMPANIES INC (THE)
TOTAL SYSTEM SERVICES INC (TSYS)
TOWERS WATSON & CO
TRAVELERS COMPANIES INC (THE)
TREEHOUSE FOODS INC
TRUSTMARK COMPANIES
TTM TECHNOLOGIES INC
TW TELECOM INC
UNDER ARMOUR INC
UNION PACIFIC CORP
UNITED NATURAL FOODS INC
UNITED PARCEL SERVICE INC (UPS)
UNITED STATES CELLULAR CORP
UNITED TECHNOLOGIES CORPORATION
UNITEDHEALTH GROUP INC
UNIVERSAL HEALTH SERVICES INC
UNIVISION COMMUNICATIONS INC
URS CORPORATION
USAA
VALASSIS COMMUNICATIONS INC
VALSPAR CORPORATION (THE)
VARIAN MEDICAL SYSTEMS INC
VCA ANTECH INC
VERIZON COMMUNICATIONS INC
VICTORIAS SECRET
VISA INC
VORNADO REALTY TRUST
WABTEC CORP
WALGREEN CO
WAL-MART STORES INC
WALT DISNEY COMPANY (THE)
WARNACO GROUP INC (THE)
WASTE MANAGEMENT INC
WATERS CORP
WATSON PHARMACEUTICALS INC
WEIGHT WATCHERS INTERNATIONAL INC
WEST PHARMACEUTICAL SERVICES INC
WESTERN DIGITAL CORP
WHOLE FOODS MARKET INC
WILLIAMS COMPANIES INC (THE)

WINDSTREAM CORPORATION
WM WRIGLEY JR COMPANY
WW GRAINGER INC
WYNDHAM WORLDWIDE
WYNN RESORTS LIMITED
XEROX CORP
YUM! BRANDS INC
ZIMMER HOLDINGS INC

Software Development
3M COMPANY
7-ELEVEN INC
ACADEMY SPORTS & OUTDOORS LTD
ACCENTURE PLC
ACOSTA SALES & MARKETING
ACTIVISION BLIZZARD INC
ADOBE SYSTEMS INC
ADVANCE AUTO PARTS INC
ADVANCED MICRO DEVICES INC (AMD)
AECOM TECHNOLOGY CORPORATION
AES CORPORATION (THE)
AFFILIATED COMPUTER SERVICES INC
AFLAC INC
AGILENT TECHNOLOGIES INC
AIR PRODUCTS & CHEMICALS INC
ALASKA AIR GROUP INC
ALLERGAN INC
ALLIANCE DATA SYSTEMS CORPORATION
ALTRIA GROUP INC
AMAZON.COM INC
AMERICAN EXPRESS CO
AMERICAN POWER CONVERSION (APC)
AMERIGROUP CORPORATION
AMERISOURCEBERGEN CORP
AMGEN INC
AMKOR TECHNOLOGY INC
AMR CORP (AMERICAN AIRLINES)
ANALOG DEVICES INC
APACHE CORP
APPLE INC
APPLIED MATERIALS INC
ARAMARK CORPORATION
ARCHER DANIELS MIDLAND CO
ARROW ELECTRONICS INC
ARTHUR J GALLAGHER & CO
ASCENA RETAIL GROUP INC
ASCENSION HEALTH
AT&T INC
AUTOMATIC DATA PROCESSING INC
AUTONATION INC
AUTOZONE INC
AVON PRODUCTS INC
AXA FINANCIAL INC
BAIN & COMPANY INC
BAKER HUGHES INC
BASS PRO SHOPS INC
BAUSCH & LOMB INC
BECHTEL GROUP INC
BECKMAN COULTER INC
BECTON DICKINSON & CO
BED BATH & BEYOND INC
BERKSHIRE HATHAWAY INC
BEST BUY CO INC
BIO RAD LABORATORIES INC
BIOGEN IDEC INC
BLACKROCK INC
BLOOMBERG LP
BMC SOFTWARE INC
BOEING COMPANY (THE)
BOOZ ALLEN HAMILTON INC
BOSTON CONSULTING GROUP INC (THE, BCG)
BRINKS COMPANY (THE)
BROADCOM CORP
BROCADE COMMUNICATIONS SYSTEMS INC
BROWN & BROWN INC
BRUKER CORP
BUCKLE INC (THE)
BUFFALO WILD WINGS INC
BURLINGTON NORTHERN SANTA FE LLC
CABLEVISION SYSTEMS CORP
CACI INTERNATIONAL INC
CADENCE DESIGN SYSTEMS INC
CAESARS ENTERTAINMENT CORPORATION
CAMERON INTERNATIONAL CORPORATION
CARMAX GROUP
CARNIVAL CORPORATION
CASH AMERICA INTERNATIONAL INC
CATERPILLAR INC
CATHOLIC HEALTH INITIATIVES
CDW CORPORATION
CELGENE CORP
CELLCO PARTNERSHIP (VERIZON WIRELESS)
CEPHALON INC
CERNER CORP
CH ROBINSON WORLDWIDE INC
CHEVRON CORPORATION
CHEVRON PHILLIPS CHEMICAL COMPANY LLC
CHICO'S FAS INC
CHIPOTLE MEXICAN GRILL INC
CHUBB CORPORATION (THE)
CIENA CORP
CIGNA CORP
CINTAS CORP
CISCO SYSTEMS INC
CITRIX SYSTEMS INC
CLEARWIRE CORP
CNA FINANCIAL CORP
COACH INC
COCA-COLA COMPANY (THE)
COGNIZANT TECHNOLOGY SOLUTIONS CORP
COLDWATER CREEK INC
COLGATE PALMOLIVE CO
COMCAST CORP
COMMUNITY HEALTH SYSTEMS INC
COMPUTER SCIENCES CORPORATION (CSC)
COMPUTER TASK GROUP INC
CONAGRA FOODS INC
CONCENTRA INC
CONOCOPHILLIPS COMPANY
CONTAINER STORE (THE)
COOPER COMPANIES INC
COSTCO WHOLESALE CORP
COVANCE INC
COX COMMUNICATIONS INC
CR BARD INC
CRACKER BARREL OLD COUNTRY STORE INC
CSX CORP
CUMMINS INC
CVS CAREMARK CORPORATION
DANAHER CORP
DARDEN RESTAURANTS INC
DAVITA INC
DEERE & CO
DELOITTE & TOUCHE USA LLP
DELOITTE CONSULTING LLP
DENTSPLY INTERNATIONAL INC

DEVRY INC
DIAMOND OFFSHORE DRILLING INC
DICK'S SPORTING GOODS INC
DIODES INC
DIRECTV
DOLLAR GENERAL CORPORATION
DTE ENERGY COMPANY
DUKE ENERGY CORP
DUPONT (E I DU PONT DE NEMOURS & CO)
EATON CORP
EBAY INC
EDISON INTERNATIONAL
EDWARDS LIFESCIENCES CORP
EMC CORP
EMERSON ELECTRIC CO
ENTERGY CORP
ENTERPRISE HOLDINGS INC
ERNST & YOUNG LLP
ESTEE LAUDER COMPANIES INC (THE)
EXELON CORPORATION
EXPEDIA INC
EXPERIAN AMERICAS
EXPRESS SCRIPTS INC
EXXON MOBIL CORPORATION (EXXONMOBIL)
EXXONMOBIL CHEMICAL
FACTSET RESEARCH SYSTEMS INC
FAIRVIEW HEALTH SERVICES
FAMILY DOLLAR STORES INC
FEDEX CORPORATION
FIDELITY NATIONAL INFORMATION SERVICES INC
FIRST ADVANTAGE CORPORATION
FIRSTENERGY CORP
FLUOR CORP
FMC TECHNOLOGIES INC
FMR CORP (FIDELITY INVESTMENTS)
FORD MOTOR CO
FOREST LABORATORIES INC
FORTUNE BRANDS INC
FOSSIL INC
FOX ENTERTAINMENT GROUP INC
FRONTIER COMMUNICATIONS CORPORATION
FTI CONSULTING INC
GAMESTOP CORP
GENENTECH INC
GENERAL ELECTRIC CO (GE)
GENERAL MILLS INC
GENERAL MOTORS COMPANY (GM)
GENESCO INC
GENWORTH FINANCIAL INC
GENZYME BIOSURGERY
GEOKINETICS INC
GILEAD SCIENCES INC
GOOGLE INC
GRANT THORNTON LLP
GROUP 1 AUTOMOTIVE INC
GSI COMMERCE INC
GUESS? INC
HALLIBURTON COMPANY
HANGER ORTHOPEDIC GROUP INC
HARRIS CORPORATION
HAWAIIAN ELECTRIC INDUSTRIES INC
HCA HOLDINGS INC
HE BUTT GROCERY COMPANY (HEB)
HEALTH CARE SERVICE CORPORATION (HCSC)
HEALTH MANAGEMENT ASSOCIATES INC
HEARTLAND PAYMENT SYSTEMS INC
HENRY SCHEIN INC
HERTZ GLOBAL HOLDINGS INC
HIBBETT SPORTS INC
HILTON HOTELS CORP
HONDA OF AMERICA MANUFACTURING INC
HUMANA INC
HYATT HOTELS CORPORATION
IAC/INTERACTIVECORP
ICF INTERNATIONAL INC
IDEXX LABORATORIES INC
IGATE CORPORATION
IMS HEALTH INC
INGRAM MICRO INC
INTEL CORP
INTERNATIONAL BUSINESS MACHINES CORP (IBM)
INTERPUBLIC GROUP OF COMPANIES INC
INTUIT INC
INVENTIV HEALTH INC
JACK HENRY & ASSOCIATES INC
JB HUNT TRANSPORT SERVICES INC
JETBLUE AIRWAYS CORPORATION
JOHNSON & JOHNSON
JOHNSON CONTROLS INC
JUNIPER NETWORKS INC
KAISER PERMANENTE
KEANE INC
KELLOGG COMPANY
KELLY SERVICES INC
KIMBERLY-CLARK CORP
KINDRED HEALTHCARE INC
KINETIC CONCEPTS INC
KLA TENCOR CORP
KOCH INDUSTRIES INC
KOHL'S CORP
KPMG LLP
KRAFT FOODS INC
KROGER CO (THE)
LABORATORY CORP OF AMERICA HOLDINGS
LAM RESEARCH CORP
LAS VEGAS SANDS CORP (THE VENETIAN)
LEAP WIRELESS INTERNATIONAL INC
LEAR CORP
LEXMARK INTERNATIONAL INC
LIBERTY GLOBAL INC
LIBERTY MEDIA CORP
LIBERTY MUTUAL GROUP INC
LIFE TECHNOLOGIES CORP
LIMITED BRANDS INC
LINCOLN NATIONAL CORPORATION
LOEWS CORPORATION
LORAL SPACE & COMMUNICATIONS LTD
MACY'S INC
MANPOWER INC
MANTECH INTERNATIONAL CORP
MARATHON OIL CORP
MARRIOTT INTERNATIONAL INC
MARS INC
MARSH & MCLENNAN COMPANIES INC
MARY KAY INC
MASSACHUSETTS MUTUAL LIFE INSURANCE CO
MATTEL INC
MAXIMUS INC
MAYO FOUNDATION FOR MEDICAL EDUCATION AND RESEARCH
MCDONALD'S CORP
MCKESSON CORPORATION
MCKINSEY & COMPANY INC
MEDCO HEALTH SOLUTIONS INC

MEDIACOM COMMUNICATIONS CORP
MEDTRONIC INC
MEIJER INC
MERCER INC
METHODIST HEALTH CARE SYSTEM
METLIFE INC
METROPCS COMMUNICATIONS INC
MICROCHIP TECHNOLOGY INC
MICRON TECHNOLOGY INC
MICROSOFT CORP
MIDAMERICAN ENERGY HOLDINGS CO
MILLIPORE CORP
MOLEX INC
MONRO MUFFLER BRAKE INC
MULTI-FINELINE ELECTRONIX INC
MYLAN INC
NATIONAL INSTRUMENTS CORP
NATIONAL OILWELL VARCO INC
NCR CORPORATION
NETAPP INC
NEW YORK LIFE INSURANCE CO
NEWS CORP
NEXTERA ENERGY INC
NII HOLDINGS INC
NIKE INC
NORFOLK SOUTHERN CORP
NORTH HIGHLAND
NORTHWESTERN MUTUAL LIFE INSURANCE CO
OCEANEERING INTERNATIONAL INC
OIL STATES INTERNATIONAL INC
OMNICOM GROUP INC
ORACLE CORP
O'REILLY AUTOMOTIVE INC
OSHKOSH CORPORATION
OWENS & MINOR INC
PACCAR INC
PANERA BREAD CO
PARAMETRIC TECHNOLOGY CORP
PAREXEL INTERNATIONAL CORP
PARK-OHIO HOLDINGS CORP
PARSONS BRINCKERHOFF INC
PATTERSON COMPANIES INC
PATTERSON-UTI ENERGY INC
PEPSICO INC
PERRIGO CO
PETCO ANIMAL SUPPLIES INC

PETSMART INC
PG&E CORPORATION
PHARMACEUTICAL PRODUCT DEVELOPMENT INC
PHILIP MORRIS INTERNATIONAL INC
PLEXUS CORP
POLO RALPH LAUREN CORP
POLYCOM INC
PRAXAIR INC
PRICESMART INC
PRICEWATERHOUSECOOPERS
PRINCIPAL FINANCIAL GROUP (THE)
PROCTER & GAMBLE CO
PROGRESSIVE CORPORATION (THE)
PROVIDENCE HEALTH & SERVICES
PRUDENTIAL FINANCIAL INC
PUBLIX SUPER MARKETS INC
QUALCOMM INC
RACKSPACE HOSTING INC
RED HAT INC
REGIS CORPORATION
RESMED INC
ROBERT HALF INTERNATIONAL INC
ROSS STORES INC
ROYAL CARIBBEAN CRUISES LTD
RYDER SYSTEM INC
SABRE HOLDINGS CORP
SAFECO INSURANCE COMPANY OF AMERICA
SAFEWAY INC
SAIC INC
SALESFORCE.COM INC
SAM'S CLUB
SANDISK CORP
SANMINA-SCI CORPORATION
SAPIENT CORPORATION
SARA LEE CORP
SAS INSTITUTE INC
SCANA CORPORATION
SCHLUMBERGER LIMITED
SEACOR HOLDINGS INC
SELECT MEDICAL HOLDINGS CORPORATION
SEMPRA ENERGY
SENSIENT TECHNOLOGIES CORPORATION
SHELL OIL CO
SHERWIN WILLIAMS COMPANY (THE)

SIGMA-ALDRICH CORP
SOUTHERN COMPANY (THE)
SOUTHWEST AIRLINES CO
SPIRIT AEROSYSTEMS HOLDINGS INC
SRA INTERNATIONAL INC
ST JUDE MEDICAL INC
STANLEY BLACK & DECKER INC
STARWOOD HOTELS & RESORTS WORLDWIDE INC
STIFEL FINANCIAL CORP
STONERIDGE INC
STREAM GLOBAL SERVICES INC
STRYKER CORP
SYMANTEC CORP
SYNTEL INC
SYSCO CORP
TARGET CORPORATION
TECH DATA CORP
TEKTRONIX INC
TELEDYNE TECHNOLOGIES INC
TELEPHONE AND DATA SYSTEMS INC (TDS)
TETRA TECH INC
THERMO FISHER SCIENTIFIC INC
THOMSON REUTERS
TIBCO SOFTWARE INC
TIFFANY & CO
TIME WARNER INC
TJX COMPANIES INC (THE)
TOTAL SYSTEM SERVICES INC (TSYS)
TOWERS WATSON & CO
TRAVELERS COMPANIES INC (THE)
TRUSTMARK COMPANIES
TW TELECOM INC
UNION PACIFIC CORP
UNITED NATURAL FOODS INC
UNITED PARCEL SERVICE INC (UPS)
UNITED STATES CELLULAR CORP
UNITED TECHNOLOGIES CORPORATION
UNITEDHEALTH GROUP INC
UNIVERSAL HEALTH SERVICES INC
UNIVISION COMMUNICATIONS INC
URS CORPORATION
USAA
VALASSIS COMMUNICATIONS INC
VALSPAR CORPORATION (THE)
VARIAN MEDICAL SYSTEMS INC

VCA ANTECH INC
VERIZON COMMUNICATIONS INC
VICTORIAS SECRET
VISA INC
WABTEC CORP
WALGREEN CO
WAL-MART STORES INC
WALT DISNEY COMPANY (THE)
WASTE MANAGEMENT INC
WATERS CORP
WATSON PHARMACEUTICALS INC
WEIGHT WATCHERS INTERNATIONAL INC
WEST PHARMACEUTICAL SERVICES INC
WESTERN DIGITAL CORP
WHOLE FOODS MARKET INC
WILLIAMS COMPANIES INC (THE)
WM WRIGLEY JR COMPANY
WW GRAINGER INC
WYNDHAM WORLDWIDE
WYNN RESORTS LIMITED
XEROX CORP
YUM! BRANDS INC
ZIMMER HOLDINGS INC

Liberal Arts

Broadcasting
CABLEVISION SYSTEMS CORP
COMCAST CORP
COX COMMUNICATIONS INC
DIRECTV
FOX ENTERTAINMENT GROUP INC
IAC/INTERACTIVECORP
LIBERTY MEDIA CORP
MEDIACOM COMMUNICATIONS CORP
NEWS CORP
TIME WARNER INC
UNIVISION COMMUNICATIONS INC
WAL-MART STORES INC
WALT DISNEY COMPANY (THE)

General Writing/Editing
3M COMPANY
7-ELEVEN INC
ABM INDUSTRIES INC
ACADEMY SPORTS & OUTDOORS LTD
ACCENTURE PLC
ACOSTA SALES & MARKETING
ACTIVISION BLIZZARD INC
ADOBE SYSTEMS INC
ADVANCE AUTO PARTS INC
ADVENTIST HEALTH SYSTEM
AES CORPORATION (THE)
AFFILIATED COMPUTER SERVICES INC
AFLAC INC
AGILENT TECHNOLOGIES INC
AIR PRODUCTS & CHEMICALS INC
ALASKA AIR GROUP INC
ALLERGAN INC
ALLIANCE DATA SYSTEMS CORPORATION
ALTRIA GROUP INC
AMAZON.COM INC
AMEDISYS INC
AMERICAN EXPRESS CO
AMERICAN POWER CONVERSION (APC)
AMERIGROUP CORPORATION
AMERISOURCEBERGEN CORP
AMGEN INC
AMR CORP (AMERICAN AIRLINES)
APACHE CORP
APPLE INC
ARAMARK CORPORATION
ARCHER DANIELS MIDLAND CO
ARROW ELECTRONICS INC
ARTHUR J GALLAGHER & CO
ASCENA RETAIL GROUP INC
ASCENSION HEALTH
AT&T INC
AUTOMATIC DATA PROCESSING INC
AUTONATION INC
AUTOZONE INC
AVON PRODUCTS INC
AXA FINANCIAL INC
BAIN & COMPANY INC
BAKER HUGHES INC
BARRETT BUSINESS SERVICES
BASS PRO SHOPS INC
BAUSCH & LOMB INC
BECHTEL GROUP INC
BECKMAN COULTER INC
BECTON DICKINSON & CO
BED BATH & BEYOND INC
BERKSHIRE HATHAWAY INC
BEST BUY CO INC
BIG 5 SPORTING GOODS CORPORATION
BIO RAD LABORATORIES INC
BLACKROCK INC
BLOOMBERG LP
BMC SOFTWARE INC
BOEING COMPANY (THE)
BOOZ ALLEN HAMILTON INC
BOSTON CONSULTING GROUP INC (THE, BCG)
BOYD GAMING CORP
BRINKS COMPANY (THE)
BROOKDALE SENIOR LIVING INC
BROWN & BROWN INC
BUCKLE INC (THE)
BUFFALO WILD WINGS INC
CABLEVISION SYSTEMS CORP
CACI INTERNATIONAL INC
CAESARS ENTERTAINMENT CORPORATION
CAMPBELL SOUP CO
CAPITAL SENIOR LIVING CORP
CARLSON COMPANIES INC
CARMAX GROUP
CARNIVAL CORPORATION
CASH AMERICA INTERNATIONAL INC
CATERPILLAR INC
CATHOLIC HEALTH INITIATIVES
CDW CORPORATION
CELLCO PARTNERSHIP (VERIZON WIRELESS)
CERNER CORP
CH ROBINSON WORLDWIDE INC
CHEMED CORPORATION
CHEVRON CORPORATION
CHEVRON PHILLIPS CHEMICAL COMPANY LLC
CHICO'S FAS INC
CHIPOTLE MEXICAN GRILL INC
CHS INC
CHUBB CORPORATION (THE)
CIGNA CORP
CINTAS CORP
CISCO SYSTEMS INC
CLEARWIRE CORP
CLOROX CO (THE)
CNA FINANCIAL CORP
COACH INC
COCA-COLA COMPANY (THE)
COGNIZANT TECHNOLOGY SOLUTIONS CORP

COLDWATER CREEK INC
COLGATE PALMOLIVE CO
COMCAST CORP
COMMUNITY HEALTH SYSTEMS INC
COMPUTER SCIENCES CORPORATION (CSC)
COMPUTER TASK GROUP INC
CONAGRA FOODS INC
CONCENTRA INC
CONOCOPHILLIPS COMPANY
CONTAINER STORE (THE)
COSTCO WHOLESALE CORP
COX COMMUNICATIONS INC
CR BARD INC
CRACKER BARREL OLD COUNTRY STORE INC
CROCS INC
CSX CORP
CUMMINS INC
CVS CAREMARK CORPORATION
DANAHER CORP
DARDEN RESTAURANTS INC
DAVITA INC
DEAN FOODS CO
DEERE & CO
DELOITTE & TOUCHE USA LLP
DELOITTE CONSULTING LLP
DELTA APPAREL INC
DENTSPLY INTERNATIONAL INC
DEVRY INC
DICK'S SPORTING GOODS INC
DIRECTV
DOLLAR GENERAL CORPORATION
DTE ENERGY COMPANY
DUKE ENERGY CORP
DUPONT (E I DU PONT DE NEMOURS & CO)
EBAY INC
EDISON INTERNATIONAL
EDWARDS LIFESCIENCES CORP
EMERITUS CORP
ENTERGY CORP
ENTERPRISE HOLDINGS INC
ERNST & YOUNG LLP
ESTEE LAUDER COMPANIES INC (THE)
EXELON CORPORATION
EXPEDIA INC
EXPERIAN AMERICAS
EXPRESS SCRIPTS INC
EXXON MOBIL CORPORATION
(EXXONMOBIL)
EXXONMOBIL CHEMICAL
FACTSET RESEARCH SYSTEMS INC
FAIRVIEW HEALTH SERVICES
FAMILY DOLLAR STORES INC
FEDEX CORPORATION
FIDELITY NATIONAL INFORMATION SERVICES INC
FIRST ADVANTAGE CORPORATION
FIRSTENERGY CORP
FLUOR CORP
FMR CORP (FIDELITY INVESTMENTS)
FORD MOTOR CO
FOREST LABORATORIES INC
FORTUNE BRANDS INC
FOSSIL INC
FOX ENTERTAINMENT GROUP INC
FRONTIER COMMUNICATIONS CORPORATION
FTI CONSULTING INC
GAMESTOP CORP
GENENTECH INC
GENERAL ELECTRIC CO (GE)
GENERAL MILLS INC
GENERAL MOTORS COMPANY (GM)
GENESCO INC
GENWORTH FINANCIAL INC
GENZYME BIOSURGERY
GOOGLE INC
GRANT THORNTON LLP
GROUP 1 AUTOMOTIVE INC
GUESS? INC
HALLIBURTON COMPANY
HANESBRANDS INC
HARRIS CORPORATION
HAWAIIAN ELECTRIC INDUSTRIES INC
HCA HOLDINGS INC
HE BUTT GROCERY COMPANY (HEB)
HEALTH CARE SERVICE CORPORATION (HCSC)
HEALTH FITNESS CORP
HEALTH MANAGEMENT ASSOCIATES INC
HEARTLAND PAYMENT SYSTEMS INC
HENRY SCHEIN INC
HERSHEY CO
HERTZ GLOBAL HOLDINGS INC
HIBBETT SPORTS INC
HILLENBRAND INC
HILTON HOTELS CORP
HONDA OF AMERICA MANUFACTURING INC
HUMANA INC
HYATT HOTELS CORPORATION
IAC/INTERACTIVECORP
ICF INTERNATIONAL INC
IGATE CORPORATION
IMS HEALTH INC
INGRAM MICRO INC
INTEL CORP
INTERNATIONAL BUSINESS MACHINES CORP (IBM)
INTERPUBLIC GROUP OF COMPANIES INC
INTUIT INC
INVENTIV HEALTH INC
JACKSON NATIONAL LIFE INSURANCE COMPANY
JARDEN CORP
JETBLUE AIRWAYS CORPORATION
JM SMUCKER CO
JOHNSON & JOHNSON
JOHNSON CONTROLS INC
JUNIPER NETWORKS INC
KAISER PERMANENTE
KEANE INC
KELLOGG COMPANY
KELLY SERVICES INC
KIMBERLY-CLARK CORP
KINDRED HEALTHCARE INC
KINETIC CONCEPTS INC
KOCH INDUSTRIES INC
KOHL'S CORP
KPMG LLP
KRAFT FOODS INC
KROGER CO (THE)
LABORATORY CORP OF AMERICA HOLDINGS
LAS VEGAS SANDS CORP (THE VENETIAN)
LEAP WIRELESS INTERNATIONAL INC
LEAR CORP
LEXMARK INTERNATIONAL INC
LIBERTY GLOBAL INC
LIBERTY MUTUAL GROUP INC
LIMITED BRANDS INC
LINCARE HOLDINGS INC
LINCOLN NATIONAL CORPORATION
LOEWS CORPORATION

MACY'S INC	PATTERSON COMPANIES INC	SODEXO INC
MANPOWER INC	PENSKE AUTOMOTIVE GROUP INC	SOUTHERN COMPANY (THE)
MARRIOTT INTERNATIONAL INC	PEPSICO INC	SOUTHWEST AIRLINES CO
MARS INC	PETCO ANIMAL SUPPLIES INC	SPECTRUM HEALTH
MARSH & MCLENNAN COMPANIES INC	PETSMART INC	SRA INTERNATIONAL INC
MARY KAY INC	PG&E CORPORATION	ST JUDE MEDICAL INC
MASSACHUSETTS MUTUAL LIFE INSURANCE CO	PHILIP MORRIS INTERNATIONAL INC	STANLEY BLACK & DECKER INC
MATTEL INC	POLO RALPH LAUREN CORP	STARWOOD HOTELS & RESORTS WORLDWIDE INC
MAXIMUS INC	PRICESMART INC	STIFEL FINANCIAL CORP
MAYO FOUNDATION FOR MEDICAL EDUCATION AND RESEARCH	PRICEWATERHOUSECOOPERS	STREAM GLOBAL SERVICES INC
MCDONALD'S CORP	PRINCIPAL FINANCIAL GROUP (THE)	STRYKER CORP
MCKESSON CORPORATION	PROCTER & GAMBLE CO	SUN HEALTHCARE GROUP INC
MCKINSEY & COMPANY INC	PROGRESSIVE CORPORATION (THE)	SUTTER HEALTH INC
MEDCO HEALTH SOLUTIONS INC	PROVIDENCE HEALTH & SERVICES	SYMANTEC CORP
MEDIACOM COMMUNICATIONS CORP	PRUDENTIAL FINANCIAL INC	SYNTEL INC
MEDTRONIC INC	PUBLIX SUPER MARKETS INC	SYSCO CORP
MEIJER INC	QUALCOMM INC	TARGET CORPORATION
MERCER INC	RACKSPACE HOSTING INC	TECH DATA CORP
METHODIST HEALTH CARE SYSTEM	RALCORP HOLDINGS INC	TELEPHONE AND DATA SYSTEMS INC (TDS)
METLIFE INC	RECREATIONAL EQUIPMENT INC (REI)	TETRA TECH INC
METROPCS COMMUNICATIONS INC	REGIS CORPORATION	THOMSON REUTERS
MICROSOFT CORP	REPUBLIC AIRWAYS HOLDINGS INC	THOR INDUSTRIES INC
MIDAMERICAN ENERGY HOLDINGS CO	RESMED INC	TIFFANY & CO
MONRO MUFFLER BRAKE INC	ROBERT HALF INTERNATIONAL INC	TIME WARNER INC
MUTUAL OF OMAHA COMPANIES (THE)	ROSS STORES INC	TJX COMPANIES INC (THE)
NCR CORPORATION	ROYAL CARIBBEAN CRUISES LTD	TOTAL SYSTEM SERVICES INC (TSYS)
NETAPP INC	SABRE HOLDINGS CORP	TOWERS WATSON & CO
NEW YORK LIFE INSURANCE CO	SAFECO INSURANCE COMPANY OF AMERICA	TRAVELERS COMPANIES INC (THE)
NEWS CORP	SAFEWAY INC	TRUSTMARK COMPANIES
NEXTERA ENERGY INC	SAIC INC	TW TELECOM INC
NII HOLDINGS INC	SAM'S CLUB	UNDER ARMOUR INC
NIKE INC	SAPIENT CORPORATION	UNITED NATURAL FOODS INC
NORFOLK SOUTHERN CORP	SARA LEE CORP	UNITED PARCEL SERVICE INC (UPS)
NORTHWESTERN MUTUAL LIFE INSURANCE CO	SAS INSTITUTE INC	UNITED STATES CELLULAR CORP
ODYSSEY HEALTHCARE INC	SCANA CORPORATION	UNITED TECHNOLOGIES CORPORATION
OMNICOM GROUP INC	SCHLUMBERGER LIMITED	UNITEDHEALTH GROUP INC
ORACLE CORP	SCOTTS MIRACLE GROW CO	UNIVISION COMMUNICATIONS INC
O'REILLY AUTOMOTIVE INC	SEACOR HOLDINGS INC	URS CORPORATION
OSHKOSH CORPORATION	SELECT MEDICAL HOLDINGS CORPORATION	USAA
OWENS & MINOR INC	SEMPRA ENERGY	VALASSIS COMMUNICATIONS INC
PANERA BREAD CO	SENECA FOODS CORPORATION	VALSPAR CORPORATION (THE)
PARAMETRIC TECHNOLOGY CORP	SENSIENT TECHNOLOGIES CORPORATION	VARIAN MEDICAL SYSTEMS INC
PAREXEL INTERNATIONAL CORP	SHELL OIL CO	VCA ANTECH INC
PARSONS BRINCKERHOFF INC	SHERWIN WILLIAMS COMPANY (THE)	VERIZON COMMUNICATIONS INC
		VICTORIAS SECRET
		VISA INC

WALGREEN CO
WAL-MART STORES INC
WALT DISNEY COMPANY (THE)
WARNACO GROUP INC (THE)
WASTE MANAGEMENT INC
WATSON PHARMACEUTICALS INC
WEIGHT WATCHERS INTERNATIONAL INC
WHOLE FOODS MARKET INC
WINDSTREAM CORPORATION
WM WRIGLEY JR COMPANY
WW GRAINGER INC
WYNDHAM WORLDWIDE
WYNN RESORTS LIMITED
XEROX CORP
YUM! BRANDS INC
ZIMMER HOLDINGS INC

Graphic Arts/Photography
3M COMPANY
7-ELEVEN INC
ACADEMY SPORTS & OUTDOORS LTD
ACCENTURE PLC
ACTIVISION BLIZZARD INC
ADOBE SYSTEMS INC
ADVANCE AUTO PARTS INC
ADVANCED MICRO DEVICES INC (AMD)
AECOM TECHNOLOGY CORPORATION
AES CORPORATION (THE)
AFFILIATED COMPUTER SERVICES INC
AFLAC INC
AGILENT TECHNOLOGIES INC
ALASKA AIR GROUP INC
ALLERGAN INC
ALLIANCE DATA SYSTEMS CORPORATION
ALTRIA GROUP INC
AMAZON.COM INC
AMEDISYS INC
AMERICAN EXPRESS CO
AMERICAN POWER CONVERSION (APC)
AMERISOURCEBERGEN CORP
AMGEN INC
AMR CORP (AMERICAN AIRLINES)
ANALOG DEVICES INC
APPLE INC
ARAMARK CORPORATION
ARCHER DANIELS MIDLAND CO
ARROW ELECTRONICS INC
ARTHUR J GALLAGHER & CO
ASCENA RETAIL GROUP INC
ASCENSION HEALTH
AT&T INC
AUTOMATIC DATA PROCESSING INC
AUTONATION INC
AUTOZONE INC
AVNET INC
AVON PRODUCTS INC
AXA FINANCIAL INC
BAIN & COMPANY INC
BAKER HUGHES INC
BASS PRO SHOPS INC
BAUSCH & LOMB INC
BECHTEL GROUP INC
BECKMAN COULTER INC
BECTON DICKINSON & CO
BED BATH & BEYOND INC
BERKSHIRE HATHAWAY INC
BEST BUY CO INC
BIG 5 SPORTING GOODS CORPORATION
BIO RAD LABORATORIES INC
BLOOMBERG LP
BOEING COMPANY (THE)
BOOZ ALLEN HAMILTON INC
BOSTON CONSULTING GROUP INC (THE, BCG)
BOYD GAMING CORP
BRINKS COMPANY (THE)
BROADCOM CORP
BROWN & BROWN INC
BUCKLE INC (THE)
BUFFALO WILD WINGS INC
BUNGE LTD
CABLEVISION SYSTEMS CORP
CACI INTERNATIONAL INC
CAESARS ENTERTAINMENT CORPORATION
CAMERON INTERNATIONAL CORPORATION
CAMPBELL SOUP CO
CAPITAL SENIOR LIVING CORP
CARMAX GROUP
CARNIVAL CORPORATION
CASH AMERICA INTERNATIONAL INC
CATERPILLAR INC
CATHOLIC HEALTH INITIATIVES
CDW CORPORATION
CELGENE CORP
CELLCO PARTNERSHIP (VERIZON WIRELESS)
CEPHALON INC
CERNER CORP
CHEMED CORPORATION
CHEVRON CORPORATION
CHICO'S FAS INC
CHIPOTLE MEXICAN GRILL INC
CHS INC
CHUBB CORPORATION (THE)
CIGNA CORP
CINTAS CORP
CISCO SYSTEMS INC
CLEARWIRE CORP
CLOROX CO (THE)
COACH INC
COCA-COLA COMPANY (THE)
COGNIZANT TECHNOLOGY SOLUTIONS CORP
COLDWATER CREEK INC
COLGATE PALMOLIVE CO
COMCAST CORP
COMMUNITY HEALTH SYSTEMS INC
CONAGRA FOODS INC
CONOCOPHILLIPS COMPANY
CONTAINER STORE (THE)
COOPER COMPANIES INC
COSTCO WHOLESALE CORP
COVANCE INC
COX COMMUNICATIONS INC
CR BARD INC
CRACKER BARREL OLD COUNTRY STORE INC
CUMMINS INC
CVS CAREMARK CORPORATION
DANAHER CORP
DARDEN RESTAURANTS INC
DEAN FOODS CO
DEERE & CO
DELOITTE & TOUCHE USA LLP
DELOITTE CONSULTING LLP
DELTA APPAREL INC
DENTSPLY INTERNATIONAL INC
DEVRY INC
DICK'S SPORTING GOODS INC
DIRECTV
DOLLAR GENERAL CORPORATION
DTE ENERGY COMPANY

DUKE ENERGY CORP
EATON CORP
EBAY INC
EDISON INTERNATIONAL
EMC CORP
EMERITUS CORP
EMERSON ELECTRIC CO
ENTERGY CORP
ENTERPRISE HOLDINGS INC
ERNST & YOUNG LLP
ESTEE LAUDER COMPANIES INC (THE)
EXELON CORPORATION
EXPEDIA INC
EXPERIAN AMERICAS
EXPRESS SCRIPTS INC
EXXON MOBIL CORPORATION (EXXONMOBIL)
FACTSET RESEARCH SYSTEMS INC
FAMILY DOLLAR STORES INC
FEDEX CORPORATION
FIRST ADVANTAGE CORPORATION
FIRSTENERGY CORP
FLUOR CORP
FMC TECHNOLOGIES INC
FMR CORP (FIDELITY INVESTMENTS)
FOREST LABORATORIES INC
FORTUNE BRANDS INC
FOSSIL INC
FOX ENTERTAINMENT GROUP INC
FRONTIER COMMUNICATIONS CORPORATION
FTI CONSULTING INC
GAMESTOP CORP
GENENTECH INC
GENERAL ELECTRIC CO (GE)
GENERAL MILLS INC
GENERAL MOTORS COMPANY (GM)
GENESCO INC
GENWORTH FINANCIAL INC
GILEAD SCIENCES INC
GOOGLE INC
GRANT THORNTON LLP
GROUP 1 AUTOMOTIVE INC
GUESS? INC
HALLIBURTON COMPANY
HARRIS CORPORATION
HAWAIIAN ELECTRIC INDUSTRIES INC
HCA HOLDINGS INC

HE BUTT GROCERY COMPANY (HEB)
HEALTH CARE SERVICE CORPORATION (HCSC)
HEALTH FITNESS CORP
HEALTH MANAGEMENT ASSOCIATES INC
HEARTLAND PAYMENT SYSTEMS INC
HENRY SCHEIN INC
HERSHEY CO
HERTZ GLOBAL HOLDINGS INC
HIBBETT SPORTS INC
HILTON HOTELS CORP
HOSPIRA INC
HUMANA INC
HYATT HOTELS CORPORATION
IAC/INTERACTIVECORP
IGATE CORPORATION
ILLINOIS TOOL WORKS INC
IMS HEALTH INC
INGRAM MICRO INC
INTEL CORP
INTERNATIONAL BUSINESS MACHINES CORP (IBM)
INTERPUBLIC GROUP OF COMPANIES INC
INTUIT INC
INVENTIV HEALTH INC
JARDEN CORP
JETBLUE AIRWAYS CORPORATION
JM SMUCKER CO
JOHNSON & JOHNSON
JOHNSON CONTROLS INC
JUNIPER NETWORKS INC
KAISER PERMANENTE
KEANE INC
KELLOGG COMPANY
KELLY SERVICES INC
KIMBERLY-CLARK CORP
KINDRED HEALTHCARE INC
KINETIC CONCEPTS INC
KOCH INDUSTRIES INC
KOHL'S CORP
KPMG LLP
KRAFT FOODS INC
KROGER CO (THE)
LABORATORY CORP OF AMERICA HOLDINGS
LAS VEGAS SANDS CORP (THE VENETIAN)
LEAP WIRELESS INTERNATIONAL

INC
LEAR CORP
LEXMARK INTERNATIONAL INC
LIBERTY GLOBAL INC
LIBERTY MEDIA CORP
LIBERTY MUTUAL GROUP INC
LIFE TECHNOLOGIES CORP
LIMITED BRANDS INC
LINCARE HOLDINGS INC
LINCOLN NATIONAL CORPORATION
LOEWS CORPORATION
MACY'S INC
MANPOWER INC
MARRIOTT INTERNATIONAL INC
MARS INC
MARSH & MCLENNAN COMPANIES INC
MARY KAY INC
MATTEL INC
MAYO FOUNDATION FOR MEDICAL EDUCATION AND RESEARCH
MCDONALD'S CORP
MCKESSON CORPORATION
MCKINSEY & COMPANY INC
MEDCO HEALTH SOLUTIONS INC
MEDIACOM COMMUNICATIONS CORP
MEDTRONIC INC
MEIJER INC
MERCER INC
METHODIST HEALTH CARE SYSTEM
METLIFE INC
METROPCS COMMUNICATIONS INC
MICROCHIP TECHNOLOGY INC
MICRON TECHNOLOGY INC
MICROSOFT CORP
MIDAMERICAN ENERGY HOLDINGS CO
MILLIPORE CORP
MONRO MUFFLER BRAKE INC
NCR CORPORATION
NEWS CORP
NEXTERA ENERGY INC
NII HOLDINGS INC
NIKE INC
ODYSSEY HEALTHCARE INC
OMNICOM GROUP INC
ORACLE CORP
O'REILLY AUTOMOTIVE INC
OSHKOSH CORPORATION

OWENS & MINOR INC
PACCAR INC
PANERA BREAD CO
PAREXEL INTERNATIONAL CORP
PARSONS BRINCKERHOFF INC
PATTERSON COMPANIES INC
PEPSICO INC
PETCO ANIMAL SUPPLIES INC
PETSMART INC
PG&E CORPORATION
PHARMACEUTICAL PRODUCT DEVELOPMENT INC
PHILIP MORRIS INTERNATIONAL INC
PLEXUS CORP
POLO RALPH LAUREN CORP
PRICESMART INC
PRICEWATERHOUSECOOPERS
PRINCIPAL FINANCIAL GROUP (THE)
PROCTER & GAMBLE CO
PROGRESSIVE CORPORATION (THE)
PRUDENTIAL FINANCIAL INC
PUBLIX SUPER MARKETS INC
QUALCOMM INC
RALCORP HOLDINGS INC
RECREATIONAL EQUIPMENT INC (REI)
REGIS CORPORATION
ROBERT HALF INTERNATIONAL INC
ROSS STORES INC
ROYAL CARIBBEAN CRUISES LTD
SABRE HOLDINGS CORP
SAFECO INSURANCE COMPANY OF AMERICA
SAFEWAY INC
SAIC INC
SAM'S CLUB
SANMINA-SCI CORPORATION
SAPIENT CORPORATION
SARA LEE CORP
SAS INSTITUTE INC
SCANA CORPORATION
SCHLUMBERGER LIMITED
SCOTTS MIRACLE GROW CO
SELECT MEDICAL HOLDINGS CORPORATION
SEMPRA ENERGY
SENECA FOODS CORPORATION
SENSIENT TECHNOLOGIES CORPORATION
SHAW GROUP INC (THE)
SHELL OIL CO
SHERWIN WILLIAMS COMPANY (THE)
SOUTHERN COMPANY (THE)
SOUTHWEST AIRLINES CO
SRA INTERNATIONAL INC
ST JUDE MEDICAL INC
STANLEY BLACK & DECKER INC
STARWOOD HOTELS & RESORTS WORLDWIDE INC
STRYKER CORP
SUN HEALTHCARE GROUP INC
SYMANTEC CORP
SYNTEL INC
SYSCO CORP
TARGET CORPORATION
TECH DATA CORP
TEKTRONIX INC
TELEDYNE TECHNOLOGIES INC
TELEPHONE AND DATA SYSTEMS INC (TDS)
TETRA TECH INC
THERMO FISHER SCIENTIFIC INC
THOMSON REUTERS
THOR INDUSTRIES INC
TIFFANY & CO
TIME WARNER INC
TJX COMPANIES INC (THE)
TOTAL SYSTEM SERVICES INC (TSYS)
TOWERS WATSON & CO
TRAVELERS COMPANIES INC (THE)
TREEHOUSE FOODS INC
TW TELECOM INC
UNDER ARMOUR INC
UNITED NATURAL FOODS INC
UNITED PARCEL SERVICE INC (UPS)
UNITED STATES CELLULAR CORP
UNITED TECHNOLOGIES CORPORATION
UNITEDHEALTH GROUP INC
UNIVISION COMMUNICATIONS INC
URS CORPORATION
USAA
VALASSIS COMMUNICATIONS INC
VALSPAR CORPORATION (THE)
VARIAN MEDICAL SYSTEMS INC
VCA ANTECH INC
VERIZON COMMUNICATIONS INC
VICTORIAS SECRET
VISA INC
WABTEC CORP
WALGREEN CO
WAL-MART STORES INC
WALT DISNEY COMPANY (THE)
WARNACO GROUP INC (THE)
WASTE MANAGEMENT INC
WATERS CORP
WATSON PHARMACEUTICALS INC
WEIGHT WATCHERS INTERNATIONAL INC
WEST PHARMACEUTICAL SERVICES INC
WESTERN DIGITAL CORP
WHOLE FOODS MARKET INC
WM WRIGLEY JR COMPANY
WW GRAINGER INC
WYNDHAM WORLDWIDE
WYNN RESORTS LIMITED
XEROX CORP
YUM! BRANDS INC
ZIMMER HOLDINGS INC

Music
ACTIVISION BLIZZARD INC
APPLE INC
CAESARS ENTERTAINMENT CORPORATION
CARNIVAL CORPORATION
FOX ENTERTAINMENT GROUP INC
INTERPUBLIC GROUP OF COMPANIES INC
LAS VEGAS SANDS CORP (THE VENETIAN)
MICROSOFT CORP
NEWS CORP
ROYAL CARIBBEAN CRUISES LTD
TIME WARNER INC
UNIVISION COMMUNICATIONS INC
WALT DISNEY COMPANY (THE)
WYNN RESORTS LIMITED

Other
3M COMPANY
7-ELEVEN INC
ACADEMY SPORTS & OUTDOORS LTD
ACCENTURE PLC
ACTIVISION BLIZZARD INC
ADOBE SYSTEMS INC

ADVENTIST HEALTH SYSTEM
AFFILIATED COMPUTER SERVICES INC
AFLAC INC
ALASKA AIR GROUP INC
AMAZON.COM INC
AMERICAN EXPRESS CO
AMERIGROUP CORPORATION
AMR CORP (AMERICAN AIRLINES)
APPLE INC
ASCENA RETAIL GROUP INC
ASCENSION HEALTH
AT&T INC
AVON PRODUCTS INC
AXA FINANCIAL INC
BAIN & COMPANY INC
BARRETT BUSINESS SERVICES
BERKSHIRE HATHAWAY INC
BEST BUY CO INC
BIG 5 SPORTING GOODS CORPORATION
BLOOMBERG LP
BOEING COMPANY (THE)
BOOZ ALLEN HAMILTON INC
BOSTON CONSULTING GROUP INC (THE, BCG)
BROWN & BROWN INC
BUCKLE INC (THE)
BUFFALO WILD WINGS INC
CABLEVISION SYSTEMS CORP
CAESARS ENTERTAINMENT CORPORATION
CAPITAL SENIOR LIVING CORP
CARLSON COMPANIES INC
CARNIVAL CORPORATION
CATHOLIC HEALTH INITIATIVES
CELLCO PARTNERSHIP (VERIZON WIRELESS)
CHEMED CORPORATION
CHICO'S FAS INC
CHIPOTLE MEXICAN GRILL INC
CHUBB CORPORATION (THE)
CIGNA CORP
CLEARWIRE CORP
COACH INC
COCA-COLA COMPANY (THE)
COGNIZANT TECHNOLOGY SOLUTIONS CORP
COLDWATER CREEK INC
COLGATE PALMOLIVE CO
COMCAST CORP

COMMUNITY HEALTH SYSTEMS INC
CONTAINER STORE (THE)
COSTCO WHOLESALE CORP
COX COMMUNICATIONS INC
CRACKER BARREL OLD COUNTRY STORE INC
CVS CAREMARK CORPORATION
DARDEN RESTAURANTS INC
DELOITTE & TOUCHE USA LLP
DELOITTE CONSULTING LLP
DEVRY INC
DICK'S SPORTING GOODS INC
DIRECTV
DOLLAR GENERAL CORPORATION
EBAY INC
EMERITUS CORP
ENTERPRISE HOLDINGS INC
ERNST & YOUNG LLP
ESTEE LAUDER COMPANIES INC (THE)
EXPEDIA INC
EXPERIAN AMERICAS
FAMILY DOLLAR STORES INC
FEDEX CORPORATION
FOSSIL INC
FOX ENTERTAINMENT GROUP INC
FTI CONSULTING INC
GAMESTOP CORP
GENERAL ELECTRIC CO (GE)
GENESCO INC
GENWORTH FINANCIAL INC
GOOGLE INC
GRANT THORNTON LLP
GSI COMMERCE INC
GUESS? INC
HCA HOLDINGS INC
HE BUTT GROCERY COMPANY (HEB)
HEALTH CARE SERVICE CORPORATION (HCSC)
HEALTH FITNESS CORP
HEALTH MANAGEMENT ASSOCIATES INC
HERTZ GLOBAL HOLDINGS INC
HILTON HOTELS CORP
HOSPIRA INC
HUMANA INC
HYATT HOTELS CORPORATION
IAC/INTERACTIVECORP
IMS HEALTH INC
INTEL CORP

INTERNATIONAL BUSINESS MACHINES CORP (IBM)
INTERPUBLIC GROUP OF COMPANIES INC
INVENTIV HEALTH INC
JACKSON NATIONAL LIFE INSURANCE COMPANY
JETBLUE AIRWAYS CORPORATION
KAISER PERMANENTE
KEANE INC
KELLY SERVICES INC
KIMBERLY-CLARK CORP
KINDRED HEALTHCARE INC
KOHL'S CORP
KPMG LLP
KROGER CO (THE)
LAS VEGAS SANDS CORP (THE VENETIAN)
LEAP WIRELESS INTERNATIONAL INC
LIBERTY MEDIA CORP
LIBERTY MUTUAL GROUP INC
LIMITED BRANDS INC
LINCOLN NATIONAL CORPORATION
LOEWS CORPORATION
MACY'S INC
MANPOWER INC
MARRIOTT INTERNATIONAL INC
MARSH & MCLENNAN COMPANIES INC
MARY KAY INC
MATTEL INC
MAYO FOUNDATION FOR MEDICAL EDUCATION AND RESEARCH
MCDONALD'S CORP
MCKINSEY & COMPANY INC
MEIJER INC
MERCER INC
METHODIST HEALTH CARE SYSTEM
METLIFE INC
METROPCS COMMUNICATIONS INC
MICROSOFT CORP
MUTUAL OF OMAHA COMPANIES (THE)
NEWS CORP
NIKE INC
NORTH HIGHLAND
ODYSSEY HEALTHCARE INC
ORACLE CORP
PEPSICO INC
PETCO ANIMAL SUPPLIES INC

PETSMART INC
POLO RALPH LAUREN CORP
PRICESMART INC
PRICEWATERHOUSECOOPERS
PRINCIPAL FINANCIAL GROUP (THE)
PROCTER & GAMBLE CO
PROGRESSIVE CORPORATION (THE)
PROVIDENCE HEALTH & SERVICES
PRUDENTIAL FINANCIAL INC
PUBLIX SUPER MARKETS INC
RED HAT INC
ROBERT HALF INTERNATIONAL INC
ROSS STORES INC
ROYAL CARIBBEAN CRUISES LTD
SABRE HOLDINGS CORP
SAFECO INSURANCE COMPANY OF AMERICA
SAFEWAY INC
SAIC INC
SAM'S CLUB
SAPIENT CORPORATION
SAS INSTITUTE INC
SELECT MEDICAL HOLDINGS CORPORATION
SOUTHWEST AIRLINES CO
SPECTRUM HEALTH
SRA INTERNATIONAL INC
STANLEY BLACK & DECKER INC
STARWOOD HOTELS & RESORTS WORLDWIDE INC
SUN HEALTHCARE GROUP INC
SUTTER HEALTH INC
SYNTEL INC
TARGET CORPORATION
THOMSON REUTERS
TIBCO SOFTWARE INC
TIFFANY & CO
TIME WARNER INC
TJX COMPANIES INC (THE)
TOWERS WATSON & CO
TRAVELERS COMPANIES INC (THE)
TRUSTMARK COMPANIES
UNITED PARCEL SERVICE INC (UPS)
UNITEDHEALTH GROUP INC
UNIVISION COMMUNICATIONS INC
USAA
VERIZON COMMUNICATIONS INC
VICTORIAS SECRET
VISA INC
WALGREEN CO
WAL-MART STORES INC
WALT DISNEY COMPANY (THE)
WARNACO GROUP INC (THE)
WEIGHT WATCHERS INTERNATIONAL INC
WHOLE FOODS MARKET INC
WINDSTREAM CORPORATION
WYNDHAM WORLDWIDE
WYNN RESORTS LIMITED
YUM! BRANDS INC

Technical Writing
3M COMPANY
ACCENTURE PLC
ACOSTA SALES & MARKETING
ACTIVISION BLIZZARD INC
ADOBE SYSTEMS INC
ADVANCED MICRO DEVICES INC (AMD)
ADVENTIST HEALTH SYSTEM
AECOM TECHNOLOGY CORPORATION
AES CORPORATION (THE)
AFFILIATED COMPUTER SERVICES INC
AFLAC INC
AGILENT TECHNOLOGIES INC
AIR PRODUCTS & CHEMICALS INC
ALASKA AIR GROUP INC
ALLERGAN INC
AMAZON.COM INC
AMEDISYS INC
AMERICAN POWER CONVERSION (APC)
AMERIGROUP CORPORATION
AMERISOURCEBERGEN CORP
AMGEN INC
AMKOR TECHNOLOGY INC
AMPHENOL CORPORATION
AMR CORP (AMERICAN AIRLINES)
AMSURG CORP
ANALOG DEVICES INC
APACHE CORP
APPLE INC
APPLIED MATERIALS INC
ARAMARK CORPORATION
ARCHER DANIELS MIDLAND CO
ARROW ELECTRONICS INC
ARTHUR J GALLAGHER & CO
ASCENSION HEALTH
AT&T INC
AUTOMATIC DATA PROCESSING INC
AVNET INC
BAIN & COMPANY INC
BAKER HUGHES INC
BASIC ENERGY SERVICES INC
BAUSCH & LOMB INC
BECHTEL GROUP INC
BECKMAN COULTER INC
BECTON DICKINSON & CO
BEMIS COMPANY INC
BERKSHIRE HATHAWAY INC
BIO RAD LABORATORIES INC
BIOGEN IDEC INC
BLOOMBERG LP
BMC SOFTWARE INC
BOEING COMPANY (THE)
BOOZ ALLEN HAMILTON INC
BOSTON CONSULTING GROUP INC (THE, BCG)
BROADCOM CORP
BROCADE COMMUNICATIONS SYSTEMS INC
BROWN & BROWN INC
BRUKER CORP
BURLINGTON NORTHERN SANTA FE LLC
CABLEVISION SYSTEMS CORP
CACI INTERNATIONAL INC
CADENCE DESIGN SYSTEMS INC
CAMERON INTERNATIONAL CORPORATION
CAPITAL SENIOR LIVING CORP
CARNIVAL CORPORATION
CATERPILLAR INC
CATHOLIC HEALTH INITIATIVES
CDW CORPORATION
CELGENE CORP
CELLCO PARTNERSHIP (VERIZON WIRELESS)
CEPHALON INC
CERNER CORP
CH ROBINSON WORLDWIDE INC
CHEMED CORPORATION
CHEVRON CORPORATION
CHEVRON PHILLIPS CHEMICAL COMPANY LLC
CHUBB CORPORATION (THE)
CIENA CORP
CIGNA CORP

CISCO SYSTEMS INC
CITRIX SYSTEMS INC
CLEARWIRE CORP
COCA-COLA COMPANY (THE)
COGNIZANT TECHNOLOGY SOLUTIONS CORP
COLGATE PALMOLIVE CO
COMCAST CORP
COMMUNITY HEALTH SYSTEMS INC
COMPUTER SCIENCES CORPORATION (CSC)
COMPUTER TASK GROUP INC
CONAGRA FOODS INC
CONCENTRA INC
CONOCOPHILLIPS COMPANY
CONSOL ENERGY INC
COOPER COMPANIES INC
COVANCE INC
COX COMMUNICATIONS INC
CR BARD INC
CSX CORP
CUMMINS INC
DANAHER CORP
DAVITA INC
DEERE & CO
DELOITTE & TOUCHE USA LLP
DELOITTE CONSULTING LLP
DENTSPLY INTERNATIONAL INC
DIAMOND OFFSHORE DRILLING INC
DIODES INC
DIRECTV
DTE ENERGY COMPANY
DUKE ENERGY CORP
DUPONT (E I DU PONT DE NEMOURS & CO)
DUPONT AGRICULTURE & NUTRITION
EATON CORP
EBAY INC
EDISON INTERNATIONAL
EDWARDS LIFESCIENCES CORP
EMC CORP
EMERITUS CORP
EMERSON ELECTRIC CO
ENDO PHARMACEUTICALS HOLDINGS INC
ENTERGY CORP
ERNST & YOUNG LLP
ESTEE LAUDER COMPANIES INC (THE)
EXELON CORPORATION

EXPEDIA INC
EXPERIAN AMERICAS
EXPRESS SCRIPTS INC
EXTERRAN HOLDINGS INC
EXXON MOBIL CORPORATION (EXXONMOBIL)
EXXONMOBIL CHEMICAL
FAIRVIEW HEALTH SERVICES
FASTENAL
FEDERAL MOGUL CORP
FEDEX CORPORATION
FIDELITY NATIONAL INFORMATION SERVICES INC
FIRST ADVANTAGE CORPORATION
FIRSTENERGY CORP
FLUOR CORP
FMC TECHNOLOGIES INC
FORD MOTOR CO
FOREST LABORATORIES INC
FORTUNE BRANDS INC
FOSSIL INC
FRONTIER COMMUNICATIONS CORPORATION
FTI CONSULTING INC
GE ENERGY INFRASTRUCTURE
GENENTECH INC
GENERAL ELECTRIC CO (GE)
GENERAL MILLS INC
GENERAL MOTORS COMPANY (GM)
GENTEX CORPORATION
GENWORTH FINANCIAL INC
GENZYME BIOSURGERY
GEOKINETICS INC
GILEAD SCIENCES INC
GOOGLE INC
GRANT THORNTON LLP
GSI COMMERCE INC
HALLIBURTON COMPANY
HANGER ORTHOPEDIC GROUP INC
HARRIS CORPORATION
HAWAIIAN ELECTRIC INDUSTRIES INC
HCA HOLDINGS INC
HEALTH CARE SERVICE CORPORATION (HCSC)
HEALTH MANAGEMENT ASSOCIATES INC
HEARTLAND PAYMENT SYSTEMS INC
HENRY SCHEIN INC
HONDA OF AMERICA MANUFACTURING INC

HOSPIRA INC
HUMANA INC
ICF INTERNATIONAL INC
IDEXX LABORATORIES INC
IGATE CORPORATION
ILLINOIS TOOL WORKS INC
IMS HEALTH INC
INGRAM MICRO INC
INSITUFORM TECHNOLOGIES
INTEGRA LIFESCIENCES HOLDINGS CORP
INTEL CORP
INTERNATIONAL BUSINESS MACHINES CORP (IBM)
INTERPUBLIC GROUP OF COMPANIES INC
INTUIT INC
INVENTIV HEALTH INC
JACK HENRY & ASSOCIATES INC
JB HUNT TRANSPORT SERVICES INC
JETBLUE AIRWAYS CORPORATION
JOHNSON & JOHNSON
JOHNSON CONTROLS INC
JUNIPER NETWORKS INC
KAISER PERMANENTE
KEANE INC
KELLOGG COMPANY
KELLY SERVICES INC
KEY ENERGY SERVICES INC
KINDRED HEALTHCARE INC
KINETIC CONCEPTS INC
KLA TENCOR CORP
KOCH INDUSTRIES INC
KPMG LLP
KRAFT FOODS INC
LABORATORY CORP OF AMERICA HOLDINGS
LAM RESEARCH CORP
LEAR CORP
LEXMARK INTERNATIONAL INC
LIBERTY GLOBAL INC
LIBERTY MUTUAL GROUP INC
LIFE TECHNOLOGIES CORP
LINCARE HOLDINGS INC
LINCOLN NATIONAL CORPORATION
LKQ CORP
LOEWS CORPORATION
LUFKIN INDUSTRIES INC
MANPOWER INC
MANTECH INTERNATIONAL CORP

MARATHON OIL CORP
MARS INC
MARSH & MCLENNAN COMPANIES INC
MASSACHUSETTS MUTUAL LIFE INSURANCE CO
MATTEL INC
MAXIMUS INC
MAYO FOUNDATION FOR MEDICAL EDUCATION AND RESEARCH
MCKESSON CORPORATION
MCKINSEY & COMPANY INC
MEDCO HEALTH SOLUTIONS INC
MEDNAX INC
MEDTRONIC INC
MERCER INC
METHODIST HEALTH CARE SYSTEM
METLIFE INC
MICROCHIP TECHNOLOGY INC
MICRON TECHNOLOGY INC
MICROSOFT CORP
MIDAMERICAN ENERGY HOLDINGS CO
MILLIPORE CORP
MOLEX INC
MONRO MUFFLER BRAKE INC
MULTI-FINELINE ELECTRONIX INC
MYLAN INC
NALCO HOLDING COMPANY
NATIONAL INSTRUMENTS CORP
NATIONAL OILWELL VARCO INC
NCR CORPORATION
NETAPP INC
NEXTERA ENERGY INC
NII HOLDINGS INC
NORFOLK SOUTHERN CORP
NORTH HIGHLAND
NORTHWESTERN MUTUAL LIFE INSURANCE CO
OCEANEERING INTERNATIONAL INC
ODYSSEY HEALTHCARE INC
OIL STATES INTERNATIONAL INC
ORACLE CORP
OSHKOSH CORPORATION
OWENS & MINOR INC
PACCAR INC
PARAMETRIC TECHNOLOGY CORP
PAREXEL INTERNATIONAL CORP
PARK-OHIO HOLDINGS CORP
PARSONS BRINCKERHOFF INC
PATTERSON COMPANIES INC
PATTERSON-UTI ENERGY INC
PEABODY ENERGY CORP
PEPSICO INC
PERRIGO CO
PG&E CORPORATION
PHARMACEUTICAL PRODUCT DEVELOPMENT INC
PLEXUS CORP
POLYCOM INC
PRAXAIR INC
PRICEWATERHOUSECOOPERS
PRINCIPAL FINANCIAL GROUP (THE)
PROCTER & GAMBLE CO
PROGRESSIVE CORPORATION (THE)
PROVIDENCE HEALTH & SERVICES
PRUDENTIAL FINANCIAL INC
QUALCOMM INC
QUANTA SERVICES INC
RED HAT INC
RESMED INC
ROBERT HALF INTERNATIONAL INC
ROYAL CARIBBEAN CRUISES LTD
SABRE HOLDINGS CORP
SAFECO INSURANCE COMPANY OF AMERICA
SAIC INC
SALESFORCE.COM INC
SANDISK CORP
SANMINA-SCI CORPORATION
SAPIENT CORPORATION
SARA LEE CORP
SAS INSTITUTE INC
SCANA CORPORATION
SCHLUMBERGER LIMITED
SCOTTS MIRACLE GROW CO
SEACOR HOLDINGS INC
SELECT MEDICAL HOLDINGS CORPORATION
SEMPRA ENERGY
SENSIENT TECHNOLOGIES CORPORATION
SHAW GROUP INC (THE)
SHELL OIL CO
SHERWIN WILLIAMS COMPANY (THE)
SIGMA-ALDRICH CORP
SKILLED HEALTHCARE GROUP INC
SOUTHERN COMPANY (THE)
SOUTHWEST AIRLINES CO
SPECTRUM HEALTH
SPIRIT AEROSYSTEMS HOLDINGS INC
SRA INTERNATIONAL INC
ST JUDE MEDICAL INC
STANLEY BLACK & DECKER INC
STERICYCLE INC
STONERIDGE INC
STREAM GLOBAL SERVICES INC
STRYKER CORP
SUN HEALTHCARE GROUP INC
SUTTER HEALTH INC
SYMANTEC CORP
SYNTEL INC
TEAM INC
TECH DATA CORP
TEKTRONIX INC
TELEDYNE TECHNOLOGIES INC
TELEPHONE AND DATA SYSTEMS INC (TDS)
TEREX CORPORATION
TETRA TECH INC
THERMO FISHER SCIENTIFIC INC
THOR INDUSTRIES INC
TIBCO SOFTWARE INC
TIME WARNER INC
TOWERS WATSON & CO
TRAVELERS COMPANIES INC (THE)
TTM TECHNOLOGIES INC
TW TELECOM INC
UNION PACIFIC CORP
UNITED PARCEL SERVICE INC (UPS)
UNITED STATES CELLULAR CORP
UNITED TECHNOLOGIES CORPORATION
UNITEDHEALTH GROUP INC
UNIVERSAL HEALTH SERVICES INC
URS CORPORATION
USAA
VALSPAR CORPORATION (THE)
VARIAN MEDICAL SYSTEMS INC
VCA ANTECH INC
VERIZON COMMUNICATIONS INC
WABTEC CORP
WASTE MANAGEMENT INC
WATERS CORP
WATSON PHARMACEUTICALS INC
WEST PHARMACEUTICAL SERVICES INC
WESTERN DIGITAL CORP

WILLIAMS COMPANIES INC (THE)
WINDSTREAM CORPORATION
WW GRAINGER INC
XEROX CORP
ZIMMER HOLDINGS INC

Management

Experienced Management
3M COMPANY
7-ELEVEN INC
ABM INDUSTRIES INC
ACADEMY SPORTS & OUTDOORS LTD
ACCENTURE PLC
ACOSTA SALES & MARKETING
ACTIVISION BLIZZARD INC
ADOBE SYSTEMS INC
ADVANCE AUTO PARTS INC
ADVANCED MICRO DEVICES INC (AMD)
ADVENTIST HEALTH SYSTEM
AECOM TECHNOLOGY CORPORATION
AES CORPORATION (THE)
AFFILIATED COMPUTER SERVICES INC
AFLAC INC
AGILENT TECHNOLOGIES INC
AIR PRODUCTS & CHEMICALS INC
ALASKA AIR GROUP INC
ALLERGAN INC
ALLIANCE DATA SYSTEMS CORPORATION
ALTRIA GROUP INC
AMAZON.COM INC
AMEDISYS INC
AMERCO
AMERICAN EXPRESS CO
AMERICAN POWER CONVERSION (APC)
AMERIGROUP CORPORATION
AMERISOURCEBERGEN CORP
AMGEN INC
AMR CORP (AMERICAN AIRLINES)
ANALOG DEVICES INC
APACHE CORP
APPLE INC
ARAMARK CORPORATION
ARCHER DANIELS MIDLAND CO
ARROW ELECTRONICS INC
ARTHUR J GALLAGHER & CO
ASCENA RETAIL GROUP INC
ASCENSION HEALTH
AT&T INC
AUTOMATIC DATA PROCESSING INC
AUTONATION INC
AUTOZONE INC
AVNET INC
AVON PRODUCTS INC
AXA FINANCIAL INC
BAIN & COMPANY INC
BAKER HUGHES INC
BALL CORP
BASS PRO SHOPS INC
BAUSCH & LOMB INC
BECHTEL GROUP INC
BECKMAN COULTER INC
BECTON DICKINSON & CO
BED BATH & BEYOND INC
BEMIS COMPANY INC
BERKSHIRE HATHAWAY INC
BEST BUY CO INC
BIG 5 SPORTING GOODS CORPORATION
BIO RAD LABORATORIES INC
BIOGEN IDEC INC
BLACKROCK INC
BLOOMBERG LP
BMC SOFTWARE INC
BOEING COMPANY (THE)
BOOZ ALLEN HAMILTON INC
BOSTON CONSULTING GROUP INC (THE, BCG)
BOYD GAMING CORP
BRINKS COMPANY (THE)
BROADCOM CORP
BROCADE COMMUNICATIONS SYSTEMS INC
BROOKDALE SENIOR LIVING INC
BROWN & BROWN INC
BUCKLE INC (THE)
BUFFALO WILD WINGS INC
BUNGE LTD
BURLINGTON NORTHERN SANTA FE LLC
CABLEVISION SYSTEMS CORP
CACI INTERNATIONAL INC
CAESARS ENTERTAINMENT CORPORATION
CAMERON INTERNATIONAL CORPORATION
CAMPBELL SOUP CO
CAPITAL SENIOR LIVING CORP
CARLSON COMPANIES INC
CARMAX GROUP
CARNIVAL CORPORATION
CASH AMERICA INTERNATIONAL INC
CATERPILLAR INC
CATHOLIC HEALTH INITIATIVES
CB RICHARD ELLIS GROUP INC (CBRE)
CDW CORPORATION
CELGENE CORP
CELLCO PARTNERSHIP (VERIZON WIRELESS)
CEPHALON INC
CERNER CORP
CH ROBINSON WORLDWIDE INC
CHEMED CORPORATION
CHEVRON CORPORATION
CHEVRON PHILLIPS CHEMICAL COMPANY LLC
CHICO'S FAS INC
CHIPOTLE MEXICAN GRILL INC
CHS INC
CHUBB CORPORATION (THE)
CIGNA CORP
CINTAS CORP
CISCO SYSTEMS INC
CITRIX SYSTEMS INC
CLEARWIRE CORP
CLOROX CO (THE)
CNA FINANCIAL CORP
COACH INC
COCA-COLA BOTTLING CO CONSOLIDATED
COCA-COLA COMPANY (THE)
COGNIZANT TECHNOLOGY SOLUTIONS CORP
COLDWATER CREEK INC
COLGATE PALMOLIVE CO
COMCAST CORP
COMMUNITY HEALTH SYSTEMS INC
COMPUTER SCIENCES CORPORATION (CSC)
COMPUTER TASK GROUP INC
CONAGRA FOODS INC
CONCENTRA INC
CONOCOPHILLIPS COMPANY
CONSOL ENERGY INC
CONTAINER STORE (THE)
COOPER COMPANIES INC

COSTCO WHOLESALE CORP
COVANCE INC
COX COMMUNICATIONS INC
CR BARD INC
CRACKER BARREL OLD COUNTRY STORE INC
CROCS INC
CSX CORP
CUMMINS INC
CVS CAREMARK CORPORATION
DANAHER CORP
DARDEN RESTAURANTS INC
DAVITA INC
DEAN FOODS CO
DEERE & CO
DELOITTE & TOUCHE USA LLP
DELOITTE CONSULTING LLP
DELTA APPAREL INC
DENTSPLY INTERNATIONAL INC
DEVRY INC
DIAMOND OFFSHORE DRILLING INC
DICK'S SPORTING GOODS INC
DIODES INC
DIRECTV
DOLLAR GENERAL CORPORATION
DTE ENERGY COMPANY
DUKE ENERGY CORP
DUPONT (E I DU PONT DE NEMOURS & CO)
EATON CORP
EBAY INC
EDISON INTERNATIONAL
EDWARDS LIFESCIENCES CORP
EMC CORP
EMERITUS CORP
EMERSON ELECTRIC CO
ENTERGY CORP
ENTERPRISE HOLDINGS INC
EQUITY LIFESTYLE PROPERTIES INC
ERNST & YOUNG LLP
ESTEE LAUDER COMPANIES INC (THE)
EXELON CORPORATION
EXPEDIA INC
EXPERIAN AMERICAS
EXPRESS SCRIPTS INC
EXXON MOBIL CORPORATION (EXXONMOBIL)
EXXONMOBIL CHEMICAL
FACTSET RESEARCH SYSTEMS INC

FAIRVIEW HEALTH SERVICES
FAMILY DOLLAR STORES INC
FEDEX CORPORATION
FIDELITY NATIONAL INFORMATION SERVICES INC
FINISAR CORPORATION
FIRST ADVANTAGE CORPORATION
FIRSTENERGY CORP
FLUOR CORP
FM GLOBAL
FMC TECHNOLOGIES INC
FMR CORP (FIDELITY INVESTMENTS)
FORD MOTOR CO
FOREST LABORATORIES INC
FORTUNE BRANDS INC
FOSSIL INC
FOX ENTERTAINMENT GROUP INC
FRONTIER COMMUNICATIONS CORPORATION
FTI CONSULTING INC
GAMESTOP CORP
GE ENERGY INFRASTRUCTURE
GENENTECH INC
GENERAL ELECTRIC CO (GE)
GENERAL MILLS INC
GENERAL MOTORS COMPANY (GM)
GENESCO INC
GENTIVA HEALTH SERVICES INC
GENWORTH FINANCIAL INC
GENZYME BIOSURGERY
GILEAD SCIENCES INC
GOODYEAR TIRE & RUBBER COMPANY (THE)
GOOGLE INC
GRANT THORNTON LLP
GROUP 1 AUTOMOTIVE INC
GROUPON INC
GUESS? INC
HALLIBURTON COMPANY
HANESBRANDS INC
HANGER ORTHOPEDIC GROUP INC
HARRIS CORPORATION
HAWAIIAN ELECTRIC INDUSTRIES INC
HCA HOLDINGS INC
HE BUTT GROCERY COMPANY (HEB)
HEALTH CARE SERVICE CORPORATION (HCSC)
HEALTH FITNESS CORP
HEALTH MANAGEMENT

ASSOCIATES INC
HEALTHSOUTH CORP
HEARTLAND PAYMENT SYSTEMS INC
HENRY SCHEIN INC
HERSHEY CO
HERTZ GLOBAL HOLDINGS INC
HIBBETT SPORTS INC
HILTON HOTELS CORP
HONDA OF AMERICA MANUFACTURING INC
HOSPIRA INC
HUMANA INC
HYATT HOTELS CORPORATION
IAC/INTERACTIVECORP
ICF INTERNATIONAL INC
IDEXX LABORATORIES INC
IGATE CORPORATION
ILLINOIS TOOL WORKS INC
IMS HEALTH INC
INGRAM MICRO INC
INSITUFORM TECHNOLOGIES
INTEGRA LIFESCIENCES HOLDINGS CORP
INTEL CORP
INTERNATIONAL BUSINESS MACHINES CORP (IBM)
INTERPUBLIC GROUP OF COMPANIES INC
INTUIT INC
INVENTIV HEALTH INC
JACK HENRY & ASSOCIATES INC
JARDEN CORP
JB HUNT TRANSPORT SERVICES INC
JETBLUE AIRWAYS CORPORATION
JM SMUCKER CO
JOHNSON & JOHNSON
JOHNSON CONTROLS INC
JONES LANG LASALLE INC
JUNIPER NETWORKS INC
KAISER PERMANENTE
KEANE INC
KELLOGG COMPANY
KELLY SERVICES INC
KIMBERLY-CLARK CORP
KINDRED HEALTHCARE INC
KINETIC CONCEPTS INC
KOCH INDUSTRIES INC
KOHL'S CORP
KPMG LLP

KRAFT FOODS INC
KROGER CO (THE)
LABORATORY CORP OF AMERICA HOLDINGS
LAS VEGAS SANDS CORP (THE VENETIAN)
LEAP WIRELESS INTERNATIONAL INC
LEAR CORP
LEXMARK INTERNATIONAL INC
LIBERTY GLOBAL INC
LIBERTY MEDIA CORP
LIBERTY MUTUAL GROUP INC
LIFE TECHNOLOGIES CORP
LIMITED BRANDS INC
LINCARE HOLDINGS INC
LINCOLN NATIONAL CORPORATION
LKQ CORP
LOEWS CORPORATION
LORAL SPACE & COMMUNICATIONS LTD
MACY'S INC
MANPOWER INC
MARATHON OIL CORP
MARRIOTT INTERNATIONAL INC
MARS INC
MARSH & MCLENNAN COMPANIES INC
MARY KAY INC
MASSACHUSETTS MUTUAL LIFE INSURANCE CO
MATTEL INC
MAXIMUS INC
MAYO FOUNDATION FOR MEDICAL EDUCATION AND RESEARCH
MCDONALD'S CORP
MCKESSON CORPORATION
MCKINSEY & COMPANY INC
MEDCO HEALTH SOLUTIONS INC
MEDIACOM COMMUNICATIONS CORP
MEDTRONIC INC
MEIJER INC
MERCER INC
METHODIST HEALTH CARE SYSTEM
METLIFE INC
METROPCS COMMUNICATIONS INC
MICROCHIP TECHNOLOGY INC
MICRON TECHNOLOGY INC
MICROSOFT CORP
MIDAMERICAN ENERGY HOLDINGS CO
MILLIPORE CORP
MOLEX INC
MONRO MUFFLER BRAKE INC
MULTI-FINELINE ELECTRONIX INC
MYLAN INC
NABORS INDUSTRIES LTD
NACCO INDUSTRIES INC
NATIONAL OILWELL VARCO INC
NCR CORPORATION
NETAPP INC
NEW YORK LIFE INSURANCE CO
NEWS CORP
NEXTERA ENERGY INC
NII HOLDINGS INC
NIKE INC
NORFOLK SOUTHERN CORP
NORTHWESTERN MUTUAL LIFE INSURANCE CO
OCEANEERING INTERNATIONAL INC
ODYSSEY HEALTHCARE INC
OIL STATES INTERNATIONAL INC
OMNICOM GROUP INC
ORACLE CORP
O'REILLY AUTOMOTIVE INC
OSHKOSH CORPORATION
OWENS & MINOR INC
PACCAR INC
PANERA BREAD CO
PARAMETRIC TECHNOLOGY CORP
PAREXEL INTERNATIONAL CORP
PARSONS BRINCKERHOFF INC
PATTERSON COMPANIES INC
PATTERSON-UTI ENERGY INC
PEABODY ENERGY CORP
PENSKE AUTOMOTIVE GROUP INC
PEPSICO INC
PERRIGO CO
PETCO ANIMAL SUPPLIES INC
PETSMART INC
PG&E CORPORATION
PHARMACEUTICAL PRODUCT DEVELOPMENT INC
PHILIP MORRIS INTERNATIONAL INC
PLEXUS CORP
POLO RALPH LAUREN CORP
PRAXAIR INC
PRICESMART INC
PRICEWATERHOUSECOOPERS
PRINCIPAL FINANCIAL GROUP (THE)
PROCTER & GAMBLE CO
PROGRESSIVE CORPORATION (THE)
PROVIDENCE HEALTH & SERVICES
PRUDENTIAL FINANCIAL INC
PUBLIX SUPER MARKETS INC
QUALCOMM INC
QUANTA SERVICES INC
RACKSPACE HOSTING INC
RALCORP HOLDINGS INC
RECREATIONAL EQUIPMENT INC (REI)
REGIS CORPORATION
REPUBLIC AIRWAYS HOLDINGS INC
ROBERT HALF INTERNATIONAL INC
ROSS STORES INC
ROWAN COMPANIES INC
ROYAL CARIBBEAN CRUISES LTD
RYDER SYSTEM INC
SABRE HOLDINGS CORP
SAFECO INSURANCE COMPANY OF AMERICA
SAFEWAY INC
SAIC INC
SALESFORCE.COM INC
SAM'S CLUB
SANDISK CORP
SANMINA-SCI CORPORATION
SAPIENT CORPORATION
SARA LEE CORP
SAS INSTITUTE INC
SCANA CORPORATION
SCHLUMBERGER LIMITED
SCOTTS MIRACLE GROW CO
SEACOR HOLDINGS INC
SELECT MEDICAL HOLDINGS CORPORATION
SEMPRA ENERGY
SENECA FOODS CORPORATION
SENSIENT TECHNOLOGIES CORPORATION
SHAW GROUP INC (THE)
SHELL OIL CO
SHERWIN WILLIAMS COMPANY (THE)
SIGMA-ALDRICH CORP
SNYDERS-LANCE INC
SODEXO INC
SOUTHERN COMPANY (THE)
SOUTHWEST AIRLINES CO

SPECTRUM HEALTH
SPIRIT AEROSYSTEMS HOLDINGS INC
SRA INTERNATIONAL INC
ST JUDE MEDICAL INC
STANLEY BLACK & DECKER INC
STARWOOD HOTELS & RESORTS WORLDWIDE INC
STIFEL FINANCIAL CORP
STREAM GLOBAL SERVICES INC
STRYKER CORP
SUN HEALTHCARE GROUP INC
SUTTER HEALTH INC
SYMANTEC CORP
SYNTEL INC
SYSCO CORP
TARGET CORPORATION
TEAM HEALTH HOLDINGS INC
TEAM INC
TECH DATA CORP
TEKTRONIX INC
TELEDYNE TECHNOLOGIES INC
TELEPHONE AND DATA SYSTEMS INC (TDS)
TENET HEALTHCARE CORPORATION
TETRA TECH INC
THERMO FISHER SCIENTIFIC INC
THOMSON REUTERS
THOR INDUSTRIES INC
TIFFANY & CO
TIME WARNER INC
TJX COMPANIES INC (THE)
TOTAL SYSTEM SERVICES INC (TSYS)
TOWERS WATSON & CO
TRAVELERS COMPANIES INC (THE)
TREEHOUSE FOODS INC
TW TELECOM INC
UNDER ARMOUR INC
UNION PACIFIC CORP
UNITED NATURAL FOODS INC
UNITED PARCEL SERVICE INC (UPS)
UNITED STATES CELLULAR CORP
UNITED TECHNOLOGIES CORPORATION
UNITEDHEALTH GROUP INC
UNIVERSAL HEALTH SERVICES INC
UNIVISION COMMUNICATIONS INC
URS CORPORATION
USAA
VALASSIS COMMUNICATIONS INC
VALSPAR CORPORATION (THE)
VARIAN MEDICAL SYSTEMS INC
VCA ANTECH INC
VERIZON COMMUNICATIONS INC
VICTORIAS SECRET
VISA INC
VORNADO REALTY TRUST
WABTEC CORP
WALGREEN CO
WAL-MART STORES INC
WALT DISNEY COMPANY (THE)
WARNACO GROUP INC (THE)
WASTE MANAGEMENT INC
WATERS CORP
WATSON PHARMACEUTICALS INC
WEIGHT WATCHERS INTERNATIONAL INC
WEST PHARMACEUTICAL SERVICES INC
WESTERN DIGITAL CORP
WHOLE FOODS MARKET INC
WILLIAMS COMPANIES INC (THE)
WM WRIGLEY JR COMPANY
WW GRAINGER INC
WYNDHAM WORLDWIDE
WYNN RESORTS LIMITED
XEROX CORP
YUM! BRANDS INC
ZIMMER HOLDINGS INC

International Business
3M COMPANY
7-ELEVEN INC
ABM INDUSTRIES INC
ACCENTURE PLC
ACOSTA SALES & MARKETING
ACTIVISION BLIZZARD INC
ADOBE SYSTEMS INC
ADVANCE AUTO PARTS INC
ADVANCED MICRO DEVICES INC (AMD)
AECOM TECHNOLOGY CORPORATION
AES CORPORATION (THE)
AFFILIATED COMPUTER SERVICES INC
AFLAC INC
AGILENT TECHNOLOGIES INC
AIR PRODUCTS & CHEMICALS INC
ALASKA AIR GROUP INC
ALLERGAN INC
ALLIANCE DATA SYSTEMS CORPORATION
ALTRIA GROUP INC
AMAZON.COM INC
AMERCO
AMERICAN EXPRESS CO
AMERICAN POWER CONVERSION (APC)
AMERISOURCEBERGEN CORP
AMGEN INC
AMKOR TECHNOLOGY INC
AMPHENOL CORPORATION
AMR CORP (AMERICAN AIRLINES)
ANALOG DEVICES INC
APACHE CORP
APPLE INC
APPLIED MATERIALS INC
ARAMARK CORPORATION
ARCHER DANIELS MIDLAND CO
ARROW ELECTRONICS INC
ARTHUR J GALLAGHER & CO
ASCENA RETAIL GROUP INC
AT&T INC
AUTOMATIC DATA PROCESSING INC
AUTOZONE INC
AVNET INC
AVON PRODUCTS INC
AXA FINANCIAL INC
BAIN & COMPANY INC
BAKER HUGHES INC
BALL CORP
BASS PRO SHOPS INC
BAUSCH & LOMB INC
BECHTEL GROUP INC
BECKMAN COULTER INC
BECTON DICKINSON & CO
BED BATH & BEYOND INC
BEMIS COMPANY INC
BERKSHIRE HATHAWAY INC
BEST BUY CO INC
BIO RAD LABORATORIES INC
BIOGEN IDEC INC
BLACKROCK INC
BLOOMBERG LP
BMC SOFTWARE INC
BOEING COMPANY (THE)
BOOZ ALLEN HAMILTON INC
BOSTON CONSULTING GROUP INC (THE, BCG)

BRINKS COMPANY (THE)
BROADCOM CORP
BROCADE COMMUNICATIONS SYSTEMS INC
BROWN & BROWN INC
BRUKER CORP
BUNGE LTD
BURLINGTON NORTHERN SANTA FE LLC
CACI INTERNATIONAL INC
CADENCE DESIGN SYSTEMS INC
CAESARS ENTERTAINMENT CORPORATION
CAMERON INTERNATIONAL CORPORATION
CAMPBELL SOUP CO
CARLSON COMPANIES INC
CARNIVAL CORPORATION
CASH AMERICA INTERNATIONAL INC
CATERPILLAR INC
CB RICHARD ELLIS GROUP INC (CBRE)
CDW CORPORATION
CELGENE CORP
CEPHALON INC
CERNER CORP
CH ROBINSON WORLDWIDE INC
CHEMED CORPORATION
CHEVRON CORPORATION
CHEVRON PHILLIPS CHEMICAL COMPANY LLC
CHICO'S FAS INC
CHIPOTLE MEXICAN GRILL INC
CHS INC
CHUBB CORPORATION (THE)
CIENA CORP
CIGNA CORP
CINTAS CORP
CISCO SYSTEMS INC
CITRIX SYSTEMS INC
CLEARWIRE CORP
CLOROX CO (THE)
CNA FINANCIAL CORP
COACH INC
COCA-COLA COMPANY (THE)
COGNIZANT TECHNOLOGY SOLUTIONS CORP
COLGATE PALMOLIVE CO
COMCAST CORP
COMPUTER SCIENCES CORPORATION (CSC)

COMPUTER TASK GROUP INC
CONAGRA FOODS INC
CONOCOPHILLIPS COMPANY
CONSOL ENERGY INC
CON-WAY INC
COOPER COMPANIES INC
COSTCO WHOLESALE CORP
COVANCE INC
COX COMMUNICATIONS INC
CR BARD INC
CROCS INC
CSX CORP
CUMMINS INC
CVS CAREMARK CORPORATION
DANAHER CORP
DARDEN RESTAURANTS INC
DEAN FOODS CO
DEERE & CO
DELOITTE & TOUCHE USA LLP
DELOITTE CONSULTING LLP
DELTA APPAREL INC
DENTSPLY INTERNATIONAL INC
DEVRY INC
DIAMOND OFFSHORE DRILLING INC
DIODES INC
DIRECTV
DUKE ENERGY CORP
DUPONT (E I DU PONT DE NEMOURS & CO)
DUPONT AGRICULTURE & NUTRITION
EATON CORP
EBAY INC
EDISON INTERNATIONAL
EDWARDS LIFESCIENCES CORP
EMC CORP
EMERITUS CORP
EMERSON ELECTRIC CO
ENTERGY CORP
ENTERPRISE HOLDINGS INC
EQUITY LIFESTYLE PROPERTIES INC
ERNST & YOUNG LLP
ESTEE LAUDER COMPANIES INC (THE)
EXPEDIA INC
EXPRESS SCRIPTS INC
EXTERRAN HOLDINGS INC
EXXON MOBIL CORPORATION (EXXONMOBIL)
EXXONMOBIL CHEMICAL

FACTSET RESEARCH SYSTEMS INC
FASTENAL
FEDERAL MOGUL CORP
FEDEX CORPORATION
FIDELITY NATIONAL INFORMATION SERVICES INC
FINISAR CORPORATION
FIRST ADVANTAGE CORPORATION
FLUOR CORP
FM GLOBAL
FMC TECHNOLOGIES INC
FMR CORP (FIDELITY INVESTMENTS)
FORD MOTOR CO
FOREST LABORATORIES INC
FORTUNE BRANDS INC
FOSSIL INC
FOX ENTERTAINMENT GROUP INC
FTI CONSULTING INC
GAMESTOP CORP
GE ENERGY INFRASTRUCTURE
GENENTECH INC
GENERAL ELECTRIC CO (GE)
GENERAL MILLS INC
GENERAL MOTORS COMPANY (GM)
GENESCO INC
GENTEX CORPORATION
GENWORTH FINANCIAL INC
GEOKINETICS INC
GILEAD SCIENCES INC
GOODYEAR TIRE & RUBBER COMPANY (THE)
GOOGLE INC
GROUP 1 AUTOMOTIVE INC
GROUPON INC
GSI COMMERCE INC
GUESS? INC
HALLIBURTON COMPANY
HANESBRANDS INC
HANGER ORTHOPEDIC GROUP INC
HARRIS CORPORATION
HCA HOLDINGS INC
HE BUTT GROCERY COMPANY (HEB)
HEALTH FITNESS CORP
HEALTHSOUTH CORP
HENRY SCHEIN INC
HERSHEY CO
HERTZ GLOBAL HOLDINGS INC
HILLENBRAND INC
HILTON HOTELS CORP

HOSPIRA INC
HUMANA INC
HYATT HOTELS CORPORATION
IAC/INTERACTIVECORP
ICF INTERNATIONAL INC
IDEXX LABORATORIES INC
IGATE CORPORATION
ILLINOIS TOOL WORKS INC
IMS HEALTH INC
INGRAM MICRO INC
INSITUFORM TECHNOLOGIES
INTEGRA LIFESCIENCES HOLDINGS CORP
INTEL CORP
INTERNATIONAL BUSINESS MACHINES CORP (IBM)
INTERPUBLIC GROUP OF COMPANIES INC
INTUIT INC
INVENTIV HEALTH INC
JB HUNT TRANSPORT SERVICES INC
JETBLUE AIRWAYS CORPORATION
JM SMUCKER CO
JOHNSON & JOHNSON
JOHNSON CONTROLS INC
JONES LANG LASALLE INC
JUNIPER NETWORKS INC
KEANE INC
KELLOGG COMPANY
KELLY SERVICES INC
KIMBERLY-CLARK CORP
KINETIC CONCEPTS INC
KLA TENCOR CORP
KOCH INDUSTRIES INC
KPMG LLP
KRAFT FOODS INC
LABORATORY CORP OF AMERICA HOLDINGS
LAM RESEARCH CORP
LAS VEGAS SANDS CORP (THE VENETIAN)
LEAR CORP
LEXMARK INTERNATIONAL INC
LIBERTY GLOBAL INC
LIBERTY MEDIA CORP
LIBERTY MUTUAL GROUP INC
LIFE TECHNOLOGIES CORP
LIMITED BRANDS INC
LINCOLN NATIONAL CORPORATION
LOEWS CORPORATION
LORAL SPACE & COMMUNICATIONS LTD
LUFKIN INDUSTRIES INC
MACY'S INC
MANPOWER INC
MANTECH INTERNATIONAL CORP
MARATHON OIL CORP
MARRIOTT INTERNATIONAL INC
MARS INC
MARSH & MCLENNAN COMPANIES INC
MARY KAY INC
MASSACHUSETTS MUTUAL LIFE INSURANCE CO
MATTEL INC
MAXIMUS INC
MAYO FOUNDATION FOR MEDICAL EDUCATION AND RESEARCH
MCDONALD'S CORP
MCKESSON CORPORATION
MCKINSEY & COMPANY INC
MEDCO HEALTH SOLUTIONS INC
MEDNAX INC
MEDTRONIC INC
MERCER INC
METLIFE INC
MICROCHIP TECHNOLOGY INC
MICRON TECHNOLOGY INC
MICROSOFT CORP
MIDAMERICAN ENERGY HOLDINGS CO
MILLIPORE CORP
MOLEX INC
MULTI-FINELINE ELECTRONIX INC
MYLAN INC
NABORS INDUSTRIES LTD
NACCO INDUSTRIES INC
NALCO HOLDING COMPANY
NATIONAL INSTRUMENTS CORP
NATIONAL OILWELL VARCO INC
NCR CORPORATION
NETAPP INC
NEW YORK LIFE INSURANCE CO
NEWS CORP
NEXTERA ENERGY INC
NII HOLDINGS INC
NIKE INC
NORFOLK SOUTHERN CORP
NORTH HIGHLAND
OCEANEERING INTERNATIONAL INC
OIL STATES INTERNATIONAL INC
OMNICOM GROUP INC
ORACLE CORP
OSHKOSH CORPORATION
PACCAR INC
PANERA BREAD CO
PARAMETRIC TECHNOLOGY CORP
PAREXEL INTERNATIONAL CORP
PARK-OHIO HOLDINGS CORP
PARSONS BRINCKERHOFF INC
PATTERSON COMPANIES INC
PATTERSON-UTI ENERGY INC
PEABODY ENERGY CORP
PENSKE AUTOMOTIVE GROUP INC
PEPSICO INC
PERRIGO CO
PETSMART INC
PG&E CORPORATION
PHARMACEUTICAL PRODUCT DEVELOPMENT INC
PHILIP MORRIS INTERNATIONAL INC
PLEXUS CORP
POLO RALPH LAUREN CORP
POLYCOM INC
PRAXAIR INC
PRICESMART INC
PRICEWATERHOUSECOOPERS
PRINCIPAL FINANCIAL GROUP (THE)
PROCTER & GAMBLE CO
PROGRESSIVE CORPORATION (THE)
PRUDENTIAL FINANCIAL INC
QUALCOMM INC
QUANTA SERVICES INC
RACKSPACE HOSTING INC
RALCORP HOLDINGS INC
RECREATIONAL EQUIPMENT INC (REI)
RED HAT INC
REGIS CORPORATION
RESMED INC
ROBERT HALF INTERNATIONAL INC
ROSS STORES INC
ROWAN COMPANIES INC
ROYAL CARIBBEAN CRUISES LTD
RYDER SYSTEM INC
SABRE HOLDINGS CORP
SAFECO INSURANCE COMPANY OF AMERICA

SAFEWAY INC
SAIC INC
SALESFORCE.COM INC
SAM'S CLUB
SANDISK CORP
SANMINA-SCI CORPORATION
SAPIENT CORPORATION
SARA LEE CORP
SAS INSTITUTE INC
SCHLUMBERGER LIMITED
SCOTTS MIRACLE GROW CO
SEACOR HOLDINGS INC
SELECT MEDICAL HOLDINGS CORPORATION
SEMPRA ENERGY
SENSIENT TECHNOLOGIES CORPORATION
SHAW GROUP INC (THE)
SHELL OIL CO
SHERWIN WILLIAMS COMPANY (THE)
SIGMA-ALDRICH CORP
SNYDERS-LANCE INC
SODEXO INC
SOUTHWEST AIRLINES CO
SPIRIT AEROSYSTEMS HOLDINGS INC
SRA INTERNATIONAL INC
ST JUDE MEDICAL INC
STANLEY BLACK & DECKER INC
STARWOOD HOTELS & RESORTS WORLDWIDE INC
STERICYCLE INC
STIFEL FINANCIAL CORP
STONERIDGE INC
STREAM GLOBAL SERVICES INC
STRYKER CORP
SYMANTEC CORP
SYNTEL INC
SYSCO CORP
TARGET CORPORATION
TEAM INC
TECH DATA CORP
TEKTRONIX INC
TELEDYNE TECHNOLOGIES INC
TEREX CORPORATION
TETRA TECH INC
THERMO FISHER SCIENTIFIC INC
THOMSON REUTERS
THOR INDUSTRIES INC
TIBCO SOFTWARE INC
TIDEWATER INC
TIFFANY & CO
TIME WARNER INC
TJX COMPANIES INC (THE)
TOTAL SYSTEM SERVICES INC (TSYS)
TOWERS WATSON & CO
TRAVELERS COMPANIES INC (THE)
TTM TECHNOLOGIES INC
UNDER ARMOUR INC
UNITED PARCEL SERVICE INC (UPS)
UNITED TECHNOLOGIES CORPORATION
UNITEDHEALTH GROUP INC
UNIVERSAL HEALTH SERVICES INC
UNIVISION COMMUNICATIONS INC
URS CORPORATION
USAA
VALASSIS COMMUNICATIONS INC
VALSPAR CORPORATION (THE)
VARIAN MEDICAL SYSTEMS INC
VERIZON COMMUNICATIONS INC
VICTORIAS SECRET
VISA INC
VORNADO REALTY TRUST
WABTEC CORP
WALGREEN CO
WAL-MART STORES INC
WALT DISNEY COMPANY (THE)
WARNACO GROUP INC (THE)
WASTE MANAGEMENT INC
WATERS CORP
WATSON PHARMACEUTICALS INC
WEIGHT WATCHERS INTERNATIONAL INC
WEST PHARMACEUTICAL SERVICES INC
WESTERN DIGITAL CORP
WHOLE FOODS MARKET INC
WILLIAMS COMPANIES INC (THE)
WM WRIGLEY JR COMPANY
WW GRAINGER INC
WYNDHAM WORLDWIDE
WYNN RESORTS LIMITED
XEROX CORP
YUM! BRANDS INC
ZIMMER HOLDINGS INC

Management Trainees
3M COMPANY
7-ELEVEN INC
ABM INDUSTRIES INC
ACADEMY SPORTS & OUTDOORS LTD
ACCENTURE PLC
ACOSTA SALES & MARKETING
ACTIVISION BLIZZARD INC
ADOBE SYSTEMS INC
ADVANCE AUTO PARTS INC
ADVANCED MICRO DEVICES INC (AMD)
ADVENTIST HEALTH SYSTEM
AECOM TECHNOLOGY CORPORATION
AES CORPORATION (THE)
AFFILIATED COMPUTER SERVICES INC
AFLAC INC
AGILENT TECHNOLOGIES INC
AIR PRODUCTS & CHEMICALS INC
ALLERGAN INC
ALLIANCE DATA SYSTEMS CORPORATION
ALTRIA GROUP INC
AMAZON.COM INC
AMEDISYS INC
AMERCO
AMERICAN EXPRESS CO
AMERICAN POWER CONVERSION (APC)
AMERIGROUP CORPORATION
AMERISOURCEBERGEN CORP
AMGEN INC
ANALOG DEVICES INC
APACHE CORP
APPLE INC
ARAMARK CORPORATION
ARCHER DANIELS MIDLAND CO
ARROW ELECTRONICS INC
ARTHUR J GALLAGHER & CO
ASCENA RETAIL GROUP INC
ASCENSION HEALTH
AT&T INC
AUTOMATIC DATA PROCESSING INC
AUTONATION INC
AUTOZONE INC
AVNET INC
AVON PRODUCTS INC
AXA FINANCIAL INC
BAKER HUGHES INC
BALL CORP

BASS PRO SHOPS INC
BAUSCH & LOMB INC
BECHTEL GROUP INC
BECKMAN COULTER INC
BECTON DICKINSON & CO
BED BATH & BEYOND INC
BERKSHIRE HATHAWAY INC
BEST BUY CO INC
BIG 5 SPORTING GOODS CORPORATION
BIO RAD LABORATORIES INC
BIOGEN IDEC INC
BLACKROCK INC
BLOOMBERG LP
BMC SOFTWARE INC
BOEING COMPANY (THE)
BOOZ ALLEN HAMILTON INC
BOYD GAMING CORP
BRINKS COMPANY (THE)
BROADCOM CORP
BROWN & BROWN INC
BUCKLE INC (THE)
BUFFALO WILD WINGS INC
BUNGE LTD
BURLINGTON NORTHERN SANTA FE LLC
CABLEVISION SYSTEMS CORP
CACI INTERNATIONAL INC
CAESARS ENTERTAINMENT CORPORATION
CAMERON INTERNATIONAL CORPORATION
CAMPBELL SOUP CO
CAPITAL SENIOR LIVING CORP
CARLSON COMPANIES INC
CARMAX GROUP
CARNIVAL CORPORATION
CASH AMERICA INTERNATIONAL INC
CATERPILLAR INC
CATHOLIC HEALTH INITIATIVES
CB RICHARD ELLIS GROUP INC (CBRE)
CDW CORPORATION
CELGENE CORP
CELLCO PARTNERSHIP (VERIZON WIRELESS)
CEPHALON INC
CERNER CORP
CH ROBINSON WORLDWIDE INC
CHEMED CORPORATION
CHEVRON CORPORATION
CHEVRON PHILLIPS CHEMICAL COMPANY LLC
CHICO'S FAS INC
CHIPOTLE MEXICAN GRILL INC
CHS INC
CHUBB CORPORATION (THE)
CIGNA CORP
CINTAS CORP
CISCO SYSTEMS INC
CLEARWIRE CORP
CLOROX CO (THE)
CNA FINANCIAL CORP
COACH INC
COCA-COLA BOTTLING CO CONSOLIDATED
COCA-COLA COMPANY (THE)
COGNIZANT TECHNOLOGY SOLUTIONS CORP
COLDWATER CREEK INC
COLGATE PALMOLIVE CO
COMCAST CORP
COMMUNITY HEALTH SYSTEMS INC
CONAGRA FOODS INC
CONOCOPHILLIPS COMPANY
CONSOL ENERGY INC
CONTAINER STORE (THE)
CON-WAY INC
COOPER COMPANIES INC
COSTCO WHOLESALE CORP
COVANCE INC
COX COMMUNICATIONS INC
CR BARD INC
CRACKER BARREL OLD COUNTRY STORE INC
CSX CORP
CUMMINS INC
CVS CAREMARK CORPORATION
DANAHER CORP
DARDEN RESTAURANTS INC
DAVITA INC
DEAN FOODS CO
DEERE & CO
DELOITTE & TOUCHE USA LLP
DELOITTE CONSULTING LLP
DENTSPLY INTERNATIONAL INC
DEVRY INC
DIAMOND OFFSHORE DRILLING INC
DICK'S SPORTING GOODS INC
DIRECTV
DOLLAR GENERAL CORPORATION
DTE ENERGY COMPANY
DUKE ENERGY CORP
DUPONT (E I DU PONT DE NEMOURS & CO)
EATON CORP
EBAY INC
EDISON INTERNATIONAL
EDWARDS LIFESCIENCES CORP
EMC CORP
EMERITUS CORP
EMERSON ELECTRIC CO
ENTERGY CORP
ENTERPRISE HOLDINGS INC
ERNST & YOUNG LLP
ESTEE LAUDER COMPANIES INC (THE)
EXELON CORPORATION
EXPEDIA INC
EXPERIAN AMERICAS
EXPRESS SCRIPTS INC
EXXON MOBIL CORPORATION (EXXONMOBIL)
EXXONMOBIL CHEMICAL
FAMILY DOLLAR STORES INC
FEDEX CORPORATION
FINISAR CORPORATION
FIRST ADVANTAGE CORPORATION
FIRSTENERGY CORP
FLUOR CORP
FMC TECHNOLOGIES INC
FMR CORP (FIDELITY INVESTMENTS)
FORD MOTOR CO
FOREST LABORATORIES INC
FORTUNE BRANDS INC
FOSSIL INC
FOX ENTERTAINMENT GROUP INC
FRONTIER COMMUNICATIONS CORPORATION
FTI CONSULTING INC
GAMESTOP CORP
GENENTECH INC
GENERAL ELECTRIC CO (GE)
GENERAL MILLS INC
GENERAL MOTORS COMPANY (GM)
GENESCO INC
GENTIVA HEALTH SERVICES INC
GENWORTH FINANCIAL INC
GENZYME BIOSURGERY
GILEAD SCIENCES INC
GOODYEAR TIRE & RUBBER COMPANY (THE)

GOOGLE INC
GRANT THORNTON LLP
GROUP 1 AUTOMOTIVE INC
GUESS? INC
HALLIBURTON COMPANY
HANGER ORTHOPEDIC GROUP INC
HARRIS CORPORATION
HAWAIIAN ELECTRIC INDUSTRIES INC
HCA HOLDINGS INC
HE BUTT GROCERY COMPANY (HEB)
HEALTH CARE SERVICE CORPORATION (HCSC)
HEALTH FITNESS CORP
HEALTH MANAGEMENT ASSOCIATES INC
HEALTHSOUTH CORP
HENRY SCHEIN INC
HERSHEY CO
HERTZ GLOBAL HOLDINGS INC
HIBBETT SPORTS INC
HILTON HOTELS CORP
HUMANA INC
HYATT HOTELS CORPORATION
IAC/INTERACTIVECORP
IDEXX LABORATORIES INC
IGATE CORPORATION
ILLINOIS TOOL WORKS INC
IMS HEALTH INC
INGRAM MICRO INC
INTEL CORP
INTERNATIONAL BUSINESS MACHINES CORP (IBM)
INTERPUBLIC GROUP OF COMPANIES INC
INTUIT INC
INVENTIV HEALTH INC
JB HUNT TRANSPORT SERVICES INC
JETBLUE AIRWAYS CORPORATION
JM SMUCKER CO
JOHNSON & JOHNSON
JOHNSON CONTROLS INC
JONES LANG LASALLE INC
JUNIPER NETWORKS INC
KAISER PERMANENTE
KEANE INC
KELLOGG COMPANY
KELLY SERVICES INC
KIMBERLY-CLARK CORP
KINDRED HEALTHCARE INC

KINETIC CONCEPTS INC
KOCH INDUSTRIES INC
KOHL'S CORP
KPMG LLP
KRAFT FOODS INC
KROGER CO (THE)
LABORATORY CORP OF AMERICA HOLDINGS
LAS VEGAS SANDS CORP (THE VENETIAN)
LEAP WIRELESS INTERNATIONAL INC
LEAR CORP
LEXMARK INTERNATIONAL INC
LIBERTY GLOBAL INC
LIBERTY MEDIA CORP
LIBERTY MUTUAL GROUP INC
LIFE TECHNOLOGIES CORP
LIMITED BRANDS INC
LINCARE HOLDINGS INC
LINCOLN NATIONAL CORPORATION
LKQ CORP
LOEWS CORPORATION
LORAL SPACE & COMMUNICATIONS LTD
MACY'S INC
MANPOWER INC
MARATHON OIL CORP
MARRIOTT INTERNATIONAL INC
MARS INC
MARSH & MCLENNAN COMPANIES INC
MARY KAY INC
MASSACHUSETTS MUTUAL LIFE INSURANCE CO
MATTEL INC
MAYO FOUNDATION FOR MEDICAL EDUCATION AND RESEARCH
MCDONALD'S CORP
MCKESSON CORPORATION
MCKINSEY & COMPANY INC
MEDCO HEALTH SOLUTIONS INC
MEDIACOM COMMUNICATIONS CORP
MEDTRONIC INC
MEIJER INC
MERCER INC
METHODIST HEALTH CARE SYSTEM
METLIFE INC
METROPCS COMMUNICATIONS INC
MICROCHIP TECHNOLOGY INC

MICRON TECHNOLOGY INC
MICROSOFT CORP
MIDAMERICAN ENERGY HOLDINGS CO
MILLIPORE CORP
MOLEX INC
MONRO MUFFLER BRAKE INC
MYLAN INC
NABORS INDUSTRIES LTD
NACCO INDUSTRIES INC
NATIONAL OILWELL VARCO INC
NCR CORPORATION
NETAPP INC
NEW YORK LIFE INSURANCE CO
NEWS CORP
NEXTERA ENERGY INC
NII HOLDINGS INC
NIKE INC
NORFOLK SOUTHERN CORP
OCEANEERING INTERNATIONAL INC
ODYSSEY HEALTHCARE INC
OIL STATES INTERNATIONAL INC
OMNICOM GROUP INC
ORACLE CORP
O'REILLY AUTOMOTIVE INC
OSHKOSH CORPORATION
OWENS & MINOR INC
PACCAR INC
PANERA BREAD CO
PARAMETRIC TECHNOLOGY CORP
PAREXEL INTERNATIONAL CORP
PARSONS BRINCKERHOFF INC
PATTERSON COMPANIES INC
PATTERSON-UTI ENERGY INC
PEABODY ENERGY CORP
PENSKE AUTOMOTIVE GROUP INC
PEPSICO INC
PERRIGO CO
PETCO ANIMAL SUPPLIES INC
PETSMART INC
PG&E CORPORATION
PHARMACEUTICAL PRODUCT DEVELOPMENT INC
PLEXUS CORP
POLO RALPH LAUREN CORP
PRAXAIR INC
PRICESMART INC
PRICEWATERHOUSECOOPERS
PRINCIPAL FINANCIAL GROUP (THE)

PROCTER & GAMBLE CO
PROGRESSIVE CORPORATION (THE)
PROVIDENCE HEALTH & SERVICES
PRUDENTIAL FINANCIAL INC
PUBLIX SUPER MARKETS INC
QUALCOMM INC
QUANTA SERVICES INC
RALCORP HOLDINGS INC
RECREATIONAL EQUIPMENT INC (REI)
REGIS CORPORATION
REPUBLIC AIRWAYS HOLDINGS INC
ROBERT HALF INTERNATIONAL INC
ROSS STORES INC
ROYAL CARIBBEAN CRUISES LTD
RYDER SYSTEM INC
SABRE HOLDINGS CORP
SAFECO INSURANCE COMPANY OF AMERICA
SAFEWAY INC
SAIC INC
SAM'S CLUB
SANMINA-SCI CORPORATION
SAPIENT CORPORATION
SARA LEE CORP
SAS INSTITUTE INC
SCANA CORPORATION
SCHLUMBERGER LIMITED
SCOTTS MIRACLE GROW CO
SEACOR HOLDINGS INC
SELECT MEDICAL HOLDINGS CORPORATION
SEMPRA ENERGY
SENSIENT TECHNOLOGIES CORPORATION
SHAW GROUP INC (THE)
SHELL OIL CO
SHERWIN WILLIAMS COMPANY (THE)
SIGMA-ALDRICH CORP
SKILLED HEALTHCARE GROUP INC
SNYDERS-LANCE INC
SODEXO INC
SOUTHERN COMPANY (THE)
SOUTHWEST AIRLINES CO
SPECTRUM HEALTH
SRA INTERNATIONAL INC
ST JUDE MEDICAL INC
STANLEY BLACK & DECKER INC
STARWOOD HOTELS & RESORTS WORLDWIDE INC
STIFEL FINANCIAL CORP
STRYKER CORP
SUN HEALTHCARE GROUP INC
SUTTER HEALTH INC
SYMANTEC CORP
SYNTEL INC
SYSCO CORP
TARGET CORPORATION
TEAM HEALTH HOLDINGS INC
TEAM INC
TECH DATA CORP
TEKTRONIX INC
TELEDYNE TECHNOLOGIES INC
TELEPHONE AND DATA SYSTEMS INC (TDS)
TENET HEALTHCARE CORPORATION
THERMO FISHER SCIENTIFIC INC
THOR INDUSTRIES INC
TIFFANY & CO
TIME WARNER INC
TJX COMPANIES INC (THE)
TOTAL SYSTEM SERVICES INC (TSYS)
TOWERS WATSON & CO
TRAVELERS COMPANIES INC (THE)
TREEHOUSE FOODS INC
TW TELECOM INC
UNION PACIFIC CORP
UNITED NATURAL FOODS INC
UNITED PARCEL SERVICE INC (UPS)
UNITED STATES CELLULAR CORP
UNITED TECHNOLOGIES CORPORATION
UNITEDHEALTH GROUP INC
UNIVERSAL HEALTH SERVICES INC
UNIVISION COMMUNICATIONS INC
URS CORPORATION
USAA
VALSPAR CORPORATION (THE)
VARIAN MEDICAL SYSTEMS INC
VCA ANTECH INC
VERIZON COMMUNICATIONS INC
VICTORIAS SECRET
VISA INC
WABTEC CORP
WALGREEN CO
WAL-MART STORES INC
WALT DISNEY COMPANY (THE)
WASTE MANAGEMENT INC
WATERS CORP
WATSON PHARMACEUTICALS INC
WEIGHT WATCHERS INTERNATIONAL INC
WEST PHARMACEUTICAL SERVICES INC
WESTERN DIGITAL CORP
WHOLE FOODS MARKET INC
WILLIAMS COMPANIES INC (THE)
WM WRIGLEY JR COMPANY
WW GRAINGER INC
WYNDHAM WORLDWIDE
WYNN RESORTS LIMITED
XEROX CORP
YUM! BRANDS INC
ZIMMER HOLDINGS INC

MBA Graduates
3M COMPANY
7-ELEVEN INC
ABM INDUSTRIES INC
ACADEMY SPORTS & OUTDOORS LTD
ACCENTURE PLC
ACOSTA SALES & MARKETING
ACTIVISION BLIZZARD INC
ADOBE SYSTEMS INC
ADVANCE AUTO PARTS INC
ADVANCED MICRO DEVICES INC (AMD)
ADVENTIST HEALTH SYSTEM
AECOM TECHNOLOGY CORPORATION
AES CORPORATION (THE)
AFFILIATED COMPUTER SERVICES INC
AFLAC INC
AGILENT TECHNOLOGIES INC
AIR PRODUCTS & CHEMICALS INC
ALASKA AIR GROUP INC
ALLERGAN INC
ALLIANCE DATA SYSTEMS CORPORATION
ALTRIA GROUP INC
AMAZON.COM INC
AMEDISYS INC
AMERCO
AMERICAN EXPRESS CO
AMERICAN POWER CONVERSION (APC)
AMERIGROUP CORPORATION
AMERISOURCEBERGEN CORP

AMGEN INC
AMKOR TECHNOLOGY INC
AMPHENOL CORPORATION
AMR CORP (AMERICAN AIRLINES)
AMSURG CORP
ANALOG DEVICES INC
APACHE CORP
APPLE INC
APPLIED MATERIALS INC
ARAMARK CORPORATION
ARCHER DANIELS MIDLAND CO
ARROW ELECTRONICS INC
ARTHUR J GALLAGHER & CO
ASCENA RETAIL GROUP INC
ASCENSION HEALTH
AT&T INC
AUTOMATIC DATA PROCESSING INC
AUTONATION INC
AUTOZONE INC
AVNET INC
AVON PRODUCTS INC
AXA FINANCIAL INC
BAIN & COMPANY INC
BAKER HUGHES INC
BALL CORP
BARRETT BUSINESS SERVICES
BASIC ENERGY SERVICES INC
BASS PRO SHOPS INC
BAUSCH & LOMB INC
BECHTEL GROUP INC
BECKMAN COULTER INC
BECTON DICKINSON & CO
BED BATH & BEYOND INC
BEMIS COMPANY INC
BERKSHIRE HATHAWAY INC
BEST BUY CO INC
BIG 5 SPORTING GOODS CORPORATION
BIO RAD LABORATORIES INC
BIOGEN IDEC INC
BLACKROCK INC
BLOOMBERG LP
BMC SOFTWARE INC
BOEING COMPANY (THE)
BOOZ ALLEN HAMILTON INC
BOSTON CONSULTING GROUP INC (THE, BCG)
BOYD GAMING CORP
BRINKS COMPANY (THE)
BROADCOM CORP

BROCADE COMMUNICATIONS SYSTEMS INC
BROOKDALE SENIOR LIVING INC
BROWN & BROWN INC
BRUKER CORP
BUCKLE INC (THE)
BUFFALO WILD WINGS INC
BUNGE LTD
BURLINGTON NORTHERN SANTA FE LLC
CABLEVISION SYSTEMS CORP
CACI INTERNATIONAL INC
CADENCE DESIGN SYSTEMS INC
CAESARS ENTERTAINMENT CORPORATION
CAMERON INTERNATIONAL CORPORATION
CAMPBELL SOUP CO
CAPITAL SENIOR LIVING CORP
CARLSON COMPANIES INC
CARMAX GROUP
CARNIVAL CORPORATION
CASH AMERICA INTERNATIONAL INC
CATERPILLAR INC
CATHOLIC HEALTH INITIATIVES
CB RICHARD ELLIS GROUP INC (CBRE)
CDW CORPORATION
CELGENE CORP
CELLCO PARTNERSHIP (VERIZON WIRELESS)
CEPHALON INC
CERNER CORP
CH ROBINSON WORLDWIDE INC
CHEMED CORPORATION
CHEVRON CORPORATION
CHEVRON PHILLIPS CHEMICAL COMPANY LLC
CHICO'S FAS INC
CHIPOTLE MEXICAN GRILL INC
CHS INC
CHUBB CORPORATION (THE)
CIENA CORP
CIGNA CORP
CINTAS CORP
CISCO SYSTEMS INC
CITRIX SYSTEMS INC
CLEARWIRE CORP
CLOROX CO (THE)
CNA FINANCIAL CORP
COACH INC

COCA-COLA BOTTLING CO CONSOLIDATED
COCA-COLA COMPANY (THE)
COGNIZANT TECHNOLOGY SOLUTIONS CORP
COLDWATER CREEK INC
COLGATE PALMOLIVE CO
COMCAST CORP
COMMUNITY HEALTH SYSTEMS INC
COMPUTER SCIENCES CORPORATION (CSC)
COMPUTER TASK GROUP INC
CONAGRA FOODS INC
CONOCOPHILLIPS COMPANY
CONSOL ENERGY INC
CONTAINER STORE (THE)
CON-WAY INC
COOPER COMPANIES INC
COSTCO WHOLESALE CORP
COVANCE INC
COX COMMUNICATIONS INC
CR BARD INC
CRACKER BARREL OLD COUNTRY STORE INC
CROCS INC
CSX CORP
CUMMINS INC
CVS CAREMARK CORPORATION
DANAHER CORP
DARDEN RESTAURANTS INC
DAVITA INC
DEAN FOODS CO
DEERE & CO
DELOITTE & TOUCHE USA LLP
DELOITTE CONSULTING LLP
DELTA APPAREL INC
DENTSPLY INTERNATIONAL INC
DEVRY INC
DIAMOND OFFSHORE DRILLING INC
DICK'S SPORTING GOODS INC
DIODES INC
DIRECTV
DOLLAR GENERAL CORPORATION
DTE ENERGY COMPANY
DUKE ENERGY CORP
DUPONT (E I DU PONT DE NEMOURS & CO)
DUPONT AGRICULTURE & NUTRITION
EATON CORP
EBAY INC

EDISON INTERNATIONAL
EDWARDS LIFESCIENCES CORP
EMC CORP
EMERITUS CORP
EMERSON ELECTRIC CO
ENDO PHARMACEUTICALS HOLDINGS INC
ENTERGY CORP
ENTERPRISE HOLDINGS INC
EQUITY LIFESTYLE PROPERTIES INC
ERNST & YOUNG LLP
ESTEE LAUDER COMPANIES INC (THE)
EXELON CORPORATION
EXPEDIA INC
EXPERIAN AMERICAS
EXPRESS SCRIPTS INC
EXTERRAN HOLDINGS INC
EXXON MOBIL CORPORATION (EXXONMOBIL)
EXXONMOBIL CHEMICAL
FACTSET RESEARCH SYSTEMS INC
FAMILY DOLLAR STORES INC
FASTENAL
FEDERAL MOGUL CORP
FEDEX CORPORATION
FIDELITY NATIONAL INFORMATION SERVICES INC
FINISAR CORPORATION
FIRST ADVANTAGE CORPORATION
FIRSTENERGY CORP
FLUOR CORP
FM GLOBAL
FMC TECHNOLOGIES INC
FMR CORP (FIDELITY INVESTMENTS)
FORD MOTOR CO
FOREST LABORATORIES INC
FORTUNE BRANDS INC
FOSSIL INC
FOX ENTERTAINMENT GROUP INC
FRONTIER COMMUNICATIONS CORPORATION
FTI CONSULTING INC
GAMESTOP CORP
GE ENERGY INFRASTRUCTURE
GENENTECH INC
GENERAL ELECTRIC CO (GE)
GENERAL MILLS INC
GENERAL MOTORS COMPANY (GM)
GENESCO INC
GENTEX CORPORATION
GENTIVA HEALTH SERVICES INC
GENWORTH FINANCIAL INC
GENZYME BIOSURGERY
GEOKINETICS INC
GILEAD SCIENCES INC
GOODYEAR TIRE & RUBBER COMPANY (THE)
GOOGLE INC
GRANT THORNTON LLP
GROUP 1 AUTOMOTIVE INC
GROUPON INC
GSI COMMERCE INC
GUESS? INC
HALLIBURTON COMPANY
HANESBRANDS INC
HANGER ORTHOPEDIC GROUP INC
HARRIS CORPORATION
HAWAIIAN ELECTRIC INDUSTRIES INC
HCA HOLDINGS INC
HE BUTT GROCERY COMPANY (HEB)
HEALTH CARE SERVICE CORPORATION (HCSC)
HEALTH FITNESS CORP
HEALTH MANAGEMENT ASSOCIATES INC
HEALTHSOUTH CORP
HEARTLAND PAYMENT SYSTEMS INC
HENRY SCHEIN INC
HERSHEY CO
HERTZ GLOBAL HOLDINGS INC
HIBBETT SPORTS INC
HILLENBRAND INC
HILTON HOTELS CORP
HONDA OF AMERICA MANUFACTURING INC
HOSPIRA INC
HUMANA INC
HYATT HOTELS CORPORATION
IAC/INTERACTIVECORP
ICF INTERNATIONAL INC
IDEXX LABORATORIES INC
IGATE CORPORATION
ILLINOIS TOOL WORKS INC
IMS HEALTH INC
INGRAM MICRO INC
INSITUFORM TECHNOLOGIES
INTEGRA LIFESCIENCES HOLDINGS CORP
INTEL CORP
INTERNATIONAL BUSINESS MACHINES CORP (IBM)
INTERPUBLIC GROUP OF COMPANIES INC
INTUIT INC
INVENTIV HEALTH INC
JACK HENRY & ASSOCIATES INC
JACKSON NATIONAL LIFE INSURANCE COMPANY
JARDEN CORP
JB HUNT TRANSPORT SERVICES INC
JETBLUE AIRWAYS CORPORATION
JM SMUCKER CO
JOHNSON & JOHNSON
JOHNSON CONTROLS INC
JONES LANG LASALLE INC
JUNIPER NETWORKS INC
KAISER PERMANENTE
KEANE INC
KELLOGG COMPANY
KELLY SERVICES INC
KEY ENERGY SERVICES INC
KIMBERLY-CLARK CORP
KINDRED HEALTHCARE INC
KINETIC CONCEPTS INC
KLA TENCOR CORP
KOCH INDUSTRIES INC
KOHL'S CORP
KPMG LLP
KRAFT FOODS INC
KROGER CO (THE)
LABORATORY CORP OF AMERICA HOLDINGS
LAM RESEARCH CORP
LAS VEGAS SANDS CORP (THE VENETIAN)
LEAP WIRELESS INTERNATIONAL INC
LEAR CORP
LEXMARK INTERNATIONAL INC
LIBERTY GLOBAL INC
LIBERTY MEDIA CORP
LIBERTY MUTUAL GROUP INC
LIFE TECHNOLOGIES CORP
LIMITED BRANDS INC
LINCARE HOLDINGS INC
LINCOLN NATIONAL CORPORATION
LKQ CORP
LOEWS CORPORATION
LORAL SPACE & COMMUNICATIONS

LTD
LUFKIN INDUSTRIES INC
MACY'S INC
MANPOWER INC
MANTECH INTERNATIONAL CORP
MARATHON OIL CORP
MARRIOTT INTERNATIONAL INC
MARS INC
MARSH & MCLENNAN COMPANIES INC
MARY KAY INC
MASSACHUSETTS MUTUAL LIFE INSURANCE CO
MATTEL INC
MAXIMUS INC
MAYO FOUNDATION FOR MEDICAL EDUCATION AND RESEARCH
MCDONALD'S CORP
MCKESSON CORPORATION
MCKINSEY & COMPANY INC
MEDCO HEALTH SOLUTIONS INC
MEDIACOM COMMUNICATIONS CORP
MEDNAX INC
MEDTRONIC INC
MEIJER INC
MERCER INC
METHODIST HEALTH CARE SYSTEM
METLIFE INC
METROPCS COMMUNICATIONS INC
MICROCHIP TECHNOLOGY INC
MICRON TECHNOLOGY INC
MICROSOFT CORP
MIDAMERICAN ENERGY HOLDINGS CO
MILLIPORE CORP
MOLEX INC
MONRO MUFFLER BRAKE INC
MULTI-FINELINE ELECTRONIX INC
MUTUAL OF OMAHA COMPANIES (THE)
MYLAN INC
NABORS INDUSTRIES LTD
NACCO INDUSTRIES INC
NALCO HOLDING COMPANY
NATIONAL INSTRUMENTS CORP
NATIONAL OILWELL VARCO INC
NCR CORPORATION
NETAPP INC
NEW YORK LIFE INSURANCE CO
NEWS CORP

NEXTERA ENERGY INC
NII HOLDINGS INC
NIKE INC
NORFOLK SOUTHERN CORP
NORTH HIGHLAND
NORTHWESTERN MUTUAL LIFE INSURANCE CO
OCEANEERING INTERNATIONAL INC
ODYSSEY HEALTHCARE INC
OIL STATES INTERNATIONAL INC
OMNICOM GROUP INC
ORACLE CORP
O'REILLY AUTOMOTIVE INC
OSHKOSH CORPORATION
OWENS & MINOR INC
PACCAR INC
PANERA BREAD CO
PARAMETRIC TECHNOLOGY CORP
PAREXEL INTERNATIONAL CORP
PARK-OHIO HOLDINGS CORP
PARSONS BRINCKERHOFF INC
PATTERSON COMPANIES INC
PATTERSON-UTI ENERGY INC
PEABODY ENERGY CORP
PENSKE AUTOMOTIVE GROUP INC
PEPSICO INC
PERRIGO CO
PETCO ANIMAL SUPPLIES INC
PETSMART INC
PG&E CORPORATION
PHARMACEUTICAL PRODUCT DEVELOPMENT INC
PHILIP MORRIS INTERNATIONAL INC
PLEXUS CORP
POLO RALPH LAUREN CORP
POLYCOM INC
PRAXAIR INC
PRICESMART INC
PRICEWATERHOUSECOOPERS
PRINCIPAL FINANCIAL GROUP (THE)
PROCTER & GAMBLE CO
PROGRESSIVE CORPORATION (THE)
PROVIDENCE HEALTH & SERVICES
PRUDENTIAL FINANCIAL INC
PUBLIX SUPER MARKETS INC
QUALCOMM INC
QUANTA SERVICES INC

RACKSPACE HOSTING INC
RALCORP HOLDINGS INC
RECREATIONAL EQUIPMENT INC (REI)
RED HAT INC
REGIS CORPORATION
REPUBLIC AIRWAYS HOLDINGS INC
RESMED INC
ROBERT HALF INTERNATIONAL INC
ROSS STORES INC
ROWAN COMPANIES INC
ROYAL CARIBBEAN CRUISES LTD
RYDER SYSTEM INC
SABRE HOLDINGS CORP
SAFECO INSURANCE COMPANY OF AMERICA
SAFEWAY INC
SAIC INC
SALESFORCE.COM INC
SAM'S CLUB
SANDISK CORP
SANMINA-SCI CORPORATION
SAPIENT CORPORATION
SARA LEE CORP
SAS INSTITUTE INC
SCANA CORPORATION
SCHLUMBERGER LIMITED
SCOTTS MIRACLE GROW CO
SEACOR HOLDINGS INC
SELECT MEDICAL HOLDINGS CORPORATION
SEMPRA ENERGY
SENECA FOODS CORPORATION
SENSIENT TECHNOLOGIES CORPORATION
SHAW GROUP INC (THE)
SHELL OIL CO
SHERWIN WILLIAMS COMPANY (THE)
SIGMA-ALDRICH CORP
SKILLED HEALTHCARE GROUP INC
SNYDERS-LANCE INC
SODEXO INC
SOUTHERN COMPANY (THE)
SOUTHWEST AIRLINES CO
SPECTRUM HEALTH
SPIRIT AEROSYSTEMS HOLDINGS INC
SRA INTERNATIONAL INC
ST JUDE MEDICAL INC
STANLEY BLACK & DECKER INC

STARWOOD HOTELS & RESORTS WORLDWIDE INC
STERICYCLE INC
STIFEL FINANCIAL CORP
STONERIDGE INC
STREAM GLOBAL SERVICES INC
STRYKER CORP
SUN HEALTHCARE GROUP INC
SUTTER HEALTH INC
SYMANTEC CORP
SYNTEL INC
SYSCO CORP
TARGET CORPORATION
TEAM INC
TECH DATA CORP
TEKTRONIX INC
TELEDYNE TECHNOLOGIES INC
TELEPHONE AND DATA SYSTEMS INC (TDS)
TENET HEALTHCARE CORPORATION
TEREX CORPORATION
TETRA TECH INC
THERMO FISHER SCIENTIFIC INC
THOMSON REUTERS
THOR INDUSTRIES INC
TIBCO SOFTWARE INC
TIDEWATER INC
TIFFANY & CO
TIME WARNER INC
TJX COMPANIES INC (THE)
TOTAL SYSTEM SERVICES INC (TSYS)
TOWERS WATSON & CO
TRAVELERS COMPANIES INC (THE)
TREEHOUSE FOODS INC
TRUSTMARK COMPANIES
TTM TECHNOLOGIES INC
TW TELECOM INC
UNDER ARMOUR INC
UNION PACIFIC CORP
UNITED NATURAL FOODS INC
UNITED PARCEL SERVICE INC (UPS)
UNITED STATES CELLULAR CORP
UNITED TECHNOLOGIES CORPORATION
UNITEDHEALTH GROUP INC
UNIVERSAL HEALTH SERVICES INC
UNIVISION COMMUNICATIONS INC
URS CORPORATION
USAA
VALASSIS COMMUNICATIONS INC
VALSPAR CORPORATION (THE)
VARIAN MEDICAL SYSTEMS INC
VCA ANTECH INC
VERIZON COMMUNICATIONS INC
VICTORIAS SECRET
VISA INC
VORNADO REALTY TRUST
WABTEC CORP
WALGREEN CO
WAL-MART STORES INC
WALT DISNEY COMPANY (THE)
WARNACO GROUP INC (THE)
WASTE MANAGEMENT INC
WATERS CORP
WATSON PHARMACEUTICALS INC
WEIGHT WATCHERS INTERNATIONAL INC
WEST PHARMACEUTICAL SERVICES INC
WESTERN DIGITAL CORP
WHOLE FOODS MARKET INC
WILLIAMS COMPANIES INC (THE)
WINDSTREAM CORPORATION
WM WRIGLEY JR COMPANY
WW GRAINGER INC
WYNDHAM WORLDWIDE
WYNN RESORTS LIMITED
XEROX CORP
YUM! BRANDS INC
ZIMMER HOLDINGS INC

Professionals

Consulting
ACCENTURE PLC
AECOM TECHNOLOGY CORPORATION
AFFILIATED COMPUTER SERVICES INC
BAIN & COMPANY INC
BECHTEL GROUP INC
BMC SOFTWARE INC
BOOZ ALLEN HAMILTON INC
BOSTON CONSULTING GROUP INC (THE, BCG)
CACI INTERNATIONAL INC
CERNER CORP
COGNIZANT TECHNOLOGY SOLUTIONS CORP
COMPUTER SCIENCES CORPORATION (CSC)
COVANCE INC
DELOITTE & TOUCHE USA LLP
DELOITTE CONSULTING LLP
ERNST & YOUNG LLP
FLUOR CORP
FM GLOBAL
FTI CONSULTING INC
GRANT THORNTON LLP
GSI COMMERCE INC
ICF INTERNATIONAL INC
IGATE CORPORATION
IMS HEALTH INC
INTERNATIONAL BUSINESS MACHINES CORP (IBM)
INTERPUBLIC GROUP OF COMPANIES INC
INVENTIV HEALTH INC
KEANE INC
KPMG LLP
MARSH & MCLENNAN COMPANIES INC
MAXIMUS INC
MCKINSEY & COMPANY INC
MERCER INC
NORTH HIGHLAND
NORTHWESTERN MUTUAL LIFE INSURANCE CO
OMNICOM GROUP INC
PAREXEL INTERNATIONAL CORP
PARSONS BRINCKERHOFF INC
PHARMACEUTICAL PRODUCT DEVELOPMENT INC
PRICEWATERHOUSECOOPERS
SAIC INC
SAPIENT CORPORATION
SAS INSTITUTE INC
SRA INTERNATIONAL INC
STREAM GLOBAL SERVICES INC
SYNTEL INC
TEAM HEALTH HOLDINGS INC
TETRA TECH INC
TOWERS WATSON & CO
URS CORPORATION

Finance/Accounting
3M COMPANY
7-ELEVEN INC
ABM INDUSTRIES INC
ACADEMY SPORTS & OUTDOORS LTD

ACCENTURE PLC
ACOSTA SALES & MARKETING
ACTIVISION BLIZZARD INC
ADOBE SYSTEMS INC
ADVANCE AUTO PARTS INC
ADVANCED MICRO DEVICES INC (AMD)
ADVENTIST HEALTH SYSTEM
AECOM TECHNOLOGY CORPORATION
AES CORPORATION (THE)
AFFILIATED COMPUTER SERVICES INC
AFLAC INC
AGILENT TECHNOLOGIES INC
AIR PRODUCTS & CHEMICALS INC
ALASKA AIR GROUP INC
ALLERGAN INC
ALLIANCE DATA SYSTEMS CORPORATION
ALTRIA GROUP INC
AMAZON.COM INC
AMEDISYS INC
AMERCO
AMERICAN EXPRESS CO
AMERICAN POWER CONVERSION (APC)
AMERIGROUP CORPORATION
AMERISOURCEBERGEN CORP
AMGEN INC
AMKOR TECHNOLOGY INC
AMPHENOL CORPORATION
AMR CORP (AMERICAN AIRLINES)
AMSURG CORP
ANALOG DEVICES INC
APACHE CORP
APPLE INC
APPLIED MATERIALS INC
ARAMARK CORPORATION
ARCHER DANIELS MIDLAND CO
ARROW ELECTRONICS INC
ARTHUR J GALLAGHER & CO
ASCENA RETAIL GROUP INC
ASCENSION HEALTH
AT&T INC
AUTOMATIC DATA PROCESSING INC
AUTONATION INC
AUTOZONE INC
AVNET INC
AVON PRODUCTS INC

AXA FINANCIAL INC
BAIN & COMPANY INC
BAKER HUGHES INC
BALL CORP
BARRETT BUSINESS SERVICES
BASIC ENERGY SERVICES INC
BASS PRO SHOPS INC
BAUSCH & LOMB INC
BECHTEL GROUP INC
BECKMAN COULTER INC
BECTON DICKINSON & CO
BED BATH & BEYOND INC
BEMIS COMPANY INC
BERKSHIRE HATHAWAY INC
BEST BUY CO INC
BIG 5 SPORTING GOODS CORPORATION
BIO RAD LABORATORIES INC
BIOGEN IDEC INC
BLACKROCK INC
BLOOMBERG LP
BMC SOFTWARE INC
BOEING COMPANY (THE)
BOOZ ALLEN HAMILTON INC
BOSTON CONSULTING GROUP INC (THE, BCG)
BOYD GAMING CORP
BRINKS COMPANY (THE)
BROADCOM CORP
BROCADE COMMUNICATIONS SYSTEMS INC
BROOKDALE SENIOR LIVING INC
BROWN & BROWN INC
BRUKER CORP
BUCKLE INC (THE)
BUFFALO WILD WINGS INC
BUNGE LTD
BURLINGTON NORTHERN SANTA FE LLC
CABLEVISION SYSTEMS CORP
CACI INTERNATIONAL INC
CADENCE DESIGN SYSTEMS INC
CAESARS ENTERTAINMENT CORPORATION
CAMERON INTERNATIONAL CORPORATION
CAMPBELL SOUP CO
CAPITAL SENIOR LIVING CORP
CARLSON COMPANIES INC
CARMAX GROUP
CARNIVAL CORPORATION

CASH AMERICA INTERNATIONAL INC
CATERPILLAR INC
CATHOLIC HEALTH INITIATIVES
CB RICHARD ELLIS GROUP INC (CBRE)
CDW CORPORATION
CELGENE CORP
CELLCO PARTNERSHIP (VERIZON WIRELESS)
CEPHALON INC
CERNER CORP
CH ROBINSON WORLDWIDE INC
CHEMED CORPORATION
CHEVRON CORPORATION
CHEVRON PHILLIPS CHEMICAL COMPANY LLC
CHICO'S FAS INC
CHIPOTLE MEXICAN GRILL INC
CHS INC
CHUBB CORPORATION (THE)
CIENA CORP
CIGNA CORP
CINTAS CORP
CISCO SYSTEMS INC
CITRIX SYSTEMS INC
CLEARWIRE CORP
CLOROX CO (THE)
CNA FINANCIAL CORP
COACH INC
COCA-COLA BOTTLING CO CONSOLIDATED
COCA-COLA COMPANY (THE)
COGNIZANT TECHNOLOGY SOLUTIONS CORP
COLDWATER CREEK INC
COLGATE PALMOLIVE CO
COMCAST CORP
COMMUNITY HEALTH SYSTEMS INC
COMPUTER SCIENCES CORPORATION (CSC)
COMPUTER TASK GROUP INC
CONAGRA FOODS INC
CONCENTRA INC
CONOCOPHILLIPS COMPANY
CONSOL ENERGY INC
CONTAINER STORE (THE)
CON-WAY INC
COOPER COMPANIES INC
COSTCO WHOLESALE CORP
COVANCE INC
COX COMMUNICATIONS INC

CR BARD INC
CRACKER BARREL OLD COUNTRY STORE INC
CROCS INC
CSX CORP
CUMMINS INC
CVS CAREMARK CORPORATION
DANAHER CORP
DARDEN RESTAURANTS INC
DAVITA INC
DEAN FOODS CO
DEERE & CO
DELOITTE & TOUCHE USA LLP
DELOITTE CONSULTING LLP
DELTA APPAREL INC
DENTSPLY INTERNATIONAL INC
DEVRY INC
DIAMOND OFFSHORE DRILLING INC
DICK'S SPORTING GOODS INC
DIODES INC
DIRECTV
DOLLAR GENERAL CORPORATION
DTE ENERGY COMPANY
DUKE ENERGY CORP
DUPONT (E I DU PONT DE NEMOURS & CO)
DUPONT AGRICULTURE & NUTRITION
EATON CORP
EBAY INC
EDISON INTERNATIONAL
EDWARDS LIFESCIENCES CORP
EMC CORP
EMERITUS CORP
EMERSON ELECTRIC CO
ENDO PHARMACEUTICALS HOLDINGS INC
ENTERGY CORP
ENTERPRISE HOLDINGS INC
EQUITY LIFESTYLE PROPERTIES INC
ERNST & YOUNG LLP
ESTEE LAUDER COMPANIES INC (THE)
EXELON CORPORATION
EXPEDIA INC
EXPERIAN AMERICAS
EXPRESS SCRIPTS INC
EXTERRAN HOLDINGS INC
EXXON MOBIL CORPORATION (EXXONMOBIL)
EXXONMOBIL CHEMICAL

FACTSET RESEARCH SYSTEMS INC
FAIRVIEW HEALTH SERVICES
FAMILY DOLLAR STORES INC
FASTENAL
FEDERAL MOGUL CORP
FEDEX CORPORATION
FIDELITY NATIONAL INFORMATION SERVICES INC
FINISAR CORPORATION
FIRST ADVANTAGE CORPORATION
FIRSTENERGY CORP
FLUOR CORP
FM GLOBAL
FMC TECHNOLOGIES INC
FMR CORP (FIDELITY INVESTMENTS)
FORD MOTOR CO
FOREST LABORATORIES INC
FORTUNE BRANDS INC
FOSSIL INC
FOX ENTERTAINMENT GROUP INC
FRONTIER COMMUNICATIONS CORPORATION
FTI CONSULTING INC
GAMESTOP CORP
GE ENERGY INFRASTRUCTURE
GENENTECH INC
GENERAL ELECTRIC CO (GE)
GENERAL MILLS INC
GENERAL MOTORS COMPANY (GM)
GENESCO INC
GENTEX CORPORATION
GENTIVA HEALTH SERVICES INC
GENWORTH FINANCIAL INC
GENZYME BIOSURGERY
GEOKINETICS INC
GILEAD SCIENCES INC
GOODYEAR TIRE & RUBBER COMPANY (THE)
GOOGLE INC
GRANT THORNTON LLP
GROUP 1 AUTOMOTIVE INC
GROUPON INC
GSI COMMERCE INC
GUESS? INC
HALLIBURTON COMPANY
HANESBRANDS INC
HANGER ORTHOPEDIC GROUP INC
HARRIS CORPORATION
HAWAIIAN ELECTRIC INDUSTRIES INC

HCA HOLDINGS INC
HE BUTT GROCERY COMPANY (HEB)
HEALTH CARE SERVICE CORPORATION (HCSC)
HEALTH FITNESS CORP
HEALTH MANAGEMENT ASSOCIATES INC
HEALTHSOUTH CORP
HEARTLAND PAYMENT SYSTEMS INC
HENRY SCHEIN INC
HERSHEY CO
HERTZ GLOBAL HOLDINGS INC
HIBBETT SPORTS INC
HILLENBRAND INC
HILTON HOTELS CORP
HONDA OF AMERICA MANUFACTURING INC
HOSPIRA INC
HUMANA INC
HYATT HOTELS CORPORATION
IAC/INTERACTIVECORP
ICF INTERNATIONAL INC
IDEXX LABORATORIES INC
IGATE CORPORATION
ILLINOIS TOOL WORKS INC
IMS HEALTH INC
INGRAM MICRO INC
INSITUFORM TECHNOLOGIES
INTEGRA LIFESCIENCES HOLDINGS CORP
INTEL CORP
INTERNATIONAL BUSINESS MACHINES CORP (IBM)
INTERPUBLIC GROUP OF COMPANIES INC
INTUIT INC
INVENTIV HEALTH INC
JACK HENRY & ASSOCIATES INC
JACKSON NATIONAL LIFE INSURANCE COMPANY
JARDEN CORP
JB HUNT TRANSPORT SERVICES INC
JETBLUE AIRWAYS CORPORATION
JM SMUCKER CO
JOHNSON & JOHNSON
JOHNSON CONTROLS INC
JONES LANG LASALLE INC
JUNIPER NETWORKS INC
KAISER PERMANENTE

KEANE INC
KELLOGG COMPANY
KELLY SERVICES INC
KEY ENERGY SERVICES INC
KIMBERLY-CLARK CORP
KINDRED HEALTHCARE INC
KINETIC CONCEPTS INC
KLA TENCOR CORP
KOCH INDUSTRIES INC
KOHL'S CORP
KPMG LLP
KRAFT FOODS INC
KROGER CO (THE)
LABORATORY CORP OF AMERICA HOLDINGS
LAM RESEARCH CORP
LAS VEGAS SANDS CORP (THE VENETIAN)
LEAP WIRELESS INTERNATIONAL INC
LEAR CORP
LEXMARK INTERNATIONAL INC
LIBERTY GLOBAL INC
LIBERTY MEDIA CORP
LIBERTY MUTUAL GROUP INC
LIFE TECHNOLOGIES CORP
LIMITED BRANDS INC
LINCARE HOLDINGS INC
LINCOLN NATIONAL CORPORATION
LKQ CORP
LOEWS CORPORATION
LORAL SPACE & COMMUNICATIONS LTD
LUFKIN INDUSTRIES INC
MACY'S INC
MANPOWER INC
MANTECH INTERNATIONAL CORP
MARATHON OIL CORP
MARRIOTT INTERNATIONAL INC
MARS INC
MARSH & MCLENNAN COMPANIES INC
MARY KAY INC
MASSACHUSETTS MUTUAL LIFE INSURANCE CO
MATTEL INC
MAXIMUS INC
MAYO FOUNDATION FOR MEDICAL EDUCATION AND RESEARCH
MCDONALD'S CORP
MCKESSON CORPORATION
MCKINSEY & COMPANY INC
MEDCO HEALTH SOLUTIONS INC
MEDIACOM COMMUNICATIONS CORP
MEDNAX INC
MEDTRONIC INC
MEIJER INC
MERCER INC
METHODIST HEALTH CARE SYSTEM
METLIFE INC
METROPCS COMMUNICATIONS INC
MICROCHIP TECHNOLOGY INC
MICRON TECHNOLOGY INC
MICROSOFT CORP
MIDAMERICAN ENERGY HOLDINGS CO
MILLIPORE CORP
MOLEX INC
MONRO MUFFLER BRAKE INC
MULTI-FINELINE ELECTRONIX INC
MUTUAL OF OMAHA COMPANIES (THE)
MYLAN INC
NABORS INDUSTRIES LTD
NACCO INDUSTRIES INC
NALCO HOLDING COMPANY
NATIONAL INSTRUMENTS CORP
NATIONAL OILWELL VARCO INC
NCR CORPORATION
NETAPP INC
NEW YORK LIFE INSURANCE CO
NEWS CORP
NEXTERA ENERGY INC
NII HOLDINGS INC
NIKE INC
NORFOLK SOUTHERN CORP
NORTH HIGHLAND
NORTHWESTERN MUTUAL LIFE INSURANCE CO
OCEANEERING INTERNATIONAL INC
ODYSSEY HEALTHCARE INC
OIL STATES INTERNATIONAL INC
OMNICOM GROUP INC
ORACLE CORP
O'REILLY AUTOMOTIVE INC
OSHKOSH CORPORATION
OWENS & MINOR INC
PACCAR INC
PANERA BREAD CO
PARAMETRIC TECHNOLOGY CORP
PAREXEL INTERNATIONAL CORP
PARK-OHIO HOLDINGS CORP
PARSONS BRINCKERHOFF INC
PATTERSON COMPANIES INC
PATTERSON-UTI ENERGY INC
PEABODY ENERGY CORP
PENSKE AUTOMOTIVE GROUP INC
PEPSICO INC
PERRIGO CO
PETCO ANIMAL SUPPLIES INC
PETSMART INC
PG&E CORPORATION
PHARMACEUTICAL PRODUCT DEVELOPMENT INC
PHILIP MORRIS INTERNATIONAL INC
PLEXUS CORP
POLO RALPH LAUREN CORP
POLYCOM INC
PRAXAIR INC
PRICESMART INC
PRICEWATERHOUSECOOPERS
PRINCIPAL FINANCIAL GROUP (THE)
PROCTER & GAMBLE CO
PROGRESSIVE CORPORATION (THE)
PROVIDENCE HEALTH & SERVICES
PRUDENTIAL FINANCIAL INC
PUBLIX SUPER MARKETS INC
QUALCOMM INC
QUANTA SERVICES INC
RACKSPACE HOSTING INC
RALCORP HOLDINGS INC
RECREATIONAL EQUIPMENT INC (REI)
RED HAT INC
REGIS CORPORATION
REPUBLIC AIRWAYS HOLDINGS INC
RESMED INC
ROBERT HALF INTERNATIONAL INC
ROSS STORES INC
ROWAN COMPANIES INC
ROYAL CARIBBEAN CRUISES LTD
RYDER SYSTEM INC
SABRE HOLDINGS CORP
SAFECO INSURANCE COMPANY OF AMERICA
SAFEWAY INC
SAIC INC
SALESFORCE.COM INC

SAM'S CLUB
SANDISK CORP
SANMINA-SCI CORPORATION
SAPIENT CORPORATION
SARA LEE CORP
SAS INSTITUTE INC
SCANA CORPORATION
SCHLUMBERGER LIMITED
SCOTTS MIRACLE GROW CO
SEACOR HOLDINGS INC
SELECT MEDICAL HOLDINGS CORPORATION
SEMPRA ENERGY
SENECA FOODS CORPORATION
SENSIENT TECHNOLOGIES CORPORATION
SHAW GROUP INC (THE)
SHELL OIL CO
SHERWIN WILLIAMS COMPANY (THE)
SIGMA-ALDRICH CORP
SKILLED HEALTHCARE GROUP INC
SNYDERS-LANCE INC
SODEXO INC
SOUTHERN COMPANY (THE)
SOUTHWEST AIRLINES CO
SPECTRUM HEALTH
SPIRIT AEROSYSTEMS HOLDINGS INC
SRA INTERNATIONAL INC
ST JUDE MEDICAL INC
STANLEY BLACK & DECKER INC
STARWOOD HOTELS & RESORTS WORLDWIDE INC
STERICYCLE INC
STIFEL FINANCIAL CORP
STONERIDGE INC
STREAM GLOBAL SERVICES INC
STRYKER CORP
SUN HEALTHCARE GROUP INC
SUTTER HEALTH INC
SYMANTEC CORP
SYNTEL INC
SYSCO CORP
TARGET CORPORATION
TEAM HEALTH HOLDINGS INC
TEAM INC
TECH DATA CORP
TEKTRONIX INC
TELEDYNE TECHNOLOGIES INC
TELEPHONE AND DATA SYSTEMS INC (TDS)
TENET HEALTHCARE CORPORATION
TEREX CORPORATION
TETRA TECH INC
THERMO FISHER SCIENTIFIC INC
THOMSON REUTERS
THOR INDUSTRIES INC
TIBCO SOFTWARE INC
TIDEWATER INC
TIFFANY & CO
TIME WARNER INC
TJX COMPANIES INC (THE)
TOTAL SYSTEM SERVICES INC (TSYS)
TOWERS WATSON & CO
TRAVELERS COMPANIES INC (THE)
TREEHOUSE FOODS INC
TRUSTMARK COMPANIES
TTM TECHNOLOGIES INC
TW TELECOM INC
UNDER ARMOUR INC
UNION PACIFIC CORP
UNITED NATURAL FOODS INC
UNITED PARCEL SERVICE INC (UPS)
UNITED STATES CELLULAR CORP
UNITED TECHNOLOGIES CORPORATION
UNITEDHEALTH GROUP INC
UNIVERSAL HEALTH SERVICES INC
UNIVISION COMMUNICATIONS INC
URS CORPORATION
USAA
VALASSIS COMMUNICATIONS INC
VALSPAR CORPORATION (THE)
VARIAN MEDICAL SYSTEMS INC
VCA ANTECH INC
VERIZON COMMUNICATIONS INC
VICTORIAS SECRET
VISA INC
VORNADO REALTY TRUST
WABTEC CORP
WALGREEN CO
WAL-MART STORES INC
WALT DISNEY COMPANY (THE)
WARNACO GROUP INC (THE)
WASTE MANAGEMENT INC
WATERS CORP
WATSON PHARMACEUTICALS INC
WEIGHT WATCHERS INTERNATIONAL INC
WEST PHARMACEUTICAL SERVICES INC
WESTERN DIGITAL CORP
WHOLE FOODS MARKET INC
WILLIAMS COMPANIES INC (THE)
WINDSTREAM CORPORATION
WM WRIGLEY JR COMPANY
WW GRAINGER INC
WYNDHAM WORLDWIDE
WYNN RESORTS LIMITED
XEROX CORP
YUM! BRANDS INC
ZIMMER HOLDINGS INC

Health Care
3M COMPANY
ADVENTIST HEALTH SYSTEM
AFLAC INC
ALASKA AIR GROUP INC
ALLERGAN INC
AMEDISYS INC
AMERIGROUP CORPORATION
AMGEN INC
AMR CORP (AMERICAN AIRLINES)
ASCENSION HEALTH
BAUSCH & LOMB INC
BECKMAN COULTER INC
BECTON DICKINSON & CO
BIO RAD LABORATORIES INC
BROOKDALE SENIOR LIVING INC
CAPITAL SENIOR LIVING CORP
CATHOLIC HEALTH INITIATIVES
CELGENE CORP
CEPHALON INC
CERNER CORP
CHEMED CORPORATION
CIGNA CORP
CNA FINANCIAL CORP
COMMUNITY HEALTH SYSTEMS INC
CONCENTRA INC
COOPER COMPANIES INC
COVANCE INC
CR BARD INC
CVS CAREMARK CORPORATION
DAVITA INC
DENTSPLY INTERNATIONAL INC
EMERITUS CORP
EXPRESS SCRIPTS INC
FAIRVIEW HEALTH SERVICES

FOREST LABORATORIES INC
GENENTECH INC
GENWORTH FINANCIAL INC
GILEAD SCIENCES INC
HANGER ORTHOPEDIC GROUP INC
HCA HOLDINGS INC
HEALTH CARE SERVICE CORPORATION (HCSC)
HEALTH MANAGEMENT ASSOCIATES INC
HENRY SCHEIN INC
HOSPIRA INC
HUMANA INC
IDEXX LABORATORIES INC
IMS HEALTH INC
INTEGRA LIFESCIENCES HOLDINGS CORP
INVENTIV HEALTH INC
JACKSON NATIONAL LIFE INSURANCE COMPANY
JETBLUE AIRWAYS CORPORATION
JOHNSON & JOHNSON
KAISER PERMANENTE
KINDRED HEALTHCARE INC
KINETIC CONCEPTS INC
LABORATORY CORP OF AMERICA HOLDINGS
LIFE TECHNOLOGIES CORP
LINCARE HOLDINGS INC
LINCOLN NATIONAL CORPORATION
MASSACHUSETTS MUTUAL LIFE INSURANCE CO
MAYO FOUNDATION FOR MEDICAL EDUCATION AND RESEARCH
MEDCO HEALTH SOLUTIONS INC
MEDNAX INC
MEDTRONIC INC
METHODIST HEALTH CARE SYSTEM
METLIFE INC
MUTUAL OF OMAHA COMPANIES (THE)
MYLAN INC
NEW YORK LIFE INSURANCE CO
ODYSSEY HEALTHCARE INC
OWENS & MINOR INC
PAREXEL INTERNATIONAL CORP
PARK-OHIO HOLDINGS CORP
PATTERSON COMPANIES INC
PERRIGO CO
PHARMACEUTICAL PRODUCT DEVELOPMENT INC
PRINCIPAL FINANCIAL GROUP (THE)
PROVIDENCE HEALTH & SERVICES
PRUDENTIAL FINANCIAL INC
RESMED INC
SELECT MEDICAL HOLDINGS CORPORATION
SOUTHWEST AIRLINES CO
SPECTRUM HEALTH
ST JUDE MEDICAL INC
STRYKER CORP
SUN HEALTHCARE GROUP INC
SUTTER HEALTH INC
TEAM HEALTH HOLDINGS INC
TENET HEALTHCARE CORPORATION
UNITEDHEALTH GROUP INC
UNIVERSAL HEALTH SERVICES INC
VARIAN MEDICAL SYSTEMS INC
VCA ANTECH INC
WALGREEN CO
WATSON PHARMACEUTICALS INC
WEIGHT WATCHERS INTERNATIONAL INC
WEST PHARMACEUTICAL SERVICES INC
ZIMMER HOLDINGS INC

Human Resources/Other
3M COMPANY
7-ELEVEN INC
ABM INDUSTRIES INC
ACADEMY SPORTS & OUTDOORS LTD
ACCENTURE PLC
ACOSTA SALES & MARKETING
ACTIVISION BLIZZARD INC
ADOBE SYSTEMS INC
ADVANCE AUTO PARTS INC
ADVANCED MICRO DEVICES INC (AMD)
ADVENTIST HEALTH SYSTEM
AECOM TECHNOLOGY CORPORATION
AES CORPORATION (THE)
AFFILIATED COMPUTER SERVICES INC
AFLAC INC
AGILENT TECHNOLOGIES INC
AIR PRODUCTS & CHEMICALS INC
ALASKA AIR GROUP INC
ALLERGAN INC
ALLIANCE DATA SYSTEMS CORPORATION
ALTRIA GROUP INC
AMAZON.COM INC
AMEDISYS INC
AMERCO
AMERICAN EXPRESS CO
AMERICAN POWER CONVERSION (APC)
AMERIGROUP CORPORATION
AMERISOURCEBERGEN CORP
AMGEN INC
AMKOR TECHNOLOGY INC
AMPHENOL CORPORATION
AMR CORP (AMERICAN AIRLINES)
AMSURG CORP
ANALOG DEVICES INC
APACHE CORP
APPLE INC
APPLIED MATERIALS INC
ARAMARK CORPORATION
ARCHER DANIELS MIDLAND CO
ARROW ELECTRONICS INC
ARTHUR J GALLAGHER & CO
ASCENA RETAIL GROUP INC
ASCENSION HEALTH
AT&T INC
AUTOMATIC DATA PROCESSING INC
AUTONATION INC
AUTOZONE INC
AVNET INC
AVON PRODUCTS INC
AXA FINANCIAL INC
BAIN & COMPANY INC
BAKER HUGHES INC
BALL CORP
BARRETT BUSINESS SERVICES
BASIC ENERGY SERVICES INC
BASS PRO SHOPS INC
BAUSCH & LOMB INC
BECHTEL GROUP INC
BECKMAN COULTER INC
BECTON DICKINSON & CO
BED BATH & BEYOND INC
BEMIS COMPANY INC
BERKSHIRE HATHAWAY INC
BEST BUY CO INC
BIG 5 SPORTING GOODS CORPORATION
BIO RAD LABORATORIES INC

BIOGEN IDEC INC
BLACKROCK INC
BLOOMBERG LP
BMC SOFTWARE INC
BOEING COMPANY (THE)
BOOZ ALLEN HAMILTON INC
BOSTON CONSULTING GROUP INC (THE, BCG)
BOYD GAMING CORP
BRINKS COMPANY (THE)
BROADCOM CORP
BROCADE COMMUNICATIONS SYSTEMS INC
BROOKDALE SENIOR LIVING INC
BROWN & BROWN INC
BRUKER CORP
BUCKLE INC (THE)
BUFFALO WILD WINGS INC
BUNGE LTD
BURLINGTON NORTHERN SANTA FE LLC
CABLEVISION SYSTEMS CORP
CACI INTERNATIONAL INC
CADENCE DESIGN SYSTEMS INC
CAESARS ENTERTAINMENT CORPORATION
CAMERON INTERNATIONAL CORPORATION
CAMPBELL SOUP CO
CAPITAL SENIOR LIVING CORP
CARLSON COMPANIES INC
CARMAX GROUP
CARNIVAL CORPORATION
CASH AMERICA INTERNATIONAL INC
CATERPILLAR INC
CATHOLIC HEALTH INITIATIVES
CB RICHARD ELLIS GROUP INC (CBRE)
CDW CORPORATION
CELGENE CORP
CELLCO PARTNERSHIP (VERIZON WIRELESS)
CEPHALON INC
CERNER CORP
CH ROBINSON WORLDWIDE INC
CHEMED CORPORATION
CHEVRON CORPORATION
CHEVRON PHILLIPS CHEMICAL COMPANY LLC
CHICO'S FAS INC
CHIPOTLE MEXICAN GRILL INC
CHS INC
CHUBB CORPORATION (THE)
CIENA CORP
CIGNA CORP
CINTAS CORP
CISCO SYSTEMS INC
CITRIX SYSTEMS INC
CLEARWIRE CORP
CLOROX CO (THE)
CNA FINANCIAL CORP
COACH INC
COCA-COLA BOTTLING CO CONSOLIDATED
COCA-COLA COMPANY (THE)
COGNIZANT TECHNOLOGY SOLUTIONS CORP
COLDWATER CREEK INC
COLGATE PALMOLIVE CO
COMCAST CORP
COMMUNITY HEALTH SYSTEMS INC
COMPUTER SCIENCES CORPORATION (CSC)
COMPUTER TASK GROUP INC
CONAGRA FOODS INC
CONCENTRA INC
CONOCOPHILLIPS COMPANY
CONSOL ENERGY INC
CONTAINER STORE (THE)
CON-WAY INC
COOPER COMPANIES INC
COSTCO WHOLESALE CORP
COVANCE INC
COX COMMUNICATIONS INC
CR BARD INC
CRACKER BARREL OLD COUNTRY STORE INC
CROCS INC
CSX CORP
CUMMINS INC
CVS CAREMARK CORPORATION
DANAHER CORP
DARDEN RESTAURANTS INC
DAVITA INC
DEAN FOODS CO
DEERE & CO
DELOITTE & TOUCHE USA LLP
DELOITTE CONSULTING LLP
DELTA APPAREL INC
DENTSPLY INTERNATIONAL INC
DEVRY INC
DIAMOND OFFSHORE DRILLING INC
DICK'S SPORTING GOODS INC
DIODES INC
DIRECTV
DOLLAR GENERAL CORPORATION
DTE ENERGY COMPANY
DUKE ENERGY CORP
DUPONT (E I DU PONT DE NEMOURS & CO)
DUPONT AGRICULTURE & NUTRITION
EATON CORP
EBAY INC
EDISON INTERNATIONAL
EDWARDS LIFESCIENCES CORP
EMC CORP
EMERITUS CORP
EMERSON ELECTRIC CO
ENDO PHARMACEUTICALS HOLDINGS INC
ENTERGY CORP
ENTERPRISE HOLDINGS INC
EQUITY LIFESTYLE PROPERTIES INC
ERNST & YOUNG LLP
ESTEE LAUDER COMPANIES INC (THE)
EXELON CORPORATION
EXPEDIA INC
EXPERIAN AMERICAS
EXPRESS SCRIPTS INC
EXTERRAN HOLDINGS INC
EXXON MOBIL CORPORATION (EXXONMOBIL)
EXXONMOBIL CHEMICAL
FACTSET RESEARCH SYSTEMS INC
FAIRVIEW HEALTH SERVICES
FAMILY DOLLAR STORES INC
FASTENAL
FEDERAL MOGUL CORP
FEDEX CORPORATION
FIDELITY NATIONAL INFORMATION SERVICES INC
FINISAR CORPORATION
FIRST ADVANTAGE CORPORATION
FIRSTENERGY CORP
FLUOR CORP
FMC TECHNOLOGIES INC
FMR CORP (FIDELITY INVESTMENTS)
FORD MOTOR CO
FOREST LABORATORIES INC
FORTUNE BRANDS INC

FOSSIL INC
FOX ENTERTAINMENT GROUP INC
FRONTIER COMMUNICATIONS CORPORATION
FTI CONSULTING INC
GAMESTOP CORP
GE ENERGY INFRASTRUCTURE
GENENTECH INC
GENERAL ELECTRIC CO (GE)
GENERAL MILLS INC
GENERAL MOTORS COMPANY (GM)
GENESCO INC
GENTEX CORPORATION
GENTIVA HEALTH SERVICES INC
GENWORTH FINANCIAL INC
GENZYME BIOSURGERY
GEOKINETICS INC
GILEAD SCIENCES INC
GOODYEAR TIRE & RUBBER COMPANY (THE)
GOOGLE INC
GRANT THORNTON LLP
GROUP 1 AUTOMOTIVE INC
GROUPON INC
GSI COMMERCE INC
GUESS? INC
HALLIBURTON COMPANY
HANESBRANDS INC
HANGER ORTHOPEDIC GROUP INC
HARRIS CORPORATION
HAWAIIAN ELECTRIC INDUSTRIES INC
HCA HOLDINGS INC
HE BUTT GROCERY COMPANY (HEB)
HEALTH CARE SERVICE CORPORATION (HCSC)
HEALTH FITNESS CORP
HEALTH MANAGEMENT ASSOCIATES INC
HEALTHSOUTH CORP
HEARTLAND PAYMENT SYSTEMS INC
HENRY SCHEIN INC
HERSHEY CO
HERTZ GLOBAL HOLDINGS INC
HIBBETT SPORTS INC
HILLENBRAND INC
HILTON HOTELS CORP
HONDA OF AMERICA MANUFACTURING INC
HOSPIRA INC
HUMANA INC
HYATT HOTELS CORPORATION
IAC/INTERACTIVECORP
ICF INTERNATIONAL INC
IDEXX LABORATORIES INC
IGATE CORPORATION
ILLINOIS TOOL WORKS INC
IMS HEALTH INC
INGRAM MICRO INC
INSITUFORM TECHNOLOGIES
INTEGRA LIFESCIENCES HOLDINGS CORP
INTEL CORP
INTERNATIONAL BUSINESS MACHINES CORP (IBM)
INTERPUBLIC GROUP OF COMPANIES INC
INTUIT INC
INVENTIV HEALTH INC
JACK HENRY & ASSOCIATES INC
JACKSON NATIONAL LIFE INSURANCE COMPANY
JARDEN CORP
JB HUNT TRANSPORT SERVICES INC
JETBLUE AIRWAYS CORPORATION
JM SMUCKER CO
JOHNSON & JOHNSON
JOHNSON CONTROLS INC
JONES LANG LASALLE INC
JUNIPER NETWORKS INC
KAISER PERMANENTE
KEANE INC
KELLOGG COMPANY
KELLY SERVICES INC
KEY ENERGY SERVICES INC
KIMBERLY-CLARK CORP
KINDRED HEALTHCARE INC
KINETIC CONCEPTS INC
KLA TENCOR CORP
KOCH INDUSTRIES INC
KOHL'S CORP
KPMG LLP
KRAFT FOODS INC
KROGER CO (THE)
LABORATORY CORP OF AMERICA HOLDINGS
LAM RESEARCH CORP
LAS VEGAS SANDS CORP (THE VENETIAN)
LEAP WIRELESS INTERNATIONAL INC
LEAR CORP
LEXMARK INTERNATIONAL INC
LIBERTY GLOBAL INC
LIBERTY MEDIA CORP
LIBERTY MUTUAL GROUP INC
LIFE TECHNOLOGIES CORP
LIMITED BRANDS INC
LINCARE HOLDINGS INC
LINCOLN NATIONAL CORPORATION
LKQ CORP
LOEWS CORPORATION
LORAL SPACE & COMMUNICATIONS LTD
LUFKIN INDUSTRIES INC
MACY'S INC
MANPOWER INC
MANTECH INTERNATIONAL CORP
MARATHON OIL CORP
MARRIOTT INTERNATIONAL INC
MARS INC
MARSH & MCLENNAN COMPANIES INC
MARY KAY INC
MASSACHUSETTS MUTUAL LIFE INSURANCE CO
MATTEL INC
MAXIMUS INC
MAYO FOUNDATION FOR MEDICAL EDUCATION AND RESEARCH
MCDONALD'S CORP
MCKESSON CORPORATION
MCKINSEY & COMPANY INC
MEDCO HEALTH SOLUTIONS INC
MEDIACOM COMMUNICATIONS CORP
MEDNAX INC
MEDTRONIC INC
MEIJER INC
MERCER INC
METHODIST HEALTH CARE SYSTEM
METLIFE INC
METROPCS COMMUNICATIONS INC
MICROCHIP TECHNOLOGY INC
MICRON TECHNOLOGY INC
MICROSOFT CORP
MIDAMERICAN ENERGY HOLDINGS CO
MILLIPORE CORP
MOLEX INC
MONRO MUFFLER BRAKE INC
MULTI-FINELINE ELECTRONIX INC

MUTUAL OF OMAHA COMPANIES (THE)
MYLAN INC
NABORS INDUSTRIES LTD
NACCO INDUSTRIES INC
NALCO HOLDING COMPANY
NATIONAL INSTRUMENTS CORP
NATIONAL OILWELL VARCO INC
NCR CORPORATION
NETAPP INC
NEW YORK LIFE INSURANCE CO
NEWS CORP
NEXTERA ENERGY INC
NII HOLDINGS INC
NIKE INC
NORFOLK SOUTHERN CORP
NORTH HIGHLAND
NORTHWESTERN MUTUAL LIFE INSURANCE CO
OCEANEERING INTERNATIONAL INC
ODYSSEY HEALTHCARE INC
OIL STATES INTERNATIONAL INC
OMNICOM GROUP INC
ORACLE CORP
O'REILLY AUTOMOTIVE INC
OSHKOSH CORPORATION
OWENS & MINOR INC
PACCAR INC
PANERA BREAD CO
PARAMETRIC TECHNOLOGY CORP
PAREXEL INTERNATIONAL CORP
PARK-OHIO HOLDINGS CORP
PARSONS BRINCKERHOFF INC
PATTERSON COMPANIES INC
PATTERSON-UTI ENERGY INC
PEABODY ENERGY CORP
PENSKE AUTOMOTIVE GROUP INC
PEPSICO INC
PERRIGO CO
PETCO ANIMAL SUPPLIES INC
PETSMART INC
PG&E CORPORATION
PHARMACEUTICAL PRODUCT DEVELOPMENT INC
PHILIP MORRIS INTERNATIONAL INC
PLEXUS CORP
POLO RALPH LAUREN CORP
POLYCOM INC
PRAXAIR INC
PRICESMART INC
PRICEWATERHOUSECOOPERS
PRINCIPAL FINANCIAL GROUP (THE)
PROCTER & GAMBLE CO
PROGRESSIVE CORPORATION (THE)
PROVIDENCE HEALTH & SERVICES
PRUDENTIAL FINANCIAL INC
PUBLIX SUPER MARKETS INC
QUALCOMM INC
QUANTA SERVICES INC
RACKSPACE HOSTING INC
RALCORP HOLDINGS INC
RECREATIONAL EQUIPMENT INC (REI)
RED HAT INC
REGIS CORPORATION
REPUBLIC AIRWAYS HOLDINGS INC
RESMED INC
ROBERT HALF INTERNATIONAL INC
ROSS STORES INC
ROWAN COMPANIES INC
ROYAL CARIBBEAN CRUISES LTD
RYDER SYSTEM INC
SABRE HOLDINGS CORP
SAFECO INSURANCE COMPANY OF AMERICA
SAFEWAY INC
SAIC INC
SALESFORCE.COM INC
SAM'S CLUB
SANDISK CORP
SANMINA-SCI CORPORATION
SAPIENT CORPORATION
SARA LEE CORP
SAS INSTITUTE INC
SCANA CORPORATION
SCHLUMBERGER LIMITED
SCOTTS MIRACLE GROW CO
SEACOR HOLDINGS INC
SELECT MEDICAL HOLDINGS CORPORATION
SEMPRA ENERGY
SENECA FOODS CORPORATION
SENSIENT TECHNOLOGIES CORPORATION
SHAW GROUP INC (THE)
SHELL OIL CO
SHERWIN WILLIAMS COMPANY (THE)
SIGMA-ALDRICH CORP
SKILLED HEALTHCARE GROUP INC
SNYDERS-LANCE INC
SODEXO INC
SOUTHERN COMPANY (THE)
SOUTHWEST AIRLINES CO
SPECTRUM HEALTH
SPIRIT AEROSYSTEMS HOLDINGS INC
SRA INTERNATIONAL INC
ST JUDE MEDICAL INC
STANLEY BLACK & DECKER INC
STARWOOD HOTELS & RESORTS WORLDWIDE INC
STERICYCLE INC
STIFEL FINANCIAL CORP
STONERIDGE INC
STREAM GLOBAL SERVICES INC
STRYKER CORP
SUN HEALTHCARE GROUP INC
SUTTER HEALTH INC
SYMANTEC CORP
SYNTEL INC
SYSCO CORP
TARGET CORPORATION
TEAM HEALTH HOLDINGS INC
TEAM INC
TECH DATA CORP
TEKTRONIX INC
TELEDYNE TECHNOLOGIES INC
TELEPHONE AND DATA SYSTEMS INC (TDS)
TENET HEALTHCARE CORPORATION
TEREX CORPORATION
TETRA TECH INC
THERMO FISHER SCIENTIFIC INC
THOMSON REUTERS
THOR INDUSTRIES INC
TIBCO SOFTWARE INC
TIDEWATER INC
TIFFANY & CO
TIME WARNER INC
TJX COMPANIES INC (THE)
TOTAL SYSTEM SERVICES INC (TSYS)
TOWERS WATSON & CO
TRAVELERS COMPANIES INC (THE)
TREEHOUSE FOODS INC
TRUSTMARK COMPANIES
TTM TECHNOLOGIES INC
TW TELECOM INC

UNDER ARMOUR INC
UNION PACIFIC CORP
UNITED NATURAL FOODS INC
UNITED PARCEL SERVICE INC (UPS)
UNITED STATES CELLULAR CORP
UNITED TECHNOLOGIES CORPORATION
UNITEDHEALTH GROUP INC
UNIVERSAL HEALTH SERVICES INC
UNIVISION COMMUNICATIONS INC
URS CORPORATION
USAA
VALASSIS COMMUNICATIONS INC
VALSPAR CORPORATION (THE)
VARIAN MEDICAL SYSTEMS INC
VCA ANTECH INC
VERIZON COMMUNICATIONS INC
VICTORIAS SECRET
VISA INC
VORNADO REALTY TRUST
WABTEC CORP
WALGREEN CO
WAL-MART STORES INC
WALT DISNEY COMPANY (THE)
WARNACO GROUP INC (THE)
WASTE MANAGEMENT INC
WATERS CORP
WATSON PHARMACEUTICALS INC
WEIGHT WATCHERS INTERNATIONAL INC
WEST PHARMACEUTICAL SERVICES INC
WESTERN DIGITAL CORP
WHOLE FOODS MARKET INC
WILLIAMS COMPANIES INC (THE)
WINDSTREAM CORPORATION
WM WRIGLEY JR COMPANY
WW GRAINGER INC
WYNDHAM WORLDWIDE
WYNN RESORTS LIMITED
XEROX CORP
YUM! BRANDS INC
ZIMMER HOLDINGS INC

Law
3M COMPANY
7-ELEVEN INC
ABM INDUSTRIES INC
ACADEMY SPORTS & OUTDOORS LTD
ACCENTURE PLC
ACTIVISION BLIZZARD INC
ADOBE SYSTEMS INC
ADVANCE AUTO PARTS INC
ADVANCED MICRO DEVICES INC (AMD)
ADVENTIST HEALTH SYSTEM
AECOM TECHNOLOGY CORPORATION
AES CORPORATION (THE)
AFFILIATED COMPUTER SERVICES INC
AFLAC INC
AGILENT TECHNOLOGIES INC
AIR PRODUCTS & CHEMICALS INC
ALASKA AIR GROUP INC
ALLERGAN INC
ALLIANCE DATA SYSTEMS CORPORATION
ALTRIA GROUP INC
AMAZON.COM INC
AMEDISYS INC
AMERCO
AMERICAN EXPRESS CO
AMERICAN POWER CONVERSION (APC)
AMERIGROUP CORPORATION
AMERISOURCEBERGEN CORP
AMGEN INC
AMKOR TECHNOLOGY INC
AMPHENOL CORPORATION
AMR CORP (AMERICAN AIRLINES)
AMSURG CORP
ANALOG DEVICES INC
APACHE CORP
APPLE INC
APPLIED MATERIALS INC
ARAMARK CORPORATION
ARCHER DANIELS MIDLAND CO
ARROW ELECTRONICS INC
ARTHUR J GALLAGHER & CO
ASCENA RETAIL GROUP INC
ASCENSION HEALTH
AT&T INC
AUTOMATIC DATA PROCESSING INC
AUTONATION INC
AUTOZONE INC
AVNET INC
AVON PRODUCTS INC
AXA FINANCIAL INC
BAIN & COMPANY INC
BAKER HUGHES INC
BALL CORP
BARRETT BUSINESS SERVICES
BASIC ENERGY SERVICES INC
BASS PRO SHOPS INC
BAUSCH & LOMB INC
BECHTEL GROUP INC
BECKMAN COULTER INC
BECTON DICKINSON & CO
BED BATH & BEYOND INC
BEMIS COMPANY INC
BERKSHIRE HATHAWAY INC
BEST BUY CO INC
BIG 5 SPORTING GOODS CORPORATION
BIO RAD LABORATORIES INC
BIOGEN IDEC INC
BLACKROCK INC
BLOOMBERG LP
BMC SOFTWARE INC
BOEING COMPANY (THE)
BOOZ ALLEN HAMILTON INC
BOSTON CONSULTING GROUP INC (THE, BCG)
BOYD GAMING CORP
BRINKS COMPANY (THE)
BROADCOM CORP
BROCADE COMMUNICATIONS SYSTEMS INC
BROOKDALE SENIOR LIVING INC
BROWN & BROWN INC
BRUKER CORP
BUCKLE INC (THE)
BUFFALO WILD WINGS INC
BUNGE LTD
BURLINGTON NORTHERN SANTA FE LLC
CABLEVISION SYSTEMS CORP
CACI INTERNATIONAL INC
CADENCE DESIGN SYSTEMS

INC
CAESARS ENTERTAINMENT CORPORATION
CAMERON INTERNATIONAL CORPORATION
CAMPBELL SOUP CO
CAPITAL SENIOR LIVING CORP
CARLSON COMPANIES INC
CARMAX GROUP
CARNIVAL CORPORATION
CASH AMERICA INTERNATIONAL INC
CATERPILLAR INC
CATHOLIC HEALTH INITIATIVES
CB RICHARD ELLIS GROUP INC (CBRE)
CDW CORPORATION
CELGENE CORP
CELLCO PARTNERSHIP (VERIZON WIRELESS)
CEPHALON INC
CERNER CORP
CH ROBINSON WORLDWIDE INC
CHEMED CORPORATION
CHEVRON CORPORATION
CHEVRON PHILLIPS CHEMICAL COMPANY LLC
CHICO'S FAS INC
CHIPOTLE MEXICAN GRILL INC
CHS INC
CHUBB CORPORATION (THE)
CIENA CORP
CIGNA CORP
CINTAS CORP
CISCO SYSTEMS INC
CITRIX SYSTEMS INC
CLEARWIRE CORP
CLOROX CO (THE)
CNA FINANCIAL CORP
COACH INC
COCA-COLA BOTTLING CO CONSOLIDATED
COCA-COLA COMPANY (THE)
COGNIZANT TECHNOLOGY SOLUTIONS CORP
COLDWATER CREEK INC
COLGATE PALMOLIVE CO
COMCAST CORP

COMMUNITY HEALTH SYSTEMS INC
COMPUTER SCIENCES CORPORATION (CSC)
COMPUTER TASK GROUP INC
CONAGRA FOODS INC
CONCENTRA INC
CONOCOPHILLIPS COMPANY
CONSOL ENERGY INC
CONTAINER STORE (THE)
CON-WAY INC
COOPER COMPANIES INC
COSTCO WHOLESALE CORP
COVANCE INC
COX COMMUNICATIONS INC
CR BARD INC
CRACKER BARREL OLD COUNTRY STORE INC
CROCS INC
CSX CORP
CUMMINS INC
CVS CAREMARK CORPORATION
DANAHER CORP
DARDEN RESTAURANTS INC
DAVITA INC
DEAN FOODS CO
DEERE & CO
DELOITTE & TOUCHE USA LLP
DELOITTE CONSULTING LLP
DELTA APPAREL INC
DENTSPLY INTERNATIONAL INC
DEVRY INC
DIAMOND OFFSHORE DRILLING INC
DICK'S SPORTING GOODS INC
DIODES INC
DIRECTV
DOLLAR GENERAL CORPORATION
DTE ENERGY COMPANY
DUKE ENERGY CORP
DUPONT (E I DU PONT DE NEMOURS & CO)
DUPONT AGRICULTURE & NUTRITION
EATON CORP
EBAY INC
EDISON INTERNATIONAL

EDWARDS LIFESCIENCES CORP
EMC CORP
EMERITUS CORP
EMERSON ELECTRIC CO
ENDO PHARMACEUTICALS HOLDINGS INC
ENTERGY CORP
ENTERPRISE HOLDINGS INC
EQUITY LIFESTYLE PROPERTIES INC
ERNST & YOUNG LLP
ESTEE LAUDER COMPANIES INC (THE)
EXELON CORPORATION
EXPEDIA INC
EXPERIAN AMERICAS
EXPRESS SCRIPTS INC
EXTERRAN HOLDINGS INC
EXXON MOBIL CORPORATION (EXXONMOBIL)
EXXONMOBIL CHEMICAL
FACTSET RESEARCH SYSTEMS INC
FAIRVIEW HEALTH SERVICES
FAMILY DOLLAR STORES INC
FASTENAL
FEDERAL MOGUL CORP
FEDEX CORPORATION
FIDELITY NATIONAL INFORMATION SERVICES INC
FINISAR CORPORATION
FIRST ADVANTAGE CORPORATION
FIRSTENERGY CORP
FLUOR CORP
FMC TECHNOLOGIES INC
FMR CORP (FIDELITY INVESTMENTS)
FORD MOTOR CO
FOREST LABORATORIES INC
FORTUNE BRANDS INC
FOSSIL INC
FOX ENTERTAINMENT GROUP INC
FRONTIER COMMUNICATIONS CORPORATION
FTI CONSULTING INC

GAMESTOP CORP
GE ENERGY INFRASTRUCTURE
GENENTECH INC
GENERAL ELECTRIC CO (GE)
GENERAL MILLS INC
GENERAL MOTORS COMPANY (GM)
GENESCO INC
GENTEX CORPORATION
GENTIVA HEALTH SERVICES INC
GENWORTH FINANCIAL INC
GENZYME BIOSURGERY
GEOKINETICS INC
GILEAD SCIENCES INC
GOODYEAR TIRE & RUBBER COMPANY (THE)
GOOGLE INC
GRANT THORNTON LLP
GROUP 1 AUTOMOTIVE INC
GROUPON INC
GSI COMMERCE INC
GUESS? INC
HALLIBURTON COMPANY
HANESBRANDS INC
HANGER ORTHOPEDIC GROUP INC
HARRIS CORPORATION
HAWAIIAN ELECTRIC INDUSTRIES INC
HCA HOLDINGS INC
HE BUTT GROCERY COMPANY (HEB)
HEALTH CARE SERVICE CORPORATION (HCSC)
HEALTH FITNESS CORP
HEALTH MANAGEMENT ASSOCIATES INC
HEALTHSOUTH CORP
HEARTLAND PAYMENT SYSTEMS INC
HENRY SCHEIN INC
HERSHEY CO
HERTZ GLOBAL HOLDINGS INC
HIBBETT SPORTS INC
HILLENBRAND INC
HILTON HOTELS CORP
HONDA OF AMERICA MANUFACTURING INC
HOSPIRA INC
HUMANA INC
HYATT HOTELS CORPORATION
IAC/INTERACTIVECORP
ICF INTERNATIONAL INC
IDEXX LABORATORIES INC
IGATE CORPORATION
ILLINOIS TOOL WORKS INC
IMS HEALTH INC
INGRAM MICRO INC
INSITUFORM TECHNOLOGIES
INTEGRA LIFESCIENCES HOLDINGS CORP
INTEL CORP
INTERNATIONAL BUSINESS MACHINES CORP (IBM)
INTERPUBLIC GROUP OF COMPANIES INC
INTUIT INC
INVENTIV HEALTH INC
JACK HENRY & ASSOCIATES INC
JACKSON NATIONAL LIFE INSURANCE COMPANY
JARDEN CORP
JB HUNT TRANSPORT SERVICES INC
JETBLUE AIRWAYS CORPORATION
JM SMUCKER CO
JOHNSON & JOHNSON
JOHNSON CONTROLS INC
JONES LANG LASALLE INC
JUNIPER NETWORKS INC
KAISER PERMANENTE
KEANE INC
KELLOGG COMPANY
KELLY SERVICES INC
KEY ENERGY SERVICES INC
KIMBERLY-CLARK CORP
KINDRED HEALTHCARE INC
KINETIC CONCEPTS INC
KLA TENCOR CORP
KOCH INDUSTRIES INC
KOHL'S CORP
KPMG LLP
KRAFT FOODS INC
KROGER CO (THE)
LABORATORY CORP OF AMERICA HOLDINGS
LAM RESEARCH CORP
LAS VEGAS SANDS CORP (THE VENETIAN)
LEAP WIRELESS INTERNATIONAL INC
LEAR CORP
LEXMARK INTERNATIONAL INC
LIBERTY GLOBAL INC
LIBERTY MEDIA CORP
LIBERTY MUTUAL GROUP INC
LIFE TECHNOLOGIES CORP
LIMITED BRANDS INC
LINCARE HOLDINGS INC
LINCOLN NATIONAL CORPORATION
LKQ CORP
LOEWS CORPORATION
LORAL SPACE & COMMUNICATIONS LTD
LUFKIN INDUSTRIES INC
MACY'S INC
MANPOWER INC
MANTECH INTERNATIONAL CORP
MARATHON OIL CORP
MARRIOTT INTERNATIONAL INC
MARS INC
MARSH & MCLENNAN COMPANIES INC
MARY KAY INC
MASSACHUSETTS MUTUAL LIFE INSURANCE CO
MATTEL INC
MAXIMUS INC
MAYO FOUNDATION FOR MEDICAL EDUCATION AND RESEARCH
MCDONALD'S CORP
MCKESSON CORPORATION
MCKINSEY & COMPANY INC
MEDCO HEALTH SOLUTIONS INC
MEDIACOM COMMUNICATIONS CORP
MEDNAX INC
MEDTRONIC INC

MEIJER INC
MERCER INC
METHODIST HEALTH CARE SYSTEM
METLIFE INC
METROPCS COMMUNICATIONS INC
MICROCHIP TECHNOLOGY INC
MICRON TECHNOLOGY INC
MICROSOFT CORP
MIDAMERICAN ENERGY HOLDINGS CO
MILLIPORE CORP
MOLEX INC
MONRO MUFFLER BRAKE INC
MULTI-FINELINE ELECTRONIX INC
MUTUAL OF OMAHA COMPANIES (THE)
MYLAN INC
NABORS INDUSTRIES LTD
NACCO INDUSTRIES INC
NALCO HOLDING COMPANY
NATIONAL INSTRUMENTS CORP
NATIONAL OILWELL VARCO INC
NCR CORPORATION
NETAPP INC
NEW YORK LIFE INSURANCE CO
NEWS CORP
NEXTERA ENERGY INC
NII HOLDINGS INC
NIKE INC
NORFOLK SOUTHERN CORP
NORTH HIGHLAND
OCEANEERING INTERNATIONAL INC
ODYSSEY HEALTHCARE INC
OIL STATES INTERNATIONAL INC
OMNICOM GROUP INC
ORACLE CORP
O'REILLY AUTOMOTIVE INC
OSHKOSH CORPORATION
OWENS & MINOR INC
PACCAR INC
PANERA BREAD CO
PARAMETRIC TECHNOLOGY CORP
PAREXEL INTERNATIONAL CORP
PARK-OHIO HOLDINGS CORP
PARSONS BRINCKERHOFF INC
PATTERSON COMPANIES INC
PATTERSON-UTI ENERGY INC
PEABODY ENERGY CORP
PENSKE AUTOMOTIVE GROUP INC
PEPSICO INC
PERRIGO CO
PETCO ANIMAL SUPPLIES INC
PETSMART INC
PG&E CORPORATION
PHARMACEUTICAL PRODUCT DEVELOPMENT INC
PHILIP MORRIS INTERNATIONAL INC
PLEXUS CORP
POLO RALPH LAUREN CORP
POLYCOM INC
PRAXAIR INC
PRICESMART INC
PRICEWATERHOUSECOOPERS
PRINCIPAL FINANCIAL GROUP (THE)
PROCTER & GAMBLE CO
PROGRESSIVE CORPORATION (THE)
PROVIDENCE HEALTH & SERVICES
PRUDENTIAL FINANCIAL INC
PUBLIX SUPER MARKETS INC
QUALCOMM INC
QUANTA SERVICES INC
RACKSPACE HOSTING INC
RALCORP HOLDINGS INC
RECREATIONAL EQUIPMENT INC (REI)
RED HAT INC
REGIS CORPORATION
REPUBLIC AIRWAYS HOLDINGS INC
RESMED INC
ROBERT HALF INTERNATIONAL INC
ROSS STORES INC
ROWAN COMPANIES INC
ROYAL CARIBBEAN CRUISES LTD
RYDER SYSTEM INC
SABRE HOLDINGS CORP
SAFECO INSURANCE COMPANY OF AMERICA
SAFEWAY INC
SAIC INC
SALESFORCE.COM INC
SAM'S CLUB
SANDISK CORP
SANMINA-SCI CORPORATION
SAPIENT CORPORATION
SARA LEE CORP
SAS INSTITUTE INC
SCANA CORPORATION
SCHLUMBERGER LIMITED
SCOTTS MIRACLE GROW CO
SEACOR HOLDINGS INC
SELECT MEDICAL HOLDINGS CORPORATION
SEMPRA ENERGY
SENECA FOODS CORPORATION
SENSIENT TECHNOLOGIES CORPORATION
SHAW GROUP INC (THE)
SHELL OIL CO
SHERWIN WILLIAMS COMPANY (THE)
SIGMA-ALDRICH CORP
SKILLED HEALTHCARE GROUP INC
SNYDERS-LANCE INC
SODEXO INC
SOUTHERN COMPANY (THE)
SOUTHWEST AIRLINES CO
SPECTRUM HEALTH
SPIRIT AEROSYSTEMS HOLDINGS INC
SRA INTERNATIONAL INC
ST JUDE MEDICAL INC
STANLEY BLACK & DECKER INC
STARWOOD HOTELS & RESORTS WORLDWIDE INC
STERICYCLE INC
STIFEL FINANCIAL CORP
STONERIDGE INC

STREAM GLOBAL SERVICES INC
STRYKER CORP
SUN HEALTHCARE GROUP INC
SUTTER HEALTH INC
SYMANTEC CORP
SYNTEL INC
SYSCO CORP
TARGET CORPORATION
TEAM HEALTH HOLDINGS INC
TEAM INC
TECH DATA CORP
TEKTRONIX INC
TELEDYNE TECHNOLOGIES INC
TELEPHONE AND DATA SYSTEMS INC (TDS)
TENET HEALTHCARE CORPORATION
TEREX CORPORATION
TETRA TECH INC
THERMO FISHER SCIENTIFIC INC
THOMSON REUTERS
THOR INDUSTRIES INC
TIBCO SOFTWARE INC
TIDEWATER INC
TIFFANY & CO
TIME WARNER INC
TJX COMPANIES INC (THE)
TOTAL SYSTEM SERVICES INC (TSYS)
TOWERS WATSON & CO
TRAVELERS COMPANIES INC (THE)
TREEHOUSE FOODS INC
TRUSTMARK COMPANIES
TTM TECHNOLOGIES INC
TW TELECOM INC
UNDER ARMOUR INC
UNION PACIFIC CORP
UNITED NATURAL FOODS INC
UNITED PARCEL SERVICE INC (UPS)
UNITED STATES CELLULAR CORP
UNITED TECHNOLOGIES CORPORATION
UNITEDHEALTH GROUP INC
UNIVERSAL HEALTH SERVICES INC
UNIVISION COMMUNICATIONS INC
URS CORPORATION
USAA
VALASSIS COMMUNICATIONS INC
VALSPAR CORPORATION (THE)
VARIAN MEDICAL SYSTEMS INC
VCA ANTECH INC
VERIZON COMMUNICATIONS INC
VICTORIAS SECRET
VISA INC
VORNADO REALTY TRUST
WABTEC CORP
WALGREEN CO
WAL-MART STORES INC
WALT DISNEY COMPANY (THE)
WARNACO GROUP INC (THE)
WASTE MANAGEMENT INC
WATERS CORP
WATSON PHARMACEUTICALS INC
WEIGHT WATCHERS INTERNATIONAL INC
WEST PHARMACEUTICAL SERVICES INC
WESTERN DIGITAL CORP
WHOLE FOODS MARKET INC
WILLIAMS COMPANIES INC (THE)
WINDSTREAM CORPORATION
WM WRIGLEY JR COMPANY
WW GRAINGER INC
WYNDHAM WORLDWIDE
WYNN RESORTS LIMITED
XEROX CORP
YUM! BRANDS INC
ZIMMER HOLDINGS INC

Training
3M COMPANY
7-ELEVEN INC
ABM INDUSTRIES INC
ACADEMY SPORTS & OUTDOORS LTD
ACCENTURE PLC
ACTIVISION BLIZZARD INC
ADOBE SYSTEMS INC
ADVANCE AUTO PARTS INC
ADVANCED MICRO DEVICES INC (AMD)
ADVENTIST HEALTH SYSTEM
AECOM TECHNOLOGY CORPORATION
AES CORPORATION (THE)
AFFILIATED COMPUTER SERVICES INC
AFLAC INC
AGILENT TECHNOLOGIES INC
AIR PRODUCTS & CHEMICALS INC
ALASKA AIR GROUP INC
ALLERGAN INC
ALLIANCE DATA SYSTEMS CORPORATION
ALTRIA GROUP INC
AMAZON.COM INC
AMEDISYS INC
AMERICAN EXPRESS CO
AMERICAN POWER CONVERSION (APC)
AMERIGROUP CORPORATION
AMERISOURCEBERGEN CORP
AMGEN INC
AMR CORP (AMERICAN AIRLINES)
AMSURG CORP
ANALOG DEVICES INC
APACHE CORP
APPLE INC
ARAMARK CORPORATION
ARCHER DANIELS MIDLAND CO
ARROW ELECTRONICS INC
ARTHUR J GALLAGHER & CO
ASCENA RETAIL GROUP INC
ASCENSION HEALTH
AT&T INC
AUTOMATIC DATA PROCESSING INC
AUTONATION INC
AUTOZONE INC
AVNET INC
AVON PRODUCTS INC
AXA FINANCIAL INC
BAKER HUGHES INC
BALL CORP
BARRETT BUSINESS SERVICES
BASIC ENERGY SERVICES INC
BASS PRO SHOPS INC

BAUSCH & LOMB INC
BECHTEL GROUP INC
BECKMAN COULTER INC
BECTON DICKINSON & CO
BED BATH & BEYOND INC
BERKSHIRE HATHAWAY INC
BEST BUY CO INC
BIG 5 SPORTING GOODS CORPORATION
BIO RAD LABORATORIES INC
BIOGEN IDEC INC
BLACKROCK INC
BLOOMBERG LP
BMC SOFTWARE INC
BOEING COMPANY (THE)
BOOZ ALLEN HAMILTON INC
BOYD GAMING CORP
BRINKS COMPANY (THE)
BROADCOM CORP
BROCADE COMMUNICATIONS SYSTEMS INC
BROWN & BROWN INC
BUCKLE INC (THE)
BUFFALO WILD WINGS INC
BUNGE LTD
BURLINGTON NORTHERN SANTA FE LLC
CABLEVISION SYSTEMS CORP
CACI INTERNATIONAL INC
CAESARS ENTERTAINMENT CORPORATION
CAMERON INTERNATIONAL CORPORATION
CAMPBELL SOUP CO
CAPITAL SENIOR LIVING CORP
CARLSON COMPANIES INC
CARMAX GROUP
CARNIVAL CORPORATION
CASH AMERICA INTERNATIONAL INC
CATERPILLAR INC
CATHOLIC HEALTH INITIATIVES
CB RICHARD ELLIS GROUP INC (CBRE)
CDW CORPORATION
CELGENE CORP
CELLCO PARTNERSHIP (VERIZON WIRELESS)
CEPHALON INC
CERNER CORP
CH ROBINSON WORLDWIDE INC
CHEMED CORPORATION
CHEVRON CORPORATION
CHEVRON PHILLIPS CHEMICAL COMPANY LLC
CHICO'S FAS INC
CHIPOTLE MEXICAN GRILL INC
CHS INC
CHUBB CORPORATION (THE)
CIGNA CORP
CINTAS CORP
CISCO SYSTEMS INC
CITRIX SYSTEMS INC
CLEARWIRE CORP
CLOROX CO (THE)
CNA FINANCIAL CORP
COACH INC
COCA-COLA BOTTLING CO CONSOLIDATED
COCA-COLA COMPANY (THE)
COGNIZANT TECHNOLOGY SOLUTIONS CORP
COLDWATER CREEK INC
COLGATE PALMOLIVE CO
COMCAST CORP
COMMUNITY HEALTH SYSTEMS INC
COMPUTER SCIENCES CORPORATION (CSC)
COMPUTER TASK GROUP INC
CONAGRA FOODS INC
CONOCOPHILLIPS COMPANY
CONSOL ENERGY INC
CONTAINER STORE (THE)
COOPER COMPANIES INC
COSTCO WHOLESALE CORP
COVANCE INC
COX COMMUNICATIONS INC
CR BARD INC
CRACKER BARREL OLD COUNTRY STORE INC
CSX CORP
CUMMINS INC
CVS CAREMARK CORPORATION
DANAHER CORP
DARDEN RESTAURANTS INC
DAVITA INC
DEAN FOODS CO
DEERE & CO
DELOITTE & TOUCHE USA LLP
DELOITTE CONSULTING LLP
DENTSPLY INTERNATIONAL INC
DEVRY INC
DIAMOND OFFSHORE DRILLING INC
DICK'S SPORTING GOODS INC
DIRECTV
DOLLAR GENERAL CORPORATION
DTE ENERGY COMPANY
DUKE ENERGY CORP
DUPONT (E I DU PONT DE NEMOURS & CO)
EATON CORP
EBAY INC
EDISON INTERNATIONAL
EDWARDS LIFESCIENCES CORP
EMC CORP
EMERITUS CORP
EMERSON ELECTRIC CO
ENTERGY CORP
ENTERPRISE HOLDINGS INC
ERNST & YOUNG LLP
ESTEE LAUDER COMPANIES INC (THE)
EXELON CORPORATION
EXPEDIA INC
EXPERIAN AMERICAS
EXPRESS SCRIPTS INC
EXXON MOBIL CORPORATION (EXXONMOBIL)
EXXONMOBIL CHEMICAL
FAMILY DOLLAR STORES INC
FEDEX CORPORATION
FIDELITY NATIONAL INFORMATION SERVICES INC
FINISAR CORPORATION
FIRST ADVANTAGE CORPORATION
FIRSTENERGY CORP
FLUOR CORP
FMC TECHNOLOGIES INC
FMR CORP (FIDELITY INVESTMENTS)
FORD MOTOR CO
FOREST LABORATORIES INC
FORTUNE BRANDS INC
FOSSIL INC
FOX ENTERTAINMENT GROUP INC
FRONTIER COMMUNICATIONS CORPORATION
FTI CONSULTING INC
GAMESTOP CORP
GENENTECH INC
GENERAL ELECTRIC CO (GE)
GENERAL MILLS INC
GENERAL MOTORS COMPANY (GM)
GENESCO INC

GENTEX CORPORATION
GENTIVA HEALTH SERVICES INC
GENWORTH FINANCIAL INC
GENZYME BIOSURGERY
GILEAD SCIENCES INC
GOODYEAR TIRE & RUBBER COMPANY (THE)
GOOGLE INC
GRANT THORNTON LLP
GROUP 1 AUTOMOTIVE INC
GUESS? INC
HALLIBURTON COMPANY
HANGER ORTHOPEDIC GROUP INC
HARRIS CORPORATION
HAWAIIAN ELECTRIC INDUSTRIES INC
HCA HOLDINGS INC
HE BUTT GROCERY COMPANY (HEB)
HEALTH CARE SERVICE CORPORATION (HCSC)
HEALTH FITNESS CORP
HEALTH MANAGEMENT ASSOCIATES INC
HEALTHSOUTH CORP
HENRY SCHEIN INC
HERSHEY CO
HERTZ GLOBAL HOLDINGS INC
HIBBETT SPORTS INC
HILTON HOTELS CORP
HONDA OF AMERICA MANUFACTURING INC
HUMANA INC
HYATT HOTELS CORPORATION
IAC/INTERACTIVECORP
IDEXX LABORATORIES INC
IGATE CORPORATION
ILLINOIS TOOL WORKS INC
IMS HEALTH INC
INGRAM MICRO INC
INTEL CORP
INTERNATIONAL BUSINESS MACHINES CORP (IBM)
INTERPUBLIC GROUP OF COMPANIES INC
INTUIT INC
INVENTIV HEALTH INC
JACK HENRY & ASSOCIATES INC
JACKSON NATIONAL LIFE INSURANCE COMPANY
JB HUNT TRANSPORT SERVICES INC

JETBLUE AIRWAYS CORPORATION
JM SMUCKER CO
JOHNSON & JOHNSON
JOHNSON CONTROLS INC
JONES LANG LASALLE INC
JUNIPER NETWORKS INC
KAISER PERMANENTE
KEANE INC
KELLOGG COMPANY
KELLY SERVICES INC
KEY ENERGY SERVICES INC
KIMBERLY-CLARK CORP
KINDRED HEALTHCARE INC
KINETIC CONCEPTS INC
KOCH INDUSTRIES INC
KOHL'S CORP
KPMG LLP
KRAFT FOODS INC
KROGER CO (THE)
LABORATORY CORP OF AMERICA HOLDINGS
LAS VEGAS SANDS CORP (THE VENETIAN)
LEAP WIRELESS INTERNATIONAL INC
LEAR CORP
LEXMARK INTERNATIONAL INC
LIBERTY GLOBAL INC
LIBERTY MEDIA CORP
LIBERTY MUTUAL GROUP INC
LIFE TECHNOLOGIES CORP
LIMITED BRANDS INC
LINCARE HOLDINGS INC
LINCOLN NATIONAL CORPORATION
LKQ CORP
LOEWS CORPORATION
LORAL SPACE & COMMUNICATIONS LTD
MACY'S INC
MANPOWER INC
MARATHON OIL CORP
MARRIOTT INTERNATIONAL INC
MARS INC
MARSH & MCLENNAN COMPANIES INC
MARY KAY INC
MASSACHUSETTS MUTUAL LIFE INSURANCE CO
MATTEL INC
MAYO FOUNDATION FOR MEDICAL EDUCATION AND RESEARCH
MCDONALD'S CORP

MCKESSON CORPORATION
MCKINSEY & COMPANY INC
MEDCO HEALTH SOLUTIONS INC
MEDIACOM COMMUNICATIONS CORP
MEDNAX INC
MEDTRONIC INC
MEIJER INC
MERCER INC
METHODIST HEALTH CARE SYSTEM
METLIFE INC
METROPCS COMMUNICATIONS INC
MICROCHIP TECHNOLOGY INC
MICRON TECHNOLOGY INC
MICROSOFT CORP
MIDAMERICAN ENERGY HOLDINGS CO
MILLIPORE CORP
MOLEX INC
MONRO MUFFLER BRAKE INC
MUTUAL OF OMAHA COMPANIES (THE)
MYLAN INC
NACCO INDUSTRIES INC
NATIONAL OILWELL VARCO INC
NCR CORPORATION
NETAPP INC
NEW YORK LIFE INSURANCE CO
NEWS CORP
NEXTERA ENERGY INC
NII HOLDINGS INC
NIKE INC
NORFOLK SOUTHERN CORP
OCEANEERING INTERNATIONAL INC
ODYSSEY HEALTHCARE INC
OIL STATES INTERNATIONAL INC
OMNICOM GROUP INC
ORACLE CORP
O'REILLY AUTOMOTIVE INC
OSHKOSH CORPORATION
OWENS & MINOR INC
PACCAR INC
PANERA BREAD CO
PARAMETRIC TECHNOLOGY CORP
PAREXEL INTERNATIONAL CORP
PARSONS BRINCKERHOFF INC
PATTERSON COMPANIES INC
PATTERSON-UTI ENERGY INC
PEABODY ENERGY CORP

PENSKE AUTOMOTIVE GROUP INC
PEPSICO INC
PERRIGO CO
PETCO ANIMAL SUPPLIES INC
PETSMART INC
PG&E CORPORATION
PHARMACEUTICAL PRODUCT DEVELOPMENT INC
PHILIP MORRIS INTERNATIONAL INC
PLEXUS CORP
POLO RALPH LAUREN CORP
PRAXAIR INC
PRICESMART INC
PRICEWATERHOUSECOOPERS
PRINCIPAL FINANCIAL GROUP (THE)
PROCTER & GAMBLE CO
PROGRESSIVE CORPORATION (THE)
PROVIDENCE HEALTH & SERVICES
PRUDENTIAL FINANCIAL INC
PUBLIX SUPER MARKETS INC
QUALCOMM INC
QUANTA SERVICES INC
RALCORP HOLDINGS INC
RECREATIONAL EQUIPMENT INC (REI)
REGIS CORPORATION
REPUBLIC AIRWAYS HOLDINGS INC
ROBERT HALF INTERNATIONAL INC
ROSS STORES INC
ROWAN COMPANIES INC
ROYAL CARIBBEAN CRUISES LTD
RYDER SYSTEM INC
SABRE HOLDINGS CORP
SAFECO INSURANCE COMPANY OF AMERICA
SAFEWAY INC
SAIC INC
SALESFORCE.COM INC
SAM'S CLUB
SANMINA-SCI CORPORATION
SAPIENT CORPORATION
SARA LEE CORP
SAS INSTITUTE INC
SCANA CORPORATION
SCHLUMBERGER LIMITED
SCOTTS MIRACLE GROW CO
SEACOR HOLDINGS INC
SELECT MEDICAL HOLDINGS CORPORATION
SEMPRA ENERGY
SENSIENT TECHNOLOGIES CORPORATION
SHAW GROUP INC (THE)
SHELL OIL CO
SHERWIN WILLIAMS COMPANY (THE)
SIGMA-ALDRICH CORP
SKILLED HEALTHCARE GROUP INC
SNYDERS-LANCE INC
SODEXO INC
SOUTHERN COMPANY (THE)
SOUTHWEST AIRLINES CO
SPECTRUM HEALTH
SRA INTERNATIONAL INC
ST JUDE MEDICAL INC
STANLEY BLACK & DECKER INC
STARWOOD HOTELS & RESORTS WORLDWIDE INC
STIFEL FINANCIAL CORP
STRYKER CORP
SUN HEALTHCARE GROUP INC
SUTTER HEALTH INC
SYMANTEC CORP
SYNTEL INC
SYSCO CORP
TARGET CORPORATION
TEAM HEALTH HOLDINGS INC
TEAM INC
TECH DATA CORP
TEKTRONIX INC
TELEDYNE TECHNOLOGIES INC
TELEPHONE AND DATA SYSTEMS INC (TDS)
TENET HEALTHCARE CORPORATION
THERMO FISHER SCIENTIFIC INC
THOMSON REUTERS
THOR INDUSTRIES INC
TIDEWATER INC
TIFFANY & CO
TIME WARNER INC
TJX COMPANIES INC (THE)
TOTAL SYSTEM SERVICES INC (TSYS)
TOWERS WATSON & CO
TRAVELERS COMPANIES INC (THE)
TREEHOUSE FOODS INC
TW TELECOM INC
UNION PACIFIC CORP
UNITED NATURAL FOODS INC
UNITED PARCEL SERVICE INC (UPS)
UNITED STATES CELLULAR CORP
UNITED TECHNOLOGIES CORPORATION
UNITEDHEALTH GROUP INC
UNIVERSAL HEALTH SERVICES INC
UNIVISION COMMUNICATIONS INC
URS CORPORATION
USAA
VALSPAR CORPORATION (THE)
VARIAN MEDICAL SYSTEMS INC
VCA ANTECH INC
VERIZON COMMUNICATIONS INC
VICTORIAS SECRET
VISA INC
WABTEC CORP
WALGREEN CO
WAL-MART STORES INC
WALT DISNEY COMPANY (THE)
WARNACO GROUP INC (THE)
WASTE MANAGEMENT INC
WATERS CORP
WATSON PHARMACEUTICALS INC
WEIGHT WATCHERS INTERNATIONAL INC
WEST PHARMACEUTICAL SERVICES INC
WESTERN DIGITAL CORP
WHOLE FOODS MARKET INC
WILLIAMS COMPANIES INC (THE)
WM WRIGLEY JR COMPANY
WW GRAINGER INC
WYNDHAM WORLDWIDE
WYNN RESORTS LIMITED
XEROX CORP
YUM! BRANDS INC
ZIMMER HOLDINGS INC

Sales/Marketing

Advertising Professionals
3M COMPANY
7-ELEVEN INC
ABM INDUSTRIES INC
ACADEMY SPORTS & OUTDOORS LTD
ACCENTURE PLC
ACOSTA SALES & MARKETING
ACTIVISION BLIZZARD INC
ADOBE SYSTEMS INC

ADVANCE AUTO PARTS INC
ADVANCED MICRO DEVICES INC (AMD)
ADVENTIST HEALTH SYSTEM
AES CORPORATION (THE)
AFLAC INC
AGILENT TECHNOLOGIES INC
ALASKA AIR GROUP INC
ALLERGAN INC
ALLIANCE DATA SYSTEMS CORPORATION
ALTRIA GROUP INC
AMAZON.COM INC
AMERICAN EXPRESS CO
AMERICAN POWER CONVERSION (APC)
AMERISOURCEBERGEN CORP
AMKOR TECHNOLOGY INC
AMPHENOL CORPORATION
AMR CORP (AMERICAN AIRLINES)
AMSURG CORP
ANALOG DEVICES INC
APPLE INC
APPLIED MATERIALS INC
ARAMARK CORPORATION
ARCHER DANIELS MIDLAND CO
ARROW ELECTRONICS INC
ARTHUR J GALLAGHER & CO
ASCENA RETAIL GROUP INC
ASCENSION HEALTH
AT&T INC
AUTOMATIC DATA PROCESSING INC
AUTONATION INC
AUTOZONE INC
AVON PRODUCTS INC
AXA FINANCIAL INC
BALL CORP
BARRETT BUSINESS SERVICES
BASIC ENERGY SERVICES INC
BASS PRO SHOPS INC
BAUSCH & LOMB INC
BECKMAN COULTER INC
BECTON DICKINSON & CO
BED BATH & BEYOND INC
BERKSHIRE HATHAWAY INC
BEST BUY CO INC
BIG 5 SPORTING GOODS CORPORATION
BIO RAD LABORATORIES INC
BLOOMBERG LP
BMC SOFTWARE INC
BOEING COMPANY (THE)
BOOZ ALLEN HAMILTON INC
BOYD GAMING CORP
BRINKS COMPANY (THE)
BROADCOM CORP
BROWN & BROWN INC
BRUKER CORP
BUCKLE INC (THE)
BUFFALO WILD WINGS INC
BURLINGTON NORTHERN SANTA FE LLC
CABLEVISION SYSTEMS CORP
CADENCE DESIGN SYSTEMS INC
CAESARS ENTERTAINMENT CORPORATION
CAMPBELL SOUP CO
CAPITAL SENIOR LIVING CORP
CARLSON COMPANIES INC
CARMAX GROUP
CARNIVAL CORPORATION
CASH AMERICA INTERNATIONAL INC
CATERPILLAR INC
CATHOLIC HEALTH INITIATIVES
CDW CORPORATION
CELLCO PARTNERSHIP (VERIZON WIRELESS)
CERNER CORP
CH ROBINSON WORLDWIDE INC
CHEVRON CORPORATION
CHICO'S FAS INC
CHIPOTLE MEXICAN GRILL INC
CHUBB CORPORATION (THE)
CIENA CORP
CIGNA CORP
CINTAS CORP
CISCO SYSTEMS INC
CITRIX SYSTEMS INC
CLEARWIRE CORP
CLOROX CO (THE)
CNA FINANCIAL CORP
COACH INC
COCA-COLA COMPANY (THE)
COLDWATER CREEK INC
COLGATE PALMOLIVE CO
COMCAST CORP
COMMUNITY HEALTH SYSTEMS INC
CONAGRA FOODS INC
CONCENTRA INC
CONOCOPHILLIPS COMPANY
CONTAINER STORE (THE)
CON-WAY INC
COOPER COMPANIES INC
COSTCO WHOLESALE CORP
COVANCE INC
COX COMMUNICATIONS INC
CR BARD INC
CRACKER BARREL OLD COUNTRY STORE INC
CROCS INC
CSX CORP
CUMMINS INC
CVS CAREMARK CORPORATION
DANAHER CORP
DARDEN RESTAURANTS INC
DEAN FOODS CO
DEERE & CO
DELOITTE & TOUCHE USA LLP
DELOITTE CONSULTING LLP
DELTA APPAREL INC
DENTSPLY INTERNATIONAL INC
DEVRY INC
DICK'S SPORTING GOODS INC
DIRECTV
DOLLAR GENERAL CORPORATION
DTE ENERGY COMPANY
DUKE ENERGY CORP
DUPONT AGRICULTURE & NUTRITION
EATON CORP
EBAY INC
EDISON INTERNATIONAL
EDWARDS LIFESCIENCES CORP
EMC CORP
EMERITUS CORP
EMERSON ELECTRIC CO
ENDO PHARMACEUTICALS HOLDINGS INC
ENTERGY CORP
ENTERPRISE HOLDINGS INC
ERNST & YOUNG LLP
ESTEE LAUDER COMPANIES INC (THE)
EXELON CORPORATION
EXPEDIA INC
EXPERIAN AMERICAS
EXPRESS SCRIPTS INC
EXTERRAN HOLDINGS INC
EXXON MOBIL CORPORATION (EXXONMOBIL)
FACTSET RESEARCH SYSTEMS INC

FAIRVIEW HEALTH SERVICES
FAMILY DOLLAR STORES INC
FASTENAL
FEDERAL MOGUL CORP
FEDEX CORPORATION
FIRSTENERGY CORP
FLUOR CORP
FMR CORP (FIDELITY INVESTMENTS)
FORD MOTOR CO
FORTUNE BRANDS INC
FOSSIL INC
FOX ENTERTAINMENT GROUP INC
FRONTIER COMMUNICATIONS CORPORATION
GAMESTOP CORP
GE ENERGY INFRASTRUCTURE
GENENTECH INC
GENERAL ELECTRIC CO (GE)
GENERAL MILLS INC
GENERAL MOTORS COMPANY (GM)
GENESCO INC
GENTEX CORPORATION
GENWORTH FINANCIAL INC
GENZYME BIOSURGERY
GEOKINETICS INC
GOODYEAR TIRE & RUBBER COMPANY (THE)
GOOGLE INC
GRANT THORNTON LLP
GROUP 1 AUTOMOTIVE INC
GROUPON INC
GSI COMMERCE INC
GUESS? INC
HALLIBURTON COMPANY
HANESBRANDS INC
HARRIS CORPORATION
HAWAIIAN ELECTRIC INDUSTRIES INC
HCA HOLDINGS INC
HE BUTT GROCERY COMPANY (HEB)
HEALTH FITNESS CORP
HEALTH MANAGEMENT ASSOCIATES INC
HEALTHSOUTH CORP
HENRY SCHEIN INC
HERSHEY CO
HERTZ GLOBAL HOLDINGS INC
HIBBETT SPORTS INC
HILLENBRAND INC
HILTON HOTELS CORP
HONDA OF AMERICA MANUFACTURING INC
HUMANA INC
HYATT HOTELS CORPORATION
IAC/INTERACTIVECORP
ILLINOIS TOOL WORKS INC
IMS HEALTH INC
INGRAM MICRO INC
INTEL CORP
INTERNATIONAL BUSINESS MACHINES CORP (IBM)
INTERPUBLIC GROUP OF COMPANIES INC
INTUIT INC
JACK HENRY & ASSOCIATES INC
JACKSON NATIONAL LIFE INSURANCE COMPANY
JARDEN CORP
JETBLUE AIRWAYS CORPORATION
JM SMUCKER CO
JOHNSON & JOHNSON
JOHNSON CONTROLS INC
JUNIPER NETWORKS INC
KAISER PERMANENTE
KEANE INC
KELLOGG COMPANY
KELLY SERVICES INC
KEY ENERGY SERVICES INC
KIMBERLY-CLARK CORP
KINDRED HEALTHCARE INC
KINETIC CONCEPTS INC
KLA TENCOR CORP
KOHL'S CORP
KPMG LLP
KRAFT FOODS INC
KROGER CO (THE)
LAM RESEARCH CORP
LAS VEGAS SANDS CORP (THE VENETIAN)
LEAP WIRELESS INTERNATIONAL INC
LEXMARK INTERNATIONAL INC
LIBERTY GLOBAL INC
LIBERTY MEDIA CORP
LIBERTY MUTUAL GROUP INC
LIMITED BRANDS INC
LINCOLN NATIONAL CORPORATION
LOEWS CORPORATION
LORAL SPACE & COMMUNICATIONS LTD
LUFKIN INDUSTRIES INC
MACY'S INC
MANPOWER INC
MANTECH INTERNATIONAL CORP
MARRIOTT INTERNATIONAL INC
MARS INC
MARSH & MCLENNAN COMPANIES INC
MARY KAY INC
MASSACHUSETTS MUTUAL LIFE INSURANCE CO
MATTEL INC
MAYO FOUNDATION FOR MEDICAL EDUCATION AND RESEARCH
MCDONALD'S CORP
MCKESSON CORPORATION
MCKINSEY & COMPANY INC
MEDCO HEALTH SOLUTIONS INC
MEDIACOM COMMUNICATIONS CORP
MEDNAX INC
MEDTRONIC INC
MEIJER INC
MERCER INC
METHODIST HEALTH CARE SYSTEM
METLIFE INC
METROPCS COMMUNICATIONS INC
MICROCHIP TECHNOLOGY INC
MICRON TECHNOLOGY INC
MICROSOFT CORP
MILLIPORE CORP
MOLEX INC
MONRO MUFFLER BRAKE INC
MUTUAL OF OMAHA COMPANIES (THE)
NACCO INDUSTRIES INC
NALCO HOLDING COMPANY
NATIONAL INSTRUMENTS CORP
NCR CORPORATION
NETAPP INC
NEW YORK LIFE INSURANCE CO
NEWS CORP
NEXTERA ENERGY INC
NII HOLDINGS INC
NIKE INC
NORFOLK SOUTHERN CORP
NORTH HIGHLAND
NORTHWESTERN MUTUAL LIFE INSURANCE CO
OMNICOM GROUP INC
ORACLE CORP
O'REILLY AUTOMOTIVE INC

OSHKOSH CORPORATION
OWENS & MINOR INC
PACCAR INC
PANERA BREAD CO
PARAMETRIC TECHNOLOGY CORP
PARK-OHIO HOLDINGS CORP
PATTERSON COMPANIES INC
PENSKE AUTOMOTIVE GROUP INC
PEPSICO INC
PETCO ANIMAL SUPPLIES INC
PETSMART INC
PG&E CORPORATION
PHILIP MORRIS INTERNATIONAL INC
PLEXUS CORP
POLO RALPH LAUREN CORP
POLYCOM INC
PRICESMART INC
PRICEWATERHOUSECOOPERS
PRINCIPAL FINANCIAL GROUP (THE)
PROCTER & GAMBLE CO
PROGRESSIVE CORPORATION (THE)
PRUDENTIAL FINANCIAL INC
PUBLIX SUPER MARKETS INC
QUALCOMM INC
RACKSPACE HOSTING INC
RECREATIONAL EQUIPMENT INC (REI)
RED HAT INC
REGIS CORPORATION
REPUBLIC AIRWAYS HOLDINGS INC
RESMED INC
ROBERT HALF INTERNATIONAL INC
ROSS STORES INC
ROYAL CARIBBEAN CRUISES LTD
RYDER SYSTEM INC
SAFECO INSURANCE COMPANY OF AMERICA
SAFEWAY INC
SALESFORCE.COM INC
SAM'S CLUB
SANMINA-SCI CORPORATION
SARA LEE CORP
SAS INSTITUTE INC
SCANA CORPORATION
SCHLUMBERGER LIMITED
SCOTTS MIRACLE GROW CO
SELECT MEDICAL HOLDINGS CORPORATION

SEMPRA ENERGY
SENECA FOODS CORPORATION
SHELL OIL CO
SHERWIN WILLIAMS COMPANY (THE)
SKILLED HEALTHCARE GROUP INC
SODEXO INC
SOUTHERN COMPANY (THE)
SOUTHWEST AIRLINES CO
SPECTRUM HEALTH
SRA INTERNATIONAL INC
ST JUDE MEDICAL INC
STANLEY BLACK & DECKER INC
STARWOOD HOTELS & RESORTS WORLDWIDE INC
STERICYCLE INC
STONERIDGE INC
STRYKER CORP
SUN HEALTHCARE GROUP INC
SUTTER HEALTH INC
SYMANTEC CORP
SYSCO CORP
TARGET CORPORATION
TECH DATA CORP
TEKTRONIX INC
TELEDYNE TECHNOLOGIES INC
TELEPHONE AND DATA SYSTEMS INC (TDS)
TEREX CORPORATION
THOMSON REUTERS
THOR INDUSTRIES INC
TIBCO SOFTWARE INC
TIDEWATER INC
TIFFANY & CO
TIME WARNER INC
TJX COMPANIES INC (THE)
TOTAL SYSTEM SERVICES INC (TSYS)
TOWERS WATSON & CO
TRAVELERS COMPANIES INC (THE)
TRUSTMARK COMPANIES
TTM TECHNOLOGIES INC
TW TELECOM INC
UNDER ARMOUR INC
UNION PACIFIC CORP
UNITED PARCEL SERVICE INC (UPS)
UNITED STATES CELLULAR CORP
UNITED TECHNOLOGIES CORPORATION
UNITEDHEALTH GROUP INC

UNIVISION COMMUNICATIONS INC
USAA
VALSPAR CORPORATION (THE)
VARIAN MEDICAL SYSTEMS INC
VERIZON COMMUNICATIONS INC
VICTORIAS SECRET
VISA INC
WALGREEN CO
WAL-MART STORES INC
WALT DISNEY COMPANY (THE)
WARNACO GROUP INC (THE)
WASTE MANAGEMENT INC
WATERS CORP
WEIGHT WATCHERS INTERNATIONAL INC
WEST PHARMACEUTICAL SERVICES INC
WESTERN DIGITAL CORP
WHOLE FOODS MARKET INC
WINDSTREAM CORPORATION
WM WRIGLEY JR COMPANY
WW GRAINGER INC
WYNDHAM WORLDWIDE
WYNN RESORTS LIMITED
XEROX CORP
YUM! BRANDS INC
ZIMMER HOLDINGS INC

Commercial/Industrial
3M COMPANY
ABM INDUSTRIES INC
ACCENTURE PLC
ADOBE SYSTEMS INC
ADVANCE AUTO PARTS INC
ADVANCED MICRO DEVICES INC (AMD)
ADVENTIST HEALTH SYSTEM
AECOM TECHNOLOGY CORPORATION
AES CORPORATION (THE)
AFFILIATED COMPUTER SERVICES INC
AFLAC INC
AGILENT TECHNOLOGIES INC
AIR PRODUCTS & CHEMICALS INC
ALASKA AIR GROUP INC
ALLERGAN INC
ALLIANCE DATA SYSTEMS CORPORATION
ALTRIA GROUP INC
AMEDISYS INC

AMERCO
AMERICAN EXPRESS CO
AMERICAN POWER CONVERSION (APC)
AMERISOURCEBERGEN CORP
AMGEN INC
AMKOR TECHNOLOGY INC
AMPHENOL CORPORATION
AMR CORP (AMERICAN AIRLINES)
AMSURG CORP
ANALOG DEVICES INC
APPLE INC
APPLIED MATERIALS INC
ARAMARK CORPORATION
ARCHER DANIELS MIDLAND CO
ARROW ELECTRONICS INC
ARTHUR J GALLAGHER & CO
AT&T INC
AUTOMATIC DATA PROCESSING INC
AUTONATION INC
AUTOZONE INC
AVNET INC
AXA FINANCIAL INC
BAIN & COMPANY INC
BAKER HUGHES INC
BALL CORP
BARRETT BUSINESS SERVICES
BASIC ENERGY SERVICES INC
BAUSCH & LOMB INC
BECHTEL GROUP INC
BECKMAN COULTER INC
BECTON DICKINSON & CO
BED BATH & BEYOND INC
BEMIS COMPANY INC
BERKSHIRE HATHAWAY INC
BEST BUY CO INC
BIO RAD LABORATORIES INC
BIOGEN IDEC INC
BLOOMBERG LP
BMC SOFTWARE INC
BOEING COMPANY (THE)
BOOZ ALLEN HAMILTON INC
BOSTON CONSULTING GROUP INC (THE, BCG)
BRINKS COMPANY (THE)
BROADCOM CORP
BROCADE COMMUNICATIONS SYSTEMS INC
BROWN & BROWN INC
BRUKER CORP
BUNGE LTD
BURLINGTON NORTHERN SANTA FE LLC
CABLEVISION SYSTEMS CORP
CACI INTERNATIONAL INC
CADENCE DESIGN SYSTEMS INC
CAESARS ENTERTAINMENT CORPORATION
CAMERON INTERNATIONAL CORPORATION
CAMPBELL SOUP CO
CARLSON COMPANIES INC
CARMAX GROUP
CARNIVAL CORPORATION
CASH AMERICA INTERNATIONAL INC
CATERPILLAR INC
CB RICHARD ELLIS GROUP INC (CBRE)
CDW CORPORATION
CELGENE CORP
CELLCO PARTNERSHIP (VERIZON WIRELESS)
CEPHALON INC
CERNER CORP
CH ROBINSON WORLDWIDE INC
CHEMED CORPORATION
CHEVRON CORPORATION
CHEVRON PHILLIPS CHEMICAL COMPANY LLC
CHS INC
CHUBB CORPORATION (THE)
CIENA CORP
CIGNA CORP
CINTAS CORP
CISCO SYSTEMS INC
CITRIX SYSTEMS INC
CLEARWIRE CORP
CLOROX CO (THE)
CNA FINANCIAL CORP
COACH INC
COCA-COLA BOTTLING CO CONSOLIDATED
COCA-COLA COMPANY (THE)
COGNIZANT TECHNOLOGY SOLUTIONS CORP
COLGATE PALMOLIVE CO
COMCAST CORP
COMPUTER SCIENCES CORPORATION (CSC)
COMPUTER TASK GROUP INC
CONAGRA FOODS INC
CONCENTRA INC
CONOCOPHILLIPS COMPANY
CONSOL ENERGY INC
CONTAINER STORE (THE)
CON-WAY INC
COOPER COMPANIES INC
COVANCE INC
COX COMMUNICATIONS INC
CR BARD INC
CROCS INC
CSX CORP
CUMMINS INC
DANAHER CORP
DAVITA INC
DEAN FOODS CO
DEERE & CO
DELOITTE & TOUCHE USA LLP
DELOITTE CONSULTING LLP
DELTA APPAREL INC
DENTSPLY INTERNATIONAL INC
DIAMOND OFFSHORE DRILLING INC
DIODES INC
DTE ENERGY COMPANY
DUKE ENERGY CORP
DUPONT (E I DU PONT DE NEMOURS & CO)
DUPONT AGRICULTURE & NUTRITION
EATON CORP
EDISON INTERNATIONAL
EDWARDS LIFESCIENCES CORP
EMC CORP
EMERSON ELECTRIC CO
ENDO PHARMACEUTICALS HOLDINGS INC
ENTERGY CORP
ENTERPRISE HOLDINGS INC
ERNST & YOUNG LLP
ESTEE LAUDER COMPANIES INC (THE)
EXELON CORPORATION
EXPEDIA INC
EXPERIAN AMERICAS
EXPRESS SCRIPTS INC
EXTERRAN HOLDINGS INC
EXXON MOBIL CORPORATION (EXXONMOBIL)
EXXONMOBIL CHEMICAL
FACTSET RESEARCH SYSTEMS INC
FAIRVIEW HEALTH SERVICES
FASTENAL

FEDERAL MOGUL CORP
FEDEX CORPORATION
FIDELITY NATIONAL INFORMATION SERVICES INC
FINISAR CORPORATION
FIRST ADVANTAGE CORPORATION
FIRSTENERGY CORP
FLUOR CORP
FMC TECHNOLOGIES INC
FMR CORP (FIDELITY INVESTMENTS)
FORD MOTOR CO
FOREST LABORATORIES INC
FORTUNE BRANDS INC
FOSSIL INC
FOX ENTERTAINMENT GROUP INC
FRONTIER COMMUNICATIONS CORPORATION
FTI CONSULTING INC
GE ENERGY INFRASTRUCTURE
GENENTECH INC
GENERAL ELECTRIC CO (GE)
GENERAL MILLS INC
GENERAL MOTORS COMPANY (GM)
GENESCO INC
GENTEX CORPORATION
GENTIVA HEALTH SERVICES INC
GENWORTH FINANCIAL INC
GENZYME BIOSURGERY
GEOKINETICS INC
GILEAD SCIENCES INC
GOOGLE INC
GRANT THORNTON LLP
GROUP 1 AUTOMOTIVE INC
GROUPON INC
GSI COMMERCE INC
HALLIBURTON COMPANY
HANESBRANDS INC
HANGER ORTHOPEDIC GROUP INC
HARRIS CORPORATION
HAWAIIAN ELECTRIC INDUSTRIES INC
HEALTH CARE SERVICE CORPORATION (HCSC)
HEALTH FITNESS CORP
HEALTHSOUTH CORP
HEARTLAND PAYMENT SYSTEMS INC
HENRY SCHEIN INC
HERSHEY CO
HERTZ GLOBAL HOLDINGS INC
HILLENBRAND INC
HILTON HOTELS CORP
HONDA OF AMERICA MANUFACTURING INC
HOSPIRA INC
HUMANA INC
HYATT HOTELS CORPORATION
IAC/INTERACTIVECORP
ICF INTERNATIONAL INC
IDEXX LABORATORIES INC
IGATE CORPORATION
ILLINOIS TOOL WORKS INC
IMS HEALTH INC
INGRAM MICRO INC
INSITUFORM TECHNOLOGIES
INTEGRA LIFESCIENCES HOLDINGS CORP
INTEL CORP
INTERNATIONAL BUSINESS MACHINES CORP (IBM)
INTERPUBLIC GROUP OF COMPANIES INC
INTUIT INC
INVENTIV HEALTH INC
JACK HENRY & ASSOCIATES INC
JARDEN CORP
JB HUNT TRANSPORT SERVICES INC
JM SMUCKER CO
JOHNSON & JOHNSON
JOHNSON CONTROLS INC
JONES LANG LASALLE INC
JUNIPER NETWORKS INC
KAISER PERMANENTE
KEANE INC
KELLOGG COMPANY
KELLY SERVICES INC
KEY ENERGY SERVICES INC
KIMBERLY-CLARK CORP
KINETIC CONCEPTS INC
KLA TENCOR CORP
KOCH INDUSTRIES INC
KPMG LLP
KRAFT FOODS INC
LABORATORY CORP OF AMERICA HOLDINGS
LAM RESEARCH CORP
LAS VEGAS SANDS CORP (THE VENETIAN)
LEAP WIRELESS INTERNATIONAL INC
LEAR CORP
LEXMARK INTERNATIONAL INC
LIBERTY GLOBAL INC
LIBERTY MEDIA CORP
LIBERTY MUTUAL GROUP INC
LIFE TECHNOLOGIES CORP
LINCARE HOLDINGS INC
LINCOLN NATIONAL CORPORATION
LKQ CORP
LOEWS CORPORATION
LORAL SPACE & COMMUNICATIONS LTD
LUFKIN INDUSTRIES INC
MANPOWER INC
MANTECH INTERNATIONAL CORP
MARATHON OIL CORP
MARRIOTT INTERNATIONAL INC
MARS INC
MARSH & MCLENNAN COMPANIES INC
MASSACHUSETTS MUTUAL LIFE INSURANCE CO
MATTEL INC
MAXIMUS INC
MCKESSON CORPORATION
MCKINSEY & COMPANY INC
MEDCO HEALTH SOLUTIONS INC
MEDNAX INC
MEDTRONIC INC
MERCER INC
METLIFE INC
METROPCS COMMUNICATIONS INC
MICROCHIP TECHNOLOGY INC
MICRON TECHNOLOGY INC
MICROSOFT CORP
MIDAMERICAN ENERGY HOLDINGS CO
MILLIPORE CORP
MOLEX INC
MULTI-FINELINE ELECTRONIX INC
MYLAN INC
NABORS INDUSTRIES LTD
NALCO HOLDING COMPANY
NATIONAL INSTRUMENTS CORP
NATIONAL OILWELL VARCO INC
NCR CORPORATION
NETAPP INC
NEW YORK LIFE INSURANCE CO
NEWS CORP
NEXTERA ENERGY INC
NII HOLDINGS INC
NIKE INC

NORFOLK SOUTHERN CORP
NORTH HIGHLAND
NORTHWESTERN MUTUAL LIFE INSURANCE CO
OCEANEERING INTERNATIONAL INC
OIL STATES INTERNATIONAL INC
OMNICOM GROUP INC
ORACLE CORP
O'REILLY AUTOMOTIVE INC
OSHKOSH CORPORATION
OWENS & MINOR INC
PACCAR INC
PARAMETRIC TECHNOLOGY CORP
PAREXEL INTERNATIONAL CORP
PARK-OHIO HOLDINGS CORP
PARSONS BRINCKERHOFF INC
PATTERSON COMPANIES INC
PATTERSON-UTI ENERGY INC
PEABODY ENERGY CORP
PEPSICO INC
PERRIGO CO
PG&E CORPORATION
PHARMACEUTICAL PRODUCT DEVELOPMENT INC
PHILIP MORRIS INTERNATIONAL INC
PLEXUS CORP
POLO RALPH LAUREN CORP
POLYCOM INC
PRAXAIR INC
PRICEWATERHOUSECOOPERS
PRINCIPAL FINANCIAL GROUP (THE)
PROCTER & GAMBLE CO
PRUDENTIAL FINANCIAL INC
QUALCOMM INC
QUANTA SERVICES INC
RACKSPACE HOSTING INC
RALCORP HOLDINGS INC
RED HAT INC
RESMED INC
ROBERT HALF INTERNATIONAL INC
ROWAN COMPANIES INC
ROYAL CARIBBEAN CRUISES LTD
RYDER SYSTEM INC
SABRE HOLDINGS CORP
SAFECO INSURANCE COMPANY OF AMERICA
SAIC INC
SALESFORCE.COM INC
SANDISK CORP
SANMINA-SCI CORPORATION
SAPIENT CORPORATION
SARA LEE CORP
SAS INSTITUTE INC
SCANA CORPORATION
SCHLUMBERGER LIMITED
SCOTTS MIRACLE GROW CO
SEACOR HOLDINGS INC
SEMPRA ENERGY
SENECA FOODS CORPORATION
SENSIENT TECHNOLOGIES CORPORATION
SHAW GROUP INC (THE)
SHERWIN WILLIAMS COMPANY (THE)
SIGMA-ALDRICH CORP
SKILLED HEALTHCARE GROUP INC
SNYDERS-LANCE INC
SODEXO INC
SOUTHERN COMPANY (THE)
SPECTRUM HEALTH
SPIRIT AEROSYSTEMS HOLDINGS INC
SRA INTERNATIONAL INC
ST JUDE MEDICAL INC
STANLEY BLACK & DECKER INC
STARWOOD HOTELS & RESORTS WORLDWIDE INC
STERICYCLE INC
STONERIDGE INC
STREAM GLOBAL SERVICES INC
STRYKER CORP
SUTTER HEALTH INC
SYMANTEC CORP
SYNTEL INC
SYSCO CORP
TEAM INC
TECH DATA CORP
TEKTRONIX INC
TELEDYNE TECHNOLOGIES INC
TELEPHONE AND DATA SYSTEMS INC (TDS)
TEREX CORPORATION
TETRA TECH INC
THERMO FISHER SCIENTIFIC INC
THOMSON REUTERS
THOR INDUSTRIES INC
TIBCO SOFTWARE INC
TIDEWATER INC
TIME WARNER INC
TOTAL SYSTEM SERVICES INC (TSYS)
TOWERS WATSON & CO
TRAVELERS COMPANIES INC (THE)
TREEHOUSE FOODS INC
TRUSTMARK COMPANIES
TTM TECHNOLOGIES INC
TW TELECOM INC
UNDER ARMOUR INC
UNION PACIFIC CORP
UNITED NATURAL FOODS INC
UNITED PARCEL SERVICE INC (UPS)
UNITED STATES CELLULAR CORP
UNITED TECHNOLOGIES CORPORATION
UNITEDHEALTH GROUP INC
UNIVISION COMMUNICATIONS INC
URS CORPORATION
VALASSIS COMMUNICATIONS INC
VALSPAR CORPORATION (THE)
VARIAN MEDICAL SYSTEMS INC
VERIZON COMMUNICATIONS INC
VISA INC
WABTEC CORP
WALT DISNEY COMPANY (THE)
WARNACO GROUP INC (THE)
WASTE MANAGEMENT INC
WATERS CORP
WATSON PHARMACEUTICALS INC
WEST PHARMACEUTICAL SERVICES INC
WESTERN DIGITAL CORP
WILLIAMS COMPANIES INC (THE)
WINDSTREAM CORPORATION
WM WRIGLEY JR COMPANY
WW GRAINGER INC
WYNDHAM WORLDWIDE
WYNN RESORTS LIMITED
XEROX CORP
ZIMMER HOLDINGS INC

Marketing Professionals
3M COMPANY
7-ELEVEN INC
ABM INDUSTRIES INC
ACADEMY SPORTS & OUTDOORS LTD
ACCENTURE PLC
ACOSTA SALES & MARKETING
ACTIVISION BLIZZARD INC

ADOBE SYSTEMS INC
ADVANCE AUTO PARTS INC
ADVANCED MICRO DEVICES INC (AMD)
ADVENTIST HEALTH SYSTEM
AECOM TECHNOLOGY CORPORATION
AES CORPORATION (THE)
AFFILIATED COMPUTER SERVICES INC
AFLAC INC
AGILENT TECHNOLOGIES INC
AIR PRODUCTS & CHEMICALS INC
ALASKA AIR GROUP INC
ALLERGAN INC
ALLIANCE DATA SYSTEMS CORPORATION
ALTRIA GROUP INC
AMAZON.COM INC
AMEDISYS INC
AMERCO
AMERICAN EXPRESS CO
AMERICAN POWER CONVERSION (APC)
AMERIGROUP CORPORATION
AMERISOURCEBERGEN CORP
AMGEN INC
AMKOR TECHNOLOGY INC
AMPHENOL CORPORATION
AMR CORP (AMERICAN AIRLINES)
AMSURG CORP
ANALOG DEVICES INC
APACHE CORP
APPLE INC
APPLIED MATERIALS INC
ARAMARK CORPORATION
ARCHER DANIELS MIDLAND CO
ARROW ELECTRONICS INC
ARTHUR J GALLAGHER & CO
ASCENA RETAIL GROUP INC
AT&T INC
AUTOMATIC DATA PROCESSING INC
AUTONATION INC
AUTOZONE INC
AVNET INC
AVON PRODUCTS INC
AXA FINANCIAL INC
BAIN & COMPANY INC
BAKER HUGHES INC
BALL CORP
BARRETT BUSINESS SERVICES
BASIC ENERGY SERVICES INC
BASS PRO SHOPS INC
BAUSCH & LOMB INC
BECHTEL GROUP INC
BECKMAN COULTER INC
BECTON DICKINSON & CO
BED BATH & BEYOND INC
BEMIS COMPANY INC
BERKSHIRE HATHAWAY INC
BEST BUY CO INC
BIG 5 SPORTING GOODS CORPORATION
BIO RAD LABORATORIES INC
BIOGEN IDEC INC
BLACKROCK INC
BLOOMBERG LP
BMC SOFTWARE INC
BOEING COMPANY (THE)
BOOZ ALLEN HAMILTON INC
BOSTON CONSULTING GROUP INC (THE, BCG)
BOYD GAMING CORP
BRINKS COMPANY (THE)
BROADCOM CORP
BROCADE COMMUNICATIONS SYSTEMS INC
BROOKDALE SENIOR LIVING INC
BROWN & BROWN INC
BRUKER CORP
BUCKLE INC (THE)
BUFFALO WILD WINGS INC
BUNGE LTD
BURLINGTON NORTHERN SANTA FE LLC
CABLEVISION SYSTEMS CORP
CACI INTERNATIONAL INC
CADENCE DESIGN SYSTEMS INC
CAESARS ENTERTAINMENT CORPORATION
CAMERON INTERNATIONAL CORPORATION
CAMPBELL SOUP CO
CAPITAL SENIOR LIVING CORP
CARLSON COMPANIES INC
CARMAX GROUP
CARNIVAL CORPORATION
CASH AMERICA INTERNATIONAL INC
CATERPILLAR INC
CATHOLIC HEALTH INITIATIVES
CB RICHARD ELLIS GROUP INC (CBRE)
CDW CORPORATION
CELGENE CORP
CELLCO PARTNERSHIP (VERIZON WIRELESS)
CEPHALON INC
CERNER CORP
CH ROBINSON WORLDWIDE INC
CHEMED CORPORATION
CHEVRON CORPORATION
CHEVRON PHILLIPS CHEMICAL COMPANY LLC
CHICO'S FAS INC
CHIPOTLE MEXICAN GRILL INC
CHS INC
CHUBB CORPORATION (THE)
CIENA CORP
CIGNA CORP
CINTAS CORP
CISCO SYSTEMS INC
CITRIX SYSTEMS INC
CLEARWIRE CORP
CLOROX CO (THE)
CNA FINANCIAL CORP
COACH INC
COCA-COLA BOTTLING CO CONSOLIDATED
COCA-COLA COMPANY (THE)
COGNIZANT TECHNOLOGY SOLUTIONS CORP
COLDWATER CREEK INC
COLGATE PALMOLIVE CO
COMCAST CORP
COMMUNITY HEALTH SYSTEMS INC
COMPUTER SCIENCES CORPORATION (CSC)
COMPUTER TASK GROUP INC
CONAGRA FOODS INC
CONCENTRA INC
CONOCOPHILLIPS COMPANY
CONSOL ENERGY INC
CONTAINER STORE (THE)
CON-WAY INC
COOPER COMPANIES INC
COSTCO WHOLESALE CORP
COVANCE INC
COX COMMUNICATIONS INC
CR BARD INC
CRACKER BARREL OLD COUNTRY STORE INC
CROCS INC

CSX CORP
CUMMINS INC
CVS CAREMARK CORPORATION
DANAHER CORP
DARDEN RESTAURANTS INC
DAVITA INC
DEAN FOODS CO
DEERE & CO
DELOITTE & TOUCHE USA LLP
DELOITTE CONSULTING LLP
DELTA APPAREL INC
DENTSPLY INTERNATIONAL INC
DEVRY INC
DIAMOND OFFSHORE DRILLING INC
DICK'S SPORTING GOODS INC
DIODES INC
DIRECTV
DOLLAR GENERAL CORPORATION
DTE ENERGY COMPANY
DUKE ENERGY CORP
DUPONT (E I DU PONT DE NEMOURS & CO)
DUPONT AGRICULTURE & NUTRITION
EATON CORP
EBAY INC
EDISON INTERNATIONAL
EDWARDS LIFESCIENCES CORP
EMC CORP
EMERITUS CORP
EMERSON ELECTRIC CO
ENDO PHARMACEUTICALS HOLDINGS INC
ENTERGY CORP
ENTERPRISE HOLDINGS INC
ERNST & YOUNG LLP
ESTEE LAUDER COMPANIES INC (THE)
EXELON CORPORATION
EXPEDIA INC
EXPERIAN AMERICAS
EXPRESS SCRIPTS INC
EXTERRAN HOLDINGS INC
EXXON MOBIL CORPORATION (EXXONMOBIL)
EXXONMOBIL CHEMICAL
FACTSET RESEARCH SYSTEMS INC
FAIRVIEW HEALTH SERVICES
FAMILY DOLLAR STORES INC
FASTENAL
FEDERAL MOGUL CORP
FEDEX CORPORATION
FIDELITY NATIONAL INFORMATION SERVICES INC
FINISAR CORPORATION
FIRST ADVANTAGE CORPORATION
FIRSTENERGY CORP
FLUOR CORP
FM GLOBAL
FMC TECHNOLOGIES INC
FMR CORP (FIDELITY INVESTMENTS)
FORD MOTOR CO
FOREST LABORATORIES INC
FORTUNE BRANDS INC
FOSSIL INC
FOX ENTERTAINMENT GROUP INC
FRONTIER COMMUNICATIONS CORPORATION
FTI CONSULTING INC
GAMESTOP CORP
GE ENERGY INFRASTRUCTURE
GENENTECH INC
GENERAL ELECTRIC CO (GE)
GENERAL MILLS INC
GENERAL MOTORS COMPANY (GM)
GENESCO INC
GENTEX CORPORATION
GENTIVA HEALTH SERVICES INC
GENWORTH FINANCIAL INC
GENZYME BIOSURGERY
GEOKINETICS INC
GILEAD SCIENCES INC
GOODYEAR TIRE & RUBBER COMPANY (THE)
GOOGLE INC
GRANT THORNTON LLP
GROUP 1 AUTOMOTIVE INC
GROUPON INC
GSI COMMERCE INC
GUESS? INC
HALLIBURTON COMPANY
HANESBRANDS INC
HANGER ORTHOPEDIC GROUP INC
HARRIS CORPORATION
HAWAIIAN ELECTRIC INDUSTRIES INC
HCA HOLDINGS INC
HE BUTT GROCERY COMPANY (HEB)
HEALTH CARE SERVICE CORPORATION (HCSC)
HEALTH FITNESS CORP
HEALTH MANAGEMENT ASSOCIATES INC
HEALTHSOUTH CORP
HEARTLAND PAYMENT SYSTEMS INC
HENRY SCHEIN INC
HERSHEY CO
HERTZ GLOBAL HOLDINGS INC
HIBBETT SPORTS INC
HILLENBRAND INC
HILTON HOTELS CORP
HONDA OF AMERICA MANUFACTURING INC
HOSPIRA INC
HUMANA INC
HYATT HOTELS CORPORATION
IAC/INTERACTIVECORP
ICF INTERNATIONAL INC
IDEXX LABORATORIES INC
IGATE CORPORATION
ILLINOIS TOOL WORKS INC
IMS HEALTH INC
INGRAM MICRO INC
INSITUFORM TECHNOLOGIES
INTEGRA LIFESCIENCES HOLDINGS CORP
INTEL CORP
INTERNATIONAL BUSINESS MACHINES CORP (IBM)
INTERPUBLIC GROUP OF COMPANIES INC
INTUIT INC
INVENTIV HEALTH INC
JACK HENRY & ASSOCIATES INC
JACKSON NATIONAL LIFE INSURANCE COMPANY
JARDEN CORP
JB HUNT TRANSPORT SERVICES INC
JETBLUE AIRWAYS CORPORATION
JM SMUCKER CO
JOHNSON & JOHNSON
JOHNSON CONTROLS INC
JONES LANG LASALLE INC
JUNIPER NETWORKS INC
KAISER PERMANENTE
KEANE INC
KELLOGG COMPANY
KELLY SERVICES INC
KEY ENERGY SERVICES INC
KIMBERLY-CLARK CORP
KINDRED HEALTHCARE INC

KINETIC CONCEPTS INC
KLA TENCOR CORP
KOCH INDUSTRIES INC
KOHL'S CORP
KPMG LLP
KRAFT FOODS INC
KROGER CO (THE)
LABORATORY CORP OF AMERICA HOLDINGS
LAM RESEARCH CORP
LAS VEGAS SANDS CORP (THE VENETIAN)
LEAP WIRELESS INTERNATIONAL INC
LEAR CORP
LEXMARK INTERNATIONAL INC
LIBERTY GLOBAL INC
LIBERTY MEDIA CORP
LIBERTY MUTUAL GROUP INC
LIFE TECHNOLOGIES CORP
LIMITED BRANDS INC
LINCARE HOLDINGS INC
LINCOLN NATIONAL CORPORATION
LKQ CORP
LOEWS CORPORATION
LORAL SPACE & COMMUNICATIONS LTD
LUFKIN INDUSTRIES INC
MACY'S INC
MANPOWER INC
MANTECH INTERNATIONAL CORP
MARATHON OIL CORP
MARRIOTT INTERNATIONAL INC
MARS INC
MARSH & MCLENNAN COMPANIES INC
MARY KAY INC
MASSACHUSETTS MUTUAL LIFE INSURANCE CO
MATTEL INC
MAXIMUS INC
MAYO FOUNDATION FOR MEDICAL EDUCATION AND RESEARCH
MCDONALD'S CORP
MCKESSON CORPORATION
MCKINSEY & COMPANY INC
MEDCO HEALTH SOLUTIONS INC
MEDIACOM COMMUNICATIONS CORP
MEDNAX INC
MEDTRONIC INC
MEIJER INC
MERCER INC
METLIFE INC
METROPCS COMMUNICATIONS INC
MICROCHIP TECHNOLOGY INC
MICRON TECHNOLOGY INC
MICROSOFT CORP
MIDAMERICAN ENERGY HOLDINGS CO
MILLIPORE CORP
MOLEX INC
MONRO MUFFLER BRAKE INC
MULTI-FINELINE ELECTRONIX INC
MUTUAL OF OMAHA COMPANIES (THE)
MYLAN INC
NABORS INDUSTRIES LTD
NACCO INDUSTRIES INC
NALCO HOLDING COMPANY
NATIONAL INSTRUMENTS CORP
NATIONAL OILWELL VARCO INC
NCR CORPORATION
NETAPP INC
NEW YORK LIFE INSURANCE CO
NEWS CORP
NEXTERA ENERGY INC
NII HOLDINGS INC
NIKE INC
NORFOLK SOUTHERN CORP
NORTH HIGHLAND
NORTHWESTERN MUTUAL LIFE INSURANCE CO
OCEANEERING INTERNATIONAL INC
ODYSSEY HEALTHCARE INC
OIL STATES INTERNATIONAL INC
OMNICOM GROUP INC
ORACLE CORP
O'REILLY AUTOMOTIVE INC
OSHKOSH CORPORATION
OWENS & MINOR INC
PACCAR INC
PANERA BREAD CO
PARAMETRIC TECHNOLOGY CORP
PAREXEL INTERNATIONAL CORP
PARK-OHIO HOLDINGS CORP
PARSONS BRINCKERHOFF INC
PATTERSON COMPANIES INC
PATTERSON-UTI ENERGY INC
PEABODY ENERGY CORP
PENSKE AUTOMOTIVE GROUP INC
PEPSICO INC
PERRIGO CO
PETCO ANIMAL SUPPLIES INC
PETSMART INC
PG&E CORPORATION
PHARMACEUTICAL PRODUCT DEVELOPMENT INC
PHILIP MORRIS INTERNATIONAL INC
PLEXUS CORP
POLO RALPH LAUREN CORP
POLYCOM INC
PRAXAIR INC
PRICESMART INC
PRICEWATERHOUSECOOPERS
PRINCIPAL FINANCIAL GROUP (THE)
PROCTER & GAMBLE CO
PROGRESSIVE CORPORATION (THE)
PROVIDENCE HEALTH & SERVICES
PRUDENTIAL FINANCIAL INC
PUBLIX SUPER MARKETS INC
QUALCOMM INC
QUANTA SERVICES INC
RACKSPACE HOSTING INC
RALCORP HOLDINGS INC
RECREATIONAL EQUIPMENT INC (REI)
RED HAT INC
REGIS CORPORATION
REPUBLIC AIRWAYS HOLDINGS INC
RESMED INC
ROBERT HALF INTERNATIONAL INC
ROSS STORES INC
ROWAN COMPANIES INC
ROYAL CARIBBEAN CRUISES LTD
RYDER SYSTEM INC
SABRE HOLDINGS CORP
SAFECO INSURANCE COMPANY OF AMERICA
SAFEWAY INC
SAIC INC
SALESFORCE.COM INC
SAM'S CLUB
SANDISK CORP
SANMINA-SCI CORPORATION
SAPIENT CORPORATION
SARA LEE CORP
SAS INSTITUTE INC
SCANA CORPORATION
SCHLUMBERGER LIMITED

SCOTTS MIRACLE GROW CO
SEACOR HOLDINGS INC
SELECT MEDICAL HOLDINGS CORPORATION
SEMPRA ENERGY
SENECA FOODS CORPORATION
SENSIENT TECHNOLOGIES CORPORATION
SHAW GROUP INC (THE)
SHELL OIL CO
SHERWIN WILLIAMS COMPANY (THE)
SIGMA-ALDRICH CORP
SKILLED HEALTHCARE GROUP INC
SNYDERS-LANCE INC
SODEXO INC
SOUTHERN COMPANY (THE)
SOUTHWEST AIRLINES CO
SPECTRUM HEALTH
SPIRIT AEROSYSTEMS HOLDINGS INC
SRA INTERNATIONAL INC
ST JUDE MEDICAL INC
STANLEY BLACK & DECKER INC
STARWOOD HOTELS & RESORTS WORLDWIDE INC
STERICYCLE INC
STIFEL FINANCIAL CORP
STONERIDGE INC
STREAM GLOBAL SERVICES INC
STRYKER CORP
SUN HEALTHCARE GROUP INC
SUTTER HEALTH INC
SYMANTEC CORP
SYNTEL INC
SYSCO CORP
TARGET CORPORATION
TEAM HEALTH HOLDINGS INC
TEAM INC
TECH DATA CORP
TEKTRONIX INC
TELEDYNE TECHNOLOGIES INC
TELEPHONE AND DATA SYSTEMS INC (TDS)
TENET HEALTHCARE CORPORATION
TEREX CORPORATION
TETRA TECH INC
THERMO FISHER SCIENTIFIC INC
THOMSON REUTERS
THOR INDUSTRIES INC
TIBCO SOFTWARE INC
TIDEWATER INC
TIFFANY & CO
TIME WARNER INC
TJX COMPANIES INC (THE)
TOTAL SYSTEM SERVICES INC (TSYS)
TOWERS WATSON & CO
TRAVELERS COMPANIES INC (THE)
TREEHOUSE FOODS INC
TRUSTMARK COMPANIES
TTM TECHNOLOGIES INC
TW TELECOM INC
UNDER ARMOUR INC
UNION PACIFIC CORP
UNITED NATURAL FOODS INC
UNITED PARCEL SERVICE INC (UPS)
UNITED STATES CELLULAR CORP
UNITED TECHNOLOGIES CORPORATION
UNITEDHEALTH GROUP INC
UNIVERSAL HEALTH SERVICES INC
UNIVISION COMMUNICATIONS INC
URS CORPORATION
USAA
VALASSIS COMMUNICATIONS INC
VALSPAR CORPORATION (THE)
VARIAN MEDICAL SYSTEMS INC
VCA ANTECH INC
VERIZON COMMUNICATIONS INC
VICTORIAS SECRET
VISA INC
WABTEC CORP
WALGREEN CO
WAL-MART STORES INC
WALT DISNEY COMPANY (THE)
WARNACO GROUP INC (THE)
WASTE MANAGEMENT INC
WATERS CORP
WATSON PHARMACEUTICALS INC
WEIGHT WATCHERS INTERNATIONAL INC
WEST PHARMACEUTICAL SERVICES INC
WESTERN DIGITAL CORP
WHOLE FOODS MARKET INC
WILLIAMS COMPANIES INC (THE)
WINDSTREAM CORPORATION
WM WRIGLEY JR COMPANY
WW GRAINGER INC
WYNDHAM WORLDWIDE
WYNN RESORTS LIMITED
XEROX CORP
YUM! BRANDS INC
ZIMMER HOLDINGS INC

Retail Sales
7-ELEVEN INC
ACADEMY SPORTS & OUTDOORS LTD
ACOSTA SALES & MARKETING
ADVANCE AUTO PARTS INC
AMAZON.COM INC
APPLE INC
ASCENA RETAIL GROUP INC
AT&T INC
AUTONATION INC
AUTOZONE INC
AVON PRODUCTS INC
BASS PRO SHOPS INC
BED BATH & BEYOND INC
BERKSHIRE HATHAWAY INC
BEST BUY CO INC
BIG 5 SPORTING GOODS CORPORATION
BUCKLE INC (THE)
CARMAX GROUP
CASH AMERICA INTERNATIONAL INC
CELLCO PARTNERSHIP (VERIZON WIRELESS)
CHICO'S FAS INC
COACH INC
COLDWATER CREEK INC
CONTAINER STORE (THE)
COSTCO WHOLESALE CORP
CVS CAREMARK CORPORATION
DICK'S SPORTING GOODS INC
DOLLAR GENERAL CORPORATION
ESTEE LAUDER COMPANIES INC (THE)
FAMILY DOLLAR STORES INC
FMR CORP (FIDELITY INVESTMENTS)
FOSSIL INC
GAMESTOP CORP
GENESCO INC
GOODYEAR TIRE & RUBBER COMPANY (THE)
GROUP 1 AUTOMOTIVE INC
GUESS? INC
HANGER ORTHOPEDIC GROUP INC
HE BUTT GROCERY COMPANY

(HEB)
HERTZ GLOBAL HOLDINGS INC
HIBBETT SPORTS INC
KOHL'S CORP
KROGER CO (THE)
LIMITED BRANDS INC
MACY'S INC
MARY KAY INC
MASSACHUSETTS MUTUAL LIFE INSURANCE CO
MEIJER INC
NACCO INDUSTRIES INC
NEW YORK LIFE INSURANCE CO
NIKE INC
O'REILLY AUTOMOTIVE INC
PENSKE AUTOMOTIVE GROUP INC
PETCO ANIMAL SUPPLIES INC
PETSMART INC
POLO RALPH LAUREN CORP
PRICESMART INC
PUBLIX SUPER MARKETS INC
RECREATIONAL EQUIPMENT INC (REI)
REGIS CORPORATION
ROSS STORES INC
RYDER SYSTEM INC
SAFEWAY INC
SAM'S CLUB
SCOTTS MIRACLE GROW CO
SHERWIN WILLIAMS COMPANY (THE)
TARGET CORPORATION
TIFFANY & CO
TJX COMPANIES INC (THE)
UNITED STATES CELLULAR CORP
VERIZON COMMUNICATIONS INC
VICTORIAS SECRET
WALGREEN CO
WAL-MART STORES INC
WHOLE FOODS MARKET INC

Sales Trainees
3M COMPANY
7-ELEVEN INC
ABM INDUSTRIES INC
ACADEMY SPORTS & OUTDOORS LTD
ADOBE SYSTEMS INC
ADVANCE AUTO PARTS INC
AFLAC INC
ALTRIA GROUP INC
AMAZON.COM INC
AMERCO
AMERICAN POWER CONVERSION (APC)
AMERISOURCEBERGEN CORP
AMGEN INC
APPLE INC
ARAMARK CORPORATION
ARROW ELECTRONICS INC
ASCENA RETAIL GROUP INC
AT&T INC
AUTOMATIC DATA PROCESSING INC
AUTONATION INC
AUTOZONE INC
AVON PRODUCTS INC
AXA FINANCIAL INC
BASS PRO SHOPS INC
BAUSCH & LOMB INC
BECHTEL GROUP INC
BED BATH & BEYOND INC
BERKSHIRE HATHAWAY INC
BEST BUY CO INC
BIG 5 SPORTING GOODS CORPORATION
BLOOMBERG LP
BRINKS COMPANY (THE)
BUCKLE INC (THE)
CABLEVISION SYSTEMS CORP
CAESARS ENTERTAINMENT CORPORATION
CARMAX GROUP
CARNIVAL CORPORATION
CASH AMERICA INTERNATIONAL INC
CDW CORPORATION
CELLCO PARTNERSHIP (VERIZON WIRELESS)
CHEMED CORPORATION
CHEVRON CORPORATION
CHICO'S FAS INC
CHUBB CORPORATION (THE)
CINTAS CORP
CISCO SYSTEMS INC
CLEARWIRE CORP
CLOROX CO (THE)
COACH INC
COCA-COLA COMPANY (THE)
COLDWATER CREEK INC
COLGATE PALMOLIVE CO
COMCAST CORP
CONOCOPHILLIPS COMPANY
CONTAINER STORE (THE)
COSTCO WHOLESALE CORP
COX COMMUNICATIONS INC
CRACKER BARREL OLD COUNTRY STORE INC
CVS CAREMARK CORPORATION
DANAHER CORP
DEAN FOODS CO
DICK'S SPORTING GOODS INC
DIRECTV
DOLLAR GENERAL CORPORATION
ENDO PHARMACEUTICALS HOLDINGS INC
ENTERPRISE HOLDINGS INC
ESTEE LAUDER COMPANIES INC (THE)
EXPEDIA INC
EXPERIAN AMERICAS
EXXON MOBIL CORPORATION (EXXONMOBIL)
FAMILY DOLLAR STORES INC
FEDEX CORPORATION
FIRST ADVANTAGE CORPORATION
FLUOR CORP
FMR CORP (FIDELITY INVESTMENTS)
FORTUNE BRANDS INC
FOSSIL INC
GAMESTOP CORP
GENENTECH INC
GENERAL MILLS INC
GENESCO INC
GENWORTH FINANCIAL INC
GOODYEAR TIRE & RUBBER COMPANY (THE)
GROUP 1 AUTOMOTIVE INC
GUESS? INC
HE BUTT GROCERY COMPANY (HEB)
HEALTH FITNESS CORP
HENRY SCHEIN INC
HERTZ GLOBAL HOLDINGS INC
HIBBETT SPORTS INC
HILTON HOTELS CORP
HYATT HOTELS CORPORATION
INGRAM MICRO INC
INTERNATIONAL BUSINESS MACHINES CORP (IBM)
JACKSON NATIONAL LIFE INSURANCE COMPANY
JARDEN CORP

JM SMUCKER CO
JOHNSON & JOHNSON
JUNIPER NETWORKS INC
KELLOGG COMPANY
KELLY SERVICES INC
KIMBERLY-CLARK CORP
KINETIC CONCEPTS INC
KOHL'S CORP
KRAFT FOODS INC
KROGER CO (THE)
LAS VEGAS SANDS CORP (THE VENETIAN)
LEAP WIRELESS INTERNATIONAL
LEXMARK INTERNATIONAL INC
LIMITED BRANDS INC
LINCOLN NATIONAL CORPORATION
LOEWS CORPORATION
MACY'S INC
MANPOWER INC
MARRIOTT INTERNATIONAL INC
MARS INC
MARY KAY INC
MASSACHUSETTS MUTUAL LIFE INSURANCE CO
MCKESSON CORPORATION
MEDTRONIC INC
MEIJER INC
METLIFE INC
METROPCS COMMUNICATIONS INC
MUTUAL OF OMAHA COMPANIES (THE)
NACCO INDUSTRIES INC
NCR CORPORATION
NEW YORK LIFE INSURANCE CO
NIKE INC
O'REILLY AUTOMOTIVE INC
OWENS & MINOR INC
PARSONS BRINCKERHOFF INC
PATTERSON COMPANIES INC
PENSKE AUTOMOTIVE GROUP INC
PEPSICO INC
PETCO ANIMAL SUPPLIES INC
PETSMART INC
PHILIP MORRIS INTERNATIONAL INC
POLO RALPH LAUREN CORP
PRICESMART INC
PRINCIPAL FINANCIAL GROUP (THE)
PROCTER & GAMBLE CO
PROGRESSIVE CORPORATION
(THE)
PRUDENTIAL FINANCIAL INC
PUBLIX SUPER MARKETS INC
RECREATIONAL EQUIPMENT INC (REI)
ROBERT HALF INTERNATIONAL INC
ROSS STORES INC
ROYAL CARIBBEAN CRUISES LTD
RYDER SYSTEM INC
SAFECO INSURANCE COMPANY OF AMERICA
SAFEWAY INC
SAM'S CLUB
SARA LEE CORP
SCOTTS MIRACLE GROW CO
SENECA FOODS CORPORATION
SHERWIN WILLIAMS COMPANY (THE)
SOUTHWEST AIRLINES CO
ST JUDE MEDICAL INC
STANLEY BLACK & DECKER INC
STARWOOD HOTELS & RESORTS WORLDWIDE INC
SYSCO CORP
TARGET CORPORATION
TECH DATA CORP
TELEPHONE AND DATA SYSTEMS INC (TDS)
TIFFANY & CO
TJX COMPANIES INC (THE)
TOTAL SYSTEM SERVICES INC (TSYS)
TRAVELERS COMPANIES INC (THE)
UNITED NATURAL FOODS INC
UNITED STATES CELLULAR CORP
USAA
VERIZON COMMUNICATIONS INC
VICTORIAS SECRET
WALGREEN CO
WAL-MART STORES INC
WALT DISNEY COMPANY (THE)
WASTE MANAGEMENT INC
WEIGHT WATCHERS INTERNATIONAL INC
WHOLE FOODS MARKET INC
WM WRIGLEY JR COMPANY
WW GRAINGER INC
WYNDHAM WORLDWIDE
WYNN RESORTS LIMITED
XEROX CORP
ZIMMER HOLDINGS INC

Technical/Scientific

Engineers, Electrical
3M COMPANY
ACCENTURE PLC
ACTIVISION BLIZZARD INC
ADOBE SYSTEMS INC
ADVANCED MICRO DEVICES INC (AMD)
AECOM TECHNOLOGY CORPORATION
AES CORPORATION (THE)
AFFILIATED COMPUTER SERVICES INC
AGILENT TECHNOLOGIES INC
AIR PRODUCTS & CHEMICALS INC
ALLERGAN INC
AMERICAN POWER CONVERSION (APC)
AMGEN INC
AMKOR TECHNOLOGY INC
AMPHENOL CORPORATION
ANALOG DEVICES INC
APACHE CORP
APPLE INC
APPLIED MATERIALS INC
AT&T INC
AUTOMATIC DATA PROCESSING INC
BAKER HUGHES INC
BASIC ENERGY SERVICES INC
BAUSCH & LOMB INC
BECHTEL GROUP INC
BECKMAN COULTER INC
BECTON DICKINSON & CO
BERKSHIRE HATHAWAY INC
BIO RAD LABORATORIES INC
BIOGEN IDEC INC
BLOOMBERG LP
BMC SOFTWARE INC
BOEING COMPANY (THE)
BROADCOM CORP
BROCADE COMMUNICATIONS SYSTEMS INC
BRUKER CORP
BURLINGTON NORTHERN SANTA FE LLC
CABLEVISION SYSTEMS CORP
CACI INTERNATIONAL INC
CADENCE DESIGN SYSTEMS INC
CAMERON INTERNATIONAL CORPORATION

CAMPBELL SOUP CO
CATERPILLAR INC
CELGENE CORP
CELLCO PARTNERSHIP (VERIZON WIRELESS)
CEPHALON INC
CERNER CORP
CHEVRON CORPORATION
CHEVRON PHILLIPS CHEMICAL COMPANY LLC
CIENA CORP
CISCO SYSTEMS INC
CITRIX SYSTEMS INC
CLEARWIRE CORP
COGNIZANT TECHNOLOGY SOLUTIONS CORP
COMCAST CORP
COMPUTER TASK GROUP INC
CONOCOPHILLIPS COMPANY
COX COMMUNICATIONS INC
CSX CORP
CUMMINS INC
DANAHER CORP
DEERE & CO
DENTSPLY INTERNATIONAL INC
DIAMOND OFFSHORE DRILLING INC
DIODES INC
DIRECTV
DTE ENERGY COMPANY
DUKE ENERGY CORP
DUPONT (E I DU PONT DE NEMOURS & CO)
EATON CORP
EBAY INC
EDISON INTERNATIONAL
EDWARDS LIFESCIENCES CORP
EMC CORP
EMERSON ELECTRIC CO
ENTERGY CORP
EXELON CORPORATION
EXPEDIA INC
EXTERRAN HOLDINGS INC
EXXON MOBIL CORPORATION (EXXONMOBIL)
EXXONMOBIL CHEMICAL
FASTENAL
FEDERAL MOGUL CORP
FEDEX CORPORATION
FINISAR CORPORATION
FIRSTENERGY CORP
FLUOR CORP
FMC TECHNOLOGIES INC
FORD MOTOR CO
FOREST LABORATORIES INC
FOSSIL INC
FOX ENTERTAINMENT GROUP INC
FRONTIER COMMUNICATIONS CORPORATION
GE ENERGY INFRASTRUCTURE
GENENTECH INC
GENERAL ELECTRIC CO (GE)
GENERAL MOTORS COMPANY (GM)
GENTEX CORPORATION
GENZYME BIOSURGERY
GEOKINETICS INC
GILEAD SCIENCES INC
GOOGLE INC
GSI COMMERCE INC
HALLIBURTON COMPANY
HANGER ORTHOPEDIC GROUP INC
HARRIS CORPORATION
HAWAIIAN ELECTRIC INDUSTRIES INC
HERSHEY CO
HONDA OF AMERICA MANUFACTURING INC
HOSPIRA INC
IAC/INTERACTIVECORP
IDEXX LABORATORIES INC
IGATE CORPORATION
IMS HEALTH INC
INSITUFORM TECHNOLOGIES
INTEGRA LIFESCIENCES HOLDINGS CORP
INTEL CORP
INTERNATIONAL BUSINESS MACHINES CORP (IBM)
INTUIT INC
JACK HENRY & ASSOCIATES INC
JETBLUE AIRWAYS CORPORATION
JOHNSON & JOHNSON
JOHNSON CONTROLS INC
JUNIPER NETWORKS INC
KEANE INC
KEY ENERGY SERVICES INC
KINETIC CONCEPTS INC
KLA TENCOR CORP
KOCH INDUSTRIES INC
LAM RESEARCH CORP
LEAP WIRELESS INTERNATIONAL INC
LEAR CORP
LEXMARK INTERNATIONAL INC
LIBERTY GLOBAL INC
LIBERTY MEDIA CORP
LIFE TECHNOLOGIES CORP
LORAL SPACE & COMMUNICATIONS LTD
LUFKIN INDUSTRIES INC
MANTECH INTERNATIONAL CORP
MARATHON OIL CORP
MATTEL INC
MEDIACOM COMMUNICATIONS CORP
MEDTRONIC INC
METROPCS COMMUNICATIONS INC
MICROCHIP TECHNOLOGY INC
MICRON TECHNOLOGY INC
MICROSOFT CORP
MIDAMERICAN ENERGY HOLDINGS CO
MILLIPORE CORP
MOLEX INC
MULTI-FINELINE ELECTRONIX INC
MYLAN INC
NABORS INDUSTRIES LTD
NALCO HOLDING COMPANY
NATIONAL INSTRUMENTS CORP
NATIONAL OILWELL VARCO INC
NCR CORPORATION
NETAPP INC
NEWS CORP
NEXTERA ENERGY INC
NII HOLDINGS INC
NORFOLK SOUTHERN CORP
OCEANEERING INTERNATIONAL INC
OIL STATES INTERNATIONAL INC
ORACLE CORP
OSHKOSH CORPORATION
PACCAR INC
PARAMETRIC TECHNOLOGY CORP
PAREXEL INTERNATIONAL CORP
PARSONS BRINCKERHOFF INC
PATTERSON-UTI ENERGY INC
PERRIGO CO
PG&E CORPORATION
PHARMACEUTICAL PRODUCT DEVELOPMENT INC
PHILIP MORRIS INTERNATIONAL INC
PLEXUS CORP
POLYCOM INC

PRAXAIR INC
QUALCOMM INC
QUANTA SERVICES INC
RACKSPACE HOSTING INC
RED HAT INC
RESMED INC
ROWAN COMPANIES INC
SABRE HOLDINGS CORP
SAIC INC
SALESFORCE.COM INC
SANDISK CORP
SANMINA-SCI CORPORATION
SAPIENT CORPORATION
SAS INSTITUTE INC
SCANA CORPORATION
SCHLUMBERGER LIMITED
SEACOR HOLDINGS INC
SEMPRA ENERGY
SHAW GROUP INC (THE)
SHELL OIL CO
SIGMA-ALDRICH CORP
SOUTHERN COMPANY (THE)
SOUTHWEST AIRLINES CO
SPIRIT AEROSYSTEMS HOLDINGS INC
SRA INTERNATIONAL INC
ST JUDE MEDICAL INC
STANLEY BLACK & DECKER INC
STONERIDGE INC
SYMANTEC CORP
SYNTEL INC
TEKTRONIX INC
TELEDYNE TECHNOLOGIES INC
TELEPHONE AND DATA SYSTEMS INC (TDS)
TEREX CORPORATION
TETRA TECH INC
THOR INDUSTRIES INC
TIBCO SOFTWARE INC
TIDEWATER INC
TIME WARNER INC
TTM TECHNOLOGIES INC
TW TELECOM INC
UNION PACIFIC CORP
UNITED PARCEL SERVICE INC (UPS)
UNITED STATES CELLULAR CORP
UNITED TECHNOLOGIES CORPORATION
UNIVISION COMMUNICATIONS INC
URS CORPORATION
VARIAN MEDICAL SYSTEMS INC
VERIZON COMMUNICATIONS INC
WABTEC CORP
WALT DISNEY COMPANY (THE)
WATERS CORP
WATSON PHARMACEUTICALS INC
WESTERN DIGITAL CORP
WILLIAMS COMPANIES INC (THE)
WINDSTREAM CORPORATION
XEROX CORP

Engineers, Other
3M COMPANY
ACCENTURE PLC
AECOM TECHNOLOGY CORPORATION
AES CORPORATION (THE)
AIR PRODUCTS & CHEMICALS INC
ALASKA AIR GROUP INC
ALLERGAN INC
AMERICAN POWER CONVERSION (APC)
AMGEN INC
AMPHENOL CORPORATION
AMR CORP (AMERICAN AIRLINES)
APACHE CORP
ARCHER DANIELS MIDLAND CO
AT&T INC
BAKER HUGHES INC
BASIC ENERGY SERVICES INC
BAUSCH & LOMB INC
BECHTEL GROUP INC
BECKMAN COULTER INC
BECTON DICKINSON & CO
BEMIS COMPANY INC
BIO RAD LABORATORIES INC
BIOGEN IDEC INC
BOEING COMPANY (THE)
BROCADE COMMUNICATIONS SYSTEMS INC
BUNGE LTD
BURLINGTON NORTHERN SANTA FE LLC
CABLEVISION SYSTEMS CORP
CAMERON INTERNATIONAL CORPORATION
CAMPBELL SOUP CO
CARNIVAL CORPORATION
CATERPILLAR INC
CELGENE CORP
CELLCO PARTNERSHIP (VERIZON WIRELESS)
CEPHALON INC
CHEVRON CORPORATION
CHEVRON PHILLIPS CHEMICAL COMPANY LLC
CLOROX CO (THE)
COCA-COLA COMPANY (THE)
COLGATE PALMOLIVE CO
COMCAST CORP
CONAGRA FOODS INC
CONOCOPHILLIPS COMPANY
CONSOL ENERGY INC
COOPER COMPANIES INC
COX COMMUNICATIONS INC
CR BARD INC
CSX CORP
CUMMINS INC
DANAHER CORP
DEAN FOODS CO
DEERE & CO
DENTSPLY INTERNATIONAL INC
DIAMOND OFFSHORE DRILLING INC
DIODES INC
DIRECTV
DTE ENERGY COMPANY
DUKE ENERGY CORP
DUPONT (E I DU PONT DE NEMOURS & CO)
DUPONT AGRICULTURE & NUTRITION
EATON CORP
EDISON INTERNATIONAL
EDWARDS LIFESCIENCES CORP
EMERSON ELECTRIC CO
ENTERGY CORP
ESTEE LAUDER COMPANIES INC (THE)
EXELON CORPORATION
EXTERRAN HOLDINGS INC
EXXON MOBIL CORPORATION (EXXONMOBIL)
EXXONMOBIL CHEMICAL
FASTENAL
FEDERAL MOGUL CORP
FIRSTENERGY CORP
FLUOR CORP
FM GLOBAL
FMC TECHNOLOGIES INC
FOREST LABORATORIES INC
FORTUNE BRANDS INC
FRONTIER COMMUNICATIONS

CORPORATION
GE ENERGY INFRASTRUCTURE
GENENTECH INC
GENERAL MILLS INC
GENTEX CORPORATION
GENTIVA HEALTH SERVICES INC
GENZYME BIOSURGERY
GEOKINETICS INC
GILEAD SCIENCES INC
HALLIBURTON COMPANY
HANGER ORTHOPEDIC GROUP INC
HAWAIIAN ELECTRIC INDUSTRIES INC
HEALTHSOUTH CORP
HERSHEY CO
HONDA OF AMERICA MANUFACTURING INC
HOSPIRA INC
IDEXX LABORATORIES INC
INSITUFORM TECHNOLOGIES
INTEGRA LIFESCIENCES HOLDINGS CORP
INTERNATIONAL BUSINESS MACHINES CORP (IBM)
JARDEN CORP
JETBLUE AIRWAYS CORPORATION
JM SMUCKER CO
JOHNSON & JOHNSON
JOHNSON CONTROLS INC
KELLOGG COMPANY
KEY ENERGY SERVICES INC
KINETIC CONCEPTS INC
KOCH INDUSTRIES INC
KRAFT FOODS INC
LIBERTY GLOBAL INC
LIFE TECHNOLOGIES CORP
LKQ CORP
LUFKIN INDUSTRIES INC
MARATHON OIL CORP
MARS INC
MEDTRONIC INC
MIDAMERICAN ENERGY HOLDINGS CO
MULTI-FINELINE ELECTRONIX INC
MYLAN INC
NALCO HOLDING COMPANY
NATIONAL OILWELL VARCO INC
NEXTERA ENERGY INC
NII HOLDINGS INC
NORFOLK SOUTHERN CORP
OCEANEERING INTERNATIONAL
INC
OIL STATES INTERNATIONAL INC
OSHKOSH CORPORATION
PACCAR INC
PARAMETRIC TECHNOLOGY CORP
PARSONS BRINCKERHOFF INC
PATTERSON-UTI ENERGY INC
PEABODY ENERGY CORP
PEPSICO INC
PERRIGO CO
PG&E CORPORATION
PHILIP MORRIS INTERNATIONAL INC
PRAXAIR INC
PROCTER & GAMBLE CO
QUANTA SERVICES INC
RALCORP HOLDINGS INC
ROWAN COMPANIES INC
ROYAL CARIBBEAN CRUISES LTD
SAIC INC
SANDISK CORP
SANMINA-SCI CORPORATION
SARA LEE CORP
SCANA CORPORATION
SCHLUMBERGER LIMITED
SCOTTS MIRACLE GROW CO
SEACOR HOLDINGS INC
SEMPRA ENERGY
SENECA FOODS CORPORATION
SENSIENT TECHNOLOGIES CORPORATION
SHAW GROUP INC (THE)
SHELL OIL CO
SIGMA-ALDRICH CORP
SOUTHERN COMPANY (THE)
SOUTHWEST AIRLINES CO
SPIRIT AEROSYSTEMS HOLDINGS INC
ST JUDE MEDICAL INC
STANLEY BLACK & DECKER INC
STRYKER CORP
TEAM INC
TEKTRONIX INC
TELEDYNE TECHNOLOGIES INC
TELEPHONE AND DATA SYSTEMS INC (TDS)
TENET HEALTHCARE CORPORATION
TEREX CORPORATION
TIDEWATER INC
TIME WARNER INC
TREEHOUSE FOODS INC
UNION PACIFIC CORP
UNITED STATES CELLULAR CORP
UNITED TECHNOLOGIES CORPORATION
URS CORPORATION
VALSPAR CORPORATION (THE)
VARIAN MEDICAL SYSTEMS INC
VERIZON COMMUNICATIONS INC
WABTEC CORP
WASTE MANAGEMENT INC
WATERS CORP
WATSON PHARMACEUTICALS INC
WEST PHARMACEUTICAL SERVICES INC
WILLIAMS COMPANIES INC (THE)
XEROX CORP
ZIMMER HOLDINGS INC

Health/Laboratory
3M COMPANY
ADVENTIST HEALTH SYSTEM
ALLERGAN INC
AMEDISYS INC
AMERIGROUP CORPORATION
AMGEN INC
AMSURG CORP
ASCENSION HEALTH
BAIN & COMPANY INC
BAUSCH & LOMB INC
BECKMAN COULTER INC
BECTON DICKINSON & CO
BIO RAD LABORATORIES INC
BIOGEN IDEC INC
BOSTON CONSULTING GROUP INC (THE, BCG)
BROOKDALE SENIOR LIVING INC
CAMPBELL SOUP CO
CATHOLIC HEALTH INITIATIVES
CELGENE CORP
CEPHALON INC
CHEMED CORPORATION
CLOROX CO (THE)
COLGATE PALMOLIVE CO
COMMUNITY HEALTH SYSTEMS INC
CONCENTRA INC
COOPER COMPANIES INC
COVANCE INC
CR BARD INC
DAVITA INC
DENTSPLY INTERNATIONAL INC

DUPONT (E I DU PONT DE NEMOURS & CO)
DUPONT AGRICULTURE & NUTRITION
EDWARDS LIFESCIENCES CORP
ENDO PHARMACEUTICALS HOLDINGS INC
FAIRVIEW HEALTH SERVICES
FORD MOTOR CO
FOREST LABORATORIES INC
GENENTECH INC
GENERAL MOTORS COMPANY (GM)
GILEAD SCIENCES INC
HCA HOLDINGS INC
HEALTH MANAGEMENT ASSOCIATES INC
HOSPIRA INC
IDEXX LABORATORIES INC
IMS HEALTH INC
JOHNSON & JOHNSON
KAISER PERMANENTE
KINDRED HEALTHCARE INC
KINETIC CONCEPTS INC
LABORATORY CORP OF AMERICA HOLDINGS
LEAR CORP
LIFE TECHNOLOGIES CORP
LINCARE HOLDINGS INC
MAYO FOUNDATION FOR MEDICAL EDUCATION AND RESEARCH
MEDTRONIC INC
METHODIST HEALTH CARE SYSTEM
MILLIPORE CORP
MYLAN INC
ODYSSEY HEALTHCARE INC
PAREXEL INTERNATIONAL CORP
PATTERSON COMPANIES INC
PERRIGO CO
PHARMACEUTICAL PRODUCT DEVELOPMENT INC
PROCTER & GAMBLE CO
PROVIDENCE HEALTH & SERVICES
RESMED INC
SELECT MEDICAL HOLDINGS CORPORATION
SPECTRUM HEALTH
ST JUDE MEDICAL INC
STRYKER CORP
SUTTER HEALTH INC
TEAM HEALTH HOLDINGS INC
UNIVERSAL HEALTH SERVICES INC
VARIAN MEDICAL SYSTEMS INC
VCA ANTECH INC
WATERS CORP
WATSON PHARMACEUTICALS INC
WEST PHARMACEUTICAL SERVICES INC
ZIMMER HOLDINGS INC

Math/Other
3M COMPANY
ADVANCED MICRO DEVICES INC (AMD)
AGILENT TECHNOLOGIES INC
ALASKA AIR GROUP INC
ALLERGAN INC
AMGEN INC
AMR CORP (AMERICAN AIRLINES)
ANALOG DEVICES INC
APPLE INC
AXA FINANCIAL INC
BAIN & COMPANY INC
BAUSCH & LOMB INC
BECHTEL GROUP INC
BECKMAN COULTER INC
BERKSHIRE HATHAWAY INC
BOEING COMPANY (THE)
BOOZ ALLEN HAMILTON INC
BOSTON CONSULTING GROUP INC (THE, BCG)
BRUKER CORP
CELGENE CORP
CEPHALON INC
CERNER CORP
CHEVRON CORPORATION
CHUBB CORPORATION (THE)
CIENA CORP
CISCO SYSTEMS INC
CNA FINANCIAL CORP
COMPUTER SCIENCES CORPORATION (CSC)
CONCENTRA INC
CONOCOPHILLIPS COMPANY
DELOITTE CONSULTING LLP
DIODES INC
DUPONT AGRICULTURE & NUTRITION
EMC CORP
EMERSON ELECTRIC CO
ENDO PHARMACEUTICALS HOLDINGS INC
EXPERIAN AMERICAS
EXXON MOBIL CORPORATION (EXXONMOBIL)
FEDEX CORPORATION
FLUOR CORP
FORD MOTOR CO
FOREST LABORATORIES INC
GENENTECH INC
GENERAL ELECTRIC CO (GE)
GENERAL MOTORS COMPANY (GM)
GENWORTH FINANCIAL INC
GEOKINETICS INC
GILEAD SCIENCES INC
HARRIS CORPORATION
HOSPIRA INC
INTEL CORP
INTERNATIONAL BUSINESS MACHINES CORP (IBM)
JOHNSON & JOHNSON
JOHNSON CONTROLS INC
JUNIPER NETWORKS INC
LIFE TECHNOLOGIES CORP
LINCOLN NATIONAL CORPORATION
LOEWS CORPORATION
MASSACHUSETTS MUTUAL LIFE INSURANCE CO
MCKINSEY & COMPANY INC
MEDTRONIC INC
METLIFE INC
MICROSOFT CORP
MILLIPORE CORP
MYLAN INC
NEW YORK LIFE INSURANCE CO
NORTHWESTERN MUTUAL LIFE INSURANCE CO
ORACLE CORP
PAREXEL INTERNATIONAL CORP
PARSONS BRINCKERHOFF INC
PERRIGO CO
POLYCOM INC
PRINCIPAL FINANCIAL GROUP (THE)
PROGRESSIVE CORPORATION (THE)
PRUDENTIAL FINANCIAL INC
QUALCOMM INC
SAS INSTITUTE INC
SCHLUMBERGER LIMITED
SHELL OIL CO
SRA INTERNATIONAL INC
SYMANTEC CORP
TEKTRONIX INC

TELEDYNE TECHNOLOGIES INC
TRAVELERS COMPANIES INC (THE)
UNITED PARCEL SERVICE INC (UPS)
UNITED TECHNOLOGIES CORPORATION
USAA
VARIAN MEDICAL SYSTEMS INC
WATSON PHARMACEUTICALS INC
WESTERN DIGITAL CORP

Petroleum/Chemicals
AIR PRODUCTS & CHEMICALS INC
ALLERGAN INC
AMGEN INC
APACHE CORP
ARCHER DANIELS MIDLAND CO
AVON PRODUCTS INC
BAKER HUGHES INC
BASIC ENERGY SERVICES INC
BECHTEL GROUP INC
CAMPBELL SOUP CO
CELGENE CORP
CEPHALON INC
CHEVRON CORPORATION
CHEVRON PHILLIPS CHEMICAL COMPANY LLC
COLGATE PALMOLIVE CO
CONOCOPHILLIPS COMPANY
CONSOL ENERGY INC
DIAMOND OFFSHORE DRILLING INC
DTE ENERGY COMPANY
DUKE ENERGY CORP
DUPONT (E I DU PONT DE NEMOURS & CO)
EDISON INTERNATIONAL
ESTEE LAUDER COMPANIES INC (THE)
EXELON CORPORATION
EXTERRAN HOLDINGS INC
EXXON MOBIL CORPORATION (EXXONMOBIL)
EXXONMOBIL CHEMICAL
FIRSTENERGY CORP
FLUOR CORP
FMC TECHNOLOGIES INC
FOREST LABORATORIES INC
GENENTECH INC
GILEAD SCIENCES INC
HALLIBURTON COMPANY
HERSHEY CO
HOSPIRA INC
JOHNSON & JOHNSON
KEY ENERGY SERVICES INC
KOCH INDUSTRIES INC
LINCARE HOLDINGS INC
MARATHON OIL CORP
MARY KAY INC
MIDAMERICAN ENERGY HOLDINGS CO
MYLAN INC
NABORS INDUSTRIES LTD
NALCO HOLDING COMPANY
NATIONAL OILWELL VARCO INC
NEXTERA ENERGY INC
OCEANEERING INTERNATIONAL INC
OIL STATES INTERNATIONAL INC
PARSONS BRINCKERHOFF INC
PATTERSON-UTI ENERGY INC
PEABODY ENERGY CORP
PERRIGO CO
PG&E CORPORATION
PRAXAIR INC
PROCTER & GAMBLE CO
ROWAN COMPANIES INC
SCANA CORPORATION
SCHLUMBERGER LIMITED
SCOTTS MIRACLE GROW CO
SEACOR HOLDINGS INC
SEMPRA ENERGY
SENSIENT TECHNOLOGIES CORPORATION
SHELL OIL CO
SHERWIN WILLIAMS COMPANY (THE)
SIGMA-ALDRICH CORP
SOUTHERN COMPANY (THE)
TIDEWATER INC
VALSPAR CORPORATION (THE)
WATSON PHARMACEUTICALS INC
WILLIAMS COMPANIES INC (THE)

Science/Research
3M COMPANY
ADVANCED MICRO DEVICES INC (AMD)
AGILENT TECHNOLOGIES INC
AIR PRODUCTS & CHEMICALS INC
ALLERGAN INC
AMGEN INC
ANALOG DEVICES INC
APPLE INC
ARCHER DANIELS MIDLAND CO
BAUSCH & LOMB INC
BECKMAN COULTER INC
BECTON DICKINSON & CO
BIO RAD LABORATORIES INC
BIOGEN IDEC INC
BOEING COMPANY (THE)
BRUKER CORP
BUNGE LTD
CELGENE CORP
CEPHALON INC
CERNER CORP
CHEVRON CORPORATION
CHEVRON PHILLIPS CHEMICAL COMPANY LLC
CISCO SYSTEMS INC
CNA FINANCIAL CORP
COLGATE PALMOLIVE CO
CONCENTRA INC
CONOCOPHILLIPS COMPANY
COVANCE INC
CR BARD INC
DAVITA INC
DUPONT (E I DU PONT DE NEMOURS & CO)
DUPONT AGRICULTURE & NUTRITION
EATON CORP
EMC CORP
EMERSON ELECTRIC CO
ENDO PHARMACEUTICALS HOLDINGS INC
ESTEE LAUDER COMPANIES INC (THE)
EXXON MOBIL CORPORATION (EXXONMOBIL)
EXXONMOBIL CHEMICAL
FAIRVIEW HEALTH SERVICES
FINISAR CORPORATION
FM GLOBAL
FMC TECHNOLOGIES INC
FMR CORP (FIDELITY INVESTMENTS)
FORD MOTOR CO
FOREST LABORATORIES INC
GENENTECH INC
GENERAL ELECTRIC CO (GE)
GENERAL MOTORS COMPANY (GM)
GILEAD SCIENCES INC
HALLIBURTON COMPANY
HARRIS CORPORATION

IDEXX LABORATORIES INC
INTEL CORP
INTERNATIONAL BUSINESS MACHINES CORP (IBM)
JOHNSON & JOHNSON
JOHNSON CONTROLS INC
JUNIPER NETWORKS INC
LABORATORY CORP OF AMERICA HOLDINGS
LIFE TECHNOLOGIES CORP
MASSACHUSETTS MUTUAL LIFE INSURANCE CO
MEDTRONIC INC
MICROCHIP TECHNOLOGY INC
MICRON TECHNOLOGY INC
MICROSOFT CORP
MILLIPORE CORP
MYLAN INC
NALCO HOLDING COMPANY
NEW YORK LIFE INSURANCE CO
ORACLE CORP
PAREXEL INTERNATIONAL CORP
PERRIGO CO
PHARMACEUTICAL PRODUCT DEVELOPMENT INC
PHILIP MORRIS INTERNATIONAL INC
PRAXAIR INC
PROCTER & GAMBLE CO
PROVIDENCE HEALTH & SERVICES
QUALCOMM INC
SAIC INC
SAS INSTITUTE INC
SCHLUMBERGER LIMITED
SCOTTS MIRACLE GROW CO
SENSIENT TECHNOLOGIES CORPORATION
SHELL OIL CO
SHERWIN WILLIAMS COMPANY (THE)
SIGMA-ALDRICH CORP
ST JUDE MEDICAL INC
STRYKER CORP
TEAM HEALTH HOLDINGS INC
TEKTRONIX INC
TELEDYNE TECHNOLOGIES INC
UNITED TECHNOLOGIES CORPORATION
VALSPAR CORPORATION (THE)
VARIAN MEDICAL SYSTEMS INC
WATERS CORP
WATSON PHARMACEUTICALS INC
WEST PHARMACEUTICAL SERVICES INC
WESTERN DIGITAL CORP
XEROX CORP